THE JERUSALEM BIBLE

General Editor
ALEXANDER JONES
L.S.S., S.T.L., I.C.B.

THE JERUSALEM BIBLE

POPULAR EDITION

with Abridged Introductions
and Notes

LONDON
DARTON, LONGMAN & TODD

Darton, Longman & Todd Ltd
89 Lille Road, London SW6 1UD

The Popular Edition with abridged introductions
and notes first published 1974

© 1966, 1967 and 1968 by Darton, Longman & Todd
Ltd and Doubleday & Company, Inc.

The abridged introductions and notes of this Bible
are based on those which appear in *La Bible de Jérusalem* (one volume edition) published by Les editions
du Cerf, Paris. The English text, though translated
from the ancient texts, owes a large debt to the work
of the many scholars who collaborated to produce
La Bible de Jérusalem, which the publishers of this
English Bible gratefully acknowledge.

Printed in Great Britain by
Hazell Watson & Viney Limited
Member of BPCC plc
Aylesbury Bucks
Bound by Dorstel Press Ltd
Harlow, Essex

Not to be sold to or in the U.S.A., Canada
or the Philippine Republic
1/16

ISBN 0 232 51283 3 (Cased Bound Edn)
ISBN 0 232 51715 0 (Paperback Bound Edn)
ISBN 0 232 51293 0 (Imitation Leather Edn)

The Jerusalem Bible Popular Edition is published
for Africa (excluding the Republic of South Africa)
by Geoffrey Chapman, 1 Vincent Square, London SW1

EDITOR'S FOREWORD

TO THE READER'S EDITION*

When the Jerusalem Bible was first published in English in 1966, the Foreword to the complete Standard edition announced its objects: to serve two pressing needs facing the Church, the need to keep abreast of the times and the need to deepen theological thought. This double programme was carried out by translating the ancient texts into the language we use today, and by providing notes to the texts which were neither sectarian nor superficial. In that Foreword also, the dependence of the translators on the original pioneer work of the School of Biblical Studies in Jerusalem was acknowledged, and the English version was offered as an entirely faithful rendering of the original texts which, in doubtful points, preserved the text established and (for the most part) the interpretation adopted by the School in the light of the most recent researches in the fields of history, archaeology and literary criticism. With the text, the Standard edition presented the full explanatory notes that would enable any student to confirm for himself the interpretations that were adopted, to appreciate the theological implications drawn from them, and to understand the complex relations between different parts of the Bible.

However the Bible is not only for students undergoing a formal course of study, and there has been an immediate demand for an edition of the Jerusalem Bible which would bring the modern clarity of the text before the ordinary reader, and open to him the results of modern researches without either justifying them at length in literary and historical notes or linking them with doctrinal studies. For this reason, the present edition has been prepared. The full Introductions of the Standard edition are here greatly abridged, to serve simply as brief explanations of the character of each book or group of books, their dates and their authorship; and the full Notes of the Standard edition have been greatly reduced in number and length, to restrict them to the minimum which are necessary for understanding the primary, literal meaning of the text; to explain terms, places, people and customs; to specify dates, and to identify the sources of quotations. In short, the brief Introductions and Notes are here only to help the ordinary reader to understand what he is reading and do not assume in him any wide literary, historical or theological knowledge or interests.

Christ's College, Liverpool   Alexander Jones
1st March 1968

*The Popular Edition reproduces the Introductions, Text and Notes of the Reader's Edition.

TYPOGRAPHICAL NOTE

Chapter numbers

The beginning of a chapter is usually marked by a large bold numeral. A smaller bold numeral is used when a chapter begins inside a paragraph.

Verse numbers

The beginning of each verse is indicated in the line by a dot • preceding the first word, except when a verse starts at the beginning of a line or begins a chapter. Where two verses begin in the same line, the verse numbers in the margin are placed one slightly above and the other slightly below the line. In a few places, the text adopted by the Editors differs from St Jerome's famous Latin version, from which the Vulgate and indirectly the A.V. are derived, but for ease of reference the verse numbering of the previous versions has wherever possible been retained. Occasionally, however, where a verse is omitted or displaced, its number will not appear in the usual sequence, and where a large or lengthy divergence is inevitable from the Vulgate and the A.V. numbering, this previous numbering is printed in italic in addition to the new numbering necessitated by the text. Italic verse numbers are also used (e.g. in Dn 3) for passages incorporated from the Greek Septuagint version where the verse numbering duplicates that of neighbouring Hebrew material.

Italics in the text

Italic type is used in the text to distinguish words which are quotations from or close allusions to another book of the Bible. The origins of such quotations or allusions are given as references in the footnotes (except in cases in which the source is obvious to any Bible-reader), and are not necessarily repeated when the same passage is quoted more than once in a single book.

Punctuation of biblical references

Chapter and verse are separated by a colon, e.g. Ex 20:17. In a succession of references, items are separated by a semi-colon, e.g. Ex 20:17; Lv 9:15. The same practice is followed in a succession of references to different chapters of one book, e.g. Ex 20:17; 21:3 or Ex 15;17;20.

Brackets in the text

In the text, round brackets are used only to indicate that the words within them are considered to be a gloss.

CONTENTS

Editor's Foreword v
Typographical Note vii
List of Abbreviations x

OLD TESTAMENT

THE PENTATEUCH

Introduction to the Pentateuch   3
GENESIS   5
EXODUS   60
LEVITICUS   106
NUMBERS   141
DEUTERONOMY   188

THE HISTORICAL BOOKS

Introduction to Joshua, Judges,
Ruth, Samuel and Kings . .   229
JOSHUA   231
JUDGES   260
RUTH   290
1 SAMUEL   295
2 SAMUEL   329
1 KINGS   360
2 KINGS   393
Introduction to Chronicles,
Ezra and Nehemiah . . .   426
1 CHRONICLES   427
2 CHRONICLES   458
EZRA and NEHEMIAH . .   496
Introduction to Tobit, Judith
and Esther   523
*TOBIT   524
*JUDITH   539
*ESTHER   556
Introduction to the Books of
Maccabees   569

*THE FIRST BOOK OF MACCABEES   570
*THE SECOND BOOK OF
MACCABEES   604

THE WISDOM BOOKS

Introduction to the Wisdom
Books   629
Introduction to Job . . .   630
JOB   631
Introduction to Psalms . .   675
PSALMS   676
Introduction to Proverbs . .   811
PROVERBS   812
Introduction to Ecclesiastes .   854
ECCLESIASTES   855
Introduction to The Song of
Songs   865
THE SONG OF SONGS . . .   866
Introduction to The Book of
Wisdom   875
*THE BOOK OF WISDOM . . .   876
Introduction to Ecclesiasticus   901
*ECCLESIASTICUS   902

THE PROPHETS

General Introduction . . .   969
Introduction to Isaiah . .   970
ISAIAH   971
Introduction to Jeremiah . .   1067
JEREMIAH   1069

LAMENTATIONS	.	. 1153	AMOS.	.	. 1280
*BARUCH	.	. 1165	OBADIAH.	.	. 1292
Introduction to Ezekiel		. 1174	JONAH	.	. 1295
EZEKIEL	.	. 1175	MICAH	.	. 1298
Introduction to Daniel		. 1230	NAHUM	.	. 1308
*DANIEL	.	. 1231	HABAKKUK	.	. 1313
Introduction to the Minor			ZEPHANIAH	.	. 1318
Prophets	.	. 1256	HAGGAI	.	. 1324
HOSEA	.	. 1258	ZECHARIAH	.	. 1326
JOEL	.	. 1273	MALACHI	.	. 1338

NEW TESTAMENT

Introduction to the Synoptic Gospels	. 3	COLOSSIANS	.	. 257
MATTHEW	. 5	1 THESSALONIANS	.	. 262
MARK	. 46	2 THESSALONIANS	.	. 266
LUKE	. 70	1 TIMOTHY	.	. 268
Introduction to the Gospel and Letters of St John	. 112	2 TIMOTHY	.	. 273
		TITUS	.	. 277
JOHN	. 114	PHILEMON	.	. 280
Introduction to the Acts of the Apostles	. 154	HEBREWS	.	. 281
ACTS	. 156	Introduction to the Letters to All Christians	.	. 294
Introduction to the Letters of St Paul	. 194	JAMES	.	. 295
		1 PETER	.	. 300
ROMANS	. 197	2 PETER	.	. 305
1 CORINTHIANS	. 214	1 JOHN	.	. 308
2 CORINTHIANS	. 230	2 JOHN	.	. 316
GALATIANS	. 240	3 JOHN	.	. 317
EPHESIANS	. 246	JUDE	.	. 318
PHILIPPIANS	. 252	Introduction to Revelation		. 320
		REVELATION	.	. 321

*Some editions of the Bible have not admitted these deuterocanonical books (or parts of books: in the case of *Esther* the passages 1:1a-1r; 3:13a-13g; 4:17a-17z; 5:1a-1f,2a,2b; 8:12a-12v; 10:3a-3l, which are here printed in italic type; and in *Daniel* the passages 3:24-90 and ch. 13-14); or have included them only as Apocrypha.

LIST OF ABBREVIATIONS

The Books of the Bible in biblical order

Genesis	Gn	Obadiah	Ob
Exodus	Ex	Jonah	Jon
Leviticus	Lv	Micah	Mi
Numbers	Nb	Nahum	Na
Deuteronomy	Dt	Habakkuk	Hab
Joshua	Jos	Zephaniah	Zp
Judges	Jg	Haggai	Hg
Ruth	Rt	Zechariah	Zc
1 Samuel	1 S	Malachi	Ml
2 Samuel	2 S		
1 Kings	1 K	Matthew	Mt
2 Kings	2 K	Mark	Mk
1 Chronicles	1 Ch	Luke	Lk
2 Chronicles	2 Ch	John	Jn
Ezra	Ezr	Acts	Ac
Nehemiah	Ne	Romans	Rm
Tobit	Tb	1 Corinthians	1 Co
Judith	Jdt	2 Corinthians	2 Co
Esther	Est	Galatians	Ga
1 Maccabees	1 M	Ephesians	Ep
2 Maccabees	2 M	Philippians	Ph
Job	Jb	Colossians	Col
Psalms	Ps	1 Thessalonians	1 Th
Proverbs	Pr	2 Thessalonians	2 Th
Ecclesiastes	Qo	1 Timothy	1 Tm
Song of Songs	Sg	2 Timothy	2 Tm
Wisdom	Ws	Titus	Tt
Ecclesiasticus	Si	Philemon	Phm
Isaiah	Is	Hebrews	Heb
Jeremiah	Jr	James	Jm
Lamentations	Lm	1 Peter	1 P
Baruch	Ba	2 Peter	2 P
Ezekiel	Ezk	1 John	1 Jn
Daniel	Dn	2 John	2 Jn
Hosea	Ho	3 John	3 Jn
Joel	Jl	Jude	Jude
Amos	Am	Revelation	Rv

The books of the Bible in alphabetical order of abbreviation

Ac	Acts	Lk	Luke
Am	Amos	Lm	Lamentations
Ba	Baruch	Lv	Leviticus
1 Ch	1 Chronicles	1 M	1 Maccabees
2 Ch	2 Chronicles	2 M	2 Maccabees
1 Co	1 Corinthians	Mi	Micah
2 Co	2 Corinthians	Mk	Mark
Col	Colossians	Ml	Malachi
Dn	Daniel	Mt	Matthew
Dt	Deuteronomy	Na	Nahum
Ep	Ephesians	Nb	Numbers
Est	Esther	Ne	Nehemiah
Ex	Exodus	Ob	Obadiah
Ezk	Ezekiel	1 P	1 Peter
Ezr	Ezra	2 P	2 Peter
Ga	Galatians	Ph	Philippians
Gn	Genesis	Phm	Philemon
Hab	Habakkuk	Pr	Proverbs
Heb	Hebrews	Ps	Psalms
Hg	Haggai	Qo	Ecclesiastes
Ho	Hosea	Rm	Romans
Is	Isaiah	Rt	Ruth
Jb	Job	Rv	Revelation
Jdt	Judith	1 S	1 Samuel
Jg	Judges	2 S	2 Samuel
Jl	Joel	Sg	Song of Songs
Jm	James	Si	Ecclesiasticus
Jn	John	Tb	Tobit
1 Jn	1 John	1 Th	1 Thessalonians
2 Jn	2 John	2 Th	2 Thessalonians
3 Jn	3 John	1 Tm	1 Timothy
Jon	Jonah	2 Tm	2 Timothy
Jos	Joshua	Tt	Titus
Jr	Jeremiah	Ws	Wisdom
Jude	Jude	Zc	Zechariah
1 K	1 Kings	Zp	Zephaniah
2 K	2 Kings		

The books of the Bible in alphabetical order of abbreviation

Ac	Acts	Lk	Luke
Am	Amos	Lam	Lamentations
Ba	Baruch	Lv	Leviticus
1 Ch	1 Chronicles	1 M	1 Maccabees
2 Ch	2 Chronicles	2 M	2 Maccabees
1 Co	1 Corinthians	Mi	Micah
2 Co	2 Corinthians	Mk	Mark
Col	Colossians	Ml	Malachi
Dn	Daniel	Mt	Matthew
Dt	Deuteronomy	Na	Nahum
Ep	Ephesians	Nb	Numbers
Est	Esther	Ne	Nehemiah
Ex	Exodus	Ob	Obadiah
Ezk	Ezekiel	1 P	1 Peter
Ezr	Ezra	2 P	2 Peter
Ga	Galatians	Ph	Philippians
Gn	Genesis	Phm	Philemon
Hab	Habakkuk	Pr	Proverbs
Heb	Hebrews	Ps	Psalms
Hg	Haggai	Qo	Ecclesiastes
Ho	Hosea	Rm	Romans
Is	Isaiah	Rt	Ruth
Jb	Job	Rv	Revelation
Jdt	Judith	1 S	1 Samuel
Jg	Judges	2 S	2 Samuel
Jl	Joel	Sg	Song of Songs
Jm	James	Si	Ecclesiasticus
Jn	John	Tb	Tobit
1 Jn	1 John	1 Th	1 Thessalonians
2 Jn	2 John	2 Th	2 Thessalonians
3 Jn	3 John	1 Tm	1 Timothy
Jon	Jonah	2 Tm	2 Timothy
Jos	Joshua	Tt	Titus
Jr	Jeremiah	Ws	Wisdom
Jude	Jude	Zc	Zechariah
1 K	1 Kings	Zp	Zephaniah
2 K	2 Kings		

THE
OLD TESTAMENT

INTRODUCTION TO
THE PENTATEUCH

The first five books of the Bible make up a group which was known to the Jews as 'The Law' and for many centuries all five of the books were attributed to Moses as the sole or principal author. However, modern study of the texts has revealed a variety of styles, a lack of sequence and such repetitions and variations in narrative that it is impossible to ascribe the whole group to a single author; four distinct literary 'traditions' can be identified and found side by side in the Pentateuch. Two of these go back to the time when Israel became a nation—a period dominated by the figure of Moses: the traditions of earlier times converging on him and the memories of what happened under his leadership together made up the national epic. One means of distinguishing between these two separate strands is their use of different names for God: one employs the name Yahweh and is known as the *Yahwist*, the other uses *Elohim* and is known as the *Elohist*. The two other identifiable written traditions are later: one known as the *Deuteronomic*, introducing additions and revisions by Levites after the fall of the kingdom of Israel; and one the work of editors after the Exile, known as the *priestly* tradition. The Mosaic religion set its enduring seal on the faith and practice of the nation, and the Mosaic law remained its standard; the modifications required by changing conditions over some seven centuries were presented as interpretations of the mind of Moses and invested themselves with his authority.

Genesis sets the history of the ancestors in a background of primordial history. The early chapters visualise the situation of all mankind in the persons of Adam and Eve and see the origins of human history in an increasing wickedness which brings the Flood as its punishment. The repopulation of the earth starts with Noah, but our attention is directed ultimately to Abraham, father of the chosen people, to whose descendants the Holy Land was promised. Chapters 15 to 50 deal with the history of the patriarchs.

The three books which follow have for their common framework the life of Moses. **Exodus** tells of the deliverance from Egyptian slavery, and the Covenant of Sinai; the journey through the Wilderness connects the two. There is added a list of ordinances controlling the practice of worship in desert conditions.

Leviticus is taken up almost entirely with legislation for the ritual of Israelite religion. It can be largely attributed to the Priestly tradition.

Numbers resumes the account of the desert journey and the first settlement of Israelite tribes in Transjordania. Within this narrative material there are groups of enactments supplementing the Sinaitic code or anticipating the time when the people will have settled in Canaan.

Deuteronomy is a code of civil and religious laws, set in three discourses of Moses. It ends with an account of the death of Moses and the appointment of Joshua as his successor.

The history of Israel is the story of God's intervention and God's promises, and the obligation of his people to keep his law. At the same time, the Pentateuch gives a faithful picture of the origin and migrations of Israel's ancestors and their moral and religious way of life, seen through the treasured memories of character and anecdote. We may put Abraham's stay in Canaan at about 1850 B.C., but from Exodus onwards, after the birth of Moses, we are dealing with a much later period; the likeliest time for the Exodus is the reign of Meneptah (1224-1214) and from this point the history begins to be much more circumstantial.

The original Ten Commandments of Moses, of which there are two distinct traditions in the Pentateuch, are certainly ancient; the rest of the large code of legislation found in the five books includes other elements of the greatest antiquity (for example, the food laws in Lv 11), but also laws from the later times of the Judges and of the Monarchy and others again which show the development in social and religious customs which is traceable to the Exile. Throughout, the hands of the Deuteronomic and Priestly editors are often to be observed, annotating and adapting.

GENESIS

I. THE ORIGIN OF THE WORLD AND OF MANKIND

1. THE CREATION AND THE FALL

The first account of the creation[a]

1 In the beginning God created the heavens and the earth. •Now the earth
was a formless void, there was darkness over the deep, and God's spirit
hovered over the water.

God said, 'Let there be light', and there was light. •God saw that light was
good, and God divided light from darkness. •God called light 'day', and darkness
he called 'night'. Evening came and morning came: the first day.

God said, 'Let there be a vault[b] in the waters to divide the waters in two'.
And so it was. •God made the vault, and it divided the waters above the vault
from the waters under the vault. •God called the vault 'heaven'. Evening came
and morning came: the second day.

God said, 'Let the waters under heaven come together into a single mass,
and let dry land appear'. And so it was. •God called the dry land 'earth' and the
mass of waters 'seas', and God saw that it was good.

God said, 'Let the earth produce vegetation: seed-bearing plants, and fruit
trees bearing fruit with their seed inside, on the earth'. And so it was. •The
earth produced vegetation: plants bearing seed in their several kinds, and trees
bearing fruit with their seed inside in their several kinds. God saw that it was
good. •Evening came and morning came: the third day.

God said, 'Let there be lights in the vault of heaven to divide day from night,
and let them indicate festivals, days and years. •Let them be lights in the vault
of heaven to shine on the earth.' And so it was. •God made the two great lights:[c]
the greater light to govern the day, the smaller light to govern the night, and the
stars. •God set them in the vault of heaven to shine on the earth, •to govern
the day and the night and to divide light from darkness. God saw that it was
good. •Evening came and morning came: the fourth day.

God said, 'Let the waters teem with living creatures, and let birds fly above
the earth within the vault of heaven'. And so it was. •God created great sea-
serpents and every kind of living creature with which the waters teem, and every
kind of winged creature. God saw that it was good. •God blessed them, saying,
'Be fruitful, multiply, and fill the waters of the seas; and let the birds multiply
upon the earth'. •Evening came and morning came: the fifth day.

God said, 'Let the earth produce every kind of living creature: cattle, reptiles,[d]
and every kind of wild beast'. And so it was. •God made every kind of wild
beast, every kind of cattle, and every kind of land reptile. God saw that it
was good.

1 a. Ascribed to the 'priestly' source (see Introduction).   b. For the ancient Semites, the 'arch'
or 'vault' of the sky was a solid dome holding the upper waters in check.   c. Their names are
omitted deliberately: the sun and the moon were worshipped by neighbouring peoples, and
here they are treated as no more than lamps to light the earth and regulate the calendar.
d. 'Things which crawl', a general term for small mammals, reptiles, amphibians and insects.

God said, 'Let us' make man' in our own image, in the likeness of ourselves, 26
and let them be masters of the fish of the sea, the birds of heaven, the cattle, all
the wild beasts and all the reptiles that crawl upon the earth'.

> God created man in the image of himself, 27
> in the image of God he created him,
> male and female he created them.

God blessed them, saying to them, 'Be fruitful, multiply, fill the earth and 28
conquer it. Be masters of the fish of the sea, the birds of heaven and all living
animals on the earth.' •God said, 'See, I give you all the seed-bearing plants that 29
are upon the whole earth, and all the trees with seed-bearing fruit; this shall be
your food. •To all wild beasts, all birds of heaven and all living reptiles on the 30
earth I give all the foliage of plants for food.' And so it was. •God saw all he had 31
made, and indeed it was very good. Evening came and morning came: the sixth
day.

2 Thus heaven and earth were completed with all their array. •On the seventh ½
day God completed the work he had been doing. He rested on the seventh day
after all the work he had been doing. •God blessed the seventh day and made it 3
holy, because on that day he had rested after all his work of creating.

Such were the origins of heaven and earth when they were created. 4

The second account of the creation.ª Paradise

At the time when Yahweh God made earth and heaven •there was as yet no 5
wild bush on the earth nor had any wild plant yet sprung up, for Yahweh God
had not sent rain on the earth, nor was there any man to till the soil. •However, 6
a flood was rising from the earth and watering all the surface of the soil. •Yahweh 7
God fashioned man of dust from the soil. Then he breathed into his nostrils a
breath of life, and thus man became a living being.

Yahweh God planted a garden in Eden which is in the east, and there he put 8
the man he had fashioned. •Yahweh God caused to spring up from the soil every 9
kind of tree, enticing to look at and good to eat, with the tree of life and the tree
of the knowledge of good and evil in the middle of the garden. •A river flowed 10
from Eden to water the garden, and from there it divided to make four streams.ᵇ
The first is named the Pishon, and this encircles the whole land of Havilah where 11
there is gold. •The gold of this land is pure; bdelliumᶜ and onyx stone are found 12
there. •The second river is named the Gihon, and this encircles the whole land 13
of Cush. •The third river is named the Tigris, and this flows to the east of Ashur. 14
The fourth river is the Euphrates. •Yahweh God took the man and settled him 15
in the garden of Eden to cultivate and take care of it. •Then Yahweh God gave 16
the man this admonition, 'You may eat indeed of all the trees in the garden.
Nevertheless of the tree of the knowledge of good and evil you are not to eat, 17
for on the day you eat of it you shall most surely die.'

Yahweh God said, 'It is not good that the man should be alone. I will make 18
him a helpmate.' •So from the soil Yahweh God fashioned all the wild beasts 19
and all the birds of heaven. These he brought to the man to see what he would
call them; each one was to bear the name the man would give it. •The man gave 20
names to all the cattle, all the birds of heaven and all the wild beasts. But no
helpmate suitable for man was found for him. •So Yahweh God made the man 21
fall into a deep sleep. And while he slept, he took one of his ribs and enclosed
it in flesh. •Yahweh God built the rib he had taken from the man into a woman, 22
and brought her to the man. •The man exclaimed: 23

> 'This at last is bone from my bones,
> and flesh from my flesh!
> This is to be called woman,ᵈ
> for this was taken from man.'

24   This is why a man leaves his father and mother and joins himself to his wife, and they become one body.

25   Now both of them were naked, the man and his wife, but they felt no shame in front of each other.

The Fall

1   **3** The serpent was the most subtle of all the wild beasts that Yahweh God had made. It asked the woman, 'Did God really say you were not to eat from
2 any of the trees in the garden?' •The woman answered the serpent, 'We may eat
3 the fruit of the trees in the garden. •But of the fruit of the tree in the middle of the garden God said, "You must not eat it, nor touch it, under pain of death".'
4 Then the serpent said to the woman, 'No! You will not die! •God knows in fact
5 that on the day you eat it your eyes will be opened and you will be like gods,
6 knowing good and evil.' •The woman saw that the tree was good to eat and pleasing to the eye, and that it was desirable for the knowledge that it could give. So she took some of its fruit and ate it. She gave some also to her husband who
7 was with her, and he ate it. •Then the eyes of both of them were opened and they realised that they were naked. So they sewed fig-leaves together to make themselves loin-cloths.

8   The man and his wife heard the sound of Yahweh God walking in the garden in the cool of the day, and they hid from Yahweh God among the trees
9 of the garden. •But Yahweh God called to the man. 'Where are you?' he asked.
10 'I heard the sound of you in the garden;' he replied 'I was afraid because I was
11 naked, so I hid.' •'Who told you that you were naked?' he asked 'Have you been
12 eating of the tree I forbade you to eat?' •The man replied, 'It was the woman you
13 put with me; she gave me the fruit, and I ate it'. •Then Yahweh God asked the woman, 'What is this you have done?' The woman replied, 'The serpent tempted me and I ate'.

14   Then Yahweh God said to the serpent, 'Because you have done this,

> 'Be accursed beyond all cattle,
> all wild beasts.
> You shall crawl on your belly and eat dust
> every day of your life.

15
> I will make you enemies of each other:
> you and the woman,
> your offspring and her offspring.
> It will crush your head
> and you will strike its heel.'

16   To the woman he said:

> 'I will multiply your pains in childbearing,
> you shall give birth to your children in pain.
> Your yearning shall be for your husband,
> yet he will lord it over you.'

17   To the man he said, 'Because you listened to the voice of your wife and ate from the tree of which I had forbidden you to eat,

> 'Accursed be the soil because of you.
> With suffering shall you get your food from it

---

e. Perhaps the plural of majesty: the common name for God was *Elohim*, a plural form. But possibly the plural form implies a discussion between God and his heavenly court.   f. Man, *adam*, is a collective noun ('mankind'); hence the plural in 'Let them be masters of. . . '. **2 a.** From the 'Yahwistic' source (see Introduction).   b. Verses 10-14 are intended to fix the locality of Eden. However, the rivers Pishon and Gihon are unknown, and the two 'lands' named are probably not the regions designated elsewhere by the same names.   c. An aromatic resin.   d. In Hebrew a play on the words *ishshah* (woman) and *ish* (man).

every day of your life.
It shall yield you brambles and thistles,   18
and you shall eat wild plants.
With sweat on your brow   19
shall you eat your bread,
until you return to the soil,
as you were taken from it.
For dust you are
and to dust you shall return.'

The man named his wife 'Eve' because she was the mother of all those who 20
live.ᵃ •Yahweh God made clothes out of skins for the man and his wife, and 21
they put them on. •Then Yahweh God said, 'See, the man has become like 22
one of us, with his knowledge of good and evil. He must not be allowed to
stretch his hand out next and pick from the tree of life also, and eat some
and live for ever.' •So Yahweh God expelled him from the garden of Eden, 23
to till the soil from which he had been taken. •He banished the man, and in 24
front of the garden of Eden he posted the cherubs, and the flame of a flashing
sword, to guard the way to the tree of life.

Cain and Abel

4 The man had intercourse with his wife Eve, and she conceived and gave birth 1
to Cain. 'I have acquired a man with the help of Yahweh'ᵃ she said. •She gave 2
birth to a second child, Abel, the brother of Cain. Now Abel became a shepherd
and kept flocks, while Cain tilled the soil. •Time passed and Cain brought some 3
of the produce of the soil as an offering for Yahweh, •while Abel for his part 4
brought the first-born of his flock and some of their fat as well. Yahweh looked
with favour on Abel and his offering. •But he did not look with favour on Cain 5
and his offering, and Cain was very angry and downcast. •Yahweh asked 6
Cain, 'Why are you angry and downcast? •If you are well disposed, ought you 7
not to lift up your head? But if you are ill disposed, is not sin at the door like
a crouching beast hungering for you, which you must master?' •Cain said to 8
his brother Abel, 'Let us go out'; and while they were in the open country,
Cain set on his brother Abel and killed him.

Yahweh asked Cain, 'Where is your brother Abel?' 'I do not know' he 9
replied. 'Am I my brother's guardian?' •'What have you done?' Yahweh 10
asked. 'Listen to the sound of your brother's blood, crying out to me from the
ground. •Now be accursed and driven from the ground that has opened its 11
mouth to receive your brother's blood at your hands. •When you till the ground 12
it shall no longer yield you any of its produce. You shall be a fugitive and a
wanderer over the earth.' •Then Cain said to Yahweh, 'My punishment is 13
greater than I can bear. •See! Today you drive me from this ground. I must 14
hide from you, and be a fugitive and a wanderer over the earth. Why, whoever
comes across me will kill me!' •'Very well, then,' Yahweh replied 'if anyone 15
kills Cain, sevenfold vengeance shall be taken for him.' So Yahweh put a mark
on Cain, to prevent whoever might come across him from striking him down.
Cain left the presence of Yahweh and settled in the land of Nod, east of Eden. 16

The descendants of Cain

Cain had intercourse with his wife, and she conceived and gave birth to Enoch. 17
He became builder of a town, and he gave the town the name of his son
Enoch. •Enoch had a son, Irad, and Irad became the father of Mehujael; 18
Mehujael became the father of Methushael, and Methushael became the father
of Lamech. •Lamech married two women: the name of the first was Adah 19
and the name of the second was Zillah. •Adah gave birth to Jabal: he was the 20
ancestor of the tent-dwellers and owners of livestock. •His brother's name was 21
Jubal: he was the ancestor of all who play the lyre and the flute. •As for Zillah, 22

she gave birth to Tubal-cain: he was the ancestor of all metalworkers, in bronze or iron. Tubal-cain's sister was Naamah.

23   Lamech said to his wives:

> 'Adah and Zillah, hear my voice,
> Lamech's wives, listen to what I say:
> I killed a man for wounding me,
> a boy for striking me.

24
> Sevenfold vengeance is taken for Cain,
> but seventy-sevenfold for Lamech.'

Seth and his descendants

25   Adam had intercourse with his wife, and she gave birth to a son whom she named Seth, 'because God has granted[b] me other offspring' she said 'in place 26 of Abel, since Cain has killed him'. •A son was also born to Seth, and he named him Enosh. This man was the first to invoke the name of Yahweh.[c]

The patriarchs before the flood

1   5 This is the roll of Adam's descendants :
2   On the day God created Adam he made him in the likeness of God. •Male and female he created them. He blessed them and gave them the name 'Man' on the day they were created.
3   When Adam was a hundred and thirty years old he became the father of 4 a son, in his likeness, as his image, and he called him Seth. •Adam lived for eight hundred years after the birth of Seth and he became the father of sons 5 and daughters. •In all, Adam lived for nine hundred and thirty years; then he died.
6   When Seth was a hundred and five years old he became the father of Enosh. 7 After the birth of Enosh, Seth lived for eight hundred and seven years, and 8 he became the father of sons and daughters. •In all, Seth lived for nine hundred and twelve years; then he died.
9
10   When Enosh was ninety years old he became the father of Kenan. •After the birth of Kenan, Enosh lived for eight hundred and fifteen years and he 11 became the father of sons and daughters. •In all, Enosh lived for nine hundred and five years; then he died.
12   When Kenan was seventy years old he became the father of Mahalalel. 13 After the birth of Mahalalel, Kenan lived for eight hundred and forty years 14 and he became the father of sons and daughters. •In all, Kenan lived for nine hundred and ten years; then he died.
15   When Mahalalel was sixty-five years old he became the father of Jared. 16 After the birth of Jared, Mahalalel lived for eight hundred and thirty years 17 and he became the father of sons and daughters. •In all, Mahalalel lived for eight hundred and ninety-five years; then he died.
18   When Jared was a hundred and sixty-two years old he became the father 19 of Enoch. •After the birth of Enoch, Jared lived for eight hundred years and 20 he became the father of sons and daughters. •In all, Jared lived for nine hundred and sixty-two years; then he died.
21   When Enoch was sixty-five years old he became the father of Methuselah. 22 Enoch walked with God. After the birth of Methuselah he lived for three 23 hundred years and he became the father of sons and daughters. •In all, Enoch 24 lived for three hundred and sixty-five years. •Enoch walked with God. Then he vanished because God took him.
25   When Methuselah was a hundred and eighty-seven years old he became

3 a. The name Eve is explained as derived from the Hebrew verb, 'to live'.
4 a. Folk-derivation of the name Cain from *qanah*, acquire.   **b.** Folk-derivation of the name Seth (*Sheth*) from *shath*, he has granted.   **c.** Other traditions put the revelation of the divine name later, in the time of Moses, Ex 3:14.

the father of Lamech. •After the birth of Lamech, Methuselah lived for seven 26
hundred and eighty-two years and he became the father of sons and daughters.
In all, Methuselah lived for nine hundred and sixty-nine years; then he died. 27

When Lamech was a hundred and eighty-two years old he became the father 28
of a son. •He gave him the name Noah because, he said, 'Here is one who will 29
give us, in the midst of our toil and the labouring of our hands, a consolation
derived from the ground that Yahweh cursed'. •After the birth of Noah, 30
Lamech lived for five hundred and ninety-five years and became the father of
sons and daughters. •In all, Lamech lived for seven hundred and seventy-seven 31
years; then he died.

When Noah was five hundred years old he became the father of Shem, Ham 32
and Japheth.

Sons of God and daughters of men

6 When men had begun to be plentiful on the earth, and daughters had been 1
born to them, •the sons of God, looking at the daughters of men, saw they 2
were pleasing, so they married as many as they chose. •Yahweh said, 'My spirit 3
must not for ever be disgraced in man, for he is but flesh; his life shall last no
more than a hundred and twenty years'. •The Nephilim were on the earth at 4
that time (and even afterwards) when the sons of God resorted to the
daughters of man, and had children by them. These are the heroes of days
gone by, the famous men.

2. THE FLOOD

The corruption of mankind

Yahweh saw that the wickedness of man was great on the earth, and that 5
the thoughts in his heart fashioned nothing but wickedness all day long. •Yahweh 6
regretted having made man on the earth, and his heart grieved. •'I will rid 7
the earth's face of man, my own creation,' Yahweh said 'and of animals also,
reptiles too, and the birds of heaven; for I regret having made them.' •But 8
Noah had found favour with Yahweh.

This is the story of Noah: 9

Noah was a good man, a man of integrity among his contemporaries, and
he walked with God. •Noah became the father of three sons, Shem, Ham and 10
Japheth. •The earth grew corrupt in God's sight, and filled with violence. •God ¹¹₁₂
contemplated the earth: it was corrupt, for corrupt were the ways of all flesh
on the earth.

Preparations for the flood

God said to Noah, 'The end has come for all things of flesh; I have decided 13
this, because the earth is full of violence of man's making, and I will efface
them from the earth. •Make yourself an ark out of resinous wood. Make it 14
with reeds and line it with pitch inside and out. •This is how to make it: the 15
length of the ark is to be three hundred cubits, its breadth fifty cubits, and its
height thirty cubits. •Make a roof for the ark... put the door of the ark high 16
up in the side, and make a first, second and third deck.

'For my part I mean to bring a flood, and send the waters over the earth, 17
to destroy all flesh on it, every living creature under heaven; everything on
earth shall perish. •But I will establish my Covenant with you, and you must 18
go on board the ark, yourself, your sons, your wife, and your sons' wives along
with you. •From all living creatures, from all flesh, you must take two of each 19
kind aboard the ark, to save their lives with yours; they must be a male and
a female. •Of every kind of bird, of every kind of animal and of every kind 20
of reptile on the ground, two must go with you so that their lives may be saved.
For your part provide yourself with eatables of all kinds, and lay in a store 21

22 of them, to serve as food for yourself and them.' •Noah did this; he did all that God had ordered him.

1 7 Yahweh said to Noah, 'Go aboard the ark, you and all your household, for you alone among this generation do I see as a good man in my judgement.
2 Of all the clean animals you must take seven of each kind, both male and
3 female; of the unclean animals you must take two, a male and its female •(and of the birds of heaven also, seven of each kind, both male and female), to
4 propagate their kind over the whole earth. •For in seven days' time I mean to make it rain on the earth for forty days and nights, and I will rid the earth of
5 every living thing that I made.' •Noah did all that Yahweh ordered.
6 Noah was six hundred years old when the flood of waters appeared on the earth.
7 Noah with his sons, his wife, and his sons' wives boarded the ark to escape
8 the waters of the flood. •(Of the clean animals and the animals that are not
9 clean, of the birds and all that crawls on the ground, •two of each kind boarded the ark with Noah, a male and a female, according to the order God gave Noah.)
10 Seven days later the waters of the flood appeared on the earth.
11 In the six hundredth year of Noah's life, in the second month, and on the seventeenth day of that month, that very day all the springs of the great deep
12 broke through, and the sluices of heaven opened. •It rained on the earth for forty days and forty nights.
13 That very day Noah and his sons Shem, Ham and Japheth boarded the ark,
14 with Noah's wife and the three wives of his sons, •and with them wild beasts of every kind, cattle of every kind, reptiles of every kind that crawls on the
15 earth, birds of every kind, all that flies, everything with wings. •One pair of
16 all that is flesh and has the breath of life boarded the ark with Noah; •and so there went in a male and a female of every creature that is flesh, just as God had ordered him.
And Yahweh closed the door behind Noah.

The flood

17 The flood lasted forty days on the earth. The waters swelled, lifting the ark
18 until it was raised above the earth. •The waters rose and swelled greatly on the
19 earth, and the ark sailed on the waters. •The waters rose more and more on the earth so that all the highest mountains under the whole of heaven were
20 submerged. •The waters rose fifteen cubits higher, submerging the mountains.
21 And so all things of flesh perished that moved on the earth, birds, cattle, wild
22 beasts, everything that swarms on the earth, and every man. •Everything with
23 the breath of life in its nostrils died, everything on dry land. •Yahweh destroyed every living thing on the face of the earth, man and animals, reptiles, and the birds of heaven. He rid the earth of them, so that only Noah was left, and those
24 with him in the ark. •The waters rose on the earth for a hundred and fifty days.

The flood subsides

1 8 But God had Noah in mind, and all the wild beasts and all the cattle that were with him in the ark. God sent a wind across the earth and the waters
2 subsided. •The springs of the deep and the sluices of heaven were stopped.
3 Rain ceased to fall from heaven; •the waters gradually ebbed from the
4 earth. After a hundred and fifty days the waters fell, •and in the seventh month, on the seventeenth day of that month, the ark came to rest on the mountains
5 of Ararat. •The waters gradually fell until the tenth month when, on the first day of the tenth month, the mountain peaks appeared.
6 At the end of forty days Noah opened the porthole he had made in the ark
7 and he sent out the raven. This went off, and flew back and forth until the
8 waters dried up from the earth. •Then he sent out the dove, to see whether
9 the waters were receding from the surface of the earth. •The dove, finding nowhere to perch, returned to him in the ark, for there was water over the whole

surface of the earth; putting out his hand he took hold of it and brought it back into the ark with him. •After waiting seven more days, again he sent out the 10 dove from the ark. •In the evening, the dove came back to him and there it was 11 with a new olive-branch in its beak. So Noah realised that the waters were receding from the earth. •After waiting seven more days he sent out the dove, 12 and now it returned to him no more.

It was in the six hundred and first year of Noah's life, in the first month and 13 on the first of the month, that the water dried up from the earth. Noah lifted back the hatch of the ark and looked out. The surface of the ground was dry!

In the second month and on the twenty-seventh day of the month the earth 14 was dry.

They disembark

Then God said to Noah, •'Come out of the ark, you yourself, your wife, 15 16 your sons, and your sons' wives with you. •As for all the animals with you, 17 all things of flesh, whether birds or animals or reptiles that crawl on the earth, bring them out with you. Let them swarm on the earth; let them be fruitful and multiply on the earth.' •So Noah went out with his sons, his wife, and his 18 sons' wives. •And all the wild beasts, all the cattle, all the birds and all 19 the reptiles that crawl on the earth went out from the ark, one kind after another.

Noah built an altar for Yahweh, and choosing from all the clean animals 20 and all the clean birds he offered burnt offerings on the altar. •Yahweh smelt 21 the appeasing fragrance and said to himself, 'Never again will I curse the earth because of man, because his heart contrives evil from his infancy. Never again will I strike down every living thing as I have done.

> 'As long as earth lasts,   22
> sowing and reaping,
> cold and heat,
> summer and winter,
> day and night
> shall cease no more.'

The new world order

9 God blessed Noah and his sons, saying to them, 'Be fruitful, multiply and 1 fill the earth. •Be the terror and the dread of all the wild beasts and all the 2 birds of heaven, of everything that crawls on the ground and all the fish of the sea; they are handed over to you. •Every living and crawling thing shall provide 3 food for you, no less than the foliage of plants. I give you everything, •with 4 this exception: you must not eat flesh with life, that is to say blood, in it. •I will 5 demand an account of your life-blood. I will demand an account from every beast and from man. I will demand an account of every man's life from his fellow men.

> 'He who sheds man's blood,   6
> shall have his blood shed by man,
> for in the image of God
> man was made.

'As for you, be fruitful, multiply, teem over the earth and be lord of it.' 7

God spoke to Noah and his sons, •'See, I establish my Covenant with you, 8 9 and with your descendants after you; •also with every living creature to be found 10 with you, birds, cattle and every wild beast with you: everything that came out of the ark, everything that lives on the earth. •I establish my Covenant with 11 you: no thing of flesh shall be swept away again by the waters of the flood. There shall be no flood to destroy the earth again.'

12   God said, 'Here is the sign of the Covenant I make between myself and you
13 and every living creature with you for all generations: •I set my bow in the
14 clouds and it shall be a sign of the Covenant between me and the earth. •When
15 I gather the clouds over the earth and the bow appears in the clouds, •I will
recall the Covenant between myself and you and every living creature of
every kind. And so the waters shall never again become a flood to destroy
16 all things of flesh. •When the bow is in the clouds I shall see it and call to mind
the lasting Covenant between God and every living creature of every kind that
is found on the earth.'
17   God said to Noah, 'This is the sign of the Covenant I have established
between myself and every living thing that is found on the earth'.

3. FROM THE FLOOD TO ABRAHAM

Noah and his sons

18   The sons of Noah who went out from the ark were Shem, Ham and
19 Japheth; Ham is the ancestor of the Canaanites. •These three were Noah's
sons, and from these the whole earth was peopled.

20
21   Noah, a tiller of the soil, was the first to plant the vine. •He drank some
of the wine, and while he was drunk he uncovered himself inside his tent.
22 Ham, Canaan's ancestor, saw his father's nakedness, and told his two brothers
23 outside. •Shem and Japheth took a cloak and they both put it over their
shoulders, and walking backwards, covered their father's nakedness; they kept
24 their faces turned away, and did not see their father's nakedness. •When Noah
awoke from his stupor he learned what his youngest son had done to him.
25 And he said:

> 'Accursed be Canaan.
> He shall be his brothers'
> meanest slave.'

26   He added:

> 'Blessed be Yahweh, God of Shem,
> let Canaan be his slave!
27 > May God extend Japheth,
> may he live in the tents of Shem,
> and may Canaan be his slave!'

28
29   After the flood Noah lived three hundred and fifty years. •In all, Noah's
life lasted nine hundred and fifty years; then he died.

The peopling of the earth[a]

1   **10** These are the descendants of Noah's sons, Shem, Ham and Japheth,
        to whom sons were born after the flood:
2   Japheth's sons: Gomer, Magog, the Medes, Javan, Tubal, Meshech, Tiras.
3 Gomer's sons: Ashkenaz, Riphath, Togarmah. •Javan's sons: Elishah,
4
5 Tarshish, the Kittim, the Dananites. •From these came the dispersal to the
islands of the nations.[b]
    These were Japheth's sons, according to their countries and each of their
languages, according to their tribes and their nations.
6   Ham's sons: Cush, Misraim, Put, Canaan. •Cush's sons: Seba, Havilah,
7
Sabtah, Raamah, Sabteca. Raamah's sons: Sheba, Dedan.
8   Cush became the father of Nimrod who was the first potentate on earth.

---

10 a. In the form of a genealogical tree, this chapter draws up a Table of Peoples, arranging
them according to their geographical and historical relationship. It sums up the knowledge of
the inhabited world possessed by Israel in Solomon's time.   **b.** The islands and the seaboard
of the Mediterranean.

He was a mighty hunter in the eyes of Yahweh, hence the saying, 'Like Nimrod, 9 a mighty hunter in the eyes of Yahweh'. •First to be included in his empire 10 were Babel, Erech and Accad, all of them in the land of Shinar. •From this 11 country came Ashur, the builder of Nineveh, Rehoboth-ir, Calah, •and Resen 12 between Nineveh and Calah (this is the great city).

Misraim became the father of the people of Lud, of Anam, Lehab, Naphtuh, 13 Pathros, Cusluh and Caphtor, from which the Philistines came. 14

Canaan became the father of Sidon, his first-born, then Heth, •and the $^{15}_{16}$ Jebusites, the Amorites, Girgashites, •Hivites, Arkites, Sinites, •Arvadites, $^{17}_{18}$ Zemarites, Hamathites; later the Canaanite tribes scattered. •The Canaanite 19 frontier stretched from Sidon in the direction of Gerar and as far as Gaza, then in the direction of Sodom, Gomorrah, Admah and Zeboim, and as far as Lesha.

These were Ham's sons, according to their tribes and languages, according 20 to their countries and nations.

Shem also was the father of children, the ancestor of all the sons of Eber 21 and the elder brother of Japheth.

Shem's sons: Elam, Asshur, Arpachshad, Lud, Aram. •Aram's sons: Uz, $^{22}_{23}$ Hul, Gether and Mash.

Arpachshad became the father of Shelah, and Shelah became the father 24 of Eber. •To Eber were born two sons: the first was called Peleg, because it was 25 in his time that the earth was divided, and his brother was called Joktan. •Joktan 26 became the father of Almodad, Sheleph, Hazarmaveth, Jerah, •Hadoram, 27 Uzal, Diklah, •Obal, Abima-el, Sheba, •Ophir, Havilah, Jobab; all these are $^{28}_{29}$ sons of Joktan. •They occupied a stretch of country from Mesha in the direction 30 of Sephar, the eastern mountain range.

These were Shem's sons, according to their tribes and languages, and 31 according to their countries and nations.

These were the tribes of Noah's sons, according to their descendants and their 32 nations. From these came the dispersal of the nations over the earth, after the flood.

The tower of Babel[a]

11 Throughout the earth men spoke the same language, with the same voca- 1 bulary. •Now as they moved eastwards they found a plain in the land of 2 Shinar[b] where they settled. •They said to one another, 'Come, let us make 3 bricks and bake them in the fire'. — For stone they used bricks, and for mortar they used bitumen. — •'Come,' they said 'let us build ourselves a town and a 4 tower with its top reaching heaven. Let us make a name for ourselves, so that we may not be scattered about the whole earth.'

Now Yahweh came down to see the town and the tower that the sons of 5 man had built. •'So they are all a single people with a single language!' said 6 Yahweh. 'This is but the start of their undertakings! There will be nothing too hard for them to do. •Come, let us go down and confuse their language 7 on the spot so that they can no longer understand one another.' •Yahweh 8 scattered them thence over the whole face of the earth, and they stopped building the town. •It was named Babel therefore, because there Yahweh 9 confused[c] the language of the whole earth. It was from there that Yahweh scattered them over the whole face of the earth.

The patriarchs after the flood

These were Shem's descendants: 10

When Shem was a hundred years old he became the father of Arpachshad, two years after the flood. •After the birth of Arpachshad, Shem lived five 11 hundred years and became the father of sons and daughters.

When Arpachshad was thirty-five years old he became the father of Shelah. 12 After the birth of Shelah, Arpachshad lived four hundred and three years and 13 became the father of sons and daughters.

14 15   When Shelah was thirty years old he became the father of Eber. •After the birth of Eber, Shelah lived four hundred and three years and became the father of sons and daughters.

16 17   When Eber was thirty-four years old he became the father of Peleg. •After the birth of Peleg, Eber lived four hundred and thirty years and became the father of sons and daughters.

18 19   When Peleg was thirty years old he became the father of Reu. •After the birth of Reu, Peleg lived two hundred and nine years and became the father of sons and daughters.

20 21   When Reu was thirty-two years old he became the father of Serug. •After the birth of Serug, Reu lived two hundred and seven years and became the father of sons and daughters.

22 23   When Serug was thirty years old he became the father of Nahor. •After the birth of Nahor, Serug lived two hundred years and became the father of sons and daughters.

24   When Nahor was twenty-nine years old he became the father of Terah.
25 After the birth of Terah, Nahor lived a hundred and nineteen years and became the father of sons and daughters.

26   When Terah was seventy years old he became the father of Abram, Nahor and Haran.

The descendants of Terah

27   These are Terah's descendants:

Terah became the father of Abram, Nahor and Haran. Haran became the
28 father of Lot. •Haran died in the presence of his father Terah in his native
29 land, Ur of the Chaldaeans. •Abram and Nahor both married: Abram's wife was called Sarai, Nahor's wife was called Milcah, the daughter of Haran, father
30 of Milcah and Iscah. •Sarai was barren, having no child.

31   Terah took his son Abram, his grandson Lot the son of Haran, and his daughter-in-law the wife of Abram, and made them leave Ur of the Chaldaeans to go to the land of Canaan. But on arrival in Haran they settled there.ᵈ
32   Terah's life lasted two hundred and five years; then he died at Haran.

II. THE STORY OF ABRAHAM

The call of Abraham

1
2 **12** Yahweh said to Abram, 'Leave your country, your family and your father's house, for the land I will show you. •I will make you a great nation; I will bless you and make your name so famous that it will be used as a blessing.

3   'I will bless those who bless you:
I will curse those who slight you.
All the tribes of the earth
shall bless themselves by you.'

4   So Abram went as Yahweh told him, and Lot went with him. Abram was
5 seventy-five years old when he left Haran. •Abram took his wife Sarai, his nephew Lot, all the possessions they had amassed and the people they had acquired in Haran. They set off for the land of Canaan, and arrived there.
6   Abram passed through the land as far as Shechem's holy place, the Oak
7 of Moreh. At that time the Canaanites were in the land. •Yahweh appeared

---

11 a. A different explanation, from another source, of the diversity of peoples and languages.
b. Babylonia.   **c.** *Babel* is derived here from a verb meaning 'to confuse', but in fact the name means 'gate of the god'.   **d.** Ur is in Lower Mesopotamia; Haran lies to the N.W. of Mesopotamia.

to Abram and said, 'It is to your descendants that I will give this land'. So
Abram built there an altar for Yahweh who had appeared to him. •From there 8
he moved on to the mountainous district east of Bethel, where he pitched his
tent, with Bethel to the west and Ai to the east. There he built an altar to
Yahweh and invoked the name of Yahweh. •Then Abram made his way stage 9
by stage to the Negeb.

Abraham in Egypt

When famine came to the land Abram went down into Egypt, to stay there 10
for the time, since the land was hard pressed by the famine. •On the threshold 11
of Egypt he said to his wife Sarai, 'Listen! I know you are a beautiful woman.
When the Egyptians see you they will say, "That is his wife", and they will 12
kill me but spare you. •Tell them you are my sister, so that they may treat me 13
well because of you and spare my life out of regard for you.' •When Abram 14
arrived in Egypt the Egyptians did indeed see that the woman was very beautiful.
When Pharaoh's officials saw her they sang her praises to Pharaoh and the 15
woman was taken into Pharaoh's palace. •He treated Abram well because of 16
her, and he received flocks, oxen, donkeys, men and women slaves, she-donkeys
and camels. •But Yahweh inflicted severe plagues on Pharaoh and his household 17
because of Abram's wife Sarai. •So Pharaoh summoned Abram and said, 'What 18
is this you have done to me? Why did you not tell me she was your wife? •Why 19
did you say, "She is my sister", so that I took her for my wife? Now, here is
your wife. Take her and go!' •Pharaoh committed him to men who escorted 20
him back to the frontier with his wife and all he possessed.

Abraham and Lot separate

13 From Egypt Abram returned to the Negeb with his wife and all he 1
possessed, and Lot with him. •Abram was a very rich man, with livestock, 2
silver and gold. •By stages he went from the Negeb to Bethel, where he had first 3
pitched his tent, between Bethel and Ai, •at the place where he had formerly 4
erected the altar. Here Abram invoked the name of Yahweh.

Lot, who was travelling with Abram, had flocks and cattle of his own, and 5
tents too. •The land was not sufficient to accommodate them both at once, 6
for they had too many possessions to be able to live together. •Dispute broke 7
out between the herdsmen of Abram's livestock and those of Lot's. (The Canaanites and the Perizzites were then living in the land.) •Accordingly Abram 8
said to Lot, 'Let there be no dispute between me and you, nor between
my herdsmen and yours, for we are brothers. •Is not the whole land open 9
before you? Part company with me: if you take the left, I will go right; if you
take the right, I will go left.'

Looking round, Lot saw all the Jordan plain, irrigated everywhere—this 10
was before Yahweh destroyed Sodom and Gomorrah—like the garden of
Yahweh or the land of Egypt, as far as Zoar.ª •So Lot chose all the Jordan 11
plain for himself and moved off eastwards. Thus they parted company: •Abram 12
settled in the land of Canaan; Lot settled among the towns of the plain, pitching
his tents on the outskirts of Sodom. •Now the people of Sodom were vicious 13
men, great sinners against Yahweh.

Yahweh said to Abram after Lot had parted company with him, 'Look 14
all round from where you are towards the north and the south, towards
the east and the west. •All the land within sight I will give to you and your 15
descendants for ever. •I will make your descendants like the dust on the ground: 16
when men succeed in counting the specks of dust on the ground, then they will
be able to count your descendants! •Come, travel through the length and 17
breadth of the land, for I mean to give it to you.'

So Abram went with his tents to settle at the Oak of Mamre, at Hebron, 18
and there he built an altar to Yahweh.

The campaign of the four great kings[a]

1,2 **14** It was in the time of Amraphel king of Shinar, Arioch king of Ellasar, Chedor-laomer king of Elam, and Tidal king of the Goiim. •These made war on Bera king of Sodom, Birsha king of Gomorrah, Shinab king of Admah, Shemeber king of Zeboiim, and the king of Bela (that is, Zoar).

3 These latter all banded together in the Valley of Siddim (that is, the Salt 4 Sea). •For twelve years they had been under the yoke of Chedor-laomer, 5 but in the thirteenth year they revolted. •In the fourteenth year Chedor-laomer arrived and the kings who were on his side. They defeated the Rephaim at Asteroth-karnaim, the Zuzim at Ham, the Emim in the plain of Kiriathaim, 6 the Horites in the mountainous district of Seir as far as El-paran, which is on 7 the edge of the wilderness. •Wheeling round, they came to the Spring of Judgement (that is, Kadesh); they conquered all the territory of the Amalekites 8 and also the Amorites who lived in Hazazon-tamar. •Then the kings of Sodom, Gomorrah, Admah, Zeboiim and Bela (that is, Zoar) marched out and took 9 up battle positions against them in the Valley of Siddim, •against Chedor-laomer king of Elam, Tidal king of the Goiim, Amraphel king of Shinar and Arioch 10 king of Ellasar: four kings against five! •Now there were many bitumen wells in the Valley of Siddim, and in their flight the kings of Sodom and Gomorrah 11 fell into them, while the rest took refuge in the mountains. •The conquerors seized all the possessions of Sodom and Gomorrah, and all their provisions, 12 and made off. •They also took Lot (the nephew of Abram) and his possessions and made off; he was living at Sodom.

13 A survivor came to tell Abram the Hebrew, who was living at the Oak of the Amorite Mamre, the brother of Eshcol and Aner; these were allies of Abram. 14 When Abram heard that his kinsman had been taken captive, he mustered his supporters, the members of his household from birth, numbering three 15 hundred and eighteen, and led them in pursuit as far as Dan. •He and his servants fell on them by night and defeated them, pursuing them as far as Hobah, north 16 of Damascus. •He recaptured all the goods, along with his kinsman Lot and his possessions, together with the women and people.

Melchizedek

17 When Abram came back after the defeat of Chedor-laomer and the kings who had been on his side, the king of Sodom came to meet him in the Valley 18 of Shaveh (that is, the Valley of the King).[b] •Melchizedek king of Salem 19 brought bread and wine; he was a priest of God Most High. •He pronounced this blessing:

20 'Blessed be Abram by God Most High, creator of heaven and earth, and blessed be God Most High for handing over your enemies to you'. And Abram gave him a tithe of everything.

21 The king of Sodom said to Abram, 'Give me the people and take the 22 possessions for yourself'. •But Abram replied to the king of Sodom, 'I raise my hand in the presence of Yahweh, God Most High, creator of heaven and earth: 23 not one thread, not one sandal strap, nothing will I take of what is yours; you 24 shall not say, "I enriched Abram". •For myself, nothing. There is only what my men have eaten, and the share belonging to the men who came with me, Eshkol, Aner and Mamre; let them take their share.'

The divine promises and Covenant

1 **15** It happened some time later that the word of Yahweh was spoken to Abram in a vision, 'Have no fear, Abram, I am your shield; your reward 2 will be very great'.

---

13 a. At the S. end of the Dead Sea.
14 a. The kings are not identifiable, but this episode finds its most natural setting in the conditions of the 19th century B.C.   **b.** According to Josephus, this was close to Jerusalem.

'My Lord Yahweh,' Abram replied 'what do you intend to give me? I go childless...' •Then Abram said, 'See, you have given me no descendants; 3 some man of my household will be my heir'. •And then this word of Yahweh 4 was spoken to him, 'He shall not be your heir; your heir shall be of your own flesh and blood'. •Then taking him outside he said, 'Look up to heaven and 5 count the stars if you can. Such will be your descendants' he told him. •Abram 6 put his faith in Yahweh, who counted this as making him justified.

'I am Yahweh' he said to him 'who brought you out of Ur of the Chaldaeans 7 to make you heir to this land.' •'My Lord Yahweh,' Abram replied 'how am I 8 to know that I shall inherit it?' •He said to him, 'Get me a three-year-old heifer, 9 a three-year-old goat, a three-year-old ram, a turtledove and a young pigeon'. He brought him all these, cut them in half and put half on one side and half 10 facing it on the other; but the birds he did not cut in half. •Birds of prey came 11 down on the carcases but Abram drove them off.

Now as the sun was setting Abram fell into a deep sleep, and terror seized 12 him. •Then Yahweh said to Abram, 'Know this for certain, that your descendants 13 will be exiles in a land not their own, where they will be slaves and oppressed for four hundred years. •But I will pass judgement also on the nation that 14 enslaves them and after that they will leave, with many possessions. •For your 15 part, you shall go to your fathers in peace; you shall be buried at a ripe old age. •In the fourth generation they will come back here, for the wickedness 16 of the Amorites is not yet ended.'

When the sun had set and darkness had fallen, there appeared a smoking 17 furnace and a firebrand that went between the halves.*ᵃ* •That day Yahweh 18 made a Covenant with Abram in these terms:

'To your descendants I give this land,
from the wadi of Egypt to the Great River,

the river Euphrates, •the Kenites, the Kenizzites, the Kadmonites, •the Hittites, ¹⁹₂₀
the Perizzites, the Rephaim, •the Amorites, the Canaanites, the Girgashites, and 21
the Jebusites'.

The birth of Ishmael

16 Abram's wife Sarai had borne him no child, but she had an Egyptian 1 maidservant named Hagar. •So Sarai said to Abram, 'Listen, now! Since 2 Yahweh has kept me from having children, go to my slave-girl. Perhaps I shall get children through her.'*ᵃ* Abram agreed to what Sarai had said.

Thus after Abram had lived in the land of Canaan for ten years Sarai took 3 Hagar her Egyptian slave-girl and gave her to Abram as his wife. •He went to 4 Hagar and she conceived. And once she knew she had conceived, her mistress counted for nothing in her eyes. •Then Sarai said to Abram, 'May this insult 5 to me come home to you! It was I who put my slave-girl into your arms but now she knows that she has conceived, I count for nothing in her eyes. Let Yahweh judge between me and you.' 'Very well,' Abram said to Sarai 'your 6 slave-girl is at your disposal. Treat her as you think fit.' Sarai accordingly treated her so badly that she ran away from her.

The angel of Yahweh*ᵇ* met her near a spring in the wilderness, the spring 7 that is on the road to Shur. •He said, 'Hagar, slave-girl of Sarai, where have 8 you come from, and where are you going?' 'I am running away from my mistress Sarai' she replied. •The angel of Yahweh said to her, 'Go back to your mistress 9 and submit to her'. •The angel of Yahweh said to her, 'I will make your 10 descendants too numerous to be counted'. •Then the angel of Yahweh said 11 to her:

'Now you have conceived, and you will bear a son,
and you shall name him Ishmael,
for Yahweh has heard*ᶜ* your cries of distress.
A wild-ass of a man he will be, 12

against every man, and every man against him,
setting himself to defy all his brothers.'

13   Hagar gave a name to Yahweh who had spoken to her: 'You are El Roi', for, she said, 'Surely this is a place where I, in my turn, have seen the one who 14 sees me?'[d] •This is why this well is called the well of Lahai Roi; it is between Kadesh and Bered.

15   Hagar bore Abram a son, and Abram gave to the son that Hagar bore the 16 name Ishmael. •Abram was eighty-six years old when Hagar bore him Ishmael.

The Covenant and circumcision

1
2   **17** When Abram was ninety-nine years old Yahweh appeared to him and said, 'I am El Shaddai.[a] Bear yourself blameless in my presence, •and I will make a Covenant between myself and you, and increase your numbers greatly.'
3
4   Abram bowed to the ground and God said this to him, •'Here now is my 5 covenant with you: you shall become the father of a multitude of nations. •You shall no longer be called Abram; your name shall be Abraham,[b] for I make 6 you father of a multitude of nations. •I will make you most fruitful. I will make 7 you into nations, and your issue shall be kings. •I will establish my Covenant between myself and you, and your descendants after you, generation after generation, a Covenant in perpetuity, to be your God and the God of your descendants 8 after you. •I will give to you and to your descendants after you the land you are living in, the whole land of Canaan, to own. in perpetuity, and I will be your God.'

9   God said to Abraham, 'You on your part shall maintain my Covenant, 10 yourself and your descendants after you, generation after generation. •Now this is my Covenant which you are to maintain between myself and you, and your 11 descendants after you: all your males must be circumcised. •You shall circumcise your foreskin, and this shall be the sign of the Covenant between myself and 12 you. •When they are eight days old all your male children must be circumcised, generation after generation of them, no matter whether they be born within 13 the household or bought from a foreigner not one of your descendants. •They must always be circumcised, both those born within the household and those who have been bought. My Covenant shall be marked on your bodies as 14 a Covenant in perpetuity. •The uncircumcised male, whose foreskin has not been circumcised, such a man shall be cut off from his people: he has violated my Covenant.'

15   God said to Abraham, 'As for Sarai your wife, you shall not call her Sarai, 16 but Sarah. •I will bless her and moreover give you a son by her. I will bless her and nations shall come out of her; kings of peoples shall descend from 17 her.' •Abraham bowed to the ground, and he laughed, thinking to himself, 'Is a child to be born to a man one hundred years old, and will Sarah have a 18 child at the age of ninety?' •Abraham said to God, 'Oh, let Ishmael live in your 19 presence!' •But God replied, 'No, but your wife Sarah shall bear you a son whom you are to name Isaac. With him I will establish my Covenant, a Covenant 20 in perpetuity, to be his God and the God of his descendants after him. •For Ishmael too I grant you your request: I bless him and I will make him fruitful and greatly increased in numbers. He shall be the father of twelve princes, and I 21 will make him into a great nation. •But my Covenant I will establish with Isaac,

15 a. In the ancient ritual of covenant, the two parties to a contract walked between the halves of a dead animal and called down on themselves the fate of the victim if they should violate the agreement. Here the firebrand symbolises Yahweh.
16 a. A recognised practice. Cf. 30:1-6 and 30:9-13.   **b.** In the most ancient texts, 'the angel of Yahweh' is not a created being, but is God himself in a form visible to men.   **c.** 'Ishmael' means 'God has heard'.   **d.** 'El Roi' means 'God of vision'.
17 a. An ancient name of God, rarely used outside the Pentateuch (except Job).   **b.** There is in fact a similarity between *Abraham* and the Hebrew expression for 'the father of many', but the name is not derived from this expression.

whom Sarah will bear you at this time next year.' •When he had finished 22
speaking to Abraham God went up from him.

Then Abraham took his son Ishmael, all those born in his household and 23
all those he had bought, in short all the males among the people of Abraham's
household, and circumcised their foreskins that same day, in accordance with
God's commands to him. •Abraham was ninety-nine years old when his 24
foreskin was circumcised. •Ishmael his son was thirteen years old when his 25
foreskin was circumcised. •That same day Abraham and his son Ishmael were 26
circumcised; •all the men of his household, both those born in the household 27
and those who had been bought, were circumcised with him.

The apparition at Mamre

18 Yahweh appeared to him at the Oak of Mamre while he was sitting by 1
the entrance of the tent during the hottest part of the day. •He looked 2
up, and there he saw three men standing near him. As soon as he saw them he
ran from the entrance of the tent to meet them, and bowed to the ground.
'My lord,' he said 'I beg you, if I find favour with you, kindly do not pass your 3
servant by. •A little water shall be brought; you shall wash your feet and lie 4
down under the tree. •Let me fetch a little bread and you shall refresh your- 5
selves before going further. That is why you have come in your servant's
direction.' They replied, 'Do as you say'.

Abraham hastened to the tent to find Sarah. 'Hurry,' he said 'knead three 6
bushels of flour and make loaves.' •Then running to the cattle Abraham took 7
a fine and tender calf and gave it to the servant, who hurried to prepare it.
Then taking cream, milk and the calf he had prepared, he laid all before them, 8
and they ate while he remained standing near them under the tree.

'Where is your wife Sarah?' they asked him. 'She is in the tent' he replied. 9
Then his guest said, 'I shall visit you again next year without fail, and your 10
wife will then have a son'. Sarah was listening at the entrance of the tent behind
him. •Now Abraham and Sarah were old, well on in years, and Sarah had ceased 11
to have her monthly periods. •So Sarah laughed to herself, thinking, 'Now 12
that I am past the age of child-bearing, and my husband is an old man, is pleasure
to come my way again!' •But Yahweh asked Abraham, 'Why did Sarah laugh 13
and say, "Am I really going to have a child now that I am old?" •Is anything 14
too wonderful for Yahweh? At the same time next year I shall visit you again
and Sarah will have a son.' •'I did not laugh' Sarah said, lying because she 15
was afraid. But he replied, 'Oh yes, you did laugh'.

Abraham intercedes

From there the men set out and arrived within sight of Sodom, with 16
Abraham accompanying them to show them the way. •Now Yahweh had 17
wondered, 'Shall I conceal from Abraham what I am going to do, •seeing that 18
Abraham will become a great nation with all the nations of the earth blessing
themselves by him? •For I have singled him out to command his sons and his 19
household after him to maintain the way of Yahweh by just and upright living.
In this way Yahweh will carry out for Abraham what he has promised him.'
Then Yahweh said, 'How great an outcry there is against Sodom and Gomorrah! 20
How grievous is their sin! •I propose to go down and see whether or not they 21
have done all that is alleged in the outcry against them that has come up to me.
I am determined to know.'

The men left there and went to Sodom while Abraham remained standing 22
before Yahweh. •Approaching him he said, 'Are you really going to destroy 23
the just man with the sinner? •Perhaps there are fifty just men in the town. 24
Will you really overwhelm them, will you not spare the place for the fifty just
men in it? •Do not think of doing such a thing: to kill the just man with the 25
sinner, treating just and sinner alike! Do not think of it! Will the judge of

26 the whole earth not administer justice?' •Yahweh replied, 'If at Sodom I find
fifty just men in the town, I will spare the whole place because of them'.
27 Abraham replied, 'I am bold indeed to speak like this to my Lord, I who
28 am dust and ashes. •But perhaps the fifty just men lack five: will you destroy
the whole city for five?' 'No,' he replied 'I will not destroy it if I find forty-five
29 just men there.' •Again Abraham said to him, 'Perhaps there will only be forty
there'. 'I will not do it' he replied 'for the sake of the forty.'
30 Abraham said, 'I trust my Lord will not be angry, but give me leave to speak:
perhaps there will only be thirty there'. 'I will not do it' he replied 'if I find
31 thirty there.' •He said, 'I am bold indeed to speak like this, but perhaps there
will only be twenty there'. 'I will not destroy it' he replied 'for the sake of the
32 twenty.' •He said, 'I trust my Lord will not be angry if I speak once
more: perhaps there will only be ten'. 'I will not destroy it' he replied 'for the
sake of the ten.'
33 When he had finished talking to Abraham Yahweh went away, and Abraham
returned home.

The destruction of Sodom

1 **19** When the two angels reached Sodom in the evening, Lot was sitting at
the gate. As soon as Lot saw them he rose to meet them and bowed to
2 the ground. •'I beg you, my lords,' he said 'please come down to your servant's
house to stay the night and wash your feet. Then in the morning you can
continue your journey.' 'No,' they replied 'we can spend the night in the open
3 street.' •But he pressed them so much that they went home with him and
entered his house. He prepared a meal for them, baking unleavened bread,
and they ate.
4 They had not gone to bed when the house was surrounded by the men of
the town, the men of Sodom both young and old, all the people without
5 exception. •Calling to Lot they said, 'Where are the men who came to you
tonight? Send them out to us so that we may abuse them.'ᵃ
6 Lot came out to them at the door, and having closed the door behind him
7
8 said, 'I beg you, my brothers, do no such wicked thing. •Listen, I have two
daughters who are virgins. I am ready to send them out to you, to treat as it
pleases you. But as for the men, do nothing to them, for they have come under
9 the shadow of my roof.' •But they replied, 'Out of the way! Here is one who
came as a foreigner, and would set himself up as a judge. Now we will treat
you worse than them.' Then they forced Lot back and moved forward to break
10 down the door. •But the men reached out, pulled Lot back into the house,
11 and shut the door. •And they struck the men who were at the door of the house
with blindness, from youngest to oldest, and they never found the doorway.
12 The men said to Lot, 'Have you anyone else here? Your sons, your daughters
13 and all your people in the town, take them out of the place. •We are about
to destroy this place, for there is a great outcry against them, and it has reached
14 Yahweh. And Yahweh has sent us to destroy them.' •Lot went to speak to
his future sons-in-law who were to marry his daughters. 'Come,' he said
'leave this place, for Yahweh is about to destroy the town.' But his sons-in-law
thought he was joking.
15 When dawn broke the angels urged Lot, 'Come, take your wife and these
two daughters of yours, or you will be overwhelmed in the punishment of the
16 town'. •And as he hesitated, the men took him by the hand, and his wife and
his two daughters, because of the pity Yahweh felt for him. They led him out
and left him outside the town.

19 a. The unnatural vice that takes its name from this incident was condemned by the Israelites
though it was common among their neighbours. However, underlying the story is a horror of
the double offence of such behaviour towards angels (as the 'men' are revealed to be), and the
breach of the law of hospitality would also be considered serious.

As they were leading him out he said, 'Run for your life. Neither look behind 17 you nor stop anywhere on the plain. Make for the hills if you would not be overwhelmed.' •'No, I beg you, my lord,' Lot said to them •'your servant has ¹⁸/₁₉ won your favour and you have shown great kindness to me in saving my life. But I could not reach the hills before this calamity overtook me, and death with it. •The town over there is near enough to flee to, and is a little one. 20 Let me make for that—is it not little?—and my life will be saved.' •He 21 answered, 'I grant you this favour too, and will not destroy the town you speak of. •Hurry, escape to it, for I can do nothing until you reach it.' That 22 is why the town is named Zoar.

As the sun rose over the land and Lot entered Zoar, •Yahweh rained on ²³/₂₄ Sodom and Gomorrah brimstone and fire from Yahweh. •He overthrew these 25 towns and the whole plain, with all the inhabitants of the towns, and everything that grew there.ᵇ •But the wife of Lot looked back, and was turned into a 26 pillar of salt.

Rising early in the morning Abraham went to the place where he had stood 27 before Yahweh, •and looking towards Sodom and Gomorrah, and across all 28 the plain, he saw the smoke rising from the land, like smoke from a furnace.

Thus it was that when God destroyed the towns of the plain, he kept 29 Abraham in mind and rescued Lot out of disaster when he overwhelmed the towns where Lot lived.

The origin of the Moabites and the Ammonites

After leaving Zoar Lot settled in the hill country with his two daughters, 30 for he dared not stay at Zoar. He made his home in a cave, himself and his two daughters.

The elder said to the younger, 'Our father is an old man, and there is not 31 a man in the land to marry us in the way they do the world over. •Come let 32 us ply our father with wine and sleep with him. In this way we shall have children by our father.' •That night they made their father drunk, and the 33 elder slept with her father though he was unaware of her coming to bed or of her leaving. •The next day the elder said to the younger, 'Last night I slept 34 with my father. Let us make him drunk again tonight, and you go and sleep with him. In this way we shall have children by our father.' •They made their 35 father drunk that night too, and the younger went and slept with him, but he was unaware of her coming to bed or of her leaving. •Both Lot's daughters 36 thus became pregnant by their father. •The elder gave birth to a son whom 37 she named Moab; and he is the ancestor of the Moabites of our own times. The younger also gave birth to a son whom she named Ben-ammi; and he is 38 the ancestor of the Bene-ammon of our own times.ᶜ

Abraham at Gerar

20 Abraham left there for the land of the Negeb, and settled between Kadesh 1 and Shur, staying for the time being at Gerar. •Of his wife Sarah, Abraham 2 said, 'She is my sister', and Abimelech the king of Gerar had Sarah brought to him. •But God visited Abimelech in a dream at night. 'You are to die' he 3 told him 'because of the woman you have taken, for she is a married woman.' Abimelech however had not gone near her; so he said, 'My Lord, would you 4 kill innocent people too? •Did he not tell me himself, "She is my sister", 5 and did not she herself say, "He is my brother"? I did this with a clear conscience and clean hands.' •'Yes I know' God replied in the dream 'that 6 you did this with a clear conscience, and it was I who prevented you from sinning against me. That was why I did not let you touch her. •Now send the 7 man's wife back; for he is a prophet and can intercede on your behalf for your life. But understand that if you do not send her back, you will most surely die, and all your people too.'

8 So Abimelech rose early next morning and summoning all his servants
9 told them the whole story, at which the men were very much afraid. •Then
summoning Abraham Abimelech said to him, 'What have you done to us?
What wrong have I done you that you bring so great a sin on me and on my
10 kingdom? You have treated me as you should not have done.' •And Abimelech
11 asked Abraham, 'What possessed you to do this?' •'Because' Abraham
replied 'I thought there would be no fear of God here; and the people would kill
12 me because of my wife. •Besides, she is indeed my sister, my father's
13 daughter though not my mother's; and she became my wife. •So when God
made me wander far from my father's home I said to her, "There is a kindness
you can do me: everywhere we go, say of me that I am your brother". '
14 Abimelech took sheep, cattle, men and women slaves, and presented them
15 to Abraham, and gave him back his wife Sarah. •And Abimelech said, 'See,
16 my land lies before you. Settle wherever you please.' •To Sarah he said, 'Look,
I am giving one thousand pieces of silver to your brother. For you this will
17 be compensation in the eyes of all those with you...' •At Abraham's prayer God
healed Abimelech, his wife and his slave-girls, so that they could have children,
18 for Yahweh had made all the women of Abimelech's household barren on
account of Sarah, Abraham's wife.

The birth of Isaac

1 **21** Yahweh dealt kindly with Sarah as he had said, and did what he had
2 promised her. •So Sarah conceived and bore a son to Abraham in his
3 old age, at the time God had promised. •Abraham named the son born to him
4 Isaac, the son to whom Sarah had given birth. •Abraham circumcised his son
5 Isaac when he was eight days old, as God had commanded him. •Abraham
6 was a hundred years old when his son Isaac was born to him. •Then Sarah
said, 'God has given me cause to laugh; all those who hear of it will laugh with
7 me'.[a] •She added:

> 'Who would have told Abraham
> that Sarah would nurse children!
> Yet I have borne him a child in his old age.'

The dismissal of Hagar and Ishmael

8 The child grew and was weaned, and Abraham gave a great banquet on
9 the day Isaac was weaned. •Now Sarah watched the son that Hagar the Egyptian
10 had borne to Abraham, playing[b] with her son Isaac. •'Drive away that slave-
girl and her son,' she said to Abraham; 'this slave-girl's son is not to share
11 the inheritance with my son Isaac.' •This greatly distressed Abraham because
12 of his son, •but God said to him, 'Do not distress yourself on account of the
boy and your slave-girl. Grant Sarah all she asks of you, for it is through Isaac
13 that your name will be carried on. •But the slave-girl's son I will also make
14 into a nation, for he is your child too.' •Rising early next morning Abraham
took some bread and a skin of water and, giving them to Hagar, he put the
child on her shoulder and sent her away.
15 She wandered off into the wilderness of Beersheba. •When the skin of water
16 was finished she abandoned the child under a bush. •Then she went and sat down
at a distance, about a bowshot away, saying to herself, 'I cannot see the child
die'. So she sat at a distance; and the child wailed and wept.

b. The story relates to a subsidence or earthquake in the southern part of the Dead Sea, a region
which is still unstable. The fate of Lot's wife, v.26, is a popular explanation of some landmark.
c. Folk-etymology; Moab is explained as from me-ab 'from my father'; Ben-ammi, 'son of my
kinsman', is associated with 'sons of Ammon'.
21 a. 'Isaac' is a form of the Hebrew for 'God has laughed'; the name recalls 17:17 and 18:12.
Both Abraham and Sarah had laughed when it was foretold that a son would be born to them.
b. If this chapter was consistent with ch. 16, Ishmael would now be over fifteen years old.
Different sources have been conflated.

But God heard the boy wailing, and the angel of God called to Hagar from 17 heaven. 'What is wrong, Hagar?' he asked. 'Do not be afraid, for God has heard the boy's cry where he lies. •Come, pick up the boy and hold him safe, for I will 18 make him into a great nation.' •Then God opened Hagar's eyes and she saw a 19 well, so she went and filled the skin with water and gave the boy a drink.

God was with the boy. He grew up and made his home in the wilderness, 20 and he became a bowman. •He made his home in the wilderness of Paran, and his 21 mother chose him a wife from the land of Egypt.

Abraham and Abimelech at Beersheba

At that time Abimelech came with Phicol, the commander of his army, to 22 speak to Abraham, 'God is with you in all you are doing. •Swear by God to me 23 here and now that you will not trick me, neither myself nor my descendants nor any of mine, and that you will show the same kindness to me and the land of which you are a guest as I have shown to you.' •'Yes,' Abraham replied 'I swear it.' 24 Abraham reproached Abimelech about a well that Abimelech's servants 25 had seized. •'I do not know who has done this' Abimelech said. 'You yourself 26 have never mentioned it to me and, for myself, I heard nothing of it till today.' Then Abraham took sheep and cattle and presented them to Abimelech and the 27 two of them made a covenant. •Abraham put seven lambs of the flock on one 28 side. •'Why have you put these seven lambs on one side?' Abimelech asked 29 Abraham. •He replied, 'You must accept these seven lambs from me as evidence 30 that I have dug this well'. •This is why they called that place Beersheba, 31 because there the two of them swore an oath.ᶜ

After they had made a covenant at Beersheba Abimelech went off with Phicol, 32 the commander of his army, and returned to the land of the Philistines. •Abraham 33 planted a tamarisk at Beersheba and there he invoked Yahweh, the everlasting God. •Abraham stayed for a long while in the land of the Philistines. 34

The sacrifice of Isaac

22 It happened some time later that God put Abraham to the test. 'Abraham, 1 Abraham' he called. 'Here I am' he replied. •'Take your son,' God said 2 'your only child Isaac, whom you love, and go to the land of Moriah.ᵈ There you shall offer him as a burnt offering, on a mountain I will point out to you.'

Rising early next morning Abraham saddled his ass and took with him two 3 of his servants and his son Isaac. He chopped wood for the burnt offering and started on his journey to the place God had pointed out to him. •On the third 4 day Abraham looked up and saw the place in the distance. •Then Abraham said to 5 his servants, 'Stay here with the donkey. The boy and I will go over there; we will worship and come back to you.'

Abraham took the wood for the burnt offering, loaded it on Isaac, and 6 carried in his own hands the fire and the knife. Then the two of them set out together. •Isaac spoke to his father Abraham, 'Father' he said. 'Yes, my son' 7 he replied. 'Look,' he said 'here are the fire and the wood, but where is the lamb for the burnt offering?' •Abraham answered, 'My son, God himself will provide 8 the lamb for the burnt offering'. Then the two of them went on together.

When they arrived at the place God had pointed out to him, Abraham built 9 an altar there, and arranged the wood. Then he bound his son Isaac and put him on the altar on top of the wood. •Abraham stretched out his hand and seized 10 the knife to kill his son.

But the angel of Yahweh called to him from heaven. 'Abraham, Abraham' 11 he said. 'I am here' he replied. •'Do not raise your hand against the boy' the 12 angel said. 'Do not harm him, for now I know you fear God. You have not refused me your son, your only son.' •Then looking up, Abraham saw a ram 13 caught by its horns in a bush. Abraham took the ram and offered it as a burnt-offering in place of his son. •Abraham called this place 'Yahweh provi- 14 des', and hence the saying today: On the mountain Yahweh provides.

¹⁵⁄₁₆ The angel of Yahweh called Abraham a second time from heaven. •'I swear by my own self—it is Yahweh who speaks—because you have done this, because

¹⁷ you have not refused me your son, your only son, •I will shower blessings on you, I will make your descendants as many as the stars of heaven and the grains of sand on the seashore. Your descendants shall gain possession of the gates^b of their

¹⁸ enemies. •All the nations of the earth shall bless themselves by your descendants, as a reward for your obedience.'

¹⁹ Abraham went back to his servants, and together they set out for Beersheba, and he settled in Beersheba.

The descendants of Nahor

²⁰ It happened some time later that Abraham received word that Milcah, too,

²¹ had now borne sons to his brother Nahor: •Uz his first-born, Buz his brother,

²²⁄₂₃ Kemuel Aram's father, •Chesed, Hazo, Pildash, Jidlaph, Bethuel •(and Bethuel was the father of Rebekah). These are the eight children Milcah gave Nahor,

²⁴ Abraham's brother. •He had a concubine named Reumah, and she too had children: Tebah, Gaham, Tahash and Maacah.

The tomb of the patriarchs

¹⁄₂ **23** The length of Sarah's life was a hundred and twenty-seven years. •She died at Kíriath-arba, or Hebron, in the land of Canaan, and Abraham went in to mourn and grieve for her.

³⁄₄ Then leaving his dead, Abraham spoke to the sons of Heth: •'I am a stranger and a settler among you' he said. 'Let me own a burial-plot among you, so that

⁵ I may take my dead wife and bury her.' •The sons of Heth gave Abraham this

⁶ answer, 'Listen, my lord, you are God's prince amongst us; bury your dead in the best of our tombs; not one of us would refuse you his tomb and keep you from burying your dead'.

⁷ Abraham rose and bowed to the ground before the people of the land, the

⁸ sons of Heth, •and spoke to them. 'If' he said 'you are willing for me to take my dead wife and bury her, then listen to me. Intercede for me with Ephron,

⁹ Zohar's son, to give me the cave he owns at Machpelah, which is on the edge of his land. Let him make it over to me in your presence at its full price, for me

¹⁰ to own as a burial-plot.' •Now Ephron was sitting among the sons of Heth, and Ephron the Hittite answered Abraham in the hearing of the sons of Heth and

¹¹ of all the citizens of the town. •'My lord, listen to me' he said. 'I give you the land and I give you the cave on it; I make this gift in the sight of the sons of my people. Bury your dead.'

¹²⁄₁₃ Abraham bowed before the people of the land •and he spoke to Ephron in the hearing of the people of the land, 'Oh, if it be you. . . But listen to me. I will pay the price of the land; accept it from me and I will bury my dead there.'

¹⁴⁄₁₅ Ephron answered Abraham, •'My lord, listen to me. A property worth four hundred shekels of silver, what is a little thing like that between me and you?

¹⁶ Bury your dead.' •Abraham agreed to Ephron's terms, and Abraham weighed out for Ephron the silver he had stipulated in the hearing of the sons of Heth, namely four hundred shekels of silver, according to the current commercial rate.

¹⁷ Thus Ephron's field at Machpelah opposite Mamre, the field and the cave that was on it, and all the trees that were on it, the whole of its extent in every

¹⁸ direction, passed •into Abraham's possession in the sight of the sons of Heth

¹⁹ and of all the citizens of the town. •After this Abraham buried his wife Sarah in the cave of the field of Machpelah opposite Mamre, in the country of

c. 'Well of the oath' and 'Well of the sheep' are two traditional explanations of the name Beersheba.

22 a. Traditionally identified with the hill on which the Temple of Jerusalem was later built.
b. I.e., the towns.

Canaan. •And so the field and the cave that was on it passed from the sons of 20
Heth into Abraham's possession to be owned as a burial-plot.

The marriage of Isaac

24 By now Abraham was an old man well on in years, and Yahweh had blessed 1
him in every way. •Abraham said to the eldest servant of his house- 2
hold, the steward of all his property, 'Place your hand under my thigh, •I would 3
have you swear by Yahweh, God of heaven and God of earth, that you will not
choose a wife for my son from the daughters of the Canaanites among whom
I live. •Instead, go to my own land and my own kinsfolk to choose a wife for my 4
son Isaac.' •The servant asked him, 'What if the woman does not want to come 5
with me to this country? Must I take your son back to the country from which
you came?' •Abraham answered, 'On no account take my son back there. 6
Yahweh, God of heaven and God of earth, took me from my father's home, and 7
from the land of my kinsfolk, and he swore to me that he would give this country
to my descendants. He will now send his angel ahead of you, so that you may
choose a wife for my son there. •And if the woman does not want to come 8
with you, you will be free from this oath of mine. Only do not take my son back
there.' •And the servant placed his hand under the thigh of his master Abraham, 9
and swore to him that he would do it.

The servant took ten of his master's camels and something of the best 10
of all his master owned, and set out for Aram Naharaiim[d] and Nahor's town.
In the evening, at the time when women go down to draw water, he made the 11
camels kneel outside the town near the well. •And he said, 'Yahweh, God of my 12
master Abraham, be with me today, and show your kindness to my master Abraham. •Here I stand by the spring as the young women from the town come out 13
to draw water. •To one of the girls I will say: Please tilt your pitcher and let me 14
drink. If she answers, "Drink, and I will water your camels too", may she be the
one you have chosen for your servant Isaac; by this I shall know you have
shown your kindness to my master.'

He had not finished speaking when Rebekah came out. She was the daughter 15
of Bethuel, son of Milcah, wife of Abraham's brother Nahor. She had a pitcher
on her shoulder. •The girl was very beautiful, and a virgin; no man had touched 16
her. She went down to the spring, filled her pitcher and came up again. •Running 17
to meet her, the servant said, 'Please give me a little water to drink from your
pitcher'. •She replied, 'Drink, my lord', and she quickly lowered her pitcher on 18
her arm and gave him a drink. •When she had finished letting him drink, she said, 19
'I will draw water for your camels, too, until they have had enough'. •She 20
quickly emptied her pitcher into the trough, and ran to the well again to draw
water, and drew water for all the camels •while the man watched in silence, 21
wondering whether Yahweh had made his journey successful or not.

When the camels had finished drinking, the man took a gold ring weighing 22
half a shekel, and put it through her nostril, and put on her arms two bracelets
weighing ten gold shekels, •and he said, 'Whose daughter are you? Please tell me. 23
Is there room at your father's house for us to spend the night?' •She answered, 24
'I am the daughter of Bethuel, the son whom Milcah bore to Nahor'. •And she 25
went on, 'We have plenty of straw and fodder, and room to lodge'. •Then the 26
man bowed down and worshipped Yahweh •saying, 'Blessed be Yahweh, God 27
of my master Abraham, for he has not stopped showing kindness and
goodness to my master. Yahweh has guided my steps to the house of my master's
brother.'

The girl ran to her mother's house to tell what had happened. •Now Rebekah 28/29
had a brother called Laban, and Laban ran out to the man at the spring. •As soon 30
as he had seen the ring and the bracelets his sister was wearing, and had heard
his sister Rebekah saying, 'This is what the man said to me', he went to the man
and found him still standing by his camels at the spring. •He said to him, 'Come 31

in, blessed of Yahweh, why stay out here when I have cleared the house and made
32 room for the camels?' •The man went to the house, and Laban unloaded the
camels. He provided straw and fodder for the camels and water for him and his
companions to wash their feet.

33   They offered him food, but he said, 'I will eat nothing before I have said what
34 I have to say'. Laban said, 'Speak'. •He said, 'I am the servant of Abraham.
35 Yahweh has overwhelmed my master with blessings, and Abraham is now very
rich. He has given him flocks and herds, silver and gold, men slaves and women
36 slaves, camels and donkeys. •Sarah, my master's wife, bore him a son in his old
37 age, and he has made over all his property to him. •My master made me take
this oath, "You are not to choose a wife for my son from the daughters of the
38 Canaanites in whose country I live. •Curse you if you do not go to my father's
39 home and to my kinsfolk to choose a wife for my son." •I said to my master:
40 Suppose the woman will not agree to come with me? •and his reply was, "Yahweh, in whose presence I have walked, will send his angel to make your journey
successful; you shall choose a wife for my son from my kinsfolk and from my
41 father's house. •So doing, you will be free from my curse: you will have gone to
42 my family, and if they refuse you, you will be free from my curse." •Arriving
today at the spring I said: Yahweh, God of my master Abraham, show me, I
43 pray, if you intend to make my journey successful. •Here I stand, by the
spring: when a girl comes out to draw water and I say to her: Please let me drink
44 a little water from your pitcher, •and she replies, "Drink by all means, and I will
draw water for your camels too", may she be the wife Yahweh has chosen for my
45 master's son: •I was still turning this over in my mind when Rebekah came out,
her pitcher on her shoulder. She came down to the spring and drew water. I said
46 to her: Please give me a drink. •Quickly she lowered her pitcher saying, "Drink,
47 and I will water your camels too". •I asked her: Whose daughter are you?
She replied, "I am the daughter of Bethuel, whom Milcah bore to Nahor". Then
48 I put this ring through her nostrils and these bracelets on her arms. •I bowed
down and worshipped Yahweh, and I blessed Yahweh, God of my master
Abraham, who had so graciously led me to choose the daughter of my master's
49 brother for his son. •Now tell me whether you are prepared to show
kindness and goodness to my master; if not, say so, and I shall know what
to do.'

50   Laban and Bethuel replied, 'This is from Yahweh; it is not in our power to
51 say yes or no to you. •Rebekah is there before you. Take her and go; and let her
52 become the wife of your master's son, as Yahweh has decreed.' •On hearing this
53 Abraham's servant prostrated himself on the ground before Yahweh. •He brought
out silver and gold ornaments and clothes which he gave to Rebekah; he also
gave rich presents to her brother and to her mother.

54   They ate and drank, he and his companions, and they spent the night there.
55 Next morning when they were up, he said, 'Let me go back to my master'. •Rebe-
kah's brother and mother replied, 'Let the girl stay with us a few days, perhaps
56 ten; after that she may go'. •But he replied, 'Do not delay me; it is Yahweh who
57 has made my journey successful; let me leave to go back to my master'. •They
58 replied, 'Let us call the girl and find out what she has to say'. •They called
Rebekah and asked her, 'Do you want to leave with this man?' 'I do' she replied.
59 Accordingly they let their sister Rebekah go, with her nurse, and Abraham's
60 servant and his men. •They blessed Rebekah in these words:

> 'Sister of ours, increase
> to thousands and tens of thousands!
> May your descendants gain possession
> of the gates of their enemies!'

24 a. 'Aram of the Rivers', Upper Mesopotamia.

Rebekah and her servants stood up, mounted the camels, and followed the man. 61
The servant took Rebekah and departed.

Isaac, who lived in the Negeb, had meanwhile come into the wilderness of 62
the well of Lahai Roi. •Now Isaac went walking in the fields as evening fell, and 63
looking up saw camels approaching. •And Rebekah looked up and saw Isaac. She 64
jumped down from her camel, •and asked the servant, 'Who is that man walking 65
through the fields to meet us?' The servant replied, 'That is my master'; then she
took her veil and hid her face. •The servant told Isaac the whole story, 66
and Isaac led Rebekah into his tent and made her his wife; and he loved her. 67
And so Isaac was consoled for the loss of his mother.

The descendants of Keturah

25 Abraham married another wife whose name was Keturah; •and she bore $\frac{1}{2}$
him Zimram, Jokshan, Medan, Midian, Ishbak and Shuah.—•Jokshan 3
was the father of Sheba and Dedan, and the sons of Dedan were the Asshurites,
the Letushim and the Leummim.—•The sons of Midian are Ephah, Epher, 4
Hanoch, Abida and Eldaah. All these are sons of Keturah.

Abraham gave all his possessions to Isaac. •To the sons of his concubines $\frac{5}{6}$
Abraham gave presents, and during his lifetime he sent them away from his son
Isaac eastward, to the east country.

The death of Abraham

The number of years Abraham lived was a hundred and seventy-five. •Then $\frac{7}{8}$
Abraham breathed his last, dying at a ripe old age, an old man who had lived
his full span of years; and he was gathered to his people. •His sons Isaac and 9
Ishmael buried him in the cave of Machpelah opposite Mamre, in the field
of Ephron the Hittite, son of Zohar. •This was the field that Abraham had bought 10
from the sons of Heth, and Abraham and his wife Sarah were buried there.
After Abraham's death God blessed his son Isaac, and Isaac lived near the well 11
of Lahai Roi.

The descendants of Ishmael

These are the descendants of Ishmael, the son of Abraham by Hagar, Sarah's 12
Egyptian maidservant. •These are the names of the sons of Ishmael in the order 13
of their birth: Ishmael's first born was Nebaioth; then Kedar, Adbeel, Mibsam,
Mishma, Dumah, Massa, •Hadad, Tema, Jetur, Naphish and Kedemah. •These $^{14,1}_{16}$
are the sons of Ishmael, and these are their names, according to their settlements
and encampments, twelve chiefs of as many tribes.

The number of years Ishmael lived was one hundred and thirty-seven. Then 17
he breathed his last, died, and was gathered to his people. •He lived in the terri- 18
tory stretching from Havilah to Shur, which is to the east of Egypt, on the way
to Assyria. He set himself to defy his brothers.

III. THE STORY OF ISAAC AND JACOB

The birth of Esau and Jacob

This is the story of Isaac son of Abraham. 19
Abraham was the father of Isaac. •Isaac was forty years old when he married 20
Rebekah, the daughter of Bethuel the Aramaean of Paddan-aram, and sister of
Laban the Aramaean. •Isaac prayed to Yahweh on behalf of his wife, for she was 21
barren. Yahweh heard his prayer, and his wife Rebekah conceived. •But the 22
children struggled with one another inside her, and she said, 'If this is the way
of it, why go on living?' So she went to consult Yahweh,ᵘ •and he said to her: 23

'There are two nations in your womb,
your issue will be two rival peoples.
One nation shall have the mastery of the other,
and the elder shall serve the younger.'[b]

24 When the time came for her confinement, there were indeed twins in her womb.
25 The first to be born was red, and as though he were completely wrapped in a hairy
26 cloak; so they named him Esau. •Then his brother was born, with his hand grasping Esau's heel; so they named him Jacob.[c] Isaac was sixty years old at the time
27 of their birth. •When the boys grew up Esau became a skilled hunter, a man of the
open country. Jacob on the other hand was a quiet man, staying at home among
28 the tents. •Isaac preferred Esau, for he had a taste for wild game; but Rebekah
preferred Jacob.

Esau gives up his birthright

29 Once, Jacob had made a soup, and Esau returned from the countryside ex-
30 hausted. •Esau said to Jacob, 'Let me eat the red soup, that red soup there; I
31 am exhausted'—hence the name given to him, Edom. •Jacob said, 'First sell me
32 your birthright,[d] then'. •Esau said, 'Here I am, at death's door; what use will my
33 birthright be to me?' •Then Jacob said, 'First give me your oath'; he gave him his
34 oath and sold his birthright to Jacob. •Then Jacob gave him bread and lentil soup,
and after eating and drinking he got up and went. That was all Esau cared for his
birthright.

Isaac at Gerar

1 **26** There was a famine in the land—a second one after the famine which took
place in the time of Abraham—and Isaac went to Abimelech, the Philistine
2 king at Gerar. •Yahweh appeared to him and said, 'Do not go down into Egypt;
3 stay in the land I shall tell you of. •Remain for the present here in this land, and I
will be with you and bless you. For it is to you and your descendants that I will give
4 all these lands, and I will fulfil the oath I swore to your father Abraham. •I will
make your descendants as many as the stars of heaven, and I will give them
all these lands; and all the nations in the world shall bless themselves by your
5 descendants •in return for Abraham's obedience; for he kept my charge, my
6 commandments, my statutes and my laws.' •So Isaac stayed at Gerar.
7 When the people of the place asked him about his wife he replied, 'She is my
sister', for he was afraid to say, 'She is my wife', in case they killed him
8 on Rebekah's account, for she was beautiful. •When he had been there some time,
Abimelech the Philistine king happened to look out of the window and saw Isaac
9 fondling his wife Rebekah. •Abimelech summoned Isaac and said to him, 'Surely
she must be your wife! How could you say she was your sister?' Isaac answered
10 him, 'Because I thought I might be killed on her account'. •Abimelech said, 'What
is this you have done to us? One of my subjects might easily have slept with your
11 wife, and then you would have made us incur guilt.' •Then Abimelech issued this
order to all the people: 'Whoever touches this man or his wife shall be put to death'.
12 Isaac sowed his crops in that land, and that year he reaped a hundredfold.
13 Yahweh blessed him •and the man became rich; he prospered more and more until
14 he was very rich indeed. •He had flocks and herds and many servants. The Philistines began to envy him.

25 a. At some recognised holy place.   **b.** A prediction of the enmity between the Edomites, as
descendants of Esau, and the Israelites, the descendants of Jacob.   **c.** A play on words connects
the names with Hebrew words for 'red' and 'heel' respectively, but the derivation is implausible.
d. By law, the firstborn son took precedence over his brothers, and on his father's death received
a double share of the inheritance and became the head of the family.

The wells between Gerar and Beersheba

The Philistines had sealed all the wells dug by his father's servants, filling them 15
with earth. These had existed from the time of his father Abraham. •Abimelech 16
said to Isaac, 'Leave us, for you have become much more powerful than we are'.
So Isaac left; he pitched camp in the Valley of Gerar and there he stayed. •Isaac 17/18
dug again the wells made by the servants of his father Abraham and
sealed by the Philistines after Abraham's death, and he gave them the same
names as his father had given them.

Isaac's servants dug in the valley and found a well of spring-water. •But the 19/20
shepherds of Gerar quarrelled with Isaac's shepherds, saying, 'That water is ours!'
So Isaac named the well Esek, because they had quarrelled with him. •They dug 21
another well, and there was a quarrel about that one too; so he named it Sitnah.
Then he left there, and dug another well, and since there was no quarrel about this 22
one, he named it Rehoboth, saying, 'Now Yahweh has made room for us, so that
we may thrive in the land'.[d]

From here he went up to Beersheba. •Yahweh appeared to him that night and 23/24
said:

'I am the God of your father Abraham.
Do not be afraid, for I am with you.
I will bless you and make your descendants many in number
on account of my servant Abraham.'

There he built an altar and invoked the name of Yahweh. There he pitched his 25
tent, and there Isaac's servants sank a well.

The alliance with Abimelech

Abimelech came from Gerar to see him, with his adviser Ahuzzath and the 26
commander of his army, Phicol. •Isaac said to them, 'Why do you come to me 27
since you hate me, and have made me leave you?' •'It became clear to us that 28
Yahweh was with you:' they replied 'and so we said, "Let there be a sworn treaty
between ourselves and you, and let us make a covenant with you". •Swear not to 29
do us any harm, since we never molested you but were unfailingly kind to you and
let you go away in peace. Now you have Yahweh's blessing.' •He then made them 30
a feast and they ate and drank.

Rising early in the morning, they exchanged oaths. Then Isaac bade them 31
farewell and they went from him in peace. •Now it was on the same day that 32
Isaac's servants brought him news of the well they had dug. 'We have found
water!' they said to him. •So he called the well Sheba, and hence the town is 33
named Beersheba to this day.

The Hittite wives of Esau

When Esau was forty years old he married Judith, the daughter of Beeri the 34
Hittite, and Basemach, the daughter of Elon the Hittite. •These were a bitter 35
disappointment to Isaac and Rebekah.

Jacob obtains Isaac's blessing by cunning

27 Isaac had grown old, and his eyes were so weak that he could no longer see. 1
He summoned his elder son Esau, 'My son!' he said to him, and the latter
answered, 'I am here'. •Then he said, 'See, I am old and do not know when I may 2
die. •Now take your weapons, your quiver and bow; go out into the country and 3
hunt me some game. •Make me the kind of savoury I like and bring it to me, 4
so that I may eat, and give you my blessing before I die.'

Rebekah happened to be listening while Isaac was talking to his son Esau. So 5
when Esau went into the country to hunt game for his father, •Rebekah 6
said to her son Jacob, 'I have just heard your father saying to your brother
Esau, •"Bring me some game and make a savoury for me. Then I shall eat, 7

8 and bless you in the presence of Yahweh before I die." •Now my son, listen to me
9 and do as I tell you. •Go to the flock, and bring me back two good kids, so that I
10 can make the kind of savoury your father likes. •Then you can take it to your
father for him to eat so that he may bless you before he dies.'

11 Jacob said to his mother Rebekah, 'Look, my brother Esau is hairy, while I am
12 smooth-skinned. •If my father happens to touch me, he will see I am cheating him,
13 and I shall bring down a curse on myself instead of a blessing.' •But his mother
answered him, 'On me be the curse, my son! Just listen to me; go and fetch me the
14 kids.' •So he went to fetch them, and he brought them to his mother, and she
15 made the kind of savoury his father liked. •Rebekah took her elder son Esau's
best clothes, which she had in the house, and dressed her younger son Jacob in
16 them, •covering his arms and the smooth part of his neck with the skins of the
17 kids. •Then she handed the savoury and the bread she had made to her
son Jacob.

18 He presented himself before his father and said, 'Father'. 'I am here;' was the
19 reply 'who are you, my son?' •Jacob said to his father, 'I am Esau your first-born;
I have done as you told me. Please get up and take your place and eat the game I
20 have brought and then give me your blessing.' •Isaac said to his son, 'How quickly
you found it, my son!' 'It was Yahweh your God' he answered 'who put it in my
21 path.' •Isaac said to Jacob, 'Come here, then, and let me touch you, my son, to
22 know if you are my son Esau or not'. •Jacob came close to his father Isaac, who
touched him and said, 'The voice is Jacob's voice but the arms are the arms of
23 Esau!' •He did not recognise him, for his arms were hairy like his brother Esau's,
24 and so he blessed him. •He said, 'Are you really my son Esau?' And he replied,
25 'I am'. •Isaac said, 'Bring it here that I may eat the game my son has brought,
and so may give you my blessing'. He brought it to him and he ate; he offered him
26 wine, and he drank. •His father Isaac said to him, 'Come closer, and kiss me, my
27 son'. •He went closer and kissed his father, who smelled the smell of his clothes.
He blessed him saying:

'Yes, the smell of my son
is like the smell of a fertile field blessed by Yahweh.
28   May God give you
dew from heaven,
and the richness of the earth,
abundance of grain and wine!
29   May nations serve you
and peoples bow down before you!
Be master of your brothers;
may the sons of your mother bow down before you!
Cursed be he who curses you;
blessed be he who blesses you!'

30 As soon as Isaac had finished blessing Jacob, and just when Jacob was leaving
31 the presence of his father Isaac, his brother Esau returned from hunting. •He too
made a savoury and brought it to his father. He said to him, 'Father, get up and
32 eat the game your son has brought and then give me your blessing!' •His father
33 Isaac asked him, 'Who are you?' 'I am your firstborn son, Esau' he replied. •At
this Isaac was seized with a great trembling and said, 'Who was it, then, that went
hunting and brought me game? Unsuspecting I ate before you came; I blessed
34 him, and blessed he will remain! •When Esau heard his father's words, he cried
35 out loudly and bitterly to his father, 'Father, bless me too!' •But he replied, 'Your
36 brother came by fraud and took your blessing'. •Esau said, 'Is it because his name
is Jacob, that he has now supplanted me twice? First he took my birthright, and
look, now he has taken my blessing! But' he added 'have you not kept a blessing

26 a. *Esek* means 'quarrel', *Sitnah* 'accusation', *Rehoboth* 'room, space'.

for me?' •Isaac answered Esau, 'See, I have made him your master; I have given 37
him all his brothers as servants, I have provided him with grain and wine. What
can I do for you, my son?' •Esau said to his father, 'Was that your only blessing, 38
father? Father, give me a blessing too.' Isaac remained silent, and Esau burst into
tears. •Then his father Isaac gave him this answer: 39

> 'Far from the richness of the earth
> shall be your dwelling-place,
> far from the dew that falls from heaven.
> You shall live by your sword, 40
> and you shall serve your brother.

But when you win your freedom, you shall shake his yoke from your neck.' [a]

Esau hated Jacob because of the blessing his father had given him, and thought 41
thus to himself, 'The time to mourn for my father will soon be here. Then I will
kill my brother Jacob.' •When the words of Esau, her elder son, were repeated to 42
Rebekah, she sent for her younger son Jacob and said to him, 'Look, your brother
Esau means to take revenge and kill you. •Now, my son, listen to me; go away 43
and take refuge with my brother Laban in Haran. •Stay with him a while, until 44
your brother's fury cools, •until your brother's anger against you cools and he 45
forgets what you have done to him. Then I will send someone to bring you back.
Why should I lose you both on the same day?'

Isaac sends Jacob to Laban

Rebekah said to Isaac, 'I am tired to death because of the daughters of Heth. 46
If Jacob marries one of the daughters of Heth like these, one of the women of the
country, what meaning is there left in life for me?'

28 Isaac summoned Jacob and blessed him; and he gave him this order: 'You 1
are not to choose a wife from the Canaanite women. •Away now to 2
Paddan-aram, the home of Bethuel, your mother's father, and there choose a wife
for yourself among the daughters of Laban, your mother's brother. •May El 3
Shaddai bless you; may he make you fruitful and make you multiply so that you
become a group of nations. •May he grant you the blessing of Abraham, and your 4
descendants after you, so that you may take possession of the land in which you
live now, which God gave to Abraham.' •Isaac sent Jacob away, and Jacob went to 5
Paddan-aram, to Laban the son of Bethuel, the Aramaean, and brother of
Rebekah, the mother of Jacob and Esau.

Another marriage of Esau

Esau saw that Isaac had blessed Jacob and sent him to Paddan-aram to choose 6
a wife there, and that in blessing him he had given him this order: 'You are not to
choose a wife from the Canaanite women', •and that in obedience to his father 7
and mother Jacob had gone to Paddan-aram. •Esau saw from this that the women 8
of Canaan were not held in favour by his father Isaac, •so he went to Ishmael and 9
chose for wife, in addition to the wives he had, Mahalath, daughter of Abraham's
son Ishmael and sister of Nebaioth.

Jacob's dream

Jacob left Beersheba and set out for Haran. •When he had reached a certain 10
place he passed the night there, since the sun had set. Taking one of the stones 11
to be found at that place, he made it his pillow and lay down where he was. •He 12
had a dream: a ladder was there, standing on the ground with its top reaching
to heaven; and there were angels of God going up it and coming down. •And 13
Yahweh was there, standing over him, saying, 'I am Yahweh, the God of Abraham
your father, and the God of Isaac. I will give to you and your descendants the land
on which you are lying. •Your descendants shall be like the specks of dust on the 14
ground; you shall spread to the west and the east, to the north and the south,

and all the tribes of the earth shall bless themselves by you and your descendants.
15 Be sure that I am with you; I will keep you safe wherever you go, and bring you
back to this land, for I will not desert you before I have done all that I have
16 promised you.' •Then Jacob awoke from his sleep and said, 'Truly, Yahweh is in
17 this place and I never knew it!' •He was afraid and said, 'How awe-inspiring
this place is! This is nothing less than a house of God; this is the gate of heaven!'
18 Rising early in the morning, Jacob took the stone he had used for his pillow, and
19 set it up as a monument, pouring oil over the top of it. •He named the place
Bethel,ᵃ but before that the town was called Luz.
20   Jacob made this vow, 'If God goes with me and keeps me safe on this journey I
21 am making, if he gives me bread to eat and clothes to wear, •and if I return home
22 safely to my father, then Yahweh shall be my God. •This stone I have set up as a
monument shall be a house of God, and I will surely pay you a tenth part of all you
give me.'

Jacob arrives at Laban's home

1
2 **29** Moving on, Jacob went to the land of the sons of the East. •He looked and
there in the fields was a well with three flocks of sheep lying beside it, for
this well was used for watering the flocks. Now the stone on the mouth of the well
3 was a large one; •so they used to gather all the flocks there, and then roll the stone
off the mouth of the well, to water the sheep; then they put the stone back in its
4 place over the mouth of the well. •Jacob said to the shepherds, 'Brothers, where
5 are you from?' They replied, 'We are from Haran'. •Then he asked them, 'Do you
6 know Laban, the son of Nahor?' 'We know him' they replied. •Then he asked
them, 'Does all go well with him?' 'Yes,' they replied 'and here comes his daugh-
7 ter Rachel with the sheep.' •Then he said, 'See, it is still broad daylight; it is not
yet time to bring the animals in. Water the sheep and go and take them back to
8 pasture.' •But they answered, 'We cannot do that until all the flocks are gathered
and they roll the stone off the mouth of the well; then we shall water the sheep'.
9   He was still talking to them, when Rachel came with the sheep belonging to
10 her father, for she was a shepherdess. •As soon as Jacob saw Rachel, the daughter
of his uncle Laban, and the sheep of his uncle Laban, he came up and, rolling the
11 stone off the mouth of the well, he watered the sheep of his uncle Laban. •Jacob
12 kissed Rachel and burst into tears. •He told Rachel he was her father's kinsman
13 and Rebekah's son, and she ran to tell her father. •As soon as he heard her speak
of his sister's son Jacob, Laban ran to meet him; and embracing him he kissed
him warmly, and brought him to his house. Jacob told Laban everything that
14 had happened, •and Laban said to him, 'Truly you are my bone and flesh!'
And Jacob stayed with him for a month.

Jacob's two marriages

15   Laban said to Jacob, 'Because you are my kinsman, are you to work for me
16 without payment? Tell me what wages you want.' •Now Laban had two daugh-
17 ters, the elder named Leah, and the younger Rachel. •There was no sparkle in
18 Leah's eyes, but Rachel was shapely and beautiful, •and Jacob had fallen in
love with Rachel. So his answer was, 'I will work for you seven years to win
19 your younger daughter Rachel'. •Laban replied, 'It is better for me to give her to
you than to a stranger; stay with me'.
20   To win Rachel, therefore, Jacob worked seven years, and they seemed to him
21 like a few days because he loved her so much. •Then Jacob said to Laban, 'Give
22 me my wife, for my time is finished, and I should like to go to her'. •Laban gather-
23 ed all the people of the place together, and gave a banquet. •But when night came
he took his daughter Leah and brought her to Jacob, and he slept with her.

27 a. This sentence, not a part of the verse, may have been added after the Edomites had regained their freedom.
28 a. The house of God.

(Laban gave his slave-girl Zilpah to be his daughter Leah's slave.) •When morn- 24
ing came, there was Leah.ᵃ So Jacob said to Laban, 'What is this you have done 25
to me? Did I not work for you to win Rachel? Why then have you tricked
me?' •Laban answered, 'It is not the custom in our country to give the younger 26
before the elder. •Finish this marriage week and I will give you the other one too 27
in return for your working with me another seven years.' •Jacob did this, and 28
when the week was over, Laban gave him his daughter Rachel as his wife.
(Laban gave his daughter Rachel his slave-girl Bilhah to be her slave.) •So Jacob 29
slept with Rachel also, and he loved Rachel more than Leah. He worked with 30
Laban another seven years.

The sons of Jacob

Yahweh saw that Leah was neglected, so he opened her womb, while Rachel 31
remained barren. •Leah conceived and gave birth to a son whom she named 32
Reuben,ᵇ 'Because' she said 'Yahweh has seen my misery; now my husband will
love me'. •Again she conceived and gave birth to a son, saying, 'Yahweh has heard 33
that I was neglected, so he has given me this one too'; and she named him Simeon.
Again she conceived and gave birth to a son, saying, 'This time my husband will 34
be united to me, for I have now borne three sons to him'; accordingly, she
named him Levi. •Again she conceived and gave birth to a son, saying, 'This 35
time I will give glory to Yahweh'; accordingly she named him Judah. Then she had
no more children.

30 Rachel, seeing that she herself gave Jacob no children, became jealous of 1
her sister. And she said to Jacob, 'Give me children, or I shall die!' •This 2
made Jacob angry with Rachel, and he retorted, 'Am I in God's place? It is he who
has refused you motherhood.' •So she said, 'Here is my slave-girl, Bilhah. Sleep 3
with her so that she may give birth on my knees; through her, then, I too shall
have children!' •So she gave him her slave-girl Bilhah as a wife. Jacob slept with 4
her, •and Bilhah conceived and gave birth to a son by Jacob. •Then Rachel said, 5/6
'God has done me justice; yes, he has heard my prayer and given me a son'.
Accordingly she named him Dan. •Again Rachel's slave-girl Bilhah conceived 7
and gave birth to a second son by Jacob. •Then Rachel said, 'I have fought God's 8
fight with my sister, and I have won'; so she named him Naphtali.

Now Leah, seeing that she had no more children, took her slave-girl Zilpah 9
and gave her to Jacob as a wife. •So Leah's slave-girl Zilpah gave birth to a son by 10
Jacob. •Then Leah exclaimed, 'What good fortune!' So she named him Gad. 11
Leah's slave-girl Zilpah gave birth to a second son by Jacob. •Then Leah said, 12/13
'What happiness! Women will call me happy!' So she named him Asher.

Going out when they were harvesting the corn, Reuben found some man- 14
drakesᵃ and brought them to his mother Leah. Rachel said to Leah, 'Please give
me some of your son's mandrakes'. •But Leah replied, 'Is it not enough to have 15
taken my husband that you should want to take my son's mandrakes too?' So
Rachel said, 'Very well, he shall sleep with you tonight in return for your son's
mandrakes'. •When Jacob came back from the fields that night, Leah went out to 16
meet him, saying, 'You must come to me, for I have hired you at the price of my
son's mandrakes'. So he slept with her that night. •God heard Leah, and she 17
conceived and gave birth to a fifth son by Jacob. •Then Leah said, 'God has paid 18
me my wages for giving my slave-girl to my husband'. So she named him Issachar.
Again Leah conceived and gave birth to a sixth son by Jacob, •saying, 'God has 19/20
given me a fine gift; now my husband will honour me, for I have borne six children
to him'. So she named him Zebulun. •Later she gave birth to a daughter and 21
named her Dinah.

Then God remembered Rachel; he heard her and opened her womb. •She 22/23
conceived and gave birth to a son, saying, 'God has taken away my shame'. •So 24
she named him Joseph, saying, 'May Yahweh give me another son!'

How Jacob becomes rich

25 When Rachel had given birth to Joseph, Jacob said to Laban, 'Release me, and
26 then I can go home to my own country. •Give me my wives for whom I have
worked for you, and my children, so that I can go. You know very well the work
27 I have done for you.' •Laban said to him, 'If I have won your friendship. . . I
28 learned from the omens that Yahweh had blessed me on your account. •So name
29 your wages,' he added 'and I will pay you.' •He answered him, 'You know very
well how hard I have worked for you, and how your stock has fared in my charge.
30 The little you had before I came has increased enormously, and Yahweh has
blessed you wherever I have been. But when am I to provide for my own House?'
31 Laban said, 'How much am I to pay you?' And Jacob replied, 'You will not have
to pay me anything: if you do for me as I propose, I will be your shepherd once
more and look after your flock.

32 'Today I will go through all your flock. Take out of it every black animal
among the sheep, and every speckled or spotted one among the goats. Such shall
33 be my wages, •and my honesty will answer for me later: when you come to check
my wages, every goat I have that is not speckled or spotted, and every sheep that is
34 not black shall rank as stolen property in my possession.' •Laban replied, 'Good!
35 Let it be as you say.' •That same day he took out the striped and speckled he-
goats and all the spotted and speckled she-goats, every one that had white on it,
36 and all the black sheep. He handed them over to his sons, •and put three days'
journey between himself and Jacob. Jacob took care of the rest of Laban's flock.

37 Jacob gathered branches in sap, from poplar, almond and plane trees, and
38 peeled them in white strips, laying bare the white on the branches. •He put the
branches he had peeled in front of the animals, in the troughs in the channels
where the animals came to drink; and the animals mated when they came to drink.
39 They mated therefore in front of the branches and so produced striped, spotted
40 and speckled young. •As for the sheep, Jacob put them apart, and he turned the
animals towards whatever was striped or black in Laban's flock. Thus he built
41 up droves of his own which he did not put with Laban's flock. •Moreover, whenever the sturdy animals mated, Jacob put the branches where the animals could see
42 them, in the troughs, so that they would mate in front of the branches. •But when
the animals were feeble, he did not put them there; thus Laban got the feeble,
43 and Jacob the sturdy, •and he grew extremely rich, and became the owner of
large flocks, with men and women slaves, camels and donkeys.

Jacob's flight

1 31 Jacob learned that the sons of Laban were saying, 'Jacob has taken everything that belonged to our father; it is at our father's expense that he
2 has acquired all this wealth'. •Jacob saw from Laban's face that things were
3 not as they had been. •Yahweh said to Jacob, 'Go back to the land of your
4 forefathers and to your kindred; and I will be with you'. •So Jacob had Rachel
5 and Leah called to the fields where his flocks were, •and he said to them, 'I can see
from your father's face that I am out of favour with him now; but the
6 God of my father has been with me. •You yourselves know that I have worked
7 for your father with all my strength. •Your father has tricked me, ten times
8 changing my wages, yet God has not allowed him to harm me. •Whenever he said,
"The spotted ones shall be your wages", all the animals produced spotted young;
whenever he said, "The striped ones shall be your wages", all the animals produced
9 striped young. •Thus God has taken your father's livestock and given it to me.
10 It happened at the time when the animals were on heat, that in a dream I looked
up and saw that the males covering the females of the flock were striped or spotted

29 a. The bride was veiled until the wedding-night.   **b.** The twelve sons born to Jacob are the
ancestors of the twelve tribes of Israel. Here their names are all explained in terms of the rivalry
between Leah and Rachel.
30 a. Mandragora, regarded as an aphrodisiac.

or piebald. •In the dream the angel of God called to me, "Jacob!" And I answered: 11
I am here. •He said, "Look up and see: all the males covering the females of the 12
flock are striped or spotted or piebald, for I have seen all that Laban has done to
you. •I am the God of Bethel where you poured oil on a monument, and where 13
you made a vow to me. Now get ready to leave this country and return to the
land of your birth." '

In answer Rachel and Leah said to him, 'Have we any share left in the inher- 14
itance of our father's House? •Does he not treat us as foreigners, for he has sold 15
us and gone on to use up all our money? •Surely all the riches God has taken 16
from our father belong to us and to our children. So do all that God has told you.'

Jacob made ready and put his children and his wives on camels, •and he drove 17
all his livestock before him—with all he had acquired, the livestock belonging 18
to him which he had acquired in Paddan-aram—to go to his father Isaac in the
land of Canaan. •When Laban had gone to shear his flock, Rachel stole the house- 19
hold idols*a* belonging to her father. •Jacob outwitted Laban the Aramaean by 20
giving him no inkling of his flight. • He fled with all he had and went away, crossing 21
the River*b* and making for Mount Gilead.

Laban pursues Jacob

Three days later Laban was told that Jacob had fled. •Taking his brothers 22
with him he pursued him for seven days and overtook him at Mount Gilead. •God 23
came by night in a dream to Laban the Aramaean and said to him, 'On no account 24
say anything whatever to Jacob'. •Laban caught up with Jacob, who had pitched 25
his tent in the hills; and Laban pitched camp on Mount Gilead.

Laban said to Jacob, 'What have you done, tricking me and driving my daugh- 26
ters off like prisoners of war? •Why did you flee in secret, stealing away without 27
letting me know so that I could send you on your way rejoicing, with songs and
the music of tambourines and lyres? •You did not even let me kiss my sons and 28
daughters. You have behaved like a fool. •It is in my power to do you harm, but 29
the God of your father said to me last night, "On no account say anything whatever to Jacob". •Now it may be you really went because you had such a longing 30
for your father's House, but why did you steal my gods?'

Jacob answered Laban, 'I was afraid, thinking you were going to snatch your 31
daughters from me. •But whoever is found in possession of your gods shall not 32
remain alive. In the presence of our brothers, examine for yourself what I have,
and take what is yours.' Now Jacob did not know that Rachel had stolen them.
Laban went into Jacob's tent, and then into Leah's tent and the tent of the two 33
slave-girls, but he found nothing. He came out of Leah's tent and went into
Rachel's. •Now Rachel had taken the household idols and put them in the camel's 34
litter, and was sitting on them. Laban went through everything in the tent but
found nothing. •Then Rachel said to her father, 'Do not look angry, my lord, 35
because I cannot rise in your presence, for I am as women are from time to time'.
Laban searched but did not find the idols.

Then Jacob lost his temper and took Laban to task. And Jacob said to Laban, 36
'What is my offence, what is my crime, that you have set on me? •You have gone 37
through all my belongings; have you found anything belonging to your House?
Produce it here in the presence of my brothers and yours, and let them decide
between the two of us. •In all the twenty years I have been with you, your ewes 38
and your she-goats have never miscarried, and I have eaten none of the rams from
your flock. •As for those mauled by wild beasts, I have never brought them back 39
to you, but have borne the loss myself; you claimed them from me, whether I was
robbed by day or robbed by night. •In the daytime the heat has consumed me, 40
and at night the cold has gnawed at me, and sleep has fled from my eyes. •These 41
twenty years I have been in your house; fourteen years I have worked for you
for your two daughters, and six years for your flock; and ten times you have
changed my wages. •If the God of my father, the God of Abraham, the Kinsman 42

of Isaac, had not been with me, you would have sent me away empty-handed. But God has seen my weariness and the work done by my hands, and last night he delivered judgement.'

A treaty between Jacob and Laban

43 Laban gave Jacob this answer, 'These daughters are my daughters and these sons are my sons; these sheep are my sheep, and all that you see belongs to me. But what can I do today about my daughters, and about the sons they have borne?
44 Come now, let us make a covenant, you and I . . ., and let it serve as a witness between us.'
45
46 Then Jacob took a stone and set it up as a monument. •Jacob said to his kinsmen, 'Collect some stones', and gathering some stones they made a cairn.
47 They had a meal there, on the cairn, and •Laban called it Jegar-sahadutha while
48 Jacob called it Galeed. •Laban said, 'May this cairn be a witness between us
49 today'. That is why he named it Galeed, •and also Mizpah, because he said, 'Let Yahweh act as watchman between us when we are no longer in sight of
50 each other. •If you ill-treat my daughters or marry other women in addition to my daughters, even though no one be with us, remember: God is witness between
51 us.'. •Then Laban said to Jacob, 'Here is this cairn I have thrown up
52 between us, and here is the monument. •This cairn is a witness, and the monument bears witness: I must not pass this cairn to attack you, and you
53 must not pass this cairn and this monument to attack me. •May the God of Abraham and the god of Nahor judge between us.' Then Jacob swore by the
54 Kinsman of his father Isaac. •He offered a sacrifice on the mountain and invited his brothers to the meal. They ate the meal, and passed the night on the mountain.

1
55
2
1
3
2
32 Laban rose early next morning, and kissing his sons and daughters he blessed them. Then Laban left to return home. •While Jacob was going on his way angels of God met him, •and on seeing them he said, 'This is God's camp', and he named the place Mahanaim.

Jacob prepares for his meeting with Esau

3
5
4 Jacob sent messengers ahead of him to his brother Esau in the land of Seir, the countryside of Edom, •with these instructions, 'Say this to my lord Esau, "Here is the message of your servant Jacob: I have been staying with Laban till
6
5 now, and have acquired oxen, beasts of burden and flocks, and men and women slaves. I send news of this to my lord in the hope of winning your approval."
7
6 The messengers returned to Jacob and told him, 'We went to your brother Esau, and he is already on his way to meet you; there are four hundred men with him'.
8
7
9
8
10
9 Jacob was greatly afraid and distressed. He divided the people with him, and the flocks and cattle, into two companies, •saying, 'If Esau comes to one of the companies and attacks it, the other company will be left to escape'. •Jacob said, 'O God of my father Abraham, and God of my father Isaac, Yahweh who said
11
10 to me, "Go back to your country and family, and I will make you prosper", •I am unworthy of all the kindness and goodness you have shown your servant. I had only my staff when I crossed the Jordan[a] here, and now I can form two companies.
12
11 I implore you, save me from my brother's clutches, for I am afraid of him; he may
13
12 come and attack us and the mothers and their children. •Yet it was you who said, "I will make you prosper, and make your descendants like the sand on
14
13 the seashore, so many that it cannot be counted".' •Then Jacob passed that night there.

15
14 From what he had with him he chose a gift for his brother Esau: •two hundred
16
15 she-goats and twenty he-goats, two hundred ewes and twenty rams, •thirty camels

---

31 a. The *teraphim* or household idols.   b. Euphrates.
32 a. But the river is the Jabbok (see v.23). Some later elaboration of the original narrative seems to have been made here, and it may be thought that the whole of Jacob's prayer is an insertion in a tersely factual story.

in milk with their calves, forty cows and ten bulls, twenty she-asses and ten donkeys. •He put them in the charge of his servants, in separate droves, and he told
his servants, 'Go ahead of me, leaving a space between each drove and the next'.
He gave the first this order: 'When my brother Esau meets you and asks, "To
whom do you belong? Where are you going? Whose are those animals that you
are driving?" •you will answer, "To your servant Jacob. They are a gift sent to
my lord Esau. Jacob himself is following." ' •He gave the same order to the second
and the third, and to all who were following the droves, 'That is what you must
say to Esau when you find him. •You must say, "Yes, your servant Jacob himself
is following".' For he argued, 'I shall conciliate him by sending a gift in advance;
so when I come face to face with him he may perhaps receive me favourably'.
The gift went ahead of him, but he himself spent that night in the camp.

Jacob wrestles with God

That same night he rose, and taking his two wives and his two slave-girls and
his eleven children he crossed the ford of the Jabbok. •He took them and sent
them across the stream and sent all his possessions over too. •And Jacob was
left alone.

And there was one that wrestled with him until daybreak •who, seeing that he
could not master him, struck him in the socket of his hip, and Jacob's hip was
dislocated as he wrestled with him. •He said, 'Let me go, for day is breaking'.
But Jacob answered, 'I will not let you go unless you bless me'. •He then asked,
'What is your name?' 'Jacob', he replied. •He said, 'Your name shall no longer
be Jacob, but Israel, because you have been strong[b] against God, you shall
prevail against men'. •Jacob then made this request, 'I beg you, tell me
your name', but he replied, 'Why do you ask my name?' And he blessed him
there.

Jacob named the place Peniel, 'Because I have seen God face to face,' he said
'and I have survived'. •The sun rose as he left Peniel, limping because of his
hip. •That is the reason why to this day the Israelites do not eat the sciatic nerve
which is in the socket of the hip; because he had struck Jacob in the socket of the
hip on the sciatic nerve.

The meeting with Esau

33 Looking up Jacob saw Esau arriving with four hundred men. Accordingly
he divided the children between Leah, Rachel and the two slave-girls. •He
put the slave-girls and their children in front, with Leah and her children following, and Rachel and Joseph behind. •He himself went ahead of them and bowed
to the ground seven times before going up to his brother. •But Esau ran to meet
him, took him in his arms and held him close and wept. •Then looking up he
saw the women and children. 'Who are these with you?' he asked. Jacob answered,
'The children whom God has bestowed on your servant'. •The slave-girls then
came up with their children, and they all bowed low. •Leah also came up along
with her children, and they all bowed low. Finally Rachel and Joseph came up
and bowed low.

Esau asked, 'What was the meaning of all the company that I have met?'
'It is to win my lord's favour' he replied. •'Brother, I have plenty,' Esau answered
'keep what is yours.' •Jacob protested,' Please, if I have found favour with you,
accept the gift I offer. To speak truly, I came into your presence as into the
presence of God, but you have received me kindly. •So accept the gift I have
brought for you; since God has been generous to me, I have all I need.' And he
urged him, and Esau accepted.

Jacob leaves Esau

Esau said, 'Let us break camp and move off; I will lead you'. •But Jacob
replied, 'My lord is aware that the children are weak, and that I must consider

the sheep and the cows that have calved. If they are driven too hard, even for one
14 day, the whole drove will die. • May it please my lord to go on ahead of his servant.
For my part, I will move at a slower pace, to suit the flock I am driving and the
15 children, until I join my lord in Seir.' • Then Esau said, 'But I must at least
leave you some of the people accompanying me'. 'Why?' Jacob asked 'All I
16 desire is to win your favour.' • So that day Esau resumed his journey to
17 Seir. • But Jacob left for Succoth, where he built himself a house and
made shelters for his livestock; that is why the place was given the name
of Succoth.ᵃ

Jacob arrives at Shechem

18   Jacob arrived safely at the town of Shechem in Canaanite territory, on his
19 return from Paddan-aram. He encamped opposite the town • and for one hundred
pieces of silver he bought from the sons of Hamor, the father of Shechem, the
20 piece of land on which he had pitched his tent. • Here he erected an altar which he
called, 'El, God of Israel'.

The rape of Dinah

1 **34** Dinah, who was Jacob's daughter by Leah went out to visit the women of
2   that region. • Shechem, the son of Hamor the Hivite, who was ruler of that
3 region, saw her, carried her off and raped her, and so dishonoured her. • But he
was captivated by Dinah, the daughter of Jacob; he fell in love with the young
4 girl and comforted her. • Accordingly Shechem said to his father Hamor, 'Get me
5 this young girl, I want to marry her'. • Meanwhile, Jacob had heard how his daughter Dinah had been dishonoured, but since his sons were out in the countryside
with his livestock, Jacob said nothing until they came back.

A matrimonial alliance with the Shechemites

6
7   Hamor the father of Shechem went out to talk to Jacob. • When Jacob's sons
returned from the countryside and heard the news, these men were outraged and
infuriated that Shechem had insulted Israel by raping Jacob's daughter—an
8 offence that could not be overlooked. • Hamor said to them, 'The heart of my son
9 Shechem is set on your daughter; I beg you, let him marry her. • Ally yourselves
with us by marriage; give us your daughters and take our daughters for yourselves.
10 Stay with us and the land shall be open to you to live in or move through or own.'
11 Shechem said to the father and brothers of the young girl, 'If only I can win your
12 favour, I will give you whatever you ask. • Demand from me a huge bridal
price and gifts; I will give you as much as you ask. Only let me marry the young
girl.'
13   Then came the answer Jacob's sons gave to Shechem and his father Hamor,
14 a crafty answer because he had dishonoured their sister Dinah. • 'We cannot do
such a thing' they said to them. 'To give our sister to an uncircumcised man would
15 be a disgrace for us. • We can agree only on one condition: that you become like
16 us by circumcising all your males. • Then we will give you our daughters, taking
17 yours for ourselves; and we will stay with you to make one nation. • But if you do
not listen to us on this matter of circumcision we shall take our daughter and
18
19 go.' • Hamor and Shechem, Hamor's son, were pleased with what they heard. • The
young man did not hesitate about doing this, for he was deeply in love with Jacob's
daughter. Moreover he was the most important person in his father's household.
20   Hamor and his son Shechem went to the gate of their town and spoke to their
21 fellow townsmen saying, • 'These men are friendly; let them stay with us in
the land, and move about as freely as they like. Let us marry their daugh-
22 ters and give our daughters to them. • But these men will agree to stay with us and

b. The probable meaning of 'Israel' is 'May God show his strength', but it is here explained as
'He has been strong against God'.
33 a. 'Shelter'.

become a single nation only on this condition: all males must be circumcised as
they are. •Will not their livestock, their goods and all their cattle belong to us, 23
if only we agree to let them stay with us?' •All the citizens of the town agreed 24
to the proposal made by Hamor and his son Shechem, and so all the males
were circumcised.

The treacherous revenge of Simeon and Levi

Now on the third day, when they were still in pain, Jacob's two sons Simeon 25
and Levi, brothers of Dinah, took their swords and marched into the town
unsuspected; they killed all the males. •They put Hamor and his son Shechem to 26
the sword, took Dinah from Shechem's house and came away. •Jacob's sons 27
attacked the wounded and pillaged the town because their sister had been dishonoured. •They took away their flocks, cattle, donkeys and whatever there 28
was in the town and in the countryside. •They carried off all their riches, all 29
their little children and their wives, and looted everything to be found in their
houses.

Jacob said to Simeon and Levi, 'You have done me harm, putting me in 30
bad odour with the people of this land, the Canaanites and the Perizzites. I have
few men, whereas they will unite against me to defeat me and destroy me and my
family.' •They retorted, 'Is our sister to be treated like a whore?' 31

Jacob at Bethel

35 God said to Jacob, 'Move on now and go to Bethel and settle there. Make 1
an altar there for the God who appeared to you when you were fleeing from
your brother Esau.'

Jacob said to his family and to all who were with him, 'Get rid of the foreign 2
gods you have with you; wash, and change your clothes. •We must move on and 3
go to Bethel. There I will make an altar for the God who heard me when I was
in distress, and gave me his help on the journey I made.' •They gave Jacob all the 4
foreign gods in their possession, and the earrings that they were wearing. Jacob
buried them under the oak tree near Shechem. •They broke camp; a divine 5
terror struck the towns round about, and no one pursued the sons of Jacob.

When Jacob arrived at Luz in the land of Canaan—Bethel, in other words— 6
and all the people with him, •he built an altar there, giving the place the name 7
Bethel, because it was there that God had appeared to him when he was fleeing
from his brother. •Deborah, who had been Rebekah's nurse, died and was buried 8
below Bethel, under the oak tree; so they named it the Oak of Tears.

Once more God appeared to Jacob on his return from Paddan-aram, and 9
blessed him. •God said to him, 'Your name is Jacob, but from now on you shall 10
be named not Jacob but Israel'. Accordingly they named him Israel.

God said to him, 'I am El Shaddai. Be fruitful and multiply. A nation, indeed 11
a group of nations shall descend from you. Even kings shall be numbered among
your descendants. •I give you this land, the land I gave to Abraham and to Isaac; 12
and I will give this land to your descendants after you.' •Then God went up from 13
him.

Jacob raised a monument in the place where he had spoken with him, a stone 14
monument, on which he made a libation and poured oil. •Jacob named the place 15
Bethel where God had spoken with him.

The birth of Benjamin and the death of Rachel

They left Bethel, and while they were still some distance from Ephrath, Rachel 16
began to be in labour, and her pains were severe. •But in her difficult delivery 17
the midwife said to her, 'Do not be afraid; you have another son here'. •At 18
the moment when she breathed her last, for she was dying, she named him Ben-oni.
His father however named him Benjamin.ᵃ •So Rachel died and was buried on the 19
road to Ephrath, at Bethlehem. •Jacob raised a monument on her grave, and this 20
is the monument of the tomb of Rachel which is still there today.

Reuben's incest

21
22   Israel left and pitched his tent beyond Migdal-eder. •While Israel was living in that district, Reuben went and slept with Bilhah his father's concubine, and Israel learned of it.

The twelve sons of Jacob

23   Jacob's sons numbered twelve. •The sons of Leah: Jacob's eldest son Reuben,
24   then Simeon, Levi, Judah, Issachar and Zebulun. •The sons of Rachel: Joseph
25
26   and Benjamin. •The sons of Bilhah, Rachel's slave-girl: Dan and Naphtali. •The sons of Zilpah, Leah's slave-girl: Gad and Asher. These are the sons born to Jacob in Paddan-aram.

Isaac's death

27   Jacob reached the house of his father Isaac at Mamre, at Kiriath-arba—or
28   Hebron—where Abraham and Isaac had stayed. •Isaac was one hundred and
29   eighty years old •when he breathed his last. He died and was gathered to his people, an old man who had enjoyed his full span of life. His sons Esau and Jacob buried him.

Esau's wives and children in Canaan

1
2
36 Here are the descendants of Esau, who is Edom. •Esau married women of Canaan: Adah, the daughter of Elon the Hittite, Oholibamah, the daughter
3   of Anah, who was the son of Zibeon the Horite, •Basemath, the daughter of
4   Ishmael and sister of Nebaioth. •Adah bore to Esau Eliphaz, Basemath bore
5   Reuel, •Oholibamah bore Jeush, Jalam and Korah. These are the sons of Esau born to him in the land of Canaan.

Esau's migration

6   Esau, taking his wives, his sons and daughters, all the members of his household, his livestock, all his cattle and all the goods he had acquired in the land of
7   Canaan, left for the land of Seir away from his brother Jacob. •For they had acquired too much to live together. The land in which they were at that time could
8   not support them both because of their livestock. •That is why Edom settled in the mountainous region of Seir. Esau is Edom.

Esau's descendants in Seir

9   Here are the descendants of Esau, the father of Edom, in the mountainous region of Seir.
10   Here are the names of Esau's sons: Eliphaz the son of Adah, Esau's wife, and Reuel the son of Basemath, Esau's wife.
11
12   The sons of Eliphaz were: Teman, Omar, Zepho, Gatam, Kenaz. •Eliphaz son of Esau had Timna for concubine and she bore him Amalek. These are the sons of Adah, Esau's wife.
13   Here are the sons of Reuel: Nahath, Zerah, Shammah, Mizzah. These are the sons of Basemath, Esau's wife.
14   Here are the sons of Esau's wife Oholibamah, daughter of Anah son of Zibeon: she bore him Jeush, Jalam and Korah.

The chiefs of Edom

15   Here are the chiefs of the sons of Esau.
      The sons of Eliphaz, first-born of Esau: chief Teman, chief Omar, chief Zepho,
16   chief Kenaz, •chief Gatam, chief Amalek. These are the chiefs of Eliphaz in the land of Edom, these are the sons of Adah.
17   And here are the sons of Reuel son of Esau: chief Nahath, chief Zerah, chief Shammah, chief Mizzah. These are the chiefs of Reuel in the land of Edom, these are the sons of Basemath, Esau's wife.

35 a. Ben-oni: 'son of my sorrow'. 'Benjamin' is 'son of the right hand = son of good omen'.

And here are the sons of Oholibamah, Esau's wife: chief Jeush, chief Jalam, 18 chief Korah. These are the chiefs of Esau's wife Oholibamah, daughter of Anah. These are the sons of Esau and these are their chiefs. This is Edom. 19

The descendants of Seir the Horite

Here are the sons of Seir the Horite,[a] natives of the land: Lotan, Shobal, 20 Zibeon, Anah, •Dishon, Ezer, Dishan, these are the chiefs of the Horites, the 21 sons of Seir in the land of Edom. •The sons of Lotan were Hori and Hemam, and 22 Lotan's sister was Timna. •Here are the sons of Shobal: Alvan, Manahath, Ebal, 23 Shepho, Onam. •Here are the sons of Zibeon: Aiah, Anah—the Anah who found 24 the hot springs in the wilderness as he pastured the donkeys of his father Zibeon. Here are the children of Anah: Dishon, Oholibamah daughter of Anah. •Here $^{25}_{26}$ are the sons of Dishon: Hemdan, Eshban, Ithran, Cheran. •Here are the sons of 27 Ezer: Bilhan, Zaavan, Akan. •Here are the sons of Dishan: Uz and Aran. 28

Here are the chiefs of the Horites: chief Lotan, chief Shobal, chief Zibeon, 29 chief Anah, •chief Dishon, chief Ezer, chief Dishan. These are the chiefs of the 30 Horites according to their clans in the land of Seir.

The kings of Edom

Here are the kings who ruled in the land of Edom before an Israelite king 31 ruled. •In Edom there ruled Bela son of Beor; his city was called Dinhabah. 32 Bela died and Jobab son of Zerah, from Bozrah, succeeded. •Jobab died and $^{33}_{34}$ Husham of the land of the Temanites succeeded. •Husham died and Hadad son 35 of Bedad succeeded; he defeated the Midianites in the country of Moab, and his city was called Avith. •Hadad died and Samlah of Masrekah succeeded. •Samlah $^{36}_{37}$ died and Shaul of Rehoboth-han-nahar succeeded. •Shaul died and Baal-hanan 38 son of Achbor succeeded. •Baal-hanan died and Hadad succeeded; his city was 39 called Pau; his wife's name was Mehetabel daughter of Matred, from Me-zahab.

More chiefs of Edom

Here are the names of the chiefs of Esau according to their clans and localities, 40 by name: chief Timna, chief Alvah, chief Jetheth, •chief Oholibamah, chief Elah, 41 chief Pinon, •chief Kenaz, chief Teman, chief Mibzar, •chief Magdiel, chief Iram. $^{42}_{43}$ These are the chiefs of Edom according to their residence in the land that was theirs. This is Esau, father of Edom.

37 But Jacob lived in the land where his father had stayed, the land of 1 Canaan.

IV. THE STORY OF JOSEPH

Joseph and his brothers

This is the story of Joseph. 2

Joseph was seventeen years old. As he was still young, he was shepherding the flock with his brothers, with the sons of Bilhah and Zilpah his father's wives. Joseph informed their father of the evil spoken about them.

Israel loved Joseph more than all his other sons, for he was the son of his old 3 age, and he had a coat with long sleeves made for him. •But his brothers, seeing 4 how his father loved him more than all his other sons, came to hate him so much that they could not say a civil word to him.

Now Joseph had a dream, and he repeated it to his brothers. •'Listen' he 5 said 'to this dream I have had. •We were binding sheaves in the countryside; and 6 my sheaf, it seemed, rose up and stood upright; then I saw your sheaves gather 7 round and bow to my sheaf.' •'So you want to be king over us,' his brothers 8 retorted 'or to lord it over us?' And they hated him still more, on account of his dreams and of what he said. •He had another dream which he told to his brothers. 9

'Look, I have had another dream' he said. 'I thought I saw the sun, the moon
10 and eleven stars, bowing to me.' •He told his father and brothers, and his father
scolded him. 'A fine dream to have!' he said to him. 'Are all of us then, myself,
your mother and your brothers, to come and bow to the ground before you?'
11 His brothers were jealous of him, but his father kept the thing in mind.

Joseph sold by his brothers

12
13   His brothers went to pasture their father's flock at Shechem. •Then Israel
said to Joseph, 'Are not your brothers with the flock at Shechem? Come, I am
14 going to send you to them.' 'I am ready' he replied. •He said to him, 'Go and
see how your brothers and the flock are doing, and bring me word'. He sent him
from the valley of Hebron, and Joseph arrived at Shechem.
15   A man found him wandering in the countryside and the man asked him, 'What
16 are you looking for?' •'I am looking for my brothers' he replied. 'Please tell me
17 where they are pasturing their flock.' •The man answered, 'They have moved on
from here; indeed I heard them say, "Let us go to Dothan" '. So Joseph went
after his brothers and found them at Dothan.
18   They saw him in the distance, and before he reached them they made a plot
19 among themselves to put him to death. •'Here comes the man of dreams' they
20 said to one another. •'Come on, let us kill him and throw him into some well;
we can say that a wild beast devoured him. Then we shall see what becomes of his
dreams.'
21   But Reuben heard, and he saved him from their violence. 'We must not take
22 his life' he said. •'Shed no blood,' said Reuben to them 'throw him into this well
in the wilderness, but do not lay violent hands on him'—intending to save him
23 from them and to restore him to his father. •So, when Joseph reached his brothers,
24 they pulled off his coat, the coat with long sleeves that he was wearing, •and
catching hold of him they threw him into the well, an empty well with no water
25 in it. •They then sat down to eat.
Looking up they saw a group of Ishmaelites who were coming from Gilead,
their camels laden with gum, tragacanth, balsam and resin, which they were taking
26 down into Egypt. •Then Judah said to his brothers, 'What do we gain by killing
27 our brother and covering up his blood?[a] •Come, let us sell him to the Ishmaelites, but let us not do any harm to him. After all, he is our brother, and our own
flesh.' His brothers agreed.
28   Now some Midianite merchants were passing, and they drew Joseph up out
of the well. They sold Joseph to the Ishmaelites for twenty silver pieces, and
29 these men took Joseph to Egypt. •When Reuben went back to the well there was
30 no sign of Joseph. Tearing his clothes, •he went back to his brothers. 'The boy
has disappeared' he said. 'What am I going to do?'
31   They took Joseph's coat and, slaughtering a goat, they dipped the coat in the
32 blood. •Then they sent back the coat with long sleeves and had it taken to their
father, with the message, 'This is what we have found. Examine it and see whether
33 or not it is your son's coat.' •He examined it and exclaimed, 'It is my son's
coat! A wild beast has devoured him. Joseph has been the prey of some animal
34 and has been torn to pieces.' •Jacob, tearing his clothes and putting on a loin-
35 cloth of sackcloth, mourned his son for a long time. •All his sons and daughters
came to comfort him, but he refused to be comforted. 'No,' he said 'I will go down
in mourning to Sheol, beside my son.' And his father wept for him.

36 a. The Horites are the ancient inhabitants of Seir, and were dispossessed by the Edomites,
Dt 2:12,22.
37 a. A murderer would cover the victim's blood so that it would not cry to heaven, Ezk 24:7.
It will be noticed that two different versions of the story are combined in this chapter. In one,
Joseph's brothers are for killing him but Reuben, hoping to rescue him later, persuades them to
abandon him in a well instead, and Midianite traders extricate him and take him to Egypt.
According to the second, Joseph's brothers are for killing him but Judah suggests selling him
to a party of Ishmaelites on their way to Egypt.

Meanwhile the Midianites had sold him in Egypt to Potiphar, one of 3ˣ
Pharaoh's officials and commander of the guard.

The story of Judah and Tamar

38 It happened at that time that Judah left his brothers, to go down and stay 1
with an Adullamite called Hirah. •There Judah saw the daughter of a 2
Canaanite called Shua. He made her his wife and slept with her. •She conceived 3
and gave birth to a son whom she named Er. •She conceived again and gave birth 4
to a son whom she named Onan. •Yet again she gave birth to a son whom she 5
named Shelah. She was at Chezib when she gave birth to him.

Judah took a wife for his first-born Er, and her name was Tamar. •But Er, ⁶₇
Judah's first-born, offended Yahweh greatly, so Yahweh brought about his
death. •Then Judah said to Onan, 'Take your brother's wife, and do your duty 8
as her brother-in-law, to produce a child for your brother'. •But Onan, knowing 9
the child would not be his, spilt his seed on the ground every time he slept with
his brother's wife, to avoid providing a child for his brother. •What he did was 10
offensive to Yahweh, so he brought about his death also. •Then Judah said to 11
his daughter-in-law Tamar, 'Return home as a widow to your father, and wait
for my son Shelah to grow up', for he was thinking, 'He must not die like his
brothers'. So Tamar went back home to her father.

A long time passed, and then Shua's daughter, the wife of Judah, died. After 12
Judah had been comforted[a] he went up to Timnah to the men who sheared his
sheep, himself and Hirah, his Adullamite friend. •This was reported to Tamar, 13
'Listen, your father-in-law is going up to Timnah for the shearing of his sheep'.
She therefore changed her widow's clothes, wrapped a veil around her, and sat 14
down, heavily swathed, where the road to Enaim branches off the road to Timnah.
Shelah had now grown up, as she saw, and yet she had not been given to him as
his wife.

Judah, seeing her, took her for a prostitute, since her face was veiled. •Going ¹⁵₁₆
up to her on the road, he said, 'Come, let me sleep with you'. He did not know
that she was his daughter-in-law. 'What will you give me to sleep with me?' she
asked. •'I will send you a kid from the flock' he answered. 'Agreed, if you give 17
me a pledge until you send it' she answered. •'What pledge shall I give you?' he 18
asked. 'Your seal, your cord and the stick you are holding' she answered. He
gave them to her and slept with her, and she conceived by him. •Then she rose 19
and left him, and taking off her veil she put on her widow's weeds.

Judah sent the kid by his Adullamite friend to recover the pledge from the 20
woman. But he did not find her. •He inquired from the men of the place, 'Where 21
is the prostitute who was by the roadside at Enaim?' 'There has been no prostitute there', they answered. •So returning to Judah he said, 'I did not find her. 22
What is more, the men of the place told me there had been no prostitute there.'
'Let her keep what she has' Judah replied 'or we shall become a laughing-stock. 23
At least I sent her this kid, even though you did not find her.'

About three months later it was reported to Judah, 'Your daughter-in-law has 24
played the harlot; furthermore, she is pregnant, as a result of her misconduct'.
'Take her outside and burn her' said Judah. •But as she was being led off she sent 25
this message to her father-in-law, 'It was the man to whom these things belong
who made me pregnant. Look at them' she said 'and see whose seal and cord
and stick these are.' •Judah examined them and then said, 'She is in the right, 26
rather than I. This comes of my not giving her to my son Shelah to be his wife.'
He had no further intercourse with her.

When the time for her confinement came she was found to have twins in her 27
womb. •During the delivery one of them put out a hand, and the midwife caught 28
it and tied a scarlet thread to it, saying, 'This is the first to arrive'. •But he drew 29
his hand back, and it was his brother who came out first. Then she said, 'What
a breach you have opened for yourself!' So he was named Perez. •Then his 30
brother came out with the scarlet thread on his hand, so he was named Zerah.

Joseph's early days in Egypt

39 ¹ Now Joseph had been taken down into Egypt. Potiphar the Egyptian, one of Pharaoh's officials and commander of the guard, bought him from the ² Ishmaelites who had brought him down there. •Yahweh was with Joseph, and everything went well with him. He lodged in the house of his Egyptian master, ³ and when his master saw how Yahweh was with him and how Yahweh made ⁴ everything succeed that he turned his hand to, •he was pleased with Joseph and made him his personal attendant; and his master put him in charge of his ⁵ household, entrusting everything to him. •And from the time he put him in charge of his household and all his possessions, Yahweh blessed the Egyptian's household out of consideration for Joseph; Yahweh's blessing extended to all his ⁶ possessions, both household and estate. •So he left Joseph to handle all his possessions, and with him at hand, concerned himself with nothing beyond the food he ate.

The attempt to seduce Joseph

⁷ Now Joseph was well built and handsome, •and it happened some time later ⁸ that his master's wife looked desirously at him and said, 'Sleep with me'. •But he refused, and answered his master's wife, 'Because of me, my master does not concern himself with what happens in the house; he has handed over all his ⁹ possessions to me. •He is no more master in this house than I am. He has withheld nothing from me except yourself, because you are his wife. How could I ¹⁰ do anything so wicked, and sin against God?' •Although she spoke to Joseph day after day he would not agree to sleep with her and surrender to her.

¹¹ But one day Joseph in the course of his duties came to the house, and there ¹² was not a servant there indoors. •The woman caught hold of him by his tunic and said, 'Sleep with me'. But he left the tunic in her hand and ran out of the ¹³⁄¹⁴ house. •Seeing he had left the tunic in her hand and left the house, •she called her servants and said to them, 'Look at this! He has brought us a Hebrew to insult us. ¹⁵ He came to me to sleep with me, but I screamed, •and when he heard me scream and shout he left his tunic beside me and ran out of the house.' ¹⁶⁄¹⁷ She put the tunic down by her side until the master came home. •Then she told him the same tale, 'The Hebrew slave you bought us came to insult me. ¹⁸ But when I screamed and called out he left his garment by my side and made ¹⁹ his escape.' •When the master heard his wife say, 'This is how your slave treated ²⁰ me', he was furious. •Joseph's master had him arrested and committed to the gaol where the king's prisoners were kept.

Joseph in gaol

²¹ And there in gaol he stayed. •But Yahweh was with Joseph. He was kind to ²² him and made him popular with the chief gaoler. •The chief gaoler put Joseph in charge of all the prisoners in the gaol, making him responsible for everything ²³ done there. •The chief gaoler did not need to interfere with Joseph's administration, for Yahweh was with him, and Yahweh made everything he undertook successful.

Joseph interprets the dreams of Pharaoh's officials

40 ¹ It happened some time later that the king of Egypt's cup-bearer and his ² baker offended their master the king of Egypt. •Pharaoh was angry with his ³ two officials, the chief cup-bearer and the chief baker, •and put them under arrest in the house of the commander of the guard, in the gaol where Joseph was a ⁴ prisoner. •The commander of the guard assigned Joseph to them to attend to their wants, and they remained under arrest for some time.

⁵ Now both of them had dreams on the same night, each with its own meaning for the cup-bearer and the baker of the king of Egypt, who were prisoners

38 a. I.e., when he had observed all the mourning rites.

in the gaol. •When Joseph came to them in the morning, he saw that they looked 6
gloomy, •and he asked the two officials who were with him under arrest in his 7
master's house, 'Why these black looks today?' •They answered him, 'We 8
have had a dream, but there is no one to interpret it'. 'Are not interpretations
God's business?' Joseph asked them. 'Come, tell me.'

So the chief cup-bearer described his dream to Joseph, telling him, 'In my 9
dream I saw a vine in front of me. •On the vine were three branches; no sooner 10
had it budded than it blossomed, and its clusters became ripe grapes. •I had 11
Pharaoh's cup in my hand; I picked the grapes and squeezed them into Pharaoh's
cup, and put the cup into Pharaoh's hand.' •'Here is the interpretation of it' 12
Joseph told him. 'The three branches are three days. •In another three days 13
Pharaoh will release you and restore you to your place. Then you will hand
Pharaoh his cup, as you did before, when you were his cup-bearer. •But be sure 14
to remember me when things go well with you, and do me the kindness of reminding Pharaoh about me, to get me out of this house. •I was kidnapped from the 15
land of the Hebrews in the first place, and even here I have done nothing to
warrant imprisonment.'

The chief baker, seeing that the interpretation had been favourable, said to 16
Joseph, 'I too had a dream; there were three trays of cakes on my head. •In the top 17
tray there were all kinds of Pharaoh's favourite cakes, but the birds ate them off
the tray on my head.' •Joseph gave him this answer, 'Here is the interpretation of 18
it: the three trays are three days. •In another three days Pharaoh will release you 19
and hang you on a gallows, and the birds will eat the flesh off your bones.'

And so it happened; the third day was Pharaoh's birthday and he gave a banquet 20
for all his officials, and he released the chief cup-bearer and the chief baker in the
presence of his officials. •The chief cup-bearer he restored to his position as cup- 21
bearer, to hand Pharaoh his cup; •the chief baker he hanged. It was as Joseph 22
had said in his interpretation. •But the chief cup-bearer did not remember Joseph: 23
he forgot him.

Pharaoh's dreams

41 Two years later it happened that Pharaoh had a dream: he was standing 1
by the Nile, •and there, coming up from the Nile, were seven cows, sleek 2
and fat, and they began to feed among the rushes. •And seven other cows, 3
ugly and lean, came up from the Nile after them; and these went over and stood
beside the other cows on the bank of the Nile. •The ugly and lean cows ate the 4
seven sleek and fat cows. Then Pharaoh awoke.

He fell asleep and dreamed a second time: there, growing on one stalk, were 5
seven ears of corn full and ripe. •And sprouting up after them came seven ears 6
of corn, meagre and scorched by the east wind. •The scanty ears of corn swallowed 7
the seven full and ripe ears of corn. Then Pharaoh awoke; it was a dream.

In the morning Pharaoh, feeling disturbed, had all the magicians and wise men 8
of Egypt summoned to him. Pharaoh told them his dream, but no one could
interpret it for Pharaoh. •Then the chief cup-bearer addressed Pharaoh, 'Today I 9
must recall my offence •Pharaoh was angry with his servants and put myself 10
and the chief baker under arrest in the house of the commander of the guard.
We had a dream on the same night, he and I, and each man's dream had a 11
meaning for himself. •There was a young Hebrew with us, one of the slaves 12
belonging to the commander of the guard. We told our dreams to him and he
interpreted them, giving each of us the interpretation of his dream. •It turned 13
out just as he interpreted for us: I was restored to my place, but the other man
was hanged.'

Then Pharaoh had Joseph summoned, and they hurried him from prison. He 14
shaved and changed his clothes, and came into Pharaoh's presence. •Pharaoh 15
said to Joseph, 'I have had a dream which no one can interpret. But I have heard
it said of you that when you hear a dream you can interpret it.' •Joseph answered 16

Pharaoh, 'I do not count. It is God who will give Pharaoh a favourable answer.'
17   So Pharaoh told Joseph, 'In my dream I was standing on the bank of the
18 Nile. •And there were seven cows, fat and sleek, coming up out of the Nile, and
19 they began to feed among the rushes. •And seven other cows came up after them,
    starved, ugly and lean; I have never seen such poor cows in all the land of Egypt.
20
21 The lean and ugly cows ate up the seven fat cows. •But when they had eaten them
    up, it was impossible to tell they had eaten them, for they remained as lean as
22 before. Then I woke up. •And then again in my dream, there, growing on one
    stalk, were seven ears of corn, beautifully ripe; •but sprouting up after them came
23 seven ears of corn, withered, meagre and scorched by the east wind. •The shrivel-
24 led ears of corn swallowed the seven ripe ears of corn. I told the magicians this,
    but no one could tell me the meaning.'
25   Joseph told Pharaoh, 'Pharaoh's dreams are one and the same: God has re-
26 vealed to Pharaoh what he is going to do. •The seven fine cows are seven years
27 and the seven ripe ears of corn are seven years; it is one and the same dream. •The
    seven gaunt and lean cows coming up after them are seven years, as are the seven
    shrivelled ears of corn scorched by the east wind: there will be seven years of
28 famine. •It is as I have told Pharaoh: God has revealed to Pharaoh what he is
29 going to do. •Seven years are coming, bringing great plenty to the whole
30 land of Egypt, •but seven years of famine will follow them, when all the plenty
31 in the land of Egypt will be forgotten, and famine will exhaust the land. •The
    famine that is to follow will be so very severe that no one will remember what
32 plenty the country enjoyed. •The reason why the dream came to Pharaoh twice is
    because the event is already determined by God, and God is impatient to bring
    it about.
33   'Pharaoh should no./ choose . man who is intelligent and wise to govern the
34 land of Egypt. •Pharaoh should take action and appoint supervisors over the
    land, and impose a tax of one-fifth on the land of Egypt during the seven years of
35 plenty •They will collect all food produced during these good years that are
    coming. They will store the corn in Pharaoh's name, and place the food in the
36 towns and hold it there. •This food will serve as a reserve for the land during the
    seven years of famine that will afflict the land of Egypt. And so the land will
    not be destroyed by the famine.'

Joseph's promotion

37
38   Pharaoh and all his ministers approved of what he had said. •Then Pharaoh
    asked his ministers, 'Can we find any other man like this, possessing the spirit of
39 God?' •So Pharaoh said to Joseph, 'Seeing that God has given you knowledge
40 of all this, there can be no one as intelligent and wise as you. •You shall be my
    chancellor, and all my people shall respect your orders; only this throne shall set
41 me above you.' •Pharaoh said to Joseph, 'I hereby make you governor of the
42 whole land of Egypt'. •Pharaoh took the ring from his hand and put it on Joseph's.
43 He clothed him in fine linen and put a gold chain round his neck. •He made him
    ride in the best chariot he had after his own, and they cried before him 'Abrek'.[a]
    This is the way he was made governor of the whole land of Egypt.
44   Pharaoh said to Joseph, 'I am Pharaoh: without your permission no one is to
45 move hand or foot throughout the whole land of Egypt'. Pharaoh named Joseph
    Zaphenath-paneah, and gave him Asenath the daughter of Potiphera, priest of
    On,[b] for his wife. Joseph travelled through the land of Egypt.
46   Joseph was thirty years old when he appeared before Pharaoh king of Egypt.
    After leaving Pharaoh's presence Joseph went through the whole land of Egypt.
47
48 During the seven years of plenty, the soil yielded generously. •He collected
    all the food of the seven years when there was an abundance in the land of Egypt,

---

41 a. 'Make way'. **b.** Heliopolis; the priests of the sun-god Ra played an important part in
the politics of the country.

and allotted food to the towns, placing in each the food from the surrounding
countryside. •Joseph stored the corn like the sand of the sea, so much that they 49
stopped reckoning, since it was beyond all estimating.

Joseph's sons

Before the year of famine came, two sons were born to Joseph: Asenath, the 50
daughter of Potiphera priest of On, bore him these. •Joseph named the first-born 51
Manasseh, 'Because' he said 'God has made me forget all my suffering and all
my father's household'. •He named the second Ephraim, 'Because' he said 'God 52
has made me fruitful in the country of my misfortune'.

Then the seven years of plenty that there had been in the land of Egypt came 53
to an end. •The seven years of famine began to come as Joseph had said. There 54
was famine in every country, but there was bread to be had throughout the land of
Egypt. •When the whole country began to feel the famine, the people cried out to 55
Pharaoh for bread. But Pharaoh told all the Egyptians, 'Go to Joseph and do what
he tells you'.—•There was famine all over the world.—Then Joseph opened all the 56
granaries and sold grain to the Egyptians. The famine grew worse in the land of
Egypt. •People came to Egypt from all over the world to buy grain from Joseph, 57
for the famine had grown severe throughout the world.

The first meeting between Joseph and his brothers

42 Jacob, seeing that there was grain for sale in Egypt, said to his sons, 'Why 1
do you stand looking at one another? •I hear' he said 'that there is grain 2
for sale in Egypt. Go down and buy grain for us there, that we may survive and
not die.' •So ten of Joseph's brothers went down to buy grain in Egypt. •But ³⁄₄
Jacob did not send Joseph's brother Benjamin with his brothers. 'Nothing must
happen to him' he said.

Israel's sons with others making the same journey went to buy grain, for there 5
was famine in the land of Canaan. •It was Joseph, as the man in authority 6
over the country, who sold the grain to all comers. So Joseph's brothers went and
bowed down before him, their faces touching the ground. •When Joseph saw his 7
brothers he recognised them. But he did not make himself known to them, and he
spoke harshly to them. 'Where have you come from?' he asked. 'From the land
of Canaan to buy food' they replied.

So Joseph recognised his brothers, but they did not recognise him. •Joseph, ⁸⁄₉
remembering the dreams he had had about them, said to them, 'You are spies.
You have come to discover the country's weak points.' •'No, my lord,' they told 10
him 'your servants have come to buy food. •We are all sons of the same man. 11
We are honest men, your servants are not spies.' •'Not so!' he replied 'It is the 12
country's weak points you have come to discover.' •'Your servants are twelve 13
brothers,' they said 'sons of the same man, from the land of Canaan. The youngest, we should explain, is at present with our father, and the other one is no more.'
Joseph answered them, 'It is as I said, you are spies. •This is the test you are to ¹⁴⁄₁₅
undergo: as sure as Pharaoh lives you shall not leave unless your youngest brother
comes here. •Send one of your number to fetch your brother; you others will re- 16
main under arrest, so that your statements can be tested to see whether or not you
are honest. If not, then as sure as Pharaoh lives you are spies.' •Then he kept 17
them all in custody for three days.

On the third day Joseph said to them, 'Do this and you shall keep your lives, 18
for I am a man who fears God. •If you are honest men let one of your brothers be 19
kept in the place of your detention; as for you, go and take grain to relieve the
famine of your families. •You shall bring me your youngest brother; this way 20
your words will be proved true, and you will not have to die!' This they did.
They said to one another, 'Truly we are being called to account for our brother. 21
We saw his misery of soul when he begged our mercy, but we did not listen to him
and now this misery has come home to us.' •Reuben answered them, 'Did I not 22

tell you not to wrong the boy? But you did not listen, and now we are brought
23 to account for his blood.' •They did not know that Joseph understood, because
24 there was an interpreter between them. •He left them and wept. Then he went
back to them and spoke to them. Of their number he took Simeon and had him
bound while they looked on.

Jacob's sons return to Canaan

25 　　Joseph gave the order to fill their panniers with corn, to put back each man's
money in his sack, and to give them provisions for the journey. This was done for
26 them. •They loaded the grain on their donkeys and went away. •But when they
27
• camped for the night one of them opened his corn-sack to give fodder to his
28 donkey and saw his money in the mouth of his sack. •He said to his brothers,
'My money has been put back; here it is in my corn-sack'. Their hearts sank, and
they looked at one another in panic, saying, 'What is this that God has done to us?'
29 　　Returning to their father Jacob in the land of Canaan, they gave him a full
30 report of what had happened to them, •'The man who is lord of the land spoke
31 harshly to us, taking us for men spying on the country. •We told him, "We are
32 honest men, we are not spies. •We are twelve brothers, sons of the same father.
One of us is no more, and the youngest is at present with our father in the land of
33 Canaan." •But the man who is lord of the land said to us, "This is how I shall
know if you are honest: leave one of your brothers with me. Take the grain your
34 families stand in need of, and go. •But bring me back your youngest brother and
then I shall know that you are not spies but honest men. Then I will hand over
your brother to you, and you can trade in the country." '
35 　　As they emptied their sacks, each discovered his bag of money in his sack. On
36 seeing their bags of money they were afraid, and so was their father. •Then their
father Jacob said to them, 'You are robbing me of my children; Joseph
is no more; Simeon is no more; and now you want to take Benjamin.
All this I must bear.'
37 　　Then Reuben said to his father, 'You may put my two sons to death if I do not
38 bring him back to you. Put him in my care and I will bring him back to you.' •But
he replied, 'My son is not going down with you, for now his brother is dead he is
the only one left. If any harm came to him on the journey you are to undertake,
you would send me down to Sheol with my white head bowed in grief.'

Jacob's sons leave again with Benjamin

$^1_2$ **43** But the country was hard-pressed by famine, •and when they had finished
eating the grain they had brought from Egypt their father said to them,
3 'Go back and buy us a little food'. •'But the man expressly warned us' Judah told
him. 'He said, "You will not be admitted to my presence unless your brother is
4 with you". •If you are ready to send our brother with us, we are willing to go
5 down and buy food for you. •But if you are not ready to send him we will not go
down, for the man told us, "You will not be admitted to my presence unless your
6 brother is with you".' •Then Israel said, 'Why did you bring this misery on me by
7 telling the man you had another brother?' •They replied, 'He kept questioning us
about ourselves and our kinsfolk, "Is your father still alive?" and, "Have you a
brother?" That is why we told him. How could we know he was going to say,
8 "Bring your brother down here"?' •Judah said to his father Israel, 'Send the boy
with me. Let us start off and go, so that we may save our lives and not die, we, you,
9 and our dependants. •I will go surety for him, and you can hold me responsible
for him.^{a} If I do not bring him back to you and set him before you, let me bear the
10 blame all my life. •Indeed, if we had not wasted so much time we should have
been back again by now!'

---

43 a. As in ch. 37, the conflation of two versions is to be noticed. Judah's offer here to be surety
for the return of Benjamin is paralleled by Reuben's offer in ch. 42.

Then their father Israel said to them, 'If it must be so, then do this: take some 11
of the land's finest products in your panniers, and carry them down to the man as
a gift, a little balsam, a little honey, gum, tragacanth, resin, pistachio nuts and
almonds. •Take double the amount of money with you and return the money put 12
back in the mouths of your sacks; it may have been a mistake. •Take your brother, 13
and go back to the man. •May El Shaddai move the man to be kind to you, 14
and allow you to bring back your other brother and Benjamin. As for me, if
I must be bereaved, bereaved I must be.'

The meeting with Joseph

The men took this gift; they took double the amount of money with them, 15
and Benjamin. They started off and went down to Egypt. They presented themselves to Joseph. •When Joseph saw Benjamin with them he said to his 16
chamberlain, 'Take these men to the house. Slaughter a beast and prepare it, for
these men are to eat with me at midday.' •The man did as Joseph had ordered, 17
and took the men to Joseph's house.

The men were afraid at being taken to Joseph's house, thinking, 'We are being 18
taken there because of the money replaced in our corn-sacks the first time. They
will set on us; they will fall on us and make slaves of us, and take our donkeys
too.' •So they went up to Joseph's chamberlain and spoke to him at the entrance 19
to the house. •'By your leave, sir,' they said 'we came down once before to buy 20
food, •and when we reached camp and opened our corn-sacks, there was each 21
man's money in the mouth of his sack, to its full amount. But we have brought it
back with us, •and we have brought more money with us to buy food. We do 22
not know who put our money in our corn-sacks.' •'Peace to you,' he replied 23
'do not be afraid. Your God and your father's God has put a treasure in your
corn-sacks. Your money reached me safely.' And he brought Simeon out to
them.

The man took the men into Joseph's house. He offered them water to wash 24
their feet, and gave their donkeys fodder. •They arranged their gift while they 25
waited for Joseph to come at midday, for they had heard they were to dine there.

When Joseph arrived at the house they offered him the gift they had with them, 26
and bowed before him to the ground. •But he greeted them kindly, asking, 'Is your 27
father well, the old man you told me of? Is he still alive?' •'Your servant our father 28
is well,' they replied 'he is still alive', and they bowed low in homage. •Looking 29
up he saw his brother Benjamin, his mother's son. 'Is this your youngest brother,'
he asked 'of whom you told me?' Then he said to him, 'God be good to you, my
son'. •Joseph hurried out, for his heart was moved at the sight of his brother 30
and he was near to weeping. He went into his room and there he wept. •After 31
bathing his face he returned and, controlling himself, gave the order: 'Serve the
meal'. •He was served separately; so were they, and so were the Egyptians who 32
ate in his household, for Egyptians cannot take food with Hebrews: they have a
horror of it. •They were placed opposite him each according to his rank, from the 33
eldest to the youngest, and the men looked at one another in amazement. •He 34
had portions carried to them from his own dish, the portion for Benjamin being
five times larger than any of the others. They drank with him and were happy.

Joseph's cup in Benjamin's sack

44 Joseph gave this order to his chamberlain: 'Fill these men's sacks with as 1
much food as they can carry, and put each man's money in the mouth of his
sack. •And put my cup, the silver one, in the mouth of the youngest one's sack as 2
well as the money for his grain.' He carried out the instructions Joseph had given.

When morning came and it was light, the men were sent off with their donkeys. 3
They had scarcely left the city, and had not gone far before Joseph said to his 4
chamberlain, 'Away now and follow those men. When you catch up with them
say to them, "Why did you reward good with evil? •Is this not the one my lord 5

uses for drinking and also for reading omens? What you have done is wrong." '

6
7   So when he caught up with them he repeated these words. •They,asked him, 'What does my lord mean? Your servants would never think of doing such a thing.
8 Look, the money we found in the mouths of our corn-sacks we brought back to you from the land of Canaan. Are we likely to have stolen silver or gold from
9 your master's house? •Whichever of your servants is found to have it shall die,
10 and we ourselves shall be slaves of my lord.' •'Very well, then,' he replied 'it shall be as you say. The one on whom it is found shall become my slave, but the rest
11 of you can go free.' •Each of them quickly lifted his corn-sack to the ground, and
12 each opened his own. •He searched them, beginning with the eldest and ending
13 with the youngest, and found the cup in Benjamin's sack. •Then they tore their clothes, and when each man had reloaded his ass they returned to the city.

14   When Judah and his brothers arrived at Joseph's house he was still there, so
15 they fell on the ground in front of him. •'What is this deed you have done?' Joseph asked them. 'Did you not know that a man such as I am is a reader of omens?'
16 'What can we answer my lord?' Judah replied 'What can we say? How can we clear ourselves? God himself has uncovered your servants' guilt. Here we are then, my lord's slaves, we no less than the one in whose possession the cup was
17 found.' •'I could not think of doing such a thing' he replied. 'The man in whose possession the cup was found shall be my slave, but you can go back safe and sound to your father.'

Judah intervenes

18   Then Judah went up to him and said, 'May it please my lord, let your servant have a word privately with my lord. Do not be angry with your servant, for you
19 are like Pharaoh himself. •My lord questioned his servants, "Have you father or
20 brother?" •And we said to my lord, "We have an old father, and a younger brother born of his old age. His brother is dead, so he is the only one left of his
21 mother, and his father loves him." •Then you said to your servants, "Bring him
22 down to me that my eyes may look on him". •We replied to my lord, "The boy
23 cannot leave his father. If he leaves him, his father will die." •But you said to your servants, "If your youngest brother does not come down with you, you will
24 not be admitted to my presence again". •When we went back to your servant my
25 father, we repeated to him what my lord had said. •So when our father said,
26 "Go back and buy us a little food", •we said, "We cannot go down. If our youngest brother is with us, we will go down, for we cannot be admitted to the man's
27 presence unless our youngest brother is with us." •So your servant our father
28 said to us, "You know that my wife bore me two children. •When one left me, I said that he must have been torn to pieces. And I have not seen him to this
29 day. •If you take this one from me too and any harm comes to him, you will
30 send me down to Sheol with my white head bowed in misery." •If I go to your servant my father now, and we have not the boy with us, he will die as soon as
31 he sees the boy is not with us, for his heart is bound up with him. •Then your servants will have sent your servant our father down to Sheol with his white head
32 bowed in grief. •Now your servant went surety to my father for the boy. I said:
33 If I do not bring him back to you, let me bear the blame before my father all my life. •Let your servant stay, then, as my lord's slave in place of the boy, I implore
34 you, and let the boy go back with his brothers. •How indeed could I go back to my father and not have the boy with me? I could not bear to see the misery that would overwhelm my father.'

Joseph makes himself known

1   **45** Then Joseph could not control his feelings in front of all his retainers, and he exclaimed, 'Let everyone leave me'. No one therefore was present with
2 him while Joseph made himself known to his brothers, •but he wept so loudly that all the Egyptians heard, and the news reached Pharaoh's palace.

Joseph said to his brothers, 'I am Joseph. Is my father really still alive?' His ³
brothers could not answer him, they were so dismayed at the sight of him.
Then Joseph said to his brothers, 'Come closer to me'. When they had come closer ⁴
to him he said, 'I am your brother Joseph whom you sold into Egypt. •But now, ⁵
do not grieve, do not reproach yourselves for having sold me here, since God
sent me before you to preserve your lives. •For this is the second year there has ⁶
been famine in the country, and there are still five years to come of no ploughing or reaping. •God sent me before you to make sure that your race would have ⁷
survivors in the land and to save your lives, many lives at that. •So it was not you ⁸
who sent me here but God, and he has made me father*a* to Pharaoh, lord of all
his household and administrator of the whole land of Egypt.

'Return quickly to your father and tell him, "Your son Joseph says this: God ⁹
has made me lord of all Egypt. Come down to me at once. •You shall live ¹⁰
in the country of Goshen*b* where you will be near me, you, your children and your
grandchildren, your flocks, your cattle and all your possessions. •I will provide ¹¹
for you there, for there are still five years of famine, and I do not want you to be
in need, you and your household and all you have." •You can see with your own ¹²
eyes, and my brother Benjamin can see too that it is my own mouth speaking to
you. •Give my father a full report of all the honour I enjoy in Egypt, and of all ¹³
you have seen. Then hurry and bring my father down here.'

Then throwing his arms round the neck of his brother Benjamin he wept; and ¹⁴
Benjamin wept on his shoulder. •He kissed all his brothers, weeping over them. ¹⁵
After which his brothers talked with him.

Pharaoh's invitation

News reached Pharaoh's palace that Joseph's brothers had come, and Pharaoh ¹⁶
was pleased to hear it, as were his servants. •Pharaoh told Joseph, 'Say to your ¹⁷
brothers, "Do this: load your beasts and go off to the land of Canaan. •Fetch ¹⁸
your father and families, and come back to me. I will give you the best the land
of Egypt offers, and you shall feed on the fat of the land." •And you, for your ¹⁹
part, give them this command: "Do this: take waggons from the land of Egypt,
for your little ones and your wives. Get your father and come. •Never mind about ²⁰
your property, for the best that the land of Egypt offers is yours." '

The return to Canaan

Israel's sons did as they were told. Joseph gave them waggons as Pharaoh ²¹
had ordered, and he gave them provisions for the journey. •To each and every ²²
one he gave a festal garment, and to Benjamin three hundred shekels of silver
and five festal garments. •And he sent his father ten donkeys laden with the ²³
best that Egypt offered, and ten she-donkeys laden with grain, bread and food for
his father's journey. •Then he sent his brothers on their way. His final words to ²⁴
them were, 'Do not be upset on the journey'.

And so they left Egypt. When they reached the land of Canaan and their ²⁵
father Jacob, •they gave him this report, 'Joseph is still alive. Indeed it is he who is ²⁶
administrator of the whole land of Egypt.' But he was as one stunned, for
he did not believe them. •However, when they told him all Joseph had said to ²⁷
them, and when he saw the waggons that Joseph had sent to fetch him, the spirit
of their father Jacob revived, •and Israel said, 'That is enough! My son Joseph ²⁸
is still alive. I must go and see him before I die.'

Jacob leaves for Egypt

46 Israel left with his possessions, and reached Beersheba. There he offered ¹
sacrifices to the God of his father Isaac. •God spoke to Israel in a vision ²
at night, 'Jacob, Jacob', he said. 'I am here', he replied. •'I am God, the God of ³
your father', he continued. 'Do not be afraid of going down to Egypt, for I will
make you a great nation there. •I myself will go down to Egypt with you. I myself ⁴

5 will bring you back again, and Joseph's hand shall close your eyes.' •Then Jacob left Beersheba. Israel's sons conveyed their father Jacob, their little children and their wives in the waggons Pharaoh had sent to fetch him.

6   Taking their livestock and all that they had acquired in the land of Canaan,
7 they went to Egypt, Jacob and all his family with him: •his sons and his grandsons, his daughters and his grand-daughters, in a word, all his children he took with him to Egypt.

Jacob's family

8   These are the names of Israel's sons who came to Egypt, Reuben, Jacob's first-
9 born, •and the sons of Reuben: Hanoch, Pallu, Hezron, Carmi. •The sons of
10 Simeon: Jemuel, Jamin, Ohad, Jachin, Zohar, and Shaul the son of the Canaanite
11 woman. •The sons of Levi: Gershon, Kohath, Merari. •The sons of Judah: Er,
12 Onan, Shelah, Perez, and Zerah (though Er and Onan died in the land of Canaan),
13 and Hezron and Hamul, sons of Perez. •The sons of Issachar: Tola, Puvah,
14 Jashub and Shimron. •The sons of Zebulun: Sered, Elon, Jahleel. •These are the
15 sons that Leah had born to Jacob in Paddan-aram, besides his daughter Dinah; in all, his sons and daughters numbered thirty-three.

16   The sons of Gad: Ziphion, Haggi, Shuni, Ezbon, Eri, Arodi, and Areli.
17 The sons of Asher: Imnah, Ishvah, Ishvi, Beriah, with their sister Serah; the sons
18 of Beriah: Heber and Malchiel. •These are the sons of Zilpah whom Laban gave to his daughter Leah; she bore these to Jacob—sixteen persons.

19   The sons of Rachel, wife of Jacob: Joseph and Benjamin. •Born to Joseph in
20 Egypt were: Manasseh and Ephraim, children of Asenath, the daughter of Poti-
21 phera priest of On. •The sons of Benjamin: Bela, Becher, Ashbel, Gera, Naaman,
22 Ehi, Rosh, Muppim, Huppim and Ard. •These are the sons that Rachel bore to Jacob—fourteen persons in all.

23   The sons of Dan: Hushim. •The sons of Naphtali: Jahzeel, Guni, Jezer and
24 Shillem. •These are the sons of Bilhah whom Laban gave to his daughter Rachel;
25 she bore these to Jacob—seven persons in all.

26   The people who went to Egypt with Jacob, of his own blood and not counting
27 the wives of Jacob's sons, numbered sixty-six all told. •Joseph's sons born to him in Egypt were two in number. The members of the family of Jacob who went to Egypt totalled seventy.ᵃ

Joseph welcomes them

28   Israel sent Judah ahead to Joseph, so that the latter might present himself
29 to him in Goshen. When they arrived in the land of Goshen, •Joseph had his chariot made ready and went up to meet his father Israel in Goshen. As soon as he appeared he threw his arms round his neck and for a long time wept on his
30 shoulder. •Israel said to Joseph, 'Now I can die, now that I have seen you again, and seen you still alive'.

31   Then Joseph said to his brothers and his father's family, 'I will go up and break the news to Pharaoh. I will tell him, "My brothers and my father's family
32 who were in the land of Canaan have come to me. •The men are shepherds and look after livestock, and they have brought their flocks and cattle and all their
33 possessions." •Thus, when Pharaoh summons you and asks, "What is your occu-
34 pation?", •you are to say, "Ever since our boyhood your servants have looked after livestock, we and our fathers before us". And so you will be able to stay in the land of Goshen.' For the Egyptians have a horror of all shepherds.

45 a. A title of the vizier.   **b.** In the Nile delta.
46 a. The total of seventy-five given by Stephen in Ac 7:14 is from the Septuagint, which adds five descendants of Ephraim and Manasseh.

Pharaoh grants an audience

47 So Joseph went and told Pharaoh, 'My father and brothers, along with 1
their flocks and cattle and all their possessions, have come from the land of
Canaan and are now in the land of Goshen'. •He had taken five of his brothers, 2
and he now presented them to Pharaoh. •Pharaoh asked his brothers, 'What 3
is your occupation?' and they gave Pharaoh the answer, 'Your servants are
shepherds, like our fathers before us'. •They went on to tell Pharaoh, 'We have 4
come to stay for the present in this land, for there is no pasture for your servants'
flocks, the land of Canaan is hard-pressed by famine. Now give your servants leave
to stay in the land of Goshen.' •Then Pharaoh said to Joseph, •'They may stay in ⁵ᵃ
the land of Goshen, and if you know of any capable men among them, put them ⁶ᵇ
in charge of my own livestock'.

Another version

Jacob and his sons went to Egypt where Joseph was. Pharaoh, king of Egypt, ⁵ᵇ
heard of this and said to Joseph, 'Your father and brothers have come to you.
The country of Egypt is open to you: settle your father and brothers in the best ⁶ᵃ
region.' •Joseph brought his father and presented him to Pharaoh. Jacob blessed 7
Pharaoh. •Pharaoh asked Jacob, 'How many years of life can you reckon?' 8
'My life of wandering has lasted one hundred and thirty years,' Jacob told 9
Pharaoh 'few years and unhappy, falling short of the years of my fathers in their
life of wandering.' •Jacob blessed Pharaoh and left Pharaoh's presence. •Joseph ¹⁰
settled his father and brothers, giving them a holding in the land of Egypt, and in ¹¹
the best region of the land, namely the land of Rameses, according to Pharaoh's
command.

Joseph provided his father, brothers and all his father's family with food 12
according to the number of their dependants.

Joseph's agrarian policy

There was no bread in the whole land, for the famine had grown so severe 13
that the land of Egypt and the land of Canaan were weakened with hunger.
Joseph accumulated all the money there was to be found in the land of Egypt and 14
in the land of Canaan, in return for the grain which men were buying, and he
brought the money to Pharaoh's palace.

When all the money in the land of Egypt and in the land of Canaan had run out, 15
the Egyptians all came to Joseph: 'Give us bread' they said. 'Have we to perish
before your eyes? For our money has come to an end.' •Joseph answered, 'Hand 16
over your livestock; I am willing to give you bread in exchange for your livestock,
if your money has come to an end'. •So they brought their livestock to Joseph, and 17
Joseph gave them bread, in exchange for horses and livestock, whether sheep or
cattle, and for donkeys. Thus he fed them that year with bread, in exchange for
all their livestock.

When that year was over, they came to him the next year, and said to him, 18
'We cannot hide it from my lord: the truth is, our money has run out and the livestock is in my lord's possession. There is nothing left for my lord except our bodies
and our land. •Have we to perish before your eyes, we and our land? Buy us 19
and our land in exchange for bread; we with our land will be Pharaoh's serfs.
But give us something to sow, that we may keep our lives and not die and the
land may not become desolate.'

Thus Joseph acquired all the land in Egypt for Pharaoh, since one by one the 20
Egyptians sold their estates, so hard-pressed were they by the famine, and the
whole country passed into Pharaoh's possession. •As for the people, he reduced 21
them to serfdom from one end of Egypt to the other. •The only land he 22
did not acquire belonged to the priests, for the priests received an allowance from
Pharaoh and lived on the allowance that Pharaoh gave them. Therefore they
did not have to sell their land.

23   Then Joseph said to the people, 'This is how we stand: I have bought you out, with your land, on Pharaoh's behalf. Here is seed for you so that you can sow the
24   land. • But when harvest comes you must give a fifth to Pharaoh. The other four-fifths you can have for sowing your fields, to provide food for yourselves and your
25   households, and food for your dependants.' • 'You have saved our lives' they
26   replied. 'If we may enjoy my lord's favour, we will be Pharaoh's serfs.' • So Joseph made a statute, still in force today, concerning the soil of Egypt: a fifth goes to Pharaoh. The land of the priests alone did not go to Pharaoh.

Jacob's last wishes

27   The Israelites stayed in the land of Egypt, in the country of Goshen. They acquired property there; they were fruitful and increased in numbers greatly.
28   Jacob lived seventeen years in the land of Egypt, and the length of his life was a
29   hundred and forty-seven years. • When Israel's time to die drew near he called his son Joseph and said to him, 'If I enjoy your favour, place your hand under my
30   thigh and promise to be kind and good to me, do not bury me in Egypt. • When I sleep with my fathers, carry me out of Egypt and bury me in their tomb.' 'I will
31   do as you say' he replied. • 'Swear to me' he insisted. So he swore to him, and Israel sank back on the pillow.

Jacob adopts Joseph's two sons and blesses them

1   **48** Some time later it was reported to Joseph, 'Your father has been taken
2   ill'. So he took with him his two sons Manasseh and Ephraim. • When Jacob was told, 'Look, your son Joseph has come to you', Israel, summoning his
3   strength, sat up in bed. • 'El Shaddai appeared to me at Luz in the country of
4   Canaan,' Jacob told Joseph 'and he blessed me, • saying to me, "I will make you fruitful and increase you in numbers. I will make you a group of peoples and give
5   this country to your descendants after you, to own in perpetuity." • Now your two sons, born to you in the land of Egypt before I came to you in Egypt, shall be
6   mine; Ephraim and Manasseh shall be as much mine as Reuben and Simeon. • But with regard to the children you have had since them, they shall be yours, and they shall be known by their brothers' names for the purpose of their inheritance.
7   'When I was on my way from Paddan, to my sorrow death took your mother Rachel from me, in the land of Canaan, on the journey while we were still some distance from Ephrath. I buried her there on the road to Ephrath at Bethlehem.'
8
9   When Israel saw Joseph's two sons, he asked, 'Who are these?' • 'They are my sons, whom God has given me here' Joseph told his father. 'Then bring them
10   to me,' he said 'that I may bless them.' • Israel's sight was failing because of his great age, and so he could not see. Joseph therefore made them come closer to
11   him and he kissed and embraced them. • Then Israel said to Joseph, 'I did not think that I should see you again, but God has let me see your family as well'.
12   Joseph took them from his lap and bowed to the ground.
13   Joseph took hold of the two of them, Ephraim with his right hand so that he should be on Israel's left, and Manasseh with his left hand, so that he should be on
14   Israel's right, and brought them close to him. • But Israel held out his right hand and laid it on the head of Ephraim, the younger, and his left on the head
15   of Manasseh, crossing his hands—Manasseh was, in fact, the elder. • Then he blessed Joseph saying:

    'May God in whose presence my fathers Abraham and Isaac walked,
        may God who has been my shepherd from my birth until this day,
16   may the angel who has been my saviour from all harm, bless these boys,
        may my name live on in them, and the names of my fathers Abraham
            and Isaac.
    May they grow and increase on the earth.'

17   Joseph saw that his father was laying his right hand on the head of Ephraim,

and this upset him. He took his father's hand and tried to shift it from the head of Ephraim to the head of Manasseh. •Joseph protested to his father, 'Not 18 like that, father! This one is the elder; put your right hand on his head.' •But his 19 father refused. 'I know, my son, I know' he said. 'He too shall become a people; he too shall be great. Yet his younger brother shall be greater than he, and his descendants shall become a multitude of nations.'

So he blessed them that day saying: 20

> 'May you be a blessing in Israel; may they say,
> "God make you like Ephraim and Manasseh!" '

In this way he put Ephraim before Manasseh.

Then Israel said to Joseph, 'Now I am about to die. But God will be with you 21 and take you back to the country of your fathers. •As for me, I give you a She- 22 chem *a* more than your brothers, the one I took from the Amorites with my sword and my bow.'

Jacob's blessings

49 Jacob called his sons and said, 'Gather together that I may declare to you 1 what lies before you in time to come.

> 'Gather round, sons of Jacob, and listen;   2
> listen to Israel your father.
>
> Reuben, you are my first-born,   3
> my vigour, and the first-fruit of my manhood,
> foremost in pride, foremost in strength,
> uncontrolled as a flood: you shall not be foremost,   4
> for you mounted your father's bed,
> and so defiled my couch, to my hurt.
>
> 'Simeon and Levi are brothers,   5
> they carried out their malicious plans.
> Let my soul not enter into their counsel   6
> nor my heart join in their company,
> for in their rage they have killed men,
> in their fury they hamstrung bulls.
> Accursed be their rage for its ruthlessness,   7
> their wrath for its ferocity.
> I will divide them among Jacob,
> I will scatter them among Israel.*a*
>
> 'Judah, your brothers shall praise you: 8
> you grip your enemies by the neck,
> your father's sons shall do you homage,
> Judah is a lion cub,   9
> you climb back, my son, from your kill;
> like a lion he crouches and lies down,
> or a lioness: who dare rouse him?
> The sceptre shall not pass from Judah,   10
> nor the mace from between his feet,
> until he come to whom it belongs,
> to whom the peoples shall render obedience.
> He ties up his young ass to the vine,   11
> to its stock the foal of his she-ass.
> He washes his coat in wine,
> his cloak in the blood of the grape;
> his eyes are cloudy with wine,   12
> his teeth are white with milk.

13   Zebulun lives by the shore of the sea,
       he is a sailor on board the ships,
       he has Sidon close by him.

14   'Issachar is a strong ass,
       lying down in the midst of the sheepfolds.

15   He saw how good it was to take his ease,
       how pleasant was the country,
       so he bowed his shoulders for the load,
       he became a slave to forced labour.[b]

16   'Dan is judge of his people
       like each one of the tribes of Israel.

17   May Dan be a serpent on the road,
       a viper on the path,
       who bites the horse on the hock
       and its rider falls backward.

18   'I trust in your salvation, Yahweh.

19   'Gad, robbers rob him,
       and he, he robs and pursues them.

20   'Asher, his bread is rich,
       he provides food fit for a king.

21   'Naphtali is a swift hind,
       dropping beautiful fawns.

22   'Joseph is a fruitful creeper near the spring,
       whose tendrils climb over the wall.

23   Bowmen provoked him,
       they drew and assailed him.

24   But their bow was broken by a mighty one,
       the sinews of their arms were parted
       by the hands of the Mighty One of Jacob,
       by the name of the Stone of Israel,

25   by the God of your father who assists you,
       by El Shaddai who blesses you:
       with blessings of heaven above,
       blessings of the deep lying below,
       blessings of breasts and womb,

26   blessings of grain and flowers,
       blessings of ancient mountains;
       bounty of the everlasting hills;
       may they descend on Joseph's head,
       on the brow of the dedicated one among his brothers.

27   'Benjamin is a ravening wolf,
       in the morning he devours his prey,
       in the evening he is still dividing the spoil.'

28   All these make up the tribes of Israel, twelve in number, and this is what their
father said to them. He blessed them, giving to each one an appropriate
blessing.

---

48 a. A play on words: Jacob is like the president of a feast or sacrificial meal handing the
shoulder (*shekem*) to the sons of Joseph. According to 33:19, he had bought a field at Shechem.
49 a. Both tribes were in fact scattered. Simeon ceased to exist and the Levites became a priestly
clan, see Dt 33.   **b.** Under the Canaanites.

Jacob's last moments and his death

Then he gave them these instructions, 'I am about to be gathered to my people. 29
Bury me near my fathers, in the cave that is in the field of Ephron the Hittite, •in 30
the cave in the field at Machpelah, opposite Mamre, in the land of Canaan, which
Abraham bought from Ephron the Hittite as a burial-plot. •There Abraham was 31
buried and his wife Sarah. There Isaac was buried and his wife Rebekah. There
I buried Leah. •I mean the field and the cave in it that were bought from the sons 32
of Heth.'

When Jacob had finished giving his instructions to his sons, he drew his feet 33
up into the bed, and breathing his last was gathered to his people.

Jacob's funeral

50 At this Joseph threw himself on his father, covering his face with tears and 1
kissing him. •Then Joseph ordered the doctors in his service to embalm his 2
father. The doctors embalmed Israel, •and it took them forty days, for embalming 3
takes forty days to complete.

The Egyptians mourned him for seventy days. •When the period of mourning 4
for him was over, Joseph said to Pharaoh's household, 'If I may presume to enjoy
your favour, please see that this message reaches Pharaoh's ears, •"My father 5
made me swear an oath: I am about to die, he said, I have a tomb which I dug for
myself in the land of Canaan, and there you must bury me. So now I seek leave
to go up and bury my father, and then I shall come back." ' •Pharaoh replied, 6
'Go up and bury your father, in accordance with the oath he made you swear'.

Joseph went up to bury his father, all Pharaoh's servants and the palace digni- 7
taries going up with him, joined by all the dignitaries of the land of Egypt, •as 8
well as all Joseph's family and his brothers, along with his father's family. They
left no one in the land of Goshen but their dependants, with their flocks and their
cattle. •Chariots also and horsemen went up with them; it was a very large retinue. 9

On arriving at Goren-ha-atad, which is across the Jordan, they performed 10
there a long and solemn lamentation, and Joseph observed three days' mourning
for his father. •When the Canaanites, the inhabitants of the land, witnessed the 11
mourning at Goren-ha-atad they exclaimed, 'This is a solemn act of mourning
for the Egyptians'. For this reason they call this place Abel-mizraim*a*—it is across
the Jordan.

His sons did what he had ordered them to do for him. •His sons carried him to 12 13
the land of Canaan and buried him in the cave in the field at Machpelah opposite
Mamre, which Abraham had bought from Ephron the Hittite as a burial-plot.

Then Joseph returned to Egypt, he and his brothers, along with all those who 14
had come up with him for his father's burial.

From the death of Jacob to that of Joseph

Seeing that their father was dead, Joseph's brothers said, 'What if Joseph 15
intends to treat us as enemies and repay us in full for all the wrong we did
him?' •So they sent this message to Joseph: 'Before your father died he gave us 16
this order: •"You must say to Joseph: Oh forgive your brothers their crime and 17
their sin and all the wrong they did you". Now therefore, we beg you,
forgive the crime of the servants of your father's God.' Joseph wept at the message
they sent to him.

His brothers came themselves and fell down before him. 'We present ourselves 18
before you' they said 'as your slaves.' •But Joseph answered them, 'Do not be 19
afraid; is it for me to put myself in God's place? •The evil you planned to do me 20
has by God's design been turned to good, that he might bring about, as indeed
he has, the deliverance of a numerous people. •So you need not be afraid; I my- 21
self will provide for you and your dependants.' In this way he reassured them
with words that touched their hearts.

So Joseph stayed in Egypt with his father's family; and Joseph lived a hundred 22

23 and ten years. •Joseph saw the third generation of Ephraim's children, as also the
24 children of Machir, Manasseh's son, who were born on Joseph's lap. •At length
Joseph said to his brothers, 'I am about to die; but God will be sure to remember
you kindly and take you back from this country to the land that he promised on
25 oath to Abraham, Isaac and Jacob'. •And Joseph made Israel's sons swear an oath,
'When God remembers you with kindness be sure to take my bones from here'.
26   Joseph died at the age of a hundred and ten; they embalmed him and laid
him in his coffin in Egypt.

50 a. Neither Goren-ha-atad ('threshing-floor of the bramble') nor Abel-mizraim (Meadow of
Egypt) is known.

EXODUS

I. THE LIBERATION FROM EGYPT

A. ISRAEL IN EGYPT

The prosperity of the Hebrews in Egypt

1 These are the names of the sons of Israel who went with Jacob to Egypt, 1 each with his family: •Reuben, Simeon, Levi and Judah, •Issachar, Zebulun ²₃ and Benjamin, •Dan and Naphtali, Gad and Asher. •In all, the descendants of ⁴₅ Jacob numbered seventy persons. Joseph was in Egypt already. •Then Joseph 6 died, and his brothers, and all that generation. •But the sons of Israel were fruitful 7 and grew in numbers greatly; they increased and grew so immensely powerful that they filled the land.

The Hebrews oppressed

Then there came to power in Egypt a new king who knew nothing of Joseph. 8 'Look,' he said to his subjects 'these people, the sons of Israel, have become so 9 numerous and strong that they are a threat to us. •We must be prudent and 10 take steps against their increasing any further, or if war should break out, they might add to the number of our enemies. They might take arms against us and so escape out of the country.' •Accordingly they put slave-drivers over the 11 Israelites to wear them down under heavy loads. In this way they built the store-cities of Pithom and Rameses[a] for Pharaoh. •But the more they were 12 crushed, the more they increased and spread, and men came to dread the sons ¹³₁₄ of Israel. •The Egyptians forced the sons of Israel into slavery, •and made their lives unbearable with hard labour, work with clay and with brick, all kinds of work in the fields; they forced on them every kind of labour.

The king of Egypt then spoke to the Hebrew midwives, one of whom was 15 named Shiphrah, and the other Puah. •'When you midwives attend Hebrew 16 women,' he said 'watch the two stones[b] carefully. If it is a boy, kill him; if a girl, let her live.' •But the midwives were God-fearing: they disobeyed the command 17 of the king of Egypt and let the boys live. •So the king of Egypt summoned the 18 midwives. 'Why' he asked them 'have you done this and spared the boys?' •'The 19 Hebrew women are not like Egyptian women,' they answered Pharaoh 'they are hardy, and they give birth before the midwife reaches them.' •God was kind 20 to the midwives. The people went on increasing and grew very powerful; •since 21 the midwives reverenced God he granted them descendants.

Pharaoh then gave his subjects this command: 'Throw all the boys born to 22 the Hebrews into the river, but let all the girls live'.

B. EARLY LIFE AND CALL OF MOSES

The birth of Moses

2 There was a man of the tribe of Levi who had taken a woman of Levi as his 1 wife. •She conceived and gave birth to a son and, seeing what a fine child he 2

3 was, she kept him hidden for three months. •When she could hide him no longer,
she got a papyrus basket for him; coating it with bitumen and pitch, she put the
4 child inside and laid it among the reeds at the river's edge. •His sister stood
some distance away to see what would happen to him.
5   Now Pharaoh's daughter went down to bathe in the river, and the girls
attending her were walking along by the riverside. Among the reeds she noticed
6 the basket, and she sent her maid to fetch it. •She opened it and looked, and
saw a baby boy, crying; and she was sorry for him. 'This is a child of one of the
7 Hebrews' she said. •Then the child's sister said to Pharaoh's daughter,
'Shall I go and find you a nurse among the Hebrew women to suckle the child
8 for you?' •'Yes, go' Pharaoh's daughter said to her; and the girl went off to find
9 the baby's own mother. •To her the daughter of Pharaoh said, 'Take this child
away and suckle it for me. I will see you are paid.' So the woman took the child
10 and suckled it. •When the child grew up, she brought him to Pharaoh's daughter
who treated him like a son; she named him Moses because, she said, 'I drew
him out of the water'.a

Moses escapes to Midian

11   Moses, a man by now, set out at this time to visit his countrymen, and he saw
what a hard life they were having; and he saw an Egyptian strike a Hebrew, one
12 of his countrymen. •Looking round he could see no one in sight, so he killed the
13 Egyptian and hid him in the sand. •On the following day he came back, and there
were two Hebrews, fighting. He said to the man who was in the wrong, 'What
14 do you mean by hitting your fellow countryman?' •'And who appointed you'
the man retorted •'to be prince over us, and judge? Do you intend to kill me as
you killed the Egyptian?' Moses was frightened. 'Clearly that business has
15 come to light' he thought. •When Pharaoh heard of the matter he would have
killed Moses, but Moses fled from Pharaoh and made for the land of Midian.b
And he sat down beside a well.
16   Now the priest of Midian had seven daughters. They came to draw water and
17 fill the troughs to water their father's sheep. •Shepherds came and drove them
18 away, but Moses came to their defence and watered their sheep for them. •When
they returned to their father Reuel, he said to them, 'You are back early today!'
19 'An Egyptian protected us from the shepherds;' they said 'yes, and he drew
20 water for us and watered the flock.' •'And where is he?' he asked his daughters.
21 'Why did you leave the man there? Ask him to eat with us.' •So Moses settled
22 with this man, who gave him his daughter Zipporah in marriage.• She gave birth
to a son, and he named him Gershom because, he said, 'I am a stranger in a
foreign land'.

THE CALL OF MOSES

God remembers Israel

23   During this long period the king of Egypt died. The sons of Israel, groaning
in their slavery, cried out for help and from the depths of their slavery their cry
24 came up to God. •God heard their groaning and he called to mind his covenant
25 with Abraham, Isaac and Jacob. •God looked down upon the sons of Israel, and
he knew...

1 a. The residence of Rameses II in the Delta; either Tanis or Qantir.   **b.** The exact meaning is uncertain.
2 a. Folk-derivation of the name Moses from *mashah*, to draw out.   **b.** Midian lies S. of Edom and E. of the Gulf of Aqaba.

The burning bush

3 Moses was looking after the flock of Jethro, his father-in-law, priest of Midian. 1 He led his flock to the far side of the wilderness and came to Horeb,ᵃ the mountain of God. •There the angel of Yahweh appeared to him in the shape 2 of a flame of fire, coming from the middle of a bush. Moses looked; there was the bush blazing but it was not being burnt up. •'I must go and look at this 3 strange sight,' Moses said 'and see why the bush is not burnt.' •Now Yahweh 4 saw him go forward to look, and God called to him from the middle of the bush. 'Moses, Moses!' he said. 'Here I am' he answered. •'Come no nearer' 5 he said. 'Take off your shoes, for the place on which you stand is holy ground. 6 I am the God of your father,' he said 'the God of Abraham, the God of Isaac and the God of Jacob.' At this Moses covered his face, afraid to look at God.

The mission of Moses

And Yahweh said, 'I have seen the miserable state of my people in Egypt. 7 I have heard their appeal to be free of their slave-drivers. Yes, I am well aware of their sufferings. •I mean to deliver them out of the hands of the Egyptians and 8 bring them up out of that land to a land rich and broad, a land where milk and honey flow, the home of the Canaanites, the Hittites, the Amorites, the Perizzites, the Hivites and the Jebusites. •And now the cry of the sons of Israel has come 9 to me, and I have witnessed the way in which the Egyptians oppress them, so come, I send you to Pharaoh to bring the sons of Israel, my people, out of 10 Egypt.'

Moses said to God, 'Who am I to go to Pharaoh and bring the sons of Israel 11 out of Egypt?' •'I shall be with you,' was the answer 'and this is the sign by which 12 you shall know that it is I who have sent you. . . After you have led the people out of Egypt, you are to offer worship to God on this mountain.'

The divine name revealed

Then Moses said to God, 'I am to go, then, to the sons of Israel and say to 13 them, "The God of your fathers has sent me to you". But if they ask me what his name is, what am I to tell them?' •And God said to Moses, 'I Am who I Am. 14 This' he added 'is what you must say to the sons of Israel: "I Am has sent me to you".' •And God also said to Moses, 'You are to say to the sons of Israel: 15 "Yahweh,ᵇ the God of your fathers, the God of Abraham, the God of Isaac, and the God of Jacob, has sent me to you". This is my name for all time; by this name I shall be invoked for all generations to come.

Moses instructed for his mission

'Go and gather the elders of Israel together and tell them, "Yahweh, the God 16 of your fathers, has appeared to me,—the God of Abraham, of Isaac, and of Jacob; and he has said to me: I have visited you and seen all that the Egyptians are doing to you. •And so I have resolved to bring you up out of Egypt where 17 you are oppressed, into the land of the Canaanites, the Hittites, the Amorites, the Perizzites, the Hivites and the Jebusites, to a land where milk and honey flow." •They will listen to your words, and with the elders of Israel you are to 18 go to the king of Egypt and say to him, "Yahweh, the God of the Hebrews, has come to meet us. Give us leave, then, to make a three days' journey into the wilderness to offer sacrifice to Yahweh our God." •For myself, knowing that 19 the king of Egypt will not let you go unless he is forced by a mighty hand, •I shall 20 show my power and strike Egypt with all the wonders I am going to work there. After this he will let you go.

The Egyptians to be plundered

I will give this people such prestige in the eyes of the Egyptians that when you 21 go, you will not go empty-handed. •Every woman will ask her neighbour and the 22 woman who is staying in her house for silver ornaments and gold. With these you will adorn your sons and daughters; you will plunder the Egyptians.'

Moses granted miraculous powers

1 Then Moses answered, 'What if they will not believe me or listen to my words
2 and say to me, "Yahweh has not appeared to you"?' •Yahweh asked him,
3 'What is that in your hand?' 'A staff' Moses said. •'Throw it on the ground' said Yahweh; so Moses threw his staff on the ground—it turned into a serpent
4 and he drew back from it. •'Put your hand out and catch it by the tail' Yahweh said to him. And he put out his hand and caught it, and in his hand the serpent
5 turned into a staff . . . •'so that they may believe that Yahweh, the God of their fathers, the God of Abraham, the God of Isaac, and the God of Jacob, has really appeared to you.'

6 Again Yahweh spoke to Moses, 'Put your hand into your bosom.' He put his hand into his bosom and when he drew it out, his hand was covered with leprosy,
7 white as snow. •'Put your hand back into your bosom.' He put his hand back into his bosom and when he drew it out, there it was restored, just like the rest
8 of his flesh. •'Even so: should they not believe you nor be convinced by the first
9 sign, the second will convince them; •but if they should believe neither of these two signs and not listen to your words, you must take water from the river and pour it on the ground, and the water you have drawn from the river will turn to blood on the ground.'

Aaron, the mouthpiece of Moses

10 Moses said to Yahweh, 'But, my Lord, never in my life have I been a man of eloquence, either before or since you have spoken to your servant. I am a
11 slow speaker and not able to speak well.' •'Who gave man his mouth?' Yahweh answered him. 'Who makes him dumb or deaf, gives him sight or leaves
12 him blind? Is it not I, Yahweh? •Now go, I shall help you to speak and tell you what to say.'
13
14 'If it please you, my Lord,' Moses replied 'send anyone you will!' •At this, the anger of Yahweh blazed out against Moses, and he said to him, 'There is your brother Aaron the Levite, is there not? I know that he is a good speaker. Here
15 he comes to meet you. When he sees you, his heart will be full of joy. •You will speak to him and tell him what message to give. I shall help you to speak, and
16 him too, and instruct you what to do. •He himself is to speak to the people in your place; he will be your mouthpiece, and you will be as the god in-
17 spiring him. •And take this staff into your hand; with this you will perform the signs.'

Moses returns to Egypt. He leaves Midian

18 Moses went away and returned to his father-in-law Jethro, and said to him, 'Give me leave to go back to my relatives in Egypt to see if they are still alive'. And Jethro said to Moses, 'Go in peace'.
19 Yahweh said to Moses in Midian, 'Go, return to Egypt, for all those who
20 wanted to kill you are dead'. •So Moses took his wife and his son and, putting them on a donkey, started back for the land of Egypt; and Moses took in his
21 hand the staff of God. •Yahweh said to Moses, 'Now that you are going back to Egypt, be prepared to perform before Pharaoh all the marvels that I have given you power to do. I myself will harden his heart, and he will not let the
22 people go. •Then you will say to Pharaoh, "This is what Yahweh says: Israel
23 is my first-born son. •I ordered you to let my son go to offer me worship. You refuse to let him go. So be it! I shall put your first-born to death". '

---

3 a. Sinai; the alternative name used in the 'Elohistic' tradition.   **b.** The formula, 'I Am who I Am' becomes, in the third person, Yahweh, 'He is'.

The son of Moses circumcised

On the journey, when Moses had halted for the night, Yahweh came to meet 24
him and tried to kill him. •At once Zipporah, taking up a flint, cut off her son's 25
foreskin and with it she touched the genitals of Moses. 'Truly, you are a bridegroom of blood to me!' she said. •And Yahweh let him live. It was then that she 26
said, 'bridegroom of blood' on account of the circumcision.

Moses meets Aaron

Yahweh said to Aaron, 'Go into the wilderness to meet Moses'. And so he 27
went, and met him at the mountain of God; and he kissed him. •Moses then 28
told Aaron all that Yahweh had said when he set him his task and all the signs
he had ordered him to perform. •Moses and Aaron then went and gathered all 29
the elders of the sons of Israel together, •and Aaron told all that Yahweh had said 30
to Moses, and in the sight of the people he performed the signs. •The people were 31
convinced, and they rejoiced that Yahweh had visited the sons of Israel and
seen their misery, and they bowed down and worshipped.

The first audience with Pharaoh

5 After this, Moses and Aaron went to Pharaoh and said to him, 'This is what 1
Yahweh, the God of Israel, has said, "Let my people go, so that they may
keep a feast in the wilderness in honour of me." ' •'Who is Yahweh,' Pharaoh 2
replied 'that I should listen to him and let Israel go? I know nothing of Yahweh,
and I will not let Israel go.' •'The God of the Hebrews has come to meet us' they 3
replied. 'Give us leave to make a three days' journey into the wilderness to offer
sacrifice to Yahweh our God, or he will come down on us with a plague or with
the sword.' •The king of Egypt said to them, 'Moses and Aaron, what do you 4
mean by taking the people away from their work? Get back to your labouring.'
And Pharaoh said, 'Now that these common folk have grown to such numbers, 5
do you want to stop them labouring?'

Instructions to the slave-drivers

That same day, Pharaoh gave this command to the people's slave-drivers and 6
to the overseers. •'Up to the present, you have provided these people with straw 7
for brickmaking. Do so no longer; let them go and gather straw for themselves.
All the same, you are to get from them the same number of bricks as before, not 8
reducing it at all. They are lazy, and that is why their cry is, "Let us go and offer
sacrifice to our God". •Make these men work harder than ever, so that they do 9
not have time to stop and listen to glib speeches.'

The people's slave-drivers went out with the overseers to speak to the people. 10
'Pharaoh has given orders' they said: ' "I will not provide you with straw. •Go 11
out and collect straw for yourselves wherever you can find it. But your output
is not to be any less." ' •So the people scattered all over the land of Egypt to 12
gather stubble for making chopped straw. •The slave-drivers harassed them. 13
'Every day you must complete your daily quota,' they said 'just as you did when
straw was provided for you.' •And the foremen who had been appointed for the 14
sons of Israel by Pharaoh's slave-drivers were flogged, and they were asked,
'Why have you not produced your full amount of bricks as before, either yesterday
or today?'

The Hebrew foremen complain

The foremen for the sons of Israel went to Pharaoh and complained. 'Why 15
do you treat your servants so?' they said. •'No straw is provided for your servants 16
and still the cry is, "Make bricks!" And now your servants have been flogged! . . .'
'You are lazy, lazy' he answered 'that is why you say, "Let us go and offer 17
sacrifice to Yahweh". •Get back to your work at once. You shall not get any 18
straw, but you must deliver the number of bricks due from you.'

The dilemma of the foremen. Moses prays

19 The foremen for the sons of Israel saw themselves in a very difficult position
20 when told there was to be no reduction in the daily number of bricks. •As they
left Pharaoh's presence they met Moses and Aaron who were waiting for them.
21 'May Yahweh see your work and punish you as you deserve!' they said to them.
'You have made us hated by Pharaoh and his court; you have put a sword into
22 their hand to kill us.' •Once more Moses turned to Yahweh. 'Lord,' he said
to him 'why do you treat this people so harshly? Why did you send me here?
23 Ever since I came to Pharaoh and spoke to him in your name, he has ill-treated
1 this nation, and you have done nothing to deliver your people.' 6 Then Yahweh
said to Moses, 'You will see now how I shall punish Pharaoh. He will be forced
to let them go; yes, he will be forced to send them out of his land.'

Another account of the call of Moses

2
3   God spoke to Moses and said to him, 'I am Yahweh. •To Abraham and Isaac
and Jacob I appeared as El Shaddai; I did not make myself known to them by
4 my name Yahweh. •Also, I made my covenant with them to give them the land
5 of Canaan, the land they lived in as strangers. •And I have heard the groaning
of the sons of Israel, enslaved by the Egyptians, and have remembered my
6 covenant. •Say this, then, to the sons of Israel, "I am Yahweh. I will free you of
the burdens, which the Egyptians lay on you. I will release you from slavery to
them, and with my arm outstretched and my strokes of power I will deliver you.
7 I will adopt you as my own people, and I will be your God. Then you shall
know that it is I, Yahweh your God, who have freed you from the Egyptians'
8 burdens. •Then I will bring you to the land I swore that I would give to Abraham,
and Isaac, and Jacob, and will give it to you for your own; I, Yahweh, will do
9 this!" ' •Moses told this to the sons of Israel, but they would not listen to him,
so crushed was their spirit and so cruel their slavery.
10
11   Yahweh then said to Moses, •'Go to Pharaoh, king of Egypt, and tell him to
12 let the sons of Israel leave his land'. •But Moses answered to Yahweh's face:
'Look,' said he 'since the sons of Israel have not listened to me, why should
13 Pharaoh listen to me, a man slow of speech?' •Yahweh spoke to Moses and
Aaron and ordered them both to go to Pharaoh, king of Egypt, and to bring the
sons of Israel out of the land of Egypt.

The genealogy of Moses and Aaron

14   These are the heads of their families:
     The sons of Reuben, Israel's first-born: Hanoch, Pallu, Hezron and Carmi:
these are the clans of Reuben.
15   The sons of Simeon: Jemuel, Jamin, Ohad, Jachin, Zohar, and Shaul, son of
the Canaanite woman: these are the clans of Simeon.
16   These are the names of the sons of Levi with their descendants: Gershon,
17 Kohath and Merari. Levi lived for a hundred and thirty-seven years. •The sons
of Gershon: Libni and Shimei and their clans.
18   The sons of Kohath: Amram, Izhar, Hebron and Uzziel. Kohath lived for
a hundred and thirty-three years.
19   The sons of Merari: Mahli and Mushi. These are the clans of Levi with their
descendants.
20   Amram married Jochebed, his aunt, who bore him Aaron and Moses. Amram
lived for a hundred and thirty-seven years.
21   The sons of Izhar were: Korah, Nepheg and Zichri.
22   And the sons of Uzziel: Mishael, Elzaphan and Sithri.
23   Aaron married Elisheba, daughter of Amminadab and sister of Nahshon,
and she bore him Nadab, Abihu, Eleazar and Ithamar.
24   The sons of Korah: Assir, Elkanah and Abiasaph. These are the clans of the
Korahites.

Eleazar, son of Aaron, married one of Putiel's daughters who bore him 25
Phinehas.

These are the heads of families of the Levites according to their clans.

It was to this same Aaron and Moses that Yahweh had said, 'Bring the sons 26
of Israel out of the land of Egypt in battle order'. •It was they who spoke with 27
Pharaoh, king of Egypt, about bringing the sons of Israel out of Egypt. It was
the same Moses and Aaron.

The narrative of Moses' call resumed

On the day when Yahweh spoke to Moses in the land of Egypt, •he said 28
this to him, 'I am Yahweh. Tell Pharaoh, king of Egypt, all that I say to you.' 29
But Moses said to Yahweh's face, 'I am slow of speech, why should Pharaoh 30
listen to me?'

7 Yahweh said to Moses, 'See, I make you as a god for Pharaoh, and Aaron 1
your brother is to be your prophet. •You yourself must tell him all I command 2
you, and Aaron your brother will tell Pharaoh to let the sons of Israel leave
his land. •I myself will make Pharaoh's heart stubborn, and perform many 3
a sign and wonder in the land of Egypt. •Pharaoh will not listen to you, and 4
so I will lay my hand on Egypt and with strokes of power lead out my armies,
my people, the sons of Israel, from the land of Egypt. •And all the Egyptians 5
shall come to know that I am Yahweh when I stretch out my hand against Egypt
and bring out the sons of Israel from their midst.' •Moses and Aaron obeyed; 6
they did what Yahweh commanded them. •Moses was eighty years old, and 7
Aaron eighty-three at the time of their audience with Pharaoh.

C. THE PLAGUES OF EGYPT ^a — THE PASSOVER

The staff turned into a serpent

Yahweh said to Moses and Aaron, •'If Pharaoh says to you, "Produce some 8
marvel", you must say to Aaron, "Take your staff and throw it down in front 9
of Pharaoh, and let it turn into a serpent" '. •To Pharaoh, then, Moses and 10
Aaron duly went, and they did as Yahweh commanded. Aaron threw down
his staff in front of Pharaoh and his court, and it turned into a serpent. •Then 11
Pharaoh in his turn called for the sages and the sorcerers, and with their
witchcraft the magicians of Egypt did the same. •Each threw his staff down and 12
these turned into serpents. But Aaron's staff swallowed up the staffs of the
magicians. •Yet Pharaoh's heart was stubborn and, as Yahweh had foretold, 13
he would not listen to Moses and Aaron.

The first plague: the water turns to blood

Then Yahweh said to Moses, 'Pharaoh is adamant. He refuses to let the 14
people go. •In the morning go to him as he makes his way to the water and 15
wait for him by the bank of the river. In your hand take the staff that turned
into a serpent. •Say to him, "Yahweh, the God of the Hebrews, has sent me 16
to say: Let my people go to offer me worship in the wilderness. Now, so far
you have not listened. •Here is Yahweh's message: That I am Yahweh you shall 17
learn by this: with the staff that is in my hand I will strike the water of the
river and it shall be changed into blood. •The fish in the river will die, and the 18
river will smell so foul that the Egyptians will not want to drink the water of it." '

Yahweh said to Moses, 'Say this to Aaron, "Take your staff and stretch out 19
your hand over the waters of Egypt, over their rivers and their canals, their
marshland, and all their reservoirs, and let them turn to blood throughout
the land of Egypt, even down to the contents of every tub or jar" '. •Moses 20
and Aaron did as Yahweh commanded. He raised his staff and in the sight
of Pharaoh and his court he struck the waters of the river, and all the water
in the river changed to blood. •The fish in the river died, and the river smelt 21

so foul that the Egyptians found it impossible to drink its water. Throughout
22 the land of Egypt there was blood. •But the magicians of Egypt used their
witchcraft to do the same, so that Pharaoh's heart was stubborn and, as Yahweh
23 had foretold, he would not listen to Moses and Aaron. •Pharaoh turned away
24 and went back into his palace, taking no notice even of this. •Meanwhile, all
the Egyptians dug holes along the banks of the river in search of drinking water;
25 they found the water of the river impossible to drink. •After Yahweh had struck
the river, seven days passed.

The second plague: the frogs

26
1   Then Yahweh said to Moses, 'Go to Pharaoh and say to him, "This is
27
2 Yahweh's message: Let my people go to offer me worship. •If you refuse to let
28
3 them go, know that I will plague the whole of your country with frogs. •The
river will swarm with them; they will make their way into your palace, into
your bedroom, on to your bed, into the houses of your courtiers and of your
29
4 subjects, into your ovens, into your kneading bowls. •The frogs will even climb
all over you, over your courtiers, and over all your subjects." '

1
5   8 Yahweh said to Moses, 'Say this to Aaron, "Stretch out your hand, with
your staff, over the rivers, the canals, the marshland, and make frogs swarm
2
6 all over the land of Egypt" '. •So Aaron stretched out his hand over the waters of
3
7 Egypt, and the frogs came up and covered the land of Egypt. •But the magicians did
the same with their witchcraft, and made frogs swarm all over the land of Egypt.
4
8   Pharaoh summoned Moses and Aaron, 'Entreat Yahweh' he said 'to rid
me and my subjects of the frogs, and I promise to let the people go and offer
5
9 sacrifice to Yahweh.' •Moses answered Pharaoh, 'Take this chance to get the
better of me! When I pray on your account and for your courtiers, and for
your subjects, what time am I to fix for the frogs to leave you and your subjects
6
10 and your houses, and stay in the river?' •'Tomorrow' Pharaoh said. 'It shall
be as you say' answered Moses. 'By this you shall learn that Yahweh our God
7
11 has no equal. •The frogs will go from you and your palaces, your courtiers
8
12 and your subjects; they will stay in the river.' •When Moses and Aaron had
gone from Pharaoh's presence, Moses pleaded with Yahweh about the frogs
9
13 with which he had afflicted Pharaoh. •And Yahweh granted Moses' prayer:
10
14 in house and courtyard and field the frogs died. •They piled them up in heaps
11
15 and the land reeked of them. •But as soon as he saw that relief had been granted,
Pharaoh became adamant again and, as Yahweh had foretold, he refused to
listen to Moses and Aaron.

The third plague: the mosquitoes

12
16   Then Yahweh said to Moses, 'Say this to Aaron, "Stretch out your rod and
strike the dust on the ground: throughout the land of Egypt it will turn into
13
17 mosquitoes" '. •Aaron stretched out his hand, with his staff, and struck the
dust on the ground. The mosquitoes attacked men and beasts; throughout the
14
18 land of Egypt the dust on the ground turned into mosquitoes. •The magicians
with their witchcraft tried to produce mosquitoes and failed. The mosquitoes
15
19 attacked men and beasts. •So the magicians said to Pharaoh, 'This is the finger
of God'. But Pharaoh's heart was stubborn and, as Yahweh had foretold, he
refused to listen to Moses and Aaron.

The fourth plague: the gadflies

16
20   Then Yahweh said to Moses, 'Get up early in the morning and wait for
Pharaoh as he makes his way to the water. Say to him, "This is Yahweh's message:
17
21 Let my people go to offer me worship. •But if you do not let my people go, I shall

---

7 a. In the narrative of the plagues we must recognise the conflation of several traditions: one,
for instance, which always ranges Aaron with Moses, and one in which Moses acts by himself.

send gadflies on you, on your courtiers and your palaces. The houses of the
Egyptians will be infested with them, and even the very ground they stand on.
But I shall set apart the land of Goshen, where my people live, on that day; $^{18}_{22}$
there will be no gadflies there, and so you may know that I, Yahweh, am in
the midst of the land. •I shall make a distinction between my people and yours. $^{19}_{23}$
This sign shall take place tomorrow." ' •Yahweh did this, and great swarms of $^{20}_{24}$
gadflies found their way into Pharaoh's palace, into the houses of his courtiers,
and into all the land of Egypt, and ruined the country.

Pharaoh summoned Moses and Aaron. 'Go' he said 'and offer sacrifice to $^{21}_{25}$
your God, but in this country!' •'That would not be right' Moses answered. $^{22}_{26}$
'We sacrifice to Yahweh our God animals which Egyptians count it sacrilege
to slaughter. If we offer in front of the Egyptians sacrifices that outrage them, will
they not stone us?^{a} •We must make a three days' journey into the wilderness to $^{23}_{27}$
offer sacrifice to Yahweh our God, as he has commanded us.' •Pharaoh replied, $^{24}_{28}$
'I will let you go to offer sacrifice to Yahweh your God in the wilderness,
provided you do not go far. And intercede for me.' •'The moment I leave you,' $^{25}_{29}$
said Moses 'I will pray to Yahweh. Tomorrow morning the gadflies will leave
Pharaoh and his courtiers and his subjects. Only, Pharaoh must not play false
again, and refuse to let the people go to offer sacrifice to Yahweh.' •So Moses $^{26}_{30}$
went out of Pharaoh's presence and prayed to Yahweh. •And Yahweh did as $^{27}_{31}$
Moses asked; the gadflies left Pharaoh and his courtiers and his subjects; not
one remained. •But Pharaoh was adamant this time too and did not let the $^{28}_{32}$
people go.

The fifth plague: death of the Egyptians' livestock

9 Then Yahweh said to Moses, 'Go to Pharaoh and say to him, "This is the 1
message of Yahweh, the God of the Hebrews: Let my people go to offer
me worship. •If you refuse to let them go and detain them any longer, •you $^2_3$
will find that the hand of Yahweh will fall on your livestock in the fields, horse
and donkey and camel, herd and flock, with a deadly plague. •Yahweh will 4
discriminate between the livestock of Israel and of Egypt: nothing shall die of
all that belongs to the sons of Israel. •Yahweh has fixed the hour. Tomorrow, 5
he has said, Yahweh will carry out this threat in all the land." •Next day Yahweh 6
kept his word; all the Egyptians' livestock died, but none owned by the sons
of Israel died. •Pharaoh had inquiries made, but it was true: none was dead of 7
the livestock owned by the sons of Israel. But Pharaoh became adamant again
and did not let the people go.

The sixth plague: the boils

Yahweh said to Moses and Aaron, 'Take handfuls of soot from the kiln, 8
and before the eyes of Pharaoh let Moses throw it in the air. •It shall spread 9
like fine dust over the whole land of Egypt and bring out boils that break into
sores on man and beast all over the land of Egypt.' •So they took soot from the 10
kiln and stood in front of Pharaoh, and Moses threw it in the air. And on man
and beast it brought out boils breaking into sores. •And the magicians could 11
not face Moses, because the magicians were covered with boils like all the other·
Egyptians. •But Yahweh made Pharaoh's heart stubborn and, as Yahweh had 12
foretold, he refused to listen to them.

The seventh plague: the hail

Then Yahweh said to Moses, 'Get up early in the morning and present yourself 13
to Pharaoh. Say to him, "This is the message of Yahweh, the God of the
Hebrews: Let my people go to offer me worship. •This time I mean to send 14
all my plagues on you and your courtiers and your subjects so that you shall
learn that there is no one like me in the whole world. •Had I stretched out my 15
hand to strike you and your subjects with pestilence, you would have been swept

16 from the earth. •But I have let you live for this: to make you see my power and
17 to have my name published throughout all the earth. •High-handed with my
18 people still, you will not let them go. •Tomorrow, therefore, at about this time,
I will let fall so great a storm of hail as was never known in Egypt from the
19 day of its foundation. •So now have your livestock, and everything that is yours
in the fields put under cover: on man and beast, on all that remains in the fields
20 and is not brought indoors, the hail will fall and they will die." ' •Some of
Pharaoh's courtiers, terrified by Yahweh's threat, brought their slaves and
21 livestock indoors, •but those who disregarded Yahweh's threat left their slaves
and livestock in the fields.

22   Yahweh said to Moses, 'Stretch out your hand towards heaven so that hail
may fall on the whole land of Egypt, on man and beast and all that grows in
23 the fields in the land of Egypt'. •Moses stretched out his staff towards heaven,
and Yahweh thundered and rained down hail. Lightning struck the earth.
24 Yahweh rained down hail on the land of Egypt. •The hail fell, and lightning
flashing in the midst of it, a greater storm of hail than had ever been known
25 in Egypt since it first became a nation. •Throughout the land of Egypt the hail
struck down everything in the fields, man and beast. It struck all the crops in
26 the fields, and it shattered every tree in the fields. •Only in the land of Goshen
where the Hebrews lived, was there no hail.

27   Pharaoh sent for Moses and Aaron. 'This time' he said 'I admit my fault.
28 Yahweh is in the right; I and my subjects are in the wrong. •Entreat Yahweh
to stop the thunder and the hail; I promise to let you go, and you shall stay
29 here no longer.' •Moses answered him, 'The moment I leave the city I will
stretch out my hands to Yahweh. The thunder will stop, and there will be no
30 more hail, so that you may know that the earth belongs to Yahweh. •But as
for you and your courtiers, I know very well that you have no fear yet of Yahweh
31 our God.' •The flax and the barley were ruined, since the barley was in the ear and
32 the flax budding. •The wheat and the spelt, being late crops, were not destroyed.

33   Moses left Pharaoh and went out of the city. He stretched out his hands to
Yahweh and the thunder and the hail stopped and the rain no longer poured
34 down on the earth. •When Pharaoh saw that rain and hail and thunder had
35 stopped, he sinned yet again. •He became adamant, he and his courtiers. The
heart of Pharaoh was stubborn and, as Yahweh had foretold through Moses,
he did not let the sons of Israel go.

The eighth plague: the locusts

1 **10** Then Yahweh said to Moses, 'Go to Pharaoh, for it is I who have made
his heart and his courtiers stubborn, so that I could work these signs of
2 mine among them; •so that you can tell your sons and your grandsons how
I made fools of the Egyptians and what signs I performed among them, to let
3 you know that I am Yahweh'. •So Moses and Aaron went to Pharaoh. They
said to him, 'This is the message of Yahweh, the God of the Hebrews, "How
much longer will you refuse to submit to me? Let my people go to offer me
4 worship. •If you refuse to let my people go, then tomorrow I will send locusts
5 over your country. •They shall cover the surface of the soil so thick that the soil
will not be seen. They shall devour the remainder that is left to you, all that has
survived from the hail; they shall devour all your trees growing in the fields;
they shall fill your palaces, the houses of your courtiers, the houses of all the
6 Egyptians. •Your forefathers and their ancestors will never have seen the like
since first they lived in the country." ' Then Moses turned away and left Pharaoh's
7 presence. •And Pharaoh's courtiers said to him, 'How much longer is this man
to be the cause of our trouble? Let the people go to offer worship to Yahweh
their God. Do you not understand that Egypt is now on the brink of ruin?'

---

8 a. In the Delta there were gods represented as rams, goats and bulls.

So Moses and Aaron were brought back to Pharaoh. 'You may go' he said 8
to them 'and offer worship to Yahweh your God. But who are to go?' •'We 9
shall take our young men and our old men' Moses answered. 'We shall take
our sons and daughters, our flocks and our herds, because for us it is a feast
of Yahweh.' •'May Yahweh be with you if ever I let you and your little ones go!' 10
Pharaoh retorted. 'It is plain you are up to no good. •Oh no! You men may 11
go and offer worship to Yahweh, since that is what you wanted.' And with
that they were dismissed from the presence of Pharaoh.

Then Yahweh said to Moses, 'Stretch out your hand over the land of Egypt 12
to bring the locusts. Let them invade the land of Egypt and devour all its
greenstuff, all that the hail has left.' •And over the land of Egypt Moses 13
stretched his staff, and Yahweh brought up an east wind over the land and it
blew all that day and night. By morning, the east wind had brought the locusts.

The locusts invaded the whole land of Egypt. On the whole territory of 14
Egypt they fell, in numbers so great that such swarms had never been seen
before, nor would be again. •They covered the surface of the soil till the ground 15
was black with them. They devoured all the greenstuff in the land and all the
fruit of the trees that the hail had left. No green was left on tree or plant in the
fields throughout the land of Egypt.

Pharaoh sent urgently for Moses and Aaron. 'I have sinned against Yahweh 16
your God,' he said 'and against yourselves. •Forgive my sin, I implore you, 17
this once, and entreat Yahweh your God just to rid me of this deadly plague.'
So Moses left Pharaoh's presence and interceded with Yahweh. •Then Yahweh ¹⁸₁₉
made the wind veer till it blew so strongly from the west that it caught up the
locusts and carried them off towards the Sea of Reeds. There was not one locust
left in the whole land of Egypt. •But Yahweh made Pharaoh's heart stubborn, 20
and he did not let the sons of Israel go.

The ninth plague: the darkness

Then Yahweh said to Moses, 'Stretch out your hand towards heaven, and 21
let darkness, darkness so thick that it can be felt, cover the land of Egypt'.
So Moses stretched out his hand towards heaven, and for three days there 22
was deep darkness over the whole land of Egypt. •No one could see anyone 23
else or move about for three days, but where the sons of Israel lived there was
light for them.

Pharaoh summoned Moses. 'Go and offer worship to Yahweh,' he said 24
'but your flocks and herds must remain here. Your children may go with you
too.' •Moses replied, 'But you must let us have means of offering sacrifices 25
and holocausts to Yahweh our God. •Our livestock, too, must go with us; 26
not one head of cattle must be left behind: it must be from our livestock that
we provide for the worship of Yahweh our God; until we reach the place, we
do not know ourselves what worship we shall have to offer Yahweh.'

But Yahweh made Pharaoh's heart stubborn, and he refused to let them go. 27
Pharaoh said to Moses, 'Out of my sight! Take care! Never appear before me 28
again, for on the day you do, you die!' •Moses replied, 'You yourself have said it: 29
never again shall I appear before you.'

Moses proclaims the death of the first-born

11 Then Yahweh said to Moses, 'One disaster more I shall bring on Pharaoh 1
and on Egypt, just one. After this he will let you go from here . . . Indeed,
he will drive you out! •Instruct the people that every man is to ask his neighbour, 2
every woman hers, for silver ornaments and gold.' •And Yahweh gave the 3
people prestige in the eyes of the Egyptians, while Moses himself was a man of
great importance in the land of Egypt, and of high prestige with Pharaoh's
courtiers and with the people.

Moses said, 'This is Yahweh's message, "Towards midnight I shall pass 4

5 through Egypt. •All the first-born in the land of Egypt shall die: from the first-born of Pharaoh, heir to his throne, to the first-born of the maidservant at the
6 mill, and all the first-born of the cattle. •And throughout the land of Egypt
7 there shall be such a wailing as never was heard before, nor will be again. •But against the sons of Israel, against man or beast, never a dog shall bark, so that
8 you may know that Yahweh discriminates between Egypt and Israel. •Then all these courtiers of yours will come down to me and bow low before me and say: Go away, you and all the people who follow you! After this, I shall go." ' And, hot with anger, Moses left Pharaoh's presence.
9   Then Yahweh said to Moses, 'Pharaoh will not listen to you; so that my
10 wonders may be multiplied in the land of Egypt'. •All these wonders Moses and Aaron worked in the presence of Pharaoh. But Yahweh made Pharaoh's heart stubborn, and he did not let the sons of Israel leave his country.

The Passover

¹/₂ **12** Yahweh said to Moses and Aaron in the land of Egypt, •'This month is to be the first of all the others for you, the first month of your year.
3 Speak to the whole community of Israel and say, "On the tenth day of this month each man must take an animal from the flock, one for each family: one
4 animal for each household. •If the household is too small to eat the animal, a man must join with his neighbour, the nearest to his house, as the number of persons requires. You must take into account what each can eat in deciding
5 the number for the animal. •It must be an animal without blemish, a male
6 one year old; you may take it from either sheep or goats. •You must keep it till the fourteenth day of the month when the whole assembly of the community
7 of Israel shall slaughter it between the two evenings.ᵃ •Some of the blood must then be taken and put on the two doorposts and the lintel of the houses where
8 it is eaten. •That night, the flesh is to be eaten, roasted over the fire; it must
9 be eaten with unleavened bread and bitter herbs. •Do not eat any of it raw
10 or boiled, but roasted over the fire, head, feet and entrails. •You must not leave any over till the morning: whatever is left till morning you are to burn.
11 You shall eat it like this: with a girdle round your waist, sandals on your feet, a staff in your hand. You shall eat it hastily: it is a passoverᵇ in honour of
12 Yahweh. •That night, I will go through the land of Egypt and strike down all the first-born in the land of Egypt, man and beast alike, and I shall deal out
13 punishment to all the gods of Egypt, I am Yahweh! •The blood shall serve to mark the houses that you live in. When I see the blood I will pass over you and
14 you shall escape the destroying plague when I strike the land of Egypt. •This day is to be a day of remembrance for you, and you must celebrate it as a feast in Yahweh's honour. For all generations you are to declare it a day of festival, for ever.

The feast of Unleavened Bread

15   "For seven days you must eat unleavened bread. On the first day you are to clean all leaven out of your houses, for anyone who eats leavened bread from
16 the first to the seventh day shall be cut off from Israel. •On the first day you are to hold a sacred gathering, and again on the seventh day. On those days no
17 work is to be done; you are allowed only to prepare your food. •The feast of Unleavened Bread must be kept because it was on that same day I brought your armies out of the land of Egypt. Keep that day from age to age: it is an
18 irrevocable ordinance. •In the first month, from the evening of the fourteenth day and until the evening of the twenty-first day, you are to eat unleavened bread.
19 For seven days no leaven must be found in your houses, because anyone who eats leavened bread will be cut off from the community of Israel, whether he be

---

12 a. I.e. either between sunset and darkness (Samaritans), or between afternoon and sunset (Pharisees).   **b.** The explanation of this word is in v.13.

stranger or native-born. •You must eat no leavened bread; wherever you live you 20
must eat unleavened bread." '

Injunctions relating to the Passover

Moses summoned all the elders of Israel and said to them, 'Go and choose 21
animals from the flock on behalf of your families, and kill the Passover victim.
Then take a spray of hyssop, dip it in the blood that is in the basin, and with 22
the blood from the basin touch the lintel and the two doorposts. Let none of
you venture out of the house till morning. •Then, when Yahweh goes through 23
Egypt to strike it, and sees the blood on the lintel and on the two doorposts,
he will pass over the door and not allow the destroyer to enter your homes
and strike. •You must keep these rules as an ordinance for all time for you 24
and your children. •When you enter the land that Yahweh is giving you, as he 25
promised, you must keep to this ritual. •And when your children ask you, 26
"What does this ritual mean?" •you will tell them, "It is the sacrifice of the 27
Passover in honour of Yahweh who passed over the houses of the sons of Israel
in Egypt, and struck Egypt but spared our houses".' And the people bowed
down and worshipped. •The sons of Israel then departed, and they obeyed. 28
They carried out the orders Yahweh had given to Moses and Aaron.

The tenth plague: death of the first-born

And at midnight Yahweh struck down all the first-born in the land of Egypt: 29
the first-born of Pharaoh, heir to his throne, the first-born of the prisoner in his
dungeon, and the first-born of all the cattle. •Pharaoh and all his courtiers and 30
all the Egyptians got up in the night, and there was a great cry in Egypt, for
there was not a house without its dead. •And it was night when Pharaoh 31
summoned Moses and Aaron. 'Get up,' he said 'you and the sons of Israel, and
get away from my people. Go and offer worship to Yahweh as you have asked
and, as you have asked, take your flocks and herds, and go. And also ask a 32
blessing on me.' •The Egyptians urged the people to hurry up and leave the 33
land because, they said, 'Otherwise we shall all be dead'. •So the people carried 34
off their dough, still unleavened, on their shoulders, their kneading bowls wrapped
in their cloaks.

The Egyptians plundered

The sons of Israel did as Moses had told them and asked the Egyptians 35
for silver ornaments and gold, and for clothing. •Yahweh gave the people such 36
prestige in the eyes of the Egyptians, that they gave them what they asked. So
they plundered the Egyptians.

Israel's departure

The sons of Israel left Rameses for Succoth, about six hundred thousand 37
on the march—all men—not counting their families. •People of various sorts 38
joined them in great numbers; there were flocks, too, and herds in immense
droves. •They baked cakes with the dough which they had brought from Egypt, 39
unleavened because the dough was not leavened; they had been driven out of
Egypt, with no time for dallying, and had not provided themselves with food
for the journey.ᶜ •The time that the sons of Israel had spent in Egypt was four 40
hundred and thirty years. •And on the very day the four hundred and thirty 41
years ended, all the array of Yahweh left the land of Egypt. •The night, when 42
Yahweh kept vigil to bring them out of the land of Egypt, must be kept as a vigil
in honour of Yahweh for all their generations.

Ordinances for the Passover

Yahweh said to Moses and Aaron, 'This is what is ordained for the Passover: 43
No alien may take part in it, •but any slave bought for money may take part 44

45 when you have had him circumcised. •No stranger and no hired servant may take
46 part in it. •It is to be eaten in one house alone, out of which not a single morsel
47 of the flesh is to be taken; nor must you break any bone of it. •The whole com-
48 munity of Israel must keep the Passover. •Should a stranger be staying with you
and wish to celebrate the Passover in honour of Yahweh, all the males of his
household must be circumcised: he may then be admitted to the celebration, for
he becomes as it were a native-born. But no uncircumcised person may take part.
49 The same law will run for the native and for the stranger resident among you.'
50 The sons of Israel all obeyed. They carried out the orders Yahweh had given
51 to Moses and Aaron. •And that same day Yahweh brought the sons of Israel
in their armies out of Egypt.

The first-born

$\frac{1}{2}$ 13 Yahweh spoke to Moses and said, •'Consecrate all the first-born to me,
the first issue of every womb, among the sons of Israel. Whether man or
beast, this is mine.'

The feast of Unleavened Bread

3 　　Moses said to the people, 'Keep this day in remembrance, the day you came
out of Egypt, from the house of slavery, for it was by sheer power that Yahweh
4 brought you out of it; no leavened bread must be eaten. •On this day, in the
5 month of Abib, you are leaving Egypt. •And so, in this same month, when
Yahweh brings you to the land of the Canaanites, the Hittites, the Amorites, the
Hivites, the Jebusites, the land he swore to your fathers he would give you, a land
6 where milk and honey flow, you are to hold this service. •For seven days you
will eat unleavened bread, and on the seventh day there is to be a feast in honour
7 of Yahweh. •During these seven days unleavened bread is to be eaten; no
leavened bread must be seen among you, no leaven among you in all your
8 territory. •And on that day you will explain to your son, "This is because of
9 what Yahweh did for me when I came out of Egypt". •The rite will serve as
a sign on your hand would serve, or a memento on your forehead, and in that
way the law of Yahweh will be ever on your lips, for Yahweh brought you out
10 of Egypt with a mighty hand. •You will observe this ordinance each year at its
appointed time.

The first-born

11 　'When Yahweh brings you to the land of the Canaanites—as he swore to
12 you and your fathers he would do—and gives it to you, •you are to make over
to Yahweh all that first issues from the womb, and every first-born cast by your
13 animals: these males belong to Yahweh. •But every first-born donkey you will
redeem with an animal from your flocks. If you do not redeem it, you must
14 break its neck. Of your sons, every first-born of men must be redeemed. •And
when your son asks you in days to come, "What does this mean?" you will tell
him, "By sheer power Yahweh brought us out of Egypt, out of the house of
15 slavery. •When Pharaoh stubbornly refused to let us go, Yahweh killed all the
first-born in the land of Egypt, of man and of beast alike. For this I sacrifice
to Yahweh every male that first issues from the womb, and redeem every first-born
16 of my sons." •The rite will serve as a sign on your hand would serve, or a circlet
on your forehead, for Yahweh brought us out of Egypt with a mighty hand.'

c. This is not, according to vv.8 and 18-20, the reason why the bread was unleavened.

D. THE CROSSING OF THE SEA OF REEDS

The departure of the Israelites

When Pharaoh had let the people go, God did not let them take the road to 17
the land of the Philistines, although that was the nearest way. God thought that
the prospect of fighting would make the people lose heart and turn back to
Egypt. •Instead, God led the people by the roundabout way of the wilderness 18
to the Sea of Reeds. The sons of Israel went out from Egypt fully armed. •Moses 19
took with him the bones of Joseph who had put the sons of Israel on solemn
oath. 'It is sure that God will visit you,' he had said 'and when that day comes
you must take my bones from here with you.'

From Succoth they moved on, and encamped at Etham, on the edge of the 20
wilderness.

Yahweh went before them, by day in the form of a pillar of cloud to show 21
them the way, and by night in the form of a pillar of fire to give them light:
thus they could continue their march by day and by night. •The pillar of cloud 22
never failed to go before the people during the day, nor the pillar of fire during
the night.

From Etham to the Sea of Reeds

14 Yahweh spoke to Moses and said, •'Tell the sons of Israel to turn back ¹⁄₂
and pitch camp in front of Pi-hahiroth, between Migdol and the sea,
facing Baal-zephon. You are to pitch your camp opposite this place, beside the
sea. •Pharaoh will think, "Look how these sons of Israel wander to and fro in 3
the countryside; the wilderness has closed in on them". •Then I shall make 4
Pharaoh's heart stubborn and he will set out in pursuit of them. But I shall win
glory for myself at the expense of Pharaoh and all his army, and the Egyptians
will learn that I am Yahweh.' And the Israelites did this.

The Egyptians pursue the Israelites

When Pharaoh, king of Egypt, was told that the people had made their 5
escape, he and his courtiers changed their minds about the people. 'What have
we done,' they said 'allowing Israel to leave our service?' •So Pharaoh had his 6
chariot harnessed and gathered his troops about him, •taking six hundred of the 7
best chariots and all the other chariots in Egypt, each manned by a picked team.
Yahweh made Pharaoh, king of Egypt, stubborn, and he gave chase to the 8
sons of Israel as they made their triumphant escape. •So the Egyptians gave 9
chase and came up with them where they lay encamped beside the sea—all the
horses, the chariots of Pharaoh, his horsemen, his army—near Pi-hahiroth,
facing Baal-zephon. •And as Pharaoh approached, the sons of Israel looked 10
round—and there were the Egyptians in pursuit of them! The sons of Israel were
terrified and cried out to Yahweh. •To Moses they said, 'Were there no graves 11
in Egypt that you must lead us out to die in the wilderness? What good have you
done us, bringing us out of Egypt? •We spoke of this in Egypt, did we not? 12
Leave us alone, we said, we would rather work for the Egyptians! Better to
work for the Egyptians than die in the wilderness!' •Moses answered the people, 13
'Have no fear! Stand firm, and you will see what Yahweh will do to save you
today: the Egyptians you see today, you will never see again. •Yahweh will do 14
the fighting for you: you have only to keep still.'

The crossing

Yahweh said to Moses, 'Why do you cry to me so? Tell the sons of Israel to 15
march on. •For yourself, raise your staff and stretch out your hand over the sea 16
and part it for the sons of Israel to walk through the sea on dry ground. I for
my part will make the heart of the Egyptians so stubborn that they will follow 17

them. So shall I win myself glory at the expense of Pharaoh, of all his army, his
18 chariots, his horsemen. •And when I have won glory for myself, at the expense of
Pharaoh and his chariots and his army, the Egyptians will learn that I am Yahweh.'

19   Then the angel of god, who marched at the front of the army of Israel,
changed station and moved to their rear. The pillar of cloud changed station
20 from the front to the rear of them, and remained there. •It came between the
camp of the Egyptians and the camp of Israel. The cloud was dark, and the night
21 passed without the armies drawing any closer the whole night long. •Moses
stretched out his hand over the sea. Yahweh drove back the sea with a strong
22 easterly wind all night, and he made dry land of the sea. The waters parted •and
the sons of Israel went on dry ground right into the sea, walls of water to right
23 and to left of them. •The Egyptians gave chase: after them they went, right into
24 the sea, all Pharaoh's horses, his chariots, and his horsemen. •In the morning
watch, Yahweh looked down on the army of the Egyptians from the pillar of
25 fire and of cloud, and threw the army into confusion. •He so clogged their
chariot wheels that they could scarcely make headway. 'Let us flee from the
Israelites,' the Egyptians cried 'Yahweh is fighting for them against the Egyp-
26 tians!' •'Stretch out your hand over the sea,' Yahweh said to Moses 'that the
waters may flow back on the Egyptians and their chariots and their horsemen.'
27 Moses stretched out his hand over the sea and, as day broke, the sea returned
to its bed. The fleeing Egyptians marched right into it, and Yahweh overthrew
28 the Egyptians in the very middle of the sea. •The returning waters overwhelmed
the chariots and the horsemen of Pharaoh's whole army, which had followed
29 the Israelites into the sea; not a single one of them was left. •But the sons of
Israel had marched through the sea on dry ground, walls of water to right and
30 to left of them. •That day, Yahweh rescued Israel from the Egyptians, and Israel
31 saw the Egyptians lying dead on the shore. •Israel witnessed the great act that
Yahweh had performed against the Egyptians, and the people venerated
Yahweh; they put their faith in Yahweh and in Moses, his servant.

Song of victory

1 **15** It was then that Moses and the sons of Israel sang this song in honour of
Yahweh:

     'Yahweh I sing: he has covered himself in glory,
     horse and rider he has thrown into the sea.
2   Yah is my strength, my song,
     he is my salvation.
     This is my God, I praise him;
     the God of my father, I extol him.
3   Yahweh is a warrior;
     Yahweh is his name.
4   The chariots and the army of Pharaoh he has hurled into the sea;
     the pick of his horsemen lie drowned in the Sea of Reeds.
5   The depths have closed over them;
     they have sunk to the bottom like a stone.
6   Your right hand, Yahweh, shows majestic in power,
     your right hand, Yahweh, shatters the enemy.
7   So great your splendour, you crush your foes;
     you unleash your fury, and it devours them like stubble.
8   A blast from your nostrils and the waters piled high;
     the waves stood upright like a dyke;
     in the heart of the sea the deeps came together.

9   "I will give chase and overtake," the enemy said
     "I shall share out the spoil, my soul will feast on it;
     I shall draw my sword, my hand will destroy them."
10   One breath of yours you blew, and the sea closed over them;

they sank like lead in the terrible waters.
Who among the gods is your like, Yahweh?   11
Who is your like, majestic in holiness,
terrible in deeds of prowess, worker of wonders?
You stretched your right hand out, the earth swallowed them!   12
By your grace you led the people you redeemed,   13
by your strength you guided them to your holy house.
Hearing of this, the peoples tremble;   14
pangs seize on the inhabitants of Philistia.
Edom's chieftains are now dismayed,   15
the princes of Moab fall to trembling,
Canaan's inhabitants are all unmanned.
On them fall terror and dread;   16
through the power of your arm they are still as stone
as your people pass, Yahweh,
as the people pass whom you purchased.
You will bring them and plant them on the   17
mountain that is your own,
the place you have made your dwelling, Yahweh,
the sanctuary, Yahweh, prepared by your own hands.
Yahweh will be king for ever and ever.'   18

Pharaoh's cavalry, both his chariots and horsemen, had indeed entered the 19
sea, but Yahweh had made the waters of the sea flow back on them, yet the sons
of Israel had marched on dry ground right through the sea.ᵃ

Miriam, the prophetess, Aaron's sister, took up a timbrel, and all the women 20
followed her with timbrels, dancing. •And Miriam led them in the refrain: 21

'Sing of Yahweh: he has covered himself in glory,
horse and rider he has thrown into the sea'.

II. ISRAEL IN THE DESERT

Marahᵇ

Moses made Israel move from their camp at the Sea of Reeds, and they made 22
for the wilderness of Shur where they travelled for three days without finding
water. •They reached Marah but the water there was so bitter they could not 23
drink it; this is why the place was named Marah. •The people grumbled at 24
Moses. 'What are we to drink?' they said. •So Moses appealed to Yahweh, and 25
Yahweh pointed out some wood to him; this Moses threw into the water, and
the water was sweetened.

There it was he charged them with statute and with ordinance,
there that he put them to the test.

Then he said, •'If you listen carefully to the voice of Yahweh your God and 26
do what is right in his eyes, if you pay attention to his commandments and keep
his statutes, I shall inflict on you none of the evils that I inflicted on the
Egyptians, for it is I, Yahweh, who give you healing'.

So they came to Elim where twelve water-springs were, and seventy palm trees; 27
and there they pitched their camp beside the water.

The manna and the quails

16 From Elim they set out again, and the whole community of the sons of 1
Israel reached the wilderness of Sin—between Elim and Sinai—on the
fifteenth day of the second month after they had left Egypt. •And the whole 2
community of the sons of Israel began to complain against Moses and Aaron in

3 the wilderness •and said to them, 'Why did we not die at Yahweh's hand in the land of Egypt, when we were able to sit down to pans of meat and could eat bread to our heart's content! As it is, you have brought us to this wilderness to starve this whole company to death!'

4 Then Yahweh said to Moses, 'Now I will rain down bread for you from the heavens. Each day the people are to go out and gather the day's portion; I propose

5 to test them in this way to see whether they will follow my law or not. •On the sixth day, when they prepare what they have brought in, this will be twice as much as the daily gathering.'

6 Moses and Aaron said to the whole community of the sons of Israel, 'In the evening you shall learn that it was Yahweh who brought you out of the land of

7 Egypt, •and in the morning you shall see the glory of Yahweh, for he has heard your complaints against him—it is not against us you complain, for what are

8 we?' •Moses said, 'In the evening Yahweh will give you meat to eat, in the morning bread to your heart's content, for Yahweh has heard the complaints you made against him; your complaining is not against us—for what are we?— but against Yahweh'.

9 Moses said to Aaron, 'To the whole community of the sons of Israel say this,

10 "Present yourselves before Yahweh, for he has heard your complaints" '. •As Aaron was speaking to the whole community of the sons of Israel, they turned towards the wilderness, and there was the glory of Yahweh appearing in the

11 12 form of a cloud. •Then Yahweh spoke to Moses and said, •'I have heard the complaints of the sons of Israel. Say this to them, "Between the two evenings you shall eat meat, and in the morning you shall have bread to your heart's content.

13 Then you will learn that I, Yahweh, am your God." ' •And so it came about: quails flew up in the evening, and they covered the camp; in the morning there

14 was a coating of dew all round the camp. •When the coating of dew lifted, there on the surface of the desert was a thing delicate, powdery, as fine as hoarfrost

15 on the ground. •When they saw this, the sons of Israel said to one another, 'What is that?' not knowing what it was. 'That' said Moses to them 'is the

16 bread Yahweh gives you to eat. •This is Yahweh's command: Everyone must gather enough of it for his needs, one omer a head, according to the number of persons in your families. Each of you will gather for those who share his tent.'

17 18 The sons of Israel did this. They gathered it, some more, some less. •When they measured in an omer what they had gathered, the man who had gathered more had not too much, the man who had gathered less had not too little. Each found he had gathered what he needed.

19 20 Moses said to them, 'No one must keep any of it for tomorrow'. •But some would not listen to Moses and kept part of it for the following day, and it bred

21 maggots and smelt foul; and Moses was angry with them. •Morning by morning they gathered it, each according to his needs. And when the sun grew hot, it dissolved.

22 Now on the sixth day they gathered twice the amount of food: two omers a

23 head. All the leaders of the community came to tell Moses, •and he said to them, 'This is Yahweh's command: Tomorrow is a day of complete rest, a sabbath sacred to Yahweh. Bake what you want to bake, boil what you want to boil;

24 put aside all that is left for tomorrow.' •So, as Moses ordered, they put it aside for the following day, and its smell was not foul nor were there maggots in it.

25 'Eat it today,' Moses said 'for today is a sabbath in honour of Yahweh; you

26 will find none in the field today. •For six days you are to gather it, but on the

27 seventh day—the sabbath—there will be none.' •On the seventh day some of

28 the people went from the camp to gather it, but they found none. •Then Yahweh said to Moses, 'How much longer will you refuse to keep my commandments

29 and my laws? •Listen! Yahweh has laid down the sabbath for you; for this

15 a. Editorial comment.   b. Bitter, bitterness.

he gives you two day's food on the sixth day; each of you is to stay where he is; on the seventh day no one is to leave his home.' •So on the seventh day the 30 people abstained from all work.

The House of Israel named it 'manna'. It was like coriander seed; it was white 31 and its taste was like that of wafers made with honey.

Moses said, 'This is Yahweh's command: Fill an omer with it, and let it be 32 kept for your descendants, to let them see the food that I fed you with in the wilderness when I brought you out of the land of Egypt'. •Moses said to Aaron, 33 'Take a jar and put in it a full omer of manna and place it before Yahweh, to be kept for your descendants'. •Accordingly, Aaron put a full omer of manna in the 34 jar, as Yahweh had ordered Moses, and placed the manna before the Testimony,ᵃ to be kept there.

The sons of Israel ate manna for forty years, up to the time they reached 35 inhabited country: they ate manna up to the time they reached the frontier of the land of Canaan. •An omer is one-tenth of an ephah. 36

The water from the rock

17 The whole community of the sons of Israel moved from their camp in the 1 desert of Zin at Yahweh's command, to travel the further stages; and they pitched camp at Rephidimᵃ where there was no water for the people to drink. •So they grumbled against Moses. 'Give us water to drink' they said. 2 Moses answered them. 'Why do you grumble against me? Why do you put Yahweh to the test?' •But tormented by thirst, the people complained against 3 Moses. 'Why did you bring us out of Egypt?' they said. 'Was it so that I should die of thirst, my children too, and my cattle?' •Moses appealed to Yahweh. 4 'How am I to deal with this people?' he said. 'A little more and they will stone me!' •Yahweh said to Moses, 'Take with you some of the elders of Israel and 5 move on to the forefront of the people; take in your hand the staff with which you struck the river, and go. •I shall be standing before you there on the rock, 6 at Horeb. You must strike the rock, and water will flow from it for the people to drink.' This is what Moses did, in the sight of the elders of Israel. •The place 7 was named Massah and Meribahᵇ because of the grumbling of the sons of Israel and because they put Yahweh to the test by saying, 'Is Yahweh with us, or not?'

A battle against the Amalekites

The Amalekitesᶜ came and attacked Israel at Rephidim. •Moses said to Joshua, 8/9 'Pick out men for yourself, and tomorrow morning march out to engage Amalek. I, meanwhile, will stand on the hilltop, the staff of God in my hand.' •Joshua did 10 as Moses told him and marched out to engage Amalek, while Moses and Aaron and Hur went up to the top of the hill. •As long as Moses kept his arms raised, 11 Israel had the advantage; when he let his arms fall, the advantage went to Amalek. But Moses' arms grew heavy, so they took a stone and put it under him and 12 on this he sat, Aaron and Hur supporting his arms, one on one side, one on the other; and his arms remained firm till sunset. •With the edge of the sword Joshua 13 cut down Amalek and his people. •Then Yahweh said to Moses, 'Write this 14 action down in a book to keep the memory of it, and say in Joshua's hearing that I shall wipe out the memory of Amalek from under heaven.' •Moses then built an 15 altar and named it Yahweh-nissi •because he said, 'Lay hold of the banner of 16 Yahweh! Yahweh is at war with Amalek from age to age!'

The meeting of Jethro and Moses

18 Jethro priest of Midian, father-in-law of Moses, heard of all that God had 1 done for Moses and for Israel his people, and how Yahweh had brought Israel out of Egypt. •So Jethro, father-in-law of Moses, brought Moses' wife 2 Zipporah—after she had been dismissed—•with her two sons. One of these was 3 named Gershom because, he had said, 'I am a stranger in a foreign land'; •the 4

name of the other was Eliezer[a] because 'The God of my father is my help and
5 has delivered me from the sword of Pharaoh.' •So Jethro, father-in-law of Moses,
came with his son-in-law's wife and children to the wilderness where his camp
6 was, at the mountain of God. •'Here is your father-in-law, Jethro, come to
7 visit you,' Moses was told 'with your wife and her two sons.' • So Moses went
out to meet his father-in-law and bowing low before him he kissed him; and when
8 each had enquired of the other's health, they went into the tent. •Then Moses
told his father-in-law all that Yahweh had done to Pharaoh and the Egyptians
for the sake of Israel, and all the hardships that had overtaken them on the way,
9 and how Yahweh had rescued them. •And Jethro rejoiced at all Yahweh's
10 goodness to Israel in rescuing them from the Egyptians' hands. •'Blessed be
Yahweh' said Jethro then 'who has rescued you from the Egyptians and from
11 Pharaoh, and has rescued the people from the grasp of the Egyptians. •Now
I know that Yahweh is greater than all the gods . . .'
12   Then Jethro, father-in-law of Moses, offered a holocaust and sacrifices to
God; and Aaron came with all the elders of Israel to share the meal with the
father-in-law of Moses in the presence of God.

The appointment of judges

13   On the following day, Moses took his seat to administer justice for the people,
14 and from morning till evening they stood round him. •Observing what labours
. he took on himself for the people's sake, the father-in-law of Moses said to him,
'Why do you take all this on yourself for the people? Why sit here alone with the
15 people standing round you from morning till evening?' •Moses answered his
father-in-law, 'Because the people come to me to bring their enquiries to God.
16 When they have some dispute they come to me, and I settle the differences
between the one and the other and instruct them in God's statutes and his
17 decisions.' •'It is not right' the father-in-law of Moses said to him 'to take this
18 on yourself. •You will tire yourself out, you and the people with you. The work
19 is too heavy for you. You cannot do it alone. •Take my advice, and God will
be with you. You ought to represent the people before God and bring their
20 disputes to him. •Teach them the statutes and the decisions; show them the way
21 they must follow and what their course must be. •But choose from the people
at large some capable and God-fearing men, trustworthy and incorruptible, and
appoint them as leaders of the people: leaders of thousands, hundreds, fifties,
22 tens. •Let these be at the service of the people to administer justice at all times.
They can refer all difficult questions to you, but all smaller questions they will
decide for themselves, so making things easier for you and sharing the burden
23 with you. •If you do this—and may God so command you—you will be able
to stand the strain, and all these people will go home satisfied.'
24
25   Moses took his father-in-law's advice and did as he said. •Moses chose capable
men from the ranks of the Israelites and set them over the people: leaders of
26 thousands, hundreds, fifties, tens. •They were at the service of the people to
administer justice at all times. They referred hard questions to Moses, and
decided smaller questions by themselves.
27   Then Moses allowed his father-in-law to go, and he made his way back to
his own country.

16 a. That is, the tablets of the Law, kept in the ark (or chest); but in the tradition from which
the main narrative comes, the tablets and the ark have not yet been instituted.
17 a. A valley in the Sinai range. A similar miracle at Kadesh is described in Nb 20:1-13.
b. 'Trial and contention'.   c. Inhabitants of the mountain country of Seir and the northern
part of the Negeb.
18 a. Eli, my God; 'ezer, help.

III. THE COVENANT AT SINAI

A. THE COVENANT AND THE DECALOGUE

The Israelites come to Sinai

19 Three months after they came out of the land of Egypt . . . on that day 1
the sons of Israel came to the wilderness of Sinai.ᵃ •From Rephidim they set 2
out again; and when they reached the wilderness of Sinai, there in the wilderness
they pitched their camp; there facing the mountain Israel pitched camp.

Yahweh promises a covenant

Moses then went up to God, and Yahweh called to him from the mountain, 3
saying, 'Say this to the House of Jacob, declare this to the sons of Israel, •"You 4
yourselves have seen what I did with the Egyptians, how I carried you on eagle's
wings and brought you to myself. •From this you know that now, if you obey my 5
voice and hold fast to my covenant, you of all the nations shall be my very own
for all the earth is mine. •I will count you a kingdom of priests, a consecrated 6
nation." Those are the words that you are to speak to the sons of Israel.' •So Moses 7
went and summoned the elders of the people, putting before them all that Yahweh
had bidden him. • Then all the people answered as one, 'All that Yahweh has 8
said, we will do.' And Moses took the people's reply back to Yahweh.

Preparing for the Covenant

Yahweh said to Moses, 'I am coming to you in a dense cloud so that the 9
people may hear when I speak to you and may trust you always'. And Moses
took the people's reply back to Yahweh.

Yahweh said to Moses, 'Go to the people and tell them to prepare themselves 10
today and tomorrow. Let them wash their clothing and •hold themselves in 11
readiness for the third day, because on the third day Yahweh will descend on
the mountain of Sinai in the sight of all the people. •You will mark out the 12
limits of the mountain and say, "Take care not to go up the mountain or to
touch the foot of it. Whoever touches the mountain will be put to death.
No one must lay a hand on him: he must be stoned or shot down by arrow, 13
whether man or beast; he must not remain alive." When the ram's horn sounds
a long blast, they are to go up the mountain.'

So Moses came down from the mountain to the people and bade them prepare 14
themselves; and they washed their clothing. •Then he said to the people, 'Be 15
ready for the third day; do not go near any woman'.

The theophany on Sinai

Now at daybreak on the third day there were peals of thunder on the 16
mountain and lightning flashes, a dense cloud, and a loud trumpet blast, and
inside the camp all the people trembled. •Then Moses led the people out of 17
the camp to meet God; and they stood at the bottom of the mountain. •The 18
mountain of Sinai was entirely wrapped in smoke, because Yahweh had descended
on it in the form of fire. Like smoke from a furnace the smoke went up, and
the whole mountain shook violently. •Louder and louder grew the sound 19
of the trumpet. Moses spoke, and God answered him with peals of thunder.
Yahweh came down on the mountain of Sinai, on the mountain top, and Yahweh 20
called Moses to the top of the mountain; and Moses went up. •Yahweh said 21
to Moses, 'Go down and warn the people not to pass beyond their bounds to
come and look on Yahweh, or many of them will lose their lives. •The priests, 22
the men who do approach Yahweh,ᵇ even these must purify themselves, or
Yahweh will break out against them.' •Moses answered Yahweh, 'The people 23
cannot come up the mountain of Sinai because you warned us yourself when

24 you said, "Mark out the limits of the mountain and declare it sacred"'. •'Go
down,' said Yahweh to him 'and come up again bringing Aaron with you.
But do not allow the priests or the people to pass beyond their bounds to come
25 up to Yahweh, or he will break out against them.' •So Moses went down to
the people and spoke to them...

The Decalogue[a]

$^1_2$ **20** Then God spoke all these words. He said, •'I am Yahweh your God who
brought you out of the land of Egypt, out of the house of slavery.
3   'You shall have no gods except me.
4   'You shall not make yourself a carved image or any likeness of anything
5 in heaven or on earth beneath or in the waters under the earth; •you shall not
bow down to them or serve them. For I, Yahweh your God, am a jealous God
and I punish the father's fault in the sons, the grandsons, and the great-grandsons
6 of those who hate me; •but I show kindness to thousands of those who love me
and keep my commandments.
7   'You shall not utter the name of Yahweh your God to misuse it,[b] for Yahweh
will not leave unpunished the man who utters his name to misuse it.
$^8_9$ 'Remember the sabbath day and keep it holy. •For six days you shall labour
10 and do all your work, •but the seventh day is a sabbath for Yahweh your God.
You shall do no work that day, neither you nor your son nor your daughter
nor your servants, men or women, nor your animals nor the stranger who lives
11 with you. •For in six days Yahweh made the heavens and the earth and the
sea and all that these hold, but on the seventh day he rested; that is why Yahweh
has blessed the sabbath day and made it sacred.
12   'Honour your father and your mother so that you may have a long life in the
land that Yahweh your God has given to you.
13   'You shall not kill.
14   'You shall not commit adultery.
15   'You shall not steal.
16   'You shall not bear false witness against your neighbour.
17   'You shall not covet your neighbour's house. You shall not covet your
neighbour's wife, or his servant, man or woman, or his ox, or his donkey, or
anything that is his.'
18   'All the people shook with fear at the peals of thunder and the lightning
flashes, the sound of the trumpet, and the smoking mountain; and they kept
19 their distance. •'Speak to us yourself' they said to Moses 'and we will listen;
20 but do not let God speak to us, or we shall die.' •Moses answered the people,
'Do not be afraid; God has come to test you, so that your fear of him, being
21 always in your mind, may keep you from sinning'. •So the people kept their
distance while Moses approached the dark cloud where God was.

B. THE BOOK OF THE COVENANT

Law concerning the altar

22   Yahweh said to Moses, 'Tell the sons of Israel this, "You have seen for your-
23 selves that I have spoken to you from heaven. •You shall not make gods of
silver or gods of gold to stand beside me; you shall not make things like this
for yourselves.

---

19 a. According to tradition, Mount Sinai was at Jebel Musa, in the southern region of the
Sinai peninsula.   **b.** But see ch. 29, which treats the investiture of priests as a later occurrence.
20 a. This is the priestly version of the Ten Commandments; another version, the Deuteronomic,
is found in Dt 5, and it is the second which has been adopted by the Church.   **b.** Either in a
false oath or irreverently.   **c.** This section probably should be read after 19:19; the Decalogue
itself is not linked to the narrative framework.

"You are to make me an altar of earth, and sacrifice on this the holocausts 24 and communion sacrifices from your flocks or herds. In every place in which I have my name remembered I shall come to you and bless you. •If you make 25 me an altar of stone, do not build it of dressed stones; for if you use a tool on it, you profane it. •You shall not go up to my altar by steps for fear you expose 26 your nakedness."

Laws concerning slaves

21 'This is the ruling you are to lay before them: •"When you buy a Hebrew $\frac{1}{2}$ slave, his service shall be for six years. In the seventh year he may leave; he shall be free, with no compensation to pay. •If he came single, he shall leave 3 single; if he came married, his wife shall leave with him. •If his master gives 4 him a wife and she bears him sons and daughters, wife and children shall belong to her master, and the man must leave alone. •But if the slave declares, "I love 5 my master and my wife and children; I renounce my freedom", •then his master 6 shall take him to God, leading him to the door or the door post. His master shall pierce his ear with an awl, and he shall be in his service for all time. •If a man 7 sells his daughter as a slave, she shall not regain her liberty like male slaves. If she does not please her master who intended her for himself, he must let 8 her be bought back: he has not the right to sell her to foreigners, thus treating her unfairly. •If he intends her for his son, he shall deal with her according to the 9 ruling for daughters. •If he takes another wife, he must not reduce the food 10 of the first or her clothing or her conjugal rights. •Should he cheat her of these 11 three things she may leave, freely, without having to pay any money.

Homicide

"Anyone who strikes a man and so causes his death, must die. •If he has not lain $\frac{12}{13}$ in wait for him but God has delivered him into his hands,ᵃ then I will appoint you a place where he may seek refuge. •But should a man dare to kill his fellow by 14 treacherous intent, you must take him even from my altar to be put to death.

"Anyone who strikes his father or mother must die. •Anyone who abducts a $\frac{15}{16}$ man—whether he has sold him or is found in possession of him—must die. Anyone who curses father or mother must die. 17

Blows and wounds

"If men quarrel and one strikes the other a blow with stone or fist so that 18 the man, though he does not die, must keep his bed, •the one who struck the 19 blow shall not be liable provided the other gets up and can go about, even with a stick. He must compensate him, however, for his enforced inactivity, and care for him until he is completely cured.

"If a man beats his slave, male or female, and the slave dies at his hands, 20 he must pay the penalty. •But should the slave survive for one or two days, 21 he shall pay no penalty because the slave is his by right of purchase.

"If, when men come to blows, they hurt a woman who is pregnant and she 22 suffers a miscarriage, though she does not die of it, the man responsible must pay the compensation demanded of him by the woman's master; he shall hand it over, after arbitration. •But should she die, you shall give life for life, •eye $\frac{23}{24}$ for eye, tooth for tooth, hand for hand, foot for foot, •burn for burn, wound 25 for wound, stroke for stroke.

"When a man strikes at the eye of his slave, male or female, and destroys 26 the use of it, he must give him his freedom to compensate for the eye. •If he 27 knocks out the tooth of his slave, male or female, he must give him his freedom to compensate for the tooth.

"When an ox gores a man or woman to death, the ox must be stoned. Its flesh 28 shall not be eaten, and the owner of the ox shall not be liable. •But if the ox 29 has been in the habit of goring before, and if its owner was warned but has not

30 kept it under control, then should this ox kill a man or woman, the ox must
be stoned and its owner put to death. •If a ransom is imposed on him, he must
31 pay whatever is imposed, to redeem his life. •If the ox gores a boy or a girl, he
32 must be treated in accordance with this same rule. •If the ox gores a slave, male
or female, the owner must pay over to their master a sum of money —thirty
shekels— and the ox must be stoned.
33   "When a man leaves a pit uncovered, or when he digs one but does not
34 cover it, should an ox, or donkey, fall into it, •then the owner of the pit shall
make up for the loss: he must pay its owner money, and the dead animal shall
35 be his own. •If one man's ox harms another's so that it dies, the owners must
sell the live ox and share the price of it; they shall also share the dead animal.
36 But if it is common knowledge that the ox has been in the habit of goring before,
and its owner has not kept it under control, he must repay ox for ox; the dead
animal shall be his own.

Theft of animals

37
1   "If a man steals an ox or a sheep and then slaughters or sells it, he must pay
five oxen for the ox, four sheep for the sheep.
1
2 **22** "If a thief is caught breaking in and is struck a mortal blow, there is to
3   be no blood-vengeance for him, •but there shall be blood-vengeance for
him if it was after dawn. Full restitution must be made; if he has not the means,
3
4 he must be sold to pay for what he has stolen. •If the stolen animal is found alive
in his possession, ox or donkey or sheep, he must pay double.

Offences demanding compensation

4
5   "When a man puts his animals out to graze in a field or vineyard and lets
his beasts graze in another's field, he must make restitution for the part of the
field that has been grazed in proportion to its yield. But if he has let the whole
field be grazed, he must make restitution in proportion to the best crop recorded in
the injured party's field or vineyard.
5
6   "When a fire spreads, setting light to thorn bushes and destroying stacked
or standing corn or the field itself, the man responsible for the fire must make
full restitution.
6
7   "When a man has entrusted money or goods to another's keeping and these
are stolen from his house, the thief, if he can be caught, must repay double.
7
8 Should the thief not be caught, the owner of the house must swear before God
that he has not laid hands on the other man's property.
8
9   "Whenever there is breach of trust in the matter of ox, donkey, sheep, clothing,
or any lost property for which it is claimed 'Yes, this is it', the dispute shall
be brought before God. The person whom God pronounces guilty[a] must pay
double to the other.
9
10   "When a man has entrusted to another's keeping a donkey, ox, sheep, or any
beast whatever, and this dies or is injured or carried off, without a witness,
10
11 an oath by Yahweh shall decide between the two parties whether one man has
laid hands on the other's property or not. The owner shall take what remains,
11
12 the other shall not have to make good the loss. •But if the animal has been
13 stolen from him, he must make restitution to the owner. •If it has been savaged
by wild beasts, he must bring the savaged remains of the animal as evidence,
and he shall not be obliged to give compensation.
13
14   "When a man borrows an animal from another, and it is injured or dies in
14
15 the owner's absence, the borrower must make full restitution. •But if the owner
has been present, the borrower will not have to make good the loss. If the owner
has hired it out, he shall settle for the price of its hire:

---

21 a. Accidents are attributed to God.
22 a. Through trial by ordeal, or oracle, or oath.

Violation of a virgin

"If a man seduces a virgin who is not betrothed and sleeps with her, he must ¹⁵ pay her price*b* and make her his wife. •If her father absolutely refuses to let ¹⁶ ¹⁷ him have her, the seducer must pay a sum of money equal to the price fixed for a virgin.

Moral and religious laws

"You shall not allow a sorceress to live. ¹⁷ ¹⁸

"Anyone who has intercourse with an animal must die. ¹⁸ ¹⁹

"Anyone who sacrifices to other gods shall come under the ban. ¹⁹ ²⁰

"You must not molest the stranger or oppress him, for you lived as strangers ²⁰ ²¹ in the land of Egypt. •You must not be harsh with the widow, or with the orphan; ²¹ ²² if you are harsh with them, they will surely cry out to me, and be sure I shall hear ²³ their cry; •my anger will flare and I shall kill you with the sword, your own wives ²⁴ will be widows, your own children orphans.

"If you lend money to any of my people, to any poor man among you, ²⁴ ²⁵ you must not play the usurer with him: you must not demand interest from him.

"If you take another's cloak as a pledge, you must give it back to him before ²⁵ ²⁶ sunset. •It is all the covering he has; it is the cloak he wraps his body ²⁶ ²⁷ in; what else would he sleep in? If he cries to me, I will listen, for I am full of pity.

"You shall not revile God nor curse a ruler of your people. ²⁷ ²⁸

First-fruits and first-born

"Do not be slow to make offering from the abundance of your threshing- ²⁸ ²⁹ floor and your winepress. You must give me the first-born of your sons; •you ²⁹ ³⁰ must do the same with your flocks and herds. The first-born must remain with its mother for seven days; on the eighth day you must give it to me.

"You are to be men consecrated to me. You must not eat the flesh of an ³⁰ ³¹ animal that has been savaged by wild beasts; you must throw it to the dogs.

Justice. Duties towards enemies

23 "You must not make false assertions. You must not support a guilty man ¹ by giving malicious evidence. •You must not take the side of the greater ² number in the cause of wrong-doing nor side with the majority and give evidence in a lawsuit in defiance of justice; •nor in a lawsuit must you show ³ partiality to the poor.

"If you come on your enemy's ox or donkey going astray, you must lead it ⁴ back to him. •If you see the donkey of a man who hates you fallen under its ⁵ load, instead of keeping out of his way, go to him to help him.

"You must not cheat any poor man of yours of his rights at law. •Keep out ⁶ ⁷ of trumped-up cases. See that the man who is innocent and just is not done to death, and do not acquit the guilty. •You must not accept a bribe, for a bribe ⁸ blinds clear-sighted men and is the ruin of the just man's cause.

"You must not oppress the stranger; you know how a stranger feels, for you ⁹ lived as strangers in the land of Egypt.

The sabbatical year and the sabbath

"For six years you may sow your land and gather its produce, •but in the ¹⁰ ¹¹ seventh year you must let it lie fallow and forego all produce from it. Those of your people who are poor may take food from it, and let the wild animals feed on what they leave. You shall do the same with your vineyard and your olive grove.

"For six days you shall do your work, but stop on the seventh day, so that your ¹² ox and your donkey may rest and the son of your slave girl have a breathing space, and the stranger too.

13   "Take notice of all I have told you and do not repeat the name of other gods:
      let it not be heard from your lips.

The great feasts

14
15   "Three times a year you are to celebrate a feast in my honour. •You must
      celebrate the feast of Unleavened Bread: you must eat unleavened bread, as
      I have commanded you, at the appointed time in the month of Abib, for in that
      month you came out of Egypt. And no one must come before me empty-handed.
16   The feast of Harvest, too, you must celebrate, the feast of the first-fruits of the
      produce of your sown fields; the feast of Ingathering also, at the end of the year
17   when you gather in the fruit of your labours from the fields. •Three times a year
      all your menfolk must present themselves before the Lord Yahweh.
18   "You must not offer unleavened bread with the blood of the victim sacrificed
      to me, nor put by the fat of my festal victim for the following day.
19   "You must bring the best of the first-fruits of your soil to the house of Yahweh
      your God.
      "You must not boil a kid in its mother's milk.[a]

Preparatory promises and instructions for the entry into Canaan

20   "I myself will send an angel before you to guard you as you go and to bring
21   you to the place that I have prepared. •Give him reverence and listen to all
      that he says. Offer him no defiance; he would not pardon such a fault,
22   for my name is in him. •If you listen carefully to his voice and do all that I say,
23   I shall be enemy to your enemies, foe to your foes. •My angel will go before
      you and lead you to where the Amorites are and the Hittites, the Perizzites,
24   the Canaanites, the Hivites, the Jebusites; I shall exterminate these. •You must
      not bow down to their gods or worship them; you must not do as they do:
25   you must destroy their gods utterly and smash their standing-stones.[b] •You are to
      worship Yahweh your God, and I shall bless your bread and water, and remove
26   sickness from among you. •In your land no woman will miscarry, none be
      barren. I shall give you your full term of life.
27   "I shall spread panic ahead of you; I shall throw into confusion all the
      people you encounter; I shall make all your enemies turn and run from you.
28   I shall send hornets in front of you to drive Hivite and Canaanite and Hittite from
29   your presence. •I shall not drive them out before you in a single year, or the
      land would become a desert where, to your cost, the wild beasts would multiply.
30   Little by little I will drive them out before you until your numbers grow and
31   you come into possession of the land. •For your frontiers I shall fix the Sea
      of Reeds and the Philistine sea, the desert and the river;[c] yes, I shall deliver the
      inhabitants of the country into your hands, and you will drive them out before
32
33   you. •You must make no pact with them or with their gods. •They must not
      live in your country or they will make you sin against me; you would come to
      worship their gods, and that would be a snare for you indeed!" '

C. THE COVENANT RATIFIED

1   **24** To Moses he had said, 'Come up to Yahweh, yourself and Aaron, Nadab
             and Abihu, and seventy of the elders of Israel and bow down in worship
2   at a distance. •Moses alone must approach Yahweh; the others must not, nor
      must the people go up with him.'
3   Moses went and told the people all the commands of Yahweh and all the
      ordinances. In answer, all the people said with one voice, 'We will observe all

b. The 'bride-price', *mohar*, paid by a betrothed man to the family of his future wife.
23 a. A Canaanite custom.   b. *Stelae*, stones or pillars with a phallic significance in the
Canaanite cult.   c. The Arabian desert and the river Euphrates. The boundaries mentioned
are those of Solomon's kingdom, 1 K 5:1.

the commands that Yahweh has decreed'. •Moses put all the commands of 4 Yahweh into writing, and early next morning he built an altar at the foot of the mountain, with twelve standing-stones for the twelve tribes of Israel. •Then 5 he directed certain young Israelites to offer holocausts and to immolate bullocks to Yahweh as communion sacrifices. •Half of the blood Moses took up and 6 put into basins, the other half he cast on the altar. •And taking the Book of 7 the Covenant he read it to the listening people, and they said, 'We will observe all that Yahweh has decreed; we will obey.' •Then Moses took the blood and 8 cast it towards the people. 'This' he said 'is the blood of the Covenant that Yahweh has made with you, containing all these rules.'

Moses went up with Aaron, Nadab and Abihu, and seventy elders of Israel. 9 They saw the God of Israel beneath whose feet there was, it seemed, a sapphire 10 pavement pure as the heavens themselves. •He laid no hand on these notables 11 of the sons of Israel: they gazed on God. They ate and they drank.

Moses on the mountain

Yahweh said to Moses, 'Come up to me on the mountain and stay there 12 while I give you the stone tablets —the law and the commandments— that I have written for their instruction'. •Accordingly Moses rose, he and his servant 13 Joshua, and they went up the mountain of God. •To the elders he had said, 14 'Wait here for us until we come back to you. You have Aaron and Hur with you; if anyone has a difference to settle, let him go to them.' •And Moses went 15 up the mountain.

The cloud covered the mountain, •and the glory of Yahweh settled on the 16 mountain of Sinai; for six days the cloud covered it, and on the seventh day Yahweh called to Moses from inside the cloud. •To the eyes of the sons of 17 Israel the glory of Yahweh seemed like a devouring fire on the mountain top. Moses went right into the cloud. He went up the mountain, and stayed there for 18 forty days and forty nights.

IV. INSTRUCTIONS ON THE BUILDING OF THE SANCTUARY AND ON ITS MINISTERS[a]

Contributions for the sanctuary

25 Yahweh spoke to Moses and said, •'Tell the sons of Israel to set aside $\frac{1}{2}$ a contribution for me; you shall accept this contribution from every man whose heart prompts him to give it. •You shall accept from them the following 3 contributions: gold, silver and bronze; •purple stuffs, of violet shade and red, 4 crimson stuffs, fine linen, goats' hair; •rams' skins dyed red, fine leather, acacia 5 wood; •oil for the lamps, spices for the chrism and for the fragrant incense; 6 onyx stones and gems to be set in ephod and pectoral. •Build me a sanctuary $\frac{7}{8}$ so that I may dwell among them. •In making the tabernacle and its furnishings 9 you must follow exactly the pattern I shall show you.

The tabernacle and its furnishings. The ark

'You are to make me an ark of acacia wood, two and a half cubits long, one 10 and a half cubits wide, one and a half cubits high.[b] •You are to plate it, inside and 11 out, with pure gold, and decorate it all round with a gold moulding. •You will 12 cast four gold rings for the ark and fix them to its four supports: two rings on one side and two rings on the other. •You will also make shafts of acacia wood 13 plated with gold •and pass the shafts through the rings on the sides of the ark, 14 to carry the ark by these. •The shafts must remain in the rings of the ark and 15 not be withdrawn. •Inside the ark you will place the Testimony that I shall 16 give you.

17   'Further, you are to make a throne of mercy, of pure gold, two and a half
18 cubits long, and one and a half cubits wide. •For the two ends of this throne
   of mercy you are to make two golden cherubs;ᶜ you are to make them of beaten
19 gold. •Make the first cherub for one end and the second for the other, and
   fasten them to the two ends of the throne of mercy so that they make one piece
20 with it. •The cherubs are to have their wings spread upwards so that they
   overshadow the throne of mercy. They must face one another, their faces towards
21 the throne of mercy. •You must place the throne of mercy on the top of the ark.
22 Inside the ark you must place the Testimony that I shall give you. •There I shall
   come to meet you; there, from above the throne of mercy, from between the
   two cherubs that are on the ark of the Testimony, I shall give you all
   my commands for the sons of Israel.

The table for the offertory bread

23   'You are to make a table of acacia wood, two cubits long, one cubit wide,
24 and one and a half cubits high. •You are to plate it with pure gold, and decorate
25 it all round with a gold moulding. •You are to fit it with struts, one hand's
26 breadth wide, and decorate these with a golden moulding. •You are to make for
27 it four gold rings and fix these at the four corners where the four legs are. •The
28 rings must lie close to the struts to hold the shafts for carrying the table. •You
   are to make the shafts of acacia wood and plate them with gold. The table is to be
29 carried by these. •You are to make dishes, cups, jars and libation bowls for it;
30 you are to make these of pure gold. •On the table, before me, you must place the
   bread of continual offering.

The lamp-stand

31   'You are to make a lamp-stand of pure gold; the lamp-stand must be of
   beaten gold, base and stem. Its cups —calyx and petals— must be of one piece
32 with it. •Six branches must extend from the sides of it, three from one side, three
33 from the other. •The first branch is to carry three cups shaped like almond
   blossoms, each with its calyx and petals; the second branch, too, is to carry
   three cups shaped like almond blossoms, each with its calyx and petals, and
34 similarly for all six branches extending from the lamp-stand. •The lamp-stand
   itself is to carry four cups shaped like almond blossoms, each with its calyx
35 and petals, •thus: one calyx under the first two branches extending from the
   lamp-stand, one under the next pair, one under the last pair: corresponding to
36 the six branches extending from the lamp-stand. •The calyxes and the branches
   must be of one piece with the lamp-stand, and the whole made from a single
37 piece of pure gold, beaten out. •Then you are to make lamps for it, seven of them,
38 and set them so that they throw their light towards the front of it. •The snuffers
39 and trays must be of pure gold. •You are to use a talent of pure gold for making
40 the lamp-stand and all its accessories. •See that you make them according
   to the pattern shown you on the mountain.

The tabernacle. Fabrics and hangings

1 **26** 'The tabernacle itself you are to make with ten sheets of fine twined linen,
         of purple stuffs, violet shade and red, and of crimson stuffs; you are to have
2 these sheets finely brocaded with cherubs. •The length of a single sheet is to
   be twenty-eight cubits, its width four cubits, all the sheets to be of the same size.
3 Five of the sheets must be joined to each other, and the other five similarly.
4 You must attach loops of violet stuff to the border of the last sheet in one set,

25 a. Ch. 25-31 define the system of worship which goes back to Moses and contain elements of
great antiquity, but with these are mixed others which reflect the development of worship
in the course of the history of Israel. The formula, 'Yahweh said to Moses' asserts the equal
authority of all the religious institutions.   **b.** A rectangular chest (3¾ ft × 2¼ ft × 2¼ ft).   **c.** Half-
human, half-animal figures, corresponding to the tutelary deities guarding Babylonian shrines.

and do the same for the border of the last sheet in the other set. •You are to ⁵
put fifty loops on the first sheet and, matching them one by one, fifty loops on
the border of the last sheet in the second set. •And you are to make fifty gold ⁶
clasps to draw the sheets together. In this way the tabernacle will be a unified
whole.

'You are to make sheets of goats' hair to form a tent over the tabernacle; ⁷
you will make eleven of these. •The length of a single sheet is to be thirty cubits, ⁸
its width four cubits, the eleven sheets to be all of the same size. •You must join ⁹
five of these sheets together into one set, the remaining six into another; the
sixth you will fold double over the front of the tent. •You must attach fifty loops ¹⁰
to the border of the last sheet in one set, and do the same for the border
of the last sheet in the second set. •You must make fifty bronze clasps and ¹¹
put them into the loops, so as to draw the tent together and make it a unified
whole.

'As one sheet of the tent will be left over, half of this extra sheet is to hang ¹²
over the back of the tabernacle. •The extra cubit on either side along the ¹³
length of the tent sheets is to hang over the sides of the tabernacle as a covering
for it.

'For the tent you will further make a covering of rams' skins dyed red, and ¹⁴
a covering of fine leather to spread over that.

The framework

'You are to make frames of acacia wood for the tabernacle, these to stand ¹⁵
upright. •Each frame is to be ten cubits long and one and a half cubits wide. ¹⁶
Each frame must be fitted with twin tenons; for all the frames of the tabernacle ¹⁷
you must do this. •You are to make the frames for the tabernacle: twenty frames ¹⁸
for the southern side, facing the south country. •You are to make forty silver ¹⁹
sockets for putting under the twenty frames thus: two sockets under the first
frame to receive its two tenons, and so on for the other frames. •The other side ²⁰
of the tabernacle, on the north, is to have twenty frames •supported by forty ²¹
silver sockets, two sockets under each frame. •For the back of the tabernacle, on ²²
the west, you must make six frames. •You are to make two frames for the corners ²³
at the back of the tabernacle. •These frames must be coupled at their lower ²⁴
end and so to the top, up to the level of the first ring; this for the two frames
that are to form the two corners. •Thus there will be eight frames with their ²⁵
sixteen silver sockets: two sockets under the first frame and so on.

'You are to make crossbars of acacia wood: five to hold together the frames ²⁶
for one side of the tabernacle, •five to hold the frames for the other side of the ²⁷
tabernacle, and five to hold the frames that form the west end of the tabernacle.
The middle bar, fixed half-way up, is to run from one end to the other. •The ²⁸/²⁹
frames are to be plated with gold, and with gold rings on them to take the crossbars which you are to plate with gold. •This is how you are to erect the tabernacle ³⁰
according to the model shown to you on the mountain.

The veil

'You are to make a veil of purple stuffs, violet shade and red, of crimson ³¹
stuffs, and of fine twined linen; you are to have it finely embroidered with cherubs.
You are to hang it on four posts of acacia wood plated with gold and furnished ³²
with golden hooks and set in four silver sockets. •You must hang the veil from ³³
the clasps and there behind the veil you must place the ark of the Testimony,
and the veil will serve you to separate the Holy Place from the Holy of Holies.
The throne of mercy you must place on top of the ark inside the Holy of Holies. ³⁴
The table you must set outside the veil, and the lamp-stand on the south side ³⁵
of the tabernacle, opposite the table. You must put the table on the north side.
For the entrance to the tent you are to make a screen of purple stuffs, violet shade ³⁶
and red, and of crimson stuffs and fine twined linen, the work of a skilled

37 embroiderer. •For this screen you are to make five posts of acacia wood plated with gold, with golden hooks; for these you are to cast five bronze sockets.

The altar of holocaust

1,2 **27** 'You are to make the altar out of acacia wood, a square five cubits long and five cubits wide, its height to be three cubits. •At its four corners you are to put horns, the horns to be of one piece with it, plating it with bronze. 3 For the altar you are to make pans for the ashes from the fat, shovels, sprinkling basins, hooks, fire pans; you must make all the vessels for the altar out of 4 bronze. •You are also to make a grating for it of bronze network, and on the 5 four corners of this fix four bronze rings. •This grating you must set under the 6 altar's ledge, below, so that it reaches half-way up the altar. •And for the altar 7 you are to make shafts of acacia wood and plate them with bronze. •These are to be passed through the rings, so that they are on either side of the altar when 8 it is carried. •You are to make the altar hollow, of boards; you will make it in the way that was shown to you on the mountain.

The court.

9 'You are to make the court of the tabernacle. Facing the south country, on the southern side, the hangings of the court are to be of fine twined linen, one 10 hundred cubits long for one side. •Their twenty bronze posts are to be set in 11 twenty bronze sockets and to have their hooks and rods of silver. •So too for the northern side there are to be hangings one hundred cubits long, and twenty 12 posts set in twenty bronze sockets, with their hooks and rods of silver. •Across the width of the court, on the western side, there are to be fifty cubits of 13 hangings, carried on ten posts set in ten sockets. •The width of the court on the 14 eastern side facing the sunrise is to be fifty cubits. •On one side of the gateway there are to be fifteen cubits of hangings, carried on three posts set in three 15 sockets. •On the other side of the gateway there are also to be fifteen cubits 16 of hangings, carried on three posts set in three sockets. •The gateway to the court is to consist of a screen twenty cubits wide made of purple stuffs, violet shade and red, of crimson stuffs and fine twined linen, the work of a skilled 17 embroiderer, carried on four posts set in their four sockets. •All the posts enclosing the court are to be connected by silver rods; their hooks are to be of 18 silver, their sockets of bronze. •The length of the court is to be one hundred cubits, its width fifty cubits, its height five cubits. All the hangings are to be 19 made of fine twined linen, and their sockets of bronze. •All the furnishings for whatever use in the tabernacle, all the pegs of it and of the court, must be of bronze.

The oil for the lamps

20 'You are to order the sons of Israel to bring you pure olive oil for the light, 21 and to keep a flame burning there perpetually. •Aaron and his sons are to set this flame in the Tent of Meeting, outside the veil that is before the Testimony. It must burn there before Yahweh from evening to morning perpetually. This is an irrevocable ordinance for their descendants, to be kept by the sons of Israel.

The priestly vestments

1 **28** 'From among the sons of Israel summon your brother Aaron and his sons to be priests in my service: Aaron, Nadab and Abihu, Eleazar and Ithamar, 2 sons of Aaron. •For Aaron your brother you are to make sacred vestments 3 to give dignity and magnificence. •You are to instruct all the ablest craftsmen, whose ability I have given them, to make Aaron's vestments for his consecration 4 to my priesthood. •These are the vestments they must make: pectoral, ephod, robe, embroidered tunic, turban and girdle. They are to make sacred vestments 5 for your brother Aaron and his sons to be priests in my service. •They must use gold, purple stuffs, violet shade and red, crimson stuffs, and fine twined linen.

The ephod

'They are to make the ephod of gold, purple stuffs, violet shade and red, crimson stuffs, and fine twined linen, the work of a skilled embroiderer. •It must have two shoulder-straps fitted to it to join its two ends together. •The woven band on it to hold it is to be of similar workmanship and form one piece with it: this must be of gold, purple stuffs, violet shade and red, crimson stuffs, and fine twined linen. •You will then take two onyx stones and engrave them with the names of the sons of Israel, •six of their names on one stone, the remaining six on the other, in the order of their birth. •With the art of a jeweller, of an engraver of seals, you are to engrave the two stones with the names of the sons of Israel, and mount them in settings of gold mesh. •You are to fasten the two stones commemorating the sons of Israel to the shoulder-straps of the ephod. In this way Aaron will bear their names on his shoulders in the presence of Yahweh, so as to commemorate them. •You must also make golden rosettes, •and two chains of pure gold twisted like cord; you are to attach these cord-like chains to the rosettes.

The pectoral of judgement

'You are to make the pectoral of judgement, finely brocaded, of the same workmanship as the ephod. You are to make it of gold, purple stuffs, violet shade and red, crimson stuffs, and fine twined linen. •It is to be square and doubled over, a span in length and a span in width. •In this you are to set four rows of stones. Sard, topaz, carbuncle, for the first row; •emerald, sapphire, diamond the second row; •the third row, hyacinth, ruby, amethyst; •the fourth row, beryl, onyx, jasper. These are to be mounted in gold settings. •They are to bear the names of the sons of Israel and, like the names on them, are to be twelve in number. They are to be engraved like seals, each with the name of one of the twelve tribes. •For the pectoral you will make chains of pure gold twisted like cords. •For the pectoral you must make two gold rings and fix them to its two upper corners. •You must fasten the two gold cords to the two rings fixed on the corners of the pectoral. •The other two ends of the cords you must fasten to the two rosettes, so that they will be attached to the shoulder-straps of the ephod, on the front. •You are to make two gold rings and fix them to the two lower corners of the pectoral, on the inner hem, next to the ephod. •You are to make two more gold rings and fix them low down on the front of the two shoulder-pieces of the ephod, close to the join, above the woven band of the ephod. •You must secure the pectoral by passing a ribbon of violet-purple through its rings and those of the ephod, so that the pectoral will sit above the woven band and not come àpart from the ephod. •Thus by means of the pectoral of judgement, when Aaron enters the sanctuary, he will bear the names of the sons of Israel on his breast to call them to mind continually in the presence of Yahweh. •To the pectoral of judgement you will add the Urim and the Thummim so that Aaron may have them on his breast when he goes into Yahweh's presence. Thus in the presence of Yahweh Aaron will continually bear on his breast the oracle of the sons of Israel.

The robe

'You are to make the robe of the ephod entirely of violet-purple. •In the centre it must have an opening for the head, the opening to have round it a border woven like the neck of a coat of mail to keep the robe from being torn. •The lower hem you are to decorate with pomegranates of purple stuffs, violet shade and red, crimson stuffs, and fine twined linen, with golden bells between: •gold bells and pomegranates alternately all round the lower hem of the robe. •Aaron is to wear it when he officiates, so that the tinkling of the bells will be heard whenever he enters the sanctuary into Yahweh's presence, or leaves it; thus he will not die.

The diadem

36 'You are to make a plate of pure gold and engrave on it "Consecrated to
37 Yahweh" as a man engraves a seal. •You will secure this to the turban with a
38 ribbon of violet-purple; it is to be placed on the front of the turban. •Aaron is to
wear it on his brow, and so take on himself any shortcomings there may be in
what the sons of Israel consecrate in any of their sacred offerings. Aaron must
always wear it on his brow, to draw down on them the goodwill of Yahweh.
39 The tunic you must weave of fine linen, and make a turban of fine linen, and a
girdle, the work of a skilled embroiderer.

The vestments of the priests

40 'For the sons of Aaron you are to make tunic and girdle and head-dress to give
41 dignity and magnificence. •You will put these on your brother Aaron and his
sons. You will then anoint and invest and consecrate them to serve me in the
42 priesthood. •You are to make them linen breeches to cover their nakedness from
43 loin to thigh. •Aaron and his sons must wear these when they go into the Tent
of Meeting and when they approach the altar to serve in the sanctuary, as a
precaution against incurring some fault that would mean death. This is an
irrevocable ordinance for Aaron and for his descendants after him.

The consecration of Aaron and his sons. Preparations

1 **29** 'This is the ritual you must use for them when you consecrate them to
serve me in the priesthood. Take one young bull and two rams without
2 blemish, •unleavened bread, unleavened cakes mixed with oil, and unleavened
3 wafers spread with oil, made from fine wheat flour. •You must put these into a
basket and present them in the basket, at the same time as the young bull and
the two rams.

Their purification, clothing, and anointing

4 'You are to bring Aaron and his sons to the entrance of the Tent of Meeting
5 and they are to be bathed. •Take the vestments and dress Aaron in the tunic,
the robe of the ephod, the ephod, and the pectoral, and gird him with the woven
6 band of the ephod. •Put the turban on his head, and on the turban fix the sacred
7 diadem. •Then take the chrism and pour it on his head, and so anoint him.
8 'Next, bring his sons and clothe them with tunics. •Pass the girdles round
9 their waists and put the head-dresses on their heads. And by irrevocable ordinance
the priesthood will be theirs. This is how you are to invest Aaron and his sons.

The offerings

10 'You are to bring the bull in front of the Tent of Meeting. Aaron and his sons
11 are to lay their hands on its head. •Immolate the bull there before Yahweh
12 at the entrance to the Tent of Meeting. •Then take some of its blood and with
your finger put it on the horns of the altar. Next, pour out the rest of the blood
13 at the foot of the altar. •And then take all the fat that covers the entrails, the
fatty mass which is over the liver, the two kidneys with their covering fat, and
14 burn them on the altar. •As for the bull's flesh, its skin and its dung, you must
burn them outside the camp, for it is a sin-offering.
15 'Next you are to take one of the rams. Aaron and his sons are to lay their
16 hands on its head. •You are to immolate the ram, take up its blood and pour it
17 out on the surrounds of the altar. •Next, divide the ram in pieces and wash
18 the entrails and legs and put them on top of the pieces and the head. •Then
burn the whole ram on the altar. This will be a burnt offering whose fragrance
will appease Yahweh; it will be a holocaust in honour of Yahweh.
19 'Next you are to take the other ram. Aaron and his sons are to lay their hands
20 on its head. •You are to immolate the ram, take some of its blood and put it on
the lobe of Aaron's right ear, on the lobes of his sons' right ears, the thumbs

of their right hands, and the big toes of their right feet, and pour out the rest of the blood on the surrounds of the altar. •Then take some of the blood 21 that remains on the altar, together with the chrism, and sprinkle it on Aáron and his vestments and on his sons and their vestments: so that he and his vestments will be consecrated and his sons too, and their vestments.

The investiture of the priests

'You are to take the fatty parts of the ram: the tail, the fat that covers the 22 entrails, the fatty mass which is over the liver, the two kidneys with their covering fat and also the right thigh, for this is a ram of investiture. •You are to take a loaf 23 of bread, a cake of bread made with oil, and a wafer, from the basket of unleavened bread placed before Yahweh, •and put it all into Aaron's hands and 24 those of his sons and make the gesture of offering before Yahweh. •Then you 25 are to take them back and burn them on the altar, on top of the holocaust, an appeasing fragrance before Yahweh. This will be a holocaust in honour of Yahweh.

'You are to take the breast of the ram of Aaron's investiture and make the 26 gesture of offering before Yahweh; this is to be your portion. •You are to conse- 27 crate the breast that has been thus offered, as also the thigh that is set aside —the breast, that is, which has been offered and the thigh that has been set aside from the ram of investiture of Aaron and his sons. •This, by perpetual 28 law, will be the portion that Aaron and his sons are to receive from the sons of Israel, since it is the portion set aside, a portion the sons of Israel are to set aside from their communion sacrifices, the portion they owe to Yahweh.

'Aaron's sacred vestments are to pass to his sons after him, and they will 29 wear them for their anointing and investiture. •The son of Aaron who succeeds 30 him in the priesthood and enters the Tent of Meeting to serve in the sanctuary must wear them for seven days.

The sacred meal

'You are to take the ram of investiture and cook its meat in a holy place. 31 Aaron and his sons will eat the meat of the ram, and also the bread that is in 32 the basket, at the entrance to the Tent of Meeting. •They are to eat what was 33 used in making atonement for them at their investiture, their consecration. No layman may eat these; they are holy things. •If any of the meat from the 34 investiture sacrifice, or the bread, should be left till morning, you must put what is left in the fire. It is not to be eaten; it is a holy thing. •For Aaron and 35 his sons you are to do exactly as I have commanded you: you are to take seven days over their investiture.

The consecration of the altar of holocaust

'On each of the days you are also to offer a bull as a sacrifice for sin, 36 in atonement; by offering an atonement sacrifice for sin you will take away sin from the altar; then you must anoint it, and so consecrate it. •For seven days 37 you are to repeat the atonement sacrifice for the altar and consecrate it. So it will excel in holiness, and whatever touches it will be holy.

The daily holocaust

'This is what you are to offer on the altar: two yearling lambs each day in 38 perpetuity. •The first lamb you must offer in the morning, the second between 39 the two evenings. •With the first lamb you must offer one-tenth of a measure 40 of fine flour mixed with one quarter of a hin of purest oil and, for a libation, one quarter of a hin of wine. •The second lamb you must offer between the two 41 evenings; do this with the same oblation and the same libation as in the morning, as an appeasing fragrance, an offering burnt in honour of Yahweh. •This is to 42 be a perpetual holocaust from generation to generation, at the entrance to the Tent of Meeting in the presence of Yahweh; that is where I shall meet you and speak to you.

⁴³₄₄   'I will meet the sons of Israel in the place consecrated by my glory. •I will consecrate the Tent of Meeting and the altar. I will consecrate Aaron too, and
45 his sons, to be priests in my service. •I will remain with the sons of Israel, and
46 I will be their God. •And so they will know that it is I, Yahweh their God, who brought them out of the land of Egypt to live among them: I, Yahweh their God.

The altar of incense

1   **30**   'You must make an altar on which to burn incense;ᵃ you are to make it out
2   of acacia wood. •It is to be one cubit long, and one cubit wide —that is to say, square— and to stand two cubits high; its horns are to be of one piece
3 with it. •The top of it, its surrounding sides, and its horns, are to be plated with
4 pure gold, and decorated with a gold moulding all round. •You are to fix two gold rings to it below the moulding on its two opposite sides: these are to take the
5 shafts used for carrying it. •These shafts you must make of acacia wood and plate
6 with gold. •You are to set up the altar before the veil that is in front of the ark of Testimony, opposite the throne of mercy that covers the Testimony, the
7 place appointed for my meeting with you. •There Aaron must burn fragrant
8 incense each morning when he trims the lamps, •and between the two evenings, when Aaron puts the lamps back, he must burn it again. You must make these offerings of incense before Yahweh unfailingly from generation to generation.
9 You must not offer profane incense on it, —no holocaust, no oblation; and you
10 must pour no libation on it. •Once a year Aaron is to perform the rite of atonement on the horns of the altar; with the blood of the sacrifice offered for sin he is to perform the rite of atonement once a year. And you shall do the same in the generations to come. This altar of supreme holiness is to be consecrated to Yahweh'.

The poll tax

¹¹₁₂   Yahweh spoke to Moses and said, •'When you take a census and make a register of the sons of Israel, each is to pay Yahweh a ransom for his life, so
13 that no plague comes on them when the census is being made. •Everyone subject to the census must pay half a shekel, reckoning by the sanctuary shekel which
14 is twenty gerahs, and this half-shekel shall be set aside for Yahweh. •Everyone subject to the census, that is to say of twenty years and over, must pay the sum
15 set aside for Yahweh. •The rich man is not to give more, nor the poor man less, than half a shekel as payment of the sum set aside for Yahweh, the ransom for
16 your lives. •You will devote this ransom money given to you by the sons of Israel to the service of the Tent of Meeting. It will remind Yahweh of the sons of Israel and will be the ransom for your lives'.

The bronze basin

¹⁷₁₈   Yahweh spoke to Moses and said, •'You must also make a bronze basin on a stand, for washing. You must place it between the Tent of Meeting and the
19 altar and put water in it. •In this Aaron and his sons must wash their hands and
20 feet. •When they are to enter the Tent of Meeting they must wash in water for fear they die, and when they have to approach the altar for their service, to burn
21 the offering burnt in honour of Yahweh. •They must wash their hands and feet for fear they die. This is a lasting ordinance for them, for Aaron and his descendants from generation to generation'.

The chrismᵇ

²²₂₃   Yahweh spoke to Moses and said, •'Take the choicest spices: of liquid myrrh five hundred shekels, half this weight of fragrant cinnamon —that is, two hundred

30 a. A separate altar from the 'high altar' or supreme altar of 27:1.   **b.** Ointment.

and fifty shekels— and of scented cane two hundred and fifty shekels; •of cassia 24
five hundred shekels (reckoning by the sanctuary shekel) and one hin of olive oil.
These you are to compound into a holy chrism, such a blend as the perfumer 25
might make; it is to be a holy chrism. •With it you are to anoint the Tent of 26
Meeting and the ark of the Testimony, •the table and all its furnishings, the 27
lamp-stand and all its accessories, the altar of incense, •the altar of holocaust 28
with all its furnishings, and the basin with its stand. •These you are to consecrate. 29
Thus they will excel in holiness, and whatever touches them will be holy. •You 30
must also anoint Aaron and his sons and consecrate them, so that they may be
priests in my service. •Then you are to say this to the sons of Israel, 'You must 31
hold this chrism holy from generation to generation. •It is not to be poured 32
on the bodies of common men, nor are you to make any other of the same
mixture. It is a holy thing; you must consider it holy. •Whoever copies the 33
composition of it or uses it on a layman shall be outlawed from his people" '.

The incense

Yahweh said to Moses, 'Take sweet spices: storax, onycha, galbanum, sweet 34
spices and pure frankincense in equal parts, •and compound an incense, such 35
a blend as the perfumer might make, salted, pure, and holy. •Crush a part of it 36
into a fine powder, and put some of this in front of the Testimony in the Tent
of Meeting, the place appointed for my meetings with you. You must regard
it as most holy. •You are not to make any incense of similar composition for 37
your own use. You must hold it to be a holy thing, reserved for Yahweh.
Whoever copies it for use as perfume shall be outlawed from his people'.

The craftsmen for the sanctuary

31 Yahweh spoke to Moses and said, •'See, I have singled out Bezalel son ${}^1_2$
of Uri, son of Hur, of the tribe of Judah. •I have filled him with the spirit 3
of God and endowed him with skill and perception and knowledge for every
kind of craft: •for the art of designing and working in gold and silver and bronze; 4
for cutting stones to be set, for carving in wood, for every kind of craft. •Here ${}^5_6$
and now I give him a partner, Oholiab son of Ahisamach, of the tribe of Dan;
and to all the men that have skill I have given more, for them to carry out all
that I have commanded you: •the Tent of Meeting; the ark of the Testimony; 7
the throne of mercy that covers it, and all the furniture of the tent; •the table 8
and all its furnishings; the pure lamp-stand and all its accessories; the altar of
incense; •the altar of holocaust with all its furnishings; the basin with its stand; 9
the sumptuous vestments —sacred vestments for Aaron the priest, and vestments 10
for his sons— for the priestly functions; •the chrism and the fragrant incense 11
for the sanctuary. In this they are to do exactly as I have directed you'.

The sabbath rest

Yahweh said this to Moses, •'Speak to the sons of Israel and say, "You must ${}^{12}_{13}$
keep my sabbaths carefully, because the sabbath is a sign between myself and
you from generation to generation to show that it is I, Yahweh, who sanctify
you. •You must keep the sabbath, then; it is to be held sacred by you. The 14
man who profanes it must be put to death; whoever does any work on that day
shall be outlawed from his people. •Work is to be done for six days, but the 15
seventh day must be a day of complete rest, consecrated to Yahweh. Whoever
does any work on the sabbath day must be put to death. •The sons of Israel are 16
to keep the sabbath, observing it from generation to generation: this is a lasting
covenant. •Between myself and the sons of Israel the sabbath is a sign for ever, 17
since in six days Yahweh made the heavens and the earth, but on the seventh
day he rested and drew breath" '.

The tablets of the Law committed to Moses

18   When he had finished speaking with Moses on the mountain of Sinai, he gave him the two tablets of the Testimony, tablets of stone inscribed by the finger of God.

V. ISRAEL'S APOSTASY. THE COVENANT RENEWED

The golden calf

1   32 When the people saw that Moses was a long time before coming down the mountain, they gathered round Aaron and said to him, 'Come, make us a god to go at the head of us; this Moses, the man who brought us up from
2 Egypt, we do not know what has become of him'. •Aaron answered them, 'Take the gold rings out of the ears of your wives and your sons and daughters, and
3 bring them to me'. •So they all took the gold rings from their ears and brought
4 them to Aaron. •He took them from their hands and, in a mould, melted the metal down and cast an effigy of a calf. 'Here is your God, Israel,' they cried
5 'who brought you out of the land of Egypt!' •Observing this, Aaron built an altar before the effigy. 'Tomorrow' he said 'will be a feast in honour of Yahweh.'
6   And so, early the next day they offered holocausts and brought communion sacrifices; then all the people sat down to eat and drink, and afterwards got up to amuse themselves.

Moses forewarned by Yahweh

7   Then Yahweh spoke to Moses, 'Go down now, because your people whom
8 you brought out of Egypt have apostasised. •They have been quick to leave the way I marked out for them; they have made themselves a calf of molten metal and have worshipped it and offered it sacrifice. "Here is your God, Israel,"
9 they have cried "who brought you up from the land of Egypt!" ' •Yahweh said
10 to Moses, 'I can see how headstrong these people are! •Leave me, now, my wrath shall blaze out against them and devour them; of you, however, I will make a great nation.'

The prayer of Moses

11   But Moses pleaded with Yahweh his God. 'Yahweh,' he said 'why should your wrath blaze out against this people of yours whom you brought out of
12 land of Egypt with arm outstretched and mighty hand? •Why let the Egyptians say, "Ah, it was in treachery that he brought them out, to do them to death in the mountains and wipe them off the face of the earth"? Leave your burning
13 wrath; relent and do not bring this disaster on your people. •Remember Abraham, Isaac and Jacob, your servants to whom by your own self you swore and made this promise: I will make your offspring as many as the stars of heaven, and all this land which I promised I will give to your descendants, and it shall be their
14 heritage for ever.' •So Yahweh relented and did not bring on his people the disaster he had threatened.

Moses breaks the tablets of the Law

15   Moses made his way back down the mountain with the two tablets of the Testimony in his hands, tablets inscribed on both sides, inscribed on the front
16 and on the back. •These tablets were the work of God, and the writing on them was God's writing engraved on the tablets.
17   Joshua heard the noise of the people shouting. 'There is the sound of battle
18 in the camp', he told Moses. •Moses answered him:

'No song of victory is this sound,
no wailing for defeat this sound;
it is the sound of chanting that I hear'.

As he approached the camp and saw the calf and the groups dancing, Moses' 19
anger blazed. He threw down the tablets he was holding and broke them at the
foot of the mountain. •He seized the calf they had made and burned it, grinding 20
it into powder which he scattered on the water; and he made the sons of Israel
drink it.ᵃ •To Aaron Moses said, 'What has this people done to you, for you 21
to bring such a·great sin on them?' •'Let not my lord's anger blaze like this' 22
Aaron answered. 'You know yourself how prone this people is to evil. •They said 23
to me, "Make us a god to go at our head; this Moses, the man who brought us
up from Egypt, we do not know what has become of him". •So I said to them, 24
"Who has gold?", and they took it off and brought it to me. I threw it into the
fire and out came this calf.'

The zeal of the Levites

When Moses saw the people so out of hand—for Aaron had allowed them to 25
lapse into idolatry with enemies all round them—•he stood at the gate of the 26
camp and shouted, 'Who is for Yahweh? To me!' And all the sons of Levi rallied
to him. •And he said to them, 'This is the message of Yahweh, the God of Israel, 27
"Gird on your sword, every man of you, and quarter the camp from gate to gate,
killing one his brother, another his friend, another his neighbour" '. •The sons 28
of Levi carried out the command of Moses, and of the people about three
thousand men perished that day. •'Today' Moses said 'you have won your- 29
selves investiture as priests of Yahweh at the cost, one of his son, another of his
brother; and so he grants you a blessing today.'

Moses prays again

On the following day Moses said to the people, 'You have committed a grave 30
sin. But now I shall go up to Yahweh: perhaps I can make atonement for your
sin.' •And Moses returned to Yahweh. 'I am grieved,' he cried 'this people has 31
committed a grave sin, making themselves a god of gold. •And yet, if it pleased 32
you to forgive this sin of theirs...! But if not, then blot me out from the book
that you have written.' •Yahweh answered Moses, 'It is the man who has sinned 33
against me that I shall blot out from my book. •Go now, lead the people to the 34
place of which I told you. My angel shall go before you but, on the day of my
visitation, I shall punish them for their sin.' •And Yahweh punished the people 35
for moulding the calf that Aaron had made.

The Israelites ordered to depart

33 Yahweh said to Moses, 'Leave this place, with the people you brought out 1
of the land of Egypt, and go to the land that I swore to Abraham, Isaac
and Jacob I would give their descendants. •I will send an angel in front of you; 2
I will drive out the Canaanites, the Amorites, the Hittites, the Perizzites, the
Hivites, the Jebusites. •Go on to the land where milk and honey flow. I shall 3
not go with you myself—you are a headstrong people—or I might exterminate
you on the way.' •On hearing these stern words the people went into mourning, 4
and no one wore his ornaments.

Then Yahweh said to Moses, 'Say to the sons of Israel, "You are a headstrong 5
people. If I were to go with you, even for a moment only, I should exterminate
you. Take off your ornaments, then, that I may know how to deal with you!" '
So, from Mount Horeb onwards, the sons of Israel stripped themselves of their 6
ornaments.

The Tent

Moses used to take the Tent and pitch it outside the camp, at some distance 7
from the camp. He called it the Tent of Meeting. Anyone who had to consult

8 Yahweh would go out to the Tent of Meeting, outside the camp. •Whenever
Moses went out to the Tent, all the people would rise. Every man would stand
9 at the door of his tent and watch Moses until he reached the Tent; •the pillar
of cloud would come down and station itself at the entrance to the Tent, and
10 Yahweh would speak with Moses. •When they saw the pillar of cloud stationed
at the entrance to the Tent, all the people would rise and bow low, each at the
11 door of his tent. •Yahweh would speak with Moses face to face, as a man speaks
with his friend.ᶜ Then Moses would turn back to the camp, but the young man
who was his servant, Joshua son of Nun, would not leave the Tent.

Moses prays

12   Moses said to Yahweh, 'See, you yourself say to me, "Make the people go
on", but you do not let me know who it is you will send with me. Yet you yourself
13 have said, "I know you by name and you have won my favour". •If indeed
I have won your favour, please show me your ways, so that I can understand
you and win your favour. Remember, too, that this nation is your own people.'
14
15 Yahweh replied, 'I myself will go with you, and I will give you rest'. •Moses
said, 'If you are not going with us yourself, do not make us leave this place.
16 By what means can it be known that I, I and my people, have won your favour,
if not by your going with us? By this we shall be marked out, I and my people,
17 from all the peoples on the face of the earth.' •Yahweh said to Moses, 'Again
I will do what you have asked, because you have won my favour and because
I know you by name'.

Moses on the mountain

18
19   Moses said, 'Show me your glory, I beg you'. •And he said, 'I will let all
my splendour pass in front of you, and I will pronounce before you the name
Yahweh. I have compassion on whom I will, and I show pity to whom I please.
20
21 You cannot see my face,' he said 'for man cannot see me and live.' •And
22 Yahweh said, 'Here is a place beside me. You must stand on the rock, •and
when my glory passes by, I will put you in a cleft of the rock and shield you
23 with my hand while I pass by. •Then I will take my hand away and you shall
see the back of me; but my face is not to be seen.'

The Covenant renewed. The tablets of the Law

1 **34** Yahweh said to Moses, 'Cut two tablets of stone like the first ones and
come up to me on the mountain, and I will inscribe on them the words
2 that were on the first tablets, which you broke. •Be ready by morning, and come
up to the mountain of Sinai at dawn; await my orders there at the top of the
3 mountain. •No one must come up with you, no one be seen anywhere on the
mountain; even the flocks and herds may not graze in front of this mountain.'
4 And so Moses cut two tablets of stone like the first and, with the two tablets
of stone in his hands, he went up the mountain of Sinai in the early morning as
5 Yahweh had commanded him. •And Yahweh descended in the form of a cloud,
and Moses stood with him there.

God appears

6   He called on the name of Yahweh. •Yahweh passed before him and proclaimed, 'Yahweh, Yahweh, a God of tenderness and compassion, slow to anger,
7 rich in kindness and faithfulness; •for thousands he maintains his kindness,
forgives faults, transgression, sin; yet he lets nothing go unchecked, punishing
the father's fault in the sons and in the grandsons to the third and fourth
8 generation'. •And Moses bowed down to the ground at once and worshipped.

32 a. Probably a trial by ordeal like that of Nb 5:11-31.
33 a. This paragraph appears to be an interpolation from another tradition. According to the
main narrative, v.20, it would be impossible for Moses to speak 'face to face' with Yahweh.

'If I have indeed won your favour, Lord,' he said 'let my Lord come with us, 9
I beg. True, they are a headstrong people, but forgive us our faults and our
sins, and adopt us as your heritage.'

The Covenant

Yahweh said, 'I am about to make a covenant with you. In the presence of 10
all your people I shall work such wonders as have never been worked in any land
or in any nation. All the people round you will see what Yahweh can do, for
what I shall do through you will be awe-inspiring. •Mark, then, what I command 11
you today. I mean to drive out the Amorites before you, the Canaanites, the
Hittites, the Perizzites, the Hivites, the Jebusites. •Take care you make no pact 12
with the inhabitants of the land you are about to enter, or this will prove a
pitfall at your very feet. •You are to tear down their altars, smash their standing- 13
stones, cut down their sacred poles.ᵃ

'You shall bow down to no other god, for Yahweh's name is the Jealous One; 14
he is a jealous God. •Make no pact with the inhabitants of the land or, when they 15
prostitute themselves to their own gods and sacrifice to them, they may invite
you and you may consent to eat from their victim; •or else you may choose wives 16
for your sons from among their daughters and these, prostituting themselves to
their own gods, may induce your sons to do the same.

'You shall make yourself no gods of molten metal.   17

'You shall celebrate the feast of Unleavened Bread: you shall eat unleavened 18
bread, as I have commanded you, at the appointed time in the month of Abib,
for in the month of Abib you came out of Egypt.

'All that first issues from the womb is mine: every male, every first-born of 19
flock or herd. •But the first-born donkey you must redeem with an animal from 20
your flocks. If you do not redeem it, you must break its neck. You must redeem
all the first-born of your sons. And no one is to come before me empty-handed.

'For six days you shall labour, but on the seventh day you shall rest, even at 21
ploughing time and harvest.

'You shall celebrate the feast of Weeks, of the first-fruits of wheat harvest, 22
and the feast of Ingathering at the close of the year.

'Three times a year all your menfolk must present themselves before the Lord 23
Yahweh, the God of Israel.

'When I have dispossessed the nations for you and extended your frontiers, 24
no one will covet your land, if you present yourselves three times in the year
before Yahweh your God.

'You must not offer the blood of the victim sacrificed to me at the same time 25
as you offer unleavened bread, nor is the victim offered at the feast of Passover
to be put aside for the following day.

'You must bring the best of the first-fruits of your soil to the house of Yahweh 26
your God.

'You must not boil a kid in its mother's milk.'

Yahweh said to Moses, 'Put these words in writing, for they are the terms of 27
the covenant I am making with you and with Israel'.

He stayed there with Yahweh for forty days and forty nights, eating and 28
drinking nothing. He inscribed on the tablets the words of the Covenant—the
Ten Words.

Moses comes down from the mountain

When Moses came down from the mountain of Sinai—as he came down 29
from the mountain, Moses had the two tablets of the Testimony in his hands—he
did not know that the skin on his face was radiant after speaking with Yahweh.
And when Aaron and all the sons of Israel saw Moses, the skin on his face 30
shone so much that they would not venture near him. •But Moses called to them, 31
and Aaron with all the leaders of the community came back to him; and he

32 spoke to them. •Then all the sons of Israel came closer, and he passed on to
33 them all the orders that Yahweh had given him on the mountain of Sinai. •And
34 when Moses had finished speaking to them, he put a veil over his face. •Whenever he went into Yahweh's presence to speak with him, Moses would remove the veil until he came out again. And when he came out, he would tell the sons of
35 Israel what he had been ordered to pass on to them, •and the sons of Israel would see the face of Moses radiant. Then Moses would put the veil back over his face until he returned to speak with Yahweh.

VI. THE FURNISHING AND BUILDING
OF THE SANCTUARY

The sabbath rest

1 35 Moses assembled the whole community of the sons of Israel and said to
2 them, 'These are the things Yahweh has ordered to be done: •Work is to be done for six days, but the seventh is to be a holy day for you, a day of complete rest, consecrated to Yahweh. Whoever does any work on that day shall
3 be put to death. •You must not light a fire on the sabbath day in any of your homes.'

The materials are collected

4 Moses spoke to the whole community of the sons of Israel. 'This' he said 'is
5 what Yahweh has commanded: •Set aside a contribution for Yahweh out of your possessions. Let all give willingly and bring this contribution for Yahweh:
6 gold, silver and bronze; •purple stuffs, of violet shade and red, crimson stuffs,
7 fine linen, goats' hair, •rams' skins dyed red and fine leather, acacia wood, •oil
8
9 for the light, spices for the chrism and for the fragrant incense; •onyx stones
10 and gems to be set in ephod and pectoral. •Let all the most skilled craftsmen
11 among you come and make all that Yahweh has commanded: •the tabernacle, its tent and its covering, its hooks and its frames, its crossbars, its posts, and its
12 sockets; •the ark with its shafts, the throne of mercy and the veil that screens it;
13 the table with its shafts and all the furnishings for it, and the loaves of offering;
14 the lamp-stand for the light, with its accessories, its lamps, and the oil for the
15 light; •the altar of incense with its shafts, the chrism, the fragrant incense, and
16 the screen for the entrance to the tent; •the altar of holocaust with its bronze
17 grating, its shafts, and all the furnishings for it, the basin and its stand; •the hangings of the court, its posts, its sockets, and the screen for the gateway to
18 the court; •the pegs of the tabernacle and of the court, together with their cords;
19 the sumptuous vestments for service in the sanctuary—sacred vestments for Aaron the priest, and his sons' vestments—for the priestly functions.'
20 Then the whole community of Israel's sons withdrew from Moses' presence.
21 And all those whose heart prompted them to give came, bringing their contribution for Yahweh for making the Tent of Meeting, for all its functions and for
22 the sacred vestments. •They came, men and women, all giving willingly, bringing brooches, rings, bracelets, necklaces, gold things of every kind, all those who
23 had vowed to Yahweh some article of gold. •All those who happened to own purple stuffs, of violet shade or red, crimson stuffs, fine linen, goats' hair, rams'
24 skins dyed red, or fine leather, brought them. •All who could contribute to the collection of silver and bronze brought their contribution for Yahweh. And all who happened to own acacia wood, suitable for any of the work to be done,
25 brought it. •All the skilled women set their hands to spinning, and brought purple stuffs, of violet shade and red, crimson stuffs and fine linen, from what
26 they had spun. •All the women willingly used their special skill and spun the
27 goats' hair. •The leaders brought onyx stones and gems to be set in ephod and

34 a. Sacred poles were the emblems of Asherah (Astarte, Ashteroth), goddess of love and fecundity.

pectoral, •and the spices and oil for the light, for the chrism and for the fragrant 28
incense. •All the men and women whose heart prompted them to contribute to 29
all the work that Yahweh had ordered through Moses to be done—the sons of
Israel brought their free offering to Yahweh.

The craftsmen for the sanctuary

Moses said to the sons of Israel, 'See, Yahweh has singled out Bezalel son of 30
Uri, son of Hur, of the tribe of Judah. •He has filled him with the spirit of God 31
and endowed him with skill and perception and knowledge for every kind of
craft: •for the art of designing and working in gold and silver and bronze; •for $^{32}_{33}$
cutting stones to be set, for carving in wood, for every kind of craft. •And on 34
him and Oholiab son of Ahisamach, of the tribe of Dan, he has bestowed the
gift of teaching. •He has filled them with skill to carry out all the crafts of 35
engraver, damask weaver, embroiderer in purple stuffs, of violet shade and red,
in crimson stuffs and fine linen, or of the common weaver; they are able to do
work of all kinds, and to do it with originality'.

36 Bezalel and Oholiab and all the skilled craftsmen whom Yahweh had 1
endowed with the skill and perception to carry out all that was required
for the building of the sanctuary, did their work exactly as Yahweh had directed.

A halt is called to the collection

Moses then summoned Bezalel and Oholiab and all the skilled craftsmen 2
whose hearts Yahweh had endowed with skill, all whose heart prompted them
to offer to do the work. •From Moses they received all that the sons of Israel 3
had brought as contributions for the work of building the sanctuary. As these
continued each morning to bring •their offerings, the skilled craftsmen, busy 4
with the various works on the sanctuary, all left their work •and went to tell 5
Moses, 'The people are bringing more than is needed for the work Yahweh has
directed us to do'. •At Moses' command, therefore, this proclamation was made 6
throughout the camp: 'Let no one, man or woman, do anything more towards
the collection for the sanctuary.' So the people were stopped from bringing any
more; •the material they had was enough, and more than enough, to complete 7
all the work.

The tabernacle

All the most skilled craftsmen among the workers made the tabernacle. He 8
made it with ten sheets of fine twined linen, of purple stuffs, violet shade and red,
and of crimson stuffs, finely brocaded with cherubs. •The length of a single sheet 9
was twenty-eight cubits, its width four cubits, all the sheets being of the same
size. •He joined five of the sheets together, and the other five similarly. •He $^{10}_{11}$
attached loops of violet stuff to the border of the last sheet in one set, and did
the same for the border of the last sheet in the other set. •He put fifty loops on 12
the first sheet and, matching them one by one, fifty loops on the border of the
last sheet in the second set. •He made fifty gold clasps and with them drew the 13
sheets together. In this way the tabernacle was a unified whole.

Next he made sheets of goats' hair to form a tent over the tabernacle; he made 14
eleven of these. •The length of a single sheet was thirty cubits, its width four 15
cubits; the eleven sheets were all of the same size. •He joined five of these sheets 16
together into one set, the remaining six into another. •He attached fifty loops to 17
the border of the last sheet in one set, and fifty loops to the border of the last
sheet in the second set. •And he made fifty bronze clasps, so as to draw the tent 18
together and make it a unified whole. •For the tent he made a covering of rams' 19
skins dyed red, and a covering of fine leather to spread over it.

The framework

For the tabernacle he made frames of acacia wood, these to stand upright. 20
Each frame was ten cubits long and one and a half cubits wide. •Each frame $^{21}_{22}$

23 was fitted with twin tenons; this he did for all the frames of the tabernacle. •He
made the frames for the tabernacle: twenty frames for the southern side, facing
24 the south country. •He made forty silver sockets for putting under the twenty
frames: two sockets under the first frame to receive its two tenons, and so on
25 for the other frames. •For the other side of the tabernacle, on the north, he made
26
27 twenty frames •and forty silver sockets, two sockets under each frame. •For the
28 back of the tabernacle, on the west, he made six frames. •And he made two frames
29 for the corners at the back of the tabernacle. •These frames were coupled at their
lower end and so to the top, up to the level of the first ring; this he did with the
30 two frames that were to form the two corners. •Thus there were eight frames
31 with their sixteen silver sockets; two sockets under each frame. •He made
crossbars of acacia wood: five to hold the frames together that were to form
32 one side of the tabernacle, •five on the other side to hold the frames that were to
33 form the end of the tabernacle on the west. •He made the middle bar, fixed
34 half-way up, to run from one end to the other. •He plated the frames with gold,
and put gold rings on them to take the crossbars which he plated with gold.

The veil

35 He made the veil of purple stuffs, violet shade and red, of crimson stuffs, and
36 of fine twined linen, skilfully embroidered with cherubs. •For hanging this veil
he made four posts of acacia wood and plated them with gold, with golden hooks,
37 and he cast four silver sockets for them. •For the entrance to the tent he made
a screen of purple stuffs, violet shade and red, and of crimson stuffs and fine
38 twined linen, the work of a skilled embroiderer. •For the hanging of this he
made five posts, and their hooks; their capitals and rods he plated with gold;
their five sockets were of bronze.

The ark

1 **37** Bezalel made the ark of acacia wood, two and a half cubits long, one and
2 a half cubits wide, one and a half cubits high. •He plated it, inside and
3 out, with pure gold, and decorated it all round with a gold moulding. •He cast
four gold rings for the ark, attaching them to its four feet: two rings on one side
4 and two rings on the other. •He also made shafts of acacia wood plating them
5 with gold; •and he passed the shafts through the rings on the sides of the ark,
6 for carrying it. •Also he made of pure gold a throne of mercy, two and a half
7 cubits long, and one and a half cubits wide. •For the two ends of this throne
8 of mercy he made two golden cherubs; he made them of beaten gold, •the first
cherub for one end and the second for the other, and fastened them to the two
9 ends of the throne of mercy so that they made one piece with it. •The cherubs
had their wings spread upwards so that they overshadowed the throne of mercy.
They faced one another, their faces towards the throne of mercy.

The table for the offertory bread

10 He made the table of acacia wood, two cubits long, one cubit wide, and one
11 and a half cubits high. •He plated it with pure gold, and decorated it all round
12 with a gold moulding. •He fitted it with struts, one hand's breadth wide, and
13 decorated these with a golden moulding. •He cast four gold rings for it and
14 fixed these at the four corners where the four legs were. •The rings lay close
15 to the struts to hold the shafts for carrying the table. •He made the shafts of
16 acacia wood and plated them with gold; these·were for carrying the table. •He
made the furnishings of pure gold for the table: dishes, cups, jars and libation bowls.

The lamp-stand

17 He made the lamp-stand of pure gold, and made the lamp-stand, base and
18 stem, of beaten gold. Its·cups—calyx and petals—were of one piece with it. •Six
branches extended from the sides of it, three from one side, three from the other.

The first branch carried three cups shaped like almond blossoms, each with its 19
calyx and petals; the second branch, too, carried three cups shaped like almond
blossoms, each with its calyx and petals, and similarly all six branches extending
from the lamp-stand. •The lamp-stand itself carried four cups shaped like almond 20
blossoms, each with its calyx and petals, •thus: one calyx under the first two 21
branches extending from the lamp-stand, one under the next pair, one under
the last pair: corresponding to the six branches extending from the lamp-stand.
The calyxes and the branches were of one piece with the lamp-stand, and the 22
whole was made from a single piece of pure gold, beaten out. •Then he made 23
the lamps for it, seven of them, and its snuffers and trays of pure gold. •He used 24
a talent of pure gold for making the lamp-stand and all its accessories.

The altar of incense. Chrism and incense

He made the altar of incense out of acacia wood. It was one cubit long, and 25
one cubit wide—that is to say, square—and two cubits high; its horns were of
one piece with it. •The top of it, its surrounding sides, and its horns, he plated 26
with pure gold, and decorated it all round with a gold moulding. •He fixed two 27
gold rings to it below the moulding on its two opposite sides, to take the shafts
used for carrying it. •These shafts he made of acacia wood and plated with gold. 28
He also made the sacred chrism and the pure, fragrant incense, blending it as 29
perfumers do.

The altar of holocaust

38 He made the altar of holocaust out of acacia wood, a square five cubits 1
long and five cubits wide, its height three cubits. •At its four corners he put 2
horns, the horns being of one piece with it, and plated it with bronze. •He made 3
all the altar vessels: pans for the ashes, shovels, sprinkling basins, hooks, fire pans;
he made all the vessels for the altar out of bronze. •He made a grating for it of 4
bronze network which he set under the ledge, below, so that it reached half-way
up the altar. •He cast four rings and fixed them on the four corners of the bronze 5
grating to take the shafts. •He made the shafts of acacia wood and plated them 6
with bronze. •He placed these through the rings fixed to the sides of the altar for 7
carrying it, and he made the altar hollow, of boards.

The bronze basin

He made the bronze basin and its bronze support from the mirrors of the 8
women who served at the entrance to the Tent of Meeting.

The court

He made the court. For the southern side of the court, facing the south country, 9
there were one hundred cubits of hangings of fine twined linen. •Their twenty 10
posts with their twenty sockets were of bronze, their hooks and rods of silver.
For the northern side there were one hundred cubits of hangings; their twenty 11
posts with their twenty sockets were of bronze, their hooks and rods of silver.
For the western side, fifty cubits of hangings, carried on ten posts set in ten 12
sockets, with their hooks and rods of silver. •Fifty cubits, too, for the eastern side 13
facing the sunrise. •On one side of the gateway there were fifteen cubits of 14
hangings, carried on three posts set in three sockets. •On the other side—either 15
side of the entrance to the court—there were fifteen cubits of hangings with their
three posts and three sockets. •All the hangings enclosing the court were of fine 16
twined linen. •The sockets for the posts were of bronze and their hooks of silver, 17
like the plating on their capitals. The posts for the court all had their rods of
silver. •The screen for the gateway of the court, the work of a skilled embroiderer, 18
was made of purple stuffs, violet shade and red, of crimson stuffs, and fine
twined linen. It was twenty cubits long and, along the width of it, five cubits high,
like the hangings of the court. •Its four posts with their four sockets were of 19

bronze. The hooks for the posts were of silver, like the plating on their capitals
20 and like their rods. •The pegs for the tabernacle and for the court enclosure were
all of bronze.

The amount of metal used

21   Here is the account of metals used for the tabernacle—the tabernacle of the
Testimony—the account drawn up by order of Moses, the work of the Levites[a]
under the direction of Ithamar son of Aaron, the priest.
22   Bezalel son of Uri, son of Hur, of the tribe of Judah, made all that Yahweh
23 had directed Moses to have made. •His partner was Oholiab son of Ahisamach,
of the tribe of Dan, engraver, damask weaver, embroiderer in purple stuffs, of
violet shade and red, in crimson stuffs and fine linen.
24   The amount of gold used in the work—the entire work for the sanctuary—(this
was gold consecrated by offering) was twenty-nine talents and seven hundred
25 and thirty shekels (reckoning by the sanctuary shekel). •The silver collected when
the census of the community was taken weighed one hundred talents and one
thousand seven hundred and seventy-five shekels (reckoning by the sanctuary
26 shekel), •one beqa per head, or half a shekel (reckoning by the sanctuary shekel)
for everyone of twenty years and over included in the census. These numbered
27 six hundred and three thousand five hundred and fifty. •The hundred talents of
silver were used for casting the sockets for the sanctuary and for the veil: one
28 hundred sockets out of the hundred talents, or one talent per socket. •With the
one thousand seven hundred and seventy-five shekels he made the hooks for the
29 posts, the plating for their capitals, and their rods. •The bronze consecrated by
offering amounted to seventy talents and two thousand four hundred shekels,
30 and with this he made the sockets for the entrance of the Tent of Meeting, the
31 bronze altar with its grating of bronze and all the furnishings for it, •the sockets
for the enclosure of the court, those for the gateway to the court, all the pegs for
the tabernacle, and all the pegs for the court enclosure.

The vestments of the high priest

1   **39** From the purple stuffs, violet shade and red, the crimson stuffs, and the
fine linen he made sumptuous vestments for service in the sanctuary. They
made the sacred vestments for Aaron, as Yahweh had directed Moses.

The ephod

2   They made the ephod of gold, purple stuffs, violet shade and red, crimson
3 stuffs, and fine twined linen. •They beat gold into thin plates, and cut these into
fine strips to weave into the purple stuffs, violet shade and red, into the crimson
4 stuffs and the fine linen, as does the weaver of damask. •For the ephod they made
5 two shoulder-straps, joined to it at its two ends. •The woven band on it to hold
it formed one piece with it and was of similar workmanship: this was of gold,
purple stuffs, violet shade and red, crimson stuffs, and fine twined linen,
6 as Yahweh had directed Moses. •They fashioned the onyx stones, mounted in
settings of gold mesh and engraved, as a seal is engraved, with the names of
7 the sons of Israel. •They fastened the stones to the shoulder-straps of the ephod,
stones commemorating the sons of Israel, as Yahweh had directed Moses.

The pectoral of judgement

8   They made the pectoral, finely brocaded, of the same workmanship as the
9 ephod, of gold, purple stuffs, violet shade and red, and fine twined linen. •It was
10 square and they doubled it over, a span in length and a span in width. •In this

38 a. A late addition: the Levites were not yet established. Later in the same section are references to a tax which had not yet been imposed, and a distinction between two shekels which
had not been made.

they set four rows of stones. Sard, topaz, carbuncle, for the first row; •emerald, 11
sapphire, diamond, the second row; •the third row, hyacinth, ruby, amethyst; 12
the fourth row, beryl, onyx, jasper. These were mounted in settings of gold mesh. 13
They bore the names of the sons of Israel and, like their names, were twelve 14
in number. They were engraved as seals are, each with the name of one of the
twelve tribes. •For the pectoral they made chains of pure gold twisted like cords. 15
They made two gold rosettes and two gold rings, •and they fastened the 16 17
two gold cords to the two rings fixed on the corners of the pectoral. •The other 18
two ends of the cords they fastened to the two rosettes; they were thus attached
to the shoulder-straps of the ephod, on the front. •They made two gold rings 19
and fixed them to the two lower corners of the pectoral, on the inner hem, next
to the ephod. •And they made two more gold rings and fixed them low down on 20
the front of the two shoulder-straps of the ephod, close to the join, above the
woven band of the ephod. •They secured the pectoral by passing a ribbon of 21
violet-purple through its rings and those of the ephod, so that the pectoral would
sit above the woven band and not come apart from the ephod, as Yahweh had
directed Moses.

The robe

Then they made the robe of the ephod woven entirely of violet-purple. •The 22 23
opening in the centre of it was like the neck of a coat of mail; round the opening
was a border to keep the robe from tearing. •The lower hem of the robe they 24
decorated with pomegranates of purple stuffs, violet shade and red, crimson
stuffs, and fine twined linen. •They also made bells of pure gold and placed 25
them all round the lower hem of the robe between the pomegranates, •bells and 26
pomegranates alternately all round the lower hem of the robe of office, as Yahweh
had directed Moses.

The vestments of the priests

Then they made the tunics of finely woven linen for Aaron and his sons, •the 27 28
turban of fine linen, the head-dresses of fine linen, the breeches of fine twined
linen, •the girdles of fine twined linen, of purple stuffs, violet shade and red, 29
and of crimson stuffs, finely embroidered, as Yahweh had directed Moses.

They also made the plate, the holy diadem, of pure gold, and engraved on 30
it 'Consecrated to Yahweh', as a man engraves a seal. •They attached to this 31
a ribbon of violet-purple to secure it to the top of the turban, as Yahweh had
directed Moses.

So all the work of the tabernacle, the Tent of Meeting, was completed. In 32
carrying it out the sons of Israel had done exactly as Yahweh had directed Moses.

The finished work presented to Moses

They brought to Moses the tabernacle, the Tent and all its furnishings: its 33
hooks, frames, crossbars, posts, sockets; •the covering of rams' skins dyed red, 34
the covering of fine leather, and the screening veil; •the ark of the testimony with 35
its shafts and the throne of mercy; •the table with all its furnishings, and the 36
loaves of offering; •the lamp-stand of pure gold with its lamps—the lamps that 37
were to be set on it—and all its accessories; the oil, too, for the light; •the golden 38
altar, the chrism, the fragrant incense, the screen for the entrance to the tent;
the bronze altar with its grating of bronze, its shafts and all its furnishings; the 39
basin and its stand; •the hangings of the court, its posts, its sockets, and the 40
screen for the gateway to the court, its cords, its pegs, and all the furniture for
the service in the tabernacle, the Tent of Meeting; •the sumptuous vestments for 41
service in the sanctuary—sacred vestments for Aaron the priest, and vestments
for his sons—for the priestly functions. •The sons of Israel had done all the work 42
exactly as Yahweh had directed Moses.

Moses examined the whole work, and he could see they had done it as Yahweh 43
had directed him. And Moses blessed them.

The sanctuary erected and consecrated

$\begin{smallmatrix}1\\2\\3\end{smallmatrix}$ **40** Yahweh spoke to Moses and said, •'On the first day of the first month you are to erect the tabernacle, the Tent of Meeting, •and place the ark of the 4 Testimony in it, screening it with the veil. •Bring in the table, arranging what is to be set in order on it. Bring in the lamp-stand, too, and set up its lamps. 5 Place the golden altar of incense in front of the ark of the Testimony, and set 6 up the screen at the entrance to the tabernacle. •Place the altar of holocaust 7 in front of the entrance to the tabernacle, the Tent of Meeting. •Place the basin 8 between the Tent of Meeting and the altar, and fill it with water. •Set up the 9 enclosure of the court and hang the screen at the gateway of the court. •Then, taking the chrism, anoint the tabernacle and everything in it, consecrating it 10 with its furniture, to make it a holy place. •Anoint the altar of holocaust with all its furnishings; and consecrate the altar which henceforth will be a most holy $\begin{smallmatrix}11\\12\end{smallmatrix}$ thing. •Anoint the basin with its stand, and consecrate it. •Bring Aaron and his 13 sons to the entrance of the Tent of Meeting and see that they bathe. •Then clothe Aaron with the sacred vestments, and anoint and consecrate him, to serve $\begin{smallmatrix}14\\15\end{smallmatrix}$ me in the priesthood. •Next, bring his sons and clothe them with tunics. •Anoint them as you have anointed their father, to serve me in the priesthood. This anointing of them is to confer the priesthood on them in perpetuity from generation to generation.'

The divine commands are carried out

$\begin{smallmatrix}16\\17\end{smallmatrix}$ Moses did this; he did exactly as Yahweh had directed him. •The tabernacle 18 was set up on the first day of the first month in the second year. •Moses erected the tabernacle. He fixed the sockets for it, put up its frames, put its crossbars 19 in position, set up its posts. •He spread the tent over the tabernacle and on 20 top of this the covering for the tent, as Yahweh had directed Moses. •He took the Testimony and placed it inside the ark. He set the shafts to the ark and 21 placed the throne of mercy on it. •He brought the ark into the tabernacle and put the screening veil in place; thus he screened the ark of Yahweh, as Yahweh 22 had directed Moses. •He placed the table in the Tent of Meeting, on the north 23 side of the tabernacle, outside the veil, •and on it arranged the loaves before 24 Yahweh, as Yahweh had directed Moses. •He put the lamp-stand in the Tent 25 of Meeting, opposite the table, on the south side of the tabernacle; •and he set 26 up the lamps before Yahweh, as Yahweh had directed Moses. •He put the 27 golden altar in the Tent of Meeting in front of the veil, •and on it burnt fragrant 28 incense, as Yahweh had directed Moses. •Then he put the screen at the entrance 29 to the tabernacle. •He put the altar of holocaust at the entrance to the tabernacle, the Tent of Meeting, and on it offered the holocaust and the oblation, as Yahweh 30 had directed Moses. •He put the basin between the Tent of Meeting and the 31 altar, and filled it with water for the ablutions; •this was for Aaron and his 32 sons to wash their hands and feet: •whenever they entered the Tent of Meeting 33 or approached the altar they washed, as Yahweh had directed Moses. •Moses then set up the court round the tabernacle and the altar and placed the screen at the gateway to the court. Thus Moses completed the work.

Yahweh takes possession of the sanctuary

34 The cloud covered the Tent of Meeting and the glory of Yahweh filled the 35 tabernacle. •Moses could not enter the Tent of Meeting because of the cloud that rested on it and because of the glory of Yahweh that filled the tabernacle.

The cloud guides the Israelites

36 At every stage of their journey, whenever the cloud rose from the tabernacle 37 the sons of Israel would resume their march. •If the cloud did not rise, they 38 waited and would not march until it did. •For the cloud of Yahweh rested on the tabernacle by day, and a fire shone within the cloud by night, for all the House of Israel to see. And so it was for every stage of their journey.

LEVITICUS

I. THE RITUAL OF SACRIFICE

Holocaust[a]

1 Yahweh called Moses, and from the Tent of Meeting addressed him, saying, 1
'Speak to the sons of Israel; say to them, "When any of you brings an offering 2
to Yahweh, he can offer an animal from either herd or flock.

"If his offering is a holocaust of an animal out of the herd, he is to offer a male 3
without blemish; it is to be offered at the entrance to the Tent of Meeting, so
that it may be accepted before Yahweh. •He is to lay his hand on the victim's 4
head, and it shall be accepted as effectual for his atonement. •Then he must immol- 5
ate the bull before Yahweh, and the sons of Aaron, the priests, shall offer the
blood. They will pour it out on the borders of the altar which stands at the
entrance to the Tent of Meeting. •Then he must skin the victim and quarter it. 6
The sons of Aaron, the priests, must put fire on the altar and arrange wood on 7
this fire. •Then the sons of Aaron, the priests, are to put the pieces, the head and 8
the fat on the wood on the altar fire. •He is to wash the entrails and legs in water, 9
and the priest is to burn all of it on the altar. This holocaust will be a burnt
offering[b] and the fragrance of it will appease Yahweh.

"If his offering is an animal out of the flock, a lamb or a goat offered as a 10
holocaust, he is to offer a male without blemish. •He must immolate it on the 11
north side of the altar, before Yahweh, and the sons of Aaron, the priests, shall
pour out the blood on the borders of the altar. •Then he is to quarter it, and the 12
priest is to arrange the quarters, as well as the head and the fat, on the wood on
the altar fire. •He is to wash the entrails and legs in water, and the priest shall 13
burn all of it on the altar. This holocaust will be a burnt offering and the fragrance
of it will appease Yahweh.

"If his offering to Yahweh is a holocaust of a bird, he is to offer a turtledove 14
or a young pigeon. •The priest shall offer it at the altar and wring off its head, 15
which he is to burn on the altar; then its blood is to be drained out on the side
of the altar. •Then he shall remove the crop and the feathers; these he is to throw 16
on the eastern side of the altar, where the ashes from the fat are placed. •He is to 17
divide it in two halves with a wing on each side, but without separating the two
parts. Then the priest shall burn it on the altar, on the wood that is on the fire.
This holocaust will be a burnt offering and its fragrance will appease Yahweh.

The Oblation[a]

2 "If anyone offers Yahweh an oblation, his offering is to consist of wheaten 1
flour on which he is to pour wine and put incense. •He shall bring it to the sons 2
of Aaron, the priests; he is to take a handful of the wheaten flour and oil and all
the incense, and the priest shall burn it on the altar as a memorial, a burnt offering
wnose fragrance will appease Yahweh. •The remainder of the oblation is to 3
revert to Aaron and his sons; a most holy portion of the burnt offerings of
Yahweh.

4   "When you are going to offer an oblation of dough baked in the oven, the wheaten flour is to be prepared either in the form of unleavened cakes mixed with oil, or in the form of unleavened wafers spread with oil.

5   "If your offering is an oblation cooked on the griddle, the wheaten flour mixed
6 with oil is to contain no leavening. •You must break it in pieces and pour oil over it. It is an oblation.

7   "If your offering is an oblation cooked in the pan, the wheaten flour is to be prepared in oil.

8   "You must bring to Yahweh the oblation that has been thus prepared, presenting
9 it to the priest, who is to bring it to the altar. •The priest shall take the memorial from the oblation and burn it on the altar, as a burnt offering whose fragrance
10 will appease Yahweh. •The remainder of the oblation will revert to Aaron and his sons, a most holy portion of Yahweh's burnt offering.

11   "None of the oblations that you offer to Yahweh is to be prepared with leaven,
12 for you must never burn leaven or honey as a burnt offering for Yahweh. •You may offer them up to Yahweh as an offering of first-fruits, but they must not go
13 up as an appeasing fragrance at the altar. •You must salt every oblation that you offer, and you must never fail to put on your oblation the salt of the Covenant with your God: to every offering you are to join an offering of salt to Yahweh
14 your God. •If you offer Yahweh an oblation of first-fruits, you must offer roasted
15 corn or bread made from ground corn. •You are to add oil to it and put incense
16 on it; it is an oblation; •and the priest is to burn the memorial from part of the bread and oil (together with all the incense) as a burnt offering for Yahweh.

The Communion Sacrifice[a]

1 **3** "If a man's sacrifice is a communion sacrifice, and if he offers an animal from the herd, male or female, whatever he offers before Yahweh must be without
2 blemish. •He is to lay his hand on the victim's head and immolate it at the entrance to the Tent of Meeting. Then the sons of Aaron, the priests, must pour
3 out the blood on the borders of the altar. •He is to offer part of the sacrifice as a burnt offering for Yahweh: the fat that covers the entrails, all the fat that
4 is on the entrails, •the two kidneys, the fat on them and on the loins, the fatty
5 mass which he is to remove from the liver and kidneys. •The sons of Aaron must burn this part on the altar, in addition to the holocaust, on the wood of the fire. It will be a burnt offering and its fragrance will appease Yahweh.

6   "If it is an animal from the flock that he offers as a communion sacrifice for Yahweh, he is to offer a male or female without blemish.

7
8   "If he offers a sheep, he is to offer it before Yahweh; •he is to lay his hand on the victim's head and immolate it in front of the Tent of Meeting; then the sons
9 of Aaron shall pour out its blood on the borders of the altar. •Of this communion sacrifice he is to offer the following as a burnt offering for Yahweh: the fat, all the tail taken off near the sacrum, the fat that covers the entrails, all the fat that
10 is on the entrails, •the two kidneys, the fat that is on them and on the loins,
11 the fatty mass which he will remove from the liver and kidneys. •The priest must burn this part on the altar as food, as a burnt offering for Yahweh.

12
13   "If his offering is a goat, he is to offer it before Yahweh: •he is to lay his hand on the victim's head and immolate it in front of the Tent of Meeting, and the
14 sons of Aaron shall pour out its blood on the borders of the altar. •Then this is what he is to offer as a burnt offering for Yahweh: the fat that covers the entrails,
15 all the fat that is on the entrails, •the two kidneys, the fat that is on them and on the loins, the fatty mass which he will remove from the liver and kidneys.

1 a. The term means 'wholly burned' (offering).   b. I.e., no part of it is to be eaten in a com-
munion-meal or set aside for the priests.
2 a. An offering of crops, cereal or vegetable produce.
3 a. A ritual meal (often called the 'peace-offering') at which part of the victim was eaten by the worshippers and part offered to God, so that the meal was 'shared' with God.

The priest must burn these pieces on the altar as food, as a burnt offering for 16 Yahweh.

"All the fat belongs to Yahweh. •This is a perpetual law for all your descendants, 17 wherever you may live: never eat either fat or blood." '

The Sacrifice for Sin[a]

4 Yahweh spoke to Moses; he said: 1
'Speak to the sons of Israel and say: 2
"A man may sin inadvertently against any one of the commandments of Yahweh and do one of the forbidden things; in such a case:

a. Sins of the high priest

"If the one who sins is the anointed priest, thus making the people guilty, 3 then for the sin which he has committed he is to offer to Yahweh a young bull, an animal from the herd without blemish, as a sacrifice for sin. •He is to bring 4 the bull before Yahweh at the entrance to the Tent of Meeting, he is to lay his hand on its head and immolate it before Yahweh. •Then the anointed priest 5 must take a little of the blood of the bull and take it into the Tent of Meeting. He shall dip his finger in the blood and sprinkle it over the veil of the sanctuary 6 seven times, before Yahweh. •Then the priest must put a little of the blood of 7 the bull on the horns of the altar of incense that smokes before Yahweh in the Tent of Meeting, and he is to pour all the rest of the bull's blood at the foot of the altar of holocaust at the entrance to the Tent of Meeting.

"Of all the fat of this bull offered as a sacrifice for sin, this is what he will 8 remove: the fat that covers the entrails, all the fat that is on the entrails, •the two 9 kidneys, the fat that is on them and on the loins, the fatty mass which he will remove from the liver and kidneys—•exactly as was done with the portion set 10 apart in the communion sacrifice—and the priest must burn these on the altar of holocaust.

"The bull's skin, all its flesh, its head, legs, entrails and dung, •the whole of 11 the bull, must be carried outside the camp to a place that is clean, the place 12 where the ashes from the fat are thrown away, and the bull must be burnt there.

b. Sins of the community of Israel

"If the whole community of Israel has sinned inadvertently, and without being 13 aware of it has done something that is forbidden by the commandments of Yahweh, •the community is to offer a young bull as a sacrifice for sin, an animal 14 of the herd without blemish, when the sin of which they have been guilty is discovered. The animal must be brought before the Tent of Meeting; •before 15 Yahweh the elders of the community shall lay their hands on the bull's head, and it must be immolated before Yahweh.

"Then the anointed priest is to carry a little of the blood of the bull into the 16 Tent of Meeting. •He is to dip his finger in the blood and sprinkle the veil before 17 Yahweh seven times. •Then he must put a little of the blood on the horns of the 18 altar that stands before Yahweh inside the Tent of Meeting, and then pour out all the rest of the blood at the foot of the altar of holocaust at the entrance to the Tent of Meeting.

"Then he is to remove all the fat from the animal and burn it on the altar. 19 He must treat this bull as he did the other for the sacrifice of sin. It is to be treated 20 in the same way; and when the priest has performed the rite of atonement over the people, they will be forgiven.

"He must have the bull taken out of the camp and burn it as he burned the 21 first one. This is the sacrifice for the sin of the community.

c. Sins of leaders in the community

"When a leader sins and inadvertently does one of the things forbidden by 22 the commandments of Yahweh his God, thus rendering himself guilty •(or if 23

anyone draws his attention to the sin thus committed), he is to bring a goat as
24 an offering, a male without blemish. •He is to lay his hand on the goat's head
and immolate it in the place where the holocausts are immolated before Yahweh.
25 This is a sacrifice for sin: •the priest is to take a little of the victim's blood on his
finger and put it on the horns of the altar of holocaust. Then he must pour out
26 its blood at the foot of the altar of holocaust •and burn all the fat on the altar,
as with the fat in the communion sacrifice. This is how the priest is to perform
the rite of atonement over this leader to free him from his sin, and he will be
forgiven.

d. Sins of private individuals

27 "If one of the people sins inadvertently and makes himself guilty by doing
28 something forbidden by the commandments of Yahweh •(or if anyone draws
his attention to the sin he has committed), he is to bring a she-goat as an offering
29 for the sin he has committed, a female without blemish. •He is to lay his hand
on the victim's head and immolate it in the place where the holocausts are
30 immolated. •The priest is to take a little of its blood on his finger and put it
on the horns of the altar of holocaust. Then he must pour out all the rest of the
31 blood at the foot of the altar. •Then he is to remove all the fat, as the fat was
removed for the communion sacrifice, and the priest shall burn it on the altar
as an appeasing fragrance for Yahweh. This is how the priest is to perform the rite
of atonement over the man, and he will be forgiven.

32 "If he wishes to bring a lamb as an offering for this kind of sacrifice, he is to
33 bring a female without blemish. •He is to lay his hand on the victim's head and
immolate it as a sacrifice for sin in the place where the holocausts are immolated.
34 The priest is to take a little of the blood of this sacrifice on his finger and put it
on the horns of the altar of holocaust. Then he must pour out all the rest of the
35 blood at the foot of the altar. •He is to remove its fat as was done for the sheep in
the communion sacrifice, and the priest shall burn it all on the altar, in addition
to the burnt offering for Yahweh. This is how the priest is to perform the rite of
atonement over the man, and he will be forgiven.

Some cases of Sacrifice for Sin

1 **5** "If anyone sins in any of these following cases:
"A man should have come forward to give evidence when he heard the
formal adjuration, having seen the incident or known the facts; but he has
not spoken out, and so bears the consequences of his fault;
2 "or else he touches something unclean, whatever it may be—the dead body of
an unclean animal, wild or tame, or of one of the unclean things that swarm—and
without realising it becomes unclean, he becomes answerable for it;
3 "or else he touches some human uncleanness, whatever it may be, and contact
with it makes him unclean; he does not notice it, then, realising it later, he
becomes answerable for it;
4 "or else a man lets slip some oath to do either evil or good, in any of those
matters on which a man may swear unthinkingly; he does not notice it, then,
realising it later, he becomes answerable for it;
5 "if he is answerable in any of those cases, he will have to confess the sin
6 committed, •and he must bring to Yahweh as a sacrifice of reparation for the sin
committed a female of the flock (sheep or goat) as a sacrifice for sin; and the
priest shall perform the rite of atonement over him to free him from his sin.

Sins of private individuals (continued)

7 "If he cannot afford an animal of the flock, he is to bring to Yahweh, as a
sacrifice of reparation for the sin he has committed, two turtledoves or two

---

4 a. The sacrifice for sin expiates ritual faults against Yahweh.

young pigeons—one for a sacrifice for sin and the other for a holocaust. •He will ⁸ bring them to the priest who is to offer first the one intended for the sacrifice for sin. The priest is to wring its neck, but not remove the head. •He must sprinkle ⁹ the side of the altar with the victim's blood, and then drain out the rest of the blood at the foot of the altar. This is a sacrifice for sin. •Of the other bird he ¹⁰ is to make a holocaust according to the ritual. This is how the priest is to perform the rite of atonement over the man for the sin he has committed, and he will be forgiven.

"If he cannot afford two turtledoves or two young pigeons, he is to bring a ¹¹ tenth of an ephah of wheaten flour as an offering for the sin committed; he must not mix oil with it or put incense on it, for it is a sacrifice for sin. •He is to bring ¹² it to the priest, who is to take a handful of it as a memorial, and burn this in addition to the burnt offering for Yahweh. This is a sacrifice for sin. •This is ¹³ how the priest is to perform the rite of atonement over the man for the sin he has committed in any of those cases, and he will be forgiven. In this case, the priest has the same rights as in the oblation." '

The Sacrifice of Reparation*

Yahweh spoke to Moses; he said: ¹⁴

'If anyone is guilty of fraud and sins inadvertently by not observing Yahweh's ¹⁵ sacred rights, he is to bring to Yahweh as a sacrifice of reparation an unblemished ram from his flock. This ram is to be valued in silver shekels according to the rate of the shekel of the sanctuary. This is a sacrifice of reparation. •He must ¹⁶ restore what his sin subtracted from the sacred rights, adding one-fifth to the value, and give it to the priest. The priest shall perform the rite of atonement over him with the ram for the sacrifice of reparation and he will be forgiven.

'If anyone sins and without realising it does one of the things forbidden ¹⁷ by the commandments of Yahweh, he must answer for it and must bear the consequences of his fault. •As a sacrifice of reparation he is to bring to the ¹⁸ priest an unblemished ram of his flock, subject to valuation. The priest shall perform the rite of atonement over him for the oversight he has committed without realising it and he will be forgiven. •This is a sacrifice of reparation; the ¹⁹ man was certainly answerable to Yahweh.'

Yahweh spoke to Moses; he said: ²⁰/₁

'If anyone sins and is guilty of fraud against Yahweh by deceiving his ²¹/₂ neighbour over a deposit or a security, or by withholding something due to him or exploiting him;

'or if he finds lost property and denies it;   ²²/₃

'or if he perjures himself about any sin that a man may commit;

'if he sins and so becomes answerable, he is to restore what he has taken or ²³/₄ demanded in excess: the deposit confided to him, the lost property that he found, or any object about which he has perjured himself. He must add one-fifth to the ²⁴/₅ principal and pay the whole to whoever held the property rights on the day when he became answerable. •Then he is to bring an unblemished ram of his ²⁵/₆ flock to Yahweh as a sacrifice of reparation: it must be valued according to the rate paid to the priest for a sacrifice of reparation. •The priest shall perform the ²⁶/₇ rite of atonement over him before Yahweh and he will be forgiven, whatever the act for which he became answerable.'

Priesthood and sacrifice
a. Holocaust

6 Yahweh spoke to Moses; he said: ¹/₈
'Give these orders to Aaron and his sons: ²/₉

"This is the ritual for holocaust (that is, the holocaust that stays on the altar brazier all night until morning and is consumed by the altar fire).

³
¹⁰ "The priest is to put on his linen tunic and cover his body with linen. Then he must remove the ashes of the fat of the sacrifice consumed by the ⁴
¹¹ altar fire and place them at the side of the altar. •Then he is to take off his clothes and put on others and carry the ashes to some place that is clean, outside the camp.

⁵
¹² "The fire that consumes the holocaust on the altar must not be allowed to go out. Every morning the priest must make it up with wood. He is to arrange the ⁶
¹³ holocaust on it and burn the fat from the communion sacrifices. •An undying fire is always to burn on the altar; it must not go out.

b. The Oblation

⁷
¹⁴ "This is the ritual for the oblation:

"One of the sons of Aaron is to bring it into the presence of Yahweh in front ⁸
¹⁵ of the altar; •he is to take a handful of the wheaten flour (with the oil and incense which have been added to it); he must burn the memorial on the altar so that its ⁹
¹⁶ fragrance will appease Yahweh; •and after all this has been done Aaron and his sons shall eat the remainder in the form of unleavened loaves. They are to eat it ¹⁰
¹⁷ in a sacred place within the precincts of the Tent of Meeting. •The portion I give them of my burnt offering must not be baked with leaven. It is a most ¹¹
¹⁸ holy portion, like the sacrifice for sin and the sacrifice of reparation. •All the males of Aaron's family may eat this portion of Yahweh's burnt offering (this is a perpetual law for all your descendants; and everyone who touches it will be consecrated)." '

¹²
¹⁹ Yahweh spoke to Moses; he said:

¹³
²⁰ 'This is the offering that Aaron and his sons are to make to Yahweh on the day of their anointing: one-tenth of an ephah of wheaten flour as a perpetual ¹⁴
²¹ oblation, half in the morning and half in the evening. •It must be prepared on the griddle and mixed with oil; you must bring the paste as an oblation in several ¹⁵
²² pieces, offering them as a fragrance that will appease Yahweh. •The priest among the sons of Aaron who is to be anointed in his place shall do the same. This is a perpetual law.

¹⁶
²³ 'This entire oblation must be burnt for Yahweh. •Every oblation made by a priest must be a total sacrifice; none of it is to be eaten.'

c. The Sacrifice for Sin

^{17,18}
^{24,25} Yahweh spoke to Moses; he said, •'Say to Aaron and his sons:

"This is the ritual for the sacrifice for sin:

"The victim for the sacrifice is to be immolated before Yahweh in the place ¹⁹
²⁶ where the holocausts are immolated. It is a most holy thing. •The priest who offers this sacrifice is to eat it. It must be eaten in a holy place within the precincts ²⁰
²⁷ of the Tent of Meeting. •Everything that touches the flesh of this victim will become consecrated; if any of the blood splashes on clothing, the stain must be ²¹
²⁸ cleaned in some holy place. •The earthenware vessel in which the meat is cooked must be broken; if a bronze vessel has been used for the cooking, it must be ²²
²⁹ scrubbed and thoroughly rinsed with water. •Any male who is a priest may eat it. ²³
³⁰ It is a most holy thing. •But no one may eat any of the victims offered for sin, the blood of which has been taken into the Tent of Meeting to make atonement inside the sanctuary. These must be thrown on the fire.

d. The Sacrifice of Reparation

¹ **7** "This is the ritual for the sacrifice of reparation:

² "It is a most holy thing. •The victim is to be immolated in the place where the holocausts are immolated, and the priest must pour out the blood on the borders ³ of the altar. •Then he is to offer all the fat: the tail, the fat that covers the entrails,

---

5 a. The sacrifice of reparation (or 'guilt-offering') was offered whenever the rights of God or of neighbour had been violated.

the two kidneys, the fat that is on them and on the loins, the fatty mass which 4
he will remove from the liver and kidneys. •The priest must burn these pieces 5
on the altar as a burnt offering for Yahweh. This is a sacrifice of reparation.
Every male who is a priest may eat it. It must be eaten in a holy place; it is a 6
most holy thing.

The rights of the priests

"As with the sacrifice for sin, so with the sacrifice of reparation—the ritual is 7
the same for both. The offering with which he has performed the rite of atonement
is to revert to the priest. •The skin of the victim presented by a man to the priest 8
to be offered as a holocaust shall revert to the priest. •Every oblation baked in 9
the oven, every oblation cooked in the pan or on the griddle shall revert to the
priest who offered it. •Every oblation, mixed with oil or dry, is to revert to all 10
the sons of Aaron without distinction.

e. The Communion Sacrifice
(i) Sacrifice with Praise

"This is the ritual for the communion sacrifice offered to Yahweh: 11

"If it is offered with a sacrifice with praise, there must be added to it an 12
offering of unleavened cakes mixed with oil, unleavened wafers spread with oil,
and wheaten flour in the form of cakes mixed with oil. •This offering, then, 13
must be added to the cakes of leavened bread and to the communion sacrifice
with praise. •One of the cakes of this offering is to be presented as an offering 14
to Yahweh; it shall revert to the priest who pours out the blood of the communion
sacrifice. •The flesh of the victim must be eaten on the day when the offering 15
is made; nothing must remain until the next morning.

(ii) Votive or Voluntary Sacrifices

"If the victim is offered as a votive or a voluntary sacrifice, it is to be eaten on 16
the day it is offered and also on the following day; •but on the third day whatever 17
remains of the victim's flesh must be thrown on the fire.

General rules

"If the flesh offered as a communion sacrifice is eaten on the third day, the 18
man who has offered it will not be accepted. He is to receive no credit for it,
it is defiled flesh, and the man who eats it shall bear the consequences of his fault.

"Flesh that has touched anything unclean cannot be eaten; it must be thrown 19
on the fire.

"Anyone who is clean may eat flesh, •but anyone unclean who eats the flesh 20
of a communion sacrifice offered to Yahweh shall be outlawed from his people.
If anyone touches anything unclean, human or animal, or any foul thing, and 21
then eats the flesh of a communion sacrifice offered to Yahweh, this man shall
be outlawed from his people."'

Yahweh spoke to Moses; he said, •'Speak to the sons of Israel, say to them: 22 23

"You must not eat the fat of ox, sheep or goat. •The fat of an animal that 24
has died a natural death or been savaged by beasts may be used for any other
purpose, but you must not eat it. •Anyone who eats the fat of an animal offered 25
as a burnt offering to Yahweh shall be outlawed from his people.

"Wherever you live, you must not eat blood, whether it be of bird or of beast. 26
Anyone who eats blood, whoever he may be, shall be outlawed from his people."' 27

The priest's portion

Yahweh spoke to Moses; he said, •'Speak to the sons of Israel, say to them: 28 29

"Anyone who offers a communion sacrifice to Yahweh is to bring him part
of his sacrifice as an offering. •He is to bring Yahweh's burnt offering—that is, 30
the fat that adheres to the breast—with his own hands. He is to bring it, and

also the breast, with which he must make the gesture of offering before Yahweh.
31 The priest must burn the fat on the altar, and the breast shall revert to Aaron and
32 his sons. •You must set aside the right thigh from your communion sacrifices and
33 give it to the priest. •This right thigh shall be the portion of the son of Aaron
34 who offers the blood and fat of the communion sacrifice. •Thus, I keep back
this breast and thigh out of the communion sacrifices offered by the sons of
Israel, and give these to Aaron the priest and to his sons: this is a perpetual law
binding the sons of Israel." '

Conclusion

35   This, then, was the portion of Aaron and of his sons in Yahweh's burnt
36 offerings on the day he presented them to Yahweh to be his priests. •This is
what the orders of Yahweh bind the sons of Israel to give them on the day
they are anointed: this is a perpetual law for all their descendants.
37   Such then is the ritual for holocaust, oblation, sacrifice for sin, sacrifices of
38 reparation, investiture and communion. •This is what Yahweh commanded
Moses on Mount Sinai when he ordered the sons of Israel to make their offerings
to Yahweh in the wilderness of Sinai.

II. THE INVESTITURE OF THE PRIESTS

Ordination rites[a]

1 Yahweh spoke to Moses; he said:
2 'Take Aaron, his sons with him, and the vestments, and the chrism, the bull
for the sacrifice for sin, the two rams and the basket of unleavened bread.
3 Then call the whole community together at the entrance to the Tent of Meeting.'
4   Moses followed the orders of Yahweh; the community gathered at the entrance
5 to the Tent of Meeting, •and Moses said to them, 'This is what Yahweh has
ordered to be done'.
6   He made Aaron and his sons come forward, and washed them with water.
7   He put the tunic on him, passed the girdle round his waist, dressed him in the
robe and put the ephod on him. Then he put round his waist the woven band
8 of the ephod with which he clothed him. •He put the pectoral on him, and
9 placed the Urim and Thummim in it. •He put the turban on his head, with the
golden plate on the front; this is the sacred diadem as Yahweh prescribed it
to Moses.
10   Then Moses took the chrism and anointed the tabernacle and everything in it,
11 to consecrate them. •He sprinkled the altar seven times, and anointed the altar
12 and its furnishing, the basin and its stand, to consecrate them. •Then he
poured the chrism on Aaron's head, consecrating him by unction.
13   Then Moses made Aaron's sons come forward; he put the tunics on them,
passed the girdles round their waists and put on their head-dress, as Yahweh
had ordered Moses.
14   Then he had the bull for the sacrifice for sin brought forward. Aaron and his
15 sons laid their hands on the victim's head •and Moses immolated it. Then he
took the blood and with his finger put some of it on the horns round the altar,
to take away its sin. Then he poured out the rest of the blood at the foot of the
16 altar, which he consecrated by performing the rite of atonement over it. •Then
he took all the fat that covers the entrails, the fatty mass which is over the liver,
17 the two kidneys and their fat; and he burnt them all on the altar. •The bull's
skin, its flesh and its dung he burnt outside the camp, as Yahweh had
ordered Moses.

8 a. The ritual for high-priestly investiture appears here as an account of the investiture of
Aaron and his sons.

Then he had the ram for holocaust brought forward. Aaron and his sons laid 18
their hands on its head •and Moses immolated it. He poured its blood out on 19
the borders of the altar. •Then he quartered the ram and burned the head, the 20
pieces and the fat. •He washed the entrails and legs, and burnt the whole ram 21
on the altar. This was a holocaust whose fragrance would appease Yahweh;
a burnt offering for Yahweh, as Yahweh had ordered Moses.

Then he had the other ram brought forward, for the sacrifice of investiture. 22
Aaron and his sons laid their hands on its head •and Moses immolated it. He 23
took some of its blood and put it on the lobe of Aaron's right ear, the thumb
of his right hand, and the big toe of his right foot. •Then he made the sons of 24
Aaron come forward and he put some of the blood on the lobes of their right
ears, the thumbs of their right hands and the big toes of their right feet. Next
Moses poured the rest of the blood on the borders of the altar. •Then he took 25
the fat: the tail, all the fat that is on the entrails, the fatty mass which is over the
liver, the two kidneys and their fat, and the right thigh. •From the basket of 26
unleavened bread placed before Yahweh, he took an unleavened cake, a cake of
bread made with oil, and a wafer; he placed these on the fat and the right thigh,
and put it all into Aaron's hands and those of his sons, and made the gesture 27
of offering before Yahweh. •Then Moses took them back and burned them on 28
the altar in addition to the holocaust. This was the sacrifice of investiture
whose fragrance would appease Yahweh, a burnt offering to Yahweh. •Then 29
Moses took the breast and made the gesture of offering before Yahweh. This
was the portion of the ram of investiture that reverted to Moses, as Yahweh had
ordered Moses.

Then Moses took the chrism and the blood that was on the altar and 30
sprinkled Aaron and his vestments with it, and his sons and their vestments.
In this way he consecrated Aaron and his vestments, and his sons and their
vestments.

Then Moses said to Aaron and his sons, 'Cook the meat at the entrance to 31
the Tent of Meeting, and eat it there, as also the bread for the sacrifice of
investiture that is in the basket, as I ordered, when I said: Aaron and his sons
are to eat it. •What remains of the meat and bread you will burn. •For seven days $^{32}_{33}$
you must not leave the entrance to the Tent of Meeting, until the time of your
investiture is complete; for your investiture will require seven days. •Yahweh has 34
ordered us to do as we have done today to perform the rite of atonement over
you; •and for seven days, day and night, you must remain at the entrance to the 35
Tent of Meeting observing Yahweh's ritual; do this, and you will not die.*b* For
this is the order I received.' •And Aaron and his sons did everything that Yahweh 36
had ordered through Moses.

The priests assume their functions

9 On the eighth day Moses summoned Aaron and his sons and the elders of 1
Israel; •he said to Aaron, 'Take a calf to offer a sacrifice for sin, and a ram 2
for a holocaust, both without blemish, and bring them before Yahweh. •Then 3
say to the sons of Israel, "Take a goat to be offered as a sacrifice for sin, and as
a holocaust a calf and a lamb both one year old and without blemish, •and for 4
communion sacrifices an ox and a ram to be immolated before Yahweh; and
finally an oblation mixed with oil. For Yahweh will appear to you today."'

They brought what Moses had commanded in front of the Tent of Meeting; 5
then the whole community came and stood before Yahweh. •Moses said, 'This is 6
what Yahweh has ordered to be done, so that his glory may be visible to you'.
Moses then addressed Aaron, 'Go to the altar and offer your sacrifice for sin 7
and your holocaust, and so perform the rite of atonement for yourself and your
family. Then present the people's offering and perform the rite of atonement
for them, as Yahweh has ordered.'

Aaron went to the altar and immolated the calf as a sacrifice for his own sin. 8

9 Then the sons of Aaron presented the blood to him; he dipped his finger in it
and put some on the horns of the altar, and then poured out the rest of the
10 blood at the foot of the altar. •The fat of the sacrifice for sin and the kidneys
and the fatty mass which is over the liver, he burned on the altar, as Yahweh had
11 commanded Moses; •the flesh and the skin he burned outside the camp.

12 Next Aaron immolated the holocaust; his sons handed him the blood and he
13 poured it on the borders of the altar. •Then they handed him the quartered
14 victim, and its head too, and he burned these on the altar. •He washed the entrails
and legs and burned them on the altar in addition to the holocaust.

15 He then presented the people's offering. He took the goat for the people's
sacrifice for sin, immolated it, and made a sacrifice for sin with it in the same
16 way as with the first. •Then he had the holocaust brought forward and proceeded
17 according to the ritual. •Next he had the oblation brought forward, took a
handful of it and burned it on the altar in addition to the morning holocaust.

18 Finally, he immolated the ox and the ram as a communion sacrifice for the
people. Aaron's sons handed him the blood and he poured it out on the borders
19 of the altar. •The fat of the ox and of the ram—the tail, the fatty covering, the
20 kidneys, the fatty mass over the liver—•all of this he laid on the breasts and
21 burned it all on the altar. •With the breasts and the right thigh Aaron made
the gesture of offering as Yahweh had ordered Moses.

22 Then Aaron raised his hands towards the people and blessed them. Having
thus performed the sacrifice for sin, the holocaust and the communion sacrifice,
23 he came down •and entered the Tent of Meeting with Moses. Then they came
out together to bless the people and the glory of Yahweh appeared to the whole
24 people—•a flame leaped forth from before Yahweh and consumed the holocaust
and the fat that was on the altar. At this sight the people shouted for joy and
fell on their faces.

Complementary legislation[a]
a. A lesson in exact observance

1 **10** Nadab and Abihu, sons of Aaron, each took his censer, put fire in it and
incense on the fire, and presented unlawful fire before Yahweh, fire which
2 he had not prescribed for them. •Then from Yahweh's presence a flame leaped
3 out and consumed them, and they perished in the presence of Yahweh. •And
Moses said to Aaron, 'That is what Yahweh meant when he said:

"In those who are close to me I show my holiness,
and before all the people I show my glory" '.[b]

Aaron remained silent.

b. Removal of bodies

4 Moses summoned Mishael and Elzaphan, sons of Aaron's uncle Uzziel, and
said to them, 'Come and take your brothers far away from the sanctuary, out
5 of the camp'. •They came and carried them away, still in their tunics, out of
the camp, as Moses had ordered.

c. Rules for priestly mourning

6 Moses said to Aaron and his sons Eleazar and Ithamar, 'Do not disorder your
hair nor tear your garments;[c] you are not going to die. It is with the whole
community that he is angry; it is the whole House of Israel that must lament
7 your brothers, the victims of Yahweh's fire. •Do not leave the entrance to the
Tent of Meeting, lest you die; for the chrism of Yahweh is on you.' And they
obeyed the words of Moses.

b. Not a promise of immortality: 'the penalty for infringing any of these ritual laws is death'.
10 a. Presented in anecdotes, as case law.   b. Holy things are reserved for priests who are
'close to' Yahweh.   c. Mourning ritual.

d. Wine forbidden

Yahweh spoke to Aaron; he said: 8

'When you come to the Tent of Meeting, you and your sons with you, do not 9 take wine or strong drink; then you will not die. This is a perpetual law for all your descendants. •And so be it too when you separate the sacred from the 10 profane, the unclean from the clean, •and when you teach the sons of Israel 11 any of the laws that Yahweh has pronounced for them through Moses.'

e. The priests' portion in offerings

Moses said to Aaron and his surviving sons, Eleazar and Ithamar, 'Take the 12 oblation that is left over from Yahweh's burnt offering. Eat the unleavened part of it beside the altar, because it is a most holy thing. •Eat it in a holy place; 13 it is the portion of Yahweh's burnt offering prescribed for you and your sons; this is the order I have received.

'The breast that was offered up and the thigh that was set aside you will eat 14 in some place that is clean, you, your sons and your daughters with you; this is the portion of the communion sacrifices of the sons of Israel that is prescribed for you and your sons. •The thigh that was set aside and the breast that was 15 offered up, when the fat was burnt, revert to you, to you and your sons with you, after they have been presented before Yahweh by the gesture of offering, in virtue of a perpetual law as Yahweh has ordered.'

f. A special regulation concerning Sacrifice for Sin

Then Moses enquired about the goat offered as a sacrifice for sin, and found 16 that they had burnt it. He was angry with Eleazar and Ithamar, Aaron's surviving sons: •'Why' he asked 'did you not eat this victim in the holy place? For it is 17 a most holy thing given to you to take away the fault of the community, by performing the rite of atonement over it before Yahweh. •Since its blood was 18 not taken inside the sanctuary, you should have eaten its flesh there, as I ordered you.' •Aaron said to Moses, 'Today they have offered their sacrifice for sin and 19 their holocaust before Yahweh. If I had been concerned, if I had eaten the victim for sin today, would that have seemed good to Yahweh?' •And when Moses 20 heard this, he was satisfied.

III. RULES CONCERNING THE CLEAN AND UNCLEAN

Clean and unclean beasts
a. On land

11 Yahweh spoke to Moses and Aaron and said to them, •'Speak to the sons ½ of Israel and say:

"Of all the beasts on the earth these are the animals you may eat:

"You may eat any animal that has a cloven hoof, divided into two parts, 3 and that is a ruminant. •The following, which either chew the cud or have a 4 cloven hoof, are the ones that you may not eat: the camel must be held unclean, because though it is ruminant, it has not a cloven hoof; •the hyrax must be held 5 unclean, because though it is ruminant, it has not a cloven hoof; •the hare must 6 be held unclean, because though it is ruminant, it has not a cloven hoof; •the 7 pig must be held unclean, because though it has a cloven hoof, divided into two parts, it is not ruminant. •You must not eat the meat of such animals nor 8 touch their dead bodies; you must hold them unclean.

b. In water

"Of all that lives in water, these you may eat: 9

"Anything that has fins and scales, and lives in the water, whether in sea or river, you may eat. •But anything in sea or river that has not fins or scales, 10

of all the small water-creatures and all the living things found there, must be
11 held detestable. •You must hold them detestable; you are not to eat their
12 flesh and you must avoid their carcases. •Anything that lives in water, but
has no fins or scales, is to be held detestable.

c. Birds

13 "Among the birds here are those you must hold detestable; they may not be
eaten, they are detestable:

14 "The tawny vulture, the griffon, the osprey, •the kite, the several kinds of
15 16 buzzard, •all kinds of raven, •the ostrich, the screech owl, the seagull, the several
17 18 kinds of hawk, •horned owl, night owl, cormorant, barn owl, •ibis, pelican,
19 white vulture, •stork, the several kinds of heron, hoopoe and bat.

d. Winged insects

20 21 "All winged insects that move on four feet[a] you must hold detestable. •Of all
these winged insects you may eat only the following: those that have legs above
22 their feet so that they can leap over the ground. •These are the ones you may
eat: the several kinds of migratory locust, solham, hargol and hagab locusts in
23 their several kinds. •But all winged insects on four feet you are to hold detestable.

Contact with unclean animals

24 "By these you will be made unclean. Anyone who touches the carcase of one
25 will be unclean until evening. •Anyone who picks up their carcases must wash
26 his clothing and will be unclean until evening. •Animals that have hoofs, but
not cloven, and that are not ruminant, you are to hold unclean; anyone
27 who touches them will be unclean. •Those four-footed animals which walk on
the flat of their foot[b] must be held unclean; anyone who touches their carcases
28 will be unclean until evening, •and anyone who picks up their carcases must wash
his clothing and will be unclean until evening. You are to hold them unclean.

e. Small ground beasts

29 "These are the small beasts crawling on the ground that you are to hold
30 unclean: the mole, the rat, the several kinds of lizard: •gecko, koah, letaah,
chameleon and tinshameth.

Further rules on contact with things unclean

31 "Of all the small beasts, these are the creatures that you are to hold unclean.
Anyone who touches them when they are dead will be unclean until evening.
32 "Any object on which one of these creatures falls when it is dead becomes
unclean: wooden utensil, clothing, skin, sackcloth—any utensil at all. It must
be dipped in water and will remain unclean until evening: then it will be clean.
33 If the creature falls into an earthenware vessel, the vessel must be broken;
34 whatever the vessel contains is unclean. •Any food that is eaten will be unclean,
even if it is steeped in water; any liquid that is drunk will be unclean, no matter
35 what its container. •Anything on which a carcase of such a creature may fall
will be unclean: oven or stove must be destroyed, for unclean they are and
36 unclean they must be for you •(although springs, wells and stretches of water
will remain clean); anyone who touches a carcase of theirs will be unclean.
37 If one of their carcases falls on any seed whatever, the seed will remain clean;
38 but if the seed has been wet, and a carcase of theirs falls on it, then you must
hold it unclean.
39 "If one of the animals that you use as food dies, then anyone who touches the
40 carcase will be unclean until evening; •anyone who eats the dead meat must

---

11 a. There are certain insects which use only four feet for walking, but the intention is probably
to distinguish between birds and insects.　　**b.** I.e., without hooves.

wash his clothing and will remain unclean until evening; anyone who picks up
the carcase must wash his clothing and will remain unclean until evening.

The religious aspect

"Any small beast that crawls on the ground is detestable; you must not 41
eat it. •Anything that moves on its belly, anything that moves on four legs or 42
more—in short all the small beasts that crawl on the ground—you must not eat
these because they are detestable. •Do not make yourself detestable with 43
all these crawling beasts; do not defile yourself with them, do not be defiled
by them. •For it is I, Yahweh, who am your God. You have been sanctified 44
and have become holy because I am holy: do not defile yourself with all these
beasts that crawl on the ground. •Yes, it is I, Yahweh, who brought you out 45
of Egypt to be your God: you therefore must be holy because I am holy." '

Conclusion

Such is the law concerning animals, birds, all living creatures that move in 46
water and every creature that crawls on the ground. •Its purpose is to separate 47
the clean from the unclean; creatures that may be eaten from those that must
not be eaten.

Purification of a woman after childbirth

12 Yahweh spoke to Moses; he said, •'Speak to the sons of Israel and say: ½
"If a woman conceives and gives birth to a boy, she is to be unclean for
seven days, just as she is unclean during her monthly periods. •On the eighth day 3
the child's foreskin must be circumcised, •and she must wait another thirty-three 4
days for her blood to be purified. She must not touch anything consecrated nor
go to the sanctuary until the time of her purification is over.

"If she gives birth to a girl, she is to be unclean for two weeks, as during her 5
monthly periods; and she must wait another sixty-six days for her blood to be
purified.

"When the period of her purification is over, for either boy or girl, she is to 6
bring to the priest at the entrance to the Tent of Meeting a lamb one year old
for a holocaust, and a young pigeon or turtledove as a sacrifice for sin. •The 7
priest is to offer this before Yahweh, perform the rite of atonement over her,
and she will be purified from her flow of blood.

"Such is the law concerning a woman who gives birth to either a boy or a girl.
If she cannot afford a lamb, she is to take two turtledoves or two young pigeons, 8
one for the holocaust and the other for the sacrifice for sin. The priest is to
perform the rite of atonement over her and she will be purified." '

Human leprosy
a. Swellings, scabs, discolorations

13 Yahweh said to Moses and Aaron, •'If a swelling or scab or shiny spot ½
appears on a man's skin, a case of leprosy of the skin is to be suspected.
The man must be taken to Aaron, the priest, or to one of the priests who are
his sons. •The priest must examine the disease on the skin. If the hair on the 3
diseased part has turned white, or if the disease bites into the skin, then it is
indeed a case of leprosy, and after examination the priest must declare the man
unclean. •But if there is a shiny spot on the skin without any visible depression 4
of the skin and without whitening of the hair, the priest is to isolate the sick
person for seven days. •On the seventh day he must examine him, and if he sees 5
with his own eyes that the disease persists though without spreading over the
skin, he is to isolate him for a further seven days •and examine him again on 6
the seventh. If he finds that the diseased part is no longer shiny and has not
spread over the skin, then the priest is to declare the man clean. It is a scab
merely. Having washed his clothing he will be clean.

7 'But if the scab spreads over the skin after the sick person has been examined by the priest and declared clean, then he must present himself again to the priest.
8 After examining him and certifying the spread of the scab over the skin, the priest must declare him unclean: it is leprosy.

b. Chronic leprosy

9
10 'When a leprous disease strikes a man, he must be taken to the priest, •who must examine him, and if he finds on the skin a whitish swelling with whitening
11 of the hair and an ulcer forming, •then it is chronic leprosy in the skin and the priest must declare him unclean. He is not to isolate him; he is unclean beyond doubt.
12 'But if the leprosy spreads all through the skin, if it covers him entirely from
13 head to foot so far as the priest can see, •then the priest must examine the sick person and, if he finds that the leprosy covers his whole body, declare the sick
14 person[a] clean. Since it has all become white, he is clean.• But as soon as an
15 ulcer appears on him, he will be unclean. •After examining the ulcer, the priest
16 is to declare him unclean: the ulcer is unclean, it is leprous. •But if the ulcer
17 becomes white again, the man must go to the priest; •the priest must examine him and if he finds that the disease has turned white, he is to declare the sick person clean: he is clean.

c. Boils

18
19 'When a boil appears on a man's skin, which, after healing, •leaves in its place a whitish swelling or a shiny spot of reddish white, the man must show
20 himself to the priest. •The priest must examine him, and if he finds a visible depression in the skin and a whitening of the hair, he is to declare him unclean:
21 it is a case of leprosy that has broken out in a boil. •But if on examination the priest finds neither white hair nor depression of the skin, but a fading of the
22 affected part, he is to isolate the sick person for seven days. •If the disease has indeed spread over the skin, he must declare him unclean: it is a case of leprosy.
23 But if the shiny spot is still restricted and has not spread, then it is the scar of a boil and the priest is to declare the man clean.

d. Burns

24 'If someone has had a burn, and on the burn an ulcer forms, a shiny spot
25 reddish-white or whitish in colour, •then the priest must examine it. If he finds a whitening of the hair or a visible depression of the mark on the skin, this means that leprosy has broken out in the burn. The priest is to declare the man
26 unclean: it is a case of leprosy. •If on the other hand the priest on examination does not find white hair on the mark or depression of the skin, but a fading of
27 the mark, then the priest is to isolate him for seven days. •On the seventh day he must examine him, and if the disease has spread on the skin, he must declare
28 him unclean: it is a case of leprosy. •If the mark is still restricted and has not spread over the skin, but has faded instead, this means that it is only a swelling due to the burn. The priest is to declare the man clean: it is merely a burn scar.

e. Diseases of the scalp and chin

29
30 'If a man or a woman has a sore on the head or chin, •the priest must examine this sore; and if he finds a depression visible in the skin, with the hair on it yellow and thin, he must declare the sick person unclean. It is tinea, that is to
31 say, leprosy of the head or chin. •If on examining this case of tinea the priest finds no visible depression in the skin nor yellow hair, he is to isolate the person
32 so affected for seven days. •He must examine the infected part on the seventh day, and if he finds that the tinea has not spread, that the hair on it is not yellow,
33 and that there is no visible depression in the skin, • the sick person will shave his hair, all except the part affected with tinea, and the priest is to isolate him

13 a. When the symptoms spread over the surface it is a sign of recovery.

again for seven days. •He must examine the infected part on the seventh day, 34
and if he finds that it has not spread over the skin, and that there is no visible
depression of the skin, the priest is to declare the sick person clean After washing
his clothes he will be clean. •But if after this purification the tinea does spread 35
over the skin, •the priest must examine him; if he finds that the tinea has indeed 36
spread over the skin, this means that the sick person is unclean, and there is no
need to verify whether the hair is yellow. •Whereas if, so far as he can see, the 37
tinea is arrested and dark hair is beginning to grow on it, this means that the
sick person is cured. He is clean, and the priest is to declare him clean.

f. Rash

'If shiny spots break out on the skin of a man or woman, and if these spots 38
are white, •the priest must examine them. If he finds that these patches are of 39
a dull white, it is a rash that has broken out on the skin: the sick person is clean.

g. Loss of hair

'If a man loses the hair of his scalp, this is baldness of the scalp but the man 40
is clean. •If he loses his hair off the front of the head, this is baldness of the 41
forehead but the man is clean. •If, however, a reddish-white sore appears on 42
scalp or forehead, this means that leprosy has broken out on the man's scalp or
forehead. •The priest must examine it, and if he finds a reddish-white swelling 43
on the scalp or forehead, of the same appearance as leprosy of the skin, •this 44
means that the man is leprous: he is unclean. The priest must declare him
unclean; he is suffering from leprosy of the head.

A regulation for lepers

'A man infected with leprosy must wear his clothing torn and his hair disor- 45
dered; he must shield his upper lip and cry, "Unclean, unclean". •As long as the 46
disease lasts he must be unclean; and therefore he must live apart: he must live
outside the camp.

Leprosy of clothes

'When a piece of clothing is infected with leprosy—woollen or linen clothing, 47
linen or woollen fabric or covering, leather or leatherwork—•and if this clothing, 48
 49
fabric, covering, leather or leatherwork appears greenish or reddish, it is a case
of leprosy to be shown to the priest. •The priest must examine the infection 50
and isolate the object for seven days. •If on the seventh day he observes that the 51
infection has spread on the garment, fabric, covering, leather or leatherwork,
whatever it may be, it is a case of contagious leprosy and the object is unclean.
He will burn this clothing, fabric, linen or woollen covering, leather article of any 52
kind, on which the infection has appeared; for it is a contagious leprosy which
must be destroyed by fire.

'But if on examination the priest finds that the infection has not spread on 53
the clothing, fabric, covering, or leather object whatever it may be, •he is to order 54
the infected article to be washed and is to isolate it again for a period of seven
days. •After the cleansing he must examine the infection and if he finds that there 55
is no change in its appearance, even though it has not spread, the article is
unclean. It must be destroyed by fire; it is infected through and through.

'But if on examination the priest finds that the infection has diminished after 56
washing, he is to cut it out of the clothing, leather, fabric or covering. •But if the 57
infection reappears on the same clothing, fabric, covering or leather article
whatever it may be, this means that the infection is active and you must destroy
by fire whatever is infected. •The clothing, fabric, covering or leather article 58
whatever it may be, from which the infection disappears after washing, is to be
clean after it has been washed a second time.

'Such is the law for a case of leprosy in a linen or woollen garment, a fabric 59 or covering or leather article whatever it may be, when it is a question of declaring them clean or unclean.'

Purification of lepers

1 14 Yahweh spoke to Moses; he said:
2 'This is the law to be applied to a leper on the day he is purified. He must
3 be taken to the priest, •and the priest must go outside the camp. If he finds on
4 examination that the leper is cured of his leprosy, •he shall order the following to be brought for the man's purification: two live birds that are clean, cedar
5 wood, scarlet and hyssop. •Then he is to give orders for one of the birds to be
6 immolated in an earthenware pot over running water. •Then he is to take the live bird, the cedar wood, the scarlet and the hyssop and he must dip all of this (including the live bird) into the blood of the bird immolated over running water.
7 Then he must sprinkle the man who is to be purified of leprosy seven times, and having declared him clean, must set the live bird free to fly off into the open
8 country. •The man who is undergoing purification is to wash his clothing, shave all his hair, and wash himself; then he will be clean. After this he may return
9 to the camp, although he must remain seven days outside his tent. •On the seventh day he must shave off all his hair—head, beard and eyebrows; he must shave off all his hair. After washing his clothing and his body he will be clean.
10 'On the eighth day, he is to take two lambs without blemish, an unblemished ewe one year old, three-tenths[a] of wheaten flour mixed with oil for the oblation,
11 and one log of oil. •The priest who is performing the purification is to station the man who is being purified, with all his offerings, at the entrance to the Tent
12 of Meeting, before Yahweh. •Then he must take one of the lambs and offer it as a sacrifice of reparation, as also the log of oil. With these he is to make the gesture
13 of offering before Yahweh. •Then he must immolate the lamb on that spot inside the sacred precincts where the victims of the sacrifice for sin and of the holocaust are immolated. This offering of reparation, like the sacrifice for sin, reverts to
14 the priest: it is a most holy thing. •The priest must take the blood of this sacrifice and put some of it on the lobe of the right ear, the thumb of the right hand, and
15 the big toe of the right foot of the man who is being purified. •Then he is to take
16 the log of oil and pour a little into the hollow of his left hand. •He must dip a finger of his right hand into the oil in the hollow of his left hand, and with this
17 oil make seven sprinklings with his finger before Yahweh. •Then he is to take a little of the oil that remains in the hollow of his hand and put it on the lobe of the right ear of the man who is being purified, and on the thumb of his right hand and on the big toe of his right foot (this in addition to the blood of the
18 sacrifice of reparation). •The rest of the oil in the hollow of his hand he is to put on the head of the man who is being purified. In this way he will have performed over him the rite of atonement before Yahweh.
19 'Then the priest must offer the sacrifice for sin, and perform the rite of atonement for uncleanness over the man who is being purified. After this he must
20 immolate the holocaust, •and send up holocaust and oblation on the altar. When the priest has performed the rite of atonement over him in this way, the man will be clean.
21 'If he is poor and cannot afford all this, he need take only one lamb, the one for the sacrifice of reparation, and it is to be presented with the gesture of offering to perform the rite of atonement over the man. And he is to take for the oblation
22 only one-tenth of wheaten flour mixed with oil, and the log of oil, •and finally two turtledoves or two young pigeons—if he can afford them—one to be used
23 as a sacrifice for sin and the other for the holocaust. •On the eighth day he must bring them to the priest at the entrance to the Tent of Meeting before Yahweh,
24 for his purification. •The priest is to take the lamb for the sacrifice of reparation

14 a. I.e., of an ephah.

and the log of oil, and present them before Yahweh with the gesture of offering. Then he must immolate the lamb for the sacrifice of reparation, take some of its 25 blood and put it on the lobe of the right ear of the man who is being purified, on the thumb of his right hand and on the big toe of his right foot. •He is to 26 pour the oil into the hollow of his left hand, •and with this oil in the hollow of 27 his left hand he must make seven sprinklings with his finger before Yahweh. He is to put some of it on the lobe of the right ear of the man who is being 28 purified, on the thumb of his right hand and on the big toe of his right foot, as he did with the blood of the sacrifice of reparation. •The remainder of the oil 29 in the hollow of his hand he must put on the head of the man who is being purified, performing the rite of atonement over him before Yahweh. •Of the 30 two turtledoves or two young pigeons—if he can afford them—he is to offer a sacrifice for sin with one, and with the other a holocaust together with an 31 oblation—if he can afford them. In this way the priest will have performed before Yahweh the rite of atonement over the person who is being purified.

'Such is the law concerning a person afflicted by leprosy who cannot afford 32 the means for his purification.'

Leprosy of houses

Yahweh spoke to Moses and Aaron; he said: 33
'When you reach the land of Canaan, which I am giving you as an 34 inheritance, if I strike a house with leprosy in the land you are to possess, •the 35 owner must come and warn the priest; he must say, "I have seen something like leprosy in the house". •The priest is to give orders for the house to be emptied 36 before he goes to examine the infection; thus nothing in the house will become unclean. Then the priest must go and look at the house; •and if on examination 37 he finds the walls of the house pitted with reddish or greenish depressions, the priest is to go out of the house, to the door, and shut it up for seven days. 38 On the seventh day he must go back again, and if on examination he finds that 39 the infection has spread over the walls of the house, •he must give orders for 40 the infected stones to be removed and thrown into some unclean place outside the town. •Then he must have all the inside of the house scraped, and the plaster 41 that comes off must be emptied out into an unclean place outside the town. •The 42 stones must be replaced by new ones and the house given a new coat of plaster.

'If the infection spreads again after the stones have been removed and the 43 house scraped and replastered, •the priest is to come and examine it. If he finds 44 that the infection has spread, this means that there is a contagious leprosy in the house: it is unclean. •It must be pulled down and the stones, woodwork and 45 all the plaster be taken to an unclean place outside the town.

'Anyone who enters the house while it is closed will be unclean until evening. 46 Anyone who sleeps there must wash his clothing. Anyone who eats there must 47 wash his clothing. •But if the priest finds, when he comes to examine the 48 infection, that it has not spread in the house since it was plastered, he is to declare the house clean, for the infection is cured.

'As a sacrifice for the sin of the house, he is to take two birds, cedar wood, 49 scarlet and hyssop. •He must immolate one of the birds in an earthenware pot 50 over running water. •Then he is to take the cedar wood, the hyssop, the scarlet 51 and the live bird, and must dip them into the blood of the bird that was immolated and into the running water. He is to sprinkle the house seven times; •and after 52 having offered a sacrifice for the sin of the house with the blood of the bird, the running water, the live bird, the cedar wood, the hyssop and the scarlet, he must set the live bird free to fly out of the town into the open country. When 53 the rite of atonement has been performed over the house in this way it will be clean.

'Such is the law for all cases of leprosy and tinea, •leprosy of clothing and 54 / 55 houses, •swellings, scabs and shiny spots. It defines the occasions when things 56 are unclean and when clean. •Such is the law on leprosy.'   57

Sexual impurities
a. Of men

1 15 Yahweh spoke to Moses and Aaron; he said:
2 'Speak to the sons of Israel and say to them:
3 "When a man has a discharge from his body, that discharge is unclean. •While the discharge continues, the nature of his uncleanness is as follows:

"Whether his body allows the discharge to flow or whether it retains it, he is unclean.

4 "Any bed the man lies on and any seat he sits on shall be unclean.

5 "Anyone who touches his bed must wash his clothing and wash himself and will be unclean until evening.

6 "Anyone who sits on a seat where the man has sat must wash his clothing and wash himself and will be unclean until evening.

7 "Anyone who touches the body of a man so affected must wash his clothing and wash himself and will be unclean until evening.

8 "If the sick man spits on someone who is clean, that person must wash his clothing and wash himself and will be unclean until evening.

9 "Any saddle the sick man travels on will be unclean.

10 "All those who touch any object that may be under him will be unclean until evening.

"Anyone who picks up such an object must wash his clothing and wash himself and will be unclean until evening.

11 "All those whom the sick man touches without washing his hands must wash their clothing and wash themselves and will be unclean until evening.

12 "Any earthenware vessel the sick man touches must be broken and any wooden utensil must be rinsed.

13 "When the man suffering from a discharge is cured, he must allow seven days for his purification. He must wash his clothing and wash his body in running
14 water and he will be clean. •On the eighth day he must take two turtledoves or two young pigeons and come before Yahweh at the entrance to the Tent of
15 Meeting, and give them to the priest. •The priest is to offer a sacrifice for sin with one of them, and with the other a holocaust. So the priest will perform the rite of atonement over him before Yahweh for his discharge.

16 "When a man has a seminal discharge, he must wash his whole body with
17 water and he shall be unclean until evening. •Any clothing or leather touched by the seminal discharge must be washed and it will be unclean until evening.
18 When a woman has slept with a man, both of them must wash and they will be unclean until evening.

b. Of women

19 "When a woman has a discharge of blood, and blood flows from her body, this uncleanness of her monthly periods shall last for seven days.

"Anyone who touches her will be unclean until evening.

20 "Any bed she lies on in this state will be unclean; any seat she sits on will be unclean.

21 "Anyone who touches her bed must wash his clothing and wash himself and will be unclean until evening.

22 "Anyone who touches any seat she has sat on must wash his clothing and
23 wash himself and will be unclean until evening. •If there is anything on the bed or on the chair on which she sat, anyone who touches it will be unclean until evening.

24 "If a man sleeps with her, he will be affected by the uncleanness of her monthly periods. He shall be unclean for seven days. Any bed he lies on will be unclean.

25 "If a woman has a flow of blood for several days outside the period, or if the period is prolonged, during the time this flow lasts she shall be in the same state
26 of uncleanness as during her monthly periods. •Any bed she lies on during the

time this flow lasts will be in the same condition as the bed she lies on during her monthly periods. Any seat she sits on will be unclean as it would be during her monthly periods. •Anyone who touches them will be unclean; he must 27 wash his clothing and wash himself and will be unclean until evening.

"When she is cured of her flow, she will let seven days pass; then she will be 28 clean. •On the eighth day she is to take two turtledoves or two young pigeons 29 and bring them to the priest at the entrance to the Tent of Meeting. •With one 30 of them the priest is to offer a sacrifice for sin and with the other a holocaust. This is the way in which the priest will perform the rite of atonement over her before Yahweh for the flow that caused her uncleanness."

Conclusion

'You must warn the sons of Israel of their uncleanness lest they should die 31 because of it, by being a defilement to my tabernacle which is set amongst them.

'Such is the law concerning a man with a discharge, anyone made unclean by 32 a seminal discharge, •a woman in the uncleanness of her monthly periods, a 33 man or a woman with a discharge, a man who sleeps with an unclean woman.'

The great Day of Atonement

16 After the death of the two sons of Aaron who died through offering 1 unlawful fire before Yahweh, •Yahweh spoke to Moses. He said: 2 'Tell Aaron your brother that he must not enter the sanctuary beyond the veil, in front of the throne of mercy that is over the ark, whenever he chooses. He may die; for I appear in a cloud on the throne of mercy.

'This is how he is to enter the sanctuary: with a young bull for a sacrifice 3 for sin and a ram for a holocaust. •He is to put on a tunic of consecrated linen, 4 wear linen on his body, a linen girdle round his waist, and a linen turban on his head. These are the sacred vestments he must put on after washing himself with water.

'He is to receive two goats for a sacrifice for sin and a ram for a holocaust from 5 the community of the sons of Israel. •After offering the bull as a sacrifice for 6 his own sin and performing the rite of atonement for himself and his family, Aaron must take the two goats and set them before Yahweh at the entrance to 7 the Tent of Meeting. •He is to draw lots for the two goats and allot one to 8 Yahweh and the other to Azazel.ᵃ •Aaron is to offer up the goat whose lot was 9 marked "For Yahweh", and offer it as a sacrifice for sin. •The goat whose lot 10 was marked "For Azazel" shall be set before Yahweh, still alive, to perform the rite of atonement over it, sending it out into the desert to Azazel.

'Aaron must offer the bull which is to be a sacrifice for his own sin, then he 11 must perform the rite of atonement for himself and for his family, and immolate the bull. •Then he is to fill a censer with live coals from the altar that stands 12 before Yahweh; and to take two handfuls of finely ground aromatic incense. He is to take these through the veil •and then to put the incense on the fire 13 before Yahweh, and with a cloud of incense he must cover the throne of mercy that is on the Testimony; if he does this, he shall not die. •Then he must take 14 some of the blood of the bull and sprinkle it with his finger on the eastern side of the throne of mercy; in front of the throne of mercy he must sprinkle this blood seven times with his finger.

'He must then immolate the goat for the sacrifice for the sin of the people, and 15 take its blood through the veil. With this blood he is to do as with the blood of the bull, sprinkling it on the throne of mercy and in front of it. •This is how 16 he is to perform the rite of atonement over the sanctuary for the uncleanness of the sons of Israel, for their transgressions and for all their sins.

'This also is how he must deal with the Tent of Meeting which remains with them, surrounded by their uncleanness. •Let no one stay in the Tent of 17 Meeting, from the moment he enters to make atonement in the sanctuary until the time he comes out.

18 'When he has made atonement for himself, for his family, and for the whole community of Israel, •he is to come out and go to the altar which is before Yahweh, and perform over it the rite of atonement. He must take some of the blood of the bull and of the goat, and put it on the horns around the altar.
19 With this blood he must sprinkle the altar seven times with his finger. This is how he will render it clean and sacred, purified and separated from the uncleannesses of the sons of Israel.

20 'When the atonement of the sanctuary, the Tent of Meeting and the altar is
21 complete, he is to bring the other goat that is still alive. •Aaron must lay his hands on its head and confess all the faults of the sons of Israel, all their transgressions and all their sins, and lay them to its charge. Having thus laid them on the goat's head, he shall send it out into the desert led by a man
22 waiting ready, •and the goat will bear all their faults away with it into a desert place.

23 'When he has sent the goat out into the wilderness, •Aaron is to return to the Tent of Meeting and remove the linen vestments he wore to enter the sanctuary.
24 He must leave them there •and wash his body in a consecrated place. Then he is to put the vestments on again and go out to offer his own and the people's holocaust. He must perform the rite of atonement for himself and for the people;
25 he must burn up the fat of the sacrifice for sin on the altar.

26 'The man who leads out the goat to Azazel must wash his clothing and his
27 body, and then he can return to the camp. •The bull and the goat offered as a sacrifice for sin, whose blood has been taken into the sanctuary for the rite of atonement, are to be taken out of the camp where their skin, flesh and dung are
28 to be burnt. •The man who burns them must wash his clothing and his body, and then he can return to the camp.

29 'This shall be a perpetual law for you.

'On the tenth day of the seventh month you must fast and refrain from work,
30 the native and the stranger who lives among you. •For this is the day on which the rite of atonement shall be performed over you, to purify you. Before Yahweh
31 you will be clean of all your sins. •It shall be a sabbath rest for you and you are to fast. This is a perpetual law.

32 'The rite of atonement must be performed by the priest who has been anointed and installed to officiate in place of his father. He is to put on the linen, the
33 sacred vestments, •and to perform the atonement of the sacred sanctuary, the Tent of Meeting and the altar. Then he must perform the rite of atonement over
34 the priests and all the people of the community. •This shall be a perpetual law for you; once a year the rite of atonement must be made over the sons of Israel for all their sins.'

And it was done as Yahweh commanded Moses.

IV. THE LAW OF HOLINESS

Immolation and sacrifice

1 **17** Yahweh spoke to Moses; he said:
2 'Speak to Aaron and his sons and all the sons of Israel and say to them: "This is the word of Yahweh, his command:

3 Any man of the House of Israel who immolates an ox, lamb or goat, whether
4 inside the camp or outside it, •must first bring it to the entrance to the Tent of Meeting to make an offering of it to Yahweh before his tabernacle; and anyone who fails to do this must answer for the blood that is spilt; he shall be
5 outlawed from his people. •Thus, the sacrifices that the sons of Israel wish to make

16 a. Azazel, in ancient Hebrew and Canaanite belief, is a demon of the desert. It will be noticed that the 'scapegoat' is not sacrificed to Azazel.

in the open country will be brought to the priest, for Yahweh, at the entrance to the Tent of Meeting, and with them they will make communion sacrifices for Yahweh. •The priest shall sprinkle the blood on the altar of Yahweh that stands 6 at the entrance to the Tent of Meeting, and he shall burn the fat, and its fragrance will appease Yahweh. •They must no longer offer their sacrifices to the satyrs*a* 7 in whose service they once prostituted themselves.*b* This is a perpetual law for them and for their descendants."

'You will also say to them, "Any man of the House of Israel or stranger living 8 among you who offers a holocaust or sacrifice •without bringing it to the entrance 9 to the Tent of Meeting to offer it to Yahweh shall be outlawed from his people.

"If any man of the House of Israel or stranger living among you eats blood 10 of any kind, I will set my face against the man who has eaten the blood and will outlaw him from his people. •The life of the flesh is in the blood. This 11 blood I myself have given you to perform the rite of atonement for your lives at the altar; for it is blood that atones for a life. •That is why I have said to 12 the sons of Israel: None of you nor any stranger living among you shall eat blood.

"If any son of Israel or any stranger living among you catches game 13 or bird that it is lawful to eat, he must pour out its blood and cover it with earth. For the life of all flesh is its blood, and I have said to the sons of Israel: You 14 must not eat the blood of any flesh, for the life of all flesh is in its blood, and anyone who eats it shall be outlawed from his people.

"Anyone, native or stranger, who eats an animal that has died a natural death 15 or been savaged by beasts must wash his clothing and wash himself; he shall be unclean until evening, then he will be clean. •But if he does not 16 wash his clothing and wash his body, he must bear the consequences of his fault." '

Rules for conjugal relationships

18 Yahweh spoke to Moses; he said: 1
'Speak to the sons of Israel and say to them: 2
"I am Yahweh your God. •You must not behave as they do in Egypt where 3 once you lived; you must not behave as they do in Canaan where I am taking you. You must not follow their laws. •You must follow my customs and keep 4 my laws; by them you must lead your life.

"I am Yahweh your God. •You must keep my laws and my customs. Whoever 5 complies with them will find life in them.

"I am Yahweh.

"None of you may approach a woman who is closely related to him, to 6 uncover her nakedness. I am Yahweh.

"You must not uncover the nakedness of your father or mother. She is your 7 mother—you must not uncover her nakedness.

"You must not uncover the nakedness of your father's wife; it is your father's 8 nakedness.

"You must not uncover the nakedness of your sister, whether she is your 9 father's or your mother's daughter. Whether she is born in the same house or elsewhere, you must not uncover her nakedness.

"You must not uncover the nakedness of the daughter of your son or daughter; 10 for their nakedness is your own.

"You must not uncover the nakedness of the daughter of your father's 11 wife, born of your father. She is your sister; you must not uncover her nakedness.

"You must not uncover the nakedness of your father's sister; for it is your 12 father's flesh.

"You must not uncover the nakedness of your mother's sister; for it is your 13 mother's flesh.

14 "You must not uncover the nakedness of your father's brother; you must therefore not approach his wife, for she is your aunt.

15 "You must not uncover the nakedness of your daughter-in-law. She is your son's wife; you must not uncover her nakedness.

16 "You must not uncover the nakedness of your brother's wife; for it is your brother's nakedness.

17 "You must not uncover the nakedness of a woman and of her daughter too; you must not take the daughter of her son or of her daughter to uncover their nakedness. They are your own flesh; it would be incest.

18 "You must not take into your harem a woman and her sister at the same time, uncovering the latter's nakedness while the former is still alive.

19 "You must not approach and uncover the nakedness of a woman who is unclean by reason of her monthly periods.

20 "You must not give your marriage bed to your neighbour's wife; you would thereby become unclean.

21 "You must not hand over any of your children to have them passed to Molech,ᵃ nor must you profane the name of your God in this way. I am Yahweh.

22 "You must not lie with a man as with a woman. This is a hateful thing.

23 "You must not lie with any animal; you would thereby become unclean. A woman must not offer herself to an animal, to have intercourse with it. This would be a foul thing.

24 "Do not make yourselves unclean by any of these practices, for it was by such things that the nations that I have expelled to make way for you made themselves unclean.

25 "The land became unclean; I exacted the penalty for its fault and the land had to vomit out its inhabitants.

26 "But you must keep my laws and customs, you must not do any of these
27 hateful things, neither native nor stranger living among you. •For all these hateful things were done by the people who inhabited this land before you,
28 and the land became unclean. •If you make it unclean, will it not vomit you out
29 as it vomited the nation that was here before you? •Yes, anyone who does one of these hateful things, whatever it may be, any person doing so must be cut
30 off from his people. •Keep to my rules; do not observe the hateful practices that were observed before you came, then you will not be made unclean by them. I am Yahweh your God." '

Worship

1 **19** Yahweh spoke to Moses; he said:
2 'Speak to the whole community of the sons of Israel and say to them:
   "Be holy, for I, Yahweh your God, am holy.

3 "Each of you must respect his father and mother.
   "And you must keep my sabbaths; I am Yahweh your God.

4 "Do not turn to idols, and cast no gods of metal. I am Yahweh your God.

5 "If you offer a communion sacrifice to Yahweh, make yourselves acceptable
6 and so offer it. •It must be eaten the same day or the day after; whatever is
7 left the day after must be burnt. •If eaten on the third day it would be a
8 corrupt offering, it would not be acceptable. •Anyone who eats it must bear the consequences of his fault, for he will have profaned the holiness of Yahweh; this person shall be outlawed from his people.

9 "When you gather the harvest of your land, you are not to harvest to the very

17 a. 'Goats', contemptuously used of the demons in animal-form thought to live in deserts and ruins, e.g. Azazel.   b. The common phrase for religious unfaithfulness.
18 a. This is generally understood as forbidding the Canaanite practice of sacrificing children by making them 'pass through' fire as an offering to the god Molech (or Melech, 'king').

end of the field. You are not to gather the gleanings of the harvest. •You are 10
neither to strip your vine bare nor to collect the fruit that has fallen in your
vineyard. You must leave them for the poor and the stranger. I am Yahweh your
God.

"You must not steal nor deal deceitfully or fraudulently with your neighbour. 11
You must not swear falsely by my name, profaning the name of your God. I am 12
Yahweh. •You must not exploit or rob your neighbour. You must not keep back 13
the labourer's wage until next morning. •You must not curse the dumb, nor put 14
an obstacle in the blind man's way, but you must fear your God. I am Yahweh.

"You must not be guilty of unjust verdicts. You must neither be partial to the 15
little man nor overawed by the great; you must pass judgement on your neighbour
according to justice. •You must not slander your own people, and you must not 16
jeopardise your neighbour's life. I am Yahweh. •You must not bear hatred for 17
your brother in your heart. You must openly tell him, your neighbour, of his
offence; this way you will not take a sin upon yourself. •You must not exact 18
vengeance, nor must you bear a grudge against the children of your people. You
must love your neighbour as yourself. I am Yahweh.

"You must keep my laws. 19

"You are not to mate your cattle with those of another kind; you are not to
sow two kinds of grain in your field; you are not to wear a garment made from
two kinds of fabric.

"If a man sleeps with a woman as though married to her, she being another's 20
concubine slave not yet purchased or given her freedom, then the man is to be
answerable for infringement of rights, but he shall not be put to death, since
she was not a free woman. •He must bring a sacrifice of reparation for Yahweh 21
to the entrance to the Tent of Meeting. This is to be a ram of reparation. •With 22
this ram of reparation the priest must perform the rite of atonement over the man
before Yahweh for the sin committed; and the sin he has committed will be
forgiven.

"Once you have entered this land and planted a fruit tree of any sort, you 23
are to regard its fruits as its foreskin.*ᵃ* For three years it shall be a thing uncircumcised, and you must not eat it. •In the fourth year, all the fruit shall be consecrated 24
to Yahweh in a feast of praise. •In the fifth year you may eat the fruit and gather 25
the produce for yourselves. I am Yahweh your God.

"You must eat nothing with blood in it. You must not practise divination or 26
magic.

ᵇ "You are not to round off your hair at the edges nor trim the edges of your 27
beard. •You are not to gash your bodies when someone dies, and you are not to 28
tattoo yourselves. I am Yahweh.

"Do not profane your daughter by making her a prostitute; thus the land will 29
not be prostituted and filled with incest.

"You must keep my sabbaths and reverence my sanctuary. I am Yahweh. 30

"Do not have recourse to the spirits of the dead or to magicians; they will 31
defile you. I am Yahweh your God.

"You are to rise up before grey hairs, you are to honour old age and fear 32
your God. I am Yahweh.

"If a stranger lives with you in your land, do not molest him. •You must 33
34
count him as one of your own countrymen and love him as yourself—for you
were once strangers yourselves in Egypt. I am Yahweh your God.

"Your legal verdicts, your measures—length, weight and capacity—must all be 35
just. •Your scales and weights must be just, a just ephah and a just hin. I am 36
Yahweh who brought you out of the land of Egypt.

"Keep all my laws and customs, put them into practice. I am Yahweh." ' 37

Penalties

a. Offences against true worship

1, 2 **20** Yahweh spoke to Moses; he said: 'Tell the sons of Israel:

"Any son of Israel or any stranger living in Israel must die if he hands over any of his children to Molech. The people of the country must stone him,
3 and I shall set my face against that man and outlaw him from his people; for in handing over his children to Molech he has defiled my sanctuary and profaned
4 my holy name. •If the people of the country choose to close their eyes to the man's action in handing over his children to Molech, and they do not put him
5 to death, •I myself shall turn my face against him and his clan. I shall outlaw them from their people, him and all those after him who prostitute themselves by following Molech.

6 "If a man has recourse to the spirits of the dead or to magicians, to prostitute himself by following them, I shall set my face against that man and outlaw him from his people.

7 "You must make yourselves holy, for I am Yahweh your God.

b. Offences against the family

8 "You must keep my laws and put them into practice, for it is I, Yahweh, who
9 make you holy. •Hence:

"Anyone who curses father or mother must die. Since he has cursed his father or mother, his blood shall be on his own head.

10 "The man who commits adultery with a married woman:

"The man who commits adultery with his neighbour's wife must die, he and his accomplice.

11 "The man who lies with his father's wife has uncovered his father's nakedness. Both of them must die, their blood shall be on their own heads.

12 "The man who lies with his daughter-in-law: both of them must die; they have defiled each other, their blood shall be on their own heads.

13 "The man who lies with a man in the same way as with a woman: they have done a hateful thing together; they must die, their blood shall be on their own heads.

14 "The man who takes a woman and her mother to wife: that is incest. They must be burnt to death—he and they: there must be no incest among you.

15 "The man who lies with an animal: he must die and the animal must be killed.

16 "The woman who approaches any animal to have intercourse with it: you shall kill the woman and the animal. They must die, their blood shall be on their own heads.

17 "The man who takes the daughter of his father or mother to wife: if he sees her nakedness and she sees his, it is a disgrace. They must be executed in public, for the man has uncovered the nakedness of his sister and he must bear the consequences of his fault.

18 "The man who lies with a woman during her monthly periods and uncovers her nakedness: he has laid bare the source of her blood, and she has uncovered the source of her blood: both of them must be outlawed from their people.

19 "You must not uncover the nakedness of your mother's sister or of your father's sister, a man has thus uncovered his own flesh, and they must bear the consequences of their fault.

20 "The man who lies with the wife of his paternal uncle: he has uncovered his uncle's nakedness, they must bear the consequences of their fault and die childless.

21 "The man who takes to wife the wife of his brother: that is impurity; he has uncovered his brother's nakedness, and they shall die childless.

---

19 a. I.e., as the sign that it is adult and no longer 'unclean' (uncircumcised).   b. Prohibition of pagan customs.

c. Appendix: the clean and the unclean

"You must keep all my laws, all my customs, and put them into practice: thus 22
you will not be vomited out by the land where I am taking you to live. •You 23
must not follow the laws of the nations that I expel to make way for you; they
practised all these things and for this I have come to detest them. •I have told 24
you already: You shall take possession of their soil, I myself will give you
possession of it, a land where milk and honey flow.

"I, Yahweh your God, have set you apart from these peoples. •Therefore you 25
must set the clean animal apart from the unclean, the unclean bird apart from
the clean. Do not defile yourselves with these animals or birds, or things that
creep on the ground: I have made you set them apart as unclean.

Conclusion

"Be consecrated to me, because I, Yahweh, am holy, and I will set you apart 26
from all these peoples so that you may be mine.

"Any man or woman who is a necromancer or magician must be put to death 27
by stoning; their blood shall be on their own heads." '

The holiness of the priesthood
a. The priests

21 Yahweh said to Moses: 1
'Speak to the priests, the sons of Aaron, and say to them:

"None of them is to make himself unclean by going near the corpse of one of
his family, •unless it be of his closest relations—father, mother, son, daughter, 2
brother. •He may also make himself unclean for his virgin sister: if she is still 3
a close relation since she has not belonged to a man. •If a husband, he 4
must not make himself unclean for his family; in doing so he would profane
himself.

"They must not wear tonsures, shave the edges of their beards, or gash their 5
bodies. •They shall be consecrated to their God and must not profane the name 6
of their God. For it is they who bring the burnt offerings to Yahweh, the food
of their God; and they must be in a holy condition.

"They must not marry a woman profaned by prostitution, or one divorced 7
by her husband; for the priest is consecrated to his God.

"You shall treat him as holy, for he offers up the food of your God, He shall 8
be a holy person to you, because I, Yahweh, am holy, who sanctify you.

"If the daughter of a man who is a priest profanes herself by prostitution, 9
she profanes her father and must be burnt to death.

b. The high priest

"The priest who is pre-eminent over his brother, on whose head the chrism 10
is poured, and who, clothed with the sacred robes, receives investiture, is not to
disorder his hair or tear his garments; •he must not go near a dead man's corpse, 11
he must not make himself unclean even for his father or mother. •He must not 12
leave the holy place, so that he may not profane the sanctuary of his God; for
he bears on himself the consecration of his God, given by the oil of anointing.
I am Yahweh.

"He must take to wife a woman who is still a virgin. •He must not marry a 13 14
woman who is a widow or divorced, or profaned by prostitution: only a virgin
from his own family may he take to wife. •He must not profane his levitical 15
descendants, for it is I, Yahweh, who have sanctified him." '

c. Impediments to the priesthood

Yahweh spoke to Moses; he said: 16
'Speak to Aaron and say: 17
"None of your descendants, in any generation, must come forward to offer

18 the food of his God if he has any infirmity—•no man must come near if he has
19 an infirmity such as blindness or lameness, if he is disfigured or deformed,
20 if he has an injured foot or arm, •if he is a hunchback or a dwarf, if he has a
disease of the eyes or of the skin, if he has a running sore, or if he is a eunuch.
21 No descendant of Aaron the priest must come forward to offer the burnt offerings
of Yahweh if he has any infirmity; if he has an infirmity, he must not come
22 forward to offer the food of his God.
23   "He may eat the food of his God, things most holy and things holy; •but he
must not go near the veil or approach the altar, because he has an infirmity, and
must not profane my holy things; for it is I, Yahweh, who have sanctified them." '
24   And Moses told this to Aaron, to his sons, and to all the sons of Israel.

Holiness in consuming the sacred meal
a. The priests

1 22 Yahweh spoke to Moses; he said:
2   'Speak to Aaron and his sons: let them be consecrated through the holy
offerings of the sons of Israel, and not profane my holy name; for my sake they
3 are to sanctify it; I am Yahweh. •Tell them this:
    "Any one of your descendants, in any generation, who in a state of uncleanness
approaches the holy offerings consecrated to Yahweh by the sons of Israel,
shall be outlawed from my presence. I am Yahweh.
4   "Anyone of Aaron's line who is afflicted with leprosy or with a discharge
must not eat holy things until he is clean. Anyone who touches something made
5 unclean by a dead body, or has a seminal discharge, •or is made unclean
by touching either some creeping thing or some man who has communicated
6 to him his own uncleanness of whatever kind, •in short, anyone who has had any
such contact shall be unclean until evening, and must not eat holy things until he
7 has washed his body. •At sunset he will be clean and may then eat holy things,
for these are his food.
8   "He must not eat an animal that has died a natural death or been savaged by
beasts; he would contract uncleanness from it. I am Yahweh.
9   "Let them keep my rules and not burden themselves with sin. If they profane
them, they shall die: it is I, Yahweh, who have sanctified them.

b. Lay people

10   "No lay person may eat holy things: neither the guest of a priest, nor his
11 hired servant. •But if the priest has acquired a slave by purchase, the slave may
eat them like anyone born in the house; for they eat his own food.
12   "If a priest's daughter marries a layman, she must not eat the holy portion set
13 aside; •but if she is widowed or divorced and, being childless, has had to return
to her father's house as when she was young, she may eat her father's food.
14 No lay person may eat of it; •if someone does eat a holy thing by inadvertence,
he shall restore it to the priest with one-fifth added.
15   "They must not profane the holy offerings which the sons of Israel have set
16 aside for Yahweh. •To eat these would lay on them a fault demanding a sacrifice
of reparation; for it is I, Yahweh,' who have sanctified these offerings." '

c. Animals sacrificed

17   Yahweh spoke to Moses; he said:

18   'Tell this to Aaron, to his sons, and to all the sons of Israel:
    "Any man of the House of Israel or any stranger living in Israel who brings
an offering either in payment of a vow or as a voluntary gift, and makes
19 a holocaust with it for Yahweh, •must, if he is to be acceptable, offer a male
20 without blemish, ox, sheep or goat. •You must not offer one that is blemished;
for it would not make you acceptable.
21   "If anyone offers to Yahweh a communion sacrifice, either to fulfil a vow

or as a voluntary offering, the animal—from the herd or from the flock—must be without blemish if it is to be acceptable; no defect must be found in it. •You 22 must not offer to Yahweh an animal that is blind, lame, mutilated, ulcerous, or suffering from skin disease or sore. No part of such an animal shall be laid on the altar as a burnt offering for Yahweh. •As a voluntary offering, you may offer 23 a bull or a lamb that is underdeveloped or deformed; but such will not be acceptable in payment of a vow. •An animal must not be offered to Yahweh 24 if its testicles have been bruised, crushed, removed or cut. You are not to do that in your country, •and you are not to accept any such from the hands of a stranger, 25 to be offered as food for your God. Their deformity is a blemish, and they would not make you acceptable." '

Yahweh spoke to Moses; he said: 26

'A calf, lamb, or kid shall stay with its dam seven days after birth. From the 27 eighth day it will be acceptable as a burnt offering to Yahweh. •But no animal, 28 whether cow or ewe, shall be immolated on the same day as its young.

'If you offer Yahweh a sacrifice with praise, do it in the acceptable manner; 29 it must be eaten the same day, with nothing left till the morning. I am Yahweh. 30

d. Final exhortation

'You must keep my commands and put them into practice. I am Yahweh. 31 You must not profane my holy name, so that I may be proclaimed holy among 32 the sons of Israel, I, Yahweh who sanctify you. •I who brought you out of the 33 land of Egypt to be your God, I am Yahweh.'

The ritual for the annual feasts

23 Yahweh spoke to Moses; he said: 1
       'Speak to the sons of Israel and say to them: 2
(the solemn festivals of Yahweh to which you summon them are sacred assemblies)
     "These are my solemn festivals.

a. Sabbath

"You may work for six days, but the seventh must be a day of complete rest, 3 a day for the sacred assembly on which you do no work at all. Wherever you live, this is a sabbath for Yahweh.

"These are Yahweh's solemn festivals, the sacred assemblies to which you are 4 to summon the sons of Israel on the appointed day.

b. The Passover and the feast of Unleavened Bread

"The fourteenth day of the first month, between the two evenings, is the 5 Passover of Yahweh; •and the fifteenth day of the same month is the feast of 6 Unleavened Bread for Yahweh. For seven days you shall eat bread without leaven. •On the first day you are to hold a sacred assembly; you must do no heavy 7 work. •For seven days you shall offer a burnt offering to Yahweh. The seventh 8 day is to be a day of sacred assembly; you must do no work." '

c. The first sheaf

Yahweh spoke to Moses; he said: 9
'Speak to the sons of Israel and say to them: 10
"When you enter the land that I give you, and gather in the harvest there, you must bring the first sheaf of your harvest to the priest, •and he is to present 11 it to Yahweh with the gesture of offering, so that you may be acceptable. The priest shall make this offering on the day after the sabbath, •and on the same day 12 as you make this offering, you are to offer Yahweh the holocaust of an unblemished lamb one year old. •The oblation for that day shall be two-tenths of wheaten 13 flour mixed with oil, a burnt offering whose fragrance will appease Yahweh. The

14 libation is to be one quarter of a hin of wine. •You are to eat no bread, roasted corn or baked bread, before this day, before making the offering to your God. This is a perpetual law for all your descendants, wherever you live.

d. The feast of Weeks

15 "From the day after the sabbath, the day on which you bring the sheaf of
16 offering, you are to count seven full weeks. •You are to count fifty days, to the day
17 after the seventh sabbath, and then you are to offer Yahweh a new oblation. •You must bring bread from your houses to present with the gesture of offering—two loaves, made of two-tenths of wheaten flour baked with leaven; these are
18 first-fruits for Yahweh. •In addition to the bread you must offer seven unblemished lambs one year old, a young bull and two rams, as a holocaust to Yahweh, together with an oblation and a libation, a burnt offering whose fragrance will
19 appease Yahweh. •You are also to offer a goat as a sacrifice for sin, and two lambs
20 one year old as a communion sacrifice. •The priest shall present them before Yahweh with the gesture of offering, in addition to the bread of the first-fruits. These, and the two lambs, are holy things for Yahweh, and will revert to the priest.
21 "This same day you are to hold an assembly; this shall be a sacred assembly for you; you will do no heavy work. This is a perpetual law for your descendants, wherever you live.
22 "When you gather the harvest in your country, you are not to harvest to the very end of your field, and you are not to gather the gleanings of the harvest. You are to leave them for the poor and the stranger. I am Yahweh your God."'

e. The First Day of the Seventh Month

23 Yahweh spoke to Moses; he said:
24 'Speak to the sons of Israel and say to them:
"The first day of the seventh month[a] shall be a day of rest for you, a sacred
25 assembly proclaimed with trumpet call. •You must not do any heavy work and you must offer a burnt offering to Yahweh."'

f. The Day of Atonement

26 Yahweh spoke to Moses; he said:
27 'But the tenth day of this seventh month shall be the Day of Atonement. You are to hold a sacred assembly. You must fast, and you must offer a burnt offering to
28 Yahweh. •You are not to do any work that day, for it is the Day of Atonement, on which the rite of atonement will be performed over you before Yahweh your
29 God. •Indeed, anyone who fails to fast that day shall be outlawed from his people;
30
31 anyone who works that day I will remove from his people. •No work must
32 be done—this is a perpetual law for your descendants wherever you live. •This is to be a day of sabbath rest for you. You must fast; on the evening of the ninth day of the month, from this to the following evening, you must cease to work.'

g. The feast of Tabernacles

33 Yahweh spoke to Moses; he said:
34 'Speak to the sons of Israel and say to them:
"The fifteenth day of this seventh month shall be the feast of Tabernacles
35 for Yahweh, lasting seven days. •The first day is a day of sacred assembly; you
36 must do no heavy work. •For seven days you must offer a burnt offering to Yahweh. On the eighth day you are to hold a sacred assembly, you must offer a burnt offering to Yahweh. It is a day of solemn meeting; you must do no heavy work.

23 a. The first day of each month (New Moon) was observed as a feast. The first day of the seventh month was a Greater Feast, and for a long time was the beginning of the new year.

Conclusion

"These are the solemn festivals of Yahweh to which you are to summon the 37
children of Israel, sacred assemblies for the purpose of offering burnt offerings,
holocausts, oblations, sacrifices and libations to Yahweh, according to the ritual
of each day, •besides the sabbaths of Yahweh and the presents, and the votive 38
and voluntary gifts that you make to Yahweh.

Recapitulation on the feast of Tabernacles

"But on the fifteenth day of the seventh month, when you have harvested the 39
produce of the land, you are to celebrate the feast of Yahweh for seven days. On
the first and eighth days there shall be a complete rest. •On the first day you shall 40
take choice fruits, palm branches, boughs of leafy trees and willows from the
river bank, and for seven days you shall rejoice in the presence of Yahweh your
God. •You are to celebrate a feast for Yahweh in this way for seven days every 41
year. This is a perpetual law for your descendants.

"You are to keep this feast in the seventh month. •For seven days you are 42
to live in shelters: all natives of Israel must live in shelters, •so that your 43
descendants may know that I made the sons of Israel live in shelters when I
brought them out of the land of Egypt. I am Yahweh your God."'

And Moses described the solemn festivals of Yahweh to the sons of Israel.   44

Complementary ritual prescriptions
a. The perpetual flame

24 Yahweh spoke to Moses; he said: 1
'Order the sons of Israel to bring you pure olive oil for the lamp-stand, and 2
keep a flame burning there continually. •Outside the veil of Testimony, in the 3
Tent of Meeting, Aaron is to see to this flame. It shall burn there before Yahweh
from evening to morning continually. This is a perpetual law for your descendants:
Aaron is to see to the lamps on the pure lamp-stand before Yahweh, continually. 4

b. The bread on the Golden Table

'You are to take wheaten flour and with it bake twelve cobs, each of two-tenths 5
of an ephah. •Then you must set them in two rows of six on the pure table that 6
stands before Yahweh. •On each row you shall place pure incense. This will be 7
the food offered as a memorial, a burnt offering for Yahweh. •Continually, 8
every sabbath they shall be set before Yahweh. The sons of Israel are to provide
them by unending covenant. •They will belong to Aaron and his sons, who shall 9
eat them in a holy place, for they are a most holy portion for him of Yahweh's
burnt offerings. This is a perpetual law.'

A case of blasphemy. The law of retaliation

There was a man whose mother was an Israelite woman and whose father 10
was an Egyptian. He came out of his house and in the camp, surrounded by the
sons of Israel, he began to quarrel with a man who was an Israelite. •Now this 11
son of the Israelite woman blasphemed the name and cursed it. So they brought
him to Moses (his mother's name was Shelomith daughter of Dibri, of the tribe
of Dan). •He was put under guard until the will of Yahweh should be made 12
clear to them.

Yahweh spoke to Moses; he said: 13
'Take the man who pronounced the curse outside the camp. Let all who have 14
heard him lay their hands on his head, and let the whole community stone
him. •Then say to the sons of Israel: 15

"Any man who curses his God shall bear the burden of his fault. •The one 16
who blasphemes the name of Yahweh must die; the whole community must
stone him. Stranger or native, if he blasphemes the name, he dies.

"If a man strikes down any human being, he must die.   17

18   "If a man strikes an animal down he must make restitution for it: a life for a life.

19   "If a man injures his neighbour, what he has done must be done to him:
20 broken limb for broken limb, eye for eye, tooth for tooth. As the injury inflicted,
21 so must be the injury suffered. •The one who strikes an animal down must
22 make restitution for it, and the one who strikes down a man must die. •The sentence you pass shall be the same whether it be on native or on stranger; for I am Yahweh your God." '

23   •When Moses had said this to the sons of Israel, they took the man who had pronounced the curse out of the camp and stoned him. In this way the sons of Israel carried out the order of Yahweh to Moses.

The Holy Years
a. The Sabbatical Year

1   **25**   Yahweh spoke to Moses on Mount Sinai; he said:
2   'Speak to the sons of Israel and say to them:
     "When you enter the land that I am giving you, the land is to keep a sabbath's
3 rest for Yahweh. •For six years you shall sow your field, for six years you shall
4 prune your vine and gather its produce. •But in the seventh year the land is to have its rest, a sabbath for Yahweh. You must not sow your field or prune your
5 vine, •or harvest your ungathered corn or gather grapes from your untrimmed
6 vine. It is to be a year of rest for the land. •The sabbath of the land will itself feed you and your servants, men and women, your hired labourer, your guest,
7 and all who live with you. •For your cattle too, and the animals on your land, all its produce will serve as food.

b. The Year of Jubilee

8   "You are to count seven weeks of years—seven times seven years, that is to say
9 a period of seven weeks of years, forty-nine years. •And on the tenth day of the seventh month you shall sound the trumpet; on the Day of Atonement you shall
10 sound the trumpet throughout the land. •You will declare this fiftieth year sacred and proclaim the liberation of all the inhabitants of the land. This is to be a jubilee for you; each of you will return to his ancestral home, each to his own
11 clan. •This fiftieth year is to be a jubilee year for you: you will not sow, you will not harvest the ungathered corn, you will not gather from the untrimmed vine.
12 The jubilee is to be a holy thing to you, you will eat what comes from the fields.
13
14   "In this year of jubilee each of you is to return to his ancestral home. •If you
15 buy or sell with your neighbour, let no one wrong his brother. •If you buy from your neighbour, this must take into account the number of years since the
16 jubilee: according to the number of productive years he will fix the price. •The greater the number of years, the higher shall be the price demanded; the less the number of years, the greater the reduction; for what he is selling you is a
17 certain number of harvests. •Let none of you wrong his neighbour, but fear your God; I am Yahweh your God.

18   "You must put my laws and customs into practice; you must keep them,
19 practise them; and so you shall be secure in your possession of the land. •The land will give its fruit, you will eat your fill and live in security.

The divine guarantee

20   "In case you should ask: What shall we eat in this seventh year if we do not
21 sow or harvest the produce? •I have ordered my blessing to be on you every
22 sixth year, which will therefore provide for you for three years." •You will have the old produce to eat while you are sowing in the eighth year and even as late

---

25 a. I.e., enough for the sabbatical year and a jubilee year which might follow it, and the next year as well, since there would be no autumn sowing in jubilee year.

as the ninth year; you will eat the old produce, while waiting for the harvest of that year.

Consequences of the holiness of land and people
a. The land: redemption of landed property

"Land must not be sold in perpetuity, for the land belongs to me, and to me 23 you are only strangers and guests. •You will allow a right of redemption on all 24 your landed property. •If your brother falls on evil days and has to sell his 25 patrimony, his nearest relation shall come to him and exercise his right of redemption on what his brother has sold. •The man who has no one to exercise this 26 right can regain his property in this way: when he has found the means to effect the redemption, •he is to calculate the number of years that the alienation would 27 have lasted, repay to the purchaser the sum due for the time still to run, and so return to his property. •If he cannot find the sum for paying the compensation, 28 the property sold shall remain in the possession of the purchaser until the jubilee year. In the jubilee year, the latter must relinquish it and return to his own property.

"If anyone sells a dwelling house that is in a walled town, he shall have the right 29 of redemption until the expiry of the year following the sale. His right of redemption is limited to the year; •and if the redemption has not been effected 30 by the end of the year, this house in the town shall be the property of the purchaser and his descendants in perpetuity; he need not relinquish it at the jubilee. •But 31 houses in villages not enclosed by walls will be considered as situated in the open country; they carry the right of redemption, and the purchaser must relinquish them at the jubilee.

"As regards the towns of the Levites, any property in the towns possessed by 32 them shall carry a perpetual right of redemption in their favour. •If it is a Levite 33 who is affected by the right of redemption, at the jubilee he must come out of the property that was sold and return to his house, to the town in which he has a title to property. For the houses in the towns of the Levites are their property in the midst of the sons of Israel, •and the arable land depending on these towns 34 cannot be sold, for it is their property for ever.

b. The people: loans and enfranchisement

"If your brother who is living with you falls on evil days and is unable to 35 support himself with you, you must support him as you would a stranger or a guest, and he must continue to live with you. •Do not make him work for you, do not 36 take interest from him; fear your God, and let your brother live with you. •You 37 are not to lend him money at interest, or give him food to make a profit out of it. I am Yahweh your God who brought you out of the land of Egypt to give you 38 the land of Canaan and to be your God.

"If your brother falls on evil days when he is with you and sells himself to 39 you, you must not impose a slave's work on him; •he shall be like a hired man or 40 a guest, and shall work with you until the jubilee year. •Then he shall leave you, 41 he and his children; he shall return to his clan and regain possession of his ancestral property. •For they are my servants, these whom I have brought out of 42 Egypt, and they must not be sold like slaves. •You must not be a hard master 43 to him, but you must fear your God.

"The servants you have, men and women, shall come from the nations round 44 you; from these you may purchase servants, men and women. •You may also 45 purchase them from the children of the strangers who live among you, and from their families living with you who have been born on your soil. They shall be your property •and you may leave them as an inheritance to your sons after you, 46 to hold in perpetual possession. These you may have for slaves; but to your brothers, the sons of Israel, you must not be hard masters.

"If some stranger or settler among you grows rich, and your brother falls 47 on evil days and is in difficulties with him and sells himself to him, to this stranger

48 or settler among you or to one of his descendants, •he shall enjoy the right of
49 redemption after sale, and one of his brothers may redeem him. •His paternal
uncle, his uncle's son, or a member of his own family may redeem him; if he has
50 the means, he may redeem himself. •By agreement with his purchaser, he must
count the number of years between the year of sale and his jubilee year; the sum
of the price of sale must be calculated at the annual rate for these years, his time
51 being valued as that of a hired man. •If there are still many years to run, in
proportion to their number he must refund part of his sale price as payment for
52 his redemption. •And if there are only a few years still to run before the jubilee
year, he must calculate in proportion to the number of these years what shall be
53 refunded for his redemption, •the calculation being made as if he were hired by
the year. You must see that the man is not hardly dealt with.
54 "If he has not been redeemed in any of these ways, he shall go free in the jubilee
55 year, he and his children with him. •For they are my servants, these sons of
Israel; they are my servants whom I have brought out of the land of Egypt. I am
Yahweh your God.

Summary: conclusion

1 **26** "You must make no idols; you must set up neither carved image nor
standing-stone, set up no sculptured stone in your land, to prostrate
2 yourselves in front of it; for it is I, Yahweh, who am your God. •You must keep
my sabbaths and reverence my sanctuary. I am Yahweh.

Blessings

3 "If you live according to my laws, if you keep my commandments and put
4 them into practice, •I will give you the rain you need at the right time; the
5 earth shall give its produce and the trees of the countryside their fruits; •you shall
thresh until vintage time and gather grapes until sowing time. You shall eat your
fill of bread and live secure in your land.
6 "I will give peace to the land, and you shall sleep with none to frighten you.
I will rid the land of beasts of prey. The sword shall not pass through your land.
7/8 You shall pursue your enemies and they shall fall before your sword; •five of
you pursuing a hundred of them, one hundred pursuing ten thousand; and your
enemies shall fall before your sword.
9 "I will turn towards you, I will make you be fruitful and multiply, and I will
uphold my Covenant with you.
10 "You shall eat your fill of last year's harvest, and still throw out the old to
make room for the new.
11/12 "I will set up my dwelling among you, and I will not cast you off. •I will
13 live in your midst; I will be your God and you shall be my people. •It is I,
Yahweh your God, who have brought you out of the land of Egypt so that you
should be their servants no longer. I have broken the yoke that bound you and
have made you walk with head held high.

Curses

14 "But if you do not listen to me, and do not observe each one of these
15 commandments, •if you refuse my laws and disregard my customs, and break
16 my Covenant by not observing each one of my commandments, •then I will deal
in like manner with you.
"I will inflict terror on you, consumption and fever that waste the eyes away
and exhaust the breath of life. You shall sow your seed in vain—your enemies
17 shall feed on it. •I will turn against you and you shall be defeated by your enemies.
Your foes shall have the mastery over you, and you shall take flight when there
is no one pursuing you.
18 "And if, in spite of this, you do not listen to me, I will still punish
19 you sevenfold for your sins. •I will break your proud strength. I will give you

a sky of iron, an earth of bronze. •You shall wear out your strength in vain, 20
your land shall not yield its produce any longer nor the trees their fruit.

"If you set yourselves against me and will not listen to me, I will heap these 21
plagues on you in sevenfold punishment for your sins. •I will let wild beasts 22
loose against you to make away with your children, destroy your cattle, and
reduce you in number until your roads are deserted.

"And if that does not reform you, and you still set yourselves against me, 23
I too will set myself against you and I will strike you with sevenfold punishment 24
for your sins. •I will send out the sword against you, to avenge the Covenant. 25
You may huddle inside your towns: I will send pestilence among you, and you
shall be delivered into the hands of the enemy. •I will take away from you your 26
bread, which is your staff, and one oven shall suffice for ten women to bake
your bread; they shall dole this bread out by weight, and you shall eat and not
be filled.

"And if, in spite of this, you do not listen to me but set yourselves against me, 27
I will set myself against you in fury and punish you sevenfold for your sins. 28
You shall eat the flesh of your own sons, and you shall eat the flesh of your 29
own daughters. •I will destroy your high places and smash your altars of 30
incense; I will pile your corpses on the corpses of your idols, and I will cast
you off. •I will reduce your cities to ruins; I will lay your sanctuaries waste; 31
I will no longer breathe the fragrance that would appease me. •I, yes I, will 32
make such a desolation of the land that your enemies who come to live there
will be appalled by it. •And I will scatter you among the nations. I will unsheathe 33
the sword against you to make your land a waste and your towns a ruin. •Then 34
the land will observe its sabbaths indeed, lying desolate there, while you are in
the land of your enemies. Then indeed the land will rest and observe its sabbaths.
And as it lies desolate it will rest, as it never did on your sabbaths when you 35
lived in it. •I will strike fear into the hearts of those of you that are left; in the 36
land of their enemies the sound of a falling leaf shall send them fleeing as men
flee from the sword, and they shall fall though there is no one pursuing them.
They shall stumble over one another as if the sword were upon them even when 37
there is no one pursuing them. You shall be powerless to stand before your enemies;
you shall perish among the nations, and the land of your enemies shall swallow 38
you up. •For their sins, those of you who are left shall perish in the lands of their 39
enemies; they shall perish too for the sins of their fathers added to their own.
Then they shall confess their sins and the sins of their fathers, sins by which 40
they betrayed me—worse, by which they set themselves against me.

"I in my turn will set myself against them and take them to the land of their 41
enemies. Then their uncircumcised heart will be humbled, then they will atone
for their sins. •I shall remember my Covenant with Jacob, and my Covenant with 42
Isaac and my Covenant with Abraham; and I shall remember the land.

"Abandoned by them, the land will keep its sabbaths, as it lies desolate when 43
they are gone. But they must atone for their sin, for they have spurned my
customs and abhorred my laws.

"Yet this is not the end. When they are in the land of their enemies, I will 44
not so spurn them or abhor them as to destroy them altogether and break my
Covenant with them; for I am Yahweh their God. •For their sake I will remember 45
the Covenant I made with those first generations that I brought out of the land
of Egypt in the sight of the nations, that I would be their God, I, Yahweh." '

These are the laws, customs and rules which Yahweh laid down between 46
himself and the sons of Israel on Mount Sinai through the mediation of Moses.

Tariffs and estimates
a. Persons

27 Yahweh spoke to Moses; he said: 1
'Speak to the sons of Israel and tell them: 2
"If anyone vows the value of a person to Yahweh and wishes to discharge the vow:

3 "a man between twenty and sixty years of age shall be valued at fifty silver
4 shekels—the sanctuary shekel; •a woman shall be valued at thirty shekels;
5 "between five and twenty years, a boy shall be valued at twenty shekels, a girl
at ten shekels;
6 "between one month and five years, a boy shall be valued at five silver shekels,
a girl at three silver shekels;
7 "at sixty years and over, a man shall be valued at fifteen shekels and a woman
at ten shekels.
8 "If the person who made the vow cannot meet this valuation, he must present
the person concerned to the priest, and the priest shall set a value proportionate
to the resources of the person who made the vow.

b. Animals

9 "If it is a question of an animal suitable for offering to Yahweh, any such
10 animal given to Yahweh shall be a consecrated thing. •It cannot be exchanged or
a substitute offered—good for bad, bad for good. If one animal is substituted
11 for another, both of them shall be consecrated. •If it is a question of an unclean
animal, and not suitable for offering to Yahweh, whatever it may be it must be
12 presented to the priest •and he shall set a value on it, judging it good or bad.
13 You must abide by his valuation; •but if the person wishes to redeem it, he must
add one-fifth to the valuation.

c. Houses

14 "If a man consecrates his house to Yahweh, the priest shall set a value on it,
judging whether its value is great or little. You must abide by the priest's valuation,
15 but if the man who has vowed his house wishes to redeem it, he must add one-
fifth to the valuation, and it shall revert to him.

d. Fields

16 "If a man consecrates one of the fields of his patrimony to Yahweh, its value
shall be calculated according to its productivity, at the rate of fifty silver shekels
to one omer of barley.
17 "If he consecrates the field during the jubilee year, he must stand by this
18 valuation. •But if he consecrates it after the jubilee, the priest shall calculate the
price on the basis of the number of years still to run until the next jubilee and the
valuation shall be reduced accordingly.
19 "If he wishes to redeem the field, he shall add one-fifth to the valuation, and the
20 field shall revert to him. •If he does not redeem it but sells it to another, the right
21 of redemption ceases; •when the buyer has to relinquish it at the jubilee year,
it becomes a thing consecrated to Yahweh, the same as a field laid under ban:
the man's property passes to the priest.
22 "If he consecrates to Yahweh a field which he has bought, but which is not
23 part of his patrimony, •the priest shall assess the valuation on the basis of the
number of years still to run before the jubilee year; and the man shall pay this
24 sum the same day, as for a thing consecrated to Yahweh. •In the jubilee year,
the field shall return to the seller, to the man to whose patrimony the land belongs.
25 All valuation must be made in sanctuary shekels, at the rate of twenty gerahs
to the shekel.

Particular rules for the redemption
a. of first-born

26 "No one, however, may consecrate the first-born of his cattle, for it belongs to
27 Yahweh by right: whether ox or sheep, it belongs to Yahweh. •But if it is an
unclean animal it may be repurchased at the valuation price with one-fifth added;
if it is not redeemed, the animal shall be sold at the valuation price.

b. of things under the ban

"Nothing, however, that a man lays under ban for Yahweh may be redeemed; 28
nothing he possesses, whether man, beasts, or fields of his patrimony. What is
laid under ban is always a most holy thing and belongs to Yahweh. •A human 29
being laid under ban cannot be redeemed, he must be put to death.

c. of tithes

"All tithes of the land, levied on the produce of the earth or the fruits of trees, 30
belong to Yahweh; they are consecrated to Yahweh. •If a man wishes to redeem 31
part of his tithe, he must add one-fifth to its value.

"In all tithes of flock or herd, the tenth animal of all that pass under the 32
herdsman's staff shall be a thing consecrated to Yahweh; •there must be no 33
picking out of good and bad, no substitution. If substitution takes place, both the
animal and its substitute shall be things consecrated without possibility of
redemption.'"

These are the commandments that Yahweh laid down for Moses on Mount 34
Sinai, for the sons of Israel.

NUMBERS

I. THE CENSUS

1 1 Yahweh spoke to Moses, in the wilderness of Sinai, in the Tent of Meeting, on the first day of the second month, in the second year after the exodus from the land of Egypt. He said:

2 'Take a census of the whole community of Israel's sons, by clans and families, 3 taking a count of the names of all the males, head by head. •Every man of Israel, twenty years of age and over, fit to bear arms, must be registered by you and 4 Aaron and assigned to his fighting station. •You are to take a man from each tribe, the head of his family, to help you in this.

The census officials

5 'These are the names of those who are to be your helpers:
For Reuben, Elizur son of Shedeur.
6 For Simeon, Shelumiel son of Zurishaddai.
7 For Judah, Nahshon son of Amminadab.
8 For Issachar, Nethanel son of Zuar.
9 For Zebulun, Eliab son of Helon.
10 Of the sons of Joseph: for Ephraim, Elishama son of Ammihud; for Manasseh, Gamaliel son of Pedahzur.
11 For Benjamin, Abidan son of Gideoni.
12 For Dan, Ahiezer son of Ammishaddai.
13 For Asher, Pagiel son of Ochran.
14 For Gad, Eliasaph son of Reuel.
15 For Naphtali, Ahira son of Enan.'
16 These were men of repute in the community; they were leaders of their ancestral clans, chiefs of Israel's hosts.

17
18 Moses and Aaron took these men who have been named, •and on the first day of the second month they mustered the whole community. The sons of Israel established their kinship by clans and families, and one by one the names 19 of all men of twenty years and over were singled out. •As Yahweh had commanded, Moses took a census of them in the wilderness of Sinai.

The census

20 When the kinship of the sons of Reuben, Israel's first-born, had been established by clans and families, the names of all the males of twenty years and 21 over, fit to bear arms, were singled out one by one. •The total of these for the tribe of Reuben was forty-six thousand five hundred.

22 When the kinship of the sons of Simeon had been established by clans and families, the names of all the males of twenty years and over, fit to bear arms, 23 were singled out one by one. •The total of these for the tribe of Simeon was fifty-nine thousand three hundred.

24 When the kinship of the sons of Gad had been established by clans and families, the names of all the males of twenty years and over, fit to bear arms,

were singled out one by one. •The total of these for the tribe of Gad was forty-five 25 thousand six hundred and fifty.

When the kinship of the sons of Judah had been established by clans and 26 families, the names of all the males of twenty years and over, fit to bear arms, were singled out one by one. •The total of these for the tribe of Judah was 27 seventy-four thousand six hundred.

When the kinship of the sons of Issachar had been established by clans and 28 families, the names of all the males of twenty years and over, fit to bear arms, were singled out one by one. •The total of these for the tribe of Issachar was 29 fifty-four thousand four hundred.

When the kinship of the sons of Zebulun had been established by clans and 30 families, the names of all the males of twenty years and over, fit to bear arms, were singled out one by one. •The total of these for the tribe of Zebulun was 31 fifty-seven thousand four hundred.

The sons of Joseph: when the kinship of the sons of Ephraim had been es- 32 tablished by clans and families, the names of all the males of twenty years and over, fit to bear arms, were singled out one by one. •The total of these for the 33 tribe of Ephraim was forty thousand five hundred. •When the kinship of the 34 sons of Manasseh had been established by clans and families, the names of all the males of twenty years and over, fit to bear arms, were singled out one by one. The total of these for the tribe of Manasseh was thirty-two thousand two hundred. 35

When the kinship of the sons of Benjamin had been established by clans and 36 families, the names of all the males of twenty years and over, fit to bear arms, were singled out one by one. •The total of these for the tribe of Benjamin was 37 thirty-five thousand four hundred.

When the kinship of the sons of Dan had been established by clans and 38 families, the names of all the males of twenty years and over, fit to bear arms, were singled out one by one. •The total of these for the tribe of Dan was sixty- 39 two thousand seven hundred.

When the kinship of the sons of Asher had been established by clans and 40 families, the names of all the males of twenty years and over, fit to bear arms, were singled out one by one. •The total of these for the tribe of Asher was forty- 41 one thousand five hundred.

When the kinship of the sons of Naphtali had been established by clans and 42 families, the names of all the males of twenty years and over, fit to bear arms, were singled out one by one. •The total of these for the tribe of Naphtali was 43 fifty-three thousand four hundred.

Such were the men registered by Moses, Aaron and the leaders of Israel, of 44 whom there were twelve, each representing his patriarchal House. •Every man of 45 Israel of twenty years and over, fit to bear arms, was counted according to his patriarchal House. •Altogether the full total was six hundred and three thousand 46 five hundred and fifty. *a*

But the Levites and their patriarchal tribe were not included in the count. 47

Statute for the Levites

Yahweh spoke to Moses and said: 48
'Do not, however, take any census of the Levites, or register them among the 49 sons of Israel. •You yourself must enrol the Levites to serve the tabernacle 50 of the Testimony and to look after its furnishings and its belongings. They are to carry the tabernacle, and all its furnishings, and they are to take care of it and pitch their camp around it. •Whenever the tabernacle is moved the Levites 51 are to be the people to dismantle it; whenever the tabernacle is set up again, they are to do this. Any layman coming near it must be put to death. •The sons of 52 Israel are to pitch their tents in formation each in their own encampment, every man by his standard. •But the Levites are to pitch their tents round the taber- 53 nacle of the Testimony. In this way the wrath will be kept from falling on the

whole community of the sons of Israel. The Levites are to be in charge of the tabernacle of the Testimony.'

54 The sons of Israel did exactly as Yahweh had ordered Moses. They did as he said.

Order of the tribes

1 2 Yahweh spoke to Moses and to Aaron. He said:

2 'The sons of Israel are to pitch their tents, every man by his own standard, under the banner of his patriarchal House. They are to pitch their tents all round the tabernacle of the Testimony, at a measured distance.

3 'Those who are to pitch their tents on the east side:

'Towards the sunrise, the standard of the camp of Judah, in battle array.
4 Leader of the sons of Judah: Nahshon son of Amminadab. •His command: seventy-four thousand six hundred men.

5 'Encamped next to him:

'The tribe of Issachar. Leader of the sons of Issachar: Nethanel son of Zuar.
6 His command: fifty-four thousand four hundred men.

7 'The tribe of Zebulun. Leader of the sons of Zebulun: Eliab son of Helon.
8 His command: fifty-seven thousand four hundred men.

9 'The assembled strength of the camp of Judah numbers in all a hundred and eighty-six thousand four hundred. These are to be first in order of breaking camp.

10 'On the south side, the standard of the camp of Reuben, in battle array. Leader
11 of the sons of Reuben: Elizur son of Shedeur. •His command: forty-six thousand five hundred men.

12 'Encamped next to him:

'The tribe of Simeon. Leader of the sons of Simeon: Shelumiel son of Zurishad-
13 dai. •His command: fifty-nine thousand three hundred men.

14
15 'The tribe of Gad. Leader of the sons of Gad: Eliasaph son of Reuel. •His command: forty-five thousand six hundred and fifty men.

16 'The assembled strength of the camp of Reuben numbers in all a hundred and fifty-one thousand four hundred and fifty. They are to be second in order of breaking camp.

17 'Next the Tent of Meeting will move, since the camp of the Levites is situated in the middle of the other camps. The order of movement is to be the order of encampment, every man under his own standard.

18 'On the west side, the standard of the camp of Ephraim, in battle array. Leader
19 of the sons of Ephraim: Elishama son of Ammihud. •His command: forty thousand five hundred men.

20 'Next to him:

'The tribe of Manasseh. Leader of the tribe of Manasseh: Gamaliel son of
21 Pedahzur. •His command: thirty-two thousand two hundred men.

22 'The tribe of Benjamin. Leader of the sons of Benjamin: Abidan son of
23 Gideoni. •His command: thirty-five thousand four hundred men.

24 'The assembled strength of the camp of Ephraim numbers in all a hundred and eight thousand one hundred. They are to be third in order of breaking camp.

25 'On the north side, the standard of the camp of Dan, in battle array. Leader
26 of the sons of Dan: Ahiezer son of Ammishaddai. •His command: sixty-two thousand seven hundred men.

27 'Encamped next to him:

28 'The tribe of Asher. Leader of the sons of Asher: Pagiel son of Ochran. •His command: forty-one thousand five hundred men.

29 'The tribe of Naphtali. Leader of the sons of Naphtali: Ahira son of Enan.
30 His command: fifty-three thousand four hundred men.

31 'The assembled strength of the camp of Dan numbers in all a hundred and

---

1 a. Not historically accurate; this figure implies that Israel's total population was 2,500,000.

fifty-seven thousand six hundred. They are to be last in order of breaking camp.'
(This concerns their stationing by standards.)

Such was the tally of the sons of Israel when the census was made according 32
to patriarchal Houses. The full count of the entire camp, grouped under the various
commands, is six hundred and three thousand five hundred and fifty. •The Levites, 33
as Yahweh had commanded Moses, were not included in this census of the sons
of Israel.

The sons of Israel did exactly as Yahweh had ordered Moses. This was 34
how they pitched camp, grouped by standards. This was how they broke camp,
each in his own clan, every man with his own family.

The tribe of Levi
a. The priests

3 These are the descendants of Aaron and Moses, at the time when Yahweh 1
spoke to Moses on Mount Sinai.

These are the names of the sons of Aaron: Nadab the eldest, then Abihu, 2
Eleazar and Ithamar.

These are the names of Aaron's sons, priests anointed and invested with the 3
powers of the priesthood. •Nadab and Abihu died in the presence of Yahweh, 4
in the wilderness of Sinai, when they offered fire that was unlawful. They left
no children and so it fell to Eleazar and Ithamar to exercise the priesthood
under their father Aaron.

b. The Levites: their duties

Yahweh spoke to Moses and said: 5
'Muster the tribe of Levi and put it at the disposal of Aaron the priest: they are 6
to be at his service. •They are to undertake the duties that are laid on him and 7
on the entire community before the Tent of Meeting, in their service of the
tabernacle. •The furnishings for the Tent of Meeting are to be in their charge, and 8
they are to undertake the duties that are laid on the sons of Israel in their service
of the tabernacle. •You are to give the Levites to Aaron and his sons as 'oblates';[a] 9
they are to be given to him by the sons of Israel.

'You are to enrol Aaron and his sons, and they are to carry out their priestly 10
duty. But any layman who comes near is to be put to death.'

c. Their divine election

Yahweh spoke to Moses and said: 11
'I myself have chosen the Levites from among the sons of Israel, in place of 12
the first-born, those who open the mother's womb among the sons of Israel;
these Levites therefore belong to me. •For every first-born belongs to me. On the 13
day when I struck all the first-born in the land of Egypt, I consecrated for my
own all the first-born of Israel, of both man and beast. They are mine; I am Yahweh.'

d. Census of the Levites

Yahweh spoke to Moses in the wilderness of Sinai. He said: 14
'You are to take a census of the sons of Levi by families and clans; all the males 15
of the age of one month and over must be counted'.

At Yahweh's word, Moses took his census, as Yahweh had ordered. •These ¹⁶₁₇
are the names of the sons of Levi: Gershon, Kohath and Merari.

These are the names of Gershon's sons by their clans: Libni and Shimei; 18
Kohath's sons by their clans: Amram, Izhar, Hebron and Uzziel; •Merari's ¹⁹₂₀
sons by their clans: Mahli and Mushi. These are the clans of Levi, grouped
according to their patriarchal families.

From Gershon are descended the Libnite and the Shimeite clans; these are 21
the Gershonite clans. •Their full number, counting the males of one month and 22
over, came to seven thousand five hundred. •The Gershonite clans pitched their 23

24 camp behind the tabernacle, on the west side. •The leader of the House of Gershon
25 was Eliasaph son of Lael. •In the Tent of Meeting the sons of Gershon had charge
of the tabernacle, the Tent and its covering, the screen for the entrance to the
26 Tent of Meeting, •the hangings in the court, the screen for the entrance to the court
surrounding the tabernacle and the altar, and the cords needed for all this work.

27 From Kohath are descended the Amramite, the Izharite, the Hebronite and
28 the Uzzielite clans; these are the Kohathite clans. •Their full number, counting the
males of one month and over, came to eight thousand three hundred. They were in
29 charge of the sanctuary. •The Kohathite clans pitched their camp on the south side
30 of the tabernacle. •The leader of the house of the Kohathite clans was Elizaphan
31 son of Uzziel. •They were in charge of the ark, the table, the lamp-stand, the
altars, the sacred vessels used in the liturgy, and the screen with all its fittings.
32 The chief of the Levite leaders was Eleazar, son of Aaron the priest. He was
the head of all those who were in charge of the sanctuary.

33 From Merari are descended the Mahlite and the Mushite clans; these are the
34 Merarite clans. •Their full number, counting the males of one month and over,
35 came to six thousand two hundred. •The leader of the house of the Merarite
clans was Zuriel, son of Abihail. They pitched their camp on the north side of
36 the tabernacle. •The sons of Merari were in charge of the framework of the
tabernacle, with its crossbars, posts and sockets, all its accessories and fittings,
37 and also the posts round the court, with their sockets, pegs and cords.

38 Finally, 'on the east side, facing the tabernacle and the Tent of Meeting,
towards the sunrise, was the camp of Moses and Aaron and his sons, who had
charge of the sanctuary on behalf of the sons of Israel. Any layman coming near
was to be put to death.

39 Altogether, the total count of Levites of the age of one month and over, whom
Moses numbered by clans as Yahweh had ordered, came to twenty-two thousand.

e. The Levites and the ransoming of the first-born

40 Yahweh said to Moses:
'Take a census of all the first-born among the sons of Israel, all the males
41 from the age of one month and over; take a census of them by name. •Then you
will present the Levites to me, Yahweh, in place of the first-born of Israel;
in the same way you will give me their cattle in place of the first-born cattle of
the sons of Israel.'
42 As Yahweh ordered, Moses took a census of all the first-born of the sons
43 of Israel. •The total count, by name, of the first-born from the age of one month
and over came to twenty-two thousand two hundred and seventy-three.

44' Then Yahweh spoke to Moses and said,
45 'Take the Levites in the place of àll the first-born of Israel's sons, and the
cattle of the Levites in place of their cattle; the Levites shall be my own, Yahweh's
46 own. •For the ransom of the two hundred and seventy-three of the first-born of
47 the sons of Israel in excess of the number of Levites, •you are to take five shekels
48 for each, reckoning by the sanctuary shekel, twenty gerahs to the shekel; •you
must then give this money to Aaron and his sons as the ransom price for this extra
number.'

49 Moses received this money as the ransom for this extra number unransomed
50 by the Levites. •He received the money for the first-born of the sons of Israel,
51 one thousand three hundred and sixty-five shekels, sanctuary shekels. •Moses
handed over this ransom money to Aaron and his sons, at the bidding of Yahweh,
as Yahweh had ordered Moses.

3 a. 'dedicated ones'.

The Levite clans

a. The Kohathites

4 Yahweh spoke to Moses and Aaron. He said: 1
'Take a census of those Levites who are sons of Kohath, by clans and families: 2
count all the men between thirty and fifty years of age, those fit to bear arms, 3
who are liable for service in the Tent of Meeting.

'These are the duties of the sons of Kohath in the Tent of Meeting: they are 4
to have charge of the most holy things.

'When camp is broken, Aaron and his sons are to come and take down the veil 5
of the screen. With it they must cover up the ark of the Testimony. •On top of 6
this they must put a covering of fine leather, and spread over the whole a cloth
all of violet. Then they are to fix the poles to the ark.

'Over the offertory table they are to spread a violet cloth, and put on it the 7
dishes, cups, bowls and libation jars; the bread of perpetual offering is also to
be on it. •Over these they must spread a cloth of scarlet and cover the whole with 8
a covering of fine leather. Then they are to fix the poles to the table.

'They are then to take a cloth of violet and cover the light-bearing lamp-stand, 9
together with the lamps, snuffers, trays and all the oil jars that belong to it.
They are to put it, with all its accessories, on a covering of fine leather and place 10
it on the litter.

'Over the golden altar they must spread a violet cloth, and cover that with 11
a covering of fine leather. Then they are to fix the poles to it.

'They are also to take all the other objects used in the service of the sanctuary. 12
They must put them all on a violet cloth, cover them with a covering of fine leather,
and place them together on the litter.

'When they have removed the ashes from the altar,ᵃ they must spread a scarlet 13
cloth over it, •and place on this all the objects used in the liturgical service, 14
the fire pans, hooks, scoops, sprinkling basins and all the altar vessels. Over the
whole they must spread a covering of fine leather. Then they are to fix the poles
to it.

'When Aaron and his sons have finished covering all the sacred objects and all 15
their accessories at the breaking of camp, the sons of Kohath are to come to
take up the burden, but without touching any of the sacred things; otherwise
they would die. This is the charge entrusted to the sons of Kohath in the Tent
of Meeting. •It is to fall to Eleazar, son of Aaron the priest, to watch over the 16
oil for the light, the fragrant incense, the perpetual oblation and the chrism; he
must watch over the whole tabernacle and everything in it: the sacred objects
and their accessories.'

Yahweh spoke to Moses and Aaron. He said: 17
'Do not cut off the tribe of the clans of Kohath from the number of the Levites. 18
But deal with them in this way, so that they may live on and not incur death 19
when they approach the most holy things: Aaron and his sons must go in and
assign to each of them his task and his burden. •In this way they can go in and 20
yet cast not their eyes, even for a moment, on any of the holy things; if they
did, they would die.'

b. The Gershonites

Yahweh spoke to Moses and said to him: 21
'Take a census also of the sons of Gershon, by families and clans: •count all 22
23
the men between thirty and fifty years of age, those fit to bear arms, who are
liable for service in the Tent of Meeting.

'These are the duties of the Gershonite clans, their functions and their burdens. 24
They are to carry the curtains of the tabernacle, the Tent of Meeting with its 25
covering and the covering of fine leather that goes over it, the screen for the
entrance to the Tent of Meeting, •the hangings of the court, the screen for the 26
entrance to the court that surrounds the tabernacle and the altar, the cords
and all the accessories, and all the necessary equipment.

27 'They are to be responsible for these things. •All the duties of the sons of
Gershon—their functions and their tasks—are to be carried out under the
28 direction of Aaron and his sons: you must see that they fulfil their charge. •Such
shall be the duties of the Gershonite clans in the Tent of Meeting. Their work
will be supervised by Ithamar, son of Aaron the priest.

c. The Merarites

29 'You are to count the sons of Merari, by clans and families. •Count all the
30 men between thirty and fifty years of age, those fit to bear arms, who are liable
for service in the Tent of Meeting.
31 'The burden they are to carry and the duties that are to fall to them in the Tent
of Meeting shall be as follows: the framework of the tabernacle, its crossbars,
32 its posts and sockets, •the posts around the court with their sockets, pegs, cords
and all their tackle. You are to draw up a list of their names with the burden that
each man must carry.
33 'These are the duties of the Merarite clans. All their duties in the Tent of
Meeting will be supervised by Ithamar, son of Aaron the priest.'

Census of the Levites

34 Moses, Aaron and the leaders of the community took a census of the sons
35 of Kohath, by clans and families: •of every man between thirty and fifty years
36 of age, fit to bear arms and liable for service in the Tent of Meeting. •The total
37 of their clans was two thousand seven hundred and fifty men. •This was the
number of the Kohathite clans, of all those who were liable for service in the Tent
of Meeting, whom Moses and Aaron counted at the bidding of Yahweh given
through Moses.
38
39 A census was taken of the sons of Gershon, by clans and families: •of every
man between thirty and fifty years of age, fit to bear arms and liable for service
40 in the Tent of Meeting. •By clans and families the total was two thousand six
41 hundred and thirty men. •This was the number of the Gershonite clans, of all
those who were liable for service in the Tent of Meeting, whom Moses and Aaron
counted at the bidding of Yahweh.
42 A census was taken of the clans of the sons of Merari, by clans and families:
43 of every man between thirty and fifty years of age, fit to bear arms and liable for
44 service in the Tent of Meeting. •The total of their clans was three thousand
45 two hundred men. •This was the number of the Merarite clans, whom Moses
and Aaron counted at the bidding of Yahweh through Moses.
46 The total number of Levites, counted according to clans and families by
47 Moses and Aaron and the leaders of Israel—•all the men between thirty and
. fifty years of age, fit to bear arms and liable for serving or carrying in the Tent
48 of Meeting—•amounted to eight thousand five hundred and eighty. •At the
49 bidding of Yahweh through Moses, the census was taken to assign to every
man his duty and his task; they were numbered as Yahweh had ordered Moses.

II. VARIOUS LAWS

Expulsion of the unclean

1 5 Yahweh spoke to Moses and said:
2 'Order the sons of Israel to put out of the camp all lepers, and all who suffer
3 from a discharge, or who have become unclean by touching a corpse. •Man or
woman, you must put them out and forbid them the camp. The sons of Israel
must not defile in this way the camp where I dwell among them.'
4 The sons of Israel did so: they put them out of the camp. The sons of Israel
did as Yahweh had ordered Moses.

4 a. 'The altar' is the altar of holocaust; 'the golden altar' of v.11 is the altar of incense.

Restitution

Yahweh spoke to Moses and said, •'Tell the sons of Israel: 5
6

"If a man or woman commits any of the sins by which men break faith with Yahweh, that person incurs guilt.

"He must confess the sin he has committed and restore in full the amount 7 for which he is liable, with one-fifth added. Payment is to be made to the person whom he has wronged.

"If, however, the latter has no kinsman to whom this restitution can be made, 8 the restitution due to Yahweh reverts to the priest, over and above the ram of atonement with which the priest makes atonement for the guilty man. •For of 9 everything consecrated by the sons of Israel and brought to the priest he has a right to the portion set aside. •Whatever a man consecrates is his own; 10 whatever is given to the priest belongs to the priest." '

Oblation in cases of jealousy

Yahweh spoke to Moses and said, •'Say this to the sons of Israel: 11
12

"If anyone has a wife who goes astray and is unfaithful to him, •if some other 13 man sleeps with the woman without the husband's knowledge, if she disgraces herself in secret in this way, without any witness against her, and without anyone catching her in the act; •then, if a spirit of jealousy comes over the husband and 14 makes him jealous for the wife who has disgraced herself, or again if this spirit of jealousy comes upon him and makes him jealous for his wife even when she is innocent: •the man must bring his wife before the priest, and on her behalf 15 make an offering of one-tenth of an ephah of barley meal. He is not to pour oil on it or put incense on it, because this is an 'oblation for jealousy', a memorial offering to record a fault.

"The priest is then to bring the woman forward and stand her before Yahweh. 16 Then he shall take living water in an earthen jar, and on the water throw dust 17 that he has taken from the floor of the tabernacle. •After he has placed the 18 woman before Yahweh, he shall unbind her hair and put in her hands the commemorative oblation (that is, the oblation for jealousy). In his own hands the priest will hold the water of bitterness and of cursing.

"He is then to put the woman on oath. He shall say to her: If it is not true that 19 a man has slept with you, that you have gone astray and disgraced yourself while under your husband's authority, then may this water of bitterness and cursing do you no harm. •But if it is true that you have gone astray, while under 20 your husband's authority, that you have disgraced yourself by sharing your bed with a man other than your husband... •Here the priest shall impose an impre- 21 catory oath on the woman. He shall say to her:... May Yahweh make of you an execration and a curse among your people, making your thigh shrivel and your belly swell! •May this water of cursing enter your bowels to swell your 22 belly and shrivel your organs!' The woman must answer: Amen! Amen!

"Then the priest shall commit these curses to writing and wash them off in the 23 water of bitterness. •He must make the woman drink this water of bitterness and 24 of cursing, and this water of cursing shall go into her and be bitter inside her.

"The priest·shall then take the oblation for jealousy from the woman's hands, 25 and hold it up before Yahweh with a gesture of offering, and so carry it up to the altar. •He shall take a handful as a memorial, and burn it on the altar. 26

"He shall then make the woman drink the water. •After he has made her drink 27 it, if it is true that she has disgraced herself, deceiving her husband, then the water of cursing that goes into her shall indeed be bitter: her belly will swell and her thigh shrivel, and she will be an execration among her people. •But if she has 28 not disgraced herself and is clean, then she will go unscathed and will bear children.

"This is the ritual in cases of jealousy, when a woman has gone astray and 29 disgraced herself while under her husband's authority, •or when a spirit of 30

jealousy has come over a man and made him jealous for his wife. When a
husband brings such a woman before Yahweh, the priest must apply this ritual
31 to her in full. •The husband shall be guiltless, but the woman must bear the
punishment for her sin." '

The nazirite

$\begin{smallmatrix} 1 \\ 2 \end{smallmatrix}$ 6 Yahweh spoke to Moses and said, •'Say this to the sons of Israel:
"If a man or a woman wishes to make a vow, the vow of the nazirite by
3 which he is pledged to Yahweh, •he shall abstain from wine and strong drink,
4 and neither drink the juice of grapes, nor eat grapes, fresh or dried. •For the
duration of his vow he shall touch nothing that comes from the vine, not even
5 verjuice or lees. •As long as he is bound by his vow, no razor shall touch his
head; until the time of his consecration to Yahweh is completed, he remains
6 under vow and shall let his hair grow free. •For the entire period of his conse-
7 cration to Yahweh he must not go near a corpse, •he must not make himself
unclean for either father or mother, for either brother or sister, should they die;
8 on his head he carries his consecration to his God. •Throughout the whole of
his nazirate he is a person consecrated to Yahweh.
9 "If anyone dies suddenly in his presence, and so makes his consecrated
hair unclean, he must shave his head on the day of his cleansing, he must shave
10 his head on the seventh day. •On the eighth day, he is to bring two turtledoves
or two young pigeons to the priest, at the entrance to the Tent of Meeting.
11 The priest must offer one as a sacrifice for sin, and the other as a holocaust;
he must then perform over this man the rite of atonement for the defilement that
he has contracted from the corpse. The man must consecrate his head that same
12 day; •he must consecrate himself to Yahweh for the period of his nazirate, and
he must bring a male yearling lamb as a sacrifice of reparation. The time already
spent shall not count, since his hair has become unclean.
13 "This is the ritual to be followed by the nazirite on the day when his period of
consecration is completed. He is to be led to the entrance of the Tent of Meeting,
14 and must make his offering to Yahweh: for holocaust, a male yearling lamb
without blemish; for sacrifice for sin, a yearling ewe lamb without blemish;
15 for communion sacrifice, a ram without blemish, •and a basket of unleavened
loaves made of fine flour mixed with oil, and of unleavened wafers spread with
16 oil, with the oblations and libations appropriate to them. •When he has brought
all this before Yahweh, the priest must offer the sacrifice for sin and the holocaust
17 for the nazirite. •The nazirite must offer up the communion sacrifice with the ram
and the unleavened bread in the basket, and the priest must offer the accom-
18 panying oblation and libation. •Then the nazirite shall shave off his consecrated
hair at the entrance to the Tent of Meeting, and taking the locks of his consecrated
19 head, he shall put them in the fire of the communion sacrifice. •The priest is to
take the shoulder of the ram, as soon as it is cooked, with an unleavened cake
from the basket, and an unleavened wafer. He is to put them into the hands of the
20 nazirite when the nazirite has shaved off his hair. •With them he must make the
gesture of offering before Yahweh; as it is a holy thing, it reverts to the priest, in
addition to the breast that has been presented and the thigh that has been set
aside. After this the nazirite may once more drink wine.
21 "Such is the ritual for the nazirite. If, besides the hair, he has also vowed a
personal offering to Yahweh, he must (apart from anything else that his means
allow) fulfil the vow that he has made, in addition to what the ritual prescribes
for his hair." '

The form of blessing

$\begin{smallmatrix} 22 \\ 23 \end{smallmatrix}$ Yahweh spoke to Moses and said, •'Say this to Aaron and his sons:
"This is how you are to bless the sons of Israel. You shall say to them:
24 May Yahweh bless you and keep you.

May Yahweh let his face shine on you and be gracious to you.   25
May Yahweh uncover his face to you and bring you peace."   26
This is how they are to call down my name on the sons of Israel, and I will   27
bless them.'

III. OFFERINGS OF THE LEADERS
AND CONSECRATION OF THE LEVITES

Offering of wagons

7 On the day Moses finished setting up the tabernacle, he anointed and conse- 1
crated it with all its furniture, as well as the altar and all its accessories. When
he had anointed and consecrated it all, •the leaders of Israel made an offering; 2
these were the heads of the patriarchal Houses, who were leaders of tribes and
had presided over the census. •They brought their offering before Yahweh: 3
six covered wagons and twelve oxen, one wagon for every two leaders and one
ox each. They brought them before the tabernacle. •Yahweh spoke to 4
Moses and said, •'Accept these from them, and let them be set apart for the 5
service of the Tent of Meeting. You are to give them to the Levites, to each as
his duties require.' •Moses took the wagons and the oxen, and gave them to 6
the Levites. •To the sons of Gershon he gave two wagons and four oxen for 7
the duties they had to perform. •To the sons of Merari he gave four wagons 8
and eight oxen, for the duties they had to perform under the direction of Ithamar,
son of Aaron the priest. •But to the sons of Kohath he gave none at all, because 9
the sacred charge entrusted to them had to be carried on their shoulders.

Dedication offering

The leaders then made an offering for the dedication of the altar, on the day 10
it was anointed. They brought their offering before the altar, •and Yahweh said 11
to Moses, 'Let the leaders each bring an offering on successive days for the
dedication of the altar'.

On the first day an offering was brought by Nahshon son of Amminadab, 12
of the tribe of Judah. •His offering consisted of: one silver bowl weighing a 13
hundred and thirty shekels, one silver sprinkling bowl weighing seventy shekels
(sanctuary shekels), both of them filled, for the oblation, with fine flour mixed
with oil, •one golden bowl weighing ten shekels, filled with incense, •one young ¹⁴₁₅
bull, one ram and one male yearling lamb for the holocaust, •one goat for the 16
sacrifice for sin, •and, for the communion sacrifice, two oxen, five rams, five 17
kids, and five male yearling lambs. This was the offering of Nahshon son of
Amminadab.

On the second day an offering was brought by Nethanel son of Zuar, leader 18
of Issachar. •His offering consisted of: one silver bowl weighing a hundred and 19
thirty shekels, one silver sprinkling bowl weighing seventy shekels (sanctuary
shekels), both of them filled, for the oblation, with fine flour mixed with oil,
one golden bowl weighing ten shekels, filled with incense, •one young bull, ²⁰₂₁
one ram and one male yearling lamb for the holocaust, •one goat for the 22
sacrifice for sin, •and, for the communion sacrifice, two oxen, five rams, five kids, 23
and five male yearling lambs. This was the offering of Nethanel son of Zuar.

On the third day an offering was brought by Eliab son of Helon, leader of 24
the sons of Zebulun. •His offering consisted of: one silver bowl weighing a 25
hundred and thirty shekels, one silver sprinkling bowl weighing seventy shekels
(sanctuary shekels), both of them filled, for the oblation, with fine flour mixed
with oil, •one golden bowl weighing ten shekels, filled with incense, •one young ²⁶₂₇
bull, one ram and one male yearling lamb for the holocaust, •one goat for the 28
sacrifice for sin, •and, for the communion sacrifice, two oxen, five rams, five 29
kids, and five male yearling lambs. This was the offering of Eliab son of Helon.

30 On the fourth day an offering was brought by Elizur son of Shedeur, leader
31 of the sons of Reuben. •His offering consisted of: one silver bowl weighing
a hundred and thirty shekels, one silver sprinkling bowl weighing seventy shekels
(sanctuary shekels), both of them filled, for the oblation, with fine flour mixed
32
33 with oil, •one golden bowl weighing ten shekels, filled with incense, •one young
34 bull, one ram, and one male yearling lamb for the holocaust, •one goat for the
35 sacrifice for sin, •and, for the communion sacrifice, two oxen, five rams, five
kids, and five male yearling lambs. This was the offering of Elizur son of Shedeur.
36 On the fifth day an offering was brought by Shelumiel son of Zurishaddai,
37 leader of the sons of Simeon. •His offering consisted of: one silver bowl weighing
a hundred and thirty shekels, one silver sprinkling bowl weighing seventy shekels
(sanctuary shekels), both of them filled, for the oblation, with fine flour mixed
38
39 with oil, •one golden bowl weighing ten shekels, filled with incense, •one young
40 bull, one ram and one male yearling lamb for the holocaust, •one goat for the
41 sacrifice for sin, •and, for the communion sacrifice, two oxen, five rams, five
kids, and five male yearling lambs. This was the offering of Shelumiel son of
Zurishaddai.
42 On the sixth day an offering was brought by Eliasaph son of Reuel, leader of
43 the sons of Gad. •His offering consisted of: one silver bowl weighing a hundred
and thirty shekels, one silver sprinkling bowl weighing seventy shekels (sanctuary
shekels), both of them filled, for the oblation, with fine flour mixed with oil,
44
45 one golden bowl weighing ten shekels, filled with incense, •one young bull,
46 one ram and one male yearling lamb for the holocaust, •one goat for the
47 sacrifice for sin, •and, for the communion sacrifice, two oxen, five rams, five kids,
and five male yearling lambs. This was the offering of Eliasaph son of Reuel.
48 On the seventh day an offering was brought by Elishama son of Ammihud,
49 leader of the sons of Ephraim. •His offering consisted of: one silver bowl
weighing a hundred and thirty shekels, one silver sprinkling bowl weighing
seventy shekels (sanctuary shekels), both of them filled, for the oblation, with
50 fine flour mixed with oil, •one golden bowl weighing ten shekels, filled with
51 incense, •one young bull, one ram and one male yearling lamb for the holocaust,
52
53 one goat for the sacrifice for sin, •and, or the communion sacrifice, two oxen,
five rams, five kids, and five male yearling lambs. This was the offering of
Elishama son of Ammihud.
54 On the eighth day an offering was brought by Gamaliel son of Pedahzur,
55 leader of the sons of Manasseh. •His offering consisted of: one silver bowl
weighing a hundred and thirty shekels, one silver sprinkling bowl weighing
seventy shekels (sanctuary shekels), both of them filled, for the oblation, with
56 fine flour mixed with oil, •one golden bowl weighing ten shekels, filled with
57 incense, •one young bull, one ram and one male yearling lamb for the holocaust,
58
59 one goat for the sacrifice for sin, •and, for the communion sacrifice, two oxen,
five rams, five kids, and five male yearling lambs. This was the offering of
Gamaliel son of Pedahzur.
60 On the ninth day an offering was brought by Abidan son of Gideoni, leader
61 of the sons of Benjamin. •His offering consisted of: one silver bowl weighing
a hundred and thirty shekels, one sprinkling bowl weighing seventy shekels
(sanctuary shekels), both of them filled, for the oblation, with fine flour mixed
62
63 with oil, •one golden bowl weighing ten shekels, filled with incense, •one young
64 bull, one ram and one male yearling lamb for the holocaust, •one goat for the
65 sacrifice for sin, •and, for the communion sacrifice, two oxen, five rams, five
kids, and five male yearling lambs. This was the offering of Abidan son of
Gideoni.
66 On the tenth day an offering was brought by Ahiezer son of Ammishaddai,
67 leader of the sons of Dan. •His offering consisted of: one silver bowl weighing
a hundred and thirty shekels, one silver sprinkling bowl weighing seventy shekels
(sanctuary shekels), both of them filled, for the oblation, with fine flour mixed

with oil, •one golden bowl weighing ten shekels, filled with incense, •one young ⁶⁸⁶⁹ bull, one ram, and one male yearling lamb for the holocaust, •one goat for the 70 sacrifice for sin, •and, for the communion sacrifice, two oxen, five rams, five 71 kids, and five male yearling lambs. This was the offering of Ahiezer son of Ammishaddai.

On the eleventh day an offering was brought by Pagiel son of Ochran, leader 72 of the sons of Asher. •His offering consisted of: one silver bowl weighing a 73 hundred and thirty shekels, one silver sprinkling bowl weighing seventy shekels (sanctuary shekels), both of them filled, for the oblation, with fine flour mixed ⁷⁴⁷⁵ with oil, •one golden bowl weighing ten shekels, filled with incense, •one young bull, one ram and one male yearling lamb for the holocaust, •one goat for the 76 sacrifice for sin, •and, for the communion sacrifice, two oxen, five rams, five 77 kids, and five male yearling lambs. This was the offering of Pagiel son of Ochran.

On the twelfth day an offering was brought by Ahira son of Enan, leader of 78 the sons of Naphtali. •His offering consisted of: one silver bowl weighing a 79 hundred and thirty shekels, one silver sprinkling bowl weighing seventy shekels (sanctuary shekels), both of them filled, for the oblation, with fine flour mixed ⁸⁰⁸¹ with oil, •one golden bowl weighing ten shekels, filled with incense, •one young bull, one ram and one male yearling lamb for the holocaust, •one goat for the 82 sacrifice for sin, •and, for the communion sacrifice, two oxen, five rams, five kids, 83 and five male yearling lambs. This was the offering of Ahira son of Enan.

These were the offerings made by the leaders of Israel for the dedication of 84 the altar on the day it was anointed: twelve silver bowls, twelve silver sprinkling bowls, and twelve golden bowls. •Each silver bowl weighed a hundred and 85 thirty shekels, and each sprinkling bowl seventy, the silver of these objects weighing in all two thousand four hundred sanctuary shekels. •The twelve 86 golden bowls filled with incense weighed ten shekels each (sanctuary shekels), the gold of these bowls weighing in all a hundred and twenty shekels.

The sum total of animals for the holocaust: twelve bulls, twelve rams, twelve 87 male yearling lambs, together with their accompanying oblations. For the sacrifice for sin, twelve goats. •The sum total of animals for the communion 88 sacrifice: twenty-four bulls, sixty rams, sixty kids, and sixty male yearling lambs.

These were the offerings for the dedication of the altar, after it had been anointed.

When Moses went into the Tent of Meeting to speak with Him, he heard 89 the voice that spoke to him from above the throne of mercy which was on the ark of the Testimony, from between the two cherubs. It was then that he spoke with Him.

The lamps for the lamp-stand

8 Yahweh spoke to Moses and said: 1 'Say this to Aaron, "When you set up the lamps, the seven lamps must throw 2 their light towards the front of the lamp-stand" '.

Aaron saw to this. He set up the lamps to the front of the lamp-stand, as 3 Yahweh had ordered Moses. •This lamp-stand was worked in beaten gold, 4 including its stem and its petals, which were also of beaten gold. This lamp-stand had been made according to the pattern Yahweh had shown to Moses.

The Levites are offered to Yahweh

Yahweh spoke to Moses and said: 5 'Separate the Levites from the sons of Israel and purify them. •This is how ⁶⁷ you are to purify them: you must sprinkle them with lustral water, and they must shave their bodies all over and wash their clothing. They will then be clean. •They 8 must next take a young bull, with the accompanying oblation of fine flour mixed with oil, and you must take a second young bull for a sacrifice for sin. •Then 9 bring the Levites before the Tent of Meeting, and call together the whole

10 community of the sons of Israel. •When you have brought the Levites before
11 Yahweh, the sons of Israel must lay their hands on them. •Aaron shall then offer
the Levites, making the gesture of offering before Yahweh on behalf of the sons
of Israel. From that time, they will be dedicated to the service of Yahweh.
12   'The Levites must then lay their hands on the heads of the bulls, one of which
you are to offer as a sacrifice for sin, and the other as a holocaust to Yahweh;
13 this is how the rite of atonement for the Levites is to be performed. •Having
brought the Levites before Aaron and his sons, you will present them to Yahweh
14 with the gesture of offering. •This is how you are to set the Levites apart from
15 the rest of the sons of Israel, so that they may be mine. •The Levites will then
begin their ministry in the Tent of Meeting.
16   'You must purify them and offer them with the gesture of offering •because
they have been made over to me from among the sons of Israel, as 'oblates'.
They are to replace those who open the womb, all the first-born; of all the sons
17 of Israel I have taken them for my own. •All the first-born among the sons of
Israel, man and beast, do indeed belong to me: the day I struck all the first-born
18 in the land of Egypt, I consecrated them to myself, •and now, in place of all
19 the first-born among the sons of Israel, I have taken the Levites. •From among
the sons of Israel I give them to Aaron and his sons, as 'oblates'; on behalf of
the sons of Israel, they will minister in the Tent of Meeting and perform the rite
of atonement over them, so that none of the sons of Israel may be struck down
for approaching the sanctuary.'
20   Moses, Aaron and the whole community of the sons of Israel dealt with
the Levites exactly as Yahweh had directed Moses concerning them; this is what
21 the sons of Israel did with them. •The Levites purified themselves and washed
their clothes, and Aaron presented them with the gesture of offering before
Yahweh. Then he performed the rite of atonement over them to purify them.
22 The Levites were then allowed to perform their ministry in the Tent of Meeting
in the presence of Aaron and his sons. As Yahweh had directed Moses concerning
the Levites, so it was done to them.

The duration of their ministry

23   Yahweh spoke to Moses and said:
24   'This concerns the Levites. From the age of twenty-five onwards, the Levite
25 must exercise his ministry and do duty in the Tent of Meeting. •After the age
of fifty, he is no longer bound to the ministry; he will have no further duties;
26 but he will still help his brothers to ensure the services in the Tent of Meeting,
though he himself will no longer have any ministry. See that this is the rule for
the ministry of the Levites.'

IV. THE PASSOVER AND THE DEPARTURE

Date of the Passover

1 9 Yahweh spoke to Moses, in the wilderness of Sinai, in the second year after
        the exodus from Egypt, in the first month. He said:
2
3   'Let the sons of Israel keep the Passover at its appointed time. •The fourteenth
day of this month, between the two evenings, is the appointed time for you
to keep it. You must keep it with all the laws and customs proper to it.'
4
5   Moses gave orders for the sons of Israel to keep the Passover. •They kept it,
in the wilderness of Sinai, in the first month, on the fourteenth day of the month,
between the two evenings. The sons of Israel did exactly as Yahweh had
ordered Moses.

Individual cases

It happened that certain men had become unclean by touching a dead body; 6
they could not keep the Passover that day. They came the same day to Moses
and Aaron, •and said to them, 'We have become unclean by touching a dead 7
body. Why should we be forbidden to bring an offering to Yahweh at the proper
time with the rest of the sons of Israel?' •Moses answered them, 'Wait there 8
till I learn what orders Yahweh gives about you'.

Yahweh spoke to Moses and said, •'Say this to the sons of Israel: 9,10
"If anyone, among you or your descendants, becomes unclean by touching
a dead body or is on a journey abroad, he can still keep a Passover for Yahweh.
Such persons shall keep it in the second month, on the fourteenth day, between 11
the two evenings. They are to eat it with unleavened bread and bitter herbs;
nothing of it must be left over until morning, nor must they break any of its 12
bones: they must keep this Passover exactly according to the paschal ritual.
But if anyone who is clean, or who has not had to go on a journey, fails to keep 13
the Passover, he shall be outlawed from his people. He has not brought the
offering to Yahweh at its appointed time, and he must bear the burden of his sin.

"If a stranger is living among you and keeps a Passover for Yahweh, he must 14
keep it in accordance with the laws and customs of the Passover. There is to
be only one law among you, for settler and native alike." '

The Cloud

On the day the tabernacle was set up, the Cloud covered the tabernacle, 15
the Tent of the Testimony. From nightfall until morning, it remained over the
tabernacle under the appearance of fire. •So the Cloud covered it continually, 16
at night taking the appearance of fire.

Whenever the Cloud lifted above the Tent, the sons of Israel broke camp; 17
whenever the Cloud halted, there the sons of Israel pitched camp. •The sons of 18
Israel set out at the command of Yahweh, and at his command they pitched camp.

The people remained encamped as long as the Cloud rested on the tabernacle.
If the Cloud stayed for many days above the tabernacle, the sons of Israel paid 19
worship to Yahweh and did not break camp. •But if the Cloud happened to 20
stay for only a few days above the tabernacle, they pitched camp at Yahweh's
command and broke camp at Yahweh's command. •If the Cloud happened to 21
remain only from evening to morning, they set out when it lifted the next
morning. Or, if it stayed for a whole day and night, they set out only when it
lifted. •Sometimes it stayed there for two days, a month, or a year; however 22
long the Cloud stayed above the tabernacle, the sons of Israel remained in camp
in the same place, and when it lifted they set out. •At Yahweh's command they 23
pitched camp, and at Yahweh's command they broke camp. They paid worship to
Yahweh, according to the orders which Yahweh had given through Moses.

The trumpets

10 Yahweh spoke to Moses and said: 1
'Make two trumpets; make them of beaten silver; and use them for 2
summoning the community, and for sounding the order to break camp. •When- 3
ever they are sounded, the whole community is to gather round you, at the
entrance to the Tent of Meeting. •But if only one trumpet is sounded, then only 4
the leaders, the chiefs of Israel's battalions, are to gather round you.

'When the trumpet blast is accompanied by a battle cry, the camps pitched 5
to the east shall set out. •At the second blast accompanied by a battle cry, the 6
camps pitched to the south shall set out. To break camp, the trumpet blast must
be accompanied by a battle cry, •but to assemble the community the trumpets 7
shall be sounded without battle cry. •The sons of Aaron, the priests, are to sound 8
the trumpets; this is a perpetual law for you and your descendants.

'In your own land when you go to war against an enemy who oppresses you, 9

you must sound the trumpet with a battle cry: Yahweh your God will remember
10 you, and you will be delivered from your enemies. •At your festivals, solemnities, or new-moon feasts, you will sound the trumpet at the time of your holocausts and your communion sacrifices, and they will call you to the remembrance of your God. I am Yahweh your God.'

The order of march

11   In the second year, in the second month, on the twentieth day of the month,
12 the Cloud lifted over the tabernacle of the Testimony. •The sons of Israel set out, in marching order, from the wilderness of Sinai. In the wilderness of Paran the Cloud came to rest.

13   These are the men who set out in the vanguard, at the order of Yahweh
14 given through Moses: •in the vanguard was the standard of the camp of the sons of Judah, in battle array. In command of Judah's force was Nahshon son of
15 Amminadab; •in command of the sons of Issachar, in battle array, was Nethanel
16 son of Zuar; •in command of the tribe of the sons of Zebulun, in battle array, was Eliab son of Helon.

17   Then, the tabernacle being dismantled, the sons of Gershon and the sons of Merari set out, carrying the tabernacle.

18   Then came the standard of the camp of the sons of Reuben, in battle array.
19 In command of Reuben's force was Elizur son of Shedeur; •in command of the tribe of the sons of Simeon, in battle array, was Shelumiel son of Zurishaddai;
20 in command of the tribe of the sons of Gad, in battle array, was Eliasaph son of Reuel.

21   Then came the sons of Kohath, who carried the sanctuary (the tabernacle was set up before their arrival).

22   Then came the standard of the camp of the sons of Ephraim, in battle array.
23 In command of Ephraim's force was Elishama son of Ammihud; •in command of the tribe of the sons of Manasseh, in battle array, was Gamaliel son of
24 Pedahzur; •in command of the tribe of the sons of Benjamin was Abidan son of Gideoni.

25   Last of all, the rearguard of all the camps, came the standard of the camp of the sons of Dan, in battle array. In command of the force of Dan was Ahiezer
26 son of Ammishaddai; •in command of the tribe of the sons of Asher, in battle
27 array, was Pagiel son of Ochran; •in command of the sons of Naphtali, in battle array, was Ahira son of Enan.

28   Such was the order of march for the sons of Israel, in battle array. So they set out.

Moses' proposal to Hobab

29   Moses said to Hobab son of Reuel the Midianite, his father-in-law, 'We are setting out for the land of which Yahweh has said: I will give it to you. Come with us, and we will treat you well, for Yahweh has promised happiness to
30 Israel.' •'I will not come with you,' he answered 'I will go to my own land and
31 my own kindred.' •'Do not leave us,' Moses replied 'for you know where we
32 can camp in the wilderness, and so you will be our eyes. •If you come with us, you will share in the blessing of the happiness with which Yahweh blesses us.'

The departure

33   They set out from the mountain of Yahweh and journeyed for three days. The ark of the covenant of Yahweh went at their head for this journey of three days, searching out a camping place for them.
34   In the daytime, the Cloud of Yahweh was over them whenever they left camp.

35   And as the ark set out, Moses would say,
        'Arise, Yahweh, may your enemies be scattered
        and those who hate you run

for their lives before you!'
And as it came to rest, he would say,　　　　　　　　36
'Come back, Yahweh,
to the thronging hosts of Israel'.

V. THE HALTS IN THE WILDERNESS

Taberah

11 Now the people set up a lament which was offensive to Yahweh's ears, 1
and Yahweh heard it. His anger blazed, and the fire of Yahweh burned
among them: it destroyed one end of the camp. •The people appealed to Moses, 2
and he interceded with Yahweh and the fire died down. •So the place was called 3
Taberah, because the fire of Yahweh had burned among them.

Kibroth-hattaavah. *a* The people complain

The rabble who had joined the people were overcome by greed, and the sons 4
of Israel themselves began to wail again, 'Who will give us meat to eat?'
they said. •'Think of the fish we used to eat free in Egypt, the cucumbers, 5
melons, leeks, onions and garlic! •Here we are wasting away, stripped of 6
everything; there is nothing but manna for us to look at!'

The manna was like coriander seed, and had the appearance of bdellium. 7
The people went round gathering it, and ground it in a mill or crushed it with 8
a pestle; it was then cooked in a pot and made into pancakes. It tasted like cake
made with oil. •When the dew fell on the camp at night-time, the manna fell 9
with it.

The prayer of Moses

Moses heard the people wailing, every family at the door of its tent. The 10
anger of Yahweh flared out, and Moses greatly worried over this. •And he 11
spoke to Yahweh:

'Why do you treat your servant so badly? Why have I not found favour
with you, so that you load on me the weight of all this nation? •Was it I who 12
conceived all this people, was it I who gave them birth, that you should say
to me, "Carry them in your bosom, like a nurse with a baby at the breast, to
the land that I swore to give their fathers"? •Where am I to find meat to give 13
to all this people, when they come worrying me so tearfully and say, "Give us
meat to eat"? •I am not able to carry this nation by myself alone; the weight 14
is too much for me. •If this is how you want to deal with me, I would rather you 15
killed me! If only I had found favour in your eyes, and not lived to see such
misery as this!'

Yahweh replies

Yahweh said to Moses, 'Gather seventy of the elders of Israel, men you 16
know to be the people's elders and scribes. Bring them to the Tent of Meeting,
and let them stand beside you there. •I will come down to speak with you; 17
and I will take some of the spirit which is on you and put it on them. So they
will share with you the burden of this nation, and you will no longer have to
carry it by yourself.

'To the people, say this, "Purify yourselves for tomorrow and you will have 18
meat to eat, now that you have wailed in the hearing of Yahweh and said: Who
will give us meat to eat? How happy we were in Egypt! So be it! Yahweh will
give you meat to eat. •You shall eat it not for one day only, or two, or five 19
or ten or twenty, •but for a full month, until you are sick of it and cannot bear 20
the smell of it, because you have rejected Yahweh who is with you, and have
wailed before him saying: Why did we ever leave Egypt?" '

21 Moses said, 'The people round me number six hundred thousand foot
22 soldiers, and you say, "I shall give them meat to eat for a whole month"! •If all
the flocks and herds were slaughtered, would that be enough for them? If all
23 the fish in the sea were gathered, would that be enough for them?' •Yahweh
answered Moses, 'Is the arm of Yahweh so short? You shall see whether the
promise I have made to you comes true or not.'

The spirit given to the elders

24 Moses went out and told the people what Yahweh had said. Then he gathered
25 seventy elders of the people and brought them round the Tent. •Yahweh came
down in the Cloud. He spoke with him, but took some of the spirit that was
on him and put it on the seventy elders. When the spirit came on them they
prophesied, but not again.
26 Two men had stayed back in the camp; one was called Eldad and the other
Medad. The spirit came down on them; though they had not gone to the Tent,
their names were enrolled among the rest. These began to prophesy in the camp.
27 The young man ran to tell this to Moses, 'Look,' he said 'Eldad and Medad
28 are prophesying in the camp'. •Then said Joshua the son of Nun, who had
29 served Moses from his youth, 'My Lord Moses, stop them!' •Moses answered
him, 'Are you jealous on my account? If only the whole people of Yahweh
30 were prophets, and Yahweh gave his Spirit to them all!' •Then Moses went back
to the camp, the elders of Israel with him.

The quails

31 A wind came from Yahweh and it drove quails in from the sea and brought
them down on the camp. They lay for a distance of a day's march either
32 side of the camp, two cubits thick on the ground. •The people were up all
that day and night and all the next day collecting quails: the least gathered
33 by anyone was ten homers; then they spread them out round the camp. •The
meat was still between their teeth, not even chewed, when the anger of Yahweh
blazed out against the people. Yahweh struck them with a very great plague.
34 The name given to this place was Kibroth-hattaavah, because it was there
that they buried the people who had indulged their greed.
35 From Kibroth-hattaavah the people set out for Hazeroth, and at Hazeroth
they pitched camp.

Hazeroth. Complaints of Miriam and Aaron

1 **12** Miriam, and Aaron too, spoke against Moses in connexion with the
Cushite woman[a] he had taken. (For he had married a Cushite woman.)
2 They said, 'Has Yahweh spoken to Moses only? Has he not spoken to us too?'
3 Yahweh heard this. •Now Moses was the most humble of men, the humblest
man on earth.

God's answer

4 Suddenly, Yahweh said to Moses and Aaron and Miriam, 'Come, all three
5 of you, to the Tent of Meeting'. They went, all three of them, •and Yahweh
came down in a pillar of cloud and stood at the entrance of the Tent. He called
6 Aaron and Miriam and they both came forward. •Yahweh said, 'Listen now
to my words:
> If any man among you is a prophet
> I make myself known to him in a vision,
> I speak to him in a dream.
7 > Not so with my servant Moses:
> he is at home in my house;

11 a. The name of the second place at which the people rebelled, explained in v.34 as 'the graves
of the greedy'.
12 a. Zipporah, the Midianite, Ex 2:21.

> I speak with him face to face,   8
> plainly and not in riddles,
> and he sees the form of Yahweh.

How then have you dared to speak against my servant Moses?'   9
   The anger of Yahweh blazed out against them. He departed, •and as soon   10
as the cloud withdrew from the Tent, there was Miriam a leper, white as snow!
Aaron turned to look at her; she had become a leper.

The prayer of Aaron and Moses

   Aaron said to Moses: 11
   'Help me, my lord! Do not punish us for a sin committed in folly of which
we are guilty. •I entreat you, do not let her be like a monster, coming from its   12
mother's womb with flesh half corrupted.'
   Moses cried to Yahweh, 'O God,' he said 'please heal her, I beg you!'   13
   Then Yahweh said to Moses, 'If her father had done no more than spit in her   14
face, would she not be a thing of shame for seven days? Let her be shut outside
the camp for seven days, and then let her be brought in again.'
   Miriam was shut outside the camp for seven days. The people did not set   15
out until she returned. •Then the people left Hazeroth, and camp was pitched   16
in the wilderness of Paran.

The reconnaissance in Canaan

13 Yahweh spoke to Moses and said, •'Send out men, one from each tribe,   1 2
to make a reconnaissance of this land of Canaan which I am giving to
the sons of Israel. Send the leader of each tribe.'
   At Yahweh's bidding, Moses sent them from the wilderness of Paran. All   3
these men were chiefs among the sons of Israel. •These were their names: 4
   For the tribe of Reuben, Shammua son of Zaccur;
   for the tribe of Simeon, Shaphat son of Hori;   5
   for the tribe of Judah, Caleb son of Jephunneh;   6
   for the tribe of Issachar, Igal son of Joseph;   7
   for the tribe of Ephraim, Hoshea son of Nun;   8
   for the tribe of Benjamin, Palti son of Raphu;   9
   for the tribe of Zebulun, Gaddiel son of Sodi;   10
   for the tribe of Joseph, for the tribe of Manasseh, Gaddi son of Susi;   11
   for the tribe of Dan, Ammiel son of Gemalli;   12
   for the tribe of Asher, Sethur son of Michael;   13
   for the tribe of Naphtali, Nahbi son of Vophsi;   14
   for the tribe of Gad, Geuel son of Machi.   15
   These were the names of the men whom Moses sent to make a reconnaissance   16
of the land. Then Moses gave to Hoshea son of Nun the name of Joshua.
   Moses sent them to reconnoitre the land of Canaan, 'Go up into the Negeb;   17
then go up into the highlands. •See what sort of country it is, and what sort   18
of people the inhabitants are, whether they are strong or weak, few or many,
what sort of country they live in, whether it is good or poor; what sort of towns   19
they have, whether they are open or fortified; •what sort of land it is, fertile   20
or barren, wooded or open. Be bold, and bring back some of the produce of
the country.'
   It was the season for early grapes. •They went up to reconnoitre the land,   21
from the wilderness of Zin to Rehob, the Pass of Hamath.ᵃ •They went up   22
by way of the Negeb as far as Hebron, where the Anakim lived, Ahiman, Sheshai
and Talmai. (Hebron was founded seven years before Tanis in Egypt.) •They   23
came to the Valley of Eshcol; there they lopped off a vine branch with a cluster
of grapes, which two of them carried away on a pole, as well as pomegranates
and figs. •This place was called the Valley of Eshcolᵇ after the cluster which   24
the sons of Israel had cut there.

The envoys' report

25 At the end of forty days, they came back from their reconnaissance of the
26 land. •They sought out Moses, Aaron and the whole community of Israel,
in the wilderness of Paran, at Kadesh. They made their report to them, and to
the whole community, and showed them the produce of the country.
27 They told them this story, 'We went into the land to which you sent us.
28 It does indeed flow with milk and honey; this is its produce. •At the same time,
its inhabitants are a powerful people; the towns are fortified and very big; yes,
29 and we saw the descendants of Anak there. •The Amalekite holds the Negeb
area, the Hittite, Amorite and Jebusite the highlands, and the Canaanite the
sea coast and the banks of the Jordan.'
30 Caleb harangued the people gathered about Moses: 'We must march in,'
31 he said 'and conquer this land: we are well able to do it'. •But the men who
had gone up with him answered, 'We are not able to march against this people;
32 they are stronger than we are'. •And they began to disparage the country they
had reconnoitred to the sons of Israel, 'The country we went to reconnoitre is a
country that devours its inhabitants. Every man we saw there was of enormous
33 size. •Yes, and we saw giants there (the sons of Anak, descendants of the Giants).
We felt like grasshoppers, and so we seemed to them.'

The rebellion of Israel

1 **14** At this, the whole community raised their voices and cried aloud, and
2 the people wailed all that night. •Then all the sons of Israel grumbled
against Moses and Aaron, and the whole community said, 'Would that we had
3 died in the land of Egypt, or at least that we had died in this wilderness! •Why
does Yahweh bring us to this land, only to have us fall by the sword, and our
wives and young children seized as booty? Should we not do better to go back to
4 Egypt?' •And they said to one another, 'Let us appoint a leader and go back to Egypt'.
5 Before the whole assembled community of the sons of Israel, Moses and
6 Aaron fell down, face to the ground. •Joshua son of Nun and Caleb son
of Jephunneh, two of those who had reconnoitred the country, tore their
7 garments; •and they said to the entire community of the sons of Israel, 'The land
8 we went to reconnoitre is a good land, an excellent land. •If Yahweh is pleased
with us, he will lead us into this land and give it to us. It is a land where milk and
9 honey flow. •Do not rebel against Yahweh. And do not be afraid of the people of
this land; we shall gobble them up. Their tutelary shadow has gone from them
so long as Yahweh is with us.[a] Do not be afraid of them.'

The anger of Yahweh. Moses makes an appeal

10 The entire community was talking of stoning them, when the glory of
11 Yahweh appeared at the Tent of Meeting to all the sons of Israel. •And Yahweh
said to Moses:
'How long will this people insult me? How long will they refuse to believe
in me despite the signs I have worked among them? •I will strike them with
pestilence and disown them. And of you I shall make a new nation, greater and
mightier than they are.'
13 Moses answered Yahweh:
'But the Egyptians already know that you, by your own power, have brought
14 this people out from their midst. •They have said as much to the inhabitants
of this country. They already know that you, Yahweh, are in the midst of this
people, and that you show yourself to them face to face; that it is you, Yahweh,
whose cloud stands over them, that you go before them in a pillar of cloud
15 by day and a pillar of fire by night. •If you destroy this people now as if it were

13 a. The extreme north of Palestine.   b. Near Hebron.
14 a. The shelter of their own tutelary gods.

one man, then the nations who have heard about you will say, • "Yahweh was 16
not able to bring this people into the land he swore to give them, and so he
has slaughtered them in the wilderness". • No, my Lord! It is now you must 17
display your power, according to those words you spoke, • "Yahweh is slow to 18
anger and rich in graciousness, forgiving faults and transgression, and yet letting
nothing go unchecked, punishing the father's fault in the sons to the third and
fourth generation". • In the abundance, then, of your graciousness, forgive the 19
sin of this people, as you have done from Egypt until now.'

Pardon and punishment

Yahweh said, 'I forgive them as you ask. • But—as I live, and as the glory 20 21
of Yahweh fills all the earth—• of all the men who have seen my glory and the 22
signs that I worked in Egypt and in the wilderness, who have put me to the test
ten times already and not obeyed my voice, • not one shall see the land I 23
swore to give their fathers. Not one of those who slight me shall see it. But
my servant Caleb is of another spirit. Because he has obeyed me perfectly, I 24
will bring him into the land he has entered, and his race shall possess it. (The
Amalekite and the Canaanite dwell in the plain.) • Tomorrow you will turn 25
about and go back into the wilderness, in the direction of the Sea of Suph.'

Yahweh spoke to Moses and Aaron. He said: 26
'How long does this perverse community, which complains against me . . .? 27
I have heard the complaints which the sons of Israel make against me. • Say 28
to them, "As I live—it is Yahweh who speaks—I will deal with you according
to the very words you have used in my hearing. • In this wilderness your dead 29
bodies will fall, all you men of the census, all you who were numbered from
the age of twenty years and over, you who have complained against me. • I swear 30
that you shall not enter the land where I swore most solemnly, to settle you.
It is Caleb son of Jephunneh, and Joshua son of Nun, • and your young children 31
that you said would be seized as booty, it is these I shall bring in to know the
land you have disdained. • As for you, your dead bodies will fall in this wilderness, 32
and your sons will be nomads in the wilderness for forty years, bearing the 33
weight of your faithlessness, until the last of you lies dead in the desert. • For 34
forty days you reconnoitred the land. Each day shall count for a year: for forty
years you shall bear the burden of your sins, and you shall learn what it means
to reject me." • I, Yahweh, have spoken: this is how I will deal with this perverse 35
community that has conspired against me. Here in this wilderness, to the last
man, they shall die.'

The men whom Moses had sent to reconnoitre the land, who on their return 36
had incited the whole community of Israel to grumble against Yahweh by
disparaging it, • these men who had disparaged the land were all struck dead 37
before Yahweh. • Of the men who had gone to reconnoitre the land, only Joshua 38
son of Nun and Caleb son of Jephunneh remained alive.

An abortive attempt by the Israelites

Moses reported these words to all the sons of Israel, and the people set up 39
a great outcry. • Then they rose early and set out for the heights of the highlands 40
saying, 'Look, we are setting out for this place, since Yahweh has told us that
we have sinned'. • Moses replied, 'Why disobey the command of Yahweh? Nothing 41
will come of it. • Do not go up, for Yahweh is not among you; do not get your- 42
selves beaten by your enemies. • Yes, there facing you are the Amalekite and the 43
Canaanite, and you will fall to their swords because you have turned away from
Yahweh, and Yahweh is not with you.' • Yet they set out presumptuously towards 44
the heights of the highlands. Neither the ark of the covenant of Yahweh nor
Moses left the camp. • The Amalekite and the Canaanite who lived in that 45
hill country came down and defeated them, and harried them all the way to
Hormah.

VI. LAWS GOVERNING SACRIFICES. POWERS
OF PRIESTS AND LEVITES

The oblation to accompany sacrifices

${}^{1}_{2}$ 15 Yahweh spoke to Moses and said, • 'Tell this to the sons of Israel:
"When you have arrived in the land where you are to live, the land I give to
3 you, •and you make burnt offering to Yahweh either as a holocaust or as a
sacrifice, whether in payment of a vow, or as a voluntary gift, or on the occasion
of one of your solemn feasts—taking from your herds and flocks to make an
4 appeasing fragrance for Yahweh—•the offerer must bring, as his personal gift to
Yahweh, an oblation of one-tenth of an ephah of fine flour mixed with one quarter
5 of a hin of oil. •You must also make a libation of wine, one quarter of a hin to
6 each lamb, in addition to the holocaust or sacrifice. •For a ram, you must make
an oblation of two-tenths of an ephah of fine flour mixed with one-third of a hin
7 of oil, •and a libation of one-third of a hin of wine, offering it as an appeasing
8 fragrance for Yahweh. •If you offer a bull as a holocaust or sacrifice, in payment of
9 a vow or as a communion sacrifice for Yahweh, •you must offer in addition to
the beast an oblation of three-tenths of an ephah of fine flour mixed with half
10 a hin of oil, •and you must offer a libation of half a hin of wine, as a burnt
11 offering, an appeasing fragrance for Yahweh. •This must be done for every
12 bull, every ram, every lamb or kid. •Whatever the number of victims you
have for sacrifice, you must do the same for each of them, however many there
are.
13 "This must be done by every man of your own people when he makes a burnt
14 offering, an appeasing fragrance for Yahweh. •Any stranger living among you, or
among your descendants, will also make a burnt offering, an appeasing fragrance
15 for Yahweh: just as you act, so must •the assembly.ᵃ There shall be only one law
for you and for the settler among you. This is a law that shall bind your descend-
16 ants always: before Yahweh, you and the settler are alike. •There is to be one law
only, and one statute for you and for the stranger who lives among you." '

The first-fruits of bread

${}^{17}_{18}$ Yahweh spoke to Moses and said, •'Speak to the sons of Israel and say to
them:
19 "When you have entered the land to which I am bringing you, •you must set
20 aside a portion for Yahweh when you eat the bread of this country. •You must
set aside one loaf as the first-fruits of your meal; you must set this offering
21 aside like the one set aside from your threshing. •You are to set aside for Yahweh
a portion of the best of your meal. This applies to your descendants.

Atonement for faults of inadvertence

22 "If through inadvertence you fail in any of these commands that Yahweh has
23 given to Moses •(every single precept that Yahweh has laid on you through
Moses, from the day he gave his commands and onwards to your descendants),
24 this is what must be done:
"If it is an inadvertence of the community, the community as a whole must
make a holocaust of a young bull, an appeasing fragrance for Yahweh, with the
prescribed accompanying oblation and libation, and a he-goat must be offered
25 as a sacrifice for sin. •The priest must perform the rite of atonement over the entire
community of the sons of Israel, and pardon will be given, since it was an inadvertence. When they have brought their offering as a burnt offering to Yahweh,
and have presented their sacrifice for sin before Yahweh to make amends for
26 their inadvertence, •pardon will be given to the entire community of the sons

15 a. I.e., the assembly of the future.

of Israel, as also to the stranger who lives among them, since the entire people has sinned through inadvertence.

"If it is an individual who has sinned by inadvertence, he must offer a yearling 27 kid in sacrifice for sin. •The priest must perform the rite of atonement before 28 Yahweh over the person who has gone astray by this sin of inadvertence; when the rite of atonement has been performed over him, he will be forgiven, •whether 29 he is a native, one of the sons of Israel, or a stranger living among them. There shall be only one law among you for the man who sins by inadvertence.

"But the man who sins deliberately, whether native or stranger, outrages 30 Yahweh himself. Such a man must be outlawed from his people; •he has despised 31 the word of Yahweh and broken his command. This man must be entirely outlawed, since his sin is inseparable from him." '

Breaking the sabbath

While the sons of Israel were in the wilderness, a man was caught gathering 32 wood on the sabbath day. •Those who caught him gathering wood brought 33 him before Moses, Aaron and the whole community. •He was kept in custody, 34 because the penalty he should undergo had not yet been fixed. •Yahweh said to 35 Moses, 'This man must be put to death. The whole community must stone him outside the camp.' •The whole community took him outside the camp and stoned 36 him till he was dead, as Yahweh had commanded Moses.

Tassels on garments

Yahweh spoke to Moses and said, •'Speak to the sons of Israel and tell them ³⁷₃₈ to put tassels on the hems of their garments, and to put a violet cord on this tassel at the hem. •You must have a tassel, then, and the sight of it will remind you 39 of all the commands of Yahweh. You are to put them into practice then, and no longer follow the desires of your heart and your eyes, which have led you to make wantons of yourselves.

'This will remind you of all my commandments; put them into practice, 40 and you will be consecrated to your God. •It is I, Yahweh your God, who have 41 brought you out of the land of Egypt so that I may be your God, I Yahweh your God.'

The rebellion of Korah, Dathan and Abiram

16 Korah son of Izhar, son of Kohath, son of Levi took . . . Dathan and 1 Abiram sons of Eliab, and On son of Peleth (Eliab and Peleth were sons of Reuben) •rebelled against Moses, together with two hundred and fifty of the 2 sons of Israel, leaders of the community, prominent in the solemn feasts, men of repute. •These joined forces against Moses and Aaron saying to them, 'You take 3 too much on yourselves! The whole community and all its members are consecrated, and Yahweh lives among them. Why set yourselves higher than the community of Yahweh?'

Moses, when he heard this, threw himself face downward on the ground. 4 Then he said to Korah and all his followers, 'Tomorrow morning Yahweh will 5 reveal who is his, who is the consecrated man that he will allow to come near him. The one he allows to come near is the one whom he has chosen. •This is what 6 you are to do: take the censers of Korah and all his followers, •fill them with fire 7 and, tomorrow, put incense in them before Yahweh. Yahweh will choose the one who is the consecrated man. Sons of Levi, you take too much on yourselves!'

Moses said to Korah, 'Listen to me now, you sons of Levi! •Is it not enough ⁸₉ for you that the God of Israel has singled you out from the community of Israel, and called you close to himself for service in the tabernacle of Yahweh, to stand before this community and perform the sacred rites on their behalf? •He has 10 called you to be near him, you and all your brother Levites with you, and now you aspire to the office of priesthood as well! •Against Yahweh himself you have 11 joined forces, you and your followers: for what is Aaron that you should complain against him?'

12 Moses summoned Dathan and Abiram, the sons of Eliab. They replied,
13 'We will not come. •Was it not enough to take us from a land where milk and honey flow to die in this wilderness, without seeking to lord it over us now?
14 There is no land flowing with milk and honey that you have brought us to, nor have you given us fields and vineyards for our inheritance. Do you expect
15 this people to be blind? We will not come.' •Moses flew into a rage and said to Yahweh, 'Pay no heed to their offering. I have not taken so much as a donkey from them, nor have I harmed any of them.'

The punishment

16 Moses said to Korah, 'You and all your followers, come tomorrow into the
17 presence of Yahweh, you and they, and Aaron too. •Let every man bring his censer, put incense in it, and carry his censer before Yahweh—two hundred and
18 fifty censers. You and Aaron also, each of you bring his censer.' •So every man took his censer, filled it with fire, and put incense in it. And they stood at the
19 entrance to the Tent of Meeting, and Moses and Aaron with them. •Then, when Korah had assembled the whole community to confront these two at the entrance to the Tent of Meeting, the glory of Yahweh appeared to the whole community.
20
21 Yahweh spoke to Moses and Aaron. He said, •'Stand apart from this assembly,
22 I am going to destroy them here and now'. •They threw themselves face downward on the ground, and cried out, 'O God, God of the spirits that give life to every living thing, will you be angry with the whole community for one man's
23
24 sin?' •Yahweh answered Moses and said, •'Say this to the community, "Stand clear of the dwelling of Korah" '.
25 Moses stood up and went to Dathan and Abiram; the elders of Israel followed
26 him. •He said to the community, 'Stand away, I beg you, from the tents of these perverse men, and touch nothing that belongs to them, for fear that with all
27 their sins you too will be swept away'. •So they moved away from the dwelling of Korah.

Dathan and Abiram had come out and were standing at their tent doors,
28 with their wives and their sons and their young children. •Moses said, 'By this you will know that Yahweh himself has sent me to perform all these tasks and
29 that this is not my doing. •If these people die a natural death such as men
30 commonly die, then Yahweh has not sent me. •But if Yahweh does something utterly new, if the earth should open its mouth and swallow them, themselves and all that belongs to them, so that they go down alive to Sheol,*a* then you will know that these men have rejected Yahweh.'
31 The moment he finished saying all these words, the ground split open under
32 their feet, •the earth opened its mouth and swallowed them, their families too, and all Korah's men and all their belongings.
33 They went down alive to Sheol, they and all their possessions. The earth
34 closed over them and they disappeared from the midst of the assembly. •At their cries all the Israelites around them ran away. For they said, 'The earth must not swallow us!'
35 A fire came down from Yahweh and consumed the two hundred and fifty men carrying incense.

The censers

1,2
36,37 **17** Yahweh spoke to Moses and said, •'Tell Eleazar, son of Aaron, the priest, to pick the censers out of these ashes and take this unlawful fire elsewhere,
3
38 for these sinful censers are sanctified, at the price of these men's lives. Since they have been brought before Yahweh and consecrated, let the metal be hammered into sheets to cover the altar. They will be an object-lesson to the sons of Israel.'
4
39 Eleazar the priest took the bronze censers which had been carried by the men

16 a. The underworld, the place of the dead.

who were destroyed by the fire. They were hammered into sheets to cover the altar. •They are a reminder to the sons of Israel that no layman, no one outside Aaron's line, may come near Yahweh with incense to burn, under pain of suffering the lot of Korah ·and his followers, according to the order given by Yahweh through Moses.
$\frac{5}{40}$

Aaron intercedes

On the following day, the entire community of the sons of Israel grumbled against Moses and Aaron, saying, 'You have brought death to the people of Yahweh'. •As the community was banding together against Moses and Aaron, these turned towards the Tent of Meeting, and there was the Cloud covering it, and the glory of Yahweh appeared. •And Moses and Aaron went to the door of the Tent of Meeting.
$\frac{6}{41}$ $\frac{7}{42}$ $\frac{8}{43}$

Yahweh spoke to Moses and said, •'Stand clear of this community; I am going to destroy them here and now'. They threw themselves face downward on the ground. •Then Moses said to Aaron, 'Take the censer, fill it with fire from the altar, put incense in it and hurry to the community to perform the rite of atonement over them. The wrath has come down from Yahweh and the plague has begun.' •Aaron did as Moses said and ran among the assembly, but the plague was already at work among them. He put in the incense and performed the rite of atonement over the people. •Then he stood between the living and the dead, and the plague stopped. •There were fourteen thousand seven hundred victims of that plague, not counting those who died because of Korah. •Then Aaron came back to Moses at the Tent of Meeting; the plague had been halted.
$\frac{9.10}{44,45}$ $\frac{11}{46}$ $\frac{12}{47}$ $\frac{13}{48}$ $\frac{14}{49}$ $\frac{15}{50}$

Aaron's branch

Yahweh spoke to Moses and said, •'Tell the sons of Israel to give you a branch, one for each patriarchal family; let their leaders together give you twelve branches for their patriarchal families. Write the name of each on his branch; and on the branch of Levi write the name of Aaron, because the leader of the families of Levi must have a branch too. •Then put them in the Tent of Meeting before the Testimony, the place where I meet you. •The man whose branch sprouts will be the one I have chosen; this is how I shall put an end to the complaints that the sons of Israel make against you.'
$\frac{16,17}{1,2}$ $\frac{18}{3}$ $\frac{19}{4}$ $\frac{20}{5}$

Moses spoke to the sons of Israel, and all their leaders gave him one branch each, twelve branches in all for their patriarchal families; Aaron's branch was among them. •Moses placed them before Yahweh in the Tent of the Testimony. On the following day Moses came to the Tent of the Testimony and there, already sprouting, was Aaron's branch, standing for the House of Levi. Buds had opened, flowers had blossomed, and almonds had already ripened. •Moses took all the branches away from before Yahweh and brought them back to all the sons of Israel; they examined them and each one took back his own branch.
$\frac{21}{6}$ $\frac{22}{7}$ $\frac{23}{8}$ $\frac{24}{9}$

Then Yahweh said to Moses, 'Put back Aaron's branch before the Testimony, where it will have its prescribed place, a sign to these rebels. It will stop them complaining to me any more, and they will not die.' •Moses did as Yahweh had ordered. That is what he did.
$\frac{25}{10}$ $\frac{26}{11}$

Atonement: the function of the priesthood

The sons of Israel said to Moses, 'We are lost! We are dead men! We are all dead men! •Anyone who goes near the tabernacle of Yahweh with an offering will die. Are we to be doomed to the last man?'
$\frac{27}{12}$ $\frac{28}{13}$

18 Then Yahweh said to Aaron:
'You and your sons, and your whole family shall bear the burden of transgressions against the sanctuary. You and your sons with you shall bear the burden of the transgressions of your priesthood. •Let your brothers of the branch of Levi, your father's tribe, come with you too. They are to join you and
1

2

3 serve you, yourselves and your sons, before the Tent of the Testimony. •They are
to be at your service and the service of the whole Tent. Provided they do not come
near the sacred vessels or the altar, they will be in no more danger of death
4 than you. •They are to join you, they are to take charge of the Tent of Meeting for
5 the entire ministry of the Tent, and no layman shall come near you. •You must
take charge of the sanctuary and charge of the altar, and the wrath will never
6 again fall on the sons of Israel. •I myself have chosen your brothers, the Levites,
from among the sons of Israel as a gift to you. As 'oblates' they will belong
7 to Yahweh, to serve at the Tent of Meeting. •You and your sons will undertake
the priestly duties in all that concerns the altar and all that lies behind the veil.*
You will perform the liturgy, the duties of which I entrust to your priesthood.
But the layman who comes near shall die.'

The priests' portion

8   Yahweh said to Aaron:
'I myself have given you charge of all that is set aside for me. Everything that
the sons of Israel consecrate I give to you as your portion, as well as to your sons,
9 by perpetual ordinance. •This is what shall be yours of the most holy things, of
the consecrated food: every offering that the sons of Israel give back to me,
whether it be an oblation or a sacrifice for sin or a sacrifice of reparation, is a
10 thing most holy; it shall belong to you and your sons. •You may eat these most
holy things. Every male may eat them. You are to count them sacred.
11   'To you also shall belong whatever is set aside from the offerings of the sons
of Israel to be held out with the gesture of offering; this I give to you, as well as
to your sons and daughters, by perpetual ordinance. Every undefiled person in
12 your house may eat it. •All the best of the oil, all the best of the wine and wheat,
13 the first-fruits made over by them to Yahweh, these I give to you. •All the first
produce of their land which they bring to Yahweh shall be yours. Every undefiled
14 person in your house may eat them. •All in Israel on which the ban is laid shall
15 be yours. •Every first-born brought to Yahweh shall be yours, of all living
creatures, whether man or beast; nevertheless you must redeem the first-born of
16 man, and you must redeem the first-born of an unclean beast. •You must redeem
it in the month in which it is born at the price of five shekels, each of sanctuary
17 weight—which is twenty gerahs. •The first-born of cow, sheep and goat, these
alone you shall not redeem. They are holy: you must sprinkle their blood on the
18 altar and burn the fat as a burnt offering, an appeasing fragrance for Yahweh; •the
meat shall be yours, together with the breast that has been presented with the
19 gesture of offering, and the right thigh. •All that the sons of Israel set aside for
Yahweh from the holy things, this I give to you, and to your sons and daughters,
by perpetual ordinance. This is a covenant of salt for ever before Yahweh, for you
and your descendants after you.'

The Levites' portion

20   Yahweh said to Aaron:
'You shall have no inheritance in their land, no portion of it among them shall
be yours. It is I who will be your portion and your inheritance among the sons
of Israel.
21   See, to the sons of Levi I give as their inheritance all the tithes collected in
Israel, in return for their services, for the ministry they render in the Tent of
22 Meeting. •The sons of Israel must no longer go near the Tent of Meeting; they
23 would be burdened with sin and die. •To Levi belongs the ministry of the Tent
of Meeting, and the Levites will bear the burden of their sin. This is a perpetual
law for all your descendants: the Levites are to have no inheritance among the sons
24 of Israel. •The tithe that the sons of Israel set aside for Yahweh, I give the Levites

---

18 a. The curtain screening the Most Holy Place.

for their inheritance. For this reason I have told them that they are to have no
inheritance among the sons of Israel.'

Tithes

Yahweh spoke to Moses and said, •'You are to say to the Levites: 25
                                                                       26
"When you receive the tithe from the sons of Israel which they must pay you
and which I am giving you as your inheritance, out of this you are to set aside a
portion for Yahweh, a tithe of the tithe. •This is to take the place of the portion 27
set aside that is due from you, like the corn from the threshing-floor and new wine
from the press. •Thus you too will set aside a portion for Yahweh, of all the 28
tithes you receive from the sons of Israel. You will give what you have set aside
for Yahweh to Aaron the priest. •Out of all the gifts you receive you will set 29
aside a portion for Yahweh. From the best of all these things you will set aside
the sacred portion."

'You are to say to them, "After you have set aside the best, all these gifts shall, 30
for the Levites, take the place of the produce of the threshing-floor and of the
wine press. •You may consume them anywhere, you and your people: this is 31
your payment for serving in the Tent of Meeting. •You will not incur the burden 32
of any sin on this account, once you have set aside the best; you will not be
profaning the things consecrated by the sons of Israel, and you will not die." '

The ashes of the red heifer^a

19 Yahweh spoke to Moses and Aaron. He said: 1
'This is a statute of the Law which Yahweh has prescribed. Say this to the 2
sons of Israel,

'They are to bring you a red heifer without fault or blemish, one that has
never borne the yoke. •You will give it to Eleazar the priest. It must be taken 3
outside the camp and slaughtered in his presence. •Then Eleazar the priest is to 4
take some of the victim's blood on his finger, and sprinkle this blood seven times
towards the entrance to the Tent of Meeting. •The heifer must then be burned in 5
his presence: hide, flesh, blood, and the dung too, must be burnt. •Then the 6
priest is to take cedar wood, hyssop and cochineal red, and throw them on the
fire where the heifer is burning. •Then he must wash his clothing and bathe his 7
body in water; after which he may go back to the camp, though he will remain
unclean until evening. •The man who has burnt the heifer must wash his 8
clothing and bathe his body in water and will remain unclean until evening. •The 9
man who gathers up the ashes of the heifer must be ritually clean; he will deposit
them outside the camp, in a clean place. They must be kept for the ritual use of the
community of the sons of Israel for making lustral water; it is a sacrifice for sin.
The man who has gathered up the ashes of the heifer must wash his clothing 10
and will remain unclean until evening. For the sons of Israel as for the stranger
living among them, this will be a perpetual law.

A case of uncleanness

'Anyone who touches a corpse, of any person whatsoever, shall be unclean 11
for seven days. •He shall purify himself with these waters on the third and the 12
seventh day, and he will be clean; but if he does not purify himself on the third
and the seventh day he will not be clean. •Anyone who touches a dead person, the 13
body of a man that has died, and has not purified himself, defiles the tabernacle
of Yahweh; such a man must be outlawed from Israel because the lustral waters
have not flowed over him; he is unclean, and his uncleanness remains in him.

This is the law when a man dies in a tent. Anyone who goes into the tent, or 14
anyone who is already there, shall be unclean for seven days. •Equally unclean 15
also shall be every open vessel that has not been closed with a lid or fastening.

Anyone in the open country who touches a man who has been killed, or a man 16
who has died, or human bones or a tomb, shall be unclean for seven days.

The ritual of lustral water

17   'For a man thus unclean, some of the ashes must be taken from the victim burnt as a sacrifice for sin. Spring water must be poured on them, in a vessel.
18   Then one who is ritually clean shall take hyssop and dip it in the water. He must then sprinkle the tent, all the vessels and everyone there, and also the man who has touched the bones, or the body of the person, whether he was killed or died
19   of natural causes, or the tomb. •The man who is clean must sprinkle the unclean on the third and the seventh day, and on the seventh day he will have freed him from his sin. The man who is unclean must then wash his clothing and bathe
20   himself in water, and by evening he will be clean. •If an unclean man fails to purify himself in this way, he must be cut off from the community, for he would defile the sanctuary of Yahweh. The lustral waters have not flowed over him, and he is unclean.
21   'This is to be a perpetual law for them. The person who sprinkles the lustral water must wash his clothing, and the person who touches these waters shall be
22   unclean until evening. •Anything that an unclean person touches shall be unclean, and anyone who touches it shall be unclean until evening.'

VII. FROM KADESH TO MOAB

The waters of Meribah

1   **20** The sons of Israel, the whole community, arrived in the first month at the desert of Zin. The people settled at Kadesh. It was there that Miriam died and was buried.
2   There was no water for the community, and they were all united against Moses
3   and Aaron. •The people challenged Moses: 'We would rather have died,' they
4   said 'as our brothers died before Yahweh! •Why did you bring the assembly of Yahweh into this wilderness, only to let us die here, ourselves and our cattle?
5   Why did you lead us out of Egypt, only to bring us to this wretched place? It is a place unfit for sowing, it has no figs, no vines, no pomegranates, and there is not even water to drink!'
6   Leaving the assembly, Moses and Aaron went to the door of the Tent of Meeting. They threw themselves face downward on the ground, and the glory
7   of Yahweh appeared to them. •Yahweh spoke to Moses and said, •'Take the
8   branch and call the community together, you and your brother Aaron. Then, in full view of them, order this rock to give water. You will make water flow for them out of the rock, and provide drink for the community and their cattle.'
9   Moses took up the branch from before Yahweh, as he had directed him. •Then
10   Moses and Aaron called the assembly together in front of the rock and addressed them, 'Listen now, you rebels. Shall we make water gush from this rock for
11   you?' •And Moses raised his hand and struck the rock twice with the branch; water gushed in abundance, and the community drank and their cattle too.

The punishment of Moses and Aaron

12   Then Yahweh said to Moses and Aaron, 'Because you did not believe that I could proclaim my holiness in the eyes of the sons of Israel, you shall not lead this assembly into the land I am giving them'.[a]
13   These are the waters of Meribah, where the sons of Israel challenged Yahweh and he proclaimed his holiness.

---

19 a. In this rite an ancient, half-magical custom is given legal status by assimilating it to an atonement sacrifice for sin.
20 a. No explanation of the offence of Moses and Aaron is given here; but in Dt 1:37 it is the abandonment of the campaign against Canaan that brings on this punishment, and it is possible that this verse should relate to ch. 14 and not to the Meribah incident.

Edom refuses right of way

Moses sent messengers from Kadesh, 'To the king of Edom. A message 14
from your brother Israel. You know well enough the extremity to which we have
been reduced. •Our ancestors went down into Egypt, and there we stayed for a 15
long time. But the Egyptians treated us badly, as they did our ancestors. •We 16
cried to Yahweh. He listened to us and sent an angel to bring us out of Egypt.
Now we are here at Kadesh, a town on the borders of your territory. •We ask 17
permission to pass through your land. We will not cross any fields or vineyards;
we will not drink any water from the wells; we will keep to the king's highway
without turning to right or left until we are clear of your frontiers.' •Edom 18
answered, 'You shall not pass through my country; if you do, I will come out to
attack you'. •The answer of the sons of Israel was, 'We will keep to the high 19
road; if we use any of your water for myself and my cattle, I will pay for it.
I am asking only to pass through on foot.' •Edom replied, 'You shall not pass', 20
and Edom marched out to meet them with many men and in great force. •At 21
Edom's refusal to allow Israel a passage through his territory, Israel turned away.

The death of Aaron

They set out from Kadesh, and the whole community of the sons of Israel 22
came to Mount Hor. •Yahweh spoke to Moses and Aaron at Mount Hor, on the 23
frontier of the land of Edom.[b] He said, •'Aaron must be gathered to his people: 24
he is not to enter the land that I am giving to the sons of Israel, since you disobeyed
my order at the waters of Meribah. •Take Aaron and Eleazar his son, and bring 25
them up Mount Hor. •There, strip Aaron of his garments and put them on 26
Eleazar his son, and Aaron will be gathered to his people: he is to die there.'

Moses did as Yahweh ordered. In the sight of the whole community they 27
went up Mount Hor. •Moses stripped Aaron of his garments and put them on 28
Eleazar his son; and Aaron died there on top of the mountain. Then Moses and
Eleazar came back down the mountain. •The whole community saw that Aaron 29
had died, and all the House of Israel wept for Aaron for thirty days.

The capture of Hormah

21 The king of Arad,[a] a Canaanite living in the Negeb, learned that Israel was 1
coming by way of Atharim. He attacked Israel and took some prisoners.
Israel then made this vow to Yahweh, 'If you deliver this people into my power, 2
I will lay their towns under ban'. •Yahweh heard the voice of Israel and delivered 3
the Canaanites into their power. And they laid them under ban, both them and
their towns. This place was given the name Hormah.

The bronze serpent

They left Mount Hor by the road to the Sea of Suph,[b] to skirt the land of 4
Edom. On the way the people lost patience. •They spoke against God and against 5
Moses, 'Why did you bring us out of Egypt to die in this wilderness? For there
is neither bread nor water here; we are sick of this unsatisfying food.'

At this God sent fiery serpents among the people; their bite brought death 6
to many in Israel. •The people came and said to Moses, 'We have sinned by 7
speaking against Yahweh and against you. Intercede for us with Yahweh to save
us from these serpents.' Moses interceded for the people, •and Yahweh answered 8
him, 'Make a fiery serpent and put it on a standard. If anyone is bitten and looks
at it, he shall live.' •So Moses fashioned a bronze serpent which he put on 9
a standard, and if anyone was bitten by a serpent, he looked at the bronze serpent
and lived.

By stages to Transjordania

The sons of Israel set out and camped at Oboth. •Then they left Oboth and 10
camped at Iye-abarim, in the wilderness that borders Moab, towards the sunrise. 11

¹²₁₃ They set out from there and camped in the wadi Zered. •They set out from there and camped beyond the Arnon...ᶜ

This wadi in the desert begins in the land of the Amorites. For the Arnon is
14 the frontier of Moab, between the Moabites and the Amorites. •Hence it is written in the Book of the Wars of Yahweh:

15   ...Waheb by Suphah and the wadi Arnon
        and the slope of the ravine
        that runs down to the site of Ar
        and leans over the frontier of Moab...

16 and from there they went on to Beer...ᵈ

It was of the well here that Yahweh had said to Moses, 'Call the people
17 together and I will give them water'. •Then it was that Israel sang this song:

        'For the well.
        Sing out for the well
18   that was sunk by the princes
        and dug by the leaders of the people
        with the sceptre, with their staves.'

19 . . . . . and from Beer to Mattanah, •and from Mattanah to Nahaliel, and from
20 Nahaliel to Bamoth, •and from Bamoth to the valley that gives on to the country of Moab, towards the heights of Pisgah which marks the edge of the desert and looks down on it.

The conquest of Transjordania

²¹₂₂ •Israel sent messengers to say to Sihon, king of the Amorites, •'I wish to pass through your land. We will not stray into fields or vineyards; we will not drink any water from the wells; we will keep to the king's highway until we are clear of your frontiers.'

23 But Sihon would not give Israel leave to pass through his land. He gathered all his people, marched into the desert to meet Israel, and reached Jahaz, where
24 he gave battle to Israel. •Israel struck him down with the edge of the sword and conquered his country from the Arnon to the Jabbok, as far as the sons of Ammon, for Jazer was the Ammonite frontier.

25 Israel took all these towns, and occupied all the Amorite towns, Heshbon
26 and all the towns under its jurisdiction, •Heshbon being the capital of Sihon, king of the Amorites. It was the same Sihon who had waged war on the first king
27 of Moab and captured all his territory as far as the Arnon. •Hence the poets sing:

        Courage, Heshbon!
        Well built and well founded,
        city of Sihon!
28   For a fire came out of Heshbon,
        a flame from the city of Sihon,
        it devoured Ar of Moab,
        it engulfed the heights of the Arnon.
29   Woe to you, Moab!
        You are lost, people of Chemosh!
        He has turned his sons into fugitives,
        his daughters into captives
        for Sihon, king of the Amorites.
30   Heshbon has destroyed

---

b. Edom included Mount Seir and the plateau east of the Arabah.
21 a. A town in southern Palestine.   b. Towards the Gulf of Aqaba.   c. This sentence is continued in v.16. A historical note on the old frontier has been inserted.   d. The sentence is continued at the end of v.18, after a parenthetical note explaining the name *Beer*, a well.

> the little children as far as Dibon,
> the women as far as Nophah,
> the men as far as Medeba.

Israel settled in the land of the Amorites. •Moses sent men to reconnoitre 31 32
Jazer, and Israel took it and all the towns in its jurisdiction and evicted the
Amorites who dwelt there.

Then they turned and marched in the direction of Bashan. Og king of Bashan 33
marched out to meet them with all his people to give battle at Edrei. •Yahweh 34
said to Moses, 'Do not be afraid of him, for I have given him into your power, him
and all his people and his country. Deal with him as you dealt with Sihon, king
of the Amorites, who lived in Heshbon.' •So they defeated him, his sons and all 35
his people; not one of them escaped. And they took possession of his country.

22 Then the sons of Israel set out and pitched their camp in the plains of 1
Moab, beyond the Jordan opposite Jericho.[a]

The king of Moab appeals to Balaam[b]

Balak son of Zippor saw all that Israel had done to the Amorites, •and Moab 2 3
was seized with panic before this people because of their immense number.

Moab was afraid of the sons of Israel; •he said to the elders of Midian, 'Here 4
is a horde now cropping everything round us as an ox crops the grass of the fields'.

Now Balak son of Zippor was king of Moab at the time. •He sent messengers 5
to summon Balaam son of Beor, at Pethor on the river,[c] in the land of the sons
of Amaw, saying, 'Look how this people coming from Egypt has overrun the
whole countryside; they have settled at my door. •Come, please, and curse this 6
people for me, for they are stronger than I am. We may then be able to defeat
them and drive them out of the country. For this I know: the man you bless is
blessed, the man you curse is accursed.'

The elders of Moab and the elders of Midian set out, taking the fee for the 7
divination with them. They found Balaam and gave him Balak's message. •He 8
said to them, 'Stay the night here, and I will answer as Yahweh directs me.'
So the chiefs of Moab stayed with Balaam. •God came to Balaam and said, 9
'Who are these men staying with you?' •Balaam gave God this answer, 'Balak 10
son of Zippor has sent me this message, •"Look how this people coming from 11
Egypt has overrun the whole countryside. Come and curse them for me; I may
then be able to defeat them and drive them out." ' •God said to Balaam, 'You are 12
not to go with them. You are not to curse this people, for they are blessed.'
In the morning Balaam rose and said to the chiefs sent by Balak, 'Go back to 13
your country, for Yahweh will not let me go with you'. •So the chiefs of Moab 14
rose and returned to Balak and said, 'Balaam would not come with us'.

And again Balak sent chiefs, more numerous and more renowned than the 15
first. •They came to Balaam and said, 'A message from Balak son of Zippor, 16
"Do not refuse, I beg you, to come to me. •I will load you with honours and do 17
whatever you say. Come, I beg you, and curse this people for me." ' •Balaam 18
answered the envoys of Balak, 'Even if Balak gave me his house full of silver and
gold, I could not go against the order of Yahweh my God in anything, great
or small. •Now please stay the night here yourselves, and I will learn what else 19
Yahweh has to tell me.' •God came to Balaam during the night and said to him, 20
'Have not these men come to summon you? Get up, go with them. But you
must do nothing except what I tell you.' •In the morning Balaam rose and 21
saddled his she-donkey and set out with the chiefs of Moab.

Balaam's donkey

His going kindled the wrath of Yahweh, and the angel of Yahweh took his 22
stand on the road to bar his way. He was riding his donkey and his two servants
were with him. •Now the donkey saw the angel of Yahweh standing on the road, 23

a drawn sword in his hand, and she turned off the road and made off across country. But Balaam beat her to turn her back on to the road.

24 The angel of Yahweh then took his stand on a narrow path among the
25 vineyards, with a wall to the right and a wall to the left. •The donkey saw the angel of Yahweh and brushed against the wall, grazing Balaam's foot. Balaam beat her again.

26 The angel of Yahweh moved and took up his stand in a place so narrow that
27 there was no room to pass, right or left. •When the donkey saw the angel of Yahweh, she lay down under Balaam. Balaam flew into a rage and beat her with his stick.

28 Then Yahweh opened the mouth of the donkey, who said to Balaam, 'What
29 have I done to you? Why beat me three times like this?' •Balaam answered the donkey, 'Because you are playing the fool with me! If I had had a sword in my
30 hand, I would have killed you by now.' •The donkey said to Balaam, 'Am I not your donkey, and have I not been your mount from your youth? In all this time, have I ever failed to serve you?' He answered, 'No'.

31 Then Yahweh opened the eyes of Balaam. He saw the angel of Yahweh standing on the road, a drawn sword in his hand; and he bowed down and fell
32 prostrate on his face. •And the angel of Yahweh said to him, 'Why did you beat your donkey three times like that? I myself had come to bar your way; while I am
33 here your road is blocked. •The donkey saw me and turned aside from me three times. You are lucky she did turn aside, or I should have killed you by now,
34 though I would have spared her.' •Balaam answered the angel of Yahweh, 'I have sinned. I did not know you were standing in my path. However, if you
35 are angry with me, I will go back.' •The angel of Yahweh answered Balaam, 'Go with these men, but only say what I tell you to say.' So Balaam went with the chiefs sent by Balak.

Balaam and Balak

36 Balak learned that Balaam was coming and went out to meet him, in the direction of Ar of Moab, at the Arnon frontier on the country's furthest bound-
37 ary. •Balak said to Balaam, 'Did I not send messengers to summon you? Why did you not come to me? Did you think, perhaps, I could confer no honours on you?'
38 Balaam answered Balak, 'Here I am at your side. May I make myself clear to you now? The word that God puts into my mouth, this I shall speak.'
39 Balaam set out with Balak. They came to Kiriath-huzoth. •Balak sacrificed
40 oxen and sheep, and offered portions to Balaam and the chiefs who were with
41 him. •Next morning Balak took Balaam and brought him up to Bamoth-baal,
1 from where he could see the end of the camp. 23 Balaam said to Balak, 'Build
2 me seven altars, and bring here to me seven bulls and seven rams'. •Balak did as Balaam asked and he offered a holocaust of one bull and one ram on each
3 altar. •Balaam then said to Balak, 'Stand beside your holocausts. I will go; perhaps Yahweh will allow me to meet him. Whatever he shows me I shall tell you.' And he withdrew to a bare hill.

The oracles of Balaam

4 God came to meet Balaam, who said to him, 'I have prepared the seven altars
5 and offered a holocaust of one bull and one ram on each altar'. •Yahweh then put a word into his mouth and said to him, 'Go back to Balak and that is what
6 you must say to him'. •So Balaam went back to him, and found him still standing
7 beside his holocaust, with all the chiefs of Moab. •Then he declaimed his poem. He said:

22 a. Moab was bounded on the south by the Zered; on the north the Moabites had been driven back to the Arnon by the Amorites.   b. In this story there are materials from two different traditions, not always consistent with one another.   c. Euphrates.

'Balak brought me from Aram,
the king of Moab from the hills of Kedem,
"Come, curse Jacob for me;
come, denounce Israel".
How shall I curse one when God does not curse?   8
How shall I denounce when God does not denounce?
Yes, from the top of the crags I see him,   9
from the hills I observe him.
See, a people dwelling apart,
not reckoned among the nations.
Who can count the dust of Jacob?   10
Who can number the cloud of Israel?
May I die the death of the just!
May my end be one with theirs!'

Balak said to Balaam, 'What have you done to me? I brought you to curse 11
my enemies, and you heap blessings on them!' •Balaam answered, 'Am I not 12
obliged to say what Yahweh puts into my mouth?' •Balak said to him, 'Come 13
with me to another place. What you see from here is only the fringe of this
people, you do not see them all. Curse them for me over there.' •He led him to 14
the Field of Spies, towards the summit of Pisgah. There he built seven altars
and offered a holocaust of one bull and one ram on each altar. •Balaam said to 15
Balak, 'Stand beside these holocausts. I will wait over there.' •God came to 16
meet Balaam, he put a word into his mouth and said to him, 'Go back to Balak
and that is what you must say to him'. •So Balaam went to him, and found him 17
still standing beside his holocaust and all the chiefs of Moab with him. 'What
did Yahweh say?' Balak asked him. •Then Balaam declaimed his poem. He said: 18

'Arise, Balak, and listen,
give ear to me, son of Zippor.
God is no man that he should lie,   19
no son of Adam to draw back.
Is it his to say and not to do,
to speak and not fulfil?
The charge laid on me is to bless,   20
I shall bless and not take it back.
I have seen no evil in Jacob   21
I marked no suffering in Israel.
Yahweh his God is with him;
in him sounds the royal acclaim.
God brings him out of Egypt,   22
he is like the wild ox's horns to him.
There is no omen against Jacob,   23
no divination against Israel.
Though men say to Jacob,
say to Israel, "What wonder has God to show?"
here is a people like a lioness rising,   24
poised like a lion to spring;
not lying down till he has devoured his prey
and drunk the blood of his victims.'

Balak said to Balaam, 'Very well! Do not curse them. But at least do not bless 25
them!' •Balaam answered Balak, 'Have I not told you: whatever Yahweh says, 26
I must do?'

Balak said to Balaam, 'Come then, let me take you somewhere else. From 27
there perhaps it will please God to curse them.' •So Balak led Balaam to the 28
summit of Peor, dominating the desert. •Then Balaam said to Balak, 'Build me 29

30 seven altars here and find me seven bulls and seven rams'. •Balak did as Balaam asked, and offered a holocaust of one bull and one ram on each altar.

1 **24** Balaam then saw that it pleased Yahweh to bless Israel. He did not go as
2 before to seek omens but turned towards the wilderness. •Raising his eyes Balaam saw Israel, encamped by tribes; the spirit of God came on him
3 and he declaimed his poem. He said:

> 'The oracle of Balaam son of Beor,
> the oracle of the man with far-seeing eyes,
4 > the oracle of one who hears the word of God.
> He sees what Shaddai makes him see,
> receives the divine answer, and his eyes are opened.
5 > How fair are your tents, O Jacob!
> How fair your dwellings, Israel!
6 > Like valleys that stretch afar,
> like gardens by the banks of a river,
> like aloes planted by Yahweh,
> like cedars beside the waters!
7 > A hero arises from their stock,
> he reigns over countless peoples.
> His king is greater than Agag,
> his majesty is exalted.
8 > God brings him out of Egypt,
> he is like the wild ox's horns to him.
> He *a* feeds on the carcase of his enemies,
> and breaks their bones in pieces.
9 > He has crouched, he has lain down,
> like a lion, like a lioness;
> who dare rouse him?
> Blessed be those who bless you,
> and accursed be those who curse you!'

10 Balak flew into a rage with Balaam. He beat his hands together and said to Balaam, 'I brought you to curse my enemies, and you bless them three times over!
11 Be off with you, and go home. I promised to load you with honours. Yahweh
12 himself has deprived you of them.' •Balaam answered Balak, 'Did I not tell the
13 messengers you sent me: •Even if Balak gave me his house full of gold and silver I could not go against the order of Yahweh and do anything of my own
14 accord, good or evil; what Yahweh says is what I will say. •Now that I am going back to my own folk, let me warn you what this people will do to your people,
15 in time to come.' •Then he declaimed his poem. He said:

> 'The oracle of Balaam son of Beor,
> the oracle of the man with far-seeing eyes,
16 > the oracle of one who hears the word of God,
> of one who knows the knowledge of the Most High.
> He sees what Shaddai makes him see,
> receives the divine answer, and his eyes are opened.
17 > I see him—but not in the present,
> I behold him—but not close at hand:
> a star from Jacob takes the leadership,
> a sceptre arises from Israel.
> It crushes the brows of Moab
> the skulls of all the sons of Sheth. *b*
18 > Edom becomes a conquered land;

24 a. Israel.   b. The Bedouin tribes. The poem goes on to enumerate those of Israel's enemies who lived on the borders of Canaan.

a conquered land is Seir.
Israel exerts his strength,   19
Jacob dominates his enemies
and destroys the fugitives from Ar.'

Balaam looked on Amalek and declaimed his poem. He said: 20

'Amalek, first among the nations!
But his posterity shall perish for ever.'

Then he looked on the Kenites and declaimed his poem. He said: 21

'Your house was firm, Kain,
and your nest^c perched high in the rock.
But the nest belongs to Beor;   22
how long will you be Asshur's captive?'

Then he looked on Og^d and declaimed his poem. He said: 23

'The Sea-people^e gather in the north,
ships from the coasts of Kittim.   24
They bear down on Asshur, they bear down on Eber;
he too shall perish for ever.'

Then Balaam rose, left and went home. Balak too went his way.   25

Israel at Peor

25 Israel settled at Shittim. The people gave themselves over to debauchery 1
with the daughters of Moab. •These invited them to the sacrifices of their 2
gods, and the people ate and bowed down before their gods. •With Israel thus 3
committed to the Baal of Peor, the anger of Yahweh blazed out against them.

Yahweh said to Moses, 'Take all the leaders of the people. Impale them for 4
Yahweh, here in the sun; then the burning anger of Yahweh will turn away from
Israel.' •Moses said to the judges in Israel, 'Every one of you must put to death 5
those of his people who have committed themselves to the Baal of Peor'.

A man of the sons of Israel came along, bringing the Midianite woman into 6
his family, under the very eyes of Moses and the whole community of the sons
of Israel as they wept at the door of the Tent of Meeting. •When he saw this, 7
Phinehas the priest, son of Eleazar son of Aaron, stood up and left the assembly,
seized a lance, •followed the Israelite into the alcove, and there ran them both 8
through, the Israelite and the woman, right through the groin. And the plague
that had struck the sons of Israel was arrested. •In the plague twenty-four 9
thousand of them had died.

Yahweh spoke to Moses and said, •'Phinehas the priest, son of Eleazar son $^{10}_{11}$
of Aaron, has turned my wrath away from the sons of Israel, because he was the
only one among them to have the same zeal as I have; for this I did not make an
end, in my zeal, of the sons of Israel. •Proclaim this, therefore: To him I now 12
grant my covenant of peace. •For him and for his descendants after him, this 13
covenant shall ensure the priesthood for ever. In reward for his zeal for his God,
he shall have the right to perform the ritual of atonement over the sons of Israel.'

The Israelite who was killed (he who had been killed with the Midianite 14
woman) was called Zimri son of Salu, leader of one of the patriarchal Houses of
Simeon. •The woman, the Midianite who was killed, was called Cozbi, daughter 15
of Zur, chief of a clan, of a patriarchal House in Midian.

Yahweh spoke to Moses and said, •'Harry the Midianites and strike them $^{16}_{17}$
down, •for they have harassed you with their guile in the Peor affair and in the 18
affair of Cozbi their sister, daughter of a prince of Midian, the woman who
was killed the day the plague came on account of Peor'.

VIII. FURTHER LEGISLATION

The census

¹⁹₁ After this plague, **26** Yahweh spoke to Moses and to Eleazar son of Aaron, the priest. He said:

² 'Take a census of all the community of the sons of Israel, by families: all those of twenty years and over, fit to bear arms'.

³ So Moses and Eleazar the priest spoke to the people in the plains of Moab, near the Jordan opposite Jericho. They counted:

⁴ (As Yahweh had ordered Moses and the sons of Israel on their coming out of the land of Egypt:) Men of twenty years and over:

⁵ Reuben, the first-born of Israel. The sons of Reuben: for Hanoch, the ⁶ Hanochite clan; for Pallu, the Palluite clan; •for Hezron, the Hezronite clan; ⁷ for Carmi, the Carmite clan. •These were the Reubenite clans. They numbered forty-three thousand seven hundred and thirty men.

⁸₉ The sons of Pallu: Eliab. •The sons of Eliab: Nemuel, Dathan and Abiram. These two, Dathan and Abiram, men of repute in the community, were the ones who challenged Moses and Aaron; they belonged to the followers of Korah ¹⁰ who challenged Yahweh. •The earth opened its mouth and swallowed them (Korah perished with his followers), when fire consumed the two hundred and ¹¹ fifty men. They were a sign. •The sons of Korah did not perish.

¹² The sons of Simeon by clans; for Nemuel, the Nemuelite clan; for Jamin, ¹³ the Jaminite clan; for Jachin, the Jachinite clan; •for Zerah, the Zerahite clan; ¹⁴ for Shaul, the Shaulite clan. •These were the Simeonite clans. They numbered twenty-two thousand two hundred men.

¹⁵ The sons of Gad by clans: for Zephon, the Zephonite clan; for Haggi, the ¹⁶ Haggite clan; for Shuni, the Shunite clan; •for Ozni, the Oznite clan; for Eri, ¹⁷₁₈ the Erite clan; •for Arod, the Arodite clan; for Areli, the Arelite clan. •These were the clans of the sons of Gad. They numbered forty thousand five hundred men.

¹⁹ The sons of Judah: Er and Onan. Er and Onan died in the land of Canaan. ²⁰ The sons of Judah became clans: for Shelah, the Shelanite clan; for Perez, the ²¹ Perezzite clan; for Zerah, the Zerahite clan. •The sons of Perez were: for Hezron, ²² the Hezronite clan; for Hamul, the Hamulite clan. •These were the clans of Judah. They numbered seventy-six thousand five hundred men.

²³ The sons of Issachar, by clans: for Tola, the Tolaite clan; for Puvah, the ²⁴ Puvite clan; •for Jashub, the Jashubite clan; for Shimron, the Shimronite clan. ²⁵ These were the clans of Issachar. They numbered sixty-four thousand three hundred men.

²⁶ The sons of Zebulun by clans: for Sered, the Seredite clan; for Elon, the ²⁷ Elonite clan; for Jahleel, the Jahleelite clan. •These were the clans of Zebulun. They numbered sixty thousand five hundred men.

²⁸ The sons of Joseph, by clans: Manasseh and Ephraim.

²⁹ The sons of Manasseh: for Machir, the Machirite clan; Machir was the father ³⁰ of Gilead: for Gilead, the Gileadite clan. •These were the clans of Gilead; for ³¹ Iezer, the Iezerite clan; for Helek, the Helekite clan; •Asriel, the Asrielite clan; ³² Shechem, the Shechemite clan; •Shemida, the Shemidaite clan; Hepher, the ³³ Hepherite clan. •Zelophehad son of Hepher had no sons but only daughters; these are the names of Zelophehad's daughters: Mahlah, Noah, Hoglah, Milcah ³⁴ and Tirzah. •These were the clans of Manasseh. They numbered fifty-two thousand seven hundred men.

³⁵ These are the sons of Ephraim by clans: for Shuthelah, the Shuthelahite clan; ³⁶ for Becher, the Becherite clan; for Tahan, the Tahanite clan. •These are the sons

---

c. *Qen* means 'a nest'. The Kenites were nomads allied to the Midianites.   d. King of Bashan, the territory of the Asshurites.   e. Philistines and other invaders. Kittim includes Cyprus and the coastal region of the eastern Mediterranean.

of Shuthelah: for Eran, the Eranite clan. •These were the clans of Ephraim. 37
They numbered thirty-two thousand five hundred men.

These were the sons of Joseph, by clans.

The sons of Benjamin, by clans: for Bela, the Belaite clan; for Ashbel, the 38
Ashbelite clan: for Ahiram, the Ahiramite clan; •for Shephupham, the Shephu- 39
phamite clan; for Hupham, the Huphamite clan. •Bela had Ard and Naaman for 40
sons: for Ard, the Ardite clan; for Naaman, the Naamite clan. •These were the 41
sons of Benjamin by clans. They numbered forty-five thousand six hundred men.

These were the sons of Dan, by clans: for Shuham, the Shuhamite clan. 42
These were the sons of Dan, by clans. •All the Shuhamite clans numbered 43
sixty-four thousand four hundred men.

The sons of Asher, by clans: for Imnah the Imnite clan; for Ishvi, the Ishvite 44
clan; for Beriah, the Beriite clan. •For the sons of Beriah: for Heber, the Heberite 45
clan; for Malchiel, the Malchielite clan. •The daughter of Asher was called 46
Serah. •These were the clans of Asher. They numbered fifty-three thousand four 47
hundred men.

The sons of Naphtali, by clans: for Jahzeel, the Jahzeelite clan; for Guni, 48
the Gunite clan; •for Jezer, the Jezerite clan; for Shillem the Shillemite clan. 49
These were the clans of Naphtali grouped by clans. The sons of Naphtali 50
numbered forty-five thousand four hundred men.

The sons of Israel numbered in all six hundred and one thousand seven 51
hundred and thirty men.

Yahweh spoke to Moses and said, •'The land is to be shared out among $\substack{52 \\ 53}$
these as a heritage, according to the number of those inscribed. •To the large in 54
number you are to give a large area of land, to the small in number a small area;
to each the heritage will be in proportion to the number registered. •The dividing 55
of the land is, however, to be done by lot. Each is to receive his inheritance
according to the number of names in the patriarchal tribes; •the inheritance of 56
each tribe is to be divided by lot, each receiving in accordance with its larger or
smaller numbers.'

Census of the Levites

These are, by clans, the Levites that were registered: for Gershon, the 57
Gershonite clan; for Kohath, the Kohathite clan; for Merari, the Merarite clan.

These are the Levite clans: the Libnite clan, the Hebronite clan, the Mahlite 58
clan, the Mushite clan, the Korahite clan.

Kohath was the father of Amram. •The wife of Amram was called Jochebed 59
daughter of Levi, born to him in Egypt. To Amram she bore Aaron, Moses and
Miriam their sister. •Aaron was the father of Nadab and Abihu, Eleazar and 60
Ithamar. •Nadab and Abihu died when they brought unlawful fire before Yahweh. 61

Altogether there were registered twenty-three thousand males of one month 62
and over. They were not registered with the sons of Israel, having received no
inheritance among them.

These were the men registered by Moses and Eleazar the priest who took 63
this census of the sons of Israel in the plains of Moab, near the Jordan, opposite
Jericho. •Not one of them was among those whom Moses and Aaron had 64
registered when they numbered the sons of Israel in the wilderness of Sinai;
for Yahweh had told them that these were to die in the wilderness and without 65
anyone remaining, except Caleb son of Jephunneh and Joshua son of Nun.

The inheritance of daughters

27 Then there came forward the daughters of Zelophehad. He was the son of 1
Hepher son of Gilead, son of Machir, son of Manasseh; he belonged to
the clans of Manasseh son of Joseph. These are the names of his daughters:
Mahlah, Noah, Hoglah, Milcah and Tirzah. •They appeared before Moses, 2
before Eleazar the priest, and before the leaders and the whole community,

3 at the entrance to the Tent of Meeting, and said, •'Our father died in the desert. He was not one of the company of those who conspired against Yahweh, Korah's
4 party; it was for his own sin that he died without sons. •Why must our father's name be lost to his clan? Since he had no son, give us some property among our father's kinsmen.'
5
6 Moses took their case before Yahweh, •and Yahweh spoke to Moses. He
7 said, •'The daughters of Zelophehad have a just case. Give them a property for their inheritance among their father's kinsmen; pass on to them their father's
8 inheritance. •Then say this to the sons of Israel, "If a man dies without sons,
9 his inheritance is to pass to his daughter. •If he has no daughter, the inheritance
10 is to go to his brothers. •If he has no brothers, it is to go to his father's brothers.
11 If his father has no brothers, it is to go to the member of his clan who is most nearly related: he is to take possession. This shall be a statutory ordinance for the sons of Israel, as Yahweh has ordered Moses." '

Joshua the head of the community

12 Yahweh said to Moses, 'Climb this mountain of the Abarim range, and look
13 on the land I have given to the sons of Israel. •After you have seen it, you will
14 be gathered to your people, as Aaron your brother was. •For you both rebelled in the wilderness of Zin when the community complained against me, when I ordered you to proclaim my holiness before their eyes by means of the water.' (These are the waters of Meribah of Kadesh, in the wilderness of Zin.)
15
16 Moses said to Yahweh, •'May Yahweh, God of the spirits that give life to
17 all living creatures, appoint a leader for this community, •to be at their head in all they do, a man who will lead them out and bring them in, so that the
18 community of Yahweh may not be like sheep without a shepherd'. •Yahweh answered Moses, 'Take Joshua son of Nun, a man in whom the spirit
19 dwells. Lay your hands on him. •Then bring him before Eleazar the priest
20 and the whole community, to give him your orders in their presence •and to give him a share of your authority, so that the whole community of the sons of
21 Israel may obey him. •He shall present himself to Eleazar the priest, who is to make inquiry for him before Yahweh, according to the rite of the Urim. At his command all the sons of Israel shall go out and come in with him, the whole community.'
22 Moses did as Yahweh had ordered. He took Joshua and brought him before
23 Eleazar the priest and the whole community, •laid his hands on him and gave him his orders, as Yahweh had directed through Moses.

Regulations for sacrifices

1
2 **28** Yahweh spoke to Moses and said, •'Give the sons of Israel this order: "Take care to bring at the appointed time my offering, my sustenance in the form of burnt offering, an appeasing fragrance for me".
3 Say to them, "These are the burnt offerings you must offer to Yahweh:

a. Daily sacrifices

"Every day, two yearling lambs without blemish, as a perpetual holocaust.
4 The first lamb you must offer in the morning, the second between the two evenings,
5 together with an oblation of one-tenth of an ephah of fine flour mixed with one
6 quarter of a hin of purest oil. •This is the perpetual holocaust made long ago
7 at Mount Sinai as an appeasing fragrance, a burnt offering to Yahweh. •The accompanying libation is to be at the rate of one quarter of a hin for each lamb; the libation of strong drink for Yahweh must be poured out in the sanctuary.
8 The second lamb you must offer as a holocaust between the two evenings; do this with the same oblation and the same libation as in the morning, as a burnt offering, an appeasing fragrance for Yahweh.

b. The sabbath

"On the sabbath day, you must offer two yearling lambs without blemish, 9
and two-tenths of an ephah of fine flour as an oblation, mixed with oil, as well
as the accompanying libation. •The sabbath holocaust is to be offered every 10
sabbath in addition to the perpetual holocaust, and the accompanying libation
similarly.

c. The feast of New Moon

"At the beginning of each of your months you must offer a holocaust to 11
Yahweh: two young bulls, one ram and seven yearling lambs without blemish;
for each bull an oblation of three-tenths of an ephah of fine flour mixed with 12
oil; for each ram, an oblation of two-tenths of fine flour mixed with oil; •for 13
each lamb, an oblation of one-tenth of fine flour mixed with oil. This is a
holocaust, an appeasing fragrance, a burnt offering to Yahweh. •The accom- 14
panying libation is to be half a hin of wine for a bull, one-third of a hin for a　．
ram, one-quarter of a hin for a lamb. This must be the monthly holocaust,
month after month, every month of the year. •In addition to the perpetual 15
holocaust a he-goat must be offered to Yahweh, as a sacrifice for sin, with its
accompanying libation.

d. The feast of Unleavened Bread

"The fourteenth day of the first month, is the Passover of Yahweh, •and 16
the fifteenth day of this month is a feast day. For seven days unleavened bread 17
must be eaten. •On the first day there will be a solemn assembly. You must 18
do no laborious work. •You shall offer to Yahweh a burnt offering as a holocaust: 19
two young bulls, a ram, seven yearling sheep without blemish. •The accompanying
oblation of fine flour mixed with oil is to be three-tenths of an ephah for the bull, 20
two-tenths for the ram, •and one-tenth for each of the seven lambs. •There 21
must also be a he-goat for the sacrifice for sin, for performing the rite of atonement 22
over you. •This must be done in addition to the morning holocaust which is a 23
perpetual holocaust. •You must do this every day for seven days. It is nourish- 24
ment, a burnt offering, an appeasing fragrance for Yahweh; it is to be offered
in addition to the perpetual holocaust and its accompanying libation. •On the 25
seventh day you must hold a solemn assembly; you will do no laborious work.

e. The feast of Weeks

"On the day of the first-fruits, when you make your offering of new fruits to 26
Yahweh at your feast of Weeks, you are to hold a solemn assembly; you must
do no laborious work. •You must offer as a holocaust, an appeasing fragrance for 27
Yahweh: two young bulls, one ram, seven yearling lambs. •The accompanying 28
oblation of fine flour mixed with oil is to be three-tenths of an ephah for each
bull, •two-tenths for the ram, and one-tenth for each of the seven lambs. •There 29
must also be a he-goat for the sacrifice for sin, for performing the rite of 30
atonement over you. •This must be done in addition to the perpetual holocaust 31
and its accompanying oblation.

f. The feast of Acclamations

29 "In the seventh month, on the first day of the month, you are to hold a 1
solemn assembly; you must do no heavy work. It shall be your day of
Acclamations. •You must offer as a holocaust, an appeasing fragrance for 2
Yahweh: one young bull, one ram, seven yearling lambs without blemish. •The 3
accompanying oblation of fine flour mixed with oil is to be three-tenths of an
ephah for the bull, two-tenths for the ram, •and one-tenth for each of the seven 4
lambs. •There must also be a he-goat for the sacrifice for sin, for performing 5
the rite of atonement over you. •All this must be done in addition to the monthly 6
holocaust and its oblation, the perpetual holocaust and its oblation, and the

accompanying libations enjoined by law,—an appeasing fragrance, a burnt offering to Yahweh.

g. The day of Atonement

7 "On the tenth day of this seventh month, you are to hold a solemn assembly.
8 You must fast and do no work. •You must offer as a holocaust to Yahweh, an appeasing fragrance: one young bull, one ram, and seven yearling lambs of your
9 choice without blemish. •The accompanying oblation of fine flour mixed with
10 oil is to be three-tenths of an ephah for the bull, two-tenths for the ram, •and
11 one-tenth for each of the seven lambs. •A he-goat must be offered for the sacrifice for sin. This is in addition to the victim for sin at the feast of Atonement, and to the perpetual holocaust with its accompanying oblation and libations.

h. The feast of Tabernacles

12 "On the fifteenth day of the seventh month you are to hold a solemn assembly, you must do no heavy work, and for the space of seven days you are to celebrate
13 a feast for Yahweh. •You must offer as a holocaust, a burnt offering, an appeasing fragrance for Yahweh: thirteen young bulls, two rams, fourteen yearling lambs
14 without blemish. •The accompanying oblation of fine flour mixed with oil is to be three-tenths of an ephah for each of the thirteen bulls, two-tenths for
15,16 each of the two rams, •one-tenth for each of the fourteen lambs; •also one he-goat as a sacrifice for sin. This is in addition to the perpetual holocaust and its oblation and libations.

17 "On the second day: twelve young bulls, two rams, fourteen yearling lambs
18 without blemish; •the accompanying oblation and libations, as prescribed, in
19 proportion to the number of bulls, rams and lambs; •also one he-goat for the sacrifice for sin. This is in addition to the perpetual holocaust with its oblation and libations.

20 "On the third day: eleven bulls, two rams, fourteen yearling lambs without
21 blemish; •the accompanying oblation and libations, as prescribed, in proportion
22 to the number of bulls, rams and lambs; •also one he-goat for the sacrifice for sin. This is in addition to the perpetual holocaust with its oblation and libations.

23 "On the fourth day: ten bulls, two rams, fourteen yearling lambs without
24 blemish; •the accompanying oblation and libations, as prescribed, in proportion
25 to the number of bulls, rams and lambs; •also one he-goat for the sacrifice for sin. This is in addition to the perpetual holocaust with its oblation and libations.

26 "On the fifth day: nine bulls, two rams, fourteen yearling lambs without
27 blemish; •the accompanying oblation and libations, as prescribed, in proportion
28 to the number of bulls, rams and lambs; •also one he-goat for the sacrifice for sin. This is in addition to the perpetual holocaust with its oblation and libations.

29 "On the sixth day: eight bulls, two rams, fourteen yearling lambs without
30 blemish; •the accompanying oblation and libations, as prescribed, in proportion
31 to the number of bulls, rams and lambs; •also one he-goat for the sacrifice for sin. This is in addition to the perpetual holocaust with its oblation and libations.

32 "On the seventh day: seven bulls, two rams, fourteen yearling lambs without
33 blemish; •the accompanying oblation and libations, as prescribed, in proportion
34 to the number of bulls, rams and lambs; •also one he-goat for the sacrifice for sin. This is in addition to the perpetual holocaust with its oblation and libations.

35,36 "On the eighth day you must all assemble. You must do no heavy work. •You must offer as a holocaust, a burnt offering, an appeasing fragrance for Yahweh:
37 one bull, one ram, seven yearling lambs without blemish; •the accompanying oblation and libations, as prescribed, in proportion to the number of bulls, rams
38 and lambs; •also one he-goat for the sacrifice for sin. This is in addition to the perpetual holocaust with its oblation and libations.

39 "This is what you are to do for Yahweh at your solemn feasts, over and above

your votive and voluntary offerings, your holocausts, oblations and libations, and your communion sacrifice." '

30 Moses told the sons of Israel exactly what Yahweh had ordered him.   1

Laws concerning vows

Moses spoke to the leaders of the tribes of the sons of Israel. He said, 'This is 2 what Yahweh has ordered:

"If a man makes a vow to Yahweh or takes a formal pledge under oath, he 3 must not break his word: whatever he promises by word of mouth he must do.

"If a woman makes a vow to Yahweh or takes a formal pledge during her 4 youth, while she is still in her father's house, •and if he hears about this vow 5 or pledge made by her and says nothing to her, her vow, whatever it may be, shall be binding, and the pledge she has taken, whatever it may be, shall be binding. •But if the father on the day he learns of it expresses his disapproval 6 of it, then none of the vows or pledges she has taken shall be binding. Yahweh will not hold her to it, since her father has expressed his disapproval.

"If, being bound by vows or by a pledge voiced without due reflection, she 7 then marries, •and if her husband hears of it but says nothing on the day he 8 learns of it, her vows shall be binding and the pledges she has taken shall be binding. •But if on the day he learns of it he expresses his disapproval to her, 9 this will annul the vow that she has made or the pledge that binds her, voiced without due reflection. Yahweh will not hold her to it.

"The vow of a widow or a divorced woman and all pledges taken by her are 10 binding on her.

"If she has made a vow or taken a pledge under oath while in her husband's 11 house, •and if when the husband learns of it he says nothing to her and does 12 not express disapproval to her, then the vow, whatever it is, shall be binding, and the pledge, whatever it is, shall be binding. •But if the husband when he hears 13 of them annuls them on the day he learns of them, no word of her mouth, vow or pledge, shall be binding. Since the husband has annulled them, Yahweh will not hold her to them.

"Every vow or oath that is binding on the wife may be endorsed or annulled 14 by the husband.

"If by the following day the husband has said nothing to her, it means that 15 he endorses her vow, whatever it may be, or her pledge, whatever it may be. He endorses them if he says nothing on the day he learns of them. •But if he 16 annuls them a longer time after he learnt of them, then he must bear the burden of the wife's fault." '

These are the laws ordained by Yahweh to Moses, concerning the relationship 17 between man and wife, and between a father and his daughter while still young and living in her father's home.

IX. BOOTY AND ITS ALLOCATION

The holy war against Midian

31 Yahweh spoke to Moses and said, •'Exact full vengeance for the sons of $\frac{1}{2}$ Israel on the Midianites. Afterwards you will be gathered to your people.'

Moses said to the people, 'Some of you must take arms to wage Yahweh's 3 campaign against Midian, to carry out the vengeance of Yahweh on Midian. •Put 4 a thousand men in the field from each of the tribes of Israel.'

In this way Israel's hosts provided twelve thousand men equipped for war, 5 one thousand from each tribe: •Moses put them in the field, one thousand from 6 each tribe, with Phinehas, son of Eleazar the priest, to go with them carrying the sacred vessels and the trumpets for sounding the alarm.

7 They waged the campaign against Midian, as Yahweh had ordered
8 Moses, and they put every male to death. •And further, they killed the kings
of Midian, Evi, Rekem, Zur, Hur and Reba, the five Midianite kings; they also
9 put Balaam son of Beor to the sword. •The sons of Israel took the Midianite
women captive with their young children, and plundered all their cattle, all their
10 flocks and all their goods. •They set fire to the towns where they lived and all
11 their encampments. •Then, taking all their booty, all that they had captured,
12 man and beast, •they took the captives, spoil and booty to Moses, Eleazar
the priest and all the community of the sons of Israel, at the camp in the plains
of Moab, near the Jordan opposite Jericho.

The slaughter of the women and purification of the booty

13 Moses, Eleazar the priest, and all the leaders of the community went out of
14 the camp to meet them. •Moses was enraged with the commanders of the army,
the captains of thousands and the captains of hundreds, who had come back
15 from this military expedition. •He said, 'Why have you spared the life of all
16 the women? •These were the very ones who, on Balaam's advice, perverted the
sons of Israel and made them renounce Yahweh in the affair at Peor: hence the
17 plague which struck the community of Israel. •So kill all the male children.
18 Kill also all the women who have slept with a man. •Spare the lives only of the
19 young girls who have not slept with a man, and take them for yourselves. •As
for you, you must camp for seven days outside the camp, all of you who have
killed a man or touched a corpse. Purify yourselves, you and your prisoners,
20 on the third and seventh days; •purify also all clothing, everything made of skin,
everything woven of goats' hair and everything made of wood.'
21 Eleazar the priest said to the soldiers who had come back from this campaign,
22 'This is a statute of the Law which Yahweh has commanded Moses. •Whereas
23 the gold, silver, bronze, iron, tin and lead, •everything that can withstand fire,
must be passed through the fire and it will be clean, yet it must still be purified
with lustral water. Whatever cannot resist fire you must pass through water.
24 'Wash your clothes on the seventh day and you will then be clean. You may
then come back to the camp.'

The allocation of the booty

25 Yahweh spoke to Moses and said:
26 'With Eleazar the priest and the heads of families in the community, count
27 the spoils and the captives, man and beast. •Then share out the spoil, half and
half, between those who fought the campaign and the rest of the community.
28 As Yahweh's portion you will set aside, from the share of the combatants who
took part in the campaign, one out of every five hundred persons, oxen, donkeys
29 and sheep. •These are to be taken from the half share which is their due, and
30 given to Eleazar the priest as an offering to Yahweh. •From the half which is
due to the sons of Israel, you will take one out of every fifty persons, oxen,
donkeys, sheep, and all other animals, and give them to the Levites who have
charge of the tabernacle of Yahweh.'
31
32 Moses and Eleazar the priest did as Yahweh had ordered Moses. •The
spoils, the remainder of the booty captured by the soldiers, came to six hundred
33 and seventy-five thousand head of small stock, •seventy-two thousand head of
34
35 cattle, •sixty-one thousand donkeys, •and in persons, women who had never
36 slept with a man, thirty-two thousand in all. •Half was assigned to those who
had taken part in the war, namely three hundred and thirty-seven thousand
37 five hundred head of small stock, •of which Yahweh's portion was six hundred
38 and seventy-five, •thirty-six thousand head of cattle, of which Yahweh's portion
39 was seventy-two. •Thirty thousand five hundred donkeys, of which Yahweh's
40 portion was sixty-one, •and sixteen thousand persons, of which Yahweh's
41 portion was thirty-two. •Moses gave Eleazar the priest the portion set aside
for Yahweh, in accordance with Yahweh's instructions to Moses.

As for the half due to the sons of Israel, which Moses had separated from 42
that of the combatants, •this half, the community's share, came to three hundred 43
and thirty-seven thousand five hundred head of small stock, •thirty-six thousand 44
head of cattle, •thirty thousand five hundred donkeys •and sixteen thousand 45/46
persons. •From this half, the share of the sons of Israel, Moses took one out 47
of every fifty, man and beast, and gave them to the Levites who had charge of
the tabernacle of Yahweh, in accordance with Yahweh's instructions to Moses.

The offerings

The commanders of the hosts who had fought the campaign, the captains 48
of thousands and the captains of hundreds, came to Moses •and said, 'Your 49
servants have numbered the soldiers under their command: not one is missing.
And further, we bring as an offering for Yahweh the gold ornaments we have 50
found, armlets and bracelets, signet rings, earrings and brooches, to have the
rite of atonement performed over us before Yahweh.' •Moses and Eleazar the 51
priest accepted this gold from them, all this jewellery. •This offering of gold 52
given by them to Yahweh amounted to sixteen thousand seven hundred and
fifty shekels, all given by the captains of thousands and the captains of hundreds.

Each of the soldiers took his own booty. •But Moses and Eleazar the priest 53/54
received the gold from the captains of thousands and of hundreds, and carried
it to the Tent of Meeting as a reminder to Yahweh of the sons of Israel.

The allocation of Transjordania

32 The sons of Reuben and the sons of Gad owned great herds of fine cattle. 1
Now they observed that the land of Jazer and the land of Gilead was an
ideal region for raising stock. •The sons of Gad and the sons of Reuben 2
therefore went to Moses, Eleazar the priest and the leaders of the community,
and said to them, •'The land of Ataroth, Dibon, Jazer, Nimrah, Heshbon, 3
Elealeh, Sebam, Nebo and Beon, •which Yahweh has conquered in the sight 4
of the community of Israel, is ideal land for raising stock, and your servants are
cattle breeders. •If we have deserved your friendship,' they said 'give this land 5
to your servants for our own; do not make us cross the Jordan.'

Moses said to the sons of Gad and the sons of Reuben, 'Your brothers are 6
off to the war—are you content to stay here? •Why do you keep the sons of 7
Israel from entering the land that Yahweh has given them? •This is what your 8
fathers did when I sent them from Kadesh-barnea to inspect the land. •They 9
went up as far as the Valley of Eshcol and inspected the land; but they kept
the sons of Israel from entering the land that Yahweh had given them. •Hence 10
the wrath of Yahweh blazed out that day and he swore this oath, •"If ever these 11
men of twenty years and over, who came out from Egypt, set eyes on the land
that I promised on oath to Abraham, Isaac and Jacob..."ᵃ For they have not
followed me faithfully, •except Caleb son of Jephunneh the Kenizzite, and 12
Joshua son of Nun: these indeed have followed Yahweh faithfully." •The wrath 13
of Yahweh blazed out against Israel and he made them wander in the wilderness
for forty years, until the generation that offended Yahweh had all disappeared.
And now you, you rise up in your father's place, offshoot of sinful stock, to add 14
still more to the burning wrath of Yahweh against Israel! •If you turn away 15
from him, he will prolong the time spent in the wilderness, and you will bring
about the ruin of all this people.'

They came to Moses and said, 'We would like to build sheepfolds here for 16
our flocks and towns for our young children. •We ourselves will take up arms 17
to lead the sons of Israel until we have brought them to the place appointed for
them: only our young children will stay in the fortified towns, safe from the
inhabitants of the country. •We will not return to our homes until every one 18
of the sons of Israel has taken possession of his inheritance. •For we shall have 19
no inheritance with them on the other bank of the Jordan or beyond, since our
inheritance has fallen to us here, east of the Jordan.'

20   Moses said to them, 'If you do as you have said, if you are prepared to fight
21 before Yahweh, •and if all those of you who bear arms cross the Jordan before
22 Yahweh, until he has driven all his enemies before him, •then, once the land has
become subject to Yahweh, you may go back; you shall be free of your obligation
towards Yahweh and Israel, and this land shall be your inheritance before
23 Yahweh. •But if you do not, you will sin against Yahweh, and be sure your
24 sin will find you out. •Build towns, then, for your young children and folds for
your flocks; but do what you have promised.'

25   The sons of Gad and the sons of Reuben said to Moses, 'Your servants will
26 do as you order, sir. •Our children, our wives, our flocks and all our livestock
27 will stay in the towns of Gilead, •but your servants, every man armed for war,
will cross over to fight before Yahweh as you have ordered.'

28   Then Moses gave directions about them to Eleazar the priest, to Joshua
son of Nun, and to the leaders of the patriarchal Houses of the tribes of Israel.
29 Moses said to them, 'If the sons of Gad and the sons of Reuben, all who bear
arms, cross the Jordan with you to fight before Yahweh, then once the land is in
30 your power, you will give them the land of Gilead for their possession. •But if
they do not cross over in arms with you, then they must have their possessions
with you in the land of Canaan.'

31   The sons of Gad and the sons of Reuben replied, 'What Yahweh has said
32 to your servants, we will do. •We will cross in arms before Yahweh into the land
of Canaan; but you must give us possession of our inheritance beyond the
33 Jordan.' •Moses gave them—the sons of Gad and the sons of Reuben and the
half-tribe of Manasseh son of Joseph—the kingdom of Sihon king of the
Amorites, the kingdom of Og king of Bashan, the land and the towns contained
within its boundaries, the frontier towns of the land.

34
35   The sons of Gad built Dibon, Ataroth, Aroer, •Atroth-shophan, Jazer,
36 Jogbehah, •Beth-nimrah, Beth-haran, fortified towns, and folds for the flocks.

37
38   The sons of Reuben built Heshbon, Elealeh, Kiriathaim, •Nebo, Baal-meon
(their names were changed), Sibmah. They gave names to the towns they had
built.

39   The sons of Machir son of Manasseh went to Gilead. They conquered it and
40 drove out the Amorites who were there. •Moses gave Gilead to Machir son of
41 Manasseh, and he settled there. •Jair son of Manasseh went and seized their
42 encampments and called them Encampments of Jair. •Nobah went and seized
Kenath with its outlying villages, and called it Nobah after himself.

The stages of the Exodus

1   **33** Here are the stages of the journey made by the sons of Israel when they
came out in a body from the land of Egypt, under the leadership of Moses
2 and Aaron. •Moses recorded their starting-points in writing whenever they broke
camp on Yahweh's orders. Here are the stages according to their starting-points.

3   They left Rameses in the first month. It was on the fifteenth day of the first
month, on the day following the Passover, that the sons of Israel set out
4 triumphantly in the sight of all Egypt. •The Egyptians· were burying those of
their own people whom Yahweh had struck down, all their first-born; Yahweh
had carried out his judgement on their gods.

5
6   The sons of Israel left Rameses and camped at Succoth. •Then they left
7 Succoth and encamped at Etham which is on the edge of the wilderness. •They
left Etham, turned back to Pi-hahiroth which faces Baal-zephon, and encamped
8 before Migdol. •They left Pi-hahiroth, crossed over the sea into the wilderness,
and after marching for three days in the desert of Etham they encamped at
9 Marah. •They left Marah and reached Elim. At Elim there are twelve springs
10 of water and seventy palm trees; they encamped there. •They left Elim and

---

32 a. The main clause of an oath is often left out, in reporting it.

encamped by the Sea of Reeds. •They left the Sea of Reeds and encamped in 11
the wilderness of Sin. •They left the wilderness of Sin and encamped at 12
Dophkah. •They left Dophkah and encamped at Alush. •They left Alush and ¹³₁₄
encamped at Rephidim; the people found no drinking water there. •They left 15
Rephidim and encamped in the wilderness of Sinai. •They left the wilderness 16
of Sinai and encamped at Kibroth-hattaavah. •They left Kibroth-hattaavah and 17
encamped at Hazeroth. •They left Hazeroth and encamped at Rithmah. •They ¹⁸₁₉
left Rithmah and encamped at Rimmon-perez. •They left Rimmon-perez and 20
encamped at Libnah. •They left Libnah and encamped at Rissah. •They left ²¹₂₂
Rissah and encamped at Kehelathah. •They left Kehelathah and encamped at 23
Mount Shepher. •They left Mount Shepher and encamped at Haradah. •They ²⁴₂₅
left Haradah and encamped at Makheloth. •They left Makheloth and encamped 26
at Tahath. •They left Tahath and encamped at Terah. •They left Terah and ²⁷₂₈
encamped at Mithkah. •They left Mithkah and encamped at Hashmonah. •They ²⁹₃₀
left Hashmonah and encamped at Moseroth. •They left Moseroth and encamped 31
at Bene-jaakan. •They left Bene-jaakan and encamped at Hor-haggidgad. •They ³²₃₃
left Hor-haggidgad and encamped at Jotbathah. •They left Jotbathah and 34
encamped at Abronah. •They left Abronah and encamped at Ezion-geber. 35
They left Ezion-geber and encamped in the wilderness of Zin; this is Kadesh. 36
They left Kadesh and encamped at Mount Hor, on the borders of the land of 37
Edom. •Aaron the priest went up Mount Hor on Yahweh's orders and it was 38
there that he died, in the fortieth year of the exodus of the sons of Israel from
the land of Egypt, in the fifth month, on the first day of the month. •Aaron was 39
a hundred and twenty-three years old when he died at Mount Hor. •The king 40
of Arad, a Canaanite who lived in the Negeb in the land of Canaan, was
informed when the sons of Israel arrived. •They left Mount Hor and encamped 41
at Zalmonah. •They left Zalmonah and encamped at Punon. •They left Punon ⁴²₄₃
and encamped at Oboth. •They left Oboth and encamped in Moabite territory 44
at Iye-abarim. •They left Iyim and encamped at Dibon-gad. •They left Dibon- ⁴⁵₄₆
gad and encamped at Almon-diblathaim. •They left Almon-diblathaim and 47
encamped in the Abarim mountains facing Nebo. •They left the Abarim 48
mountains and encamped in the plains of Moab, near the Jordan opposite
Jericho. •They encamped near the Jordan between Beth-ha-jeshimoth and Abel- 49
hash-shittim, in the plains of Moab.

The allocation of Canaan. God's order

Yahweh spoke to Moses in the plains of Moab, near the Jordan opposite 50
Jericho. He said:

'Say this to the sons of Israel: 51

"When you have crossed the Jordan into the land of Canaan, •you must drive 52
all the inhabitants of the country before you. You must destroy their sculptured
stones, you must destroy all their statues of cast metal, and you must demolish all
their high places. •You will take possession of this land and you will stay in it, 53
for I have given it to you for your own. •You are to divide it by lot among your 54
clans. To a large clan you will give a greater inheritance, to a small clan a lesser
one. Where the lot falls for each, that will be his. Make this apportionment
according to patriarchal tribes. •But if you do not drive the inhabitants of the 55
country before you, then those you have spared will be barbs in your eyes and
thorns in your side, they will harass you in the land where you live •and I will 56
deal with you as I meant to deal with them."'

The boundaries of Canaan

34 Yahweh spoke to Moses and said, •'Give the sons of Israel this order: ½
"When you go into the land (of Canaan), this is the territory that will be
your inheritance. This is the land of Canaan defined by its boundaries.

"The southern part of your country will stretch from the wilderness of Zin, 3

on the borders of Edom. Your southern boundary will start on the east at the
4 end of the Salt Sea. •It will then turn south towards the Ascent of the Scorpions
and go by Zin to end in the south at Kadesh-barnea. Then it will go towards
5 Hazar-addar and pass through Azmon. •From Azmon the boundary will turn
towards the wadi of Egypt and end at the Sea.
6 "Your seaboard will be the Great Sea; this will be your western boundary.
7 "This will be your northern boundary. You will draw a line from the Great
8 Sea to Mount Hor, •then from Mount Hor you will draw a line to the Pass
9 of Hamath, and the boundary will end at Zedad. •From there it will go on to
Ziphron and end at Hazar-enan. This will be your northern boundary.
10 "You will then draw your eastern boundary from Hazar-enan to Shepham.
11 The boundary will go down from Shepham towards Riblah on the east side of
Ain. Further down it will keep to the eastern shore of the Sea of Chinnereth.[a]
12 The frontier will then follow the Jordan and end at the Salt Sea.
"This will be your land with the boundaries surrounding it." '
13 Moses then laid this charge on the sons of Israel:
'This is the land you are to apportion by lot, which Yahweh has ordered to
14 be made over to the nine tribes and the half-tribe. •The tribe of the sons of
Reuben with its patriarchal Houses and the tribe of the sons of Gad with its
patriarchal Houses have already been given their heritage; the half-tribe of
15 Manasseh has also been given its heritage. •These two tribes and the half-tribe
have been given their heritage beyond the Jordan opposite Jericho, to the east,
towards the sunrise.'

The leaders in charge of the allocation

16 Yahweh spoke to Moses and said:
17 'These are the names of those who will share out the land: Eleazar the priest
18 and Joshua son of Nun, •and you will take one leader from each tribe to share out
19 the land. Here are the names of these men:
For the tribe of Judah, Caleb son of Jephunneh;
20 for the tribe of the sons of Simeon, Shemuel son of Ammihud;
21 for the tribe of Benjamin, Elidad son of Chislon;
22 for the tribe of the sons of Dan, the leader Bukki son of Jogli;
23 for the sons of Joseph: for the tribe of Manasseh, the leader Hanniel son
of Ephod;
24 and for the tribe of the sons of Ephraim, the leader Kemuel son of Shiphtan;
25 for the tribe of the sons of Zebulun, the leader Elizaphan son of Parnach;
26 for the tribe of the sons of Issachar, the leader Paltiel son of Azzan;
27 for the tribe of the sons of Asher, the leader Ahihud son of Shelomi;
28 for the tribe of the sons of Naphtali, the leader Pedahel son of Ammihud.'
29 These are the men whom Yahweh ordered to divide the land of Canaan
among the sons of Israel.

The portion of the Levites

1 **35** Yahweh spoke to Moses in the plains of Moab, near the Jordan opposite
Jericho. He said:
2 'Direct the sons of Israel to make over to the Levites, out of the inheritance
they possess, towns in which to live and pasture land round the towns. Give
3 these to the Levites. •The towns are to be their homes and the surrounding
4 pasture land is to be for their cattle, their possessions and all their animals. •The
pasture land surrounding the towns that you make over to the Levites shall
extend, from the walls of the towns, for a thousand cubits all round.
5 'Outside the town, measure two thousand cubits to the east side, two thousand
cubits to the south, two thousand cubits to the west and two thousand cubits

34 a. The Lake of Gennesareth.

to the north, the town lying in the centre: this is to be the pasture-land for these towns. •The towns you hand over to the Levites will be the six cities of refuge, 6 ceded by you as sanctuary for men who cause another's death; and you are to hand over forty-two towns in addition. •Altogether you will make over forty- 7 eight towns to the Levites, towns together with their pasturage. •Of the towns 8 that you grant out of the possession of the sons of Israel, more will be taken from those who hold more, and less from those who hold less. Everyone will make over towns to the Levites in proportion to the inheritance he himself has received.'

Cities of refuge

Yahweh spoke to Moses and said: 9

'Say this to the sons of Israel: 10

"When you cross the Jordan and reach the land of Canaan, •you are to select 11 towns which you will make into cities of refuge where a man who has killed accidentally may find sanctuary. •These towns will be your refuge from the 12 avenger of blood, so that the killer may not die without being brought to judgement before the community. •The towns you make over will serve you as 13 six cities of refuge: •the three that you make over beyond the Jordan and the 14 three that you make over in the land of Canaan are to be cities of refuge. These six towns will be a refuge, for the sons of Israel as well as for the stranger 15 and the settler among you, where anyone who has killed accidentally may find sanctuary.

"But if he has struck the person with an iron object so as to cause death, 16 he is a murderer. The murderer must be put to death. •If he struck him with a 17 stone capable of killing, and has killed him, he is a murderer. The murderer must be put to death. •Or if he has struck him with a wooden instrument capable 18 of killing, and has killed him, he is a murderer. The murderer must be put to death. •The avenger of blood must put the murderer to death. When he meets 19 him he must put him to death.ᵃ

"If the killer has maliciously manhandled his victim, or thrown some lethal 20 missile to strike him down, •or out of enmity dealt him the death-blow with 21 his fist, then he who struck the blow must die; he is a murderer; the avenger of blood must put him to death when he meets him. •If, however, he has 22 manhandled his victim by chance, without malice, or thrown some missile at him not meaning to hit him, •or without seeing him dropped a stone on him 23 capable of causing death and so killed him, so long as he bore him no malice and wished him no harm, •then the community must decide in accordance with 24 these rules between the one who struck the blow and the avenger of blood, •and 25 so rescue the killer from the avenger of blood. They will send him back to the city of refuge where he had sought sanctuary, and there he will stay until the death of the high priest who has been anointed with the holy oil. •If the killer 26 should leave the bounds of the city of refuge where he has sought sanctuary and the avenger of blood encounters him outside the bounds of his city of refuge, 27 the avenger of blood may kill him without fear of reprisal; •since the killer 28 should stay in his city of refuge until the death of the high priest; only after the death of the high priest is he free to go back to the land where he has his home. •These regulations shall have force of law for you and your descendants, 29 wherever you may be.

"In any case of homicide, the evidence of witnesses must determine whether 30 the murderer is to be put to death; but the evidence of a single witness is not sufficient to uphold a capital charge. •You are not to accept ransom for the life 31 of a murderer condemned to death; he must die. •Nor are you to accept ransom 32 for anyone who, having sought sanctuary in his city of refuge, wishes to come back and live at home before the death of the high priest. •You must not profane 33 the land you live in. Blood profanes the country, and there is no other expiation

34 for the country for bloodshed than the blood of the one who shed it. •You must not defile the land you inhabit, the land in which I live; for I, Yahweh, live among the sons of Israel." '

A wife's inheritance

1 **36** Then the heads of families in the clan of the sons of Gilead, son of Machir, son of Manasseh, one of the clans of Joseph's sons, came forward.

2 They spoke before Moses and the leaders, the heads of families of Israel's sons, and said:

'Yahweh has ordered my lord to give the land to the sons of Israel, sharing it out by lot; and my lord has been ordered by Yahweh to give the
3 inheritance of our brother Zelophehad to his daughters. •Now, if they marry someone from another tribe in the sons of Israel, their property will be taken away from the inheritance of our fathers. The property of the tribe to which they will
4 belong will be increased, and the property allotted to us diminished. •And when the jubilee comes round for the sons of Israel, the property of these women will be added to the inheritance of the tribe to which they then belong, and lost to the inheritance of our own patriarchal tribe.'

5 Moses, at Yahweh's bidding, gave the following ruling to the sons of Israel. He said:

6 'The tribe of the sons of Joseph is in the right. •This is Yahweh's ruling for the daughters of Zelophehad: "They may marry whom they please, providing
7 they marry into a clan of their father's tribe. •The heritage of the sons of Israel is not to be transferred from tribe to tribe; every man of the sons of Israel is to
8 remain bound to the heritage of his patriarchal tribe. •Every daughter who has a heritage in one of the tribes of the sons of Israel must marry into a clan of her own paternal tribe, so that the sons of Israel may each preserve the heritage of
9 his father. •No heritage may be transferred from one tribe to another: every tribe of the sons of Israel will stay bound to its own heritage."'

10 The daughters of Zelophehad did as Yahweh had ordered Moses.
11 Mahlah, Tirzah, Hoglah, Milcah and Noah, daughters of Zelophehad, married
12 the sons of their father's brothers. •Since they married into the clans of the sons of Manasseh son of Joseph, their heritage reverted to the tribe of their father's clan.

Conclusion

13 These are the commandments and laws that Yahweh laid down for the sons of Israel through Moses in the plains of Moab near the Jordan opposite Jericho.

---

35 a. 'The avenger of blood' is the victim's nearest relation.

DEUTERONOMY

I. INTRODUCTORY DISCOURSES

A. THE FIRST DISCOURSE OF MOSES

Its time and place

1 These are the words spoken beyond Jordan to the whole of Israel. (In the ¹ wilderness, in the Arabah facing Suph, between Paran and Tophel, Laban, Hazeroth and Dizahab. •It is eleven day's march from Horeb by way of Mount ² Seir to Kadesh-barnea.)ᵃ •It was in the fortieth year, on the first day of the ³ eleventh month, that Moses spoke to the sons of Israel as Yahweh had ordered. He had defeated Sihon king of the Amorites, who lived at Heshbon, and Og ⁴ king of Bashan, who lived at Ashtaroth and Edrei. •There, in the land of Moab ⁵ beyond the Jordan, Moses set himself to expound this Law. He said:

The final instructions at Horeb

'Yahweh our God said to us at Horeb, "You have stayed long enough at this ⁶ mountain. •Move on from here, continue your journey, go to the highlands of ⁷ the Amorites, to those who make their home in the Arabah, in the highlands, in the lowlands, in the Negeb and in the coastland; go into the land of Canaan and to Lebanon as far as the great river Euphrates. •This is the land I have made ⁸ over to you; go and take possession of the land that Yahweh swore to give to your fathers, Abraham, Isaac and Jacob, and to their descendants after them."

'It was then that I told you: I cannot carry the burden of you by myself. ⁹ Yahweh your God has multiplied you, till now you are like the stars of heaven ¹⁰ in number. •And Yahweh your God is going to increase you a thousand times ¹¹ more, and bless you as he promised. •So how can I carry the heavy burden ¹² of you and your bickerings, all by myself? •Bring me wise men, shrewd and ¹³ tested, out of each of your tribes, therefore, and I will make them your leaders. And you answered me, "Your plan is a good one". •And so I selected tribal leaders ¹⁴/¹⁵ for you, wiseᵇ men and tested, and appointed them to lead you: captains of thousands, hundreds, fifties, tens, and scribes for your tribes too. •At that same ¹⁶ time I told your judges: You must give your brothers a fair hearing and see justice done between a man and his brother or the stranger who lives with him. •You ¹⁷ must be impartial in judgement and give an equal hearing to small and great alike. Do not be afraid of any man, for the judgement is God's. Should a case be too difficult, bring it to me and I will hear it. •And I gave you directions at that ¹⁸ time for everything you were to do.

Kadesh: the Israelites lose faith

'So we left Horeb and came to the vast and terrible wilderness you have seen. ¹⁹ We made for the highlands of the Amorites, as Yahweh our God had ordered, and arrived at Kadesh-barnea. •It was then that I said to you: Now you have ²⁰ reached these Amorite highlands which Yahweh our God is giving to us. •See, ²¹ Yahweh your God has made over this land to you. March in, take possession of it as Yahweh the God of your fathers ordered you; do not be afraid or discouraged. •Then you all came to me and said, "Let us send men ahead of us ²²

to explore the country; they will report to us which way we must go and what
23 towns we shall come to". •This seemed good advice to me and I selected twelve
24 of your men, one from each tribe. •These men made towards the highlands and
25 went up into them; they reached the Valley of Eshcol and reconnoitred it. •They
collected some of the fruit of the country and brought it down to us; and they
made us this report, "It is a prosperous land that Yahweh our God has given us".
26 Yet you refused to go up into it and you rebelled against the voice of Yahweh
27 your God. •You grumbled in your tents; "It is because he hates us" you said
"that Yahweh brought us out of the land of Egypt to put us under the power of
28 the Amorites and so destroy us. •What kind of place are we making for? Our
own brothers have made us lose heart: It is a people, they say, bigger and
stronger than we are; their cities are immense, with walls reaching to the sky.
And we saw Anakim there too."

29
30 'And I said to you: Do not take fright, do not be afraid of them. •Yahweh
your God goes in front of you and will be fighting on your side as you saw him
31 fight for you in Egypt. •In the wilderness, too, you saw him: how Yahweh
carried you, as a man carries his child, all along the road you travelled on the
32 way to this place. •But for all this, you put no faith in Yahweh your God, •who
33 had gone in front of you on the journey to find you a camping ground, by night
in the fire to light your path, by day in the cloud.

Yahweh's instructions at Kadesh

34
35 'Yahweh heard this talk of yours and, in his anger, took this oath, •"Not one
of these men, this perverse generation, shall see the rich land that I swore to give
36 to your fathers, •except Caleb son of Jephunneh. He shall see it. To him and to
his sons I will give the land he has set foot on, for he has followed Yahweh in all
37 things". •Yahweh was angry with me too, on your account. "You shall not go
38 in either" he said. •"Your servant Joshua son of Nun, he shall be the one to enter.
Give him encouragement, for it is he who shall bring Israel to take possession of
39 the land. •But your little ones who, you said, would be seized as booty, these
children of yours who do not yet know good from evil, these shall go in there;
40 I will give it to them and they shall possess it. •As for you, turn round, go back
into the wilderness, in the direction of the Sea of Suph."

41 'You answered me then, "We have sinned against Yahweh our God. We will
go up and fight as Yahweh our God has ordered us." And each one of you
42 buckled on his arms and blithely marched up into the highlands. •But Yahweh
said to me, "Tell them this: Do not go up and fight. I am not among you. You
43 will be defeated by your enemies." •And I did tell you, but you would not listen,
and you rebelled against the voice of Yahweh: you still dared to go up into the
44 highlands. •The Amorites, who live in that country of hills, came swarming out
against you like bees, pursued you and struck you down in Seir and as far away
45 as Hormah. •And when you returned you shed tears in the presence of Yahweh,
46 but he did not listen to your cries and paid no heed to you. •For many a day you
had to stay at Kadesh, your full tally of days.

Israel's relations with Edom and Moab

1 2 'We turned round, therefore, and made for the wilderness, in the direction of
the Sea of Suph, as Yahweh had ordered me. For many days we wandered
2 about the highlands of Seir. •Yahweh then said to me, •"You have wandered
3
4 long enough in these highlands. Go north. •And give the people this order: You
are about to pass through the territory of your kinsmen, the sons of Esau who
5 live in Seir. They are frightened of you; but take care •not to provoke them. For
I will give you none of their land, no, not so much as a foot's length of it. I have
6 given the highlands of Seir to Esau as his domain. •Pay them in money for

---

1 a. The parenthesis sums up the stages of the Israelites' journey from Sinai. The eleven days'
march is only the last stage.   **b.** Or 'practical'.

what food you eat; and pay them in money for all the water you drink. •Yahweh 7
your God has blessed you in all you do; he has watched over your journeying
through this vast wilderness. Yahweh your God has been with you these forty
years and you have never been in want."

'So we passed beyond those kinsmen of ours, the sons of Esau who live in 8
Seir, by the Arabah and Elath and Ezion-geber road; then, changing direction,
we took the road towards the wilderness of Moab. •And Yahweh said to me, 9
"Make no attack on Moab and do not provoke him to fight, for I will give you
none of his land. I have given Ar into the possession of the sons of Lot.' •(At one 10
time the Emim lived there, a great and numerous people, tall as the Anakim;*
and, like the Anakim, they were accounted Rephaim, though the Moabites call 11
them Emim. •The Horites,* too, lived in Seir at one time; these, however, were 12
dispossessed and exterminated by the sons of Esau who settled there in place
of them, just as Israel did in their own land, the heritage they received from
Yahweh.) •'Forward, then! Cross the wadi Zered!" 13

The arrival in Transjordania

'And so we crossed the wadi Zered. •Now from Kadesh-barnea to the wadi 14
Zered our wanderings had taken thirty-eight years, so that the whole generation
of men fit for war was lost to the camp, as Yahweh had sworn to them. •The 15
hand of Yahweh fell upon them in the camp until they had perished entirely.
When all the men fit for war had been carried off by death from among the people, 16
down to the last man, •Yahweh said this to me, •"You are now about to cross Ar, 17 18
the land of Moab, •and to approach the frontier of the sons of Ammon. Make 19
no attack on them and do not provoke them, for I will give you none of the
land belonging to the sons of Ammon. I have given it to the sons of Lot as
their domain.' •(This also was accounted a land of Rephaim; at one time the 20
Rephaim lived there, though the Ammonites call them Zamzummim, •a great 21
and numerous people, tall as the Anakim. Yahweh exterminated them before
the advancing Ammonites who dispossessed them and settled there in place of
them, •just as he had exterminated the Horites in front of the sons of Esau who 22
live in Seir, so that they dispossessed them and settled there in place of them and
are still there now. •It was the same with the Avvites who had their encampments 23
as far as Gaza: the Caphtorim, coming from Caphtor,* exterminated them, settling
there in place of them.) •'Break camp, set out and cross the wadi Arnon. See, 24
I am putting Sihon the Amorite, king of Heshbon, at your mercy, and his country
too. Set about the conquest; engage him in battle. •Today and henceforth 25
I spread the terror and fear of you among the peoples under all heaven: all who
hear the sound of your coming will tremble and be in dread."

The conquest of Sihon's kingdom

'So from the wilderness of Kedemoth I sent envoys to Sihon king of Heshbon 26
with this message of peace: •I mean to pass through your land. I shall go my 27
way, straying neither right nor left. •What food I eat, sell me in return for money; 28
and I will pay for all the water I drink. Only give me leave to march through,
just as the sons of Esau who live in Seir gave me leave, and the Moabites who live 29
in Ar, until I cross the Jordan into the land that Yahweh our God is giving to us.

'But Sihon king of Heshbon would not give us leave to pass through his land: 30
Yahweh your God has made his spirit obstinate and his heart stubborn, so as to
leave him at your mercy, as he still is. •And Yahweh said to me, "You see, I have 31
begun to deliver Sihon and his land over to you. Set about the conquest; seize
his land." •Sihon then, with all his people, marched out against us to give battle 32
at Jahaz. •And Yahweh our God delivered him over to us: we defeated him, with 33
his sons and all his people. •Then we captured all his cities and laid whole towns 34
under ban, men, women, children; we spared nothing •but the livestock which 35
we took as our spoil, as also the plunder from the towns we captured. •From 36

Aroer on the height above the wadi Arnon, and from the town at the bottom of the ravine, as far as Gilead, not one town was beyond our reach; Yahweh our
37 God delivered them all over to us. •The country of the Ammonites alone you did not go near, neither the region of wadi Jabbok nor the towns of the hill country, nor anywhere forbidden us by Yahweh our God.

The end of the stay in Transjordania

1 **3** 'We then turned in the direction of Bashan and went up there. And Og king of Bashan marched out against us, he and all his people, to give battle at Edrei.
2 And Yahweh said to me, "Do not be afraid of him, for I have put him at your mercy, with all his people and his land. Deal with him as you dealt with Sihon
3 the king of the Amorites who lives in Heshbon." •So Yahweh our God put Og king of Bashan at our mercy too, with all his people. We struck him down and
4 not a thing remained to him. •We captured all his towns at that time; there was not a town of theirs we did not take: sixty towns, the whole confederation of
5 Argob, Og's capital in Bashan, •all strongholds enclosed in high walls and fortified with gates and bars, not to mention the Perizzite*a* towns, which were
6 very many. •We laid them under ban as we had done with Sihon king of Heshbon,
7 laying the whole town, men, women, children, under the ban; •but we seized the livestock and the spoil from these towns as our plunder.

8 'So at that time we took the land of the two Amorite kings beyond Jordan,
9 from the wadi Arnon to Mount Hermon •(the Sidonians call Hermon Sirion
10 and the Amorites call it Senir): •all the towns of the tableland, all Gilead, and
11 all Bashan as far as Salecah and Edrei, the capital cities of Og in Bashan. •(Og king of Bashan was the last survivor of the Rephaim; his bed was the bed of iron*b* that can be seen at Rabbah-of-the-Ammonites, nine cubits long and four wide, in the common cubit.)

12 'At that time, therefore, we occupied this land, onwards from Aroer on the wadi Arnon. To Reuben and Gad I gave half the highlands of Gilead with its
13 towns. •To the half-tribe of Manasseh I gave the rest of Gilead and the whole of Bashan, Og's kingdom. (The whole confederation of Argob and the whole of
14 Bashan is called the country of the Rephaim. •Since Jair son of Manasseh occupied the whole confederation of Argob as far as the frontiers of the Geshurites and Maacathites, he gave his name to those towns that are still called the Encamp-
15 ments of Jair.) •To Machir I gave Gilead. •To the Reubenites and the Gadites
16 I gave the region from Gilead to the wadi Arnon, the middle of the ravine marking the boundary, and up as far as the Jabbok, the wadi marking the frontier of the
17 Ammonites. •The Arabah and the Jordan serve as frontiers from Chinnereth down to the Sea of the Arabah (the Salt Sea), at the foot of the slopes of Pisgah on the east.

The last instructions of Moses

18 'Then I gave you this command: Yahweh your God has given you this land for your own. All you fighting men must take up arms and march at the head
19 of your brothers, the sons of·Israel. •Only your wives, your children and your flocks (you have many flocks, I know) shall stay behind in the towns I have given
20 you, •until such time as Yahweh settles your brothers as he has settled you, and they too occupy the land that Yahweh your God is giving them beyond the
21 Jordan; then you shall return, each to the domain I have given you. •I then gave Joshua this order: You can see with your own eyes all that Yahweh has done to

2 a. The Anakim were remnants of the prehistoric inhabitants of Palestine and Transjordania. Tradition associated them with the legendary Nephilim, and they were supposed to have built the megalithic monuments. The Emim, Rephaim, Zamzummim and Zuzim were similar remnants from prehistory. **b.** Possibly the survivors of the Hurrites, a non-semitic race; as the text says, the Horites were absorbed by the Edomites. **c.** Philistines.
3 a. Perizzite towns were unfortified. **b.** Possibly one of the cromlechs near Amman.

these two kings; Yahweh will do the same to all the kingdoms through which you pass. •Do not be afraid of them: Yahweh your God himself is fighting for you. 22

'And I pleaded then with Yahweh. •My Lord Yahweh, I said, you that 23 24 have begun to reveal your greatness and your power to your servant, you whose works and mighty deeds no one in heaven or on earth can rival, •may I not go 25 across and see this prosperous land beyond the Jordan, this prosperous country of hills, and Lebanon? •But because of you, Yahweh was angry with me and would 26 take no notice of me. "Enough!" he said "Speak to me no more of this. •Climb to 27 the top of Pisgah; let your eyes turn towards the west, the north, the south, the east. Look well, for across this Jordan you shall not go. •Give Joshua your 28 instructions; encourage him, strengthen him; for it is he who shall go across at the head of his people; it is he who shall put them in possession of the land that you will see."

'So we stayed in the valley close to Beth-peor. 29

The apostasy at Peor. Where true wisdom lies

4 'And now, Israel, take notice of the laws and customs that I teach you today, 1 and observe them, that you may have life and may enter and take possession of the land that Yahweh the God of your fathers is giving you. •You must add 2 nothing to what I command you, and take nothing from it, but keep the commandments of Yahweh your God just as I lay them down for you. •You can see 3 with your own eyes what Yahweh has done at Baal-peor; all the followers of the Baal of Peor have been wiped out from among you by Yahweh your God; but all of you who stayed faithful to Yahweh your God are still alive today. 4 See, as Yahweh my God has commanded me, I teach you the laws and customs 5 that you are to observe in the land you are to enter and make your own. •Keep 6 them, observe them, and they will demonstrate to the peoples your wisdom and understanding. When they come to know of all these laws they will exclaim, "No other people is as wise and prudent as this great nation". •And indeed, 7 what great nation is there that has its gods so near as Yahweh our God is to us whenever we call to him? •And what great nation is there that has laws and 8 customs to match this whole Law that I put before you today?

The revelation at Horeb; its demands

'But take care what you do and be on your guard. Do not forget the things 9 your eyes have seen, nor let them slip from your heart all the days of your life; rather, tell them to your children and to your children's children. •The day you 10 stood at Horeb in the presence of Yahweh your God, Yahweh said to me, "Call the people round me that I may let them hear my words, that they may learn to fear me all the days they live on earth, and teach this to their children". •So you 11 came and stood at the foot of the mountain, and the mountain flamed to the very sky, a sky darkened by cloud, murky and thunderous. •Then Yahweh spoke to 12 you from the midst of the fire; you heard the sound of words but saw no shape, there was only a voice. •And Yahweh revealed his covenant to you and com- 13 manded you to observe it, the Ten Sayings which he inscribed on two tablets of stone. •He ordered me then to teach you the laws and customs that you were to 14 observe in the land towards which you are going to make it your own. *a*

'Take great care what you do, therefore: since you saw no shape on that day 15 at Horeb when Yahweh spoke to you from the midst of the fire, •see that you do 16 not act perversely, making yourselves a carved image in the shape of anything at all: whether it be in the likeness of man or of woman, •or of any beast on the 17 earth, or of any bird that flies in the heavens, •or of any reptile that crawls on 18 the ground, or of any fish in the waters under the earth. •When you raise your 19 eyes to heaven, when you see the sun, the moon, the stars, all the array of heaven, do not be tempted to worship them and serve them. Yahweh your God has allotted them to all the peoples under heaven, •but as for you, Yahweh has taken you, 20 and brought you out from the furnace of iron, from Egypt, to be a people all his own, as you still are today.

Of punishment to come, and of conversion

21 'Yahweh has been angry with me on your account; he has sworn that I shall not cross the Jordan or enter the prosperous land which Yahweh your God is 22 giving you as your heritage. •Yes, I am to die in this country; I shall not go 23 across this Jordan; you will go over and take possession of that rich land. •Take care therefore not to forget the covenant which Yahweh your God has made with you, by making a carved image of anything that Yahweh your God has forbidden 24 you; •for Yahweh your God is a consuming fire, a jealous God.

25 'When you have begotten children and grandchildren and you have lived long in the land, if you act perversely, making a carved image in one shape or another, 26 doing what displeases Yahweh and angers him, •on that day I will call heaven and earth to witness against you; and at once you will vanish from the land which you are crossing the Jordan to possess. You shall not live there long; you 27 shall be utterly destroyed. •Yahweh will scatter you among the peoples, and only a small number of you will remain among the nations where Yahweh will have 28 driven you. •There you will pay service to gods that human hands have made, of wood and of stone, that cannot see or hear, eat or smell.

29 'But you will seek Yahweh your God from there, and if you seek him with all 30 your heart and with all your soul, you shall find him. •In your distress, all that I have said will overtake you, but at the end of days[b] you will return to Yahweh 31 your God and listen to his voice. •For Yahweh your God is a merciful God and will not desert or destroy you or forget the covenant he made on oath with your fathers.

The splendour of the divine election

32 'Put this question, then, to the ages that are past, that went before you, from the time God created man on earth: Was there ever a word so majestic, from one 33 end of heaven to the other? Was anything ever heard? •Did ever a people hear the voice of the living God speaking from the heart of the fire, as you heard it, and 34 remain alive? •Has any god ventured to take to himself one nation from the midst of another by ordeals, signs, wonders, war with mighty hand and outstretched arm, by fearsome terrors—all this that Yahweh your God did for you before your eyes in Egypt?

35 'This he showed you so that you might know that Yahweh is God indeed and 36 that there is no other. •He let you hear his voice out of heaven for your instruction; on earth he let you see his great fire, and from the heart of the fire you heard 37 his word. •Because he loved your fathers and chose their descendants after them, he brought you out from Egypt, openly showing his presence and his great power, 38 driving out in front of you nations greater and more powerful than yourself, and brought you into their land to give it you for your heritage, as it is still today.

39 'Understand this today, therefore, and take it to heart: Yahweh is God indeed, 40 in heaven above as on earth beneath, he and no other. •Keep his laws and commandments as I give them to you today, so that you and your children may prosper and live long in the land that Yahweh your God gives you for ever.'

B. THE SECOND DISCOURSE OF MOSES

Its time and place

41
42
Then Moses set apart three cities to the east, beyond the Jordan, •where a man might find refuge who had killed his fellow unwittingly and with no previous feud

---

4 a. 'The laws and customs' given by Moses, as distinct from the Ten Commandments.
b. The end of the era; the beginning of a new age.

against him: by taking flight to one of these cities he could save his life. •These 43 were, for the Reubenites, Bezer in the wilderness on the tableland; for the Gadites, Ramoth in Gilead; for the Manassites, Golan in Bashan.

This is the Law which Moses put before the sons of Israel. •These are the 44 45 decrees and laws and customs that Moses proclaimed to the sons of Israel when they came out of Egypt, •beyond the Jordan in the valley near Beth-peor, in the 46 land of Sihon the Amorite king who lived at Heshbon. Moses and the sons of Israel had defeated him when they came out of Egypt, •and had taken possession 47 of his land and of the land of Og king of Bashan—two kings of the Amorites to the east beyond the Jordan, •from Aroer on the height above the wadi Arnon 48 as far as Mount Sirion (which is Hermon)—•and of all the Arabah east of the 49 Jordan as far as the Sea of the Arabah, at the foot of the slopes of Pisgah.

5 Moses called the whole of Israel together and said to them: 1

The Ten Commandments

'Listen, Israel, to the laws and customs that I proclaim in your hearing today. Learn them and take care to observe them.

'Yahweh our God made a covenant with us at Horeb. •It was not with our 2 3 fathers that Yahweh made this covenant, but with us, with us who are here, all living today. •On the mountain, from the heart of the fire, Yahweh spoke to you 4 face to face, •and I stood all the time between Yahweh and yourselves to tell you 5 of Yahweh's words, for you were afraid of the fire and had not gone up the mountain. He said:

"I am Yahweh your God who brought you out of the land of Egypt, out of the 6 house of slavery.

"You shall have no gods except me.   7

"You shall not make yourself a carved image or any likeness of anything in 8 heaven above or on earth beneath or in the waters under the earth; •you shall 9 not bow down to them or serve them. For I, Yahweh your God, am a jealous God and I punish the fathers' fault in the sons, the grandsons and the great-grandsons of those who hate me; •but I show kindness to thousands, to those 10 who love me and keep my commandments.

"You shall not utter the name of Yahweh your God to misuse it, for Yahweh 11 will not leave unpunished the man who utters his name to misuse it.

"Observe the sabbath day and keep it holy, as Yahweh your God has com- 12 manded you. •For six days you shall labour and do all your work, •but the 13 14 seventh day is a sabbath for Yahweh your God. You shall do no work that day, neither you nor your son nor your daughter nor your servants, men or women, nor your ox nor your donkey nor any of your animals, nor the stranger who lives with you. Thus your servant, man or woman, shall rest as you do. •Remember 15 that you were a servant in the land of Egypt, and that Yahweh your God brought you out from there with mighty hand and outstretched arm; because of this, Yahweh your God has commanded you to keep the sabbath day.

"Honour your father and your mother, as Yahweh your God has commanded 16 you, so that you may have long life and may prosper in the land that Yahweh your God gives to you.

"You shall not kill.   17

"You shall not commit adultery.   18

"You shall not steal.   19

"You shall not bear false witness against your neighbour.   20

"You shall not covet your neighbour's wife, you shall not set your heart on 21 his house, his field, his servant—man or woman—his ox, his donkey or anything that is his."

'These are the words Yahweh spoke to you when you were all assembled on 22 the mountain. With a great voice he spoke to you from the heart of the fire, in cloud and thick darkness. He added nothing, but wrote them on two tablets of stone which he gave to me.

Moses the mediator

23 'Now when you had heard this voice coming out of the darkness, while the mountain was all on fire, you came to me, all of you, heads of tribes and elders,
24 and said, "See how Yahweh our God has shown us his glory and his greatness and we have heard his voice from the middle of the fire. Today we have seen that
25 God can speak with man and man still live. •Why should we die now, when this great fire is ready to devour us, and when we are sure to perish if we hear
26 the voice of Yahweh our God a second time? •For what creature of flesh could possibly live after hearing, as we have heard, the voice of the living God speaking
27 from the heart of the fire? •You, then, go near and hear everything Yahweh our God will say and tell us all that Yahweh our God says to you; we will listen and observe it."

28 'Yahweh heard the words you spoke to me, and he said to me, "I have heard
29 this people's words. All they have spoken is well said. •If only their heart were always so, set on the fear of me and the keeping of my commandments, so that
30 they and their children might prosper for ever! •Go and say to them: Return
31 to your tents. •But you will stand here by me and I shall tell you all the commandments, the laws and the customs that you must teach them, which they must observe in the land I am giving them for their possession."

To love Yahweh is the essence of the Law

32 'Keep this, observe it. This is what Yahweh our God has commanded you.
33 Stray neither to right nor to left. •Follow the whole way that Yahweh has marked for you and you shall live, you shall prosper and shall live long in the land you are to possess.

1 6 'These then are the commandments, the laws and the customs[a] which Yahweh your God has instructed me to teach you that you may observe them in the
2 land which you are going to make your own. •Thus, if you fear Yahweh your God all the days of your life and if you keep all his laws and commandments which I lay on you, you will have a long life, you and your son and your grandson.
3 Listen then, Israel, keep and observe what will make you prosper and give you great increase, as Yahweh the God of your fathers has promised you, giving you a land where milk and honey flow.

4
5 'Listen, Israel: Yahweh our God is the one Yahweh. •You shall love Yahweh
6 your God with all your heart, with all your soul, with all your strength. •Let
7 these words I urge on you today be written on your heart. •You shall repeat them to your children and say them over to them whether at rest in your house
8 or walking abroad, at your lying down or at your rising; •you shall fasten them
9 on your hand as a sign and on your forehead as a circlet; •you shall write them on the doorposts of your house and on your gates.

10 'When Yahweh has brought you into the land which he swore to your fathers Abraham, Isaac and Jacob that he would give you, with great and prosperous
11 cities not of your building, •houses full of good things not furnished by you, wells you did not dig, vineyards and olives you did not plant, when you have
12 eaten these and had your fill, •then take care you do not forget Yahweh who
13 brought you out of the land of Egypt, out of the house of slavery. •You must fear Yahweh your God, you must serve him, by his name you must swear.

An appeal for loyalty

14
15 'Do not follow other gods, gods of the peoples round you, •for Yahweh your God who dwells among you is a jealous God; his anger could blaze out against

6 a. 'The laws and customs' begin at 12:1.

you and wipe you from the face of the earth. •Do not put Yahweh your God 16
to the test as you tested him at Massah. •Keep the commandments of Yahweh 17
your God and his decrees and laws that he has laid down for you, •and do 18
what is right and good in the eyes of Yahweh so that you may prosper and take
possession of the rich land which Yahweh swore to give to your fathers, •driving 19
out your enemies before you; this was the promise of Yahweh.

'In times to come, when your son asks you, "What is the meaning of the 20
decrees and laws and customs that Yahweh our God has laid down for you?" •you 21
shall tell your son, "Once we were Pharaoh's slaves in Egypt, and Yahweh brought
us out of Egypt by his mighty hand. •Before our eyes Yahweh worked great and 22
terrible signs and wonders against Egypt, against Pharaoh and all his House.
And he brought us out from there to lead us into the land he swore to our 23
fathers he would give to us. •And Yahweh commanded us to observe all these 24
laws and to fear Yahweh our God, so as to be happy for ever and to live, as
he has granted us to do until now. •For us right living will mean this: to keep 25
and observe all these commandments before Yahweh our God as he has
directed us."

Israel a people apart

7 'When Yahweh your God has led you into the land you are entering to make 1
your own, many nations will fall before you: Hittites, Girgashites, Amorites,
Canaanites, Perizzites, Hivites and Jebusites,ª seven nations greater and stronger
than yourselves. •Yahweh your God will deliver them over to you and you will 2
conquer them. You must lay them under ban. You must make no covenant with
them nor show them any pity. •You must not marry with them: you must not 3
give a daughter of yours to a son of theirs, nor take a daughter of theirs for a son
of yours, •for this would turn away your son from following me to serving other 4
gods and the anger of Yahweh would blaze out against you and soon
destroy you. •Instead, deal with them like this: tear down their altars, 5
smash their standing-stones, cut down their sacred poles and set fire to their
idols. •For you are a people consecrated to Yahweh your God; it is you that 6
Yahweh our God has chosen to be his very own people out of all the peoples
on the earth.

God's election and his favour

'If Yahweh set his heart on you and chose you, it was not because you out- 7
numbered other peoples: you were the least of all peoples. •It was for love of you 8
and to keep the oath he swore to your fathers that Yahweh brought you out with
his mighty hand and redeemed you from the house of slavery, from the power
of Pharaoh king of Egypt. •Know then that Yahweh your God is God indeed, 9
the faithful God who is true to his covenant and his graciousness for a thousand
generations towards those who love him and keep his commandments, •but who 10
punishes in their own persons those that hate him. He is not slow to destroy the
man who hates him; he makes him work out his punishment in person. •You are 11
therefore to keep and observe the commandments and statutes and ordinances
that I lay down for you today.

'Listen to these ordinances, be true to them and observe them, and in return 12
Yahweh your God will be true to the covenant and the kindness he promised
your fathers solemnly. •He will love you and bless you and increase your numbers; 13
he will bless the fruit of your body and the produce of your soil, your corn, your
wine, your oil, the issue of your cattle, the young of your flock, in the land he
swore to your fathers he would give you. •You will be more blessed than all 14
peoples. No man or woman among you shall be barren, no male or female of
your beasts infertile. •Yahweh will keep all sickness far from you; he will not 15
afflict you with those evil plagues of Egypt which you have known, but will
save them for all those who hate you.

16 'Devour, then, all these peoples whom Yahweh your God delivers over to you, show them no pity, do not serve their gods, for otherwise you would be ensnared.

The power of Yahweh

17 'You may say in your heart, "These nations outnumber me; how shall I be able
18 to dispossess them?" •Do not be afraid of them: remember how Yahweh your
19 God dealt with Pharaoh and all Egypt, •the great ordeals your own eyes have seen, the signs and wonders, the mighty hand and outstretched arm with which Yahweh your God has brought you out. So will Yahweh your God deal with all
20 the peoples whom you fear to face. •And what is more, Yahweh your God will send hornets to destroy those who remain and hide from you.

21 'Do not be afraid of them, for Yahweh your God is among you, a God who
22 is great and terrible. •Little by little Yahweh your God will destroy these nations before you; you will not be able to make an end of them at once, or the wild
23 beasts would grow too many for you. •But Yahweh your God will deliver them
24 over to you and will harass them until they are destroyed. •He will deliver their kings into your hands and you will blot out their names from under heaven; none shall withstand you, until you have destroyed them all.

25 'You must set fire to all the carved images of their gods, not coveting the gold and silver that covers them; take it and you will be caught in a snare: it is
26 detestable to Yahweh your God. •You must not bring any detestable thing into your house or you, like it, will come under the ban too. You must regard them as unclean and loathsome, for they are under the ban.

The ordeal in the wilderness

1   **8** 'All the commandments I enjoin on you today you must keep and observe so that you may live and increase in numbers and enter into the land that Yahweh
2 promised on oath to your fathers, and make it your own. •Remember how Yahweh your God led you for forty years in the wilderness, to humble you, to test you and know your inmost heart—whether you would keep his com-
3 mandments or not. •He humbled you, he made you feel hunger, he fed you with manna which neither you nor your fathers had known, to make you understand that man does not live on bread alone but that man lives on everything that comes
4 from the mouth of Yahweh. •The clothes on your back did not wear out and your feet were not swollen, all those forty years.

5 'Learn from this that Yahweh your God was training you as a man trains
6 his child, •and keep the commandments of Yahweh your God, and so follow his ways and reverence him.

The Promised Land and its temptations

7 'But Yahweh your God is bringing you into a prosperous land, a land of streams and springs, of waters that well up from the deep in valleys and hills,
8 a land of wheat and barley, of vines, of figs, of pomegranates, a land of olives,
9 of oil, of honey, •a land where you will eat bread without stint, where you will want nothing, a land where the stones are of iron, where the hills may be quarried
10 for copper. •You will eat and have all you want and you will bless Yahweh your God in the rich land he has given you.

11 'Take care you do not forget Yahweh your God, neglecting his commandments
12 and customs and laws which I lay on you today. •When you have eaten and
13 had all you want, when you have built fine houses to live in, •when you have seen your flocks and herds increase, your silver and gold abound and all your
14 possessions grow great, •do not become proud of heart. Do not then forget Yahweh your God who brought you out of the land of Egypt, out of the house
15 of slavery: •who guided you through this vast and dreadful wilderness, a land

---

7 a. Conventional list of pre-Israelite peoples of Palestine; but 'Hittites' (properly meaning a people of Asia Minor) is used in a vague sense of non-semitic inhabitants.

of fiery serpents, scorpions, thirst; who in this waterless place brought you water
from the hardest rock; •who in this wilderness fed you with manna that your 16
fathers had not known, to humble you and test you and so make your future the
happier. •Beware of saying in your heart, "My own strength and the might of my 17
own hand won this power for me". •Remember Yahweh your God: it was he who 18
gave you this strength and won you this power, thus keeping the covenant then,
as today, that he swore to your fathers. •Be sure that if you forget Yahweh your 19
God, if you follow other gods, if you serve them and bow down before them
—I warn you today— you will most certainly perish. •Like the nations Yahweh 20
is to destroy before you, so you yourselves shall perish, for not having listened
to the voice of Yahweh your God.

The victory comes from Yahweh, not from Israel's merits

9 'Listen, Israel; today you are about to cross the Jordan, to go and dispossess 1
nations greater and stronger than yourself, to capture great cities fortified to
the sky. •A people great and tall, these Anakim, as you know; you have heard 2
the saying: Who can stand up to the sons of Anak? •Be therefore sure today 3
that Yahweh your God himself will go in front of you, a devouring fire that will
destroy them, and he himself will subdue them for you; so you will dispossess
them and destroy them quickly as Yahweh has promised you. •Do not say in 4
your heart, when Yahweh your God has driven them before you, "It is for my
own goodness that Yahweh has brought me to possession of this land"; when
it is for their wickedness that Yahweh dispossesses these nations for you. •It is 5
not for any goodness or sincerity of yours that you are entering their land to
possess it; no, it is for the wickedness of these nations that Yahweh your God is
dispossessing them for you, and to keep the word that he swore to your fathers,
Abraham, Isaac and Jacob. •Be in fact sure, then, that it is not for any goodness 6
of yours that Yahweh gives you this rich land to possess, for you are a headstrong
people.

Israel's conduct at Horeb; Moses intercedes

'Remember; never forget how you provoked Yahweh your God in the wilder- 7
ness. From the day you came out of the land of Egypt you have been rebels against
Yahweh. •At Horeb you provoked Yahweh, and Yahweh was so angry with 8
you that he was ready to destroy you. •I had gone up the mountain to receive 9
the tablets of stone, the tablets of the covenant that Yahweh was making with
you. I stayed forty days and forty nights on the mountain, eating no bread,
drinking no water. •Yahweh gave me the two stone tablets inscribed by the 10
finger of God, and all the words on them that Yahweh had spoken to you on the
mountain from the midst of the fire on the day of the Assembly. •At the end of 11
the forty days and forty nights, after he had given me the two tablets of stone,
the tablets of the covenant, •Yahweh said to me, "Leave this place, go down 12
quickly, for your people whom you brought out of Egypt have broken faith.
They have been quick to leave the way I marked out for them; they have made
themselves an idol of cast metal." •Then Yahweh said to me, "I have seen this 13
people, and what a headstrong people they are! •Let me destroy them, and wipe 14
out their name from under heaven, and make out of you a nation mightier and
greater than they."

'So I went down the mountain again and it was blazing with fire, and in my 15
hands were the two tablets of the covenant. •And I looked and there you were, 16
you had been sinning against Yahweh your God. You had made yourself a
calf of cast metal; you had been quick to leave the way Yahweh marked out
for you. •I seized the two tablets and with my two hands threw them down and 17
broke them before your eyes. •Then I fell prostrate before Yahweh; as before, 18
I passed forty days and forty nights eating no bread and drinking no water, for
all the sin you had committed in doing what was displeasing to Yahweh, thus

19 arousing his anger. •For I was afraid of this anger, of the fury which so roused Yahweh against you that he was ready to destroy you. And once more Yahweh
20 heard my prayer. •Yahweh was enraged with Aaron too and was ready to destroy
21 him, and I pleaded for Aaron also. •That work of sin, the calf you had made, I took and burned and broke to pieces, and grinding it to fine dust I threw its dust into the stream that comes down from the mountain.

Israel sins again. A prayer of Moses

22 'At Taberah too and at Massah and Kibroth-hattaavah you provoked Yahweh.
23 And when Yahweh wanted you to leave Kadesh-barnea, saying, "Go up and take possession of the land I have given you", you rebelled against the command of
24 Yahweh your God and did not believe him or listen to his voice. •You have been rebels against Yahweh from the day he first knew you.

25 'So I fell prostrate before Yahweh and lay there these forty days and forty
26 nights, for Yahweh had said he would destroy you. •And I pleaded with Yahweh. My Lord Yahweh, I said, do not destroy your people, your heritage whom in your greatness you have redeemed, whom you have brought out of Egypt with
27 your mighty hand. •Remember your servants, Abraham, Isaac, and Jacob; take
28 no notice of this people's stubbornness, their wickedness, and their sin, •so that it may not be said in the land from which you brought us, "Yahweh was not able to bring them to the land he promised them. It was because he hated them
29 that he brought them out, to die in the wilderness." •But they are your people and your heritage whom you brought out by your great power and your outstretched arm.

The ark of the covenant; the choice of Levi

1   **10** 'Yahweh then said to me, "Cut two stone tablets like the first, and come
2 up to me on the mountain. Make an ark of wood; •on the tablets I shall inscribe the words that were on the first tablets, which you broke, and you will
3 put them in the ark." •So I made an ark of acacia wood, cut two stone tablets
4 like the first and went up the mountain with the two tablets in· my hand. •And he inscribed the tablets as he had inscribed them before with the Ten Sayings that Yahweh had spoken to you on the mountain from the middle of the fire on
5 the day of the Assembly. Then Yahweh gave them to me. •I came down the mountain again and put the tablets in the ark I had made, and there they stayed as Yahweh had commanded me.

6   *ᵃ* 'The sons of Israel left the wells of the Bene-jaakan for Moserah, where Aaron died; he was buried there, and his son Eleazar succeeded him in the
7 priesthood. •From there they set out for Gudgodah, and from Gudgodah for
8 Jotbathah, a land of water-streams. •Yahweh then set apart the tribe of Levi to carry the ark of Yahweh's covenant, to stand in the presence of Yahweh, to do him service and in his name to pronounce blessing as they still do today.
9 Levi therefore has no share or inheritance with his brothers: Yahweh is his inheritance, as Yahweh your God told him.

10 'And I, as before, stayed on the mountain forty days and forty nights. And
11 again Yahweh heard my prayer and agreed not to destroy you. •And Yahweh said to me, "Now go on your way at the head of this people, that they may go and take possession of the land I swore to their fathers I would give them".

Circumcision of the heart

12 'And now, Israel, what does Yahweh your God ask of you? Only this: to fear Yahweh your God, to follow all his ways, to love him, to serve Yahweh your God
13 with all your heart and all your soul, •to keep the commandments and laws of Yahweh that for your good I lay down for you today.

---

10 a. Vv.6-9 interrupt the narrative and are probably a later addition, dissociating the Levites from Aaron's sin.

'To Yahweh your God belong indeed heaven and the heaven of heavens, the 14
earth and all it contains; •yet it was on your fathers that Yahweh set his heart 15
for love of them, and after them of all the nations chose their descendants, you
yourselves, up to the present day. •Circumcise your heart then and be obstinate 16
no longer; •for Yahweh your God is God of gods and Lord of lords, the great 17
God, triumphant and terrible, never partial, never to be bribed. •It is he who 18
sees justice done for the orphan and the widow, who loves the stranger and gives
him food and clothing. •Love the stranger then, for you were strangers in the 19
land of Egypt. •It is Yahweh your God you must fear and serve; you must cling 20
to him; in his name take your oaths. •He it is you must praise, he is your God: for 21
you he has done these great and terrible things you have seen with your own eyes;
and though your fathers numbered only seventy when they went down to Egypt, 22
Yahweh your God has made you as many as the stars of heaven.

Israel's lessons

11 'You must love Yahweh your God and always keep his injunctions, his 1
laws, his customs, his commandments. •Mark, this day, how it was you 2
who received the instruction, not your sons. They have not known or seen the
lessons of Yahweh your God, his greatness, the might of his hand, the strength
of his arm, •the signs and the deeds he performed in Egypt itself against Pharaoh 3
and all his land; •what he did to the armies of Egypt, to their horses and their 4
chariots, how he poured the waters of the Sea of Reeds over them as they pursued
you, leaving no trace of them to this day; •what he did for you in the wilderness 5
before you reached this place; •what he did to Dathan and Abiram, the sons of 6
Eliab the Reubenite, how, right in the midst of all Israel, the earth opened its
mouth and swallowed them with their households, their tents and all their retinue.
It is your eyes that have seen all this great work that Yahweh has done. 7

Promises and warnings

'You must keep all the commandments I enjoin on you today, so that you may 8
have the strength to conquer the land into which you are to cross to make it your
own, •and to live long in the land which Yahweh swore to give to your fathers 9
and their descendants, a land where milk and honey flow.

'For the land which you are to enter and make your own is not like the land 10
of Egypt from which you came, where you sowed your seed and watered it by
tread*a* like a vegetable garden. •No, the land into which you are to cross to 11
make it your own is a land of hills and valleys watered by the rain from heaven.
Yahweh your God takes care of this land, the eyes of Yahweh your God are on 12
it always, from the year's beginning to its end. •And it is most sure that if you 13
faithfully obey the commandments I enjoin on you today, loving Yahweh your
God and serving him with all your heart and all your soul, •"I will give your 14
land rain in season, autumn rain and spring, so that you may harvest your corn,
your wine, your oil; •I shall provide grass in the fields for your cattle, and you 15
will eat and have all you want". •Take care your heart is not seduced, that you 16
do not go astray, serving other gods and worshipping them, •or the anger of 17
Yahweh will blaze out against you, he will shut up the heavens and there will be
no rain, the land will not yield its produce and you will quickly die in the
prosperous land that Yahweh is giving you.

Conclusion

'Let these words of mine remain in your heart and in your soul; fasten them 18
on your hand as a sign and on your forehead as a circlet. •Teach them to your 19
children and say them over to them, whether at rest in your house or walking
abroad, at your lying down or at your rising. •Write them on the doorposts of 20
your house and on your gates, •so that you and your children may live long in 21
the land that Yahweh swore to your fathers he would give them for as long as
there is a sky above the earth.

22   'For if you faithfully keep and observe all these commandments that I enjoin
on you today, loving Yahweh your God, following all his ways and clinging to
23 him, •Yahweh will dispossess all these nations for you, and you shall dispossess
24 nations greater and more powerful than yourselves. •Wherever the sole of your
foot treads shall be yours; your territory shall stretch from the wilderness and
25 from Lebanon, from the river, the river Euphrates, to the Western Sea. •No man
will be able to stand against you; Yahweh your God will make you feared and
dreaded throughout the land that you tread, just as he promised you.
26
27   'See, I set before you today a blessing and a curse: •a blessing, if you obey
28 the commandments of Yahweh our God that I enjoin on you today; •a curse,
if you disobey the commandments of Yahweh your God and leave the way I have
29 marked out for you today, by going after other gods you have not known. •And
when Yahweh your God has brought you into the land which you are to enter
and make your own, you shall set the blessing on Mount Gerizim and the curse
30 on Mount Ebal. •These mountains, as you know, are beyond the Jordan on the
westward road, in the land of the Canaanites who live in the Plain, opposite
31 Gilgal, near the Oak of Moreh. •You shall indeed cross the Jordan to enter and
make the land your own that Yahweh your God is giving you. You shall possess
32 it and you shall live in it, •and you must keep and observe all the laws and
customs that I set before you today.

II. THE DEUTERONOMIC CODE

1   **12** 'Now these are the laws and customs that you must keep and observe,
in the land that Yahweh the God of your fathers has granted you to possess,
for as long as you live in that land.

A. RELIGIOUS OBSERVANCES

The place of worship

2   'You must destroy completely all the places where the nations you dispossess
have served their gods, on high mountains, on hills, under any spreading tree;
3   you must tear down their altars, smash their pillars, cut down their sacred poles,
set fire to the carved images of their gods and wipe out their name from that
place.
4
5   'Not so are you to behave towards Yahweh your God. •You must seek Yahweh
your God only in the place he himself will choose from among all your tribes,
6   to set his name there and give it a home. •There you shall bring your holocausts
and your sacrifices, your tithes, the offerings from your hands, your votive
offerings and your voluntary offerings, the first-born of your herd and flock;
7   there you will eat in the presence of Yahweh your God and be thankful for all
that your hands have presented, you and your households blessed by Yahweh
your God.[a]
8   'You must not act as we do here today: every man does what seems right to
9   him, •for as yet you have not come to the resting place and the inheritance that
10 Yahweh your God is giving you. •You are about to cross the Jordan and live in
the land that Yahweh your God grants you to inherit; he will give you relief
11 from all the enemies that surround you, and you shall live in security. •To the
place chosen by Yahweh your God as a home for his name, to that place you
are to bring all that I command you: your holocausts and your sacrifice, your

---

11 a. Probably with a waterwheel worked by a treadle.
12 a. The centralising of the nation's worship in one place (ultimately Jerusalem), though
attributed to Moses, did not in fact take place until after the time of Solomon, 1 K 3:4.

tithes, the offerings from your hands, and all the best of your possessions that
you vow to Yahweh. •There you shall rejoice in the presence of Yahweh your 12
God, you and your sons and daughters, your serving men and women, and the
Levite who lives in your towns, since he has no share or inheritance with you.

Regulations concerning sacrifice

'Take care you do not offer your holocausts in all the sacred places you see; 13
only in the place that Yahweh chooses in one of your tribes may you offer 14
your holocausts and do all I command you.

'Still, whenever you want you may slaughter and eat flesh in any of your 15
towns, as much as the blessing of Yahweh affords you. Clean or unclean may
eat it, just as if it were gazelle or deer. •Only you must not consume the blood 16
but pour it out like water on the ground.

'In your towns you may not consume the tithes of your corn, your wine or 17
your oil, or the first-born of your herd or flock, or any of your votive offerings,
or voluntary offerings, or anything your hands have presented. •You must eat 18
these in the presence of Yahweh your God in the place Yahweh your God
chooses and there alone, you and your son and daughter, your serving man or
woman and the Levite who lives in your towns. You shall rejoice in the presence
of Yahweh your God over all that your hands have presented. •In your land 19
take care never to neglect the Levite.

'When Yahweh your God enlarges your territory as he has promised you, and 20
you say, "I should like to eat meat", if you want to eat meat you may eat as much
as you like. •If the place in which Yahweh your God chooses to set his name is 21
too far away, you may slaughter any of your herd or flock that Yahweh has
given you in the way that I have laid down for you; you may eat in your towns
as much as you will. •But you must eat it as you would gazelle or deer; clean 22
or unclean alike may eat it. •Only take care not to consume the blood, for the 23
blood is the life, and you must not consume the life with the flesh. •You must 24
not consume it but pour it out like water on the ground. •You must not consume 25
it, and then you and your sons after you will prosper, doing what is right in the
eyes of Yahweh. •But the holy things you have and those you have vowed you 26
must go and take to the place that Yahweh chooses. •The holocaust of flesh and 27
blood you must offer on the altar of Yahweh your God; and, in your sacrifices,
the blood must be poured out on the altar of Yahweh your God; the flesh you
may eat yourselves. •Be faithful in keeping all the instructions that I give you and 28
obey them, so that you and your sons after you may be happy for always, doing
what is good and right in the eyes of Yahweh your God.

Against Canaanite cults

'When Yahweh your God has annihilated in front of you the nations that you 29
are to dispossess, and when you have dispossessed them and made your home
in their country, •be careful you are not caught in a trap: do not imitate them 30
once they have been destroyed in front of you, or go enquiring after their gods,
saying, "How did these nations worship their gods? I will go and do the same."
This is not the way for you to behave towards Yahweh your God. For Yahweh 31
detests all this and hates what they have done for their gods, even burning their
sons and daughters in the fire for their gods.

13 'All I command you, you must keep and observe, adding nothing to it, ¹₃₂
taking nothing away.

Against the enticements of idolatry

'If a prophet or a dreamer of dreams arises among you and offers to do a sign ²⁄₇
or a wonder for you, •and the sign or wonder comes about; and if he then says ³⁄₂
to you, "Come, then, let us follow other gods (whom you have not known) and
serve them", •you are not to listen to the words of that prophet or to the dreams ⁴⁄₃

of that dreamer. Yahweh your God is testing you to know if you love Yahweh
your God with all your heart and all your soul. •Yahweh your God you shall
follow, him you shall fear, his commandments you shall keep, his voice you shall
obey, him shall you serve, to him shall you cling. •That prophet or that dreamer
of dreams must be put to death, for he has preached apostasy from Yahweh
your God who brought you out of the land of Egypt and redeemed you from
the house of slavery, and he would have made you turn aside from the way
that Yahweh your God marked out for you. You must banish this evil from
among you.

'If your brother, the son of your father or of your mother, or your son or
daughter, or the wife you cherish, or the friend with whom you share your life,
if one of these secretly tries to entice you, saying. "Come, let us serve other gods",
whom neither you nor your fathers have known, •gods from among those of the
peoples far or near surrounding you, from one end of the earth to the other,
you must not give way to him, nor listen to him, you must show him no pity, you
must not spare him, you must not conceal his guilt. •No, you must kill him; your
hand is to be the first raised against him in putting him to death, the hand of
all the people will come next. •You must stone him to death, for he has tried
to lure you away from Yahweh your God who brought you out of the land of
Egypt, from the house of slavery. •All Israel shall hear of it and be afraid and
never again commit such wickedness among you.

'If you hear that in one of the towns which Yahweh your God has given you
for a home, •there are men, scoundrels from your own stock, who have led
fellow citizens astray, saying "Come, let us serve other gods" whom you have
not known, •it is your duty to look into the matter, examine it and inquire
most carefully. If it is proved and confirmed that such a hateful thing has taken
place among you, •then you must kill all the inhabitants of that town without
giving any quarter; you must lay it under ban, the town and all it contains.
You must gather all the wealth of it in the public square, and set fire to the town
and all its goods, offering it all to Yahweh your God. It shall be a ruin for all
time, never to be built again. •From what is thus banned you must keep nothing
back, so that Yahweh may turn from the ferocity of his anger and show you
mercy, and have pity on you and increase your numbers as he swore to your
fathers; •that is, provided you listen to the voice of Yahweh your God, keeping
all the commandments of his that I enjoin on you today, and doing what is right
in the eyes of Yahweh your God.

Against an idolatrous practice

14 'You are sons of Yahweh your God. You must not gash yourselves or
shave your foreheads for one who is dead.[a] •For you are a people consecrated to Yahweh your God, and Yahweh has chosen you to be his very own
people out of all the peoples on the earth.

Clean and unclean animals

'You must eat nothing that is detestable. •These are the animals you may
eat: ox, sheep, goat, •deer, gazelle, roebuck, ibex, antelope, oryx, mountain
sheep. •You may eat any animal that has a divided and cloven hoof and that
is a ruminant. •Of those, however, that are ruminant and those that have a divided
and cloven hoof you may not eat the following: the camel, the hare and the
hyrax, which are ruminant but have no cloven hoof; you must hold them unclean.
So also the pig, which though it has a cloven hoof is not ruminant; you must
hold it unclean. You must not eat the meat of such animals nor touch their
dead bodies.

---

14 a. Since the prophets do not appear to doubt the lawfulness of these practices as a ritual of
domestic mourning, it may be that the 'one who is dead' is the god Baal, whose death was
commemorated annually when the vegetation withered.

'Of all that lives in water you may eat the following: whatever has fins and 9
scales may be eaten. • But you must not eat anything that has not fins and scales: 10
you must hold it unclean.

'You may eat all clean birds, • but the following birds you must not eat: the ¹¹₁₂
tawny vulture, the griffon, the osprey, • the kite and the several kinds of buzzard, 13
all kinds of raven, • the ostrich, the screech owl, the seagull, the several kinds ¹⁴₁₅
of hawk, • owl, barn owl, ibis, • pelican, white vulture, cormorant, • stork, the ¹⁶,¹⁷₁₈
several kinds of heron, hoopoe and bat. • You are to hold all winged insects to be 19
unclean and must not eat them. • You may eat anything winged that is clean. 20

'You must not eat any animal that has died a natural death. You may give 21
it for food to the alien who lives in your towns, or sell it to a foreigner.

'You are not to boil a kid in its mother's milk.

The annual tithe

'Every year you must take a tithe of all that your sowing yields on the land, 22
and in the presence of Yahweh your God, in the place he chooses to give his 23
name a home, you are to eat the tithe of your corn, your wine and your oil and
the first-born of your herd and flock; so shall you learn to fear Yahweh your
God always.

'If the road is too long for you, if you cannot bring your tithe because the 24
place in which Yahweh chooses to make a home for his name is too far, when
Yahweh your God has blessed you, • you must turn your tithe into money, and 25
with the money clasped in your hand you must go to the place chosen by Yahweh;
there you may spend the money on whatever you like, oxen, sheep, wine, strong 26
drink, anything your heart desires. You are to eat there in the presence of Yahweh
your God and rejoice, you and your household. • Do not neglect the Levite who 27
lives in your towns, since he has no share or inheritance with you.

The third-year tithe

'At the end of every three years you must take all the tithes of your harvests 28
for that year and deposit them at your doors. • Then the Levite (since he has no 29
share or inheritance with you), the stranger, the orphan and the widow who live
in your towns may come and eat and have all they want. So shall Yahweh your
God bless you in all the work that your hands undertake.

The sabbatical year

15 'At the end of every seven years you must grant a remission. • Now the ¹₂
nature of the remission is this: every creditor who holds the person of his
neighbour in bond*ᵃ* must grant him remission; he may not exact payment from
his fellow or his brother once the latter appeals to Yahweh for remission. • From 3
a foreigner you may exact payment, but you must remit whatever claim you have
on your brother. • Let there be no poor among you then. For Yahweh will bless 4
you in the land Yahweh your God gives you for your inheritance • only if you 5
pay careful attention to the voice of Yahweh your God, keeping and observing
all these commandments that I enjoin on you today. • If Yahweh your God 6
blesses you as he promised, you will be creditors to many nations and debtors
to none; you will rule over many nations and be ruled by none.

'Is there a poor man among you, one of your brothers, in any town of yours 7
in the land that Yahweh your God is giving you? Do not harden your heart or
close your hand against that poor brother of yours, • but be open-handed with 8
him and lend him enough for his needs. • Do not allow this mean thought in 9
your heart, "The seventh year, the year of remission is near", and look coldly
on your poor brother and give him nothing; he could appeal against you to
Yahweh and it would be a sin for you. • When you give to him, you must give 10
with an open heart; for this Yahweh your God will bless you in all you do and
in all your giving. • Of course there will never cease to be poor in the land; 11

I command you therefore: Always be open-handed with your brother, and with anyone in your country who is in need and poor.

Slaves

12 'If your fellow Hebrew, man or woman, is sold to you, he can serve you for
13 six years. In the seventh year you must set him free, •and in setting him free you
14 must not let him go empty-handed. •You must make him a generous provision from your flock, your threshing-floor, your winepress; as Yahweh your God has
15 blessed you, so you must give to him. •Remember that you were a slave in the land of Egypt and that Yahweh your God redeemed you; that is why I lay this charge on you today.

16 'But if he says to you, "I do not want to leave you", if he loves you and your
17 household and is happy with you, •you are to take an awl and drive it through his ear into the door and he shall be your servant for all time. You are to do the same for your maidservant.

18 'Do not think it hard on you to have to give him his freedom; he is worth twice the cost of a hired servant and has served you for six years. So shall Yahweh your God bless you in all you do.

The first-born

19 'You must consecrate every first-born male from your herd and flock to Yahweh your God. You must not put the first-born of your herd to work nor
20 shear the first-born of your flock. •You are to eat it, you and your household, each year, in the presence of Yahweh your God, in the place Yahweh chooses.
21 If it has a blemish, if it is lame or blind, or has any serious defect at all, you
22 must not sacrifice it to Yahweh your God. •You must eat it at home, unclean
23 and clean together, as you would gazelle or deer; •only you must not consume the blood, but pour it out like water on the ground.

The feasts: Passover and Unleavened Bread

1 **16** 'Observe the month of Abib and celebrate the Passover for Yahweh your God, because it was in the month of Abib that Yahweh your God brought
2 you out of Egypt by night. •You must sacrifice a passover from your flock or herd for Yahweh your God in the place where Yahweh chooses to give his name
3 a home. •You must not eat leavened bread with this; for seven days you must eat it with unleavened bread, the bread of emergency, for it was in great haste that you came out of the land of Egypt; so you will remember, all the days of your
4 life, the day you came out of the land of Egypt. •For seven days no leaven must be found in any house throughout your territory, nor must any of the meat that you sacrifice in the evening of the first day be kept overnight until morning.
5 You may not sacrifice the passover in any of the towns that Yahweh your God
6 gives you; •but only in the place where Yahweh your God chooses to give his name a home, there you must sacrifice the passover, in the evening at sunset,
7 at the hour at which you came out of Egypt. •You must cook it and eat it in the place Yahweh your God chooses, and in the morning you are to return and
8 go to your tents. •For six days you shall eat unleavened bread; on the seventh day there shall be an assembly for Yahweh your God; and you must do no work.

Other feasts

9 'You are to count seven weeks, counting these seven weeks from the time you
10 begin to put your sickle into the standing corn. •You must then celebrate the feast of Weeks for Yahweh your God with the gift of a voluntary offering from your hand in proportion to the way that Yahweh your God has blessed you.
11 You must rejoice in the presence of Yahweh your God in the place where Yahweh

---

15 a. The case of a debtor who has bound himself by contract to work for his creditor in the event of non-payment.

your God chooses to give his name a home, you and your son and daughter, your serving men and women, the Levite who lives in your towns, the stranger, the orphan and the widow who live among you. •Remember that you were a 12 slave in Egypt, and carefully observe these laws.

'You must celebrate the feast of Tabernacles for seven days, at the time when 13 you gather in the produce of your threshing-floor and winepress. •You must 14 rejoice at your feast, you and your son and daughter, your serving men and women, the Levite, the stranger, the orphan and the widow who live in your towns. For seven days you are to celebrate the feast for Yahweh your God in the place 15 Yahweh chooses, for Yahweh your God will bless you in all your harvest and all your handiwork, and you will be filled with joy.

'Three times a year all your menfolk are to appear before Yahweh your God 16 in the place he chooses: at the feast of Unleavened Bread, at the feast of Weeks, at the feast of Tabernacles. No one must appear before Yahweh empty-handed, but every man must give what he can, in proportion to the blessing that Yahweh 17 your God gives you.

Judges

'You are to appoint judges and scribes in each of the towns that Yahweh is 18 giving you, for all your tribes; these must administer an impartial judgement to the people. •You must not pervert the law; you must be impartial, you must take 19 no bribes, for a bribe blinds wise men's eyes and jeopardises the cause of the just. Strict justice must be your ideal, so that you may live in rightful possession of 20 the land that Yahweh your God is giving you.

Abuses in worship

'You must not plant a sacred pole of any wood whatsoever beside the altar 21 that you put up for Yahweh your God; •nor must you set up a standing-stone, 22 a thing Yahweh your God would abhor. 17 To Yahweh your God you must 1 sacrifice nothing from herd or flock that has any blemish or defect whatsoever, for Yahweh your God holds this detestable.

'If there is anyone, man or woman, among you in any of the towns Yahweh 2 your God is giving you, who does what is displeasing to Yahweh your God by violating his covenant, •who goes and serves other gods and worships them, or 3 the sun or the moon or any of heaven's array—a thing I have forbidden—•and 4 this person is denounced to you; if after careful inquiry it is found true and confirmed that this hateful thing has been done in Israel, •you must take the 5 man or woman guilty of this evil deed outside your city gates, and there you must stone that man or woman to death. •A man may be put to death only on 6 the word of two witnesses or three; and no man may be put to death on the word of one witness alone. •The witnesses shall be the first to raise their hands 7 against him in putting him to death, then all the people shall follow. You must banish this evil from your midst.

Levitical judges

'If a case comes before you which is too difficult for you, a case of murder, 8 legal rights or assault, or any dispute at all in your towns, you must make your way to the place Yahweh your God chooses, •and approach the levitical priests 9 and the judge then in office. They will hold an inquiry and give a decision for you. •You must abide by the decision they pronounce for you in that place 10 which Yahweh chooses, and you must take care to carry out all their instructions. You must abide by the verdict they give you and by the decision they declare to 11 you, swerving neither right nor left of the sentence they have pronounced for you. •If anyone presumes to disobey either the priest who is there in the service 12 of Yahweh your God, or the judge, that man must die. You must banish this evil from Israel. •And all the people shall hear of it and be afraid and not act 13 presumptuously a second time.

Kings

14 'When you reach the land that Yahweh your God gives you, and take possession of it and live there, if you say to yourself, "I will appoint a king over
15 me like all the surrounding nations", •it must be a king of Yahweh's choosing whom you appoint over you; it must be one from among your brothers that is appointed king over you; you are not to give yourself a foreign king who is no brother of yours.

16 'Ensure that he does not increase the number of his horses, or make the people go back to Egypt to increase his cavalry, for Yahweh said to you, "You must
17 never go back that way again". •Nor must he increase the number of his wives, for that could lead his heart astray. Nor must he increase his gold and silver
18 excessively. •When he is seated on his royal throne he must write a copy of this
19 Law on a scroll for his own use at the dictation of the levitical priests. •It must never leave him and he must read it every day of his life and learn to fear Yahweh
20 his God by keeping all the words of this Law and observing these laws. •So his heart will not look down on his brothers and he will swerve neither right nor left from these commandments. If he does this, he will have long days on his throne, he and his sons, in Israel.

The levitical priesthood

1 **18** 'The levitical priests, that is to say the whole of the tribe of Levi, shall have no share or inheritance with Israel; they shall live on the foods offered to
2 Yahweh and on his dues. •This tribe is to have no inheritance among their brothers; Yahweh will be their inheritance as he promised them.

3 'These are the priests' dues from the people, from those who offer an ox or a sheep in sacrifice: the priest is to be given the shoulder, the cheeks and the
4 stomach. •You must give him the first-fruits of your corn, your wine, your oil,
5 as well as the first of your sheep's shearing. •For Yahweh your God has chosen him out of all your tribes to stand before Yahweh your God, to do the duties of the sacred ministry, and to bless in Yahweh's name, him and his sons for all time.

6 'If the Levite living in one of your towns anywhere in Israel decides to come
7 to the place Yahweh chooses, •he shall minister there in the name of Yahweh his God like all his fellow Levites who stand ministering there in the presence of
8 Yahweh, •and shall eat equal shares with them, no count being taken of the claims he has on the levitical families for the goods he has sold.

Prophets

•9 'When you come into the land Yahweh your God gives you, you must not
10 fall into the habit of imitating the detestable practices of the natives. •There must never be anyone among you who makes his son or daughter pass through
11 fire, who practises divination, who is soothsayer, augur or sorcerer, •who uses
12 charms, consults ghosts or spirits, or calls up the dead. •For the man who does these things is detestable to Yahweh your God; it is because of these detestable practices that Yahweh your God is driving these nations before you.

13
14 'You must be entirely faithful to Yahweh your God. •For these nations whom you are dispossessing may listen to soothsayers and diviners, but this is not the
15 gift that Yahweh your God gives to you: •Yahweh your God will raise up for you a prophet like myself, from among yourselves, from your own brothers;
16 to him you must listen. •This is what you yourselves asked of Yahweh your God at Horeb on the day of the Assembly. "Do not let me hear again" you said "the voice of Yahweh my God, nor look any longer on this great fire, or I shall die";
17
18 and Yahweh said to me, "All they have spoken is well said. •I will raise up a prophet like yourself for them from their own brothers; I will put my words into
19 his mouth and he shall tell them all I command him. •The man who does not listen to my words that he speaks in my name, shall be held answerable to me

for it. •But the prophet who presumes to say in my name a thing I have not 20
commanded him to say, or who speaks in the name of other gods, that prophet
shall die."

'You may say in your heart, "How are we to know what word was not spoken 21
by Yahweh?" •When a prophet speaks in the name of Yahweh and the thing 22
does not happen and the word is not fulfilled, then it has not been spoken by
Yahweh. The prophet has spoken with presumption. You have nothing to fear
from him.

B. ON THE LAW OF RETALIATION

Homicide and cities of refuge

19 'When Yahweh your God has annihilated the nations whose land Yahweh 1
your God gives you, and you have dispossessed them and you live in their
towns and in their houses, •you are to set aside three cities in the land Yahweh is 2
giving you for your possession. •You must keep the approaches to them in good 3
order and divide into three parts the area of the land Yahweh your God is giving
into your possession, so that any homicide may be able to find a refuge in them.
Here is the case of how a man may save his life by taking refuge there.   4

'If anyone has struck his fellow accidentally, not having any previous feud
with him •(for example, he goes with his fellow into the forest to cut wood; his 5
arm swings the axe to fell a tree; the head slips off the handle and strikes his
companion dead), that man may take refuge in one of these cities and save his
life. •It must not be allowed that the avenger of blood, in the heat of his anger, 6
should pursue the killer and that the length of the road should help him to
overtake and fatally wound him; for the man has not deserved to die, having
had no previous feud with his companion.

'I command you therefore: You are to set aside three cities, •and if Yahweh 7/8
your God enlarges your territory, as he swore to your fathers he would, and gives
you the whole land he promised to give your fathers—•provided you keep and 9
observe all the commandments I enjoin on you today, loving Yahweh your God
and always following his ways—then to those three cities you will add three more.
In this way, innocent blood will not be shed in the land Yahweh your God gives 10
for your inheritance; otherwise there would be blood-guilt on you.

'But if it happens that a man has a feud with his fellow and lies in wait for 11
him and falls on him and wounds him fatally and he dies, and the man takes
refuge in one of these cities, •the elders of his own town shall send to have him 12
seized and hand him over to the avenger of blood to die. •You are to show him 13
no pity. You must banish the shedding of innocent blood from Israel, and then
you will prosper.

Boundaries

'You must not displace your neighbour's boundary mark, set by your forbears, 14
in the inheritance you receive in the land Yahweh is giving into your possession.

Witnesses

'A single witness cannot suffice to convict a man of a crime or offence of any 15
kind; whatever the misdemeanour, the evidence of two witnesses or three is
required to sustain the charge.

'If a malicious witness appears against a man to accuse him of rebellion, 16
both parties to this dispute before Yahweh must be brought before the priests 17
and judges then in office. •The judges must make a careful inquiry, and if it turns 18
out that the witness who accused his brother is a lying witness, •you must deal 19
with him as he would have dealt with his brother. You must banish this evil from
your midst. •Others will hear of it and be afraid and never again do such an evil 20
thing among you. •You are to show no pity.   21

The 'lex talionis'

'Life for life, eye for eye, tooth for tooth, hand for hand, foot for foot.

War and combatants

1 20 'When you go to war against your enemies and see horses and chariots and
an army greater than your own, you must not be afraid of them; Yahweh

2 your God is with you, who brought you out of the land of Egypt. •When you
are about to join battle the priest is to come forward and address the people.

3 He is to say to them, "Listen, Israel; now that you are about to join battle against
your enemies, do not be faint-hearted. Let there be no fear or trembling or alarm

4 as you face them. •Yahweh your God goes with you to fight for you against your
enemies and to save you."

5 Then the scribes are to address the people in words like these:
"Is there any man here who has built a new house and not yet dedicated it?
Let him go home lest he die in battle and another perform the dedication.

6 "Is there any man here who has planted a vineyard and not yet enjoyed its
fruit? Let him go home lest he die in battle and another enjoy its fruit.

7 Is there any man here who has betrothed a wife and not yet taken her? Let
him go home lest he die in battle and another take her."

8 'The scribes shall also address the people like this:
"Is there any man here who is fearful and faint of heart? Let him go home
lest he make his fellows lose heart too."

9 'And when the scribes have finished speaking to the people, commanders will
be appointed to lead them.

Captured towns

10 'When you advance to the attack on any town, first offer it terms of peace.

11 If it accepts these and opens its gates to you, all the people to be found in it shall

12 do forced labour for you and be subject to you. •But if it refuses peace and offers

13 resistance, you must lay siege to it. •Yahweh your God shall deliver it into your

14 power and you are to put all its menfolk to the sword. •But the women, the
children, the livestock and all that the town contains, all its spoil, you may take
for yourselves as booty. You will devour the spoil of your enemies which Yahweh
your God has delivered to you.

15 'That is how you will treat the far-distant towns not belonging to the nations

16 near you. •But as regards the towns of those peoples which Yahweh your God
gives you as your own inheritance, you must not spare the life of any living thing.

17 Instead, you must lay them under ban, the Hittites, Amorites, Canaanites,

18 Perizzites, Hivites and Jebusites, as Yahweh your God commanded, •so that they
may not teach you to practise all the detestable practices they have in honour
of their gods and so cause you to sin against Yahweh your God.

19 'If, when attacking a town, you have to besiege it for a long time before you
capture it, you must not destroy its trees by taking an axe to them: eat their
fruit but do not cut them down. Is the tree in the fields human that you should

20 besiege it too? •Any trees, however, which you know are not fruit trees, you
may mutilate and cut down and use to build siege-works against the hostile town
until it falls.

The unidentified murderer

1 21 'In the land Yahweh is giving you as your possession, if a murdered man
is discovered lying in open country and it is not known who killed him,

2 your elders and scribes must go and measure the distance between the victim and

3 the surrounding towns, •and establish which town is nearest the victim. Then
the elders of that town are to take a heifer that has not yet been put to work or

4 used as a draught animal under the yoke. •And the elders of that town must
bring the heifer down to a watercourse that is never dry at a spot that has been

neither ploughed nor sown, and there by the watercourse they must break the heifer's neck. •And the priests, the sons of Levi, shall then come forward, for 5 these are the men Yahweh your God has chosen to do him service and to bless in the name of Yahweh, and it is their business to settle all cases of dispute or of violence. •All the elders of the town nearest the murdered man shall then wash 6 their hands in the watercourse, over the slaughtered heifer. •They are to pro- 7 nounce these words, "Our hands did not shed this blood and our eyes saw nothing. •Cover your people Israel whom you have redeemed, Yahweh, and let 8 no innocent blood be shed among your people Israel." So they will be covered against blood-vengeance. •You must banish all shedding of innocent blood from 9 among you if you mean to do what is right in the eyes of Yahweh.

C. ON MARRIAGE

Women taken in war

'When you go to war against your enemies and Yahweh your God delivers 10 them into your power and you take prisoners, •if you see a beautiful woman 11 among the prisoners and find her desirable, you may make her your wife •and 12 bring her to your home. She is to shave her head and cut her nails •and take off 13 her prisoner's garb; she is to stay inside your house and must mourn her father and mother for a full month. Then you may go to her and be a husband to her, and she shall be your wife. •Should she cease to please you, you will let her go 14 where she wishes, not selling her for money: you are not to make any profit out of her, since you have had the use of her.

Birthright

'If a man has two wives, one loved and the other unloved, and the loved one 15 and the unloved both bear him children, and if the first-born son is of the unloved wife, •then when the man comes to bequeath his goods to his sons, he may not 16 treat the son of the wife whom he loves as the first-born at the expense of the son of the wife he does not love, the true first-born. •He must acknowledge as 17 first-born the son of the wife he does not love and give to him a double share of his estate, for this son is the first-fruit of his strength, and the right of the first-born is his.

The rebellious son

'If a man has a stubborn and rebellious son who will not listen to the voice 18 of his father or the voice of his mother, and even when they punish him still will not pay attention to them, •his father and mother shall take hold of him and bring 19 him out to the elders of the town at the gate of that place. •And they shall 20 say to the elders of his town, "This son of ours is stubborn and rebellious and will not listen to us; he is a wastrel and a drunkard". •Then all his fellow citizens 21 shall stone him to death. You must banish this evil from your midst. All Israel will hear of it and be afraid.

Various rulings

'If a man guilty of a capital offence is put to death and you hang him on a tree, 22 his body must not remain on the tree overnight; you must bury him the same 23 day, for one who has been hanged is accursed of God, and you must not defile the land that Yahweh your God gives you for an inheritance.

22 'If you see your brother's ox or one of his sheep straying there must be no 1 evasion: you must take them back to your brother. •And if he is not close 2 at hand or you do not know who he is, you must take them home with you and keep them by you until your brother comes for them; you will then return them to him.

3   'You are to do the same with his donkey, the same with his cloak, the same with anything your brother loses and that you find; there must be no evasion.

4   'You must not make off when you see your brother's ox or donkey fall on the road, but must help your brother to put it on its feet again.

5   'A woman must not wear men's clothes nor a man put on women's dress; anyone who does this is detestable to Yahweh your God.

6   'If, when out walking, you come across a bird's nest, in a tree or on the ground, with chicks or eggs and the mother bird sitting on the chicks or the eggs, you
7 must not take the mother who is brooding the chicks. •Let the mother go; the young you may take for yourself. So shall you prosper and have a long life.

8   'When you build a new house you are to give your roof a parapet; then your house will not incur blood-vengeance through anyone falling from it.

9   'You must not sow any other seed in your vineyard lest the whole of its produce become consecrated, both the crop you have sown and the produce of your vineyard.

10   'You must not plough with ox and donkey together.

11   'You must not wear clothing woven part of wool, part of linen.

12   'You are to make tassels for the four corners of the cloak in which you wrap yourself.

A young wife's reputation

13   'If a man marries a wife, and sleeps with her and then turns against her,
14 and taxes her with misconduct and publicly defames her by saying, "I married this woman and when I slept with her I did not find the evidence of her virginity",
15 the girl's father and mother must take her and produce the evidence of her
16 virginity before the elders of the town at the gate. •The girl's father shall then declare to the elders, "I gave this man my daughter for a wife and he has turned
17 against her, •and now he taxes her with misconduct: I found no evidence of virginity in your daughter, he says. But the evidence of my daughter's virginity
18 is here." And they shall spread the cloth out before the elders of the town. •Then
19 the elders of the town shall take the man and flog him •and fine him one hundred silver shekels for publicly defaming a virgin of Israel, and give this money to the girl's father. She shall remain his wife and as long as he lives he may not repudiate her.

20   'But if the accusation that the girl cannot show the evidence of virginity is
21 substantiated, •they shall take her to the door of her father's house and her fellow citizens shall stone her to death for having committed an infamy in Israel by disgracing her father's House. You must banish this evil from your midst.

Adultery and fornication

22   'If a man is caught sleeping with another man's wife, both must die, the man who has slept with her and the woman herself. You must banish this evil from Israel.

23   'If a virgin is betrothed and a man meets her in the city and sleeps with her,
24 you shall take them both out to the gate of the town and stone them to death; the girl, because she did not cry for help in the town; the man, because he has
25 violated the wife of his fellow. You must banish this evil from your midst. •But if the man has met the betrothed girl in the open country and has taken her by
26 force and lain with her, only the man who lay with her shall die; •you must do nothing to the girl, for hers is no capital offence. The case is like that of a man
27 who attacks and kills his fellow; •for he came across her in the open country and the betrothed girl could have cried out without anyone coming to her rescue.

28   'If a man meets a virgin who is not betrothed and seizes her and lies with
29 her and is caught in the act, •the man who has lain with her must give the girl's

father fifty silver shekels; she shall be his wife since he has violated her, and as
long as he lives he may not repudiate her.

23 'A man must not take his father's wife, and must not withdraw the skirt ¹⁄₃₀
of his father's cloak from her.ᵃ

Some who are excluded from public worship

'A man whose testicles have been crushed or whose male member has been ²⁄₁
cut off is not to be admitted to the assembly of Yahweh. •No bastardᵇ is to be ³⁄₂
admitted to the assembly of Yahweh. •No Ammonite or Moabite is to be admitted ⁴⁄₃
to the assembly of Yahweh; not even their descendants to the tenth generation
may be admitted to the assembly of Yahweh, and this is for all time; •because ⁵⁄₄
they did not come to meet you with bread and water when you were on your way
out of Egypt, and because they hired Balaam son of Beor from Pethor in Aram
of the Two Rivers to curse you. •But Yahweh your God refused to listen to ⁶⁄₅
Balaam, and Yahweh your God turned the curse into a blessing for you, because
Yahweh your God loved you. •Never, as long as you live, shall you seek their ⁷⁄₆
welfare or their prosperity.

'You are not to regard the Edomite as detestable, for he is your brother; nor ⁸⁄₇
the Egyptian, because you were a stranger in his land. •The third generation of ⁹⁄₈
children born to these may be admitted to the assembly of Yahweh.

The camp and legal purity

'When you are in camp, at war with your enemies, you must keep clear of all ¹⁰⁄₉
evil. •If any man among you is unclean by reason of a nocturnal emission, he ¹¹⁄₁₀
must go out of the camp and not come into it again; •towards evening he must ¹²⁄₁₁
wash himself, and he may return to the camp at sunset.

'You must have a latrine outside the camp, and go out to this; •and you ¹³,¹⁴⁄₁₂,₁₃
must have a mattock among your equipment, and with this mattock, when you
go outside to ease yourself, you must dig a hole and cover your excrement. •For ¹⁵⁄₁₄
Yahweh your God goes about within your camp to guard you and to deliver
your enemies to you. Your camp must therefore be a holy place; Yahweh must
not see anything improper among you or he would turn away from you.

D. ON PROTECTING THE WEAK

Protection of the Israelite

'You must not allow a master to imprison a slave who has escaped from him ¹⁶⁄₁₅
and come to you. •He shall live with you, among you, wherever he pleases in any ¹⁷⁄₁₆
one of your towns he chooses; you are not to molest him.

'There must be no sacred prostitute among the daughters of Israel, and no ¹⁸⁄₁₇
sacred prostitute among the sons of Israel. •You must not bring to the house ¹⁹⁄₁₈
of Yahweh your God the wages of a prostitute or the earnings of a dog,ᶜ whatever
vow you may have made, for both are detestable to Yahweh your God.

'You must not lend on interest to your brother, whether the loan be of money ²⁰⁄₁₉
or food or anything else that may earn interest. •You may demand interest on ²¹⁄₂₀
a loan of a foreigner, but you must not demand interest from your brother; so
that Yahweh your God may bless you in all your giving in the land you are to
enter and make your own.

'If you make a vow to Yahweh your God, you must not be lazy in keeping it; ²²⁄₂₁
be sure that Yahweh your God requires it, and to withold it would be a sin.
But if you had refrained from making a vow, there would be no sin for you. ²³⁄₂₂
Whatever passes your lips you must keep to, and the vow that you have freely ²⁴⁄₂₃
made with your own mouth to Yahweh your God must be fulfilled.

'If you go through your neighbour's vineyard, you may eat your fill of grapes, ²⁵⁄₂₄
as many as you wish, but you must not put any in your basket. •If you go through ²⁶⁄₂₅

your neighbour's standing corn, you may pick the ears with your hand, but you must not put a sickle into your neighbour's corn.

Divorce

1 **24** 'Supposing a man has taken a wife and consummated the marriage; but she has not pleased him and he has found some impropriety of which to accuse her; so he has made out a writ of divorce for her and handed it to her 2 and then dismissed her from his house; •she leaves his home and goes away to 3 become the wife of another man. •If this other man takes a dislike to her and makes out a writ of divorce for her and hands it to her and dismisses her from his 4 house (or if this other man who took her as his wife happens to die), •her first husband, who has repudiated her, may not take her back as his wife now that she has been defiled in this way. For that is detestable in the sight of Yahweh, and you must not bring guilt on the land that Yahweh your God gives for your inheritance.

More protective measures

5 'If a man is newly married, he shall not join the army nor is he to be pestered at home; he shall be left at home free of all obligations for one year to bring joy to the wife he has taken.

6 'No man may take a mill or a millstone in pledge; that would be to take life itself in pledge.

7 'If anyone is found kidnapping one of his brothers, one of the sons of Israel, whether he makes him his slave or sells him, that thief must die. You must banish this evil from your midst.

8 'In a case of leprosy, take care you faithfully observe and follow exactly all that the levitical priests direct you to do. You are to keep and observe all that I have 9 commanded them. •Remember what Yahweh your God did to Miriam when you were on your way out of Egypt.

10 'If you are making your fellow a loan on pledge, you are not to go into his 11 house and seize the pledge, whatever it may be. •You must stay outside, and the 12 man to whom you are making the loan shall bring the pledge out to you. •And if the man is poor, you are not to go to bed with his pledge in your possession; 13 you must return it to him at sunset so that he can sleep in his cloak and bless you; and it will be a good action on your part in the sight of Yahweh your God.

14 'You are not to exploit the hired servant who is poor and destitute, whether 15 he is one of your brothers or a stranger who lives in your towns. •You must pay him his wage each day, not allowing the sun to set before you do, for he is poor and is anxious for it; otherwise he may appeal to Yahweh against you, and it would be a sin for you.

16 'Fathers may not be put to death for their sons, nor sons for fathers. Each is to be put to death for his own sin.

17 'You must not pervert justice in dealing with a stranger or an orphan, nor 18 take a widow's garment in pledge. •Remember that you were a slave in Egypt and that Yahweh your God redeemed you from there. That is why I lay this charge on you.

19 'When reaping the harvest in your field, if you have overlooked a sheaf in that field, do not go back for it. Leave it for the stranger, the orphan and the widow, so that Yahweh your God may bless you in all your undertakings.

20 'When you beat your olive trees you must not go over the branches twice. Let anything left be for the stranger, the orphan and the widow.

23 a. 'To spread the fold (of the cloak)' over' a woman signifies marriage. Thus 'to withdraw the fold' here expresses the violation of the husband's rights.   **b.** An imprecise term; possibly the offspring of a mixed marriage between Hebrew and Philistine.   **c.** Male prostitute.

'When you harvest your vineyard you must not pick it over a second time. 21
Let anything left be for the stranger, the orphan and the widow.

'Remember that you were a slave in the land of Egypt. That is why I lay this 22
charge on you.

25 'If men have any dispute they must go to court for the judges to decide 1
between them; these must declare the one who is right to be in the right,
the one who is wrong to be in the wrong. •If the one who is in the wrong deserves 2
a flogging, the judge shall make him lie down and have him flogged in his presence
with the number of strokes proportionate to his offence. •He may impose forty 3
strokes but no more, lest the flogging be too severe and your brother be degraded
in your eyes.

'You must not muzzle an ox when it is treading out the corn. 4

The levirate law

'If brothers live together and one of them dies childless, the dead man's wife 5
must not marry a stranger outside the family. Her husband's brother must come
to her and, exercising his levirate, make her his wife, •and the first son she bears 6
shall assume the dead brother's name; and so his name will not be blotted out
in Israel. •But if the man declines to take his brother's wife, she must go to the 7
elders at the gate and say, "I have no levir willing to perpetuate the name of his
brother in Israel; he declines to exercise his levirate in my favour". •The elders 8
of the town shall summon the man and talk to him. If he appears before them,
and shall say, "I refuse to take her", •then she to whom he owes levirate shall 9
go up to him in the presence of the elders, take the sandal off his foot, spit in
his face, and pronounce the following words, "This is what we do to the man
who does not restore his brother's house", •and the man shall be surnamed in 10
Israel, House-of-the-Unshod.

Modesty in brawls

'When two men are fighting together, if the wife of one intervenes to protect 11
her husband from the other's blows by putting out her hand and seizing the
other by the private parts, •you shall cut her hand off and show no pity. 12

Appendices

'You are not to keep two different weights in your bag, one heavy, one light. 13
You are not to keep two different measures in your house, one large, one small. 14
You must keep one weight, full and accurate, so that you may have a long life 15
in the land that Yahweh your God is giving you. •For anyone who does things 16
of this kind and acts dishonestly is detestable to Yahweh your God.

'Remember how Amalek treated you when you were on your way out of 17
Egypt. •He met you on your way and, after you had gone by, he fell on you from 18
the rear and cut off the stragglers; when you were faint and weary he had no
fear of God. •When Yahweh your God has granted you peace from all the enemies 19
surrounding you in the land Yahweh your God is giving you to possess as an
inheritance, you are to blot out the memory of Amalek from under heaven.
Do not forget.

E. RITUAL PRESCRIPTIONS

First-fruits

26 'When you come to the land Yahweh your God is giving you for an inherit- 1
ance, when you have taken possession of it and are living in it, •you must 2
set aside the first-fruits of all the produce of the soil raised by you in the land
Yahweh is giving you. You must put them in a pannier and go to the place where
Yahweh your God chooses to give his name a home. •You must go to the priest 3

then in office and say to him, "Today I declare to Yahweh my God that I have come to the land Yahweh swore to our fathers he would give us".

4 'The priest shall then take the pannier from your hand and lay it before the
5 altar of Yahweh your God. •Then, in the sight of Yahweh your God, you must make this pronouncement:

"My father was a wandering Aramaean. He went down into Egypt to find refuge there, few in numbers; but there he became a nation, great, mighty, and
6 strong. •The Egyptians ill-treated us, they gave us no peace and inflicted harsh
7 slavery on us. •But we called on Yahweh the God of our fathers. Yahweh heard
8 our voice and saw our misery, our toil and our oppression; •and Yahweh brought us out of Egypt with mighty hand and outstretched arm, with great terror, and
9 with signs and wonders. •He brought us here and gave us this land, a land where
10 milk and honey flow. •Here then I bring the first-fruits of the produce of the soil that you, Yahweh, have given me".

'You must then lay them before Yahweh your God, and bow down in the sight
11 of Yahweh your God. •Then you are to feast on all the good things Yahweh has given you, you and your household, and with you the Levite and the stranger who lives among you.

The third-year tithe

12 'In the third year, the tithing year, when you have finished reckoning the tithe of all your produce and have given it to the Levite, the stranger, the orphan and
13 the widow, and they have eaten it in your towns and had their fill, •you are to say in the sight of Yahweh your God:

"I have cleared my house of all that was consecrated. Yes, I have given it to the Levite, the stranger, the orphan and the widow, in accordance with all the commandments you laid on me, not going beyond your commandments, not
14 forgetting them. •I have not eaten any bread of mourning; I have consumed nothing that was unclean; I have offered nothing to the dead. I have obeyed
15 the voice of Yahweh my God and I have done all as you commanded me. •Look down from the dwelling place of your holiness, from heaven, and bless your people Israel and the soil you have given us as you swore to our fathers, a land where milk and honey flow".

III. CONCLUDING DISCOURSE

A. END OF THE SECOND DISCOURSE

Israel, the people of Yahweh

16 'Yahweh your God today commands you to observe these laws and customs; you must keep and observe them with all your heart and with all your soul.

17 'You have today made this declaration about Yahweh; that he will be your God, but only if you follow his ways, keep his statutes, his commandments, his
18 ordinances, and listen to his voice. •And Yahweh has today made this declaration about you: that you will be his very own people as he promised you, but
19 only if you keep all his commandments; •then for praise and renown and honour he will set you high above all the nations he has made, and you will be a people consecrated to Yahweh, as he promised.'

The writing of the Law

1 **27** Moses and the elders of Israel gave the people this command: 'Keep all the
2 commandments I enjoin on you today. •After you have crossed the Jordan into the land Yahweh your God is giving you, you are to set up tall stones and
3 coat them with lime •and write on them all the words of this Law, the moment you cross to enter the land Yahweh your God is giving you, a land where milk and honey flow, as Yahweh the God of your fathers promised you.

'And when you have crossed the Jordan, you are to set up these stones on 4 Mount Ebal, as today I command you, and you are to coat them with lime. There you must build Yahweh your God an altar of stones that no iron tool has 5 worked. •You must build the altar to Yahweh your God of undressed stone, 6 and on this altar you will offer holocausts to Yahweh your God, •and immolate 7 communion sacrifices and eat them there, rejoicing in the sight of Yahweh your God. •On these stones you must write all the words of this Law; cut them 8 carefully.'

Then Moses and the levitical priests said to all Israel: 9

'Be silent, Israel, and listen. Today you have become a people for Yahweh your God. •You must listen to the voice of Yahweh your God and observe the 10 commandments and laws I enjoin on you today.'

And the same day Moses gave the people this order: •'When you have crossed ¹¹₁₂ the Jordan, the following tribes shall stand on Mount Gerizim to bless the people: Simeon and Levi, Judah and Issachar, Joseph and Benjamin. •And the following 13 tribes shall stand on Mount Ebal for the curse: Reuben, Gad and Asher, Zebulun, Dan and Naphtali. •The Levites shall then speak, and proclaim loudly to all the 14 Israelites:

"A curse on the man who carves or casts an idol, a thing detestable to Yahweh, 15 the work of a craftsman's hands, and sets it up in secret." And all the people shall answer saying: Amen.

"A curse on him who treats his father or mother dishonourably." And all the 16 people shall say: Amen.

"A curse on him who displaces his neighbour's boundary mark." And all the 17 people shall say: Amen.

"A curse on him who leads a blind man astray on the road." And all the people 18 shall say: Amen.

"A curse on him who tampers with the rights of the stranger, the orphan and 19 the widow." And all the people shall say: Amen.

"A curse on him who sleeps with his father's wife and withdraws the skirt of 20 his father's cloak from her." And all the people shall say: Amen.

"A curse on him who lies with any kind of animal." And all the people shall 21 say: Amen.

"A curse on him who sleeps with his sister, the daughter of his father or of his 22 mother." And all the people shall say: Amen.

"A curse on him who sleeps with his mother-in-law." And all the people shall 23 say: Amen.

"A curse on him who strikes down his neighbour in secret." And all the 24 people shall say: Amen.

"A curse on him who accepts a bribe to take an innocent life." And all the 25 people shall say: Amen.

"A curse on him who does not maintain the words of the Law by observing 26 them." And all the people shall say: Amen.

Promised blessings

28 'But if you obey the voice of Yahweh your God faithfully, keeping and 1 observing all those commandments of his that I enjoin on you today, Yahweh your God will set you high above all the nations of the earth. •All the 2 blessings that follow shall come up with you and overtake you if only you obey the voice of Yahweh your God.

'You will be blessed in the town and blessed in the country. •Blessed will be ³₄ the fruit of your body, the produce of your soil, the issue of your livestock, the increase of your cattle, the young of your flock. •Blessed will be your pannier 5 and your bread bin. •Blessed will you be coming in, and blessed going out. 6 The enemies that rise against you Yahweh will conquer for your sake; they will 7 come at you by one way and flee before you by seven. •Yahweh will summon 8 a blessing for you in your barns and in all your undertakings, and will bless you in the land that Yahweh is giving you.

9 'Yahweh will make of you a people consecrated to himself as he has sworn to you, if you keep the commandments of Yahweh your God and follow his ways.
10 All the peoples of the earth will see that you bear the name of Yahweh and will
11 go in fear of you. •Yahweh will give you great store of good things, the fruit of your body, the fruit of your cattle and the produce of your soil, in the land he
12 swore to your fathers he would give you. •Yahweh will open the heavens to you, his rich treasure house, to give you seasonable rain for your land and to bless all the work of your hands. You will make many nations your subjects, yet you will
13 be subject to none. •Yahweh will put you at the head, not at the tail; you will always be on top and never underneath, if you obey the commandments of
14 Yahweh your God that I enjoin on you today, keeping and observing them, •not swerving to right or left from any of the works I enjoin on you today by following any other gods and serving them.

Curses

15 'But if you do not obey the voice of Yahweh your God nor keep and observe all those commandments and statutes of his that I enjoin on you today, then all the curses that follow shall come up with you and overtake you.
16
17 'You will be accursed in the town and accursed in the country. •Accursed will
18 be your pannier and your bread bin. •Accursed will be the fruit of your body, the produce of your soil, the increase of your cattle, the young of your flock.
19 Accursed will you be coming in, and accursed going out.

20 'Yahweh will send on you curses, frustration, imprecation in return for all your offerings, until you are destroyed and speedily perish for your perverse
21 behaviour, and for deserting me. •Yahweh will infect you with the plague until it has consumed you on the land which you are entering to make your own.
22 Yahweh will strike you down with consumption, fever, inflammation, burning
23 fever, drought, blight, mildew, and these will pursue you to your ruin. •The
24 heavens above you will be brass, the earth beneath you iron. •Yahweh will turn the rain on your land to dust and sand; it will fall on you from the heavens until
25 you perish. •Yahweh will have you defeated in front of your enemies; you will come at them by one way and flee before them by seven; and you will become a
26 thing of horror for all the kingdoms of the earth. •Your carcase will be carrion for all the birds of heaven and all the beasts of the earth, with no one to scare them away.

27 'Yahweh will strike you down with Egyptian boils, with swellings in the groin,
28 with scurvy and the itch for which you will find no cure. •Yahweh will strike you
29 down with madness, blindness, distraction of mind, •until you grope your way at noontide like a blind man groping in the dark, and your steps will lead you nowhere.

'You will never be anything but exploited and plundered continually, and no
30 one will come to your help. •Betroth a wife, another man will have her; build a house, you will not live in it; plant a vineyard, you will not gather its first-fruits.
31 Your ox will be killed before your eyes and you will eat none of it; your donkey will be carried off in your presence and not be restored to you; your sheep will be
32 given to your enemies, and no one will come to your help. •Your sons and daughters will be handed over to another people, and every day you will wear
33 your eyes out watching eagerly for them, while your hands are powerless. •A nation you do not know will eat the fruit of your soil and of your labour. You
34 will never be anything but exploited and crushed continually. •You will be driven
35 mad by the sights your eyes will see. •Yahweh will strike you down with foul boils on knee and leg, for which you will find no cure, from the sole of your foot to the top of your head.

36 'Yahweh will send you and the king you set over you, to a nation that

neither you nor your fathers have known, and there you will serve other gods of wood and of stone. •You will become a thing of horror, a proverb, and a 37 byword to all the peoples among whom Yahweh takes you.

'You will cast seed in plenty on the fields but harvest little, for the locust will 38 devour it. •You will plant and till your vineyards but not drink wine or gather 39 grapes, for the grub will eat them up. •You will grow olive trees throughout your 40 territory but not anoint yourself with oil, for your olive trees will be cut down. You will father sons and daughters but they will not be yours, for they will go 41 into captivity. •All your trees and all the produce of your soil will become the 42 prey of insects.

'The stranger living among you will rise higher and higher at your expense, 43 and you yourselves sink lower and lower. •He will make you his chattel, you 44 will not make him yours; he it is who will be at the head, and you at the tail.

'All these curses will come up with you, will pursue you and overtake you 45 until you perish for not obeying the voice of Yahweh your God by keeping those· commandments and laws of his that he enjoined on you. •They will be a sign 46 and a wonder over you and your descendants for ever.

Of war and exile to come

'For failing to serve Yahweh your God in the joy and happiness that come 47 from an abundance of all things, •you will submit to the enemies that Yahweh 48 will send against you, in hunger, thirst, nakedness, utter destitution. He will put an iron yoke on your neck until you perish.

'Yahweh will raise against you a far-off nation from the ends of the earth, 49 like an eagle taking wing. This will be a nation whose language you do not understand, •a nation grim of face, with neither respect for the old, nor pity for 50 the young. •They will eat the offspring of your cattle and the produce of your 51 soil until you perish, leaving you neither corn nor wine nor oil nor increase of your cattle nor young of your flock, until they make an end of you. •They will 52 besiege you in all your towns until your loftiest and most strongly fortified walls collapse, the walls on which you relied within your frontiers. They will besiege you in all the towns that Yahweh gives you. •During the siege and in the distress 53 to which your enemies will reduce you, you will eat the fruit of your body, the flesh of those sons and daughters of yours whom Yahweh has given you. •The 54 tenderest and most fastidious among you will glower at his brother, even at the wife he cherishes and at the children that are left to him, •grudging them a share 55 in the flesh of those children of his that he is eating, for during the siege and in the distress to which your enemies will reduce you in all your towns, there will be nothing left to him. •The tenderest and most fastidious woman among you, 56 so tender, so fastidious that she has never ventured to set the sole of her foot to the ground, will glower at the husband she cherishes, even at her son and her daughter, •and hide from them the afterbirth of her womb and the child she bears 57 to eat them, so utter will be the destitution during the siege and in the distress to which your enemies will reduce you in all your towns.

'If you do not keep and observe all the words of this Law that are written in 58 this book, in the fear of this name of glory and awe: Yahweh your God, •Yahweh 59 will strike you down with monstrous plagues, you and your descendants: with plagues grievous and lasting, diseases pernicious and enduring. •Once more he 60 will bring on you the diseases of Egypt that you dreaded, and they will infect you. Further, Yahweh will bring on you every sickness, every plague, not mentioned 61 in the Book of this Law, until you perish. •There will be only a handful of you 62 left, you who were as many as the stars of heaven.

'For not obeying the voice of Yahweh your God, •just as Yahweh took delight 63 in giving you prosperity and increase, so now he will take delight in bringing you ruin and destruction. You will be torn from the land which you are entering to make your own. •Yahweh will scatter you among all peoples, from one end of the 64

65 earth to the other; there you will serve other gods of wood and of stone that neither you nor your fathers have known. •Among these nations there will be no repose for you, no rest for the sole of your foot; Yahweh will give you a
66 quaking heart, weary eyes, halting breath. •Your life from the outset will be
67 a burden to you; night and day you will go in fear, uncertain of your life. •In the morning you will say, "How I wish it were evening!", and in the evening, "How I wish it were morning!", such terror will grip your heart, such sights your
68 eyes will see. •Yahweh will take you back to Egypt by sea and by land, though I had promised you: You will not see it again. And there you will want to sell yourselves to your enemies as serving men and women, but no one will buy you.'

Conclusion

69
1   These are the words of the covenant which Yahweh ordered Moses to make with the sons of Israel in the land of Moab, in addition to the covenant he had made with them at Horeb.

B. THE THIRD AND LAST DISCOURSE

The exodus and the covenant recalled

1
2 **29** Moses called the whole of Israel together and said to them:
'You have seen all that Yahweh did before your eyes in the land of Egypt,
2
3 to Pharaoh, to his servants and to his whole land, •the great ordeals your own
3
4 eyes witnessed, the signs and those great wonders. •But until today Yahweh has given you no heart to understand, no eyes to see, no ears to hear.
4
5 'For forty years I led you in the wilderness; the clothes on your back did not
5
6 wear out and your sandals did not wear off your feet. •You had no bread to eat, you drank no wine, no strong drink, learning thus that I, Yahweh, am your God.
6
7 When you reached this place, Sihon king of Heshbon and Og king of Bashan
7
8 came out against us to do battle, but we defeated them. •We conquered their land and gave it as an inheritance to Reuben, Gad and the half-tribe of Manasseh.
8
9 'Keep the words of this covenant and observe them and you will thrive in all
9
10 you do. •All of you stand here today in the presence of Yahweh your God: your
10
11 heads of tribes, your elders, your scribes, all the men of Israel, •with your children and your wives (and the stranger too who is in your camp, whether he cuts wood
11
12 or draws water for you), •and you are about to enter into the covenant of Yahweh your God, a covenant ratified with dire sanctions, which he has made
12
13 with you today, •and by which, today, he makes a nation of you and he himself becomes a God to you, as he has promised and as he has sworn to your fathers Abraham, Isaac and Jacob.

The covenant and generations to come

13
14
15 'Not with you alone do I make this covenant today and pronounce these
14
15 sanctions, •but with him also who is not here today, as well as with him who stands with us here in the presence of Yahweh our God.
15
16
17 'Yes, you know those among whom we lived in Egypt, those through whose
16
17 lands we journeyed, the nations through whom we have passed. •You have seen their abominations and their idols, the wood, the stone, the silver and gold they have in their countries.
17
18 'Let there be no man or woman among you, no clan or tribe, whose heart turns away from Yahweh your God today to go and serve the gods of those nations. Let there be no root among you bearing fruit that is poisonous and
18
19 bitter. •If, after hearing these sanctions, such a man should bless himself in his heart and say, "I may follow the dictates of my own heart and still lack nothing;
19
20 much water drives away thirst", •Yahweh will not pardon him. The wrath and jealousy of Yahweh will blaze against such a man; every curse written in this book will fall on him, and Yahweh will blot out his name from under heaven.

Yahweh will single him out from all the tribes of Israel to his destruction, in ²⁰⁄₂₁ accordance with all the curses of the covenant written in the Book of this Law.

'The future generation, your children who are to come after you, as also the ²¹⁄₂₂ stranger from a distant country, will see the plagues of that land and the diseases Yahweh will inflict on it, and will exclaim, •"Sulphur, salt, scorched earth, the ²²⁄₂₃ whole land through! No one will sow, nothing grow, no grass spring ever again. Like this, Sodom and Gomorrah were overthrown, Admah and Zeboiim, which Yahweh overthrew in his anger and his wrath." •And all the nations will exclaim, ²³⁄₂₄ "Why has Yahweh treated this land like this? Why this great blaze of anger?" And people will say, "Because they deserted the covenant of Yahweh, the God of ²⁴⁄₂₅ their fathers, the covenant he made with them when he brought them out of the land of Egypt; •because they went and served other gods and worshipped them, ²⁵⁄₂₆ gods they had not known, gods that were no part of their heritage from him, •for ²⁶⁄₂₇ this the anger of Yahweh has blazed against this land, bringing on it all the curses written in this book. •In anger, in fury, in fierce wrath Yahweh has torn ²⁷⁄₂₈ them from their country and flung them into another land where they are today."

Return from exile and repentance

'Things hidden belong to Yahweh our God but things revealed are ours and ²⁸⁄₂₉ our children's for all time, so that we may observe all the words of this Law. 30 And when all these words come true for you, the blessing and the curse 1 I have set before you, if you meditate on them in your heart wherever among the nations Yahweh your God drives you, •if you return to Yahweh your God, 2 if you obey his voice with all your heart and soul in everything I enjoin on you today, you and your children, •then Yahweh your God will bring back your 3 captives, he will have pity on you and gather you once again out of all the peoples where Yahweh your God has scattered you. •Had you wandered to the ends of 4 the heavens, Yahweh your God would gather you even from there, would come there to reclaim you •and bring you back to the land your fathers possessed, so 5 that you in your turn might make it your own, prospering there and increasing even more than your fathers.

'Yahweh your God will circumcise your heart and the heart of your descend- 6 ants, until you love Yahweh your God with all your heart and soul, and so have life. •Yahweh your God will make all these curses recoil on your foes 7 and on your enemies who have persecuted you. •And once again you will obey 8 the voice of Yahweh your God and keep all those commandments of his that I enjoin on you today. •Yahweh your God will give you great prosperity in all 9 your undertakings, in the fruit of your body, the fruit of your cattle and in the produce of your soil. For once again Yahweh will take delight in your prosperity as he took delight in the prosperity of your fathers, •if only you obey the voice 10 of Yahweh your God, keeping those commandments and laws of his that are written in the Book of this Law, and if you return to Yahweh your God with all your heart and soul.

'For this Law that I enjoin on you today is not beyond your strength or beyond 11 your reach. •It is not in heaven, so that you need to wonder, "Who will go up 12 to heaven for us and bring it down to us, so that we may hear it and keep it?" Nor is it beyond the seas, so that you need to wonder, "Who will cross the seas 13 for us and bring it back to us, so that we may hear it and keep it?" •No, the Word 14 is very near to you, it is in your mouth and in your heart for your observance.

The two ways

'See, today I set before you life and prosperity, death and disaster. •If you ¹⁵⁄₁₆ obey the commandments of Yahweh your God that I enjoin on you today, if you love Yahweh your God and follow his ways, if you keep his commandments, his laws, his customs, you will live and increase, and Yahweh your God will bless you in the land which you are entering to make your own. •But if your heart 17

strays, if you refuse to listen, if you let yourself be drawn into worshipping other
18 gods and serving them, •I tell you today, you will most certainly perish; you will
19 not live long in the land you are crossing the Jordan to enter and possess. •I call
heaven and earth to witness against you today: I set before you life or death,
blessing or curse. Choose life, then, so that·you and your descendants may live,
20 in the love of Yahweh your God, obeying his voice, clinging to him; for in this
your life consists, and on this depends your long stay in the land which Yahweh
swore to your fathers Abraham, Isaac and Jacob he would give them.'

IV. THE LAST DAYS OF MOSES

Joshua and his mission

1
2 **31** Moses proceeded to address these words to the whole of Israel, •'I am
one hundred and twenty years old now, and can no longer come and go
3 as I will. Yahweh has said to me, "You shall not cross this Jordan". •It is Yahweh
your God who will cross it at your head to destroy these nations facing you
and dispossess them; and Joshua too shall cross at your head, as Yahweh has
4 said. •Yahweh will treat them as he treated Sihon and Og the Amorite kings
5 and their land, destroying them. •Yahweh will hand them over to you, and you
will deal with them in exact accordance with the commandments I have enjoined
6 on you. •Be strong, stand firm, have no fear of them, no terror, for Yahweh
your God is going with you; he will not fail you or desert you.'
7   Then Moses summoned Joshua and in the presence of all Israel said to him,
'Be strong, stand firm; you are going with this people into the land Yahweh swore
to their fathers he would give them; you are to give it into their possession.
8 Yahweh himself will lead you; he will be with you; he will not fail you or desert
you. Have no fear, do not be disheartened by anything.'

The ritual reading of the Law

9   Moses committed this Law to writing and gave it to the priests, the sons of
Levi, who carried the ark of Yahweh's covenant, and to all the elders of Israel.
10 And Moses gave them this command: 'At the end of every seven years, at the
11 time fixed for the year of remission, at the feast of Tabernacles, •when the whole
of Israel comes to look on the face of Yahweh your God in the place he chooses,
12 you must proclaim this Law in the hearing of all Israel. •Call the people together,
men, women, children, and the stranger who lives with you, for them to hear
it and learn to fear Yahweh your God and keep and observe all the words of this
13 Law. •Their children, who as yet do not know it, shall hear it and learn to fear
Yahweh your God for as long as you live in the land that you are crossing the
Jordan to possess.'

Yahweh's instructions

14   Yahweh said to Moses, 'And now the time draws near when you must die.
Summon Joshua and take your stand at the Tent of Meeting, that I may give him
his orders.' And Moses and Joshua came and took their stand at the Tent of
15 Meeting. •And Yahweh showed himself at the Tent in a pillar of cloud; the
pillar of cloud stood at the door of the Tent.
16   Yahweh said to Moses, 'And now you will soon be sleeping with your fathers.
This people will start playing the harlot, following the alien gods of the land they
are invading. They will desert me and break this covenant of mine that I have
17 made with them. •On that day my anger shall blaze against them; I will forsake
them and hide my face from them. A host of disasters and misfortunes will
overtake them to devour them, and when that day comes they will say, "If
18 such disasters overtake me, surely Yahweh my God cannot be with me?" •Yes
indeed, I shall hide my face that day for all the evil they have done by turning to
other gods.

The song of witness

'Now write down this song which you must use; teach it to the sons of Israel, 19
put it into their mouths that it may be a witness on my behalf against the sons of
Israel; •against Israel whom I am bringing into the land I swore to his fathers 20
I would give him, a land where milk and honey flow; against Israel who will eat
and take his fill and grow fat, then turn to other gods to serve them, and despise
me and break my covenant. •When a host of disasters and misfortunes overtake 21
him, this song shall stand as witness against him, for his descendants must not
forget it. Yes, even today, before I have brought him to the land I promised on
oath, I know what plans he has in mind.' •So on that same day, Moses wrote 22
out this song and taught it to the sons of Israel.

He gave Joshua son of Nun this order: 'Be strong and stand firm, for you are 23
to bring the sons of Israel to the land I swore I would give them, and I myself will
be with you.'

The Law placed beside the ark

When Moses had finished writing in a book the words of this Law to the very 24
end, •he gave this command to the Levites who carried the ark of Yahweh's 25
covenant: •'Take this Book of the Law and put it beside the ark of the covenant 26
of Yahweh your God. Let it lie there as a witness against you. •For I know how 27
defiant you are and how stubborn. If today while I am still alive and with you,
you defy Yahweh, how much more will you defy him after my death!

Israel assembles to hear the song

'Gather round me all the elders of your tribes, and your scribes, so that I may 28
let them hear these words and call heaven and earth to witness against them.
For I know that after my death you are sure to act perversely; you will leave the 29
way I have marked out for you; in days to come disaster will fall on you for doing
what is displeasing to Yahweh, provoking him by your behaviour.'

Then in the hearing of Israel's full assembly Moses spoke the words of this 30
song to the very end:

A. THE SONG OF MOSES

32   'Listen, heavens, while I speak;   1
     earth, hear the words that I am saying.
     May my teaching fall like the rain,   2
     may my word drop down like the dew,
     like showers on fresh grass
     and light rain on the turf.
     For I proclaim the name of Yahweh.   3
     Oh, tell the greatness of our God!

     'He is the Rock, his work is perfect,   4
     for all his ways are Equity.
     A God faithful, without unfairness,
     Uprightness itself and Justice.
     They have acted perversely, those he begot without blemish,   5
     a deceitful and underhand brood.
     Is this the return you make to Yahweh?   6
     O foolish, unwise people!
     Is not this your father, who gave you being,
     who made you, by whom you subsist?
     Think back on the days of old,   7
     think over the years, down the ages.
     Ask of your father, let him teach you;

of your elders, let them enlighten you.

8   When the Most High gave the nations their inheritance,
when he divided the sons of men,
he fixed their bounds according to the number of the sons of God;*a*

9   but Yahweh's portion was his people,
Jacob his share of inheritance.

10   'In the waste lands he adopts him,
in the howling desert of the wilderness.
He protects him, rears him, guards him
as the pupil of his eye.

11   Like an eagle watching its nest,
hovering over its young,
he spreads out his wings to hold him,
he supports him on his pinions.

12   'Yahweh alone is his guide,
with him is no alien god.

13   He gives him the heights of the land to ride,
he feeds him on the yield of the mountains,
he gives him honey from the rock to taste,
and oil from the flinty crag;

14   curds from the cattle, milk from the flock,
with rich food of the pastures,
rams of Bashan's breed, and goats,
rich food of the wheat's ear,
and blood of the fermenting grape for drink.

15   'Jacob ate and had his fill,
Jeshurun grew fat, turned restive.
(You grew fat, gross, bloated.)
He disowned the God who made him,
dishonoured the Rock, his salvation.

16   They roused him to jealousy with alien gods,
with things detestable they angered him.

17   They sacrificed to demons who are not God,
to gods they did not know,
newcomers of yesterday
whom their fathers had never feared.

18   (You forget the Rock who begot you,
unmindful now of the God who fathered you.)

19   Yahweh has seen this, and in his anger
cast off his sons and his daughters.

20   "I shall hide my face from them," he says
"and see what becomes of them.
For they are a deceitful brood,
children with no loyalty in them.

21   They have roused me to jealousy with what is no god,
they have angered me with their beings of nothing;
I, then, will rouse them to jealousy with what is no people,
I will anger them with an empty-headed nation.

22   Yes, a fire has blazed from my anger,
it will burn to the depths of Sheol;
it will devour the earth and all its produce,
it will set fire to the foundations of the mountains.

---

32 a. I.e. the angels, meaning the guardian angels of the nations, cf. Dn 10:13. But Yahweh himself takes care of Israel.

I will hurl disasters on them,
and on them I will spend all my arrows. 23

For weapons I shall have barns of famine,
fever and consumption for poison. 24

I will send the sharp teeth of the wild beast,
and the venom of creeping things against them.

Outside, the sword shall carry off their children,
and terror shall reign within. 25

Youth and maid alike shall perish,
suckling and greybeard both together.

I should crush them to dust, I said, 26
I should wipe out their memory among men,
did I not fear the boasting of the enemy. 27

But let not their foes be mistaken!
Let them not say: Our own power wins the victory,
Yahweh plays no part in this.

What a nation of short sight it is; 28
in them there is no understanding.

Were they wise, they would succeed, 29
they would be able to read their destiny.

How else could one man rout a thousand, 30
how could two put ten thousand to flight,
were it not that their Rock has sold them,
that Yahweh has delivered them up?

"But their rock is not like our Rock; 31
our enemies are no intercessors. [b]

For their stock springs from the vinestock of Sodom 32
and from the groves of Gomorrah:
their grapes are poisonous grapes,
their clusters are envenomed;

their wine is the poison of serpents, 33
the vipers' cruel venom.

But he, is he not something precious to me, 34
sealed inside my treasury?

Vengeance is mine, and requital, 35
for the time when they make a false step.

For it is close, the day of their ruin;
their doom comes at speed.

(For Yahweh will see his people righted, 36
he will take pity on his servants.)

For he will see to it that their power fails,
that, serf or freeman, there is not one remaining.

Where are their gods? he will ask then, 37
the rock where they thought to take refuge,

who ate the fat of their sacrifices 38
and drank the wine of their libations?

Let these arise and help you,
let these be the shelter above you!

See now that I, I am He, 39
and beside me there is no other god.

It is I who deal death and life;
when I have struck it is I who heal
(and none can deliver from my hand).

"Yes, I lift up my hand to heaven, 40
and I say: As surely as I live for ever,

41   when I have whetted my flashing sword
    I will take up the cause of Right,
    I will give my foes as good again,
    I will repay those who hate me.
42   I will make my arrows drunk with blood,
    and my sword shall feed on flesh:
    the blood of wounded and captives,
    the skulls of the enemy leaders."

43   'Heavens, rejoice with him,
    let the sons of God pay him homage!
    Nations, rejoice with his people,
    let God's envoys tell of his power!
    For he will avenge the blood of his servants,
    he will give his foes as good again,
    he will repay those who hate him
    and purify the land of his people.'

44   Moses came with Joshua son of Nun and recited all the words of this song in the people's hearing.

The Law, the source of life

45
46   When Moses had finished reciting these words[c] to all Israel, •he said to them, 'Take all these words to heart; I call them to witness against you today. You must
47 order your children to keep and observe all the words of this Law. •It is no idle thing you will be doing, for the Law is your life, and by its means you will live long in the land that you are crossing the Jordan to possess.'

Moses' death foretold

48
49   Yahweh spoke to Moses that same day and said to him, •'Climb Mount Nebo, that mountain of the Abarim range, in the land of Moab, opposite Jericho, and view the land of Canaan which I am giving the sons of Israel as their domain.
50 Die on the mountain you have climbed, and be gathered to your people, as your
51 brother Aaron died on Mount Hor and was gathered to his people. •Because you broke faith with me among the sons of Israel that time at Meribath-kadesh in the wilderness of Zin, because you did not display my holiness among the sons
52 of Israel, •you may see this land only from afar; you cannot enter it, this land that I am giving to the sons of Israel.'

Moses blesses the tribes

1
2 **33** This is the blessing that Moses, the man of God, pronounced over the sons of Israel before he died. •He said:

    'Yahweh came from Sinai.
    For them, after Seir, he rose on the horizon,
    after Mount Paran he shone forth.
    For them he came, after the mustering at Kadesh,
    from his zenith as far as the foothills.

3   'You who have such love for the forefathers,
    in your hand are all the holy ones.
    At your feet they fell,
    under your guidance went swiftly on.

4   (Moses enjoined a law on us.)
    The assembly of Jacob comes into its inheritance;
5   there was a king in Jeshurun

b. Because the gods to whom they pray are no gods.   c. 'The words' of the Law, not of the canticle; this verse continues 31:27.

when the heads of the people foregathered
and the tribes of Jacob were all assembled.

'May Reuben live and not die,
live too, his small band of warriors!'   6

Of Judah he said this: 7

'Listen, Yahweh, to the voice of Judah
and bring him back to his people.
That his hands may defend his rights,
come to his help against his foes.'

Of Levi he said: 8

'Grant to Levi*a* your Urim,
your Thummim to the one you favoured
after you had tested him at Massah
and striven with him at the waters of Meribah.
He says of his father and mother,   9
"I have not seen them".
His brothers he does not know,
nor does he know his children.
Yes, they have kept your word,
they hold firmly to your covenant.
They teach your customs to Jacob,   10
your Law to Israel.
They send incense rising to your nostrils,
place the holocaust on your altar.
Yahweh, bless his worthiness,   11
and accept the work of his hands.
Crush the loins of his enemies
and of his foes, till they rise no more.'

Of Benjamin he said: 12

'Beloved of Yahweh, he rests in safety.
The Most High*b* protects him day after day
and dwells between his hillsides.'

Of Joseph he said: 13

'His land is blessed by Yahweh.
For him the best of heaven's dew
and of the deep that lies below,
the best of what the sun makes grow,   14
of what springs with every month,
the first-fruits of the ancient mountains,   15
the best from the hills of old,
the best of the land and all it holds,   16
the favour of him who dwells in the Bush.
May the hair grow thick on the head of Joseph,
of the consecrated one among his brothers!
First-born of the bull, his the glory.   17
His horns are the wild ox's horns,
with them he tosses the peoples
to the very ends of the earth.
Such are the myriads of Ephraim,
such are the thousands of Manasseh.'

Of Zebulun he said: 18

'Prosper, Zebulun, in your voyages abroad,
and you, Issachar, in your tents!

19 On the mountain where the people come to pray
they offer sacrifices for success,
for they taste the riches of the seas,
and the treasures hidden in the sands.'

20 Of Gad he said:

'Blessed be he who gives Gad space enough!
He lies there like a lioness;
he has savaged arm and face and head.
21 Then he took the first portion for himself;
he saw that there a leader's share was kept for him.
He came as leader of the people,
having executed the justice of Yahweh
and his sentences on Israel.'

22 Of Dan he said:

'Dan is a lion cub
leaping from Bashan.'

23 Of Naphtali he said:

'Naphtali, sated with favours,
filled with the blessings of Yahweh:
the Sea and the South are his domain.'

24 Of Asher he said:

'Most blessed of the sons may Asher be!
Let him be privileged among his brothers
and bathe his feet in oil!
25 Be your bolts of iron and of bronze
26 and your security as lasting as your days!

There is none like the God of Jeshurun:
he rides the heavens to your rescue,
27 rides the clouds in his majesty.
The God of old, he is your refuge.
Here below, he is the age-old arm
driving the enemy before you;
28 it is he who cries, "Destroy!"
Israel rests in safety.
The well spring of Jacob is chosen out
for a land of corn and wine;
29 there heaven itself rains down dew.
Happy are you, O Israel!
Who is like you, a victorious people?
In Yahweh is the shield that protects you
and the marching sword leading to your triumph.
Your enemies will try to corrupt you,
but you yourself shall trample on their backs.'

33 a. Urim and Thummim: the sacred lots, worn in the breastplate of the high priest, see Ex 28:30 and Lv 8:8. **b.** The blessings given to the tribes are allusions (though some are obscure) to their future enjoyment of the promised land. Benjamin's hillside is Jerusalem; Joseph's 'hills of old' are the places where the patriarchs once lived; Zebulun and Issachar became trading communities; Gad and Reuben were the first tribes to settle; Dan was on the borders of Bashan; Naphtali's 'sea' is Gennesareth; Assher grew olives.

The death of Moses

34 Then, leaving the plains of Moab, Moses went up Mount Nebo, the 1
peak of Pisgah opposite Jericho, and Yahweh showed him the whole land;
Gilead as far as Dan, •all Naphtali, the land of Ephraim and Manasseh, all the 2
land of Judah as far as the Western Sea, •the Negeb, and the stretch of the Valley 3
of Jericho, city of palm trees, as far as Zoar." •Yahweh said to him, 'This is the 4
land I swore to give to Abraham, Isaac and Jacob, saying: I will give it to your
descendants. I have let you see it with your own eyes, but you shall not cross
into it.' •There in the land of Moab, Moses the servant of Yahweh died as 5
Yahweh decreed; •he buried him in the valley, in the land of Moab, opposite 6
Beth-peor; but to this day no one has ever found his grave. •Moses was a 7
hundred and twenty years old when he died, his eye undimmed, his vigour
unimpaired. •The sons of Israel wept for Moses in the plains of Moab for thirty 8
days. The days of weeping for the mourning rites of Moses came to an end.
Joshua son of Nun was filled with the spirit of wisdom, for Moses had laid his 9
hands on him. It was he that the sons of Israel obeyed, carrying out the order
that Yahweh had given to Moses.

Since then, never has there been such a prophet in Israel as Moses, the man 10
Yahweh knew face to face. •What signs and wonders Yahweh caused him to 11
perform in the land of Egypt against Pharaoh and all his servants and his whole
land! •How mighty the hand and great the fear that Moses wielded in the sight 12
of all Israel!

34 a. To the south of the Dead Sea.

INTRODUCTION TO THE BOOKS OF
JOSHUA, JUDGES, RUTH,
SAMUEL AND KINGS

In these books the history of Israel is continued from the death of Moses at the end of the book Deuteronomy, and a constant theme is the recurring disobedience of the nation, and often its rulers, to the laws of God revealed by Moses and served by the prophets.

Oral traditions and written documents of varying ages and characteristics were brought together to form the books as we know them, and these appear to have given continuity and a general consistency by successive editors profoundly influenced by the outlook of Deuteronomy, between the time of Josiah's reform (622 B.C.) and the return from Exile (538).

The Book of Joshua describes the conquest of the Promised Land and the partition of the territory between the tribes, and ends with the last discourse of Joshua. All is centred on the one heroic figure, and the complex history of the times is presented in a simplified picture: here the conquest is shown as the collective action of a united nation, whereas the first chapter of Judges depicts each of the tribes as fighting to win its own territory.

Judges contains the traditions of the century and a half during which 'there was no king in Israel' and groups of tribes were led in war and ruled in peace by governors. The short book, Ruth, is placed with it because its story is set in the same period, but it does not form a part of the single conspectus of national history which runs from Joshua to the end of Kings.

The First and Second Books of Samuel mingle, or place side by side, various traditions relating to the beginnings of the monarchical period; the prophet Samuel, through whom God chooses Saul as the first of the kings, is represented as the last of the 'judges'. The history of David's family and the disputed succession includes much eye-witness material which goes back to the time of his son Solomon, and the books contain other cycles and groups of stories which were probably combined before 700 B.C. The period covered, roughly the century ended by David's death in 970, saw the war of liberation against the Philistine invaders and the unification of national territory under Jerusalem as capital. For later generations, the reign of David remained the golden age, and the promises made to the House of David, from Nathan's prophecy onwards, sustained and nourished the messianic hope.

The two Books of Kings open with the concluding chapters of the history of David's family, begun in 2 Samuel 9, and are a continuation of Israel's national story up to the destruction of Jerusalem in 587. This includes the reign of Solomon and the building of his Temple; after his death, the divided kingdoms of Israel and Judah are treated separately until Israel is extinguished by the Assyrians. The history of Judah alone is mainly concerned with two reigns, each remarkable for a national revival, invasion by foreign armies, and religious reform: the reigns of Hezekiah and Josiah. Only these two, of all the kings of Israel and Judah, are given unqualified praise for fidelity to Yahweh's commands: the discovery of Deuteronomy in the reign of Josiah and the religious reform inspired by it mark the climax of the entire history.

THE BOOK OF JOSHUA

I. THE CONQUEST OF THE PROMISED LAND

A. THE PREPARATIONS

The summons to enter the Promised Land

1 ¹ When Moses the servant of Yahweh was dead,ᵃ Yahweh spoke to Joshua son
² of Nun, Moses' adjutant. He said, •'Moses my servant is dead; rise—it is
time—and cross the Jordan here, you and all this people with you, into the
³ land which I am giving the sons of Israel. •Every place you tread with the soles
⁴ of your feet I shall give you as I declared to Moses that I would. •From the
wilderness and Lebanon to the great river Euphrates and to the Great Sea
⁵ westwards, this shall be your territory.ᵇ •As long as you live, no one shall be able
to stand in your way: I will be with you as I was with Moses; I will not leave
you or desert you.

Faithfulness to the Law is a condition of God's aid

⁶ 'Be strong and stand firm, for you are the man to give this people possession
⁷ of the land that I swore to their fathers I should give to them. •Only be strong
and stand firm and be careful to keep all the Law which my servant Moses laid
on you. Never swerve from this to right or left, and then you will be happy in
⁸ all you do. •Have the book of this Law always on your lips; meditate on
it day and night, so that you may carefully keep everything that is written in it.
⁹ Then you will prosper in your dealings, then you will have success. •Have I not
told you: Be strong and stand firm? Be fearless then, be confident, for go where
you will, Yahweh your God is with you.'

Aid from the tribes beyond the Jordan

¹⁰
¹¹ Then Joshua gave the officers of the people this order: •'Go through the camp
and say to the people, "Get provisions ready, for in three days you will cross
the Jordan here and go on to take possession of the land which Yahweh your
¹² God is giving you as your very own"'. •Then to the Reubenites and Gadites
¹³ and the half-tribe of Manasseh, Joshua said, •'Remember what Yahweh's servant
Moses told you, "Yahweh your God, granting you a place to find rest, has given
¹⁴ you this land". •Your wives, your little ones and your cattle may remain in the
land that Moses gave you beyond the Jordan. But all you who are fighting men
must go over with your weapons in front of your brothers and fight with them
¹⁵ till Yahweh grants rest, to your brothers and you alike, when they too have
taken possession of the land that Yahweh your God is giving them. Then you
may go back again to the land that is yours to hold, which Yahweh's servant
¹⁶ Moses gave you eastwards beyond the Jordan.' •Then they answered Joshua,

---

1 a. The book is introduced as the continuation of Dt.   b. These boundaries go far beyond
those of the country partitioned in ch. 13-19.

'We will do all that you have told us, and wherever you send us we will go. •We 17
obeyed Moses in all things, and now we will obey you. Only may Yahweh your
God be with you as he was with Moses! •If anyone rebels against your direction 18
and does not obey whatever orders you lay on him, let him be put to death.
Only be strong and stand firm.'

Joshua's spies at Jericho

2 Joshua son of Nun sent out two spies secretly from Shittim.ᵃ He said, 'Go out 1
and explore the country at Jericho'. They went, and they entered the house
of a harlot called Rahab; there they lodged. •Word of this was brought to the 2
king of Jericho, 'Take notice, some men from the Israelites have come here
tonight to reconnoitre the country'. •Then the king of Jericho sent a message 3
to Rahab, 'Send out the men who came to you and are lodging in your house,
for they have come to reconnoitre the whole country'. •But the woman took 4
the two men and hid them; and she answered, 'True, the men came to me, but
I did not know where they came from. •When the city gate was about to be 5
closed at nightfall, the men went out and I cannot say where they went. Follow
them quickly, you may still overtake them.'
    She had taken them up to the roof and hidden them under stalks of flax she 6
had heaped up there. •The king's men pursued them towards the Jordan, as far 7
as the fords, and the gate was shut once the pursuers had gone through.

The pact between Rahab and the spies

    The others had not yet lain down when Rahab came up to them on the roof. 8
She said to them, 'I know that Yahweh has given you this land, that we ourselves 9
are afraid of you and that all who live in this territory have been seized with
terror at your approach; •for we have heard how Yahweh dried up the Sea of 10
Reeds before you when you came out of Egypt and what you did with the two
Amorite kings across the Jordan, Sihon and Og, whom you put under the ban.
When we heard this, our hearts failed us, and no courage is left in any of us to 11
stand up to you, because Yahweh your God is God both in heaven above and
on earth beneath. •Swear to me now by Yahweh, then, since I myself have 12
shown you kindness, that you too will show kindness to the people of my father's
house, and will give me a sure sign of this; •that you will spare the lives of my 13
father and mother, my brothers and sisters and all who belong to them, and
will preserve us from death.' •Then the men answered her, 'If we do not, it is 14
we, not you, who will deserve to die, unless you tell of our agreement. When
Yahweh has given us the land, we will deal with you kindly and faithfully.'
Rahab let them down from the window by a rope, for her house was against the 15
city wall and she lived inside the wall itself. •She said, 'You must make for the 16
hills, to escape your pursuers. Hide there for three days till the pursuers have
returned, and then go on your way.' •The men answered, 'We for our part will 17
be free of the oath you made us swear, except on these conditions. •When we 18
enter your land you must use this sign: you must tie this scarlet cord to the
window from which you let us down, and you must gather with you in your
house your father and mother and brothers and all your family. •If anybody 19
passes through the doors of your house to go out, his blood shall be on his own
head and we are not to blame; but the blood of all who stay with you in the
house shall be on our heads if a hand is laid on any of them. •If you make this 20
talk of ours known, we shall be free of the oath that you made us swear.' •She 21
replied, 'Let it be as you say'. She let them go, and they left. Then she tied the
scarlet cord to the window.ᵇ

The spies return

    They left her and made for the hills. They stayed there for three days, till 22
the pursuers had returned, having scoured the countryside without finding them.

23 Then the two men came down again from the hills, crossed the river and came
24 to Joshua son of Nun; and they told him all that had happened to them. •They
said to Joshua, 'Yahweh has delivered the whole country into our hands, and
its inhabitants all tremble already at the thought of us'.

B. THE CROSSING OF THE JORDAN

Before the crossing

1 **3** Early in the morning, Joshua struck camp and set out from Shittim with all
the Israelites. They reached the Jordan and camped there before they crossed.
2
3 Three days later, the officers went through the camp •and gave the people these
instructions, 'When you see the ark of the covenant of Yahweh your God and
the levitical priests carrying it, you must leave the place where you are standing
4b and follow the ark, •so that you know which way to take; you have never gone
4a this way before. •Between you and the ark, however, keep a distance of some
5 thousand cubits;ᵃ do not go near it.' •Joshua said to the people, 'Sanctify yourselves for tomorrow, because tomorrow Yahweh will work wonders among you'.
6 Then he said to the priests, 'Take up the ark of the covenant, and cross at the
head of the people'. They took up the ark of the covenant and moved to the
front of the people.

The final instructions

7 Yahweh said to Joshua, 'This very day I will begin to make you a great man
in the eyes of all Israel, to let them be sure that I am going to be with you
8 even as I was with Moses. •As for you, give this order to the priests carrying
the ark of the covenant: "When you have reached the brink of the waters of the
9 Jordan, you are to stand still in the Jordan itself" .' •Then Joshua said to the
10 Israelites, 'Come closer and hear the words of Yahweh your God'. •Joshua said,
'By this you shall know that a living God is with you and without a doubt will
expel the Canaanite, the Hittite, the Hivite, the Perizzite, the Girgashite, the
11 Amorite and the Jebusite. •Look, the ark of Yahweh, the Lord of the whole
12 earth, is about to cross the Jordan at your head. •Choose twelve men at once
13 from the tribes of Israel, one man from each tribe. •As soon as the priests with
the ark of Yahweh, the Lord of the whole earth, have set their feet in the
waters of the Jordan, the upper waters of the Jordan flowing down will be
stopped in their course and stand still in one mass.'

The river crossed

14 Accordingly, when the people struck camp to cross the Jordan, the priests
15 carried the ark of the covenant in front of the people. •As soon as the bearers
of the ark reached the Jordan and the feet of the priests who carried it touched
the waters (the Jordan overflows the whole length of its banks throughout the
16 harvest season) •the upper waters stood still and made one heap over a wide
space—from Adam to the fortress of Zarethan—while those flowing down to
the Sea of the Arabah, that is, the Salt Sea, stopped running altogether. The
17 people crossed opposite Jericho. •The priests who carried the ark of the covenant
of Yahweh stood still on dry ground in mid-Jordan, and all Israel continued
to cross dry-shod till the whole nation had finished its crossing of the river.

The twelve memorial stones

1 **4** When the whole nation had finished crossing the Jordan, Yahweh spoke to
2 Joshua, •'Choose out twelve men from the people, one man from each tribe,
3 and give them this command: "Take from here, from mid-Jordan, twelve stones;

2 a. Shittim (the acacias) is a region north-east of the Dead Sea.   b. Vv.17-21 seem to be inter-
polated from a different tradition; there is no further mention of the scarlet cord.
3 a. About half a mile.

carry them with you and set them down in the camp where you pass the night" '. Joshua called the twelve men he had marked out among the Israelites, one man 4 for each tribe, •and told them, 'Pass on before the ark of Yahweh your God 5 into mid-Jordan, and each of you take one stone on his shoulder, matching the number of the tribes of Israel, •to make a memorial of this in your midst; for 6 when in days to come your children ask you, "What do these stones mean for you?", •you will tell them, "The waters of the Jordan separated in front 7 of the ark of the covenant of Yahweh, and when it crossed the Jordan, the waters of the river vanished. These stones are an everlasting reminder of this to the Israelites." ' •The Israelites did as Joshua told them; they took twelve stones 8 from mid-Jordan to match the number of the tribes of Israel, as Yahweh had told Joshua; they carried them over to the camp and set them down there. •Then 9 Joshua set up twelve stones in mid-Jordan in the spot where the feet of the priests who carried the ark had rested; they are there even now.*

The crossing ends

The priests carrying the ark stood still in mid-Jordan until everything was 10 done that Yahweh had directed Joshua to tell the people, all as Moses had instructed Joshua; and the people hurried across. •When they were all over, 11 the ark of Yahweh then crossed, with the priests at the head of the people. •The 12 Reubenites, the Gadites and the half-tribe of Manasseh crossed over armed in front of the Israelites, as Moses had ordered them. •They were some forty 13 thousand warriors in arms, and they crossed before Yahweh, ready for battle, towards the plain of Jericho. •That day Yahweh made Joshua great in the sight 14 of all Israel, and they honoured him as they had honoured Moses as long as he lived. •Yahweh said to Joshua, •'Tell the priests carrying the ark of the $^{15}_{16}$ testimony to come up from the Jordan'. •And Joshua commanded the priests: 17 'Come up from the Jordan!' •Now when the priests carrying the ark of the 18 covenant of Yahweh came up from the Jordan, their feet had no sooner touched the bank than the waters of the Jordan returned to their bed and ran on overflowing as before.

Gilgal is reached

It was the tenth day of the first month when the people came up from the 19 Jordan and made their camp at Gilgal, east of Jericho. •As for the twelve stones 20 that had been taken from the Jordan, Joshua set them up at Gilgal. •Then he 21 said to the Israelites, 'When your children in days to come ask their fathers, "What is the meaning of these stones?" •tell them this, "You see the Jordan. 22 Israel crossed over it dry-shod, •because Yahweh your God dried up the waters 23 of the Jordan in front of you until you had crossed, just as Yahweh your God had done with the Sea of Reeds, which he dried up before us till we had crossed it; •so that all the peoples of the earth may recognise how mighty the hand of 24 Yahweh is, and that you yourselves may always stand in awe of Yahweh your God." '

The peoples west of the Jordan are terrified

5 When all the kings of the Amorites in the country west of Jordan and all 1 the kings of the Canaanites in the coastal region heard that Yahweh had dried up the waters of the Jordan before the Israelites until they had crossed it, their hearts grew faint and their spirit failed them as the Israelites drew near.

The Hebrews are circumcised at Gilgal

At this time Yahweh said to Joshua, 'Make knives of flint and circumcise 2 the Israelites again'. •Joshua made knives of flint and circumcised the Israelites 3 on the Hill of Foreskins.

The reason why Joshua circumcised them was this. All the males of the people 4

who had come out of Egypt of age to bear arms had died in the wilderness on their
5 journey after leaving Egypt. •Now all the people who came out had been circumcised; but those who had been born in the wilderness—in the journey through
6 it when Egypt was left behind—none of these had been circumcised, •because
for forty years the Israelites travelled through the wilderness, until all the nation
had died out, that is, the men who had come out of Egypt of age to bear arms;
they had not obeyed the voice of Yahweh, and Yahweh had sworn to them never
to let them see the land that he had sworn to our fathers to give us, a land where
7 milk and honey flow. •But in place of these he set their sons, and these it was
that Joshua circumcised, for they were uncircumcised, since they could not be
8 circumcised on the journey. •When the circumcising of the whole nation was
9 over, they stayed to rest in the camp till they were well again; •and Yahweh
said to Joshua, 'Today I have taken the shame of Egypt away from you'. Hence
that place has been called Gilgal until now.ᵃ

The Passover kept

10   The Israelites pitched their camp at Gilgal and kept the Passover there on
11 the fourteenth day of the month, at evening in the plain of Jericho. •On the
morrow of the Passover they tasted the produce of that country, unleavened
12 bread and roasted ears of corn, that same day. •From that time, from their
first eating of the produce of that country, the manna stopped falling. And
having manna no longer, the Israelites fed from that year onwards on what the
land of Canaan yielded.

C. THE CONQUEST OF JERICHO

Prelude: a theophany

13   When Joshua was near Jericho, he raised his eyes and saw a man standing
there before him, grasping a naked sword. Joshua walked towards him and said
14 to him, 'Are you with us or with our enemies?' •He answered, 'No, I am captain
of the army of Yahweh, and now I come. . .' Joshua fell on his face to the ground
and worshipped him and said, 'What are my Lord's commands to his servant?'
15 The captain of the army of Yahweh answered Joshua, 'Take your sandals off
your feet, for the place you are standing on is holy'. And Joshua obeyed.

The taking of Jerichoᵃ

1 **6** Now Jericho had been carefully barricaded against the Israelites; no one came
2 out, no one went in. •Then Yahweh said to Joshua, 'Now I am delivering
3 Jericho and its king into your hands. All you fighters, •valiant warriors, will
march round the town and make the circuit once, and for six days you will do
4 the same thing. •(But seven priests will carry seven trumpets in front of the ark.)
On the seventh day you will go seven times round the town (and the priests will
5 blow their trumpets). •When the ram's horn rings out (when you hear the sound
of the trumpet), the whole people must utter a mighty war cry and the town
wall will collapse then and there; then the people can storm the town, each man
going straight ahead.'
6   Joshua son of Nun (called the priests and said to them, 'Take up the ark
of the covenant, and seven priests are to carry seven trumpets of ram's horn in
7 front of the ark of Yahweh'. •He) said to the people, 'Forward! March round

---

4 a. The narrative shows signs of two distinct traditions; in the first the stones are set up at
Gilgal, and the circles of stones that were to be seen there were thus related to the crossing;
in the second, the twelve stones were set up in the Jordan. *Gilgal* means 'stone circle'.
5 a. Play on words: Gilgal is connected with *galal* ('take away').
6 a. Two narratives are conflated here. In the first, the Israelites march round the walls in silence
until they are told to raise the great war cry; in the second, there is a procession with the ark to
the sound of the priests' trumpets. In the text, the second account is bracketed.

the town (and let the vanguard march before the ark of Yahweh).' •All was done 8 as Joshua ordered the people. (Seven priests carrying the seven trumpets of ram's horn in front of Yahweh moved onwards and blew their trumpets; the ark of the covenant of Yahweh came behind them, •the vanguard marched in 9 front of the priests with their trumpets, the rearguard followed behind the ark; the men marched, the trumpets sounded.)

Joshua had given the people the following order: 'Do not shout, do not utter 10 even a word; let nothing be heard from you till the day when I say: Raise the war cry. Then you are to shout.'

(At Joshua's command, the ark of Yahweh went round the town and made 11 the circuit once; then they returned to the camp and spent the night there.) Joshua rose early (and the priests took up the ark of Yahweh. •Bearing the $^{12}_{13}$ seven ram's horn trumpets, the seven priests walked before the ark of Yahweh sounding their trumpets as they went, while the vanguard marched before them and the rearguard behind the ark of Yahweh, and the march went on to the sound of the trumpet.)

They marched once round the town (on the second day) and returned to the 14 camp, and so on for six days. •On the seventh day they rose at dawn and marched 15 seven times round the town in the same manner. Only on that day did they march round seven times. •At the seventh time (the priests blew their trumpets and) 16 Joshua said to the people, 'Raise the war cry, because Yahweh has given the town into your hands.

Jericho placed under the ban

'The town and everything inside it must be set apart for Yahweh under a ban; 17 only the life of Rahab the harlot is to be spared, with all who are in her house, since she hid the messengers we sent. •But beware of the ban yourselves; do not 18 be covetous and take anything that is under the ban; that would lay the whole camp of Israel open to the same ban and bring disaster on it. •All the 19 silver and all the gold, all the things of bronze and things of iron are consecrated to Yahweh and must be put into his treasury.'

The people shouted, the trumpets sounded. When they heard the sound of the 20 trumpet, the people raised a mighty war cry and the wall collapsed then and there. At once the people stormed the town, every man going straight ahead; and they captured the town. •They enforced the ban on everything in the 21 town: men and women, young and old, even the oxen and sheep and donkeys, massacring them all.

Rahab's house preserved

Joshua said to the two men who had reconnoitred the country, 'Go into the 22 harlot's house, and bring out the woman with all who belong to her, so as to keep your oath to her'. •The young men who had been spies went in and brought 23 out Rahab and her father and mother and brothers and all who belonged to her. They brought out all her clansmen too and set them in safety outside the camp of Israel. •They burned the town and all within it except the silver and gold and 24 things of bronze and iron; these they put into the treasury of Yahweh's house. But Rahab the harlot, her father's household and all who belonged to her, these 25 Joshua spared. She has dwelt among Israel until now, because she concealed the messengers Joshua sent to reconnoitre Jericho.

A curse upon Jericho's restorer

At that time Joshua made them take this oath before Yahweh: 26

'Cursed be any man who comes forth
and builds this town up again!
On his eldest son he shall lay its foundations,
on his youngest set up its gates.'

Yahweh was with Joshua, and Joshua's fame spread all through the country. 27

The ban defied

1 7 But the sons of Israel incurred guilt by violating the ban. Achan son of Carmi, son of Zabdi, son of Zerah, of the tribe of Judah, laid his hands on something that fell under the ban, and the anger of Yahweh flared out against the Israelites.

The sacrilege punished by a repulse at Ai

2 Now Joshua sent men from Jericho to Ai,ᵃ east of Bethel; his command was: 'Go up and reconnoitre the country'. The men went up and reconnoitred Ai.
3 They came back to Joshua and said, 'There is no need for all the people to go up; let some two or three thousand men go and attack Ai. Spare the whole people
4 such a toil; the enemy are not many.' •Some three thousand men of the people
5 marched up to Ai, but broke before the townsmen. •These killed some thirty-six of them and drove the men back from the town gate to Shebarim; there on the slope they made havoc of them. Then the people lost heart and their courage melted away.

Joshua's prayer

6 Joshua tore his garments and prostrated himself before the ark of Yahweh till nightfall; the elders of Israel did as he did, and all poured dust on their heads.
7 And Joshua said, 'Alas, Lord Yahweh, why did you bring this nation across the Jordan only to deliver us into the power of the Amorite and destroy us?
8 I wish we had won a place to live in on the other side of the Jordan! •Forgive me, Lord, but what can I say, now that Israel has turned its back on the enemy?
9 The Canaanites will hear of it, and all the inhabitants of the country; they will unite against us to wipe our name off the face of the earth. What are you going to do for your great name?'

Yahweh's answer

10 Yahweh answered Joshua, 'Stand up! Why are you lying prostrate like this?
11 Israel has sinned; they have violated the covenant I ordained for them. Yes, they have taken what was under the ban, stolen and hidden it and put it into
12 their baggage. •That is why the sons of Israel cannot stand up to their foes; why they have turned their backs on their enemies, because they have come under the ban themselves. I will be with you no longer unless you remove what is under the ban from among you.
13 'Rise and call the people together and say to them, "Sanctify yourselves for tomorrow, because Yahweh the God of Israel declares: The ban is now among you, Israel; you can never stand up to your enemies until you take what is under
14 the ban from among you". •In the morning therefore you will come forward tribe by tribe, and then the tribe that Yahweh marks out by lot will come forward, clan by clan, and the clan that Yahweh marks out by lot will come forward family by family, and the family that Yahweh marks out by lot will come
15 forward man by man. •And then the man taken with the thing that is banned is to be delivered over to the fire, he and all that belongs to him, because he has violated the covenant with Yahweh and committed an infamy in Israel.'

The culprit brought to light and punished

16 Joshua rose early; he made Israel come forward tribe by tribe, and the lot
17 marked out the tribe of Judah. •He called up to him the clans of Judah, and the lot marked out the clan of Zerah. He called up the clan of Zerah, family by
18 family, and Zabdi was marked out. •Then Joshua called up the family of Zabdi, man by man, and it was Achan son of Carmi, son of Zabdi, son of Zerah, of the tribe of Judah, who was chosen by the lot.
19 Then Joshua said to Achan, 'My son, give glory to Yahweh the God of Israel,

7 a. Now et-Tell ('ruin').

and pay him homage; tell me what you have done and hide nothing from me'. Achan answered Joshua, 'Yes, I am the man who has sinned against Yahweh 20 the God of Israel, and this is what I have done. •When I saw among the spoil 21 a fine robe from Shinar and two hundred shekels of silver and an ingot of gold weighing fifty shekels, I coveted them and took them. They are hidden there in the ground inside my tent, and the silver is underneath.'

Joshua sent out messengers; they ran to the tent, and the robe was indeed 22 hidden inside the tent, and the silver was underneath. •They took everything 23 from inside the tent and brought it to Joshua and the elders of Israel and laid it out before Yahweh.

Then Joshua took Achan son of Zerah, with the silver and the robe and the 24 ingot of gold and led him up to the Vale of Achor—and with him his sons and daughters, his oxen and donkeys and sheep, his tent and everything that belonged to him. All Israel went with him.

Joshua said, 'Why did you bring evil on us? May Yahweh bring evil on you 25 today!' And all Israel stoned him.

A great cairn was reared over him,[b] which is still there today. Then Yahweh 26 ceased from his burning anger. It was then that the place was given the name, the Vale of Achor,[c] which it is still called now.

D. THE TAKING OF AI

The command given to Joshua

8 Then Yahweh said to Joshua, 'Be fearless now, and be confident. Take all 1 your fighting men with you, and march out against Ai. I will put into your power the king of Ai, his people, his town and his territory. •You are to do with 2 Ai and its king as you did with Jericho and its king. As regards booty, you may take the goods and the cattle—no more. Take up a concealed position against the city, to the rear of it.'

Joshua's stratagem

Joshua prepared to march against Ai with all the fighting men. He chose 3 thirty thousand men from among the bravest and sent them out by night •after 4 giving them these instructions, 'Listen! You are to take up a concealed position against the town, but at the rear not far from the town, and mind you all keep alert! •I and all the people with me will go forward till we are near the town, and 5 when the people of Ai come out against us as they did the first time, we will run before them. •Then they will follow close behind us, and we shall draw them 6 away from the town, because they will think, "They are running from us as they did last time". •Then you will rise from your concealed position and seize the 7 town; Yahweh your God will deliver it into your hands. •When you have captured 8 the town, set fire to it. These orders must be carried out. See to it! The orders come from me.' •Joshua sent them off, and they made their way to the concealed 9 position, at a point between Bethel and Ai, to the west of Ai. Joshua spent the night among the people, •then, rising early next day, mustered the people and 10 marched on Ai; he and the elders of Israel marched at the head of the people. All the warriors with him marched up towards the front of the town; they pitched 11 camp north of Ai, with the ravine between Joshua and the town. •He took some 12 five thousand men and concealed these between Bethel and Ai, to the west of the town. •The people pitched their camp north of the town, while the concealed 13 position lay to the west. Joshua spent that night in the valley itself.

The battle of Ai

When the king of Ai saw how things lay, he and all his people hurried out 14 to engage Israel on the slope facing the Arabah; he did not know that an ambush

15 had been laid against him to the rear of the town. •Joshua and all Israel with him
16 let themselves be driven back, taking flight towards the wilderness. •All the
people who were in the town followed them in loud pursuit, and in pursuing
17 Joshua they left the town itself unguarded. •Not a man was left behind in Ai,
all had gone out in pursuit of Israel; and in pursuing Israel they left the town
undefended.
18   Then Yahweh said to Joshua, 'Point the javelin in your hand at Ai; for
I am about to put the town in your power'. Then Joshua pointed the javelin
19 in his hand towards the town. •No sooner had he stretched out his hand than
the men in ambush rose quickly from their position, ran forward and entered
the town; they captured it and quickly set it on fire.

Disaster for the people of Ai

20   When the men of Ai looked back, they saw smoke rising from the town into
the sky. None of them had the chance to run one way rather than another, for the
21 people fleeing towards the wilderness turned back on their pursuers. •For when
Joshua and all Israel saw that the town had been seized by the men in ambush, and
saw the smoke rising from the town into the sky, they turned round and attacked
22 the men of Ai. •The others came out from the town to engage them, so that the
men of Ai found themselves surrounded by Israelites, some on this side and
some on that. These set about them till not one was alive and none left to flee;
23
24 but the king of Ai was captured alive, and brought to Joshua. •When Israel
had finished killing all the inhabitants of Ai in the open ground and where they
followed them into the wilderness, and when all to a man had fallen by the edge
25 of the sword, all Israel returned to Ai and slaughtered all its people •The
number of those who fell that day, men and women together, was twelve thousand,
all people of Ai.

The ban; the destruction of the town

26   Joshua did not draw back the hand with which he had pointed the
javelin until he had dealt with all the dwellers in Ai as with men under a ban.
27 For booty, Israel took only the cattle and the spoils of the town, according to the
28 order Yahweh had given to Joshua. •Then Joshua burned Ai, making it
29 a ruin for evermore, a desolate place even today. •He hanged the king of Ai
from a tree till evening; but at sunset Joshua ordered his body to be taken down
from the tree. It was then thrown down at the entrance to the town gate and
a great cairn was reared over it; and that is still there today.

E. SACRIFICE ON MOUNT EBAL: THE LAW READ THERE

The altar of undressed stones

30   Then Joshua built an altar to Yahweh the God of Israel on Mount Ebal,
31 as Moses, Yahweh's servant, had ordered the sons of Israel, as is written
in the Book of the Law of Moses, 'an altar of undressed stones that no iron tool
has ever worked'. On this they offered holocausts to Yahweh and offered
communion sacrifices as well.

The reading of the Law

32   There Joshua wrote on the stones a copy of the Law which Moses had written
33 for the Israelites. •Then, on both sides of the ark, and facing the levitical priests
who carried the ark of the covenant of Yahweh, all Israel with their elders and
scribes and judges—strangers as well as Israelites born—all took their places,
half of them in front of Mount Gerizim and half in front of Mount Ebal, as

b. To mark the grave of a criminal or outlaw.   c. Here derived from 'achar, 'to bring misfortune'

Moses the servant of Yahweh had ordered originally for the blessing of the people of Israel. •After this, Joshua read all the words of the Law—the blessing 34 and the cursing—exactly as it stands written in the Book of the Law. •Of every 35 word laid down by Moses there was not one left unread by Joshua in the presence of the full assembly of Israel, with the women and children there, and the strangers living among the people.

F. THE TREATY BETWEEN ISRAEL AND THE GIBEONITES

A coalition against Israel

9 Hearing these things, all the kings on this side of the Jordan, in the highlands 1 and in the lowlands, all along the coast of the Great Sea towards Lebanon, the Hittites, the Amorites, the Canaanites, the Perizzites, the Hivites and the Jebusites, •formed an alliance to fight together against Joshua and Israel. 2

The ruse of the Gibeonites[a]

When the inhabitants of Gibeon heard what Joshua had done to Jericho and 3 to Ai, •they decided to resort to trickery. They set out provided with supplies, 4 having loaded their donkeys with old sacks and with old wineskins that had burst and been sewn up again. •The sandals on their feet were worn out and 5 patched, the garments they wore were threadbare. The bread they took with them to eat was all dry and crumbling.

They came to Joshua in the camp at Gilgal, and speaking to him and the men 6 of Israel, they said, 'We come from a distant country, so make a treaty with us'. The men of Israel answered these Hivites, 'It may be that you live in our neigh- 7 bourhood; how then can we make a treaty with you?' •They answered Joshua, 8 'We are your servants'. But Joshua asked them, 'Who are you and where do you come from?' •They answered, 'Your servants have come from a country very 9 far away, because of the fame of Yahweh your God; for we have heard of him and all that he has done in Egypt •and all that he has done to the two Amorite 10 kings whose realm was beyond the Jordan, Sihon the king of Heshbon and Og the king of Bashan who lived at Ashtaroth. •Then our elders and all the 11 people of our country said to us, "Take provisions with you for the journey; go to meet them and say to them: We are your servants; so make a treaty with us". •Here is our bread; it was warm when we took it from home for our journey 12 the day we set out to come to you, and now you see it is dry and crumbling. •These wineskins were new when we filled them; you see they have 13 burst; and our clothes and sandals are all worn out from travelling such a long way.'

The leaders partook of the provisions they offered and did not consult the 14 oracle of Yahweh. •Joshua granted them peace and made a treaty with 15 them guaranteeing their lives, and the leaders of the community ratified it by oath.

Now it so happened that three days after the treaty had been made, it became 16 known that they were a neighbouring people whose home was in the midst of Israel. •The Israelites set out from the camp and came to their towns, which 17 were Gibeon, Chephirah, Beeroth and Kiriath-jearim. •The Israelites did not 18 attack them because the leaders of the community had sworn to them by Yahweh the God of Israel, but the community grumbled at the leaders.

The Gibeonites' place in the community

All the leaders declared in full assembly, 'Since we have sworn an oath to 19 them by Yahweh the God of Israel, we cannot touch them. •This is what we 20 will do with them: we will let them live, lest otherwise we bring the wrath on ourselves because of the oath we swore to them.' •The leaders went on, 'Let 21 them live, but let them be wood-cutters and water-carriers in the service

22 of the whole community'. The community did as the leaders had said. •Joshua sent for the Gibeonites and asked them, 'Why did you trick us with those words,
23 "We live very far away", when in fact you live right among us? •From now you are accursed, and you shall never cease being serfs, wood-cutters
24 and water-carriers in the house of my God.' •They answered Joshua, 'We did it because your servants had become convinced that Yahweh your God had ordered Moses his servant to give you this whole country and destroy all its inhabitants before you; also because, as you advanced on us, we were extremely
25 afraid that you would kill us. That was why we did this. •Now, see, we are in
26 your power; do with us whatever you think right and good.' •What he did with them was this. He saved them from the hands of the Israelites, and they did not
27 kill them. •But from that day forward, Joshua made them wood-cutters and water-carriers for the community, and bound them, down to the present day, to wait on Yahweh's altar wherever Yahweh might choose.

G. FIVE AMORITE KINGS FORM A COALITION[a]
THE SOUTH OF PALESTINE IS SUBDUED

Five kings make war on Gibeon

1 **10** Now it happened that Adoni-zedek the king of Jerusalem was told that Joshua had conquered Ai and put the town under a ban, dealing with Ai and its king as he had dealt earlier with Jericho and its king; and also that the inhabitants of Gibeon had made their peace with Israel and entered their
2 community. •There was consternation at this, since Gibeon was as important a town as one of the royal towns themselves, and larger than Ai, while all its citizens
3 were fighting men. •Then Adoni-zedek the king of Jerusalem sent word to Hoham the king of Hebron, Piram the king of Jarmuth, Japhia the king of Lachish and
4 Debir the king of Eglon, •'Join me and help me to conquer Gibeon, because
5 it has made peace with Joshua and the Israelites'. •The five Amorite kings joined forces and set off together, that is, the king of Jerusalem, the king of Hebron, the king of Jarmuth, the king of Lachish and the king of Eglon, they and all their armies with them; they besieged Gibeon and attacked it.

Joshua comes to the rescue of Gibeon

6 The men of Gibeon sent word to Joshua in the camp at Gilgal, 'Do not desert your servants; come up here quickly to save us and help us, because all the Amorite kings living in the mountains have allied themselves against us'.
7 Joshua came up from Gilgal in person, bringing all the fighting men and all the
8 bravest of his army with him. •Yahweh said to Joshua, 'Do not be afraid of these men; I have delivered them into your power; not one of them will be
9 able to stand against you'. •Having marched from Gilgal throughout the night, Joshua caught them unawares.

Aid from on high

10 Yahweh drove them headlong before Israel, defeating them completely at Gibeon; furthermore, he pursued them towards the descent of Beth-horon and
11 harassed them as far as Azekah, and as far as Makkedah. •And as they fled from Israel down the descent of Beth-horon, Yahweh hurled huge hailstones from heaven on them all the way to Azekah, which killed them. More of them

9 a. The Gibeonites, living in the four places listed in v.17, constituted an isolated enclave in Canaan.
10 a. Ch. 10 and 11 describe the conquest of the whole south, and later of the whole north of the land, in expeditions against the coalition of Canaanite kings by all the united tribes led by Joshua. Ch. 13-15 and 17 show the conquest as slow and incomplete, with each tribe acting by itself, and this is closer to the historical fact.

died under the hailstones than at the edge of Israel's sword. •Then Joshua spoke 12
to Yahweh, the same day that Yahweh delivered the Amorites to the Israelites.
Joshua declared:[b]

> 'Sun, stand still over Gibeon,
> and, moon, you also, over the Vale of Aijalon'.
> And the sun stood still, and the moon halted, 13
> till the people had vengeance on their enemies.

Is this not written in the Book of the Just?[c] The sun stood still in the middle
of the sky and delayed its setting for almost a whole day. •There was never a 14
day like that before or since, when Yahweh obeyed the voice of a man, for
Yahweh was fighting for Israel. •Then Joshua, and all Israel with him, returned 15
to the camp at Gilgal.[d]

The five kings in the cave at Makkedah

As for those five kings, they had fled and hidden in the cave of Makkedah, 16
and news of this was brought to Joshua. 'The five kings' the message ran 'have 17
been found hiding in the cave at Makkedah.' •Joshua answered, 'Roll great 18
stones to the mouth of the cave and post men there to keep guard. •And you, 19
do not stay there idle; pursue the enemy, cut off their line of retreat and do not
let them enter their towns, for Yahweh your God has put them in your power.'
When Joshua and the sons of Israel had routed them completely and were near 20
to slaughtering the last of them, the survivors who had escaped alive took refuge
in their fortresses. •The people came back to Joshua's camp at Makkedah; they were 21
all safe and sound, and no one dared to attempt anything against the Israelites.
Then Joshua said, 'Clear the mouth of the cave, and bring the five kings out 22
to me'. •They did so, bringing him the five kings from the cave; the king of 23
Jerusalem, the king of Hebron, the king of Jarmuth, the king of Lachish and
the king of Eglon. •When these kings had been brought to him, Joshua assembled 24
all the men of Israel and said to the officers of the men of war who had fought
with him, 'Come forward and put your feet on the necks of these kings!' They
came forward and put their feet on their necks. •'Do not be afraid; have 25
confidence,' Joshua went on 'be resolute, for this is how Yahweh shall deal
with all the enemies you fight.' •With this Joshua struck and killed them and 26
had them hanged on five trees; they hung there till evening.
At the hour of sunset Joshua gave his order; they were taken down from 27
the trees and thrown into the cave where they had been hiding. Great stones
were laid at the mouth of the cave, and these are still there today.

The conquest of the southern towns of Canaan

The same day, Joshua took Makkedah, striking the town and its king with 28
the edge of the sword; he delivered them over to the ban, with every living
creature there, and let no one escape; and he treated the king of Makkedah
as he had treated the king of Jericho.
Joshua, and all Israel with him, went on from Makkedah to Libnah and 29
attacked it. •This, too, with its king, Yahweh gave into the power of Israel; 30
and Israel struck every living creature there with the edge of the sword, and
left none alive, and treated its king like the king of Jericho.
Joshua, and all Israel with him, went on from Libnah to Lachish, and besieged 31
it and attacked it. •Yahweh gave Lachish into the power of Israel and Israel 32
took it on the second day and struck it and every living creature there with the
edge of the sword, as they had treated Libnah. •Then Horam the king of Gezer 33
marched up to help Lachish, but Joshua struck him and his people down until
not one was left alive.
Joshua, and all Israel with him, went on from Lachish to Eglon. They besieged 34
it and attacked it. •They took it the same day and struck it with the edge of the 35

sword. Every living creature there he delivered over to the ban that day, as he had treated Lachish.

36 Joshua, and all Israel with him, went on up from Eglon to Hebron. They
37 attacked it, •took it and struck it with the edge of the sword, with its king, all the places belonging to it and every living creature in it. As he had treated Eglon, so here, he left not a man alive. He delivered it over to the ban, with every living creature in it.

38
39 Joshua, and all Israel with him, turned aside to Debir and attacked it. •He took it and its king and all the places belonging to it; they struck them with the edge of the sword, and every living creature there they delivered over to the ban. He left none alive. As he had treated Hebron, as he had treated Libnah and its king, so he treated Debir and its king.

The southern conquests recapitulated

40 Thus Joshua subdued the whole land: the highlands, the Negeb, the lowlands, the hillsides, and all the kings in them. He left not a man alive and delivered every single soul over to the ban, as Yahweh the God of Israel had commanded.
41 Joshua conquered them from Kadesh-barnea to Gaza, and the whole region
42 of Goshen as far as Gibeon. •All these kings and their kingdoms Joshua mastered
43 in one campaign, because Yahweh the God of Israel fought for Israel. •And then Joshua, and all Israel with him, returned to the camp at Gilgal.

H. THE CONQUEST OF THE NORTH

A coalition of northern kings

1 **11** When Jabin the king of Hazor heard these things, he sent word of them to Jobab the king of Madon, to the king of Shimron, the king of Achshaph
2 and the kings in the northern highlands and in the valley south of Chinneroth,
3 and those of the lowlands and the hillsides of Dor westwards. •Eastwards and westwards lived the Canaanite; in the highlands the Amorite and Hivite and
4 Perizzite and Jebusite; under Hermon the Hittite, in the land of Mizpah. •They set out with all their troops, a horde as countless as the sands of the sea, with innumerable horses and chariots.

The victory at Merom

5 These kings, having all agreed on a meeting place, came and encamped near
6 one another at the waters of Merom, to fight against Israel. •Then Yahweh said to Joshua, 'Have no fear of these men, for by this time tomorrow Israel shall see them all cut to pieces; you shall hamstring their horses and burn their chariots'.
7 Joshua and all his warriors caught them unawares by the waters of Merom
8 and fell on them. •Yahweh delivered them into the power of Israel, who defeated them and pursued them to Sidon the Great and to Misrephoth-maim westwards and to the Vale of Mizpah eastwards; Israel harried them till not one was left
9 to escape. •Joshua treated them as Yahweh had ordered; he hamstrung their horses and burned their chariots.

The capture of Hazor and of the other northern towns

10 Joshua then came back and captured Hazor, putting its king to the sword.
11 Hazor in earlier days was the capital of all these kingdoms. •And they put to the sword every living creature there, because of the ban. Not a soul was left
12 there, and lastly Hazor was burned. •Joshua conquered all these royal cities

b. Lines from a popular song, appealing for time to secure a victory, are here adapted to the author's purpose. **c.** An ancient collection now lost; it is quoted also in 2 S 1:18. **d.** But cf. v.21. This chapter draws on various sources.

and their kings and struck them with the edge of the sword because of the ban, as Moses the servant of Yahweh had ordered.

Yet of all these towns standing on their mounds Israel burned none, apart from 13 Hazor which Joshua gave to the flames. •As for the spoils of these towns and 14 the cattle, the Israelites took them for themselves. But they struck all the human beings with the edge of the sword, and wiped them all out; they did not leave one living soul.

The orders of Moses carried out by Joshua

What Yahweh had ordered his servant Moses, Moses in turn had ordered 15 Joshua, and Joshua carried it out, leaving nothing unaccomplished that Yahweh had ordered Moses. •Thus Joshua mastered the whole country: the 16 highlands, the whole Negeb and the whole land of Goshen, the lowlands, the Arabah, the highlands and the lowlands of Israel.

From Mount Halak, which rises towards Seir, to Baal-gad in the Vale of 17 Lebanon below Mount Hermon, he captured all their kings, struck them down and slaughtered them. •For many a day Joshua had made war on all these kings; 18 no city had made peace with the Israelites except the Hivites who lived at Gibeon; 19 all the rest they conquered in battle. •For Yahweh had ordained that the hearts 20 of these men should be stubborn enough to fight against Israel, so that they might be mercilessly delivered over to the ban and be wiped out, as Yahweh had ordered Moses.ᵃ

The Anakim wiped out

Then Joshua came and wiped out the Anakim from the highlands, from 21 Hebron, from Debir, from Anab, from all the highlands of Judah and all the highlands of Israel; he delivered them and their towns over to the ban. •No more 22 Anakim were left in Israelite territory except at Gaza, Gath and Ashdod. •Joshua 23 mastered the whole country, just as Yahweh had told Moses, and he gave it to Israel as an inheritance according to their division by tribes.

And the country had rest from war.

I. RECAPITULATION

The kings conquered east of the Jordan

12 These are the kings of the country whom the Israelites conquered and 1 despoiled of their kingdoms, beyond Jordan eastwards, from the wadi Arnon to the mountain country of Hermon, with all the Arabah eastwards: Sihon the king of the Amorites who lived at Heshbon ruled from Aroer on the 2 edge of the gorge of the Arnon (and with this went the bed of the gorge) over half of Gilead to the wadi Jabbok, the boundary of the Ammonites, •and 3 eastwards over the Arabah to the Sea of Chinneroth on the one side, and to the Sea of the Arabah, the Salt Sea, towards Beth-jeshimoth where you come to the foothills of Pisgah on the south.

Og, the king of Bashan, one of the last of the Rephaim, who lived at Ashtaroth 4 and Edrei, •ruled over Mount Hermon and over Salecah, and over the whole 5 of Bashan as far as the boundary of the Geshurites and the Maacathites, and over half of Gilead to the boundary of Sihon the king of Heshbon. •Moses, the 6 servant of Yahweh, and with him the Israelites, had conquered these kings, and Moses, the servant of Yahweh, had given their possessions to the Reubenites, the Gadites and the half-tribe of Manasseh.

The kings conquered west of the Jordan

And these are the kings of the country whom Joshua and the Israelites 7 conquered westwards of the Jordan, from Baal-gad in the Vale of Lebanon to

Mount Halak rising towards Seir, and Joshua allotted their inheritance to the
8 tribes of Israel according to their divisions: •in the highlands and lowlands, in
the Arabah and on the hillsides, in the wilderness and the Negeb: in the territories
of Hittite, Amorite, Canaanite, Perizzite, Hivite and Jebusite:

9	the king of Jericho,	one;
	the king of Ai near Bethel,	one;
10	the king of Jerusalem,	one;
	the king of Hebron,	one;
11	the king of Jarmuth,	one;
	the king of Lachish,	one;
12	the king of Eglon,	one;
	the king of Gezer,	one;
13	the king of Debir,	one;
	the king of Geder,	one;
14	the king of Hormah,	one;
	the king of Arad,	one;
15	the king of Libnah,	one;
	the king of Adullam,	one;
16	the king of Makkedah,	one;
	the king of Bethel,	one;
17	the king of Tappuah,	one;
	the king of Hepher,	one;
18	the king of Aphek,	one;
	the king of Sharon,	one;
19	the king of Madon,	one;
	the king of Hazor,	one;
20	the king of Symoon,	one;
	the king of Achshaph,	one;
21	the king of Taanach,	one;
	the king of Megiddo,	one;
22	the king of Kedesh,	one;
	the king of Jokneam in Carmel,	one;
23	the king of Dor on the hillsides of Dor,	one;
	the king of Goiim in Galilee,	one;
24	the king of Tirzah,	one;
	Total number of all these kings:	thirty-one.

II. THE APPORTIONING OF THE LAND
AMONG THE TRIBES

Lands remaining unconquered

1 13 Now Joshua had grown old and advanced in years. Yahweh said to him,
'You are old now and advanced in years, yet much of the country still
2 remains to be subdued. •This is the country remaining:

'All the regions of the Philistines[a] and the whole country of the Geshurites;
3 from the Shihor, east of Egypt, to the boundary of Ekron northwards, the land
is counted as Canaanite. (The five chiefs of the Philistines are those of Gaza,
4 Ashdod, Ashkelon, Gath and Ekron; the Avvites are in •the south.) The whole
country of the Canaanites from Arah, which the Sidonians hold, to Aphekah

11 a. See Dt 7:2f and 20:16-18.
13 a. The Philistines settled in the coastal plain of Palestine about 1200. In the time of the Judges
and of Saul they were bitter enemies of Israel; they were driven back by David but maintained
control of the coastal districts.

and the boundary of the Amorites, •and then the country of the Gebalites with 5 all Lebanon eastwards from Baal-gad at the foot of Mount Hermon to the Pass of Hamath.

'All who live in the highlands from Lebanon to Misrephoth-maim 6 westwards—all the Sidonians—I myself will drive out before the Israelites. In the meantime, share out the land by lot among the Israelites as I have ordered you. •The time has come to divide this land among the nine tribes and the 7 half-tribe of Manasseh: from the Jordan to the Great Sea westwards you shall give it to them; the Great Sea will mark their boundary.'

A. THE TRIBES BEYOND THE JORDAN DESCRIBED

A general survey

As for the other half-tribe of Manasseh, this and the Reubenites and Gadites 8 had already received the allotted inheritance given them by Moses beyond the Jordan eastwards; Moses the servant of Yahweh had then assigned them the country onward from Aroer, which lies on the edge of the wadi Arnon, 9 and from the town within the gorge itself; all the tableland from Medeba to Dibon; •all the towns of Sihon the king of the Amorites, who had reigned in 10 Heshbon, to the boundary of the Ammonites. •Then Gilead and the territory 11 of the Geshurites and Maacathites with all the highlands of Hermon and with the whole of Bashan, including Salecah; •and in Bashan the whole kingdom 12 of Og, who had reigned in Ashtaroth and Edrei and was the last survivor of the Rephaim. Moses had conquered and dispossessed these two kings. •But the 13 Israelites did not dispossess the Geshurites or the Maacathites, and therefore Geshur and Maacah even now still form part of Israel. •To the tribe of Levi 14 alone no inheritance was given; Yahweh the God of Israel was their inheritance, as he had told them.

The tribe of Reuben

Moses had given the tribe of the sons of Reuben a portion according to their 15 clans. •Thus the land they received stretched from Aroer, on the edge of the 16 wadi Arnon, and the town within the gorge itself, and all the tableland up to Medeba, •and Heshbon and all the towns on the tableland: Dibon, Bamoth-baal, 17 Beth-baal-meon, •Jahaz, Kedemoth, Mephaath, •Kiriathaim, Sibmah and ¹⁸₁₉ Zereth-shahar in the highlands of Gor; •Beth-peor, the slopes of Pisgah, 20 Beth-jeshimoth, •all the towns on the tableland and the whole kingdom of Sihon 21 the king of the Amorites, who reigned in Heshbon; he had been defeated by Moses, and with him the princes of Midian, Evi, Rekem, Zur, Hur and Reba, vassals of Sihon who used to live in this country. •As for Balaam son of Beor, 22 the soothsayer, the Israelites had put him to the sword with others they had slaughtered. •Thus the land of the Reubenites stretched to the Jordan. This was 23 the inheritance of the sons of Reuben according to their clans, with the towns and their outlying villages.

The tribe of Gad

Moses had given the tribe of Gad, the sons of Gad, a portion according to 24 their clans. •The land they received was Jazer, all the towns of Gilead, half the 25 country of the Ammonites as far as Aroer facing Rabbah, •and from Heshbon 26 to Ramath-mizpeh and Betonim, and from Mahanaim as far as the territory of Lo-debar, •and lastly, in the valley: Beth-haram, Beth-nimrah, Succoth, and 27 Zaphon, the rest of the kingdom of Sihon the king of Heshbon. The Jordan was their boundary to the lower end of the Sea of Chinnereth, on the eastern side of the Jordan. •This was the inheritance of the sons of Gad according to their 28 clans, with the towns and their outlying villages.

The half-tribe of Manasseh

29   Moses had given the half-tribe of the sons of Manasseh a portion according
30 to their clans. •The land they received stretched from Mahanaim right through
Bashan, with the whole kingdom of Og the king of Bashan and all the Encamp-
31 ments of Jair in Bashan, sixty towns. •Half of Gilead, with Ashtaroth and Edrei,
the royal cities of Og in Bashan, were allotted to the sons of Machir son of
Manasseh, to half of the sons of Machir according to their clans.
32   This was the apportioning made by Moses in the plains of Moab, beyond the
33 Jordan and facing Jericho eastwards. •But to the tribe of Levi Moses had given
no inheritance; Yahweh the God of Israel is their inheritance, as he has told
them.

B. THE THREE GREAT TRIBES WEST OF JORDAN DESCRIBED

Introduction

1   **14** These are the portions that the Israelites received as an inheritance in the
      land of Canaan, assigned to them by Eleazar the priest and by Joshua son
2 of Nun and by the heads of the families of the tribes of Israel. •They made the
apportionment by lot, as Yahweh had ordered through Moses for the nine
3 tribes and the half-tribe. •Moses had given the two-and-a-half tribes beyond the
Jordan their own inheritance but had given the Levites no inheritance among
4 them. •The sons of Joseph were two tribes, Manasseh and Ephraim. No portion
in the land was given the Levites except certain towns to live in, with the pasture
5 lands adjoining for their cattle and property. •In apportioning the land, the
Israelites did as Yahweh had ordered Moses to do.

The portion of Caleb

6   Certain sons of Judah came to Joshua at Gilgal, and Caleb son of Jephunneh
the Kenizzite said to him, 'You know what Yahweh said to Moses the man
7 of God at Kadesh-barnea concerning you and me. •I was forty years old when
Moses the servant of Yahweh sent me from Kadesh-barnea to reconnoitre this
8 country, and of this I most faithfully made report to him. •But the brothers who
had gone up with me discouraged the people, whereas I myself did the whole
9 will of Yahweh my God. •That day Moses swore this oath, "Be sure of this,
that the land your foot has trodden shall be an inheritance for you and your
children for ever, because you have done the whole will of Yahweh my God".
10 From then till now, Yahweh has kept me alive in accordance with his promise.
It is forty-five years since Yahweh made this promise to Moses (it was while
Israel was journeying through the wilderness), and now I am eighty-five years
11 old. •Today I am still as strong as the day when Moses sent me out on that
12 errand; for fighting, for going and coming, I am as strong now as then. •It is
time you gave me the highlands that Yahweh promised me then. You heard
then how it was peopled by the Anakim and how its towns were great and
strong. If Yahweh is with me, I shall drive them out as Yahweh said.'
13   Joshua blessed Caleb son of Jephunneh and gave him Hebron as an inheritance.
14 And hence Hebron down to the present day has remained the possession of
Caleb son of Jephunneh the Kenizzite, because he did the whole will of Yahweh
15 the God of Israel. •The name of Hebron in earlier times was Kiriath-arba. Arba
had been the greatest man of the Anakim.
    And the country had rest from war.

The tribe of Judah

1   **15** The portion falling to the tribe of the sons of Judah according to their
      clans was near the boundary of Edom, from the wilderness of Zin to
2 Kadesh south-westwards. •Their southern boundary began at the end of the
3 Salt Sea, at the bay that faces south; •it proceeded south of the Ascent of Akrabbim,

crossed through Zin and up to the south of Kadesh-barnea, passed Hezron, went up to Addar and from there turned to Karka, •skirted Azmon, came out 4 at the wadi of Egypt and ended at the sea. This will be your southern boundary. Eastwards, the boundary was the Salt Sea as far as the mouth of the Jordan. 5 The boundary to the north began at the bay at the mouth of the Jordan. •This 6 boundary went up to Beth-hoglah, passed along north of Beth-arabah and reached the Stone of Bohan son of Reuben. •The boundary went up to Debir 7 from the Vale of Achor and turned towards the circle of stones opposite the Ascent of Adummim, south of the wadi; the boundary went on to the waters of En-shemesh and ended at En-rogel. •Then it went on up the wadi Ben- 8 hinnom, coming from the south to the flank of the Jebusite, that is to say Jerusalem, and climbed to the crest of the mountain barring the wadi Hinnom, westward and at the northern end of the plain of Rephaim. •From the mountain 9 top the boundary bent towards the source of the Waters of Nephtoah, passed from there towards Mount Ephron and then turned towards Baalah, that is to say, Kiriath-jearim. •From Baalah the boundary bent westwards to the mountain 10 country of Seir, skirted the northern slope of Mount Jearim, that is to say Chesalon, went down to Beth-shemesh and through Timnah, •reached the north 11 side of Ekron, turned towards Shikkeron, passed by the Hill of Baalah, then on to Jabneel, and ended at the sea. •The western boundary was the Great Sea 12 itself. This was the boundary that enclosed the lands assigned to the clans of the sons of Judah.

The Calebites occupy the territory of Hebron

Caleb son of Jephunneh was given a portion among the sons of Judah in 13 accordance with the order given by Yahweh to Joshua. Joshua gave him Kiriath-arba,[a] the chief city of the Anakim, which is now Hebron. •Caleb drove 14 the three sons of Anak out of it: Sheshai, Ahiman and Talmai, descended from Anak. •From there he marched up against the inhabitants of Debir, the name 15 of which was once Kiriath-sepher. •Then Caleb said, 'To the man who conquers 16 and captures Kiriath-sepher, I will give my daughter Achsah to wife'. •The man 17 who captured it was Othniel son of Kenaz, Caleb's brother; Caleb gave him his daughter Achsah to wife. •When she came to her husband, he urged her 18 to ask her father for a field. Then she jumped down from her donkey, and Caleb asked her, 'What do you want?' •She answered, 'Grant me a favour; since you 19 have banished me to the wilderness of the Negeb, at least grant me some springs of water'. So he gave her the upper springs and the lower springs.

This was the inheritance of the tribe of the sons of Judah according to their 20 clans.

Names of places possessed by the tribe of Judah

These are the furthermost towns of the tribe of the sons of Judah, towards 21 the boundary of Edom in the Negeb: Kabzeel, Eder, Jagur, •Kinah, Dimon, 22 Adadah, •Kedesh, Hazor, Ithnan, •Ziph, Telem, Bealoth, •Hazor-hadattah, 23,24 25 Kerioth-hezron (that is to say, Hazor), •Amam, Shema, Moladah, •Hazar- 26 27 gaddah, Heshmon, Beth-pelet, •Hazar-shual, Beersheba, Biziothiah, •Baalah, Iim, 28 29 Ezem, •Eltolad, Chesil, Hormah, •Ziklag, Madmannah, Sansannah, •Lebaoth, 30,31 32 Shilhim, En-rimmon.

In all, twenty-nine towns, with their outlying villages.

In the lowlands: 33 Eshtaol, Zorah, Ashnah, •Zanoah, En-gannim, Tappuah, Enam, •Jarmuth, 34 35 Adullam, Socoh, Azekah, •Shaaraim, Adithaim, Gederah, Gederothaim; fourteen 36 towns with their villages. Zenan, Hadashah, Migdal-gad, •Dilean, Mizpeh, Joktheel, •Lachish, Bozkath, 37,31 39 Eglon, •Cabbon, Lahmas, Chitlish, •Gederoth, Beth-dagon, Naamah, Makkedah: 40 41 sixteen towns with their villages.

42,43,44 Libnah, Ether, Ashan, •Iphtah, Ashnah, Nezib, •Keilah, Achzib, Mareshah: nine towns with their villages.

45,46 Ekron, with its towns and outlying villages. •From Ekron to the sea, everything 47 to the side of Ashdod, with its villages. •Ashdod with its towns and outlying villages; Gaza with its towns and outlying villages as far as the wadi of Egypt; the Great Sea marks the boundary.

48   In the highlands:

49,50 Shamir, Jattir, Socoh, •Dannah, Kiriath-sannah, which is now Debir, •Anab, 51 Eshtemoh, Anim, •Goshen, Holon, Giloh: eleven towns with their villages.

52,53,54 Arab, Dumah, Eshan, •Janum, Beth-tappuah, Aphekah, •Humtah, Kiriath-arba, 55 which is now Hebron, Zior: nine towns with their villages. •Maon, Carmel, 56,57 Ziph, Juttah, •Jezreel, Jokdeam, Zanoah, •Kain, Gibeah, Timnah: ten towns with their villages.

58,59 Halhul, Beth-zur, Gedor, •Maarath, Beth-anoth, Eltekon: six towns with their villages.

Tekoa, Ephrathah, which is now Bethlehem, Peor, Etam, Kulon, Tatam, Sores, Carem, Gallim, Bether, Manach: eleven towns with their villages.

60 Kiriath-baal, which is now Kiriath-jearim, and Rabbah: two towns with their villages.

61   In the wilderness:

62 Beth-arabah, Middin, Secacah, •Nibshan, the City of Salt and Engedi: six towns with their villages.

63 But the sons of Judah could not drive out the Jebusites who lived in Jerusalem; the Jebusites lived in Jerusalem side by side with the sons of Judah, as they still do today.

The tribe of Ephraim

1 **16** The portion awarded by lot to the sons of Joseph stretched from the Jordan opposite Jericho eastwards. From Jericho onwards the boundary climbed 2 the highlands to the wilderness of Bethel; •it left Bethel-luz and went on 3 towards the boundary of the Archites at Ataroth; •then passed downwards and westwards to the boundary of the Japhletites as far as the border of Lower 4 Beth-horon, as far as Gezer, and from there it reached the sea. •This was the inheritance of the sons of Joseph, Manasseh and Ephraim.

5   As regards the territory of the sons of Ephraim according to their clans, the boundary of their inheritance to the east was Ataroth-addar as far as Upper 6 Beth-horon, •and it ended at the sea . . . Michmethath to the north; and the boundary turned east to Tanaath-shiloh and ran beyond it on the east to Janoah; 7 it went down from Janoah to Ataroth and Naarah, then touched Jericho and 8 ended at the Jordan. •From Tappuah the boundary went westwards to the wadi Kanah and ended at the sea. This was the inheritance of the tribe of Ephraim 9 according to their clans, •as well as the towns set apart for the Ephraimites inside the inheritance of the sons of Manasseh, all those towns and their villages. 10 The Canaanites living in Gezer were not driven out; they have remained in Ephraim to the present day, but are obliged to do forced labour.

The tribe of Manasseh

1 **17** A portion was awarded by lot to Manasseh, because he was Joseph's first-born son. To Machir, Manasseh's eldest son and father of Gilead, there fell, as was right for a fighting man, the country of Gilead and Bashan. 2 And portions were also given to Manasseh's other sons, according to their clans: to the sons of Abiezer, the sons of Helek, the sons of Asriel, the sons of Shechem, the sons of Hepher, the sons of Shemida: these were the clans of the male children 3 of Manasseh son of Joseph. •Zelophehad son of Hepher, son of Gilead, son

---

15 a. 'Town of the four', though *Arba* is explained as a proper name, 14:15.

of Machir, son of Manasseh, had no sons, only daughters, whose names are these: Mahlah, Noah, Hoglah, Milcah and Tirzah. •These came to the priest 4 Eleazar and to Joshua the son of Nun and to the leaders, and said, 'Yahweh ordered Moses to give us an inheritance among our brothers'. According to Yahweh's order, therefore, they were given an inheritance among the brothers of their father. •In this way there fell to Manasseh ten portions besides 5 the country of Gilead and Bashan which lies across the Jordan, •since Manasseh's 6 daughters received an inheritance as well as his sons. The country of Gilead itself belonged to Manasseh's other sons. •The boundary of Manasseh was, on 7 the side of Asher, Michmethath, which is opposite Shechem, and thence continued to the right to Jashib at the spring of Tappuah. The territory of Tappuah 8 belonged to Manasseh, but Tappuah on Manasseh's border belonged to the sons of Ephraim. •The boundary passed down to the wadi Kanah (south of the 9 wadi were the Ephraimite towns, besides those which Ephraim had among the towns of Manasseh, the territory of Manasseh being north of the wadi), and it ended at the sea. •Southwards Ephraim, northwards Manasseh, both bounded 10 by the sea; they touched Asher to the north and Issachar to the east. •In Issachar 11 and in Asher, Manasseh had Beth-shean and its dependent towns, Ibleam and its dependent towns, the inhabitants of Dor and En-dor and their dependent towns, the inhabitants of Taanach and Megiddo and their dependent towns, and a third of the Nepheth. •But because the sons of Manasseh could not take 12 possession of these towns, the Canaanites managed to hold their own in the country. •However, when the Israelites became stronger, they put the Canaanites 13 to forced labour, though they never drove them out.

The sons of Joseph occupy forest country

The House of Joseph spoke thus to Joshua, 'Why have you given me for 14 inheritance only one share, only one portion, when my people are many because Yahweh has so blessed me?' •Joshua answered, 'If your people are so many, 15 go up to the woodland region and clear yourselves the forest of the country of the Perizzites and the Rephaim, since the highlands of Ephraim are too small for you'. •The sons of Joseph answered, 'The highlands are not enough 16 for us, and what is more, all the Canaanites living in the plain have iron chariots, and so have those in Beth-shean and its dependent towns, and those in the plain of Jezreel'. •Joshua said to the House of Joseph, to Ephraim and Manasseh, 17 'You are a large population and one of great strength; you shall not have one share only •but a mountain shall be yours; it is covered with woods, but you 18 must clear it, and its boundaries shall be yours, since you cannot drive out the Canaanite because of his iron chariots and his superior strength'.

C. THE SEVEN OTHER TRIBES DESCRIBED

The land survey for these seven tribes

18 The whole community of the Israelites assembled at Shiloh, and the Tent 1 of Meeting was set up there; the whole country was now subdued and at their disposal. •But among the Israelites there were still seven tribes left which 2 had not received their inheritance. •Then Joshua said to them, 'How much more 3 time will you waste before taking possession of the land which Yahweh the God of your fathers has given to you? •Choose three men from each tribe, for me to 4 send up and down the country so that they can make a survey with a view to its apportioning, and then come back to me. •They must divide the land into seven 5 portions. Judah will remain in his territory to the south, and those of the House of Joseph will remain in their territory to the north. •You are to survey the land 6 in seven sections and bring your findings to me here, so that I can cast lots for you before Yahweh our God. •For the Levites have no portion with the rest 7

of you; the priesthood of Yahweh is to be their inheritance; and Gad and Reuben and the half-tribe of Manasseh have received their inheritance beyond the Jordan eastwards, as Moses, Yahweh's servant, gave it to them.'

8　The men set off. To those who were to survey the country Joshua gave this order: 'Off you go, survey and map the whole country, and then come back here 9　to me; I shall cast lots for you before Yahweh at Shiloh'. •So the men left, and went up and down the country, making a sevenfold list in writing of all the towns and bringing it back to Joshua in the camp at Shiloh.

10　Joshua cast lots for them before Yahweh at Shiloh, and there Joshua apportioned the land among the Israelites according to their groupings.

The tribe of Benjamin

11　One portion fell to the tribe of the sons of Benjamin according to their clans: their territory lay, as it proved, between that of the sons of Judah and the sons 12　of Joseph. •Their northern boundary began at the Jordan, climbed to the northern flank of Jericho, rose through the highlands westwards and ended at the 13　wilderness of Beth-aven. •Thence it continued towards Luz, southwards to the flank of Luz, which is now Bethel; then downwards to Ataroth-addar, on the 14　mountain south of Lower Beth-horon. •The boundary curved, and on the western side turned southward, from the mountain that faces Beth-horon from the south and ended at Kiriath-baal, which is now Kiriath-jearim, a city of the 15　sons of Judah. This was the western side. •On the south side the boundary ran from the edge of Kiriath-jearim towards Gasin, emerged by the waters of the 16　spring of Nephtoah, •continued to the skirts of the mountain facing the Vale of Ben-hinnom, north of the plain of the Rephaim, then down into the Vale 17a　of Hinnom, south of the flank of the Jebusite and reaching En-rogel. •It then curved northwards, going on to En-shemesh; it came out at the circles of stones 18　facing the Ascent of Adummim, •then went on to Cheteph in sight of the Arabah 17b 19　and down to the Arabah and •the Stone of Bohan son of Reuben, •then reached the flank of Beth-hoglah to the north. The boundary stopped at the northern bay of the Salt Sea, at the southern end of the Jordan. This was the southern 20　border. •The Jordan itself was the eastern border. Such was the inheritance of the sons of Benjamin, with the boundaries defining it.

The towns of Benjamin

21　The towns of the tribe of the sons of Benjamin, according to their clans, were 22 23　Jericho, Beth-hoglah, Emek-keziz; •Beth-arabah, Zemaraim, Bethel; •Avvim, 24　Parah, Ophrah; •Chephar-ammoni, Ophni, Geba: twelve towns and their villages. 25,26 27　Gibeon, Ramah, Beeroth; •Mizpeh, Chephirah, Mozah; •Rekem, Irpeel, 28　Taralah; •Zela Haeleph, Jerusalem, Gibeah and Kiriath: fourteen towns with their villages. This was the inheritance of the sons of Benjamin, according to their clans.

The tribe of Simeon

1　**19** The second portion awarded by lot came to Simeon, the tribe of the sons of Simeon, according to their clans; their inheritance was encircled by the 2　inheritance of the sons of Judah. •For their portion they had Beersheba, Shema, 3,4 5　Moladah; •Hazar-shual, Balah, Ezem; •Eltolad, Bethul, Hormah; •Ziklag, 6　Beth-marcaboth, Hazar-susah; •Beth-lebaoth and Sharuhen: thirteen towns and 7　their villages; •Ain, Rimmon, Ether and Ashan: four towns and their villages. 8　With these go all the villages lying outside these towns as far as Baalath-beer, Ramah of the Negeb. This was the inheritance of the tribe of the sons of Simeon 9　according to their clans. •The inheritance of the sons of Simeon was taken out of the portion of the sons of Judah, because the share of the sons of Judah was too large for them; this is why it was within the inheritance of the sons of Judah that the sons of Simeon were given theirs.

The tribe of Zebulun

The third portion fell to the sons of Zebulun according to their clans; the 10
territory of their inheritance reached as far as Sarid; •their boundary climbed 11
westwards to Maraalah, touching Dabbesheth first and then the wadi facing
Jokneam. •But eastwards and towards the sunrise the boundary went from 12
Sarid to the boundary of Chisloth-tabor, then towards Dobrath and upwards
to Japhia. •Thence it went on, eastwards and towards the sunrise, to Gath- 13
hepher and Ittah-kazin; it came out at Rimmon and turned towards Neah.
Then northwards the boundary bent towards Hannathon and ended at the plain 14
of Iphtahel. •Besides this, there were Kattath, Nahalal, Shimron, Iralah and 15
Bethlehem: twelve towns with their villages. •This was the inheritance of the 16
sons of Zebulun according to their clans: these towns and their villages.

The tribe of Issachar

The fourth portion came to Issachar, to the sons of Issachar, according to 17
their clans. •Their territory reached to Jezreel and included Chesulloth and 18
Shunem; •Hapharaim, Shion, Anaharath; •Dobrath, Kishion, Ebez; •Remeth 19,20
and En-gannim, En-haddah and Beth-pazzez. •Their boundary touched Tabor 22
and Shahazimah and Beth-shemesh, and ended at the Jordan: sixteen towns
with their villages. •This was the inheritance of the tribe of the sons of Issachar, 23
according to their clans: the towns with their villages.

The tribe of Asher

The fifth portion came to the tribe of the sons of Asher, according to their 24
clans. •Within their territory were Helkath, Hali, Beten, Achshaph, •Allam- 25 26
melech, Amad and Mishal; on the west it touched Carmel and the streams of the
Libnath; •on the other side it went eastwards to Beth-dagon, touching Zebulun 27
and the Vale of Iphtahel northwards, then Beth-emek and Neiel beyond; it
ended at Cabul. To the north it took in •Abdon, Rehob, Hammon and Kanah 28
as far as Sidon the Great. •The boundary then turned back towards Ramah 29
and on to the stronghold of Tyre and Hosah, and ended at the sea. Mahalab,
Achzib, •Acco, Aphek, Rehob: twenty-two towns with their villages. •This was 30 31
the inheritance of the tribe of the sons of Asher, according to their clans; these
towns with their villages.

The tribe of Naphtali

To the sons of Naphtali came the sixth portion, to the sons of Naphtali 32
according to their clans. •Their territory went from Heleph and the Oak of 33
Zanaannim to Adami-negeb, to Jabneel as far as Lakkum, and ended at the
Jordan. •The westward boundary ran to Aznoth-tabor and thence passed on to 34
Hukkok, touching Zebulun southwards, Asher westwards and the Jordan east-
wards. •The fortified towns were Ziddim, Zer, Hammath, Rakkath, Chinnereth; 35
Adamah, Ramah, Hazor; •Kedesh, Edrei, En-hazor; •Yiron, Migdalel, Horem, 36,37 38
Beth-anath, Beth-shemesh: nineteen towns with their villages. •This was the 39
inheritance of the sons of Naphtali according to their clans; the towns with their
villages.

The tribe of Dan [a]

To the tribe of the sons of Dan came the seventh portion according to their 40
clans. •Within the territory of their inheritance were Zorah, Eshtaol, Irshemesh; 41
Sha-alabbin, Aijalon, Ithlah; •Elon, Timnah, Ekron, •Eltekeh, Gibbethon, 42,43 44
Baalath; Jehud, Bene-berak, Gath-rimmon; •Me-jarkon and Rakkon with the 45 46
territory facing Joppa.

But the territory of the sons of Dan resisted them; and therefore the sons of 47
Dan went up and attacked Leshem and captured it and put it to the sword.
Having seized the town they settled in it, and changed the name of Leshem to

48 Dan after Dan their ancestor. •This was the inheritance of the tribe of the sons of Dan, according to their clans: these towns with their villages.

49 So ended the drawing of lots for the country and the apportioning of it.
50 And the Israelites gave Joshua son of Nun an inheritance among them; •at the command of Yahweh, they gave him the city he had asked for, Timnath-serah in the highlands of Ephraim; he rebuilt the city and settled there.

51 These are the inheritances which Eleazar the priest, Joshua son of Nun, and the heads of each family apportioned by lot among the tribes of Israel at Shiloh, in Yahweh's presence, at the door of the Tent of Meeting; and thus the apportioning of the land was finished.

D. PRIVILEGED CITIES

The cities of refuge

1
2 **20** Yahweh said to Joshua, •'Speak to the Israelites and say to them, "Choose
3 the cities of refuge of which I spoke to you through Moses, •towns where a man who has killed accidentally, unwittingly, may find sanctuary; they
4 are to be your refuge from the avenger of blood. •The man who has killed may seek sanctuary in one of these towns; he must stop at the entrance of the town gate and explain his case to the elders of the place. They shall let him enter
5 the town and assign him a place to live with them. •If he is pursued by the avenger of blood, they are not to give him up to him, since he has killed his neighbour
6 unwittingly, with no long-cherished hatred against him. •The man who has killed must remain in that town until he has appeared for judgement before the community, until the death of the high priest then in office. Only then may the man who has killed go back to his own town and his own house, to the town from which he has fled." '

7 For this purpose they designated Kedesh in Galilee, in the highlands of Naphtali, Shechem in the highlands of Ephraim, and Kiriath-arba,
8 which is now Hebron, in the highlands of Judah. •Across the Jordan and on the east facing Jericho, in the wilderness on the tableland, they chose Bezer of the tribe of Reuben, Ramoth-gilead of the tribe of Gad, and Golan
9 in Bashan of the tribe of Manasseh. •These were the towns marked out for all the Israelites and for the stranger living among them, so that any man might find sanctuary there if he had killed accidentally, and might escape the hand of the avenger of blood until he had appeared for judgement before the community.

The levitical cities

1 **21** Then the heads of families among the Levites came to Eleazar the priest and to Joshua son of Nun and the heads of families of the tribes of Israel—
2 they were then at Shiloh in the land of Canaan. They said to them, 'Yahweh ordered through Moses that we should be given towns to live in, with the
3 adjoining pasture lands for our cattle'. •So because of Yahweh's order the Israelites gave the Levites these towns from their inheritance, and with them
4 the adjoining pasture lands. •Lots were cast for the clans of the Kohathites. To the Levites, the sons of Aaron the priest, fell thirteen towns from the tribes
5 of Judah, Simeon and Benjamin; •the other sons of Kohath received, clan by
6 clan, ten towns from the tribes of Ephraim, Dan, and the half-tribe of Manasseh. To the sons of Gershon, clan by clan, fell thirteen towns from the tribes of Issachar,
7 Asher, Naphtali and the half-tribe of Manasseh in Bashan. •To the sons of Merari, clan by clan, fell twelve towns from the tribes of Reuben, Gad and Zebulun.
8 These towns and the adjoining pasture land, the Israelites gave by lot to the Levites, as Yahweh had ordered through Moses.

19 a. Most of the Danites emigrated northwards to the sources of the Jordan, Jg 18. Part of Dan's original territory was repopulated by Calebites, 1 Ch 2:42-50.

The portion of the Kohathites

From the tribe of Judah and the tribe of Simeon they gave the towns named 9 below; •this was the portion of the sons of Aaron from the clans of the Koha- 10 thites, of the sons of Levi; for theirs was the first portion. •They gave them 11 Kiriath-arba, the chief city of the Anakim, which is now Hebron, in the highlands of Judah, with the pasture lands round it. •But the fields and villages of this 12 town they gave into the possession of Caleb son of Jephunneh as his property. To the sons of Aaron the priest they gave Hebron, the city of refuge for men 13 who had killed, and the adjoining pasture lands; also Libnah with its pasture lands, •and Jattir, Eshtemoa, •Holon, Debir, •Ashan, Juttah and Beth-shemesh, 14,15 each with its pasture lands: nine towns taken from these two tribes. •From 17 the tribe of Benjamin, Gibeon and Geba with their pasture lands, •and Anathoth 18 and Almon with theirs: four towns. •The towns of the priests, the sons of 19 Aaron, were thirteen towns in all, with their pasture lands.

To the clans of the sons of Kohath, to the remaining Levites of the sons of 20 Kohath, the lot assigned towns belonging to the tribe of Ephraim. •They were 21 given the city of refuge, Shechem, with its pasture lands, in the highlands of Ephraim, together with Gezer, •Kibzaim and Beth-horon, each with its 22 pasture lands: four towns. •From the tribe of Dan, Elteke, Gibbethon, •Aijalon 23 24 and Gath-rimmon with their pasture lands: four towns. •From the half-tribe 25 of Manasseh, Taanach and Jibleam with their pasture lands: two towns. •In all: 26 ten towns with their pasture lands for the remaining clans of the sons of Kohath.

The portion of the sons of Gershon

To the sons of Gershon who were of levitical clans were given the city of 27 refuge Golan in Bashan and also Ashtaroth, each with its pasture lands: two towns, both from the half-tribe of Manasseh. •From the tribe of Issachar, 28 Kishion, Dobrath, •Jarmuth and En-gannim, each with its pasture lands: four 29 towns. •From the tribe of Asher, Mishal, Abdon, •Helkath and Rehob, each 30 31 with its pasture lands: four towns. •From the tribe of Naphtali, Kedesh the city 32 of refuge in Galilee, Hammoth-dor and Rakkath, each with its pasture lands: three towns. •The towns for the Gershonites according to their clans were thirteen 33 towns in all with their pasture lands.

The portion of the sons of Merari

To the clans of the sons of Merari, the remainder of the Levites, fell four 34 towns with their pasture lands from the tribe of Zebulun, Jokneam, Kartah, Rimmon and Nahalal; •from beyond the Jordan and from the tribe of Reuben, 35 36 the city of refuge Bezer in the wilderness on the tableland, Jahaz, •Kedemoth 37 and Mephaath, each with its pasture lands: four towns; •from the tribe of Gad 38 the city of refuge Ramoth-gilead, Mahanaim, •Heshbon and Jazer, each with 39 its pasture lands: four towns. •The towns allotted clan by clan to the sons of 40 Merari, to the remainder of the levitical clans, were twelve towns in all.

The towns thus granted to the Levites in Israelite territory were in all forty- 41 eight, with their pasture lands. •For all these towns, the town itself and the 42 pasture land round it went together. This was true of every town named.

The end of the apportioning

So it was that Yahweh gave the Israelites all the land he had sworn to give 43 their fathers. They took possession of it and settled there. •Yahweh granted 44 them peace on all their frontiers just as he had sworn to their fathers, and of all their enemies not one had managed to stand against them. Yahweh had given all their enemies into their hands. •Of all the promises that Yahweh had made to 45 the House of Israel, not one failed; all were fulfilled.

III. JOSHUA FINISHES HIS COURSE

A. THE RETURN OF THE EASTERN TRIBES.
THE QUESTION OF THEIR ALTAR

The tribes from across the Jordan are sent home

1 22 Then Joshua summoned the Reubenites, the Gadites and the half-tribe of
2 Manasseh •and said to them, 'You have faithfully observed all that Moses
the servant of Yahweh ordered you, and whenever I have given you an
3 order you have obeyed me. •Despite the fact that the campaign has lasted such
a very long time, you have never deserted your brothers; at every point you
4 have obeyed the orders of Yahweh your God. •Now that Yahweh your God
has granted your brothers the rest he promised them, go back to your tents,
to the land given into your possession by Moses the servant of Yahweh, beyond
5 the Jordan. •But take great care to practise the commandments and the Law
which Moses the servant of Yahweh gave you: love Yahweh your God, follow
his paths always, keep his commandments, be loyal to him and serve him with
all your heart and soul.'
6 Joshua blessed them and sent them away; they went home to their tents.
7 Moses had given a territory in Bashan to one half of the tribe of Manasseh; to
the other half Joshua gave another among their brothers on the west bank of the
8 Jordan. As Joshua sent them home to their tents he blessed them •and said to
them, 'You are going back to your tents with great wealth, with cattle in plenty,
with silver and gold, bronze and iron and great quantities of clothing; share
these spoils of your enemies with your brothers'.

An altar is built beside the Jordan

9 The Reubenites, the Gadites and the half-tribe of Manasseh went home again;
they left the Israelites at Shiloh in the land of Canaan, and made their way back
to the land of Gilead, the territory which belonged to them and where they had
settled in accordance with the order of Yahweh given through Moses.
10 When they came to the circles of stones at the Jordan which are in Canaanite
territory, the Reubenites, the Gadites and the half-tribe of Manasseh built an
11 altar there beside the Jordan, an imposing altar of great size. •This came to the
ears of the Israelites. 'See,' the word went round 'the Reubenites, the Gadites
and the half-tribe of Manasseh have built this altar facing the land of
Canaan near the circles of stones at the Jordan, beyond the territory of the
Israelites.'
12 At this news, the whole community of the children of Israel mustered at
Shiloh, ready to march against them and make war on them.

The eastern tribes rebuked

13 The Israelites sent the priest Phinehas son of Eleazar to the Reubenites, the
14 Gadites and the half-tribe of Manasseh, in the land of Gilead, •and with him
ten leading men, one leader and head of his family from each tribe in Israel;
15 every one of them was head of his family among the clans of Israel. •When they
came to the Reubenites, the Gadites and the half-tribe of Manasseh in the land
of Gilead, this is what they said to them:
16 'This is our message to you from the whole community of Yahweh: What
do you mean by this treachery committed against the God of Israel? Why turn
aside from Yahweh today, building yourselves an altar, an act of rebellion today
against Yahweh himself?
17 'Was the sin at Peor not enough, the sin from which we are not cleansed
even now, in spite of the plague that ravaged the whole community of Yahweh?
18 Since then, you have stopped following Yahweh today, since you set yourselves

in revolt against him today, tomorrow his anger will be roused against the whole community of Israel.

'Do you think your territory is unclean? Then cross over into the territory 19 of Yahweh, where his tabernacle is, and choose a home among us. But do not rebel against Yahweh or make us accomplices in rebellion by building an altar to vie with the altar of Yahweh our God. •When Achan son of Zerah betrayed 20 his trust in the matter of the ban, did not the wrath come down on the whole community of Israel, although he was only one man? Did he not have to die for his sin?'

The tribes from across the Jordan clear their name

The Reubenites, the Gadites and the half-tribe of Manasseh spoke in their 21 turn and answered the heads of the clans of Israel:

'The God of gods, Yahweh, the God of gods, Yahweh well knows, and 22 let Israel know it too: if there has been defiance or treachery on our part against Yahweh, let him not save us today; •or if we have built an altar to turn 23 away from Yahweh and offer holocaust and oblation and communion sacrifice on it, let Yahweh punish us for it! •The truth is, we acted from fear and for 24 this reason: one day your children might say to ours, "What link have you with Yahweh the God of Israel? •Has not Yahweh set the boundary of the Jordan 25 between us and you, you sons of Reuben and sons of Gad? You have no share in Yahweh." Thus your children might be the cause of stopping ours from paying reverence to Yahweh.

'So we said to each other, "Let us build this altar, not for holocausts or other 26 sacrifices •but as a witness between us and you and among our descendants 27 after us, proving that we do indeed worship Yahweh with our holocausts, our victims and our communion sacrifices in his presence. So that one day your children will not be able to say to ours: You have no share in Yahweh. •But 28 if ever it were to happen that they said such a thing to us or to our descendants in the future, we should say to them: Look at this structure, Yahweh's altar, made by our ancestors not for holocausts or other sacrifices but as a witness between us and you." •We have no intention of defying Yahweh or turning 29 away from serving him today by building an altar for holocausts or oblations or sacrifices to vie with the altar of Yahweh our God that stands before his tabernacle!'

Peace restored

When Phinehas the priest, the leaders of the community and the heads of the 30 clans of Israel who were with him heard the words spoken by the sons of Gad and of Reuben and of Manasseh, they approved of them. •Then the priest 31 Phinehas son of Eleazar said to the sons of Reuben and sons of Gad and sons of Manasseh, 'Now we clearly see that Yahweh is among us, because you have not committed any treachery against him; this means you have saved the children of Israel from the punishment of Yahweh'.

The priest Phinehas son of Eleazar and the leaders left the Reubenites and 32 the Gadites and returned from the land of Gilead to the land of Canaan and the Israelites, to whom they brought back this answer. •The Israelites were 33 pleased to hear this; they gave thanks to God and spoke no more of marching against them and making war and ravaging the country where the sons of Reuben and of Gad had settled. •The Reubenites and the Gadites named the altar. . ., 34 'Because' they said 'it will be a witness between us that Yahweh is God'.

B. JOSHUA'S LAST WORDS TO THE PEOPLE

Joshua sums up his work

23 Long after Yahweh had given Israel rest from all the enemies round 1 them—Joshua was old now, far advanced in years—•Joshua summoned 2

all Israel, their elders, chief men, judges and scribes, and said to them, 'I myself
3 am old, far advanced in years; •you for your part have witnessed all that Yahweh
your God has done to all these nations before your eyes; Yahweh your God
4 himself has fought for you. •Now as an inheritance for your tribes, I have apportioned you by lot the peoples who still remain to be conquered, no less than
those that I have wiped out between the Jordan and the Great Sea in the west.
5 Yahweh your God will himself drive them out before you; he will cast them out
before you and you will take possession of their country as Yahweh your God
promised you.

A rule of life among foreign peoples

6   'Therefore stand firm to keep and fulfil all that is written in the Book of the
7 Law of Moses, never turning aside from it to right or left, •never mingling with
the peoples who are still left beside you. Do not utter the names of their gods,
do not swear by them, do not serve them and do not bow down before them.
⁸₉ No; you must be loyal to Yahweh your God as you have been till now. •Because
of this, Yahweh has driven out great and powerful nations before you, and no
10 one so far has been able to resist you. •One man of you could rout a thousand
of them, because Yahweh your God himself fought for you as he had promised
11 you. •Be very careful, as you value your life, to love Yahweh your God.
12   'But if you prove faithless, if you make friends with the remnant of those
peoples who are still left beside you, if you form kinships with them and inter-
13 marry, •then know for certain that Yahweh your God will no longer drive these
peoples before you; instead, they will be a snare and a pitfall for you, a scourge
to your sides and thorns in your eyes, till you vanish from this good land which
Yahweh your God has given you.
14   'And now today I must go the way of all the earth. Acknowledge with all
your heart and soul that of all the promises of good that Yahweh your God has
made you, not one has failed: all have been fulfilled, and not one has failed.
15   'But just as every promise of good made to you by Yahweh your God has
been fulfilled for you, so also will Yahweh fulfil against you all his threats
of evil, even to driving you out of the good land that Yahweh your God has
given you.
16   'For if you violate the covenant which Yahweh your God has demanded of
you, if you go and serve other gods and bow down before them, then Yahweh's
anger will be roused against you and you will quickly vanish from the good land
that he has given you.'

C. THE GREAT ASSEMBLY AT SHECHEM[a]

Israel's vocation set forth once more

1 **24** Joshua gathered all the tribes of Israel together at Shechem; then he called
the elders, leaders, judges and scribes of Israel, and they presented
2 themselves before God. •Then Joshua said to all the people:
   'Yahweh the God of Israel says this, "In ancient days your ancestors lived
beyond the River—such was Terah the father of Abraham and of Nahor—and
3 they served other gods. •Then I brought your father Abraham from beyond the
River and led him through all the land of Canaan. I increased his descendants
4 and gave him Isaac. •To Isaac I gave Jacob and Esau. To Esau I gave the mountain
country of Seir as his possession. Jacob and his sons went down into Egypt.
5 Then I sent Moses and Aaron and plagued Egypt with the wonders that I worked
6 there. So I brought you out of it. •I brought your ancestors out of Egypt, and

24 a. The pact at Shechem confirmed the religious unity, and thus preserved the political unity,
of the tribes.

you came to the Sea; the Egyptians pursued your ancestors with chariots and horsemen as far as the Sea of Reeds. •There they called to Yahweh, and he 7 spread a thick fog between you and the Egyptians, and made the sea go back on them and cover them. You saw with your own eyes the things I did in Egypt. Then for a long time you lived in the wilderness, •until I brought you into the 8 land of the Amorites who lived beyond the Jordan; they made war on you and I gave them into your hands; you took possession of their country because I destroyed them before you. •Next, Balak son of Zippor the king of Moab 9 arose to make war on Israel, and sent for Balaam son of Beor to come and curse you. •But I would not listen to Balaam; instead, he had to bless you, and I saved 10 you from his hand.

"When you crossed the Jordan and came to Jericho, those who held Jericho 11 fought against you, as did the Amorites and Perizzites, the Canaanites, Hittites, Girgashites, Hivites and Jebusites, but I put them all into your power. •I sent 12 out hornets in front of you, which drove the two Amorite kings before you; this was not the work of your sword or your bow. •I gave you a land where you 13 never toiled, you live in towns you never built; you eat now from vineyards and olivegroves you never planted."

Israel chooses Yahweh

'So now, fear Yahweh and serve him perfectly and sincerely; put away the 14 gods that your ancestors served beyond the River and in Egypt, and serve Yahweh. •But if you will not serve Yahweh, choose today whom you wish to serve, 15 whether the gods that your ancestors served beyond the River, or the gods of the Amorites in whose land you are now living. As for me and my House, we will serve Yahweh.'

The people answered, 'We have no intention of deserting Yahweh and 16 serving other gods! •Was it not Yahweh our God who brought us and our 17 ancestors out of the land of Egypt, the house of slavery, who worked those great wonders before our eyes and preserved us all along the way we travelled and among all the peoples through whom we journeyed? •What is more, Yahweh 18 drove all those peoples out before us, as well as the Amorites who used to live in this country. We too will serve Yahweh, for he is our God.'

Then Joshua said to the people, 'You cannot serve Yahweh, because he is 19 a holy God, he is a jealous God who will not forgive your transgressions or your sins. •If you desert Yahweh to follow alien gods he in turn will afflict and destroy 20 you after the goodness he has shown you.' •The people answered Joshua, 'No; 21 it is Yahweh we wish to serve'. •Then Joshua said to the people, 'You are 22 witnesses against yourselves that you have chosen Yahweh, to serve him'. They answered, 'We are witnesses'. •'Then cast away the alien gods among you and 23 give your hearts to Yahweh the God of Israel!' •The people answered Joshua, 24 'It is Yahweh our God we choose to serve; it is his voice that we will obey'.

The covenant at Shechem

That day, Joshua made a covenant for the people; he laid down a statute and 25 ordinance for them at Shechem. •Joshua wrote these words in the Book of the 26 Law of God. Then he took a great stone and set it up there, under the oak in the sanctuary of Yahweh, •and Joshua said to all the people, 'See! This stone 27 shall be a witness against us because it has heard all the words that Yahweh has spoken to us: it shall be a witness against you in case you deny your God.' Then Joshua sent the people away, and each returned to his own inheritance. 28

D. TWO ADDITIONS
The death of Joshua

After these things Joshua son of Nun, the servant of Yahweh, died; he was 29 a hundred and ten years old. •They buried him on the estate he had received 30

for inheritance, at Timnath-serah which lies in the highlands of Ephraim, north
31 of Mount Gaash. •Israel served Yahweh throughout the lifetime of Joshua and
the lifetime of those elders who outlived Joshua and had known all the deeds that
Yahweh had done for the sake of Israel.

The bones of Joseph. The death of Eleazar

32   The bones of Joseph, which the sons of Israel had brought from Egypt, were
buried at Shechem in the portion of ground that Jacob had bought for a hundred
pieces of money from the sons of Hamor, the father of Shechem, which had
33 become the inheritance of the sons of Joseph. •Then Eleazar son of Aaron died
and was buried at Gibeah, the town of his son Phinehas, which had been given
him in the highlands of Ephraim.

THE BOOK OF JUDGES

I. FIRST INTRODUCTION[a]

A. SUMMARY ACCOUNT OF THE SETTLEMENT IN CANAAN

The settlement of Judah, Simeon, Caleb and the Kenites

1 After the death of Joshua the Israelites consulted Yahweh, 'Which of us 1
shall march up first against the Canaanites to attack them?' •And Yahweh 2
answered, 'Judah is to attack first; I am delivering the country straight into his
hands'. •Then Judah said to Simeon his brother,[b] 'March with me into the 3
territory allotted to me; we will attack the Canaanite, and then I in my turn
will march with you into your allotted territory'. And Simeon marched with
him. •So Judah marched up, and Yahweh delivered the Canaanites and Periz- 4
zites into their hands, and they routed ten thousand men at Bezek. •They came 5
on Adoni-zedek at Bezek, joined battle with him and routed the Canaanites
and Perizzites. •Adoni-zedek took to flight, but they followed and captured 6
him and cut off his thumbs and big toes. •Then Adoni-zedek said, 'Seventy 7
kings with their thumbs and big toes cut off used to pick up the crumbs under
my table. As I did to others, so God does to me.' He was taken to Jerusalem,[c]
and there he died. •(The sons of Judah attacked Jerusalem and took it: they 8
put its people to the sword and set fire to the city.)[d]

After this the sons of Judah went down to attack those Canaanites living 9
in the highlands and in the Negeb and the lowlands. •Then Judah marched 10
against the Canaanites in Hebron—in earlier times the name of Hebron was
Kiriath-arba—and they overcame Sheshai and Ahiman and Talmai. •From there 11
they marched against the inhabitants of Debir—in earlier times the name of
Debir was Kiriath-sepher. •Caleb said, 'To the man who conquers and captures 12
Kiriath-sepher, I will give my daughter Achsah to wife'. •The man who captured 13
it was Othniel son of Kenaz, Caleb's younger brother; Caleb gave him his
daughter Achsah to wife. •When she came to her husband, he urged her to 14
ask her father for a field. Then she jumped down from her donkey, and Caleb
asked her, 'What do you want?' •She answered, 'Grant me a favour; since you 15
have banished me to the wilderness of Negeb, at least grant me some springs
of water'. So Caleb gave her the upper springs and the lower springs.

The sons of Hobab the Kenite, father-in-law of Moses, went up with the 16
sons of Judah from the city of palms into the wilderness in the Negeb of Judah
at the Ascent of Arad; they went and lived with the Amalekites.

Then Judah set out with his brother Simeon. They overcame the Canaanites 17
who lived in Zephath and delivered it over to the ban; hence the town was
given the name of Hormah. •But Judah did not take Gaza with its territory 18
or Ashkelon with its territory or Ekron with its territory; •they could not 19b
drive out the inhabitants of the plain, because they had iron chariots. •Yahweh 19a
was with Judah, and Judah subdued the highlands.

20   As Moses had directed, Hebron was given to Caleb, and he drove the three
21 sons of Anak out of it. •As regards the Jebusites living in Jerusalem, the sons
    of Benjamin did not drive them out, and even now the Jebusites are still living
    in Jerusalem with the sons of Benjamin.

The settlement of the House of Joseph

22   In the same way, the House of Joseph went up against Bethel, and Yahweh
23 was with them. •The House of Joseph made a reconnaissance of Bethel. The
24 name of the city used to be Luz. •The scouts saw a man coming out of the city,
25 and said to him, 'If you show us how to enter the city, we will spare you'. •He
    showed them a way into the city. They put the inhabitants to the sword but
26 let the man go, and all his clan with him. •The man went off to the country
    of the Hittites and built a town which he called Luz; that is its name even yet.

The settlement of the northern tribes and the Edomites

27   Manasseh did not subdue Beth-shean and its outlying villages, or Taanach
    and its villages. He did not drive out the inhabitants of Dor and its outlying
    villages, or of Ibleam and its villages, or of Megiddo and its villages; in those
28 parts the Canaanites held their ground. •But when the Israelites became stronger,
    they subjected the Canaanites to forced labour, though they did not drive them
29 out. •Nor did Ephraim drive out the Canaanites in Gezer;ᶜ thus the Canaanites
30 went on living there among them. •Zebulun did not drive out the inhabitants
    of Kitron or of Nahalol. The Canaanites remained among Zebulun, but were
31 subjected to forced labour. •Asher did not drive out the inhabitants of Acco
32 or of Sidon or Ahlab, or Achzib . . . or Aphik or Rehob. •So the Asherites
    lived among the Canaanite inhabitants of the country, for they did not drive
33 them out. •Naphtali did not drive out the inhabitants of Beth-shemesh or of
    Beth-anath; they settled among the Canaanite inhabitants of the country; but
    the inhabitants of Beth-shemesh and of Beth-anath were compelled to do forced
34 labour for them. •The Amorites drove back the Danites into the highlands
35 and would not allow them to enter the plain below. •The Amorites held
    their ground at Har-heres and Shaalbim, but when the hand of the House of
    Jacob grew heavier, they were subjected to forced labour.
36   The territory of the Edomites begins at the Ascent of Akrabbim, runs to
    the Rock and continues on upwards.

The angel of Yahweh tells Israel of ills to come

1 2 The angel of Yahweh went up from Gilgal to Bethel and came to the
        House of Israel; and he said, '. . . and I brought you out of Egypt and led
    you into this land which I swore to give your fathers. I said: I shall never break
2 my covenant with you. •You for your part must make no covenant with the
    inhabitants of this country; you must destroy their altars. But you have not
3 obeyed my orders. What is it that you have done? •Very well, I now say this:
    I am not going to drive out these nations before you. They shall become your
4 oppressors, and their gods shall be a snare for you.' •When the angel of
    Yahweh had spoken these words to all the Israelites, the people began to groan
5 and weep. •And they called the name of the place Bochim,ᵃ and offered sacrifices
    to Yahweh there.

---

1 a. In this general view of the situation after the death of Joshua, the Israelites are seen establishing themselves slowly and painfully in the highlands and having little success against the
towns in the plain; tribes, and even clans, fight as isolated units.   b. The tribes are personified
under the names of their ancestors.   c. To his own people.   d. A gloss: it was David who
captured Jersualem, 2 S 5:6f.   e. On the Jerusalem-Jaffa road. The southern tribes were thus
almost completely cut off from the northern.
2 a. 'The Weepers'.

II. SECOND INTRODUCTION

GENERAL REFLECTIONS ON THE AGE
OF THE JUDGES

The end of Joshua's life

Then Joshua told the people to go, and the Israelites went away, each to his 6 own possession, to occupy the land. •The people served Yahweh throughout the 7 lifetime of Joshua and the lifetime of those elders who outlived Joshua and had known all the great deeds that Yahweh had done for the sake of Israel. •Joshua 8 son of Nun, the servant of Yahweh, died when he was a hundred and ten years old. •They buried him on the estate he had received for inheritance, at Timnath- 9 heres in the highlands of Ephraim, north of Mount Gaash. •And when 10 that generation too had been gathered to its fathers, another generation followed it which knew neither Yahweh nor the deeds that he had done for the sake of Israel.

The unfaithfulness of succeeding generations; their punishment

Then the sons of Israel did what displeases Yahweh and served the 11 Baals. •They deserted Yahweh, the God of their ancestors, who had brought them 12 out of the land of Egypt, and followed other gods from the gods of the peoples round them. They bowed down to these; they provoked Yahweh; •they deserted 13 Yahweh to serve Baal and Astarte.b •Then Yahweh's anger flamed out against 14 Israel. He handed them over to pillagers who plundered them; he delivered them to the enemies surrounding them, and they were not able to resist them. In every warlike venture, the hand of Yahweh was there to foil them, as 15 Yahweh had warned, as Yahweh had sworn to them. Thus he reduced them to dire distress.

The judges. No lasting conversion

Then Yahweh appointed judgesc for them, and rescued the men of Israel from 16 the hands of their plunderers. •But they would not listen to their judges. They 17 prostituted themselves to other gods, and bowed down before these. Very quickly they left the path their ancestors had trodden in obedience to the orders of Yahweh; they did not follow their example. •When Yahweh appointed 18 judges for them, Yahweh was with the judge and rescued them from the hands of their enemies as long as the judge lived, for Yahweh felt pity for them as they groaned under the iron grip of their oppressors. •But once the judge 19 was dead, they relapsed and behaved even worse than their ancestors. They followed other gods; they served them and bowed before them, and would not give up the practices and stubborn ways of their ancestors at all.

Why foreign nations were left in the land

Then Yahweh's anger flamed out against Israel, and he said, 'Since this 20 people has broken the covenant I laid down for their ancestors, since they have not listened to my voice, •in future I will not evict any of the nations that Joshua 21 left in the land when he died'; •this was to test them by means of these nations, 22 to see whether Israel would or would not tread the paths of Yahweh as once their ancestors had trodden them. •So Yahweh allowed these nations to remain; 23 he did not hurry to drive them out, and did not deliver them into the hands of Joshua.

The peoples who remained

3 These are the nations that Yahweh let remain, to use them to test all those 1 in Israel who had never known war in Canaan •(this was only in the interest 2

of the generations of the sons of Israel, to teach them the art of war, those at
3 least who had never known the former wars): •the five chiefs of the Philistines,
all the Canaanites, the Sidonians, and the Hittites who lived in the range of
4 Lebanon, from the uplands of Baal-hermon to the Pass of Hamath. •They
were used to put Israel to the test and see if they would keep the orders that
5 Yahweh had given their fathers through Moses. •The Israelites lived among the
Canaanites and Hittites and Amorites, the Perizzites, Hivites and Jebusites;
6 they married the daughters of these peoples, gave their own daughters in marriage
to their sons, and served their gods.

III. THE STORY OF THE JUDGES
TOLD IN EPISODES

A. OTHNIEL

7   The Israelites[a] did what displeases Yahweh. They forgot Yahweh their God
8 and served the Baals and the Asherahs. •Then Yahweh's anger flamed out
against Israel: he handed them over to Cushan-rishathaim the king of Edom,
and the Israelites were enslaved by Cushan-rishathaim for eight years.
9   The Israelites cried to Yahweh, and Yahweh raised up for the Israelites a
deliverer who rescued them, Othniel son of Kenaz, Caleb's younger brother.
10 The spirit of Yahweh came on him; he became judge in Israel and set out
to fight. Yahweh delivered the king of Edom, Cushan-rishathaim, into his
11 hands, and he overcame Cushan-rishathaim. •Then the land enjoyed rest for forty
years.

B. EHUD

12   When Othniel son of Kenaz died, •once again the men of Israel began to do
what displeases Yahweh, and Yahweh gave Eglon the king of Moab power over
13 Israel, because they had done what displeases Yahweh. •Eglon in alliance with
the sons of Ammon and Amalek marched against Israel and conquered them
14 and took possession of the city of palms.[b] •The Israelites were enslaved by
Eglon the king of Moab for eighteen years.
15   Then the Israelites cried to Yahweh, and Yahweh raised up a deliverer for
them, Ehud the son of Gera the Benjaminite; he was left-handed. The men of
16 Israel appointed him to take their tribute to Eglon the king of Moab. •Ehud
made a dagger—it was double-edged and a cubit long—and strapped it on under
17 his clothes, over his right thigh. •He presented the tribute to Eglon the king
18 of Moab. This Eglon was a very fat man. •Having presented the tribute, Ehud
19 went off again with the men who had carried it; •but he himself, on reaching the
Idols of Gilgal,[c] turned and went back and said, 'I have a secret message for
you, O king'. The king replied, 'Silence!' and all who were with him went out.
20 Then Ehud went in. The king sat in the cool retreat of his upper room; he was
alone. Ehud said to him, 'I have a message from God for you, O king'. The
21 king immediately stood up from his seat. •Then Ehud, using his left hand, drew
the dagger he was carrying on his right thigh and thrust it into the king's belly.
22 The hilt too went in after the blade, and the fat closed over the blade, for Ehud
23 left the dagger in his belly; then he went out through the window. •Ehud went
out by the porch; he had shut and locked the doors of the upper room behind
him.

b. 'Baal and Astarte' or 'the Baals and Astartes' is the common expression for the gods of the
Canaanites.   c. The 'judges', regarded as divinely chosen, were rules and governors who led
a tribe or group of tribes in war rather than administrators of justice.
3 a. Here indicating only the southern tribes, Judah and Simeon.   b. Jericho.   c. The ring of
stones mentioned in Jos 4:19.

When he had gone, the servants came back and looked; the doors of the 24 upper room were locked. They thought, 'He is probably covering his feet^d in the inner part of the cool room'. •They waited until they no longer knew what to 25 think, for he still did not open the doors of the upper room. At length they took the key and unlocked the room; their master lay on the ground, dead.

While they were waiting, Ehud had fled. He passed the Idols and escaped 26 to safety in Seirah. •When he reached the territory of Israel he sounded the 27 horn in the highlands of Ephraim, and the Israelites came down with him from the hills, with him at their head. •And he said to them, 'Follow 28 me, because Yahweh has delivered your enemy Moab into your hands'. So they followed him, cut Moab off from crossing the fords of the Jordan and let no one across. •On that occasion they beat the Moabites, some ten thousand men, 29 all tough and seasoned fighters, and not one escaped. •That day, Moab was 30 humbled under the hand of Israel, and the land enjoyed rest for eighty years.

C. SHAMGAR

After him came Shamgar son of Anath. He routed six hundred of the Phil- 31 istines with an ox-goad; he too was a deliverer of Israel.

D. DEBORAH AND BARAK

Israel oppressed by the Canaanites

4 When Ehud died, once again the Israelites began to do what displeases 1 Yahweh, •and Yahweh handed them over to Jabin the king of Canaan 2 who reigned at Hazor. The commander of his army was Sisera, who lived in Harosheth-ha-goiim.

Then the Israelites cried to Yahweh; for Jabin had nine hundred chariots 3 plated with iron and had cruelly oppressed the Israelites for twenty years.

Deborah

At this time Deborah was judge in Israel, a prophetess, the wife of Lappidoth. 4 She used to sit under Deborah's Palm between Ramah and Bethel in the 5 highlands of Ephraim, and the Israelites would come to her to have their disputes decided. •She sent for Barak son of Abinoam from Kedesh in 6 Naphtali. She said to him, 'This is the order of Yahweh, the God of Israel: "March to Mount Tabor and take with you ten thousand men from the sons of Naphtali and the sons of Zebulun. •I will entice Sisera, the commander of 7 Jabin's army, to encounter you at the wadi Kishon with his chariots and troops; and I will put him into your power." ' •Barak answered her, 'If you 8 come with me, I will go; if you will not come, I will not go, for I do not know how to choose the day when the angel of Yahweh will grant me success'. 'I will go with you then,' she said 'but, the way you are going about it, the 9 glory will not be yours; for Yahweh will deliver Sisera into the hands of a woman.' Then Deborah stood up and went with Barak to Kedesh, ••and there 10 Barak summoned Zebulun and Naphtali. Ten thousand men marched behind him, and Deborah marched with him.

Heber the Kenite

Heber the Kenite had cut himself off from the tribe of Kain and the clan 11 of the sons of Hobab, the father-in-law of Moses; he had pitched his tent near the Oak of Zaanannim, not far from Kedesh.

Sisera routed

When Sisera heard that Barak son of Abinoam was encamped on Mount 12 Tabor, •he called for all his chariots—nine hundred chariots plated with 13

iron—and all the troops he had. He summoned them from Harosheth-ha-goiim
14 to the wadi Kishon. •Deborah said to Barak, 'Up! For today is the day Yahweh
has put Sisera into your power. Yes, Yahweh marches at your head.' And
Barak charged down from Mount Tabor with ten thousand men behind him.
15 At Barak's advance, Yahweh struck terror into Sisera, all his chariots and all
16 his troops. Sisera leapt down from his chariot and fled on foot. •Barak pursued
the chariots and the army as far as Harosheth-ha-goiim. Sisera's whole army
fell by the edge of the sword; not one man escaped.

Sisera slain

17   Sisera meanwhile fled on foot towards the tent of Jael, the wife of Heber
the Kenite. For there was peace between Jabin the king of Hazor and the family
18 of Heber the Kenite. •Jael came out to meet Sisera and said to him, 'My lord,
stay here with me; do not be afraid!' He stayed there in her tent, and she covered
19 him with a rug. •He said to her, 'Please give me a little water to drink, for I am
thirsty'. She opened the skin that had milk in it, gave him some to drink and
20 covered him up again. •Then he said to her, 'Stand at the tent door, and if anyone
21 comes and questions you—if he asks, "Is there a man here?", say, "No".' •But
Jael the wife of Heber took a tent-peg, and picked up a mallet; she crept up
softly to him and drove the peg into his temple right through to the ground. He
22 was lying fast asleep, worn out; and so he died. •And now Barak came up
in pursuit of Sisera. Jael went out to meet him and said, 'Come in, and I will
show you the man you are looking for'. He went into her tent; Sisera lay dead,
with the tent-peg through his temple.

Israel delivered

23   Thus God that day humbled Jabin the king of Canaan before the Israelites.
24 And the Israelites bore down more and more heavily on Jabin the king of
Canaan, until he was utterly destroyed.

THE SONG OF DEBORAH AND BARAK

1 5 They sang a song that day, Deborah and Barak son of Abinoam, and the
   words were:

2   'That warriors in Israel unbound their hair,
              that the people came forward with a will,
              for this, bless Yahweh!

3   'Listen, you kings! Give ear, you princes!
              From me, from me comes a song for Yahweh.
              I will glorify Yahweh, God of Israel.

4   'Yahweh, when you set out from Seir,ᵃ
              as you trod the land of Edom,
              earth shook, the heavens quaked,
              the clouds dissolved into water.

5   The mountains melted before Yahweh,
              before Yahweh, the God of Israel.

6   'In the days of Shamgar the son of Anath,
              in the days of Jael,
              every highroad was forsaken;
              those who went forth on their travels
              through by-paths took their way.

d. Euphemism: relieving nature.
5 a. Here meaning Sinai.

'Dead, dead were Israel's villages
until you rose up, O Deborah,
you rose up, a mother in Israel.   7

'Those that should stand for God were dumb.
From five cities, not one shield!
Not one spear from forty thousand in Israel!   8

'My heart beats fast for Israel's chieftains,
with those of the people who stood forth boldly.
For this, bless Yahweh!   9

'You who ride on white she-asses,   10
you with caparisons beneath you,
and you who walk the highways, sing
to the shouts of a rejoicing people   11
gathered about the watering places.
There they extol Yahweh's blessings,
the blessings of his reign in Israel.
(Yahweh's people marched down to the gates.)

'Awake, awake, Deborah!   12
Awake, awake, declaim a song!
Take heart, arise Barak,
capture your captors, son of Abinoam!

'Then Israel marched down to the gates;   13
Yahweh's people, like heroes, marched down to fight for him.

'Ephraim's princes are in the valley.   14
Your brother Benjamin joins your ranks.
From Machir, captains have come down;
from Zebulun, those with the staff of office.
The princes of Issachar are with Deborah;   15
Naphtali in the vale with Barak has sped forward to follow him.

'Where the streams of Reuben are,
men hold their long debate.
Why did you linger among the sheepfolds   16
listening to pipes amid the flocks?
(Where the streams of Reuben are,
men hold their long debate.)

'Gilead stayed beyond the Jordan.   17
Why is Dan in the ships of strangers?[b]
Asher kept by the sea coast,
dwelling at ease within his harbours.

'The tribe of Zebulun fronted death,   18
Naphtali too, on the rising ground.

'The kings came, they stood in line of battle;   19
then they fought, those kings of Canaan,
at Taanach, by Megiddo's waters,
yet bore away no silver spoils.

'From high in heaven fought the stars,   20
fought from their orbits against Sisera.

'The torrent of Kishon swept them away,   21
the sacred torrent, the torrent of Kishon.
Trample, my soul, with might and main!

22   'The horses' hoofs beat the ground;
      galloping, galloping go his steeds.

23   "Curse Meroz," says Yahweh's angel
      "curse, curse the dwellers in it;
      for they never came to Yahweh's aid,
      to Yahweh's aid among the warriors."

24   'Blessed be Jael among women
      (the wife of Heber the Kenite);
      among all women that dwell in tents may she be blessed.

25   'He asked for water; she gave him milk;
      in a precious bowl she brought him cream.

26   She stretched out her hand to seize the peg,
      her right hand to seize the workman's mallet.

      'She struck Sisera, crushed his head,
      pierced his temple and shattered it.

27   At her feet he tumbled, he fell, he lay;
      at her feet he tumbled, he fell.
      Where he tumbled, there he fell dead.

28   'Through her window she leans and looks,
      Sisera's mother, through the lattice:
      "Why is his chariot long in coming?
      Why are the harnessed horses slow?"

29   'Among her princesses the wisest one answers,
      and she to herself repeats,

30   "They are gathering, doubtless, sharing the spoil:
      a girl, two girls for each man of war;
      a garment, two dyed garments for Sisera;
      a scarf, two embroidered scarves for me!"

31   'So perish all your enemies, Yahweh!
      And let those who love you be like the sun
      when he arises in all his strength!'

And the land enjoyed rest for forty years.

E. GIDEON AND ABIMELECH
1. THE CALLING OF GIDEON

Israel oppressed by the Midianites

1   6 The Israelites did what displeases Yahweh; Yahweh gave them over for seven
2   years into the hands of Midian, •and Midian bore down heavily on Israel.
To escape from Midian the Israelites used the mountain clefts and the caves
3 and shelters. •Whenever Israel sowed seed, Midian would march up with Amalek
4 and the sons of the East; they would march up against Israel •and encamp
on their territory and destroy the produce of the country as far as Gaza. They
5 left Israel nothing to live on, not a sheep or ox or donkey, •for they came
up as thick as locusts with their own cattle and their tents; they and their camels
6 were past counting, they overran and pillaged the country. •Thus Midian brought
Israel to great distress, and the Israelites cried to Yahweh.

b. By this time Dan had emigrated, and apparently the men of the tribe hired out their labour
to Phoenician shipmasters.

A message from a prophet

When the Israelites cried to Yahweh because of Midian, •Yahweh sent a 7 8 prophet to the Israelites. This was his message, 'Thus Yahweh speaks, the God of Israel. "It was I who brought you out of Egypt and led you out of a house of slavery. •I rescued you from the power of the Egyptians and the power of 9 all who oppressed you. I drove them out before you and gave you their land, and I said to you: I am Yahweh your God. Do not reverence the gods of the 10 Amorites in whose land you now live. But you have not listened to my words."'

The angel of Yahweh appears to Gideon

The angel of Yahweh came and sat under the terebinth at Ophrah which 11 belonged to Joash of Abiezer. Gideon his son was threshing wheat inside the winepress to keep it hidden from Midian, •when the angel of Yahweh appeared 12 to him and said, 'Yahweh is with you, valiant warrior!' •Gideon answered him, 13 'Forgive me, my lord, but if Yahweh is with us, then why is it that all this is happening to us now? And where are all the wonders our ancestors tell us of when they say, "Did not Yahweh bring us out of Egypt?" But now Yahweh has deserted us; he has abandoned us to Midian.'

At this Yahweh turned to him and said, 'Go in the strength now upholding 14 you, and you will rescue Israel from the power of Midian. Do I not send you myself?' •Gideon answered him, 'Forgive me, my lord, but how can I deliver 15 Israel? My clan, you must know, is the weakest in Manasseh and I am the least important in my family.' •Yahweh answered him, 'I will be with you and you shall 16 crush Midian as though it were a single man'. •Gideon said to him, 'If I 17 have found favour in your sight, give me a sign that it is you who speak to me. •I beg you, do not go away until I come back, I will bring you my 18 offering and set it down before you.' And he answered, 'I will stay until you return'.

Gideon went away and prepared a young goat and made unleavened cakes 19 with an ephah of flour. He put the meat into a basket and the broth into a pot, then brought it all to him under the terebinth. As he came near, •the angel of 20 Yahweh said to him, 'Take the meat and unleavened cakes, put them on this rock and pour the broth over them'. Gideon did so. •Then the angel of Yahweh 21 reached out the tip of the staff in his hand and touched the meat and unleavened cakes. Fire sprang from the rock and consumed the meat and unleavened cakes, and the angel of Yahweh vanished before his eyes. •Then Gideon knew this 22 was the angel of Yahweh, and he said, 'Alas, my Lord Yahweh! I have seen the angel of Yahweh face to face!' •Yahweh answered him, 'Peace be with you; 23 have no fear; you will not die'. •Gideon built an altar there to Yahweh and 24 called it Yahweh-Peace. This altar still stands at Ophrah of Abiezer.

Gideon and Baal [a]

Now that night Yahweh said to Gideon, 'Take your father's fattened calf, 25 and pull down the altar to Baal belonging to your father and cut down the sacred post at the side of it. •Then, on the top of this bluff, build a carefully 26 constructed altar to Yahweh your God. Then take the fattened calf and burn it as a holocaust on the wood of the sacred post you have cut down.' •Then Gideon 27 chose ten of his servants and did as Yahweh had ordered him. But since he stood too much in fear of his family and the townspeople to do this by day, he did it by night. •Next morning, when the townspeople got up, the altar to 28 Baal had been destroyed, the sacred post that had stood beside it was now cut down, and the fattened calf had been burnt as a holocaust on the newly-built altar. •Then they said to each other, 'Who has done this?' They searched, made 29 enquiries and declared, 'Gideon son of Joash has done it'. •Then the townspeople 30 said to Joash, 'Bring out your son for he must die, since he has destroyed the altar to Baal and cut down the sacred post that stood beside it'. •Joash answered 31

all those mustered round him, 'Would you plead for Baal? Would you champion his cause? (Let anyone who pleads for Baal be put to death before dawn.) If he is a god, let him plead for himself, now that Gideon has destroyed his altar.'
32 That day Gideon was given the name of Jerubbaal,[b] because, they said, 'Baal must plead against him, seeing that he has destroyed his altar'.

The call to arms

33   Then all Midian and Amalek and the sons of the East joined forces, crossed
34 the Jordan and encamped in the plain of Jezreel. •And the spirit of Yahweh
35 came on Gideon; he sounded the horn and Abiezer rallied behind him. •He sent messengers throughout Manasseh, and Manasseh too rallied behind him; he sent messengers to Asher, Zebulun and Naphtali, and they too marched out to meet him.

The trial with the fleece

36   Gideon said to God, 'If you really mean to deliver Israel by my hand, as you
37 have declared, •see now, I spread out a fleece on the threshing-floor; if there is dew only on the fleece and all the ground is left dry, then I shall know that
38 you will deliver Israel by my hand, as you have declared'. •And so it happened. Gideon rose the next morning, squeezed the fleece and wrung enough dew out
39 of the fleece to fill a drinking cup. •Then Gideon spoke to God again, 'Do not be angry with me if I speak once again. Let me make trial with the fleece just once more. Let the fleece alone be dry, and let there be dew on the ground
40 all round it.' •And God did so that night. The fleece alone stayed dry, and there was dew on the ground all round it.

2. GIDEON MAKES WAR WEST OF THE JORDAN

Yahweh cuts down the numbers of Gideon's army

1 7 Jerubbaal (that is, Gideon) got up very early, as did all the people with him; he pitched camp at En-harod; the camp of Midian was north of his, under
2 the Hill of Moreh in the valley. •Then Yahweh said to Gideon, 'There are too many people with you for me to put Midian into their power; Israel might claim the credit for themselves at my expense: they might say, "My own hand
3 has rescued me". •Therefore, make this proclamation now to the people: "Let anyone who is frightened or fearful go home!" ' Gideon put them to the test. Twenty-two thousand men went home, and ten thousand were left.
4   Yahweh said to Gideon, 'There are still too many people. Take them down to the waterside and I will sift them there. If I say of a man: He is to go with you, that man is to go with you. And if I say of a man: He is not to go
5 with you, that man is not to go.' •So Gideon took the people down to the waterside, and Yahweh said to him, 'All those who lap the water with their tongues, as a dog laps, place these on one side. And all those who kneel down
6 to drink, place these on the other side.' •The number of those who lapped with their tongues was three hundred; all the rest of the people had knelt to drink.
7 Then Yahweh said to Gideon, 'With the three hundred who lapped the water I will rescue you and put Midian into your power. Let all the others go back,
8 every man to his own home.' •Gideon made the people give him what pitchers and horns they had, then sent away all the Israelites, each to his own tent, keeping only the three hundred with him. The camp of Midian was below his own in the valley.

---

6 a. A second account of the call of Gideon.   b. Folk-derivation: the name in fact has the opposite sense, 'Baal defend him'.

An omen of victory

Now it came about that in the night Yahweh said to him, 'Get up and go 9
down to the camp. I am putting it into your power. •However, if you are afraid 10
to make the assault, go down first to the camp with your servant Purah; •listen 11
to what they are saying; you will be encouraged by it and then you will march
against the camp.' So with his servant Purah he went down to the outposts of
the camp.

Midian and Amalek and all the sons of the East stretched through the valley 12
as thick as locusts; their camels were innumerable like the sand on the seashore.
Gideon came up just as a man was telling his comrade a dream; he was 13
saying, 'I had a dream: a cake made of barley bread came rolling through
the camp of Midian; it reached the tent, struck against it and turned it upside
down'. •His comrade answered, 'This can be nothing else than the sword of 14
Gideon son of Joash the Israelite. God has put Midian and all the camp into
his power.' •When Gideon heard the dream thus told and interpreted, he fell 15
to his knees; then he returned to the camp of Israel and said, 'On your feet,
for Yahweh has put the camp of Midian into your power!'

The surprise attack

Gideon then divided his three hundred men into three companies. To each 16
man he gave a horn and an empty pitcher, with a torch inside each pitcher.
He said to them, 'Watch me, and do as I do. When I reach the edge of the 17
camp, whatever I do, you do too. •When I sound the horn, I and those with me, 18
then you too must sound your horns all round the camp and shout, "For Yahweh
and for Gideon!" '

Gideon and his hundred companions reached the edge of the camp at the 19
beginning of the middle watch, when the new sentries had just been posted;
they sounded their horns and smashed the pitchers in their hands. •The three 20
companies sounded their horns and smashed their pitchers; with their left hands
they grasped the torches, with their right hands the horns ready to blow; and
they shouted, 'For Yahweh and for Gideon!' •And they stood still, spaced out 21
all round the camp. Then the whole camp woke and the Midianites fled,
shouting. •While the three hundred kept sounding their horns, Yahweh made 22
every man in the camp turn his sword against his comrade. They all fled as far
as Beth-shittah towards Zarethan, as far as the bank of Abel-meholah opposite
Tabbath.

The pursuit

The men of Israel mustered from Naphtali, Asher and all Manasseh, and 23
pursued Midian. •Gideon sent messengers throughout the highlands of 24
Ephraim to say, 'Come down and fight Midian, seize the water-points as far as
Beth-barah and the Jordan before they reach them'. All the men of Ephraim
mustered and seized the water-points as far as Beth-barah and the Jordan. •They 25
captured the two Midianite chieftains, Oreb and Zeeb; they killed Oreb at
Oreb's Rock and Zeeb at Zeeb's Winepress. They pursued Midian; and they
brought Gideon the heads of Oreb and of Zeeb beyond the Jordan.

The Ephraimites take offence

8 Now, the men of Ephraim said to Gideon, 'What do you mean by treating 1
us like this, not summoning us when you went to fight with Midian?' And
they reproached him bitterly. •He answered, 'What have I done when compared 2
to you? Is not the gleaning of Ephraim's grapes better than the vintage of
Abiezer? •Into your power Yahweh has given the chieftains of Midian, Oreb 3
and Zeeb. Can what I managed to do compare with what you have done?' And
at these words their anger left them.

3. GIDEON MAKES WAR BEYOND THE JORDAN. GIDEON'S END

Gideon pursues the enemy beyond the Jordan

4 Gideon reached the Jordan and crossed it, but he and his three hundred
5 companions were tired out and famished. •So he said to the men of Succoth,
'Please give my followers a few loaves of bread, because they are tired out, and
6 I am pursuing Zebah and Zalmunna,ᵃ the kings of Midian'. •The chieftains of
Succoth answered, 'Give bread to your army? Are the hands of Zebah and
7 Zalmunna already in your grasp?' •And Gideon answered, 'Very well! When
Yahweh has put Zebah and Zalmunna into my power, I will tear your flesh
8 with desert thorn and briar.' •From there he went up to Penuel and asked the
men of Penuel the same thing; they answered as those of Succoth had done.
9 And to those of Penuel he made a similar reply, 'When I return victorious,
I will destroy this tower'.

The defeat of Zebah and Zalmunna

10 Zebah and Zalmunna were in Karkor with their army, about fifteen thousand
men, all who remained of the army of the sons of the east. Those who had
11 fallen were a hundred and twenty thousand fighting men. •Gideon went up the
nomads' way, eastwards of Nobah and Jogbehah, and routed the army when
12 it thought itself in safety. •Zebah and Zalmunna fled. He pursued them; he
took the kings of Midian prisoner, both Zebah and Zalmunna. And he utterly
destroyed the army.

Gideon's acts of vengeance

13
14 After the battle, Gideon returned by the Ascent of Heres. •He seized a young
man, one of the people of Succoth, and questioned him, and the young man
wrote down the names of the chieftains and elders of Succoth for him—seventy-
15 seven men. •Then Gideon came to the people of Succoth and said, 'Here you
see Zebah and Zalmunna, about whom you taunted me and said, "Are the
hands of Zebah and Zalmunna already in your grasp, for us to give bread to
16 your tired troops?"' •Then he seized the elders of the city, and took desert thorn
17 and briar and tore the men of Succoth with them. •He destroyed the tower
18 of Penuel and slaughtered the townsmen. •Then he said to Zebah and Zalmunna,
'The men you killed at Tabor—what were they like?' They answered, 'They
19 looked like you. Every one of them carried himself like the son of a king.' •Gideon
replied, 'They were my brothers, the sons of my own mother; as Yahweh lives,
20 if you had spared their lives I would not kill you'. •Then he ordered Jether his
eldest son: 'Stand up and kill them'. But the boy did not draw his sword; he
21 dared not; he was still only a lad. •Then Zebah and Zalmunna said, 'Stand up
yourself, and strike us down; for as a man is, so is his strength'. Then Gideon
stood up and killed Zebah and Zalmunna; and he took the crescents from round
their camels' necks.

Gideon triumphant. His end

22 The men of Israel said to Gideon, 'Rule over us, you and your sons and
23 your grandson,ᵇ because you have rescued us from the power of Midian'. •But
Gideon answered them, 'It is not I who shall rule over you, nor my son; Yahweh
24 must be your lord'. •But Gideon went on, 'Let me make one request of you.
Let every man of you give me one of the rings out of his spoils'—for the
25 vanquished army had golden rings, because they were Ishmaelites. •They
answered, 'Gladly'. So he spread out his cloak, and on it they threw, every man
26 of them, a ring taken from their spoils. •The weight of the golden rings he had

---

8 a. Mocking distortions of the kings' names, cf. 7:25.   b. Gideon refuses the title but accepts the authority; not, in fact, over all Israel but over Shechem and a few tribes.

asked for reached seventeen hundred shekels of gold, besides the crescents and the earrings and purple garments worn by the kings of Midian, and besides the collars round their camels' necks, too. •Of all this, Gideon made an ephod^c and 27 put it in his own city of Ophrah. After him, all Israel prostituted themselves to it, and it was a snare for Gideon and his family.

Thus Midian was humbled before the Israelites. They did not lift up their 28 heads again, and the land enjoyed rest for forty years, as long as Gideon lived. So Jerubbaal son of Joash withdrew and lived in his own house. •Gideon had 29 30 seventy sons begotten by him, for he had many wives. •His concubine, who 31 lived in Shechem, bore him a son too, whom he called Abimelech. •Gideon 32 son of Joash was blessed in his old age; he died, and was buried in the tomb of Joash his father, at Ophrah of Abiezer.

Israel relapses into idolatry

After Gideon's death, the people of Israel again began to prostitute themselves 33 to the Baals, and took Baal-berith for their god. •The Israelites no longer 34 remembered Yahweh their God, who had rescued them from all the enemies round them. •And towards the family of Jerubbaal—Gideon—they remained 35 ungrateful for all its good deeds to Israel.

4. THE REIGN OF ABIMELECH

Abimelech becomes king

9 Abimelech son of Jerubbaal came to his mother's brothers at Shechem and 1 said to them and the whole clan of his mother's family, •'Please put this 2 question to the leading men of Shechem: Which is better for you, to be ruled by seventy—I mean all the sons of Jerubbaal—or to be ruled by one? Remind yourselves also that I am your own flesh and blood.' •His mother's brothers 3 spoke of him to all the leading men of Shechem in these terms, and their hearts inclined towards Abimelech, for they told themselves, 'He is our brother'. So they gave him seventy shekels of silver from the temple of Baal-berith, and 4 with this Abimelech paid worthless scoundrels to follow him. •Then he went 5 to his father's house at Ophrah and murdered his brothers, the seventy sons of Jerubbaal, on the selfsame stone. Only the youngest son of Jerubbaal escaped, for he had gone into hiding; this was Jotham. •Then all the leading men of 6 Shechem and all Beth-millo gathered, and proclaimed Abimelech king by the terebinth of the pillar at Shechem.

Jotham's fable

News of this was brought to Jotham. He came and stood on the top of Mount 7 Gerizim and shouted aloud for them to hear:

> 'Hear me, leaders of Shechem,
> that God may also hear you!

> 'One day the trees went out 8
> to anoint a king to rule over them.
> They said to the olive tree, "Be our king!"

> 'The olive tree answered them, 9
> "Must I forego my oil
> which gives honour to gods and men,
> to stand swaying above the trees?"

> 'Then the trees said to the fig tree, 10
> "Come now, you be our king!"

> 'The fig tree answered them, 11
> "Must I forego my sweetness,

forego my excellent fruit,
to stand swaying above the trees?"

12   'Then the trees said to the vine,
"Come now, you be our king!"

13   'The vine answered them,
"Must I forego my wine
which cheers the heart of gods and men,
to stand swaying above the trees?"

14   'Then all the trees said to the thorn bush,
"Come now, you be our king!"

15   'And the thorn bush answered the trees,
"If in all good faith you anoint me king to reign over you,
then come and shelter in my shade.
If not, fire will come from the thorn bush
and devour the cedars of Lebanon."

16   'In the same way, therefore, if you have acted in sincerity and good faith
in making Abimelech king, if you have dealt honourably with Jerubbaal and
17   his family, and have acted towards him as his own deeds deserve....ᵃ •My father
on his side fought for you, risked his life, rescued you from the power of Midian;
18   you on your side have risen today against my father's family, you have murdered
his seventy sons on the selfsame stone; and to rule the leading men of Shechem
you have set up Abimelech, the son of his slave-girl, because he is your brother.
19   If, I say, you have acted in sincerity and good faith towards Jerubbaal and his
20   family, then may Abimelech be your joy and may you be his. •If not, may fire
come out of Abimelech and devour the leading men of Shechem and Beth-millo,
and fire come out of the leading men of Shechem and Beth-millo to devour
Abimelech.'

21   Then Jotham took flight; he escaped and made his way to Beer; and there
he remained, to be out of the reach of his brother Abimelech.

The men of Shechem revolt against Abimelech

22   Abimelech ruled over Israel for three years.ᵇ •Then God sent a spirit of
23   discord between Abimelech and the leaders of Shechem, and the leaders of
24   Shechem rebelled against Abimelech. •And this was so that the crime committed
against Jerubbaal's seventy sons should be avenged, and their blood recoil on
their brother Abimelech who had murdered them and on those leaders of
25   Shechem who had helped him to murder his brothers. •To spite him, the leaders
of Shechem put men in ambush on the mountain tops, and these robbed anyone
26   travelling their way. Abimelech was told of this. •Gaal son of Ebed, with his
brothers, happened to pass through Shechem and won the confidence of the
27   leaders of Shechem. •They went out into the countryside to harvest their
vineyards; they trod the grapes and held rejoicings and went into the temple
28   of their god. They ate and drank there and cursed Abimelech. •Then Gaal son
of Ebed exclaimed, 'Who is Abimelech, and what is Shechem, that we should
be his slaves? Would it not be more fitting for the son of Jerubbaal and Zebul
his delegate to serve the men of Hamor, the father of Shechem? Why should
29   we be his slaves? •Who will put this people under my command? Then I would
drive Abimelech out and say to him: Reinforce your army and come and
30   fight.' •Zebul the governor of the city was told what Gaal son of Ebed had

c. Apparently some kind of religious emblem which later became the object of idolatrous
worship. In other passages, the ephod is a receptacle for the sacred lots and is worn by the priests.
9 a. The interrupted construction is resumed in v.19.   b. I.e., over Shechem and a few Israelite
clans.

said, and he was furious. •He sent messengers to Abimelech at Arumah, bidding ³¹
them tell him, 'Listen! Gaal son of Ebed has come to Shechem with his brothers,
and they are stirring up the town against you. •Move, therefore, under cover ³²
of dark, you and the men you have with you, and take up concealed positions
in the countryside; •then in the morning at sunrise leave them quickly and ³³
advance against the town. When Gaal and his men come out to meet you, do
with him as occasion serves.' •So Abimelech set off under cover of dark with ³⁴
all the men he had and took up concealed positions opposite Shechem, in four
companies. •And as Gaal son of Ebed came out and paused at the entrance ³⁵
to the gate of the town, Abimelech and the men with him rose from their ambush.
Gaal saw these men and said to Zebul, 'Look, there are men coming down from ³⁶
the tops of the mountains!' Zebul answered, 'You mistake the shadow of the
mountains for men'. •But Gaal said again, 'Look, there are men coming down ³⁷
from the Navel of the Land, and another band is on its way from Diviners'
Oak'. •Then Zebul said to him, 'What has become of your boasting now, you ³⁸
who said, "Who is Abimelech that we should be his slaves?" Are not these the
men you made light of? Sally out now, then, and fight them.' •So Gaal ³⁹
sallied out at the head of the leaders of Shechem and fought with Abimelech.
But Abimelech drove Gaal before him; Abimelech went in pursuit of Gaal who ⁴⁰
fled before him, and many of his men fell dead before they reached the town
gate. •Then Abimelech went back to Arumah, and Zebul drove out Gaal and ⁴¹
his brothers and prevented them from living in Shechem.

Shechem destroyed and Migdal-shechem taken

Next day the people went out into the country, and Abimelech was told of ⁴²
this. •He took his men, divided them into three companies and lay in wait in ⁴³
the fields. When he saw the people leaving the town, he bore down on them and
cut them to pieces. •While Abimelech and the company with him advanced and ⁴⁴
took up their post at the entrance to the town gate, the two other companies
fell on everyone in the fields and slaughtered them. •All that day Abimelech ⁴⁵
attacked the town. He stormed it and slaughtered the people inside, razed the
town and sowed it with salt. •On hearing this, the leading men of Migdal- ⁴⁶
shechem took refuge in the crypt of the temple of El-berith. •As soon as ⁴⁷
Abimelech heard that all the leaders of Migdal-shechem had gathered there,
he went up to Mount Zalmon with all his men. Then taking an axe in his hands, ⁴⁸
he cut off the branch of a tree, picked it up and put it on his shoulder, and said
to the men with him, 'Do what you have seen me do, and do it quickly'. •So ⁴⁹
all his men set to work cutting down branches, one each; then they followed
Abimelech and heaped the branches on the crypt, and set it on fire over those
inside.ᶜ All the inhabitants of Migdal-shechem perished too, about a thousand
men and women.

The siege of Thebez: the death of Abimelech

Then Abimelech marched against Thebez, besieged it and stormed it. •In the ⁵⁰₅₁
middle of the town there was a fortified tower in which all the men and women
and all the leading men of the town took refuge. They locked the door behind them
and climbed up to the roof of the tower. •Abimelech reached the tower and ⁵²
attacked it. As he was approaching the door of the tower to set it on fire,
a woman threw down a millstone on his head and crushed his skull. •He called ⁵³₅₄
his armour-bearer at once and said to him, 'Draw your sword and kill me, that
no one may say of me, "A woman killed him"'. His armour-bearer ran
him through, and he died. •When the men of Israel saw that Abimelech ⁵⁵
was dead, they withdrew, each to his own home.

Thus God made the evil recoil on Abimelech that he had done to his father ⁵⁶
by murdering his seventy brothers, •as God made all the wickedness of the ⁵⁷
people of Shechem recoil on their own heads too. And so the curse of Jotham
son of Jerubbaal came true for them.

JEPHTHAH AND THE LESSER JUDGES

F. TOLA

1 **10** After Abimelech, Tola son of Puáh, son of Dodo, rose to deliver Israel. He belonged to Issachar and lived at Shamir in the mountain country of 2 Ephraim. •He was judge in Israel for twenty-three years; then he died and was buried at Shamir.

G. JAIR

3
4 After him rose Jair of Gilead, who judged Israel for twenty-two years. •He had thirty sons who rode on thirty donkeys' colts; and they possessed thirty towns, 5 which are still called the Encampments of Jair, in the land of Gilead. •Then Jair died and was buried at Kamon.

H. JEPHTHAH

Oppression by the Ammonites

6 Again the Israelites began to do what displeases Yahweh. They served the Baals and the Astartes, and the gods of Aram and Sidon, the gods of Moab and those of the Ammonites and Philistines. They deserted Yahweh and served 7 him no more. •Then Yahweh's anger flamed out against Israel and he gave them over into the power of the Philistines and the power of the Ammonites, 8 who from that year onward crushed and oppressed the men of Israel for eighteen years—all the Israelites who lived beyond the Jordan, in the Amorite country 9 in Gilead. •The Ammonites also crossed the Jordan to fight Judah, Benjamin 10 and the House of Ephraim, and Israel's distress was very great. •Then the Israelites cried to Yahweh and said, 'We have sinned against you, because we 11 have turned from Yahweh our God to serve the Baals'. •And Yahweh said to the Israelites, 'When the Egyptians and the Amorites, the Ammonites and the 12 Philistines, •the Sidonians and Amalek and Midian oppressed you and you 13 cried to me, did I not rescue you from their power? •But you on your part have turned from me and served other gods; and so I shall rescue you no more. 14 Go and cry to the gods you have chosen. Let them rescue you in your time of 15 trouble.' •The Israelites answered Yahweh, 'We have sinned. Do with us as you 16 think fit; only do rescue us today.' •They got rid of the foreign gods that they had, and served Yahweh, and he could bear Israel's suffering no longer.

17 The Ammonites mustered and pitched their camp in Gilead. The Israelites 18 rallied and camped at Mizpah. •Then the people, the chieftains of Gilead, said to each other, 'Who will volunteer to fight the sons of Ammon? He shall be made leader of all the inhabitants of Gilead.'

Jephthah lays down his terms

1 **11** Jephthah the Gileadite was a valiant warrior. He was the son of a harlot. 2 Gilead was Jephthah's father, •but Gilead's wife also bore him sons, and the sons of this wife, when they grew up, drove Jephthah out, saying, 'You are to have no share in our father's inheritance, because you are the son of an alien 3 woman'. •Jephthah fled from his brothers and made his home in the land of Tob. Worthless followers gathered round him and used to go raiding with him.

4
5 Some time after this, the Ammonites took up arms against Israel. •And when the Ammonites had attacked Israel, the elders of Gilead went to fetch Jephthah 6 from the land of Tob. ••'Come' they said 'and be our commander, and we can

---

c. Thus avoiding the sacrilege of spilling blood in a consecrated sanctuary.

fight the Ammonites.' •But Jephthah answered the elders of Gilead, 'Was it not 7
you who hated me and drove me out of my father's house? Why come to me
when you are in trouble?' •The elders of Gilead answered Jephthah, 'That is 8
exactly why we have come back to you. Come with us; fight the Ammonites and
be our leader, leader of all the inhabitants of Gilead.' •Jephthah answered the 9
elders of Gilead, 'If you take me home to fight the Ammonites and Yahweh puts
them at my mercy, I am to be your leader?' •The elders of Gilead answered 10
Jephthah, 'Yahweh be witness between us. May we be accursed if we do not
do as you have said!' •So Jephthah set off with the elders of Gilead. The people 11
set him at their head as leader and commander; and Jephthah repeated all his
conditions at Mizpah in Yahweh's presence.

Jephthah negotiates with the Ammonites

Jephthah sent messengers to the king of the Ammonites to say to him, 'What 12
is the trouble between us, for you to come and make war on my country?' •The 13
king of the Ammonites answered Jephthah's messengers, 'The reason is that
when Israel came up from Egypt, they seized my land from the Arnon to the
Jabbok and the Jordan. Give it back peaceably now.' •Jephthah sent messengers 14
to the king of the Ammonites •with this answer, 'Jephthah says this: "Israel 15
seized neither the land of Moab nor the land of the Ammonites. •When Israel 16
came out of Egypt, they passed through the wilderness to the Sea of Reeds
and reached Kadesh. •Then Israel sent messengers to the king of Edom to say 17
to him: Please let us pass through your country, but the king of Edom would
not listen. They sent similarly to the king of Moab, but he refused, and Israel
remained at Kadesh; •later they made their way through the wilderness, going 18
round the countries of Edom and Moab until they were to the east of Moab
territory. The people encamped beyond the Arnon but did not cross the border
of Moab, for the Arnon itself is the boundary there. •Then Israel sent messengers 19
to Sihon the king of the Amorites, who ruled at Heshbon. Israel's message was:
Please let us pass through your country to our destination. •But Sihon would 20
not let Israel pass through his territory; he mustered his whole army; they
encamped at Jahaz, and he then joined battle with Israel. •Yahweh the God 21
of Israel delivered Sihon and his whole army into the power of Israel; Israel
defeated them and took possession of the whole country of the Amorites who
lived in that region. •Thus they came to occupy the whole country of the 22
Amorites, from the Arnon to the Jabbok and from the wilderness to the Jordan.
And now that Yahweh the God of Israel has driven the Amorites out before 23
his people Israel, will one such as you dispossess us? •Do you not possess all 24
that Chemosh your god took from its owners?" In the same fashion, whatever
Yahweh our God took from its owners, that we possess too. •Are you a better 25
man than Balak son of Zippor, the king of Moab? Did he challenge Israel?
Did he make war against them? •When Israel settled in Heshbon and its 26
outlying villages, or in Jazer and its villages, or in any of the towns on the banks
of the Jordan (three hundred years), why did you not recover those places
then? •I for my part have committed no sin against you, rather, you for your 27
part are wronging me by making war on me. Let Yahweh the Judge give judgement
today between the sons of Israel and the king of the Ammonites." ' •But the king 28
of the Ammonites took no notice of the message Jephthah had sent him.

Jephthah's vow and his victory

The spirit of Yahweh came on Jephthah, who crossed Gilead and Manasseh, 29
passed through to Mizpah in Gilead, and from Mizpah in Gilead made his way
to the rear of the Ammonites. •And Jephthah made a vow to Yahweh, 'If you 30
deliver the Ammonites into my hands, •then the first person to meet me from 31
the door of my house when I return in triumph from fighting the Ammonites
shall belong to Yahweh, and I will offer him up as a holocaust'.ᵇ •Jephthah 32

marched against the Ammonites to attack them, and Yahweh delivered them
33 into his power. •He harassed them from Aroer almost to Minnith (twenty towns)
and to Abel-keramim. It was a very severe defeat, and the Ammonites were
humbled before the Israelites.

34   As Jephthah returned to his house at Mizpah, his daughter came out from
it to meet him; she was dancing to the sound of timbrels. This was his only
35 child; apart from her he had neither son nor daughter. •When he saw her, he
tore his clothes and exclaimed, 'Oh my daughter, what sorrow you are bringing
me! Must it be you, the cause of my ill-fortune! I have given a promise to Yahweh,
36 and I cannot unsay what I have said.' •She answered him, 'My father, you
have given a promise to Yahweh; treat me as the vow you took binds you to,
since Yahweh has given you vengeance on your enemies the Ammonites.'
37 Then she said to her father, 'Grant me one request. Let me be free for two months.
I shall go and wander in the mountains, and with my companions bewail my
38 virginity.' •He answered, 'Go', and let her depart for two months. So she went
39 away with her companions and bewailed her virginity in the mountains. •When
the two months were over, she returned to her father, and he treated her as the
vow that he had uttered bound him. She had never known a man. From this
40 comes this custom in Israel •for the daughters of Israel to leave home every
year and to lament the daughter of Jephthah the Gileadite for four days every
year.

War between Ephraim and Gilead. The death of Jephthah

1 12 The men of Ephraim mobilised; they crossed the Jordan, making for
Zaphon, and said to Jephthah, 'Why did you go to fight the Ammonites
2 without asking us to go with you? We shall burn you and your house.' •Jephthah
answered them, 'My people and I were hard put to it, the Ammonites pressed
us hard. I summoned you to help me, but you did not rescue me from their
3 hands. •When I saw that no one came to my help, I took my life in my hands
and marched against the Ammonites, and Yahweh handed them over to me.
4 Why then today come up against me to make war on me?' •Then Jephthah
mustered all the men of Gilead and joined battle with Ephraim, and the men
of Gilead routed Ephraim, because these kept saying, 'You are no more than
deserters from Ephraim, you Gileadites in the heart of Ephraim and Manasseh'.
5 Then Gilead cut Ephraim off from the fords of the Jordan, and whenever an
Ephraimite fugitive said, 'Let me cross', the men of Gilead asked him, 'Are you
6 an Ephraimite?' If he answered 'No', •they said, 'Then say Shibboleth'. He
would say 'Sibboleth', since he could not pronounce the word correctly. Thereupon they seized and slaughtered him by the fords of the Jordan. There
perished in this way forty-two thousand men of Ephraim.
7   Jephthah was judge in Israel for six years. Then Jephthah the Gileadite died,
and was buried in his own town, Mizpah in Gilead.

I. IBZAN

8
9   After him, Ibzan of Bethlehem[a] was judge in Israel. •He had thirty sons and
thirty daughters. He gave his daughters in marriage outside his clan, and brought
in thirty brides from outside for his sons. He was judge in Israel for seven years.
10 Then Ibzan died and was buried in Bethlehem.

11 a. Milcom was in fact the god of Ammonites; Chemosh was the principal god of the
Moabites.   b. Human sacrifice was forbidden by the Law but made its way into Israel through
Canaanite influence.
12 a. Bethlehem of Zebulun.

J. ELON

After him, Elon of Zebulun was judge in Israel. He was judge in Israel for 11 ten years. •Then Elon of Zebulun died and was buried at Elon in the land of 12 Zebulun.

K. ABDON

After him, Abdon son of Hillel of Pirathon was judge in Israel. •He had 13 14 forty sons and thirty grandsons who rode on seventy donkeys' colts. He was judge in Israel for eight years. •Then Abdon son of Hillel of Pirathon died, and 15 he was buried at Pirathon in the mountain country of Ephraim, in the land of Shaalim.

L. SAMSON

Samson's birth foretold

13 Again the Israelites began to do what displeases Yahweh, and Yahweh 1 delivered them into the hands of the Philistines for forty years.

There was a man of Zorah of the tribe of Dan, called Manoah. His wife 2 was barren, she had borne no children. •The angel of Yahweh appeared to this 3 woman and said to her, 'You are barren and have had no child. •But from now 4 on take great care. Take no wine or strong drink, and eat nothing unclean. For you will conceive and bear a son. No razor is to touch his head, for the 5 boy shall be God's nazirite from his mother's womb. It is he who will begin to rescue Israel from the power of the Philistines.' •Then the woman went and 6 told her husband, 'A man of God has just come to me; his presence was like the presence of the angel of God, he was so majestic. I did not ask him where he came from, and he did not reveal his name to me. •But he said to me, "You 7 will conceive and bear a son. From now on, take no wine or strong drink, and eat nothing unclean. For the boy shall be God's nazirite from his mother's womb to his dying day." '

The angel appears a second time

Then Manoah pleaded with Yahweh and said, 'I beg you, Lord, let the man 8 of God that you sent come to us once again and instruct us in what we must do with the boy when he is born'. •Yahweh heard Manoah's prayer for favour, 9 and the angel of Yahweh visited the woman again as she was sitting in the field; her husband Manoah was not with her. •The woman ran quickly and told 10 her husband: 'Look,' she said 'the man who came to me the other day has appeared to me again'. •Manoah rose and followed his wife, and he came to the man and 11 said to him, 'Are you the man who spoke to this woman?' He answered, 'I am'. Manoah went on, 'When your words are fulfilled, what is to be the boy's rule 12 of life? How must he behave?' •And the angel of Yahweh answered Manoah, 13 'The things that I forbade this woman, let him refrain from too. •Let him taste 14 nothing that comes from the vine, let him take no wine or strong drink, let him eat nothing unclean, let him obey all the orders I gave this woman.' •Manoah 15 then said to the angel of Yahweh, 'Do us the honour of staying with us while we prepare a kid for you'. •For Manoah did not know this was the angel 16b of Yahweh. •The °angel of Yahweh said to Manoah, 'Even if I did stay 16a with you, I would not eat your food; but if you wish to prepare a holocaust, offer it to Yahweh'. •Manoah then said to the angel of Yahweh, 'What is your 17 name, so that we may honour you when your words are fulfilled?' •The angel 18 of Yahweh replied, 'Why ask my name? It is a mystery.' •Then Manoah took 19 the kid and the oblation and offered it as a holocaust on the rock to Yahweh

20 who works mysteries. •As the flame went up heavenwards from the altar, the angel of Yahweh ascended in the flame in the sight of Manoah and his wife,
21 and they fell face downwards on the ground. •After this, the angel of Yahweh did not appear any more to Manoah and his wife, by which Manoah understood
22 that this had been the angel of Yahweh. •And Manoah said to his wife, 'We
23 are certain to die, because we have seen God'. •His wife answered him, 'If Yahweh had meant to kill us, he would not have accepted a holocaust and
24 oblation from our hands; he would not have told us all these things.' •The woman gave birth to a son and called him Samson. The child grew, and Yahweh blessed
25 him; •and the spirit of Yahweh began to move him in the Camp of Dan, between Zorah and Eshtaol.

Samson marries

1   **14** Samson went down to Timnah, and there he noticed one of the daughters
2 of the Philistines. •He came up again and told his father and mother this. 'At Timnah' he said 'I noticed one of the daughters of the Philistines. Get
3 her for me, then, to be my wife.' •His father and mother said to him, 'Is there no woman among those of your own clan or among your whole nation, for you to seek a wife among these uncircumcised Philistines?' But Samson answered
4 his father, 'Get this one for me; get her, because I like her'. •His father and mother did not know that all this came from Yahweh, who was seeking an occasion for quarrelling with the Philistines; since at this time the Philistines had Israel in their power.

5 Samson went down to Timnah, and as he reached the vineyards of Timnah
6 he saw a young lion coming roaring towards him. •The spirit of Yahweh seized on him, and though he had no weapon in his hand he tore the lion in pieces as a
7 man tears a kid; but he did not tell his father or mother what he had done. •He
8 went down and talked to the woman, and he liked her. •Not long after this, Samson came back to marry her. He went out of his way to look at the carcase
9 of the lion, and there was a swarm of bees in the lion's body, and honey. •He took up some honey in his hand and ate it as he went along. On returning to his father and mother, he gave some to them, which they ate too, but he did not
10 tell them he had taken it from the lion's carcase. •Then he went down to the woman, and they made a feast for Samson for seven days there, for such is
11 the custom of young men. •But because they were frightened of him, they chose thirty companions to stay with him.

Samson's riddle

12 Then Samson said to them, 'Let me ask you a riddle. If you find the answer within the seven days of the feast, I will give you thirty pieces of fine linen and
13 thirty festal robes. •But if you cannot find the answer, then you in your turn must give me thirty pieces of fine linen and thirty festal robes.' 'Ask your riddle,'
14 they replied 'we are listening.' •So he said to them:

'Out of the eater came what is eaten,
and out of the strong came what is sweet'.

But three days went by and they could not solve the riddle.
15 On the fourth day they said to Samson's wife. 'Cajole your husband into telling you the answer to the riddle, or we will burn you and your father's house
16 together. Did you invite us here to rob us?' •Then Samson's wife fell on his neck in tears and said, 'You only hate me, you do not love me. You have asked my fellow countrymen a riddle and not even told me the answer.' He said to her,
17 'I have not even told my father or mother, why should I tell you?' •She wept on his neck for the seven days their feast lasted. She was so persistent that on the seventh day he told her the answer, and she in turn told her fellow countrymen what the answer to the riddle was.

So on the seventh day, before Samson entered the bridal room, the men 18
of the town said to him:

> 'What is sweeter than honey,
> and what stronger than a lion?'

He retorted:

> 'If you had not ploughed with my heifer,
> you would never have guessed my riddle'.

Then the spirit of Yahweh seized on him. He went down to Ashkelon, killed 19
thirty men there, took what they wore and gave the festal robes to those who
had answered the riddle, then burning with rage returned to his father's house.
Then Samson's wife was given to the companion who had been his best man.   20

Samson sets fire to the crops of the Philistines

15 Not long after this, at the time of the wheat harvest, Samson went back 1
to see his wife; he had brought a kid for her; he said, 'I wish to go to my
wife in her room'. But her father would not let him enter. •'I felt sure' he said 2
'that you had taken a real dislike to her, so I gave her to your companion. But
would not her younger sister suit you better? Have her instead of the other.'
Samson answered them, 'I can only get my own back on the Philistines now 3
by doing them some damage'. •So Samson went off and caught three hundred 4
foxes, then took torches and turning the foxes tail to tail put a torch between
each pair of tails. •He lit the torches and set the foxes free in the Philistines' 5
cornfields. In this way he burned both sheaves and standing corn, and the vines
and olive trees as well.

The Philistines asked, 'Who has done this?' and received the answer, 'Samson, 6
who married the Timnite's daughter; his father-in-law took the wife back again
and gave her to his companion instead'. Then the Philistines went up and burned
the woman and her family to death. •Samson said to them, 'Since this is how 7
you behave, I swear I will not rest till I have had my revenge on you'. •And he 8
fell on them for all he was worth and caused great havoc. Then he went down
to the cave in the Rock of Etam, and stayed there.

The donkey's jawbone

The Philistines came up and encamped in Judah and made a foray against 9
Lehi.

The men of Judah said to them, 'Why are you attacking us?' They 10
answered, 'We have come to seize Samson and to do to him what he did to us'.
Then three thousand of the men of Judah went down to the cave in the Rock 11
of Etam and said to him, 'Do you not know that the Philistines have us in their
power? Now what have you done to us?' He answered, 'What they did to me
I did to them'. •Then they said to him, 'We have come down to take you, to 12
hand you over to the Philistines'. He said to them, 'Swear to me not to kill me
yourselves'. •They answered, 'No; we only want to bind you and hand you 13
over to them; we certainly do not want to kill you'. Then they bound him
with two new ropes and brought him up from the Rock.

As he approached Lehi, and the Philistines came running towards him with 14
triumphant shouts, the spirit of Yahweh seized on Samson; the ropes on his
arms became like burnt strands of flax and the bonds melted off his hands.
Catching sight of the fresh jawbone of a donkey, he reached out and snatched 15
it up; then with it he struck down a thousand men. •And Samson said: 16

> 'With the jawbone of a donkey I have thrashed them;[a]
> with the jawbone of a donkey I have struck down a thousand men'.

And with this, he hurled the jawbone from him; and that is why the place was 17
called Ramath-lehi. •And as he was thirsty, he called on Yahweh and said, 18

'You yourself have worked this great victory by the hand of your servant; and
19 now must I die of thirst and fall into the hands of the uncircumcised?' •Then
God opened a hollow in the ground, the hollow there is at Lehi, and water
gushed out of it. Samson drank; his vigour returned and he revived. And therefore
20 this spring was called En-hakkore; it is still at Lehi today. •Samson was judge
in Israel in the days of the Philistines for twenty years.

The gates of Gaza

1 **16** From here Samson went on to Gaza, and seeing a harlot there he went
2   into her house. •The news was told to the men of Gaza, 'Samson has
arrived'. They surrounded the place and kept watch for him at the gate of
the town. All that night they made no move, thinking, 'We will wait till daybreak;
3 then we will kill him'. •Samson however stayed in bed till midnight, and rising
at midnight, he seized the doors of the town gate and the two posts as well; he
tore them up, bar and all, hoisted them on to his shoulders and carried them
to the top of the hill facing Hebron and there he left them.

Samson is betrayed by Delilah

4   After this, Samson fell in love with a woman in the Vale of Sorek; she was
5 called Delilah. •The chiefs of the Philistines visited her and said to her, 'Cajole
him and find out where his great strength comes from, and how we can master
him and bind him and reduce him to helplessness. In return we will each
give you eleven hundred silver shekels.'
6   Delilah said to Samson, 'Please tell me where your great strength comes
7 from, and what would be needed to bind you and tame you'. •Samson answered,
'If I were bound with seven new bowstrings that had not yet been dried, I should
8 lose my strength and become like any other man'. •The chiefs of the Philistines
brought Delilah seven new bowstrings that had not yet been dried and she took
9 them and bound him with them. •She had men concealed in her room, and she
shouted, 'The Philistines are on you, Samson!' Then he snapped the bowstrings
as a strand of tow snaps at a touch of the fire. So the secret of his
strength remained unknown.
10   Then Delilah said to Samson, 'You have been laughing at me and telling me
11 lies. But now please tell me what would be needed to bind you.' •He answered,
'If I were bound tightly with new ropes that have never been used, I should lose
12 my strength and become like any other man'. •Then Delilah took new ropes
and bound him with them, and she shouted, 'The Philistines are on you, Samson!'
She had men concealed in her room, but he snapped the ropes round his arms
like thread.
13   Then Delilah said to Samson, 'Up to now you have been laughing at me
and telling me lies. Tell me what would be needed to bind you.' He answered,
'If you wove the seven locks of my hair into the warp of the web and fixed the
14 peg firmly, I should lose my strength and become like any other man.' •She
lulled him to sleep, then wove the seven locks of his hair into the warp, fixed
the peg and shouted, 'The Philistines are on you, Samson!' He woke from his
sleep and pulled out both stuff and peg. So the secret of his strength remained
unknown.
15   Delilah said to him, 'How can you say you love me when you do not trust
me? Three times now you have laughed at me and have not told me where your
16 great strength comes from.' •And day after day she persisted with her questions,
17 and allowed him no rest, till he grew tired to death of it. •At last he told her
his whole secret; he said to her, 'A razor has never touched my head, because
I have been God's nazirite from my mother's womb. If my head were shorn, then

15 a. A play on the words 'donkey' and 'thrash' is lost in translation; similarly the place-name
Ramath-lehi is here explained as 'jawbone thrown'.

my power would leave me and I should lose my strength and become like any
other man.' •Then Delilah realised he had told his whole secret to her; she 18
had the chiefs of the Philistines summoned and given this message, 'Come just
once more: he has told his whole secret to me'. And the chiefs of the
Philistines came to her with the money in their hands. •She lulled Samson to 19
sleep in her lap, and summoned a man who sheared the seven locks off his head.
Then he began to lose his strength, and his power left him. •She cried, 'The 20
Philistines are on you, Samson!' He awoke from sleep, thinking, 'I shall break
free as I did before and shake myself clear'. But he did not know that Yahweh
had turned away from him. •The Philistines seized him, put out his eyes and 21
took him down to Gaza. They fettered him with a double chain of bronze, and
he spent his time turning the mill in the prison.

But the hair that had been shorn off began to grow again.   22

Samson's revenge and death

The chiefs of the Philistines assembled to offer a great sacrifice to Dagon 23
their god and to rejoice. They said:

> 'Into our hands our god has delivered
> Samson our enemy'.

And as soon as the people saw their god, they acclaimed him, shouting his 24
praises:

> 'Into our hands our god has delivered
> Samson our enemy,
> the man who laid our country waste
> and killed so many of us'.

And as their hearts were full of joy, they shouted, 'Send Samson out to amuse us'. 25
So Samson was brought out of prison, and he performed feats for them; then
he was put to stand between the pillars. •But Samson said to the boy who was 26
leading him by the hand, 'Lead me where I can touch the pillars supporting the
building, so that I can lean against them'. •Now the building was crowded with 27
men and women. All the chiefs of the Philistines were there, while about three
thousand men and women were watching Samson's feats from the roof. •Samson 28
called on Yahweh and cried out, 'Lord Yahweh, I beg you, remember me; give
me strength again this once, and let me be revenged on the Philistines at one blow
for my two eyes'. •And Samson put his arms round the two middle pillars 29
supporting the building, and threw all his weight against them, his right arm
against one and his left arm against the other; •and he cried out, 'May I die 30
with the Philistines!' He thrust now with all his might, and the building fell on
the chiefs and on all the people there. Those he killed at his death outnumbered
those he had killed in his life. •His brothers and his father's whole family came 31
down and carried him away. They took him up and buried him between Zorah
and Eshtaol in the tomb of Manoah his father. He had been judge in Israel
for twenty years.

IV. ADDITIONS

A. THE SANCTUARY OF MICAH AND THE SANCTUARY OF DAN

The household shrine of Micah

17 In the highlands of Ephraim there was a man called Micayehu. •He 1
said to his mother, 'The eleven hundred silver shekels which were taken 2a
from you and concerning which you uttered a curse, going on to say—I heard it
with my own ears—•"I solemnly declare that of my own free will I consecrate 3b

this silver to Yahweh, to make a carved image (and an idol of cast metal)"—
2b
3c I myself have that silver; I was the one who took it, •and now I give it back
2c
3a to you'. •His mother answered, 'May my son be blessed by Yahweh!' •And
Micayehu gave her back the eleven hundred silver shekels.

4   Then his mother took two hundred silver shekels and gave them to the metal-
worker. From them he made a carved image (and an idol of cast metal), and
5 this was placed in the house of Micah, •who built a shrine for it, and then made
an ephod and teraphim, and installed one of his sons to act as priest for him.
6 In those days there was no king in Israel, and every man did as he pleased.

7   There was a young man of Bethlehem in Judah, of the clan of Judah, who
8 was a Levite and resided there as a stranger. •This man left the town of Bethlehem
in Judah to look for a place where he could find a home. In his travels he
9 came to the highlands of Ephraim and to Micah's house. •Micah asked him,
'Where do you come from?' The other answered him, 'I am a Levite from
Bethlehem in Judah. I am travelling and looking for a place where I can find a
10 home.' •Micah said to him, 'Stay here with me; be a father and a priest for me,
and I will give you ten silver shekels a year, and food and clothing'; and he
11 urged the Levite. •The Levite agreed to remain in the man's house, and the
12 young man became like one of his sons to him. •Micah installed the Levite;
13 the young man became Micah's priest and stayed in his house. •And Micah
said, 'Now I know that Yahweh will prosper me, because I have this Levite as
my priest'.

The Danites go in search of a territory

1 **18** In those days there was no king in Israel.
     Now in those days the tribe of Dan was in search of a territory to live in,
because up till then no territory had fallen to them among the tribes of Israel.
2 From their clan the Danites sent five brave men from Zorah and Eshtaol to
reconnoitre the country and explore it. They said to them, 'Go and explore the
country'. The five men came to the highlands of Ephraim and to Micah's
3 house, and spent the night there. •When they were near Micah's house, they
recognized the voice of the young Levite, and turning that way they said to
him, 'Who brought you here? What are you doing here? What is keeping you
4 here?' •He answered, 'Micah has done such and such for me. He pays me a wage
5 and I act as his priest.' •They replied, 'Then consult God and find out for us
6 whether the journey we are making will be successful'. •The priest replied,
7 'Go in peace; the journey you are making is under the eye of Yahweh'. •So the
five men set out, and came to Laish. They saw that the people there lived in
security like the Sidonians, peaceful and trusting, that nothing lacked there of
all that the earth yields, and that they were far from the Sidonians and had no
8 relations with the Aramaeans. •Then they went back to their kinsfolk at Zorah
9 and Eshtaol, and when these asked them, 'What can you tell us?' •they
answered, 'We went and passed through the country as far as Laish. We saw
that the people there live in security like the Sidonians. They are far from Sidon
and have no relations with Aram. Up, and let us march against them, for we
have seen the country and it is very good. But you—why stand there speechless?
10 Set out for Laish without delay and take possession of the country. •When you
reach it, you will find a defenceless people. The country is wide; God has put in
your power a place where there is nothing lacking of all that man can want on
earth.'

The migration of the Danites

11   So men of the tribe of Dan set out from Zorah and Eshtaol, six hundred
12 of them, armed for war. •They went up and camped at Kiriath-jearim in Judah;
and for this reason the place is still called the Camp of Dan today. It lies west
13 of Kiriath-jearim. •From there they entered the highlands of Ephraim and
came to Micah's house.

Then the five men who had been to explore the country spoke to their brothers 14 and said, 'Do you know that there is an ephod in these houses, and teraphim and a carved image (and an idol in cast metal)? So now think what you have to do.' •They turned aside and went to the young Levite's dwelling in Micah's 15 house, and greeted him. •While the six hundred men of the Danites, armed 16 for war, stood at the threshold of the gate, •the five who had set out to explore 17 the country went on into the house and took the carved image and ephod and teraphim (and the idol of cast metal), while the priest remained at the threshold of the gate with the six hundred men armed for war. •These men, having entered 18 Micah's house, took the carved image, the ephod and the teraphim (and the idol of cast metal). But the priest said, 'What are you doing?' •They answered, 19 'Hush! Put your hand over your mouth and come with us. You shall be a father and a priest for us. Is it better for you to be priest for one man's household, or to be priest for a tribe and clan in Israel?' •The priest was overjoyed; he took the 20 ephod and teraphim and the carved image and set off in the middle of the band of men.

They left by the way they came, putting the women, children, cattle and 21 valuables in front of them. •They had gone some way from Micah's home when 22 the neighbours with houses next to his gave the alarm and set off in pursuit of the Danites. •And as they shouted after them, the Danites turned round and 23 asked Micah, 'What is all this shouting about?' •He answered, 'You have taken 24 away the god I made for myself; you have taken away the priest as well. You go on your way, and what is left for me? How can you ask me, "What is this about?" ' The Danites answered, 'Let us hear no more from you, or men may lose their 25 tempers and fall on you. You may bring about your own destruction and that of your household.' •So the Danites went on their way; and since Micah saw 26 they were the stronger, he turned and went home.

Laish taken. Dan and its sanctuary founded

So taking with them the god that Micah had made and the priest who had 27 served him, the Danites marched against Laish, against a peaceful and trusting people. They slaughtered all the inhabitants and set the town on fire. •There 28 was no one to help the town because it was a long way from Sidon and had no relations with the Aramaeans. It lay in the valley running towards Beth-rehob. They rebuilt the town and settled in it, •and called it Dan after Dan their father 29 who had been born to Israel, although the town was originally called Laish. The Danites erected the carved image for their own use. Jonathan son of Gershom, 30 son of Moses, and his sons after him were priests for the tribe of Dan till the day when the inhabitants of the country were carried away into exile. •The carved 31 image that Micah had made they enshrined for their own use, and there it stayed as long as the house of God remained at Shiloh.ᵃ

B. THE CRIME AT GIBEAH AND THE WAR AGAINST BENJAMINᵃ

The Levite of Ephraim and his concubine

19 In those days, when there was no king in Israel, there was a man, a Levite, 1 whose home was deep in the highlands of Ephraim. He took as concubine a woman from Bethlehem in Judah. •In a fit of anger his concubine 2 left him and returned to her father's house at Bethlehem in Judah, and she stayed there for some four months. •Her husband set out to visit her, to reason with 3 her and fetch her back; he had his servant and two donkeys with him. As he approached the house of the girl's father, the father saw him and came very joyfully to meet him. •His father-in-law, the father of the girl, made him his 4 guest; and he stayed with him for three days; they ate and drank and spent the night there. •On the fourth day they got up early, and the Levite was preparing 5

to leave when the girl's father said to his son-in-law, 'Have a bite of food to
6 fortify yourself; you can leave later'. •So they sat down and began eating and
drinking, the two of them together; then the girl's father said to the young man,
7 'Come, say you will spend· tonight here too, and enjoy yourself'. •And when
the man got up to leave, the father-in-law pressed him again, and he spent
8 another night there. •On the fifth morning, the Levite got up early to leave,
but the girl's father said to him, 'Eat something first, I beg you'. So they whiled
away the time till the day began to decline, and the two of them ate together.
9 The husband was preparing· to leave with his concubine and his servant when
his father-in-law, the father of the girl, said to him, 'Look, the day is drawing
towards evening. Spend the night here and enjoy yourself. Early tomorrow you
10 can go and return to your tent.' •But the man would not stay the night there;
he got up and set off and came within sight of Jebus—that is, Jerusalem. He
had with him two donkeys saddled, and his concubine and his servant.

The crime of the men of Gibeah

11   By the time they were near Jerusalem, the day was fast going. The servant
said to his master, 'Please let us leave the road now and enter this Jebusite
12 town and spend the night there'. •His master answered, 'We will not enter
a town of foreigners, of people who are not Israelites; we will go on to Gibeah
13 instead'. •He went on to say to the servant, 'Come on, we will try to reach one
or other of those places, either Gibeah or Ramah, and spend the night there'.
14 So they kept on, continuing their journey. As they approached Gibeah in
15 Benjamin the sun was already setting. •So they turned that way to spend the
night in Gibeah. Inside the town, the Levite sat down in the middle of the public
square, but no one offered to take them into his house for the night.
16   But an old man came their way, who was returning at nightfall from his
work in the fields. He was a man from the highlands of Ephraim, and a
17 foreigner resident in Gibeah, the men of the place being Benjaminites. •Raising
his eyes, he saw the traveller sitting in the public square of the town; the old man
18 asked him, 'Where have you come from? Where are you going?' •The other
answered, 'We are on our way from Bethlehem in Judah to a place deep in
the highlands of Ephraim. That is where I come from. I have been to Bethlehem in Judah and now I am going home, but no one has offered to take me
19 into his house, •although we have straw and provender for our donkeys, and
I have bread and wine as well for myself and this maidservant and the young
20 man who is travelling with your servant; we are short of nothing.' •The old
man answered, 'Welcome to you! Let me see to all your needs; you cannot spend
21 the night in the public square.' •So he took him into his house and gave the
donkeys provender. The travellers washed their feet, then ate and drank.
22   As they were at their cheerful meal, some men from the town, scoundrels,
came crowding together round the house; they battered on the door and said
to the old man, the master of the house, 'Send out the man who has come
23 into your house, so that we can abuse him'. •Then the master of the
house went out to them and said, 'No, my brothers; I implore you, do not
commit this crime. This man has become my guest; do not commit
24 such an infamy.[a] •Here is my daughter, she is a virgin; I will give her
to you. Possess her, do what you please with her, but do not commit such an
25 infamy against this man.' •The men would not listen to him. So the Levite
took his concubine and brought her out to them. They had intercourse with her
and outraged her all night till morning; when dawn was breaking they let her go.
26   At daybreak the girl came and fell on the threshold of her husband's host,
27 and she stayed there till it was full day. •In the morning her husband got up and

---

18 a. It was still in being, 2 K 10:29, after the one at Shiloh had been destroyed, 1 S 4.
19 a. It is the violation of the sacred duty of hospitality which is considered a grave infamy.

opened the door of the house; he was coming out to continue his journey when
he saw the woman who had been his concubine lying at the door of the house
with her hands on the threshold. •He said to her, 'Stand up; we must go'. There 28
was no answer. Then he laid her across his donkey and began the journey home.
Having reached his house, he picked up his knife, took hold of his concubine, 29
and limb by limb cut her into twelve pieces; then he sent her all through the land
of Israel. •He instructed his messengers as follows, 'This is what you are to 30
say to all the Israelites, "Has any man seen such a thing from the day the Israelites
came out of the land of Egypt, until this very day? Ponder on this, discuss it;
then give your verdict." ' And all who saw it declared, 'Never has such a
thing been done or been seen since the Israelites came out of the land of
Egypt'.

The Israelites pledge themselves to avenge the crime at Gibeah

20 So all the sons of Israel came out, and the whole community, from Dan 1
to Beersheba and the land of Gilead, gathered together as one man in the
presence of Yahweh at Mizpah. •The leaders of all the people and all the tribes 2
of Israel were present at this assembly of the people of God, four hundred
thousand foot soldiers who could handle the sword. •The Benjaminites heard 3
that the sons of Israel had gone up to Mizpah... Then the sons of Israel said,
'Tell us how this crime was committed'. •The Levite, the husband of the murdered 4
woman, spoke in reply and said, 'I had come with my concubine to Gibeah
in Benjamin, to spend the night there. •The men of Gibeah rose against me and 5
in the night surrounded the house where I was lodging; as for me, they wanted
to kill me, and as for my concubine, they raped her to death. •Then I took my 6
concubine, cut her in pieces and sent her throughout all the territory that Israel
inherited because these men have committed an infamy in Israel. •You have all 7
met together here, men of Israel. Discuss the matter and make your decision here
and now.' •All the people stood up as one man and said, 'Not one of us will 8
return to his tent, not one of us will go back to his house. •Now, this is what we 9
shall do to Gibeah. We will cast lots, •and select ten men from every hundred 10
from each of the tribes of Israel, and a hundred from every thousand, and
a thousand from every ten thousand; they will collect food for the army, for
those who will go and punish Gibeah in Benjamin for the infamy they have
committed in Israel.' •So all the men of Israel mustered against that town, united 11
as one man.

The Benjaminites remain stubborn

The tribes of Israel sent messengers out through the whole tribe of Benjamin, 12
saying, 'What is this crime that has been committed among you? •Come now, 13
give up these men, these scoundrels from Gibeah, so that we may put them to
death and banish wickedness from the midst of Israel.' But the Benjaminites
would not listen to their brother Israelites.

The first encounters

The Benjaminites left their towns and mustered at Gibeah to fight the 14
Israelites. •The Benjaminites from these various towns had counted their numbers 15
that day, and in all there were twenty-five thousand men who could handle the
sword, besides the inhabitants of Gibeah. •In this great army were seven hundred 16
picked men who could fight with both hands; every one of these could sling
a stone at a hair and not miss it. •The men of Israel also took a count. Without 17
Benjamin, there were four hundred thousand of them who could handle the
sword; all experienced fighters. •They set off and went up to Bethel to consult 18
God. The Israelites put the question, 'Which of us should go out first to
attack the Benjaminites?' And Yahweh answered, 'Judah shall go first'.
In the morning the Israelites marched out and pitched their camp facing 19
Gibeah. •Then advancing to engage Benjamin they drew up their line in front 20

21 of the town. •But the Benjaminites sallied out from Gibeah and that day killed
23 twenty-two thousand Israelites, who were left on the field. •The Israelites went
and wept before Yahweh until evening; then they consulted Yahweh; they
asked, 'Shall we join battle again with the sons of our brother Benjamin?' Yahweh
22 answered, 'March against him'. •Then the army of the people of Israel took
heart afresh; and again they drew up their line for battle in the same place as
24 the day before. •This second day the Israelites advanced on the Benjaminites;
25 but again this second day Benjamin sallied out from Gibeah against them and
killed eighteen thousand Israelites, who were left on the field; they were all
26 experienced fighters who could handle the sword. •Then all the Israelites and
the whole people went up to Bethel; they wept and sat in Yahweh's presence;
they fasted all day till the evening and offered holocausts and communion
27 sacrifices before Yahweh; •then the Israelites consulted Yahweh. The ark of the
28 covenant of God was there in those days, •and Phinehas son of Eleazer son of
Aaron was the priest who ministered at it at that time. They said, 'Ought we to
go again and fight the sons of our brother Benjamin, or should we stop?'
Yahweh answered, 'March; for tomorrow I shall deliver him into your power'.

Benjamin is conquered and wiped out

29
30   Then Israel stationed men in ambush round Gibeah. •On the third day the
Israelites marched against the Benjaminites and, just as before, they drew up
31 their line in front of the town. •The Benjaminites made a sally against them
and let themselves be drawn away from the town. As before, they began by
killing those of the people who were on the road that runs up to Bethel and on
the road that runs up to Gibeon; and there in the open country they killed
32 about thirty men of Israel. •The Benjaminites thought, 'They have had to fall
back in front of us as before'; but the Israelites decided, 'Let us take to flight
33 and draw them away from the town along the highroads. •Then the main body
of the army of Israel, leaving its position, will form up for battle at Baal-tamar,
but meanwhile the Israelites in ambush will rush forward from their position
34 west of Geba.' •Then ten thousand picked men, chosen from the whole of
Israel, appeared before Gibeah. The battle was fierce. The Benjaminites did not
35 suspect the disaster hanging over them. •Yahweh defeated Benjamin before
Israel, and on that day the Israelites killed twenty-five thousand one hundred
36 men of Benjamin, all men who could handle the sword. •The Benjaminites,
seeing themselves defeated... [a]
    The men of Israel had given ground to Benjamin because they relied on the
37 ambush they had set against Gibeah. •The men in ambush quickly poured out
38 and reached Gibeah and put the whole town to the sword. •For it had been
. agreed between the Israelite army and the troops in ambush that these should
39 raise a smoke signal from the town, •whereupon the Israelites in the thick of the
battle would turn about. Now Benjamin had begun by killing men of the Israelite
army, about thirty of them; so they were thinking, 'Plainly we have routed them
40 now as we did before'. •But the signal, a column of smoke, began to rise from
the town, and the Benjaminites looking back saw the whole town going up in
41 flames to the sky. •Then the Israelites turned about, and the Benjaminites were
seized with terror, for they saw that disaster was imminent.
42   They retreated before Israel, making for the wilderness, but the main body
of Israel pressed them hard, while the others coming out of the town surprised
43 and slaughtered them from the rear. •They hemmed the Benjaminites in, pursued
44 them relentlessly and crushed them opposite Geba on the east. •Eighteen
45 thousand men of Benjamin fell, all of them brave men. •The survivors turned
and ran, and fled into the wilderness and towards the Rock of Rimmon. On

20 a. The sentence is concluded in v.45. It is evident that two documents have been placed side
by side; the next paragraph begins a second account of the same battle that has just been described.

the highroads the Israelites caught five thousand men. Then they pursued the
Benjaminites to Geba and killed two thousand of them. •The total number of 46
Benjaminites who fell that day was twenty-five thousand men who could handle
the sword, all of them brave men. •Six hundred men had escaped into the 47
wilderness, to the Rock of Rimmon, and there they stayed for four months.
The men of Israel went back to the Benjaminites, and put all the males in the 48
towns to the sword, the cattle too, and all that came their way. And they set on
fire all the towns that they came to in Benjamin.

The Israelites relent*

21 The men of Israel had sworn this oath at Mizpah, 'Not one of us will give 1
his daughter in marriage to Benjamin'. •The people went to Bethel and 2
stayed there until evening, sitting before God with groans and bitter weeping.
They said, 'Yahweh, God of Israel, why must this be Israel's lot, to lose one 3
of its tribes today?' •The next day the people got up early and built an altar 4
there; they offered holocausts and communion sacrifices. •Then the Israelites 5
said, 'Which of all the tribes of Israel has not come to the assembly in Yahweh's
presence?' For they had sworn a solemn oath threatening death to anyone who
would not come into Yahweh's presence at Mizpah.

Now the Israelites were sorry for Benjamin their brother; 'Today,' they said 6
'one tribe has been cut off from Israel. •What shall we do to find wives for those 7
who are left, since we have sworn by Yahweh not to give them any of our own
daughters in marriage?'

The maidens of Jabesh given to the Benjaminites

Then they asked the question, 'Which of the tribes of Israel has not come into 8
Yahweh's presence at Mizpah?' It was discovered that no one from Jabesh-gilead
had come to the camp for the assembly; •for the people had been counted over, 9
and not one of the inhabitants of Jabesh-gilead was there. •Then the community 10
sent twelve thousand of their bravest men there, with these orders: 'Go and
slaughter all the inhabitants of Jabesh-gilead, the women and children too. •This 11
is what you must do. You are to put all the males and all women who have
slept with a male under the ban, but you are to spare the maidens.' They obeyed
the orders. •Among the inhabitants of Jabesh-gilead they found four hundred 12
young virgins who had never slept with a man, and brought them to the camp (at
Shiloh, which is in the land of Canaan).

Then the whole community sent messengers to offer peace to the Benjaminites 13
who were at the Rock of Rimmon. •Benjamin returned, and they were given 14
those women from Jabesh-gilead who had been left alive; but there were not
enough for all.

•The daughters of Shiloh are carried off

The people were sorry for Benjamin because Yahweh had made a breach in 15
the tribes of Israel. •And the elders of the community said, 'What shall we do 16
to find wives for the survivors, since the women of Benjamin have been
wiped out?' •They went on, 'How can we preserve a remnant for Benjamin so 17
that a tribe may not be blotted out from Israel? •We ourselves cannot give them 18
our own daughters in marriage.' For the Israelites had sworn this oath, 'Cursed
be any man who gives a wife to Benjamin!'

'But yet' they said 'there is Yahweh's feast which is held every year at Shiloh.' 19
(This town lies north of Bethel, east of the highway that runs from Bethel up to
Shechem, and south of Lebonah.) •So they gave this advice to the Benjaminites, 20
'Place yourselves in ambush in the vineyards. •Keep watch there, and when the 21
daughters of Shiloh come out to dance in groups together, you too come out
of the vineyards: seize a wife, each one of you, from the daughters of Shiloh and
make for the land of Benjamin. •If their fathers or brothers come to complain 22

to you, we shall say to them, "Forgive them because each one of them has taken a wife for himself, as men do in war. For if you had given them brides, you would

23 have broken your oath, and so would have sinned." ' •The Benjaminites did this, and from the dancers they had captured, they chose as many wives as there were men; then they set off, returned to their inheritance, rebuilt their towns and settled in them.

24 Then the Israelites went away, each to rejoin his own tribe and clan, and returned from Shiloh each to his own inheritance.

25 In those days there was no king in Israel, and every man did as he pleased.

21 a. Ch. 21 contains several traditions put together by· an editor; hence repetitions will be noticed.

THE BOOK OF
RUTH

I. RUTH AND NAOMI

1 In the days of the Judges famine came to the land and a certain man from 1
Bethlehem of Judah went—he, his wife and his two sons—to live in the country
of Moab. •The man was called Elimelech, his wife Naomi and his two sons, 2
Mahlon and Chilion;ᵃ they were Ephrathites from Bethlehem of Judah. They came
to the country of Moab and settled there. •Elimelech, Naomi's husband, died, 3
and she and her two sons were left. •These married Moabite women: one was 4
named Orpah and the other Ruth. They lived there about ten years. •Then 5
both Mahlon and Chilion also died and the woman was bereft of her two sons
and her husband. •So she and her daughters-in-law prepared to return from 6
the country of Moab, for she had heard that Yahweh had visited his people and
given them food. •So, with her daughters-in-law, she came away from the place 7
where she was living and they took the road back to the land of Judah.

Naomi said to her two daughters-in-law, 'Go back, each of you to her mother's 8
house. May Yahweh be kind to you as you have been to those who have died
and to me. •Yahweh grant that you find rest, each of you, in the house of a 9
husband.' And she kissed them. But they wept aloud •and said to her, 'No, we 10
will go back with you to your people'. •And Naomi said, 'You must return, my 11
daughters; why come with me? Have I any more sons in my womb to make
husbands for you?ᵇ •Return my daughters, go, for I am too old now to marry again. 12
Even if I said there is still hope for me, even if I were to have a husband this very
night and bear sons, •would you be prepared to wait until they were grown up? 13
Would you refuse to marry for this? No, my daughters, I should then be deeply
grieved for you, for the hand of Yahweh has been raised against me.' •And once 14
more they started to weep aloud. Then Orpah kissed her mother-in-law and
went back to her people. But Ruth clung to her.

Naomi said to her, 'Look, your sister-in-law has gone back to her people 15
and to her god. You must return too; follow your sister-in-law.'

But Ruth said, 'Do not press me to leave you and to turn back from your 16
company, for

> 'wherever you go, I will go,
> wherever you live, I will live.
> Your people shall be my people,
> and your God, my God.
> Wherever you die, I will die 17
> and there I will be buried.
> May Yahweh do this thing to me
> and more also,ᶜ
> if even death should come between us!'

Seeing that she was determined to go with her, Naomi said no more. 18

19 The two of them went on until they came to Bethlehem. Their arrival there
20 set the whole town astir, and the women said, 'Can this be Naomi?' •But she
said to them, 'Do not call me Naomi, call me Mara,ᵈ for Shaddai has marred
me bitterly.

21   'Filled full I departed,
                       Yahweh brings me back empty.
                       Why call me Naomi, then,
                       since Yahweh has given witness against me
                       and Shaddai has afflicted me?'

22 This was how Naomi, she who returned from the country of Moab, came
back with Ruth the Moabitess her daughter-in-law. And they came to Bethlehem
at the beginning of the barley harvest.

II. RUTH IN THE FIELDS OF BOAZ

1 2 Now Naomi had a kinsman on her husband's side, well-to-do and of
      Elimelech's clan. His name was Boaz.
2 Ruth the Moabitess said to Naomi, 'Let me go into the fields and glean
among the ears of cornᵃ in the footsteps of some man who will look on me with
3 favour'. And she said to her, 'Go, my daughter'. •So she set out and went to
glean in the fields after the reapers. And it chanced that she came to that part
4 of the fields which belonged to Boaz of Elimelech's clan. •Now Boaz, as it
happened, had just come from Bethlehem. 'Yahweh be with you!' he said to
5 the reapers. 'Yahweh bless you!' they replied. •Boaz said to a servant of his who
6 was in charge of the reapers, 'To whom does this young woman belong?' •And
the servant in charge of the reapers replied, 'The girl is the Moabitess, the one
7 who came back with Naomi from the country of Moab, •and she said, "Please
let me glean and gather the ears of corn after the reapers". So she came and has
been on her feet from morning till now.'
8 Boaz said to Ruth, 'Listen, my daughter, and understand this. You are not
9 to glean in any other field, do not leave here but stay with my servants. •Keep
your eyes on whatever part of the field they are reaping and follow behind.
I have ordered my servants not to molest you. And if you are thirsty, go to the
10 pitchers and drink what the servants have drawn.' •Then she fell on her face,
bowing to the ground. And she said to him, 'How have I so earned your favour that
11 you take notice of me, even though I am a foreigner?' •And Boaz answered her,
'I have been told all you have done for your mother-in-law since your husband's
death, and how you left your own father and mother and the land where you
were born to come among a people whom you knew nothing about before you
12 came here. •May Yahweh reward you for what you have done! May rich
recompense be made to you by Yahweh, the God of Israel, to whom you have
13 come, to find shelter beneath his wings.' •Then she said, 'May I find favour in
your eyes, my lord, since you have given me courage and spoken kindly to your
maidservant, though indeed I am not the equal of one maidservant of yours'.
14 When it was time to eat Boaz said to her, 'Come, eat some of this bread and
dip your piece in the wine'. Ruth sat with the reapers and Boaz made a heap
of roasted grain for her and she ate till her hunger was satisfied, and she had some
15 left over. •Then she got up to glean and Boaz gave orders to his servants, 'Let her
16 glean among the sheaves themselves,' he said 'and do not check her. •And see

---

1 a. The names may be fictitious and chosen for their meaning: Mahlon is 'sickness', Chilion 'pining away', Orpah 'she who turns away', Ruth 'the beloved', Naomi 'my fair one' and Elimelech 'my God is king'. **b.** In accordance with levirate law the husband's brother takes the widow as his own wife, Dt 25. **c.** This formula is used to avoid repeating the actual words of the oath and thus incurring the danger of calling it down. **d.** 'Bitter'.
2 a. The Law gave this right to the poor, but its exercise depended on the landowner's goodwill.

you pull a few ears of corn from the bundles and let them fall. Let her glean them, and do not scold her.' •So she gleaned in the field till evening. Then she beat out 17 what she had gleaned and it came to about an ephah of barley.

And taking it with her, she went into the town. She showed her mother-in-law 18 what she had gleaned and also showed her the food she had set aside after satisfying her hunger, and gave it to her. •And her mother-in-law said to her, 19 'Where did you glean today? Where have you been working? Blessed be the man who took notice of you!' Then Ruth told her mother-in-law in whose field she had worked, 'The name of the man with whom I have been working today' she said 'is Boaz. •Then Naomi said to her daughter-in-law, 'May he be blessed 20 by Yahweh who does not withhold his kindness from living or dead! This man' Naomi added 'is a relative of ours. He is one of those who has the right of redemption over us.' •Then Ruth said to her mother-in-law, 'He also said to me, 21 "Stay with my servants until they have gathered in all my harvest" '. •And 22 Naomi said to Ruth, her daughter-in-law, 'It is better for you, my daughter, to go with his servants than to go to some other field where you might be molested'. So Ruth stayed with the servants of Boaz and gleaned until the barley and 23 wheat harvests were done. And she went on living with her mother-in-law.

III. BOAZ SLEEPS

3 Then Naomi, her mother-in-law, said to her, 'My daughter, is it not my duty 1 to see you happily settled? •And is not Boaz, with whose servants you were, 2 our kinsman? Now tonight he is winnowing the barley at the threshing-floor. Come, wash and anoint and dress yourself. Then go down to the threshing-floor. 3 Do not make yourself known to him before he has finished eating and drinking. But when he settles down to sleep, take careful note of the place where he lies, 4 then go and turn back the covering at his feet and lie there yourself. He will tell you what to do.' •And Ruth said to her, 'I will do all you say'. 5

So she went down to the threshing-floor and did all that her mother-in-law 6 had told her. •When Boaz had eaten and drunk, he was in a happy mood and 7 went to lie down by the heap of barley. Then she came quietly and turned back the covering at his feet and lay there. •In the middle of the night the man started 8 up and looked about him; and there lying at his feet was a woman. •'Who are 9 you?' he said; and she replied, 'I am Ruth, your maidservant. Spread the skirt of your cloak over your servant for you have right of redemption over me.'ᵃ 'May Yahweh bless you, my daughter,' said Boaz 'for this last act of kindness 10 of yours is greater than the first, since you have not gone after young men, poor or rich. •Have no fear then, my daughter, I will do whatever you ask, for the 11 people of Bethlehem all know your worth. •But, though it is true I have right of 12 redemption over you, you have a kinsman closer than myself. •Stay here for 13 tonight, and in the morning if he wishes to exercise his right over you, very well, let him redeem you. But if he does not wish to do so, then as Yahweh lives, I will redeem you. Lie here till morning.' •So she lay at his feet till morning. Boaz 14 rose before the hour when one man can recognise another, 'For' said he 'it must not be known that this woman came to the threshing-floor'. •Then he said 15 to her, 'Bring the cloak you are wearing and hold it out'. She held it out while he put six measures of barley into it and then gave it to her to carry. And she went into the town.

When Ruth came back, her mother-in-law asked her, 'How did things go with 16 you, my daughter?' Then she told her all that the man had done for her. •'He 17 gave me these six measures of barley,' she added 'and he said to me, "You must not go back to your mother-in-law empty-handed". ' •Naomi replied, 'Wait, my 18 daughter, and see how things will go, for he will not rest until it is settled, and settled today'.

IV. BOAZ MARRIES RUTH

¹ 4 Meanwhile Boaz had gone up to the gate of the town and sat down, and the relative of whom he had spoken chanced to come past. Boaz said to him, 'Come ² here, man, and sit down'; and he came and sat down. •Then Boaz picked out ten of the town's elders and said to them, 'Sit down here', and they sat down. ³ Then Boaz said to the man who had right of redemption, 'Naomi, who has come back from the country of Moab, is selling the piece of land that belonged to our ⁴ brother, Elimelech. •I thought I should tell you about this and say: Buy it in the presence of the men who are sitting here and in the presence of the elders of my people. If you want to use your right of redemption, redeem it; if you do not, tell me so and I shall know, for there is no one but you to redeem it except me, ⁵ though I come after you, myself.' And he said, 'I am willing to redeem it'. •But Boaz continued, 'On the day you purchase the land from Naomi, you purchase Ruth the Moabitess also, the wife of the dead man,ᵃ and so restore his name to ⁶ his inheritance'. •And the man with right of redemption said, 'Then I cannot use my right of redemption, without jeopardising my own inheritance. As I cannot ⁷ use my right of redemption, exercise the right yourself.' •Now in former times it was the custom in Israel, in matters of redemption or exchange, to confirm the transaction by one of the parties removing his sandal and giving it to the other. In Israel this was the form of ratification in the presence of witnesses. ⁸ So when the man with right of redemption said to Boaz, 'Purchase it for yourself', he took off his sandal.

⁹ Then Boaz said to the elders and all the people, 'You are witnesses this day that I buy from Naomi all that belonged to Elimelech, to Chilion and to ¹⁰ Mahlon. •You are witnesses too that I buy Ruth the Moabitess, Mahlon's widow, to be my wife, to keep the name of the dead man in his inheritance, so that the dead man's name may not die out among his brothers and at the gate of ¹¹ his town.' •All the people at the gate said, 'We are witnesses'; and the elders said, 'May Yahweh make the woman who is to enter your House like Rachel and Leah who together built up the House of Israel.

> 'Grow mighty in Ephrathah,
> be renowned in Bethlehem.

¹² And through the children Yahweh will give you by this young woman, may your House become like the House of Perez whom Tamar bore to Judah.'

¹³ So Boaz took Ruth and she became his wife. And when they came together, ¹⁴ Yahweh made her conceive and she bore a son. •And the women said to Naomi, 'Blessed be Yahweh who has not left the dead man without next of kin this day ¹⁵ to perpetuate his name in Israel. •The child will be a comfort to you and the prop of your old age, for your daughter-in-law who loves you and is more to ¹⁶ you than seven sons has given him birth.' •And Naomi took the child to her own bosom and she became his nurse.ᵇ

¹⁷ And the women of the neighbourhood gave him a name. 'A son has been born for Naomi' they said; and they named him Obed. This was the father of David's father, Jesse.

---

3 a. This is asking Boaz to take her as his wife. Because it is her purpose to have a son who will be the legal descendant of her father-in-law Elimelech, this request is called 'an act of kindness' or filial piety.
4 a. Elimelech, the head of the family. Though Ruth is actually the widow of Mahlon, she ranks in this matter as Elimelech's widow.   **b.** Naomi is the child's legal mother and Elimelech his legal father.

THE GENEALOGY OF DAVID[c]

These are the descendants of Perez. Perez was the father of Hezron, •Hezron [18][19]
of Ram, Ram of Amminadab, •Amminadab of Nahshon, Nahshon of Salmon, [20]
Salmon of Boaz, Boaz of Obed, •Obed of Jesse, and Jesse of David. [21][22]

---

c. This genealogy cannot be the work of the same author, since the whole point of the story is
that Elimelech's name is perpetuated; but here Boaz is named as the father of Obed.

THE BOOKS OF SAMUEL

THE FIRST BOOK OF SAMUEL

I. SAMUEL

A. THE CHILDHOOD OF SAMUEL

The pilgrimage to Shiloh

1 There was a man of Ramathaim, a Zuphite from the highlands of Ephraim whose name was Elkanah son of Jeroham, son of Elihu, son of Tohu, son of 2 Zuph, an Ephraimite. •He had two wives, one called Hannah, the other Peninnah; 3 Peninnah had children but Hannah had none. •Every year this man used to go up from his town to worship and to sacrifice to Yahweh Sabaoth[a] in Shiloh.[b] The two sons of Eli, Hophni and Phinehas, were there as priests of Yahweh.

4 One day Elkanah offered sacrifice. He used to give portions to Peninnah and 5 to all her sons and daughters; •to Hannah, however, he would give only one 6 portion, although he loved her more, since Yahweh had made her barren. •Her rival would taunt her to annoy her, because Yahweh had made her barren. 7 And this went on year after year; every time they went up to the temple of Yahweh she used to taunt her. And so Hannah wept and would not eat. 8 Then Elkanah her husband said to her, 'Hannah, why are you crying and why are you not eating? Why so sad? Am I not more to you than ten sons?'

The prayer of Hannah

9 Now after they had eaten in the hall, Hannah rose and took her stand before Yahweh, while Eli the priest was sitting on his seat by the doorpost of the temple 10 of Yahweh. •In the bitterness of her soul she prayed to Yahweh with many 11 tears •and made a vow, saying, 'Yahweh Sabaoth! If you will take notice of the distress of your servant, and bear me in mind and not forget your servant and give her a man-child, I will give him to Yahweh for the whole of his life and no razor shall ever touch his head'.

12 While she prayed before Yahweh which she did for some time, Eli was watching 13 her mouth, •for she was speaking under her breath; her lips were moving but 14 her voice could not be heard. He therefore supposed that she was drunk •and said to her, 'How long are you going to be in this drunken state? Rid yourself 15 of your wine.' •'No, my lord,' Hannah replied 'I am a woman in great trouble; I have taken neither wine nor strong drink—I was pouring out my soul before 16 Yahweh. •Do not take your maidservant for a worthless woman; all this time

1 a. 'Yahweh of armies': not only of the armies of Israel on earth, but of the 'armies of heaven', the stars, angels and 'powers'.   b. Seilun, about 12 m. S. of Nablus, where the ark of the covenant was kept. The annual pilgrimage was made on the feast of Tabernacles.

I have been speaking from the depth of my grief and my resentment.' •Then Eli 17
answered her: 'Go in peace,' he said 'and may the God of Israel grant what you
have asked of him'. And she said, •'May your maidservant find favour in your 18
sight'; and with that the woman went away; she returned to the hall and ate
and was dejected no longer.

The birth and consecration of Samuel

They rose early in the morning and worshipped before Yahweh and then set 19
out and returned to their home in Ramah. Elkanah had intercourse with Hannah
his wife and Yahweh was mindful of her. •She conceived and gave birth to a son, 20
and called him Samuel 'since' she said 'I asked Yahweh for him.'

When a year had gone by, •the husband Elkanah went up again with all his 21
family to offer the annual sacrifice to Yahweh and to fulfil his vow. •Hannah, 22
however, did not go up, having said to her husband, 'Not before the child is
weaned. Then I will bring him and present him before Yahweh and he shall stay
there for ever.' •Elkanah her husband then said to her, 'Do what you think fit; 23
wait until you have weaned him. May Yahweh bring about what you have
said.' So the woman stayed behind and nursed her child until his weaning.

When she had weaned him, she took him up with her together with a three- 24
year old bull, an ephah of flour and a skin of wine, and she brought him to the
temple of Yahweh at Shiloh; and the child was with them. •They slaughtered the 25
bull and the child's mother came to Eli. •She said, 'If you please, my lord. As 26
you live, my lord, I am the woman who stood here beside you, praying to
Yahweh. •This is the child I prayed for, and Yahweh granted me what I asked 27
him. •Now I make him over to Yahweh for the whole of his life. He is made over 28
to Yahweh.'

There she left him, for Yahweh.

The song of Hannah

2 Then Hannah said this prayer: 1

'My heart exults in Yahweh,
    my horn is exalted in my God,
    my mouth derides my foes,
    for I rejoice in your power of saving.

There is none as holy as Yahweh,   2
    (indeed, there is no one but you)
    no rock like our God.

Do not speak and speak with haughty words,   3
    let not arrogance come from your mouth.
For Yahweh is an all-knowing God
    and his is the weighing of deeds.

The bow of the mighty is broken   4
    but the feeble have girded themselves with strength.
The sated hire themselves out for bread   5
    but the famished cease from labour;
    the barren woman bears sevenfold,
    but the mother of many is desolate.

Yahweh gives death and life,   6
    brings down to Sheol and draws up;
Yahweh makes poor and rich,   7
    he humbles and also exalts.

He raises the poor from the dust,   8
    he lifts the needy from the dunghill

to give them a place with princes,
and to assign them a seat of honour;
for to Yahweh the props of the earth belong,
on these he has poised the world.

9   He safeguards the steps of his faithful
but the wicked vanish in darkness
(for it is not by strength that man triumphs).
10 The enemies of Yahweh are shattered,
the Most High thunders in the heavens.

Yahweh judges the ends of the earth,
he endows his king with power,
he exalts the horn of his Anointed.'

11   Then she left for Ramah, but the boy stayed to minister to Yahweh in the
presence of Eli the priest.

The sons of Eli

12
13   Now the sons of Eli were scoundrels; they cared nothing for Yahweh •nor
for the rights of the priests as regards the people. Whenever a man offered a
sacrifice, the priest's servant would come with a three-pronged fork in his hand
14 while the meat was being cooked; •he would thrust this into cauldron or pan,
or dish or pot, and the priest claimed for his own whatever the fork brought up.
That was how they behaved with all the Israelites who came there to Shiloh.
15 The priest's servant would even come up before the fat had been burnt and say
to the man who was making the sacrifice, 'Give the priest meat for him to roast.
16 He will not take boiled meat from you, but raw.' •Then if the man replied,
'Let them first burn the fat and then take for yourself whatever you wish', he
17 would retort, 'No! You must give it to me now or I will take it by force'. •This
sin of the young men was very great in the sight of Yahweh, because they
treated the offering made to Yahweh with contempt.

Samuel at Shiloh

18   Samuel was in the service of Yahweh; the boy wore a linen loincloth round
19 him. •His mother used to make him a little tunic which she brought him each
20 year when she came up with her husband to offer the yearly sacrifice. •Then Eli
would bless Elkanah and his wife and say, 'May Yahweh grant you an heir
by this woman in place of the one she has made over to Yahweh.' And then they
21 would go home. •Yahweh visited Hannah; she conceived and gave birth to
three sons and two daughters. Meanwhile the boy Samuel grew up in the
presence of Yahweh.

More about the sons of Eli

22   Though now very old, Eli came to hear of everything that his sons were
23 doing to all Israel. •And he said to them, 'Why do you do these things I hear
24
25 from all the people? •No, my sons! The reports I hear are not good . . . •If man
sins against man, God will be the arbiter, but if he sins against Yahweh, who
will intercede for him?' But they did not listen to their father's words, for
Yahweh was determined to bring them to their deaths.
26   Meanwhile the boy Samuel went on growing in stature and in favour both
with Yahweh and with men.

Future punishment is announced

27   A man of God came to Eli and said to him, 'Yahweh says this,
"Did I not reveal myself to your father's[a] House when they were in Egypt,

2 a. Levi.

slaves of the household of Pharaoh. •I chose them out of all the tribes of Israel 28
to be my priests, to go up to my altar, to burn incense, to carry the ephod;ᵇ and
to your father's House I granted all the burnt offerings of the sons of Israel.
Why do you look with envious eyes on the sacrifice and the offering I have 29
ordered, honouring your sons more than me, by letting them grow fat on the
best part of all the offerings of my people Israel? •Whereas—it is Yahweh the 30
God of Israel who speaks—I had said that your House and your father's House
would walk in my presence for ever, now, however,—it is Yahweh who speaks—
far be this from me. For those who honour me I honour in my turn, and those
who despise me are esteemed as nothing. •So, the days are coming when I 31
will break your strength and the strength of your father's House, till there is
not one old man left in your House. •Like an envious enemy you will look on 32
all the good that I shall do to Israel, but there shall be not one old man left in
your House for ever. •One of you I will keep at my altar for his eyes to perish 33
and his soul to wither, but the bulk of your House shall perish by the sword of
men. •What happens to your two sons Hophni and Phinehas shall be a sign for 34
you: on the one day both shall die. •I will raise up a faithful priest for myself; 35
he shall do whatever I plan and whatever I desire. I will build him an
enduring House and he will walk in the presence of my Anointed for ever. •And 36
all that survive of your House will come and beg him on their knees for a silver
piece or a loaf of bread and say: Please give me some priestly task, so that I can
have a scrap of bread to eat."ᶜ

God calls Samuel

3 Now the boy Samuel was ministering to Yahweh in the presence of Eli; 1
it was rare for Yahweh to speak in those days; visions were uncommon.
One day, it happened that Eli was lying down in his room. His eyes were 2
beginning to grow dim; he could no longer see. •The lamp of God had not 3
yet gone out, and Samuel was lying in the sanctuary of Yahweh where the ark
of God was, •when Yahweh called, 'Samuel! Samuel!' He answered, 'Here I am'. 4
Then he ran to Eli and said, 'Here I am, since you called me'. Eli said, 'I did 5
not call. Go back and lie down.' So he went and lay down. •Once again Yahweh 6
called, 'Samuel! Samuel!' Samuel got up and went to Eli and said, 'Here I am,
since you called me'. He replied, 'I did not call you, my son; go back and lie
down'. •Samuel had as yet no knowledge of Yahweh and the word of Yahweh 7
had not yet been revealed to him. •Once again Yahweh called, the third time. 8
He got up and went to Eli and said, 'Here I am, since you called me'. Eli then
understood that it was Yahweh who was calling the boy, •and he said to Samuel, 9
'Go and lie down, and if someone calls say, "Speak, Yahweh, your servant is
listening" '. So Samuel went and lay down in his place.

Yahweh then came and stood by, calling as he had done before, 'Samuel! 10
Samuel!' Samuel answered, 'Speak, Yahweh, your servant is listening'. •Then 11
Yahweh said to Samuel, 'I am about to do such a thing in Israel as will make
the ears of all who hear it ring. •On that day, I will carry out against Eli 12
everything I have spoken about his House, from beginning to end. •You are to 13
tell him that I condemn his House for ever because he has known that his
sons have been cursing God, yet he has not corrected them. •Therefore—I swear 14
it to the House of Eli—neither sacrifice nor offering shall ever expiate the guilt
of the House of Eli.'

Then Samuel lay still until the morning, when he opened the doors of 15
Yahweh's temple. He was afraid to tell the vision to Eli, •but Eli called him and 16
said, 'Samuel, my son'. 'Here I am' he answered. •'What message did he give 17
you?' Eli asked; 'Do not hide it from me. May God do this to you, and more,
if you keep back anything of what he said to you.' •Samuel then told him 18
everything, keeping nothing back from him. Eli said, 'He is Yahweh; let him
do what he thinks good'.

19 Samuel grew up and Yahweh was with him and let no word of his fall to
20 the ground. •All Israel from Dan to Beersheba came to know that Samuel was
21 accredited as a prophet of Yahweh. •Yahweh continued to appear in Shiloh, for
1   he revealed himself to Samuel, 4 and the word of Samuel went out to all
Israel. By then, Eli was very old and his sons still persisted in their wicked
behaviour towards Yahweh.

B. THE ARK IN PHILISTINE HANDS

The defeat of the Israelites and capture of the ark

It happened at that time that the Philistines mustered to fight Israel and
Israel went out to meet them in battle, encamping near Ebenezer while the
2 Philistines were encamped at Aphek. •The Philistines drew up their battle line
against Israel, the battle was hotly engaged, and Israel was defeated by the
Philistines and about four thousand of their army were killed on the field.
3 The troops returned to the camp and the elders of Israel said, 'Why has Yahweh
allowed us to be defeated today by the Philistines? Let us fetch the ark of our
God from Shiloh so that it may come among us and rescue us from the power
4 of our enemies.' •So the troops sent to Shiloh and brought away the ark of
Yahweh Sabaoth, he who is seated on the cherubs; the two sons of Eli, Hophni
5 and Phinehas, came with the ark. •When the ark of Yahweh arrived in the camp,
6 all Israel gave a great shout so that the earth resounded. •When the Philistines
heard the noise of the shouting, they said, 'What can this great shouting in the
Hebrew camp mean?' And they realised that the ark of Yahweh had come into
7 the camp. •At this the Philistines were afraid; and they said, 'God has come to
8 the camp'. 'Alas!' they cried 'This has never happened before. •Alas! Who
will save us from the power of this mighty God? It was he who struck down
9 Egypt with every kind of plague! •But take courage and be men, Philistines,
or you will become slaves to the Hebrews as they have been slaves to you. Be
10 men and fight.' •So the Philistines joined battle and Israel was defeated, each
man fleeing to his tent. The slaughter was great indeed, and there fell of the
11 Israelites thirty thousand foot soldiers. •The ark of God was captured too, and
the two sons of Eli died, Hophni and Phinehas.

The death of Eli

12 A Benjaminite ran from the battle line, reaching Shiloh that same day, his
13 clothes torn and dust on his head. •When he arrived, Eli was there, sitting on
his seat beside the gate watching the road, for his heart trembled for the ark
of God. This man, then, came to the town bringing the news, whereupon cries
14 filled the town. •Eli heard the uproar and asked, 'What does this great outcry
15 mean?' The man made haste and told Eli. —•Eli was ninety-eight years old;
16 his gaze was fixed; he was blind.—•The man said to Eli, 'I have come
from the camp. I escaped from the ranks today'. 'My son,' said Eli 'what has
17 happened?' •The messenger replied, 'Israel has fled before the Philistines; the
army has been utterly routed. What is worse, your two sons are dead and the
18 ark of God has been captured.' •When he mentioned the ark of God, Eli fell
backward off his seat by the gate; his neck was broken and he died, for he was
old and heavy. He had ruled Israel for forty years.

The death of the wife of Phinehas

19 Now his daughter-in-law, the wife of Phinehas, was with child and near her
time. When she heard the news that the ark of God had been captured and that
her father-in-law and husband were dead she crouched down and gave birth,

b. The container of the sacred lots.

for her labour pains came on. •When she was at the point of death, the women 20
standing round her said, 'Do not be afraid; you have given birth to a son'. But
she did not answer and took no notice. •She named the boy Ichabod,ᵃ saying, 21
'The glory has gone from Israel', thinking of her father-in-law and husband and
of the capture of the ark of God. •She said, 'The glory has gone from Israel, 22
because the ark of God has been captured'.

The ark brings disaster to the Philistines

5 When the Philistines had captured the ark of God they brought it from 1
Ebenezer to Ashdod. •Taking the ark of God, the Philistines put it in the 2
temple of Dagon, setting it down beside Dagon. •Next morning the people 3
of Ashdod went to the temple of Dagon and there lay Dagon face down on
the ground before the ark of Yahweh. They picked Dagon up and put him back
in his place. •But early next morning there lay Dagon face down again on the 4
ground before the ark of Yahweh, and Dagon's head and two hands were lying
severed on the threshold; only the trunk of Dagon was left in its place.
This is why the priests of Dagon and indeed all who enter Dagon's temple do 5
not step on the threshold of Dagon in Ashdod to the present day.

The hand of Yahweh weighed heavily on the people of Ashdod and struck 6
terror into them, afflicting them with tumours, in Ashdod and its territory.
When the men of Ashdod saw what was happening they said, 'The ark of the God 7
of Israel must not stay here with us, for his hand lies heavy on us and on Dagon
our god'. •So they summoned all the Philistine chiefs to them, and said, 'What 8
shall we do with the ark of the God of Israel?' They decided, 'The ark of the
God of Israel must go away to Gath'. So they took the ark of the God of Israel
to Gath. •But after they had taken it there, the hand of Yahweh lay heavy on 9
that town and a great panic broke out; the people of the town, from youngest to
oldest, were struck with tumours that he brought out on them. •They then sent 10
the ark of God to Ekron, but when it came to Ekron the Ekronites shouted,
'They have brought us the ark of the God of Israel to bring death to us and
our people'. •They summoned all the Philistine chiefs and said, 'Send the ark 11
of the God of Israel away; let it go back to where it belongs and not bring death
to us and our people'—for there was mortal panic throughout the town; the
hand of God was very heavy there. •The people who did not die were struck 12
with tumours and the wailing from the town went up to heaven.

The return of the ark

6 The ark of Yahweh was in Philistine territory for seven months. •Then the ¹₂
Philistines called for their priests and diviners and asked, 'What shall we do
with the ark of Yahweh? Tell us how to send it back to where it belongs.' •They 3
replied, 'If you do send the ark of the God of Israel away, you must not send
it away empty; you must pay him a guilt-offering. Then you will be healed and
you will know why his hand would not turn away from you.' •They then asked, 4
'What guilt-offering ought we to pay him?' They answered, 'In proportion to
the number of the Philistine chiefs, five golden tumours and models of your
rats, for the plague was the same for you all as for your chiefs. •So you must 5
make models of your tumours and models of the rats that ravage your country,
and you must pay honour to the God of Israel. Then perhaps he will lighten
his hand on you and your gods and your country. •Why should you be as 6
stubborn as Egypt and Pharaoh were? After he had brought evil on them, did they
not let them leave? •Now, then, take and fit out a new cart, and two milch cows 7
that have never borne the yoke. Then harness the cows to the cart and take
their calves back to the byre. •Then take the ark of Yahweh, place it on the 8
cart, and put the golden objects which you are paying him as guilt-offering in
a box beside it; then let it go its own way. •Watch it; if it goes up the road to 9
its own territory, to Beth-shemesh, then it was he who did us this great harm;

but if not, then we will know it was not his hand that struck us, but that this happened to us by chance.'

10 The people did this. They took two milch cows and harnessed them to the
11 cart and shut up their calves in the byre. •Then they placed the ark of Yahweh on the cart, with the box and the golden rats and the models of their tumours.
12 The cows made straight for Beth-shemesh keeping to the one road, lowing as they went and turning neither to right nor to left. The Philistine chiefs followed them as far as the boundaries of Beth-shemesh.

The ark at Beth-shemesh

13 The people of Beth-shemesh were reaping the wheat harvest in the plain
14 when, raising their eyes, they saw the ark and went joyfully to meet it. •When the cart came to the field of Joshua of Beth-shemesh it stopped. There was a large stone*ᵃ* there, and they cut up the wood of the cart and offered the cows as
15 a holocaust to Yahweh. •The Levites had taken down the ark of Yahweh and the box containing the golden objects beside it, and placed all this upon the large stone. The men of Beth-shemesh offered holocausts that day and offered
16 sacrifices to Yahweh. •When the five Philistine chiefs had seen this, they went
17 back to Ekron the same day. •These were the golden tumours the Philistines paid as guilt-offering to Yahweh: one for Ashdod, one for Gaza, one for
18 Ashkelon, one for Gath, one for Ekron; •as also the golden rats to the number of all the Philistine towns of the five chiefs, from fortified towns to open villages. The large stone on which they placed the ark of Yahweh is a witness
19 to the present day in the field of Joshua of Beth-shemesh. •Of the people of Beth-shemesh the sons of Jeconiah had not rejoiced when they saw the ark of Yahweh, and he struck down seventy of them. The people mourned because Yahweh had struck them so fiercely.

The ark at Kiriath-jearim

20 The men of Beth-shemesh then said, 'Who can stand his ground before
21 Yahweh this holy God; to whom shall we let him go up, away from us?' •So they sent messengers to the inhabitants of Kiriath-jearim saying, 'The Philistines have sent back the ark of Yahweh; come down and take it up to your town'.
1 **7** The men of Kiriath-jearim came and, taking up the ark of Yahweh, brought it to the house of Abinadab on the hill, and consecrated Eleazar his son to guard the ark of Yahweh.

Samuel, judge and liberator

2 From the day the ark settled in Kiriath-jearim a long time passed, twenty
3 years, and the whole House of Israel longed for Yahweh. •Then Samuel said to the whole House of Israel, 'If you are returning to Yahweh with all your heart, put aside the foreign gods you now have, and the Astartes too, and set your heart on Yahweh and serve him alone; and he will deliver you from
4 the hand of the Philistines'. •And the Israelites put aside the Baals and Astartes and served Yahweh alone.
5 Then Samuel said, 'Muster all Israel at Mizpah and I will plead with
6 Yahweh for you'. •So they mustered at Mizpah and drew water and poured it out before Yahweh. They fasted that day and declared, 'We have sinned against Yahweh'. And it was at Mizpah that Samuel was judge over the Israelites.
7 The Philistines came to hear that the children of Israel had mustered at Mizpah and the Philistine chiefs marched against Israel. The Israelites heard
8 of this and grew afraid of the Philistines. •They said to Samuel, 'Do not cease
9 calling on Yahweh our God to save us from the power of the Philistines'. •Then

4 a. 'Where is the glory?'
6 a. Which could serve as an altar.

Samuel took a sucking lamb and offered it as a holocaust to Yahweh, and he called on Yahweh on behalf of Israel and Yahweh answered his prayer. •While 10 Samuel was offering the holocaust the Philistines approached to give Israel battle, but Yahweh thundered with a great noise that day against the Philistines and threw them into a panic, and so they were routed before Israel. •The men 11 of Israel then went out from Mizpah in pursuit of the Philistines and struck them down as far as below Beth-car. •Then Samuel took a stone and erected 12 it between Mizpah and Jeshanah and gave it the name Ebenezer,ᵃ saying, 'Thus far has Yahweh aided us'.

So the Philistines were humbled and no longer came into Israelite territory; 13 the hand of Yahweh lay on the Philistines all Samuel's lifetime. •The towns the 14 Philistines had taken from Israel were given back to them, from Ekron to Gath, and Israel freed their territory from the power of the Philistines. There was peace, too, between Israel and the Amorites.

Samuel was judge over Israel as long as he lived. •Each year he went on ¹⁵₁₆ circuit through Bethel and Gilgal and Mizpah and judged Israel in all these places. •He would then return to Ramah, for his home was there; there too he 17 judged Israel. And there he built an altar to Yahweh.

II. SAMUEL AND SAUL

A. THE INSTITUTION OF THE MONARCHYᵃ

The people ask for a king

8 When Samuel grew old, he appointed his two sons as judges over Israel. 1 The name of the first-born was Joel, that of the younger Abijah; they were 2 judges in Beersheba. •But his sons did not follow his ways; they wanted money, 3 taking bribes and perverting justice. •Then all the elders of Israel gathered 4 together and came to Samuel at Ramah. •'Look,' they said to him 'you are 5 old, and your sons do not follow your ways. So give us a king to rule over us, like the other nations.' •It displeased Samuel that they should say, 6 'Let us have a king to rule us', so he prayed to Yahweh. •But Yahweh said to 7 Samuel, 'Obey the voice of the people in all that they say to you, for it is not you they have rejected; they have rejected me from ruling over them. •All they have 8 done to me from the day I brought them out of Egypt until now—they deserted me and served other gods—they are doing now to you. •Well then, obey their 9 voice; only, you must warn them solemnly and instruct them in the rights of the king who is to reign over them.'

The disadvantages of the monarchy

All that Yahweh had said Samuel repeated to the people who were asking 10 him for a king •He said, 'These will be the rights of the king who is to reign 11 over you. He will take your sons and assign them to his chariotry and cavalry, and they will run in front of his chariot. •He will use them as leaders of a 12 thousand and leaders of fifty; he will make them plough his ploughland and harvest his harvest and make his weapons of war and the gear for his chariots. He will also take your daughters as perfumers, cooks and bakers. •He will take ¹³₁₄ the best of your fields, of your vineyards and olive groves and give them to his officials. •He will tithe your crops and vineyards to provide for his eunuchs and 15 his officials. •He will take the best of your manservants and maidservants, of 16 your cattle and your donkeys, and make them work for him. •He will tithe your 17 flocks, and you yourselves will become his slaves. •When that day comes, you 18 will cry out on account of the king you have chosen for yourselves, but on that day God will not answer you.'

19   The people refused to listen to the words of Samuel. They said, 'No! We
20 want a king, •so that we in our turn can be like the other nations; our king
21 shall rule us and be our leader and fight our battles.' •Samuel listened to all
22 that the people had to say and repeated it in the ears of Yahweh. •Yahweh then
said to Samuel, 'Obey their voice and give them a king'. Samuel then said to the
men of Israel, 'Go back, each to your own town'.

Saul and his father's she-donkeys

1   Among the men of Benjamin there was a man named Kish son of Abiel,
9 son of Zeror, son of Becorath, son of Aphiah; a Benjaminite and a man of
2 rank. •He had a son named Saul, a handsome man in the prime of life. Of all
the Israelites there was no one more handsome than he; he stood head and
3 shoulders taller than the rest of the people. •Now some of the she-donkeys of
Saul's father Kish had strayed, so Kish said to Saul, 'My son, take one of the
4 servants with you and be off; go and look for the she-donkeys'. •They passed
through the highlands of Ephraim and passed through the land of Shalishah,
but did not find them; they passed through the land of Shaalim, they were not
5 there; they passed through the land of Benjamin, but did not find them. •When
they came to the land of Zuph, Saul said to the servant who was with him,
'Come, let us go back or my father will stop worrying over the she-donkeys and
6 start being anxious about us'. •He answered, 'Look, there is a man of God in
this town, a man held in honour; everything he says comes true. Let us go
there, then; perhaps he will be able to guide us on the journey we have
7 undertaken.' •Saul replied to the servant, 'But if we do go, what can we take to
the man? The bread in our sacks has gone, and we have no present to offer
8 the man of God. What can we give him?' •Again the servant answered Saul,
'Look,' he said 'I have a quarter of a silver shekel here; I will give it to the man
10 of God and he shall tell us our road.' •Then Saul said to his servant, 'Well said!
Come, let us go.' And they went off to the town where the man of God was.

Saul meets Samuel

11   As they were going up the slope to the town they came across some girls going
9 out to draw water, and said to them, 'Is the seer there?'—•Formerly in Israel
when a man used to go to consult God he would say, 'Come, let us go to the
12 seer', for a man who is now called a 'prophet' was formerly called a 'seer'.—•The
girls replied, 'Yes, the seer is ahead of you. He has just come into the town,
13 for the people are having a sacrifice today on the high place. •You will meet
him as soon as you enter the town before he goes up to the high place for
the meal. The people will not eat until he comes, since he must bless the
sacrifice; then the people invited eat afterwards. Go up now and you will soon
find him.'

14   So they went up to the town, and as they were going through the gate Samuel
15 came out in their direction on his way to the high place. •Now Yahweh had
16 given Samuel a revelation the day before Saul came, saying, •'About this time
tomorrow I will send to you a man from the land of Benjamin; you are to
anoint him as prince over my people Israel, and he will save my people from the
power of the Philistines; for I have seen the distress of my people and their
17 crying has come to me'. •When Samuel saw Saul, Yahweh told him, 'That is the
18 man of whom I told you; he shall rule my people'. •Saul accosted Samuel in the
19 gateway and said, 'Tell me, please, where the seer's house is?' •Samuel replied
to Saul, 'I am the seer. Go up ahead of me to the high place. You are to

---

7 a. 'Stone of help'.
8 a. Two versions of this key episode in the history of Israel will be found alternating in the
next five chapters: one by an anti-royalist in ch. 8, 10:17-24, and ch. 12, and a royalist version
in ch. 9-10:16 and ch. 11

eat with me today. In the morning I shall take leave of you and tell you all that is in your heart. •As regards the she-donkeys you lost three days ago, do not 20 worry about them; they have been found already. Besides, for whom is all the wealth of Israel destined, if not for you and all your father's House?' •Saul 21 then replied, 'Am I not a Benjaminite, from the smallest of Israel's tribes? And is not my family the least of all the families of the tribe of Benjamin? Why do you say such words to me?'

Samuel then took Saul and his servant and brought them into the hall and 22 gave them a place at the head of those invited; there were about thirty of them. Samuel said to the cook, 'Serve the portion I gave you, which I told you to 23 put on one side'. •The cook then took up the leg and the tail and set it in front 24 of Saul, saying, 'There! The part that has been kept is set before you. Eat!'. . . So, Saul ate that day with Samuel.

From the high place they came down to the town. On the housetop they 25 spread out coverlets for Saul and he lay down.

The consecration of Saul

At the break of day Samuel called to Saul on the housetop, 'Get up; I must 26 take leave of you'. Saul got up, and the two of them, he and Samuel, went out into the street. •They had walked as far as the end of the town when Samuel 27 said to Saul, 'Tell the servant to go on ahead of us, but you stand still for a moment and I shall make known to you the word of God'.

10 Samuel took a phial of oil and poured it on Saul's head; then he kissed 1 him, saying, 'Has not Yahweh anointed you prince over his people Israel? You are the man who must rule Yahweh's people, and who must save them from the power of the enemies surrounding them. This shall be the sign for you that Yahweh has appointed you prince of his heritage: •when you leave 2 me now, you will meet two men near the tomb of Rachel, on the frontiers of Benjamin . . . and they will say to you, "The she-donkeys you went in search of have been found and your father has lost interest in the donkeys and is worrying about you, thinking, What am I to do about my son?" •Going further 3 from there you will come to the Oak of Tabor where three men will meet you, going up to God at Bethel; one will be carrying three kids, one three loaves of bread and the third a skin of wine. •They will greet you and give you two loaves 4 of bread which you must accept from them. •After this you will go to Gibeah of 5 God (where the Philistine pillar is) and as you come to the town you will meet a group of prophets coming down from the high place, headed by harp, tambourine, flute and lyre; they will be in an ecstasy. •Then the spirit of Yahweh 6 will seize on you, and you will go into an ecstasy with them, and be changed into another man. •When these signs are fulfilled for you, act as occasion serves, 7 for God is with you. •You must go down before me to Gilgal; I will join you 8 there to offer holocausts and communion sacrifices. You are to wait seven days for me to come to you, and then I will show you what you are to do.'

The return of Saul

As soon as Saul had turned his back to leave Samuel, God changed his heart 9 and all these signs were accomplished that same day. •From there they came 10 to Gibeah, and there was a group of prophets coming to meet him; the spirit of God seized on him and he fell into ecstasy in their midst. •When all who knew 11 him previously saw him prophesying with the prophets, the people said to each other, 'What has happened to the son of Kish? Is Saul one of the prophets too?' One of the group retorted, 'And who is their father?' And this is the origin of 12 the proverb: Is Saul one of the prophets too?

When Saul's ecstasy had passed he went back into the house •and his uncle $^{13}_{14}$ asked him and his servant, 'Where have you been?' He replied, 'In search of the she-donkeys; and when we saw we could not find them, we went to Samuel.'

¹⁵
¹⁶ Saul's uncle then said, 'Tell me, now, what did Samuel say to you?' •Saul said to his uncle, 'He only told us that the donkeys were already found', but he said nothing to him about the kingship of which Samuel had spoken.

Saul is chosen king by lot

¹⁷
¹⁸ Samuel called the people together to Yahweh at Mizpah •and said to the Israelites, 'Yahweh the God of Israel has spoken and says, "I brought Israel out of Egypt and delivered you from the power of the Egyptians and of all the
¹⁹ kingdoms that were oppressing you". •But today you have rejected your God, he who saved you from all your calamities and desperate straits; and you have said, "No, you must set a king over us". Well then, take your positions before Yahweh according to your tribes and clans.'

²⁰ Samuel then made all the tribes of Israel come forward, and the lot fell to
²¹ the tribe of Benjamin. •He then made the tribe of Benjamin come forward clan by clan, and the lot fell to the clan of Matri; he then made the clan of Matri come forward man by man, and the lot fell to Saul son of Kish. They looked for him but he was not to be found.

²² Once again they consulted Yahweh, 'Has the man come here?' 'There he is,'
²³ Yahweh answered 'hidden among the baggage'. •So they ran and brought him out and, as he stood among the people, he was head and shoulders taller than
²⁴ them all. •Then Samuel said to all the people, 'Have you seen the man Yahweh has chosen? Of all the people there is none to equal him.' And all the people acclaimed him, shouting, 'Long live the king!'

²⁵ Samuel explained the royal constitution to the people and inscribed it in a book which he placed before Yahweh. He then dismissed all the people, each
²⁶ to his own home. •Saul too went home to Gibeah and with him went the mighty
²⁷ men whose hearts God has touched. •But there were some scoundrels who said, 'How can this fellow save us?' They despised him, and offered him no present.

Victory over the Ammonites

¹ About a month later, **11** Nahash the Ammonite marched up and laid siege to Jabesh-gilead. All the men of Jabesh said to Nahash, 'Make a
² treaty with us and we will be your subjects'. •But Nahash the Ammonite said to them, 'I will make a treaty with you on this condition, that I put out all your
³ right eyes; I shall inflict this disgrace on the whole of Israel'. •The elders of Jabesh said to him, 'Give us seven days' grace while we send messengers throughout the territory of Israel, and if no one comes to our help, we will go
⁴ over to you'. •The messengers came to Gibeah of Saul, and reported this to the people, and all the people began to lament and weep.

⁵ Now Saul was just then coming in from the fields behind his oxen, and he said, 'What is wrong? Why are the people weeping?' They explained to him
⁶ what the men of Jabesh had said. •And the spirit of Yahweh seized on Saul
⁷ when he heard these words, and his fury was stirred to fierce flame. •He took a yoke of oxen and cut them in pieces which he sent by messengers throughout the territory of Israel with these words: 'If anyone will not march with Saul, this shall be done with his oxen!' At this, a dread of Yahweh fell on the people
⁸ and they marched out as one man. •He inspected them at Bezek; there were
⁹ three hundred thousand Israelites and thirty thousand of Judah. •He then said to the messengers who had come, 'This is what you must say to the men of Jabesh-gilead, "Tomorrow by the time the sun is hot help will reach you" '. The messengers went and reported this to the men of Jabesh who were overjoyed;
¹⁰ they said to Nahash, 'Tomorrow we will go over to you and you can do what you like to us'.

¹¹ The next day, Saul disposed the army in three companies; they burst into the middle of the camp in the last watch of the night and struck down the

Ammonites until high noon. The survivors were so scattered that not two of them were left together.

Saul is proclaimed king

The people then said to Samuel, 'Who said, "Is Saul to reign over us?" Hand 12 the men over for us to put them to death.' •'No one is to be put to death today' 13 Saul replied 'for today Yahweh has brought victory to Israel.' •Then Samuel 14 said to the people, 'Come, let us go to Gilgal and reaffirm the monarchy there'.

So all the people went to Gilgal and there they proclaimed Saul king before 15 Yahweh at Gilgal. They offered communion sacrifices there before Yahweh; and Saul and all the men of Israel rejoiced greatly.

Samuel gives way to Saul

12 Samuel said to all Israel, 'I have faithfully done all you asked of me, and 1 I have appointed a king over you. •In future it is the king who will 2 lead you. As for me, I am old and grey, and my sons are here among you. I have led you from my youth until today. •Here I am. Testify against me before 3 Yahweh and before his anointed. Whose ox have I taken? Whose donkey have I taken? Have I ever wronged or oppressed anyone? Have I ever taken a bribe from anyone? If so I will here and now requite you.' •'You have neither wronged 4 nor oppressed us' they said 'nor accepted a bribe from anyone.' •He said to them, 5 'Yahweh is witness against you and his anointed is witness today that you have found nothing in my hands?' 'He is witness' they replied.

Samuel then said to the people, 'Yahweh is witness, he who raised up 6 Moses and Aaron and who brought your ancestors out of the land of Egypt. •So 7 now stand here while I argue with you before Yahweh and remind you of all the saving works he performed for you and for your ancestors. •When Jacob came 8 to Egypt the Egyptians oppressed them, and your ancestors cried to Yahweh who sent Moses and Aaron; they brought your ancestors out of Egypt and gave them a settled home here. •Then they forgot Yahweh their God and he sold 9 them into the power of Sisera, general of the army of Hazor, as also into the power of the Philistines and of the king of Moab who fought against them. They cried to Yahweh, "We have sinned, for we have deserted Yahweh; we 10 have served the Baals and the Astartes. Rescue us now from the power of our enemies, and we will serve you". •Then Yahweh sent Jerubbaal, Barak, Jephthah, 11 and Samuel. He rescued you from the power of the enemies surrounding you, and you lived in security.

'But when you saw Nahash, king of the Ammonites, come to attack you, 12 you said to me, "No, a king must rule over us"—although Yahweh your God himself is your king. •Here then is the king you have chosen; Yahweh has set a 13 king over you. •If you reverence and serve Yahweh and obey his voice and do 14 not rebel against his order, and if both you and the king who rules over you follow Yahweh your God, all will be well. •But if you do not obey the voice 15 of Yahweh, if you rebel against his order, his hand will be against you and against your king.

'Stand here, then, and watch the great wonder Yahweh will do before your 16 eyes. •It is now wheat harvest, is it not?ª I will call on Yahweh and he shall 17 send thunder and rain. Consider then and see what a very wicked thing you have done in the sight of Yahweh by asking to have a king.' •Samuel then called 18 on Yahweh, and Yahweh sent thunder and rain the same day, and all the people held Yahweh and Samuel in great awe. •They all said to Samuel, 'Plead for 19 your servants with Yahweh your God that we may not die, for we have added to all our sins this evil of asking to have a king'.

Samuel said to the people, 'Do not be afraid; you have indeed done all 20 this evil, yet do not turn aside from following Yahweh, but serve Yahweh with all your hearts. •Do not turn aside after empty idols which, being empty, are 21

22 useless and cannot save, •since for the sake of his great name Yahweh will
23 not desert his people, for it has pleased Yahweh to make you his people. •For
my part, far be it from me that I should sin against Yahweh by ceasing to plead
24 for you or to instruct you in the good and right way. •Only reverence and
serve Yahweh faithfully with all your heart, for you see the great wonder he
25 has done among you. •But if you persist in wickedness, you and your king will
perish.'

B. THE BEGINNING OF SAUL'S REIGN

Revolt against the Philistines

1
2 **13** ... •Saul chose three thousand men from Israel; there were two thousand
with Saul at Michmash and in the highlands of Bethel, and a thousand
with Jonathan at Geba of Benjamin; the rest of the people Saul sent home,
each man to his own tent.

3 　　Jonathan smashed the Philistine pillar which was at Gibeah and the Philistines
learned that the Hebrews had risen in revolt. Saul had the trumpet sounded
4 throughout the country, •and the whole of Israel heard the news: Saul has
smashed the Philistine pillar, and now Israel has incurred the enmity of the
5 Philistines. So all the people rallied behind Saul at Gilgal. •The Philistines
mustered to do battle with Israel, three thousand chariots, six thousand horse
and a force as numerous as the sand on the seashore. They came up and pitched
6 camp at Michmash, to the east of Beth-aven.ᵃ •When the men of Israel saw
that their situation was desperate, since they were hard pressed, they hid in
7 caves, in holes, in crevices, in vaults, in wells. •Many, too, crossed over the
Jordan fords into the territory of Gad and Gilead.

Samuel breaks with Saul

　　Saul was still at Gilgal and all the people who followed him were trembling.
8 He waited for seven days, the period Samuel had fixed, but Samuel did not
9 come to Gilgal and the army, deserting Saul, was dispersed. •So Saul said,
'Bring me the holocaust and the communion sacrifices'; and he offered the
10 holocaust. •Just as he was completing the offering of the holocaust Samuel
11 came, and Saul went out to meet him and greet him, •but Samuel said, 'What
have you done?' Saul replied, 'I saw the army deserting me and dispersing,
and you had not come at the time fixed, while the Philistines were mustering
12 at Michmash. •So I thought: Now the Philistines are going to fall on me at
Gilgal and I have not implored the favour of Yahweh. So I felt obliged to act
13 and I offered the holocaust myself.' •Samuel answered Saul, 'You have acted
like a fool. If you had carried out the order Yahweh your God commanded
14 you, Yahweh would have confirmed your sovereignty over Israel for ever. •But
now your sovereignty will not last; Yahweh has searched out a man for himself
after his own heartᵇ and designated him leader of his people, since you have
15 not carried out what Yahweh ordered you.' •Samuel then rose and left Gilgal
to continue his journey.

　　Those of the people who remained followed Saul as he went to join the
warriors, and went from Gilgal to Geba of Benjamin. Saul inspected the force
that was with him; there were about six hundred men.

Preparations for war

16 　　Saul, his son Jonathan, and the force that was with them took up their quarters
17 in Geba of Benjamin while the Philistines camped at Michmash. •The raiding
contingent came out from the Philistine camp in three companies: one made
18. for Ophrah in the land of Shual; •another for Beth-horon; and the third for the

---

12 a. The dry season.
13 a. Bethel.　b. David.

height overhanging the Valley of the Hyenas, towards the wilderness.

There was not a single smith in the whole land of Israel, because the 19
Philistines had reasoned: We must prevent the Hebrews from forging swords or
spears. •Hence all the Israelites were in the habit of going down to the Philistines 20
to sharpen every ploughshare, axe, mattock or goad. •The price was two-thirds 21
of a shekel for ploughshares and axes, and one-third for sharpening mattocks
and straightening goads. •So it was that on the day of the battle of Michmash 22
no one in the whole army with Saul and Jonathan had either sword or spear
in his hand, except, however, Saul and his son Jonathan.

A Philistine outpost left for the Pass of Michmash.   23

Jonathan attacks the outpost

14 One day, Jonathan son of Saul said to his armour-bearer, 'Come on, let us 1
go across to the Philistine outpost in the pass'. But he did not warn his
father. •Saul was on the outskirts of Geba, sitting under the pomegranate tree 2
that stands near the threshing-floor; the force with him numbered about six
hundred men. •Ahijah son of Ahitub, brother of Ichabod son of Phinehas, son 3
of Eli, the priest of Yahweh at Shiloh, was wearing the ephod. The force did
not know that Jonathan had left.

In the pass that Jonathan was trying to cross to reach the Philistine outpost 4
there is a rocky spur on one side and a rocky spur on the other; one is called
Bozez, the other Seneh. •The first spur stands to the north facing Michmash, 5
the other to the south facing Geba. •Jonathan said to his armour-bearer, 'Come 6
on, let us go across to the outpost of these uncircumcised men; perhaps Yahweh
will do something for us, for nothing can prevent Yahweh from giving us victory,
whether there are many or few of them'. •His armour-bearer said to him, 'Do 7
just as your heart tells you; as for me, my heart is with you'. •Jonathan 8
then said, 'Look, we will go across to these people and let ourselves be seen.
If they say to us, "Do not move till we come to you" we shall stay where we are 9
and not go up to them. •But if they say, "Come up to us" we will go up, for 10
that will be the sign for us that Yahweh has given them into our power.'

When they both let themselves be seen by the Philistine post, the Philistines 11
said, 'Look, the Hebrews are coming out of the holes where they have been
hiding'. •The men of the post then hailed Jonathan and his armour-bearer. 12
'Come up to us,' they said 'we have something to tell you.' Jonathan then said
to his armour-bearer, 'Follow me up; Yahweh has given them into the power
of Israel'. •Jonathan climbed up, hands and feet, with his armour-bearer behind 13
him. The Philistines fell before Jonathan, and his armour-bearer, coming behind,
finished them off. •This first blow that Jonathan and his armour-bearer struck 14
accounted for about twenty men...

Battle is engaged

There was panic in the camp and in the countryside; all the men in the 15
outpost, and the raiding contingent too, were terrified; the earth shook; it was
a very panic of God. •Saul's lookout men in Geba of Benjamin could see the 16
camp scattering in all directions. •Saul then said to the force that was with him, 17
'Call the roll and see who has left us'. So they called the roll, and Jonathan
and his armour-bearer were missing.

Saul then said to Ahijah, 'Bring the ephod'; for it was he who carried the 18
ephod in the presence of Israel.ᵃ •But while Saul was speaking to the priest, 19
the turmoil in the Philistine camp grew worse and worse; and Saul said to the
priest, 'Withdraw your hand'. •Then Saul and the whole force with him formed 20
up and advanced to where the fighting was, where men were all drawing their
swords on each other in wild confusion. •The Hebrews who had earlier taken 21
service with the Philistines and had accompanied them into camp, themselves
defected to the Israelites with Saul and Jonathan. •All the Israelites in hiding 22

in the highlands of Ephraim, hearing that the Philistines were on the run, chased
23 after them and joined in the fight. •That day Yahweh gave Israel the victory,
and the battle spread beyond Beth-horon.

Jonathan defies Saul's orders

24   Saul had imposed a great fast that day, laying the people under an oath,
'Cursed be the man who eats food before evening, before I have had my revenge
on my enemies!' So no one so much as tasted food.

25
26   Now there was a honeycomb lying on the ground; •but when the people
came up to the honeycomb, though the swarm had gone no one put a hand
27 to his mouth for fear of the oath. •But Jonathan, not having heard his father lay
the oath on the people, put out the end of the stick he was holding, thrust it
into the honeycomb and put his hand to his mouth; then his eyes brightened.
28 But one of the men spoke up. 'Your father' he said 'has bound the people with
a strict oath to the effect that anyone who eats food today will be accursed.'
29 Jonathan replied, 'My father has done the nation a disservice. See how much
30 brighter my eyes are now that I have eaten this mouthful of honey. •By the same
token, if the people had eaten their fill of the booty they took from the enemy
today, would not the defeat of the Philistines have been all the greater?'

The people commit a ritual fault

31   They struck at the Philistines that day from Michmash as far as Aijalon
32 until the people were utterly weary. •They flung themselves on the booty and,
taking sheep, oxen and calves, slaughtered them there on the ground and ate
33 them with the blood. •News of this came to Saul. 'Look,' they said 'the people
are sinning against Yahweh, eating with the blood.' At which he replied to those
34 who brought the news, 'Roll me a large stone here'.[b] •Then he said, 'Scatter
through the people and say to them, "Let each man bring me his ox or his sheep;
slaughter them here and eat, not sinning against Yahweh by eating with the
blood". All the people then brought what each one had that night, and they
35 slaughtered them there. •Saul built an altar to Yahweh; it was the first altar
he had built to Yahweh.

The guilt of Jonathan is discovered, but he is saved by the people

36   Saul said, 'Let us go down under cover of darkness and pursue and plunder
the Philistines until dawn; we shall not leave one of them alive'. 'Do whatever
you think right' they replied. But the priest said, 'Let us approach God here'.
37 Saul consulted God, 'Shall I go down and pursue the Philistines? Will you
38 give them into Israel's power?' But he gave him no reply that day. •Then Saul
said, 'Come forward, all you leaders of the people; consider carefully where
39 today's sin may lie; •for as Yahweh lives who gives victory to Israel, even if it
be in Jonathan my son, he shall be put to death'. And not one of all the people
40 answered him. •Then to all Israel he said, 'Stand on one side, and I and
Jonathan my son will stand on the other'. And the people replied to Saul, 'Do
41 as you think right'. •Then Saul said, 'Yahweh, God of Israel, why did you not
answer your servant to-day? If the fault lies on me or on my son Jonathan,
O Yahweh, God of Israel, give Urim: if the fault lies on your people Israel, give
42 Thummim.'[c] Jonathan and Saul were indicated and the people went free. •Saul
said, 'Cast the lot between me and my son Jonathan'; and Jonathan was
indicated.
43   Saul then said to Jonathan, 'Tell me what you have done'. Jonathan said,
'I only ate a mouthful of honey off the end of the stick I was holding. Here I am.

---

14 a. Saul means to consult Yahweh by means of the sacred lots. The next verse, however,
shows that he stopped the priest from revealing them.   b. To serve as an altar.   c. This is the
use of the ephod: Urim and Thummim are the name of the two objects used as lots.

I am ready to die.' •Saul said, 'May God do this to me and more if you do not 44
die, Jonathan'. •But the people said to Saul, 'Must Jonathan die after winning 45
this great victory for Israel? Never let it be so! As Yahweh lives, not one hair
of his head shall fall to the ground, for his deeds today have been done with
the help of God.' And so the people ransomed Jonathan and he was not put
to death.

Saul decided not to pursue the Philistines, and the Philistines returned to 46
their own territory.

Summary of Saul's reign

Saul consolidated his rule over Israel and fought against all his enemies 47
everywhere: against Moab, the Ammonites, Edom, Beth-rehob, the king of
Zobah, the Philistines; wherever he turned he was victorious. •He did great 48
deeds of valour; he defeated the Amalekites and delivered Israel from the power
of their plunderers.

The sons of Saul were: Jonathan, Ishvi[d] and Malchishua. The names of his 49
two daughters were: the elder, Merab, and the younger, Michal. •The name 50
of Saul's wife was Ahinoam daughter of Ahimaaz. The name of his army
commander was Abner son of Ner; he was Saul's uncle. •Kish the father of 51
Saul, and Ner the father of Abner were the sons of Abiel.

There was fierce war against the Philistines throughout Saul's lifetime. Any 52
strong man or man of valour that caught Saul's eye he recruited into his service.[c]

The holy war against the Amalekites

15 Samuel said to Saul, 'I am the man whom Yahweh sent to anoint you 1
king over his people, over Israel, so now listen to the words of Yahweh.
Thus speaks Yahweh Sabaoth, "I will repay what Amalek did to Israel when they 2
opposed them on the road by which they came up out of Egypt. •Now, go and 3
strike down Amalek; put him under the ban with all that he possesses. Do not
spare him, but kill man and woman, babe and suckling, ox and sheep, camel
and donkey".'

Saul summoned the people and reviewed them at Telaim: two hundred 4
thousand foot soldiers (and ten thousand men of Judah). •Saul went to the city 5
of Amalek and lay in ambush in the river bed. •Saul said to the Kenites, 'Go, 6
leave your homes among the Amalekites or I may destroy you with them, for
you were friendly to all the sons of Israel when they came up from Egypt'.
So the Kenites moved away from the Amalekites.

Saul then defeated the Amalekites, starting from Havilah in the direction of 7
Shur, which is to the east of Egypt. •He took Agag king of the Amalekites 8
alive and, executing the ban, put all the people to the sword. •But Saul and the 9
army spared Agag with the best of the sheep and cattle, the fatlings and lambs
and all that was good. They did not want to put those under the ban; they only
put under the ban what was poor and worthless.

Saul is rejected by Yahweh

The word of Yahweh came to Samuel, •'I regret having made Saul king, 10
for he has turned away from me and has not carried out my orders'. Then 11
Samuel was deeply moved, and all night long he cried out to Yahweh.

In the morning Samuel went to meet Saul; word was brought him that Saul 12
had gone to Carmel to raise himself a monument, and had passed on again
and gone down to Gilgal. •When Samuel reached Saul, Saul said to him, 'Blessed 13
may you be by Yahweh! I have carried out Yahweh's orders'. •But Samuel 14
replied, 'Then what is the meaning of this bleating of sheep in my ears, and the
lowing of oxen I hear?' •Saul said, 'They have brought them from Amalek 15
because the people spared the best of the sheep and oxen to sacrifice them to
Yahweh, your God; the rest we put under the ban'.

16 Then Samuel said to Saul, 'Stop! Let me tell you what Yahweh said to me
17 last night.' Saul said, 'Tell me'. •Samuel continued, 'Small as you may be in
your own eyes, are you not head of the tribes of Israel? Yahweh has anointed
18 you king over Israel. •Yahweh sent you on a mission and said to you, "Go, put
these sinners, the Amalekites, under the ban and make war on them until they
19 are exterminated". •Why then did you not obey the voice of Yahweh? Why did
20 you fall on the booty and do what is displeasing to Yahweh?' •Saul replied to
Samuel, 'But I did obey the voice of Yahweh. I went on the mission which
Yahweh gave me; I brought back Agag king of the Amalekites; I put the
21 Amalekites under the ban. •From the booty the people took the best sheep and
oxen of what was under the ban to sacrifice them to Yahweh your God in
22 Gilgal.' •But Samuel replied:

'Is the pleasure of Yahweh in holocausts and sacrifices
or in obedience to the voice of Yahweh?
Yes, obedience is better than sacrifice,
submissiveness better than the fat of rams.
23 Rebellion is a sin of sorcery,
presumption a crime of teraphim.ᵃ

'Since you have rejected the word of Yahweh, he has rejected you as king.'

Saul vainly asks for pardon

24 Then Saul said to Samuel, 'I have sinned, for I have transgressed the
order of Yahweh and your directions, being afraid of the people and doing
25 what they said. •Now, I pray you, forgive my sin; come back with me and I will
26 worship Yahweh.' •But Samuel answered Saul, 'I will not come back with you,
for you have rejected the word of Yahweh and he has rejected you as king of
27 Israel'. •As Samuel turned to go away, Saul caught at the hem of his garment
28 and it tore, •and Samuel said to him, 'Today Yahweh has torn the kingdom
of Israel from you and given it to a neighbour of yours who is better than you'.
29 (And yet the glory of Israel will not lie or go back on his word, for he is not
30 a man to go back on his word.) •'I have sinned,' Saul said 'but please still
show me respect in front of the elders of my people and in front of Israel,
31 and come back with me, so that I can worship Yahweh your God.' •Samuel
followed Saul back and Saul worshipped Yahweh.

Agag's death and Samuel's departure

32 Then Samuel said, 'Bring me Agag the king of the Amalekites', and Agag
33 came to him reluctantly. 'Truly, death is a bitter thing' he said. •Samuel said:

'As your sword has made women childless,
so shall your mother be made childless among women.'

Then Samuel butchered Agag before Yahweh at Gilgal.
34
35 Samuel left for Ramah, and Saul went up home to Gibeah of Saul. •Samuel
did not see Saul again to the day of his death;ᵇ Samuel was very sorry for Saul,
but Yahweh regretted having made Saul king of Israel.

III. SAUL AND DAVID

A. DAVID AT COURT

David is anointed

1 **16** Yahweh said to Samuel, 'How long will you go on mourning over Saul when
I have rejected him as king of Israel? Fill your horn with oil and go.

---

d. I.e. 'man of Yahweh'. The same person is called Ishbaal in 1 Ch 8, and Ishbosheth in 2 S 2.
e. The beginnings of a professional army.
15 a. 'False gods'; teraphim were household idols.   b. But 19:22-24 records a different
tradition.

I am sending you to Jesse of Bethlehem, for I have chosen myself a king among
his sons.' •Samuel replied, 'How can I go? When Saul hears of it he will kill me.' 2
Then Yahweh said, 'Take a heifer with you and say, "I have come to sacrifice
to Yahweh". •Invite Jesse to the sacrifice, and then I myself will tell you what 3
you must do; you must anoint to me the one I point out to you.'

Samuel did what Yahweh ordered and went to Bethlehem. The elders 4
of the town came trembling to meet him and asked, 'Seer, have you come with
good intentions towards us?' •'Yes,' he replied 'I have come to sacrifice to 5
Yahweh. Purify yourselves and come with me to the sacrifice.' He purified Jesse
and his sons and invited them to the sacrifice.

When they arrived, he caught sight of Eliab and thought, 'Surely Yahweh's 6
anointed one stands there before him', •but Yahweh said to Samuel, 'Take no 7
notice of his appearance or his height for I have rejected him; God does not
see as man sees; man looks at appearances but Yahweh looks at the heart'.
Jesse then called Abinadab and presented him to Samuel, who said, 'Yahweh 8
has not chosen this one either'. •Jesse then presented Shammah, but Samuel said, 9
'Yahweh has not chosen this one either'. •Jesse presented his seven sons to 10
Samuel, but Samuel said to Jesse, 'Yahweh has not chosen these'. •He then 11
asked Jesse, 'Are these all the sons you have?' He answered, 'There is still one
left, the youngest; he is out looking after the sheep'. Then Samuel said to Jesse,
'Send for him; we will not sit down to eat until he comes'. •Jesse had him sent 12
for, a boy of fresh complexion, with fine eyes and pleasant bearing. Yahweh
said, 'Come, anoint him, for this is the one'. •At this, Samuel took the horn of 13
oil and anointed him where he stood with his brothers; and the spirit of Yahweh
seized on David and stayed with him from that day on. As for Samuel, he rose
and went to Ramah.

David takes service with Saul[a]

Now the spirit of Yahweh had left Saul and an evil spirit from Yahweh 14
filled him with terror. •Saul's servants said to him, 'Look, an evil spirit of God 15
is the cause of your terror. •Let our lord give the order, and your servants 16
who wait on you will look for a skilled harpist; when the evil spirit of God
troubles you, the harpist will play and you will recover.' •Saul said to his 17
servants, 'Find me a man who plays well and bring him to me'. •One of the 18
soldiers then spoke up. 'I have seen one of the sons of Jesse the Bethlehemite'
he said; 'he is a skilled player, a brave man and a fighter, prudent in speech,
a man of presence, and Yahweh is with him.' •At this, Saul sent messengers to 19
Jesse, saying, 'Send me David your son who is with the sheep'. •Jesse took five 20
loaves, a skin of wine and a kid, and sent them to Saul by David his son. •And so 21
David came to Saul and entered his service; Saul loved him greatly and David
became his armour-bearer. •Then Saul sent to Jesse saying, 'Let David enter 22
my service; he has won my favour'. •And whenever the spirit from God troubled 23
Saul, David took the harp and played; then Saul grew calm, and recovered, and
the evil spirit left him.

Goliath defies the Israelite army

17 The Philistines mustered their troops for war; they assembled at Socoh, 1
which is a town of Judah, and pitched camp between Socoh and Azekah, in
Ephes-dammim. •Saul and the Israelites also mustered, pitching camp in the 2
Valley of the Terebinth, and drew up their battle line to meet the Philistines.
These took their stand on the hills one side and the Israelites on the hills the 3
other side, with the valley between them.

One of their shock-troopers stepped out from the Philistine ranks; his name 4
was Goliath, from Gath; he was six cubits and one span tall. •On his head was 5
a bronze helmet and he wore a breastplate of scale-armour; the breastplate
weighed five thousand shekels of bronze. •He had bronze greaves on his legs and 6

7 a bronze javelin across his shoulders. •The shaft of his spear was like a weaver's beam, and the head of his spear weighed six hundred shekels of iron. A shield-bearer walked in front of him.

8 He took his stand in front of the ranks of Israel and shouted, 'Why come out and range yourselves for battle? Am I not a Philistine and are you not the

9 slaves of Saul? Choose a man and let him come down to me. •If he wins in a fight with me and kills me, we will be your slaves; but if I beat him and kill him, you

10 shall become our slaves and be servants to us.' •The Philistine then said, 'I challenge the ranks of Israel today. Give me a man and we will fight in single combat.'

11 When Saul and all Israel heard these words of the Philistine they were dismayed and terrified.

David arrives in the camp

12 David was the son of an Ephrathite from Bethlehem of Judah whose name was Jesse; Jesse had eight sons and, by Saul's time, he was old and well on in

13 years. •The three eldest sons of Jesse followed Saul to the war. The names of the three sons who went to the war were: the first-born Eliab, the second Abinadab

14 and the third Shammah. •David was the youngest; the three eldest followed Saul.

15 (David alternated between serving Saul and looking after his father's sheep at

16 Bethlehem. •Morning and evening for forty days the Philistine advanced and

17 took his stand.) •Jesse said to David his son, 'Take your brothers this ephah of

18 roasted grain and these ten loaves, and hurry to your brothers' camp. •And take these ten cheeses to their commanding officer; ask after your brothers' health and

19 bring some token from them; •they are with Saul and all the Israelites in the Valley of the Terebinth fighting the Philistines.'

20 David rose early in the morning and, leaving the sheep with someone to guard them, took up his load and went off as Jesse had ordered him; he came to the encampment just as the troops were leaving to take up battle stations, shouting

21 the war cry. •Israel and the Philistines drew up their lines facing one another.

22 David left the bundle in charge of the baggage guard, ran to the battle line and went to ask his brothers how they were.

23 While he was talking to them, the shock-trooper (his name was Goliath, the Philistine from Gath) came up from the Philistine ranks and made his usual

24 speech, and David heard it. •As soon as the Israelites saw this man, they all

25 ran away from him and were terrified. •The Israelites said, 'Have you seen this man coming up now? He is coming to challenge Israel. The king will lavish riches on the man who kills him and give him his daughter in marriage and grant his father's House the freedom of Israel.'

26 Then David asked the men who were standing near him, 'What reward will the man have who kills this Philistine and removes the disgrace from Israel? Who is this uncircumcised Philistine who dares insult the armies of the living God?'

27 The people replied as before, 'That is how the man will be rewarded who kills

28 him'. •Now Eliab his elder brother heard him talking to the men and his anger flared up against David. 'Why have you come down here?' he said. 'Whom have you left in charge of those few sheep out there in the wilderness? I know your

29 insolence and your wicked heart; you have come to watch the battle.' •David

30 retorted, 'What have I done? Must I not even speak?' •And he turned away from him to address another and asked the same question; and the people answered

31 as before. •But David's words were noted and reported to Saul, who sent for him.

David volunteers to accept the challenge

32 David said to Saul, 'Let no one lose heart on his account; your servant will

33 go and fight this Philistine'. •But Saul answered David, 'You cannot go and fight

---

16 a. The next chapter contains a different tradition of David's early association with Saul.

the Philistine; you are only a boy and he has been a warrior from his youth'.

David said to Saul, 'Your servant used to look after the sheep for his father 34 and whenever a lion or a bear came out and took a sheep from the flock, •I used 35 to follow him up and strike him down and rescue it from his mouth; if he turned on me I seized him by the hair at his jaw and struck him down and killed him. Your servant has killed both lion and bear, and this uncircumcised Philistine shall 36 be like one of them, for he has dared to insult the armies of the living God. Yahweh who rescued me from the claws of lion and bear' David said 'will 37 rescue me from the power of this Philistine.' Then Saul said to David, 'Go, and Yahweh be with you!'

Saul made David put on his own armour and put a bronze helmet on his 38 head and gave him a breastplate to wear, •and over David's armour he buckled 39 his own sword; but not being used to these things David found he could not walk. 'I cannot walk with these,' he said to Saul 'I am not used to them.' So they took them off again.

David and Goliath

He took his staff in his hand, picked five smooth stones from the river bed, 40 put them in his shepherd's bag, in his pouch, and with his sling in his hand he went to meet the Philistine. •The Philistine, his shield-bearer in front of him, 41 came nearer and nearer to David; •and the Philistine looked at David, and what 42 he saw filled him with scorn, because David was only a youth, a boy of fresh complexion and pleasant bearing. •The Philistine said to him, 'Am I a dog for 43 you to come against me with sticks?' And the Philistine cursed David by his gods. •The Philistine said to David, 'Come over here and I will give your flesh 44 to the birds of the air and the beasts of the field'. •But David answered the 45 Philistine, 'You come against me with sword and spear and javelin, but I come against you in the name of Yahweh Sabaoth, the God of the armies of Israel that you have dared to insult. •Today Yahweh will deliver you into my hand 46 and I shall kill you; I will cut off your head, and this very day I will give your dead body and the bodies of the Philistine army to the birds of the air and the wild beasts of the earth, so that all the earth may know that there is a God in Israel, •and that all this assembly may know that it is not by sword or by spear 47 that Yahweh gives the victory, for Yahweh is lord of the battle and he will deliver you into our power.'

No sooner had the Philistine started forward to confront David than 48 David left the line of battle and ran to meet the Philistine. •Putting his hand 49 in his bag, he took out a stone and slung it and struck the Philistine on the forehead; the stone penetrated his forehead and he fell on his face to the ground. Thus David triumphed over the Philistine with a sling and a stone and struck 50 the Philistine down and killed him. David had no sword in his hand. •Then David 51 ran and, standing over the Philistine, seized his sword and drew it from the scabbard, and with this he killed him, cutting off his head.

The Philistines saw that their champion was dead and took to flight. •The 52 men of Israel and of Judah started forward, shouting their war cry, and pursued the Philistines as far as the approaches of Gath and the gates of Ekron. The Philistine wounded lay all along the road from Shaaraim as far as Gath and Ekron. •From their determined pursuit of the Philistines the Israelites returned 53 and plundered their camp. •And David took the Philistine's head and brought 54 it to Jerusalem; the man's armour he kept in his own tent.

David the conqueror of Goliath is presented to Saul

When Saul saw David going to engage the Philistine he said to Abner, his 55 army commander, 'Abner, whose son is that boy?' 'On your life, O king,' Abner replied 'I do not know.' •So the king said, 'Find out whose son the lad is'.   56

When David came back after killing the Philistine, Abner took him and 57

58 brought him before Saul, with the Philistine's head in his hand. •Saul asked him, 'Whose son are you, young man?' David replied, 'The son of your servant Jesse of Bethlehem'.

1 **18** After David had finished talking to Saul, Jonathan's soul became closely
2 bound to David's and Jonathan came to love him as his own soul. •Saul kept him by him from that day forward and would not let him go back to his
3 father's house. •Jonathan made a pact with David to love him as his own soul;
4 he took off the cloak he was wearing and gave it to David, and his armour too,
5 even his sword, his bow and his belt. •Whenever David went out, on whatever mission Saul sent him, he was successful, and Saul put him in command of the fighting men; he stood well in the people's eyes and in the eyes of Saul's officers too.

The first stirrings of jealousy in Saul

6 On their way back, as David was returning after killing the Philistine, the women came out to meet King Saul from all the towns of Israel, singing and
7 dancing to the sound of tambourine and lyre and cries of joy; •and as they danced the women sang:

> 'Saul has killed his thousands,
> and David his tens of thousands.'

8 Saul was very angry; the incident was not to his liking. 'They have given David the tens of thousands,' he said 'but me only the thousands; he has all but the
9 kingship now.' •And Saul turned a jealous eye on David from that day forward.
10 On the following day an evil spirit from God seized on Saul and he fell into a fit of frenzy while he was in his house. David was playing the harp as on other
11 days and Saul had his spear in his hand. •Saul brandished the spear; 'I am going to pin David to the wall' he said. But David twice evaded him.
12 Saul feared David, for Yahweh was with him but had turned away from Saul.
13 So Saul dismissed him from his presence, making him commander of a thousand;
14 he marched at the head of the people. •In all his enterprises David was successful,
15 and Yahweh was with him. •And seeing how well he succeeded, Saul was fright-
16 ened of him. •But all Israel and Judah loved David, because he was their leader in all their exploits.

David's marriage

17 Saul said to David, 'Here is my elder daughter Merab; I will give her to you in marriage; but you must serve me bravely and fight the battles of Yahweh'—for Saul had made up his mind, 'Let it be not my hand that strikes him down, but
18 the hand of the Philistines!' •David replied to Saul, 'Who am I and what is my ancestry and my father's family in Israel, that I should be the king's son-in-law?'
19 But when the time came for Merab the daughter of Saul to be given to David, she was given in marriage to Adriel of Meholah.
20 Now Michal the daughter of Saul fell in love with David. When Saul heard
21 this he was pleased. •He thought, 'Yes, I will give her to him, but she will prove a snare for him and the hand of the Philistines will strike him'. (Twice Saul said
22 to David, 'Now you shall be my son-in-law'.) •Saul then gave this command to his servants, 'Talk secretly to David and say, "Look, the king is pleased with you and all his servants love you; it is time you became the king's son-in-law"'.
23 The king's servants repeated these words in David's ear, and David replied, 'Does it strike you as an easy thing for me to become the king's son-in-law, poor
24 and of humble position as I am?' •Saul's servants then reported back what
25 David had said. •Saul replied, 'Tell David this, "The king desires no settlement except a hundred foreskins of the Philistines, for vengeance on the king's enemies"'. Saul was planning that David should fall by the hand of the Philistines.
26 His servants brought this message to David and he was delighted at the
27 thought of becoming the king's son-in-law. The time had not yet expired •when

David rose and set off, he and his men, and killed two hundred of the Philistines. David brought back their foreskins and counted them out before the king so that he could be the king's son-in-law. Saul then gave him his daughter Michal in marriage.

Saul now realised that Yahweh was with David, and that all the House of 28 Israel loved him; •then Saul feared David all the more and became David's 29 lasting enemy. •The leaders of the Philistines went out to battle, but every time 30 they went out to battle David was more successful than all Saul's officers, and his name was held in great honour.

Jonathan intervenes on behalf of David

19 Saul told Jonathan his son and all his servants of his intention to kill 1 David. Now Jonathan, Saul's son, held David in great affection; •and so 2 Jonathan warned David; 'My father Saul is looking for a way to kill you,' he said 'so be on your guard tomorrow morning; hide away in some secret place. Then I will go out and keep my father company in the fields where you are hiding, 3 and will talk to my father about you; I will find out what the situation is and let you know.'

So Jonathan spoke well of David to Saul his father; he said, 'Let not the king 4 sin against his servant David, for he has not sinned against you, and what he has done has been greatly to your advantage. •He took his life in his hands 5 when he killed the Philistine, and Yahweh brought about a great victory for all Israel. You saw it yourself and rejoiced; why then sin against innocent blood in killing David without cause?' •Saul was impressed by Jonathan's words and 6 took an oath, 'As Yahweh lives, I will not kill him'. •Jonathan called David 7 and told him all these things. Then Jonathan brought him to Saul, and David attended on him as before.

B. THE FLIGHT OF DAVID

Saul's attempt on David's life

War broke out again and David went out to fight against the Philistines; he 8 inflicted a great defeat on them and they fled before him. •An evil spirit from 9 Yahweh came on Saul while he was sitting in his house with his spear in his hand; David was playing the harp. •Saul tried to pin David to the wall with his spear, 10 but he avoided Saul's thrust and the spear stuck in the wall. David fled and made good his escape.

David is saved by Michal

That same night •Saul sent agents to watch David's house, intending to kill 11 him in the morning. But Michal, David's wife, warned him, 'If you do not escape tonight, you will be a dead man tomorrow'. •Then Michal let David down 12 through the window, and he made off and took to flight and so escaped.

Michal then took the teraphim, laid it on the bed, put a tress of goats' hair on 13 its head and covered it with a garment. •When Saul sent the agents to arrest 14 David, she said, 'He is ill'. •Saul, however, sent the agents back to see David, 15 saying, 'Bring him to me on his bed for me to kill him'. •So they went in, and 16 there on the bed was the teraphim with the tress of goats' hair on its head! •Then 17 Saul said to Michal, 'Why have you deceived me like this and let my enemy go, and so make his escape?' Michal answered Saul, 'He said to me, "Let me go or I will kill you"'.

Saul and David at Ramah with Samuel

So David fled and made his escape, and he went to Samuel at Ramah and told 18 him all that Saul had done to him; he and Samuel went and lived in the huts.

19
20 Word was brought to Saul, 'David is in the huts at Ramah'. •Saul accordingly
sent agents to capture David; when they saw the company of prophets prophesying, and Samuel there as their leader, the spirit of God came on Saul's agents,
21 and they too fell into an ecstasy. •Word of this was brought to Saul and he sent
other agents, and they, too, fell into an ecstasy; Saul then sent a third group of
agents, and they fell into an ecstasy too.
22   He then went to Ramah himself and, coming to the well of the threshing-floor
on the bare hill, asked, 'Where are Samuel and David?' And someone answered,
23 'Why, they are in the huts at Ramah'. •He went on from there to the huts at
Ramah and the spirit of God came on him too, and he went on his way in an ecsta-
24 sy until he came to the huts at Ramah. •He too stripped off his clothes and he too
fell into an ecstasy in the presence of Samuel, and falling down lay there naked
all that day and night. Hence the saying: Is Saul one of the prophets too?

Jonathan helps David to return

1 20 David then fled from the huts at Ramah. And he went and talked to
Jonathan, 'What have I done, what is my guilt and what is my sin
2 against your father that he is seeking my life?' •He answered, 'You must not think
that. He will not kill you. Look, my father does nothing, important or unimpor-
tant, without confiding it to me; why should he hide this from me? It is not true.'
3 But David swore this solemn oath, 'Your father knows very well that I enjoy your
favour, and thinks, "Jonathan must not come to know of this or he will be
grieved". But as Yahweh lives and as you yourself live, there is only a step
between me and death.'
4   Then Jonathan said to David, 'What do you want me to do for you?'
5 David replied, 'Look, tomorrow is New Moon and I should be sitting at table
6 with the king, but you must let me go and hide in the fields till evening. •If your
father notices my absence, you must say, "David asked urgent leave of me to
hurry off to Bethlehem, his own town, because they are holding the annual
7 sacrifice there for all the clan". •If he says, "Very well", your servant is safe, but
8 if he is angry, you may be sure he is set on evil. •Do this favour for your servant,
since you have united yourself with him by a pact in Yahweh's name. But if
9 I am guilty, then kill me yourself—why take me to your father?' •Jonathan
replied, 'You must not think that. If I had certain knowledge that my father
10 was set on bringing evil upon you, would I not tell you?' •David then said to
Jonathan, 'Who will let me know if your father gives you a harsh answer?'
11   'Come,' Jonathan said to David 'let us go out into the fields.' So the pair of
12 them went out into the fields. •Then Jonathan said to David, 'Yahweh the God
of Israel be witness! I will sound my father this time tomorrow; if all is well
13 as concerns David and I do not then inform him, •then may Yahweh do this to
Jonathan and more! If my father thinks fit to do you some harm, I will inform
you and send you away, and you will go unharmed. And may Yahweh be with
14 you as he used to be with my father. •If I am still alive, show me Yahweh's own
15 kindness; if I die, •never withdraw your own kindness from my House. When
16 Yahweh cuts off every one of David's enemies from the face of the earth, •let
not the name of Jonathan be cut off with the House of Saul, or Yahweh will
17 demand a reckoning of David.' •Once again Jonathan swore the solemn oath
to David because he loved him as his own soul.
18   Jonathan said to him, 'Tomorrow is New Moon; your absence will be noticed,
19 for your place will be empty. •The day after tomorrow your absence will be very•
marked, and you must go to the place where you hid on the day of the deed,
20 and you must stay beside the heap of stones there. •For my part, the day after
21 tomorrow I shall be shooting arrows towards it as though at a target. •Then
I shall send a servant to say, "Go and find the arrow". If I say to the servant,
"The arrow is this side of you, get it", come by all means, because it will be safe
22 for you and there will be nothing to fear as sure as Yahweh lives. •But if I say

to the youth, "The arrow is ahead of you", then be off, for Yahweh himself sends
you away. •And as regards the agreement we made, you and I, why, Yahweh is 23
witness between us for ever.'

So David hid in the fields; New Moon came and the king sat down to his 24
meal. •He sat in his usual place, the place by the wall, with Jonathan seated 25
facing him and Abner sitting next to Saul; but David's place was empty. •Saul 26
said nothing that day, thinking, 'Something has happened; he is unclean'. •On 27
the day after New Moon, the second day, David's place was still empty. •Saul 28
said to his son Jonathan, 'Why did not the son of Jesse come to the meal either
yesterday or today?' •Jonathan answered Saul, 'David asked urgent leave of 29
me to go to Bethlehem. "Please let me go," he said "for we are holding the clan
sacrifice in the town and my brothers have ordered me to attend. So now if
you approve of this, let me take my leave and see my brothers." That is why he
has not come to the king's table'.

Then Saul's anger flared up against Jonathan and he said to him, 'You son 30
of a wanton! Do I not know that you are in league with the son of Jesse to your
own disgrace and the disgrace of your mother's nakedness? •As long as the son 31
of Jesse lives on the earth neither your person nor your royal rights are secure. •
Now, send and bring him to me; he is condemned to death.' •Jonathan answered 32
Saul his father and said, 'Why should he die? What has he done?' •But Saul 33
brandished his spear at him to strike him down, and Jonathan knew then that
his father had already made up his mind that David should die. •Hot with 34
anger Jonathan rose from the table and took no food that second day of the
New Moon, being grieved on David's account because his father had insulted him.

Next morning Jonathan went out into the fields for the agreed meeting with 35
David, taking a young servant with him. •He said to his servant, 'Run and find 36
the arrows I am going to shoot', and the servant ran while Jonathan shot an arrow
ahead of him. •When the servant reached the place where Jonathan had shot 37
the arrow, Jonathan shouted after him, 'Is not the arrow ahead of you?' •Again 38
Jonathan shouted after the servant, 'Be quick, hurry, do not stand about'.
Jonathan's servant picked up the arrow and brought it back to his master. •The 39
servant suspected nothing; only Jonathan and David knew what was meant.

Jonathan then gave his weapons to his servant and said, 'Go and carry them 40
to the town'. •When the servant went off, David rose from beside the hillock 41
and fell with his face to the ground and bowed down three times. Then they
kissed each other and both shed many tears. •Then Jonathan said to David, 42
'Go in peace. And as regards the oath that both of us have sworn in the name
of Yahweh, may Yahweh be witness between you and me, between your descendants and mine for ever.' 21 David then rose and left, and Jonathan went $^1_{43}$
back to the town.

David and the priest at Nob

David went to Nob, to Ahimelech the priest. Ahimelech came out trembling $^2_1$
to meet David and said, 'Why are you alone and no one with you?' •David replied $^3_2$
to Ahimelech the priest, 'The king has given me an order and said to me, "Let
no one know anything of the mission I am sending you on, nor of the order I am
giving you". As regards my soldiers, I have arranged to meet them at such and
such a place. •Meanwhile if you have five loaves of bread to hand, give them $^4_3$
to me, or whatever there is.' •The priest replied to David, 'I have no ordinary $^5_4$
bread to hand; there is only consecrated bread—provided your soldiers have
kept themselves from women?'

David replied to the priest, 'Certainly, women are forbidden us, as always $^6_5$
when I set off on a campaign. The soldiers' things are pure. Though this is a
profane journey, they are certainly pure today as far as their things are concerned.' •The priest then gave him what had been consecrated, for the only $^7_6$
bread there was the bread of offering which is taken away from the presence of
Yahweh to be replaced by warm bread when it is removed.

8/7   Now one of Saul's servants happened to be there that day, detained in the presence of Yahweh; his name was Doeg the Edomite and he was the chief of Saul's guardsmen.

9/8   David then said to Ahimelech, 'Have you no spear or sword here to hand? I did not bring either my sword or my weapons with me, because the king's
10/9   business was pressing.' •The priest replied, 'The sword of Goliath the Philistine whom you killed in the Valley of the Terebinth is over there wrapped up in a cloth behind the ephod; if you wish to take it, do so, for there is no other here'. David said, 'There is none like it; give it to me'.

David with the Philistines

11/10 That day David left, fleeing from Saul and went to Achish the king of Gath.
12/11 But the servants of Achish said, 'Is not this David, the king of the country? Was it not of him they sang in the dance:

> "Saul has killed his thousands,
> and David his tens of thousands"?'

13/12 David pondered these words and became very frightened of Achish the king
14/13 of Gath. •When their eyes were on him he played the madman and, when they held him, feigned lunacy. He would drum on the doors of the gate and let his spittle run down his beard.

15/14 Achish said to his servants, 'You can see this man is mad. Why bring him
16/15 to me? •Have I not enough madmen without your bringing me this one to weary me with his antics? Is he to join my household?'

C. DAVID THE OUTLAW

David begins his wanderings

1   **22** David left there and took refuge in the Cave of Adullam; his brothers
2   and all his father's family heard of it and joined him there. •All the oppressed, those in distress, all those in debt, anyone who had a grievance, gathered round him and he became their leader. There were about four hundred men with him.

3   David went from there to Mizpah in Moab and said to the king of Moab, 'Allow my father and mother to stay with you until I know what God intends
4   to do for me'. •He left them with the king of Moab and they stayed with him all the time that David was in the stronghold.

5   But the prophet Gad said to David, 'Do not stay in the stronghold; go and make your way into the land of Judah.' So David went away and came to the forest of Hereth.

The massacre of the priests of Nob

6   Saul came to hear that David and the men with him had been discovered. Saul was at Gibeah, seated under the tamarisk on the high place, spear in hand,
7   with his officers standing round him. •'Listen, men of Benjamin,' Saul said to his officers standing round him, 'is the son of Jesse ready to give you all fields and vineyards and to make all of you commanders of thousands and commanders
8   of hundreds •that you all conspire against me? No one told me when my son made a pact with the son of Jesse; none of you felt sorry for me or told me when my son incited my servant to become my enemy, as is now the case.'

9   Doeg the Edomite then spoke up—he was standing near Saul's officers: 'I saw the son of Jesse come to Nob,' he said 'to Ahimelech son of Ahitub.
10   This man consulted Yahweh for him, gave him provisions and also the sword
11   of Goliath the Philistine.' •Then the king sent and summoned the priest Ahimelech son of Ahitub and his whole family, the priests of Nob; they all came to the king

Saul said, 'Now listen, son of Ahitub'. He answered, 'I am here, my lord'. 12
'Why have you conspired against me,' Saul said 'you and the son of Jesse, 13
giving him bread and a sword and consulting God on his behalf, for him to rebel
against me as is now the case?' •Ahimelech answered the king, 'Who among all 14
your servants is as faithful as David, son-in-law to the king, captain of your
bodyguard, honoured in your household? •Was today the first time I ever 15
consulted God on his behalf? Far be it from me to do otherwise! Let not the
king bring any charge against his servant or against his whole family, for your
servant knew nothing whatever of the whole affair.' •But the king answered, 16
'Most surely you shall die, Ahimelech, you and your whole family'.

The king said to the guardsmen who were standing beside him, 'Step forward 17
and put the priests of Yahweh to death, for they too have supported David,
they knew he was making his escape yet did not tell me'. But the king's servants
would not lift a hand to strike the priests of Yahweh. •The king then said to 18
Doeg, 'You step forward and strike the priests'. Doeg the Edomite stepped
forward and struck the priests himself, that day killing eighty-five men who wore
the linen ephod. •As for Nob, the town of the priests, Saul put it to the sword, 19
men and women, children and infants, cattle and donkeys and sheep.

One son only of Ahimelech son of Ahitub escaped. His name was Abiathar, 20
and he fled away to join David •and told him that Saul had slaughtered the 21
priests of Yahweh. •David said to Abiathar, 'I knew that day, when Doeg the 22
Edomite was there, he would be sure to inform Saul. I am responsible for the
death of all your kinsmen. •Stay with me, have no fear, for he who seeks your life 23
seeks mine too; you will be safe with me.'

David at Keilah

23 They brought the news to David, 'The Philistines are fighting against Keilah 1
and are plundering the threshing-floors'. •David consulted Yahweh, 'Shall 2
I go and fight these Philistines?' Yahweh answered David, 'Go and fight the
Philistines and save Keilah'. •But David's men said to him, 'We go in fear here 3
in Judah; how much more, then, if we go to Keilah to fight against the Philistines?'
So David consulted Yahweh again and Yahweh replied, 'Be on your way; go 4
down to Keilah for I will give the Philistines into your power'. •So David and 5
his men went to Keilah and fought the Philistines, and carried off their cattle
and inflicted a great defeat on them. Thus David saved the inhabitants of Keilah.
Now when Abiathar son of Ahimelech took refuge with David, he went down to 6
Keilah with the ephod in his hand.

When word was brought to Saul that David had gone to Keilah he said, 'God 7
has delivered him into my power, for he has walked into a trap by going into
a town with gates and bars'. •Saul called all the people to arms, to go down to 8
Keilah and besiege David and his men. •David, however, was aware that Saul 9
was plotting evil against him and said to Abiathar the priest, 'Bring the ephod'.
David said, 'Yahweh, God of Israel, your servant has heard that Saul is preparing 10
to come to Keilah and destroy the town because of me. •Will Saul come down 11
as your servant has heard? Yahweh, God of Israel, I beg you, let your servant
know.' Yahweh replied, 'He will come down'. •Then David asked, 'Will the 12
townsmen of Keilah hand me and my men over to Saul?' Yahweh replied, 'They
will hand you over'. •At this, David made off with his men, about six hundred in 13
number; they left Keilah and went where they could. When the news was brought to
Saul that David had escaped from Keilah, he abandoned the expedition.

David stayed in the wilderness, in the strongholds; he stayed in the mountains, 14
in the wilderness of Ziph; Saul searched for him continually, but God did not
deliver him into his power.

David at Horesh. A visit from Jonathan

David was afraid because Saul had mounted an expedition to take his life. 15
At that time he was at Horesh in the wilderness of Ziph. •Jonathan son of 16

Saul set off and went to David at Horesh and encouraged him in the name of
17 God. •'Have no fear,' he told him 'for the hand of my father Saul will not reach
you; you are the one who is to reign over Israel, and I shall be second to you.
18 Saul my father is himself aware of this.' •And the two made a pact in the presence
of Yahweh. David stayed at Horesh and Jonathan went home.

David has a narrow escape from Saul

19   Now some men of Ziph went up to Saul at Gibeah. 'Is not David in hiding
among us' they said 'in the strongholds at Horesh, on the Hill of Hachilah
20 to the south of the wastelands? •Now whenever you wish to go down, O king,
21 do so; it will be our task to deliver him into the king's power.' •Saul replied,
22 'May you be blessed by Yahweh, for coming to help me. •Go now, make surer
still. Find out and note the place his footsteps hurry to, for I have been told
23 he is very cunning. •Take careful notice of all the hiding places where he lurks,
and come back to me when you are certain. I will then come to you; and if he
is in the country, I will track him down through all the clans of Judah.'
24   So they set off and went to Ziph ahead of Saul. Meanwhile, David and his
men were in the wilderness of Maon, in the plain to the south of the wastelands.
25 When Saul and his men set out in search of him, David was informed of it and
went down to the rock that is in the wilderness of Maon. Saul heard of this
26 and pursued David into the wilderness of Maon. •Saul and his men proceeded
along one side of the mountain, David and his men along the other. David was
hurrying to get away from Saul, while Saul with his men was trying to outflank
27 David and his men and so capture them, •when a messenger came to Saul and
28 said, 'Come at once, the Philistines have invaded the country'. •So Saul broke
off his pursuit of David and went to fight the Philistines. This is why that place
is called the Rock of Divisions.

David spares Saul

1 **24** David went away from there, and stayed in the strongholds of Engedi.
2 When Saul returned from pursuing the Philistines, he was told, 'David is
3 now in the wilderness of Engedi'. •Saul thereupon took three thousand men
chosen from the whole of Israel and went in search of David and his men east
4 of the Rocks of the Wild Goats. •He came to the sheepfolds along the route
where there was a cave, and went in to cover his feet.ᵃ Now David and his men
5 were sitting in the recesses of the cave; •David's men said to him, 'Today is the
day of which Yahweh said to you, "I will deliver your enemy into your power,
do what you like with him" '. David stood up and, unobserved, cut off the
6 border of Saul's cloak. •Afterwards David reproached himself for having cut off
7 the border of Saul's cloak. •He said to his men, 'Yahweh preserve me from
doing such a thing to my lord and raising my hand against him, for he is the
8 anointed of Yahweh'. •David gave his men strict instructions, forbidding them
to attack Saul.
9   Saul then left the cave and went on his way. •After this, David too left the
cave and called after Saul, 'My lord king!' Saul looked behind him and David
10 bowed to the ground and did homage. •Then David said to Saul, 'Why do you
11 listen to the men who say to you, "David means to harm you"? •Why, your
own eyes have seen today how Yahweh put you in my power in the cave
and how I refused to kill you, but spared you. "I will not raise my hand
12 against my lord," I said "for he is the anointed of Yahweh." •O my father, see,
look at the border of your cloak in my hand. Since I cut off the border of your
cloak, yet did not kill you, you must acknowledge frankly that there is neither
malice nor treason in my mind. I have not offended against you, yet you hunt
13 me down to take my life. •May Yahweh be judge between me and you, and may
14 Yahweh avenge me on you; but my hand shall not be laid on you. •(As the old

24 a. The common euphemism for 'to relieve himself'.

proverb says: Wickedness goes out from the wicked, and my hand will not be laid on you.) •On whose trail has the king of Israel set out? On whose trail 15 are you in hot pursuit? On the trail of a dead dog! On the trail of a single flea! May Yahweh be the judge and decide between me and you; may he take up my 16 cause and defend it and give judgement for me, freeing me from your power.'

When David had finished saying these words to Saul, Saul said, 'Is that your 17 voice, my son David?' And Saul wept aloud. •'You are a more upright man 18 than I,' he said to David 'for you have repaid me with good while I have repaid you with evil. •Today you have crowned your goodness toward me since 19 Yahweh had put me in your power yet you did not kill me. •When a man 20 comes on his enemy, does he let him go unmolested? May Yahweh reward you for the goodness you have shown me today. •Now I know you will indeed 21 reign and that the sovereignty in Israel will be secure in your hands. •Now 22 swear to me by Yahweh that you will not cut off my descendants after me nor blot out my name from my family.' •This David swore to Saul and Saul went 23 home while David and his men with him went back to the stronghold.

The death of Samuel

25 Samuel died and the whole of Israel assembled to mourn him. They buried 1 him at his home in Ramah.

The story of Nabal and Abigail

David then set off and went down to the wilderness of Maon.

Now there was a man in Maon whose business was at Carmel, a man of 2 means who owned three thousand sheep and a thousand goats. He was engaged in shearing his sheep at Carmel. •The man's name was Nabal and his wife's 3 Abigail. She was a woman of intelligence and beauty, but the man was brutish and ill-mannered. He was a Calebite.

When David learned in the wilderness that Nabal was at his sheepshearing, 4 he sent ten soldiers, saying to them,ᵃ 'Go up to Carmel, visit Nabal and greet 5 him in my name. •You are to say this to my brother, "Peace to you, peace 6 to your House, peace to all that is yours! •I hear that you have the shearers; 7 now your shepherds were with us and we did not molest them, nor did they find anything missing all the time they were at Carmel. •Ask your soldiers and they 8 will tell you. May these soldiers win your favour, for we come on a day of feasting. Whatever you have to hand please give to your servants and to David your son." '

David's soldiers came and said all this to Nabal in David's name, and waited. 9 Then Nabal answered David's soldiers, 'Who is David? Who is the son of Jesse? 10 There are many servants nowadays who run away from their masters. •Am I to 11 take my bread and my wine and the meat I have slaughtered for my shearers and give it to men who come from I do not know where?' •David's soldiers 12 turned away and went back the way they had come, and they told all this to David. Then David said to his men, 'Every man buckle on his sword!' And they 13 buckled on their swords, and David buckled on his too; about four hundred men followed David while two hundred remained with the baggage.

Now one of the servants had brought the news to Abigail, Nabal's wife. 14 He said, 'David sent messengers from the wilderness to greet our master, but he flared out at them. •Now these men were very good to us; they did not molest 15 us and we did not find anything missing all the time we were out in the fields while we were in their neighbourhood. •They were a protection to us night and 16 day, all the time we were in their neighbourhood minding the sheep. •Now bear 17 this in mind and see what you can do, for the ruin of our master and of his whole House is decided on, and he is so ill-tempered no one can say a word to him.'

Abigail hastily took two hundred loaves, two skins of wine, five sheep ready 18 prepared, five measures of roasted grain, a hundred bunches of raisins and two

19 hundred cakes of figs and loaded them on donkeys. •She said to her servants, 'Go on ahead of me, I will follow you'—but she did not tell her husband.

20 As she was riding her donkey down behind a spur of the mountain, David and his men happened to be coming down in her direction; and she met 21 them. •Now David had decided, 'It was a waste of time guarding all this man's property in the wilderness. Nothing was missing of all he had, and yet he 22 returned evil for good. •May God do this to David and more if by morning 23 I leave one male alive of all those who belong to him!' •As soon as Abigail saw David she quickly dismounted from the donkey and, falling on her face 24 before David, bowed down to the ground. •She fell at his feet and said, 'Let me take the blame, my lord. Let your servant speak in your ear; listen to the words 25 of your servant. •Pay no attention to this ill-tempered man Nabal for his nature is like his name; "Brute" is his name and brutish his character. 26 But I your servant did not see the soldiers my lord had sent. •And now, my lord, as Yahweh lives and as your soul lives, by Yahweh who kept you from the crime of bloodshed and from taking vengeance with your own hand, may your 27 enemies, and all those who plan evil against my lord become like Nabal. •As for the present your servant brings my lord, let it be given to the soldiers of 28 my lord's own following. •I ask you to forgive your servant's fault, for then Yahweh will grant my lord a lasting dynasty, for my lord is fighting the battles of Yahweh, and in all your life there is no wickedness to be found in you. 29 Should men set out to hunt you down and try to take your life, my lord's life will be kept close in the satchel of life with Yahweh your God, while as for the 30 lives of your enemies he will fling them away, as from a sling. •When Yahweh has done for my lord all the good he has promised you, when he has made you 31 prince over Israel, •you do not want to have any reason to grieve or feel remorse at having shed blood needlessly and avenged yourself with your own hand. And when Yahweh has shown his goodness to my lord, then remember your servant.'

32 David said to Abigail, 'Blessed be Yahweh, the God of Israel, who sent you 33 to meet me today! •Blessed be your wisdom and blessed you yourself for restraining me today from the crime of bloodshed and from avenging myself 34 with my own hand! •But as Yahweh the God of Israel lives, he who kept me from harming you, had you not hurried out to meet me, I swear that 35 Nabal would not have had one male left alive by the morning.' •David then accepted from her what she had brought him and said, 'Go home in peace; see, I have listened to you and have granted your request'.

36 Abigail returned to Nabal. He was holding a feast, a princely feast, in his house; Nabal was in high spirits, and as he was very drunk she told him nothing 37 at all till it was daylight. •In the morning then, when the wine had left him, his wife told him all that had happened and his heart died inside him and he 38 became like a stone. •About ten days later Yahweh struck Nabal, and he died.

39 When David heard that Nabal was dead, he said, 'Blessed be Yahweh who has avenged the insult I received at Nabal's hands and has restrained his servant from doing evil; Yahweh has brought Nabal's wickedness down on his own head.'

40 David then sent Abigail an offer of marriage. •When David's servants came to Abigail at Carmel, they said, 'David has sent us to you to take you to him 41 as his wife.' •She rose and bowed down her face to the ground. 'Consider your 42 servant a slave' she said 'to wash the feet of my lord's servants.' •Quickly Abigail stood up again and mounted a donkey; followed by five of her slave-girls she followed David's messengers and became his wife.

43
44 David had also married Ahinoam of Jezreel and he kept them both as wives. •Saul had given Michal his daughter, the wife of David, to Palti son of Laish, from Gallim.

25 a. Shearing is a time of festival when the owner of the flock should be generous; David is choosing the best time to make the levy on neighbouring villages customarily made by nomads under 'the law of brotherhood'.

David spares Saul

26 Now the men of Ziph came to Saul at Gibeah. 'Is not David in hiding' 1
they said 'on the Hill of Hachilah on the edge of the wastelands?' •So Saul 2
set off and went down to the wilderness of Ziph, accompanied by three thousand
men chosen from Israel to search for David in the wilderness of Ziph. •Saul 3
pitched camp on the Hill of Hachilah, which is on the edge of the wastelands,
by the roadside. David was then living in the wilderness and saw that Saul was
coming after him there. •Accordingly, David sent out spies and learned that Saul 4
had indeed arrived. •Setting off, David went to the place where Saul had pitched 5
camp. He saw the place where Saul and Abner son of Ner commander of his army
were lying. Saul was lying inside the camp with the troops bivouacking round him.

Speaking to Ahimelech the Hittite and Abishai son of Zeruiah and brother of 6
Joab, David said, 'Who will come down with me into the camp of Saul?' Abishai
answered, 'I will go down with you'. •So in the dark David and Abishai made 7
their way towards the force, where they found Saul lying asleep inside the camp,
his spear stuck in the ground beside his head, with Abner and the troops lying
round him.

Then Abishai said to David, 'Today God has put your enemy in your 8
power; so now let me pin him to the ground with his own spear. Just one
stroke! I will not need to strike him twice.' •David answered Abishai, 'Do not 9
kill him, for who can lift his hand against Yahweh's anointed and be without
guilt? •As Yahweh lives,' David said 'Yahweh himself will strike him down, 10
whether his time to die comes, or he goes out to battle and perishes then.
Yahweh forbid that I should raise my hand against Yahweh's anointed! But now 11
take the spear beside his head and the pitcher of water and let us go away.'
David took the spear and the pitcher of water from beside Saul's head, and 12
they made off. No one saw, no one knew, no one woke up; they were all asleep,
for a deep sleep from Yahweh had fallen on them.

David crossed to the other side and halted on the top of the mountain a 13
long way off; there was a wide space between them. •David then called out to 14
the troops and to Abner son of Ner, 'Abner, will you not answer?' Abner replied,
'Who is that calling?' •David said to Abner, 'Are you not a man? Who is your 15
like in Israel? Why did you not guard your lord the king then? Some man of
the people came to kill the king your lord. •What you did was not well done. 16
As Yahweh lives, you all deserve to die since you did not guard your lord,
Yahweh's anointed. Look where the king's spear is now, and the pitcher of
water that was beside his head.'

Then Saul recognised David's voice and said, 'Is that your voice, my son 17
David?' David answered, 'It is my voice, my lord king. •Why does my lord 18
pursue his servant?' he said. 'What have I done? What evil am I guilty of? •May 19
my lord king now listen to the words of his servant: if Yahweh himself has
incited you against me, let him accept an offering; but if men have done it,
may they be accursed before Yahweh, for now they have driven me out so that
I have no share in the heritage of Yahweh. They have said, "Go and serve other
gods".*a* •So now, do not let my blood fall to the ground out of the presence 20
of Yahweh; for the king of Israel has gone out in quest of my life as a man
hunts a partridge on the mountains.'

Saul replied, 'I have sinned. Come back, my son David; I will never harm 21
you again since you have shown such respect for my life today. Yes, my course
has been folly and my error grave.' •David answered, 'Here is the king's spear. 22
Let one of the soldiers come across and take it. •Yahweh repays everyone for 23
his uprightness and loyalty. Today Yahweh put you in my power, but
I would not raise my hand against Yahweh's anointed. •Just as today your life 24
counted for much in my sight, so shall my life count for much in the sight of
Yahweh and he will deliver me from all distress.'

Then Saul said to David, 'May you be blessed, my son David! You will do 25
great things and will succeed.' Then David went on his way and Saul returned home.

D. DAVID AMONG THE PHILISTINES

He takes refuge at Gath

27 ¹ 'One of these days' David thought 'I shall perish at the hand of Saul. I can do no better than escape to the land of the Philistines; then Saul will give up tracking me through the length and breadth of Israel and ² I shall be safe from him.' •So David set off and went, he and the six hundred ³ men who were with him, down to Achish son of Maoch the king of Gath. •He settled at Gath with Achish, he and his men, each with his family and David with his two wives, Ahinoam of Jezreel and Abigail the wife of Nabal from ⁴ Carmel. •When news reached Saul that David had fled to Gath, he stopped searching for him.

David as vassal of the Philistines

⁵ David said to Achish, 'If you will grant me a favour, let me be given a place in one of the country towns for me to settle in. Why should your servant live ⁶ in the royal city with you?' •So that day Achish gave him Ziklag, and for this reason Ziklag has been the property of the kings of Judah to the present day. ⁷ The length of time that David stayed in Philistine territory was a year and four months.

⁸ David and his men went out on raids against the Geshurites, Girzites and Amalekites, for these are the tribes inhabiting the region that goes from Telam ⁹ in the direction of Shur and as far as the land of Egypt. •David laid the country-side waste and left neither man nor woman alive but took the sheep and oxen, ¹⁰ donkeys, camels and garments and came back, bringing them to Achish. •Achish would ask, 'Where did you go raiding today?' David would reply, 'Against the Negeb of Judah', or 'the Negeb of Jerahmeel', or 'the Negeb of the Kenites.'ᵃ ¹¹ But David never brought a man or woman back alive to Gath 'in case' as he thought 'they inform against us and say, "David did such and such"'. This ¹² was David's practice all the time he stayed in Philistine territory. •Achish trusted David. 'He has made himself hated by his own people Israel' he thought 'and so will be my servant for ever.'

The Philistines go to war against Israel

28 ¹ At that time the Philistines mustered their forces for war to fight Israel, and Achish said to David, 'It is understood that you join forces with me, ² you and your men?' •David answered Achish, 'In that case, you will soon see what your servant can do.' Achish replied to David, 'Right, I shall appoint you as my permanent bodyguard.'

Saul and the witch of En-dor

³ Now Samuel was dead, and all Israel had mourned him and buried him at Ramah, his own town. Saul had expelled the necromancers and wizards from the country.

⁴ Meanwhile the Philistines had mustered and pitched camp at Shunem. ⁵ Saul mustered all Israel and they encamped at Gilboa. •When Saul saw the Philistine camp he was afraid and there was a great trembling in his heart. ⁶ Saul consulted Yahweh, but Yahweh gave him no answer, either by dream or ⁷ oracle or prophet. •Then Saul said to his servants, 'Find a woman who is a necromancer for me to go and consult her'. His servants replied, 'There is a necromancer at En-dor'.

⁸ And so Saul, disguising himself and changing his clothes, set out accompanied by two men; their visit to the woman took place at night. 'Disclose the

26 a. To be exiled was to be outside Yahweh's territory.
27 a. In fact, none of the raids was against the men of Judah or their allies such as the Kenites.

future to me' he said 'by means of a ghost. Conjure up the one I shall name
to you.' •The woman answered, 'Look, you know what Saul has done, how he 9
has swept the necromancers and wizards out of the country; why are you setting
a trap for my life, then, to have me killed?' •But Saul swore to her by Yahweh, 10
'As Yahweh lives,' he said 'no blame shall attach to you for this business.'
Then the woman asked, 'Whom shall I conjure up for you?' He replied, 'Conjure 11
up Samuel'.

Then the woman saw Samuel and, giving a great cry, she said to Saul, 12
•Why have you deceived me? You are Saul. •The king said, 'Do not be afraid! 13
What do you see?' The woman answered Saul, 'I see a ghost rising up from the
earth'. •'What is he like?' he asked. She answered, 'It is an old man coming up; 14
he is wrapped in a cloak'. Then Saul knew it was Samuel and he bowed down
his face to the ground and did homage.

Then Samuel said to Saul, 'Why have you disturbed my rest, conjuring me up?' 15
Saul replied, 'I am in great distress; the Philistines are waging war against me,
and God has abandoned me and no longer answers me either by prophet or
dream; and so I have summoned you to tell me what I must do'. •Samuel said, 16
'And why do you consult me, when Yahweh has abandoned you and is with
your neighbour? •Yahweh has done to you as he foretold through me; he has 17
snatched the sovereignty from your hand and given it to your neighbour, David,
because you disobeyed the voice of Yahweh and did not execute his fierce anger 18
against Amalek. That is why Yahweh treats you like this now. •What is more, 19
Yahweh will deliver Israel and you, too, into the power of the Philistines.
Tomorrow you and your sons will be with me; and Israel's army, too, for
Yahweh will deliver it into the power of the Philistines.'

Saul was overcome and fell full-length on the ground. He was terrified by 20
what Samuel had said and, besides this, he was weakened by having eaten
nothing at all that day and all that night. •The woman then came to Saul, and seeing 21
his terror said, 'Look, your servant has obeyed your voice; I have taken my life
in my hands, and have obeyed the command you gave me. •So now you in your 22
turn listen to what your servant says. Let me set a little food before you for
you to eat and get some strength for your journey.' •But he refused. 'I will 23
not eat' he said. His servants however pressed him, and so did the woman.
Allowing himself to be persuaded by them, he rose from the ground and sat
on the divan. •The woman owned a fattened calf which she quickly slaughtered, 24
and she took some flour and kneaded it and with it baked cakes of unleavened
bread; •she put these before Saul and his servants; and after they had eaten 25
they set off and left the same night.

David is sent away by the Philistine leaders

29 The Philistines mustered all their forces at Aphek while the Israelites 1
were encamped near the spring which is in Jezreel. •The Philistine lords 2
paraded in their groups of a hundred and a thousand, with David and his men
bringing up the rear with Achish. •The Philistine leaders asked, 'Who are these 3
Hebrews?' Achish replied to the Philistine leaders, 'Why, this is David the
servant of Saul, king of Israel, who has been with me for the last one or two
years. I have had no fault to find with him from the day he gave himself up
to me to the present time.' •But the Philistine leaders were angry with him. 4
'Send the man back,' they said 'let him return to the place you assigned him.
He must not go down with us to battle, in case he turns on us once battle is
joined. Would there be a better way for the man to regain his master's favour
than with the heads of these men here? •Is not this the David of whom they 5
sang in the dance:

> "Saul has killed his thousands,
> David his tens of thousands"?'

6 So Achish called David and said, 'As Yahweh lives, you are loyal, and to
me it seems only right you should accompany me in the campaign, for I have
found nothing wrong in you from the day you came to me to the present time.
7 But you are not acceptable to the leaders. •So go back, and go in peace, rather
than antagonise the leaders of the Philistines.'

8 'But what have I done,' David asked Achish 'what fault have you had to
find with your servant from the day I entered your service to the present time,
for me not to be allowed to go and fight the enemies of my lord the king?'
9 Achish answered, 'You know that in my sight you are as blameless as an angel
of God; but the Philistine leaders have said, "He must not go out with us to
10 battle". •So now, get up early in the morning, you and your master's servants
who came with you, and go to the place I assigned you. Let there be no rancour
in your heart, for to me you are blameless. You must get up early in the
morning and when it is light enough you must be off.'

11 So David rose early, he and his men, and set off in the morning to return
to the land of the Philistines. The Philistines went up to Jezreel.

The campaign against the Amalekites

1 **30** Now by the time David and his men reached Ziklag on the third day, the
Amalekites had raided the Negeb and Ziklag; they had stormed Ziklag and
2 burnt it down. •They had taken the women captive with all those who were
there, both small and great. They had not killed anyone, but taken the prisoners
3 and gone on their way. •When David and his men arrived, they found the town
4 burnt down and their wives and sons and daughters taken captive. •Then David
and the people with him wept aloud till they were too weak to weep any more.
5 David's two wives had been taken captive, Ahinoam of Jezreel and Abigail the
wife of Nabal from Carmel.

6 David was in great trouble, for the people were talking of stoning him; all
the people were bitter in soul, each for his sons and daughters. But David took
7 courage from Yahweh his God. •To the priest Abiathar son of Ahimelech David
8 said, 'Bring me the ephod'. Abiathar brought the ephod to David. •Then David
consulted Yahweh, 'Am I to go in pursuit of these raiders? Shall I overtake them?'
The answer was, 'Go in pursuit; you will certainly overtake them and rescue the
9 captives'. •David accordingly set off with the six hundred men who were with
10 him, and reached the wadi Besor. •David then continued the pursuit with four
hundred men, two hundred staying behind who were too exhausted to cross the
wadi Besor.

11 Out in the country they found an Egyptian and brought him to David. They
12 gave him bread which he ate, and water to drink; •they also gave him a piece
of fig cake and two bunches of raisins; he ate these and his spirits revived, for
he had neither eaten bread nor drunk water for three days and three nights.
13 David then said to him, 'Whose man are you and where do you come from?' He
answered, 'I am a young Egyptian, the slave of an Amalekite; my master aban-
14 doned me because I fell sick three days ago. •We raided the Negeb of the
Cherethites, and the Negeb of Judah, and the Negeb of Caleb too, and we burnt
15 Ziklag down.' •David said, 'Will you lead me down to these raiders?' He replied,
'Swear to me by God not to kill me or hand me over to my master and I will lead
you down to these raiders'.

16 And when he led him down there they were, scattered over the whole
countryside, eating, drinking and rejoicing, because of the enormous booty they
17 had taken from the land of the Philistines and from the land of Judah. •David
struck them down from dawn till evening, putting them under the ban. None
18 escaped except for four hundred soldiers who mounted camels and fled. •David
set free all whom the Amalekites had captured. David set his two wives free also.
19 Nothing was missing, whether small or great, booty or sons and daughters,
20 everything that had been captured; David brought all back. •They captured the

flocks and herds as well and drove them in front of him. 'This is David's booty' they shouted.

Then David came to the two hundred men who had been too exhausted to 21 follow him, those he had left at the wadi Besor; they came out to meet David and the troops with him, and, approaching David and the troops, asked how they had fared. •But all the rogues and scoundrels among the men who had 22 gone with David said, 'They did not go with us so we will not give them any of the booty we have rescued, though each can take his wife and children away and go'. •But David said, 'Do not act like this after what Yahweh has done 23 for us; he has protected us, delivering into our hands the raiders who set on us. Who would agree with you on this? No: 24

'As the share is of him who goes down to the battle,
    so is the share of him who stays with the baggage.

'They must share alike.' •And from that day forward he made this a statute 25 and an ordinance for Israel which obtains to the present day.

When David came to Ziklag he sent parts of the booty to the elders of Judah, 26 proportionate to their towns, with this message, 'Here is a present for you from the booty taken from the enemies of Yahweh':

for those in Bethel,   27
for those in Ramoth of the Negeb,
for those in Jattir,   28
for those in Aroer,
for those in Siphmoth,
for those in Eshtemoa,
for those in Carmel,   29
for those in the towns of Jerahmeel,
for those in the towns of the Kenites,
for those in Hormah,   30
for those in Borashan,
for those in Athach,
for those in Hebron   31

and for all the places which David and his men had frequented.

The battle of Gilboa and the death of Saul

31 The Philistines made war on Israel and the men of Israel fled from 1 the Philistines and were slaughtered on Mount Gilboa. •The Philistines 2 pressed Saul and his sons hard and killed Jonathan, Abinadab and Malchishua, the sons of Saul. •The fighting grew heavy about Saul; the bowmen took him 3 off his guard, so that he fell wounded by the bowmen. •Then Saul said to his 4 armour-bearer, 'Draw your sword and run me through with it; I do not want these uncircumcised men to come and gloat over me'. But his armour-bearer was afraid and would not do it. So Saul took his own sword and fell on it. •His 5 armour-bearer, seeing that Saul was dead, fell on his sword too and died with him. •And so Saul and his three sons and his armour-bearer died together 6 that day. •When the Israelites who were on the other side of the valley saw that 7 the men of Israel had taken flight and that Saul and his sons were dead, they abandoned their towns and fled. The Philistines then came and occupied them.

When the Philistines came on the following day to strip the dead, they found 8 Saul and his three sons lying on Mount Gilboa. •They cut off his head and, 9 stripping him of his armour, had it carried round the land of the Philistines to proclaim the good news to their idols and their people. •They placed his 10 armour in the temple of Astarte; they fastened his body to the wall of Beth-shan.

11 When the inhabitants of Jabesh-gilead[a] heard what the Philistines had done
12 to Saul, •all the warriors set out, marching throughout the night, and took the
bodies of Saul and his sons off the wall of Beth-shan, and bringing them to
13 Jabesh they burned them there. •Then they took their bones and buried them
under the tamarisk of Jabesh, and fasted for seven days.

THE SECOND BOOK OF SAMUEL

David learns of Saul's death

1 After the death of Saul, David returned from his rout of the Amalekites and
2 spent two days in Ziklag. •On the third day a man came from the camp
where Saul had been, his garments torn and earth on his head. When he came
3 to David, he fell to the ground and did homage. •'Where do you come from?'
4 David asked him. 'I have escaped from the Israelite camp' he said. •David said
to him, 'What happened? Tell me.' He replied, 'The people have fled from the
battlefield and many of them have fallen. Saul and his son Jonathan are dead
too.'
5 David then asked the young soldier who brought the news, 'How do you
6 know that Saul and his son Jonathan are dead?' •'I happened to be on Mount
Gilboa,' the young soldier replied 'and there was Saul, leaning on his spear,
7 with the chariots and the cavalry pressing him hard. •Then he turned round
8 and saw me, and shouted to me. I answered, "Here I am". •He said, "Who are
9 you?" "An Amalekite" I replied. •Then he said, "Stand over me and kill me, for
10 a giddiness has come on me, though my life is wholly in me still". •So I stood
over him and killed him, because I knew that once he fell he could not survive.
Then I took the crown he wore on his head and the bracelet on his arm, and
I have brought them here to my lord.'
11 Then David took hold of his garments and tore them, and all the men with
12 him did the same. •They mourned and wept and fasted until the evening for
Saul and his son Jonathan, for the people of Yahweh and for the House of
Israel, because they had fallen by the sword.
13 David said to the young soldier who had brought the news, 'Where are you
14 from?' 'I am the son of a resident alien,' he answered 'an Amalekite.' •David
said, 'How is it you were not afraid to lift your hand to destroy Yahweh's
15 anointed?' •Then David called one of his soldiers. 'Come here,' he said 'strike
16 him down.' The man struck him and he died. •'Your blood be on your own
head,' David said 'for your own lips gave evidence against you when you
said, "I killed Yahweh's anointed".'

David's elegy over Saul and Jonathan

17
18 Then David made this lament over Saul and his son Jonathan. •It is written
in the Book of the Just,[a] so that it may be taught to the sons of Judah. It runs:

19 Alas, the glory of Israel has been slain on your heights!
How did the heroes fall?

20 Do not speak of it in Gath,
nor announce it in the streets of Ashkelon,
or the daughters of the Philistines will rejoice,
the daughters of the uncircumcised will gloat.

31 a. They had been rescued by Saul, ch. 11.
1 a. A lost collection of traditional verse.

O mountains of Gilboa,   21
let there be no dew or rain on you;
treacherous fields,
for there the hero's shield was dishonoured!

The shield of Saul was anointed not with oil
but with blood of the wounded, fat of the warriors;   22
the bow of Jonathan did not turn back,
nor the sword of Saul return idle.

Saul and Jonathan, loved and lovely,   23
neither in life, nor in death, were divided.
Swifter than eagles were they,
stronger were they than lions.

O daughters of Israel, weep for Saul   24
who clothed you in scarlet and fine linen,
who set brooches of gold
on your garments.

How did the heroes fall   25
in the thick of the battle?

O Jonathan, in your death I am stricken,   26
I am desolate for you, Jonathan my brother.
Very dear to me you were,
your love to me more wonderful
than the love of a woman.

How did the heroes fall   27
and the battle armour fail?

I. DAVID

A. DAVID KING OF JUDAH

David consecrated king at Hebron

2 After this David consulted Yahweh. 'Shall I go up to one of the towns of 1
Judah?' he asked. Yahweh answered, 'Go up'. 'Which shall I go to?' David
asked. 'To Hebron' was the reply. •So David went up, with his two wives, 2
Ahinoam of Jezreel and Abigail the wife of Nabal from Carmel. •The men who 3
were with him, David made go up too, each with his family, and they settled
in the towns of Hebron. •There the men of Judah came and anointed David 4
king over the House of Judah.

David's message to Jabesh

They told David that the people of Jabesh-gilead had given Saul burial,
so David sent messengers to the men of Jabesh-gilead. 'May you be blessed by 5
Yahweh' he said 'for doing this kindness to Saul your lord, and for burying
him. •And now may Yahweh show kindness and faithfulness to you! I too shall 6
treat you well because you have done this. •And now take courage and be men 7
of valour. Saul your lord is dead, but the House of Judah has anointed me to be
their king.'

Abner makes Ishbaal king over Israel

Abner son of Ner, Saul's army commander, had taken Ishbaal son of Saul 8
and brought him over to Mahanaim. •He had made him king over Gilead, 9
over the Ashurites, over Jezreel and Ephraim and Benjamin, and indeed over

10 all Israel. •Ishbaal son of Saul was forty years old when he became king of
Israel, and he reigned for two years. Only the House of Judah supported David.
11 The length of David's reign over Judah in Hebron was seven years and six months.

War between Israel and Judah. The battle of Gibeon

12 Abner son of Ner with Ishbaal's followers marched out from Mahanaim to
13 Gibeon. •Joab son of Zeruiah with David's followers also marched out,
encountering them by the Pool of Gibeon. There they halted, one party on one
side of the pool, and the other opposite.
14 Then Abner said to Joab, 'Let the young soldiers come forward and hold
15 a contest before us'. 'Let them come forward' Joab replied. •So they came
forward and were numbered off, twelve from Benjamin for Ishbaal son of Saul,
16 and twelve of David's followers. •Each caught his adversary by the head and
drove his sword into his side so that they all fell together. Hence the place was
called the Field of Sides; it is at Gibeon.
17 That day a very fierce battle took place, and Abner and the men of Israel
18 were beaten by David's followers. •The three sons of Zeruiah were there, Joab,
19 Abishai, and Asahel. Now Asahel was as swift-footed as a wild gazelle. •Asahel
set off in pursuit of Abner turning neither to right nor to left as he went in pursuit
20 of him. •Abner turned. 'Asahel,' he said 'is that you?' He answered, 'It is'.
21 'Turn to your right or your left,' Abner said 'catch one of the soldiers and take
22 his spoil.' But Asahel would not break off the pursuit. •Again Abner spoke to
Asahel, 'Stop pursuing me, unless you want me to strike you to the ground;
23 and then how could I look your brother Joab in the face again?' •But he refused
to turn away, so Abner struck him in the belly with the butt of his spear so that
the spear came out at his back; and he fell there and died on the spot. On coming
to the place where Asahel had fallen and died, everyone halted.
24 Joab and Abishai took up the pursuit of Abner and at sunset reached the
25 Hill of Ammah, which is to the east of the valley, on the road to Giah. •The
Benjaminites gathered behind Abner in close formation and halted at the top
26 of the Hill of Ammah. •Abner called out to Joab, 'Is the sword to go on eating
its fill for ever?' he said. 'Do you not know that this will end in disaster? How
long will it be before you order these people to stop pursuing their brothers?'
27 'As Yahweh lives,' Joab replied 'if you had not spoken, these men would not
28 have given up the pursuit of their brothers until morning.' •Joab then sounded
the trumpet and all the troops halted; they pursued Israel no further and fought
no more.
29 All that night Abner and his men made their way through the Arabah;[a] they
crossed the Jordan and, marching throughout the morning, came to Mahanaim.
30 Joab, giving up the pursuit of Abner, mustered his whole force; David's followers
31 had lost nineteen men in addition to Asahel, •but had killed three hundred and
32 sixty of Benjamin, Abner's men. •They took up Asahel and buried him in his
father's tomb, which is at Bethlehem. Then Joab and his men marched throughout
the night and day dawned as they reached Hebron.
1 3 So the war dragged on between the House of Saul and the House of David,
but David grew steadily stronger, and the House of Saul ever weaker.

The sons born to David at Hebron

2 Sons were born to David at Hebron: his first-born Amnon, by Ahinoam of
3 Jezreel; •his second Chileab, by Abigail the wife of Nabal from Carmel; the
4 third Absalom the son of Maacah, daughter of Talmai king of Geshur; •the
5 fourth Adonijah the son of Haggith; the fifth Shephatiah the son of Abital; •the
sixth Ithream, by Eglah wife of David. These were born to David at Hebron.

2 a. Here meaning the Jordan valley.

The rift between Abner and Ishbaal

This is what took place during the war between the House of Saul and the 6
House of David. Abner took complete control in the House of Saul. •Now there 7
was a concubine of Saul's named Rizpah, the daughter of Aiah, and Abner took
her. Ishbaal said to Abner, 'Why have you slept with my father's concubine?'
At these words of Ishbaal Abner flew into a rage. 'Am I a dog's head?' he 8
shouted. 'Here am I full of goodwill towards the House of Saul your father,
his brothers and his friends, not leaving you to the hands of David, and now
you find fault with me about a woman! •May God do this to Abner and more 9
if I do not bring about what Yahweh has promised on oath to David, •to take 10
the sovereignty from the House of Saul, and set up the throne of David over
Israel and Judah, from Dan to Beersheba.' •Ishbaal dared not say a single 11
word in answer to Abner, because he was afraid of him.

Abner negotiates with David

Abner sent messengers to say to David, '. . . Come to an agreement with 12
me and I will give you my support to win all Israel over to you'. •'Very well,' 13
David said 'I will come to an agreement with you. I impose one condition
however; you will not be admitted to my presence unless you bring me Michal,
Saul's daughter, when you come to see me.' •David then sent messengers to 14
Ishbaal son of Saul. 'Give me back my wife Michal,' he said 'whom I won with
a hundred foreskins of the Philistines.' •So Ishbaal sent for her to be taken from 15
her husband Paltiel son of Laish. •Her husband set off with her and followed 16
her, weeping, as far as Bahurim; but Abner said to him, 'Go back', and he
went.

Now Abner had conferred with the elders of Israel. 'For a long time now' 17
he said 'you have wanted David for your king. •Now you must take action; 18
Yahweh has given this promise about David, "By the hand of my servant David
I will deliver my people Israel from the hands of the Philistines and all their
enemies'." •Abner also spoke to the men of Benjamin, and then went to 19
Hebron to tell David all that had been agreed by Israel and the House of
Benjamin.

Abner accompanied by twenty men came to David at Hebron, and David 20
held a feast for Abner and the men who were with him. •Then Abner said to 21
David, 'I must be off. I am going to rally all Israel to my lord the king. They
will make an alliance with you, and you will reign over all that you desire.'
So David allowed Abner to go, and he went unmolested.

The murder of Abner

The followers of David were just then coming back with Joab from a raid, 22
bringing a great amount of booty with them. Abner was no longer with David
at Hebron, since David had allowed him to go, and he had gone unmolested.
When Joab arrived and the whole force that was with him, Joab was told, 'Abner 23
son of Ner has been to the king and he has allowed Abner to go away unmolested'.
Then Joab went to the king. 'What have you done?' he said. 'Abner comes to 24
you and you allow him to go unmolested? Why? •Do you not know Abner son 25
of Ner? He came to trick you, to know your every move, to find out what you
are doing.'

Joab left David's presence and sent messengers after Abner and these, 26
unknown to David, brought him back from the Well of Sirah. •When Abner 27
reached Hebron, Joab drew him apart to the side of the gate as if to have a word
with him in private, and there struck him in the belly. And so, for the blood
of Joab's brother Asahel, he died. •Afterwards when David heard of this, he 28
said, 'I and my kingdom are innocent for ever before Yahweh of the blood of
Abner son of Ner; •may it fall on the head of Joab and on all his family! May 29
the House of Joab never lack men with the discharge or the leprosy, or only

30 fit to hold a distaff, or falling by the sword, or short of bread!' •(Joab and his
brother Abishai had murdered Abner because he killed their brother Asahel
31 at the battle of Gibeon.) •David then said to Joab and all the troops who were
with him, 'Tear your garments, put on sackcloth, and mourn before Abner';
32 and King David walked behind the bier. •They buried Abner at Hebron, and the
33 king wept aloud at Abner's grave, and the people all wept too. •The king made
this lament over Abner:

'Should Abner have died as a fool dies?
34   Your hands were not tied, your feet not chained;
          you fell as a man falls at the hands of criminals.'

And all the people wept once more over him.

35   They all tried then to persuade David to have some food while it was still
daylight, but David took this oath, 'May God do this to me and more if I taste
36 bread or anything whatever until the sun is down!' •All the people took note
of this and it pleased them; indeed, everything the king did pleased the people.
37 That day all the people and all Israel understood that the king had no part
in the death of Abner son of Ner.
38   The king said to his officers, 'Do you not know that in Israel a prince, a great
39 man, has fallen today? •I, though I am king by anointing, am weak at this
present time, and these men, the sons of Zeruiah, are too ruthless for me. May
Yahweh pay back the wrong-doer in proportion to the wrong he has done.'

The murder of Ishbaal

1 4 When Ishbaal son of Saul heard the news that Abner had died at Hebron,
2   his heart failed him, and the whole of Israel was alarmed. •Now Ishbaal
son of Saul had two freebooting chieftains; one was called Baanah, the other
Rechab. They were the sons of Rimmon of Beeroth, and Benjaminites—for
3 Beeroth is regarded as belonging to Benjamin. •The people of Beeroth had
taken refuge in Gittaim where they have remained to this day as resident aliens.
4   Jonathan son of Saul had a son with crippled feet. He was five years old
when the news about Saul and Jonathan came from Jezreel. His nurse picked him
up and fled, but as she hurried away he fell and was lamed. His name was
Meribbaal.
5   The sons of Rimmon of Beeroth, Rechab and Baanah, set out; they came
to Ishbaal's house at the hottest part of the day when he was taking his midday
6 rest. •The woman who kept the door had been cleaning wheat, and she had
7 drowsed off to sleep. Rechab and his brother Baanah stole by •and entered the
house where Ishbaal was lying in his bedroom on his bed. They struck and killed
him and cut off his head; and taking the head with them, they travelled all night
8 by the road of the Arabah. •They brought Ishbaal's head to David at Hebron.
'Here' they said to the king 'is the head of Ishbaal son of Saul, your enemy,
who sought your life. Yahweh has avenged my lord the king today on Saul
and on his offspring.'
9   But David answered Rechab and his brother Baanah by saying, 'As Yahweh
10 lives, who has delivered me from all adversity, •the man who thought to bring
me good news when he told me Saul was dead, this man I seized and killed
11 at Ziklag, rewarding him for his good news. •How much more when bandits
have killed an honest man in his house, and on his bed! Am I not bound to
12 demand account of his blood from you, and wipe you from the earth?' •Then
David gave an order to his soldiers, who put them to death, cut off their hands
and feet, and hung them up beside the Pool of Hebron. Ishbaal's head
they took and buried in Abner's grave at Hebron.

B. DAVID KING OF JUDAH AND OF ISRAEL

David is anointed king of Israel

5 All the tribes of Israel then came to David at Hebron. 'Look' they said 1
'we are your own flesh and blood. •In days past when Saul was our king, 2
it was you who led Israel in all their exploits; and Yahweh said to you, "You are
the man who shall be shepherd of my people Israel, you shall be the leader of
Israel". ' •So all the elders of Israel came to the king at Hebron, and King David 3
made a pact with them at Hebron in the presence of Yahweh, and they anointed
David king of Israel.

David was thirty years old when he became king, and he reigned for 4
forty years. •He reigned in Hebron over Judah for seven years and six months; 5
then he reigned in Jerusalem over all Israel and Judah for thirty-three years.

The capture of Jerusalem

David and his men marched on Jerusalem against the Jebusites living there. 6
These said to David, 'You will not get in here. The blind and the lame will hold
you off.' (That is to say: David will never get in here.) •But David captured the 7
fortress of Zion, that is, the Citadel of David. •That day David said, 'Whoever 8
strikes the Jebusites and goes up by the conduit. . .' As for the blind and the
lame, David hated them in his soul. (Hence the saying: the blind and the lame
shall not enter the Temple.) •David went to live in the fortress and called it the 9
Citadel of David. David then built a wall round it, from the Millo going
inwards. •David grew greater and greater, and Yahweh, God of Sabaoth, was 10
with him.

Hiram king of Tyre sent envoys to David with cedar wood and carpenters 11
and stonemasons, who built David a palace. •David then knew that Yahweh 12
had confirmed him as king over Israel, and for the sake of his people Israel was
making his reign glorious.

The sons born to David in Jerusalem

After coming from Hebron, David took other concubines and wives in 13
Jerusalem, and sons and daughters were born to him. •These are the names 14
of those born to him in Jerusalem: Shammua, Shobab, Nathan, Solomon,
Ibhar, Elishua, Nepheg, Japhia, •Elishama, Eliada, Eliphelet. ¹⁵/₁₆

Victory over the Philistines

When the Philistines heard that David had been anointed king of all Israel, 17
they all marched up to seek him out. On hearing this, David went down to the
stronghold.ᵃ •When the Philistines arrived they deployed in the Valley of the 18
Rephaim. •David consulted Yahweh; 'Shall I attack the Philistines?' he asked. 19
'Will you deliver them into my power?' Yahweh answered David, 'Attack!
I will most surely deliver the Philistines into your power.' •Accordingly David 20
went to Baal-perazim and there defeated them. David said, 'Yahweh has made
a breach in my enemies for me like a breach the waters make'. For this reason
that place was called Baal-perazim. •They had left their gods behind them 21
there, and David and his men carried them off.

Again the Philistines marched up and deployed in the Valley of the Rephaim. 22
David consulted Yahweh, who answered, 'Do not attack them from the front; 23
go round to their rear and engage them opposite the balsam trees. •When you 24
hear the sound of steps in the tops of the balsam trees, advance, for that will
be Yahweh going out ahead of you to rout the army of the Philistines.' •David 25
did as Yahweh had ordered and routed the Philistines from Gibeon as far as
the Pass of Gezer.

The ark in Jerusalem

6 ¹David again mustered all the picked troops of Israel, thirty thousand men. ²Setting off with the whole force then with him, David went to Baalah of Judah, to bring up from there the ark of God which bears the name of Yahweh ³Sabaoth who is seated on the cherubs. •They placed the ark of God on a new cart, and brought it from Abinadab's house which is on the hill. Uzzah and ⁴Ahio, the sons of Abinadab, were leading the cart, •Uzzah walked alongside ⁵the ark of God and Ahio went in front. •David and all the House of Israel danced before Yahweh with all their might, singing to the accompaniment of ⁶lyres, harps, tambourines, castanets, and cymbals. •When they came to the threshing-floor of Nacon, Uzzah stretched his hand out to the ark of God and ⁷steadied it, as the oxen were making it tilt. •Then the anger of Yahweh blazed out against Uzzah, and for this crime God struck him down on the spot, and ⁸he died there beside the ark of God. •David was displeased that Yahweh had broken out against Uzzah, and that place was called Perez-uzzah, as it still is now. ⁹David went in fear of Yahweh that day. 'However can the ark of Yahweh ¹⁰come to me?' he said. •So David decided not to take the ark into the Citadel ¹¹of David and took it to the house of Obed-edom of Gath. •The ark of Yahweh remained in the house of Obed-edom of Gath for three months, and Yahweh blessed Obed-edom and his whole family.

¹²Word was brought to King David that Yahweh had blessed the family of Obed-edom and all that belonged to him on account of the ark of God. David accordingly went and brought the ark of God up from Obed-edom's house to ¹³the Citadel of David with great rejoicing. •When the bearers of the ark of Yahweh ¹⁴had gone six paces, he sacrificed an ox and a fat sheep. •And David danced whirling round before Yahweh with all his might, wearing a linen loincloth ¹⁵round him. •Thus David and all the House of Israel brought up the ark of ¹⁶Yahweh with acclaim and the sound of the horn. •Now as the ark of Yahweh entered the Citadel of David, Michal the daughter of Saul was watching from the window and saw King David leaping and dancing before Yahweh; and she ¹⁷despised him in her heart. •They brought the ark of Yahweh in and put it in position inside the tent that David had pitched for it; and David offered holo-¹⁸causts before Yahweh, and communion sacrifices. •And when David had finished offering holocausts and communion sacrifices, he blessed the people in the name ¹⁹of Yahweh Sabaoth. •He then distributed among all the people, among the whole multitude of Israelites, men and women, a roll of bread to each, a portion of dates, and a raisin cake. Then they all went away, each to his own house.

²⁰As David was coming back to bless his household Michal, the daughter of Saul, went out to meet him. 'What a fine reputation the king of Israel has won himself today,' she said 'displaying himself under the eyes of his servant-²¹maids, as any buffoon might display himself.' •David answered Michal, 'I was dancing for Yahweh, not for them. As Yahweh lives, who chose me in preference to your father and his whole House to make me leader of Israel, Yahweh's ²²people, I shall dance before Yahweh •and demean myself even more. In your eyes I may be base, but by the maids you speak of I shall be held in honour.' ²³And to the day of her death Michal, the daughter of Saul, had no children.

The prophecy of Nathan

7 ¹Once David had settled into his house and Yahweh had given him rest from ²all the enemies surrounding him, •the king said to the prophet Nathan, 'Look, I am living in a house of cedar while the ark of God dwells in a tent'. ³Nathan said to the king, 'Go and do all that is in your mind, for Yahweh is with you'.

⁴But that very night the word of Yahweh came to Nathan:

5 a. Perhaps Adullam; Jerusalem was not yet captured.

'Go and tell my servant David, "Thus Yahweh speaks: Are you the man to 5 build me a house to dwell in? •I have never stayed in a house from the day I 6 brought the Israelites out of Egypt until today, but have always led a wanderer's life in a tent. •In all my journeying with the whole people of Israel, did I say 7 to any one of the judges of Israel, whom I had appointed as shepherds of Israel ny people: Why have you not built me a house of cedar?" •This is what you 8 must say to my servant David, "Yahweh Sabaoth says this: I took you from the pasture, from following the sheep, to be leader of my people Israel; I have been with you on all your expeditions; I have cut off all your enemies 9 before you. I will give you fame as great as the fame of the greatest on earth. •I will provide a place for my people Israel; I will plant them there and 10 they shall dwell in that place and never be disturbed again; nor shall the wicked continue to oppress them as they did, •in the days when I appointed judges over 11 my people Israel; I will give them rest from all their enemies. Yahweh will make you great; Yahweh will make you a House. •And when your days are 12 ended and you are laid to rest with your ancestors, I will preserve the offspring of your body after you and make his sovereignty secure. •(It is he who shall 13 build a house for my name, and I will make his royal throne secure for ever.) I will be a father to him and he a son to me; if he does evil, I will punish him 14 with the rod such as men use, with strokes such as mankind gives. •Yet I will 15 not withdraw my favour from him, as I withdrew it from your predecessor. Your House and your sovereignty will always stand secure before me and your 16 throne be established for ever." '

Nathan related all these words to David and this whole revelation.   17

David's prayer

King David then went in and, seated before Yahweh, said: 18

'Who am I, Lord Yahweh, and what is my House, that you have led me as far as this? •Yet in your sight, Lord Yahweh, this is still not far enough, and 19 you make your promises extend to the House of your servant for a far-distant future... •What more can David say to you, when you yourself have singled 20 out your servant, Lord Yahweh? •For your servant's sake, this dog of yours, 21 you have done so great a thing by revealing this to your servant. •In this is your 22 greatness, Lord Yahweh, there is none like you, no God but you alone, as our own ears have heard. •Is there another people on the earth like your people Israel, 23 with a God setting out to redeem them and make them his people, make them renowned, work great and terrible things on their behalf, drive nations out and gods before his people? •You have constituted your people Israel to be your 24 own people for ever; and you, Yahweh, have become their God. •Now, Lord 25 Yahweh, always keep the promise you have made your servant and his House, and do as you have said. •Your name will be exalted for ever and men will say, 26 "Yahweh Sabaoth is God over Israel." The House of your servant David will be made secure in your presence, •since you yourself, Yahweh Sabaoth, God 27 of Israel, have made this revelation to your servant, "I will build you a House"; hence your servant has ventured to offer this prayer to you. •Yes, Lord Yahweh, 28 you are God indeed, your words are true and you have made this fair promise to your servant. •Be pleased, then, to bless the House of your servant, that it 29 may continue for ever in your presence; for you, Lord Yahweh, have spoken; and with your blessing the House of your servant will be for ever blessed.'

The wars of David

8 After this, David defeated the Philistines and subdued them. From the hands 1 of the Philistines he took... •He also defeated the Moabites, and making 2 them lie down on the ground measured them off by the line; he measured out two lines to be put to death and one full line to have their lives spared. The Moabites became subject to David, paying him tribute.

3 David defeated Hadadezer son of Rehob, king of Zobah, on his way to
4 extend his power over the river.ᵃ •David captured one thousand seven hundred
charioteers and twenty thousand foot soldiers from him; David hamstrung all
5 the chariot teams, keeping only a hundred of them. •The Aramaeans of
Damascus came to the help of Hadadezer king of Zobah, but David killed
6 twenty-two thousand men of the Aramaeans. •Then David imposed governors on
Aram of Damascus, and the Aramaeans became subject to David, paying him
7 tribute. Wherever David went, Yahweh gave him victory. •David took the
golden shields carried by the guards of Hadadezer and brought them to Jerusalem.
8 From Betah and Berothai, towns belonging to Hadadezer, King David took a
great quantity of bronze.

9   When Tou king of Hamath heard that David had defeated Hadadezer's
10 entire army, •he sent his son Hadoram to King David to greet him and to
congratulate him on fighting and defeating Hadadezer, since Hadadezer was the
enemy of Tou. Hadoram brought with him articles of silver, gold and bronze,
11 which King David also consecrated to Yahweh as he had already consecrated
12 the silver and gold taken from all the nations he had subjugated: •Edom, Moab,
the Ammonites, the Philistines, Amalek; from the spoil, too, of Hadadezer son
of Rehob, king of Zobah.

13   Thus David won fame for himself. On his return he defeated the Edomites
14 in the Valley of Salt,ᵇ eighteen thousand of them. •He imposed governors on
Edom and all the Edomites became subject to David. Wherever David went,
Yahweh gave him victory.

The administration of the kingdom

15
16   David ruled over all Israel, administering law and justice to all his people. •Joab
son of Zeruiah was in command of the army; Jehoshaphat son of Ahilud was
17 recorder; •Zadok son of Ahitub and Abiathar son of Ahimelech were priests;
18 Seraiah was secretary; •Benaiah son of Jehoiada was in command of the Cherethites and Pelethites;ᶜ David's sons were priests.

C. DAVID'S FAMILY AND THE INTRIGUES FOR THE SUCCESSION

1. MERIBBAAL

David's kindness to Jonathan's son

1 **9** David asked, 'Is there anyone still left of Saul's family so that I can show him
2   kindness for Jonathan's sake?' •Now there was a servant of Saul's household
whose name was Ziba, and they called him to David. 'You are Ziba?' the king
3 asked. 'At your service' he answered. •The king said, 'Is there no one still left
of Saul's family for me to show him God's kindness?' 'There is still one of
4 Jonathan's sons,' Ziba answered the king 'a man with crippled feet.' •'Where
is he?' the king asked. Ziba replied, 'He is living in the household of Machir son
5 of Ammiel at Lo-debar'. •So King David sent to have him brought from the
house of Machir son of Ammiel at Lo-debar.

6   On entering David's presence, Meribbaal son of Jonathan, son of Saul, fell
on his face and did homage. David said, 'Meribbaal!' He answered, 'I am at
7 your service'. •Then David said, 'Do not be afraid; I intend to show you kindness
for your father Jonathan's sake. I will restore all the land of Saul your father
8 to you and you shall always eat at my table.' •And Meribbaal did homage.
'What is your servant' he said 'that you should show favour to a dead dog
like me?'

9   Then the king called Ziba, Saul's servant, and said, 'Everything belonging to
10 Saul and his family I give to your master's son. •You must work the land for him,

---

8 a. The Euphrates.   **b.** Probably the Arabah, the valley running S. from the Dead Sea.
c. David's bodyguard of mercenaries from Philistia.

you and your sons and your slaves; you must harvest the produce to provide food for your master's family to eat. But Meribbaal, your master's son, shall always take his meals at my table.' Now Ziba had fifteen sons and twenty slaves. •Ziba 11 said to the king, 'Your servant will do everything my lord the king has ordered his servant'.

So Meribbaal ate at David's table like one of the king's sons. •Meribbaal had 12 a young son whose name was Mica. All those who lived in Ziba's house became Meribbaal's servants. •Meribbaal lived in Jerusalem, since he always ate at the 13 king's table. He was crippled in both feet.

2. THE AMMONITE WAR — BIRTH OF SOLOMON

David's ambassadors are insulted

10 After this, the king of the Ammonites died and his son Hanun succeeded 1 him. •David thought, 'I will show the same kindness for Hanun son of 2 Nahash as his father showed me'. And through his servants David sent him his condolences on his father's death. But when David's servants reached the land of the Ammonites, •the Ammonite leaders said to Hanun their master, 'Do you 3 imagine David means to honour your father when he sends you messengers of sympathy? On the contrary, the reason why David has sent his servants to you is to explore the city,ᵃ to reconnoitre it and so overthrow it.' •Whereupon Hanun 4 seized David's servants, shaved off half of each man's beard, cut their clothes half-way up to the buttocks, and sent them away. •When David was told, he 5 sent someone to meet them, for the men were covered with shame. 'Stay in Jericho' the king said 'until your beards have grown again, and come back then.'

The first Ammonite campaign

The Ammonites saw that they had incurred the enmity of David and accord- 6 ingly sent messengers to hire the Aramaeans of Beth-rehob and the Aramaeans of Zobah, twenty thousand foot; also the king of Maacah with one thousand men, and the men of Tob, twelve thousand men. •When David heard this, he 7 sent Joab with all the common soldiers and the champions.ᵇ •The Ammonites 8 marched out and drew up their line of battle at the approaches to the gate, while the Aramaeans of Zobah and of Rehob and the men of Tob and Maacah kept their distance in the open country. •Joab, seeing that he had to fight on two 9 fronts, to his front and to his rear, chose the best of Israel's picked men and drew them up in line facing the Aramaeans. •He entrusted the rest of the army to his 10 brother Abishai, and drew them up in line facing the Ammonites. •'If the Ara- 11 maeans prove too strong for me,' he said 'you must come to my help; if the Ammonites prove too strong for you, I will go to yours. •Take courage and 12 stand firm for the sake of our people and the towns of our God. And may Yahweh do as he thinks right.' •Joab and the force with him joined battle with the 13 Aramaeans, who fled before him. •When the Ammonites saw that the Aramaeans 14 had taken flight, they too fled before Abishai and withdrew into their town. Then Joab returned from the war with the Ammonites and came back to Jerusalem.

Victory over the Aramaeans

Seeing that they had been defeated by Israel, the Aramaeans consolidated 15 their forces. •Hadadezer sent messengers and mobilised the Aramaeans from 16 beyond the river. They came to Helam with Shobach, commander of Hadadezer's army, at their head. •Word of this was brought to David, who mustered all 17 Israel, crossed the Jordan and reached Helam. The Aramaeans drew up in line facing David and engaged him. •But the Aramaeans gave ground before 18 Israel, and David killed seven hundred of their chariot teams and forty thousand men; he also struck down Shobach their general, who died then and there. •When 19 all the vassal kings of Hadadezer saw that they had been defeated by Israel, they made peace with the Israelites and became subject to them. The Aramaeans were afraid to give any more help to the Ammonites.

The second Ammonite campaign. David's sin

1 **11** At the turn of the year,[a] the time when kings go campaigning, David sent Joab and with him his own guards and the whole of Israel. They massacred the Ammonites and laid siege to Rabbah. David however remained in Jerusalem.

2 It happened towards evening when David had risen from his couch and was strolling on the palace roof, that he saw from the roof a woman bathing; the 3 woman was very beautiful. •David made inquiries about this woman and was told, 'Why, that is Bathsheba, Eliam's daughter, the wife of Uriah the Hittite'.[b] 4 Then David sent messengers and had her brought. She came to him, and he slept with her; now she had just purified herself from her courses. She then went home 5 again. •The woman conceived and sent word to David, 'I am with child'.

6 Then David sent Joab a message, 'Send me Uriah the Hittite', whereupon 7 Joab sent Uriah to David. •When Uriah came into his presence, David asked 8 after Joab and the army and how the war was going. •David then said to Uriah, 'Go down to your house and enjoy yourself'. Uriah left the palace, and was 9 followed by a present from the king's table. •Uriah however slept by the palace door with his master's bodyguard and did not go down to his house.

10 This was reported to David; 'Uriah' they said 'did not go down to his house'. So David asked Uriah, 'Have you not just arrived from a journey? Why do you 11 not go to your home?' •But Uriah answered, 'Are not the ark and the men of Israel and Judah lodged in tents; and my master Joab and the bodyguard of my lord, are they not in the open fields? Am I to go to my house, then, and eat and drink and sleep with my wife?[c] As Yahweh lives, and as you yourself 12 live, I will do no such thing!' •Then David said to Uriah, 'Stay on here today; 13 tomorrow I shall send you back'. So Uriah stayed that day in Jerusalem. •The next day David invited him to eat and drink in his presence and made him drunk. In the evening Uriah went out and lay on his couch with his master's bodyguard, but he did not go down to his house.

14
15 Next morning David wrote a letter to Joab and sent it by Uriah. •In the letter he wrote, 'Station Uriah in the thick of the fight and then fall back behind 16 him so that he may be struck down and die'. •Joab, then besieging the town, 17 posted Uriah in a place where he knew there were fierce fighters. •The men of the town sallied out and engaged Joab; the army suffered casualties, including some of David's bodyguard; and Uriah the Hittite was killed too.

18
19 Joab sent David a full account of the battle. •To the messenger he gave this order: 'When you have finished telling the king all the details of the battle, 20 the king's anger may be provoked; he may say, "Why did you go so near the 21 town to fight? Did you not know they would shoot from the ramparts? •Who killed Abimelech son of Jerubbaal? Was it not a woman who dropped a mill-stone on him from the ramparts, causing his death at Thebez? Why did you go so near the ramparts?" If so, you are to say, "Your servant Uriah the Hittite has been killed too".'

22 So the messenger left, and on his arrival told David all that Joab had instructed him to say. David was angry with Joab. 'Why did you go so near the ramparts?' he said to the messenger. 'Who killed Abimelech son of Jerubbaal? Was it not a woman who dropped a millstone on him from the ramparts, causing 23 his death at Thebez? Why did you go so near the ramparts?' •The messenger answered David, 'Because their men made a show of force against us and sallied out against us in the open. We drove them back to the approaches of the gate,

10 a. Rabbah, the capital, now Amman. b. I.e., the mercenaries of the king's bodyguard. **11** a. The Spring equinox. b. A foreign mercenary. c. Continence while on active service was a religious obligation.

but the bowmen shot at your bodyguard from the ramparts; some of the king's 24
bodyguard perished, and your servant Uriah the Hittite was killed too.'

Then David said to the messenger, 'Say this to Joab, "Do not take the matter 25
to heart; the sword devours now one and now another. Storm the town in
greater force and overthrow it." That is the way to encourage him.' •When 26
Uriah's wife heard that her husband Uriah was dead, she mourned for her
husband. •When the period of mourning was over, David sent to have her 27
brought to his house; she became his wife and bore him a son. But what David
had done displeased Yahweh.

David is rebuked by Nathan. His repentance

12 Yahweh sent Nathan the prophet to David. He came to him and said: 1

'In the same town were two men,
     one rich, the other poor.
The rich man had flocks and herds   2
     in great abundance;
the poor man had nothing but a ewe lamb,   3
     one only, a small one he had bought.
This he fed, and it grew up with him and his children,
     eating his bread, drinking from his cup,
     sleeping on his breast; it was like a daughter to him.
When there came a traveller to stay, the rich man   4
     refused to take one of his own flock or herd
     to provide for the wayfarer who had come to him.
Instead he took the poor man's lamb
     and prepared it for his guest.'

David's anger flared up against the man. 'As Yahweh lives,' he said to Nathan 5
'the man who did this deserves to die! •He must make fourfold restitution for 6
the lamb, for doing such a thing and showing no compassion.'

Then Nathan said to David, 'You are the man. Yahweh the God of Israel 7
says this, "I anointed you king over Israel; I delivered you from the hands of
Saul; •I gave your master's house to you, his wives into your arms; I gave you 8
the House of Israel and of Judah; and if this were not enough, I would add as
much again for you. •Why have you shown contempt for Yahweh, doing what 9
displeases him? You have struck down Uriah the Hittite with the sword, taken
his wife for your own, and killed him with the sword of the Ammonites. •So now 10
the sword will never be far from your House, since you have shown contempt
for me and taken the wife of Uriah the Hittite to be your wife."

'Thus Yahweh speaks, "I will stir up evil for you out of your own House. 11
Before your very eyes I will take your wives and give them to your neighbour,
and he shall lie with your wives in the sight of this sun. •You worked in 12
secret, I will work this in the face of all Israel and in the face of the sun."'

David said to Nathan, 'I have sinned against Yahweh'. Then Nathan said 13
to David, 'Yahweh, for his part, forgives your sin; you are not to die. •Yet 14
because you have outraged Yahweh by doing this, the child that is born to
you is to die.' •Then Nathan went home.   15

The death of Bathsheba's child. The birth of Solomon

Yahweh struck the child that Uriah's wife had borne to David and it fell
gravely ill. •David pleaded with Yahweh for the child; he kept a strict fast and 16
went home and spent the night on the bare ground, covered with sacking. •The 17
officials of his household came and stood round him to get him to rise from the
ground, but he refused, nor would he take food with them. •On the seventh day 18
the child died. David's officers were afraid to tell him the child was dead. 'Even
when the child was alive' they thought 'we reasoned with him and he would

not listen to us. How can we tell him the child is dead? He will do something
19 desperate.' •David, however, noticed that his officers were whispering among
themselves, and realised that the child was dead. 'Is the child dead?' he asked
the officers. They answered, 'He is dead'.
20 David got up from the ground, bathed and anointed himself and put
on fresh clothes. Then he went into the sanctuary of Yahweh•and prostrated
himself. On returning to his house he asked for food to be set before him, and
21 ate. •His officers said, 'Why are you acting like this? When the child was alive
22 you fasted and wept; now the child is dead you get up and take food.' •'When
the child was alive' he answered 'I fasted and wept because I kept thinking, "Who
23 knows? Perhaps Yahweh will take pity on me and the child will live." •But
now he is dead, why should I fast? Can I bring him back again? I shall go to
him but he cannot come back to me.'
24 David consoled his wife Bathsheba. He went to her and slept with her. She
conceived and gave birth to a son whom she named Solomon. Yahweh loved
25 him •and made this known through the prophet Nathan who named him Jedidiah
in accordance with the word of Yahweh.[a]

The capture of Rabbah

26 Joab attacked Rabbah of the Ammonites and captured the water town.
27 He then sent messengers to tell David, 'I have stormed Rabbah and captured
28 the water town. •So now muster the rest of the troops and pitch camp against
the town and take it, unless you want me to capture the town and give it my
29 name.' •So David mustered the whole army and marched on Rabbah; he stormed
30 the town and captured it. •He took the crown from the head of Milcom;[b] it
weighed one talent of gold, and in it was set a precious stone which made an
ornament for David's head. He carried off great quantities of spoil from the
31 town. •He brought away its population and set them to work with saws, iron
picks and iron axes, and employed them in brickmaking. He treated all the
Ammonite towns in the same way. Then David and the whole army returned to
Jerusalem.

3. ABSALOM

Amnon violates Tamar his sister

1 **13** After this, the following events took place. Absalom son of David had
a beautiful sister whose name was Tamar; Amnon son of David fell in love
2 with her. •Amnon was so obsessed with his sister Tamar that it made him ill,
for she was a virgin and it seemed to Amnon impossible to do anything to her.
3 But Amnon had a friend called Jonadab son of Shimeah, David's brother, and
4 Jonadab was a very shrewd man. •'Son of the king,' he said 'tell me why, morning
after morning, you look so worn? Will you not tell me?' Amnon answered, 'I am
5 in love with Tamar, my brother Absalom's sister'. •Then Jonadab said, 'Lie down
on your bed, pretend to be ill and when your father comes to visit you, say,
"Let my sister Tamar come and give me something to eat; let her prepare the
6 food before my eyes for me to see; only at her hands will I eat" '. •So Amnon
lay down and pretended to be ill. Then the king came to visit him and Amnon
said to the king, 'Let my sister Tamar come and make a cake or two; I will eat
7 at her hands'. •David then sent word to Tamar at the palace, 'Go to your brother
8 Amnon's house and prepare some food for him'. •Tamar went to the house of
her brother Amnon who was lying there in bed. She took dough and kneaded it,
9 and she made cakes there before his eyes and baked the cakes. •Then she took
the pan and dished them up in front of him, but he refused to eat. 'Let everyone
10 leave me' he said; so they all withdrew. •Then Amnon said to Tamar, 'Bring

---

12 a. Jedidiah is 'beloved of Yahweh'.   **b.** The Ammonite idol.

the food to the inner room so that I can eat at your hands'. So Tamar took the
cakes she had made and brought them to her brother Amnon in the inner room.
And as she was offering the food to him, he caught hold of her and said, 'Come; 11
lie with me, my sister'. •But she answered, 'No, my brother! Do not violate me. 12
This is not a thing men do in Israel. Do not commit such an outrage. •Wherever 13
should I go, bearing my shame? While you would become an outcast in Israel.
Go now and speak to the king; he will not refuse to give me to you.'ᵃ •But he 14
would not listen to her; he overpowered her and, raping her, lay with her.

Then Amnon was seized with extreme hatred for her; the hatred he now felt 15
for her was greater than his earlier love. 'Get up and go' he said. •'No, my 16
brother,' she said 'to send me away would be a greater wrong than the other
you have done me.' But he would not listen to her. •He called the soldier who 17
was his servant. 'Get rid of this woman for me,' he said 'throw her out and bolt
the door after her.' •(She was wearing a long-sleeved gown, for this was what 18
the king's unmarried daughters wore in days gone by.) So the servant put her
out and bolted the door after her.

Tamar took dust and put it on her head, tore the long-sleeved gown she was 19
wearing, laid her hand on her head, and went away uttering cries as she went.
Her brother Absalom said to her, 'Has Amnon your brother been with you? 20
Be quiet now, my sister; he is your brother; do not take this so much to heart.'
But Tamar remained disconsolate in her brother Absalom's house.

When King David heard the whole story, he was very angry; but he had no 21
wish to harm his son Amnon, since he loved him; he was his first-born. •Absalom 22
however would not so much as speak to Amnon, for he hated Amnon for having
raped his sister Tamar.

Absalom kills Amnon and flees

Two years later, when Absalom had the sheep-shearers at Baal-hazor, which 23
is near Ephraim, he invited the entire royal household. •Absalom went to the 24
king and said, 'At this moment your servant has the sheep-shearers. Will the
king and his officers be pleased to come with your servant?' •'No, my son,' the 25
king replied 'we must not all come and be a burden to you.' And though Absalom
was insistent, he would not go but dismissed him. •Absalom persisted, 'Then 26
at least let my brother Amnon come with us'. The king said, 'Why should he
go with you?' •But Absalom insisted, so he allowed Amnon and all the king's 27
sons to go with him.

Absalom prepared a royal banquet •and then gave this order to his servants: 28
'Listen carefully; when Amnon's heart is merry with wine and I say, "Strike
Amnon down", then kill him. Have no fear. I myself have given you the order.
Take courage, be brave.' •Absalom's servants treated Amnon as Absalom had 29
ordered. Then all the king's sons started up, mounted their mules and took flight.

While they were on the road, a rumour reached David, 'Absalom has killed 30
all the king's sons; not one of them is left'. •The king rose and tore his garments 31
and lay down on the ground. All his officers in attendance tore their garments
too. •But Jonadab son of Shimeah, David's brother, spoke up. 'Let not my lord 32
imagine' he said 'that they have killed all the young men, the sons of the king;
Amnon alone is dead, for Absalom's face gave warning of this ever since Amnon
violated his sister Tamar. •Let not my lord the king imagine that all the king's 33
sons are dead; Amnon alone is dead •and Absalom has taken flight.' 34

The soldier on sentry duty looked up and saw a large troop advancing down
the slope on the Bahurim road. The sentry came to tell the king. 'I saw men'
he said 'coming down the Bahurim road on the mountainside.' •Then Jonadab 35
said to the king, 'Here come the king's sons; it has turned out just as your servant
said'. •He had scarcely finished speaking when the king's sons arrived, and they 36
cried aloud and wept; the king and all his officers wept bitterly too. •Absalom 37a
however had taken flight and gone to Talmai son of Ammihud, king of Geshur,

38b
37b where he stayed for three years. •And all that time the king observed mourning
for his son.

Joab negotiates the return of Absalom

39   The king's heart was now no longer set against Absalom, once he had
1 recovered from Amnon's death. **14** Now Joab son of Zeruiah observed that
2 the heart of the king was again turning to Absalom, •so he sent to Tekoa*a* for
a quick-witted woman. 'Pretend to be in mourning' he said. 'Put on mourning
garments; do not anoint yourself with oil; act like a woman who has long been
3 mourning for the dead. •Go then to the king and say this to him.' And Joab
put into her mouth the words she had to say.

4   So the woman of Tekoa went to the king and fell with her face to the ground
5 and did homage. 'Help, O king! she said. •The king said, 'What is the matter?'
6 'Alas,' she replied 'I am a widow; my husband is dead. •Your servant had two
sons and out in the fields, where there was no one to intervene, they quarrelled
7 with each other. And one of them struck the other and killed him. •And now
the whole clan has risen against your servant. "Give up the man who killed his
brother" they say. "For the life of the brother he murdered we will have his
death, and so destroy the heir too." By this means they will put out what embers
remain to me, and leave my husband neither name nor survivor on the face of
8 the earth.' •The king then said to the woman, 'Go to your house; I myself will
9 give orders concerning your case'. •The woman of Tekoa said to the king, 'My
lord king! May the guilt be on me and on my family; the king and his throne
10 are innocent of it.' •'Bring me the man who threatened you,' the king replied
11 'and he shall never hurt you again.' •Then she said, 'Let the king be pleased to
pronounce the name of Yahweh his God, so that the avenger of blood may not
do greater harm and destroy my son'. 'As Yahweh lives,' he said 'not one hair
of your son shall fall to the ground.'

12   Then the woman said, 'Permit your servant to say something else to my lord
13 the king.' 'Go on' he said. •'Why then' the woman said 'has the king—who
in making this decision convicts himself—so conspired against God's people by
14 not bringing back home the one he has banished? •We must all die; we are like
water spilt on the ground that can never be gathered up again, nor does God
raise up a corpse; let the king make plans then for the one who has
been banished not to remain far away from him in exile.

15   'Now the reason why I have come to speak about this to my lord the king
is because people have frightened me, and your servant thought, "I will speak
16 to the king; perhaps the king will do what his servant asks. •For the king will
consent to deliver his servant from the hands of the man who would cut us off,
17 myself and my son with me, from God's heritage. •May the word of my lord
the king" your servant thought "set me at rest. For my lord the king is like
the angel of God for discerning good and evil." May Yahweh your God be
with you!'

18   Answering her the king said, 'Please do not evade the question I am about
19 to ask you'. The woman said, 'Let my lord the king ask his question'. •'Is not
the hand of Joab behind you in all this?' the king asked. The woman replied,
'As surely as you live, my lord king, I cannot get away from the things which my
lord the king has said. Yes, it was your servant Joab who asked me to
20 do this; he put all these words into your servant's mouth. •Your servant Joab
acted in this way to disguise the matter, but my lord has the wisdom of the
angel of God; he knows all that takes place on earth.'

21   The king then said to Joab, 'Very well, the suit is granted. Go and bring the
22 young man Absalom back.' •Joab fell with his face to the ground, did homage

13 a. By ancient custom, Amnon could have married his half-sister. Such marriages were
forbidden by the laws of Lv 18 and Dt 27.
14 a. About 11 m. S. of Jerusalem.

and blessed the king. 'My lord king,' Joab said 'your servant knows now that
he has won your favour, since the king has done what his servant asked.' •Joab 23
then set off and went to Geshur, and brought Absalom back to Jerusalem. •The 24
king, however, said, 'Let him retire to his own house; he is not to appear in my
presence'. So Absalom retired to his own house and was not received by the king.

Some details about Absalom

In the whole of Israel there was no man who could be praised for his beauty as 25
much as Absalom; from the sole of his foot to the crown of his head there
was not a blemish on him. •When he cut the hair of his head—and he would 26
cut it every year; he would cut it then because it grew too heavy for him—he
would weigh the hair; two hundred shekels, king's weight. •To Absalom were 27
born three sons and one daughter called Tamar; she was a beautiful woman.

Absalom obtains his pardon

Absalom lived in Jerusalem for two years without being received by the king. 28
Then Absalom sent for Joab to send him to the king, but Joab would not come 29
to him. He sent for him a second time, but Joab would not come. •So he said 30
to his servants, 'Look, Joab's field is next to mine and he has barley in it;
go and set fire to it'. Absalom's servants set fire to the field. •At this, Joab went 31
off to Absalom at his house. 'Why' he asked him 'have your servants set fire
to the field belonging to me?' •Absalom answered Joab, 'Look now, I sent word 32
to you to say I wanted you to go to the king with this message, "Why did
I come back from Geshur? Better for me to be there still. Now I wish to be
received by the king, and if I am guilty, let him put me to death."' •Joab went 33
to the king and told him this. He then summoned Absalom who went to the
king and bowed low before him, throwing himself on his face to the ground
before the king. And the king kissed Absalom.

Absalom's intrigues

15 After this, Absalom procured a chariot and horses, with fifty men to run 1
ahead of him. •He would rise early and stand beside the road leading to 2
the gate; and whenever a man with some lawsuit had to come before the king's
court, Absalom would call out to him and ask, 'What town are you from?' He
would answer, 'Your servant is from one of the tribes in Israel'. •Then Absalom 3
would say, 'Look, your case is sound and just, but there is not one deputy of the
king's who will listen to you'. •Absalom would go on to say, 'Oh, who will 4
appoint me judge in the land? Then anyone with a lawsuit or a plea could come
to me and I would see he had justice.' •And whenever anyone came up to do 5
homage to him, he would stretch out his hand and take him and kiss him.
Absalom acted in this way with all the Israelites who came to the king for 6
justice, and so Absalom seduced the hearts of the men of Israel.

Absalom's rebellion

At the end of four years Absalom said to the king, 'Allow me to go to Hebron*ᵃ* 7
to fulfil the vow I made to Yahweh; •for when I was at Geshur in Aram, your 8
servant made this vow: "If Yahweh brings me back to Jerusalem," I said "I will
offer worship to Yahweh in Hebron".' •The king said to him, 'Go in peace'. 9
So he set off and went to Hebron.
Absalom sent couriers throughout the tribes of Israel saying, 'When you hear 10
the trumpet sound you are to say, "Absalom is king at Hebron!"' •With Absalom 11
there went two hundred men from Jerusalem; they were invited guests and came
in all innocence, quite unaware. •Absalom sent for Ahithophel the Gilonite, 12
David's counsellor, from Giloh his town, and had him with him while he was
offering the sacrifices. The conspiracy grew in strength and Absalom's supporters
grew in number.

David's flight

13   A messenger came to tell David, 'The hearts of the men of Israel are now
14 with Absalom.' •So David said to all his officers who were with him in Jerusalem,
'Let us be off, let us fly, or we shall never escape from Absalom. Leave as quickly
as you can in case he mounts a surprise attack and worsts us and puts the city
15 to the sword.' •The king's officers answered, 'Whatever my lord the king decides,
16 we are at your service'. •The king left on foot with all his household, leaving
17 ten concubines to look after the palace. •The king left on foot with all the people
18 and stopped at the last house. •All his officers stood at his side. All the Cherethites and all the Pelethites, with Ittai and all the six hundred Gittites who had
19 come in his retinue from Gath, marched past the king. •The king said to Ittai
the Gittite, 'You, why are you coming with us? Go back and stay with the king,
20 for you are a foreigner, an exile too from your homeland. •You came only
yesterday; should I take you wandering today with us, when I do not know
myself where I am going? Go back, take your fellow countrymen with you, and
21 may Yahweh show you kindness and faithfulness.' •But Ittai answered the king,
'As Yahweh lives, and as my lord the king lives, wherever my lord the king
22 may be, for death or life, there will your servant be too'. •So David said to
Ittai, 'Go then, pass on'. And Ittai of Gath passed on with all his men and
23 retinue. •All the people wept aloud. The king took his stand in the wadi Kidron,
and all the people marched past him towards the wilderness.

The ark leaves the city

24   Zadok was there too and all the Levites carrying the ark of God. They set
down the ark of God beside Abiathar until the people had all passed out of the
25 city. •Then the king said to Zadok, 'Take the ark of God back to the city. Should
I win the favour of Yahweh, he will bring me back and permit me to see it and
26 its dwelling place again. •But should he say, "I take no pleasure in you", then
27 here I am, let him deal with me as he likes.' •The king said to Zadok the
priest, 'Look, you and Abiathar go back in peace to the city, with your two
28 sons, your own son and Jonathan son of Abiathar. •I intend to wait in the
29 plains of the wilderness until word comes from you bringing me news.' •So
Zadok and Abiathar took the ark of God back to Jerusalem and remained there.

Hushai undertakes to work for David

30   David then made his way up the Mount of Olives, weeping as he went, his
head covered and his feet bare. And all the people with him had their heads
31 covered and made their way up, weeping as they went. •Then David was
told that Ahithophel was among the conspirators with Absalom. David said,
'Yahweh, turn Ahithophel's counsels to folly.'
32   As David reached the summit, where God is worshipped, he saw Hushai
the Archite, the companion of David, coming to meet him with his tunic torn
33 and with earth on his head. •David said, 'If you go on with me, you will be
34 a burden to me. •But if you go back to the city and say to Absalom, "I will be
your servant, my lord king; once I was in your father's service, but now I will
35 serve you", you will be able to thwart the counsels of Ahithophel for me. •Will
not the priests Zadok and Abiathar be with you? Anything you hear from the
36 palace you must report to the priests Zadok and Abiathar. •With them, you
will find, are their two sons, Zadok's son Ahimaaz, and Abiathar's son Jonathan;
37 through them you are to send me word of all you hear.' •Hushai, the companion
of David, re-entered the city just as Absalom was reaching Jerusalem.

---

15 a. Having already curried favour with the northern tribes, he is now seeking support in the
south.

David and Ziba

16 When David had passed a little beyond the summit, Ziba the servant of 1
Meribbaal came to meet him with a pair of donkeys, saddled and laden with
two hundred loaves of bread, a hundred bunches of raisins, a hundred of the
season's fruits, and a skin of wine. •The king said to Ziba, 'What are you going 2
to do with that?' 'The donkeys' Ziba replied 'are for the king's family to ride,
the bread and the fruit for the soldiers to eat, the wine is for drinking by those
who grow weary in the wilderness.' •'And where is your master's son?' the king 3
asked. Ziba answered the king, 'Why, he has stayed in Jerusalem because, he
says, "The House of Israel will give me back my father's kingdom today" '.
Then the king said to Ziba, 'All that Meribbaal owns is now yours'. Ziba said, 4
'My homage, lord king! May I deserve your favour!'

Shimei curses David

As David was reaching Bahurim, out came a man of the same clan as Saul's 5
family. His name was Shimei son of Gera, and as he came he uttered curse after
curse •and threw stones at David and at all King David's officers, though the 6
whole army and all the champions flanked the king right and left. •The words 7
of his curse were these, 'Be off, be off, man of blood, scoundrel! •Yahweh has 8
brought on you all the blood of the House of Saul*a* whose sovereignty you have
usurped; and Yahweh has transferred that same sovereignty to Absalom your
son. Now your doom has overtaken you, man of blood that you are.' •Abishai 9
son of Zeruiah said to the king, 'Is this dead dog to curse my lord the king?
Let me go over and cut his head off.' •But the king replied, 'What business is 10
it of mine and yours, sons of Zeruiah? Let him curse. If Yahweh said to him,
"Curse David", what right has anyone to say, "Why have you done this?" '
David said to Abishai and all his officers, 'Why, my own son, sprung from my 11
body, is now seeking my life; so now how much the more this Benjaminite?
Let him curse on if Yahweh has told him to. •Perhaps Yahweh will look on my 12
misery and repay me with good for his curse today.' •So David and his men 13
went on their way. But Shimei continued along the mountainside opposite him,
cursing as he went, throwing stones and flinging earth. •The king and all the 14
people who were with him arrived exhausted at...*b* where he refreshed himself.

Hushai with Absalom

Absalom entered Jerusalem with all the men of Israel; with him was Ahitho- 15
phel. •When Hushai the Archite, the companion of David, came to Absalom, 16
Hushai said to Absalom, 'Long live the king! Long live the king!' •'Is this your 17
affection for your friend?' Absalom said to Hushai. 'Why did you not leave
with your friend?' •Hushai answered Absalom, 'No, I belong to the man whom 18
Yahweh and these people and all the men of Israel have chosen, and on his side
I will remain. •Besides, whom should I serve, if not his son? As I served your 19
father, so I shall serve you.'

Absalom and David's concubines

Absalom said to Ahithophel, 'Think carefully. What shall we do?' •Ahithophel 20/21
answered Absalom, 'Go to your father's concubines whom he left to look after
the palace; then all Israel will hear that you have incurred your father's enmity,
and the resolution of all your supporters will be strengthened'. •So they pitched 22
a tent for Absalom on the housetop and in the sight of all Israel Absalom went
to his father's concubines. •In those days the advice Ahithophel gave was like 23
an oracle asked from God; and so was all Ahithophel's advice respected, as by
David, so by Absalom.

Hushai thwarts Ahithophel's plans

1,2 **17** Ahithophel said to Absalom, 'Let me choose twelve thousand men and set off this very night in pursuit of David. •I shall fall on him while he is tired and dispirited; I shall strike terror into him, and all the people who are
3 with him will take flight. Then I shall strike down the king alone •and bring all the people back to you, as a bride returns to her husband. You seek the life
4 of only one man; the rest of the people will go unharmed.' •The suggestion appealed to Absalom and all the elders of Israel.
5 'Next call Hushai the Archite' Absalom said. 'Let us hear what he too has
6 to say.' •When Hushai came to Absalom, Absalom said, 'This is what Ahithophel
7 says. Are we to do as he suggests? If not, say something yourself.' •Hushai answered Absalom, 'On this occasion the advice Ahithophel has offered is not
8 good. •You know' Hushai went on 'that your father and his men are champions and as angry as a wandering bear robbed of her cubs. Your father is used to
9 warfare; he will not let the army rest during the night. •At this very moment he is hiding in a hollow or somewhere else. If at the outset there are casualties among our troops, word will go round of disaster to the army supporting
10 Absalom. •And then even the valiant, with a heart like the heart of a lion, will be quite unmanned; for all Israel knows that your father is a champion and
11 that the men with him are valiant. •For my part, I offer this advice: Let all Israel, from Dan to Beersheba, muster round you, numerous as the sand on the
12 seashore, with your royal person marching in their midst. •We shall come up with him wherever he is to be found; we shall fall on him as the dew falls on the
13 ground, and not leave him or one of the men with him alive. •Should he retire into a town, all Israel will bring ropes to that town, and we will drag it into
14 the wadi until not a pebble of it is to be found.' •Then Absalom and all the people of Israel said, 'The advice of Hushai the Archite is better than the advice of Ahithophel'. Yahweh had determined to thwart Ahithophel's shrewd advice and so to bring disaster on Absalom.
15 Hushai then told the priests Zadok and Abiathar, 'Ahithophel gave such and such advice to Absalom and the elders of Israel, but I advised so and so.
16 Now send quickly and tell David this, "Do not camp in the plains of the wilderness tonight but cross to the other side as fast as you can, or the king and all the army with him will be annihilated" .'

David is warned and crosses the Jordan

17 Jonathan and Ahimaaz were stationed at the Fuller's Spring; a maidservant was to go and warn them and they in turn were to warn King David, for they
18 dared not let themselves be seen entering the town. •A young man saw them nonetheless and told Absalom. Then both of them hastily made off and came to the house of a man of Bahurim. In his courtyard was a cistern and they got
19 down into it. •The woman took a covering and, spreading it over the mouth of the cistern, scattered crushed grain on it so that nothing showed.
20 Absalom's servants came to the woman in the house and said, 'Where are Ahimaaz and Jonathan?' 'They have gone further on towards the water' the woman answered. They searched, but finding nothing went back to Jerusalem.
21 When they had gone, the men climbed out of the cistern and went to warn King David. 'Be on your way' they told David 'and cross the water quickly,
22 for Ahithophel has given such and such advice about you.' •So David and all the troops with him set off and crossed the Jordan. By dawn no one was left who had not crossed the Jordan.
23 When Ahithophel saw that his advice had not been followed, he saddled his donkey and set off and went home to his own town. Then having set his house in order, he strangled himself and so died. He was buried in his father's tomb.

---

16 a. Probably an allusion to the massacre of 21:1-14.   **b.** A place-name has dropped out of the text.

Absalom crosses the Jordan. David at Mahanaim

David had reached Mahanaim when Absalom crossed the Jordan with all 24 the men of Israel. •Absalom had put Amasa in command of the army in place 25 of Joab. This Amasa was the son of a man called Ithra the Ishmaelite, who had married Abigail the daughter of Jesse and sister of Zeruiah, Joab's mother. Israel and Absalom pitched camp in the land of Gilead. 26

When David reached Mahanaim, Shobi son of Nahash from Rabbah of the 27 Ammonites, Machir son of Ammiel from Lodebar, and Barzillai the Gileadite from Rogelim •brought mattresses, rugs, bowls and crockery, wheat, barley, 28 meal, roasted grain, beans, lentils, •honey, curds and cheese, sheep and oxen, 29 which they presented to David and the people with him for them to eat. 'The army' they said 'has been hungry and tired and thirsty in the wilderness.'

The defeat of Absalom's party

18 David reviewed the troops that were with him, and appointed commanders 1 of thousands and commanders of hundreds to lead them. •David divided 2 the army into three groups, one under the command of Joab, another under the command of Abishai son of Zeruiah, Joab's brother, and the third under the command of Ittai the Gittite. Then David said to the troops, 'I too will march with you in person'. •But the troops replied, 'You must not go. 3 If we are routed, they will not give us a thought; and if half of us die, they will not give us a thought; but you, you are the equal of ten thousand of us. Besides, it is better for you to be ready to reinforce us from the town.' •David said, 4 'I will do as you think best'. And the king stood by the gate as the troops marched 5 out by their hundreds and their thousands. •The king gave orders to Joab, Abishai and Ittai, 'For my sake treat young Absalom gently'. And all the troops heard that the king had given these orders about Absalom to all the commanders. So the troops marched out to take the field against Israel, and battle was joined 6 in the Forest of Ephraim. •There Israel's army was beaten by David's followers; 7 it was a great defeat that day, with twenty thousand casualties. •The fighting 8 spread throughout the region and, of the troops, the forest claimed more victims that day than the sword.

The death of Absalom

Absalom happened to run into some of David's followers. Absalom was 9 riding a mule and the mule passed under the thick branches of a great oak. Absalom's head caught fast in the oak and he was left hanging between heaven and earth, while the mule he was riding went on. •Someone saw this and told 10 Joab. 'I have just seen Absalom' he said 'hanging from an oak.' •Joab said 11 to the man who told him, 'If you saw him, why did you not strike him to the ground then and there? I would have taken it on myself to give you ten silver shekels and a belt too.' •But the man answered Joab, 'Even were I to feel the 12 weight of a thousand silver shekels in my hand, I would not lift my hand against the king's son. In our own hearing the king gave you and Abishai and Ittai these orders, "For my sake spare young Absalom". •Had I acted treacherously, thus 13 endangering my life, nothing is hidden from the king, and you yourself would have stood by idle.' •Then Joab said, 'I cannot waste my time with you 14 like this'. And he took three lances in his hand and thrust them into Absalom's heart while he was still alive there in the oak tree. •Then ten soldiers, Joab's 15 armour-bearers, stepped forward, cut Absalom down and finished him off.

Then Joab had the trumpet sounded and the troops stopped pursuing Israel, 16 for Joab held the troops back. •They took Absalom, flung him into a deep pit 17 in the forest and reared a great cairn over him. All the Israelites had fled, each man to his tent.

Now Absalom during his lifetime had undertaken the erection of the pillar 18 to himself which is in the Valley of the King. 'I have no son' he said 'to preserve

the memory of my name.' So he had given the pillar his name, and it is called
to this day the Pillar of Absalom.

The news is brought to David

19 Ahimaaz son of Zadok said, 'I must run and tell the good news to the king
20 that Yahweh has vindicated his cause by ridding him of his enemies'. •But Joab
said, 'Today you would be no bearer of good news, some other day you will
be; but today you would not be bringing good news, for the king's son is dead'.
21 Then Joab said to the Cushite, 'Go and tell the king what you have seen'. The
22 Cushite bowed to Joab and ran off. •But Ahimaaz son of Zadok persisted.
'Come what may,' he said to Joab 'I must myself run after the Cushite.' 'My son,'
23 Joab said 'why run? You will get no reward for your news.' •But he replied,
'Come what may, I am going to run'. 'Then run' Joab said. And Ahimaaz
set off to run by way of the plain and passed the Cushite.
24 David was sitting between the two gates. The lookout had gone up to the roof
of the gate, on the ramparts; he looked up and saw a man running all by himself.
25 The watch called out to the king and told him. The king said, 'If he is by himself,
26 he has good news to tell'. As the man drew still nearer, •the watch saw another
man running, and the watch who was on top of the gate called out, 'Here comes
another man running by himself'. David said, 'He too is a bearer of good
27 news'. •The watchman said, 'I recognise the way the first man runs; Ahimaaz
son of Zadok runs like that'. 'He is a good man' the king said 'and he comes
with good news.'
28 Ahimaaz approached the king. 'All hail!' he said, and bowed down before
the king with his face to the earth. 'Blessed be Yahweh your God' he said
29 'who has handed over the men who rebelled against my lord the king!' •'Is all
well with young Absalom?' the king asked. Ahimaaz replied, 'I saw there was a
great uproar when Joab despatched your servant, but I do know what it was'.
30 The king said, 'Move aside and stand there'. He moved aside and stood waiting.
31 Then the Cushite arrived. 'Good news for my lord the king!' cried the Cushite.
'Yahweh has vindicated your cause today by ridding you of all who rebelled
32 against you.' •'Is all well with young Absalom?' the king asked the Cushite.
'May the enemies of my lord the king' the Cushite answered 'and all who
rebelled against you to your hurt, share the lot of that young man.'

David mourns for Absalom

¹
₃₃ **19** The king shuddered. He went up to the room over the gate and burst into
tears, and weeping said, 'My son Absalom! My son! My son Absalom!
²
₁ Would I had died in your place! Absalom, my son, my son!' •Word was brought
³
₂ to Joab, 'The king is now weeping and mourning for Absalom'. •And the day's
victory was turned to mourning for all the troops, because they learned that
⁴
₃ the king was grieving for his son. •And the troops returned stealthily that day
⁵
₄ to the town, as troops creep back ashamed when routed in battle. •The king
had veiled his face and was crying aloud, 'My son Absalom! Absalom, my son,
my son!'
⁶
₅ Then Joab went indoors to the king. 'Today' he said 'you are covering the
faces of all your servants with shame when they have saved your life today, and
the lives of your sons and daughters, of your wives too and your concubines,
⁷
₆ all because you love those who hate you and hate those who love you. Today
you have made it plain that commanders and soldiers mean nothing to you,
since now I see that if Absalom were alive today and we all dead, you would
⁸
₇ be pleased. •Now get up, come out and reassure your soldiers, for if you do not
come I swear by Yahweh not one man will stay with you tonight; and this will
be a worse misfortune for you than all that has happened to you from your youth
⁹
₈ until now.' •So the king rose and took his seat at the gate. All the troops soon
heard the news: 'The king' they say 'has taken his seat at the gate'. And the
whole army assembled in front of the king.

Preparations for David's return

Israel had fled, each man to his tent. •Throughout the tribes of Israel all [9] [10] were quarrelling. 'The king' they said 'delivered us from the power of our enemies, he saved us from the hands of the Philistines, and now he himself has had to flee the country to escape from Absalom; •while Absalom, whom we [11]/[10] had anointed to reign over us, has now died in battle. So now why not do something about bringing the king back?'

Word of what was being said throughout Israel reached the king. •Then [12b]/[12a] King David sent word to the priests Zadok and Abiathar, 'Say to the elders of Judah, "Why should you be the last to bring the king home? •You are my [13]/[12] brothers, you are my own flesh and blood, why should you be the last to bring the king back?" •Say to Amasa*a* too, "Are you not my own flesh and blood? May God [14]/[13] do this to me and more, if you are not my army commander from now on, in place of Joab." ' •Then all the men of Judah were won over as one man, [15]/[14] sending word to the king, 'Come back, you and all who serve you'.

Episodes connected with David's return: Shimei

So the king turned about and reached the Jordan. Judah, coming to meet [16]/[15] the king to escort the king across the Jordan, had arrived at Gilgal. •Shimei son [17]/[16] of Gera the Benjaminite from Bahurim hurried down with the men of Judah to meet King David. •With him were a thousand men from Benjamin. Ziba, the [18]/[17] servant of the House of Saul, with his fifteen sons and twenty servants, arrived at the Jordan before the king •and worked manfully ferrying the king's family [19]/[18] across and doing whatever he wanted.

While the king was crossing the Jordan, Shimei son of Gera fell at his feet [20]/[19] and said to the king, 'Let not my lord hold me guilty. Do not remember the wrong your servant did, the day my lord the king left Jerusalem. Put it out of your mind. •For your servant admits that he has sinned, and here I am today, [21]/[20] first of all the House of Joseph to come down and meet my lord the king.'

Then Abishai son of Zeruiah spoke out. 'Does not Shimei deserve death for [22]/[21] cursing Yahweh's anointed?' •But David said, 'What is there between me and [23]/[22] you, sons of Zeruiah, for you to be my enemies today? On such a day, could anyone in Israel be put to death? Today I know for sure that I am king over Israel. •Your life is spared' the king said. And the king gave him his oath.*b* [24]/[23]

Meribbaal

Meribbaal son of Saul had also gone down to meet the king. He had not [25]/[24] cared for his feet or his hands, he had neither trimmed his moustache nor washed his clothes from the day the king left to the day he came back in peace. When he arrived from Jerusalem to greet the king, the king asked him, 'Why [26]/[25] did you not come with me, Meribbaal?' •'My lord king,' he answered 'my [27]/[26] servant deceived me. Your servant said to him, "Saddle my donkey; I shall ride it and go with the king", for your servant is lame. •He has slandered your [28]/[27] servant to my lord the king. But my lord the king is like the angel of God; do as you think right. •For all my father's family earned no better than death from [29]/[28] the hands of my lord the king, and yet you have admitted your servant among those who eat at your table. What right have I to make further appeal to the king?' •The king said, 'Why say any more? I rule that you and Ziba are to share [29]/[29] the property.' •'Let him take it all,' Meribbaal said to the king 'since my lord [31]/[30] the king has come home in peace.'

Barzillai

Barzillai the Gileadite, too, had gone down from Rogelim and had stayed with [32]/[31] the king to escort him as far as the Jordan. •Barzillai was a man of great age; [33]/[32] he was eighty years old. He had kept the king in provisions during his stay at Mahanaim, for he was a very rich man. •'Come with me' the king said to [34]/[33]

35
34 Barzillai 'and I will provide for your old age in Jerusalem with me.' •But
Barzillai answered the king, 'How many years have I left to live, for me to go
36
35 up to Jerusalem with the king? •I am eighty years old now; can I tell the good
from the bad? Has your servant any taste for his food and drink? Can I still
hear the voices of men and women singers? Why should your servant be a further
37
36 burden to my lord the king? •Your servant will just cross the Jordan with the
38
37 king; why should the king grant me such reward? •Allow your servant to go
back to die in my own town near the grave of my father and mother. But here
is your servant Chimham;[c] let him go with my lord the king; treat him as
39
38 you think right.' •The king said, 'Let Chimham go with me then; I will do
things for him that will please you, and anything you request I will do for him
40
39 for your sake'. •All the people then crossed the Jordan and the king crossed too;
he kissed Barzillai and blessed him, and the latter returned to his home.

Judah and Israel dispute over the king

41
40   The king went on to Gilgal and Chimham stayed with him. All the people
42
41 of Judah accompanied the king and half the people of Israel too. •Then all the
men of Israel came to the king. 'Why' they asked the king 'have our brothers,
the men of Judah, carried you off and brought the king and his family across
43
42 the Jordan, and all David's men with him?' •All the men of Judah retorted to
the men of Israel, 'Because the king is more closely related to us. Why do you
take offence at this? Have we eaten at the king's expense or levied portions for
44
43 ourselves?' •The men of Israel replied to the men of Judah, 'We have ten shares
in the king. We are your elder too. Why have you despised us then? Were we
not the first to speak of bringing back the king?' But the language of the men
of Judah was more vehement than that of the men of Israel.

The revolt of Sheba

1
20 Now there happened to be a scoundrel there called Sheba son of Bichri,
a Benjaminite, who sounded the trumpet and cried:

> 'We have no share in David,
> we have no inheritance in the son of Jesse.
> Every man to his tents, Israel!'

2 At this all the men of Israel deserted David and followed Sheba son of Bichri.
But the men of Judah stayed with their king on his way from Jordan to
Jerusalem.

3   So David came to his palace at Jerusalem. He took the ten concubines he
had left to look after the palace and put them under guard. He provided for
their upkeep but never went to them again; they were shut away until the day
they died, widows, as it were, of a living man.

The assassination of Amasa

4   The king said to Amasa, 'Summon the men of Judah to me, and be here yourself
5 within three days'. •Amasa went to summon Judah, but he delayed beyond the
6 time David had fixed. •David then said to Abishai, 'Sheba son of Bichri is more
dangerous to us than ever Absalom was, so take your master's guards and be
7 after him, or he may reach fortified towns and elude us'. •Behind Abishai marched
Joab, the Cherethites, the Pelethites and all the champions, marching from
8 Jerusalem in pursuit of Sheba son of Bichri. •They were near the great stone
at Gibeon when Amasa came face to face with them. Joab was wearing his
uniform, over which he had buckled on a sword hanging from his waist in its
9 scabbard; the sword came out and fell. •Joab said to Amasa, 'Are you well,
my brother?' And with his right hand he took Amasa by the beard to kiss him.

---

19 a. The military commander of the rebellion, 17:25.   **b.** But he made sure that vengeance
was exacted after his death, 1 K 2:8f.   **c.** Barzillai's son.

Amasa paid no attention to the sword Joab was holding, and Joab struck him 10
with it in the belly and spilled his entrails on the ground. He did not need to
strike a second blow; and so Amasa died. Joab and Abishai hurried on in pursuit
of Sheba son of Bichri.

One of Joab's soldiers stood on guard beside Amasa. 'Whoever is on Joab's 11
side,' he said 'whoever is for David, let him follow Joab.' •Meanwhile Amasa 12
lay in the middle of the road in pools of his blood. Seeing that everyone was
stopping, the man dragged Amasa off the road into the field and threw a cloak
over him, because he saw that everyone stopped on reaching him. •When 13
Amasa had been taken off the road, the men all went on their way, following
Joab in pursuit of Sheba son of Bichri.

The rebellion ends

The latter went all through the tribes of Israel as far as Abel of Beth-maacah 14
and all the Bichrites. . . . They mustered and went in after him. •Besieging him 15
in Abel of Beth-maacah, they threw up earthworks against the city. •As all the 16
troops who were with Joab were sapping the wall to bring it down, a quick-
witted woman stood on the outer wall and shouted from the town, 'Listen!
Listen! Say to Joab, "Come here, I want to speak to you". ' •He came forward, 17
and the woman said, 'Are you Joab?' 'I am' he answered. She said to him,
'Listen to what your servant says'. 'I am listening' he replied. •Then she spoke. 18
'In olden days' she said 'they used to say, "Let them ask in Abel and in Dan
if all is over •with what Israel's faithful ones have laid down". Yet you are trying 19
to destroy a town, yes a mother city, in Israel. Why do you wish to devour the
heritage of Yahweh?' •'Far, far be it from me' Joab said. 'I neither wish to 20
devour nor to destroy. •This is not the issue; but a man of the highlands 21
of Ephraim called Sheba son of Bichri has revolted against the king, against
David. Hand that one man over and I will raise the siege of the town.' 'Very
well,' the woman said to Joab 'his head shall be thrown over the wall to you.'
The woman went back into the town and spoke to all the people as her intel- 22
ligence dictated. They cut off the head of Sheba son of Bichri and threw it down
to Joab. He had the trumpet sounded and they withdrew from the town, each
man to his tents. Joab himself returned to the king in Jerusalem.

David's officials

Joab commanded the whole army; Benaiah son of Jehoiada commanded the 23
Cherethites and Pelethites; •Adoram was in charge of forced labour; Jehoshaphat 24
son of Ahilud was recorder; •Sheva, secretary; Zadok and Abiathar, priests. 25
Ira the Jairite was also a priest of David. 26

II. SUPPLEMENTARY INFORMATION

The great famine and the execution of Saul's descendants[a]

21 In the time of David there was a famine lasting for three whole years. 1
David consulted Yahweh, and Yahweh said, 'There is blood on Saul and his
family because he put the Gibeonites to death'. •The king then summoned the 2
Gibeonites and said to them—now the Gibeonites were not Israelites, they were
a remnant of the Amorites to whom the Israelites had bound themselves by
oath; but Saul in his zeal for the Israelites and for Judah had tried to crush
them—•'What must I do for you?' David therefore asked the Gibeonites, 'how 3
make amends, for you to call down a blessing on the heritage of Yahweh?'
The Gibeonites answered, 'It is no mere matter of silver or gold between 4
ourselves and Saul and his family; nor is it for us to have any man in Israel put
to death'. David said, 'Say what you want and I will do it for you'. •So they 5
told the king, 'It is about the man who decimated us and planned to annihilate

6 us so that we should no longer exist anywhere in Israelite territory. •Let seven of his sons be handed over to us, for us to impale them before Yahweh at Gibeon 7 on the mountain of Yahweh.' 'I will hand them over' the king said. •The king spared Meribbaal son of Jonathan, son of Saul, on account of the oath by Yahweh 8 that bound them together, David and Jonathan son of Saul. •But the king took the two sons that Rizpah the daughter of Aiah had borne Saul, Armoni and Meribbaal; also the five sons that Merab the daughter of Saul had borne Adriel 9 son of Barzillai, of Meholah. •He handed these over to the Gibeonites who impaled them on the mountain before Yahweh. The seven of them perished together; they were put to death in the first days of the harvest, at the beginning of the barley harvest.

10 Rizpah the daughter of Aiah took sackcloth and spread it for herself on the rock from the beginning of the barley harvest until the rain fell from the sky on them;[b] she did not allow the birds of heaven to come at them by day nor the 11 wild beasts by night. •David was told what Rizpah the daughter of Aiah, Saul's 12 concubine, had done. •David went and took the bones of Saul and his son Jonathan from the chief men of Jabesh-gilead. These had stolen them from the square in Beth-shan where the Philistines had hung them when the Philistines 13 had defeated Saul at Gilboa. •David brought the bones of Saul and his son Jonathan from there and put them together with the bones of those who had been 14 impaled. •They buried the bones of Saul, of his son Jonathan, and of those who had been impaled, in the land of Benjamin at Zela in the tomb of Saul's father, Kish. They did all that the king ordered; and after that, God took pity on the country.

Various exploits against the Philistines

15 Once again the Philistines made war on Israel. David went down with his guards; they pitched camp at Gob and fought the Philistines. Then there arose 16 Dodo •son of Joash, a descendant of Rapha. His spear weighed three hundred shekels of bronze; he was wearing a new sword and was confident he could kill 17 David. •But Abishai son of Zeruiah went to his rescue; he struck down the Philistine and killed him. It was then that David's men urged him, 'You must never again go into battle with us' they said 'in case you put out the lamp of Israel.'

18 After this, war with the Philistines broke out at Gob again. This was when Sibbecai of Hushah killed Saph, a descendant of Rapha.

19 Again war with the Philistines broke out at Gob, and Elhanan son of Jair from Bethlehem killed Goliath of Gath, the shaft of whose spear was like a 20 weaver's beam. •There was another battle at Gath, where there was a man of huge stature with six fingers on each hand and six toes on each foot, twenty-four 21 in all. He too was a descendant of Rapha. •Jonathan, son of David's brother, Shimeah, killed him when he defied Israel.

22 These four were descended from Rapha of Gath and fell at the hands of David and his guards.

A psalm of David

1 **22** David addressed the words of this song to Yahweh when Yahweh had
2 delivered him from all his enemies and from the hands of Saul. •He said:

> Yahweh is my rock and my bastion,
3 >   my deliverer is my God.
>   I take refuge in him, my rock,
>   my shield, my horn of salvation,

21 a. This narrative is detached from its context and the events are probably to be placed before 9:1. The whole of the next four chapters of 'Supplementary Information' interrupt the long story of David's family, which is resumed in 1 K. **b.** The sign that the expiation is accepted and the famine (see v.1) will soon be over.

my stronghold and my refuge.
From violence you rescue me.
He is to be praised; on Yahweh I call   4
and am saved from my enemies.

The waves of death encircled me,   5
the torrents of Belial burst on me;
the cords of Sheol girdled me,   6
the snares of death were before me.

In my distress I called to Yahweh   7
and to my God I cried;
from his Temple he heard my voice,
my cry came to his ears.

Then the earth quivered and quaked,   8
the foundations of the heavens trembled
(they quivered because he was angry);
from his nostrils a smoke ascended,   9
and from his mouth a fire that consumed
(live embers were kindled at it).

He bent the heavens and came down,   10
a dark cloud under his feet;
he mounted a cherub and flew,   11
and soared on the wings of the wind.

Darkness he made a veil to surround him,   12
his tent a watery darkness, dense cloud;
before him a flash enkindled   13
hail and fiery embers.

Yahweh thundered from heaven,   14
the Most High made his voice heard;
he let his arrows fly and scattered them,
launched the lightnings and routed them.   15

The bed of the seas was revealed,   16
the foundations of the world were laid bare
at Yahweh's muttered threat,
at the blast of his nostrils' breath.

He sends from on high and takes me,   17
he draws me from deep waters,
he delivers me from my powerful enemy,
from foes too strong for me.   18

They assailed me on my day of disaster,   19
but Yahweh was my support;
he freed me, set me at large,   20
he rescued me, since he loves me.

Yahweh requites me as I act justly,   21
as my hands are pure so he repays me,
since I have kept the ways of Yahweh,   22
and not fallen away from my God.

His judgements are all before me,   23
his statutes I have not put from me;
I am blameless in his presence,
I keep sin at arm's length.   24

25   And Yahweh repays me as I act justly,
as my purity is in his sight.

26   Faithful you are with the faithful,
blameless with the blameless,

27   pure with the one who is pure,
but crafty with the devious,

28   you save a people that is humble
and humiliate eyes that are haughty.

29   Yahweh, you yourself are my lamp,
my God lights up my darkness;

30   with you I storm the barbican,
with my God I leap the rampart.

31   This God, his way is blameless,
the word of Yahweh is without dross.
He it is who is the shield
of all who take refuge in him.

32   Who else is God but Yahweh,
who else a rock save our God?

33   This God who girds me with strength
and makes my way without blame,

34   who makes my feet like the hinds'
and holds me from falling on the heights,

35   who trains my hands for battle,
my arms to bend a bow of bronze.

36   You give me your saving shield
and your armour covers me over.

37   Wide room you have made for my steps under me;
my feet have never faltered.

38   I pursue my enemies and destroy them,
nor turn back till an end is made of them;

39   I strike them down, and they do not rise,
they fall, they are under my feet.

40   You have girt me with strength for the fight,
bent down my assailants beneath me,

41   made my enemies turn their backs to me;
and those who hate me I destroy.

42   They cry out, there is no one to save,
to Yahweh, but there is no reply;

43   I crush them fine as the dust of the squares,
trample them like the mud of the streets.

44   You deliver me from a people in revolt,
you place me at the head of the nations,
a people I did not know are now my servants,

45   foreigners come wooing my favour,
no sooner do they hear than they obey me,

46   foreigners grow faint of heart,
they come trembling out of their fastnesses.

47   Life to Yahweh! Blessed be my rock!
Exalted be the God of my salvation,

> the God who gives me vengeance   48
> and crushes the peoples beneath me,
>
> who rescues me from my enemies.   49
> You lift me high above those who attack me,
> you deliver me from the man of violence.
>
> For this I will praise you, Yahweh, among the heathen,   50
> and sing praise to your name.
> His king he saves and saves again,   51
> displays his love for his anointed,
> for David and his heirs for ever.

The last words of David

23 These are the last words of David: 1

> Oracle of David son of Jesse,
> oracle of the man raised to eminence,
> the anointed of the God of Jacob,
> the singer of the songs of Israel.
>
> The spirit of Yahweh speaks through me,   2
> his word is on my tongue;
> the God of Jacob has spoken,   3
> the Rock of Israel has said to me:
>
> He who rules men with justice,
> who rules in the fear of God,
> is like morning light at sunrise   4
> (on a cloudless morning)
> making the grass of the earth sparkle after rain.
>
> Yes, my House stands firm with God: 5
> he has made an everlasting covenant with me,
> all in order, well assured;
> does he not bring to flower all that saves me, all I desire?
>
> But godless men are all like desert thorns,   6
> for these are never gathered by hand:
> no one touches them   7
> unless with iron or the shaft of a spear,
> and then they are burnt in the fire.

David's champions

These are the names of David's champions: Ishbaal the Hachmonite, leader 8
of the three; it was he who wielded his battle-axe against eight hundred whom
he killed at one time. •After him there was Eleazar son of Dodo, the Ahohite, 9
one of the three champions. He was with David at Pas-dammim when the Philistines mustered for battle there and the men of Israel retreated before them.
But he stood his ground and struck down the Philistines until his hand was so 10
numb that it stuck to the sword. Yahweh brought about a great victory that
day, and though the army rallied behind Eleazar it was only to plunder. •After 11
him there was Shamma son of Elah, the Hararite. The Philistines had mustered
at Lehi. There was a field full of lentils there; the army took flight before the
Philistines, •but he positioned himself in the middle of the field, defended it, 12
and struck down the Philistines. So Yahweh brought about a great victory.

13   Three out of the thirty went down at the beginning of the harvest and came to David at the Cave of Adullam while a company of Philistines was encamped
14 in the Valley of the Rephaim. •David was then in the stronghold, and there was
15 a Philistine garrison in Bethlehem. •'Oh,' David sighed 'if someone would fetch
16 me a drink of water from the well that stands by the gate at Bethlehem!' •At this the three champions, forcing their way through the Philistine camp, drew water from the well that stands by the gate of Bethlehem, and bringing it away presented it to David. But he would drink none of it and poured it out as a libation to
17 Yahweh. •'Yahweh keep me' he said 'from drinking this! This is the blood of men who went at the risk of their lives.' And so he would not drink. Such were the deeds of the three champions.

18   Abishai, the brother of Joab and son of Zeruiah, was leader of the thirty. It was he who wielded his spear against three hundred whom he killed, winning
19 himself a name among the thirty. •He was more famous than the thirty and became their captain, but he was no rival for the three.

20   Benaiah son of Jehoiada, a hero from Kabzeel, a man of many exploits, struck down the two champions of Moab and, one snowy day, went down and
21 killed the lion in the cistern. •He was also the man who killed an Egyptian of great stature. The Egyptian had a spear in his hand, but he went down against him with a staff, tore the spear from the Egyptian's hand and killed the man
22 with it. •Such were the exploits of Benaiah son of Jehoiada, winning him a name
23 among the thirty champions. •He was more famous than the thirty, but he was no rival for the three. David put him in command of his bodyguard.

24   Asahel the brother of Joab was one of the thirty;
        Elhanan son of Dodo, from Bethlehem;
25   Shammah from Harod;
        Elika from Harod;
26   Helez from Beth-pelet;
        Ira son of Ikkesh, from Tekoa;
27   Abiezer from Anathoth;
        Sibbecai from Hushah;
28   Zalmon from Ahoh;
        Maharai from Netophah;
29   Heled son of Baanah, from Netophah;
        Ittai son of Ribai, from Gibeah of Benjamin;
30   Benaiah from Pirathon;
        Hiddai from the wadis of Gaash;
31   Abialbon from Beth-arabah;
        Azmaveth from Bahurim;
32   Eliahba from Shaalbon;
        Jashen from Gimzo;
33   Jonathan •son of Shammah, from Harar;
        Ahiam son of Sharar, from Harar;
34   Eliphelet son of Ahasbai, from Beth-maacah;
        Eliam son of Ahithophel, from Gilo;
35   Hezro from Carmel;
        Paarai from Arab;
36   Igal son of Nathan, from Zobah;
        Bani the Gadite;
37   Zelek the Ammonite;
        Naharai, from Beeroth, armour-bearer to Joab son of Zeruiah;
38   Ira from Jattir;
        Gareb from Jattir;
39   Uriah the Hittite—

thirty-seven in all.

The census

24 The anger of Yahweh once again blazed out against the Israelites and he ¹
incited David against them. 'Go,' he said 'take a census of Israel and
Judah.' •The king said to Joab and to the senior army officers who were with ²
him, 'Now go throughout the tribes of Israel from Dan to Beersheba and take
a census of the people; I wish to know the size of the population.' •Joab said ³
to the king, 'May Yahweh your God multiply the people a hundred times while
my lord the king still has eyes to see it, but why should my lord the king be so
set on this?' •But the king enforced his order on Joab and the senior officers, ⁴
and Joab and the senior officers went from the king's presence to take a census
of the people of Israel.

They crossed the Jordan and made a start with Aroer and the town that is ⁵
in the middle of the wadi, moving on to the Gadites and towards Jazer. •They ⁶
then went to Gilead and to Kadesh in the land of the Hittites; next they went
on to Dan and from Dan made their way round towards Sidon. •They then ⁷
came to the fortress of Tyre and to all the towns of the Hivites and Canaanites,
ending up in the Negeb of Judah at Beersheba. •Having covered the whole ⁸
country, they returned to Jerusalem at the end of nine months and twenty days.
Joab gave the king the figures for the census of the people; Israel numbered ⁹
eight hundred thousand armed men capable of drawing sword, and Judah five
hundred thousand men.

The pestilence. God's forgiveness

But afterwards David's heart misgave him for having taken a census of the ¹⁰
people. 'I have committed a grave sin' David said to Yahweh. 'But now, Yahweh,
I beg you to forgive your servant for this fault. I have been very foolish.' •But ¹¹
when David got up next morning, the following message had come from Yahweh
to the prophet Gad, David's seer, •'Go and say to David, "Yahweh says this: ¹²
I offer you three things; choose one of them for me to do to you" '.

So Gad went to David and told him. 'Are three years of famine to come on ¹³
you in your country' he said 'or will you flee for three months before your
pursuing enemy, or would you rather have three days' pestilence in your country?
Now think, and decide how I am to answer him who sends me.' •David said to ¹⁴
Gad, 'This is a hard choice. But let us rather fall into the power of Yahweh,
since his mercy is great, and not into the power of men.' •So David chose ¹⁵
pestilence.

It was the time of the wheat harvest. Yahweh sent a pestilence on Israel from
the morning till the time appointed and plague ravaged the people, and from
Dan to Beersheba seventy thousand men of them died. •The angel stretched out ¹⁶
his hand towards Jerusalem to destroy it, but Yahweh thought better of this
evil, and he said to the angel who was destroying the people, 'Enough! Now
withdraw your hand.' The angel of Yahweh was beside the threshing-floor of
Araunah the Jebusite. •When David saw the angel who was ravaging the people, ¹⁷
he spoke to Yahweh. 'It was I who sinned;' he said 'I who did this wicked thing.
But these, this flock, what have they done? Let your hand lie heavy on me then,
and on my family.'

An altar is built

Gad went to David that day and said, 'Go up and erect an altar to Yahweh ¹⁸
on the threshing-floor of Araunah the Jebusite'. •So at Gad's bidding David ¹⁹
went up as Yahweh had ordered him. •When Araunah looked down and ²⁰
saw the king and his officers advancing towards him—Araunah was threshing
the wheat—he came forward and with his face to the ground did the king
homage. •'Why has my lord the king come to his servant?' Araunah asked. ²¹
David answered, 'To buy the threshing-floor from you, in order to build an
altar to Yahweh, so that the plague may leave the people'. •'Let my lord the king ²²

take it' Araunah said to David 'and offer up what he thinks right. Here are the oxen for the holocaust, the threshing-sled and the oxen's yoke for the wood.

23 The servant of my lord the king gives all this to the king. And' Araunah said to the king 'may Yahweh your God accept your offering.'

24 But the king said to Araunah, 'No, I must pay you money for it; I will not offer Yahweh my God holocausts that have cost me nothing'. So David paid

25 fifty shekels in silver for the threshing-floor and oxen. •David built an altar to Yahweh there and offered holocausts and communion sacrifices. Then Yahweh took pity on the country and the plague was turned away from Israel.

THE BOOKS OF THE

KINGS

THE FIRST BOOK OF THE KINGS

I. THE DAVIDIC SUCCESSION

David's last days. The intrigues of Adonijah

1 King David was an old man well on in years and though they laid coverlets 1
over him he could not keep warm. •So his servants said to him, 'Let some 2
young girl be found for my lord the king, to wait on the king and look after him;
she shall lie on your breast and this will keep my lord the king warm'. •Having 3
searched for a beautiful girl throughout the territory of Israel, they found Abishag
of Shunem and brought her to the king. •The girl was of great beauty. She 4
looked after the king and waited on him but the king had no intercourse with her.
Now Adonijah, Haggith's son, was ambitious; he thought he might be king; 5
accordingly he procured a chariot and team with fifty men to run in front of
him. •At no time in his life had his father ever crossed him by asking, 'Why do you 6
behave like this?' He was also very handsome; his mother had given birth to him
after Absalom. •He conferred with Joab son of Zeruiah and with the priest 7
Abiathar*a* who rallied to Adonijah's cause; •but neither Zadok the priest, nor 8
Benaiah son of Jehoiada, nor the prophet Nathan, nor Shimei and his companions, David's champions, supported Adonijah.
One day when Adonijah was sacrificing sheep and oxen and fattened calves 9
at the Sliding Stone which is beside the Fuller's Spring, he invited all his brothers,
the royal princes, and all the men of Judah in the king's service; •but he did not 10
invite the prophet Nathan, or Benaiah, or the champions, or his brother Solomon.

The intrigues of Nathan and Bathsheba

Then Nathan said to Bathsheba, Solomon's mother, 'Have you not heard that 11
unknown to our lord David, Adonijah, Haggith's son, has become king? •Well, 12
this is my advice to you if you want to save your own life and the life of
your son Solomon. •Go straight in to King David and say, "My lord king, did 13
you not make your servant this promise on oath: Your son Solomon is to be
king after me; he is the one who is to sit on my throne? How is it, then, that
Adonijah is king?" •And while you are still there talking to the king, I will 14
come in after you and confirm what you say.'
So Bathsheba went to the king in his room (he was very old and Abishag of 15
Shunem was in attendance on him). •She knelt down and did homage to the 16
king, and the king said, 'What is your wish?' •'My lord,' she answered 'you swore 17
this to your servant by Yahweh your God, "Your son Solomon is to be king after
me; he is the one who is to sit on my throne". •And now here is Adonijah king 18
and you, my lord king, knowing nothing about it. •He has sacrificed quantities 19'
of oxen and fattened calves and sheep, and invited all the royal princes, the

priest Abiathar, and Joab the army commander; but he has not invited your
20 servant Solomon. •Yet you are the man, my lord king, to whom all Israel looks,
21 to name for them the successor of my lord the king.ᵇ •And when my lord the
king sleeps with his fathers, my son Solomon and I will be made to suffer for
this.'

22
23 She was still speaking when the prophet Nathan entered. •'The prophet
Nathan is here' they told the king; and he came into the king's presence and
24 bowed down to the ground on his face before the king. •'My lord king,' said
Nathan 'is this, then, your decree: "Adonijah is to be king after me; he is the
25 one who is to sit on my throne"? •For he has gone down today and sacrificed
quantities of oxen and fattened calves and sheep, and invited all the royal princes,
the army chiefs, and the priest Abiathar; and they are there now, eating and
26 drinking in his presence and shouting, "Long live King Adonijah!" •He has not,
however, invited me your servant, Zadok the priest, Benaiah son of Jehoiada, or
27 your servant Solomon. •Is this with my lord the king's approval? Or have you
not told those loyal to you who is to succeed to the throne of my lord the king?'

Solomon is consecrated king at David's nomination

28 Then King David spoke. 'Call Bathsheba to me' he said. And she came into
29 the king's presence and stood before him. •Then the king swore this oath, 'As
30 Yahweh lives, who has delivered me from all adversity, •just as I swore to you
by Yahweh the God of Israel that your son Solomon should be king after me and
31 take my place on the throne, so I will bring it about this very day'. •Bathsheba
knelt down, her face to the ground, and did homage to the king. 'May my lord
32 King David live for ever!' she said. •Then King David said, 'Summon Zadok
the priest, the prophet Nathan and Benaiah son of Jehoiada'. So they came
33 into the king's presence. •'Take the royal guard with you,' said the king 'mount
34 my son Solomon on my own mule and escort him down to Gihon. •There Zadok
the priest and the prophet Nathan are to anoint him king of Israel; then sound
35 the trumpet and shout, "Long live King Solomon!" •Then you are to follow him
up and he is to come and take his seat on my throne and be king in place of me,
36 for he is the man I have appointed as ruler of Israel and of Judah.' •Benaiah son
of Jehoiada answered the king. 'Amen!' he said 'And may Yahweh too say
37 Amen to the words of my lord the king! •As Yahweh has been with my lord the
king, so may he be with Solomon and make his throne even greater than the
throne of my lord King David!'

38 Then Zadok the priest, the prophet Nathan, Benaiah son of Jehoiada, and
the Cherethites and Pelethites went down; they mounted Solomon on King
39 David's mule and escorted him to Gihon. •Zadok the priest took the horn of oil
from the Tent and anointed Solomon. They sounded the trumpet and all the
40 people shouted, 'Long live King Solomon!' •The people all followed him up, with
pipes playing and loud rejoicing and shouts to split the earth.

Adonijah is afraid

41 Adonijah and his guests, who had by then finished their meal, all heard the
noise. Joab too heard the sound of the trumpet and said, 'What is that noise of
42 uproar in the city?' •While he was still speaking, Jonathan the son of Abiathar
the priest arrived. 'Come in,' Adonijah said 'you are an honest man, so you
43 must be bringing good news.' •'Yes,' Jonathan answered 'our lord King David
44 has made Solomon king. •The king sent Zadok the priest with him, and the
prophet Nathan and Benaiah son of Jehoiada and the Cherethites and Pelethites;
45 they mounted him on the king's mule, •and Zadok the priest and the prophet
Nathan anointed him king at Gihon; and they went up from there with shouts

---

1 a. Joab, see 2 S 19; Abiathar, see 1 S 22.   b. The king was expected to choose his successor
from among his sons.

of joy and the city is now in an uproar; that was the noise you heard. •What is 46
more, Solomon is seated on the royal throne. •And further, the king's officers 47
have been to congratulate our lord King David with the words, "May your God
make the name of Solomon more glorious even than yours, and his throne more
exalted than your own!" And the king bowed down on his bed, •and then said, 48
"Blessed be Yahweh, the God of Israel, who has allowed my eyes to see one of
my descendants sitting on my throne today".'

At this, all Adonijah's guests, taking fright, rose and made off in their several 49
directions. •Adonijah, in terror of Solomon, rose too and ran off to cling to 50
the horns of the altar. •Solomon was told, 'You should know that Adonijah is in 51
terror of King Solomon and is now clinging to the horns of the altar, saying,
"Let King Solomon first swear to me that he will not have his servant put to the
sword"'. •'Should he bear himself honourably,' Solomon answered 'not one 52
hair of his shall fall to the ground; but if he is found malicious, he shall die.'
King Solomon then sent for him to be brought down from the altar; he came 53
and did homage to King Solomon; Solomon said to him, 'Go to your house'.

David's testament. His death

2 As David's life drew to its close he laid this charge on his son Solomon, 1
'I am going the way of all the earth. Be strong and show yourself a man. 2
Observe the injunctions of Yahweh your God, following his ways and keeping 3
his laws, his commandments, his customs and his decrees, as it stands written
in the Law of Moses, that so you may be successful in all you do and undertake,
so that Yahweh may fulfil the promise he made me, "If your sons are careful 4
how they behave, and walk loyally before me with all their heart and soul, you
shall never lack for a man on the throne of Israel".

'You know too what Joab son of Zeruiah did to me, and what he did to the 5
two commanders of the army of Israel, Abner son of Ner and Amasa son of
Jether; how he murdered them, how in time of peace he took vengeance for
blood shed in war, staining the belt round my waist and the sandals on my feet
with innocent blood. •You will be wise not to let his grey head go down to 6
Sheol in peace. •As regards the sons of Barzillai of Gilead, treat them kindly, 7
let them be among those who eat at your table, for they were as kind to me when
I was fleeing from your brother Absalom. •You also have with you Shimei son 8
of Gera, the Benjaminite from Bahurim. He called down a terrible curse on me
the day I left for Mahanaim, but he came down to meet me at the Jordan and
I swore to him by Yahweh I would not put him to the sword. •But you, you 9
must not let him go unpunished; you are a wise man and will know how to deal
with him to bring his grey head down to Sheol in blood.'

So David slept with his ancestors and was buried in the Citadel of David. 10
David's reign over Israel lasted forty years: he reigned in Hebron for seven years, 11
and in Jerusalem for thirty-three.

The death of Adonijah

Solomon was seated upon the throne of David, and his sovereignty was 12
securely established.

Adonijah, Haggith's son, went to Bathsheba the mother of Solomon and 13
bowed down before her. 'Do you bring peace?' she asked. He answered, 'Yes,
peace'. •Then he said, 'I have something to say to you'. 'Speak' she replied. 14
'You know' he said 'that the kingdom should have come to me,ᵃ and that all 15
Israel expected me to be king; but the crown eluded me and fell to my brother,
since it came to him from Yahweh. •Now I have one request to make you; 16
do not refuse me.' 'Speak' she said. •He went on, 'Please ask King Solomon—for 17
he will not refuse you—to give me Abishag of Shunem in marriage'. •'Very well,' 18
Bathsheba replied 'I will speak to the king about you.' •So Bathsheba went to 19
King Solomon to speak to him about Adonijah; the king rose to meet her and

bowed before her; he then sat down on his throne; a seat was brought for the
20 mother of the king, and she sat down at his right hand. •She said, 'I have one
small request to make you; do not refuse me'. 'My mother,' the king answered
21 'make your request, for I will not refuse you.' •'Let Abishag of Shunem' she
22 said 'be given in marriage to your brother Adonijah.' •King Solomon answered
his mother. 'And why' he said 'do you request Abishag of Shunem for Adonijah?
You might as well request the kingdom for him,[b] since he is my elder brother
23 and Abiathar the priest and Joab son of Zeruiah are on his side.' •And King
Solomon swore by Yahweh: 'May God do this to me and more' he said 'if
24 Adonijah does not pay for these words of his with his life! •As Yahweh lives
who has set me securely on the throne of David my father, and who, as he
promised, has given him a dynasty, Adonijah shall be put to death this very
25 day.' •And King Solomon commissioned Benaiah son of Jehoiada to strike him
down, and he died.

The fate of Abiathar and Joab

26 As for Abiathar the priest, the king said to him, 'Go to Anathoth[c] to your
estate. You deserve to die, but I am not going to put you to death now, since
you carried the ark of Yahweh in the presence of David my father and shared
27 all my father's hardships.' •Solomon deprived Abiathar of the priesthood of
Yahweh, thus fulfilling the oracle Yahweh had uttered against the House of
Eli at Shiloh.

28 When the news reached Joab—for Joab had lent his support to Adonijah,
though he had not supported Absalom—he fled to the Tent of Yahweh and
29 clung to the horns of the altar. •King Solomon was told, 'Joab has fled to the
Tent of Yahweh; he is there beside the altar'. Then Solomon sent word to Joab,
'What reason did you have for fleeing to the altar?' Joab replied, 'I was afraid
of you and fled to Yahweh'. Then Solomon sent Benaiah son of Jehoiada.
30 'Go' he said 'and strike him down.' •Accordingly Benaiah went to the Tent
of Yahweh. 'By order of the king,' he said 'come out!' 'No,' he said 'I will die
here.' So Benaiah brought back word to the king, 'This is what Joab said, and
31 the answer he gave me'. •'Do as he says' the king replied. 'Strike him down
and bury him, and so rid me and my family today of the innocent blood Joab
32 has shed. •Yahweh will bring his blood down on his own head, because he struck
down two more honourable and better men than he, and put to the sword,
without my father David's knowledge, Abner son of Ner, commander of the army
33 of Israel, and Amasa son of Jether, commander of the army of Judah. •May their
blood come down on the head of Joab and his descendants for ever, but may
David, his descendants, his dynasty, his throne, have peace for ever from Yahweh.'
34 Whereupon Benaiah son of Jehoiada went out, struck Joab down and put him
35 to death; he was buried at his home in the wilderness. •In his place as head of
the army the king appointed Benaiah son of Jehoiada and, in place of Abiathar,
Zadok the priest.

The disobedience and death of Shimei

36 The king had Shimei summoned to him. 'Build yourself a house in Jerusalem,'
37 he told him 'you are to live there; do not move anywhere else. •The day you go out
and cross the wadi Kidron, be sure you will certainly die. Your blood will be
38 on your own head.' •'Very well,' Shimei answered the king 'your servant will
do as my lord the king orders.' And for a long time Shimei lived in Jerusalem.
39 But when three years had gone by, it happened that two of Shimei's slaves
ran away to Achish son of Maacah, king of Gath; Shimei was told, 'Your slaves
40 are in Gath'. •At this, Shimei set about saddling his donkey and went to Achish at

2 a. He was the elder.   b. To take the wife of a dead or deposed king gave a title to succession.
c. Levitical town near Jerusalem.

Gath to find his slaves. He went off and brought his slaves back from Gath.
Solomon was informed that Shimei had gone from Jerusalem to Gath and had 41
come back.

The king had Shimei summoned to him. 'Did I not make you swear by 42
Yahweh,' he said 'and did I not solemnly warn you: The day you go out to go
anywhere else, be sure you will certainly die? •Why did you not keep the oath 43
of Yahweh and the order I laid on you? •You know all the evil you did to my 44
father David' the king went on. 'Yahweh will bring your wickedness down on
your own head. •But may King Solomon be blessed, and may the throne of 45
David be kept secure before Yahweh for ever.' •The king gave orders to Benaiah 46
son of Jehoiada; he went out and struck down Shimei; and he died.

And now the sovereignty was securely in the hands of Solomon.

II. SOLOMON IN ALL HIS GLORY

A. SOLOMON THE SAGE

Introduction

3 Solomon allied himself by marriage with Pharaoh*ᵃ* king of Egypt; he married 1
Pharaoh's daughter, and took her to the Citadel of David until he could
complete the building of his palace and the Temple of Yahweh and the wall
surrounding Jerusalem. •The people, however, were still sacrificing on the high 2
places, because at that time a dwelling place for the name of Yahweh had not
yet been built. •Solomon loved Yahweh: he followed the precepts of David his 3
father, except that he offered sacrifice and incense on the high places.

Solomon's dream at Gibeon

The king went to Gibeon to sacrifice there, since that was the greatest of the 4
high places—Solomon offered a thousand holocausts on that altar. •At Gibeon 5
Yahweh appeared in a dream to Solomon during the night. God said, 'Ask what
you would like me to give you'. •Solomon replied, 'You showed great kindness 6
to your servant David, my father, when he lived his life before you in faithfulness
and justice and integrity of heart; you have continued this great kindness to
him by allowing a son of his to sit on his throne today. •Now, Yahweh my God, 7
you have made your servant king in succession to David my father. But I am
a very young man, unskilled in leadership. •Your servant finds himself in the 8
midst of this people of yours that you have chosen, a people so many its number
cannot be counted or reckoned. •Give your servant a heart to understand 9
how to discern between good and evil, for who could govern this people of yours
that is so great?' •It pleased Yahweh that Solomon should have asked for this. 10
'Since you have asked for this' Yahweh said 'and not asked for long life for 11
yourself or riches or the lives of your enemies, but have asked for a discerning
judgement for yourself, •here and now I do what you ask. I give you a heart 12
wise and shrewd as none before you has had and none will have after you. •What 13
you have not asked I shall give you too: such riches and glory as no other king
ever had. •And I will give you a long life, if you follow my ways, keeping my 14
laws and commandments, as your father David followed them.' •Then Solomon 15
awoke; it was a dream. He returned to Jerusalem and stood before the ark of the
covenant of Yahweh; he offered holocausts and communion sacrifices, and
held a banquet for all his servants.

The judgement of Solomon

Then two prostitutes came to the king and stood before him. •'If it please 16
17
you, my lord,' one of the women said 'this woman and I live in the same house,
and while she was in the house I gave birth to a child. •Now it happened on the 18
third day after my delivery that this woman also gave birth to a child. We were
alone together; there was no one else in the house with us; just the two of us

19
20 in the house. •Now one night this woman's son died; she overlaid him. •And in
the middle of the night she got up and took my son from beside me while your
servant was asleep; she put him to her breast and put her own dead son to mine.
21 When I got up to suckle my child, there he was, dead. But in the morning
22 I looked at him carefully, and he was not the child I had borne at all.' •Then
the other woman spoke. 'That is not true! My son is the live one, yours is the
dead one'; and the first retorted, 'That is not true! Your son is the dead one,
23 mine is the live one.' And so they wrangled before the king. •'This one says,' the
king observed ' "My son is the one who is alive; your son is dead", while the
other says, "That is not true! Your son is the dead one, mine is the live one."
24 Bring me a sword' said the king; and a sword was brought into the king's
25 presence. •'Cut the living child in two,' the king said 'and give half to one,
26 half to the other.' •At this the woman who was the mother of the living child
addressed the king, for she burned with pity for her son. 'If it please you, my
lord,' she said 'let them give her the child; only do not let them think of killing
27 it!' But the other said, 'He shall belong to neither of us. Cut him up.' •Then
the king gave his decision. 'Give the child to the first woman,' he said 'and
28 do not kill him. She is his mother.' •All Israel came to hear of the judgement
the king had pronounced, and held the king in awe, recognising that he possessed
divine wisdom for dispensing justice.

Solomon's high officials

1
2 **4** King Solomon was king over all Israel, •and these were his high officials:
     Azariah son of Zadok, priest.
3   Elihoreph and Ahijah, sons of Shisha, secretaries.
     Jehoshaphat son of Ahilud, recorder.
4   (Benaiah son of Jehoiada, commander of the army.
     Zadok and Abiathar, priests.)
5   Azariah son of Nathan, chief administrator.
     Zabud son of Nathan, Friend of the King,
6   and his brother, master of the palace.
     Eliab son of Joab, commander of the army.
     Adoram son of Abda, in charge of forced labour.

Solomon's administrators

7 Solomon had twelve administrators for the whole of Israel who saw to the
provisioning of the king and his household; each had to provide for one month
in the year.
8 These are their names:
...son of Hur, in the mountain country of Ephraim.
9 ...son of Deker, in Makaz, Shaalbim, Beth-shemesh,
     Aijalon as far as Beth-hanan.
10 ...son of Hesed, in Arubboth; his district was Socoh
     and all the land of Hepher.
11 ...son of Abinadab: the whole region of Dor.
     Taphath, Solomon's daughter, was his wife.
12 Baana son of Ahilud, in Taanach and Megiddo
     as far as the other side of Jokmeam, and
     all Beth-shean below Jezreel, from Beth-shean
     as far as Abel Meholah, which is beside Zarethan.
13 ...son of Geber, in Ramoth-gilead: his district was
     the Encampments of Jair, son of Manasseh, which
     are in Gilead; he had the region of Argob, which
     is in Bashan, sixty fortified towns, walled-in
     and with bolts of bronze.

3 a. Probably Psusennis, last king of the 21st dynasty.

Ahinadab son of Iddo, in Mahanaim.   14
Ahimaaz in Naphtali; he too married a daughter of Solomon, Basemath.   15
Baana son of Hushai, in Asher and in the highlands.   16
Jehoshaphat son of Paruah, in Issachar.   17
Shimei son of Ela, in Benjamin.   18
Geber son of Uri, in the land of Gad, the land of Sihon   19
       king of the Amorites and of Og king of Bashan.
In addition, there was one governor in the land.*

5   These administrators provided the food for Solomon and for all those who ⁷₄:₂₇
    were admitted by him to the royal table, each for the period of a month; they
saw to it that nothing was wanting. •They also provided the barley and straw ⁸₂₈
for the horses and draught animals, where required, each according to his own
assignment. •The daily provisions for Solomon were: thirty measures of fine ²₂₂
flour and sixty measures of meal, •ten fattened oxen, twenty free-grazing oxen, ³₂₃
one hundred sheep, besides deer and gazelles, roebucks and fattened cuckoos.
For he was master of all Transeuphrates*—of all the kings of Transeuphrates from ⁴₂₄
Tiphsah to Gaza—and he enjoyed peace on all his frontiers. •Judah and Israel ⁵₂₅
lived in security, each man under his vine and his fig tree, from Dan as far as
Beersheba, throughout the lifetime of Solomon.
4 Judah and Israel were like the sand by the sea for number; they ate and drank 20
and lived happily. 5 Solomon extended his power over all the kingdoms ¹₄:₂₁
from the river to the land of the Philistines and the Egyptian border. They
brought tribute and served him all his life long. •For his chariots Solomon had ⁶₂₆
four thousand stalls and twelve thousand horses.

Solomon's fame

    Yahweh gave Solomon immense wisdom and understanding, and a heart ⁹₂₉
as vast as the sand on the seashore. •The wisdom of Solomon surpassed ¹⁰₃₀
the wisdom of all the sons of the East, and all the wisdom of Egypt. •He was ¹¹₃₁
wiser than any other, wiser than Ethan the Ezrahite,* wiser than Heman and
Calcol and Darda, the cantors. •He composed three thousand proverbs, and his ¹²₃₂
songs numbered a thousand and five. •He could talk about plants from the cedar ¹³₃₃
in Lebanon to the hyssop growing on the wall; and he could talk of animals,
and birds and reptiles and fish. •Men from all nations came to hear Solomon's ¹⁴₃₄
wisdom, and he received gifts from all the kings of the world, who had heard
of his wisdom.

B. SOLOMON THE BUILDER

Preparations for building the Temple

Hiram the king of Tyre sent an embassy to Solomon, having learnt that he ¹⁵₁
had been anointed king in succession to his father and because Hiram had
always been a friend of David. •And Solomon sent this message to Hiram, ¹⁶₂
'You are aware that David my father was unable to build a temple for the name of ¹⁷₃
Yahweh, his God, because his enemies waged war on him from all sides, until
Yahweh should put them under his control. •But now Yahweh my God has ¹⁸₄
given me rest on every side: not one enemy, no calamities. •I therefore plan ¹⁹₅
to build a temple for the name of Yahweh my God, just as Yahweh said to
David my father, "Your son whom I will place on your throne to succeed you
shall be the man to build a temple for my name". •So now have cedars of ²⁰₆
Lebanon cut down for me; my servants will work with your servants, and I will
pay for the hire of your servants at whatever rate you fix. As you know, we have
no one as skilled in felling trees as the Sidonians.' •When Hiram* heard what ²¹₇
Solomon had said, he was delighted. 'Now blessed be Yahweh' he said 'who
has given David a wise son to rule over this great people!' •And Hiram sent ²²₈

word to Solomon, 'I have received your message. For my part, I will supply
all you want in the way of cedar wood and juniper. •Your servants will bring
these down from Lebanon to the sea, and I shall have them towed by sea to any
place you name; I shall discharge them there, and you will take them over.
For your part, you will see to the provisioning of my household as I direct.
So Hiram provided Solomon with all the cedar wood and juniper he wanted,
while Solomon gave Hiram twenty thousand kors of wheat to feed his household,
and twenty thousand kors of pure oil. Solomon gave Hiram this every year.
Yahweh gave Solomon wisdom as he had promised him; good relations persisted
between Solomon and Hiram, and the two of them concluded a treaty.

King Solomon raised a levy throughout Israel for forced labour: the levy
numbered thirty thousand men. •He sent these to Lebanon in relays, ten thousand
a month; they spent one month in Lebanon and two months at home. Adoram
was in charge of the forced labour. •Solomon also had seventy thousand porters
and eighty thousand quarrymen in the mountains, •as well as the administrators'
officials who supervised the work, three thousand three hundred of them in
charge of the men employed in the work. •At the king's orders they quarried huge
stones, special stones, for the laying of the temple foundations, dressed stones.
Solomon's workmen and Hiram's workmen and the Giblites cut and assembled
the wood and stone for the building of the Temple.

The Temple building

6 In the four hundred and eightieth year after the Israelites came out of the
land of Egypt,ᵃ in the fourth year of Solomon's reign over Israel, in the month
of Ziv, which is the second month, he began to build the Temple of Yahweh.
2 The Templeᵇ that King Solomon built for Yahweh was sixty cubits long, twenty
3 cubits wide and twenty-five in height. •The Ulam in front of the Hekal of the
Temple was twenty cubits long across the width of the Temple and ten cubits
4 wide along the length of the Temple. •He made windows for the Temple with
5 frames and latticework. •He also built an annex against the Temple wall,
6 round the Hekal and the Debir, and made side tiers all round. •The lower story
was five cubits wide, the middle one six cubits, and the third seven cubits, for
round the Temple on the outside he had placed offsets so that this was not
7 attached to the Temple walls. •(The building of the Temple was done with
quarry-dressed stone; no sound of hammer or pick or any iron tool was to be
8 heard in the Temple while it was being built.) •The entrance to the lower story
was at the right-hand corner of the Temple, and access to the middle story above
9 was by trap-doors, and so from the middle story to the third. •He built the
10 Temple, completed it, and covered it with cedar wood. •He built the annex on
to the whole length of the Temple; it was five cubits high and was attached to the
11 Temple by beams of cedar wood. •And the word of Yahweh came to Solomon,
12 'This house you are building . . . if you follow my statutes and obey my ordinances
and faithfully follow my commandments, I will fulfil that promise I made about
13 you to your father David. •And I will make my home among the sons of Israel,
14 and never forsake Israel my people.' •Solomon built the Temple, and completed
it.

Interior furnishings. The Holy of Holies

15 He lined the inside of the Temple walls with panels of cedar wood—panelling
them on the inside from the floor of the Temple to the rafters in the roof—and
16 laid the floor of the Temple with juniper planks. •The twenty cubits measured

---

4 a. 'The land' is the royal territory of Judah.
5 a. The area between the Euphrates and the Mediterranean; the term shows that this verse
was added during the Persian period.   b. To whom Ps 89 is attributed.   c. Hiram was king
of Tyre and Sidon.
6 a. In fact about 960 B.C.   b. An oblong building consisting of three compartments: *Ulam*,
the Porch; *Hekal*, the Great Chamber for worship, later called the Holy Place; *Debir*, the
sanctuary, later called the Most Holy Place.

from the end of the Temple he built of cedar planks from floor to rafters, and this part was reserved as the Debir, the Holy of Holies. •The Temple measured 17 forty cubits—the Hekal—in front of the Debir. •There was cedar wood round 18 the inside of the Temple, ornamentally carved with gourds and rosettes; all was cedar wood, with no stone showing. •In the inner part of the Temple he designed 19 a Debir, to contain the ark of the covenant of Yahweh. •The Debir was twenty 20 cubits long, twenty cubits wide, and twenty high, and he plated it on the inside with pure gold. He made an altar of cedar wood •in front of the Debir and 21 plated it with gold. •He plated the whole Temple with gold, the whole Temple 22 entirely.

The cherubs

In the Debir he made two cherubs of olive wood ... It was ten cubits high. 23 One cherub's wing was five cubits long and the other wing five cubits: ten cubits 24 from wing tip to wing tip. •The other cherub also measured ten cubits; both 25 cherubs had the same measurements and the same shape. •The height of one 26 cherub was the same as the other's. •He placed the cherubs in the middle of the 27 inner chamber; their wings were spread out so that the wing of one touched one of the walls and the wing of the other touched the other wall, while their wings met in the middle of the chamber, wing to wing. •And he plated the 28 cherubs with gold. •All round the Temple walls he carved figures of cherubs, 29 palm trees and rosettes, both inside and outside. •He plated the floor of the 30 Temple with gold, both inside and outside.

The doors. The court

He made the door of the Debir with uprights of olive wood, and five-sided 31 door jambs, •and the two leaves of olive wood. He carved figures of cherubs, 32 palm trees and rosettes which he plated with gold; he put a gold surface on the cherubs and palm trees. •Similarly, he made uprights of olive wood for the door 33 of the Hekal, and four-sided door jambs, •and the two leaves of juniper: one 34 leaf had two ribs binding it, and the other had two ribs binding it. •He carved 35 cherubs, palm trees and rosettes, which he plated with gold laid evenly over the carvings.

He built the wall of the inner court in three courses of dressed stone and one 36 course of cedar beams.

The date

In the fourth year, in the month of Ziv, the foundations of the Temple were 37 laid; •in the eleventh year, in the month of Bul—that is, the eighth month—the 38 Temple was completed exactly as it had been planned and designed. Solomon took seven years to build it.

Solomon's palace

7 As regards his palace, Solomon spent thirteen years on it before the building 1 was completed. •He built the Hall of the Forest of Lebanon, a hundred 2 cubits long, fifty cubits wide, and thirty cubits high, on four rows of cedar wood pillars with cedar capitals on the pillars. •It was panelled in cedar on the upper 3 part as far as the planks above the pillars. •There were three rows of architraves, 4 forty-five in all, that is, fifteen in each row, facing one another from three sides. All the doors and uprights were of rectangular design, facing one another from 5 three sides. •And he made the Hall of Pillars, fifty cubits long and thirty cubits 6 wide... with a porch in front. •He also made the Hall of the Throne where he 7 used to dispense justice, that is, the Hall of Justice; it was panelled in cedar from floor to rafters. •His own living quarters, in the other court and inwards 8 from the Hall, were of the same construction. And there was a house similar to this Hall for the daughter of Pharaoh whom he had taken in marriage.

9   All these buildings were of special stones cut to measure, trimmed on the inner and outer sides with the saw, right from the foundations to the wood course
10 —their foundations were of special stones, huge stones, stones of ten and eight
11
12 cubits, •and, above these, special stones, cut to measure, and cedar wood—•and, on the outside, the great court had three courses of dressed stone round it and one course of cedar beams; so also had the inner court of the Temple of Yahweh and the vestibule of the Temple.

Hiram, the bronzeworker

13
14 King Solomon sent for Hiram of Tyre; •he was the son of a widow of the tribe of Naphtali but his father had been a Tyrian, a bronzeworker. He was a highly intelligent craftsman, skilled in all types of bronzework. He came to King Solomon and did all this work for him:

The bronze pillars

15 He cast two bronze pillars; the height of one pillar was eighteen cubits, and a cord twelve cubits long gave the measurement of its girth; so also was the second
16 pillar. •He made two capitals of cast bronze for the tops of the pillars; the
17 height of one capital was five cubits, and the height of the other five cubits. • He made two sets of filigree to cover the moulding of the two capitals surmounting the pillars, one filigree for one capital and one filigree for the other capital.
18
19b He also made pomegranates: two rows of them round each filigree, •four
20 hundred in all, •applied on the raised moulding behind the filigree; there were two hundred pomegranates round one capital and the same round the other
19a
21 capital. •The capitals surmounting the pillars were flower-shaped. •He set up the pillars in front of the vestibule of the sanctuary; he set up the right-hand pillar and named it Jachin; he set up the left-hand pillar and named it Boaz.
22 So the work on the pillars was completed.

The bronze 'Sea'

23 He made the Sea of cast metal, ten cubits from rim to rim, circular in shape and five cubits high; a cord thirty cubits long gave the measurement of its girth.
24 Under its rim and completely encircling it were gourds; they went round the Sea over a length of thirty cubits; the gourds were in two rows, of one and
25 the same casting with the rest. •It rested on twelve oxen, three facing north, three facing west, three facing south, three facing east; on these, their hind-
26 quarters all turned inwards, stood the Sea. •It was a hand's breadth in thickness, and its rim was shaped like the rim of a cup, like a flower. It held two thousand baths.

The wheeled stands and the bronze basins

27 He made the ten stands of bronze; each stand was four cubits long, four
28 cubits wide, and three high. •They were designed as follows: they had an under-
29 carriage and crosspieces to the undercarriage. •On the crosspieces of the undercarriage were lions and bulls and cherubs, and on top of the undercarriage was a support; under the lions and oxen there were scrolls in the style of...
30 Each stand had four bronze wheels with bronze axles; its four feet had shoulder-
31 ings under the basin, and the shoulderings were cast.... •Its mouth measured one and a half cubits from where the shoulderings met to the top; its mouth was round like a rest for a vessel, and on the mouth there were engravings too;
32 the crosspieces, however, were rectangular and not round. •The four wheels were under the crosspieces. The axles of the wheels were inside the stands;
33 the height of the wheels was one and a half cubits. •The wheels were designed like chariot wheels: their axles, felloes, spokes and naves had all been cast.
34 There were four shoulderings at the four corners of each stand: the stand and the
35 shoulderings were all of a piece. •At the top of the stand there was a support,

circular in shape and half a cubit high; and on top of the stand there were lugs. The crosspieces were of a piece with the stand. •On the bands he engraved cherubs 36 and lions and palm leaves . . . and scrolls right round. •He made the ten stands 37 like this: the same casting and the same measurements for all.

He made ten bronze basins; each basin held forty baths and each basin 38 measured four cubits, one basin to each of the ten stands. •He arranged the 39 stands, five on the right-hand side of the Temple, five on the left-hand side of the Temple; the Sea he placed on the right-hand side of the Temple to the south-east.

The utensils. Summary

Hiram made the ash containers, the scoops and the sprinkling bowls. He 40 finished all the work that he did for King Solomon on the Temple of Yahweh:

two pillars; the two mouldings of the capitals surmounting the pillars; the 41 two sets of filigree to cover the two mouldings of the capitals surmounting the pillars; •the four hundred pomegranates for the two sets of filigree; the pome- 42 granates of each set of filigree were in two rows;

the ten stands and the ten basins on the stands;   43

the one Sea and the twelve oxen beneath the Sea;   44

the ash containers, the scoops, the sprinkling bowls.   45

All these furnishings made by Hiram for King Solomon for the Temple of Yahweh were of burnished bronze. •He made them by the process of sand 46 casting, in the Jordan area between Succoth and Zarethan. •There were so 47 many of them, that the weight of the bronze was never calculated.

Solomon placed all the furnishings he had made in the Temple of Yahweh: 48 the golden altar and the table for the loaves of offering, which was of gold; the lamp-stands, five on the right and five on the left in front of the Debir, of 49 pure gold; the floral work, the lamps, the extinguishers, of gold; •the basins, 50 knives, sprinkling bowls, incense boats, censers, of pure gold; the door sockets for the inner shrine—that is, the Holy of Holies—and for the Hekal, of gold.

So all the work that King Solomon did for the Temple of Yahweh was 51 completed, and Solomon brought what his father David had consecrated, the silver and the gold and the vessels, and put them in the treasury of the Temple of Yahweh.

The ark brought to the Temple

8 Then Solomon called the elders of Israel together in Jerusalem to bring the 1 ark of the covenant of Yahweh up from the Citadel of David, which is Zion. All the men of Israel assembled round King Solomon in the month of Ethanim, 2 at the time of the feast *a* (that is, the seventh month), •and the priests took up 3 the ark •and the Tent of Meeting with all the sacred vessels that were in it. 4 In the presence of the ark, King Solomon and all Israel sacrificed sheep and oxen, 5 countless, innumerable. •The priests brought the ark of the covenant of Yahweh 6 to its place, in the Debir of the Temple, that is, in the Holy of Holies, under the cherubs' wings. •For there where the ark was placed the cherubs spread out 7 their wings and sheltered the ark and its shafts. •These were long enough for 8a their ends to be seen from the Holy Place in front of the Debir, but not from outside. •There was nothing in the ark except the two stone tablets Moses had 9 placed in it at Horeb, the tablets of the covenant which Yahweh had made with the Israelites when they came out of the land of Egypt; •they are still there today. 8b

The Lord takes possession of his Temple

Now when the priests came out of the sanctuary, the cloud filled the Temple 10 of Yahweh, •and because of the cloud the priests could no longer perform their 11 duties: the glory of Yahweh filled Yahweh's Temple.

Then Solomon said: 12

'Yahweh has chosen to dwell in the thick cloud.
13   Yes, I have built you a dwelling,
a place for you to live in for ever.'

Solomon addresses the people

14   Then the king turned and blessed the whole assembly of Israel, while the whole
15 assembly of Israel stood. •He said, 'Blessed be Yahweh, the God of Israel, who
has carried out by his hand what he promised with his mouth to David my father
16 when he said, •"From the day I brought my people Israel out of Egypt I chose
no city, in any of the tribes of Israel, to have a house built where my name might
17 make its home; but I chose David, to rule over Israel my people". •My father
David had set his heart on building a house for the name of Yahweh, the God
18 of Israel, •but Yahweh said, "You have set your heart on building a house for
19 my name, and in this you have done well; •and yet, you are not the man to build
the house; your son, born of your own body, shall build the house for my name".
20 Yahweh has kept the promise he made: I have succeeded David my father and
am seated on the throne of Israel, as Yahweh promised; I have built the house
21 for the name of Yahweh, the God of Israel, •and have made a place in it for the
ark containing the covenant that Yahweh made with our fathers when he brought
them out of the land of Egypt.'

Solomon's prayer for himself

22   Then (in the presence of the whole assembly of Israel) Solomon stood before
23 the altar of Yahweh and, stretching out his hands towards heaven, •said, 'Yahweh,
God of Israel, not in heaven above nor on earth beneath is there such a God
as you, true to your covenant and your kindness towards your servants when
24 they walk wholeheartedly in your way. •You have kept the promise you made
to your servant David my father; what you promised with your mouth, today
25 you have carried out by your hand. •And now, Yahweh, God of Israel, keep
the promise you made to your servant David when you said, "You shall never
lack for a man to sit before me on the throne of Israel, if only your sons are
26 careful how they behave, walking before me as you yourself have done". •So
now, God of Israel, let the words come true which you spoke to your servant
27 David my father. •Yet will God really live with men on the earth? Why, the
heavens and their own heavens cannot contain you. How much less this house
28 that I have built! •Listen to the prayer and entreaty of your servant, Yahweh my
29 God; listen to the cry and to the prayer your servant makes to you today. •Day
and night let your eyes watch over this house, over this place of which you have
said, "My name shall be there". Listen to the prayer that your servant will offer
in this place.

Solomon's prayer for the people

30   'Hear the entreaty of your servant and of Israel your people as they pray in
this place. From heaven where your dwelling is, hear; and, as you hear, forgive.
31   'If a man sins against his neighbour, and the neighbour calls down a curse
32 on him and makes him swear an oath before your altar in this Temple, •hear
from heaven, and act; decide between your servants: pronounce the wicked one
guilty, bringing his conduct down on his own head; and vindicate the innocent,
rewarding him as his innocence deserves.
33   'When your people Israel are defeated by the enemy because they have sinned
against you, if they return to you and praise your name and pray to you and
34 entreat you in this Temple, •hear from heaven; forgive the sin of your people
Israel, and bring them back to the land you gave to their ancestors.
35   'When the heavens are shut and there is no rain because they have sinned

8 a. 'The feast' is the feast of Tents, or Tabernacles.

against you, if they pray in this place and praise your name and, having been humbled by you, repent of their sin, •hear from heaven and forgive the sin of 36 your servant and of your people Israel—show them the good way they ought to follow—and send rain on your land which you have given your people for an inheritance.

'Should there be famine in the land, or pestilence, blight or mildew, locust 37 or caterpillar; should this people's enemy lay siege to one of its city gates; if there is any plague or sickness; •if anyone should feel remorse in his own heart and 38 pray or make entreaty, stretching out his hands towards this Temple, •hear from 39 heaven where your home is; forgive and act, dealing with each as his conduct deserves; for you know every heart,—you alone know the hearts of all mankind— and so they may come to revere you as long as they live in the land you gave to 40 our fathers.

Supplementary section

'And the foreigner too, not belonging to your people Israel, if he comes from 41 a distant country for the sake of your name—•for men will hear of your name, 42 of your mighty hand and outstretched arm—if he comes and prays in this Temple, hear from heaven where your home is, and grant all the foreigner asks, so that 43 all the peoples of the earth may come to know your name and, like your people Israel, revere you, and know that your name is given to the Temple I have built.

'If your people go out to war against their enemies on the way that you send 44 them, and if they turn towards the city you have chosen and towards the Temple I have built for your name, and pray to Yahweh, •hear from heaven their prayer 45 and their entreaty, and uphold their cause.

'If they sin against you—for there is no man who does not sin—and you 46 are angry with them and deliver them to the enemy, and their conquerors lead them captive to a country far or near, •if in the land of their exile they come 47 to themselves and repent, and in the country of their conquerors they entreat you saying, "We have sinned, we have acted perversely and wickedly", •and if 48 they turn again to you with all their heart and soul in the country of the enemies who have deported them, and pray to you, turning towards the land you gave to their ancestors, towards the city you have chosen, and towards the Temple I have built for your name, •hear from heaven where your home is, •forgive $\begin{smallmatrix}49\\50\end{smallmatrix}$ your people the sins they have committed against you and all the crimes they have been guilty of, grant them to win favour with their conquerors so that they may have pity on them; •for they are your people and your heritage whom you brought 51 out of Egypt, that iron furnace.

Conclusion of the prayer and blessing of the people

'Be always watchful for the entreaty of your servant and of your people 52 Israel, always hearing them when they call to you. •For it was you who set them 53 apart from all the peoples of the earth to be your own heritage, as you declared through Moses your servant when you brought our ancestors out of Egypt, Lord Yahweh.'

When Solomon had finished offering this whole prayer and entreaty, he rose 54 from where he was kneeling with hands stretched out towards heaven before the altar of Yahweh, •and stood erect. And in a loud voice he blessed the whole 55 assembly of Israel. •'Blessed be Yahweh' he said 'who has granted rest to 56 his people Israel, keeping all his promises; of all the promises of good that he made through Moses his servant, not one has failed. •May Yahweh our God be 57 with us, as he was with our ancestors; may he never desert us or cast us off. May he turn our hearts towards him so that we may follow all his ways and 58 keep the commandments, and laws, and ordinances he gave to our ancestors. May these words of mine, of my entreaty before Yahweh, be present with Yahweh 59 our God day and night, that he may uphold the cause of his servant and the

60 cause of Israel his people, as each day requires, •so that all the peoples of the earth may come to know that Yahweh is God indeed, and that there is no other.
61 May your hearts be wholly with Yahweh our God, following his laws and keeping his commandments as at this present day.'

The sacrifices on the feast of Dedication

62 63 The king and all Israel with him offered sacrifice before Yahweh. •Solomon offered twenty-two thousand oxen and a hundred and twenty thousand sheep as communion sacrifices to Yahweh; and so the king and all the Israelites
64 dedicated the Temple of Yahweh. •On the same day the king consecrated the middle of the court lying in front of the Temple of Yahweh; and there he offered the holocaust, oblations and fatty parts of the communion sacrifices, since the bronze altar that stood before Yahweh was too small to hold the holocaust,
65 oblation and the fatty parts of the communion sacrifices. •And so at that time, Solomon celebrated the feast, and all the Israelites with him, a great gathering from the Pass of Hamath to the wadi of Egypt, before Yahweh our God for
66 seven days.[b] •Then, on the eighth day, he dismissed the people, who blessed the king and went to their homes, rejoicing and happy in heart for all the goodness Yahweh had shown to David and to his people Israel.

Yahweh appears a second time

1 **9** When Solomon had finished building the Temple of Yahweh and the royal
2 palace and all he had a mind to build, •Yahweh appeared to Solomon a
3 second time, as he had appeared to him at Gibeon. •Yahweh said to him, 'I grant your prayer and the entreaty you have made before me. I consecrate this house you have built: I place my name there for ever; my eyes and my heart shall
4 be always there. •For your part, if you walk before me with innocence of heart and in honesty, like David your father, if you do all I order you and keep my
5 laws and my ordinances, •I will make your royal throne secure over Israel for ever, as I promised David your father when I said: You shall never lack for a
6 man on the throne of Israel. •But if you turn away from me, you or your sons, and do not keep the commandments and laws I have set before you, and go
7 and serve other gods and worship them, •then I will cut Israel off from the land I have given them, and I will cast out from my presence this Temple that I have consecrated for my name, and Israel shall become a proverb and a byword
8 among all the nations. •As for this exalted Temple, all who pass by will be astounded; they will whistle and say, "Why has Yahweh treated this country
9 and this Temple like this?" •And the answer will be, "Because they deserted Yahweh their God who brought their ancestors out of the land of Egypt, and they adopted other gods and worshipped them and served them; that is why Yahweh has brought all these disasters on them".'

The bargain with Hiram

10 At the end of the twenty years it took Solomon to erect the two buildings,
11 the Temple of Yahweh and the royal palace •(Hiram king of Tyre had provided Solomon with as much cedar wood, juniper wood and gold as he had wanted),
12 King Solomon gave Hiram twenty towns in the land of Galilee. •But when Hiram came from Tyre to view the towns Solomon had given him, he was not
13 pleased with them. •He said, 'What kind of towns are these you have given me,
14 my brother?' And to this day they are called 'the land of Cabul'. •Hiram sent the king one hundred and twenty talents of gold.

Forced labour for Solomon's building programme

15 This is an account of the forced labour King Solomon levied for the building of the Temple of Yahweh, his own palace, the Millo[a] and the wall of Jerusalem,

b. The duration of the feast of Tabernacles, Dt 16:13-15.
9 a. The 'filling' of earth that levelled the uneven ground round the Temple and the Palace.

Hazor, Megiddo, Gezer •(Pharaoh king of Egypt went up and captured Gezer, 16 he burnt it down and massacred the Canaanites living there; he then gave the town as a dowry to his daughter, Solomon's wife, •and Solomon rebuilt Gezer), 17 Lower Beth-horon, •Baalath, Tamar in the wilderness, inside the country, •all ¹⁸₁₉ the garrison towns owned by Solomon, all the towns for his chariots and horses, and all it pleased Solomon to build in Jerusalem, in Lebanon and in all the countries subject to him. •All those who survived of the Amorite, Hittite, Perizzite, 20 Hivite and Jebusite peoples, who were not Israelites, •their descendants who were 21 left in the country after them, those on whom the Israelites had not been able to enforce the ban, these Solomon conscripted as slave-labourers, as they are still. •However, Solomon did not impose slave-labour on the Israelites;ᵇ these 22 served as fighting men: they were his guards, officers, equerries, chariot and cavalry commanders. •These were the administrators' officials who supervised 23 Solomon's work: five hundred and fifty of them in charge of the people employed in the work. •After Pharaoh's daughter had moved from the Citadel of David 24 to the house which he had built for her, he then built the Millo.

The maintenance of the Temple

Three times a year Solomon offered holocausts and communion sacrifices 25 on the altar he had built for Yahweh. . . and he kept the Temple in good repair.

C. SOLOMON THE TRADER

Solomon as ship-owner

King Solomon equipped a fleet at Ezion-geber, which is near Elath on the 26 shores of the Red Sea, in the land of Edom. •For this fleet Hiram sent men of 27 his, sailors who knew the sea, to serve with Solomon's men. •They went to Ophir 28 and from there they brought back four hundred and twenty talents of gold, which they delivered to King Solomon. ᶜ

The queen of Sheba visits Solomon

10 The fame of Solomon having reached the queen of Sheba. . . ᵈ she came 1 to test him with difficult questions. •She brought immense riches to Jerusa- 2 lem with her, camels laden with spices, great quantities of gold, and precious stones. On coming to Solomon, she opened her mind freely to him; •and Solomon 3 had an answer for all her questions, not one of them was too obscure for the king to expound. •When the queen of Sheba saw all the wisdom of Solomon, 4 the palace he had built, •the food at his table, the accommodation for his officials, 5 the organisation of his staff and the way they were dressed, his cup-bearers, and the holocausts he offered in the Temple of Yahweh, it left her breathless, •and 6 she said to the king, 'What I heard in my own country about you and your wisdom was true, then! •Until I came and saw it with my own eyes I could not 7 believe what they told me, but clearly they told me less than half: for wisdom and prosperity you surpass the report I heard. •How happy your wives are! How 8 happy are these servants of yours who wait on you always and hear your wisdom! Blessed be Yahweh your God who has granted you his favour, setting you on 9 the throne of Israel! Because of Yahweh's everlasting love for Israel, he has made you king to deal out law and justice.' •And she presented the king with 10 a hundred and twenty talents of gold and great quantities of spices and precious stones; no such wealth of spices ever came again as those given to King Solomon by the queen of Sheba. •And the fleet of Hiram, which carried gold from Ophir, 11 also brought great cargoes of almuggim wood and precious stones. •The king 12 made supports with the almuggim wood for the Temple of Yahweh and for the royal palace, and lyres and harps for the musicians; no more of this almuggim wood has since come or been seen to this day. •And King Solomon in his turn, 13

presented the queen of Sheba with all she expressed a wish for, besides those presents he made her out of his royal bounty. Then she went home, she and her servants, to her own country.

Solomon's wealth

14　The weight of gold coming to Solomon in one year was six hundred and
15　sixty-six talents of gold, •not counting what came in from merchants' dues and traders' profits, and from all the foreign kings and the governors of the country.
16　King Solomon made three hundred great shields of beaten gold, and plated each
17　shield with six hundred shekels of gold; •also three hundred small shields of beaten gold, and plated each of these with three minas of gold; and he put them
18　in the Hall of the Forest of Lebanon. •The king also made a great ivory throne,
19　and plated it with refined gold. •The throne had six steps, and bulls' heads at the back of it, and arms at either side of the seat; two lions stood beside the arms,
20　and twelve lions stood on either side of the six steps. No throne like this was ever made in any other kingdom.
21　All King Solomon's drinking vessels were of gold, and all the furnishings in the Hall of the Forest of Lebanon were of pure gold; silver was thought little of in
22　the time of Solomon. •And the king also had a fleet of Tarshish at sea with Hiram's fleet, and once every three years the fleet of Tarshish would come back
23　laden with gold and silver, ivory, apes and baboons. •For riches and for wisdom
24　King Solomon outdid all the kings of the earth. •The whole world sought audience
25　of Solomon to hear the wisdom God had implanted in his heart •and each would bring his own present: gold vessels, silver vessels, robes, armour, spices, horses and mules; and this went on year after year.

Solomon's chariots

26　Solomon built up a force of chariots and horses; he had one thousand four hundred chariots and twelve thousand horses; these he stationed in the chariot
27　towns and near the king in Jerusalem. •In Jerusalem the king made silver common
28　as pebbles, and cedars plentiful as the sycamores of the Lowlands. •Solomon's horses were imported from Cilicia; the king's agents took delivery of them from
29　Cilicia at a fixed rate. •A chariot was imported from Egypt for six hundred shekels, a horse for a hundred and fifty. These were exported through the king's agents to all the kings of the Hittites and to the kings of Aram in the same way.

D. HIS DECLINE

Solomon's wives

1
2　**11** King Solomon loved many foreign women: not only Pharaoh's daughter but Moabites, Edomites, Sidonians and Hittites, •from those peoples of whom Yahweh had said to the Israelites, 'You are not to go to them nor they to you, or they will surely sway your hearts to their own gods'. But Solomon
3　was deeply attached to them. •He had seven hundred wives of royal rank, and
4　three hundred concubines. •When Solomon grew old his wives swayed his heart to other gods; and his heart was not wholly with Yahweh his God as his
5　father David's had been. •Solomon became a follower of Astarte, the goddess
6　of the Sidonians, and of Milcom, the Ammonite abomination. •He did what was displeasing to Yahweh, and was not a wholehearted follower of Yahweh, as his
7　father David had been. •Then it was that Solomon built a high place for Chemosh the god of Moab on the mountain to the east of Jerusalem, and to Milcom the

b. But see 5:27 and 11:28.　　c. Ophir was probably on the W. coast of Arabia. Ezion-geber was near Aqaba.
10 a. Sheba was in the Arabian peninsula, but this was probably the queen of one of the Sabaean settlements in North Africa.

god of the Ammonites. •He did the same for all his foreign wives, who offered 8
incense and sacrifice to their gods.

Yahweh was angry with Solomon because his heart had turned from Yahweh 9
the God of Israel who had twice appeared to him •and who had then forbidden 10
him to follow other gods; but he did not carry out Yahweh's order. •Yahweh 11
therefore said to Solomon, 'Since you behave like this and do not keep my
covenant or the laws I laid down for you, I will most surely tear the kingdom
away from you and give it to one of your servants. •For your father David's sake, 12
however, I will not do this during your lifetime, but will tear it out of your son's
hands. •Even so, I will not tear the whole kingdom from him. For the sake of 13
my servant David, and for the sake of Jerusalem which I have chosen, I will
leave your son one tribe.'ᵃ

Solomon's foreign enemies

Yahweh raised an enemy against Solomon, Hadad the Edomite, of the 14
kingly stock of Edom. •After David had crushed Edom, Joab, the commander 15
of the army, had gone to bury the dead and he had slaughtered the entire male
population of Edom •(Joab stayed there with all Israel for six months until he 16
had exterminated the entire male population of Edom), •but Hadad with a 17
number of Edomites in his father's service had fled to Egypt. Hadad had been
only a boy at the time. •They set out from Midian, and on reaching Paran, 18
took a number of men from Paran with them and went on to Egypt, to Pharaoh,
the king of Egypt, who provided him with a house, undertook to maintain him,
and assigned him an estate. •Hadad became a great favourite of Pharaoh who 19
gave him his own wife's sister in marriage, the sister of the Great Lady Tahpenes.
The sister of Tahpenes bore him Genubath his son whom Tahpenes brought up 20
in Pharaoh's palace, Genubath living with Pharaoh's children. •But when news 21
reached Hadad in Egypt that David slept with his ancestors and that Joab the
commander of the army was dead, he said to Pharaoh, 'Give me leave to return
to my own country'. •'Do you want for anything here with me' said Pharaoh 22
'that you now ask to return to your own country?' 'No,' he replied 'but please let
me go.' •This is where the harm of Hadad comes from: he loathed Israel and 25b
ruled Edom.

God raised a second enemy against Solomon, Rezon son of Eliada. He had 23
fled from his master, Hadadezer king of Zobah. •A number of men having rallied 24
to him, he had become leader of a marauding band (which was then massacred
by David). Rezon captured Damascus and settled there and became king of
Damascus. •He was hostile to Israel as long as Solomon lived. 25a

The revolt of Jeroboam

Jeroboam was the son of Nebat, an Ephraimite from Zeredah; the name of 26
his mother, a widow, was Zeruah; he was in Solomon's service but revolted
against the king. •This is the account of his revolt. 27

Solomon was building the Millo and closing the breach in the Citadel of
David his father. •Now this Jeroboam was a man of rank; Solomon, noticing 28
how the young man set about his work, put him in charge of all the forced
labour of the House of Joseph. •One day when Jeroboam had gone out of 29
Jerusalem, the prophet Ahijah of Shiloh accosted him on the road. Ahijah was
wearing a new cloak; the two of them were in the open country by themselves.
Ahijah took the new cloak he was wearing and tore it into twelve strips, •saying ³⁰₃₁
to Jeroboam, 'Take ten strips for yourself, for thus Yahweh speaks, the God of
Israel, "I am going to tear the kingdom from Solomon's hand and give ten tribes
to you. •He shall keep one tribeᵇ for the sake of my servant David and for the 32
sake of Jerusalem, the city I have chosen out of all the tribes of Israel; •for he 33
has forsaken me to worship Astarte the goddess of the Sidonians, Chemosh the
god of Moab, Milcom the god of the Ammonites; he has not followed my ways

by doing what is right in my eyes or keeping my laws and ordinances as his
34 father David did. •But I will not take the kingdom out of his own hands, since
I have made him a prince for as long as he lives, for the sake of my servant David
35 who kept my commandments and laws. •I will, however, take the kingdom
36 from the hand of his son, giving the ten tribes to you. •I will keep one tribe to
give to his son, so that my servant David may always have a lamp in my presence
37 in Jerusalem, the city I have chosen as a dwelling place for my name. •You
nonetheless I will take to rule over as much as you wish, and you shall be king
38 of Israel. •If you listen to all my orders and follow my ways, by doing what
is right in my eyes and keeping my laws and commandments as my servant
David did, then I will be with you and will build you as enduring a House as
39 the one I built for David. I will give Israel to you, •thus humbling the descendants
of David; but not for ever." '
40 Solomon tried to kill Jeroboam but he made off and fled to Egypt, to Shishak
king of Egypt, and he remained in Egypt until Solomon's death.

The end of the reign of Solomon

41 The rest of the history of Solomon, his entire career, his wisdom, is not all
42 this recorded in the Book of the Acts of Solomon? •Solomon's reign in Jerusalem
43 over all Israel lasted forty years. •Then Solomon slept with his ancestors and was
buried in the Citadel of David his father; Rehoboam his son succeeded him.

III. THE POLITICAL AND RELIGIOUS SCHISM

The assembly at Shechem

2 **12** As soon as Jeroboam son of Nebat heard the news—he was still in Egypt,
where he had taken refuge from King Solomon—he returned from Egypt.
1 Rehoboam went to Shechem, for it was to Shechem that all Israelᵃ had gone to
3 proclaim him king, •and they said this to him, •'Your father gave us a heavy
4 burden to bear; lighten your father's harsh tyranny now, and the weight of the
5 burden he laid on us, and we will serve you'. •He said to them, 'Go away for three
days and then come back to me'. And the people went away.
6 King Rehoboam consulted the elders, who had been in the service of his
father Solomon while he was alive. 'What reply' he asked 'do you advise me to
7 give to this people?' •'Act as servant of this people now,' they said 'humour
8 them, treat them fairly, and they will be your servants for ever.' •But he rejected
the advice given him by the elders and consulted the young men who had grown
9 up with him and were in his service. •'How do you advise us' he asked 'to answer
this people who have said to me, "Lighten the burden your father imposed
10 on us"?' •The young men who had grown up with him replied, 'Give this answer
to these people who have said, "Your father gave us a heavy burden to bear, you
must lighten it for us", say this to them, "My little finger is thicker than my father's
11 loins! •So then, my father made you bear a heavy burden. I will make it heavier
still. My father beat you with whips; I am going to beat you with loaded
scourges." '
12 On the third day all the people came to Rehoboam in obedience to the
13 king's command: 'Come back to me on the third day'. •The king, rejecting the
14 advice given him by the elders, gave the people a harsh answer, •speaking to
them as the young men had recommended. 'My father made you bear a heavy
burden,' he said 'but I will make it heavier still. My father beat you with whips;

11 a. Solomon's marriages with foreign wives were made for political reasons and the pagan
shrines were set up for his wives and for visiting traders. The writer interprets the situation in
the spirit and language of Dt.   b. Judah, the one tribe left to Solomon, had absorbed the
twelfth tribe, Simeon.
12 a. I.e. the northern tribes as distinct from Judah. See v.20.

I am going to beat you with loaded scourges.' •The king in fact took no notice 15
of the people's wishes, and this was brought about by Yahweh to carry out the
promise he had spoken through Ahijah of Shiloh to Jeroboam son of Nebat.
When all Israel saw that the king took no notice of their wishes, they gave him 16
this answer:

> 'What share have we in David?
> We have no inheritance in the son of Jesse.
> To your tents, Israel!
> Henceforth look after your own house, David!'

And Israel went off to their tents. •Rehoboam, however, reigned over those 17
sons of Israel who lived in the towns of Judah. •King Rehoboam sent Adoram 18
who was in charge of forced labour, but the Israelites stoned him to death;
whereupon King Rehoboam was obliged to mount his chariot and escape to
Jerusalem. •And Israel has been separated from the House of David until the 19
present day.

The political schism

When all Israel heard that Jeroboam had returned, they summoned him 20
to the assembly and made him king of all Israel; no one remained loyal to the
House of David, except the tribe of Judah.

Rehoboam went to Jerusalem and mustered the whole House of Judah and the 21
tribe of Benjamin, a hundred and eighty thousand picked warriors, to fight the
House of Israel and win back the kingdom for Rehoboam son of Solomon.
But the word of Yahweh came to Shemaiah the man of God, •'Say this to $^{22}_{23}$
Rehoboam son of Solomon, king of Judah, to the whole House of Judah, to
Benjamin and to the rest of the people, •"Yahweh says this: Do not go to 24
fight against your brothers, the sons of Israel; let everyone go home, for what
has happened is my doing"'.

Jeroboam fortified Shechem in the mountain country of Ephraim, and lived 25
there. Then, leaving there, he fortified Penuel.

The religious schism

Jeroboam thought to himself, 'As things are, the kingdom will revert to 26
the House of David. •If this people continues to go up to the Temple of 27
Yahweh in Jerusalem to offer sacrifices, the people's heart will turn back again
to their lord, Rehoboam king of Judah, and they will put me to death.' •So the 28
king thought this over and then made two golden calves; he said to the people,
'You have been going up to Jerusalem long enough. Here are your gods, Israel;
these brought you up out of the land of Egypt!' •He set up one in Bethel •and $^{29}_{30}$
the people went in procession all the way to Dan in front of the other. •He set 31
up the temple of the high places and appointed priests from ordinary families,
who were not of the sons of Levi. •Jeroboam also instituted a feast in the eighth 32
month, on the fifteenth of the month, like the feast that was kept in Judah,
and he went up to the altar.[b] That was how he behaved in Bethel, sacrificing
to the calves he had made; and at Bethel he put the priests of the high
places he had established. •On the fifteenth of the eighth month, the month he 33
had deliberately chosen, he went up to the altar he had made; he instituted a feast
for the Israelites, and went up to the altar to offer incense.

The condemnation of the altar in Bethel

13 There came to Bethel at Yahweh's command a man of God from Judah, 1
just as Jeroboam was standing by the altar to offer the sacrifice, •and at 2
Yahweh's command this man denounced the altar. 'Altar, altar,' he said
'Yahweh says this, "A son shall be born to the House of David, Josiah by name,
who shall immolate on you the priests of the high places who have offered sacrifice

3 on you, and on you shall he burn the bones of men".' •At the same time he gave
a sign. 'This is the sign' he said 'that Yahweh has spoken, "This altar here will
4 burst apart and the ashes that are on it will be scattered".' •When the king
heard how the man of God denounced the altar of Bethel, he stretched out his
hand from the altar, saying, 'Seize him!' But the hand he stretched out against
5 the man withered, and he could not draw it back, •and the altar burst apart
and the ashes from the altar were scattered, in accordance with the sign given by
6 the man of God at Yahweh's command. •The king said to the man of God, 'I beg
you to placate Yahweh your God, and so restore me the use of my hand'.
The man of God placated Yahweh; the king's hand was restored as it had been
7 before. •The king then said to the man of God, 'Come home with me and refresh
8 yourself, and I will give you a present'; •but the man of God answered the king,
'Were you to give me half your house, I would not go with you. I will eat and
9 drink nothing here, •for I have had Yahweh's order: "You are to eat or drink
10 nothing, nor to return by the way you came".' •And he left by another road and
did not return by the way he had come to Bethel.

The man of God and the prophet[a]

11   Now there was an old prophet living in Bethel and his sons came to tell him
all that the man of God had done in Bethel that day; and the words he had said
12 to the king, they told these to their father too. •'Which road did he take?' their
father asked. His sons showed him the road that the man of God who came from
13 Judah had taken. •'Saddle the donkey for me' he said to his sons; they saddled
14 the donkey for him and he mounted. •He followed the man of God and found
him sitting under a terebinth. 'Are you the man of God' he said 'who came from
15 Judah?' 'I am' he replied. •'Come home with me' he said 'and take some food.'
16
17 'I cannot go back with you', he answered 'or eat or drink anything here, •for
I have received Yahweh's order: "You are to eat or drink nothing there, nor
18 to return by the way you came".' •'I too am a prophet like you,' the other replied
'and an angel told me this by Yahweh's order: "Bring him back with you to
19 your house to eat and drink".' He was lying to him. •The man of God went
back with him; he ate and drank at his house.

20   As they were sitting at table a word of Yahweh came to the prophet who had
21 brought him back, •and he addressed the man of God who came from Judah.
'Yahweh says this,' he said ' "Since you have defied Yahweh's command and
22 not obeyed the orders Yahweh your God gave you, •but have come back and
eaten and drunk where he forbade you to eat or drink, your corpse will never
23 reach the tomb of your ancestors".' •After he had eaten and drunk, the prophet
24 saddled the donkey for him, and he turned about and went away. •A lion met
him on the road and killed him; his corpse lay stretched out on the road; the
25 donkey stood there beside it; the lion stood by the corpse too. •People going
by saw the corpse lying on the road and the lion standing by the corpse, and went
26 and spoke about it in the town where the old prophet lived. •When the prophet
who had made the man turn back heard about it, he said, 'That is the man of God
who defied Yahweh's command! Yahweh has handed him over to the lion, which
27 has mauled and killed him, just as Yahweh had foretold it would.' •He said
28 to his sons, 'Saddle the donkey for me', and they saddled it. •He set off and
found the man's corpse lying on the road with the donkey and the lion standing
beside the corpse; the lion had neither eaten the corpse nor mauled the donkey.
29 The prophet lifted the corpse of the man of God and put it on the donkey and
brought it back to the town where he lived to hold mourning for him and bury
30 him. •He laid the corpse in his own tomb, and they raised the mourning cry
31 for him, 'Alas, my brother!' •After burying him, the prophet said to his sons,
'When I die, bury me in the same tomb as the man of God, lay my bones beside

b. The new temple, like Solomon's Temple, is dedicated on the feast of Tabernacles.
13 a. At this time, the 'prophet' is of a lower grade than the 'man of God'.

his. •For the word he uttered at Yahweh's command against the altar of Bethel 32
and against all the shrines of the high places in the towns of Samaria will certainly
come true.'

Jeroboam did not give up his wicked ways after this incident, but went on 33
appointing priests for the high places from the common people. He consecrated
as priests of the high places any who wished to be. •Such conduct made the 34
House of Jeroboam a sinful House, and caused its ruin and extinction from the
face of the earth.

IV. THE TWO KINGDOMS UNTIL ELIJAH

Continuation of the reign of Jeroboam I (931-910)

14 At that time Abijah, Jeroboam's son, fell sick, •and Jeroboam said to his $\frac{1}{2}$
wife, 'Come, please disguise yourself so that no one will recognise you as
Jeroboam's wife, and go to Shiloh; the prophet Ahijah is there, the man who
said I was to be king over this people. •Go to him, and take ten loaves and some 3
savoury food and a jar of honey; he will tell you what will happen to the child.'
Jeroboam's wife did this: she set out, went to Shiloh and came to Ahijah's house. 4
Now Ahijah could not see, his eyes were dimmed with age, •but Yahweh had told 5
him, 'Jeroboam's wife is now on her way to ask you for an oracle about her son,
as he is sick. You will tell her such and such. When she comes, she will pretend
to be some other woman.' •So when Ahijah heard her footsteps at the door, he 6
called, 'Come in, wife of Jeroboam; why pretend to be someone else? I have
bad news for you. •Go and tell Jeroboam, "Yahweh says this, the God of 7
Israel: I raised you from the people and made you leader of my people Israel;
I tore the kingdom from the House of David and gave it to you. But you have 8
not been like my servant David who kept my commandments and followed me
with all his heart doing only what is right in my eyes; •you have done more 9
evil than all your predecessors, you have gone and made yourself other gods,
idols of cast metal, provoking my anger, and you have turned your back on
me. •For this I will bring disaster on the House of Jeroboam, I will wipe out 10
every male belonging to the family of Jeroboam, fettered or free in Israel, I will
sweep away the House of Jeroboam as a man sweeps dung away till none is left.
Those of Jeroboam's family who die in the city, the dogs will eat; and those 11
who die in the open country, the birds of the air will eat, for Yahweh has spoken."
Now get up and go home; at the moment your feet enter the town, the child 12
will die. •All Israel will mourn for him, and bury him; and he alone of Jeroboam's 13
household will go to the tomb, for it is in him alone of the House of Jeroboam
that anything pleasing to Yahweh, the God of Israel, is found. •Yahweh will 14
raise up a king for himself over Israel to wipe out the House of Jeroboam.
Yahweh will make Israel shake as a reed shakes in the water, he will uproot 15
Israel from this prosperous land which he gave to their ancestors and scatter
them beyond the river for provoking Yahweh to anger by making their sacred
poles. •He will abandon Israel for the sins Jeroboam has committed and made 16
Israel commit.' •Jeroboam's wife rose and left. She arrived at Tirzah,ª and when 17
she crossed the threshold of the house, the child was already dead. •They buried 18
him, and all Israel mourned him, just as Yahweh had foretold through his servant
Ahijah the prophet.

The rest of the history of Jeroboam, what wars he waged, how he governed, 19
these may be found recorded in the Book of the Annals of the Kings of Israel.
Jeroboam's reign lasted twenty-two years; then he slept with his ancestors; his son 20
Nadab succeeded him.

The reign of Rehoboam (931-913)

In Judah Rehoboam son of Solomon became king; he was forty-one years old 21
when he came to the throne and he reigned for seventeen years in Jerusalem,

the city which Yahweh had chosen out of all the tribes of Israel, to give his
22 name a home there. His mother's name was Naamah, the Ammonitess. •He did
what is displeasing to Yahweh, arousing his resentment more than his ancestors
23 did by all the sins they committed, •they who had built themselves high places,
and had set up pillars and sacred poles on every high hill and under every spread-
24 ing tree. •There were even men in the country who were sacred prostitutes. He
copied all the shameful practices of the nations whom Yahweh had dispossessed
for the sons of Israel.

25   In the fifth year of Rehoboam, Shishak the king of Egypt marched on
26 Jerusalem. •He took all the treasures from the Temple of Yahweh and the
treasures from the royal palace, he took everything, including all the golden
27 shields that Solomon had made; •in place of them King Rehoboam had bronze
shields made, entrusting them to the care of the officers of the guard who
28 guarded the king's palace gate. •Whenever the king went to the Temple of
Yahweh, the guards would carry them, returning them to the guardroom afterwards.

29   The rest of the history of Rehoboam, his entire career, is not all this recorded
30 in the Book of the Annals of the Kings of Judah? •Rehoboam and Jeroboam were
31 at war with each other throughout their reigns. •Then Rehoboam slept with his
ancestors and was buried in the Citadel of David; his son Abijam succeeded him.

The reign of Abijam in Judah (913-911)

1   **15** In the eighteenth year of King Jeroboam son of Nebat, Abijam became king
2   of Judah •and reigned for three years in Jerusalem. His mother's name
3 was Maacah, daughter of Absalom. •He followed the sinful example of his father
before him in everything; his heart was not wholly with Yahweh his God, as the
4 heart of David his ancestor had been. •However, for David's sake, Yahweh his
God gave him a lamp in Jerusalem, assuring him sons after him and keeping
5 Jerusalem secure; •for David had done what is right in the eyes of Yahweh and
had never in all his life disobeyed whatever he ordered him.
(6)7   The rest of the history of Abijam, his entire career, is not all this recorded in
the Book of the Annals of the Kings of Judah? Abijam and Jeroboam were at
8 war with each other. •Then Abijam slept with his ancestors and they buried him in
the Citadel of David; his son Asa succeeded him.

The reign of Asa in Judah (911-870)

9   In the twentieth year of Jeroboam king of Israel, Asa became king of Judah
10 and reigned for forty-one years in Jerusalem. His mother's name was Maacah,
11 daughter of Absalom. •Asa did what is right in the eyes of Yahweh, as his
12 ancestor David had done. •He drove out of the country the men who had been
13 sacred prostitutes and cleared away all the idols his ancestors had made. •He
even deprived his grandmother of the dignity of queen mother for making an
obscenity for Asherah; Asa cut down her obscenity and burned it in the wadi
14 Kidron. •Though the high places were not abolished, the heart of Asa was
15 wholly with Yahweh throughout his life. •He deposited the offerings dedicated
by his father and his own offerings too, in the Temple of Yahweh, silver and gold
and furnishings.

16   Asa and Baasha king of Israel were at war with each other as long as they
17 lived. •Baasha king of Israel marched on Judah and fortified Ramah to blockade
18 Asa king of Judah. •Asa then took the remaining silver and gold from the
treasuries of the Temple of Yahweh and the royal palace. Entrusting this to
his servants, he sent them with the following message to Ben-hadad son of
19 Tabrimmon son of Hezion, the king of Aram who lived in Damascus, •'An

14 a. The capital of the kingdom of Israel before Samaria was built.

alliance between myself and you, as between my father and your father! With this I send you a gift of silver and gold. Come, break off your alliance with Baasha king of Israel, and he will have to retire from my territory.' •Ben-hadad 20 agreed, and sent his generals against the towns of Israel; he conquered Ijon, Dan, Abel-beth-maacah, all Chinneroth, and the whole land of Naphtali too. When Baasha heard this he gave up fortifying Ramah and returned to Tirzah. 21 King Asa then summoned the whole of Judah, no one was exempt; they took 22 away the stones and timber with which Baasha had been fortifying Ramah, and with them the king fortified Geba of Benjamin and Mizpah.

The rest of the history of Asa, all his valour, his entire career, is not all this 23 recorded in the Book of the Annals of the Kings of Judah? In his old age, however, he suffered from a disease of the feet. •Then Asa slept with his ancestors 24 and was buried in the Citadel of David his ancestor; his son Jehoshaphat succeeded him.

The reign of Nadab in Israel (910-909)

Nadab son of Jeroboam became king of Israel in the second year of Asa king 25 of Judah, and he reigned over Israel for two years. •He did what is displeasing 26 to Yahweh; he copied his father's example and the sin into which he had led Israel. •Baasha son of Ahijah, of the House of Issachar, plotted against him 27 and murdered him at Gibbethon, a Philistine town which Nadab and all Israel were besieging. •Baasha killed Nadab and succeeded him in the third year of 28 Asa king of Judah. •No sooner was he king than he butchered the entire House 29 of Jeroboam, not sparing a soul, and wiped it out, just as Yahweh had foretold through his servant Ahijah of Shiloh, •because of the sins into which he had 30 led Israel, and because he had provoked the anger of Yahweh, the God of Israel.

The rest of the history of Nadab, his entire career, is not all this recorded 31 in the Book of the Annals of the Kings of Israel?ᵃ (32)

The reign of Baasha in Israel (909-886)

In the third year of Asa king of Judah, Baasha son of Ahijah became king 33 of Israel at Tirzah for twenty-four years. •He did what is displeasing to Yahweh; 34 he copied the example of Jeroboam and the sin into which he had led Israel.

16 The word of Yahweh came to Jehu son of Hanani against Baasha, •'I raised ¹₂ you from the dust and made you leader of my people Israel, but you have followed Jeroboam's example and led my people Israel into sins that provoke my anger. •Now I will sweep away Baasha and his House; I will make your 3 House like the House of Jeroboam son of Nebat. •Those of Baasha's family 4 who die in the city, the dogs will eat; and those who die in the open country, the birds of the air will eat.'

The rest of the history of Baasha, his career, his valour, is not all this 5 recorded in the Book of the Annals of the Kings of Israel? •Then Baasha slept 6 with his ancestors and was buried in Tirzah; his son Elah succeeded him.

Furthermore, the word of Yahweh was delivered through the prophet Jehu 7 son of Hanani against Baasha and his House, firstly because of all the evil he did in the sight of Yahweh, provoking him to anger by his actions and becoming like the House of Jeroboam; secondly because he destroyed that House.

The reign of Elah in Israel (886-885)

In the twenty-sixth year of Asa king of Judah, Elah son of Baasha became 8 king of Israel at Tirzah, for two years. •Zimri, one of his officers, captain of 9 half his chariotry, plotted against him. While he was at Tirzah, drinking himself senseless in the house of Arza who was master of the palace in Tirzah, •Zimri 10 came in, struck him down and killed him in the twenty-seventh year of Asa king of Judah, and succeeded him. •On his accession, as soon as he was seated 11

on the throne, he butchered Baasha's entire family, not leaving him a single
12 male, or any relations, or friends. •Zimri destroyed the whole House of Baasha,
in accordance with the word which Yahweh had spoken through the prophet
13 Jehu, •because of all the sins of Baasha and his son Elah into which they
had led Israel, provoking the anger of Yahweh, the God of Israel, with their
useless idols.
14   The history of Elah, his entire career, is not all this recorded in the Book
of the Annals of the Kings of Israel?

The reign of Zimri in Israel (885)

15   In the twenty-seventh year of Asa king of Judah, Zimri became king for
seven days, in Tirzah. The people were then encamped in front of Gibbethon,
16 a Philistine town. •When news reached the camp of how Zimri had not only
plotted against but actually killed the king, all Israel proclaimed Omri, their
17 general, king of Israel in the camp the same day. •Omri, and all Israel with him,
18 raised the siege of Gibbethon and laid siege to Tirzah. •When Zimri saw that
the town was captured, he went into the keep of the royal palace, burned
19 the palace over his own head, and died. •This was because of the sin he
committed by doing what is displeasing to Yahweh, by copying the example of
Jeroboam and the sin into which he had led Israel.
20   The rest of the history of Zimri and the plot he hatched, is not all this
recorded in the Book of the Annals of the Kings of Israel?
21   The people of Israel then split into two factions: one half following Tibni
22 son of Ginath to make him king, the other half following Omri. •But the faction
of Omri proved stronger than that of Tibni son of Ginath; Tibni died, and Omri
became king.

The reign of Omri in Israel (885-874)

23   In the thirty-first year of Asa king of Judah, Omri became king of Israel and
24 reigned for twelve years. He reigned for six years in Tirzah. •Then for two
talents of silver he bought a hill from Shemer and on it built a town which
25 he named Samaria after Shemer who had owned the hill. •Omri did what is
26 displeasing to Yahweh, and was worse than all his predecessors. •In every way
he copied the example of Jeroboam son of Nebat and the sins into which he
had led Israel, provoking the anger of Yahweh, the God of Israel, with their
useless idols.
27   The rest of the history of Omri, his career, his valour, is not all this recorded
28 in the Book of the Annals of the Kings of Israel? •Then Omri slept with his
ancestors and was buried in Samaria; his son Ahab succeeded him.

Introduction to the reign of Ahab (874-853)

29   Ahab son of Omri became king of Israel in the thirty-eighth year of Asa king
30 of Judah, and reigned over Israel for twenty-two years in Samaria. •Ahab son
of Omri did what is displeasing to Yahweh, and was worse than all his prede-
31 cessors. •The least that he did was to follow the sinful example of Jeroboam
son of Nebat: he married Jezebel, the daughter of Ethbaal king of the Sidonians,ᵃ
32 and then proceeded to serve Baal and worship him. •He erected an altar to him
33 in the temple of Baal which he built in Samaria. •Ahab also put up a sacred
pole and committed other crimes as well, provoking the anger of Yahweh, the
God of Israel, more than all the kings of Israel who were his predecessors.
34 It was in his time that Hiel of Bethel rebuilt Jericho; he laid its foundations
at the price of Abiram, his first-born; its gates he erected at the price of his
youngest son Segub,ᵇ just as Yahweh had foretold through Joshua son of Nun.

15 a. V.32 simply repeats v.16, and is here omitted.
16 a. Ethbaal, a priest of Astarte, seized power in Tyre at the same time as Omri in Israel; the
two sealed an alliance by a family marriage.   b. The sons were killed as a foundation sacrifice.

V. THE ELIJAH CYCLE

A. THE GREAT DROUGHT

Elijah foretells the drought

17 Elijah the Tishbite, of Tishbe in Gilead said to Ahab, 'As Yahweh lives, 1 the God of Israel whom I serve, there shall be neither dew nor rain these years except at my order'.

At the wadi Cherith

The word of Yahweh came to him, •'Go away from here, go eastwards, and ²₃ hide yourself in the wadi Cherith which lies east of Jordan. •You can drink 4 from the stream, and I have ordered the ravens to bring you food there.' •He did 5 as Yahweh had said; he went and stayed in the wadi Cherith which lies east of Jordan. •The ravens brought him bread in the morning and meat in the 6 evening, and he quenched his thirst at the stream.

At Zarephath. The miracle of the flour and the oil

But after a while the stream dried up, for the country had no rain. And then ⁷₈ the word of Yahweh came to him, •'Up and go to Zarephath, a Sidonian town, 9 and stay there. I have ordered a widow there to give you food.' •So he went 10 off to Sidon. And when he reached the city gate, there was a widow gathering sticks; addressing her he said, 'Please bring a little water in a vessel for me to drink'. •She was setting off to bring it when he called after her. 'Please' he said 11 'bring me a scrap of bread in your hand.' •'As Yahweh your God lives,' she 12 replied 'I have no baked bread, but only a handful of meal in a jar and a little oil in a jug; I am just gathering a stick or two to go and prepare this for myself and my son to eat, and then we shall die.' •But Elijah said to her, 'Do not be afraid, 13 go and do as you have said; but first make a little scone of it for me and bring it to me, and then make some for yourself and for your son. •For thus Yahweh 14 speaks, the God of Israel:

"Jar of meal shall not be spent,
jug of oil shall not be emptied,
before the day when Yahweh sends
rain on the face of the earth".'

The woman went and did as Elijah told her and they ate the food, she, himself 15 and her son. •The jar of meal was not spent nor the jug of oil emptied, just as 16 Yahweh had foretold through Elijah.

The widow's son raised to life

It happened after this that the son of the mistress of the house fell sick; 17 his illness was so severe that in the end he had no breath left in him. •And the 18 woman said to Elijah, 'What quarrel have you with me, man of God? Have you come here to bring my sins home to me and to kill my son?' •'Give me your son' 19 he said, and taking him from her lap, carried him to the upper room where he was staying and laid him on his own bed. •He cried out to Yahweh, 'Yahweh 20 my God, do you mean to bring grief to the widow who is looking after me by killing her son?' •He stretched himself on the child three times and cried out to 21 Yahweh, 'Yahweh my God, may the soul of this child, I beg you, come into him again!' •Yahweh heard the prayer of Elijah and the soul of the child 22 returned to him again and he revived. •Elijah took the child, brought him down 23 from the upper room into the house, and gave him to his mother. 'Look,' Elijah said 'your son is alive.' •And the woman replied, 'Now I know you are a man 24 of God and the word of Yahweh in your mouth is truth itself'.

Elijah and Obadiah

1 **18** A long time went by, and the word of Yahweh came to Elijah in the third
year, 'Go, present yourself to Ahab; I am about to send down rain on the
2 land'. •So Elijah set off to present himself to Ahab.

3   As the famine was particularly severe in Samaria, •Ahab summoned Obadiah,
4 the master of the palace—Obadiah held Yahweh in great reverence: •when
Jezebel was butchering the prophets of Yahweh, Obadiah took a hundred of
them and hid them, fifty at a time, in a cave, and kept them provided with food
5 and water—•and Ahab said to Obadiah, 'Come along, we must scour the
country, all the springs and all the wadis in the hope of finding grass to keep
6 horses and mules alive, or we shall have to slaughter some of our stock'. •They
divided the country for the purpose of their survey; Ahab went one way by
7 himself and Obadiah went another way by himself. •While Obadiah was on his
way, whom should he meet but Elijah; recognising him he fell on his face and
8 said, 'So it is you, my lord Elijah!' •'Yes,' he replied 'go and tell your master,
9 "Elijah is here".' •But Obadiah said, 'What sin have I committed, for you to
10 put your servant in Ahab's power and cause my death? •As Yahweh your God
lives, there is no nation or kingdom where my master has not sent in search
of you; and when they said, "He is not there", he made the kingdom or nation
11 swear on oath that they did not know where you were. •And now you say to me,
12 "Go and tell your master: Elijah is here". •But as soon as I leave you, the spirit
of Yahweh will carry you away and I shall not know where; I shall come and
tell Ahab; he will not be able to find you, and will kill me. Yet from his youth
13 your servant has revered Yahweh. •Has no one told my lord what I did when
Jezebel butchered the prophets of Yahweh, how I hid a hundred of them in
14 a cave, fifty at a time, and kept them provided with food and water? •And now
you say to me, "Go and tell your master: Elijah is here". Why, he will kill me!'
15 Elijah replied, 'As Yahweh Sabaoth lives, whom I serve, I shall present myself
before him today!'

Elijah and Ahab

16   Obadiah went to find Ahab and tell him the news, and Ahab then went to
17 find Elijah. •When he saw Elijah, Ahab said, 'So there you are, you scourge of
18 Israel!' •'Not I,' he replied 'I am not the scourge of Israel, you and your family
19 are; because you have deserted Yahweh and gone after the Baals. •Now give
orders for all Israel to gather round me on Mount Carmel, and also the four
hundred prophets of Baal who eat at Jezebel's table.'

The sacrifice on Carmel

20   Ahab called all Israel together and assembled the prophets on Mount
21 Carmel. •Elijah stepped out in front of all the people. 'How long' he said
'do you mean to hobble first on one leg then on the other? If Yahweh is God,
22 follow him; if Baal, follow him.' But the people never said a word. •Elijah
then said to them, 'I, I alone, am left as a prophet of Yahweh, while the prophets
23 of Baal are four hundred and fifty. •Let two bulls be given us; let them
choose one for themselves, dismember it and lay it on the wood, but not set
24 fire to it. I in my turn will prepare the other bull, but not set fire to it. •You
must call on the name of your god, and I shall call on the name of mine; the
god who answers with fire, is God indeed.' The people all answered, 'Agreed!'
25 Elijah then said to the prophets of Baal, 'Choose one bull and begin, for there
26 are more of you. Call on the name of your god but light no fire.' •They took
the bull and prepared it, and from morning to midday they called on the name
of Baal. 'O Baal, answer us!' they cried, but there was no voice, no answer,
27 as they performed their hobbling dance round the altar they had made. •Midday
came, and Elijah mocked them. 'Call louder,' he said 'for he is a god: he is
preoccupied or he is busy, or he has gone on a journey; perhaps he is asleep

and will wake up.' •So they shouted louder and gashed themselves, as their 28
custom was, with swords and spears until the blood flowed down them. •Midday 29
passed, and they ranted on until the time the offering is presented; *a* but there
was no voice, no answer, no attention given to them.

Then Elijah said to all the people, 'Come closer to me', and all the people 30
came closer to him. He repaired the altar of Yahweh which had been broken
down. •Elijah took twelve stones, corresponding to the number of the tribes 31
of the sons of Jacob, to whom the word of Yahweh had come, 'Israel shall be
your name', •and built an altar in the name of Yahweh. Round the altar he 32
dug a trench of a size to hold two measures of seed. •He then arranged the 33
wood, dismembered the bull, and laid it on the wood. •Then he said, 'Fill four 34
jars with water and pour it on the holocaust and on the wood'; this they did.
He said, 'Do it a second time'; they did it a second time. He said, 'Do it a third
time'; they did it a third time. •The water flowed round the altar and the trench 35
itself was full of water. •At the time when the offering is presented, Elijah 36
the prophet stepped forward. 'Yahweh, God of Abraham, Isaac and Israel,'
he said 'let them know today that you are God in Israel, and that I am your
servant, that I have done all these things at your command. •Answer me, 37
Yahweh, answer me, so that this people may know that you, Yahweh, are God
and are winning back their hearts.'

Then the fire of Yahweh fell and consumed the holocaust and wood and 38
licked up the water in the trench. •When all the people saw this they fell on their 39
faces. 'Yahweh is God,' they cried 'Yahweh is God.' •Elijah said, 'Seize the 40
prophets of Baal: do not let one of them escape'. They seized them, and Elijah
took them down to the wadi Kishon, and he slaughtered them there.

The drought ends

Elijah said to Ahab, 'Go back, eat and drink; for I hear the sound of rain'. 41
While Ahab went back to eat and drink, Elijah climbed to the top of Carmel 42
and bowed down to the earth, putting his face between his knees. •'Now go up,' 43
he told his servant 'and look out to the sea.' He went up and looked. 'There
is nothing at all' he said. 'Go back seven times' Elijah said. •The seventh time, 44
the servant said, 'Now there is a cloud, small as a man's hand, rising from the
sea'. Elijah said, 'Go and say to Ahab, "Harness the chariot and go down before
the rain stops you" '. •And with that the sky grew dark with cloud and 45
storm, and rain fell in torrents. Ahab mounted his chariot and made for Jezreel.
The hand of Yahweh was on Elijah, and tucking up his cloak he ran in front of 46
Ahab as far as the outskirts of Jezreel.

B. ELIJAH AT HOREB

The journey to Horeb

19 When Ahab told Jezebel all that Elijah had done, and how he had put 1
all the prophets to the sword, •Jezebel sent a messenger to Elijah to say, 2
'May the gods do this to me and more, if by this time tomorrow I have not made
your life like the life of one of them!' •He was afraid and fled for his 3
life. He came to Beersheba, a town of Judah, where he left his servant. •He 4
himself went on into the wilderness, a day's journey, and sitting under a furze
bush wished he were dead. 'Yahweh,' he said 'I have had enough. Take my life;
I am no better than my ancestors.' •Then he lay down and went to sleep. But an 5
angel touched him and said, 'Get up and eat'. •He looked round, and there at 6
his head was a scone baked on hot stones, and a jar of water. He ate and drank
and then lay down again. •But the angel of Yahweh came back a second time 7
and touched him and said, 'Get up and eat, or the journey will be too long for
you'. •So he got up and ate and drank, and strengthened by that food he walked 8
for forty days and forty nights until he reached Horeb, the mountain of God.

The encounter with God

9 There he went into the cave[a] and spent the night in it. Then the word of
10 Yahweh came to him saying, 'What are you doing here, Elijah?' •He replied,
'I am filled with jealous zeal for Yahweh Sabaoth, because the sons of Israel
have deserted you, broken down your altars and put your prophets to the sword.
11 I am the only one left, and they want to kill me.' •Then he was told, 'Go out
and stand on the mountain before Yahweh'. Then Yahweh himself went by.
There came a mighty wind, so strong it tore the mountains and shattered the
rocks before Yahweh. But Yahweh was not in the wind. After the wind came an
12 earthquake. But Yahweh was not in the earthquake. •After the earthquake
came a fire. But Yahweh was not in the fire. And after the fire there came the
13 sound of a gentle breeze. •And when Elijah heard this, he covered his face
with his cloak and went out and stood at the entrance of the cave. Then a voice
14 came to him, which said, 'What are you doing here, Elijah?' •He replied, 'I am
filled with jealous zeal for Yahweh Sabaoth, because the sons of Israel have
deserted you, broken down your altars and put your prophets to the sword.
I am the only one left and they want to kill me.'
15 'Go,' Yahweh said 'go back by the same way to the wilderness of Damascus.
16 You are to go and anoint Hazael as king of Aram. •You are to anoint Jehu son
of Nimshi as king of Israel, and to anoint Elisha son of Shaphat, of Abel
17 Meholah, as prophet to succeed you. •Anyone who escapes the sword of Hazael
will be put to death by Jehu; and anyone who escapes the sword of Jehu will be
18 put to death by Elisha. •But I shall spare seven thousand in Israel: all the knees
that have not bent before Baal, all the mouths that have not kissed him.'

The call of Elisha

19 Leaving there, he came on Elisha son of Shaphat as he was ploughing
behind twelve yoke of oxen, he himself being with the twelfth. Elijah passed
20 near to him and threw his cloak over him. •Elisha left his oxen and ran after
Elijah. 'Let me kiss my father and mother, then I will follow you' he said.
21 Elijah answered, 'Go, go back; for have I done anything to you?' •Elisha turned
away, took the pair of oxen and slaughtered them. He used the plough for
cooking the oxen, then gave to his men, who ate. He then rose, and followed
Elijah and became his servant.

C. THE ARAMAEAN WARS

The siege of Samaria

20 Ben-hadad king of Aram[a] mustered his whole army—thirty-two kings
were with him, and horses and chariots—and went up to lay siege to
2 Samaria and storm it. •He sent messengers into the city to Ahab king of Israel
3 to tell him, 'Thus says Ben-hadad, "Your silver and gold are mine; you may
4 keep your wives and children".' •The king of Israel replied, 'As you command,
my lord king. Myself and all I have are yours.'
5 But the messengers came back and said, 'Ben-hadad says this, "I sent you
this order: Hand over your silver and your gold, your wives and your children.
6 Count on it that this time tomorrow I will send my servants to search your
house and your servants' houses and lay hands on all they fancy and take
it away." '
7 The king of Israel summoned all the elders of the land and said, 'You can
see clearly how this man intends to ruin us. He now claims my wives and my

---

18 a. I.e. until the late afternoon; this is merely an indication of the time of day.
19 a. The 'crevice' where Moses crouched when God appeared, Ex 33:22.
20 a. Ben-hadad II, successor to the Ben-hadad of 1 K 15:18.

children, although I have not refused him my silver and my gold.' •All the elders 8
and all the people said, 'Take no notice. Do not consent'. •So he gave this answer 9
to Ben-hadad's messengers, 'Say to my lord the king, "All you first required
of your servant I will do, but this I cannot do" '. And the messengers went back
with the answer.

Ben-hadad then sent him the following message, 'May the gods do this to 10
me and more if there are enough handfuls of rubble in Samaria for all the people
in my following'. •But the king of Israel returned this answer, 'The proverb 11
says: The man who puts on his armour is not the one who can boast, but the
man who takes it off'. •When Ben-hadad heard this message—he was under the 12
awnings drinking with the kings—he gave orders to his servants, 'Take post!'
And they took up their positions against the city.

Victory for Israel

A prophet then arrived, looking for Ahab king of Israel. 'Yahweh says 13
this' he said. 'You have seen this mighty army? This very day I will deliver
it into your hands, and you shall know that I am Yahweh.' •'By whose means?' 14
asked Ahab. The prophet replied, 'Yahweh says this, "By means of the young
soldiers of the district governors" '. 'Who is to open the attack?' Ahab asked.
'Yourself' the prophet answered.

So Ahab inspected the young soldiers of the district governors: there were 15
two hundred and thirty-two. After these he reviewed the whole army, all the
Israelites: there were seven thousand. •They made a sortie at midday, when 16
Ben-hadad was drinking himself senseless under the awnings, he and the thirty-
two kings who were his allies. •The young soldiers of the district governors led 17
the sortie. Ben-hadad was informed, 'Some men have come out of Samaria'.
He said, 'If they have come out for peace, take them alive; if they have come 18
out for war, take them alive too'. •So they made a sortie from the town, the 19
young soldiers of the district governors and behind them the army, •and each 20
struck down his man. Aram took to flight and Israel pursued; Ben-hadad king
of Aram escaped on a chariot horse. •Then the king of Israel came out, capturing 21
horses and chariots and inflicting a great defeat on Aram.

Respite

The prophet went up to the king of Israel. 'Come,' he said to him 'take 22
courage and think carefully what you should do, for at the turn of the year
the king of Aram will march against you.'

The servants of the king of Aram said to him, 'Their god is a god of the 23
mountains; that is why they have proved stronger than us. But if we fight them
on level ground, we will certainly beat them. •This is what you must do: remove all 24
these kings from their posts and appoint commanders instead. •You, for your 25
part, must recruit an army as large as the one that deserted you, with as many
horses and as many chariots; then if we fight them on level ground, we will
certainly beat them.' He listened to their advice and acted accordingly.

The victory of Aphek

At the turn of the year, Ben-hadad mustered the Aramaeans and went up 26
to Aphek to fight Israel. •The Israelites had also mustered, and marched out 27
to meet them. Encamped opposite them, the Israelites looked like two herds of
goats, whereas the Aramaeans filled the countryside.

The man of God accosted the king of Israel. 'Yahweh says this' he said. 28
' "Since Aram has said that Yahweh is a god of the mountains and not a god of
the plains, I will put all this mighty host into your power, and you shall know
that I am Yahweh." ' •For seven days they were encamped opposite each other. 29
On the seventh day battle was joined and the Israelites slaughtered the
Aramaeans, a hundred thousand foot soldiers[b] in one day. •The rest fled to 30

Aphek, into the town itself, but the walls fell down on the twenty-seven thousand who remained.

31 Now Ben-hadad had fled and taken refuge within the town in an inner room. 'Look,' his servants said to him 'we have heard that the kings of Israel are merciful kings. Let us put sackcloth round our waists and ropes on our heads 32 and go out to the king of Israel; perhaps he will spare your life.' •So they wrapped sackcloth round their waists and put ropes on their heads and went to the king of Israel, and said, 'Your servant Ben-hadad says, "Spare my life" '. 33 'So he is still alive?' he answered. 'He is my brother.'^{c} •The men took this for a good omen and quickly seized on his words. 'Yes,' they said 'Ben-hadad is your brother.' Ahab said, 'Go and fetch him'. Then Ben-hadad came out to 34 him and Ahab made him get up into his chariot. •Ben-hadad said, 'I will restore the towns my father took from your father and you may set up bazaars for yourself in Damascus as my father did in Samaria. Myself, by the terms of this treaty, you will set free.' So Ahab made a treaty with him and let him go free.

A prophet condemns Ahab's policy

35 At Yahweh's order a member of the brotherhood of prophets said to 36 a companion of his, 'Strike me', but the man refused to strike him. •So he said to him, 'Since you have disobeyed the order of Yahweh, the very moment you leave me a lion will kill you'. And no sooner had he left him than he met 37 a lion, which killed him. •The prophet then went to find another man and said, 38 'Strike me', and the man struck him and wounded him. •The prophet then went and stood waiting for the king on the road, disguising himself with his 39 headband over his eyes. •As the king passed, he called out to him, 'Your servant was making his way to where the fight was thickest when someone left the fighting to bring a man to me, and said, "Guard this man; if he is found missing, your life will pay for his, or else you will have to pay one talent of 40 silver". •But while your servant was busy with one thing and another, the man disappeared.' The king of Israel said, 'That is your sentence, then. You have 41 pronounced it yourself.' •At this the man quickly pulled off the headband covering his eyes, and the king of Israel recognised him as one of the prophets.^{d} 42 He said to the king, 'Yahweh says this, "Since you have let the man escape who was under my ban, your life will pay for his, your people for his people" '. 43 And off went the king of Israel, gloomy and out of temper, on his way back to Samaria.

D. NABOTH'S VINEYARD

Naboth refuses to hand over his vineyard

1 21 This is what happened next: Naboth of Jezreel had a vineyard close by 2 the palace of Ahab king of Samaria, •and Ahab said to Naboth, 'Give me your vineyard to be my vegetable garden, since it adjoins my house; I will give you a better vineyard for it or, if you prefer, I will give you its worth in 3 money'. •But Naboth answered Ahab, 'Yahweh forbid that I should give you the inheritance of my ancestors!'

Ahab and Jezebel

4 Ahab went home gloomy and out of temper at the words of Naboth of Jezreel, 'I will not give you the inheritance of my fathers'. He lay down on 5 his bed and turned his face away and refused to eat. •His wife Jezebel came to 6 him. 'Why are you so dispirited' she said 'that you will not eat?' •He said,

---

b. Not an accurate figure.   c. Ahab declines his homage.   d. Members of the brotherhood of prophets may have worn a distinguishing mark on their foreheads.

'I have been speaking to Naboth of Jezreel; I said: Give me your vineyard either for money or, if you prefer, for another vineyard in exchange. But he said, "I will not give you my vineyard".' •Then his wife Jezebel said, 'You make 7 a fine king of Israel, and no mistake! Get up and eat; cheer up, and you will feel better; I will get you the vineyard of Naboth of Jezreel myself.'

Naboth is murdered

So she wrote letters in Ahab's name and sealed them with his seal, sending 8 them to the elders and nobles who lived where Naboth lived. •In the letters 9 she wrote, 'Proclaim a fast, and put Naboth in the forefront of the people. Confront him with a couple of scoundrels who will accuse him like this, "You 10 have cursed God and the king" Then take him outside and stone him to death.' The men of Naboth's town, the elders and nobles who lived in his town, 11 did what Jezebel ordered, what was written in the letters she had sent them. They proclaimed a fast and put Naboth in the forefront of the people. •Then ¹²⁄₁₃ the two scoundrels came and stood in front of him and made their accusation, 'Naboth has cursed God and the king'. They led him outside the town and stoned him to death. •They then sent word to Jezebel, 'Naboth has been stoned 14 to death'. •When Jezebel heard that Naboth had been stoned to death, she said 15 to Ahab, 'Get up! Take possession of the vineyard which Naboth of Jezreel would not give you for money, for Naboth is no longer alive, he is dead.' •When Ahab 16 heard that Naboth was dead, he got up to go down to the vineyard of Naboth of Jezreel and take possession of it.

Elijah pronounces God's sentence

Then the word of Yahweh came to Elijah the Tishbite, •'Up! Go down to ¹⁷⁄₁₈ meet Ahab king of Israel, in Samaria. You will find him in Naboth's vineyard; he has gone down to take possession of it. •You are to say this to him, 19 "Yahweh says this: You have committed murder; now you usurp as well. For this—and Yahweh says this—in the place where the dogs licked the blood of Naboth, the dogs will lick your blood too."' •Ahab said to Elijah, 'So you have 20 found me out, O my enemy!' Elijah answered, 'I have found you out. For your double dealing, and since you have done what is displeasing to Yahweh, •I will 21 now bring disaster down on you; I will sweep away your descendants, and wipe out every male belonging to the family of Ahab, fettered or free in Israel. I will treat your House as I treated the House of Jeroboam son of Nebat and 22 of Baasha son of Ahijah, for provoking my anger and leading Israel into sin. (Against Jezebel too Yahweh spoke these words: The dogs will eat Jezebel in 23 the Field of Jezreel.) •Those of Ahab's family who die in the city, the dogs 24 will eat; and those who die in the open country, the birds of the air will eat.' And indeed there never was anyone like Ahab for double dealing and for 25 doing what is displeasing to Yahweh, urged on by Jezebel his wife. •He behaved 26 in the most abominable way, adhering to idols, just as the Amorites used to do whom Yahweh had dispossessed for the sons of Israel.

Ahab repents

When Ahab heard these words, he tore his garments and put sackcloth next 27 his skin and fasted; he slept in the sackcloth; he walked with slow steps. •Then 28 the word of Yahweh came to Elijah the Tishbite, •'Have you seen how Ahab 29 has humbled himself before me? Since he has humbled himself before me, I will not bring the disaster in his days; I will bring the disaster down on his House in the days of his son.'

E. ANOTHER WAR WITH ARAM

Ahab plans a campaign against Ramoth-gilead

1 22 There was a lull of three years, with no fighting between Aram and Israel.
2   Then, in the third year, Jehoshaphat king of Judah paid a visit to the
3 king of Israel. •The king of Israel said to his officers, 'You are aware that
Ramoth-gilead belongs to us? And yet we do nothing to wrest it away from
4 the king of Aram.' •He said to Jehoshaphat, 'Will you come with me to fight
at Ramoth-gilead?' Jehoshaphat answered the king of Israel, 'I am as ready as
you, my men as your men, my horses as your horses'.

The spurious prophets predict success

5   Jehoshaphat, however, said to the king of Israel, 'First, please consult the
6 word of Yahweh'. •So the king of Israel called the prophets together, about four
hundred of them. 'Should I march to attack Ramoth-gilead' he asked 'or
should I refrain?' 'March,' they replied 'Yahweh will deliver it into the power
7 of the king.' •But Jehoshaphat said, 'Is there no other prophet of Yahweh here
8 for us to consult?' •The king of Israel answered Jehoshaphat, 'There is one more
man through whom we can consult Yahweh, but I hate him because he never
has a favourable prophecy for me, only unfavourable ones; he is Micaiah son
9 of Imlah'. 'The king should not say such things' Jehoshaphat said. •Accordingly
the king of Israel summoned one of the eunuchs and said, 'Bring Micaiah son
of Imlah immediately'.

10   The king of Israel and Jehoshaphat king of Judah were both sitting on their
thrones in full regalia, at the threshing-floor outside the gate of Samaria, with
11 all the prophets raving in front of them. •Zedekiah son of Chenaanah had
made himself iron horns. 'Yahweh says this' he said. ' "With these you
12 will gore the Aramaeans till you make an end of them." ' •And all the prophets
prophesied the same. 'March to Ramoth-gilead' they said 'and conquer. Yahweh
will deliver it into the power of the king.'

The prophet Micaiah predicts defeat

13   The messenger who had gone to summon Micaiah said, 'Here are all the
prophets as one man speaking favourably to the king. Try to speak like one of
14 them and foretell success.' •But Micaiah answered, 'As Yahweh lives, what
15 Yahweh says to me, that will I utter!' •When he came to the king, the king said,
'Micaiah, should we march to attack Ramoth-gilead, or should we refrain?' He
answered, 'March and conquer. Yahweh will deliver it into the power of the
16 king.' •But the king said, 'How often must I put you on oath to tell me nothing
17 but the truth in the name of Yahweh?' •Then Micaiah spoke:

> 'I have seen all Israel scattered on the mountains
> like sheep without a shepherd.
> And Yahweh said, "These have no master,
> let each go home unmolested".'

18   At this the king of Israel said to Jehoshaphat, 'Did I not tell you that he never
19 gives me favourable prophecies, but only unfavourable ones?' •Micaiah went
on, 'Listen rather to the word of Yahweh. I have seen Yahweh seated on his
throne; all the array of heaven stood in his presence, on his right and on his left.
20 Yahweh said, "Who will trick Ahab into marching to his death at Ramoth-
21 gilead?" At which some answered one way, and some another. •Then the spirit
came forward and stood before Yahweh. "I," he said "I will trick him." "How?"
22 Yahweh asked. •He replied, "I will go and become a lying spirit in the mouths
of all his prophets". "You shall trick him," Yahweh said "you shall succeed.
23 Go and do it." •Now see how Yahweh has put a lying spirit into the mouths
of all your prophets here. But Yahweh has pronounced disaster on you.'

Then Zedekiah son of Chenaanah came up and struck Micaiah on the jaw. 24
'Which way' he asked 'did the spirit of Yahweh leave me, to talk to you?' •'That 25
is what you will find out,' Micaiah retorted 'the day you flee to an inner room
to hide.' •The king of Israel said, 'Seize Micaiah and hand him over to Amon, 26
governor of the city, and to Prince Joash, •and say, "These are the king's orders: 27
Put this man in prison and feed him on nothing but bread and water until I come
back safe and sound" '. •Micaiah said, 'If you come back safe and sound, Yahweh 28
has not spoken through me'.

Ahab falls at Ramoth-gilead

The king of Israel and Jehoshaphat king of Judah went up against Ramoth- 29
gilead. •The king of Israel said to Jehoshaphat, 'I will disguise myself to go 30
into battle, but I want you to wear your royal uniform'. The king of Israel went
into battle disguised. •The king of Aram had given his chariot commanders the 31
following order: 'Do not attack anyone of whatever rank, except the king of
Israel'. •When the chariot commanders caught sight of Jehoshaphat, they said, 32
'That is obviously the king of Israel'. And they wheeled to the attack. But
Jehoshaphat shouted his war cry •and the chariot commanders, realising that 33
he was not the king of Israel, called off their pursuit.

Now one of the men, drawing his bow at random, hit the king of Israel 34
between the corslet and the scale-armour of his breastplate. 'Turn about' the
king said to his charioteer. 'Get me out of the battle; I have been hurt.' •But 35
the battle grew fiercer as the day went on; the king was held upright in his chariot
facing the Aramaeans, and in the evening he died; the blood from the wound
flowed into the bottom of the chariot. •At sundown a shout ran through the 36
camp, 'Every man back to his town, every man back to his country; •the king 37
is dead!' They went to Samaria, and in Samaria they buried the king. •They 38
washed the chariot at the Pool of Samaria; the dogs licked up the blood, and
the prostitutes washed in it, in accordance with the word that Yahweh had spoken.

F. AFTER THE DEATH OF AHAB

The end of the reign of Ahab

The rest of the history of Ahab, his entire career, the ivory house he erected, 39
all the towns he built, is not all this recorded in the Book of the Annals of the
Kings of Israel? •Then Ahab slept with his ancestors; his son Ahaziah succeeded 40
him.

The reign of Jehoshaphat in Judah (870-848)

Jehoshaphat son of Asa became king of Judah in the fourth year of Ahab 41
king of Israel. •Jehoshaphat was thirty-five years old when he came to the 42
throne, and he reigned for twenty-five years in Jerusalem. His mother's name
was Azubah, daughter of Shilhi. •In every way he followed the example of his 43
father Asa undeviatingly, doing what is right in the eyes of Yahweh. •The high 44
places, however, were not abolished; the people still offered sacrifice and incense
on the high places. •Jehoshaphat was at peace with the king of Israel. 45
The rest of the history of Jehoshaphat, the valour he showed, the wars he 46
waged, is not all this recorded in the Book of the Annals of the Kings of Judah?
The remaining male sacred prostitutes of those who had lived in the time of his 47
father Asa, he swept out of the country. •There was no king in Edom, •and ⁴⁸₄₉
King Jehoshaphat built a ship of Tarshish to go to Ophir for gold, but his ship
never reached there: it was wrecked at Ezion-geber. •Then Ahaziah son of 50
Ahab said to Jehoshaphat, 'Let my men man the ships with yours'. But
Jehoshaphat would not agree. •Then Jehoshaphat slept with his ancestors and was 51
buried in the Citadel of David, his ancestor; his son Jehoram succeeded him.

King Ahaziah of Israel and the prophet Elijah (853-852)

52 Ahaziah son of Ahab became king of Israel in Samaria in the seventeenth
53 year of Jehoshaphat king of Judah, and reigned over Israel for two years. •He
did what is displeasing to Yahweh, by following the example of his father and
54 mother, and of Jeroboam son of Nebat who had led Israel into sin. •He served
Baal and worshipped him, and provoked the anger of Yahweh the God of Israel
just as his father had done.

THE SECOND BOOK OF THE KINGS

1   1 After the death of Ahab Moab rebelled against Israel.
2   Ahaziah had fallen from the balcony of his upper room in Samaria, and
was lying ill; so he sent messengers, saying to them, 'Go and consult Baalzebub
3 the god of Ekron and ask whether I shall recover from my illness'. •But the
angel of Yahweh said to Elijah the Tishbite, 'Up! Go and intercept the messengers of the king of Samaria. Say to them, "Is there no God in Israel, for you
4 to go and consult Baalzebub the god of Ekron? •Yahweh says this: The
bed you have got into you will not get out of; you are certainly going to die." '
And Elijah set out.
5   The messengers returned to the king, who said, 'Why have you come back?'
6 'A man came to meet us' they answered 'and said, "Go back to the king who
sent you and tell him: Yahweh says this: Is there no God in Israel for you
to go and consult Baalzebub the god of Ekron? For this, the bed you have
7 got into you will not get out of; you are certainly going to die." ' •He said, 'This
8 man who met you and said all this, what was he like?' •'A man wearing a hair
cloak' they answered 'and a leather loincloth.' 'It was Elijah the Tishbite'
he said.
9   He then sent a captain of fifty soldiers with his contingent to Elijah, whom
they found sitting on top of the hill; the captain went up to him and said, 'Man
10 of God, the king says, "Come down" '. •Elijah answered the captain, 'If I am
a man of God, let fire come down from heaven and destroy both you and your
fifty men'. And fire came down from heaven and destroyed him and his fifty
11 men. •The king sent a second captain of fifty to him, again with fifty men, and
he too went up and said, 'Man of God, this is the king's order: "Come down
12 at once" '. •Elijah answered them, 'If I am a man of God, let fire come down
from heaven and destroy both you and your fifty men'. And fire came down
13 from heaven and destroyed him and his fifty men. •Then the king sent a third
captain of fifty to him, with another fifty men. The third captain of fifty came
up to Elijah, fell on his knees before him and pleaded with him. 'Man of God,'
he said 'let my life and the lives of these fifty servants of yours have some value
14 in your eyes. •Fire has fallen from heaven and destroyed two captains of fifties,
15 but let my life have some value now in your eyes.' •The angel of Yahweh said
to Elijah, 'Go down with him; do not be afraid of him'. He rose and accom-
16 panied him down to the king, •and said to him, 'Yahweh says this, "Since
you sent messengers to consult Baalzebub the god of Ekron, the bed you have
got into you will not get out of; you are certainly going to die" '.
17   And, in accordance with the word of Yahweh that Elijah had uttered, he died.
Since he had no son, his brother Jehoram succeeded him, in the second year
18 of Jehoram son of Jehoshaphat, king of Judah. •The rest of the history of
Ahaziah, and his career, is not all this recorded in the Book of the Annals of the
Kings of Israel?

VI. THE ELISHA CYCLE

A. ITS OPENING

Elijah is taken up and Elisha succeeds him

2 This is what happened when Yahweh took Elijah up to heaven in the 1
whirlwind: Elijah and Elisha set out from Gilgal, •and Elijah said to Elisha, 2
'Please stay here, for Yahweh is only sending me to Bethel'. But Elisha replied,
'As Yahweh lives and as you yourself live, I will not leave you!' and they went
down to Bethel. •The brotherhood of prophets who live at Bethel came out 3
to meet Elisha and said, 'Do you know that Yahweh is going to carry your lord
and master away today?' 'Yes, I know,' he said 'be quiet.' •Elijah said, 'Elisha, 4
please stay here, Yahweh is only sending me to Jericho'. But he replied, 'As
Yahweh lives and as you yourself live, I will not leave you!' and they went on
to Jericho. •The brotherhood of prophets who live at Jericho went up to Elisha 5
and said, 'Do you know that Yahweh is going to carry your lord and master
away today?' 'Yes, I know,' he said 'be quiet.' •Elijah said, 'Elisha, please stay 6
here, Yahweh is only sending me to the Jordan'. But he replied, 'As Yahweh lives
and as you yourself live, I will not leave you!' And they went on together.

Fifty of the brotherhood of prophets followed them, halting some distance 7
away as the two of them stood beside the Jordan. •Elijah took his cloak, rolled 8
it up and struck the water; and the water divided to left and right, and the two
of them crossed over dry-shod. •When they had crossed, Elijah said to Elisha, 9
'Make your request. What can I do for you before I am taken from you?' Elisha
answered, 'Let me inherit a double share of your spirit'.*a* •'Your request is a 10
difficult one' Elijah said. 'If you see me while I am being taken from you, it shall
be as you ask; if not, it will not be so.' •Now as they walked on, talking as 11
they went, a chariot of fire appeared and horses of fire, coming between the
two of them; and Elijah went up to heaven in the whirlwind. •Elisha saw it, and 12
shouted, 'My father! My father! Chariot of Israel and its chargers!' Then he
lost sight of him, and taking hold of his clothes he tore them in half. •He picked 13
up the cloak of Elijah which had fallen, and went back and stood on the bank
of the Jordan.

He took the cloak of Elijah and struck the water. 'Where is Yahweh, the 14
God of Elijah?' he cried. He struck the water, and it divided to right and left,
and Elisha crossed over. •The brotherhood of prophets saw him in the distance, 15
and said, 'The spirit of Elijah has come to rest on Elisha'; they went to meet
him and bowed to the ground before him. •'Look,' they said 'your servants 16
have fifty strong men with them; let them go and look for your master; the
spirit of Yahweh may have taken him up and thrown him down on a mountain
or into a valley.' 'Send no one' he replied. •But they so shamed him with their 17
insistence that he consented. So they sent fifty men who searched for three days
without finding him. •They then came back to Elisha who had stayed in Jericho; 18
he said, 'Did I not tell you not to go?'

Two miracles of Elisha

The men of the town said to Elisha, 'The town is pleasant to live in, as my 19
lord indeed can see, but the water is foul and the country suffers from
miscarriages'. •'Bring me a new bowl,' he said 'and put some salt in it.' They 20
brought it to him. •Then he went to the place the water came from and threw 21
salt into it. 'Thus Yahweh speaks,' he said ' "I make this water wholesome:
neither death nor miscarriage shall come from it any more". ' •And the water 22
was made wholesome, and is so today, exactly as Elisha had said it would be.

From there he went up to Bethel, and while he was on the road up, some 23
small boys came out of the town and jeered at him. 'Go up, baldhead!' they
shouted 'Go up, baldhead!' •He turned round and looked at them; and he 24

cursed them in the name of Yahweh. And two she-bears came out of the wood
25 and savaged forty-two of the boys. •From there he went on to Mount Carmel,
and then returned to Samaria.

B. THE MOABITE WAR

Introduction to the reign of Jehoram in Israel (852-841)

1 Jehoram son of Ahab became king of Israel in Samaria in the eighteenth year
2 3 of Jehoshaphat king of Judah, and reigned for twelve years.ᵃ •He did what is
displeasing to Yahweh, though not like his father and mother, for he did away
3 with the pillar of Baal that his father had made. •Nonetheless, he continued
to practise the sins into which Jeroboam son of Nebat had led Israel, and did
not give them up.

The expedition of Israel and Judah against Moab

4 Mesha king of Moab was a sheep-breeder and used to pay the king of Israel
a hundred thousand lambs and the wool of a hundred thousand rams in tribute.
5 But when Ahab died, the king of Moab rebelled against the king of Israel.
6 At once King Jehoram went out of Samaria and mustered all Israel.. After
7 this he sent word to the king of Judah, 'The king of Moab has rebelled
against me. Will you join with me fighting Moab?' 'I will' he replied. 'I am as
8 ready as you, my men as your men, my horses as your horses,' •and added
'which way are we to attack?' 'Through the wilderness of Edom' the other
answered.
9 So they set out, the king of Israel, the king of Judah and the king of Edom.
They followed a devious route for seven days, until there was no water left for
10 the troops or for the beasts in their baggage train. •'Alas!' the king of Israel
exclaimed 'Yahweh has summoned us three kings, only to put us into the power
11 of Moab.' •But the king of Judah said, 'Is there no prophet of Yahweh here
for us to consult Yahweh through him?' One of the king of Israel's servants
answered, 'Elisha son of Shaphat is here, who used to pour water on the hands
12 of Elijah'. •'The word of Yahweh is with him' the king of Judah said. So they
13 went to him, the king of Israel, the king of Judah and the king of Edom. •But
Elisha said to the king of Israel, 'What business have you with me? Go to the
prophets of your father and your mother.' 'No,' the king of Israel answered
'Yahweh has summoned us three kings, only to put us into the power of Moab.'
14 Elisha replied, 'As Yahweh Sabaoth lives, whom I serve, if I did not respect
Jehoshaphat king of Judah, I should not take any notice of you, or so much
15 as look at you. •Now bring me someone who can play the lyre.'ᵇ And as the
16 musician played, the hand of Yahweh was laid on him •and he said, 'Yahweh
17 says this, "Dig ditch on ditch in this wadi", •for Yahweh says, "You
shall see neither wind nor rain, but this wadi shall be filled with water, and
18 you and your troops and your baggage animals shall drink". •But this is only
a little thing in the sight of Yahweh, for he will put Moab itself into your power.
19 You shall storm every fortified town, fell every sound tree, block every water-
20 spring, ruin all the best fields with stones.' •Next morning at the time when
the oblation was being offered, water came from the direction of Edom, and the
country was filled with it.
21 When the Moabites learned that the kings had come up to fight against
them, all who were of age to bear arms were called up; they took up position
22 on the frontier. •In the morning when they got up, the sun was shining on the
23 water; and in the distance the Moabites saw the water as red as blood.ᶜ •'This is

2 a. I.e. 'Let me succeed you as your principal heir, having the eldest son's portion.'
3 a. By the most reliable dating, Jehoram reigned for eight years.   b. To stimulate a prophetic
ecstasy.   c. Perhaps owing to the red sand of Edom in the wadi el Hesa.

blood!' they said. 'The kings must have fought among themselves and killed one another. So now for the booty, Moab!'

But when they reached the Israelite camp, the Israelites launched their attack 24 and the Moabites fled before them, and as they advanced they cut the Moabites to pieces. •They laid the towns in ruins, and each man threw a stone into all 25 the best fields to fill them up, and they blocked every water-spring and felled every sound tree. In the end, there was only Kir-hareseth left, which the slingers surrounded and battered. •When the king of Moab saw that the battle had turned 26 against him, he mustered seven hundred swordsmen in the hope of breaking a way out and going to the king of Aram, but he failed. •Then he took his eldest 27 son who was to succeed him and offered him as a sacrifice on the city wall. There was bitter indignation against the Israelites, who then withdrew, retiring to their own country.

C. SOME MIRACLES OF ELISHA

The widow's oil

4 The wife of a member of the prophetic brotherhood appealed to Elisha. 1 'Your servant my husband is dead,' she said 'and you know how your servant revered Yahweh. A creditor has now come to take my two children and make them his slaves.' •Elisha said, 'What can I do for you? Tell me, what have you 2 in the house?' 'Your servant has nothing in the house,' she replied 'except a pot of oil.' •Then he said, 'Go outside and borrow jars from all your neighbours, 3 empty jars and not too few. •When you come back, shut the door on yourself 4 and your sons, and pour the oil into all these jars, putting each aside when it is full.' •So she left him; and she shut the door on herself and her sons; they passed 5 her the jars and she went on pouring. •When the jars were full, she said to her 6 son, 'Pass me another jar'. 'There are no more' he replied. Then the oil stopped flowing. •She went and told the man of God, who said, 'Go and sell the oil 7 and redeem your pledge; you and your children can live on the remainder'.

The woman of Shunem and her son

One day as Elisha was on his way to Shunem, a woman of rank who lived 8 there pressed him to stay and eat there. After this he always broke his journey for a meal when he passed that way. •She said to her husband, 'Look, I am 9 sure the man who is constantly passing our way must be a holy man of God. Let us build him a small room on the roof, and put him a bed in it, and a table 10 and chair and lamp; whenever he comes to us he can rest there.' •One day when 11 he came, he retired to the upper room and lay down. •He said to his servant 12 Gehazi, 'Call our Shunammitess'. He called her, and she came and stood before him. •'Tell her this,' Elisha said ' "Look, you have gone to all this trouble for 13 us, what can we do for you? Is there anything you would like said for you to the king or to the commander of the army?" ' But she replied, 'I live with my own people about me'. •'What can be done for her then?' he asked. Gehazi 14 answered, 'Well, she has no son and her husband is old'. •Elisha said, 'Call her'. 15 The servant called her and she stood at the door. •'This time next year,' he said 16 'you will hold a son in your arms.' But she said, 'No, my lord, do not deceive your servant'. •But the woman did conceive, and she gave birth to a son at the 17 time Elisha had said she would.

The child grew up; one day he went out to his father who was with the reapers, 18 and exclaimed to his father, 'Oh, my head! My head!' The father told a servant 19 to carry him to his mother. •He lifted him up and took him to his mother, and 20 the boy sat on her knee until midday, when he died. •She went upstairs, laid 21 him on the bed of the man of God, shut the door on him and went out. •She 22 called her husband and said, 'Send me one of the servants with a donkey. I must

23 hurry to the man of God and back.' •'Why go to him today?' he asked 'It is
24 not New Moon or sabbath.' But she answered, 'Never mind'. •She had the
donkey saddled, and said to her servant, 'Lead on, go! Do not draw rein until
25 I give the order.' •She set off and came to the man of God at Mount Carmel;
when he saw her in the distance, he said to his servant Gehazi, 'Look, here
26 comes our Shunammitess! •Now run and meet her and ask her, "Are you well?
27 Is your husband well? Your child well?"' She answered, 'Yes'. •When she came
to the man of God there on the mountain, she took hold of his feet. Gehazi
stepped forward to push her away, but the man of God said, 'Leave her; there
is bitterness in her soul and Yahweh has hidden it from me, he has not told me'.
28 She said, 'Did I ask my lord for a son? Did I not say: Do not deceive me?'
29 Elisha said to Gehazi, 'Tuck up your cloak, take my staff in your hand and go.
If you meet anyone, do not greet him; if anyone greets you, do not answer him.
30 You are to stretch out my staff over the child.' •But the child's mother said, 'As
Yahweh lives and as you yourself live, I will not leave you'. Then he stood up
31 and followed her. •Gehazi had gone ahead of them and had stretched out the
staff over the child, but there was no sound or response. He went back to meet
32 Elisha and told him. 'The child has not woken up' he said. •Elisha then went to
33 the house, and there on his bed lay the child, dead. •He went in and shut the door
34 on the two of them and prayed to Yahweh. •Then he climbed on to the bed and
stretched himself on top of the child, putting his mouth on his mouth, his eyes
to his eyes, and his hands on his hands, and as he lowered himself on to him,
35 the child's flesh grew warm. •Then he got up and walked to and fro inside the
house, and then climbed on to the bed again and lowered himself on to the child
36 seven times in all; then the child sneezed and opened his eyes. •He then summoned Gehazi. 'Call our Shunammitess' he said; and he called her. When she
37 came to him, he said, 'Take up your son'. •She went in and, falling at his feet,
bowed down to the ground; and taking up her son went out.

The poisoned soup

38 Elisha went back to Gilgal while there was famine in the country. As the
brotherhood of prophets were sitting with him, he said to his servant, 'Put the
39 large pot on the fire and cook some soup for the brotherhood'. •One of them
went into the fields to gather herbs and came on some wild vine off which he
gathered enough gourds to fill his lap. On his return, he cut them up into the
40 pot of soup; they did not know what they were. •They then poured the soup out
for the men to eat, but they had no sooner tasted the soup than they cried, 'Man
41 of God, there is death in the pot!' And they could not eat it. •'Bring some meal
then' Elisha said. This he threw into the pot, and said, 'Pour out for these men,
and let them eat'. And there was nothing harmful in the pot.

The multiplication of loaves

42 A man came from Baal-shalishah, bringing the man of God bread from the
first-fruits, twenty barley loaves and fresh grain in the ear. 'Give it to the people
43 to eat', Elisha said. •But his servant replied, 'How can I serve this to a hundred
men?' 'Give it to the people to eat' he insisted 'for Yahweh says this, "They
44 will eat and have some left over".' •He served them; they ate and had some
left over, as Yahweh had said

Naaman is healed

1 **5** Naaman, army commander to the king of Aram, was a man who enjoyed
his master's respect and favour, since through him Yahweh had granted
2 victory to the Aramaeans. But the man was a leper. •Now on one of their
raids, the Aramaeans had carried off from the land of Israel a little girl who had
3 become a servant of Naaman's wife. •She said to her mistress, 'If only my master
would approach the prophet of Samaria. He would cure him of his leprosy.'

Naaman went and told his master. 'This and this' he reported 'is what the girl 4
from the land of Israel said.' •'Go by all means,' said the king of Aram 'I will 5
send a letter to the king of Israel.' So Naaman left, taking with him ten talents
of silver, six thousand shekels of gold and ten festal robes. •He presented the 6
letter to the king of Israel. It read: 'With this letter, I am sending my servant
Naaman to you for you to cure him of his leprosy'. •When the king of Israel 7
read the letter, he tore his garments. 'Am I a god to give death and life,' he said
'that he sends a man to me and asks me to cure him of his leprosy? Listen to this,
and take note of it and see how he intends to pick a quarrel with me.'

When Elisha heard that the king of Israel had torn his garments, he sent word 8
to the king, 'Why did you tear your garments? Let him come to me, and he will
find there is a prophet in Israel.' •So Naaman came with his team and chariot 9
and drew up at the door of Elisha's house. •And Elisha sent him a messenger 10
to say, 'Go and bathe seven times in the Jordan, and your flesh will become clean
once more'. •But Naaman was indignant and went off, saying, 'Here was I 11
thinking he would be sure to come out to me, and stand there, and call on the
name of Yahweh his God, and wave his hand over the spot and cure the leprous
part. •Surely Abana and Pharpar, the rivers of Damascus, are better than 12
any water in Israel? Could I not bathe in them and become clean?' And he turned
round and went off in a rage. •But his servants approached him and said, 'My 13
father, if the prophet had asked you to do something difficult, would you not
have done it? All the more reason, then, when he says to you, "Bathe, and you
will become clean".' •So he went down and immersed himself seven times in the 14
Jordan, as Elisha had told him to do. And his flesh became clean once more
like the flesh of a little child.

Returning to Elisha with his whole escort, he went in and stood before him. 15
'Now I know' he said 'that there is no God in all the earth except in Israel.
Now, please, accept a present from your servant.' •But Elisha replied, 'As Yahweh 16
lives, whom I serve, I will accept nothing'. Naaman pressed him to accept, but
he refused. •Then Naaman said, 'Since your answer is "No", allow your servant 17
to be given as much earth as two mules may carry, because your servant will no
longer offer holocaust or sacrifice to any god except Yahweh. •Only—and may 18
Yahweh forgive your servant—when my master goes to the temple of Rimmon
to worship there, he leans on my arm, and I bow down in the temple of Rimmon
when he does;ᵃ may Yahweh forgive your servant this act!' •'Go in peace' 19
Elisha answered.

Naaman had gone a small distance, •when Gehazi, the servant of Elisha, 20
said to himself, 'My master has let this Aramaean Naaman off lightly, by not
accepting what he offered. As Yahweh lives, I will run after him and get
something out of him.' •So Gehazi set off in pursuit of Naaman. When Naaman 21
saw him running after him, he jumped down from his chariot to meet him.
'Is all well?' he asked. •'All is well' he said. 'My master has sent me to say, 22
"This very moment two young men of the prophetic brotherhood have arrived
from the highlands of Ephraim. Be kind enough to give them a talent of
silver." ' •'Please accept two talents' Naaman replied, and pressed him, tying 23
up the two talents of silver in two bags and consigning them to two of his
servants who carried them in front of Gehazi. •When he reached Ophel, he took 24
them from their hands and put them away in the house. He then dismissed the
men, who went away.

He, for his part, went and presented himself to his master. Elisha said, 'Gehazi, 25
where have you been?' 'Your servant has not been anywhere' he replied. •But 26
Elisha said to him, 'Was not my heart present there when someone left his
chariot to meet you? Now you have taken the money, you can buy gardens with
it, and olive groves, sheep and oxen, male and female slaves. •But Naaman's 27
leprosy will cling to you and to your descendants for ever.' And Gehazi left his
presence a leper, white as snow.

The axe lost and found

1 6 The brotherhood of prophets said to Elisha, 'Look, the place where we live
2 side by side with you is too confined for us. •Let us go to the Jordan, then,
and each of us cut a beam there, and we will make our living quarters there.'
3 He replied, 'Go'. •'Be good enough to go with your servants' one of them said.
4 'I will go' he answered, •and went with them. On reaching the Jordan they
5 cut down timber. •But, as one of them was felling his beam, the iron axehead
fell into the water. 'Alas, my lord,' he exclaimed 'and it was a borrowed one
6 too!' •'Where did it fall?' the man of God asked; and he showed him the spot.
Then, cutting a stick, Elisha threw it in at that point and made the iron axehead
7 float. •'Lift it out' he said; and the man stretched out his hand and took it.

D. THE ARAMAEAN WARS

Elisha captures an armed band of Aramaeans

8 The king of Aram was at war with Israel. He conferred with his officers,
9 and said, 'You are to attack at such and such a place'. •But Elisha sent word
to the king of Israel, 'Be on your guard at this place, because the Aramaeans
10 are going to attack it'. •The king of Israel accordingly sent men to the place
Elisha had named. And he kept warning the king, and the king stayed on the
alert; and this happened more than once or twice.
11 The king of Aram was disturbed in mind at this; he summoned his officers,
12 and said, 'Tell me which of you is betraying us to the king of Israel'. •'No, my
lord king,' one of his officers replied 'it is Elisha, the prophet in Israel, who
13 reveals to the king of Israel the words you speak in your bedchamber.' •'Go and
find out where he is,' the king said 'so that I can send people to capture him.'
14 Word was brought to him, 'He is now in Dothan'. •So he sent horses and chariots
there, and a large force; and these, arriving during the night, surrounded the town.
15 Next day, Elisha rose early and went out; and there surrounding the town
was an armed force with horses and chariots. 'Oh, my lord,' his servant said
16 'what are we to do?' •'Have no fear,' he replied 'there are more on our side than
17 on theirs.' •And Elisha prayed. 'Yahweh,' he said 'open his eyes and make him
see.' Yahweh opened the servant's eyes, and he saw the mountain covered with
horses and chariots of fire surrounding Elisha.
18 As the Aramaeans came down towards him, Elisha prayed to Yahweh,
'I beg you to strike this people with blindness'. And at the word of Elisha he
19 struck them blind. •Then Elisha said to them, 'This is not the road, nor is this
the town. Follow me; I will lead you to the man you are looking for.' But he
20 led them to Samaria. •As they entered Samaria, Elisha said, 'Yahweh, open the
eyes of these men, and let them see'. Yahweh opened their eyes and they saw;
they were inside Samaria.
21 When the king of Israel saw them, he said to Elisha, 'Shall I kill them, my
22 father?' •'Do not kill them' he answered. 'Do you put prisoners to death when
you have taken them with your sword and your bow? Offer them bread and
23 water for them to eat and drink, and let them go back to their master.' •So the
king provided a great feast for them; and when they had eaten and drunk, he
sent them off and they returned to their master. Aramaean raiding parties never
invaded the territory of Israel again.

Samaria besieged; the famine

24 It happened after this that Ben-hadad king of Aram mustered his whole
25 army and came to lay siege to Samaria. •In Samaria there was great famine,

---

5 a. Rimmon is Hadad, god of storms, chief deity of Damascus.

and so strict was the siege that the head of a donkey sold for eighty shekels of silver, and one quarter-kab of wild onions for five shekels of silver.

Now as the king was passing along the city wall, a woman shouted, 'Help, 26 my lord king!' • 'May Yahweh leave you helpless!' he retorted. 'Where can 27 I find help for you? From the threshing-floor? From the winepress? • Then the 28 king asked, 'What is the matter?' 'This woman here' she answered 'has said to me, "Give up your son; we will eat him today, and eat my son tomorrow". So we cooked my son and ate him. Next day, I said to her, "Give up your son 29 for us to eat". But she has hidden her son.' • On hearing the woman's words, 30 the king tore his garments; the king was walking on the wall, and the people saw that underneath he was wearing sackcloth next his body. • 'May God do 31 this to me and more,' he said 'if the head of Elisha son of Shaphat remains on his shoulders today!'

Elisha foretells imminent relief

Elisha was sitting in his house, and the elders were sitting with him. The king 32 sent a messenger ahead but, before the man arrived, Elisha had said to the elders, 'Do you see how this born assassin has given orders to cut off my head? Look, when the messenger comes, shut the door; hold the door against him. Is not the sound of his master's step following behind him?' • Even as he spoke, the king 33 arrived. 'This misery plainly comes from Yahweh,' he said 'why should I still trust in Yahweh?' **7** 'Listen to the word of Yahweh' Elisha said. 'Yahweh says 1 this, "By this time tomorrow a measure of finest flour will sell for one shekel, and two measures of barley for one shekel, at the gate of Samaria".' • The 2 equerry on whose arm the king was leaning retorted to Elisha, 'Even if Yahweh made windows in the sky, could this come true?' 'You will see it with your own eyes,' Elisha answered 'though you will eat none of it.'

The Aramaean camp is found abandoned

Now at the entrance to the gate—for they were lepers—there were four men 3 and they debated among themselves, 'Why sit here waiting for death? • If we 4 decide to go into the town, what with the famine in it, we shall die there; if we stay here we shall die just the same. Come on, let us go over to the Aramaean camp; if they spare our lives, we live; if they kill us, well then we die.' • So at 5 dusk they set out and made for the Aramaean camp, but when they reached the confines of the camp there was not a soul there. • For Yahweh had caused the 6 Aramaeans in their camp to hear a noise of chariots and horses, the noise of a great army; and they had said to one another, 'Hark! The king of Israel has hired the Hittite kings against us and the kings of Egypt to attack us.' • So 7 in the dusk they had made off and fled, abandoning their tents, their horses and their donkeys; leaving the camp just as it was, they had fled for their lives. The lepers, then, reached the confines of the camp. They went into one of the 8 tents and ate and drank, and from it carried off silver and gold and clothing; these they went and hid. Then they came back and, entering another tent, looted it too, and went and hid their booty.

The siege at an end; the famine ceases

Then they said to one another, 'We are doing wrong. This is a day of good 9 news, yet we are holding our tongues! If we wait till morning, we shall surely be punished. Come on, let us go and take the news to the palace.' • Off they 10 went, called the city guards, and said, 'We have been to the Aramaean camp. There was not a soul there, no sound of anyone, only tethered horses and tethered donkeys, and their tents just as they were.' • The gatekeepers shouted the news, 11 which was reported inside the palace.

The king got up while it was still dark and said to his officers, 'I can tell you 12 what the Aramaeans have done to us. They know we are starving, so they have

left the camp to hide in the open country. "They will come out of the town,"
13 they think "we will catch them alive and get into the town." ' •One of his officers
replied, 'Five of the surviving horses still left us had better be taken—they
14 would die in any case like all the rest. Let us send them and see.' •So they took
two chariot teams and the king sent them after the Aramaean army, saying,
15 'Go and see'. •They tracked them as far as the Jordan, finding the whole way
strewn with clothes and gear that the Aramaeans had thrown away in their
panic. The scouts returned and informed the king.
16   Then the people went out and plundered the Aramaean camp: a measure
of finest flour sold for one shekel, and two measures of barley for one shekel,
17 as Yahweh had promised they would be. •The king had detailed the equerry,
on whose arm he leaned, as commander of the guard on the gate, but the people
trampled on him in the gateway and he died, as the man of God had foretold
18 when the king had come down to him. •(What Elisha had said to the king came
true, 'Two measures of barley will sell for one shekel, and a measure of finest
19 flour for one shekel, by this time tomorrow at the gate of Samaria'. •The equerry
had retorted to Elisha, 'Even if Yahweh made windows in the sky, could this
come true?' 'You will see it with your own eyes,' Elisha had answered 'though you
20 will eat none of it.' •And this is what happened to him: the people trampled
on him in the gateway and he died.)

Epilogue to the story of the woman of Shunem

1   8 Elisha had said to the woman whose son he had raised to life, 'Move away with
your ιamily, and live where you can in some foreign country, for Yahweh has
called up a famine—it is coming on the country already—for seven years.'
2 The woman hurried to do what the man of God had told her: she set out, she
3 and her family, and for seven years she lived in the land of the Philistines. •When
the seven years were over, the woman came back from the land of the Philistines
and went to lodge a claim with the king for her house and lands.
4   Now the king was talking to Gehazi, the servant of the man of God. 'Tell me'
5 he was saying 'all the great things Elisha has done.' •Gehazi was just telling the
king how Elisha had raised the dead child to life, when the woman whose son
Elisha had raised lodged her claim with the king for her house and lands. 'My lord
king,' Gehazi said 'this is the very woman, and that is her son whom Elisha
6 raised to life.' •The king questioned the woman, who told him the story. The
king then referred her to one of the eunuchs, giving him this order: 'See that all
her property is restored to her, and all the revenue from her land from the day
she left the country until now'.

Elisha and Hazael of Damascus

7   Elisha came to Damascus. Ben-hadad the king of Aram was ill, and was
8 told, 'The man of God has come all the way to us'. •Then the king said to Hazael,
'Take a present with you and go to meet the man of God; consult Yahweh
through him, and find out if I shall recover from my illness'.
9   So Hazael went to meet Elisha, taking with him as a present the best Damascus
could offer, a load for forty camels. He came and standing before him said,
'Your son Ben-hadad has sent me to ask you, "Shall I recover from my illness?" '
10 Elisha answered, 'Go and tell him, "You will certainly recover", though Yahweh
11 has shown me that he will certainly die'. •Then his face went rigid and his look
12 grew fixed, and the man of God wept. •'Why' Hazael asked 'does my lord
weep?' 'Because I know' Elisha replied 'all the harm you will do the Israelites:
you will burn down their fortresses, put their picked warriors to the sword,
13 dash their little children to pieces, rip open their pregnant women.' •'But
what is your servant?' Hazael said. 'How could this dog achieve anything so
great?' 'In a vision from Yahweh,' Elisha replied 'I have seen you king of
Aram.'

Leaving Elisha, Hazael went back to his master who asked, 'What did Elisha 14
say to you?' He answered, 'He told me you would certainly recover'. •Next day 15
he took a blanket, soaked it in water, and spread it over his face.ª So died Ben-
hadad, and Hazael succeeded him.

The reign of Jehoram in Judah (848-841)

In the fifth year of Jehoram son of Ahab king of Israel, Jehoram son of 16
Jehoshaphat became king of Judah. •He was thirty-two years old when he came 17
to the throne, and he reigned for eight years in Jerusalem. •He followed the 18
example of the kings of Israel as the family of Ahab had done, having taken a wife
from the familyᵇ of Ahab; he did what is displeasing to Yahweh. •Yahweh, 19
however, did not intend to destroy Judah, because of his servant David, and was
faithful to the promise he had made to leave him a lamp for ever in his presence.
In his time Edom threw off the domination of Judah and set up a king for 20
itself. •Jehoram crossed to Zair, and with him all the chariots . . . He rose 21
during the night and, with his chariot commanders, broke through the
Edomites encircling him; the people fled to their tents. •Thus Edom threw off 22
the domination of Judah, remaining free to the present day. Libnah also
revolted. At that time...
The rest of the history of Jehoram, his entire career, is not all this recorded 23
in the Book of the Annals of the Kings of Judah? •Then Jehoram slept with his 24
ancestors and was buried with his ancestors in the Citadel of David; his son
Ahaziah succeeded him.

The reign of Ahaziah in Judah (841)

In the twelfth year of Jehoram son of Ahab king of Israel, Ahaziah son of 25
Jehoram became king of Judah. •Ahaziah was twenty-two years old when he 26
came to the throne, and he reigned for one year in Jerusalem. His mother's name
was Athaliah, daughter of Omri king of Israel. •He followed the example of the 27
family of Ahab and did what is displeasing to Yahweh as the family of Ahab
had done, to whom he was related by marriage.
He went with Jehoram son of Ahab to fight against Hazael king of Aram 28
at Ramoth-gilead, but the Aramaeans wounded Jehoram. •King Jehoram 29
returned to Jezreel to recover from the wounds which he had received at Ramah,
fighting against Hazael king of Aram. Ahaziah son of Jehoram king of Judah
went down to Jezreel to visit Jehoram son of Ahab because he was ill.

E. THE HISTORY OF JEHU

A disciple of Elisha anoints Jehu king

9 Elisha the prophet summoned a member of the prophetic brotherhood to 1
him, 'Tuck up your cloak, take this flask of oil, and go to Ramoth-gilead.
When you arrive there, look for Jehu son of Jehoshaphat son of Nimshi. Then, 2
when you find him, tell him to get up and leave his companions, and take
him into an inner room. •Take the flask of oil then and pour it over his head, 3
and say, "This is Yahweh's word: I have anointed you king of Israel". Then
throw open the door and escape as fast as you can.'
The young man left for Ramoth-gilead •and when he arrived, he found the ⁴⁄₅
senior officers of the army sitting together. 'I have a message for you, commander'
he said. 'For which of us?' asked Jehu. 'For you, commander' he answered.
Then Jehu got up and went into the house. And the young man poured the oil 6
on his head, saying, 'Yahweh the God of Israel says this, "I have anointed
you king over the people of Yahweh, king of Israel. •You are to strike down the 7
family of Ahab your master, and I will avenge the blood of my servants the
prophets and of all the servants of Yahweh on Jezebel •and the whole family of 8

Ahab. I will wipe out every male belonging to the family of Ahab, fettered or
9 free in Israel. •I will make the family of Ahab like the family of Jeroboam son
10 of Nebat and of Baasha son of Ahijah. •As for Jezebel, the dogs shall eat her in
the territory of Jezreel; no one will bury her." ' With this, he opened the door
and made his escape.

Jehu proclaimed king

11   Jehu came out to the officers of his master. 'Is all well?' they asked him. 'Why
did this madman come to you?' 'You know the fellow and how he talks' he
12 answered. •'Evasion!' they cried 'Come on, tell us.' He replied, 'His drift was
this— he said, "Yahweh says this: I have anointed you king of Israel" '.
13 Whereupon they all took their cloaks and spread them under him on the bare
steps; they sounded the trumpet and shouted, 'Jehu is king!'

Jehu prepares to usurp power

14   Jehu son of Jehoshaphat son of Nimshi plotted against Jehoram. (Jehoram,
with all Israel, was at that time defending Ramoth-gilead against Hazael king
15 of Aram, •although Jehoram had returned to Jezreel to recover from the wounds
which he had received from the Aramaeans while he was fighting against Hazael
king of Aram.) 'If this is how you feel,' Jehu said 'let no one escape from the
16 town to go and take the news to Jezreel. •Jehu then mounted his chariot and
left for Jezreel; Jehoram had taken to his bed there, and Ahaziah king of Judah
had gone down to visit him.

17   The lookout posted on the tower of Jezreel saw Jehu's troop approaching,
'I can see a body of men' he shouted. Jehoram gave the order: 'Have a horseman
18 sent to meet them and ask, "Is all well?" ' •The horseman went to meet Jehu
and said, 'The king says, "Is all well?" ' 'What has it to do with you whether
all is well?' Jehu replied. 'Fall in behind me.' The lookout reported, 'The messenger
19 has reached them and is not coming back'. •The king sent a second horseman
who reached them and said, 'The king says, "Is all well?" ' 'What has it to do
20 with you whether all is well?' Jehu replied. 'Fall in behind me.' •The lookout
reported, 'He has reached them and is not coming back. The manner of driving
21 is like that of Jehu son of Nimshi: he drives like a madman.' •'Harness!' Jehoram
cried; and they harnessed his chariot. Then Jehoram king of Israel and Ahaziah
king of Judah, each in his chariot, set out to meet Jehu. They reached him in the
field of Naboth of Jezreel.

The assassination of Jehoram

22   As soon as Jehoram saw Jehu he asked, 'Is all well, Jehu?' 'What a question!'
he replied 'when all the while the prostitutions[a] and countless sorceries of your
23 mother Jezebel go on.' •At this, Jehoram wheeled and fled, saying to Ahaziah,
24 'Treason, Ahaziah!' •But Jehu had drawn his bow; he struck Jehoram between
the shoulder-blades, the arrow went through the king's heart, and he sank down
25 in his chariot. •'Pick him up,' Jehu said to Bidkar, his equerry 'and throw him
into the field of Naboth of Jezreel. Remember how, when you and I both rode
26 behind Ahab his father, Yahweh pronounced this sentence against him: •"This
I swear. Yesterday I saw the blood of Naboth and the blood of his sons—it is
Yahweh who speaks. In this same field I will requite you—it is Yahweh who
speaks." So pick him up, and throw him into the field, as Yahweh declared
should happen.'

The assassination of Ahaziah

27   When Ahaziah king of Judah saw this, he fled along the Beth-haggan road,
but Jehu went in pursuit of him. 'Strike him down too' he said. And they wounded

8 a. Presumably murder by Hazael, not suicide by Ben-hadad.   b. Ahab's sister Athaliah.
9 a. The primary meaning is metaphorical: spiritual unfaithfulness in worshipping other gods.
But there may be an allusion to sacred prostitution.

him in his chariot at the slope of Gur, which is near Ibleam, and he took refuge in Megiddo, where he died. •His servants carried him in a chariot to Jerusalem 28 and buried him in his tomb in the Citadel of David. •Ahaziah had become king 29 of Judah in the eleventh year of Jehoram son of Ahab.

The assassination of Jezebel

Jehu went back to Jezreel and Jezebel heard of it. She made up her eyes with 30 kohl and adorned her head and appeared at the window. •As Jehu came through 31 the gateway she said, 'Is all well, Zimri, you murderer of your master?'[b] •Jehu 32 looked up to the window and said, 'Who is on my side? Who?' And two or three eunuchs looked down at him. •'Throw her down' he said. They threw her down, 33 and her blood spattered the walls and the horses; and Jehu rode over her. •He 34 went in and ate and drank, then said, 'See to this accursed woman, and give her burial; after all, she was a king's daughter'. •But when they went to bury her, 35 they found nothing but her skull, feet and hands. •They came back and told 36 Jehu, who said, 'This is the word of Yahweh which he spoke through his servant Elijah the Tishbite, "The dogs will eat the flesh of Jezebel in the territory of Jezreel; •the corpse of Jezebel will be like dung spread on the fields, so that no 37 one will be able to say: This was Jezebel" '.

The massacre of the royal family of Israel

10 There were seventy sons of Ahab in Samaria.[a] Jehu sent to Samaria, to the 1 authorities of the city, to the elders and to the guardians of the children of Ahab. He said, •'At this time, when this letter reaches you, you have your 2 master's sons with you; you also have chariots and horses, fortified towns and weapons. •See which of your master's sons is the best and worthiest, put him 3 on his father's throne and fight for the dynasty of your master.' •They were 4 utterly terrified. 'We have seen how the two kings could not stand up to him,' they said 'so how could we do so?' •Consequently the master of the palace, the 5 governor of the city, the elders and the guardians sent word to Jehu, 'We are your servants. We will do whatever you order us. We will not proclaim a king; act as you think best.'

Jehu then wrote them a second letter. He said, 'If you are for me and if you 6 are prepared to accept orders from me, take the heads[b] of the men of your master's house and come to me at Jezreel by this time tomorrow'. (There were seventy sons of the king being educated there by the leading men of the city.) •When this 7 letter reached them, they took the king's sons and butchered all seventy of them, put their heads in baskets and sent them to him at Jezreel.

The messenger came and told Jehu, 'They have brought the heads of the 8 king's sons'. 'Leave them in two heaps at the entrance to the gate until morning' he replied. •When morning came, he went out and, standing, said to all the people, 9 'Be guiltless! I certainly plotted against my master and murdered him; but who killed all these? •Know, then, nothing will fail to be fulfilled of the oracle uttered 10 by Yahweh against the family of Ahab: Yahweh has done what he said through his servant Elijah.' •Jehu then killed everyone of the House of Ahab surviving 11 in Jezreel, all his leading men, his close friends, his priests; he did not leave a single one alive.

The massacre of the princes of Judah

Jehu then set out and went to Samaria. As he was on his way •he met, at 12 Beth-eked of the Shepherds, the brothers of Ahaziah king of Judah. 'Who are 13 you?' he asked. 'We are brothers of Ahaziah,' they answered 'and we are going down to pay our respects to the sons of the king and the sons of the queen.' 'Take them alive' he said. They took them alive, and he slaughtered them at the 14 cistern of Beth-eked, forty-two of them; he did not spare a single one.

Jehu and Jehonadab

15 Leaving there, he came upon Jehonadab son of Rechab who was on his way to meet him. He greeted him and said, 'Is your heart true to mine, as my heart is to yours?' Jehonadab replied, 'Yes'. 'If so,' Jehu said 'give me your hand.' Jehonadab gave him his hand, and Jehu took him up beside him in his chariot. 16 'Come with me,' he said 'and witness my zeal for Yahweh', and drove him on 17 in his chariot. •When he entered Samaria, he killed all the survivors of Ahab's family in Samaria; he wiped it out, as Yahweh had told Elijah it would happen.

The destruction of the adherents and temple of Baal

18 Then Jehu assembled all the people. 'Ahab did Baal some small service,' 19 he said 'but Jehu will do him a great one. •Now call me all the prophets of Baal and all his priests. Let no one be missing: I have a great sacrifice to offer to Baal. If anyone is missing, he shall forfeit his life.' This was a trick on Jehu's part to 20 destroy the devotees of Baal. •'Summon a sacred assembly for Baal' he com- 21 manded; and they summoned it. •Jehu sent messengers throughout Israel, and all the devotees of Baal arrived, not a man was left who did not attend. They 22 packed into the temple of Baal until it was full from wall to wall. •Jehu then said to the keeper of the wardrobe, 'Bring out vestments for all the devotees of Baal'; 23 he brought out the vestments for them. •Jehu then went into the temple of Baal with Jehonâdab son of Rechab and said to the devotees of Baal, 'Make quite sure there are no devotees of Yahweh in here with you, but only devotees of 24 Baal'. •He then proceeded to offer sacrifices and holocausts.

Now Jehu had stationed eighty of his men outside, having said, 'If any of you lets anyone of those I am handing over to you escape, his life will pay for 25 the life of the other'. •When he had finished offering the holocaust, he gave the order to the guards and squires: 'Go in, strike them down! Let no one out!' The guards and squires went in, putting everyone to the sword, until they had 26 reached the sanctuary of the temple of Baal. •They took the sacred pole out 27 of the temple of Baal and burned it. •They demolished the altar of Baal, and demolished the temple of Baal too, making it into a latrine, which it still is today.

The reign of Jehu in Israel (841-814)

28
29 Thus Jehu rid Israel of Baal. •Even so, Jehu did not give up the sins into which Jeroboam son of Nebat had led Israel, the golden calves of Bethel and 30 Dan. •Yahweh said to Jehu, 'Since you have done properly what was pleasing in my sight, and have achieved all I set my heart on against Ahab's family, your 31 sons shall sit on the throne of Israel down to the fourth generation'. •But Jehu did not follow the law of Yahweh, the God of Israel faithfully and wholeheartedly: he did not give up the sins into which Jeroboam son of Nebat had led Israel.

32 At that time, Yahweh began to whittle Israel down, and Hazael defeated the 33 Israelites throughout the territory •from the Jordan eastwards: all the land of Gilead, of the Gadites, the Reubenites and the Manassites, from Aroer which is by the wadi Arnon, Gilead and Bashan.

34 The rest of the history of Jehu, his entire career, all his prowess, is not all this 35 recorded in the Book of the Annals of the Kings of Israel? •Then he slept with his ancestors, and they buried him in Samaria; his son Jehoahaz succeeded him. 36 Jehu's reign over Israel in Samaria lasted twenty-eight years.

b. Zimri assassinated King Elah, 1 K 16:9; the sting in this taunt is that he reigned for only eight days.
10 a. I.e., sons and grandsons, and seventy is the conventional number used to indicate the entire offspring.   b. An ambiguous word; Jehu claims in v.9 that he is not responsible for the deaths.
c. All Israel's Transjordanian territory.

F. FROM THE REIGN OF ATHALIAH TO THE DEATH OF ELISHA

Athaliah (841-835)

11 When Athaliah the mother of Ahaziah learned that her son was dead, she [1] promptly did away with all those of royal stock. •But Jehosheba, daughter [2] of King Jehoram and sister of Ahaziah, secretly took away Jehoash, her brother's son, from among the sons of the king who were being murdered, and put him with his nurse in the sleeping quarters; in this way she hid him from Athaliah, and he was not put to death. •He stayed with her for six years, hidden in the Temple [3] of Yahweh, while Athaliah governed the country.

In the seventh year, Jehoiada[a] sent for the commanders of hundreds of the [4] Carians[b] and of the guards, and had them brought to him in the Temple of Yahweh. He made a pact with them and, putting them under oath, showed them the king's son. •He gave them this order: 'This is what you must do: one third of [5] you, those who are off duty on the sabbath, are to mount guard at the royal [6] palace, •while the other two thirds of you, mounting guard at the Temple of [7] Yahweh, •are to surround the king, each with his weapons in his hand; anyone [8] who tries to break through your ranks is to be put to death. Wherever the king goes or comes, you are to escort him.'

The commanders of hundreds did everything as Jehoiada the priest had [9] ordered. They brought their men, those coming off duty on the sabbath together with those mounting guard on the sabbath, and came to Jehoiada the priest. The priest equipped the commanders of hundreds with King David's spears and [10] shields which were in the Temple of Yahweh. •The guards formed up, each man [11] with his weapon in his hand, from the south corner to the north corner of the Temple, surrounding the altar and the Temple. •Then Jehoiada brought out: [12] the king's son, put the crown and armlets on him, and he anointed him king. They clapped their hands and shouted, 'Long live the king!'

Athaliah, on hearing the shouts of the people, made for the Temple of [13] Yahweh where the people were. •When she saw the king standing there beside [14] the pillar, as the custom was, with the captains and trumpeters at the king's side, and all the country people rejoicing and sounding trumpets, Athaliah tore her garments and shouted, 'Treason, treason!' •Then Jehoiada the priest gave [15] the order to the army officers: 'Take her outside the precincts and put to death anyone who follows her'. 'For' the priest had reasoned 'she must not be put to death in the Temple of Yahweh.' •They seized her, and when she had reached [16] the palace through the Entry of the Horses, she was put to death there.

Jehoiada made a covenant between Yahweh and king and people, by which [17] the latter undertook to be the people of Yahweh; and also between king and people. •All the country people then went to the temple of Baal and demolished [18] it; they smashed his altars and his images and killed Mattan, priest of Baal, in front of the altars.

The priest posted sentries to guard the Temple of Yahweh. •He then took the [19] commanders of hundreds, the Carians, the guards and all the country people and made them escort the king down from the Temple of Yahweh and through the Gate of the Guards into the palace. Jehoash took his seat on the throne of the kings. •All the country people were delighted, and the city made no move. [20] And they put Athaliah to death in the royal palace.

The reign of Jehoash in Judah (835-796)

12 Jehoash was seven years old when he came to the throne. •Jehoash became [1,2] king in the seventh year of Jehu, and reigned for forty years in Jerusalem. [21,1] His mother's name was Zibiah, of Beersheba. •Jehoash did what is pleasing to [3] Yahweh all his life, having been instructed by Jehoiada the priest. •The high [4] places, however, were not abolished, and the people still offered sacrifices and [3] incense on the high places.

⁵/₄ Jehoash said to the priests, 'All the money from the sacred dues brought to the Temple of Yahweh, the money from personal taxes, and the money given ⁶/₅ spontaneously to the Temple • is to be accepted by the priests, from people of their acquaintance, and the priests are to carry out all repairs to the Temple as ⁷/₆ required'. • Now in the twenty-third year of King Jehoash, the priests had done ⁸/₇ no repairs to the Temple; • so King Jehoash summoned Jehoiada the priest and the other priests. 'Why are you not repairing the Temple?' he asked. 'You are no longer to accept money from people of your acquaintance, but are to hand it ⁹/₈ over for the Temple repairs.' • The priests agreed to accept no money from the people and no longer to be responsible for repairs to the Temple.

¹⁰/₉ Jehoiada the priest procured a chest, bored a hole in the lid of it, and placed it beside the pillar, to the right as you enter the Temple of Yahweh; in it the priests who guarded the threshold put all the money that was given for the ¹¹/₁₀ Temple of Yahweh. • Whenever they saw that there was a lot of money in the chest, the king's secretary would come, and they would melt down and reckon ¹²/₁₁ the money then in the Temple of Yahweh. • Once checked, they paid this money over to the masters of works attached to the Temple of Yahweh, and these in turn spent it on carpenters and builders working on the Temple of Yahweh, ¹³/₁₂ on masons and stonecutters, and on buying wood and dressed stone to be used for repairs to the Temple of Yahweh; in short, for all the costs of the Temple ¹⁴/₁₃ repairs. • No silver basins, however, no knives, sprinkling bowls, trumpets, no gold or silver objects whatever were made for the Temple of Yahweh out of the ¹⁵/₁₄ money presented, • for this was all given to the workmen who used it for repairing ¹⁶/₁₅ the Temple of Yahweh. • No accounts were kept with the men to whom the money was paid over to be spent on the workmen, since they were honest in ¹⁷/₁₆ their dealings. • Money offered in expiation of an offence or of a sin was not given to the Temple of Yahweh; that was for the priests.

¹⁸/₁₇ At that time Hazael king of Aram went to war against Gath, and captured it; ¹⁹/₁₈ he then prepared to attack Jerusalem. • Jehoash king of Judah took all the sacred offerings dedicated by his ancestors, the kings of Judah, Jehoshaphat, Jehoram and Ahaziah, with those that he himself had dedicated, and all the gold that was to be found in the treasuries of the Temple of Yahweh and of the royal palace; he sent it all to Hazael king of Aram, who retired from Jerusalem.

²⁰/₁₉ The rest of the history of Jehoash, his entire career, is not all this recorded in ²¹/₂₀ the Book of the Annals of the Kings of Judah? • His officers rebelled and hatched a ²²/₂₁ plot; they struck Jehoash down at Beth-millo... • Jozacar son of Shimeath and Jehozabad son of Shomer were the two who struck him down and killed him. They buried him with his ancestors in the Citadel of David; his son Amaziah succeeded him.

The reign of Jehoahaz in Israel (814-798)

¹ **13** In the twenty-third year of Joash son of Ahaziah, king of Judah, Jehoahaz son of Jehu became king of Israel in Samaria. He reigned for seventeen ² years. • He did what is displeasing to Yahweh and persisted in the sin into which Jeroboam had led Israel; he did not give it up.

³ Then the anger of Yahweh blazed out against the Israelites, and he delivered them without respite into the power of Hazael king of Aram and of Ben-hadad[a] ⁴ son of Hazael. • Jehoahaz, however, tried to placate Yahweh, and Yahweh heard him, for he had seen the oppression the king of Aram was inflicting on ⁵ them. • Yahweh gave Israel a saviour who freed them from the grip of Aram, ⁶ and the Israelites lived in their tents as in the past. • But they did not give up the sin into which Jeroboam had led Israel; they persisted in it, and even the ⁷ sacred pole remained in Samaria. • Yahweh left of the army of Jehoahaz only

11 a. Chief priest in Jerusalem.   b. Mercenaries from Asia Minor.
13 a. Ben-hadad III.

fifty horsemen, ten chariots and ten thousand foot soldiers. The king of Aram had destroyed them, making them like the dust that is trampled under foot.

The rest of the history of Jehoahaz, his entire career, his prowess, is not all 8 this recorded in the Book of the Annals of the Kings of Israel? •Then Jehoahaz 9 slept with his ancestors, and they buried him in Samaria; his son Joash succeeded him.

The reign of Jehoash in Israel (798-783)

In the thirty-seventh year of Joash king of Judah, Jehoash, son of Jehoahaz, 10 became king of Israel in Samaria. He reigned for sixteen years. •He did what is 11 displeasing to Yahweh, he did not give up the sin into which Jeroboam son of Nebat had led Israel; he persisted in it.

The rest of the history of Joash, his entire career, his prowess, how he waged 12 war on Amaziah king of Judah, is not all this recorded in the Book of the Annals of the Kings of Israel? •Then Joash slept with his ancestors, and Jeroboam 13 ascended his throne. Joash was buried in Samaria with the kings of Israel.

The death of Elisha

When Elisha had fallen ill of the illness he was to die of, Joash king of Israel 14 went down to him and shedding tears over him said, 'My father! My father! Chariot of Israel and its chargers!' •Elisha said to him, 'Bring bow and arrows'; 15 and he sent for a bow and arrows. •Then Elisha said to the king, 'Draw the bow'; 16 and he drew it. Elisha put his hands over the hands of the king, •then he said, 17 'Open the window towards the east', and he opened it. Then Elisha said, 'Arrow of victory over Aram! You will defeat Aram at Aphek completely.'

Elisha said, 'Take the arrows'; and he took them. Then he said to the king, 18 'Strike the ground'; and he struck it three times, then stopped. •At this, the man 19 of God grew angry with him. 'You should have struck half a dozen times' he said 'and you would have beaten Aram completely; now you will only beat Aram three times.'

Elisha died, and was buried. Now bands of Moabites were making incursions 20 into the country every year. •Some people happened to be carrying a man out 21 for burial; at the sight of one of these bands, they flung the man into the tomb of Elisha and made off. The man had no sooner touched the bones of Elisha than he came to life and stood up on his feet.

Victory over the Aramaeans

Hazael king of Aram had oppressed the Israelites throughout the lifetime of 22 Jehoahaz, •but Yahweh was kind and took pity on them. Because of the covenant 23 he had made with Abraham, Isaac and Jacob, he relented towards them; he had no wish to destroy them, he did not cast them out of his presence. •Hazael king 24 of Aram died, and his son Ben-hadad succeeded him. •Jehoash son of Jehoahaz 25 recaptured from Ben-hadad son of Hazael the towns which Hazael had seized from his father Jehoahaz by force of arms. Joash defeated him three times and recovered the Israelite towns.

VII. THE TWO KINGDOMS TO THE FALL OF SAMARIA

The reign of Amaziah in Judah (796-781)

14 In the second year of Joash son of Jehoahaz, king of Israel, Amaziah son 1 of Joash became king of Judah. •He was twenty-five years old when he 2 came to the throne, and he reigned for twenty-nine years in Jerusalem. His mother's name was Jehoaddin, of Jerusalem. •He did what is pleasing to Yahweh, 3 though not like his ancestor David; he imitated his father Joash in all respects.

4 The high places, however, were not abolished, and the people still offered sacrifices and incense on the high places.

5 Once the kingdom was firmly under his control, he killed those of his officers 6 who had murdered the king his father. •But he did not put the murderers' sons to death, in accordance with what is written in the Book of Moses, where Yahweh has ordered: 'Fathers must not be put to death for sons, nor sons for fathers; every one must be put to death for his own sin'.

7 It was he who defeated the Edomites in the Valley of Salt, ten thousand of them, and who took the Rock by assault; he gave it the name Joktheel, which it bears to this present day.

8 Then Amaziah sent messengers to Jehoash son of Jehoahaz son of Jehu, king 9 of Israel, saying, 'Come and make a trial of strength!' •Jehoash king of Israel sent word to Amaziah king of Judah, 'The thistle of Lebanon sent a message to the cedar of Lebanon, "Give my son your daughter in marriage"; but the wild 10 animals of Lebanon trampled down the thistle as they passed. •You have conquered Edom, and now hold your head in the air; boast on, but stay at home. Why challenge disaster, to your own ruin and the ruin of Judah?'

11 But Amaziah would not listen, and Jehoash king of Israel marched to the attack. And at Beth-shemesh, which belongs to Judah, they made their trial of strength, 12 Jehoash and Amaziah king of Judah. •Judah was defeated by Israel, and everyone 13 fled to his tent. •The king of Judah, Amaziah son of Jehoash, son of Ahaziah, was taken prisoner at Beth-shemesh by Joash king of Israel who led him off to Jerusalem, where Joash demolished the city wall from the Gate of Ephraim to 14 the Gate of the Corner for a distance of four hundred cubits. •He took all the gold and silver, and all the furnishings to be found in the Temple of Yahweh and in the treasury of the royal palace, and hostages besides, and then returned to Samaria.

15 The rest of the history of Jehoash, his entire career, his prowess, how he waged war on Amaziah king of Judah, is not all this recorded in the Book of the 16 Annals of the Kings of Israel? •Then Jehoash slept with his ancestors, and was buried in Samaria with the kings of Israel; his son Jeroboam succeeded him.

17 Amaziah son of Joash, king of Judah, lived for fifteen years after the death of Jehoash son of Jehoahaz, king of Israel.

18 The rest of the history of Amaziah, is not all this recorded in the Book of 19 the Annals of the Kings of Judah? •A plot having been hatched against him in Jerusalem, he fled to Lachish; but he was followed to Lachish where he was 20 put to death. •He was brought back by horse, and buried in Jerusalem with 21 his ancestors in the Citadel of David. •All the people of Judah chose Uzziah, then sixteen years old, and made him king in succession to his father Amaziah. 22 It was he who rebuilt Elath and recovered it for Judah, after the king had slept with his ancestors.

The reign of Jeroboam II in Israel (783-743)

23 In the fifteenth year of Amaziah son of Joash, king of Judah, Jeroboam son of Joash became king of Israel in Samaria. He reigned for forty-one years. 24 He did what is displeasing to Yahweh and did not give up any of the sins into which Jeroboam son of Nebat had led Israel.

25 It was he who recovered the territory of Israel from the Pass of Hamath as far as the Sea of the Arabah, in accordance with the word that Yahweh, the God of Israel, had spoken through his servant Jonah[a] son of Amittai, the 26 prophet from Gath-hepher. •For Yahweh had seen how very bitter the affliction of Israel was, with no one, neither fettered nor free, to come to the help of Israel. 27 But Yahweh had resolved not to blot out the name of Israel from under heaven; he rescued them by means of Jeroboam son of Joash.

14 a. This prophet is made the central figure of the Book of Jonah.

The rest of the history of Jeroboam, his entire career, his prowess, what 28
wars he waged, how he . . . is not all this recorded in the Book of the Annals
of the Kings of Israel? •Then Jeroboam slept with his ancestors. They buried him 29
in Samaria with the kings of Israel; his son Zechariah succeeded him.

The reign of Uzziah in Judah (781-740)

15 In the seventeenth year of Jeroboam king of Israel, Uzziah son of Amaziah 1
became king of Judah. •He was sixteen years old when he came to the 2
throne, and he reigned for fifty-two years in Jerusalem. His mother's name was
Jecoliah, of Jerusalem. •He did what is pleasing to Yahweh, just as his father 3
Amaziah had done. •The high places, however, were not abolished, and the 4
people still offered sacrifices and incense on the high places.

But Yahweh struck the king, and he became a leper till his dying day. He lived 5
confined to his room; his son Jotham was master of the palace and ruled the
country.

The rest of the history of Uzziah, his entire career, is not all this recorded 6
in the Book of the Annals of the Kings of Judah? •Then Uzziah slept with 7
his ancestors, and they buried him in the Citadel of David; his son Jotham
succeeded him.

The reign of Zechariah in Israel (743)

In the thirty-eighth year of Uzziah king of Judah, Zechariah son of Jeroboam 8
became king of Israel in Samaria for six months. •He did what is displeasing 9
to Yahweh, as his fathers had done; he did not give up the sins into which
Jeroboam son of Nebat had led Israel.

Shallum son of Jabesh plotted against him, murdered him at Ibleam, and 10
succeeded him.

The rest of the history of Zechariah is recorded in the Book of the Annals 11
of the Kings of Israel. •It happened as Yahweh had said to Jehu, 'Your sons will 12
sit on the throne of Israel to the fourth generation'. And so it turned out.

The reign of Shallum in Israel (743)

Shallum son of Jabesh became king in the thirty-ninth year of Uzziah king 13
of Judah, and reigned for one month in Samaria.

Then Menahem son of Gadi went up from Tirzah, entered Samaria, murdered 14
Shallum son of Jabesh there, and succeeded him.

The rest of the history of Shallum, and the plot he hatched, all this is recorded 15
in the Book of the Annals of the Kings of Israel. •It was at that time that 16
Menahem sacked Tappush—killing all who were in it—and its territory from
Tirzah onwards, because it had not opened its gates to him; he sacked the town
and ripped open all the pregnant women.

In the thirty-ninth year of Uzziah king of Judah, Menahem son of Gadi 17
became king of Israel. He reigned for ten years in Samaria. •He did what is 18
displeasing to Yahweh, he did not give up the sins into which Jeroboam son
of Nebat had led Israel.

In his times, •Pul[a] king of Assyria invaded the country, Menahem gave Pul 19
a thousand talents of silver in return for his support in strengthening his hold
on the royal power. •Menahem levied this sum from Israel, from all the men 20
of rank, at the rate of fifty shekels a head, to be given to the king of Assyria,
who then withdrew, and did not stay in the country.

The rest of the history of Menahem, his entire career, is not all this recorded 21
in the Book of the Annals of the Kings of Israel? •Then Menahem slept with 22
his ancestors; his son Pekahiah succeeded him.

The reign of Pekahiah in Israel (738-737)

In the fiftieth year of Uzziah king of Judah, Pekahiah son of Menahem 23
became king of Israel in Samaria. He reigned for two years. •He did what is 24

displeasing to Yahweh; he did not give up the sins into which Jeroboam son of Nebat had led Israel.

25 Pekah son of Remaliah, his equerry, plotted against him and struck him down in Samaria, in the keep of the royal palace... He had fifty men of Gilead with him. He killed the king, and succeeded him.

26 The rest of the history of Pekahiah, his entire career, all this is recorded in the Book of the Annals of the Kings of Israel.

The reign of Pekah in Israel (737-732)

27 In the fifty-second year of Uzziah king of Judah, Pekah son of Remaliah
28 became king of Israel in Samaria. He reigned for twenty years. •He did what is displeasing to Yahweh; he did not give up the sins into which Jeroboam son of Nebat had led Israel.

29 In the days of Pekah king of Israel, Tiglath-pileser king of Assyria came and captured Ijon, Abel-beth-maacah, Janoah, Kedesh, Hazor, Gilead and Galilee,
30 all the land of Naphtali, and deported the population to Assyria.[b] •Hoshea son of Elah hatched a plot against Pekah son of Remaliah; he murdered the king, and succeeded him.

31 The rest of the history of Pekah, and his entire career, is not all this recorded in the Book of the Annals of the Kings of Israel?

The reign of Jotham in Judah (740-736)

32 In the second year of Pekah son of Remaliah, king of Israel, Jotham son of
33 Uzziah became king of Judah. •He was twenty-five years old when he came to the throne, and he reigned for sixteen years in Jerusalem. His mother's name was
34 Jerusha, daughter of Zadok. •He did what is pleasing to Yahweh, just as his
35 father Uzziah had done. •The high places, however, were not abolished, and the people still offered sacrifices and incense on the high places.

It was he who built the Upper Gate of the Temple of Yahweh.

36 The rest of the history of Jotham, his entire career, is not all this recorded
37 in the Book of the Annals of the Kings of Judah? •At that time, Yahweh began
38 sending Rezin king of Aram and Pekah son of Remaliah against Judah. •Then Jotham slept with his ancestors, and was buried in the Citadel of David, his ancestor; his son Ahaz succeeded him.

The reign of Ahaz in Judah (736-716)

1 **16** In the seventeenth year of Pekah son of Remaliah, Ahaz son of Jotham
2 became king of Judah. •Ahaz was twenty years old when he came to the throne, and he reigned for sixteen years in Jerusalem. He did not do what is
3 pleasing to Yahweh his God, as his ancestor David had done. •He followed the example of the kings of Israel, even causing his son to pass through fire, copying the shameful practices of the nations which Yahweh had dispossessed for the sons
4 of Israel. •He offered sacrifices and incense on the high places, on the hills and under every spreading tree.

5 It was then that Rezin king of Aram and Pekah son of Remaliah, king of Israel, launched their campaign against Jerusalem. They besieged it but could
6 not reduce it. •(At that time, the king of Edom recovered Elath for Edom; he drove out the men of Judah from Elath, and the Edomites occupied it and
7 live there to this present day.) •Then Ahaz sent messengers to Tiglath-pileser king of Assyria to say, 'I am your servant and your son. Come and rescue me from the king of Aram and the king of Israel who are making war against me.'
8 And Ahaz took the silver and gold that was found in the Temple of Yahweh and in the treasury of the royal palace, and sent this as a present to the king

---

15 a. Tiglath-Pileser III (745-727) took this name when he assumed power in Babylon in 729.
b. The first Israelite deportation. 'All Naphtali' was subdued in the Assyrian campaign against Philistia in 734; Gilead and Galilee were conquered in the campaign against Damascus, 733-732.

of Assyria. •The king of Assyria granted his request and, going up against 9
Damascus, captured it; he deported its population to Kir, and put Rezin to
death.

When King Ahaz went to Damascus to meet Tiglath-pileser king of Assyria, 10
he saw the altar that was in Damascus. He then sent the measurements and a
model of the altar with the detail of its workmanship to Uriah the priest.
Uriah the priest constructed the altar; all the instructions sent by King Ahaz 11
from Damascus were carried out by Uriah the priest before King Ahaz returned
from Damascus. •When the king arrived from Damascus, he inspected the altar, 12
he approached it and ascended it. •He burned his holocaust and his oblation; 13
he poured out his libation and sprinkled the blood of his communion sacrifice.
The altar that used to stand before Yahweh he removed from the front of the 14
Temple, where it had stood between the new altar and the Temple of Yahweh,
and placed it at the north side of the new altar. •King Ahaz gave this order to 15
Uriah the priest: 'In future you will burn the morning holocaust, the evening
oblation, the king's holocaust and his oblation, the holocaust, the oblation and
the libations of all people on the great altar; on it you will pour out all the blood
of the holocausts and sacrifices. As regards the altar of bronze, I shall see to
that.' •Uriah the priest did everything that King Ahaz had ordered.   16

King Ahaz dismantled the wheeled stands, removed the crosspieces and the 17
basins from them, and took the bronze Sea off the oxen supporting it, and rested
it on the stone pavement. •In deference to the king of Assyria, he removed 18
from the Temple of Yahweh the dais for the throne, which had been set up
there, and the royal entry on the outside.

The rest of the history of Ahaz, his entire career, is not all this recorded in 19
the Book of the Annals of the Kings of Judah? •Then Ahaz slept with his an- 20
cestors, and was buried in the Citadel of David; his son Hezekiah succeeded him.

The reign of Hoshea in Israel (732-724)

17 In the twelfth year of Ahaz king of Judah, Hoshea son of Elah became 1
king of Israel in Samaria, and reigned for nine years. •He did what is 2
displeasing to Yahweh, though not like the preceding kings of Israel.

Shalmaneser king of Assyria made war on Hoshea who submitted to him 3
and paid him tribute. •But the king of Assyria discovered that Hoshea was 4
playing a double game with him: he had sent messengers to So, king of Egypt,
and had not, as in previous years, handed over the tribute to the king of Assyria.
For this the king of Assyria imprisoned him, in chains.

The fall of Samaria (721)

The king of Assyria invaded the whole country and, coming to Samaria, laid 5
siege to it for three years. •In the ninth year of Hoshea, the king of Assyria 6
captured Samaria and deported the Israelites to Assyria. He settled them in
Halah on the Habor, a river of Gozan,ᵃ and in the cities of the Medes.ᵇ

Observations on the fall of the Northern Kingdom

This happened because the Israelites had sinned against Yahweh their God 7
who had brought them out of the land of Egypt, out of the grip of Pharaoh
king of Egypt. They worshipped other gods, •they followed the practices of the 8
nations that Yahweh had dispossessed for them. •The Israelites, and the kings 9
they had made for themselves, plotted wicked schemes against their God. They
built high places for themselves wherever they lived, from watchtower to fortified
town. •They set up pillars and sacred poles for themselves on every high hill 10
and under every spreading tree. •They sacrificed there after the manner of the 11
nations that Yahweh had expelled before them, and did wicked things there,
provoking the anger of Yahweh. •They served idols, although Yahweh had told 12
them, 'This you must not do'.

13   And yet through all the prophets and all the seers, Yahweh had given Israel and Judah this warning, 'Turn from your wicked ways and keep my commandments and my laws in accordance with the entire Law I laid down for your
14   fathers and delivered to them through my servants the prophets'. •But they would not listen, they were more stubborn than their ancestors had been who
15   had no faith in Yahweh their God. •They despised his laws and the covenant he had made with their ancestors, and the warnings he had given them. They pursued emptiness, and themselves became empty through copying the nations round them although Yahweh had ordered them not to act as they did.
16   They rejected all the commandments of Yahweh their God and made idols of cast metal for themselves, two calves; they made themselves sacred poles, they
17   worshipped the whole array of heaven, and they served Baal. •They made their sons and daughters pass through fire, they practised divination and sorcery, they sold themselves to evil-doing in the sight of Yahweh, provoking his anger.
18   For this, Yahweh was enraged with Israel and thrust them away from him. There was none left but the tribe of Judah only.
19   Judah did not keep the commandments of Yahweh their God either, but
20   copied the practices that Israel had introduced. •Yahweh rejected the whole race of Israel; he brought them low, delivering them into the hands of marauders,
21   until at length he thrust them away from him. •And indeed he had torn Israel away from the House of David, and they had made Jeroboam son of Nebat king; Jeroboam had drawn Israel away from Yahweh and led them into a great
22   sin. •The Israelites copied the sin Jeroboam had committed; they did not
23   give it up, •until at length Yahweh thrust Israel away from him, as he had foretold through all his servants the prophets; he deported the Israelites from their own country to Assyria, where they still are today.

The origin of the Samaritans

24   The king of Assyria brought people from Babylon, Cuthah, Avva, Hamath and Sepharvaim, and settled them in the towns of Samaria to replace the Israelites; they took possession of Samaria and lived in its towns.
25   When they first came to live there, they did not worship Yahweh, so Yahweh
26   sent lions against them, which killed a number of them. •They said to the king of Assyria, 'The nations you deported and settled in the towns of Samaria do not know how to worship the god of the country, and he has sent lions against them; and now these are killing them because they do not know how to worship
27   the god of the country'. •So the king of Assyria gave this order: 'Send back one of the priests whom I deported from there; let him go and live there and
28   teach them how to worship the god of the country'. •Accordingly, one of the priests they had deported from Samaria came to live in Bethel; he taught them how to worship Yahweh.
29   Each national group made idols representing its own gods and put them in the temples of the high places made by the Samaritans; each national group
30   did this in the towns allocated to it. •The men of Babylon had made a Succoth-
31   benoth, the men of Cuthah a Nergal, the men of Hamath an Ashima, •the Avvites a Nibhaz and a Tartak; while the Sepharvites burnt their children in the fire in honour of Adrammelech and of Anammelech, gods of Sepharvaim.
32   They worshipped Yahweh as well, and they appointed priests out of their own number for the high places who officiated for them in the temples of the high
33   places. •They worshipped Yahweh and served their own gods at the same time,
34   with the rites of the countries from which they had been deported. •They still follow their old rites even now.
    They did not worship Yahweh[c] and did not conform to his statutes or ritual, or the law or the commandments, which Yahweh had laid down for the

17 a. Near Haran.   b. E. of Mesopotamia.   c. This paragraph returns to the general description of the unfaithfulness of the Israelites.

sons of Jacob to whom he gave the name Israel. •Yahweh had made a covenant 35
with them and had given them this command: 'You are not to worship alien
gods, you are not to bow down to them or serve them or offer them sacrifices.
You are to bow down and offer sacrifice to Yahweh who brought you out of 36
the land of Egypt with great power and outstretched arm. •You are to observe 37
the statutes and ritual, the law and the commandments which he has given you
in writing and to which you are always to conform; you are not to worship
alien gods. •Do not forget the covenant I have made with you, and do not 38
venerate alien gods. •Venerate Yahweh alone, your God, and he will deliver 39
you out of the power of all your enemies.' •But they would not listen, and still 40
followed their old rites.

These nations, then, worshipped Yahweh and served their carved images as 41
well, their children, too, and their children's children still behave today as their
fathers behaved in the past.

VIII. THE LAST YEARS OF THE KINGDOM OF JUDAH

A. HEZEKIAH, THE PROPHET ISAIAH; ASSYRIA

Introduction to the reign of Hezekiah (716-687)

18 In the third year of Hoshea son of Elah, king of Israel, Hezekiah son of 1
Ahaz became king of Judah. •He was twenty-five years old when he came 2
to the throne, and he reigned for twenty-nine years in Jerusalem. His mother's
name was Abijah daughter of Zechariah. •He did what is pleasing to Yahweh, 3
just as his ancestor David had done. •It was he who abolished the high places, 4
broke the pillars, cut down the sacred poles and smashed the bronze serpent
that Moses had made; for•up to that time the Israelites had offered sacrifice
to it; it was called Nehushtan. •He put his trust in the God of Israel. No king 5
of Judah after him could be compared with him—nor any of those before him.
He was devoted to Yahweh, never turning from him, but keeping the command- 6
ments that Yahweh had laid down for Moses. •And so Yahweh was with him, 7
and he was successful in all that he undertook. He rebelled against the king of
Assyria and refused to serve him. •It was he who harassed the Philistines as far 8
as Gaza, laying their territory waste from watchtower to fortified town.

The fall of Samaria; recapitulation

In the fourth year of Hezekiah, which was the seventh year of Hoshea son 9
of Elah, king of Israel, Shalmaneser king of Assyria made war on Samaria and
laid siege to it. •He captured it after three years. Samaria fell in the sixth year 10
of Hezekiah, which was the ninth year of Hoshea king of Israel. •The king of 11
Assyria deported the Israelites to Assyria and settled them in Halah on the
Habor, a river of Gozan, and in the cities of the Medes. •This happened because 12
they had not obeyed the voice of Yahweh their God and had broken his
covenant, violating all that Moses the servant of Yahweh had laid down. They
neither listened to it nor put it into practice.

Sennacherib's invasion [a]

In the fourteenth year of King Hezekiah, Sennacherib king of Assyria attacked 13
the fortified towns of Judah and captured them. •Then Hezekiah king of Judah 14
sent this message to the king of Assyria at Lachish, 'I have been at fault. Call
off the attack, and I will submit myself to whatever you impose on me.' The
king of Assyria exacted three hundreds talents of silver and thirty talents of
gold from Hezekiah king of Judah, •and Hezekiah gave him all the silver in 15
the Temple of Yahweh and in the treasury of the royal palace. •It was then that 16

Hezekiah stripped the facing from the leaves and jambs of the doors of the Temple of Yahweh, which . . . king of Judah had plated, and gave it to the king of Assyria.

The embassy of the cupbearer-in-chief

17 From Lachish the king of Assyria sent the cupbearer-in-chief with a large force to King Hezekiah in Jerusalem. He went up to Jerusalem, and when he arrived, he took a position near the conduit of the upper pool which is on the
18 road to the Fuller's Field. •He summoned the king. The master of the palace, Eliakim son of Hilkiah, Shebnah the secretary and the herald Joah son of
19 Asaph went out to him. •The cupbearer-in-chief said to them, 'Say to Hezekiah, "Thus speaks the great king, the king of Assyria: What makes you so confident?
20 Do you think empty words are as good as strategy and military strength? Who
21 are you relying on, to dare to rebel against me? •We know you are relying on that broken reed Egypt, which pricks and pierces the hand of the man who leans on it.—That is what Pharaoh king of Egypt is like to all who rely
22 on him.—•You may say to me: We rely on Yahweh our God, but are they not his high places and altars that Hezekiah has suppressed, saying to the people of Judah and Jerusalem: This in Jerusalem, is the altar, before which you must
23 worship? •Come, make a wager with my lord the king of Assyria: I will give
24 you two thousand horses if you can find horsemen to ride them. •How could you repulse a single one of the least of my master's servants? And yet you have
25 relied on Egypt for chariots and horsemen. •And lastly, have I come up against this place to lay it waste without warrant from Yahweh? Yahweh himself said to me: March against this country and lay it waste." '
26 Eliakim, Shebnah and Joah said to the cupbearer-in-chief, 'Please speak to your servants in Aramaic, for we understand it; do not speak to us in the
27 Judaean language within earshot of the people on the ramparts'. •But the cupbearer-in-chief said, 'Do you think my lord sent me here to say these things to your master or to you? On the contrary, it was to the people sitting on the ramparts who, like you, are doomed to eat their own dung and drink their own urine.'
28 Then the cupbearer-in-chief stood erect and, shouting loudly in the Judaean language, called out, 'Listen to the word of the great king, the king of Assyria.
29 Thus the king speaks: "Do not let Hezekiah delude you. He will be powerless
30 to save you from my hands. •Do not let Hezekiah persuade you to rely on Yahweh by saying: Yahweh is sure to save us; this city will not fall into the
31 power of the king of Assyria. •Do not listen to Hezekiah, for the king of Assyria says this: Make peace with me, surrender to me, and every one of you will eat the fruit of his own vine and of his own fig tree and drink the water
32 of his own cistern •until I come and deport you to a country like your own, a land of corn and good wine, a land of bread and of vineyards, a land of oil and of honey, so that you may not die but live. Do not listen to Hezekiah who is
33 deluding you when he says: Yahweh will save us. •Has any god of any nation
34 saved his country from the power of the king of Assyria? •Where are the gods of Hamath and Arpad? Where are the gods of Sepharvaim and Hena and Ivvah? Where are the gods of the land of Samaria? Did they save Samaria from me?
35 Tell me which, of all the gods of any country, have saved their countries from my hands, for Yahweh to be able to save Jerusalem?" '
36 They kept silence and said nothing in reply, since such was the king's order:
37 'Do not answer him' he had said. •The master of the palace, Eliakim son of Hilkiah, Shebnah the secretary and the herald Joah son of Asaph, with their garments torn, went to Hezekiah and reported what the cupbearer-in-chief had said.

18 a. 701 B.C.

The prophet Isaiah is consulted

19 On hearing this, King Hezekiah tore his garments, covered himself with 1
sackcloth and went to the Temple of Yahweh. •He sent the master of the 2
palace, Eliakim, Shebnah the secretary and the elders of the priests, covered in
sackcloth, to the prophet Isaiah son of Amoz. •They said to him, 'This is what 3
Hezekiah says, "Today is a day of suffering, of punishment, of disgrace. Children
come to birth, and there is no strength to bring them forth. •May Yahweh 4
your God hear the words of the cupbearer-in-chief whom his master, the king
of Assyria, has sent to insult the living God, and may Yahweh your God punish
the words he has heard. Offer your prayer for the remnant that is left." '
When the ministers of King Hezekiah had come to Isaiah, •he replied, 'Say ⁵₆
to your master, "Yahweh says this: Do not be afraid of the words you have
heard or the blasphemies the minions of the king of Assyria have uttered against
me. •I am going to put a spirit in him, and when he hears a rumour he will 7
return to his own country, and in that country I will bring him down with the
sword." '

The cupbearer returns to his master

The cupbearer went back and rejoined the king of Assyria at Libnah, 8
which he was attacking. The cupbearer had already learnt that the king of Assyria
had left Lachish, •since he had received this news about Tirhakah*a* king of Cush, 9
'He has set out to fight you'.

Sennacherib's letter to Hezekiah

Sennacherib sent messengers to Hezekiah again, saying, •'Tell this to Hezekiah 10
king of Judah, "Do not let your God on whom you are relying deceive you,
when he says: Jerusalem shall not fall into the power of the king of Assyria.
You have learnt by now what the kings of Assyria have done to every country, 11
putting them all under the ban. Are you likely to be spared? •What power to 12
help did the gods have of those nations my fathers destroyed, Gozan, Haran,
Rezeph and the Edenites who were in Tel Basar? •Where are the king of Hamath, 13
the king of Arpad, the kings of Sepharvaim, of Hena, of Ivvah?" '
Hezekiah took the letter from the hands of the messenger and read it; he then 14
went up to the Temple of Yahweh and spread it out before Yahweh. •Hezekiah 15
said this prayer in the presence of Yahweh, 'Yahweh Sabaoth, God of Israel,
enthroned on the cherubs, you alone are God of all the kingdoms of the earth,
you have made heaven and earth.

> 'Give ear, Yahweh, and listen.   16
> Open your eyes, Yahweh, and see.
> Hear the words of Sennacherib
> who has sent to insult the living God.

'It is true, Yahweh, that the kings of Assyria have exterminated all the nations, 17
they have thrown their gods on the fire, for these were not gods but the work 18
of men's hands, wood and stone, and hence they have destroyed them. •But 19
now, Yahweh our God, save us from his hand, I pray you, and let all the kingdoms of the earth know that you alone are God, Yahweh.'

Isaiah intervenes

Then Isaiah son of Amoz sent to Hezekiah. 'Yahweh, the God of Israel' he 20
said 'says this, "I have heard the prayer you have addressed to me about
Sennacherib king of Assyria". •Here is the oracle that Yahweh has pronounced 21
against him:

"She despises you, she scorns you,
the virgin, daughter of Zion;
she tosses her head behind you,
the daughter of Jerusalem.

22   Whom have you insulted, whom did you blaspheme?
Against whom raised your voice
and lifted your haughty eyes?
Against the Holy One of Israel!

23   Through your envoys you have insulted the Lord,
you have said: With my many chariots
I have climbed the tops of mountains,
the utmost peaks of Lebanon.
I have felled its tall forest of cedars,
its finest cypresses.
I have reached its furthest recesses,
its forest garden.

24   Yes, I have dug wells
and drunk of alien waters;
I have put down my feet,
and I have dried up all the rivers of Egypt.

25   "Do you hear? Long ago
I planned for it,
from days of old I designed it,
now I carry it out.
Your part was to bring down in heaps of ruins
fortified cities.

26   Their inhabitants, hands feeble,
dismayed, discomfited,
were like plants of the field,
like tender grass,
like grass of housetop and meadow
under the east wind.

27   But I am there whether you rise or sit;
whether you go out, or you come in, I know it.

28   Because you have raved against me
and your insolence has come to my ears,
I will put my ring through your nostrils,
my bit between your lips,
to make you return by the road
on which you came.

A sign for Hezekiah

29   "This shall be the sign for you:
this year will be eaten the self-sown grain,
next year what sprouts in the fallow,
but in the third year sow and reap,
plant vineyards and eat their fruit.

30   The surviving remnant of the House of Judah shall bring forth
new roots below and fruits above;

31   for a remnant shall go out from Jerusalem,
and survivors from Mount Zion.
The jealous love of Yahweh Sabaoth shall accomplish this."

32   'This, then, is what Yahweh says about the king of Assyria:

19 a. Pharaoh, 690-664, called 'king of Cush' because he was of Ethiopian descent (Cush is Ethiopia).

"He will not enter this city,
he will let fly no arrow against it,
confront it with no shield,
throw up no earthwork against it.
By the road that he came on he will return;   33
he shall not enter this city. It is Yahweh who speaks.
I will protect this city and save it   34
for my own sake and for the sake of my servant David." '

Sennacherib is punished

That same night the angel of Yahweh went out and struck down a hundred 35
and eighty-five thousand men in the Assyrian camp. In the early morning when
it was time to get up, there they lay, so many corpses.

Sennacherib struck camp and left; he returned home and stayed in Nineveh. 36
One day when he was worshipping in the temple of his god Nisroch, his sons 37
Adrammelech and Sharezer struck him down with the sword and escaped into
the land of Ararat.ᵇ His son Esarhaddon succeeded him.

The illness and cure of Hezekiah

20 In those days Hezekiah fell ill and was at the point of death. The prophet 1
Isaiah son of Amoz came and said to him, 'Yahweh says this, "Put
your affairs in order, for you are going to die, you will not live" '. •Hezekiah 2
turned his face to the wall and addressed this prayer to Yahweh, •'Ah, Yahweh, 3
remember I beg you, how I have behaved faithfully and with sincerity of heart
in your presence and done what is right in your eyes'. And Hezekiah shed many
tears.

Isaiah had not left the middle court, before the word of Yahweh came to 4
him, •'Go back and say to Hezekiah, prince of my people, "Yahweh, the God of 5
David your ancestor, says this : I have heard your prayer and seen your tears.
I will cure you: in three days' time you shall go up to the Temple of Yahweh.
I will add fifteen years to your life. I will save you and this city from the hands 6
of the king of Assyria, I will protect this city for my own sake and the sake
of my servant David." '

'Bring a fig poultice' Isaiah said; they brought one, applied it to the ulcer, 7
and the king recovered.

Hezekiah said to Isaiah, 'What is the sign to tell me that Yahweh will cure 8
me and that I shall be going up to the Temple of Yahweh in three days?' •'Here' 9
Isaiah replied 'is the sign from Yahweh that he will do what he has said; would
you like the shadow to go forward ten steps, or to go back ten steps?' •'It is easy 10
for the shadow to lengthen ten steps,' Hezekiah answered 'no, I would rather
the shadow went back ten steps.' •The prophet Isaiah then called on Yahweh 11
who made the shadow go back ten steps on the steps of Ahaz.

The Babylonian embassy

At that time the king of Babylon, Merodach-baladan son of Baladan, sent 12
letters and a gift to Hezekiah, for he had heard of his illness and his recovery.
Hezekiah was delighted at this and showed the messengers his treasure-house, 13
the silver, gold, spices, precious oil, his armoury too, and everything there was
in his storehouses. There was nothing Hezekiah did not show them in his palace
or in his whole domain.

Then the prophet Isaiah came to King Hezekiah and asked him, 'What have 14
these men said, and where have they come from?' Hezekiah answered, 'They
have come from a faraway country, from Babylon'. •Isaiah said, 'What have 15
they seen in your palace?' 'They have seen everything in my palace' Hezekiah
answered. 'There is nothing in my storehouses that I have not shown them.'
Then Isaiah said to Hezekiah, 'Listen to the word of Yahweh, •"The days ¹⁶₁₇

are coming when everything in your palace, everything that your ancestors have
amassed until now, will be carried off to Babylon. Not a thing will be left" says
18 Yahweh. •"Sons sprung from you, sons begotten by you, will be chosen to be
19 eunuchs in the palace of the king of Babylon." ' •Hezekiah said to Isaiah, 'This
word of Yahweh that you announce is reassuring', for he was thinking, 'And
why not? So long as there is peace and security during my own lifetime.'

The end of the reign of Hezekiah

20   The rest of the history of Hezekiah, all his prowess, how he constructed
the pool and the conduit to bring water into the city, is not all this recorded in
21 the Book of the Annals of the Kings of Judah? •Then Hezekiah slept with his
fathers; his son Manasseh succeeded him.

B. TWO WICKED KINGS

The reign of Manasseh in Judah (687-642)

1 **21** Manasseh was twelve years old when he came to the throne, and he reigned
2   **21** for fifty-five years in Jerusalem. His mother's name was Hephzibah. •He
did what is displeasing to Yahweh, copying the shameful practices of the nations
3 whom Yahweh had dispossessed for the sons of Israel. •He rebuilt the high
places that his father Hezekiah had destroyed, he set up altars to Baal and made
a sacred pole as Ahab king of Israel had done, he worshipped the whole array
4 of heaven and served it. •He built altars in the Temple of Yahweh of which
Yahweh had said, 'Jerusalem is where I will give my name a home'.
5   He built altars to the whole array of heaven in the two courts of the
6 Temple of Yahweh. •He caused his son to pass through the fire. He practised
soothsaying and magic and introduced necromancers and wizards. He did very
7 many more things displeasing to Yahweh, thus provoking his anger. •He placed
the carved image of Asherah which he had made in the Temple, of which
Yahweh had said to David and his son Solomon, 'In this Temple and in
Jerusalem, the city I chose out of all the tribes of Israel, I will give my name
8 a home for ever. •I will no longer make Israel's footsteps wander from the
land I gave their fathers, provided they observe all I have ordered them in accord-
9 ance with the whole Law that my servant Moses prescribed for them.' •But
they did not listen, Manasseh led them astray, so that they did more evil than
those nations Yahweh had destroyed before the sons of Israel.
10
11   Then Yahweh spoke through his servants the prophets, •'Since Manasseh
king of Judah has done these shameful deeds, acting more wickedly than all the
Amorites did before him, and has led Judah itself into sin with his idols,
12 Yahweh, the God of Israel, says this, "Look, I will bring such disaster as to
13 make the ears of all who hear of it tingle. •I will stretch over Jerusalem the same
measuring line as over Samaria, the same plumb-rule as for the House of Ahab;
I will scour Jerusalem as a man scours a dish and, having scoured it, turns it
14 upside down. •I will cast away the remnant of my inheritance, delivering them
into the power of their enemies, and making them serve as prey and booty to
15 all their enemies, •because they have done what is displeasing to me and have
provoked my anger from the day their ancestors came out of Egypt until now." '
16   Manasseh shed innocent blood, too, in such great quantity that he flooded
Jerusalem from end to end, apart from the sins into which he led Judah by
doing what is displeasing to Yahweh.
17   The rest of the history of Manasseh, his entire career, the sins he committed,
18 is not all this recorded in the Book of the Annals of the Kings of Judah? •Then
Manasseh slept with his ancestors, and was buried in the garden of his palace,
the garden of Uzza; his son Amon succeeded him.

b. He was assassinated in 681.

The reign of Amon in Judah (642-640)

Amon was twenty-two years old when he came to the throne, and he reigned 19 for two years in Jerusalem. His mother's name was Meshullemeth, daughter of Haruz, of Jotbah. •He did what is displeasing to Yahweh, as Manasseh his 20 father had done. •In every respect he followed the example of his father, serving 21 the idols his father had served, and worshipping them. •He abandoned Yahweh, 22 the God of his ancestors; he did not follow the way of Yahweh.

Amon's officers plotted against the king and killed him in his palace. •But $^{23}_{24}$ the country people struck down all those who had plotted against king Amon, and proclaimed his son Josiah as his successor.

The rest of the history of Amon, his entire career, is not all this recorded in 25 the Book of the Annals of the Kings of Judah? •He was buried in his father's 26 tomb in the garden of Uzza; his son Josiah succeeded him.

C. JOSIAH AND THE RELIGIOUS REFORM

Introduction to the reign of Josiah (640-609)

22 Josiah was eight years old when he came to the throne, and he reigned for 1 thirty-one years in Jerusalem. His mother's name was Jedidah, daughter of Adaiah, of Bozkath. •He did what is pleasing to Yahweh, and in every respect 2 followed the example of his ancestor David, not deviating from it to right or left.

The Book of the Law discovered

In the eighteenth year of King Josiah, the king sent the secretary Shaphan 3 son of Azaliah son of Meshullam to the Temple of Yahweh. •'Go to Hilkiah 4 the high priest,' he told him 'and tell him to melt down the silver that has been brought to the Temple of Yahweh and that those who guard the threshold have collected from the people. •Let him hand it over to the masters of works 5 attached to the Temple of Yahweh, for them to spend on the workmen working on the repairs to the Temple of Yahweh, •on the carpenters, builders and masons, 6 and on buying wood and dressed stone for the Temple repairs. •But they are 7 not to be asked to render account of the money handed over to them, since they are honest in their dealings.'

The high priest Hilkiah said to Shaphan the secretary, 'I have found the 8 Book of the Law in the Temple of Yahweh'.^{a} And Hilkiah gave the book to Shaphan, who read it. •Shaphan the secretary went to the king and reported 9 to him as follows, 'Your servants' he said 'have melted down the silver which was in the Temple and have handed it over to the masters of works attached to the Temple of Yahweh'. •Then Shaphan the secretary informed the king, 'Hilkiah 10 the priest has given me a book'; and Shaphan read it aloud in the king's presence.

Huldah the prophetess is consulted

On hearing the contents of the Book of the Law, the king tore his garments, and gave the following order to Hilkiah the priest, Ahikam son of Shaphan, 11 Achbor son of Micaiah, Shaphan the secretary and Asaiah the king's minister: 12 'Go and consult Yahweh, on behalf of me and the people, about the contents of this book that has been found. Great indeed must be the anger of Yahweh 13 blazing out against us because our ancestors did not obey what this book says by practising everything written in it.'

Hilkiah the priest, Ahikam, Achbor, Shaphan and Asaiah went to Huldah 14 the prophetess, wife of Shallum son of Tikvah, son of Harhas, the keeper of the wardrobe; she lived in Jerusalem in the new town. They put the matter to her, •and she replied, 'Yahweh, the God of Israel, says this, "To the man 15 who sent you to me say this: •Yahweh says this: I am bringing disaster 16 on this place and those who live in it, carrying out everything said in the book

17 the king of Judah has read, •because they have deserted me and sacrificed to other gods, to provoke my anger by everything they did. My anger blazes out
18 against this place; it will not be extinguished. •And you are to say to the king of Judah who sent you to consult Yahweh: Yahweh, the God of Israel, says
19 this: The words you have heard... •But since your heart has been touched and you have humbled yourself before Yahweh on hearing what I have decreed against this place and those who live in it, how they will become an object of horror and cursing; and since you have torn your garments and wept before me,
20 I for my part have heard—it is Yahweh who speaks. •For this reason I will gather you to your ancestors, you shall be gathered into your grave in peace; your eyes will not see all the disasters that I mean to bring on this place." ' They took this answer to the king.

The covenant renewed

1 23 The king then had all the elders of Judah and of Jerusalem summoned to
2 him, •and the king went up to the Temple of Yahweh with all the men of Judah and all the inhabitants of Jerusalem, priests, prophets and all the people, of high or low degree. In their hearing he read out everything that was said
3 in the book of the covenant found in the Temple of Yahweh. •The king stood beside the pillar, and in the presence of Yahweh he made a covenant to follow Yahweh and keep his commandments and decrees and laws with all his heart and soul, in order to enforce the terms of the covenant as written in that book. All the people gave their allegiance to the covenant.

Religious reform in Judah

4 The king ordered Hilkiah with the priest next in rank and the guardians of the threshold to remove all the cult objects that had been made for Baal, Asherah and the whole array of heaven; he burnt them outside Jerusalem in
5 the fields of the Kidron and had the ashes taken to Bethel. •He did away with the spurious priests whom the kings of Judah had appointed and who offered sacrifice on the high places, in the towns of Judah and the neighbourhood of Jerusalem; also those who offered sacrifice to Baal, to the sun, the moon, the
6 constellations and the whole array of heaven. •From the Temple of Yahweh he removed the sacred pole right out of Jerusalem to the wadi Kidron, and in the wadi Kidron he burnt it; he reduced it to ashes and threw its ashes on the
7 common burying-ground. •He pulled down the house of the sacred male prostitutes which was in the Temple of Yahweh and where the women wove clothes for Asherah.

8 He brought all the priests in from the towns of Judah, and from Geba to Beersheba he desecrated the high places where these priests had offered sacrifice. He pulled down the shrine of the goats[a] which stood at the gate of Joshua,
9 the governor of the city, to the left as you enter the city gate. •The priests of the high places, however, could not go up to the altar of Yahweh in Jerusalem,
10 but they ate unleavened bread in the company of their brother priests. •He desecrated the furnace in the Valley of Ben-hinnom, so that no one could make
11 his son or daughter pass through fire in honour of Molech. •He did away with the horses that the kings of Judah had dedicated to the sun at the entrance to the Temple of Yahweh, near the apartment of Nathan-melech the eunuch,
12 in the precincts, and he burned the chariot of the sun. •The altars on the roof that the kings of Judah had built, with those that Manasseh had built in the two courts of the Temple of Yahweh, the king pulled down, and broke them to pieces on the spot, then carried them away and threw their rubble into the wadi
13 Kidron. •The king desecrated the high places facing Jerusalem, to the south

22 a. The sacred Law of the Temple, included in Deuteronomy, which had been hidden or lost during the reign of Manasseh.
23 a. Deities represented as satyrs.

of the Mount of Olives, which Solomon king of Israel had built for Astarte
the Sidonian abomination, for Chemosh the Moabite abomination, and for
Milcom the Ammonite abomination. •He also smashed the sacred pillars, cut 14
down the sacred poles, and covered the places where they had stood with human
bones.ᵇ

The reform is extended to the former Northern Kingdom

Similarly, as regards the altar that was at Bethel, the high place built by 15
Jeroboam son of Nebat who had led Israel into sin, this altar and this high
place he also demolished, breaking up its stones and reducing them to powder.
The sacred pole he burned.

As he looked around, Josiah saw the tombs there on the hillside; he had the 16
bones fetched from the tombs and burned them on the altar. Thus he desecrated it,
in accordance with the word of Yahweh which the man of God had proclaimed
when Jeroboam was standing by the altar at the time of the feast. As he looked
around, Josiah caught sight of the tomb of the man of God who had foretold
these things. •'What is that monument I see?' he asked. The townspeople replied, 17
'It is the tomb of the man of God who came from Judah and foretold what
you have done to the altar'. •'Let him rest,' the king said 'and let no one disturb 18
his bones.' So they left his bones untouched, with the bones of the prophet
who was from Samaria.

Josiah also did away with all the temples of the high places that the kings 19
of Israel had built in the towns of Samaria, provoking the anger of Yahweh;
he treated these places exactly as he had treated the one at Bethel. •All the 20
priests of the high places who were there he slaughtered on the altars, and on
those altars burned human bones. Then he returned to Jerusalem.

The Passover celebrated

The king gave this order to the whole people: 'Celebrate a Passover in honour 21
of Yahweh your God, as prescribed in this book of the covenant'. •No Passover 22
like this one had ever been celebrated since the days when the judges ruled
Israel or throughout the entire period of the kings of Israel and the kings of
Judah. •The eighteenth year of King Josiah was the only time when such a 23
Passover was celebrated in honour of Yahweh at Jerusalem.

Last words on the religious reform

What is more, the necromancers and wizards, the household gods and idols, 24
and all the abominations to be seen in the land of Judah and in Jerusalem, all
these were swept away by Josiah to give effect to the words of the Law written
in the book found by Hilkiah the priest in the Temple of Yahweh. •No king 25
before him had turned to Yahweh as he did, with all his heart, all his soul,
all his strength, in perfect loyalty to the Law of Moses; nor was any king like him
seen again.

Yet Yahweh did not renounce the heat of his great anger which blazed out 26
against Judah because of all the provocation Manasseh had offered him.
Yahweh decreed, 'I will thrust Judah away from me too, as I have already thrust 27
Israel; I will cast away Jerusalem, this city I had chosen, and the Temple of which
I had said: There my name shall be.'

The end of the reign of Josiah

The rest of the history of Josiah, his entire career, is not all this recorded 28
in the Book of the Annals of the Kings of Judah?

During his reign Pharaoh Neco king of Egypt was on his way to the king 29
of Assyria at the river Euphrates when King Josiah intercepted him; but Neco
killed him at Megiddo in the first encounter. •His servants carried his body 30
from Megiddo by chariot; they brought him to Jerusalem, and buried him in

his own tomb. The country people took Jehoahaz son of Josiah and anointed him, proclaiming him king in succession to his father.

D. THE DESTRUCTION OF JERUSALEM

The reign of Jehoahaz in Judah (609)

31 Jehoahaz was twenty-three years old when he came to the throne, and he reigned for three months in Jerusalem. His mother's name was Hamutal, daughter 32 of Jeremiah, from Libnah. •He did what is displeasing to Yahweh, just as his ancestors had done.

33 Pharaoh Neco put him in chains at Riblah, in the territory of Hamath, and imposed a levy of a hundred talents of silver and ten talents of gold on the 34 country. •Pharaoh Neco made Eliakim son of Josiah king in succession to Josiah his father, and changed his name to Jehoiakim. Jehoahaz he took and carried away into Egypt, where he died.

35 Jehoiakim paid over the silver and gold to Pharaoh, but first had to tax the country before he could raise the sum that Pharaoh demanded: he levied the silver and gold to be paid over to Pharaoh Neco from each according to his means.

The reign of Jehoiakim in Judah (609-598)

36 Jehoiakim was twenty-five years old when he came to the throne, and he reigned for eleven years in Jerusalem. His mother's name was Zebidah, daughter 37 of Pedaiah, from Rumah. •He did what is displeasing to Yahweh, just as his ancestors had done.

1 **24** During his time Nebuchadnezzar*a* king of Babylon invaded, and Jehoiakim became his vassal for three years, but then rebelled against him a second 2 time. •So he sent armed bands of Chaldaeans, Aramaeans, Moabites and Ammonites against him; he sent these against Judah to destroy it, in accordance with the word that Yahweh had spoken through his servants the prophets. 3 That this happened in Judah was due entirely to the anger of Yahweh: he had resolved to thrust them away from him because of the sins of Manasseh and 4 all that he had done, •and also because of the innocent blood that he had shed, flooding Jerusalem from end to end with innocent blood. Yahweh would not forgive.

5 The rest of the history of Jehoiakim, his entire career, is not all this recorded 6 in the Book of the Annals of the Kings of Judah? •Then Jehoiakim slept with his ancestors; his son Jehoiachin succeeded him.

7 The king of Egypt did not leave his own country again, because the king of Babylon had conquered everywhere belonging to the king of Egypt, from the wadi of Egypt to the river Euphrates.*b*

Introduction to the reign of Jehoiachin (598)

8 Jehoiachin was eighteen years old when he came to the throne, and he reigned for three months in Jerusalem. His mother's name was Nehushta, daughter of 9 Elnathan, from Jerusalem. •He did what is displeasing to Yahweh, just as his father had done.

The first deportation

10 At that time the troops of Nebuchadnezzar king of Babylon marched on 11 Jerusalem, and the city was besieged. •Nebuchadnezzar king of Babylon himself

---

b. To desecrate them once and for all; cf. vv.16 and 20.
24 a. He ruled the Chaldaean (Neo-Babylonian) empire from 605 to 562. This invasion took place about 602.   **b.** The Egyptians were defeated at Carcemish, 605.

came to attack the city while his troops were besieging it. •Then Jehoiachin king 12 of Judah surrendered to the king of Babylon, he, his mother, his officers, his nobles and his eunuchs, and the king of Babylon took them prisoner. This was in the eighth year of King Nebuchadnezzar.

The latter carried off all the treasures of the Temple of Yahweh and the 13 treasures of the royal palace, and broke up all the golden furnishings that Solomon king of Israel had made for the sanctuary of Yahweh, as Yahweh had foretold. He carried off all Jerusalem into exile, all the nobles and all the notables, ten 14 thousand of these were exiled, with all the blacksmiths and metalworkers; only the poorest people in the country were left behind. •He deported Jehoiachin to 15 Babylon, as also the king's mother, his eunuchs and the nobility of the country; he made them all leave Jerusalem for exile in Babylon. •All the men of distinction, 16 seven thousand of them, the blacksmiths and metalworkers, one thousand of them, all of them men capable of bearing arms, were led into exile in Babylon by the king of Babylon.

The king of Babylon made Mattaniah, Jehoiachin's uncle, king in succession 17 to him, and changed his name to Zedekiah.

Introduction to the reign of Zedekiah in Judah (598-587)

Zedekiah was twenty-one years old when he came to the throne, and he reigned 18 for eleven years in Jerusalem. His mother's name was Hamital, daughter of Jeremiah, from Libnah. •He did what is displeasing to Yahweh, just as Jehoiakim 19 had done. •That this happened in Jerusalem and Judah was due to the anger of 20 Yahweh, with the result that in the end he cast them away from him.

The siege of Jerusalem

Zedekiah rebelled against the king of Babylon. **25** In the ninth year of his 1 reign,*a* in the tenth month, on the tenth day of the month, Nebuchadnezzar king of Babylon came with his whole army to attack Jerusalem; he pitched camp in front of the city and threw up earthworks round it. •The city lay under siege 2 till the eleventh year of King Zedekiah. •In the fourth month, on the ninth day 3 of the month, when famine was raging in the city and there was no food for the populace, •a breach was made in the city wall. At once, the king made his 4 escape under cover of dark, with all the fighting men, by way of the gate between the two walls, which is near the king's garden—the Chaldaeans had surrounded the city—and made his way towards the Arabah.*b* •The Chaldaean troops pursued 5 the king and caught up with him in the plains of Jericho, where all his troops deserted. •The Chaldaeans captured the king and took him to the king of Babylon 6 at Riblah, who passed sentence on him. •He had the sons of Zedekiah slaughtered 7 before his eyes, then put out Zedekiah's eyes and, loading him with chains, carried him off to Babylon.

The sack of Jerusalem. The second deportation

In the fifth month, on the seventh day of the month—it was in the nineteenth 8 year of Nebuchadnezzar king of Babylon—Nebuzaradan, commander of the guard, an officer of the king of Babylon, entered Jerusalem. •He burned down the 9 Temple of Yahweh, the royal palace and all the houses in Jerusalem. •The 10 Chaldaean troops who accompanied the commander of the guard demolished the walls surrounding Jerusalem. •Nebuzaradan, commander of the guard, 11 deported the remainder of the population left behind in the city, the deserters who had gone over to the king of Babylon, and the rest of the common people. The commander of the guard left some of the humbler country people as vineyard 12 workers and ploughmen.

The Chaldaeans broke up the bronze pillars from the Temple of Yahweh, the 13 wheeled stands and the bronze Sea that were in the Temple of Yahweh, and took the bronze away to Babylon. •They also took the ash containers, the scoops, 14

the knives, the incense boats, and all the bronze furnishings used in worship.
15 The commander of the guard took the censers and the sprinkling bowls, everything
16 that was made of gold and everything made of silver. •As regards the two pillars,
the one Sea and the wheeled stands, which Solomon had made for the Temple
of Yahweh, there was no reckoning the weight of bronze in all these objects.
17 The height of one pillar was eighteen cubits, and on it stood a capital of bronze,
the height of the capital being five cubits; round the capital were filigree and
pomegranates, all in bronze. So also for the second pillar...
18   The commander of the guard took prisoner Seraiah the chief priest, Zephaniah
19 the priest next in rank, and the three guardians of the threshold. •In the city he
took prisoner a eunuch who was in command of the fighting men, five of the
king's personal friends who were discovered in the city, the secretary to the army
commander, responsible for military conscription, and sixty men of distinction
20 discovered in the city. •Nebuzaradan, commander of the guard, took these men
21 and brought them to the king of Babylon at Riblah, •and at Riblah, in the land
of Hamath, the king of Babylon had them put to death. Thus Judah was deported
from its land.

Gedaliah, governor of Judah

22   As regards the people who remained in the land of Judah whom Nebuchadnezzar king of Babylon had left behind, he appointed Gedaliah son of Ahikam
23 son of Shaphan as their governor. •When the commanders of the troops and their
men all heard that the king of Babylon had appointed Gedaliah as governor,
they went to him at Mizpah: Ishmael son of Nethaniah, Johanan son of Kareah,
Seraiah son of Tanhumeth, the Netophathite, Jaazaniah the Maacathite, they
24 and their men. •To them and to their men Gedaliah swore an oath. 'Do not be
afraid of the Chaldaeans,' he said 'live in the country, obey the king of Babylon,
and all will go well with you.'
25   But in the seventh month, Ishmael son of Nethaniah son of Elishama, who
was of royal descent, and ten men with him, came and murdered Gedaliah, as
26 well as the Judaeans and Chaldaeans who were with him at Mizpah. •Then the
people, of high and low degree, with the commanders of the troops, all set out
and made for Egypt, in fear of the Chaldaeans.

King Jehoiachin pardoned

27   In the thirty-seventh year of the exile of Jehoiachin king of Judah, in the
twelfth month, on the twenty-seventh day of the month, Evil-merodach king
of Babylon, in the year he came to the throne, pardoned Jehoiachin king of Judah
28 and released him from prison. •He treated him kindly and allotted him a seat
29 above those of the other kings who were with him in Babylon. •So Jehoiachin
laid aside his prisoner's garb, and for the rest of his life always ate at the king's
30 table. •And his upkeep was permanently ensured by the king, day after day,
for the rest of his life.

25 a. December 589.   b. The Jordan valley.

INTRODUCTION TO THE BOOKS OF
CHRONICLES,
EZRA AND NEHEMIAH

The two Books of Chronicles, the Book of Ezra and the Book of Nehemiah, are a continuous work by the same hand. This work was compiled in the 3rd century B.C. and the author was very probably a Jerusalem Levite.

The part of this work known as 'Chronicles' is a revision of the history of Israel which is contained in the earlier books, from Joshua to Kings, supplemented from other sources which are lost to us. The author treats his sources with great freedom in order to provide a lesson for his contemporaries, and in his book the whole period is viewed as leading up to the ideal kingdom of David and the building of the Temple under his son Solomon. There is great stress on the part played by the religious orders, not only priests but Levites and the lesser orders of cantors and gatekeepers, and the ritual organisation of the author's own time is projected into the age of David. Chronicles ends, like Kings, with the deportation of the Israelites into the Babylonian Exile.

The history is continued in Ezra and Nehemiah, with the return from Exile, the repopulation of Jerusalem and the rebuilding of the Temple in 538 to 515 B.C. Though the date of these two books is the same as that of Chronicles, they make use of original records and documents, including Ezra's report of his own mission and Nehemiah's memoir, and they are a valuable complement to the information on the Jewish Restoration which is incidentally contained in the books of the prophets Haggai, Zechariah and Malachi. The different documents are, however, arranged in a baffling order in which incidents appear to be classified by subjects rather than chronologically.

THE BOOKS OF CHRONICLES

THE FIRST BOOK OF CHRONICLES

I. DAVID AND HIS ENTOURAGE:
THE GENEALOGIES

A. FROM ADAM TO ISRAEL[a]

The origin of the three ethnic groups

1,2
3   1 Adam, Seth, Enosh, •Kenan, Mahalalel, Jared, •Enoch, Methuselah, Lamech,
4   Noah, Shem, Ham and Japheth.

The Japhethites

5   Sons of Japheth: Gomer, Magog, the Medes, Javàn, Tubal, Meshech, Tiras.
6
7   Sons of Gomer: Ashkenaz, Diphath, Togarmah. •Sons of Javan: Elishah,
Tarshish, the Kittim, the Dananites.

The Hamites

8   Sons of Ham: Cush, Misraim, Put, Canaan.
9   Sons of Cush: Seba, Havilah, Sabta, Raama, Sabteca. Sons of Raamah: Sheba,
10 Dedan. •Cush became father of Nimrod, the first potentate on earth.
11   Misraim became father of the people of Lud, of Anam, of Lehab, of Naphtuh,
12
13 of Pathros, Casluh and Caphtor, from which the Philistines came. •Canaan
14 became father of Sidon, his first-born, then Heth, •and the Jebusites, the Amorites,
15
16 Girgashites, •Hivites, Arkites, Sinites, •Arvadites, Zemarites, Hamathites.

The Semites

17   Sons of Shem: Elam, Asshur, Arpachshad, Lud, Aram.
     Sons of Aram: Uz, Hul, Gether and Meshech.
18   Arpachshad became father of Shelah, and Shelah became father of Eber.
19 To Eber were born two sons; the first was called Peleg, because it was in his
time the earth was divided, and his brother was called Joktan.
20
21   Joktan became father of Almodad, Sheleph, Hazarmaveth, Jerah, •Hadoram,
22
23 Uzal, Diklah, •Ebal, Abimael, Sheba, •Ophir, Havilah, Jobab; all these are
sons of Joktan.

---

1 a. The long lists of Gn 5 and 11 are abbreviated and supplemented from Gn 10 to concentrate all interest on the Semites. David, with his retinue of priests, Levites and cantors, is the author's subject.

From Shem to Abraham

Arpachshad, Shelah, •Eber, Peleg, •Reu, •Serug, Nahor, Terah, •Abram, _{24,25} _{26,27} that is, Abraham. •Sons of Abraham: Isaac and Ishmael. •These are their ₂₈ ₂₉ descendants:

The Ishmaelites

The first-born of Ishmael, Nebaioth; then Kedar, Adbeel, Mibsam, •Mishma, 30 Dumah, Massa, Hadad, Tema, •Jetur, Naphish and Kedemah. These are the 31 sons of Ishmael.

Sons of Keturah, Abraham's concubine: she gave birth to Zimran, Jokshan, 32 Medan, Midian, Ishbak, and Shuah. Sons of Jokshan: Sheba and Dedan. •Sons 33 of Midian: Ephah, Epher, Hanoch, Abida, Eldaah. All these are sons of Keturah.

Isaac and Esau

Abraham became father of Isaac. Sons of Isaac: Esau and Israel. 34

Sons of Esau: Eliphaz, Reuel, Jeush, Jalam and Korah. •Sons of Eliphaz: ₃₅ ₃₆ Teman, Omar, Zephi, Gatam, Kenaz, Timna, Amalek. •Sons of Reuel: Nahath, 37 Zerah, Shammah, Mizzah.

Seir

Sons of Seir: Lotan, Shobal, Zibeon, Anah, Dishon, Ezer, Dishan. •Sons of ₃₈ ₃₉ Lotan: Hori and Homam. Sister of Lotan: Timna. •Sons of Shobal: Alian, 40 Manahath, Ebal, Shephi, Onam. Sons of Zibeon: Aiah and Anah. •Son of 41 Anah: Dishon. Sons of Dishon: Hamran, Eshban, Ithran, Cheran. •Sons of 42 Ezer: Bilhan, Zaavan, Jaakan. Sons of Dishan: Uz and Aran.

The kings of Edom

Here are the kings who ruled in the land of Edom before an Israelite king 43 ruled: Bela son of Beor; his city was called Dinhabah. •Bela died and Jobab 44 son of Zerah, from Bozrah, succeeded. •Jobab died and Husham of the land of 45 the Temanites succeeded. •Husham died and Hadad son of Bedad succeeded; 46 he defeated the Midianites in the country of Moab, and his city was called Avith. Hadad died and Samlah of Masrekah succeeded. •Samlah died and Shaul of ₄₇ ₄₈ Rehoboth-han-nahar succeeded. •Shaul died and Baal-hanan son of Achbor 49 succeeded. •Baal-hanan died and Hadad succeeded. His city was called Pai; 50 his wife's name was Mehetabel daughter of Matred, from Mezahab.

The chiefs of Edom

Hadad died, and then there were chiefs in Edom: Chief Timna, Chief Aliah, 51 Chief Jetheth, •Chief Oholibamah, Chief Elah, Chief Pinon, •Chief Kenaz, Chief ₅₂ ₅₃ Teman, Chief Mibzar, •Chief Magdiel, Chief Iram. These are the chiefs of Edom. 54

B. JUDAH

The sons of Israel

2 These are the sons of Israel: Reuben, Simeon, Levi, Judah, Issachar, and 1 Zebulun, •Dan, Joseph, and Benjamin, Naphtali, Gad, and Asher. 2

The descendants of Judah

Sons of Judah: Er, Onan and Shelah. These three were born to him by Bath-shua 3 the Canaanite woman. Er, Judah's first-born, displeased Yahweh who put him to death. •Tamar, Judah's daughter-in-law, bore him Perez and Zerah. Judah 4 had five sons in all.

5　Sons of Perez: Hezron and Hamul.
6　Sons of Zerah: Zimri, Ethan, Heman, Calcol and Dara, five in all.
7　Sons of Carmi: Achar, who brought trouble on Israel by violating the ban.
8　Sons of Ethan: Azariah.

The ancestors of David

9　Sons of Hezron: there were born to him Jerahmeel, Ram, Chelubai.
10　Ram became father of Amminadab, Amminadab father of Nahshon, prince
11　of the sons of Judah, •Nahshon became father of Salma, Salma father of Boaz.
12
13　Boaz became father of Obed, Obed father of Jesse. •Jesse became father of Eliab,
14　his first-born, of Abinadab second, Shimea third, •Nethanel fourth, Raddai
15
16　fifth, •Ozem sixth, David seventh. •Their sisters were Zeruiah and Abigail. Sons
17　of Zeruiah: Abishai, Joab and Asahel: three. •Abigail gave birth to Amasa; the
father of Amasa was Jether the Ishmaelite.

Caleb

18　Caleb son of Hezron became father of Azubah, Ishshah and Jerioth; these
19　are the sons: Jesher, Shobab and Ardon. •Azubah died, and Caleb took Ephrath,
20　who bore him Hur. •Hur became father of Uri, Uri father of Bezalel.
21　Then Hezron married the daughter of Machir, father of Gilead; he took her
22　when he was sixty years old and she bore him Segub. •Segub became father of
23　Jair who held twenty-three towns in the land of Gilead. •Then from Geshur
and Aram he won the Encampments of Jair, Kenath and its outlying villages,
sixty towns. All this belonged to the sons of Machir, father of Gilead.
24　After Hezron's death, Caleb married Ephrathah, wife of Hezron his father,
who bore him Ashhur, father of Tekoa.

Jerahmeel

25　Jerahmeel, Hezron's eldest son had sons: Hezron, his first-born, Ram, Bunah,
26　Oren, Ozem, Ahijah. •Jerahmeel had another wife called Atarah; she was the
mother of Onam.
27　Sons of Ram, Jerahmeel's first-born: Maaz, Jamin and Eker.
28　Sons of Onam: Shammai and Jada, Sons of Shammai: Nadab and Abishur.
29
30　Abishur's wife was called Abihail; she bore him Ahban and Molid. •Sons of
31　Nadab: Seled and Ephraim. Seled died leaving no son. •Sons of Ephraim: Ishi;
32　sons of Ishi: Sheshan; sons of Sheshan: Ahlai. •Sons of Jada, Shammai's brother:
33　Jether and Jonathan. Jether died leaving no sons. •Sons of Jonathan: Peleth and
Zaza.
These are the sons of Jerahmeel.
34
35　Sheshan had no sons,ᵃ only daughters. He had an Egyptian slave Jarha •to
36　whom Sheshan gave his daughter in marriage. She bore him Attai. •Attai became
37　father of Nathan, Nathan father of Zabad, •Zabad father of Ephlal, Ephlal
38
39　father of Obed, •Obed father of Jehu, Jehu father of Azariah, •Azariah father of
40　Helez, Helez father of Eleasah, •Eleasah father of Sismai, Sismai father of
41　Shallum, •Shallum father of Jekamiah, Jekamiah father of Elishama.

Calebᵇ

42　Sons of Caleb, Jerahmeel's brother: Mesha, his first-born, who was the father
43　of Ziph. His son was Mareshah, father of Hebron. •Sons of Hebron: Korah,
44　Tappuah, Rekem and Shema. •Shema became father of Raham, Jorkeam's
45　father. Rekem became father of Shammai. •Shammai's son was Maon, and Maon
became father of Bethzur.

2 a. But see v.31, which must follow a different tradition.　b. Genealogies were often deduced
from relationships between clans. This reconstruction of the descendants of Caleb may differ
from the list in vv.18-24 because it was made at a date when alliances between clans were
different.

Ephah, Caleb's concubine, gave birth to Haran, Moza and Gazez. Haran 46 became father of Gazez.

Sons of Jahdai: Regem, Jotham, Geshan, Pelet, Ephah and Shaaph. 47

Maacah, Caleb's concubine, gave birth to Sheber and Tirhanah. •She gave 48 49 birth to Shaaph, father of Madmannah, and Sheva, father of Machbenah and father of Gibea.

The daughter of Caleb was Achsah.

These are the sons of Caleb. 50

Hur

Sons of Hur, the first-born of Ephrathah: Shobal, father of Kiriath-jearim, Salma, father of Bethlehem, Hareph, father of Beth-gader. •Shobal, father of 51 52 Kiriath-jearim had sons: Haroeh, that is, half of the Manahathites, •and the 53 clans of Kiriath-jearim: the Ithrites, Puthites, Shumathites and Mishraites. Their descendants are the people of Zorah and Eshtaol.

Sons of Salma: Bethlehem, the Netophathites, Atroth-beth-joab, half of the 54 Manahathites, the Zorathites, •the Sophrite clans living at Jabez, the Tirathites, 55 the Shimeathites, the Sucathites. These are the Kenites who came from Hammath; their descendants are the House of Rechab.

C. THE HOUSE OF DAVID

The sons of David

3 These are the sons of David who were born to him in Hebron: the first-born 1 Amnon, by Ahinoam of Jezreel; second, Daniel, by Abigail of Carmel; •third, 2 Absalom son of Maacah the daughter of Talmai king of Geshur; fourth, Adonijah son of Haggith; •fifth, Shephatiah by Abital; sixth, Ithream by his wife Eglah. 3 Six, therefore, were born to him in Hebron, where he reigned for three years 4 and six months.

He reigned for thirty-three years in Jerusalem. •These are the sons who were 5 born to him in Jerusalem: Shimea, Shobab, Nathan, Solomon, the four of them children of Bath-shua, the daughter of Ammiel; •Ibhar, Elishama, Eliphelet, 6 7 Nogah, Nepheg, Japhia, •Elishama, Eliada, Eliphelet: nine. 8

These are all the sons of David, not counting the sons of the concubines. Tamar 9 was their sister.

The kings of Judah [a]

.Sons of Solomon: Rehoboam; Abijah his son, Asa his son, Jehoshaphat his 10 son, •Joram his son, Ahaziah his son, Joash his son, •Amaziah his son, Azariah 11 12 his son, Jotham his son, •Ahaz his son, Hezekiah his son, Manasseh his son, 13 Amon his son, Josiah his son. •Sons of Josiah: Johanan, the first-born, 14 15 Jehoiakim second, Zedekiah third, Shallum fourth. •The sons of Jehoiakim: 16 Jeconiah his son, Zedekiah his son.

The royal line after the exile

Sons of Jeconiah the captive: Shealtiel. His sons: •Malchiram, Pedaiah, 17 18 Shenazzar, Jekamiah, Hoshama, Nedabiah. •Sons of Pedaiah: Zerubbabel and 19 Shimei. Sons of Zerubbabel: Meshullam and Hananiah; Shelomith was their sister. •Sons of Meshullam: Hashubah, Ohel, Berechiah, Hasadiah, Jushab-hesed: 20 five. •Sons of Hananiah: Pelatiah; Jeshaiah his son, Rephaiah his son, Arnan 21 his son, Obadiah his son, Shecaniah his son. •Sons of Shecaniah: Shemaiah, 22 Hattush, Igal, Bariah, Neariah, Shaphat: six. •Sons of Neariah: Elioenai, 23 Hizkiah, Azrikam: three. •Sons of Elioenai: Hodaviah, Eliashib, Pelaiah, 24 Akkub, Johanan, Delaiah, Anani: seven.

D. THE SOUTHERN TRIBES

Judah. Shobal

1 4 Sons of Judah: Perez, Hezron, Carmi, Hur, Shobal.
2 Reaiah son of Shobal became father of Jahath, and Jahath father of Ahumai and Lahad. These are the Zorathite clans.

Hur

3 These are Abi-etam, Jezreel, Ishma, and Idbash, whose sister was called Hazzelelponi.
4 Penuel became father of Gedor, Ezer father of Hushah.
These are the sons of Hur, the first-born of Ephrathah, father of Bethlehem.

Ashhur

5 Ashhur, father of Tekoa, had two wives: Helah and Naarah.
6 Naarah bore him Ahuzzam, Hepher, the Timnites, and the Ahashtarites. These are the sons of Naarah.
7 Sons of Helah: Zereth, Zohar, Ethnan.
8 Koz became father of Anub, Hazzobebah and the clans of Aharhel son of
9 Harum. •Jabez won himself more honour than his brothers. His mother gave
10 him the name Jabez, 'because' she said 'in distress I gave birth to him'. •Jabez called on the God of Israel. 'If you truly bless me,' he said 'you will extend my lands, your hand will be with me, you will keep harm away and my distress will cease.' God granted him what he had asked.

Caleb

11 Chelub, Shuhah's brother, became father of Mehir, who was the father of
12 Eshton. •Eshton became father of Bethrapha, Paseah and Tehinnah father of Irnahash, brother of Eselon the Kenizzite. These are the men of Recah.
13 Sons of Kenaz: Othniel and Seraiah. Sons of Othniel: Hathath and
14 Meonothai, •who became father of Ophrah. Seraiah became father of Joab, father of Geharashim—and they were in fact craftsmen.[a]
15 Sons of Caleb son of Jephunneh: Iru, Elah and Naam. Sons of Elah: Kenaz.
16 Sons of Jehallelel: Ziph, Ziphah, Tiri-a, Asarel.
17 Sons of Ezrah: Jether, Mered, Epher, Jalon. Then she conceived Miriam,
18 Shammai, and Ishbah, the father of Eshtemoa, •whose Judaean wife gave birth to Jered father of Gedor, Heber father of Soco, and Jekuthiel, father of Zanoah. These are the sons of Bithiah, the daughter of Pharaoh whom Mered married.
19 The sons of the wife of Hodiah, the sister of Naham father of Keilah the Garmite and of Eshtemoa the Maacathite.
20 Sons of Shimon: Amnon, Rinnah, Ben-hanan, Tilon.
Sons of Ishi: Zoheth and Ben-zoheth.

Shelah

21 Sons of Shelah son of Judah: Er father of Lecah, Laadah father of Mareshah,
22 and the clans of linenworkers at Beth-ashbea, •Jokim, the men of Cozeba, Joash and Saraph who went to Moab to take wives before returning to Bethlehem.
23 (Events, these, of long ago.) •These were potters and lived at Netaim and Gederah; they stayed with the king there, employed in his workshop.

Simeon

24
25 Sons of Simeon: Nemuel, Jamin, Jarib, Zerah, Shaul; •Shallum was his son,
26 Mibsam his son, Mishma his son. •The sons of Mishma: Hammuel his son,

---

3 a. The list is from Kings; Shallum is the Jehoahaz of Kings.
4 a. The name means 'Valley of Craftsmen'.

Zaccur his son, Shimei his son. •Shimei had sixteen sons and six daughters, 27
but his brothers did not have many children, and the sum of their clans did not
multiply as the sons of Judah did.

They lived in Beersheba, Moladah and Hazar-shual, •Bilhah, Ezem and 28
Tolad, •Bethuel, Hormah and Ziklag, •Beth-marcaboth, Hazar-susim, Beth-biri, 30
Shaaraim. These were their towns until the reign of David. •Their outlying 32
villages were: Etam, Ain, Rimmon, Tochen and Ashan, five towns, •with all 33
the outlying villages round these towns as far as Baalath. Here they had their
settlements and sorted themselves into their various groups.

Meshobab, Jamlech, Joshah son of Amaziah, •Joel, Jehu son of Joshibiah, 34 35
son of Seraiah, son of Asiel, •Elioenei, Jaakobah, Jeshohaiah, Asaiah, Adiel, 36
Jesimiel, Benaiah, •Ziza, Ben-shiphi, Ben-allon, Ben-jedaiah, Ben-shimri, Ben- 37
shemaiah, •These men here named came with their clans and families; they grew 38
in number and spread. •In search of pasture for their flocks they travelled from 39
the Gerar pass to the eastern end of the valley, •where they found good, fat 40
pasture; the land was broad, untroubled, peaceful. Hamites[b] had been living there
before them.

The Simeonites, registered by name, arrived there in the time of Hezekiah 41
king of Judah; they overran their tents and the dwellings they found there. They
put them under a ban still in force today and settled in their place, since there
was pasturage for their flocks.

Some of them, belonging to the sons of Simeon, reached Mount Seir: five 42
hundred men led by Pelatiah, Neariah, Rephaiah, and Uzziel, the sons of Ishi.
They defeated the surviving fugitives of Amalek and still live there today. 43

E. THE TRANSJORDANIAN TRIBES

Reuben

5 Sons of Reuben, first-born of Israel. He was indeed the first-born but, when 1
he violated his father's couch, his birthright was given to the sons of Joseph
son of Israel.

The group of Reuben forfeited the birthright •because Judah proved more 2
powerful than his brothers—a prince having come from him—with Joseph
having the birthright.

Sons of Reuben, first-born of Israel: Hanoch, Pallu, Hezron, Carmi. 3

Joel

Sons of Joel: Shemaiah his son, Gog his son, Shimei his son, •Micah his 4 5
son, Reaiah his son, Baal his son, •Beerah his son, whom Tiglath-pileser king 6
of Assyria carried off into exile. He was a prince of the Reubenites.

His kinsmen, by clans, grouped according to their kinship: Jeiel, the chief, 7
Zechariah, •Bela son of Azaz, son of Shema, son of Joel. 8

Reuben's territory

Reuben, having settled at Aroer, spread as far as Nebo and Baal-meon. •To 9
the east his lands stretched to the beginning of the desert that ends at the river
Euphrates, for he had many herds in the land of Gilead.

During the reign of Saul they waged war on the Hagrites; they suffered 10
defeat at their hands and the Hagrites occupied their tents throughout the
region east of Gilead.

Gad[a]

The sons of Gad lived next to them, inhabiting the land of Bashan as far as 11
Salecah: •Joel, the chief, Shapham second, then Janai and Shaphat in Bashan. 12

13   Their kinsmen, by families: Michael, Meshullam, Sheba, Jorai, Jacan, Zia, Eber: seven.

14   These are the sons of Abihail: Ben-huri, Ben-jaroah, Ben-gilead, Ben-michael,
15 Ben-jeshishai, Ben-jahdo, Ben-buz. •Ahi son of Abdiel, son of Guni, was head of their family.

16   They had settled in Gilead, in Bashan and its dependencies, as well as
17 throughout the pasturages of Sharon to their furthest limit. •They sorted themselves into their various groups in the days of Jotham king of Judah.

18   The sons of Reuben, the sons of Gad, the half-tribe of Manasseh, a number of their fighting men, men who carried shield and spear and could handle the bow, men used to warfare, forty-four thousand seven hundred and sixty of them fit
19 for service, •waged war against the Hagrites, against Jetur, Naphish and Nodab.
20 God came to their help against them, and the Hagrites with all their allies fell into their hands, for they had called on God as they fought, and because they put
21 their trust in him their prayer was heard. •They carried off of the Hagrites' live-stock fifty thousand camels, two hundred and fifty thousand sheep, two thousand
22 donkeys and a hundred thousand people, •for, God directing the battle, the greater part had been killed. And they settled in what had been Hagrite territory until the exile.

The half-tribe of Manasseh

23   The sons of the half-tribe of Manasseh settled in the country between Bashan and Baal-hermon, Senir and Mount Hermon.
24   They were numerous. •These are the heads of their families: Epher, Ishi, Eliel, Azriel, Jeremiah, Hodaviah, Jahdiel. These were stout fighting men, men of renown, heads of their families.
25   But they were unfaithful to the God of their ancestors and prostituted themselves to the gods of the peoples of the land whom God had destroyed before them.
26 So the God of Israel roused the hostility of Pul[b] king of Assyria and of Tiglath-pileser king of Assyria. He deported Reuben, Gad and the half-tribe of Manasseh, taking them off to Halah near Habor and the river Gozan. They are still there today.

F. LEVI

The lineage of the high priests

27,28
6:1,2   Sons of Levi: Gershom, Kohath and Merari. •Sons of Kohath: Amram, Izhar,
29
3 Hebron, Uzziel. •Children of Amram: Aaron, Moses and Miriam. Sons of Aaron: Nadab and Abihu, Eleazar and Ithamar.

30,31
4,5   Eleazar became father of Phinehas, Phinehas father of Abishua, •Abishua
32 father of Bukki, Bukki father of Uzzi. •Uzzi father of Zerahiah, Zerahiah
33
7 father of Meraioth, •Meraioth father of Amariah, Amariah father of Ahitub,
34,35
8,9 Ahitub father of Zadok, Zadok father of Ahimaaz. •Ahimaaz father of Azariah,
36
10 Azariah father of Johanan, •Johanan father of Azariah. It was he who officiated
37
11 as priest in the Temple that Solomon built in Jerusalem. •Azariah became father
38
12 of Amariah, Amariah father of Ahitub, •Ahitub father of Zadok, Zadok father
39,40
13,14 of Shallum, •Shallum father of Hilkiah, Hilkiah father of Azariah, •Azariah
41
15 father of Seraiah, Seraiah father of Jehozadak, •and Jehozadak had to go into exile when, at the hands of Nebuchadnezzar, Yahweh exiled Judah and Jerusalem.

---

b. Non-Israelite peoples living to the S. of Palestine.
5 a. The list of families and their settlements, for Gad and the half-tribe of Manasseh, does not tally with the sources in early books of the O.T. and probably reflects the disposition of these tribes at the time of the Exile.   b. Cf. 2 K 15:19.

The line of Levi

6 Sons of Levi: Gershom, Kohath and Merari. •These are the names of the sons of Gershom: Libni and Shimei. •Sons of Kohath: Amram, Izhar, Hebron, Uzziel. •Sons of Merari: Mahli and Mushi. These are the clans of Levi grouped according to their fathers.

For Gershom: Libni his son, Jahath his son, Zimmah his son, •Joah his son, Iddo his son, Zerah his son, Jeatherai his son.

Sons of Kohath: Amminadab his son, Korah his son, Assir his son, •Elkanah his son, Ebiasaph his son, Assir his son, •Tahath his son, Uriel his son, Uzziah his son, Shaul his son. •Sons of Elkanah: Amasai and Ahimoth. •Elkanah his son, Zophai his son, Nahath his son, •Eliab his son, Jeroham his son, Elkanah his son. •Sons of Elkanah: Samuel his first-born, the second Abijah.

Sons of Merari: Mahli, Libni his son, •Shimei his son, Haggiah his son, Asaiah his son.

The cantors

These are the men David nominated to lead the singing in the Temple of Yahweh when the ark had come to rest there. •They were responsible for the singing before the tabernacle of the Tent of Meeting until Solomon had built the Temple of Yahweh in Jerusalem, and in accordance with the rules laid down for them they did their office.

These are the men who were in office, and their sons:

Of the sons of Kohath: Heman the cantor, the son of Joel, son of Samuel, son of Elkanah, son of Jeroham, son of Eliel, son of Toah, •son of Zuph, son of Elkanah, son of Mahath, son of Amasai, •son of Elkanah, son of Joel, son of Azariah, son of Zephaniah, •son of Tahath, son of Assir, son of Ebiasaph, son of Korah, •son of Izhar, son of Kohath, son of Levi, son of Israel.

His brother Asaph stood at his right hand: Asaph son of Berechiah, son of Shimea, •son of Michael, son of Baaseiah, son of Malchijah, •son of Ethni, son of Zerah, son of Adaiah, •son of Ethan, son of Zimmah, son of Shimei, son of Jahath, son of Gershom, son of Levi.

At the left hand, the sons of Merari: Ethan son of Kishi, son of Abdi, son of Malluch, •son of Hashabiah, son of Amaziah, son of Hilkiah, •son of Amzi, son of Bani, son of Shemer, •son of Mahli, son of Mushi, son of Merari, son of Levi.

The other Levites

Their brothers the Levites were completely dedicated to the service of the tabernacle of the Temple of Yahweh. •Aaron and his sons burned the offerings on the altar of holocaust and on the altar of incense; they were concerned exclusively with the most holy things and with the ritual of atonement for Israel, in accordance with all that Moses the servant of God had laid down.

These are the sons of Aaron: Eleazar his son, Phinehas his son, Abishua his son, •Bukki his son, Uzzi his son, Zerahiah his son, •Meraioth his son, Amariah his son, Ahitub his son, •Zadok his son, Ahimaaz his son.

Where these lived
a. The Aaronitic priests

These are the places they lived in, according to the boundaries of their settlements:

To the sons of Aaron of the Kohath clan (for to these the lot fell) •they gave Hebron in the land of Judah and the pasture lands adjoining. •The fields and villages of this town they gave to Caleb son of Jephunneh, •but to the sons of Aaron they gave the cities of refuge, Hebron, Libnah with its pasture lands, Jattir, Eshtemoa with its pasture lands, •Hilen, Debir, •Ashan, Beth-shemesh each with its pasture lands. •From the tribe of Benjamin they gave Geba, Alemeth and Anathoth, each with its pasture lands. In all, their clans took in thirteen towns.

b. Other Levites

⁴⁶
⁶¹
⁴⁷
⁶² The remaining sons of Kohath were allotted ten towns taken from the clans of the tribe, from the half-tribe, the half of Manasseh. •The sons of Gershom and their clans were allotted thirteen towns taken from the tribe of Issachar, the tribe of Asher, the tribe of Naphtali and the tribe of Manasseh ⁴⁸
⁶³ in Bashan. •The sons of Merari and their clans were allotted twelve towns taken from the tribe of Reuben, the tribe of Gad and the tribe of Zebulun. ⁴⁹
⁶⁴ The sons of Israel gave these towns with their pasture lands to the Levites.

⁵⁰
⁶⁵ Also from the tribes of the sons of Judah, the sons of Benjamin and the sons of Simeon, they allotted the towns to which they gave their names.

⁵¹
⁶⁶
⁵²
⁶⁷ Towns from the tribe of Ephraim also were assigned to the territory of some clans of the sons of Kohath. •They were given the following cities of refuge: Shechem with its pasture lands in the highlands of Ephraim, together with ^{53,54}
^{68,69} Gezer and its pasture lands, •Jokmeam, Beth-horon, •Aijalon and Gath-rimmon, ⁵⁵
⁷⁰ each with its pasture lands, •and from the half-tribe of Manasseh: Aner and Bileam, each with its pasture lands. This for the clan of the remaining sons of Kohath.

⁵⁶
⁷¹
⁵⁷
⁷²
^{58,59}
^{73,74}
^{60,61}
^{75,76} The sons of Gershom were given, from the half-tribe of Manasseh: Golan in Bashan, and Ashtaroth, each with its pasture lands; •from the tribe of Issachar: Kedesh, Daberath, •Ramoth, Anem, each with its pasture lands; •from the tribe of Asher: Mashal, Abdon, •Hukok, Rehob, each with its pasture lands; •from the tribe of Naphtali: Kedesh in Galilee, Hammon, Kiriathaim, each with its pasture lands.

⁶²
⁷⁷
⁶³
⁷⁸
⁶⁴
⁷⁹
⁶⁵
⁸⁰
⁶⁶
⁸¹ To the remainder of the sons of Merari: from the tribe of Zebulun: Rimmono, Tabor, each with its pasture lands; •beyond the Jordan near Jericho, east of Jordan, from the tribe of Reuben: Bezer in the wilderness, Jahzah, •Kedemoth, Mephaath, each with its pasture lands; •from the tribe of Gad: Ramoth in Gilead, Mahanaim, •Heshbon, Jazer, each with its pasture lands.

G. THE NORTHERN TRIBES

Issachar

¹ **7** For the sons of Issachar: Tola, Puah, Jashub, Shimron: four.
² Sons of Tola: Uzzi, Rephaiah, Jeriel, Jahmai, Ibsam, Shemuel, heads of the families of Tola. In the time of David these numbered twenty-two thousand six hundred stout fighting men, grouped according to their kinship.
³ Sons of Uzzi: Izrahiah. Sons of Izrahiah: Michael, Obadiah, Joel, Isshiah.
⁴ Five chiefs in all, •answerable for a battle force numbering thirty-six thousand men, grouped according to their kinship and families; for there were many
⁵ women and children. •They had kinsmen belonging to all the clans of Issachar, eighty-seven thousand stout fighting men, all belonging to one related group.

Benjamin

⁶ Benjamin: Bela, Becher, Jediael: three.
⁷ Sons of Bela: Ezbon, Uzzi, Uzziel, Jerimoth and Iri: five, heads of families, stout fighting men, forming a related group of twenty-two thousand and thirty-four men.
⁸ Sons of Becher: Zemirah, Joash, Eliezer, Elioenai, Omri, Jeremoth, Abijah,
⁹ Anathoth, Alemeth, all these were the sons of Becher; •the heads of their families, stout fighting men, formed a related group, according to their kinship, of twenty thousand two hundred men.
¹⁰ Sons of Jediael: Bilhan. Sons of Bilhan: Jeush, Benjamin, Ehud, Chenaanah,
¹¹ Zethan, Tarshish, Ahishahar. •All these sons of Jediael became heads of families,

stout fighting men, numbering seventeen thousand two hundred men fit for
active service.

Shuppim and Huppim. Sons of Ir: Hushim; his son: Aher.   12

Naphtali

Sons of Naphtali: Jahziel, Guni, Jezer, Shallum. They were the sons of 13
Bilhah.

Manasseh

Sons of Manasseh: Asriel, born of his Aramaean concubine. She gave birth 14
to Machir, father of Gilead. •Machir took a wife for Huppim and Shuppim. 15
His sister's name was Maacah.

The name of the second was Zelophehad. Zelophehad had daughters.

Maacah the wife of Machir gave birth to a son whom she called Peresh. 16
His brother was called Sheresh and his sons Ulam and Rakem.

Sons of Ulam: Bedan. These were the sons of Gilead son of Machir, son of 17
Manasseh.

His sister was Malchath. She gave birth to Ishhod, Abiezer and Mahlah.   18

Shemida had sons: Ahian, Shechem, Likhi and Aniam.   19

Ephraim

Sons of Ephraim: Shuthelah, Bered his son, Tahath his son, Eleadah his son, 20
Tahath his son, •Zabad his son, Shuthelah his son, Ezer and Elead.   21

The men of Gath killed them because they had come down to raid their
cattle. •Ephraim their father mourned long for them and his brothers came to 22
comfort him. •Then Ephraim went to his wife, and she conceived and gave birth 23
to a son whom she called Beriah, 'because' she said 'in my house one is in
misfortune.' [a] •He had a daughter, Sheerah, who built both Lower and Upper 24
Beth-horon and Uzzen-sheerah.

Rephah his son, Shuthelah his son, Tahan his son, •Ladan his son, Ammihud 25 26
his son, Elishama his son, •Nun his son, Joshua his son.   27

They had lands and settlements in Bethel and its outlying towns, in Naaran 28
to the east, in Gezer and its outlying towns to the west, Shechem and its outlying
towns, as far as Ayyah and its outlying towns. •Beth-shean, Taanach, Megiddo, 29
Dor, each with its outlying towns, were in the hands of the sons of Manasseh.
There lived the sons of Joseph son of Israel.

Asher

Sons of Asher: Imnah, Ishvah, Ishvi, Beriah; their sister Serah.   30

Sons of Beriah: Heber and Malchiel. He was the father of Birzaith. •Heber 31 32
became father of Japhlet, Shomer, Hotham and their sister Shua.

Sons of Japhlet: Pasach, Bimhal and Ashvath. These are the sons of Japhlet. 33

Sons of Shomer his brother: Rohgah, Hubbah and Aram.   34

Sons of Helem his brother: Zophah, Imna, Shelesh and Amal. •Sons of 35 36
Zophah: Suah, Harnepher, Shual, Beri and Imrah, •Bezer, Hod, Shamma, 37
Shilshah, Ithran and Beerah. •Sons of Ithran: Jephunneh, Pispa, Ara.   38

Sons of Ulla: Arah, Hanniel, Rizia.   39

All these were sons of Asher, heads of families, stout fighting men; when 40
numbered, they formed a related group of twenty-six thousand men for active
service.

H. BENJAMIN AND JERUSALEM

The line of Benjamin [a]

8 Benjamin became father of Bela, his first-born, Ashbel second, Ahiram third, 1
Nohah fourth, Rapha fifth. •Bela had sons: Addar, Gera father of Ehud, 2 3
Abishua, Naaman and Ahoah, •Gera, Shephuphan and Huram.   4 5

In Geba

6 These are the sons of Ehud. They were heads of families of the inhabitants
7 of Geba and led them into exile at Manahath: •Naaman, Ahijah and Gera.
It was he who led them into exile; he became the father of Uzza and Ahihud.

In Moab

8 He became father of Shaharaim in the plains of Moab after he had dismissed
9 his wives, Hushim and Baara. •By his new wife he had sons: Jobab, Zibia,
10 Mesha, Malcam, •Jeuz, Sachia, Mirmah. These were his sons, heads of families.

In Ono and Lud

11
12 By Hushim he had sons: Abitub and Elpaal. •Sons of Elpaal: Eber, Misham
and Shemed: it was he who built Ono, and Lud with its outlying towns.

In Aijalon

13 Beriah and Shema. They were heads of families of the inhabitants of Aijalon
and put the inhabitants of Gath to flight.
14 His brother: Shashak.

In Jerusalem [b]

15
16 Jeremoth, •Zebadiah, Arad, Eder, •Michael, Ishpah, Joha were sons of
Beriah.
17
18 Zebadiah, Meshullam, Hizki, Haber, •Ishmerai, Izliah, Jobab were sons of
Elpaal.
19,20
21 Jakim, Zichri, Zabdi, •Elioenai, Zille-thai, Eliel, •Adaiah, Beraiah, Shimrath
were sons of Shimei.
22,23
24 Ishpan, Eber, Eliel, •Abdon, Zichri, Hanan, •Hananiah, Elam, Anthothijah,
25 Iphdeiah, Penuel were sons of Shashak.
26
27 Shamsherai, Shehariah, Athaliah, •Jaareshaiah, Elijah, Zichri were sons of
Jeroham.
28 These were the heads of families, grouped according to their kinship. They
lived in Jerusalem.

In Gibeon

29
30 At Gibeon lived Abi-gibeon, whose wife was called Maacah. •His first-born
31
32 son was Abdon, then Zur, Kish, Baal, Ner, Nadab, •Gedor, Ahio, Zecher •and
Mikloth who became father of Shimeah. These also, near their kinsmen, lived
with their kinsmen in Jerusalem.

Saul and his family

33 Ner became father of Kish, Kish father of Saul, Saul father of Jonathan,
34 Malchi-shua, Abinadab and Eshbaal. •Son of Jonathan: Meribbaal. Meribbaal
35
36 became father of Micah. •Sons of Micah: Pithon, Melech, Tarea, Ahaz. •Ahaz
became father of Jehoaddah, Jehoaddah father of Alemeth, Azmaveth and
37 Zimri. Zimri became father of Moza, •Moza father of Binea.
38 Raphah his son, Eleasah his son, Azel his son. •Azel had six sons, whose
names were these: Azrikam, his first-born, then Ishmael, Sheariah, Obadiah,
Hanan. All these were sons of Azel.
39 Sons of Eshek his brother: Ulam, his first-born, Jeush second, Eliphelet third.
40 Ulam had sons, stout fighting men and bowmen. They had numerous sons and
grandsons, a hundred and fifty of them.
All these were sons of Benjamin.

7 a. Connecting the name Beriah with *raah*, 'in misfortune'.
8 a. This list differs from the list of Benjamin's descendants in ch. 7; the purpose of treating
Benjamin again is to lead up to Jerusalem and David's preparations for the Temple.   b. A list
of families made after the repopulation of Jerusalem at the end of the Exile; cf. Ne 11:4-9.

Jerusalem, the holy city of Israel

9 All the Israelites were classified in related groups, and these were already ¹
listed in the Book of the Kings of Israel and Judah when they were deported
to Babylon for their faithlessness. •The first to take up residence in their towns ²
and their estates were the Israelites, the priests, the Levites and the oblates;
in Jerusalem lived Judaeans, Benjaminites, Ephraimites and Manassites. ³

Uthai son of Ammihud, son of Omri, son of Imri, son of Bani, one of the ⁴
sons of Perez son of Judah. •Of the Shilonites: Asaiah, the first-born, and his ⁵
sons. •Of the sons of·Zerah: Jeuel. Also their kinsmen: six hundred and ninety. ⁶

Of the sons of Benjamin: Sallu son of Meshullam, son of Hodaviah, son of ⁷
Hassenuah; •Ibneiah son of Jeroham; Elah son of Uzzi, son of Michri; ⁸
Meshullam son of Shephatiah, son of Reuel, son of Ibnijah. •They had nine ⁹
hundred and fifty-six kinsmen, grouped according to their kinship. All these men
were heads, each of his family.

Of the priests: Jedaiah, Jehoiarib, Jachin, •Azariah son of Hilkiah, son of ¹⁰ ¹¹
Meshullam, son of Zadok, son of Meraioth, son of Ahitub, ruler of the house
of God. •Adaiah son of Jeroham, son of Pashhur, son of Malchijah, Maasai ¹²
son of Adiel, son of Jahzerah, son of Meshullam, son of Meshillemith, son of
Immer. •They had kinsmen, heads of families, one thousand seven hundred and ¹³
sixty stout fighting men who undertook the duties of the Temple of God.

Of the Levites: Shemaiah son of Hasshub, son of Azrikam, son of Hashabiah ¹⁴
of the sons of Merari, •Bakbakkar, Heresh, Galal, Mattaniah son of Mica, son ¹⁵
of Zichri, son of Asaph, •Obadiah son of Shemaiah, son of Galal, son of Jeduthun, ¹⁶
and Berechiah son of Asa, son of Elkanah who lived in the villages of the Netophathites.

The keepers of the gate: Shallum, Akkub, Talmon, Ahiman and their kinsmen. ¹⁷
Shallum, their head, •still keeps station at the royal gate, to the east. These were ¹⁸
the gatekeepers of the camps of the Levites. •Shallum son of Kore, son of ¹⁹
Ebiasaph, son of Korah, with his brother Korahites, of the same family, were
responsible for the liturgical service; they were keepers of the threshold for the
Tent, as their fathers, in charge of the camp of Yahweh, had guarded the entrance
to it. •At one time, Phinehas son of Eleazar had ruled them (may Yahweh ²⁰
be with him!). •Zechariah son of Meshelemiah was keeper of the gate at the ²¹
entrance to the Tent of Meeting. •All the keepers of the gate at the thresholds ²²
were picked men; there were two hundred and twelve of them. They were grouped
by relationship in their various villages. These were confirmed in office by David
and Samuel the seer because of their loyalty. •They and their sons had the ²³
guardianship of the gates of the Temple of Yahweh, the house of the Tent.ᵃ
On the four sides stood the keepers of the gate, east, west, north, and south. ²⁴
Their kinsmen in their villages would come to join them for a week from time ²⁵
to time, •since the four head gatekeepers themselves lived there permanently. ²⁶
They were the Levites responsible for the chambers and treasuries of the house
of God. •They spent the night in the precincts of the house of God, their duties ²⁷
being to guard it and open it every morning.

Some of them were responsible for the furnishings of worship; they counted ²⁸
them whenever they put them away and took them out. •Certain others were in ²⁹
charge of the furniture and all the sacred furnishings, the fine flour, the wine,
the oil, the incense, the spices, •while those who prepared the mixture for the ³⁰
spices were priests.

One of the Levites, Mattithiah—he was the first-born of Shallum the ³¹
Korahite—was, because of his loyalty, made responsible for making the offerings that were baked on the pan. •Some of their kinsmen the Kohathites were ³²
responsible for the loaves to be set out in rows sabbath by sabbath.

These are the cantors, heads of the levitical families. When free from service ³³
they lived in the Temple chambers, because they were on duty day and night.

These were the heads of the levitical families, grouped according to their ³⁴
kinship. These heads lived in Jerusalem.

I. SAUL, DAVID'S PREDECESSOR

The ancestors of Saul

35 At Gibeon lived Abi-gibeon and Jeiel, whose wife was called Maacah,
36,37 His first-born son was Abdon, then Zur, Kish, Baal, Ner, Nadab, •Gedor, Ahio.
38 Zechariah and Mikloth. •Mikloth became father of Shimeam. These also, near
their kinsmen, lived with their kinsmen in Jerusalem.

39 Ner became father of Kish, Kish father of Saul, Saul father of Jonathan,
40 Malchi-shua, Abinadab and Eshbaal. •Son of Jonathan: Meribbaal. Meribbaal
41,42 became father of Micah. •Sons of Micah: Pithon, Melech, Tahrea.• Ahaz
became father of Jarah, Jarah father of Alemeth, Azmaveth and Zimri; Zimri
43 became father of Moza, •Moza father of Binea.

44 Rephaiah his son, Eleasah his son, Azel his son. •Azel had six sons; their
names were these: Azrikam, his first-born, then Ishmael, Bocheru, Sheariah,
Obadiah, Hanan. These were the sons of Azel.

The death of Saul

1,2 **10** The Philistines made war on Israel, and the Israelites fled from the
Philistines and were slaughtered on Mount Gilboa. •The Philistines pressed
Saul and his sons hard and killed Jonathan, Abinadab and Malchi-shua, the
3 sons of Saul. •The fighting grew heavy about Saul; the bowmen took him off
4 his guard, so that he fell wounded by the bowmen. •Then Saul said to his
armour-bearer, 'Draw your sword and run me through with it. I do not want
these uncircumcised men to come and gloat over me'. But his armour-bearer was
5 afraid and would not do it. So Saul took his own sword and fell on it. •His
armour-bearer, seeing that Saul was dead, fell on his sword too and died with
6 him. •And so Saul died, he and his three sons and all his House together.
7 When all the Israelites who were in the valley saw that the men of Israel had
taken to flight and that Saul and his sons were dead, they abandoned their towns
and fled away. The Philistines then came in and occupied them.

8 When the Philistines came on the following day to strip the dead, they found
9 Saul and his sons lying on Mount Gilboa. •They stripped him and, taking his
head and his armour, had them carried round the land of the Philistines to
10 proclaim the good news to their idols and their people. •They placed his armour
in the temple of their god, but his head they nailed up in the temple of Dagon.

11 When all the inhabitants of Gilead heard all that the Philistines had done
12 to Saul, •all the warriors set off; and they took the bodies of Saul and his sons
away and, bringing them to Jabesh, they buried their bones under the tamarisk
of Jabesh; and they fasted for seven days.

13 Saul died because he had shown himself unfaithful to Yahweh: he had not
kept the word of Yahweh; he had even questioned and consulted a necromancer.
14 He had not consulted Yahweh, who therefore put him to death and transferred
the monarchy to David son of Jesse.

II. DAVID, FOUNDER OF THE TEMPLE WORSHIP

A. DAVID THE KING

David is anointed king

1,2 **11** All the tribes of Israel then rallied to David at Hebron. 'Look,' they said
'we are your own flesh and blood. •In days past when Saul was our king,
it was you who led Israel in all their exploits; and Yahweh your God said to

---

9 a. At this time, the tabernacle was at Gibeon, but in this chapter the Chronicler anticipates
various developments known to his own times, e.g. the use of the word 'Temple', the office of
cantors, the Levites as residents of Jerusalem.

you, "You are the man who shall be shepherd of my people Israel, you shall
be the leader of my people Israel". ' •So all the elders of Israel came to the king 3
at Hebron, and David made a pact with them at Hebron in the presence of
Yahweh, and they anointed David king of Israel, in accordance with the word
of Yahweh through Samuel.

The capture of Jerusalem

David with all Israel marched on Jerusalem (that is to say, Jebus); the 4
inhabitants of the country were Jebusites. •The inhabitants of Jebus said to 5
David, 'You will not get in here'. But David captured the fortress of Zion,
that is, the Citadel of David. •David said, 'The first to strike down a Jebusite 6
shall become leader and commander'. Joab son of Zeruiah was first to go up,
and became leader. •David went to live in the fortress, and that is how it came 7
to be called the Citadel of David. •He then built a wall round the city, and the 8
Millo as well as the surrounding wall, while Joab restored the rest of the city.
David grew greater and greater, and Yahweh Sabaoth was with him.   9

David's champions

These are the principal champions of David, those who in his reign grew in 10
power with him and who, with all Israel, had made him king in accordance
with the word of Yahweh concerning Israel. •This is the roll of David's 11
champions: Jashobeam the Hachmonite, leader of the Thirty; it was he who
wielded his battle-axe against three hundred whom he killed at one time.

After him there was Eleazar son of Dodo, the Ahohite, one of the three 12
champions. •He was with David at Pas-dammim when the Philistines mustered 13
for battle there. There was a field full of barley there; the army took flight before
the Philistines, •but they positioned themselves in the middle of the field, defended it 14
and struck down the Philistines. So Yahweh brought about a great victory.

Three out of the Thirty went down to David at the rock near the Cave of 15
Adullam while a company of Philistines was encamped in the Valley of the
Rephaim. •David was then in the stronghold and there was a Philistine garrison 16
in Bethlehem. •'Oh' David sighed 'if someone would fetch me a drink of water from 17
the well that stands by the gate at Bethlehem!' •At this the three champions, forcing 18
their way through the Philistine camp, drew water from the well that stands by
the gate of Bethlehem and, bringing it away, presented it to David. But David
would drink none of it and poured it out as a libation to Yahweh. •'God keep 19
me' he said 'from doing this! Am I to drink the blood of these men? For at
the risk of their lives they brought it.' And so he would not drink. Such were
the deeds of the three champions.

Abishai, the brother of Joab, was leader of the Thirty. It was he who wielded 20
his spear against three hundred whom he killed, winning himself a name among
the Thirty. •He was more famous than the Thirty and became their captain, 21
but he was no rival for the Three.

Benaiah son of Jehoiada, a hero from Kabzeel, a man of many exploits, 22
struck down the two champions of Moab and, one snowy day, went down and
killed the lion in the cistern. •He was also the man who killed an Egyptian, 23
a huge man five cubits tall. The Egyptian had a spear in his hand like a weaver's
beam, but he went down against him with a staff, tore the spear from the
Egyptian's hand and killed the man with it. •Such were the exploits of Benaiah 24
son of Jehoiada, winning him a name among the thirty champions. •He was more 25
famous than the Thirty, but he was no rival for the Three. David put him in
command of his bodyguard.

The valiant champions: 26
Asahel the brother of Joab.
Elhanan son of Dodo, from Bethlehem.
Shammoth from Harod.   27

Helez the Pelonite.

28 Ira son of Ikkesh, from Tekoa.
Abiezer from Anathoth.

29 Sibbecai from Hushah.
Ilai from Ahoh.

30 Maharai from Netophah.
Heled son of Baanah, from Netophah.

31 Ithai son of Ribai, from Gibeah of Benjamin.
Benaiah from Pirathon.

32 Hurai from the wadis of Gaash.
Abiel from Beth-ha-arabah.

33 Azmaveth from Baharum.
Eliahba from Shaalbon.

34 Bene-hashem from Gizon.
Jonathan son of Shagee, from Harar.

35 Ahiam son of Sachar, from Harar.
Eliphelet son of Ur.

36 Hepher from Mecherah.
Ahijah the Pelonite.

37 Hezro from Carmel.
Naarai son of Ezbai.

38 Joel the brother of Nathan.
Mibhar son of Hagri.

39 Zelek the Ammonite.
Naharai from Beeroth, armour-bearer to Joab son of Zeruiah.

40 Ira from Jattir.
Gareb from Jattir.

41 Uriah the Hittite.
Zabad son of Ahlai.

42 Adina son of Shiza the Reubenite, leader of the Reubenites and over the Thirty.

43 Hanan son of Maacah.
Joshaphat the Mithnite.

44 Uzzia from Ashteroth.
Shama and Jeiel, sons of Hotham the Aroerite.

45 Jediael son of Shimri, and Joha his brother, the Tizite.

46 Eliel the Mahavite.
Jeribai and Joshaviah, sons of Elnaam.
Ithmah the Moabite.

47 Eliel, Obed, and Jaasiel from Zoba.

David's first supporters

1 **12** These are the men who rallied to David at Ziklag when he was still kept from the presence of Saul son of Kish; they were champions, a standby 2 in battle, ·who could handle the bow with right hand or with left, who could use stones or arrows.

3 Of the kinsmen of Saul the Benjaminite: ·Ahiezer the leader, and Joash, sons of Hasshemar from Gibeah, Jeziel and Pelet, sons of Azmaveth, Beracah and 4 Jehu from Anathoth, ·Ishmaiah from Gibeon, a champion among the Thirty,
5 and over the Thirty; ·Jeremiah, Jahaziel, Johanan and Jozabad from Gederoth,
6,7 Eluzai, Jerimoth, Bealiah, Shemariah, Shephatiah from Hariph, ·Elkanah,
5,6
8 Isshiah, Azarel, Joezer, Jashobeam, Korahites, ·Joelah, Zebadiah, sons of
9 Jeroham from Gedor.

9 Some Gadites seceded to David in the stronghold in the wilderness. They
8 were stout fighting men and trained, well used to shield and spear. Lions they
10 were in aspect, and, for speed, gazelles on the mountains. ·Ezer was the leader,
9

Obadiah second, Eliab third, •Mishmannah fourth, Jeremiah fifth, •Attai sixth, 11,12 / 10,11
Eliel seventh, •Johanan eighth, Elzabad ninth, •Jeremiah tenth, Machbannai 13,14 / 12,13
eleventh. •These sons of Gad were troop commanders, each one in command, 14
the lesser of a hundred, the greater of a thousand. •These are the men who 16 / 15
crossed the Jordan in the first month, when it overflows its course, and put to
flight all who lived on its banks, both east and west.

Certain Benjaminites, too, and Judaeans came to David in the stronghold. 17 / 16
David went forward to them and addressed them. 'If you come to me as friends' 18 / 17
he said 'to give me help, then I am ready to join with you. But if it is to betray
me to my enemies, when I have done no wrong, then may the God of our
ancestors take note and give judgement.'

Then the spirit took possession of Amasai, leader of the Thirty: 19 / 18

> 'Go forth, David! Peace be with you, son of Jesse!
> Peace to you, peace to him that helps you,
> for your help is your God.'

David accepted them and added them to his other company commanders. 20 / 19

Certain Manassites deserted to David as he was setting out with the 20 / 19
Philistines to fight Saul. But he gave them no help because the Philistine chiefs,
after consultation, dismissed him. 'If he deserted to his master Saul' they said
'it would cost us our heads.' •He was on his way to Ziklag when these 21 / 20
Manassites deserted to him: Adnah, Jozabad, Jediael, Michael, Jozabad, Elihu,
Zillethai, commanders of thousands in Manasseh. •This was a reinforcement 22 / 21
for David and his troops, since they were all valiant champions and became
officers in the army.

Indeed reinforcements reached David every day, so that his camp grew into 23 / 22
a camp of prodigious size.

The warriors who assured David's kingship

These are the figures from the roll of warriors equipped for battle who joined 24 / 23
David at Hebron to transfer Saul's kingship to him in accordance with the
order of Yahweh:

Sons of Judah carrying shield and spear: six thousand eight hundred warriors 25 / 24
equipped for battle;

of the sons of Simeon; seven thousand one hundred champions valiant in war; 26 / 25

of the sons of Levi: four thousand six hundred, •in addition to Jehoiada, 27,28 / 26,27
in command of the Aaronites, with three thousand seven hundred of these,
Zadok, a young and valiant champion, and twenty-two commanders of his family; 29 / 28

of the sons of Benjamin: three thousand kinsmen of Saul, most of them 30 / 29
hitherto in the service of the House of Saul;

of the sons of Ephraim: twenty thousand eight hundred valiant champions, 31 / 30
men famous in their families;

of the half-tribe of Manasseh: eighteen thousand men assigned by name to 32 / 31
go and proclaim David king;

of the sons of Issachar, sound judges of the times when Israel should take 33 / 32
action, and the way to do it: two hundred chiefs and all their kinsmen under
their command;

of Zebulun: fifty thousand men fit for service, marshalled for battle, with 34 / 33
warlike weapons of every kind, staunch-hearted auxiliaries;

of Naphtali: a thousand commanders, and with them thirty-seven thousand 35 / 34
men armed with shield and spear;

of the Danites: twenty-eight thousand six hundred men marshalled for battle; 36 / 35

of Asher: forty thousand men fit for service, marshalled for battle; 37 / 36

from Transjordania: a hundred and twenty thousand men of Reuben, Gad 38 / 37
and the half-tribe of Manasseh, with warlike weapons of every kind.

³⁹⁄₃₈ All these fighting men, marshalled reinforcements, came to Hebron with the purpose and determination to proclaim David king over all Israel; and the rest of ⁴⁰⁄₃₉ Israel, too, were all of one mind in making David king. •For three days they stayed there, eating and drinking with David.

⁴¹⁄₄₀ Their kinsmen had made preparations for them; •furthermore, from as far as Issachar and Zebulun and Naphtali their neighbours brought provisions, by donkey and camel, mule and ox—flour cakes, fig cakes, bunches of raisins, wine, oil, quantities of oxen and sheep; for there was joy in Israel.

The ark brought back from Kiriath-jearim

1 **13** David conferred with the commanders of thousands and of hundreds and
2 with all the leaders. •To the whole assembly of Israel David said, 'If this has your approval, and if Yahweh our God wills it so, we will send messengers to the rest of our brothers throughout the territories of Israel, and also to the priests and Levites in their towns and adjacent lands, bidding them join us.
3 We will then recover the ark of our God, for in the time of Saul we neglected it.'

4 The whole assembly agreed to this, for in the eyes of all the people it was
5 the right thing to do. •So David gathered all the people together from the Shihor of Egypt to the Pass of Hamath to bring the ark of God from Kiriath-
6 jearim. •Then David and all Israel went up to Baalah, to Kiriath-jearim in Judah, to bring up from there the ark of God which bears the name of Yahweh
7 who is seated on the cherubs. •At Abinadab's house they placed the ark of God
8 on a new cart. Uzzah and Ahio were leading the cart. •David and all Israel danced before God with all their might, singing to the accompaniment of lyres,
9 harps, tambourines, cymbals, trumpets. •When they came to the threshing-floor of the Javelin, Uzzah stretched his hand out to hold the ark, as the oxen
10 were making it tilt. •Then the anger of Yahweh blazed out against Uzzah and he struck him down because he had laid his hand on the ark, and he died there
11 in the presence of God. •David was displeased that Yahweh had broken out against Uzzah, and that place was called Perez-uzzah as it still is now.

12 David went in fear of God that day. 'However can I bring the ark of God
13 to my home?' he said. •So David did not take the ark home to the Citadel of
14 David, but took it to the house of Obed-edom of Gath. •The ark of God remained with the family of Obed-edom, in his house, for three months, and Yahweh blessed the family of Obed-edom and everything that belonged to him.

David at Jerusalem, his palace, his children

1 **14** Hiram king of Tyre sent envoys to David with cedar wood and stone-
2 masons and carpenters to build him a palace. •David then knew that Yahweh had confirmed him as king over Israel, and that for the sake of his people Israel his reign was being made glorious.

3 At Jerusalem David took more wives and fathered more sons and daughters.
4 These are the names of the children born to him in Jerusalem: Shammua, Shobab,
^{5,6}⁄₇ Nathan, Solomon, •Ibhar, Elishua, Elpelet, •Nogah, Nepheg, Japhia, •Elishama, Beeliada, Eliphelet.

Victories over the Philistines

8 When the Philistines heard that David had been anointed king of all Israel, they all marched up to seek him out. On hearing this, David went out to meet
9 them. •When the Philistines arrived they deployed in the Valley of the Rephaim.
10 David consulted God; 'Shall I attack the Philistines?' he asked. 'Will you deliver them into my power?' Yahweh answered him, 'Attack! I will deliver them into
11 your power.' •Accordingly they went up to Baal-perazim and there David defeated them. David said, 'Through me God has made a breach in my enemies like a breach the waters make'. For this reason that place was called Baal-perazim.

They had left their gods behind them there, and David ordered them to be burnt. 12

Again the Philistines deployed in the valley. •David again consulted God, 13 14 and God answered, 'Do not attack them from the front; go round and engage them opposite the balsam trees. •When you hear the sound of steps in the tops 15 of the balsam trees, launch your attack, for that will be God going out ahead of you to rout the army of the Philistines.' •David did as God had ordered, and 16 they routed the Philistine army from Gibeon as far as Gezer.

The fame of David spread into every region, and Yahweh made him feared 17 by every nation.

B. THE ARK IN THE CITADEL OF DAVID

Preparations for moving the ark

15 He put up buildings for himself in the Citadel of David and prepared 1 a place for the ark of God, and he pitched a tent for it. •Then he said, 2 'The ark of God may be moved only by the Levites, since Yahweh has chosen them to carry the ark of Yahweh and to serve him always'.

Then David gathered all Israel together in Jerusalem to bring the ark of 3 God up to the place he had prepared for it. •David called together the sons of 4 Aaron and the sons of Levi: •of the sons of Kohath: Uriel the chief and his 5 hundred and twenty kinsmen; •of the sons of Merari: Asaiah the chief and his 6 two hundred and twenty kinsmen; •of the sons of Gershom: Joel the chief and 7 his hundred and thirty kinsmen; •of the sons of Elizaphan: Shemaiah the chief 8 and his two hundred kinsmen; •of the sons of Hebron: Eliel the chief and eighty 9 kinsmen; •of the sons of Uzziel: Amminadab the chief and his hundred and 10 twelve kinsmen.

David summoned the priests Zadok and Abiathar, and the Levites Uriel, 11 Asaiah, Joel, Shemaiah, Eliel and Amminadab. •To these he said, 'You are 12 the heads of the levitical families. Sanctify yourselves,[a] you and your kinsmen, and bring the ark of Yahweh, the God of Israel, up to the place I have prepared for it. •It was because you were not there the first time that Yahweh our God 13 broke out against us,[b] because we did not approach him in the right way.' •So the 14 priests and the Levites sanctified themselves to bring up the ark of Yahweh, the God of Israel, •and the Levites carried the ark of God with the shafts on 15 their shoulders, as Moses had ordered in accordance with the word of Yahweh.

David then told the heads of the Levites to assign duties for their kinsmen 16 as cantors, with their various instruments of music, harps and lyres and cymbals, to play joyful tunes. •The Levites then appointed Heman son of Joel, Asaph 17 son of Berechiah, one of his brothers, Ethan son of Kushaiah, one of their Merarite kinsmen; •and with them, next in rank, their kinsmen: Zechariah son 18 of Jaaziel, Shemiramoth, Jehiel, Unni, Eliab, Benaiah, Maaseiah, Mattithiah, Eliphelehu, Mikneiah, Obed-edom, Jeiel, keepers of the gate. •Heman, Asaph 19 and Ethan, the cantors, were to clash the cymbals of bronze; •Zechariah, 20 Jaaziel, Shemiramoth, Jehiel, Unni, Eliab, Maaseiah and Benaiah were to play the keyed harp. •Mattithiah, Eliphelehu, Mikneiah, Obed-edom, Jeiel and 21 Azaziah, giving the beat, were to play the octave lyre. •Chenaniah, a chief of 22 the Levites and versed in divine oracles, was to expound these, being expert in them. •Berechiah and Elkanah were to be gatekeepers to the ark. •The priests 23 24 Shebaniah, Joshaphat, Nethanel, Amasai, Zechariah, Benaiah and Eliezer were to sound the trumpet before the ark of God. Obed-edom and Jehiah were to be gatekeepers to the ark.[c]

The ark is brought to Jerusalem

So David, with the elders of Israel and the commanders of thousands, went 25 to bring up the ark of the covenant of Yahweh from Obed-edom's house with great rejoicing. •And since God was helping the Levites who carried the ark of 26

27 the covenant of Yahweh, they sacrificed seven bulls and seven rams. •David was wearing a cloak of fine linen, like all the Levites who carried the ark, the cantors and Chenaniah, the officer in charge of its transportation. David also
28 wore the linen ephod. •Thus all Israel brought up the ark of the covenant of Yahweh with acclaim, to the sound of the horn, of trumpets, of cymbals, making
29 harp and lyre resound. •Now as the ark of the covenant of Yahweh entered the Citadel of David, Michal the daughter of Saul was watching from the window and saw King David dancing and exultant; and she despised him in her heart.

1　**16** They brought the ark of God in and put it inside the tent that David had pitched for it; and they offered holocausts before God, and communion
2 sacrifices. •And when David had finished offering holocausts and communion
3 sacrifices, he blessed the people in the name of Yahweh. •He then distributed to all the Israelites, men and women, a loaf of bread each, a portion of dates, and a raisin cake.

The service of the Levites before the ark

4　David appointed some of the Levites as ministers before the ark of Yahweh,
5 to commemorate, glorify and praise Yahweh, the God of Israel: •first Asaph, second Zechariah, then Uzziel, Shemiramoth, Jehiel, Mattithiah, Eliab, Benaiah, Obed-edom, Jeiel. These were to play the harp and the lyre, Asaph was to clash
6 the cymbals. •The priests Benaiah and Jahaziel were to keep sounding the
7 trumpet before the ark of the covenant of Yahweh. •That day, David, foremost in praising Yahweh, entrusted this song of praise [a] to Asaph and his kinsmen:

8　　Give thanks to Yahweh, call his name aloud,
　　　proclaim his deeds to the peoples.
9　　Sing to him, play to him,
　　　tell over all his marvels.
10　　Glory in his holy name,
　　　let the hearts that seek Yahweh rejoice!

11　　Seek Yahweh and his strength,
　　　seek his face untiringly;
12　　remember the marvels he has done,
　　　his wonders, the judgements from his mouth.
13　　Stock of Israel his servant,
　　　sons of Jacob his chosen one,
14　　he is Yahweh our God;
　　　his authority is over all the earth.

15　　Remember his covenant for ever,
　　　his word of command for a thousand generations,
16　　the pact he made with Abraham,
　　　his oath to Isaac.

17　　He established it as a statute for Jacob,
　　　an everlasting covenant for Israel.
18　　'I give you a land,' he said
　　　'Canaan, your allotted heritage,
19　　'there where you were easily counted,
　　　'few in number, strangers to the country.'

20　　They went from nation to nation,
　　　from one kingdom to another people,

---

15 a. By the ceremonies of purification.　b. When he struck Uzzah dead, 13:10-11.　c. Three lists are combined in this chapter: first, the three famous cantors; second, twelve keepers of the gate; third, a list of seven priests and two gatekeepers to the ark which corresponds with the situation in the Chronicler's own day.
16 a. Mainly consisting of extracts from Ps 105, 96 and 106.

he let no man oppress them,   21
he punished kings on their behalf.
'Do not touch my anointed ones,' he said   22
'do not harm my prophets.'

Sing to Yahweh, all the earth.   23
Proclaim his salvation day after day,
tell of his glory among the nations,   24
tell his marvels to every people.

Yahweh is great, loud must be his praise,   25
he is to be feared beyond all gods.
Nothingness, all the gods of the nations.   26
Yahweh himself made the heavens;
in his presence are splendour and majesty,   27
in his sanctuary power and joy.

Pay tribute to Yahweh, families of the peoples,   28
tribute to Yahweh of glory and power,
tribute to Yahweh of his name's due glory.   29

Bring out the offering, bear it before him,
worship Yahweh in his sacred court,
tremble before him, all the earth!   30

Firm has he made the world, and unshakeable.
Let the heavens be glad, let earth rejoice!   31
Say among the nations, 'Yahweh is king!'
Let the sea thunder and all that it holds,   32
let the fields exult and all that is in them,
let all the woodland trees cry out for joy,   33
at the presence of Yahweh;
for he comes to judge the earth.

Give thanks to Yahweh, for he is good,   34
his love is everlasting.

Say, 'God of our salvation, save us,   35
gather us, rescue us from among the heathen,
to give thanks to your holy name
and to find our happiness in praising you.'

Blessed be Yahweh the God of Israel   36
from all eternity and for ever!
And let all the people say, 'Amen!'
Alleluia!

There before the ark of the covenant of Yahweh David left Asaph and his 37 kinsmen to maintain a permanent ministry before the ark as each day's ritual required, •and also Obed-edom, with his sixty-eight kinsmen. Obed-edom son 38 of Jeduthun, and Hosah were to be keepers of the gate.

Zadok the priest and the priests, his kinsmen, he left before the tabernacle 39 of Yahweh on the high place at Gibeon •to offer holocausts to Yahweh 40 unfailingly, morning and evening, on the altar of holocaust, and to carry out all that is written in the Law of Yahweh laid down for Israel. •With them were 41 Heman and Jeduthun and the rest of those who were chosen and assigned by name to give praise to God, 'for his love is everlasting'. •With them were Heman 42 and Jeduthun who were to sound the trumpets, cymbals and musical instruments accompanying the hymns to God. The sons of Jeduthun were given charge of the gate.

43   Then all went away, each to his own house, and David returned to bless his household.

The prophecy of Nathan

17 Once David had settled into his house, he said to the prophet Nathan, 'Here am I living in a house of cedar, while the ark of Yahweh's covenant
2 is still beneath the awning of a tent'. •Nathan said to David, 'Do all that is in your mind, for God is with you'.

3   But that very night the word of Yahweh came to Nathan,

4   'Go and tell my servant David, "Yahweh says this: You are not the man
5 to build me a house to dwell in. •I have never stayed in a house from the day I brought Israel out until today, but went from tent to tent, from one shelter
6 to another. •In all my journeying with the whole of Israel, did I say to any one of the judges of Israel, whom I had appointed as shepherds of my people: Why
7 have you not built me a house of cedar? •This is what you must say to my servant David: Yahweh Sabaoth says this: I took you from the pasture,
8 from following the sheep, to be leader of my people Israel. •I have been with you on all your expeditions; I have cut off all your enemies before you. I will
9 give you fame as great as the fame of the greatest on earth. •I will provide a place for my people Israel; I will plant them there and they shall live in that place and never be disturbed again; nor shall the wicked continue to destroy
10 them, as they did •in the days when I appointed judges over my people Israel; I will subdue all their enemies. I will make you great; Yahweh will make
11 you a House. •And when your days are ended and you must go to your ancestors, I will preserve your offspring after you, a son of your own, and make
12 his sovereignty secure. •It is he who shall build a house for me and I will make
13 his throne firm for ever. •I will be a father to him and he a son to me. I will not withdraw my favour from him, as I withdrew it from your predecessor.
14 I will preserve him for ever in my house and in my kingdom; and his throne shall be established for ever." '

15   Nathan related all these words to David and this whole revelation.

David's prayer

16   King David then went in and, seated before Yahweh, said:
'Who am I, Yahweh God, and what is my House, that you have led me as
17 far as this? •Yet in your eyes, O God, this is still not far enough, and you make your promises extend to your servant's House into the distant future. You show
18 me as it were a line of men, and it is Yahweh God, who promises it. •What more can David say to you for the honour you have given to your servant?
19 You yourself have singled out your servant. •For your servant's sake, this dog of yours, you have done such a great thing by revealing all this greatness to come.
20 There is none like you, no God except you alone, that we have ever heard of.
21 Is there another people on the earth like your people Israel, with a God setting out to redeem it and make it his people, giving yourself a name for great and terrible things by driving nations out before your people whom you redeemed
22 from Egypt? •You made your people Israel your own people for ever; and you,
23 Yahweh, have become their God. •Now, Yahweh, let the promise you have made to your servant and to his House be always kept, and do as you have said.
24 May this promise hold good and your name be exalted for ever; may they say, "Yahweh Sabaoth is the God of Israel, he is God for Israel." The House of your
25 servant David will be made secure in your presence, •since you yourself, my God, have made the revelation to your servant that you would build him a House; and so your servant has ventured to offer this prayer in your presence.
26 Yes, Yahweh, you are God indeed, and you have made this kind promise to your
27 servant. •Be pleased, then, to bless the House of your servant, that it may continue for ever in your presence; for what you, Yahweh, have blessed is blessed for ever.'

The wars of David

18 After this, David defeated the Philistines and subdued them. From the 1 hands of the Philistines he took Gath and its outlying villages. •He also 2 defeated the Moabites; the Moabites became subject to David, paying him tribute.

At Hamath David defeated Hadadezer king of Zobah on his way to 3 consolidate his power over the river Euphrates. •David captured one thousand 4 chariots, seven thousand charioteers and twenty thousand foot soldiers from him; David hamstrung all the chariot teams, keeping only a hundred of them. The Aramaeans of Damascus came to the help of Hadadezer king of Zobah, 5 but David killed twenty-two thousand men of the Aramaeans. •Then David 6 imposed governors on Aram of Damascus, and the Aramaeans became subject to David, paying him tribute. Wherever David went, God gave him victory. David took the golden shields carried by the guards of Hadadezer and brought 7 them to Jerusalem. •From Tibhath and from Cun, towns belonging to Hadadezer, 8 David took a great quantity of bronze; with this Solomon made the bronze Sea and the bronze pillars and furnishings.

When Tou king of Hamath heard that David had defeated the entire army 9 of Hadadezer king of Zobah, •he sent his son Hadoram to King David to greet 10 him and to congratulate him on fighting and defeating Hadadezer, since Hadadezer was the enemy of Tou. He sent articles of every kind in gold, silver and bronze, •which King David also consecrated to Yahweh together with the 11 silver and gold he had levied from all the nations: Edom, Moab, Ammonites, Philistines, Amalek.

Abishai son of Zeruiah defeated the Edomites in the Valley of Salt, eighteen 12 thousand of them. •He imposed governors on Edom, and all the Edomites 13 became subject to David. Wherever David went, God gave him victory.

The exploits of David's commanders

David ruled over all Israel, administering law and justice to all his people. •Joab 14
son of Zeruiah was in command of the army; Jehoshaphat son of Ahilud was 15
recorder; •Zadok son of Ahitub and Abiathar son of Ahimelech were priests; 16
Shavsha was secretary; •Benaiah son of Jehoiada was in command of the 17
Cherethites and Pelethites; David's sons held the first place at the king's side.ᵃ

19 After this, Nahash king of the Ammonites died and his son Hanun suc- 1 ceeded him. •David thought, 'I will show kindness to Hanun son of Nahash 2 since his father was kind to me'. And David sent messengers with his condo-lences on his father's death. But when David's servants reached Hanun in the land of the Ammonites to present these condolences, •the Ammonite leaders, 3 said to Hanun, 'Do you imagine David means to honour your father when he sends you messengers of sympathy? On the contrary, the reason why his servants have come to you is to explore, overthrow and reconnoitre the country.' Whereupon Hanun seized David's servants, shaved them, cut their clothes half- 4 way up to the buttocks, and sent them away. •David was soon told what had 5 happened to these men; he sent someone to meet them, for the men were covered with shame. 'Stay in Jericho' the king said 'until your beards have grown again, and come back then.'

The Ammonites saw that they had incurred the enmity of David, and 6 accordingly Hanun and the Ammonites sent a thousand talents of silver to hire chariots and charioteers from the Aramaeans of Upper Mesopotamia, of Maacah and of Zobah. •They hired thirty-two thousand chariots; also the king 7 of Maacah with his army. These came and encamped before Medeba, while the Ammonites, having left their towns and mustered, were advancing to the war. •When David heard this, he sent Joab with all the common soldiers and 8 the champions. •The Ammonites marched out and drew up their line of battle 9 at the approaches to the town, but the kings who had come kept their distance in the open country. •Joab, seeing that he had to fight on two fronts, to his 10

front and to his rear, chose the best of Israel's picked men and drew them up
11 in line facing the Aramaeans. •He entrusted the rest of the army to his brother
12 Abishai, and drew them up in line facing the Ammonites. •'If the Aramaeans
prove too strong for me,' he said 'you must come to my help; if the Ammonites
13 prove too strong for you, I will come to yours. •Take courage and stand firm
for the sake of our people and the towns of our God. And may Yahweh do as he
14 thinks right.' •Joab and the force with him joined battle with the Aramaeans,
15 who fled before him. •When the Ammonites saw that the Aramaeans had taken
flight, they too fled before Abishai, Joab's brother, and withdrew into their
town. Then Joab came back to Jerusalem.

16   Seeing that they had been defeated by Israel, the Aramaeans sent messengers
and mobilised the Aramaeans from beyond the river, with Shophach, commander
17 of Hadadezer's army, at their head. •Word of this was brought to David, who
mustered all Israel, crossed the Jordan, made contact with them and took up
position near them. David drew up his line of battle facing the Aramaeans, who
18 then engaged him. •But the Aramaeans gave ground before Israel, and David
killed seven thousand of their chariot teams and forty thousand foot soldiers.
19 He also killed Shophach their general. •When the vassals of Hadadezer saw
that they had been defeated by Israel, they made peace with David and became
subject to him. The Aramaeans were reluctant to give any more help to the
Ammonites.

1 **20** At the turn of the year, the time when kings go campaigning, Joab led out
the troops and ravaged the land of the Ammonites and went to lay siege
to Rabbah. David, however, remained in Jerusalem. Joab reduced Rabbah and
2 dismantled it. •David took the crown from the head of Milcom and found that
it weighed a talent of gold; in it was set a precious stone which made an
ornament for David's head. He carried off a great quantity of spoil from the
3 town. •He brought away its population and set them to work with saws, iron
picks and axes. David treated all the Ammonite towns in the same way. Then
David and the whole army returned to Jerusalem.

4   After this, war with the Philistines was resumed at Gezer. This was when
Sibbecai of Hushah killed Sippai, a descendant of the Rephaim. The Philistines
were subdued.

5   War with the Philistines broke out again, and Elhanan son of Jair killed
Lahmi, the brother of Goliath of Gath, the shaft of whose spear was like a
weaver's beam.

6   There was another battle at Gath, where there was a man of huge stature
with six fingers on each hand and six toes on each foot, twenty-four in all. He
7 too was a descendant of Rapha. •Jonathan, son of David's brother Shimea,
killed him when he defied Israel.

8   These men were descended from Rapha of Gath and they fell at the hands
of David and his guards.

C. PRELUDE TO THE BUILDING OF THE TEMPLE

The census

1 **21** Satan rose against Israel and incited David to take a census of the
2   Israelites. •David said to Joab and to the senior army officers, 'Go, and
take a census of Israel, from Beersheba to Dan, then come back and tell me the
3 total.' •Joab said, 'May Yahweh multiply the people a hundred times! My lord
king, are they not all servants of my lord? Why should my lord make this
4 enquiry? Why should guilt be brought on Israel?' •But the king enforced his

---

18 a. According to 2 S they were priests; for the Chronicler, priests are of levitical and not
Judaean descent.

order on Joab, and Joab went away, covered the whole of Israel, and then returned
to Jerusalem. •Joab gave David the figures for the census of the people: the 5
whole of Israel numbered one million one hundred thousand men capable of
drawing sword, and Judah four hundred and seventy thousand capable of
drawing sword. •Joab had found the king's command so distasteful that he had 6
taken no census of Levi or of Benjamin.

The pestilence. God's forgiveness

God looked with displeasure on these proceedings, and he struck Israel. 7
Then David said to God, 'I have committed a grave sin by doing this. But now 8
I beg you to forgive your servant for this fault. I have been very foolish.' •Then 9
Yahweh spoke to Gad, David's seer, •'Go and say to David, "Yahweh 10
says this: I offer you three things; choose one of them for me to do to you".'
So Gad went to David and said, 'Yahweh, says this, "Take your choice: 11
three years of famine, three months of disaster at the hands of your enemies, 12
with the sword of your enemies thrusting at you, or the sword of Yahweh and
three days' pestilence in the country, with the angel of Yahweh ravaging all the
territory of Israel". Now decide how I am to answer him who sends me.'
'This is a hard choice' David said to Gad. 'But let me rather fall into the power 13
of Yahweh, since his mercy is very great; and not into the power of men.'
So Yahweh sent a pestilence on Israel, and seventy thousand men of the 14
Israelites died. •Then God sent the angel to Jerusalem to destroy it, but as he 15
was about to destroy it, Yahweh looked and thought better of this evil; and
he said to the destroying angel, 'Enough! Now withdraw your hand.' The angel
of Yahweh was standing beside the threshing-floor of Ornan the Jebusite.
David, raising his eyes, saw the angel of Yahweh standing between earth and 16
heaven, a drawn sword in his hand stretched out towards Jerusalem. Then
David and the elders, clothed in sackcloth, fell on their faces. •'Was it not I who 17
sinned, who did this most wicked thing? But these, this flock, what have they
done? Yahweh my God, let your hand lie heavy on me and on my family; but
let your people escape the plague.'

The altar is built

The angel of Yahweh then said to Gad, 'David must go up and erect an altar 18
to Yahweh on the threshing-floor of Ornan the Jebusite.' •So David went up 19
at the word which Gad had spoken in the name of Yahweh. •Now Ornan, as 20
he turned, had seen the angel and had hidden, with his four sons. Ornan was
threshing wheat •when David came to him. Ornan looked down, saw David, came 21
off the threshing-floor and with his face to the ground did homage to David.
Then David said to Ornan, 'Let me have the site of this threshing-floor, to build 22
an altar to Yahweh. Let me have it at its full price. For then the plague will
be turned away from the people.' •'Take it' Ornan said to David 'and let my 23
lord the king do as he thinks right. Look, I will give you the oxen for holocausts,
the threshing-sled for the wood and the wheat for the oblation. I give them all.'
But King David said to Ornan, 'No. I must buy it from you at the full price; 24
I will not take for Yahweh what belongs to you, offering holocausts that cost
me nothing.' •So David gave Ornan six hundred shekels of gold by weight for 25
the site.
David built an altar there to Yahweh and offered holocausts and communion 26
sacrifices. He called on Yahweh, and Yahweh answered him with fire from
heaven on the altar of holocaust •and ordered the angel to sheathe his sword. 27
Then it was, seeing that Yahweh had answered him on the threshing-floor of 28
Ornan the Jebusite, that David offered sacrifice there. •The tabernacle of Yahweh 29
that Moses had made in the wilderness and the altar of holocaust were at that
time on the high place at Gibeon, •but David had not been able to go into 30
God's presence there to consult him, so fearful was he of the sword of the angel

1 of Yahweh. **22** Then David said, 'Here is the house of Yahweh God; and this shall be the altar of holocaust for Israel'.

Preparations for the building of the Temple[a]

2 David gave orders for the gathering of all the strangers living in the land of Israel and set stonecutters preparing dressed stones for building the house of
3 God. •David furthermore stored up great quantities of iron to make nails for the leaves of the doors and for clamps, and more bronze than could be weighed;
4 logs of cedar too, beyond number, the Sidonians and Tyrians having brought cedar logs to David in great quantities.
5 Then David said, 'My son Solomon is young, of tender years, and the house to be built for Yahweh must be of great splendour, renowned for its magnificence in every country. I will make preparations for him.' And so, before he
6 died, David made ample preparations. •He then summoned his son Solomon
7 and instructed him to build a house for Yahweh, the God of Israel. •'My son,' David said to Solomon 'my heart was set on building a house for the name
8 of Yahweh my God. •But the word of Yahweh came to me, "You have shed much blood and fought great battles; it is not for you to build a house for my
9 name, since you have shed so much blood on the earth in my presence. •But now a son is born to you. He shall be a man of peace, and I will give him peace from all the enemies that surround him; for Solomon is his name,[b] and in his
10 days I will give Israel peace and quiet. •He shall build a house for my name; he shall be a son to me and I a father to him, and I will make his royal throne
11 secure in Israel for ever." •Now, my son, may Yahweh be with you and give you success in building a house for Yahweh your God, as he has said concerning
12 you. •Yet may he give you discretion and discernment, may he give you his orders for Israel so that you may observe the Law of Yahweh your God.
13 Success will be yours if you carefully observe the statutes and the ordinances that Yahweh has prescribed to Moses for Israel. Be strong and stand fast, be
14 fearless, be dauntless. •Poor as I am, I have set aside for the house of Yahweh one hundred thousand talents of gold, a million talents of silver and more bronze and iron than can be weighed; I have stored up wood and stone too,
15 to which you must add more. •You will have many workmen, stonecutters,
16 masons, carpenters, skilled artisans of every kind, •while your gold and silver, bronze and iron, will be beyond reckoning. Set to work, then, and may Yahweh be with you!'
17 David then ordered all the Israelite leaders to help his son Solomon.
18 'Is not Yahweh your God with you?' he said. 'He has given you peace on all sides, since he has put the inhabitants of the country into my power and
19 the land has been subdued for Yahweh and for his people. •So now devote heart and soul to the search for Yahweh your God. Set to and build the sanctuary of Yahweh your God, so that you can bring the ark of the covenant of Yahweh and the holy things of God to the house that is built for the name of Yahweh.'

The orders and functions of the Levites

1 **23** David, an old man now with his fill of days, made his son Solomon king
2 over Israel. •He gathered all the Israelite leaders together, with the priests and Levites.
3 A census was taken of those Levites thirty years old and upwards. On a
4 count of heads their number was thirty-eight thousand; •twenty-four thousand of these were responsible for the services[a] of the house of Yahweh; six thousand
5 were scribes and judges; •four thousand were keepers of the gate; four thousand praised Yahweh on the instruments David had made for that purpose.

---

22 a. The author's sources for the remaining chapters of 1 Ch are not in the Bible.   **b.** Peace is *shalom*; 'Solomon' is derived from it.
23 a. As cantors.

Then David divided the Levites into orders: Gershon, Kohath and Merari. 6
For the Gershonites: Ladan and Shimei. •Sons of Ladan: Jehiel first, ⁷⁄₈
Zetham, Joel; three in all. •Sons of Shimei: Shelomoth, Haziel, Haran; three 9
in all. These are the heads of families of Ladan. •Sons of Shimei: Jahath, Zina, 10
Jeush, Beriah; these were the sons of Shimei; four in all. •Jahath was the eldest, 11
Zizah the second, then Jeush and Beriah, who had not many children and were
reckoned as one family.
Sons of Kohath: Amram, Izhar, Hebron, Uzziel; four in all. •Sons of Amram: ¹²⁄₁₃
Aaron and Moses. Aaron was set apart to consecrate the most holy things, he
and his sons for ever, to burn incense in the presence of Yahweh, to serve him
and to bless in his name for ever. •Moses was a man of God whose sons were 14
given the name of the tribe of Levi. •Sons of Moses: Gershom and Eliezer. 15
Sons of Gershom: Shebuel, the first. •Eliezer had sons: Rehabiah, the first. ¹⁶⁄₁₇
Eliezer had no other sons, but the sons of Rehabiah were very numerous. •Sons 18
of Izhar: Shelomith, the first. •Sons of Hebron: Jeriah first, Amariah second, 19
Jahaziel third, Jekameam fourth. •Sons of Uzziel: Micah first, Isshiah second. 20
Sons of Merari: Mahli and Mushi. Sons of Mahli: Eleazar and Kish. •Eleazar ²¹⁄₂₂
died leaving no sons but only daughters; their kinsmen, the sons of Kish, married
these. •Sons of Mushi: Mahli, Eder, Jeremoth; three in all.   23
These were the sons of Levi by their families, the heads of families, and those 24
registered by name, individually; whoever was twenty years old or upwards had
his function in the service of the Temple of Yahweh.
For David had said, 'Yahweh, the God of Israel, has given peace to his peo- 25
ple; and he dwells in Jerusalem for ever. •The Levites are no longer required 26
to carry the tabernacle or any thing used in its service.' •For, according to the 27
last words of David, the Levites who had been registered were of twenty years
and upwards. •Their duty is to be at the disposal of the sons of Aaron for the 28
service of the Temple of Yahweh, in the courts and chambers, to purify
everything consecrated; their duty is to serve the Temple of God. •They are 29
also responsible for the loaves set out in rows, and for the flour for the oblation,
the wafers of unleavened bread, the cakes baked on the griddle or mixed, and
with the various measures of volume and of length.ᵇ •They have to be present 30
every morning to give glory and praise to Yahweh, and also in the evening, •and 31
at every offering of holocaust to Yahweh on the sabbath, New Moon or solemn
feast—a set number of them laid down by rule. This is a perpetual obligation
for them in the presence of Yahweh. •In serving the Temple of Yahweh they 32
observe the ritual of the Tent of Meeting, the ritual of the sanctuary and the
ritual of their kinsmen, the sons of Aaron.

The classification of the priests

24 Orders of the sons of Aaron: Sons of Aaron: Nadab, Abihu, Eleazar, 1
Ithamar. •Nadab and Abihu died in their father's lifetime leaving no 2
children, so Eleazar and Ithamar became priests. •David divided them into 3
orders with the help of Zadok, one of Eleazar's sons, and Ahimelech, one of
the sons of Ithamar, and made a register of them according to their duties.
The sons of Eleazar were found to have more leading men than the sons of 4
Ithamar; accordingly, from the heads of families of the sons of Eleazar they
made sixteen orders, and from those of the sons of Ithamar, eight. •They divided 5
them, both parties, by lot: there were consecrated officials, officials of God,
among the sons of Eleazar, as among the sons of Ithamar. •One of the Levites, 6
the scribe Shemaiah son of Nethanel, recorded them in the presence of the king,
his officers, Zadok the priest, Ahimelech son of Abiathar and the heads of the
priestly and levitical families. They drew lots for each family of the sons of
Eleazar and for the sons of Ithamar, turn and turn about.
The first lot fell to Jehoiarib, to Jedaiah the second, •Harim the third, ⁷⁄₈
Seorim the fourth, •Malchijah the fifth, Mijamin the sixth, •Hakkoz the seventh, ⁹⁄₁₀

11,12 Abijah the eighth, •Jeshua the ninth, Shecaniah the tenth, •Eliashib the eleventh,
13,14 Jakim the twelfth, •Huppah the thirteenth, Ishbaal the fourteenth, •Bilgah the
15 fifteenth, Immer the sixteenth, •Hezir the seventeenth, Happizzez the eighteenth,
16,17 Pethahiah the nineteenth, Jehezkel the twentieth, •Jachin the twenty-first, Gamul
18 the twenty-second, •Delaiah the twenty-third, Maaziah the twenty-fourth.

19   These were the men as registered by their various duties, to enter the Temple
of Yahweh in conformity to their rule handed on by Aaron their father as
Yahweh, the God of Israel, had laid it down for him.

20   As regards the rest of the sons of Levi:
21   For the sons of Amram: Shubael. For the sons of Shubael: Jehdeiah. •For
22 Rehabiah, for the sons of Rehabiah: the eldest, Isshiah. •For the Izharites:
23 Shelomoth; for the sons of Shelomoth: Jahath. •The sons of Hebron: Jeriah
24 the first, Amariah the second, Jahaziel the third, Jekameam the fourth. •Sons
25 of Uzziel: Micah; for the sons of Micah: Shamir; •the brother of Micah: Isshiah;
26 for the sons of Micah: Isshiah, Zechariah. •Sons of Merari: Mahli and Mushi.
27 Sons of Jaaziah: his son; •sons of Merari: for Jaaziah his son: Shoham, Zaccur,
28,29 Ibri; •for Mahli: Eleazar who had no sons; •for Kish: the sons of Kish:
30 Jerahmeel. •Sons of Mushi: Mahli, Eder, Jerimoth.
31   These were the sons of Levi by their families. •Like their kinsmen, the sons
of Aaron, these families, senior and junior, drew lots in the presence of king
David, Zadok, Ahimelech, and the heads of the priestly and levitical families.

The cantors

1   **25** For the liturgy, David and the senior army officers set apart the sons of
Asaph, of Heman and of Jeduthun, prophets who accompanied themselves with lyre and harp and cymbal, and a list was made of those with these
duties to perform.
2   For the sons of Asaph: Zaccur, Joseph, Nethaniah, Asharelah; the sons of
Asaph were under the direction of Asaph who prophesied at the king's direction.
3   For Jeduthun: sons of Jeduthun: Gedaliah, Zeri, Jeshaiah, Hashabiah,
Mattithiah; there were six of them under the direction of their father Jeduthun
who, to the sound of the lyre, prophesied to the glory and praise of Yahweh.
4   For Heman: sons of Heman: Bukkiah, Mattaniah, Uzziel, Shebuel, Jerimoth,
Hananiah, Hanani, Eliathah, Giddalti, Romamti-ezer, Joshbekashah, Mallothi,
5 Hothir, Mahazioth. •All these were sons of Heman, the king's seer; these
sounded the trumpet to accompany God's words. God gave Heman fourteen
6 sons and three daughters; •all of them sang in the Temple of Yahweh under
their father's direction to the sound of cymbal, harp and lyre, for the liturgy
in the house of Yahweh at the king's direction.
7   Asaph, Jeduthun and Heman, •these who had learnt to sing to Yahweh,
were registered with their kinsmen; the total of those so trained was two hundred
8 and eighty-eight. •Junior and senior, master and pupil alike, they drew lots for
9 their term of duty. •The first to whom the lot fell was the Asaphite, Joseph.
10 The second was Gedaliah, twelve with his sons and brothers. •The third was
11 Zaccur, twelve with his sons and brothers. •The fourth was Izri, twelve with
12 his sons and brothers. •The fifth was Nethaniah, twelve with his sons and brothers.
13,14 The sixth was Bukkiah, twelve with his sons and brothers. •The seventh was
15 Jesharelah, twelve with his sons and brothers. •The eight was Jeshaiah, twelve
16 with his sons and brothers. •The ninth was Mattaniah, twelve with his sons and
17,18 brothers. •The tenth was Shimei, twelve with his sons and brothers. •The
19 eleventh was Azarel, twelve with his sons and brothers. •The twelfth was
20 Hashabiah, twelve with his sons and brothers. •The thirteenth was Shubael,
21 twelve with his sons and brothers. •The fourteenth was Mattithiah, twelve with
22 his sons and brothers. •The fifteenth was Jeremoth, twelve with his sons and

b. The 'sanctuary shekel' and probably the special cubit.

brothers. •The sixteenth was Hananiah, twelve with his sons and brothers. •The $^{23}_{24}$
seventeenth was Joshbekashah, twelve with his sons and brothers. •The eighteenth 25
was Hanani, twelve with his sons and brothers. •The nineteenth was Mallothi, 26
twelve with his sons and brothers. •The twentieth was Eliathah, twelve with his 27
sons and brothers. •The twenty-first was Hothir, twelve with his sons and brothers. 28
The twenty-second was Giddalti, twelve with his sons and brothers. •The twenty- $^{29}_{30}$
third was Mahazioth, twelve with his sons and brothers. •The twenty-fourth 31
was Romamti-ezer, twelve with his sons and brothers.

The keepers of the gate

26 As regards the orders of the gatekeepers: 1
For the Korahites: Meshelemiah son of Kore, one of the sons of Ebiasaph.
Meshelemiah had sons: Zechariah the first-born, Jediael the second, Zebadiah 2
the third, Jathniel the fourth, •Elam the fifth, Jehohanan the sixth, Eliehoenai 3
the seventh.
Obed-edom had sons: Shemaiah the first-born, Jehozabad the second, Joah 4
the third, Sacar the fourth, Nethanel the fifth, •Ammiel the sixth, Issachar the 5
seventh, Peullethai the eighth; God had indeed blessed him. •To his son 6
Shemaiah sons were born who had authority in their families, for they were
stout fighting men. •Sons of Shemaiah: Othni, Rephael, Obed, Elzabad and his 7
brothers Elihu and Semachiah, brave men. •All these were sons of Obed-edom. 8
These and their sons and brothers were well fitted for their task. For Obed-edom,
sixty-two.
Meshelemiah had sons and brothers: eighteen brave men.   9
Hosah, one of the sons of Merari, had sons: Shimri was the first, for although 10
he was not the first-born his father had made him the chief. •Hilkiah was the 11
second, Tebaliah the third, Zechariah the fourth. The sons and brothers of Hosah
were thirteen in all.
These, as keepers of the gate, had their orders, and the leaders of these heroes 12
had duties corresponding to those of their kinsmen in the service of the Temple
of Yahweh. •They drew lots, junior and senior family alike, for each gate. •For $^{13}_{14}$
the east side the lot fell to Shelemiah, whose son Zechariah was a shrewd counsellor; when they drew lots, the lot for the north side fell to the latter. •To 15
Obed-edom went the south, and to his sons the storehouse. •To Shuppim and 16
Hosah went the west with the Gate of the Felled Tree-trunk on the upper road.
The watch, turn and turn about: •on the east, six daily; on the north, four daily; 17
on the south, four daily; at the storehouse, two each side; •for the Parbar 18
on the west: four at the road, two at the Parbar. •These were the orders of the 19
gatekeepers among the Korahites and Merarites.

Other levitical duties

The Levites, their kinsmen, were responsible for those in charge of the 20
treasuries of the Temple of God and in charge of the treasuries of votive offerings:
The sons of Ladan, sons, through Ladan, of Gershon, had the Jehielites for 21
heads of the families of Ladan the Gershonite. •The Jehielites, Zetham and Joel 22
his brother, were responsible for the treasuries of the Temple of Yahweh.
As regards the Amramites, Izharites, Hebronites, and Uzzielites: 23
Shebuel son of Gershom, son of Moses, was the officer responsible for the 24
treasuries. •His kinsmen through Eliezer: Rehabiah his son, Jeshaiah his son, 25
Joram his son, Zichri his son, Shelomoth his son. •This Shelomoth and his 26
kinsmen were responsible for all the treasuries of votive offerings dedicated by
King David and by the heads of families as officers of thousands, of hundreds,
or other senior officers, •(they had dedicated a part of the spoils of war to make 27
the house of Yahweh more impressive), •and also for all that Samuel the seer 28
had dedicated, and Saul son of Kish, Abner son of Ner, and Joab son of Zeruiah.
All that had been dedicated was the responsibility of Shelomoth and his kinsmen.

29   For the Izharites: Chananiah and his sons were assigned to outside duties for Israel[a] as scribes and judges.

30   For the Hebronites: Hashabiah and his kinsmen, one thousand seven hundred fighting men to guard Israel west of Jordan in all that had to do with Yahweh and
31 in the service of the king. •For the Hebronites: Jerijah the chief. In the fortieth year of David's reign, the pedigrees of the Hebronite families were investigated
32 and stout fighting men were found belonging to them at Jazer in Gilead. •King David nominated two thousand seven hundred fighting men, kinsmen to Jerijah and heads of families, as overseers of the Reubenites, the Gadites and the half-tribe of Manasseh in all the business of God and of the king.

Military and civil organisation

1   27 The sons of Israel; their enumeration. The heads of families, the commanders of thousands and hundreds, their scribes, these performed their duties among the people. The orders played their part in all royal business. There was one on duty for a month, every month of the year. Each order was made up of twenty-four thousand men.

2   The commissioner for the first order detailed for the first month was Jashobeam
3 son of Zabdiel. He had charge of an order of twenty-four thousand men. •He was a son of Perez and chief of all the officers of the group detailed for the first month.

4   The commissioner for the order for the second-month was Dodai the Ahohite. He had charge of an order of twenty-four thousand men.

5   The officer of the third group detailed for the third month was Benaiah son of Jehoiada, the chief priest. He had charge of an order of twenty-four thousand
6 men. •This was the Benaiah who was champion of the Thirty, and who was commissioner for the Thirty and for his order. Ammizabad was his son.

7   The fourth, detailed for the fourth month, was Asahel, the brother of Joab; his son Zebadiah succeeded him. He had charge of an order of twenty-four thousand men.

8   The fifth, detailed for the fifth month, was the officer Shamhuth the Izrahite. He had charge of an order of twenty-four thousand men.

9   The sixth, detailed for the sixth month, was Ira son of Ikkesh of Tekoa. He had charge of an order of twenty-four thousand men.

10   The seventh, detailed for the seventh month, was Helez the Pelonite, one of the sons of Ephraim. He had charge of an order of twenty-four thousand men.

11   The eighth, detailed for the eighth month, was Sibbecai of Hushah, a Zerahite. He had charge of an order of twenty-four thousand men.

12   The ninth, detailed for the ninth month, was Abiezer of Anathoth, a Benjaminite. He had charge of an order of twenty-four thousand men.

13   The tenth, detailed for the tenth month, was Maharai of Netophah, a Zerahite. He had charge of an order of twenty-four thousand men.

14   The eleventh, detailed for the eleventh month, was Benaiah of Pirathon, a son of Ephraim. He had charge of an order of twenty-four thousand men.

15   The twelfth, detailed for the twelfth month, was Heldai from Netophah, of Othniel. He had charge of an order of twenty-four thousand men.

16   Commissioners for the tribes of Israel: Eliezer son of Zichri was chief officer
17 for the Reubenites, Shephatiah son of Maacah for the Simeonites, •Hashabiah
18 son of Kemuel for the Levites, Zadok for the Aaronites, •Elihu, one of David's
19 brothers, for the Judaeans, Omri son of Michael for the Issacharites, •Ishmaiah son of Obadiah for the Zebulunites, Jeremoth son of Azriel for the Naphtalites,
20 Hoshea son of Azaziah for the Ephraimites, Joel son of Pedaiah for the half-tribe
21 of Manasseh, •Iddo son of Zechariah for the half-tribe of Manasseh in Gad,
22 Jaasiel son of Abner for the Benjaminites, •Azarel son of Jeroham for the Danites. These were the officials for the tribes of Israel.

26 a. I.e., outside the sanctuary, and possibly outside the city.

David took no census of those who were twenty years old and under, since 23 Yahweh had promised to make Israel as numerous as the stars of heaven. •Joab 24 son of Zeruiah began a census, though he did not finish it. That is why the wrath came on Israel, and the figure never reached the figure found in the Annals of King David.ᵃ

Commissioner for the king's stores: Azmaveth son of Adiel. Commissioner 25 for the stores in provincial towns, villages, castles: Jonathan son of Uzziah. Commissioner for the agricultural workers employed on the land: Ezri son of 26 Chelub. •Commissioner for the vineyards: Shimei of Ramah. Commissioner for 27 those in the vineyards who looked after the wine cellars: Zabdi of Shepham. Commissioner for the olives and sycamores in the lowlands: Baal-hanan of 28 Geder. Commissioner for the stores of oil: Joash. •Commissioner for cattle in 29 pasture at Sharon: Shitrai of Sharon. Commissioner for cattle in the valleys: Shaphat son of Adlai. •Commissioner for camels: Obil the Ishmaelite. Commis- 30 sioner for donkeys: Jehdeiah of Meranoth. •Commissioner for flocks: Jaziz the 31 Hagrite. All these were bailiffs for King David's property.

Jonathan, David's uncle, who was a councillor, a shrewd man and a scribe, 32 had charge of the royal children, with Jehiel son of Hachmoni. •Ahithophel was 33 the king's counsellor. Hushai the Archite was Friend of the King. •Jehoiada son 34 of Benaiah, and Abiathar ᵇ succeeded Ahithophel. Joab was commander of the king's armies.

David's instructions for the Temple

28 David held a meeting in Jerusalem of all the officials of Israel, the commis- 1 sioners for the tribes, and the officials of the orders in the royal service, the commanders of thousands, the commanders of hundreds, the bailiffs for all the property and livestock of the king and his sons, together with the eunuchs and champions and all the stout fighting men. •Then King David rose to his 2 feet and said:

'My brothers and my people, listen to me. I had set my heart on building a settled home for the ark of the covenant of Yahweh, as a footstool for our God. I have made preparations for building, •but God has said to me, "You are 3 not to build a house for my name, for you have been a man of war and have shed blood".

'Of all my father's House it was I whom Yahweh, the God of Israel, chose 4 to be king over Israel for ever. He chose Judah for leader, my family within the House of Judah, and of my father's sons myself, in his good pleasure, he gave to all Israel as king. •Of all my sons—and many sons Yahweh has granted 5 me—he has chosen my son Solomon to sit on the sovereign throne of Yahweh over Israel. •He said to me, "Solomon your son is the man to build my house 6 and my courts, for I have chosen him to be a son to me and I will be a father to him. •I will make his sovereignty secure for ever if he sturdily maintains my 7 commandments and my ordinances, as they are now."

'So now in the sight of all Israel and of the assembly of Yahweh, and in the 8 hearing of our God, observe and make sure you understand all the commandments of Yahweh your God, so that you may possess this prosperous land and leave it to your children after you as an inheritance for ever.

'And you, Solomon my son, know the God of your father, serve him with 9 an undivided heart and a willing mind; for Yahweh searches every heart, and knows every plan it devises. If you seek him, he will let you find him; once forsake him, and he casts you off for ever. •Think at this moment how Yahweh has 10 chosen you to build a house for his sanctuary. Be strong and set to work.'

David gave his son Solomon the plans for the vestibule, the buildings, the 11 treasuries, the upper rooms, the inner apartments and the room for the throne of mercy; •he also gave him a description of all he had in mind for the courts 12 of the Temple of Yahweh, all the surrounding apartments, the treasuries of the

13 Temple of God and the treasuries of votive offerings; •also of the orders of
14 priests and Levites, the liturgical duties in the Temple of Yahweh, •the gold
bullion, gold for every article for whatever function, the silver bullion for all
15 the silver articles, for every article for whatever function, •the bullion for the
golden lamp-stands and their lamps, the gold bulllion for each lamp-stand and
its lamps, the bullion for the silver lamp-stands, for the lamp-stand and its lamps
16 according to the requirements for each lamp-stand, •gold bullion for the tables
on which the rows of bread were set, for each of these tables, the silver for the
17 silver tables, •the forks, the sprinkling bowls, basins of pure gold, the gold
18 bullion for the bowls, for each of the bowls, •the bullion of refined gold for the
altar of incense. He gave him the plans for the chariot,ᵃ for the golden cherubs
19 with wings outspread covering the ark of the covenant of Yahweh—•all this in
accordance with what Yahweh with his hand had written in order to make the
whole work clear for which he was providing the plans.
20 　　Then David said to his son Solomon, 'Be strong, stand firm; be fearless, be
dauntless and set to work, because Yahweh God, my God, is with you. He will
not fail you or forsake you before you have finished all the work to be done
21 for the house of Yahweh. •Here are the orders of priests and Levites for all the
duties of the house of God; every willing man of any aptitude will help you in
all this work; the officials and all the people are entirely at your command.'

The voluntary offerings

1 29 Then King David said to the whole assembly, 'Solomon my son, whom
　　alone Yahweh has chosen, is young, of tender years, and the work is great;
2 this palace is not for man but for Yahweh God. •With all the resources I have,
I have provided for the house of my God, adding gold to gold, silver to silver,
bronze to bronze, iron to iron, wood to wood, onyx, inlaid stones, coloured and
3 striped stones, precious stones of every kind, masses of alabaster. •What is
more; what gold and silver I have in my own treasury I give out of love for the
house of my God, over and above what I have provided already for the holy
4 Temple—•three thousand talents of gold, gold of Ophir, seven thousand talents
5 of refined silver for plating the walls of the buildings. •Whatever gold you have,
whatever silver, or workmanship of the craftsman's hand, which of you today
will undertake to consecrate it to Yahweh?'
6 　　Then the heads of families, the officials for the tribes of Israel, the commanders
of thousands and of hundreds, and those who managed the king's affairs,
7 undertook •to give for the service of the house of God five thousand talents of
gold, ten thousand darics, ten thousand talents of silver, eighteen thousand
8 talents of bronze, a hundred thousand talents of iron. •All this, with what there
were in the way of stones, they paid into the treasury of the house of Yahweh,
9 for Jehiel the Gershonite to administer. •The people rejoiced at what these had
given so readily, since their generous gift to Yahweh had been made whole-
10 heartedly. King David too was filled with joy. •In sight of the whole assembly
David blessed Yahweh and said:
　　'May you be blessed, Yahweh, the God of Israel our ancestor, for ever and
11 for ever! •Yours, Yahweh, is the greatness, the power, splendour, length of days,
glory, for all that is in the heavens and on the earth is yours. Yours is the
12 sovereignty, Yahweh; you are exalted over all, supreme. •Riches and honour
go before you, you are ruler of all, in your hand lie strength and power; in your
13 hand it is to give greatness and strength to all. •At this time, our God, we give you
14 glory, we praise the splendour of your name. •For who am I and what is my
people to have the means to give so generously? All comes from you; from your

27 a. I.e., why the figures in 1 Ch 21 are lower than those in 2 S 24:9.　　b. Probably Abiathar
the priest, 1 S 22; the Chronicler traces the succession of the priesthood through Zadok.
28 a. The ark represented a throne, not a chariot. In the vision of Ezekiel, the place in which
'the glory of God' is guarded by cherubs is described as a chariot, Ezk 10.

own hand we have given them to you. •For we are strangers before you, settlers 15
only, as all our ancestors were; our days on earth pass like a shadow, and there is
no hope. •Yahweh our God, this store we have provided to build a house for 16
your holy name, all comes from your hand, all is yours. •O my God, you search 17
the heart, I know, and delight in honesty, and with honesty of heart I have
willingly given all this; and now with joy I have seen your people here offer
you their gifts willingly. •Yahweh, God of our ancestors, of Abraham, of 18
Isaac, of Israel, watch over this for ever, shape the purpose of your people's
heart and direct their hearts to you. •Give Solomon my son a heart determined 19
to keep your commandments, your decrees, your statutes; may he practise
them all, and build this palace I have prepared for you.'

Then David said to the whole assembly, 'Bless now Yahweh your God!' And 20
the whole assembly blessed Yahweh, the God of their ancestors, and went on
their knees to do homage to Yahweh and to the king.

The accession of Solomon and the end of the reign of David

On the day following this, the Israelites offered sacrifices and holocausts to 21
Yahweh: a thousand bulls, a thousand rams, a thousand lambs with their libations,
as well as many sacrifices for the whole of Israel. •They ate and drank that day 22
in Yahweh's presence with great joy. Then having made Solomon son of David
their second king, they anointed him leader in the name of Yahweh, and anointed
Zadok as priest. •Solomon took his seat on the throne of Yahweh, to reign in 23
succession to David his father. He prospered, and all Israel obeyed him. •All the 24
officials, all the champions, and even all the sons of King David, pledged allegiance
to King Solomon. •Yahweh brought Solomon's greatness to its height in the 25
sight of all Israel, and gave him a reign of such splendour as none that had
reigned over Israel before him had ever known.

David son of Jesse had reigned over the whole of Israel. •His reign over Israel ²⁶₂₇
had lasted forty years; he had reigned in Hebron for seven years, and in Jerusalem
for thirty-three. •He died in happy old age, with his fill of days, of riches, of 28
honour. Then his son Solomon succeeded him. •The history of King David, from 29
first to last, is not all this recorded in the Annals of Samuel the seer, the Annals
of Nathan the prophet, and the Annals of Gad the seer, •with his entire reign, 30
his prowess, and the turns of fortune that came to him and to Israel and to all
the kingdoms of the other countries?

THE SECOND BOOK OF CHRONICLES

III. SOLOMON AND THE BUILDING OF THE TEMPLE

Solomon's gift of wisdom

1 Solomon son of David made himself secure on the throne. Yahweh his God 1
was with him and brought his greatness to its height. •Solomon then spoke 2
to all Israel, to the commanders of thousands and of hundreds, to the judges,
and to all the princes of all Israel, the heads of families. •Then Solomon, and 3
with him the whole assembly, went to the high place of Gibeon, where God's
Tent of Meeting was, which Moses, the servant of God, had made in the
wilderness; •David, however, had brought the ark of God from Kiriath- 4
jearim to the place he had prepared for it, having pitched a tent for it in Jerusalem.
The bronze altar that Bezalel son of Uri, son of Hur, had made stood there 5
in front of the tabernacle of Yahweh; to this went Solomon, with the
assembly. •And there Solomon, in Yahweh's presence, ascended the bronze altar 6

that was by the Tent of Meeting, and on it he offered a thousand holocausts.

7 That night, God appeared to Solomon and said, 'Ask what you would like
8 me to give you'. •Solomon replied to God, 'You showed great kindness to
9 David my father; and you have made me king in succession to him. •Yahweh
God, the promise you made to David my father has now been fulfilled, since you
have made me king over a people like the dust of the earth for number.
10 Therefore now give me wisdom and knowledge to act as leader of this people,
for who could govern a people so great as yours?'
11 'Since that is what you want,' God said to Solomon 'since you have asked,
not for riches, treasure, honour, the lives of your enemies, or even for a long
life, but for wisdom and knowledge to govern my people of whom I have made
12 you king, •therefore wisdom and knowledge are granted you. I give you riches
too, and treasure, and honour such as none of the kings had that were before
you, nor shall any have that come after you.'

13 Solomon left the high place of Gibeon for Jerusalem, away from the Tent
14 of Meeting. He reigned over Israel. •Solomon built up a force of chariots and
horses; he had one thousand four hundred chariots and twelve thousand horses;
15 these he stationed in the chariot towns and with the king in Jerusalem. •In
Jerusalem the king made silver common as pebbles, and cedars plentiful as the
16 sycamores of the lowlands. •Solomon's horses were imported from Cilicia;
17 the king's agents took delivery of them from Cilicia at a fixed rate. •They imported
chariots from Egypt at six hundred shekels apiece, and horses at one hundred
and fifty shekels. These men acted in a similar capacity for all the kings of
the Hittites and the kings of Aram.

The final preparations. Huram of Tyre

18
2:1
Solomon decided to build a house for the name of Yahweh and another
for himself and his court.

1
2
2 He impressed seventy thousand men for carrying loads, eighty thousand to
quarry in the hill country, and three thousand six hundred overseers in charge
2
3
of them. •Solomon then despatched this message to Huram king of Tyre, 'Deal
with me as you dealt with my father David when you sent him cedars for him
3
4
to build a house to live in. •I am now building a house for the name of Yahweh
my God, to acknowledge his holiness, by burning incense of scented spices in
his presence, by the loaves that are perpetually set out, by offering holocausts
morning and evening, on the sabbath, New Moon, and the solemn festivals
4
5
of Yahweh our God—and this for ever in Israel. •The house I am building will
6
be large, for our God is greater than all gods. •Who would have the means to
build him a house when the heavens and their own heavens cannot contain him?
And I, for what purpose could I build him a house other than to burn incense
6
7
in his presence? •So send me a man skilled in the use of gold, silver, bronze,
iron, scarlet, crimson, violet,[a] and the art of engraving too; he is to work with
my skilled men here in Judah and Jerusalem, men my father David provided.
7
8
From Lebanon send me cedar wood, juniper and algummim, since I know your
servants know the art of felling the trees of Lebanon. My servants will work
8
9
with yours.'•They will prepare wood in bulk for me, since the house I wish to
9
10
build is to be of astounding size. •For the woodmen who are to fell the trees
I assign twenty thousand kors of grain, twenty thousand kors of barley, twenty
thousand baths of wine, and twenty thousand baths of oil—this is for the
maintenance of your servants.'
10
11
In a letter sent to King Solomon, Huram king of Tyre replied, 'Because
11
12
Yahweh loves his people he has made you king. •Blessed be Yahweh, the God
of Israel' Huram went on to say. 'He has made the heavens and the earth, and

---

2 a. These materials are from the description of the tabernacle, e.g. Ex 28:5, not that of Solomon's
Temple, 1 K 10:11.

given King David a wise son, endowed with discretion and discernment, who is
going to build a house for Yahweh and another for himself and his court. •And ¹²⁄₁₃
I am also sending you a skilled craftsman, Huram-abi, •the son of a ¹³⁄₁₄
Danite woman by a Tyrian father. He is skilled in the use of gold, silver,
bronze, iron, stone, wood, scarlet, violet, fine linen, crimson, in engraving of all
kinds, and in the execution of any design suggested to him. Let him be put to
work with your craftsmen and those of my lord David, your father. •So now ¹⁴⁄₁₅
let my lord send his servants the wheat, barley, oil and wine, as already
suggested.

'For our part, we will fell all the wood you need from Lebanon, and bring ¹⁵⁄₁₆
it you in rafts by sea to Joppa, and it will be your responsibility to transport it to
Jerusalem.'

The construction

Solomon took a count of all the aliens resident in the land of Israel, following ¹⁶⁄₁₇
the census that David his father had taken; it was found there were a hundred
and fifty-three thousand six hundred. •He impressed seventy thousand of these ¹⁷⁄₁₈
for carrying loads, eighty thousand for quarrying in the hill country, and three
thousand six hundred as overseers to make sure the people worked.

3 Solomon then began to build the house of Yahweh in Jerusalem on Mount ₁
Moriah where David his father had a vision. It was the place prepared by
David, the threshing-floor of Ornan the Jebusite. •Solomon began building in ₂
the second month of the fourth year of his reign, on the second day. •Now the ₃
structure of the house of God founded by Solomon was sixty cubits long—cubits
of the old standard—and twenty cubits wide. •The Ulam in front of the Hekal ₄
of the Temple was twenty cubits long across the width of the house, and its
height was a hundred and twenty cubits. He plated it on the inside with pure
gold. •The Great Hall he faced with juniper which he plated with pure gold, ₅
and on it set palms and festoons. •He adorned the hall with precious stones ₆
of great beauty; the gold was gold from Parvaim, •and with this he faced the ₇
hall, the rafters, thresholds, walls and doors; on the walls he carved cherubs.

He then built the hall of the Holy of Holies; its length, across the width of ₈
the Great Hall, was twenty cubits, and its width twenty cubits. He plated it with
six hundred talents of fine gold; •the gold nails weighed fifty shekels. He also ₉
plated the upper rooms with gold. •In the hall of the Holy of Holies he made ₁₀
two cherubs of wrought metal work and plated them with gold. •The total span ₁₁
of the cherubs' wings was twenty cubits, each being five cubits long, with one
wing touching the wall of the hall, while the other touched that of the other
cherub. •One wing of a cherub, five cubits long, touched the wall of the apartment; ₁₂
the second, five cubits long, touched the wing of the other cherub. •The spread ₁₃
of these cherubs' wings was twenty cubits. They stood on their feet, facing the
Hall.

He made the Veil of violet, scarlet, crimson and fine linen; he worked ₁₄
cherubs on it.

In front of the hall he made two pillars thirty-five cubits high, and on the ₁₅
top of each a capital measuring five cubits. •In the Debir he made festoons, ₁₆
setting them at the tops of the pillars, and a hundred pomegranates which he
placed on the festoons. •He set up the pillars in front of the Hekal, one on the ₁₇
right, the other on the left; the one on the right he called Jachin, the one on the
left Boaz.

4 He made an altar of bronze, twenty cubits long, twenty cubits wide and ten ₁
high. •He made the Sea of cast metal, ten cubits from rim to rim, circular ₂
in shape and five cubits high; a cord thirty cubits long gave the measurement
of its girth. •Under it and completely encircling it were animals shaped like oxen; ₃
they went round the Sea over a length of thirty cubits; the oxen were in two
rows, of one and the same casting with the rest. •It rested on twelve oxen, three ₄

facing north, three facing west, three facing south, three facing east; on these,
5 their hindquarters all turned inwards, stood the Sea. •It was a hand's breadth
in thickness, and its rim was shaped like the rim of a cup, like a flower. It could
hold three thousand baths.

6   He made ten basins, arranging five on the right-hand side, five on the left-hand
side, for washing the victim for the holocaust which was purified there; but the
7 Sea was for the priests to wash in. •He made the ten golden lamp-stands in the
way prescribed and placed them in the Hekal, five on the right and five on the
8 left. •He made ten tables and placed them in the Hekal, five on the right and
five on the left. He made a hundred golden sprinkling bowls.

9   He made the court of the priests[a] and the great court with its gates and
10 plated the gates with bronze. •He placed the Sea some distance from the right-hand
side, to the south-east.

11   Huram made the ash containers, the scoops and the sprinkling bowls. He
finished all the work that he did for King Solomon on the Temple of God:
12   the two pillars; the two mouldings of the capitals surmounting the pillars;
     the two sets of filigree to cover the two mouldings of the capitals surmounting
13   the pillars; •the four hundred pomegranates for the two sets of filigree; the
     pomegranates of each set of filigree were in two rows;
14   the ten stands and the ten basins on the stands;
15   the one Sea and the twelve oxen beneath it;
16   the ash containers, the scoops, the forks, and all their accessories made by
Huram-abi of burnished bronze for King Solomon, for the Temple of Yahweh.
17 The king made them by the process of sand casting, in the Jordan area between
18 Succoth and Zeredah. •Solomon made all these articles in great quantities, no
reckoning being made of the weight of bronze.

19   Solomon placed all the furnishings he had made in the Temple of God:
20 the golden altar and the tables for the loaves of offering; •the lamp-stands with
21 their lamps to burn, as prescribed, in front of the Debir, of pure gold; •the floral
22 work, the lamps, the extinguishers, of gold (and it was pure gold); •the knives,
the sprinkling bowls, incense boats, of fine gold; the door of the Temple, the
inner doors (for the Holy of Holies) and the Temple doors (for the Hekal),
of gold.

1 **5** So all the work that Solomon did for the Temple of Yahweh was
completed, and Solomon brought what his father David had consecrated,
the silver and the gold and the vessels, and put them in the treasury of the
Temple of God.

The ark is brought to the Temple

2   Then Solomon called the elders of Israel together in Jerusalem to bring the
ark of the covenant of Yahweh up from the Citadel of David, which is Zion.
3 All the men of Israel assembled round the king in the seventh month, at the time
4 of the feast. •All the elders of Israel came, and the Levites took up the ark
5 and the Tent of Meeting with all the sacred vessels that were in it; the levitical
priests brought them up.

6   King Solomon, and all the community of Israel gathering with him in front
7 of the ark, sacrificed sheep and oxen, countless, innumerable. •The priests
brought the ark of the covenant of Yahweh to its place, in the Debir of the
8 Temple, that is, in the Holy of Holies, under the cherubs' wings. •For there
where the ark was placed the cherubs spread out their wings and sheltered the
9a ark and its shafts. •These were long enough for their ends to be seen from the
10 Holy Place in front of the Debir, but not from outside. •There was nothing
in the ark except the two tablets that Moses had placed in it at Horeb, where

4 a. The inner court of Solomon's Temple. It was not reserved to the priests until the time of
Ezekiel, Ezk 42:13.

Yahweh had made a covenant with the Israelites when they came out of Egypt;
they are still there today.   9b

The Lord takes possession of his Temple[a]

Now when the priests came out of the sanctuary, •a cloud filled the sanctuary,   11a
the Temple of Yahweh.   13b
Now all the priests present, whatever order they belonged to, had sanctified   11b
themselves. •The entire body of levitical cantors, Asaph, Heman and Jeduthun   12
with their sons and brothers, was stationed to the east of the altar, robed in fine
linen and playing cymbals, harps, and lyres. A hundred and twenty priests
accompanied them on the trumpet. •All those who played the trumpet, or who   13a
sang, united in giving praise and glory to Yahweh. Lifting their voices to the
sound of the trumpet and cymbal and instruments of music, they gave praise to
Yahweh, 'for he is good, for his love is everlasting'.
Because of the cloud the priests could no longer perform their duties: the   14
glory of Yahweh filled the Temple of God.

6 Then Solomon said: 1

'Yahweh has chosen to dwell in the thick cloud.
Yes, I have built you a dwelling,
a place for you to live in for ever.'   2

Solomon addresses the people

Then the king turned and blessed the whole assembly of Israel, while the   3
whole assembly of Israel stood. •He said, 'Blessed be Yahweh, the God of   4
Israel, who has carried out by his hand what he promised with his mouth to
David, my father, when he said, •"From the day I brought my people out of   5
the land of Egypt I chose no city, in any of the tribes of Israel, to have a house
built where my name might make its home, and chose no man to be prince of
my people Israel; •but I chose Jerusalem for my name to make its home there,   6
and I chose David to rule over Israel my people". •My father David had set his   7
heart on building a house for the name of Yahweh, the God of Israel, •but   8
Yahweh said, "You have set your heart on building a house for my name, and
in this you have done well; •and yet, you are not the man to build the house;   9
your son, born of your own body, shall build the house for my name". •Yahweh   10
has kept the promise he made: I have succeeded David my father and am seated
on the throne of Israel, as Yahweh promised; I have built the house for the
name of Yahweh, the God of Israel, •and have placed in it the ark containing   11
the covenant that Yahweh made with the sons of Israel.'

Solomon's prayer for himself

Then in the presence of the whole assembly of Israel Solomon stood before   12
the altar of Yahweh and stretched out his hands. •Now Solomon had made a bronze 13
pedestal and had placed it in the middle of the court; it was five cubits long,
five cubits wide and five cubits high. Solomon mounted it, and knelt down on
it in the presence of the whole assembly of Israel; he stretched out his hands
to heaven, •and said, 'Yahweh, God of Israel, not in heaven nor on earth is   14
there such a God as you, true to your covenant and your graciousness towards
your servants when they walk wholeheartedly in your way. •You have kept the   15
promise you made to your servant David my father; what you promised with
your mouth, today you have carried out by your hand. •And now, Yahweh,   16
God of Israel, keep the promise you made your servant David when you
said, "You shall never lack for a man seated before me on the throne of Israel,
if only your sons are careful how they behave, following my law as you yourself
have done". •So now, God of Israel, let the words come true which you spoke   17
to your servant David my father. •Yet will God really live with men on the   18
earth? Why, the heavens and their own heavens cannot contain you! How much

19 less this house that I have built! •Listen to the prayer and entreaty of your servant,
Yahweh my God; listen to the cry and to the prayer your servant makes to you.
20 Day and night let your eyes watch over this house, over this place in which you
have promised to make a home for your name. Listen to the prayer that your
servant will offer in this place.

Solomon's prayer for the people

21 'Hear the entreaties of your servant and of Israel your people as they pray
in this place. From heaven where your dwelling is, hear; and, as you hear,
forgive.

22 'If a man sins against his neighbour, and the neighbour calls down a curse
23 on him and makes him swear an oath before your altar in this Temple, •hear from
heaven, and act; decide between your servants: punish the wicked one, bringing
his conduct down on his own head; and vindicate the innocent, rewarding him
as his innocence deserves.

24 'If Israel your people are defeated by the enemy because they have sinned
against you, if they return to you and praise your name and pray to you and
25 entreat you in this Temple, •hear from heaven; forgive the sin of your
people Israel, and bring them back to the land you gave to them and their
ancestors.

26 'When the heavens are shut and there is no rain because they have sinned
against you, if they pray in this place and praise your name and, having been
27 humbled by you, repent of their sin, •hear from heaven and forgive the sin of
your servant and of your people Israel; show them the good way they ought to
follow; and send rain on your land which you have given your people as an
inheritance.

28 'Should there be famine in the land or pestilence, blight or mildew, locust
or caterpillar, should this people's enemies lay siege to one of its city gates,
29 if there is any plague or sickness, •if any one man, or all Israel your people,
should feel remorse and sorrow and pray or make entreaty, stretching out his
30 hands towards this Temple, •hear from heaven where your home is; forgive,
and deal with each as his conduct deserves, for you know each heart—you
31 alone know the hearts of all mankind—•that they may come to revere you and
follow your ways as long as they live in the land you gave to our ancestors.

32 'And the foreigner too, not belonging to your people Israel, if he comes from
a distant country for the sake of your name and of your mighty hand and
33 outstretched arm, if he comes and prays in this Temple, •hear from heaven where
your home is, and grant all the foreigner asks, so that all the peoples of the
earth may come to know your name and, like your people Israel, revere you,
and know that your name is given to the Temple I have built.

34 'If your people go out to war against their enemies on the way you send
them, and if they turn towards the city you have chosen and towards the Temple
35 I have built for your name and pray to you, •hear from heaven their prayer
and their entreaty, and uphold their cause.

36 'If they sin against you—for there is no man who does not sin—and you are
angry with them and deliver them to the enemy, and they are led away captive
37 to a land far or near, •if in the land of their exile they come to themselves and
repent, and in the country of their captivity they entreat you saying, "We have
38 sinned, we have acted perversely and wickedly", •and if they turn again to you
with all their heart and soul in the country of their captivity to which they have
been deported, and pray, turning towards the land you gave their ancestors,
towards the city you have chosen, and towards the Temple I have built for your
39 name, •hear from heaven where your home is, hear their prayer and their

---

5 a. An elaboration of the narrative in 1 K, with emphasis on the part played in the ceremonies
by psalms and music.

entreaty, uphold their cause, and forgive your people the sins they have committed against you.

Conclusion of the prayer

'Now, O my God, may your eyes be open and your ears attentive to the 40 prayer offered in this place. •And now 41

Rise Yahweh God, come to your resting place,
you and the ark of your power.
Your priests, Yahweh God, are vested in salvation,
your faithful rejoice in prosperity.
Yahweh God, do not turn away from the face of your anointed; 42
remember your favours to David your servant.'

The dedication

7 When Solomon had finished his prayer, fire came down from heaven and 1 consumed the holocaust and the sacrifices; and the glory of Yahweh filled the Temple. •The priests could not enter the house of Yahweh, because the glory 2 of Yahweh filled the house of Yahweh. •All the sons of Israel, seeing the fire 3 come down and the glory of Yahweh resting on the Temple, bowed down on the pavement with their faces to the earth; they worshipped and gave praise to Yahweh, 'for he is good, for his love is everlasting'. •Then the king and all the 4 people offered sacrifice before Yahweh. •King Solomon offered twenty-two 5 thousand oxen and a hundred and twenty thousand sheep in sacrifice; and so the king and all the people dedicated the Temple of Yahweh. •The priests stood 6 in their places, while the Levites gave praise to Yahweh on the instruments that David had made to accompany the canticles of Yahweh, 'for his love is everlasting'. These performed the hymns of praise that David had composed. By their side were the priests sounding the trumpet, while all Israel stood.

Solomon consecrated the middle of the court that is in front of the Temple 7 of Yahweh; he offered the holocaust there and the fatty parts of the communion sacrifices, since the bronze altar Solomon had made could not hold the holocaust, the oblation and the fatty parts. •Solomon then celebrated the feast for seven 8 days and all the Israelites gathered together with him in enormous numbers from the Pass of Hamath to the wadi of Egypt. •On the eighth day they held 9 a propitiation ceremony, for they had been seven days dedicating the altar and seven days celebrating the feast. •On the twenty-third day of the seventh month 10 Solomon dismissed the people to their homes, rejoicing and with happy hearts for the goodness Yahweh had shown to David and to Solomon and to his people Israel.

Yahweh appears and gives a warning

Solomon finished the Temple of Yahweh and the royal palace and successfully 11 concluded all he had set his heart on doing in the house of Yahweh and in his own. •Then Yahweh appeared to Solomon in the night and said, 'I grant your 12 prayer. I choose this place for myself to be a house of sacrifice. •When I close 13 the skies and there is no rain, when I command the locust to devour the land, when I send pestilence among my people, •then if my people who bear my name 14 humble themselves, and pray and seek my presence and turn from their wicked ways, I myself will hear from heaven and forgive their sins and restore their land. •Now and for the future my eyes are open and my ears attentive to the 15 prayer that is offered in this place. •Now and for the future I have chosen and 16 consecrated this house for my name to be there for ever; my eyes and my heart will be there for ever. •For your part, if you walk before me as David your father 17 did, if you do all that I order you and keep my statutes and my ordinances, I will make your royal throne secure, according to the compact I made with 18 David your father when I said: You shall never lack for a man to rule in Israel. But if you turn away from me and forsake the commandments and statutes 19

20 I have set before you, and go and serve other gods and worship them, •then I will tear the Israelites from the land I have given them, and I will reject from my presence this Temple that I have consecrated for my name and make it a
21 proverb and a byword among all the nations. •As for this Temple, now so exalted, all who pass by will be astounded; they will whistle and say, "Why has
22 Yahweh treated this country and this Temple like this?" •And the answer will be, "Because they forsook Yahweh, the God of their ancestors, who brought them out of the land of Egypt, and they adopted other gods and worshipped them and served them; that is why he has brought all these disasters on them". '

Conclusion. The completion of the building programme

1 8 At the end of the twenty years which it took Solomon to build the Temple
2 of Yahweh and his own palace, •he rebuilt the towns that Huram had given
3 him and settled Israelites in them. •He then went to Hamath of Zobah, which
4 he captured; •he rebuilt Tadmor in the wilderness*a* and all the garrison towns
5 he had built in Hamath. •He rebuilt Upper Beth-horon and Lower Beth-horon,
6 fortified towns with walls and gates and bars, •also Baalath and all the garrison towns owned by Solomon, all the towns for his chariots and horses, and all it pleased Solomon to build in Jerusalem, in Lebanon and in all the countries
7 subject to him. •All those who survived of the Hittite, Amorite, Perizzite, Hivite
8 and Jebusite peoples, who were not Israelites •and whose descendants were left in the country after them, and not exterminated by the Israelites, these Solomon
9 levied for forced labour, as they are levied still. •On the Israelites, however, Solomon did not impose slave-labour; these served as fighting men: they were
10 officers of his equerries and his chariot and cavalry commanders. •These were the administrators' officials in the service of King Solomon: two hundred and fifty in charge of the people.
11 Solomon brought Pharaoh's daughter from the Citadel of David up to the house he had built for her. 'It is not for me' he said 'to let a woman live in the palace of David king of Israel; these are holy places, where the ark of Yahweh has been.'
12 Solomon then offered holocausts to Yahweh on Yahweh's altar which he had
13 built in front of the porch. •Observing the daily rule for holocausts laid down in the commandment of Moses for sabbath, New Moon and the three annual feasts: the feast of Unleavened Bread, the feast of Weeks and the feast of
14 Tabernacles, •he maintained the regulations of his father David, as also the priestly orders in their duties, the rules affecting the Levites who offered praise and served with the priests according to the daily ritual, and the different orders of gatekeepers at each gate, for such had been the commandments of David,
15 the man of God. •They did not deviate in anything, not even in the matter of the treasuries, from the royal ordinances applying to the priests and the Levites.
16 And all Solomon's work which, until the day when the foundations of the Temple of Yahweh were laid, had been only in preparation, was completed when the Temple of Yahweh was finished.

Solomon in his glory

17 Then Solomon went as far as Ezion-geber and Elath on the shores of the sea,
18 in the land of Edom. •Huram sent him ships manned by his own men, and experienced sailors. These went with Solomon's men to Ophir and from there they brought back four hundred and fifty talents of gold, which they delivered to King Solomon.
1 9 The fame of Solomon having reached the queen of Sheba, she came to Jerusalem to test him with difficult questions. She came with immense riches, camels laden with spices, great quantities of gold and precious stones. On
2 coming to Solomon, she opened her mind freely to him; •and Solomon had an

8 a. Tadmor is the city of Palmyra. Here the name is a mistake for the Tamar of 1 K.

answer for all her questions, not one was too recondite for Solomon to expound.
When the queen of Sheba saw the wisdom of Solomon, the palace he had built, 3
the food at his table, the accommodation for his officials, the organisation of his 4
staff and the way they were dressed, his cupbearers and the holocausts he offered
in the Temple of Yahweh, it left her breathless, •and she said to the king, 'What 5
I heard in my own country about you and your wisdom was true, then! •Until 6
I came and saw it with my own eyes I could not believe what they told me, but
evidently what they told me was less than half the real extent of your wisdom;
you surpass the report I heard. •How happy your wives are! How happy these 7
servants of yours who wait on you always and hear your wisdom! •Blessed be 8
Yahweh your God who has granted you his favour, setting you on his throne
as king in the name of Yahweh your God. Because your God loves Israel and
means to uphold him for ever, he has made you king over them to administer law
and justice.' •And she presented the king with a hundred and twenty talents 9
of gold and great quantities of spices and precious stones. There never were
spices like those the queen of Sheba gave to King Solomon. •Similarly the servants 10
of Huram and the servants of Solomon, who carried gold from Ophir, brought
algummim wood and precious stones. •Of the algummim wood the king made 11
floorboards for the Temple of Yahweh and for the royal palace, and lyres and
harps for the musicians; the like of them had never been seen before in the land
of Judah. •And King Solomon, in his turn, presented the queen of Sheba with 12
everything she expressed any wish for, besides returning what she had brought to
the king. Then she went home, she and her servants, to her own country.

The weight of gold coming to Solomon in one year was six hundred and 13
sixty-six talents of gold, •not counting the merchants' dues that the import 14
agents brought in; all the kings of Arabia and the governors of the country also
brought gold and silver to Solomon. •King Solomon made two hundred great 15
shields of beaten gold, and plated each shield with six hundred shekels of gold.
Also three hundred small shields of beaten gold, and plated each of these with 16
three hundred shekels of gold; and he put them in the Hall of the Forest of
Lebanon. •The king also made a great ivory throne, and plated it with purest 17
gold. •The throne had six steps, and at the back of it a lamb in gold, and arms 18
at either side of the seat; two lions stood beside the arms, •and twelve lions stood 19
on either side of the six steps. No throne like this was ever made in any other
kingdom.

All King Solomon's drinking vessels were of gold, and all the furnishings in 20
the Hall of the Forest of Lebanon were of pure gold; silver was thought little
of in the time of Solomon. •And the king also had ships that went to Tarshish 21
with Huram's men, and once every three years the ships of Tarshish would come
back laden with gold and silver, ivory, apes and baboons. •For riches and for 22
wisdom King Solomon outdid all the kings of the earth. •All the kings of the 23
earth sought audience of Solomon to hear the wisdom God had implanted in
his heart, •and each would bring his own present: gold vessels, silver vessels, 24
robes, armour, spices, horses and mules; and this went on year after year.

Solomon had four thousand stalls for his horses and chariots, and twelve 25
thousand horses; these he stationed in the chariot towns and near the king in
Jerusalem. •Solomon extended his power over all the kingdoms from the river 26
to the land of the Philistines and the Egyptian border. •In Jerusalem the king 27
made silver common as pebbles, and cedars plentiful as the sycamores of the
Lowlands. •Horses were imported for Solomon from Cilicia and all the other 28
countries too.

The death of Solomon

The rest of the history of Solomon, from first to last, is not all this recorded 29
in the History of Nathan the prophet, in the Prophecy of Ahijah of Shiloh, and
in the Vision of Iddo the seer concerning Jeroboam son of Nebat? •Solomon 30

31 reigned in Jerusalem for forty years over all Israel. •Then Solomon slept with his ancestors and was buried in the Citadel of David his father; his son Rehoboam succeeded him.

IV. FIRST REFORMS OF THE MONARCHICAL PERIOD

A. REHOBOAM AND THE REGROUPING OF THE LEVITES

The schism

1
2 **10** Rehoboam went to Shechem, for it was to Shechem that all Israel had gone to proclaim him king. •As soon as Jeroboam son of Nebat heard the news—he was still in Egypt, where he had taken refuge from King Solomon—he
3 returned from Egypt. •They sent and summoned him, and he came, with the whole assembly.

4   And they said this to Rehoboam, •'Your father gave us a heavy burden to bear; lighten your father's harsh tyranny now, and the weight of the burden he
5 laid on us, and we will serve you'. •He said, 'Come back to me in three days'. And the people went away.

6   King Rehoboam consulted the elders, who had been in the service of his father Solomon while he was alive. 'What reply' he asked 'do you advise me
7 to give to this people?' •'If you are kind to these people,' they said 'if you are pleasant to them and treat them fairly, then they will be your servants for ever.'
8 But he rejected the advice given him by the elders and consulted the young men
9 who had grown up with him and were in his service. •'How do you advise us' he asked 'to answer these people who have said to me, "Lighten the burden your
10 father imposed on us"?' •The young men who had grown up with him replied, 'Give this answer to these people who have said, "Your father gave us a heavy burden to bear, you must lighten it for us", say this to them, "My little finger is
11 thicker than my father's loins! •So then, my father made you bear a heavy burden; I will make it heavier still! My father beat you with whips; I am going to beat you with loaded scourges!" '

12   On the third day all the people came to Rehoboam in obedience to the king's
13 command: 'Come back to me on the third day'. •The king gave them a harsh
14 answer. King Rehoboam, rejecting the advice of the elders, •spoke to them as the young men had recommended. 'My father made you bear a heavy burden,' he said 'but I will make it heavier still. My father beat you with whips; I am
15 going to beat you with loaded scourges!' •The king in fact took no notice of the people's wishes, and this was brought about by God to carry out the promise Yahweh had spoken through Ahijah of Shiloh to Jeroboam son of Nebat.
16 When all Israel saw that the king took no notice of their wishes, they gave him this answer:

> 'What share have we in David?
> We have no inheritance in the son of Jesse.
> To your tents, Israel, each one of you.
> Henceforth look after your own House, David!'

17   And all Israel went off to their tents. •Rehoboam however ruled over those
18 sons of Israel who lived in the towns of Judah. •King Rehoboam sent Adoram who was in charge of forced labour, but the Israelites stoned him to death; whereupon King Rehoboam was obliged to mount his chariot and escape to
19 Jerusalem. •And Israel has remained separated from the House of David until the present day.

The activities of Rehoboam

11 Rehoboam went to Jerusalem and mustered the House of Judah with 1
Benjamin, a hundred and eighty thousand picked warriors, to fight the
House of Israel and win back the kingdom of Rehoboam. •But the word of 2
Yahweh came to Shemaiah the man of God, •'Say this to Rehoboam son of 3
Solomon, king of Judah, and to all the Israelites in Judah and Benjamin,
"Yahweh says this: Do not set out to fight against your brothers; let everyone go 4
home, for what has happened is my doing"'. They obeyed Yahweh's command
and went back instead of marching against Jeroboam.

Rehoboam lived in Jerusalem and built fortified towns in Judah. •He rebuilt 5,6
Bethlehem, Etam, Tekoa, •Beth-zur, Soco, Adullam, •Gath, Mareshah, Ziph, 7,8
Adoraim, Lachish, Azekah, •Zorah, Aijalon, Hebron; these were fortified towns 9,10
in Judah and Benjamin. •He fortified them strongly and put commanders in 11
them with stores of food, oil and wine. •In each of these towns were shields 12
and spears. He made them very strong to keep Judah and Benjamin under
control.

Rehoboam's relations with the priests and Levites

The priests and the Levites throughout Israel left their districts to take up 13
residence near him. •The Levites, indeed, abandoned their pasture lands and 14
their holdings, and came to Judah and Jerusalem, since Jeroboam and his sons
had excluded them from the priesthood of Yahweh, •and had set up for himself 15
a priesthood of the high places, for the satyrs and the calves he had made.
Members of all the tribes of Israel, men wholeheartedly devoted to the worship 16
of Yahweh the God of Israel, followed them and came to Jerusalem to sacrifice
to Yahweh, the God of their ancestors. •These added strength to the kingdom of 17
Judah, and gave their support to Rehoboam son of Solomon for three years,
because during three years he followed the example of David and Solomon.

Rehoboam turns unfaithful

Rehoboam took as wife Mahalath the daughter of Jerimoth son of David, 18
and of Abihail, daughter of Eliab son of Jesse, •and she bore him sons: Jeush, 19
Shemariah and Zaham. •After her, he married Maacah daughter of Absalom, 20
who bore him Abijah, Attai, Ziza and Shelomith. •Rehoboam loved Maacah, 21
daughter of Absalom, more than all his other wives and concubines. He had
in fact a total of eighteen wives and sixty concubines and had twenty-eight sons and
sixty daughters. •Rehoboam appointed Abijah, Maacah's son, as head of the 22
family, to be prince among his brothers, with a view to making him king. •He 23
built more and demolished more than any of his descendants throughout the
territories of Judah and Benjamin and in all the fortified towns, which he equipped
with numerous granaries.

But he consulted the many gods of his wives, 12 and no sooner was his 1
royal authority securely consolidated than he, and all Israel with him, abandoned
the Law of Yahweh. •In the fifth year of Rehoboam, Shishak the king of Egypt 2
marched on Jerusalem, since it had been unfaïhful to Yahweh. •With twelve 3
hundred chariots and sixty thousand horses and a countless army of Libyans,
Sukkiim and Ethiopians who came from Egypt with him, •he captured the 4
fortified towns of Judah and reached Jerusalem. •Rehoboam and the Judaean 5
captains, at the advance of Shishak, had mustered near Jerusalem; to them came
Shemaiah the prophet. 'Yahweh says this' he said to them. '"You have
abandoned me, now I have abandoned you into the hands of Shishak."' •Then 6
the Israelite captains and the king humbled themselves. 'Yahweh is just!' they
said. •When Yahweh saw that they had humbled themselves, the word of Yahweh 7
came to Shemaiah. 'They have humbled themselves,' it said 'I will not destroy
them. In a little while I will grant them deliverance; my wrath shall not fall
on Jerusalem through the power of Shishak. •Nevertheless they shall become his 8

slaves, so that they may come to understand the difference between serving me and serving the kingdoms of foreign countries.'

9   Shishak the king of Egypt marched on Jerusalem. He took all the treasures from the Temple of Yahweh and the treasures from the royal palace, he took
10 everything, including the golden shields that Solomon had made; •in place of them King Rehoboam had bronze shields made, entrusting them to the care
11 of the officers of the guard who guarded the king's palace gate. •Whenever the king went to the Temple of Yahweh, the guards would come out carrying them, and return them to the guardroom afterwards.

12   Since he had humbled himself, the wrath of Yahweh turned away from him
13 and did not destroy him altogether. Indeed, things went well in Judah, •and King Rehoboam was able to strengthen his position in Jerusalem and to govern. Now Rehoboam was forty-one years old when he came to the throne and he reigned for seventeen years in Jerusalem, the city chosen by Yahweh out of all the tribes of Israel, in which to give his name a home. His mother's name was
14 Naamah the Ammonitess. •He did evil, because he had not set his heart on seeking Yahweh.

15   The history of Rehoboam, from first to last, is not all this recorded in the Annals of Shemaiah the prophet and of Iddo the seer concerning the grouping of the Levites and the incessant warfare between Rehoboam and Jeroboam?
16 Then Rehoboam slept with his ancestors and was buried in the Citadel of David; his son Abijah succeeded him.

B. ABIJAH AND LOYALTY TO THE LEGITIMATE PRIESTHOOD

War

1
2 **13** In the eighteenth year of King Jeroboam, Abijah became king of Judah and reigned for three years in Jerusalem. His mother's name was Micaiah,
3 daughter of Uriel, from Gibeah. Abijah and Jeroboam were at war. •Abijah went into battle with an army of brave fighters, four hundred thousand picked men, while Jeroboam drew up his battle line against him with eight hundred thousand picked men, stout fighters.

Abijah addresses the Israelites

4   Abijah took his stand on Mount Zemaraim, in the highlands of Ephraim.
5 'Jeroboam and all Israel' he cried 'listen to me! •Do you not know that Yahweh the God of Israel has given the sovereignty of Israel to David for
6 ever? It is an inviolable covenant for him and for his sons. •Yet Jeroboam son of Nebat, a servant of Solomon son of David, has risen in revolt against
7 his lord; •worthless men, scoundrels, have rallied to him and forced their will on Rehoboam the son of Solomon, on Rehoboam, then a young man and timid,
8 powerless to resist them. •Now you talk of resisting the sovereignty of Yahweh, which belongs to the sons of David, and you stand there in a great horde, with
9 your golden calves that Jeroboam made you for gods! •Have you not driven out the priests of Yahweh, the sons of Aaron and the Levites, to make priests of your own like the peoples of foreign countries? Anyone who comes with a bull and seven rams to get himself consecrated can become priest of what is no god
10 at all! •But for our part, our God is Yahweh, and we have not abandoned him: our priests are sons of Aaron who minister to Yahweh, and those who serve
11 are Levites. •Every morning, every evening, we burn holocausts to Yahweh our God; we have the incense of sweet spices, the loaves set out in rows on the pure table, the golden lamp-stand with its lamps that burn each evening; for we
12 observe the ritual of Yahweh our God, but you have abandoned him. •See how God is with us, at our head; see his priests with the trumpets, who will sound them to raise the war cry against you. Sons of Israel, do not fight against Yahweh, the God of our ancestors, for you will not succeed.'

The battle

Jeroboam outflanked the Judaeans by setting an ambush in their rear; the 13 Judaeans were facing the Israelites with the ambush in their rear. •The Judaeans, 14 turning about, found themselves attacked in front and rear. They called on Yahweh, the priests sounded the trumpets, •and the men of Judah raised the war cry, and 15 as they raised the cry God scattered Jeroboam and all Israel before Abijah and Judah. •The Israelites fled before Judah and God delivered them into the power 16 of the Judaeans. •Abijah and his army inflicted a crushing defeat on them: five 17 hundred thousand of Israel's chosen men fell killed. •So the sons of Israel 18 were humbled on that occasion, and the sons of Judah reassured since they had relied on Yahweh, the God of their ancestors.

The end of the reign of Abijah

Abijah pursued Jeroboam and captured certain towns from him: Bethel with 19 its outlying villages, Jeshanah with its outlying villages and Ephron with its outlying villages. •So in the lifetime of Abijah, Jeroboam could no longer 20 maintain his power; and Yahweh struck him down, and he died. •But Abijah 21 grew in strength; he took fourteen wives and had twenty-two sons and sixteen daughters. •The rest of the history of Abijah, his conduct and his deeds, is not 22 all this recorded in the Midrash of the prophet Iddo? •Then Abijah slept with 23 / 14:1 his fathers and they buried him in the Citadel of David; his son Asa succeeded him.

C. ASA AND HIS REFORM OF PUBLIC WORSHIP

Peace under Asa

In his time the country was at peace for ten years.

14 Asa did what is good and right in the eyes of Yahweh. •He abolished 1:2 / 2:3 the foreign altars and the high places, broke the pillars, cut down the sacred poles, •and urged the Judaeans to look to Yahweh, the God of their 3/4 ancestors, and to observe law and commandment. •He abolished the high 4/5 places and the altars of incense in every town of Judah. The kingdom was at peace under his rule. •He rebuilt the fortified towns of Judah, since the country 5/6 was at peace and free of war during those years, Yahweh having granted him peace.

'Let us rebuild these towns,' he told Judah 'let us surround them with wall 6/7 and tower, with gate and bar; we shall be left in this land, since we have looked to Yahweh our God; and he has looked to us and given us peace on every side.' They built and prospered. •Asa had an army of three hundred thousand 7/8 Judaeans armed with buckler and spear, and two hundred and eighty thousand Benjaminites bearing shield and wielding the bow, all of them valiant champions.

Zerah's invasion

Zerah the Cushite and an army one million strong with three hundred chari- 8/9 ots made an incursion, and penetrated to Mareshah. •Asa marched out to 9/10 intercept him and drew up his battle line in the Valley of Zephathah, at Mareshah. He called on Yahweh, his God. 'Yahweh,' he said 'no one but you can stand 10/11 up for the powerless against the powerful. Come to our help, Yahweh our God! We rely on you, and confront this horde in your name. Yahweh, you are our God. Let man leave everything to you!'

Yahweh defeated the Cushites before Asa and the Judaeans, the Cushites 11/12 fled, •and Asa pursued them with his army as far as Gerar. So many of the 12/13 Cushites fell that recovery was impossible, for they had been shattered before Yahweh and his army. They collected great quantities of booty, •they conquered 13/14 all the towns in the area of Gerar, for the terror of Yahweh had fallen on these;

¹⁴⁄₁₅ they plundered them all since they were full of loot. •They also set on the enclosures of livestock and carried off great numbers of sheep and camels; then they returned to Jerusalem.

The prophecy of Azariah and the oath of fidelity

¹⁄₂ 15 The spirit of God came on Azariah son of Oded; •he went out to meet Asa and said, 'Listen to me, Asa, and all you of Judah and of Benjamin. Yahweh is with you so long as you are with him. When you seek him, he lets ³ you find him; when you desert him, he deserts you. •Many a day Israel will ⁴ spend without a faithful God, without priest to teach, without law; •but in their distress they will return to Yahweh, the God of Israel; they will seek him, and ⁵ he will let them find him. •When that time comes no grown man will know peace, ⁶ for many troubles will afflict all the inhabitants of the country. •Nation will be shattered by nation, city shattered by city, since God will afflict them with every ⁷ kind of distress. •But for your part, take courage, do not let your hands weaken, for your deeds will be rewarded.'

⁸ When Asa heard these words and this prophecy, he was emboldened to remove all the abominable idols throughout the land of Judah and Benjamin, and in the towns he had captured in the highlands of Ephraim; he then ⁹ repaired the altar of Yahweh that stood in front of the Porch of Yahweh.ᵃ •He gathered all Judah and Benjamin together, and also the Ephraimites, Manassites and Simeonites who had settled with them, since great numbers of Israelites had ¹⁰ gone over to Asa when they saw that Yahweh was with him. •In the third month ¹¹ of the fifteenth year of Asa they assembled in Jerusalem; •and they sacrificed to Yahweh that day seven hundred oxen and seven thousand sheep out of the ¹² spoil they had brought back. •They made a compact to seek Yahweh, the God of ¹³ their ancestors, with all their heart and soul; •anyone who would not seek Yahweh the God of Israel was to be put to death, whether of high or low degree, man ¹⁴ or woman. •They pledged their oath to Yahweh aloud with shouts to the sound ¹⁵ of trumpet and horn; •all Judah rejoiced at the oath they had wholeheartedly taken. They sought Yahweh so earnestly that he let them find him, and granted them peace on every side.

Further activities of Asa

¹⁶ Maacah herself, the mother of King Asa, was deprived by him of the dignity of queen mother for making an obscenity for Asherah; Asa cut down her obscenity ¹⁷ and burnt it in the wadi Kidron. •Though the high places were not abolished ¹⁸ in Israel,ᵇ the heart of Asa was blameless all his life. •He deposited the offerings dedicated by his father and his own offerings too, in the Temple of God, silver and gold and furnishings.

¹⁹⁄₁ Up to the thirty-fifth year of Asa's reign there was no war. 16 In the thirty-sixth year of Asa's reign, Baasha king of Israel marched on Judah and fortified ² Ramah to blockade Asa king of Judah. •Asa then took the silver and gold from the treasuries of the Temple of Yahweh and the royal palace, and sent this with the following message to Ben-hadad king of Aram who lived in Damascus, ³ 'An alliance between myself and you, as between my father and your father! With this I send you silver and gold. Come, break off your alliance with Baasha king ⁴ of Israel, and he will have to retire from my territory.' •Ben-hadad agreed, and sent his generals against the towns of Israel; he conquered Ijon, Dan, Abel-⁵ maim and all the garrison towns of Naphtali. •When Baasha heard this he gave ⁶ up fortifying Ramah, abandoning this work. •King Asa then brought all Judah; they took away the stones and timber with which Baasha had been fortifying Ramah, and the king used them to fortify Geba and Mizpah.

---

15 a. Asa, who is credited at the beginning of this chapter with measures exactly like those taken by Josiah, 2 K 22, is credited here with Hezekiah's restoration of the altar, 2 K 16.
b. The Chronicler follows 1 K without harmonising it with 2 Ch 14.

It was then that Hanani the seer came to Asa king of Judah and said, 'Since 7
you have relied on the king of Aram and not on Yahweh your God, the army
of the king of Aram will slip through your fingers. •Did not the Cushites and 8
Libyans form a vast army with great numbers of chariots and horses? And were
they not delivered into your power because you relied on Yahweh? •Since the 9
eyes of Yahweh rove to and fro across the whole world to display his might
on behalf of those whose hearts are wholly his, you have acted on this occasion
like a fool; and from now on you will have war.' •Enraged with the seer, Asa 10
had him put in the stocks in prison, he was so angry with him for this; at the
same time Asa began treating part of the population harshly too.

The end of the reign of Asa

The history of Asa, from first to last, is recorded in the Book of the Kings 11
of Judah and Israel. •A disease attacked Asa from head to foot in the thirty- 12
ninth year of his reign; and, what is more, he turned in his sickness, not to
Yahweh, but to doctors. •Then Asa slept with his ancestors, dying in the 13
forty-first year of his reign. •They buried him in the tomb he had ordered to 14
be dug for himself in the Citadel of David. They laid him on a couch entirely
covered with spices and varied ointments, products of the perfumer's skill, and
lit a huge fire for him.

D. JEHOSHAPHAT AND HIS GOVERNMENT

His power

17 His son Jehoshaphat succeeded him and consolidated his power over Israel. 1
He put troops in all the fortified towns in Judah, and appointed governors 2
in the land of Judah and in all the towns of Ephraim captured by his father Asa.

His observance of the Law

Yahweh was with Jehoshaphat because he followed the example of his father's 3
earlier days and did not have recourse to the Baals; •he sought the God of his 4
father, following his commandments and not following the example of Israel.
Yahweh made the kingship secure in his hands; all Judah paid tribute to Jehosha- 5
phat, and ample riches and honour were his. •His heart advanced in the ways 6
of Yahweh, and once again he did away with the high places and sacred poles
in Judah.

In the third year of his reign he sent his officers: Ben-hail, Obadiah, Zechariah, 7
Nethanel and Micaiah, to give instruction in the towns of Judah. •With them 8
went the Levites: Shemaiah, Nethaniah, Zebadiah, Asahel, Shemiramoth,
Jehonathan, Adonijah and Toḅijah, the Levites, together with the priests,
Elishama and Jehoram. •They gave instruction in Judah, having with them the 9
book of the Law of Yahweh, and went round all the towns of Judah instructing
the people. •The terror of Yahweh fell on all the kingdoms of the land 10
surrounding Judah; they did not make war on Jehoshaphat. •Some of the 11
Philistines brought him gifts and silver in tribute; the Arabs^a themselves brought
him, in small stock, seven thousand seven hundred rams and seven thousand
seven hundred he-goats. •Jehoshaphat became more and more powerful. 12
He built fortresses and garrison towns in Judah.

The army

He had strong formations in the towns of Judah and a garrison of valiant 13
champions in Jerusalem. •This was their disposition by families: for Judah, 14
commanders of thousands: Adnah, the commanding officer, with three hundred
thousand valiant champions; •under his command, Jehohanan with two hundred 15

16 and eighty thousand; •under his command, Amasiah son of Zichri, who had volunteered for Yahweh's service, with two hundred thousand valiant champions.
17 From Benjamin: the valiant champion Eliada with two hundred thousand,
18 armed with bow and shield; •under his command, Jehozabad with a hundred and eighty thousand equipped for war.
19 These were the men who served the king, not counting those the king had put in the fortified towns throughout Judah.

The alliance with Ahab; the prophets' attitude

1 18 Jehoshaphat, then, enjoyed great wealth and honour, and allied himself
2   by marriage to Ahab. •After some years he went to visit Ahab in Samaria. Ahab slaughtered for him and for his retinue great numbers of sheep and oxen
3 to induce him to attack Ramoth-gilead. •'Will you come with me to Ramoth-gilead?' Ahab king of Israel asked Jehoshaphat king of Judah. Jehoshaphat answered the king of Israel, 'I am as ready for battle as you, my men as your men'.

The spurious prophets predict success

4 Jehoshaphat, however, said to the king of Israel, 'First, please consult the
5 word of Yahweh'. •So the king of Israel called the prophets together, four hundred of them. 'Should we march to attack Ramoth-gilead,' he asked 'or should I refrain?' 'March,' they replied 'Yahweh will deliver it into the power of the
6 king.' •But Jehoshaphat said, 'Is there no other prophet of Yahweh here for
7 us to consult?' •The king of Israel answered Jehoshaphat, 'There is one more man through whom we can consult Yahweh, but I hate him because he never has a favourable prophecy for me, always unfavourable ones; he is Micaiah son
8 of Imlah'. 'The king should not say such things' Jehoshaphat said. •Accordingly the king of Israel summoned one of the eunuchs and said, 'Bring Micaiah son of Imlah immediately'.
9 The king of Israel and Jehoshaphat king of Judah were both sitting on their thrones in full regalia; they sat at the threshing-floor outside the gate of Samaria,
10 with all the prophets raving in front of them. •Zedekiah son of Chenaanah had made himself iron horns. 'Yahweh says this' he said. ' "With these you will
11 gore the Aramaeans till you make an end of them." ' •And all the prophets prophesied the same. 'March to Ramoth-gilead,' they said 'and conquer. Yahweh will deliver it into the power of the king.'
12 The messenger who had gone to summon Micaiah said, 'Here are all the prophets as one man in speaking favourably to the king. Try to speak like one
13 of them and foretell success.' •But Micaiah answered, 'As Yahweh lives, what
14 my God says, that will I utter!' •When he came to the king, the king said, 'Micaiah, should we march to attack Ramoth-gilead, or should I refrain?' He
15 answered, 'March and conquer. They will be delivered into your power.' •But the king said, 'How often must I put you on oath to tell me nothing but the
16 truth in the name of Yahweh?' •Then Micaiah spoke:

> 'I have seen all Israel scattered on the mountains
> like sheep without a shepherd.
> And Yahweh said, "These have no master,
> let each one go home unmolested".'

17 At this the king of Israel said to Jehoshaphat, 'Did I not tell you that he
18 never gives me favourable prophecies, but only unfavourable ones?' •Micaiah went on, 'Listen rather to the word of Yahweh. I have seen Yahweh seated on
19 his throne; all the array of heaven stood to his right and to his left. •Yahweh said, "Who will trick Ahab king of Israel into marching to his death at Ramoth-

17 a. Nomadic settlers in Edom and Moab.

gilead?" At which some answered one way, and some another. •Then the spirit 20
came forward and stood before Yahweh. "I," he said "I will trick him." "How?"
Yahweh asked. •He replied, "I will go and become a lying spirit in the mouths 21
of all his prophets". "You shall trick him," Yahweh said "you shall succeed.
Go and do it." •Now see how Yahweh has put a lying spirit into the mouths 22
of your prophets here. But Yahweh has pronounced disaster on you.'

Then Zedekiah son of Chenaanah came up and struck Micaiah on the jaw. 23
'Which way' he asked 'did the spirit of Yahweh leave me, to talk to you?'
'This is what you will find out,' Micaiah retorted 'the day you flee to an inner 24
room to hide.' •The king of Israel said, 'Seize Micaiah and hand him over to 25
Amon, governor of the city, and to Prince Joash, •and say, "This is the king's 26
order: Put this man in prison and feed him on nothing but bread and water
until I come back safe and sound" '. •Micaiah said, 'If you come back safe 27
and sound, Yahweh has not spoken through me'.

The king of Israel and Jehoshaphat king of Judah went up against Ramoth- 28
gilead. •The king of Israel said to Jehoshaphat, 'I will disguise myself to go 29
into battle, but I want you to wear your royal uniform.' The king of Israel
disguised himself, and they went into battle. •The king of Aram had given his 30
chariot commanders the following order: 'Do not attack anyone of whatever
rank, except the king of Israel'. •When the chariot commanders caught sight 31
of Jehoshaphat, they said, 'That is the king of Israel'. And they wheeled to the
attack. But Jehoshaphat gave a shout and Yahweh came to his help, God drew
them away from him, •for the chariot commanders, realising that he was not 32
the king of Israel, called off their pursuit.

Now one of the men, drawing his bow at random, hit the king of Israel 33
between the corslet and the scale-armour of his breastplate. 'Turn about,' the
king said to his charioteer 'get me out of the battle; I have been hurt.' •But 34
the battle grew fiercer as the day went on; until evening the king held himself
upright in his chariot facing the Aramaeans, and at sunset he died.

19 Jehoshaphat came back safe and sound to Jerusalem. •Jehu, son of Hanani $\frac{1}{2}$
the seer, went to meet him and said to King Jehoshaphat, 'Should a man
give help to the wicked? Should you love those who hate Yahweh and so bring
his wrath on you? •There is some good in you, however, since you have removed 3
the sacred poles from the land and have set your heart on seeking God.'

Measures taken to spread the true religion of Yahweh

After a stay in Jerusalem, Jehoshaphat made another progress through his 4
people, from Beersheba to the highlands of Ephraim, to bring them back to
Yahweh, the God of their ancestors. •He appointed judges in the country in 5
every one of all the fortified towns of Judah. •He said to these judges, 'Give 6
due thought to your duties, since you are not judging in the name of men but in
the name of Yahweh, who is with you whenever you pronounce sentence. •May 7
the fear of Yahweh now be on you. Keep the Law, apply it, for Yahweh our
God has no part in fraud or partiality or the taking of bribes.'

In addition, Jehoshaphat appointed priests, Levites and heads of Israelite 8
families in Jerusalem to pronounce the verdicts of Yahweh and to judge disputed
cases. They lived in Jerusalem •and Jehoshaphat gave them the following 9
instructions, 'You are to perform these duties in the fear of Yahweh, faithfully
and with all your heart. •Whatever dispute comes before you from your brothers 10
living in their towns: a question of blood-vengeance, of the Law, of some commandment, of statute, or of ordinance, you are to clarify these matters for them
so that they do not incur guilt before Yahweh, whose wrath will otherwise come
on you and your brothers. Do this and you will incur no guilt.

'Amariah, the chief priest, will preside over you in all religious matters, and 11
Zebadiah son of Ishmael, controller of the House of Judah, in all matters
affecting the king. The Levites will serve as your scribes. Be resolute, carry out
these instructions, and Yahweh will be there to bring success.'

An act of faith and song of praise in the war against Edom

1 **20** After this the Moabites and Ammonites, with some of the Meunites*
2 started to make war on Jehoshaphat. •Jehoshaphat received the following
intelligence, 'A vast horde is advancing against you from Edom, from the other
side of the sea; they are already at Hazazon-tamar, that is, En-gedi'.

3 Jehoshaphat was alarmed and resolved to have recourse to Yahweh; he
4 proclaimed a fast for all Judah. •Judah assembled to seek help from Yahweh;
they came seeking Yahweh from every single town in Judah.

5 At this assembly of the people of Judah and Jerusalem in the Temple of
6 Yahweh, Jehoshaphat stood before the new court •and said, 'Yahweh, God of
our ancestors, are you not the God who dwells in the heavens? Do you not rule
over all the kingdoms of the nations? Such power and might are in your hands
7 that no one can resist you. •Are you not our God, you who have dispossessed the
inhabitants of this land for Israel your people, and given it to the descendants of
8 Abraham whom you will love for ever? •They have settled in it and built a
9 sanctuary there for your name, •saying, "Should calamity befall us, or war,
punishment, pestilence, or famine, then we shall stand before this Temple and
before you, for your name is in this Temple. From the depths of our distress
we shall cry to you, and you will hear and save us."

10 'Here now are the Ammonites and Moab and the mountain folk of Seir;
when Israel came out of the land of Egypt you would not let Israel invade them;
11 instead, Israel turned away from them and did not destroy them; •and this
is how they reward us, by coming to drive us out of the possessions you have
12 given us as our inheritance. •Will you our God not execute judgement on them,
since we are helpless against this vast horde attacking us? We ourselves do not
know what to do; we look to you.'

13 All the men of Judah, even down to their youngest children and their wives,
14 stood in the presence of Yahweh. •In the middle of the assembly the spirit of
Yahweh came on Jahaziel son of Zechariah, son of Benaiah, son of Jeiel, son
15 of Mattaniah the Levite, one of the sons of Asaph. •'Listen all you men of
Judah,' he cried 'and you who live in Jerusalem, and you, King Jehoshaphat!
Yahweh says this to you, "Do not be afraid, do not be daunted by this vast
16 horde; this battle is not yours but God's. •March out against them tomorrow;
they are coming up by the Slope of Ziz and you will come on them in the Valley
17 of Soph, near the wilderness of Jeruel. •You will not need to fight here. Take
up your position, stand firm, and see what salvation Yahweh has in store for
you. Judah and Jerusalem, be fearless, be dauntless; march out against them
tomorrow and Yahweh will be with you." '

18 Jehoshaphat bent his head, his face to the ground, and all Judah with those
19 who lived in Jerusalem fell down before Yahweh, worshipping him. •Then the
Levites—Kohathites and Korahites—began praising Yahweh the God of Israel
at the tops of their voices.

20 They rose early in the morning and left for the wilderness of Tekoa. As they
were setting out, Jehoshaphat stood and said, 'Listen to me Judah and all who
live in Jerusalem! Have faith in Yahweh your God and you will be secure; have
21 faith in his prophets and you will be successful.' •Then, having held a conference
with the people, he set the cantors of Yahweh in sacred vestments at the head of
the army, to sing praises to him. 'Give praise to Yahweh,' they sang 'for his love is
22 everlasting.' •As they began to sing their joy and their praise, Yahweh laid an
ambush for the Ammonites and Moab and the mountain folk of Seir who had
23 come to attack Judah, and routed them. •The Ammonites and Moabites turned
on the mountain folk of Seir to inflict the ban on them and destroy them
altogether, but they only helped each other to their own undoing.

24 When the men of Judah reached the spot that looks out on the wilderness

20 a. Meon is in Edom, near Petra.

and turned to face the horde, they found only corpses lying on the ground; no one had escaped. •Jehoshaphat came with his troops to plunder them, and 25 found quantities of cattle, goods, clothing and valuables; they collected more than they could take away; the booty was so plentiful they were three days gathering it. •On the fourth day they mustered in the Valley of Beracah; 26 and there they did indeed bless Yahweh,ᵇ hence the name of the Valley of Beracah by which the place is still called today. •Then all the men of Judah and Benjamin, 27 with Jehoshaphat at their head, went back joyfully to Jerusalem, for Yahweh had given them cause to rejoice over their enemies. •To the music of harp and 28 lyre and trumpet they came to Jerusalem and to the Temple of Yahweh, •and 29 the Terror of God came on all the kingdoms of foreign countries when they came to hear how Yahweh had fought against the enemies of Israel. •The kingdom 30 of Jehoshaphat was calm, his God granting him peace on all his frontiers.

The end of the reign of Jehoshaphat

Jehoshaphat reigned over Judah. He was thirty-five years old when he came 31 to the throne and he reigned for twenty-five years in Jerusalem. His mother's name was Azubah, daughter of Shilhi. •He followed the example of his father Asa 32 undeviatingly, doing what is right in the eyes of Yahweh. •The high places, 33 however, were not abolished; the people had still not turned their hearts to the God of their ancestors. •The rest of the history of Jehoshaphat, from first to last, 34 is recorded in the Annals of Jehu son of Hanani which have been transcribed into the Book of the Kings of Israel.

After this, Jehoshaphat king of Judah allied himself with Ahaziah king of 35 Israel, who led him into evil ways. •He combined with him to build ships that 36 would sail to Tarshish; they built them at Ezion-geber. •Eliezer son of Dodavahu 37 of Mareshah then made a prophecy against Jehoshaphat. 'Because you have allied yourself with Ahaziah,' he said 'Yahweh has broken your work.' The ships broke up and were never fit to sail for Tarshish.

21 Jehoshaphat slept with his ancestors and was buried in the Citadel of 1 David; his son Jehoram succeeded him.

E. IMPIETY AND DISASTERS UNDER JEHORAM, AHAZIAH, ATHALIAH AND JOASH

The accession and crime of Jehoram

Jehoram had six brothers, sons of Jehoshaphat: Azariah, Jehiel, Zechariah, 2 Azariahu, Michael and Shephatiah; these are all the sons of Jehoshaphat king of Israel. •Their father had made them many gifts of silver, gold and jewels, 3 and of fortified towns in Judah, but he bequeathed the throne to Jehoram since he was the first-born. •Jehoram, having maintained his hold over his father's 4 kingdom and secured his own position, put all his brothers to the sword and some officials of Israel too.

Jehoram was thirty-two years old when he came to the throne and he reigned 5 for eight years in Jerusalem. •He followed the example of the kings of Israel 6 as the family of Ahab had done, having married one of Ahab's daughters; and he did what is displeasing to Yahweh. •Yahweh however did not intend 7 to destroy the House of David, because of the covenant he had made with David, and was faithful to the promise he had made to leave a lamp for him and his sons for ever.

The punishment

In his time Edom threw off the domination of Judah and set up a king for 8 itself. •Jehoram crossed the frontier with his commanders and all his chariots. 9 He rose during the night and broke through the Edomites encircling him and

10 his chariot commanders. •Thus Edom threw off the domination of Judah, and
has remained free to the present day. Libnah threw off Jehoram's domination
at the same time.

11   He had indeed deserted Yahweh, the God of his ancestors. •He also set up
high places in the highlands of Judah and caused the inhabitants of Jerusalem
12 to prostitute themselves, and Judah to go astray. •Then something written by the
prophet Elijah came into his hands. It ran, 'This is the word of Yahweh, the
God of David your ancestor. "Since you have not followed the example of
13 your father Jehoshaphat or of Asa king of Judah, •but the example of the
kings of Israel, and have caused Judah and the inhabitants of Jerusalem to
prostitute themselves, just as the House of Ahab did, and since you have also
14 murdered your brothers, your own family, better men than yourself, •Yahweh
will strike you with a great calamity, your people, your descendants, your wives
15 and all your property. •You yourself shall suffer dire diseases, and a disease of
your bowels so severe that within two years it will make your bowels drop out." '

16   Yahweh roused against Jehoram the hostility of the Philistines, and of the
17 Arabs bordering on the Cushites. •They attacked Judah, invading it and carrying
off all the property they found belonging to the king's household, including his
sons and his wives; the only son left him was Ahaziah, the youngest of them.
18 And after all this, Yahweh struck him down with an incurable disease of the
19 bowels; •it lasted for more than one year, and when two years were over and
his last hour had come, his bowels dropped out with disease and he died in great
pain. The people did not light a fire for him as they had for his father.

20   He was thirty-two years old when he came to the throne and he reigned
for eight years in Jerusalem. He passed away with no one to regret him, and
they buried him in the Citadel of David, though not in the tombs of the kings.

Ahaziah and his policy

1 **22** The population of Jerusalem made his youngest son Ahaziah king in
   succession to him, since the armed band that had broken into the camp
with the Arabs had killed all the elder sons. That was why Ahaziah son of Jehoram
2 became king of Judah. •Ahaziah was twenty years old when he came to the
throne and he reigned for one year in Jerusalem. His mother's name was Athaliah,
3 daughter of Omri. •He too followed the example of Ahab's family, since his
4 mother gave him wicked advice. •He did what is displeasing to Yahweh as
Ahab's family had done, for these were his advisers after his father's death, to
5 his undoing. •He also put their policy into practice and went with Jehoram son
of Ahab, king of Israel, to fight against Hazael king of Aram at Ramoth-gilead.
6 But the Aramaeans wounded Jehoram, •who returned to Jezreel to recover from
the wounds that he had received at Ramoth, fighting against Hazael king
of Aram. Ahaziah son of Jehoram, king of Judah, went down to Jezreel to visit
7 Jehoram son of Ahab because he was ill. •Through this visit to Jehoram Yahweh
brought ruin to Ahaziah. On his arrival he went out with Jehoram to meet Jehu
son of Nimshi whom Yahweh had anointed to make an end of the House of
8 Ahab. •While Jehu was busy executing justice on the House of Ahab, he came
across the officials of Judah and the nephews of Ahaziah who were in the king's
9 service; he killed them, •and then went in search of Ahaziah. The latter was
captured while trying to hide in Samaria, and taken to Jehu who put him to
death. But they gave him burial. 'This was a son of Jehoshaphat,' they said
'who sought Yahweh with all his heart.'

The crime of Athaliah

10   There was no one left in the House of Ahaziah strong enough to reign. •As soon
as Athaliah the mother of Ahaziah learned that her son was dead, she promptly
11 did away with all the royal stock of the House of Judah. •But Jehosheba,

b. *Beracah* means 'blessing'.

daughter of the king, secretly took away Joash, her brother's son, from among the sons of the king who were being murdered, and put him with his nurse in the sleeping quarters; in this way Jehosheba the daughter of King Joram and wife of Jehoiada the priest (a sister, too, of Ahaziah) hid him from Athaliah, and prevented her from killing him. •He stayed with them for six years, hidden in 12 the Temple of God, while Athaliah governed the country.

The ministers of the Temple oppose Athaliah

23 In the seventh year Jehoiada took strong measures. He sent for the com- 1 manders of hundreds, Azariah son of Jeroham, Ishmael son of Jehohanan, Azariah son of Obed, Maaseiah son of Adaiah and Elishaphat son of Zichri, and made a pact with them. •They went through Judah, gathering the Levites 2 from all the towns of Judah, and the heads of the Israelite families.ᵃ They came to Jerusalem, •and this whole assembly made a pact with the king in the Temple 3 of God. 'Here is the son of the king' Jehoiada told them. 'Let him reign, as Yahweh has promised of the sons of David! •This is what you must do: one 4 third of you, priests, Levites and keepers of the gate, must come in for the sabbath, •one third must be at the royal palace, one third at the Gate of Foun- 5 dation, and all the people will be in the court of the Temple of Yahweh. •Let no 6 one enter the Temple of Yahweh except the priests and the Levites on duty, since they are consecrated and may enter. The people must all observe the injunctions of Yahweh. •The Levites must surround the king, each with his 7 weapons in his hand; anyone who tries to enter the Temple is to be put to death. Wherever the king comes or goes, you must escort him.'

The Levites and all Judah carried out all the orders of Jehoiada the priest. 8 Each brought his men, those coming off duty on the sabbath together with those mounting guard on the sabbath, for Jehoiada the priest had exempted none of the orders. •Then Jehoiada the priest issued the commanders of hundreds with 9 King David's spears and large and small shields, which were in the Temple of God. •He drew all the people up, each man with his weapon in his hand, 10 from the south corner to the north corner of the Temple, surrounding the altar and the Temple, to form a circle round the king. •Then Jehoiada brought out 11 the king's son, crowned him, and imposed the Law on him; and they proclaimed him king, Jehoiada and his sons then anointed him and shouted, 'Long live the king!'

Athaliah, on hearing the shouts of the people rushing to the king and 12 acclaiming him, made for the Temple of Yahweh where the people were. •When 13 she saw the king standing there at the entrance beside the pillar, with the captains and trumpeters at the king's side, and all the country people rejoicing and sounding trumpets, and the cantors with their musical instruments leading the hymns, Athaliah tore her garments and shouted, 'Treason, treason!' •Then 14 Jehoiada the priest called out the military officers. 'Take her outside the precincts,' he ordered 'and put anyone to the sword who follows her.' For the priest had said, 'You must not put her to death in the Temple of Yahweh'. •They seized 15 her, and when she had reached the palace at the entry to the Gate of the Horses, they put her to death there.

The reforms by Jehoiada

Jehoiada made a covenant between the king and all the people, by which 16 they undertook to be the people of Yahweh. •All the people then went to the 17 temple of Baal and demolished it; they smashed his altars and his images and killed Mattan, priest of Baal, in front of the altars.

Jehoiada posted sentries to guard the Temple of Yahweh under the authority 18 of the levitical priests. David had given the Temple of Yahweh to these as their portion, so that they could offer the holocausts of Yahweh as is laid down in the Law of Moses, with joy and song, in accordance with the orders of

19 David. •He stationed gatekeepers at the gates of the Temple of Yahweh so that
20 no one who was in any way unclean might enter. •Then taking the commanders of hundreds, the notables, those holding public positions, and all the country people, he escorted the king down from the Temple of Yahweh. They entered the royal palace through the middle arch of the Upper Gate and seated
21 the king on the royal throne. •All the country people were delighted, and the city made no move. Athaliah was put to death.

Joash repairs the Temple

1 24 Joash was seven years old when he came to the throne and he reigned for forty years in Jerusalem. His mother's name was Zibiah of Beersheba.
2 Joash did what is pleasing to Yahweh throughout the lifetime of Jehoiada the
3 priest. •Jehoiada found him two wives and he had sons and daughters. •Subse-
4 quently, Joash made up his mind to repair the Temple of Yahweh.
5   Calling the priests and the Levites together, he said, 'Go out to the towns of Judah, and collect enough money from all the Israelites to make possible annual repairs to the Temple of Yahweh. Do this quickly.' But the Levites
6 were in no hurry, •so the king summoned Jehoiada their leader, and said, 'Why have you not insisted on the Levites collecting from Judah and Jerusalem what Moses the servant of Yahweh levied from the community of Israel for the Tent
7 of the Testimony? •Athaliah and her sons, whom she perverted, not only damaged the Temple of God but even assigned the sacred revenues of the Temple of
8 Yahweh to the Baals.' •The king ordered them to make a chest and to place
9 it outside the gate of the Temple of Yahweh. •Proclamation was then made in Judah and in Jerusalem that what Moses the servant of God had levied from
10 Israel in the wilderness should be brought to Yahweh. •All the officials and all the people came joyfully with their contribution, dropping it into the chest until all was paid.
11   When the chest was taken to the royal office of control, run by the Levites, these would check the amount of money in it; then the king's secretary would come with a representative of the chief priest; they would take up the chest, carry it away, and later return it to its place. They did this every day, and collected
12 a large sum of money. •The king and Jehoiada handed it over to the master of works attached to the Temple of Yahweh. The hired men, masons and carpenters, set about restoring the Temple of Yahweh; craftsmen in iron and
13 bronze also worked on the repairing of it. •The masters of works having once made a start, the repairs went ahead under their supervision; they rebuilt the
14 Temple of God to its former state and strengthened the fabric. •When they had finished, they brought the balance of the money to the king and Jehoiada, and with this furnishings were made for the Temple of Yahweh, vessels for the liturgy and for the holocausts, incense boats and objects of gold and silver.
     So, for as long as Jehoiada lived they offered perpetual holocaust in the
15 Temple of Yahweh. •Then Jehoiada, growing old, had his fill of days and died.
16 He died at the age of a hundred and thirty years, •and they buried him with the kings in the Citadel of David because he had served God and his Temple well in Israel.

Joash falls away and is punished

17   After the death of Jehoiada, the officials of Judah came to pay court to the
18 king, and the king now turned to them for advice. •The Judaeans abandoned the Temple of Yahweh, the God of their ancestors, for the worship of sacred poles and idols. Because of their guilt, God's anger fell on Judah and Jerusalem.

23 a. Comparison of this chapter with 2 K 11 shows how the Chronicler adapts his source to maintain the Temple regulations of his own time, and loses no opportunity to emphasise the part of priests and Levites: a *coup d'état* has become a liturgical act, even to the hymns led by cantors in v.13.

He sent them prophets to bring them back to Yahweh, but when these gave 19 their message, they would not listen. •The spirit of God took possession of 20 Zechariah son of Jehoiada the priest. He stood up before the people and said, 'God says this, "Why do you transgress the commandments of Yahweh to no good purpose? You have deserted Yahweh, now he deserts you." ' •They 21 then plotted against him and by order of the king stoned him in the court of the Temple of Yahweh. •King Joash, forgetful of the kindness that Jehoiada, 22 the father of Zechariah, had shown him, killed Jehoiada's son who cried out as he died, 'Yahweh sees and he will avenge!'

When a year had gone by, the Aramaean army made war on Joash. They 23 reached Judah and Jerusalem, and executed all the officials among the people, sending back to the king at Damascus all that they had plundered from them. Though the Aramaean army had by no means come in force, Yahweh delivered 24 into its power an army of great size for having deserted him, the God of their ancestors.

The Aramaeans treated Joash as he had deserved, •and when they retired 25 they left him a very sick man; and his officers, plotting against him to avenge the death of the son of Jehoiada the priest, murdered him in his bed. So he died, and they buried him in the Citadel of David, though not in the tombs of the kings. •These were the conspirators: Zabad son of Shimeath the Ammonite 26 woman, and Jehozabad son of Shimrith the Moabitess. •As regards his sons, 27 the heavy tribute imposed on him, and the restoration of the Temple of God, this is all recorded in the Midrash on the Book of the Kings. His son Amaziah succeeded him.

F. THE HALF-HEARTED PIETY AND PARTIAL SUCCESS
OF AMAZIAH, UZZIAH AND JOTHAM

The religious policy of Amaziah

25 Amaziah was twenty-five years old when he came to the throne and he 1 reigned for twenty-nine years in Jerusalem. His mother's name was Jehoaddan of Jerusalem. •He did what is pleasing to Yahweh, though not 2 wholeheartedly. •Once the kingdom was firmly under his control, he killed 3 those of his officers who had murdered the king his father. •But he did not put 4 their sons to death, in obedience to what is written in the Law, in the book of Moses, where Yahweh has ordered, 'Fathers must not be put to death for sons, nor sons for fathers; each one must be put to death for his own sin'.

Amaziah called the men of Judah together and organised them in families 5 with commanders of thousands and of hundreds for all Judah and Benjamin. He took a census of those who were twenty years old and upwards, and found there were three hundred thousand of them, eligible and fit for military service, with spear and shield to hand. •Next, he enrolled one hundred thousand valiant 6 champions from Israel as mercenaries, for a hundred talents of silver. •A man 7 of God then came to him. 'O king,' he said 'the troops of Israel must not march with you, for Yahweh is not with Israel, nor with anyone from Ephraim. •For 8 if they come, no matter how brave your conduct in the fight, God will still bring you down before your enemies, for God's is the power to uphold or to throw down.' •Amaziah answered the man of God, 'And what about the hundred 9 talents I have given the Israelite contingent?' 'Yahweh can give you far more than that' the man of God replied. •At this, Amaziah dismissed from his army 10 the troops that had come to him from Ephraim and sent them home; these men were furious with Judah and went home in a great rage.

His infidelity after the Edomite campaign

11 Amaziah decided to lead out his troops and, having reached the Valley of
12 Salt, defeated ten thousand of the sons of Seir. •The men of Judah took ten
thousand captives alive and, taking them to the summit of the Rock, threw
13 them off the top; they were all dashed to pieces. •Then the contingent which
Amaziah had dismissed and not allowed to fight with him raided the towns of
Judah, from Samaria as far as Beth-horon, beating a force of three thousand
strong and capturing great quantities of plunder.

14 On returning from his defeat of the Edomites, Amaziah brought the gods
of the sons of Seir with him; he set these up as gods for himself, bowing down
15 before them and burning incense to them. •The anger of Yahweh blazed out
against Amaziah; he sent him a prophet, who said, 'Why do you resort to this
people's gods, to gods who could not save their own people from your hands?'
16 He was still speaking when Amaziah interrupted him. 'Have we appointed you
a royal counsellor? If you do not want to be hurt, be quiet!' The prophet paused;
then he said, 'I know that God has determined to destroy you, since you have
behaved like this and have refused to listen to my advice'.

The disaster at Beth-shemesh

17 After consulting his advisers, Amaziah king of Judah sent a message to Joash
son of Jehoahaz son of Jehu, king of Israel, saying, 'Come and make a trial of
18 strength!' •Joash king of Israel sent back word to Amaziah king of Judah, 'The
thistle of Lebanon sent a message to the cedar of Lebanon, saying, "Give my
son your daughter in marriage"; but the wild animals of Lebanon trampled the
19 thistle down as they passed. •"Look at me, the conqueror of Edom" you say,
and now hold your head in the air; boast on, but stay at home. Why challenge
disaster, to your own ruin and the ruin of Judah?'

20 But Amaziah would not listen, and this was God's doing: he intended to
21 hand them over to their enemies for resorting to the gods of Edom. •And at
Beth-shemesh, which belongs to Judah, they made their trial of strength, Joash
22 and Amaziah king of Judah. •Judah was defeated by Israel, and everyone fled
23 to his tent. •The king of Judah, Amaziah son of Joash, son of Ahaziah, was
taken prisoner at Beth-shemesh by Joash king of Israel who led him off to
Jerusalem, where Joash demolished the city wall from the Gate of Ephraim to
24 the Gate of the Corner for a distance of four hundred cubits. •He took all the
gold and silver, and all the furnishings to be found with Obed-edom in the
Temple of God, the treasures of the royal palace, and hostages besides, and
then returned to Samaria.

The end of the reign of Amaziah

25 Amaziah son of Joash, king of Judah, lived for fifteen years after the death
of Joash son of Jehoahaz, king of Israel.

26 The rest of the history of Amaziah, from first to last, is not all this recorded
27 in the Book of the Kings of Judah and Israel? •After the time when Amaziah
rejected Yahweh, a plot was hatched against him in Jerusalem; he fled to Lachish;
28 but he was followed to Lachish and was put to death there. •He was brought
back by horse, and buried with his ancestors in the Citadel of David.

The beginning of the reign of Uzziah

1 **26** All the people of Judah chose Uzziah, who was sixteen years old, and
2 made him king in succession to his father Amaziah. •It was he who rebuilt
Elath and recovered it for Judah, after the king was sleeping with his ancestors.
3 Uzziah was sixteen years old when he came to the throne and he reigned for
4 fifty-two years in Jerusalem. His mother's name was Jecoliah, of Jerusalem. •He
5 did what is pleasing to Yahweh, just as his father Amaziah had done; •he
sought God devotedly throughout the lifetime of Zechariah, who had advanced

so far in the fear of God. And for as long as he sought Yahweh, God gave him prosperity.

His military strength

He went out to fight the Philistines, demolished the walls of Gath, Jabneh 6 and Ashdod, then rebuilt the towns in the area of Ashdod and in Philistine territory. •God helped him against the Philistines, the Arabs, the inhabitants 7 of Gur-baal[a] and the Meunites. •The Ammonites paid tribute to Uzziah. His 8 fame spread as far as the approaches of Egypt, since he had become very powerful indeed.

Uzziah built towers in Jerusalem, at the Gate of the Corner, at the Gate of 9 the Valley and at the Angle; and he fortified these. •He built towers in the 10 wilderness too, and dug a great many cisterns, for he had large herds in the lowlands and on the tableland; and he had farmers and vine dressers in the hills and on the fertile lands; he was fond of agriculture.

Uzziah had a professional army ready to go on campaign, divided into 11 contingents manned as detailed by the scribe Jeiel and the registrar Maaseiah, and commanded by Hananiah, one of the king's officers. •The total number 12 of heads of families of these valiant champions was two thousand six hundred. Under their command was a trained army of three hundred and seven thousand 13 five hundred fighting men, a powerful force to support the king against the enemy. Uzziah provided them with shields, spears, helmets, coats of mail, bows and 14 sling stones, for each campaign. •In Jerusalem he constructed engines, invented 15 by experts, which were mounted on the towers and at the corners to fire arrows and great stones. His fame spread far and wide; he owed his strength to a help nothing short of miraculous.

Pride and its punishment

But, as his power increased, his heart grew proud, and this was his ruin: 16 he broke faith with Yahweh his God. He entered the great hall of the Temple of Yahweh to burn incense on the altar of incense. •Azariah the priest followed 17 King Uzziah in, with eighty brave priests of Yahweh, •to resist him. 'Uzziah,' 18 they said 'it is not for you to burn incense to Yahweh, but for the priests, the sons of Aaron, consecrated for the purpose. Leave the sanctuary; you have broken faith; the glory from Yahweh God, is no longer yours.' •Uzziah, censer 19 in hand for the burning of incense, flew into a rage. But while he was raging at the priests, leprosy broke out on his forehead in the presence of the priests, in the Temple of Yahweh, there by the altar of incense. •Azariah the chief priest 20 and all the other priests turned towards him and saw the leprosy on his forehead. They quickly hurried him out, and he himself was anxious to go, since Yahweh had struck him.

King Uzziah was a leper till his dying day. He lived confined to his room, 21 a leper, excluded from the Temple of Yahweh. Jotham, his son, was master of the palace, and ruled the people of the country.

The rest of the history of Uzziah, from first to last, has been written by the 22 prophet Isaiah son of Amoz. •Then Uzziah slept with his ancestors and they 23 buried him with his fathers in the burial ground of the kings,[b] for they said, 'He is a leper'. His son Jotham succeeded him.

The reign of Jotham

27 Jotham was twenty-five years old when he came to the throne and he reigned 1 for sixteen years in Jerusalem. His mother's name was Jerushah, daughter of Zadok. •He did what is pleasing to Yahweh, just as his father Uzziah had 2 done. But he did not enter the sanctuary of Yahweh. As for the people, they were still corrupt.

It was he who built the Upper Gate of the Temple of Yahweh and carried 3

4 out considerable work on the wall of the Ophel. •He built towns in the highlands
of Judah, and fortified places and towers in the arable lands.

5   He fought against the king of the Ammonites. [a] He defeated these, and that
year the Ammonites had to give him a hundred talents of silver, ten thousand
kors of wheat and ten thousand of barley. This was the amount that the
6 Ammonites had to pay him, and the same for the second and third years. •Jotham
became powerful because he kept an even course in the presence of Yahweh his
God.

7   The rest of the history of Jotham, all his wars and his policy, are recorded in
8 the Book of the Kings of Israel and Judah. •He was twenty-five years old when
9 he came to the throne and he reigned for sixteen years in Jerusalem. •Then
Jotham slept with his ancestors, and they buried him in the Citadel of David; his
son Ahaz succeeded him.

V. THE GREAT REFORMS UNDER HEZEKIAH AND JOSIAH

A. THE SINS OF AHAZ, FATHER OF HEZEKIAH

Summary of the reign

1 28 Ahaz was twenty years old when he came to the throne and he reigned
for sixteen years in Jerusalem. He did not do what is pleasing to Yahweh,
2 as his ancestor David had done. •He followed the example of the kings of Israel,
3 even having idols cast for the Baals; •he offered incense in the Valley of the
Sons of Hinnom[a] and caused his sons to pass through fire, copying the shameful
practices of the nations which Yahweh had dispossessed for the sons of Israel.
4 He offered sacrifices and incense on the high places, on the hills and under every
spreading tree.

The invasion

5   Yahweh his God delivered him into the power of the king of the Aramaeans
who defeated him and took great numbers of his people captive, carrying them
off to Damascus. He was also delivered into the power of the king of Israel,
6 who inflicted a crushing defeat on him. •In a single day, Pekah son of Remaliah
killed a hundred and twenty thousand in Judah, all stout fighting men; this was
7 because they had deserted Yahweh, the God of their ancestors. •Zichri, an
Ephraimite champion, killed Maaseiah, son of the king, Azrikam the controller
8 of the palace, and Elkanah the king's second-in-command. •The Israelites took
two hundred thousand of their brothers captive, with wives, sons, daughters;
they also took quantities of booty, carrying everything off to Samaria.

The Israelites obey the prophet Oded

9   A prophet of Yahweh was there named Oded, who went out to meet the
troops returning to Samaria and said, 'Yahweh, the God of your ancestors, was
angry with Judah and so he delivered them into your power, but you have
10 slaughtered with such fury as reaches to heaven. •And now you propose to
reduce these children of Judah and Jerusalem to being your serving men and
women! And are you not all the while the ones who are guilty before Yahweh
11 your God? •Now listen to me: release the prisoners you have taken of your
brothers, for the fierce anger of Yahweh hangs over you.'
12   Some of the Ephraimite chieftains then protested to those who were returning
from the expedition: Azariah son of Jehohanan, Berechiah son of Meshillemoth,

26 a. 'The home of Baal', perhaps Samaria: the list is very like that of the enemies of Nehemiah,
Ne 4:1.   b. But not in the tomb itself.
27 a. Possibly the Meunites of ch. 20 are meant.
28 a. The Valley of Gehenna, S. of Jerusalem.

Jehizkiah son of Shallum and Amasa son of Hadlai. •'You must not bring 13
the captives in here,' they said 'or we should be guilty before Yahweh. You are
proposing to add to our sins and to our guilt, but our guilt is already heavy and
the fierce anger of Yahweh is hanging over Israel.' So in the presence of the 14
officials and of the whole assembly the army gave up the captives and the booty.
Men expressly nominated for the purpose saw to the relief of the prisoners. 15
From the booty they clothed all those of them who were naked; they gave them
clothing and sandals and provided them with food, drink and shelter. They
mounted all those who were infirm on donkeys and took them back to their
kinsmen at Jericho, the city of palm trees. Then they returned to Samaria.

The sins of Ahaz

It was then that King Ahaz sent asking the kings of Assyria to come to his 16
assistance.

The Edomites once again invaded and defeated Judah, and carried off 17
prisoners. •The Philistines encroached on the towns in the lowlands and in the 18
Negeb of Judah. They took Beth-shemesh, Aijalon, Gederoth, and Soco with
its outlying villages, Timnah with its outlying villages, Gimzo with its outlying
villages, and they settled in them. •For Yahweh humbled Judah on account of 19
Ahaz king of Israel, since he neglected Judah and was unfaithful to Yahweh.
Tiglath-pileser king of Assyria attacked and besieged him but could not 20
overcome him. •Ahaz however had to take part of the goods in the Temple 21
of Yahweh and in the palaces of the king and princes, to hand over to the king
of Assyria, yet he received no help from him. •During the time he was under siege 22
he made his faithlessness graver still, this King Ahaz, •by offering sacrifices to 23
the gods of Damascus who had defeated him. 'Since the gods of the kings of
Aram' he said 'have been of help to them, I will sacrifice to them in the hope
that they may be of help to me.' But they proved his downfall and that of Israel.
Ahaz collected a number of the furnishings of the Temple of God, and 24
dismantled others; he closed the doors of the Temple of Yahweh and put
up altars at every street corner in Jerusalem; •he set up high places in every 25
town of Judah to offer incense to other gods, and so provoked the anger of
Yahweh, the God of his ancestors.
The rest of his history, his whole policy, from first to last, is recorded in the 26
Book of the Kings of Judah and Israel. •Then Ahaz slept with his ancestors, and 27
they buried him in the Citadel, in Jerusalem, though he was not taken into the
tombs of the kings of Israel. His son Hezekiah succeeded him.

B. REFORM UNDER HEZEKIAH

Summary of the reign

29 Hezekiah came to the throne when he was twenty-five years old and reigned 1
for twenty-nine years in Jerusalem. His mother's name was Abijah, daughter
of Zechariah. •He did what is pleasing to Yahweh, just as his ancestor David 2
had done.

The Temple is purified

It was he who, in the first month of the first year of his reign, threw open 3
the doors of the Temple of Yahweh and repaired them. •Then he brought the 4
priests and the Levites, assembled them in the eastern square, •and said to them. 5
'Listen to me, Levites! Sanctify yourselves now and consecrate the Temple
of Yahweh, the God of our ancestors, and eject what is impure from the sanctuary.
Your ancestors have been unfaithful and done what is displeasing to Yahweh 6
our God. They have deserted him; they have turned their faces away from the
place Yahweh has made his home, they have turned their backs on him. •They 7
have even closed the doors of the Vestibule, they have put out the lamps and

8 offered no incense, no holocaust, to the God of Israel in the holy place. •So the anger of Yahweh has fallen on Judah and Jerusalem; he has made them an object of terror, astonishment and derisive whistling, as you can see for your-
9 selves. •This is why our ancestors have fallen by the sword, and our sons,
10 our daughters, our wives, been taken captive. •I am now determined to make a covenant with Yahweh, the God of Israel, so that his fierce anger may be
11 turned away from us. •My sons, be negligent no longer, for Yahweh has chosen you to stand in his presence and serve him, to conduct his worship, and offer him incense.'

12 The Levites set to work: Mahath son of Amasai and Joel son of Azariah, of the sons of Kohath; of the Merarites: Kish son of Abdi and Azariah son of Jehallelel; of the Gershonites: Joah son of Zimmah and Eden son of Joah;
13 of the sons of Elizaphan: Shimri and Jeuel; of the sons of Asaph: Zechariah
14 and Mattaniah; •of the sons of Heman: Jehiel and Shimei; of the sons of
15 Jeduthun: Shemaiah and Uzziel. •They gathered their brothers together, they sanctified themselves, and in obedience to the king's order, in accordance with the words of Yahweh, they began purifying the Temple of Yahweh.
16 The priests went inside the Temple of Yahweh to purify it. They brought out everything unclean they found in the sanctuary of Yahweh, out into the court of the Temple of Yahweh, and the Levites collected it and carried it outside,
17 into the wadi Kidron. •They began this consecration on the first day of the first month, and were able to enter the Vestibule of Yahweh on the eighth of the month; they then took eight days to consecrate the Temple of Yahweh, and finished on the sixteenth day of the first month.

The sacrifice of Atonement

18 They then waited on King Hezekiah and said, 'We have purified the whole Temple of Yahweh, the altar of holocaust with all its furnishings, and the tables
19 on which the rows of bread are set with all its furnishings. •All the furnishings King Ahaz cast aside during his sacrilegious reign we have put back and conse-crated; they are now in front of the altar of Yahweh.'

20 King Hezekiah lost no time but called the officials of the city together and
21 went up to the Temple of Yahweh. •They brought seven bulls, seven rams and seven lambs, with seven he-goats as a sacrifice for sin on behalf of the royal house, of the sanctuary, and of Judah. The king then told the priests, the sons
22 of Aaron, to offer the holocaust on the altar of Yahweh. •They slaughtered the bulls and the priests took up the blood and poured it on the altar. They then slaughtered the rams and poured their blood on the altar; and they slaughtered
23 the lambs and poured their blood on the altar. •Then they brought the he-goats, the sacrifice for sin, before the king and the assembly who laid their hands on
24 them. •The priests slaughtered them, and with their blood on the altar offered a sacrifice for sin, to perform the ritual of atonement for all Israel—since the king had ordered the holocaust and the sacrifice for sin on behalf of all Israel.

25 He then positioned the Levites in the Temple of Yahweh with cymbals, harps and lyres, in accordance with the ordinances of David, of Gad the king's seer and of Nathan the prophet; the order had in fact come from Yahweh
26 through his prophets. •When the Levites had taken their places with David's
27 musical instruments, and the priests with their trumpets, •Hezekiah ordered the holocaust to be offered on the altar. And as the holocaust began, the hymns of Yahweh began too, and the trumpets sounded, to the accompaniment of the
28 instruments of David king of Israel. •The whole assembly worshipped, cantors singing, trumpets sounding, until the holocaust was over.

29 The offering at an end, the king and all there with him fell to their knees
30 and worshipped. •Then King Hezekiah and the officials told the Levites to sing praise to Yahweh in the words of David and of Asaph the seer; they sang most
31 fervently and then fell down and worshipped. •Hezekiah spoke again, 'Now you

are dedicated to the service of Yahweh. Come forward, bring the sacrifices of communion and praise into the Temple of Yahweh.' The assembly brought sacrifices of communion and praise, and every kind of holocaust as votive offerings. •The number of victims for these holocausts was seventy bulls, a 32 hundred rams and two hundred lambs, all as holocausts for Yahweh; •six 33 hundred bulls and three thousand sheep were consecrated. •The priests were 34 too few, however, and could not dismember all the holocausts, so the Levites helped them until the work was done and the priests were sanctified; for the Levites had been more conscientious about sanctifying themselves than the priests had. •There was, in addition, an abundant holocaust of fatty parts of the 35 communion sacrifices, and numerous libations in association with the holocaust. And so the liturgy of Yahweh's Temple was restored. •Hezekiah and all the 36 people rejoiced that God had disposed the people to act so promptly.

The Passover assembly

30 Hezekiah sent messengers to all Israel and Judah, and also wrote letters 1 to Ephraim and Manasseh, bidding them come to the Temple of Yahweh in Jerusalem to celebrate a Passover in honour of Yahweh, the God of Israel. The king and his officials and all the assembly in Jerusalem had agreed to celebrate 2 it in the second month, •being unble to celebrate it at the proper time, since 3 the priests had not purified themselves in sufficient number, and the people had not assembled in Jerusalem. •This arrangement seemed fitting to the king and 4 to all the assembly. •It was resolved to send a proclamation throughout Israel, 5 from Dan to Beersheba, calling on the people to come to Jerusalem and celebrate a Passover in honour of Yahweh, the God of Israel, for few had observed the prescribed regulations. •Couriers set out with letters from the hands of the king 6 and his officials for every part of Israel and Judah. They had orders from the king to say, 'Sons of Israel, come back to Yahweh, the God of Abraham, of Isaac, of Israel, and he will come back to those of you who are left and have escaped the grasp of the kings of Assyria. •Do not be like your fathers and 7 brothers who were unfaithful to Yahweh, the God of their ancestors, and whom he handed over to destruction, as you can see. •Do not be stubborn now as 8 your ancestors were. Yield to Yahweh, come to his sanctuary which he has consecrated for ever, serve Yahweh your God and he will turn his fierce anger from you. If you come back sincerely to Yahweh, your brothers and your sons will win favour 9 with their conquerors and return to this land, for Yahweh your God is gracious and merciful. If you come back to him, he will not turn his face from you.'

The couriers went from town to town through the land of Ephraim and 10 Manasseh, but the people laughed and scoffed at them, •though a few men from 11 Asher and Manasseh and Zebulun were humble enough to come to Jerusalem. It was in Judah, rather, that the hand of God worked to inspire them with a 12 united will to obey the order of the king and the officials as contained in the word of Yahweh. •A great number of people gathered in Jerusalem to celebrate 13 the feast of Unleavened Bread in the second month. A very great assembly set to work removing the altars that were in Jerusalem and all the altars for 14 burning incense, and throwing them into the wadi Kidron.

The Passover and feast of Unleavened Bread

They slaughtered the passover on the fourteenth day of the second month. 15 The priests and the Levites were ashamed; they sanctified themselves and so were able to bring holocausts into the Temple of Yahweh. •Then they took up 16 their positions as ordained for them according to the Law of Moses, the man of God. The priests poured out the blood handed to them by the Levites, •since 17 there were many people in the assembly who had not sanctified themselves; the Levites were given the task of slaughtering the Passover victims on behalf of those who lacked the requisite purity to consecrate their victims to Yahweh.

18 In point of fact, most of the people, many from Ephraim, Manasseh, Issachar and Zebulun, had not purified themselves; they had eaten the Passover without observing the prescribed regulations. But Hezekiah interceded for them, saying,
19 'May Yahweh in his goodness cover up the fault of •anyone who sets his heart to seeking God, Yahweh the God of his ancestors, even if he lacks the purity requisite
20 for holy things'. •Yahweh heard Hezekiah and left the people unharmed.
21   For seven days and with great rejoicing the Israelites in Jerusalem celebrated the feast of Unleavened Bread, while each day the Levites and the priests praised
22 Yahweh with all their might. •The words of Hezekiah encouraged the Levites who all showed how versed they were in the things of Yahweh, and for seven days they ate their portion in the feast, offering communion sacrifices with praise
23 to Yahweh, the God of their ancestors. •Then all the assembly agreed to continue the celebrations for a further seven days and made of them seven days of rejoicing,
24 since Hezekiah king of Judah had provided a thousand bulls and seven thousand sheep for the assembly, and the officials another thousand bulls and ten thousand
25 sheep. The priests sanctified themselves in great numbers, •and the whole assembly of Judah rejoiced, the priests too, and the Levites, and all who had come from
26 Israel, the refugees who came from Israel and those who lived in Judah. •There was great rejoicing in Jerusalem, for since the time of Solomon son of David,
27 king of Israel, nothing comparable had ever occurred in Jerusalem. •The levitical priests began to bless the people. Their voices were heard and their prayer received in heaven, his holy dwelling place.

Idolatrous worship abolished

1 **31** When all this was over, all the Israelites who were there set off for the towns of Judah to smash the pillars, cut down the sacred poles, wreck the high places and the altars, and so do away with them altogether throughout Judah, Benjamin, Ephraim, and Manasseh. Then all the Israelites returned to their towns, each man to his holding.

The reorganisation of the priests and Levites

2   Hezekiah re-established the priestly and levitical orders, each man in his proper order according to his duties, whether priest or Levite, whether for holocaust, communion sacrifice, liturgical service, thanksgiving or praise, within
3 the gates of the camp of Yahweh. •The king set aside a portion of his own possessions for the morning and evening holocausts, and the holocausts of sabbath, New Moon, and solemn feast, as laid down in the Law of Yahweh.
4 He then told the people, the inhabitants of Jerusalem, to give the priests and the Levites their share so that they might devote themselves to the Law of Yahweh.
5 As soon as the order had been promulgated, the Israelites amassed the first fruits of corn, wine, oil, honey, and all agricultural produce, and brought in a generous
6 tithe of everything. •The Israelites and Judaeans living in the towns of Judah also brought in the tithe of cattle and sheep, and the tithe of the holy things
7 dedicated to Yahweh their God, piling them up, heap after heap. •They began making these heaps in the third month and finished them in the seventh.
8 Hezekiah and his officials came to inspect the heaps and blessed Yahweh and
9 his people Israel. •Hezekiah questioned the priests and the Levites about the
10 heaps, •and Azariah, the chief priest, of the family of Zadok, answered him. 'Since the contributions were first brought to the Temple of Yahweh,' he said, 'we have had enough to eat and still have plenty left over, for Yahweh has blessed his people; this huge pile is what is left.'
11   Hezekiah then ordered them to have rooms prepared in the Temple of
12 Yahweh. They did this, •and then brought in the contributions, tithes and consecrated things, to keep them in a safe place. Conaniah the Levite was officer
13 in charge of them, with Shimei his brother as his second. •Jehiel, Azaziah, Nahath, Asahel, Jerimoth, Jozabad, Eliel, Ismachiah, Mahath, and Benaiah were

appointed overseers under the command of Conaniah and his brother Shimei, by order of King Hezekiah and of Azariah, ruler of the house of God. •Kore 14 son of Imnah the Levite, keeper of the eastern gate, was made responsible for the voluntary offerings to God; he provided the portion set aside for Yahweh and the most holy offerings. •Under his command he had Eden, Miniamin, 15 Jeshua, Shemaiah, Amariah and Shecaniah, who resided permanently in the towns of the priests to carry out the distributions to their kinsmen according to their orders whether more or less important.

Further to this, there was the organisation by related groups of all those 16 men thirty years old and upwards who went to the Temple of Yahweh, by daily rotation, to perform the ritual duties appropriate to their orders. •There was 17 also the organisation of priests by families; as also that of Levites twenty years old and upwards, by duties and orders. •There was also the organisation of all 18 their families, wives, sons and daughters for the whole assembly, since they had an obligation to sanctify themselves faithfully by means of the holy things. As regards the priests, the sons of Aaron, who lived in the pasture lands belonging 19 to their towns, or in the towns themselves, there were men expressly named for the purpose of distributing portions to every male among the priests. Each group was organised by the Levites.

Hezekiah enforced these arrangements throughout Judah. He did what is 20 good and right and loyal before Yahweh his God. •All he undertook in the 21 service of the Temple of God as concerning law or commandments, he performed while seeking God with all his heart, and he prospered.

Sennacherib's invasion

32 After these loyal acts of service came the invasion of Sennacherib king 1 of Assyria. He invaded Judah, pitched camp before the fortified towns and gave orders for them to be taken by storm. •Realising that Sennacherib's advance 2 was the preliminary to an attack on Jerusalem, Hezekiah •and his officers and 3 champions decided to cut off the water supply from the springs situated outside the city. His military staff supported this plan •and numbers of people banded 4 together to block all the springs and cut off the watercourse flowing through the fields. 'Why' they said 'should the kings of Assyria find plenty of water when they arrive?' •Hezekiah strengthened his defences: he had the broken parts of 5 the wall repaired, built towers on it, constructed a second wall on the outer side, strengthened the Millo of the Citadel of David and made quantities of missiles and shields. •He then appointed generals to command the people, 6 summoned them to him in the square by the city gate and spoke as follows to encourage them, •'Be strong and stand firm; be fearless, be undaunted when 7 you face the king of Assyria and the whole horde he brings with him, since he that is with us is stronger than he that is with him. •He has only an arm of 8 flesh, but we have Yahweh our God to help us and fight our battles.' The people took heart at the words of Hezekiah king of Judah.

The blasphemies of Sennacherib

Next, Sennacherib king of Assyria, who was then outside Lachish with 9 all his forces, sent his servants to Jerusalem, to Hezekiah king of Judah, and to all the Judaeans who were in Jerusalem. They said, •'Hear the message from 10 Sennacherib king of Assyria, "What gives you the confidence to stay in Jerusalem under siege? •Is not Hezekiah deluding you? Is he not condemning you to die 11 of hunger and thirst when he says: Yahweh our God will save us from the king of Assyria? •Is not Hezekiah the very man who has suppressed his 12 high places and his altars, and given the order to Judah and to Jerusalem: Before one altar only are you to worship, and on that alone offer incense? Do you not know what I have done, I and my ancestors, to all the peoples 13 of other countries? Have the gods of any single nation in those countries ever

14 been able to save them from me? •Of all the gods of those nations devoted to the ban by my father, name a single one who has been able to save his people
15 from me! So how could your god save you? •Do not let Hezekiah deceive you. Do not let him delude you like this. Do not believe him, for no god of any nation or kingdom has been able to save his people from me or from my
16 ancestors. No more will your god be able to save you from me."' •The envoys
17 were still maligning Yahweh God, and his servant Hezekiah, •when Sennacherib wrote a letter insulting Yahweh the God of Israel. This is what he said about him, 'Just as the gods of the nations in other countries have failed to save their
18 peoples from me, so will the god of Hezekiah fail to save his people'. •They shouted this out in the language of Judah, to the people of Jerusalem on the ramparts, to confuse and frighten them, and so that they might capture the city;
19 they spoke of the God of Jerusalem as of one of the gods of the peoples of the world, the work of men's hands.

The prayer of Hezekiah is heard

20 Faced with this situation, King Hezekiah and the prophet Isaiah son of Amoz
21 prayed and cried out to heaven. •Yahweh sent an angel who massacred all the mighty warriors, commanders and officers in the camp of the king of Assyria. Covered with disgrace he retired to his own country. He went into the temple of his god, and there some of his own children struck him down with the sword.
22 So Yahweh saved Hezekiah and the inhabitants of Jerusalem from the power of Sennacherib king of Assyria and of everyone else, and he gave them peace
23 on every side. •Many people brought oblations to Yahweh in Jerusalem and gifts for Hezekiah king of Judah; after what had happened, he stood high in the esteem of all the nations.

24 In those days, Hezekiah fell ill and was at the point of death. He prayed to
25 Yahweh, who heard him and granted him a sign. •But Hezekiah made no return for the benefit he received; his heart grew proud and the wrath came
26 on him and on Judah and Jerusalem. •Hezekiah did however humble the pride of his heart, and so did the inhabitants of Judah and Jerusalem; hence the wrath
27 of Yahweh did not come on them in the lifetime of Hezekiah. •Hezekiah enjoyed immense riches and honour. He built himself treasuries for gold, silver, precious
28 stones, spices, gems and every sort of valuable. •He had storehouses for his returns of corn, wine and oil, buildings for his different sorts of cattle, and
29 sheep-runs for his sheep, •and, further, acquired donkeys and enormous herds and flocks. God had indeed given him immense possessions.

Summary of the reign; its end

30 It was Hezekiah who stopped the upper outlet of the waters of Gihon and directed them down to the west side of the Citadel of David. Hezekiah succeeded
31 in all he undertook. •Even in the affair of the messengers from the authorities in Babylon, sent to him to inquire about the extraordinary thing that had taken place in the country, God only deserted him to test him, and to discover the secrets of his heart.

32 The rest of the history of Hezekiah, and his deeds of piety, are recorded in the Vision of the prophet Isaiah son of Amoz, in the Book of the Kings of Judah
33 and Israel. •Then Hezekiah slept with his ancestors, and they buried him on the slope going up to the tombs of the sons of David. At his death, all Judah and the inhabitants of Jerusalem did him honour. His son Manasseh succeeded him.

C. THE SINS OF MANASSEH AND OF AMON

Manasseh undoes the work of Hezekiah

1
2 **33** Manasseh was twelve years old when he came to the throne and he reigned for fifty-five years in Jerusalem. •He did what is displeasing to Yahweh,

copying the shameful practices of the nations whom Yahweh had dispossessed for the sons of Israel. •He rebuilt the high places that his father Hezekiah had 3 demolished, he set up altars to the Baals and made sacred poles, he worshipped the whole array of heaven and served it. •He built altars in the Temple of Yahweh, 4 the Temple of which Yahweh had said, 'In Jerusalem my name shall be for ever'. He built altars to the whole array of heaven in the two courts of the Temple 5 of Yahweh. •He caused his sons to pass through the fire in the Valley of Ben- 6 hinnom. He practised soothsaying, magic and witchcraft, and introduced necro- mancers and wizards. He did very many more things displeasing to Yahweh, thus provoking his anger. •He placed the image of the idol he had made in the 7 Temple of which God had said to David and to his son Solomon, 'In this Temple and in Jerusalem, the city I chose out of all the tribes of Israel, I will give my name a home for ever. •I will no longer turn Israel's footsteps away from the 8 land I assigned to their fathers, provided they observe all I have ordered them in accordance with the whole Law, the statutes and the ordinances, given through Moses.' •Manasseh led Judah and the inhabitants of Jerusalem astray, 9 so that they did more evil than those nations Yahweh had destroyed before the sons of Israel. •Yahweh spoke to Manasseh and his people, but they paid no attention. 10

The conversion of Manasseh[a]

Then Yahweh sent the generals of the king of Assyria against them, who 11 captured Manasseh with hooks, put him in chains and led him away to Babylon.[b] In his distress he sought to appease Yahweh his God, humbling himself deeply 12 before the God of his ancestors; •he prayed to him, and God relented at his prayer, 13 hearing his plea and bringing him back to Jerusalem and his kingdom. Manasseh realised then that Yahweh is God. •After this he rebuilt the outer wall of the 14 Citadel of David, west of Gihon in the wadi, as far as the Fish Gate; it encircled the Ophel, and he increased its height very considerably. He stationed military governors in all the fortified towns of Judah.

Next he removed the alien gods and the idol from the Temple of Yahweh, 15 and all the altars he had built on the mountain of the Temple of Yahweh and in Jerusalem, and threw them out of the city. •He rebuilt the altar of Yahweh 16 and offered sacrifices of communion and of praise on it, and ordered Judah to offer worship to Yahweh the God of Israel; •however, the people continued to 17 sacrifice on the high places, although only to Yahweh their God.

The rest of the history of Manasseh, his prayer to his God,[c] and the words 18 of the seers who spoke to him in the name of Yahweh the God of Israel, can be found in the Annals of the Kings of Israel. •His prayer and how God relented 19 at his prayer, all his sins, his unfaithfulness, the sites where he built high places and set up sacred poles and idols before he humbled himself, are recorded in the Annals of Hozai. •Then Manasseh slept with his ancestors, and they buried him 20 in his palace. His son Amon succeeded him.

The obduracy of Amon

Amon was twenty-two years old when he came to the throne and he reigned 21 for two years in Jerusalem. •He did what is displeasing to Yahweh, as Manasseh 22 his father had done. Amon offered sacrifice and worship to all the idols Manasseh his father had made. •He did not humble himself before Yahweh like Manasseh 23 his father; it was this very Amon who made the guilt of Judah so grave. •His 24 officers plotted against him and killed him in his palace. •But the country people 25 struck down all those who had plotted against King Amon and proclaimed his son Josiah as his successor.

D. REFORM UNDER JOSIAH

Summary of the reign

1,2 **34** Josiah was eight years old when he came to the throne and he reigned for thirty-one years in Jerusalem. •He did what is pleasing to Yahweh, and followed the example of his ancestor David, not deviating from it to right or left.

The first reforms

3 In the eighth year of his reign, when he was still a youth, he began to seek the God of his ancestor David. In the twelfth year he began to purge Judah and
4 Jerusalem of high places, sacred poles and carved or cast idols. •He looked on as the altars of the Baals were demolished; he tore down the altars of incense standing on them, he smashed the sacred poles and the carved and cast idols; he reduced them to dust, scattering it over the graves of those who had offered
5 them sacrifices. •He burned the bones of their priests on their altars, and so
6 purified Judah and Jerusalem; •he did the same in the towns of Manasseh, Ephraim, Simeon, and even Naphtali, and in the ravaged districts round them.
7 He demolished the altars and sacred poles, smashed the idols and ground them to powder, and tore down all the altars of incense throughout the land of Israel. Then he returned to Jerusalem.

Work on the Temple

8 In the eighteenth year of his reign, with the object of purifying land and Temple, he sent Shaphan son of Azaliah, Maaseiah governor of the city and
9 the herald Joah son of Joahaz, to repair the Temple of Yahweh his God. •These went to the high priest Hilkiah and handed over the money that had been brought to the Temple of God and that the Levites, the guardians of the threshold, had collected; the money had come from Manasseh, Ephraim and all the rest of
10 Israel, and from all the Judaeans and Benjaminites who lived in Jerusalem. •They handed it over to the masters of works attached to the Temple of Yahweh, and
11 these used it for the repair and restoration of the Temple. •They gave it to the carpenters and builders for buying dressed stone, and wood for the coupling and the rafters of the buildings which the kings of Judah had allowed to fall into ruin.
12 The men were conscientious in doing their work; to supervise them they had Jahath and Obadiah, Levites of the sons of Merari; Zechariah and Meshullam of the sons of Kohath, who were masters of works; Levites who were all skilled
13 liturgical musicians; •others who were in charge of the carriers; others who gave instructions to the masters of works of the various undertakings; and lastly a number of Levites who were scribes, clerks and gatekeepers.

The Book of the Law discovered

14 When they took out the money that had been brought to the Temple of Yahweh, Hilkiah the high priest found the book of the Law given through
15 Moses. •At once Hilkiah told Shaphan the secretary, 'I have found the Book of the Law in the Temple of Yahweh'. And Hilkiah gave the book to Shaphan.
16 Shaphan took the book to the king, and reported to him: 'Your servants' he
17 said 'are carrying out the commissions you gave them: •they have melted down the silver which was in the Temple of Yahweh and have handed it over to the
18 overseers and masters of works,' •after which Shaphan the secretary informed

---

33 a. This narrative is peculiar to Ch; 2 K 21 condemns the reign of Manasseh in the words used here of Amon in vv.21-23.   **b.** Manasseh of Judah was a vassal of Esarhaddon (680-669) and of Assurbanipal (668-633).   **c.** 'The Prayer of Manasseh' is found in some editions of the Apocrypha.

the king, 'Hilkiah the priest has given me a book'; and Shaphan read from it in the king's presence.

On hearing the contents of the Law, the king tore his garments, •and gave ¹⁹ ²⁰ the following order to Hilkiah, Ahikam son of Shaphan, Abdon son of Micah, Shaphan the secretary and Asaiah the king's minister, •'Go and consult Yahweh, ²¹ on behalf of me and those left in Israel and Judah, about the contents of the book that has been found. Great indeed must be the anger of Yahweh pouring down on us because our ancestors did not observe the word of Yahweh by practising everything written in this book.'

Huldah the prophetess is consulted

Hilkiah and the king's men went to Huldah the prophetess, wife of Shallum ²² son of Tokhath, son of Hasrah, the keeper of the wardrobe; she lived in Jerusalem in the new town. They spoke to her about this, •and she replied, 'Yahweh, ²³ the God of Israel says this, "To the man who sent you to me say this: Yahweh says this: I am bringing disaster on this place and those who live in it, ²⁴ carrying out all the curses written in the book that has been read in the presence of the king of Judah, •because they have deserted me and sacrificed to other gods, ²⁵ to provoke my anger by everything they did. My anger blazes out against this place; it will not be extinguished. •And you will say to the king of Judah who ²⁶ sent you to consult Yahweh, Yahweh, the God of Israel says this: The words you have heard. . . •But since your heart has been touched and you have humbled ²⁷ yourself before God on hearing what he has threatened against this place and those who live in it, since you have humbled yourself before me and torn your garments and wept before me, I for my part have heard—it is Yahweh who speaks. •I will ²⁸ gather you to your ancestors, you shall be gathered into your grave in peace; your eyes will not see all the disasters that I mean to bring on this place and on those who live in it." ' They took this answer to the king.

The covenant renewed

The king then had all the elders of Judah and of Jerusalem summoned, •and ²⁹ ³⁰ the king went up to the Temple of Yahweh, with all the men of Judah and all the inhabitants of Jerusalem, priests, Levites and all the people, of high or low degree. In their hearing he read out everything that was said in the book of the covenant found in the Temple of Yahweh. •The king stood beside the pillar, ³¹ and in the presence of Yahweh he made a covenant to follow Yahweh and to enforce the terms of the covenant as written in that book with all his heart and soul. •He allotted a station to everyone there in Jerusalem or in Benjamin; and ³² the inhabitants of Jerusalem complied with the covenant of God, the God of their ancestors. •Josiah removed all the abominations throughout the territories ³³ belonging to the sons of Israel. His whole life long he made sure that every member of Israel served their God. They did not fail to follow Yahweh, the God of their ancestors.

The preparation for the Passover

35 Josiah then celebrated a Passover in honour of Yahweh in Jerusalem and ¹ they slaughtered the passover on the fourteenth day of the first month.

He re-established the priests in their functions and made it possible for them ² to discharge the duties of the Temple of Yahweh. •Then he said to the Levites, ³ whose understanding was at the disposal of all Israel and who were consecrated to Yahweh, 'Place the holy ark in the Temple built by Solomon son of David, king of Israel. It is no longer a burden for your shoulders. Now serve Yahweh your God and Israel his people. •Take your places by families according to your ⁴ orders, in compliance with the written decree of David king of Israel and his son Solomon. •Stand in the sanctuary at the disposal of the family groupings, ⁵ at the disposal of your brothers the laity; the Levites are to have a portion in

6 the family. •Slaughter the passover, sanctify yourselves, and be at the disposal of your brothers in acting in accordance with the word of Yahweh which was spoken through Moses.'

The celebration of the Passover

7 Josiah then provided for the laity lambs and kids from the flocks to the number of thirty thousand, all as Passover victims for all who were present, and three thousand bulls as well; all these animals came from the king's possessions.
8 His officials, for their part, made provision for the voluntary offerings on behalf of the people, the priests and the Levites. The senior officials gave the priests of the Temple of God, Hilkiah, Zechariah and Jehiel, two thousand six hundred
9 lambs and kids and three hundred bulls as Passover victims. •The heads of the Levites, Conaniah, Shemaiah and his brother Nathanel, Hashabiah, Jeiel and Jozabad, provided five thousand lambs and kids and five hundred bulls as
10 Passover victims for the Levites. •The order of the service was arranged, the priests at their places and the Levites in their orders, in compliance with the
11 king's order. •They slaughtered the passover, and the priests sprinkled the
12 blood as they received it from the Levites, and the Levites dismembered the victims. •They put the holocaust on one side to give it to the family groupings among the laity as each made its offering to Yahweh, as is written in the Book
13 of Moses; they did the same with the bulls. •They roasted the passover, as ordained, and the sacred foods in pots, dishes, pans, carrying them speedily
14 to the laity. •Afterwards they prepared the passover for themselves and for the priests—the priests, the sons of Aaron, having been busy till nightfall offering the holocaust and the fatty parts; that was why the Levites prepared the passover
15 for themselves and for the priests, the sons of Aaron. •The cantors, the sons of Asaph, were at their places, in accordance with the ordinances of David; neither Asaph, Heman, Jeduthun the king's seer, nor the keepers of each gate, had to leave their duties, since their brothers the Levites made all the preparations for them.
16 So the whole liturgical service of Yahweh was arranged that day to celebrate the Passover and to offer holocausts on the altar of Yahweh, in accordance with
17 the ordinances of King Josiah. •And so it was that the Israelites who were present celebrated the Passover and, for seven days, the feast of Unleavened Bread.
18 No Passover like this one had ever been celebrated in Israel since the days of the prophet Samuel; no king of Israel had ever celebrated a Passover like the one celebrated by Josiah with the priests, the Levites, all of Judah and of Israel who were present, and the inhabitants of Jerusalem.

The tragic end of the reign

19 This Passover was celebrated in the eighteenth year of the reign of Josiah.
20 After everything had been done by Josiah to set the Temple in order, Neço king of Egypt came up to fight at Carchemish on the Euphrates. When Josiah marched out
21 to intercept him, •Neco sent him messengers to say, 'What quarrel is there between me and you, king of Judah? I have not come today to attack you; my quarrel is with another dynasty, and God has told me to hurry. Do not oppose the God
22 who is with me any more, or else he may destroy you.' •But Josiah continued to challenge him; he was in fact determined to fight him, and would not listen to the words of Neco from God's own mouth. He gave battle in the plain of
23 Megiddo; •the bowmen fired on King Josiah, and the king said to his followers,
24 'Take me away; I am badly wounded'. •His servants lifted him out of his own chariot, transferred him to another one and took him back to Jerusalem, where he died. He was buried in the tombs of his ancestors. All Judah and Jerusalem
25 mourned for Josiah. •Jeremiah composed a lament for Josiah which all the singing men and singing women still recite today when they lament for Josiah; this has become a custom in Israel; the dirges are recorded in the Lamentations.ᵃ

35 a. Probably Jr 22:10,15,18.

The rest of the history of Josiah, his deeds of piety conforming to everything 26
written in the Law of Yahweh, •his history from first to last, are recorded in the 27
Book of the Kings of Israel and Judah.

E. ISRAEL IN THE CLOSING YEARS OF THE MONARCHY

Jehoahaz

36 The country people took Jehoahaz son of Josiah and made him king in 1
Jerusalem in succession to his father. •Jehoahaz was twenty-three years 2
old when he came to the throne and he reigned for three months in Jerusalem.
The king of Egypt carried him off from Jerusalem and imposed a levy of a hundred 3
talents of silver and one talent of gold on the country. •The king of Egypt then 4
made Eliakim, brother of Jehoahaz, king of Judah and Jerusalem, and changed
his name to Jehoiakim. Neco took his brother Jehoahaz and carried him off
to Egypt.

Jehoiakim

Jehoiakim was twenty-five years old when he came to the throne and he reigned 5
for eleven years in Jerusalem. He did what is displeasing to Yahweh his God.
Nebuchadnezzar king of Babylon attacked him, loaded him with chains and 6
carried him off to Babylon. •To Babylon Nebuchadnezzar also carried off part 7
of the furnishings of the Temple of Yahweh and put them in his palace at
Babylon. •The rest of the history of Jehoiakim, the shameful things he did and 8
those discovered to his discredit, these are recorded in the Book of the Kings of
Israel and Judah. His son Jehoiachin succeeded him.

Jehoiachin

Jehoiachin was eight years old when he came to the throne and he reigned for 9
three months and ten days in Jerusalem. He did what is displeasing to Yahweh.
At the turn of the year, King Nebuchadnezzar sent for him and had him taken 10
to Babylon, with the precious furnishings of the Temple of Yahweh, and made
Zedekiah his brother*a* king of Judah and Jerusalem in his place.

Zedekiah

Zedekiah was twenty-one years old when he came to the throne and he reigned 11
for eleven years in Jerusalem. •He did what is displeasing to Yahweh his God. 12
He did not listen humbly to the prophet Jeremiah, accredited by Yahweh himself.
He also rebelled against King Nebuchadnezzar to whom he had sworn allegiance 13
by God. He became stubborn, and obstinately refused to return to Yahweh
the God of Israel.

The nation as a whole

Furthermore, all the heads of the priesthood, and the people too, added 14
infidelity to infidelity, copying all the shameful practices of the nations and
defiling the Temple that Yahweh had consecrated for himself in Jerusalem.
Yahweh, the God of their ancestors, tirelessly sent them messenger after messenger, 15
since he wished to spare his people and his house. •But they ridiculed the 16
messengers of God, they despised his words, they laughed at his prophets, until
at last the wrath of Yahweh rose so high against his people that there was no
further remedy.

The end

He summoned against them the king of the Chaldaeans who put their young 17
warriors to the sword within their sanctuary; he spared neither youth nor virgin,
neither old man nor aged cripple; God handed them all over to him. •All 18

the furnishings of the Temple of God, large and small, the treasures of the Temple of Yahweh, the treasures of the king and his officials, he carried everything off
19 to Babylon. •They burned down the Temple of God, demolished the walls of Jerusalem, set fire to all its palaces, and destroyed everything of value in it.
20 The survivors were deported by Nebuchadnezzar to Babylon; they were to
21 serve him and his sons until the kingdom of Persia came to power. •This is how the word of Yahweh was fulfilled that he spoke through Jeremiah, 'Until this land has enjoyed its sabbath rest, until seventy years have gone by, it will keep sabbath throughout the days of its desolation'.

Looking to the future

22   And in the first year of Cyrus king of Persia, to fulfil the word of Yahweh that was spoken through Jeremiah, Yahweh roused the spirit of Cyrus king of Persia to issue a proclamation and to have it publicly displayed throughout his
23 kingdom: •'Thus speaks Cyrus king of Persia, "Yahweh, the God of heaven, has given me all the kingdoms of the earth; he has ordered me to build him a Temple in Jerusalem, in Judah. Whoever there is among you of all his people, may his God be with him! Let him go up." '

36 a. His uncle, 2 K 24:17.

THE BOOK OF
EZRA AND NEHEMIAH

EZRA

I. THE RETURN FROM EXILE
AND THE REBUILDING OF THE TEMPLE

The return of the exiles

1 Now in the first year of Cyrus king of Persia,[a] to fulfil the word of 1
Yahweh that was spoken through Jeremiah,[b] Yahweh roused the spirit of
Cyrus king of Persia to issue a proclamation and to have it publicly displayed
throughout his kingdom: •'Thus speaks Cyrus king of Persia, "Yahweh, the 2
God of heaven, has given me all the kingdoms of the earth; he has ordered me
to build him a Temple in Jerusalem, in Judah. •Whoever there is among you 3
of all his people, may his God be with him! Let him go up to Jerusalem in
Judah to build the Temple of Yahweh, the God of Israel––he is the God who
is in Jerusalem. •And let each survivor, wherever he lives, be helped by the 4
people of that place with silver and gold, with goods and cattle, as well as
voluntary offerings for the Temple of God which is in Jerusalem." '

Then the heads of families of Judah and of Benjamin, the priests and the 5
Levites, in fact all whose spirit had been roused by God, prepared to go and
rebuild the Temple of Yahweh in Jerusalem; •and all their neighbours gave them 6
every assistance with silver, gold, goods, cattle, quantities of costly gifts and
with voluntary offerings of every kind.

King Cyrus took the vessels of the Temple of Yahweh which Nebuchadnezzar 7
had carried away from Jerusalem and dedicated to the temple of his god. •Cyrus, 8
king of Persia, handed them over to Mithredath, the treasurer, who counted
them out to Sheshbazzar, the prince of Judah. •The inventory was as follows: 9
thirty golden bowls for offerings; one thousand and twenty-nine silver bowls
for offerings; •thirty golden bowls; four hundred and ten silver bowls; one 10
thousand other vessels. •In all, five thousand four hundred vessels of gold and 11
silver. Sheshbazzar took all these with him when the exiles travelled back from
Babylon to Jerusalem.

The list of the returning exiles

2 These were the people of the province who returned from captivity and exile. 1
After being deported to Babylon by Nebuchadnezzar king of Babylon, they
returned to Jerusalem and to Judah, each to his own town. •They arrived with 2
Zerubbabel, Jeshua, Nehemiah, Seraiah, Reelaiah, Nahamani, Mordecai,
Bilshan, Mispar, Bigvai, Rehum and Baanah.

The list of the men of the people of Israel: •sons of Parosh, two thousand 3
one hundred and seventy-two; •sons of Shephatiah, three hundred and seventy- 4
two; •sons of Arah, seven hundred and seventy-five; •sons of Pahath-moab, ⁵⁄₆

that is to say the sons of Jeshua and Joab, two thousand eight hundred and twelve; •
sons of Elam, one thousand two hundred and fifty-four; •sons of Zattu, nine
hundred and forty-five; •sons of Zaccai, seven hundred and sixty; •sons of
Bani, six hundred and forty-two; •sons of Bebai, six hundred and twenty-three;
sons of Azgad, one thousand two hundred and twenty-two; •sons of Adonikam,
six hundred and sixty-six; •sons of Bigvai, two thousand and fifty-six; •sons of
Adin, four hundred and fifty-four; •sons of Ater, that is to say of Hezekiah,
ninety-eight; •sons of Bezai, three hundred and twenty-three; •sons of Jorah,
one hundred and twelve; •sons of Hashum, two hundred and twenty-three;
sons of Gibbar, ninety-five; •men of Bethlehem, one hundred and twenty-three;
men of Netophah, fifty-six; •men of Anathoth, one hundred and twenty-eight;
men of Beth-azmaveth, forty-two; •men of Kiriath-jearim, Chephirah and
Beeroth, seven hundred and forty-three; •men of Ramah and Geba, six hundred
and twenty-one; •men of Michmas, one hundred and twenty-two; •men of Bethel
and Ai, two hundred and twenty-three; •sons of Nebo, fifty-two; •sons of
Magbish, one hundred and fifty-six; •sons of another Elam, one thousand two
hundred and fifty-four; •sons of Harim, three hundred and twenty; •men of
Lod, Hadid and Ono, seven hundred and twenty-five; •men of Jericho, three
hundred and forty-five; •sons of Senaah, three thousand six hundred and thirty.

The priests: sons of Jedaiah, that is to say the House of Jeshua, nine hundred
and seventy-three; •sons of Immer, one thousand and fifty-two; •sons of Pashhur,
one thousand two hundred and forty-seven; •sons of Harim, one thousand and
seventeen.

The Levites: sons of Jeshua, that is to say Kadmiel, Binnui, Hodaviah,
seventy-four.

The cantors: sons of Asaph, one hundred and twenty-eight.

The gatekeepers: sons of Shallum, sons of Ater, sons of Talmon, sons of
Akkub, sons of Hatita, sons of Shobai: in all, one hundred and thirty-nine.

The oblates: sons of Ziha, sons of Hasupha, sons of Tabbaoth, •sons of
Keros, sons of Siaha, sons of Padon, •sons of Lebanah, sons of Hagabah, sons
of Akkub, •sons of Hagab, sons of Shamlai, sons of Hanan, •sons of Giddel,
sons of Gahar, sons of Reaiah, •sons of Rezin, sons of Nekoda, sons of Gazzam,
sons of Uzza, sons of Paseah, sons of Besai, •sons of Asnah, sons of the Meunites,
sons of the Nephisites, •sons of Bakbuk, sons of Hakupha, sons of Harhur,
sons of Bazluth, sons of Mehida, sons of Harsha, •sons of Barkos, sons of Sisera,
sons of Temah, •sons of Neziah, sons of Hatipha.

The sons of Solomon's slaves: sons of Sotai, sons of Hassophereth, sons of
Peruda, •sons of Jaalah, sons of Darkon, sons of Giddel, •sons of Shephatiah,
sons of Hattil, sons of Pochereth-haz-zebaim, sons of Ami. •The total of the
oblates and the sons of Solomon's slaves: three hundred and ninety-two.

The following, who came from Tel-melah, Tel-harsha, Cherub, Addan and
Immer, could not prove that their families and ancestry were of Israelite origin:
sons of Delaiah, sons of Tobiah, sons of Nekoda: six hundred and fifty-two.
And among the priests: sons of Habaiah, sons of Hakkoz, sons of Barzillai, who
had married one of the daughters of Barzillai, the Gileadite, whose name he
adopted. •These people searched in their ancestral registers but could not be
located in them, so they were excluded from the priesthood as unclean •and His
Excellency[a] forbade them to eat the sacred foods until a priest could be found
for the Urim and Thummim.[b]

The whole assembly numbered forty-two thousand three hundred and sixty
people, •not counting their slaves and maidservants to the number of seven
thousand three hundred and thirty-seven. They also had two hundred male and

---

1 a. His reign over the Babylonian Empire began in 538.   b. Jeremiah foretold seventy years
of captivity.
2 a. The governor (a Persian title); presumably Sheshbazzar.   b. The sacred lots by which God
could be consulted; a high priest has not yet been invested.

female singers. •Their horses numbered seven hundred and thirty-six, their mules 66
two hundred and forty-five, •their camels four hundred and thirty-five and their 67
donkeys six thousand seven hundred and twenty.

When they arrived at the Temple of Yahweh in Jerusalem, a certain number 68
of heads of families made voluntary offerings for the Temple of God, for its
rebuilding on its site. •In accordance with their means they gave sixty-one 69
thousand gold drachmas, five thousand silver minas and one hundred priestly
robes to the sacred funds.

The priests, Levites and part of the people settled in Jerusalem; the gatekeepers, 70
cantors, oblates and all the other Israelites, in their own towns.

The resumption of worship

3 When the seventh month came and the sons of Israel were in their own towns, 1
they all gathered as one man in Jerusalem. •Jeshua son of Jozadak, with his 2
brother priests, and Zerubbabel son of Shealtiel, with his brothers, began to
rebuild the altar of the God of Israel, to offer holocausts there, as it is written
in the Law of Moses the man of God. •The altar was set up on its old site, 3
despite their fear of the surrounding peoples, and on it they offered holocausts
to Yahweh, holocausts morning and evening; •they celebrated the feast of 4
Tabernacles, according to the written Law, with as many daily holocausts as are
ordained for each day; •then, in addition to the perpetual holocaust, they offered 5
those prescribed for the sabbaths, New Moon feasts and all the solemnities
sacred to Yahweh, as well as those voluntary offerings made by individuals
to Yahweh. •From the first day of the seventh month they began offering 6
holocausts to Yahweh, though the foundations of the sanctuary of Yahweh had
not yet been laid.

Then they gave money to the masons and carpenters; to the Sidonians and 7
Tyrians they gave food, drink and oil, so that they would bring cedar wood from
Lebanon by sea to Jaffa, for which Cyrus king of Persia had given permission.
It was in the second month of the second year after their arrival at the Temple 8
of God in Jerusalem that Zerubbabel son of Shealtiel and Jeshua son of Jozadak,
with the rest of their brothers, the priests, the Levites and all the people who
had returned to Jerusalem from captivity, began the work; they appointed the
Levites who were twenty years old or more to superintend the work on the
Temple of Yahweh. •So Jeshua, his sons and his brothers, with Kadmiel, Binnui 9
and Hodaviah, agreed to superintend the workmen at the Temple of God.
When the builders had laid the foundations of the sanctuary of Yahweh, the 10
priests in fine linen came with trumpets, and the Levites, the sons of Asaph,
with cymbals, to praise Yahweh according to the ordinances of David king of
Israel; •they chanted praise and thanksgiving to Yahweh, 'For he is good, for 11
his love for Israel is everlasting'. And all the people shouted aloud the praises of
Yahweh, since the foundations of the Temple of Yahweh had now been laid.
True, many priests and Levites, many heads of families, who were then old and 12
had seen with their own eyes the earlier Temple on its foundations, wept aloud,
but many others raised their voices in shouts of joy. •And nobody could distinguish 13
the shouts of joy from the sound of the people's weeping; for the people shouted
so loudly that the noise could be heard far away.

An indictment of the Samaritans: their tactics under Cyrus

4 But when the enemies of Judah and Benjamin heard that the exiles were 1
building a sanctuary for Yahweh, the God of Israel, •they came to Zerubbabel 2
and Jeshua and the heads of families and said, 'We would like to build with
you, for we seek your God as you do and we have sacrificed to him since the
time of Esarhaddon king of Assyria, who brought us here'. •Zerubbabel, 3
Jeshua, and the other heads of Israelite families replied, 'It is not right that you
should join us in building a Temple for our God; we alone may build for

Yahweh, the God of Israel, as we were ordered by Cyrus king of Persia'.
4 Then the people of the country[a] set out to dishearten and frighten the people of
5 Judah from building any further; •they lured counsellors against them, to defeat
their purpose. This lasted throughout the reign of Cyrus king of Persia and
until the reign of Darius king of Persia.

Samaritan tactics under Xerxes and Artaxerxes

6   At the beginning of the reign of Xerxes[b] they lodged a complaint against
the inhabitants of Judah and Jerusalem.
7   In the time of Artaxerxes,[c] Mithredath, Tabeel and the rest of their colleagues
denounced Jerusalem in writing to Artaxerxes king of Persia. The text of the
document was in the Aramaic script and the Aramaic language.
8   Then Rehum the governor[d] and Shimshai the secretary wrote the following
9 letter denouncing Jerusalem to King Artaxerxes—•Rehum the governor and
Shimshai the secretary and the rest of their colleagues, the judges and legates,
Persian officials, the people of Uruk, Babylon and Susa—that is, the Elamites—
10 and the other peoples whom Assurbanipal the Great deported and settled in the
towns of Samaria and in the rest of Transeuphrates.[e]
11   This is a copy of the letter they sent:
'To King Artaxerxes, from your servants, the people of Transeuphrates:
12   'Whereas •the king should be informed that the Jews, who have come up from
your country to Jerusalem, are now rebuilding that rebellious and wicked city;
they are working to restore the walls, and the foundations are already laid,
13 and whereas the king should be informed that if this city is rebuilt and the walls
are restored, they will refuse to pay tribute, customs or tolls, and that in short
14 this city will damage the authority of the kings, •and whereas, because we eat
the salt of the palace, it does not seem proper to us to see this affront offered
15 to the king; we therefore send this information to the king •so that a search
may be made in the archives of your ancestors: in which archives you will find it
proved that this city is a rebellious city, the bane of the kings and the provinces,
and that sedition has been stirred up there from ancient times; which is why this
16 city was destroyed. •We inform the king that if this city is rebuilt and its walls
are restored, you will soon have no territories left in Transeuphrates.'
17   The king sent this reply:
'To Rehum the governor, to Shimshai the secretary, and to the rest of their
colleagues resident in Samaria and elsewhere in Transeuphrates, peace!
18   'Whereas •the document you sent to me has been translated and read before
19 me, •and by my orders search has been made, and it has been found that from
ancient times this city has risen against kings and that rebellion and sedition
20 have been contrived in it; •and that powerful kings have reigned in Jerusalem,
21 who dominated all Transeuphrates, exacting tribute, customs and tolls, •you
must now order the work of these men to cease immediately: this city is not to
22 be rebuilt until I give further orders. •Beware of negligence in this matter
lest further harm be done to the king's interests.'
23   As soon as the copy of King Artaxerxes' document had been read before
Rehum the governor, Shimshai the secretary and their colleagues, they hurried
to the Jews in Jerusalem and stopped their work by force of arms.

The building of the Temple (520-515 B.C.)

24   Thus the work on the Temple of God in Jerusalem was brought to a standstill;
it remained interrupted until the second year of the reign of Darius king of
Persia.

4 a. The Samaritan settlers established in the district.   b. 486-485 B.C.   c. Artaxerxes I, 465-
424.   d. Of Samaria, the capital of the province which included Judah.   e. This list includes
the highest authorities in the province and the heads of the various national groups of settlers.

5 Then the prophets Haggai and Zechariah son of Iddo began to prophesy to 1
the Jews of Judah and Jerusalem in the name of the God of Israel who was
with them. •At this, Zerubbabel son of Shealtiel and Jeshua son of Jozadak 2
started again to build the Temple of God in Jerusalem; the prophets of God
were with the people, giving them courage. •It was then that Tattenai, satrap 3
of Transeuphrates, Shethar-bozenai and their colleagues came to them and
asked, 'Who gave you authority to build this Temple and to do this woodwork?
What are the names of the men responsible for this building?' •But the eyes $\frac{4}{5}$
of their God were on the elders of the Jews; they were not compelled to
stop while a report on the matter was sent to Darius and an official edict
awaited.

Copy of the letter that Tattenai, satrap of Transeuphrates, Shethar-bozenai 6
and his colleagues, the officials in Transeuphrates, sent to King Darius. •They 7
sent a report to him which ran as follows:

'To King Darius, all peace! •The king should be informed that we went to 8
the district of Judah, to the Temple of the great God: it is being built of blocks
of stone; the walls are being panelled with wood; the work is being done with
great care and makes progress in their hands. •Questioning the elders, we asked, 9
"Who gave you authority to build this Temple and to do this woodwork?"
We also asked their names so that you might be informed; hence we have been 10
able to list the names of those who are superintending these men.

'They gave us this answer, "We are the servants of the God of heaven and 11
earth; we are rebuilding a Temple which until recently had been standing for
many years and which was built and finished by a great king of Israel. •But our 12
ancestors angered the God of heaven and he delivered them into the power of
Nebuchadnezzar the Chaldaean, king of Babylon, who destroyed that Temple and
deported the people to Babylon. •In the first year of Cyrus king of Babylon, 13
however, King Cyrus authorised the rebuilding of this Temple of God; •further- 14
more, those vessels of gold and silver belonging to the Temple of God, which
Nebuchadnezzar had removed from the sanctuary in Jerusalem and taken to
that of Babylon, King Cyrus in turn removed from the sanctuary in Babylon and
handed back to a man called Sheshbazzar, whom he appointed high commissioner, •with the words: Take these vessels; go and return them to the 15
sanctuary in Jerusalem and let the Temple of God be rebuilt on its original site;
the aforesaid Sheshbazzar therefore came and laid the foundations of the Temple 16
of God in Jerusalem; they have been building it ever since, and it is still not
finished."

'Wherefore, if it please the king, let search be made in the king's muniment 17
rooms in Babylon, to find out if it is true that King Cyrus gave permission for
the rebuilding of this Temple of God in Jerusalem. And let the king's decision
on this matter be sent to us.'

6 Then, on the order of King Darius, a search was made in Babylonia in the 1
muniment rooms where the archives were kept; •at Ecbatana, the fortress 2
situated in the province of Media, a scroll was found which ran thus:

'Memorandum.

'In the first year of Cyrus the king, King Cyrus decreed: 3

"Temple of God in Jerusalem.

"The Temple will be rebuilt as a place at which sacrifices are offered and to
which offerings are brought to be burnt. Its height is to be sixty cubits, its width
sixty cubits. •There are to be three thicknesses of stone blocks and one of wood. 4
The expense is to be met by the king's household. •Furthermore, the vessels 5
of gold and silver from the Temple of God which Nebuchadnezzar took from
the sanctuary in Jerusalem and brought to Babylon are to be restored so that
everything may be restored to the sanctuary in Jerusalem and be put back in
the Temple of God."

'Wherefore, Tattenai, satrap of Transeuphrates, Shethar-bozenai and you, 6

7 their colleagues, the officials of Transeuphrates, withdraw from there; •leave the high commissioner of Judah and the elders of the Jews to work on this
8 Temple of God; they are to rebuild this Temple of God on its ancient site. •This, I decree, is how you must assist the elders of the Jews in the reconstruction of this Temple of God: the expenses of these people are to be paid, promptly and without fail, from the royal revenue—that is, from the tribute of Transeuphrates.
9 What they need for holocausts to the God of heaven: young bulls, rams and lambs, as also wheat, salt, wine and oil, is to be supplied to them daily, without
10 fail, as required by the priests of Jerusalem, •so that they may offer acceptable sacrifices to the God of heaven and pray for the lives of the king and his sons.
11 I also decree this: If anyone disobeys this edict, a beam is to be torn from his house, he is to be pilloried upright on it and his house is to be made into a dung
12 heap for this crime. •May the God who causes his name to live there overthrow any king or people who dares to defy this and destroy the Temple of God in Jerusalem! I, Darius, have issued this decree. Let it be obeyed to the letter!'
13 Then Tattenai, satrap of Transeuphrates, Shethar-bozenai and their colleagues
14 obeyed to the letter the instructions sent by King Darius. •The elders of the Jews, for their part, prospered with their building, inspired by Haggai the prophet and Zechariah son of Iddo. They finished the building in accordance with the
15 order of the God of Israel and the order of Cyrus and of Darius. •This Temple was finished on the twenty-third day of the month of Adar; it was
16 the sixth year of the reign of King Darius.[a] •The Israelites—the priests, the Levites and the remainder of the exiles—joyfully dedicated this Temple of God;
17 for the dedication of this Temple of God they offered one hundred bulls, two hundred rams, four hundred lambs and, as a sacrifice for sin for the whole of Israel, twelve he-goats, corresponding to the number of the tribes of Israel.
18 Then they installed the priests according to their orders in the service of the Temple of God in Jerusalem, as is written in the Book of Moses.

The Passover of 515 B.C.

19 The exiles celebrated the Passover on the fourteenth day of the first month.
20 The Levites, as one man, had purified themselves; all were pure, so they sacrificed the passover for all the exiles, for their brothers the priests and for themselves.
21 The following ate the passover: the Israelites who had returned from exile and all those who, having broken with the impurity of the surrounding peoples,
22 joined them to seek Yahweh, the God of Israel. •For seven days they joyfully celebrated the feast of Unleavened Bread, for Yahweh had given them cause to rejoice, having moved the heart of the king of Assyria to encourage their work on the Temple of God, the God of Israel.

II. THE ORGANISATION

OF THE COMMUNITY BY EZRA AND NEHEMIAH

The mission and personality of Ezra

1 7 After these events, in the reign of Artaxerxes king of Persia, Ezra son of
2 Seraiah, son of Azariah, son of Hilkiah, •son of Shallum, son of Zadok, son
3 of Ahitub, •son of Amariah, son of Azariah, son of Meraioth, •son of Zerahiah,
4
5 son of Uzzi, son of Bukki, •son of Abishua, son of Phinehas, son of Eleazar,
6 son of the chief priest Aaron, •this man Ezra came up from Babylon. He was a scribe versed in the Law of Moses, which had been given by Yahweh, the God of Israel. As the favour of his God, Yahweh, was with him, the king gave him all
7 he asked. •A certain number of Israelites, priests, Levites, cantors, gatekeepers

6 a. 1st April 515.

and oblates went up to Jerusalem in the seventh year of the reign of King Artaxerxes. •He arrived in Jerusalem in the fifth month: it was the seventh year of 8
the king's reign, •for he had decided to depart from Babylon on the first day of 9
the first month, and he arrived in Jerusalem on the first day of the fifth month;
the kindly favour of his God was certainly with him. •For Ezra had devoted 10
himself to the study of the Law of Yahweh, to practising it and to teaching
Israel its laws and customs.

The edict of Artaxerxes

This is a copy of the document which King Artaxerxes handed to Ezra, 11
the priest-scribe, the scribe who was especially learned in the text of Yahweh's
commandments and his laws relating to Israel:

'Artaxerxes, king of kings, to the priest Ezra, scribe of the Law of the 12
God of heaven, perfect peace.

'Here then are my orders: Anyone in my kingdom who is of the people 13
of Israel, of their priests or their Levites and who freely chooses to go to Jerusalem, may go with you. •For you are sent by the king and his seven counsellors 14
to make an inspection of Judah and Jerusalem according to the Law of your
God, which is in your possession, •and also to carry the silver and gold which the 15
king and his counsellors have voluntarily offered to the God of Israel who dwells
in Jerusalem, •as well as all the silver and gold you find in the whole province 16
of Babylonia, together with those voluntary offerings given by the people and
the priests for the Temple of their God in Jerusalem. •Further, with this money 17
take pains to buy bulls, rams and lambs, as well as the oblations and libations
which go with them; you must offer them on the altar of the Temple of your God in
Jerusalem. •The gold and silver left over you may spend as you and your brothers 18
think right, according to the will of your God. •Place the vessels that have been 19
given you for the service of the Temple of your God before your God in Jerusalem.
For anything else necessary for the Temple of your God, which you may find 20
occasion to provide, you may draw on the royal treasury. •I, King Artaxerxes, 21
give this command to all the treasurers of Transeuphrates: Whatever the priest
Ezra, scribe of the Law of the God of heaven, may ask of you must be instantly
allowed: •up to one hundred talents of silver, one hundred measures of wheat, 22
one hundred baths of wine, one hundred baths of oil, and salt as requested.
Everything that the God of heaven commands must be carried out zealously for 23
the Temple of the God of heaven, lest the wrath should come on the realm of
the king and of his sons. •You are also informed that it is forbidden to impose 24
tribute, customs or tolls on any of the priests, Levites, cantors, gatekeepers,
oblates; in short, on the servants of this Temple of God.

'And you, Ezra, by virtue of the wisdom of your God, which is in your posses- 25
sion,*a* you are to appoint scribes and judges to administer justice for the whole
people of Transeuphrates, that is, for all who know the Law of your God. You
must teach those who do not know it. •If anyone does not obey the Law of 26
your God—which is the law of the king—let judgement be strictly executed on
him: death, banishment, confiscation or imprisonment.'

The journey of Ezra from Babylonia to Palestine

Blessed be Yahweh, the God of our ancestors, who moved the king's heart in 27
this way to glorify the Temple of Yahweh in Jerusalem •and who won for me 28
the favour of the king, his counsellors and all the most powerful of the king's
officials. For my part, I took courage, for the favour of Yahweh my God
was with me, and I gathered the leading men of Israel together to set out with
me.

8 These, with their genealogies, are the heads of families who set out from 1
Babylon with me in the reign of King Artaxerxes:

Of the sons of Phinehas: Gershom; of the sons of Ithamar: Daniel; of the 2
sons of David: Hattush •son of Shecaniah; of the sons of Parosh: Zechariah, 3

4 with whom one hundred and fifty males were registered; •of the sons of Pahath-
5 moab: Eliehoenai son of Zerahiah, and with him two hundred males; •of the
sons of Zattu: Shecaniah son of Jahaziel, and with him three hundred males;
⁶₇ of the sons of Adin: Ebed son of Jonathan, and with him fifty males; •of the
8 sons of Elam: Jeshaiah son of Athaliah, and with him seventy males; •of the
9 sons of Shephatiah: Zebadiah son of Michael, and with him eighty males; •of
the sons of Joab: Obadiah son of Jehiel, and with him two hundred and eighteen
10 males; •of the sons of Bani: Shelomith son of Josiphiah, and with him a hundred
11 and sixty males; •of the sons of Bebai: Zechariah son of Bebai, and with him
12 twenty-eight males; •of the sons of Azgad: Johanan son of Hakkatan, and with
13 him a hundred and ten males; •of the sons of Adonikam: the younger sons,
whose names are: Eliphelet, Jeiel and Shemaiah, and with them sixty
14 males; •and of the sons of Bigvai: Uthai son of Zabud, and with him seventy
males.

15   I assembled them near the river that runs to Ahava, where we camped for
16 three days. Observing them I saw laymen and priests, but no Levites. •So
I dispatched Eliezer, Ariel, Shemaiah, Elnathan, Jarib, Elnathan, Nathan,
17 Zechariah and Meshullam, men of judgement, •and sent them to Iddo, the
leading man in the region of Casiphia; I told them the words they were
to say to Iddo and his kinsmen, living in the region of Casiphia, to provide
18 us with servants for the Temple of our God. •Then, thanks to the kindly favour
of our God which was with us, they sent us a capable man, of the sons of Mahli
son of Levi son of Israel, Sherebiah with his sons and kinsmen: eighteen men;
19 also Hashabiah and with him his brother Jeshaiah of the sons of Merari, as
20 well as their sons: twenty men; •and of the oblates whom David and his notables
had assigned to serve the Levites: two hundred and twenty oblates. All were
registered by name.

21   There, beside the river of Ahava, I proclaimed a fast: we were to humble
ourselves before our God and pray to him for a successful journey for us, our
22 children and our belongings; •since I should have been ashamed to ask the
king for an armed guard and cavalry to protect us from an enemy on the road,
for we had already told the king, 'The hand of our God is held out in blessing over
all who seek him, his power and his anger over all who turn away from him'.
23 So we fasted, pleading with our God for this favour, and he answered our
prayers.

24   I chose twelve of the leading priests, and then Sherebiah and Hashabiah
25 and with them ten of their kinsmen; •I weighed out for them the silver, the gold
and the vessels, the offerings that the king, his counsellors, his nobles and all
26 the Israelites present had presented for the Temple of our God. •So I weighed
out and handed over to them six hundred and fifty talents of silver, one hundred
27 silver vessels worth two talents, one hundred talents of gold, •twenty golden
bowls worth a thousand darics and two vessels of fine gilded bronze which
28 were as valuable as gold. •I told them, 'You are consecrated to Yahweh; these
vessels are sacred; the silver and gold are voluntary offerings to Yahweh, the God
29 of your ancestors. •Take charge of them and guard them until you weigh them
before the leading priests, the Levites and the heads of families of Israel in
30 Jerusalem in the chambers of the Temple of Yahweh.' •The priests and Levites
then took charge of the silver, the gold and the vessels thus weighed, to take
them to Jerusalem to the Temple of our God.

31   On the twelfth day of the first month we left the river of Ahava to go to
Jerusalem; the favour of our God was with us and protected us on the road from
32 enemies and thieves. •We arrived in Jerusalem and stayed there, resting, for
33 three days. •On the fourth day the silver, the gold and the vessels were weighed
in the Temple of our God and handed over to the priest Meremoth son of Uriah

7 a. The Mosaic Law is given the force of state law, not only in Palestine but for the Jewish
communities west of the Euphrates as well.

and, with him, Eleazar son of Phinehas; with them were the Levites Jozabad son of Jeshua and Noadiah son of Binnui. •Number and weight, all was there. 34 The total weight was put on record.

At that time •those who came back from captivity, the exiles, offered 35 holocausts to the God of Israel: twelve bulls for all Israel, ninety-six rams, seventy-two lambs, twelve he-goats for sin; the whole as a holocaust to Yahweh.

The king's instructions were notified to the king's satraps and the governors 36 of Transeuphrates, who then assisted the people and the Temple of God.

The marriages with foreigners dissolved

9 Once this was done, the leaders approached me to say, 'The people of Israel, 1 the priests and the Levites, have not broken with the natives of the countries who are steeped in abominations—Canaanites, Hittites, Perizzites, Jebusites, Ammonites, Moabites, Egyptians and Amorites—•but have found wives among 2 these foreign women for themselves and for their sons; the holy race has been mingling with the natives of the countries; in this act of treachery the chief men and officials have led the way'. •At this news I tore my garment and my 3 cloak; I tore hair from my head and beard and sat down, quite overcome. •All 4 who trembled at the words of the God of Israel gathered round me, when faced by this treachery of the exiles. For my part, I went on sitting there, overcome, until the evening oblation. •At the evening sacrifice I came out of my stupor 5 and falling on my knees, with my garment and cloak torn, I stretched out my hands to Yahweh my God, •and said: 6

'My God, I am ashamed, I blush to lift my face to you, my God. For our crimes have increased, until they are higher than our heads, and our sin has piled up to heaven. •From the days of our ancestors until now our guilt has been 7 great; on account of our crimes we, our kings and our priests, were given into the power of the kings of other countries, given to the sword, to captivity, to pillage and to shame, as is the case today. •But now, suddenly, Yahweh our God 8 by his favour has left us a remnant and granted us a refuge in his holy place; this is how our God has cheered our eyes and given us a little respite in our slavery. For we are slaves; but God has not forgotten us in our slavery; he has 9 shown us kindness in the eyes of the kings of Persia, obtaining permission for us to rebuild the Temple of our God and restore its ruins, and he has found us safety and shelter in Judah and in Jerusalem. •But now what can we say, my 10 God, if after this kindness we have deserted your commandments, •which, 11 through your servants the prophets, you ordained in these words, "The land you are entering to possess is a land unclean because of the foulness of the natives of the countries and of the abominations with which their impurities have infected it from end to end. •So you must not give your daughters to their 12 sons nor take their daughters for your sons; you must not be concerned for their peace or their prosperity, so that you yourselves may grow strong, eat the best of what the country produces and leave it as an inheritance to your sons for ever."

'Now after all that has come upon us on account of our evil deeds and our great 13 fault—although you, our God, have rated our crimes less than their wickedness and left us this remnant here—•are we to break your commandments again and 14 intermarry with these people who practise such abominations? Would you not be provoked to the point of destroying us, so that not even the smallest remnant would survive? •Yahweh, God of Israel, by your justice we survive 15 as the remnant we are today; here we are before you with our sin. And because of it, no one can survive in your presence.'

10 While Ezra, weeping and prostrate before the Temple of God, prayed 1 and confessed, a great crowd of Israelites gathered round him, men, women and children, weeping bitterly too. •Then Shecaniah son of Jehiel, one of the 2 sons of Elam, spoke up and said to Ezra, 'We have betrayed our God by marrying

foreign women, taken from the natives of the countries. But, in spite of this,
3 there is still some hope for Israel. •We will make a solemn promise before our God
to put away our foreign wives and the children born to them, as my lord and
those who tremble at the commandment of our God may advise. Let us act in
4 accordance with the Law. •Up! This is for you to decide, but we will support
5 you. Take courage; to work!' •Then Ezra stood up and put the leading priests
and Levites and all Israel on oath to do what had been said. They took the oath.
6 Ezra left his place before the Temple of God and went to the room of Jehohanan
son of Eliashib, where he spent the night without eating bread or drinking
water; he was in mourning for the exiles' treachery.

7 A proclamation was issued in Judah and in Jerusalem to all the exiles that
8 they were to assemble in Jerusalem: •anyone who did not come within three
days—such was the warning of the leaders and elders—would have all his goods
9 seized and would himself be excluded from the community of the exiles. •As
a result, all the men of Judah and Benjamin assembled in Jerusalem within the
three days; it was the ninth month, the twentieth day of the month; all the people
gathered in the square before the Temple of God; the occasion itself, and the
10 heavy rain, had them trembling. •Then Ezra the priest stood up and spoke,
'You have committed treason by marrying foreign women; you have added
11 to the sin of Israel. •But now give thanks to Yahweh, the God of your ancestors,
and do his will, by separating from the natives of the country and from your
12 foreign wives.' •In a loud voice the whole assembly answered, 'Yes, our duty
13 is to do as you say. •But there are a great many people here and it is the
rainy season; we cannot stay out in the open; besides, this is not something that
can be dealt with in one or two days, since many of us have sinned in this respect.
14 Our leaders could represent the full assembly; all those from our towns who
have foreign wives could come at stated times, accompanied by elders and judges
from each town, until we have turned away God's anger which has been thus
15 roused against us.' •Only Jonathan son of Asahel and Jahzeiah son of Tikvah,
supported by Meshullam and Shabbethai the Levite, were opposed to this
16 procedure. •The exiles acted on this suggestion. Ezra the priest chose as
helpers the heads of families for each House, all designated by name. The session
for investigating individual cases began on the first day of the tenth month.
17 And by the first day of the first month they had dealt with all the men who had
married foreign women.

The list of the guilty

18 Among the members of the priesthood, these are the names of those who
were found to have married foreign women: among the sons of Jeshua son of
19 Jozadak and among his brothers: Maaseiah, Eliezer, Jarib and Gedaliah; •they
pledged their word to put their wives away and, for their sin, offered a ram as
a sacrifice of reparation;
20 among the sons of Immer: Hanani and Zebadiah;
21 among the sons of Harim: Maaseiah, Elijah, Shemaiah, Jehiel and Uzziah;
22 among the sons of Pashhur: Elioenai, Maaseiah, Ishmael, Nethanel, Jozabad
and Elasah.
23 Among the Levites: Jozabad, Shimei, Kelaiah—that is, Kelita—Pethahiah,
Judah, and Eliezer.
24 Among the cantors: Eliashib and Zaccur.
Among the gatekeepers: Shallum, Telem and Uri.
25 And among the Israelites:
of the sons of Parosh: Ramiah, Izziah, Malchijah, Mijamin, Eleazar,
Malchijah and Benaiah;
26 of the sons of Elam: Mattaniah, Zechariah, Jehiel, Abdi, Jeremoth and Elijah;
27 of the sons of Zattu: Elioenai, Eliashib, Mattaniah, Jeremoth, Zabad and
Aziza;

of the sons of Bebai: Jehohanan, Hananiah, Zabbai, Athlai;   28

of the sons of Bigvai: Meshullam, Malluch, Jedaiah, Jashub, Sheal, Jeremoth;   29

of the sons of Pahath-moab: Adna, Chelal, Benaiah, Maaseiah, Mattaniah,   30
Bezalel, Binnui and Manasseh;

of the sons of Harim: Eliezer, Isshijah, Malchijah, Shemaiah, Shimeon,   31
Benjamin, Malluch, Shemariah;   32

of the sons of Hashum: Mattenai, Mattattah, Zabad, Eliphelet, Jeremai,   33
Manasseh, Shimei;

of the sons of Bani: Maadai, Amram, Uel, •Benaiah, Bediah, Cheluhi,   34 35
Vaniah, Meremoth, Eliashib, •Mattaniah, Mattenai and Jaasau;   36 37

of the sons of Binnui: Shimei, •Shelemiah, Nathan and Adaiah;   38 39

of the sons of Zaccai: Shashai, Sharai, •Azarel, Shelemiah, Shemariah,   40 41
Shallum, Amariah, Joseph;   42

of the sons of Nebo: Jeiel, Mattithiah, Zabad, Zebina, Jaddai, Joel, Benaiah.   43

All these had married foreign wives; they put them away, both women and   44
children.

NEHEMIAH

The call of Nehemiah: his mission to Judah

1 The words of Nehemiah son of Hacaliah. In the month of Chislev, in the   1
twentieth year of King Artaxerxes,ᵃ when I was in the citadel of Susa, •one   2
of my kinsmen, Hanani, arrived with some men from Judah. I asked them
about the Jews—the remnant rescued from captivity—and about Jerusalem.
'Those who escaped from captivity,' they replied 'who are back there in the   3
province, are in great trouble and humiliation: the walls of Jerusalem are in
ruins and its gates burnt down.' •On hearing this I sank down and wept; for   4
several days I mourned, fasting and praying before the God of heaven.

And I said, 'Yahweh, God of heaven, great God who must be feared,   5
maintaining covenant and kindness with those who love you and obey your
commandments, •let your ear be listening, and your eyes open, to hear your   6
servant's prayer. I am making this to you now day and night on behalf of the
sons of Israel, your servants; and I confess the sins of the sons of Israel which
we have committed against you: I and my father's House have sinned. •We have   7
acted very wickedly towards you: we have not kept the commandments, laws
and customs you laid down for Moses your servant. •Remember, I beg you,   8
the charge you gave to Moses your servant: "If you prove faithless, I will
scatter you among the peoples; •but if you come back to me and keep my   9
commandments and practise them, even if your outcasts were at the very sky's
end, I would gather them from there and bring them back to the place I have
chosen for my name to dwell in". •Now these are your servants, your own people: 10
you have redeemed them with your mighty power and outstretched arm.
O Lord, let your ear be attentive to your servant's prayer and to the prayer   11
of your servants who delight to reverence your name. I beg you, let your servant
be successful today; make him acceptable to this man.'

At that time I was cupbearer to the king.

2 In the month of Nisan, in the twentieth year of King Artaxerxes,ᵃ the wine   1
being my concern, I took up the wine and offered it to the king. Now I had
never been downcast before. •So the king said, 'Why is your face so sad? You   2
are not sick, surely? This must be a sadness of the heart.' A great fear came over
me •and I said to the king, 'May the king live for ever! How could my face be   3
other than sad when the city where the tombs of my ancestors are lies in ruins,
and its gates have been burnt down?' •'What' the king asked 'is your request?'   4
I called on the God of heaven •and made this reply to the king, 'If it pleases   5

the king, and if you are satisfied with your servant, give me leave to go to Judah,
6 to the city of my ancestors' tombs, and rebuild it'. •The king, with the queen sitting there beside him, said, 'How long will your journey take, and when will you return?' So I named a date that seemed acceptable to the king and he gave
7 me leave to go. •I spoke to the king once more, 'If it please the king, could letters be given me for the governors of Transeuphrates to allow me to pass through
8 to Judah? •And also a letter for Asaph, keeper of the king's park, to supply me with timber for the gates of the citadel of the Temple, for the city walls and for the house I am to occupy?' This the king granted me, for the kindly favour of my God was with me.
9   So I travelled to the governors of Transeuphrates, and handed them the king's letters. The king had given me an escort of army officers and cavalry.
10   When Sanballat the Horonite and Tobiah the Ammonite slave[b] came to know of this, they were much displeased that anyone should come to promote the welfare of the sons of Israel.

The decision to rebuild the walls of Jerusalem

11
12   And so I reached Jerusalem and stayed there for three days. •Then I rose in the night, with a few other men, not having told anyone what work God had inspired me to do for Jerusalem, and having no animal with me but my own
13 mount. •At night, therefore, leaving by the Valley Gate, I went by way of the Well of the Dragon to the Dung Gate; I examined the walls of Jerusalem with
14 their gaps and burnt-out gates. •I went on to the Fountain Gate and the King's
15 Pool, but found no further path for my mount. •So I returned, in the dark, through the wadi, still examining the walls, and came in again by the Valley
16 Gate. And so I returned •without the officials knowing where I had gone or what I was doing. So far I had said nothing to the Jews: either to the priests,
17 the authorities, the officials or any other responsible persons. •Then I said to them, 'You see the trouble we are in: Jerusalem is in ruins, its gates have been burnt down. Come, let us rebuild the walls of Jerusalem and suffer this indignity
18 no longer.' •And I told them how the kindly favour of God had been with me, and also repeated the words the king had said to me. 'Let us start!' they exclaimed 'Let us build'; and with willing hands they set about the good work.
19   When Sanballat the Horonite and Tobiah the Ammonite slave, and Geshem the Arab came to know of this, they ridiculed us, and came and asked, 'What
20 are you doing? Are you planning to revolt against the king?' •But I gave them this answer, 'The God of heaven will give us success. We, his servants, are going to build; you have neither share nor rights nor memorial in Jerusalem.'

The volunteer builders

1 **3** Eliashib the high priest and his brother priests set about building the Sheep Gate; they constructed its framework and set its doors, bolts and bars in
2 place, and proceeded as far as the Tower of Hananel. •The men of Jericho
3 built next to them; Zaccur son of Imri built next to them. •The sons of Hassenaah built the Fish Gate; they constructed its framework and set its doors,
4 bolts and bars in place. •Meremoth son of Uriah, son of Hakkoz carried out repairs next to them; Meshullam son of Berechiah, son of Meshezabel carried
5 out repairs next to him. •The men of Tekoa carried out repairs next to him,
6 though their chiefs refused to bow their necks and work for their lords. •Joiada son of Paseah and Meshullam son of Besodeiah repaired the gate of the new

---

1 a. December 446.
2 a. March-April 445.   b. Sanballat was governor of Samaria; Tobiah was probably an official under him.

quarter:^a they constructed its framework and set its doors, bolts and bars in place. •Next to them repairs were carried out by Melatiah of Gibeon and Jadon 7 of Meronoth, and also by the men of Gibeon and Mizpah, on behalf of the governors of Transeuphrates. •Next to them repairs were carried out by Uzziel, 8 a member of the goldsmiths' guild, and next to him repairs were carried out by Hananiah, of the perfumers' guild: they strengthened Jerusalem as far as the Wall of the Square. •Next to them repairs were carried out by Rephaiah 9 son of Hur, ruler of half the district of Jerusalem. •Next to them Jedaiah son 10 of Harumaph carried out repairs opposite his own house; next to him repairs were carried out by Hattush son of Hashabneiah. •Malchijah son of Harim 11 and Hasshub son of Pahath-moab repaired the next section as far as the Tower of the Furnaces. •Next to them repairs were carried out by Shallum son of 12 Hallohesh, ruler of half the district of Jerusalem, by him and his sons. •Hanun 13 and the inhabitants of Zanoah repaired the Valley Gate; they restored it, constructed its framework and set its doors, bolts and bars in place, and repaired a thousand cubits of wall up to the Dung Gate. •Malchijah son of Rechab, 14 ruler of the district of Beth-hac-cherem, repaired the Dung Gate, he and his sons: he set its doors, bolts and bars in place.

Shallum son of Col-hozeh, ruler of the district of Mizpah, repaired the 15 Fountain Gate; he restored it, covered it, and set its doors, bolts and bars in place. He also rebuilt the wall of the conduit cistern, adjoining the king's garden, as far as the steps coming down from the Citadel of David. •Next to him, 16 Nehemiah son of Azbuk, ruler of half the district of Beth-zur, carried out repairs up to a point opposite the tombs of David, the artificial pool and the House of Heroes.^b •Next to him repairs were carried out by the Levites: Rehum son 17 of Bani; next to him Hashabiah, ruler of half the district of Keilah, carried out repairs for his own district. •Next to him repairs were carried out by their 18 brothers: Binnui son of Henadad, ruler of half the district of Keilah; •next to 19 him, Ezer son of Jeshua, ruler of Mizpah, repaired another section opposite the slope up to the Armoury, towards the Angle.

Next to him Baruch son of Zabbai repaired another section from the Angle as 20 far as the door of the house of Eliashib the high priest. •Next to him Meremoth 21 son of Uriah, son of Hakkoz repaired another section from the door of Eliashib's house to its farther end. •Next to him repairs were carried out by the priests 22 who lived locally in the country. •Next to them repairs were carried out by 23 Benjamin and Hasshub, opposite their own houses. Next to them repairs were carried out by Azariah son of Maaseiah, son of Ananiah, beside his own house. Next to him Binnui son of Henadad repaired another section from the house of 24 Azariah as far as the Angle. •Next to him Palal son of Uzai carried out repairs 25 opposite the corner of the tower jutting out over the upper palace of the king and standing in the prison courtyard. Next to him Pedaiah son of Parosh carried out repairs •as far as the Water Gate, in an easterly direction and 26 up to a point opposite the projecting tower. •Next to him the men of Tekoa 27 repaired another section opposite the great projecting tower as far as the wall of Ophel.

From the Horse Gate onwards repairs were carried out by the priests, each 28 opposite his own house. •Next to them repairs were carried out by Zadok son 29 of Immer opposite his own house. Next to him repairs were carried out by Shemaiah son of Shecaniah, keeper of the East Gate. •Next to him Hananiah 30 son of Shelemiah and Hanun sixth son of Zalaph repaired another section. Next to him repairs were carried out by Meshullam son of Berechiah opposite where he lived. •Next to him Malchijah, of the goldsmiths' guild, repaired as ³¹⁄₃₀ far as the quarters of the oblates and of the merchants, opposite the Watch Gate as far as the high chamber of the corner. •And between the high chamber ³²⁄₃₁ of the corner and the Sheep Gate repairs were carried out by the goldsmiths and the merchants.

The effect on the Jews' opponents

³³^{4:1} When Sanballat heard that we were rebuilding the walls he flew into a rage,
³⁴² beside himself with anger. He ridiculed the Jews •and in front of his kinsmen
and the wealthy men of Samaria he exclaimed, 'What are these pathetic Jews
trying to do?... Do they expect to finish in one day? Do they think they can
put new life into these charred stones, salvaged from the heaps of rubble?'
³⁵³ Tobiah the Ammonite was standing beside him. 'Let them build,' he said
³⁶⁴ 'a jackal jumping on their wall will soon knock the stones down again.' •See,
our God, how we are despised! Make their sneers fall back on their own heads.
³⁷⁵ Give them over to shame in a land of exile. •Do not hide their guilt or let their
sin be blotted out before you, for heaping insults on the builders.
³⁸⁶ Meanwhile we were rebuilding the wall which was soon finished all the way
round to mid-height, since the people put their hearts into the work.

¹⁷ 4 When news reached Sanballat, Tobiah, the Arabs, the Ammonites and the
Ashdodites, that repairs to the walls of Jerusalem were going forward—since
²⁸ the gaps were beginning to be made good—they were furious, •and conspired
together to come and attack Jerusalem and upset my plans.
³⁹ Then we called on our God and set a watch against them, day and night,
⁴¹⁰ to guard the city. •Judah, however, was saying, 'The strength of the carriers is
failing and the amount of rubble enormous; we shall never finish the wall'.
⁵¹¹ And our enemies were saying, 'We will appear among them before they know
or see anything; then we will cut them down and put an end to the business'.
⁶¹² Now on ten occasions Jews who lived near them gave us warning, 'They are
⁷¹³ coming up against us from every place they live in'. •So we took up positions
down behind the wall where the place was clear; I posted the people by
⁸¹⁴ families with their swords, spears and bows. •I had seen their fear and
I stood up and addressed the authorities, the officials and the rest of the people,
'Do not be afraid of them. Keep your minds on the Lord, who is great and to
be feared, and fight for your kinsmen, your sons, your daughters, your wives
⁹¹⁵ and your homes.' •Learning, however, that we were forewarned, and that God
had thwarted their plan, our enemies withdrew, and we all went back, everyone
to his work on the wall.
¹⁰¹⁶ But from that day onwards only half of my men continued the work; the
rest, with spears, shields, bows and breastplates, stood behind all the House
¹¹¹⁷ of Judah •who were building the wall. The carriers, too, were armed so that
each did his work with one hand while gripping his weapon with the other.
¹²¹⁸ And as each builder worked, he wore his sword at his side. Beside me stood a
¹³¹⁹ trumpeter. •I addressed the authorities, the officials and the rest of the people,
'The work is important and extensive, and we are deployed along the wall at
¹⁴²⁰ some distance from each other. •Rally round us wherever you hear the trumpet
¹⁵²¹ sounding, and our God will fight for us.' •So we went on with the work from
¹⁶²² break of day till the stars appeared. •Then I spoke to the people again, 'Let
each man, with his servant, spend the night inside Jerusalem: in this way we can
¹⁷²³ employ the night in watching and the day in working'. •But none of us, neither
myself, my kinsmen, my servants, nor the members of my personal guard, ever
took off our clothes; every man kept his weapon to hand.

The social problems of Nehemiah. He vindicates his administration

¹ 5 The ordinary people and their wives began complaining loudly against their
² brother Jews. •Some said, 'We are having to barter our sons and daughters
³ to get enough corn to eat and keep us alive'. •Others said, 'We are having to
mortgage our fields, our vineyards, our houses to get corn during the famine'.
⁴ Still others said, 'We have had to borrow money on our fields and our vineyards
⁵ to pay the king's tax; •and though we are of the same flesh as our brothers, and

3 a. Called 'the gate of Ephraim' in Ne 12:39.   b. Once the barracks of the king's bodyguard.

our children as good as theirs, we are having to sell our sons and our daughters into slavery; some of our daughters have even been raped! We can do nothing about it, since our fields and our vineyards are now the property of others.'

When I heard their complaints and these words I was very angry. •Having ⁶₇ turned the matter over in my mind, I reprimanded the authorities and officials. 'What a burden you impose,' I said 'every one of you on his brother!' Summoning a great assembly to deal with them, •I said to them, 'To the best 8 of our power, we have redeemed our brother Jews who had been sold to foreigners, and now you in turn are selling our brothers for us to redeem them!' They were silent and could find nothing to say. •'What you are doing' I went 9 on 'is wrong. Do you not want to walk in the fear of our God and escape the sneers of the nations, our enemies? •I too, my kinsmen, and my servants have 10 lent them money and corn. Let us cancel this debt. •Return them their fields, 11 their vineyards, their olive groves and their houses forthwith, and remit the debt on the money, corn, wine and oil which you have lent them.' •'We will make 12 restitution,' they replied 'we will claim nothing more from them; we will do as you say.' At once I summoned the priests and made them swear to do as they had promised. •Then I shook out the lap of my gown with the words, 'May 13 God do this, and shake out of his house and property any man who does not keep this promise; may he be shaken out like this and left empty!' And the whole assembly answered, 'Amen' and gave praise to Yahweh. And the people kept this promise.

What is more, from the day the king appointed me governor in the land of 14 Judah, from the twentieth to the thirty-second year of King Artaxerxes, for twelve years, neither I nor my kinsmen ever ate governor's bread.ᵃ •Now the 15 former governors, my predecessors, had been a burden on the people, from whom they took forty silver shekels each day as their subsistence allowance, while their servants oppressed the people too. But I, fearing God, never did this.

And furthermore I worked on this wall all the time, though I owned no land; 16 and my servants also were all employed on the work.

Leaders and officials to the number of a hundred and fifty ate at my table, 17 not to mention those who came to us from the surrounding nations. •Every day, 18 one ox, six fine sheep, and poultry, were prepared at my expense; every ten days skins of wine were brought in bulk. But even so, I never claimed the governor's subsistence allowance, since the people already had burden enough to bear.

In my favour, my God, remember all I have done for this people.   19

The intrigues of Nehemiah's enemies. The wall is finished

6 When Sanballat, Tobiah, Geshem the Arab and our other enemies heard 1 that I had rebuilt the wall and that not a single gap was left—though at that time I had not fixed the doors to the gates—•Sanballat and Geshem sent me a 2 message, 'Come and meet us at Hac-chepirim in the Vale of Ono'. Now they intended some harm to me. •So I sent messengers to them to say, 'I am engaged 3 in a great undertaking and so cannot come down. The work would come to a halt if I left it to come down to you.' •Four times they sent me the 4 same invitation and I made them the same reply. •The fifth time, with the same 5 purpose in mind, Sanballat sent me his servant bearing an open letter. •It ran, 6 'There is a rumour among the nations, so Gashmu ᵃ says, that you and the Jews are thinking of rebelling, which is why you are building the wall; that you yourself are to become their king; •that you have even briefed prophets in 7 your own interest in Jerusalem to proclaim: "Judah has a king". These rumours will soon be reaching the king; so you had better come and talk things over with us.' •To this, however, I replied, 'As regards what you say, nothing of the 8

9 sort has occurred; it is a figment of your own imagination'. •For they were trying to frighten us, thinking, 'Their hands will tire of the work, and it will never be finished'. But I meanwhile was making my hands even stronger.

10   I had been to visit Shemaiah son of Delaiah, son of Mehetabel, since he was prevented from coming to me. He said:

> 'Let us meet at the Temple of God,
>   in the innermost part of the sanctuary;
>   let us shut the sanctuary doors,
>   for they are coming to kill you,
>   they are coming to kill you tonight'.

11   But I retorted, 'Is a man like me to run away? A man in my position to go
12 into the sanctuary to save his life? I will not go.' •I realised that God had not sent him to say this, but that he had pronounced this oracle over me because Tobiah
13 was paying him •to frighten me into doing this, and so committing a sin as as a result of which they would have been able to blacken my reputation and ridicule
14 me. •Remember Tobiah, my God, for what he has done; and Noadiah the prophetess, and the other prophets who tried to frighten me.

15   The wall was finished within fifty-two days, on the twenty-fifth of Elul.[b]
16 When all our enemies heard about it, and all the surrounding nations had seen it, they were deeply impressed and acknowledged that this work had been accomplished by the power of our God.

17   During this same period several of the authorities of Judah kept sending letter
18 after letter to Tobiah, and letters from Tobiah kept arriving for them; •for he had many sworn to his interest in Judah, since he was son-in-law to Shecaniah son of Arah, and his son Jehohanan had married the daughter of Meshullam
19 son of Berechiah. •They even cried up his good deeds in my presence, and they reported what I said back to him. And Tobiah kept on sending letters to frighten me.

1 7 When the wall had been rebuilt and I had set the doors in place, keepers
2   were appointed for the gates (besides cantors and Levites). •I entrusted the administration of Jerusalem to my brother Hanani, and to Hananiah the commander of the citadel, for he was a trustworthy man and God-fearing above the
3 ordinary. •I said to them, 'The gates of Jerusalem must not be opened until the sun gets hot; and you are to shut and bar the doors while it is still high; and detail guard pickets from the inhabitants of Jerusalem, some for the lookout posts, and others for duty outside their own houses'.

The repopulation of Jerusalem

4   The city was large and spacious but the population was small, and no new
5 families were growing up. •My God therefore inspired me to assemble the authorities, the officials and the people for the purpose of taking a census by families. I discovered the genealogical register of those who had returned in the first group, and there I found entered:

A list of the first exiles to return

6   These are the people of the province who returned from captivity and exile. After being deported by Nebuchadnezzar king of Babylon, they returned to
7 Jerusalem and to Judah, each to his own town. •They arrived with Zerubbabel, Jeshua, Nehemiah, Azariah, Raamiah, Nahamani, Mordecai, Bilshan, Mispereth, Bigvai, Nehum, Baanah.

---

5 a. I.e., never drew the governor's subsistence allowance, raised by taxes.
6 a. Geshem the Arab of 2:19. b. October 445.

The number of the men of the people of Israel: •sons of Parosh, two thousand 8
one hundred and seventy-two; •sons of Shephatiah, three hundred and seventy- 9
two; •sons of Arah, six hundred and fifty-two; •sons of Pahath-moab, that is 10 11
to say sons of Jeshua and Joab, two thousand eight hundred and eighteen;
sons of Elam, one thousand two hundred and fifty-four; •sons of Zattu, eight 12 13
hundred and forty-five; •sons of Zaccai, seven hundred and sixty; •sons of 14 15
Binnui, six hundred and forty-eight; •sons of Bebai, six hundred and twenty- 16
eight; •sons of Azgad, two thousand three hundred and twenty-two; •sons of 17 18
Adonikam, six hundred and sixty-seven; •sons of Bigvai, two thousand and 19
sixty-seven; •sons of Adin, six hundred and fifty-five; •sons of Ater, that is to 20 21
say of Hezekiah, ninety-eight; •sons of Hashum, three hundred and twenty- 22
eight; •sons of Bezai, three hundred and twenty-four; •sons of Hariph, one 23 24
hundred and twelve; •men of Gibeon, ninety-five; •men of Bethlehem and 25 26
Netophah, one hundred and eighty-eight; •men of Anathoth, one hundred and 27
twenty-eight; •men of Beth-azmaveth, forty-two; •men of Kiriath-jearim, 28 29
Chephirah and Beeroth, seven hundred and forty-three; •men of Ramah and 30
Geba, six hundred and twenty-one; •men of Michmas, one hundred and 31
twenty-two; •men of Bethel and Ai, one hundred and twenty-three; •men of 32 33
Nebo, fifty-two; •sons of another Elam, one thousand two hundred and fifty- 34
four; •sons of Harim, three hundred and twenty; •men of Jericho, three hundred 35 36
and forty-five; •men of Lod, Hadid and Ono, seven hundred and twenty-one; 37
sons of Senaah, three thousand nine hundred and thirty. 38

The priests: sons of Jedaiah, that is to say the House of Jeshua, nine hundred 39
and seventy-three; •sons of Immer, one thousand and fifty-two; •sons of 40 41
Pashhur, one thousand two hundred and forty-seven; •sons of Harim, one 42
thousand and seventeen.

The Levites: sons of Jeshua, that is to say of Kadmiel, Binnui, Hodiah, 43
seventy-four.

The cantors: sons of Asaph, one hundred and forty-eight. 44

The gatekeepers: sons of Shallum, sons of Ater, sons of Talmon, sons of 45
Akkub, sons of Hatita, sons of Shobai, one hundred and thirty-eight.

The oblates: sons of Ziha, sons of Hasupha, sons of Tabbaoth, •sons of 46 47
Keros, sons of Sia, sons of Padon, •sons of Lebana, sons of Hagaba, sons of 48
Shalmai, •sons of Hanan, sons of Giddel, sons of Gahar, •sons of Reaiah, 49 50
sons of Rezin, sons of Nekoda, •sons of Gazzam, sons of Uzza, sons of Paseah, 51
sons of Besai, sons of the Meunites, sons of the Nephusites, •sons of Bakbuk, 52 53
sons of Hakupha, sons of Harhur, •sons of Bazlith, sons of Mehida, sons of 54
Harsha, •sons of Barkos, sons of Sisera, sons of Temah, •sons of Neziah, sons 55 56
of Hatipha.

The sons of Solomon's slaves: sons of Sotai, sons of Sophereth, sons of 57
Perida, •sons of Jaala, sons of Darkon, sons of Giddel, •sons of Shephatiah, 58 59
sons of Hattil, sons of Pochereth-haz-zebaim, sons of Amon. •The total of the 60
oblates and the sons of Solomon's slaves: three hundred and ninety-two.

The following, who came from Tel-melah, Tel-harsha, Cherub, Addon and 61
Immer, could not prove that their families and ancestry were of Israelite origin:
sons of Delaiah, sons of Tobiah, sons of Nekoda: six hundred and forty-two. 62
And among the priests: sons of Hobaiah, sons of Hakkoz, sons of Barzillai—who 63
had married one of the daughters of Barzillai, the Gileadite, whose name he
adopted. •These people searched in their ancestral registers but could not be 64
located in them, so they were excluded from the priesthood as unclean, •and 65
His Excellency forbade them to eat the sacred foods until a priest could be found
for the Urim and Thummim.

The whole assembly numbered forty-two thousand three hundred and sixty 66
people, •not counting their slaves and maidservants to the number of seven 67
thousand three hundred and thirty-seven. They also had two hundred and
forty-five male and female singers. •They had (seven hundred and thirty-six 68

horses, two hundred and forty-five mules) four hundred and thirty-five camels and six thousand seven hundred and twenty donkeys.

69 A certain number of heads of families gave offerings for the building. His Excellency contributed one thousand gold drachmas, fifty bowls, thirty priestly
70 robes and five hundred (silver minas) to the fund. •And heads of families gave twenty thousand gold drachmas and two thousand two hundred silver
71 minas to the building fund. •The gifts made by the rest of the people amounted to twenty thousand gold drachmas, two thousand silver minas, and sixty-seven priestly robes.

72a The priests, Levites and part of the people settled in Jerusalem; the gate-keepers, cantors, oblates and all the other Israelites, in their own towns.

Judaism is born. Ezra reads the Law. The feast of Tabernacles

72b
1 When the seventh month came, 8 all the people gathered as one man on the square before the Water Gate. They asked Ezra the scribe to bring the Book
2 of the Law of Moses which Yahweh had prescribed for Israel. •Accordingly Ezra the priest brought the Law before the assembly, consisting of men, women, and children old enough to understand. This was the first day of the seventh
3 month. •On the square before the Water Gate, in the presence of the men and women, and children old enough to understand, he read from the book from early morning till noon; all the people listened attentively to the Book of the Law.
4 Ezra the scribe stood on a wooden dais erected for the purpose; beside him stood, on his right, Mattithiah, Shema, Anaiah, Uriah, Hilkiah and Maaseiah; on his left, Pedaiah, Mishael, Malchijah, Hashum, Hashbaddanah, Zechariah,
5 and Meshullam. •In full view of all the people—since he stood higher than all the people—Ezra opened the book; and when he opened it all the people stood
6 up. •Then Ezra blessed Yahweh, the great God, and all the people raised their hands and answered, 'Amen! Amen!'; then they bowed down and, face to the
7 ground, prostrated themselves before Yahweh. •(Jeshua, Bani, Sherebiah, Jamin, Akkub, Shabbethai, Hodiah, Maaseiah, Kelita, Azariah, Jozabab, Hanan, Pelaiah, who were Levites, explained the Law to the people while the people
8 remained standing.) •And Ezra read from the Law of God, translating and giving the sense, so that the people understood what was read.
9 Then (Nehemiah—His Excellency—and) Ezra, priest and scribe (and the Levites who were instructing the people) said to all the people, 'This day is sacred to Yahweh your God. Do not be mournful, do not weep.' For the people were all in tears as they listened to the words of the Law.
10 He then said, 'Go, eat the fat, drink the sweet wine, and send a portion to the man who has nothing prepared ready. For this day is sacred to our Lord.
11 Do not be sad: the joy of Yahweh is your stronghold.' •And the Levites calmed
12 all the people, saying, 'Be at ease; this is a sacred day. Do not be sad.' •And all the people went off to eat and drink and give shares away and begin to enjoy themselves since they had understood the meaning of what had been proclaimed to them.
13 On the second day the heads of families of the whole people, and the priests
14 and Levites, gathered round Ezra the scribe to study the words of the Law. •And written in the Law that Yahweh had prescribed through Moses they found this, 'The sons of Israel are to live in shelters during the feast of the seventh month'.
15 As soon as they heard this, they issued a proclamation in all their towns and in Jerusalem: 'Go into the hills and bring branches of olive, pine, myrtle, palm
16 and other leafy trees to make shelters, as it says in the book'. •The people went; they brought back branches and made themselves shelters, each man on his own roof, in their courtyards, in the precincts of the Temple of God, on the square
17 of the Water Gate and the square of the Gate of Ephraim. •The whole assembly, all who had returned from captivity, put up shelters and lived in them; the sons

of Israel had never done such a thing from the days of Joshua son of Nun till the present.ᵃ And there was great merrymaking.

Each day, from the first day to the last, Ezra read from the Book of the 18 Law of God. They celebrated the feast for seven days; on the eighth day, as prescribed, there was a solemn assembly.

The ceremony of atonement

9 On the twenty-fourth day of this month the Israelites, in sackcloth and with 1 dust on their heads, assembled for a fast. •Those of Israelite stock separated 2 themselves from all those of foreign origin; they stood confessing their sins and the transgressions of their ancestors. •(Standing, each man in his right position, 3 they read from the Book of the Law of Yahweh their God for one quarter of the day; for another quarter they confessed their sins and prostrated themselves before Yahweh their God.)ᵃ •(On the Levites' platform stood Jeshua, Binnui, 4 Kadmiel, Shebaniah, Bunni, Sherebiah, Bani and Chenani, calling loudly to Yahweh their God; •and the Levites, Jeshua, Kadmiel, Bani, Hashabneiah, 5 Sherebiah, Hodiah, Shebaniah and Pethahiah said, 'Arise and bless Yahweh our God'.)

> Blessed be you, Yahweh our God,
> from everlasting to everlasting.
> And blessed be your name of glory
> that surpasses all blessing and praise.

> Yahweh, you are the only one.   6
> You made the heavens, the heaven of heavens, with all their array,
> the earth and all it bears,
> the seas and all they hold.
> To all of these you give life
> and the array of the heavens bows down before you.

> Yahweh, you are the God   7
> who chose Abram,
> brought him out from Ur in Chaldaea,
> and gave him the name of Abraham.
> Finding him faithful of heart before you,   8
> you made a covenant with him,
> to give him the land of the Canaanite,
> of the Hittite and Amorite,
> of the Perizzite, Jebusite, Girgashite,
> to him and his posterity.
> And you kept your promise
> because you are just.

> You saw the distress of our fathers in Egypt,   9
> you heard their cry by the Sea of Reeds.
> You worked portents and miracles against Pharaoh,   10
> against his servants and all the people of his land;
> for you knew how they treated them with arrogance.
> You won a reputation which you keep to this day.
> You divided the sea in front of them: 11
> they passed through the deep sea dry-shod.
> Into the depths you hurled their pursuers
> like a stone into rushing waters.
> With a pillar of cloud you led them by day,   12
> with a pillar of fire by night:
> to light the way ahead of them
> by which they should go.

13   You came down on Mount Sinai
and spoke with them from heaven;
you gave them
ordinances that are just,
laws that are sure,
good statutes and commandments;

14   you taught them to know
your holy sabbath,
laid down for them commandments (statutes) and Law
through Moses your servant.

15   For their hunger you gave them bread from heaven,
for their thirst you brought them water spurting from the rock.
You bade them go in
and take possession of the land
that you had sworn
to give to them.

16   But our fathers grew proud,
were obstinate, and flouted your commands.

17   They refused to obey, forgetful of the wonders
that you had worked for them;
they became obstinate, they even thought
of going back to Egypt and their slavery.
But you are a God of forgiveness,
gracious and loving,
slow to anger, abounding in goodness,
you did not forsake them.

18   When they cast themselves a calf
out of molten metal
and said, 'This is your God
who brought you up from Egypt'
(and were guilty of grave blasphemies),

19   you, so greatly loving,
still did not forsake them in the wilderness:
the pillar of cloud did not leave them
that led them on their path by day,
nor the pillar of fire by night,
to light the way ahead of them
by which they should go.

20   You gave them your good spirit
to make them wise,
you did not withhold your manna from their mouths,
you gave them water for their thirst.

21   Forty years you cared for them in the wilderness:
they went short of nothing,
their clothes did not wear out,
their feet were not swollen.

22   You gave to them kingdoms and peoples,
allotted them these as frontier regions;
they occupied the land of Sihon king of Heshbon,
and of Og king of Bashan.

23   You multiplied their sons

8 a. Ho 12:10 seems to attest this feast in the 8th century. According to 2 Ch. 7:8;8: it was celebrated from the time of Solomon.
9 a. This gloss makes the gathering resemble the liturgical penitential gatherings of the Chronicler's own day.

as the stars of heaven
and led them to the land that you had told their fathers
to enter and possess.
The sons invaded and conquered the land,   24
and before them you humbled
the land's inhabitants, the Canaanites,
whom you gave into their hands;
with their kings and the population of that country,
to be treated just as they pleased;
they captured fortified towns   25
and a fertile countryside,
took possession of houses stocked with all kinds of goods,
of cisterns ready-hewn, of vineyards and olive groves,
of fruit trees in profusion;
they ate, ate their fill,
regaling themselves on the good things you lavished on them.

But, disobedient as they were and rebellious towards you,   26
they thrust the Law behind their backs,
they killed the prophets who admonished them
to bring them back to you
(and were guilty of grave blasphemies).
So you delivered them into the hands of their oppressors   27
who oppressed them.
In the days of their oppression they cried to you,
and from heaven you heard them
and, greatly loving, you granted them saviours
who freed them from the hands of their oppressors.
But, once at peace, again they did wrong before you   28
and you gave them over to the hands of their enemies who treated
        them tyrannically.
And once more they cried to you
and from heaven you heard them:
how often are you, so loving, to deliver them?
You admonished them to bring them back to your Law;   29
but they grew proud, they did not obey your commandments,
they sinned against your ordinances
in which a man finds life if he observes them;
they shrugged their shoulders,
they were obstinate, they would not obey.
You were patient with them   30
for many years;
you admonished them by your spirit
through your prophets,
but they would not listen.
You delivered them then into the hands of the natives of the countries.
But, greatly loving,   31
you did not make an end of them,
you did not forsake them,
for you are a gracious and a loving God.
Now therefore, our God,   32
great and mighty God who must be feared,
maintaining your covenant and your kindness,
count as no small thing this misery
that has happened to us, our kings, our leaders,
our priests, our prophets, and all your people

from the time of the kings of Assyria
to the present day.

33
You have been just
in all that has happened to us,
for you have shown your faithfulness,
we our wickedness:

34
our kings, our leaders, our priests and our fathers
have not kept your Law,
they have been unmindful of your commandments and the warnings
that you gave them.

35
While they were in their kingdom
with the good things you lavished on them,
in the wide and fertile land
that you had set before them,
they did not renounce their evil deeds.

36
Here are we now, enslaved;
here in the land you gave our fathers
to enjoy its fruits and its good things,
we are slaves.

37
Its rich fruits swell the profit of the kings
whom for our sins you have set over us,
who dispose as they please of our bodies and our cattle.
Such the distress we endure!

A record of the promises made by the community[a]

38 / 1
10 ...As a result of all this we make a firm agreement, in writing. Our leaders, our Levites, and our priests have put their names to the document under seal...

2 / 1
On the sealed document were the names of: Nehemiah son of Hacaliah,
3,4 / 2,3 and Zedekiah, •Seraiah, Azariah, Jeremiah, •Pashhur, Amariah, Malchijah,
5-7 / 4-6 Hattush, Shebaniah, Malluch, •Harim, Meremoth, Obadiah, •Daniel, Ginnethon,
8,9 / 7,8 Baruch, •Meshullam, Abijah, Mijamin, •Maaziah, Bilgai, Shemaiah: these are
the priests.

10 / 9
Then the Levites: Jeshua son of Azaniah, Binnui of the sons of Henadad,
11 / 10 Kadmiel, •and their kinsmen Shebaniah, Hodaviah, Kelita, Pelaiah, Hanan,
12-14 / 11-13 Mica, Rehob, Hashabiah, •Zaccur, Sherebiah, Shebaniah, •Hodiah, Bani, Chenani.
15,16 / 14,15 The leaders of the people: Parosh, Pahath-moab, Elam, Zattu, Bani, •Bunni,
17-19 / 16-18 Azgad, Bebai, •Adonijah, Bigvai, Adin, •Ater, Hezekiah, Azzur, •Hodiah,
20,21 / 19,20 Hashum, Bezai, •Hariph, Anathoth, Nebai, •Magpiash, Meshullam, Hezir,
22-24 / 21-23 Meshezabel, Zadok, Jaddua, •Pelatiah, Hanan, Anaiah, •Hoshea, Hananiah,
25-27 / 24-26 Hasshub, •Hallohesh, Pilha, Shobek, •Rehum, Hashabnah, Maaseiah, •Ahiah,
28 / 27 Hanan, Anan, •Malluch, Harim, Baanah.

29 / 28
...but also the rest of the people, priests and Levites—gatekeepers, cantors, oblates—in short, all who have broken with the natives of the countries to adhere to the Law of God; as also their wives, sons and daughters, all those
30 / 29 who are old enough to understand, •join with their kinsmen and leaders and undertake, under curse and oath, to walk according to the Law of God given through Moses, the servant of God, and to observe and practise all the commandments of Yahweh our Lord, his customs and his laws.

31 / 30
In particular: we will not give our daughters to the natives of the land nor take their daughters for our sons.

32 / 31
If the natives of the land bring goods or any foodstuff whatever to sell on the sabbath day, we will buy nothing from them on sabbath or holy day.

---

10 a. During Nehemiah's second mission, described in ch. 13, he had to correct various religious abuses; this is an official report of the community's undertaking to reform, though the Chronicler has linked it with the reading of the Law, ch. 8-9.

We will forego the fruits of the soil in the seventh year, and all debts. ³³⁄₃₂

We recognise the following obligations:

to give one third of a shekel yearly for the liturgical requirements of the ³⁴⁄₃₃ Temple of our God: •for the loaves set out, for the perpetual oblation, for the perpetual holocaust, for the sacrifices on sabbaths, on New Moon feasts and on solemnities, for sacred foods, for sacrifices for sin to atone for Israel; in short, for all the services of the Temple of our God;

and further, to bring yearly to the Temple of our God the first-fruits of our ³⁶⁄₃₅ soil and the first-fruits of every fruit of every tree, •also the first-born of our ³⁷⁄₃₆ sons and of our cattle, as is written in the Law—those first-born of our herds and flocks taken to the Temple of our God being intended for the priests officiating in the Temple of our God. •Furthermore, we will bring to the priests, ³⁸⁄₃₇ to the chambers of the Temple of our God, the best of our meal, the fruit of every tree, new wine and oil; and to the Levites the tithe on our soil—the Levites themselves will collect the tithes from all our agricultural towns; •a priest, a son ³⁹⁄₃₈ of Aaron, is to accompany the Levites when they collect the tithes, and the Levites will pay a tenth part of the tithes into the Temple of our God, into the treasury offices; •since these rooms are where the Israelites and the Levites ⁴⁰ᵃᵇ⁄₃₉ₐᵦ bring the contributions of corn, wine and oil, and where the supplies are kept for the sanctuary, the officiating priests, the gatekeepers and cantors.

Furthermore, as regards deliveries of wood for burning on the altar of our ³⁵⁄₃₄ God as is written in the Law, we have arranged, by drawing lots among the priests, Levites and people, that these deliveries are to be made at the Temple of our God by each family in turn at stated times every year.

We will no longer neglect the Temple of our God. ⁴⁰ᶜ⁄₃₉ᶜ

The repopulation policy of Nehemiah. Various lists

11 ...Then the leaders of the people settled in Jerusalem. The rest of the ¹ people drew lots: one man in ten was to come and live in Jerusalem, the holy city, while the remaining nine were to stay in their towns. •And the people ² blessed all those who volunteered to live in Jerusalem.

These are the provincial leaders who settled in Jerusalem—and those who ³ settled in the towns of Judah. So Israel, the priests, the Levites, the oblates and the sons of Solomon's slaves, made their homes in their appropriate towns, each man on his own property.

The Jewish population in Jerusalem

In Jerusalem there lived some of the sons of Judah and some of the sons ⁴ of Benjamin.

Of the sons of Judah: Athaiah son of Uzziah, son of Zechariah, son of Amariah, son of Shephatiah, son of Mehalalel, of the descendants of Perez; Maaseiah son of Baruch, son of Col-hozeh, son of Hazaiah, son of Adaiah, son ⁵ of Joiarib, son of Zechariah, descendant of Shelah. •The total number of the de- ⁶ scendants of Perez living in Jerusalem was four hundred and sixty-eight adult men.

These are the sons of Benjamin: Sallu son of Meshullam, son of Joed, son ⁷ of Pedaiah, son of Kolaiah, son of Maaseiah, son of Ithiel, son of Jeshaiah, and his kinsmen, adult men: nine hundred and twenty-eight. ⁸

Joel son of Zichri was in charge of them, and Judah son of Hassenuah was ⁹ second in command of the city.

Of the priests: Jedaiah son of Joiakim, son of •Seraiah, son of Hilkiah, ¹⁰⁄₁₁ son of Meshullam, son of Zadok, son of Meraioth, son of Ahitub, prefect of the Temple of God, •and his kinsmen who were responsible for the Temple ¹² liturgy: eight hundred and twenty-two; Adaiah son of Jeroham, son of Pelaliah, son of Amzi, son of Zechariah, son of Pashhur, son of Malchijah, •and his ¹³ kinsmen, heads of families: two hundred and forty-two; and Amashai son of Azarel, son of Ahzai, son of Meshillemoth, son of Immer, •and his kinsmen, ¹⁴ adult men: one hundred and twenty-eight.

Zabdiel son of Haggadol was in charge of them.

15 Of the Levites: Shemaiah son of Hasshub, son of Azrikam, son of Hashabiah,
16 son of Bunni; •Shabbethai and Jozabad, the levitical leaders responsible for
17 the outside work of the Temple of God; •Mattaniah son of Mica, son of Zabdi,
son of Asaph, who directed the hymns and, at prayer, intoned the thanksgiving;
Bakbukiah, the second in rank among his kinsmen; Obadiah son of Shammua,
18 son of Galal, son of Jeduthun. •The total number of Levites in the holy city:
two hundred and eighty-four.

19 The gatekeepers: Akkub, Talmon and their kinsmen, who kept watch at the
gates: one hundred and seventy-two.

Supplementary notes

21 The oblates lived at Ophel; Ziha and Gishpa were in charge of the oblates.
22 —The head of the Levites in Jerusalem was Uzzi son of Bani, son of Hashabiah,
son of Mattaniah, son of Mica; he belonged to the sons of Asaph who were
23 responsible for the chanted parts of the liturgy in the Temple of God; •there
was a royal decree relating to the cantors, embodying regulations for their
24 attendance day by day.—•Pethahiah son of Meshezabel, belonging to the sons
of Zerah son of Judah, was the king's commissioner for all such matters as
concerned the people.

20 The rest of the Israelites, priests and Levites made their homes throughout
25 the towns of Judah, each man in his own inheritance, •and in the hamlets situated
in rural districts of their own.

The Jewish population outside Jerusalem

Some of the sons of Judah made their homes in Kiriath-arba and its outlying
villages, in Dibon and its outlying villages, in Jekabzeel and its outlying hamlets,
26
27 in Jeshua, Moladah, Beth-pelet, •Hazar-shual, in Beersheba and its villages,
28,29
30 in Ziklag, in Meconah and its villages, •in Enrimmon, Zorah, Jarmuth, •Zanoah,
Adullam and their hamlets, Lachish and its countryside, Azekah and its villages:
thus, they settled from Beersheba as far as the Valley of Hinnom.

31 Some of the sons of Benjamin made their homes in Geba, Michmash, Aija,
32
33 in Bethel and its villages, •Anathoth, Nob, Ananiah, •Hazor, Ramah, Gittaim,
34
35 Hadid, Zeboim, Neballat, •Lod and Ono, and the Valley of the Craftsmen.
36 Some groups of Levites settled in Judah as well as in Benjamin.

Priests and Levites who returned under Zerubbabel and Jeshua

1 ㅤ12 These are the priests and the Levites who came back with Zerubbabel son
ㅤ ㅤ of Shealtiel, and Jeshua:
2
3 Seraiah, Jeremiah, Ezra, •Amariah, Malluch, Hattush, •Shecaniah, Harim,
4,5
6 Meremoth, •Iddo, Ginnethoi, Abijah, •Mijamin, Maadiah, Bilgah, •Shemaiah;
7a also: Joiarib, Jedaiah, •Sallu, Amok, Hilkiah, Jedaiah.
8 And the Levites: Jeshua, Binnui, Kadmiel, Sherebiah, Judah, Mattaniah—
9 this last, with his kinsmen, directed the hymns of thanksgiving •while Bakbukiah,
Unno and their kinsmen in their respective orders formed an alternate choir.
7b These were the heads of the priests and of their kinsmen in the days of Jeshua.

Genealogical list of high priests

10 Jeshua was the father of Joiakim, Joiakim father of Eliashib, Eliashib father
11 of Joiada, •Joiada father of Johanan, and Johanan father of Jaddua.

Priests and Levites in the time of the High Priest Joiakim

12 In the days of Joiakim the heads of the priestly families were: family of
13 Seraiah, Meraiah; of Jeremiah, Hananiah; •of Ezra, Meshullam; of Amariah,
14
15 Jehohanan; •of Malluchi, Jonathan; of Shebaniah, Joseph; •of Harim, Adna;
16
17 of Meremoth, Helkai; •of Iddo, Zechariah; of Ginnethon, Meshullam; •of

Abijah, Zichri; of Miniamin, ...; of Moadiah, Piltai; •of Bilgah, Shammua; 18
of Shemaiah, Jehonathan; •also: of Joiarib, Mattenai; of Jedaiah, Uzzi; •of 19 20
Sallai, Kallai; of Amok, Eber; •of Hilkiah, Hashabiah; of Jedaiah, Nethanel. 21

In the days of Eliashib, Joiada, Johanan and Jaddua, the heads of the priestly 22
families had been recorded in the Book of the Chronicles[a] up to the reign of
Darius the Persian.

The sons of Levi. 23

The heads of families were recorded in the Book of the Chronicles, but only
up to the time of Johanan, grandson of Eliashib.

The heads of the Levites: Hashabiah, Sherebiah, Jeshua, Binnui, Kadmiel; 24
and their kinsmen forming an alternate choir for the hymns of praise and
thanksgiving, in accordance with the ordinances of David the man of God, in
corresponding groups, •these were: Mattaniah, Bakbukiah and Obadiah. The 25
gatekeepers, Meshullam, Talmon and Akkub stood guard at the storehouses
near the gates.

These lived in the days of Joiakim son of Jeshua, son of Jozadak, and in the 26
days of Nehemiah the governor and of Ezra, priest and scribe.

The dedication of the wall of Jerusalem

At the dedication of the wall of Jerusalem the Levites were sent for, wherever 27
they lived, to come to Jerusalem: the dedication was to be celebrated joyfully
with songs of thanksgiving, with cymbal, lute and lyre. •Accordingly the cantors, 28
sons of Levi, assembled from the countryside round Jerusalem, from the villages
of the Netophathites, •from Beth-gilgal, from the districts of Geba and 29
Azmaveth; since the cantors had built themselves villages all round Jerusalem.
And the priests and Levites purified themselves, then purified the people, the 30
gates and the wall.

I then made the leaders of Judah come on to the top of the wall, and 31
organized two great choirs. The first made its way along the top of the wall,
right-handed, towards the Dung Gate; •bringing up the rear were Hoshaiah 32
and half the leaders of Judah, •and also Azariah, Ezra, Meshullam, •Judah, 33 34
Mijamin, Shemaiah and Jeremiah, •selected from the priests and carrying 35
trumpets; then Zechariah son of Jonathan, son of Shemaiah, son of Mattaniah,
son of Micaiah, son of Zaccur, son of Asaph, •with his kinsmen, Shemaiah, 36
Azarel, Milalai, Gilalai, Maai, Nethanel, Judah, Hanani, carrying the musical
instruments of David the man of God. And Ezra the scribe walked at their head.
At the Fountain Gate they went straight on up, near the steps of the Citadel 37
of David, along the top of the wall and along the ascent of the Palace of David
as far as the Water Gate, on the east.

The second choir made its way left-handed; I followed it, with half the leaders 38
of the people, along the top of the wall, above the Tower of the Furnaces and
as far as the wall of the Square, •then over the Gate of Ephraim, the Fish 39
Gate, the Tower of Hananel, as far as the Sheep Gate; they came to a halt at
the Watch Gate.

The two choirs then took their places in the Temple of God. I had half of 40
the officials with me, •as well as the priests, Eliakim, Maaseiah, Miniamin, 41
Micaiah, Elioenai, Zechariah, Hananiah, carrying trumpets, •also Maaseiah, 42
Shemaiah, Eleazar, Uzzi, Jehohanan, Malchijah, Elam and Ezer. The cantors
sang under the direction of Jezrahiah. •There were great sacrifices offered that 43
day and the people rejoiced, God having given them good cause for rejoicing;
the women and children rejoiced too, and the joy of Jerusalem could be heard
from far away.

A golden age

For the chambers intended for the stores, contributions, first-fruits and tithes, 44
supervisors were then appointed whose business it would be to collect in them

those portions from the town lands awarded by the Law to the priests and
45 Levites. For Judah rejoiced in the officiating priests and Levites. •It was they
who performed the liturgy of their God and the duties of purification—and the
cantors and gatekeepers too—in accordance with the ordinances of David and
46 his son Solomon. •For from ancient times, from the days of David and Asaph,
there had been guilds of cantors and canticles of praise and thanksgiving to God.
47 And so, in the days of Zerubbabel and in the days of Nehemiah, the whole of
Israel used to give the cantors and gatekeepers their due portion for each day.
They set aside for the Levites their sacred dues, and the Levites would set theirs
aside for the sons of Aaron.

1 **13** At that time they were reading from the Book of Moses to the people,
when they found this written in it, 'The Ammonite and the Moabite shall
2 never be admitted to the assembly of God, •since they did not come to meet
the sons of Israel with bread and water. They hired Balaam *against them* to curse
3 *them,*[a] but *our God* turned the curse into a blessing.' •As soon as the people
had heard the Law they excluded all of foreign descent from Israel.

The second mission of Nehemiah

4 Now before this, Eliashib the priest had been appointed supervisor of the
5 chambers of the Temple of our God. A connection of Tobiah's, •he had
furnished a spacious chamber for him where the oblations, incense, utensils,
tithes of corn, wine and oil had previously been kept, that is to say the portions
of the Levites, cantors and gatekeepers, and what was set aside for the priests.
6 While all this was going on I was away from Jerusalem, for in the thirty-second
year of Artaxerxes king of Babylon[b] I had gone to see the king. But after some
7 time I asked the king for permission to leave, •and returned to Jerusalem. It was
then that I heard the wicked thing that Eliashib had done for Tobiah, furnishing
8 a chamber for him inside the court of the Temple of God. •This made me very
9 angry. I threw all Tobiah's household furniture out of the chamber, •gave
orders for the chambers to be purified, and had the utensils of the Temple of
God, the oblations and the incense, all put back.

10 I also discovered that the portions of the Levites were not being delivered
and that they, the Levites and the cantors responsible for the liturgy, had all
11 gone off home to their fields. •I reprimanded the officials. 'Why is the Temple
of God deserted?' I asked. And I collected them together again and sent them
12 back to their duties. •Then the whole of Judah brought the tithe of corn, wine
13 and oil to the storehouses. •As supervisors of the storehouses I appointed
Shelemiah the priest, Zadok the scribe, Pedaiah one of the Levites and, as their
assistants, Hanan son of Zaccur, son of Mattaniah, since they were considered
14 reliable; their duty was to make the distributions to their kinsmen. •Remember
me for this, my God; do not blot out the pious deed I have done for the Temple
of my God and for its liturgy.

15 In those days I saw people in Judah treading winepresses on the sabbath, and
others taking sheaves of corn and loading them on donkeys with wine, grapes,
figs and every kind of load which they meant to bring into Jerusalem on the
16 sabbath day. I warned them not to sell the foodstuffs. •In Jerusalem itself,
Tyrians who lived in the city were bringing in fish and every sort of merchandise
17 to sell them on the sabbath day. •I reprimanded the authorities of Judah,
18 'What a wicked way to behave, profaning the sabbath day! •Did not your ancestors
do just this, with the result that our God brought all this misery on us and on
this city? Do you want to bring fresh wrath on Israel, by profaning the
19 sabbath?' •So just before the sabbath[c] as the shadows were falling on the gates

---

12 a. A claim that the foregoing lists are based on reliable records. 'Darius' is Darius II, d. 405.
13 a. Free quotations from Dt 23 and Nb 22.   b. Nehemiah's first mission had thus lasted
from 445 to 433.   c. The sabbath began on Friday at sunset.

of Jerusalem, I gave orders for the doors to be shut, and said, 'Do not open them again until the sabbath is over'. I stationed a few of my servants at the gates to see that no load was brought in on the sabbath day. •Once or twice 20 merchants and traders in goods of all kinds spent the night outside Jerusalem, but I gave them this warning, 'Why are you spending the night by the wall? 21 Do it again, and I will punish you.' After that, they did not come on the sabbath any more. •I ordered the Levites to purify themselves and to come and 22 supervise the gates, so that the sabbath day might be kept holy. For this too remember me, my God, and as your mercy is great, so pity me.

At that time I again saw Jews who had married women from Ashdod, 23 Ammon and Moab. •As regards their children, half of them spoke the language 24 of Ashdod[d] or the language of one of the other peoples, but could not speak the language of Judah. •I reprimanded them and called down curses on them; 25 I struck several of them and tore out their hair and made them swear by God, 'You shall not give your daughters to their sons or take their daughters either for your sons or for yourselves. •Is this not how Solomon king of Israel sinned? 26 Among all the nations there was never a king like him; he was loved by his God; God made him king of all Israel; and yet for him, foreign women were causes of sin. •Must we then hear it said that you too are committing this grave 27 crime: playing traitor to our God by marrying foreign women?'

One of the sons of Jehoiada, son of the high priest Eliashib, was son-in-law 28 to Sanballat the Horonite, and I expelled him from my presence. •Remember 29 these, O my God, for the degradation they have brought on the priesthood and on the covenant of the priests and Levites.

And so I purged them of everything foreign; I drew up regulations for the 30 priests and Levites defining each man's duty, •and regulations for the deliveries 31 of wood at stated times, and for the first-fruits.

Remember me, my God, for my happiness.

d. An Aramaic dialect, contrasted with Hebrew.

INTRODUCTION TO
TOBIT, JUDITH AND ESTHER

Although these three books have the literary form of historical stories, the events of which they tell are not attested from other sources and the books are found to treat the facts of history and geography with a good deal of freedom. Plainly they were written to teach lessons of another kind, and some of the early Greek Bibles include them with the wisdom writings.

Tobit, the story of a dutiful son who is given miraculous help by an angel, was written among the Jews of the dispersion, possibly in Egypt, between the 4th and 5th centuries B.C., though the setting of the story is some two hundred years earlier. The book was not accepted into the Hebrew Bible and was recognised by the Church only after a certain hesitancy in the patristic period. In the new translations of the Bible made at the Reformation, it was put in the Apocrypha.

The same treatment was given to the Book of **Judith**, the story of the defeat of Nebuchadnezzar's armies through a woman's single-handed assassination of their commander. It was written about 100 B.C.

The theme of **Esther** is similarly the deliverance of the nation by the actions of a woman. The Hebrew version was probably written about 300 B.C.; the Greek version, which is longer and contains some important additions, is later. In this text, additions adopted from the Greek version are printed in italics. Although the book of Esther has been read and quoted from early days, the Greek passages are 'deuterocanonical', their history being the same as that of Tobit and Judith.

TOBIT

1 The tale of Tobit[a] son of Tobiel, son of Ananiel, son of Aduel, son of Gabael, 1
of the lineage of Asiel and tribe of Naphtali. •In the days of Shalmaneser, 2
king of Assyria, he was exiled from Thisbe, which is south of Kedesh-Naphtali
in Upper Galilee, above Hazor, some distance to the west, north of Shephat.

I. TOBIT THE EXILE

I, Tobit, have walked in paths of truth and in good works all the days of my 3
life. I have given much in alms to my brothers and fellow countrymen, exiled
like me to Nineveh in the country of Assyria. •In my young days, when I still 4
was at home in the country of Israel, the whole tribe of Naphtali my ancestor
broke away from the House of David and from Jerusalem. Yet this was the city
chosen out of all the tribes of Israel for their sacrifices; in this the Temple—God's
dwelling place—had been built and hallowed for all generations to come. •But 5
all my brothers and the House of Naphtali offered sacrifice to the calf that
Jeroboam the king of Israel had made at Dan, on the mountains of Galilee.

Often I was quite alone in making the pilgrimage to Jerusalem, fulfilling the 6
law that binds all Israel perpetually. I would hurry to Jerusalem with the first
yield of fruits and beasts, the tithe of cattle and the sheep's first shearings. •I would 7
give these to the priests, the sons of Aaron, for the altar. To the Levites
ministering at Jerusalem I would give my tithe of wine and corn, olives, pomegranates and other fruits. Six years in succession I took the second tithe in money
and went and paid it at Jerusalem. •I gave the third to orphans and widows and 8
to the strangers who live among the Israelites; I brought it them as a gift every
three years. When we ate, we obeyed both the ordinances of the Law of Moses
and the exhortations of Deborah, the mother of our father Ananiel; for my
father had died and left me an orphan. •When I came to man's estate, I married 9
a woman from our kinsmen whose name was Anna; she bore me a son whom
I called Tobias.

When the banishment into Assyria came, I was taken away and went to 10/11
Nineveh. All my brothers and the men of my race ate the food of the heathen,
but for my part I would not eat the food of the heathen.[b] •And because I had 11,12/12,13
kept faith with my God with my whole heart, •the Most High granted me the 13
favour of Shalmaneser, and I became the king's purveyor. •Until his death 14/16
I used to travel to Media, where I transacted business on his behalf; and
I deposited sacks of silver worth ten talents with Gabael, the brother of Gabrias,
at Rhages in Media.

On the death of Shalmaneser his son Sennacherib succeeded; the roads into 15/18
Media were barred, and I could no longer go there. •In the days of Shalmaneser 16
I had often given alms to the brothers of my race; •I gave my bread to the hungry 17/20
and clothes to the naked; and I buried, when I saw them, the bodies of my
countrymen thrown over the walls of Nineveh.

I also buried those who were killed by Sennacherib (for when he retreated 18/21
from Judaea in disorder, after the King of heaven had punished his blasphemies,

in his anger Sennacherib killed a great number of Israelites). So I stole their bodies to bury them; Sennacherib looked for them and could not find them. ¹⁹₂₂ A Ninevite went and told the king it was I who had buried them secretly. When I knew that the king had been told about me and saw myself being hunted by men who would put me to death, I was afraid and fled. •All my goods were seized; they were all confiscated by the treasury; nothing was left me but my wife Anna and my son Tobias.

²¹₂₄   Less than forty days after this, the king was murdered by his two sons, who then fled to the mountains of Ararat. His son Esarhaddon succeeded. Ahikar,^c the son of my brother Anael, was appointed chancellor of the exchequer for the kingdom and given the main ordering of affairs. •Ahikar then interceded for me and I was allowed to return to Nineveh, since Ahikar had been chief cupbearer, keeper of the signet, administrator and treasurer under Sennacherib, king of Assyria, and Esarhaddon had kept him in office. He was a relation of mine; he was my nephew.

II. TOBIT BLINDED

¹ **2** In the reign of Esarhaddon, therefore, I returned home, and my wife Anna was restored to me with my son Tobias. At our feast of Pentecost (the feast of Weeks)['] there was a good dinner. I took my place for the meal; •the table was brought to me and various dishes were brought. Then I said to my son Tobias, 'Go, my child, and seek out some poor, loyal-hearted man among our brothers exiled in Nineveh, and bring him to share my meal. I will wait until you come back, my child.' •So Tobias went out to look for some poor man among our brothers, but he came back again and said, 'Father!' I answered, 'What is it, my child?' He went on, 'Father, one of our nation has just been murdered; he has been strangled and then thrown down in the market place; he is there still'. •I sprang up at once, left my meal untouched, took the man from the market place and laid him in one of my rooms, waiting until sunset to bury him. •I came in again and washed myself and ate my bread in sorrow, remembering the words of the prophet Amos concerning Bethel:

> Your feasts will be turned to mourning,
> and all your songs to lamentation.

⁷ And I wept. When the sun was down, I went and dug a grave and buried him. ⁸ My neighbours laughed and said, 'See! He is not afraid any more.' (You must remember that a price had been set on my head earlier for this very thing.) 'The time before this he had to flee, yet here he is, beginning to bury the dead again.'

⁹₁₀₁₁   That night I took a bath; then I went into the courtyard and lay down by the courtyard wall. Since it was hot I left my face uncovered. •I did not know that there were sparrows in the wall above my head; their hot droppings fell into my eyes. White spots then formed, which I was obliged to have treated by the doctors. But the more ointments they tried me with, the more the spots blinded me, and in the end I became blind altogether. I remained without sight four years; all my brothers were distressed; and Ahikar provided for my upkeep for two years, till he left for Elymais.

¹¹₁₉   My wife Anna then undertook woman's work; she would spin wool and take cloth to weave; •she used to deliver whatever had been ordered from her and then receive payment. Now on March the seventh she finished a piece of work

---

1 a. This translation follows the Greek. In places where the verse numbering differs from the Vulgate Latin text, the Vulgate verse numbers are added in italic.   **b.** Food prepared without regard for the Law's regulations.   **c.** A famous chancellor to Sennacherib and Esarhaddon, kings of Assyria.

and delivered it to her customers. They paid her all that was due, and into the ²⁰
bargain presented her with a kid for a meal. •When the kid came into my house, ¹³ ²¹
it began to bleat. I called to my wife and said, 'Where does this creature come
from? Suppose it has been stolen! Quick, let the owners have it back; we have
no right to eat stolen goods.' •She said, 'No, it was a present given me over and ¹⁴
above my wages'. I did not believe her, and told her to give it back to the owners
(I blushed at this in her presence). Then she answered, 'What about your own ²²
alms? What about your own good works? Everyone knows what return you
have had for them.' **3** Then, sad at heart, I sighed and wept, and began this ¹
prayer of lamentation:

'You are just, O Lord,   ²
    and just are all your works.
All your ways are grace and truth,
    and you are the Judge of the world.

'Therefore, Lord,   ³
    remember me, look on me.
Do not punish me for my sins
    or for my heedless faults
    or for those of my fathers.

'For we have sinned against you   ⁴
    and broken your commandments;
and you have given us over to be plundered,
    to captivity and death,
to be the talk, the laughing-stock and scorn
    of all the nations among whom you have dispersed us.

'Whereas all your decrees are true   ⁵
    when you deal with me as my faults deserve,
and those of my fathers,
    since we have neither kept your commandments
nor walked in truth before you;
    so now, do with me as you will;   ⁶
be pleased to take my life from me;
    I desire to be delivered from earth
and to become earth again.
For death is better for me than life.
I have been reviled without a cause
and I am distressed beyond measure.

'Lord, I wait for the sentence you will give
    to deliver me from this affliction.
Let me go away to my everlasting home;
    do not turn your face from me, O Lord.
For it is better to die than still to live
    in the face of trouble that knows no pity;
I am weary of hearing myself traduced.'

III. SARAH

It chanced on the same day that Sarah the daughter of Raguel, who lived in ⁷
Media at Ecbatana, also heard insults from one of her father's maids. •You must ⁸
know that she had been given in marriage seven times, and that Asmodeus,
that worst of demons, had killed her bridegrooms one after another before ever
they had slept with her as man with wife. The servant-girl said, 'Yes, you kill

your bridegrooms yourself. That makes seven already to whom you have been
9 given, and you have not once been in luck yet. •Just because your bridegrooms
have died, that is no reason for punishing us. Go and join them, and may we be
10 spared the sight of any child of yours!' •That day, she grieved, she sobbed, and
went up to her father's room intending to hang herself. But then she thought,
'Suppose they blamed my father! They will say, "You had an only daughter
whom you loved, and now she has hanged herself for grief". I cannot cause my
father a sorrow which would bring down his old age to the dwelling of the dead.
I should do better not to hang myself, but to beg the Lord to let me die and
11 not live to hear any more insults.' •And at this, by the window with outstretched
arms she said this prayer:

> 'You are blessed, O God of mercy!
> May your name be blessed for ever,
> and may all things you have made
> bless you everlastingly.

12
14
> 'And now, I lift up my face
> and to you I turn my eyes.

13
15
> Let your word deliver me from earth;
> I can hear myself traduced no longer.

14
16
> 'O Lord, you know
> that I have remained pure;
> no man has touched me;

15
17
> I have not dishonoured your name
> or my father's name
> in this land of exile.

> 'I am my father's only daughter,
> he has no other child as heir;
> he has no brother at his side,
> nor has he any kinsman left
> for whom I ought to keep myself.

> 'Already I have lost seven husbands;
> why should I live any longer?
> If it does not please you to take my life,
> then look on me with pity;
> I can hear myself traduced no longer.'

16
24
17
25
    This time the prayer of each of them found favour before the glory of God,
and Raphael was sent to bring remedy to them both. He was to take the white
spots from the eyes of Tobit, so that he might see God's light with his own eyes;
and he was to give Sarah, the daughter of Raguel, as bride to Tobias son of
Tobit, and to rid her of Asmodeus, that worst of demons. For it was to Tobias
before all other suitors that she belonged by right. Tobit was coming back from
the courtyard into the house at the same moment as Sarah, the daughter of
Raguel, was coming down from the upper room.

IV. TOBIAS

1 **4** The same day, Tobit remembered the silver that he had left with Gabael
2 at Rhages in Media •and thought, 'I have come to the point of praying for
death; I should do well to call my son Tobias and tell him about the money
3 before I die'. •He summoned his son Tobias and told him:

'When I die, give me an honourable burial. Honour your mother, and never abandon her all the days of your life. Do all that she wants, and give her no reason for sorrow. •Remember, my child, all the risks she ran for your sake when you were in her womb. And when she dies, bury her at my side in the same grave. ⁴/₅

'My child, be faithful to the Lord all your days. Never entertain the will to sin or to transgress his laws. Do good works all the days of your life, never follow ways that are not right; •for if you act in truthfulness, you will be successful in all your actions, as all men are if they practise what is right. ⁵/₆ ⁶

'Set aside part of your goods for almsgiving. Never turn your face from any poor man and God will never turn his from you. •Measure your alms by what you have; if you have much, give more; if you have little, give less, but do not be mean in giving alms. •By doing so, you will lay up for yourself a great treasure for the day of necessity. •For almsgiving delivers from death and saves men from passing down to darkness. •Alms is a most effective offering for all those who give it in the presence of the Most High. ⁷ ⁸ ⁹ ⁹/₁₀ ¹⁰/₁₁ ¹¹/₁₂

'My child, avoid all loose conduct. Choose a wife of your father's stock. Do not take a foreign wife outside your father's tribe, because we are the sons of the prophets. Remember Noah, Abraham, Isaac and Jacob, our ancestors from the beginning. All of them took wives from their own kindred, and they were blessed in their children, and their race will inherit the earth. •You, too, my child, must prefer your own brothers; never presume to despise your brothers, the sons and daughters of your people; choose your wife from among them. For pride brings ruin and much worry; idleness causes need and poverty, for the mother of famine is idleness. ¹² ¹³ ¹⁴

'Do not keep back until next day the wages of those who work for you; pay them at once. If you serve God you will be rewarded. Be careful, my child, in all you do, well-disciplined in all your behaviour. •Do to no one what you would not want done to you. Do not drink wine to the point of drunkenness; do not let excess be your travelling companion. ¹⁴/₁₅ ¹⁵/₁₆

'Give your bread to those who are hungry, and your clothes to those who are naked. Whatever you own in plenty, devote a proportion to almsgiving; and when you give alms, do not do it grudgingly. •Be generous with bread and wine on the graves of virtuous men, but not for the sinner. ¹⁶/₁₇ ¹⁷/₁₈

'Ask advice of every wise person; never scorn any profitable advice. •Bless the Lord God in everything; beg him to guide your ways and bring your paths and purposes to their end. For wisdom is not given to every nation; the Lord himself gives all good things. At his will he lifts up or he casts down to the depths of the dwelling of the dead. So now, my child, remember these precepts and never let them fade from your heart. ¹⁸,¹⁹ ¹⁹,²⁰

'Now, my child, I must tell you I have left ten talents of silver with Gabael son of Gabrias, at Rhages in Media. •Do not be afraid, my child, if we have grown poor. You have great wealth if you fear God, if you shun every kind of sin and if you do what is pleasing to the Lord your God.' ²⁰/₂₁ ²¹/₂₃

V. THE FELLOW TRAVELLER OF TOBIAS

5 Tobias then answered his father Tobit, 'Father, I will do everything you have told me. •But how am I to recover the money from him? He does not know me, nor I him. What token am I to give him for him to believe me and hand me over the silver? And besides, I do not know what roads to take for this journey into Media.' •Then Tobit answered his son Tobias, 'Each of us set his signature to a note which I cut in two, so that each could keep half of it. I took one piece, and put the other with the silver. To think it was twenty years ago I left this silver in his keeping! And now, my child, find some trustworthy man ¹ ² ³ ⁴

to travel with you—we will pay him for his time until you arrive back—and then go and collect the money from Gabael.'

⁴/₅   Tobias went out to look for a man who knew the way to go with him to Media. Outside he found Raphael the angel standing facing him (though he ⁵/₆ did not guess he was an angel of God). •He said, 'Where do you come from, ₇ friend?' The angel replied, 'I am one of your brother Israelites; I have come to these parts to look for work'. Tobias asked, 'Do you know the road to Media?' ⁶/₈ The other replied, 'Certainly I do. I have been there many times; I know all the ways by heart. I have often been to Media and stayed with Gabael, one of our kinsmen who lives at Rhages in Media. It usually takes two full days to get from Ecbatana to Rhages; Rhages lies in the mountains, and Ecbatana is in ⁷/₉ the middle of the plain.'ᵃ •Tobias said, 'Wait for me, friend, while I go and ₈ tell my father; I need you to come with me; I will pay you for your time'. •The other replied, 'Good; I will wait; but do not be long'.

⁹/₁₀   Tobias went in and told his father that he had found one of their brother Israelites. And the father said, 'Fetch him in; I want to find out about his family and tribe. I must see if he is going to be a reliable companion for you, my child.' So Tobias went out and called him. 'Friend,' he said 'my father wants you.'

¹⁰/₁₁   The angel came into the house; Tobit greeted him, and the other answered, ₁₂ wishing him happiness. Tobit replied, 'Can I ever be happy again? I am a blind man; I no longer see the light of heaven; I am sunk in darkness like the dead who see the light no more. I am a man buried alive; I hear men speak but cannot ₁₃ see them.' The angel said, 'Take comfort; before long God will heal you. Take ₁₄ comfort.' Tobit said, 'My son Tobias wishes to go to Media. Will you join him as his guide? Brother, I will pay you.' He replied, 'I am willing to go with him; I know all the ways; I have often been to Media, I have crossed all its ¹¹/₁₆ plains and mountains, and I know all the roads'. •Tobit said, 'Brother, what ¹²/₁₇ family and what tribe do you belong to? Will you tell me, brother?' •'What does my tribe matter to you?' the angel said. Tobit said, 'I want to be quite sure ¹³/₁₈ whose son you are and what your name is'. •The angel said, 'I am Azarias, son ¹⁴/₁₉ of the great Ananias, one of your kinsmen'. •'Welcome and greetings, brother! Do not be offended at my wanting to know the name of your family; I find you are my kinsman, of a good and honourable line. I know Ananias and Jathan, the two sons of the great Shemaiah. They used to go to Jerusalem with me; we have worshipped together there, and they have never strayed from the right path. Your brothers are worthy men; you come of good stock; welcome.'

₁₅   He went on, 'I engage you at a drachma a day, with your expenses, like my ₁₆ own son. Complete the journey with my son, •and I will go beyond the agreed ₂₀ wage.' The angel replied, 'I will complete the journey with him. Do not be afraid. On the journey outward all will be well; on the journey back all will be well; ₁₇ the road is safe.' •Tobit said, 'Blessings on you, brother!' Then he turned to his son. 'My child,' he said 'prepare what you need for the journey, and set off with ₂₁ your brother. May God in heaven protect you abroad and bring you both back to me safe and sound! May his angel go with you and protect you, my child!'

₂₂   Tobias left the house to set out and kissed his father and mother. Tobit said, ¹⁸/₂₃ 'A happy journey!' •His mother burst into tears and said to Tobit, 'Why must you send my child away? Is he not the staff of our hands, with his errands to ¹⁹/₂₄ and fro for us? •Surely money is not the only thing that matters? Surely it is not ²⁰/₂₅ as precious as our child? •The way of life God had already given us was good ²¹/₂₆ enough. •He said, 'Do not think such thoughts. Going away and coming back, all will be well with our child. On the day of his homecoming you will see for yourself how all is still well with him. Do not think such thoughts; do not worry ²²/₂₇ on their account, my sister. •A good angel will go with him; he will have a good ¹/₂₈ journey and come back to us well and happy. ₆ And she dried her tears.

---

5 a. The geography is inexact.

VI. THE FISH

The boy left with the angel, and the dog followed behind. The two walked on, 1 and when the first evening came they camped beside the Tigris. •The boy had 2 gone down to the river to wash his feet, when a great fish leapt out of the water and all but swallowed his foot. The boy gave a shout •and the angel said, 'Catch 3,4 the fish; do not let it go'. The boy mastered the fish and pulled it on to the bank. The angel said, 'Cut it open; take out the gall, the heart and the liver; set these 5 aside and throw the entrails away, for the gall and heart and liver have curative properties'. •The boy cut the fish open and took out the gall and heart and liver. 6 He fried part of the fish for his meal and kept some for salting. Then they walked on again together until they were nearly in Media.

Then the boy asked the angel this question, 'Brother Azarias, what can the 7 fish's heart, liver and gall cure?' •He replied, 'You burn the fish's heart and 8 liver, and their smoke is used in the case of a man or woman plagued by a demon or evil spirit; any such affliction disappears for good, leaving no trace. •As 9 regards the gall, this is used as an eye ointment for anyone having white spots on his eyes; after using it, you only have to blow on the spots to cure them.'

They entered Media and had nearly reached Ecbatana •when Raphael said 10 to the boy, 'Brother Tobias'. 'Yes?' he answered. The angel went on, 'Tonight 11 we shall be staying with Raguel, who is a kinsman of yours. He has a daughter called Sarah, •but apart from Sarah he has no other son or daughter. Now you 12 are her next of kin; she belongs to you before anyone else and you may claim her father's inheritance. She is a thoughtful, courageous and very lovely girl, and her father loves her dearly. •You have the right to marry her. Listen, brother; 13 this very evening I will speak about the girl to her father and arrange for her to be betrothed to you, and when we come back from Rhages we can celebrate the marriage. I assure you, Raguel has no right whatever to refuse you or to betroth her to anyone else. That would be asking for death, as prescribed in the Book of Moses, once he was aware that kinship gives you the pre-eminent right to marry his daughter. So listen, brother. This very evening we will speak about the girl and ask for her hand in marriage. When we come back from Rhages we will fetch her and take her home with us.'

Tobias answered Raphael, 'Brother Azarias, I have been told that she has 14 already been given in marriage seven times and that each time her bridegroom has died in the bridal room. He died the same night as he entered her room; and I have heard people say it was a demon that killed them, •and this makes 15 me a little afraid. He does no harm to her, of course, because he loves her; but as soon as a man tries to approach her, he kills him. I am my father's only son, and I have no wish to die; I shrink from causing my father and mother a grief that would bring them to the grave; they have no other son to bury them.' •The 16 angel said, 'Are you going to forget your father's advice? After all, he urged you to choose a wife from your father's family. Listen then, brother. Do not worry about the demon; take her. This very evening, I promise, she will be given you as your wife. •Then once you are in the bridal room, take the heart and 17 liver of the fish and lay a little of it on the burning incense. The reek will rise, the demon will smell it and flee, and there is no danger that he will ever be found 18 near the girl again. Then, before you sleep together, first stand up, both of you, and pray. Ask the Lord of heaven to grant you his grace and protection. Do not be afraid; she was destined for you from the beginning, and it is you who will save her. She will follow you, and I pledge my word she will give you children who will be like brothers to you. Do not hesitate.' And when Tobias heard Raphael say this, when he understood that Sarah was his sister, a kinswoman of his father's family, he fell so deeply in love with her that he could no longer call his heart his own.

VII. RAGUEL

7 ¹ As they entered Ecbatana, Tobias said, 'Brother Azarias, take me at once to our brother Raguel's'. And he showed him the way to the house of Raguel, whom they found sitting beside his courtyard door. They greeted him first, and he replied, 'Welcome and greetings, brothers'. And he took them into his house. ²⁄₃ He said to his wife Edna, 'How like my brother Tobit this young man is!' •Edna asked them where they came from; they said, 'We are sons of Naphtali exiled ⁴⁄₅ in Nineveh'. •'Do you know our brother Tobit?' 'Yes.' 'How is he?' •'He is ⁶ still alive and he is well.' And Tobias added, 'He is my father'. •Raguel leapt ⁷ to his feet and kissed him and wept. •Then finding words, he said, 'Blessings on you, child! You are the son of a noble father. How sad it is that someone so virtuous and full of good deeds should have gone blind!' He fell on the neck ⁸ of his kinsman Tobias and wept. •And his wife Edna wept for him, and so did ⁹ his daughter Sarah. •Raguel killed a sheep from the flock, and they gave them a warmhearted welcome.

They washed and bathed and sat down to table. Then Tobias said to Raphael, ¹⁰ 'Brother Azarias, will you ask Raguel to give me my sister Sarah?' •Raguel overheard the words, and said to the young man, 'Eat and drink, and make the most of your evening; no one else has the right to take my daughter Sarah—no one but you, my brother. In any case I, for my own part, am not at liberty to give her to anyone else, since you are her next of kin. However, my boy, I must ¹¹ be frank with you: •I have tried to find a husband for her seven times among our kinsmen, and all of them have died the first evening, on going to her room. But for the present, my boy, eat and drink; the Lord will grant you his grace and peace.' Tobias spoke out, 'I will not hear of eating and drinking till you have come to a decision about me'. Raguel answered, 'Very well. Since, as prescribed by the Book of Moses, she is given to you, heaven itself decrees she shall be yours. I therefore entrust your sister to you. From now you are her brother and she is your sister. She is given to you from today for ever. The Lord of heaven favour you tonight, my child, and grant you his grace and peace.' ¹² Raguel called for his daughter Sarah, took her by the hand and gave her to Tobias with these words, 'I entrust her to you; the law and the ruling recorded in the Book of Moses assign her to you as your wife. Take her; take her home to your father's house with a good conscience. The God of heaven grant you ¹³ a good journey in peace.' •Then he turned to her mother and asked her to fetch ¹⁶ him writing paper. He drew up the marriage contract, how he gave his daughter as bride to Tobias according to the ordinance in the Law of Moses.

¹⁴,¹⁵ ¹⁷,¹⁸ After this they began to eat and drink. •Raguel called his wife Edna and ¹⁶ ¹⁹ said, 'My sister, prepare the second room and take her there'. •She went and made the bed in this room as he had ordered, and took her daughter to it. She ²⁰ wept over her, then wiped away her tears and said, 'Courage, daughter! May the Lord of heaven turn your grief to joy! Courage, daughter!' And she went out.

VIII. THE GRAVE

8 ¹ When they had finished eating and drinking and it seemed time to go to bed, ² the young man was taken from the dining room to the bedroom. •Tobias remembered Raphael's advice; he went to his bag, took the fish's heart and liver ³ out of it and put some on the burning incense. •The reek of the fish distressed the demon, who fled through the air to Egypt. Raphael pursued him there, and bound and shackled him at once.

⁴ The parents meanwhile had gone out and shut the door behind them. Tobias rose from the bed, and said to Sarah, 'Get up, my sister! You and I must pray

and petition our Lord to win his grace and his protection.' •She stood up, and ⁵⁄₆
they began praying for protection, and this was how he began: ⁷

> 'You are blessed, O God of our fathers;
> blessed, too, is your name
> for ever and ever.
> Let the heavens bless you
> and all things you have made
> for evermore.

> It was you who created Adam, ⁶⁄₈
> you who created Eve his wife
> to be his help and support;
> and from these two the human race was born.
> It was you who said,
> *"It is not good that the man should be alone;*
> *let us make him a helpmate like himself"*.
> And so I do not take my sister ⁷⁄₉
> for any lustful motive;
> I do it in singleness of heart.
> Be kind enough to have pity on her and on me
> and bring us to old age together.'

And together they said, 'Amen, Amen', •and lay down for the night. ⁸⁄₉
  But Raguel rose and called his servants, who came and helped him to dig ¹¹
a grave. •He had thought, 'Heaven grant he does not die! We should be over- ¹⁰⁄₁₂
whelmed with ridicule and shame.' •When the grave was finished, Raguel went ¹¹⁄₁₃
back to the house, called his wife •and said, 'Will you send a maid to the room ¹²⁄₁₄
to see if Tobias is still alive? For if he is dead, we may be able to bury him without
anyone else knowing.' •The maid was called, the lamp lit and the door opened; ¹³⁄₁₅
the maid went in. She found the two fast asleep; •she came out again and ¹⁴⁄₁₆
whispered, 'He is not dead; all is well'. •Then Raguel blessed the God of heaven ¹⁵⁄₁₇
with these words:

> 'You are blessed, my God,
> with every blessing that is pure;
> may you be blessed for evermore!

> 'You are blessed for having made me glad. ¹⁶
> What I feared has not happened;
> instead you have treated us
> with mercy beyond all measure.

> 'You are blessed for taking pity ¹⁷⁄₁₉
> on this only son, this only daughter.
> Grant them, Master, your grace and your protection;
> let them live out their lives
> in happiness and in grace.'

And he made his servants fill the grave in before dawn broke. ¹⁸⁄₂₀
  He told his wife to make plenty of bread; he went to his flock, brought back ¹⁹
two oxen and four sheep and gave orders for them to be cooked; and preparations
began. •He called Tobias and said, 'I will not hear of your leaving here for ²⁰⁄₂₃
a fortnight. You are to stay where you are, eating and drinking, with me. You
will make my daughter happy again after all her troubles. •After that, take away ²¹⁄₂₄
a half of all I have, and go without let or hindrance back to your father. When
my wife and I are dead you will have the other half. Courage, my boy! I am your
father, and Edna is your mother. We are your parents in future, as we are your
sister's. Courage, my son!'

IX. THE WEDDING FEAST

1
2 **9** Then Tobias turned to Raphael. •'Brother Azarias,' he said 'take four servants
3 and two camels and leave for Rhages. •Go to Gabael's house, give him the
receipt and see about the money; then invite him to come with you to my wedding
4 feast. •You know that my father must be counting the days and that I cannot
5 lose a single one without worrying him. •You see what Raguel has pledged
6 himself to do; I am bound by his oath.' So Raphael left for Rhages in Media
with the four servants and two camels. They stayed with Gabael, and Raphael
7 showed him the receipt. He told him about the marriage of Tobias son of Tobit
and gave him his invitation to the wedding feast. Gabael started counting out
the sacks to him—the seals were intact—and they loaded them on to the camels.
6
8 Early in the morning they set off together for the feast, and reached Raguel's
house where they found Tobias dining. He rose to greet Gabael, who burst
into tears and blessed him with the words, 'Excellent son of a father beyond
9 reproach, just and generous in his dealings! The Lord give heaven's blessing
to you, to your wife, to the father and mother of your wife! Blessed be God for
granting me the sight of this living image of my cousin Tobit!'

1 **10** Every day, meanwhile, Tobit kept reckoning the days required for the
journey there and the journey back. The full number went by, and still
2 his son had not come. •Then he thought, 'I hope he has not been delayed there!
I hope Gabael is not dead! Perhaps no one was there to give him the money.'
3
4 And he began to worry. •His wife Anna kept saying, 'My son is dead! He is no
longer among the living!' And she began to weep and mourn over her son. She
5 kept saying, •'Alas! I let you leave me, my child, you, the light of my eyes.'
6 And Tobit would reply, 'Hush, my sister! Do not think such thoughts. All is well
with him. Something has happened there to delay them. His companion is
someone we can trust, one of our kinsmen at that. Do not lose heart, my sister.
7 He will be here soon.' •But she only said, 'Leave me alone; do not try to deceive
me. My child is dead.' And every day she would go abruptly out to watch the
road by which her son had left. She trusted no eyes but her own. Once the sun
had set she would come home again, only to weep and moan all night, unable
to sleep.

After the fourteen days of feasting that Raguel had sworn to keep for his
daughter's marriage, Tobias came to him and said, 'Let me go now; my father
and mother must have lost all hope of seeing me again. So I beg you, father,
to let me return to my father's house; I have told you the plight he was in when
8 I left him.' •Raguel said to Tobias, 'Stay, my son, stay with me. I will send
9 messengers to your father Tobit to give him news of you.' •But Tobias pressed
10 him, 'No. I ask your permission to go back to my father's house.' •Without
more ado, Raguel committed Sarah his bride into his keeping. He gave Tobias
half his wealth, menservants and maidservants, oxen and sheep, donkeys and
11 camels, clothes and money and household things. •And so he let them leave
happily. To Tobias he said these parting words, 'Good health, my son, and
a happy journey! May the Lord of heaven be gracious to you and to your wife
12
13 Sarah! I hope to see your children before I die.' •To his daughter Sarah he said,
'Go now to your father-in-law's house, since henceforward they are as much
your parents as those who gave you life. Go in peace, my daughter, I hope to
hear nothing but good of you, as long as I live.' He said goodbye to them and let
them go.

Edna in her turn said to Tobias, 'Dear son and brother, may it please the
Lord to bring you back again! I hope to live long enough to see the children
of you and my daughter Sarah before I die. In the sight of the Lord I give my
daughter into your keeping. Never make her unhappy as long as you live. Go in
peace, my son. Henceforward I am your mother and Sarah is your sister. May

we all live happily all the days of our lives!' And she kissed them both and saw 12
them set out happily.

Tobias left Raguel's house with his mind at ease. In his gladness he blessed 13
the Lord of heaven and earth, the King of all that is, for the happy issue of his
travels. He gave this blessing to Raguel and his wife Edna, 'May it be my
happiness to honour you all the days of my life!'

X. TOBIT'S SIGHT RESTORED

11 They were nearly at Kaserin, opposite Nineveh, •when Raphael said, 'You ¹₂
know the plight in which we left your father; •let us go on ahead of your 3
wife and prepare the house ourselves while she travels behind with the others'.
They went on together (Raphael had warned Tobias to take the gall with him) 4
and the dog followed them.

Anna was sitting, watching the road by which her son would come. •She was ⁵₆
sure at once it must be he and said to the father, 'Here comes your son, with
his companion'.

Raphael said to Tobias before he reached his father, 'I give you my word 7
that your father's eyes will open. •You must put the fish's gall to his eyes; the 8
medicine will smart and will draw a filmy white skin off his eyes. And your
father will be able to see and look on the light.'

The mother ran forward and threw her arms round her son's neck. 'Now 9
I can die,' she said 'I have seen you again.' And she wept. •Tobit rose to his 10
feet and stumbled across the courtyard through the door. Tobias came on towards
him •(he had the fish's gall in his hand). He blew into his eyes and said, steadying ¹¹₁₃
him, 'Take courage, father!' With this he applied the medicine, left it there
a while, •then with both hands peeled away a filmy skin from the corners of his ¹²₁₄
eyes. •Then his father fell on his neck •and wept. He exclaimed, 'I can see, ¹³₁₄
my son, the light of my eyes!' And he said:

'Blessed be God!   17
Blessed be his great name!
Blessed be all his holy angels!
Blessed be his great name
for evermore!
For he had scourged me   15
and now has had pity on me
and I see my son Tobias.'

Tobias went into the house, and with a loud voice joyfully blessed God. Then
he told his father everything: how his journey had been successful and he had
brought the silver back; how he had married Sarah, the daughter of Raguel;
how she was following him now, close behind, and could not be far from the
gates of Nineveh.

Tobit set off to the gates of Nineveh to meet his daughter-in-law, giving joyful 16
praise to God as he went. When the people of Nineveh saw him walking without
a guide and stepping forward as briskly as of old, they were astonished. •Tobit 17
described to them how God had taken pity on him and had opened his eyes.
Then Tobit met Sarah, the bride of his son Tobias, and blessed her in these
words, 'Welcome, daughter! Blessed be your God for sending you to us, my
daughter. Blessings on your father, blessings on my son Tobias, blessings on
yourself, my daughter. Welcome now to your own house in joyfulness and in
blessedness. Come in, my daughter.' He held a feast that day for all the Jews of
Nineveh, •and his cousins Ahikar and Nadab came to share in Tobit's happiness. ¹⁸₂₀

XI. RAPHAEL

1 **12** When the feasting was over, Tobit called his son Tobias and said, 'My son, you ought to think about paying the amount due to your fellow traveller; 2 give him more than the figure agreed on'. •'Father,' he replied 'how much am I to give him for his help? Even if I give him half the goods he brought back with 3 me, I shall not be the loser. •He has brought me back to you safe and sound, he has cured my wife, he has brought the money back too, and now he has 4 cured you as well. How much am I to give him for all this?' •Tobit said, 'He has 5 richly earned half of what he brought back'. •So Tobias called his companion and said, 'Take half of what you brought back, in payment for all you have done, and go in peace'.

6 Then Raphael took them both aside and said, 'Bless God, utter his praise before all the living for all the favours he has given you. Bless and extol his name. Proclaim before all men the deeds of God as they deserve, and never tire 7 of giving him thanks. •It is right to keep the secret of a king, yet right to reveal and publish the works of God. Thank him worthily. Do what is good, and no evil can befall you.

8 'Prayer with fasting and alms with right conduct are better than riches with 9 iniquity. Better to practise almsgiving than to hoard up gold. •Almsgiving saves from death and purges every kind of sin. Those who give alms have their fill 10 of days; •those who commit sin and do evil, bring harm on themselves.

11 'I am going to tell you the whole truth, hiding nothing from you. I have already told you that it is right to keep the secret of a king, yet right too to reveal 12 in worthy fashion the works of God. •So you must know that when you and Sarah were at prayer, it was I who offered your supplications before the glory 13 of the Lord and who read them; so too when you were burying the dead. •When you did not hesitate to get up and leave the table to go and bury a dead man, 14 I was sent to test your faith, •and at the same time God sent me to heal you 15 and your daughter-in-law Sarah. •I am Raphael, one of the seven[a] angels who stand ever ready to enter the presence of the glory of the Lord.'

16 They were both overwhelmed with awe; they fell on their faces in terror. 17 But the angel said, 'Do not be afraid; peace be with you. Bless God for ever. 18 As far as I was concerned, when I was with you, my presence was not by any decision of mine, but by the will of God; it is he whom you must bless throughout 19 your days, he that you must praise. •You thought you saw me eating, but that 20 was appearance and no more. •Now bless the Lord on earth and give thanks to God. I am about to return to him above who sent me. Write down all that has 21 21,22 happened.' And he rose in the air. •When they stood up again, he was no longer visible. They praised God with hymns; they thanked him for having performed such wonders; had not an angel of God appeared to them?

XII. ZION

1 **13** And he said:

'Blessed be God who lives for ever,
for his reign endures throughout all ages!

2 By turns he punishes and pardons;
he sends men down to the depths of the underworld
and draws them up from supreme Destruction;
no one can escape his hand.

3 Declare his praise before the nations,

---

12 a. Only three are named in the Bible: Gabriel, Michael, Raphael.

you who are the sons of Israel!
For if he has scattered you among them,
there too he has shown you his greatness. 4
Extol him before all the living;
he is our Master
and he is our God
and he is our Father
and he is God for ever and ever.

'Though he punishes you for your iniquities, 5
he will take pity on you all;
he will gather you from every nation
wherever you have been scattered.
If you return to him 6
with all your heart and all your soul,
behaving honestly towards him,
then he will return to you
and hide his face from you no longer.
Consider how well he has treated you;
loudly give him thanks.
Bless the Lord of justice
and extol the King of the ages.
I for my part sing his praise 7
in the country of my exile;
I make his power and greatness known
to a nation that has sinned.
Sinners, return to him; 8
let your conduct be upright before him;
perhaps he will be gracious to you
and take pity on you.
I for my part extol God 7
and my soul rejoices 9
in the King of heaven.
Let his greatness be in all men's mouths, 8
his praises be sung in Jerusalem.

'Jerusalem, Holy City, 9
God scourged you for your handiwork 11
yet still will take pity on the sons of the upright.
Thank the Lord as he deserves 10
and bless the King of the ages, 12
that your Temple may be rebuilt with joy within you
and within you he may comfort every exile,
and within you he may love all those who are distressed,
for all generations to come.

'A bright light shall shine 11
over all the regions of the earth; 13
many nations shall come from far away, 14
from all the ends of the earth,
to dwell close to the holy name of the Lord God,
with gifts in their hands for the King of heaven.
Within you, generation after generation
shall proclaim their joy,
and the name of her who is Elect shall endure
through the generations to come.

'Cursed be any who affront you, 12
16

cursed be any who destroy you,
who throw down your walls,
who raze your towers,
who burn your houses!
Blessed for ever be all who build you!

13
17 Then you will exult, and rejoice
over the sons of the upright,
for they will all have been gathered in
and will bless the Lord of the ages.

14
18 'Happy are those who love you,
happy those who rejoice over your peace,
happy those who have mourned
over all your punishment!
For they will soon rejoice within you,
witnessing all your blessedness in days to come.

15
19 My soul blesses the Lord, the great King,
16 because Jerusalem shall be built anew
and his house for ever and ever.

20 'What bliss if one of my blood is left
to see your glory and praise the King of heaven!

21 The gates of Jerusalem shall be built
of sapphire and of emerald,
and all your walls of precious stone;
the towers of Jerusalem shall be built of gold
and their battlements of pure gold.

17 The streets of Jerusalem shall be paved
with ruby and with stones from Ophir;
the gates of Jerusalem will resound
with songs of exultation;
and all her houses will say,

23 "Alleluia! Blessed be the God of Israel."
Within you they will bless the holy name
for ever and for ever.'

1 **14** The end of the hymns of Tobit.

XIII. NINEVEH

2 Tobit died in peace when he was a hundred and twelve years old and received
2
3 an honourable burial in Nineveh. •He was sixty-two when he went blind; and
4 after his cure he lived from then on in comfort, practising almsgiving and
3
5 continually praising God and extolling his greatness. •When he was at the
point of death he summoned his son Tobias and gave him these instructions,
4 'My son, take your children •and hurry away to Media, since I believe the word
6 of God pronounced over Nineveh by Nahum. Everything will come true,
everything happen that the emissaries of God, the prophets of Israel, have
predicted against Assyria and Nineveh; not one of their words shall prove empty.
It will all take place in due time. You will be safer in Media than in Assyria
or in Babylonia. Since I for my part know and believe that everything God has
said will come true; so it will be, and not a word of the prophecies shall fail.

'A census will be taken of our brothers living in the land of Israel and they
will be exiled far from their own fair country. The entire territory of Israel will
become a desert, and Samaria and Jerusalem will become a desert, and the

house of God, for a time, will be laid waste and burnt. •Then once again God 5
will take pity on them and bring them back to the land of Israel. They will rebuild
his house, although it will be less beautiful than the first, until the time has fully
come. But after this, all will return from captivity and rebuild Jerusalem in all
her glory, and the house of God will be rebuilt within her as the prophets of
Israel have foretold. •And all the people of the whole earth will be converted 6
and will fear God with all sincerity. All will renounce their false gods who have
led them astray into error, •and will bless the God of the ages by upright conduct. 7
All the Israelites spared in those days will remember God in sincerity of heart.
They will come and gather in Jerusalem and thereafter dwell securely in the
land of Abraham, which shall be their own. And those who sincerely love God
shall rejoice. And those who commit sin and wickedness shall vanish from the
earth.

'And now, my children, I lay this duty on you: serve God sincerely, and do $\frac{8}{10}$
what is pleasing to him. And lay on your children the obligation to behave 11
uprightly, to give alms, to keep God in mind and to bless his name always,
sincerely and with all their might.

'So then, my son, leave Nineveh; do not stay here. •As soon as you have $\frac{9,10}{12}$
buried your mother next to me, go the same day, whenever it may be, and do 13
not linger in this country where I see wickedness and perfidy unashamedly
triumphant. Consider, my child, all that Nadab did to his fosterfather Ahikar.
Was he not forced to go underground, though still a living man? But God made
the criminal pay for his outrage before the eyes of his victim, since Ahikar came
back to the light of day, while Nadab went down to everlasting darkness in
punishment for plotting against Ahikar's life. Because of his good works Ahikar
escaped the deadly snare Nadab had laid for him, and Nadab fell into it to his
own ruin. •So, my children, you see what comes of almsgiving, and what wicked- 11
ness leads to, I mean to death. But now breath fails me.'

They laid him back on his bed; he died and was buried with honour.

When his mother died, Tobias buried her beside his father. Then he left for $\frac{12}{14}$
Media with his wife and children. He lived in Ecbatana with Raguel, his father-
in-law. •He treated the aging parents of his wife with every care and respect, $\frac{13}{15}$
and later buried them in Ecbatana in Media. Tobias inherited the patrimony
of Raguel besides that of his father Tobit. •Much honoured, he lived to the age $\frac{14}{16}$
of a hundred and seventeen years. •Before he died he witnessed the ruin of 15
Nineveh. He saw the Ninevites taken prisoner and deported to Media by Cyaxares
king of Media. He blessed God for everything he inflicted on the Ninevites and
Assyrians. Before his death he had the opportunity of rejoicing over the fate
of Nineveh, and he blessed the Lord God for ever and ever. Amen.

JUDITH

I. THE CAMPAIGN OF HOLOFERNES

Nebuchadnezzar and Arphaxad[a]

1 It was the twelfth year of Nebuchadnezzar[b] who reigned over the Assyrians in the great city of Nineveh. Arphaxad was then reigning over the Medes at
2 Ecbatana. •He surrounded this city with walls of dressed stones three cubits thick and six cubits long, making the rampart seventy cubits high and fifty
3 cubits wide. •At the gates he placed towers one hundred cubits high and, at the
4 foundations, sixty cubits wide, •the gates themselves being seventy cubits high and forty wide to allow his forces to march out in a body and his infantry to parade freely.

5 Now at this time King Nebuchadnezzar gave battle to King Arphaxad in the
6 great plain lying in the territory of Ragae. •Supporting him were all the peoples from the highlands, all from the Euphrates and Tigris and Hydaspes, and those from the plains who were subject to Arioch, king of the Elymaeans. Thus many nations had mustered to take part in the battle of the sons of Cheleoud.[c]

7 Nebuchadnezzar king of the Assyrians sent a message to all the inhabitants of Persia, to all the inhabitants of the western countries, Cilicia, Damascus,
8 Lebanon, Anti-Lebanon, to all those along the coast, •to the peoples of Carmel,
9 Gilead, Upper Galilee, the great plain of Esdraelon, •to the men of Samaria and its outlying towns, to those beyond Jordan, as far away as Jerusalem, Bethany, Chelous, Kadesh, the river of Egypt, Tahpanhes, Rameses and the
10 whole territory of Goshen, •beyond Tanis, too, and Memphis, and to all the
11 inhabitants of Egypt as far as the frontiers of Ethiopia. •But the inhabitants of these countries ignored the summons of Nebuchadnezzar king of the Assyrians and did not rally to him to make war. They were not afraid of him, since in their view he appeared isolated. Hence they sent his ambassadors back with nothing
12 achieved and in disgrace. •Nebuchadnezzar was furious with all these countries. He swore by his throne and kingdom to take revenge on all the territories of Cilicia, Damascene and Syria, of the Moabites and of the Ammonites, of Judaea and Egypt as far as the limits of the two seas, and to ravage them with the sword.

The campaign against Arphaxad

13 In the seventeenth year he and his forces gave battle to King Arphaxad and in this battle defeated him. He routed Arphaxad's entire army and all his cavalry
14 and chariots; •he occupied his towns and advanced on Ecbatana; he seized its towers and plundered its market places, reducing its former magnificence to a
15 mockery. •He later captured Arphaxad in the mountains of Ragae and, thrusting him through with his spears, destroyed him once and for all.

---

1 a. This translation follows the Greek. In places where the verse numbering differs from the Vulgate Latin text, the Vulgate verse numbers are added in italic.   b. Nebuchadnezzar stands for 'the enemy of God's people, Israel'; historically he was king of Babylon and was never styled 'king of Assyria', and Nineveh was not his capital city.   c. Probably the Chaldaeans.

He then retired with his troops and all who had joined forces with him: 16
a vast horde of armed men. Then, carefree, he and his army gave themselves up
to feasting for a hundred and twenty days.

The campaign in the west

2 In the eighteenth year,ᵃ on the twenty-second day of the first month, a rumour 1
ran through the palace that Nebuchadnezzar king of the Assyrians was to
have his revenge on the whole world, as he had threatened. •Summoning his 2
general staff and senior officers he held a secret conference with them, and
with his own lips pronounced utter destruction on all these countries. •It was 3
then decreed that everyone should be put to death who had not answered the
king's appeal.

When the council was over, Nebuchadnezzar king of the Assyrians sent for 4
Holofernes,ᵇ general-in-chief of his armies and subordinate only to himself.
He said to him, •'Thus speaks the Great King, lord of the whole world:ᶜ 5
"Be on your way; take men of proved valour, about a hundred and twenty
thousand foot soldiers and a strong contingent of horse with twelve thousand
cavalrymen; •then advance against the western lands, since these people have 6
disregarded my call. •Bid them have earth and water ready, because in my rage I 7
am about to march on them; the feet of my soldiers will cover the whole face of the
earth, and I will plunder it. •Their wounded will fill the valleys and the torrents 8
and rivers, blocked with their dead, will overflow. •I will lead them captive 9
to the ends of the earth. •Now go! Begin by conquering this whole region for me. 10
If they surrender to you, hold them for me until the time comes to punish them.
But if they resist, look on no one with clemency. Hand them over to slaughter 11
and plunder throughout the territory entrusted to you. •For by my life and 12
by the living power of my kingdom, I have spoken. All this I will do indeed.
And you, neglect none of your master's commands, act strictly according to my 13
orders without further delay."'

Leaving the presence of his sovereign, Holofernes immediately summoned ¹⁴⁄₇
all the marshals, generals and officers of the Assyrian army •and detailed the 15
picked troops as his master had ordered, about a hundred and twenty thousand
men and a further twelve thousand mounted bowmen. •He organised these in the 16
normal battle formation. •He then secured vast numbers of camels, donkeys ¹⁷⁄₈
and mules to carry the baggage, and innumerable sheep, oxen and goats for
food supplies. •Every man received full rations and a generous sum of gold ¹⁸⁄₁₀
and silver from the king's purse.

He then set out for the campaign with his whole army, in advance of King ¹⁹⁄₁₁
Nebuchadnezzar, to overwhelm the whole western region with his chariots, his
horsemen and his picked body of foot. •A composite corps brought up the rear, 20
as numerous as locusts or the grains of sand on the ground; there was no
counting their multitude.

The stages of Holofernes' advance

Thus they set out from Nineveh and marched for three days towards the plain ²¹⁄₁₂
of Bectileth. From Bectileth they went on to pitch camp near the mountains
that lie to the north of Upper Cilicia. •From there Holofernes advanced into 22
the highlands with his whole army, infantry, horsemen, chariots. •He cut his ²³⁄₁₃
way through Put and Lud, stripped all the sons of Rassis and sons of Ishmael
living on the verge of the desert south of Cheleon, •marched along the Euphrates, ²⁴⁄₁₄
crossed Mesopotamia, razed all the fortified towns controlling the wadi Abron
and reached the sea. •Next he attacked the territories of Cilicia, butchering ²⁵⁄₁₅
all who offered him resistance, advanced on the southern frontiers of Japheth,
facing Arabia, •completely encircled the Midianites, burned their tents and ²⁶⁄₁₆
plundered their sheep-runs, •made his way down to the Damascus plain in the ²⁷⁄₁₇
time of the wheat harvest, set fire to the fields, destroyed the flocks and herds,

sacked the towns, laid the countryside waste and put all the young men to the
²⁸/₁₈ sword. •Fear and trembling seized all the coastal peoples. The populations of
Sidon and Tyre, of Sur, Ocina, Jamnia, Azotus, Ascalon, were panic-stricken.

¹/₂ **3** They therefore sent envoys to him to sue for peace and say, •'We are servants
of the great King Nebuchadnezzar and we lie prone before you. Treat us as
3 you think fit. •Our cattle farms, all our land, all our wheat fields, our flocks
and herds, all the sheep-runs in our encampments are at your disposal. Do with
4 them as you please. •Our towns and their inhabitants, too, are at your service;
5 go and advance against them if such is your good pleasure.' •These men came to
Holofernes and delivered the message as above.

⁶/₇ He then made his way down to the coast with his army and stationed
8 garrisons in all the fortified towns, levying outstanding men there as auxiliaries.
⁷/₉ The people of these cities and of all the other towns in the neighbourhood
10 welcomed him, wearing garlands and dancing to the sound of tambourines.
⁸/_{11,12} Notwithstanding this, he demolished their shrines and cut down their sacred
13 trees, carrying out his commission to destroy all local gods and to force the nations
to worship Nebuchadnezzar alone and to compel men of every language and
nationality to hail him as a god. *

9 Thus he reached the edge of Esdraelon, in the neighbourhood of Dothan,
10 a village facing the great ridge of Judaea. •He pitched camp between Geba and
Scythopolis and stayed there a full month to replenish his supplies.

Judaea on the alert

1 **4** When the Israelites living in Judaea heard how Holofernes, general-in-chief
of Nebuchadnezzar king of the Assyrians, had treated the various nations,
2 first plundering their temples and then destroying them, •they were thoroughly
alarmed at his approach and trembled for Jerusalem and the Temple of the
3 Lord their God. •They had returned from captivity only a short time before,
and the resettlement of the people in Judaea and the reconsecration of the sacred
furnishings, of the altar, and of the Temple, which had been profaned, were of
recent date. *

⁴/₃ They therefore alerted the whole of Samaria, Kona, Beth-horon, Belmain,
5 Jericho, Choba, Aesora and the Salem valley. •They occupied the summits of
4 the highest mountains and fortified the villages on them; they laid in supplies
⁶/₅ for the coming war, as the fields had just been harvested. •Joakim the high
priest, resident in Jerusalem at the time, wrote to the inhabitants of Bethulia
and of Betomesthaim, two towns facing Esdraelon, towards the plain of
⁷/₆ Dothan. •He ordered them to occupy the mountain passes, the only means of
access to Judaea, for there it would be easy for them to halt an attacking force,
the narrowness of the approach not allowing men to advance more than two
⁸/₇ abreast. •The Israelites carried out the orders of Joakim the high priest and of
the people's Council of Elders in session at Jerusalem.

A nation at prayer

⁹/₈ All the men of Israel cried most fervently to God and humbled themselves
¹⁰/₉ before him. •They, their wives, their children, their cattle, all their resident
11 aliens, hired or slave, wrapped sackcloth round their loins. •All the Israelites in
Jerusalem, including the women and children, lay prone in front of the Temple,
12 and with ashes on their heads stretched out their hands before the Lord. •They
draped the very altar in sackcloth and fervently joined together in begging the
God of Israel not to let their little ones be massacred, their wives carried off,

2 a. The 18th year of his reign was 587, in which he captured Jerusalem.   b. The name of an
officer under King Artaxerxes III.   c. Title of the Persian kings.
3 a. Neither Assyrian nor Babylonian kings claimed divine honours.
4 a. Historically, the return from Exile and the repopulation of Jerusalem were in 539-400.
Nebuchadnezzar had died in 562.

the towns of their heritage destroyed, the Temple profaned and desecrated for the heathen to gloat over it. •The Lord heard them and looked kindly on their 13 distress.

The people fasted for many days throughout Judaea as well as in Jerusalem before the sanctuary of the Lord Almighty. •Joakim the high priest and all 14 who stood before the Lord, the Lord's priests and ministers, wore sackcloth round their loins as they offered the perpetual holocaust and the votive and voluntary offerings of the people. •With ashes on their turbans they earnestly 15 called on the Lord to look kindly on the House of Israel.

A council of war in Holofernes' camp

5 Holofernes, general-in-chief of the Assyrian army, received the intelligence 1 that the sons of Israel were preparing for war; that they had closed the mountain passes, fortified the high peaks and laid obstructions in the plains. Holofernes was furious. He summoned all the princes of Moab, all the generals 2 of Ammon and all the satraps of the coastal regions. •'Men of Canaan,' he said 3 'tell me: what people is this that occupies the highlands? What towns does it inhabit? How large is its army? What are the sources of its power and strength? Who is the king who rules it and commands its army? •Why have these not 4 condescended to wait on me, as all the western peoples have done?'

Achior,[a] leader of all the Ammonites, replied, 'May my lord please listen 5 to what your servant is going to say. I will give you the facts about these mountain folk whose home lies close to you. You will hear no lie from the mouth of your servant. •These people are descended from the Chaldaeans. 6 They once came to live in Mesopotamia, because they did not want to follow 7 the gods of their ancestors who lived in Chaldaea. •They abandoned the way of 8 their ancestors to worship the God of heaven, the God they had learnt to acknowledge. Banished from the presence of their own gods, they fled to Mesopotamia where they lived for a long time. •When God told them to leave 9 their home and set out for Canaan, they settled there and accumulated gold and silver and great herds of cattle. •Next, famine having overwhelmed the land of 10/9 Canaan, they went down to Egypt where they stayed as long as food could be found there. There they became a great multitude, a race beyond counting. But the king of Egypt turned against them and exploited them by forcing them 11/10 to make bricks; he degraded them, reducing them to slavery. •They cried to 12 their God, who struck the entire land of Egypt with incurable plagues, and the 11 Egyptians expelled them. •God dried up the Red Sea before them •and led 13,14/12 them forward by way of Sinai and Kadesh-barnea. Having driven off all the inhabitants of the desert, •they settled in the land of the Amorites and, such 15 was their strength, exterminated the inhabitants of Heshbon. Then, having crossed the Jordan, they took possession of all the highlands, •driving out the 16/20 Canaanites before them and the Perizzites, Jebusites, Shechemites and all the Girgashites, and lived there for many years. •All the while they did not sin 17/21 before their God, prosperity was theirs, for they have a God who hates wickedness. •But when they turned from the path he had marked out for them, 18/22 some were exterminated in a succession of battles, others taken captive to a foreign land. The Temple of their God was razed to the ground and their towns were seized by their enemies. •Then having turned once again to their God, 19/23 they came back from the places to which they had been dispersed and scattered, regained possession of Jerusalem, where they have their Temple, and reoccupied the highlands which had been left deserted. •So now, master and lord, if this 20/24 people has committed any fault, if they have sinned against their God, let us first make sure that they have offended in this way, and then let us advance and attack them. •But if their nation is guiltless, my lord would do better to abstain, 21/25 for fear that their Lord and God should protect them; we should then become the laughing-stock of the whole world.'

²²₂₆   When Achior had ended this speech, all the people crowding round the tent began protesting. Holofernes' own senior officers, as well as all the coastal
²³₂₇ peoples and the Moabites, threatened to tear him limb from limb. •'Why should
²⁸ we be afraid of the Israelites? They are a weak and powerless people, quite
²⁴ unable to stand a stiff attack. •Forward! Advance! Your army, Holofernes our master, will swallow them in one mouthful!'

Achior handed over to the Israelites

¹   6 When the uproar of those crowding round the council had subsided, Holofernes, general-in-chief of the Assyrian army, reprimanded Achior in
² front of the whole crowd of foreigners and Ammonites. •'Achior, who do you think you are, you and the Ammonite mercenaries, playing the prophet like this with us today, and trying to dissuade us from making war on the people of Israel? You claim their God will protect them. And who is their God if not Nebuchadnezzar? He himself will display his power and wipe them off the face
³ of the earth, and their God will certainly not save them. •But we, his servants, shall destroy them as easily as a single individual. They can never resist the
⁴ strength of our cavalry. •We shall burn them all. Their mountains will be drunk with their blood and their plains filled with their corpses. Far from being able to resist us, every one of them will die; thus says King Nebuchadnezzar, lord of the whole world. For he has spoken, and his words will not prove empty.
⁵ As for you, Achior, you Ammonite mercenary, who in a rash moment said these words, you shall not see my face again until the day when I have taken
⁶₄ my revenge on this brood of fugitives from Egypt. •And then the swords of my soldiers and the spears of my officers will pierce your sides. You will fall
⁷ among the wounded, the moment I turn on Israel. •My servants will now take
⁸ you into the highlands and leave you near one of the towns in the passes; •you
⁹₅ will not die, until you share their ruin. •No need to look so sad if you cherish the secret hope that they will not be captured! I have spoken; none of my words will prove idle.'

¹⁰₇   Holofernes having commanded his tent-orderlies to seize Achior, to take him
¹¹₈ to Bethulia and to hand him over to the Israelites, •the orderlies took him, escorted him out of the camp and across the plain, and then, making for the
¹² highlands, reached the springs below Bethulia. •As soon as the men of the town sighted them, they snatched up their weapons, left the town and made for the mountain tops, while all the slingers pelted them with stones to prevent
¹³₉ them from coming up. •However, they managed to take cover at the foot of the slope, where they bound Achior and left him lying at the bottom of the mountain and returned to their master.

¹⁴₁₀   The Israelites then came down from their town, stopped by him, unbound him and took him to Bethulia, where they brought him before the chief men
¹⁵₁₁ of the town, •who at that time were Uzziah son of Micah of the tribe of Simeon,
¹⁶ Chabris son of Gothoniel and Charmis son of Melchiel. •These summoned all the elders of the town. The young men and the women also hurried to the assembly. Achior was made to stand with all the people surrounding him and
¹⁷₁₂ Uzziah questioned him about what had happened. •He answered by telling them what had been said at Holofernes' council, and what he himself had said in the
¹³ presence of the Assyrian leaders, and how Holofernes had bragged of what he
¹⁸₁₄ would do to the House of Israel. •At this the people fell to the ground and
¹⁹₁₅ worshipped God. •'Lord God of heaven,' they cried 'take notice of their arrogance and have pity on the humiliation of our race. Look kindly today on
²⁰₁₆ those who are consecrated to you.' •They then spoke reassuringly to Achior
²¹₁₉ and praised him warmly. •After the assembly Uzziah took him home and gave a banquet for the elders; all that night they called on the God of Israel for help.

---

5 a. Possibly modelled on Ahikar, the virtuous pagan sage mentioned in Tb 1:21.

II. BETHULIA UNDER SIEGE

The campaign against Israel

7 The following day Holofernes issued orders to his whole army and to the 1
  whole host of auxiliaries who had joined him to break camp and march on
Bethulia, to occupy the mountain passes and so open the campaign against the
Israelites. •The troops broke camp that same day. The actual fighting force 2
numbered one hundred and twenty thousand infantry and twelve thousand
cavalry, not to mention the baggage train with the vast number of men on foot
concerned with that. •They penetrated the valley in the neighbourhood of 3
Bethulia, near the spring, and deployed on a wide front from Dothan to Balbaim
and, in depth, from Bethulia to Cyamon, which faces on Esdraelon. •When the 4
Israelites saw this horde, they were all appalled and said to each other, 'Now
they will lick the whole country clean. Not even the loftiest peaks, the gorges
or the hills will be able to stand the weight of them.' •Each man snatched up 5
his arms; they lit beacons on their towers and spent the whole night on watch.

On the second day Holofernes deployed his entire cavalry in sight of the 6
Israelites in Bethulia. •He reconnoitred the slopes leading up to the town, located ⁷₆
the water-points, seized them and posted pickets over them and returned to the
main body. •The chiefs of the sons of Esau, the leaders of the Moabites*a* and 8
the generals of the coastal district then came to him and said, •'If our master 9
will please listen to us, his forces will not sustain a single wound. •The 10
Israelites do not rely so much on their spears as on the height of the mountains
where they live. And admittedly it is not at all easy to scale these heights
of theirs.   11

'This being the case, master, do not engage them in a pitched battle, and then 12
you will not lose a single man. •Stay in camp, keep all your troops there too, 9
while your servants seize the spring which rises at the foot of the mountain, 13
since that is what provides the population of Bethulia with their water supply.
Thirst will then force them to surrender their town. Meanwhile, we and our
men will climb the nearest mountain tops and form advance posts there to
prevent anyone from leaving the town. •Hunger will waste them with their 14
wives and children, and before the sword can reach them they will already be
lying in the streets outside their houses. •And you will make them pay dearly 15
for their defiance and their refusal to meet you peaceably.'

Their words pleased Holofernes as well as all his officers and he decided to ¹⁶₁₀
do as they suggested. •Accordingly a troop of Moabites moved forward with a 17
further five thousand Assyrians. They penetrated the valley and seized the
Israelites' waterpoints and springs. •Meanwhile the Edomites and Ammonites 18
went and took up positions in the highlands opposite Dothan, sending some
of their men to the south-east opposite Egrebel, near Chous on the wadi Mochmur.
The rest of the Assyrian army took up positions in the plain, covering every
inch of the earth; their tents and equipment made an immense encampment,
so vast were their numbers.

The Israelites called on the Lord their God, dispirited because the enemy 19
had surrounded them and cut all line of retreat. •For thirty-four days the Assyrian ²⁰₁₁
army, infantry, chariots, cavalrymen, had them surrounded. Every water jar the
inhabitants of Bethulia had was empty, •their wells were drying up; on no day 21
could a man quench his thirst, since their water was rationed. •Their little 22
children pined away, the women and young men grew weak with thirst; they
collapsed in the streets and gateways of the town; they had no strength left.

Young men, women, children, the whole people thronged clamouring round ²³₁₂
Uzziah and the chief men of the town, shouting in the presence of the assembled
elders, •'May God be judge between you and us! For you have done us great ²⁴₁₃
harm, by not suing for peace with the Assyrians. •And now there is no one to ²⁵₁₄

help us. God has delivered us into their hands to be prostrated before them in
26 thirst and utter helplessness. •Call them in at once; hand the whole town over
15
27 to be sacked by Holofernes' men and all his army. •After all, we should be much
16
better off as their booty than we are now; no doubt we shall be enslaved, but at
least we shall be alive and not see our little ones dying before our eyes or our
28 wives and children perishing. •By heaven and earth and by our God, the Lord
17
of our fathers who is punishing us for our sins and the sins of our ancestors, we
29 implore you to take this course now, today.' •Bitter lamentations rose from the
18
whole assembly, and they all cried loudly to the Lord God.

30 Then Uzziah spoke to them, 'Take heart, brothers! Let us hold out five days
23
24 more. By then the Lord our God will take pity on us, for he will not desert us
31 altogether. •At the end of this time, if there is no help forthcoming, I will do
25
32 as you have said.' •With that he dismissed the people to their various quarters.
The men went to man the walls and towers of the town, sending the women
and children home. The town was full of despondency.

III. JUDITH

A portrait of Judith

1 8 Judith[a] was informed at the time of what had happened. She was the daughter
of Merari son of Ox, son of Joseph, son of Oziel, son of Elkiah, son of Ananias,
son of Gideon, son of Raphaim, son of Ahitub, son of Elijah, son of Hilkiah,
son of Eliab, son of Nathanael, son of Salamiel, son of Sarasadai, son of Israel.
2 Her husband Manasseh, of her own tribe and family, had died at the time of
3 barley harvest. •He was supervising the men as they bound up the sheaves in
the field when he caught sunstroke and had to take to his bed. He died in Bethulia,
his home town, and was buried with his ancestors in the field that lies between
4 Dothan and Balamon. •As a widow, Judith stayed inside her home for three
5 years and four months. •She had had an upper room built for herself on the
6 roof. She wore sackcloth round her waist and dressed in widow's weeds. •She
fasted every day of her widowhood except for the sabbath eve, the sabbath itself,
the eve of New Moon, the feast of New Moon and the festival days of the House
7 of Israel. •Now, she was very beautiful, charming to see. Her husband Manasseh
had left her gold and silver, menservants and maidservants, cattle and lands;
8 and she lived among all her possessions •without anyone finding a word to say
against her, so devoutly did she fear God.

Judith and the elders

9 Hearing how the water shortage had demoralised the people and how they
had complained bitterly to the headman of the town, and being also told what
Uzziah had said to them and how he had given them his oath to surrender the
10 town to the Assyrians in five days' time, •Judith immediately sent her woman
of affairs who managed her property to summon Chabris and Charmis, two elders
11 of the town. •When these came in she said:
'Listen to me, leaders of the people of Bethulia. You were wrong to speak to
the people as you did today and to bind yourself by oath, in defiance of God, to
surrender the town to our enemies if the Lord did not come to your help within
12 a set number of days. •Who are you, to put God to the test today, you, out
11
13 of all mankind, to set yourselves above him? •You of all people to put the Lord
14 Almighty to the test! You do not understand anything, and never will. •If you
cannot sound the depths of the heart of man or unravel the arguments of his
mind, how can you fathom the God who made all things, or sound his mind

7 a. 'The sons of Esau' are the Edomites; they and the Moabites are traditional enemies of
Israel.
8 a. The name means 'the Jewess'.

or unravel his purposes? No, brothers, do not provoke the anger of the Lord our God. •Although it may not be his will to help us within the next five days, he 15 has the power to protect us for as many days as he pleases, just as he has the power to destroy us before our enemies. •But you have no right .to demand 16 guarantees where the designs of the Lord our God are concerned. For God is *15* not to be coerced as man is, nor is he, like mere man, to be cajoled. •Rather, 17 as we wait patiently for him to save, let us plead with him to help us. He will hear our voice if such is his good pleasure.

'And indeed of recent times and still today there never has been one tribe 18 of ours, or family, or village, or town that has worshipped gods made with human hands, as once was done, •and that was the reason why our ancestors were 19 delivered over to sword and sack, and perished in misery at the hands of our enemies. We for our part acknowledge no other God than him; and so we may 20 hope he will not look on us disdainfully or desert our nation.

'If indeed they capture us, as you expect, then all Judaea will be captured too, 21 and our holy places plundered, and we shall answer with our blood for their profanation. •The slaughter of our brothers, the exile of our country, the 22 unpeopling of our heritage, will recoil on our own heads among the nations whose slaves we will become, and our new masters will look down on us as an outrage and a disgrace; •for our surrender will not reinstate us in their favour; 23 no, the Lord our God will make it a thing to be ashamed of. •So now, brothers, 24 let us set an example to our brothers, since their lives depend on us and our most sacred possessions—Temple and altar—rest on us.

'All this being so, let us rather give thanks to the Lord our God who, as he $^{25}_{21}$ tested our ancestors, is now testing us. •Remember how he treated Abraham, all $^{26}_{22}$ the ordeals of Isaac, all that happened to Jacob in Syrian Mesopotamia while he kept the sheep of Laban, his mother's brother. •For as these ordeals were 27 intended by him to search their hearts, so now this is not vengeance God exacts against us, but a warning inflicted by the Lord on those who are near his heart.'

Uzziah replied, 'Everything you have said has been spoken from sincerity 28 of heart and no one will contradict a word of it. •Not that today is the first time 29 your wisdom has been displayed; from your earliest years all the people have known how shrewd you are and of how sound a heart. •But, parched with 30 thirst, the people forced us to act as we had promised them and to bind ourselves by an inviolable oath. •You are a devout woman; pray to the Lord, then, to $^{31}_{29}$ send us a downpour to fill our cisterns, so that our faintness may pass.'

Judith replied, 'Listen to me. I intend to do something, the memory of which 32 will be handed down to the children of our race from age to age. •Tonight you $^{33}_{32}$ must be at the gate of the town: I shall make my way out with my attendant. Before the time fixed by you for surrendering the town to our enemies, the Lord will make use of me to rescue Israel. •You must not ask what I intend to do; $^{34}_{33}$ I will not tell you until I have done it.' •Uzziah and the chief man said, 'Go in $^{35}_{34}$ peace. May the Lord show you a way to take revenge on our enemies.' •And 36 leaving the upper room they went back to their posts.

Judith's prayer

9 Judith threw herself face to the ground, scattered ashes on her head, uncovered 1 the sackcloth she was wearing and cried loudly to the Lord. At the same time in Jerusalem the evening incense was being offered in the Temple of God. Judith said:

'Lord, God of my father Simeon, 2
you armed him with a sword to take vengeance on the foreigners
who had undone a virgin's girdle to her shame,
laid bare her thigh to her confusion,
violated her womb to her dishonour,

since though you said, "This must not be", they did it.

3   For this you handed their leaders over to slaughter,
their bed, defiled by their deceit, to blood.
You struck the slaves down with the chiefs
and the chiefs with their servants.

4
3   You left their wives to be carried off,
their daughters to be taken captive,
and their spoils to be shared out
among the sons you loved,
who had been so zealous for you,
had loathed the stain put on their blood
and called on you for help.

'God, my God,
now hear this widow too;

5
4   for you have made the past,
and what is happening now, and what will follow.
What is, what will be, you have planned;
what has been, you designed.

6   Your purposes stood forward;
"See, we are here!" they said.

5   For all of your ways are prepared
and your judgements delivered with foreknowledge.

7
6   'See the Assyrians, boasting in their army,
glorying in their horses and their riders,
exulting in the strength of their infantry.

9   Trust as they may in shield and spear,
in bow and sling,

10   in you they have not recognised
the Lord, the shatterer of war;

8   yours alone the title of Lord.

11   'Break their violence with your might,
in your anger bring down their strength.
For they plan to profane your holy places,
to defile the tabernacle, the resting place of your glorious name,
and to throw down with iron the horn of your altar.

9
12   Observe their arrogance,
send your fury on their heads,
give the needful courage
to this widow's hand.

10   By guile of my lips
strike slave down with master,
and master with his servant.

15   Break their pride
by a woman's hand.

11
16   'Your strength does not lie in numbers,
nor your might in violent men;
since you are the God of the humble,
the help of the oppressed,
the support of the weak,
the refuge of the forsaken,
the saviour of the despairing.

12   Please, please, God of my father,
God of the heritage of Israel,

> Master of heaven and earth,   17
> Creator of the waters,
> King of your whole creation,
> hear my prayer.
> Give me a beguiling tongue   13
> to wound and kill   18
> those who have formed such cruel designs
> against your covenant,
> against your holy dwelling place,
> against Mount Zion,
> against the house belonging to your sons.
> And demonstrate to every nation, every tribe,   14
> that you are Yahweh, God almighty, all-powerful,   19
> and that the race of Israel
> has you for sole protector.'

IV. JUDITH AND HOLOFERNES

Judith goes to the camp of Holofernes

10 Thus Judith called on the God of Israel. When she had finished praying, 1
she rose from where she lay, summoned her attendant and went down into 2
the rooms which she used on sabbath days and feasts. •There she removed the 3
sackcloth she was wearing and, taking off her widow's dress, she washed all
over, anointed herself with costly perfumes, dressed her hair, wrapped a turban
round it and put on the dress she used to wear on joyful occasions when her
husband Manasseh was alive. •She put sandals on her feet, put on her necklaces, 4
bracelets, rings, earrings and all her jewellery, and made herself beautiful enough
to catch the eye of every man who saw her. •Then she handed her attendant 5
a skin of wine and a flask of oil, filled a bag with barley girdle cakes, cakes of
dried fruit and pure loaves, and wrapping all these provisions up gave them
to her as well. •They then went out, making for the town gate of Bethulia. There 6
they found Uzziah waiting with the two elders of the town, Chabris and Charmis.
When they saw Judith, her face so changed and her clothes so different, they were 7
lost in admiration of her beauty. They said to her:

> 'May the God of our ancestors keep you in his favour!   8
> May he grant your purposes fulfilment
> to the glory of the sons of Israel,
> to the greater glory of Jerusalem!'

Judith worshipped God, and then she said, 'Have the town gate opened for me 9
so that I can go out and make all your wishes come true'. They did as she asked
and gave orders to the young men to open the gate for her. •This done, Judith 10
went out accompanied by her maid, while the men of the town watched her all
the way down the mountain and across the valley, until they lost sight of her.

As the women were making straight through the valley, an advance unit of 11
Assyrians intercepted them, •and seizing Judith began questioning her. 'Which 12
side are you on? Where do you come from? Where are you going?' 'I am
a daughter of the Hebrews,' she replied 'and I am fleeing from them since they
will soon be your prey. •I am on my way to see Holofernes, the general of your 13
army, to give him trustworthy information. I will show him the road to take
if he wants to capture all the highlands without losing one man or one life.'
As the men listened to what she was saying, they stared in astonishment at the 14
sight of such a beautiful woman. •'It will prove the saving of you,' they said 15
to her 'coming down to see our master of your own accord. You had better
go to his tent; some of our men will escort you and hand you over to him. •Once 16

you are in his presence do not be afraid. Tell him what you have just told us and
17 you will be well treated.' •They then detailed a hundred of their men as escort
for herself and her attendant, and these led them to the tent of Holofernes.

18 News of her coming had already spread through the tents, and there was a
general stir in the camp. She was still outside the tent of Holofernes waiting to
19 be announced, when a crowd began forming round her. •They were immensely
18 impressed by her beauty and impressed with the Israelites because of her. 'Who
could despise a people having women like this?' they kept saying. 'Better not
leave one man of them alive; let any go and they would twist the whole world
round their fingers!'

20 Then the bodyguard and adjutants of Holofernes came out and led Judith
21
19 into the tent. •Holofernes was resting on his bed under a canopy of purple and
22 gold studded with emeralds and precious stones. •The men announced her and
he came out to the open part of the tent, with silver torches carried before him.
23
20 When Judith confronted the general and his adjutant, the beauty of her
face astonished them all. She fell on her face and did homage to him, but his
servants raised her from the ground.

The first meeting of Judith with Holofernes

1 **11** 'Courage, woman,' Holofernes said 'do not be afraid. I have never hurt
anyone who chose to serve Nebuchadnezzar, king of the whole world.
2 Even now, if your nation of mountain dwellers had not insulted me, I would
3 not have raised a spear against them. This was their fault, not mine. •But tell
me, why have you fled from them and come to us?... Anyhow, this will prove
the saving of you. Courage! You will live through this night, and many after.
4 No one shall hurt you. No, you shall be treated as well as all those who serve
my lord King Nebuchadnezzar.'
5
4 Judith said, 'Please listen favourably to what your slave has to say. Permit
your servant to speak in your presence. I will speak no word of a lie in my lord's
6 presence tonight. •You have only to follow your servant's advice and God will
bring your work to a successful conclusion; in what my lord undertakes he shall
7
5 not fail. •Long life to Nebuchadnezzar, king of the whole world, who has sent
you to set every living soul to rights; may his power endure! Since, thanks to
you, he is served not only by men, but through your compulsion the wild animals
themselves, the cattle, and the birds of the air are to live in the service of Nebuchadnezzar and his whole House.
8
6 'We have indeed heard of your genius and adroitness of mind. It is known
everywhere in the world that throughout the empire you have no rival for ability,
9
7 wealth of experience and brilliance in waging war. •We have also heard what
Achior said in his speech to your council. The men of Bethulia having spared
10 him, he has told them everything that he said to you. •Now, master and lord,
8 do not disregard what he said; keep it in your mind, since it is true; our nation
will not be punished, the sword will indeed have no power over them, unless
11
9 they sin against their God. •But as it is, my lord need expect no repulse or
setback, since death is about to fall on their heads, for sin has gained a hold
over them, provoking the anger of their God each time that they commit it.
12
10.11 As they are short of food and their water is giving out, they have resolved to
fall back on their cattle and decided to make use of all the things that God has,
13
12 by his laws, forbidden them to eat. •Not only have they made up their minds
to eat the first-fruits of corn and the tithes of wine and oil, though these have
been consecrated by them and set apart for the priests who serve in Jerusalem
in the presence of our God and may not, lawfully, even be touched by the
14 people, •but they have even sent men to Jerusalem—where the inhabitants are
doing much the same—to bring them back authorisation from the Council of
15 Elders. •Now this will be the outcome: when the permission arrives and they act
on it, that very day they shall be delivered over to you for destruction.

'When I, your servant, came to know all this, I fled from them. God has sent 16/13 me to do things with you at which the world will be astonished when it hears. Your servant is a devout woman; she honours the God of heaven day and night. 17/14 I therefore propose, my lord, to stay with you. I, your servant, will go out 15 every night into the valley and pray to God to let me know when they have committed their sin. •I will then come and tell you, so that you can march out 18 with your whole army; and none of them will be able to resist you. •I will 19 be your guide right across Judaea until you reach Jerusalem; there I will enthrone you in the very middle of the city. Then you shall lead them like sheep and never a dog dare open its mouth to bark at you. Foreknowledge tells me this; this 16 has been foretold to me and I have been sent to reveal it to you.' 17

Her words pleased Holofernes and all his adjutants. Full of admiration at 20/18 her wisdom they exclaimed, •'There is no woman like her from one end of the 21/19 earth to the other, so lovely of face and so wise of speech!' •Holofernes said, 22/20 'God has done well to send you ahead of your people. Strength will be ours, and ruin theirs who have insulted my lord. •As for you, you are as beautiful as 23/21 you are eloquent; if you do as you have promised, your god shall be my god, and you yourself shall make your home in the palace of King Nebuchadnezzar and be famous throughout the world.'

12 With that he had her brought in to where his silver dinner service was 1 already laid, and had his own food served to her and his own wine poured out for her. •But Judith said, 'I would rather not eat this, in case I incur some 2 fault. What I have brought will be enough for me.' •'Suppose your provisions 3 run out,' Holofernes asked 'how could we get more of the same sort? We have no one belonging to your race here.' •'Never fear, my lord,' Judith answered 4 'the Lord will have used me to accomplish his plan, before your servant has finished these provisions.' •Then the adjutants of Holofernes took her to a tent 5 where she slept till midnight. A little before the morning watch she rose. •She 6 had already sent this request to Holofernes, 'Let my lord kindly give orders for your servant to be allowed to go out and pray', •and Holofernes had ordered 7 his guards not to prevent her. She stayed in the camp for three days; she went 7 out each night to the valley of Bethulia and washed at the spring where the picket had been posted. •As she came up again she prayed to the Lord God of 8 Israel to guide her in her plan to relieve the children of her people. •Having 9 purified herself, she would return and stay in her tent until her meal was brought her in the evening.

Judith at the banquet of Holofernes

On the fourth day Holofernes gave a banquet, inviting only his own staff 10 and none of the other officers. •He said to Bagoas, the eunuch in charge of his 11 personal affairs, 'Go and persuade that Hebrew woman you are looking after to come and join us and eat and drink in our company. •We shall be disgraced 12/11 if we let a woman like this go without knowing her better. If we do not seduce her, everyone will laugh at us!' •Bagoas then left Holofernes and went to see 13/12 Judith. 'Would this young and lovely woman condescend to come to my lord?' he asked. 'She shall occupy the seat of honour opposite him, drink the joyful wine with us and be treated today like one of the Assyrian ladies-in-waiting in the palace of Nebuchadnezzar. •'Who am I' Judith replied 'to resist my lord? 14/13 I will not hesitate to do whatever he wishes, and doing this will be my joy to my 14 dying day.'

At this she rose and put on her dress and all her feminine adornments. Her 15 maid preceded her, and on the floor in front of Holofernes spread the fleece which Bagoas had given Judith for her daily use to lie on as she ate.

Judith entered and took her place. The heart of Holofernes was ravished at 16 the sight; his very soul was stirred. He was seized with a violent desire to sleep with her; and indeed since the first day he saw her, he had been waiting for an

17 opportunity to seduce her. •'Drink, drink!' Holofernes said 'Enjoy yourself
18 with us!' •'I am delighted to do so, Lord, for since my birth I have never felt
19 my life more worthwhile than today.' •She took what her maid had prepared,
20 and ate and drank facing him. •Holofernes was so enchanted with her that he
drank far more wine than he had drunk on any other day in his life.

1   **13** It grew late and his staff hurried away. Bagoas closed the tent from the
outside, having shown out those who still lingered in his lord's presence.
3,4 2 They went to their beds wearied with all their drinking, •and Judith was left
alone in the tent with Holofernes who had collapsed wine-sodden on his bed.
3/5 Judith then told her maid to stay just outside the bedroom and wait for her to
come out, as she did every morning. She had let it be understood she would be
going out to her prayers and had also spoken of her intention to Bagoas.

4   By now everyone had left Holofernes and no one, either important or unim-
6 portant, was left in the bedroom. Standing beside the bed, Judith murmured
to herself:

7   'Lord God, to whom all strength belongs,
                    prosper what my hands are now to do
                    for the greater glory of Jerusalem,
5   now is the time to recover your heritage
                    and further my designs
                    to crush the enemies arrayed against us'.

6/8 With that she went up to the bedpost by Holofernes' head and took down his
7/9 scimitar; •coming closer to the bed she caught him by the hair and said, 'Make
8/10 me strong today, Lord God of Israel!' •Twice she struck at the nape of his neck
9 with all her strength and cut off his head. •She then rolled his body off the
11 bed and tore the canopy down from the bedposts. Soon after, she went out
10 and gave the head of Holofernes to her attendant •who put it in her food bag.
12 The two then left the camp together, as they always did when they went to pray.
Once they were out of the camp, they skirted the ravine, climbed the slope to
Bethulia and made for the gates.

Judith brings the head of Holofernes to Bethulia

11/13 From a distance, Judith shouted to the guards on the gates, 'Open the gate!
Open! For the Lord our God is with us still, displaying his strength in Israel
12/14 and his might against our enemies, as he has today!' •Hearing her voice, the
13/15 townsmen hurried down to the town gate and summoned the elders. •Everyone,
16 great and small, came running down, since her arrival was unexpected. They
threw the gate open, welcomed the women, lit a fire to see by and crowded
14/17,18 round them. •Then Judith raised her voice and said, 'Praise God! Praise him!
Praise the God who has not withdrawn his mercy from the House of Israel,
15/19 but has shattered our enemies by my hand tonight!' •She pulled the head out
of the bag and held it for them to see. 'This is the head of Holofernes, general-
in-chief of the Assyrian army; here is the canopy under which he lay drunk!
16/20 The Lord has struck him down by the hand of a woman! •Glory to the Lord
who has protected me in the course I took! My face seduced him, only to his
own undoing; he committed no sin with me to shame me or disgrace me.'
17/22 Overcome with emotion, the people all fell on their knees and worshipped
God, exclaiming as one man, 'Blessings on you, O our God, for confounding
18/23 your people's enemies today!' •Uzziah then said to Judith:

                    'May you be blessed, my daughter, by God Most High,
                    beyond all women on earth;
24   and may the Lord God be blessed,
                    the Creator of heaven and earth,
                    by whose guidance you cut off the head

of the leader of our enemies.
The trust you have shown   19 25
shall not pass from the memories of men,
but shall ever remind them
of the power of God.
God grant you to be always held in honour,   20
and rewarded with blessings,
since you did not consider your own life
when our nation was brought to its knees,
but warded off our ruin,
walking undeterred before our God.'

All the people answered, 'Amen! Amen!'   26

V. TRIUMPH

The Jews attack the Assyrian camp

14 Judith said, 'Listen to me, brothers. Take this head and hang it on your 1 battlements. •When morning comes and the sun is up, let every man take 2 his arms and every able-bodied man leave the town. Appoint a leader for these, as if you meant to march down to the plain against the Assyrian advance post. But you must not do this. •The Assyrians will gather up their equipment, make 3 for their camp and wake up their commanders; they in turn will rush to the 4 tent of Holofernes and not be able to find him. They will then be seized with panic and flee at your advance. •All you and the others who live in the territory 4 5 of Israel will have to do is to give chase and slaughter them as they retreat.

'But before you do this, call me Achior the Ammonite for him to see the 5 man who thought so meanly of the House of Israel and recognise this as the man who sent him to us as a man already doomed to die.' (13)ᵃ So they had Achior 6 27,28 brought from the house of Uzziah. No sooner had he arrived and seen the 29 head of Holofernes held by a member of the people's assembly than he fell down on his face in a faint. •They lifted him up. He then threw himself at the 7 30 feet of Judith, and prostrate before her exclaimed:

'May you be blessed in all the tents of Judah   31
and in every nation;
at the sound of your name
men will be seized with dread.

'Now tell me exactly what you have been doing in these past few days.' And 8 surrounded by all the people Judith told him everything she had done from the day she left Bethulia to the moment when she was speaking. •When she came 9 to the end, the people cheered at the tops of their voices until the town echoed. (14) •Achior, recognising the mighty works of the God of Israel, believed 10 6 ardently in him and, accepting circumcision, was incorporated in the House of Israel forever.

At daybreak they hung the head of Holofernes on the ramparts. Every man 11 7 took his arms and they all went out in groups to the slopes of the mountain. Seeing this, the Assyrians sent word to their leaders, who in turn reported to 12 8 the generals, the captains of thousands and all the other officers; •and these 13 9,11 in their turn reported to the tent of Holofernes. 'Rouse our master,' they said to his major-domo 'these slaves have dared to march down on us to attack— 12 and to be wiped out to a man!' •Bagoas went inside and clapped his hands in 14 13 front of the curtain dividing the tent, thinking that Holofernes was sleeping with Judith. •But as no one seemed to hear, he drew the curtain and went into 15 14 the bedroom, to find him thrown down dead on the threshold and the head

16 gone from his body. •He gave a great shout, wept, sobbed, shrieked and rent
17
15 his clothes. •He then went into the tent which Judith had occupied and could
18
16 not find her either. Then, rushing out to the men, he shouted, •'Those slaves
have duped us! One Hebrew woman has brought shame on the House of
Nebuchadnezzar. Holofernes is lying dead on the ground, with his head cut off!'
19
17 When they heard this, the leaders of the Assyrian army tore their tunics in
18 consternation, and the camp rang with their wild cries and their shouting.

1 **15** When the men who were still in their tents heard the news they were
2   appalled. •They were so gripped with panic and dread that no two men
could keep together: the rout was complete. They fled along every track across
3 the plain or through the mountains. •The men who had been bivouacking in
the mountains round Bethulia were fleeing too. Then all the Israelite warriors
4 charged down on them. •Uzziah sent messengers to Betomasthaim, Bebai,
Choba, Kola and through all the highlands of Israel, to inform them of what
had happened and to urge them all to hurl themselves on the enemy and
5 annihilate them. •As soon as the Israelites heard the news, they fell on them as
one man and massacred them all the way to Choba. The men of Jerusalem and
the entire mountain country also rallied to them, once they had been informed
of the events in the enemy camp. Then the men of Gilead and Galilee attacked
them on the flank and struck at them fiercely till they neared Damascus and
6
7 its territory. •The rest, who had stayed in Bethulia, fell upon the Assyrian camp
7
8 and looted it to their great profit. •The Israelites returning from the slaughter
seized what was left. The hamlets and villages of the mountain country and the
plain also captured a great deal of booty, since there were vast stores of it.

Israel gives thanks

8
9   Joakim the high priest and the Council of Elders of Israel, who were in
Jerusalem, came to gaze on the benefits that the Lord had lavished on Israel
9
10 and to see Judith and congratulate her. •On coming to her house they blessed
her with one accord, saying:

> 'You are the glory of Jerusalem!
> You are the great pride of Israel!
> You are the highest honour of our race!

10
11
> 'By doing all this with your own hand
> you have deserved well of Israel,
> and God has approved what you have done.

> 'May you be blessed by the Lord Almighty
> in all the days to come!'

12 All the people answered, 'Amen!'
11
13,14   The people looted the camp for thirty days. They gave Judith the tent of
Holofernes, all his silver plate, his divans, his drinking bowls and all his furniture.
She took this, loaded her mule, harnessed her carts and heaped the things into
12
15 them. •All the women of Israel, hurrying to see her, formed choirs of dancers
in her honour. Judith distributed branches to the women who accompanied her;
13 she and her companions put on wreaths of olive. Then she took her place at
the head of the procession and led the women as they danced. All the men of
14
1 Israel, armed and garlanded, followed them, singing hymns. •With all Israel
round her, Judith broke into this song of thanksgiving and the whole people
sang this hymn aloud:

1
2 **16**   'Praise my God with the tambourine,
                      sing to the Lord with the cymbal,
                      let psalm and canticle mingle for him,

14 a. This incident is included in ch. 13 in the Latin Vulgate.

extol his name, invoke it!
For the Lord is a God who shatters war; | 2 / 3
he has pitched his camp in the middle of his people | 4
to deliver me from the hands of my enemies.

'Assyria came down from the mountains of the north, | 3 / 5
came with tens of thousands of his army.
Their multitude blocked the wadis,
their horses covered the hills.
He promised to burn up my country, | 4 / 6
destroy my young men with the sword,
dash my sucklings to the ground,
make prey of my little ones,
carry off my maidens;
but the Lord Almighty has thwarted them | 5 / 7
by a woman's hand.
For their hero did not fall at the young men's hands, | 6 / 8
it was not sons of Titans who struck him down,
no proud giants made that attack,
but Judith, the daughter of Merari,
who disarmed him with the beauty of her face.
She laid aside her widow's dress | 7 / 9
to rally those who were oppressed in Israel;
she anointed her face with perfume, | 10
bound her hair under a turban, | 8
put on a linen gown to seduce him.
Her sandal ravished his eye, | 9 / 11
her beauty took his soul prisoner...
and the scimitar cut through his neck!

'The Persians trembled at her boldness, | 10 / 12
the Medes were daunted by her daring.
These were struck with fear when my lowly ones shouted, | 11 / 13
these were seized with terror when my weak ones shouted louder,
and when they shouted loudest, these gave ground.
The children of mere girls ran them through, | 12 / 14
pierced them like the offspring of deserters.
They perished in the battle of my Lord!

'I will sing a new song to my God. | 13 / 15
Lord, you are great, you are glorious, | 16
wonderfully strong, unconquerable.
May your whole creation serve you! | 14 / 17
For you spoke and things came into being,
you sent your breath and they were put together,
and no one can resist your voice.

'Should mountains topple | 15 / 18
to mingle with the waves,
should rocks melt
like wax before your face,
to those who fear you, | 19
you would still be merciful.

'A little thing indeed | 16
is a sweetly smelling sacrifice,
still less the fat
burned for you in holocaust;

> but whoever fears the Lord
> is great for ever.

¹⁷
²⁰
> 'Woe to the nations
> who rise against my race!
> The Lord Almighty
> will punish them on judgement day.

²¹
> He will send fire and worms in their flesh
> and they shall weep with pain for evermore.'

¹⁸
²² When they reached Jerusalem they fell on their faces before God and, once the people were purified, they offered their holocausts and voluntary offerings ¹⁹
²³ and gifts. •All Holofernes' property given her by the people and the canopy she herself had stripped from his bed, Judith vowed to God as a dedicated offering. ²⁰
²⁴ For three months the people gave themselves up to rejoicings in Jerusalem before the Temple, where Judith stayed with them.

Judith lives to old age. Her death

²¹
²⁵   When this was over, everyone returned home. Judith went back to Bethulia and lived on her estate; as long as she lived, she enjoyed a great reputation ²²
²⁶ throughout the country. •She had many suitors, but all her days, from the time her husband Manasseh died and was gathered to his people, she never gave ²³ herself to another man. •Her fame spread more and more the older she grew ²⁸ in her husband's house; she lived to the age of a hundred and five years.^a She emancipated her maid, then died in Bethulia and was buried in the cave where ²⁴
²⁹ Manasseh her husband lay. •The House of Israel mourned her for seven days. Before her death she had distributed her property among her own relations and those of her husband Manasseh.

²⁵
³⁰   Never again during the lifetime of Judith, nor indeed for long after her death, did anyone trouble the sons of Israel.

16 a. And thus qualifies to be ranked with the heroes of the patriarchal age.

ESTHER

INTRODUCTORY

Mordecai's dream[a]

1 *In the second year of the reign of the great King Ahasuerus,[b] on the first day*   1a
11:2
of Nisan, a dream came to Mordecai son of Jair, son of Shimei, son of Kish,
of the tribe of Benjamin, •*a Jew living at Susa and holding high office at the royal*   1b
3
court. •*He was one of the captives whom Nebuchadnezzar, king of Babylon, had*   1c
4
deported from Jerusalem with Jeconiah, king of Judah.[c]

  This was his dream. There were cries and noise, thunder and earthquakes, and   1d
5
disorder over the whole earth. •*Then two great dragons came forward, each ready*   1e
6
for the fray, and set up a great roar. •*At the sound of them every nation made ready*   1f
7
to wage war against the nation of the just. •*A day of darkness and gloom, of affliction*   1g
8
and distress, oppression and great disturbance on earth! •*The righteous nation was*   1h
9
thrown into consternation at the fear of the evils awaiting them, and prepared for
death, crying out to God. •*Then from their cry, as from a little spring, there grew*   1i
10
a great river, a flood of water. •*Light came as the sun rose, and the humble*   1k
11
were raised up and devoured the mighty.

  On awakening from this dream and vision of God's designs, Mordecai thought   1l
12
deeply on the matter, trying his best all day to discover what its meaning might be.

A plot against the king

  Lodging at court with Bigthan and Teresh, two of the king's eunuchs who   1m
12:1
guarded the palace, •*Mordecai got wind of their intentions and uncovered their*   1n
2
plot. Learning that they were preparing to assassinate King Ahasuerus, he warned
the king against them. •*The king gave orders for the two eunuchs to be tortured;*   1o
3
they confessed and were executed. •*The king then had these events recorded in his*   1p
4
Chronicles, while Mordecai himself also wrote an account of them. •*The king then*   1q
5
appointed Mordecai to an office at court and rewarded him with presents. •*But*   1r
6
Haman son of Hammedatha, the Agagite, who enjoyed high favour with the king,
determined to injure Mordecai in revenge for the king's two eunuchs.

I. AHASUERUS AND VASHTI

Ahasuerus' banquet

1 It was in the days of Ahasuerus, the Ahasuerus whose empire stretched from 1
  India to Ethiopia and comprised one hundred and twenty-seven provinces.
In those days, when King Ahasuerus was sitting on his royal throne in the 2
citadel of Susa, •in the third year of his reign, he gave a banquet at his court 3
for all his administrators and ministers, chiefs of the army of Persia and Media,
nobles and governors of provinces. •Thus he displayed the riches and splendour 4
of his empire and the pomp and glory of his majesty; the festivities went on for
a long time, a hundred and eighty days.

5 When this period was over, for seven days the king gave a banquet for all the people living in the citadel of Susa, to high and low alike, in the enclosure 6 adjoining the king's palace. •There were white and violet hangings fastened with cords of fine linen and purple thread to silver rings on marble columns, couches of gold and silver on a pavement of porphyry, marble, mother-of-pearl and 7 precious stones. •For drinking there were golden cups of various design and 8 the royal wine in plenty according to the king's bounty. •By royal command, however, drinking was not obligatory, the king having instructed the officials of his household to treat each guest according to his own wishes.

The affair of Vashti

9 Queen Vashti,*d* too, had given a banquet for the women in the royal palace 10 of King Ahasuerus. •On the seventh day, when the king was merry with wine, he commanded Mehuman, Biztha, Harbona, Bigtha, Abagtha, Zethar and Carkas, the seven eunuchs in attendance on the person of King Ahasuerus, 11 to bring Queen Vashti before the king crowned with her royal diadem, in order to display her beauty to the people and the administrators, for she was very 12 beautiful. •But Queen Vashti refused to come at the king's command delivered 13 by the eunuchs. The king was very angry at this and his rage grew hot. •He then consulted the wise men who were versed in the law, since it was the practice 14 to refer matters affecting the king to expert lawyers and jurists. •He summoned Carshena, Shethar, Admatha, Tarshish, Meres, Marsena and Memucan, the seven administrators of Persia and Media who had privileged access to the royal 15 presence and occupied the leading positions in the kingdom. •'According to law,' he said 'what is to be done to Queen Vashti for not obeying the command 16 of King Ahasuerus delivered by the eunuchs?' •In the presence of the king and of the administrators Memucan answered, 'Vashti has wronged not only the king, but also all the administrators and nations inhabiting the provinces of King 17 Ahasuerus. •The queen's conduct will soon become known to all the women and encourage them in a contemptuous attitude towards their husbands, since they will say, "King Ahasuerus ordered Queen Vashti to appear before him and 18 she did not come". •The wives of all the Persian and Median administrators will hear of the queen's answer before the day is out, and will start talking to the king's administrators in the same way; that will mean contempt and anger 19 all round. •If it is the king's pleasure, let him issue a royal edict, to be irrevocably incorporated into the laws of the Persians and Medes, to the effect that Vashti is never to appear again before King Ahasuerus, and let the king confer her royal 20 dignity on a worthier woman. •Let this edict issued by the king be proclaimed throughout the length and breadth of his realm, and all the women will henceforth bow to the authority of their husbands, both high and low alike.'

21 This speech pleased the king and the administrators and the king did as 22 Memucan advised. •He sent letters to all the provinces of the kingdom, to each province in its own script and to each nation in its own language, ensuring that every husband should be master in his own house.

II. MORDECAI AND ESTHER

Esther becomes queen

1 **2** Some time after this, when the king's wrath had abated, Ahasuerus remembered Vashti, how she had behaved, and the measures taken against her.

1 a. Passages found in the Greek text but not contained in the Hebrew are printed in italic. In places where the verse numbering differs from the Vulgate Latin text, the Vulgate verse numbers are added in italic.   b. 'Ahasuerus' is the Hebrew transliteration of the Persian name which in Greek is rendered Xerxes.   c. The chronological details cannot be harmonised: Mordecai is a courtier of Ahasuerus (about 480) and was exiled in the reign of Jeconiah (about 598).   d. She is unknown to history.

The king's courtiers-in-waiting said, 'Let beautiful girls be selected for the king. 2
Let the king appoint commissioners throughout the provinces of his realm to 3
bring all these beautiful young virgins to the citadel of Susa, to the harem under
the authority of Hegai the king's eunuch, custodian of the women. Let him
provide them with what they need for their adornment, •and let the girl who 4
pleases the king take Vashti's place as queen.' This advice pleased the king
and he acted on it.

Now in the citadel of Susa there lived a Jew called Mordecai son of Jair, son 5
of Shimei, son of Kish, of the tribe of Benjamin, •who had been deported from 6
Jerusalem among the captives taken away with Jeconiah king of Judah by
Nebuchadnezzar king of Babylon. •He had brought up Hadassah, otherwise 7
called Esther,ª his uncle's daughter, who had lost both father and mother; the
girl had a good figure and a beautiful face, and on the death of her parents
Mordecai had adopted her as his daughter.

Following the promulgation of the king's edict, a great number of girls were 8
brought to the citadel of Susa where they were entrusted to Hegai. Esther also
was taken to the king's palace and entrusted to Hegai, the custodian of the
women. •The girl pleased him and won his favour. Not only did he quickly 9
provide her with all she needed for her dressing room and her meals, but he
gave her seven special maids from the king's household and transferred her and
her maids to the best part of the harem. •Esther did not reveal her race or 10
kindred, since Mordecai had forbidden her to do so. •Mordecai walked up 11
and down in front of the courtyard of the harem every day, to learn how Esther
was and how she was being treated.

Each girl had to appear in turn before King Ahasuerus, after a delay of 12
twelve months fixed by the regulations for the women; this preparatory period
was occupied as follows: six months with oil of myrrh, and six months with
spices and lotions commonly used for feminine beauty treatment. •Before going 13
into the king, each girl was allowed to take with her from the harem to the king's
palace whatever she chose. •She went there in the evening, and the following 14
morning returned to another harem entrusted to the care of Shaashgaz, the king's
eunuch, custodian of the concubines. She did not go to the king any more, unless
he was particularly pleased with her and had her summoned by name.

But when it was the turn of Esther, the daughter of Abihail whose nephew 15
Mordecai had adopted her as his own daughter, to go into the king's presence,
she did not ask for anything beyond what had been assigned her by Hegai, the
king's eunuch, custodian of the women. And Esther soon won the admiration of
all who saw her. •She was brought to King Ahasuerus in his royal palace in the 16
tenth month, which is called Tebeth, in the seventh year of his reign; •and the 17
king liked Esther better than any of the other women; none of the other girls
found so much favour and approval with him. So he set the royal diadem on her
head and proclaimed her queen instead of Vashti.

Then the king gave a great banquet, Esther's banquet, for all his administrators 18
and ministers, decreed a holiday for all the provinces and distributed largesse
with royal prodigality.

Mordecai and Haman

When Esther, like the other girls, had been transferred to the second harem, 19
she had not revealed her kindred or race, in obedience to the orders of Mordecai, 20
whose instructions she continued to follow as when she had been under his care.
At this time Mordecai was attached to the Chancellery and two malcontents, 21
Bigthan and Teresh, king's eunuchs belonging to the Guardians of the Threshold,
plotted to assassinate King Ahasuerus. •Mordecai came to hear of this and 22
informed Queen Esther, who in turn, on Mordecai's authority, told the king.
The matter was investigated and proved to be true. The two conspirators were 23
sent to the gallows, and the incident was recorded in the Book of the Chronicles
in the presence of the king.

3 Shortly afterwards, King Ahasuerus singled out Haman son of Hammedatha, from the land of Agag,ª for promotion. He raised him in rank and precedence
2 above all his colleagues, the other officers of state, •and gave orders that all the officials employed at the Chancellery were to bow down and prostrate themselves
3 before Haman. Mordecai refused either to bow or prostrate himself. •'Why do you flout the royal command?' the officials of the Chancellery asked Mordecai.
4 They asked him this day after day, but he took no notice of them. In the end they reported the matter to Haman, wishing to see whether Mordecai would
5 persist in his attitude, since he had told them he was a Jew. •When Haman had seen for himself that Mordecai did not bow or prostrate himself before him, he
6 was seized with fury. •Having been told what race Mordecai belonged to, he could not be content with murdering Mordecai but made up his mind to wipe out all the members of Mordecai's race, the Jews, throughout the empire of Ahasuerus.

III. THE JEWS IN PERIL

The decree of extermination against the Jews

7 In the first month, that is the month of Nisan, of the twelfth year of King Ahasuerus, they cast the pur (that is, the lot) before Haman for the day and
8 the month. The lot falling on the twelfth month, which is Adar, •Haman said to King Ahasuerus, 'There is a certain unassimilated nation scattered among the other nations throughout the provinces of your realm; their laws are different from those of all the other nations and they ignore the royal edicts; hence it
9 is not in the king's interests to tolerate them. •If it please the king to decree their destruction, I am prepared to pay ten thousand talents of silver to the king's receivers, to be credited to the royal treasury.'
10 The king then took his signet ring off his hand and gave it to Haman son of
11 Hammedatha, the Agagite, the persecutor of the Jews. •'Keep the money,' he said 'and you can have the people too; do what you like with them.'
12 Then on the thirteenth day of the first month the royal scribes were summoned, and copies were made of the orders addressed by Haman to the king's satraps, to the governors ruling each province and to the principal officials of each people, to each province in its own script and to each people in its own language. The edict was signed in the name of King Ahasuerus and sealed with his ring,
13 and letters were sent by runners to every province of the realm ordering the destruction, slaughter and annihilation of all Jews, young and old, women and children, on the one day, the thirteenth day of the twelfth month, which is Adar, and the seizing of their possessions.

13a   *The text of the letter was as follows:*
13:1   *'The great King, Ahasuerus, to the governors of the hundred and twenty-seven provinces stretching from India to Ethiopia, and to their subordinate district commissioners.*

13b
2   *'Being placed in authority over many nations and ruling the whole world, I have resolved never to be carried away by the insolence of power, but always to rule with moderation and clemency, so as to assure for my subjects a life ever free from storms and, offering my kingdom the benefits of civilisation and free transit from*
13c
3   *end to end, to restore that peace which all men desire. •In consultation with our advisers as to how this aim is to be effected, we have been informed by one of them, eminent among us for prudence and well proved for his unfailing devotion and unshakeable trustworthiness, and in rank second only to our majesty, Haman by*

2 a. Probably a Babylonian name (Ishtar), like Mordecai (Marduk).
3 a. Country not known; the name is that of an Amalekite king conquered by Saul.

name, •*that there is, mingled among all the tribes of the earth a certain ill-disposed* ${}^{13d}_{4}$
people, opposed by its laws to every other nation and continually defying the royal
ordinances, in such a way as to obstruct that form of government assured by us
to the general good.

'*Considering therefore that this people, unique of its kind, is in complete oppos-* ${}^{13e}_{5}$
ition to all mankind from which it differs by its outlandish system of laws, that
it is hostile to our interests and that it commits the most heinous crimes, to the
point of endangering the stability of the realm:

'*We command that the people designated to you in the letters written by Haman,* ${}^{13f}_{6}$
appointed to watch over our interests and a second father to us, are all, including
women and children, to be destroyed root and branch by the swords of their enemies,
without any pity or mercy, on the fourteenth day of the twelfth month, Adar, of
the present year, •*so that, these past and present malcontents being in one day* ${}^{13g}_{7}$
forcibly thrown down to Hades, our government may henceforward enjoy perpetual
stability and peace.'

The text of this decree, to be promulgated as law in each province, was 14
published to the various peoples, so that each might be ready for the day afore-
mentioned. •At the king's command, the runners set out with all speed; the 15
decree was first promulgated in the citadel of Susa.

While the king and Haman gave themselves up to feasting and drinking,
consternation reigned in the city of Susa.

Mordecai and Esther try to avert the danger

4 When Mordecai learned what had happened, he tore his garments and put on 1
sackcloth and ashes. Then he went right through the city, wailing loud and
bitterly, •until he arrived in front of the Chancellery, which no one clothed in 2
sackcloth was allowed to enter. •And in every province, no sooner had the royal 3
edict been read than among the Jews there was great mourning, fasting, weeping
and wailing, and many lay on sackcloth and ashes.

When Queen Esther's maids and eunuchs came and told her, she was overcome 4
with grief. She sent clothes for Mordecai to put on instead of his sackcloth,
but he refused them. •Then Esther summoned Hathach, a eunuch whom the 5
king had appointed to wait on her, and ordered him to go to Mordecai and
enquire what was the matter and why he was acting in this way.

Hathach went out to Mordecai, who was still in the city square in front of 6
the Chancellery, •and Mordecai told him what had happened to him personally, 7
and also about the sum of money which Haman had offered to pay into the
royal treasury as compensation for the destruction of the Jews. •He also gave 8
him a copy of the edict of extermination published in Susa for him to show
Esther for her information, with the message that she was to go to the king and ${}^{15:1}$
implore his favour and plead with him for her people. •'*Remember your humbler* ${}^{8a}_{2}$
circumstances,' he said '*when you were fed by my hand. Since Haman, the second*
person in the realm, has petitioned the king for our deaths, •*invoke the Lord,* ${}^{8b}_{3}$
speak to the king for us and save us from death!'

Hathach came back and told Esther what Mordecai had said; •and she ${}^{9}_{10}$
replied with the following message for Mordecai, •'All the king's servants and 11
the people of his provinces know that for a man or woman who approaches the
king in the inner court without being summoned there is one penalty: death,
unless, by pointing his golden sceptre towards him, the king grants him his life.
And I have not been summoned to the king for the last thirty days.'

These words of Esther were reported to Mordecai, •who sent back the ${}^{12}_{13}$
following reply, 'Do not suppose that, because you are in the king's palace, you
are going to be the one Jew to escape. •No; if you persist in remaining silent 14
at such a time, relief and deliverance will come to the Jews from another place,ᵈ
but both you and the House of your father will perish. Who knows? Perhaps you
have come to the throne for just such a time as this.'

¹⁵
¹⁶   Whereupon Esther sent this reply to Mordecai, •'Go and assemble all the Jews now in Susa and fast for me. Do not eat or drink day or night for three days. For my part, I and my maids will keep the same fast, after which I shall
¹⁷ go to the king in spite of the law; and if I perish, I perish.' •Mordecai went away and carried out Esther's instructions.

Mordecai's prayer

^{17a}
^{13:8}   *Then calling to mind all the wonderful works of the Lord, he offered this prayer:*

^{17b}
⁹   'Lord, Lord, King and Master of all things,
> *everything is subject to your power,*
> *and there is no one who can withstand you*
> *in your will to save Israel.*

^{17c}
¹⁰   *'Yes, you have made heaven and earth,*
> *and all the marvels that are under heaven.*

¹¹   *You are the Lord of all,*
> *and there is none who can resist you, Lord.*

^{17d}
¹²   *'You know all things;*
> *you know, Lord, you know,*
> *that no insolence, arrogance, vainglory*
> *prompted me to this,*
> *to this refusal to bow down*
> *before proud Haman.*

¹³   *I would readily have kissed his feet*
> *for the safety of Israel.*

^{17e}
¹⁴   *'But what I did, I did*
> *rather than place the glory of a man*
> *above the glory of God;*
> *and I will not bow down to any*
> *but to you, Lord;*
> *in so refusing I will not act in pride.*

^{17f}
¹⁵   *'And now, Lord God,*
> *King, God of Abraham,*
> *spare your people!*
> *For men are seeking our ruin*
> *and plan to destroy your ancient heritage.*

^{17g}
¹⁶   *Do not overlook your inheritance,*
> *which you redeemed for your own out of the land of Egypt.*

^{17h}
¹⁷   *Hear my supplication,*
> *have mercy on your heritage,*
> *and turn our grief into rejoicing,*
> *that we may live to hymn your name, Lord.*
> *Do not suffer the mouths*
> *of those who praise you to perish.'*

¹⁷ⁱ
¹⁸   *And all Israel cried out with all their might, for they were faced with death.*

Esther's prayer

^{17k}
^{14:1}   *Queen Esther also took refuge with the Lord in the mortal peril which had*
² *overtaken her. She took off her sumptuous robes and put on sorrowful mourning. Instead of expensive perfumes she covered her head with ashes and dung. She humbled her body severely, and the former scenes of her happiness and elegance*

---

4 a. The author of the Hebrew text avoids using the name of God.

were now littered with tresses torn from her hair. She besought the Lord God of 3
Israel in these words:

'My Lord, our King, the only one,   17*l*
come to my help, for I am alone
and have no helper but you
and am about to take my life in my hands.   4

'I have been taught from my earliest years, in the bosom of my family,   17m
that you, Lord, chose   5
Israel out of all the nations
and our ancestors out of all the people of old times
to be your heritage for ever;
and that you have treated them as you promised.

'But then we sinned against you,   17n
and you handed us over to our enemies   6
for paying honour to their gods.
Lord, you are just.   7

'But even now they are not satisfied   17o
with the bitterness of our slavery: 8
they have put their hands in the hands of their idols[b]
to abolish the decree that your own lips have uttered,   9
to blot out your heritage,
to stop the mouths of those who praise you,
to quench your altar and the glory of your House,
and instead to open the mouths of the heathen,   17p
to sing the praise of worthless idols   10
and forever to idolise a king of flesh.

'Do not yield your sceptre, Lord,   17q
to non-existent beings.   11
Never let men mock at our ruin.
Turn their designs against themselves,
and make an example of him who leads the attack on us.
Remember, Lord; reveal yourself   17r
in the time of our distress.   12

'As for me, give me courage,
King of gods and master of all power.
Put persuasive words into my mouth   17s
when I face the lion;   13
change his feeling into hatred for our enemy,
that the latter and all like him may be brought to their end.

'As for ourselves, save us by your hand,   17t
and come to my help, for I am alone   14
and have no one but you, Lord.
You have knowledge of all things,   17u
and you know that I hate honours from the godless,   15
that I loathe the bed of the uncircumcised,
of any foreigner whatever.
You know I am under constraint,   17w
that I loathe the symbol of my high position   16
bound round my brow when I appear at court;
I loathe it as if it were a filthy rag
and do not wear it on my days of leisure.
Your handmaid has not eaten at Haman's table,   17x
                                                                    17

> nor taken pleasure in the royal banquets,
> nor drunk the wine of libations.
>
> 17y
> 18   Nor has your handmaid found pleasure
> from the day of her promotion until now
> except in you, Lord, God of Abraham.
>
> 17z
> 19   O God, whose strength prevails over all,
> listen to the voice of the desperate,
> save us from the hand of the wicked,
> and free me from my fear.'

Esther presents herself at the palace

1a
15:4   5 On the third day, *when she had finished praying, she took off her suppliant's*
5   *mourning attire* and dressed herself in her full splendour. *Radiant as she then appeared, she invoked God who watches over all men and saves them. Then*
6 *she took two maids with her. With a delicate air she leaned on one, while the other accompanied her carrying her train. She leaned on the maid's arm as though*
7 *languidly, but in fact because her body was too weak to support her; the other*
1b
8 *maid followed her mistress, lifting her robes which swept the ground.* •*Rosy with the full flush of her beauty, her face radiated joy and love; but her heart shrank*
1c
9 *with fear.* •Having passed through door after door, she found herself in the presence of the king. He was seated on the royal throne, *dressed in all his robes*
1d
10 *of state, glittering with gold and precious stones—a formidable sight.* •*Raising his face, afire with majesty, he looked on her, blazing with anger. The queen sank down. She grew faint and the colour drained from her face, and she leaned her*
1e
11 *head against the maid who accompanied her.* •*But God changed the king's heart, inducing a milder spirit. He sprang from his throne in alarm and took her in his*
1f
12 *arms until she recovered, comforting her with soothing words.* •'*What is the matter,*
13 *Esther?*' he said 'I *am your brother. Take heart; you will not die; our order only*
2
14,15 *applies to ordinary people. Come to me.*' •And raising his golden sceptre he laid
2a
16 it on her neck, *embraced her and said, 'Speak to me*'. •'*My lord,*' she said '*you looked to me like an angel of God, and my heart was moved with fear of your*
17 *majesty. For you are a figure of wonder, my lord, and your face is full of*
2b
18,19 *graciousness.*' •*But as she spoke she fell down in a faint. The king was distressed,*
3 *and all his attendants tried their best to revive her.* •'What is the matter, Queen Esther?' the king said. 'Tell me what you desire; even if it is half my kingdom,
4 I grant it you.' •'Would the king be pleased' Esther replied 'to come with Haman
5 today to the banquet I have prepared for him?' •The king said, 'Tell Haman to come at once, so that Esther may have her wish'.

6   So the king and Haman came to the banquet that Esther had prepared. •As they drank their wine, the king again said to Esther, 'Tell me what you request; I grant it to you. Tell me what you desire; even if it is half my kingdom, it is yours
7
8 for the asking.' •'What do I desire, what do I request?' Esther replied. •'If I have found favour in the king's eyes, and if it is his pleasure to grant what I ask and to agree to my request, let the king and Haman come to the other banquet I intend to give them tomorrow, and then I will do as the king says.'

9   Haman left full of joy and high spirits that day; but when he saw Mordecai at the Chancellery, neither standing up nor stirring at his approach, he felt
10 a gust of anger. •He restrained himself, however. Returning home, he sent for
11 his friends and Zeresh his wife •and held forth to them about his dazzling wealth, his many children, how the king had raised him to a position of honour and
12 promoted him over the heads of the king's administrators and ministers. •'What is more,' he added 'Queen Esther just invited me and the king—no one else except me—to a banquet she was giving, and better still she has invited me and
13 the king again tomorrow. •But what do I care about all this when all the while
14 I see Mordecai the Jew sitting there at the Chancellery?' •'Have a fifty-cubit

b. Gesture of taking an oath.

gallows run up,' Zeresh his wife and all his friends said 'and in the morning
ask the king to have Mordecai hanged on it. Then accompany the king to the
feast without a care in the world!' Delighted with this advice, Haman had the
gallows erected.

IV. THE JEWS' REVENGE

The discomfiture of Haman

6 That night, the king could not sleep; he called for the Record Book, the ¹
Chronicles, to be brought and read to him. •They contained an account of ²
how Mordecai had denounced Bigthan and Teresh, two of the king's eunuchs
serving as Guardians of the Threshold, who had plotted to assassinate king
Ahasuerus. •'And what honour and dignity' the king asked 'was conferred on ³
Mordecai for this?' 'Nothing has been done for him' the courtiers in attendance
replied. •Then the king said, 'Who is on duty in the antechamber?' Haman had ⁴
at that moment entered the outer antechamber of the king's palace to ask the
king to have Mordecai hanged on the gallows which he had just put up for the
purpose. •So the king's courtiers replied, 'Haman is waiting in the antechamber'. ⁵
'Bring him in' the king said, •and went on to ask as soon as Haman had entered, ⁶
'What is the right way to treat a man whom the king wishes to honour?' 'Whom'
thought Haman 'would the king wish to honour, if not me?' •So he replied, 'If ⁷
the king wishes to honour someone, •have royal robes brought, which the ⁸
king has worn, and a horse which the king has ridden, with a royal diadem on
its head. •The robes and horse should be handed to one of the noblest of the ⁹
king's officers, and he should array the man whom the king wishes to honour
and lead him on horseback through the city square, proclaiming before him:
"This is the way to treat a man whom the king wishes to honour".' •'Hurry,' the ¹⁰
king said to Haman 'take the robes and the horse, and do everything you have
just said to Mordecai the Jew, who works at the Chancellery. On no account
leave anything out that you have mentioned.'

So taking the robes and the horse, Haman arrayed Mordecai and led him on ¹¹
horseback through the city square, proclaiming before him: 'This is the way to
treat a man whom the king wishes to honour'. •After this Mordecai returned ¹²
to the Chancellery, while Haman went hurrying home dejected, covering his
face. •He told his wife Zeresh and all his friends what had just happened. His ¹³
wife Zeresh and his friends said, 'Thanks to Mordecai, you have just had a fall;
if he happens to belong to the Jewish race, you will never recover the upper
hand again. Far from it; once having begun, thanks to him you will fall and
fall again.'

Haman at Esther's banquet

While they were still talking, the king's eunuchs arrived in a hurry to escort ¹⁴
Haman to the banquet that Esther had prepared. 7 When the king and Haman ¹
were seated at the banquet with Queen Esther •this second day, the king again ²
said to Esther as they drank their wine, 'Tell me what you request, Queen Esther?
I grant it to you. Tell me what you desire; even if it is half my kingdom, it is yours
for the asking.' •'If I have found favour in your eyes, O king,' Queen Esther ³
replied 'and if it please your majesty, grant me my life—that is what I request;
and the lives of my people—that is what I desire. •For we are doomed, I and ⁴
my people, to destruction, slaughter and annihilation; if we had merely been
condemned to become slaves and servant-girls, I would have said nothing; but
as things are, it will be beyond the means of the persecutor to make good the
loss that the king is about to sustain.' •King Ahasuerus interrupted Queen ⁵
Esther, 'Who is this man?' he exclaimed. 'Where is he, the schemer of such an
outrage?' •Esther replied, 'The persecutor, the enemy? Why, this wretch Haman!' ⁶
Haman quaked with terror in the presence of the king and queen. •In a rage ⁷

the king rose and left the banquet to go into the palace garden; while Haman, realising that the king was determined on his ruin, stayed behind to beg Queen Esther for his life.

8   When the king returned from the palace garden into the banqueting hall, he found Haman huddled across the couch where Esther was reclining. 'What!' the king exclaimed. 'Is he going to rape the queen before my eyes in my own palace?' The words were scarcely out of his mouth than a veil was thrown over

9 Haman's face. •Harbona, one of the eunuchs attending the king, was present. He said, 'How convenient! There is that fifty-cubit gallows which Haman ran up for Mordecai, whose report saved the king's life. It is all ready at his house.'

10 'Hang him on it' said the king. •So Haman was hanged on the gallows which he had erected for Mordecai, and the king's wrath subsided.

The royal favour passes to the Jews

1   That same day King Ahasuerus gave Queen Esther the house of Haman, the
     persecutor of the Jews. Mordecai was presented to the king, Esther having

2 revealed their mutual relationship. •The king, who had recovered his signet ring from Haman, took it off and gave it to Mordecai, while Esther gave Mordecai charge of Haman's house.

3   Esther again went to speak to the king. She fell at his feet, weeping and imploring his favour, to frustrate the wicked scheme devised by Haman the

4 Agagite and his plot against the Jews. •The king held out the golden sceptre

5 to her, whereupon Esther rose and stood face to face with him. •'If such is the king's good pleasure,' she said 'and if I have found favour before him, if my petition seems proper to him and if I myself am pleasing to his eyes, may he be pleased to issue a written revocation of the letters which Haman son of Hamme-datha, the Agagite, contrived to have written to procure the destruction of the

6 Jews in every province of the realm. •For how can I look on, while my people suffer what is in store for them? How can I bear to witness the extermination of my race?'

7   King Ahasuerus said to Queen Esther and to Mordecai the Jew, 'I for my part have given Esther Haman's house, and have had him hanged on the gallows

8 for planning to destroy the Jews. •You are free now to write to them as you judge best, in the king's name, and seal what you write with the king's signet; for an order written in the king's name and sealed with his signet is irrevocable.'

9 The royal scribes summoned at once—it was the third month, the month of Sivan, on the twenty-third day—and at Mordecai's dictation an order was written to the Jews, the satraps, governors and administrators of the provinces stretching from India to Ethiopia, a hundred and twenty-seven provinces, to each province in its own script, and to each people in its own language, and to

10 the Jews in their own script and language. •These letters, written in the name of King Ahasuerus and sealed with the king's signet, were carried by couriers

11 mounted on horses from the king's own stud-farms. •In them the king granted the Jews, in whatever city they lived, the right to assemble in self-defence, with permission to destroy, slaughter and annihilate any armed force of any people or province that might attack them, together with their women and children,

12 and to plunder their possessions, •with effect from the same day throughout the provinces of King Ahasuerus—the thirteenth day of the twelfth month, which is Adar.

The decree of rehabilitation

12a
16:1   *The text of the letter was as follows:*

12b   *'The great King, Ahasuerus, to the satraps of the hundred and twenty-seven provinces which stretch from India to Ethiopia, to the provincial governors and to all our loyal subjects, greeting.*

12c
2   *'Many men, repeatedly honoured by the extreme bounty of their benefactors,*

only grow the more arrogant. It is not enough for them to seek our subjects' ³
*injury, but unable as they are to support the weight of their own surfeit they turn
to scheming against their benefactors themselves.* • *Not content with banishing* ¹²ᵈ
gratitude from the human heart, but elated by the plaudits of men unacquainted ⁴
*with goodness, notwithstanding that all is for ever under the eye of God, they
vainly expect to escape his justice, so hostile to the wicked.* • *Thus it has often* ¹²ᵉ
happened to those placed in authority that, having entrusted friends with the conduct ⁵
*of affairs and allowed themselves to be influenced by them, they find themselves
sharing with these the guilt of innocent blood and involved in irremediable misfortunes,* • *the upright intentions of rulers having been misled by false arguments of* ¹²ᶠ
the evilly disposed. • *This may be seen without recourse to the history of earlier times* ⁶
to which we have referred; you have only to look at what is before you, at the crimes ¹²ᵍ
perpetrated by a plague of unworthy officials. • *For the future we will exert our* ⁷
efforts to assure the tranquillity and peace of the realm for all, • *by adopting new* ¹²ʰ
policies and by always judging matters that are brought to our notice in the most ⁸
equitable spirit. ¹²ⁱ
⁹

'*Thus Haman son of Hammedatha, a Macedonian, without a drop of Persian* ¹²ᵏ
blood and far removed from our goodness, enjoyed our hospitality • *and was treated* ¹⁰
by us with the benevolence which we show to every nation, even to the extent of ¹²ˡ
being proclaimed our 'father' and being accorded universally the prostration of ¹¹
respect as second in dignity to the royal throne. • *But he, unable to keep within his* ¹²ᵐ
own high rank, schemed to deprive us of our realm and of our life. • *Furthermore, by* ¹²
tortuous wiles and arguments, he would have had us destroy Mordecai, our saviour ¹²ⁿ
and constant benefactor, with Esther the blameless partner of our majesty, and ¹³
their whole nation besides. • *He thought by these means to leave us without support* ¹²ᵒ
and so to transfer the Persian empire to the Macedonians. ¹⁴

'*But we find that the Jews, marked out for annihilation by this arch-scoundrel,* ¹²ᵖ
are not criminals; they are in fact governed by the most just of laws. • *They are sons* ¹⁵
of the Most High, the great and living God to whom we and our ancestors owe ¹²ᑫ
the continuing prosperity of our realm. • *You will therefore do well not to act on* ¹⁶
the letters sent by Haman son of Hammedatha with his whole household: a well-earned punishment which ¹²ʳ
God, the ruler of all things, has speedily inflicted on him. • *Put up copies of this letter* ¹⁷,¹⁸
everywhere, allow the Jews freedom to observe their own customs, and come to ¹²ˢ
their help against anyone who attacks them on the day originally chosen for their ¹⁹
maltreatment, that is the thirteenth day of the twelfth month, which is Adar. • *For* ²⁰
the all-powerful God has made this day a day of joy and not of ruin for his chosen ¹²ᵗ
people. • *Jews, for your part, among your solemn festivals celebrate this as a special* ²¹
day with every kind of feasting, so that now and in the future, for you and for ¹²ᵘ
Persians of good will it may commemorate your rescue, and for your enemies may ²²
stand as a reminder of their ruin. ²³

'*Every city and, more generally, every country, which does not follow these* ¹²ᵛ
instructions, will be mercilessly devastated with fire and sword, and made not only ²⁴
inaccessible to men but hateful to wild animals and even birds for ever.'

The text of this edict, to be promulgated as law in each province, was published ¹³
to the various peoples, so that the Jews could be ready on the day stated to
avenge themselves on their enemies. • The couriers, mounted on the king's horses, ¹⁴
set out in great haste and urgency at the king's command. The edict was also
published in the citadel of Susa. • Mordecai left the royal presence in a princely ¹⁵
gown of violet and white, with a great golden crown and a cloak of fine linen
and purple. The city of Susa shouted for joy. • For the Jews there was light and ¹⁶
gladness, joy and honour. • In every province and in every city, wherever the ¹⁷
king's command and decree arrived, there was joy and gladness among the Jews,
with feasting and holiday-making. Of the country's population many became
Jews, since now the Jews were feared.

The great day of Purim

9 ¹ The king's command and decree came into force on the thirteenth day of the twelfth month, Adar, and the day on which the enemies of the Jews had hoped to crush them produced the very opposite effect: the Jews it was who ² crushed their enemies. •In their towns throughout the provinces of King Ahasuerus, the Jews assembled to strike at those who had planned to injure them. No one resisted them, since the various peoples were now all afraid of ³ them. •Provincial administrators, satraps, governors and officers of the king, all ⁴ supported the Jews for fear of Mordecai. •And indeed Mordecai was a power in the palace, and his fame was spreading through all the provinces; Mordecai was steadily growing more powerful.

⁵ So the Jews struck down all their enemies with the sword, with resulting ⁶ slaughter and destruction, and worked their will on their opponents. •In the ⁷ citadel of Susa alone the Jews put five hundred men to death, •notably Parshan-⁸ datha, Dalphon, Aspatha, •Poratha, Adalia, Aridatha, •Parmashta, Arisai, ⁹ ¹⁰ Aridai and Jezatha, •the ten sons of Haman son of Hammedatha, the persecutor of the Jews. But they took no plunder.

¹¹ The number of those killed in the citadel of Susa was reported the same day ¹² to the king, •who said to Queen Esther, 'In the citadel of Susa the Jews have killed five hundred men and also the ten sons of Haman. What must they have done in the other provinces of the realm? Tell me what you request; I grant it to you. ¹³ Tell me what else you desire; it is yours for the asking.' •'If such is the king's pleasure,' Esther replied 'let the Jews of Susa be allowed to enforce today's decree tomorrow as well. And as for the ten sons of Haman, let their bodies ¹⁴ be hanged on the gallows.' •Whereupon the king ordered this to be done; the ¹⁵ edict was issued in Susa and the ten sons of Haman were hanged. •Thus the Jews of Susa reassembled on the fourteenth day of the month of Adar and killed three hundred men in the city. But they took no plunder.

¹⁶ The other Jews who lived in the king's provinces also assembled to defend their lives and rid themselves of their enemies. They slaughtered seventy-five ¹⁷ thousand of their opponents. But they took no plunder. •This was on the thirteenth day of the month of Adar. On the fourteenth day they rested and ¹⁸ made it a day of feasting and gladness. •But for the Jews of Susa, who had assembled on the thirteenth and fourteenth days, the fifteenth was the day they ¹⁹ rested, making that a day of feasting and gladness. •This is why Jewish country people, those who live in undefended villages, keep the fourteenth day of the month of Adar as a day of gladness, feasting and holiday-making, and exchange ¹⁹ᵃ portions with one another, •*whereas for those who live in cities the day of rejoicing and exchanging portions with their neighbours is the fifteenth day of Adar.*

V. THE FEAST OF PURIM

The official institution of the feast of Purim

²⁰ Mordecai committed these events to writing. Then he sent letters to all the ²¹ Jews throughout the provinces of King Ahasuerus, both near and far, •enjoining them to celebrate the fourteenth and fifteenth days of the month of Adar every ²² year, •as the days on which the Jews had rid themselves of their enemies, and the month in which their sorrow had been turned into gladness, and mourning into a holiday. He therefore told them to keep these as days of festivity and gladness when they were to exchange portions and make gifts to the poor.

²³ Once having begun to observe them, the Jews undertook to continue these ²⁴ practices about which Mordecai had written these words to them, •'Haman son of Hammedatha, the Agagite, the persecutor of all the Jews, had plotted their destruction and had cast the pur, that is, the lot, for their overthrow and ruin.

But when he went again to the king to ask him to order the hanging of Mordecai, 25 the wicked scheme which he had devised against the Jews recoiled on his own head, and both he and his sons were hanged on the gallows. •That is why these 26 days were called Purim, from the word pur.' And so, because of what was written in this letter, because of what they had seen for themselves and because of what had happened to them, •the Jews vowed and took on themselves and their 27 descendants and on all who should join them, to celebrate these two days without fail, in the manner prescribed and at the time appointed, year after year. Thus commemorated and celebrated from generation to generation, in each 28 family, each province and each city, these days of Purim shall never be abrogated among the Jews, nor shall their memory die out among their race.

Queen Esther, the daughter of Abihail, wrote with full authority to ratify 29 this second letter, •and sent letters to all the Jews of the hundred and twenty- 30 seven provinces of the realm of Ahasuerus in terms of kindness and friendship enjoining them to observe these days of Purim at the appointed time, as Mordecai 31 the Jew had recommended, and in the manner prescribed for themselves and their descendants, with additional ordinances for fasts and lamentations. •The 32 ordinance of Esther fixed this observance of Purim and it was recorded in writing.

Praise of Mordecai

10 King Ahasuerus levied tribute from the continent and the islands of the 1 sea. •All his mighty acts of power and the account of the high honour 2 to which he raised Mordecai, is not all this recorded in the Book of the Annals of the Kings of Media and Persia? •How 'Mordecai the Jew was next in rank 3 to King Ahasuerus. He was a man held in respect among the Jews, esteemed by thousands of his brothers, a man who sought the good of his people and cared for the welfare of his entire race.'

And Mordecai said, 'All this is God's doing. •I remember the dream I had about 3a 10:4,5 *these matters, nothing of which has failed to come true: •the little spring that* 3c 6 *became a river, the light that shone, the sun, the flood of water. Esther is* *the river—she whom the king married and made queen. •The two dragons are* 3d 7 *Haman and myself. •The nations are those that banded together to blot out the* 3e 8 *name of Jew. •The single nation, mine, is Israel, those who cried out to God and* 3f 9 *were saved. Yes, the Lord has saved his people, the Lord has delivered us from* *all these evils, God has worked such signs and great wonders as have never happened* *among the nations.*

'Two destinies he appointed, one for his own people, one for the nations at 3g 10 *large. •And these two destinies were worked out at the hour and time and day laid* 3h 11 *down by God involving all the nations. •In this way God has remembered his people* 3i 12 *and vindicated his heritage; •and for them these days, the fourteenth and fifteenth* 3k 13 *of the month of Adar, are to be days of assembly, of joy and of gladness before* *God, through all generations and for ever among his people Israel.'*

Note on the Greek translation of the book

In the fourth year of the reign of Ptolemy and Cleopatra, Dositheus, who 3l 11:1 affirmed that he was a priest and Levite, and Ptolemy his son brought the foregoing letter concerning the Purim. They maintained it as being authentic, the translation having been made by Lysimachus son of Ptolemy, a member of the Jerusalem community.

INTRODUCTION TO THE BOOKS OF
MACCABEES

The First and Second Books of Maccabees were not in the Jewish Canon of scripture and have sometimes been relegated to the Apocrypha. The Church nevertheless gave recognition to them after a period of doubt and there is much to be learnt from them about late developments in Jewish belief before the incarnation, and about the position of the Jewish nation between Greeks and Romans in the 2nd century B.C.

The background of both books is the fight of the resistance movement against the hellenisation of the Jewish nation by the Seleucid kings. The First Book of Maccabees covers the forty years from 175 to 134 B.C., and must have been written before 63 B.C. As a history of the times it is invaluable, but allowances must be made for the author's intention of writing a religious history modelled on the ancient chronicles of Israel.

The Second Book of Maccabees covers a part of the same period. It was written about the same date, in Greek and in a formal didactic style, incorporating documents which may well be genuine but are not always placed appropriately. The book was addressed to the expatriate Jews of Alexandria, to rouse their concern for the dangers threatening the Temple of Jerusalem, and it selects and arranges historical incidents for this purpose.

These books provide the setting in which the Book of Daniel was written.

THE FIRST BOOK OF
MACCABEES

I. INTRODUCTION

Alexander and the Diadochoi

1 Alexander of Macedon, son of Philip, had come from the land of Kittim[a] 1
and defeated Darius, king of the Persians and Medes, whom he succeeded
as ruler, at first of Hellas. •He undertook many campaigns, gained possession 2
of many fortresses, and put the local kings to death. •So he advanced to the 3
ends of the earth, plundering nation after nation; the earth grew silent before
him, and his ambitious heart swelled with pride. •He assembled very powerful 4,5
forces and subdued provinces, nations and princes, and they became his
tributaries. •But the time came when Alexander took to his bed, in the knowledge 5,6
that he was dying. •He summoned his comrades, noblemen who had been 7
brought up with him from his youth, and divided his kingdom among them
while he was still alive. •Alexander had reigned twelve years when he died.[b] 7,8
Each of his comrades established himself in his own region. •All assumed crowns 8,9,10
after his death, they and their heirs after them for many years, bringing increasing
evils on the world.

Antiochus Epiphanes: Israel infected with hellenism

From these there grew a sinful offshoot, Antiochus Epiphanes, son of King 10,11
Antiochus; once a hostage in Rome,[c] he became king in the one hundred and
thirty-seventh year of the kingdom of the Greeks.[d] •It was then that there emerged 11,12
from Israel a set of renegades who led many people astray. 'Come,' they said
'let us reach an understanding with the pagans surrounding us, for since we
separated ourselves from them many misfortunes have overtaken us.' •This 12,13
proposal proved acceptable, •and a number of the people eagerly approached 13,14
the king, who authorised them to practise the pagan observances. •So they 14,15
built a gymnasium in Jerusalem, such as the pagans have, •disguised their 15,16
circumcision, and abandoned the holy covenant, submitting to the heathen rule
as willing slaves of impiety.

Antiochus Epiphanes despoils the Temple, and persecutes Jews remaining faithful to the Law

Once Antiochus had seen his authority established, he determined to make 16,17
himself king of Egypt, and the ruler of both kingdoms. •He invaded Egypt 17,18
in massive strength, with chariots and elephants and a great fleet. •He engaged 18,19
Ptolemy, king of Egypt, in battle, and Ptolemy turned back and fled before his
advance, leaving many casualties. •The fortified cities of the land of Egypt 19,20
were captured, and Antiochus plundered the country. •After his conquest of 20,21
Egypt, in the year one hundred and forty-three, Antiochus turned about and 22
advanced on Israel and Jerusalem in massive strength. •Insolently breaking into 21,23
the sanctuary, he removed the golden altar and the lamp-stand for the light

22 with all its fittings, •together with the table for the loaves of offering, the libation
vessels, the cups, the golden censers, the veil, the crowns, and the golden decora-
23
24 tion on the front of the Temple, which he stripped of everything. •He made
off with the silver and gold and precious vessels, he discovered the secret treasures
24
25 and seized them, •and removing all of these, he went back to his own country,
leaving the place a shambles and uttering words of extreme arrogance.

25
26   Then there was deep mourning for Israel throughout the country:

26
27   Rulers and elders groaned;
        girls and young men wasted away;
        the women's beauty suffered a change;
27
28   every bridegroom took up a dirge,
        the bride sat grief-stricken on her marriage-bed.
28
29   The very land quaked for its inhabitants
        and the whole House of Jacob was clothed with shame.

29
30   The days passed, and after two years the king sent the mysarch[e] through
30
31 the cities of Judah. He came to Jerusalem with an impressive force, •and
addressing them with what appeared to be peaceful words, he gained their
32 confidence; •then suddenly he fell on the city dealing it a terrible blow, and
31
33 destroying many of the people of Israel. •He pillaged the city and set it on fire,
32
34 tore down its houses and encircling wall, •took the women and children captive
33
35 and commandeered the cattle. •Then they fortified the City of David with a great
34
36 strong wall and strong towers, and made this their Citadel. •There they installed
35
37 an army of sinful men, renegades, who fortified themselves inside it, •storing
arms and provisions, and depositing there the loot they had collected from
Jerusalem; they were to prove a great trouble.

36
38   It became an ambush for the sanctuary,
        an evil adversary for Israel at all times.
37
39   They shed innocent blood all round the sanctuary
        and defiled the sanctuary itself.
38
40   The citizens of Jerusalem fled because of them,
        she became a dwelling place of strangers;
        estranged from her own offspring,
        her children forsook her.
39
41   Her sanctuary became as deserted as a wilderness,
        her feasts were turned into mourning,
        her sabbaths into a mockery,
        her honour into reproach.
40
42   Her dishonour now fully matched her former glory,
        her greatness was turned into grief.

41
43   Then the king issued a proclamation to his whole kingdom that all were
42
44 to become a single people, each renouncing his particular customs. •All the pagans
43
45 conformed to the king's decree, •and many Israelites chose to accept his
44
46 religion, sacrificing to idols and profaning the sabbath. •The king also sent
instructions by messenger to Jerusalem and the towns of Judah directing them
45
47 to adopt customs foreign to the country, •banning holocausts, sacrifices and
46
48, 49 libations from the sanctuary, profaning sabbaths and feasts, •defiling the
47
50 sanctuary and the sacred ministers, •building altars, precincts and shrines for
48
51 idols, sacrificing pigs and unclean beasts, •leaving their sons uncircumcised,
49 and prostituting themselves to all kinds of impurity and abomination, •so
50
52 that they should forget the Law and revoke all observance of it. •Anyone not

---

1 a. Cyprus; but the name is used vaguely of more distant countries.   b. 324 B.C. The empire
was not finally divided until 301.   c. Handed over to the Romans by his father, Antiochus the
Great, after his defeat at Magnesia.   d. 175 B.C., the 137th year of the Seleucid era.   e. Commander of the Mysian mercenaries.

obeying the king's command was to be put to death. •Writing in such terms to ⁵¹₅₃
every part of his kingdom, the king appointed inspectors for the whole people,
and directed all the towns of Judah to offer sacrifice one after another. ⁵⁴
Many of the people—that is, every apostate from the Law—rallied to them, ⁵²₅₅
and so committed evil in the country, •forcing Israel into hiding in all their ⁵³₅₆
places of refuge. •On the fifteenth day of Chislev in the year one hundred and ⁵⁴₅₇
forty-five ͟ the king erected the abomination of desolation ͟ above the altar; and
altars were built in the surrounding towns of Judah •and incense offered at ⁵⁵₅₈
the doors of houses and in the streets. •Any books of the Law that came to ⁵⁶₅₉
light were torn up and burned. •Whenever anyone was discovered possessing ⁵⁷₆₀
a copy of the covenant or practising the Law, the king's decree sentenced him
to death. •Having might on their side they took action month after month ⁵⁸₆₁
against any offenders they discovered in the towns of Israel. •On the twenty- ⁵⁹₆₂
fifth day of the month sacrifice was offered on the altar erected over the altar
of holocaust. •Women who had had their children circumcised were put to ⁶⁰₆₃
death according to the edict •with their babies hung round their necks, and ⁶¹₆₄
the members of their household and those who had performed the circumcision
were executed with them.

Yet there were many in Israel who stood firm and found the courage to ⁶²₆₅
refuse unclean food. •They chose death rather than contamination by such fare ⁶³₆₆
or profanation of the holy covenant, and they were executed. •It was a dreadful ⁶⁴₆₇
wrath that visited Israel.

II. MATTATHIAS UNLEASHES THE HOLY WAR

Mattathias and his sons

2 In those days Mattathias son of John, son of Simeon, a priest of the line ₁
of Joarib, left Jerusalem and settled in Modein. •He had five sons, John ₂
known as Gaddi, •Simon called Thassi, •Judas called Maccabaeus, •Eleazar, ₃,₄,₅
called Avaran, and Jonathan called Apphus. •When he saw the blasphemies being ₆
committed in Judah and Jerusalem, •he said, 'Alas that I should have been ₇
born to witness the overthrow of my people, and the overthrow of the Holy
City, and to sit by while she is delivered over to her enemies, and the sanctuary
into the hand of foreigners.

'Her Temple has become like a man of no repute,   ₈
the vessels that were her glory have been carried off as booty,   ₉
her babies have been slaughtered in her streets,
her young men by the enemy's sword.
Is there a nation that has not claimed a share of her royal prerogatives, ₁₀
that has not taken some of her spoils?
All her ornaments have been snatched from her,   ₁₁
her former freedom has become slavery.
See how our Holy Place, our beauty, our glory, is now laid waste,   ₁₂
profaned by the pagans.
What have we left to live for?'   ₁₃

Mattathias and his sons tore their garments, put on sackcloth, and observed ₁₄
deep mourning.

The ordeal of the sacrifice at Modein

The king's commissioners who were enforcing the apostasy came to the ₁₅
town of Modein to make them sacrifice. •Many Israelites gathered round them, ₁₆
but Mattathias and his sons drew apart. •The king's commissioners then ₁₇
addressed Mattathias as follows, 'You are a respected leader, a great man in
this town; you have sons and brothers to support you. •Be the first to step ₁₈

forward and conform to the king's decree, as all the nations have done, and the leaders of Judah and the survivors in Jerusalem; you and your sons shall be reckoned among the Friends of the King, you and your sons shall be honoured
19 with gold and silver and many presents.' •Raising his voice, Mattathias retorted, 'Even if every nation living in the king's dominions obeys him, each forsaking
20 its ancestral religion to conform to his decrees, •I, my sons and my brothers
21 will still follow the covenant of our ancestors. •Heaven preserve us from for-
22 saking the Law and its observances. •As for the king's orders, we will not follow
23 them: we will not swerve from our own religion either to right or to left.' •As he finished speaking, a Jew came forward in the sight of all to offer sacrifice on the
24 altar in Modein as the royal edict required. •When Mattathias saw this, he was fired with zeal; stirred to the depth of his being, he gave vent to his legitimate
25 anger, threw himself on the man and slaughtered him on the altar. •At the same time he killed the king's commissioner who was there to enforce the sacrifice,
26 and tore down the altar. •In his zeal for the Law he acted as Phinehas did against
27 Zimri son of Salu. •Then Mattathias went through the town, shouting at the top of his voice, 'Let everyone who has a fervour for the Law and takes his stand
28 on the covenant come out and follow me'. •Then he fled with his sons into the hills, leaving all their possessions behind in the town.

The ordeal of the sabbath in the desert

29 At this many who were concerned for virtue and justice went down to the
30 desert and stayed there, •taking with them their sons, their wives and their
31 cattle, for the burden of their wrongs had become unendurable. •But word was brought to the king's men and the garrison in Jerusalem, in the City of David, that the men who had repudiated the king's edict had gone down to hiding
32 places in the desert. •A strong detachment went after them, and when it came up with them ranged itself against them in battle formation, preparing to attack
33 them on the sabbath day. •But first they challenged them, 'Enough of this!
34 Come out and do as the king orders and you shall be spared'. •But they an-swered, 'We refuse to come out, and we are not going to obey the king's orders
35 and so profane the sabbath day'. •The others at once went into action, •but they
36 offered no opposition; not a stone was thrown, there was no barricading of the
37 hiding places. •They only said, 'Let us all die innocent; let heaven and earth
38 bear witness that you are massacring us with no pretence of justice'. •The attack was pressed home on the sabbath itself, and they were slaughtered, with their wives and children and cattle, to the number of one thousand persons.

The activity of Mattathias and his associates

39 When the news reached Mattathias and his friends, they mourned bitterly
40 for the victims, •and said to one another, 'If we all do as our brothers have done, and refuse to fight the pagans for our lives and institutions, they
41 will only destroy us the sooner from the earth'. •So then and there they came to this decision, 'If anyone attacks us on the sabbath day, whoever he may be, we will resist him; we must not all be killed, as our brothers were in the hiding places'.
42 Soon they were joined by a community of Hasidaeans,[a] stout fighting men
43 of Israel, each one a volunteer on the side of the Law. •All the refugees from
44 the persecution rallied to them, giving them added support. •They organised themselves into an armed force, striking down the sinners in their anger, and the renegades in their fury, and those who escaped them fled to the pagans
45 for safety. •Mattathias and his friends made a tour, overthrowing the altars

f. 8th December 167.   g. The altar or symbol of Baal Shamem, or the Olympian Zeus.
2 a. 'The Devout': a Jewish party devoted to the Law who had already opposed pagan influ-ences. Both the Pharisees and the Essenes derive from them.

and forcibly circumcising all the boys they found uncircumcised in the territories 46
of Israel. •They hunted down the upstarts, and managed their campaign to good 47
effect. •They wrested the Law out of the control of the pagans and the 48
kings, and robbed sinful men of their advantage.

The testament and death of Mattathias

As the days of Mattathias were drawing to a close, he said to his sons, 49
'Arrogance and outrage are now in the ascendant; it is a period of turmoil
and bitter hatred. •This is the time, my children, for you to have a burning 50
fervour for the Law and to give your lives for the covenant of our ancestors.

'Remember the deeds performed by our ancestors, each 51
    in his generation,
and you shall win great honour and everlasting renown.
Was not Abraham tried and found faithful, 52
    was that not counted as making him just?
Joseph in the time of his distress maintained the Law, 53
    and so became lord of Egypt.
Phinehas, our father, in return for his burning fervour 54
    received a covenant of everlasting priesthood.
Joshua, for carrying out his task, 55
    became judge of Israel.
Caleb, for his testimony before the assembled people, 56
    received an inheritance in the land.
David for his generous heart 57
    inherited the throne of an everlasting kingdom.
Elijah for his consuming fervour for the Law 58
    was caught up to heaven itself.
Hananiah, Azariah and Mishael, for their fidelity, 59
    were saved from the flame.
Daniel for his singleness of heart 60
    was rescued from the lion's jaw.
Consider, then, how in generation after generation 61
    all who hope in him will not be found to falter.
Do not fear the threats of the sinner, 62
    all his brave show must come to the dunghill and the worms.
Exalted today, tomorrow he is nowhere to be found, 63
    for he has returned to the dust he came from
    and his scheming is brought to nothing.
My children, play the man and be courageous for the Law, 64
    for it will bring you glory.

'Here is your brother Simeon, I know he is a man of sound judgement. Listen 65
to him all your lives; let him take your father's place. •Judas Maccabaeus, 66
strong and brave from his youth, let him be your general and conduct the war
against the pagans. •The rest of you are to enrol in your ranks all those who 67
keep the Law, and to exact vengeance for your people. •Pay back the pagans 68
to the full, and hold fast to the ordinance of the Law.' •Then he blessed them 69
and was laid with his ancestors. •He died in the year one hundred and forty-six 70
and was buried in his ancestral tomb at Modein, and all Israel mourned him
deeply.

III. JUDAS MACCABAEUS, LEADER OF THE JEWS

(166-160 B.C.)

The eulogy of Judas Maccabaeus

$^1_2$ 3 Then his son Judas, called Maccabaeus, took over his command. •All his brothers, and all who had attached themselves to his father, supported him, and they fought for Israel with a will.

3   He extended the fame of his people.
He put on the breastplate like a giant
and girded on his war harness;
he engaged in battle after battle,
protecting the ranks with his sword.

4   He was like a lion in his exploits,
like a lion's whelp roaring over its prey.

5   He pursued and tracked down the renegades,
he consigned those who troubled his people to the flames.

6   Renegades were abashed for terror of him,
all evil-doers were utterly confounded,
and deliverance went forward under his leadership.

7   He brought bitterness to many a king
and rejoicing to Jacob by his deeds,
his memory is blessed for ever and ever.

8   He went through the towns of Judah
and utterly destroyed the infidels in them,
turning wrath away from Israel.

9   His name resounded to the ends of the earth
and he rallied those who were on the point of perishing.

The first successes of Judas

10   But Apollonius[a] mustered the pagans and a large force from Samaria to fight
11 against Israel. •When Judas learned of it, he went out to meet him and routed
12 and killed him. Many fell wounded, and the survivors took to flight. •Their
spoils were seized and the sword of Apollonius was taken by Judas, who used
13 it to fight with throughout his life. •On hearing that Judas had raised a mixed force
14 of believers and seasoned fighters, •Seron, commander of the Syrian troops,
said, 'I will make a name for myself and gain honour in the kingdom if I fight
Judas and those supporters of his who are so contemptuous of the king's orders'.
15 He therefore launched another expedition, with a strong army of infidels to
16 support him in taking revenge on the Israelites. •He had nearly reached the
descent of Beth-horon when Judas went out to confront him with a handful
17 of men. •But as soon as these saw the force advancing to meet them they said
to Judas, 'How can we, few as we are, engage such overwhelming numbers?
18 We are exhausted as it is, not having had anything to eat today.' •'It is easy'
Judas answered 'for a great number to be routed by a few; indeed in the sight
19 of heaven deliverance, whether by many or by few, is all one; •for victory in
war does not depend on the size of the fighting force; it is from heaven 'that
20 strength comes. •They are coming against us in full-blown insolence and law-
21 lessness to destroy us, our wives and our children, and to plunder us; •but we
22 are fighting for our lives and our laws, •and he will crush them before our
23 eyes; do not be afraid of them.' •When he had finished speaking, he made a sudden
24 sally against Seron and his force and overwhelmed them. •Judas pursued him
down from Beth-horon as far as the plain. About eight hundred of their men

3 a. 'The mysarch' of 1:29.

fell, and the rest took refuge in the country of the Philistines. •Judas and his 25
brothers began to be feared, and alarm seized the surrounding peoples. •His 26
name even reached the king's ears, and in every nation there was talk of Judas
and his battles.

Preparations for expeditions in Persia and Judaea. The regency of Lysias

The news of these events infuriated Antiochus, and he ordered mobilisation 27
of all the forces in his kingdom, a very powerful army. •Opening his treasury, 28
he distributed a year's pay to his troops, telling them to be prepared for any
eventuality. •He then found that the money in his coffers had run short and that 29
the tribute of the province had decreased, as a result of the dissension and
disaster brought upon the country by his own abrogation of laws that had
been in force from antiquity. •He began to fear that, as had happened more than 30
once, he would not have enough to cover the expenses and the lavish bounties
he had previously been accustomed to make on a larger scale than his predecessors
on the throne. •In this grave quandary he resolved to visit Persia, in order to 31
levy tribute on the provinces and so accumulate substantial funds. •Lysias, 32
a nobleman belonging to the royal family, was left in charge of the king's affairs
from the river Euphrates to the Egyptian frontier, •and was to be responsible 33
for the education of his son Antiochus until his return. •Antiochus made over 34
to him half his forces, with the elephants, and gave him instructions about all
his policies, particularly about the inhabitants of Judaea and Jerusalem, •against 35
whom he was to send a force, to crush and destroy the power of Israel and the
remnant of Jerusalem, to wipe out their very memory from the place, •to settle 36
the sons of foreigners in all parts of their territory and to distribute their land
by lot. •The king took with him the remaining half of his forces and set out 37
from Antioch, the capital of his kingdom, in the year one hundred and forty-
seven;[b] he crossed the river Euphrates and made his way along the upper
provinces.

Gorgias and Nicanor lead the Syrian army into Judaea

Lysias chose Ptolemy son of Dorymenes, with Nicanor and Gorgias, 38
influential men from among the Friends of the King, •and despatched under their 39
command forty thousand foot and seven thousand horse to invade the land
of Judah and devastate it, as the king had ordered. •The entire force set out 40
and reached the neighbourhood of Emmaus in the Lowlands, where they pitched
camp. •When the merchants of the province heard who they were, they came 41
to the camp, bringing with them a large amount of gold and silver, and fetters
as well, proposing to buy the Israelites as slaves; they were accompanied by a
contingent from Idumaea and the Philistine country. •Judas and his brothers 42
saw that the situation was going from bad to worse and that armies were camping
in their territory; they were also well aware that the king had ordered the people's
total destruction. •So they said to each other, 'Let us restore the ruins of our 43
people and fight for our people and our sanctuary.' •They mustered their people 44
to prepare for war, and to offer prayer and implore compassion and mercy.

> Jerusalem was left uninhabited like a desert, 45
> there was none left to go in or out, of all her children.
> The sanctuary was trodden underfoot,
> with men of an alien race in the Citadel,
> now a lodging place for pagans.
> There was no more rejoicing for Jacob,
> flute and zither were mute.

The Jews muster at Mizpah

After mustering, they made their way to Mizpah, opposite Jerusalem, since 46
Mizpah was traditionally a place of prayer for Israel. •That day they fasted 47

and put on sackcloth, covering their heads with ashes and tearing their garments.
48 For the guidance that the heathen would have sought from the images of their
49 false gods,' they opened the Book of the Law. •They also brought out the priestly
vestments, with first-fruits and tithes, and marshalled the nazirites who had
50 completed the period of their vow. •Then, raising their voices to heaven, they
cried, 'What shall we do with these people, and where are we to take them?ᶜ
51 Your sacred precincts have been trampled underfoot and defiled, your priests
52 mourn in their humiliation, •and now the pagans are allied together to destroy
53 us: you know what they have in mind for us. •How can we stand up and face them
54 if you do not come to our aid?' •Then they sounded the trumpets and made a
great outcry.

55   Next Judas appointed leaders for the people, to command a thousand, a
56 hundred, fifty or ten men. •He told those who were building houses, or about
to be married, or planting vineyards, or who were simply afraid, to go home
57 every one of them, as the Law allowed. •Then the formation marched off and
58 took up a position south of Emmaus. •'Stand to your arms,' Judas told them
'acquit yourselves bravely, be ready to fight in the morning against these pagans
59 massed against us to destroy us and our sanctuary. •Better for us to die in battle
60 than to watch the ruin of our nation and our holy place. •Whatever be the
will of heaven, he will perform it.'

The battle of Emmaus

1 **4** Gorgias took with him five thousand foot and a thousand picked cavalry,
2   and the force moved off by night •with the object of attacking the Jewish
position and dealing them an unexpected blow; the men from the Citadel were
3 there to guide them. •Judas got wind of it and himself moved off with his fighters
4 to strike at the king's forces in Emmaus, •while their fighting troops had been
5 moved away from the encampment. •And so, when Gorgias reached the camp of
Judas, he found nobody and he began to search for the Jews in the mountains,
6 exclaiming, 'They are running away from us'. •First light found Judas in the
plain with three thousand men, although these lacked the armour and swords
7 they could have wished. •They could now see the heathen encampment with
its strong fortifications and cavalry surrounding it, clearly people who understood warfare.

8   Judas said to his men, 'Do not be afraid of their numbers, and do not flinch at
9 their attack. •Remember how our ancestors were delivered at the Red Sea when
0 Pharaoh was pursuing them in force. •And now let us implore heaven to be kind
to us and to remember his covenant with our ancestors and to destroy this army
confronting us today; •then all the nations will know for certain that there is one
who saves and delivers Israel.'

    The foreigners looked up and, seeing the Jews advancing against them,
came out of the camp to join battle. Judas' men sounded the trumpet •and
engaged them. The pagans were routed and fled towards the plain •and all the
stragglers fell by the sword. The pursuit continued as far as Gezer and the plains
of Idumaea, Azotus and Jamnia, and the enemy lost about three thousand men.

    Breaking off the pursuit, Judas returned with his men •and said to the people,
'Never mind the booty, for we have another battle ahead of us. •Gorgias and
his forces are still in the mountains not far from us. First stand up to our enemies
and fight them, and then you can collect as much booty as you like.' •The words
were hardly out of Judas' mouth when an enemy patrol appeared on the mountainside. •This patrol, observing that their own troops had been routed and that
the camp had been fired, for the smoke, which was clearly visible, told them
what had happened, •were panic-stricken at the sight; and when they also saw

---

b. 165 B.C.   c. When the time of a vow was completed, the nazirite had to offer sacrifice in
the Temple. But now the Temple was desecrated.

the forces of Judas drawn up on the plain in battle formation, •they all fled
into Philistine territory. •Judas now turned back to plunder the camp, and
they carried off a large sum in gold and silver, with violet and sea-purple stuffs,
and many other valuables. •On their return, the Jews chanted praises to heaven,
'For he is good, and his mercy is everlasting'. •That day had seen a remarkable
deliverance in Israel.

The first campaign of Lysias

Those of the foreigners who had escaped came and gave Lysias an account
of all that had happened. •The news shocked and dismayed him, for affairs
in Israel had not gone as he intended, and the results were very different from
the instructions given him by the king. •The next year he mobilised sixty thousand
picked troops and five thousand cavalry with the intention of putting the Jews out
of action. •They advanced into Idumaea and made their base at Bethzur,ᵃ
where Judas met them with ten thousand men. •When he saw their military
strength he offered this prayer, 'Blessed are you, saviour of Israel, who shattered
the might of the Philistine champion by the hand of your servant David, and
delivered their camp into the hands of Jonathan son of Saul, and his armour-
bearer. •Crush this expedition in the same way at the hands of your people
Israel; make them ashamed of their forces and their cavalry. •Make cowards of
them, undermine their confidence in their own strength, and may they reel at their
defeat. •Overthrow them by the sword of those who love you, and all who acknowledge your name will sing your praises.' •The two forces engaged, and five
thousand men of Lysias' troops fell in hand-to-hand fighting. •Seeing the
rout of his army and the courage of Judas' troops and their readiness to live
or die as soldiers should, Lysias withdrew to Antioch, where he recruited
mercenaries for a further invasion of Judaea in even greater strength.

The purification of the Temple and its dedication

Then Judas and his brothers said, 'Now that our enemies have been defeated,
let us go up to purify the sanctuary and dedicate it'. •So they marshalled the whole
army, and went up to Mount Zion. •There they found the sanctuary a wilderness, the altar desecrated, the gates burnt down, and vegetation growing in
the courts as it might in a wood or on some mountain, while the storerooms
were in ruins. •They tore their garments and mourned bitterly, putting dust
on their heads. •They prostrated themselves on the ground, and when the
trumpets gave the signal they cried aloud to heaven.

Then Judas ordered his men to engage the garrison in the Citadel until he
had purified the sanctuary. •Next, he selected priests who were blameless in
observance of the Law •to purify the sanctuary and remove the stones of the
abomination to an unclean place.

They discussed what should be done about the altar of holocausts which had
been profaned, •and very properly decided to pull it down, that it might never
become a reproach to them, from its defilement by the pagans. They therefore
demolished it •and deposited the stones in a suitable place on the Temple hill
to await the appearance of a prophet who should give a ruling about them.
They took unhewn stones, as the Law prescribed, and built a new altar on the
lines of the old one. •They restored the Holy Place and the interior of the house,
and purified the courts. •They made new sacred vessels, and brought the lamp-
stand, the altar of incense, and the table into the Temple. •They burned incense
on the altar and lit the lamps on the lamp-stand, and these shone inside the
Temple. •They set out the loaves on the table and hung the curtains and completed
all the tasks they had undertaken.

On the twenty-fifth of the ninth month, Chislev, in the year one hundred and
forty-eight, they rose at dawn •and offered a lawful sacrifice on the new altar
of holocausts which they had made. •The altar was dedicated, to the sound of

zithers, harps and cymbals, at the same time of year and on the same day on which
55 the pagans had originally profaned it. •The whole people fell prostrate in
56 adoration, praising to the skies him who had made them so successful. •For eight
days they celebrated the dedication of the altar, joyfully offering holocausts,
57 communion sacrifices and thanksgivings. •They ornamented the front of the
Temple with crowns and bosses of gold, repaired the gates and the storerooms
58 and fitted them with doors. •There was no end to the rejoicing among the people,
59 and the reproach of the pagans was lifted from them. •Judas, with his brothers
and the whole assembly of Israel, made it a law that the days of the dedication
of the altar should be celebrated yearly at the proper season, for eight days
beginning on the twenty-fifth of the month Chislev, with rejoicing and gladness.
60 They then proceeded to build high walls with strong towers round Mount
Zion, to prevent the pagans from coming and riding roughshod over it as in the
61 past. •Judas stationed a garrison there to guard the mount; he also fortified
Bethzur, to give the people a fortress against Idumaea.

The expedition against the Idumaeans and Ammonites

1 5 When the surrounding nations heard that the altar had been rebuilt and the
2   sanctuary restored to what it had been before, they became very angry, •and
determined to destroy the whole race of Jacob living among them; they began
murdering and evicting Jewish citizens.
3 Judas made war on the sons of Esau in Idumaea,[a] in the region of Akrabattene
where they held the Israelites under siege. He inflicted a crushing defeat on
4 them, and plundered them. •He also remembered the wickedness of the sons
of Baean who were a menace and a trap for the people with their ambushes
5 on the roads. •Having blockaded them in their towers and besieged them, he
vowed them to the ban; then he set fire to their towers and burned them down
6 with everyone inside. •Next, he crossed over to the Ammonites where he found
a strong fighting force and a numerous people with Timotheus for their leader.
7 He engaged them in many encounters, routed them and cut them to pieces.
8 After capturing Jazer and its outlying villages, he retired to Judaea.

The opening of campaigns in Galilee and Gilead

9 The pagans in Gilead now banded together against the Israelites living on
their territory, to destroy them. But they took refuge in the fortress of Dathema,
10 and sent the following letter to Judas and his brothers, 'The pagans round us
11 have banded themselves together against us to wipe us out, •and they are preparing to storm the fortress in which we have taken refuge; Timotheus is in command
12 of their forces. •Come at once and rescue us from their clutches, for we have
13 already suffered great losses. •All our countrymen living among the Tubians
have been put to death, their women and children have been taken into captivity,
their property has been seized, and a force about a thousand strong has been
14 wiped out there.' •While the letter was being read, other messengers arrived
15 from Galilee with their garments torn bearing similar news, •'The people of
Ptolemais,[b] Tyre and Sidon have joined forces with the whole of heathen Galilee
16 to destroy us!' •When Judas and the people heard this, a great assembly was
held to decide what should be done for their oppressed countrymen who were
17 under attack from their enemies. •Judas said to his brother Simon, 'Pick your
men and go and relieve your countrymen in Galilee, while my brother Jonathan
18 and I make our way into Gilead'. •He left Joseph son of Zechariah and the
people's leader Azariah with the remainder of the army in Judaea to guard it,
19 and gave them these orders: 'Take charge of this people, and do not engage the

---

4 a. 18 m. S. of Jerusalem.
5 a. Edomite country S. of Palestine; the Akrabattene region lay to the S.W. of the Dead Sea.
b. Acre.

pagans until we return'. •Simon was allotted three thousand men for the exped- 20
ition into Galilee, Judas eight thousand for Gilead.

The expeditions in Galilee and Gilead

Simon advanced into Galilee, engaged the pagans in several battles and 21
drove them off in disorder; •he pursued them to the gate of Ptolemais, and they 22
lost about three thousand men, whose spoils he collected. •He took away with 23
him the Jews of Galilee and Arbatta,ᶜ with their wives and children and all
their possessions, and brought them into Judaea with great rejoicing.

Meanwhile Judas Maccabaeus and his brother Jonathan crossed the Jordan 24
and made a three days' march through the desert, •where they encountered 25
the Nabataeans,ᵈ who came to an understanding with them and gave them
an account of all that had happened to their brothers in Gilead. •Many of 26
them, they said, were shut up in Bozrah and Bosor, Alema, Chaspho, Maked
and Carnaim, all large fortified towns. •Others were blockaded in the other 27
towns of Gilead, and the enemy planned to attack and capture these strongholds
the very next day, and wipe out all the people inside them in a single day.

Judas and his army at once turned off by the desert road to Bozrah; having 28
captured the town, he put the entire male population to the sword, plundered
the town and set it on fire. •When night came, he left the place, and they 29
continued their march until they reached the fortress.ᵉ •In the light of dawn 30
they saw an innumerable horde, setting up ladders and engines to capture the
fortress; the assault was just beginning. •When Judas saw that the attack had 31
begun and that the war cry was rising to heaven, mingled with trumpet calls
and a great clamour, •he said to the men of his army, 'You must fight today, 32
fight for your countrymen'. •Dividing them into three commands, he advanced 33
on the enemy's rear, with trumpets sounding and prayers shouted aloud. •The 34
troops of Timotheus, recognising that this was Maccabaeus, fled before his
advance; Maccabaeus dealt them a crushing defeat; about eight thousand of their
men fell that day. •Then, wheeling on Alema, he attacked and captured it, put its 35
male population to death, plundered it and burned the place down. •From 36
there he moved on and took Chaspho, Maked, Bosor and the remaining towns
of Gilead. •After these events, Timotheus mustered another force and pitched 37
camp opposite Raphon, on the far side of the wadi. •Judas sent men to recon- 38
noitre the camp, and these reported back as follows, 'With him are massed
all the pagans surrounding us, making a very numerous army, •with Arab 39
mercenaries as auxiliaries; they are encamped on the far side of the wadi, and
ready to launch an attack on you.' Judas then advanced to engage them, •and 40
was approaching the watercourse with his troops when Timotheus told the
commanders of his army, 'If he crosses first we shall not be able to resist him,
because he will have the advantage of us. •But if he is afraid and camps on the 41
other side of the stream we will cross over to him and the advantage will then
be ours.'

As soon as he reached the watercourse Judas posted the scribes of the people 42
along the wadi, giving them this order: 'Do not let anyone pitch his tent; all
are to go into battle!' •He was himself the first across to the enemy side, with 43
all the people following. Driven before them, the pagans all tore off their armour
and ran for refuge in the sacred precinct of Carnaim. •The Jews first captured 44
the town, and then burned down the precinct with everyone inside. And so
Carnaim was overthrown, and the enemy could offer no further resistance to
Judas.

Next, Judas assembled all the Israelites living in Gilead, from the least to the 45
greatest, with their wives, children and belongings, an enormous muster, to
take them into the land of Judah. •They reached Ephron, a large town straddling 46
the road and strongly fortified. As it was impossible to by-pass it on the right or
the left, there was nothing for it but to march straight through. •But the 47

people of the town denied them passage and barricaded the gates with stones.
48 Judas sent them a conciliatory message in these terms, 'Let us go through your territory to reach our own; no one will do you any harm, we only want to march
49 through'. But they would not open up for him. •So Judas sent an order down
50 the column for everyone to halt where he stood. •The fighting men took up their positions; Judas attacked the town all day and night, and it was delivered
51 into his hands. •He put all the male inhabitants to the sword, razed it to the ground, plundered it and marched through the town over the bodies of the
52 dead. •The Jews now crossed the Jordan into the great plain, opposite Bethshan,
53 Judas all the time rallying the stragglers and encouraging the people the whole
54 way until they reached the land of Judah. •They climbed Mount Zion in joy and gladness, and offered holocausts because they had returned safe and sound without having lost a single man.

A setback at Jamnia

55 While Judas and Jonathan were in the land of Gilead and Simon his brother
56 in Galilee before Ptolemais, •Joseph son of Zechariah, and Azariah, who were in command of the army, heard of their exploits and how well they had done in
57 battle, •and said, 'Let us make a name for ourselves too and go and fight the
58 nations around us'. •So they issued orders to the men of the forces under them
59 and marched on Jamnia. •But Gorgias came out from the town with his men
60 to engage them. •Joseph and Azariah were routed and pursued as far as the frontiers of Judaea. That day about two thousand Israelites lost their lives.
61 And so the people met with a great reverse, because they had not listened
62 to Judas and his brothers, but had relied on their own prowess. •These were not of the same mould as those to whom the deliverance of Israel had been entrusted.

Successes in Idumaea and Philistia

63 But that hero Judas and his brothers were held in high honour throughout
64 Israel and among all the nations wherever their name was heard, •and men
65 gathered round them to acclaim them. •Judas marched out with his brothers to fight the Edomites in the country towards the south; he stormed Hebron and its outlying villages, threw down its fortifications and burned its circle of towers.
66 Leaving there, he made for the country of the Philistines and passed through
67 Marisa.*ᶠ* •Among the fallen in that day's fighting were some priests who sought
68 to prove their courage there by joining in the battle, a foolhardy venture. •Judas next turned towards Azotus, a Philistine district; he overthrew their altars, burned down the carved images of their gods, and withdrew to the land of Judah, leaving their towns utterly despoiled.

The last days of Antiochus Epiphanes

1 **6** Meanwhile King Antiochus was making his way across the upper provinces; he had heard that in Persia there was a city called Elymais, renowned for
2 its riches, its silver and gold, •and its very wealthy temple containing golden armour, breastplates and weapons, left there by Alexander son of Philip, the
3 king of Macedon, the first to reign over the Greeks. •He therefore went and attempted to take the city and pillage it, but without success, since the citizens
4 learnt of his intention, •and offered him a stiff resistance, whereupon he
5 turned about and retreated, disconsolate, in the direction of Babylon. •But while he was still in Persia news reached him that the armies that had invaded
6 the land of Judah had been defeated, •and that Lysias in particular had advanced in massive strength, only to be forced to turn and flee before the Jews; these

---

c. On the coast of Samaria.   d. Nomad people of Transjordania.   e. Dathema, v.9.   f. On the road from Hebron to Philistia.

had been strengthened by the acquisition of arms, supplies and abundant spoils
from the armies they had cut to pieces; •they had overthrown the abomination 7
he had erected over the altar in Jerusalem, and had encircled the sanctuary
with high walls as in the past, and had fortified Bethzur, one of his cities. •When 8
the king heard this news he was amazed and profoundly shaken; he threw
himself on his bed and fell into a lethargy from acute disappointment, because
things had not turned out for him as he had planned. •And there he remained 9
for many days, subject to deep and recurrent fits of melancholy, until he understood that he was dying. •Then summoning all his Friends, he said to them, 10
'Sleep evades my eyes, and my heart is cowed by anxiety. •I have been asking 11
myself how I could have come to such a pitch of distress, so great a flood as that
which now engulfs me—I who was so generous and well-loved in my heyday.
But now I remember the wrong I did in Jerusalem when I seized all the vessels of 12
silver and gold there, and ordered the extermination of the inhabitants of Judah
for no reason at all. •This, I am convinced, is why these misfortunes have over- 13
taken me, and why I am dying of melancholy in a foreign land.'

The accession of Antiochus V

He summoned Philip, one of his Friends, and made him regent of his whole 14
kingdom. •He entrusted him with his diadem, his robe and his signet, on the 15
understanding that he was to educate his son Antiochus and train him for the
throne. •Then King Antiochus died, in the year one hundred and forty-nine.ᵃ 16
Lysias, learning that the king was dead, established his son Antiochus on the 17
throne in succession to him, having brought him up from childhood—and
styled him Eupator.

The siege of the Citadel of Jerusalem by Judas Maccabaeus

The men from the Citadel were a threat to Israel in the neighbourhood 18
of the sanctuary, seeking every opportunity of harming them, and proving a
strong support to the pagans. •Judas decided that they must be destroyed, 19
and he mobilised the whole people to besiege them. •They assembled, and 20
laid siege to the Citadel in the year one hundred and fifty, building firing platforms and siege-engines. •But some of the besieged broke through the blockade, 21
and to these a number of renegades from Israel attached themselves. •They 22
made their way to the king and said, 'How much longer are you going to wait
before you see justice done and avenge our fellows? •We were content to 23
serve your father, to comply with his orders, and to obey his edicts. •As a 24
result our own people will have nothing to do with us; what is more, they have
killed all those of us they could catch, and have plundered our heritages. •Nor 25
is it on us alone that their blows have fallen, but on all your dominions. •At this 26
moment they are laying siege to the Citadel of Jerusalem, to capture it, and they have
fortified the sanctuary and Bethzur. •Unless you forestall them at once, they will 27
go on to even bigger things, and then you will never be able to control them.'

The expedition of Antiochus V and Lysias. The battle of Bethzechariah

The king was furious when he heard this, and summoned all his Friends, 28
the generals of his forces and the cavalry commanders. •He recruited mer- 29
cenaries from other kingdoms and the islands of the seas. •His forces numbered 30
a hundred thousand foot soldiers, twenty thousand cavalry and thirty-two
elephants with experience of battle conditions. •They advanced through Idumaea 31
and besieged Bethzur, pressing the attack for days on end; they also constructed
siege-engines, but the defenders made a sortie and set these on fire, putting
up a brave resistance.

At this Judas raised the siege of the Citadel and pitched camp at Beth- 32
zechariahᵇ opposite the royal encampment. •The king rose at daybreak and 33
marched his army at top speed down the road to Bethzechariah, where his

34 forces took up their battle formations and sounded the trumpets. •The elephants
were shown a syrup of grapes and mulberries to prepare them for the battle.
35 They distributed these animals among the phalanxes, allocating to each elephant
a thousand men dressed in coats of mail with bronze helmets on their heads;
36 five hundred picked horsemen were also assigned to each beast. •The horsemen
anticipated every move their elephant made; wherever it went they went with
37 it, and never separated from it. •On each elephant, to protect it, was a stout
wooden tower, kept in position by girths, each with its team fighting from their
38 mounted position, as well as its driver. •The remainder of the cavalry was
stationed on one or other of the two flanks of the army, to harass the enemy
and cover the phalanxes.
39 When the sun glinted on the bronze and golden shields the mountains caught
40 the glint and gleamed like fiery torches. •One part of the king's army was deployed
high up in the mountains and others on the valley floor, all advancing con-
41 fidently and in good order. •Everyone trembled at the noise made by this vast
multitude, the thunder of the troops on the march and the clanking of their
42 armour, for it was an immense and mighty army. •Judas and his army advanced
43 to give battle, and six hundred of the king's army were killed. •Eleazar, called
Avaran, noticing that one of the elephants was royally caparisoned and was also
taller than all the others, and supposing that the king was mounted on it,
44
45 sacrificed himself to save his people and win an imperishable name. •Boldly
charging towards the creature through the thick of the phalanx, dealing death to
46 right and left, so that the enemy scattered on either side at his onslaught, •he
darted in under the elephant, ran his sword into it and killed it. The beast
47 collapsed on top of him, and he died on the spot. •The Jews saw how strong the
king was, and the ferocity of the royal troops, and retired before them.

The capture of Bethzur and siege of Mount Zion by the Syrians

48 The royal army moved up to encounter them before Jerusalem, and the
49 king began to blockade Judaea and Mount Zion. •He granted peace terms
to the people of Bethzur, who evacuated the town; it lacked store of provisions
50 to withstand a siege, since the land was enjoying a sabbatical year. •Having
51 occupied Bethzur, the king stationed a garrison there to hold it. •He besieged
the sanctuary for a long time, erecting firing platforms and siege-engines, fire-
52 throwers and ballistas, scorpions to discharge arrows, and catapults. •The
defenders countered these by constructing their own engines, and were thus
53 able to prolong their resistance. •But they had no stocks of provisions, because
it was the seventh year, and those who had taken refuge in Judaea from the
54 pagans had eaten up the last of their reserves. •Only a few men were left in
the Holy Place, owing to the severity of the famine; the rest had dispersed
and gone home.

The king grants the Jews religious freedom

55 Meanwhile Philip, whom King Antiochus before his death had appointed
56 to train his son Antiochus for the throne, •had returned from Persia and Media
with the forces that had accompanied the king, and was planning to seize
57 control of affairs. •On hearing this, Lysias at once decided to leave, and said
to the king, the generals of the army and the men, 'We are growing weaker
every day, we are short of food, and the place we are besieging is well fortified;
58 moreover the affairs of the kingdom demand our attention. •Let us offer the
hand of friendship to these men and make peace with them and with their whole
59 nation. •Let us grant them permission to follow their own customs as before,
since it is our abolition of these customs that provoked them into acting like
60 this.' •The king and his commanders approved this argument, and he sent
61 the Jews an offer of peace, which they accepted. •The king and the generals

6 a. 163 B.C.　　**b.** 6 m. N. of Bethzur.

ratified the treaty by oath, and the besieged accordingly left the fortress. •The 62
king then entered Mount Zion, but on seeing how impregnable the place was,
he broke the oath he had sworn and gave orders for the encircling wall to be
demolished. •He then hurriedly struck camp and retired to Antioch, where 63
he found Philip already master of the city. Antiochus fought him and took
the city by storm.

Demetrius I becomes king, and sends Bacchides and Alcimus to Judaea

7 In the year one hundred and fifty Demetrius, son of Seleucus, escaped from 1
Rome and arrived with a few men at a town on the coast, where he began
to hold court. •As he was entering the crown lands of his ancestors his army 2
arrested Antiochus and Lysias, intending to bring them before him. •But when 3
he heard of this he said, 'Keep them out of my sight'. •So the army killed 4
them and Demetrius ascended the throne of his kingdom. •Then there came to 5
him all the renegades and godless men in Israel, led by Alcimus, whose ambition
it was to become high priest. •They denounced the people before the king. 6
'Judas and his brothers' they said 'have killed all your friends, and he has driven
us out of our country. •Send someone now whom you can trust; let him go and 7
see the wholesale ruin Judas has brought on us and on the king's dominions,
and let him punish the wretches and all who assist them.'

The king chose Bacchides, one of the Friends of the King, governor of the 8
country beyond the river,ᵃ a great man in the kingdom and loyal to the king.
He sent him with the godless Alcimus, whom he established as high priest, 9
with orders to exact retribution from the Israelites. •So they set out with a 10
large force, and on reaching the land of Judah they sent messengers to Judas and
his brothers with treacherous proposals of peace. •But these did not trust them, 11
seeing that they had come with a large force. •Nevertheless a commission of 12
scribes presented themselves before Alcimus and Bacchides, to sue for just
terms. •The first among the Israelites to ask them for peace-terms were the 13
Hasidaeans, •who reasoned like this, 'This is a priest of Aaron's line who has 14
come with the armed forces; he will not wrong us'. •He did in fact discuss 15
peace-terms with them and gave them his oath, 'We will not attempt to injure
you or your friends'. •They believed him, but he arrested sixty of them and 16
put them to death in one day, fulfilling the words of scripture: •*They have scattered* 17
the flesh of your devout, and shed their blood all round Jerusalem, and no one
to dig a grave! •At this, fear and dread gripped the whole people. 'There is 18
no truth or virtue in them;' they said 'they have broken their agreement and
their sworn oath.'

Bacchides then left Jerusalem and encamped at Bethzaith,ᵇ and from there 19
sent and arrested many of the men who had deserted him, and some of the people,
and killed them, throwing them into the great cistern. •Then he put Alcimus 20
in charge of the province, leaving an army with him to support him; Bacchides
himself returned to the king. •Alcimus continued his struggle to become high 21
priest, •and all who were disturbing the peace of their own people rallied to 22
him; gaining control of the land of Judah, they worked great havoc in Israel.
Seeing that all the wrongs done to the Israelites by Alcimus and his supporters 23
exceeded what the pagans had done, •Judas went right round the whole territory 24
of Judaea to take vengeance on those who had deserted him and prevent their
free movement about the country.

When Alcimus saw how strong Judas and his supporters had grown, he 25
realised that he had not the strength to resist them, and returned to the king
where he laid criminal charges against them.

Nicanor in Judaea. The battle of Capharsalama

The king sent Nicanor, one of his generals ranking as Illustrious and a bitter 26
enemy of Israel, with orders to exterminate the people. •Reaching Jerusalem 27

with a large force, Nicanor sent envoys to Judas and his brothers with treacherous
28 proposals of peace: •'Let us have no fighting' he said 'between me and you;
29 I will come with a small escort and meet you face to face in peace.' •And he
came to Judas and they greeted each other peaceably enough; however,
30 the enemy had made preparations to abduct Judas. •When Judas became aware
of Nicanor's treacherous purpose in coming to see him, he took fright and
31 refused any further meeting. •Nicanor then realised that his plan had been
discovered, and went out to meet Judas in battle near Capharsalama.
32 About five hundred of Nicanor's men fell; the rest took refuge in the City of
David.

Threats against the Temple

33   After these events Nicanor went up to Mount Zion. Some of the priests
came out from the Holy Place with some elders, to welcome him peacefully
34 and to show him the holocaust that was being offered for the king. •But he
mocked them and laughed in their faces, defiled them and used insolent language,
35 swearing in his rage, 'Unless Judas is handed over to me this time with his army,
as soon as I am safely back, I promise you, I will burn this building down!'
36 Then he went off in a fury. •At this the priests went in again, and stood in tears
37 before the altar and the sanctuary, saying, •'You chose this house to be called
38 by your name, to be a house of prayer and petition for your people. •Take
vengeance on this man and on his army, and let them fall by the sword; remember
their blasphemies and give them no respite.'

The 'Day of Nicanor' at Adasa

39   Nicanor left Jerusalem and encamped at Beth-horon, where he was joined
40 by an army from Syria. •Meanwhile Judas camped at Adasa[c] with three thousand
41 men, and offered this prayer, •'When the Assyrian king's envoys blasphemed,
your angel went out and struck down one hundred and eighty-five thousand
42 of his men. •In the same way let us see you crush this army today, so that the
rest may know that this man has spoken blasphemously against your sanctuary:
judge him according to his wickedness.'
43   The armies met in battle on the thirteenth of the month Adar, and Nicanor's
44 army was crushed, he himself being the first to fall in the battle. •When his troops
45 saw that Nicanor had fallen, they threw down their arms and fled. •The Jews
pursued them a day's journey, from Adasa to the approaches of Gezer; they
46 sounded their trumpets in warning as they followed them, •and people came
out from all the surrounding villages of Judaea and blocked their flight, so
that they turned back on their own men, and all fell by the sword, not one being
47 left alive. •Collecting the spoils and booty, they cut off Nicanor's head and
the right hand he had stretched out in a display of insolence; these were taken
48 and displayed within sight of Jerusalem. •The people were overjoyed, and
49 kept that day as a great holiday: •indeed they decided to celebrate it annually
50 on the thirteenth of Adar. •The land of Judah was at peace for a short time.

A eulogy of the Romans

1 **8** Now, Judas had heard of the reputation of the Romans, their military strength
and their benevolence towards all who made common cause with them; they
2 wanted to establish friendly relations with anyone who approached them, •be-
cause of their military strength. He was told of their wars and of their prowess
3 among the Gauls,[a] whom they had conquered and put under tribute; •and of all
they had done in the province of Spain to gain possession of the silver and gold
4 mines there, •making themselves masters of the whole country by their deter-

7 a. Euphrates.   b. About 4 m. N. of Bethzur.   c. Between Beth-horon and Jerusalem.
8 a. 200-189 B.C.

mination and perseverance, despite its great distance from their own; of the kings who came from the ends of the earth to attack them, only to be crushed by them and overwhelmed with disaster, and of others who paid them annual tribute; •Philip, Perseus king of the Kittim, and others who had dared to make 5 war on them, had been defeated and reduced to subjection, •while Antiochus the 6 Great, king of Asia, who had advanced to attack them with a hundred and twenty elephants, cavalry, chariots and a very large army, had also suffered defeat at their hands; •they had taken him alive and imposed on him and his 7 successors the payment of an enormous tribute, the surrender of hostages, and the cession •of the Indian territory, with Media, Lydia, and some of their best 8 provinces, which they took from him and gave to King Eumenes. •Judas was 9 also told how, when the Greeks planned an expedition to destroy them, •the 10 Romans got wind of it and sent against them a single general, fought a campaign in which they inflicted heavy casualties, carried off their women and children into captivity, pillaged their goods, subdued their country, tore down their fortresses and reduced them to a slavery lasting to this very day; •and how all 11 other kingdoms and islands that had ever resisted them were also destroyed and enslaved.

But where their friends and those who relied on them were concerned, they 12 had always stood by their friendship. They had subdued kings far and near, and all who heard their name went in terror of them. •One man, if they deter- 13 mined to help him and advance him to a throne, would certainly occupy it, while another, if they so determined, would find himself deposed; their influence was paramount. •In spite of all this not one of them had assumed a crown or 14 put on the purple for his own aggrandisement. •They had set up a senate, where 15 three hundred and twenty councillors deliberated daily, constantly debating how best to regulate public affairs. •They entrusted their government to one man 16 for a year at a time, with absolute power over their whole empire, and this man was obeyed by all without any envy or jealousy.

The alliance between the Jews and Romans

Having chosen Eupolemus son of John, of the family of Accos, and Jason 17 son of Eleazar, Judas sent them to Rome to make a treaty of friendship and alliance with these people, •who would surely lift the yoke from their shoulders 18 once they understood that the kingdom of the Greeks was reducing Israel to slavery. •The envoys made the lengthy journey to Rome and presented themselves 19 before the Senate with their formal proposal, •'Judas Maccabaeus and his 20 brothers, with the Jewish people, have sent us to you to conclude a treaty of alliance and peace with you, and to enrol ourselves as your allies and friends'. The proposal met with the approval of the senators, •and this is a copy of the $^{21}_{22}$ rescript which they engraved on bronze tablets and sent to Jerusalem to be kept there by the Jews as a record of peace and alliance:

'Good fortune attend the Romans and the Jewish nation by sea and land 23 for ever; may sword or enemy be far from them! •If war comes first to Rome or 24 any of her allies throughout her dominions, •the Jewish nation is to take action 25 as her ally, as occasion may require, and do it wholeheartedly. •They are not 26 to give or supply to the aggressor any grain, arms, money or ships; this is the Roman decision, and they are to honour their obligations without recompense. In the same way, if war comes first to the Jewish nation the Romans are to support 27 them energetically as occasion may offer, •and the aggressor shall not be furnished 28 with grain, arms, money or ships; this is the Roman decision, and they will honour these obligations unreservedly. •These are the terms laid down by the 29 Romans for the Jewish people. •If when they have come into force either party 30 should wish to make any addition or deletion, they shall be free to do so, and any such addition or deletion shall be binding.[b]

'As regards the wrongs done to them by King Demetrius, we have written 31

to him in these terms: Why have you made your yoke lie heavy on our friends
32 and allies the Jews? •If they appeal against you again we will uphold their rights
and make war on you by sea and land.'

The battle of Beerzeth and death of Judas Maccabaeus

1 9 Demetrius heard that Nicanor and his army had fallen in battle,
and he sent Bacchides and Alcimus a second time into the land of Judah, and
2 with them the right wing of his army. •They took the road to Galilee and
besieged Mesaloth in Arbela,ᵃ and captured it, putting many people to death.
3 In the first month of the year one hundred and fifty-two they set up camp
4 before Jerusalem; •they then moved on, making their way to Beerzethᵇ with
5 twenty thousand foot and two thousand horse. •Judas lay in camp at Elasa,
6 with three thousand picked men. •When they saw the huge size of the enemy
forces they were terrified, and many slipped out of the camp, until no more
7 than eight hundred of the force were left. •When Judas saw that his army had
melted away and that attack was imminent, he was aghast, for he had no time
8 to rally them. •Yet, dismayed as he was, he said to those who were left, 'Up!
9 Let us face the enemy; we may yet have the strength to fight them.' •His men
tried to dissuade him, declaring, 'We have no strength for anything but to escape
with our lives this time; then we can come back with our brothers to fight them;
10 by ourselves we are too few'. •'God forbid' Judas retorted 'that I should do
such a thing as run away from them! If our time has come, at least let us die
like men for our countrymen, and leave nothing to tarnish our reputation.'
11   The enemy forces then marched out of the camp, and the Jews took up their
position in readiness to engage them. The cavalry was ordered into two squadrons;
the slingers and archers marched in the van of the army with the shock-troops,
12 all stout fighters; •Bacchides was on the right wing. The phalanx advanced
from between the two squadrons, sounding the trumpets; the men on Judas'
13 side blew their trumpets also, •and the earth shook with the noise of the armies.
The engagement lasted from morning until evening.
14   Judas saw that Bacchides and the main strength of his army lay on the right;
15 all the stout-hearted rallied to him, •and they broke the right wing and pursued
16 them to the furthest foothills of the range. •But when the Syrians on the left
wing saw that the right had been broken, they turned and followed hot on the
17 heels of Judas and his men to take them in the rear. •The fight became desperate,
18 and there were many casualties on both sides. •Judas himself fell, and the remnant
fled.

The funeral of Judas Maccabaeus

19   Jonathan and Simon took up their brother Judas and buried him in his
20 ancestral tomb at Modein. •All Israel wept and mourned him deeply and for
21 many days they repeated this dirge, •'What a downfall for the strong man,
22 the man who saved Israel single-handed!' •The other deeds of Judas, the battles
he fought, the exploits he performed, and all his titles to greatness have not been
recorded; but they were very many.

IV. JONATHAN, LEADER OF THE JEWS AND HIGH PRIEST

(160-142 B.C.)

The triumph of the Greek party. Jonathan leads the resistance

23   After the death of Judas the renegades came out of hiding throughout Israel
24 and all the evil-doers reappeared. •At that time there was a severe famine, and

---

b. The text of the treaty ends here, and the next paragraph is a summary of the verbal answer to
the envoys.
9 a. The Mesaloth were fortified caves.   b. About 12 m. N. of Jerusalem.

the country went over to their side. •Bacchides deliberately chose the enemies 25
of religion and set them up as governors of the country. •These traced and 26
searched out the friends of Judas and brought them before Bacchides, who
took revenge on them and humiliated them. •A terrible oppression began in Israel; 27
there had been nothing like it since the disappearance of prophecy among them.

Then all the friends of Judas came together and said to Jonathan, •'Since $^{28}_{29}$
your brother Judas died, there has been no one like him to head the resistance
to the enemy, Bacchides and those who hate our nation. •Accordingly, we have 30
today chosen you to take his place as our ruler and leader and to fight our
campaigns.' •From that day Jonathan accepted the leadership and took over 31
the command from his brother Judas.

Jonathan in the desert of Tekoa. Bloody encounters round Medeba

Bacchides, when he heard the news, made plans to kill Jonathan. •But this $^{32}_{33}$
became known to Jonathan, his brother Simon and all his supporters, and they
took refuge in the desert of Tekoa, camping by the water of the cistern at
Asphar. •(Bacchides came to know of this on the sabbath day, and he too crossed 34
the Jordan with his entire army.)

Jonathan sent his brother, who was in charge of the convoy, to request his 35
friends the Nabataeans to store their considerable baggage for them. •But 36
the sons of Jambri from Medeba^c raided them, captured John and everything
he had and made off with their prize. •After this had happened it was reported 37
to Jonathan and his brother Simon that the sons of Jambri were celebrating a
great wedding, and were escorting the bride, a daughter of one of the great
notables of Canaan, from Nadabath with a large retinue. •Remembering the 38
bloody end of their brother John, they went up and hid under cover of the
mountain. •As they were keeping watch, there came into sight a noisy procession 39
with a great deal of baggage, and the bridegroom, with his groomsmen and
his family, came out to meet it with tambourines and a band, and military display.
The Jews rushed down on them from their ambush and killed them, inflicting 40
heavy casualties; the survivors escaped to the mountain, leaving their entire
baggage train to be captured. •And so the wedding was turned into mourning 41
and the music of their band into a dirge. •Having in this way avenged in full the 42
blood of their brother they returned to the marshes of the Jordan.

Crossing the Jordan

As soon as Bacchides heard this, he came on the sabbath day with a 43
considerable force to the steep banks of the Jordan. •Jonathan said to his men, 44
'Up! Let us fight for our lives, for today is not like yesterday and the day before.
You can see, we shall have to fight on our front and to our rear, we have the 45
waters of the Jordan on one side, the marsh and scrub on the other, and we
have no line of withdrawal. •This is the moment to call on heaven for your 46
deliverance from the hand of our enemies.' •The engagement was begun by 47
Jonathan, who aimed a blow at Bacchides, but the Syrian disengaged himself
and withdrew, •whereupon Jonathan and his men leapt into the Jordan and swam 48
to the other bank, but the enemy did not cross the Jordan in pursuit. •That 49
day Bacchides lost about a thousand men.

Bacchides builds fortifications. The death of Alcimus

Bacchides returned to Jerusalem and built strongholds in Judaea, the fortress 50
in Jericho, Emmaus, Beth-horon, Bethel, Timnath, Pharathon and Tephon,
with high walls and barred gates, •and stationed a garrison in each of them to 51
harass Israel. •He also fortified the town of Bethzur, Gezer and the Citadel, 52
and placed troops in them with supplies of provisions. •He took the sons of 53
the leading men of the country as hostages, and had them placed under guard
in the Citadel of Jerusalem.

54 In the year one hundred and fifty-three, in the second month, Alcimus ordered the demolition of the wall of the inner court of the sanctuary, destroying
55 the work of the prophets.ᵈ Alcimus had just begun the demolition •when he suffered a stroke, and his work was interrupted. His mouth became obstructed, and his paralysis made him incapable of speaking at all or giving directions
56 to his household; •it was not long before he died in great agony. •When Bacchides
57 saw that Alcimus was dead he returned to the king; and the land of Judah was left in peace for two years.

The siege of Bethbasi

58 All the renegades then agreed on a plan. 'Now is the time,' they said 'while Jonathan and his supporters are living in peace and are full of confidence, for
59 us to bring back Bacchides; he can arrest them all in one night.' •So they went
60 to him and reached an understanding. •Bacchides at once set out with a large force, and sent secret instructions to all his allies in Judaea to seize Jonathan and his supporters. But they were unable to do this because their plan became
61 known, •and Jonathan and his men arrested some fifty of the men of the country who were ringleaders in the plot, and put them to death.
62 Jonathan and Simon then retired with their partisans into the wilderness
63 to Bethbasi; they rebuilt the ruinous parts of the place and fortified it. •When Bacchides heard this, he mustered his whole force and notified his adherents
64 in Judaea. •He then proceeded to lay siege to Bethbasi, attacking it for many
65 days and constructing siege-engines. •But Jonathan, leaving his brother Simon
66 in the town, broke out into the countryside with a handful of men. •He attacked Odomera and his brothers, and the sons of Phasiron in their tents; and these
67 went over to the attack, joining forces with him. •Meanwhile Simon and his
68 people made a sortie from the town and set fire to the siege-engines. •Taking the offensive against Bacchides, they routed him. He was greatly disconcerted
69 to find that his plan and his assault had come to nothing, •and vented his anger on those renegades who had induced him to enter the country, putting many
70 of them to death; then he decided to return to his own country. •Discovering this, Jonathan sent envoys to negotiate peace-terms and the release of prisoners
71 with him. •Bacchides agreed to this, accepting his proposals and swearing
72 never to seek occasion to harm him all the days of his life. •After surrendering to Jonathan the prisoners he had earlier taken in the land of Judah, he turned about and withdrew to his own country, and never again came near their frontiers.
73 The sword no longer hung over Israel, and Jonathan settled in Michmash, where he began to judge the people and to rid Israel of the godless.

Alexander Balas competes for Jonathan's support, and appoints him high priest

1 **10** In the year one hundred and sixty Alexander styled Epiphanes, son of Antiochus, landed at Ptolemais and occupied it. He was well received,
2 and held court there. •On hearing this, King Demetrius assembled a very large
3 army and marched out to meet him in battle. •Demetrius furthermore sent
4 Jonathan a conciliatory letter designed to enhance his dignity, •for, as he said, 'We had better move first to come to terms with these people before he makes
5 common cause with Alexander against us; •he will not have forgŏtten all the
6 wrongs we inflicted on him and his brothers, and on his nation'. •He therefore authorised him to raise an army and manufacture arms, and to describe himself as his ally, and ordered the hostages in the Citadel to be surrendered to him.
7 Jonathan went straight to Jerusalem and read the letter in the hearing of
8 the whole people and of the men in the Citadel. •Everyone was awestruck when
9 they heard that the king had given him authority to raise an army. •The men

c. In Transjordania, S.W. of Amman.   d. The wall, dividing the inner court from the Court of the Gentiles; Haggai and Zechariah had laboured for this and Ezekiel provided the model.

in the Citadel surrendered the hostages to Jonathan, who handed them back to
their parents. •Jonathan then took up residence in Jerusalem and began the 10
rebuilding and restoration of the city. •He ordered those responsible for the 11
work to build the walls and the defences round Mount Zion in square hewn stones
to make them stronger, and this was done. •The foreigners in the fortresses 12
built by Bacchides abandoned them, •one after another leaving his post to go 13
back to his own country. •Only at Bethzur were a few left of those who had 14
forsaken the Law and the commandments, since this served them as a place
of refuge.

King Alexander heard of all the promises Demetrius had sent to Jonathan, 15
and he was also given an account of the battles and exploits of this man and
his brothers and the trials they had endured. •'Shall we ever find another man 16
like him?' he exclaimed. 'Let us be quick to make a friend and ally of him!' •He 17
therefore wrote him a letter, addressing him in these terms, •'King Alexander 18
to his brother Jonathan, greetings. •You have been brought to our notice as 19
a strong man of action, and one disposed to be our friend. •Accordingly we 20
have today appointed you high priest of your nation, with the title of 'Friend
of the King'—he also sent him a purple robe and a golden crown—'and you
are to study our interests and maintain friendly relations with us.'

Jonathan put on the sacred vestments in the seventh month of the year one 21
hundred and sixty, on the feast of Tabernacles; he then set about raising troops
and manufacturing arms in quantity.

A letter from Demetrius I to Jonathan

Demetrius was displeased when he heard what had happened. •'What have 22 23
we done' he said 'that Alexander should have forestalled us in gaining the
friendship of the Jews to strengthen his position? •I will address an appeal to 24
them too offering them advancement and riches as an inducement to support
me.' •And he wrote to them as follows: 25

'King Demetrius to the Jewish nation, greetings. •We have heard how you 26
have kept your agreement with us and have maintained friendly relations with
us and have not gone over to our enemies, and it has given us great satisfaction.
If you now continue to keep faith with us, we will make you a handsome return 27
for what you do on our behalf. •We will accord you many exemptions and 28
grant you privileges. •Henceforth I release you and exempt all the Jews from 29
the tribute, the salt dues and the crown levies, •and whereas I am entitled to 30
levy the equivalent of one third of the sowing and one half of the fruit of the
trees, I release from this levy, from today and for the future, the land of Judah
and the three districts annexed to it from Samaria-Galilee, from this day in perpetuity. •Jerusalem shall be sacred and exempt, with its territory, tithes and 31
dues. •I relinquish control of the Citadel in Jerusalem and make it over to the 32
high priest, so that he may man it with a garrison of his own choosing. •Every 33
Jewish person taken from the land of Judah into captivity in any part of my
kingdom I set free without ransom, and decree that all shall be exempt from
taxes, even on their livestock. •All festivals, sabbaths, new moons and days 34
of special observance, and the three days before and three days after a festival,
shall all be days of exemption and quittance for all the Jews in my kingdom,
and no one shall have the right to pursue or molest any of them for any matter 35
whatsoever. •Jews shall be enrolled in the king's forces to the number of thirty 36
thousand men, and receive maintenance on the same scale as the rest of the
king's forces. •Some of them shall be stationed in the king's major fortresses, 37
and from among others appointments shall be made to positions of trust
in the kingdom. Their officers and commanders shall be appointed from their
own number, and shall live under their own laws, as the king has prescribed for
the land of Judah. •As regards the three districts annexed to Judaea from the 38
province of Samaria, they shall be integrated into Judaea and considered as

coming under one governor, obeying the high priest's authority and no other.
39 I have made over Ptolemais and its environs as a free gift to the sanctuary in
40 Jerusalem, to meet the necessary expenses of public worship. •And I make a
personal grant of fifteen thousand silver shekels annually chargeable to the
41 royal revenue from appropriate places. •And the entire surplus, which has
not been paid in by the officials as in previous years, shall henceforth be paid
42 over by them for work on the Temple. •In addition, the sum of five thousand
silver shekels, levied annually on the profits of the sanctuary, as shown in the
annual accounts, is also relinquished as the perquisite of the priests who perform
43 the liturgy. •Anyone who takes refuge in the Temple in Jerusalem or any of its
precincts, when in debt to the royal exchequer or otherwise, shall be discharged
44 in full possession of all the goods he owns in my kingdom. •As regards the
building and restoration of the sanctuary, the expense of the work shall be
45 met from the royal exchequer. •The reconstruction of the walls of Jerusalem
and the fortification of the perimeter shall also be a charge on the royal exchequer,
and so also the reconstruction of other city walls in Judaea.'

Jonathan rejects Demetrius' offers

46   When Jonathan and the people heard these proposals they put no faith
in them and refused to accept them, because they remembered the great wrongs
47 Demetrius had done in Israel and how cruelly he had oppressed them. •They
decided in favour of Alexander, since they regarded him as their outstanding
48 benefactor, and they became his constant allies. •King Alexander now mustered
49 large forces and took up a position confronting Demetrius, •and the two kings
met in battle. Alexander's army was routed, and Demetrius pursued him and
50 defeated his troops. •He continued the battle with vigour until sunset, but
Demetrius himself was killed that day.

Alexander's marriage with Cleopatra. Jonathan as military commissioner and governor-general

51   Alexander sent ambassadors to Ptolemy king of Egypt, with this message,
52 'Now that I have returned to my kingdom and ascended the throne of my
ancestors, and have established my authority by crushing Demetrius, so gaining
53 control of our country—•for I fought him and we destroyed both him and his
54 army and now occupy the throne of his kingdom—•now, therefore, let us make
a treaty of mutual friendship. Give me your daughter in marriage, and I will
become your son-in-law and give you, and her, presents which are worthy of you.'
55   King Ptolemy replied as follows, 'Happy the day when you returned to
56 the land of your ancestors and ascended their royal throne! •I will do at once for
you what your letter proposes; but meet me at Ptolemais, so that we can see
one another, and I will become your father-in-law, as you have asked.'
57   Ptolemy[a] left Egypt with his daughter Cleopatra, and reached Ptolemais
58 in the year one hundred and sixty-two. •King Alexander went to meet him, and
Ptolemy gave him the hand of his daughter Cleopatra and celebrated her wedding
59 in Ptolemais with great magnificence, as kings do. •King Alexander then wrote
60 to Jonathan to come and meet him. •Jonathan made his way in state to Ptolemais,
and met the two kings; he gave them and their friends silver and gold, and
61 many gifts, and made a favourable impression on them. •A number of scoundrels
from Israel[b] combined to denounce him, but the king paid no attention to
62 them. •In fact the king commanded that Jonathan should be divested of his
63 own garments and clothed in the purple, which was done. •The king then seated
him by his side and said to his officers, 'Escort him into the centre of the city
and proclaim that no one is to bring charges against him on any count; no one is
64 to molest him for any reason.' •And so, when his accusers saw the honour

10 a. Ptolemy VI Philometor.   b. The Jews sympathetic to hellenisation.

done him by this proclamation, and Jonathan himself invested in the purple, they all fled. •The king did him the honour of enrolling him among the First 65 Friends, and appointed him military commissioner and governor-general. Jonathan then returned to Jerusalem in peace and gladness.   66

Demetrius II. Apollonius, governor of Coele-Syria, defeated by Jonathan

In the year one hundred and sixty-five,ᶜ Demetrius son of Demetrius came 67 from Crete to the land of his ancestors. •When King Alexander heard of it he was 68 plunged in gloom and retired to Antioch. •Demetrius appointed Apollonius 69 as governor of Coele-Syria; the latter assembled a large force, and from his camp at Jamnia sent the following message to Jonathan the high priest:

'You are entirely alone in rising against us, and now I find myself ridiculed 70 and reproached on your account. Why do you use your authority to our disadvantage in the mountains? •If you are so confident in your forces, come down 71 now to meet us on the plain and let us take each other's measure there; on my side I have the strength of the towns. •Ask and learn who I am and who are 72 the others supporting us. Men will tell you that you cannot stand up to us, because your ancestors were twice routed on their own ground,ᵈ •nor will you 73 now be able to withstand the cavalry or so great an army on the plain, where there is neither stone nor outcrop nor cover of any kind.'

When Jonathan heard the message of Apollonius his spirit was roused; 74 he picked ten thousand men and left Jerusalem, and his brother Simon joined him with reinforcements. •He drew up his forces before Joppa; the citizens had 75 shut him out as Apollonius had a garrison in Joppa. When they began the attack, •the citizens took fright and opened the gates, and Jonathan occupied 76 Joppa. •Hearing this, Apollonius marshalled three thousand cavalry and a large 77 army and made his way to Azotus as though intending to march through, while in fact pressing on into the plain, since he had a great number of cavalry on which he was relying. •Jonathan pursued him as far as Azotus, where the armies 78 joined battle. •Now Apollonius had left a thousand horsemen in concealment 79 behind them. •Jonathan knew of this ambush behind him; the horsemen 80 surrounded his army and shot their arrows into the people from morning till evening. •But the people stood firm, as Jonathan had ordered, while the enemy's 81 horses tired. •So Simon was able to throw in his force and close with the 82 phalanx, which he cut to pieces and routed. •The cavalry scattered over the 83 plain and fled to Azotus, where they entered Beth-dagon, the temple of their idol, to take shelter there. •But Jonathan set fire to Azotus and the surrounding 84 towns, plundered them, and burned down the temple of Dagon, with all the fugitives who had crowded into it. •The enemy losses, counting those who 85 fell by the sword and those burnt to death, totalled about eight thousand men. Then Jonathan left there and encamped opposite Askalon, whose citizens came 86 out to meet him with great ceremony. •Jonathan then returned to Jerusalem 87 with his followers, laden with booty. •In the event, when King Alexander heard 88 what had happened, he awarded Jonathan fresh honours: •he sent him a golden 89 brooch, of the kind customarily presented to the Cousins of the King, and gave him proprietary rights over Ekron with all its lands.

Ptolemy VI supports Demetrius II but dies at the same time as Alexander Balas

11 The king of Egypt then assembled an army as numerous as the sands 1 of the seashore, with many ships, and attempted to take possession of Alexander's kingdom by a ruse and add it to his own kingdom. •He set off for 2 Syria with protestations of peace, and the people of the towns opened their gates to him and came out to meet him, since King Alexander's orders were to welcome him, Ptolemy being his father-in-law. •On entering the towns, however, 3 Ptolemy quartered troops as a garrison in each one. •When he reached Azotus 4 he was shown the burnt-out temple of Dagon, with Azotus and its suburbs

in ruins, corpses scattered here and there, and the charred remains of those whom Jonathan had burnt to death in the battle, piled into heaps along his
5 route. •They explained to the king what Jonathan had done, hoping for his
6 disapproval; but the king said nothing. •Jonathan then went to receive the king in state at Joppa, where they greeted each other and spent the night.
7 Jonathan accompanied the king as far as the river called Eleutherus,ᵃ and then
8 returned to Jerusalem. •King Ptolemy for his part occupied the coastal towns as far as the maritime quarter of Seleucia,ᵇ all the while maturing his wicked
9 designs against Alexander. •He sent envoys to King Demetrius, saying, 'Come, let us make a treaty with each other; I will give you my daughter, whom Alexander
10 now has, and you shall rule your father's kingdom. •I regret having given my
11 daughter to that man, who has attempted to kill me.' •He made this accusation
12 because he coveted his kingdom. •Having carried off his daughter and bestowed her on Demetrius, he broke with Alexander, and their enmity became open.
13 Ptolemy next entered Antioch and assumed the crown of Asia; he now wore on
14 his head the two crowns of Egypt and Asia. •Meanwhile, King Alexander was
15 in Cilicia, since the people of those parts had risen in revolt, •but when he heard the news, he advanced on his rival to give battle, while Ptolemy for his part also
16 took the field, met him with a strong force and routed him. •Alexander fled to
17 Arabia for refuge, and King Ptolemy held victory celebrations. •Zabdiel the Arab
18 cut off Alexander's head and sent it to Ptolemy. •Three days later King Ptolemy died, and the Egyptian garrisons in the strongholds were killed by the local
19 inhabitants. •So Demetrius became king in the year one hundred and sixty-seven.

Early relations between Demetrius and Jonathan

20   At the same time Jonathan mustered the men of Judaea for an assault on the Citadel in Jerusalem, and they constructed many siege-engines for use against it.
21 But some renegades who hated their nation made their way to the king and told
22 him that Jonathan was besieging the Citadel. •The king was angered by the news. No sooner had he been informed than he set out and came to Ptolemais. He wrote to Jonathan, telling him to raise the siege and to meet him for a conference
23 in Ptolemais as soon as possible. •When Jonathan heard this he gave orders for the siege to continue; then he selected a deputation from the elders of Israel
24 and the priests, and took the deliberate risk •of taking silver and gold, clothing and numerous other presents, and going to Ptolemais to face the king, whose
25 favour he succeeded in winning; •and although one or two renegades of his
26 nation brought charges against him, •the king treated him as his predecessors
27 had treated him, and promoted him in the presence of all his friends. •He confirmed him in the high-priesthood and whatever other distinctions he already
28 held, and had him ranked among the First Friends. •Jonathan claimed that the king should exempt Judaea from tribute, with the three Samaritan provinces,
29 promising him three hundred talents in return. •The king consented, and wrote Jonathan a rescript covering the whole matter, in these terms:

A new charter favouring the Jews

30   'King Demetrius to Jonathan his brother, and to the Jewish nation, greeting.
31 We have written to Lasthenes our cousin concerning you, and now send you
32 this copy of our rescript for your own information: •King Demetrius to his
33 father Lasthenes, greeting. •The nation of the Jews are our friends and fulfil their obligations to us, and in view of their goodwill towards us we have decided
34 to show them our bounty. •We confirm them in their possession of the territory of Judaea and the three districts of Aphairema, Lydda and Ramathaim;ᶜ these

---

c. 147-146 B.C.   d. By the Philistines, 1 S 4:1-11;31:1-7.
11 a. N. of Tripoli.   b. The port of Antioch.   c. Extending the boundaries of Judaea by about 12 m. to N. and W.

were annexed to Judaea from Samaritan territory, with all their dependencies, in favour of all who offer sacrifice in Jerusalem, instead of the royal dues which the king formerly received from them every year, from the yield of the soil and the fruit crops. •As regards our other rights over the tithes and taxes due to us, 35 over the salt marshes, and the crown taxes due to us, as from today we release them from them all. •No single one of these grants shall be set aside, from 36 today in perpetuity. •It shall be your responsibility to have a copy of this 37 made, to be given to Jonathan and displayed on the holy mountain in a conspicuous place.'

Demetrius II rescued by Jonathan's troops at Antioch

When King Demetrius saw that the country was at peace under his rule and 38 that no resistance was offered him, he dismissed his forces, and sent all the men home, except for the foreign troops that he had recruited in the islands of the nations, thus incurring the enmity of the veterans who had served his ancestors. Now Trypho, one of Alexander's former supporters, seeing that all the troops 39 were muttering against Demetrius, approached Iamleku the Arab, who was bringing up Antiochus, Alexander's young son, •and repeatedly urged him 40 to let him have the boy, so that he might succeed his father as king; he told him of Demetrius' decision and the resentment it had aroused among his troops. He spent a long time there. •Meanwhile Jonathan sent to ask King Demetrius 41 to withdraw the troops in the Citadel from Jerusalem and to remove the garrisons from the strongholds, since they were constantly fighting Israel. •Demetrius 42 sent back word to Jonathan, 'Not only will I do this for you and for your nation, but I will heap honours on you and your nation if I find a favourable opportunity. For the present, you would do well to send me reinforcements, for all my troops 43 have deserted.' •Jonathan sent off three thousand experienced soldiers to him 44 in Antioch; when they reached the king, he was delighted at their arrival. •The 45 citizens crowded together in the centre of the city, to the number of some hundred and twenty thousand, intending to kill the king. •The king took refuge in the 46 palace, while the citizens occupied the thoroughfares of the city and began to attack. •The king then called on the Jews for help; and these all rallied round 47 him in a body, then spread out through the city, and that day killed about a hundred thousand of its inhabitants. •They fired the city, seizing a great deal 48 of plunder at the same time, and secured the king's safety. •When the citizens 49 saw that the Jews had the city at their mercy their courage failed them, and they made an abject appeal to the king, •'Give us the right hand of peace, and 50 let the Jews stop their fight against us and the city'. •They threw down their 51 arms and made peace. The Jews were covered in glory, in the eyes of the king and of everyone else in his kingdom. Having won renown in his kingdom they returned to Jerusalem laden with booty. •King Demetrius continued to occupy the throne 52 of his kingdom, and the country was quiet under his government. •But he gave 53 the lie to all the promises he had made, and fell out with Jonathan, giving nothing in return for the services Jonathan had rendered him, but thwarting him at every turn.

Jonathan opposes Demetrius II. Simon retakes Bethzur. The Hazor affair

After this Trypho came back with the little boy Antiochus,^d who became 54 king and was crowned. •All the troops that Demetrius had summarily dismissed 55 rallied to Antiochus, and made war on Demetrius, and he turned tail and fled. Trypho captured the elephants and seized Antioch. 56

Young Antiochus then wrote Jonathan the following letter, 'I confirm you 57 in the high-priesthood and set you over the four districts^e and appoint you one of the Friends of the King'. •He sent him a service of gold plate, and granted 58 him the right to drink from gold vessels, and to wear the purple and the golden brooch. •He appointed his brother Simon as military commissioner of the 59

60 region from the Ladder of Tyre to the frontiers of Egypt. •Jonathan then set out
and made a progress through Transeuphrates and its towns, and the entire Syrian
army rallied to his support. He came to Askalon and was received in state by
61 the inhabitants. •From there he proceeded to Gaza, but the people of Gaza
shut him out, so he laid siege to it, burning down its suburbs and plundering them.
62 The people of Gaza then pleaded with Jonathan, and he made peace with them;
but he took the sons of their chief men as hostages and sent them away to
Jerusalem. He then travelled through the country as far as Damascus.
63   Jonathan now learned that Demetrius' generals had arrived at Kadesh in
64 Galilee with a great army, with the object of diverting him from his mission, •and
65 he went to meet them, leaving his brother Simon inside the country. •Simon
laid siege to Bethzur, attacking it day after day, and blockading the inhabitants
66 till they sued for peace, which he granted them, though he expelled them from
67 the town and occupied it, stationing a garrison there. •Meanwhile Jonathan
and his army, having pitched camp by the Lake of Gennesaret, rose early, and by
68 morning were already in the plain of Hazor. •The foreigners' army advanced
to fight them on the plain, after laying first an ambush for him in the mountains.
69 While the main body was advancing directly towards the Jews, •the troops in
70 ambush broke cover and attacked first. •All the men with Jonathan fled; no
one was left, except Mattathias son of Absalom and Judas son of Chalphi, the
71 generals of his army. •At this Jonathan tore his garments, put dust on his head,
72
73 and prayed. •Then he returned to the fight and routed the enemy, who fled. •When
the fugitives from his own forces saw this they came back to him and joined
in the pursuit as far as Kadesh where the enemy encampment was, and there they
74 themselves pitched camp. •About three thousand of the foreign troops fell
that day. Jonathan then returned to Jerusalem.

Jonathan's relations with the Spartans

1 12 When Jonathan saw that circumstances were working in his favour he sent
a select mission to Rome to confirm and renew his treaty of friendship
2 with the Romans. •He also sent letters to the same effect to the Spartans and
3 to other places.ᵃ •The envoys made their way to Rome and entered the Senate,
where they made this announcement: 'Jonathan the high priest and the Jewish
nation have sent us to renew your treaty of friendship and alliance with them
4 as before'. •The Romans gave them letters to the authorities of each place, to
procure their safe conduct to the land of Judah.
5   The following is the copy of the letter Jonathan wrote to the Spartans:
6   'Jonathan the high priest, the senate of the nation, the priests and the rest
7 of the Jewish people to the Spartans their brothers, greetings. •In the past,
a letter was sent to Onias, the high priest, from Areios, one of your kings, stating
8 that you are indeed our brothers, as the copy subjoined attests. •Onias received
the envoy with honour, and accepted the letter, in which a clear reference was
9 made to friendship and alliance. •For our part, though we have no need of
10 these, having the consolation of the holy books in our possession, •we venture
to send to renew our fraternal friendship with you, so that we may not become
11 strangers to you, for a long time has elapsed since you sent us the letter.ᵇ •We
may say that constantly on every occasion, at our festivals and on other appointed
days, we make a remembrance of you in the sacrifices we offer and in our prayers,
12 as it is right and fitting to remember brothers. •We rejoice in your renown.
13 As for ourselves, we have been involved in many trials, many battles, and the
14 surrounding kings have fought against us. •We were unwilling to trouble you
15 or our other allies and friends during these wars. •But now, having the support
of heaven to help us, we have been delivered from our enemies, and it is they

---

d. Antiochus VI Dionysos.   e. The three listed in v.34, and Akrabatta.
12 a. Listed in ch. 15.   b. 150 years. Onias I was high priest from 323 to 300.

who have been brought low, •and so we have chosen Numenius son of Antiochus, 16
and Antipater son of Jason, and sent them to the Romans to renew our former
treaty of friendship and alliance, •and we have ordered them to make their way to 17
you also, to greet you, and deliver to you this letter of ours concerning the
renewal of our brotherhood; •we shall be grateful for an answer to it.' 18

The following is the copy of the letter sent to Onias: 19

'Areios king of the Spartans, to Onias the high priest, greetings. •It has 20
been discovered in a document concerning the Spartans and Jews that they 21
are brothers, and of the race of Abraham. •Now that this has come to our 22
knowledge, we shall be obliged if you will send us news of your welfare. •Our 23
own message to you is this: your flocks and your possessions are ours, and
ours are yours, and we are instructing our envoys to give you a message to
this effect.'

Jonathan in Coele-Syria. Simon in Philistia

Jonathan learned that Demetrius' generals had returned with a larger army 24
than before to make war on him. •For that reason he left Jerusalem and went 25
to face them in the region of Hamath, giving them no respite in which to mount
an invasion of his own country. •He sent spies into their camp, who told him 26
on their return that the enemy were taking up positions for a night attack on
the Jews. •At sunset Jonathan ordered his men to keep watch with their weapons 27
at hand, in readiness to fight at any time during the night, and posted advance
guards all round the camp. •When they knew that Jonathan and his men were 28
ready to fight, the enemy became afraid, and with quaking hearts they kindled
fires in their camp. •Jonathan and his men, watching the glow of the fires, were 29
unaware of their withdrawal until morning, •and although Jonathan pursued 30
them, he failed to overtake them, for they had already crossed the river Eleutherus. •So Jonathan wheeled round on the Arabs called Zabadaeans, defeated 31
them and plundered them; •then, breaking camp, he went to Damascus, and 32
travelled through the whole province. •Meanwhile Simon had also set out and 33
had penetrated as far as Askalon and the neighbouring strongholds. He then
turned on Joppa and moved quickly to occupy it, •for he had heard of their 34
intention to hand over this strong point to the supporters of Demetrius; he
stationed a garrison there to hold it.

Building work in Jerusalem

On Jonathan's return he called a meeting of the elders of the people and 35
decided with them to build fortresses in Judaea •and to heighten the walls of 36
Jerusalem and erect a high barrier between the Citadel and the city, to separate
it from the city and isolate it, to prevent the occupants from buying or selling.
They gathered together to rebuild the city. Part of the wall over the eastern 37
ravine had fallen, and he restored the quarter called Chaphenatha. •Meanwhile 38
Simon rebuilt Adida in the Lowlands, fortifying it, and erecting gates with
bolts.

Jonathan falls into the hands of his enemies

Trypho's ambition was to become king of Asia, assume the crown, and 39
overpower King Antiochus. •He was apprehensive that Jonathan might not allow 40
him to do so, and might even make war on him, so he set out and came to Beth-
shan, in the hopes of finding some pretext for his arrest and execution.

Jonathan went out to intercept him, with forty thousand picked men in 41
battle order, and arrived at Bethshan. •When Trypho saw him there with 42
a large force, he hesitated to make any move against him. •He even received 43
him with honour, commended him to all his friends and presented gifts to him,
and told his friends and his troops to obey him as they would himself. •He said 44
to Jonathan, 'Why have you made all these people so tired, when there is no

45 threat of war between us? •Send them back home; pick yourself a few men as your bodyguard, and come with me to Ptolemais. I will hand it over to you, with the other fortresses and the remaining troops and all the officials; then I will take the road for home, for that was my purpose in coming here.'
46 Jonathan trusted him and did as he said; he dismissed his forces, who returned
47 to the land of Judah. •With him he retained three thousand men, of whom
48 he left two thousand in Galilee, while a thousand accompanied him. •But as soon as Jonathan had entered Ptolemais the people of Ptolemais closed the gates, seized him, and put all those who had entered with him to the sword.
49 Trypho sent troops and cavalry into Galilee and the Great Plain to wipe out all
50 Jonathan's supporters. •These, concluding that he had been taken, and had perished with his companions, encouraged one another, marching with closed
51 ranks and ready to give battle, •and when their pursuers saw that they would
52 fight for their lives, they turned back. •They all reached the land of Judah safe and sound, but lamenting Jonathan and his companions, and in a state of alarm;
53 all Israel was plunged into mourning. •All the surrounding pagans were now looking for ways of destroying them: 'They have no leader,' they said 'no ally; we have only to attack them now, and we shall blot out their very memory from mankind'.

V. SIMON, HIGH PRIEST AND ETHNARCH OF THE JEWS

(142-134 B.C.)

Simon takes command

1
2 13 Simon heard that Trypho had collected a large army to invade and devastate the land of Judah, •and when he saw how the people were quaking with
3 fear, he went up to Jerusalem, called the people together, •and exhorted them thus, 'You know yourselves how much I and my brothers and my father's family have done for the laws and the sanctuary; you know what wars and hardships
4 we have experienced. •That is why my brothers are all dead, for Israel's sake,
5 and I am the only one left. •Far be it from me, then, to be sparing of my own life in any time of oppression, for I am not worth more than my brothers.
6 Rather will I avenge my nation and the sanctuary and your wives and children,
7 now that all the pagans have united in their malice to destroy us.' •The spirit
8 of the people rekindled as they listened to his words, •and they shouted back at
9 him, 'You are our leader in place of Judas and your brother Jonathan. •Fight
10 our battles for us, and we will do whatever you tell us.'•So he assembled all the fighting men and hurried on the completion of the walls of Jerusalem, forti-
11 fying the whole perimeter. •He sent a considerable force to Joppa under Jonathan, son of Absalom, who drove out the inhabitants and remained there in occupation.

Simon repels Trypho from Judaea

12 Trypho now left Ptolemais with a large army to invade the land of Judah,
13 taking Jonathan with him under guard. •Simon pitched camp in Adida, facing
14 the plain. •When Trypho learned that Simon had stepped into the place of his brother Jonathan, and that he intended to join battle with him, he sent envoys
15 to him with this message, •'Your brother Jonathan was in debt to the royal
16 exchequer for the offices he held; that is why we are detaining him. •If you send a hundred talents of silver and two of his sons as hostages, to make sure
17 that on his release he does not revolt against us, we will release him.' •Although Simon was aware that the message was a ruse, he sent for the money and the
18 boys for fear of incurring great hostility from the people, •who would have said that Jonathan died because Simon did not send Trypho the money and
19 the boys. •He therefore sent both the boys and the hundred talents, but Trypho
20 broke his word and did not release Jonathan. •Next, Trypho set about the invasion

and devastation of the country; he made a detour along the Adora road, but Simon and his army confronted him wherever he attempted to go. •The men 21 in the Citadel kept sending messengers to Trypho, urging him to get through to them by way of the wilderness and send them supplies. •Trypho organised 22 his entire cavalry to go, but that night it snowed so heavily that he could not get through for the snow, so he struck camp and moved off into Gilead. •As 23 he approached Baskama*a* he killed Jonathan, and he was buried there. •Trypho 24 turned back and regained his own country.

Jonathan is buried in the mausoleum built by Simon at Modein

Simon sent and recovered the bones of his brother Jonathan, and buried 25 him in Modein, the town of his ancestors. •All Israel kept solemn mourning for 26 him, bewailing him for many days. •Over the tomb of his father and brothers 27 Simon raised a monument high enough to catch the eye, using dressed stone back and front. •He erected seven pyramids facing each other, for his father 28 and mother and his four brothers, •raising them on plinths and surrounding 29 them with tall columns on which he had trophies of arms carved to their ever-lasting memory and, beside the armour, sculptured ships to be seen by all who sailed the sea. •Such was the monument he constructed at Modein, and it is 30 still there today.

The favours of Demetrius II to Simon

Trypho treated the young King Antiochus treacherously and put him to 31 death. •He usurped his throne, assuming the crown of Asia, and brought great 32 havoc on the country. •Simon built up the fortresses of Judaea, surrounding 33 them with high towers, great walls and gates with bolts, and stocked these fortresses with food. •He also sent a delegation to King Demetrius to induce 34 him to grant relief to the province, because all that Trypho did was to confiscate. •King Demetrius replied to his request in a letter framed as follows: 35

'King Demetrius to Simon, high priest and Friend of Kings, and to the elders 36 and nation of the Jews, greetings. •It has pleased us to accept the golden crown 37 and the palm you have sent us, and we are disposed to make a general peace with you, and to write to the officials to grant you remissions. •Everything that 38 we have decreed concerning you remains in force, and the fortresses you have built are to remain in your hands. •We pardon all offences, unwitting or inten- 39 tional, committed up to this day, as well as the crown tax which you owe, and any other duty that used to be paid in Jerusalem shall no longer be payable. If any of you are suitable for enrolment in our bodyguard, let them be enrolled, 40 and let there be peace between us.' •It was in the year one hundred and seventy, 41 that the rule of the pagans was lifted from Israel, •and the people began to 42 engross their documents and contracts, 'In the year one of Simon, great high priest, military commissioner, and leader of the Jews.'

The capture of Gezer by Simon

At that time Simon went to lay siege to Gezer and surrounded it with his 43 troops. He constructed a mobile tower, brought it up to the city, opened a breach in one of the bastions and took it. •The men in the mobile tower sprang 44 out into the city, where great confusion ensued. •The citizens, accompanied 45 by their wives and children, mounted the ramparts with their garments torn and loudly implored Simon to make peace with them: •'Treat us' they said 'not 46 as our wickedness deserves, but as your mercy prompts you'. •Simon came to 47 terms with them and stopped the fighting; but he expelled them from the city, purified the houses which contained idols, and then made his entry with songs of praise. •He banished all uncleanness from it, settled men in it who observed 48 the Law, and having fortified it, built a residence there for himself.

Simon occupies the Citadel in Jerusalem

49 The men in the Citadel in Jerusalem, prevented as they were from going out into the country and back to buy and sell, were in desperate want of food, and 50 numbers of them were carried off by starvation. •They begged Simon to make peace with them, and he granted this, though he expelled them and purified the 51 Citadel from its pollutions. •The Jews made their entry on the twenty-third day of the second month in the year one hundred and seventy-one, with acclamations and carrying palms, to the sound of harps, cymbals and zithers, chanting hymns and canticles, since a great enemy had been crushed and thrown out of 52 Israel. •Simon made it a day of annual rejoicing. He strengthened the fortifications of the Temple hill by the side of the Citadel, and took up residence there 53 with his men. •Seeing that his son John had come to manhood, Simon appointed him commander of all the forces, with his residence in Gezer.

A eulogy of Simon

14 In the year one hundred and seventy-two King Demetrius assembled his forces and marched into Media to muster help, in order to fight Trypho. 2 When Arsaces[a] king of Persia and Media heard that Demetrius had entered his 3 territory, he sent one of his generals to capture him alive. •The general went and defeated the army of Demetrius, seized him and brought him to Arsaces, 4 who put him in prison. •The country was at peace throughout the days of Simon.

> He sought the good of his nation
> and they were well pleased with his authority,
> and his magnificence throughout his life.
>
> 5 And to crown all his magnificence
> he took Joppa and made it his harbour,
> gaining access to the islands of the sea.
>
> 6 He enlarged the frontiers of his nation,
> keeping his mastery over the homeland,
> 7 and resettled a host of the captives.
> He conquered Gezer, Bethzur, and the Citadel
> and cast out the unclean things from it;
> and no one could resist him.
>
> 8 They farmed their land in peace,
> the land gave its produce,
> the trees of the plain their fruit.
>
> 9 The elders sat at ease in the streets,
> all their talk was of their prosperity;
> the young men wore finery and armour.
>
> 10 He kept the towns supplied with provisions
> and furnished with fortifications;
> until his fame resounded to the ends of the earth.
>
> 11 He established peace in the land,
> and Israel knew great joy.
>
> 12 Each man sat under his own vine and his own fig tree,
> and there was no one to make them afraid.
>
> 13 No enemy was left in the land to fight them,
> and the kings in those days were crushed.
>
> 14 He gave strength to all the humble folk among his people
> and cleared away every renegade and wicked man.
> He strove to observe the Law,
> 15 and gave new splendour to the Temple,
> replenishing it with sacred vessels.

13 a. N.E. of Lake Tiberias.
14 a. Mithridates I, whose dynastic name was Arsaces VI.

Renewal of the alliances with Sparta and with Rome

When it became known in Rome and later in Sparta that Jonathan was ¹⁶ dead, people were deeply grieved. •But as soon as they heard that his brother ¹⁷ Simon had succeeded him as high priest and was master of the country and the cities in it, •they wrote to him on bronze tablets to renew the treaty of ¹⁸ friendship and alliance which they had made with his brothers, Judas and Jonathan, •and the document was read out before the assembly in Jerusalem. ¹⁹ This is the copy of the letter sent by the Spartans: ²⁰

'The rulers and the city of Sparta to Simon the high priest and to the elders and priests and the rest of the people of the Jews, greetings. •The ambassadors ²¹ whom you sent to our people informed us of your glory and honour, and we were delighted by their visit. •We recorded their declarations in the minutes ²² of our public assemblies, as follows, "Numenius son of Antiochus, and Antipater son of Jason, ambassadors of the Jews, came to us to renew their friendship with us. •And it was the people's pleasure to receive these personages with honours ²³ and to deposit a copy of their statements in the public archives, so that the people of Sparta may preserve a record of them; they also made a copy for Simon the high priest." '

After this Simon sent Numenius to Rome as the bearer of a large gold shield ²⁴ weighing a thousand minas, to confirm the alliance with them.

Official honours decreed for Simon

When these events were reported to the people they said, 'What mark of ²⁵ appreciation shall we give to Simon and his sons? •He stood firm, he and ²⁶ his brothers and his father's House; he fought off the enemies of Israel and secured its freedom.' So they recorded an inscription on bronze tablets and set it up on pillars on Mount Zion. •This is a copy of the text: ²⁷

'On the eighteenth of Elul in the year one hundred and seventy-two, which is the third year of Simon the great high priest, in Asaramel, •in the grand ²⁸ assembly of priests and people, leaders of the nation and elders of the country, we were notified as follows:

'When there was frequent fighting in the country, Simon. son of Mattathias, ²⁹ a scion of the line of Joarib, and his brothers courted danger and withstood the enemies of their nation to safeguard the integrity of their sanctuary and the Law, and so brought their nation great glory. •Jonathan rallied his nation ³⁰ and became their high priest, and was then gathered to his people. •Their ³¹ enemies planned to invade their country in order to devastate their territory and lay hands on their sanctuary. •Simon then arose to fight for his nation. ³² He spent much of his own wealth on arming the nation's fighting men and providing their pay; •he fortified the cities of Judaea and Bethzur on the frontier ³³ of Judaea, where the enemy arsenal had formerly been, and stationed there a garrison of Jewish soldiers. •He also fortified Joppa on the coast and Gezer ³⁴ on the borders of Azotus, a place formerly inhabited by the enemy; he founded a Jewish settlement there, providing everything they needed to set them on their feet. •The people saw Simon's faith and the glory he had resolved to win ³⁵ for his nation; they made him their leader and high priest because of all these achievements of his and the justice and faithfulness he had maintained towards his own nation, and because he sought every means to enhance the honour of his people. •In his day and under his guidance they succeeded in rooting ³⁶ out the pagans from their country, including those in the City of David in Jerusalem, who had converted it into a citadel for their own use from which they would sally out to defile the surroundings of the sanctuary and violate its sacred character. •He settled Jewish soldiers in it and fortified it as a protection ³⁷ for the country and city, and heightened the walls of Jerusalem. •In consequence ³⁸ of this, King Demetrius confirmed him in the high-priestly office, •made him one ³⁹ of his Friends and advanced him to high honours; •he had heard that the Romans ⁴⁰

41 named the Jews friends, allies and brothers, and that they had given Simon's ambassadors an honourable reception; •and further, that the Jews and the priests had agreed that Simon should be their perpetual leader and high priest until a

42 trustworthy prophet should arise; •he was also to be their commissioner and to be responsible for the sanctuary and for the appointment of officials to supervise the fabric, to administer the country, and to control the arsenal and fortresses;

43 he was to take charge of the sanctuary, and everyone had to obey him; all official documents in the country were to be drawn up in his name; he was to assume

44 the purple and wear golden ornaments. •No member of the public or the priesthood was to be allowed to set aside any one of these articles or contest his decisions, or convene a meeting anywhere in the country without his leave,

45 or assume the purple or wear the golden brooch. •Anyone contravening or

46 rejecting any of these articles was to be liable at law. •All the people consented

47 to grant Simon the right to act on these decisions. •And Simon accepted and consented to assume the high-priestly office and to act as military commissioner and ethnarch[b] of the Jews and their priests, and to preside over all.'

48 They ordered that this decree should be inscribed on bronze tablets and

49 set up in the Temple precinct in a prominent place, •and that copies should be deposited in the treasury, and made available to Simon and his sons.

Antiochus VII recognises Simon's titles, and besieges Trypho in Dor

15 Antiochus, son of King Demetrius, addressed a letter from the islands of the sea to Simon, priest and ethnarch of the Jews, and to the whole

2 nation; •this was how it read:

'King Antiochus to Simon, high priest and ethnarch, and to the Jewish

3 nation, greetings. •Whereas certain scoundrels have seized control of the kingdom of our fathers, and I propose to claim back the kingdom so that I may re-establish it as it was before, and whereas I have accordingly recruited very

4 large forces and fitted out warships, •intending to make a landing in the country and deal with the men who have ruined it and laid waste many towns in my

5 kingdom, •now therefore I confirm in your favour all the remissions of tribute that my royal predecessors granted you, with any other concessions that they

6 granted to you. •I hereby authorise you to mint your own coinage as legal tender

7 for your own country. •I declare Jerusalem and the sanctuary exempt; all the arms

8 you have manufactured and the fortresses you have built and now occupy are to remain yours. •All debts to the royal treasury, present or future, shall be

9 cancelled from henceforth in perpetuity. •When we have gained possession of our kingdom we will bestow such great honour on yourself, your nation and the Temple as shall exhibit your glory to the whole world.'

10 In the year one hundred and seventy-four Antiochus mounted his expedition against the land of his ancestors, and all the troops rallied to him, so that few

11 remained with Trypho. •Antiochus pursued the usurper, who took refuge

12 in Dor on the coast, •knowing that misfortunes were piling up on him and

13 that his troops had deserted him. •Antiochus pitched camp before Dor with

14 a hundred and twenty thousand fighting men and eight thousand cavalry. •He laid siege to the city while the ships closed in from the sea, so that he had the city under attack from land and sea, and allowed no one to go in or come out.

The ambassadors return from Rome to Judaea; the alliance with Rome proclaimed

15 Meanwhile Numenius and his companions arrived from Rome carrying letters addressed to various kings and states, in the following terms:

16
17 'Lucius,[a] consul of the Romans, to King Ptolemy, greetings. •The Jewish ambassadors have come to us as our friends and allies to renew our original

b. The recognised head of a racial unit within the empire.
15 a. Probably Lucius Calpurnius Piso, consul in 130.

friendship and alliance in the name of the high priest Simon and the Jewish people. •They have brought a gold shield worth a thousand minas. •Accordingly ¹⁸ we have decided to write to various kings and states, warning them not to molest them nor to attack them or their towns or their country, nor ally themselves with any such aggressors. •We have decided to accept the shield from them. 20 If then any scoundrels have fled their country to take refuge with you, hand them 21 over to Simon the high priest to be punished by him according to their law.'

The consul sent the same letter to King Demetrius, to Attalus, Ariarathes 22 and Arsaces, •and to all states, including Sampsames, the Spartans, Delos, 23 Myndos, Sicyon, Caria, Samos, Pamphylia, Lycia, Halicarnassus, Rhodes, Phaselis, Cos, Side, Aradus, Gortyna, Cnidus, Cyprus and Cyrene. •They 24 also drew up a copy for Simon the high priest.

Antiochus VII, besieging Dor, becomes hostile to Simon and sends him a reprimand

Meanwhile Antiochus, from his positions on the outskirts of Dor, was 25 continually throwing detachments against the town. He constructed siege-engines, and blockaded Trypho, preventing movement in or out. •Simon sent 26 him two thousand picked men to support him in the fight, with silver and gold and plenty of equipment. •But Antiochus would not accept them; instead, 27 he repudiated all his previous agreements with Simon, and completely changed his attitude to him. •He sent him Athenobius, one of his friends, for an interview 28 at which he was to say, 'You are now occupying Joppa and Gezer and the Citadel in Jerusalem, which are towns in my kingdom. •You have laid waste 29 their territory and done immense harm to the country; and you have seized many localities belonging to my kingdom. •Now either surrender the towns 30 you have taken, with the revenue from the localities you have seized beyond the limits of Judaea, •or else pay me five hundred talents of silver in compensation 31 for them and for the destruction you have done, and another five hundred talents for the revenues of the towns; otherwise we shall come and make war on you.' •When Athenobius, one of the Friends of the King, reached Jerusalem 32 and saw Simon's magnificence, his cabinet of gold and silver plate, and his large retinue, he was dumbfounded. He delivered the king's message, •but Simon 33 gave him this answer, 'It is not any foreign land that we have taken, nor any foreign property that we have seized, but the inheritance of our ancestors, for some time unjustly wrested from us by our enemies; •now that we have a 34 favourable opportunity, we are merely recovering the inheritance of our ancestors. •As for Joppa and Gezer, which you claim, these were towns that did 35 great harm to the people and laid waste the countryside; we are prepared to give a hundred talents for them.' Without so much as a word in answer, •the 36 envoy went back to the king in a rage and reported on Simon's answer and his magnificence, and on everything he had seen, at which the king fell into a fury.

Cendebaeus, governor of the Littoral, harasses Judaea

Trypho now boarded a ship and escaped to Orthosia. •The king appointed ³⁷ Cendebaeus commander-in-chief of the coastal region and allotted him a force ³⁸ of infantry and cavalry. •He ordered him to deploy his men facing Judaea, 39 and instructed him to strengthen Kedron and fortify its gates, and to make war on the people, while the king himself went in pursuit of Trypho. •Cendebaeus 40 arrived at Jamnia and began to harry the people forthwith, invading Judaea, imprisoning the people and massacring them. •He strengthened Kedron and 41 stationed cavalry and troops there to make sorties and patrol the roads of Judaea, as the king had instructed him.

The victory of Simon's sons over Cendebaeus

16 John then went up from Gezer and reported to his father Simon what 1 Cendebaeus was busy doing. •At this, Simon summoned his two elder 2 sons, Judas and John, and said to them, 'I and my brothers and my father's

House have fought the enemies of Israel from our youth until today; the enterprises we directed have been successful, and many a time have we brought Israel
3 deliverance. •But now I am an old man, while you, mercifully, are old enough;
take my place and my brother's, go out and fight for our nation, and may the
4 support of heaven be with you.' •Then he selected from the country twenty
thousand fighting men and cavalry, and these marched against Cendebaeus,
5 spending the night at Modein. •Making an early start, they marched into the
plain, to find a large army opposing them, both infantry and cavalry; there was,
6 however, a wadi in between. •John drew up facing them, he and his people,
and seeing that the men were afraid to cross the wadi he crossed over first
7 himself. When his men saw this, they too crossed after him. •He divided his
army into two bodies of foot, with the horse in the centre, the enemy's cavalry
8 being very numerous. •The trumpets rang out, and Cendebaeus was routed
with his army; many of them fell mortally wounded, and the remainder took
9 refuge in the fortress. •It was then that Judas, John's brother, was wounded,
but John pursued them until Cendebaeus reached Kedron, which he had
10 strengthened. •Their flight took them as far as the towers in the countryside
of Azotus, and John burnt these down. The enemy losses amounted to ten
thousand men; John returned safely to Judaea.

Simon's tragic death at Dok. His son John succeeds him

11   Ptolemy son of Abubus had been appointed military commissioner for the
12 plain of Jericho; he owned much silver and gold, •and was the high priest's
13 son-in-law. •His ambition was fired; he hoped to make himself master of the
14 whole country, and began to plot the ruin of Simon and his sons. •Simon,
who was inspecting the towns up and down the country and attending to their
administration, had come down to Jericho with his sons Mattathias and Judas,
in the year one hundred and seventy-seven, in the eleventh month, the month
15 of Shebat. •The son of Abubus lured them into a small fortress called Dok,ᵃ
which he had built, where he offered them a great banquet, having men concealed
16 about the place. •When Simon and his sons were drunk, Ptolemy leapt to his
feet with his men, and, grasping their weapons, they rushed on Simon in the
banqueting hall and killed him with his two sons and some of his servants.
17 So he committed a great act of treachery, and rendered evil for good.
18 Ptolemy wrote a report of the affair and sent it to the king, in the expectation
of being sent reinforcements and having the cities and the province made over to
19 him. •He sent other men to Gezer to murder John, and sent written orders
to the military commanders to come to him so that he could present them
20 with silver and gold and gifts; •he also sent others to take possession of Jerusalem
21 and the Temple hill. •But someone had been too quick for him and had already
informed John in Gezer that his father and brothers had perished, adding, 'He
22 is also sending people to kill you too!' •Overcome as he was by the news, John
arrested the men who had come to kill him and put them to death, since he
23 already knew their murderous design. •The rest of John's acts, the battles he
fought and the exploits he performed, the city walls he built, and all his other
24 achievements, •are to be found recorded in the Annals of his pontificate from
the day he succeeded his father as high priest.

16 a. On a clifftop above the plain of Jericho.

THE SECOND BOOK OF
MACCABEES

I. LETTERS TO THE JEWS OF EGYPT

FIRST LETTER

1 Greetings to their brothers, the Jews in Egypt, from their brothers, the 1
Jews in Jerusalem and in the country of Judaea, and prosperity and peace.
May God prosper you, remembering his covenant with Abraham, Isaac and 2
Jacob, his faithful servants. •May he give you all a heart to worship him and 3
to do his will with a generous mind and a willing spirit. •May he open your 4
hearts to his Law and his precepts, and give you peace. •May he hear your 5
prayers and be reconciled with you, and not abandon you in time of evil. •Here 6
we are now praying for you. •When Demetrius was king, in the year one hundred 7
and sixty-nine, we Jews wrote to you as follows, 'In the desperate affliction
that has come on us in these years since Jason and his associates betrayed the
Holy Land and the kingdom, •they burned the Temple gateway and shed innocent 8
blood. Then we prayed to the Lord and were heard; we offered a sacrifice with
wheat-flour, kindled the lamps and set out the loaves'. •And we now recommend 9
you to keep the feast of Tabernacles of the month of Chislev. In the year one
hundred and eighty-eight.*

SECOND LETTER*b*

Address

The people of Jerusalem and of Judaea, the senate and Judas,*c* to Aristobulus, 10
tutor to King Ptolemy and one of the family of the anointed priests, and to the
Jews in Egypt, greetings and good health.

Thanksgiving for the punishment of Antiochus

Since we have been rescued by God from great dangers, we give him great 11
thanks for championing our cause against the king, •for it was He who drove out 12
those who had taken up arms against the Holy City. •For when their leader 13
reached Persia with his seemingly irresistible army, he was cut to pieces in the
temple of Nanaea,*d* as the result of a ruse employed by the priests who served that
goddess. •On the pretext of making a marriage with Nanaea, Antiochus came 14
to the place with his friends, intending to take its many treasures as a dowry.
The priests of Nanaea had put these on display, and he entered the sacred 15
precincts with a small retinue. As soon as Antiochus was inside they closed the
temple, •opened the secret door in the ceiling and struck down the leader and 16
his party by hurling stones like thunderbolts. They then dismembered them,
cut off their heads and flung them to those outside. •Blessed in all things be our 17
God, who has given the godless their deserts!

The miraculous preservation of the sacred fire

18 As we shall be celebrating the purification of the Temple on the twenty-fifth of Chislev, we consider it proper to notify you, so that you may celebrate the feast of Tabernacles and of the fire that appeared when Nehemiah, the 19 builder of the Temple and the altar, offered sacrifice. •For when our ancestors were being deported to Persia the devout priests of the time took some of the fire from the altar and hid it secretly in the hollow of a dry well, where they 20 concealed it in such a way that the place was unknown to anyone. •When some years had elapsed, in God's good time, Nehemiah, commissioned by the king of Persia, sent the descendants of the priests who had hidden the fire to recover it; but they notified us that they had found not fire but a thick liquid. Nehemiah 21 ordered them to draw some out and bring it back. •When the materials for the sacrifice had been set out, Nehemiah ordered the priests to pour the liquid over 22 the wood and what lay on it. •When this had been done, and when in due course the sun, which had previously been clouded over, shone out, a great fire flared 23 up, to the astonishment of all. •While the sacrifice was being burned, the priests and all those present with the priests offered prayer, Jonathan intoning 24 and the rest responding with Nehemiah. •The prayer took this form: 'Lord, Lord God, creator of all things, dreadful, strong, just, merciful, the only king 25 and benefactor, •the only provider, who alone are just, almighty and everlasting, the deliverer of Israel from every evil, who made our fathers your chosen ones 26 and sanctified them, •accept this sacrifice on behalf of all your people Israel, and 27 protect your heritage and consecrate it. •Bring together those cf us who are dispersed, set free those in slavery among the heathen, look favourably on those held in contempt or abhorrence, and let the heathen know that you are 28/29 our God. •Punish those who oppress us and affront us by their insolence, •and plant your people firmly in your Holy Place, as Moses promised.'

30/31 The priests then chanted hymns. •When the sacrifice was all burned, Nehemiah 32 ordered the remaining liquid to be poured over large stones, •and when this was done a flame flared up, to be absorbed in the corresponding blaze of light 33 from the altar. •When the matter became known and the king of the Persians heard that in the place where the exiled priests had hidden the fire a liquid had appeared, with which Nehemiah and his people had purified the materials of the 34 sacrifice, •the king after verifying the facts, had the place enclosed and 35 pronounced sacred. •The king exchanged many valuable presents with those 36 who enjoyed his favour. •Nehemiah and his people termed this stuff 'nephtar', which means 'purification', but it is generally called 'naphtha'.

Jeremiah conceals the tabernacle, ark and altar

1 2 We find in the archives that the prophet Jeremiah,[a] when he had given the 2 deportees the order to take the fire, as we have described, •in giving them the Law warned the deportees never to forget the Lord's precepts, nor to let their thoughts be tempted by the sight of gold and silver statues or the finery 3 adorning them. •Among other similar admonitions he urged them not to 4 let the Law depart from their hearts. •The document also described how the prophet, warned by an oracle, gave orders for the tabernacle and the ark to go with him when he set out for the mountain which Moses had climbed to survey 5 God's heritage. •On his arrival Jeremiah found a cave-dwelling, into which he brought the tabernacle, the ark and the altar of incense, afterwards blocking

up the entrance. •Some of his companions came up to mark out the way, but 6 were unable to find it. •When Jeremiah learned this, he reproached them: 'The 7 place is to remain unknown' he said 'until God gathers his people together again and shows them his mercy. •Then the Lord will bring these things once 8 more to light, and the glory of the Lord will be seen, and so will the cloud, as it was revealed in the time of Moses and when Solomon prayed that the Holy Place might be gloriously hallowed.' •It was also recorded how Solomon in his wisdom 9 offered the sacrifice of the dedication and completion of the sanctuary. •As 10 Moses had prayed to the Lord and fire had come down from heaven and burned up the sacrifice, so Solomon also prayed, and the fire from above burned up the holocausts. •Moses had said, 'It is because it had not been eaten 11 that the sin-offering was burned up'. •Solomon kept the feast in the same way 12 for eight days.

Nehemiah's library

In addition to the above, it was also recorded, both in the archives and in the 13 Memoirs of Nehemiah,[b] how he founded a library and made a collection of the books dealing with the kings and the prophets, the writings of David and the letters of the kings on the subject of offerings. •In the same way Judas made a 14 complete collection of the books dispersed in the late war, and these we still have. •If you need any of them, send someone to fetch copies for you.   15

An invitation to the dedication

To conclude, since we are now about to celebrate the purification of the 16 Temple, we are writing to you requesting you to observe the same days. •God, 17 who has saved his whole people, conferring on all the heritage, kingdom, priesthood and sanctification •as he promised through the Law, will surely, as 18 our hope is in him, be swift to show us mercy and gather us together from everywhere under heaven to the Holy Place, since he has rescued us from great evils and has purified the Temple.

II. COMPILER'S PREFACE

The story of Judas Maccabaeus and his brothers, the purification of the great 19 Temple, the dedication of the altar, •together with the wars against Antiochus 20 Epiphanes and his son Eupator, •and the manifestations from heaven that 21 came to hearten the brave champions of Judaism, so that, few though they were, they despoiled the whole country, routed the barbarian hordes, •recovered 22 the sanctuary renowned the whole world over, liberated the city and re-established the laws which were all but abolished, the Lord showing his favour by all his gracious help to them—•all this, already related in five books by Jason of 23 Cyrene, we shall attempt to condense into a single digest. •Considering the spate of 24 figures and the difficulty encountered, because of the mass of material, by those who wish to immerse themselves in historical records, •we have aimed at providing 25 diversion for those who merely want something to read, a saving of labour for those who enjoy committing things to memory, and profit for each and all. For us who have undertaken the drudgery of this abridgement, this has been 26 no easy task but a matter of sweat and midnight oil, •comparable to the exacting 27 task of a man organising a banquet, whose aim is to satisfy a variety of tastes; nevertheless, for the sake of rendering a general service we remain glad to endure this drudgery, •leaving accuracy of detail to the historian and concen- 28 trating our effort on tracing the outlines in this condensed version. •Just as the 29 architect of a new house is responsible for the construction as a whole, while the man undertaking the ceramic painting is responsible for estimating the decorative requirements, so, I think, it is with us. •To make the subject his own, 30

31 to explore its by-ways, to be meticulous about details, is the business of the
original historian, •but the man making the adaptation must be allowed to aim
at conciseness of expression and to forgo any exhaustive treatment of his
subject.

32 So now let us begin our narrative, without adding any more to what has been
said above; there would be no sense in expanding the preface to the history and
curtailing the history itself.

III. THE STORY OF HELIODÓRUS

The arrival of Heliodorus in Jerusalem

1 3 While the Holy City was inhabited in all peace and the laws were observed
as perfectly as possible, through the piety of Onias the high priest and his
2 hatred of wickedness, •it came about that the kings themselves honoured the
Holy Place and enhanced the glory of the Temple with the most splendid
3 offerings, •even to the extent that Seleucus* king of Asia defrayed from his own
4 revenues all the expenses arising out of the sacrificial services. •But a certain
Simon, of the tribe of Bilgah, on being appointed administrator of the Temple,
came into conflict with the high priest over the regulation of the city markets.
5 Unable to get the better of Onias, he went off to Apollonius of Tarsus,
6 who at that time was military commissioner for Coele-Syria and Phoenicia, •and
made out to him that the Treasury in Jerusalem was groaning with untold
wealth, that the amount contributed was incalculable and out of all proportion
to expenditure on the sacrifice, but that it could all be brought under the control
7 of the king. •Apollonius met the king and told him about the wealth that had
been disclosed to him; whereupon the king selected Heliodorus, his chancellor,
and sent him with instructions to effect the removal of the reported wealth.
8 Heliodorus lost no time in setting out, ostensibly to inspect the towns of Coele-
9 Syria and Phoenicia, but in fact to accomplish the king's purpose. •On his arrival
in Jerusalem, and after a hospitable reception from the high priest and the city,
he announced what had been disclosed, thus revealing the reason for his presence,
10 and asked if this was indeed the true situation. •The high priest explained that
·1 there were funds set aside for widows and orphans, •with some belonging to
Hyrcanus son of Tobias, a man occupying a very exalted position, and that the
whole sum, in contrast to what the evil Simon had alleged, amounted to four
12 hundred talents of silver and two hundred of gold. •He added also that it was
entirely out of the question that an injustice should be done to those who had put
their trust in the sanctity of the place and the inviolable majesty of a Temple
venerated throughout the entire world.

Consternation in Jerusalem

13 But Heliodorus, because of his instructions from the king, peremptorily insisted
14 that the funds must be confiscated for the royal exchequer. •Fixing a day for
the purpose, he went in to draw up an inventory of the funds. There was
15 consternation throughout the city; •the priests in their sacred vestments prostrated
themselves before the altar and called upon heaven, the author of the law
16 governing deposits, to preserve these funds intact for the depositors. •The
appearance of the high priest was enough to pierce the heart of the beholder,
17 his expression and his altered colour betraying the anguish of his soul; •the man
was so overwhelmed by fear and bodily trembling that those who saw him
18 could not possibly mistake the distress he was suffering. •People rushed headlong from the houses intent on making public supplication because of the

b. An uncanonical book, not the memoir included in Ezra-Nehemiah.
3 a. Seleucus IV, who ruled 186-175 B.C.

indignity threatening the Holy Place. •Women thronged the streets swathed in 19
sackcloth below their breasts; girls secluded indoors ran together, some to the
doorways, some to the city walls, while others leaned out of the windows, •all 20
stretching out their hands to heaven in entreaty. •It was pitiful to see the 21
people crowding together to prostrate themselves and the foreboding of the high
priest in his deep anguish. •While they were calling on the all-powerful Lord to 22
preserve the deposits intact for the depositors, in full security, •Heliodorus 23
carried on with his appointed task.

The punishment of Heliodorus

He had already arrived with his bodyguard near the Treasury, when the 24
Sovereign of spirits and of every power caused so great an apparition that all
who had dared to accompany Heliodorus were dumbfounded at the power of
God, and were reduced to abject terror. •Before their eyes appeared a horse 25
richly caparisoned and carrying a fearsome rider. Rearing violently, it struck at
Heliodorus with its forefeet. The rider was seen to be accoutred entirely in gold.
Two other young men of outstanding strength and radiant beauty, magnificently 26
apparelled, appeared to him at the same time, and taking their stand on either
side of him flogged him unremittingly, inflicting stroke after stroke. •Suddenly 27
Heliodorus fell to the ground, enveloped in thick darkness. His men came to
his rescue and placed him in a litter, •this man who but a moment before had made 28
his way into the Treasury, as we said above, with a great retinue and his whole
bodyguard; and as they carried him away, powerless to help himself, they openly
acknowledged the sovereign power of God.
While Heliodorus lay prostrate under the divine visitation, speechless and 29
bereft of all hope of deliverance, •the Jews blessed the Lord who had miraculously 30
glorified his own Holy Place. And the Temple, which a little while before had
been filled with terror and commotion, now overflowed with joy and gladness
at the manifestation of the almighty Lord. •Some of Heliodorus' companions 31
quickly begged Onias to call upon the Most High, to bestow life on a man lying
at the very point of death.
The high priest, afraid that the king might suspect the Jews of some foul 32
play concerning Heliodorus, did indeed offer a sacrifice for the man's recovery.
And while the high priest was performing the rite of atonement, the same young 33
men again appeared to Heliodorus wearing the same apparel, and standing
beside him said, 'Be very grateful to Onias the high priest, since it is for his
sake that the Lord has granted you your life. •As for you, who have been 34
scourged from heaven, you must proclaim to all men the grandeur of God's
power.' So saying, they vanished.

The conversion of Heliodorus

Heliodorus offered sacrifice to the Lord and made most solemn vows to the 35
preserver of his life, and then took courteous leave of Onias and marched his forces
back to the king. •He openly testified to all men of the works of the supreme God 36
which he had seen with his own eyes. •When the king asked Heliodorus what 37
sort of man would be the right person to send to Jerusalem on a second occasion,
he replied, •'If you have some enemy or a rebel against the government, send 38
him there, and you will get him back well flogged, if he survives at all, for there
is certainly some peculiar power of God about that place. •He who has his 39
dwelling in heaven watches over the place and defends it, and he strikes down and
destroys those who come to harm it.' •This was the outcome of the affair of 40
Heliodorus and the preservation of the Treasury.

IV. HELLENISTIC PROPAGANDA
AND PERSECUTION UNDER ANTIOCHUS EPIPHANES

The misdeeds of Simon, administrator of the Temple

1 4 The Simon mentioned above as the informer against the funds and his own country began to slander Onias, insinuating that it was the high priest who had treated Heliodorus so harshly and had himself contrived these startling 2 events. •Simon now had the effrontery to name this benefactor of the city, this protector of his compatriots, this zealot for the laws, as an enemy of the public 3 good. •This hostility reached such proportions that murders were actually 4 committed by some of Simon's agents, •and at this point Onias, recognising how mischievous this rivalry was, and aware that Apollonius son of Menestheus, military commissioner for Coele-Syria and Phoenicia, was encouraging Simon 5 in his malice, •went to see the king, not to play the accuser of his fellow citizens, but having the public and private welfare of the entire people at heart. 6 He saw that without some intervention by the king an orderly administration would no longer be possible, nor would Simon be forced to put a stop to his folly.

Jason, the high priest, introduces hellenism

7 When Seleucus had departed this life and Antiochus styled Epiphanes had succeeded to the kingdom, Jason, brother of Onias,[a] usurped the high-priesthood 8 by underhand methods; •he approached the king with a promise of three hundred and sixty talents of silver, with eighty talents to come from some other 9 source of revenue. •He further committed himself to guarantee another hundred and fifty if he was allowed to use his authority to establish a gymnasium and a 10 youth centre, and to enrol men in Jerusalem as Antiochists. •When the king gave his assent, Jason set about introducing his fellow countrymen to the Greek 11 way of life as soon as he was in power. •He suppressed the existing royal concessions to the Jews, granted at the instance of John, father of that Eupolemus who was later to be sent on the embassy of friendship and alliance with the Romans, and, overthrowing the lawful institutions, introduced new usages 12 contrary to the Law. •He went so far as to plant a gymnasium at the very foot of 13 the Citadel, and to fit out the noblest of his cadets in the petasos.[b] •Godless wretch that he was and no true high priest, Jason set no bounds to his impiety; indeed the 14 hellenising process reached such a pitch •that the priests ceased to show any interest in the services of the altar; scorning the Temple and neglecting the sacrifices, they would hurry to take part in the unlawful exercises on the training 15 ground as soon as the signal was given for the discus. •They disdained all that 16 their ancestors had esteemed, and set the highest value on hellenic honours. •But all this brought its own retribution; the very people whose way of life they envied, whom they sought to resemble in everything, proved to be their enemies and 17 executioners. •It is no small thing to violate the divine laws, as the period that followed will demonstrate.

18 On the occasion of the quinquennial games at Tyre in the presence of the 19 king, •the vile Jason sent some Antiochists from Jerusalem as official spectators; these brought with them three hundred silver drachmae for the sacrifice to Hercules. But even those who brought the money thought it should not be spent on the sacrifice—this would not be right—and decided to reserve it for some other 20 item of expenditure; •and so what the sender had intended for the sacrifice to Hercules was in fact applied, at the suggestion of those who brought it, to the construction of triremes.

---

4 a. Joshua, brother of Onias; the change of his name to Jason is evidence of his sympathies with hellenisation.   b. The hat of Hermes, worn by athletes.

Antiochus Epiphanes is acclaimed in Jerusalem

Apollonius son of Menestheus had been sent to Egypt to attend the 21
enthronement of King Philometor. Learning that the king had become hostile
to his policies, Antiochus began to think of his own safety; and so he left Joppa
and moved to Jerusalem. •He was given a magnificent welcome by Jason and the 22
city, and was received with torches and acclamations; following this, he withdrew
his army to Phoenicia.

Menelaus becomes high priest

When three years had passed, Jason sent Menelaus, brother of the Simon 23
mentioned above, to convey the money to the king and get his decisions on
various essential matters made effective. •But Menelaus, on being presented to 24
the king, flattered him by his own appearance of authority, and so secured the
high-priesthood for himself, outbidding Jason by three hundred talents of silver.
He returned with the royal mandate, bringing nothing worthy of the high- 25
priesthood and supported only by the fury of a cruel tyrant and the rage of a
savage beast. •Thus Jason, who had supplanted his own brother, was in turn 26
supplanted by a third, and obliged to take refuge in Ammonite territory. •As for 27
Menelaus, he retained his high office, but he defaulted altogether on the sums
promised to the king, •although Sostratus, the commandant of the Citadel, 28
whose business it was to collect the revenue, kept demanding payment. The pair
of them in consequence were summoned before the king, •Menelaus leaving his 29
brother Lysimachus as deputy high priest, while Sostratus left Crates, the
commander of the Cypriots, to act for him.

The murder of Onias

While all this was going on, it happened that the people of Tarsus and Mallus 30
revolted, because their towns had been given as a present to Antiochis, the
king's concubine. •The king therefore hurried off to settle the affair, leaving 31
Andronicus, one of his dignitaries, to act as his deputy. •Thinking he had found 32
a favourable opportunity, Menelaus abstracted a number of golden vessels
from the Temple and presented them to Andronicus, and managed to sell others
to Tyre and the surrounding cities. •On receiving clear evidence to this effect, 33
Onias retired to a place of sanctuary at Daphne near Antioch and then taxed him
with it. •Thereupon Menelaus, taking Andronicus aside, urged him to murder 34
Onias. Andronicus sought out Onias and, after deceitfully reassuring him by
offering him his right hand on oath, succeeded in persuading him, in spite of
his lingering suspicions, to leave the sanctuary; whereupon he immediately put
him to death, in defiance of all justice. •The result was that not only the Jews 35
but many of the other nations were appalled and indignant at this impious murder.
On the king's return from the region of Cilicia, the Jews of the capital, and 36
those Greeks who shared their hatred of the crime, appealed to him about the
insensate murder of Onias. •Antiochus was profoundly grieved and filled with 37
pity, and he wept for the prudence and great moderation of the dead man. •His 38
indignation was roused, and he immediately stripped Andronicus of the purple,
tore his garments off him, and, parading him through the length of the city, rid the
world of the assassin on the very spot where he had laid impious hands on Onias,
the Lord dealing out to him the punishment he deserved.

Lysimachus killed in an insurrection

Now Lysimachus, with the connivance of Menelaus, had committed many 39
sacrilegious thefts in the city, and when the facts had become widely known,
the populace rose against Lysimachus, who had already disposed of many
pieces of gold plate. •The infuriated mob was becoming menacing, and 40
Lysimachus armed nearly three thousand men and took aggressive action; the
troops were led by a certain Auranus, a man advanced in years and no less in

41 folly. •Recognising this act of aggression as the work of Lysimachus, some
snatched up stones, others cudgels, while others scooped up handfuls of ashes lying
42 at hand, and all hurled everything indiscriminately at Lysimachus' men, •to such
effect that they wounded many of them, even killing a few, and routed them all;
the Temple robber himself they killed outside the treasury.

Menelaus buys his acquittal

43
44   As a result of this, legal proceedings were taken against Menelaus. •When
the king came down to Tyre, the three men sent by the elders maintained the
45 justice of their case in his presence. •Menelaus, seeing he was already defeated,
promised a substantial sum to Ptolemy son of Dorymenes if he would
46 influence the king in his favour. •Ptolemy then took the king aside into a
47 colonnade for some fresh air, and persuaded him to change his mind; •the king
actually dismissed the charges against Menelaus, the cause of all this evil, while
he condemned to death the other poor wretches who, had they pleaded before
48 even Scythians, would have been let off scot-free. •No time was lost in carrying out
this unjust punishment on those who had championed the cause of the city, the
49 rural communities and the sacred vessels. •Some Tyrians even were so outraged
50 by the crime that they provided sumptuously for their funeral, •while as a result of
the greed of those in high places Menelaus retained his high office, growing
in wickedness and establishing himself as the chief enemy of his fellow citizens.

Menelaus and Jason

1 5 About this time Antiochus undertook his second expedition[a] against Egypt.
2   It then happened that all over the city for nearly forty days there were
apparitions of horsemen galloping through the air, in cloth of gold, troops of
3 lancers fully armed, •squadrons of cavalry in order of battle, attacks and charges
this way and that, a flourish of shields, a forest of pikes, brandishing of swords,
hurling of missiles, a glitter of golden accoutrements and armour of all kinds.
4 So everyone prayed that this manifestation might prove a good omen.
5   Then on the strength of a false report that Antiochus was dead, Jason took
at least a thousand men and launched an unexpected attack on the city. The
troops manning the wall were forced back, and Menelaus, with the city all but
6 captured, took refuge in the Citadel. •Jason, however, was still making a pitiless
slaughter of his own fellow citizens, not stopping to consider that success against
his own countrymen was the greatest of disasters, but rather picturing himself
as setting up trophies won from some enemy, not from his own flesh and blood.
7 Even so, he did not succeed in seizing power; in the end his conspiracy brought
him nothing but disgrace, and once again he took refuge in Ammonite territory.
8 His career of wickedness was thus brought to a halt. Kept under restraint by
Aretas the Arab despot, fleeing from town to town, the quarry of all men, hated
as a rebel against the laws, abhorred as the butcher of his country and his
9 countrymen, he drifted to Egypt, •and at last this man, who had exiled so many
from their fatherland, himself perished on foreign soil, having travelled to Sparta
10 in the hope that for kinship's sake they might harbour him. •So many carcases
he had thrust out to lie unburied; now he himself had none to mourn him, no
funeral rites, no place in the tomb of his ancestors.

Antiochus Epiphanes plunders the Temple

11   When the king came to hear of what had happened, he concluded that Judaea
was in revolt. He therefore marched from Egypt, raging like a wild beast, and
12 began by storming the city. •He then ordered his soldiers to cut down without
mercy everyone they encountered, and to butcher all who took refuge in their

5 a. The author dates this event in 168; but 1 Maccabees should preferably be followed, and this
dates the sack of the Temple after the first expedition in 169.

houses. •It was a massacre of young and old, a slaughter of women and children, 13
a butchery of virgins and infants. •There were eighty thousand victims in the 14
course of those three days, forty thousand dying by violence and as many again
being sold into slavery. •Not satisfied with this, he had the audacity to enter the 15
holiest Temple in the entire world, Menelaus, that traitor to the laws and to his
country, acting as his guide; •with his unclean hands he seized the sacred vessels; 16
and his impious hands swept away what other kings had presented for the
advancement, the glory and the honour of the place. •Antiochus, so much above 17
himself, did not realise that the Lord was angry for the moment at the sins of the
inhabitants of the city, hence his unconcern for the Holy Place. •Had it not 18
happened that they were entangled in many sins, Antiochus too, like Heliodorus
when King Seleucus sent him to inspect the Treasury, would have been flogged
the moment he arrived and checked in his presumption. •However, the Lord 19
had not chosen the people for the sake of the place, but the place for the sake
of the people; •and so the place itself, having shared the disasters that befell the 20
people, in due course also shared their good fortune; forsaken by the Almighty
in the time of his anger, it was reinstated in all its glory, once the great Sovereign
had been reconciled.

High commissioners in Judaea

Antiochus went off with eighteen hundred talents he had stolen from the 21
Temple, and hurried back to Antioch; in his arrogance he would have undertaken
to make the dry land navigable and the sea passable on foot, so high his ambition
soared. •But he left high commissioners to plague the nation: in Jerusalem, 22
Philip, a Phrygian by race,[b] and by nature more barbarous than the man who
appointed him; on Mount Gerizim, Andronicus; and besides these Menelaus, 23
who lorded it over his countrymen worse than all the others. In his rooted
hostility to the Jews, •the king also sent the mysarch Apollonius at the head of 24
an army twenty-two thousand strong, with orders to put to death all men in their
prime and to sell the women and children. •Arriving in Jerusalem and posing as 25
a man of peace, this man waited until the holy day of the sabbath and then,
taking advantage of the Jews as they rested from work, ordered his men to
parade fully armed; •all those who came out to watch he put to the sword; 26
then, running through the city with his armed troops, he cut down an immense
number of people.

Judas called Maccabaeus, however, with about nine others, withdrew into 27
the wilderness, and lived like wild animals in the hills with his companions,
eating nothing but wild plants to avoid contracting defilement.

Pagan cults imposed

6 Shortly afterwards, the king sent an old man from Athens to compel the 1
Jews to abandon their ancestral customs and live no longer by the laws of
God; •and to profane the Temple in Jerusalem and dedicate it to Olympian Zeus, 2
and that on Mount Gerizim to Zeus, patron of strangers, as the inhabitants had
requested.[a] •The imposition of this evil was oppressive and altogether intolerable. 3
The Temple was filled with revelling and debauchery by the pagans, who took 4
their pleasure with prostitutes and had intercourse with women in the sacred
precincts, introducing other indecencies besides. •The altar of sacrifice was loaded 5
with victims proscribed by the laws as unclean. •A man might neither keep the 6
sabbath nor observe the traditional feasts, nor so much as admit to being a
Jew. •People were driven by harsh compulsion to eat the sacrificial entrails at 7
the monthly celebration of the king's birthday; and when a feast of Dionysus
occurred they were forced to wear ivy wreaths and walk in the Dionysiac
procession. •A decree was issued at the instance of the people of Ptolemais for 8
the neighbouring Greek cities, enforcing the same conduct on the Jews there,
obliging them to share in the sacrificial meals, •and ordering the execution 9

of those who would not voluntarily conform to Greek customs. So it became clear that disaster was imminent.

10 For example, there were two women charged with having circumcised their children. They were paraded publicly round the town, with their babies hung at
11 their breasts, and then hurled over the city wall. •Other people who had assembled in the caves to keep the seventh day without attracting attention were denounced to Philip and all burned together, since their consciences would not allow them to defend themselves, out of respect for the holiness of the day.

Providential interpretation of the persecution

12 Now I urge anyone who may read this book not to be dismayed at these calamities, but to reflect that such visitations are not intended to destroy our
13 race but to discipline it. •Indeed when evil-doers are not left for long to their
14 own devices but incur swift retribution, it is a sign of great benevolence. •In the case of the other nations the Master waits patiently for them to attain the full measure of their sins before he punishes them, but with us he has decided
15 to deal differently, •rather than have to punish us later, when our sins come to
16 a head. •And so he never entirely withdraws his mercy from us; he may discipline
17 us by some disaster, but he does not desert his own people. •Let this be said simply by way of reminder; we must return to our story without more ado.

The martyrdom of Eleazar

18 Eleazar, one of the foremost teachers of the Law, a man already advanced in years and of most noble appearance, was being forced to open his mouth
19 wide to swallow pig's flesh. •But he, resolving to die with honour rather than
20 to live disgraced, went to the block of his own accord, •spitting the stuff out, the plain duty of anyone with the courage to reject what it is not lawful to taste,
21 even from a natural tenderness for his own life. •Those in charge of the impious banquet, because of their long-standing friendship with him, took him aside and privately urged him to have meat brought of a kind he could properly use, prepared by himself, and only pretend to eat the portions of sacrificial meat as
22 prescribed by the king; •this action would enable him to escape death, by availing
23 himself of an act of kindness prompted by their long friendship. •But having taken a noble decision worthy of his years and the dignity of his great age and the well earned distinction of his grey hairs, worthy too of his impeccable conduct from boyhood, and above all of the holy legislation established by God himself, he publicly stated his convictions, telling them to send him at once to Hades.
24 'Such pretence' he said 'does not square with our time of life; many young people would suppose that Eleazar at the age of ninety had conformed to the
25 foreigners' way of life, •and because I had played this part for the sake of a paltry brief spell of life might themselves be led astray on my account; I should
26 only bring defilement and disgrace on my old age. •Even though for the moment I avoid execution by man, I can never, living or dead, elude the grasp of the
27 Almighty. •Therefore if I am man enough to quit this life here and now I shall
28 prove myself worthy of my old age, •and I shall have left the young a noble example of how to make a good death, eagerly and generously, for the venerable and holy laws.'
29 With these words he went straight to the block. •His escorts, so recently well disposed towards him, turned against him after this declaration, which they
30 regarded as sheer madness. •Just before he died under the blows, he groaned aloud and said, 'The Lord whose knowledge is holy sees clearly that, though I might have escaped death, whatever agonies of body I now endure under this bludgeoning, in my soul I am glad to suffer, because of the awe which he inspires in me'.

b. 'Philip the Phrygian', not the Philip of 1 M 6:14.
6 a. 'The inhabitants' are the Samaritans.

This was how he died, leaving his death as an example of nobility and a 31
record of virtue not only for the young but for the great majority of the nation.

The martyrdom of the seven brothers

7 There were also seven brothers who were arrested with their mother. The 1
king tried to force them to taste pig's flesh, which the Law forbids, by
torturing them with whips and scourges. •One of them, acting as spokesman for 2
the others, said, 'What are you trying to find out from us? We are prepared to
die rather than break the laws of our ancestors.' •The king, in a fury, 3
ordered pans and cauldrons to be heated over a fire. •As soon as they were 4
red-hot he commanded that this spokesman of theirs should have his tongue cut
out, his head scalped and his extremities cut off, while the other brothers and
his mother looked on. •When he had been rendered completely helpless, the 5
king gave orders for him to be brought, still breathing, to the fire and fried alive
in a pan. As the smoke from the pan drifted about, his mother and the rest
encouraged one another to die nobly, with such words as these, •'The Lord 6
God is watching, and surely he takes pity on us, as in the song in which Moses
bore witness against the people to their face, proclaiming that "he will certainly
take pity on his servants" '.

When the first had left the world in this way, they led on the second for their 7
brutal amusement. After stripping the skin from his head, hair and all, they asked
him, 'Will you eat, before your body is tortured limb by limb?' •But he retorted 8
in the language of his ancestors, 'Never!' And so he too was put to the torture in
his turn. •With his last breath he exclaimed, 'Inhuman fiend, you may discharge 9
us from this present life, but the King of the world will raise us up, since
it is for his laws that we die, to live again for ever'.

After him, they amused themselves with the third, who on being asked for 10
his tongue promptly thrust it out and boldly held out his hands, •with these 11
honourable words, 'It was heaven that gave me these limbs; for the sake of his
laws I disdain them; from him I hope to receive them again'. •The king and his 12
attendants were astounded at the young man's courage and his utter indifference
to suffering.

When this one was dead they subjected the fourth to the same savage torture. 13
When he neared his end he cried, 'Ours is the better choice, to meet death at 14
men's hands, yet relying on God's promise that we shall be raised up by him;
whereas for you there can be no resurrection, no new life'. •

Next they brought forward the fifth and began torturing him. •But he looked ¹⁵⁄₁₆
at the king and said, 'You have power over men, mortal as you are, and can
act as you please. But do not think that our race has been deserted by God.
Only wait, and you shall see in your turn how his mighty power will torment 17
you and your race.'

After him they led out the sixth, and his dying words were these, 'Do not 18
delude yourself: we are suffering like this through our own fault, having sinned
against our own God; the result has been terrible, •but do not think you yourself 19
will go unpunished for attempting to make war on God'.

But the mother was especially admirable and worthy of honourable remem- 20
brance, for she watched the death of seven sons in the course of a single day,
and endured it resolutely because of her hopes in the Lord. •Indeed she 21
encouraged each of them in the language of their ancestors; filled with noble
conviction, she reinforced her womanly argument with manly courage, saying
to them, •'I do not know how you appeared in my womb; it was not I who 22
endowed you with breath and life, I had not the shaping of your every part.
It is the creator of the world, ordaining the process of man's birth and presiding 23
over the origin of all things, who in his mercy will most surely give you back
both breath and life, seeing that you now despise your own existence for the sake
of his laws.'

24 Antiochus thought he was being ridiculed, suspecting insult in the tone of her voice;[a] and as the youngest was still alive he appealed to him not with mere words but with promises on oath to make him both rich and happy if he would abandon the traditions of his ancestors; he would make him his Friend and entrust
25 him with public office. •The young man took no notice at all, and so the king then appealed to the mother, urging her to advise the youth to save his life.
26 After a great deal of urging on his part she agreed to try persuasion on her son.
27 Bending over him, she fooled the cruel tyrant with these words, uttered in the language of their ancestors, 'My son, have pity on me; I carried you nine months in my womb and suckled you three years, fed you and reared you to the age you
28 are now (and cherished you). •I implore you, my child, observe heaven and earth, consider all that is in them, and acknowledge that God made them out
29 of what did not exist, and that mankind comes into being in the same way. •Do not fear this executioner, but prove yourself worthy of your brothers, and make death welcome, so that in the day of mercy I may receive you back in your brothers' company.'
30 She had scarcely ended when the young man said, 'What are you all waiting for? I will not comply with the king's ordinance; I obey the ordinance of the
31 Law given to our ancestors through Moses. •As for you, sir, who have contrived every kind of evil against the Hebrews, you will certainly not escape the hands
32/33 of God. •We are suffering for our own sins; •and if, to punish and discipline us, our living Lord vents his wrath upon us, he will yet be reconciled with his own
34 servants. •But you, unholy wretch, bloodiest villain of all mankind, do not be carried away with senseless elation, crowing with false confidence as you raise
35 your hand against his servants, •for you have not yet escaped the judgement of
36 God the almighty, the all-seeing. •Our brothers already, after enduring their brief pain, now drink of ever-flowing life, by virtue of God's covenant, while you, by God's judgement, will have to pay the just penalty for your arrogance.
37 I too, like my brothers, surrender my body and life for the laws of my ancestors, calling on God to show his kindness to our nation and that soon, and by trials and
38 afflictions to bring you to confess that he alone is God, •so that with my brothers and myself there may be an end to the wrath of the Almighty, rightly let loose on our whole nation.'
39 The king fell into a rage and treated this one more cruelly than the others,
40 for he was himself smarting from the young man's scorn. •And so the last brother
41 met his end undefiled and with perfect trust in the Lord. •The mother was the last to die, after her sons.
42 But let this be sufficient account of the ritual meals and excessive torments.

V. THE VICTORY OF JUDAISM

THE DEATH OF THE PERSECUTOR
AND PURIFICATION OF THE TEMPLE

Judas Maccabaeus and the resistance

1 8 Judas Maccabaeus and his companions made their way secretly among the villages, rallying their kinsfolk; they recruited those who remained loyal
2 to Judaism, and assembled about six thousand. •They called upon the Lord to have regard for the people oppressed on all sides, to take pity on the Temple
3 profaned by the godless, •to have mercy on the city falling into ruin and nearly levelled to the ground, to hear the blood of the victims that cried aloud to him,
4 to remember the criminal slaughter of innocent babies and to avenge the
5 blasphemies perpetrated against his name. •As soon as Maccabaeus had an

7 a. He did not understand Aramaic.

organised force he at once proved invincible to the pagans, the Lord's anger having turned into compassion. •Making surprise attacks on towns and villages, 6 he fired them; he captured favourable positions and inflicted a number of reverses on the enemy, •generally availing himself of the cover of night for such enter- 7 prises. The fame of his valour spread far and wide.

Early exploits

When Philip saw Judas was making steady progress and winning more and 8 more frequent successes, he wrote to Ptolemy, the military commissioner for Coele-Syria and Phoenicia, asking for reinforcements in the royal interest. Ptolemy appointed Nicanor son of Patroclus, one of the king's First Friends, 9 and sent him without delay at the head of an international force of at least twenty thousand men, to exterminate the entire Jewish race. As his associate he appointed Gorgias, a professional general of wide military experience. •Nicanor 10 determined to raise the two thousand talents of tribute money owed by the king to the Romans, by the sale of Jewish prisoners of war. •He lost no time in 11 sending the seaboard towns an invitation to come and buy Jewish manpower, promising delivery of ninety head for one talent; but he did not reckon on the judgement from the Almighty that was soon to overtake him.

When news reached Judas of Nicanor's advance, he warned his men of the 12 enemy's approach, •whereupon the fainthearted and those who lacked confidence 13 in the justice of God took to their heels and ran away. •The rest sold all their 14 remaining possessions, at the same time praying the Lord to deliver them from the godless Nicanor, who had sold them even in advance of any encounter—•if 15 not for their own sakes, then at least out of consideration for the covenants made with their ancestors, and because they themselves bore his sacred and majestic name.

Maccabaeus marshalled his men, who numbered about six thousand, and 16 exhorted them not to be dismayed at the enemy or discouraged at the vast horde of pagans wickedly advancing against them, but to fight bravely, •keeping 17 before their eyes the criminal outrage inflicted by these men on the Holy Place, and the agony of the humiliated city, not to mention the destruction of their traditional way of life. •'They may put their trust in their weapons and their 18 exploits,' he said 'but our confidence is in almighty God, who is able with a nod to overthrow both those marching on us and the whole world with them.' •He 19 reminded them of the occasions on which their forbears had received help: that time when, under Sennacherib, a hundred and eighty-five thousand men had perished; •that time in Babylonia when in the battle with the Galatians 20 the Jewish combatants numbered only eight thousand and four thousand Macedonians, yet when the Macedonians were hard pressed, the eight thousand wiped out a hundred and twenty thousand because of the help they received from heaven, and won incalculable gains.

Having so roused their courage by these words that they were ready to die 21 for the laws and their country, he then divided his army roughly into four, putting his brothers, Simon, Joseph and Jonathan in command of one division 22 each, and assigning them fifteen hundred men apiece. •Next, he ordered Esdrias*a* 23 to read the sacred book aloud, and gave them their watchword 'Help from God'; then he put himself at the head of the first division and joined battle with Nicanor. •With the Almighty for their ally, they slaughtered over nine thousand 24 of the enemy, wounded and crippled the greater part of Nicanor's army and put them all to flight. •The money of their prospective purchasers fell into their 25 hands. After pursuing them for a good while, they turned back, since time was pressing: •it was the eve of the sabbath, and for that reason they did not prolong 26 their pursuit. •They collected the enemy's weapons and stripped them of their 27 spoils, and then celebrated the sabbath with heartfelt praise and thanks to the Lord, who had reserved that day for distilling on them the first dew of his mercy.

28 When the sabbath was over they distributed some of the booty among the victims
of the persecution and the widows and orphans; the rest they divided among
29 themselves and their children. •They then joined in public supplication, imploring
the merciful Lord to be fully reconciled with his servants.

The defeat of Timotheus and Bacchides

30   They also challenged the forces of Timotheus and Bacchides and wiped out
over twenty thousand of them, gaining possession of several high fortresses.
They divided their enormous booty into two equal shares, one for themselves,
the other for the victims of the persecution and the orphans and widows, not
31 forgetting the aged. •They carefully collected the enemy's weapons and stored
32 them in convenient places. The rest of the spoils they took to Jerusalem. •They
killed the officer commanding Timotheus' bodyguard, an extremely wicked man
33 who had done great harm to the Jews. •In the course of their victory celebrations
in Jerusalem they burned the men that had fired the holy gates, who with
Callisthenes had taken refuge in one small house; so these received a fitting
reward for the sacrilege.

The flight and testimony of Nicanor

34   The triple-dyed scoundrel Nicanor, who had brought the thousand merchants
35 to buy the Jews, •finding himself humbled, with the Lord's help, by men he had
himself reckoned as of very little account, stripped off his robes of state, and
made his way across country unaccompanied, like a runaway slave, reaching
Antioch by a singular stroke of fortune, considering that his army was destroyed.
36 Thus the man who had promised the Romans to make good their tribute money
by selling the prisoners from Jerusalem testified that the Jews had a defender,
and that on this account the Jews were invulnerable, because they followed the
laws which that defender had ordained.

The last days of Antiochus Epiphanes

1 9 About that time, as it happened, Antiochus had retreated in disorder from
2   the country of Persia. •He had entered the city called Persepolis, planning
to rob the temple and occupy the city; but the population at once sprang to arms to
defend themselves, with the result that Antiochus was routed by the inhabitants
3 and forced to beat a humiliating retreat. •On his arrival in Ecbatana he learned
4 what had happened to Nicanor and to Timotheus' forces. •Flying into a
passion, he resolved to make the Jews pay for the disgrace inflicted by those who
had routed him, and with this in mind he ordered his charioteer to drive without
stopping and get the journey over. But the condemnation of heaven travelled
with him. He had said in his pride, 'When I reach Jerusalem I will turn it into
5 a mass grave for the Jews'. •But the all-seeing Lord, the God of Israel, struck
him with an incurable and unseen complaint. The words were hardly out of his
mouth when he was seized with an incurable pain in his bowels and with
6 excruciating internal torture; •and this was only right, since he had inflicted many
7 barbaric tortures on the bowels of others. •Even so he in no way diminished
his arrogance; still bursting with pride, breathing fire in his wrath against the
Jews, he was in the act of ordering an even keener pace when he suddenly
hurtled from his chariot, and the violence of his headlong fall racked every bone
8 in his body. •He who only a little while before had thought in his superhuman
boastfulness to command the waves of the sea, he who imagined he could weigh
mountain peaks in a balance, found himself flat on the ground, borne in a
9 litter, a visible demonstration to all of the power of God, •in that the very
eyes of this godless man teemed with worms and his flesh rotted away while he
lingered on in agonising pain, and the stench of his decay sickened the whole

8 a. The Azariah of 1 M 5:18.

army. •A short while beforehand he had thought to grasp the stars of heaven; 10
now no one could bring himself to act as his bearer, for the stench was
unbearable.

In consequence he began there and then, in his shattered state, to shed his 11
excessive pride and to come to his senses under the divine lash, for he was tormented with pain all the time. •His stench became unendurable even to himself, 12
and he exclaimed, 'It is right to submit to God; no mortal should aspire to
equality with the godhead'. •The wretch began to pray to the Master, who would 13
never take pity on him now, declaring •that the Holy City, towards which he had 14
been speeding to raze it to the ground and turn it into a mass grave, should be
,declared free; •as for the Jews, whom he had considered as not even worth 15
burying, so much carrion to be thrown out with their children for birds and
beasts to prey on, he would make them all the equals of the citizens of Athens;
the holy Temple which he had once plundered he would now adorn with the 16
finest offerings; he would restore all the sacred vessels many times over; he
would defray from his personal revenue the expenses incurred for the sacrifices;
and to crown it all he would himself turn Jew and visit every place where men 17
lived, proclaiming the power of God.

Antiochus writes to the Jews

Finding no respite at all from his suffering, because God had punished him 18
with his righteous sentence, he abandoned all hope for himself and wrote the
Jews the letter transcribed below, which takes the form of an appeal in these
terms:

'To the excellent Jews his citizens, Antiochus, king and commander-in-chief, 19
sends hearty greetings, wishing them all health and prosperity. •If you and your 20
children are well and your affairs are as you would wish, then I am profoundly
thankful. •For my part, though prostrate with sickness, I cherish tender memories 21
of you. On my return from the country of Persia I fell seriously ill, and thought
it necessary to make provision for the common security of all. •Not that I despair 22
of my condition, for I have great hope of shaking off the malady, •but considering 23
how my father, whenever he was making an expedition into the uplands, would
designate his successor, •so that in case of any unforeseen event or disquieting 24
rumour the people of the provinces might know to whom he had left the conduct
of affairs and thus remain undisturbed: •furthermore, being well aware that the 25
princes on our frontiers and neighbours of our realm are watching for opportunities and waiting to see what will happen, I have designated as king my son
Antiochus, whom I have more than once entrusted and commended to most of
you when I was setting out for the upland satrapies; a transcript of my letter to
him is appended hereto. •I therefore urge and require you to remember past 26
favours both public and personal, and to persist, each one of you, in your existing
goodwill towards myself and my son. •I am confident that he will pursue my 27
own policy with benevolence and humanity, and will prove accommodating to
your interests.'

And so this murderer and blasphemer, having endured the same terrible 28
suffering as he had made others endure, met his pitiable fate, and ended his life
among the remote and inhospitable mountains. •His comrade Philip brought back 29
his body, and then, fearing Antiochus's son, withdrew to Egypt, to the court of
Ptolemy Philometor.

The purification of the Temple^a

10 Maccabaeus and his companions, under the Lord's guidance, restored 1
the Temple and the city, •and pulled down the altars erected by the 2
foreigners in the market place, as well as the sacred enclosures. •They purified 3
the sanctuary and built another altar; then striking fire from flints and using
this fire, they offered the first sacrifice for two years, burning incense, lighting the

4 lamps and setting out the loaves. •When they had done this they threw themselves
flat on the ground, and implored the Lord never again to let them fall into such
adversity, but if they should ever sin, to correct them with moderation and not to
5 deliver them over to blasphemous and barbarous nations. •This day of the
purification of the Temple fell on the very day on which the Temple had been
6 profaned by the foreigners, the twenty-fifth of the same month, Chislev. •They
kept eight festal days with rejoicing, in the manner of the feast of Tabernacles,
remembering how, not long before at the time of the feast of Tabernacles, they
7 had been living in the mountains and caverns like wild beasts. •Then, carrying
branches, leafy boughs and palms, they offered hymns to him who had brought
8 the cleansing of his own Holy Place to a happy outcome. •They also decreed by
public edict, ratified by vote, that the whole Jewish nation should celebrate those
same days every year.

VI. THE STRUGGLE OF JUDAS
AGAINST THE NEIGHBOURING PEOPLES,
AND AGAINST LYSIAS, EUPATOR'S HIGH COMMISSIONER

The disgrace of Ptolemy Macron

9   Such were the circumstances attending the death of Antiochus styled
10 Epiphanes. •Our task now is to unfold the history of Antiochus Eupator, son
11 of that godless man, and relate briefly the evil effects of the wars. •On coming
to the throne, this prince put at the head of affairs a certain Lysias, high
12 commissioner for Coele-Syria and Phoenicia. •Now Ptolemy, Macron as he was
styled, the first governor to treat the Jews with any justice, had done his best to
govern them peacefully to make up for the wrongs inflicted on them in the past.
13 Denounced to Eupator by the Friends of the King, he heard himself called traitor
at every turn for having abandoned Cyprus, which had been entrusted to him
by Philometor, and for going over to Antiochus Epiphanes; having shed no
lustre on his illustrious office, he committed suicide by poisoning himself.

Gorgias and the Idumaean fortresses

14   Gorgias now became military commissioner for that region; he maintained
15 a force of mercenaries and a continual state of war with the Jews. •At the same
time the Idumaeans, who controlled important fortresses, were exerting pressure
on the Jews, welcoming outlaws from Jerusalem and endeavouring to maintain
16 a state of war. •Maccabaeus and his men, after making public supplication to
God, entreating him to support them, hurled themselves against the Idumaean
17 fortresses. •Vigorously pressing home their attack, they seized possession of
these vantage points, beating off all who fought on the ramparts; they slaughtered
18 all who fell into their hands, accounting for not less than twenty thousand. •Nine
thousand at least took refuge in two exceptionally strong castles with everything
19 they needed to withstand a siege, •whereupon Maccabaeus left Simon and Joseph,
with Zacchaeus and his forces, in sufficient numbers to besiege them, and himself
20 went off to other places demanding his attention. •But Simon's men were greedy
for money and allowed themselves to be bribed by some of the men in the
castles; accepting seventy thousand drachmae, they let a number of them escape.
21 When Maccabaeus was told what had happened, he summoned the people's
commanders and accused the offenders of having sold their brothers for money
22 by setting free men who were at war with them. •Having executed them as
23 traitors, he at once proceeded to capture both castles. •Successful in all that he
undertook by force of arms, in these two fortresses he slaughtered more than
twenty thousand men.

10 a. This incident took place (December 164) before the death of Antiochus (Spring 163).

Judas defeats Timotheus and captures Gezer

Timotheus, who had been beaten by the Jews once before, now assembled 24 an enormous force of mercenaries, mustering cavalry from Asia in considerable numbers, and appeared in Judaea, expecting to conquer it by force of arms. At his approach Maccabaeus and his men made their supplications to God, 25 sprinkling earth on their heads and putting sackcloth round their waists. •Pros- 26 trating themselves on the terrace before the altar, they begged him to support them and to show himself the enemy of their enemies, the adversary of their adversaries, as the Law clearly states.

After these prayers they armed themselves and advanced a fair distance 27 from the city, halting when they were close to the enemy. •As the first light of 28 dawn began to spread, the two sides joined battle, the one having as their pledge of success and victory not only their own valour but their recourse to the Lord, the other making their own ardour their mainstay in the fight. •When the battle 29 was at its height the enemy saw five magnificent men appear from heaven on horses with golden bridles and put themselves at the head of the Jews; •sur- 30 rounding Maccabaeus and screening him with their own armour, they kept him unscathed, while they rained arrows and thunderbolts on the enemy until, blinded and confused, they scattered in complete disorder. •Twenty thousand five 31 hundred infantry and six hundred cavalry were slaughtered. •Timotheus himself 32 fled to a strongly guarded citadel called Gezer, where Chaereas was in command. For four days Maccabaeus and his men eagerly besieged the fortress, •while 33 34 the defenders, confident in the security of the place, hurled fearful blasphemies and godless insults at them. •At daybreak on the fifth day, twenty young men 35 of Maccabaeus' forces, fired with indignation at the blasphemies, bravely stormed the wall, and cut down with brutal fury everyone they encountered. Others, in a similar scaling operation, took the defenders in the rear, and set 36 fire to the towers, lighting pyres on which they burned the blasphemers alive. Others broke down the gates and let in the rest of the army, and were the first to occupy the town. •Timotheus had hidden in a cistern, but they killed him, 37 with his brother Chaereas, and Apollophanes. •When all this was over, they 38 blessed with hymns and thanksgiving the Lord, who had shown such great kindness to Israel and given them the victory.

The first campaign of Lysias

11 Almost immediately afterwards, Lysias, the king's tutor and cousin and 1 his visier, much disturbed at the turn of events, •mustered about eighty 2 thousand foot soldiers and his entire cavalry and advanced against the Jews, intending to make the Holy City a place for Greeks to live in, •to levy a tax on 3 the Temple as was done with other national shrines, and to put the office of high priest up for sale every year; •he took no account at all of the power of 4 God, being sublimely confident in his tens of thousands of infantrymen, his thousands of cavalry, and his eighty elephants.

Invading Judaea, he approached Bethzur, a fortified position about twenty 5 miles from Jerusalem, and began to subject it to strong pressure. •When 6 Maccabaeus and his men learned that Lysias was besieging the fortresses, they and the populace with them begged the Lord with lamentation and tears to send a good angel to save Israel. •Maccabaeus himself was the first to take up 7 his weapons, and he urged the rest to risk their lives with him in support of their brothers; so they sallied out resolutely, as one man. •They were still near 8 Jerusalem when a rider attired in white appeared at their head brandishing golden accoutrements. •With one accord they all blessed the God of mercy, and 9 found themselves filled with such courage that they were ready to lay low not men only but the fiercest beasts and walls of iron. •They advanced in battle order 10 with the aid of their celestial ally, the Lord having had mercy on them. •Charging 11 like lions on the enemy, they laid low eleven thousand of the infantry and 12 sixteen hundred horsemen, and routed all the rest. •Of those, the majority got away, wounded and weaponless. Lysias himself escaped only by ignominious flight.

Lysias makes peace with the Jews. Four letters concerning the treaty

13 Now Lysias was not lacking in intelligence, and as he reflected on the reverse he had suffered he realised that the Hebrews were invincible because the mighty
14 God fought for them. He therefore sent to them •suggesting a reconciliation on just terms all round, and promising to induce even the king to become their
15 friend. •Maccabaeus, thinking only of the common good, agreed to all that Lysias proposed, and whatever Maccabaeus submitted to Lysias in writing concerning the Jews was granted by the king.

16 Here is the text of the letter Lysias wrote to the Jews, 'From Lysias to the
17 Jewish people, greetings. •John and Absalom, your envoys, have delivered to me the communication transcribed below, requesting me to approve its provisions.
18 Anything requiring the king's attention I have put before him; anything coming
19 within my own competence I have granted. •Provided you maintain your good will towards the administration I will do my best in the future to promote
20 your advantage. •As for the details, I have given orders for your envoys and my
21 own officials to discuss these with you. •May you prosper. The year one hundred and forty-eight, the twenty-fourth day of the month of Dioscoros.'

22 The king's letter was as follows, 'King Antiochus to his brother Lysias,
23 greetings. •Now that our father has taken his place among the gods our will is that the subjects of the realm be left undisturbed to attend to their own affairs.
24 We understand that the Jews do not approve our father's policy, the adoption of Greek customs, but prefer their own way of life and ask to be allowed to
25 observe their own laws. •Accordingly, since we intend this people to be free from vexation like any other, our ruling is that the Temple be restored to them and
26 that they conduct their affairs according to the customs of their ancestors. •It will therefore be your concern to send them a mission of friendship, so that on learning our policy they may have confidence and proceed happily about their own affairs.'

27 The king's letter to the Jewish nation was in these terms, 'King Antiochus
28 to the Jewish senate and the rest of the Jews, greetings. •If you are well, that is
29 as we would wish; we ourselves are in good health. •Menelaus informs us that
30 you wish to return home and attend to your own affairs. •Accordingly, all those who return before the thirtieth day of Xanthicus may rest assured that they have
31 nothing to fear. •The Jews may make use of their own kind of food and their own laws as formerly, and none of them is to be molested in any way for any
32 unwitting offences. •I am in fact sending Menelaus to set your minds at rest.
33 Farewell. In the hundred and forty-eighth year, the fifteenth of Xanthicus.'

34 The Romans also sent the Jews a letter, which read as follows, 'Quintus Memmius, Titus Manius, ambassadors of the Romans, to the people of the Jews,
35 greetings. •Whatever Lysias, the king's cousin, has granted you we also approve.
36 As for the matters he decided to refer to the king, consider them carefully and send someone without delay, if we are to interpret them to your advantage,
37 because we are leaving for Antioch. •Lose no time, therefore, in sending us
38 those who can tell us what your intentions are. •Farewell. In the hundred and forty-eighth year, the fifteenth of Xanthicus.'

Incidents at Joppa and Jamnia

1 **12** After these agreements had been concluded Lysias returned to the king
2 while the Jews went back to their farming. •Among the local military commissioners, Timotheus and Apollonius son of Gennaeus, as also Hieronymus and Demophon, and Nicanor the Cypriarch as well, would not allow the Jews to live in peace and quiet.

3 The people of Joppa went so far as to perpetrate the following outrage: they

invited the Jews living among them to go aboard some boats they had lying ready, taking their wives and children. There was no hint of any intention to harm them; •there had been a public vote by the citizens, and the Jews accepted, 4 as well they might, being peaceable people with no reason to suspect anything. But once out in the open sea they were all sent to the bottom, a company of at least two hundred.

When Judas heard of the cruel fate of his countrymen, he issued his orders 5 to his men •and after invoking God, the just judge, he attacked his brothers' 6 murderers. Under cover of dark he set fire to the harbour, burned the boats and put to the sword everyone who had taken refuge there. •As the town gates were 7 closed, he withdrew, intending to come back and wipe out the whole community of Joppa. •But hearing that the people of Jamnia were planning to treat their 8 resident Jews in the same way, •he made a night attack on the Jamnites and 9 fired the harbour with its fleet; the glow of the flames was seen as far off as Jerusalem, thirty miles away.

The expedition in Gilead

When they had left the town over a mile behind them in their advance on 10 Timotheus, Judas was attacked by an Arab force of at least five thousand foot soldiers, with five hundred cavalry. •A fierce engagement followed, and with 11 God's help Judas' men won the day; the defeated nomads begged Judas to offer them the right hand of friendship, and promised to surrender their herds and make themselves generally useful to him. •Realising that they might indeed 12 prove valuable in many ways, Judas consented to make peace with them and after an exchange of pledges the Arabs withdrew to their tents.

Judas also attacked a certain fortified town, enclosed by ramparts and 13 inhabited by a medley of races; its name was Caspin. •Confident in the strength 14 of their walls and their stock of provisions, the besieged adopted an insolent attitude to Judas and his men, reinforcing their insults with blasphemies and profanity. •But Judas and his men invoked the great Sovereign of the world 15 who without battering-ram or siege-engine overthrew Jericho in the days of Joshua; they then made a furious assault on the wall. •Capturing the city by the 16 will of God, they made such indescribable slaughter that the nearby lake, two furlongs across, seemed filled to overflowing with blood.

The battle of Carnaim

Ninety-five miles further on from there, they reached the Charax, in the 17 country of Jews known as Tubians. •They did not find Timotheus himself in 18 that neighbourhood; he had already left the district, having achieved nothing apart from leaving a very strong garrison at one point. •Dositheus and Sosipater, 19 two of the Maccabaean generals, marched out and destroyed the force Timotheus had left behind in the fortress, amounting to more than ten thousand men. Maccabaeus himself divided his army into cohorts to which he assigned com- 20 manders, and then hurried in pursuit of Timotheus, whose troops numbered one hundred and twenty thousand infantry and two thousand five hundred cavalry. •Timotheus's first move on learning of Judas' advance was to send 21 away the women and children and the rest of the baggage train to the place called Carnaim, since it was an impregnable position, difficult of access owing to the narrowness of all the approaches. •When the first of Judas' cohorts came into 22 sight, the enemy were seized with fright; panic-stricken at this manifestation of the All-seeing, they fled headlong in all directions, so that they were often wounded by their own men, running on the points of one another's swords. Judas pursued them with a will, cutting the sinners to pieces and killing something 23 like thirty thousand men. •Timotheus himself, having fallen into the hands of 24 Dositheus and Sosipater and their men, very craftily pleaded with them to let him go with his life, on the grounds that he had the parents of most and the

brothers of some in his power, and that these could otherwise expect short shrift.
25 When at long last he convinced them that he would honour his promise and return these people safe and sound, they let him go for the sake of saving their brothers.
26   Reaching Carnaim and the Atargateion,ᵃ Judas slaughtered twenty-five thousand men.

The return by way of Ephron and Scythopolis

27   After the rout of these enemies he led his army against Ephron, a fortified town, where Lysias was living. Stalwart young men drawn up outside the walls offered vigorous resistance, while inside there were quantities of war-engines
28 and missiles in reserve. •But the Jews, invoking the Sovereign who by his power shatters enemies' defences, gained control of the city, and cut down nearly
29 twenty-five thousand of the people inside. •Moving off from there, they pressed
30 on to Scythopolis,ᵇ seventy-five miles from Jerusalem. •But as the Jews who had settled there assured Judas that the people of Scythopolis had always treated them well and had been particularly kind to them when times had been at their
31 worst, •he and his men thanked them and urged them to extend the same friendship to his race in the future.
They reached Jerusalem shortly before the feast of Weeks.

The campaign against Gorgias

32   After Pentecost, as it is called, they marched against Gorgias, the military
33 commissioner for Idumaea. •He came out at the head of three thousand infantry
34 and four hundred cavalry; •in the course of the ensuing battle a few Jews lost their lives.
35   A man called Dositheus, one of the Tubians, who was on horseback and a powerful man, grasped Gorgias, taking him by the cloak, and was forcibly dragging him along, intending to take the accursed man alive, but one of the Thracian cavalry, hurling himself on Dositheus, slashed his shoulder, and
36 Gorgias escaped to Marisa. •Meanwhile since Esdrias and his men had been fighting for a long time and were exhausted, Judas called on the Lord to show them he was their ally and leader in battle.
37   Then, chanting the battle cry and other hymns at the top of his voice in the language of his ancestors, he routed Gorgias' troops.

The sacrifice for the fallen

38   Judas then rallied his army and moved on to the town of Adullam, and since the seventh day of the week had arrived they purified themselves according to
39 custom and kept the sabbath in that place. •The next day they came to Judas (since the necessity was by now urgent) to have the bodies of the fallen taken up
40 and laid to rest among their relatives in their ancestral tombs. •But when they found on each of the dead men, under their tunics, amulets of the idols taken from Jamnia, which the Law prohibits to Jews, it became clear to everyone that
41 this was why these men had lost their lives. •All then blessed the ways of the
42 Lord, the just judge who brings hidden things to light, •and gave themselves to prayer, .begging that the sin committed might be fully blotted out. Next, the valiant Judas urged the people to keep themselves free from all sin, having
43 seen with their own eyes the effects of the sin of those who had fallen; •after this he took a collection from them individually, amounting to nearly two thousand drachmae, and sent it to Jerusalem to have a sacrifice for sin offered, an altogether fine and noble action, in which he took full account of the resur-
44 rection. •For if he had not expected the fallen to rise again it would have been
45 superfluous and foolish to pray for the dead, •whereas if he had in view the

___

12 a. Temple of Atargatis, a Syrian goddess. Carnaim appears to be a temple of the horned Astarte.   **b.** Beth-shan.

splendid recompense reserved for those who make a pious end, the thought was holy and devout. This was why he had this atonement sacrifice offered for the dead, so that they might be released from their sin.

Antiochus V and Lysias. The fate of Menelaus

13 In the year one hundred and forty-nine Judas and his men discovered 1 that Antiochus Eupator was advancing in force against Judaea, ·and 2 with him Lysias his tutor and vizir; he had moreover a Greek force of one hundred and ten thousand infantry, five thousand three hundred cavalry, twenty-two elephants, and three hundred chariots fitted with scythes.

Menelaus sided with them, and with great duplicity kept encouraging 3 Antiochus, not for the welfare of his own country but in the hope of being confirmed in office. ·But the King of kings stirred up the anger of Antiochus 4 against the guilty wretch, and when Lysias made it clear to the king that Menelaus was the cause of all the troubles, Antiochus gave orders for him to be taken to Beroea and there put to death by the local method of execution. ·In that 5 place there is a tower fifty cubits high, filled with ash, with a circular construction sloping steeply down from all sides towards the ashes. ·If anyone is convicted of 6 sacrilegious theft or notoriously guilty of certain other crimes, they take him up to the top and thrust him down to perish. ·In such a manner was the renegade 7 fated to die; Menelaus had not even the privilege of burial. ·Deserved justice, 8 this; since he had committed many sins against the altar whose fire, whose very ashes were holy, it was in ashes that he met his death.

The prayers and success of the Jews near Modein

The king, then, was advancing, his mind filled with barbarous designs, to 9 give the Jews a demonstration of far worse things than anything that had happened under his father. ·When Judas heard of this he ordered the people to 10 call day and night upon the Lord, now if ever, for this once at least, to come to the help ·of those who were in peril of being deprived of the Law, their 11 fatherland and the holy Temple, and not to allow the people, just when they were beginning to breathe again, to fall into the power of the blaspheming pagans. ·When they had all, as one man, obeyed his instructions and had made 12 their petitions to the merciful Lord, weeping, fasting and prostrating themselves for three days continuously, Judas spoke words of encouragement and told them to keep close to him. ·After separate consultation with the elders he resolved not 13 to wait for the king's army to invade Judaea and take possession of the city, but to march out and bring the whole matter to a decision with the help of God.

Leaving the outcome to the creator of the world, and exhorting his soldiers 14 to fight bravely to the death for the laws, the Temple, the city, their country and their way of life, he halted his army near Modein. ·Leaving his men with 15 the watchword 'Victory from God', he made a night attack on the king's pavilion with a picked band of the bravest young men. Inside the camp he destroyed about two thousand, and his men cut down the largest of the elephants with its driver; ·in the end they filled the whole camp with terror and confusion before 16 withdrawing in triumph. ·Dawn was just breaking as this was brought to an end, 17 through the protection of the Lord watching over Judas.

Antiochus in treaty with the Jews

The king, having had a taste of Jewish daring, now tried to attack their 18 positions strategically. ·He advanced on Bethzur, a strong fortress of the Jews, 19 but was repulsed, and so checked and worsted.

Judas sent in to the garrison what they needed, ·but Rhodocus, of the Jewish 20 21 army, supplied the enemy with secret information; the man was identified, arrested, and dealt with. ·For the second time the king parleyed with the garrison 22 of Bethzur; he offered and accepted pledges of amity, retired, then attacked Judas

23 and his men, but came off worst. •He was then told that Philip, left in charge of
affairs at Antioch, had made a desperate move. He was stunned by this, opened
negotiations with the Jews, capitulated, and swore to abide by all reasonable
conditions. He reached an agreement, offered sacrifice, honoured the Temple,
and made generous gifts to the Holy Place.

24 He received Maccabaeus kindly, then left Hegemonides behind as military com-
25 missioner from Ptolemais to the territory of the Gerrenians, •and went to
Ptolemais. The inhabitants of the place disapproved of the treaty; they voiced
26 their resentment and wanted to annul its articles. •Lysias mounted the rostrum
and made a persuasive defence of the articles which convinced and calmed them,
and so won their good will. He then withdrew to Antioch.

So much for the episode of the king's offensive and retreat.

VII. THE CONFLICT WITH NICANOR,
GENERAL OF DEMETRIUS I.
THE DAY OF NICANOR

Alcimus the high priest intervenes

1 **14** Three years after this, Judas and his men learned that Demetrius son
of Seleucus had landed at the port of Tripolis with a strong army and
2 a fleet, •and that he had occupied the country and had killed Antiochus and
3 his tutor Lysias. •A certain Alcimus, a former high priest, had wilfully incurred
defilement at the time of the insurrection; realising that whichever way he turned
4 there was no security for him, nor any further access to the holy altar, •he went
to King Demetrius in about the year one hundred and fifty-one and presented
him with a golden crown and a palm, together with the traditional olive branches
from the Temple; there, for that day, he let the matter rest.

5 Presently he found an opportunity that suited his perverse purpose. When
Demetrius called him into his council and questioned him about the dispositions
6 and intentions of the Jews, he replied, •'Those Jews called Hasidaeans, who
are led by Judas Maccabaeus, are warmongers and rebels who are preventing
7 the kingdom from finding stability. •That is why, after being deprived of my
8 hereditary dignity, I mean the high-priesthood, I have come here now, •first,
out of genuine concern for the king's interests, and secondly, out of a regard for
our own fellow citizens, because the irresponsible behaviour of those I have
9 mentioned has brought great degradation on our entire race. •When your
majesty has taken note of all these points, may it please you to make provision
for the welfare of our country and our oppressed nation, as befits the gracious
10 benevolence you extend to all; •for as long as Judas remains alive the state will
never enjoy peace.'

11 When Alcimus had finished this speech, the rest of the Friends of the King,
who hated Judas, seized the occasion to arouse Demetrius' anger against him.
12 He at once selected Nicanor, who had been commander of the elephants,
13 promoted him military commissioner for Judaea and despatched him •with
instructions to dispose of Judas, disperse his followers and instal Alcimus as high
14 priest of the greatest of temples. •The pagans in Judaea, who had fled before
Judas, flocked to join Nicanor, thinking that the misfortunes and troubles of
the Jews would be to their own advantage.

Nicanor comes to terms with Judas

15 When the Jews heard that Nicanor was coming and that the pagans were
about to attack, they sprinkled dust over themselves and made supplication to
him who had established his people for ever and had never failed to support his
16 own heritage by his direct intervention. •On their leader's orders they at once

left the place where they were and came upon the enemy at the village of
Dessau.ᵃ •Simon, brother of Judas, had engaged Nicanor, but because of the 17
unexpected arrival of his adversaries had suffered a slight check. •However, 18
Nicanor had heard how brave Judas and his men were and how resolutely they
always fought for their country, and he did not dare allow bloodshed to decide the
issue. •And so he sent Posidonius, Theodotus and Mattathias to offer the Jews 19
pledges of friendship and to accept theirs.

After careful consideration of his terms, the leader communicated them to 20
his troops, and since they were all clearly of one mind they agreed to the treaty.
A day was fixed on which the respective leaders were to meet privately on 21
neutral ground: a litter came out from either side and seats were set up. •Judas 22
had posted armed men on the alert in advantageous positions in case of a sudden
treacherous move by the enemy. The leaders held their conference and reached
agreement. •Nicanor took up residence in Jerusalem and did nothing out of 23
place there; he even sent away the crowds that had flocked to join him. •He kept 24
Judas constantly with him, becoming deeply attached to him •and he encouraged 25
him to marry and have children. Judas married, settled down and led a normal
life.

Alcimus renews hostilities, and Nicanor threatens the Temple

When Alcimus saw how friendly the two men had become, he went to 26
Demetrius with a copy of the treaty they had signed and told him that Nicanor
was holding ideas against the interests of the state, and was planning that Judas,
an enemy of the realm, should fill the next vacancy among the Friends of the
King.

The king flew into a rage; roused by the calumnies of this arch-villain, he 27
wrote to Nicanor, telling him of his strong displeasure at the treaty and ordering
him to send Maccabaeus to Antioch in chains immediately.

When the letter reached Nicanor he was very much upset, for it went against 28
the grain with him to break his agreement with a man who had done nothing
wrong. •However, there was no question of opposing the king, so he waited 29
for an opportunity to carry out the order by a stratagem. •Maccabaeus began 30
to notice that Nicanor was treating him more sharply and that his manner
of speaking to him was more abrupt than it had been, and he concluded that
such severity could have no very good motive. He therefore collected a considerable number of his followers and withdrew from Nicanor. •The latter, realising 31
that the man had well and truly outmanoeuvred him, went to the great and
holy Temple at a time when the priests were offering the customary sacrifices,
and ordered them to surrender Judas. •When they protested on oath that 32
they did not know where the wanted man could be, •he stretched out his right 33
hand towards the Temple and swore this oath, 'If you do not hand Judas over
to me as prisoner, I will raze this sanctuary of God to the ground, I will demolish
the altar, and on this very spot I will erect a splendid temple to Dionysus'.
With these words he left them. The priests stretched out their hands to heaven, 34
calling on him who has at all times done battle for our nation; this was their
prayer: •'O Lord, you who stand in need of nothing at all, it has pleased you that 35
there should be in our midst a Temple for your dwelling place. •Now therefore, 36
holy Lord of all holiness, preserve for ever from all profanation this house, so
newly purified.'

The death of Razis

Now, a certain Razis, one of the elders of Jerusalem, was denounced to 37
Nicanor. He was a man who loved his countrymen and stood high in their
esteem, and he was known as the father of the Jews because of his kindness.
In the earlier days of the insurrection he had been convicted of Judaism, and he 38
had risked both body and life for Judaism with the utmost zeal. •By way of 39

demonstrating the enmity he had for the Jews, Nicanor sent over five hundred
40 soldiers to arrest him, •reckoning that if he eliminated this man he would be
41 dealing them a severe blow. •When the troops were on the point of capturing the
tower and were forcing the courtyard gate and calling for fire to set the doors
alight, Razis, finding himself completely surrounded, fell on his own sword,
42 nobly resolving to die rather than fall into the clutches of these villains and suffer
43 outrages unworthy of his noble birth. •But in the heat of conflict he missed his
thrust, and while the troops swarmed in through the doorways, he ran up with
44 alacrity on to the wall and bravely threw himself down among the troops. •But
as they instantly drew back some distance, he fell into the middle of the empty
45 space. •Still breathing, and blazing with anger, he struggled to his feet, blood
spurting in all directions, and despite his terrible wounds ran right through the
46 crowd; then, taking his stand on a steep rock, •although he had now lost every
drop of blood, he tore out his entrails and taking them in both hands flung them
among the troops, calling on the Master of his life and spirit to give them back to
him one day. Such was the manner of his passing.

Nicanor's blasphemies

1 **15** Nicanor heard that Judas and his men were in the neighbourhood of
Samaria, so he decided to attack them, at no risk to himself, on the day of
2 rest. •Those Jews who had been compelled to follow him said, 'You must not
massacre them in such a savage, barbarous way, but give its proper honour to the
3 day on which the All-seeing has conferred a special holiness'. •At this the triple-
dyed scoundrel asked if there was in heaven a sovereign who had ordered the
4 keeping of the sabbath day. •When they answered, 'It is the living Lord himself,
the heavenly sovereign, who has ordered the observance of the seventh day', •
5 he retorted, 'And it is I myself as sovereign on earth who order you to take up
arms and carry through this business of the king'. For all that, he never
managed to carry through his savage plan.

Judas harangues his men. His dream

6 While Nicanor, in his unlimited boastfulness and pride, was planning to erect
7 a public trophy with the spoils taken from Judas and his men, •Maccabaeus
8 remained firm in his confident conviction that the Lord would stand by him. •He
urged his men not to be dismayed by the attacks of the pagans but, keeping
in mind the help that had come to them from heaven in the past, to be confident
9 that this time also victory would be theirs with the help of the Almighty. •He
put fresh heart into them, citing the Law and the Prophets, and by stirring
up memories of the battles they had already won he filled them with new
•10 enthusiasm. •Having thoroughly roused their courage, he ended his speech
by detailing the treachery of the heathen and their violation of their oaths.

11 Having armed each one of them not so much with the safety given by shield
and lance as with that confidence that springs from noble language, he encouraged
12 them all by describing to them a convincing dream—a vision, as it were. •What
he had seen was this: Onias, the former high priest, that paragon of men, modest
of bearing and gentle of manners, suitably eloquent and trained from boyhood
in the practice of every virtue—Onias was stretching out his hands and praying
13 for the whole nation of the Jews. •Next there appeared a man equally remarkable
for his great age and dignity and invested with a marvellous and impressive
14 air of majesty. •Onias began to speak: 'This is a man' he said 'who loves his
brothers and prays much for the people and the Holy City—Jeremiah, the
15 prophet of God'. •Jeremiah then stretched out his right hand and presented
16 Judas with a golden sword, saying as he gave it, •'Take this holy sword as a gift
from God; with it you shall strike down enemies'.

14 a. Adasa. Compare the very similar incident at Capharsalama (which is nearby) in 1 M 7.

The disposition of the combatants

Encouraged by the noble words of Judas, which had the power to inspire 17 valour and give the young the spirit of grown men, they decided not to pitch camp but to make a spirited attack and settle the matter fighting hand to hand with all their courage, since the city, their holy religion and the Temple were in danger. •Their concern for their wives and children, their brothers and 18 relatives, had shrunk to minute importance; their chief and greatest fear was for the consecrated Temple. •Those left behind in the city felt a similar 19 anxiety, alarmed as they were about the forthcoming encounter in the open country. •Everyone now awaited the coming issue. The enemy had already 20 concentrated their forces and stood formed up in order of battle, with the elephants drawn up in a strategic position and the cavalry disposed on the wings. Maccabaeus took note of these masses confronting him, the glittering array of 21 armour and the fierce aspect of the elephants; then, raising his hands to heaven, he called on the Lord who works miracles, in the knowledge that it is not by force of arms, but as he sees fit to decide, that victory is granted by him to such as deserve it. •His prayer was worded thus: 'You, Master, sent your angel in 22 the days of Hezekiah king of Judaea, and destroyed no less than one hundred and eighty-five thousand of Sennacherib's army; •now once again, Sovereign of 23 heaven, send a good angel before us to spread terror and dismay. •May these men 24 be struck down by the might of your arm, since they have come with blasphemy on their lips to attack your holy people.' With this, he brought his prayer to an end.

The defeat and death of Nicanor

Nicanor and his men advanced to the sound of trumpets and war songs, 25 but the men of Judas closed with the enemy uttering invocations and prayers. 26 Fighting with their hands and praying to God in their hearts, they cut down at 27 least thirty-five thousand men and were greatly cheered by this divine manifestation. •When the engagement was ended and they were withdrawing in 28 triumph they recognised Nicanor, lying dead in full armour.

With shouting and confusion all around, they blessed the sovereign Master 29 in the language of their ancestors. •The man who had devoted himself entirely, 30 body and soul, to the service of his countrymen, and had always preserved the love he had felt even in youth for those of his own race, gave orders for Nicanor's head to be cut off, together with his arm and shoulder, and taken to Jerusalem. When he arrived there himself, he called together his countrymen and the priests; 31 then standing in front of the altar he sent for the people from the Citadel. •He 32 showed them the head of the infamous Nicanor, and the hand which the blasphemer had stretched out so insolently against the holy house of the Almighty. •Then, cutting out the tongue of the godless Nicanor, he gave orders 33 for it to be fed piecemeal to the birds, and for the reward of his folly to be hung up in sight of the Temple. •At this everyone sent blessings heavenward to the glorious 34 Lord, saying, 'Blessings on him who has preserved his own dwelling from pollution!'

He hung Nicanor's head from the Citadel,[a] a clear and evident sign to all 35 of the help of the Lord. •They all passed a decree by unanimous vote never to 36 let that day go by unobserved, but to celebrate the thirteenth day of the twelfth month, called Adar in Aramaic, the eve of the day of Mordecai.[b]

Compiler's epilogue

So ends the episode of Nicanor, and as, since then, the city has remained 37 in the possession of the Hebrews, I shall bring my own work to an end here too. If it is well composed and to the point, that is just what I wanted. If it is trashy 38 and mediocre, that is all I could manage. •Just as it is injurious to drink wine 39 by itself, or again water, whereas wine mixed with water is pleasant and produces a delightful sense of well-being, so skill in presenting the incidents is what delights the understanding of those who read the story. On that note I will close.

15 a. This is an anachronism; the Citadel was still in the hands of the Syrians at this date.
b. Called the Day of Nicanor, 1 M 7:48. The Day of Mordecai is the Purim of Est 9:20.

INTRODUCTION TO
THE WISDOM WRITINGS

Wisdom literature flourished throughout the ancient East, ignoring national boundaries and often little affected by religious beliefs. It is essentially the wisdom of experience, offering a recipe for successful living, and this wisdom is itself respected as a cultural accomplishment.

The earliest wisdom writings of Israel are like those of neighbouring races. The five books of the Old Testament known as 'the wisdom books' are Job, Proverbs, Ecclesiastes, Ecclesiasticus and Wisdom; with them is grouped the Song of Songs owing to its reputed connection with Solomon the wise king, and characteristic wisdom writing is also found in some Psalms and in parts of the books of Tobit and Baruch.

In the latest of these books, Ecclesiastes and Wisdom, we find a combination of the typical worldly prudence with a return to the great themes of the Old Testament: like their pagan counterparts, the sages of Israel may still be absorbed in the individual and his destiny, but they see the world under the providence of Yahweh who has given so many wise men to Israel in the past. And now wisdom itself is exalted and celebrated as the supreme gift of God.

INTRODUCTION
TO THE BOOK OF
JOB

The Book of Job is the literary masterpiece of the wisdom movement. The main character, Job, is a famous figure from ancient history, traditionally regarded as a model of virtue; he is used by the author to exemplify the problem of the good man who is punished by misfortune and sickness.

The form of the book is that of a long dialogue poem, with a prose prologue and epilogue. In the course of the dialogue, Job's friends offer him all the answers that piety and wisdom can suggest; Job is not reconciled, and the final word is with Yahweh, whose speeches assert a majesty that may not be questioned.

In spite of the ancient setting of the story, the book dates from after the Exile, and a likely date is the beginning of the 5th century B.C. From differences of style and anomalies in the sequence of the speeches, it has sometimes been suspected that editors have added to the original text: the speeches of Elihu, in particular, may be a later addition. But these, too, make a contribution to the book.

THE BOOK OF
JOB

I. PROLOGUE

Satan tests Job

1 There was once a man in the land of Uz*a* called Job: a sound and honest
2 man who feared God and shunned evil. •Seven sons and three daughters
3 were born to him. •And he owned seven thousand sheep, three thousand camels,
five hundred yoke of oxen and five hundred she-donkeys, and many servants
besides. This man was indeed a man of mark among all the people of the East.*b*
4 It was the custom of his sons to hold banquets in each other's houses, one after
the other, and to send and invite their three sisters to eat and drink with them.
5 Once each series of banquets was over, Job would send for them to come and
be purified, and at dawn on the following day he would offer a holocaust for
each of them. 'Perhaps' Job would say 'my sons have sinned and in their hearts
affronted God.' So that was what he used to do after each series.

6 One day the Sons of God*c* came to attend on Yahweh, and among them was
7 Satan. •So Yahweh said to Satan, 'Where have you been?' 'Round the earth,'
8 he answered 'roaming about.' •So Yahweh asked him, 'Did you notice my
servant Job? There is no one like him on the earth: a sound and honest man
9 who fears God and shuns evil.' •'Yes,' Satan said 'but Job is not God-fearing
10 for nothing, is he? •Have you not put a wall round him and his house and all
his domain? You have blessed all he undertakes, and his flocks throng the
11 countryside. •But stretch out your hand and lay a finger on his possessions:
12 I warrant you, he will curse you to your face.' •'Very well,' Yahweh said to
Satan 'all he has is in your power. But keep your hands off his person.' So
Satan left the presence of Yahweh.

13 On the day when Job's sons and daughters were at their meal and drinking
14 wine at their eldest brother's house, •a messenger came to Job. 'Your oxen'
15 he said 'were at the plough, with the donkeys grazing at their side, •when the
Sabaeans*d* swept down on them and carried them off. Your servants they put
16 to the sword: I alone escaped to tell you.' •He had not finished speaking
when another messenger arrived. 'The fire of God' he said 'has fallen from
the heavens and burnt up all your sheep, and your shepherds too: I alone escaped
17 to tell you.' •He had not finished speaking when another messenger arrived.
'The Chaldaeans,' he said 'three bands of them, have raided your camels and
made off with them. Your servants they put to the sword: I alone escaped to
18 tell you.' •He had not finished speaking when another messenger arrived.
'Your sons and daughters' he said 'were at their meal and drinking wine at
19 their eldest brother's house, •when suddenly from the wilderness a gale sprang

---

1 a. Probably in the S. of Edom. **b.** I.e., of Edomite or Arab territory to the E. of Palestine.
c. The angels who make up his Council. **d.** Predatory nomads. So are the Chaldaeans of
v.17.

up, and it battered all four corners of the house which fell in on the young
people. They are dead: I alone escaped to tell you.'

Job rose and tore his gown and shaved his head.ᶜ Then falling to the ground   20
he worshipped •and said: 21

> 'Naked I came from my mother's womb,
> naked I shall return.
> Yahweh gave, Yahweh has taken back.
> Blessed be the name of Yahweh!'

In all this misfortune Job committed no sin nor offered any insult to God.   22

2 Once again the Sons of God came to attend on Yahweh, and among them was   1
Satan. •So Yahweh said to Satan, 'Where have you been?' 'Round the earth,'   2
he answered 'roaming about.' •So Yahweh asked him, 'Did you notice my   3
servant Job? There is no one like him on the earth: a sound and honest man who
fears God and shuns evil. His life continues blameless as ever; in vain you
provoked me to ruin him.' •'Skin for skin!' Satan replied. 'A man will give   4
away all he has to save his life. •But stretch out your hand and lay a finger on 5
his bone and flesh; I warrant you, he will curse you to your face.' •'Very well,' 6
Yahweh said to Satan 'he is in your power. But spare his life.' •So Satan left   7
the presence of Yahweh.

He struck Job down with malignant ulcers from the sole of his foot to the
top of his head. •Job took a piece of pot to scrape himself, and went and sat   8
in the ashpit. •Then his wife said to him, 'Do you now still mean to persist   9
in your blamelessness? Curse God, and die.' •'That is how foolish women   10
talk' Job replied. 'If we take happiness from God's hand, must we not take
sorrow too?' And in all this misfortune Job uttered no sinful word.

The news of all the disasters that had fallen on Job came to the ears of three of 11
his friends. Each of them set out from home—Eliphaz of Teman, Bildad of Shuah
and Zophar of Naamathᵃ—and by common consent they decided to go and offer
him sympathy and consolation. •Looking at him from a distance, they could   12
not recognise him; they wept aloud and tore their garments and threw dust over
their heads. •They sat there on the ground beside him for seven days and seven 13
nights. To Job they spoke never a word, so sad a sight he made.

II. THE DIALOGUE

A. FIRST SERIES OF SPEECHES

Job curses the day of his birth

3 In the end it was Job who broke the silence and cursed the day of his birth. 1
This is what he said: 2

> May the day perish when I was born,   3
> and the night that told of a boy conceived.
> May that day be darkness,   4
> 　may God on high have no thought for it,
> 　may no light shine on it.
> May murk and deep shadow claim it for their own,   5
> 　clouds hang over it,
> 　eclipse swoop down on it.
> Yes, let the dark lay hold of it,   6
> 　to the days of the year let it not be joined,
> 　into the reckoning of months not find its way.
> May that night be dismal,   7
> 　no shout of joy come near it.

8 Let them curse it who curse the day,
who are prepared to rouse Leviathan.[a]

9 Dark be the stars of its morning,
let it wait in vain for light
and never see the opening eyes of dawn.

10 Since it would not shut the doors of the womb on me
to hide sorrow from my eyes.

11 Why did I not die new-born,
not perish as I left the womb?

12 Why were there two knees to receive me,
two breasts for me to suck?

13 Had there not been, I should now be lying in peace,
wrapped in a restful slumber,

14 with the kings and high viziers of earth
who build themselves vast vaults,

15 or with princes who have gold and to spare
and houses crammed with silver.

16 Or put away like a still-born child that never came to be,
like unborn babes that never see the light.

17 Down there,[b] bad men bustle no more,
there the weary rest.

18 Prisoners, all left in peace,
hear no more the shouts of the gaoler.

19 Down there, high and low are all one,
and the slave is free of his master.

20 Why give light to a man of grief?
Why give life to those bitter of heart,

21 who long for a death that never comes,
and hunt for it more than for a buried treasure?

22 They would be glad to see the grave-mound
and shout with joy if they reached the tomb.

23 Why make this gift of light to a man who does not see his way,
whom God baulks on every side?

24 My only food is sighs,
and my groans pour out like water.

25 Whatever I fear comes true,
whatever I dread befalls me.

26 For me, there is no calm, no peace;
my torments banish rest.

Confidence in God

1 **4** Eliphaz of Teman spoke next. He said:

2 If one should address a word to you, will you endure it?
Yet who can keep silent?

3 Many another, once, you schooled,
giving strength to feeble hands;

4 your words set right whoever wavered,
and strengthened every failing knee.

5 And now your turn has come, and you lose patience too;
now it touches you, and you are overwhelmed.

e. Mourning ritual.
2 a. The three towns are in Idumaean and Arab territory. Edom and 'the East' were proverbially the homeland of the sages.
3 a. The dragon of primeval chaos; he might be roused by a curse against the present order.
b. In Sheol, the underworld.

Does not your piety give you confidence,   6
    your blameless life not give you hope?
Can you recall a guiltless man that perished,   7
    or have you ever seen good men brought to nothing?
I speak of what I know: those who plough iniquity   8
    and sow the seeds of grief reap a harvest of the same kind.
A breath from God will bring them to destruction,   9
    a blast of his anger will wipe them out.
The lion's roar, his savage growls,   10
    like the fangs of lion cubs are broken off.
For lack of prey the lion dies at last,   11
    and the whelps of his lioness are scattered.

Now, I have had a secret revelation,   12
    a whisper has come to my ears.
At the hour when dreams master the mind,   13
    and slumber lies heavy on man,
a shiver of horror ran through me,   14
    and my bones quaked with fear.
A breath slid over my face,   15
    the hairs of my body bristled.
Someone stood there—I could not see his face,   16
    but the form remained before me.
    Silence—and then I heard a Voice,
'Was ever any man found blameless in the presence of God,   17
    or faultless in the presence of his Maker?
In his own servants, God puts no trust,   18
    and even with his angels he has fault to find.
What then of those who live in houses of clay,   19
    who are founded on dust?
They are crushed as easily as a moth,
    one day is enough to grind them to powder.   20
    They vanish for ever, and no one remembers them.
Their tent-peg is snatched from them,   21
    and they die for lack of wisdom.'

5   Make your appeal then. Will you find an answer?   1
    To which of the Holy Ones will you turn?
Resentment kills the senseless,   2
    and anger brings death to the fool.
I myself have seen how such a one took root,   3
    until a swift curse fell on his House.
His sons at a single blow lose their prop and stay,   4
    ruined at the gate^a with no one to defend them;
their harvest goes to feed the hungry,   5
    God snatches it from their mouths,
    and thirsty men hanker after their goods.
Grief does not grow out of the earth,   6
    nor sorrow spring from the ground.
It is man who breeds trouble for himself   7
    as surely as eagles fly to the height.

If I were as you are, I should appeal to God,   8
    and lay my case before him.
His works are great, past all reckoning,   9
    marvels, beyond all counting.
He sends down rain to the earth,   10
    pours down water on the fields.

11   If his will is to rescue the downcast,
          or raise the afflicted to the heights of joy,
12   he wrecks the plans of the artful,
          and brings to naught their intrigues.
13   He traps the crafty in the snare of their own shrewdness,
          turns subtle counsellors to idiots.
14   In daylight they come against darkness,
          and grope their way as if noon were night.
15   He rescues the bankrupt from their jaws,
          and the poor man from the hands of the violent.
16   Thus the wretched can hope again
          and wickedness must shut its mouth.

17   Happy indeed the man whom God corrects!
          Then do not refuse this lesson from Shaddai.[b]
18   For he who wounds is he who soothes the sore,
          and the hand that hurts is the hand that heals.
19   Six times he will deliver you from sorrow,
          and the seventh, evil shall not touch you.
20   In time of famine, he will save you from death,
          and in wartime from the stroke of the sword.
21   You shall be safe from the lash of the tongue,
          and see the approach of the brigand without fear.
22   You shall laugh at drought and frost,
          and have no fear of the beasts of the earth.
23   You shall have a pact with the stones of the field,
          and live in amity with wild beasts.
24   You shall find your tent secure,
          and your sheepfold untouched when you come.
25   You shall see your descendants multiply,
          your offspring grow like the grass in the fields.
26   In ripe age you shall go to the grave,
          like a wheatsheaf stacked in due season.
27   All this, we have observed: it is true.
          Heed it, and do so to your profit.

Only the sufferer knows his own grief

1 **6** Job spoke next. He said:
2   If only my misery could be weighed,
          and all my ills be put on the scales!
3   But they outweigh the sands of the seas:
          what wonder then if my words are wild?
4   The arrows of Shaddai stick fast in me,
          my spirit absorbs their poison,
          God's terrors stand against me in array.
5   Does a wild donkey bray when it finds soft grass,
          or an ox ever low when its fodder is in reach?
6   Can tasteless food be taken without salt,
          or is there flavour in the white of an egg?
7   The very dishes which I cannot stomach,
          these are my diet in my sickness.
8   Oh may my prayer find fulfilment,
          may God grant me my hope!

5·a. The town gate, at which justice was dispensed.   b. Name for God in the patriarchal period, here a deliberate archaism.

May it please God to crush me,   9
     to give his hand free play and do away with me!

This thought, at least, would give me comfort   10
     (a thrill of joy in unrelenting pain),
     that I had not denied the Holy One's decrees.

But have I the strength to go on waiting?   11
     What use is life to me, when doomed to certain death?

Is mine the strength of stone,   12
     or is my flesh bronze?

Can any power be found within myself,   13
     has not all help deserted me?

Grudge pity to a neighbour,   14
     and you forsake the fear of Shaddai.

My brothers have been fickle as a torrent,   15
     as the course of a seasonal stream.

Ice is the food of their dark waters,   16
     they swell with the thawing of the snow;

but in the hot season they dry up,   17
     with summer's heat they vanish.

Caravans leave the trail to find them,   18
     go deep into desert, and are lost.

The caravans of Tema look to them,   19
     and on them Sheba's convoys build their hopes.

Their trust proves vain,   20
     they reach them only to be thwarted.

So, at this time, do you behave to me: 21
     one sight of me, and then you flee in fright.

Have I said to you, 'Give me this or that,   22
     bribe someone for me at your own cost,

snatch me from the clutches of an enemy,   23
     or ransom me from a tyrant's hand'?

Put me right, and I will say no more;   24
     show me where I have been at fault.

Fair comment can be borne without resentment,   25
     but what is the basis for your strictures?

Do you think mere words deserve censure,   26
     desperate speech that the wind blows away?

Soon you will be casting lots for an orphan,   27
     and selling your friend at bargain prices!

Come, I beg you, look at me: 28
     as man to man, I will not lie.

Relent, and grant me justice;   29
     relent, my case is not yet tried.

Is falsehood to be found on my lips?   30
     Cannot my palate tell the taste of misfortune?

7   Is not man's life on earth nothing more than pressed service,   1
     his time no better than hired drudgery?

Like the slave, sighing for the shade,   2
     or the workman with no thought but his wages,

months of delusion I have assigned to me,   3
     nothing for my own but nights of grief.

Lying in bed I wonder, 'When will it be day?'   4
     Risen I think, 'How slowly evening comes!'
     Restlessly I fret till twilight falls.

5　　Vermin cover my flesh, and loathsome scabs;
　　　　my skin is cracked and oozes pus.

6　　Swifter than a weaver's shuttle my days have passed,
　　　　and vanished, leaving no hope behind.

7　　Remember that my life is but a breath,
　　　　and that my eyes will never again see joy.

8　　The eye that once saw me will look on me no more,
　　　　your eyes will turn my way, and I shall not be there.

9　　As a cloud dissolves and is gone,
　　　　so he who goes down to Sheol never ascends again.

10　　He never comes home again,
　　　　and his house knows him no more.

11　　No wonder then if I cannot keep silence;
　　　　in the anguish of my spirit I must speak,
　　　　lament in the bitterness of my soul.

12　　Am I the Sea, or the Wild Sea Beast,[a]
　　　　that you should keep me under watch and guard?

13　　If I say, 'My bed will comfort me,
　　　　my couch will soothe my pain',

14　　you frighten me with dreams
　　　　and terrify me with visions.

15　　Strangling I would welcome rather,
　　　　and death itself, than these my sufferings.

16　　I waste away, my life is not unending;
　　　　leave me then, for my days are but a breath.

17　　What is man that you should make so much of him,
　　　　subjecting him to your scrutiny,

18　　that morning after morning you should examine him
　　　　and at every instant test him?

19　　Will you never take your eyes off me
　　　　long enough for me to swallow my spittle?

20　　Suppose I have sinned, what have I done to you,
　　　　you tireless watcher of mankind?
　　　　Why do you choose me as your target?
　　　　Why should I be a burden to you?

21　　Can you not tolerate my sin,
　　　　nor overlook my fault?
　　　　It will not be long before I lie in earth;
　　　　then you will look for me, but I shall be no more.

The unswerving course of God's justice

1　8　Bildad of Shuah spoke next. He said:

2　　Is there no end to these words of yours,
　　　　to your long-winded blustering?

3　　Can God deflect the course of right
　　　　or Shaddai falsify justice?

4　　If your sons sinned against him,
　　　　they have paid for their sins;

6a　　so you too, if so pure and honest,

5　　　　must now seek God, plead with Shaddai.

7 a. In the Babylonian cosmogonies, the Sea (personified as Tiamat) was conquered and controlled by one of the gods. In popular imagery influenced by this story, Yahweh became the conqueror who held the sea under his control.

Without delay he will restore his favour to you,   6b
    will see that the good man's house is rebuilt.

Your former state will seem to you as nothing   7
    beside your new prosperity.

Question the generation that has passed,   8
    meditate on the experience of its fathers.

We sons of yesterday know nothing;   9
    our life on earth passes like a shadow.

But they will teach you, they will tell you,   10
    and these are the words they will speak from the heart,

'Does papyrus flourish, except in marshes?   11
    Without water, can the rushes grow?

Pluck them even at their freshest: 12
    fastest of all plants they wither.

Such is the fate of all who forget God;   13
    so perishes the hope of the godless man.

His trust is only a thread,   14
    his assurance a spider's web.

Let him lean on his house; it will not stand firm;   15
    cling to it, it will not hold.

Like some lush plant in the sunlight,   16
    he sprouted his early shoots over the garden;

but his roots were twined in a heap of stones,   17
    he drew his life among the rocks.

Snatch him from his bed,   18
    and it denies it ever saw him.

Now he rots on the roadside,   19
    and from that soil spring others.

Believe me, God neither spurns a stainless man,   20
    nor lends his aid to the evil.

Once again your cheeks will fill with laughter,   21
    from your lips will break a cry of joy.

Your enemies shall be covered with shame,   22
    and the tent of the wicked folk shall vanish.'

God's justice is above all law

9 Job spoke next. He said: 1

Indeed, I know it is as you say: 2
    how can man be in the right against God?

If any were so rash as to challenge him for reasons,   3
    one in a thousand would be more than they could answer.

His heart is wise, and his strength is great: 4
    who then can successfully defy him?

He moves the mountains, though they do not know it;   5
    he throws them down when he is angry.

He shakes the earth, and moves it from its place,   6
    making all its pillars tremble.

The sun, at his command, forbears to rise,   7
    and on the stars he sets a seal.

He and no other stretched out the skies,   8
    and trampled the Sea's tall waves.

The Bear, Orion too, are of his making,   9
    the Pleiades and the Mansions of the South.

His works are great, beyond all reckoning,   10
    his marvels, past all counting.

11   Were he to pass me, I should not see him,
> nor detect his stealthy movement.

12   Were he to snatch a prize, who could prevent him,
> or dare to say, 'What are you doing?'

13   God never goes back on his anger,
> Rahab's minions still lie at his feet.[a]

14   How dare I plead my cause, then,
> or choose arguments against him?

15   Suppose I am in the right, what use is my defence?
> For he whom I must sue is judge as well.

16   If he deigned to answer my citation,
> could I be sure that he would listen to my voice?

17   He, who for one hair crushes me,
> who, for no reason, wounds and wounds again,

18   leaving me not a moment to draw breath,
> with so much bitterness he fills me.

19   Shall I try force? Look how strong he is!
> Or go to court? But who will summon him?

20   Though I think myself right, his mouth may condemn me;
> though I count myself innocent, it may declare me a hypocrite.

21   But am I innocent after all? Not even I know that,
> and, as for my life, I find it hateful.

22   It is all one, and this I dare to say:
> innocent and guilty, he destroys all alike.

23   When a sudden deadly scourge descends,
> he laughs at the plight of the innocent.

24   When a country falls into a tyrant's hand,
> it is he who blindfolds the judges.
> Or if not he, who else?

25   My days run hurrying by,
> seeing no happiness in their flight,

26   skimming along like a reed canoe,
> or the flight of an eagle after its prey.

27   If I resolve to stifle my moans,
> change countenance, and wear a smiling face,

28   fear comes over me, at the thought of all I suffer,
> for such, I know, is not your treatment of the innocent.

29   And if I am guilty,
> why should I put myself to useless trouble?

30   No use to wash myself with snow,
> or bleach my hands pure white;

31   for you will plunge me in dung
> until my very clothes recoil from me.

32   Yes, I am man, and he is not; and so no argument,
> no suit between the two of us is possible.

33   There is no arbiter between us,
> to lay his hand on both,

34   to stay his rod from me,
> or keep away his daunting terrors.

35   Nonetheless, I shall speak, not fearing him:
> I do not see myself like that at all.

10   1   Since I have lost all taste for life,
> I will give free rein to my complaints;

---

9 a. Rahab stands for Chaos, the first enemy conquered by God.

I shall let my embittered soul speak out.
I shall say to God, 'Do not condemn me,   2
   but tell me the reason for your assault.
Is it right for you to injure me,   3
   cheapening the work of your own hands
   and abetting the schemes of the wicked?
Have you got human eyes,   4
   do you see as mankind sees?
Is your life mortal like man's,   5
   do your years pass as men's days pass?
You, who inquire into my faults   6
   and investigate my sins,
you know very well that I am innocent,   7
   and that no one can rescue me from your hand.
Your own hands shaped me, modelled me;   8
   and would you now have second thoughts, and destroy me?
You modelled me, remember, as clay is modelled,   9
   and would you reduce me now to dust?
Did you not pour me out like milk,   10
   and curdle me then like cheese;*
clothe me with skin and flesh,   11
   and weave me of bone and sinew?
And then you endowed me with life,   12
   watched each breath of mine with tender care.
Yet, after all, you were dissembling;   13
   biding your time, I know,
to mark if I should sin   14
   and to let no fault of mine go uncensured.
Woe to me, if I am guilty;   15
   if I am innocent, I dare not lift my head,
   so wholly abject, so drunk with pain am I.
And if I make a stand, like a lion you hunt me down,   16
   adding to the tale of your triumphs.
You attack, and attack me again,   17
   with stroke on stroke of your fury,
   relentlessly your fresh troops assail me.

'Why did you bring me out of the womb?   18
   I should have perished then, unseen by any eye,
a being that had never been,   19
   to be carried from womb to grave.
The days of my life are few enough: 20
   turn your eyes away, leave me a little joy,
before I go to the place of no return,   21
   the land of murk and deep shadow,
where dimness and disorder hold sway,   22
   and light itself is like the dead of night.'

Job must acknowledge God's wisdom

11 Zophar of Naamath spoke next. He said: 1

Is babbling to go without an answer?   2
   Is wordiness in man a proof of right?
Do you think your talking strikes men dumb,   3
   will you jeer with no one to refute you?
These were your words, 'My way of life is faultless,   4
   and in your eyes I am free from blame'.

5   But if God had a mind to speak,
           to open his lips and give you answer,

6   were he to show you the secrets of wisdom
           which put all cleverness to shame —
           you would know it is for sin he calls you to account.

7   Can you claim to grasp the mystery of God,
           to understand the perfection of Shaddai?

8   It is higher than the heavens: what can you do?
           It is deeper than Sheol: what can you know?

9   Its length is longer than the earth,
           its breadth is broader than the sea.

10   If he passes, who can stop him,
           or make him yield once he has seized?

11   For he detects the worthlessness in man,
           he sees iniquity and marks it well.

12   And so the idiot grows wise,
           thus a young wild donkey grows tame.

13   Come, you must set your heart right,
           stretch out your hands to him.

14   Renounce the iniquity that stains your hands,
           let no injustice live within your tents.

15   Then you may face the world in innocence,
           unwavering and free from fear.

16   You will forget your sufferings,
           remember them as waters that have passed away.

17   Your life, more radiant than the noonday,
           will make a dawn of darkness.

18   Full of hope, you will live secure,
           dwelling well and safely guarded.

19   No one will dare disturb you,
           and many a man will seek your favour.

20   But the wicked will look round with weary eyes,
           and finding no escape,
           the only hope they have is life's last breath.

God's wisdom is best seen in the dreadful works of his omnipotence

1 **12** Job spoke next. He said:

2   Doubtless, you are the voice of the people,
           and when you die, wisdom will die with you!

3   I can reflect as deeply as ever you can,
           I am no way inferior to you.
           And who, for that matter, has not observed as much?

4   A man becomes a laughing-stock to his friends
           if he cries to God and expects an answer.
           The blameless innocent incurs only mockery.

5   'Add insult to injury,' think the prosperous
           'strike the man now that he is staggering!'

6   And yet, the tents of brigands are left in peace,
           and those who challenge God live in safety,
           and make a god of their two fists!

7   If you would learn more, ask the cattle,
           seek information from the birds of the air.

10 a. The contemporary belief was that an embryo was formed by the congealing of the mother's blood.

The creeping things of earth will give you lessons, 8
and the fishes of the sea will tell you all.
There is not one such creature but will know 9
this state of things is all of God's own making.
He holds in his power the soul of every living thing, 10
and the breath of each man's body.

The ear is a judge of speeches, is it not, 11
just as the palate can tell one food from another?
Wisdom is found in the old, 12
and discretion comes with great age.
But in him there is wisdom, and power, too, 13
and decision no less than discretion.
What he destroys, none can rebuild; 14
whom he imprisons, none can release.
Is there a drought? He has checked the waters. 15
Do these play havoc with the earth? He has let them loose.
In him is strength, in him resourcefulness, 16
beguiler and beguiled are both alike his slave.
He robs the country's counsellors of their wits, 17
turns judges into fools.
His hands untie the belt of kings, 18
and bind a rope about their loins.
He makes priests walk barefoot, 19
and overthrows the powers that are established.
He strikes the cleverest speakers dumb, 20
and robs old men of their discretion.
He pours contempt on the nobly born, 21
and unties the girdle of the strong.
He robs the depths of their darkness, 22
brings deep shadow to the light.
He builds a nation up, then strikes it down, 23
or makes a people grow, and then destroys it.
He strips a country's leaders of their judgement, 24
and leaves them to wander in a trackless waste,
to grope about in unlit darkness, 25
and totter like a man in liquor.

13 I have seen all this with my own eyes, 1
heard with my own ears, and understood.
Whatever you know, I know too; 2
I am no way inferior to you.
But my words are intended for Shaddai; 3
I mean to remonstrate with God.
As for you, you are only charlatans, 4
physicians in your own estimation.
I wish someone would teach you to be quiet 5
—the only wisdom that becomes you!
Kindly listen to my accusation, 6
pay attention to the pleading of my lips.
Will you plead God's defence with prevarication, 7
his case in terms that ring false?
Will you be partial in his favour, 8
and act as his advocates?
For you to meet his scrutiny, would this be well? 9
Can he be duped as men are duped?
Harsh rebuke you would receive from him 10

for your covert partiality.

11 Does his majesty not affright you,
    dread of him not fall on you?

12 Your old maxims are proverbs of ash,
    your retorts, retorts of clay.

13 Silence! Now I will do the talking,
    whatever may befall me.

14 I put my flesh between my teeth,
    I take my life in my hands.

15 Let him kill me if he will; I have no other hope
    than to justify my conduct in his eyes.

16 This very boldness gives promise of my release,
    since no godless man would dare appear before him.

17 Listen carefully to my words,
    and lend your ears to what I have to say.

18 You shall see, I will proceed by due form of law,
    persuaded, as I am, that I am guiltless.

19 Who comes against me with an accusation?
    Let him come! I am ready to be silenced and to die.

20 But grant me these two favours:
    if not, I shall not dare to confront you.

21 Take your hand away, which lies so heavy on me,
    no longer make me cower from your terror.

22 Then arraign me, and I will reply;
    or rather, I will speak and you shall answer me.

23 How many faults and crimes have I committed?
    What law have I transgressed, or in what have I offended?

24 Why do you hide your face
    and look on me as your enemy?

25 Will you intimidate a wind-blown leaf,
    will you chase the dried-up chaff;

26 you list bitter accusations against me,
    taxing me with the faults of my youth,

27 after putting my feet in the stocks,
    watching my every step,
    and measuring my footprints;

28 while my life is crumbling like rotten wood,
    or a moth-eaten garment.

14

1 Man, born of woman,
    has a short life yet has his fill of sorrow.

2 He blossoms, and he withers, like a flower;
    fleeting as a shadow, transient.

3 And is this what you deign to turn your gaze on,
    him that you would bring before you to be judged?

4 Who can bring the clean out of the unclean?
    No man alive!

5 Since man's days are measured out,
    since his tale of months depends on you,
    since you assign him bounds he cannot pass,

6 turn your eyes from him, leave him alone,
    like a hired drudge, to finish his day.

7 There is always hope for a tree:
    when felled, it can start its life again;
    its shoots continue to sprout.

8 Its roots may be decayed in the earth,
    its stump withering in the soil,

but let it scent the water, and it buds,　　　　9
　　and puts out branches like a plant new set.
But man? He dies, and lifeless he remains;　　10
　　man breathes his last, and then where is he?
The waters of the seas may disappear,　　　　11
　　all the rivers may run dry or drain away;
but man, once in his resting place, will never rise again.　　12
　　　The heavens will wear away before he wakes,
　　　before he rises from his sleep.

If only you would hide me in Sheol,　　　　13
　　and shelter me there until your anger is past,
fixing a certain day for calling me to mind—
　　for once a man is dead can he come back to life?—　　14
　　day after day of my service I would wait
　　for my relief to come.
Then you would call, and I should answer,　　15
　　you would want to see the work of your hands once more.
Now you count every step I take,　　　　16
　　but then you would cease to spy on my sins;
you would seal up my crime in a bag,　　　　17
　　and whiten my fault over.

But no! Soon or late the mountain falls,　　18
　　the rock moves from its place,
water wears away the stones,　　　　　　19
　　the cloudburst erodes the soil;
　　just so do you destroy man's hope.
You crush him once for all, and he is gone;　　20
　　you mar him, and then you bid him go.
Let his sons achieve honour, he does not know of it,　　21
　　humiliation, he gives it not a thought.
He feels no pain for anything but his own body,　　22
　　makes no lament, save for his own life.

B. SECOND SERIES OF SPEECHES

Job's own words condemn him

15 Eliphaz of Teman spoke next. He said:　　1

　　Does a wise man answer with airy reasonings,　　2
　　　or feed himself on an east wind?
　　Does he defend himself with empty talk　　3
　　　and ineffectual wordiness?
　　You do worse: you flout piety,　　　　4
　　　you repudiate meditation in God's presence.
　　A guilty conscience prompts your words,　　5
　　　you adopt the language of the cunning.
　　Your own mouth condemns you, and not I;　　6
　　　your own lips bear witness against you.

　　Are you the first-born of the human race,　　7
　　　brought into the world before the hills?
　　Have you been a listener at God's council,　　8
　　　or established a monopoly of wisdom?

9 What knowledge have you that we have not,
    what understanding that is not ours too?

10 A grey-haired man, and an ancient, are of our number;
    these have seen more summers than your father.

11 Do you scorn the comfort that God gives,
    and the moderation we have used in speaking?

12 See how passion carries you away!
    How evil you look,

13 when you thus loose your anger on God
    and utter speeches such as these!

14 How can any man be clean?
    Born of woman, can he ever be good?

15 In his own Holy Ones God puts no trust,
    and the heavens themselves are not, in his eyes, clean.

16 Then how much less this hateful, corrupt thing,
    mankind, that drinks iniquity like water!

17 Listen to me, I have a lesson for you:
    I will tell you of my own experience,

18 and of the teaching of the sages,
    those faithful guardians of the tradition of their fathers,

19 to whom alone the land was given,
    , with never a foreigner to mix with them.

20 The life of the wicked is unceasing torment,
    the years allotted to the tyrant are numbered.

21 The danger signal ever echoes in his ear,
    in the midst of peace the marauder swoops on him.

22 He has no hope of fleeing from the darkness,
    but knows that he is destined for the sword,

23 marked down as meat for the vulture.
    He knows that his ruin is at hand.

24 The hour of darkness makes him terrified;
    distress and anguish close in on him,
    as though some king were mounting an attack.

25 He raised his hand against God,
    he ventured to defy Shaddai.

26 Blindly he bore down on him
    from behind his massive shield.

27 His face had grown full and fat,
    and his thighs too heavy with flesh.

28 He had taken possession of ruined towns
    and made his dwelling in deserted houses.

    But all his careful building will go once more to ruin;

29   not for him increase of wealth, his riches will not last,
    no longer will he cast his shadow over the land.

30 A flame will wither up his tender buds;
    the wind will carry off his blossom.

31 But he should not trust in his great stature,
    if he would not trust in vain.

32 His boughs will wither before their time,
    and his branches never again be green.

33 Like a vine he will let his unripe clusters fall,
    like an olive shed his blossom.

34 Ah yes, the sinner's brood is barren,
    and fire consumes the tents of the venal.

35 Conceive mischief, and you breed disaster,
    and carry in yourself deceitfulness.

The injustice of man and the justice of God

16
Job spoke next. He said: 1

How often have I heard all this before!   2
  What sorry comforters you are!
Is there never to be an end of airy words?   3
  What a plague your need to have the last word is!
I too could talk like you,   4
  were your soul in the plight of mine.
I too could overwhelm you with sermons,
  I could shake my head over you,
and speak words of encouragement,   5
  until my lips grew tired.
But, while I am speaking, my suffering remains;   6
  and when I am not, do I suffer any the less?
And now ill-will drives me to distraction,   7
  and a whole host molests me,   8
rising, like some witness for the prosecution,
  to utter slander to my very face.
In tearing fury it pursues me,   9
  with gnashing teeth.
My enemies whet their eyes on me,
  and open gaping jaws.   10
Their insults strike like slaps in the face,
  and all set on me together.
Yes, God has handed me over to the godless,   11
  and cast me into the hands of the wicked.

I lived at peace, until he shattered me,   12
  taking me by the neck to dash me to pieces.
He has made me a target for his archery,
  shooting his arrows at me from every side.   13
Pitiless, through the loins he pierces me,
  and scatters my gall on the ground.
Breach after breach he drives through me,   14
  bearing down on me like a warrior.
I have sewn sackcloth over my skin   15
  and rubbed my brow in the dust.
My face is red with tears,   16
  and a veil of shadow hangs on my eyelids.
This notwithstanding, my hands are free of violence,   17
  and my prayer is undefiled.
Cover not my blood, O earth,*a*   18
  afford my cry no place to rest.
Henceforth I have a witness in heaven,   19
  my defender is there in the height.
My own lament is my advocate with God,   20
  while my tears flow before him.
Let this plead for me as I stand before God,   21
  as a man will plead for his fellows.
For the years of my life are numbered,   22
  and I shall soon take the road of no return.

17
My breath grows weak,   1
  and the gravediggers are gathering for me.
I am the butt of mockers,   2
  and all my waking hours I brood on their spitefulness.

3   You yourself must take my own guarantee,
        since no one cares to clap his hand on mine. *a*

4   For you have shut their hearts to reason,
        and not a hand is lifted.

5   Like a man who invites his friends to share his property
        while the eyes of his own sons languish,

6   I have become a byword among the people,
        and a creature on whose face to spit.

7   My eyes grow dim with grief,
        and my limbs wear away like a shadow.

8   At this, honest men are shocked, *b*
        and the guiltless man rails against the godless;

9   just men grow more settled in their ways,
        those whose hands are clean add strength to strength.

10   Come, then, all of you: set on me once more!
        I shall not find a single sage among you.

11   My days have passed, far otherwise than I had planned,
        and every fibre of my heart is broken.

12   Night, they say, makes room for day,
        and light is near at hand to chase the darkness.

13   All I look forward to is dwelling in Sheol,
        and making my bed in the dark.

14   I tell the tomb, 'You are my father',
        and call the worm my mother and my sister.

15   Where then is my hope?
        Who can see any happiness for me?

16   Will these come down with me to Sheol,
        or sink with me into the dust?

Anger is powerless against the course of justice

1 **18** Bildad of Shuah spoke next. He said:

2   Will you never learn to check such words?
        Do you think we shall be slow to speak?

3   Why do you regard us as beasts,
        look on us as dumb animals?

4   Tear yourself to pieces if you will,
        but the world, for all your rage, will not turn to desert,
        the rocks will not shift from their places.

5   The wicked man's light must certainly be put out,
        his brilliant flame cease to shine.

6   In his tent the light is dimmed,
        the lamp that shone on him is snuffed.

7   His vigorous stride grows cramped,
        his own cunning brings him down.

8   For into the net his own feet carry him,
        he walks among the snares.

9   A spring grips him by the heel,
        a trap snaps shut, and he is caught.

10   Hidden in the earth is a noose to snare him,
        pitfalls lie across his path.

11   Terrors attack him on every side,
        and follow behind him step for step.

12   Hunger becomes his companion,

16 a. Blood, if not covered with earth, cries to heaven for vengeance.
17 a. I.e., to go surety for me.   b. Assuming that such suffering is a punishment for guilt.

by his side Disaster stands.
Disease devours his flesh,   13
    Death's First-Born*a* gnaws his limbs.
He is torn from the shelter of his tent,   14
    and dragged before the King of Terrors.
The Lilith*b* makes her home under his roof,   15
    while people scatter brimstone on his holding.
His roots grow withered below,   16
    and his branches are blasted above.
His memory fades from the land,   17
    his name is forgotten in his homeland.
Driven from light into darkness,   18
    he is an exile from the earth,
without issue or posterity among his own people,   19
    none to live on where he has lived.
His tragic end appals the West,   20
    and fills the East with terror.
A fate like his awaits every sinful house,   21
    the home of every man who knows not God.

Faith at its height in desertion by God and man

19 Job spoke next. He said: 1

Will you never stop tormenting me,   2
    and shattering me with speeches?
Ten times, no less, you have insulted me,   3
    ill-treating me without a trace of shame.
Suppose that I have gone astray,   4
    suppose I am even yet in error:
it is still true, though you think you have the upper hand of me   5
    and feel that you have proved my guilt,
that God, you must know, is my oppressor,   6
    and his is the net that closes round me.
If I protest against such violence, there is no reply;   7
    if I appeal against it, judgement is never given.
He has built a wall across my path which I cannot pass,   8
    and covered my way with darkness.
He has stolen my honour away,   9
    and taken the crown from my head.
On every side he breaks through my defences, and I succumb.   10
    As a man a shrub, so he uproots my hope.
His anger flares against me,   11
    and he counts me as his enemy.
His troops have come in force,   12
    they have mounted their attack against me,
    laid siege to my tent.

My brothers stand aloof from me,   13
    and my relations take care to avoid me.
My kindred and my friends have all gone away,   14
    and the guests in my house have forgotten me.
The serving maids look on me as a foreigner,   15
    a stranger, never seen before.
My servant does not answer when I call him,   16
    I am reduced to entreating him.
To my wife my breath is unbearable,   17
    for my own brothers I am a thing corrupt.

18 Even the children look down on me,
    ever ready with a jibe when I appear.
19 All my dearest friends recoil from me in horror:
    those I loved best have turned against me.
20 Beneath my skin, my flesh begins to rot,
    and my bones stick out like teeth.
21 Pity me, pity me, you, my friends,
    for the hand of God has struck me.
22 Why do you hound me down like God,
    will you never have enough of my flesh?

23 Ah, would that these words of mine were written down,
    inscribed on some monument
24 with iron chisel and engraving tool,
    cut into the rock for ever.
25 This I know: that my Avenger*a* lives,
    and he, the Last, will take his stand on earth.
26 After my awaking, he will set me close to him,
    and from my flesh I shall look on God.
27 He whom I shall see will take my part:
    these eyes will gaze on him and find him not aloof.
    My heart within me sinks...
28 You, then, that mutter, 'How shall we track him down,
    what pretext shall we find against him?'
29 may well fear the sword on your own account.
    There is an anger stirred to flame by evil deeds;
    you will learn that there is indeed a judgement.

The course of justice admits of no exception

1 **20** Zophar of Naamath spoke next. He said:

2 To this my thoughts are eager to reply:
    no wonder if I am possessed by impatience.
3 I found these admonitions little to my taste,
    but my spirit whispers to me how to answer them.
4 Do you not know, that since time began
    and man was set on the earth,
5 the triumph of the wicked has always been brief,
    and the sinner's gladness has never lasted long?
6 Towering to the sky he may have been,
    with head touching the clouds;
7 but he vanishes, like a phantom, once for all,
    while those who saw him now ask, 'Where is he?'
8 Like a dream that leaves no trace he takes his flight,
    like a vision in the night he flies away.
9 The eye that looked on him will never see him more,
    his house nevermore sets eyes on him.
10 His sons must recoup his victims,
    and his children pay back his riches.
11 With the vigour of youth his bones were filled,
    now it lies in the dust with him.
12 Evil was sweet to his mouth,
    he hid it beneath his tongue;

18 a. The principal disease, probably plague.   b. A female demon of popular legend.
19 a. 'Avenger' and 'take his stand' are technical legal terms.

unwilling to let it go,   13
  he let it linger on his palate.

Such food goes bad in his belly,   14
  working inside him like the poison of a viper.

Now he must bring up all the wealth that he has swallowed,   15
  God makes him disgorge it.

He sucked 'poison of vipers':   16
  and the tongue of the adder kills him.

He will know no more of streams that run with oil,   17
  or the torrents of honey and cream.

Gone that glad face at the sight of his gains,   18
  those comfortable looks when business was thriving.

Since he once destroyed the huts of poor men,   19
  and stole other's houses when he should have built his own,

since his avarice could never be satisfied,   20
  now his hoarding will not save him;

since there was nothing ever escaped his greed,   21
  now his prosperity will not last.

His abundance at its full, want seizes him,   22
  misery descends on him in all its force.

On him God looses all his burning wrath,   23
  hurling against his flesh a hail of arrows.

No use to run away from the iron armoury,   24
  for the bow of bronze will shoot him through.

Out through his back an arrow sticks,   25
  from his gall a shining point.

An arsenal of terrors falls on him,
  and all that is dark lies in ambush for him.   26

A fire unlit by man devours him,
  and consumes what is left in his tent.

The heavens lay bare his iniquity,   27
  the earth takes its stand against him.

A flood sweeps his house away,   28
  and carries it off in the Day of Wrath.

Such is the fate God allots to the wicked,   29
  such his inheritance assigned by God.

Facts give the lie

21 Job spoke next. He said: 1

Listen, only listen to my words;   2
  this is the consolation you can offer me.

Let me have my say;   3
  you may jeer when I have spoken.

Do you think I bear a grudge against man?   4
  Have I no reason to be out of patience?

Hear what I have to say, and you will be dumbfounded,   5
  will place your hands over your mouths.

I myself am appalled at the very thought,   6
  and my flesh begins to shudder.

Why do the wicked still live on,   7
  their power increasing with their age?

They see their posterity ensured,   8
  and their offspring grow before their eyes.

The peace of their houses has nothing to fear,   9
  the rod that God wields is not for them.

10 No mishap with their bulls at breeding-time,
      nor miscarriage with their cows at calving.

11 They let their infants frisk like lambs,
      their children dance like deer.

12 They sing to the tambourine and the lyre,
      and rejoice to the sound of the flute.

13 They end their lives in happiness
      and go down in peace to Sheol.

14 Yet these were the ones who said to God, 'Go away!
      We do not choose to learn your ways.

15 What is the point of our serving Shaddai?
      What profit should we get from praying to him?'

16 Is it not true, they held their fortune in their own two hands,
      and in their counsels, left no room for God?

17 Do we often see a wicked man's light put out,
      or disaster overtaking him,
      or all his goods destroyed by the wrath of God?

18 How often do we see him harassed like a straw before the wind,
      or swept off like chaff before a gale?

19 God, you say, reserves the man's punishment for his children.
      No! Let him bear the penalty himself, and suffer under it!

20 Let him see his ruin with his own eyes,
      and himself drink the anger of Shaddai.

21 When he has gone, how can the fortunes of his House affect him,
      when the number of his months is cut off?

22 But who can give lessons in wisdom to God,
      to him who is judge of those on high?

23 And again: one man dies in the fulness of his strength,
      in all possible happiness and ease,

24 with his thighs all heavy with fat,
      and the marrow of his bones undried.

25 Another dies with bitterness in his heart,
      never having tasted happiness.

26 Together now they lie in the dust
      with worms for covering.

27 I know well what is in your mind,
      the spiteful thoughts you entertain about me.

28 'What has become of the great lord's house,' you say
      'where is the tent where the wicked lived?'

29 Have you never asked those that have travelled,
      or have you misunderstood the tale they told,

30 'The wicked man is spared for the day of disaster,
      and carried off in the day of wrath'?

31 But who is there then to accuse him to his face for his deeds,
      and pay him back for what he has done,

32 when he is on his way to his burial,
      when men are watching at his grave.

33 The clods of the valley are laid gently on him,
      and a whole procession walks behind him.

34 So what sense is there in your empty consolation?
      What nonsense are your answers!

C. THIRD SERIES OF SPEECHES

God punishes only to vindicate justice

22 Eliphaz of Teman spoke next. He said: | 1

Can a man be of any use to God, | 2
when even the wise man's wisdom is of use only to himself?

Does Shaddai derive any benefit from your integrity, | 3
or profit from your blameless conduct?

Would he punish you for your piety, | 4
and hale you off to judgement?

No, rather for your manifold wickednesses, | 5
for your unending iniquities!

You have exacted needless pledges from your brothers, | 6
and men go naked now through your despoiling;

you have grudged water to the thirsty man, | 7
and refused bread to the hungry;

you have narrowed the lands of the poor man down to nothing | 8
to set your crony in his place,

sent widows away empty-handed | 9
and crushed the arms of orphans.

No wonder, then, if snares are all around you, | 10
or sudden terrors make you afraid.

Light has turned to darkness and it blinds you, | 11
and a flood of water overwhelms you.

Does not God live at the height of heaven, | 12
and see the zenith of the stars?

Because he is far above, you said, 'What does God know? | 13
Can he peer through the shadowed darkness?'

The clouds, to him, are an impenetrable veil, | 14
and he prowls on the rim of the heavens.

And will you still follow the ancient trail | 15
trodden by the wicked?

Those men who were borne off before their time, | 16
with rivers swamping their foundations,

because they said to God, 'Go away! | 17
What can Shaddai do to us?'

Yet he himself had filled their houses with good things, | 18
while these wicked men shut him out of their counsels.

At the sight of their ruin, good men rejoice, | 19
and the innocent deride them:

'See how their greatness is brought to nothing! | 20
See how their wealth has perished in the flames!'

Well then! Make peace with him, be reconciled, | 21
and all your happiness will be restored to you.

Welcome the teaching from his lips, | 22
and keep his words close to your heart.

If you return, humbled, to Shaddai | 23
and drive all injustice from your tents,

if you reckon gold as dust | 24
and Ophir as the pebbles of the torrent,

then you will find Shaddai worth bars of gold | 25
or silver piled in heaps.

Then Shaddai will be all your delight, | 26
and you will lift your face to God.

27 You will pray, and he will hear;
    you will have good reason to fulfil your vows.

28 Whatever you undertake will go well,
    and light will shine on your path;

29 for he that casts down the boasting of the braggart
    is he that saves the man of downcast eyes.

30 If a man is innocent, he will bring him freedom,
    and freedom for you if your hands are kept unstained.

God is far off, and evil is victorious

23 1 Job spoke next. He said:

2 My lament is still rebellious,
    that heavy hand of his drags groans from me.

3 If only I knew how to reach him,
    or how to travel to his dwelling!

4 I should set out my case to him,
    my mouth would not want for arguments.

5 Then I could learn his defence, every word of it,
    taking note of everything he said to me.

6 Would he use all his strength in this debate with me?
    No, he would have to give me a hearing.

7 He would see he was contending with an honest man,
    and I should surely win my case.

8 If I go eastward, he is not there;
    or westward—still I cannot see him.

9 If I seek him in the north, he is not to be found,
    invisible still when I turn to the south.

10 And yet he knows of every step I take!
    Let him test me in the crucible: I shall come out pure gold.

11 My footsteps have followed close in his,
    I have walked in his way without swerving;

12 I have kept every commandment of his lips,
    cherishing the words from his mouth in my breast.

13 But once he has decided, who can change his mind?
    Whatever he plans, he carries out.

14 No doubt, then, but he will carry out my sentence,
    like so many other decrees that he has made.

15 That is why I am full of fear before him,
    and the more I think, the greater grows my dread of him.

16 God has made my heart sink,
    Shaddai has filled me with fear.

17 For darkness hides me from him,
    and the gloom veils his presence from me.

24 1 Why has not Shaddai his own store of times,
    and why do his faithful never see his Days?[a]

2 The wicked move boundary-marks away,
    they carry off flock and shepherd.

3 Some drive away the orphan's donkey,
    and take the widow's ox for a security.

4 Beggars, now, avoid the roads,
    and all the poor of the land must go into hiding.

---

24 a. A 'store of times' could be used to lengthen a man's life and provide the opportunity to complete his punishment; 'his Days' would be like 'the Day of Yahweh', a time when he would assert his sovereignty in universal retribution.

Like wild donkeys in the desert, they go out,   5
  driven by the hunger of their children,
  to seek food on the barren steppes.
They must do the harvesting in the scoundrel's field,   6
  they must do the picking in the vineyards of the wicked.
They go about naked, lacking clothes,   10
  and starving while they carry the sheaves.
They have no stones for pressing oil,   11
  they tread the winepresses, yet they are parched with thirst.
They spend the night naked, lacking clothes,   7
  with no covering against the cold.
Mountain rainstorms cut them through,   8
  shelterless, they hug the rocks.
Fatherless children are robbed of their lands,   9
  and poor men have their cloaks seized as security.
From the towns come the groans of the dying   12
  and the gasp of wounded men crying for help.
    Yet God remains deaf to their appeal!

Others of them hate the light,   13
  know nothing of its ways,
  avoid its paths.
When all is dark the murderer leaves his bed   14
  to kill the poor and needy.
All night long prowls the thief,
  breaking into houses while the darkness lasts.   16a
The eye of the adulterer watches for twilight,   15
  'No one will see me' he mutters
  as he masks his face.
In the daytime they go into hiding,   16b
  these folk who have no love for the light.
For all of them, morning is their darkest hour,   17
  because they know its terrors.
Is this not so? Who can prove me a liar   25
  or show that my words have no substance?

A hymn to God's omnipotence

25 Bildad of Shuah spoke next. He said: 1

What sovereignty, what awe, is his   2
  who keeps the peace in his heights!
Can anyone number his armies,   3
  or boast of having escaped his ambushes?
Could any man ever think himself innocent, when confronted by God?   4
  Born of woman, how could he ever be clean?
The very moon lacks brightness,   5
  and the stars are unclean as he sees them.
What, then, of man, maggot that he is,   6
  the son of man, a worm?

26 The Shades tremble beneath the earth;   5
  the waters and their denizens are afraid.
Before his eyes, Sheol is bare,   6
  Perdition^a itself is uncovered.
He it was who spread the North^b above the void,   7
  and poised the earth on nothingness.
He fastens up the waters in his clouds—   8
  the mists do not tear apart under their weight.

9   He covers the face of the moon at the full,
    his mist he spreads over it.

10   He has traced a ring on the surface of the waters,
    at the boundary between light and dark.

11   The pillars of the heavens tremble,
    they are struck with wonder when he threatens them.

12   With his power he calmed the Sea,
    with his wisdom struck Rahab down.

13   His breath made the heavens luminous,
    his hand transfixed the Fleeing Serpent.

14   All this but skirts the ways he treads,
    a whispered echo is all that we hear of him.
    But who could comprehend the thunder of his power?

Bildad's words are empty

1   Job spoke next. He said:

2   To one so weak, what a help you are,
    for the arm that is powerless, what a rescuer!

3   What excellent advice you give the unlearned,
    never at a loss for a helpful suggestion!

4   But who are they aimed at, these speeches of yours,
    and what spirit is this that comes out of you?

Job reaffirms his innocence while acknowledging God's power

1 **27** And Job continued his solemn discourse. He said:

2   I swear by the living God who denies me justice,
    by Shaddai who has turned my life sour,

3   that as long as a shred of life is left in me,
    and the breath of God breathes in my nostrils,

4   my lips shall never speak untruth,
    nor any lie be found on my tongue.

5   Far from ever admitting you to be in the right:
    I will maintain my innocence to my dying day.

6   I take my stand on my integrity, I will not stir:
    my conscience gives me no cause to blush for my life.

7   May my enemy meet a criminal's end,
    and my opponent suffer with the guilty.

8   For what hope, after all, has the godless when he prays,
    and raises his soul to God?

9   Is God likely to hear his cries
    when disaster descends on him?

10   Did he make Shaddai all his delight,
    calling on him at every turn?

11   No: I am showing you how God's power works,
    making no secret of Shaddai's designs.

12   And if you all had understood them for yourselves,
    you would not have wasted your breath in empty words.

The speech of Zophar: the accursed

13   Here is the fate that God has in store for the wicked,
    and the inheritance with which Shaddai endows the man of violence.

14   A sword awaits his sons, however many they may be,
    and their children after them will go unfed.

---

26 a. 'Abaddon', perhaps originally a deity, here a synonym for Sheol, the underworld.
b. The 'fixed quarter' of the vault of the sky, on which the heavens were believed to revolve.

Plague will bury those he leaves behind him,   15
   and their widows will have no chance to mourn them.

He may collect silver like dust,   16
   and gather fine clothes like clay.

Let him gather! Some good man will wear them,   17
   while his silver is shared among the innocent.

He has built himself a spider's web,   18
   made himself a watchman's shack.

He goes to bed a rich man, but never again: 19
   he wakes to find not a penny left.

Terrors attack him in broad daylight,   20
   and at night a whirlwind sweeps him off.

An east wind picks him up and drags him away,   21
   snatching him up from his homestead.

Pitilessly he is turned into a target,   22
   and forced to flee from the hands that menace him.

His downfall is greeted with applause,   23
   and hissing meets him on every side.

24   Headlong he flees from the daylight,   18acb
   he shrinks from the road which runs on the heights.

The lands of his home are under a curse,
   for heat and drought dry up the waters   19
   and scorch what is left of his corn.

The womb that shaped him forgets him   20
   and his name is recalled no longer.

Thus wickedness is blasted as a tree is struck.

He used to be harsh to the barren, childless woman,   21
   and show no kindness to the widow.

But he who lays mighty hold on tyrants   22
   rises up to take away that life which seemed secure.

He let him build his hopes on false security,   23
   but kept his eyes on every step he took.

The man had his time of glory, now he vanishes,   24
   drooping like a mallow plucked from its bed,
   and withering like an ear of corn.

D. A HYMN IN PRAISE OF WISDOM

Wisdom is beyond man's reach

28
Silver has its mines,   1
   and gold a place for refining.

Iron is extracted from the earth,   2
   the smelted rocks yield copper.

Man makes an end of darkness   3
   when he pierces to the uttermost depths
   the black and lightless rock.

Mines the lamp-folk dig   4
   in places where there is no foothold,
   and hang suspended far from mankind.

That earth from which bread comes   5
   is ravaged underground by fire.

Down there, the rocks are set with sapphires,   6
   full of spangles of gold.

Down there is a path unknown to birds of prey,   7
   unseen by the eye of any vulture;

8　　a path not trodden by the lordly beasts,
　　　　where no lion ever walked.

9　　Man attacks its flinty sides,
　　　　upturning mountains by their roots,

10　　driving tunnels through the rocks,
　　　　on the watch for anything precious.

11　　He explores the sources of rivers, [a]
　　　　and brings to daylight secrets that were hidden.

12　　But tell me, where does wisdom come from?
　　　　Where is understanding to be found?

13　　The road to it is still unknown to man,
　　　　not to be found in the land of the living.

14　　'It is not in me' says the Abyss;
　　　　'Nor here' replies the Sea.

15　　It cannot be bought with solid gold,
　　　　not paid for with any weight of silver,

16　　nor be priced by the standard of the gold of Ophir,
　　　　or of precious onyx or sapphire.

17　　No gold, no glass can match it in value,
　　　　nor for a fine gold vase can it be bartered.

18　　Nor is there need to mention coral, nor crystal;
　　　　beside wisdom pearls are not worth the fishing.

19　　Topaz from Cush is worthless in comparison,
　　　　and gold, even refined, is valueless.

20　　But tell me, where does wisdom come from?
　　　　Where is understanding to be found?

21　　It is outside the knowledge of every living thing,
　　　　hidden from the birds in the sky.

22　　Perdition and Death can only say,
　　　　'We have heard reports of it'.

23　　God alone has traced its path
　　　　and found out where it lives.

24　　(For he sees to the ends of the earth,
　　　　and observes all that lies under heaven.)

25　　When he willed to give weight to the wind
　　　　and measured out the waters with a gauge,

26　　when he made the laws and rules for the rain
　　　　and mapped a route for thunderclaps to follow,

27　　then he had it in sight, and cast its worth,
　　　　assessed it, fathomed it.

28　　And he said to man,
　　　　'Wisdom? It is fear of the Lord.
　　　　Understanding?—avoidance of evil.'

E. CONCLUSION OF THE DIALOGUE

Job's lament and final defence
a. His former happiness

1　**29**　And Job continued his solemn discourse. He said:

2　　　Who will bring back to me the months that have gone,
　　　　and the days when God was my guardian,

---

28 a. In 'the waters under the earth', cf. 26:5.

when his lamp shone over my head,   3
and his light was my guide in the darkness?
Shall I ever see my autumn days again   4
when God hedged round my tent;
when Shaddai dwelt with me,   5
and my children were around me;
when my feet were plunged in cream,   6
and streams of oil poured from the rocks?

When I went out to the gate of the city,   7
when I took my seat in the square,
as soon as I appeared, the young men stepped aside,   8
while the older men rose to their feet.
Men of note interrupted their speeches,   9
and put their fingers on their lips;
the voices of rulers were silenced,   10
and their tongues stayed still in their mouths.
They waited anxiously to hear me,   21
and listened in silence to what I had to say.
When I paused, there was no rejoinder,   22
and my words dropped on them, one by one.
They waited for me, as men wait for rain,   23
open-mouthed, as if to catch the year's last showers.
If I smiled at them, it was too good to be true,   24
they watched my face for the least sign of favour.
In a lordly style, I told them which course to take,   25
and like a king amid his armies,
I led them where I chose.

My praises echoed in every ear,   11
and never an eye but smiled on me;
because I freed the poor man when he called,   12
and the orphan who had no one to help him.
When men were dying, I it was who had their blessing;   13
if widows' hearts rejoiced, that was my doing.
I had dressed myself in righteousness like a garment;   14
justice, for me, was cloak and turban.
I was eyes for the blind,   15
and feet for the lame.
Who but I was father of the poor?   16
The stranger's case had a hearing from me.
I used to break the fangs of wicked men,   17
and snatch their prey from between their jaws.

So I thought to myself, 'I shall die in honour,   18
my days like a palm tree's for number.
My roots thrust out to the water,   19
my leaves freshened by the falling dew at night.
My reputation will never fade,   20
and the bow in my hands will gain new strength.'

b. His present misery

30   And now I am the laughing-stock   1
of my juniors, the young people,
whose fathers I did not consider fit
to put with the dogs that looked after my flock.
The strength of their hands would have been useless to me,   2

3 enfeebled as they were,
    worn out by want and hunger.
They used to gnaw the roots of desert plants,
    and brambles from abandoned ruins;
4 and plucked mallow, and brushwood leaves,
    making their meals off roots of broom.
5 Outlawed from the society of men,
    who, as against thieves, raised hue and cry against them,
6 they made their dwellings on ravines' steep sides,
    in caves or clefts in the rock.
7 You could hear them wailing from the bushes,
    as they huddled together in the thistles.
8 Their children are as worthless a brood as they were,
    nameless people, outcasts of society.
9 And these are the ones that now sing ballads about me,
    and make me the talk of the town!
10 To them I am loathsome, they stand aloof from me,
    do not scruple to spit in my face.
11 Because he has unbent my bow and chastened me
    they cast the bridle from their mouth.
12 That brood of theirs rises to right of me,
    stones are their weapons,
    and they take threatening strides towards me.
13 They have cut me off from all escape,
    there is no one to check their attack.
14 They move in, as though through a wide breach,
    and I am crushed beneath the rubble.
15 Terrors turn to meet me,
    my confidence is blown away as if by the wind;
    my hope of safety passes like a cloud.

16 And now the life in me trickles away,
    days of grief have gripped me.
17 At night-time, sickness saps my bones,
    I am gnawed by wounds that never sleep.
18 With immense power it has caught me by the clothes,
    clutching at the collar of my coat.
19 It has thrown me into the mud
    where I am no better than dust and ashes.

20 I cry to you, and you give me no answer;
    I stand before you, but you take no notice.
21 You have grown cruel in your dealings with me,
    your hand lies on me, heavy and hostile.
22 You carry me up to ride the wind,
    tossing me about in a tempest.
23 I know it is to death that you are taking me,
    the common meeting place of all that lives.

24 Yet have I ever laid a hand on the poor
    when they cried out for justice in calamity?
25 Have I not wept for all whose life is hard,
    felt pity for the penniless?
26 I hoped for happiness, but sorrow came;
    I looked for light, but there was darkness.
27 My stomach seethes, is never still,
    for every day brings further suffering.

Sombre I go, yet no one comforts me,   28
     and if I rise in the council, I rise to weep.

I have become the jackal's brother   29
     and the ostrich's companion.

My skin has turned black on me,   30
     my bones are burnt with fever.

My harp is tuned to funeral wails,   31
     my flute to the voice of mourners.

Job's apologia[a]

31

I made a pact with my eyes,   1
     not to linger on any virgin.

Now, what shares does God deal out on high,   2
     what lots does Shaddai assign from heaven,

if not disaster for the wicked,   3
     and calamities for the iniquitous?

But surely he sees how I behave,   4
     does he not count all my steps?

Have I been a fellow traveller with falsehood,   5
     or hastened my steps towards deceit?

If he weighs me on honest scales,   6
     being God, he cannot fail to see my innocence.

If my feet have wandered from the rightful path,   7
     or if my eyes have led my heart astray,
     or if my hands are smirched with any stain,

let another eat what I have sown,   8
     and let my young shoots all be rooted out.

If I ever lost my heart to any woman,   9
     or lurked at my neighbour's door,

let my wife grind corn that is not mine,   10
     let her sleep between others' sheets.

For I should have committed a sin of lust,   11
     a crime punishable by the law,

and should have lit a fire burning till Perdition,   12
     which would have devoured all my harvesting.

If ever I have infringed the rights of slave   13
     or maidservant in legal actions against me—

what shall I do, when God stands up?   14
     What shall I say, when he holds his assize?

They, no less than I, were created in the womb   15
     by the one same God who shaped us all within our mothers.

If my land calls down vengeance on my head   38
     and every furrow runs with tears,

if without payment I have eaten fruit grown on it   39
     or given those who toiled there cause to groan,

let brambles grow where once was wheat,   40a
     and foul weeds where barley thrived.

Have I been insensible to poor men's needs,   16
     or let a widow's eyes grow dim?

Or taken my share of bread alone,   17
     not giving a share to the orphan?

I, whom God has fostered father-like, from childhood,   18
     and guided since I left my mother's womb.

Have I ever seen a wretch in need of clothing,   19
     or a beggar going naked,

20   without his having cause to bless me from his heart,
          as he felt the warmth of the fleece from my lambs?

21   Have I raised my hand against the guiltless,
          presuming on my credit at the gate?

22   If so, then let my shoulder fall from its socket,
          my arm be shattered at the joint.

23   God's terror would indeed descend on me;
          how could I hold my ground before his majesty?

24   Have I put all my trust in gold,
          from finest gold sought my security?

25   Have I ever gloated over my great wealth,
          or the riches that my hands have won?

26   Or has the sight of the sun in its glory,
          or the glow of the moon as it walked the sky,

27   stolen my heart, so that my hand
          blew them a secret kiss?

28   That too would be a criminal offence,
          to have denied the supreme God.

29   Have I taken pleasure in my enemies' misfortunes,
          or made merry when disaster overtook them,

30   I who allowed my tongue to do no wrong,
          by cursing them or vowing them to death?

31   The people of my tent, did they not say,
          'Is there a man he has not filled with meat?'

32   No stranger ever had to sleep outside,
          my door was always open to the traveller.

33   Have I ever hidden my sins from men,
          keeping my iniquity secret in my breast?

34   Have I ever stood so in fear of common gossip,
          or so dreaded any family's contempt,
          that I have been reduced to silence, not venturing out of doors?

35   Who can get me a hearing from God?
          I have had my say, from A to Z; now let Shaddai answer me.
          When my adversary has drafted his writ against me

36   I shall wear it on my shoulder,
          and bind it round my head like a royal turban.

37   I will give him an account of every step of my life,
          and go as boldly as a prince to meet him.

40b   End of the words of Job.

III. THE SPEECHES OF ELIHU

Elihu joins the discussion

1 **32** These three men said no more to Job, because he was convinced of his
2   innocence. •But another man was infuriated—Elihu son of Barachel the
   Buzite, of the clan of Ram. He fumed with rage against Job for thinking that
3 he was right and God was wrong; •and he was equally angry with the three
   friends for giving up the argument and thus admitting that God could be unjust.
4 While they were speaking, Elihu had held himself back, because they were older
5 than he was; •but when he saw that the three men had not another word to say
6 in answer, his anger burst out. •Thus Elihu son of Barachel the Buzite spoke
   next. He said:

31 a. The form of this declaration, 'a conditional imprecation', is that required by law from an
accused person pleading 'not guilty'.

Prologue

        I am still young,
           and you are old,
        so I was shy, afraid,
           to tell you what I know.
        I told myself, 'Old age should speak,   7
           advancing years will utter wisdom'.
        But now I know that it is a breath in man,   8
           the inspiration of Shaddai, that gives discernment.
        Great age does not give wisdom,   9
           nor longevity sound judgement.
        And so I ask you for a hearing;   10
           now it is my turn to tell what I know.
        There was a time when I hoped for much from your speeches: 11
           I gave your reasonings a ready hearing,
           and watched you choose your words.
         I gave you all my attention,   12
           and I can say that no one gave Job the lie,
           not one of you disproved his statements.
        So do not dare to say that you have found wisdom,   13
           or that your teaching is from God not man.
        I am not going to follow the same line of argument;   14
           my reply to Job will be couched in different terms.

        They have been nonplussed, baffled for an answer,   15
           words have failed them.
        I have been waiting. Since they are silent,   16
           and have abandoned all efforts to reply,
        now I will have my say,   17
           my turn has come to say what I know.
        For I am filled with words,   18
           choked by the rush of them within me.
        I have a feeling in my heart like new wine seeking a vent,   19
           and bursting a brand-new wineskin.
        Nothing will bring relief but speech,   20
           I will open my mouth and give my answer.
        I shall not show any partiality towards anyone,   21
           nor heap on any fulsome flatteries.
        I have no skill in flattery,   22
           my creator would soon silence me otherwise.

Job's presumption

33   Now, Job, be kind enough to listen to my words,   1
           and attend to all I have to say.
        Now as I open my mouth,   2
           and my tongue shapes words against my palate,
        my heart shall utter sayings full of wisdom,   3
           and my lips speak the honest truth.
        Refute me, if you can.   5
           Prepare your ground to oppose me.
        See, I am your fellow man, not a god;   6
           like you, I was fashioned out of clay.
        God's breath it was that made me,   4
           the breathing of Shaddai that gave me life.
        Thus, no fear of me need disturb you,   7
           my hand will not lie heavy over you.

8 How could you say in my hearing—
    for the sound of your words did not escape me—

9 'I am clean, and sinless,
    I am pure, free of all fault.

10 Yet he is inventing grievances against me,
    and imagining me his enemy.

11 He puts me in the stocks,
    he watches my every step'?

12 In saying so, I tell you, you are wrong:
    God does not fit man's measure.

13 Why do you rail at him
    for not replying to you, word for word?

14 God speaks first in one way,
    and then in another, but no one notices.

15 He speaks by dreams, and visions that come in the night,
    when slumber comes on mankind,
    and men are all asleep in bed.

16 Then it is he whispers in the ear of man,
    or may frighten him with fearful sights,

17 to turn him away from evil-doing,
    and make an end of his pride;

18 to save his soul from the pit
    and his life from the pathway to Sheol.

19 With suffering, too, he corrects man on his sick-bed,
    when his bones keep trembling with palsy;

20 when his whole self is revolted by food,
    and his appetite spurns dainties;

21 when his flesh rots as you watch it,
    and his bare bones begin to show;

22 when his soul is drawing near to the pit,
    and his life to the dwelling of the dead.

23 Then there is an Angel by his side,
    a Mediator, chosen out of thousands,
    to remind a man where his duty lies,

24   to take pity on him and to say,
'Release him from descent into the pit,
    for I have found a ransom for his life';

25 his flesh recovers the bloom of its youth,
    he lives again as he did when he was young.

26 He prays to God who has restored him to favour,
    and comes, in happiness, to see his face.
He publishes far and wide the news of his vindication,

27   singing before his fellow men this hymn of praise,
'I sinned and left the path of right,
    but God has not punished me as my sin deserved.

28 He has spared my soul from going down into the pit,
    and is allowing my life to continue in the light.'

29 All this God does
    again and yet again for man,

30 rescuing his soul from the pit,
    and letting the light of life shine bright on him.

31 Job, give me your attention, listen well;
    keep silence: I have more to say.

32 If you have anything to say, refute me,
    speak out, for I would gladly recognise your innocence.

> If you have not, then listen:
>> keep silence, while I teach you wisdom.   33

The three Sages have failed to justify God

34 Elihu continued his speech. He said: 1

> You men of wisdom, listen to my words: 2
>> lend me your ears, you learned men.
> The ear is a judge of speeches,   3
>> just as the palate can tell one food from another.
> Let us discover together where justice lies,   4
>> and settle among us what is best.
> Now Job has said, 'I am in the right,   5
>> and God refuses to grant me justice.
> The judge who judges me is ill-disposed,   6
>> and though I have not sinned, my wounds are past all cure.'
> Are there many men like Job,   7
>> who drink scurrility like water,
> who keep company with evil-doers,   8
>> and march in step with the wicked?
> Did he not say it was useless   9
>> for man to try to please God?

> Listen then to me, like intelligent men.   10
> So far is God removed from wickedness,
>> and Shaddai from injustice,
> that he requites a man for what he does,   11
>> treating each one as his way of life deserves.
> God never does wrong, do not doubt that!   12
>> Shaddai does not deflect the course of right.
> It is not as if someone else had given him the earth in trust,   13
>> or confided the whole universe to his care.
> Were he to recall his breath,   14
>> to draw his breathing back into himself,
> things of flesh would perish all together,   15
>> and man would return to dust.
> If you have any intelligence, listen to this,   16
>> and lend your ear to what I have to say.
> Could an enemy of justice ever govern?   17
>> Would you dare condemn the Just One, the Almighty,
> who can tell kings that they are good for nothing,   18
>> and treat noblemen like criminals,
> who shows no partiality to princes   19
>> and makes no distinction between the rich and the poor,
> all alike being made by his own hands?
>> They die, they are gone in an instant,   20
> great though they are, they perish in the dead of night;
>> it costs him no effort to remove a tyrant.
> His eyes, you see, keep watch on all men's ways,   21
>> and he observes their every step.
> Not darkness, nor the deepest shadow,   22
>> can hide the wrong-doer.
> He serves no writ on men   23
>> summoning them to appear before God's court:
> he smashes great men's power without enquiry   24
>> and sets up others in their places.
> He knows well enough what they are about,   25

and one fine night he throws them down for men to trample on.

26   He strikes them down for their wickedness,
       and makes them prisoners for all to see.

27   You may say, 'They have so turned from him,
       and so ignored his ways,

28   that the poor have cried out to him against them
       and the wailing of the humble has assailed his ears,

29   yet he is unmoved, and nothing can touch him;
       he hides his face and nobody can see him'.

       But nonetheless he does take pity on nations and on men,
30   freeing the godless man from the meshes of distress.

31   If such a man says to God,
       'I was led astray, I will sin no more.

32   If I did wrong, tell me about it,
       if I have been unjust, I will be so no more'—

33   in such a case, do you think he ought to punish him,
       you who reject his decisions?
       Since it is you who make this choice, not I,
       let us all share your knowledge!

34   But this is what all sensible folk will say,
       and any wise man among my hearers,

35   'There is no wisdom in Job's speech,
       his words lack sense.

36   Put him unsparingly to the proof
       since his retorts are the same as those that the wicked make.

37   For to sin he adds rebellion,
       calling justice into question in our midst
       and heaping abuse on God.'

God is not indifferent to what happens on earth

1 **35** Elihu continued his speech. He said:

2   Do you presume to maintain that you are in the right,
       to insist on your innocence before God,

3   even to ask him, 'How does it affect you,
       what harm has it done you if I have sinned?'

4   Well then, this is how I will answer you,
       and your friends as well.

5   Look up at the skies, look at them well,
       and see how high the clouds are above you.

6   If you sin, what do you achieve against him?
       If you heap up crimes, what is the injury you do him?

7   If you are just, what do you give him,
       what benefit does he receive at your hands?

8   Your fellow men are the ones to suffer from your crimes,
       humanity is the gainer if you are good.

9   When people groan under the weight of oppression,
       or cry out under the tyranny of the mighty,

10   no one thinks to ask, 'Where is God, my maker,
       who makes glad songs ring out at dead of night,

11   who makes us cleverer than the earth's wild beasts,
       wiser than the birds in the sky?'

12   Then they cry aloud, but he does not answer
       because of man's base pride.

How idle to maintain that God is deaf,   13
    that Shaddai notices nothing!

You even claim, 'He does not see me: 14
    my cause is exposed before him, and yet I wait and wait'.

Or even, 'His anger never punishes,   15
    he does not seem to know of men's rebellion'.

Hence when Job opens his mouth, it is for idle talk: 16
    his spate of words comes out of ignorance.

The real meaning of Job's sufferings

36 Elihu went on speaking. He said: 1

Be patient with me a little longer while I explain,   2
    for I have more to say on God's behalf.

I will range far afield for my arguments   3
    to prove my Maker just.

What I say contains no fallacies, I assure you,   4
    you see before you an enlightened man.

God does not spurn the blameless man   5
    or let the sinner live on in all his power.   6

He accords justice to the poor,
    and upholds the good man's rights.   7

When he raises kings to thrones,
    if they grow proud of their unending sway,

then he fetters them with chains,   8
    binding them in the bondage of distress.

He shows them all that they have done,   9
    and all the sins of pride they have committed.

He whispers a message in their ears,   10
    urging them to amend themselves.

If they listen and do as he says,   11
    their days end in happiness,
    and their closing years are full of ease.

If not, then a thunderbolt destroys them,   12
    and death comes on them unawares.

Yes the stubborn who cherish anger,   13
    and when he shackles them, do not ask for help:

they die in their youth,   14
    or lead a life despised by all.

The wretched, however, he saves by their very wretchedness,   15
    and uses distress to open their eyes.

For you, no less, he plans relief from sorrow.   16
Once you lived in luxury unbounded,
    with rich food piled high on your table.

But you did not execute justice on the wicked,   17
    you cheated orphaned children of their rights.

In future beware of being led astray by riches,   18
    or corrupted by fat bribes.

Prosecute the rich, not merely the penniless;   19
    strong-armed men as well as those who are powerless.

Do not trample on those you do not know   20
    to install your relations in their place.

Avoid any tendency to wrong-doing,   21
    for such has been the true cause of your trials.

A hymn to God's wisdom and omnipotence

22   Look, by reason of his power God is supreme,
      what teacher can be compared with him?

23   Who has ever told him which course to take,
      or dared to say to him, 'You have done wrong'?

24   Turn your mind rather to praising his works,
      a theme that many men have sung:

25   a sight that everyone can see,
      that man may gaze on from afar.

26   Yes, the greatness of God exceeds our knowledge,
      the number of his years is past computing.

27   He it is who keeps the raindrops back,
      dissolving the showers into mist,

28   which otherwise the clouds would spill
      in floods over all mankind.

31   Thanks to them he nourishes the nations
      with generous gifts of food.

29   And who can fathom how he spreads the clouds,
      or why such crashes thunder from his tent?

30   He spreads out the mist, wrapping it about him,
      and covers the tops of the mountains.

32   He gathers up the lightning in his hands,
      choosing the mark it is to reach;

33   his thunder gives warning of its coming:
      wrath overtakes iniquity.

37

1   At this my own heart quakes,
      and leaps from its place.

2   Listen, oh listen, to the blast of his voice
      and the sound that blares from his mouth.

3   He hurls his lightning below the span of heaven,
      it strikes to the very ends of the earth.

4   After it comes the roar of his voice,
      the peal of God's majestic thunder.
      He does not check his thunderbolts
      until his voice resounds no more.

5   No doubt of it, but God reveals wonders,
      and does great deeds that we cannot understand.

6   When he says to the snow, 'Fall on the earth'
      or tells the rain to pour down in torrents,

7   he brings all men's strivings to a standstill
      so that each must acknowledge his hand at work.

8   All the beasts go back to their dens,
      taking shelter in their lairs.

9   The storm wind comes from the Mansion of the South,
      and the north winds usher in the cold.

10   God breathes, and the ice is there,
      the surface of the waters freezes over.

11   He weighs the clouds down with moisture,
      and the storm clouds radiate his lightning.

12   He himself guides their wheeling motion
      directing all their seasonal changes:
      they carry out his orders to the letter
      all over his inhabited world.

13   Whether for punishing earth's peoples
      or for a work of mercy, he despatches them.

14   Listen to all this Job: no backsliding now!

Meditate on God's wonders.

Can you tell how God controls them   15
     or how his clouds make the lightning flash?
Can you tell how he holds the clouds in balance: 16
     a miracle of consummate skill?
When your clothes are hot to your body   17
     and the earth lies still under the south wind,
can you help him to spread the vault of heaven,   18
     or temper that mirror of cast metal?
Tell me what to say to him: 19

. . . .

Can my words carry weight with him?   20
     Do man's commands reach his ears?
There are times when the light vanishes   21
     behind darkening clouds;
then comes the wind, sweeping them away,
     and brightness spreads from the north.   22
God is clothed in fearful splendour:
     he, Shaddai, is far beyond our reach.   23
Supreme in power, in equity,
     excelling in justice, yet no oppressor—
no wonder that men fear him,   24
     and thoughtful men hold him in awe.

IV. THE SPEECHES OF YAHWEH

FIRST SPEECH

Job must bow to the creator's wisdom

38 Then from the heart of the tempest Yahweh gave Job his answer. 1
He said:

Who is this obscuring my designs   2
     with his empty-headed words?
Brace yourself like a fighter;   3
     now it is my turn to ask questions and yours to inform me.
Where were you when I laid the earth's foundations?   4
     Tell me, since you are so well-informed!
Who decided the dimensions of it, do you know?   5
     Or who stretched the measuring line across it?
What supports its pillars at their bases?   6
     Who laid its cornerstone
when all the stars of the morning were singing with joy,
     and the Sons of God in chorus were chanting praise?   7
Who pent up the sea behind closed doors   8
     when it leapt tumultuous out of the womb,
when I wrapped it in a robe of mist   9
     and made black clouds its swaddling bands;
when I marked the bounds it was not to cross   10
     and made it fast with a bolted gate?
Come thus far, I said, and no farther: 11
     here your proud waves shall break.

Have you ever in your life given orders to the morning   12
     or sent the dawn to its post,
telling it to grasp the earth by its edges   13

and shake the wicked out of it,

14   when it changes the earth^a to sealing clay
    and dyes it as a man dyes clothes;

15   stealing the light from wicked men^b
    and breaking the arm raised to strike?

16   Have you journeyed all the way to the sources of the sea,
    or walked where the Abyss is deepest?

17   Have you been shown the gates of Death
    or met the janitors of Shadowland?

18   Have you an inkling of the extent of the earth?
    Tell me all about it if you have!

19   Which is the way to the home of the light,
    and where does darkness live?

20   You could then show them the way to their proper places,
    or put them on the path to where they live!

21   If you know all this, you must have been born with them,
    you must be very old by now!

22   Have you ever visited the place where the snow is kept,
    or seen where the hail is stored up,

23   which I keep for times of stress,
    for days of battle and war?

24   From which direction does the lightning fork
    when it scatters sparks over the earth?

25   Who carves a channel for the downpour,
    and hacks a way for the rolling thunder,

26   so that rain may fall on lands where no one lives,
    and the deserts void of human dwelling,

27   giving drink to the lonely wastes
    and making grass spring where everything was dry?

28   Has the rain a father?
    Who begets the dewdrops?

29   What womb brings forth the ice,
    and gives birth to the frost of heaven,

30   when the waters grow hard as stone
    and the surface of the deep congeals?

31   Can you fasten the harness of the Pleiades,
    or untie Orion's bands?

32   Can you guide the morning star season by season
    and show the Bear and its cubs which way to go?

33   Have you grasped the celestial laws?
    Could you make their writ run on the earth?

34   Can your voice carry as far as the clouds
    and make the pent-up waters do your bidding?

35   Will lightning flashes come at your command
    and answer, 'Here we are'?

36   Who gave the ibis wisdom
    and endowed the cock with foreknowledge?^c

37   Whose skill details every cloud
    and tilts the flasks of heaven,

38   until the soil cakes into a solid mass
    and clods of earth cohere together?

---

38 a. The 'clay' is red in colour.   **b.** The light, or natural element, of the wicked, is the darkness of night.   **c.** Both birds credited with foresight: the ibis heralds the flooding of the Nile, the cock announces the dawn.

Do you find a prey for the lioness   39
    and satisfy the hunger of her whelps
when they crouch in their dens   40
    and lurk in their lairs?
Who makes provision for the raven   41
    when his squabs cry out to God
    and crane their necks in hunger?

39

Do you know how mountain goats give birth,   1
    or have you ever watched the hinds in labour?
How many months do they carry their young?   2
    At what time do they give birth?
They crouch to drop their young,   3
    and let their burdens fall in the open desert;
and when the calves have grown and gathered strength   4
    they leave them, never to return.

Who gave the wild donkey his freedom,   5
    and untied the rope from his proud neck?
I have given him the desert as a home,   6
    the salt plains as his own habitat.
He scorns the turmoil of the town: 7
    there are no shouts from a driver for him to listen for.
The mountains are the pastures that he ranges   8
    in quest of any type of green blade or leaf.

Is the wild ox willing to serve you   9
    or spend a night beside your manger?
If you tie a rope round his neck   10
    will he harrow the furrows for you?
Can you rely on his massive strength   11
    and leave him to do your heavy work?
Can you depend on him to come home   12
    carrying your grain to your threshing-floor?

Can the wing of the ostrich be compared   13
    with the plumage of the stork or falcon?
She leaves her eggs on the ground   14
    with only earth to warm them;
forgetting that a foot may tread on them   15
    or a wild beast may crush them.
Cruel to her chicks as if they were not hers,   16
    little she cares if her labour goes for nothing.
God, you see, has made her unwise,   17
    and given her no share of common sense.
Yet, if she bestirs herself to use her height,   18
    she can make fools of horse and rider too.

Are you the one who makes the horse so brave   19
    and covers his neck with flowing hair?
Do you make him leap like a grasshopper?   20
    His proud neighing spreads terror far and wide.
Exultantly he paws the soil of the valley,   21
    and prances eagerly to meet the clash of arms.
He laughs at fear; he is afraid of nothing,   22
    he recoils before no sword.
On his back the quiver rattles,   23
    the flashing spear and javelin.

24　　Quivering with impatience, he eats up the miles;
　　　　when the trumpet sounds, there is no holding him.
25　　At each trumpet blast he shouts 'Hurrah!'
　　　　He scents the battle from afar,
　　　　hearing the thundering of chiefs, the shouting.

26　　Does the hawk take flight on your advice
　　　　when he spreads his wings to travel south?
27　　Does the eagle soar at your command
　　　　to make her eyrie in the heights?
28　　She spends her nights among the crags
　　　　with an unclimbed peak as her redoubt
29　　from which she watches for prey,
　　　　fixing it with her far-ranging eye.
30　　She feeds her young on blood:
　　　　wherever men fall dying, there she is.

31/1　**40** Then Yahweh turned to Job, and he said:

32/2　　Is Shaddai's opponent willing to give in?
　　　　Has God's critic thought up an answer?

33/3　Job replied to Yahweh:

34/4　　My words have been frivolous: what can I reply?
　　　　I had better lay my finger on my lips.
35/5　　I have spoken once... I will not speak again;
　　　　more than once... I will add nothing.

SECOND SPEECH

God is master of the forces of evil

6/1　Yahweh gave Job his answer from the heart of the tempest. He said:

7/2　　Brace yourself like a fighter,
　　　　now it is my turn to ask questions and yours to inform me.
8/3　　Do you really want to reverse my judgement,
　　　　and put me in the wrong to put yourself in the right?
9/4　　Has your arm the strength of God's,
　　　　can your voice thunder as loud?
10/5　　If so, assume your dignity, your state,
　　　　robe yourself in majesty and splendour.
11/6　　Let the spate of your anger flow free;
　　　　humiliate the haughty at a glance!
12/7　　Cast one look at the proud and bring them low,
　　　　strike down the wicked where they stand.
13/8　　Bury the lot of them in the ground,
　　　　shut them, silent-faced, in the dungeon.
14/9　　I myself will be the first to acknowledge
　　　　that your own right hand can assure your triumph.

Behemoth

15/10　　Now think of Behemoth;
　　　　he eats greenstuff like the ox.
16/11　　But what strength he has in his loins,
　　　　what power in his stomach muscles!
17/12　　His tail is as stiff as a cedar,
　　　　the sinews of his thighs are tightly knit.

His vertebrae are bronze tubing,
    his bones as hard as hammered iron.   18 / 13

He is the masterpiece of all God's work,
    but his Maker threatened him with the sword,   19 / 14

forbidding him the mountain regions
    where all the wild beasts have their playground.   20 / 15

So he lies beneath the lotus,
    and hides among the reeds in the swamps.   21 / 16

The leaves of the lotus give him shade,
    the willows by the stream shelter him.   22 / 17

Should the river overflow on him, why should he worry?
    A Jordan could pour down his throat without his caring.   23 / 18

So who is going to catch him by the eyes
    or drive a peg through his nostrils?   24 / 19

Leviathan

Leviathan, too! Can you catch him with a fish-hook
    or run a line round his tongue?   25 / 20

Can you put a ring through his nose
    or pierce his jaw with a hook?   26 / 21

Will he plead and plead with you,
    will he coax you with smooth words?   27 / 22

Will he strike a bargain with you
    to become your slave for life?   28 / 23

Will you make a pet of him, like a bird,
    keep him on a lead to amuse your maids?   29 / 24

Is he to be sold by the fishing guild
    and then retailed by merchants?   30 / 25

Riddle his hide with darts?
    Prod his head with a harpoon?   31 / 26

You have only to lay a finger on him
    never to forget the struggle or risk it again!   32 / 27

41

Any hopes you might have would prove vain,
    for the mere sight of him would stagger you.   1 / 28

When roused, he grows ferocious,
    no one can face him in a fight.   2 / 1

Who can attack him with impunity?
    No one beneath all heaven.   3 / 2

Next I will talk of his limbs
    and describe his matchless strength.   4 / 3

Who can unloose the front of his coat
    or pierce the double armour of his breastplate?   5 / 4

Who dare open the gates of his mouth?
    Terror dwells in those rows of teeth!   6 / 5

His back is like rows of shields,
    sealed with a seal of stone,   7 / 6

touching each other so close
    that not a breath could pass between;   8 / 7

sticking to one another
    to make an indivisible whole.   9 / 8

When he sneezes, light leaps forth,
    his eyes are like the eyelids of the dawn.   10 / 9

From his mouth come fiery torches,
    sparks of fire fly out of it.   11 / 10

His nostrils belch smoke
    like a cauldron boiling on the fire.   12 / 11

13/12	His breath could kindle coals,
	so hot a flame issues from his mouth.
14/13	Strength has made a home in his neck,
	fear leaps before him as he goes.
17/16	When he stands up, the waves themselves take fright,
	the billows of the sea retreat.
15/14	The folds of his flesh stick together,
	firmly set in it, immovable.
16/15	His heart is as hard as rock
	unyielding as a millstone.
18/17	Sword may strike him, but cannot pierce him;
	no more can spear, javelin or lance.
19/18	Iron means no more to him than straw,
	nor bronze than rotten wood.
20/19	The arrow does not make him run,
	sling stones he treats as wisps of hay.
21/20	A club strikes him like a reed,
	he laughs at the whirring javelin.
22/21	He has sharp potsherds underneath,
	and moves across the slime like a harrow.
23/22	He churns the depths into a seething cauldron,
	he makes the sea fume like a scent burner.
24/23	Behind him he leaves a glittering wake—
	a white fleece seems to float on the deeps.
25/24	He has no equal on earth,
	being created without fear.
26/25	He looks the haughtiest in the eye;
	of all the sons of pride he is the king.

Job's final answer

1 **42** This was the answer Job gave to Yahweh:

2 I know that you are all-powerful:
  what you conceive, you can perform.

3 I am the man who obscured your designs
  with my empty-headed words.
  I have been holding forth on matters I cannot understand,
  on marvels beyond me and my knowledge.

4 (Listen, I have more to say,
  now it is my turn to ask questions and yours to inform me.)

5 I knew you then only by hearsay;
  but now, having seen you with my own eyes,

6 I retract all I have said,
  and in dust and ashes I repent.

V. EPILOGUE

Yahweh rebukes the three Sages

7 When Yahweh had said all this to Job, he turned to Eliphaz of Teman.
'I burn with anger against you and your two friends' he said 'for not speaking
8 truthfully about me as my servant Job has done. •So now find seven bullocks
and seven rams, and take them back with you to my servant Job and offer a
holocaust for yourselves, while Job, my servant, offers prayers for you. I will
listen to him with favour and excuse your folly in not speaking of me properly
9 as my servant Job has done.' •Eliphaz of Teman, Bildad of Shuah and Zophar

of Naamath went away to do as Yahweh had ordered, and Yahweh listened to Job with favour.

Yahweh restores Job's fortunes

Yahweh restored Job's fortunes, because he had prayed for his friends. 10 More than that, Yahweh gave him double what he had before. •And all his 11 brothers and all his sisters and all his friends of former times came to see him and sat down at table with him. They showed him every sympathy, and comforted him for all the evils Yahweh had inflicted on him. Each of them gave him a silver coin, and each a gold ring. •Yahweh blessed Job's new fortune 12 even more than his first one. He came to own fourteen thousand sheep, six thousand camels, a thousand yoke of oxen and a thousand she-donkeys. •He had 13 seven sons and three daughters; •his first daughter he called 'Turtledove', the 14 second 'Cassia' and the third 'Mascara'. •Throughout the land there were no 15 women as beautiful as the daughters of Job. And their father gave them inheritance rights like their brothers.

After his trials, Job lived on until he was a hundred and forty years old, and 16 saw his children and his children's children up to the fourth generation. •Then 17 Job died, an old man and full of days.

INTRODUCTION TO
THE PSALMS

The Psalter, or Book of Psalms, is a collection of hymns used in the liturgical worship of the Temple; it is arranged in five 'books' or parts. Some of the psalms can be identified as written for one or other of the great festivals (for example the group called 'Songs of Ascents', which are for the annual pilgrimage); others cannot be so simply defined, and it may well be that the liturgical use of them changed during the eventful years of Israel's history.

The 150 psalms represent the work of several centuries. There are some which can be dated from the Exile and some after the return to Jerusalem, and others which are clearly allied to the wisdom writings of later times; but there are also psalms which belong to the period of the kings and among these there may be psalms as early as David himself, traditionally the writer and singer of songs. Although the inscriptions appear to ascribe many of the psalms to David, it should be noted that these inscriptions actually refer to different collections of the hymns made at different times or places; it is the existence of these separate collections which explains the duplication of a few Psalms in the Psalter. Nevertheless, an early editor accepted some of the inscriptions as indications of authorship, and added annotations on the probable occasion of their writing.

The psalms have for so long been used in Christian worship that their early origins are often overlooked; like all lyrical poetry, they express passion—and in their own time there was nothing improper about violent curses against enemies and oppressors or against the unfaithful, nor about a frank longing for revenge and massacre. These are notes which can be found in the psalms and, like the name Yahweh, must be accepted as a part of the world of the psalmists. But the principal kinds of psalms which can be distinguished by their subjects include: hymns of praise, often recalling the mighty works of God in the past history of the nation; prayers of entreaty or penitence, either personal or collective; thanksgivings; wisdom psalms and praise of the Law; prophetic oracles; royal psalms. The royal psalms are addressed to kings, the successors of David, and often include prophecies of their future glory; after the end of the monarchy, these oracles together with the prophecies of the renewal of Zion became a focus of the messianic hope, and they are commonly accepted as such by the writers of the New Testament.

THE PSALMS

PSALM 1

The two ways

Happy the man
who never follows the advice of the wicked,
or loiters on the way that sinners take,
or sits about with scoffers,
but finds his pleasure in the Law of Yahweh,
and murmurs his law day and night.

He is like a tree that is planted
by water streams,
yielding its fruit in season,
its leaves never fading;
success attends all he does.

It is nothing like this with the wicked, nothing like this!

No, these are like chaff
blown away by the wind.
The wicked will not stand firm when Judgement comes,
nor sinners when the virtuous assemble.
For Yahweh takes care of the way the virtuous go,
but the way of the wicked is doomed.

PSALM 2

The messianic drama

Why this uproar among the nations?
Why this impotent muttering of pagans—
kings on earth rising in revolt,
princes plotting against Yahweh and his Anointed,
'Now let us break their fetters!
Now let us throw off their yoke!'

The One whose throne is in heaven sits laughing,
Yahweh derides them.
Then angrily he addresses them,
in a rage he strikes them with panic,
'This is my king, installed by me
on Zion, my holy mountain'.

Let me proclaim Yahweh's decree;
he has told me, 'You are my son,
today I have become your father.
Ask and I will give you the nations for your heritage,

1

2

3

4

5

6

1

2

3

4

5

6

7

8

the ends of the earth for your domain.
9   With iron sceptre you will break them,
   shatter them like potter's ware.'

10   So now, you kings, learn wisdom,
   earthly rulers, be warned:
11   serve Yahweh, fear him,
12   tremble and kiss his feet,
   or he will be angry and you will perish,
   for his anger is very quick to blaze.

   Happy all who take shelter in him.

PSALM 3

Morning prayer of the virtuous man under persecution

Psalm   Of David   When he was escaping from his son Absalom

1   Yahweh, more and more are turning against me,
   more and more rebelling against me,
2   more and more saying about me,
   'There is no help for him in his God'.   *Pause*

3   But, Yahweh, my encircling shield,
   my glory, you help me hold up my head.
4   Loudly I cry to Yahweh,
   and he answers me from his holy mountain.   *Pause*

5   Now I can lie down and go to sleep
   and then awake, for Yahweh has hold of me:
6   no fear now of those tens of thousands
   posted against me wherever I turn.

7   Rise, Yahweh!
      Save me, my God!
   You hack all my enemies to the cheekbone,
   you break the teeth of the wicked.
8   From Yahweh, rescue.
      On your people, blessing!   *Pause*

PSALM 4

Evening prayer

For the choirmaster   For strings   Psalm   Of David

1   God, guardian of my rights, you answer when I call,
      when I am in trouble, you come to my relief;
      now be good to me and hear my prayer.

2   You men, why shut your hearts so long,
   loving delusions, chasing after lies.   *Pause*

3   Know this, Yahweh works wonders for those he loves,
   Yahweh hears me when I call to him.

Tremble: give up sinning,   4
spend your night in quiet meditation.   *Pause*
Offer sacrifice in a right spirit, and trust Yahweh.   5

'Who will give us sight of happiness?' many say.   6
Show us the light of your face, turned towards us!

Yahweh, •you have given more joy to my heart   7
than others ever knew, for all their corn and wine.

In peace I lie down, and fall asleep at once,   8
since you alone, Yahweh, make me rest secure.

PSALM 5

Morning Prayer

For the choirmaster   For flutes   Psalm   Of David

Yahweh, let my words come to your ears,   1
     spare a thought for my sighs.
Listen to my cry for help,   2
     my King and my God!

I say this prayer to you, •Yahweh,   3
     for at daybreak you listen for my voice;
and at dawn I hold myself in readiness for you,
     I watch for you.

You are not a God who is pleased with wickedness,   4
     you have no room for the wicked;
boasters collapse   5
     under your scrutiny.

You hate all evil men,
     liars you destroy;   6
murderers and frauds
     Yahweh detests.

But I, so great is your love,   7
     may come to your house,
and before your holy Temple bow down
     in reverence to you.

Yahweh, lead me in the path of your righteousness,   8
     for there are men lying in wait for me;
make your way plain before me.

Not a word from their lips can be trusted,   9
     deep within them lies ruin,
their throats are yawning graves;
     they make their tongues so smooth!

Pronounce them guilty, God,   10
     make their intrigues their own downfall!
Hound them for their countless crimes,
     since they have rebelled against you.

But joy for all who take shelter in you,   11
     endless shouts of joy!
Since you protect them, they exult in you,
     those who love your name.

12 It is you who bless the virtuous man, Yahweh;
your favour is like a shield covering him.

PSALM 6

Prayer in ordeal

For the choirmaster   For strings, for the octachord   Psalm   Of David

1 Yahweh, do not punish me in your rage,
or reprove me in the heat of anger.
2 Pity me, Yahweh, I have no strength left,
heal me, my bones are in torment,
3 my soul is in utter torment.
Yahweh, how long will you be?

4 Come back, Yahweh, rescue my soul,
save me, if you love me;
5 for in death there is no remembrance of you:
who can sing your praises in Sheol?

6 I am worn out with groaning,
every night I drench my pillow
and soak my bed with tears;
7 my eye is wasted with grief,
I have grown old with enemies all round me.

8 Away from me, all you evil men!
For Yahweh has heard the sound of my weeping;
9 Yahweh has heard my petition,
Yahweh will accept my prayer.
10 Let all my enemies, discredited, in utter torment,
fall back in sudden confusion.

PSALM 7

Prayer of the virtuous under persecution

Lamentation   Of David, who sang it to Yahweh about Cush the Benjaminite

1 Yahweh my God, I take shelter in you;
from all who hound me, save me, rescue me,
2 or, like a lion, he will carry me off
and tear me to pieces where no one can save me.

3 Yahweh my God, if I ever
soiled my hands with fraud,
4 repaid a friend evil for good,
spared a man who wronged me,[a]
5 then let the enemy hound me down and catch me,
let him stamp my life into the ground,
and leave my entrails lying in the dust!   Pause

7 a. The *lex talionis*, cf. Ex 21:25, required that evil should be rendered for evil, just as good for good.

Rise, Yahweh, in anger,
  awake, my God!   6
Confront the raging of my enemies,
  you who demand that justice shall be done.
Let the nations muster round you in a body,   7
  and then return, high over them.
(Yahweh is arbiter of nations.)*b*   8

Give judgement for me, Yahweh: as my virtue
  and my integrity deserve.
Bring the maliciousness of evil men to an end,   9
  set the virtuous on his feet,
    you righteous God,
assessor of mind and heart.

God is the shield that protects me,   10
  he preserves upright hearts,
God the righteous judge   11
  is slow to show his anger,
but he is a God who is always enraged
  by those who refuse to repent.   12

The enemy may sharpen his sword,
he may bend his bow and take aim,
but the weapons he prepares will kill himself   13
and his arrows turn into firebrands.
Look at him, pregnant with wickedness,   14
conceiving Spite, he gives birth to Mishap.
He dug a pit, hollowed it out,   15
only to fall into his own trap!
His spite recoils on his own head,   16
his brutality falls back on his own skull.

I give thanks to Yahweh for his righteousness,   17
I sing praise to the name of the Most High.

PSALM 8

The munificence of the creator

*For the choirmaster   On the ...of Gath*a *Psalm   Of David*

Yahweh, our Lord,   1
how great your name throughout the earth!

Above the heavens is your majesty chanted
by the mouths of children, babes in arms.   2
You set your stronghold firm against your foes
to subdue enemies and rebels.

I look up at your heavens, made by your fingers,   3
at the moon and stars you set in place—
ah, what is man that you should spare a thought for him,   4
the son of man that you should care for him?

Yet you have made him little less than a god,   5
you have crowned him with glory and splendour,

6　　　　　made him lord over the work of your hands,
　　　　　　set all things under his feet,

7　　　　　sheep and oxen, all these,
　　　　　　yes, wild animals too,
8　　　　　birds in the air, fish in the sea
　　　　　　travelling the paths of the ocean.

9　　　　　Yahweh, our Lord,
　　　　　　how great your name throughout the earth!

PSALM 9-10

God crushes the wicked and saves the humble[a]

For the choirmaster　For oboe and harp　Psalm　Of David

1　*Aleph*　　I thank you, Yahweh, with all my heart;
　　　　　　I recite your marvels one by one,
2　　　　　I rejoice and exult in you,
　　　　　　I sing praise to your name, Most High.

3　*Beth*　　My enemies are in retreat,
　　　　　　stumbling, perishing as you confront them:
4　　　　　you have upheld the justice of my cause
　　　　　　from the throne where you sit as righteous judge.

5　*Ghimel*　You have checked the nations, you have crushed the wicked,
　　　　　　blotted out their name for ever and ever;
6　　　　　the enemy is finished, in everlasting ruin,
　　　　　　you have overthrown cities, their memory has perished.

7　*He*　　See, •Yahweh is enthroned for ever,
　　　　　　he sets up his throne for judgement;
8　　　　　he is going to judge the world with justice,
　　　　　　and pronounce a true verdict on the nations.

9　*Waw*　　May Yahweh be a stronghold for the oppressed,
　　　　　　a stronghold when times are hard.
10　　　　　Those who acknowledge your name can rely on you,
　　　　　　you never desert those who seek you, Yahweh.

11　*Zain*　To Yahweh with his home in Zion, sing praise,
　　　　　　tell the nations of his mighty actions;
12　　　　　he, the avenger of blood, remembers them,
　　　　　　he does not ignore the cry of the wretched.

13　*Heth*　Take pity on me, Yahweh, look on my suffering,
　　　　　　you who lift me back from the gates of death,
14　　　　　that in the gates of the daughter of Zion
　　　　　　I may recite your praises one by one, rejoicing that you have
　　　　　　　　saved me.

15　*Teth*　The nations have sunk into a pit of their own making,
　　　　　　they are caught by the feet in the snare they set themselves.

b. This gloss indicates that the peoples are gathered for judgement.
8 a. A musical instrument, or the name of a tune.
9 a. Ps 9 and 10 were originally one poem; it is 'alphabetical' (i.e., an acrostic), but in the present text there are several letters without their strophes.

Yahweh has made himself known, has given judgement, 16
he has trapped the wicked in the work of their own hands.

Muted music

May the wicked return to Sheol, *Pause* 17
all the nations forgetful of God.

Kaph   For the needy is not always forgotten, 18
the hope of the poor is never brought to nothing.

Rise, Yahweh, let not man have the upper hand, 19
let the nations stand trial before you!
Strike terror into them, Yahweh, 20
let the nations know they are only men! *Pause* **10**

Lamed   Yahweh, why do you stand aside, 1
why hide from us now the times are hard?
The poor man is devoured by the pride of the wicked, 2
he is caught in the wiles that the other has devised.

(Mem)   The evil man boasts of his soul's desires, 3
the grasping man blasphemes, the wicked spurns Yahweh.
(Nun)   'His anger is up there, he will not make me pay! 4
There is no God!' This is the way his mind works.

At every moment his course is assured, 5
your rulings are too lofty for his notice;
his rivals? He sneers at them all.

'Nothing can shake me' he assures himself. 6
Himself untouched by disaster, ·he curses others. 7

(Samek)   Fraud and oppression fill his mouth,
Pe   spite and iniquity are under his tongue;
there in the reeds he lies in ambush 8
to kill the innocent where no one can see.

Ain   Peering and prying for the out-of-luck,
lurking unseen like a lion in his hide, 9
lurking to capture the poor man,
the poor man seized, he drags him away in his net.

(Sade)   Questing of eye, he stoops, he crouches, 10
and the luckless wretch falls into his power
as he thinks to himself, 'God forgets, 11
he hides his face, he does not see at all'.

Qoph   Rise, Yahweh, God raise your hand, 12
do not forget the poor!
Why does the wicked man spurn God, 13
assuring himself, 'He will not make me pay'?

Resh   You yourself have seen the distress and the grief, 14
you watch and then take them into your hands;
the luckless man commits himself to you,
you, the orphan's certain help.

Shin   Break the power of the wicked, of the evil man, 15
seek out his wickedness till there is none to be found!
Yahweh is king for ever and ever, 16
the pagans are doomed to vanish from his country.

17 *Tau*   Yahweh, you listen to the wants of the humble,
          you bring strength to their hearts, you grant them a hearing,
18   judging in favour of the orphaned and exploited,
          so that earthborn man may strike fear no longer.

PSALM 11   V 10

The confidence of the virtuous

For the choirmaster   *Of David*

1   In Yahweh I take shelter.
          How can you say to me,
          'Bird, fly back to your mountain:
2   'see how the wicked are bending their bows
          and fitting their arrows to the string,
          ready to shoot the upright from the shadows.
3   When foundations fall to ruin, what can the virtuous do?'
4   Yahweh is in his holy Temple,
          Yahweh whose throne is in heaven;
          his eyes look down at the world,
          his searching gaze scans all mankind.

5   The virtuous and the wicked are under Yahweh's scrutiny,
          and his soul hates anyone who loves brutality.
6   He rains coals of fire and brimstone on the wicked,
          he serves them a scorching wind to swallow down.
7   Yahweh is righteous, he loves virtue,
          upright men will contemplate his face.

PSALM 12   V 11

Against a deceitful world

For the choirmaster   *For the octachord*   *Psalm*   *Of David*

1   Save us, Yahweh! There are no devout men left,
          fidelity has vanished from mankind.
2   All they do is lie to one another,
          flattering lips, talk from a double heart.
3   May Yahweh slice off every flattering lip,
          each tongue so glib with boasts,
4   those who say, 'In our tongue lies our strength,
          our lips have the advantage; who can master us?'
5   'For the plundered poor, for the needy who groan,
          now will I act' says Yahweh.
          ' I will grant them the safety they sigh for.'
6   The words of Yahweh are without alloy,
          nature's silver coming from the earth seven times refined.
7   And you, Yahweh, hold us in your keeping,
          against that breed protect us always.
8   The wicked prowl on every side,
          baseness stands high among the sons of men.

---

10 a. Lit. 'blesses', the customary euphemism.

PSALM 13   V 12

A confident appeal

For the choirmaster   Psalm   Of David

How much longer will you forget me, Yahweh? For ever?   1
How much longer will you hide your face from me?
How much longer must I endure grief in my soul,   2
and sorrow in my heart by day and by night?
How much longer must my enemy have the upper hand of me?
Look and answer me, Yahweh my God!   3

Give my eyes light, or I shall sleep in death,
and my enemy will say, 'I have beaten him',   4
and my oppressors have the joy of seeing me stumble.
But I for my part rely on your love, Yahweh;   5
let my heart rejoice in your saving help.
Let me sing to Yahweh for the goodness he has shown me.

PSALM 14   V 13

The godless men

For the choirmaster   Of David

The fool says in his heart,   1
'There is no God!'
Their deeds are corrupt and vile,
there is not one good man left.
Yahweh is looking down from heaven   2
at the sons of men,
to see if a single one is wise,
if a single one is seeking God.

All have turned aside,   3
all alike are tainted;
there is not one good man left,
not a single one.

Are they so ignorant, all these evil men   4
who swallow my people
as though they were eating bread,
and never invoke Yahweh?

They will be struck with fear,   5
fear without reason,
since God takes the side of the virtuous:
deride as you may the poor man's hopes,   6
Yahweh is his shelter.

Who will bring Israel salvation from Zion?   7
When Yahweh brings his people home,
what joy for Jacob, what happiness for Israel!

PSALM 15

The guest of Yahweh

Psalm   Of David

1   Yahweh, who has the right to enter your tent,
     or to live on your holy mountain?

2   The man whose way of life is blameless,
     who always does what is right,
     who speaks the truth from his heart,
3   whose tongue is not used for slander,

     who does no wrong to his fellow,
     casts no discredit on his neighbour,
4   looks with contempt on the reprobate,
     but honours those who fear Yahweh;

     who stands by his pledge at any cost,
5   does not ask interest on loans,
     and cannot be bribed to victimise the innocent.
     —If a man does all this, nothing can ever shake him.

PSALM 16

Yahweh, my heritage

Miktam   Of David

1   Look after me, God, I take shelter in you.

2   To Yahweh you say, 'My Lord,
     you are my fortune, nothing else but you',
3   yet to those pagan deities in the land,
     'My princes, all my pleasure is in you'.

4   Their idols teem, after these they run:
     shall I pour their blood-libations?—not I!
     Take their names on my lips?—never!

5   Yahweh, my heritage, my cup,
     you, and you only, hold my lot secure;
6   the measuring line marks out delightful places for me,
     for me the heritage is superb indeed.
7   I bless Yahweh, who is my counsellor,
     and in the night my inmost self instructs me;
8   I keep Yahweh before me always,
     for with him at my right hand nothing can shake me.

9   So my heart exults, my very soul rejoices,
     my body, too, will rest securely,
10   for you will not abandon my soul to Sheol,
     nor allow the one you love to see the Pit;
11   you will reveal the path of life to me,
     give me unbounded joy in your presence,
     and at your right hand everlasting pleasures.

PSALM 17 V 16

The innocent man pleads his cause

Prayer   Of David

Yahweh, hear the plea of virtue,   1
    listen to my appeal,
lend an ear to my prayer,
    my lips free from dishonesty.
From your presence will my sentence come,   2
    your eyes are fixed on what is right.

You probe my heart, examine me at night,   3
you test me yet find nothing, no murmuring from me:
my mouth has never sinned •as most men's do.   4

No, I have treasured the words from your lips;
in the path prescribed •walking deliberately   5
in your footsteps, so that my feet do not slip.

I invoke you, God, and you answer me;   6
turn your ear to me, hear what I say,
display your marvellous kindness, saviour of fugitives!   7

From those who revolt against you
guard me like the pupil of your eye;   8
hide me in the shadow of your wings
from the onslaughts of the wicked.   9

My enemies cluster round me, breathing hostility;
entrenched in their fat, their mouths utter   10
arrogant claims; •now they are closing in,   11
they have eyes for nothing but to see me overthrown.
They look like a lion eager to tear to pieces,   12
like a young lion crouching in its hide.

Rise, Yahweh, subdue him face to face,   13
rescue my soul from the wicked with your sword,
with your hand, Yahweh, rescue me from men,   14
from the sort of men whose lot is here and now.

Cram their bellies from your stores,
    give them all the sons that they could wish for,
let them have a surplus to leave their children!
For me the reward of virtue is to see your face,   15
and, on waking, to gaze my fill on your likeness.

PSALM 18 V 17

Song of triumph for the king

For the choirmaster. Of David, the servant of Yahweh, who addressed the words of this song to Yahweh at the time when Yahweh delivered him from the power of his enemies and of Saul. He said:

I love you, Yahweh, my strength   1
(my saviour, you rescue me from violence.)
Yahweh is my rock and my bastion,   2
my deliverer is my God.

I take shelter in him, my rock,
my shield, my horn of salvation,
my stronghold and my refuge.
From violence you rescue me.

3   He is to be praised; on Yahweh I call
and am saved from my enemies.

4   The waves of death encircled me,
the torrents of Belial burst on me;
5   the cords of Sheol girdled me,
the snares of death were before me.

6   In my distress I called to Yahweh
and to my God I cried;
from his Temple he heard my voice,
my cry came to his ears.

7   Then the earth quivered and quaked,
the foundations of the mountains trembled
(they quivered because he was angry);
8   from his nostrils a smoke ascended,
and from his mouth a fire that consumed
(live embers were kindled at it).

9   He bent the heavens and came down,
a dark cloud under his feet;
10 he mounted a cherub and flew,
and soared on the wings of the wind.

11 Darkness he made a veil to surround him,
his tent a watery darkness, dense cloud;
12 before him a flash enkindled
hail and fiery embers.

13 Yahweh thundered from heaven,
the Most High made his voice heard;
14 he let his arrows fly and scattered them,
launched the lightnings and routed them.

15 The bed of the seas was revealed,
the foundations of the world were laid bare,
at your muttered threat, Yahweh,
at the blast of your nostrils' breath.

16 He sends from on high and takes me,
he draws me from deep waters,
17 he delivers me from my powerful enemy,
from a foe too strong for me.

18 They assailed me on my day of disaster,
but Yahweh was my support;
19 he freed me, set me at large,
he rescued me, since he loves me.

20 Yahweh requites me as I act justly,
as my hands are pure so he repays me,
21 since I have kept the ways of Yahweh,
nor fallen away from my God.

22 His judgements are all before me,
his statutes I have not put from me;

I am blameless in his presence,   23
I keep sin at arm's length.

And Yahweh repays me as I act justly,   24
as my purity is in his sight.
Faithful you are with the faithful,   25
blameless with the blameless,
pure with the one who is pure,   26
but crafty with the devious,
you save a people that is humble   27
and humiliate eyes that are haughty.

Yahweh, you yourself are my lamp,   28
my God lights up my darkness;
with you I storm the barbican,   29
with my God I leap the rampart.

This God, his way is blameless;   30
the word of Yahweh is without dross.
He it is who is the shield
of all who take shelter in him.

Who else is God but Yahweh,   31
who else a rock save our God?
This God who girds me with strength   32
and makes my way without blame,

who makes my feet like the hinds'   33
and holds me from falling on the heights,
who trains my hands for battle,   34
my arms to bend a bow of bronze.

You give me your saving shield   35
(your right hand upholds me), with care you train me,
wide room you make for my steps under me,   36
my feet have never faltered.

I pursue my enemies and overtake them,   37
nor turn back till an end is made of them;
I strike them down, and they cannot rise,   38
they fall, they are under my feet.

You have girt me with strength for the fight,   39
bent down my assailants beneath me,
made my enemies turn their backs to me;   40
and those who hate me I destroy.

They cry out, there is no one to save,   41
to Yahweh, but there is no reply;
I crush them fine as dust before the wind,   42
trample them like the mud of the streets.

You deliver me from a people in revolt,   43
you place me at the head of the nations,
a people I did not know are now my servants,

foreigners come wooing my favour,   44
no sooner do they hear than they obey me,
foreigners grow faint of heart,   45
they come trembling out of their fastnesses.

46 Life to Yahweh! Blessed be my rock!
Exalted be the God of my salvation,
47 the God who gives me vengeance
and subjects the peoples to me,

48 who rescues me from my raging enemies.
You lift me high above those who attack me,
you deliver me from the man of violence.

49 For this I will praise you, Yahweh, among the heathen
and sing praise to your name.

50 His king he saves and saves again,
displays his love for his anointed,
for David and his heirs for ever.

PSALM 19

V 18

Yahweh, the sun of righteousness

For the choirmaster   Psalm   Of David

1 The heavens declare the glory of God,
the vault of heaven proclaims his handiwork;
2 day discourses of it to day,
night to night hands on the knowledge.

3 No utterance at all, no speech,
no sound that anyone can hear;
4 yet their voice goes out through all the earth,
and their message to the ends of the world.

High above, he pitched a tent for the sun,
5 who comes out of his pavilion like a bridegroom,
exulting like a hero to run his race.

6 He has his rising on the edge of heaven,
the end of his course is its furthest edge,
and nothing can escape his heat.

7 The Law of Yahweh is perfect,
new life for the soul;
the decree of Yahweh is trustworthy,
wisdom for the simple.

8 The precepts of Yahweh are upright,
joy for the heart;
the commandment of Yahweh is clear,
light for the eyes.

9 The fear of Yahweh is pure,
lasting for ever;
the judgements of Yahweh are true,
righteous, every one,

10 more desirable than gold,
even than the finest gold;
his words are sweeter than honey,.
even than honey that drips from the comb.

Thus your servant is formed by them,   11
    observance brings great reward.
But who can detect his own failings?   12
    Wash out my hidden faults.

And from pride preserve your servant,   13
    never let it dominate me.
So shall I be above reproach,
    free from grave sin.

May the words of my mouth always find favour,   14
    and the whispering of my heart,
in your presence, Yahweh,
    my Rock, my Redeemer!

PSALM 20   V 19

Prayer for the king

For the choirmaster   Psalm   Of David

May Yahweh answer you in time of trouble,   1
    may the name of the God of Jacob protect you!

May he send you help from the sanctuary,   2
    give you support from Zion,
remember all your oblations   3
    and find your holocaust acceptable;   *Pause*
may he grant you your heart's desire,   4
    and crown all your plans with success;
may we shout with joy for your victory,   5
    and plant our banners in the name of our God!

May Yahweh grant all your petitions!

Now I know that Yahweh   6
    saves his anointed,
and answers him from his holy heaven
    with mighty victories from his own right hand.

Some boast of chariots, some of horses,   7
    but we boast about the name of Yahweh our God;
theirs to crumple and fall,   8
    but we shall stand, and stand firm!

Yahweh, save the king,   9
    answer us when we call.

PSALM 21   V 20

Thanksgiving for the king

For the choirmaster   Psalm   Of David

Yahweh, the king rejoices in your power;   1
    what great joy your saving help gives him!
You have granted him his heart's desire,   2
    not denied him what his lips entreated.   *Pause*

3 For you have met him with choicest blessings,
put a crown of pure gold on his head;
4 he asked for life, and you gave it him,
length of days for ever and ever.

5 Great his glory through your saving help,
you have loaded him with splendour and majesty;
6 yes, you confer on him everlasting blessings,
you gladden him with the joy of your presence.

7 Yes, the king puts his trust in Yahweh,
by grace of the Most High he reigns unshaken.

8 Your hand will unmask all your enemies,
your right hand all who hate you;
9 you will make them like a blazing furnace,
the day that you appear,

Yahweh will engulf them in his anger,
and fire will devour them;
10 you will wipe their children from the earth,
their descendants from among the sons of men.

11 Plot though they do to harm you
and weave their plan as they may, they cannot win;
12 since you will make them turn tail,
by shooting your arrows in their faces.

13 Rise, Yahweh, in your power!
We will sing and play in honour of your strength.

PSALM 22   V 21

The sufferings and hope of the virtuous man

For the choirmaster   To the 'Doe of the Dawn'   Psalm   Of David

1 My God, my God, why have you deserted me?
How far from saving me, the words I groan!
2 I call all day, my God, but you never answer,
all night long I call and cannot rest.
3 Yet, Holy One, you
who make your home in the praises of Israel,
4 in you our fathers put their trust,
they trusted and you rescued them;
5 they called to you for help and they were saved,
they never trusted you in vain.

6 Yet here am I, now more worm than man,
scorn of mankind, jest of the people,
7 all who see me jeer at me,
they toss their heads and sneer,
8 'He relied on Yahweh, let Yahweh save him!
If Yahweh is his friend, let Him rescue him!'

9 Yet you drew me out of the womb,
you entrusted me to my mother's breasts;
10 placed on your lap from my birth,
from my mother's womb you have been my God.

Do not stand aside: trouble is near,   11
I have no one to help me!

A herd of bulls surrounds me,   12
strong bulls of Bashan close in on me;
their jaws are agape for me,   13
like lions tearing and roaring.

I am like water draining away,   14
my bones are all disjointed,
my heart is like wax,
melting inside me;
my palate is drier than a potsherd   15a
and my tongue is stuck to my jaw.   15b

A pack of dogs surrounds me,   16
a gang of villains closes me in;
they tie me hand and foot
and leave me lying in the dust of death.   15c

I can count every one of my bones,   17
and there they glare at me, gloating;
they divide my garments among them   18
and cast lots for my clothes.

Do not stand aside, Yahweh.   19
O my strength, come quickly to my help;
rescue my soul from the sword,   20
my dear life from the paw of the dog,
save me from the lion's mouth,   21
my poor soul from the wild bulls' horns!

Then I shall proclaim your name to my brothers,   22
praise you in full assembly:
you who fear Yahweh, praise him!   23
Entire race of Jacob, glorify him!
Entire race of Israel, revere him!

For he has not despised   24
or disdained the poor man in his poverty,
has not hidden his face from him,
but has answered him when he called.

You are the theme of my praise in the Great Assembly,   25
I perform my vows in the presence of those who fear him.
The poor will receive as much as they want to eat.   26
Those who seek Yahweh will praise him.
Long life to their hearts!

The whole earth, from end to end, will remember and come   27
        back to Yahweh;
all the families of the nations will bow down before him.
For Yahweh reigns, the ruler of nations!   28
Before him all the prosperous of the earth will bow down,   29
before him will bow all who go down to the dust.
And my soul will live for him, •my children will serve him;   30
men will proclaim the Lord to generations •still to come,   31
his righteousness to a people yet unborn. All this he has done.

PSALM 23

The Good Shepherd

Psalm   *Of David*

1   Yahweh is my shepherd,
     I lack nothing.

2   In meadows of green grass he lets me lie.
     To the waters of repose he leads me;
3   there he revives my soul.

     He guides me by paths of virtue
      for the sake of his name.

4   Though I pass through a gloomy valley,
     I fear no harm;
     beside me your rod and your staff
      are there, to hearten me.

5   You prepare a table before me
     under the eyes of my enemies;
   you anoint my head with oil,
     my cup brims over.

6   Ah, how goodness and kindness pursue me,
     every day of my life;
   my home, the house of Yahweh,
     ' as long as I live!

PSALM 24

Antiphonal psalm for solemn entry into the sanctuary

Psalm   *Of David*

1   To Yahweh belong earth and all it holds,
     the world and all who live in it;
2   he himself founded it on the ocean,
     based it firmly on the nether sea.

3   Who has the right to climb the mountain of Yahweh,
     who the right to stand in his holy place?
4   He whose hands are clean, whose heart is pure,
     whose soul does not pay homage to worthless things
     and who never swears to a lie.

5   The blessing of Yahweh is his,
     and vindication from God his saviour.
6   Such are the people who seek him,
     who seek your presence, God of Jacob!   *Pause*

7   Gates, raise your arches,
     rise, you ancient doors,
     let the king of glory in!

8   Who is this king of glory?
     Yahweh the strong, the valiant,
     Yahweh valiant in battle!

Gates, raise your arches,
rise, you ancient doors,
let the king of glory in!　　　　　　　　　　9

Who is this king of glory?　　　　　　　　10
He is Yahweh Sabaoth,
King of glory, he!　　　　　　　　　　　Pause

PSALM 25　　　　　　V 24

Prayer in danger

Of David

Aleph	To you, Yahweh, I lift up my soul,	1
	O my God.	2
Beth	I rely on you, do not let me be shamed,	
	do not let my enemies gloat over me!	
Ghimel	No, those who hope in you are never shamed,	3
	shame awaits disappointed traitors.	
Daleth	Yahweh, make your ways known to me,	4
	teach me your paths.	
He	Set me in the way of your truth, and teach me,	5
	for you are the God who saves me.	
Waw	All day long I hope in you	
	because of your goodness, Yahweh.	7c
Zain	Remember your kindness, Yahweh,	6
	your love, that you showed long ago.	
Heth	Do not remember the sins of my youth;	7a
	but rather, with your love remember me.	7b
Teth	Yahweh is so good, so upright,	8
	he teaches the way to sinners;	
Yod	in all that is right he guides the humble,	9
	and instructs the poor in his way.	
Kaph	All Yahweh's paths are love and truth	10
	for those who keep his covenant and his decrees.	
Lamed	For the sake of your name, Yahweh,	11
	forgive my guilt, for it is great.	
Mem	Everyone who fears Yahweh	12
	will be taught the course a man should choose;	
Nun	his soul will live in prosperity,	13
	his children have the land for their own.	
Samek	The close secret of Yahweh belongs to them who fear him,	14
	his covenant also, to bring them knowledge.	
Ain	My eyes are always on Yahweh,	15
	for he releases my feet from the net.	
Pe	Turn to me, take pity on me,	16
	alone and wretched as I am!	
Sade	Relieve the distress of my heart,	17
	free me from my sufferings.	
Qoph	See my misery and pain,	18
	forgive all my sins!	

19	Resh	See how my enemies multiply,
		and how violent their hatred has grown.
20	Shin	Watch over my soul, rescue me;
		let me not be shamed: I take shelter in you.
21	Tau	Let innocence and integrity be my protection,
		since my hope is in you, Yahweh.

Redeem Israel, God,
from all his troubles.

PSALM 26   V 25

Prayer of the blameless

Of David

1 Yahweh, be my judge!
I go my way in my innocence,
My trust in Yahweh never wavers.
2 Test me, Yahweh, and probe me,
put me to the trial, loins and heart;
3 for your love is before my eyes,
and I live my life in loyalty to you.

4 No sitting with wastrels for me,
no associating with hypocrites;
5 I hate the society of evil men,
I refuse to sit down with the wicked.

6 I wash my hands in innocence
and join the procession round your altar,
7 singing a hymn of thanksgiving,
proclaiming all your wonders.
8 I love the house where you live,
the place where your glory makes its home.

9 Do not let my soul share the fate of sinners,
or my life the doom of men of blood,
10 men with guilt on their hands,
whose right hands are heavy with bribes.

11 But I live my life in innocence,
redeem me, Yahweh, take pity on me;
12 my foot is set on the right path,
I bless you, Yahweh, at the Assemblies.

PSALM 27   V 26

In God's company there is no fear

Of David

1 Yahweh is my light and my salvation,
whom need I fear?
Yahweh is the fortress of my life,
of whom should I be afraid?

When evil men advance against me
  to devour my flesh,
they, my opponents, my enemies,
  are the ones who stumble and fall.   **2**

Though an army pitched camp against me,
  my heart would not fear;
though war were waged against me,
  my trust would still be firm.   **3**

One thing I ask of Yahweh,
  one thing I seek:
to live in the house of Yahweh
  all the days of my life,
to enjoy the sweetness of Yahweh
  and to consult him in his Temple.   **4**

For he shelters me under his awning
  in times of trouble;
he hides me deep in his tent,
  sets me high on a rock.   **5**

And now my head is held high
  over the enemies who surround me,
in his tent I will offer
  exultant sacrifice.   **6**

I will sing, I will play for Yahweh!

Yahweh, hear my voice as I cry!
  Pity me! Answer me!   **7**
My heart has said of you,
  'Seek his face'.   **8**
Yahweh, I do seek your face;
  do not hide your face from me.   **9**

Do not repulse your servant in anger;
  you are my help.
Never leave me, never desert me,
  God, my saviour!
If my father and mother desert me,
  Yahweh will care for me still.   **10**

Yahweh, teach me your way,   **11**
lead me in the path of integrity
  because of my enemies;
do not abandon me to the will of my foes—   **12**
false witnesses have risen against me,
  and breathe out violence.

This I believe: I shall see the goodness of Yahweh,   **13**
  in the land of the living.
Put your hope in Yahweh, be strong, let your heart be bold,   **14**
  put your hope in Yahweh.

PSALM 28

Petition and thanksgiving

Of David

1　　　　I cry to you, Yahweh,
　　　　　　my Rock! Do not be deaf to me,
　　　　for if you are silent, I shall go
　　　　　　down to the Pit like the rest.

2　　　　Hear my voice, raised in petition,
　　　　　　as I cry to you for help,
　　　　as I raise my hands, Yahweh,
　　　　　　toward your Holy of Holies.

3　　　　Do not drag me away with the wicked,
　　　　　　away with the evil men
　　　　who talk of peace to their neighbours
　　　　　　while malice is in their hearts.

4　　　　Repay them for their actions, Yahweh,
　　　　　　for the evil they commit,
　　　　for their handiwork repay them,
　　　　　　let them have what they deserve!

5　　　　How blind they are to the works of Yahweh,
　　　　　　to his own handiwork!
　　　　May he pull them down and not rebuild them!

6　　　　Blessed be Yahweh, for he hears
　　　　　　the sound of my petition!

7　　　　Yahweh is my strength, my shield,
　　　　　　my heart puts its trust in him;
　　　　I have been helped, my flesh has bloomed again,
　　　　　　I thank him with all my heart.

8　　　　Yahweh is the strength of his people,
　　　　　　a saving fortress for his anointed.

9　　　　Save your people! Bless your heritage!
　　　　　　Shepherd them; carry them for ever!

PSALM 29

Hymn to the lord of the storm

Psalm   Of David

1　　　　Pay tribute to Yahweh, you sons of God,[a]
　　　　　　tribute to Yahweh of glory and power,
2　　　　tribute to Yahweh of the glory of his name,
　　　　　　worship Yahweh in his sacred court.

3a　　　The voice of Yahweh over the waters!
3c　　　Yahweh over the multitudinous waters!

29 a. The angels, who make up the 'sacred court' of v.2.

The voice of Yahweh in power!   4
The voice of Yahweh in splendour!

The voice of Yahweh shatters the cedars,   5
Yahweh shatters the cedars of Lebanon,
making Lebanon leap like a calf,   6
Sirion[b] like a young wild bull.

The voice of Yahweh sharpens lightning shafts!   7

The voice of Yahweh sets the wilderness shaking.   8
Yahweh shakes the wilderness of Kadesh.
The voice of Yahweh sets the terebinths shuddering,   9a
stripping the forests bare.   9b

The God of glory thunders.   3b
In his palace everything cries, 'Glory!'   9c
Yahweh sat enthroned for the Flood,   10
Yahweh sits enthroned as a king for ever.

Yahweh gives strength to his people,   11
Yahweh blesses his people with peace.

PSALM 30   V 29

Thanksgiving after mortal danger

Psalm   Canticle for the Dedication of the House   Of David

High praise, Yahweh, I give you, for you have helped me up,   1
and not let my enemies gloat over me.
Yahweh, my God, I cried to you for help, and you have   2
healed me.
Yahweh, you have brought my soul up from Sheol,   3
of all those who go down to the Pit you have revived me.

Play music in Yahweh's honour, you devout,   4
remember his holiness, and praise him.
His anger lasts a moment, his favour a lifetime;   5
in the evening, a spell of tears, in the morning, shouts of joy.

In my prosperity, I used to say,   6
'Nothing can ever shake me!'
Your favour, Yahweh, stood me on a peak impregnable;   7
but then you hid your face and I was terrified.

Yahweh, I call to you,   8
I beg my God to pity me,
'What do you gain by my blood[a] if I go down to the Pit?   9
Can the dust praise you or proclaim your faithfulness?

'Hear, Yahweh, take pity on me;   10
Yahweh, help me!'
You have turned my mourning into dancing,   11
you have stripped off my sackcloth and wrapped me in gladness;
and now my heart, silent no longer, will play you music;   12
Yahweh, my God, I will praise you for ever.

PSALM 31

Prayer in time of ordeal

For the choirmaster   Psalm   Of David

1
In you, Yahweh, I take shelter;
never let me be disgraced.
In your righteousness deliver me, rescue me,

2
turn your ear to me, make haste!

Be a sheltering rock for me,
a walled fortress to save me!

3
For you are my rock, my fortress;
for the sake of your name, guide me, lead me!

4
Pull me out of the net they have spread for me,
for you are my refuge;

5
into your hands I commit my spirit,
you have redeemed me, Yahweh.

6
God of truth, •you hate
those who serve worthless idols;
but I put my trust in Yahweh:

7
I will exult, and rejoice in your love!

You, who have seen my wretchedness,
and known the miseries of my soul,

8
have not handed me over to the enemy,
you have given my feet space and to spare.

9
Take pity on me, Yahweh,
    I am in trouble now.
Grief wastes away my eye,
    my throat, my inmost parts.

10
For my life is worn out with sorrow,
    my years with sighs;
my strength yields under misery,
    my bones are wasting away.

11
To every one of my oppressors
    I am contemptible,
loathsome to my neighbours,
    to my friends a thing of fear.

Those who see me in the street
    hurry past me;

12
I am forgotten, as good as dead in their hearts,
    something discarded.

13
I hear their endless slanders,
    threats from every quarter,
as they combine against me,
    plotting to take my life.

b. Another name for Lebanon.
30 a. I.e., my death.

But I put my trust in you, Yahweh,   14
  I say, 'You are my God'.
My days are in your hand, rescue me   15
  from the hands of my enemies and persecutors;
let your face smile on your servant,   16
  save me in your love.

I invoke you, Yahweh; do not let me be disgraced,   17
  let the disgrace fall on the wicked!
May they go speechless to Sheol,
  their lying lips struck dumb   18
for those insolent slurs on the virtuous,
  for that arrogance and contempt.

Yahweh, how great your goodness,   19
  reserved for those who fear you,
bestowed on those who take shelter in you,
  for all mankind to see!

Safe in your presence you hide them   20
  far from the wiles of men;
inside your tent you shelter them
  far from the war of tongues.

Blessed be Yahweh, who performs   21
  marvels of love for me
  (in a fortress-city)!
In my alarm I exclaimed,   22
  'I have been snatched out of your sight!'
Yet you heard my petition
  when I called to you for help.

Love Yahweh, all you devout: 23
  Yahweh, protector of the faithful,
will repay the arrogant
  with interest.
Be strong, let your heart be bold,   24
  all you who hope in Yahweh!

PSALM 32   V 31

Candid admission of sin

Of David Poem

Happy the man whose fault is forgiven,   1
  whose sin is blotted out;
happy the man whom Yahweh   2
  accuses of no guilt,
  whose spirit is incapable of deceit!

All the time I kept silent, my bones were wasting away   3
  with groans, day in, day out;
day and night your hand   4
  lay heavy on me;
my heart grew parched as stubble
  in summer drought.   *Pause*

5　At last I admitted to you I had sinned;
　　　no longer concealing my guilt,
　I said, 'I will go to Yahweh
　　　and confess my fault'.
　And you, you have forgiven the wrong I did,
　　　have pardoned my sin.　　　　　　　*Pause*

6　That is why each of your servants prays to you
　　　in time of trouble;
　even if floods come rushing down,
　　　they will never reach him.

7　You are a hiding place for me,
　　　you guard me when in trouble,
　you surround me with songs of deliverance.　　*Pause*

8　I will instruct you, and teach you the way to go;
　I will watch over you and be your adviser.

9　Do not be like senseless horse or mule
　　that need bit and bridle to curb their spirit
　　(to let you get near them).

10　Many torments await the wicked,
　　but grace enfolds the man who trusts in Yahweh.

11　Rejoice in Yahweh,
　　　exult, you virtuous,
　　　shout for joy, all upright hearts.

PSALM 33

V 32

Hymn to Providence

1　Shout for joy to Yahweh, all virtuous men,
　　praise comes well from upright hearts;
2　give thanks to Yahweh on the lyre,
　　play to him on the ten-string harp;
3　sing a new song in his honour,
　　play with all your skill as you acclaim*a* him!
4　The word of Yahweh is integrity itself,
　　all he does is done faithfully;
5　he loves virtue and justice,
　　Yahweh's love fills the earth.

6　By the word of Yahweh the heavens were made,
　　their whole array by the breath of his mouth;
7　he collects the ocean waters as though in a wineskin,
　　he stores the deeps in cellars.

8　Let the whole world fear Yahweh,
　　let all who live on earth revere him!
9　He spoke, and it was created;
　　he commanded, and there it stood.

10　Yahweh thwarts the plans of nations,
　　frustrates the intentions of peoples;
11　but Yahweh's plans hold good for ever,
　　the intentions of his heart from age to age.

33 a. 'Hail him with the war cry'; but after the Exile, the war cry has assumed a ceremonial and liturgical character in thanksgivings and processions.

Happy the nation whose God is Yahweh, 12
the people he has chosen for his heritage.

Yahweh looks down from heaven, 13
he sees the whole human race;
from where he sits he watches 14
all who live on the earth,
he who moulds every heart 15
and takes note of all men do.

A large army will not keep a king safe, 16
nor does the hero escape by his great strength;
it is delusion to rely on the horse for safety, 17
for all its power, it cannot save.

But see how the eye of Yahweh is on those who fear him, 18
on those who rely on his love,
to rescue their souls from death 19
and keep them alive in famine.

Our soul awaits Yahweh, 20
he is our help and shield;
our hearts rejoice in him, 21
we trust in his holy name.
Yahweh, let your love rest on us 22
as our hope has rested in you.

PSALM 34   V 33

In praise of God's justice

Of David. When, after pretending to be mad in front of Abimelech, he was dismissed by him and made his escape

Aleph   I will bless Yahweh at all times, 1
his praise shall be on my lips continually;
Beth   my soul glories in Yahweh, 2
let the humble hear and rejoice.

Ghimel Proclaim with me the greatness of Yahweh, 3
together let us extol his name.
Daleth I seek Yahweh, and he answers me 4
and frees me from all my fears.

He   Every face turned to him grows brighter 5
and is never ashamed.
Zain   A cry goes up from the poor man, and Yahweh hears, 6
and helps him in all his troubles.

Heth   The angel of Yahweh pitches camp 7
round those who fear him; and he keeps them safe.
Teth   How good Yahweh is—only taste and see! 8
Happy the man who takes shelter in him.

Yod   Fear Yahweh, you his holy ones: 9
those who fear him want for nothing.
Kaph   The young lion may go empty and hungry, 10
but those who seek Yahweh lack nothing good.

11 *Lamed*	Come, my sons, listen to me,
	I will teach you the fear of Yahweh.
12 *Mem*	Which of you wants to live to the full,
	who loves long life and enjoyment of prosperity?
13 *Nun*	Malice must be banished from your tongue,
	deceitful conversation from your lips;
14 *Samek*	never yield to evil, practise good,
	seek peace, pursue it.
16 *Pe*	The face of Yahweh frowns on evil men,
	to wipe their memory from the earth;
15 *Ain*	the eyes of Yahweh are turned towards the virtuous,
	his ears to their cry.
17 *Sade*	They cry for help and Yahweh hears
	and rescues them from all their troubles;
18 *Qoph*	Yahweh is near to the broken-hearted,
	he helps those whose spirit is crushed.
19 *Resh*	Hardships in plenty beset the virtuous man,
	but Yahweh rescues him from them all;
20 *Shin*	taking care of every bone,
	Yahweh will not let one be broken.
21 *Tau*	Evil will bring death to the wicked,
	those who hate the virtuous will have to pay;
22 *(Waw)*	while Yahweh himself ransoms the souls of his servants,
	and those who take shelter in him have nothing to pay.

PSALM 35   V 34

Prayer of a virtuous man under oppression

Of David

1	Accuse my accusers, Yahweh,
	attack my attackers;
2	grip shield and buckler,
	up, and help me;
3	brandish lance and pike
	in the faces of my pursuers.
	Tell my soul, 'I am your salvation'.
4	Shame and dishonour on those
	who are out to kill me!
	Back with them! Cover with confusion
	those who plot my downfall!
5	May they be like chaff before the wind,
	with the angel of Yahweh to chase them!
6	May their way be dark and slippery,
	with the angel of Yahweh to hound them!
7	Unprovoked they spread their net for me,
	they dug a pit for me;
8	but Ruin creeps on them unawares,
	the net they have spread will catch them instead,
	and into their own pit will they fall.

Then my soul will rejoice in Yahweh,   9
    exult that he has saved me.
All my bones will exclaim, 'Yahweh,   10
    who can compare with you
in rescuing the poor man from the stronger,
    the needy from the man who exploits him?'

Lying witnesses take the stand,   11
    questioning me on things I know nothing about;
they repay my kindness with evil,   12
    there is desolation in my soul.

Yet, when they were sick, I put sackcloth on,   13
    I humbled my soul with fasting,
murmuring prayers to my own breast
    as though for a friend or brother;   14
and, like a person mourning his mother,
    went about dejected and sorrowing.

Now I have fallen, they crowd round delighted,   15
    flocking to jeer at me;
strangers I never even knew
    with loud cries tear me to pieces,
riddling me with gibe after gibe,   16
    grinding their teeth at me.

How much longer, Lord, will you look on?   17
Rescue my soul from their onslaughts,
    my dear life from these lions.
I will give thanks in the Great Assembly,   18
    praise you where the people throng.

Do not let my lying enemies   19
    gloat over me,
do not let those who hate me for no reason
    exchange sly glances.

Peace is not what they discuss   20
    with the peaceloving people of the land;
they think out false accusations,
    their mouths wide to accuse me,   21
'Aha! Aha!' they say
    'With our own eyes we saw it!'

Now break your silence, Yahweh, you were looking too,   22
    Lord, do not stand aside,
up, wake up, come to my defence,   23
    Lord my God side with me!
Yahweh my God, you are righteous, so give verdict for me,   24
    and do not let them gloat over me.

Do not let them think, 'Just as we hoped!'   25
    Do not let them say, 'Now we have got him down!'
Shame and dishonour on all   26
    who gloat over my misfortune;
shame and discredit cover all
    who profit at my expense!

But shouts of joy and gladness for all   27
    who take pleasure in my virtue;

give them constant cause to say,
   'Great is Yahweh,
who likes to see his servant at peace!'

28   Then my tongue will shout your goodness,
      and sing your praises all day long.

PSALM 36

The wickedness of the sinner, the goodness of God

For the choirmaster   *Of the servant of Yahweh, David*

1   The wicked man's oracle is Sin
      in the depths of his heart;
    there is no fear of God
      before his eyes.

2   He sees himself with too flattering an eye
      to detect and detest his guilt;
3   all he says tends to mischief and deceit,
      he has turned his back on wisdom.

4   How best to work ·mischief he plots,
      even when he is in bed;
    he persists in his evil course,
      he never rejects what is bad.

5   Your love, Yahweh, reaches to the heavens,
      your faithfulness to the clouds;
6   your righteousness is like the mountains of God,
      your judgements like the mighty deep.

    Yahweh, protector of man and beast,
7   how precious, God, your love!
    Hence the sons of men
      take shelter in the shadow of your wings.

8   They feast on the bounty of your house,
      you give them drink from your river of pleasure;
9   yes, with you is the fountain of life,
      by your light we see the light.

10   Do not stop loving those who know you,
      or being righteous to upright hearts.
11   Do not let arrogant feet crush me
      or wicked hands expel me.

12   The evil men have fallen, there they lie,
      beaten down, never to stand again!

PSALM 37

The fate of the virtuous and the wicked

Of David

1 *Aleph*   Do not worry about the wicked,
         do not envy those who do wrong.
2   Quick as the grass they wither,
         fading like the green in the field.

Beth	Trust in Yahweh and do what is good,	3
	make your home in the land and live in peace;	
	make Yahweh your only joy	4
	and he will give you what your heart desires.	
Ghimel	Commit your fate to Yahweh,	5
	trust in him and he will act:	
	making your virtue clear as the light,	6
	your integrity as bright as noon.	
Daleth	Be quiet before Yahweh, and wait patiently for him,	7
	not worrying about men who make their fortunes,	
	about men who scheme	
	to bring the poor and needy down.	14c
He	Enough of anger, leave rage aside,	8
	do not worry, nothing but evil can come of it:	
	for the wicked will be expelled,	9
	while those who hope in Yahweh shall have the land for their own.	
Waw	A little longer, and the wicked will be no more,	10
	search his place well, he will not be there;	
	but the humble shall have the land for their own	11
	to enjoy untroubled peace.	
Zain	The wicked man plots against the virtuous,	12
	and grinds his teeth at him;	
	but the Lord only laughs at the man,	13
	knowing his end is in sight.	
Heth	Though the wicked draw the sword,	14a
	and bend their bow, to kill the upright,	14b
	their swords will only pierce their own hearts	15
	and their bows will be smashed.	
Teth	The little the virtuous possesses	16
	outweighs all the wealth of the wicked,	
	since the arms of the wicked are doomed to break,	17
	and Yahweh will uphold the virtuous.	
Yod	Yahweh takes care of good men's lives,	18
	and their heritage will last for ever;	
	they will not be at a loss when bad times come,	19
	in time of famine they will have more than they need.	
Kaph	As for the wicked—they will perish,	20
	these enemies of Yahweh;	
	they will vanish like the beauty of the meadows,	
	they will vanish in smoke.	
Lamed	The wicked man borrows without meaning to repay,	21
	but a virtuous man is generous and open-handed;	
	those he blesses will have the land for their own,	22
	those he curses will be expelled.	
Mem	Yahweh guides a man's steps,	23
	they are sure, and he takes pleasure in his progress;	
	he may fall, but never fatally,	24
	since Yahweh supports him by the hand.	
Nun	Now I am old, but ever since my youth	25
	I never saw a virtuous man deserted,	

		or his descendants forced to beg their bread;
26		he is always compassionate, always lending:
		his children will be blessed.
27	Samek	Never yield to evil, practise good
		and you will have an everlasting home,
28		for Yahweh loves what is right,
		and never deserts the devout.
	Ain	Those who do wrong will perish once and for all,
		and the children of the wicked shall be expelled;
29		the virtuous will have the land for their own,
		and make it their home for ever.
30	Pe	The mouth of the virtuous man murmurs wisdom,
		and his tongue speaks what is right;
31		with the Law of his God in his heart
		his steps can never falter.
32	Sade	The wicked man spies on the virtuous,
		seeking to kill him;
33		Yahweh will never leave him in those clutches,
		or let him be condemned under trial.
34a	Qoph	Put your hope in Yahweh, keep his way,
40b		and he will save you from the wicked,
34b		raising you until you make the land your own
		and see the wicked expelled.
35	Resh	I have seen the wicked in his triumph
		towering like a cedar of Lebanon;
36		but when next I passed, he was not there,
		I looked for him and he was nowhere to be found.
37	Shin	Observe the innocent man, consider the upright:
		for the man of peace there are descendants,
38		but sinners shall be destroyed altogether,
		the descendants of the wicked shall be wiped out.
39	Tau	The salvation of the virtuous comes from Yahweh,
		he is their shelter when trouble comes;
40a		Yahweh helps and rescues them,
		he saves them because they take shelter in him.

PSALM 38

V 37

Prayer in distress

Psalm	Of David	In commemoration
1		Yahweh, do not punish me in your rage,
		or reprove me in the heat of anger.
2		Your arrows have pierced deep,
		your hand has pressed down on me;
3		no soundness in my flesh now you are angry,
		no health in my bones, because of my sin.
4		My guilt is overwhelming me,
		it is too heavy a burden;
5		my wounds stink and are festering,

the result of my folly;
bowed down, bent double, overcome,   6
I go mourning all the day.

My loins are burnt up with fever,   7
there is no soundness in my flesh:
numbed and crushed and overcome,   8
my heart groans, I moan aloud.

Lord, all that I long for is known to you,   9
my sighing is no secret from you;
my heart is throbbing, my strength deserting me,   10
the light of my eyes itself has left me.

My friends and my companions shrink from my wounds,   11
even the dearest of them keep their distance;
men intent on killing me lay snares,   12
others, hoping to hurt me, threaten my ruin,
hatching treacherous plots all day.

But I am like the deaf, I do not hear,   13
like the dumb man who does not open his mouth;
I am like the man who, hearing nothing,   14
gives no sharp answer in return.

For I put my trust in you, Yahweh,   15
and leave you to answer for me, Lord my God.
I have already said, 'Stop them gloating over me,   16
do not let them take advantage of me if my foot should slip'.

And now my fall is upon me,   17
there is no relief from my pains;
yes, I admit my guilt,   18
I am sorry for having sinned.

There are more and more to hurt me for no reason,   19
There are more to hate me unprovoked,
repaying my kindness with evil,   20
arraigning me for trying to do right.

Yahweh, do not desert me,   21
do not stand aside, my God!
Come quickly to my help,   22
Lord, my saviour!

PSALM 39   V 38

The insignificance of man before God

For the choirmaster   For Jeduthun   Psalm   Of David

I said, 'I will watch how I behave,   1
and not let my tongue lead me into sin;
I will keep a muzzle on my mouth
as long as the wicked man is near me'.
I stayed dumb, silent, speechless,   2
though the sight of him thriving made torment increase.

My heart had been smouldering inside me,   3
but it flared up at the thought of this

and the words burst out,

4　　'Tell me, Yahweh, when my end will be,
how many days are allowed me,
show me how frail I am.

5　　'Look, you have given me an inch or two of life,
my life-span is nothing to you;
each man that stands on earth is only a puff of wind,　　*Pause*
6　　every man that walks, only a shadow,
and the wealth he amasses is only a puff of wind—
he does not know who will take it next.'

7　　So tell me, Lord, what can I expect?
My hope is in you.
8　　Free me from all my sins,
do not make me the butt of idiots.
9　　I am dumb, I speak no more,
since you yourself have been at work.

10　　Lay your scourge aside,
I am worn out with the blows you deal me.
11　　You punish man with the penalties of sin,
like a moth you eat away all that gives him pleasure—
man is indeed only a puff of wind!　　*Pause*

12　　Yahweh, hear my prayer,
listen to my cry for help,
do not stay deaf to my crying.
I am your guest, and only for a time,
a nomad like all my ancestors.
13　　Look away, let me draw breath,
before I go away and am no more!

PSALM 40

V 39

Song of praise and prayer for help

For the choirmaster　Psalm　Of David

1　　I waited and waited for Yahweh,
now at last he has stooped to me
and heard my cry for help.

2　　He has pulled me out of the horrible pit,
out of the slough of the marsh,
has settled my feet on a rock
and steadied my steps.

3　　He has put a new song in my mouth,
a song of praise to our God;
dread will seize many at the sight,
and they will put their trust in Yahweh.

4　　Happy the man who puts
his trust in Yahweh,
and does not side with rebels
who stray after false gods.

How many wonders you have done for us,
Yahweh, my God!

How many plans you have made for us;
    you have no equal!
I want to proclaim them, again and again,
    but they are more than I can count.

You, who wanted no sacrifice or oblation,   6
    opened my ear,
you asked no holocaust or sacrifice for sin;
    then I said, 'Here I am! I am coming!'   7

In the scroll of the book am I not commanded
    to obey your will?   8
My God, I have always loved your Law
    from the depths of my being.

I have always proclaimed the righteousness of Yahweh   9
    in the Great Assembly;
nor do I mean to stop proclaiming,
    as you know well.

I have never kept your righteousness to myself,   10
    but have spoken of your faithfulness and saving help;
I have made no secret of your love and faithfulness
    in the Great Assembly.

For your part, Yahweh, do not withhold   11
    your kindness from me!
May your love and faithfulness
    constantly preserve me.

More misfortunes beset me   12
    than I can count,
my sins close in on me
    until I can hardly see,
they outnumber the hairs on my head;
    my courage is running out.

Oh come and rescue me, Yahweh,   13
Yahweh come quickly and help me!
Shame and dishonour on all   14
who are out to kill, to destroy me!

Down with them! Disgrace on those
    who enjoy my misfortune!
May they be aghast with shame,   15
    those who say to me, 'Aha! Aha!'

But joy and gladness   16
    for all who seek you!
To all who love your saving power
    give constant cause to say, 'God is great!'

To me, poor wretch,   17
    come quickly, Lord!
My helper, my saviour, my God,
    come and do not delay!

PSALM 41

Prayer of a sick and lonely man

For the choirmaster   Psalm   Of David

1   Happy the man who cares for the poor and the weak:
if disaster strikes, Yahweh will come to his help.

2   Yahweh will guard him, give him life and happiness in the land;
ah, do not let his enemies treat him as they please!

3   Yahweh will be his comfort on his bed of sickness;
most carefully you make his bed when he is sick.

4   I for my part said, 'Yahweh, take pity on me!
Cure me, for I have sinned against you.'

5   My enemies say of me with malice,
'How long before he dies and his name perishes?'

6   They visit me, their hearts full of spite,
they offer hollow comfort, and go out to spread the news.

7   All who hate me whisper to each other about me,
reckoning I deserve the misery I suffer,

8   'This sickness is fatal that has overtaken him,
he is down at last, he will never get up again'.

9   Even my closest and most trusted friend,
who shared my table, rebels against me.

10   But Yahweh, take pity on me!
Raise me up, and I will pay them back;

11   and by this I shall know that I enjoy your favour,
if my enemy fails to triumph over me;

12   and I, whom you uphold, go unscathed,
set by you in your presence for ever.

13   Blessed be Yahweh, the God of Israel,
from all eternity and for ever!
Amen. Amen![a]

PSALM 42-43

Lament of a Levite in exile

For the choirmaster   Poem   Of the sons of Korah

1   As a doe longs
for running streams,
so longs my soul
for you, my God.

2   My soul thirsts for God,
the God of life;
when shall I go to see
the face of God?[a]

3   I have no food but tears,
day and night;

41 a. This doxology ends the first book of the Psalter.
42 a. To find the presence of God in the Temple at Jerusalem.

and all day long men say to me,
'Where is your God?'

I remember, and my soul 　　　　　　　　　　　4
　　melts within me:
I am on my way to the wonderful Tent,
　　to the house of God,
among cries of joy and praise
　　and an exultant throng.

Why so downcast, my soul, 　　　　　　　　　5
　　why do you sigh within me?
Put your hope in God: I shall praise him yet,
　　my saviour, •my God. 　　　　　　　　　6

When my soul is downcast within me,
　　I think of you;
from the land of Jordan and of Hermon,
　　of you, humble mountain!ᵇ

Deep is calling to deep 　　　　　　　　　　7
　　as your cataracts roar;
all your waves, your breakers,
　　have rolled over me.

In the daytime may Yahweh 　　　　　　　　8
　　command his love to come,
and by night may his song be on my lips,
　　a prayer to the God of my life!

Let me say to God my Rock, 　　　　　　　　9
　　'Why do you forget me?
Why must I walk
　　so mournfully, oppressed by the enemy?'

Nearly breaking my bones 　　　　　　　　　10
　　my oppressors insult me,
as all day long they ask me,
　　'Where is your God?'

Why so downcast, my soul, 　　　　　　　　　11
　　why do you sigh within me?
Put your hope in God: I shall praise him yet,
　　my saviour, my God.

43

Defend me, take up my cause 　　　　　　　　1
　　against people who have no pity;
from the treacherous and cunning man
　　rescue me, God.

It is you, God, who are my shelter: 　　　　　2
　　why do you abandon me?
Why must I walk
　　so mournfully, oppressed by the enemy?

Send out your light and your truth, 　　　　　3
　　let these be my guide,
to lead me to your holy mountain
　　and to the place where you live.

Then I shall go to the altar of God, 　　　　　4
　　to the God of my joy,

I shall rejoice, I shall praise you on the harp,
Yahweh, my God.

5 Why so downcast, my soul,
why do you sigh within me?
Put your hope in God: I shall praise him yet,
my saviour, my God.

PSALM 44

V 43

National lament

For the choirmaster   Of the sons of Korah   Psalm

1 God, we have heard with our own ears,
our ancestors have told us
of the deeds you performed in their days,
2 in days long ago, •by your hand.

To put them in the land you dispossessed the nations,
you harried the peoples to make room for them;
3 it was not by their swords they won the land,
it was not by their arms they gained the victory:
it was your right hand, your arm
and the light of your face—because you loved them.

4 You it was, my King, my God,
who won those victories for Jacob;
5 through you we trampled down our enemies,
through your name we subdued our aggressors.

6 My trust was not in my bow,
my sword did not gain me victory:
7 we conquered our enemies through you,
you, who defeated all who hated us—
8 our boast was always of God,
we praised your name without ceasing.   *Pause*

9 Yet now you abandon and scorn us,
you no longer march with our armies,
10 you allow the enemy to push us back,
and let those who hate us raid us when it suits them.

11 You let us go to the slaughterhouse like sheep,
you scatter us among the nations;
12 you sell your people for next to nothing,
and make no profit from the bargain.

13 Thanks to you, our neighbours insult us,
all those around us make us their butt and laughing-stock;
14 you make us a byword to pagans,
a thing to make them toss their heathen heads.

15 All day long I brood on this disgrace,
my face covered in shame,
16 under a shower of insult and blasphemy,
a display of hatred and revenge.

b. Mount Zion.

All this happened to us though we had not forgotten you,   17
though we had not been disloyal to your covenant;
though our hearts had not turned away,   18
though our steps had not left your path:
yet you crushed us in the place where the jackals live,   19
and threw the shadow of death over us.

Had we forgotten the name of our own God   20
and stretched out our hands to a foreign one,
would not God have found this out,   21
he who knows the secrets of the heart?
No, it is for your sake we are being massacred daily,   22
and counted as sheep for the slaughter.

Wake up, Lord! Why are you asleep?   23
Awake! Do not abandon us for good.
Why do you hide your face,   24
and forget we are wretched and exploited?

For we are bowed in the dust,   25
our bodies crushed to the ground.
Rise! Come to our help!   26
Redeem us for the sake of your love.

PSALM 45   V 44

Royal wedding song

For the choirmaster   Tune: 'Lilies...'   Of the sons of Korah
Poem   Love song

My heart is stirred by a noble theme: 1
I address my poem to the king;
my tongue as ready as the pen of a busy scribe.

Of all men you are the most handsome,   2
your lips are moist with grace,
for God has blessed you for ever.

Hero, strap your sword at your side,   3
in majesty and splendour; •on, ride on,   4
in the cause of truth, religion and virtue!

Stretch the bowstring tight,
lending terror to your right hand.
Your arrows are sharp; nations lie at your mercy,   5
the king's enemies are losing heart.

Your throne, God, shall last for ever and ever,   6
your royal sceptre is a sceptre of integrity:
virtue you love as much as you hate wickedness.   7

This is why God, your God, has anointed you
with the oil of gladness, above all your rivals;
myrrh and aloes waft from your robes.   8

From palaces of ivory harps entertain you,
daughters of kings are among your maids of honour;
on your right stands the queen, in gold from Ophir.   9

10 Listen, daughter, pay careful attention:
forget your nation and your ancestral home,
11 then the king will fall in love with your beauty.
He is your master now, bow down to him.

12 The daughter of Tyre will solicit your favour with gifts,
13 the wealthiest nations, •with jewels set in gold.

14 Dressed •in brocades, the king's daughter
is led in to the king, with bridesmaids in her train.

Her ladies-in-waiting follow
15 and enter the king's palace to general rejoicing.

16 Your ancestors will be replaced by sons
whom you will make lords of the whole world.

17 I shall immortalise your name,
nations will sing your praises for ever and ever.

PSALM 46

V 45

God is on our side

For the choirmaster   Of the sons of Korah   For oboe   Song

1 God is our shelter, our strength,
ever ready to help in time of trouble,
2 so we shall not be afraid when the earth gives way,
when mountains tumble into the depths of the sea,
3 and its waters roar and seethe,
the mountains tottering as it heaves.

(Yahweh Sabaoth is on our side,
our citadel, the God of Jacob!)   *Pause*

4 There is a river whose streams refresh the city of God,
and it sanctifies the dwelling of the Most High.
5 God is inside the city, she can never fall,
at crack of dawn God helps her;
6 to the roaring of nations and tottering of kingdoms,
when he shouts, the world disintegrates.

7 Yahweh Sabaoth is on our side,
our citadel, the God of Jacob!   *Pause*

8 Come, think of Yahweh's marvels,
the astounding things he has done in the world;
9 all over the world he puts an end to wars,
he breaks the bow, he snaps the spear,
he gives shields to the flames.
10 'Pause a while and know that I am God,
exalted among the nations, exalted over the earth!'

11 Yahweh Sabaoth is on our side,
our citadel, the God of Jacob!   *Pause*

PSALM 47

Yahweh, king of Israel, lord of the world

For the choirmaster   Of the sons of Korah   Psalm

> Clap your hands, all you peoples,   **1**
> acclaim God with shouts of joy;
> for Yahweh, the Most High, is to be dreaded,   **2**
> the Great King of the whole world.
>
> He brings the peoples under our dominion,   **3**
> he puts the nations under our feet;
> for us he chooses our heritage—   **4**
> the pride of Jacob, whom he loved.
>
> God rises to shouts of acclamation,   **5**
> Yahweh rises to a blast of trumpets,
> let the music sound for our God, let it sound,   **6**
> let the music sound for our King, let it sound!
>
> God is king of the whole world: **7**
> play your best in his honour!
> God is king of the nations,   **8**
> he reigns on his holy throne.
>
> The leaders of the nations rally   **9**
> to the people of the God of Abraham.
> Every shield in the world belongs to God.
> He reigns supreme.

PSALM 48

Zion, the mountain of God

Song   Psalm   Of the sons of Korah

> Yahweh is great and supremely to be praised   **1**
>   in the city of our God,
> the holy mountain, •beautiful where it rises,   **2**
>   joy of the whole world;
>
> Mount of Zion, deep heart of the North,
>   city of the Great King;
> here among her palaces,   **3**
>   God proved to be her fortress.
>
> There was a rallying, once, of kings,   **4**
>   advancing together along a common front;
> they looked, they were amazed,   **5**
>   they panicked, they ran!
>
> There they shuddered and writhed   **6**
>   like women in labour,
> it was the east wind, that wrecker   **7**
>   of ships of Tarshish!ª

8   What we had heard we saw for ourselves
         in the city of our God,
     the city of Yahweh Sabaoth,
         God-protected for ever.   *Pause*

9   God, in your Temple
         we reflect on your love:
10   God, your praise, like your name,
         reaches to the ends of the world.

     Your right hand holds the victory;
11   Mount Zion rejoices,
     the daughters of Judah exult
         to have your rulings.

12   Go through Zion, walk round her,
         counting her towers,
13   admiring her walls,
         reviewing her palaces;

     then tell the next generation
14   that God is here,
     our God and leader,
         for ever and ever.

PSALM 49

The futility of riches   V 48

For the choirmaster   Of the sons of Korah   Psalm

1   Hear this, all nations,
         pay attention all who live on earth,
2   important people, ordinary people,
         rich and poor alike!

3   My lips have wisdom to utter,
         my heart whispers sound sense;
4   I turn my attention to a proverb,
         and set my solution to the harp.

5   Why should I be afraid in evil times,
         when malice dogs my steps and hems me in,
6   of men who trust in their wealth
         and boast of the profusion of their riches?

7   But man could never redeem himself
         or pay his ransom to God:
8   it costs so much to redeem his life,
9   it is beyond him; •how then could he live on for ever
         and never see the Pit—

10   when all the time he sees that wise men die,
         that foolish and stupid perish both alike,
         and leave their fortunes to others.

48 a. 'Ships capable of sailing to Ṭarshish', the common phrase for sea-going vessels.

Their tombs are their eternal home,   11
their lasting residence,
though they owned estates that bore their names.

Man when he prospers forfeits intelligence: 12
he is one with the cattle doomed to slaughter.
So on they go with their self-assurance,   13
with men to run after them when they raise their voice.   *Pause*

Like sheep to be penned in Sheol,   14
Death will herd them to pasture
and the upright will have the better of them.

Dawn will come and then the show they made will disappear,
Sheol the home for them!
But God will redeem my life   15
from the grasp of Sheol, and will receive me.   *Pause*

Do not be afraid when a man grows rich,   16
when the glory of his House increases;
when he dies he can take nothing with him,   17
his glory cannot follow him down.

The soul he made so happy while he lived   18
— 'look after yourself and men will praise you' —
will join the company of his ancestors   19
who will never see the light of day again.

Man in his prosperity forfeits intelligence: 20
he is one with the cattle doomed to slaughter.

PSALM 50

V 49

Worship in spirit and truth

ᵖsalm   Of Asaph

Yahweh, God of gods,   1
speaks, he summons the earth.
From east to west,
from Zion, perfection of beauty, he shines.   2

Let our God come, and be silent no more!   3

Preceding him, a devouring fire,
round him, a raging storm;
he summons the heavens above   4
and the earth, to his people's trial:

'Assemble my faithful before me   5
who sealed my covenant by sacrifice!'
Let the heavens proclaim his righteousness   6
when God himself is judge!   *Pause*

'Listen, my people, I am speaking;   7a
Israel, I am giving evidence against you!   7b
I charge, I indict you to your face,   21c
I, God, your God.   7c

8 'I am not finding fault with your sacrifices,
   those holocausts constantly before me;
9 I do not claim one extra bull from your homes,
   nor one extra goat from your pens,

10 'since all the forest animals are already mine,
    and the cattle on my mountains in their thousands;
11 I know all the birds of the air,
    nothing moves in the field that does not belong to me.

12 'If I were hungry, I should not tell you,
    since the world and all it holds is mine.
13 Do I eat the flesh of bulls,
    or drink goats' blood?

14 'No, let thanksgiving be your sacrifice to God,
    fulfil the vows you make to the Most High;
15 then you can invoke me in your troubles
    and I will rescue you, and you shall honour me.'

16 But to the wicked man God says:

    'What business have you reciting my statutes,
    standing there mouthing my covenant,
17 since you detest my discipline
    and thrust my words behind you?

18 'You make friends with a thief as soon as you see one,
    you feel at home with adulterers,
19 your mouth is given freely to evil
    and your tongue to inventing lies.

20 'You sit there, slandering your own brother,
    you malign your own mother's son.
21 You do this, and expect me to say nothing?
21b Do you really think I am like you?

22 'You are leaving God out of account; take care!
    Or I will tear you to pieces where no one can rescue you!
23 Whoever makes thanksgiving his sacrifice honours me;
    to the upright man I will show how God can save.'

PSALM 51   V 50

Miserere

*For the choirmaster   Psalm   Of David   When the prophet Nathan came to him
because he had been with Bathsheba*

1 Have mercy on me, O God, in your goodness,
   in your great tenderness wipe away my faults;
2 wash me clean of my guilt,
   purify me from my sin.

3 For I am well aware of my faults,
   I have my sin constantly in mind,
4 having sinned against none other than you,
   having done what you regard as wrong.

You are just when you pass sentence on me,
blameless when you give judgement.
You know I was born guilty,   5
a sinner from the moment of conception.

Yet, since you love sincerity of heart,   6
teach me the secrets of wisdom.
Purify me with hyssop*a* until I am clean;   7
wash me until I am whiter than snow.

Instil some joy and gladness into me,   8
let the bones you have crushed rejoice again.
Hide your face from my sins,   9
wipe out all my guilt.

God, create a clean heart in me,   10
put into me a new and constant spirit,
do not banish me from your presence,   11
do not deprive me of your holy spirit.

Be my saviour again, renew my joy,   12
keep my spirit steady and willing;
and I shall teach transgressors the way to you,   13
and to you the sinners will return.

Save me from death, God my saviour,   14
and my tongue will acclaim your righteousness;
Lord, open my lips,   15
and my mouth will speak out your praise.

Sacrifice gives you no pleasure,   16
were I to offer holocaust, you would not have it.
My sacrifice is this broken spirit,   17
you will not scorn this crushed and broken heart.

Show your favour graciously to Zion,   18
rebuild the walls of Jerusalem.*b*
Then there will be proper sacrifice to please you   19
—holocaust and whole oblation—
and young bulls to be offered on your altar.

PSALM 52   V 51

The fate of cynics

*For the choirmaster   Poem   Of David   When Doeg the Edomite went and
warned Saul, 'David has gone to Ahimelech's house'*

Why make a boast of your wickedness,   1
     you champion in villainy,
all day •plotting destruction?   2
Your tongue is razor-sharp,
     you artist in perfidy!

You prefer evil to good,   3
     lying to honest speech;   *Pause*
you love the destructive word,   4
     perfidious tongue!

5   That is why God will crush you,
     snatch you away for good,
     tear you out of your tent,
    uproot you from the land of the living.   *Pause*

6   Dread will seize the virtuous at the sight,
     they will laugh at his fate:
7   'So much for the man who refused
     to make God his fortress,
    but relied on his own great wealth
     and drew his strength from crime!'

8   I, for my part, like an olive tree
     growing in the house of God,
    put my trust in God's love
     for ever and ever.

9   I mean to thank you constantly
     for doing what you did,
    and put my hope in your name, that is so full of kindness,
     in the presence of those who love you.

PSALM 53   V 52

The godless man[a]

For the choirmaster In sickness Poem Of David

1   The fool says in his heart,
     'There is no God!'
    They are false, corrupt, vile,
     there is not one good man left.

2   God is looking down from heaven
     at the sons of men,
    to see if a single one is wise,
     if a single one is seeking God.

3   All have turned aside,
     all alike are tainted
    There is not one good man left,
     not a single one.

4   Are they so ignorant, these evil men
     who swallow my people
    as though they were eating bread,
     and never invoke God?

5   They will be struck with fear,
     fear without reason,
    since God scatters the bones of the apostate,
     they are disgraced, for God rejects them.

6   Who will bring Israel salvation from Zion?
    When God brings his people home,
    what joy for Jacob, what happiness for Israel!

51 a. Plant used in ceremonial purification by sprinkling. **b.** In spite of the inscription at the beginning of this psalm, this stanza at least speaks of a time after the return from Exile.
53 a. An edition of Ps 14 by an 'Elohistic' editor.

PSALM 54   V 53

An appeal to the God of justice

For the choirmaster   On stringed instruments   Poem   Of David   When the Ziphites went to Saul and said, 'Is not David hiding with us?'

God, save me by your name,   1
by your power see justice done to me;
God, hear my prayer,   2
listen to what I am saying!

Arrogant men are attacking me,   3
brutes who are hounding me to death,
people to whom God means nothing.   *Pause*

But now God himself comes to help me,   4
the Lord, supporter of my life.
May their wickedness recoil on themselves,   5
Yahweh, ever faithful, destroy my enemies!

How gladly will I offer sacrifice to you   6
and praise your name, that is so full of kindness.
He has rescued me from all my troubles,   7
and let me see my enemies defeated.

PSALM 55   V 54

Prayer in persecution

For the choirmaster   For strings   Poem   Of David

God, hear my prayer,   1
   do not hide from my petition,
give me a hearing, answer me,   2
   I cannot rest for complaining.

I shudder •at the enemy's shouts,   3
   at the howling of the wicked;
they bring misery crashing down on me,
   and vent their fury on me.

My heart aches in my breast,   4
Death's terrors assail me,
fear and trembling descend on me,   5
   horror overwhelms me.

And I say,   6
'Oh for the wings of a dove
to fly away and find rest'.
How far I would take my flight,   7
   and make a new home in the desert!   *Pause*

There I should soon find shelter   8
   from the raging wind,
and from the tempest, •Lord, that destroys,   9
   and from their malicious tongues.

I can see how Violence
    and Discord fill the city;
10   day and night they stalk together
      along the city walls.

Sorrow and Misery live inside,
11   Ruin is an inmate;
Tyranny and Treachery are never absent
    from its central square.

12   Were it an enemy who insulted me,
      I could put up with that;
had a rival got the better of me,
      I could hide from him.

13   But you, a man of my own rank,
      a colleague and a friend,
14   to whom sweet conversation bound me
      in the house of God!

    May they recoil in disorder,
15   may Death descend on them,
may they go down, still living, to Sheol—
    since Evil shares their homes.

16   I, for myself, appeal to God
      and Yahweh saves me;
17   evening, morning, noon,
      I complain, I groan;
      he will hear me calling.

18   His peace can ransom me
      from the war being waged on me.
How many are ranged against me!
19   But God will hear me.

Sovereign from the first, he will humble them;   *Pause*
no change of heart for them,
    since they do not fear God.

20   He[a] has attacked his friends,
      he has gone back on his word;
21   though his mouth is smoother than butter,
      he has war in his heart;
his words may soothe more than oil,
    but they are naked swords.

22   Unload your burden on to Yahweh,
      and he will support you;
he will never permit
    the virtuous to falter.

23   As for these murderous, these treacherous men,
      you, God, will push them
down to the deepest Pit
    before half their days are out.

For my part, I put my trust in you.

---

55 a. The 'friend' of v.13.

PSALM 56

Reliance on God

For the choirmaster Tune: 'Dove of the distant gods' Of David Miktam
When the Philistines held him in Gath

Take pity on me, God, as they harry me, 1
pressing their attacks home all day.
All day my opponents harry me, 2
hordes coming in to the attack.

Raise me up •when I am most afraid, 3
I put my trust in you;
in God, whose word*a* I praise, 4
in God I put my trust, fearing nothing;
what can men do to me?

All day long they twist what I say, 5
all they think of is how to harm me,
they conspire, lurk, spy on my movements, 6
determined to take my life.

Are they to go unpunished for such a crime? 7
God, in fury bring the nations down!
You have noted my agitation, 8
now collect my tears in your wineskin!
Then my enemies will have to fall back 9
   as soon as I call for help.

This I know: that God is on my side.
In God whose word I praise, 10
in Yahweh, whose word I praise,
in God I put my trust, fearing nothing; 11
what can man do to me?

I must fulfil the vows I made you, God; 12
I shall pay you my thank-offerings,
for you have rescued me from Death 13
to walk in the presence of God
   in the light of the living.

PSALM 57

Among ferocious enemies

For the choirmaster Tune: 'Do not destroy' Of David Miktam When he
escaped from Saul, in the cave

Take pity on me, God, take pity on me, 1
in you my soul takes shelter;
I take shelter in the shadow of your wings
until the destroying storm is over.

I call on God the Most High, 2
on God who has done everything for me:
to send from heaven and save me, 3
to check the people harrying me, *Pause*
may God send his faithfulness and love.

4   I lie surrounded by lions
     greedy for human prey,
     their teeth are spears and arrows,
     their tongue a sharp sword.

5   Rise high above the heavens, God,
     let your glory be over the earth!
6   They laid a net where I was walking
     when I was bowed with care;
     they dug a pitfall for me
     but fell into it themselves!   *Pause*

7   My heart is ready, God,
     my heart is ready;
     I mean to sing and play for you,
8   awake, my muse,
     awake, lyre and harp,
     I mean to wake the Dawn!

9   Lord, I mean to thank you among the peoples;
     to play music to you among the nations;
10   your love is high as heaven,
     your faithfulness as the clouds.
11   Rise high above the heavens, God,
     let your glory be over the earth!

PSALM 58   V 57

The Judge of earthly judges

For the choirmaster   *Tune: 'Do not destroy'*   *Of David*   *Miktam*

1   Gods[a] you may be, but do you give the sentences you should,
     and dispense impartial justice to mankind?
2   On the contrary, in your hearts you meditate oppression,
     with your hands you dole out tyranny on earth.

3   Right from the womb these wicked men have gone astray,
     these double talkers have been in error since their birth;
4   their poison is the poison of the snake,
     they are deaf as the adder that blocks its ears
5   so as not to hear the magician's music
     and the clever snake-charmer's spells.

6   God, break their teeth in their mouths,
     Yahweh, wrench out the fangs of these savage lions!
7   May they drain away like water running to waste,
     may they wither like trodden grass,
8   like a slug that melts as it moves,
     like an abortion, denied the light of day!

9   Before they sprout thorns like the bramble,
     green or scorched, may the wrath whirl them away!
10   What joy for the virtuous, seeing this vengeance,

56 a. I.e., promise.
58 a. The judges and rulers addressed in these two verses.

bathing their feet in the blood of the wicked!
'So' people will say 'the virtuous do have their harvest;   11
so there is a God who dispenses justice on earth!'

PSALM 59   V 58

Against the wicked

For the choirmaster   Tune: 'Do not destroy'   Of David   Miktam   When
Saul sent spies to his house to have him killed

Rescue me from my enemies, my God,   1
protect me from those attacking me,
rescue me from these evil men,   2
save me from these murderers!

Look at them lurking to ambush me,   3
they are strong and united against me;
for no fault, no sin, • no offence of mine,   4
Yahweh, how they hurry into position!

Wake up, stand by me and look,
Yahweh, God of Sabaoth, God of Israel,   5
up, now, and punish these pagans,
show no mercy to these villains and traitors!   *Pause*

    Back they come at nightfall,   6
    snarling like curs,
    prowling through the town.

See how they slaver at the mouth,   7
with swords between their teeth,
'There is no one listening'.

Yahweh, you laugh at them,   8
you make fun of these pagans.
My Strength, I look to you.   9

My citadel is God himself,
the God who loves me is coming,   10
God will show me my enemies defeated.

Slaughter them, God, before my people forget!   11
Harry them with your power and strike them down,
    Lord, our shield!

Sin is in their mouths, sin on their lips,   12
so let them be caught in their pride!
For the curses and lies they utter,

destroy them in anger, destroy, until they are finished,   13
until God is acknowledged as ruler in Jacob
to the remotest parts of the earth!   *Pause*

    Back they come at nightfall,   14
    snarling like curs,
    prowling through the town;
scavenging for food,   15
growling till they are full.

16   I, for my part, celebrate your strength,
      I sing of your love morning by morning;
      you have always been my citadel,
      a shelter when I am in trouble.

17   My Strength, I play for you,
      my citadel is God himself,
      the God who loves me.

PSALM 60   V 59

National prayer after defeat

For the choirmaster   Tune: 'The decree is a lily'   Miktam   Of David   For instruction   When he was at war with Aram-naharaim and Aram-zobah, and Joab marched back to destroy twelve thousand Edomites in the Valley of Salt

1   God, you have rejected us, broken us;
     you have been angry, come back to us!

2   You have made the earth tremble, torn it apart;
     now mend the rifts, it is tottering still!

3   You have allowed your people to suffer,
     to drink a wine that makes us reel.

4   Hoist the standard to rally those who fear you,
     to put them out of range of bow and arrow.   *Pause*

5   To bring rescue to those you love,
     save with your right hand and answer us!

6   God promised us once from his sanctuary,
     'I the Victor will parcel out Shechem,
     and share out the Valley of Succoth.

7   'Gilead is mine, Manasseh mine,
     Ephraim is my helmet,
     Judah, my marshal's baton.

8   'Moab a bowl for me to wash in!
     I throw my sandal*a* over Edom.
     Now shout "Victory", Philistia!'*b*

9   Who is there now to take me into the fortified city,
     to lead me into Edom?

10   God, can you really have rejected us?
     You no longer march with our armies.

11   Help us in this hour of crisis,
     the help that man can give is worthless.

12   With God among us we shall fight like heroes,
     he will trample on our enemies.

60 a. The symbolic action of taking possession.   b. Ironical.

PSALM 61

Prayer of an exile

For the choirmaster   For strings   Of David

God, hear my cry for help,
  listen to my prayer! 1

From the end of the earth I call to you,
  with sinking heart. 2

To the rock too high for me,
  lead me!
For you are my refuge, 3
  a strong tower against the enemy.

Let me stay in your tent for ever, 4
  taking refuge in the shelter of your wings. *Pause*
You, God, accept my vows, 5
you grant me the heritage of those who fear your name.

Let the king live on and on, 6
  prolong his years, generation on generation.
May he sit enthroned in God's presence for ever! 7
Assign your Love and Faithfulness to guard him!

So I shall always sing of your name, 8
fulfilling the vows I have taken, day after day.

PSALM 62

Hope in God alone

For the choirmaster...   Jeduthun   Psalm   Of David

In God alone there is rest for my soul, 1
  from him comes my safety;
with him alone for my rock, my safety, 2
  my fortress, I can never fall.

How many times will you come rushing at a man, 3
  all of you, to bring him down
like a wall already leaning over,
  like a rampart undermined?

Deceit their sole intention, 4
  their delight is to mislead;
with lies on their lips they bless aloud,
  while cursing inwardly. *Pause*

Rest in God alone, my soul! 5
  He is the source of my hope;
with him alone for my rock, my safety, 6
  my fortress, I can never fall;
rest in God, my safety, my glory, 7
  the rock of my strength.

In God, I find shelter; •rely on him, 8
  people, at all times;
unburden your hearts to him,
  God is a shelter for us. *Pause*

9 Ordinary men are only a puff of wind,
      important men*a* delusion;
  put both in the scales and up they go,
      lighter than a puff of wind.

10 Put no reliance on extortion,
      no empty hopes in robbery;
  though riches may increase,
      keep your heart detached.

11 God has spoken once,
      twice I have heard this:
  it is for God to be strong,
12   for you, Lord, to be loving;
  and you yourself repay
      man as his works deserve.

PSALM 63

V 62

Desire for God

Psalm Of David When he was in the wilderness of Judah

1 God, you are my God, I am seeking you,
  my soul is thirsting for you,
  my flesh is longing for you,
  a land parched, weary and waterless;
2 I long to gaze on you in the Sanctuary,
  and to see your power and glory.

3 Your love is better than life itself,
  my lips will recite your praise;
4 all my life I will bless you,
  in your name lift up my hands;
5 my soul will feast most richly,
  on my lips a song of joy and, in my mouth, praise.

6 On my bed I think of you,
  I meditate on you all night long,
7 for you have always helped me.
  I sing for joy in the shadow of your wings;
8 my soul clings close to you,
  your right hand supports me.

9 But may those now hounding me to death
  go down to the earth below,
10 consigned to the edge of the sword,
  and left as food for jackals.
11 Then will the king rejoice in God,
  and all who swear by him be able to boast
  once these lying mouths are silenced.

62 a. Lit. 'Sons of Adam' (ordinary men) . . . 'sons of persons' (important men).

PSALM 64

The punishment for slanderers

For the choirmaster   Psalm.   Of David

> God, hear me as I make my plea,   1
> protect me from this frightening enemy,
> hide me from the wicked and their schemes,   2
> from this mob of evil men,
>
> sharpening their tongues like swords,   3
> shooting bitter words like arrows,
> shooting them at the innocent from cover,   4
> shooting suddenly, without warning.
>
> Urging each other on to their wicked purpose,   5
> they discuss where to hide their snares.
> 'Who is going to see us?' they say
>   'Who can probe our secrets?'   6
> Who? He who probes the inmost mind
>   and the depths of the heart.
>
> God will shoot them with his own arrow,   7
> wound them without warning.
> He will destroy them for that tongue of theirs,   8
> and all who see them fall will shake their heads.
>
> Then all will feel afraid,   9
> will tell others what God has done;
>   they will understand why he has done it.
> The virtuous will rejoice in Yahweh,   10
>   will make him their refuge;
> and upright hearts will be able to boast.

PSALM 65

Thanksgiving hymn

For the choirmaster   Of David   Song

> Praise is rightfully yours,   1
>   God, in Zion.
> Vows to you must be fulfilled,
>   for you answer prayer.   2
>
> All flesh must come to you
>   with all its sins;
> though our faults overpower us,   3
>   you blot them out.
>
> Happy the man you choose, whom you invite   4
>   to live in your courts.
> Fill us with the good things of your house,
>   of your holy Temple.
>
> Your righteousness repays us with marvels,   5
>   God our saviour,
> hope of all the ends of the earth
>   and the distant islands.

6   Your strength holds the mountains up,
          such is the power that wraps you;
7   you calm the clamour of the ocean,
          the clamour of its waves.

8   The nations are in uproar, ·in panic
          those who live at the ends of the world,
      as your miracles bring shouts of joy
          to the portals of morning and evening.

9   You visit the earth and water it,
          you load it with riches;
      God's rivers brim with water
          to provide their grain.

10   This is how you provide it:
      by drenching its furrows, by levelling its ridges,
      by softening it with showers, by blessing the first-fruits.
11   You crown the year with your bounty,
      abundance flows wherever you pass;
12   the desert pastures overflow,
      the hillsides are wrapped in joy,
13   the meadows are dressed in flocks,
      the valleys are clothed in wheat,
      what shouts of joy, what singing!

PSALM 66   V 65

Corporate act of thanksgiving

For the choirmaster   Song   Psalm

1   Acclaim God, all the earth,
2   play music to the glory of his name,
          glorify him with your praises,
3   say to God, 'What dread you inspire!'

      Your achievements are the measure of your power.
      Your enemies cringe in your presence;
4   all the earth bows down to you,
          playing music for you, playing in honour of your name.   *Pause*

5   Come and see what marvels God has done,
      so much to be feared for his deeds among mankind:
6   he turned the sea into dry land,
          they crossed the river on foot!

      So let us rejoice in him,
7   who rules for ever by his power:
      his eyes keep watch on the nations,
          let no rebel raise his head!   *Pause*

8   You nations, bless our God
      and make his praise resound,
9   who brings our soul to life
      and keeps our feet from faltering.

10   You tested us, God,
      you refined us like silver,
11   you let us fall into the net,

you laid heavy burdens on our backs,
you let people drive over our heads;   12
but now the ordeal by fire and water is over,
and you allow us once more to draw breath.

I bring holocausts to your house,   13
I bring them to fulfil those vows
that rose to my lips,   14
those vows I spoke when in trouble.

I offer you fat holocausts   15
and the smoke of burning rams,
I offer you bullocks and he-goats.   *Pause*

Come and listen, all you who fear God,   16
while I tell you what he has done for me:
when I uttered my cry to him   17
and high praise was on my tongue,
had I been guilty in my heart,   18
the Lord would never have heard me.
But God not only heard me,   19
he listened to my prayer.

Blessed be God,   20
who neither ignored my prayer
nor deprived me of his love.

PSALM 67   V 66

Harvest song

For the choirmaster   For strings   Psalm   Song

May God show kindness and bless us,   1
and make his face smile on us!   *Pause*
For then the earth will acknowledge your ways   2
and all the nations will know of your power to save.

Let the nations praise you, O God,   3
let all the nations praise you!

Let the nations shout and sing for joy,   4
since you dispense true justice to the world;
you dispense strict justice to the peoples,
on earth you rule the nations.   *Pause*

Let the nations praise you, God,   5
let all the nations praise you!

The soil has given its harvest,   6
God, our God, has blessed us.
May God bless us, and let him be feared   7
to the very ends of the earth.

PSALM 68

National song of triumph

For the choirmaster   Of David   Psalm   Song

1   Let God arise, let his enemies be scattered,
    let those who hate him flee before him!
2   As smoke disperses, they disperse;
    as wax melts when near the fire,
    so the wicked perish when God approaches.

3   But at God's approach, the virtuous rejoice,
    exulting and singing for joy.
4   Sing to Yahweh, play music to his name,
    build a road for the Rider of the Clouds,
    rejoice in Yahweh, exult at his coming!

5   Father of orphans, defender of widows,
    such is God in his holy dwelling;
6   God gives the lonely a permanent home,
    makes prisoners happy by setting them free,
    but rebels must live in an arid land.

7   God, when you set out at the head of your people,
8   and marched across the desert, •the earth rocked,   *Pause*
    the heavens deluged at God's coming,
    at the coming of God, the God of Israel.

9   God, you rained a downpour of blessings,
    when your heritage was faint you gave it strength;
10 your family found a home, where you
    in your goodness, God, provided for the needy.

11a The Lord gives his couriers the news,
14a 'Shaddai has scattered •a huge army'.
11b
12 Kings are in flight, armies in flight,
    the women at home take their pick of the loot.

13 Meanwhile you others were lolling in the sheepfolds.
    There were dove-wings covered with silver,
    on their pinions the sheen of green gold;
14b jewels were there like snow on Dark Mountain.

15 That peak of Bashan, a mountain of God?
    Rather, a mountain of pride, that peak of Bashan!
16 Peaks of pride, have you the right to look down on
    a mountain where God has chosen to live,
    where Yahweh is going to live for ever?

17 With thousands of myriads of divine chariots
    the Lord has left Sinai for his sanctuary.
18 God, you have ascended to the height, and captured prisoners,
    you have taken men as tribute,
    yes, taken rebels to your dwelling, Yahweh!

19 Blessed be the Lord day after day,
    the God who saves us and bears our burdens!

This God of ours is a God who saves,   20
to the Lord Yahweh belong the ways of escape from death;
but God will smash the heads of his enemies,   21
the hairy skull of the man who parades his guilt.

The Lord has promised, 'I will bring them back from Bashan,   22
I will bring them back from the bottom of the sea,
for your feet to wade in blood,   23
for the tongues of your dogs to lap their share of the enemy'.

God, your procession can be seen,   24
my God's, my king's procession to the sanctuary,
with cantors marching in front, musicians behind,   25
and between them maidens playing tambourines.

> Bless God in your choirs,   26
> bless the Lord, you who spring from Israel!

Benjamin, the youngest, is there in the lead,   27
the princes of Judah in brocaded robes,
the princes of Zebulun, the princes of Naphtali.

Take command, God, as befits your power,   28
that power, God, you have wielded on our behalf
from your Temple high above Jerusalem!   29
Kings will come to you, bringing presents.

Rebuke the Beast of the Reeds,[a]   30
that herd of bulls, those calves, that people,
until, humbled, they bring gold and silver.
Scatter those warmongering pagans!

Ambassadors will come from Egypt,   31
Ethiopia will stretch out her hands to God.

Sing to God, you kingdoms of the earth,   32
play for •the Rider of the Heavens, the ancient heavens!   *Pause* 33
Listen to him shouting, to his thundering,
and acknowledge the power of God!   34

Over Israel his splendour, in the clouds his power,
God in his sanctuary is greatly to be feared.   35
He, the God of Israel,
gives power and strength to his people.

> Blessed be God.

PSALM 69   V 68

Lament

For the choirmaster   Tune: 'Lilies...'   Of David

> Save me, God! The water   1
> is already up to my neck!

2 I am sinking in the deepest swamp,
  there is no foothold;
 I have stepped into deep water
  and the waves are washing over me.

3 Worn out with calling, my throat is hoarse,
 my eyes are strained, looking for my God.

4 More people hate me for no reason
  than I have hairs on my head,
 more are groundlessly hostile
  than I have hair to show.
 (They ask me to give back what I never took.)

5 God, you know how foolish I have been,
 my offences are not hidden from you;

6 but let those who hope in you not blush for me,
  Yahweh Sabaoth![a]
 Let those who seek you not be ashamed of me,
  God of Israel!

7 It is for you I am putting up with insults
 that cover me with shame,

8 that make me a stranger to my brothers,
 an alien to my mother's other sons;

9 zeal for your house devours me,
 and the insults of those who insult you fall on me.

10 If I mortify myself with fasting,
 they make this a pretext for insulting me;

11 if I dress myself in sackcloth,
 I become their laughing-stock,

12 the gossip of people sitting at the city gate,
 and the theme of drunken songs.

13 For my part, I pray to you, Yahweh,
  at the time you wish;
 in your great love, answer me, God,
  faithful in saving power.

14 Pull me out of this swamp; let me sink no further,
  let me escape those who hate me,
  save me from deep water!

15 Do not let the waves wash over me,
  do not let the deep swallow me
 or the Pit close its mouth on me.

16 In your loving kindness, answer me, Yahweh,
 in your great tenderness turn to me;

17 do not hide your face from your servant,
 quick, I am in trouble, answer me;

18 come to my side, redeem me,
 from so many enemies ransom me.

19a You know all the insults I endure,
19c every one of my oppressors is known to you;
20a the insults have broken my heart,

68 a. Egypt.
69 a. 'Lord of the armies', not only Lord of the Nation of Israel at arms, but also of 'the hosts of heaven'.

my shame and disgrace ·are past cure;   19b / 20b
I had hoped for sympathy, but in vain,
I found no one to console me.   20c

They gave me poison to eat instead,   21
when I was thirsty they gave me vinegar to drink.

May their own table prove a trap for them,   22
and their plentiful supplies, a snare!
may their eyes grow dim, go blind,   23
strike their loins with chronic palsy!

Vent your fury on them,   24
let your burning anger overtake them;
may their camp be reduced to ruin,   25
and their tents left unoccupied:
for hounding a man after you had struck him,   26
for adding more wounds to those which you inflicted.

Charge them with crime after crime,   27
deny them further access to your righteousness,
blot them out of the book of life,   28
strike them off the roll of the virtuous!

For myself, wounded wretch that I am,   29
by your saving power, God, lift me up!
I will praise the name of God with a song,   30
I will extol him with my thanksgiving,
more pleasing to Yahweh than any ox   31
or bull with horn and hoof.

Then, seeing this, the humble can rejoice: 32
long life to your hearts, all you who seek for God!
Yahweh will always hear those who are in need,   33
will never scorn his captive people.
Let heaven and earth acclaim him,   34
the oceans and all that moves in them!

For God will save Zion,   35
and rebuild the towns of Judah:
they will be lived in, owned,
handed down to his servants' descendants,   36
and lived in by those who love his name.

PSALM 70   V 69

A cry of distress[a]

For the choirmaster   Of David   For commemoration

Oh come and rescue me, God,   1
    Yahweh come quickly and help me!
Shame and dishonour on those   2
    who are out to kill me!

Down with them! Disgrace on those
    who enjoy my misfortune!
May they be aghast with shame,   3
    those who say to me, 'Aha! Aha!'

4 But joy and gladness
    for all who seek you!
  To all who love your saving power
    give constant cause to say, 'God is great!'

5 To me, poor wretch,
    come quickly, God!
  My helper, my saviour, Yahweh,
    come without delay!

PSALM 71

V 70

An old man's prayer

1 In you, Yahweh, I take shelter;
  never let me be disgraced.
2 In your righteousness rescue me, deliver me,
  turn your ear to me and save me!

3 Be a sheltering rock for me,
  a walled fortress to save me!
  For you are my rock, my fortress.
4 My God, rescue me from the hands of the wicked,
  from the clutches of rogue and tyrant!

5 For you alone are my hope, Lord,
  Yahweh, I have trusted you since my youth,
6 I have relied on you since I was born,
  you have been my portion from my mother's womb,
  and the constant theme of my praise.

7 To many I have seemed an enigma,
  but you are my firm refuge.
8 My mouth is full of your praises,
  filled with your splendour all day long.

9 Do not reject me now I am old,
  nor desert me now my strength is failing,
10 for my enemies are uttering threats,
  spies hatching their conspiracy:

11 'Hound him down now that God has deserted him,
  seize him, there is no one to rescue him!'
12 God, do not stand aside,
  my God, come quickly and help me!

13 Shame and ruin on those
    who attack me;
  may insult and disgrace cover those
    whose aim is to hurt me!

14 I promise that, ever hopeful,
    I will praise you more and more,
15 my lips shall proclaim your righteousness
    and power to save, all day long.

16 I will come in the power of Yahweh
  to commemorate your righteousness, yours alone.

70 a. Doublet of Ps 40:13-17.

God, you taught me when I was young,
and I am still proclaiming your marvels.   17

Now that I am old and grey,   18
God, do not desert me;
let me live to tell the rising generation
about your strength and power,
about your heavenly righteousness, God.   19

You have done great things;
who, God, is comparable to you?
You have sent me misery and hardship,   20
but you will give me life again,
you will pull me up again from the depths of the earth,
prolong my old age, and once more comfort me.   21

I promise I will thank you on the lyre,   22
   my ever-faithful God,
I will play the harp in your honour,
   Holy One of Israel.

My lips shall sing for joy as I play to you,   23
   and this soul of mine which you have redeemed.
And all day long, my tongue   24
   shall be talking of your righteousness.
Shame and disgrace on those
   whose aim is to hurt me!

PSALM 72   V 71

The promised king

Of Solomon

God, give your own justice to the king,   1
   your own righteousness to the royal son,
so that he may rule your people rightly   2
   and your poor with justice.

Let the mountains and hills   3
   bring a message of peace for the people.
Uprightly •he will defend the poorest,   4
he will save the children of those in need,
   and crush their oppressors.

Like sun and moon he will endure,   5
   age after age,
welcome as rain that falls on the pasture,   6
   and showers to thirsty soil.

In his days virtue will flourish,   7
   a universal peace till the moon is no more;
his empire shall stretch from sea to sea,   8
   from the river to the ends of the earth.

The Beast[a] will cower before him   9
   and his enemies grovel in the dust;
the kings of Tarshish and of the islands   10
   will pay him tribute.

The kings of Sheba and Seba
will offer gifts;
11   all kings will do him homage,
all nations become his servants.

12   He will free the poor man who calls to him,
and those who need help,
13   he will have pity on the poor and feeble,
and save the lives of those in need;

14   he will redeem their lives from exploitation and outrage,
their lives will be precious in his sight.
15   (Long may he live, may gold from Sheba be given him!)
Prayer will be offered for him constantly,
blessings invoked on him all day long.

16   Grain everywhere in the country,
even on the mountain tops,
abundant as Lebanon its harvest,
luxuriant as common grass!
17   Blessed be his name for ever,
enduring as long as the sun!
May every race in the world be blessed in him,
and all the nations call him blessed!

18   Blessed be Yahweh, the God of Israel,
who alone performs these marvels!
19   Blessed for ever be his glorious name,
may the whole world be filled with his glory!
Amen. Amen!

20   End of the prayers of David, son of Jesse. *b*

PSALM 73

V 72

The triumph of justice

Psalm   Of Asaph

1   God is indeed good to Israel,
the Lord is good to pure hearts.

2   My feet were on the point of stumbling,
a little further and I should have slipped,
3   envying the arrogant as I did,
and watching the wicked get rich.

4   For them, no such thing as pain,
their bodies are healthy and strong,
5   they do not suffer as other men do,
no human afflictions for them!

72 a. A word for a demon or a dangerous wild animal of the desert, used here for the heathen neighbouring nations.   **b.** As this note indicates, the doxology (vv.18,19) ends the second book of the Psalter

So pride is their chain of honour,   6
violence the garment that covers them;
their spite oozes like fat,   7
their hearts drip with slyness.

Cynical advocates of evil,   8
lofty advocates of force,
they think their mouth is heaven   9
and their tongue can dictate on earth.

This is why my people turn to them   10
and lap up all they say,
asking, 'How will God find out?   11
Does the Most High know everything?
Look at them: these are the wicked,   12
well-off and still getting richer!'

After all, why should I keep my own heart pure,   13
and wash my hands in innocence,
if you plague me all day long   14
and discipline me every morning?

Had I said, 'That talk appeals to me',   15
I should have betrayed your children's race.
Instead, I tried to analyse the problem,   16
hard though I found it—

until the day I pierced the mystery   17
and saw the end in store for them:
they are on a slippery slope, you put them there,   18
you urge them on to ruin,

until suddenly they fall,   19
done for, terrified to death.
When you wake up, Lord, you shrug them off   20
like the phantoms of a morning dream.

When my heart had been growing sourer   21
with pains shooting through my loins,
I had simply failed to understand,   22
my stupid attitude to you was brutish.

Even so, I stayed in your presence,   23
you held my right hand;
now guide me with advice   24
and in the end receive me into glory.

I look to no one else in heaven,   25
I delight in nothing else on earth.
My flesh and my heart are pining with love,   26
my heart's Rock, my own, God for ever!

So then: those who abandon you are doomed,   27
you destroy the adulterous deserter;[a]
whereas my joy lies in being close to God.   28
I have taken shelter in the Lord,
continually to proclaim what you have done.

Lament on the destruction of the Temple

Poem   *Of Asaph*

1 God, have you finally rejected us,
   raging at the flock you used to pasture?

2 Remember the people you long since made your own,
   your hereditary tribe whom you redeemed,
   and this Mount Zion where you came to live.

3 Pick your steps over these endless ruins:
   the enemy have sacked everything in the sanctuary.

4 They roared where your Assemblies used to take place,
   they stuck their enemy emblems over the entrance, *a*

5 emblems •we had never seen before.

6 Axes deep in the wood, •hacking at the panels,
   they battered them down with mallet and hatchet;

7 then, God, setting fire to your sanctuary,
   they profanely razed the house of your name to the ground.

8 Determined to destroy us once and for all,
   they burned down every shrine of God in the country.

9 Deprived of signs, with no prophets left,
   who can say how long this will last?

10 How much longer, God, is the oppressor to blaspheme,
    is the enemy to insult your name for ever?

11 Why hold back your hand,
    why keep your right hand hidden?

12 Yet, God, my king from the first,
    author of saving acts throughout the earth,

13 by your power you split the sea in two,
    and smashed the heads of monsters on the waters.

14 You crushed Leviathan's heads,
    leaving him for wild animals to eat,

15 you opened the spring, the torrent,
    you dried up inexhaustible rivers.

16 You are master of day and night,
    you instituted light and sun,

17 you fixed the boundaries of the world,
    you created summer and winter.

18 Now, Yahweh, remember the enemy's blasphemy,
    how frenzied people dare to insult your name.

19 Do not betray your turtledove to the beast,
    do not forget your wretched people for good.

20 Respect the covenant! We can bear no more—
    every cave in the country is the scene of violence!

21 Do not let the hard-pressed retreat in confusion,
    give the poor and needy cause to praise your name.

73 a. As in the prophets, the expression refers to religious unfaithfulness.
74 a. Probably a description of the destruction of the Temple by 'the mad king', Antiochus
Epiphanes; if so, he is the 'madman' of v.22.

Rise, God, say something on your own behalf,   22
do not forget the madman's day-long blaspheming,
remember the shouting of your enemies,   23
this ever-rising clamour of your adversaries.

PSALM 75   V 74

To the divine judge

For the choirmaster   Tune: 'Do not destroy'   Psalm   Of Asaph   Song

We give thanks to you, God,   1
we give thanks as we invoke your name,
as we recount your marvels.

'At the moment I decide   2
I will dispense strict justice;
the earth shall quake and all its inhabitants,   3
it is I who poised its columns.

'I said to the boastful: Enough of boasting!   4
and to the wicked: How dare you raise your horn,
how dare you raise your horn like that,   5
how dare you speak so boldly!'

Not from the east, nor from the west,   6
not from the desert, nor from the mountains,
but from God the judgement comes,   7
lowering one, raising another.

Yahweh is holding a cup   8
of frothing wine, heavily drugged;
he pours it out, they drain it to the dregs,
all drink of it, the wicked of the earth.

But I will never stop proclaiming the God of Jacob   9
or playing in his honour;
I will cut off the horns of all the wicked   10
and raise the horns of the virtuous.

PSALM 76   V 75

Ode to God the awe-inspiring[a]

For the choirmaster   For strings   Psalm   Of Asaph

God is renowned in Judah,   1
his name is great in Israel;
his tent is pitched in Salem,   2
his home is in Zion;
there he has broken the lightning-swift arrow,   3
the shield, the sword and the line of battle.   *Pause*

You the Illustrious and Majestic: 4
mountains of spoil •have been captured;   5
heroes are now sleeping their last sleep,
the warriors' arms have failed them;
at your reproof, God of Jacob,   6
chariot and horse stand spellbound.

7 You the Terrible! Who can oppose you
and your furious onslaught?

8 When your verdicts thunder from heaven,
earth stays silent with dread;

9 when God stands up to give judgement
and to save all the humble of the earth.   *Pause*

10 Man's wrath only adds to your glory;
the survivors of your wrath you will draw like a girdle
around you;

11 fulfil the promises you make to Yahweh your God,
make offerings to the Terrible, you who surround him;

12 he snuffs out the lives of princes,
he is terrible to the kings of the earth.

PSALM 77

V 76

Meditation on Israel's past

For the choirmaster...   Jeduthun   Of Asaph   Psalm

1 Loudly I cry to God,
loudly to God who hears me.

2 When in trouble I sought the Lord,
all night long I stretched out my hands,
my soul refusing to be consoled.

3 I thought of God and sighed,
I pondered and my spirit failed me.

4 You stopped me closing my eyes,
I was too distraught to speak;

5 I thought of the olden days,

6 years long past ·came back to me,
I spent all night meditating in my heart,
I pondered and my spirit asked this question:

7 'If the Lord has rejected you, is this final?
If he withholds his favour, is this for ever?

8 Is his love over for good
and the promise void for all time?

9 Has God forgotten to show mercy,
or has his anger overcome his tenderness?   *Pause*

10 'This' I said then 'is what distresses me:
that the power of the Most High is no longer what it was.'

11 Remembering Yahweh's achievements,
remembering your marvels in the past,

12 I reflect on all that you did,
I ponder on all your achievements.

13 God, your ways are holy!
What god so great as God?

14 You are the God who did marvellous things
and forced nations to acknowledge your power,

15 with your own arm redeeming your people,
the sons of Jacob and Joseph.   *Pause*

76 a. Apparently related to the defeat of Sennacherib, 2 K 19.

When the waters saw it was you, God,   16
when the waters saw it was you, they recoiled,
shuddering to their depths.
The clouds poured down water,   17
the sky thundered,
your arrows darted out.

Your thunder crashed as it rolled,   18
your lightning lit up the world,
the earth shuddered and quaked.
You strode across the sea,   19
you marched across the ocean,
but your steps could not be seen.

You guided your people like a flock   20
by the hands of Moses and Aaron.

PSALM 78   V 77

The lessons of Israelite history

Psalm   Of Asaph

Listen to this Law, my people,   1
pay attention to what I say;
I am going to speak to you in parable   2
and expound the mysteries of our past.

What we have heard and known for ourselves,   3
and what our ancestors have told us,
must not be withheld from their descendants,   4
but be handed on by us to the next generation;

that is: the titles of Yahweh, his power
and the miracles he has done.
When he issued the decrees for Jacob   5
and instituted a Law in Israel,

he gave our ancestors strict orders
to teach it to their children;
the next generation was to learn it,   6
the children still to be born,

and these in their turn were to tell their own children
so that they too would put their confidence in God,   7
never forgetting God's achievements,
and always keeping his commandments,

and not becoming, like their ancestors,   8
a stubborn and unruly generation,
a generation with no sincerity of heart,
in spirit unfaithful to God.

The sons of Ephraim, who were bowmen,   9
turned tail when the time came to fight;
they had not kept God's covenant,   10
they refused to follow his Law;

they had forgotten his achievements,   11
the marvels he had shown them:

12   he had worked wonders for their ancestors
      in the plains of Zoan, down in Egypt:

13   dividing the sea, bringing them through,
      making the waters stand up like dikes,
14   leading them with a cloud by day
      and with a fiery glow at night,

15   splitting rocks in the wilderness,
      quenching their thirst with unlimited water,
16   conjuring streams from the rock
      and bringing down water in torrents.

17   They only sinned against him more than ever,
      defying the Most High in the desert,
18   deliberately challenging God
      by demanding their favourite food.

19   They blasphemed against God,
      'Is it likely' they said 'that God
      could give a banquet in the wilderness?

20   'Admittedly, when he struck the rock,
      ᵗwaters gushed, torrents streamed out,
      but bread now, can he give us that,
      can he provide meat for his people?'

21   Yahweh was enraged when he heard them,
      a fire flared at Jacob,
      the wrath attacked Israel
22   for having no faith in God,
      no trust in his power to save.

23   He gave orders to the skies above,
      he opened the doors of heaven,
24   he rained down manna to feed them,
      he gave them the wheat of heaven;
25   men ate the bread of Immortals,
      he sent them more food than they could eat.

26   He stirred up an east wind in the heavens,
      he conjured up a south wind by his power,
27   he rained down meat on them like dust;
      birds as thick as sand on the seashore
28   he sent tumbling into their camp,
      in all directions round their tents.

29   They all had enough and to spare,
      he having provided what they wanted;
30   but they had hardly satisfied their craving,
      the food was still in their mouths,

31   when the wrath of God attacked them,
      slaughtering their strongest men
      and laying the flower of Israel low.

32   Despite all this they went on sinning,
      and put no faith in his marvels;
33   for which he blasted their days
      and their years in a flash.

Whenever he slaughtered them they sought him,   34
they came to their senses and sought him earnestly
remembering that God was their rock,   35
God the Most High, their redeemer.

But though they outwardly flattered him   36
and used their tongues to lie to him,
in their hearts they were not true to him,   37
they were unfaithful to his covenant.

Compassionately, however,   38
he forgave their guilt instead of killing them,
repeatedly repressing his anger
instead of rousing his full wrath,
remembering they were creatures of flesh,   39
a puff of wind that passes and does not return.

How often they defied him in the wilderness,   40
how often they outraged him in the desert,
repeatedly challenging God,   41
provoking the Holy One of Israel—
entirely oblivious of his hand   42
and of the time he saved them from the oppressor:

by imposing his signs on Egypt,   43
by displaying his wonders in the plains of Zoan,
by turning their rivers into blood   44
to stop them drinking from their streams,

by sending horseflies to eat them   45
and frogs to devastate them,
by consigning their crops to the caterpillar   46
and their hard-won harvest to the locust,

by killing their vines with hail   47
and their sycamore trees with frost,
by condemning their cattle to plague   48
and their flocks to feverish pests,

by unleashing his fierce anger, rage,   49
indignation and hardship on them,
a mission of angels of disaster,
by giving his anger free rein,   50

by not even exempting them from death,
by condemning them to plague,
by striking down all the first-born in Egypt,   51
the first-fruits of their virility in the tents of Ham,

by driving his people out like sheep,   52
by leading them through the wilderness like a flock,
by guiding them safe and unafraid   53
while the sea engulfed their enemies,

by bringing them to his sacred frontier,   54
the highlands conquered by his own right hand,
by expelling the pagans in front of them   55
and by marking out a heritage for each,
in which the tribes of Israel could pitch their tents.

Even so, they went on challenging God the Most High,   56
rebelliously disregarding his decrees;

57   as perverse and disloyal as their ancestors,
treacherous as a bow with a warp,
58   provoking him with their high places
and rousing his jealousy with their idols.

59   God was enraged when he heard them,
he rejected Israel out of hand,
60   he left his home in Shiloh,
that tent where he once lived with men.

61   He consigned his power to captivity,
his splendour*a* to the enemy's clutches;
62   he condemned his own people to the sword,
he raged at his heritage,

63   whose young men were then burnt to death—
no brides left to hear the wedding song;
64   whose priests fell by the sword—
no widows left to raise the dirge.

65   Then, like a sleeper, like a hero
fighting-mad with wine, the Lord woke up
66   to strike his enemies on the rump
and put them to everlasting shame.

67   Rejecting the tent of Joseph,
not choosing the tribe of Ephraim,
68   instead he chose the tribe of Judah
and his well-loved mountain of Zion,
69   where he built his sanctuary, a copy of high heaven,
founding it firm as the earth for ever.

70   Choosing David as his servant,
he took him from the sheepfolds,
71   called him from tending ewes in lamb
to pasture his people Jacob
and Israel his heritage:
72   who did this with unselfish care
and led them with a sensitive hand.

PSALM 79

V 78

National lament*a*

Psalm   Of Asaph

1   God, the pagans have invaded your heritage,
they have desecrated your holy Temple;
they have reduced Jerusalem to a pile of ruins,
2   they have left the corpses of your servants
to the birds of the air for food,
and the flesh of your devout to the beasts of the earth.

3   They have shed blood like water
throughout Jerusalem, not a gravedigger left!
4   we are now insulted by our neighbours,

78 a. I.e., the ark of the covenant, 2 Ch 6:41.
79 a. Possibly relating to the capture of Jerusalem by the Chaldaeans in 587.

butt and laughing-stock of all those around us.
How much longer will you be angry, Yahweh? For ever?   5
Is your jealousy to go on smouldering like a fire?

Pour out your anger on the pagans,   6
    who do not acknowledge you,
and on those kingdoms
    that do not call on your name,
for they have devoured Jacob   7
    and reduced his home to desolation.

Do not hold our ancestors' crimes against us,   8
in tenderness quickly intervene,
we can hardly be crushed lower;
help us, God our saviour,   9
for the honour of your name;
Yahweh, blot out our sins,
rescue us for the sake of your name.

Why should the pagans ask, 'Where is their God?'   10
May we soon see the pagans learning what vengeance
you exact for your servants' blood shed here!
May the groans of the captive reach you;   11
by your mighty arm rescue those doomed to die!

Pay our neighbours sevenfold, strike to the heart   12
for the monstrous insult proffered to you, Lord!
And we your people, the flock that you pasture,   13
    giving you everlasting thanks,
    will recite your praises for ever and ever.

PSALM 80   V 79

Prayer for the restoration of Israel

For the choirmaster   Tune: 'The decrees are lilies'   Of Asaph   Psalm

Shepherd of Israel, listen,   1
you who lead Joseph like a flock;
enthroned on the cherubs, shine
on Ephraim, Benjamin and Manasseh;*   2
rouse your strength,
come to us and save us!

Yahweh Sabaoth, bring us back,   3
let your face smile on us and we shall be safe.

Yahweh Sabaoth, how much longer   4
will you smoulder at your people's prayer?
Having fed us on the bread of tears,   5
having made us drink them in such measure,
you now let our neighbours quarrel over us   6
and our enemies deride us.

Yahweh Sabaoth, bring us back,   7
let your face smile on us and we shall be safe.

8   There was a vine: you uprooted it from Egypt;
        to plant it, you drove out other nations,
9   you cleared a space where it could grow,
        it took root and filled the whole country.

10   It covered the mountains with its shade,
        the cedars of God with its branches,
11   its tendrils extended to the sea,
        its offshoots all the way to the river.[b]

12   Why have you destroyed its fences?
        Now anyone can go and steal its grapes,
13   the forest boar can ravage it
        and wild animals eat it.

14   Please, Yahweh Sabaoth, relent!
        Look down from heaven, look at this vine,
15   visit it, •protect
        what your own right hand has planted.
16   They threw it on the fire like dung,
        but one look of reproof from you
        and they will be doomed.

17   May your hand protect the man at your right,
        the son of man who has been authorised by you.
18   We shall never turn from you again;
        our life renewed, we shall invoke your name.

19   Yahweh Sabaoth, bring us back,
        let your face smile on us and we shall be safe.

PSALM 81

For the feast of Tabernacles[a]

For the choirmaster   On the... of Gath   Of Asaph

1   Shout for joy to honour God our strength,
        shout to acclaim the God of Jacob!

2   Start the music, sound the drum,
        the melodious lyre and the harp;
3   sound the New Moon trumpet,
        at the full moon, on our feastday!

4   This is a statute binding on Israel,
        an ordinance of the God of Jacob,
5   this decree he imposed on Joseph
        when he went to war against Egypt.

        I can hear a voice I no longer recognise,
6   'It was I who relieved your shoulder of the burden,
        your hands could drop the labourer's basket;
7   you called in your trouble, so I rescued you.

80 a. The principal tribes of the North.   b. Euphrates.
81 a. The greatest feast of the year, commemorating the period in the desert and the giving of the Law at Sinai.

'Hidden in the storm, I answered you,
I tested you at the waters of Meribah. *Pause*
Listen, you are my people, let me warn you. 8
Israel, if you would only listen to me!

'Tolerate no foreign god, 9
worship no alien god;
I, Yahweh, am your God, 10
I who brought you here from Egypt;
you have only to open your mouth for me to fill it.

'My people refused to listen to me, 11
Israel refused to obey me,
so I left them to their stubborn selves 12
to do whatever they pleased.

'If only my people would listen, 13
if Israel would follow my ways,
at one blow I would defeat their enemies 14
and strike at all who attack them.

'Then those who hate Yahweh would cringe, 15
their doom being sealed for ever;
while I would feed you on pure wheat 16
and satisfy you with the wild rock honey.'

PSALM 82

V 81

Against corrupt judges

Psalm Of Asaph

God stands in the divine assembly, 1
among the gods he dispenses justice:

'No more mockery of justice, 2
no more favouring the wicked! *Pause*
Let the weak and the orphan have justice, 3
be fair to the wretched and destitute;
rescue the weak and needy, 4
save them from the clutches of the wicked!'

Ignorant and senseless, they carry on blindly, 5
undermining the very basis of earthly society.
I once said, 'You too are gods, 6
sons of the Most High, all of you',
but all the same, you shall die like other men; 7
as one man, princes, you shall fall.

Rise, God, dispense justice throughout the world, 8
since no nation is excluded from your ownership.

PSALM 83

Against the enemies of Israel

Song   Psalm   Of Asaph

1   God, do not remain silent;
     do not be unmoved, O God, or unresponsive!
2   See how your enemies are stirring,
     see how those who hate you rear their heads.

3   Weaving a plot against your people,
4   conspiring against those you protect, ·they say,
     'Come, we will finish them as a nation,
     the name of Israel shall be forgotten!'

5   Unanimous in their plot,
     they seal a treaty against you:
6   the tents of Edom and the Ishmaelites,
     Moab and the Hagrites,

7   Gebal, Ammon, Amalek,
     Philistia and the Tyrians;
8   and now Assur*a* has joined them
     to reinforce the sons of Lot.   *Pause*

9   Treat them like Midian and Sisera,
     like Jabin at the river Kishon,
10   wiped out at En-dor,
     they served to dung the ground.

11   Treat their generals like Oreb and Zeeb,
     their commanders like Zebah and Zalmunna,
12   those who once said, 'Let us take for ourselves
     possession of the Dwellings of God!'

13   My God, bowl them along like tumbleweed,
     like chaff at the mercy of the wind;
14   as fire devours the forest,
     as the flame licks up the mountains,

15   drive them on with your whirlwind,
     rout them with your tornado;
16   cover their faces with shame,
     until they seek your name, Yahweh.

17   Shame and panic be always theirs,
18   disgrace and death; ·and let them know this:
     you alone bear the name Yahweh,
     Most High over the whole world.

---

83 a. The names are those of ten traditional enemies of Israel. Three of them are not immediately familiar from the historical books: 'Hagrites', the sons of Hagar, are Transjordanian nomads; 'Gebal' is Gabalene in Idumaea; 'Assur' may be either Assyria or the Asshurite tribe.

PSALM 84

V 83

Pilgrimage song

For the choirmaster   On the... of Gath   Of the sons of Korah   Psalm

How I love your palace,
    Yahweh Sabaoth!   1

How my soul yearns and pines   2
    for Yahweh's courts!
My heart and my flesh sing for joy
    to the living God.

The sparrow has found its home at last,   3
    the swallow a nest for its young,
your altars, Yahweh Sabaoth,
    my king and my God.

Happy those who live in your house   4
    and can praise you all day long;   *Pause*
and happy the pilgrims inspired by you   5
    with courage to make the Ascents!

As they go through the Valley of the Weeper,[a]   6
    they make it a place of springs,
clothed in blessings by early rains.
Thence they make their way from height to height,   7
soon to be seen before God on Zion.

Yahweh Sabaoth, hear my prayer,   8
listen, God of Jacob;   *Pause*
God our shield, now look on us   9
and be kind to your anointed.

A single day in your courts   10
    is worth more than a thousand elsewhere;
merely to stand on the steps of God's[b] house
    is better than living with the wicked.

For God is battlement and shield,   11
    conferring grace and glory;
Yahweh withholds nothing good
    from those who walk without blame.

    Yahweh Sabaoth,   12
happy the man who puts his trust in you!

PSALM 85

V 84

Prayer for peace

For the choirmaster   Of the sons of Korah   Psalm

Yahweh, you favour your own country,   1
you bring back the captives of Jacob,
you take your people's guilt away,   2
you blot out all their sins,   *Pause*
you retract all your anger,   3
you abjure your fiery rage.

4   Bring us back, God our saviour,
        master your resentment against us.

5   Do you mean to be angry with us for ever,
        to prolong your wrath age after age?

6   Will you not give us life again,
        for your people to rejoice in you?

7   Yahweh, show us your love,
        grant us your saving help.

8   I am listening. What is Yahweh saying?
        What God is saying means peace
        for his people, for his friends,
        if only they renounce their folly;

9   for those who fear him, his saving help is near,
        and the glory will then live in our country.

10   Love and Loyalty now meet,
        Righteousness and Peace now embrace;

11   Loyalty reaches up from earth
        and Righteousness leans down from heaven.

12   Yahweh himself bestows happiness
        as our soil gives its harvest,

13   Righteousness always preceding him
        and Peace following his footsteps.

PSALM 86

V 85

Prayer in ordeal

Prayer   *Of David*

1   Listen to me, Yahweh, and answer me,
        poor and needy as I am;

2   keep my soul: I am your devoted one,
        save your servant who relies on you.

3   You are my God, •take pity on me, Lord,
        I invoke you all day long;

4   give your servant reason to rejoice,
        for to you, Lord, I lift my soul.

5   Lord, you are good and forgiving,
        most loving to all who invoke you;

6   Yahweh, hear my prayer,
        listen to me as I plead.

7   Lord, in trouble I invoke you,
        and you answer my prayer;

8   there is no god to compare with you,
        no achievement to compare with yours.

9   All the pagans will come and adore you, Lord,
        all will glorify your name,

10   since you alone are great, you perform marvels,
        you God, you alone.

84 a. The balsam tree: this valley was the last stage of the pilgrimage to Jerusalem.   **b.** The 'sons of Korah' (see inscription) were the order of gatekeepers at the Temple.

Yahweh, teach me your way,
how to walk beside you faithfully,
make me single-hearted in fearing your name.   11

I thank you with all my heart, Lord my God,   12
I glorify your name for ever,
your love for me has been so great,   13
you have rescued me from the depths of Sheol.

Now arrogant men, God, are attacking me,   14
a brutal gang hounding me to death:
people to whom you mean nothing.

Lord God, you who are always merciful and tender-hearted,   15
slow to anger, always loving, always loyal,
turn to me and pity me.   16

Give me your strength, your saving help,
me your servant, this son of a pious mother,
give me one proof of your goodness.   17

Yahweh, make my opponents ashamed,
show them that you are my help and consolation.

PSALM 87   V 86

Zion, mother of nations

Of the sons of Korah   Psalm   Song

Yahweh loves •his city   2a / 1
founded on the holy mountain;
he prefers the gates of Zion   2b
to any town in Jacob.   2c
He has glorious predictions to make of you,   3
city of God!   *Pause*

'I will add Egypt and Babylon   4
to the nations that acknowledge me.
Of Philistia, Tyre, Ethiopia,
"Here so and so was born" men say.
But all call Zion "Mother",   5
since all were born in her.'

It is he who makes her what she is,
he, the Most High, •Yahweh;   6
and as he registers the peoples,
'It was here' he writes 'that so and so was born'.   *Pause*
And there will be princes dancing there.ᵃ   7
All find their home in you.

PSALM 88   V 87

Lament

*Song   Psalm   Of the sons of Korah   For the choirmaster   In sickness or
suffering   Poem   For Heman the native-born*

Yahweh my God, I call for help all day,   1
I weep to you all night;

2   may my prayer reach you
hear my cries for help;

3   for my soul is all troubled,
my life is on the brink of Sheol;

4   I am numbered among those who go down to the Pit,
a man bereft of strength:

5   a man alone, down among the dead,
among the slaughtered in their graves,
among those you have forgotten,
those deprived of your protecting hand.

6   You have plunged me to the bottom of the Pit,
to its darkest, deepest place,

7   weighted down by your anger,
drowned beneath your waves.   *Pause*

8   You have turned my friends against me
and made me repulsive to them;
in prison and unable to escape,

9   my eyes are worn out with suffering.

Yahweh, I invoke you all day,
I stretch out my hands to you:

10   are your marvels meant for the dead,
can ghosts rise up to praise you?   *Pause*

11   Who talks of your love in the grave,
of your faithfulness in the place of perdition?

12   Do they hear about your marvels in the dark,
about your righteousness in the land of oblivion?

13   But I am here, calling for your help,
praying to you every morning:

14   why do you reject me?
Why do you hide your face from me?

15   Wretched, slowly dying since my youth,
I bore your terrors—now I am exhausted;

16   your anger overwhelmed me,
you destroyed me with your terrors

17   which, like a flood, were round me, all day long,
all together closing in on me.

18   You have turned my friends and neighbours against me,
now darkness is my one companion left.

PSALM 89

Hymn and a prayer to God's faithfulness

Poem   *For Ethan the native-born*

1   I will celebrate your love for ever, Yahweh,
age after age my words shall proclaim your faithfulness;

2   for I claim that love is built to last for ever
and your faithfulness founded firmly in the heavens.

87 a. In the ceremonial celebrations in the Temple.

'I have made a covenant with my Chosen,   3
I have given my servant David my sworn word:
I have founded your dynasty to last for ever,   4
I have built you a throne to outlast all time.'   *Pause*

Yahweh, the assembly of holy ones in heaven   5
applaud the marvel of your faithfulness.
Who in the skies can compare with Yahweh?   6
Which of the heaven-born can rival him?

God, dreaded in the assembly of holy ones,   7
great and terrible to all around him,
Yahweh, God of Sabaoth, who is like you?—   8
mighty Yahweh, clothed in your faithfulness!

You control the pride of the ocean,   9
when its waves ride high, you calm them;
you split Rahab[a] in two like a carcase   10
and scattered your enemies with your mighty arm.

The heavens are yours and the earth is yours,   11
you founded the world and all it holds,
you created north and south;   12
Tabor and Hermon hail your name with joy.

Yours was the arm, and yours the prowess,   13
mighty and exalted your right hand;
Righteousness and Justice support your throne,   14
Love and Faithfulness are your attendants.

Happy the people who learn to acclaim you!   15
Yahweh, they will live in the light of your favour;
   they will rejoice in your name all day   16
   and exult in your righteousness.

   You are their glory and their strength,   17
   you, by your kindness, raise our fortunes,
   since both our shield and our king   18
   belong to Yahweh, the Holy One of Israel.

   Once you spoke in vision   19
   and said to your friends,[b]
   'I have conferred the crown on a hero,
   and promoted one chosen from my people.

   'I have selected my servant David   20
   and anointed him with my holy oil;
   my hand will be constantly with him,   21
   he will be able to rely on my arm.

   'No enemy will be able to outwit him,   22
   no wicked man to worst him,
   I myself will crush his opponents,   23
   I will strike dead all who hate him.

   'With my faithfulness and love,   24
   his fortunes shall rise in my name.
   I will give him control of the sea,   25
   complete control of the rivers.

   'He will invoke me, "My father,   26
   my God and rock of my safety",

27   and I shall make him my first-born,
       the Most High for kings on earth.

28   'I will keep my love for him always,
       my covenant with him shall stand,
29   I have founded his dynasty to last for ever,
       his throne to be as lasting as the heavens.

30   'Should his descendants desert my Law
       and disregard my rulings,
31   should they violate my statutes
       and not keep my commandments,

32   'I will punish their sins with the rod
       and their crimes with the whip,
33   but never withdraw my love from him
       or fail in my faithfulness.

34   'I will not break my covenant,
       I will not revoke my given word;
35   I have sworn on my holiness, once for all,
       and cannot turn liar to David.

36   'His dynasty shall last for ever,
       I see his throne like the sun,
37   enduring for ever like the moon,
       that faithful witness in the sky.'   *Pause*

38   And yet you have rejected, disowned
       and raged at your anointed;
39   you have repudiated the covenant with your servant
       and flung his crown dishonoured to the ground.

40   You have pierced all his defences,
       and laid his forts in ruins;
41   anyone may go and loot him,
       his neighbours treat him with scorn.

42   You have let his opponents get the upper hand,
       and made all his enemies happy,
43   you have snapped his sword on a rock
       and failed to support him in battle.

44   You have stripped him of his glorious sceptre,
       and toppled his throne to the ground,
45   you have aged him before his time
       and covered him in shame.   *Pause*

46   Yahweh, how much longer will you hide? For ever?
       How much longer must your anger smoulder like a fire?
47   Remember me, the short time I have left
       and the void to which you destine mankind.
48   What man can cling to life and not see death?
       Who can evade the clutches of Sheol?   *Pause*

49   Lord, where are those earlier signs of your love?
       You swore your oath to David on your faithfulness!
50   Lord, do not forget how your servant was insulted,

---

89 a. A demon or monster personifying water, the element of chaos; sometimes used for Egypt.
b. Samuel and Nathan.

how I take these pagans' taunts to heart,
insults, Yahweh, that your enemies have offered,   51
insults to your anointed wherever he goes.

> Blessed be Yahweh for ever.
> Amen. Amen!ᶜ

PSALM 90   V 89

The human condition

Prayer   *Of Moses, man of God*

Lord, you have been   1
our refuge age after age.

Before the mountains were born,   2
before the earth or the world came to birth,
you were God from all eternity and for ever.

You can turn man back into dust   3
by saying, 'Back to what you were, you sons of men!'
To you, a thousand years are a single day,   4
a yesterday now over, an hour of the night.

You brush men away like waking dreams,   5
they are like grass
sprouting and flowering in the morning,   6
withered and dry before dusk.

We too are burnt up by your anger   7
and terrified by your fury;
having summoned up our sins   8
you inspect our secrets by your own light.

Our days dwindle under your wrath,   9
our lives are over in a breath
—our life lasts for seventy years,   10
eighty with good health,

but they all add up to anxiety and trouble—
over in a trice, and then we are gone.
Who yet has felt the full force of your fury,   11
or learnt to fear the violence of your rage?

Teach us to count how few days we have   12
and so gain wisdom of heart.
Relent, Yahweh! How much longer do we have?   13
Take pity on your servants!

Let us wake in the morning filled with your love   14
and sing and be happy all our days;
make our future as happy as our past was sad,   15
those years when you were punishing us.

Let your servants see what you can do for them,   16
let their children see your glory.
May the sweetness of the Lord be on us!   17
Make all we do succeed.

PSALM 91

God's protection

1　If you live in the shelter of Elyon[a]
　and make your home in the shadow of Shaddai,
2　you can say to Yahweh, 'My refuge, my fortress,
　my God in whom I trust!'

3　He rescues you from the snares
　of fowlers hoping to destroy you;
4a　he covers you with his feathers,
4b　and you find shelter underneath his wings.

5　You need not fear the terrors of night,
　the arrow that flies in the daytime,
6　the plague that stalks in the dark,
　the scourge that wreaks havoc in broad daylight.

7　Though a thousand fall at your side,
　ten thousand at your right hand,
　you yourself will remain unscathed,
4c　with his faithfulness for shield and buckler.

8　You have only to look around
　to see how the wicked are repaid,
9　you who can say, 'Yahweh my refuge',
　and make Elyon your fortress.

10　No disaster can overtake you,
　no plague come near your tent:
11　he will put you in his angels' charge
　to guard you wherever you go.

12　They will support you on their hands
　in case you hurt your foot against a stone;
13　you will tread on lion and adder,
　trample on savage lions and dragons.

14　'I rescue all who cling to me,
　I protect whoever knows my name,
15　I answer everyone who invokes me,
　I am with them when they are in trouble;
　I bring them safety and honour.
16　I give them life, long and full,
　and show them how I can save.'

PSALM 92

The virtuous man rejoices

Psalm　Song　For the sabbath

1　It is good to give thanks to Yahweh,
　to play in honour of your name, Most High,

c. The doxology ends the third book of the Psalter.
91 a. Four names for God are used in this strophe: Elyon, Shaddai, Yahweh and Elohim. They
can be rendered, the Most High, the God of heaven, the Lord, God.

to proclaim your love at daybreak   2
and your faithfulness all through the night
to the music of the zither and lyre,   3
to the rippling of the harp.

I am happy, Yahweh, at what you have done;   4
at your achievements I joyfully exclaim,
'Great are your achievements, Yahweh,   5
immensely deep your thoughts!'
Stupid men are not aware of this,   6
fools can never appreciate it.

The wicked may sprout as thick as weeds   7
and every evil-doer flourish,
but only to be everlastingly destroyed,
whereas you are supreme for ever.   8
See how your enemies perish,   9
how all evil men are routed.

You raise my horn as if I were a wild ox,   10
you pour fresh oil on my head;
I was able to see those who were spying on me,   11
to overhear what the wicked were whispering,
so the virtuous flourish like palm trees   12
and grow as tall as the cedars of Lebanon.

Planted in the house of Yahweh,   13
they will flourish in the courts of our God,
still bearing fruit in old age,   14
still remaining fresh and green,
to proclaim that Yahweh is righteous,   15
my rock in whom no fault is to be found!

PSALM 93   V 92

The majesty of God

Yahweh is king, robed in majesty,   1
Yahweh is robed in power,
he wears it like a belt.

You have made the world firm, unshakeable;
your throne has stood since then,   2
you existed from the first, Yahweh.

Yahweh, the rivers raise,   3
the rivers raise their voices,
the rivers raise their thunders;

greater than the voice of ocean,   4
transcending the waves of the sea,
Yahweh reigns transcendent in the heights.

Your decrees will never alter;   5
holiness will distinguish your house,
Yahweh, for ever and ever.

PSALM 94

The justice of God

1 Yahweh, God of revenge,
God of revenge, appear!
2 Rise, judge of the world,
give the proud their deserts!

3 Yahweh, how much longer are the wicked,
how much longer are the wicked to triumph?
4 Are these evil men to remain unsilenced,
boasting and asserting themselves?

5 Yahweh, they crush your people,
they oppress your hereditary people,
6 murdering and massacring
widows, orphans and guests.

7 'Yahweh sees nothing,' they say
'the God of Jacob takes no notice.'
8 You most stupid of men, you fools,
think this over and learn some sense.

9 Is the inventor of the ear unable to hear?
The creator of the eye unable to see?
10 The punisher of the pagans unable to punish?
Yahweh the teacher of mankind
11 knows exactly how men think,
how their thoughts are a puff of wind.

12 Yahweh, happy the man whom you instruct,
the man whom you teach through your law;
13 his mind is at peace though times are bad,
while a pit is being dug for the wicked.

14 For Yahweh has not abandoned
or deserted his hereditary people;
15 for verdict will return to righteousness again,
and, in its wake, all upright hearts.

16 No one ever stood up for me against the wicked,
not a soul took a stand to save me from evil men;
17 without Yahweh's help, I should, long ago,
have gone to the Home of Silence.

18 I need only say, 'I am slipping',
and your love, Yahweh, immediately supports me;
19 and in the middle of all my troubles
you console me and make me happy.

20 You never consent to that corrupt tribunal
that imposes disorder as law,
21 that takes the life of the virtuous
and condemns the innocent to death.

22 No! Yahweh is still my citadel,
my God is a rock where I take shelter;
23 he will pay them back for all their sins,
he will silence their wickedness,
Yahweh our God will silence them.

PSALM 95

Psalm for daily use

Come, let us praise Yahweh joyfully,
acclaiming the Rock of our safety;
let us come into his presence with thanksgiving,
acclaiming him with music.

For Yahweh is a great God,
a greater King than all other gods;
from depths of earth to mountain top
everything comes under his rule;
the sea belongs to him, he made it,
so does the land, he shaped this too.

Come in, let us bow, prostrate ourselves,
and kneel in front of Yahweh our maker,
for this is our God,
and we are the people he pastures,
the flock that he guides.

If only you would listen to him today,
'Do not harden your hearts as at Meribah,
as you did that day at Massah in the wilderness,ᵃ
when your ancestors challenged me, tested me,
although they had seen what I could do.

'For forty years that generation repelled me,
until I said: How unreliable these people
who refuse to grasp my ways!
And so, in anger, I swore that not one
would reach the place of rest I had for them.'

1
2

3
4

5

6

7

8

9

10

11

PSALM 96

Yahweh, king and judge

Sing Yahweh a new song!
Sing to Yahweh, all the earth!
Sing to Yahweh, bless his name.

Proclaim his salvation day after day,
tell of his glory among the nations,
tell his marvels to every people.

Yahweh is great, loud must be his praise,
he is to be feared beyond all gods.
Nothingness, all the gods of the nations.

Yahweh himself made the heavens,
in his presence are splendour and majesty,
in his sanctuary power and beauty.

Pay tribute to Yahweh, families of the peoples,
tribute to Yahweh of glory and power,
tribute to Yahweh of his name's due glory.

1
2

3

4

5

6

7

8

Bring out the offering, bear it before him,
9   worship Yahweh in his sacred court,
tremble before him, all the earth!

10   Say among the nations, 'Yahweh is king!'
Firm has he made the world, and unshakeable;
he will judge each nation with strict justice.

11   Let the heavens be glad, let earth rejoice,
let the sea thunder and all that it holds,
12   let the fields exult and all that is in them,
let all the woodland trees cry out for joy,

13   at the presence of Yahweh, for he comes,
he comes to judge the earth,
to judge the world with justice
and the nations with his truth.

PSALM 97   V 96

The triumph of Yahweh

1   Yahweh is king! Let earth rejoice,
the many isles be glad!
2   Cloud and Darkness surround him,
Righteousness and Justice support his throne.

3   A fire precedes him as he goes,
devouring all enemies around him;
4   his lightning lights up the world,
earth observes and quakes.

5   The mountains melt like wax
at the coming of the Master of the world;
6   the heavens proclaim his righteousness,
all nations see his glory.

7   Shame on those who worship images,
who take pride in their idols:
bow down as he passes, all you gods!

8   Zion hears and rejoices,
the daughters of Judah exult
at the rulings you utter, Yahweh.

9   For you are Yahweh
Most High over the world,
far transcending all other gods.

10   Yahweh loves those who repudiate evil,
he guards the souls of the devout,
rescuing them from the clutches of the wicked.

11   Light dawns for the virtuous,
and joy, for upright hearts.
12   Rejoice in Yahweh, you virtuous,
remember his holiness, and praise him!

95 a. 'The place was named Massah and Meribah', Ex 17:7. The names mean 'Temptation' and 'Dispute'

PSALM 98

The judge of the world"

Psalm

Sing Yahweh a new song   1
   for he has performed marvels,
his own right hand, his holy arm,
   gives him the power to save.

Yahweh has displayed his power;   2
has revealed his righteousness to the nations,
mindful of his love and faithfulness   3
   to the House of Israel.

The most distant parts of the earth have seen
   the saving power of our God.
Acclaim Yahweh, all the earth,   4
   burst into shouts of joy!

Sing to Yahweh, sing to the music of harps,   5
   and to the sound of many instruments;
to the sound of trumpet and horn   6
   acclaim Yahweh the King!

Let the sea thunder and all that it holds,   7
   and the world, with all who live in it;
let all the rivers clap their hands   8
   and the mountains shout for joy,

at the presence of Yahweh, for he comes   9
   to judge the earth,
to judge the world with righteousness
   and the nations with strict justice.

PSALM 99

God, righteous and holy king

Yahweh is king, the nations tremble;   1
he is enthroned on the cherubs, earth quakes;
   Yahweh is great in Zion.   2

He is high over all nations;
may they praise your great and terrible name,   3
   'Holy is he, •and mighty!'   4

You are a king who loves justice,
insisting on honesty, justice, virtue,
   as you have done for Jacob.

   Let us extol Yahweh our God,   5
   and worship at his footstool,
     'Holy is he!'

6   Moses, Aaron one of his priests, and Samuel
      his votary, all invoked Yahweh:
        and he answered them.

7   He talked with them in the pillar of cloud;
      they obeyed his decrees, the Law he gave them.

8   Yahweh our God, you responded to them,
      a God of forgiveness for them,
        in spite of punishing their sins.

9   Extol Yahweh our God,
      worship at his holy mountain,
      'Holy is Yahweh our God!'

PSALM 100

V 99

Invitation to praise God

Psalm   For thanksgiving

1   Acclaim Yahweh, all the earth,
2   serve Yahweh gladly,
      come into his presence with songs of joy!

3   Know that he, Yahweh, is God,
      he made us and we belong to him,
      we are his people, the flock that he pastures.

4   Walk through his porticos giving thanks,
      enter his courts praising him,
      give thanks to him, bless his name!

5   Yes, Yahweh is good,
      his love is everlasting,
      his faithfulness endures from age to age.

PSALM 101

V 100

The ideal ruler

Of David   Psalm

1   My song is about kindness and justice;
      Yahweh, I sing it to you.
2   I mean to make good progress, as the blameless do:
      when will you come to me?

      In my household, I will advance
        in purity of heart;
3   I will not let my eyes rest
        on any misconduct.

      I hate the practices of the apostate,
        they have no appeal for me;
4   perverted hearts must keep their distance,
        the wicked I disregard.

98 a. Almost a doublet of Ps 96 and, like that psalm, owing much to the closing chapters of Is.

The man who secretly slanders his neighbour   5
   I reduce to silence;
haughty looks, proud heart,
   I cannot tolerate these.

I look to my religious countrymen   6
   to compose my household;
only the man who makes progress, as the blameless do,
   can be my servant.

There is no room in my house   7
   for any hypocrite;
no liar keeps his post
   where I can see him.

Morning after morning[a] I reduce to silence   8
   all who are wicked in this country,
banishing from the city of Yahweh
   all evil men.

PSALM 102   V 101

Prayer in misfortune

Prayer of the downtrodden telling Yahweh their troubles at a moment of distress

Yahweh, hear my prayer,   1
let my cry for help reach you;
do not hide your face from me   2
when I am in trouble;
bend down to listen to me,
when I call, be quick to answer me!

For my days are vanishing like smoke,   3
my bones smouldering like logs,
my heart shrivelling like scorched grass   4
and my appetite has gone;
whenever I heave a sigh,   5
my bones stick through my skin.

I live in a desert like the pelican,   6
in a ruin like the screech owl,
I stay awake, lamenting   7
like a lone bird on the roof;
my enemies insult me all day long,   8
those who used to praise me now use me as a curse.

Ashes are the bread I eat,   9
what I drink I lace with tears,
under your furious anger,   10
since you only picked me up to throw me down;
my days dwindle away like a shadow,   11
I am as dry as hay.

Whereas, Yahweh, you remain for ever;   12
each generation in turn remembers you!

Rise, take pity on Zion!—   13
the time has come to have mercy on her,
the hour has come;

14   for your servants prize her stones
               and are moved to pity by her dust.

15   Then will the nations fear the name of Yahweh
               and all kings on earth respect your glory;
16   when Yahweh builds Zion anew,
               he will be seen in his glory;
17   he will answer the prayer of the abandoned,
               he will not scorn their petitions.

18   Put this on record for the next generation,
               so that a race still to be born can praise God:
19   Yahweh has leaned down from the heights of his sanctuary,
               has looked down at earth from heaven,
20   to hear the sighing of the captive,
               and to set free those doomed to die.

28   Your servants' sons will have a permanent home,
               and their descendants be in your presence always,
21   to proclaim the name of Yahweh in Zion,
               his praise in Jerusalem;
22   nations and kingdoms will be united
               and offer worship to Yahweh together.

23a   My strength has already run out;
24a
23b   tell me •how much longer I have left.
24b   Do not take me prematurely,
               when your own life lasts for ever.

25   Aeons ago, you laid earth's foundations,
               the heavens are the work of your hands;
26   all will vanish, though you remain,
               all wear out like a garment,
               like clothes that need changing you will change them;
27   but yourself, you never change, and your years are unending.

PSALM 103   V 102

God is love

Of David

1   Bless Yahweh, my soul,
               bless his holy name, all that is in me!
2   Bless Yahweh, my soul,
               and remember all his kindnesses:

3   in forgiving all your offences,
               in curing all your diseases,
4   in redeeming your life from the Pit,
               in crowning you with love and tenderness,
5   in filling your years with prosperity,
               in renewing your youth like an eagle's.ᵃ

6   Yahweh, who does what is right,
               is always on the side of the oppressed;

---

101 a. Morning is the time for administering justice.
103 a. I.e., like an eagle recovering strength and vigour after moulting.

he revealed his intentions to Moses,　　　　　7
his prowess to the sons of Israel.

Yahweh is tender and compassionate,　　　　　8
slow to anger, most loving;
his indignation does not last for ever,　　　　9
his resentment exists a short time only;
he never treats us, never punishes us,　　　　10
as our guilt and our sins deserve.

No less than the height of heaven over earth　　11
is the greatness of his love for those who fear him;
he takes our sins farther away　　　　　　12
than the east is from the west.

As tenderly as a father treats his children,　　13
so Yahweh treats those who fear him;
he knows what we are made of,　　　　　14
he remembers we are dust.

Man lasts no longer than grass,　　　　　15
no longer than a wild flower he lives,
one gust of wind, and he is gone,　　　　16
never to be seen there again;

yet Yahweh's love for those who fear him　　17
lasts from all eternity and for ever,
like his goodness to their children's children,
as long as they keep his covenant　　　　18
and remember to obey his precepts.

Yahweh has fixed his throne in the heavens,　　19
his empire is over all.
Bless Yahweh, all his angels,　　　　　20
heroes mighty to enforce his word,
attentive to his word of command.

Bless Yahweh, all his armies,　　　　　21
servants to enforce his will.
Bless Yahweh, all his creatures　　　　22
in every part of his empire!

Bless Yahweh, my soul.

PSALM 104　　　　　　　　　　　V 103

The glories of creation

Bless Yahweh, my soul.　　　　　　　1
Yahweh my God, how great you are!
Clothed in majesty and glory,
wrapped in a robe of light!　　　　　2

You stretch the heavens out like a tent,
you build your palace on the waters above;　　3
using the clouds as your chariot,
you advance on the wings of the wind;
you use the winds as messengers　　　　4
and fiery flames as servants.

5   You fixed the earth on its foundations,
    unshakeable for ever and ever;
6   you wrapped it with the deep as with a robe,
    the waters overtopping the mountains.

7   At your reproof the waters took to flight,
    they fled at the sound of your thunder,
8   cascading over the mountains, into the valleys,
    down to the reservoir you made for them;
9   you imposed the limits they must never cross again,
    or they would once more flood the land.

10 You set springs gushing in ravines,
    running down between the mountains,
11 supplying water for wild animals,
    attracting the thirsty wild donkeys;
12 near there the birds of the air make their nests
    and sing among the branches.

13 From your palace you water the uplands
    until the ground has had all that your heavens have to offer;
14 you make fresh grass grow for cattle
    and those plants made use of by man,
    for them to get food from the soil:
15 wine to make them cheerful,
    oil to make them happy
    and bread to make them strong.

16 The trees of Yahweh get rain enough,
    those cedars of Lebanon he planted;
17 here the little birds build their nest
    and, on the highest branches, the stork has its home.
18 For the wild goats there are the mountains,
    in the crags rock-badgers hide.

19 You made the moon to tell the seasons,
    the sun knows when to set:
20 you bring darkness on, night falls,
    all the forest animals come out:
21 savage lions roaring for their prey,
    claiming their food from God.

22 The sun rises, they retire,
    going back to lie down in their lairs,
23 and man goes out to work,
    and to labour until dusk.
24 Yahweh, what variety you have created,
    arranging everything so wisely!
    Earth is completely full of things you have made:

25 among them vast expanse of ocean,
    teeming with countless creatures,
    creatures large and small,
26 with the ships going to and fro
    and Leviathan whom you made to amuse you.

27 All creatures depend on you
    to feed them throughout the year;
28 you provide the food they eat,
    with generous hand you satisfy their hunger.

You turn your face away, they suffer,   29
you stop their breath, they die
and revert to dust.
You give breath, fresh life begins,   30
you keep renewing the world.

Glory for ever to Yahweh!   31
May Yahweh find joy in what he creates,
at whose glance the earth trembles,   32
at whose touch the mountains smoke!

I mean to sing to Yahweh all my life,   33
I mean to play for my God as long as I live.
May these reflections of mine give him pleasure,   34
as much as Yahweh gives me!
May sinners vanish from the earth   35
and the wicked exist no more!

Bless Yahweh, my soul.

PSALM 105   V 104

The wonderful history of Israel

Alleluia!

Give thanks to Yahweh, call his name aloud,   1
proclaim his deeds to the peoples!
Sing to him, play to him,   2
tell over all his marvels!
Glory in his holy name,   3
let the hearts that seek Yahweh rejoice!

Seek Yahweh and his strength,   4
seek his face untiringly;
remember the marvels he has done,   5
his wonders, the judgements from his mouth.

Stock of Abraham his servant,   6
sons of Jacob his chosen one!
He is Yahweh our God,   7
his authority is over all the earth.

Remember his covenant for ever,   8
his word of command for a thousand generations,
the pact he made with Abraham,   9
his oath to Isaac.

He established it as a statute for Jacob,   10
an everlasting covenant for Israel.
'I give you a land,' he said   11
'Canaan, your allotted heritage.

'There where you were easily counted,   12
few in number, strangers to the country.'
They went from nation to nation,   13
from one kingdom to another people;

he let no man oppress them,   14
he punished kings on their behalf.

15   'Do not touch my anointed ones,' he said
       'do not harm my prophets!'

16   Next, he called down famine on the country,
       he broke their staff, that is, their bread;
17   he sent a man ahead of them,
       Joseph, sold as a slave.

18   They tortured his feet with fetters,
       they put his neck in irons;
19   time passed, Joseph's oracle came true,
       Yahweh's word proved him right.

20   The king gave orders to release him,
       that master of nations set him free,
21   putting him in charge of his household,
       in control of all he possessed,

22   to train his officials as he thought fit
       and convert his elders into sages.
23   Israel then migrated to Egypt,
       Jacob settled in the land of Ham.

24   He made his people fertile
       and more vigorous than their oppressors,
25   whose hearts he then disposed to hatred of his people
       and double-dealing with his servants.

26   He sent his servant Moses,
       and Aaron, the man of his choice;
27   there they displayed his signs,
       his wonders in the land of Ham.

28   He sent darkness, darkness fell,
       but still they defied his word.
29   He turned their rivers into blood,
       thus killing all their fish.

30   Their country was overrun with frogs
       even in the royal apartments;
31   he spoke: flies and mosquitoes
       swarmed throughout the country.

32   He sent them hail instead of rain,
       fire swept across their land;
33   he blasted their vines and fig trees,
       he shattered the trees throughout the country.

34   He spoke: there came locusts,
       grasshoppers, more than you could count,
35   eating every scrap of greenstuff,
       every blade their soil produced.

36   Next, he struck down all the first-born in their land,
       the entire first-fruits of their fertility;
37   then he led Israel out with gold and silver,
       and not one man of their tribes was left behind.

38   Egypt was glad to see them go,
       they had filled her with alarm;
39   he spread a cloud to cover them,
       and a fire to glow at night.

They demanded food, he sent them quails,   40
he satisfied them with the bread of heaven;
he opened the rock, the waters gushed   41
to flow through the desert like a river.

Yes, faithful to the sacred promise   42
given to his servant Abraham,
he led his happy people forward,   43
to joyful shouts from his chosen,

and gave them the pagans' territories.   44
Where others had toiled, they took possession,
on condition that they kept his statutes   45
and remained obedient to his laws.

PSALM 106   V 105

National confession

Alleluia!

Give thanks to Yahweh, for he is good,   1
his love is everlasting!
Who can count all Yahweh's triumphs?   2
Who can praise him enough?

Happy are we if we exercise justice   3
and constantly practise virtue!
Yahweh, remember me,   4
for the love you bear your people,
come to me as a saviour,
let me share the happiness of your chosen,   5
the joys of your nation
and take pride in being one of your heirs.

We have sinned quite as much as our fathers,   6
we have been wicked, we are guilty;
our ancestors in Egypt never grasped   7
the meaning of your marvels.

They failed to appreciate your great love,
they defied the Most High at the Sea of Reeds.
For the sake of his name, he saved them   8
to demonstrate his power.

One word from him dried up the Sea of Reeds,   9
he led them across the sea bed like dry land,
he saved them from the grasp of those who hated them   10
and rescued them from the clutches of the enemy.

And the waters swallowed their oppressors,   11
not one of them was left.
Then, having faith in his promises,   12
they immediately sang his praises.

They forgot his achievements as quickly,   13
going on before asking his advice;
their desires overcame them in the desert,   14
they challenged God in the wilds.

15 He granted them what they asked for,
then struck them with a wasting fever;

16 in camp, they grew jealous of Moses
and Aaron, Yahweh's holy one.

17 The earth opened, swallowing Dathan,
closing on Abiram's faction,

18 fire flamed out against their faction,
the renegades went up in flames.

19 They made a calf at Horeb,
performed prostrations to a smelted thing,

20 exchanging the one who was their glory
for the image of a grass-eating ox.

21 They forgot the God who had saved them
by performing such feats in Egypt,

22 such wonders in the land of Ham,
such fearful things at the Sea of Reeds.

23 He talked of putting an end to them
and would have done, if Moses his chosen
had not stood in the breach, confronting him,
and deflecting his destructive anger.

24 They refused a land of delight,
having no faith in his promise;

25 they stayed in their camp and grumbled,
they would not listen to Yahweh's voice.

26 So, raising his hand, he swore
to make them fall dead in the desert

27 and their descendants to fall to the heathen,
and to disperse them throughout those countries.

28 They accepted the yoke of Baal-peor
and ate sacrifices to the dead.

29 They provoked him by their behaviour;
plague broke out among them.

30 Then up stood Phinehas to intervene,
and the plague was checked;

31 hence his reputation for virtue
through successive generations for ever.

32 They enraged him at the waters of Meribah;
as a result, things went wrong for Moses,

33 since they had embittered his spirit
and he spoke without stopping to think.

34 They did not destroy the pagans
as Yahweh had told them to do,

35 but, intermarrying with them,
adopted their practices instead.

36 Serving the pagans' idols,
they found themselves trapped

37 into sacrificing their own sons
and daughters to demons.

38 They shed innocent blood,
the blood of their sons and daughters,

offering them to the idols of Canaan,
they polluted the country with blood.

They defiled themselves by such actions,   39
their behaviour was that of a whore.
Yahweh's anger blazed out at his people,   40
he came to loathe his heirs.

He handed them over to the pagans,   41
those who hated them became their masters;
their enemies tyrannised over them,   42
crushing them under their rule.

Time and again he rescued them,   43
but they went on defying him deliberately
and plunging deeper into wickedness;
even so, he took pity on their distress   44
each time he heard them calling.

For their sake, he remembered his covenant,   45
he relented in his great love,
making their captors mitigate   46
the harshness of their treatment.

Yahweh our God and saviour,   47
gather us from among the pagans,
to give thanks to your holy name
and to find our happiness in praising you.

Blessed be Yahweh the God of Israel,   48
from all eternity and for ever!
Here, all the people are to say, 'Amen'.ᵃ

PSALM 107   V 106

God, a refuge in all dangers

Alleluia!

Give thanks to Yahweh, for he is good,   1
his love is everlasting:

let these be the words of Yahweh's redeemed,   2
those he has redeemed from the oppressor's clutches,
by bringing them home from foreign countries,   3
from east and west, from north and south.

Some had lost their way in the wilds and the desert,   4
not knowing how to reach an inhabited town;
they were hungry and desperately thirsty,   5
their courage was running low.

Then they called to Yahweh in their trouble   6
and he rescued them from their sufferings,
guiding them by a route leading   7
direct to an inhabited town.

Let these thank Yahweh for his love,   8
for his marvels on behalf of men;
satisfying the hungry,   9
he fills the starving with good things.

10	Some were living in gloom and darkness,
	fettered in misery and irons
11	for defying the orders of God,
	for scorning the advice of the Most High;
12	who bent them double with hardship,
	to breaking point, with no one to help them.

13	Then they called to Yahweh in their trouble
	and he rescued them from their sufferings;
14	releasing them from gloom and darkness,
	shattering their chains.

15	Let these thank Yahweh for his love,
	for his marvels on behalf of men;
16	breaking bronze gates open,
	he smashes iron bars.

17	Some, driven frantic by their sins,
	made miserable by their own guilt
18	and finding all food repugnant,
	were nearly at death's door.

19	Then they called to Yahweh in their trouble
	and he rescued them from their sufferings;
20	sending his word and curing them,
	he snatched them from the Pit.

21	Let these thank Yahweh for his love,
	for his marvels on behalf of men.
22	Let them offer thanksgiving sacrifices
	and proclaim with shouts of joy what he has done.

23	Others, taking ship and going to sea,
	were plying their business across the ocean;
24	they too saw what Yahweh could do,
	what marvels on the deep!

25	He spoke and raised a gale,
	lashing up towering waves.
26	Flung to the sky, then plunged to the depths,
	they lost their nerve in the ordeal,
27	staggering and reeling like drunkards
	with all their seamanship adrift.

28	Then they called to Yahweh in their trouble
	and he rescued them from their sufferings,
29	reducing the storm to a whisper
	until the waves grew quiet,
30	bringing them, glad at the calm,
	safe to the port they were bound for.

31	Let these thank Yahweh for his love,
	for his marvels on behalf of men.
32	Let them extol him at the Great Assembly
	and praise him in the Council of Elders.

33	Sometimes he turned rivers into desert,
	springs of water into arid ground,
34	or a fertile country into salt-flats,
	because the people living there were wicked.

106 a. The doxology ends the fourth book of the Psalter, and is followed by a rubric

Or again, he turned a desert into sheets of water,   35
and an arid country into flowing springs,
where he gave the hungry a home   36
in which to found a habitable town.

There, they sow the fields and plant their vines,   37
there, they show a profitable harvest.
He blesses them, they grow in number,   38
he sees that their livestock does not decrease.

Their numbers had fallen, they had grown weak   39
under pressure of disaster and hardship.
Pouring his contempt upon the nobly born,   40
he left them to wander in a trackless waste.

But now, he lifts the needy out of their misery,   41
and gives them a flock of new families;
at the sight of which, upright hearts rejoice   42
and wickedness must hold its tongue.

If you are wise, study these things   43
and realise how Yahweh shows his love.

PSALM 108   V 107

Morning hymn and national prayer[a]

Song   Psalm   Of David

My heart is ready, God   1
—I mean to sing and play.
   Awake, my muse,
awake, lyre and harp,   2
   I mean to wake the Dawn!

Yahweh, I mean to thank you among the peoples,   3
   to play music to you among the nations;
your love is high as heaven,   4
   your faithfulness as the clouds.
Rise high above the heavens, God,   5
   let your glory be over the earth!

To bring rescue to those you love   6
save with your right hand and answer us!

God promised us once from his sanctuary,   7
'I the Victor will parcel out Shechem,
and share out the Valley of Succoth.

'Gilead is mine, Manasseh mine,   8
Ephraim is my helmet,
Judah, my marshal's baton.

'Moab a bowl for me to wash in!   9
I throw my sandal over Edom
and shout: Victory! over Philistia.'

Who is there now to take me into the fortified city,   10
to lead me into Edom?
God, can you really have rejected us?   11
You no longer march with our armies.

12   Help us in this hour of crisis,
       the help that man can give is worthless.
13   With God among us, we shall fight like heroes,
       he will trample on our enemies.

PSALM 109

V 108

An appeal against enemies

For the choirmaster   *Of David*   *Psalm*

1   God whom I praise, break your silence,
2   now that the wicked and the false
        are both accusing me.
     They are defaming me,
3   saying malicious things about me,
        attacking me for no reason.

4   In return for my friendship, they denounce me,
        though all I had done was pray for them;
5   they pay me back evil for kindness
        and hatred for friendship.

6   'Give him a venal judge,
     find someone to frame the charge;
7   let him be tried and found guilty,
     let his prayer be construed as a crime!

8   'Let his life be cut short,
     let someone else take his office;
9   may his children be orphaned
     and his wife widowed!

10   'May his children be homeless vagabonds,
     beggared and hounded from their hovels;
11   may the creditor seize his possessions
     and foreigners swallow his profits!

12   'May no one be left to show him kindness,
     may no one look after his orphans,
13   may his family die out,
     its name disappear in one generation!

14   'May the crimes of his fathers be held against him
     and his mother's sin never be effaced;
15   may Yahweh bear these constantly in mind,
     to wipe their memory off the earth!'

16   That wretch never thought of being kind,
     but hounded the poor, the needy
     and the broken-hearted to death.
17   He loved cursing, may it recoil on him,
     had no taste for blessing, may it shun him!

18   He used to wrap curses round him like a cloak,
     let them soak right into him like water,
     deep into his bones like oil.
19   May they now envelop him like a gown,
     be tied round his waist for ever!

108 a. Made from Ps 57:7-11 and Ps 60:5-12, with a few minor variations.

May Yahweh pay all my accusers, 20
all my detractors like this!
Yahweh, defend me for the sake of your name, 21
rescue me, since your love is generous!

Reduced to weakness and poverty, 22
my heart is sorely tormented;
I am dwindling away like a shadow, 23
they have brushed me off like a locust.

My knees are weak for lack of food, 24
my body is thin for lack of oil;
I have become an object of derision, 25
people shake their heads at me in scorn.

Help me, Yahweh my God, 26
save me since you love me,
and let them know that you have done it, 27
that it was you, Yahweh, who did it.

Counter their curses with your blessing, 28
shame my aggressors, make your servant glad!
Clothe my accusers in disgrace, 29
cover them with a cloak of shame.

I will give thanks aloud to Yahweh 30
and praise him in the Assembly,
for conducting the poor man's defence 31
against those who would have sentenced him to death.

PSALM 110 V 109

The Messiah: king and priest

Of David   Psalm

Yahweh's oracle to you, my Lord, 'Sit at my right hand 1
and I will make your enemies a footstool for you'.

Yahweh will force all your enemies 2
under the sway of your sceptre in Zion.

Royal dignity was yours from the day you were born, on the 3
holy mountains,
royal from the womb, from the dawn of your earliest days.

Yahweh has sworn an oath which he never will retract, 4
'You are a priest of the order of Melchizedek, and for ever.

The Lord is at your right hand. 5
When he grows angry he shatters kings,
he gives the nations their deserts, 6
smashing their skulls, he heaps the wide world with corpses.
Drinking from the stream as he goes, 7
he can hold his head high in victory.

PSALM 111   V 110

In praise of the divine attributes

1   Alleluia!

Aleph   I give thanks to Yahweh with all my heart
Beth   where the virtuous meet and the people assemble.

2 *Ghimel*   The works of Yahweh are sublime,
Daleth   those who delight in them are right to fix their eyes on them.

3 *He*   Every work that he does is full of glory and majesty,
Waw   and his righteousness can never change.

4 *Zain*   He allows us to commemorate his marvels.
Heth   Yahweh is merciful and tenderhearted,

5 *Teth*   he provides food for those who fear him;
Yod   he never forgets his covenant.

6 *Kaph*   He reminds his people of the power that he wields
Lamed   by giving them the inheritance of the nations.

7 *Mem*   All that he does is done in faithfulness and justice,
Nun   in all ways his precepts are dependable,

8 *Samek*   ordained to last for ever and ever,
Ain   framed in faithfulness and integrity.

9 *Pe*   Quickly he comes to his people's rescue,
Sade   imposing his covenant once and for all;
Qoph   so holy his name, commanding our dread.

10 *Resh*   This fear of Yahweh is the beginning of wisdom,
Shin   they have sound sense who practise it.
Tau   His praises will be sung for ever.

PSALM 112   V 111

In praise of the virtuous

1   Alleluia!

Aleph   Happy the man who fears Yahweh
Beth   by joyfully keeping his commandments!

2 *Ghimel*   Children of such a man will be powers on earth,
Daleth   descendants of the upright will always be blessed.

3 *He*   There will be riches and wealth for his family,
Waw   and his righteousness can never change.

4 *Zain*   For the upright he shines like a lamp in the dark,
Heth   he is merciful, tenderhearted, virtuous.

5 *Teth*   Interest is not charged by this good man,
Yod   he is honest in all his dealings.

6 *Kaph*   Kept safe by virtue, he is ever steadfast,
Lamed   and leaves an imperishable memory behind him;

Mem	with constant heart, and confidence in Yahweh,	7
Nun	he need never fear bad news.	
Samek	Steadfast in heart he overcomes his fears:	8
Ain	in the end he will triumph over his enemies.	
Pe	Quick to be generous, he gives to the poor,	9
Sade	his righteousness can never change,	
Qoph	men such as this will always be honoured,	
Resh	though this fills the wicked with fury	10
Shin	until, grinding their teeth, they waste away,	
Tau	vanishing like their vain hopes.	

PSALM 113

V 112

To God the glorious, the merciful

Alleluia!   1

You servants of Yahweh, praise,
praise the name of Yahweh!
Blessed be the name of Yahweh,   2
henceforth and for ever!
From east to west,   3
praised be the name of Yahweh!

High over all nations, Yahweh!   4
His glory transcends the heavens!
Who is like Yahweh our God?—   5
enthroned so high, he needs to stoop
to see the sky and earth!   6

He raises the poor from the dust;   7
he lifts the needy from the dunghill
to give them a place with princes,   8
with the princes of his people.
He enthrones the barren woman in her house   9
by making her the happy mother of sons.

PSALM 114

V 113A

Hymn for the Passover

Alleluia!

When Israel came out of Egypt,   1
the House of Jacob from a foreign nation,
Judah became his sanctuary   2
and Israel his domain.

The sea fled at the sight,   3
the Jordan stopped flowing,
the mountains skipped like rams,   4
and like lambs, the hills.

Sea, what makes you run away?   5
Jordan, why stop flowing?

6   Why skip like rams, you mountains,
     why like lambs, you hills?

7   Quake, earth, at the coming of your Master,
     at the coming of the God of Jacob,
8   who turns rock into pool
     flint into fountain.

PSALM 115

The one true God

1   Not by us, Yahweh, not by us,
     by you alone is glory deserved,
     by your love and your faithfulness!
2   Do the pagans ask, 'Where is their God?'

3   Ours is the God whose will is sovereign
     in the heavens and on earth,
4   whereas their idols, in silver and gold,
     products of human skill,

5   have mouths, but never speak,
     eyes, but never see,
6   ears, but never hear,
     noses, but never smell,

7   hands, but never touch,
     feet, but never walk,
     and not a sound from their throats.
8   Their makers will end up like them,
     and so will anyone who relies on them.

9   House of Israel, rely on Yahweh,
     on him, our help and shield!
10   House of Aaron, rely on Yahweh,
     on him, our help and shield!
11   You who fear Yahweh, rely on Yahweh,
     on him, our help and shield!

12   Yahweh remembers us, he will bless,
     he will bless the House of Israel,
     he will bless the House of Aaron,
13   he will bless those who fear Yahweh,
     without distinction of rank.ᵃ

14   May Yahweh add to your numbers,
     yours and your children's too!
15   May you be blessed by Yahweh,
     maker of heaven and earth!
16   Heaven belongs to Yahweh,
     earth he bestows on man.

17   The dead cannot praise Yahweh,
     they have gone down to silence;
18   but we, the living, bless Yahweh
     henceforth and evermore.

115 a. Between the Israelites by birth, the priestly house of Aaron, and the 'God-fearers' who are proselytes.

PSALM 116

Thanksgiving

Alleluia!

I love! For Yahweh listens to my entreaty;	1
he bends down to listen to me when I call.	2

Death's cords were tightening round me,   3
    the nooses of Sheol;
distress and anguish gripped me,
    I invoked the name of Yahweh: 4

'Yahweh, rescue me!'

Yahweh is righteous and merciful,   5
    our God is tenderhearted;
Yahweh defends the simple,   6
    he saved me when I was brought to my knees.

Return to your resting place, my soul,   7
    Yahweh has treated you kindly.
He has rescued (me from death) my eyes from tears   8
    and my feet from stumbling.

(I will walk in Yahweh's presence   9
    in the land of the living.)*a*

I have faith, even when I say,   10
    'I am completely crushed'.
In my alarm, I declared,   11
    'No man can be relied on'.

What return can I make to Yahweh   12
    for all his goodness to me?
I will offer libations to my saviour,   13
    invoking the name of Yahweh.

(I will pay what I vowed to Yahweh;   14
    may his whole nation be present!)

The death of the devout   15
    costs Yahweh dear.
Yahweh, I am your servant,   16
your servant, son of a pious mother,
    you undo my fetters.

I will offer you the thanksgiving sacrifice,   17
    invoking the name of Yahweh.
I will walk in Yahweh's presence   9
    in the land of the living.

I will pay what I vowed to Yahweh;   18
    may his whole nation be present,
in the courts of the house of Yahweh,   19
    in your heart, Jerusalem.

PSALM 117

Summons to praise

Alleluia!

1 Praise Yahweh, all nations,
    extol him, all you peoples!
2 For his love is strong,
    his faithfulness eternal.

PSALM 118

Processional hymn for the feast of Tabernacles[a]

Alleluia!

1 Give thanks to Yahweh, for he is good,
    his love is everlasting!
2 Let the House of Israel say it,
    'His love is everlasting!'

3 Let the House of Aaron say it,
    'His love is everlasting!'
4 Let those who fear Yahweh say it,
    'His love is everlasting!'

5 Hard-pressed, I invoked Yahweh,
    he heard me and came to my relief.
6 With Yahweh on my side, I fear nothing:
    what can man do to me?
7 With Yahweh on my side, best help of all,
    I can triumph over my enemies.

8 I would rather take refuge in Yahweh
    than rely on men;
9 I would rather take refuge in Yahweh
    than rely on princes.

10 The pagans were swarming round me,
    in the name of Yahweh I cut them down;
11 they swarmed round me closer and closer,
    in the name of Yahweh I cut them down;

12 they swarmed round me like bees,
    they blazed like a thorn-fire,
    in the name of Yahweh I cut them down.

13 I was pressed, pressed, about to fall,
    but Yahweh came to my help;
14 Yahweh is my strength and my song,
    he has been my saviour.

15 Shouts of joy and safety
    in the tents of the virtuous:
    Yahweh's right hand is wreaking havoc,

116 a. This verse (and the bracketed words in v.8) have been added by an editor or copyist to assimilate this passage to the parallel Ps 56:13. In this psalm, v.9 should be read after v.17.
118 a. The last of the six 'Hallel' (Praise) psalms which began with Ps 113.

Yahweh's right hand is winning,   16
Yahweh's right hand is wreaking havoc!

No, I shall not die, I shall live   17
   to recite the deeds of Yahweh;
though Yahweh has punished me often,   18
   he has not abandoned me to Death.

Open the gates of virtue to me,   19
   I will come in and give thanks to Yahweh.
This is Yahweh's gateway,   20
   through which the virtuous may enter.
I thank you for having heard me,   21
   you have been my saviour.

It was the stone rejected by the builders   22
that proved to be the keystone;
this is Yahweh's doing   23
and it is wonderful to see.
This is the day made memorable by Yahweh,   24
what immense joy for us!

Please, Yahweh, please save us.   25
Please, Yahweh, please give us prosperity.
Blessings on him who comes in the name of Yahweh!   26
We bless you from the house of Yahweh.
Yahweh is God, he smiles on us.   27
With branches in your hands draw up in procession
as far as the horns of the altar,

You are my God, I give you thanks,   28
   I extol you, my God;
I give you thanks for having heard me,
   you have been my saviour.
Give thanks to Yahweh, for he is good,   29
   his love is everlasting!

PSALM 119   V 118

In praise of the divine Law

Aleph   Ah, how happy those of blameless life   1
   who walk in the Law of Yahweh!
How happy those who respect his decrees,   2
   and seek him with their whole heart,
and, doing no evil,   3
   walk in his ways!
You yourself have made your precepts known,   4
   to be faithfully kept.
Oh, may my behaviour be constant   5
   in keeping your statutes.
If I concentrate on your every commandment,   6
   I can never be put to shame.
I thank you from an upright heart,   7
   schooled in your rules of righteousness.
I mean to observe your statutes;   8
   never abandon me.

Beth   How can a youth remain pure?   9
   By behaving as your word prescribes.

10	I have sought you with all my heart,
	do not let me stray from your commandments.
11	I have treasured your promises in my heart,
	since I have no wish to sin against you.
12	How blessed are you, Yahweh!
	Teach me your statutes!
13	With my lips I have repeated them,
	all these rulings from your own mouth.
14	In the way of your decrees lies my joy,
	a joy beyond all wealth.
15	I mean to meditate on your precepts
	and to concentrate on your paths.
16	I find my delight in your statutes,
	I do not forget your word.

17 *Ghimel*	Be good to your servant and I shall live,
	I shall observe your word.
18	Open my eyes: I shall concentrate
	on the marvels of your Law.
19	Exile though I am on earth,
	do not hide your commandments from me.
20	My soul is overcome
	with an incessant longing for your rulings.
21	You reprove the arrogant, the accursed
	who stray from your commandments.
22	Avert their insults and contempt from me,
	since I respect your decrees.
23	Though princes put me on trial,
	your servant will meditate on your statutes,
24	since your decrees are my delight,
	your statutes are my counsellors.

25 *Daleth*	Down in the dust I lie prostrate:
	revive me as your word has guaranteed.
26	I admitted my behaviour, you answered me,
	now teach me your statutes.
27	Explain to me how to keep your precepts,
	that I may meditate on your marvels.
28	I am sleepless with grief:
	raise me as your word has guaranteed.
29	Turn me from the path of delusion,
	grant me the grace of your Law.
30	I have chosen the way of fidelity,
	I have set my heart on your rulings.
31	I cling to your decrees:
	Yahweh, do not disappoint me.
32	I run the way of your commandments,
	since you have set me free.

33 *He*	Expound to me the way of your statutes, Yahweh,
	and I will always respect them.
34	Explain to me how to respect your Law
	and how to observe it wholeheartedly.
35	Guide me in the path of your commandments,
	since my delight is there.
36	Turn my heart to your decrees
	and away from getting money.

	Avert my eyes from lingering on inanities,	37
	give me life by your word.	
	Keep your promise to your servant,	38
	so that others in turn may fear you.	
	Avert the insults that I fear,	39
	in the kindness of your rulings.	
	Look how I yearn for your precepts:	40
	give me life by your righteousness.	

Waw   For, Yahweh, visited by your love   41
and saving help, as you have promised,

I can find an answer to the insults,   42
since I rely on your word.

Do not deprive me of that faithful word,   43
since my hope has always lain in your rulings.

Let me observe your Law unfailingly   44
for ever and ever.

So, having sought your precepts,   45
I shall walk in all freedom.

I shall proclaim your decrees to kings   46
without fear of disgrace.

Your commandments fill me with delight,   47
I love them deeply.

I stretch out my hands to your beloved commandments,   48
I meditate on your statutes.

Zain   Remember the word you pledged your servant,   49
on which you have built my hope.

This has been my comfort in my suffering: 50
that your promise gives me life.

Endlessly the arrogant have jeered at me,   51
but I have not swerved from your Law.

Remembering your rulings in the past,   52
Yahweh, I take comfort.

Fury grips me when I see the wicked   53
abandoning your Law.

Where I live in exile,   54
your statutes are psalms for me.

All night, Yahweh, I remember your name   55
and observe your Law.

Surely it will count to my credit: 56
that I respect your precepts.

Heth   Have I not said, Yahweh, that my task   57
is to observe your words?

Wholeheartedly I now entreat you,   58
take pity on me as you have promised!

After reflecting on my behaviour,   59
I turn my feet to your decrees.

Wasting no time, I hurry   60
to observe your commandments.

Though the nooses of the wicked tighten round me,   61
I do not forget your Law.

I get up at midnight to thank you   62
for the righteousness of your rulings.

I am a friend to all who fear you   63
and observe your precepts.

64   Yahweh, your love fills the earth:
            teach me your statutes.

65 *Teth*   In accordance with your word, Yahweh,
            you have been good to your servant.

66   Teach me good sense and knowledge,
            for I rely on your commandments.

67   In earlier days I had to suffer, I used to stray,
            but now I remember your promise.

68   You, so good and kind,
            teach me your statutes!

69   Though the arrogant tell foul lies about me,
            I wholeheartedly respect your precepts.

70   Their hearts are gross as fat,
            but my delight is in your Law.

71   It was good for me to have to suffer,
            the better to learn your statutes.

72   I put the Law you have given
            before all the gold and silver in the world.

73 *Yod*   Yahweh, my maker, my preserver,
            explain your commandments for me to learn.

74   Seeing me, those who fear you will be glad,
            since I put my hope in your word.

75   I know that your rulings are righteous, Yahweh,
            that you make me suffer out of faithfulness.

76   Now, please let your love comfort me,
            as you have promised your servant.

77   Treat me tenderly, and I shall live,
            since your Law is my delight.

78   Shame seize the arrogant who defame me,
            when I meditate on your precepts!

79   May those who fear you rally to me,
            all those familiar with your decrees!

80   Blameless in your statutes be my heart:
            no such shame therefore for me!

81 *Kaph*   Keeping my hope in your word,
            I have worn myself out waiting for you to save me,

82   and have strained my eyes waiting for your promise:
            when, I want to know, will you console me?

83   Though smoked as dry as a wineskin,
            I do not forget your statutes.

84   How much longer has your servant to live,
            when will you condemn my persecutors?

85   The arrogant have dug pitfalls for me
            in defiance of your Law.

86   Your commandments epitomise faithfulness;
            when liars hound me, you must help me.

87   Though these wretches have almost done for me,
            I have never abandoned your precepts.

88   Lovingly intervene, give me life,
            and I will observe your decrees.

89 *Lamed*   Lasting to eternity, your word,
            Yahweh, unchanging in the heavens:

90   your faithfulness lasts age after age;

you founded the earth to endure.

Creation is maintained by your rulings,   91
    since all things are your servants.

Had your Law not been my delight   92
    I should have perished in my suffering.

I shall never forget your precepts;   93
    by these you have kept me alive.

I am yours, save me,   94
    since I study your precepts.

The wicked may hope to destroy me,   95
    but I am scrupulous about your decrees.

I have noticed limitations to all perfection,   96
    but your commandment has no limits at all.

Mem

Meditating all day on your Law,   97
    how I have come to love it!

By your commandment, ever mine,   98
    how much wiser you have made me than my enemies!

How much subtler than my teachers,   99
    through my meditating on your decrees!

How much more perceptive than the elders,   100
    as a result of my respecting your precepts!

I refrain my feet from every evil path,   101
    the better to observe your word.

I do not turn aside from your rulings,   102
    since you yourself teach me these.

Your promise, how sweet to my palate!   103
    Sweeter than honey to my mouth!

Your precepts endow me with perception;   104
    I hate all deceptive paths.

Nun

Now your word is a lamp to my feet,   105
    a light on my path.

I have sworn to observe, I shall maintain,   106
    your righteous rulings.

Yahweh, though my suffering is acute,   107
    revive me as your word has guaranteed.

Yahweh, accept the homage that I offer,   108
    teach me your rulings.

I would lay down my life at any moment,   109
    I have never yet forgotten your Law.

The wicked have tried to trap me,   110
    but I have never yet veered from your precepts.

Your decrees are my eternal heritage,   111
    they are the joy of my heart.

I devote myself to obeying your statutes—   112
    compensation enough for ever!

Samek

Odious, those whose allegiance is divided;   113
    I love your Law!

You, my refuge and shield,   114
    I put my hope in your word.

Away from me, you wicked people!   115
    I will respect the commandments of my God.

Support me as you have promised, and I shall live,   116
    do not disappoint me of my hope.

Uphold me, and I shall be safe   117
    with your statutes constantly before my eyes.

118   You spurn all who stray from your statutes,
         their notions being delusion.

119   You scour the wicked off the earth like rust;
         that is why I love your decrees.

120   My whole being trembles before you,
         your rulings fill me with fear.

121 *Ain*   Persevering in justice and virtue,
         must I now be abandoned to my oppressors?

122   Guarantor of your servant's well-being,
         forbid the arrogant to oppress me!

123   My eyes are worn out looking for your saving help
         for your promise of righteousness to come.

124   Treat your servant lovingly,
         teach me your statutes.

125   I am your servant; if you will explain,
         I shall embrace your decrees.

126   Yahweh, now is the time to act,
         your Law is being broken.

127   Yes, I love your commandments
         more than gold, than purest gold.

128   Yes, I rule myself by all your precepts;
         I hate all deceptive paths.

129 *Pe*   Your decrees are so wonderful
         my soul cannot but respect them.

130   As your word unfolds, it gives light,
         and the simple understand.

131   I open my mouth, panting
         eagerly for your commandments.

132   Turn to me please, pity me,
         as you should those who love your name.

133   Direct my steps as you have promised,
         let evil win no power over me.

134   Rescue me from human oppression;
         I will observe your precepts.

135   Treat your servant kindly,
         teach me your statutes.

136   My eyes stream with tears,
         because others disregard your Law.

137 *Sade*   Righteous, indeed, Yahweh!
         And all your rulings correct!

138   The decrees you impose, how righteous,
         how absolutely faithful!

139   Zeal for your house devours me,
         since my oppressors forget your word.

140   But your promise is well tested,
         and your servant holds it dear.

141   Puny and despised as I am,
         I do not forget your precepts.

142   Your righteousness is eternal righteousness,
         your Law holds true for ever.

143   Though distress and anguish grip me,
         your commandments are my delight.

144   Eternally righteous, your decrees—
         explain them to me, and I shall live.

Qoph

Sincere, my call—Yahweh, answer me!   145
     I will respect your statutes.

I invoke you, save me,   146
     I will observe your decrees.

I am up before dawn to call for help,   147
     I put my hope in your word.

I lie awake throughout the night,   148
     to meditate on your promise.

In your love, Yahweh, listen to my voice,   149
     let your rulings give me life.

My cruel persecutors are closing in,   150
     how remote they are from your Law!

But, Yahweh, you are closer still   151
     and all your commandments are true.

Long have I known that your decrees   152
     were founded to last for ever.

Resh

Take note of my suffering and rescue me,   153
     for I do not forget your Law.

Take up my cause, defend me,   154
     give me life as you have promised.

You will never save the wicked,   155
     if they do not study your statutes,

but many are your mercies to me, Yahweh,   156
     by your rulings give me life.

Many hound me and oppress me,   157
     but I do not swerve from your decrees.

The sight of these renegades disgusts me,   158
     they do not observe your promise;

but, Yahweh, see how I love your precepts,   159
     and lovingly give me life.

Faithfulness is the essence of your word,   160
     your righteous rulings hold good for ever.

Shin

Unjustifiably though princes hound me,   161
     your word is what fills me with dread.

I rejoice in your promise,   162
     like someone on finding a vast treasure.

I hate, I detest, delusion;   163
     your Law is what I love.

Seven times daily I praise you   164
     for your righteous rulings.

Universal peace for those who love your Law,   165
     no stumbling-blocks for them!

Waiting for you, Yahweh, my saviour,   166
     I fulfil your commandments.

My soul observes your decrees;   167
     these I wholly love.

I observe your precepts, your decrees;   168
     you know how I keep to your paths.

Tau

Yahweh, may my cry approach your presence;   169
     let your word endow me with perception!

May my entreaty reach your presence;   170
     rescue me as you have promised.

May my lips proclaim your praise,   171
     since you teach me your statutes.

172   May my tongue recite your promise,
  since all your commandments are righteous.
173   May your hand be there to help me,
  since I have chosen your precepts.
174   I long for you, Yahweh, my saviour,
  your Law is my delight.
175   Long may my soul live to praise you,
  long be your rulings my help!
176   I am wandering like a lost sheep:
  come and look for your servant.

No, I have never forgotten your commandments.

PSALM 120   V 119

The enemies of peace

Song of Ascents

1   When I am in trouble, I call to
  Yahweh, and he answers me.
2   Yahweh, save me from these lying lips
  and these faithless tongues!
3   How will he pay back the false oath
  of a faithless tongue?
4   With war arrows hardened
  over red-hot charcoal!
5   This is worse than a life in Meshech,[a]
  or camping in Kedar!
6   Too long have I lived
  among people who hate peace,
7   who, when I propose peace,
  are all for war.

PSALM 121   V 120

The guardian of Israel

Song of Ascents

1   I lift my eyes to the mountains:
  where is help to come from?
2   Help comes to me from Yahweh,
  who made heaven and earth.
3   No letting our footsteps slip!
  This guard of yours, he does not doze!
4   The guardian of Israel
  does not doze or sleep.
5   Yahweh guards you, shades you.
  With Yahweh at your right hand
6   sun cannot strike you down by day,
  nor moon at night.

120 a. In the Caucasus. The Arabs of Kedar lived in the Syrian desert. Both are regarded by the psalmist as uncivilised

Yahweh guards you from harm,   7
    he guards your lives,
he guards you leaving, coming back,   8
    now and for always.

PSALM 122   V 121

Hail, Jerusalem!

Song of Ascents   *Of David*

How I rejoiced when they said to me,   1
    'Let us go to the house of Yahweh!'
And now our feet are standing   2
    in your gateways, Jerusalem.

Jerusalem restored! The city,   3
    one united whole!
Here the tribes come up,   4
    the tribes of Yahweh,

they come to praise Yahweh's name,
    as he ordered Israel,
here where the tribunals of justice are,   5
    the royal tribunals of David.

Pray for peace in Jerusalem,   6
    'Prosperity to your houses!
Peace inside your city walls!   7
    Prosperity to your palaces!'

Since all are my brothers and friends,   8
    I say 'Peace be with you!'
Since Yahweh our God lives here,   9
    I pray for your happiness.

PSALM 123   V 122

Prayer of the distressed

Song of Ascents

I lift my eyes to you,   1
    to you who have your home in heaven,
eyes like the eyes of slaves   2
    fixed on their master's hand;

like the eyes of a slave-girl
    fixed on the hand of her mistress,
so our eyes are fixed on Yahweh our God,
    for him to take pity on us;

pity us, Yahweh, take pity on us,   3
    we have had more than our share of scorn,
more than our share   4
    of jeers from the complacent,
    of scorn from the proud.

PSALM 124

The saviour of Israel

Song of Ascents   *David*

1   If Yahweh had not been on our side
         —let Israel repeat it—
2   if Yahweh had not been on our side
         when they attacked us,
3   they would have swallowed us alive
         and burnt us to death in their rage.

4   The waters would have closed over us,
         the torrent have swept us away,
5   either would have drowned us
         in their turbulent waves.

6   Blessed be Yahweh who did not let us fall
         a victim to those teeth,
7   who let us escape like birds
         from the fowler's net.

     He tore the net
         and we escaped;
8   our help is in the name of Yahweh,
         who made heaven and earth.

PSALM 125

God protects his faithful

Song of Ascents

1   Those who trust in Yahweh are like Mount Zion,
         unshakeable, standing for ever.
2   Jerusalem! Encircled by mountains,
     as Yahweh encircles his people
         now and for always.

3   No wicked sceptre shall rule
         this heritage of the virtuous,
     or the virtuous in their turn
         might take to evil.

4   Yahweh, be good to the good,
         to those of upright heart.
5   But the perverts, those who follow twisting paths—
         may Yahweh send them to join the evil-doers!

     Peace to Israel!

PSALM 126

Song of the returning exiles

Song of Ascents

1   When Yahweh brought Zion's captives home,
         at first it seemed like a dream;

then our mouths filled with laughter
  and our lips with song.

Even the pagans started talking
  about the marvels Yahweh had done for us!
What marvels indeed he did for us,   3
  and how overjoyed we were!

Yahweh, bring all our captives back again   4
  like torrents in the Negeb!
Those who went sowing in tears   5
  now sing as they reap.

They went away, went away weeping,   6
  carrying the seed;
they come back, come back singing,
  carrying their sheaves.

PSALM 127   V 126

Trust in Providence

Song of Ascents   Solomon

If Yahweh does not build the house,   1
  in vain the masons toil;
if Yahweh does not guard the city,
  in vain the sentries watch.

In vain you get up earlier,   2
and put off going to bed,
sweating to make a living,
since he provides for his beloved as they sleep.

Sons are a bounty from Yahweh,   3
he rewards with descendants:
like the arrows in a hero's hand   4
are the sons you father when young.

Happy the man who has filled his quiver   5
with arrows of this sort;
in dispute with his enemies at the gate,^{a}
he will not be worsted.

PSALM 128   V 127

Blessing for the devout

Song of Ascents

Happy, all those who fear Yahweh   1
  and follow in his paths.

You will eat what your hands have worked for,   2
  happiness and prosperity will be yours.
Your wife: a fruitful vine   3
  on the inner walls of your house.
Your sons: round your table
  like shoots round an olive tree.

4   Such are the blessings that fall
       on the man who fears Yahweh.
5a   May Yahweh bless you from Zion
5c   all the days of your life!
5b   May you see Jerusalem prosperous
6   and live to see your children's children!

    Peace to Israel!

PSALM 129

Against the enemies of Zion

Song of Ascents

1   Hard as they have harried me since I was young
    —let Israel repeat it—
2   hard as they have harried me since I was young,
    they have not overcome me.

3   Ploughmen have ploughed on my back
    longer and longer furrows,
4   but now Yahweh the Righteous has shattered
    the yoke of the wicked.

5   May they all be thrown into confusion, be routed,
    who have hated Zion,
6   be blasted by winds from the east like grass
    sprouting on the roof!

7   Roof-grass never yet filled
    reaper's arm or binder's lap—
8   and no one passing them will ever say,
    'Yahweh's blessing on you!'

    We bless you in the name of Yahweh.

PSALM 130

From the depths

Song of Ascents

1   From the depths I call to you, Yahweh,
2   Lord, listen to my cry for help!
    Listen compassionately
    to my pleading!

3   If you never overlooked our sins, Yahweh,
    Lord, could anyone survive?
4   But you do forgive us:
    and for that we revere you.

5   I wait for Yahweh, my soul waits for him,
    I rely on his promise,
6   my soul relies on the Lord
    more than a watchman on the coming of dawn.

127 a. The city gate, at which all business matters and disputes are settled.

Let Israel rely on Yahweh   7
     as much as the watchman on the dawn!
For it is with Yahweh that mercy is to be found,
and a generous redemption;
it is he who redeems Israel   8
     from all their sins.

PSALM 131   V 130

Childlike trust in God

Song of Ascents   Of David

Yahweh, my heart has no lofty ambitions,   1
     my eyes do not look too high.
I am not concerned with great affairs
     or marvels beyond my scope.
Enough for me to keep my soul tranquil and quiet   2
     like a child in its mother's arms,
as content as a child that has been weaned.

Israel, rely on Yahweh,   3
     now and for always!

PSALM 132   V 131

The ark is taken to Zion: anniversary hymn

Song of Ascents

Yahweh, remember David   1
and all the hardships he suffered,
and the oath he swore to Yahweh,   2
his vow to the Mighty One of Jacob:

not to enter tent or house,   3
not to climb into bed,
not to allow himself to sleep,   4
not even to close his eyes,
until he had found a place for Yahweh,   5
a home for the Mighty One of Jacob!

Listen: we heard it was in Ephrathah,   6
we found it at Fields-of-the-Forest!
Let us go where he is waiting   7
and worship at his footstool.

Yahweh, go up to your resting place,   8
you and your ark of power.
Your priests are vesting in virtue   9
and your devout are shouting for joy.
For the sake of your servant David,   10
do not banish your anointed.

Yahweh swore to David   11
and will remain true to his word,
'I promise that your own son
shall succeed you on the throne.

12   'If your sons observe my covenant,
the decrees that I have taught them,
their sons too shall succeed you
on the throne for evermore.'

13   For Yahweh has chosen Zion,
desiring this to be his home,
14   'Here I will stay for ever,
this is the home I have chosen.

15   'I will bless her virtuous with riches,
provide her poor with food,
16   vest her priests in salvation
and her devout shall shout for joy.

17   'Here, I will make a horn sprout for David,
here, I will trim a lamp for my anointed,
18   whose enemies I shall clothe in shame,
while his crown bursts into flower.'

PSALM 133   V 132

Brotherly love

Song of Ascents   Of David

1   How good, how delightful it is
for all to live together like brothers:

2   fine as oil on the head,
running down the beard,
running down Aaron's beard
to the collar of his robes;

3   copious as a Hermon dew
falling on the heights of Zion,
where Yahweh confers his blessing,
everlasting life.

PSALM 134   V 133

Night hymn

Song of Ascents

1   Come, bless Yahweh,
all you who serve Yahweh,
serving in the house of Yahweh,

in the courts of the house of our God!
2   Stretch out your hands towards the sanctuary,
bless Yahweh night after night!

3   May Yahweh bless you from Zion,
he who made heaven and earth!^a

134 a. This blessing ends the series of pilgrim psalms ('Songs of Ascents') which began with Ps 120.

PSALM 135

Hymn of praise

Alleluia!   1

Praise the name of Yahweh,
praise Yahweh, you who serve him,
serving in the house of Yahweh,   2
in the courts of the house of our God!

Praise Yahweh, for Yahweh is good.   3
Play for his name, for he inspires love;
since Yahweh has chosen Jacob,   4
Israel as his own.

I have learnt for myself that Yahweh is great,   5
that our Lord surpasses all other gods.
In the heavens, on the earth,   6
in the ocean, in the depths,
Yahweh's will is sovereign.

He raises up clouds from the boundaries of earth,   7
makes the lightning flash for the downpour
and brings the wind out of his storehouse.

He struck down the first-born of Egypt,   8
of man and beast alike,
he sent signs and wonders   9
among you, Egypt,
against Pharaoh and his officials.

He struck the pagans down in droves,   10
he slaughtered mighty kings,
Sihon, king of the Amorites,   11
and Og, the king of Bashan,
and all the kingdoms of Canaan;
he gave their lands as a legacy,   12
a legacy to his people Israel.

Yahweh, your name endures for ever!   13
Yahweh, your memory is always fresh!
Since Yahweh vindicates his people,   14
and cares for those who serve him;

whereas pagans' idols, in silver and gold,   15
products of human skill,
have mouths, but never speak,   16
eyes, but never see,

ears, but never hear,   17
and not a breath in their mouths.
Their makers will end up like them   18
and so will anyone who relies on them.

House of Israel, bless Yahweh,   19
House of Aaron, bless Yahweh,
House of Levi, bless Yahweh,   20
you who fear Yahweh, bless Yahweh!

Blessed be Yahweh in Zion,   21
in Jerusalem his home!

PSALM 136

Litany of thanksgiving

Alleluia!

1. Give thanks to Yahweh, for he is good,
   his love is everlasting!
2. Give thanks to the God of gods,
   his love is everlasting!
3. Give thanks to the Lord of lords,
   his love is everlasting!

4. He alone performs great marvels,
   his love is everlasting!
5. His wisdom made the heavens,
   his love is everlasting!
6. He set the earth on the waters,
   his love is everlasting!

7. He made the great lights,
   his love is everlasting!
8. The sun to govern the day,
   his love is everlasting!
9. Moon and stars to govern the night,
   his love is everlasting!

10. He struck down the first-born of Egypt,
    his love is everlasting!
11. And brought Israel out,
    his love is everlasting!
12. With mighty hand and outstretched arm,
    his love is everlasting!

13. He split the Sea of Reeds,
    his love is everlasting!
14. Led Israel through the middle,
    his love is everlasting!
15. Drowned Pharaoh and his army,
    his love is everlasting!

16. He led his people through the wilderness,
    his love is everlasting!
17. He struck down mighty kings,
    his love is everlasting!
18. He slaughtered famous kings,
    his love is everlasting!
19. Sihon, king of the Amorites,
    his love is everlasting!
20. And Og, the king of Bashan,
    his love is everlasting!

21. He gave their lands as a legacy,
    his love is everlasting!
22. A legacy to his servant Israel,
    his love is everlasting!
23. He remembered us when we were down,
    his love is everlasting!

And snatched us from our oppressors,   24
   his love is everlasting!

He provides for all living creatures,   25
   his love is everlasting!
Give thanks to the God of Heaven,   26
   his love is everlasting!

PSALM 137   V 136

Ballad of the exiles

Beside the streams of Babylon   1
we sat and wept
at the memory of Zion,
leaving our harps   2
hanging on the poplars there.

For we had been asked   3
to sing to our captors,
to entertain those who had carried us off:
'Sing' they said
'some hymns of Zion'.

How could we sing   4
one of Yahweh's hymns
in a pagan country?
Jerusalem, if I forget you,   5
may my right hand wither!

May I never speak again,   6
if I forget you!
If I do not count Jerusalem
the greatest of my joys!

Yahweh, remember   7
what the Sons of Edom did
on the day of Jerusalem,[a]
how they said, 'Down with her!
Raze her to the ground!'

Destructive Daughter of Babel,   8
a blessing on the man who treats you
as you have treated us,
a blessing on him who takes and dashes   9
your babies against the rock!

PSALM 138   V 137

Hymn of thanksgiving

Of David

I thank you, Yahweh, with all my heart,   1
because you have heard what I said.
In the presence of the angels I play for you,
and bow down towards your holy Temple.   2

I give thanks to your name for your love and faithfulness;
your promise is even greater than your fame.

3 The day I called for help, you heard me
and you increased my strength.

4 Yahweh, all kings on earth give thanks to you,
for they have heard your promises;

5 they celebrate Yahweh's actions,
'Great is the glory of Yahweh!'

6 From far above, Yahweh sees the humble,
from far away he marks down the arrogant.

7 Though I live surrounded by trouble,
you keep me alive—to my enemies' fury!
You stretch your hand out and save me,

8 your right hand •will do everything for me.
Yahweh, your love is everlasting,
do not abandon us whom you have made.

PSALM 139
V 138

In praise of God's omniscience

For the choirmaster   Of David   Psalm

1 Yahweh, you examine me and know me,

2 you know if I am standing or sitting,
you read my thoughts from far away,

3 whether I walk or lie down, you are watching,
you know every detail of my conduct.

4 The word is not even on my tongue,
Yahweh, before you know all about it;

5 close behind and close in front you fence me round,
shielding me with your hand.

6 Such knowledge is beyond my understanding,
a height to which my mind cannot attain.

7 Where could I go to escape your spirit?
Where could I flee from your presence?

8 If I climb the heavens, you are there,
there too, if I lie in Sheol.

9 If I flew to the point of sunrise,
or westward across the sea,

10 your hand would still be guiding me,
your right hand holding me.

11 If I asked darkness to cover me,
and light to become night around me,

12 that darkness would not be dark to you,
night would be as light as day.

13 It was you who created my inmost self,
and put me together in my mother's womb;

14 for all these mysteries I thank you:
for the wonder of myself, for the wonder of your works.

137 a. At the destruction of Jerusalem, 587 B.C., the neighbouring nation of the Edomites joined forces with the besieging army. The prophets denounce them far more bitterly than they denounce the Chaldaean invaders.

You know me through and through,
from having watched my bones take shape   15
when I was being formed in secret,
knitted together in the limbo of the womb.

You had scrutinised my every action,   16
all were recorded in your book,
my days listed and determined,
even before the first of them •occurred.   17

God, how hard it is to grasp your thoughts!
How impossible to count them!
I could no more count them than I could the sand,   18
and suppose I could, you would still be with me.

God, if only you would kill the wicked!   19
Men of blood, away from me!
They talk blasphemously about you,   20
regard your thoughts as nothing.

Yahweh, do I not hate those who hate you,   21
and loathe those who defy you?
I hate them with a total hatred,   22
I regard them as my own enemies.

God, examine me and know my heart,   23
probe me and know my thoughts;
make sure I do not follow pernicious ways,   24
and guide me in the way that is everlasting.

PSALM 140   V 139

Against the wicked

For the choirmaster   Psalm   Of David

Yahweh, rescue me from evil people,   1
    defend me from men of violence,
from people plotting evil,   2
    forever intent on stirring up strife,
who make their tongues as sharp as serpents'   3
    with viper's venom on their lips.   *Pause*

Yahweh, guard me from attacks by the wicked,   4
    defend me from those who love force,
from people plotting to make me stumble,
    forever laying snares where I walk,   5b
insolent wretches, concealing pitfall and noose   5a
    to trap me as I pass.   *Pause* 5c

I have told Yahweh, 'You are my God'.   6
    Yahweh, listen to my cry for help.
Yahweh, my Lord, my saving strength,   7
    shielding my head when I have to fight,
Yahweh, do not grant their wicked wishes,   8
    do not let their plots succeed.

May those besieging me not •win,   *Pause* 9
    may their own cruel words overtake them,
may red-hot embers rain down on them,   10

may they be flung into the abyss for good,
11 may evil hound the man of violence to death
   and the slanderer not hold his own on earth.

12 I know Yahweh will avenge the wretched,
   and see justice done for the poor.
13 The virtuous shall have good cause to thank your name,
   and the upright to find a home with you.

PSALM 141

V 140

Against the attractions of evil

Psalm Of David

1 Yahweh, I am calling, hurry to me,
   listen to me, I am invoking you.
2 My prayers rise like incense,
   my hands like the evening offering.

3 Yahweh, set a guard at my mouth,
   a watcher at the gate of my lips.
4 Let me feel no impulse to do wrong,
   to share the godlessness of evil-doers.

No, I will not sample their delights.
5 A virtuous man may strike me in reproof, for my own good,
   but a wicked one shall never anoint my head with oil!
   Daily I counter their malice with prayer.
6 When their judges are flung on jagged rock,
   they will learn how mild my words have been,
7 'Like a millstone smashed on the ground,
   our bones are scattered at the mouth of Sheol'.

8 To you, Yahweh my Lord, I turn my eyes.
   I take shelter in you, do not leave me exposed!
9 Keep me out of traps that are set for me,
   from the bait laid for me by evil men.
10 Let the wicked fall into their own net,
   while I go on my way.

PSALM 142

V 141

Prayer of a hunted man

Poem Of David When he was in the cave Psalm

1 To Yahweh, my cry! I plead.
  To Yahweh, my cry! I entreat.
2 I pour out my supplications,
  I unfold all my troubles;
3 my spirit fails me,
  but you, you know my path.

On the path I follow
  they have concealed a trap.
4 Look on my right[a] and see,

142 a. The place for a man's advocate to stand.

there is no one to befriend me.
All help is denied me,
no one cares about me.

I invoke you, Yahweh,   5
I affirm that you are my refuge,
my heritage in the land of the living.
Listen to my cries for help,   6
I can hardly be crushed lower.

Rescue me from persecutors
stronger than I am!
Free me from this imprisonment,   7
and I will thank your name once more
in the Assembly of the virtuous,
for the goodness you show me.

PSALM 143   V 142

A humble entreaty

Psalm   Of David

Yahweh, hear my prayer,   1
listen to my pleading,
answer me faithfully, righteously;
do not put your servant on trial,   2
no one is virtuous by your standards.

An enemy who hounds me   3
to crush me into the dust,
forces me to dwell in darkness
like the dead of long ago;
my spirit fails me   4
and my heart is full of fear.

I recall the days of old,   5
I reflect on all that you did,
I ponder your deeds;
I stretch out my hands,   6
like thirsty ground I yearn for you.   *Pause*

Quick, Yahweh, answer me   7
before my spirit fails;
if you hide your face much longer,
I shall go down to the Pit like the rest.

Let dawn bring proof of your love,   8
for one who relies on you;
let it show the right road,
to one who lifts up his soul to you.

Yahweh, rescue me from my enemies,   9
I have fled to you for shelter;
teach me to obey you,   10
since you are my God;
may your good spirit guide me
on to level ground.

11   Yahweh, for the sake of your name,
      keep your promise to save me;
      protect me from oppression,
12   love me, kill my enemies,
      destroy my oppressors,
      for I am your servant.

PSALM 144

War hymn and the fruits of victory

David

1   Blessed be Yahweh, my rock,
     who trains my hands for war
     and my fingers for battle,
2   my love, my bastion,
     my citadel, my saviour,
     I shelter behind him, my shield,
     he makes the nations submit to me.

3   Yahweh, what is man, that you should notice him?
     A human being, that you should think about him?
4   Man's life, a mere puff of wind,
     his days, as fugitive as shadows.

5   Yahweh, lower your heavens, come down to us!
     Touch the mountains, make them smoke,
6   flash your lightning—scatter them,
     shoot your arrows—rout them.

7   Reach down your hand from above,
     save me, rescue me from deep waters,
     from the power of aliens
8   who tell nothing but lies,
     who are prepared to swear to falsehood!

9   God, I have made a new song for you
     to be played on the ten-string lyre,
10   you who give victory to kings
     and safety to your servant David.

11   From peril of sword ·save me,
     rescue me from the power of aliens
     who tell nothing but lies,
     who are prepared to swear to falsehood!

12   May our sons be like plants
         growing strong from their earliest days,
     our daughters like corner-statues,*a*
         carvings fit for a palace;
13   may our barns overflow
         with every possible crop,
     may the sheep in our fields be counted
         in their thousands and tens of thousands,

144 a. Presumably caryatids.

may our cattle be stout and strong;
　　and may there be an end of raids and exile,
and of panic in our streets.

14

Happy the nation of whom this is true,
happy the nation whose God is Yahweh!

15

PSALM 145

Hymn of praise to Yahweh the king

Hymn	*Of David*	
Aleph	I sing your praises, God my King,	1
	I bless your name for ever and ever,	
Beth	blessing you day after day,	2
	and praising your name for ever and ever.	
Ghimel	Can anyone measure the magnificence	3
	of Yahweh the great, and his inexpressible grandeur?	
Daleth	Celebrating your acts of power,	4
	one age shall praise your doings to another.	
He	Oh, the splendour of your glory, your renown!	5
	I tell myself the story of your marvellous deeds.	
Waw	Men will proclaim your fearful power	6
	and I shall assert your greatness;	
Zain	they will celebrate your generous kindness	7
	and joyfully acclaim your righteousness.	
Heth	He, Yahweh, is merciful, tenderhearted,	8
	slow to anger, very loving,	
Teth	and universally kind; Yahweh's tenderness	9
	embraces all his creatures.	
Yod	Yahweh, all your creatures thank you,	10
	and your faithful bless you.	
Kaph	Kingly and glorious they proclaim you,	11
	they affirm your might.	
Lamed	Let mankind learn your acts of power,	12
	and the majestic glory of your sovereignty!	
Mem	Your sovereignty is an eternal sovereignty,	13
	your empire lasts from age to age.	
(Nun)	Always true to his promises,	
	Yahweh shows love in all he does.[a]	
Samek	Only stumble, and Yahweh at once supports you,	14
	if others bow you down, he will raise you up.	
Ain	Patiently all creatures look to you	15
	to feed them throughout the year;	
Pe	quick to satisfy every need,	16
	you feed them all with a generous hand.	
Sade	Righteous in all that he does,	17
	Yahweh acts only out of love,	
Qoph	standing close to all who invoke him,	18
	close to all who invoke Yahweh faithfully.	

| 19 | *Resh* | Those who fear him need only to ask to be answered;
he hears their cries for help and saves them. |
| 20 | *Shin* | Under his protection the pious are safe,
but Yahweh is destruction to the wicked. |

| 21 | *Tau* | Yahweh's praise be ever in my mouth,
and let every creature bless his holy name
    for ever and ever! |

PSALM 146

V 145

Hymn to the God of help

1   Alleluia!

Praise Yahweh, my soul!
2   I mean to praise Yahweh all my life,
I mean to sing to my God as long as I live.

3   Do not put your trust in men in power,
or in any mortal man—he cannot save,
4   he yields his breath and goes back to the earth he came from,
and on that day all his schemes perish.

5   Happy the man who has the God of Jacob to help him,
whose hope is fixed on Yahweh his God,
6   maker of heaven and earth,
and the sea, and all that these hold!

Yahweh, forever faithful,
7   gives justice to those denied it,
gives food to the hungry,
gives liberty to prisoners.

8a   Yahweh restores sight to the blind,
8b   Yahweh straightens the bent,
9a   Yahweh protects the stranger,
9b   he keeps the orphan and widow.

8c   Yahweh loves the virtuous,
9c   and frustrates the wicked.
10   Yahweh reigns for ever,
your God, Zion, from age to age.

PSALM 147

V 146-147

Hymn to the Almighty

Alleluia!

1   Praise Yahweh—it is good to sing
in honour of our God—sweet is his praise.

2   Yahweh, Restorer of Jerusalem!
He brought back Israel's exiles,
3   healing their broken hearts,
and binding up their wounds.

145 a. This verse is missing from the Hebrew and has been preserved in the versions

He decides the number of the stars 4
and gives each of them a name;
our Lord is great, all-powerful, 5
of infinite understanding.

Yahweh, who lifts up the humble, 6
humbles the wicked to the ground.

Sing to Yahweh in gratitude, 7
play the lyre for our God:

who covers the heavens with clouds, 8
to provide the earth with rain,
to produce fresh grass on the hillsides
and the plants that are needed by man,
who gives their food to the cattle 9
and to the young ravens when they cry.

The strength of the war horse means nothing to him, 10
it is not infantry that interests him.
Yahweh is interested only in those who fear him, 11
in those who rely on his love.

Praise Yahweh, Jerusalem, 12
Zion, praise your God:

for strengthening the bars of your gates, 13
for blessing your citizens,
for granting you peace on your frontiers, 14
for feeding you on the finest wheat.

He gives an order; 15
his word flashes to earth:
to spread snow like a blanket, 16
to strew hoarfrost like ashes,

to drop ice like breadcrumbs, 17
and when the cold is unbearable,
he sends his word to bring the thaw 18
and warm wind to melt the snow.

He reveals his word to Jacob, 19
his statutes and rulings to Israel:
he never does this for other nations, 20
he never reveals his rulings to them.

PSALM 148

Cosmic hymn of praise

Alleluia! 1

Let heaven praise Yahweh:
praise him, heavenly heights,
praise him, all his angels, 2
praise him, all his armies!

Praise him, sun and moon, 3
praise him, shining stars,
praise him, highest heavens, 4
and waters above the heavens!

Let them all praise the name of Yahweh, 5
at whose command they were created;

6 he has fixed them in their place for ever,
   by an unalterable statute.

7 Let earth praise Yahweh:
   sea-monsters and all the deeps,

8 fire and hail, snow and mist,
   gales that obey his decree,

9 mountains and hills,
   orchards and forests,

10 wild animals and farm animals,
   snakes and birds,

11 all kings on earth and nations,
   princes, all rulers in the world,

12 young men and girls,
   old people, and children too!

13 Let them all praise the name of Yahweh,
   for his name and no other is sublime,
   transcending earth and heaven in majesty,

14 raising the fortunes of his people,
   to the praises of the devout,
   of Israel, the people dear to him.

PSALM 149

Song of triumph

1 Alleluia!

   Sing Yahweh a new song,
   let the congregation of the faithful sing his praise!

2 Let Israel rejoice in his maker,
   and Zion's children exult in their King;

3 let them dance in praise of his name,
   playing to him on strings and drums!

4 For Yahweh has been kind to his people,
   conferring victory on us who are weak;

5 the faithful exult in triumph,
   prostrate before God they acclaim him

6 with panegyrics on their lips,
   and a two-edged sword in their hands

7 to exact vengeance on the pagans,
   to inflict punishment on the heathen,

8 to shackle their kings with chains
   and their nobles with fetters,

9 to execute the preordained sentence.*a*
   Thus gloriously are the faithful rewarded!

PSALM 150

Final chorus of praise*a*

1 Alleluia!

   Praise God in his Temple on earth,

149 a. In the prophetic books.
150 a. A grand doxology to close the Psalter.

praise him in his temple in heaven,
praise him for his mighty achievements,   2
praise him for his transcendent greatness!

Praise him with blasts of the trumpet,   3
praise him with lyre and harp,
praise him with drums and dancing,   4
praise him with strings and reeds,
praise him with clashing cymbals,   5
praise him with clanging cymbals!
Let everything that breathes praise Yahweh!   6

Alleluia!

INTRODUCTION
TO THE BOOK OF
PROVERBS

'The Book of Proverbs' is a compilation that includes works representing several centuries of thought. The main body of the book consists of a collection of short aphorisms introduced as 'Proverbs of Solomon' with an appendix of 'sayings' of other wise men, and a second collection of 'Further Proverbs of Solomon'. This part of the book (ch.10-29) can safely be dated before the Exile; much of it may well go back to Solomon's time and it may include some of the three thousand proverbs which the king is said to have invented (1 K 5:12).

However, the appendix to the second collection, 'sayings of Agur, numerical proverbs, sayings of Lemuel', appears to be later; and the long prologue to the book, commending wisdom, is post-exilic and probably dates from the 5th century B.C. The acrostic poem in praise of the ideal wife, which ends the book, is of unknown date. It will be noticed that the later writings show some development of doctrine beyond the predominantly worldly wisdom of the short aphorisms.

THE PROVERBS

Title and purpose of the book

1 The proverbs of Solomon son of David, king of Israel: 1

> for learning what wisdom and discipline are,   2
> for understanding words of deep meaning,
> for acquiring an enlightened attitude of mind   3
> —virtue, justice and fair-dealing;
> for teaching sound judgement to the ignorant,   4
> and knowledge and sense to the young;
> for perceiving the meaning of proverbs and obscure sayings,   6
> the sayings of the sages and their riddles.
> Let the wise listen and he will learn yet more,   5
> and the man of discernment will acquire the art of guidance.

> The fear of Yahweh is the beginning of knowledge;   7
> fools spurn wisdom and discipline.

I. PROLOGUE

A COMMENDATION OF WISDOM

The sage speaks: avoid bad company

> Listen, my son, to your father's instruction,   8
> do not reject your mother's teaching:
> they will be a crown of grace for your head,   9
> a circlet for your neck.
> My son, if sinners try to seduce you,   10
> do not give way.
> If they say, 'Come with us: 11
> there is blood to be had if we lie in wait for it,
> if we plan an ambush for the innocent;
> we can swallow them alive, like Sheol,   12
> alive and whole like those who go down to the Pit.
> We shall find treasures of every sort,   13
> we shall fill our houses with plunder;
> throw in your lot with us: 14
> one purse between us all.'
> My son, do not follow them in their way,   15
> keep your steps out of their path
> (for their feet hasten to evil,   16
> they are quick to shed blood);
> the net is always spread in vain   17
> if the bird is watching.

18   It is for their own blood these men lie in wait,
          their own selves they lie in ambush for.
19   To this come all men who are after dishonest gain,
          which robs of their lives all those who take it for their own.

Wisdom speaks: a warning to the heedless

20   Wisdom calls aloud in the streets,
          she raises her voice in the public squares;
21   she calls out at the street corners,
          she delivers her message at the city gates,
22   'You ignorant people, how much longer will you cling to
              your ignorance?
          How much longer will mockers revel in their mocking
          and fools hold knowledge contemptible?
23   Pay attention to my warning:
          now I will pour out my heart to you,
          and tell you what I have to say.
24   Since I have called and you have refused me,
          since I have beckoned and no one has taken notice,
25   since you have ignored all my advice
          and rejected all my warnings,
26   I, for my part, will laugh at your distress,
          I will jeer at you when calamity comes,
27   when calamity bears down on you like a storm
          and your distress like a whirlwind,
          when disaster and anguish bear down on you.
28   Then they shall call to me, but I will not answer,
          they shall seek me eagerly and shall not find me.
29   They despised knowledge,
          they had no love for the fear of Yahweh,
30   they would take no advice from me,
          and spurned all my warnings:
31   so they must eat the fruits of their own courses,
          and choke themselves with their own scheming.
32   For the errors of the ignorant lead to their death,
          and the complacency of fools works their own ruin;
33   but whoever listens to me may live secure,
          he will have quiet, fearing no mischance.'

Wisdom, a safeguard against bad company

1 **2**   My son, if you take my words to heart,
          if you set store by my commandments,
2   tuning your ear to wisdom,
          and applying your heart to truth:
3   yes, if your plea is for clear perception,
          if you cry out for discernment,
4   if you look for it as if it were silver,
          and search for it as for buried treasure,
5   you will then understand what the fear of Yahweh is,
          and discover the knowledge of God.
6   For Yahweh himself is giver of wisdom,
          from his mouth issue knowledge and discernment.
7   He keeps his help for honest men,
          he is the shield of those whose ways are honourable;
8   he stands guard over the paths of justice,
          he keeps watch on the way of his devoted ones.

Then you will understand what virtue is, justice, and fair dealing,   9
    all paths that lead to happiness.

When wisdom comes into your heart   10
    and knowledge is a delight to you,
then prudence will be there to watch over you,   11
    and discernment be your guardian
to keep you from the way that is evil,   12
    from the man whose speech is deceitful,
from those who leave the paths of honesty   13
    to walk the roads of darkness:
men who find their joy in doing wrong,   14
    and their delight in deceitfulness,
whose tracks are twisted,   15
    and the paths that they tread crooked.
Keeping you also from the alien woman,   16
    from the stranger, with her wheedling words;
she has left the partner of her younger days,   17
    she has forgotten the covenant of God;
towards death her house is declining,   18
    down to the Shades her paths go.
Of those who go to her not one returns,   19
    they never regain the paths of life.

So you will pursue the way of good men,   20
    persisting in the paths of the virtuous.
For the land will be for honest men to live in   21
    the innocent will have it for their home;
while the wicked will be cut off from the land,   22
    and the faithless rooted out of it.

How to acquire wisdom

3 My son, do not forget my teaching,   1
    let your heart keep my principles,
for these will give you lengthier days,   2
    longer years of life, and greater happiness.

Let kindliness and loyalty never leave you: 3
    tie them round your neck,
    write them on the tablet of your heart.
So shall you enjoy favour and good repute   4
    in the sight of God and man.
Trust wholeheartedly in Yahweh,   5
    put no faith in your own perception;
in every course you take, have him in mind: 6
    he will see that your paths are smooth.
Do not think of yourself as wise,   7
    fear Yahweh and turn your back on evil:
health-giving, this, to your body,   8
    relief to your bones.
Honour Yahweh with what goods you have   9
    and with the first-fruits of all your returns;
then your barns will be filled with wheat,   10
    your vats overflowing with new wine.

My son, do not scorn correction from Yahweh,   11
    do not resent his rebuke;
for Yahweh reproves the man he loves,   12
    as a father checks a well-loved son.

The joys of wisdom

13   Happy the man who discovers wisdom,
         the man who gains discernment:

14   gaining her is more rewarding than silver,
         more profitable than gold.

15   She is beyond the price of pearls,
         nothing you could covet is her equal.

16   In her right hand is length of days;
         in her left hand, riches and honour.

17   Her ways are delightful ways,
         her paths all lead to contentment.

18   She is a tree of life for those who hold her fast,
         those who cling to her live happy lives.

19   By wisdom, Yahweh set the earth on its foundations,
         by discernment, he fixed the heavens firm.

20   Through his knowledge the depths were carved out,
         and the clouds rain down the dew.

21   My son, hold to sound judgment and to prudence,
         do not let them out of your sight;

22   they will prove the life of your soul,
         an ornament round your neck.

23   You will go on your way in safety,
         your feet will not stumble.

24   When you sit down, you will not be afraid,
         when you lie down, sweet will be your sleep.

25   Have no fear of sudden terror
         or of assault from wicked men,

26   since Yahweh will be your guarantor,
         he will keep your steps from the snare.

27   Do not refuse a kindness to anyone who begs it,
         if it is in your power to perform it.

28   Do not say to your neighbour, 'Go away! Come another time!
         I will give it you tomorrow', if you can do it now.

29   Do not plot harm against your neighbour
         as he lives unsuspecting next door.

30   Do not pick a groundless quarrel with a man
         who has done you no harm.

31   Do not emulate the man of violence,
         never model your conduct on his;

32   for the wilful wrong-doer is abhorrent to Yahweh,
         who confides only in honest men.

33   Yahweh's curse lies on the house of the wicked,
         but he blesses the home of the virtuous.

34   He mocks those who mock,
         but accords his favour to the humble.

35   Honour is the portion of the wise,
         all that fools inherit is disgrace.

On choosing wisdom

1   **4**   Listen, my sons, to a father's instruction;
         pay attention, and learn what clear perception is.

2   What I am commending to you is sound doctrine:
         do not discard my teaching.

3   I too was once a son with a father,
         in my mother's eyes a tender child, unique.

This was what he used to teach me,   4
'Let your heart treasure what I have to say,
    keep my principles and you shall live;
acquire wisdom, acquire perception,   5
    never forget her, never deviate from my words.
Do not desert her, she will keep you safe,   6
    love her, she will watch over you.
The beginning of wisdom? The acquisition of wisdom;   7
    at the cost of all you have, acquire perception.
Hold her close, and she will make you great;   8
    embrace her, and she will be your pride;
she will set a crown of grace on your head,   9
    present you with a glorious diadem.'

Listen, my son, take my words to heart,   10
    and the years of your life shall be multiplied.
I have educated you in the ways of wisdom,   11
    I have guided you along the paths of honesty.
As you walk, your going will be unhindered,   12
    as you run, you will not stumble.
Hold fast to discipline, never let her go,   13
    keep your eyes on her, she is your life.
Never set your foot on the path of the wicked,   14
    do not walk the way that the evil go.
Avoid it, do not take it,   15
    turn your back on it, pass it by.
For they cannot sleep unless they have first done wrong,   16
    they miss their sleep if they have not brought someone down;
wickedness is the bread they eat,   17
    and violence the wine they drink.

The path of the virtuous is like the light of dawn,   18
    its brightness growing to the fulness of day;
the way of the wicked is as dark as night,   19
    they cannot tell what it is they stumble over.

My son, pay attention to my words,   20
    listen carefully to the words I say;
do not let them out of your sight,   21
    keep them deep in your heart.
They are life to those who grasp them,   22
    health for the entire body.
More than all else, keep watch over your heart,   23
    since here are the wellsprings of life.
Turn your back on the mouth that misleads,   24
    keep your distance from lips that deceive.
Let your eyes be fixed ahead,   25
    your gaze be straight before you.
Let the path you tread be level   26
    and all your ways made firm.
Turn neither to right nor to left,   27
    keep your foot clear of evil.

Flight from the seductress. Where the wise man's love should be

5   My son, pay attention to my wisdom,   1
    listen carefully to what I know,
and so have prudence and knowledge to protect you;   2
    these will keep a guard on your lips.

Take no notice of a loose-living woman,
3   for the lips of this alien drip with honey,
        her words are smoother than oil,
4   but their outcome is bitter as wormwood,
        sharp as a two-edged sword.
5   Her feet go down to death,
        her steps lead down to Sheol;
6   far from following the path of life,
        her ways are undirected, irresponsible.

7   And now, my son, listen to me,
        never deviate from what I say:
8   set your course as far from her as possible,
        go nowhere near the door of her house,
9   or you will surrender your honour to others,
        your years to one who has no pity,
10   and strangers will batten on your property,
        your labours going to some alien house,
11   and, at your ending,
        when body and flesh are consumed,
12   you will groan •and exclaim,
     'Alas, I hated discipline,
        my heart spurned all correction;
13   I would not hear the voice of my masters,
        I would not listen to those who tried to teach me.
14   Now I am all but reduced to the depths of misery,
        in the presence of the whole community.'

15   Drink the water from your own cistern,
        fresh water from your own well.*a*
16   Do not let your fountains flow to waste elsewhere,
        nor your streams in the public streets.
17   Let them be for yourself alone,
        not for strangers at the same time.
18   And may your fountain-head be blessed!

     Find joy with the wife you married in your youth,
19   fair as a hind, graceful as a fawn.
        Let hers be the company you keep,
        hers the breasts that ever fill you with delight,
        hers the love that ever holds you captive.
20   Why be seduced, my son, by an alien woman,
        and fondle the breast of a woman who is a stranger?
21   For the eyes of Yahweh observe a man's ways
        and survey all his paths.
22   The wicked man is snared in his own misdeeds,
        is caught in the meshes of his own sin.
23   For want of discipline, he dies,
        and is lost through his own excessive folly.

On surety rashly offered

1
6   My son, if you have gone surety for your neighbour,
        if you have guaranteed the bond of a stranger,
2   if you have committed yourself with your own lips,
        if through words of yours you have been entrapped,

---

5 a. I.e., keep to your lawful wife.

do this, my son, to extricate yourself—　　　　　　3
　since you have put yourself in the power of your neighbour:
go, go quickly, and plead with your neighbour,
give your eyes no sleep,　　　　　　　　　　　　4
　your eyelids no rest,
break free like a gazelle from the trap,　　　　　　5
　like a bird from the snare.

The idler and the ant

Idler, go to the ant;　　　　　　　　　　　　6
　ponder her ways and grow wise:
no one gives her orders,　　　　　　　　　　　7
　no overseer, no master,
yet all through the summer she makes sure of her food,　8
　and gathers her supplies at harvest time.
How long do you intend to lie there, idler?　　　　9
　When are you going to rise from your sleep?
A little sleep, a little drowsiness,　　　　　　　10
　a little folding of the arms to take life easier,
and like a vagrant, poverty is at your elbow　　　　11
　and, like a beggar, want.

Portrait of a scoundrel

A scoundrel, a vicious man,　　　　　　　　　12
　he goes with a leer on his lips,
winking his eye, shuffling his foot,　　　　　　　13
　beckoning with his finger.
Deceit in his heart, always scheming evil,　　　　14
　he sows dissension.
Disaster will overtake him sharply for this,　　　　15
　suddenly, irretrievably, his fall will come.

Seven things hateful to God*a*

There are six things that Yahweh hates,　　　　　16
　seven that his soul abhors:
a haughty look, a lying tongue,　　　　　　　　17
　hands that shed innocent blood,
a heart that weaves wicked plots,　　　　　　　18
　feet that hurry to do evil,
a false witness who lies with every breath,　　　　19
　a man who sows dissension among brothers.

More fatherly advice

Keep your father's principle, my son,　　　　　20
　do not spurn your mother's teaching.
Bind them ever to your heart,　　　　　　　　21
　tie them round your neck.
When you walk, these will guide you,　　　　　22
　when you lie down, watch over you,
　when you wake, talk with you.

For this principle is a lamp,　　　　　　　　　23
　this teaching is a light;
correction and discipline are the way to life,
preserving you from the woman subject to a husband,　24
　from the smooth tongue of the woman who is a stranger

25   Do not covet her beauty in your heart
      or let her captivate you with the play of her eyes;

26   a harlot can be bought for a hunk of bread,
      but the adulteress is aiming to catch a precious life.

27   Can a man hug fire to his breast
      without setting his clothes alight?

28   Can a man walk on red-hot coals
      without burning his feet?

29   So it is the man who consorts with his neighbour's wife:
      no one who touches her will go unpunished.

30   Men attach small blame to the thief
      who in hunger steals to fill his belly;

31   though, once caught, he must pay back sevenfold,
      and has to hand over all his family resources.

32   But the adulterer has no sense;
      act like him, and court your own destruction.

33   All he gets is blows and insults,
      and disgrace that will not be blotted out.

34   For jealousy inflames the husband
      who will show no mercy when the day comes for revenge,

35   he will not consider any compensation,
      lavish what gifts you may, he will not be placated.

7

1   My son, keep my words,
      and treasure my principles,

2   keep my principles and you will live,
      keep my teaching as the apple of your eye.

3   Bind these to your fingers,
      write them on the tablet of your heart.

4   To Wisdom say, 'My sister!'
      Call Perception your dearest friend,

5   to preserve you from the alien woman,
      from the stranger, with her wheedling words.

6   From the window of her house
      she looked out on the street,

7   to see if among the men, young and callow,
      there was one young man who had no sense at all.

8   And now he passes down the lane, and comes near her corner,
      reaching the path to her house

9   at twilight when day is declining,
      at dead of night and in the dark.

10   But look, the woman comes to meet him,
      dressed like a harlot, wrapped in a veil.

11   She is loud and brazen;
      her feet cannot rest at home.

12   Now in the street, now in the square,
      she is on the look-out at every corner.

13   She catches hold of him, she kisses him,
      the bold-faced creature says to him,

14   'I had to offer sacrifices:
      I discharged my vows today,

15   that is why I came out to meet you,
      to look for you, and now I have found you.

16   I have made my bed gay with quilts,
      spread the best Egyptian sheets,

---

6 a. 'Numerical proverb', a favourite form; there is a series of them in ch.30.

I have sprinkled my bed with myrrh, 17
  with aloes and with cinnamon.
Come, let us drink deep of love until the morning, 18
  and abandon ourselves to delight.
For my husband is not at home, 19
  he has gone on a very long journey,
taking his moneybags with him; 20
  he will not be back until the moon is full.'
With her persistent coaxing she entices him, 21
  draws him on with her seductive patter.
Bemused, he follows her 22
  like an ox being led to the slaughter,
like a stag caught in a noose,
  till he is pierced to the liver by an arrow, 23
like a bird darting into a snare
  not knowing its life is at stake.
And now, my son, listen to me, 24
  pay attention to the words I have to say:
do not let your heart stray into her ways, 25
  or wander into her paths;
she has done so many to death, 26
  and the strongest have all been her victims.
Her house is the way to Sheol, 27
  the descent to the courts of death.

Wisdom again personified

8 Does Wisdom not call meanwhile? 1
  Does Discernment not lift up her voice?
On the hilltop, on the road, 2
  at the crossways, she takes her stand;
beside the gates of the city, 3
  at the approaches to the gates she cries aloud,
'O men! I am calling to you; 4
  my cry goes out to the sons of men.
You ignorant ones! Study discretion; 5
  and you fools, come to your senses!
Listen, I have serious things to tell you, 6
  from my lips come honest words.
My mouth proclaims the truth, 7
  wickedness is hateful to my lips.
All the words I say are right, 8
  nothing twisted in them, nothing false,
all straightforward to him who understands, 9
  honest to those who know what knowledge means.
Accept my discipline rather than silver, 10
  knowledge in preference to pure gold.
For wisdom is more precious than pearls, 11
  and nothing else is so worthy of desire.

Wisdom sings her own praises. Wisdom, the guide of kings

'I, Wisdom, am mistress of discretion, 12
  the inventor of lucidity of thought.
Good advice and sound judgement belong to me, 14
  perception to me, strength to me.
(To fear Yahweh is to hate evil.) 13
  I hate pride and arrogance,

	wicked behaviour and a lying mouth.
17	I love those who love me;
	those who seek me eagerly shall find me.
15	By me monarchs rule
	and princes issue just laws;
16	by me rulers govern,
	and the great impose justice on the world.
18	With me are riches and honour,
	lasting wealth and justice.
19	The fruit I give is better than gold, even the finest,
	the return I make is better than pure silver.
20	I walk in the way of virtue,
	in the paths of justice,
21	enriching those who love me,
	filling their treasuries.

Wisdom as creator

22	'Yahweh created me when his purpose first unfolded,
	before the oldest of his works.
23	From everlasting I was firmly set,
	from the beginning, before earth came into being.
24	The deep*a* was not, when I was born,
	there were no springs to gush with water.
25	Before the mountains were settled,
	before the hills, I came to birth;
26	before he made the earth, the countryside,
	or the first grains of the world's dust.
27	When he fixed the heavens firm, I was there,
	when he drew a ring on the surface of the deep,
28	when he thickened the clouds above,
	when he fixed fast the springs of the deep,
29	when he assigned the sea its boundaries
	—and the waters will not invade the shore—
	when he laid down the foundations of the earth,
30	I was by his side, a master craftsman,
	delighting him day after day,
	ever at play in his presence,
31	at play everywhere in his world,
	delighting to be with the sons of men.

The great invitation

32a	'And now, my sons, listen to me;
33	listen to instruction and learn to be wise,
	do not ignore it.
32b	Happy those who keep my ways!
34	Happy the man who listens to me,
	who day after day watches at my gates
	to guard the portals.
35	For the man who finds me finds life,
	he will win favour from Yahweh;
36	but he who does injury to me does hurt to his own soul,
	all who hate me are in love with death.'

8 a. 'The waters under the earth'.

Wisdom as hostess

9

Wisdom has built herself a house,
    she has erected her seven pillars,   1

she has slaughtered her beasts, prepared her wine,   2
    she has laid her table.

She has despatched her maidservants   3
    and proclaimed from the city's heights:

'Who is ignorant? Let him step this way.'   4
    To the fool she says,

'Come and eat my bread,   5
    drink the wine I have prepared!

Leave your folly and you will live,   6
    walk in the ways of perception.'

Against cynics

Correct a mocker and you make an enemy;   7
    rebuke a wicked man, you get insult in return.

Do not rebuke the mocker, he will only hate you,   8
    rebuke a wise man and he will love you for it.

Be open with the wise, he grows wiser still,   9
    teach a virtuous man, he will learn yet more.

The fear of Yahweh is the beginning of wisdom;   10
    the knowledge of the Holy One—perception indeed!

For days are multiplied by me   11
    and years of life increased.

Are you wise? It is to your advantage.   12
    A mocker? The burden is yours alone.

Dame Folly apes Wisdom

Dame Folly acts on impulse,   13
    is childish and knows nothing.

She sits at the door of her house,   14
    on a throne commanding the city,

inviting the passers-by   15
    as they pass on their lawful occasions,

'Who is ignorant? Let him step this way.'   16
    To the fool she says,

'Stolen waters are sweet,   17
    and bread tastes better when eaten in secret'.

The fellow does not realise that here the Shades are gathered,   18
    that her guests are heading for the valleys of Sheol.

II. THE MAJOR COLLECTION ATTRIBUTED
TO SOLOMON[a]

10 The proverbs of Solomon.   1

A wise son is his father's joy,
    a foolish son his mother's grief.

Treasures wickedly come by give no benefit,   2
    but right conduct brings delivery from death.

Yahweh does not leave the virtuous man hungry,   3
    but he thwarts the greed of the wicked.

4   The slack hand brings poverty,
       but the diligent hand brings wealth.

5   Gathering in summer is the mark of the prudent,
       sleeping at harvest is the sign of the shameless.

6   The blessings of Yahweh are on the head of the virtuous man,
       premature mourning stops the mouths of the wicked.

7   The virtuous man is remembered with blessings,
       the wicked man's name rots away.

8   The heart that is wise is obedient to instruction,
       the gabbling fool is heading for ruin.

9   He walks secure whose ways are honourable,
       but he who follows crooked ways is soon discovered.

10   A wink of the eye and a man makes trouble,
       a bold rebuke, and a man makes peace.

11   The mouth of the virtuous man is a life-giving fountain,
       violence lurks in the mouth of the wicked.

12   Hatred provokes disputes,
       love covers over all offences.

13   On the lips of a discerning man is wisdom found,
       on the back of a fool, the stick.

14   Wise men store up knowledge,
       but the mouth of a fool makes ruin imminent.

15   The rich man's wealth is his stronghold,
       poverty is the poor man's undoing.

16   The virtuous man's wage affords him life,
       but destruction is all the wicked man earns.

17   The path of life is to abide by discipline,
       and he who ignores correction goes astray.

18   The lips of just men silence hatred,
       he who voices slander is a fool.

19   A flood of words is never without its fault,
       he who has his lips controlled is a prudent man.

20   The virtuous man's tongue is purest silver,
       the heart of the wicked is of trumpery value.

21   The lips of the virtuous man nourish a multitude,
       but fools die in poverty.

22   The blessing of Yahweh is what brings riches,
       to this hard toil has nothing to add.

23   The joy of the fool lies in doing wrong,
       but the joy of the man of discernment in acquiring wisdom.

24   What the wicked man fears overtakes him,
       what the virtuous desires comes to him as a present.

10 a. Probably the oldest collection in the book.

When the storm is over, the wicked man is no more,   25
    but the virtuous stands firm for ever.

As vinegar to the teeth, smoke to the eyes,   26
    so the sluggard to the one who sends him.

The fear of Yahweh adds length to life,   27
    the years of the wicked will be cut short.

The hope of virtuous men is all joy,   28
    the expectations of the wicked are frustrated.

Yahweh is a stronghold for the man of honest life,   29
    for evildoers nothing but ruin.

The virtuous man will never be moved from his own place,   30
    but the land will offer no home for the wicked.

The mouth of the virtuous man utters wisdom,   31
    the deceitful tongue shall be torn out.

The lips of the virtuous man drip with kindness,   32
    the mouth of the wicked with deceit.

11   A false balance is abhorrent to Yahweh,   1
    a just weight is pleasing to him.

Pride comes first, disgrace comes after;   2
    with the humble is wisdom found.

Honest men have their own honesty for guidance,   3
    treacherous men are ruined by their own perfidy.

In the day of wrath riches will be of no advantage,   4
    but virtuous conduct delivers from death.

The virtues of the blameless man smooth the way before him,   5
    the wicked man founders in his own wickedness.

Their virtuous conduct sets honest men free,   6
    treacherous men are imprisoned by their own desires.

The hope of the wicked perishes with death,   7
    the expectation of the godless is frustrated.

The virtuous man escapes misfortune,   8
    the wicked man incurs it instead.

Through his mouth the godless man is the ruin of his neighbour,   9
    but by knowledge the virtuous are safeguarded.

When virtuous men prosper the city rejoices,   10
    there are glad cries, too, when the wicked are ruined.

A city is raised on the blessing of honest men,   11
    and demolished by the mouth of the wicked.

Who scoffs at his neighbour is a fool;   12
    the man of discernment holds his tongue.

A tittle-tattler lets secrets out,   13
    a trustworthy man keeps things hidden.

For want of guidance a people fails,   14
    safety lies in many advisers.

15 He who goes bail for a stranger will rue it,
the man who hates going surety is safe.

16 A gracious woman brings honour to her husband,
she who has no love for justice is dishonour enthroned.

The indolent lack resources,
men of enterprise grow rich.

17 The generous man is his own benefactor,
a cruel man injures his own flesh.

18 The livelihood won by the wicked is illusory,
he who sows virtue reaps a solid reward.

19 A virtuous man may count on life,
the pursuer of evil on death.

20 Men of depraved heart are abhorrent to Yahweh,
dear to him, those whose ways are blameless.

21 Be sure of it, a wicked man will not go unpunished,
but the race of the virtuous will come to no harm.

22 A golden ring in the snout of a pig
is a lovely woman who lacks discretion.

23 The desire of the virtuous ends in happiness,
the hope of the wicked is in vain.

24 One is extravagant, yet his riches grow,
another excessively mean, but only grows the poorer.

25 The generous soul will prosper,
he who waters, will be watered.

26 The people's curse is on the man who hoards the wheat,
a blessing on him who sells it.

27 He who strives after good is striving after favour,
he who looks for evil will have evil come to him.

28 He who trusts in riches will have his fall,
the virtuous will flourish like the leaves.

29 He who misgoverns his house inherits the wind,
and the fool becomes slave to the wise.

30 From fruits of virtue grows a tree of life;
the wicked are carried off before their time.

31 If here on earth the virtuous man gets his due,
how much more the wicked, how much the sinner!

12

1 He who loves discipline, loves knowledge,
stupid is the man who hates correction.

2 The good man wins the favour of Yahweh,
but he condemns the man who is a schemer.

3 No man is made secure by wickedness,
but nothing shakes the roots of virtuous men.

4 A good wife, her husband's crown,
a shameless wife, a cancer in his bones.

5 The plans of virtuous men are honest,
the intrigues of the wicked are nothing if not deceit.

The words of wicked men are snares to shed blood, 6
    but honest men have an answer and elude them.

Once thrown down, the wicked are no more, 7
    but the house of virtuous men stands firm.

The praise of a man is in proportion to his prudence, 8
    men of depraved heart are held in contempt.

Better a common man who does his own work 9
    than one who plays the lord and goes short of bread.

The virtuous man looks after the lives of his beasts, 10
    but the wicked man's heart is ruthless.

He who tills his land shall have bread and to spare, 11
    he who chases fantasies has no sense.

The desires of the godless are sickly, 12
    the roots of the devout are firmly set.

His own lips are to blame when the wicked man is entrapped, 13
    the virtuous man finds his own way out of misfortune.

When a man is filled with good things, it is the fruit of his own words, 14
    each man's labour brings its own return.

In the eyes of a fool the way he goes is right, 15
    the wise man listens to advice.

The fool shows his displeasure straight away, 16
    the discreet man overlooks the insult.

To tell the truth is to further justice, 17
    a false witness is nothing but deceit.

There are some whose thoughtless words pierce like a sword, 18
    but the tongue of the wise brings healing.

Lips that tell the truth abide firm for ever, 19
    the tongue that lies lasts only for a moment.

Bitterness is in the heart of the schemer, 20
    joy with those who give counsels of peace.

No harm can come to the virtuous man, 21
    but the wicked have their fill of troubles.

Lips that lie are abhorrent to Yahweh; 22
    dear to him those who speak the truth.

The man of discretion keeps his knowledge hidden, 23
    the heart of fools proclaims their folly.

For the diligent hand, authority; 24
    for the slack hand, forced labour.

Worry makes a man's heart heavy, 25
    a kindly word makes it glad.

An impartial arbiter is his own best friend; 26
    the way of the wicked leads them astray.

The idle man has no game to roast: 27
    diligence is a man's most precious possession.

28   Life lies along the path of virtue,
        the way of the vicious leads to death.

13

1   A wise son loves discipline,
        a mocker will not listen to reproof.

2   When a man has good things to eat, it is the fruit of his own words,
        but the appetite of the treacherous feeds on violence.

3   He keeps his life who guards his mouth,
        he who talks too much is lost.

4   The idler yearns, but there is no food for him;
        hard workers get their fill.

5   The virtuous man hates lying words,
        but the wicked man slanders and defames.

6   Virtue preserves the man of honest life,
        wickedness proves the ruin of the sinner.

7   There are some who, on nothing, pretend to be rich,
        some, with great wealth, pretend to be poor.

8   A man's wealth may ransom his life,
        but the poor man sees no threat.

9   The light of virtuous men burns bright,
        the lamp of the wicked goes out.

10   Insolence breeds disputes;
        with the humble is wisdom found.

11   A sudden fortune will dwindle away,
        he grows rich who accumulates little by little.

12   Hope deferred makes the heart sick,
        desire fulfilled is a tree of life.

13   He who despises the word will destroy himself,
        he who respects the commandment will be safe.

14   The wise man's teaching is a life-giving fountain,
        for eluding the snares of death.

15   Intelligent prudence secures favour,
        the way of the treacherous is hard.

16   Every man of discretion acts by the light of knowledge,
        the fool parades his folly.

17   A malicious messenger means a fall into misfortune,
        a trusty envoy heals.

18   For the man who rejects discipline: poverty and disgrace;
        for the man who accepts correction: honour.

19   Desire fulfilled is sweet to the soul;
        fools are loth to turn from evil.

20   Make the wise your companions and you grow wise yourself;
        make fools your friends and suffer for it.

21   Misfortune dogs the sinner;
        good fortune rewards the virtuous.

22   The good man bequeaths his heritage to his children's children,
        the wealth of the sinner is stored up for the virtuous.

The poor man's fallow yields food in plenty;　　　　　23
　　there are some who perish when justice fails.

The man who fails to use the stick hates his son;　　　24
　　the man who is free with his correction loves him.

The virtuous man eats to his heart's content,　　　　25
　　the belly of the wicked goes empty.

14

Wisdom builds herself a house;　　　　　　　　　　1
　　with her own hands Folly pulls it down.

He whose course is honest fears Yahweh,　　　　　　2
　　he whose paths are crooked scorns him.

The fool's mouth contains a rod of pride,　　　　　3
　　the wise man's lips watch over him.

No oxen, no cattle-feed;　　　　　　　　　　　　4
　　stout ox, rich crop.

The truthful witness tells no lies,　　　　　　　　5
　　the false witness lies with every breath.

In vain the mocker looks for wisdom,　　　　　　　6
　　knowledge comes easy to the discerning man.

Keep well clear of the fool,　　　　　　　　　　7
　　you will not find wise lips there.

To the man of discretion, wisdom means a watch on his own conduct, 8
　　but the folly of fools is delusion.

God mocks the wicked,　　　　　　　　　　　　9
　　he shows favour to honest men.

The heart knows its own grief best,　　　　　　　10
　　nor can a stranger share its joy.

The house of the wicked shall be destroyed,　　　　11
　　the tent of honest men will stand firm.

There is a way that some think right,　　　　　　12
　　but it leads in the end to death.

Even in laughter the heart finds sadness,　　　　　13
　　and joy makes way for sorrow.

The unstable heart is satisfied with its own ways,　　14
　　the good man with his own hard work.

The simpleton believes what he is told,　　　　　　15
　　the man of discretion watches how he treads.

The wise man sees evil coming and avoids it,　　　16
　　the fool is rash and presumptuous.

A quick-tempered man commits rash acts,　　　　　17
　　the prudent man will be long-suffering.

Simpletons have folly for their portion,　　　　　18
　　men of discretion knowledge for their crown.

The evil bow down before the good,　　　　　　　19
　　the wicked, at the gates of the virtuous.

20 The poor man is detestable even to his neighbour,
      but the rich man has friends and to spare.

21 He who looks down on his neighbour sins,
      blessed is he who takes pity on the poor.

22 To be a schemer, is this not evil?
      Lay worthy plans, and kindliness and loyalty await you.

23 Hard work always yields its profit,
      idle talk brings only want.

24 Sound judgement is the crown of the wise,
      folly the diadem of fools.

25 A truthful witness is a saver of lives,
      he who utters lies is an impostor.

26 Fear of Yahweh gives good grounds for confidence,
      in him his children find a refuge.

27 The fear of Yahweh is a life-giving spring,
      for eluding the snares of death.

28 A king's majesty shows in the numbers of his people,
      with few to rule, a prince is ruined.

29 The equable man is full of discernment,
      the hasty is more than foolish.

30 The life of the body is a tranquil heart,
      but envy is a cancer in the bones.

31 To oppress the poor is to insult his creator,
      to be kind to the needy is to honour him.

32 The wicked man is overthrown by his own malice,
      the virtuous finds shelter in his integrity.

33 In the hearts of discerning men wisdom makes her home,
      within the fool she has no place at all.

34 Virtue makes a nation great,
      by sin whole races are disgraced.

35 A clever servant enjoys the favour of the king,
      he uses his shrewdness to avoid disgrace.

15

1 A mild answer turns away wrath,
     sharp words stir up anger.

2 The tongue of wise men distils knowledge,
     the mouth of fools spews folly.

3 The eyes of Yahweh are everywhere:
     observing the evil and the good.

4 The tongue that soothes is a tree of life;
     the barbed tongue, a breaker of hearts.

5 He who spurns his father's discipline is a fool,
     he who accepts correction is discreet.

6 In the house of the virtuous there is no lack of treasure,
     the earnings of the wicked are fraught with anxiety.

Wise men's lips keep guard on knowledge,   7
not so the heart of fools.

The sacrifice of the wicked is abhorrent to Yahweh,   8
dear to him is the prayer of honest men.

The conduct of the wicked is abhorrent to Yahweh,   9
but he loves the man who makes virtue his goal.

Correction is severe for him who leaves the way;   10
he who hates being reprimanded will die.

Sheol and Perdition lie open to Yahweh;   11
how much more the hearts of mankind!

The mocker does not care to be reprimanded,   12
he will not choose the wise for his companions.

Glad heart means happy face,   13
where the heart is sad the spirit is broken.

The heart of the discerning makes knowledge its search,   14
the mouth of fools feeds on folly.

For the sorrowing every day is evil,   15
for the joyous heart it is festival always.

Better to have little and with it fear of Yahweh   16
than to have treasure and with it anxiety.

Better a dish of herbs when love is there   17
than a fattened ox and hatred to go with it.

The hot-headed man provokes disputes,   18
the equable man allays dissension.

The way of the lazy is strewn with thorns,   19
the path of the industrious is a broad highway.

A wise son is his father's joy,   20
a foolish man despises his mother.

Folly appeals to a man with no sense,   21
the man of discernment goes straight forward.

Without deliberation plans come to nothing,   22
where counsellors are many plans succeed.

When a man has a ready answer he has joy too: 23
how satisfying is the apt reply!

The upward path to life is for the wise man,   24
that he may avoid Sheol below.

Yahweh pulls down the house of the proud,   25
but he keeps the widow's boundaries intact.

Wicked scheming is abhorrent to Yahweh,   26
but words that are kind are pure.

He who seeks dishonest gain brings trouble on his house,   27
he who hates bribes shall have life.

The heart of the virtuous man contemplates kind actions,   28
the mouth of wicked men spews out malice.

29   Yahweh stands far from the wicked,
        but he listens to the prayers of the virtuous.

30   A kindly glance gives joy to the heart,
        good news lends strength to the bones.

31   The ear attentive to wholesome correction
        finds itself at home in the company of the wise.

32   He who rejects discipline despises his own self;
        he who listens to correction wins discernment.

33   The fear of Yahweh is a school of wisdom,
        humility goes before honour.

16

1   Man's heart makes the plans,
        Yahweh gives the answer.

2   A man's conduct may strike him as pure,
        Yahweh, however, weighs the motives.

3   Commend what you do to Yahweh,
        and your plans will find achievement.

4   Yahweh made everything for its own purpose,
        yes, even the wicked for the day of disaster.

5   The arrogant heart is abhorrent to Yahweh,
        be sure it will not go unpunished.

6   By kindliness and loyalty atonement is made for sin;
        with the fear of Yahweh goes avoidance of evil.

7   Let Yahweh be pleased with a man's way of life
        and he makes his very enemies into friends.

8   Better have little and with it virtue,
        than great revenues and no right to them.

9   A man's heart plans out his way
        but it is Yahweh who makes his steps secure.

10   The lips of the king utter oracles,
        he does not err when he speaks in judgement.

11   To Yahweh belong the balance and scales,
        all the weights in the bag are of his making.

12   Evil-doing is abhorrent to kings,
        since virtue is the throne's foundation.

13   Virtuous lips are welcome to a king,
        he loves a man of honest words.

14   The king's wrath is the herald of death,
        but a wise man will appease it.

15   When the king's face brightens it spells life,
        his favour is like the rain in spring.

16   Better gain wisdom than gold,
        choose discernment rather than silver.

17   To turn from evil is the way of honest men;
        he keeps his life safe who watches where he goes.

Pride goes before destruction,   18
    a haughty spirit before a fall.

Better be humble among the lowly   19
    than share the booty with the proud.

He who listens closely to the word shall find happiness;   20
    he who puts his trust in Yahweh is blessed.

He whose heart is wise is proclaimed discerning;   21
    sweetness of speech makes words the more persuasive.

Shrewdness is a fountain of life for its possessor,   22
    the folly of fools is their own punishment.

The wise man's heart lends shrewdness to his mouth   23
    and makes his words more persuasive.

Kindly words are a honeycomb,   24
    sweet to the taste, wholesome to the body.

There is a way that some think right,   25
    but it leads in the end to death.

A worker's appetite works on his behalf,   26
    his hungry mouth drives him on.

A scoundrel digs deep for mischief-making,   27
    on his lips is a fire that scorches.

A troublemaker sows strife,   28
    a talebearer divides friend from friend.

A violent man lures his neighbour astray   29
    and leads him by a way that is not good.

He who closes his eyes meditates mischief;   30
    he who purses his lips has already done wrong.

White hairs are a crown of honour,   31
    they are found in the paths of virtue.

Better an equable man than a hero,   32
    a man master of himself than one who takes a city.

On the breast the lot is drawn,^a   33
    from Yahweh the decision comes.

17   Better a dry crust and with it peace   1
    than a house where feast and dispute go together.

Where the son is profligate the shrewd slave is master,   2
    with the other brothers, he will share the inheritance.

A crucible for silver, a furnace for gold,   3
    but Yahweh for the testing of hearts!

An evil-doer pays attention to malicious lips,   4
    a liar listens to a slanderous tongue.

To mock the poor is to insult his creator,   5
    he who laughs at distress shall not go unpunished.

The crown of the aged is their children's children;   6
    the children's glory is their father.

7   Fine words do not become the foolish,
      false words become a prince still less.

8   A gift works like a talisman for him who gives it:
      he prospers whichever way he turns.

9   He who covers an offence promotes love,
      he who raises the matter again divides friends.

10   On a man of discernment a reproof makes more impression
      than a hundred strokes on a fool.

11   The wicked man thinks of nothing but rebellion,
      hence a cruel messenger will be sent against him.

12   Rather come on a bear robbed of her cubs
      than on a fool in his folly.

13   He who returns evil for good
      will not rid his house of evil.

14   As well loose a flood as initiate legal proceedings;
      break off before the dispute begins.

15   To absolve the guilty and condemn the virtuous,
      both alike are abhorrent to Yahweh.

16   What good is money in a foolish hand?
      To purchase wisdom, when he has no sense?

17   A friend is a friend at all times,
      it is for adversity that a brother is born.

18   He lacks sense who offers guarantees
      and goes surety for his neighbour.

19   He who has a taste for dispute has a taste for blows,
      the man of haughty speech courts destruction.

20   The contrary heart does not find happiness,
      the deceitful tongue falls into distress.

21   He who begets a stupid son begets him to his sorrow,
      the father of a fool knows no joy.

22   A glad heart is excellent medicine,
      a spirit depressed wastes the bones away.

23   Under cover of the cloak a venal man takes the gift
      to pervert the course of justice.

24   The man of discernment has wisdom there before him,
      but the eyes of the fool range to the ends of the earth.

25   A foolish son is his father's sorrow,
      and the grief of her who gave him birth.

26   To fine the innocent is not right,
      to strike the noble is still worse.

27   A man who can control his tongue has knowledge,
      a man of discernment keeps his temper cool.

---

16 a. The *ephod* worn on the high priest's breast is identified with the *ephod* that held the sacred lots.

If a fool can hold his tongue, even he can pass for wise,   28
and pass for clever if he keeps his lips tight shut.

18

Who lives by himself follows his own whim,   1
he is angered by advice of any kind.

The fool has no love for reflection   2
but only for airing his opinion.

When wickedness comes, contempt comes too,   3
and, with disgrace, dishonour.

Deep waters, such are the words of man: 4
a swelling torrent, a fountain of life.

It is not good to show partiality for the wicked   5
and so to deprive the virtuous when giving judgement.

The lips of the fool draw him into arguments   6
and his mouth pleads for a beating.

The mouth of the fool works his own ruin,   7
his lips are a snare for his own life.

The words of a talebearer are tasty morsels   8
that go right down into the belly.

The man who is idle at work   9
is blood-brother to the destroyer.

The name of Yahweh is a strong tower;   10
the virtuous man runs to it and is secure.

The rich man's wealth is his stronghold,   11
a high wall, as he supposes.

The human heart is haughty until destruction comes,   12
humility goes before honour.

To retort without first listening   13
is folly to work one's own confusion.

Sickness the spirit of man can endure,   14
but when the spirit is broken, who can bear this?

The heart of the discerning gains in knowledge,   15
the ear of the wise man searches for knowledge.

A present opens every door for you   16
and wins you access to the great.

The first to plead is adjudged to be right,   17
in comes his opponent, then the trial begins.

The lot puts an end to disputes   18
and decides between men of power.

Brother helped by brother is a fortress,   19
friends are like the bars of a keep.

When a man's stomach is full, it is the fruit of his own mouth,   20
it is the yield of his lips that fills him.

Death and life are in the gift of the tongue,   21
those who indulge it must eat the fruit it yields.

22   Who finds a wife finds happiness,
      receiving a mark of favour from Yahweh.

23   The poor man's language is entreaty,
      the rich man's answer harshness.

24   There are friends who lead one to ruin,
      others are closer than a brother.

19

1   Better a poor man living an honest life
      than the adept at double-talk who is a fool.

2   Where reflection is wanting, zeal is not good;
      he who goes too quickly misses his way.

3   It is man's folly that spoils his fortunes,
      yet it is against Yahweh that his heart rages.

4   Wealth multiplies friends,
      but the one friend the poor man has is taken from him!

5   The false witness will not go unpunished,
      the man who utters lies will not go free.

6   The generous man has many to court his favour,
      to one who gives, everyone is friend.

7   The poor man's brothers hate him, every one;
      his friends—how much the more do these desert him!

      He goes in search of words, but there are none to be had.

8   He who obtains wisdom works his own good,
      he who cares about discernment finds happiness.

9   The false witness shall not go unpunished,
      the man who utters lies will meet his end.

10   It is not fitting for a fool to live in luxury,
      still less for a slave to govern princes.

11   A man's shrewdness shows in equanimity,
      his self-respect in overlooking an offence.

12   Like the roaring of a lion, the anger of a king,
      but like dew on the grass his favour.

13   A foolish son is the ruin of his father,
      a woman's scolding is like a dripping gutter.

14   From fathers comes inheritance of house and wealth,
      from Yahweh a wife who is discreet.

15   Idleness lulls a man to sleep,
      the feckless soul will go hungry.

16   He who keeps the commandment is keeper of himself,
      but he who despises the word shall die.

17   The man who is kind to the poor lends to Yahweh:
      he will repay him for what he has done.

18   All the while there is hope, chastise your son,
      but do not set out to destroy him altogether.

19   A violent man lays himself open to a penalty;
      spare him, and you aggravate your own misfortune.

Listen to advice, accept correction,
  to be the wiser in the time to come.   20

Plans multiply in the human heart,
  but the purpose of Yahweh stands firm.   21

A man's attraction lies in his kindness,
  better a poor man than a liar.   22

The fear of Yahweh leads to life,
  a man has food and shelter, and no evil to fear.   23

Into the dish the idler dips his hand,
  but bring it back to his mouth he cannot.   24

Strike a mocker and the ignorant will be more wary,
  correct a man of discernment and he will listen to reason.   25

He who dispossesses his father and drives out his mother
  is a son as shameless as depraved.   26

Give up listening to instruction, my son,
  and ignoring what knowledge has to say.   27

A witness of bad character holds justice in contempt;
  the mouth of the wicked gorges on iniquity.   28

The stick was created for mockers,
  and beating for the backs of fools.   29

20

Wine is reckless, strong drink quarrelsome;
  unwise is he whom it seduces.   1

Like the roaring of a lion the fury of a king;
  whoever provokes his anger wrongs his own life.   2

It is to a man's honour if he avoids quarrels,
  but fools never exercise self-control.   3

Autumn is over but the idler does not plough,
  at harvest time he looks—nothing there!   4

Deep in water are the purposes in human hearts,
  the discerning man has only to draw them out.   5

Many describe themselves as kindly men,
  but who can find a man really to be trusted?   6

A virtuous man whose ways are blameless—
  happy his children after him!   7

A king enthroned on the judgement seat
  with one look scatters all that is evil.   8

What man can say, 'I have cleansed my heart,
  I am purified of my sin'?   9

One weight here, another there; here one measure, there another:
  both alike are abhorrent to Yahweh.   10

Even at play a child reveals
  whether his actions will be pure and right.   11

Ear that hears, eye that sees,
  Yahweh has made both of these.   12

13 Do not love sleep or you will know poverty;
    keep your eyes open and have bread and to spare.

14 'No good, no good!' says the buyer,
    but he goes off congratulating himself.

15 There is gold, and profusion of pearls,
    but lips that speak of knowledge, that is the priceless ornament.

16 Take the man's clothes! He has gone surety for a stranger.
    Seize him to the profit of persons unknown!

17 A man finds bread sweet when it is got by fraud,
    but later his mouth is full of grit.

18 Weigh your plans in consultation,
    with sound guidance wage your war.

19 The bearer of gossip lets out secrets;
    have nothing to do with chatterers.

20 Whoever curses father or mother
    in blackest darkness shall have his lamp snuffed out.

21 Property quickly come by at first
    will not be blessed in the end.

22 Do not say, 'I will repay evil';
    put your hope in Yahweh and he will keep you safe.

23 One weight here, another there: this is abhorrent to Yahweh,
    false scales are not good.

24 Yahweh guides a man's steps:
    how could man discern the way he goes?

25 A man is trapped when he shouts 'Dedicated!'
    and only begins to reflect after the vow.

26 A wise king winnows the wicked,
    and makes their spite recoil on themselves.

27 Man's spirit is the lamp of Yahweh,
    searching his deepest self.

28 Kindness and loyalty mount guard over the king,
    his throne is founded on kindness.

29 The glory of the young is their strength,
    the dignity of the old, grey hairs.

30 Wounding strokes are good medicine for evil,
    blows bring healing to the deepest self.

1 **21** Like flowing water is the heart of the king in the hand of Yahweh,
    who turns it where he pleases.

2 A man's conduct may strike him as upright,
    Yahweh, however, weighs the heart.

3 To act virtuously and with justice
    is more pleasing to Yahweh than sacrifice.

4 Haughty eye, proud heart,
    lamp of the wicked, nothing but sin.

The hardworking man is thoughtful, and all is gain;   5
   too much haste, and all that comes of it is want.

To make a fortune with the help of a lying tongue,   6
   such the idle fantasy of those who look for death.

The marauding of the wicked entraps them   7
   through their refusal to do what is right.

The way of the felon is devious,   8
   the conduct of the innocent straightforward.

Better the corner of a loft to live in   9
   than a house shared with a scolding woman.

The wicked man's soul is intent on evil,   10
   he looks on his neighbour with dislike.

When a mocker is punished, the ignorant man grows wiser,   11
   when a wise man is instructed he acquires more knowledge.

The Just One watches the house of the wicked: 12
   he hurls the wicked to destruction.

He who shuts his ear to the poor man's cry   13
   shall himself plead and not be heard.

Anger is mollified by a covert gift,   14
   raging fury by a bribe under cover of the cloak.

For the virtuous man it is a joy to execute justice,   15
   but it brings dismay to evil-doers.

The man who strays from the way of prudence   16
   will rest where the Shades gather round him.

Pleasure-lovers stay poor,   17
   he will not grow rich who loves wine and good living.

The wicked man is the price to be paid for the virtuous,   18
   the deceiver for the upright.

Better to live in a desert land   19
   than with a scolding and irritable woman.

If in a wise man's dwelling there is precious treasure and oil,   20
   the fool will gobble it up.

He who pursues virtue and kindness   21
   shall find life and honour too.

The wise man can scale a citadel of warriors   22
   and throw down the rampart it trusted in.

He who keeps watch over his mouth and his tongue   23
   preserves himself from disaster.

Arrogant, haughty, his name is 'Mocker';   24
   overweening pride marks his behaviour.

The idler's desires are the death of him,   25
   since his hands will do no work.

The godless is forever coveting,   26
   the virtuous man gives without ever refusing.

27   The sacrifice of wicked men is abhorrent,
         above all when they offer for bad motives.

28   The false witness will meet his doom,
         but the speech of the obedient will always be heard.

29   The wicked man assumes an air of confidence,
         the honest man gives his own conduct careful thought.

30   Neither wisdom, nor prudence, nor advice,
         can stand in Yahweh's presence.

31   The horse is caparisoned for the day of battle,
         but to Yahweh the victory belongs.

1 **22**   A good name is more desirable than great wealth,
         the respect of others is better than silver or gold.

2   Rich and poor are found together,
         Yahweh has made them all.

3   The discreet man sees danger and takes shelter,
         the ignorant go forward and pay for it.

4   The reward of humility is the fear of Yahweh,
         riches, honour and life.

5   Thorns and snares line the path of the wilful,
         he who values his life will keep his distance.

6   Instruct a child in the way he should go,
         and when he grows old he will not leave it.

7   The rich man lords it over the poor,
         the borrower is the lender's slave.

8   He who sows injustice reaps disaster,
         and the rod of his anger falls on himself.

9   A blessing awaits the man who is kindly,
         since he shares his bread with the poor.

10   Expel the mocker and strife goes too,
         dispute and abuse die down.

11   Yahweh loves the pure in heart,
         friend to the king is the man of gracious speech.

12   The eyes of Yahweh see knowledge safe preserved,
         but he confounds the words of liars.

13   'There is a lion outside,' says the idler
         'I shall be killed in the street!'

14   The mouth of alien women is a deep pit,
         into it falls the man whom Yahweh detests.

15   Innate in the heart of a child is folly,
         judicious beating will rid him of it.

16   Oppress the poor and you enrich him,
         give to the rich and you make him poor.

III. A COLLECTION OF THE SAGES

Sayings of the sages.   17

Give ear to my words
and apply your heart to knowing them;
for it will be a delight to keep them deep within you   18
to have them all ready on your lips.
So that your trust may be in Yahweh,   19
today I propose to make your way known to you.

Have I not written for you thirty chapters*a*   20
of advice and knowledge,
for you to be able to expound the truth   21
and with sound words to answer those who question you?

Because a man is poor, do not therefore cheat him,   22
nor, at the city gate,*b* oppress anybody in affliction;
for Yahweh takes up their cause,   23
and extorts the life of their extortioners.

Make friends with no man who gives way to anger,   24
make no hasty-tempered man a companion of yours,
for fear you learn from his behaviour   25
and in this risk the loss of your own life.

Do not be one of those who go guarantor,   26
who go surety for debts:
if you have no means of paying   27
you will find your bed taken from under you.
Do not displace the ancient landmark,   28
set by your ancestors.

You see some man sharp at business?   29
He will come to serve kings.
Not for him the service of obscure people.

23 If you take your seat at a great man's table,   1
take careful note of what you have before you;
put a knife to your throat   2
if you are prone to gluttony.
Do not crave his choice food,   3
for it is doubtful nourishment.

Do not weary yourself with getting rich,   4
and have nothing to do with dishonest gain.
You fix your gaze on this, and it is there no longer,   5
for it is able to sprout wings
like an eagle that flies off to the sky.

Do not dine with a niggardly man,   6
do not crave his choice food.
It would be like a tempest in his throat.   7
'Eat and drink', he tells you, but his heart is not in it.
You will spit out what little you have eaten   8
and find your compliments wasted.

Do not waste words on a fool,   9
he will not appreciate the shrewdness of your remarks.

10   Do not displace the ancient landmark
      or encroach on orphans' lands,
11   for he who avenges them is strong
      and will take up their cause against you.

12   Apply your heart to discipline,
      and your ears to words that are wise.

13   Do not be chary of correcting a child,
      a stroke of the cane is not likely to kill him.
14   A stroke of the cane
      and you save him from Sheol.

15   My son, if your heart is wise,
      then my own heart is glad,
16   and my inmost self rejoices
      when from your lips come honest words.

17   Do not let your heart be envious of sinners
      but be steady every day in the fear of Yahweh;
18   for there is a morrow,
      and your hope will not be nullified.

19   Listen, my son, and learn to be wise,
      and guide your heart in the way...

20   Do not be one of those forever tippling wine
      nor one of those who gorge themselves with meat;
21   for the drunkard and glutton impoverish themselves,
      and a drowsy head makes a wearer of rags.

22   Listen to your father who begot you,
      do not despise your mother in her old age.

23   Truth you must purchase, never sell;
      this is wisdom, discipline, and discernment.

24   The father of the virtuous man will rejoice indeed,
      he who fathers a wise man will have joy of it.

25   May you be the joy of your father,
      the gladness of her who bore you!
26   My son, attend to me,
      keep your eyes fixed on my advice:
27   a harlot is a deep pit,
      a narrow well, the woman who is a stranger.
28   Yes, like a robber she is on the watch
      and many are the men she dupes.

29   For whom is everybody's pity and everyone's contempt,
      for whom is strife reserved, for whom dissatisfaction,
      for whom blows struck from all sides,
      for whom the clouded eye?
30   For those who linger over wine too long,
      ever on the look-out for the well-blended wine.
31   Never relish how red it is, this wine,
      how sparkling in the cup,
      how smooth its flow.

---

22 a. Probably an illusion to *The Wisdom of Amenemophis*, on which this whole passage is based.
b. Where cases were judged.

In the end its bite is like a serpent's,   32
     its sting as sharp as an adder's.
Your eyes will see strange things,   33
     distorted words will come from your heart.
You will be like one sleeping in mid-ocean,   34
     like one asleep at the mast-head.
'Struck me, have they? But I'm not hurt.   35
     Beaten me? I don't feel anything.
When shall I wake up?...
     I'll ask for more of it!'

24 Do not be envious of wicked men   1
     or wish for their company,
for their hearts are scheming violence,   2
     their lips talking of mischief.

By wisdom a house is built,   3
     by discernment the foundation is laid;
by knowledge its storerooms filled   4
     with riches of every kind, rare and desirable.

Better the wise man than the strong,   5
     the man with knowledge than the brawny fellow;
for war is won by sound thinking   6
     and victory rests in having many counsellors.

Wisdom is coral[a] to the fool: 7
     at the city gate he does not open his mouth.

The man intent on evil-doing   8
     is called a rank intriguer.

The foolish scheme nothing but sin,   9
     the mocker is abhorrent to men.

If you lose heart,   10
     when adversity comes your strength will only be weakness.

Rescue those being led away to death,   11
     hold back those who are being dragged to the slaughter.
Will you object, 'But look, we did not know'?   12
     Has he who weighs the heart no understanding,
he who scans your soul no knowledge?
     He himself will repay a man as his deeds deserve.

Eat honey, my son, since it is good;   13
     honey that drips from the comb is sweet to the taste:
and such is knowledge of wisdom for your soul: 14
find it, and there will be a morrow,
     and your hope will not be in vain.

Do not lurk, wicked man, round the virtuous man's dwelling,   15
     do not despoil his house.
For though the virtuous man falls seven times, he stands up again;   16
     the wicked are the ones who stumble in adversity.

Should your enemy fall, do not rejoice,   17
     when he stumbles do not let your heart exult;
for fear that at the sight Yahweh will be displeased   18
     and turn his anger away from him.

Do not be indignant about the wicked,   19
     do not be envious of evil men,

20   since there is no morrow for the wicked man;
           the lamp of the wicked will be snuffed out.

21   Fear Yahweh, my son, and fear the king;
           do not rebel against either of them;
22   for suddenly their vengeance will arise,
           and then who knows what ruin both of them will send?

IV. ANOTHER COLLECTION OF THE SAGES

23   The following are also taken from the sages:

       To show partiality in judgement is not good.
24   The man who says, 'You are innocent' to the guilty;
           the peoples will have only curses for him, and the nations horror;
25   but those who deal out punishment have cause for satisfaction,
           on them a blessing rests.

26   He who returns an honest answer
           plants a kiss on the lips.

27   On the open ground, plan what you have to do,
           make your preparation in the field;
       then you may go
           and build your house.

28   Do not bear witness lightly against your neighbour,
           nor with your lips deceive.

29   Do not say, 'I will treat him as he has treated me;
           I will repay each man as he deserves'.

30   By the idler's field I was passing,
           by the vineyard of a man who had no sense,
31   there it all lay, deep in thorns,
           entirely overgrown with nettles,
           and its stone wall broken down.
32   And as I gazed I pondered,
           I drew this lesson from the sight,
33   'A little sleep, a little drowsiness,
           a little folding of the arms to take life more easily,
34   and like a vagrant, poverty is at your elbow
           and, like a beggar, want'.

V. THE SECOND COLLECTION ATTRIBUTED
TO SOLOMON

1 **25** The following also are proverbs of Solomon transcribed by Hezekiah,
        king of Judah.

2   To conceal a matter, this is the glory of God,
           to sift it thoroughly, the glory of kings.
3   High though the heavens are, deep the earth,
           there is no fathoming the heart of kings.

4   From silver remove the dross
           and it emerges wholly purified;

24 a. Too delicate for him to appreciate.

from the king's presence remove the wicked   5
     and on virtue his throne is founded.

In the presence of the king do not give yourself airs,   6
     do not put yourself where the great are standing;
better to be invited, 'Come up here'   7
     than be humiliated in the presence of the prince.

What your eyes have witnessed
     do not come out with too quickly at the trial,   8
for what are you to do at the end
     should your neighbour confute you?

Have the quarrel out with your neighbour,   9
     but do not disclose another's secret,
or someone, hearing, will reproach you with it,   10
     and so you lose your reputation.

Like apples of gold in a silver setting   11
     is a word that is aptly spoken.
A golden ring, an ornament of finest gold,   12
     is a wise rebuke to an attentive ear.

The coolness of snow in harvest time,   13
     such is the trusty messenger to those who send him:
     he revives the soul of his master.

Clouds and gusts and yet no rain,   14
     such is the man whose promises are princely but never kept.

With patience a judge may be cajoled: 15
     a soft tongue breaks bones.

Eat to your satisfaction what honey you may find,   16
     but not to excess or you will bring it up again.

Do not set foot too often in your neighbour's house,   17
     for fear he tires of you and comes to hate you.

A mace, a sword, a keen arrow,   18
     such is the man who bears false witness against his neighbour.

Decaying tooth, lame foot,   19
     such is the fickle man when trusted in time of trouble.
As well take off your coat in bitter weather.   20

It is to treat a wound with vinegar
     to sing songs to a sorrowing heart.

If your enemy is hungry, give him something to eat;   21
     if thirsty, something to drink.
By this you heap red-hot coals on his head,   22
     and Yahweh will reward you.

The rain is born of the north wind,   23
     the ravaged face of a backbiting tongue.

Better the corner of a loft to live in   24
     than a house shared with a scolding woman.

Cold water to a thirsty throat: 25
     such is good news from a distant land.

26 A churned up spring, and the fountain fouled:
   such is the virtuous man trembling before the wicked.

27 It is not good to eat too much honey,
   or to be taken in by fawning words.

28 An open town, and without defences:
   such is the man lacking self-control.

26

1 Snow no more befits the summer, or rain the harvest-time,
  than honours befit a fool.

2 As the sparrow escapes, and the swallow flies away,
  so the undeserved curse will never hit its mark.

3 A whip for the horse, a bridle for the donkey,
  and for the backs of fools, the stick.

4 Do not answer a fool in the terms of his folly
  for fear you grow like him yourself.

5 Answer a fool in the terms of his folly
  for fear he imagines himself wise.

6 ...He drinks a bitter draught
  who sends a message by a fool.

7 Unreliable as a lame man's legs:
  so is a proverb in the mouth of fools.

8 Like fixing a stone tight in the sling,
  so is giving honours to a fool.

9 A thorn branch in a drunkard's hand:
  such is a proverb in the mouth of fools.

10 An archer wounding all who pass:
   such is the man who employs a fool.

11 As a dog returns to its vomit,
   so a fool reverts to his folly.

12 You see some man who thinks himself wise?
   More hope for a fool than for him!

13 'There is a lion in the street,' says the idler
   'a lion in the square!'

14 The door turns on its hinges,
   the idler, on his bed.

15 Into the dish the idler dips his hand
   but is too tired to bring it back to his mouth.

16 The idler thinks himself wiser
   than seven men who answer with discretion.

17 Like catching a stray dog by the tail,
   so is interfering in the quarrels of others.

18 Like a madman hurling firebrands,
   arrows and death,

19 so is the man who lies to his neighbour
   and then says, 'It was all a joke'.

No wood, and the fire goes out;   20
    no talebearer, and quarrelling dies down.

Charcoal for live embers, wood for fire,   21
    for kindling strife a quarrelsome man.

The words of a talebearer are tasty morsels   22
    that go right down into the belly.

A glaze applied to an earthen pot: 23
    such are smooth lips and wicked heart.

Where hatred is there are dissembling lips,   24
    but deep within lies treachery;
do not trust him if the man be fair of speech,   25
    since in his heart lurk seven abominations.
Hatred may well disguise itself with guile,   26
    only to unmask its spite before the community.

The man who digs a pit falls into it,   27
    the stone comes back on him that rolls it.

The lying tongue hates the truth,   28
    the fawning mouth brings ruin.

27   Do not boast about tomorrow,   1
    since you do not know what today will bring forth.

Let the other man praise you, but not your own mouth.   2
    A stranger, but not your lips.

Heaviness of stone, weight of sand,   3
    heavier than both: annoyance from a fool.

Cruelty of wrath, surge of anger.   4
    But jealousy, who can withstand that?

Better open reproof   5
    than voiceless love.

From one who loves, wounds are well-intentioned;   6
    from one who hates, kisses are ominous.

The gorged throat revolts at honey,   7
    the hungry throat finds all bitterness sweet.

Like a bird that strays from its nest,   8
    so is the man who strays from where he belongs.

Fragrant oil gladdens the heart,   9
    friendship's sweetness comforts the soul.

Do not abandon friend, or father's friend;   10
    when trouble comes, do not go running to your brother's house.
Better a friend near than a brother far away.

Learn to be wise, my son, and gladden my heart,   11
    that I may have an answer for the man who insults me.

The discreet man sees danger and takes shelter,   12
    the ignorant go forward and pay for it.

Take the man's clothes! He has gone surety for a stranger.   13
    Seize him to the profit of persons unknown!

14   He who at dawn loudly blesses his neighbour
       is accounted to curse.

15   The steady dripping of a gutter on a rainy day
       and a scolding woman are alike.

16   Whoever can restrain her, can restrain the wind,
       and with his right hand grasp oil.

17   Iron is made the finer by iron,
       a man is refined by contact with his neighbour.

18   He who tends the fig tree eats its figs,
       he who looks after his master shall be honoured.

19   As no two faces are ever alike,
       unlike, too, are the hearts of men.

20   Sheol and Perdition are never satisfied,
       nor are the eyes of man ever satisfied.

21   A crucible for silver, a furnace for gold,
       a man for testing the words of flatterers.

22   Pound the fool in a mortar as you may,
       you will not separate him from his folly.

23   Know your flocks' condition well,
       take good care of your herds;

24   since riches do not last for ever,
       wealth is not handed down from age to age.

25   The grass once gone, the aftergrowth appearing,
       the hay gathered in from the mountains,

26   you should have lambs to clothe you,
       goats to pay for your fields,

27   goat's milk sufficient to feed you,
       and to provide for your serving girls.

28

1   The wicked man flees when no one is after him,
       the virtuous man is bold as a lion.

2   The fault lies with the headstrong when quarrels flare up,
       the discreet man quenches them.

3   A wicked man who oppresses the poor:
       here is a devastating rain—and farewell, bread!

4   Those who forsake the law have a good word for the wicked,
       those who observe the law have no time for such.

5   The wicked do not know what justice means,
       those who fear Yahweh understand everything.

6   Better a poor man living an honest life
       than a man of devious ways, rich though he be.

7   A discerning son is he who keeps the Law;
       an associate of profligates brings shame on his father.

8   He who increases his wealth by usury and interest
       amasses it for someone else who will bestow it on the poor.

9   He who turns his ear away from listening to the Law,
       his prayer is an abomination.

He who seduces honest men to evil ways
  will fall into his own pit.
Blameless men are the heirs to happiness.   10

The rich man may think himself wise,
  but a poor man with sense will unmask him.   11

When the virtuous triumph, there is great rejoicing;
  when the wicked are in the ascendant, men take cover.   12

He who conceals his faults will not prosper,
  he who confesses and renounces them will find mercy.   13

Happy the man who is never without fear,
  he who hardens his heart will fall into distress.   14

A roaring lion, a hungry bear,
  such is the bad ruler of a poor people.   15

A prince lacking sense is rich in rapacity,
  he who hates avarice will lengthen his days.   16

A man wanted for murder
  will be a fugitive until death. Do not lay hands on him.   17

He who lives an honest life will be safe,
  he who wavers between two ways falls down in one of them.   18

He who tills his land shall have bread and to spare,
  he who chases fantasies, poverty in plenty.   19

A trustworthy man will be overwhelmed with blessings,
  but he who tries to get rich quickly will not go unpunished.   20

It is not good to show partiality,
  but men will do wrong for a mouthful of bread.   21

He chases after wealth, the man of greedy eye,
  not knowing that want is overtaking him.   22

He who reproves another will enjoy more favour
  in the end than the flatterer.   23

He who robs his father (and his mother) saying, 'No wrong here!'
  is comrade for a brigand.   24

The covetous man provokes disputes,
  he who trusts in Yahweh shall prosper.   25

He who trusts his own promptings is a fool,
  he whose ways are wise will be safe.   26

He who gives to the poor shall never want,
  he who closes his eyes to them will bear many a curse.   27

When the wicked are in the ascendant, men take cover,
  but when they perish, virtuous men multiply.   28

29 The man often rebuked but stubborn still:
  suddenly, irretrievably, his fall will come.   1

When virtuous men are in power, the people are joyful,
  when the wicked rule, the people groan.   2

The lover of Wisdom makes his father glad,
  but the patron of harlots fritters his wealth away.   3

4   A king gives a country stability by justice,
        an extortioner brings it to ruin.

5   The man who flatters his neighbour
        spreads a net for his feet.

6   Under the feet of the wicked man there is a snare,
        but the virtuous runs on rejoicing.

7   The virtuous man is concerned for the rights of the poor,
        the wicked knows no such concern.

8   Scoffers set cities in a ferment,
        but wise men moderate anger.

9   Let a wise man argue with a fool,
        be he angry or good-humoured he will not gain his end.

10   Men of blood hate the blameless man,
        but honest men cherish his life.

11   The fool comes out with all his angry feelings,
        but the wise man subdues and restrains them.

12   When a ruler listens to false reports,
        all his ministers will be scoundrels.

13   Poor man and usurer are found together,
        Yahweh gives light to the eyes of both.

14   The king who judges the poor with equity
        sees his throne set firm for ever.

15   The stick and the reprimand bestow wisdom,
        a child left to himself brings shame on his mother.

16   When the wicked are in power, sin multiplies,
        but the virtuous shall witness their downfall.

17   Correct your son, and he will give you peace of mind;
        he will delight your soul.

18   Where there is no vision the people get out of hand;
        blessed are they who keep the Precept.[a]

19   Not by words is a slave corrected:
        even if he understands, he will take no notice.

20   You see some man too ready of speech?
        More hope for a fool than for him.

21   If a man's slave is pampered from childhood,
        he will prove ungrateful in the end.

22   A bad-tempered man provokes disputes,
        a man prone to anger is a great cause of sin.

23   A man's pride brings him humiliation,
        he who humbles himself will win honour.

24   Complicity with thieves and a wrong to oneself:
        to hear the curse[b] and make no disclosure.

29 a. 'Vision' is probably the prophetic gift; 'the Precept' may be the prophet's teaching, or else the Law.   **b.** The curse pronounced against the unidentified criminal or on witnesses who refuse to come forward.

> To be afraid of men is a snare,   25
> he who puts his trust in Yahweh is secure.

> Many a man seeks a ruler's favour,   26
> but the rights of each come from Yahweh.

> Abhorrent to the virtuous is the sinful man,   27
> abhorrent to the wicked is the man of honour.

VI. THE SAYINGS OF AGUR

30 The sayings of Agur son of Jakeh, of Massa. Oracle of this man for 1
Ithiel, for Ithiel and for Ucal.[a]

> Surely I must be the most stupid of men,   2
> bereft of human intelligence,
> I have not learnt wisdom,   3
> and I lack the knowledge of the Holy Ones.
> Who has mounted to the heavens, then descended?   4
> Who has gathered the wind in the clasp of his hand?
> Who has wrapped the waters in his cloak?
> Who has set all the ends of the earth firm?
> What is his name, or the name of his son,
> if you know it?

> Every word of God is unalloyed,   5
> he is the shield of those who take refuge in him.
> To his words make no addition,   6
> lest he reprove you and know you for a fraud.

> Two things I beg of you,   7
> do not grudge me them before I die:
> keep falsehood and lies far from me,   8
> give me neither poverty nor riches,
> grant me only my share of bread to eat,
> for fear that surrounded by plenty, I should fall away   9
> and say, 'Yahweh—who is Yahweh?'
> or else, in destitution, take to stealing
> and profane the name of my God.

> Do not denounce a slave to his master,   10
> lest he curse you, and you suffer for it.

> There is a breed of man who curses his father   11
> and does not bless his mother;
> a breed that, laying claim to purity,   12
> has yet not been cleansed of its filth;
> a breed haughty of eye,   13
> with disdain in every glance;
> a breed with swords for teeth,   14
> with knives for jaws,
> with which to devour the poor and rid the earth of them,
> to devour the needy and rid mankind of them.

VII. NUMERICAL PROVERBS

> The leech has two daughters: 'Give, give!' their cry.   15

> There are three insatiable things,
>> four, indeed, that never say, 'Enough!'
16 Sheol, the barren womb,
>> earth which can never have its fill of water,
>> fire which never says, 'Enough!'

17 The eye which looks jeeringly on a father,
>> and scornfully on an ageing mother,
>> shall be pecked out by the ravens of the valley,
>> and eaten by the vultures.

18 There are three things beyond my comprehension,
>> four, indeed, that I do not understand:
19 the way of an eagle through the skies,
>> the way of a snake over the rock,
>> the way of a ship in mid-ocean,
>> the way of a man with a girl.

20 This is how the adulteress behaves:
>> when she has eaten,
>> she wipes her mouth clean and says,
>>> 'I have done nothing wrong'.

21 There are three things at which the earth trembles,
>> four, indeed, which it cannot endure:
22 a slave become king,
>> a churlish man full-fed,
23 a jilted girl wed at last,
>> a maid supplanting mistress.

24 There are four creatures little on the earth,
>> though wisest of the wise:
25 the ants, a race with no strength,
>> yet in the summer they make sure of their food;
26 the rock rabbits, a race with no defences,
>> yet they make their home in the rocks;
27 the locusts, these have no king,
>> and yet they all march in good order;
28 the lizard which you can catch in your hand,
>> yet it frequents the palaces of kings.

29 There are three things of stately tread,
>> four, indeed, of stately bearing:
30 the lion, bravest of beasts,
>> he will draw back from nothing;
31 the cock that proudly struts among the hens,
>> the he-goat, leader of the flock,
>> and the king when he harangues his people.

32 If you have been foolish enough to fly into a passion
>> and now have second thoughts, lay your hand on your lips.
33 For by churning the milk you produce butter,
>> by wringing the nose you produce blood,
>> and by whipping up anger you produce strife.

30 a. This heading is obscure. Massa is the name of an Ishmaelite tribe of N. Arabia, credited with 'the wisdom of the East', but it may not be correct to take this word, and the other capitalised words, as proper names.

VIII. THE SAYINGS OF LEMUEL

31 The sayings of Lemuel king of Massa,*a* taught him by his mother: 1

What, my son! What, son of my womb!   2
     What, son of my vows!
Do not spend all your energy on women,   3
     nor your loins on these destroyers of kings.

Not for kings, O Lemuel,   4
     not for kings the drinking of wine,
     not for princes to love strong drink,
for fear that in liquor they forget what they have decreed   5
     and override the rights of all in distress.

Procure strong drink for a man about to perish,   6
     wine for the heart that is full of bitterness:
let him drink and forget his misfortune,   7
     and remember his misery no more.

Speak, yourself, on behalf of the dumb,   8
     on behalf of all the unwanted;
speak, yourself, pronounce a just verdict,   9
     uphold the rights of the poor, of the needy.

IX. ALPHABETIC POEM ON THE PERFECT WIFE

Aleph   A perfect wife—who can find her?   10
     She is far beyond the price of pearls.

Beth   Her husband's heart has confidence in her,   11
     from her he will derive no little profit.

Ghimel   Advantage and not hurt she brings him   12
     all the days of her life.

Daleth   She is always busy with wool and with flax,   13
     she does her work with eager hands.

He   She is like a merchant vessel   14
     bringing her food from far away.

Waw   She gets up while it is still dark   15
     giving her household their food,
     giving orders to her serving girls.

Zain   She sets her mind on a field, then she buys it;   16
     with what her hands have earned she plants a vineyard.

Heth   She puts her back into her work   17
     and shows how strong her arms can be.

Teth   She finds her labour well worth while;   18
     her lamp does not go out at night.

Yod   She sets her hands to the distaff,   19
     her fingers grasp the spindle.

Kaph   She holds out her hand to the poor,   20
     she opens her arms to the needy.

21	*Lamed*	Snow may come, she has no fears for her household, with all her servants warmly clothed.
22	*Mem*	She makes her own quilts, she is dressed in fine linen and purple.
23	*Nun*	Her husband is respected at the city gates, taking his seat among the elders of the land.
24	*Samek*	She weaves linen sheets and sells them, she supplies the merchant with sashes.
25	*Ain*	She is clothed in strength and dignity, she can laugh at the days to come.
26	*Pe*	When she opens her mouth, she does so wisely; on her tongue is kindly instruction.
27	*Sade*	She keeps good watch on the conduct of her household, no bread of idleness for her.
28	*Qoph*	Her sons stand up and proclaim her blessed, her husband, too, sings her praises:
29	*Resh*	'Many women have done admirable things, but you surpass them all!'
30	*Shin*	Charm is deceitful, and beauty empty; the woman who is wise is the one to praise.
31	*Tau*	Give her a share in what her hands have worked for, and let her works tell her praises at the city gates.

31 a. Massa: see note on the heading at 30:1.

INTRODUCTION TO
ECCLESIASTES

The name means 'the Preacher'. In the first chapter, the Preacher is called
'son of David and king in Jerusalem'; but this is a literary device for
commending the author's wisdom to readers under the name of the proverbially wise King Solomon. In fact, the book may perhaps be a compilation
by several hands, and it certainly dates from after the Exile.

A main theme of these aphorisms and meditations is the utter emptiness
of human existence and the futility of a life in which the good and the bad
must come to exactly the same end. There are affinities with Greek thinking,
and the 3rd century B.C. is the likeliest time of composition. The book
represents a transitional stage in the religious development of Israel and
exposes the need of a new revelation.

ECCLESIASTES

¹ ² ³ **1** The words of Qoheleth[a] son of David, king in Jerusalem. •Vanity of vanities, Qoheleth says. Vanity of vanities. All is vanity! •For all his toil, his toil under the sun, what does man gain by it?

PART ONE

Prologue

⁴ A generation goes, a generation comes, yet the earth stands firm for ever.
⁵ ⁶ The sun rises, the sun sets; then to its place it speeds and there it rises. •Southward goes the wind, then turns to the north; it turns and turns again; back then to its
⁷ circling goes the wind. •Into the sea all the rivers go, and yet the sea is never
⁸ filled, and still to their goal the rivers go. •All things are wearisome. No man
⁹ can say that eyes have not had enough of seeing, ears their fill of hearing. •What was will be again; what has been done will be done again; and there is nothing
¹⁰ new under the sun. •Take anything of which it may be said, 'Look now, this
¹¹ is new'. Already, long before our time, it existed. •Only no memory remains of earlier times, just as in times to come next year itself will not be remembered.

The career of Solomon

¹² ¹³ I, Qoheleth, have reigned in Jerusalem over Israel. •With the help of wisdom I have been at pains to study all that is done under heaven; oh, what a weary
¹⁴ task God has given mankind to labour at! •I have seen everything that is done under the sun, and what vanity it all is, what chasing of the wind!

¹⁵ What is twisted cannot be straightened,
what is not there cannot be counted.

¹⁶ I thought to myself, 'I have acquired a greater stock of wisdom than any of my predecessors in Jerusalem. I have great experience of wisdom and learning.'
¹⁷ Wisdom has been my careful study; stupidity, too, and folly. And now I have come to recognise that even this is chasing of the wind.

¹⁸ Much wisdom, much grief,
the more knowledge, the more sorrow.

¹ **2** I thought to myself, 'Very well, I will try pleasure and see what enjoyment
² has to offer'. And there it was: vanity again! •This laughter, I reflected, is a
³ madness, this pleasure no use at all. •I resolved to have my body cheered with wine, my heart still devoted to wisdom; I resolved to embrace folly to see what made mankind happy, and what men do under heaven in the few days they
⁴ ⁵ have to live. •I did great things: built myself palaces, planted vineyards; •made
⁶ myself gardens and orchards, planting every kind of fruit tree in them. •I had
⁷ pools made for watering the plantations; •bought men slaves, women slaves; had home-born slaves as well; herds and flocks I had too, more than anyone

---

1 a. 'The president, or the preacher, of the assembled Church (*qahal*).' The name Ecclesiastes is a Greek equivalent. The ascription of the book to Solomon is a literary fiction.

in Jerusalem before me. •I amassed silver and gold, the treasures of kings and 8
provinces; acquired singing men and singing women and every human luxury,
chest on chest of it. •So I grew great, greater than anyone in Jerusalem before 9
me; nor did my wisdom leave me. •I denied my eyes nothing they desired, 10
refused my heart no pleasure, a heart that found all my hard work a pleasure;
such was the return I got for all my efforts. •I then reflected on all that my hands 11
had achieved and on all the effort I had put into its achieving. What vanity it
all is, and chasing of the wind! There is nothing to be gained under the sun.

My reflections then turned to wisdom, stupidity, folly. For instance, what 12
can the successor of a king do? What has been done already. •More is to be 13
had from wisdom than from folly, as from light than from darkness; this, of
course, I see:

> The wise man sees ahead,   14
> the fool walks in the dark.

No doubt! But I know, too, that one fate awaits them both. •'The fool's fate' 15
I thought to myself 'will be my fate too. Of what use my wisdom, then? This,
too,' I thought 'is vanity.' •Since there is no lasting memory for wise man or 16
for fool, and in the days to come both will be forgotten; wise man, alas, no
less than fool must die. •Life I have come to hate, for what is done under the 17
sun disgusts me, since all is vanity and chasing of the wind. •All I have toiled 18
for and now bequeath to my successor I have come to hate; •who knows whether 19
he will be a wise man or a fool? Yet he will be master of all the work into which
I have put my efforts and wisdom under the sun. That, too, is vanity. •And 20
hence I have come to despair of all the efforts I have expended under the sun.
For so it is that a man who has laboured wisely, skilfully and successfully must 21
leave what is his own to someone who has not toiled for it at all. This, too,
is vanity and great injustice; •for what does he gain for all the toil and strain 22
that he has undergone under the sun? •What of all his laborious days, his cares 23
of office, his restless nights? This, too, is vanity.

There is no happiness for man but to eat and drink and to be content with 24
his work. This, too, I see as something from God's hand, •since plenty and 25
penury both come from God; •wisdom, knowledge, joy, he gives to the man 26
who pleases him; on the sinner lays the task of gathering and storing up for
another who is pleasing to God. This, too, is vanity and chasing of the wind.

Death

3 There is a season for everything, a time for every occupation under heaven: 1

> A time for giving birth,   2
> a time for dying;
> a time for planting,
> a time for uprooting what has been planted.
> A time for killing,   3
> a time for healing;
> a time for knocking down,
> a time for building.
> A time for tears,   4
> a time for laughter;
> a time for mourning,
> a time for dancing.
> A time for throwing stones away,   5
> a time for gathering them up;
> a time for embracing,
> a time to refrain from embracing.
> A time for searching,   6

a time for losing;
a time for keeping,
a time for throwing away.

7 A time for tearing,
a time for sewing;
a time for keeping silent,
a time for speaking,

8 A time for loving,
a time for hating;
a time for war,
a time for peace.

9
10 What does a man gain for the efforts that he makes? •I contemplate the task
11 that God gives mankind to labour at. •All that he does is apt for its time; but though he has permitted man to consider time in its wholeness, man cannot comprehend the work of God from beginning to end.

12 I know there is no happiness for man except in pleasure and enjoyment while
13 he lives. •And when man eats and drinks and finds happiness in his work, this is a gift from God.

14 I know that what God does he does consistently. To this nothing can be
15 added, from this nothing taken away; yet God sees to it that men fear him. •What is, already was; what is to be, has been already; yet God cares for the persecuted.
16 But I still observe that under the sun crime is where law should be, the criminal
17 where the good should be. •'God' I thought to myself 'will judge both virtuous
18 and criminal, because there is a time here for all that is purposed or done.' •I also thought that mankind behaves like this so that God may show them up for what
19 they are, and expose them for the brute beasts they are to each other. •Indeed, the fate of man and beast is identical; one dies, the other too, and both have the selfsame breath; man has no advantage over the beast, for all is vanity.
20 Both go to the same place; both originate from the dust and to the dust both
21 return. •Who knows if the spirit of man mounts upward or if the spirit of the beast goes down to the earth?

22 I see there is no happiness for man but to be happy in his work, for this is the lot assigned him. Who then can bring him to see what is to happen after his time?

Society

1 **4** I come again to contemplate all the oppression that is committed under the sun. Take for instance the tears of the oppressed, with no one to protect
2 them; the power their oppressors wield. No one to protect them! •So, rather than the living who still have lives to live, I salute the dead who have already
3 met death; •happier than both of these is he who is yet unborn and has not seen
4 the evil things that are done under the sun. •I see that all effort and all achievement spring from men's mutual jealousy. This, too, is vanity and chasing of the wind.

5 The fool folds his arms
and eats his own flesh away.

6 —Better one handful of repose
than two hands full of effort

7
8 in chasing the wind. •And I observe another vanity under the sun: •a man is quite alone—no son, no brother; and yet there is no end to his efforts, his eyes can never have their fill of riches. For whom, then, do I work so hard and grudge myself pleasure? This, too, is vanity, a sorry business.

9 Better two than one by himself, since thus their work is really profitable.
10 If one should fall, the other helps him up; but woe to the man by himself with
11 no one to help him up when he falls down. •Again: they keep warm who sleep

two together, but how can a man keep warm alone? •Where one alone would be 12
overcome, two will put up resistance; and a threefold cord is not quickly broken.

> Better a lad beggarly yet wise,   13
> than a king old yet foolish

who will no longer take advice. •The lad may well step from prison to the throne, 14
or have been born a beggar in the kingdom he now owns. •I observe that all who 15
live and move under the sun side with that lad, the usurper who has succeeded.
He takes his place at the head of innumerable subjects; sad, if later no one has 16
cause to be glad of him. This too, most certainly, is vanity and chasing of the
wind.

When you go to the Temple, be on your guard. Go near so that you can 17
hear; the sacrifice is more valuable than the offering of fools, even if they are
unaware of doing wrong.

5 Be in no hurry to speak; do not hastily declare yourself before God; for God 1
is in heaven, you on earth. Be sparing, then, of speech:

> Dreaming comes from much worrying,   2
> foolish talk from a multiplicity of words.

If you make a vow to God, discharge it without delay, for God has no love for 3
fools. Discharge your vow. •Better a vow unmade than made and not discharged. 4
Do not allow your own words to bring guilt on you, nor tell your angel afterwards 5
it was unintentional. Why should a word of yours give God occasion to be
angry, and destroy what your hands have worked for?

> For every dream, a vanity to match;   6
> too many words, a chasing of the wind.

Therefore, fear God.

If in a province you see the poor oppressed, right and justice violated, do not 7
be surprised. You will be told that officials are under the supervision of superiors,
who are supervised in turn; •you will hear talk of 'the common good' and 'the 8
service of the king'.

Money

> He who loves money never has money enough,   9
> he who loves wealth never has enough profit;

this, too is vanity.

> Where goods abound,   10
> parasites abound;

and what is the good of them to their owner? That he can feast his eyes on
them. •The labourer's sleep is sweet, whether he has eaten little or much; but 11
the rich man's wealth will not let him sleep at all. •There is a great injustice 12
that I observe under the sun: riches stored and turning to loss for their owner.
One unlucky venture, and those riches are lost; a son is born to him, and he has 13
nothing to leave him. •Naked from his mother's womb he came, as naked as 14
he came he will depart again; nothing to take with him after all his efforts. •This 15
is a grievous wrong, that as he came, so must he go; what profit can he show
after toiling to earn the wind, •as he spends the rest of his days in darkness, 16
grief, worry, sickness and resentment?

This, then, is my conclusion: the right happiness for man is to eat and drink 17
and be content with all the work he has to do under the sun, during the few
days God has given him to live, since this is the lot assigned him. •And whenever 18
God gives a man riches and property, with the ability to enjoy them and to find
contentment in his work, this is a gift from God. •He will not need to brood, 19
at least, over the duration of his life so long as God keeps his heart occupied
with joy.

$\frac{1}{2}$ 6 There is an evil I observe under the sun, that weighs men down: •suppose a man has received from God riches, property, honours—nothing at all left him to wish for. Yet God does not give him the chance to enjoy them, but some 3 stranger enjoys them. There is vanity here, and grievous suffering. •Or perhaps a man has had a hundred sons and as many daughters and lived for many years, and then derives no benefit from his estate, not even a tomb to call his own. Why then I say, better the untimely-born than he:

4   In darkness arriving,
          in darkness departing;
    even his name is wrapped in darkness.

5   Never seeing the sun,
          never knowing rest;

6 the one no more than the other. •Even if the man had lived a thousand years twice over, without deriving profit from his estate, do not both alike go to the same place?

7   Man toils but to eat,
          yet his belly is never filled.

8 What advantage has the wise man over the fool? And what about the pauper 9 who keeps up appearances before his fellow men? •Do appearances count more than the condition of the belly? This, too, is vanity and chasing of the wind. 10 What has been already has a name; and what man is, is known; he cannot 11 dispute with one stronger than himself. •The more words, the greater the vanity of it all; and what does man get from it?

$\frac{12}{1}$ Who knows what is good for man in his lifetime, in those few days he lives so vainly, days that like a shadow he spends? Who can tell a man what will happen under the sun after his time?

PART TWO

Prologue

$\frac{1}{2}$ 7   Better a good name than costly oil,
          the day of death than the day of birth.
$\frac{2}{3}$ Better go to the house of mourning
          than to the house of feasting;
        for to this end all men come,
          let the living take this to heart.
$\frac{3}{4}$ Better sadness than laughter,
          a severe face confers some benefit.
$\frac{4}{5}$ The heart of the wise is in the house of mourning,
          the heart of fools in the house of gaiety.
$\frac{5}{6}$ Better attend to a wise man's reprimand
          than listen to a song sung by a fool.
$\frac{6}{7}$ For like the crackling of thorns under the cauldron
          is the laughter of fools:
        this is vanity, too.
$\frac{7}{8}$ For laughter makes a fool of the wise man
          and merriment corrupts the heart.

Sanctions

$\frac{8}{9}$ Better the end of a matter than its beginning,
          better patience than pride.

$\frac{9}{10}$
$\frac{10}{11}$ Do not be hasty with your resentment, for resentment is found in the heart of fools. •Do not ask why earlier days were better than these, for that is not

a question prompted by wisdom. •Wisdom is a precious legacy, a boon for those on whom the sun shines. •For as money gives protection, so does wisdom; and the good that knowledge imparts is this: its possessor finds that wisdom keeps him safe.

Consider the work of God; who can set straight what he has made crooked? When times are prosperous, enjoy your happiness; when times are bad, consider this: the one is God's doing, as is the other, in order that man may know nothing of his destiny. •In this fleeting life of mine I have seen so much: the virtuous man perishing for all his virtue, for all his godlessness the godless living on.

> Do not be over-virtuous
> nor play too much the sage;

why drive yourself too hard?

> Do not be wicked to excess,
> and do not be a fool;

why die before your time? •The best thing is to hold the one and not let go the other, for both of these will happen to the God-fearing man.

Wisdom lends more strength to the wise than ten rulers in a city. •There is no virtuous man on earth who, doing good, is ever free of sin. •Another thing: pay no attention to telltales; you may hear that your servant has reviled you; •your own heart knows how often you have reviled others.

I have put all this to the test by wisdom, claiming to be wise; but wisdom has been beyond my reach. •Reality lies beyond my grasp; and deep, so deep, who can discover it?

Once again I was at pains to study wisdom and retribution, to see wickedness as folly, and foolishness as madness. •I find woman more bitter than death; she is a snare, her heart a net, her arms are chains;

> He who is pleasing to God eludes her,
> but the sinner is her captive.

This then you must know, says Qoheleth, is the sum of my investigation, putting this and that together. •I have made other researches too, without result.

> One man in a thousand I may find,
> but never a woman better than the rest.

This, however, you must know: I find that God made man simple; man's complex problems are of his own devising.

8   Who is like the sage?
      Who else can solve a problem?
      The wisdom of a man lends brightness to his face;
      his face, once grim, is altered.

This I say: Obey the command of the king, for the sake of the oath of God; do not rashly transgress it; do not be stubborn when the cause is not a good one, since he acts as he thinks fit; •for the word of the king is paramount, and who dare say to him, 'Why do that?'

> He who obeys the command will come to no harm,
> and the wise man knows there will be a time of judgement.

For there is a time of judgement for everything; and man runs grave risks, since he does not know what is going to happen; and who can tell him when it will happen? •No man can master the wind so as to hold it back, nor control the day of death. There is no discharge in time of war; no more can wickedness set its author free. •All this I observe as I consider all that is done under the sun, whenever man tyrannises over man to his hurt.

10 And then I see the wicked brought to burial and people come from the Temple to honour them in the city for having been the men they were. This, too, is
11 vanity. •Since the sentence on wrong-doing is not carried out at once, men's inmost
12 hearts are intent on doing wrong. •The sinner who does wrong a hundred times survives even so. I know very well that happiness is reserved for those who fear
13 God, because they fear him; •that there will be no happiness for the wicked man and that he will only eke out his days like a shadow, because he does not fear God.
14 But there is a vanity found on earth; the good, I mean, receive the treatment the wicked deserve; and the wicked the treatment the good deserve. This, too, I say, is vanity.
15 Joy, then, is the object of my praise, since under the sun there is no happiness for man except in eating, drinking and pleasure. This is his standby in his toil through the days of life God has given him under the sun.

Love

16 Wisdom having been my careful study, I came to observe the business that goes on here on earth. And certainly the eyes of man never rest, day and night.
17 And I look at all the work of God: plainly no one can discover what the work is that goes on under the sun or explain why man should toil to seek yet never discover. Not even a sage can discover it, though he may claim to know.
1 9 For I have reflected on all this and come to understand that the virtuous and the wise with all they do are in the hand of God.
2 Man does not know what love is, or hate, and both of these in his eyes •are vanity.

Just as one fate comes to all, to virtuous as to wicked, to clean and unclean, to him who sacrifices and him who does not sacrifice, so it is with the good man
3 and the sinner, with him who takes an oath and him who shrinks from it. •This is the evil that inheres in all that is done under the sun: that one fate comes to all; further, that the hearts of men should be full of malice; that they should practise
4 such extravagances towards the living in their lifetime and the dead thereafter. For anyone who is linked with all that live still has some hope, a live dog being
5 better than a dead lion. •The living know at least that they will die, the dead know nothing; no more reward for them, their memory has passed out of mind.
6 Their loves, their hates, their jealousies, these all have perished, nor will they ever again take part in whatever is done under the sun.

7. Go, eat your bread with joy
and drink your wine with a glad heart;
for what you do God has approved beforehand.

8 Wear white all the time,
do not stint your head of oil.

9 Spend your life with the woman you love, through all the fleeting days of the life that God has given you under the sun; for this is the lot assigned to you in life
10 and in the efforts you exert under the sun. •Whatever work you propose to do, do it while you can, for there is neither achievement, nor planning, nor knowledge, nor wisdom in Sheol where you are going.

Chance

11 I see this too under the sun: the race does not go to the swift, nor the battle to the strong; there is no bread for the wise, wealth for the intelligent, nor favour
12 for the learned; all are subject to time and mischance. •Man does not know his hour; like fish caught in the treacherous net, like birds taken in the snare, so is man overtaken by misfortune suddenly falling on him.
13
14 I observe another evil under the sun, to me a grave one. •There was a small town, with only a few inhabitants; a mighty king marched against it,
15 laid siege to it and built great siege-works round it. •But a poverty-stricken sage

confronted him and by his wisdom saved the town. No one remembered this poor man afterwards. •Now I say: wisdom is better than strength, but a poor 16 man's wisdom is never valued and his words are disregarded. •The gentle words 17 of the wise are heard above the shouts of a king of fools.

Better wisdom than warlike weapons, but one mistake undoes a deal of 18 good. 10 Dead flies spoil a bowl of perfumed oil; a little folly is stronger than 1 wisdom and honour.

> The wise man's heart leads him aright, 2
> the fool's heart leads him astray.

A fool has only to walk along the road and, having no sense, he makes plain 3 to all what a fool he is.

With the anger of the ruler mounting against you, do not leave your post; 4 composure avoids many a fault. •There is an evil I observe under the sun, 5 the type of misjudgement to which rulers are prone: •folly promoted to high 6 dignities, rich men taking the lowest place. •Slaves I see on horseback, princes 7 going on foot like slaves.

> He who digs a pit may fall into it; 8
> a man saps a wall, the serpent bites him.
> He who quarries stones may be hurt by them; 9
> he who chops wood takes a risk.

If for want of sharpening the axe is blunt, you have to strike very hard, but the 10 reward given by wisdom is success. •If the snake bites before it is charmed, 11 what is the use of the charmer?

> Words from a wise man's mouth are pleasing, 12
> but a fool's lips procure his own ruin.

Of the words he speaks folly is the beginning, sheer madness the end. •A fool 13 14 is a great spender of words; man does not know the future; so who can tell him what is to happen after his time?

> Fools find hard work irksome; 15
> he who does not know the way cannot go to town.

A bad outlook for you, country with a lad for king, and where princes feast 16 in the morning. •Happy the country whose king is nobly born, where princes 17 eat at a respectable hour to keep themselves strong, not to make themselves drunk.

> Owing to neglect the roof-tree gives way; 18
> for want of care the house lets in the rain.

-But meals are made for laughter. Wine gives joy to life. Money is the answer 19 to everything.*a*

> Do not curse the king, even in thought; 20
> do not curse the rich, even in your bedroom,
> for a bird of the air will carry the news;
> indiscretion sprouts wings.

11 Cast your bread on the water; at long last you will find it again. •Share ½ with seven, yes with eight, for you never know what disaster may occur on earth. •When clouds are full of rain, they empty it out on the earth. Let the 3 tree fall south or north, where the tree falls there it lies.

4   Keep watching the wind and you will never sow,
             stare at the clouds and you will never reap.

5 Just as you do not know the way of the wind or the mysteries of a woman with
child, no more can you know the work of God who is behind it all.

6   In the morning sow your seed,
             do not let your hands lie idle in the evening.

For which will prove successful, this or that, you cannot tell; and it may be that
both will turn out well together.

Old age

7
8   Light is sweet; at sight of the sun the eyes are glad. •However great the number
of the years a man may live, let him enjoy them all, and yet remember that dark
days will be many. All that is to come is vanity.

9   Rejoice in your youth, you who are young;
             let your heart give you joy in your young days.
             Follow the promptings of your heart
             and the desires of your eyes.

But this you must know: for all these things God will bring you to judgement.

10   Cast worry from your heart,
             shield your flesh from pain.

1 Yet youth, the age of dark hair, is vanity. **12** And remember your creator in
the days of your youth, before evil days come and the years approach when
2 you say, 'These give me no pleasure', •before sun and light and moon and stars
grow dark, and the clouds return after the rain;

3   the day when those who keep the house tremble*a*
             and strong men are bowed;
             when the women grind no longer at the mill,
             because day is darkening at the windows
4   and the street doors are shut;
             when the sound of the mill is faint,
             when the voice of the bird is silenced,
             and song notes are stilled,
5   when to go uphill is an ordeal
             and a walk is something to dread.

             Yet the almond tree is in flower,
             the grasshopper is heavy with food
             and the caper bush bears its fruit,

while man goes to his everlasting home. And the mourners are already walking
to and fro in the street

6   before the silver cord has snapped,
             or the golden lamp been broken,
             or the pitcher shattered at the spring,
             or the pulley cracked at the well,

7 or before the dust returns to the earth as it once came from it, and the breath
to God who gave it.
8   Vanity of vanities, Qoheleth says. All is vanity.

10 a. Probably to be read after v.16, as the answer given by the 'princes'.
12 a. These lines are a picture of old age.

Epilogue

Besides being a sage, Qoheleth also taught his knowledge to the people, having weighed, studied and amended a great many proverbs. •Qoheleth tried to write in an attractive style and to set down truthful thoughts in a straightforward manner.

The words of the sages are like goads, like pegs driven deep; a shepherd uses these for the good of his flocks.

One last thing, my son, be warned that writing books involves endless hard work, and that much study wearies the body.

To sum up the whole matter: fear God, and keep his commandments, since this is the whole duty of man. •For God will call all hidden deeds, good or bad, to judgement.

INTRODUCTION TO
THE SONG OF SONGS

This is a series of love poems in which the two lovers are now united, now divided, now sought, now found. In places the man is called 'king' and 'Solomon', and the whole work is ascribed to Solomon by Hebrew tradition; however, the vocabulary and style of the writing tell us that it is a later composition and dates from after the Exile.

It has been accepted as an elaborate allegory of the love-story of God and his people Israel; and, indeed, it is possible to find many correspondences between the changing fortunes of the bride in the poems and the sequence in Israel's history of conversion, hope, disillusion and hope renewed. On the other hand the book has been explained as a collection of poems about true love and marriage in which any apparent allusions to Israel's history are accidental. Neither interpretation exactly and satisfactorily accounts for every detail in the book.

THE SONG OF SONGS

TITLE AND PROLOGUE

1 The Song of Songs, which is Solomon's.   1

THE BRIDE   Let him kiss me with the kisses of his mouth.   2
              Your love is more delightful than wine;
              delicate is the fragrance of your perfume,   3
              your name is an oil poured out,
              and that is why the maidens love you.
              Draw me in your footsteps, let us run.   4
              The King has brought me into his rooms;
              you will be our joy and our gladness.
              We shall praise your love above wine;
              how right it is to love you.

FIRST POEM

THE BRIDE   I am black but lovely, daughters of Jerusalem,   5
              like the tents of Kedar,
              like the pavilions of Salmah.
              Take no notice of my swarthiness,   6
              it is the sun that has burnt me.
              My mother's sons turned their anger on me,
              they made me look after the vineyards.
              Had I only looked after my own!

              Tell me then, you whom my heart loves: 7
              Where will you lead your flock to graze,
              where will you rest it at noon?
              That I may no more wander like a vagabond
              beside the flocks of your companions.

THE CHORUS   If you do not know this, O loveliest of women,   8
              follow the tracks of the flock,
              and take your kids to graze
              close by the shepherds' tents.

THE BRIDEGROOM To my mare harnessed to Pharaoh's chariot   9
              I compare you, my love.
              Your cheeks show fair between their pendants   10
              and your neck within its necklaces.
              We shall make you golden earrings   11
              and beads of silver.

DIALOGUE OF   —While the King rests in his own room   12
THE BRIDE AND my nard yields its perfume.
BRIDEGROOM   My Beloved is a sachet of myrrh   13

lying between my breasts.
14   My Beloved is a cluster of henna flowers
among the vines of Engedi.

15   —How beautiful you are, my love,
how beautiful you are!
Your eyes are doves.

16   —How beautiful you are, my Beloved,
and how delightful!
All green is our bed.

17   —The beams of our house are of cedar,
the panelling of cypress.

2

1   —I am the rose of Sharon,
the lily of the valleys.
2   —As a lily among the thistles,
so is my love among the maidens.
3   —As an apple tree among the trees of the orchard,
so is my Beloved among the young men.
In his longed-for shade I am seated
and his fruit is sweet to my taste.
4   He has taken me to his banquet hall,
and the banner he raises over me is love.
5   Feed me with raisin cakes,
restore me with apples,
for I am sick with love.

6   His left arm is under my head,
his right embraces me.

7   —I charge you,
daughters of Jerusalem,
by the gazelles, by the hinds of the field,
not to stir my love, nor rouse it,
until it please to awake.

SECOND POEM

8   THE BRIDE   I hear my Beloved.
See how he comes
leaping on the mountains,
bounding over the hills.
9   My Beloved is like a gazelle,
like a young stag.

See where he stands
behind our wall.
He looks in at the window,
he peers through the lattice.

10   My Beloved lifts up his voice,
he says to me,
'Come then, my love,
my lovely one, come.
11   For see, winter is past,
the rains are over and gone.
12   The flowers appear on the earth.

The season of glad songs has come,
the cooing of the turtledove is heard
in our land.
The fig tree is forming its first figs   13
and the blossoming vines give out their fragrance.
Come then, my love,
my lovely one, come.
My dove, hiding in the clefts of the rock,   14
in the coverts of the cliff,
show me your face,
let me hear your voice;
for your voice is sweet
and your face is beautiful.'

Catch the foxes for us,   15
the little foxes
that make havoc of the vineyards,
for our vineyards are in flower.

My Beloved is mine and I am his.   16
He pastures his flock among the lilies.

Before the dawn-wind rises,   17
before the shadows flee,
return! Be, my Beloved,
like a gazelle,
a young stag,
on the mountains of the covenant.

3   On my bed, at night, I sought him   1
whom my heart loves.
I sought but did not find him.
So I will rise and go through the City;   2
in the streets and the squares
I will seek him whom my heart loves.
... I sought but did not find him.

The watchmen came upon me   3
on their rounds in the City:
'Have you seen him whom my heart loves?'

Scarcely had I passed them   4
than I found him whom my heart loves.
I held him fast, nor would I let him go
till I had brought him
into my mother's house,
into the room of her who conceived me.

THE BRIDEGROOM   I charge you,   5
daughters of Jerusalem,
by the gazelles, by the hinds of the field,
not to stir my love, nor rouse it,
until it please to awake.

THIRD POEM

What is this coming up from the desert   6
like a column of smoke,
breathing of myrrh and frankincense
and every perfume the merchant knows?

7
See, it is the litter of Solomon.
Around it are sixty champions,
the flower of the warriors of Israel;
8
all of them skilled swordsmen,
veterans of battle.
Each man has his sword at his side,
against alarms by night.

9
King Solomon
has made himself a throne
of wood from Lebanon.
10
The posts he has made of silver,
the canopy of gold,
the seat of purple;
the back is inlaid with ebony.

11
Daughters of Zion,
come and see
King Solomon,
wearing the diadem with which his mother crowned him
on his wedding day,
on the day of his heart's joy.

1 **4** THE BRIDEGROOM
How beautiful you are, my love,
how beautiful you are!
Your eyes, behind your veil,
are doves;
your hair is like a flock of goats
frisking down the slopes of Gilead.
2
Your teeth are like a flock of shorn ewes
as they come up from the washing.
Each one has its twin,
not one unpaired with another.
3
Your lips are a scarlet thread
and your words enchanting.
Your cheeks, behind your veil,
are halves of pomegranate.
4
Your neck is the tower of David
built as a fortress,
hung round with a thousand bucklers,
and each the shield of a hero.
5
Your two breasts are two fawns,
twins of a gazelle,
that feed among the lilies.

6
Before the dawn-wind rises,
before the shadows flee,
I will go to the mountain of myrrh,
to the hill of frankincense.

7
You are wholly beautiful, my love,
and without a blemish.

8
Come from Lebanon, my promised bride,
come from Lebanon, come on your way.
Lower your gaze, from the heights of Amana,
from the crests of Senir and Hermon,
the haunt of lions,
the mountains of leopards.

You ravish my heart,   9
my sister,[a] my promised bride,
you ravish my heart
with a single one of your glances,
with one single pearl of your necklace.
What spells lie in your love,   10
my sister, my promised bride!
How delicious is your love, more delicious than wine!
How fragrant your perfumes,
more fragrant than all other spices!
Your lips, my promised one,   11
distil wild honey.
Honey and milk
are under your tongue;
and the scent of your garments
is like the scent of Lebanon.

She is a garden enclosed,   12
my sister, my promised bride;
a garden enclosed,
a sealed fountain.
Your shoots form an orchard of pomegranate trees,   13
the rarest essences are yours:
nard and saffron,   14
calamus and cinnamon,
with all the incense-bearing trees;
myrrh and aloes,
with the subtlest odours.
Fountain that makes the gardens fertile,   15
well of living water,
streams flowing down from Lebanon.

THE BRIDE   Awake, north wind,   16
come, wind of the south!
Breathe over my garden,
to spread its sweet smell around.
Let my Beloved come into his garden,
let him taste its rarest fruits.

5 THE BRIDEGROOM   I come into my garden,   1
my sister, my promised bride,
I gather my myrrh and balsam,
I eat my honey and my honeycomb,
I drink my wine and my milk.
Eat, friends, and drink,
drink deep, my dearest friends.

FOURTH POEM

THE BRIDE   I sleep, but my heart is awake.   2
I hear my Beloved knocking.
'Open to me, my sister, my love,
my dove, my perfect one,
for my head is covered with dew,
my locks with the drops of night.'
—'I have taken off my tunic,   3
am I to put it on again?

I have washed my feet,
am I to dirty them again?'

4   My Beloved thrust his hand
'hrough the hole in the door;
ı trembled to the core of my being.

5   Then I rose
to open to my Beloved,
myrrh ran off my hands,
pure myrrh off my fingers,
on to the handle of the bolt.

6   I opened to my Beloved,
but he had turned his back and gone!
My soul failed at his flight.
I sought him but I did not find him,
I called to him but he did not answer.

7   The watchmen came upon me
as they made their rounds in the City.
They beat me, they wounded me,
they took away my cloak,
they who guard the ramparts.

8   I charge you,
daughters of Jerusalem,
if you should find my Beloved,
what must you tell him ... ?
That I am sick with love.

9   THE CHORUS   What makes your Beloved better than other lovers,
O loveliest of women?
What makes your Beloved better than other lovers,
to give us a charge like this?

10   THE BRIDE   My Beloved is fresh and ruddy,
to be known among ten thousand.

11   His head is golden, purest gold,
his locks are palm fronds
and black as the raven.

12   His eyes are doves
at a pool of water,
bathed in milk,
at rest on a pool.

13   His cheeks are beds of spices,
banks sweetly scented.
His lips are lilies,
distilling pure myrrh.

14   His hands are golden, rounded,
set with jewels of Tarshish.
His belly a block of ivory
covered with sapphires.

15   His legs are alabaster columns
set in sockets of pure gold.
His appearance is that of Lebanon,
unrivalled as the cedars.

16   His conversation is sweetness itself,
he is altogether lovable.

4 a. An expression borrowed from Egyptian love poetry.

Such is my Beloved, such is my friend,
O daughters of Jerusalem.

6 THE CHORUS　　Where did your Beloved go, $\frac{1}{17}$
O loveliest of women?
Which way did your Beloved turn
so that we can help you to look for him?

THE BRIDE　　My Beloved went down to his garden, $\frac{2}{1}$
to the beds of spices,
to pasture his flock in the gardens
and gather lilies.
I am my Beloved's, and my Beloved is mine. $\frac{3}{2}$
He pastures his flock among the lilies.

FIFTH POEM

THE BRIDEGROOM　　You are beautiful as Tirzah, my love, $\frac{4}{3}$
fair as Jerusalem.
Turn your eyes away, $\frac{5}{4}$
for they hold me captive.
Your hair is like a flock of goats
frisking down the slopes of Gilead.
Your teeth are like a flock of sheep $\frac{6}{5}$
as they come up from the washing.
Each one has its twin,
not one unpaired with another.
Your cheeks, behind your veil, $\frac{7}{6}$
are halves of pomegranate.

There are sixty queens $\frac{8}{7}$
and eighty concubines
(and countless maidens).
But my dove is unique, $\frac{9}{8}$
mine, unique and perfect.
She is *the darling of her mother*,
the favourite of the one who bore her.
The maidens saw her, *and proclaimed her blessed*,
queens and concubines *sang her praises*:
'Who is this arising like the dawn, $\frac{10}{9}$
fair as the moon,
resplendent as the sun,
terrible as an army with banners?'

I went down to the nut orchard $\frac{11}{10}$
to see what was sprouting in the valley,
to see if the vines were budding
and the pomegranate trees in flower.
Before I knew ... my desire had hurled me $\frac{12}{11}$
on the chariots of my people, as their prince.

7 THE CHORUS　　Return, return, O maid of Shulam, $\frac{1}{12}$
return, return, that we may gaze on you!

THE BRIDEGROOM　　Why do you gaze on the maid of Shulam   *1*
dancing as though between two rows of dancers?

2

     How beautiful are your feet in their sandals,
     O prince's daughter!
     The curve of your thighs is like the curve of a necklace,
     work of a master hand.

3
2

     Your navel is a bowl well rounded
     with no lack of wine,
     your belly a heap of wheat
     surrounded with lilies.

4
3

     Your two breasts are two fawns,
     twins of a gazelle.

5
4

     Your neck is an ivory tower.
     Your eyes, the pools of Heshbon,
     by the gate of Bath-rabbim.
     Your nose, the Tower of Lebanon,
     sentinel facing Damascus.

6
5

     Your head is held high like Carmel,
     and its plaits are as dark as purple;
     a king is held captive in your tresses.

7
6

     How beautiful you are, how charming,
     my love, my delight!

8
7

     In stature like the palm tree,
     its fruit-clusters your breasts.

9
8

     'I will climb the palm tree,' I resolved,
     'I will seize its clusters of dates.'
     May your breasts be clusters of grapes,
     your breath sweet-scented as apples,

10
9

     your speaking, superlative wine.

THE BRIDE   Wine flowing straight to my Beloved,
     as it runs on the lips of those who sleep.

11
10

     I am my Beloved's,
     and his desire is for me.

12
11

     Come, my Beloved,
     let us go to the fields.
     We will spend the night in the villages,

13
12

     and in the morning we will go to the vineyards.
     We will see if the vines are budding,
     if their blossoms are opening,
     if the pomegranate trees are in flower.
     Then I shall give you
     the gift of my love.

14
13

     The mandrakes yield their fragrance, [a]
     the rarest fruits are at our doors;
     the new as well as the old,
     I have stored them for you, my Beloved.

1 **8**   Ah, why are you not my brother,
     nursed at my mother's breast!
     Then if I met you out of doors, I could kiss you
     without people thinking ill of me.

2

     I should lead you, I should take you
     into my mother's house, and you would teach me!
     I should give you spiced wine to drink,
     juice of my pomegranates.

3

     His left arm is under my head
     and his right embraces me.

7 a. The mandrake was thought to be aphrodisiac, and to promote fertility.

THE BRIDEGROOM   I charge you,   4
                  daughters of Jerusalem,
                  not to stir my love, nor rouse it,
                  until it please to awake.

CONCLUSION

THE CHORUS   Who is this coming up from the desert   5
                  leaning on her Beloved?

THE BRIDEGROOM   I awakened you under the apple tree,
                  there where your mother conceived you,
                  there where she who gave birth to you conceived you.

                  Set me like a seal on your heart,   6
                  like a seal on your arm.
                  For love is strong as Death,
                  jealousy relentless as Sheol.[a]
                  The flash of it is a flash of fire,
                  a flame of Yahweh himself.
                  Love no flood can quench,   7
                  no torrents drown.

APPENDICES

Aphorism of a sage

Were a man to offer all the wealth of his house to buy love, contempt is all he would purchase.

Two epigrams[b]

Our sister is little: her breasts are not yet formed. What shall we do for our sister on the day she is spoken for? •If she is a rampart, on the crest we will 8 build a battlement of silver; if she is a door, we will board her up with planks 9 of cedar.

— I am a wall, and my breasts represent its towers. And under his eyes I have found true peace.   10

Solomon had a vineyard at Baal-hamon. He entrusted it to overseers, and each one was to pay him the value of its produce, a thousand shekels of 11 silver. •But I look after my own vineyard myself. You, Solomon, may have your thousand shekels, and those who oversee its produce their two hundred.   12

Final additions

You[c] who dwell in the gardens, my companions listen for your voice; deign 13 to let me hear it.

                  Haste away, my Beloved.   14
                  Be like a gazelle,
                  a young stag,
                  on the spicy mountains.[d]

---

8 a. Sheol (the underworld) is personified here and more or less an equivalent of Death.
b. Written in criticism of the worldly wisdom of a Jewish ruler, probably John Hyrcanus, 135–105 B.C. In the first, Jerusalem answers that she has no need of the costly fortifications proposed by 'her brothers', the Sadducees. The second seems to protest that the modern Solomon's officers are taking a large commission on the taxes which they do nothing to earn.
c. Wisdom.   **d.** An answer by a different author.

INTRODUCTION
TO THE BOOK OF
WISDOM

Wisdom, like Ecclesiastes, is attributed inside the book to King Solomon; but it is a late book, written in the last century B.C., in the expressive Greek of a well-educated hellenised Jew.

The three main divisions in this well-constructed book are distinguished in the present translation by headings:

I. Wisdom and Man's Destiny, ch.1-5.
II. The Origin, Nature and Effects of Wisdom, ch.6-9.
III. Wisdom and God in History, ch.10-19.

The last section concentrates attention on the Exodus from Egypt as the supreme work of God's provident wisdom, and it includes a long digression on idolatry.

This book was not included in the canon of Hebrew scripture. However, it was known to the writers of the New Testament, who make use of it in several places.

THE BOOK OF
WISDOM

I. WISDOM AND MAN'S DESTINY

On seeking God and rejecting evil

1 Love virtue, you who are judges on earth, [a]   1
   let honesty prompt your thinking about the Lord,
   seek him in simplicity of heart;
   since he is to be found by those who do not put him to the test,   2
   he shows himself to those who do not distrust him.
   But selfish intentions divorce from God;   3
   and Omnipotence, put to the test, confounds the foolish.
   No, Wisdom will never make its way into a crafty soul   4
   nor stay in a body that is in debt to sin;
   the holy spirit of instruction shuns deceit,   5
   it stands aloof from reckless purposes,
   is taken aback when iniquity appears.

   Wisdom is a spirit, a friend to man,   6
   though she will not pardon the words of a blasphemer,
   since God sees into the innermost parts of him,
   truly observes his heart,
   and listens to his tongue.
   The spirit of the Lord, indeed, fills the whole world,   7
   and that which holds all things together knows every word that is said.
   The man who gives voice to injustice will never go unnoticed,   8
   nor shall avenging Justice pass him by.
   For the godless man's deliberations will be examined,   9
   and a report of his words will reach the Lord
   to convict him of his crimes.
   There is a jealous ear that overhears everything,   10
   not so much as a murmur of complaint escapes it.
   Beware, then, of complaining about nothing,   11
   and keep your tongue from finding fault;
   since the most secret word will have repercussions,
   and a lying mouth deals death to the soul.

   Do not court death by the errors of your ways,   12
   nor invite destruction through your own actions.
   Death was not God's doing,   13
   he takes no pleasure in the extinction of the living.
   To be—for this he created all;   14
   the world's created things have health in them,
   in them no fatal poison can be found,
   and Hades[b] holds no power on earth;
   for virtue is undying.   15

Life as the godless see it

16 But the godless call with deed and word for Death,
counting him friend, they wear themselves out for him,
with him they make a pact,
and are fit to be his partners.

2 1 For they say to themselves, with their misguided reasoning:

'Our life is short and dreary,
nor is there any relief when man's end comes,
nor is anyone known who can give release from Hades.

2 By chance we came to birth,
and after this life we shall be as if we had never been.
The breath in our nostrils is a puff of smoke,
reason a spark from the beating of our hearts;

3 put this out and our body turns to ashes,
and the spirit melts away like idle air.

4 In time, our name will be forgotten,
nobody will remember what we have done;
our life will pass away like wisps of cloud,
dissolve like the mist
that the sun's rays drive away
and the heat of it overwhelms.

5 Yes, our days are the passing of a shadow,
from our death there is no turning back,
the seal is set: no one returns.

6 'Come then, let us enjoy what good things there are,
use this creation with the zest of youth:

7 take our fill of the dearest wines and perfumes,
let not one flower of springtime pass us by,

8 before they wither crown ourselves with roses.

9 Let none of us forgo his part in our orgy,
let us leave the signs of our revelry everywhere,
this is our portion, this the lot assigned us.

10 'As for the virtuous man who is poor, let us oppress him;
let us not spare the widow,
nor respect old age, white-haired with many years.

11 Let our strength be the yardstick of virtue,
since weakness argues its own futility.

12 Let us lie in wait for the virtuous man, since he annoys us
and opposes our way of life,
reproaches us for our breaches of the law
and accuses us of playing false to our upbringing.

13 He claims to have knowledge of God,
and calls himself a son of the Lord.

14 Before us he stands, a reproof to our way of thinking,
the very sight of him weighs our spirits down;

15 his way of life is not like other men's,
the paths he treads are unfamiliar.

16 In his opinion we are counterfeit;
he holds aloof from our doings as though from filth;
he proclaims the final end of the virtuous as happy
and boasts of having God for his father.

17 Let us see if what he says is true,

---

1 a. 'Judges' is equivalent to 'men in authority'; the book is written as though by Solomon for his fellow-kings.   b. I.e., Death; the Greek word represents the Hebrew *sheol*.

let us observe what kind of end he himself will have.
If the virtuous man is God's son, God will take his part   18
and rescue him from the clutches of his enemies.
Let us test him with cruelty and with torture,   19
and thus explore this gentleness of his
and put his endurance to the proof.
Let us condemn him to a shameful death   20
since he will be looked after—we have his word for it.'

The godless gravely mistaken

This is the way they reason, but they are misled,   21
their malice makes them blind.
They do not know the hidden things of God,   22
they have no hope that holiness will be rewarded,
they can see no reward for blameless souls.
Yet God did make man imperishable,   23
he made him in the image of his own nature;
it was the devil's envy that brought death into the world,   24
as those who are his partners will discover.

The destinies of good and bad men compared

3   But the souls of the virtuous are in the hands of God,   1
no torment shall ever touch them.
In the eyes of the unwise, they did appear to die,   2
their going looked like a disaster,
their leaving us, like annihilation;   3
but they are in peace.
If they experienced punishment as men see it,   4
their hope was rich with immortality;
slight was their affliction, great will their blessings be.   5
God has put them to the test
and proved them worthy to be with him;
he has tested them like gold in a furnace,   6
and accepted them as a holocaust.
When the time comes for his visitation they will shine out;   7
as sparks run through the stubble, so will they.
They shall judge nations, rule over peoples,   8
and the Lord will be their king for ever.
They who trust in him will understand the truth,   9
those who are faithful will live with him in love;
for grace and mercy await those he has chosen.

But the godless will be duly punished for their reasoning,   10
for neglecting the virtuous man and deserting the Lord.
Yes, wretched are they who scorn wisdom and discipline:[a]   11
their hope is void,
their toil unavailing,
their achievements unprofitable;
their wives are reckless,   12
their children depraved,
their descendants accursed.

Better be barren than have godless children

Blessed the barren woman[b] if she be blameless,   13
she who has known no guilty bed;
her fruitfulness will be seen at the scrutiny of souls.

14   Blessed, too, the eunuch[c] whose hand has committed no crime,
who has contemplated no wrong against the Lord;
for his loyalty special favour will be granted him,
a most desirable portion in the temple of the Lord.

15   For the fruit of honest labours is glorious,
and the root of understanding does not decay.

16   But children of adulterers,[d] these shall have no future,
the offspring of an unlawful bed must vanish.

17   Even if they live long, they will count for nothing,
their old age will go unhonoured at the last;

18   while if they die early, they have neither hope
nor comfort on the day of doom.

19   Yes, harsh is the fate of a race of evil-doers.

4

1   Better to have no children yet to have virtue,
since immortality perpetuates its memory
and God and men both think highly of it.

2   Present, we imitate it,
absent, we long for it;
crowned, it holds triumph through eternity,
having striven for blameless prizes and emerged the victor.

3   But the swarming brood of the godless shall bring no advantage;
offspring of bastard stock, it will never strike deep roots,
never put down firm foundations.

4   Branch out for a time they may;
but, frailly rooted, they will sway in the wind,
be torn up by the violence of the storm;

5   hardly grown, their branches will be snapped off,
their fruit be useless,
too unripe to eat,
fit for nothing.

6   For children begotten of unlawful intercourse
witness, when God judges them, to the wrong their parents did.

The premature death of the virtuous man

7   The virtuous man, though he die before his time, will find rest.

8   Length of days is not what makes age honourable,
nor number of years the true measure of life;

9   understanding, this is man's grey hairs,
untarnished life, this is ripe old age.

10   He has sought to please God, so God has loved him;
as he was living among sinners, he has been taken up.

11   He has been carried off so that evil may not warp his understanding
or treachery seduce his soul;

12   for the fascination of evil throws good things into the shade,
and the whirlwind of desire corrupts a simple heart.

13   Coming to perfection in so short a while, he achieved long life;

14   his soul being pleasing to the Lord,
he has taken him quickly from the wickedness around him.

---

3 a. This wisdom is practical—life directed by wisdom; for this, discipline is necessary.
b. Until now, it had been axiomatic that sterility was a disgrace or a punishment.   **c.** Eunuchs
were excluded from the community of Israel (Dt 23:2), and therefore from the blessings promised
to the Chosen People.   **d.** The word may bear the usual sense; or indicate Jews married to
pagans, or simply renegade Jews.

Yet people look on, uncomprehending;
it does not enter their heads
that grace and mercy await the chosen of the Lord,   15
and protection, his holy ones.
The virtuous man who dies condemns the godless who survive,   16
and youth's untimely end the protracted age of the wicked.
These people see the wise man's ending   17
without understanding what the Lord has in store for him
or why he has taken him to safety;
they look on and sneer,   18
but the Lord will laugh at them.
Soon they will be corpses without honour,   19
objects of scorn among the dead for ever.
The Lord will dash them down headlong, dumb.
He will tear them from their foundations,
they will be utterly laid waste,
anguish will be theirs,
and their memory shall perish.

Virtuous men and godless at the judgement

They will come trembling to the reckoning of their sins,   20
and their crimes, confronting them, will accuse them.

5 Then the virtuous man stands up boldly   1
to face those who have oppressed him,
those who thought so little of his sufferings.
And they, at the sight of him, will shake with cowards' fear,   2
amazed he should be saved so unexpectedly.
Stricken with remorse, each will say to the other,   3
say with a groan and in distress of spirit:

'This is the man we used to laugh at once,   4
a butt for our sarcasm, fools that we were!
His life we regarded as madness,
his ending as without honour.
How has he come to be counted as one of the sons of God?   5
How does he come to be assigned a place among the saints?
Clearly we have strayed from the way of truth;   6
the light of justice has not shone for us,
the sun never rose on us.
We have left no path of lawlessness or ruin unexplored,   7
we have crossed deserts where there was no track,
but the way of the Lord is one we have never known.
Arrogance, what advantage has this brought us?   8
Wealth and boasting, what have these conferred on us?
All those things have passed like a shadow,   9
passed like a fleeting rumour.
Like a ship that cuts through heaving waves —   10
leaving no trace to show where it has passed,
no wake from its keel in the waves.
Or like a bird flying through the air —   11
leaving no proof of its passing;
it whips the light air with the stroke of its pinions,
tears it apart in its whirring rush,
drives its way onward with sweeping wing,
and afterwards no sign is seen of its passage.
Or like an arrow shot at a mark,   12

the pierced air closing so quickly on itself,
there is no knowing which way the arrow has passed.
13 So with us: scarcely born, we have ceased to be;
of virtue not a trace have we to show,
we have spent ourselves on wickedness instead.'

14
15 Yes, the hope of the godless is like chaff carried on the wind,
like fine spray driven by the gale;
it disperses like smoke before the wind,
goes like the memory of a one-day guest.

15
16 But the virtuous live for ever,
their recompense lies with the Lord,
the Most High takes care of them.

16
17 So they shall receive the royal crown of splendour,
the diadem of beauty from the hand of the Lord;
for he will shelter them with his right hand
and shield them with his arm.

17
18 For armour he will take his jealous love,
he will arm creation to punish his enemies;

18
19 he will put on justice as a breastplate,
and for helmet wear his undissembling judgement;

19
20 he will take up invincible holiness for shield,
20
21 he will forge a biting sword of his stern wrath,
and the universe will march with him to fight the reckless.

21
22 Bolts truly aimed, the shafts of lightning will leap,
and from the clouds, as from a full-drawn bow, fly to their mark;

22
23 and the catapult will hurl hailstones charged with fury.
The waters of the sea will rage against them,
the rivers engulf them without pity.

23
24 The breath of Omnipotence will blow against them
and winnow them like a hurricane.
So lawlessness will bring the whole earth to ruin
and evil-doing bring the thrones of the mighty down.

II. THE ORIGIN, NATURE AND EFFECTS OF WISDOM
HOW IT IS TO BE HAD

The duty of kings to cultivate wisdom

1
2 **6** ᵃListen then, kings, and understand;
rulers of remotest lands, take warning;
2
3 hear this, you who have thousands under your rule,
who boast of your hordes of subjects.
3
4 For power is a gift to you from the Lord,
sovereignty is from the Most High;
he himself will probe your acts and scrutinise your intentions.

4
5 If, as administrators of his kingdom, you have not governed justly
nor observed the law,
nor behaved as God would have you behave,
5
6 he will fall on you swiftly and terribly.
Ruthless judgement is reserved for the high and mighty;
6
7 the lowly will be compassionately pardoned,

6 a. The Latin Vulgate begins this chapter with an additional maxim numbered as v.1.

the mighty will be mightily punished.
For the Lord of All does not cower before a personage, 7 / 8
he does not stand in awe of greatness,
since he himself has made small and great
and provides for all alike;
but strict scrutiny awaits those in power. 8 / 9

Yes, despots, my words are for you, 9 / 10
that you may learn what wisdom is and not transgress;
for they who observe holy things holily will be adjudged holy, 10 / 11
and, accepting instruction from them, will find their defence in them.
Look forward, therefore, to my words; 11 / 12
yearn for them, and they will instruct you.

Wisdom sought is Wisdom found

Wisdom is bright, and does not grow dim. 12 / 13
By those who love her she is readily seen,
and found by those who look for her.
Quick to anticipate those who desire her, she makes herself 13 / 14
known to them.
Watch for her early and you will have no trouble; 14 / 15
you will find her sitting at your gates.
Even to think about her is understanding fully grown; 15 / 16
be on the alert for her and anxiety will quickly leave you.
She herself walks about looking for those who are worthy of her 16 / 17
and graciously shows herself to them as they go,
in every thought of theirs coming to meet them.

Of her the most sure beginning is the desire for discipline, 17 / 18
care for discipline means loving her,
loving her means keeping her laws, 18 / 19
obeying her laws guarantees incorruptibility,
incorruptibility brings near to God; 19 / 20
thus desire for Wisdom leads to sovereignty. 20 / 21
If then, despots of nations, you delight in throne and sceptre, 21 / 22
honour Wisdom, thus to reign for ever.

Solomon sets out to describe Wisdom

What Wisdom is and how she came to be, I will now declare, 22 / 24
I will hide none of the secrets from you;
I will trace her right from the beginning
and set out knowledge of her, plainly,
not swerving from the truth.
Neither will I take blighting Envy as my travelling companion, 23 / 25
for she has nothing in common with Wisdom.
In the greatest number of wise men lies the world's salvation, 24 / 26
in a sagacious king the stability of a people.
Learn, therefore, from my words; the gain will be yours. 25 / 27

Solomon a man like other men

7 Like all the others, I too am a mortal man, 1
descendant of the first being fashioned from the earth,
I was modelled in flesh within my mother's womb,
for ten months*a* taking shape in her blood 2
by means of virile seed and pleasure, sleep's companion.
I too, when I was born, drew in the common air, 3
I fell on the same ground that bears us all,

a wail my first sound, as for all the rest.
4   I was nurtured in swaddling clothes, with every care.
5   No king has known any other beginning of existence;
6   for all there is one way only into life, as out of it.

Solomon's respect for Wisdom

7   And so I prayed, and understanding was given me;
       I entreated, and the spirit of Wisdom came to me.
8   I esteemed her more than sceptres and thrones;
       compared with her, I held riches as nothing.
9   I reckoned no priceless stone to be her peer,
       for compared with her, all gold is a pinch of sand,
       and beside her silver ranks as mud.
10   I loved her more than health or beauty,
       preferred her to the light,
       since her radiance never sleeps.
11   In her company all good things came to me,
       at her hands riches not to be numbered.
12   All these I delighted in, since Wisdom brings them,
       but as yet I did not know she was their mother.
13   What I learned without self-interest, I pass on without reserve;
       I do not intend to hide her riches.
14   For she is an inexhaustible treasure to men,
       and those who acquire it win God's friendship,
       commended as they are to him by the benefits of her teaching.

The appeal to divine inspiration

15   May God grant me to speak as he would wish
       and express thoughts worthy of his gifts,
       since he himself is the guide of Wisdom,
       since he directs the sages.
16   We are indeed in his hand, we ourselves and our words,
       with all our understanding, too, and technical knowledge.
17   It was he who gave me true knowledge of all that is,[b]
       who taught me the structure of the world and the properties
          of the elements,
18   the beginning, end and middle of the times,
       the alternation of the solstices and the succession of the seasons,
19   the revolution of the year and the positions of the stars,
20   the natures of animals and the instincts of wild beasts,
       the powers of spirits and the mental processes of men,
       the varieties of plants and the medical properties of roots.
21   All that is hidden, all that is plain, I have come to know,
       instructed by Wisdom who designed them all.

In praise of Wisdom

22   For within her is a spirit intelligent, holy,
       unique, manifold, subtle,
       active, incisive, unsullied,
       lucid, invulnerable, benevolent, sharp,
23   irresistible, beneficent, loving to man,
       steadfast, dependable, unperturbed,
       almighty, all-surveying,

7 a. Ten lunar months.   **b.** The outline of knowledge and science which follows reflects the interests of the hellenistic schools of the author's own day.

penetrating all intelligent, pure
and most subtle spirits;
for Wisdom is quicker to move than any motion;   24
she is so pure, she pervades and permeates all things.

She is a breath of the power of God,   25
pure emanation of the glory of the Almighty;
hence nothing impure can find a way into her.
She is a reflection of the eternal light,   26
untarnished mirror of God's active power,
image of his goodness.

Although alone, she can do all;   27
herself unchanging, she makes all things new.
In each generation she passes into holy souls,
she makes them friends of God and prophets;
for God loves only the man who lives with Wisdom.   28
She is indeed more splendid than the sun,   29
she outshines all the constellations;
compared with light, she takes first place,
for light must yield to night,   30
but over Wisdom evil can never triumph.

8 She deploys her strength from one end of the earth to the other, 1
ordering all things for good.

From Wisdom comes all that is desirable

She it was I loved and searched for from my youth;   2
I resolved to have her as my bride,
I fell in love with her beauty.
Her closeness to God lends lustre to her noble birth, 3
since the Lord of All has loved her.
Yes, she is an initiate in the mysteries of God's knowledge, 4
making choice of the works he is to do.
If in this life wealth be a desirable possession,   5
what is more wealthy than Wisdom whose work is everywhere?
Or if it be the intellect that is at work,   6
where is there a greater than Wisdom, designer of all?
Or if it be virtue you love,   7
why, virtues are the fruit of her labours,
since it is she who teaches temperance and prudence,
justice and fortitude;
nothing in life is more serviceable to men than these.
Or if you are eager for wide experience,   8
she knows the past, she forecasts the future;
she knows how to turn maxims, and solve riddles;
she has foreknowledge of signs and wonders,
of the unfolding of the ages and the times.

Wisdom indispensable to rulers

I therefore determined to take her to share my life, 9
knowing she would be my counsellor in prosperity,
my comfort in cares and sorrow.
Through her, I thought, I shall be acclaimed where people gather 10
and honoured, while still a youth, among the elders.
I shall be reckoned shrewd when I sit in judgement,   11
in presence of the great I shall be admired.
They will wait on my silences,   12

and pay attention when I speak;
if I speak at some length, they will lay their hand on their lips.

13 By means of her, immortality shall be mine,
I shall leave an everlasting memory to my successors.

14 I shall govern peoples and nations will be subject to me;

15 at the sound of my name fearsome despots will be afraid;
I shall show myself kind to my people and valiant in battle.

16 When I go home I shall take my ease with her,
for nothing is bitter in her company,
when life is shared with her there is no pain,
gladness only, and joy.

Solomon prepares to ask for Wisdom

17 Inwardly revolving these thoughts,
and considering in my heart
that immortality is found in being kin to Wisdom

18 pure contentment in her friendship,
inexhaustible riches in what she does,
intelligence in the cultivation of her society,
and renown in the fellowship of her conversation,
I went in all directions seeking by what means I might make her mine.

19 I was a boy of happy disposition,
I had received a good soul as my lot,

20 or rather, being good, I had entered an undefiled body;
but knowing I could not master Wisdom but by the gift of God
—a mark itself of understanding, to know whose the bounty was—
I turned to the Lord and entreated him,
with all my heart I said:

A prayer for Wisdom

1 9 'God of our ancestors, Lord of mercy,
who by your word have made all things,

2 and in your wisdom have fitted man
to rule the creatures that have come from you,

3 to govern the world in holiness and justice
and in honesty of soul to wield authority,

4 grant me Wisdom, consort of your throne,
and do not reject me from the number of your children.

5 'For I am your servant, son of your serving maid,
a feeble man, with little time to live,
with small understanding of justice and the laws.

6 Indeed, were anyone perfect among the sons of men,
if he lacked the Wisdom that comes from you, he would still
count for nothing.

7 You yourself have chosen me[a] to be king over your people,
to be judge of your sons and daughters.

8 You have bidden me build a temple on your holy mountain,
an altar in the city where you have pitched your tent,
a copy of that sacred tabernacle which you prepared
from the beginning.

9 With you is Wisdom, she who knows your works,
she who was present when you made the world;
she understands what is pleasing in your eyes

9 a. Solomon was preferred to Absalom or Adonijah, 2 S 3:2-5.

and what agrees with your commandments.
Despatch her from the holy heavens,   10
send her forth from your throne of glory
to help me and to toil with me
and teach me what is pleasing to you,
since she knows and understands everything.   11
She will guide me prudently in my undertakings
and protect me by her glory.
Then all I do will be acceptable,   12
I shall govern your people justly
and shall be worthy of my father's[b] throne.

'What man indeed can know the intentions of God?   13
Who can divine the will of the Lord?
The reasonings of mortals are unsure   14
and our intentions unstable;
for a perishable body presses down the soul,   15
and this tent of clay weighs down the teeming mind.
It is hard enough for us to work out what is on earth,   16
laborious to know what lies within our reach;
who, then, can discover what is in the heavens?
As for your intention, who could have learnt it, had you not   17
    granted Wisdom
and sent your holy spirit from above?
Thus have the paths of those on earth been straightened   18
and men been taught what pleases you,
and saved, by Wisdom.'

III. WISDOM AND GOD IN HISTORY

From Adam to Moses

10   The father of the world, the first being to be fashioned,   1
created alone, he had her for his protector
and she delivered him from his fault;[a]
she gave him the strength to subjugate all things.   2
But when a sinner[b] in his wrath deserted her,   3
he perished in his fratricidal fury.

When because of him the earth was drowned, it was Wisdom   4
    again who saved it,
piloting the virtuous man[c] on a paltry piece of wood.
Again, when, concurring in wickedness, the nations had been   5
    thrown into confusion,
it was she who singled out the virtuous man,[d] preserved him
    blameless before God
and fortified him against pity for his child.
It was she who, while the godless perished, saved the virtuous man[e]   6
as he fled from the fire raining down on the Five Cities,
in witness against whose evil ways   7
a desolate land still smokes,
where shrubs bear fruit that never ripens
and where, monument to an unbelieving soul, there stands a pillar
    of salt.
For, by neglecting the path of Wisdom,   8
not only were they kept from knowledge of the good,

they actually left the world a memorial of their folly,
so that their crimes might not escape notice.

9   But Wisdom delivered her servants from their ordeals.
10 The virtuous man,[f] fleeing from the anger of his brother,
was led by her along straight paths.
She showed him the kingdom of God
and taught him the knowledge of holy things.
She brought him success in his toil
and gave him full return for all his efforts;
11 she stood by him against grasping and oppressive men
and she made him rich.
12 She guarded him closely from his enemies
and saved him from the traps they set for him.
In an arduous struggle she awarded him the prize,
to teach him that piety is stronger than all.

13 She did not forsake the virtuous man when he was sold,[g]
but kept him free from sin;
14 she went down to the dungeon with him;
she would not abandon him in his chains,
but procured for him the sceptre of a kingdom
and authority over his despotic masters,
thus exposing as liars those who had traduced him,
and giving him honour everlasting.

The Exodus

15 A holy people and a blameless race,
this she delivered from a nation of oppressors.
16 She entered the soul of a servant of the Lord,[h]
and withstood fearsome kings with wonders and signs.
17 To the saints she gave the wages of their labours;
she led them by a marvellous road;
she herself was their shelter by day
and their starlight through the night.
18 She brought them across the Red Sea,
led them through that immensity of water,
19 while she swallowed their enemies in the waves
then spat them out from the depths of the abyss.
20 So the virtuous despoiled the godless;
Lord, they extolled your holy name,
and with one accord praised your protecting hand,
21 for Wisdom opened the mouths of the dumb
and gave speech to the tongues of babes.

1   **11** At the hand of a holy prophet[a] she gave their actions success.
2   They journeyed through an unpeopled wilderness
and pitched their tents in inaccessible places.
3   They stood firm against their enemies, fought off their foes.
4   On you[b] they called when they were thirsty,
and from the rocky cliff water was given them,
from hard stone their thirst was quenched.

b. David.
10 a. It was common doctrine of contemporary Judaism that Adam was 'delivered by
repentance and atonement.   b. Cain.   c. Noah.   d. Abraham.   e. Lot.   f. Jacob.
g. Joseph.   h. Moses.
11 a. Moses.   b. God; much of the rest of the book is directly addressed to him (e.g. continuously from here to 12:14) and Wisdom is scarcely mentioned again.

How water proved the ruin of Egypt and the saving of Israel

Thus, what served to punish their enemies   5
became a benefit for them in their distress.   5,6

You gave them not that ever-flowing source of river water   6
turbid with defiling floods,   7

stern answer for their decree of infanticide,[c]   7
but, against all hope, water in abundance,   8

showing by the thirst that then was raging   8
how severely you punished their enemies.   9

From their ordeals, which were no more than the reproofs of Mercy,   9
they learned what tortures a sentence of wrath inflicts on the godless;   10

you tested them indeed, correcting them like a father,   10
but the others you strictly examined, like a severe king who condemns.   11

Near or far away,[d] they were equally worn down,   11
double indeed was the grief that seized on them,   12

double the groaning at the memory of the past;   12
hearing that what punished them[e] had set the others rejoicing,   13

they saw the Lord in it,   13
and for him whom long ago they had cast out, exposed, and   14
    later mockingly rebuffed,[f]   15

they felt only amazement when all was done;
the thirst of the virtuous and theirs had worked so differently.

God's forbearance with Egypt

As their foolish and wicked notions led them astray   15
into worshipping mindless reptiles and contemptible beasts,   16

you sent hordes of mindless creatures to punish them
and teach them that the instruments of sin are instruments   16
    of punishment.   17

And indeed your all-powerful hand did not lack means   17
—the hand that from formless matter created the world —   18

to unleash a horde of bears or savage lions on them
or unknown beasts, newly created, full of rage,   18
exhaling fiery breath,   19

ejecting swirls of stinking smoke
or flashing fearful sparks from their eyes,

beasts not only able to crush them with a blow,   19
but also to destroy them by their terrifying appearance.   20

But even without these, they could have dropped dead at a single breath,   20
pursued by your justice,   21

whirled away by the breath of your power.
But no, you ordered all things by measure, number, weight.

This forbearance explained

For your great strength is always at your call;   21
who can withstand the might of your arm?   22

In your sight the whole world is like a grain of dust that tips the scales,   22
like a drop of morning dew falling on the ground.   23

Yet you are merciful to all, because you can do all things   23
and overlook men's sins so that they can repent.   24

Yes, you love all that exists, you hold nothing of what you have   24
    made in abhorrence,   25

for had you hated anything, you would not have formed it.
And how, had you not willed it, could a thing persist,   25
how be conserved if not called forth by you?   26

You spare all things because all things are yours, Lord, lover of life,   26
    27

1
2 **12** you whose imperishable spirit is in all.
Little by little, therefore, you correct those who offend,
you admonish and remind them of how they have sinned,
so that they may abstain from evil and trust in you, Lord.

God's forbearance with Canaan

3 The ancient inhabitants of your holy land
4 you hated for their loathsome practices,
their deeds of sorcery and unholy rites,
5 hated as ruthless murderers of children,
as eaters of entrails at feasts of human flesh,
initiated while the bloody orgy goes on, [a]
6 as murderous parents of defenceless beings.
You determined to destroy them at our fathers' hands,
7 so that this land, dearer to you than any other,
might receive a colony of God's children worthy of it.

8 Even so, since these were men, you treated them leniently,
sending hornets as forerunners of your army,
to destroy them bit by bit.
9 Not that you could not hand the godless over to the virtuous in
pitched battle
or destroy them at once by savage beasts or one stern word from you;
10 but, by condemning them piece by piece, you gave them the chance
to repent,
although you knew very well they were inherently evil,
innately wicked
11 and fixed in their cast of mind;
for they were a race accursed from the beginning.

This forbearance explained

Nor was it from awe of anyone that you left them unpunished
12 for their sins.
Who would venture to say, 'What have you done?'
Who would dare to defy your sentence?
Who arraign you for destroying nations which you have created?
What champion of guilty men dare come to confront you
and challenge you?
13 For there is no god, other than you, who cares for every thing,
to whom you might have to prove that you never judged unjustly;
14 as for those you punished, no king, no despot, dare reproach you
with it to your face.
15 Being just yourself, you order all things justly,
holding it unworthy of your power
to condemn a man who has not deserved to be punished.
16 Your justice has its source in strength,
your sovereignty over all makes you lenient to all.
17 You show your strength when your sovereign power is questioned
and you expose the insolence of those who know it;
18 but, disposing of such strength, you are mild in judgement,
you govern us with great lenience,
for you have only to will, and your power is there.

c. According to Ex 7, the turning of the Nile water into blood was a threat to persuade
Pharoah to release the Israelites; here it is represented as retribution for the decree of Ex 1.
d. The Egyptians, 'near' while Israel was among them, 'far' after the Exodus.   e. Water.
f. Moses; as a baby he had been 'exposed' on the Nile waters.
12 a. Human sacrifice was known in Canaan, but nothing is known of cannibalism; the author
is borrowing from his knowledge of hellenistic mystery religions.

What is to be learned from God's forbearance

By acting thus you have taught a lesson to your people   19
how the virtuous man must be kindly to his fellow men,
and you have given your sons the good hope
that after sin you will grant repentance.
If with such care and such indulgence you have punished   20
the enemies of your children,
when death was what they deserved,
and given them time and room to rid themselves of wickedness,
with what exact attention have you not judged your sons,   21
to whose ancestors you made such fair promises by oaths
     and covenants.
Thus, while you correct us, you flog our enemies ten thousand   22
     times harder,
to teach us, when we judge, to reflect on your kindness
and when we are judged, to look for mercy.

God follows clemency with severity

This is why, against those who were leading wicked and foolish lives,   23
you turned their own abominations to torment them;
they had indeed strayed too far from paths that strayed already,   24
and came to regard the vilest, most contemptible animals as gods,
being deceived, like silly little children.
So, as to children with no sense,   25
you sent them a punishment to mock them,
but they who took no warning from such mocking correction   26
were soon to experience a punishment worthy of God.
Worn down by what they suffered from these beasts,   27
those beasts they had taken for gods, now the means of
     their punishment,
they saw straight, and acknowledged as true God
him they had hitherto refused to know.
That is why the extreme penalty was inflicted on them.

Astral and nature cults

13 Yes, naturally stupid are all men who have not known God   1
and who, from the good things that are seen, have not been
     able to discover Him-who-is,
or, by studying the works, have failed to recognise the Artificer.
Fire however, or wind, or the swift air,   2
the sphere of the stars, impetuous water, heaven's lamps,
are what they have held to be the gods who govern the world.

If, charmed by their beauty, they have taken things for gods,   3
let them know how much the Lord of these excels them,
since the very Author of beauty has created them.
And if they have been impressed by their power and energy,   4
let them deduce from these how much mightier is he that has
     formed them,
since through the grandeur and beauty of the creatures   5
we may, by analogy, contemplate their Author.

Small blame, however, attaches to these men,   6
for perhaps they only go astray
in their search for God and their eagerness to find him;
living among his works, they strive to comprehend them   7
and fall victim to appearances, seeing so much beauty.

8   Even so, they are not to be excused:
9   if they are capable of acquiring enough knowledge
    to be able to investigate the world,
    how have they been so slow to find its Master?

The cults of idols

10 But wretched are they—in dead things putting their hopes—
    who have given to things made by human hands the title of gods,
    gold and silver, finely worked,
    likenesses of animals,
    or some useless stone, carved by some hand long ago.

11 Take a woodcutter. He fells a suitable tree,
    neatly strips off the bark all over
    and then with admirable skill
    works the wood into an object useful in daily life.

12 The bits left over from his work
    he uses for cooking his food, then eats his fill.

13 There is still a good-for-nothing bit left over,
    a gnarled and knotted billet:
    he picks it up, whittles it with the concentration of leisure,
    he shapes it with the skill of relaxation,
    he gives it a human shape

14 or perhaps he makes it into some vile animal,
    smears it with ochre, paints its surface red,
    coats over all its blemishes.

15 He next makes a worthy home for it,
    lets it into the wall, fixes it with an iron clamp.

16 Thus he makes sure that it will not fall down—
    he is well aware it cannot help itself:
    it is only an image, and it needs to be helped.

17 And yet, if he wishes to pray for his goods, for marriages,
            for his children,
    he does not blush to harangue this lifeless thing—
    for health he invokes weakness,

18 for life he pleads with death,
    for help he goes begging to utter inexperience,
    for his travels, to something that cannot stir a foot;

19 for his profits and plans and success in pursuing his craft,
    he asks skill from something whose hands have no skill whatever

14
1   Or someone else, taking ship to cross the raging sea,
    invokes a log[a] even frailer than the vessel that bears him.

2   No doubt that ship is the product of a craving for gain,
    its building embodies the wisdom of the shipwright,

3   but your providence, Father, is what steers it,
    you having opened a pathway even through the sea,
    a safe way over the waves,

4   showing that you can save, whatever happens,
    so that even without skill a man may sail abroad.

5   It is not your will that the works of your Wisdom lie idle,
    and hence men entrust their lives to the smallest piece of wood,
    cross the high seas on a raft and come safe to port.

6   Why, in the beginning even, while the proud giants were perishing,

b. False gods.
14 a. A wooden image on the prow or the poop.

the hope of the world took refuge on a raft [b]
and, steered by your hand, preserved the germ of a new
    generation for the ages to come.

For blessed is the wood which serves the cause of virtue, 7
but accursed that hand-made thing and its maker, 8
he for having made it, the perishable thing itself because it
    has been called god.
Yes, God holds the godless and his godlessness in equal hatred; 9
work and workman alike shall be punished. 10
Hence judgement shall fall on the idols themselves of the heathen, 11
since, although part of God's creation, they have become
    an abomination,
snares for the souls of men,
a pitfall for the feet of the reckless.

The origin of the cult of idols

The invention of idols was the origin of fornication, [c] 12
their discovery the corrupting of life.
They did not exist at the beginning, they will not exist for ever; 13
through human vanity they came into the world 14
and hence a sudden end has been designed for them.

A father afflicted by untimely mourning 15
makes an image of his child so swiftly taken,
and now he honours as a god what yesterday had only
    been a dead man,
bequeathing mysteries and initiations to his dependents.
Then in the course of time the godless custom hardens, and is 16
    observed as law
and, by command of princes, the carved images receive worship. 17

Of those who lived too far away to be honoured in person
men would make a portrait from a distance
and produce a visible image of the king they honoured,
meaning, by such zeal, to flatter the absent as if he were with them.
Even people who did not know him 18
were stimulated into spreading his cult by the idealism of the artist;
for the latter, doubtless wishing to please the ruler, 19
exerted all his skill to make the likeness finer than reality
and the crowd, carried away by the beauty of the work, 20
accorded divine honours to him whom only recently they
    had honoured as a man.
And this became a pitfall for life, 21
that men, whether slaves to misfortune or princely power,
should have bestowed the incommunicable name on sticks
    and stones.

The consequences of idolatry

Soon it is not enough for them that their knowledge of God 22
    should be at fault;
in the great struggle to which ignorance condemns their lives
they next give such massive ills the name of peace.
With their child-murdering initiations, their secret mysteries, 23
their orgies with outlandish ceremonies, [d]
they no longer retain any purity in their lives or their marriages, 24
one treacherously murdering the next or doing him injury
    by adultery.

25   Everywhere a welter of blood and murder, theft and fraud,
        corruption, treachery, riots, perjury,
26   disturbance of decent people, forgetfulness of favours,
        pollution of souls, sins against nature,
        disorder in marriage, adultery, debauchery.
27   For the worship of unnamed[e] idols
        is the beginning, cause, and end of every evil.
28   Either that, or they rave in ecstasy,
        or utter false oracles,
        or lead lives of great wickedness,
        or perjure themselves without hesitation;
29   for since they put their trust in lifeless idols
        they do not reckon their false oaths can harm them.

30   But justice will overtake them on two counts:
        as idolaters, for degrading the concept of God,
        as frauds, for swearing in despite of truth,
        in defiance of all that is holy.
31   For it is not the power of the things by which men swear
        but the retribution due to sinners
        that always overtakes the offence of the guilty.

Israel not idolatrous

15

1   But you, our God, are kind, loyal and slow to anger,
        and you govern all things with mercy.
2   If we sin, we still are yours, since we acknowledge your power,
        but, knowing you acknowledge us as yours, we will not sin.
3   To acknowledge you is indeed the perfect virtue,
        to know your power is the root of immortality.
4   No invention of perverted human skill has led us astray,
        no painter's sterile labour,
        no figure daubed with assorted colours,
5   the sight of which sets fools yearning
        and reverencing the lifeless form of some unbreathing image.
6   Lovers of evil and worthy of such hopes,
        are those who make them, those who reverence them and those
                who worship them.

The makers of idols are fools

7   Take a potter, now, laboriously working the soft earth,
        shaping all sorts of things for us to use.
        Out of the same clay, even so, he models
        vessels intended for clean purposes
        and the contrary sort, all alike;
        but which of these two uses each will have
        is for the potter himself to decide.
8   Then—effort very evilly spent—of the same clay he shapes
                a futile god—
        he who, so recently made out of earth himself,
        will shortly return to what he was taken from,
        once he is called to give an account of his life.

9   Even so he wastes no thought on imminent death
        or on the shortness of his life.

b. Noah's ark; the 'proud giants' are the Nephilim of Gn 6.   c. Probably in the sense of religious infidelity.   d. Such as the orgies of the Bacchanalian rites and the Phrygian mystery religions.   e. I.e., either 'unreal' or 'unspeakable'.

Far from it, he strives to outdo the goldsmiths and silversmiths,
apes the bronzeworkers too,
and takes pride in the spurious models that he makes.
Ashes, his heart,   10
meaner than dirt his hope,
his life more ignoble than clay,
since he misconceives the One who shaped him,   11
who breathed an active soul into him
and inspired a living spirit.
What is more, he looks on this life of ours as a kind of game,   12
and our time here like a fair, full of bargains.
'However foul the means,' he says 'a man must make a living.'
He, more than any other, knows he is sinning,   13
he who from the same earthly material makes both breakable
      vessel and idol.

The folly of the Egyptians; their indiscriminate idolatry

But most foolish, more pitiable even than the soul of a little child,   14
are the enemies who once played the tyrant with your people,
and have taken all the idols of the heathen for gods,   15
which can use neither their eyes for seeing
nor their nostrils for breathing the air
nor their ears for hearing
nor the fingers on their hands for handling;
while their feet are no use for walking,
since a human being made them,   16
a creature of borrowed breath gave them shape.
Now no man can shape a god as good as himself;
subject to death, his impious hands can only produce something dead.   17
He himself is worthier than the things he worships;
he will at least have lived, but never they.
Even the most hateful animals are worshipped,   18
worse than the rest in their degree of stupidity.
With no trace of beauty to prompt the inclination—as some   19
      animals might have—
the praise and blessing of God do not come their way.

Egypt and Israel: harmful animals, quails

16 Thus they were appropriately punished by similar creatures   1
and were tormented by hordes of brutes.
In contrast to this punishment, you treated your own people   2
      with kindness
and, to satisfy their sharp appetite,
you provided for their food quails, a luscious rarity.
Thus the Egyptians, at the repulsive sight of the creatures sent   ?
      against them,[a]
were to find, though they longed for food,
that even their natural appetite had revolted.
While your own people, after a short privation,
were to have a rare relish for their portion.
Inevitable that relentless want should seize on the former,   4
      the oppressors;
enough for the latter to be shown how their enemies were
      being tortured.

Egypt and Israel: the plague of locusts, the bronze serpent

5   When the savage rage of wild animals overtook them
       and they were perishing from the bites of writhing snakes,
       your wrath did not continue to the end.

6   It was by way of reprimand, lasting a short time, that they
                   were distressed,
       for they had a saving token to remind them of the commandment
           of your Law.

7   Whoever turned to it was saved, not by what he looked at,
       but by you, the universal saviour.

8   And by such means you proved to our enemies
       that it is you who deliver from every evil;

9   since the bites of locusts and flies proved fatal to them
       and no remedy could be found to save them—
       and well they deserved to be punished by such creatures.

10   But, for your sons, not even the fangs of venomous serpents
                   could bring them down;
       your mercy came to their help and cured them.

11   One sting—how quickly healed!—to remind them of your oracles
       rather than that, by sinking into deep forgetfulness,
       they should be cut off from your kindness.

12   No herb, no poultice cured them,
       but it was your word, Lord, which heals all things.

13   For you have power of life and death,
       you bring down to the gates of Hades and bring back again.

14   Man in his malice may put to death,
       he does not bring the departed spirit back
       or free the soul that Hades has once received.

Egypt and Israel: the elements

15   It is not possible to escape your hand.

16   The godless who refused to acknowledge you
       were scourged by the strength of your arm,
       pursued by no ordinary rains, hail and unrelenting downpours,
       and consumed by fire.

17   Even more wonderful, in the water—which quenches all—
       the fire raged fiercer than ever;
       for the elements fight for the virtuous.

18   At one moment the flame would die down,
       to avoid consuming the animals sent against the godless
       and to make clear to them by that sight, that the sentence
                   of God was pursuing them;

19   at another, in the very heart of the water, it would burn more fiercely
                   than fire
       to ruin the harvests of a guilty land.

20   How differently with your people! You gave them the food of angels,[b]
       from heaven untiringly sending them bread already prepared,
       containing every delight, satisfying every taste.

21   And the substance you gave demonstrated your sweetness towards
                   your children,
       for, conforming to the taste of whoever ate it,
       it transformed itself into what each eater wished.

22   Snow and ice endured the fire, without melting;

16 a. Frogs, Ex 7-8.   b. Manna, Ex 16.

by which they were to know that, to destroy the harvests
  of their enemies,
fire would burn even in hail and flare in falling rain,
whereas, on the other hand, it would even forget its own virtue   23
in the service of feeding the virtuous.

For creation, in obedience to you, its maker,   24
exerts itself to punish the wicked
and slackens for the benefit of those who trust in you.
Thus it became, by a total transformation,   25
the agent of your all-nourishing bounty,
conforming to the wish of those in need,
so that your beloved children, Lord, might learn   26
that the various crops are not what nourishes man,
but your word which preserves all who trust in you.
For that, which fire could not destroy   27
melted in the heat of a single fleeting sunbeam,
to show that, to give you thanks, we must rise before the sun   28
and pray to you when light begins to dawn;
for the hope of the ungrateful will melt like winter's frost   29
and flow away like water running to waste.

Egypt and Israel: darkness and light

17 Your judgements are indeed great and inexpressible,   1
which is why undisciplined souls have gone astray.
When impious men imagined they had the holy nation in their power,   2
they themselves lay prisoners of the dark,ᵃ in the fetters of long night,
confined under their own roofs, banished from eternal providence.
While they thought to remain unnoticed with their secret sins,   3
curtained by dark forgetfulness,
they were scattered in fearful dismay,
terrified by apparitions.
The hiding place sheltering them could not ward off their fear;   4
terrifying noises echoed round them;
and gloomy, grim-faced spectres haunted them.
No fire had power enough to give them light,   5
nor could the brightly blazing stars
illuminate that dreadful night—
only a great blaze, burning of its own accord,   6
that, full of dread, shone through to them;
and in their terror, once that sight had vanished,
they thought what they had seen more terrible than ever.
Their magic arts proved utterly unavailing,   7
their boasted cunning was ignominiously confounded;
for those who professed to drive out fears and disorders from   8
    sick souls,
themselves fell sick of a ridiculous terror.
Even when there was nothing frightful to scare them,   9
the prowling of beasts and the hissing of reptiles terrified them;
they died convulsed with fright,
refusing so much as to look at the air, which cannot be eluded anyhow!
Wickedness is confessedly very cowardly, and it condemns itself;   10
under pressure from conscience it always assumes the worst.
Fear, indeed, is nothing other   11
than the abandonment of the supports offered by reason;
the less you rely within yourself on these,   12

the more alarming it is not to know the cause of your suffering.

13 And they, all locked in the same sleep,
while that darkness lasted, which was in fact quite powerless
and had issued from the depths of equally powerless Hades,

14 were now chased by monstrous spectres,
now paralysed by fainting of their souls;
for a sudden, unexpected terror had swept over them.

15 And thus, whoever it might be that fell there
stayed clamped to the spot in this prison without bars.

16 Whether he was ploughman or shepherd,
or someone working by himself,
he was still overtaken and suffered the inevitable fate,
for all had been bound by the one same chain of darkness.

17 The soughing of the wind,
the tuneful noise of birds in the spreading branches,
the measured beat of water in its powerful course,
the harsh din of the rocky avalanche,

18 the invisible, swift course of bounding animals,
the roaring of the savagest wild beasts,
the echo rebounding from the clefts in the mountains,
all held them paralysed with fear.

19 The whole world was shining with brilliant light
and, unhindered, went on with its work;

20 over them alone there spread a heavy darkness,
image of the dark that would receive them.
But heavier than the darkness, the burden they were to themselves.

18

1 But for your holy ones all was great light.
The Egyptians who could hear their voices, though not see
their shapes,
called them fortunate because they had not suffered too;

2 they thanked them for doing no injury in return for previous
wrongs
and asked forgiveness for their past ill-will.

3 In contrast to the darkness, you gave your people a pillar of
blazing fire,
to guide them on their unknown journey,
a mild sun for their ambitious migration.

4 But well they deserved, those others, to be deprived of light
and imprisoned in darkness,
for having kept in captivity your children,
by whom the imperishable light of the Law was to be given
to the world.

Egypt and Israel: the Destroyer

5 As they had resolved to kill the infants of the holy ones,
and as of those exposed only one child had been saved,
to punish them, you made away with thousands of their children,
and destroyed them all together in the wild waves.

6 That night had been foretold to our ancestors,
so that, once they saw what kind of oaths they had put their
trust in, they would joyfully take courage.

7 This was the expectation of your people,
the saving of the virtuous and the ruin of their enemies;

17 a. The ninth plague, Ex 10, was darkness.

for by the same act with which you took vengeance on our foes　8
you made us glorious by calling us to you.
The devout children of worthy men offered sacrifice *a* in secret　9
and this divine pact they struck with one accord:
that the saints would share the same blessings and dangers alike;
and forthwith they had begun to chant the hymns of the fathers.*b*

In echo came the discordant cries of their enemies　10
and the pitiful sound rang out of those lamenting their children.
The same punishment struck slave and master alike,　11
commoner and king suffered the selfsame loss.
All had innumerable dead alike,　12
struck by the same death.
There were not enough living left to bury them,
for in a moment the flower of their race had perished.
They who, thanks to their sorceries, had been wholly incredulous,　13
at the destruction of their first-born now acknowledged
this people to be son of God.

When peaceful silence lay over all,　14
and night had run the half of her swift course,
down from the heavens, from the royal throne, leapt your　15
　　all-powerful Word;
into the heart of a doomed land the stern warrior leapt.
Carrying your unambiguous command like a sharp sword,
he stood, and filled the universe with death;　16
he touched the sky, yet trod the earth.
Immediately, dreams and gruesome visions overwhelmed　17
　　them with terror,
unexpected fears assailed them.
Hurled down, some here, some there, half dead,　18
they proclaimed why it was they were dying;
for the dreams that had troubled them had warned them　19
　　why beforehand,
so that they might not perish without knowing why they had
　　been struck down.

But the virtuous, too, felt the touch of death;　20
a multitude was struck down in the wilderness.
But the wrath did not last long,
for a blameless man *c* hastened to champion their cause.　21
Wielding the weapons of his sacred office,
prayer and atoning incense,
he took his stand against the Anger and put an end to the calamity,
showing that he was indeed your servant.
He conquered the bitter plague, not by physical strength,　22
not by force of arms;
but by word he prevailed over the Punisher,
by recalling the oaths made to the Fathers, and the covenants.
Already the corpses lay piled in heaps,　23
when he interposed and beat back the wrath
and cut off its approach to the living.
For the whole world was on his flowing robe, *d*　24
the glorious names of the Fathers on the four rows of stones,
and your Majesty on the diadem on his head.
From these the Destroyer recoiled, he was afraid of these;　25
a mere taste of the wrath had been enough.

Egypt and Israel: the Red Sea

19

1 But the godless were assailed by merciless anger to the very end,
for God knew beforehand what they would do,

2 how, after letting his people leave and hastening their departure,
they would change their minds and set out in pursuit.

3 They were actually still conducting their mourning rites
and lamenting at the tombs of their dead,
when another mad scheme entered their heads,
and they set out to pursue as fugitives the very people they had
begged to go away.

4 A well-deserved fate urged them to this extreme
and made them forget what had already happened,
so that to all their torments they might add the one penalty
still outstanding

5 and, while your people accomplished a miraculous journey,
themselves meet an extraordinary death.

6 For, to keep your children from all harm,
the whole creation, obedient to your commands,
was once more, and newly, fashioned in its nature.

7 Overshadowing the camp there was the cloud,
where water had been, dry land was seen to rise,
the Red Sea became an unimpeded way,
the tempestuous flood a green plain;

8 sheltered by your hand, the whole nation passed across,
gazing at these amazing miracles.

9 They were like horses at pasture,
they skipped like lambs,
singing your praises, Lord, their deliverer.

Nature refashioned for Israel

10 They still remembered the events of their exile,
how the land, not bearing animals, had bred mosquitoes instead,
how, instead of fish, the river had disgorged innumerable frogs.

11 Later they saw a new method of birth for birds
when, goaded by hunger, they asked for food they could relish,

12 and quails came out of the sea to satisfy them.

Egypt more blameworthy than Sodom

13 On the sinners, however, punishments rained down
not without violent thunder as early warning;
and deservedly they suffered for their crimes,
since they evinced such bitter hatred towards strangers.

14 Others[a] had refused to welcome unknown men on their arrival,
but these had made slaves of guests and benefactors.

15 The former, moreover—and this will be to their credit –
had shown the foreigners hostility from the start;

16 not so the latter: these welcomed your people with feasting
and after granting them equal rights with themselves
then afflicted them with forced labour.

17 Thus they were struck with blindness

18 a. The Passover meal, a sacrifice celebrated inside the houses.   b. In the author's time, the Psalms of Praise (Hallel) were sung at the Passover.   c. Aaron.   d. In these three lines, the author is describing the high priest's robe of his own day: 'the whole world' is a symbolic representation of the three-storey universe; 'the Fathers' are the twelve ancestors of the tribes: 'the Majesty of the Lord' is the gold plate of dedication.
19 a. The inhabitants of Sodom, Gn 19.

like the former at the door of the virtuous man,[b]
when, yawning darkness all around them,
each had to grope his way through his own door.

Nature refashioned at the Exodus

Thus the elements interchanged their qualities,   18
as on a harp the notes may change their rhythm,
though all the while preserving their tone;
this clearly appears from a scrutiny of the events.
Creatures that live on land became aquatic,[c]   19
and those that swim emerged on land.
Fire increased its own virtue in the water,   20
water forgot its property of extinguishing.
Flames, on the other hand, would not scorch the flesh   21
of animals, however frail, that ventured into them;
nor would they melt that heavenly food
like hoarfrost, and as easily melted.

Conclusion

Yes, Lord, in every way you have made your people great and glorious;   22
you have never disdained them, but stood by them always
and everywhere.

---

b. Lot, see 10:6.   c. The Israelites and their cattle 'took to the water'; frogs left the water
for the land.

INTRODUCTION TO
ECCLESIASTICUS

This book was originally written in Hebrew; as its foreword says, it was translated into Greek by the author's grandson in 132 B.C. The translation was adopted into the Greek Bible, in which it was subtitled, 'The Wisdom of Jesus Ben Sirach'. It does not appear in the Jewish canon of scripture, and its Latin title, 'Ecclesiasticus'—the Church's book—may call attention to the fact that the Church adopted it although the Synagogue did not.

Much of the book consists of maxims and aphorisms of worldly wisdom and social prudence, but there is also a strong note of respect and love for the Law of Moses and a veneration of the great figures of the Old Testament from Enoch to Nehemiah.

ECCLESIASTICUS

TRANSLATOR'S FOREWORD

Many and wonderful are the gifts we have been granted by means of the 1
Law and the Prophets •and the others that followed them, •an education in 2 3
wisdom on which Israel is indeed to be complimented. •But it is not enough 4
merely for those who read the scriptures to be learned in them; •students should 5
also be able to be of use to people outside •by what they say and write. •So it 6 7
was that my grandfather Jesus, having devoted himself more and more to reading
the Law •and the Prophets and •the other volumes of the fathers, •and having 8.9 10.11
gained ability enough in these matters, •was brought to the point of himself 12
writing down some of the things that have a bearing on education in wisdom,
in order that those studiously inclined and with obligations in these matters 13
might make all the more progress in living according to the Law. 14

You are therefore asked •to read this book •with good will and attention 15 16.17
and to show indulgence •in those places where, notwithstanding our efforts 18 19
at interpretation, we may seem •to have failed to give an adequate rendering 20
of this or that expression; •the fact is that you cannot find an equivalent •for 21 22
things originally written in Hebrew when you come to translate them into
another language; •what is more, •you will find on examination that the Law 23 24
itself, the Prophets •and the other books •differ considerably in translation 25 26
from what appears in the original text.

It was in the thirty-eighth year of the late King Euergetes, *a* •when after my 27 28
arrival in Egypt I had already spent some time there, •that I found a work 29
of more than common instructional worth, •which convinced me of the urgency 30
of applying myself in my turn with pains and diligence to the translation of the
book that follows; •and I spent much time and learning on it •in the course of 31 32
this period, •to complete the work and to publish the book •for the benefit 33 34
especially of those who, domiciled abroad, wish to study how to fit themselves
and their manners for living according to the Law. 35

I. COLLECTIONS OF SAYINGS

The mystery of wisdom

1

All wisdom is from the Lord, 1
and it is his own for ever.
The sand of the sea and the raindrops, 2
and the days of eternity, who can assess them?
The height of the sky and the breadth of the earth, 3
and the depth of the abyss, who can probe them?
Before all other things wisdom was created, 4
shrewd understanding is everlasting.
For whom has the root of wisdom ever been uncovered? 6
Her resourceful ways, who knows them?
One only is wise, terrible indeed, 8
seated on his throne, •the Lord. 9

He himself has created her, looked on her and assessed her,
    and poured her out on all his works

10   to be with all mankind as his gift,
    and he conveyed her to those who love him.

The fear of God

11   The fear of the Lord is glory and pride,
    and happiness and a crown of joyfulness.

12   The fear of the Lord will gladden the heart
    giving happiness and joy and long life.

13   With him who fears the Lord it will be well at the last,
    and he will be blessed on the day of his death.

14
16   To fear the Lord is the beginning of wisdom,
    she was created with the faithful in their mothers' womb;

15
19   she has made a nest among men, an age-old foundation,
    and to their offspring she will cling faithfully.

16
20   To fear the Lord is the perfection of wisdom;
    she intoxicates them with her fruits;

17
21   she fills their whole house with their heart's desire,
    and their storerooms with her produce.

18
22   The fear of the Lord is the crown of wisdom;
    it makes peace and health to flourish.

19
23   The Lord has looked on her and assessed her,
24   he has showered down learning and discernment,
    and exalted the renown of those who hold her close.

20
25   To fear the Lord is the root of wisdom,
    and her branches are long life.

Patience and self-control

22
28   The rage of the wicked man cannot justify him,
    for the weight of his rage is his downfall.

23
29   The patient man will hold out till the time comes,
    but his joy will break out in the end.

24
30   He will hide his words till the time comes,
    and stories of his discernment will be on many lips.

Wisdom and uprightness

25
31   In wisdom's treasuries there are learned sayings,
32   but reverence for God is loathsome to the sinner.

26
33   If you desire wisdom, keep the commandments,
    and the Lord will convey her to you.

27
34   For wisdom and instruction mean the fear of the Lord,
35   and what pleases him is faithfulness and gentleness.

28
36   Do not be unsubmissive to the fear of the Lord,
    do not practise it with a double heart.

29
37   Do not act a part in public,
    and keep a watch over your lips.

30
38   Do not raise yourself up, in case you fall
    and bring disgrace on yourself,

39   for the Lord would then reveal your secrets
    and humiliate you before the whole community

40   for not having attained the fear of the Lord,
    and for having a heart full of deceit.

F a. Probably Ptolemy VII Euergetes Physkon (170-117 B.C.), in which case the date would
be 132 B.C.

The fear of God in time of ordeal

2

My son, if you aspire to serve the Lord,
   prepare yourself for an ordeal.   1

Be sincere of heart, be steadfast,
   and do not be alarmed when disaster comes.   2

Cling to him and do not leave him,
   so that you may be honoured at the end of your days.   3

Whatever happens to you, accept it,
   and in the uncertainties of your humble state, be patient,   4

since gold is tested in the fire,
   and chosen men in the furnace of humiliation.   5

Trust him and he will uphold you,
   follow a straight path and hope in him.   6

You who fear the Lord, wait for his mercy;
   do not turn aside in case you fall.   7

You who fear the Lord, trust him,
   and you will not be baulked of your reward.   8

You who fear the Lord hope for good things,
   for everlasting happiness and mercy.   9

Look at the generations of old and see:
   who ever trusted in the Lord and was put to shame?   10 / 11

Or who ever feared him steadfastly and was left forsaken?
   Or who ever called out to him, and was ignored?   12

For the Lord is compassionate and merciful,
   he forgives sins, and saves in days of distress.   11 / 13

Woe to faint hearts and listless hands,
   and to the sinner who treads two paths.   12 / 14

Woe to the listless heart that has no faith,
   for such will have no protection.   13 / 15

Woe to you who have lost the will to endure;
   what will you do at the Lord's visitation?   14 / 16 / 17

Those who fear the Lord do not disdain his words,
   and those who love him keep his ways.   15 / 18

Those who fear the Lord do their best to please him,
   and those who love him find satisfaction in his Law.   16 / 19

Those who fear the Lord keep their hearts prepared
   and humble themselves in his presence.   17 / 20 / 21

Let us fall into the hands of the Lord, not into the hands of men;
   for as his majesty is, so too is his mercy.   18 / 22b / 23

Duties towards parents

3

Children, listen to me your father,
   do what I tell you, and so be safe;   1 / 2

for the Lord honours the father in his children,
   and upholds the rights of a mother over her sons.   2 / 3

Whoever respects his father is atoning for his sins,
   he who honours his mother is like someone amassing a fortune.   3 / 4 / 5

Whoever respects his father will be happy with children of his own,
   he shall be heard on the day when he prays.   5 / 6

Long life comes to him who honours his father,
   he who sets his mother at ease is showing obedience to the Lord.   6 / 7

He serves his parents as he does his Lord.   7b / 8b

Respect your father in deed as well as word,
   so that blessing may come on you from him;   8 / 9 / 10

since a father's blessing makes the houses of his children firm,   9 / 11 while a mother's curse tears up their foundations.

10
12 Do not make a boast of disgrace overtaking your father,
    your father's disgrace reflects no honour on you;

11
13 for a man's honour derives from the respect shown to his father,
    and a mother held in dishonour is a reproach to her children.

12
14 My son, support your father in his old age,
    do not grieve him during his life.

13
15 Even if his mind should fail, show him sympathy,
    do not despise him in your health and strength;

14
17 for kindness to a father shall not be forgotten
    but will serve as reparation for your sins.

15 In the days of your affliction it will be remembered of you,
    like frost in sunshine, your sins will melt away.

16
18 The man who deserts his father is no better than a blasphemer,
    and whoever angers his mother is accursed of the Lord.

Humility

17
19 My son, be gentle in carrying out your business,
    and you will be better loved than a lavish giver.

18
20 The greater you are, the more you should behave humbly,
    and then you will find favour with the Lord;

20
21 for great though the power of the Lord is,
    he accepts the homage of the humble.

21
22 Do not try to understand things that are too difficult for you,
    or try to discover what is beyond your powers.

22 Concentrate on what has been assigned you,
    you have no need to worry over mysteries.

23
24 Do not meddle with matters that are beyond you;
25   what you have been taught already exceeds the scope of the
        human mind.

24
26 For many have been misled by their own presumption,
    and wrong-headed opinions have warped their ideas.

Pride

26
27 A stubborn heart will come to a bad end at last,
    and whoever loves danger will perish in it.

27
29 A stubborn heart is weighed down with troubles,
    the sinner heaps sin on sin.

28
30 There is no cure for the proud man's malady,
    since an evil growth has taken root in him.

29
31 The heart of a sensible man will reflect on parables,
    an attentive ear is the sage's dream.

Charity to the poor

30
33 Water quenches a blazing fire,
    almsgiving atones for sins.

31
34 Whoever gives favours in return is mindful of the future;
    at the moment of his fall he will find support.

1 **4** My son, do not refuse the poor a livelihood,
    do not tantalise the needy.

2 Do not add to the sufferings of the hungry,
    do not bait a man in distress.

3 Do not aggravate a heart already angry,
    nor keep the destitute waiting for your alms.

4 Do not repulse a hard-pressed beggar,
    nor turn your face from a poor man.

Do not avert your eyes from the destitute,   5
    give no man occasion to curse you;
for if a man curses you in the bitterness of his soul,   6
    his maker will hear his imprecation.
Gain the love of the community,   7
    bow your head to a man of authority.
To the poor man lend an ear,   8
    and return his greeting courteously.
Save the oppressed from the hand of the oppressor,   9
    and do not be mean-spirited in your judgements.
Be like a father to orphans,   10
    and as good as a husband to widows.
And you will be like a son to the Most High,   11
    whose love for you will surpass your mother's.

Wisdom as educator

Wisdom brings up her own sons,   11 / 12
    and cares for those who seek her.
Whoever loves her loves life,   12 / 13
    those who wait on her early will be filled with happiness.
Whoever holds her close will inherit honour,   13 / 14
    and wherever he walks the Lord will bless him.
Those who serve her minister to the Holy One,   14 / 15
    and the Lord loves those who love her.
Whoever obeys her judges aright,   15 / 16
    and whoever pays attention to her dwells secure.
If he trusts himself to her he will inherit her,   16 / 17
    and his descendants will remain in possession of her;
for though she takes him at first through winding ways,   17 / 18
    bringing fear and faintness on him,   19
plaguing him with her discipline until she can trust him,
    and testing him with her ordeals,
in the end she will lead him back to the straight road,   18 / 20
    and reveal her secrets to him.   21
If he wanders away she will abandon him,   19 / 22
    and hand him over to his fate.

Shame and human respect

My son, bide your time and be on your guard against evil,   20 / 23
    and have no cause to be ashamed of yourself;   24
for there is a shame that leads to sin,   21 / 25
    as well as a shame that is honourable and gracious.
Do not show partiality, to your own detriment,   22 / 26
    or deference, to your own downfall.   27
Do not refrain from speech at an opportune time,   23 / 28
    and do not hide your wisdom;
for wisdom shall be recognised in speech,   24 / 29
    and instruction by what the tongue utters.
Do not contradict the truth,   25 / 30
    rather blush for your own ignorance.
Do not be ashamed to confess your sins,   26 / 31a
    do not strive against the current of a river.   32b
Do not grovel to a foolish man,   27 / 31b
    do not show partiality to a man of influence.   32a
Fight to the death for truth,   28 / 33
    and the Lord God will war on your side.

<table>
<tr><td>29
34</td><td>Do not be bold of tongue,
yet idle and slack in deed;</td></tr>
<tr><td>30
35</td><td>do not be like a lion at home,
or a coward before your servants.</td></tr>
<tr><td>31
36</td><td>Do not let your hands be outstretched to receive,
yet closed when the time comes to give back.</td></tr>
</table>

Wealth and presumption

<table>
<tr><td>1</td><td>**5** Do not give your heart to your money,
or say, 'With this I am self-sufficient'.</td></tr>
<tr><td>2</td><td>Do not be led by your appetites and energy
to follow the passions of your heart.</td></tr>
<tr><td>3</td><td>And do not say, 'Who has authority over me?'
for the Lord will certainly be avenged on you.</td></tr>
<tr><td>4</td><td>Do not say, 'I sinned, and what happened to me?'
for the Lord's forbearance is long.</td></tr>
<tr><td>5</td><td>Do not be so sure of forgiveness
that you add sin to sin.</td></tr>
<tr><td>6</td><td>And do not say, 'His compassion is great,
he will forgive me my many sins';</td></tr>
<tr><td>7</td><td>for with him are both mercy and wrath,
and his rage bears heavy on sinners.</td></tr>
<tr><td>7
8</td><td>Do not delay your return to the Lord,
do not put it off day after day;</td></tr>
<tr><td>9</td><td>for suddenly the Lord's wrath will blaze out,
and at the time of vengeance you will be utterly destroyed.</td></tr>
<tr><td>8
10</td><td>Do not set your heart on ill-gotten gains,
they will be of no use to you on the day of disaster.</td></tr>
</table>

Straightforwardness and self-possession

<table>
<tr><td>9
11</td><td>Do not winnow in every wind,
or walk along every by-way
(such is the practice of the deceitful sinner).</td></tr>
<tr><td>10
12</td><td>Be steady in your convictions,
sincere in your speech.</td></tr>
<tr><td>11
13</td><td>Be quick to listen,
and deliberate in giving an answer.</td></tr>
<tr><td>12
14</td><td>If you understand the matter, give your neighbour an answer,
if not, put your hand over your mouth.</td></tr>
<tr><td>13
15</td><td>Both honour and disgrace come from talking,
a man's tongue can cause his downfall.</td></tr>
<tr><td>14
16</td><td>Do not get a name for scandal-mongering,
do not set traps with your tongue;</td></tr>
<tr><td>17</td><td>for as shame lies in store for the thief,
so harsh condemnation awaits the deceitful.</td></tr>
<tr><td>15
18</td><td>Avoid offences in great as in small matters,
and do not become an enemy where you should stay a friend;</td></tr>
<tr><td>1</td><td>**6** for a bad name will earn you shame and reproach,
as happens to the deceitful sinner.</td></tr>
<tr><td>2</td><td>Do not give in to the promptings of your temper,
in case it gores your soul like a mad bull;</td></tr>
<tr><td>3</td><td>in case it gobbles up your leaves and you lose your fruits,
and are left like a withered tree.</td></tr>
<tr><td>4</td><td>An evil temper destroys the man who has it
and makes him the laughing-stock of his enemies.</td></tr>
</table>

Friendship

A kindly turn of speech multiplies a man's friends,   5
and a courteous way of speaking invites many a friendly reply.
Let your acquaintances be many,   6
but your advisers one in a thousand.
If you want to make a friend, take him on trial,   7
and be in no hurry to trust him;
for one kind of friend is only so when it suits him   8
but will not stand by you in your day of trouble.
Another kind of friend will fall out with you   9
and to your dismay make your quarrel public,
and a third kind of friend will share your table,   10
but not stand by you in your day of trouble:
when you are doing well he will be your second self,   11
ordering your servants about;
but if ever you are brought low he will turn against you   12
and will hide himself from you.
Keep well clear of your enemies,   13
and be wary of your friends.
A faithful friend is a sure shelter,   14
whoever finds one has found a rare treasure.
A faithful friend is something beyond price,   15
there is no measuring his worth.
A faithful friend is the elixir of life,   16
and those who fear the Lord will find one.
Whoever fears the Lord makes true friends,   17
for as a man is, so is his friend.

Apprenticeship to wisdom

My son, from your earliest youth choose instruction,   18
and till your hair is white you will keep finding wisdom.
Cultivate her like the ploughman and the sower,   19
and wait for her fine harvest,
for in tilling her you will toil a little while,   20
but very soon you will be eating her crops.
How very harsh she is to the undisciplined!   20/21
The senseless man does not stay with her for long:
she will weigh on him like a heavy stone,   21/22
and he will lose no time in throwing her off;
for discipline is true to her name,   22/23
she is not accessible to many.
Listen, son, and take my warning,   23/24
do not reject my advice:
put your feet into her fetters,   24/25
and your neck into her harness;
give your shoulder to her yoke,   25/26
do not be restive in her reins;
court her with all your soul,   26/27
and with all your might keep in her ways;
go after her and seek her; she will reveal herself to you;   27/28
once you hold her, do not let her go.
For in the end you will find rest in her   28/29
and she will take the form of joy for you:
her fetters you will find are a strong defence,   29/30
her harness, a robe of honour.
Her yoke will be a golden ornament,   30/31

	her reins, purple ribbons;
31 32	you will wear her like a robe of honour,
	you will put her on like a crown of honour.
32 33	If you wish, my son, you can acquire instruction,
	if you give your mind to it, subtlety will be yours.
33 34	If you love listening you will learn,
	if you lend an ear, wisdom will be yours.
34 35	Attend the gathering of elders;
	if there is a wise man there, attach yourself to him.
35	Listen willingly to any discourse coming from God,
	do not let shrewd proverbs escape you.
36	If you see a man of understanding, visit him early,
	let your feet wear out his doorstep.
37	Reflect on the injunctions of the Lord,
	busy yourself at all times with his commandments.
	He will strengthen your mind,
	and the wisdom you desire will be granted you.

Miscellaneous advice

7

1
2
Do no evil, and evil will not befall you;
shun wrong, and it will avoid you.

3 Son, do not sow in the furrows of wrong-doing,
or you may reap it seven times over.

4 Do not ask the Lord for the highest place,
or the king for a seat of honour.

5 Do not parade your virtue before the Lord,
or your wisdom before the king.

6 Do not scheme to be appointed judge,
in case you are not strong enough to stamp out injustice,
in case you let yourself be swayed by an influential man,
and so risk the loss of your integrity.

7 Do not wrong the general body of citizens
and so lower yourself in popular esteem.

8 Do not be drawn to sin twice over,
for you will not go unpunished even once.

9
11
Do not say, 'God will consider the great number of my gifts;
when I make my offerings to the Most High God he will
accept them'.

10
9
10
Do not be impatient in prayer;
do not neglect to give alms.

11
12
Do not laugh at a man when he is sad of heart,
for he who brings him low can lift him high.

12
13
Do not draw up a lying indictment against your brother,
do not do it against a friend either.

13
14
Mind you tell no lies,
for no good can come of it.

14
15
Do not make long-winded speeches in the gathering of elders,
and do not repeat yourself at your prayers.

15
16
Do not shirk wearisome labour,
or farm work, which the Most High created.

16
17
18
Do not swell the ranks of the sinners,
remember that the wrath will not delay.

Be very humble,
   since the punishment for the godless is fire and worms.   17 / 19

Do not barter a friend for profit,
   nor a real brother for the gold of Ophir.   18 / 20
Do not turn against a wise and good wife,
   for her charm is worth more than gold.   19 / 21
Do not ill-treat a slave who is an honest worker,
   or a wage-earner who does his best for you.   20 / 22
Love an intelligent slave like your own self,
   and do not deny him his freedom.   21 / 23

Children

Have you cattle? Look after them;
   if they are making you a profit, keep them.   22 / 24
Have you children? Educate them,
   make them bow the neck from childhood.   23 / 25
Have you daughters? Take care of their bodies,
   but do not be over-indulgent.   24 / 26
Marry a daughter off, and you have finished a great work;
   but give her to a man of sense.   25 / 27
Have you a wife to your liking? Do not turn her out;
   but if you dislike her, never trust her.   26 / 28

Parents

With all your heart honour your father,
   never forget the birthpangs of your mother.   27 / 29
Remember that you owe your birth to them;
   how can you repay them for what they have done for you?   28 / 30

Priests

With all your soul hold the Lord in awe,
   and revere his priests.   29 / 31
With all your might love him who made you,
   and do not abandon his ministers.   30 / 32
Fear the Lord and honour the priest   31 / 33
   and give him the portion enjoined on you: 34
first-fruits and sacrifices of reparation and the shoulder-gift,
   the sacrifice of sanctification, and first-fruits of the holy things.   35

The poor and afflicted

Stretch your hand out also to the poor man,
   that your blessing may be perfect.   32 / 36
Be generous in your gifts to all the living,
   do not withhold your favour even from the dead.   33 / 37
Do not fail those who weep,
   but share the grief of the grief-stricken.   34 / 38
Do not shrink from visiting the sick;
   in this way you will make yourself loved.   35 / 39
In everything you do, remember your end,
   and you will never sin.   36 / 40

Prudence and commonsense

8

Do not try conclusions with an influential man,
   in case you later fall into his clutches.   1
Do not quarrel with a rich man,
   in case he turns the scales against you;   2

3

for gold has destroyed many,
and has swayed the hearts of kings.

3
4

Do not quarrel with a man of quick tongue,
do not pile logs on his fire.

4
5

Do not jest with an ill-mannered man,
in case you hear your ancestry insulted.

5
6

Do not revile a repentant sinner;
remember that we all are guilty.

6
7

Do not despise a man in his old age;
after all, some of us too are growing old.

7
8

Do not gloat over a man's death;
remember that we all must die.

Tradition

8
9

Do not ignore the talk of the wise,
be conversant with their proverbs,

10

since from these you will learn the theory and art
of serving the great.

9
11

Do not underrate the talk of old men,
after all, they themselves learned it from their fathers;

12

from them you will learn how to think,
and the art of the timely answer.

Prudence

10
13

Do not kindle the coals of the sinner,
in case you scorch yourself in his blaze.

11
14

Refuse to be drawn by an arrogant man,
for fear he tries to trap you in your words.

12
15

Do not lend to anyone who is stronger than you are—
if you do lend, resign yourself to loss.

13
16

Do not stand surety beyond your means;
if you do stand surety, be prepared to pay up.

14
17

Do not go to law with a judge,
since judgement will be given in his favour.

15
18

Do not travel with a reckless fellow,
in case he imposes on you;
he will act as the whim takes him,
and you will both be ruined by his folly.

16
19

Do not argue with a quick-tempered man,
or travel with him through the wilderness;
since blood counts for nothing in his eyes,
and where no help is to be had, he will strike you down.

17
20

Do not ask a fool for advice,
since he will not be able to keep a confidence.

18
21

In a stranger's presence do nothing that should be kept secret,
since you cannot tell what use he will make of it.

19
22

Do not open your heart to every man,
or solicit favours from all comers.

Women

1

9

Do not be jealous of the wife you love,
or teach her lessons in evil to your detriment.

2

Do not give your soul to a woman,
for her to trample on your strength.

Do not keep company with a harlot,   3
    in case you get entangled in her snares.
Do not dally with a singing girl,   4
    in case you get caught by her wiles.
Do not stare at a virgin,   5
    in case you and she incur the same punishment.
Do not give your soul to whores,   6
    or you will ruin your inheritance.
Keep your eyes to yourself in the streets of a town,   7
    do not prowl about its unfrequented quarters.
Turn your eyes away from a handsome woman,   8
    do not stare at the beauty that belongs to someone else.
Woman's beauty has led many astray;   9
    it kindles desire like a flame.
Never sit down with a married woman,   9 / 12
    or sit at table with her drinking wine,   13
in case you succumb to her charms,
    and in your ardour you slide down to your ruin.

Relations with men

Do not desert an old friend;   10 / 14
    the new one will not be his match.
New friend, new wine;   15
    when it grows old, you drink it with pleasure.

Do not envy the sinner his success;   11 / 16
    you do not know what turn his career will take.
Do not take pleasure in what pleases the godless;   12 / 17
    remember they will not go unpunished to their grave.

Keep your distance from the man who has the power to put to death,   13 / 18
    and you will not be haunted by the fear of dying.
If you do approach him, make no false move,   19
    or he may take your life.
Realise that you are treading among trip-lines,   20
    that you are strolling on the battlements.

Cultivate your neighbours as far as you can,   14 / 21
    and consult with wise men.
For conversation seek intelligent men,   15 / 22
    let all your discussions bear on the law of the Most High.
Have virtuous men for your table companions,   16 / 23
    and let your pride be in fearing the Lord.

Work from skilled hands will earn its praise,   17 / 24
    but a leader of the people must be shrewd of speech.
A phrase-maker is a terror to his town,   18 / 25
    a loose talker is detested.

Government

10

The wise magistrate will be strict with his people,   1
    and the government of a prudent man will be well-regulated.
As the magistrate is, so will his officials be,   2
    as the governor is, so will be the inhabitants of his city.
An uneducated king will be the ruin of his people,   3
    a city owes its prosperity to the intelligence of its leading men.
The government of the earth is in the hands of the Lord,   4
    he sets the right man over it at the right time.

5
> A man's success is in the hands of the Lord,
> it is he who invests the lawgiver with honour.

Against pride

6
> Do not resent your neighbour's every offence,
> and never act in a fit of passion.

7
> Pride is hateful to God and man,
> and injustice is abhorrent to both.

8
> Empire passes from nation to nation
> because of injustice, arrogance and money.

9
10b
> What has dust and ashes to pride itself on?
> Even in life its guts are repellent.

10
12
> A long illness mocks the doctor;
> a king today is a corpse tomorrow.

11
13
> When a man comes to die,
> his inheritance will be creeping things, beasts of prey, worms.

12
14
15
> The beginning of human pride is to desert the Lord,
> and to turn one's heart away from one's maker.

13
> Since the beginning of pride is sin,
> whoever clings to it will pour forth filth.

16
> For which reason the Lord inflicted extraordinary punishments
>   on them
> and utterly overthrew them.

14
17
> The Lord has thrown down rulers' thrones,
> and seated the humble in their place.

15
18
> The Lord has plucked up proud men by the roots,
> and planted the lowly in their place.

16
19
> The Lord has overthrown the lands of the heathens
> and destroyed them to the very foundations of the earth.

17
20
> He has taken some of them away and destroyed them,

21
> and blotted out their memory from the earth.

18
22
> Pride was not created for men,
> nor furious rage for those born of woman.

Persons deserving honour

19
23
> What race deserves honour? The human race.
> What race deserves honour? Those who fear the Lord.
> What race deserves contempt? The human race.
> What race deserves contempt? Those who break the commandments.

20
24
> Among brothers the leader of them deserves honour,
> and those who fear the Lord deserve honour in his sight.

22
25
> Let rich and noble and poor
> take pride in fearing the Lord.

23
26
> It is not right to despise a poor but intelligent man,
> and it is not good to honour a man who is a sinner.

24
27
> Ruler, magistrate, influential man, all are to be honoured,
> but none of them is greater than him who fears the Lord.

25
28
> A wise slave will have free men waiting on him,
> and the man of sense will not grumble.

Frankness and humility

26
29
> Do not try to be smart when you do your work,
> do not put on airs when you are in difficulties.

Better a hardworking man who has plenty of everything,　　27
    than a pretentious man at a loss for a meal.　　　　　　30

My son, be modest in your self-esteem,　　　　　　　　28
    and value yourself at your proper worth.　　　　　　31

Who can justify a man who runs himself down,　　　　29
    or respect a man who despises himself?　　　　　　32

A poor man is honoured for his wits,　　　　　　　　30
    and a rich man for his wealth.　　　　　　　　　　33

Honoured in poverty, how much the more in wealth!　　31
    Dishonoured in wealth, how much the more in poverty!　34

Do not go by appearances

11   The poor man's wisdom keeps his head erect,　　　　1
    and gives him a place with the great.

Do not praise a man for his good looks,　　　　　　2
    nor dislike anybody for his appearance.

Small among winged creatures is the bee　　　　　3
    but her produce is the sweetest of the sweet.

Do not preen yourself on your fine clothes,　　　　4
    nor be swollen headed on your day of glory;
for the Lord's deeds are marvellous,
    though hidden from mankind.

Many monarchs have been made to sit on the ground,　5
    and the man nobody thought of has worn the crown.

Many influential men have been utterly disgraced,　　6
    and prominent men have fallen into the power of others.

Deliberation and reflection

Do not find fault before making thorough inquiry;　　7
    first reflect, then give a reprimand.

Listen before you answer,　　　　　　　　　　　8
    and do not interrupt a speech in the middle.

Do not wrangle about something that does not concern you,　9
    nor interfere in the squabbles of sinners.

My son, do not take on a great amount of business;　　10
    if you multiply your interests, you are bound to suffer for it;
hurry as fast as you can, yet you will never arrive,
    nor will you escape by running away.

A man labours and toils and forges ahead,　　　　11
    only to find himself the more out-distanced.

Trust in God alone

Another man is a poor creature begging for assistance,　12
    badly off for support, but rich in poverty,
and the Lord turns a favourable eye on him,
    sets him on his feet out of his abject condition,
and enables him to hold his head high,　　　　　　13
    to the utter amazement of many.

Good and bad, life and death,　　　　　　　　　14
    poverty and wealth, all come from the Lord.

The Lord's gift remains constant to the devout,　　17
    and his goodwill means a good journey for ever.

A man grows rich by his sharpness and grabbing,　18
    and here is the reward he receives for it:

19	he says, 'I have found rest, and now I can enjoy my goods';
20	but he does not know how long this will last; he will have to leave his goods for others and die.
20 21	Persevere at your duty, take pleasure in doing it, and grow old at your work.
21 22	Do not be astonished at the sinner's achievements; trust the Lord and keep to your duty;
23	since it is a trifle in the eyes of the Lord, in a moment, suddenly to make a poor man rich.
22 24	The devout man receives the Lord's blessing as his reward, in a moment God brings his blessing to flower.
23 25	Do not say, 'What are my needs, what will be my profits in future?'
24 26	And do not say, 'I am self-supporting, what losses can I suffer in future?'
25 27	In a time of profit, losses are forgotten, and in a time of loss, no one remembers profits.
26 28	Yet it is a trifle for the Lord on the day a man dies to repay him as his conduct deserves.
27 29	A moment's adversity, and pleasures are forgotten; in a man's last hour his deeds will stand revealed.
28 30	Call no man fortunate before his death; it is by his end that a man will be known.

Distrust the wicked

29 31	Do not bring every man home with you, for many are the traps of the crafty.
30 32	Like a decoy partridge in a basket, such is the proud man's heart; like a spy he watches for your downfall.
31 33	The slanderer twists good into evil, will cast a slur on what deserves most praise.
32 34	A hearthful of glowing coals starts from a single spark, and the sinner lurks for the chance to spill blood.
33 35	Beware of a scoundrel and his evil contrivances, in case he puts a smear on you for ever.
34 36	Bring a stranger home with you and he will start trouble, and estrange you from your own family.

Rules for doing good[a]

1 **12**	If you do a good turn, know for whom you are doing it, and your good deeds will not go to waste.
2	Do good to a devout man, and you will receive a reward, if not from him, then certainly from the Most High.
3	No good will come to a man who persists in evil, or who refuses to give alms.
4	Give to a devout man, do not go to the help of a sinner.

5	Do good to a humble man,
	   give nothing to a godless one.
	Refuse him bread, do not give him any,
	   it might make him stronger than you are;
	then you would be repaid evil twice over
	   for all the good you had done him.

12 a. The worldly wisdom of this section may be contrasted with the ethics of the Gospel.

For the Most High himself detests sinners,　　　　　6
　　　and will repay the wicked with a vengeance.
Give to the good man,　　　　　7
　　　and do not go to the help of a sinner.

True and false friends

In prosperity you cannot always tell a true friend,　　　　　8
　　　but in adversity you cannot mistake an enemy.
When a man is doing well his enemies are sad,　　　　　9
　　　when he is doing badly, even a friend will keep his distance.
Do not ever trust an enemy;　　　　　10
　　　as bronze tarnishes, so does his malignity.
Even if he behaves humbly and comes bowing and scraping,　　　　　11
　　　maintain your reserve and be on your guard against him.
Behave towards him as if you were polishing a mirror,
　　　you will find that his tarnish cannot last.
Do not stand him beside you　　　　　12
　　　in case he thrusts you out and takes your place.
Do not seat him at your right hand,
　　　or he will be after your position,
and you will end up by admitting the truth of my words,
　　　and feeling the sting in them.
Who feels sorry for a snake-charmer bitten by a snake,　　　　　13
　　　or for those who take risks with savage animals? —
just so for someone consorting with a sinner,　　　　　14
　　　and being accomplice to his sins.　　　　　13b
As long as you maintain your stand he will not reveal himself,　　　　　15
　　　but if you once give way he will press his advantage.　　　　　14
An enemy may have sweetness on his lips,　　　　　16
　　　and in his heart a scheme to throw you in the ditch.　　　　　15
An enemy may have tears in his eyes,　　　　　16
　　　but if he gets a chance not even blood will satisfy him.
If you meet with misfortune, you will find him there before you,　　　　　17
　　　and, pretending to help you, he will trip you up.
He will wag his head and clap his hands,　　　　　18
　　　he will whisper a lot and his expression will change.　　　　　19

Mix with your equals

13 Whoever touches pitch will be defiled,　　　　　1
　　　and anyone who associates with a proud man will come to be
　　　　　like him.
Do not try to carry a burden too heavy for you,　　　　　2
　　　do not associate with someone more powerful and wealthy
　　　　　than yourself.
Why put the clay pot next to the iron cauldron?　　　　　3
　　　It will only break when they collide.
The rich man wrongs a man and puts on airs,　　　　　3
　　　while the poor man is wronged and apologises.　　　　　4
If you are useful he will exploit you,　　　　　4
　　　if you cannot keep up with him he will desert you.　　　　　5
Are you well off?—he will live with you,　　　　　5
　　　he will clean you out without a single qualm.　　　　　6
Does he need you?—he will hoodwink you,　　　　　6
　　　smile at you and raise your hopes;　　　　　7
he will speak to you with smooth words
　　　and say, 'I wonder what you would like?'

7
8

And he will put you to shame with his grand dinners,
    until he has cleaned you out two or three times over,
    and he will finish by making you ridiculous.
When he sees you afterwards he will snub you,
    and wag his head about you.

8
11

Take care you are not hoodwinked
    and thus humiliated through your own stupidity.

9
12

When an influential man invites you, show reluctance,
    and he will press his invitation all the more.

10
13

Do not thrust yourself forward, in case you are pushed aside,
    but do not stand aloof, or you will be overlooked.

11
14

Do not affect to treat him as an equal,
    do not trust his flow of words;
since all this talking is expressly meant to test you,
    under cover of geniality he will be weighing you up.

12
15

Pitiless is the man who is too free with his words,
    he will not spare you either blows or chains.

13
16

Be wary, take very great care,
    because you are walking with your own downfall.

15
19

Every living thing loves its own sort,
    and every man his neighbour.

16
20

Every creature mixes with its kind,
    and man sticks to his own sort.

17
21

How can wolf and lamb agree?—
    Just so with sinner and devout.

18
22

What peace can there be between hyena and dog?
    And what peace between rich man and poor?

19
23

Wild donkeys are the prey of desert lions;
    so too, the poor are the quarry of the rich.

20
24

The proud man thinks humility abhorrent;
    so too, the rich abominate the poor.

21
25

When the rich man stumbles he is supported by friends;
    when the poor man falls, his friends push him away.

22
26

When the rich man slips, there are many hands to catch him,
    if he talks nonsense he is congratulated.

27

The poor man slips, and is blamed for it,
    he may talk good sense, but no room is made for him.

23
28

The rich man speaks and everyone stops talking,
    and then they praise his discourse to the skies.

29

The poor man speaks and people say, 'Who is this?'
    and if he staggers they push him down.

24
30

Wealth is good where there is no sin,
    poverty is evil, the godless say.

25
31

A man's heart moulds his expression
    whether for better or worse.

26
32

The mark of a good heart is a cheerful expression;
    inventing proverbs is weary work.

True happiness

1

14

Happy the man who has not sinned in speech
    and who need feel no remorse for sins.

2

Happy the man whose own soul does not accuse him,
    and who has never given up hope.

Envy and greed

Wealth is not the right thing for a niggardly man,   3
   and what use are possessions to a covetous one?
A man who hoards by stinting himself is hoarding for others,   4
   and others will live sumptuously on his riches.

If a man is mean to himself, to whom will he be good?   5
   He does not even enjoy what is his own.
No one is meaner than the man who is mean to himself,   6
   and this is how his wickedness pays him back.
If he does good at all, he does it without intending to,   7
   and in the end he himself reveals his wickedness.
Evil is the man who has a grudging eye,   8
   averting his face, and careless of others' lives.

The eye of the grasping man is not content with his portion,   9
   greed shrivels up the soul.

The miser is grudging of bread,   10
   there is famine at his table.

My son, treat yourself as well as you can afford,   11
   and bring worthy offerings to the Lord.
Remember that death will not delay,   12
   and that the covenant of Sheol*a* has not been revealed to you.
Be kind to your friend before you die,   13
   treat him as generously as you can afford.
Do not refuse yourself the good things of today,   14
   do not let your share of what is lawfully desired pass you by.
Will you not have to leave your fortune to another,   15
   and the fruit of your labour to be divided by lot?
Then give and receive, and take your ease,   16
   for in Sheol you cannot look for pleasure.   17
Every living thing grows old like a garment,.   17/18
   the age-old law is 'Death must be'.
Like foliage growing on a bushy tree,   18
   some leaves falling, others growing,   19
so are the generations of flesh and blood:
   one dies, another is born.
Every achievement rots away and perishes,   19/20
   and with it goes its author.

The happiness of the sage

Happy the man who meditates on wisdom,   20/22
   and reasons with good sense,
who studies her ways in his heart,   21/23
   and ponders her secrets.
He pursues her like a hunter,   22
   and lies in wait by her path;
he peeps in at her windows,   23/24
   and listens at her doors;
he lodges close to her house,   24/25
   and fixes his peg in her walls;
he pitches his tent at her side,   25
   and lodges in an excellent lodging;
he sets his children in her shade,   26
   and camps beneath her branches;

27   he is sheltered by her from the heat,
      and in her glory he makes his home.

15

1   Whoever fears the Lord will act like this,
      and whoever grasps the Law will obtain wisdom.

2   She will come to meet him like a mother,
      and receive him like a virgin bride.

3   She will give him the bread of understanding to eat,
      and the water of wisdom to drink.

4   He will lean on her and will not fall,
      he will rely on her and not be put to shame.

5   She will raise him high above his neighbours,
      and in full assembly she will open his mouth.

6   He will find happiness and a crown of joy,
      he will inherit an everlasting name.

7   Foolish men will not gain possession of her,
      nor will sinful men set eyes on her.

8   She stands remote from pride,
      and liars cannot call her to mind.

9   Praise is unseemly in a sinner's mouth,
      since it has not been put there by the Lord.

10   For praise should only be uttered in wisdom,
      and the Lord himself then prompts it.

Man is free

11   Do not say, 'The Lord was responsible for my sinning',
      for he is never the cause of what he hates.

12   Do not say, 'It was he who led me astray',
      for he has no use for a sinner.

13   The Lord hates all that is foul,
      and no one who fears him will love it either.

14   He himself made man in the beginning,
      and then left him free to make his own decisions.

15
16   If you wish, you can keep the commandments,
      to behave faithfully is within your power.

16
17   He has set fire and water before you;
      put out your hand to whichever you prefer.

17
18   Man has life and death before him;
      whichever a man likes better will be given him.

18
19   For vast is the wisdom of the Lord;
      he is almighty and all-seeing.

19
20   His eyes are on those who fear him,
      he notes every action of man.

20
21   He never commanded anyone to be godless,
      he has given no one permission to sin.

Curses reaped by the wicked

16

1   Do not long for a brood of worthless children,
      and take no pleasure in godless sons.

2   However many you have, take no pleasure in them,
      unless the fear of the Lord lives among them.

3   Do not count on their having long life,
      do not put too much faith in their future;
      for better have one than a thousand,
4   better die childless than have godless ones.

14 a. Probably the decree assigning the date of death.

One man of sense can populate a city,   4/5
   but the race of lawless men will be destroyed.

My eyes have seen many such things,   5/6
   my ears have heard things still more impressive.

Fire will be kindled in a community of sinners;   6/7
   the wrath was kindled in a disobedient nation.

God did not pardon the giants of old   7/8
   who, confident in their strength, rebelled.

He did not spare the people with whom Lot lived,   8/9
   whom he abhorred for their pride.

He had no pity on that people doomed to destruction,   9/10
   who were wiped out in their sins,

nor on the six hundred thousand men on the march   10/11
   who banded together in their obstinacy.ᵃ

Had there been even only one stubborn man,   11/12
   it would have been astonishing if he had escaped unpunished,

since mercy and wrath alike belong to the Lord
   who is mighty to forgive and to pour out wrath.

His mercy is great, but his severity is as great;   12/13
   he judges every man as his deeds deserve:

the sinner shall not escape with his ill-gotten gains,   13/14
   nor the devout man's patience go for nothing.

He allows free play to his mercy;   14/15
   yet every man shall be treated as his deeds deserve.

Certainty of retribution

Do not say, 'I will hide from the Lord,   17/16
   who will remember me up there?

I shall certainly not be noticed among so many;   17
   what am I in the immensity of creation?'

Why look, the sky and the heavens above the sky,   18
   the deep and the earth tremble at his visitation.

The mountains and the base of the earth together   19
   quail and tremble when he looks at them.

But who bothers his head about such things?   20
   Who attempts to understand the way he moves?

The storm wind itself is invisible,   21
   and most of what he does goes undetected.

'Who will report whether justice has been done?   22
   Who will be expecting it? The covenant is far away.'

Such are the thoughts of the man of little sense,   23
   the rash misguided man who loves his illusions.

Man in creation

Listen to me, my son, and learn knowledge,   24
   and give your whole mind to my words.

I will expound discipline to a nicety,   25
   and proclaim knowledge with precision.

When God created his works in the beginning,   26
   he allotted them their portions as soon as they were made.

He determined his works for all time,   27
   from their beginnings to their distant future.

They know neither hunger nor weariness,
   and they never desert their duties.

None has ever jostled its neighbour,   28
   they will never disobey his word.ᵇ   29

29 30	And afterwards the Lord looked at the earth,
30 31	and filled it with his good things.
	He covered its surface with every kind of animal,
	and to it they will return.

17

1 — The Lord fashioned man from the earth,
to consign him back to it.

2 — He gave them so many days' determined time,
he gave them authority over everything on earth.

3 — He clothed them with strength like his own,
and made them in his own image.

4 — He filled all living things with dread of man,
making him master over beasts and birds.

6 5 — He shaped for them a mouth and tongue, eyes and ears,
and gave them a heart to think with.

7 6 — He filled them with knowledge and understanding,
and revealed to them good and evil.

8 7 — He put his own light in their hearts
to show them the magnificence of his works.

10 8 — They will praise his holy name,
as they tell of his magnificent works.

11 9 — He set knowledge before them,
he endowed them with the law of life.

12 10 — He established an eternal covenant with them,
and revealed his judgements to them.

13 11 — Their eyes saw his glorious majesty,
and their ears heard the glory of his voice.

14 — He said to them, 'Beware of all wrong-doing';
12 — he gave each a commandment concerning his neighbour.

The divine judge

15 13 — Their ways are always under his eye,
they cannot be hidden from his sight.

17 14 — Over each nation he has set a governor,
15 — but Israel is the Lord's own portion.[a]

19 16 — All their works are as the sun to him,
and his eyes rest constantly on their ways.

20 17 — Their iniquities are not hidden from him,
all their sins are before the Lord.

22 18 — A man's almsgiving is like a signet ring to him,
he cherishes a man's generosity like the pupil of his eye.

23 19 — One day he will rise and reward them,
he will pay back their deserts on their own heads.

24 20 — But to those who repent he permits return,
and he encourages those who were losing hope.

Exhortation to repentance

25 21 — Return to the Lord and leave sin behind,
22 — plead before his face and lessen your offence.

26 23 — Come back to the Most High and turn away from iniquity,
and hold in abhorrence all that is foul.

27 (26) — Who will praise the Most High in Sheol,
if the living do not do so by giving glory to him?

---

16 a. Those who died in the wilderness and did not reach Canaan; Ex 12:37; Nb 11:21.
b. The reference is to the stars and planets.
17 a. Israel had no king in the author's time.

To the dead, as to those who do not exist, praise is unknown,   28
(27)
    only those with life and health can praise the Lord.
How great is the mercy of the Lord,   29
28
    his pardon on all those who turn towards him!
Man cannot have everything,   30
29
    since the son of man is not immortal.
What is brighter than the sun? Yet it suffers eclipse.   31
30
    Flesh and blood think of nothing but evil.
He surveys the armies of the lofty sky,   32
31
    while all men are no more than dust and ashes.

The greatness of God

18   He who lives for ever created all the universe.   1
    The Lord alone will be found righteous.   2
He has given no one the power to proclaim his works,   4
2
    and who can fathom his magnificent deeds?   3
Who can assess his magnificent strength,   5
4
    and who can go further and tell of his mercies?
Nothing can be added to them, nothing subtracted,   6
5
    it is impossible to fathom the marvels of the Lord.
When a man finishes he is only beginning,   7
6
    and when he stops he is as puzzled as ever.

The nothingness of man

What is man, what purpose does he serve?   8
7
    What is the good in him, and what the bad?
Take the number of a man's days; a hundred years is very long.   9
8
Like a drop of water from the sea, or a grain of sand,   10
    such are these few years compared with eternity.
For this reason the Lord shows them forbearance,   11
9
    and pours out his mercy on them.
He sees and recognises how wretched their end is,   12
10
    and so he makes his forgiveness the greater.   11
Man's compassion extends to his neighbour,   13
12
    but the compassion of the Lord extends to everything that lives;   13
rebuking, correcting and teaching,
    bringing them back as a shepherd brings his flock.
He has compassion on those who accept correction,   14
    and who fervently look for judgements.

The art of giving

My son, do not temper your favours with disparagement,   15
    nor any of your gifts with words that hurt.
Does not dew relieve the heat?   16
    In the same way a word is worth more than a gift.
Why surely, a word is better than a good present,   17
    but a generous man is ready with both.
A fool will offer nothing but insult,   18
    and a grudging man's gift makes the eyes smart.

Reflection and foresight

Learn before you speak,   19
    take care of yourself before you fall ill.
Examine yourself before judgement comes,   20
    and on the day of visitation you will find yourself acquitted.
Humble yourself before you fall ill,   21

and when you sin, repent.

22   Let nothing prevent your discharging a vow in good time,
      and do not wait till death before setting matters to rights.
23   Prepare yourself before making a vow,
      and do not be like a man who tempts the Lord.
24   Bear the wrath of the last days in mind,
      the time of vengeance when God averts his face.
25   In a time of plenty remember times of famine,
      poverty and want in days of wealth.
26   The time slips by between dawn and dusk,
      all things pass swiftly in the presence of the Lord.
27   A wise man will be cautious in everything,
      and in sinful days he will take care not to offend.
28   Every man of sense recognises wisdom,
      and will respect anyone who has found her.
29   Those who understand sayings have themselves grown wise
      and have poured out apt proverbs.

Self-control

30   Do not follow your lusts,
      restrain your desires.
31   If you allow yourself to satisfy your desires,
      this will make you the laughing-stock of your enemies.
32   Do not indulge in luxurious living,
      nor get involved in such society.
33   Do not beggar yourself by banqueting on credit
      when there is nothing in your pocket.

19

1   Behave like that and you will never grow rich;
      he who despises trifles will sink down little by little.
2   Wine and women corrupt sensible men,
      the customer of whores loses all sense of shame.
3   Grubs and worms will have him as their legacy,
      and the man who knows no shame shall lose his life.

Against loose talk

4   Being too ready to trust shows shallowness of mind,
      by committing sin a man does wrong to himself.
5   Taking pleasure in evil earns condemnation,
6   by hating gossip a man avoids evil.
7   Never repeat what you are told
      and you will come to no harm;
8   whether to friend or foe, do not talk about it,
      unless it would be sinful not to, do not reveal it;
9   you would be heard out, then mistrusted,
      and in due course you would be hated.
10   Have you heard something? Let it die with you.
      Courage! It will not burst you!
11   A fool will suffer birthpangs over something told him,
      like a woman labouring with child.
12   Like an arrow stuck in the flesh of the thigh,
      such is a piece of news inside a fool.

Do not trust everything you hear

13   Question your friend, he may have done nothing at all,
      and if he has done anything, he will not do it again.
14   Question your neighbour, he may have said nothing at all,
      and if he has said anything, he will not say it again.

Question your friend, for slander is very common,   15
   do not believe all you hear.   16

A man sometimes makes a slip, without meaning what he says;   16
   and which of us has never sinned by speech?   17

Question your neighbour before you threaten him,   17
   and leave scope for the Law of the Most High.   18

True and false wisdom

Wisdom consists entirely in fearing the Lord,   20
   and wisdom is entirely constituted by the fulfilling of the Law.

But being learned in evil is not wisdom,   22 / 19
   and there is no shrewd judgement in the advice of sinners.

There is a cleverness that is foul,   23 / 20
   he who does not have wisdom is a fool.

Better be short of sense and full of fear,   24 / 21
   than abound in shrewdness and violate the Law.

There is an adroit sort of cleverness promoting injustice,   25 / 22
   there is the man who will abuse favours to establish his case.   23

There is the man who will walk bowed down with grief,   26
   when inwardly this is nothing but deceit:

he hides his face and pretends to be deaf,   27 / 24
   and when you are off your guard he takes advantage of you.

This man may think he lacks the power to sin,   28 / 25
   but he will do wrong when he gets the chance.

You can tell a man by his appearance,   29 / 26
   you can tell a thinking man by the look on his face.

A man's dress tells you what he does,   30 / 27
   and a man's walk tells you what he is.

Silence and speech

20

There is the rebuke that is untimely,   1 / 28
   and there is the man who keeps quiet, and he is the shrewd one.

But how much better to rebuke than to fume!   2 / 1
   The man who acknowledges a fault wards off punishment.   3

Like a eunuch longing to take a girl's virginity   4 / 2
   so is he who uses force to argue cases.   3

There is the man who keeps quiet and is considered wise,   5
   another incurs hatred for talking too much.

There is the man who keeps quiet, not knowing how to answer,   6
   another keeps quiet, because he knows when to speak.

A wise man will keep quiet till the right moment,   7
   but a garrulous fool will always misjudge it.

The man who talks too much will get himself disliked,   8
   and the self-appointed oracle will make himself hated.

Paradoxes

There is the man who finds misfortune the saving of him,   9
   and the lucky find that turn to loss.

There is the gift that affords you no profit,   10
   and the gift that repays you double.

There is the honour that leads to humiliation,   11
   and there are men in a low state who raise their heads.

12   There is the man who buys much for little,
         yet pays for it seven times over.

13   The wise man will win love by his words,
         while fools may shower favours in vain.

14   A stupid man's gift will bring you no advantage,
         his eyes look for seven times as much in return.

15   He gives little and reviles much,
         he opens his mouth like the town crier,

16   he lends today and demands payment tomorrow;
         he is a detestable fellow.

16
17   The fool will say, 'I have no friends,
         I get no gratitude for my good deeds;

17
18   those who eat my bread have malicious tongues'.
         How often he will be laughed at, and by how many!

Inappropriate talk

18
20   Better a slip on the pavement than a slip of the tongue;
         this is how ruin takes the wicked by surprise.

19
21   A coarse-grained man is like an indiscreet story
         endlessly retold by the ignorant.

20
22   A maxim is rejected when coming from a fool,
         since he does not utter it on the apt occasion.

21
23   Take a man who is prevented from sinning by poverty;
         no qualms of conscience disturb his rest.

22
24   Take a man who destroys himself out of false shame,
         destroys himself for the sake of a fool's opinion.

23
25   Take a man who, out of false shame, makes promises to a friend,
         and so makes an enemy for nothing.

Lying

24
26   Lying is an ugly blot on a man,
         and ever on the lips of the ignorant.

25
27   A thief is preferable to an inveterate liar,
         but both are heading for ruin.

26
28   Lying is an abominable habit,
         so that disgrace is the liar's for ever.

The wise man: his dignity and his dangers

27
29   A wise man advances himself by his words,
         a shrewd man will please princes.

28
30   He who tills the soil will have a full harvest,
         he who pleases princes will secure pardon for his offences.

29
31   Presents and gifts blind wise men's eyes
         and stifle rebukes like a muzzle on the mouth.

30
32   Wisdom concealed, and treasure undiscovered,
         what use is either of these?

31
33   Better a man who conceals his folly
         than a man who conceals his wisdom.

Various sins

<h1 style="display:inline">21</h1>

My son, have you sinned? Do not do it again,   1
    and ask forgiveness for your previous faults.
Flee from sin as from a snake,   2
    if you approach it, it will bite you;
its teeth are lion's teeth,   3
    they deprive men of their lives.
All law-breaking is like a two-edged sword,   3 / 4
    the wounds it inflicts are beyond cure.

Panic and violence make havoc of palaces,   4 / 5
    similarly, desolation overtakes the houses of the proud.
A plea from a poor man's mouth goes straight to the ear of God,   5 / 6
    whose judgement comes without delay.

Whoever resents reproof walks in the sinner's footsteps;   6 / 7
    the man who fears the Lord bears repentance in his heart.

The glib speaker is known far and wide,   7 / 8
    but when he makes a slip the thinking man detects it.

To build your house on other people's money   8 / 9
    is like collecting stones for your own tomb.

A meeting of lawless men is like a heap of tow :   9 / 10
    they will end in a blazing fire.
The sinner's road is smoothly paved,   10 / 11
    but it ends at the pit of Sheol.

The wise man and the fool

Whoever keeps the Law will master his instincts;   11 / 12
    the fear of the Lord is made perfect in wisdom.   13

The man who lacks intelligence cannot be taught,   12 / 14
    but intelligence can increase a man's bitterness.   15

The wise man's knowledge will increase like a flood,   13 / 16
    and his advice is like a living spring.
The heart of a fool is like a broken jar,   14 / 17
    it will not hold any knowledge.
If a cultured man hears a wise saying,   15 / 18
    he praises it and caps it with another;
if an imbecile hears it, he laughs at it,
    and tosses it behind his back.

The talk of a fool is like a load on a journey,   16 / 19
    but it is a pleasure to listen to an intelligent man.
The shrewd man's utterance will be eagerly awaited in the assembly,   17 / 20
    what he says will be given serious consideration.

The wisdom of a fool is like the wreckage of a house,   18 / 21
    the knowledge of a dolt is incoherent talk.

To the senseless fellow instruction is like fetters on his feet,   19 / 22
    like manacles on his right hand.

A fool laughs at the top of his voice,   20 / 23
    but a man of intelligence quietly smiles.

To the shrewd man instruction is like a golden ornament,   21 / 24
    like a bracelet on his right arm.

<table>
<tr><td>22
25</td><td>The foot of a fool goes straight into a house,
  but a man of much experience is respectful in his approach;</td></tr>
<tr><td>23
26</td><td>a stupid man peeps inside through the door,
  a well-bred man waits outside.</td></tr>
<tr><td>24
27</td><td>Listening at doors is a sign of bad upbringing,
  a perceptive man would be ashamed to do so.</td></tr>
<tr><td>25
28</td><td>The lips of gossips repeat the words of others,
  the words of wise men are carefully weighed.</td></tr>
<tr><td>26
29</td><td>The heart of fools is exposed in their words;
  the words of wise men reveal their heart.</td></tr>
<tr><td>27
30</td><td>When a godless man curses his enemy,
  he is cursing himself.</td></tr>
<tr><td>28
31</td><td>The scandal-monger sullies himself
  and earns the hatred of the neighbourhood.</td></tr>
</table>

The idler

22

1 An idler is comparable to a stone covered in filth,
   everyone whistles at his disgrace.

2 An idler is comparable to a lump of dung,
   anyone picking it up shakes it off his hand.

Degenerate children

3 It is a disgrace to have fathered a badly brought-up son,
   and the birth of a daughter is a loss.

4 A sensible daughter is a treasure to her husband,
   but a shameless one is a grief to her father.

5 An insolent daughter puts father and mother to shame,
   and will be disowned by both.

6 An untimely remonstrance is like music at a funeral,
   but a thrashing and correction are wisdom at all times.

Wisdom and folly

<table>
<tr><td>9
7</td><td>You are gluing the broken pieces of a pot together if you try
    to teach a fool,</td></tr>
<tr><td>8</td><td>you are rousing a man who is besotted with sleep.</td></tr>
<tr><td>10
9</td><td>A fool is the same as a drowsing man if you have to explain
    anything to him,
  when you have finished he will say, 'What is it all about?'</td></tr>
<tr><td>11
10</td><td>Shed tears for the dead man, since he has left the light behind;
  shed tears for the fool, since he has left his wits behind;</td></tr>
<tr><td>11</td><td>shed quieter tears for the dead, since he is at rest.</td></tr>
<tr><td>12</td><td>For the fool, life is sadder than death.</td></tr>
<tr><td>12
13</td><td>Mourning for the dead lasts seven days,
  for the foolish and ungodly all the days of their lives.</td></tr>
<tr><td>13
14</td><td>Do not waste many words on a stupid man,
  do not go near a dolt.</td></tr>
<tr><td>15</td><td>Beware of him, or he will give you trouble,
  and will leave you soiled by contact with him.</td></tr>
<tr><td>16</td><td>Avoid him, and you will find rest
  and not be exasperated by his folly.</td></tr>
<tr><td>14
17</td><td>What is heavier than lead,
  and what is its name if not 'fool'?</td></tr>
<tr><td>15
18</td><td>Sand, and salt, and a lump of iron
  are all easier to bear than a dolt.</td></tr>
</table>

A tie-beam bonded into a building   16
     19
    will not be dislodged by an earthquake;
so too, a heart resolved after due reflection   20
    will not flinch at the critical moment.

A heart founded on intelligent reflection   17
    is like a stucco decoration on a smooth wall.

Pebbles placed on top of a wall   18
     21
    will not stand up to the wind;
no more can the heart of a fool frightened at his own thoughts   22
    stand up to fear.

Friendship

Prick an eye and you will draw a tear,   19
     24
    prick a heart and you bring its feelings to light.
Throw stones at birds and you scare them away,   20
     25
    revile a friend and you break up friendship.

If you have drawn your sword on a friend,   21
     26
    do not despair; there is a way back.
If you have opened your mouth against your friend,   22
     27
    do not worry; there is hope for reconciliation;
but insult, arrogance, betrayal of secrets, and the stab in the back—
    in these cases any friend will run away.

Win your neighbour's confidence when he is poor,   23
     28
    so that you may enjoy his later good fortune with him;
stand by him in times of trouble,   29
    in order to have your share when he comes into a legacy.

Fire is heralded by the reek of the furnace and smoke,   24
     30
    so too bloodshed by insults.
I will not be ashamed to shelter a friend,   25
     31
    nor will I hide from his face;
and if evil comes to me through him,   26
    everyone who hears about it will beware of him.   32

Vigilance

Who will set a guard on my mouth,   27
     33
    and a seal of prudence on my lips,
to keep me from falling,
    and my tongue from causing my ruin?

23   Lord, father and master of my life,   1
    do not abandon me to their whims,
    do not let me fall because of them.
Who will lay whips to my thoughts,   2
    and the discipline of wisdom to my heart,
to be unmerciful to my errors,
    and let none of my sins go unchecked
in case my errors multiply,   3
    and my sins increase in number,
and I fall before my adversaries,
    and my enemy gloats over me?
Lord, father and God of my life,   4
    do not give me proud eyes,
turn lust away from me,   5
do not let lechery and lust grip me,   6
    do not give me over to shameless desire.

Swearing

7   Listen, children, to the instruction I have to give;
      whoever keeps it will not be caught out.
8   The sinner is ensnared by his own lips,
      both the abusive and the proud man are tripped by them.
9   Do not accustom your mouth to swearing,
(10)   nor get into the habit of naming the Holy One;
10
11 for just as a slave who is constantly overseen
      will never be without bruises,
    so too the man who is continually swearing oaths and uttering
          the name
      will not be exempt from sin.
11
12 A man forever swearing is full of iniquity,
      and the scourge will not depart from his house.
13 If he offends, his sin will be on him,
      if he swears lightly, he sins twice over;
14 if he swears a false oath, he will not be treated as innocent,
      for his house will be filled with calamities.

Foul talk

12
15 There is a manner of talking that is fraught with death;
      let it not be found in the inheritance of Jacob,
16 for devout men will keep all that far from them,
      they will not wallow in sin.
13
17 Do not habituate your mouth to coarseness and foul language,
      for this means sinful talk.
14
18 Remember your father and mother
      when you are sitting among princes,
19 in case you forget yourself in their presence,
      and behave like a fool,
    and then wish you had not been born,
      and curse the day of your birth.
15
20 A man in the habit of using improper words
      will never break himself of it however long he lives.

Incest and adultery

16
21 Two kinds of men multiply sins,
      and a third draws down wrath:
17
22 there is a desire that, blazing like a furnace,
      cannot be quenched until it is slaked;
23 there is the man who lusts for his own flesh:
      he will not give up until the fire consumes him;
24 to a fornicator all food is sweet,
      and he will not weary of it until he dies.
18
25 The man who sins against his own marriage bed,
      and says to himself, 'Who can see me?
26 There is darkness all round me, the walls hide me,
      nobody sees me; why should I worry?
    The Most High will not call my sins to mind':
27 what he fears is the eyes of men,
19
28 he does not realise that the eyes of the Lord
      are ten thousand times brighter than the sun,
    observing every aspect of human behaviour,
      seeing into the most secret corners.
20
29 All things were known to him before they were created,
      and are still, now that they are finished.

This man will be punished in view of the whole town,   21 / 30
and will be seized where he least expects it.

The adulteress

Similarly the woman who deserts her husband,   22 / 32
and provides him with an heir by another man:
first, she has disobeyed the Law of the Most High;   23 / 33
secondly, she has been false to her husband;
and thirdly, she has gone whoring in adultery
and conceived children by another man.
She will be led before the assembly,   24 / 34
an enquiry will be held about her children.
Her children will strike no root,   25 / 35
her branches will bear no fruit.
She will leave an accursed memory behind her,   26 / 36
her shame will never be wiped out.
And those who survive her will recognise   27 / 37
that nothing is better than fearing the Lord,
and nothing sweeter than adherence to the Lord's commandments.

Discourse of Wisdom

24

Wisdom speaks her own praises,   1
in the midst of her people she glories in herself.
She opens her mouth in the assembly of the Most High,   2
she glories in herself in the presence of the Mighty One;
'I came forth from the mouth of the Most High,   3 / 5
and I covered the earth like mist.   6
I had my tent in the heights,   4 / 7
and my throne in a pillar of cloud.
Alone I encircled the vault of the sky,   5 / 8
and I walked on the bottom of the deeps.
Over the waves of the sea and over the whole earth,   6 / 9
and over every people and nation I have held sway.   10
Among all these I searched for rest,   7 / 11
and looked to see in whose territory I might pitch camp.
Then the creator of all things instructed me,   8 / 12
and he who created me fixed a place for my tent.
He said, "Pitch your tent in Jacob,   13
make Israel your inheritance".
From eternity, in the beginning, he created me,   9 / 14
and for eternity I shall remain.
I ministered before him in the holy tabernacle,   10
and thus was I established on Zion.   15
In the beloved city he has given me rest,   11
and in Jerusalem I wield my authority.
I have taken root in a privileged people,   12 / 16
in the Lord's property, in his inheritance.
I have grown tall as a cedar on Lebanon,   13 / 17
as a cypress on Mount Hermon;
I have grown tall as a palm in Engedi,   14 / 18
as the rose bushes of Jericho;
as a fine olive in the plain,   19
as a plane tree I have grown tall.
I have exhaled a perfume like cinnamon and acacia,   15 / 20
I have breathed out a scent like choice myrrh,

21
like galbanum, onycha and stacte,
  like the smoke of incense in the tabernacle.

16
22
I have spread my branches like a terebinth,
  and my branches are glorious and graceful.

17
23
I am like a vine putting out graceful shoots,
  my blossoms bear the fruit of glory and wealth.

19
26
Approach me, you who desire me,
  and take your fill of my fruits,

20
27
28
for memories of me are sweeter than honey,
  inheriting me is sweeter than the honeycomb.

21
29
They who eat me will hunger for more,
  they who drink me will thirst for more.

22
30
Whoever listens to me will never have to blush,
  whoever acts as I dictate will never sin.'

Wisdom and the Law

23
32
All this is no other than the book of the covenant of the
  Most High God,

33
  the Law that Moses enjoined on us,
an inheritance for the communities of Jacob.

25
35
That is what makes wisdom brim like the Pishon,[a]
  like the Tigris in the season of fruit,

26
36
what makes understanding brim over like the Euphrates,
  like the Jordan at harvest time;

27
37
and makes discipline flow like the Nile,
  like the Gihon at the time of vintage.

28
38
The first man never managed to grasp her entirely,
  nor has the most recent one fully comprehended her;

29
39
for her thoughts are wider than the sea,
  and her designs more profound than the abyss.

30
40
And I, like a conduit from a river,
  like a watercourse running into a garden,

31
42
I said, 'I am going to water my orchard,
  I intend to irrigate my flower beds'.

43
And see, my conduit has grown into a river,
  and my river has grown into a sea.

32
44
Now I shall make discipline shine out,
  I shall send its light far and wide.

33
46
I shall pour out teaching like prophecy,
  as a legacy to all future generations.

34
47
Observe that I have not toiled for myself alone,
  but for all who are seeking wisdom.

Proverbs

1
25
There are three things my soul delights in,
  and which are delightful to God and to men:

2
concord between brothers, friendship between neighbours,
  and a wife and husband who live happily together.

2
3
There are three sorts of people my soul hates,
  and whose existence I consider an outrage:

4
a poor man swollen with pride, a rich man who is a liar
  and an adulterous old man who has no sense.

24 a. The Jordan and the Nile are grouped here with the four rivers of Eden, Gn 2:10f.

Old men

If you have gathered nothing in your youth,　　　　　　3
　　how can you find anything in your old age?　　　　　5
How fine a thing: sound judgement with grey hairs,　　4
　　and for greybeards to know how to advise!　　　　6
How fine a thing: wisdom in the aged,　　　　　　　5
　　and considered advice coming from men of distinction!　7
The crown of old men is ripe experience,　　　　　6
　　their true glory, the fear of the Lord.　　　　8

Numerical proverbs

There are nine things I can think of which strike me as happy,　7
　　and a tenth which is now on my tongue:　　　　9
a man whose joy is in his children,　　　　　　　10
　　he who lives to see the downfall of his enemies;
happy the man who keeps house with a sensible wife;　8
　　he who does not toil with ox and donkey;[a]　　11
he who has never sinned with his tongue;
　　he who does not serve a man less worthy than himself;
happy the man who has acquired good sense　　　9
　　and can find attentive ears for what he has to say;　12
how great the man is who has acquired wisdom;　　10
　　but no one excels the man who fears the Lord.　13
The fear of the Lord surpasses everything;　　　11
　　what can compare with a man who has mastered that?　14
　　　　　　　　　　　　　　　　　　　　　　15

Women

Any wound rather than a wound of the heart!　　　13
　　Any spite rather than the spite of woman!　　17
Any evil rather than an evil caused by an enemy!　　14
　　Any vengeance rather than the vengeance of a foe!　18
　　　　　　　　　　　　　　　　　　　　　　19
There is no poison worse than the poison of a snake,　15
　　there is no fury worse than the fury of an enemy.　22
　　　　　　　　　　　　　　　　　　　　　　23
I would sooner keep house with a lion or a dragon　16
　　than keep house with a spiteful wife.

A woman's spite changes her appearance　　　　17
　　and makes her face as grim as any bear's.　　24
When her husband goes out to dinner with his neighbours,　18
　　he cannot help heaving bitter sighs.　　　　25

No wickedness comes anywhere near the wickedness of a woman,　19
　　may a sinner's lot be hers!　　　　　　　26

As climbing up a sandhill is for elderly feet　　　20
　　such is a garrulous wife for a quiet husband.　27
Do not be taken in by a woman's beauty,　　　21
　　never lose your head over a woman.　　　　28

Bad temper, insolence and shame hold sway　　22
　　where the wife supports the husband.　　　29
Low spirits, gloomy face, stricken heart:　　　23
　　such the achievements of a spiteful wife.　　31
Slack hands and sagging knees　　　　　　　32
　　indicate a wife who makes her husband wretched.

Sin began with a woman,　　　　　　　　24
　　and thanks to her we all must die.　　　　33

25
34 Do not let water find a leak,
 do not allow a spiteful woman free rein for her tongue.
26
35 If she will not do as you tell her,
36 get rid of her.[b]

26

1 Happy the husband of a really good wife;
 the number of his days will be doubled.
2 A perfect wife is the joy of her husband,
 he will live out the years of his life in peace.
3 A good wife is the best of portions,
 reserved for those who fear the Lord;
4 rich or poor, they will be glad of heart,
 cheerful of face, whatever the season.

5 There are three things my heart dreads,
 and a fourth which terrifies me:
6 slander by a whole town, the gathering of a mob,
7 and a false accusation—these are all worse than death;
6
8 but a woman jealous of a woman means heartbreak and sorrow,
9 and all this is the scourge of the tongue.

7
10 A bad wife is a badly fitting ox yoke,
 trying to master her is like grasping a scorpion.
8
11 A drunken wife will goad anyone to fury,
 she makes no effort to hide her degradation.

9
12 A woman's wantonness shows in her bold look,
 and can be recognised by her sidelong glances.
10
13 Keep a headstrong daughter under firm control,
 or she will abuse any indulgence she receives.
11
14 Keep a strict watch on her shameless eye,
 do not be surprised if she disgraces you.
12
15 Like a thirsty traveller she will open her mouth
 and drink any water she comes across;
 she will sit in front of every peg,
 and open her quiver to any arrow.

13
16 The grace of a wife will charm her husband,
17 her accomplishments will make him the stronger.
14
18 A silent wife is a gift from the Lord,
 no price can be put on a well-trained character.
15
19 A modest wife is a boon twice over,
20 a chaste character cannot be weighed on scales.
16
21 Like the sun rising over the mountains of the Lord
 is the beauty of a good wife in a well-kept house.
17
22 Like the lamp shining on the sacred lamp-stand
 is a beautiful face on a well-proportioned body.
18
23 Like golden pillars on a silver base
 are shapely legs on firm-set heels.

Depressing things

28
25 There are two things which grieve my heart
 and a third arouses my anger:
26 a warrior wasting away through poverty,
 intelligent men treated with contempt,
27 a man turning back from virtue to sin—
 the Lord marks this man out for a violent death.

25 a. I.e., work with an uneven team. b. The Mosaic Law allowed divorce, Dt 24:1-4.

Commerce

It is difficult for a merchant to avoid doing wrong   29
and for a salesman not to incur sin.   28

27 Many have sinned for the sake of profit,   1
he who hopes to be rich must be ruthless.

A peg will stick in the joint between two stones,   2
and sin will wedge itself between selling and buying.

If a man does not hold earnestly to the fear of the Lord,   3
his House will soon be overthrown.   4

Speech

In a shaken sieve the rubbish is left behind,   4
so too the defects of a man appear in his talk.   5

The kiln tests the work of the potter,   5
the test of a man is in his conversation.   6

The orchard where the tree grows is judged on the quality of its fruit,   6
similarly a man's words betray what he feels.   7

Do not praise a man before he has spoken,   7
since this is the test of men.   8

Virtue

If you pursue justice you will achieve it   8
and put it on like a festal gown.   9

Birds consort with their kind,   9
justice comes home to those who practise it.   10

The lion lies in wait for its prey,   10
so does sin for those who do wrong.   11

The devout man's conversation is wisdom at all times,   11
but the fool is as changeable as the moon.   12

Among stupid people look for your opportunity to leave,   12
but among thoughtful men take your time.   13

The conversation of fools is disgusting,   13
raucous their laughter at their sinful orgies.   14

The talk of hard-swearing men makes your hair stand on end,   14
their brawls make you stop your ears.   15

A quarrel between proud men leads to bloodshed,   15
their abuse is painful to hear.   16

Secrets

A betrayer of secrets forfeits all esteem   16
and will never find the kind of friend he wants.   17

Be fond of a friend and keep faith with him,   17
but if you have betrayed his secrets, do not pursue him any more;   18
                    19

for as a man destroys his enemy,   18
so you have destroyed the friendship of your neighbour,   20

and as you let a bird slip through your fingers,   19
so you have let your friend go, and will not catch him.   21

Do not go after him—he is far away,   20
he has fled like a gazelle from the snare.   22

For a wound can be bandaged and abuse forgiven,   21
but for the man who has betrayed a secret there is no hope.   23
                    24

Hypocrisy

22
25
    The man with a sly wink is plotting mischief,
        no one can dissuade him from it.

23
26
    Honey-tongued to your face,
        he is lost in admiration at your words;
    but behind your back he has other things to say,
        and makes your own words sound offensive.

24
27
    I have found many things to hate, but nothing to equal this man,
        and the Lord hates him too.

25
28
    The man who throws a stone in the air, throws it on to his own head;
        a treacherous blow cuts both ways.

26
29
    The man who digs a pit falls into it,
        he who sets a snare will be caught by it.

27
30
    On the man who does evil, evil will recoil,
        though where it came from he will not know.

28
31
    Sarcasm and abuse are the mark of an arrogant man,
        but vengeance lies in wait like a lion for him.

29
32
    The trap will close on all who rejoice in the downfall of the devout,
        and pain will eat them up before they die.

Resentment

30
33
    Resentment and anger, these are foul things too,
        and both are found with the sinner.

1
28
    He who exacts vengeance will experience the vengeance of the Lord,
        who keeps strict account of sin.

2
    Forgive your neighbour the hurt he does you,
        and when you pray, your sins will be forgiven.

3
    If a man nurses anger against another,
        can he then demand compassion from the Lord?

4
    Showing no pity for a man like himself,
        can he then plead for his own sins?

5
    Mere creature of flesh, he cherishes resentment;
        who will forgive him his sins?

6
    Remember the last things, and stop hating,

7
        remember dissolution and death, and live by the commandments.

7
8
    Remember the commandments, and do not bear your
        neighbour ill-will;

9
    remember the covenant of the Most High, and overlook
        the offence.

Quarrels

8
10
    Avoid quarrelling and you will sin less;

11
        for a hot-tempered man provokes quarrels,

9
    a sinner sows trouble between friends,
        introducing discord among men at peace.

10
12
    The way a fire burns depends on its fuel,
        a quarrel spreads in proportion to its violence;
    a man's rage depends on his strength,
        his fury grows fiercer in proportion to his wealth.

11
13
    A sudden quarrel kindles fire,
        a hasty dispute leads to bloodshed.

12
14
    Blow on a spark and up it flares,
        spit on it and out it goes;
        both are the effects of your mouth.

The tongue

A curse on the scandal-monger and the deceitful,   13/15
    he has ruined many who lived in concord.
That third tongue has shaken many,*   14/16
    and driven them from nation to nation;
it has pulled down fortified cities,   17
    and overturned the houses of princes.
The third tongue has driven virtuous wives out of house and home,   15/19
    and deprived them of the due reward for their hard work.
Anyone who listens to it will never know peace of mind,   16/20
    will never live in peace again.
A stroke of the whip raises a weal,   17/21
    but a stroke of the tongue breaks bones.
Many have fallen by the edge of the sword,   18/22
    but many more have fallen by the tongue.
Happy the man who has been sheltered from it,   19/23
    and has not experienced its fury,
who has not dragged its yoke about,
    or been bound in its chains;
for its yoke is an iron yoke, .   20/24
    its chains are bronze chains;
the death it inflicts is a miserable death,   21/25
    Sheol is preferable to it.
It cannot gain a hold over the devout,   22/26
    they are not burnt by its flames.
Those who desert the Lord will fall into it,   23/27
    it will flare up inextinguishably among them,
it will be let loose against them like a lion,
    it will tear them like a leopard.
Look, fence your property round with a quickthorn hedge,   24/28
    lock away your silver and gold;
then make scales and weights for your words,   25/29
    and put a door with bolts across your mouth.
Take care you take no false step through it,   26/30
    in case you fall a prey to him who lies in wait.

Loans

29

Making your neighbour a loan is an act of mercy,   1
    to lend him a helping hand is to keep the commandments.
Lend to your neighbour in his time of need,   2
    and in your turn repay your neighbour on time.
Be as good as your word and keep faith with him,   3
    and you will find your needs met every time.
Many treat a loan as a windfall,   4
    and embarrass those who have come to their rescue.
Until he gets something, a man will kiss his neighbour's hand,   5
    and refer to his wealth in respectful tones;
but when the loan falls due, he puts this off,   6
    he repays with offhand words,
    and pleads the inconvenience of the time.
Even if he can be made to pay, his creditor will barely recover half,   6/7
    and consider even that a windfall.
But otherwise he will be cheated of his money,   8
    and undeservedly gain himself an enemy;
the man will pay him back in curses and recriminations,   9
    and instead of respect will have contempt for him.

7
10

Many, not out of malice, refuse to lend;
    they are merely anxious not to be cheated for nothing.

Generosity

8
11

Nevertheless, be patient with those who are badly-off,
    do not keep them waiting on your generosity.

9
12

For the commandment's sake go to the poor man's help,
    do not turn him away empty-handed in his need.

10
13

Better let your silver go on brother or friend,
    do not let it go to waste, rusting under a stone.

11
14

Invest your treasure as the Most High orders,
    and you will find it more profitable than gold.

12
15

Deposit generosity in your storerooms
    and it will release you from every misfortune.

13
16

Better than sturdy shield or weighty spear,

17

    it will fight for you against the enemy.

Securities

14
18

A good man will go surety for his neighbour;
    a man has lost all shame if he fails him.

15
19

Do not forget the favour your guarantor has done you;
    he has given his life for you.

16
21

A sinner is careless of his guarantor's prosperity,
    an ungrateful man forgets the one who saved him.

17
23

Going surety has ruined many prosperous men
    and rocked them like a wave of the sea.

18
24

It has driven powerful men from home
    to wander among foreign nations.

19
25

The sinner who involves himself with guarantees,
    in pursuit of a deal, will find himself involved in lawsuits.

20
26

Come to your neighbour's help as far as you can,
    but take care not to fall into the same plight.

Home and hospitality

21
27

The first thing in life is water, and bread, and clothing,
    and a house for the sake of privacy.

22
28

Better a poor man's life under a roof of planks,
    than lavish fare in the house of another.

23
29

Whether you have little or much, be content with it,
    and you will not be dubbed an intruder.

24
30

It is a miserable life, going from house to house;
    wherever you stay, not daring to open your mouth;

25
31

you are a stranger, you know the taste of humiliation,
    not to mention the sound of embittering words,

26
32

'Come along, stranger, lay the table,
    if you have anything with you, give it to me to eat'.

27
33

'Go away, stranger, make room for someone important;
    my brother is coming to stay, I need the house.'

28
34

It is hard for a cultured man
    to hear himself begrudged hospitality
    and treated like an undischarged debtor.

---

28 a. From the context, it seems that the 'first' man is slandered to a 'second' man by 'the third tongue'.

Bringing up children

30

A man who loves his son will beat him frequently   1
    so that in after years the son may be his comfort.

A man who is strict with his son will reap the benefit,   2
    and be able to boast of him to his acquaintances.

A man who educates his son will be the envy of his enemy,   3
    and will be proud of him among his friends.

Even when the father dies, he might well not be dead,   4
    since he leaves his likeness behind him.
In life he has had the joy of his company,   5
    dying, he has no anxieties.
He leaves an avenger against his enemies,   6
    and a rewarder of favours for his friends.

A man who coddles his son will bandage his wounds,   7
    his heart will turn over at every shout.
A horse badly broken-in turns out stubborn,   8
    an uncontrolled son turns out headstrong.
Pamper your child, and he will give you a fright,   9
    play with him, and he will bring you sorrow.

Do not share his laughter, if you do not wish to share his sorrow   10
    and to end by grinding your teeth.
Allow him no independence in childhood,   11
    and do not wink at his mistakes.
Bend his neck in youth,   12
    bruise his ribs while he is a child,
or else he will grow stubborn and disobedient,
    and hurt you very deeply.
Be strict with your son, and persevere with him,   13
    or you will rue his insolence.

Health

Better a poor man healthy and fit   14
    than a rich man tormented in body.
Health and strength are better than any gold,   15
    a robust body than untold wealth.
No riches can outweigh bodily health,   16
    no enjoyment surpass a cheerful heart.
Better death than a wretched life,   17
    and everlasting rest than chronic illness.
Good things lavished on a closed mouth   18
    are like food offerings put on a grave.
What use is an offering to an idol   19
    which can neither eat nor smell?
How describe a man pursued by the Lord's displeasure?[a]   20
    He looks and sighs   20 / 21
as a eunuch embracing a virgin sighs.

Happiness

Do not abandon yourself to sorrow,   21 / 22
    do not torment yourself with brooding.
Gladness of heart is life to a man,   22 / 23
    joy is what gives him length of days.

23
24

Beguile your cares, console your heart,
   chase sorrow far away;

25

for sorrow has been the ruin of many,
   and is no use to anybody.

24
26

Jealousy and anger shorten your days,
   and worry brings premature old age.

25
27

A genial heart makes a good trencherman,
   one who benefits from his food.

Riches

31

1

The sleeplessness brought by wealth makes a man lose weight,
   the worry it causes drives away sleep.

2

The worries of the daytime interfere with slumber,
   as a serious illness drives away sleep.

3

The rich man toils, piling up money,
   and when he leaves off, he stuffs himself with luxuries;

4

the poor man toils, his livelihood dwindling,
   and when he leaves off, is destitute.

5

The man who loves gold will not be reckoned virtuous,
   the man who chases after profit will be caught out by it.

6

Many have gone to their ruin for the sake of gold,
   though their destruction stared them in the face;

7

it is a snare for those who sacrifice to it,
   and every fool will be caught in it.

8

Happy the rich man who is found to be blameless
   and does not go chasing after gold.

9

Who is he, for us to congratulate him,
   since he has achieved wonders among his kind?

10

Who has been through this test and emerged perfect?
   He may well be proud of that!
Who has had the power to sin and has not sinned,
   to wrong another and not done it?

11

His fortune will be firmly based
   and the assembly will acclaim his generosity.

Dinner parties

12

Have you sat down at a lavish table?
   Do not gape at it,
   do not say, 'What a feast!'

13
13
14
15

Remember how bad it is to have a greedy eye;
   is anything in creation greedier than the eye?
   That is why it waters on every occasion.

14
16
17

Do not reach out for anything your host has his eye on,
   do not jostle him at the dish.

15
18

Judge your fellow guest's needs by your own,
   be thoughtful in every way.

16
19

Eat what is offered you like a well brought-up person,
   do not wolf your food or you will earn dislike.

17
20

For politeness' sake be the first to stop;
   do not act the glutton, or you will give offence,

18
21

and if you are sitting with a large party,
   do not help yourself before the others do.

19
22

A little is quite enough for a well-bred person;

30 a. The sick man, who can eat nothing.

　　　　his breathing is easy when he gets to bed.
A moderate diet ensures sound sleep, ₂₀ ₂₄
　　　a man gets up early, in the best of spirits.
Sleeplessness, biliousness and gripe ₂₃
　　　are what the glutton has to endure.
If you are forced to eat too much, ₂₁ ₂₅
　　　get up, go and be sick, and you will feel better.
Listen to me my son, do not disregard me, ₂₂ ₂₆
　　　eventually you will see the force of my words.
Be moderate in all your activities ₂₇
　　　and illness will never overtake you.

People praise the man who keeps a splendid table, ₂₃ ₂₈
　　　and their opinion of his munificence is sound;
similarly, the man who keeps a mean table will be notorious ₂₄ ₂₉
　　　　　throughout the town,
　　　and their opinion of his meanness is not doubtful either.

Wine

Do not play the valiant at your wine, ₂₅ ₃₀
　　　for wine has been the undoing of many.
The furnace proves the temper of steel, ₂₆ ₃₁
　　　and wine proves hearts in the drinking bouts of braggarts.
Wine is life for man ₂₇ ₃₂
　　　if drunk in moderation.
What is life worth without wine? ₃₃
　　　It was created to make men happy.
Drunk at the right time and in the right amount, ₂₈ ₃₆
　　　wine makes for a glad heart and a cheerful mind. ₃₇
Bitterness of soul comes of wine drunk to excess ₂₉ ₃₉
　　　out of temper or bravado.
Drunkenness excites the stupid man to a fury to his own harm, ₃₀ ₄₀
　　　it reduces his strength while leading to blows.
Do not rebuke your neighbour at a wine feast, ₃₁ ₄₁
　　　do not slight him when he is enjoying himself,
do not speak reproachfully to him, ₄₂
　　　or annoy him by reclaiming money owing.

Banquets

32

Have they made you president?[a] Do not let it go to your head, 1
　　　behave like everyone else in the party,
　　　see that they are happy and then sit down yourself.
Having discharged your duties, take your place 2
　　　and enjoy yourself with the others,
　　　and receive the crown for your competence. 3

Speak, old men, it is proper that you should; 3 4
　　　but know what you are talking about, and do not interrupt 5
　　　　the music.
If entertainment is provided, do not keep up a running commentary, 4 6
　　　and do not play the sage at the wrong moment.
A carbuncle seal on a precious stone, 5 7
　　　such is a concert of music at a wine feast.
An emerald seal in a golden setting, 6 8
　　　such are strains of music with a vintage wine.

7 9,10	Speak, young men, if you have to;
11	but twice at most, and then only if questioned.
8 12	Keep to the point, say much in few words;
	give the impression of knowing but not wanting to speak.
9 13	Among eminent men do not behave as though you were their equal;
	do not make frivolous remarks when someone else is speaking.
10 14	Lightning comes before the thunder,
	favour goes ahead of a modest man.
11 15	Rise in good time to take your leave, do not bring up the rear;
	hurry home without loitering.
12 16	There amuse yourself, and do what you have a mind to,
	but do not sin by arrogant talk.
13 17	And for all this bless him who made you
	and plies you with his good things.

The fear of God

14 18	The man who fears the Lord will accept his correction;
	those who eagerly look for him will win his favour.
15 19	The man who seeks the Law will be nourished by it,
	the hypocrite will find it a stumbling-block.
16 20	Those who fear the Lord will have justice done them,
	and make their good deeds shine like a light.
17 21	The sinner waves reproof aside,
	he finds excuses to do what he wants.
18 22	A sensible man never scorns a suggestion;
	a proud and godless man will be immune to fear.
19 24	Never act without reflection,
	and you will have nothing to regret when you have done it.
20 25	Do not venture on a rough road,
	for fear of stumbling over the stones.
21 22 26 23 27	Do not be over confident on an even road,
	and beware of your own children.
	Watch yourself in everything you do,
	this is what keeping the commandments means.
24 28	The man who trusts in the Law pays attention to the commandments,
	the man who has confidence in the Lord will come to no harm.

1	**33**	If a man fears the Lord, evil will not come his way,
		again and again he will be rescued in his trials.
2		The man who hates the Law is not wise,
		if hypocritical in observance, he is like a ship in a storm.
3		A man of understanding will put his faith in the Law,
		for him the Law is as dependable as an oracle.
4		Prepare what you have to say and you will get a hearing,
		marshal your information before you answer.
5		The feelings of a fool are like a cart-wheel,
		his thought revolves like a turning axle.
6		A rutting stallion is like a sarcastic friend;
		he neighs, whoever rides him.

Inequality

7	Why is one day better than another,
	when each day's light throughout the year comes from the sun?
8	They have been differentiated in the mind of the Lord,

32 a. Chairman or host of the feast.

who has diversified the seasons and feasts;
some he has made more important and hallowed,   9
    others he has made ordinary days.
All men come from the ground,   10
    Adam himself was formed out of earth;
in the fulness of his wisdom the Lord has made distinctions   11
      between them,
    and diversified their conditions.
Some he has blessed and made more important,   12
    some he has hallowed and set near him;
others he has cursed and humiliated
    by degrading them from their positions.
Like clay in the hands of the potter   13
    to mould as it pleases him,
so are men in the hands of their Maker
    to reward as he judges right.
Opposite evil stands good,   14
    opposite death, life;
so too, opposite the devout man stands the sinner.
This is the way to view all the works of the Most High;   15
    they go, in pairs, by opposites.

I myself have been the last to keep watch,   16
    like a gleaner following the vintagers.
By the blessing of the Lord I have come in first,   17
    and, like a vintager, filled the winepress.
Observe that I have not toiled for myself only,   18
    but for all who seek instruction.

Listen to me, you princes of the people,   19
    leaders of the assembly, lend ear.

Independence

Neither to son nor wife, brother nor friend,   20
    give power over yourself during your own lifetime.
And do not give your property to anyone else,
    in case you regret it and have to ask for it back.
As long as you live and there is breath in your body,   21
    do not yield power over yourself to anyone;
since it is better for your children to be your suppliants,   22
    than for you to have to look to the generosity of your sons.
In all you do be the master,   23
    and do not spoil the honour that is rightly yours.
The day your life draws to a close,   24
    when death is approaching, is the time to distribute your
      inheritance.

Slaves

Fodder, the stick and burdens for a donkey,   25
    bread, discipline and work for a slave.
Work your servant hard, and you will know peace of mind;   26
    leave his hands idle, and he will start thinking of his freedom.
Yoke and harness will bow the neck,   27
    for a criminal slave there is the rack and torture.
Keep him occupied, or he will idle;   28
    idleness teaches all sorts of mischief.
Keep him at his duties, where he should be,   29

30   if he is disobedient, clap him in irons.
      But do not be over-exacting with anyone,
          and do nothing contrary to justice.
31   You have only one slave? Treat him like yourself,
          since you have acquired him with blood.
32   You have only one slave? Treat him as a brother,
          since you need him as you need yourself.
33   If you ill-treat him and he runs away,
          which way will you go to look for him?

Dreams

1   **34** Vain and deceptive hopes are for the foolish,
              and dreams put fools in a flutter.
2   As well clutch at shadows and chase the wind
          as put any faith in dreams.
3   Mirror and dream are similar things:
          confronting a face, the reflection of that face.
4   What can be cleansed by uncleanness,
          what can be verified by falsehood?
5   Divinations, auguries and dreams are nonsense,
          like the delirious fancies of a pregnant woman.
6   Unless sent as emissaries from the Most High,
          do not give them a thought;
7   for dreams have led many astray,
          and those building their hopes on them have been disappointed.
8   Fulfilling the Law requires no such falsehood,
          and wisdom is most perfectly expressed by truthful lips.

Travelling

9   A much travelled man knows many things,
          and a man of great experience will talk sound sense.
10   Someone who has never had his trials knows little;
          but the travelled man is master of every situation.
11
12   I have seen many things on my travels,
          I have understood more than I can put into words.
12
13   I have often been in danger of death,
          but I have been spared, and this is why:
13
14   the spirit of those who fear the Lord can survive,
15   for their hope is in someone with power to save them.
14
16   The man who fears the Lord will not be faint-hearted,
          will not be daunted since the Lord is his hope.
15
17   Happy the soul of the man who fears the Lord.
18   On whom does he rely? Who supports him?
16
19   The eyes of the Lord watch over those who love him,
          he is their powerful protection and their strong support,
          their screen from the desert wind, their shelter from the midday sun,
20   a guard against stumbling, an assurance against a fall.
17   He revives the spirit and brightens the eyes,
          he gives healing, life and blessing.

Sacrifices

18
21   The sacrifice of an offering unjustly acquired is a mockery;
          the gifts of impious men are unacceptable.
19
23   The Most High takes no pleasure in offerings from the godless,
          multiplying sacrifices will not gain his pardon for sin.
20
24   Offering sacrifice from the property of the poor

is as bad as slaughtering a son before his father's very eyes.

A meagre diet is the very life of the poor, 21/25
he who withholds it is a man of blood.

A man murders his neighbour if he robs him of his livelihood, 22/26
sheds blood if he withholds an employee's wages. 27

If one man builds while another pulls down, 23/28
what else do they gain but trouble?

If one man prays and another calls down a curse, 24/29
whose voice will the master listen to?

If a man washes after touching a corpse, and then touches it again, 25/30
what is the good of his washing?

Just so with a man who fasts for his sins, 26/31
and then goes off and commits them again.
Who will listen to his prayers?
What is the good of his self-abasement?

The Law and sacrifices

35 A man multiplies offerings by keeping the Law; 1
he offers communion sacrifices by following the commandments. 2/3
By showing gratitude he makes an offering of fine flour, 2
by giving alms he offers a sacrifice of praise. 4
Withdraw from wickedness and the Lord will be pleased, 3
withdraw from injustice and you make atonement. 5
Do not appear empty-handed in the Lord's presence; 4/6
for all these things are due under the commandment. 7
A virtuous man's offering graces the altar, 5/8
and its savour rises before the Most High.
A virtuous man's sacrifice is acceptable, 6/9
its memorial will not be forgotten.
Honour the Lord with generosity, 7/10
do not stint the first-fruits you bring.
Add a smiling face to all your gifts, 8/11
and be cheerful as you dedicate your tithes.
Give to the Most High as he has given to you, 9/12
generously as your means can afford;
for the Lord is a good rewarder, 10/13
he will reward you seven times over.

The justice of God

Offer him no bribe, he will not accept it, 11/14
do not put your faith in an unvirtuous sacrifice; 15
since the Lord is a judge 12
who is no respecter of personages.
He shows no respect of personages to the detriment of a poor man, 13/16
he listens to the plea of the injured party.
He does not ignore the orphan's supplication, 14/17
nor the widow's as she pours out her story.
Do the widow's tears not run down her cheeks, 15/18
as she cries out against the man who caused them?
The man who with his whole heart serves God will be accepted, 16/20
his petitions will carry to the clouds.
The humble man's prayer pierces the clouds, 17/21
until it arrives he is inconsolable,
nor will he desist until the Most High takes notice of him, 18
acquits the virtuous and delivers judgement.
And the Lord will not be slow, 19/22

nor will he be dilatory on their behalf,
20   until he has crushed the loins of the merciless
23   and exacted vengeance on the nations,
21   until he has eliminated the hordes of the arrogant
       and broken the sceptres of the wicked,
22
24   until he has repaid each as his deeds deserve
       and human actions as their intentions merit,
23
25   until he has judged the case of his people
       and made them rejoice in his mercy.
24
26   Mercy is welcome in time of trouble,
       like rain clouds in time of drought.

Prayer for the deliverance and restoration of Israel

1
2   **36**   Have mercy on us, Master, Lord of all, and look on us,
       cast the fear of yourself over every nation.
2
3   Raise your hand against the foreign nations
       and let them see your might.
3
4   As in their sight you have proved yourself holy before us,
       so now in our sight prove yourself great before them.
4
5   Let them acknowledge you, just as we have acknowledged
       that there is no God but you, Lord.
5
6   Send new portents, do fresh wonders,
7   win glory for your hand and your right arm.
6
8   Rouse your fury, pour out your rage,
9   destroy the opponent, annihilate the enemy.
7
10   Hasten the day, remember the oath,
       and let men tell of your mighty deeds.
8
11   Let fiery wrath swallow up the survivor,
       and destruction overtake those who use your people badly.
9
12   Crush the heads of hostile rulers
       who say, 'There is nobody else but us!'
10
13   Gather together all the tribes of Jacob,
       restore them their inheritance as in the beginning.[a]
11
14   Have mercy, Lord, on the people who have invoked your name,
       on Israel whom you have treated as a first-born.
12
15   Show compassion on your holy city,
       on Jerusalem the place of your rest.
13
16   Fill Zion with songs of your praise,
       and your sanctuary with your glory.
14
17   Bear witness to those you created in the beginning,
       and bring about what has been prophesied in your name.
15
18   Give those who wait for you their reward,
       and let your prophets be proved worthy of belief.
16   Grant, Lord, the prayer of your servants,
19   in accordance with Aaron's blessing on your people,
17   so that all the earth's inhabitants may acknowledge
       that you are the Lord, the everlasting God.

Discrimination

18
20   The stomach takes in all kinds of food
       but some foods are better than others.
19
21   As the palate discerns the flavour of game,
       so a shrewd man detects lying words.

---

36 a. The situation implied in this Prayer is that of the year 190 B.C., just before the Maccabean revolt.

> A perverse heart causes sorrow,   20
> an experienced man knows how to pay him back.   22

Choosing

> A woman will accept any husband,   21
> but some daughters are better than others.   23
> A woman's beauty delights the beholder,   22
> a man likes nothing better.   24
> If her tongue is kind and gentle,   23
> her husband has no equal among the sons of men.   25
> The man who takes a wife has the makings of a fortune,   24
> a helper that suits him, and a pillar to lean on.   26
> If a property has no fence, it will be plundered.   25
> When a man has no wife, he is aimless and querulous.   27
> Will anyone trust a man carrying weapons   26
> who flits from town to town?   28
> So it is with the man who has no nest,   27
> and lodges wherever night overtakes him.

False friends

37
> Any friend will say, 'I am your friend too',   1
> but some friends are only friends in name.
> Is it not a deadly sorrow,   2
> when a comrade or a friend turns enemy?
> O evil inclination, why were you created,   3
> to cover the earth with deceit?
> One sort of comrade takes advantage of his friend's good fortune,   4
> but in time of trouble turns against him.
> Another sort of comrade shares his friend's hardships out of concern, 5
> when it comes to a fight, he springs to arms.
> Do not forget the friend who fought your battles,   6
> do not put him out of mind once you are rich.

Advisers

> Any adviser will offer advice,   7
> but some are governed by self-interest.   8
> Beware of a man who offers advice,   8
> first find out what he wants himself—   9
> since his advice coincides with his own interest—
> in case he has designs on you   10
> and tells you, 'You are on the right road',   9
> but stands well clear to see what will happen to you.   11
> Do not consult a man who looks at you askance,   10
> conceal your plans from people jealous of you.   12
> Do not consult a woman about her rival,   11
> or a coward about war,
> a merchant about prices,
> or a buyer about selling,
> a mean man about gratitude,
> or a selfish man about kindness,   13
> a lazy fellow about any sort of work,
> or a casual worker about finishing a job,   14
> an idle servant about a major undertaking—
> do not rely on these for any advice.
> But constantly have recourse to a devout man,   12
> whom you know to be a keeper of the commandments,   15

16	whose soul matches your own,
	and who, if you go wrong, will be sympathetic.
13 17	Finally, stick to the advice your own heart gives you,
	no one can be truer to you than that;
14 18	since a man's soul often forewarns him better
	than seven watchmen perched on a watchtower.
15 19	And besides all this beg the Most High
	to guide your steps in the truth.

True and false wisdom

16 20	Reason must be the beginning of every activity,
	reflection must come before any undertaking.
17 21	Thoughts are rooted in the heart,
	and this sends out four branches:
18	good and evil, life and death,
	and always mistress of them all is the tongue.
19 22	Think of a clever man who teaches many people,
	but does no good at all to himself.
20 23	Think of a man, a ready enough speaker, yet he is detested
	and will end up by starving,
21 24	not having won the favour of the Lord,
	and being destitute of all wisdom.
22 25	Think of a man who is wise in his own eyes,
	and the fruits of his understanding are, if you take his word
	for it, certain.
23 26	The truly wise will instruct his own people,
	the fruits of his understanding are certain.
24 27	This wise man will be filled with blessing,
	and those who see him will call him happy.
25 28	A man's life lasts a number of days,
	but the days of Israel are beyond counting.
26 29	The wise man will earn confidence among his people,
	his name will live for ever.

Moderation

27 30	My son, in the course of your life test your constitution,
	and do not allow it what you see is harmful to it;
28 31	for everything does not suit everybody,
	nor does everybody take pleasure in everything.
29 32	Do not be insatiable over any delicacy,
	do not be greedy over food,
30 33	for overeating leads to sickness,
	and gluttony brings on biliousness.
31 34	Many have died of gluttony;
	beware of this and you will prolong your life.

Medicine and illness

1	**38** Honour the doctor with the honour that is his due
	in return for his services;
	for he too has been created by the Lord.
2	Healing itself comes from the Most High,
	like a gift from a king.
3	The doctor's learning keeps his head high,
	he is regarded with awe by potentates.
4	The Lord has brought medicines into existence from the earth,
	and the sensible man will not despise them.

Did not a piece of wood once sweeten the water,   5
  thus giving proof of its virtue?[a]
He has also given men learning   6
  so that they may glory in his mighty works.
He uses them[b] to heal and to relieve pain,   7
  the chemist makes up a mixture from them.
Thus there is no end to his activities,   8
  and through him health extends across the world.

My son, when you are ill, do not be depressed,   9
  but pray to the Lord and he will heal you.
Renounce your faults, keep your hands unsoiled,   10
  and cleanse your heart from all sin.
Offer incense and a memorial of fine flour,   11
  and make as rich an offering as you can afford.
Then let the doctor take over—the Lord created him too—   12
  and do not let him leave you, for you need him.
Sometimes success is in their hands,   13
  since they in turn will beseech the Lord   14
to grant them the grace to relieve
  and to heal, that life may be saved.
If a man sins in the eyes of his Maker,   15
  may he fall under the care of the doctor.

Mourning

My son, shed tears over a dead man,   16
  and intone the lament to show your own deep grief;
bury his body with due ceremonial,
  and do not neglect to honour his grave.
Weep bitterly, wail most fervently;   17
  observe the mourning the dead man deserves,   18
one day, or two, to avoid comment,
  and then be comforted in your sorrow;
for grief can lead to death,   18 / 19
  a grief-stricken heart undermines your strength.
Let grief end with the funeral;   19 / 20
  a life of grief oppresses the mind.
Do not abandon your heart to grief,   20 / 21
  drive it away, bear your own end in mind.
Do not forget, there is no going back;   21 / 22
  you cannot help the dead, and you will harm yourself.
'Remember my doom, since it will be yours too;   22 / 23
  yesterday was my day, today is yours.'
Once the dead man is laid to rest, let his memory rest too,   23 / 24
  do not fret for him, once his spirit departs.

Trades and crafts

Leisure is what gives the scribe the opportunity to acquire wisdom;   24 / 25
  the man with few business affairs grows wise.
How can the ploughman become wise,   25 / 26
  whose sole ambition is to wield the goad;
driving his oxen, engrossed in their work,
  his conversation is of nothing but cattle?
His mind is fixed on the furrows he traces,   26 / 27
  and his evenings pass in fattening his heifers.
So it is with every workman and craftsman,   27 / 28
  toiling day and night;

those who engrave seals,
    always trying to think of new designs:
they set their heart on producing a good likeness,
    and stay up perfecting the work.

28
29 So it is with the blacksmith sitting by his anvil;
    he considers what to do with the pig-iron,
the breath of the fire scorches his skin,
    as he contends with the heat of the furnace;

30 he batters his ear with the din of the hammer,
    his eyes are fixed on the pattern;

31 he sets his heart on completing his work,
    and stays up putting the finishing touches.

29
32 So it is with the potter, sitting at his work,
    turning the wheel with his feet;
constantly on the alert over his work,
    each flick of the finger premeditated;

30
33 he pummels the clay with his arm,
    and puddles it with his feet;

34 he sets his heart on perfecting the glaze,
    and stays up cleaning the kiln.

31
35 All these put their trust in their hands,
    and each is skilled at his own craft.

32
36 A town could not be built without them,
37   there would be no settling, no travelling.

33 But they are not required at the council,
    they do not hold high rank in the assembly.

38 They do not sit on the judicial bench,
    and have no grasp of the law.

34 They are not remarkable for culture or sound judgement,
    and are not found among the inventors of maxims.

39 But they give solidity to the created world,
    while their prayer is concerned with what pertains to their trade.

The scholar

1
39 It is otherwise with the man who devotes his soul
    to reflecting on the Law of the Most High.

1 He researches into the wisdom of all the Ancients,
    he occupies his time with the prophecies.

2 He preserves the discourses of famous men,
    he is at home with the niceties of parables.

3 He researches into the hidden sense of proverbs,
    he ponders the obscurities of parables.

4 He enters the service of princes,
    he is seen in the presence of rulers.

5 He travels in foreign countries,
    he has experienced human good and human evil.

5
6 At dawn and with all his heart
    he resorts to the Lord who made him;
he pleads in the presence of the Most High,

7   he opens his mouth in prayer
    and makes entreaty for his sins.

6
8 If it is the will of the great Lord,
    he will be filled with the spirit of understanding,

9 he will shower forth words of wisdom,

38 a. Ex 15:25   b. The medicines of v.4.

R.E.—Q

and in prayer give thanks to the Lord.

He will grow upright in purpose and learning,   7
     10
     he will ponder the Lord's hidden mysteries.

He will display the instruction he has received,   8
     11
     taking his pride in the Law of the Lord's covenant.

Many will praise his understanding,   9
     12
     and it will never be forgotten.

His memory will not disappear,   13
     generation after generation his name will live.

Nations will proclaim his wisdom,   10
     14
     the assembly will celebrate his praises.

If he lives long, his name will be more glorious than a thousand others,   11
     15
     and if he dies, that will satisfy him just as well.

Invitation to praise God

I wish to develop my reflections further,   12
     16
     they fill me as full as the moon at the full.

Listen to me, devout children, and blossom   13
     17
     like the rose that grows on the bank of a watercourse.

Give off a sweet smell like incense,   14
     18
     flower like the lily, spread your fragrance abroad,   19

sing a song of praise
     blessing the Lord for all his works.

Declare the greatness of his name,   15
     20
     proclaim his praise

with song and with lyre,
     and this is how you must sing his praises:

how wonderful they are, all the works of the Lord!   16
     21
     All that he orders is promptly carried out.

You must not say, 'What is this? Why is that?'
     All will be studied in due time.

At his word water stops running and piles up,   17
     22
     waters are stored at a word from his mouth.

At his bidding, all his pleasure is accomplished,   18
     23
     no one can diminish his power to save.

The actions of every creature are before him,   19
     24
     there is no hiding from his eyes;

his gaze stretches from eternity to eternity,   20
     25
     and nothing can astonish him.

You must not say, 'What is this? Why is that?'   21
     26
     All things have been created for their proper functions.

As his blessing covers the dry land like a river   22
     27
     and soaks it like a flood,   28

so wrath is his legacy to the nations,   23
     (29)
     just as he has turned fresh waters to salt.

His ways are as smooth for devout men,   24
     as they are full of obstacles for the wicked.

Good things were created from the beginning for good men,   25
     30
     as evils were for sinners.

The prime needs of mankind for living   26
     31
     are water and fire, iron and salt,

wheat-flour, milk and honey,
     the juice of the grape, oil and clothing.

All these things are good for people who are good,   27
     32
     just as they turn into bad for sinners.

28
33   Some winds were created to punish;
       he has made them the scourge of his anger;

34   on the day of doom they unleash their force,
       and appease the anger of him who made them.

29
35   Fire and hail, famine and death,
       all these were created to punish.

30
36   The teeth of savage animals, scorpions, adders,
       and the avenging sword to destroy the godless,

31
37   all these exult in obeying his orders,
       they are ready on earth when he requires,
       and when the time comes they will not disobey his order.

32
38   That is why I was determined from the outset,
       I have pondered and I have written it down,

33
39   'All the works of the Lord are good,
       and he will supply every want in due time.

34
40   You must not say, "This is worse than that",
       for everything will prove its value in its time.

35
41   So now, sing with all your heart and voice,
       and bless the name of the Lord!'

The wretchedness of man

1 **40**   Much hardship has been made for every man,
       a heavy yoke lies on the sons of Adam
    from the day they come out of their mother's womb,
       till the day they return to the mother of them all.

2   What fills them with brooding and their hearts with fear
       is dread of the day of death.

3   From the man who sits on a glorious throne
       to the wretch on dust and ashes,

4   from the man who wears purple and a crown
       to the man clothed in sacking,
    all is fury and jealousy, turmoil and unrest,
       fear of death, rivalry, strife.

5   And even at night while he rests on his bed
       his sleep only gives a new twist to his worries:

6   scarcely has he lain down to rest,
       than in his sleep, as if in broad daylight,
    he is shaken by terrible sights
       like a man running away from a battle.

7   At the moment of rescue he awakens,
       astonished that his fear was imaginary.

8   For all creatures, from men to animals—
       and seven times more for sinners—

9   there is death and blood and strife and the sword,
       disasters, famine, affliction, plague.

10   All these were created for the godless,
       through them came the Flood.

11   All that comes from the earth returns to the earth,
       what comes from the water returns to the sea.

Various maxims

12   All bribery and injustice will be blotted out,
       but good faith will stand for ever.

13   The wealth of wrong-doers will dry up like a torrent,
       will crash like a clap of thunder in a downpour.

When he opens his hands he rejoices,   14
    by the same token defaulters will come to utter ruin.
The offshoots of the godless will not have many branches,   15
    unclean roots only find hard rock.
The reeds by every lake and river's edge   16
    will be pulled up before any other grass.
Graciousness is like a paradise of blessing,   17
    and generosity stands firm for ever.

Comparisons

For the man of private means and the man who works hard,   18
    life is pleasant,
    better off than either, he who finds a treasure.
Children and the building of a city make a man's reputation;   19
    better than either, the discovery of wisdom.
Cattle and vineyards make you well known;
    better valued than either, a perfect wife.
Wine and music cheer the heart;   20
    better than either, the love of wisdom.
Flute and harp add sweetness to a song;   21
    better than either, a sweet voice.
The eye longs for grace and beauty;   22
    better than either, the green of spring corn.
Friend or comrade — it is always well met;   23
    better than either, a wife and husband.
Brothers and allies are good in times of trouble;   24
    better than either, generosity to the rescue.
Gold and silver will steady your feet;   25
    better valued than either, good advice.
Money and strength make a confident heart;   26
    better than either, the fear of the Lord.
With the fear of the Lord a man lacks nothing;   27
    with that he need seek no ally.
The fear of the Lord is like a paradise of blessing,   27 / 28
    it clothes a man with more than glory.

On begging

My son, do not live by begging from others,   28 / 29
    better be dead than a beggar.
The life of a man ever eyeing the table of another   29 / 30
    cannot be reckoned as a life at all.
He defiles his gullet with other people's food;
    a man of culture and breeding will never do this.   31
Begging comes easily to the lips of the shameless man,   30 / 32
    but eventually it will set fire to his belly.

Death

41

O death, how bitter it is to remember you   1
    for a man at peace among his goods,
to a man without worries, who prospers in everything,   2
    and still has the strength to feed himself.

O death, your sentence is welcome   2 / 3
    to a man in want, whose strength is failing,
to a man worn out with age, worried about everything,   4
    disaffected and beyond endurance.

³⁄₅ Do not dread death's sentence;
 remember those who came before you and those who will
  come after.

⁴⁄₆ This is the sentence passed on all living creatures by the Lord,
 so why object to what seems good to the Most High?

⁷ Whether your life lasts ten or a hundred or a thousand years,
 its length will not be held against you in Sheol.

The fate of the wicked

⁵⁄₈ Hateful brats, such are the children of sinners,
 who forgather in the haunts of the godless.

⁶⁄₉ The inheritance of sinners' children is doomed to perish,
 their posterity will endure lasting reproach.

⁷⁄₁₀ A godless father will be blamed by his children
 for the reproach he has brought on them.

⁸⁄₁₁ A bad outlook for you, godless men,
 who have forsaken the Law of God Most High.

⁹⁄₁₂ When you were born, you were born to be accursed,
 and when you die, that curse will be your portion.

¹⁰⁄₁₃ All that comes from the earth returns to the earth,
 so too the wicked proceed from curse to destruction.

¹¹⁄₁₄ Men go into mourning for their dead,
 but the worthless name of sinners will be blotted out.

¹²⁄₁₅ Be careful of your reputation, for it will last you longer
 than a thousand great hoards of gold.

¹³⁄₁₆ A good life lasts a certain number of days,
 but a good reputation lasts for ever.

A sense of shame

¹⁴⁄₁₇ Keep my instructions and be at peace, my children.

 Wisdom hidden away and treasure undisplayed,
  what use are either of these?

¹⁵⁄₁₈ Better a man who hides his folly
 than one who hides his wisdom.

¹⁶⁄₁₉ Now, keep your sense of shame with respect to what I am going to say,
²⁰ for not every kind of shame is right to harbour,
 nor is every situation correctly appraised by all.

¹⁷⁄₂₁ Be ashamed, before father and mother, of licentious behaviour,
 and before prince or potentate of telling lies;

¹⁸⁄₂₂ of wrong-doing before judge or magistrate,
 and of impiety before the assembly of the people;

¹⁹⁄₂₃ of sharp practice before your companion and your friend,
²⁴ and of theft before the neighbourhood you live in.

²⁰ Before the truth and covenant of God,
 be ashamed of leaning elbows on the table,

²¹ of making gifts before those who despise them,
²⁵ and of ignoring those who greet you:

²² of gazing at a loose woman
²⁶ and of turning your back on a relation,

²³ of misappropriating another's portion or gift,
²⁷ of paying court to another man's wife,

²⁴ of carrying on with his servant-girl
 —do not go near her bed—

²⁵⁄₂₈ of words of abuse before your friends
 —do not follow up a gift with a taunt—

of repeating and retailing gossip   26/1
     and of betraying confidences.
Then you will know what true shame is,   27
     and you will find yourself in every man's graces.

42

These are the things you should not be ashamed of,   1
     and do not sin from fear of what others think:
of the Law of the Most High and the covenant,   2
     of a verdict that acquits the godless,
of keeping strict accounts with a travelling companion,   3
     of settling property on your friends,
of being accurate over scales and weights,   4
     of making small and large profits,
of gaining from commercial transactions,   5
     of disciplining your children strictly,
     of lashing a wicked slave till you draw blood.
With an interfering wife, it is as well to use your seal,   6
     and where there are many hands, lock things up.
Whatever stores you issue, do it by number and weight,   7
     spendings and takings, put everything in writing.
Do not be ashamed to correct a stupid man or a fool,   8
     or an old dotard who bickers with young people.
Then you will show yourself really educated
     and win the approval of everyone.

The cares of a father over his daughter

Unknown to her, a daughter keeps her father awake,   9
     the worry she gives him drives away his sleep :
in her youth, in case she never marries,
     married, in case she should be disliked,
as a virgin, in case she should be defiled   10
     and found with child in her father's house,
having a husband, in case she goes astray,
     married, in case she should be barren.
Your daughter is headstrong? Keep a sharp look-out   11
     that she does not make you the laughing-stock of your enemies,
the talk of the town, the object of common gossip,
     and put you to public shame.

Women

Do not stare at any man for his good looks,   12
     do not sit down with the women;
for moth comes out of clothes,   13
     and woman's spite out of woman.
A man's spite is preferable to a woman's kindness;   14
     women give rise to shame and reproach.

II. THE GLORY OF GOD

A. IN NATURE

Next, I will remind you of the works of the Lord,   15
     and tell of what I have seen.
By the words of the Lord his works come into being
     and all creation obeys his will.
As the sun in shining looks on all things,   16
     so the work of the Lord is full of his glory.

17 The Lord has not granted to the holy ones[a]
     to tell of all his marvels
  which the Almighty Lord has solidly constructed
     for the universe to stand firm in his glory.

18 He has fathomed the deep and the heart,
     and seen into their devious ways;
  for the Most High knows all the knowledge there is,
     and has observed the signs of the times.

19 He declares what is past and what will be,
     and uncovers the traces of hidden things.

20 Not a thought escapes him,
     not a single word is hidden from him.

21 He has imposed an order on the magnificent works of his wisdom,
     he is from everlasting to everlasting,

22 nothing can be added to him, nothing taken away,
     he needs no one's advice.

22
23 How desirable are all his works,
     how dazzling to the eye!

23
24 They all live and last for ever,
     whatever the circumstances all obey him.

24
25 All things go in pairs, by opposites,
     and he has made nothing defective;

25
26 the one consolidates the excellence of the other,
     who could ever be sated with gazing at his glory?

The sun

1
43
  Pride of the heights, shining vault,
     so, in a glorious spectacle, the sky appears.

2 The sun, as he emerges, proclaims at his rising,
     'A thing of wonder is the work of the Most High!'

3 At his zenith he parches the land,
     who can withstand his blaze?

4 A man must blow a furnace to produce any heat,
     the sun burns the mountains three times as much;
  breathing out blasts of fire,
     flashing his rays he dazzles the eyes.

5 Great is the Lord who made him,
     and whose word speeds him on his course.

The moon

6 And then the moon, always punctual,
     to mark the months and make division of time:

7 the moon it is that signals the feasts,
     a luminary that wanes after her full.

8 The month derives its name from hers,
     she waxes wonderfully in her phases,

9 banner of the hosts on high,
     shining in the vault of heaven.

The stars

9
10 The glory of the stars makes the beauty of the sky,
     a brilliant decoration to the heights of the Lord.

10
11 At the words of the Holy One they stand as he decrees,
     and never grow slack at their watch.

42 a. The angels.

The rainbow

See the rainbow and praise its maker,
   so superbly beautiful in its splendour.

Across the sky it forms a glorious arc
   drawn by the hands of the Most High.

The wonders of nature

By his command he sends the snow,
   he speeds the lightning as he orders.

In the same way, his treasuries open
   and the clouds fly out like birds.

In his great might he banks up the clouds,
   and shivers them into fragments of hail.

At sight of him the mountains rock,
   at the roar of his thunder the earth writhes in labour.

At his will the south wind blows,
   or the storm from the north and the whirlwind.

He sprinkles snow like birds alighting,
   it comes down like locusts settling.

The eye marvels at the beauty of its whiteness,
   and the mind is amazed at its falling.

Over the earth, like salt, he also pours hoarfrost,
   which, when it freezes, bristles like thorns.

The cold wind blows from the north,
   and ice forms on the water,
settling on every watery expanse,
   and water puts it on like a breastplate.

He swallows up the mountains and scorches the desert,
   like a fire he consumes the vegetation.

But the mist heals everything in good time,
   after the heat falls the reviving dew.

By his own resourcefulness he has tamed the abyss,
   and planted it with islands.

Those who sail the sea tell of its dangers,
   their accounts fill our ears with amazement:

for there too there are strange and wonderful works,
   animals of every kind and huge sea creatures.

Thanks to him all ends well,
   and all things hold together by means of his word.

We could say much more and still fall short;
   to put it concisely, 'He is all'.

Where shall we find sufficient power to glorify him,
   since he is the Great One, above all his works,

the awe-inspiring Lord, stupendously great,
   and wonderful in his power?

Exalt the Lord in your praises
   as high as you may—still he surpasses you.

Exert all your strength when you exalt him,
   do not grow tired—you will never come to the end.

Who has ever seen him to give a description?
   Who can glorify him as he deserves?

Many mysteries remain even greater than these,
   for we have seen only a few of his works,
the Lord himself having made all things—
   and having given wisdom to devout men.

B. IN HISTORY

Eulogy of the ancestors

44

1 Next let us praise illustrious men,
   our ancestors in their successive generations.

2 The Lord has created an abundance of glory,
   and displayed his greatness from earliest times.

3 Some wielded authority as kings
   and were renowned for their strength;
   others were intelligent advisers
   and uttered prophetic oracles.

4 Others directed the people by their advice,
   by their understanding of the popular mind,
   and by the wise words of their teaching;

5 others composed musical melodies,
   and set down ballads;

6 others were rich and powerful,
   living peacefully in their homes.

7 All these were honoured by their contemporaries,
   and were the glory of their day.

8 Some of them left a name behind them,
   so that their praises are still sung.

9 While others have left no memory,
   and disappeared as though they had not existed,
   they are now as though they had never been,
   and so too, their children after them.

10 But here is a list of generous men
    whose good works have not been forgotten.

11 In their descendants there remains
    a rich inheritance born of them.

12 Their descendants stand by the covenants
    and, thanks to them, so do their children's children.

13 Their offspring will last for ever,
    their glory will not fade.

14 Their bodies have been buried in peace,
    and their name lives on for all generations.

15 The peoples will proclaim their wisdom,
    the assembly will celebrate their praises.

Enoch

16 Enoch pleased the Lord and was taken up,
    an example for the conversion of all generations.

Noah

17 Noah was found perfectly virtuous,
    in the time of wrath he became the scion:

18 because of him a remnant was preserved for the earth
    at the coming of the Flood.

18
19 Everlasting covenants were made with him
    that never again should every living creature perish by flood.

Abraham

19
20 Abraham, the great forefather of a host of nations,
    no one was ever his equal in glory.

He observed the Law of the Most High,　　　　20
　　and entered into a covenant with him.
He confirmed the covenant in his own flesh,　　21
　　and proved himself faithful under ordeal.
The Lord therefore promised him on oath　　21
　　to bless the nations through his descendants,　　22
to multiply him like the dust on the ground,
　　to exalt his descendants like the stars,　　23
and give them the land for their inheritance,
　　from sea to sea,
from the River to the ends of the earth.

Isaac and Jacob

To Isaac too, for the sake of Abraham his father,　　22
he assured •the blessing of all mankind;　　24
　　　　　　　　　　　　　　　　　　　　　　　23
　　he caused the covenant to rest on the head of Jacob.　　25
He confirmed him in his blessings　　26
　　and gave him the land for his inheritance;
he divided it into portions,
　　and shared it out among the twelve tribes.

Moses

45

From him he produced a generous man　　1
　　who found favour in the eyes of all mankind,[a]　　27
beloved by God and men,　　1
　　Moses, of blessed memory.
He made him the equal of the holy ones in glory　　2
　　and made him strong, to the terror of his enemies.
At the word of Moses he made the miracles stop,　　3
　　he raised him high in the respect of kings;
he gave him commandments for his people,
　　and showed him something of his glory.
For his loyalty and gentleness he sanctified him,　　4
　　choosing him alone out of all mankind;
he allowed him to hear his voice,　　5
　　and led him into the darkness;
he gave him the commandments face to face,　　6
　　the law of life and knowledge,
to teach Jacob his ordinances
　　and Israel his decrees.

Aaron

He raised up Aaron, a holy man like Moses,　　6
　　his brother, of the tribe of Levi.　　7
He made an everlasting covenant with him,　　7
　　and gave him the priesthood of the people.　　8
He adorned him with impressive vestments,
　　he dressed him in a robe of glory.　　9
He clothed him in glorious perfection　　8
　　and invested him with emblems of authority:
　　the breeches, the long robe, the ephod.　　10
To go round the robe he gave him pomegranates,　　9
　　and many gold bells all round
to chime at every step,　　11
　　for their sound to be heard in the Temple
　　as a reminder to the sons of his people;

<table>
<tr><td>10
12</td><td>and a sacred vestment of gold and purple, violet shade
    and red, the work of an embroiderer;
the pectoral of judgement, the Urim and Thummim, [b]</td></tr>
</table>

10
12 and a sacred vestment of gold and purple, violet shade
    and red, the work of an embroiderer;
the pectoral of judgement, the Urim and Thummim, [b]

13 of plaited crimson, the work of a craftsman;

11 precious stones cut like seals
    mounted in gold, the work of a jeweller,
as a reminder with their engraved inscriptions
    of the number of the tribes of Israel;

12
14 and a golden diadem on his turban,
    engraved with the seal of consecration;
superb ornamentation, magnificent work,
    adornment to delight the eye.

13
15 There had never been such lovely things before him,
16   and no one else has ever put them on,
but only his own sons,
    and his descendants for all time.

14
17 His sacrifices were to be burnt entirely,
    twice each day and for ever.

15
18 Moses consecrated him
    and anointed him with holy oil;

19 and this was an everlasting covenant for him,
    and for his descendants as long as the heavens endure,
that he should preside over worship, act as priest,
    and bless his people in the name of the Lord,

16
20 who chose him out of all the living
    to offer sacrifice to the Lord,
incense and an appeasing fragrance as a memorial
    to make atonement for the people.

17
21 He entrusted him with his commandments,
    committed to him the statutes of the Law
to teach Jacob his decrees,
    and enlighten Israel on his Law.

18
22 Others joined forces against him,
    they were jealous of him in the wilderness,
Dathan and Abiram and their men,
    Korah and his crew in fury and rage.

19
23 The Lord saw it and was displeased,
    his raging fury made an end of them;

24 he overwhelmed them with miracles
    and consumed them with his flaming fire.

20
25 And he added to Aaron's glory,
    he gave him an inheritance;
he allotted him the prime of the first-fruits,

26   before all else ensured him bread in abundance.

21 Thus they eat the sacrifices of the Lord
    which he gave to him and his posterity.

22
27 But of the people's territory he inherits nothing,
    he alone of all the people has no share,
    the Lord is his share and inheritance.

Phinehas

23
28 Phinehas son of Eleazar is third in glory
    because of his zeal in the fear of the Lord,

---

45 a. In the text as preserved, these two lines refer to Moses; possibly they referred originally to Joseph. b. See note *a* of Dt 33; also Ex 28:30, Lv 8:8.

because he stood firm when the people revolted,   *29*
    with a staunch and courageous heart;
    and in this way atoned for Israel.
Hence a covenant of peace was sealed with him,   *24*
    making him governor of both sanctuary and people,   *30*
and securing to him and his descendants
    the high priestly dignity for ever.
There was also a covenant with David   *25*
    son of Jesse, of the tribe of Judah,   *31*
a royal succession from father to one son exclusively,
    but the succession of Aaron passes to all his descendants.
May God endow your hearts with wisdom[c]   *26*
    to judge his people virtuously,
so that the virtues of your ancestors may never fade,
    and their glory may pass to all their descendants.

Joshua

46

Mighty in war was Joshua son of Nun,   *1*
    successor to Moses in the prophetic office,
who well deserved his name,[a]
    and was a great saviour of the Chosen People,   *2*
wreaking vengeance on the enemies who opposed him,
    and so bringing Israel into its inheritance.
How splendid he was when he raised his arms   *2*
    to brandish his sword against cities!   *3*
Who had ever shown such determination as his?   *3*
    He himself waged the wars of the Lord.   *4*
Was not the sun held back by his hand,   *4*
    and one day drawn out into two?   *5*
He called on God the Most High,   *5*
    as he pressed the enemy on every side;   *6*
and the great Lord answered him
    with hard and violent hailstones.
He fell on that enemy nation,   *6*
    and at the Descent he destroyed all resistance;   *7*
that the nations might acknowledge his warlike prowess   *8*
    and know that their foe was the Lord.

Caleb

For he was a follower of the Mighty One,   *7*
    and in the time of Moses he did devoted service,   *9*
he and Caleb son of Jephunneh,
    by opposing the whole community,
by preventing the people from sinning,
    and by silencing the mutters of rebellion.
Hence these two alone were preserved   *8*
    out of six hundred thousand men on the march,   *10*
and brought into their inheritance,
    into a land where milk and honey flow.
The Lord gave Caleb the strength—   *9*
    which he retained right into old age—   *11*
to tread the highlands of the country
    which his descendants still hold as their inheritance,
for all the sons of Israel to see   *10*
    that it is good to follow the Lord.   *12*

The judges

11	
13	The judges too, each when he was called,

The judges too, each when he was called,
  all men whose hearts were never disloyal,
who never turned their backs on the Lord—
14
    may their memory be blessed!
12
May their bones flower again from the tomb,
15
    and may the names of those illustrious men
live again in their sons.

Samuel

13
16
Samuel was the beloved of his Lord;
    prophet of the Lord, he instituted the kingdom,
    and anointed rulers over his people.
14
17
In the Law of the Lord he judged the assembly,
    and the Lord watched over Jacob.
15
18
By his loyalty he was recognised as a prophet,
    by his words he was known to be a trustworthy seer.
16
19
He called on the Lord, the Mighty One,
    when his enemies pressed him on every side,
    by offering a sucking lamb.
17
20
And the Lord thundered from heaven,
    and made his voice heard in a rolling peal;
18
21
he massacred the leaders of the enemy,
    and all the rulers of the Philistines.
19
22
Before the time of his everlasting rest
    he bore witness before the Lord and his anointed,
'Of no property, not even a pair of sandals,
    have I ever deprived a soul'.
    Nor did anyone accuse him.
20
23
And after he fell asleep he prophesied again,
    warning the king of his death;
he lifted up his voice from the earth in prophecy,
    to blot out the wickedness of the people.

Nathan

1
47
After him arose Nathan,
    to prophesy in the time of David.

David

2
As the fat is set apart from the communion sacrifice,
    so David was chosen out of all the sons of Israel.
3
He played with lions as though with kids,
    and with bears as though with lambs of the flock.
4
While still a boy, did he not slay the giant,
    and relieve the people of their shame,
5
by putting out a hand to sling a stone
    which brought down the arrogance of Goliath?
5
6
For he called on the Lord Most High,
    who gave strength to his right arm
to put a mighty warrior to death,
    and lift up the horn of his people.
6
7
Hence they gave him credit for ten thousand,
    and praised him while they blessed the Lord,

c. Addressed to the contemporary 'succession of Aaron'.
46 a. Joshua means 'Yahweh-saves'. The Greek form of the same name is Jesus.

by offering him a crown of glory;
  for he massacred enemies on every side,   7
he annihilated his foes the Philistines,   8
  and crushed their horn to this very day.
In all his activities he gave thanks   8 / 9
  to the Holy One, the Most High, in words of glory; [a]
he put all his heart into his songs   10
  out of love for his Maker.
He placed harps before the altar   9 / 11
  to make the singing sweeter with their music;
he gave the feasts their splendour,   10 / 12
  the festivals their solemn pomp,
causing the Lord's holy name to be praised
  and the sanctuary to resound from dawn.
The Lord took away his sins,   11 / 13
  and exalted his horn for ever;
he gave him a royal covenant,
  and a glorious throne in Israel.

Solomon

A wise son succeeded him,   12 / 14
  who lived spaciously, thanks to him.
Solomon reigned in a time of peace,   13 / 15
  and God gave him peace all round
so that he could raise a house to his name
  and prepare an everlasting sanctuary.
How wise you were in your youth,   14
  brimming over with understanding like a river!   16
Your mind ranged the earth,   15
  you filled it with mysterious sayings.   17
Your name reached the distant islands,   16
  and you were loved for your peace. [b]
Your songs, your proverbs, your sayings   17 / 18
  and your retorts made you the wonder of the world.
In the name of the Lord God,   18 / 19
  of him who is called the God of Israel,
you amassed gold like so much tin,   20
  and made silver as common as lead.
You abandoned your body to women,   19 / 21
  you became the slave of your appetites.
You stained your honour,   20 / 22
  you profaned your stock,
so bringing wrath on your children
  and grief on your posterity:
the sovereignty was split in two,   21 / 23
  from Ephraim arose a rebel kingdom.
But the Lord would not go back on his mercy,   22 / 24
  or undo any of his words,
he would not obliterate the issue of his elect,
  nor destroy the stock of the man who loved him;
and so he granted a remnant to Jacob,   25
  and to David a root springing from him.

Rehoboam

Solomon rested with his ancestors,   23 / 26
  leaving one of his stock as his successor,   27

28   the stupidest member of the nation,
                brainless Rehoboam, whose policy drove the nation to rebel.

Jeroboam

24
29   Next, Jeroboam son of Nebat, who made Israel sin,
                and set Ephraim on the way of evil;
            from then on their sins multiplied so excessively
30   as to drive them out of their country;
25
31   for they tried out every kind of wickedness,
                until vengeance overtook them.

Elijah

1
48   Then the prophet Elijah arose like a fire,
                his word flaring like a torch.
2   It was he who brought famine on them,
                and who decimated them in his zeal.
3   By the word of the Lord, he shut up the heavens,
                he also, three times, brought down fire.
4   How glorious you were in your miracles, Elijah!
                Has anyone reason to boast as you have?—
5   rousing a corpse from death,
                from Sheol by the word of the Most High;
6   dragging kings down to destruction,
                and high dignitaries from their beds;
7   hearing reproof on Sinai,
                and decrees of punishment on Horeb;
8   anointing kings as avengers,
                and prophets to succeed you;
9   taken up in the whirlwind of fire,
                in a chariot with fiery horses;
10   designated in the prophecies of doom
                to allay God's wrath before the fury breaks,
            to turn the hearts of fathers towards their children,[a]
                and to restore the tribes of Jacob.
11   Happy shall they be who see you,
                and those who have fallen asleep in love;
12   for we too will have life.

Elisha

12
13   Elijah was shrouded in the whirlwind,
                and Elisha was filled with his spirit;
            throughout his life no ruler could shake him,
                and no one could subdue him.
13
14   No task was too hard for him,
                and even in death his body prophesied.
14
15   In his lifetime he performed wonders,
                and in death his works were marvellous.

Infidelity and punishment

15
16   Despite all this the people did not repent,
                nor did they give up their sins,
            until they were herded out of their country
                and scattered all over the earth;

47 a. The Psalms.   b. Solomon means 'man of peace'.
48 a. Ml 3:24.

only a few of the people were left,　　　　　　　　　16
　　with a ruler of the House of David.　　　　　　　17
Some of them did what pleased the Lord,　　　　　　18
　　others piled sin on sin.

Hezekiah

Hezekiah fortified his city,　　　　　　　　　　　17
　　and laid on a water supply inside it;　　　　　　19
with iron he tunnelled through the rock
　　and constructed cisterns.
In his days Sennacherib invaded　　　　　　　　　18
　　and sent Rabshakeh;[b]　　　　　　　　　　　20
he lifted his hand against Zion,
　　and boasted loudly in his arrogance.
Then their hearts and hands trembled,　　　　　　19
　　they felt the pangs of a woman in labour,　　　21
but they called on the merciful Lord,　　　　　　20
　　stretching out their hands towards him.　　　22
Swiftly the Holy One heard them from heaven,
　　and delivered them by the hand of Isaiah,　　23
he struck the camp of the Assyrians　　　　　　　21
　　and his angel massacred them.　　　　　　　　24

Isaiah

For Hezekiah did what is pleasing to the Lord,　22
　　and was steadfast in the ways of David his father,　25
enjoined on him by the prophet Isaiah,
　　a great man trustworthy in his vision.
In his days the sun moved back;　　　　　　　　23
　　he prolonged the life of the king.　　　　　　26
In the power of the spirit he saw the last things,　24
　　he comforted the mourners of Zion,　　　　　27
he revealed the future to the end of time,　　　25
　　and hidden things long before they happened.　28

Josiah

49

The memory of Josiah is like blended incense　　1
　　prepared by the perfumer's art;
it is as sweet as honey to all mouths,　　　　　2
　　and like music at a wine feast.
He took the right course, of converting the people,　3
　　he rooted out the iniquitous abominations,
he set his heart on the Lord,　　　　　　　　　3
　　in godless times he upheld the cause of religion.　4

The last kings and prophets

Apart from David, Hezekiah and Josiah,　　　　4
　　they all heaped wrong on wrong;　　　　　　5
since they disregarded the Law of the Most High,　6
　　the kings of Judah disappeared;
since they gave their strength to others　　　5
　　and their honour to a foreign nation.　　　7
The holy, chosen city was burnt down,　　　　6
　　her streets were left deserted,　　　　　　8
as Jeremiah had predicted; for they had ill-treated him　7
　　though consecrated a prophet in his mother's womb　9

> *to tear up* and afflict *and destroy,*
>> but also *to build up and to plant.* [a]

8
10
Ezekiel it was who saw a vision of glory
>> which God showed to him above the chariot of the Cherubs,
9
11
for he remembered the enemies with torrential rain [b]
>> to the advantage of those who follow the right way.

10
12
As for the twelve prophets,
>> may their bones flower again from the tomb,
> since they have comforted Jacob
>> and redeemed him in faith and hope.

Zerubbabel and Joshua

11
13
How shall we extol Zerubbabel?
>> He was like a signet ring on the right hand,
12
14
so too was Jeshua son of Jozadak;
>> they who in their days built the Temple,
> and raised to the Lord a holy people,
>> destined to everlasting glory.

Nehemiah

13
15
Great too is the memory of Nehemiah,
>> who rebuilt our walls which lay in ruins,
> erected the gates and bars
>> and rebuilt our houses.

Retrospect

14
16
No one else has ever been created on earth to equal Enoch,
>> for he was taken up from earth.
15
17
And no one else ever born has been like Joseph,
>> the leader of his brothers, the prop of his people;
18
>> his bones were honoured.
16
19
Shem and Seth were honoured among men,
>> but above every living creature is Adam.

Simon the high priest

1
50
It was the High Priest Simon son of Onias
>> who repaired the Temple during his lifetime
>> and in his day fortified the sanctuary.
2
He laid the foundations of the double height,
>> the high buttresses of the Temple precincts.
3
In his day the water cistern was excavated,
>> a reservoir as huge as the sea.
4
Anxious to save the people from ruin,
>> he fortified the city against siege.
5
How splendid he was with the people thronging round him,
>> when he emerged from the curtained shrine, [a]
6
like the morning star among the clouds,
>> like the moon at the full,
7
like the sun shining on the Temple of the Most High,
8
>> like the rainbow gleaming against brilliant clouds,
8
like roses in the days of spring,
>> like lilies by a freshet of water,

---

b. Ben Sira's translator has made a proper name out of *rab shakeh* ('the chief cupbearer').
49 a. Jr 1:10.   **b.** Possibly an allusion to Ezk 38:22.
50 a. At the ceremonies of the feast of the Atonement.

like a sprig of frankincense in summer-time,
    like fire and incense in the censer,   9
like a vessel of beaten gold   10
    encrusted with every kind of precious stone,
like an olive tree loaded with fruit,   10 / 11
    like a cypress soaring to the clouds;
when he put on his splendid vestments,   11
    and clothed himself in glorious perfection,
when he went up to the holy altar,   12
    and filled the sanctuary precincts with his grandeur;
when he received the portions from the hands of the priests,   12 / 13
    himself standing by the altar hearth,
surrounded by a crowd of his brothers,
    like a youthful cedar of Lebanon
as though surrounded by the trunks of palm trees.   14
    When all the sons of Aaron in their glory,   13
with the offerings of the Lord in their hands,   15
    stood before the whole assembly of Israel,
while he completed the rites at the altars,   14
    presenting in due order the offering for the Most High, the Almighty,
reaching out his hand to the cup,[b]   15 / 16
    and pouring a libation of the juice of the grape,
pouring it at the foot of the altar,   17
    an appeasing fragrance to the Most High, the King of all,
then the sons of Aaron would shout   16 / 18
    and blow their trumpets of beaten metal,
making a mighty sound ring out
    as a reminder before the Most High;
and immediately the people all together   17 / 19
    would fall on their faces to the ground,
in adoration of their Lord,
    the Almighty, God Most High,
and with the cantors chanting their hymns of praise: 18 / 20
    sweet was the melody of all these voices,
as the people pleaded with the Lord Most High,   19 / 21
    and prayed in the presence of the Merciful,
until the service of the Lord was completed
    and the ceremony at an end.
Then he would come down and raise his hands   20 / 22
    over the whole concourse of the sons of Israel,
to give them the Lord's blessing from his lips,
    being privileged to pronounce his name;[c]
and once again the people would bow low   21 / 23
    to receive the blessing from the Most High.

Exhortation

And now bless the God of all things,   22 / 24
    the doer of great deeds everywhere,
who has exalted our days from the womb
    and acted towards us in his mercy.
May he grant us cheerful hearts   23 / 25
    and bring peace in our time,
    in Israel for ages on ages.
May his mercy be faithfully with us,   24 / 26
    may he redeem us in our time.

Numerical proverb

25 27	There are two nations that my soul detests, the third is not a nation at all:
26 28	the inhabitants of Mount Seir, and the Philistines, and the stupid people living at Shechem.*d*

Conclusion

27 29	Instruction in wisdom and knowledge has been committed to writing in this book by Jesus son of Sira, Eleazar, of Jerusalem, who has rained down wisdom from his heart.
28 30	Happy is he who busies himself with these things, and grows wise by taking them to heart.
29 31	If he practises them he will be strong enough for anything, since the light of the Lord is his path.

APPENDICES

A hymn of thanksgiving

1	**51**	I will give thanks to you, Lord and King, and praise you, God my saviour,
2		I give thanks to your name;
2		for you have been protector and support to me,
3		and redeemed my body from destruction,
		from the snare of the lying tongue, from lips that fabricate falsehood; and in the presence of those around me you have been my support, you have redeemed me,
3 4		true to the greatness of your mercy and of your name, from the fangs of those who would devour me,
5		from the hands of those seeking my life, from the many ordeals which I have endured,
4 6		from the stifling heat which hemmed me in, from the heart of a fire which I had not kindled,
5 7		from deep in the belly of Sheol, from the unclean tongue and the lying word—
6		the perjured tongue slandering me to the king.
8		My soul has been close to death,
9		my life had gone down to the brink of Sheol.
7 10		They were surrounding me on every side, there was no one to support me; I looked for someone to help—in vain.
8 11		Then I remembered your mercy, Lord, and your deeds from earliest times,
12		how you deliver those who wait for you patiently, and save them from the clutches of their enemies.
9 13		And I sent up my plea from the earth, I begged to be delivered from death,
10 14		I called on the Lord, the father of my Lord, 'Do not desert me in the days of ordeal, in the time of my helplessness against the proud.

---

b. A libation not described in Lv.   c. The holy name was pronounced only at the feast of the Atonement, as a blessing over the people.   d. The Samaritans.

I will praise your name unceasingly,   15
  and gratefully sing its praises.'
And my plea was heard,   11
  for you saved me from destruction,   16
  you delivered me from that time of evil.
And therefore I will thank you and praise you, 12
  and bless the name of the Lord.   17

A poem on the quest for wisdom[a]

When I was still a youth, before I went travelling,   13
  in my prayers I asked outright for wisdom.   18
Outside the sanctuary I would pray for her,   14
  and to the last I will continue to seek her.   19
From her blossoming to the ripening of her grape   15
  my heart has taken its delight in her.   20
My foot has pursued a straight path,
  I have been following her steps ever since my youth.
By bowing my ear a little I have received her,   16
  and have found much instruction.   21
                                                       22
Thanks to her I have advanced;   17
  the glory be to him who has given me wisdom!   23
For I am determined to put her into practice,   18
  I have earnestly pursued what is good, I will not be put to shame. 24
My soul has fought to possess her,   19
  I have been scrupulous in keeping the Law;   25
I have stretched out my hands to heaven   26
  and bewailed my ignorance of her;
I have directed my soul towards her,   20
  and in purity have found her;   27
having my heart fixed on her from the outset,   28
  I shall never be deserted;
my very core having yearned to discover her,   21
  I have now acquired a good possession.   29
In reward the Lord has given me a tongue   22
  with which I shall sing his praises.   30

Come close to me, you uninstructed,   23
  take your place in my school.   31
Why complain about lacking these things   24
  when your souls are so thirsty for them?   32
I have opened my mouth and spoken: 25
'Buy her without money,   33
  put your necks under her yoke,   26
and let your souls receive instruction;   34
  she is not far to seek.
See for yourselves: how slight my efforts have been   27
  to win so much peace.   35
Buy instruction with a large sum of silver,   28
  thanks to her you will gain much gold.   36
May your souls rejoice in the mercy of the Lord,   29
  may you never be ashamed of praising him.   37
Do your work before the appointed time   30
  and he in his time will give you your reward.'   38

[Subscript:] Wisdom of Jesus son of Sira.

51 a. This was an 'alphabetical' (acrostic) poem, and is no longer complete.

INTRODUCTION TO
THE PROPHETS

The nature of prophecy

The prophet in Israel is a mouthpiece; he has no doubt that 'the word of God' has come to him and that he must pass it on to others. In whatever way the divine message comes to him, and whatever method he uses to convey it, he is a man to whom the holiness and the will of God have been revealed. He contemplates present and future through the eyes of God and is a man sent to remind the nation of its duty to God and to bring them back to obedience and love.

Moses is accounted the father of them all, and prophets play a part in the whole history of the nation, whether in confraternities or singly as influential persons. At times the prophet may be powerful enough to reprove a king or direct national policy; at other times he may be in lonely opposition and his message takes the form of a tissue of menaces and reproaches against the ruling powers.

The prophetic books

Great prophets can be found in the historical books, but the men of whom we know most are those whose prophecies were collected into separate books bearing their names and sometimes including biographical incidents, and these books are grouped together in the Hebrew scriptures. Traditionally, they are arranged without regard for chronological order: the four 'Major Prophets' (distinguished only for the great length of their books)—Isaiah, Jeremiah, Ezekiel and Daniel—coming before the rest, who are called 'Minor Prophets'. With Jeremiah, the Greek Bible added Lamentations and Baruch as associated works, though the Hebrew Bible put Lamentations with 'the Writings' and did not include Baruch; it is the order of the Greek which is followed here.

The great age of prophecy lasted less than two centuries, from the mid-8th century to the Exile; it is dominated by the figures of Isaiah and Jeremiah, though it also saw the works of Amos, Hosea, Nahum, Zephaniah and Habakkuk. With Ezekiel, the prophet of Exile, spontaneity and verve decline, interest in 'the last days' increases, and apocalyptic literary form is beginning to make its appearance. The great tradition of Isaiah is continued for a while by his disciples, but the other prophets of the Return from Exile are prepossessed by the rebuilding of the Temple. In later prophets, we find a greater literary freedom: there is apocalyptic writing and the parabolic teaching style known as midrash; there is also a growing note of messianic hope. In Daniel, images of past and future come together in one great vision, and at this point it seems that the high inspiration of the prophets is exhausted and Israel must await a new outpouring of the Spirit.

Introductions

Separate introductions to the four longer books of the 'Major Prophets' are included in this edition of the Bible. Before the book of Hosea, there are short introductions to each of the books included in the 'Minor Prophets'.

INTRODUCTION
TO THE BOOK OF
ISAIAH

Isaiah the prophet belongs to the last years of the kingdom of Judah. His vocation to prophecy came 'in the year that King Uzziah died', 740 B.C., and it was his mission to announce the fall of Israel and of Judah as the due punishment for the whole nation's unfaithfulness. At this time, the kingdom of Judah, living under the threat of Assyrian invasion, was looking for military alliances to preserve its independence; Isaiah resisted all such human expedients as showing a lack of faith in God and his purposes. When eventually the armies under Sennacherib reached the walls of Jerusalem and called for the surrender of the city, Isaiah advised the king not to capitulate and in fact the city was saved without a battle. This is the background to the prophecies in the first part of the book, which ends with a history of the period written by his disciples, at chapter 39. The prophecies show Isaiah as a man of lofty vision with a strong sense of the transcendence of God; beyond the destined fall of his nation he sees a coming age in which a remnant of the people will survive to rebuild peace and justice under a future descendant of David.

In the same part of the book, some prophecies from the time of the Exile, about a hundred years later, have been included. These include oracles against Babylon (ch.13-14), an apocalypse (ch.24-27) and some poems (ch.33-35).

Towards the end of the Exile, some very fine and profound prophecies were made by an unnamed writer with a new depth of theology, looking forward to the coming time when God would comfort his people and restore them to Jerusalem. These prophecies, in a collection known as 'the Book of the Consolation of Israel' form chapters 40 to 55 of the book, and embedded in them are the four 'Songs of the Servant of Yahweh' who suffers to atone for the sins of his people.

Chapters 56-66 contain prophecies which appear to date from different times throughout the whole age, from the call of Isaiah to the restoration in Jerusalem after the Exile.

ISAIAH

I. THE FIRST PART OF ISAIAH

A. ORACLES BEFORE THE SYRO-EPHRAIMITE WAR

Title

1 1 The vision of Isaiah son of Amoz concerning Judah and Jerusalem, which
he saw in the reigns of Uzziah, Jotham, Ahaz and Hezekiah, kings of Judah.

Against a thoughtless people

2　　　Listen, you heavens; earth, attend
　　　for Yahweh is speaking,
　　　'I reared sons, I brought them up,
　　　but they have rebelled against me.
3　　　The ox knows its owner
　　　and the ass its master's crib,
　　　Israel knows nothing,
　　　my people understands nothing.'

The punishment of Judah

4　　　A sinful nation, a people weighed down with guilt,
　　　a breed of wrong-doers, perverted sons.
　　　They have abandoned Yahweh, despised the Holy One of Israel,
　　　they have turned away from him.

5　　　Where shall I strike you next,
　　　since you heap one betrayal on another?
　　　The whole head is sick, the whole heart grown faint;
6　　　from the sole of the foot to the head there is not a sound spot:
　　　wounds, bruises, open sores
　　　not dressed, not bandaged,
　　　not soothed with oil.

7　　　Your land is desolate, your towns burnt down,
　　　your fields—strangers lay them waste before your eyes;
　　　all is desolation, as after the fall of Sodom.[a]

8　　　The daughter of Zion is left
　　　like a shanty in a vineyard,
　　　like a shed in a melon patch,
　　　like a besieged city.
9　　　Had Yahweh not left us a few survivors,
　　　we should be like Sodom,
　　　we should now be like Gomorrah.

1 a. The occasion of this prophecy is probably the siege of Jerusalem, 735.

Against religious hypocrisy

Hear the word of Yahweh,   10
you rulers of Sodom;
listen to the command of our God,
you people of Gomorrah.

'What are your endless sacrifices to me?   11
says Yahweh.
I am sick of holocausts of rams
and the fat of calves.
The blood of bulls and of goats revolts me.
When you come to present yourselves before me,   12
who asked you to trample over my courts?
Bring me your worthless offerings no more,   13
the smoke of them fills me with disgust.
New Moons, sabbaths, assemblies—
I cannot endure festival and solemnity.
Your New Moons and your pilgrimages   14
I hate with all my soul.
They lie heavy on me,
I am tired of bearing them.
When you stretch out your hands   15
I turn my eyes away.
You may multiply your prayers,
I shall not listen.
Your hands are covered with blood,
wash, make yourselves clean.   16

'Take your wrong-doing out of my sight.
Cease to do evil.
Learn to do good,   17
search for justice,
help the oppressed,
be just to the orphan,
plead for the widow.

'Come now, let us talk this over,   18
says Yahweh.
Though your sins are like scarlet,
they shall be as white as snow;
though they are red as crimson,
they shall be like wool.

'If you are willing to obey,   19
you shall eat the good things of the earth.
But if you persist in rebellion,   20
the sword shall eat you instead.'
The mouth of Yahweh has spoken.

Lament for Jerusalem

What a harlot she has become,   21
the faithful city,
Zion, that was all justice!
Once integrity lived there,
but now assassins.

Your silver has turned into dross,   22
your wine is watered.

23　　　Your princes are rebels,
　　　　accomplices of thieves.

　　　　All are greedy for profit
　　　　and chase after bribes.
　　　　They show no justice to the orphan,
　　　　the cause of the widow is never heard.

24　　　Therefore—it is the Lord Yahweh Sabaoth who speaks,
　　　　the Mighty One of Israel,
　　　　'Ah, I will outdo my enemies,
　　　　avenge myself on my foes.

25　　　'I will turn my hand against you,
　　　　I will smelt away your dross in the furnace,
　　　　I will remove all your base metal from you.

26　　　'I will restore your judges as of old,
　　　　your counsellors as in bygone days.
　　　　Then you will be called City of Integrity,
　　　　Faithful City.'

27　　　Zion will be redeemed by justice,
　　　　and her penitents by integrity.

28　　　Rebels and sinners together will be shattered,
　　　　and those who abandon Yahweh will perish.

Against tree worship [b]

29　　　Yes, you will be ashamed of the terebinths
　　　　which give you such pleasure;
　　　　you will blush for the gardens
　　　　that charm you.

30　　　Since you will be like a terebinth
　　　　with faded leaves,
　　　　like a garden
　　　　without water.

31　　　The man of high estate will be tinder,
　　　　his handiwork a spark.
　　　　Both will burn together
　　　　and no one put them out.

Everlasting peace

1　2　The vision of Isaiah son of Amoz, concerning Judah and Jerusalem.

2　　　In the days to come
　　　　the mountain of the Temple of Yahweh
　　　　shall tower above the mountains
　　　　and be lifted higher than the hills.
　　　　All the nations will stream to it,

3　　　peoples without number will come to it; and they will say:
　　　　'Come, let us go up to the mountain of Yahweh,
　　　　to the Temple of the God of Jacob
　　　　that he may teach us his ways
　　　　so that we may walk in his paths;
　　　　since the Law will go out from Zion,
　　　　and the oracle of Yahweh from Jerusalem'.

4　　　He will wield authority over the nations

b. A pagan practice; possibly the prophecy is against Samaria.

and adjudicate between many peoples;
these will hammer their swords into ploughshares,
their spears into sickles.
Nation will not lift sword against nation,
there will be no more training for war.

O House of Jacob, come,   5
let us walk in the light of Yahweh.

The coming of Yahweh

Yes, you have cast off your people,   6
the House of Jacob;
the land is full of soothsayers,
full of sorcerers like the Philistines;
they clap foreigners by the hand.

His land is full of silver and gold   7
and treasures beyond counting;
his land is full of horses
and chariots without number;
his land is full of idols...   8
They bow down before the work of their hands,
before the thing their fingers have made.

The mortal will be humbled, man brought low;   9
do not forgive them.
Get among the rocks,   10
hide in the dust,
at the sight of the terror of Yahweh,
at the brilliance of his majesty,
when he arises
to make the earth quake.

Human pride will lower its eyes,   11
the arrogance of men will be humbled.
Yahweh alone shall be exalted,
on that day.
Yes, that will be the day of Yahweh Sabaoth   12
against all pride and arrogance,
against all that is great, to bring it down,
against all the cedars of Lebanon   13
and all the oaks of Bashan,
against all the high mountains   14
and all the soaring hills,
against all the lofty towers   15
and all the sheer walls,
against all the ships of Tarshish[a]   16
and all things of price...

Human pride will be humbled,   17
the arrogance of men will be brought low.
Yahweh alone will be exalted,
on that day,
and all idols thrown down.   18

Go into the hollows of the rocks,   19
into the caverns of the earth,
at the sight of the terror of Yahweh,
at the brilliance of his majesty,

> when he arises
> to make the earth quake.

20   That day man will fling to moles and bats the idols of silver and the idols of
gold that he made for worship,

21   and go into the crevices of the rocks
                and the rifts of the crag,
                at the sight of the terror of Yahweh,
                at the brilliance of his majesty,
                when he arises
                to make the earth quake.

22   ⁷rust no more in man,
                he has but a breath in his nostrils.
                How much is he worth?

Anarchy in Jerusalem

1   **3**   Yes, see how the Lord Yahweh-Sabaoth
                is taking from Jerusalem and Judah
                support of every kind
                (support of bread and support of water):
2   hero, man-at-arms, judge, prophet,
3   diviner, elder, •captain, noble,
                counsellor, sorcerer, soothsayer.
4   'I give them boys for princes,
                raw lads to rule over them.'
5   The people bully each other,
                neighbour and neighbour;
                a youth can insult his elder,
                a lout abuse a noble,
6   so that everyone tries to catch his brother
                in their father's house, to say,
                'You have a cloak, so you be leader,
                and rule this heap of ruins'.

7   When that day comes the other will protest,
                'I am no doctor,
                in my house is neither bread nor cloak;
                do not make me leader of the people'.
8   Yes, Jerusalem is falling into ruins
                and Judah is in collapse,
                since their words and their deeds affront the Lord,
                insulting his glory.

9   Their insolent airs bear witness against them,
                they parade their sin like Sodom.
                To their own undoing, they do not hide it,
                they are preparing their own downfall.

10   Tell them, 'Happy is the virtuous man,
                for he will feed on the fruit of his deeds;
11   woe to the wicked, evil is on him,
                he will be treated as his actions deserve'.

12   O my people, oppressed by a lad,

2 a. Tarshish is Tartessos in Spain—'the ends of the earth'. 'Ships of Tarshish' means 'great
ocean-going vessels'.

ruled by women.[a]
O my people, your rulers mislead you
and destroy the road you walk on.

Yahweh rises from his judgement seat,   13
he stands up to arraign his people.
Yahweh calls to judgement   14
the elders and the princes of his people:

'You are the ones who destroy the vineyard
and conceal what you have stolen from the poor.
By what right do you crush my people   15
and grind the faces of the poor?'
It is the Lord Yahweh Sabaoth who speaks.

A warning to the women of Jerusalem

Yahweh said: Because of the haughtiness   16
of the daughters of Zion,
the way they walk with their heads held high
and enticing eyes,
the way they mince along,
tinkling the bangles on their feet,
the Lord will give the daughters of Zion itching heads   17
and uncover their nakedness.

That day the Lord will take away the ankle ornaments, tiaras, pendants 18
and bracelets, the veils, •headbands, foot chains and belts, the scent bottles and 19 20
amulets, •signet rings and nose rings, •the expensive dresses, mantles, cloaks 21 22
and purses, •the mirrors, linen garments, turbans and mantillas. 23

Instead of scent, a stink;   24
instead of belt, a rope;
instead of hair elaborately done, a shaven scalp,
and instead of gorgeous dress, a sack;
and brand marks instead of beauty.

The widows of Jerusalem

Your men will fall by the sword,   25
your heroes in the fight.
The gates will moan and mourn;   26
you will sit on the ground desolate.

4 And seven women will fight   1
over a single man that day:[a]
'We will eat our own food,
and wear our own clothing,' they will say
'let us just bear your name;
take our disgrace away'.

The remnant of Jerusalem

That day, the branch of Yahweh   2
shall be beauty and glory,
and the fruit of the earth
shall be the pride and adornment
of Israel's survivors.
Those who are left of Zion   3
and remain of Jerusalem
shall be called holy
and those left in Jerusalem, noted down for survival.

The future restoration

4 When the Lord has washed away
the filth of the daughter of Zion
and cleansed Jerusalem of the blood shed in her
with the blast of judgement and the blast of destruction,

5 Yahweh will come and rest
on the whole stretch of Mount Zion
and on those who are gathered there,
a cloud by day, and smoke,
and by night the brightness of a flaring fire.
For, over all, the glory of Yahweh

6 will be a canopy •and a tent
to give shade by day from the heat,
refuge and shelter from the storm and the rain.

The song of the vineyard

1 **5** Let me sing to my friend
the song of his love for his vineyard.

My friend had a vineyard
on a fertile hillside.

2 He dug the soil, cleared it of stones,
and planted choice vines in it.
In the middle he built a tower,
he dug a press there too.
He expected it to yield grapes,
but sour grapes were all that it gave.

3 And now, inhabitants of Jerusalem
and men of Judah,
I ask you to judge
between my vineyard and me.

4 What could I have done for my vineyard
that I have not done?
I expected it to yield grapes.
Why did it yield sour grapes instead?

5 Very well, I will tell you
what I am going to do to my vineyard:
I will take away its hedge for it to be grazed on,
and knock down its wall for it to be trampled on.

6 I will lay it waste, unpruned, undug;
overgrown by the briar and the thorn.
I will command the clouds
to rain no rain on it.

7 Yes, the vineyard of Yahweh Sabaoth
is the House of Israel,
and the men of Judah
that chosen plant.
He expected justice, but found bloodshed,
integrity, but only a cry of distress.

3 a. The 'lad' is possibly the young king Ahaz, at the start of his reign, 736.
4 a. The army has been destroyed; the circumstances are those of the first or second siege of Jerusalem, 735 or 701.

Curses

Woe to those who add house to house   8
and join field to field
until everywhere belongs to them
and they are the sole inhabitants of the land.
Yahweh Sabaoth has sworn this in my hearing,   9
'Many houses shall be brought to ruin,
great and fine, but left untenanted;
ten acres of vineyard will yield only one barrel,   10
ten bushel of seed will yield only one bushel'.

Woe to those who from early morning   11
chase after strong drink,
and stay up late at night
inflamed with wine.
Nothing but harp and lyre,   12
tambourine and flute,
and wine for their drinking bouts.

Never a thought for the works of Yahweh,
never a glance for what his hands have done.
My people will go into exile,   13
for want of perception;
her dignitaries dying of hunger,
her populace parched with thirst.

[a] . . . Yes, Sheol opens wide his throat   14
and gapes with measureless jaw
to swallow up her thronging nobility
as they are shouting for joy.
The mortal humbled, man brought low,   15
proud eyes will be cast down.
Yahweh Sabaoth will increase his glory by his sentence,   16
the holy God will display his holiness by his integrity.
Lambs will graze as at pasture,   17
fatlings and kids browse in the ruins.

Woe to those who draw down punishment on themselves   18
with an ox's halter,
and sin
as with a chariot's traces:
and to those who say, 'Quick! Let him hurry his work   19
so that we can see it;
these plans of the Holy One of Israel,
let them happen and come true
so that we can know what they are.'

Woe to those who call evil good, and good evil,   20
who substitute darkness for light
and light for darkness,
who substitute bitter for sweet
and sweet for bitter.

Woe to those who think themselves wise   21
and believe themselves cunning.
Woe to the heroes of drinking bouts,   22

23   Woe to those who for a bribe acquit the guilty
     and cheat the good man of his due.

24   For this, as stubble is prey for the flames
     and as straw vanishes in the fire,
       so their root will rot,
     their blossom be carried off like dust,
     for rejecting the Law of Yahweh Sabaoth,
     and despising the word of the Holy One of Israel.

The anger of Yahweh

25   So, Yahweh aflame with anger against his people
     has raised his hand to strike them;
     he has killed the princes, their corpses lie
     like dung in the streets.
     Yet his anger is not spent,
     still his hand is raised to strike.

The Assyrian invasion

26   He hoists a signal for a distant nation,
     he whistles it up from the ends of the earth;
     and look, it comes, swiftly, promptly.

27   None of them faint or weary,
     none sleeping or drowsy,
     none of them with belt loose,
     none with sandal-straps broken.

28   Its arrows are sharpened,
     its bows all bent,
     the hoofs of its horses are like flint,
     its chariot-wheels like tornadoes.

29   Its roar is the roar of a lioness,
     like a lion cub it roars,
     it growls and seizes its prey,
     it bears it off, and no one can snatch it back.

30   Growling against it, that day,
     like the growling of the sea.
     Only look at the country: darkness and distress,
     and the light flickers out in shadows.

B. THE BOOK OF IMMANUEL

The call of Isaiah

1 **6** In the year of King Uzziah's death [a] I saw the Lord Yahweh seated on a high
2 throne; his train filled the sanctuary; •above him stood seraphs, each one
with six wings: two to cover its face, two to cover its feet and two for flying.

3   And they cried out one to another in this way,
     'Holy, holy, holy is Yahweh Sabaoth.
     His glory fills the whole earth.'

4   The foundations of the threshold shook with the voice of the one who cried out.
5 and the Temple was filled with smoke. •I said:

5 a. Vv. 14-16 are out of place and should perhaps be read with 2:6-22.
6 a. 740 B.C.

> 'What a wretched state I am in! I am lost,
> for I am a man of unclean lips
> and I live among a people of unclean lips,
> and my eyes have looked at the King, Yahweh Sabaoth.'

Then one of the seraphs flew to me, holding in his hand a live coal which he 6
had taken from the altar with a pair of tongs. •With this he touched my mouth 7
and said:

> 'See now, this has touched your lips,
> your sin is taken away,
> your iniquity is purged'.

Then I heard the voice of the Lord saying: 8

> 'Whom shall I send? Who will be our messenger?'

I answered, 'Here I am, send me'. •He said: 9

> 'Go, and say to this people,
> "Hear and hear again, but do not understand;
> see and see again, but do not perceive".
> Make the heart of this people gross,   10
> its ears dull;
> shut its eyes,
> so that it will not see with its eyes,
> hear with its ears,
> understand with its heart,
> and be converted and healed.'

Then I said, 'Until when, Lord?' He answered: 11

> 'Until towns have been laid waste and deserted,
> houses left untenanted,
> countryside made desolate,
> and Yahweh drives the people out.   12
> There will be a great emptiness in the country
> and, though a tenth of the people remain,   13
> it will be stripped like a terebinth
> of which, once felled, only the stock remains.
> The stock is a holy seed.'

The first warning to Ahaz

7 In the reign of Ahaz son of Jotham, son of Uzziah, king of Judah, Razon the 1
king of Aram went up against Jerusalem with Pekah son of Remaliah, king
of Israel, to lay siege to it; but he was unable to capture it.

The news was brought to the House of David. 'Aram' they said 'has reached 2
Ephraim.' Then the heart of the king and the hearts of the people shuddered
as the trees of the forest shudder in front of the wind. •Yahweh said to Isaiah, 3
'Go with your son Shear-jashub,*a* and meet Ahaz at the end of the conduit of
the upper pool on the Fuller's Field road, •and say to him: 4

> "Pay attention, keep calm, have no fear,
> do not let your heart sink
> because of these two smouldering stumps of firebrands,*b*
> or because Aram, Ephraim and the son of Remaliah   5
> have plotted to ruin you, and have said:
> Let us invade Judah and terrorise it   6
> and seize it for ourselves,
> and set up a king there,
> the son of Tabeel.

7   The Lord Yahweh says this:
It shall not come true; it shall not be.

8a   The capital of Aram is Damascus,
the head of Damascus, Razon;

9a   the capital of Ephraim, Samaria,
the head of Samaria, the son of Remaliah.

8b   Six or five years more
and a shattered Ephraim shall no longer be a people.

9b   But if you do not stand by me,
you will not stand at all." '

The second warning to Ahaz. The sign of Immanuel

10
11   Once again Yahweh spoke to Ahaz and said, •'Ask Yahweh your God for
a sign for yourself coming either from the depths of Sheol or from the heights
12 above'. •'No,' Ahaz answered 'I will not put Yahweh to the test.'
13   Then he said:

Listen now, House of David:
are you not satisfied with trying the patience of men
without trying the patience of my God, too?

14   The Lord himself, therefore,
will give you a sign.
It is this: the maiden is with child
and will soon give birth to a son
whom she will call Immanuel.

15   On curds and honey will he feed
until he knows how to refuse evil
and choose good.

16   For before this child knows how to refuse evil
and choose good,
the land whose two kings terrify you
will be deserted.

17   Yahweh will bring times for you
and your people and your father's House,
such as have not come
since Ephraim broke away from Judah
(the king of Assyria).

18   That day Yahweh will whistle up mosquitoes
from the Delta of the Egyptian Niles,
and bees from the land of Assyria,

19   to come and settle
on the steep ravine, on the rocky cleft,
on the thorn bush and on every pasture.

20   On that day the Lord will shave
with a blade hired from beyond the River[c]
(the king of Assyria),
the head and hairs of the body,
and take off the beard, too.

21   That day each man will raise
one heifer and two sheep,

22   and because of the abundance of milk they give,
all who are left in the country
will feed on curds and honey.

23   That day, where a thousand vines used to be,

7 a. The name means 'a remnant will return'.   **b.** The kings of Damascus and Israel.
c. Euphrates.

worth one thousand pieces of silver,
all will be briar and thorn.
Men will enter it with arrows and bow,   24
since the whole country will revert to briar and thorn.
On any hillside hoed with the hoe,   25
no one will come
for fear of briars and thorns;
it will be pasture for cattle and grazing for sheep.

The birth of a son to Isaiah

8 Yahewh said to me, 'Take a large seal and scratch on it in ordinary writing 1
MAHER-SHALAL-HASH-BAZ.ᵃ •Then find me reliable witnesses, Uriah the 2
priest and Zechariah son of Jeberechiah.'

I went to the prophetess, she conceived and gave birth to a son. Yahweh 3
said to me, 'Call him Maher-shalal-hash-baz, •for before the child knows how 4
to say father or mother, the wealth of Damascus and the booty of Samaria
will be carried off before the king of Assyria'.

Shiloah and the Euphrates

Yahweh spoke to me again and said: 5

Because this people has refused the waters of Shiloahᵇ   6
which flow in tranquillity,
and trembles before Razon
and the son of Remaliah,
the Lord will bring up against you   7
the mighty and deep waters of the River
(the king of Assyria and all his glory),
and it will overflow out of its bed
bursting all its banks;
it will inundate Judah, flow over, pour out,   8
flooding it up to the neck,
and its wings will be spread
over the whole breadth of your country, O Immanuel.

Terror for the invaders

Know this, peoples, you will be crushed;   9
listen, far-off nations,
arm yourselves, yet you will be crushed.
Devise a plan, it is thwarted;   10
put forward an argument, there is no substance in it,
for God is with us.ᶜ

Yahweh a stone in the way

Yes, Yahweh spoke to me like this   11
when his hand seized hold of me
to turn me from walking in the path
that this people follows.
Do not call conspiracy   12
all that this people calls conspiracy;
do not fear what they fear,
do not be afraid of them.
It is Yahweh Sabaoth,   13
whom you must hold in veneration,
him you must fear,
him you must dread.
He is the sanctuary and the stumbling-stone   14

and the rock that brings down
the two Houses of Israel;
a trap and a snare
for the inhabitants of Jerusalem.

15   By it many will be brought down,
many fall and be broken,
be trapped and made captive.

Isaiah addresses his disciples

16   I bind up this testimony,
I seal this revelation,
in the heart of my disciples.

17   I wait for Yahweh
who hides his face from the House of Jacob;
in him I hope.

18   I and the children whom Yahweh has given me
are signs and portents in Israel
from Yahweh Sabaoth
who dwells on Mount Zion.

19   And should men say to you, 'Consult ghosts
and wizards that whisper and mutter' —
by all means a people must consult its gods
and, on behalf of the living, consult the dead.

20   To obtain a revelation and a testimony,
without doubt this is how they will talk,
since there is no dawn for them.

Wandering in the night

21   Distressed and starving he will wander through the country
and, starving, he will become frenzied,
blaspheming his king and his God;
turning his gaze upward,

22   then down to the earth,
he will find only distress and darkness,
the blackness of anguish,
and will see nothing but night.

23   Is not all blackness where anguish is?

Epiphany

1   In days past he humbled the land of Zebulun and the land of Naphtali, but
in days to come he will confer glory on the Way of the Sea on the far side of
Jordan, province of the nations.

1 **9**   The people that walked in darkness
has seen a great light;
on those who live in a land of deep shadow
a light has shone.

2   You have made their gladness greater,
you have made their joy increase;
they rejoice in your presence
as men rejoice at harvest time,
as men are happy when they are dividing the spoils.

3
4   For the yoke that was weighing on him,

---

8 a. 'Speedy-spoil-quick-booty'.   **b.** The only spring of water in Jerusalem.   **c.** The meaning
of the name Immanuel.

the bar across his shoulders,
the rod of his oppressor,
these you break as on the day of Midian.

For all the footgear of battle,   4/5
every cloak rolled in blood,
is burnt,
and consumed by fire.

For there is a child born for us,   5/6
a son given to us
and dominion is laid on his shoulders;
and this is the name they give him:
Wonder-Counsellor, Mighty-God,
Eternal-Father, Prince-of-Peace.
Wide is his dominion   6/7
in a peace that has no end,
for the throne of David
and for his royal power,
which he establishes and makes secure
in justice and integrity.
From this time onwards and for ever,
the jealous love of Yahweh Sabaoth will do this.

The vengeance of Yahweh

The Lord hurls a word against Jacob,   7/8
it falls on Israel.
All the people of Ephraim and all the inhabitants of Samaria know it.   8/9
In their pride they have said,
speaking in the arrogance of their heart,
'The bricks have fallen down, then we will build with dressed stone;   9/10
the sycamores have been cut down, we will put cedars in their place'.
But Yahweh is marshalling his people's enemies against them,   10/11
he is stirring up their foes:
to the east, Aram, to the west, the Philistines   11/12
devour Israel with gaping jaw.
Yet his anger is not spent,
still his hand is raised to strike.

But the people have not come back to him who struck them,   12/13
they have not come looking for Yahweh Sabaoth;
hence Yahweh has cut head and tail from Israel,   13/14
palm branch and reed in a single day.
(The 'head' is the elder and the man of rank;   14/15
the 'tail', the prophet with lying vision.)
This people's leaders have taken the wrong turning,   15/16
and those who are led are lost.
And so the Lord will not spare their young men,   16/17
will have no pity for their orphans and widows.
Since the whole people is godless and evil,
its speech is madness.
Yet his anger is not spent,
still his hand is raised to strike.
Yes, wickedness burns like a fire: 17/18
it consumes briar and thorn,
it sets the forest thickets alight
and columns of smoke go rolling upwards.

18
19

The land is set aflame by the wrath of Yahweh Sabaoth
and the people are food for the fire.
Not one spares his brother,

19b each devours the flesh of his neighbour.
On the right side they carve and still are hungry,
on the left they devour and are not satisfied.

19a
20 Manasseh devours Ephraim, Ephraim Manasseh,
and both hurl themselves on Judah.

21 Yet his anger is not spent,
still his hand is raised to strike.

10

1 Woe to the legislators of infamous laws,
to those who issue tyrannical decrees,

2 who refuse justice to the unfortunate
and cheat the poor among my people of their rights,
who make widows their prey
and rob the orphan.

3 What will you do on the day of punishment,
when, from far off, destruction comes?
To whom will you run for help?
Where will you leave your riches?

4 Nothing for it but to crouch with the captives
and to fall with the slain.
Yet his anger is not spent,
still his hand is raised to strike.

Against a king of Assyria[a]

5 Woe to Assyria, the rod of my anger,
the club brandished by me in my fury!

6 I sent him against a godless nation;
I gave him commission against a people that provokes me,
to pillage and to plunder freely
and to stamp down like the mud in the streets.

7 But he did not intend this,
his heart did not plan it so.
No, in his heart was to destroy,
to go on cutting nations to pieces without limit.

8 He said, 'Are not my officers all kings?

9 Is not Calno like Carchemish,
Hamath like Arpad,[b]
Samaria like Damascus?

10 As my hand has reached out to the kingdoms of the idols,
richer in sculptured images than Jerusalem and Samaria,

11 as I have dealt with Samaria and her idols,
shall I not treat Jerusalem and her images the same?'

12 When the Lord has completed all his work on Mount Zion and in Jerusalem,
he will punish what comes from the king of Assyria's boastful heart, and his
arrogant insolence.

13 For he has said:

'By the strength of my own arm I have done this
and by my own intelligence, for understanding is mine;

10 a. Probably Sennacherib at the end of his invasion, 701.   **b.** Calno (N. Syria) captured
by Tiglath-pileser, 738; Carchemish (Hittite) taken by Sargon, 717; Hamath (Syria) captured
by Sargon, 720; Arpad (near Aleppo) captured, 728.

I have pushed back the frontiers of peoples
and plundered their treasures.
I have brought their inhabitants down to the dust.
As if they were a bird's nest, my hand has seized　　　　14
the riches of the peoples.
As people pick up deserted eggs
I have picked up the whole earth,
with not a wing fluttering,
not a beak opening, not a chirp.'

Does the axe claim more credit than the man who wields it,　　15
or the saw more strength than the man who handles it?
It would be like the cudgel controlling the man who raises it,
or the club moving what is not made of wood!
And so Yahweh Sabaoth is going to send　　　　16
a wasting sickness on his stout warriors;
beneath his plenty, a burning will burn
like a consuming fire.
The light of Israel will become a fire　　　　17
and its Holy One a flame
burning and devouring thorns
and briars in a single day.
He will destroy the luxuriance of his forest　　　　18
and his orchard, soul and body too;
that will be like a sick man passing away;
the remnant of his forest trees will be so easy to count　　19
that a child could make the list.

The name Shear-jashub [c]

That day,　　　　20
the remnant of Israel and the survivors of the House of Jacob
will stop relying on the man who strikes them
and will truly rely on Yahweh,
the Holy One of Israel.
A remnant will return, the remnant of Jacob,　　　　21
to the mighty God.

A prophecy of destruction

Israel, your people may be like the sand on the seashore, but only a remnant　22
will return. A destruction has been decreed that will bring inexhaustible integrity.
Yes, throughout the country the Lord Yahweh Sabaoth will carry out the　23
destruction he has decreed.

Oracle

And so Yahweh Sabaoth says this:　　　　24
My people who live in Zion,
do not be afraid of Assyria who strikes you with the club
and lifts up the rod against you.

A little longer, a very little,　　　　25
and fury will come to an end,
my anger will destroy them.
Yahweh Sabaoth will whirl the whip against him,　　　26
like the time he struck Midian at the Rock of Oreb,
like the time he stretched out his rod against the sea
and raised it over the road from Egypt.

27   That day,
      his burden will fall from your shoulder,
      his yoke will cease to weigh on your neck.

The invader [d]

      He advances from the district of Rimmon,
28   he reaches Aiath,
      he passes through Migron,
      he leaves his baggage train at Michmash.
29   They file through the defile,
      they bivouac at Geba.
      Ramah quakes,
      Gibeah of Saul takes flight.
30   Bath-gallim, cry aloud!
      Laishah, hear her!
      Anathoth, answer her!
31   Madmenah is running away,
      the inhabitants of Gebim are fleeing.
32   This very day he will halt at Nob.
      He will shake his fist against the mount of the daughter of Zion,
      against the hill of Jerusalem.
33   See, the Lord Yahweh Sabaoth
      hews down the boughs with a crash.
      The topmost heights are cut off,
      the proudest are brought down.
34   The forest thickets fall beneath the axe.
      Lebanon and its splendours collapse.

The coming of the virtuous king

11

1   A shoot springs from the stock of Jesse,
      a scion thrusts from his roots:
2   on him the spirit of Yahweh rests,
      a spirit of wisdom and insight,
      a spirit of counsel and power,
      a spirit of knowledge and of the fear of Yahweh.
      (The fear of Yahweh is his breath.)
3   He does not judge by appearances,
      he gives no verdict on hearsay,
4   but judges the wretched with integrity,
      and with equity gives a verdict for the poor of the land.
      His word is a rod that strikes the ruthless,
      his sentences bring death to the wicked.

5   Integrity is the loincloth round his waist,
      faithfulness the belt about his hips.

6   The wolf lives with the lamb,
      the panther lies down with the kid,
      calf and lion cub feed together
      with a little boy to lead them.
7   The cow and the bear make friends,
      their young lie down together.
      The lion eats straw like the ox.
8   The infant plays over the cobra's hole;

c. See 7:3.   **d.** The invasion route of this Assyrian enemy is not actually the way taken by Sennacherib in 701; the towns are chosen because their names suggest appropriate puns or recall past battles.

into the viper's lair
the young child puts his hand.
They do no hurt, no harm,   9
on all my holy mountain,
for the country is filled with the knowledge of Yahweh
as the waters swell the sea.

The return of the exiles

That day, the root of Jesse   10
shall stand as a signal to the peoples.
It will be sought out by the nations
and its home will be glorious.
That day, the Lord will raise his hand once more   11
to ransom the remnant of his people,
left over from the exile of Assyria, of Egypt,
of Pathros, of Cush, of Elam,
of Shinar, of Hamath, of the islands of the sea.ᵃ
He will hoist a signal for the nations   12
and assemble the outcasts of Israel;
he will bring back the scattered people of Judah
from the four corners of the earth.
Then Ephraim's jealousy will come to an end   13
and Judah's enemies be put down;
Ephraim will no longer be jealous of Judah
nor Judah any longer the enemy of Ephraim.
They will sweep down westwards on the Philistine slopes,   14
together they will pillage the sons of the East,
extend their sway over Edom and Moab,
and make the Ammonites their subjects.
And Yahweh will dry up the gulf of the Sea of Egypt   15
with the heat of his breath,
and stretch out his hand over the River,
and divide it into seven streams,
for men to cross dry-shod,
to make a pathway for the remnant of his people   16
left over from the exile of Assyria,
as there was for Israel
when it came up out of Egypt.

Two hymns of thanksgiving

12 That day, you will say: 1
I give thanks to you, Yahweh,
you were angry with me
but your anger is appeased
and you have given me consolation.
See now, he is the God of my salvation   2
I have trust now and no fear,
for Yahweh is my strength, my song,
he is my salvation.
And you will draw water joyfully   3
from the springs of salvation.

That day, you will say: 4
Give thanks to Yahweh,
call his name aloud.
Proclaim his deeds to the people,

declare his name sublime.

5 Sing of Yahweh, for he has done marvellous things,
let them be made known to the whole world.

6 Cry out for joy and gladness,
you dwellers in Zion,
for great in the midst of you
is the Holy One of Israel.

C. ORACLES ON FOREIGN NATIONS

Against Babylon

1 **13** Oracle on Babylon, seen by Isaiah son of Amoz.

2 On a bare hill hoist a signal,
sound the war cry.
Beckon them to come
to the Nobles' Gate.

3 I, for my part, issue orders
to my sacred warriors,
I summon my knights to serve my anger,
my proud champions.

4 Listen! A rumbling in the mountains
like a great crowd.
Listen! The din of kingdoms,
of nations mustering.
It is Yahweh Sabaoth
marshalling the troops for battle.

5 They come from a distant country,
from the far horizons,
Yahweh and the instruments of his fury
to lay the whole earth waste.

6 Howl! For the day of Yahweh is near,
bringing devastation from Shaddai.

7 At this, every arm falls limp . . .
The heart of each man fails him,

8 they are terrified,
pangs and pains seize them,
they writhe like a woman in labour.
They look at one another
with feverish faces.

9 The day of Yahweh is coming, merciless,
with wrath and fierce anger,
to reduce the earth to desert
and root out the sinners from it.

10 For the stars of the sky and Orion
shall not let their light shine;
the sun shall be dark when it rises,
and the moon not shed her light.

11 I will punish the world for its evil-doing,
and the wicked for their crimes,
to put an end to the pride of arrogant men
and humble the pride of despots.

12 I will make men scarcer than pure gold,

11 a. The places to which the inhabitants of the Jerusalem area had dispersed after the destruction of the city.

human life scarcer than the gold of Ophir.
This is why I am going to shake the heavens—   13
and make the earth reel from its place,
before the wrath of Yahweh Sabaoth,
the day when his anger flares.
Then like a startled gazelle,   14
like sheep that no one shepherds,
each man will return to his people,
each take flight to his native land.
All those caught are slaughtered,   15
all those captured fall by the sword,
their babies are dashed to pieces before their eyes,   16
their houses plundered,
their wives raped.
See now, I stir up against them the Medes,   17
who think nothing of silver,
who take no pleasure in gold.
The baby boys all cut to pieces,   18
the baby girls all crushed.
They have no mercy on the fruit of the womb,
no pity in their eyes for children.
Babylon, that pearl of kingdoms,   19
the jewel and boast of Chaldaeans,
like Sodom and Gomorrah
shall be overthrown by God.
Never more will anyone live there or be born there   20
from generation to generation.
No Arab will pitch his tent there,
nor shepherds feed their flocks.
But beasts of the desert will lie there,   21
and owls fill its houses.
Ostriches will make their home there
and satyrs have their dances there.
Hyenas will call to each other in its keeps,   22
jackals in the luxury of its palaces...
Its time is almost up,
its days will not last long.

The return from the Exile

14 Yes, Yahweh will have pity on Jacob, he will choose Israel once more 1
and settle them in their own country. The foreigner will join them and
attach himself to the House of Jacob. •Nations will take them and lead them 2
to the place they came from, and the House of Israel will adopt them in the land
of Yahweh as slaves and slave-girls. They will capture those who captured them
and master their oppressors.

A satire on the death of a tyrant

The day Yahweh gives you rest after your suffering and torment and the 3
grim servitude to which you were forcibly enslaved, •you are to recite this satire 4
on the king of Babylon:

What was the end of the tyrant?
What was the end of his arrogance?
Yahweh has broken the staff of the wicked   5
and the sceptre of tyrants—
which angrily thrashed the peoples   6

with blow after blow,
which furiously tyrannised over the nations,
persecuting without respite.

7 The whole earth is at rest, it is calm,
shouting for joy.

8 The cypresses, the cedars of Lebanon
rejoice at your fate,
'Now that you have been laid low,
no one comes up to fell us'.

9 On your account Sheol beneath us
is astir to greet your arrival.
To honour you he rouses the ghosts
of all the rulers of the world.
He makes all the kings of the nations
get up from their thrones.

10 Each has something to say
and what they will say to you is this,
'So you too have been brought to nothing, like ourselves.
You, too, have become like us.

11 Your magnificence has been flung down to Sheol
with the music of your harps;
underneath you a bed of maggots,
and over you a blanket of worms.

12 How did you come to fall from the heavens,
Daystar, son of Dawn?
How did you come to be thrown to the ground,
you who enslaved the nations?

13 You who used to think to yourself,
"I will climb up to the heavens;
and higher than the stars of God
I will set my throne.
I will sit on the Mount of Assembly
in the recesses of the north.

14 I will climb to the top of thunderclouds,
I will rival the Most High."

15 What! Now you have fallen to Sheol
to the very bottom of the abyss!'

16 All who see you will gaze at you,
will stare at you,
'Is this the man who made the earth tremble,
and overthrew kingdoms,

17 who made the world a desert
and levelled cities,
who never to his captives
opened the prison gates?'

18 All the kings of the nations lie honourably,
each in his tomb.

19 But you, you have been expelled from your grave
like loathsome dung,
buried under the slaughtered,
under those cut down by the sword,
and thrown on the stones of the ditch
like a mangled carcase.

20 You are never going to rejoin them in the grave,
for you have brought your country to ruin

and destroyed your people.
The offspring of the wicked
will leave no name behind them.
Start slaughtering the sons   21
for the guilt of their fathers!
Never again must they rise to conquer the earth
and spread across the face of the world.

Oracle against Babylon

I will rise against them—it is Yahweh Sabaoth who speaks—and wipe out 22
name and remnant from Babylon. No offspring, no posterity—it is Yahweh
who speaks. •I will turn it into marshland, into a place for hedgehogs. I will 23
sweep it with the broom of destruction—it is Yahweh Sabaoth who speaks.

Assyria will be destroyed

Yahweh Sabaoth has sworn it, saying: Yes,   24
what I have planned shall happen,
what I have decided shall be fulfilled—

to break Assyria in my country,   25
to crush him on my mountains.
His yoke will slip from them,
his burden from their shoulder.

This is the decision taken   26
against the whole world;
this, the hand stretched out
against all the nations.

When Yahweh Sabaoth has made a decision,   27
who would dare cancel it?
When he stretches out his hand,
who can make him withdraw it?

A warning to the Philistines

In the year Ahaz died[a] this oracle was pronounced: 28

Do not rejoice, whole country of Philistia,   29
because the rod that beat you has broken,
since the serpent's stock can still produce a basilisk
and the offspring of that will be a flying dragon.

But the poor are going to feed in my pastures   30
and beggars rest in safety,
while I let your posterity die out through hunger,
killing off any that survive.

Howl, Gate; cry, City;   31
shudder, whole country of Philistia!
For a smoke is coming from the north,
and there are no deserters in those battalions.

What reply will be given then   32
to the messengers of that nation?
'Yahweh has laid the foundations of Zion,
and there the poor of his people shall find refuge.'

Lament for Moab

15 ¹ Oracle on Moab:

The night when Ar was ravaged
Moab collapsed.
The night when Kir was ravaged
Moab collapsed.

² People climb to the temple of Dibon,
climb high places to weep;
on Nebo and in Medeba
Moab laments.

Every head shaven,
every beard clipped;
³ they wear sackcloth in the streets,
and wail on the housetops.

All in the squares are lamenting
and bursting into tears.
⁴ Heshbon and Elealeh are howling,
their noise can be heard as far as Jahaz.
That is why the loins of Moab are shivering,
why its soul is shuddering;
⁵ why the heart of Moab is groaning,
why its fugitives are as far afield as Zoar (Eglath Shelishiyah).

Ah, slopes of Luhith,
they climb them weeping.
On the road to Horonaim
they utter heartrending cries.

⁶ Ah, the waters of Nimrim
are a waste land,
the grass dried up, the turf all withered,
nothing green any more.

⁷ That is why they are busily preparing . . .
And they transport their possessions
across the wadi of the Willows.

⁸ Ah, the shrieking rings round
the whole territory of Moab;
its wailing resounds right to Eglaim,
echoes as far as Beer-elim.

⁹ Ah, the waters of Dibon are swollen with blood,
and worse disasters are still in store for Dibon,
a lion to pounce on anyone who escapes from Moab,
and on the few survivors of that country.

The Moabites take refuge in Judah

16 ¹ Send lambs
to the king of the country
from Sela, by way of the desert,
to the mountain of the daughter of Zion.

² Flying backwards and forwards
like bewildered nestlings,

14 a. In spite of this heading, 'the rod that beat' Philistia must have been Sargon II (died 705).

such are the daughters of Moab
at the ford of the Arnon.

'Advise us what to do,   3
decide for us.

'Spread your shadow as if it were night
at the height of noon.
Hide those who have been driven out,
do not let the refugee be seen.

'Let those who have been driven out of Moab   4
stay with you;
be their refuge
against the destroyer.'

Once the oppression is over,
and the destroyer is no more,
and those now trampling the country underfoot have gone away,
the throne will be made secure in gentleness,   5
and on it there will sit in all fidelity,
within the tent of David,
a judge careful for justice
and eager for integrity.

Lament for Moab

We have heard of the pride of Moab,   6
an excessive pride—
of his conceit, his pride, his arrogance;
his pretensions are empty.

And so the Moabites must mourn for Moab,   7
all of them lamenting together.
For the raisin cakes of Kir-hareseth
they mourn, in their utter bewilderment.

For blighted are the fields of Heshbon,   8
and the vine of Sibmah
whose clusters proved too strong
for the overlords of the nations;

it once reached all the way to Jazer,
had even wound its way into the desert,
and its shoots had spread
even beyond the sea.

And so I weep, as Jazer weeps,   9
for the vine of Sibmah.
I water you with my tears,
Heshbon and Elealeh.

For over your fruit and your vintage
a cheer has been heard;
joy and gladness   10
have vanished from the orchards.

No more revelry in the vineyards,
no more happy shouting;
no more wine trodden out in the presses,
the shouting all silenced.

11   And so for Moab my whole being
         quivers like lyre strings,
         my inmost self, for Kir-hareseth.

12   In vain may Moab go
         to wear himself out at high places,
         to come and pray in his temple;
         he can do nothing.

Oracle on Moab

13
14   Such was the sentence once pronounced against Moab by Yahweh. •Now
Yahweh proclaims, 'Within three years, as a wage-earner reckons them, the
glorious power of Moab, despite his teeming population, will cease to command
respect, and what remains of him will be slight, feeble, impotent'.

Oracle on Damascus

1   **17**   Oracle against Damascus:

         Damascus is going to cease to be a city,
         she will become a heap of ruins.

2   Her towns, abandoned for ever,
         will be pastures for flocks.
         There they will rest with no one to frighten them away.

3   Ephraimª will lose his defences
         and Damascus her sovereignty;
         the remnant of Aram will be treated
         in the same way as the glory of the Israelites.
         It is Yahweh Sabaoth who speaks.

4   That day, the glory of Jacob will be diminished,
         from being fat he will grow lean;

5   as when a reaper hugs an armful of standing corn
         and slices off the ears,
         or when they glean the ears in the Valley of Rephaim:

6   nothing remains but gleanings;
         or when an olive tree is beaten:
         two or three berries left on the topmost bough,
         four or five on the branches of the tree.
         It is Yahweh, the God of Israel, who speaks.

An end to idolatry

7   That day, man will look to his creator and his eyes will turn to the Holy
8 One of Israel. •He will no longer look after the altars, his own handiwork, nor
gaze at what his hands have made: the sacred poles and the solar pillars.

Against the gardens of Adonis

9   That day, your cities will be abandoned
         as were those of the Amorites and the Hivites
         in the path of the children of Israel.
         They will be a desert

10   because you have forgotten the God of your salvation,
         and failed to keep in remembrance the Rock of your strength.
         For you are planting plants for Adonis,
         you put in sprigs of foreign gods,

11   you make them flower the same day as you plant them,
         as soon as it is light your seedlings blossom,

17 a. The kingdom of Israel.

> but all that you pick will vanish on the day of trouble,
> and the evil will be incurable.

The upsurge of the nations

> Vast hordes thundering,   12
> with thunder like thundering seas,
> the roaring of nations roaring
> like the roar of mighty waters.
> (Nations roaring like the roar of many waters.)   13
> He rebukes them
> and far away they flee, driven off
> like chaff on the mountains before the wind,
> like an eddy of dust before the storm.
>
> At evening all was terror;   14
> before morning comes they are no more.
> Such was the lot of our plunderers,
> such, the fate of our despoilers.

Oracle against Cush[a]

18   Country of whirring wings   1
         beyond the rivers of Cush,
> who send ambassadors by sea,   2
> in papyrus skiffs over the waters.
>
> Go, swift messengers
> to a people tall and bronzed,
> to a nation always feared,
> a people mighty and masterful,
> in the country criss-crossed with rivers.
>
> All you who inhabit the world,   3
> you who people the earth,
> the signal is being hoisted on the mountains, look!
> The horn is being sounded, listen!
>
> For thus Yahweh speaks to me: 4
> From where I am I gaze, untroubled,
> like the clear heat produced by light,
> like a dewy mist in the heat of harvest.
>
> For, before the vintage, once the flowering is over   5
> and blossom turns into ripening grape,
> the tendrils are cut back with a pruning knife,
> the shoots taken off, cut away.
>
> They will all be abandoned together   6
> to the birds of prey in the mountains
> and to the beasts of the earth.
> The birds of prey will summer on them,
> and all the beasts of the earth winter on them.

At that time, offerings will be brought to Yahweh Sabaoth on behalf of the   7
tall and bronzed nation, on behalf of the nation always feared, on behalf of the
mighty and masterful people in the country criss-crossed with rivers, to the place
where the name of Yahweh Sabaoth dwells, on Mount Zion.

Against Egypt

19   Oracle against Egypt:

> See! Yahweh, riding a swift cloud,

comes to Egypt.
The idols of Egypt tremble before him,
and the hearts of the Egyptians sink within them.

2　　I will stir up the Egyptians against each other
and they shall fight every man against his brother,
friend against friend, city against city,
kingdom against kingdom.

3　　Egypt is going to be demoralised,
for I shall confound all their wits.
They will consult idols and wizards,
necromancers and sorcerers.

4　　I mean to hand the Egyptians over
to a hard master;
a cruel king will rule them.
It is Yahweh Sabaoth who speaks.

5　　The waters will ebb from the Nile,
the river bed be parched and dry,

6　　the canals grow foul,
the Niles of Egypt sink and dry up.

Rush and reed will droop,
7　　the plants on the banks of the Nile;
all the Nile vegetation will dry up,
blow away, and be seen no more.

8　　The fishermen will groan,
all who cast hook in the Nile will mourn;
those who throw nets on the waters
will lament.

9　　The flax workers will be baffled,
the carders too, and weavers of white cloth

10　　The weavers will be dismayed
and all the workmen dejected.

11　　The princes of Zoan are utter fools,
and Pharaoh's wisest counsellors are stupid;
how can you say to Pharaoh,
'I am a disciple of the sages,
a disciple of bygone kings'?

12　　Where are these sages of yours?
Let them come forward now,
let them explain to you
what Yahweh Sabaoth has decided
to do with Egypt.

13　　The princes of Zoan are fools,
the princes of Noph,[b] self-deceivers;
Egypt is led astray
by the governors of her provinces.

14　　On them Yahweh has poured out

18 a. Egypt, denounced under the ancient name for Ethiopia.
19 a. Probably at the time (718-701) when Egypt was seeking an alliance against Assyria.
b. Memphis.

a spirit of giddiness.
They have Egypt slithering in all she undertakes
as a drunkard slithers in his vomit.

And Egypt will never succeed in anything   15
undertaken by head or by tail, by palm or reed.

The conversion of Egypt and Assyria

That day, the Egyptians will become like women, fearful, terrified, when they 16
see the uplifted hand that Yahweh Sabaoth will raise against them. •The land of 17
Judah will become the terror of Egypt. Whenever Egypt is reminded of this,
she will be terrified, because of the fate Yahweh Sabaoth has prepared for her.
That day, in the land of Egypt there will be five towns speaking the language 18
of Canaan and swearing oaths in the name of Yahweh Sabaoth; Ir Haheres
will be one of them. •That day, there will be an altar to Yahweh in the centre 19
of the land of Egypt and, close to the frontier, a pillar to Yahweh, •which will 20
be both sign and witness of Yahweh Sabaoth in the land of Egypt. When in
oppression the Egyptians cry to Yahweh he will send them a saviour to protect
and deliver them. •Yahweh will reveal himself to them, and that day the Egyptians 21
will acknowledge Yahweh and worship him with sacrifices and offerings. They
will make vows to Yahweh and perform them. •Then, though Yahweh has 22
struck the Egyptians harshly, he will heal them. They will turn to Yahweh who
will listen to them and heal them. •That day, there will be a road from Egypt to 23
Assyria. Assyria will have access to Egypt and Egypt have access to Assyria.
Egypt will serve Assyria.

That day, Israel, making the third with Egypt and Assyria, will be blessed 24
in the centre of the world. •Yahweh Sabaoth will give his blessing in the words, 25
'Blessed be my people Egypt, Assyria my creation, and Israel my heritage'.

Prophecy of the capture of Ashdod[a]

20 The year the cupbearer-in-chief, sent by Sargon king of Assyria, came to 1
Ashdod and stormed and captured it: •at that time Yahweh had spoken 2
through Isaiah son of Amoz. He had said to him, 'Go and undo the sackcloth
round your waist and take the sandals off your feet'. The latter had done so, and
walked about, naked and barefoot. •Yahweh then said, 'As my servant Isaiah has 3
been walking about naked and barefoot for the last three years—a sign and portent
for Egypt and Cush—•so will the king of Assyria lead away captives from 4
Egypt and exiles from Cush, young and old, naked and barefoot, their buttocks
bared, to the shame of Egypt. •You will be frightened and ashamed about 5
Cush in which you trusted, and about Egypt of which you boasted. •And the 6
inhabitants of this coast will say, "Look what has happened to those in whom
we trusted and to whom we fled for help and safety from the king of Assyria!
And now, how are we going to escape?"'

The fall of Babylon

21 Oracle on the maritime plain: 1

     As whirlwinds
     sweeping over the Negeb
     come from the desert,
     from a land of horror
     —a harsh vision has been shown me—   2
     the plunderer plunders,
     the destroyer destroys.

     'Go up, Elam,
     lay siege, Media.

I am putting an end
to groaning.'

3 This is why my loins
are wracked with shuddering;
I am seized with pains
like the pains of a woman in labour;
I am too distressed to hear,
too afraid to see.

4 My heart flutters,
dread makes me tremble,
the twilight I longed for
has become my horror.

5 They spread the table,
cover it with a cloth;
they eat, they drink...
Up, captains,
grease the shield!

6 For this is what the Lord has said to me,
'Go and post the watchman,
and let him report what he sees.

7 'If he sees cavalry,
horsemen two by two,
men mounted on donkeys,
men mounted on camels,
let him observe,
closely observe.'

8 The look-out shouts,
'On a watchtower, Lord,
I stand all day;
and at my post
I keep guard all night'.

9 Look, here come the cavalry,
horsemen two by two.
They spoke to me; they said,
'Fallen, fallen is Babylon,
and all the images of her gods
are shattered on the ground'.

10 You who are threshed,
you who are winnowed,
what I have learnt
from Yahweh Sabaoth,
from the God of Israel,
I am telling you now.

Answer to the Edomites

11 Oracle on Edom:

Someone shouts to me from Seir,
'Watchman, what time of night?
Watchman, what time of night?'

12 The watchman answers,
'Morning is coming, then night again.

20 a. A Philistine town captured in 711.

> If you want to, why not ask,
> turn round, come back?'

Oracle on the Arabs

Oracle in the wastelands.   13

> You who pass the night in the scrublands, in the wastelands,
> you caravans of Dedanites,[a]
> bring water
> for the thirsty.   14
> You inhabitants of Tema
> go and meet the fugitive
> and give him bread;
> since these are fleeing from the swords,   15
> from biting swords,
> from bent bows,
> from the stress of battle.

Against Kedar

Yes, the Lord said this to me, 'In one year's time as a wage-earner reckons   16
it, all the glorious power of Kedar will be finished. • Of the bowmen, of the 17
hardiest sons of Kedar, hardly any will be left, for Yahweh God of Israel has
decreed this.'

Against untimely rejoicing in Jerusalem

22 Oracle against the Valley of Hinnom: 1

> What is the matter now that you are all climbing
> with one accord to the housetops,
> you the uproarious, the boisterous town, the joyful city?   2
> Your slain were not slain by the sword,
> your dead have not fallen in battle;
> your rulers have all fled away   3
> and been captured before bending their bows;
> and the bravest among you have been taken prisoner,
> they have fled far away.
> That is why I say, 'Turn your eyes away from me,   4
> let me weep bitterly;
> do not try to comfort me
> over the destruction of the daughter of my people'.

> For this, a day of panic and rout,   5
> is from the Lord Yahweh Sabaoth.
> In the Valley of Hinnom a wall is thrown down,
> they are shouting for help on the mountains.
> Elam takes up his quiver,   6
> Aram mounts his horse
> and Kir[a] fetches out his shield.
> Your fairest valleys   7
> are filled with chariots
> and the horsemen take up positions at the gates;
> thus falls the defence of Judah.   8

Against military preparations

> You turned your gaze that day
> to the armoury of the House of the Forest.
> You saw how many breaches there were   9
> in the Citadel of David.

You collected the waters
of the lower pool.

10 You counted
the houses of Jerusalem,
and you pulled down houses
to strengthen the wall.

11 In the middle you made a reservoir between the two walls
for the waters of the old pool.
But you had no thought for the Maker,
no eyes for him who shaped everything long ago.

12 The Lord Yahweh Sabaoth called you
that day
to weep and mourn,
to shave your heads, to put on sackcloth;

13 instead, there is joy and amusement,
killing of oxen, slaughtering of sheep,
eating of meat, drinking of wine,
'Let us eat and drink,
for tomorrow we may be dead'.

14 My ears have had this revelation
from Yahweh Sabaoth:
'Most certainly this sin will not be atoned for,
until you die'
says the Lord Yahweh Sabaoth.

Against Shebna

15 Thus says the Lord Yahweh Sabaoth:
Now go to this steward,
to Shebna, the master of the palace,

16 who is hewing a tomb for himself high up,
carving out a room for himself in the rock,
'What right have you here, and what relatives have you here
for you to hew yourself a tomb in this place?

17 See, Yahweh hurls you down,
down with a single throw;
then with a strong grip he grips you,

18 and he winds you up into a ball
and hurls you into an immense country.
There you will die,
and there will be sent the chariots you were so proud of,
you, the disgrace of your master's palace.'

Another oracle against Shebna

19 I dismiss you from your office,
I remove you from your post,

20 and the same day I call on my servant
Eliakim son of Hilkiah.

21 I invest him with your robe,
gird him with your sash,
entrust him with your authority;
and he shall be a father
to the inhabitants of Jerusalem
and to the House of Judah.

21 a. A tribe of Bedouin.
22 a. Three nations defeated by Sennacherib are now providing soldiers for his army.

I place the key of the House of David   22
on his shoulder;
should he open, no one shall close,
should he close, no one shall open.
I drive him like a peg   23
into a firm place;
he will become a throne of glory
for his father's house.

The calamity of the family of Eliakim

On it they will hang all the glory of his father's house, offspring and issue, 24
all the least of vessels from cups to pitchers. •That day—it is Yahweh Sabaoth 25
who speaks—the peg driven into a firm place will give way. It will be torn out
and will fall. And the whole load hanging on it will be shattered, for Yahweh
has spoken.

On Tyre and Sidon

23 Oracle on Tyre: 1

Howl, ships of Tarshish, [a]
for your fortress has been destroyed.
They learn the news
on their way from the land of Kittim. [b]
Be struck dumb, you inhabitants of the coast,   2
you merchants of Sidon,
whose goods travelled over the sea,
over wide oceans.   3
The grain of Nile, the harvest of the river,
formed her revenues,
as she marketed it throughout the world.
Blush, Sidon,   4
for thus speaks the sea,
'I have not laboured nor given birth,
not reared young men
nor brought up young girls'.

When the Egyptians learn the fate of Tyre,   5
they will be appalled.
Take ship for Tarshish, howl,   6
you inhabitants of the coast.

Is this your joyful city   7
founded far back in the past?
Whose footsteps led her abroad
to found her own colonies?
Who took this decision   8
against imperial Tyre,
whose traders were princes,
whose merchants, the great ones of the world?
Yahweh Sabaoth took this decision   9
to humble the pride of all her beauty
and humiliate the great ones of the world.
Till the soil, daughter of Tarshish,   10
the harbour is no more,
He has stretched his hand over the sea   11
to overthrow its kingdoms;
Yahweh has ordained the destruction
of the fortresses of Canaan.

12   He has said: Rejoice no more,
                 ravished one,
                 virgin daughter of Sidon.
             Get up and take ship for Kittim;
                 no respite for you there, either.
13   Look at the land of Kittim. . . .
             They have set up towers.
             They have demolished its bastions
                 and reduced it to ruins.
14   Howl, ships of Tarshish,
                 for your fortress has been destroyed.

The subjection of Tyre

15   That day, Tyre will be forgotten for seventy years. But in the reign of another
         king, at the end of the seventy years, Tyre will become like the whore in the
         song:

16   Take your lyre, walk the town,
                 forgotten whore.
             Play your sweetest, sing your songs again,
                 to make them remember you.

17   At the end of the seventy years Yahweh will visit Tyre. Once again she will
         begin to receive the pay for her whoring. She will play the whore with all the
18   kingdoms on the surface of the earth. •But her profits and wages will be dedicated
         to Yahweh and not stored or hoarded. Her profits will go to buy abundant food
         and splendid clothes for those who live in the presence of Yahweh.

D. APOCALYPSE

The sentence

1   **24**   See how Yahweh lays the earth waste,
                 makes it a desert, buckles its surface,
                 scatters its inhabitants,
2   priest and people alike, master and slave,
                 mistress and maid, seller and buyer,
                 lender and borrower, creditor and debtor.
3   Ravaged, ravaged the earth,
                 despoiled, despoiled,
                 as Yahweh has said.
4   The earth is mourning, withering,
                 the world is pining, withering,
                 the heavens are pining away with the earth.
5   The earth is defiled
                 under its inhabitants' feet,
                 for they have transgressed the law, violated the precept,
                 broken the everlasting covenant.
6   So a curse consumes the earth
                 and its inhabitants suffer the penalty,
                 that is why the inhabitants of the earth are burnt up
                 and few men are left.

The city in ruins

7   The wine is mourning, the vine is pining away,
                 all glad hearts are sighing.

23 a. See note on 2:16.   **b.** Cyprus.

The merry tambourines are silent,   8
the sound of revelling is over,
the merry lyre is silent.
They no longer sing over their wine,   9
the drunkard finds strong drink revolting.
The city of emptiness is in ruins,   10
the entrance to every house is shut.
There is lamentation in the streets: no wine,   11
joy quite gone,
gladness banished from the country.
Nothing but rubble in the city,   12
the gate smashed to pieces;
and so it will be on earth,   13
among the peoples,
as at the beating of the olive trees,
as at the gleaning of the grapes
when the grape harvest is over.

They lift up their voices, singing for joy;   14
they acclaim the majesty of Yahweh from the sea.
Therefore in the islands they give glory to Yahweh,   15
in the islands of the sea, to the name of Yahweh, the God of Israel.
From remotest earth we hear songs, 'Honour to the upright one'.   16

But 'Enough, enough!' I say.
'Woe to the traitors who betray,
to the traitors who treacherously betray!'
Terror, the pit, the snare   17
for you, inhabitants of the earth:
the man who runs away at the cry of terror   18
shall fall into the pit,
and the man who climbs out of the pit
shall be caught in the snare.

Continuation of the poem on the sentence

Yes, the sluicegates above will open,
and the foundations of the earth will rock.   19
The earth will split into fragments,
the earth will be riven and rent.
The earth will shiver and shake,   20
the earth will stagger like a drunkard,
sway like a shanty;
so heavy will be its sin on it, it will fall
never to rise again.   21
That day, Yahweh will punish
above, the armies of the sky,
below, the kings of the earth;
they will be herded together,   22
shut up in a dungeon,
confined in a prison
and, after long years, punished.
The moon will hide her face, the sun be ashamed,   23
for Yahweh Sabaoth will be king
on Mount Zion, in Jerusalem,
and his glory will shine in the presence of his elders.

A prayer of thanksgiving

25

1 Yahweh, you are my God,
I extol you, I praise your name;
for you have carried out your excellent design,
long planned, trustworthy, true.

2 For you have made the town a heap of stones,
the fortified city a ruin.
The citadel of the proud is a city no longer,
it will never be rebuilt.

3 Hence a mighty people gives you glory,
the city of pitiless nations holds you in awe;

4 for you are a refuge for the poor,
a refuge for the needy in distress,
a shelter from the storm,
a shade from the heat;
while the breath of pitiless men
is like the winter storm.

5 Like drought in a dry land
you will repress the clamour of the proud;
like heat by the shadow of a cloud
the singing of the despots will be subdued.

The messianic banquet

6 On this mountain,
Yahweh Sabaoth will prepare for all peoples
a banquet of rich food, a banquet of fine wines,
of food rich and juicy, of fine strained wines.

7 On this mountain he will remove
the mourning veil covering all peoples,
and the shroud enwrapping all nations,

8 he will destroy Death for ever.
The Lord Yahweh will wipe away
the tears from every cheek;
he will take away his people's shame
everywhere on earth,
for Yahweh has said so.

9 That day, it will be said: See, this is our God
in whom we hoped for salvation;
Yahweh is the one in whom we hoped.
We exult and we rejoice
that he has saved us;

10 for the hand of Yahweh
rests on this mountain.
Moab is trodden down where he stands
as straw is trodden in the dung pit;

11 and there he stretches out his hands
like a swimmer stretching out his hands to swim.
But Yahweh curbs his pride
and whatever his hands attempt.

12 Your arrogant, lofty walls
he destroys, he overthrows,
he flings them in the dust.

Song of victory

26

1 That day, this song will be sung in the land of Judah:
We have a strong city;

to guard us he has set
wall and rampart about us.
Open the gates! Let the upright nation come in,   2
she, the faithful one
whose mind is steadfast, who keeps the peace,   3
because she trusts in you.
Trust in Yahweh for ever,   4
for Yahweh is the everlasting Rock;
he has brought low those who lived high up   5
in the steep citadel;
he brings it down, brings it down to the ground,
flings it down in the dust:
the feet of the lowly, the footsteps of the poor   6
trample on it.

A psalm

The path of the upright man is straight,   7
you smooth the way of the upright.
Following the path of your judgements,   8
we hoped in you, Yahweh,
your name, your memory are all my soul desires.

At night my soul longs for you   9
and my spirit in me seeks for you;
when your judgements appear on earth
the inhabitants of the world learn the meaning of integrity.

If favour is shown to the wicked,   10
he does not learn the meaning of integrity.
He does evil in the land of uprightness,
he fails to see the majesty of Yahweh.

Yahweh, your hand is raised,   11
but they do not see it.
Let them see your jealous love for this people and be ashamed,
let the fire prepared for your enemies consume them.

Yahweh, you are giving us peace,   12
since you treat us
as our deeds deserve.

Yahweh our God,   13
other lords than you have ruled us,
but we acknowledge no one other than you,
no other name than yours.

The dead will not come to life,   14
their ghosts will not rise,
for you have punished them, annihilated them,
and wiped out their memory.

Enlarge the nation, Yahweh, enlarge it,   15
to the nation grant glory,
extend all the frontiers of the country.

Distressed, we search for you, Yahweh;   16
the misery of oppression was your punishment for us.
As a woman with child near her time   17
writhes and cries out in her pangs,

so are we, Yahweh, in your presence:

18 we have conceived, we writhe
    as if we were giving birth;
    we have not given the spirit of salvation to the earth,
    no more inhabitants of the world are born.

19 Your dead will come to life,
    their corpses will rise;
    awake, exult,
    all you who lie in the dust,
    for your dew is a radiant dew
    and the land of ghosts will give birth.

Oracle

20 Go into your rooms, my people,
    shut your doors behind you.
    Hide yourselves a little while
    until the wrath has passed.

21 For, see, Yahweh will soon come out of his dwelling,
    to punish all the inhabitants of earth for their crimes.
    The earth will reveal its blood
    and no longer hide its slain.

1 **27** That day, Yahweh will punish,
    with his hard sword, massive and strong,
    Leviathan the fleeing serpent,
    Leviathan the twisting serpent:
    he will kill the sea-dragon.

The vineyard of Yahweh

2   That day,
    sing of the delightful vineyard!
3   I, Yahweh, am its keeper;
    every moment I water it
    for fear its leaves should fall;
    night and day I watch over it.

4   I am angry no longer.
    If thorns and briars come
    I will declare war on them,
    I will burn them every one.
5   Or if they would shelter under my protection,
    let them make their peace with me,
    let them make their peace with me.

Pardon for Jacob; punishment for the oppressor

6   In the days to come, Jacob will put out shoots,
    Israel will bud and blossom
    and fill the whole world with fruit.
7   Has he beaten her as he beat those who beat her?
    Has he murdered her as he murdered those who murdered her?
8   You have punished it with expulsion and exile;
    he pursued it with a blast as fierce as the wind from the east.
9   Now here is how Jacob's guilt will be atoned for,
    here is the ransom for its sin:
    he treats all the altar stones
    like lumps of chalk that are ground to powder.

Sacred poles and solar pillars stand no longer,
for the fortified city is abandoned now,
it lies deserted,
forsaken as a wilderness.
There the herd grazes,
there it rests and browses on the branches.
The boughs are dry and broken,
women come and use them for firewood;
for this is a nation without understanding
and so its Maker will have no pity for it,
he that shaped it will show it no favour.

Oracle

That day, Yahweh will start his threshing
from the course of the River to the wadi of Egypt,
and you will be gathered one by one,
sons of Israel.
That day, the great trumpet will be sounded,
and those lost in the land of Assyria will come,
and those exiled to the land of Egypt,
and they will worship Yahweh
on the holy mountain, in Jerusalem.

E. POEMS ON ISRAEL AND JUDAH

A warning to Samaria

28

Woe to the haughty crown of Ephraim's drunkards,
to the fading flower of its proud splendour
overlooking the lush valley,
to those prostrated by wine!
See, a strong and mighty one, sent by the Lord,
like a storm of hail, a destroying tempest,
like a storm of torrential, overflowing waters;
with his hand he throws them to the ground.
There will be trampled underfoot
the haughty crown of Ephraim's drunkards,
and the faded flower of its proud splendour
overlooking the lush valley.
Just like a fig before summer comes:
whoever notices it, picks it,
no sooner in the hand than swallowed.

That day, Yahweh Sabaoth
will be a crown of glory
and a diadem of splendour
for the remnant of his people,
a spirit of justice
for him who sits in judgement,
and a spirit of courage
for him who thrusts back the attacker to the gate.

Against the priests and the false prophets

These, too, are reeling with wine,
staggering from strong drink.
Priest and prophet are reeling
from strong drink,

they are muddled with wine;
strong drink makes them stagger,
they totter when they are having visions,
they stumble when they are giving judgement.

8   Yes, all the tables are covered with vomit,
not a place left clean.

9   'Who does he think he is lecturing?
Who does he think his message is for?
Babies just weaned?
Babies just taken from the breast?

10   With his
sav lasav, sav lasav,
kav lakav, kav lakav,
zeer sham, zeer sham !'ᵃ

11   Yes, certainly with stammering lips
and in a foreign language,
he will talk to this nation,

12   he who once told them: Here is rest;
let the weary rest.
Here is repose.
—But they would not listen.

13   That is why Yahweh now says:
kav lakav, kav lakav,
sav lasav, sav lasav,
zeer sham, zeer sham.
So that when they walk they may fall over backwards
and be broken, snared and made captive.

Against evil counsellors

14   Listen to the word of Yahweh,
you scoffers,
rulers of this people
in Jerusalem.

15   You say, 'We have made
a covenant with Mot,ᵇ
and with Sheol
we have made a pact.
The destructive whip, as it goes by,
will not catch us,
for we have made lies our refuge,
and falsehood our shelter.'

Oracle

16   That is why the Lord Yahweh says this:
See how I lay in Zion
a stone of witness,
a precious cornerstone, a foundation stone:
The believer shall not stumble.

17   And I will make justice the measure,
integrity the plumb-line.

28 a. Described in the next verse as 'stammering and in a foreign language': the impression
made by Isaiah's preaching on his hearers.   **b.** Phoenician god, known to the Egyptians as
Osiris.

Continuation of the poem against evil counsellors

But hail will sweep away the refuge of lies
and floods overwhelm the shelter;
your covenant with Mot will be broken   18
and your pact with Sheol annulled.
When the destructive whip goes by
it will crush you;
each time it goes by,   19
it will seize you.
It will go by, morning after morning,
both day and night;
what panic there would be
if you were to understand what it meant!
The bed is too short to stretch in,   20
the blanket too narrow for covering.
Yes, as Yahweh did on Mount Perazim, he is going to rise,   21
as he did in the Valley of Gibeon he is going to stir himself
to do the deed, his extraordinary deed,
to work the work, his mysterious work.

Stop scoffing, then,   22
or your bonds will be tightened further;
for I have listened to the warrant of destruction
issued against the whole country
by the Lord Yahweh Sabaoth.

The parable of the farmer

Listen closely to my words,   23
be attentive and understand what I am saying.
Does the ploughman do nothing but plough   24
and turn the soil and harrow it?
Will he not, after he has levelled it,   25
scatter fennel, sow cummin,
put in wheat and barley
and, on the edges, spelt?
He has been taught this discipline   26
by his God who instructs him.

For fennel must not be crushed,   27
nor a drag be rolled over cummin;
fennel must be beaten with a stick,
and cummin with a flail.
Does a man crush wheat? No;   28
he does not thresh it endlessly.
When he has rolled the drag over it
he winnows it without crushing it.
This too comes from Yahweh Sabaoth,   29
whose advice is always admirable,
whose deeds are very great.

Oracle on Ariel[a]

29

Woe, Ariel, Ariel,   1
city where David encamped.
Let a year or two pass,
let the feasts make their full round
then I will lay siege to Ariel,   2
and there will be moaning and bemoaning.

You will be an Ariel for me,
3   like David I will encamp against you,
     I will blockade you with palisades,
     and mount siege-works against you.

4   Thrown down—you will speak from the ground,
     your words will come muffled by dust.
     Your voice will rise from the earth like a ghost's,
     you will speak from the dust in a whisper.

5c   Suddenly, unexpectedly,
6   you shall be visited by Yahweh Sabaoth
     with thunder, earthquake, mighty din,
     hurricane, tempest, flame of devouring fire.

5ab The horde of your enemies shall be scattered like fine dust,
     the tyrant horde like flying chaff;
     the horde of all the nations at war with Ariel
7   shall vanish like a dream, like a vision at night.

     And all those fighting against her,
     the entrenchments besieging her,
8   shall be like the hungry man who dreams he eats,
     and wakes with an empty belly,

     like the thirsty man who dreams he drinks
     and wakes exhausted, his throat parched;
     so shall it be with the horde of all the nations
     making war on Mount Zion.

9   Be stupefied and stunned,
     go blind, unseeing,
     drunk but not on wine,
     staggering but not through liquor.

10   For on you has Yahweh poured
     a spirit of lethargy,
     he has closed your eyes (the prophets),
     he has veiled your heads (the seers).

Secrecy of the revelation

11   For you every vision has become like the words of a sealed book. You give
     it to someone able to read and say, 'Read that'. He replies, 'I cannot, because
12   the book is sealed'. •Or else you give the book to someone who cannot read,
     and say, 'Read that'. He replies, 'I cannot read'.

Oracle

13   Yahweh has said: Because this people
     approaches me only in words,
     honours me only with lip-service
     while its heart is far from me,
     and my religion, as far as it is concerned,
     is nothing but human commandment, a lesson memorised,
14   very well, I shall have to go on
     being prodigal of prodigious prodigies with this people.
     The wisdom of its sages shall decay,
     the intelligence of its intelligent men shall be shrouded.

29 a. Ariel is 'lion of God'; here it signifies Jerusalem.

Against evil counsellors

Woe to those who hide from Yahweh   15
to conceal their plans,
who scheme in the dark
and say, 'Who can see us? Who can recognise us?'

What perversity this is!   16
Is the potter no better than the clay?
Can something that was made say of its maker,
'He did not make me'?
Or a pot say of the potter,
'He is a fool'?

In a short time, a very short time,   17
shall not Lebanon become fertile land
and fertile land turn into forest?
The deaf, that day,   18
will hear the words of a book
and, after shadow and darkness,
the eyes of the blind will see.

But the lowly will rejoice in Yahweh even more   19
and the poorest exult in the Holy One of Israel;
for tyrants shall be no more, and scoffers vanish,   20
and all be destroyed who are disposed to do evil:

those who gossip to incriminate others,   21
those who try at the gate to trip the arbitrator
and get the upright man's case dismissed for groundless reasons.

Therefore Yahweh speaks,   22
the God of the House of Jacob,
Abraham's redeemer:
No longer shall Jacob be ashamed,
no more shall his face grow pale,
for he shall see what my hands have done in his midst,   23
he shall hold my name holy.
They will hallow the Holy One of Jacob,
stand in awe of the God of Israel.
Erring spirits will learn wisdom   24
and murmurers accept instruction.

Against the embassy to Egypt

30 Woe to those rebellious sons!   1
—it is Yahweh who speaks.
They carry out plans that are not mine
and make alliances not inspired by me,
and so add
sin to sin.

They have left for Egypt,   2
without consulting me,
to take refuge in Pharaoh's protection,
to shelter in Egypt's shadow.
Pharaoh's protection will be your shame,   3
the shelter of Egypt's shadow your confounding.
For his ministers have gone to Zoan,   4
his ambassadors have already reached Hanes.ᵃ
All are carrying gifts   5

to a nation that will be of no use to them,
that will bring them neither aid, nor help,
nothing but shame and disgrace.

A second oracle against the embassy

6   Oracle on the beasts of the Negeb.

Through the land of distress and of anguish,
of lioness and roaring lion,
of viper and flying serpent,

they bear their riches on donkeys' backs,
their treasures on camels' humps,
to a nation that is of no use to them,

7   to Egypt who will prove futile and empty to them;
and so I call her
Rahab-do-nothing.

The testament of Isaiah

8   Now go and inscribe this on a tablet,
write it in a book,
that it may serve in the time to come
as a witness for ever:

9   This is a rebellious people,
they are lying sons,
sons who will not listen
to Yahweh's orders.

10   To the seers they say,
'See no visions';
to the prophets,
'Do not prophesy the truth to us,

'tell us flattering things,
have illusory visions;

11   turn aside from the way, leave the path,
take the Holy One out of our sight'.

12   So the Holy One of Israel says:
Since you reject this warning
and prefer to trust in wile and guile
and to rely on these,

13   then your guilt will prove
to be for you
a breach on the point of collapse,
the bulge at the top of the city wall

which suddenly and all at once
comes crashing down,

14   irretrievably shattered,
smashed like an earthenware pot
—so that of the fragments not one shard remains big enough to carry
a cinder from the hearth or scoop water from the cistern.

15   For thus says the Lord Yahweh, the Holy One of Israel:
Your salvation lay in conversion and tranquillity,
your strength, in complete trust;

30 a. Zoan and Hanes are Tanis and Anusis, in the Egyptian delta.

and you would have none of it.

'No,' you said 'we will flee on horses.'   16
So be it, flee then!
And you add, 'In swift chariots'.
So be it, your pursuers will be swift too.

A thousand will flee at the threat of one   17
and when five threaten you will flee,
until what is left of you will be
like a flagstaff on a mountain top,
like a signal on a hill.

But Yahweh is waiting to be gracious to you,   18
to rise and take pity on you,
for Yahweh is a just God;
happy are all who hope in him.

The coming prosperity

Yes, people of Zion, you will live in Jerusalem and weep no more. He will 19
be gracious to you when he hears your cry; when he hears he will answer. •When 20
the Lord has given you the bread of suffering and the water of distress, he who
is your teacher will hide no longer, and you will see your teacher with your own
eyes. •Whether you turn to right or left, your ears will hear these words 21
behind you, 'This is the way, follow it'. •You will regard your silvered idols 22
and gilded images as unclean. You will throw them away like the polluted things
they are, shouting after them, 'Good riddance!' •He will send rain for the seed 23
you sow in the ground, and the bread that the ground provides will be rich and
nourishing. Your cattle will graze, that day, in wide pastures. •Oxen and donkeys 24
that till the ground will eat a salted fodder, winnowed with shovel and fork.
On every lofty mountain, on every high hill there will be streams and watercourses, 25
on the day of the great slaughter when the strongholds fall. •Then moonlight will 26
be bright as sunlight and sunlight itself be seven times brighter—like the light
of seven days in one—on the day Yahweh dresses the wound of his people and
heals the bruises his blows have left.

Assyria will be sacrificed

See, the name of Yahweh comes from afar,   27
blazing is his anger, heavy his exaction.
His lips brim with fury,
his tongue is like a devouring fire.
His breath is like a river in spate   28
coming up to the neck.
He comes to sift the nations with the sieve of destruction,
to put the bit of his bridle between the jaws of the nations.
Yahweh will make his majestic voice be heard   30
and display his arm falling to strike,
in the ferocity of his anger, in the glare of a devouring fire,
in cloudburst, downpour, hailstones.

For at the voice of Yahweh Assyria will be battered   31
and beaten with the rod.
Each time he will feel the punishing rod   32
that Yahweh will lay on him.

The song you sing will be like that on a festal night   29
when hearts are gay,
or when to the sound of flute men make

a pilgrimage to the mountain of Yahweh,
to the rock of Israel,

32b
with music of tambourine and harp
and with dancing...

33
For in Topheth there has been prepared beforehand, [b]
yes, made ready for Molech,
a pit deep and wide
with straw and wood in plenty.
The breath of Yahweh, like a stream of brimstone,
will set fire to it.

Against Egypt

1
31
Woe to those who go down to Egypt
to seek help there,
who build their hopes on cavalry,
who rely on the number of chariots
and on the strength of mounted men,
but never look to the Holy One of Israel
nor consult Yahweh.

2
Yet he too is skilled in working disaster,
and he has not gone back on his word;
he will rise against the house of the wicked,
and against the protectors of evil men.

3
The Egyptian is a man, not a god,
his horses are flesh, not spirit;
Yahweh will stretch out his hand
to make the protector stumble;
the protected will fall
and all will perish together.

Yahweh wages war against Assyria

4
Yes, this is what Yahweh has said to me:
As a lion or lion cub
growls over its prey,
and even when a whole band of shepherds
gathers against him,
he is not frightened by their shouting
or alarmed by the noise they make,
just so will Yahweh Sabaoth descend to fight
on Mount Zion and on its hill.

5
Like hovering birds
so will Yahweh Sabaoth protect Jerusalem,
he will protect it, rescue it,
spare it and save it.

6
Come back to the one you have so wickedly betrayed,
sons of Israel.

7
Yes, that day, every one of you will throw away the silver idols and gold
idols which you have made with your guilty hands.

8
Assyria will fall by a sword that is not man's,
will be devoured by a sword that is more than human,
he will flee before the sword

b. Topheth is the place where human sacrifice was offered to Molech.

and his young warriors will be enslaved.
In his terror he will abandon his rock,   9
and his panic-stricken leaders desert their standard.
It is Yahweh who speaks, whose fire is in Zion,
and his furnace in Jerusalem.

The integrity of the king

32   A king reigns by integrity   1
and princes rule by law;
each is like a shelter from the wind,   2
a refuge from the storm,
like streams of water in dry places,
like the shade of a great rock in a thirsty land.
The eyes of those who see will no longer be closed,   3
the ears of those who hear will be alert,
the heart of the hasty will learn to judge,   4
the tongue of stammerers will speak clearly,
the fool will no more be called noble,   5
nor the villain be styled honourable.

Contrasts between fool and noble

For the fool speaks folly,   6
and his heart meditates wickedness,
that he may practise godlessness
and speak wild words about Yahweh,
and leave the hungry man's craving unsatisfied,
and refuse drink to the thirsty.

And the villain—his villainies are evil;   7
he devises wicked plots
to ruin the poor with lies
even when the cause of these lowly ones is just;
but the noble man plans only noble things   8
and bears himself nobly.

A warning to idle women

Stand up, you idle women,   9
listen to my words;
you over-confident daughters,
pay attention to what I say.

Within one year and a few days   10
you will tremble, you over-confident women;
the grape harvest will be over,
gathering will not come again.

Shudder, you idle women,   11
tremble, you over-confident women;
strip, undress,
put sackcloth round your waists.

Beat your breasts,   12
for the pleasant fields,
for the fruitful vine,
for the soil of my people   13
where thorns and briars grow,
for all the happy houses,
for the gay city.

14 Since the palace has been abandoned
and the noisy city deserted,
Ophel and Keep become
caverns for ever,
the playground of wild asses
and the pasture of flocks.

Salvation from Yahweh

15 Once more there will be poured on us
the spirit from above;
then shall the wilderness be fertile land
and fertile land become forest.

16 In the wilderness justice will come to live
and integrity in the fertile land;
17 integrity will bring peace,
justice give lasting security.

18 My people will live in a peaceful home,
in safe houses,
in quiet dwellings
19 —the forest shall be beaten down and the city laid low.
20 Happy will you be, sowing by every stream,
letting ox and donkey roam free.

Psalm of hope in Yahweh

33

1 Woe to you, ravager never ravaged,
plunderer never plundered!
When your ravaging is over, you shall be ravaged;
when your plundering is done, you shall be plundered.

2 Yahweh, have pity on us,
we hope in you.
Be our strong arm each morning,
our salvation in time of distress.

3 At the sound of your threat peoples flee,
when you rise nations scatter,
4 they gather loot as the grasshopper gathers,
they leap on it as locusts leap.

5 Yahweh is exalted, for he is enthroned above,
and fills Zion with justice and integrity.

6 Your continuance is assured;
wisdom and knowledge are riches that save,
the fear of Yahweh is his treasure.

The intervention of Yahweh

7 Look, Ariel is lamenting in the streets,
the ambassadors of peace weep bitterly.

8 The highways are deserted,
no travellers use the roads.
Treaties are broken, witnesses despised,
there is respect for no one.

9 The land mourns, it pines away,
Lebanon is withered with shame,
Sharon is a desert,
Bashan and Carmel are stripped bare.

'Now I stand up,' says Yahweh　　　　　　　　　10
'now I rise to my full height.
You have conceived chaff, you will give birth to straw,　　11
my breath shall devour you like fire.

'The peoples will be reduced to lime,　　　　　　　12
like cut thorns they will be burnt in the fire.
You who are far away, listen to what I have done,　　13
and you who are near, realise my strength.'

Sinners in Zion are struck with horror　　　　　14
and fear seizes on the godless.
Which of us can live with this devouring fire,
which of us exist in everlasting flames?

—He who acts with integrity,　　　　　　　15
who speaks sincerely
and rejects extortionate profit,
who waves away bribes from his hands,
shuts suggestions of murder out of his ears
and closes his eyes against crime;

this man will dwell in the heights,　　　　　16
he will find refuge in a citadel built on rock,
bread will be given him, he shall not want for water.

The glorious future

Your eyes are going to look on a king in his beauty,　　17
they will see an immense country;
your heart will look back on its fears:　　　　　18
where is he who counted,
where is he who weighed out,
where is he who counted the precious stones?
You will no longer see the overweening people,　　19
the people of obscure, unintelligible speech,
of barbarous, senseless tongue.

Look on Zion, city of our feasts,　　　　　20
your eyes will see Jerusalem
as a home that is secure,
a tent not to be moved:
its pegs not pulled out,
not one of its ropes broken.

There Yahweh is princely to us,　　　　　21
on the banks of broad-spreading rivers,
where there rows no galley,
there passes no majestic ship:
its tackle hangs loose,　　　　　　　23a
it supports the mast no longer,
it does not hoist the pennon.
For Yahweh is our judge, Yahweh our lawgiver,　　22
Yahweh our King and our saviour.
Then immense booty shall be shared out,　　23b
even the lame fall to plundering,
no one living there shall say, 'I am sickly';　　24
the people who live there will be forgiven all their faults.

The end of Edom

34

1 Come near and listen, all you races,
pay attention all you nations,
listen, earth and all that you hold,
world and all that comes from you.

2 Yahweh is angry with all the nations,
enraged with all their hordes.
He has vowed them to destruction,
and marked them down for slaughter.

3 Their dead are thrown into the streets,
a stench comes up from their corpses,
the mountains run with their blood,

4 the armies of heaven rot.

The heavens are rolled up like a scroll
and their armies all drop like leaves,
like vine leaves falling,
like falling fig leaves.

5 For my sword has drunk deep in the heavens...
See now how it slashes through Edom,
through the people I have condemned to be punished.

6 The sword of Yahweh is gorged with blood,
it is glutted with fat,
the blood of lambs and goats,
the fat of the saddle of rams.

For Yahweh has a sacrifice in Bozrah,
a great slaughter in the land of Edom.

7 But instead of wild oxen, nations fall,
in place of bulls, a race of mighty men.

Their land is drenched with blood,
its dust is sodden with fat,

8 for this is the day of Yahweh's vengeance,
the year of revenge for the defender of Zion.

9 Its streams turn into pitch,
its dust into brimstone,
its land becomes blazing pitch...

10 Never quenched night or day,
its smoke goes up for ever,
it shall lie waste age after age,
no one will pass through it.

11 It will be the haunt of pelican and hedgehog,
the owl and the raven will live there;
over it Yahweh will stretch the measuring line of chaos
and the plumb-line of emptiness.

12 The satyrs will make their home there,
its nobles will be no more,
kings will not be proclaimed there,
all its princes will be brought to nothing.

13 Thorns will grow in the palaces there,
thistles and nettles in its fortresses,
it will be a lair for jackals,

a lodging for ostriches.

Wild cats will meet hyenas there,
the satyrs will call to each other,
there too will Lilith take cover
seeking rest.

14

The viper will nest and lay eggs there,
will brood and hatch its eggs;
kites will gather there
and make it their meeting place.

15

16c

Search in the book of Yahweh, and read,
not one of these is missing;
for his mouth has ordained it,
and his spirit has brought them together.

16ab

He has drawn lots for the share of each,
his hand has divided the land with the line.
They shall possess it for ever,
and live there age after age.

17

The judgement of God

35 Let the wilderness and the dry-lands exult,
let the wasteland rejoice and bloom,
let it bring forth flowers like the jonquil,
let it rejoice and sing for joy.

1

2

The glory of Lebanon is bestowed on it,
the splendour of Carmel and Sharon;
they shall see the glory of Yahweh,
the splendour of our God.

Strengthen all weary hands,
steady all trembling knees
and say to all faint hearts,
'Courage! Do not be afraid.

3

4

'Look, your God is coming,
vengeance is coming,
the retribution of God;
he is coming to save you.'

Then the eyes of the blind shall be opened,
the ears of the deaf unsealed,
then the lame shall leap like a deer
and the tongues of the dumb sing for joy;

5

6

for water gushes in the desert,
streams in the wasteland,
the scorched earth becomes a lake,
the parched land springs of water.

7

The lairs where the jackals used to live
become thickets of reed and papyrus...

And through it will run a highway undefiled
which shall be called the Sacred Way;
the unclean may not travel by it,
nor fools stray along it.

8

9 No lion will be there
  nor any fierce beast roam about it,
  but the redeemed will walk there,
10 for those Yahweh has ransomed shall return.

They will come to Zion shouting for joy,
everlasting joy on their faces;
joy and gladness will go with them
and sorrow and lament be ended.

APPENDIX

Sennacherib's invasion

1 **36** In the fourteenth year of King Hezekiah, Sennacherib king of Assyria
2 attacked all the fortified towns of Judah and captured them. •From Lachish
the king of Assyria sent the cupbearer-in-chief with a large force to King Hezekiah
in Jerusalem. The cupbearer-in-chief took up a position near the conduit of the
3 upper pool on the road to the Fuller's Field. •The master of the palace, Eliakim
son of Hilkiah, Shebna the secretary and the herald Joah son of Asaph went
4 out to him. •The cupbearer-in-chief said to them, 'Say to Hezekiah, "The great
5 king, the king of Assyria, says to you: What makes you so confident? •Do you
think empty words are as good as strategy and military strength? Who are you
6 relying on, to dare to rebel against me? • We know you are relying on that broken
reed—Egypt—which pricks and pierces the hand of the man who leans on it.
7 — That is what Pharaoh, king of Egypt, is like to all who rely on him. — •You
may say to me: We rely on Yahweh our God, but are they not his high places
and altars that Hezekiah has suppressed, saying to the people of Judah and
8 Jerusalem: Here is the altar before which you must worship? •Come, make
a wager with my lord the king of Assyria: I will give you two thousand horses
9 if you can find horsemen to ride them. •How could you repulse a single one
of the least of my master's servants? And yet you have relied on Egypt for chariots
10 and horsemen. •And lastly, have I come up against this country to lay it waste
without warrant from Yahweh? Yahweh himself said to me: March against
this country and lay it waste."' '

11 Eliakim, Shebna and Joah said to the cupbearer-in-chief, 'Please speak to
your servants in Aramaic, for we understand it; do not speak to us in the
12 Judaean language within earshot of the people on the ramparts'. •But the
cupbearer-in-chief said, 'Do you think my lord sent me here to say these things
to your master or to you? On the contrary, it was to the people sitting on the
ramparts who, like you, are doomed to eat their own dung and drink their own
urine.'
13 Then the cupbearer-in-chief stood erect and, shouting loudly in the Judaean
language, called out, 'Listen to the words of the great king, the king of Assyria.
14 The king says to you: "Do not let Hezekiah delude you! He will be powerless
15 to save you. •Do not let Hezekiah persuade you to rely on Yahweh by saying:
Yahweh is sure to save us; this city will not fall into the power of the king of
16 Assyria." •Do not listen to Hezekiah, for the king of Assyria says: Make
17 peace with me, •surrender to me, and every one of you will eat the fruit of his
own vine and of his own fig tree and drink the water of his own cistern until
I come and deport you to a country like your own, a land of corn and good wine,
18 a land of bread and of vineyards. •Do not let Hezekiah delude you by saying:
Yahweh will save you. Has any god of any nation saved his country from
19 the power of the king of Assyria? •Where are the gods of Hamath and Arpad?
Where are the gods of Sepharvaim? Where are the gods of the land of Samaria?
20 Did they save Samaria from me? •Tell me which of all the gods of these countries

have saved their countries from my hands, for Yahweh to be able to save Jerusalem?"

They kept silence and said nothing in reply, since this was the king's order: 21 'Do not answer him' he had said. •The master of the palace, Eliakim son of 22 Hilkiah, Shebna the secretary and the herald Joah son of Asaph, with their garments torn, went to Hezekiah and reported what the cupbearer-in-chief had said.

The prophet Isaiah is consulted

37 On hearing this, King Hezekiah tore his garments, covered himself with 1 sackcloth and went to the Temple of Yahweh. •He sent the master of the 2 palace, Eliakim, Shebna the secretary and the elders of the priests, covered in sackcloth, to the prophet Isaiah son of Amoz. •They said to him, 'This is 3 what Hezekiah says, "Today is a day of suffering, of punishment, of disgrace. Children come to birth and there is no strength to bring them forth. •May Yahweh 4 your God hear the words of the cupbearer-in-chief whom his master, the king of Assyria, has sent to insult the living God, and may Yahweh your God punish the words he has heard! Offer your prayer for the remnant that is left." '

When the ministers of King Hezekiah had come to Isaiah, •he replied, 'Say $^5_6$ to your master, "Yahweh says this: Do not be afraid of the words you have heard or the blasphemies the minions of the king of Assyria have uttered against me. •I am going to put a spirit in him, and when he hears a rumour he will 7 return to his own country and in that country I will bring him down with the sword." '

The cupbearer returns to his master

The cupbearer went back and rejoined the king of Assyria at Libnah, which he 8 was attacking. The cupbearer had already learnt that the king of Assyria had left Lachish, •since he had received this news about Tirhakah king of Cush: 'He has 9 set out to fight you'.

Second account of Sennacherib's activities

Sennacherib sent messengers to Hezekiah again, saying, •'Tell this to 10 Hezekiah king of Judah, "Do not let your God on whom you are relying deceive you when he says: Jerusalem shall not fall into the power of the king of Assyria. You have learnt by now what the kings of Assyria have done to every country, 11 putting them all under the ban. Are you likely to be spared? •What power to 12 help did the gods have of those nations my fathers destroyed, Gozen, Haran, Rezeph and the Edenites who were in Tel Basar? •Where are the king of 13 Hamath, the king of Arpad, the kings of Sepharvaim, of Hena, of Ivvah?" '

Hezekiah took the letter from the hands of the messengers and read it; he 14 then went up to the Temple of Yahweh and spread it out before Yahweh. Hezekiah said this prayer in the presence of Yahweh, •'Yahweh Sabaoth, God $^{15}_{16}$ of Israel, enthroned on the cherubs, you alone are God of all the kingdoms of the earth, you have made heaven and earth.

'Give ear, Yahweh, and listen.   17
Open your eyes, Yahweh, and see.
Hear the words of Sennacherib
who has sent to insult the living God.

'It is true, Yahweh, that the kings of Assyria have exterminated all the nations 18 and their countries, •they have thrown their gods on the fire, for these were 19 not gods but the work of men's hands, wood and stone, and hence they have destroyed them. •But now, Yahweh our God, save us from his hand, and let 20 all the kingdoms of the earth know that you alone are God, Yahweh.'

Isaiah intervenes

21   Then Isaiah son of Amoz sent to Hezekiah. 'This' he said 'is what Yahweh, the God of Israel, says in answer to the prayer you have addressed to me about
22   Sennacherib king of Assyria. •Here is the oracle that Yahweh has pronounced against him:

23   "She despises you, she scorns you,
           the virgin, daughter of Zion;
           she tosses her head behind you,
           the daughter of Jerusalem.
           Whom have you insulted, whom did you blaspheme?
           Against whom raised your voice
           and lifted your insolent eyes?
           Against the Holy One of Israel.

24   Through your minions you have insulted the Lord;
           you have said: With my many chariots
           I have climbed the tops of mountains,
           the utmost peaks of Lebanon.
           I have felled its tall forest of cedars,
           its finest cypresses.
           I have reached its furthest recesses,
           its forest garden.

25   Yes I have dug wells and drunk
           of alien waters;
           I have put down my feet, and have dried up
           all the rivers of Egypt.

26   "Do you hear? Long ago
           I planned for it,
           from days of old I designed it,
           now I carry it out.
           Your part was to bring down in heaps of ruins
           fortified cities.

27   Their inhabitants, hands feeble,
           dismayed, discomfited,
           were like plants of the field,
           like tender grass,
           like grass of housetop and meadow,
           under the east wind.

28   I know whenever you rise •and whenever you sit,
           your going out, your coming in.

29   Because you have raved against me
           and your insolence has come to my ears,
           I will put my ring through your nostrils,
           my bit between your lips,
           to make you return by the road
           on which you came.

A sign for Hezekiah

30   "This shall be the sign for you:
           This year will be eaten the self-sown grain,
           next year what sprouts in the fallow,
           but in the third year sow and reap,
           plant vineyards and eat their fruit.

31   The surviving remnant of the House of Judah shall bring forth
           new roots below and fruits above.

32   For a remnant shall go out from Jerusalem,

and survivors from Mount Zion.
The jealous love of Yahweh Sabaoth will accomplish this.

An oracle on Assyria

'This, then, is what Yahweh says about the king of Assyria: 33

"He will not enter this city,
he will let fly no arrow against it,
confront it with no shield,
throw up no earthwork against it.
By the road that he came on he will return;   34
he shall not enter this city. It is Yahweh who speaks.
I will protect this city and save it   35
for my own sake and for the sake of my servant David." '

Sennacherib is punished

That same night the angel of Yahweh went out and struck down a hundred 36
and eighty-five thousand men in the Assyrian camp. In the early morning, when
it was time to get up, there they lay, so many corpses.

Sennacherib struck camp and left; he returned home and stayed in Nineveh. 37
One day when he was worshipping in the temple of his god Nisroch, his sons 38
Adrammelech and Sharezer struck him down with the sword and escaped into
the land of Ararat. His son Esarhaddon succeeded him.

The illness and cure of Hezekiah

38 In those days Hezekiah fell ill and was at the point of death. The prophet 1
Isaiah son of Amoz came and said to him, 'Yahweh says this, "Put your
affairs in order, for you are going to die, you will not live"'. •Hezekiah turned 2
his face to the wall and addressed this prayer to Yahweh, •'Ah, Yahweh, remem- 3
ber, I beg you, how I have behaved faithfully and with sincerity of heart in your
presence and done what is right in your eyes'. And Hezekiah shed many tears.

Then the word of Yahweh came to Isaiah, •'Go and say to Hezekiah, $\frac{4}{5}$
"Yahweh, the God of David your ancestor, says this: I have heard your prayer
and seen your tears. I will cure you: in three days' time you shall go up to the
Temple of Yahweh. I will add fifteen years to your life. •I will save you from the 6
hands of the king of Assyria, I will protect this city."'

'Bring a fig poultice,' Isaiah said 'apply it to the ulcer and he will recover.' 21
Hezekiah said, 'What is the sign to tell me that I shall be going up to the Temple 22
of Yahweh?' •'Here' Isaiah replied 'is the sign from Yahweh that he will do 7
what he has said. •Look, I shall make the shadow cast by the declining sun 8
go back ten steps on the steps of Ahaz.' And the sun went back the ten steps
by which it had declined.

The canticle of Hezekiah

Canticle of Hezekiah king of Judah after his illness and recovery.   9

I said: In the noon of my life   10
I have to depart
for the gates of Sheol,
I am deprived of the rest of my years.

I said: I shall never see Yahweh again   11
in the land of the living,
never again look on any man
of those who inhabit the earth.

My tent is pulled up, and thrown away   12
like the tent of a shepherd;

like a weaver you roll up my life
to cut it from the loom.

13   From dawn to night you are compassing my end,
I cry aloud until the morning;
like a lion he crushes all my bones,
from dawn to night you are compassing my end.

14   I am twittering like a swallow,
I am moaning like a dove,
my eyes turn to the heights,
take care of me, be my safeguard.

15   What can I say? Of what can I speak to him?
It is he who is at work;
I will give glory to you all the years of my life
for my sufferings.

16   Lord, my heart will live for you,
my spirit will live for you alone.
You will cure me and give me life,
17   my suffering will turn to health.

It is you who have kept my soul
from the pit of nothingness,
you have thrust all my sins
behind your back.

18   For Sheol does not praise you,
Death does not extol you;
those who go down to the pit do not go on trusting
in your faithfulness.

19   The living, the living are the ones who praise you,
as I do today.
Fathers tell their sons
about your faithfulness.

20   Yahweh, come to my help
and we will make our harps resound
all the days of our life
in front of the Temple of Yahweh.

The Babylonian embassy

1 **39** At that time, the king of Babylon, Merodach-baladan son of Baladan, sent
letters and a gift to Hezekiah, for he had heard of his illness and recovery.
2 Hezekiah was delighted at this and showed the messengers his treasure-house,
the silver, gold, spices, precious oil, his armoury too, and everything there was
in his storehouses. There was nothing Hezekiah did not show them in his palace
or in his whole domain.
3   Then the prophet Isaiah came to King Hezekiah and asked him, 'What have
these men said, and where have they come from?' Hezekiah answered, 'They
4 have come from a faraway country, from Babylon'. •Isaiah said, 'What have
they seen in your palace?' 'They have seen everything in my palace' Hezekiah
answered. 'There is nothing in my storehouses that I have not shown them.'
5   Then Isaiah said to Hezekiah, 'Listen to the word of Yahweh Sabaoth, •"The
6
days are coming when everything in your palace, everything that your ancestors
have amassed until now, will be carried off to Babylon. Not a thing will be left"
7 says Yahweh. •"Sons sprung from you, sons begotten by you, will be chosen
8 to be eunuchs in the palace of the king of Babylon." ' •Hezekiah said to Isaiah,

'This word of Yahweh that you announce is reassuring', for he was thinking, 'There is going to be peace and security during my own lifetime.'

II. THE BOOK OF THE CONSOLATION OF ISRAEL

The calling of the prophet

40   'Console my people, console them'   1
    says your God.
    'Speak to the heart of Jerusalem   2
    and call to her
    that her time of service is ended,
    that her sin is atoned for,
    that she has received from the hand of Yahweh
    double punishment for all her crimes.'

    A voice cries, 'Prepare in the wilderness   3
    a way for Yahweh.
    Make a straight highway for our God
    across the desert.
    Let every valley be filled in,   4
    every mountain and hill be laid low,
    let every cliff become a plain,
    and the ridges a valley;
    then the glory of Yahweh shall be revealed   5
    and all mankind shall see it;
    for the mouth of Yahweh has spoken.'
    A voice commands: 'Cry!'   6
    and I answered, 'What shall I cry?'
    —'All flesh is grass
    and its beauty like the wild flower's.
    The grass withers, the flower fades   7
    when the breath of Yahweh blows on them.
    (The grass is without doubt the people.)
    The grass withers, the flower fades,   8
    but the word of our God remains for ever.'

Prophecy of the theophany

    Go up on a high mountain,   9
    joyful messenger to Zion.
    Shout with a loud voice,
    joyful messenger to Jerusalem.
    Shout without fear,
    say to the towns of Judah,
    'Here is your God'.

    Here is the Lord Yahweh coming with power,   10
    his arm subduing all things to him.
    The prize of his victory is with him,
    his trophies all go before him.
    He is like a shepherd feeding his flock,   11
    gathering lambs in his arms,
    holding them against his breast
    and leading to their rest the mother ewes.

The majesty of God

12   Who was it measured the water of the sea in the hollow of his hand
     and calculated the dimensions of the heavens,
     gauged the whole earth to the bushel,
     weighed the mountains in scales,
     the hills in a balance?

13   Who could have advised the spirit of Yahweh,
     what counsellor could have instructed him?

14   Whom has he consulted to enlighten him,
     and to learn the path of justice
     and discover the most skilful ways?

15   See, the nations are like a drop on the pail's rim,
     they count as a grain of dust on the scales.
     See, the islands weigh no more than fine powder.

16   Lebanon is not enough for the fires
     nor its beasts for the holocaust.

17   All the nations are as nothing in his presence,
     for him they count as nothingness and emptiness.

18   To whom could you liken God?
     What image could you contrive of him?

19   A craftsman casts the figure,
     a goldsmith plates it with gold
     and casts silver chains for it.

20c   For it a clever sculptor seeks
20a   precious palm wood,
20b   selects wood that will not decay
20d   to set up a sturdy image.

21   Did you not know,
     had you not heard?
     Was it not told you from the beginning?
     Have you not understood how the earth was founded?

22   He lives above the circle of the earth,
     its inhabitants look like grasshoppers.
     He has stretched out the heavens like a cloth,
     spread them like a tent for men to live in.

23   He reduces princes to nothing,
     he annihilates the rulers of the world.

24   Scarcely are they planted, scarcely sown,
     scarcely has their stem taken root in the earth,
     than he blows on them. Then they wither
     and the storm carries them off like straw.

25   'To whom could you liken me
     and who could be my equal?' says the Holy One.

26   Lift your eyes and look.
     Who made these stars
     if not he who drills them like an army,
     calling each one by name?
     So mighty is his power, so great his strength,
     that not one fails to answer.

The might of Providence

27   How can you say, Jacob,
     how can you insist, Israel,

'My destiny is hidden from Yahweh,
my rights are ignored by my God'?
Did you not know?
Had you not heard?　　　　　　　　　　　　28

Yahweh is an everlasting God,
he created the boundaries of the earth.
He does not grow tired or weary,
his understanding is beyond fathoming.
He gives strength to the wearied,
he strengthens the powerless.　　　　　29
Young men may grow tired and weary,
youths may stumble,　　　　　　　　30
but those who hope in Yahweh renew their strength,
they put out wings like eagles.　　　　31
They run and do not grow weary,
walk and never tire.

The calling of Cyrus[a]

41 Islands, keep silence before me,
let the people renew their strength.
Let them come forward and speak,
let us appear together for judgement.　　1

'Who roused from the east
him that victory hails at every step?　　2
Who presents him with nations,
subdues kings to him?

'His sword makes dust of them
and his bow scatters them like straw.
He pursues them and advances unhindered,　　3
his feet scarcely touching the road.

'Who is the author of this deed
if not he who calls the generations from the beginning?　　4
I, Yahweh, who am the first
and shall be with the last.'

The islands see him and take fright,
the limits of the earth tremble:　　　　5
they approach, they are here.

Men help one another,　　　　　　　　6
they say to each other, 'Take heart!'
The craftsman encourages the goldsmith,　　7
the man who beats out with the hammer encourages the man who
strikes the anvil.
Of the soldering he says, 'It is sound',
and fastens the idol with nails
to keep it steady.[b]

God is with Israel

You, Israel, my servant,
Jacob whom I have chosen,　　　　　　8
descendant of Abraham my friend.

You whom I brought from the confines of the earth　　9
and called from the ends of the world;

you to whom I said, 'You are my servant,
I have chosen you, not rejected you',

10 do not be afraid, for I am with you;
stop being anxious and watchful, for I am your God.
I give you strength, I bring you help,
I uphold you with my victorious right hand.

11 Yes, all those who raged against you,
shall be put to shame and confusion;
they who fought against you
shall be destroyed, and perish.

12 You will seek but never find them,
those enemies of yours.
They shall be destroyed and brought to nothing,
those who made war on you.

13 For I, Yahweh, your God,
I am holding you by the right hand;
I tell you, 'Do not be afraid,
I will help you'.

14 Do not be afraid, Jacob, poor worm,
Israel, puny mite.
I will help you—it is Yahweh who speaks—
the Holy One of Israel is your redeemer.

15 See, I turn you into a threshing-sled,
new, with doubled teeth;
you shall thresh and crush the mountains,
and turn the hills to chaff.

16 You shall winnow them and the wind will blow them away,
the gale will scatter them.
But you yourself will rejoice in Yahweh,
and glory in the Holy One of Israel.

Miracles of the new Exodus

17 The poor and needy ask for water, and there is none,
their tongue is parched with thirst.
I, Yahweh, will answer them,
I, the God of Israel, will not abandon them.

18 I will make rivers well up on barren heights,
and fountains in the midst of valleys;
turn the wilderness into a lake,
and dry ground into waterspring.

19 In the wilderness I will put cedar trees,
acacias, myrtles, olives.
In the desert I will plant juniper,
plane tree and cypress side by side;

20 so that men may see and know,
may all observe and understand
that the hand of Yahweh has done this,
that the Holy One of Israel has created it.

41 a. The king who freed the people of Judah from their captivity in the Babylonian exile.
b. V. 6 and 7 are in interpolation, and belong with 40:19-20.

Yahweh is the only God

'Produce your defence', says Yahweh   21
'present your case' says Jacob's king.
'Let them come foward and tell us   22
what is going to happen next.
What could they tell us of the past
to make it worth our notice?
Or will you discourse to us of future things
and let us know their outcome?
Tell us what is to happen in the future,   23
and so convince us you are gods.
Do something at least
so that we can note it and all see it.
No, you are nothing and your works are nothingness;   24
to choose you would be an outrage.'

Yahweh foretells victory for Cyrus

I roused him from the north to come,   25
from the rising sun I summoned him by name.
He has trampled the satraps like mortar,
like a potter treading clay.
Who predicted this from the beginning so we might know it,   26
who foretold it long ago so we might say, 'It is right'?
No one predicted it,
no, no one proclaimed it,
no, no one heard you speak.
I had said in Zion beforehand, 'Here they come!'   27
I had sent a bearer of good news to Jerusalem.
I looked, but there was no one,   28
there was not a single counsellor among them
who, if I asked, could give an answer.
Taken altogether they are nothing;   29
their works are nothingness,
their images wind and emptiness.

First song of the servant of Yahweh: part one

42 Here is my servant whom I uphold,   1
my chosen one in whom my soul delights.
I have endowed him with my spirit
that he may bring true justice to the nations.

He does not cry out or shout aloud,   2
or make his voice heard in the streets.
He does not break the crushed reed,   3
nor quench the wavering flame.

Faithfully he brings true justice;
he will neither waver, nor be crushed   4
until true justice is established on earth,
for the islands are awaiting his law.

Part two

Thus says God, Yahweh,   5
he who created the heavens and spread them out,
who gave shape to the earth and what comes from it,

who gave breath to its people
and life to the creatures that move in it:

6   I, Yahweh, have called you to serve the cause of right;
I have taken you by the hand and formed you;
I have appointed you as covenant of the people and light of the
nations,

7   to open the eyes of the blind,
to free captives from prison,
and those who live in darkness from the dungeon.

8   My name is Yahweh,
I will not yield my glory to another,
nor my honour to idols.

9   See how former predictions have come true.
Fresh things I now foretell;
before they appear I tell you of them.

Hymn of triumph

10   Sing a new hymn to Yahweh!
Let his praise resound from the ends of the earth,
let the sea and all that it holds sing his praises,
the islands and those who inhabit them.

11   Let the desert and its cities raise their voice,
the camp where Kedar lives.
Let the inhabitants of Sela cry aloud
and shout from the mountain tops.

12   Let them give glory to Yahweh
and let the people of the islands voice his praise.

13   Yahweh advances like a hero,
his fury is stirred like a warrior's.
He gives the war shout, raises the hue and cry,
marches valiantly against his foes.

14   'From the beginning I have been silent,
I have kept quiet, held myself in check.
I groan like a woman in labour,
I suffocate, I stifle.

15   'I will turn mountain and hill to desert,
wither all their greenery,
turn rivers to pools
and dry up lakes.

16   'But I will make the blind walk along the road
and lead them along paths.
I will turn darkness into light before them
and rocky places into level tracks.

'These things I will do,
and not leave them undone.'

17   All who trust in idols
shall withdraw in shame,
all those who say to images of cast metal,
'You are our gods'.

The blinding of the people

Listen, you deaf!   18
Look and see, you blind!
Who so blind as my servant,   19
so deaf as the messenger I send?
(Who so blind as my envoy,
so deaf as the servant of Yahweh?)
You have seen many things but not observed them;   20
your ears are open but you do not hear.
It is Yahweh's will, for the sake of his integrity,   21
to make his Law great and glorious.
But this is a people all pillaged and plundered,   22
trapped in caves,
hidden in dungeons.
They are looted, with no one to rescue them,
robbed, with no one to say, 'Give it back!'
Which of you listening to this,   23
will pay attention and mark it, against the time to come?

Who handed Jacob over to the robber,   24
Israel to the pillagers?
Was it not Yahweh? We had sinned against him,
we had refused to follow his ways
or obey his Law.

On him he poured out the blaze of his anger   25
and the furies of war.
It enveloped him in flames and he did not notice,
it burned him up, and he gave it no thought.

The liberation of Israel

43   But now, thus says Yahweh,   1
          who created you, Jacob,
          who formed you, Israel:

Do not be afraid, for I have redeemed you;
I have called you by your name, you are mine.
Should you pass through the sea, I will be with you;   2
or through rivers, they will not swallow you up.
Should you walk through fire, you will not be scorched
and the flames will not burn you.
For I am Yahweh, your God,   3
the Holy One of Israel, your saviour.

I give Egypt for your ransom,
and exchange Cush and Seba for you.
Because you are precious in my eyes,   4
because you are honoured and I love you,
I give men in exchange for you,
peoples in return for your life.
Do not be afraid, for I am with you.   5

I will bring your offspring from the east,
and gather you from the west.
To the north I will say, 'Give them up'   6
and to the south, 'Do not hold them'.
Bring back my sons from far away,
my daughters from the end of the earth,

7
    all those who bear my name,
    whom I have created for my glory,
    whom I have formed, whom I have made.

Yahweh alone is God

8
    Bring forward the people that is blind, yet has eyes,
    that is deaf and yet has ears.
9
    Let all the nations muster
    and assemble with every race.
    Which of them ever declared this
    or foretold this in the past?
    Let them bring their witnesses to prove them right,
    let men hear them so that they may say, 'It is true'.
10
    You yourselves are my witnesses—it is Yahweh who speaks—
    my servants whom I have chosen,
    that men may know and believe me
    and understand that it is I.
    No god was formed before me,
    nor will be after me.
11
    I, I am Yahweh,
    there is no other saviour but me.
12
    It is I who have spoken, have saved, have made the proclamation,
    not any strangers among you.
    You are my witnesses—it is Yahweh who speaks—
13
    and I, I am your God, •I am he from eternity.
    No one can deliver from my hand,
    I act and no one can reverse it.

Babylon will be destroyed

14
    Thus says Yahweh,
    your redeemer, the Holy One of Israel:

    For your sake I send an army against Babylon;
    I will knock down the prison bars
    and the Chaldaeans will break into laments.
15
    I am Yahweh, your Holy One,
    the creator of Israel, your king.

Miracles of the new Exodus

16
    Thus says Yahweh,
    who made a way through the sea,
    a path in the great waters;
17
    who put chariots and horse in the field
    and a powerful army,
    which lay there never to rise again,
    snuffed out, put out like a wick:

18
    No need to recall the past,
    no need to think about what was done before.
19
    See, I am doing a new deed,
    even now it comes to light; can you not see it?
    Yes, I am making a road in the wilderness,
    paths in the wilds.

20
    The wild beasts will honour me,
    jackals and ostriches,
    because I am putting water in the wilderness
    (rivers in the wild)

to give my chosen people drink.
The people I have formed for myself   21
will sing my praises.

The ingratitude of Israel

Jacob, you have not invoked me,   22
you have not troubled yourself, Israel, on my behalf.
You have not brought me your sheep for holocausts,   23
nor honoured me with sacrifices.
I have never burdened you with oblations,
nor troubled you for incense.
You have spent no money on fragrant cane for me,   24
you have not filled me with the fat of your sacrifices.
Instead you have burdened me with your sins,
troubled me with your iniquities.
I it is, I it is, who must blot out everything   25
and not remember your sins.

Cast your mind back, let us judge this together;   26
state your own case and prove your innocence.
Your first father *a* sinned,   27
your mediators have rebelled against me.
Your princes have profaned my sanctuary.   28
So I have handed Jacob over to the ban,
and Israel to insults.

The blessing for Israel

44 But now listen, Jacob my servant,   1
Israel whom I have chosen.   2
Thus says Yahweh who made you,
who formed you from the womb, who is your help:
Do not be afraid, Jacob my servant,
Jeshurun whom I have chosen.

For I will pour out water on the thirsty soil,   3
streams on the dry ground.
I will pour my spirit on your descendants,
my blessing on your children.
They shall grow like grass where there is plenty of water,   4
like poplars by running streams.

One man will say, 'I belong to Yahweh',   5
another will call himself by Jacob's name.
On his hand another will write 'Yahweh'
and be surnamed 'Israel'.

Monotheism without compromise

Thus says Israel's king   6
and his redeemer, Yahweh Sabaoth:
I am the first and the last;
there is no other God besides me.
Who is like me? Let him stand up and speak,   7
let him show himself and argue it out before me.
Who from the very beginning foretold the future?
Let them tell us what is yet to come.
Have no fear, do not be afraid: 8
have I not told you and revealed it long ago?

You are my witnesses, is there any other God besides me?
There is no Rock; I know of none.

A satire on idolatry

9 They are all makers of idols; they are nothing and the works they prize are useless. Their servants see nothing, they understand nothing, and so they will
10 be put to shame. • Who ever fashioned a god or cast an image without hope of
11 gain? • Watch how its devotees will be put to shame, how its sculptors will blush. Let them all come together, let them appear in court. They will be both terrified and ashamed.

12 The blacksmith works on it over the fire and beats it into shape with a hammer. He works on it with his strong arm till he is hungry and tired; drinking no water, he is exhausted.

13 The wood carver takes his measurements, outlines the image with chalk, carves it with chisels, following the outline with dividers. He shapes it to human
14 proportions, and gives it a human face, for it to live in a temple. • He cut down a cedar, or else took a cypress or an oak which he selected from the trees in the
15 forest, or maybe he planted a cedar and the rain made it grow. • For the common man it is so much fuel; he uses it to warm himself, he also burns it to bake his bread. But this fellow makes a god of it and worships it; he makes an idol of it
16 and bows down before it. • Half of it he burns in the fire, on the live embers he roasts meat, eats it and is replete. He warms himself too. 'Ah!' says he 'I am
17 warm; I have a fire here!' • With the rest he makes his god, his idol; he bows down before it and worships it and prays to it. 'Save me,' he says 'because you are my god.'

18 They know nothing, understand nothing. Their eyes are shut to all seeing,
19 their heart to all reason. • They never think, they lack the knowledge and wit to say, 'I burned half of it on the fire, I baked bread on the live embers, I roasted meat and ate it, and am I to make some abomination of what remains? Am I to bow down before a block of wood?'

20 A man who hankers after ashes has a deluded heart and is led astray. He will never free his soul, or say, 'What I have in my hand is nothing but a lie!'

Oracle

21 Remember these things, Jacob,
and that you are my servant, Israel.
I have formed you, you are my servant;
Israel, I will not forget you.

22 I have dispelled your faults like a cloud,
your sins like a mist.
Come back to me, for I have redeemed you.

Song of joy

23 Shout for joy, you heavens, for Yahweh has been at work!
Shout aloud, you earth below!
Shout for joy, you mountains,
and you, forest and all your trees!
For Yahweh has redeemed Jacob
and displayed his glory in Israel.

The might of Yahweh

24 Thus says Yahweh, your redeemer,
he who formed you in the womb:
I, myself, Yahweh, made all things,

43 a. Jacob, Gn 27:1-29.

I alone spread out the heavens.
When I gave the earth shape, did anyone help me?

I am he who foils the omens of wizards   25
and makes fools of diviners,
who makes sages recant
and shows the nonsense of their knowledge,
who confirms the word of my servant   26
and makes the plans of my envoys succeed.

I am he who says of Jerusalem, 'Let her be inhabited',
of the towns of Judah, 'Let them be rebuilt',
and I will raise their ruins once more.
I am he who says to the ocean, 'Be dry.   27
I will dry up your rivers.'

I am he who says of Cyrus, 'My shepherd—   28
he will fulfil my whole purpose,
saying of Jerusalem, "Let her be rebuilt",
and of the Temple, "Let your foundation be laid" '.

Oracle in favour of Cyrus

45 Thus says Yahweh to his anointed, to Cyrus,   1
whom he has taken by his right hand
to subdue nations before him
and strip the loins of kings,*a*
to force gateways before him
that their gates be closed no more:

I will go before you   2
levelling the heights.
I will shatter the bronze gateways,
smash the iron bars.
I will give you the hidden treasures,   3
the secret hoards,
that you may know that I am Yahweh,
the God of Israel, who calls you by your name.

It is for the sake of my servant Jacob,   4
of Israel my chosen one,
that I have called you by your name,
conferring a title though you do not know me.
I am Yahweh, unrivalled;   5
there is no other God besides me.
Though you do not know me, I arm you
that men may know from the rising to the setting of the sun   6
that, apart from me, all is nothing.

Oracle of salvation

I am Yahweh, unrivalled,
I form the light and create the dark.   7
I make good fortune and create calamity,
it is I, Yahweh, who do all this.

Send victory like a dew, you heavens,   8
and let the clouds rain it down.
Let the earth open
for salvation to spring up.
Let deliverance, too, bud forth
which I, Yahweh, shall create.

The supreme power of Yahweh

9   Can it argue with the man who fashioned it,
          one vessel among earthen vessels?
          Does the clay say to its fashioner, 'What are you making?',
          does the thing he shaped say, 'You have no skill'?

10   Woe to him who says to a father, 'What have you begotten?'
          or to a woman, 'To what have you given birth?'

11   Thus says Yahweh,
          the Holy One, he who fashions Israel:
          Is it for you to question me about my children
          and to dictate to me what my hands should do?

12   I it was who made the earth,
          and created man who is on it.
          I it was who spread out the heavens with my hands
          and now give orders to their whole array.

13   I it was who roused him to victory,
          I levelled the way for him.
          He will rebuild my city,
          will bring my exiles back
          without ransom or indemnity,
          so says Yahweh Sabaoth.

The heathen will rally to Yahweh

14   Thus says Yahweh:
          The peasants of Egypt and the traders of Cush,
          and the tall men of Seba,
          will submit to you and be yours;
          they will follow you in chains.
          They will bow down before you,
          they will pray to you:
          'With you alone is God, and he has no rival;
          there is no other god'.

15   Truly, God is hidden with you,
          the God of Israel, the saviour.

16   Those who opposed you will be disgraced and humiliated;
          the makers of idols will go away confounded.

17   Israel will be saved by Yahweh,
          saved everlastingly.
          You will never be disgraced or humiliated
          for ever and ever.

Evidence of the work of Yahweh

18   Yes, thus says Yahweh,
          creator of the heavens,
          who is God,
          who formed the earth and made it,
          who set it firm,
          created it no chaos,
          but a place to be lived in:

          'I am Yahweh, unrivalled,

19   I have not spoken in secret
          in some corner of a darkened land.
          I have not said to Jacob's descendants,

45 a. I.e. leaving them no weapons in their belts.

"Seek me in chaos".
I, Yahweh, speak with directness
I express myself with clarity.'

Yahweh is the God of all

Assemble, come, gather together,   20
survivors of the nations.
They are ignorant, those who carry about
their idol of wood,
those who pray to a god
that cannot save.
Speak up, present your case,   21
consult with each other.
'Who foretold this
and revealed it in the past?
Am I not Yahweh?
There is no other god besides me,
a God of integrity and a saviour;
there is none apart from me.
Turn to me and be saved,   22
all the ends of the earth,
for I am God unrivalled.

'By my own self I swear it;   23
what comes from my mouth is truth,
a word irrevocable:
before me every knee shall bend,
by me every tongue shall swear,
saying, "From Yahweh alone   24
come victory and strength".
To him shall come, ashamed,
all who raged against him.
Victorious and glorious through Yahweh shall be   25
all the descendants of Israel.'

The fall of Bel

46

Bel is crouching. Nebo cringing.[a]   1
Their idols are being loaded on animals, on beasts of burden,
carried off like bundles on weary beasts.
They are cringing and crouching together,   2
powerless to save the ones who carry them,
as they themselves go off into captivity.

'Listen to me, House of Jacob,   3
all you who remain of the House of Israel,
you who have been carried since birth,
whom I have carried since the time you were born.

'In your old age I shall be still the same,   4
when your hair is grey I shall still support you.
I have already done so, I have carried you,
I shall still support and deliver you.'

Yahweh is without equal

To whom can you compare me, equate me,   5
to whom claim I am similar, or comparable?
These prodigals weigh out gold from their purses   6
and silver on the scales.

They engage a goldsmith to make a god
then worship and prostrate themselves before it.

7   They lift it on their shoulders and carry it,
and put it where it is meant to stand.
It never moves from the spot.
You may invoke it, it never replies,
It never saves anyone in trouble.

Yahweh is lord of the future

8   Remember this and be dismayed,
stir your memories again, you sinners,
9   remember things long past.
I am God unrivalled
God who has no like.
10   From the beginning I foretold the future,
and predicted beforehand what is to be.

I say: My purpose shall last;
I will do whatever I choose.
11   I call a bird of prey from the east,
my man of destiny from a far country.
No sooner is it said than done,
no sooner planned than performed.
12   Listen to me, faint hearts,
who feel far from victory.
13   I bring my victory near, already it is close,
my salvation will not be late.
I will give salvation to Zion,
my glory shall be for Israel.

Lament for Babylon

1 **47** Down with you! Sit in the dust,
virgin, daughter of Babylon.
Sit on the ground, dethroned,
daughter of the Chaldaeans.
Never again will you be called
tender and delicate.
2   Take the millstones, grind the meal.
Remove your veil,
tie up your skirt, uncover your legs.
Wade through rivers.
3   Let your nakedness be seen,
and your shame exposed.
I am going to take vengeance
and no one can stop me.

4   Our redeemer, Yahweh Sabaoth his name,
the Holy One of Israel, says:
5   Sit in silence and creep into shadows,
daughter of the Chaldaeans,
for you will no longer be called
sovereign lady of the kingdoms.

6   I was angry with my people,
I had profaned my heritage.
I had surrendered it into your hands,

46 a. Gods of the Babylonians, defeated by Cyrus.

but you showed them no mercy.
On the aged you laid
your crushing yoke.
You said, 'For ever　　　　　　　　　　　　　　　7
I shall be sovereign lady'.
You never took these things to heart
or pondered on their outcome.

So listen now, voluptuous woman,　　　　　　8
lolling at ease
and saying to yourself,
'I, and none besides me.
I shall never be widowed,
never know loss of children.'
Yet both these things shall happen to you　　9
both suddenly and on the same day.
Loss of children, widowhood, at once
will come to you;
in spite of all your witchcraft
and the power of all your spells.

You were bold in your wickedness and said,　10
'There is no one to see me'.
That wisdom and knowledge of yours
led you astray.
You said to yourself,
'I, and none besides me'.
A calamity shall fall on you　　　　　　　11
which you will not be able to charm away,
a disaster shall overtake you
which you will not be able to avert,
unforeseen ruin
will suddenly descend on you.

Keep to your spells then,　　　　　　　　12
and all your sorceries,
for which you have worn yourself out since your youth.
Do you think they will help you?
Do you think they will make anyone nervous?
You have spent weary hours with your many advisers.　13
Let them come forward now
and save you, these who analyse the heavens,
who study the stars
and announce month by month
what will happen to you next.

Oh, they will be like wisps of straw　　　　14
and the fire will burn them.
They will not save their lives
from the power of the flame.
No embers these, for baking,
no fireside to sit by.
This is what your wizards will be for you,
those men for whom you have worn yourself out since your youth.　15
They will all go off, each his own way,
powerless to save you.

Yahweh acts alone and is sole master of the future

48

1 Listen to this, House of Jacob,
you who bear the name of Israel,
and have sprung from the seed of Judah;
you who swear by the name of Yahweh
and invoke the God of Israel
though not in good faith or uprightness—

2 calling yourselves after the holy city
and bolstering yourselves on the God of Israel,
whose name is Yahweh Sabaoth.

3 Things now past I once revealed long ago,
they went out from my mouth and I proclaimed them;
then suddenly I acted and they happened.

4 For I knew you to be obstinate,
your neck an iron bar,
your forehead bronze.

5 And so I revealed things beforehand,
before they happened I announced them to you,
so that you could not say, 'My idol was the one that performed them,
it was my carved image, my image of cast metal, that decreed them'.

6 You have heard and seen all this,
will you not admit it?

Now I am revealing new things to you,
things hidden and unknown to you,

7 created just now, this very moment,
of these things you have heard nothing until now,
so that you cannot say, 'Oh yes, I knew all this'.

8 You had never heard,
you did not know,
I had not opened your ear beforehand;
for I knew how treacherous you were,
and that you have deserved the name of rebel from your birth.

9 For the sake of my name I deferred my anger,
for the sake of my honour I curbed it; I did not destroy you.

10 And now I have put you in the fire like silver,
I have tested you in the furnace of distress.

11 For my sake and my sake only have I acted—
is my name to be profaned?
Never will I yield my glory to another.

Cyrus is the beloved of Yahweh

12 Listen to me, Jacob,
Israel whom I have called:
I am the first,
I am also the last.

13 My hand laid the foundations of earth
and my right hand spread out the heavens.
I summon them
and they all come forward together.

14 Assemble, all of you, and listen;
which of them has foretold this?
'My beloved will perform my pleasure
with Babylon and the offspring of the Chaldaeans.'

15 I, yes I myself, have spoken and summoned him,

brought him and prospered his plans.
Come near and listen to this: 16
from the beginning I have never spoken to you obscurely,
and all the time these things have been happening, I have been present.
—And now the Lord Yahweh, with his spirit,
sends me.

What Yahweh had intended for Israel

Thus says Yahweh, your redeemer, the Holy One of Israel: 17
I, Yahweh, your God, teach you what is good for you,
I lead you in the way that you must go.
If only you had been alert to my commandments,   18
your happiness would have been like a river,
your integrity like the waves of the sea.
Your children would have been numbered like the sand,   19
your descendants as many as its grains.
Never would your name have been cut off or blotted out before me.

A song of departure from Babylon

Go away from Babylon! Flee from the Chaldaeans!   20
Declare this with cries of joy and proclaim it,
send it out to the ends of the earth.
Say, 'Yahweh has redeemed his servant Jacob'.

Those he led through the deserts never went thirsty;   21
he made water spring for them from the rock,
he split the rock and water flowed.
There is no happiness, says Yahweh, for the wicked.   22

Second song of the servant of Yahweh

49

Islands, listen to me,   1
pay attention, remotest peoples.
Yahweh called me before I was born,
from my mother's womb he pronounced my name.

He made my mouth a sharp sword,   2
and hid me in the shadow of his hand.
He made me into a sharpened arrow,
and concealed me in his quiver.

He said to me, 'You are my servant (Israel)   3
in whom I shall be glorified';
while I was thinking, 'I have toiled in vain,   4
I have exhausted myself for nothing';

and all the while my cause was with Yahweh,
my reward with my God.
I was honoured in the eyes of Yahweh,   5b
my God was my strength.

And now Yahweh has spoken,   5a
he who formed me in the womb to be his servant,
to bring Jacob back to him,
to gather Israel to him:

'It is not enough for you to be my servant,   6
to restore the tribes of Jacob and bring back the survivors of Israel;
I will make you the light of the nations
so that my salvation may reach to the ends of the earth'.

The marvellous epic of the return

7
> Thus says Yahweh,
> the redeemer of Israel and his Holy One,
> to him whose life is despised, whom the nations loathe,
> to the slave of despots:
> Kings will stand up when they see you,
> and princes will bow,
> for the sake of Yahweh who has been faithful,
> the Holy One of Israel who has chosen you.

8
> Thus says Yahweh:
> At the favourable time I will answer you,
> on the day of salvation I will help you.
> (I have formed you and have appointed you
> as covenant of the people.)
> I will restore the land
> and assign you the estates that lie waste.

9
> I will say to the prisoners, 'Come out',
> to those who are in darkness, 'Show yourselves'.
>
> On every roadway they will graze,
> and each bare height shall be their pasture.

10
> They will never hunger or thirst,
> scorching wind and sun shall never plague them;
> for he who pities them will lead them
> and guide them to springs of water.

11
> I will make a highway of all the mountains,
> and the high roads shall be banked up.

12
> Some are on their way from afar,
> others from the north and the west,
> others from the land of Sinim.ᵃ

13
> Shout for joy, you heavens; exult, you earth!
> You mountains, break into happy cries!
> For Yahweh consoles his people
> and takes pity on those who are afflicted.

14
> For Zion was saying, 'Yahweh has abandoned me,
> the Lord has forgotten me'.

15
> Does a woman forget her baby at the breast,
> or fail to cherish the son of her womb?
> Yet even if these forget,
> I will never forget you.

16
> See, I have branded you on the palms of my hands,
> Your ramparts are always under my eye.

17
> Your rebuilders make haste,
> and your destroyers and despoilers depart.

18
> Look round about you, look,
> all are assembling, coming to you.
> By my life—it is Yahweh who speaks—
> you will wear these as your jewels,
> they will adorn you as brides are adorned;

19
> for your desolate places and your ruins
> and your devastated country
> will now be too small for all your inhabitants,

49 a. Assuan in S. Egypt.

now that your devourers are far away.
Once more they will speak in your hearing,   20
those sons you thought were lost,
'This place is too small for me,
give me more space to live in'.
You will then say in your heart,   21
'Who has borne me these?
I was childless and barren,
who has brought these up?

I was left all alone,
and now, where do these come from?'
Thus speaks the Lord Yahweh: 22
I beckon to the nations
and hoist my signal for the peoples.
They will bring back your sons in the cloak,
they will take your daughters on their shoulders.
Kings will be your fosterfathers,   23
their queens your nursing mothers.
They will fall prostrate before you, faces to the ground,
and lick the dust at your feet.
You shall then know that I am Yahweh;
and that those who hope in me will not be put to shame.

Can spoil be snatched from heroes,   24
or captives escape from a soldier?
Yes, thus says Yahweh: 25
The hero's captive will be snatched away,
the soldier's spoil escape.
I myself will fight with those who fight you,
and I myself will save your children.
I will make your oppressors eat their own flesh,   26
they shall get as drunk on their own blood as on new wine.
Then all mankind shall know
that I, Yahweh, am your saviour
and that your redeemer is the Mighty One of Jacob.

The offer of salvation remains open

50

Thus says Yahweh: 1
Where is your mother's writ of divorce
by which I dismissed her?
Or to which of my creditors
have I sold you?
You were sold for your own crimes,
for your own faults your mother was dismissed.

Why did I find no one when I came?   2
Why did no one answer when I called?
Is my hand too short to redeem?
Have I not strength to save?
With one threat I can dry the sea,
and turn rivers to desert;
so that their fish shrivel up for want of water
and die of thirst.
I dress the heavens in black,   3
make sackcloth their covering.

Third song of the servant of Yahweh
a. The servant speaks

4

The Lord Yahweh has given me
a disciple's tongue.
So that I may know how to reply to the wearied
he provides me with speech.
Each morning he wakes me to hear,
to listen like a disciple.

5

The Lord Yahweh has opened my ear.

For my part, I made no resistance,
neither did I turn away.

6

I offered my back to those who struck me,
my cheeks to those who tore at my beard;
I did not cover my face
against insult and spittle.

7

The Lord Yahweh comes to my help,
so that I am untouched by the insults.
So, too, I set my face like flint;
I know I shall not be shamed.

8

My vindicator is here at hand. Does anyone start proceedings
against me?
Then let us go to court together.
Who thinks he has a case against me?
Let him approach me.

9

The Lord Yahweh is coming to my help,
who dare condemn me?
They shall all go to pieces like a garment
devoured by moths.

b. Exhortation to follow the servant

10

Let anyone who fears Yahweh among you
listen to the voice of his servant!
Whoever walks in darkness,
and has no light shining for him,
let him trust in the name of Yahweh,
let him lean on his God.

11

But you, you are all setting light to a fire,
and fanning embers.
Then in with you to the flames of your fire,
to the embers that you are lighting.
So will my hand deal with you
and you shall lie down in torments.

The salvation of the sons of Abraham

1 **51**

Listen to me, you who pursue integrity,
who seek Yahweh.
Consider the rock you were hewn from,
the quarry from which you were cut.

2

Consider Abraham your father
and Sarah who gave you birth.
For he was all alone when I called him,
but I blessed and increased him.

Yes, Yahweh has pity on Zion,   3
    has pity on all her ruins;
turns her desolation into an Eden,
    her wasteland into the garden of Yahweh.
Joy and gladness shall be found in her,
    thanksgiving and the sound of music.

Yahweh will soon judge the world

Pay attention to me, you peoples,   4
    listen to me, you nations.
For from me comes the Law
    and my justice shall be the light of the peoples,
I will establish •my integrity speedily,   5
    my salvation shall come like the light,
    my arm shall judge the peoples.
The islands put their hope in me,
    put their trust in my strength.

Lift up your eyes to the heavens,   6
    look down at the earth.
The heavens will vanish like smoke,
    the earth wear out like a garment,
and its inhabitants die like vermin,
but my salvation shall last for ever
    and my justice have no end.

Listen to me, you who know what integrity means,   7
    people who take my laws to heart:
do not fear the taunts of men,
    nor be dismayed by their insults,
for the moth shall eat them like garments,   8
    the grub devour them like wool,
but my integrity will remain for ever,
    and my salvation for all generations.

The awakening of Yahweh

Awake, awake! Clothe yourself in strength,   9
    arm of Yahweh.
Awake, as in the past,
    in times of generations long ago.
Did you not split Rahab in two,
    and pierce the Dragon through?
Did you not dry up the sea,   10
    the waters of the great Abyss,
to make the seabed a road
    for the redeemed to cross?

Those whom Yahweh has ransomed return,   11
    they come to Zion shouting for joy,
everlasting joy in their faces;
joy and gladness go with them,
    sorrow and lament are ended.

Yahweh is the all-powerful consoler

I, I am your consoler.   12
How then can you be afraid
    of mortal man, of son of man,
    whose fate is the fate of grass?

13 You have forgotten Yahweh who made you,
    who spread out the heavens and laid the earth's foundations,
    why still go in daily dread
    of the oppressor's fury,
    when he sets out to destroy you?
    What has happened to the fury of oppressors?

Salvation

14 The captive is soon to be set free; he will not die in a deep dungeon nor will
15 his bread run out. •I am Yahweh your God who stirs the sea, making its waves
16 roar, my name is Yahweh Sabaoth. •I put my words into your mouth, I hid
    you in the shadow of my hand, when I spread out the heavens and laid the
    earth's foundations and said to Zion, 'You are my people'.

The awakening of Jerusalem

17 Awake, awake!
    To your feet, Jerusalem!
    You who from Yahweh's hand have drunk
    the cup of his wrath.
    The chalice of stupor
    you have drained to the dregs.

18 She has not one to guide her
    of all the sons she has borne,
    not one to take her by the hand
    of all the sons she has reared.

19 These two calamities have befallen you
    —who is there to mourn for you?
    Devastation and ruin, famine and sword
    —who is there to console you?

20 Your sons lie helpless
    (at every street corner)
    like an antelope trapped in a net,
    sodden with the wrath of Yahweh,
    with the threats of your God.

21 Listen then to this, prostrated one,
    drunk, though not with wine.
22 Thus says your Lord Yahweh,
    your God, defender of your people.

    See, I take out of your hand
    the cup of stupor,
    the chalice of my wrath;
    you shall drink it no longer.

23 I will put it into the hand of your tormentors,
    of those who said to you,
    'Bow down that we may walk over you';
    while of your back you made a pavement,
    a street for them to walk on.

52 1 Awake, awake!
    Clothe yourself in strength, Zion.
    Put on your richest clothes,
    Jerusalem, holy city;
    since no longer shall there enter you
    either the uncircumcised or the unclean.

> Shake off your dust; to your feet,   2
> captive Jerusalem!
> Free your neck from its fetters,
> captive daughter of Zion.

The nation in captivity

Yes, Yahweh says this: You were sold for nothing and you will be redeemed 3
without money. •Yes, Yahweh says this: Once my people went to Egypt to 4
settle there, then Assyria bitterly oppressed them. •But now what is there for 5
me here?—it is Yahweh who speaks—now that my people have been carried
off for nothing, and their masters shout their triumph—it is Yahweh who speaks—
all day long my name is constantly blasphemed. •My people will therefore know 6
my name; that day they will understand that it is I who say, 'I am here'.

The awakening of Yahweh and of Jerusalem

> How beautiful on the mountains,   7
> are the feet of one who brings good news,
> who heralds peace, brings happiness,
> proclaims salvation,
> and tells Zion,
> 'Your God is king!'

> Listen! Your watchmen raise their voices,   8
> they shout for joy together,
> for they see Yahweh face to face,
> as he returns to Zion.

> Break into shouts of joy together,   9
> you ruins of Jerusalem;
> for Yahweh is consoling his people,
> redeeming Jerusalem.

> Yahweh bares his holy arm   10
> in the sight of all the nations,
> and all the ends of the earth shall see
> the salvation of our God.

> 'Go away, go away, leave that place,   11
> touch nothing unclean.
> Get out of her,[a] purify yourselves,
> you who carry the vessels of Yahweh.

> 'But you are not to hurry away,   12
> you are not to leave like fugitives.
> No, Yahweh will go in front of you,
> and the God of Israel will be your rearguard.'

Fourth song of the servant of Yahweh

> See, my servant will prosper,   13
> he shall be lifted up, exalted, rise to great heights.

> As the crowds were appalled on seeing him   14
> —so disfigured did he look
> that he seemed no longer human—
> so will the crowds be astonished at him,   15
> and kings stand speechless before him;
> for they shall see something never told
> and witness something never heard before:

53
> 'Who could believe what we have heard,   1
> and to whom has the power of Yahweh been revealed?'

2   Like a sapling he grew up in front of us,
like a root in arid ground.
Without beauty, without majesty (we saw him),
no looks to attract our eyes;

3   a thing despised and rejected by men,
a man of sorrows and familiar with suffering,
a man to make people screen their faces;
he was despised and we took no account of him.

4   And yet ours were the sufferings he bore,
ours the sorrows he carried.
But we, we thought of him as someone punished,
struck by God, and brought low.

5   Yet he was pierced through for our faults,
crushed for our sins.
On him lies a punishment that brings us peace,
and through his wounds we are healed.

6   We had all gone astray like sheep,
each taking his own way,
and Yahweh burdened him
with the sins of all of us.

7   Harshly dealt with, he bore it humbly,
he never opened his mouth,
like a lamb that is led to the slaughter-house,
like a sheep that is dumb before its shearers
never opening its mouth.

8   By force and by law he was taken;
would anyone plead his cause?
Yes, he was torn away from the land of the living;
for our faults struck down in death.

9   They gave him a grave with the wicked,
a tomb with the rich,
though he had done no wrong
and there had been no perjury in his mouth.

10   Yahweh has been pleased to crush him with suffering.
If he offers his life in atonement,
he shall see his heirs, he shall have a long life
and through him what Yahweh wishes will be done.

11   His soul's anguish over
he shall see the light and be content.
By his sufferings shall my servant justify many,
taking their faults on himself.

12   Hence I will grant whole hordes for his tribute,
he shall divide the spoil with the mighty,
for surrendering himself to death
and letting himself be taken for a sinner,
while he was bearing the faults of many
and praying all the time for sinners.

The fertility of Jerusalem

54   1   Shout for joy, you barren women who bore no children!
Break into cries of joy and gladness, you who were never in labour!

52 a. Babylon: the returning exiles are to be ritually purified because they will carry with them
the sacred vessels of the Temple, restored to them by Cyrus, Ezr 1:7f.

For the sons of the forsaken one are more in number
than the sons of the wedded wife, says Yahweh.

Widen the space of your tent,   2
stretch out your hangings freely,
lengthen your ropes, make your pegs firm;
for you will burst out to right and to left.   3
Your race will take possession of the nations,
and people the abandoned cities.

The love of Yahweh

Do not be afraid, you will not be put to shame,   4
do not be dismayed, you will not be disgraced;
for you will forget the shame of your youth
and no longer remember the curse of your widowhood.
For now your creator will be your husband,   5
his name, Yahweh Sabaoth;
your redeemer will be the Holy One of Israel,
he is called the God of the whole earth.
Yes, like a forsaken wife, distressed in spirit,   6
Yahweh calls you back.
Does a man cast off the wife of his youth?
says your God.

I did forsake you for a brief moment,   7
but with great love will I take you back.
In excess of anger, for a moment   8
I hid my face from you.
But with everlasting love I have taken pity on you,
says Yahweh, your redeemer.

I am now as I was in the days of Noah   9
when I swore that Noah's waters
should never flood the world again.
So now I swear concerning my anger with you
and the threats I made against you;
for the mountains may depart,   10
the hills be shaken,
but my love for you will never leave you
and my covenant of peace with you will never be shaken,
says Yahweh who takes pity on you.

The new Jerusalem

Unhappy creature, storm-tossed, disconsolate,   11
see, I will set your stones on carbuncles
and your foundations on sapphires.
I will make rubies your battlements,   12
your gates crystal,
and your entire wall precious stones.
Your sons will all be taught by Yahweh.   13
The prosperity of your sons will be great.
You will be founded on integrity;   14
remote from oppression, you will have nothing to fear;
remote from terror, it will not approach you.
Should anyone attack you, that will not be my doing,   15
and whoever attacks you, for your sake will fall.
I it was created the smith   16

who blows on the çoal fire
and from it takes the weapons to work on.
But I also created the destroyer who renders them useless.

17   Not a weapon forged against you will succeed.
Every tongue that accuses you in judgement will be refuted.
Such will be the lot of the servants of Yahweh,
the triumphs I award them—it is Yahweh who speaks.

The food of the poor

1   **55**   Oh, come to the water all you who are thirsty;
though you have no money, come!
Buy corn without money, and eat,
and, at no cost, wine and milk.

2   Why spend money on what is not bread,
your wages on what fails to satisfy?
Listen, listen to me, and you will have good things to eat
and rich food to enjoy.

3   Pay attention, come to me;
listen, and your soul will live.

The covenant

With you I will make an everlasting covenant
out of the favours promised to David.

4   See, I have made of you a witness to the peoples,
a leader and a master of the nations.

5   See, you will summon a nation you never knew,
those unknown will come hurrying to you,
for the sake of Yahweh your God,
of the Holy One of Israel who will glorify you.

The nearness and remoteness of Yahweh

6   Seek Yahweh while he is still to be found,
call to him while he is still near.

7   Let the wicked man abandon his way,
the evil man his thoughts.
Let him turn back to Yahweh who will take pity on him,
to our God who is rich in forgiving;

8   for my thoughts are not your thoughts,
my ways not your ways—it is Yahweh who speaks.

9   Yes, the heavens are as high above earth
as my ways are above your ways,
my thoughts above your thoughts.

The word of Yahweh cannot fail

10   Yes, as the rain and the snow come down from the heavens and do not return
without watering the earth, making it yield and giving growth to provide seed
11 for the sower and bread for the eating, •so the word that goes from my mouth
does not return to me empty, without carrying out my will and succeeding in
what it was sent to do.

Conclusion of the Book of Consolation

12   Yes, you will leave with joy
and be led away in safety.
Mountains and hills will break into joyful cries before you
and all the trees of the countryside clap their hands.

13   Cypress will grow instead of thorns,

myrtle instead of briars.
And this will make Yahweh famous,
a sign for ever, ineffaceable.

III. THIRD PART OF THE BOOK OF ISAIAH

Yahweh welcomes converts from paganism

56 Thus says Yahweh: Have a care for justice, act with integrity, for soon 1
my salvation will come and my integrity be manifest.

Blessed is the man who does this and the son of man who clings to it: observing 2
the sabbath, not profaning it, and keeping his hand from every evil deed.

Let no foreigner who has attached himself to Yahweh say, 'Yahweh will 3
surely exclude me from his people'. Let no eunuch say, 'And I, I am a dried-up
tree'.

For Yahweh says this: To the eunuchs who observe my sabbaths, and 4
resolve to do what pleases me and cling to my covenant, •I will give, in my 5
house and within my walls, a monument and a name better than sons and
daughters; I will give them an everlasting name that shall never be effaced.

Foreigners who have attached themselves to Yahweh to serve him and to 6
love his name and be his servants—all who observe the sabbath, not profaning
it, and cling to my covenant—•these I will bring to my holy mountain. I will 7
make them joyful in my house of prayer. Their holocausts and their sacrifices
will be accepted on my altar, for my house will be called a house of prayer for
all the peoples.

It is the Lord Yahweh who speaks, who gathers the outcasts of Israel: there 8
are others I will gather besides those already gathered.

The unworthiness of the leaders of Judah

Come and gorge, all you wild beasts,   9
all you beasts of the forest.
Our watchmen are all blind,   10
they notice nothing.

Dumb watchdogs all,
unable to bark,
they dream, lie down,
and love to sleep.

Greedy dogs that are never satisfied.   11
Shepherds who know nothing.
They all go their own way,
each after his own interest.

'Come, let me fetch wine;   12
we will get drunk on strong drink,
tomorrow will be just as wonderful as today
and even more so!'

57 The upright perish   1
and no one cares.
Devout men are taken off
and no one gives it a thought.

Yes, on account of evil the upright man is taken off
to enter peace.   2
They lie on their beds
those who followed the right way.

3   But you, you sons of a witch, come here,
          offspring of the adulterer and the whore.

4   At whom are you jeering, and making faces,
          and sticking out your tongue?
          Are you not the spawn of sin,
          children of lies?

5   Lusting among the terebinths,
          and under every spreading tree,
          sacrificing children in the wadis
          and in rocky clefts.

Prophetic elegy against idolatry

6   The smooth stones of the wadis, these are your share,
          these, these your portion.
          To these you pour libations,
          bring oblations.
          Can all this appease me?

7   On a mountain high and lofty
          you have put your bed.
          Thither, too, you have climbed
          to offer sacrifice.

8   Behind door and doorpost
          you have set up your sign.[a]
          Yes, far removed from me, you unroll your bedding,
          climb into it and spread it wide.

          You have struck a pact with those
          whose bed you love,
          whoring with them often
          with your eyes on the sacred symbol.

9   With oil you made yourself look your best for Molech,
          lavishing your scents;
          you sent your envoys far afield,
          down to Sheol itself.[b]

10   Tired with so much journeying,
          you never said, 'I give up'.
          Finding your strength revived,
          you never weakened.

11   Who was it you dreaded, and feared,
          that you should disown me
          and not remember me,
          and refuse me a place in your heart?

          Meanwhile I kept silent and shut my eyes, did I not?
          So you cannot have been afraid of me.

12   But now I will expose this integrity of yours
          and your futile actions.

13   When you cry, let your hateful idols save you!
          The wind will carry them all away,
          a breath will take them off.

57 a. A domestic idol.   b. By sacrificing children.

But whoever trusts in me shall inherit the land
and own my holy mountain.

A poem of consolation

It shall be said: 14
Open up, open up, clear the way,
remove all obstacles from the way of my people.
For thus speaks the Most High,   15
whose home is in eternity,
whose name is holy:

'I live in a high and holy place,
but I am also with the contrite and humbled spirit,
to give the humbled spirit new life,
to revive contrite hearts.

'For I will not quarrel for ever   16
nor be always angry,
for then the spirit would give way before me,
the very souls I have made.

'Angered by his wicked brutality,   17
I hid my face and struck him in anger.
Like a rebel he went the way of his choice;
but I have seen the way he went.   18

'But I will heal him, and console him,
I will comfort him to the full,
both him and his afflicted fellows,
bringing praise to their lips.   19
Peace, peace to far and near,
I will indeed heal him' says Yahweh.

The wicked however are like the restless sea   20
that cannot be still,
and washes up mud and slime.
'No peace' says my God 'for the wicked.'   21

Fasting

58

Shout for all you are worth,   1
raise your voice like a trumpet.
Proclaim their faults to my people,
their sins to the House of Jacob.

They seek me day after day,   2
they long to know my ways,
like a nation that wants to act with integrity
and not ignore the law of its God.

They ask me for laws that are just,
they long for God to draw near:
'Why should we fast if you never see it,   3
why do penance if you never notice?'

Look, you do business on your fastdays,
you oppress all your workmen;
look, you quarrel and squabble when you fast   4
and strike the poor man with your fist.

Fasting like yours today
will never make your voice heard on high.

5   Is that the sort of fast that pleases me,
     a truly penitential day for men?

     Hanging your head like a reed,
     lying down on sackcloth and ashes?
     Is that what you call fasting,
     a day acceptable to Yahweh?

6   Is not this the sort of fast that pleases me
     —it is the Lord Yahweh who speaks—
     to break unjust fetters
     and undo the thongs of the yoke,

     to let the oppressed go free,
     and break every yoke,
7   to share your bread with the hungry,
     and shelter the homeless poor,

     to clothe the man you see to be naked
     and not turn from your own kin?
8   Then will your light shine like the dawn
     and your wound be quickly healed over.

     Your integrity will go before you
     and the glory of Yahweh behind you.
9   Cry, and Yahweh will answer;
     call, and he will say, 'I am here'.

     If you do away with the yoke,
     the clenched fist, the wicked word,
10   if you give your bread to the hungry,
     and relief to the oppressed,

     your light will rise in the darkness,
     and your shadows become like noon.
11   Yahweh will always guide you,
     giving you relief in desert places.

     He will give strength to your bones
     and you shall be like a watered garden,
     like a spring of water
     whose waters never run dry.

12   You will rebuild the ancient ruins,
     build up on the old foundations.
     You will be called 'Breach-mender',
     'Restorer of ruined houses'.

The sabbath

13   If you refrain from trampling the sabbath,
     and doing business on the holy day,
     if you call the sabbath 'Delightful',
     and the day sacred to Yahweh 'Honourable',
     if you honour it by abstaining from travel,
     from doing business and from gossip,
14   then shall you find your happiness in Yahweh
     and I will lead you triumphant over the heights of the land.
     I will feed you on the heritage of Jacob your father.
     For the mouth of Yahweh has spoken.

59

No, the hand of Yahweh is not too short to save,
nor his ear too dull to hear.   1

But your iniquities have made a gulf   2
between you and your God.
Your sins have made him veil his face
so as not to hear you,
since your hands are stained with blood,   3
your fingers with crime,
your lips utter lies,
your tongues murmur treachery.
No one makes just accusations   4
or pleads sincerely.
All rely on nothingness, utter falsehood,
conceive harm and give birth to misery.

They are hatching adders' eggs   5
and weaving a spider's web;
eat one of their eggs and you die,
crush one and a viper emerges.
Their webs are no good for clothing,   6
their plots no use for covering.
Their plans are sinful plots,
violence is their only method.
Their feet run to do evil,   7
are quick to shed innocent blood.
Their thoughts are sinful thoughts,
wherever they go there is havoc and ruin.
They know nothing of the way of peace,   8
there is no equity in their paths.
Twisty trails they clear for themselves
and no one who follows them knows any peace.

So justice is removed far away from us,   9
and integrity keeps its distance.
We looked for light and all is darkness,
for brightness and we walk in the dark.
Like the blind we feel our way along walls   10
and hesitate like men without eyes.
We stumble as though noon were twilight
and dwell in the dark like the dead.
We growl, all of us, like bears,   11
and moan like doves,
waiting for the justice that never comes,
for salvation that is removed far away from us.

For our faults in your sight have been many   12
and our sins are a witness against us.
And indeed our faults are present to our minds,
and we know our iniquities:
rebellion and denial of Yahweh,   13
turning our back on our God,
talking treachery and revolt,
murmuring lies in our heart.
Justice is withheld   14
and integrity stands aloof;
in the public square sincerity is brought to its knees
and uprightness forbidden to enter.

Fragments of an apocalypse

15   Sincerity is missing
and he who avoids evil is robbed.
Yahweh has seen this, and is indignant
that there is no justice to be seen.

16   He saw there was no one
and wondered there was no one to intervene.
So he made his own arm his mainstay,
his own integrity his support.

17   He put integrity on like a breastplate,
and on his head the helmet of salvation.
He put vengeance on like a tunic
and wrapped himself in ardour like a cloak.

18   To each he will pay his due,
wrath to his enemies, reprisals on his foes.

19   In the west men will see the name of Yahweh
and in the east his glory;
for he shall come like a pent-up stream
impelled by the breath of Yahweh.

20   But for Zion he will come as Redeemer,
for those of Jacob who turn from their faults.
It is Yahweh who speaks.

Oracle

21   For my part, this is my covenant with them, says Yahweh. My spirit with
which I endowed you, and my words that I have put in your mouth, will not
disappear from your mouth, nor from the mouths of your children, nor from
the mouths of your children's children for ever and ever, says Yahweh.

The glorious resurrection of Jerusalem

1 **60** Arise, shine out, for your light has come,
the glory of Yahweh is rising on you,

2   though night still covers the earth
and darkness the peoples.

Above you Yahweh now rises
and above you his glory appears.

3   The nations come to your light
and kings to your dawning brightness.

4   Lift up your eyes and look round:
all are assembling and coming towards you,
your sons from far away
and your daughters being tenderly carried.

5   At this sight you will grow radiant,
your heart throbbing and full;
since the riches of the sea will flow to you,
the wealth of the nations come to you;

6   camels in throngs will cover you,
and dromedaries of Midian and Ephah;
everyone in Sheba will come,
bringing gold and incense
and singing the praise of Yahweh.

7   All the flocks of Kedar will gather inside you,

the rams of Nebaioth*a* will be at your service.
They will come up, for acceptance, to my altar,
to adorn the Temple of my glory.

Who are these flying like a cloud,   8
like doves to their cote?
Yes, for me the ships are assembling,   9
vessels of Tarshish in the front,

to bring your sons from far away,
and their silver and gold with them,
for the sake of the name of Yahweh your God,
for the sake of the Holy One of Israel who has made you glorious.

Foreigners will rebuild your walls   10
and their kings will be your servants.
For though I struck you in anger,
in mercy I have pitied you.

And your gates will lie open continually,   11
shut neither by day nor by night,
for men to bring you the wealth of the nations
with their kings leading them;
for the nation and kingdom that refuses to serve you shall perish,   12
such nations shall be utterly ruined.

The glory of Lebanon*b* will come to you,   13
with cypress and plane and box,
to adorn the site of my sanctuary,
to glorify the resting place of my feet.

The sons of your oppressors will come to you bowing,   14
at your feet shall fall all who despised you.
They will call you 'City of Yahweh',
'Zion of the Holy One of Israel'.

Though you have been abandoned,   15
and hated and shunned,
I will make you an eternal pride,
a joy for ever and ever.

You will be suckled on the milk of nations,   16
suckled on the riches of kings,
and you shall know that I, Yahweh, am your saviour,
that your redeemer is the Mighty One of Jacob.

For bronze I will bring gold;   17
for iron, silver;
and bronze for wood;
and iron for stone;
I will put Peace in as magistrate,
and Integrity as the government.

Violence will no longer be heard of in your country,   18
nor devastation and ruin within your frontiers.
You will call your walls 'Salvation'
and your gates 'Praise'.

No more will the sun give you daylight,   19
nor moonlight shine on you,
but Yahweh will be your everlasting light,
your God will be your splendour.

20   Your sun will set no more
nor your moon wane,
but Yahweh will be your everlasting light
and your days of mourning will be ended.

21   Your people will all be upright,
possessing the land for ever;
a shoot that Yahweh has planted,
my handiwork, designed for beauty.

22   The least among you will become a clan
and the smallest a mighty nation.
I, Yahweh, have spoken;
in due time I shall act with speed.

The mission of the prophet

1 **61**   The spirit of the Lord Yahweh has been given to me,
for Yahweh has anointed me.
He has sent me to bring good news to the poor,
to bind up hearts that are broken;

to proclaim liberty to captives,
freedom to those in prison;

2   to proclaim a year of favour from Yahweh,
a day of vengeance for our God,

3   to comfort all those who mourn •and to give them
for ashes a garland;
for mourning robe the oil of gladness,
for despondency, praise.
They are to be called 'terebinths of integrity',
planted by Yahweh to glorify him.

4   They will rebuild the ancient ruins,
they will raise what has long lain waste,
they will restore the ruined cities,
all that has lain waste for ages past.

5   Strangers will be there to feed your flocks,
foreigners as your ploughmen and vinedressers;

6   but you, you will be named 'priests of Yahweh',
they will call you 'ministers of our God'.
You will feed on the wealth of nations
and array yourselves in their magnificence.

7   For their shame was twofold,
disgrace and spitting their lot.
Twofold therefore shall they possess in their land,
everlasting joy is theirs.

8   For I, Yahweh, love justice,
I hate robbery and all that is wrong.
I reward them faithfully
and make an everlasting covenant with them.

9   Their race will be famous throughout the nations,
their descendants throughout the peoples.
All who see them will admit
that they are a race whom Yahweh has blessed.

60 a. Kedar, a bedouin tribe; Nebaioth, a tribe of Arabia.   b. Cedar wood.

'I exult for joy in Yahweh,
my soul rejoices in my God,
for he has clothed me in the garments of salvation,
he has wrapped me in the cloak of integrity,
like a bridegroom wearing his wreath,
like a bride adorned in her jewels.

'For as the earth makes fresh things grow,
as a garden makes seeds spring up,
so will the Lord Yahweh make both integrity and praise
spring up in the sight of the nations.'

Second poem on the glorious resurrection of Jerusalem

62

About Zion I will not be silent,
about Jerusalem I will not grow weary,
until her integrity shines out like the dawn
and her salvation flames like a torch.

The nations then will see your integrity,
all the kings your glory,
and you will be called by a new name,
one which the mouth of Yahweh will confer.
You are to be a crown of splendour in the hand of Yahweh,
a princely diadem in the hand of your God;
no longer are you to be named 'Forsaken',
nor your land 'Abandoned',
but you shall be called 'My Delight'
and your land 'The Wedded';
for Yahweh takes delight in you
and your land will have its wedding.

Like a young man marrying a virgin,
so will the one who built you wed you,
and as the bridegroom rejoices in his bride,
so will your God rejoice in you.

On your walls, Jerusalem,
I set watchmen.
Day or night
they must never be silent.

You who keep Yahweh mindful
must take no rest.
Nor let him take rest
till he has restored Jerusalem,
and made her
the boast of the earth.

Yahweh has sworn it by his right hand
and by his mighty arm:
Never again shall I give your corn
to feed your enemies.
Never again will foreigners drink your wine
that you laboured for.

But those who gather the harvest will eat it
and praise Yahweh.
Those who gathered the grapes will drink
in the courts of my sanctuary.

Conclusion

10   Pass through, pass through the gates.
    Make a way for the people.
    Bank up, bank up the highway,
    clear it of stones.
    Hoist the signal for the peoples.

11   This Yahweh proclaims
    to the ends of the earth:

    Say to the daughter of Zion, 'Look,
    your saviour comes,
    the prize of his victory with him,
    his trophies before him'.

12   They shall be called 'The Holy People',
    'Yahweh's Redeemed'.
    And you shall be called 'The-sought-after',
    'City-not-forsaken'.

An apocalyptic poem on the vengeance of Yahweh

63

1   Who is this coming from Edom,
    from Bozrah in garments stained with crimson,
    so richly clothed,
    marching so full of strength?
    —It is I, who speak of integrity
    and am powerful to save.

2   —Why are your garments red,
    your clothes as if you had trodden the winepress?

3   —I have trodden the winepress alone.
    Of the men of my people not one was with me.
    In my anger I trod them down,
    trampled them in my wrath.
    Their juice spattered my garments,
    and all my clothes are stained.

4   For in my heart was a day of vengeance,
    my year of redemption had come.

5   I looked: there was no one to help;
    aghast: not one could I find to support me.
    My own arm then was my mainstay,
    my wrath my support.

6   I crushed the people in my fury,
    trampled them in my anger,
    and made the juice of them run all over the ground.

A psalm

7   Let me sing the praises of Yahweh's goodness,
    and of his marvellous deeds,
    in return for all that he has done for us
    and for the great kindness
    he has shown us in his mercy
    and in his boundless goodness.

8   He said, 'Truly they are my people,
    sons and no rogues'.
    He proved himself their saviour

in all their troubles.   9
It was neither messenger nor angel
but his Presence that saved them.
In his love and pity
he redeemed them himself,
he lifted them up, carried them,
throughout the days of old.
But they rebelled, they grieved   10
his holy spirit.
Then he turned enemy,
and himself waged war on them.
They remembered the days of old,   11
of Moses his servant.
Where is he who brought out of the sea
the shepherd of his flock?
Where is he who endowed him
with his holy spirit,
who at the right hand of Moses   12
set to work with his glorious arm,
who divided the waters before them
to win himself everlasting renown,
who made them walk through the ocean   13
as easily as a horse through the desert?
They stumbled as little •as an ox   14
going down to the plain.
The spirit of Yahweh led them to rest.
This is how you guided your people
to win yourself glorious renown.

Look down from heaven, look down   15
from your holy and glorious dwelling.
Where is your ardour, your might,
the yearning of your inmost heart?
Do not let your compassion go unmoved,
for you are our Father.   16
For Abraham does not own us
and Israel^a does not acknowledge us;
you, Yahweh, yourself are our Father,
Our Redeemer is your ancient name.
Why, Yahweh, leave us to stray from your ways   17
and harden our hearts against fearing you?
Return, for the sake of your servants,
the tribes of your inheritance.
Why have the wicked set foot in your sanctuary,   18
why are our enemies trampling your sanctuary?
We have long been like people you do not rule,   19
people who do not bear your name.

Oh, that you would tear the heavens open and come down   1
—at your Presence the mountains would melt,   2

64

as fire sets brushwood alight,   1
as fire causes water to boil—
to make known your name to your enemies,
and make the nations tremble at your Presence,
working unexpected miracles   2
such as no one has ever heard of before.   3
    4
No ear has heard,

no eye has seen
any god but you act like this
for those who trust him.

4
5
You guide those who act with integrity
and keep your ways in mind.
You were angry when we were sinners;
we had long been rebels against you.

5
6
We were all like men unclean,
all that integrity of ours like filthy clothing.
We have all withered like leaves
and our sins blew us away like the wind.

6
7
No one invoked your name
or roused himself to catch hold of you.
For you hid your face from us
and gave us up to the power of our sins.

7
8
And yet, Yahweh, you are our Father;
we the clay, you the potter,
we are all the work of your hand.

8
9
Do not let your anger go too far, Yahweh,
or go on thinking of our sins for ever.
See, see, we are all your people;

9
10
your holy cities are a wilderness,
Zion a wilderness,
Jerusalem a desolation,

10
11
our holy and glorious Temple,
in which our fathers prayed to you,
is burnt to the ground;
all that gave us pleasure lies in ruins.

11
12
Yahweh, can you go unmoved by all of this,
oppressing us beyond measure by your silence?

A diatribe against idolatry; eschatological discourse

1 65 I was ready to be approached by those who did not consult me, ready to
be found by those who did not seek me. I said, 'I am here, I am here',
2 to a nation that did not invoke my name. •Each day I stretched out my hand to
3 a rebellious people who went by evil ways, following their own whims, •a people
who provoked me to my face incessantly, sacrificing in gardens, burning incense
4 on bricks, •living in tombs, spending nights in dark corners, eating the meat
5 of pigs, using unclean foods in their kitchens. •'Keep off,' they say 'do not
come near me, or I might sanctify you.' Such men are smoke in my nostrils,
6 an ever burning fire. •See, it is inscribed in front of me; I will not be silent until
7 I have settled my account with them •for their sins and their fathers' sins, says
Yahweh, those men who burned incense on the mountains and insulted me on
the hills. I will pay them back in full all they deserve.

8 Yahweh says this: When new wine is found in a bunch of grapes people
say, 'Do not destroy it, it contains a blessing'. I shall do the same for the sake
9 of those who serve me. I refuse to destroy the whole. •I will create a race from
Jacob, and heirs to my mountains from Judah. My chosen shall inherit them,
10 my servants live in them. •Sharon will be a pasture for flocks, the Valley
of Achor a feeding ground for oxen, for those of my people who have sought me.

11
But you who have abandoned Yahweh,
and forgotten my holy mountain,
who lay the table for Gad,
who fill a cup for Meni,[a]

---

63 a. The patriarch Jacob.
65 a. Gad and Meni are pagan gods.

> I commit you to the sword,   12
> all of you to fall in the slaughter.
> For I called and you would not answer,
> I spoke and you would not listen.
> You did what I consider evil,
> you chose to do what displeases me.
> Therefore, thus speaks   13
> the Lord Yahweh:
> You shall see my servants eat
> while you go hungry.
> You shall see my servants drink
> while you go thirsty.
> You shall see my servants rejoice
> while you are put to shame.
> You shall hear my servants sing   14
> for joy of heart,
> while you will moan
> for sadness of heart;
> you will wail for distress of spirit.

My chosen ones will use as a curse the name you leave behind: May the Lord 15 Yahweh strike you dead. But my servants are to be given a new name. Whoever asks to be blessed on earth will ask to be blessed by the God of 16 truth, and whoever takes oath on earth will take oath by the God of truth, for past troubles will be forgotten and hidden from my eyes. •For now I create 17 new heavens and a new earth, and the past will not be remembered, and will come no more to men's minds. •Be glad and rejoice for ever and ever for what I am 18 creating, because I now create Jerusalem 'Joy' and her people 'Gladness'. •I shall 19 rejoice over Jerusalem and exult in my people. No more will the sound of weeping or the sound of cries be heard in her; •in her, no more will be found the infant living 20 a few days only, or the old man not living to the end of his days. To die at the age of a hundred will be dying young; not to live to be a hundred will be the sign of a curse. •They will build houses and inhabit them, plant vineyards and 21 eat their fruit. •They will not build for others to live in, or plant so that others 22 can eat. For my people shall live as long as trees, and my chosen ones wear out what their hands have made. •They will not toil in vain or beget children to 23 their own ruin, for they will be a race blessed by Yahweh, and their children with them. •Long before they call I shall answer; before they stop speaking 24 I shall have heard. •The wolf and the young lamb will feed together, *the lion* 25 *eat straw like the ox*, and dust will be the serpent's food. *They will do no hurt, no harm on all my holy mountain*, says Yahweh.[b]

Oracle

66

> Thus says Yahweh: 1
> With heaven my throne
> and earth my footstool,
> what house could you build me,
> what place could you make for my rest?
> All of this was made by my hand   2
> and all of this is mine—it is Yahweh who speaks.
> But my eyes are drawn to the man
> of humbled and contrite spirit,
> who trembles at my word.

Against the intrusion of idolatrous practice

> Some immolate an ox, some slaughter a man,   3
> some sacrifice a lamb, some strangle a dog.

> Some offer oblations of pig's blood,
> some burn memorial incense, some consecrate idols
> Since they elect to follow their own ways
> and their souls delight in their abominations,

4
> I in my turn will select hardships for them
> and bring them what they dread;
> for I called and no one would answer,
> I spoke and they would not listen.
> They did what I consider evil,
> they chose to do what displeases me.

An apocalyptic poem

5
> Listen to the word of Yahweh,
> you who tremble at his word.
> Your brothers say, who hate you,
> who reject you because of my name,
> 'Let Yahweh show his glory,
> let us witness your joy!'
> But they shall be put to shame.

6
> Listen. An uproar from the city!
> A voice from the Temple!
> The voice of Yahweh bringing
> retribution on his enemies.

7
> Long before being in labour
> she has given birth.
> Before being overtaken by birth pangs,
> she has been delivered of a boy.

8
> Who ever heard of such a thing,
> who ever saw anything like this?
> Is a country born
> in one day?
>
> Is a nation brought forth
> all at once,
> that Zion only just in labour
> should bring forth sons?

9
> Am I to open the womb and not bring to birth?
> says Yahweh.
> Or I, who bring to birth, am I to close it?
> says your God.

10
> Rejoice, Jerusalem,
> be glad for her, all you who love her!
> Rejoice, rejoice for her,
> all you who mourned her!

11
> That you may be suckled, filled,
> from her consoling breast,
> that you may savour with delight
> her glorious breasts.

12
> For thus says Yahweh:
> Now towards her I send flowing
> peace, like a river,
> and like a stream in spate
> the glory of the nations.

b. The quotations are from the poem which is ch. 11.

At her breast will her nurslings be carried
and fondled in her lap.
Like a son comforted by his mother   13
will I comfort you.
(And by Jerusalem you will be comforted.)

At the sight your heart will rejoice,   14
and your bones flourish like the grass.
To his servants Yahweh will reveal his hand,
but to his enemies his fury.

For see how Yahweh comes in fire,   15
his chariots like the tempest,
to assuage his anger with burning,
his threats with flaming fire.

For by fire will Yahweh execute judgement,   16
and by his sword, against all mankind.
The victims of Yahweh will be many.

A fragment condemning pagan mysteries

As for those who sanctify themselves and purify themselves to enter 17
     the gardens,
following the one in the centre,
who eat the flesh of pigs, reptiles, rats:
their deeds and their thoughts shall end all at once
—it is Yahweh who speaks.

An eschatological discourse

I am coming to gather the nations of every language. They shall come to 18
witness my glory. •I will give them a sign and send some of their survivors 19
to the nations: to Tarshish, Put, Lud, Moshech, Rosh, Tubal, and Javan, to the
distant islands[a] that have never heard of me or seen my glory. They will proclaim
my glory to the nations. •As an offering to Yahweh they will bring all your 20
brothers, on horses, in chariots, in litters, on mules, on dromedaries, from all
the nations to my holy mountain in Jerusalem, says Yahweh, like Israelites
bringing oblations in clean vessels to the Temple of Yahweh. •And of some 21
of them I will make priests and Levites, says Yahweh.

For as the new heavens   22
and the new earth I shall make
will endure before me—it is Yahweh who speaks—
so will your race and name endure.

From New Moon to New Moon,   23
from sabbath to sabbath,
all mankind will come to bow down
in my presence, says Yahweh.

And on their way out they will see   24
the corpses of men
who have rebelled against me.
Their worm will not die
nor their fire go out;
they will be loathsome to all mankind.

---

66 a. Of these distant places, Rosh is unknown; the other names represent: Tartessos (Spain),
Somaliland, Libya, two regions of Asia Minor and Ionia.

INTRODUCTION TO THE BOOKS OF

JEREMIAH,

LAMENTATIONS AND BARUCH

Jeremiah

Jeremiah, a man of peace, was called to prophesy strife and disaster. In the years which saw the ruin and the end of the kingdom of Judah, he contended against kings, priests, false prophets and the nation itself, maintaining that resistance to the Chaldaean invader was vain resistance to the inexorable will of Yahweh. As the biographical anecdotes included in the book show, he was not a popular figure in his own time and barely escaped the death penalty.

However the prophecies collected by his secretary Baruch continued to be studied, meditated and interpreted; and after his death he grew steadily in stature. The truth of his message was eventually proved by history; his book reflects a warm personal religion and a confidence that there will be a covenant written in the heart; and by the Maccabean period, we find Jeremiah considered a protector of the nation, almost a patron saint.

The various oracles in the book are not in their chronological order and they include certain prophecies of a later date altogether. Nevertheless, the body of the work is undoubtedly made up of the oracles dictated to Baruch in 605 (as recounted in the book) and rewritten and supplemented afterwards, when the king had ordered the burning of the first scroll.

Lamentations

The subject-matter of this short book certainly reflects the lifetime of Jeremiah, to whom the Lamentations have traditionally been ascribed. Chapters 1, 2 and 4 take the form of a dirge for the dead, and were written in Palestine after the fall of Jerusalem in 587.

However, the conscious literary forms seem foreign to the direct sincerity of Jeremiah in his prophecies, and the poems contain judgements which contradict some of his decided views. The book remains a classic of repentance with a striking pathos.

Baruch

This short collection testifies to the enduring reputation of Jeremiah. Commended under the name of Baruch, it actually contains a prayer, a 'wisdom' poem, a prophetic passage, and a letter setting out the argument against idolatry. The letter is of the Greek period; the other sections are difficult to date and may be as late as the 2nd or 1st century B.C.

JEREMIAH

Title

¹ **1** The words of Jeremiah son of Hilkiah, of a priestly family living at Anathoth*ᵃ*
² in the territory of Benjamin. •The word of Yahweh was addressed to him in
the days of Josiah son of Amon, king of Judah, in the thirteenth year of his
³ reign;*ᵇ* •then in the days of Jehoiakim son of Josiah, king of Judah, until the end
of the eleventh year of Zedekiah son of Josiah, king of Judah, until the
deportation of Jerusalem which occurred in the fifth month.*ᶜ*

I. ORACLES AGAINST JUDAH AND JERUSALEM

A. IN THE REIGN OF JOSIAH

The call of Jeremiah

⁴ The word of Yahweh was addressed to me, saying,

⁵ 'Before I formed you in the womb I knew you;
before you came to birth I consecrated you;
I have appointed you as prophet to the nations'.

⁶ I said, 'Ah, Lord Yahweh; look, I do not know how to speak: I am a child!'

⁷ But Yahweh replied,
'Do not say, "I am a child".
Go now to those to whom I send you
and say whatever I command you.

⁸ Do not be afraid of them,
for I am with you to protect you—
it is Yahweh who speaks!'

⁹ Then Yahweh put out his hand and touched my mouth and said to me:

'There! I am putting my words into your mouth.
¹⁰ Look, today I am setting you
over nations and over kingdoms,
to tear up and to knock down,
to destroy and to overthrow,
to build and to plant.'

¹¹ The word of Yahweh was addressed to me asking, 'Jeremiah, what do you
¹² see?' 'I see a branch of the Watchful Tree'*ᵈ* I answered. •Then Yahweh said,
'Well seen! I too watch over my word to see it fulfilled.'

¹³ A second time the word of Yahweh was spoken to me, asking, 'What do you
see?' 'I see a cooking pot on the boil,' I answered 'with its contents tilting from
¹⁴ the North.' •Then Yahweh said:

---

1 a. Near Jerusalem.   b. 626 B.C.   c. That is, from 608 to July 587.   d. The almond, the
earliest to flower.

'The North is where disaster is boiling over
for all who live in this land;
since I am now going to summon all the kingdoms of the North—   15
it is Yahweh who speaks.
They are going to come, and each will set his throne
in front of the gates of Jerusalem,
all round outside its walls,
and outside all the towns of Judah.
I am going to pronounce my judgements against them   16
for all their wickedness; since they have abandoned me
to offer incense to other gods
and worship what their own hands have made.

'So now brace yourself for action.   17
Stand up and tell them
all I command you.
Do not be dismayed at their presence,
or in their presence I will make you dismayed.
I, for my part, today will make you   18
into a fortified city,
a pillar of iron,
and a wall of bronze
to confront all this land:
the kings of Judah, its princes,
its priests and the country people.
They will fight against you   19
but shall not overcome you,
for I am with you to deliver you—
it is Yahweh who speaks.'

The earliest preaching of Jeremiah: the apostasy of Israel

2 The word of Yahweh was addressed to me, saying, •'Go and shout this in ½
the hearing of Jerusalem:

"Yahweh says this:
I remember the affection of your youth,
the love of your bridal days:
you followed me through the wilderness,
through a land unsown.
Israel was sacred to Yahweh,   3
the first-fruits of his harvest;
anyone who ate of this had to pay for it,
misfortune came to them—
it is Yahweh who speaks." '
Listen to the word of Yahweh, House of Jacob,   4
and all you families of the House of Israel.
Thus says Yahweh,   5
'What shortcoming did your fathers find in me
that led them to desert me?
Vanity they pursued,
vanity they became.
They never said, "Where is Yahweh,   6
who brought us out of the land of Egypt
and led us through the wilderness,
through a land arid and scored,
a land of drought and darkness,
a land where no one passes,

and no man lives?"

7 I brought you to a fertile country
to enjoy its produce and good things;
but no sooner had you entered than you defiled my land,
and made my heritage detestable.

8 The priests have never asked, "Where is Yahweh?"
Those who administer the Law have no knowledge of me.
The shepherds[a] have rebelled against me;
the prophets have prophesied in the name of Baal,
following things with no power in them.

9 So I must put you on trial once more
—it is Yahweh who speaks—
and your children's children too.

10 Now take ship for the islands of Kittim[b]
or send to Kedar to enquire.
Take careful notice and observe
if anything like this has happened.

11 Does a nation change its gods?
—and these are not gods at all!
Yet my people have exchanged their Glory
for what has no power in it.

12 You heavens, stand aghast at this,
stand stupefied, stand utterly appalled
—it is Yahweh who speaks.

13 Since my people have committed a double crime:
they have abandoned me,
the fountain of living water,
only to dig cisterns for themselves,
leaky cisterns
that hold no water.

14 'Is Israel then a slave,
or born to serfdom,
for him to be preyed on like this?

15 Lions have roared at him,
loudly they have roared.
They have reduced his land to a desert;
his towns lie burnt and desolate.

16 The people of Noph and Tahpanhes
have even shaved your skull![c]

17 Have you not brought this on yourself,
by abandoning Yahweh your God?

18 What is the good of going to Egypt now
to drink the water of the Nile?
What is the good of going to Assyria
to drink the water of the river?

19 Your own wickedness is punishing you,
your own apostasies are rebuking you:
consider carefully
how evil and bitter it is for you
to abandon Yahweh your God
and not to stand in awe of me
—it is Yahweh Sabaoth who speaks.

---

2 a. The rulers.   **b.** Properly Cyprus; but here the term must include the coasts and islands of the Mediterranean, to the west of Palestine. *Kedar*, in the next line, a Transjordanian tribe, represents the East.   **c.** Allusion to Egyptian intervention, 608–605; the two towns are Egyptian.

'It is long ago now since you broke your yoke,　　　20
burst your bonds
and said, "I will not serve!"
Yet on every high hill
and under every spreading tree
you have lain down like a harlot.
Yet I had planted you, a choice vine,　　　21
a shoot of soundest stock.
How is it you have become a degenerate plant,
you bastard Vine?
Should you launder yourself with potash　　　22
and put in quantities of lye,
I should still detect the stain of your guilt
—it is the Lord Yahweh who speaks.
How dare you say, "I am not defiled,　　　23
I have not run after the Baals?"
Look at your footprints in the Valley,
and acknowledge what you have done.
A frantic she-camel running in all directions
bolts for the desert,　　　24
snuffing the breeze in desire;
who can control her when she is on heat?
Whoever looks for her will have no trouble,
he will find her with her mate!
Beware! Your own foot may soon go unshod,　　　25
your own throat may grow dry.
But "Who cares?" you said
"For I am in love with strangers
and they are the ones I follow".

'Like a thief in the disgrace of being caught,　　　26
so will the House of Israel be:
they, their kings, their princes,
their priests and their prophets,
who say to a piece of wood, "You are my father",　　　27
to a stone, "You have begotten me".
They turn their backs to me,
never their faces;
but when trouble comes they shout,
"Get up! Save us!"
Where are those gods of yours you made for yourself?　　　28
Let them get up to save you when trouble comes!
For you have as many gods
as you have towns, Judah,
as many altars for Baal
as Jerusalem has streets.
What case can you make against me?　　　29
You have all apostatised from me
—it is Yahweh who speaks.
In vain I have struck down your sons,　　　30
you did not accept correction:
your sword devoured your prophets
like a destructive lion.
What a brood you are! Listen, this is the word of Yahweh:　　　31
Have I been a desert for Israel
or a land of deepest gloom?
Then why do my people say,

> "We will go our own way,
> we will no longer come to you?"

32   Does a girl forget her ornaments,
> a bride her sash?
> And yet my people have forgotten me,
> for days beyond number.

33   'How well you know the way
> in pursuit of love!
> Yes, you have even accustomed your steps
> to walk with crime,

34   to the point when your hands display
> the stains from the blood of innocent men.
> —You never caught them trying to break and enter!
> Yes, for all these you will have to answer.

35   You say, "I am blameless,
> his anger has turned away from me".
> And here I am passing sentence on you
> because you say, "I have not sinned".

36   'How frivolously you undertake
> a change of course!
> But you will be disappointed by Egypt
> just as you were by Assyria.

37   You will have to leave there too
> with your hands on your head,
> for Yahweh has rejected those that you rely on,
> you will come to no good with them.'

The conversion

3   1 The word of Yahweh was addressed to me saying:

> 'If a man divorces his wife
> and she leaves him
> to marry someone else,
> may she still go back to him?
> Has not that piece of land
> been totally polluted?
> And you, who have prostituted yourself with so many lovers,
> you would come back to me?—it is Yahweh who speaks.

2   'Lift your eyes to the bare heights and look!
> Is there a single place where you have not offered your body?
> You waited by the roadside for clients
> like an Arab in the desert.
> You have polluted the country
> with your prostitution and your vices:

3   this is why the showers have been withheld,
> the late rains have not come.

> 'And you maintained a prostitute's bold front,
> never thinking to blush.

4   Even then did you not cry to me, "My father!
> You, the friend of my youth!

5   Will he keep his resentment for ever,
> will he maintain his wrath to the end?"
> That was what you said, and still you went on sinning,
> you were so obstinate.'

The Northern Kingdom urged to repent

In the days of King Josiah, Yahweh said to me, 'Have you seen what disloyal 6
Israel has done? How she has made her way up every high hill and to every
spreading tree, and has prostituted herself there? •I thought: After doing all 7
this she will come back to me. But she did not come back. Her faithless sister
Judah saw this. •She also saw that I had repudiated disloyal Israel for all her 8
adulteries and given her her divorce papers. Her faithless sister Judah, however,
was not afraid: she too went and played the whore. •So shameless was her 9
whoring that at last she polluted the country; she committed adultery with lumps
of stone and pieces of wood. •Worse than all this: Judah, her faithless sister, has 10
not come back to me in sincerity, but only in pretence—it is Yahweh who speaks.'

And Yahweh said to me, 'Beside faithless Judah, disloyal Israel seems virtuous. 11
So go and shout these words towards the North: 12

> "Come back, disloyal Israel—it is Yahweh who speaks—
> I shall frown on you no more,
> since I am merciful—it is Yahweh who speaks.
> I shall not keep my resentment for ever.
> Only acknowledge your guilt: 13
> how you have apostatised from Yahweh your God,
> how you have flirted with strangers
> and have not listened to my voice—it is Yahweh who speaks.

Zion in the messianic age

"Come back, disloyal children—it is Yahweh who speaks—for I alone am 14
your Master. I will take one from a town, two from a clan, and bring you to
Zion. •I will give you shepherds after my own heart, and these shall feed you on 15
knowledge and discretion. •And when you have increased and become many 16
in the land, then—it is Yahweh who speaks—no one will ever say again: Where
is the ark of the covenant of Yahweh? There will be no thought of it, no memory
of it, no regret for it, no making of another.ᵃ •When that time comes, Jerusalem 17
shall be called: The Throne of Yahweh; all the nations will gather there in the
name of Yahweh and will no longer follow the dictates of their own stubborn
hearts.

"In those days the House of Judah will unite with the House of Israel; 18
together they will come from the land of the North to the land I gave your
ancestors for a heritage.

Continuation of the poem on the conversionᵇ

> "And I was thinking: 19
> How I wanted to rank you with my sons,
> and give you a country of delights,
> the fairest heritage of all the nations!
> I had thought you would call me: My father,
> and would never cease to follow me.
> But like a woman betraying her lover, 20
> the House of Israel has betrayed me—
> it is Yahweh who speaks." '

> A noise is heard on the bare heights: 21
> the weeping and entreaty of the sons of Israel,
> because they have gone so wildly astray,
> and forgotten Yahweh their God.
> 'Come back, disloyal sons, 22
> I want to heal your disloyalty.'
> 'We are here, we are coming to you,
> for you are Yahweh our God.

23   The heights are a delusion after all,
        so is the tumult of the mountains.

        'Yahweh our God is, after all,
        the saving of Israel.

24   The Thing of Shame[c] has devoured what our ancestors worked for
        since our youth
        (their flocks and herds, their sons and daughters).

25   Let us lie down in our shame, let our dishonour be our covering,
        for we have sinned against Yahweh our God

('we and our ancestors since our youth until today; and we have not listened to
the voice of Yahweh our God).'

1   **4**   'If you wish to come back, Israel—it is Yahweh who speaks—
                  it is to me you must return.
                  Do away with your abominations
                  and you will have no need to avoid me.

2   If you swear, "As Yahweh lives!"
        truthfully, justly, honestly,
        the nations will bless themselves by you,
        and glory in you.

3   For thus speaks Yahweh
        to the men of Judah and to the inhabitants of Jerusalem:
        Clean your ground thoroughly,
        sow nothing among thorns.

4   Circumcise yourselves for Yahweh; off with the foreskin of your hearts
        (men of Judah and inhabitants of Jerusalem),
        lest my wrath should leap out like a fire,
        and burn with no one to quench it,
        in return for the wickedness of your deeds.'

Invasion from the North

5   Announce it in Judah,
        proclaim it in Jerusalem!
        Sound the trumpet in the countryside,
        shout the message aloud:
        Mobilise!
        Take to the fortified towns!

6   Signpost the way to Zion;
        Run! Do not delay!
        I am bringing you disaster from the North,
        an immense calamity.

7   The lion is up from his thicket,
        the destroyer of nations is on his way,
        he has come from his home
        to reduce your land to a desert;
        your towns will be in ruins, deserted.

8   So wrap yourselves in sackcloth,
        lament and wail,
        since the burning anger of Yahweh
        has not turned away from us.

9   'That day—it is Yahweh who speaks—
        the king's heart will fail him,

---

3 a. The ark was destroyed with the Temple by the Chaldaeans in 587.   **b.** Continued from
v.5.   **c.** The false god, Baal.

the princes' hearts will fail them too,
the priests will stand aghast,
the prophets stupefied.
People will say, "Ah, Lord Yahweh,   10
how utterly you deceived us
by saying: You will have peace,*—
even when the sword is at our throats!"
When that time comes, this will be said   11
to this people and to Jerusalem:
From the bare heights a scorching wind
blows from the desert on the daughter of my people
—and not to winnow or to cleanse!
A wind, full of threats, comes at my command.   12
Now I myself am going to pronounce
sentence on them!

"Look, he is advancing like the clouds,   13
his chariots like a hurricane,
his horses swifter than eagles.
Trouble is coming! We are lost!"
Wash your heart clean of wickedness, Jerusalem,   14
and so be saved.
How long will you harbour in your breast
your pernicious thoughts?
For a voice from Dan shouts the news,   15
proclaims disaster from the highlands of Ephraim.
Give warning of it, announce it in Judah,   16
proclaim it to Jerusalem:
"Enemies are coming from a distant country,
shouting their war cry against the towns of Judah;
they surround Jerusalem like watchmen round a field   17
because she has apostatised from me—it is Yahweh who speaks.
Your own behaviour and actions   18
have brought this on you.
This is your fate! How bitter!
How it pierces your heart!" '

I am in anguish! I writhe with pain!   19
Walls of my heart!
My heart is throbbing!
I cannot keep quiet,
for I have heard the trumpet call
and the cry of war.
Ruin on ruin is the news: 20
the whole land is laid waste,
my tents are suddenly destroyed,
in one moment all that sheltered me is gone.
How long must I see the standard   21
and hear the trumpet call?
'This is because my people are stupid,   22
they do not know me,
they are slow-witted children,
they have no understanding:
they are clever enough at doing wrong,
but do not know how to do right.'

I looked to the earth, to see a formless waste;   23
to the heavens, and their light had gone.

24 I looked to the mountains, to see them quaking
and all the heights astir.
25 I looked, to see no man at all,
the very birds of heaven had fled.
26 I looked, to see the wooded country a wilderness,
all its towns in ruins,
at the presence of Yahweh,
at the presence of his burning anger.
27 Yes, thus speaks Yahweh,
'The whole land shall be laid waste,
I will make an end of it once for all;
28 at which the earth will go into mourning,
and the heavens above grow dark.
For I have spoken and will not change my mind,
I have decided and will not go back on it.'
29 At the cry 'Horsemen and bowmen!'
the whole country takes flight:
some plunge into the thickets,
others scale the rocks;
every town is abandoned,
no one is left there.
30 And you, what are you going to do?
You may dress yourself in scarlet,
put on ornaments of gold,
enlarge your eyes with paint
but you make yourself pretty in vain.
Your lovers disdain you,
your life is what they are seeking.
31 Yes, I hear screams like those of a woman in labour,
anguish like that of a woman giving birth to her first child;
they are the screams of the daughter of Zion, gasping,
hands outstretched,
'Ah, I despair! I am fainting away
with murderers surrounding me.'

The invasion well deserved

1 5 'Rove to and fro through the streets of Jerusalem,
look, now, and learn,
search her squares;
if you can find a man,
one man who does right
and seeks the truth,
then I will pardon her,
says Yahweh.'

3a Yahweh, do not your eyes desire to look on truth?
2 But though they say, 'As Yahweh lives',
they are, in fact, uttering a false oath.
3b You have struck them; they have not felt it.
You have crushed them; they have ignored the lesson.
They have set their faces harder than rock,
they have refused to repent.
4 'Only the ordinary people' I thought 'behave stupidly,
because they do not know what Yahweh requires,
nor the ruling of their God.

4 a. The promise of the false prophets. See 6:14.

I will approach the men in power   5
and speak to them,
for these will know what Yahweh requires,
and the ruling of their God.'
But these, too, had broken the yoke,
had burst the bonds.

And this is why a lion from the forest strikes them down,   6
a desert wolf makes havoc of them,
a leopard lurks round their towns:
whoever goes out is torn to pieces—
because of their countless crimes,
their ever increasing apostasies.

'Why should I pardon you?   7
Your sons have abandoned me,
to swear by gods that are not gods at all.
I fed them full, and they became adulterers,
they haunted the brothel.
They were well-fed, lusty stallions,   8
each neighing for his neighbour's wife.
And am I not to punish them for such things   9
—it is Yahweh who speaks—
or from such a nation
exact my vengeance?
Scale her terraces! Destroy!   10
Make an end of her!
Strip off her branches,
Yahweh does not own them.
Treacherously indeed has she betrayed me,   11
this House of Israel—it is Yahweh who speaks.

'They have disowned Yahweh: 12
they have said, "He is nothing;
no evil will overtake us,
we shall not see sword or famine.
And the prophets? Nothing but wind;   13a
the word is not in them!"
Hence—so says Yahweh,   14a
the God of Sabaoth—
this is what is going to happen to them   13b
for saying this: 14b
now I will make my words
a fire in your mouth,
and make this people wood,
for the fire to devour.
Now I will bring on you all   15
a nation from afar, House of Israel
—it is Yahweh who speaks—
an invincible nation,
an ancient nation,
a nation whose tongue you do not know,
whose language you cannot understand.
Their quiver is an open tomb;   16
heroes all of them.
They will devour your harvest and your food,   17
devour your sons and daughters,
devour your flocks and herds,

> devour your vines and fig trees,
> bring down your fortified towns
> in which you put your trust.

Two supplementary paragraphs

18 'Yet even in those days—it is Yahweh who speaks—I shall not completely destroy you.

19 'And when they ask, "Why has Yahweh our God done all this to us?" you are to give them this answer, "As you abandoned me to serve alien gods in your own land, so you must serve aliens in a land that is not your own".

In a time of famine (?)

20 'Announce this in the House of Jacob,
> proclaim it in Judah, and say:

21 "Now listen to this,
> stupid and thoughtless people
> —they have eyes and do not see,
> they have ears and do not hear!

22 Have you no fear of me?—it is Yahweh who speaks—
> Will you not tremble at my presence,
> who set the sands as limit to the sea,
> as an everlasting barrier it can not pass?
> It storms but can do nothing.
> its waves may roar but do not pass beyond.

23 But this people
> has a rebellious, unruly heart;
> they have rebelled—being good at this!

24 They have not said in their hearts:
> Come, we must fear Yahweh our God
> who gives the rain, the early rain
> and the later, at the right time of year,
> who assures us
> of weeks appointed for harvest.

25 Your crimes have made all this go wrong,
> your sins have deprived you of these favours.

Resumption of the theme of the invasion

26 "Yes, there are wicked men among my people
> who spread their nets;
> like fowlers they set snares,
> but it is men they catch.

27 Like a cage full of birds
> so are their houses full of loot;
> they have grown rich and powerful because of it,

28 fat and sleek.
> Yes, in wickedness they go to any lengths,
> they have no respect for rights,
> for orphans' rights, to support them;
> they do not uphold the cause of the poor.

29 And must I not punish them for such things
> —it is Yahweh who speaks—
> or from such a nation
> exact my vengeance?

30 Monstrous, horrible things
> are happening in the land:

31 the prophets prophesy falsely,

the priests teach whatever they please.
And my people love it!
But when the end comes, what will you do?

More about the invasion

6 "Save yourselves, men of Benjamin,　　　　　　　1
from the heart of Jerusalem!
Sound the trumpet in Tekoa!ᵃ
Set up a standard on Beth-hac-cherem!
For disaster threatens from the North,
an immense calamity.
Shall we compare the daughter of Zion　　　　　　2
to a tender pasture?
Shepherds advance on her　　　　　　　　　　　　3
with their flocks.
They have pitched their tents all round her,
each grazes the part he chooses.
Prepare for battle against her!　　　　　　　　　　4
To arms! We will launch the attack in broad daylight.
Despair! The daylight is fading already,
the evening shadows lengthen.
To arms! We will launch the attack under cover of dark　5
and destroy her palaces.
For thus says Yahweh Sabaoth:　　　　　　　　　　6
Cut down the trees,
throw up an earthwork outside Jerusalem:
she is the City of Falsehood,
with nothing but oppression in her.
As a well keeps its water fresh　　　　　　　　　　7
so she keeps her wickedness fresh.
Violence and ruin are what you hear in her,
diseases and wounds are always before me.
Be warned, Jerusalem,　　　　　　　　　　　　　8
lest I should turn away from you,
and reduce you to a desert,
a land without people.
"Yahweh Sabaoth says this:　　　　　　　　　　　9
Glean, glean, as a vine is gleaned,
what is left of Israel;
like a grape-picker pass your hand again
over the branches!" '
To whom am I to speak,　　　　　　　　　　　　10
whom can I urge to hear?
Plainly their ears are uncircumcised,
they cannot listen.
Plainly the word of Yahweh is for them something contemptible,
they have no taste for it.
But I am full of the wrath of Yahweh,　　　　　　11
I am weary of holding it in.
'Then pour it on the children in the streets,
and where young men gather, too.
All shall be taken: husband and wife,
the greybeard and the man weighed down with years.
Their houses shall pass to other men,　　　　　　12
so also their fields and their wives.
Yes, I will stretch my hand

over those living in this land—it is Yahweh who speaks.

13 For all, least no less than greatest,
    all are out for dishonest gain;
    prophet no less than priest,
    all practise fraud.

14 They dress my people's wound
    without concern: "Peace! Peace!" they say,
    but there is no peace.

15 They should be ashamed of their abominable deeds
    But not they! They feel no shame,
    they have forgotten how to blush.
    And so as others fall, they too shall fall;
    they shall be thrown down when I come to deal with them
    —says Yahweh.

16 'Yahweh says this:
    Put yourselves on the ways of long ago
    enquire about the ancient paths:
    which was the good way? Take it then,
    and you shall find rest.
    Instead they have said, "We will not take it".

17 I posted look-outs on their behalf:
    Listen to the sound of the trumpet!
    But they answered, "We will not listen".

18 Then hear, you nations,
    and know, assembly,
    what I will do to them.

19 Hear, earth!
    I am bringing a disaster
    on this people:
    it is the fruit of their apostasy,
    since they have not listened to my words
    and, as for my Law, they have rejected that.

20 What do I care about incense
    imported from Sheba,
    or fragrant cane
    from a distant country?
    Your holocausts are not acceptable,
    your sacrifices do not please me.

21 Therefore—thus says Yahweh:
    In front of this people I will now lay blocks
    for them to stumble over;
    father as well as son,
    neighbour and friend, all shall perish.

22 'Yahweh says this:
    Now a people is coming from the land of the North,
    from the far ends of the earth a mighty nation stirs:

23 they are armed with bow and spear,
    they are cruel and pitiless;
    their noise is like the roaring of the sea;
    they are riding horses,
    each man equipped for war
    on you, daughter of Zion!

24 We have heard the news,
    our hands fall limp,

6 a. 5 m. S. of Bethlehem.

anguish has gripped us,
pain like a woman's labour.
Do not go out into the countryside,   25
do not venture on the roads,
for the enemy's sword is there,
there is terror on every side.
Wrap yourself in sackcloth, daughter of my people,   26
roll in ashes;
mourn as for an only son,
a very bitter dirge.
For on us suddenly
the destroyer is coming.

'I have appointed you as assayer of my people,   27
to learn and to assay how they behave.
They are apostates, all of them, promiscuous slanderers,   28
all of them corrupt.
The bellows blast away   29
to make the fire burn away the lead.
In vain: the smelter does his work,
but the dross is not purged out.
Silver-reject, men call them,   30
and indeed Yahweh has rejected them!'

B. ORACLES MAINLY IN THE REIGN OF JEHOIAKIM

True worship
a. Against the Temple

7 The word that was addressed to Jeremiah by Yahweh, •'Go and stand at the $\frac{1}{2}$ gate of the Temple of Yahweh and there proclaim this message. Say, "Listen to the word of Yahweh, all you men of Judah who come in by these gates to worship Yahweh. •Yahweh Sabaoth, the God of Israel, says this: Amend 3 your behaviour and your actions and I will stay with you here in this place. Put no trust in delusive words like these: This is the sanctuary of Yahweh, the 4 sanctuary of Yahweh, the sanctuary of Yahweh! •But if you do amend your 5 behaviour and your actions, if you treat each other fairly, •if you do not exploit 6 the stranger, the orphan and the widow (if you do not shed innocent blood in this place), and if you do not follow alien gods, to your own ruin, •then here 7 in this place I will stay with you, in the land that long ago I gave to your fathers for ever. •Yet here you are, trusting in delusive words, to no purpose! 8 Steal, would you, murder, commit adultery, perjure yourselves, burn incense 9 to Baal, follow alien gods that you do not know?—•and then come presenting 10 yourselves in this Temple that bears my name, saying: Now we are safe—safe to go on committing all these abominations! •Do you take this Temple that 11 bears my name for a robbers' den? I, at any rate, am not blind—it is Yahweh who speaks.

Now go to my place in Shiloh^a where at first I gave my name a home; see 12 what I have done to it because of the wickedness of my people Israel! •And 13 now, since you have committed all these sins—it is Yahweh who speaks—and have refused to listen when I spoke so urgently, so persistently, or to answer when I called you, •I will treat this Temple that bears my name, and in which 14 you put your trust, and the place I have given to you and your ancestors, just as I treated Shiloh. •I will drive you out of my sight, as I drove all your kinsmen, 15 the entire race of Ephraim."

b. Alien gods

16 'You, for your part, must not intercede for this people, nor raise either plea or
17 prayer on their behalf; do not plead with me, for I will not listen to you. •Cannot
you see what they are doing in the towns of Judah and in the streets of Jerusalem?
18 The children collect the wood, the fathers light the fire, the women knead the
dough, to make cakes for the Queen of Heaven;[b] and, to spite me, they pour
19 libations to alien gods. •Is it really me they spite—it is Yahweh who speaks—
20 is it not in fact themselves, to their own confusion? •Therefore, the Lord
Yahweh says this: My anger and my wrath shall be poured out on this place,
over man and beast, trees of the countryside, fruits of the soil; it shall burn, and
not be quenched.

c. Worship without sincerity

21 'Yahweh Sabaoth, the God of Israel, says this: Add your holocausts to
22 your sacrifices and eat all the meat. •For when I brought your ancestors out of
the land of Egypt, I said nothing to them, gave them no orders, about holocaust
23 and sacrifice. •These were my orders: Listen to my voice, then I will be your
God and you shall be my people. Follow right to the end the way that I mark
24 out for you, and you will prosper. •But they did not listen, they did not pay
attention; they followed the dictates of their own evil hearts, refused to face me,
25 and turned their backs on me. •From the day your ancestors came out of the land
of Egypt until today, day after day I have persistently sent you all my servants
26 the prophets. •But they have not listened to me, have not paid attention; they
27 have grown stubborn and behaved worse than their ancestors. •You may say all
these words to them: they will not listen to you; you may call them: they will
28 not answer. •So tell them this, "Here is the nation that will not listen to the
voice of Yahweh its God nor take correction. Sincerity is no more, it has
vanished from their mouths.

d. More about idolatrous worship: a threat of exile

29   "Cut off your tresses, throw them down.
                On the bare heights raise a dirge.
                For Yahweh has rejected, has abandoned,
                a brood that he detests."

30 'Yes, the sons of Judah have done what displeases me—it is Yahweh who
speaks. They have put their abominations in the Temple that bears my name,
31 to defile it; •they have built the high place of Topheth in the Valley of Ben-
hinnom, to burn their sons and daughters; a thing I never commanded, a thing
32 that never entered my thoughts. •So now the days are coming—it is Yahweh
who speaks—when people will no longer talk of Topheth or of the Valley of
Ben-hinnom, but of the Valley of Slaughter. Topheth will become a burial ground,
33 for lack of other space; •the corpses of this people will feed the birds of heaven
34 and the beasts of the earth, and there shall be no one to drive them away. •I will
silence the shouts of rejoicing and mirth, the voices of bridegroom and bride,
in the towns of Judah and in the streets of Jerusalem, for the whole land will be
1 reduced to desert. 8 When that time comes—it is Yahweh who speaks—the
bones of the kings of Judah, and of the princes, of the priests, of the prophets,
2 of the inhabitants of Jerusalem, will be taken from their tombs. •They will be
spread out before the sun, the moon, the whole array of heaven, whom they have
loved and served, followed, consulted and worshipped.[a] They will not be
3 gathered or reburied but stay lying on the surface like dung. •And death will

7 a. The shrine at Shiloh had been destroyed by Philistines.   b. Ishtar, the Assyrian goddess
of fertility.
8 a. Worship of the heavenly bodies was practised in the reigns of Manasseh and Amon.

seem preferable to life to all the survivors of this wicked race, wherever I have
driven them—it is Yahweh Sabaoth who speaks.

Threats, lamentations, advice. The perversity of Israel

'You are to tell them, "Yahweh says this:　　　　　　　　　　4
If you fall, can you not stand up again,
if you stray can you never find your way back?
Why does this people persist in apostasy,　　　　　　　　　　5
in continuous apostasy?
They cling to illusion,
they refuse to come back.
I have listened attentively,　　　　　　　　　　6
they are not saying what they ought to:
not one repents of his wickedness
saying: What have I done?
All go astray as they pursue their course
like a horse charging into battle.
Even the stork in the sky　　　　　　　　　　7
knows the appropriate season;
turtledove, swallow, crane,
observe their time of migration.
And my people do not know
the ruling of Yahweh!

The Law as administered by the priests

"How dare you say: We are wise,　　　　　　　　　　8
and we possess the Law of Yahweh?
But look how it has been falsified
by the lying pen of the scribes!
The wise shall be shamed,　　　　　　　　　　9
caught out, confounded.
Look how they have rejected the word of Yahweh!
So what use is their wisdom to them?

Repetition of an earlier threat

"So I will give their wives to other men,　　　　　　　　　　10
their fields to new masters,
for all, least no less than greatest,
all are out for dishonest gain;
prophet no less than priest,
all practise fraud.
They dress my people's wound　　　　　　　　　　11
without concern: Peace! Peace! they say,
but there is no peace.
They should be ashamed of their abominable deeds.　　　　　　　　　　12
But not they! They feel no shame,
they have forgotten how to blush.
And so as others fall, they too shall fall;
they shall be thrown down when I come to deal with them
—says Yahweh.

Threats against Judah the Vine

"I would like to go harvesting there, says Yahweh.　　　　　　　　　　13
But there are no grapes on the vine,
no figs on the fig tree:
even the leaves are withered.

This is because I have brought them
ravagers to ravage them." '

14   'Why do we sit still?
Mobilise!
Let us take to the fortified towns
and perish there,
since Yahweh our God wants us to perish:
giving us poisoned water to drink
because we have sinned against him.

15   We were hoping for peace—no good came of it!
For the time of healing—nothing but terror!

16   From Dan you can hear
the snorting of their horses;
at the sound of their stallions' neighing
the whole countryside quakes:
they come to devour the land and all it holds,
the town and those that live in it.'

17   'Yes, now I send you
serpents, adders,
against which no charm exists;
they will bite you—it is Yahweh who speaks—

18   incurably.

A lamentation of the prophet during a famine

'Sorrow overtakes me,
my heart fails me.

19   Listen, the cry of the daughter of my people
sounds throughout the land,
"Yahweh no longer in Zion?
Her King no longer in her?"
(Why have they provoked me with their carved images,
with these Nothings from foreign countries?)

20   "The harvest is over, summer at an end,
and we have not been saved!"

21   The wound of the daughter of my people wounds me too,
all looks dark to me, terror grips me.

22   Is there not balm in Gilead any more?
Is there no doctor there?
Then why does it make no progress,
this cure of the daughter of my people?

23   Who will turn my head into a fountain,
1   and my eyes into a spring for tears,
so that I may weep all day, all night,
for all the dead out of the daughter of my people?

The moral corruption of Judah

1   **9** 'Who will find me a wayfarer's shelter
2   in the desert,
for me to quit my people,
and leave them far behind?
For all of them are adulterers,
a conspiracy of traitors.

2   They bend their tongue like a bow;
3   not truth but falsehood
predominates in the land;
yes, they go from crime to crime.

But Yahweh, they do not acknowledge him.
Let each be on his guard against his friend,   3/4
be mistrustful of your brother,
for every brother is a very Jacob,
and every friend a diligent slanderer.
Each deceives the other,   4/5
they do not speak the truth,
they have accustomed their tongues to lying,
they are corrupt, incapable of •repentance.   5/6
Fraud after fraud! Deceit after deceit!
They refuse to acknowledge Yahweh.
And so—Yahweh Sabaoth says this: 6/7
Look, I will now test them in the crucible
—but how am I to deal with their wickedness?
Their tongue is a deadly arrow,   7/8
the words they utter are deceitful;
"Peace!" each says to his neighbour,*
while in his heart plotting a trap for him.
And am I not to punish them for such things   8/9
—it is Yahweh who speaks—
or from such a nation
exact, my vengeance?

Lamentation in Zion

'Raise the wail and lamentation for the mountains,   9/10
the dirge for the desert pastures,
for they have been burnt: no one passes there,
the sound of flocks is heard no more.
Birds of the sky and animals,
all have fled, all are gone.
I mean to make Jerusalem a heap of ruins,   10/11
a jackal's lair,
and the towns of Judah
an uninhabited wasteland.'

Who is wise enough to understand this? Who has been charged by Yahweh's 11/12
own mouth to tell

why the land lies in ruins,
burnt like the desert where no one passes?

Yahweh has said, 'This is because they have forsaken my Law which I put 12/13
before them and have not listened to my voice or followed it, •but have followed 13/14
the dictates of their own stubborn hearts, followed the Baals as their ancestors
taught them. •And so this is what Yahweh Sabaoth, the God of Israel says: 14/15
Now I am going to give this people wormwood for their food and poisoned
water to drink. •I am going to scatter them throughout nations unknown to 15/16
their ancestors or to them; and I am going to pursue them with the sword until
I have exterminated them.'

You, there! Call the mourning women! Let them come!   16/17
Send for those who are best at it! Let them come!
Let them lose no time in raising the lament for us!   17/18
Let our eyes rain tears,
our eyelids run with weeping!
Yes, the wail is to be heard from Zion,   18/19
'What ruin is ours,
what utter shame!

> For we must leave the land,
> abandon our homes!'

19
20
> And you, women, now hear the word of Yahweh,
> let your ears take in the word his own mouth speaks.
> Teach your daughters how to wail,
> teach one another what dirge to sing,

20
21
> 'Death has climbed in at our windows,
> and made its way into our palaces;
> it has cut down the children in the street,
> the youths in the square.

21
22
> Men's corpses lie
> like dung in the open field,
> like sheaves left by the reaper,
> with no one to gather them.'

True wisdom

22
23
> Thus says Yahweh,
> 'Let the sage boast no more of his wisdom,
> nor the valiant of his valour,
> nor the rich man of his riches!

23
24
> But if anyone wants to boast, let him boast of this:
> of understanding and knowing me.
> For I am Yahweh, I rule with kindness,
> justice and integrity on earth;
> yes, these are what please me
> —it is Yahweh who speaks.

Circumcision, a false guarantee

24
25
25
26
'See, the days are coming—it is Yahweh who speaks—when I am going to punish all who are circumcised only in the flesh: •Egypt, Judah, the sons of Ammon, Moab, and all the Crop-Heads^b who live in the desert. For all these nations, and the whole House of Israel too, are uncircumcised at heart.'

Idols and the true God

1
2
10 Listen, House of Israel, to the word that Yahweh addresses to you. •Thus says Yahweh:

> 'Do not adopt the ways of the nations
> or take alarm at the heavenly signs,
> alarmed though the nations may be at them.

3
> Yes, the Dread of the peoples is a nothing,
> wood, nothing more, cut out of a forest,
> worked with a blade by a carver's hand,

4a
> then embellished with silver and gold

9
> —silver leaf from Tarshish,
> and gold from Ophir—
> work of a carver and a goldsmith's hand:
> all some craftsman's work;
> they dress them up in violet and purple;

4b
> they fix them with nail and hammer
> to prevent them from falling.

5
> Scarecrows in a melon patch, and dumb as these,
> they have to be carried, cannot walk themselves.
> Have no fear of them: they can do no harm
> —nor any good either!'

9 a. The customary greeting.   **b.** Arabs.

Yahweh, there is no one like you, 6
so great are you,
so great your mighty name.
Who would not revere you, King of nations? 7
Yes, this is your due.
Since of all the wise among the nations,
and in all their kingdoms,
there is not a single one like you.

The whole lot of them are brutish and stupid: 8
the teaching given by these Nothings is void of sense.
But Yahweh is the true God. 10
He is the living God,
the everlasting King.
The earth quakes when he is wrathful,
the nations cannot endure his fury.

('Tell them this, "The gods who did not make the heavens and the earth, 11
will vanish from the earth and from under the heavens".')

By his power he made the earth, 12
by his wisdom set the world firm,
by his discernment spread out the heavens.
When he thunders 13
there is a tumult of water in the heavens;
he raises clouds from the boundaries of earth,
makes the lightning flash for the downpour,
and brings the wind from his storehouse.
At this all men stand stupefied, uncomprehending, 14
every goldsmith blushes for the idol he has made,
since his images are nothing but delusion,
with no breath in them.
They are a Nothing, a laughable production; 15
when the time comes for them to be punished, they will vanish.
'The Portion of Jacob' is not like these, 16
for he is the maker of everything,
and Israel is the tribe that is his heritage.
His name is Yahweh Sabaoth.

Panic in the country

Pack up! Flee the country, 17
you the besieged!
For Yahweh says this, 18
'Now I will throw out
the inhabitants of the land
this time,
and bring distress on them,
to see if they will find me then!'
I despair for this wound of mine! 19
My injury is incurable!
I told myself
this was an affliction that could be borne,
but now my tent is destroyed, 20
all my ropes are snapped,
my sons have left me and are no more;
no one is left to put my tent up again,
or to hang the side-cloths.

21 The shepherds are the ones who have been stupid:
they have not searched for Yahweh.
This is why they have not prospered
and why their whole flock has been dispersed.

22 News! News has come!
A mighty uproar coming from the land of the North
to reduce the towns of Judah
to desert, to a jackal's lair.

A prayer of Jeremiah

23 Well you know, Yahweh,
the course of man is not in his control,
nor is it in man's power as he goes his way
to guide his steps.

24 Correct us, Yahweh, gently,
not in your anger or you will reduce us to nothing.

25 Pour out your anger on the pagans,
who do not acknowledge you,
and on those races
that do not call on your name,
for they have devoured Jacob and made an end of him,
and reduced his home to desolation.

Jeremiah and observance of the covenant

$\begin{smallmatrix}1\\2\\3\end{smallmatrix}$ **11** The word that was addressed to Jeremiah by Yahweh, •'Speak to the men of Judah and to the inhabitants of Jerusalem. •Tell them, "Yahweh, the God of Israel, says this: Cursed be the man who will not listen to the words
4 of this covenant •which I ordained for your ancestors when I brought them out of the furnace of iron, out of the land of Egypt. Listen to my voice, I told them, carry out all my orders, then you shall be my people and I will be your God,
5 to confirm the oath I swore to your fathers, that I would give them a land where
6 milk and honey flow—as it still does today." ' I replied, 'Yahweh, I will'. •Then Yahweh said to me, 'Proclaim all this in the towns of Judah and in the streets
7 of Jerusalem: "Listen to the words of this covenant and obey them. •For when I brought your ancestors out of the land of Egypt, I solemnly warned them,
8 and have persistently warned them until today: Listen to my voice. •But they did not listen, did not pay attention; everyone followed the dictates of his own evil heart. So, I fulfilled against them all the words of this covenant which I had ordained for them to obey and which they had not obeyed." '
9 Yahweh said to me, 'Plainly there is conspiracy among the men of Judah
10 and the citizens of Jerusalem. •They have reverted to the crimes of their ancestors who refused to listen to my words: they too are following alien gods and serving them. The House of Israel and the House of Judah have broken
11 my covenant which I made with their ancestors. •And so —Yahweh says this— I will now bring them a disaster which they cannot escape; if they invoke me
12 I will not listen to them. •The towns of Judah and the citizens of Jerusalem can go and invoke the gods to whom they burn incense, but these will be no help at all to them in the time of their distress.

13 'For you have as many gods
as you have towns, O Judah.
You have built as many incense altars to Baal
as Jerusalem has streets.

14 'You, for your part, must not intercede for this people, nor raise either plea or prayer on their behalf, for I will not listen when they call to me in the time of their distress.

Rebuke to the frequenters of the Temple

'What is my beloved doing in my house?   15
She is playing the hypocrite!
Can vows and consecrated meat
rid you of your guilt?
Am I to make you clean because of this?
A spreading olive tree so fair, so sturdy,   16
was Yahweh's name for you.
With the roar of a great wind
he sets its foliage on fire;
its branches burn.

'And Yahweh Sabaoth, who planted you, has decreed disaster for you because 17
of the crime the House of Israel and the House of Judah have committed,
provoking me by burning incense to Baal.'

Jeremiah persecuted in his own town

Yahweh revealed it to me; I was warned. Yahweh, that was when you opened 18
my eyes to their scheming. 12 'Yes, even your own brothers and your own 6
family play you false. Behind your back, they too criticise you openly. Put no
reliance on them when they seem to be friendly.' 11 I for my part was like a 19
trustful lamb being led to the slaughter-house, not knowing the schemes they were
plotting against me, 'Let us destroy the tree in its strength, let us cut him off from
the land of the living, so that his name may be quickly forgotten!'

But you, Yahweh Sabaoth, who pronounce a just sentence,   20
who probe the loins and heart,
let me see the vengeance you will take on them,
for I have committed my cause to you.

This is how Yahweh has spoken against the men of Anathoth who are 21
determined to kill me and have warned me, 'Do not prophesy in the name of
Yahweh or you will die at our hands!' •This is how I will punish them. Their 22
young men shall die by the sword, their sons and daughters by famine. •No one 23
will be left when I bring disaster on the men of Anathoth, when the year comes
for their punishment.'

The prosperity of the wicked

12

You have right on your side, Yahweh,   1
when I complain about you.
But I would like to debate a point of justice with you.
Why is it that the wicked live so prosperously?
Why do scoundrels enjoy peace?
You plant them, they take root,   2
and flourish, and even bear fruit.
You are always on their lips,
yet so far from their hearts.
You know me, Yahweh, you see me,   3
you probe my heart, it is in your hands.
Drag them off like sheep for the slaughter-house,
reserve them for the day of butchery.

(How long will the land be in mourning, and the grass wither all over the 4
countryside? The animals and birds are dying as a result of the wickedness of
the inhabitants.)

For they say,
'God does not see our behaviour'.

5   If you find it exhausting to race against men on foot,
      how will you compete against horses?
      If you are not secure in a peaceful country,
      how will you manage in the thickets along the Jordan?

Yahweh laments his ravaged inheritance

7   'I have abandoned my house,
      left my heritage,
      I have delivered what I dearly loved
      into the hands of its enemies.

8   For me my heritage has become
      a lion in the forest,
      it roars at me ferociously:
      so I now hate it.

9   Or is my heritage a speckled bird
      for the birds to flock on her thus from all directions?
      Come on, all you wild beasts, gather round,
      fall on the quarry!

10   Many shepherds have laid my vineyard waste,
      have trampled down my inheritance,
      reducing my pleasant inheritance
      to a deserted wilderness.

11   They have made it a mournful, desolate place,
      desolate before me.
      The whole land has been devastated
      and no one takes it to heart.

12   The devastators have arrived
      on all the bare heights of the desert
      (for Yahweh wields a sword that devours):
      from end to end of the land
      there is no peace for any living thing.

13   Wheat they have sown, thorns they reap:
      they have worn themselves out, to no profit.
      They are disappointed in their harvests,
      through the fury of Yahweh.

The neighbouring peoples: their judgement and salvation

14   'Thus says Yahweh: As for all my evil neighbours who have laid hands on the
      heritage I granted my people Israel I will now tear them from their countries.
15   (But I will tear the House of Judah out of their hands.) •But, once torn out, I will
      take pity on them again and bring them back each to his heritage, each to his own
16   country. •And if they take care to learn my people's way and to swear by my
      name, "As Yahweh lives", as my people learned from them to swear by Baal,
17   then they shall have a place among my people. •But if any nation refuses to
      listen, I will tear it up by the roots and destroy it—it is Yahweh who speaks.'

The symbol of the loincloth

1 **13** Yahweh said this to me, 'Go and buy a linen loincloth and put it round
2   your waist. But do not dip it in water.' •And so, as Yahweh had ordered,
3 I bought a loincloth and put it round my waist. •A second time the word of
4 Yahweh was spoken to me, •'Take the loincloth that you have bought and are
   wearing round your waist; up! Go to the Euphrates and hide it in a hole in the
5 rock.' •So I went and hid it near the Euphrates as Yahweh had ordered me.
6 Many days afterwards Yahweh said to me, 'Get up and go to the Euphrates and fetch
7 the loincloth I ordered you to hide there'. •So I went to the Euphrates, and I
   searched, and I took the loincloth from the place where I had hidden it. The

loincloth was spoilt, good for nothing. •Then the word of Yahweh was addressed 8
to me, •'Thus says Yahweh: In the same way I will spoil the arrogance of 9
Judah and Jerusalem. •This evil people who refuse to listen to my words, who 10
follow the dictates of their own hard hearts, who have followed alien gods, and
served them and worshipped them, let them become like this loincloth, good
for nothing. •For just as a loincloth clings to a man's waist, so I had intended 11
the whole House of Judah to cling to me—it is Yahweh who speaks—to be my
people, my glory, my honour and my boast. But they have not listened.

The symbol of the shattered wine jugs

'Tell this people, "Any jug can be filled with wine". And if they answer you, 12
"Do you think we do not know that any jug can be filled with wine?" •you are to 13
say, "Thus says Yahweh: I am now going to fill all the inhabitants of this
land with drunkenness, the kings who occupy the throne of David, the priests
and the prophets, and all the citizens of Jerusalem. •And I will smash them 14
one against the other, father and son together—it is Yahweh who speaks.
Mercilessly, relentlessly, pitilessly, I will destroy them." '

A vision of exile

Listen, pay attention, away with pride—   15
Yahweh is speaking!
Give glory to Yahweh our God   16
before he brings darkness down
and your feet stumble
on the darkened mountains.
You hope for light,
but he will turn it into deep shadow,
change it into gloom.
If you do not listen to this warning,   17
I will bewail your pride in secret,
tears will flood my eyes,
for Yahweh's flock is led into captivity.

Jehoiachin threatened

Tell the king and the queen mother,   18
'Sit in a lower place,
since your glorious crown
has fallen from your head'.
The towns of the Negeb are shut off *a*   19
with no one to give access to them.
All Judah has been deported,
deported wholesale.

An admonition to impenitent Jerusalem

'Raise your eyes, Jerusalem, and look at these   20
now coming from the North.
Where is the flock once entrusted to you,
the flock that was your boast?
What will you say when they descend on you   21
as conquerors,
those you yourself taught
to be your friends?
Will not anguish grip you
like a woman in labour?
You may ask yourself,
"Why has all this happened to me?"   22

Because of your great wickedness your skirts have been pulled up,[b]
and you have been manhandled.

23   Can the Ethiopian change his skin,
or the leopard his spots?
And you, can you do what is right,
you so accustomed to wrong?

24   I will scatter you like chaff
driven by the desert wind.

25   This is your share, the wage of your apostasy.
This comes from me—it is Yahweh who speaks—
because you have forgotten me
and put your trust in a Delusion.

26   I will also pull your skirts up as high as your face
and let your shame be seen.

27   Oh! Your adulteries, your shrieks of pleasure,
your vile prostitution!
On the hills, in the countryside,
I have seen your Abominations.
Woe to you, Jerusalem, unclean still!
How much longer will you go on like this?'

The great drought

1   **14** The word of Yahweh that was addressed to Jeremiah on the occasion of the drought.

2   'Judah is in mourning,
her towns are disconsolate,
they sink to the ground;
a cry goes up from Jerusalem.

3   The nobles send the lesser men for water,
they come to the cisterns,
and find no water,
and return with their pitchers empty.

4   The ground refuses its yield,
for the country has had no rain;
in dismay the ploughmen
cover their heads.[a]

5   Even the doe abandons her new-born fawn in open country,
for there is no grass;

6   the wild donkeys standing on the bare heights
gasp for air like jackals:
their eyes grow dim
for lack of pasture.'

7   If our crimes are witness against us,
then, Yahweh, for your name's sake act!
Yes, our apostasies have been many,
we have sinned against you!

8   Yahweh, hope of Israel,
its saviour in time of distress,
why are you like a stranger in this land,
like a traveller who stays only for a night?

9   Why are you like someone bemused,

---

13 a. Probably by the Edomites.   **b.** Men were led naked into captivity, women with their skirts above their knees.
14 a. Sign of mourning.

like a warrior who has no power to rescue?
Yet, Yahweh, you are in our midst,
we are called by your name.
Do not desert us!

Yahweh says this regarding this people, 'They take such pleasure in 10
wandering, they cannot control their feet!' But Yahweh accepts them no longer;
now he recalls their crime and will punish their sins. •Yahweh said to me, 11
'Do not intercede for this people or their welfare. •If they fast, I will not listen 12
to their plea; if they offer holocaust and oblation, I will not accept them. Rather,
I mean to exterminate them by sword, famine and pestilence.'

'Ah, Lord Yahweh,' I answered 'here are the prophets telling them, "You 13
will not see the sword, famine will not touch you; I promise you unbroken peace
in this place". '

Then Yahweh said to me, 'The prophets are prophesying lies in my name; 14
I have not sent them, I gave them no orders, I never spoke to them. Delusive
visions, hollow predictions, daydreams of their own, that is what they prophesy
to you. •Therefore, Yahweh says this: The prophets who prophesy in my 15
name when I have not sent them, and tell you there will be no sword or famine
in this land, these same prophets are doomed to perish by sword and famine.
And as for the people to whom they prophesy, they will be tossed into the 16
streets of Jerusalem, victims of famine and the sword, with not a soul to bury
them: neither them nor their wives, nor their sons, nor their daughters. I will pour
down on them their own wickedness.

'Say this word to them, 17
"Tears flood my eyes
night and day, unceasingly,
since a crushing blow falls on the daughter of my people,
a most grievous injury.
If I go into the countryside, 18
there lie men killed by the sword;
if I go into the city,
I see people sick with hunger;
even prophets and priests
plough the land: they are at their wit's end." '

'Have you rejected Judah altogether? 19
Does your very soul revolt at Zion?
Why have you struck us down without hope of cure?
We were hoping for peace—no good came of it!
For the moment of cure—nothing but terror!
Yahweh, we do confess our wickedness 20
and our fathers' guilt:
we have indeed sinned against you.
For your name's sake do not reject us, 21
do not dishonour the throne of your glory.
Remember us; do not break your covenant with us.
Can any of the pagan Nothings make it rain? 22
Can the heavens produce showers?
No, it is you, Yahweh.
O our God, you are our hope,
since it is you who do all this.'

15 Yahweh said to me, 'Even if Moses and Samuel were standing in my 1
presence I could not warm to this people! Drive them out of my sight;
away with them! •And if they ask you, "Where shall we go?" tell them this, 2
"Yahweh says this:

> Those for the plague, to the plague;
> those for the sword, to the sword;
> those for famine, to famine;
> those for captivity, into captivity!"

3 Four kinds of doom I consign them to: the sword to kill, the dogs to drag away,
4 the birds of heaven and beasts of earth to devour and to destroy. •I will make
them an object of horror to all the kingdoms of the earth, because of Manasseh
son of Hezekiah, king of Judah, for his misdeeds in Jerusalem.

The horrors of war

5   'Who is there to pity you, Jerusalem,
        who to grieve for you,
        who to pause
        and ask how you are?

6   You yourself have rejected me—it is Yahweh who speaks—
        you have turned your back on me;
        so I have stretched my hand over you to destroy you.
        I am tired of relenting.

7   And so I have winnowed them with a fork
        in the towns of their land:
        I deprive my people of children, I exterminate them
        since they refuse to leave their ways.

8   Their widows have become more
        than the sand of the seas.
        On the mothers of young warriors
        I bring the destroyer in broad daylight.
        Suddenly I bring down
        anguish and terror on them.

9   The mother of seven sons grows faint,
        and breathes her last.
        It is still day, but already her sun has set,
        shame and disgrace are hers...
        And the remainder of them I shall hand over to their enemies
        to be cut to pieces—it is Yahweh who speaks.'

The call of Jeremiah renewed

10   Woe is me, my mother, for you have borne me
        to be a man of strife and of dissension for all the land.
        I neither lend nor borrow,
        yet all of them curse me.

11   Truthfully, Yahweh, have I not done my best to serve you,
        interceded with you for my enemy
        in the time of his disaster, his distress?

15a   You know I have!

12   Can a man break iron,
        iron from the north, or bronze?

13   'Your wealth and your treasures
        I will hand over to plunder,
        as payment for all your sins
        throughout your territory.

14   I will enslave you to your enemies
        in a country which you do not know,
        for my anger has kindled a fire
        that will burn you up.'

15b   Yahweh, remember me, take care of me,

and avenge me on my persecutors.
Your anger is very slow: do not let me be snatched away.
Realise that I suffer insult for your sake.
When your words came, I devoured them: 16
your word was my delight
and the joy of my heart;
for I was called by your name,
Yahweh, God of Sabaoth.
I never took pleasure in sitting in scoffers' company;   17
with your hand on me I held myself aloof,
since you had filled me with indignation.
Why is my suffering continual,   18
my wound incurable, refusing to be healed?
Do you mean to be for me a deceptive stream
with inconstant waters?

To which Yahweh replied,   19
'If you come back,
I will take you back into my service;
and if you utter noble, not despicable, thoughts,
you shall be as my own mouth.
They will come back to you,
but you must not go back to them.
I will make you   20
a bronze wall fortified against this people.
They will fight against you
but they will not overcome you,
because I am with you
to save you and to deliver you
—it is Yahweh who speaks.
I mean to deliver you from the hands of the wicked   21
and redeem you from the clutches of the violent.'

The prophet's life is itself symbolic

16 The word of Yahweh was addressed to me as follows: 1
'You must not take a wife or have son or daughter in this place. •For 2
3
Yahweh says this regarding the sons and daughters to be born in this place, about
the mothers who give birth to them, and about the fathers who beget them in
this land: •They will die of deadly diseases, unlamented and unburied; they   4
will be like dung spread on the ground; they will meet their end by sword and
famine, and their corpses will be food for the birds of heaven and the beasts
of earth.

'Yes, Yahweh says this: Go into no house where there is mourning, do 5
not go to lament or grieve with them; for I have withdrawn my peace from
this people—it is Yahweh who speaks—have withdrawn love and pity. •High or 6
low, they will die in this land, without burial or lament; there will be no gashing,
no shaving of the head for them. •No bread will be broken for the mourner 7
to comfort him for the dead; no cup of consolation will be offered him for
father or for mother.

'And do not enter a house where there is feasting, to sit with them and 8
eat and drink. •For Yahweh Sabaoth, the God of Israel, says this: Now 9
before your eyes, in your own days, I will silence the shouts of rejoicing and
mirth, and the voices of bridegroom and bride.

'When you tell this people all these words and they ask you, "Why has 10
Yahweh decreed this appalling disaster for us? What is our crime? What sin have
we committed against Yahweh our God?" •then you are to answer, "It is because 11

your ancestors abandoned me—it is Yahweh who speaks—and followed alien gods, and served and worshipped them. They abandoned me and did not keep my Law.

12 And you for your part have behaved even worse than your ancestors. Look, each of you follows the dictates of his hardened, wicked heart and will not listen to

13 me. •And so, I am going to eject you from this land into a country unknown to you and to your ancestors; there you will serve alien gods, day and night, for I shall show you no more favour."

The return of the scattered Israelites

14 'See, then, that the days are coming—it is Yahweh who speaks—when people will no longer say, "As Yahweh lives who brought the sons of Israel out of

15 the land of Egypt!" •but, "As Yahweh lives who brought the sons of Israel out of the land of the North and back from all the countries to which he had dispersed them". I will bring them back to the very soil I gave their ancestors.

The invasion foretold

16 'I will now send many fishermen—it is Yahweh who speaks—and these will fish them up; next, I will send many huntsmen, and these will hunt them

17 out of every mountain, every hill, out of the holes in the rocks. •For my eyes watch all their ways, these are not hidden from me, and their guilt does not

18 escape my gaze. •I will requite their guilt and their sin twice over, since they have polluted my land with the corpses of their Horrors, and filled my heritage with their Abominations.'

The conversion of the nations

19   Yahweh, my strength, my stronghold,
         my refuge in the day of distress!
         To you the nations will come
         from the confines of earth and say,
         'Our fathers inherited nothing but Delusion,
         Nothings void of all power.

20   Can man make his own gods?
         If so, these are not gods!'

21   'Now listen, I am going to make them acknowledge,
         this time I am going to make them acknowledge
         my hand and my might;
         and then they will know that Yahweh is my name.

Judah's contaminated worship

1
17   'The sin of Judah is written
         with an iron pen,
         engraved with a diamond point
         on the tablet of their heart
         and on the horns of their altars,

2   as evidence against them
(their altars and their sacred poles, by every spreading tree, on the high hills,

3 on the mountains, in the open countryside).

         'Your wealth and your treasures
         I will hand over to plunder
         as payment for all your sins
         throughout your territory.

4   You will have to relinquish your heritage
         which I gave you;
         I will enslave you to your enemies
         in a country which you do not know,
         for my anger has kindled a fire
         that will burn for ever.

A group of wisdom sayings

'Yahweh says this:　　　　　　　　　　　　　　　　　5

'A curse on the man who puts his trust in man,
who relies on things of flesh,
whose heart turns from Yahweh.
He is like dry scrub in the wastelands:　　　　　　6
if good comes, he has no eyes for it,
he settles in the parched places of the wilderness,
a salt land, uninhabited.

'A blessing on the man who puts his trust in Yahweh,　　7
with Yahweh for his hope.
He is like a tree by the waterside　　　　　　　　8
that thrusts its roots to the stream:
when the heat comes it feels no alarm,
its foliage stays green;
it has no worries in a year of drought,
and never ceases to bear fruit.

'The heart is more devious than any other thing,　　9
perverse too: who can pierce its secrets?
I, Yahweh, search to the heart,　　　　　　　　10
I probe the loins,
to give each man what his conduct
and his actions deserve.

'The partridge will hatch eggs it has not laid.　　11
Similarly, the man who wins his wealth unjustly:
his days half done, he must leave it,
proving a fool after all.'

Confidence in the Temple and in Yahweh

A glorious throne, set high from the beginning,　　12
such is our Holy Place.
Hope of Israel, Yahweh!　　　　　　　　　13
All who abandon you will be put to shame,
those who turn from you will be uprooted from the land,
since they have abandoned the fountain of living water.

A prayer for vengeance

Heal me, Yahweh, and I shall be really healed,　　14
save me, and I shall be saved,
for you alone are my hope.
Look, they keep saying to me,　　　　　　　15
'Where is the word of Yahweh? Let it come true then!'
But I, I have never urged you to do evil,　　16
the day of disaster was no desire of mine,
this you know;
what came from my lips was not concealed from you.
Do not be a terror to me,　　　　　　　　17
you, my refuge in the day of disaster.
Let my persecutors be confounded, not I,　　18
let them, not me, be terrified.
On them bring the day of disaster,
destroy them, destroy them twice over!

Observance of the sabbath

19 Yahweh said this to me, 'Go and stand at the Gate of the Sons of the People by which the kings of Judah go in and out—and at all the gates of
20 Jerusalem. •Say to them, "Listen to the word of Yahweh, you kings of Judah, all you people of Judah too, and all you citizens of Jerusalem who pass
21 through these gates. •Yahweh says this: As you value your lives, on no account carry a burden on the sabbath day or bring it in through the gates of
22 Jerusalem. •Bring no burden out of your houses on the sabbath day, and do no
23 work. Keep the sabbath day holy, as I commanded your ancestors. •They would not hear, would not pay attention, grew so stubborn they would not listen,
24 and would not accept instruction. •But if you listen carefully to me—it is Yahweh who speaks—and bring no burden in through the gates of this city on the
25 sabbath day, if you keep the sabbath holy and do no work on that day, •then, through the gates of this city, kings occupying the throne of David will continue to make their entry, mounted on chariots and horses, they and their ministers, with the men of Judah and the citizens of Jerusalem. And this city will be
26 inhabited for ever. •They will come from the towns of Judah, from the districts round Jerusalem, from the land of Benjamin, from the lowlands, from the highlands, from the Negeb, to offer holocaust and sacrifice, oblation, incense
27 and thanksgiving sacrifice in the Temple of Yahweh. •But if you do not listen to my command to keep the sabbath day holy, and not to enter the gates of Jerusalem with burdens on the sabbath day, then I will set fire to its gates; it shall devour the palaces of Jerusalem and not be quenched." '

Jeremiah visits the potter

¹₂ **18** The word that was addressed to Jeremiah by Yahweh, •'Get up and make your way down to the potter's house; there I shall let you hear what I have
3 to say'. •So I went down to the potter's house; and there he was, working at the
4 wheel. •And whenever the vessel he was making came out wrong, as happens with the clay handled by potters, he would start afresh and work it into another vessel,
⁵₆ as potters do. •Then this word of Yahweh was addressed to me, •'House of Israel, can not I do to you what this potter does?—it is Yahweh who speaks. Yes, as
7 the clay is in the potter's hand, so you are in mine, House of Israel. •On occasion, I decree for some nation, for some kingdom, that I will tear up, knock down,
8 destroy; •but if this nation, against which I have pronounced sentence, abandons its wickedness, I then change my mind about the evil which I had intended to
9 inflict on it. •On another occasion, I decree for some nation, for some kingdom,
10 that I will build up and plant; •but if that nation does what displeases me, refusing to listen to my voice, I then change my mind about the good which
11 I had intended to confer on it. •So now, say this to the men of Judah and the citizens of Jerusalem, "Yahweh says this: Listen, I have been preparing a disaster for you, I have been working out a plan against you. So now, each one of you, turn back from your evil ways, amend your conduct and actions."
12 They, however, will say, "What is the use of talking? We prefer to do as we please; we mean to behave, each of us, as his wicked heart dictates."

Israel repudiates Yahweh

13   'Therefore—Yahweh says this:
         Ask, if you will, among the nations
         if anyone has heard anything like this.
         She has done a deed of horror,
         the Virgin of Israel.
14   Does the snow of Lebanon
         vanish from the lofty crag?
         Do the proud waters run dry,
         so coolly flowing?

And yet my people have forgotten me!   15
They burn their incense to a Nothing!
They have lost their footing in their ways,
on the roads of former times,
to walk in tortuous paths,
a way unmarked.

They will make their country desolate,   16
everlastingly derided:
every passer-by will be appalled at it
and shake his head.

Like the east wind, I will scatter them   17
before the enemy.
I will turn my back to them and not my face
on the day of their disaster.'

A plot against Jeremiah

'Come on,' they said 'let us concoct a plot against Jeremiah; the priest will   18
not run short of instruction without him, nor the sage of advice, nor the prophet
of the word. Come on, let us hit at him with his own tongue; let us listen
carefully to every word he says.'

Listen to me, Yahweh,   19
hear what my adversaries are saying.
Should evil be returned for good?   20
(For they are digging a pit for me.)
Remember how I stood in your presence
to plead on their behalf,
to turn your wrath away from them.

Then hand their sons over to famine,   21
abandon them to the edge of the sword.
May their wives become
childless and widowed.
May their husbands die of plague,
their young men be cut down by the sword in battle.

Let cries re-echo from their houses   22
as you bring raiders suddenly on them.
For they have dug a pit to catch me,
they have laid snares to trap my feet.

But you, Yahweh,   23
know all their murderous plots against me.
Do not forgive their crime,
do not efface their sin from your sight.
Keep their destruction always in mind,
when the time for your anger comes deal with them.

The broken jug and the altercation with Pashhur

19 Then Yahweh said to Jeremiah, 'Go and buy an earthenware jug. Take   1
some of the elders of the people and some priests with you. •Go out   2
towards the Valley of Ben-hinnom, as far as the entry of the Gate of the
Potsherds. There proclaim the words I shall speak to you. •You are to say,   3
"Kings of Judah, citizens of Jerusalem! Listen to the word of Yahweh!
Yahweh Sabaoth, the God of Israel, says this: I am bringing down such a disaster
on this place that the ears of every one who hears of it will ring. •This is because   4
they have abandoned me, have profaned this place, have offered incense here
to alien gods which neither they, nor their ancestors, nor the kings of Judah, ever
knew before. They have filled this place with the blood of the innocent. •They   5
have built high places for Baal to burn their sons there, which I had never

6 ordered or decreed, which had never entered my thoughts. •So now the days are coming—it is Yahweh who speaks—when people will no longer call this place Topheth, or the Valley of Ben-hinnom, but Valley of Slaughter.

7 Because of this place, I mean to drainᵃ Judah and Jerusalem of sound advice; I will make them fall by the sword before their enemies, fall by the hand of people determined to kill them; I will give their corpses as food to the birds of heaven

8 and the beasts of earth. •And I will make this city a desolation, a derision; every passer-by will be appalled at it, and whistle in amazement at such calamity.

9 I will make them eat the flesh of their own sons and daughters: they shall eat each other during the siege, in the shortage to which their enemies, in their determination to kill them, will reduce them."

10
11 'You are to break this jug in front of the men who are with you, •and say to them, "Yahweh Sabaoth says this: I am going to break this people and this city just as one breaks a potter's pot, irreparably.

12 Topheth will become a burial ground, for lack of other space. •That is how I will treat this place—it is Yahweh who speaks. And I mean to make this city

13 like Topheth; •the houses of Jerusalem and those of the kings of Judah will be unclean,ᵇ like this place Topheth: all these houses on the roofs of which they offered incense to the whole array of heaven and poured their libations to alien gods." '

14 When Jeremiah came back from Topheth where Yahweh had sent him to prophesy, he went and stood in the court of the Temple of Yahweh and addressed

15 all the people. •'Yahweh Sabaoth, the God of Israel, says this, "Yes, I am going to bring down every disaster I have threatened on this city and on all its outlying towns, since they have grown so stubborn and refused to listen to my words". '

1 **20** Now the priest Pashhur son of Immer, who was in charge of the police in
2 the Temple of Yahweh, heard Jeremiah making this prophecy. •Pashhur had Jeremiah the prophet beaten and then put in the stocks at the Gate of Benjamin,

3 the upper gate leading into the Temple of Yahweh. •Next day, Pashhur had Jeremiah taken out of the stocks; Jeremiah said to him, 'Not Pashhur but Terror

4 is Yahweh's name for you. •For Yahweh says this, "I am going to hand you over to terror, you and all your friends; they shall fall by the sword of their enemies; your own eyes shall see it. The whole of Judah, too, I will hand over to the king of Babylon; he will carry them off captives to Babylon and put them

5 to the sword. •And all the wealth of this city, all its stores, all its valuables, all the treasures of the kings of Judah, I will hand over to their enemies who will

6 plunder them, round them up and carry them off to Babylon. •As for you, Pashhur, and your whole household, you shall go into captivity; you shall go to Babylon; there you will die, and there be buried, you and all your friends to whom you have prophesied lies." '

Selections from the 'Confessions' of Jeremiah

7   You have seduced me, Yahweh, and I have let myself be seduced;
      you have overpowered me: you were the stronger.
      I am a daily laughing-stock,
      everybody's butt.

8   Each time I speak the word, I have to howl
      and proclaim: 'Violence and ruin!'
      The word of Yahweh has meant for me
      insult, derision, all day long.

9   I used to say, 'I will not think about him,
      I will not speak in his name any more'.
      Then there seemed to be a fire burning in my heart,

19 a. In Hebr. 'drain' has a similar sound to 'jug'; this is another association of the jug parable.
b. Polluted by the presence of corpses.

imprisoned in my bones.
The effort to restrain it wearied me,
I could not bear it.
I hear so many disparaging me,   10
' "Terror from every side!"
Denounce him! Let us denounce him!'
All those who used to be my friends
watched for my downfall,
'Perhaps he will be seduced into error.
Then we will master him
and take our revenge!'
But Yahweh is at my side, a mighty hero;   11
my opponents will stumble, mastered,
confounded by their failure;
everlasting, unforgettable disgrace will be theirs.
But you, Yahweh Sabaoth, you who probe with justice,   12
who scrutinise the loins and heart,
let me see the vengeance you will take on them,
for I have committed my cause to you.
Sing to Yahweh,   13
praise Yahweh,
for he has delivered the soul of the needy
from the hands of evil men.

A curse on the day when I was born,   14
no blessing on the day my mother bore me!
A curse on the man who brought my father the news,   15
'A son, a boy has been born to you!'
making him overjoyed.
May this man be like the towns   16
that Yahweh overthrew without mercy;
may he hear alarms in the morning,
the war cry in broad daylight,
since he did not kill me in the womb;   17
my mother would have been my tomb
while her womb was swollen with me.
Why ever did I come out of the womb   18
To live in toil and sorrow
and to end my days in shame!

C. ORACLES MAINLY LATER THAN THE REIGN OF JEHOIAKIM

Jeremiah answers the envoys of Zedekiah[a]

21 The word that was addressed to Jeremiah by Yahweh when King Zedekiah 1
sent Pashhur son of Malchiah to him, with the priest Zephaniah son of Maaseiah, to say this, •'Please consult Yahweh for us, since Nebuchadnezzar king 2
of Babylon is making war on us: perhaps Yahweh will work all his wonders on
our behalf, so that the enemy will have to withdraw'. •Jeremiah said to them, 3
'Take this answer to Zedekiah, •"Yahweh, the God of Israel, says this: I am 4
going to bring back the weapons of war which you are now carrying, and with
which you are fighting the king of Babylon and the Chaldaeans now besieging
your walls; I am going to stack them in the centre of this city. •And I am going 5
to fight against you myself with outstretched hand and mighty arm, in anger,
fury and great wrath. •I am going to strike the inhabitants of this city, man 6
and beast, with a frightful plague: they will die. •After which—it is Yahweh 7

who speaks—I am going to deliver Zedekiah king of Judah with his servants and the people of this city who escape the plague, the sword, or the famine, into the hands of Nebuchadnezzar king of Babylon, into the hands of their enemies and of those determined to kill them; mercilessly, relentlessly, pitilessly, he will put them to the sword."

8 'And you are to say to this people, "Yahweh says this: Look, I now set
9 in front of you the way of life and the way of death. •Those who stay in this city will die by sword, by famine, or by plague; but anyone who leaves it and surrenders to the Chaldaeans now besieging it will live; he shall escape with
10 his life. •For I have turned my face against this city for its ruin, not for its prosperity—it is Yahweh who speaks. It is to be delivered into the hands of the king of Babylon, and he will burn it down." '

Address to the royal family of Judah

11
12 To the royal House of Judah. Listen to the word of Yahweh, •House of David! Yahweh says this:

> 'Each morning give sound judgement,
> rescue the man who has been wronged
> from the hands of his oppressor,
> or else my wrath will leap out like a fire,
> it will burn and no one will be able to quench it.

13
> My quarrel is with you,
> you that have gone to live at Rock-in-the-Plain[b]
> —it is Yahweh who speaks—
> with you that say, "Who would dare attack us
> and penetrate our fastness?"

14
> (I will punish you as your actions deserve
> —it is Yahweh who speaks.)
> I will set fire to its forest;
> it will devour the whole district.'

1
2
22 Yahweh said this, 'Go down to the palace of the king of Judah and there deliver this message, •"Listen to the word of Yahweh, king of Judah sitting on the throne of David, you, your servants too, and your people who go
3 through these gates. •Yahweh says this: Practise honesty and integrity; rescue the man who has been wronged from the hands of his oppressor; do not exploit the stranger, the orphan, the widow; do no violence; shed no innocent blood
4 in this place. •For if you are scrupulous in obeying this command, then kings occupying the throne of David will continue to make their entry through the gates of this palace mounted on chariots and horses, they, their servants and
5 their people. •But if you do not listen to these words, then I swear by myself —it is Yahweh who speaks—this palace shall become a ruin!
6 Yes, this is what Yahweh says about the royal palace of Judah:

> You were like a Gilead to me,
> like a peak of Lebanon.
> All the same, I will reduce you to a desert,
> to an uninhabited town.

7
> I have dedicated men to destroy you,
> each man with his axe;
> they will cut down your finest cedars
> and throw them on the fire.

8 When the hordes of the nations pass this city, they will say to each other:
9 Why has Yahweh treated such a great city like this? •And the answer will be:

21 a. During the siege of Jerusalem, 588.   **b.** Probably the royal palace built on Ophel.

Because they abandoned the covenant of Yahweh their God to worship alien gods and serve them." '

Oracles against various kings: against Jehoahaz

> Do not weep for the man who is dead,ᵃ   10
> do not raise the dirge for him.
> Weep bitterly for the man who has gone away,
> since he will never come back,
> never see his native land again.

For this is what Yahweh has said about Shallum son of Josiah, king of Judah, 11 who succeeded Josiah his father and was forced to leave this place, 'He will never come back to it •but will die in the place to which he has been taken captive; 12 and he will never see this country again.

Against Jehoiakim

> 'Doom for the man who founds his palace on anything but integrity, 13
> his upstairs rooms on anything but honesty,
> who makes his fellow man work for nothing,
> without paying him his wages,
> who says, "I will build myself an imposing palace   14
> with spacious rooms upstairs",
> who pierces lights in it,
> panels it with cedar, and paints it vermilion.
> Are you more of a king   15
> for outrivalling others with cedar?
> Your father ate and drank, like you,
> but he practised honesty and integrity,
> so all went well for him.
> He used to examine the cases of poor and needy,   16
> then all went well.
> Is not that what it means to know me?—it is Yahweh who speaks.
> You on the other hand have eyes and heart for nothing   17
> but your own interests,
> for shedding innocent blood
> and perpetrating violence and oppression.'

So Yahweh has said this about Jehoiakim son of Josiah, king of Judah: 18

> 'Doom for that man!
> Raise no dirge for him,
> "Mourn for my brother! Mourn for my sister!"
> Raise no dirge for him,
> "Mourn for his highness. Mourn for his majesty"
> He will receive the funeral honours of a donkey,   19
> —dragged away and thrown
> out of the gates of Jerusalem.

Against Jehoiachin

> 'Go up to Lebanon and shriek,   20
> let your voice be heard on Bashan,
> shriek from Abarim,ᵇ
> for all your loversᶜ have been ruined!
> I spoke to you in your prosperity,   21
> but you said, "I will not listen!"

from your youth this has been how you behaved,
refusing to listen to my voice.

22 The wind will blow all your shepherds away to other pastures,
your lovers will go into captivity.
Yes, now you may well be ashamed and confounded
at the thought of all your wickedness.

23 You who made Lebanon your home,
who made your nest among the cedars,
how you will groan when anguish overtakes you,
and pain like that of a woman in labour!

24 'As I live—it is Yahweh who speaks—even if Coniah son of Jehoiakim, king of Judah, were the signet ring on my right hand, I would still wrench him off.
25 I will deliver you into the hands of those determined to kill you, into the hands of those you dread, the hands of Nebuchadnezzar king of Babylon, the hands
26 of the Chaldaeans. •You and the mother who bore you, I will thrust you both out into another country; you were not born there but you will both die there.
27 They will not return to the country to which they so long to return.'

28 Is he a shoddy broken pot,
this man Coniah,
a crock that no one wants?
Why are they ejected, he and his descendants,
thrown into a country
they know nothing of?
29 O land, land, land,
listen to the word of Yahweh!
30 Yahweh says this,
'List this man as: Childless;
a man who made a failure of his life,
since none of his descendants will have the fortune
to sit on the throne of David,
or to rule in Judah again.

Messianic oracles. The future king

1
2 23 'Doom for the shepherds who allow the flock of my pasture to be destroyed and scattered—it is Yahweh who speaks! •This, therefore, is what Yahweh, the God of Israel, says about the shepherds in charge of my people: You have let my flock be scattered and go wandering and have not taken care of them. Right, I will take care of you for your misdeeds—it is Yahweh who speaks!
3 But the remnant of my flock I myself will gather from all the countries where I have dispersed them, and will bring them back to their pastures: they shall
4 be fruitful and increase in numbers. •I will raise up shepherds to look after them and pasture them; no fear, no terror for them any more; not one shall be lost—it is Yahweh who speaks!

5 'See, the days are coming—it is Yahweh who speaks—
when I will raise a virtuous Branch for David,
who will reign as true king and be wise,
practising honesty and integrity in the land.
6 In his days Judah will be saved
and Israel dwell in confidence.
And this is the name he will be called:
Yahweh-our-integrity.

22 a. Josiah; 'the man who has gone away' is Jehoahaz, summoned by the Pharaoh Neco, and exiled in Egypt.   b. The mountain range to the E. of Jordan.   c. The kings and leaders of Judah are the 'lovers' of Jerusalem.

'So, then, the days are coming—it is Yahweh who speaks—when people will 7 no longer say, "As Yahweh lives who brought the sons of Israel out of the land of Egypt!" •but, "As Yahweh lives who led back and brought home the 8 descendants of the House of Israel out of the land of the North and from all the countries to which he had dispersed them, to live on their own soil". '

A tract against the false prophets

On the prophets.   9

My heart is broken within me,
I tremble in all my bones
I am like a drunken man,
a man overcome with wine—
because of Yahweh
and his holy words,
'The land is full of adulterers   10

(yes, because of these men the land is in mourning and the desert pastures have dried up);

'they are quick only at doing wrong
and powerful only in crime.
Yes, even prophet and priest are godless,   11
I have found their wickedness even in my own House
—it is Yahweh who speaks.
Because of this their way will prove   12
treacherous going for them;
in the darkness where they are driven,
there they will fall.
For I will bring disaster down on them
when the year comes for me to deal with them—
it is Yahweh who speaks.

'In the prophets of Samaria   13
I have seen nauseating things:
they prophesied in the name of Baal
and led my people Israel astray.
But in the prophets of Jerusalem   14
I have seen horrors:
adultery, persistent lying,
such abetting of evil men,
that no one renounces his evil-doing;
to me they are all like Sodom,
its inhabitants all like Gomorrah.
So this is what Yahweh Sabaoth says about the prophets: 15
Now I will give them wormwood for their food,
and poisoned water to drink,
since from the prophets of Jerusalem
godlessness has spread throughout the land.

'Yahweh Sabaoth says this: 16
Do not listen to what those prophets say:
they are deluding you,
they retail visions of their own,
and not what comes from the mouth of Yahweh;
to those who reject the word of Yahweh they say,   17
"Peace will be yours",

and to those who follow the dictates of a hardened heart,
"No misfortune will touch you". '

18   (But who has been present at the council of Yahweh? Who has seen it and heard his word? Who has paid attention to his word in order to proclaim it?)

19   Now a storm of Yahweh breaks,
       a tempest whirls,
       it bursts over the head of the wicked;
20   the anger of Yahweh will not turn aside
       until he has performed, and has carried out,
       the decision of his heart.

     You will understand this clearly in the days to come.

21   'I have not sent those prophets,
       yet they are running;
       I have not spoken to them,
       yet they are prophesying.
22   Have they been present at my council?
       If so, let them proclaim my words to my people
       and turn them from their evil way
       and from the wickedness of their deeds!

23   'Am I a God when near—it is Yahweh who speaks—
       and not one when far away?
24   Can anyone hide in a dark corner
       without my seeing him?—it is Yahweh who speaks.
       Do I not fill
       heaven and earth?—it is Yahweh who speaks.

25   'I have heard what the prophets say who make their lying prophecies in my
26 name. "I have had a dream," they say "I have had a dream!" •How long will they retain this notion in their hearts, these prophets prophesying lies, who
27 announce their private delusions as prophetic? •They hope, by means of the dreams that they keep telling each other, to make my people forget my name,
28 just as their fathers forgot my name in favour of Baal. •Let the prophet who has had a dream tell his dream as his own! And let him who receives a word from me, deliver it accurately!

       'What have straw and wheat in common?
       —it is Yahweh who speaks.
29   Does not my word burn like fire
       —it is Yahweh who speaks—
       is it not like a hammer shattering a rock?

30   'So, then, I have a quarrel with the prophets—it is Yahweh who speaks—
31 that steal my words from one another. •I have a quarrel with the prophets—it is Yahweh who speaks—who have only to move their tongues to utter oracles.
32 I have a quarrel with the prophets who make prophecies out of lying dreams —it is Yahweh who speaks—who recount them, and lead my people astray with their lies and their pretensions. I certainly never sent them or commissioned them, and they serve no good purpose for this people—it is Yahweh who speaks.

33   'And when these people, either a prophet or a priest, ask you, "What is the Burden of Yahweh?"[a] you are to answer, "You, you are the burden of Yahweh; yes, you, and I mean to be rid of you! It is Yahweh who speaks."

---

23 a. *Massa*, a burden, also means 'an oracle'. The second sense is distinguished here by a capital initial.

'And the prophet, priest, or anyone else, who says, "Burden of Yahweh", 34 I will punish that man, and his household too. •This is the way you ought 35 to talk, neighbour to neighbour, brother to brother, "What answer has Yahweh given?" or "What has Yahweh said?" •But do not go on using the expression 36 burden of Yahweh or, for the man who uses it, burdensome it will certainly prove, since you twist the words of the living God, of Yahweh Sabaoth, our God. •This is the way to speak to a prophet, "What answer has Yahweh given?" 37 or "What has Yahweh said?" •But if you say, "Burden of Yahweh", then thus 38 speaks Yahweh: Since you use these words, "Burden of Yahweh", when I have warned you to stop saying, "Burden of Yahweh", •I myself will pick you up 39 and fling you out of my sight, both you and the city I gave to you and to your ancestors. •I will bring down everlasting shame on you, everlasting and unfor- 40 gettable disgrace.'

The two baskets of figs

24 Yahweh gave me a vision: placed in front of the Temple of Yahweh stood 1 two baskets of figs.ᵃ This was after Nebuchadnezzar king of Babylon had led away Jeconiah son of Jehoiakim, king of Judah, into exile from Jerusalem, with all the nobles of Judah, and the blacksmiths and metalworkers, and had taken them to Babylon. •One basket contained excellent figs, like those that ripen 2 first; the other contained very bad figs, so bad they were uneatable. •Yahweh 3 said to me, 'What do you see, Jeremiah?' 'Figs,' I answered 'the good ones excellent, the bad ones very bad, so bad as to be uneatable.' •Then the word 4 of Yahweh was addressed to me, •'Yahweh, the God of Israel, says this: 5 As these figs are good, so I mean to concern myself with the welfare of the exiles of Judah whom I have sent from this place to the land of the Chaldaeans. •My 6 eyes will watch over them for their good, to bring them back to this land, to build them up and not to break them down, to plant them and not to tear them up. •I will give them a heart to acknowledge that I am Yahweh. They shall 7 be my people and I will be their God, for they will return to me with all their heart. •As for the bad figs, the figs so bad as to be uneatable—yes, Yahweh 8 says this—that is how I will treat Zedekiah king of Judah, his nobles and the remnant of Jerusalem: those who have stayed in this land, as also those living in the land of Egypt. •I will make them an object of horror to all the kingdoms 9 of the earth, a thing of shame, a byword, a laughing-stock, a curse in every place where I shall disperse them. •Sword, famine and plague I will send against them 10 until they have vanished from the soil I gave to them and to their ancestors.'

D. BABYLON THE SCOURGE OF YAHWEHᵃ

25 The word that was addressed to Jeremiah about all the people of Judah 1 in the fourth year of Jehoiakim son of Josiah, king of Judah (that is to say the first year of Nebuchadnezzar king of Babylon). •The prophet Jeremiah 2 proclaimed it before all the people of Judah and all the citizens of Jerusalem: 'For twenty-three years, from the thirteenth year of Josiah son of Amon, 3 king of Judah, until today, the word of Yahweh has been addressed to me and I have persistently spoken to you (but you have not listened. •Furthermore, 4 Yahweh has persistently sent you all his servants the prophets, but you have not listened, or paid attention.) •The message was this, "Turn back, each of you, from 5 your evil behaviour and your evil actions, and you will stay on the soil Yahweh long ago gave to you and to your ancestors for ever. •(And do not follow alien 6 gods to serve and worship them, do not provoke me by what your own hands have made; then I will not harm you.) •But you have not listened to me (it is 7 Yahweh who speaks—so that you have now provoked me by what your own hands have made, and thus harmed yourselves).

8 "So—this is what Yahweh Sabaoth says: Since you have not listened to my
9 words, •I will now send for all the clans of the North (it is Yahweh who speaks—
referring to Nebuchadnezzar king of Babylon, my servant) and bring them
down on this land and its inhabitants (and on all these surrounding nations):
I will lay the ban on them and make them an object of horror, of scorn, of
10 lasting shame. •I will put an end for them to the shouts of rejoicing and
mirth, to the voices of bridegroom and bride, to the sound of the millstone and
11 to the light of the lamp. •The whole land shall be devastated and reduced to a
desert, while they will stay in slavery among the nations for seventy years.
12 (But when the seventy years are over, I will punish the king of Babylon and
that nation—it is Yahweh who speaks—for the wrong they have done; and
13 punish the land of the Chaldaeans too, and make it a desert for ever.) •I will
bring down on that country all the words I have pronounced against it, all that
is written in this book." '

II. ORACLES AGAINST THE NATIONS

A. INTRODUCTION

The vision of the cup   (LXX 33:13-38)

What Jeremiah prophesied against all the nations.

14   ('For these in their turn are to be enslaved to powerful nations and great
kings, and I will pay them back as their deeds and their handiwork deserve.')
15   Yahweh the God of Israel said this to me, 'Take this cup of wine from
16 my hand and make all the nations to whom I send you drink it, •let them drink
17 and reel and lose their wits at the sword I am sending among them'. •I took the
cup from the hand of Yahweh and made all the nations to whom Yahweh sent
18 me drink it •(Jerusalem and the towns of Judah, its kings and its nobles, to
make them into a desolation and a waste, a thing of scorn, a curse, as is so today):
19
20 Pharaoh king of Egypt, with his servants, his nobles, and all his people, •the
whole crowd of foreigners besides (all the kings of the land of Uz); all the kings
of the country of the Philistines, Ashkelon, Gaza, Ekron and what still remains
21
22 of Ashdod; •Edom, Moab and the sons of Ammon; •(all) the kings of Tyre,
23 (all) the kings of Sidon, the kings of the islands across the sea; •Dedan, Tema,
24
25 Buz, all the Crop-Heads, •all the kings of Arabia who live in the desert; •(all
26 the kings of Zimri) and all the kings of Elam, and all the kings of Media; •all
the kings of the north, near and far, one after another; and all the kingdoms
that are on the face of the earth. (As for the king of Sheshak, he shall drink
last of all.)
27   'You are to say to them, "Yahweh Sabaoth, the God of Israel, says this:
Drink! Get drunk! Vomit! Fall, never to rise, at the sword that I am sending
28 among you!" •If they refuse to take the cup from your hand and drink, you are
29 to say to them, "Yahweh Sabaoth says this: You must drink! •Since I am now
making a beginning of disaster with the city that bears my name, do you think
you are likely to go unpunished? You certainly shall not, for I will next summon a
sword against all the inhabitants of the earth—it is Yahweh Sabaoth who speaks."
30   'Let your prophecy to them contain all these words, and tell them:

"Yahweh roars from on high,
he makes his voice heard from his holy dwelling place,
he roars loud against his sheepfold,

---

24 a. Offered to the Temple as first-fruits.
25 a. The brackets in this section, and in the four chapters which follow, indicate passages
which appear to be glosses and additions by a later hand; several of these are absent from the
Greek text.

he shouts aloud like those who tread the grape.
The sound reaches all the inhabitants of the earth,
to the far ends of the world.   31
For Yahweh is indicting the nations,
arraigning all flesh for judgement;
the wicked he abandons to the sword
—it is Yahweh who speaks.
Yahweh Sabaoth says this: 32
See! The disaster spreads
from nation to nation,
a mighty tempest rises
from the far ends of the world.

"Those slaughtered by Yahweh that day will be scattered across the world 33
from end to end. No dirge will be raised for them; no one will gather them or
bury them; they will stay lying on the surface like dung.

"Howl, shepherds, shriek,   34
roll on the ground, you lords of the flock,
for the days have arrived for your slaughter,
like the finest rams you will fall.
No refuge now for the shepherds,   35
no escape for the lords of the flock!
Listen! A shout from the shepherds,   36
a howl from the lords of the flock!
For Yahweh has laid their pastures waste,
their quiet sheepfolds are in ruins.   37
The lion has left his lair,   38
their land is a wasteland now,
thanks to the destroying sword,
and the fierce anger of Yahweh." '

III. PROPHECIES OF HAPPINESS

A. INTRODUCTION: JEREMIAH THE TRUE PROPHET

Jeremiah's discourse against the Temple: his arrest and condemnation (LXX 33)

26 At the beginning of the reign of Jehoiakim son of Josiah, king of Judah, 1
this word was addressed to Jeremiah by Yahweh, •'Yahweh says this: 2
Stand in the court of the Temple of Yahweh. To all the people of the towns of
Judah who come to worship in the Temple of Yahweh you must speak all the
words I have commanded you to tell them; do not omit one syllable. •Perhaps 3
they will listen and each turn from his evil way: if so, I shall relent and not bring
the disaster on them which I intended for their misdeeds. •Say to them, "Yahweh 4
says this: If you will not listen to me by following my Law which I put
before you, •by paying attention to the words of my servants the prophets 5
whom I send so persistently to you, without your ever listening to them, •I will 6
treat this Temple as I treated Shiloh, and make this city a curse for all the
nations of the earth". '
The priests and prophets and all the people heard Jeremiah say these words 7
in the Temple of Yahweh. •When Jeremiah had finished saying everything that 8
Yahweh had ordered him to say to all the people, the priests and prophets
seized hold of him and said, 'You shall die! •Why have you made this prophecy 9
in the name of Yahweh, "This Temple will be like Shiloh, and this city will be
desolate, and uninhabited"?' And the people were all crowding round Jeremiah in
the Temple of Yahweh. •Hearing of this, the officials of Judah went up from 10

the royal palace to the Temple of Yahweh and took their seats at the entry of the New Gate of the Temple of Yahweh.

11   The priests and prophets then addressed the officials and all the people, 'This man deserves to die, since he has prophesied against this city, as you have
12 heard with your own ears'. •Jeremiah, however, replied to the people as follows, 'Yahweh himself sent me to say all the things you have heard against
13 this Temple and this city. •So now amend your behaviour and actions, listen to the voice of Yahweh your God: if you do, he will relent and not bring down
14 on you the disaster he has pronounced against you. •For myself, I am as you
15 see in your hands. Do whatever you please or think right with me. •But be sure of this, that if you put me to death, you will be bringing innocent blood on yourselves, on this city and on its citizens, since Yahweh has truly sent me to you to say all these words in your hearing.'

16   The officials and all the people then said to the priests and prophets, 'This man does not deserve to die: he has spoken to us in the name of Yahweh our
17 God'. •Some of the elders of the land had risen to address all the assembled
18 people. •'Micah of Moresheth,' they said 'who prophesied in the days of Hezekiah king of Judah, had this to say to all the people of Judah, "Yahweh says this:

> Zion will become ploughland,
> Jerusalem a heap of rubble,
> and the mountain of the Temple a wooded height".[a]

19   'Did Hezekiah king of Judah and all of Judah put him to death for this? Did they not rather, fearing Yahweh, entreat his favour, to make him relent and not bring the disaster on them which he had pronounced against them? Are we now to burden our souls with such a crime?'

20   There was another man, too, who used to prophesy in the name of Yahweh, Uriah son of Shemaiah, from Kiriath-jearim. He prophesied exactly the same
21 things against this city and this land as Jeremiah. •When King Jehoiakim with all his ministers and officials heard what he said, he wished to put him to death.
22 Learning this, Uriah took fright and escaped to Egypt. •King Jehoiakim, however,
23 sent Elnathan son of Achbor to Egypt with others, •who brought Uriah back from Egypt and took him to King Jehoiakim, who had him put to the sword and
24 his body thrown into the common burying ground. •But Jeremiah had a protector in Ahikam son of Shaphan,[b] so he was not handed over to the people to be put to death.

B. THE PAMPHLET FOR THE EXILES

The symbolic yoke and the message to the kings of the west   (LXX 34)

1 **27** (At the beginning of the reign of Zedekiah son of Josiah, king of Judah,
2 this word was addressed to Jeremiah by Yahweh:) •Yahweh said this to
3 me, 'Make yourself ropes and a yoke and put them on your neck. •Then send word to the king of Edom, the king of Moab, the king of the Ammonites, the king of Tyre, and the king of Sidon, through their envoys accredited
4 to Zedekiah king of Judah in Jerusalem. •Give them the following message for their masters, "Yahweh Sabaoth, the God of Israel, says this: You must tell
5 your masters this: •I by my great power and outstretched arm made the earth,
6 man and the animals that are on earth. And I can give it to whom I please. •For the present, I have handed all these countries over to Nebuchadnezzar king of
7 Babylon, my servant; I have even put the wild animals at his service. •(All the

---

26 a. Mi 3:12.   **b.** The king's scribe, who had supported the reform under Josiah. His grandson, Gedaliah, was also to be a protector of Jeremiah, Jr 40:5-6.

nations will be subject to him, to his son and to his grandson, until the time for his own country comes in its turn, when mighty nations and great kings will enslave him.) •Any nation or kingdom that will not submit to Nebuchad- 8 nezzar king of·Babylon, and will not bow its neck to the yoke of the king of Babylon, I shall punish with sword, famine and plague—it is Yahweh who speaks—until I have delivered it into his power. •For your own part, do not 9 listen to your prophets, your diviners, dreamers, soothsayers, or sorcerers, who tell you: You will not be subjects of the king of Babylon. •They prophesy lies 10 to you, the result of which will be that you will be banished from your soil, that I shall expel you, and you will perish. •The nation, however, that bends its neck 11 to the yoke of the king of Babylon and submits to him, I shall leave in peace on its own soil—it is Yahweh who speaks—to farm it and stay in it." '

To Zedekiah king of Judah I had the same to say. 'Bend your necks,' I told 12 him 'to the yoke of the king of Babylon; submit to him and to his people and you will live. •(Why so anxious to die, you and your ·people, by sword, famine 13 and plague, with which Yahweh has threatened the nation that will not submit to the king of Babylon?) •Do not listen to the words the prophets say to you, 14 "You will not be subjects of the king of Babylon". They prophesy lies to you. Since I have not sent them—it is Yahweh who speaks—they prophesy untruths 15 in my name. The result will be that I shall expel you, you will perish, and so will the prophets who prophesy to you.'

Next I spoke to the priests and all the people as follows, 'Yahweh says this, 16 "Do not listen to the words of your prophets who prophesy to you as follows: Look, the vessels of the Temple of Yahweh will (soon) be brought back from Babylon: they prophesy lies to you. •(Do not listen to them; submit to the 17 king of Babylon and you will live; why should this city become a waste?) •If 18 they were prophets, if they had the word of Yahweh, they would now be praying to Yahweh Sabaoth that the remaining vessels in the Temple of Yahweh, in the royal palace of Judah and in Jerusalem should not go to Babylon. •For this 19 is what Yahweh Sabaoth says about (the pillars, the Sea, the stands and) the other vessels still remaining in this city, •those not carried off by Nebuchadnezzar 20 king of Babylon when he led away Jeconiah son of Jehoiakim, king of Judah, into exile from Jerusalem to Babylon (with all the leading men of Judah and Jerusalem). •Yes, this is what Yahweh Sabaoth, the God of Israel, says about 21 the vessels still remaining in the Temple of Yahweh, in the royal palace of Judah, and in Jerusalem: •They will be carried off to Babylon (and stay there 22 until the day I fetch them)—it is Yahweh who speaks. (Then I shall bring them back and restore them to this place)." '

The dispute with Hananiah   (LXX 35)

28 That same year, at the beginning of the reign of Zedekiah king of Judah in 1 the fifth month of the fourth year, the prophet Hananiah son of Azzur, a Gibeonite, spoke as follows to Jeremiah in the Temple of Yahweh in the presence of the priests and of all the people. •'Yahweh, the God of Israel, says this, 2 "I have broken the yoke of the king of Babylon. •In two years' time I will bring 3 back all the vessels of the Temple of Yahweh which Nebuchadnezzar king of Babylon carried off from this place and took to Babylon. •And I will also bring 4 back Jeconiah son of Jehoiakim, king of Judah, and all the exiles of Judah who have gone to Babylon—it is Yahweh who speaks. Yes, I am going to break the yoke of the king of Babylon." '

The prophet Jeremiah then replied to the prophet Hananiah in front of the 5 priests and all the people there in the Temple of Yahweh. •'I hope so' 6 the prophet Jeremiah said. 'May Yahweh do so. May he fulfil the words that you have prophesied and bring the vessels of the Temple of Yahweh and all the exiles back to this place from Babylon. •Listen carefully, however, to this word 7 that I am now going to say for you and all the people to hear: •From remote 8

times, the prophets who preceded you and me prophesied war, famine and
9 plague for many countries and for great kingdoms; •but the prophet
who prophesies peace can only be recognised as one truly sent by Yahweh when
his word comes true.'

10 The prophet Hananiah then took the yoke off the neck of the prophet Jeremiah
11 and broke it. •In front of all the people Hananiah then said, 'Yahweh says
this, "This is how, two years hence, I will break the yoke of Nebuchadnezzar
king of Babylon and take it off the necks of all the nations" '. At this, the
prophet Jeremiah went away.

12 After the prophet Hananiah had broken the yoke which he had taken off
the neck of the prophet Jeremiah the word of Yahweh was addressed to Jeremiah,
13 'Go to Hananiah and tell him this, "Yahweh says this: You can break
14 wooden yokes? Right, I will make them iron yokes instead! •For Yahweh
Sabaoth, the God of Israel, says this: An iron yoke is what I now lay on the
necks of all these nations to subject them to Nebuchadnezzar king of Babylon.
(They will be subject to him; I have even given him the wild animals.)" '

15 The prophet Jeremiah said to the prophet Hananiah, 'Listen carefully,
Hananiah: Yahweh has not sent you; and thanks to you this people are
16 now relying on what is false. •Hence—Yahweh says this, "I am going to throw
you off the face of the earth: you are going to die this year (since you have
preached apostasy from Yahweh)".'

17 The prophet Hananiah died the same year, in the seventh month.

The letter to the exiles   (LXX 36:1-23)

1 **29** This is the text of the letter that the prophet Jeremiah sent from Jerusalem
to those elders carried off into exile, to the priests, the prophets and all the
people whom Nebuchadnezzar had led away into exile from Jerusalem to Babylon.
2 This was after King Jeconiah had left Jerusalem with the queen mother, the
eunuchs, the nobility of Judah and Jerusalem, and the blacksmiths and metal-
3 workers. •The letter was entrusted to Elasah son of Shaphan and to Gemariah
son of Hilkiah, whom Zedekiah king of Judah had sent to Babylon, to Nebuchadnezzar king of Babylon. The letter said:

4 'Yahweh Sabaoth, the God of Israel, says this to all the exiles deported
5 from Jerusalem to Babylon, •"Build houses, settle down; plant gardens and eat
6 what they produce; •take wives and have sons and daughters; choose wives for
your sons, find husbands for your daughters so that these can bear sons and
7 daughters in their turn; you must increase there and not decrease. •Work for
the good of the country to which I have exiled you; pray to Yahweh on its
10 behalf, since on its welfare yours depends. •For Yahweh says this: Only
when the seventy years granted to Babylon are over, will I visit you and fulfil
11 my promise in your favour by bringing you back to this place. •I know the plans
I have in mind for you—it is Yahweh who speaks—plans for peace, not disaster,
12 reserving a future full of hope for you. •Then when you call to me, and come
13 to plead with me, I will listen to you. •When you seek me you shall find me,
14 when you seek me with all your heart; •I will let you find me (–it is Yahweh
who speaks. I will restore your fortunes and gather you from all the nations
and all the places where I have dispersed you—it is Yahweh who speaks. I will
bring you back to the place from which I exiled you.)

15
8 "You may say: Yahweh has raised up prophets for us in Babylon, •but
thus says Yahweh Sabaoth, the God of Israel: Do not be deceived by the
prophets among you or by your diviners; do not listen to the dreams they
9 dream, •since they prophesy lies to you in my name. I have not sent them—
it is Yahweh who speaks.

16 "For this is what Yahweh says about the king now seated on the throne of
David and all the people who live in this city, your brothers who did not go

with you into exile: •Thus says Yahweh Sabaoth: I am now going to send 17
them sword, famine and plague; I will make them like rotten figs, so bad as
to be uneatable. •I will pursue them with sword, famine and plague, and 18
make them an object of horror to all the kingdoms of the earth, a curse, a thing
of wonder, scorn, derision, for all the nations where I have dispersed them;
because they have refused to listen to my words—it is Yahweh who speaks— 19
although I have persistently sent them all my servants the prophets. However,
they would not listen—it is Yahweh who speaks. •But all you exiles, whom 20
I have sent from Jerusalem to Babylon, listen to the word of Yahweh.

"This is what Yahweh Sabaoth, the God of Israel, says about Ahab son of 21
Kolaiah, and Zedekiah son of Maaseiah, who prophesy lies to you in my name:
I shall hand them over now to Nebuchadnezzar king of Babylon who will strike
them before your eyes. •This curse, based on their fate, will be used by all the 22
exiles of Judah in Babylon: May Yahweh treat you like Zedekiah and Ahab,
roasted alive by the king of Babylon! •Such is the fate of those who perpetrate 23
infamies in Israel, committing adultery with other men's wives, speaking words
in my name without orders from me. I know all the same; I see—it is Yahweh
who speaks." '

An exile objects to Jeremiah's letter   (LXX 36:24-32)

Shemaiah of Nehelam sent a letter of his own (to all the people in Jerusalem) 24 25
to the priest Zephaniah son of Maaseiah (and to all the priests), which said:
'Yahweh has appointed you priest in succession to Jehoiada to keep order in 26
the Temple of Yahweh; in the case of a madman who acts the prophet, your
duty is to put him in the stocks and iron collar. •This being the case, why have 27
you not disciplined Jeremiah of Anathoth, who poses as a prophet to you?
—since on the strength of this pretension he has sent a message to us in Babylon 28
to say, "It will be a long time. Build houses, settle down; plant gardens and eat
what they produce." '

The priest Zephaniah read this letter aloud to the prophet Jeremiah. •The 29 30
word of Yahweh, however, was addressed to Jeremiah, •'Send this message to all 31
the exiles, "This is what Yahweh says about Shemaiah of Nehelam: Since
Shemaiah has prophesied to you without my sending him, and since it is due
to him that you are now relying on what is false, •now therefore—thus says 32
Yahweh—I will punish Shemaiah of Nehelam and his descendants; no male
member of his family shall survive among this people to see the happiness that
I will bestow on my people (—it is Yahweh who speaks—since he has preached
apostasy from Yahweh)." '

C. THE BOOK OF CONSOLATION

Promise of recovery for the northern kingdom of Israel   (LXX 37:1-38:22)

30 The word addressed to Jeremiah by Yahweh: •Yahweh, the God of Israel 1 2
says this: Write all the words I have spoken to you in a book. •For see, 3
the days are coming—it is Yahweh who speaks—when I will restore the fortunes
of my people Israel (and Judah), Yahweh says, and bring them back to possess
the land I gave to their ancestors.

These are the words Yahweh spoke about Israel (and Judah):   4

> Yahweh says this: 5
> I have heard a cry of panic,
> of terror, not of peace.
> Now ask, consider: 6
> can men bear children?
> Then why do I see each man

with his hands on his loins like a woman in labour?
Why has every face changed,
turned pale?

7   This is indeed a great day,
no other like it:
a time of distress for Jacob;
but he will be freed from it.

8   On that day—it is Yahweh Sabaoth who speaks—I will break the yoke
on their necks, and snap their chains. They will be no longer the servants of
9 aliens, •but will serve Yahweh their God, and David their king whom I will
raise up for them.

10   So do not be afraid, my servant Jacob
—it is Yahweh who speaks—
Israel, do not be alarmed:
look, I will rescue you from distant countries
and your descendants from the country where they are captive.
Jacob will have quiet again
and live at ease, with no one to trouble him.

11   For I am with you to save you:
I will make an end of all the nations
where I have scattered you;
I will not make an end of you,
only discipline you in moderation,
so as not to let you go entirely unpunished.

12   Yes, Yahweh says this:
Your wound is incurable,
your injury past healing.

13   There is no one to care for your sore,
no medicine to make you well again.

14   All your lovers have forgotten you,
they look for you no more.
Yes, I have struck you as an enemy strikes,
with harsh punishment
(so great is your guilt, so many your sins).

15   Why bother to complain about your wound?
Your pain is incurable.
So great is your guilt, so many your sins,
that I have done all this to you.

16   But all those who devoured you shall themselves be devoured,
all your oppressors go into captivity,
those who despoiled you shall be despoiled,
and all who preyed on you I will make into prey.

17b   For they used to call you 'The Outcast',
'Our booty whom no one cares about!'

17a   But I will restore you to health
and heal your wounds—it is Yahweh who speaks.

18   Yahweh says this:
Now I will restore the tents of Jacob,
and take pity on his dwellings:
the city shall be rebuilt on its ruins,
the citadel restored on its site.

19   From them will come thanksgiving
and shouts of joy.
I will make them increase, and not diminish them,

make them honoured, and not disdained.
Their sons shall be as once they were,   20
their community fixed firm in my presence,
and I will punish all their oppressors.
Their prince will be one of their own,   21
their ruler come from their own people.
I will let him come freely into my presence and he can come close to me;
who else, indeed, would risk his life
by coming close to me?—it is Yahweh who speaks.

And you shall be my people and I will be your God.   22
Now a storm of Yahweh breaks,   23
a tempest whirls,
it bursts over the head of the wicked;
the anger of Yahweh will not turn aside   24
until he has performed and carried out,
the decision of his heart.
You will understand this in the days to come.

31 When that time comes—it is Yahweh who speaks—I will be the God   1
of all the clans of Israel: they shall be my people.

Yahweh says this: 2
They have found pardon in the wilderness,
those who have survived the sword.
Israel is marching to his rest.
Yahweh has appeared to him from afar: 3
I have loved you with an everlasting love,
so I am constant in my affection for you.
I build you once more; you shall be rebuilt,   4
virgin of Israel.
Adorned once more, and with your tambourines,
you will go out dancing gaily.
You will plant vineyards once more   5
on the mountains of Samaria
(the planters have done their planting: they will
gather the fruit).
Yes, a day will come when the watchmen shout   6
on the mountains of Ephraim,
'Up! Let us go up to Zion,
to Yahweh our God!'

For Yahweh says this: 7
Shout with joy for Jacob!
Hail the chief of nations!
Proclaim! Praise! Shout:
'Yahweh has saved his people,
the remnant of Israel!'
See, I will bring them back   8
from the land of the North
and gather them from the far ends of earth;
all of them: the blind and the lame,
women with child, women in labour:
a great company returning here.
They had left in tears,   9
I will comfort them as I lead them back;
I will guide them to streams of water,
by a smooth path where they will not stumble.

For I am a father to Israel,
and Ephraim is my first-born son.

10   Listen, nations, to the word of Yahweh.
Tell this to the distant islands,
'He who scattered Israel gathers him,
he guards him as a shepherd guards his flock'.

11   For Yahweh has ransomed Jacob,
rescued him from a hand stronger than his own.

12   They will come and shout for joy on the heights of Zion,
they will throng towards the good things of Yahweh:
corn and oil and wine,
sheep and oxen;
their soul will be like a watered garden,
they will sorrow no more.

13   The virgin will then take pleasure in the dance,
young men and old will be happy;
I will change their mourning into gladness,
comfort them, give them joy after their troubles,

14   refresh my priests with rich food,
and see my people have their fill of my good things
— it is Yahweh who speaks.

15   Thus speaks Yahweh:
A voice is heard in Ramah,
lamenting and weeping bitterly:
it is Rachel*a* weeping for her children,
refusing to be comforted for her children,
because they are no more.

16   Yahweh says this:
Stop your weeping,
dry your eyes,
your hardships will be redressed:
they shall come back from the enemy country.

17   There is hope for your descendants:
your sons will come home to their own lands.

18   I plainly hear the grieving of Ephraim,
'You have disciplined me, I accepted the discipline
like a young bull untamed.
Bring me back, let me come back,
for you are Yahweh my God!

19   Yes, I turned away, but have since repented;
I understood, I beat my breast.
I was deeply ashamed, covered with confusion;
yes, I still bore the disgrace of my youth'.

20   Is Ephraim, then, so dear a son to me,
a child so favoured,
that after each threat of mine
I must still remember him,
still be deeply moved for him,
and let my tenderness yearn over him?
It is Yahweh who speaks.

21   Set up signposts,
raise landmarks;
mark the road well,
the way by which you went.

31 a. The mother of Ephraim and Manasseh; her tomb was at Ramah.

> Come home, virgin of Israel,
> come home to these towns of yours.
> How long will you hesitate, disloyal daughter?   22
> For Yahweh is creating something new on earth:
> the Woman sets out to find her Husband again.

Promise of restoration to Judah   (LXX 38:23-26)

Yahweh Sabaoth, the God of Israel, says this: In the land of Judah and 23
in its towns, they will use these words again, once I have restored their fortunes:

> 'Yahweh grant you his blessing,
> you pasture of justice,
> you holy mountain!'

Judah and all his towns, the farmers and those who tend the flock will live 24
in this land. •For I refresh the wearied soul and satisfy every sorrowing soul. 25
And hence:^b 26

> I awoke and was refreshed,
> and my sleep was peaceful.

Israel and Judah   (LXX 38:27-28)

See, the days are coming—it is Yahweh who speaks—when I am going to sow 27
the seed of men and cattle on the House of Israel and on the House of Judah.
And as I once watched them to tear up, to knock down, to overthrow, destroy 28
and bring disaster, so now I shall watch over them to build and to plant. It is
Yahweh who speaks.

Individual retribution

In those days people will no longer say: 29

> 'The fathers have eaten unripe grapes;
> the children's teeth are set on edge'.

But each is to die for his own sin. Every man who eats unripe grapes is to have 30
his own teeth set on edge.

The new covenant   (LXX 38:31-34)

See, the days are coming—it is Yahweh who speaks—when I will make a new 31
covenant with the House of Israel (and the House of Judah), •but not a covenant 32
like the one I made with their ancestors on the day I took them by the hand
to bring them out of the land of Egypt. They broke that covenant of mine, so
I had to show them who was master. It is Yahweh who speaks. •No, this is 33
the covenant I will make with the House of Israel when those days arrive—it is
Yahweh who speaks. Deep within them I will plant my Law, writing it on
their hearts. Then I will be their God and they shall be my people. •There 34
will be no further need for neighbour to try to teach neighbour, or brother to
say to brother, 'Learn to know Yahweh!' No, they will all know me, the least
no less than the greatest—it is Yahweh who speaks—since I will forgive their
iniquity and never call their sin to mind.

Israel will endure   (LXX 38:35-37)

> Yahweh who provides the sun for light by day,   35
> the moon and stars for light by night,
> who stirs the sea, making its waves roar,
> he whose name is Yahweh Sabaoth, says this:
> Were this established order ever to pass away   36
> from my presence—it is Yahweh who speaks—
> only then would the race of Israel also cease

to be a nation in my presence for ever.
37   Were the heavens above ever to be measured,
          the foundations of the earth below ever to be fathomed,
          only then would I reject the race of Israel
          for all that they have done. It is Yahweh who speaks.

Jerusalem magnificently rebuilt

38   See, the days are coming—it is Yahweh who speaks—when the city of
Yahweh will be rebuilt from the Tower of Hananel to the Gate of the Corner.
39 Then once again the measuring line will stretch straight to the Hill of Gareb,
40 turning then to Goah.ᶜ •And the whole valley, with its dead and its ashes, and
all the fields beside the wadi Kidron as far as the corner of the Horse Gate,
eastwards, will be consecrated to Yahweh. It shall never again be destroyed,
or laid under the ban.

D. ADDITIONS TO THE BOOK OF CONSOLATION

Jeremiah buys a field in token of his confidence in the future of Judah   (LXX 39)

1 32 The word that was addressed to Jeremiah by Yahweh in the tenth
     year of Zedekiah king of Judah, which was the eighteenth year of
2 Nebuchadnezzar. •The army of the king of Babylon was at that time besieging
Jerusalem, and the prophet Jeremiah was confined to the Court of the Guard
3 in the royal palace of Judah, •where Zedekiah king of Judah had imprisoned
him. 'Why' he had asked 'do you make a prophecy like this, "Yahweh says
this: I am now going to deliver this city into the hands of the king of Babylon,
4 for him to capture it; •and Zedekiah king of Judah will not escape the power of
the Chaldaeans, but will inevitably be delivered into the hands of the king of
5 Babylon, speak to him personally and see him face to face. •He will take
Zedekiah to Babylon and he will stay there (until I visit him—it is Yahweh who
speaks. If you fight the Chaldaeans you will not succeed!)"'?
6   Jeremiah said, 'The word of Yahweh has been addressed to me as follows,
7 "Look, Hanamel the son of your uncle Shallum will come to you and say:
Buy my field at Anathoth, for you have the right of redemptionᵈ to purchase it".
8 And, as Yahweh had said, my cousin Hanamel came to me, in the Court of
the Guard. He said to me, "Buy my field at Anathoth, for you have the
right of inheritance and redemption; buy it". I knew then that this was
9 Yahweh's order. •Accordingly, I bought the field from my cousin Hanamel of
10 Anathoth and paid him the price: seventeen silver shekels. •I drew up the deed
and sealed it, called in witnesses and weighed out the money on the scales.
11 I then took both the sealed deed of purchase and its open copy, in accordance
12 with the requirements of the law, •and handed over the deed of purchase to
Baruch son of Neriah, son of Mahseiah, in the presence of my cousin Hanamel,
of the witnesses who had signed the deed of purchase, and of all the Jews who
13 then happened to be in the Court of the Guard. •In their presence I gave
14 Baruch these instructions: •Take these deeds, the sealed deed of purchase
and its open copy, and put them in an earthenware pot, so that they may be
15 preserved for a long time. •For Yahweh Sabaoth, the God of Israel, says this,
"People will buy fields and vineyards in this land again".
16   'After I had entrusted the deed of purchase to Baruch son of Neriah, I prayed
17 thus to Yahweh: •Ah, Lord Yahweh, you have made the heavens and
the earth with your great power and outstretched arm. To you nothing is
18 impossible. •You show kindness to thousands but repay the fathers' guilt in

b. A quotation, probably from a song.   c. The same measurements of those of the old
city destroyed by the Chaldaeans.
32 a. By blood-relationship with the late owner.

full to their children after them. Great and mighty God, whose name is Yahweh Sabaoth! •Great in purpose, mighty in execution, whose eyes are open on all 19 the ways of men, rewarding each man as his ways and the results of his actions deserve! •You performed signs and wonders in the land of Egypt and do the same 20 today, in Israel and among mankind. You have won the name that is yours today. •You brought your people Israel out of the land of Egypt with signs 21 and wonders, with mighty hand and outstretched arm and fearsome terror; then you gave them this land which you promised on oath to their ancestors, 22 a land where milk and honey flow; •and in due course they entered it and took 23 possession. But they would not listen to your voice or follow your Law: they would do nothing you ordered them to do; and so you made all these disasters happen to them. •See how the earthworks grow nearer to the city for 24 the assault! Sword, famine, and plague will deliver the city into the hands of the attacking Chaldaeans. What you have said is now fulfilled, as you see. Yet you yourself, Lord Yahweh, told me, "Buy the field with money in front 25 of witnesses"—and even now the city is falling into the hands of the Chaldaeans!

'The word of Yahweh was addressed to me as follows, •"See, I am Yahweh, $^{26}_{27}$ the God of all mankind: is anything impossible to me?

"Therefore—Yahweh says this: I am now putting this city into the power of 28 the Chaldaeans, into the power of Nebuchadnezzar king of Babylon, and he will capture it; •the Chaldaeans attacking this city will come and set fire to it; 29 they will burn the houses on the roofs of which incense was offered to Baal and libations were poured to alien gods, to provoke me. •For the sons of Israel and 30 of Judah have done nothing but displease me from their youth up (the sons of Israel in fact have done nothing but provoke me by their actions—it is Yahweh who speaks). •Yes, from the day when it was built until today, this 31 city has been such cause of anger and of wrath to me that I mean to remove it from my sight, •because of all the wickedness the sons of Israel and the sons 32 of Judah have committed to provoke me: they, their kings, their nobles, their priests and their prophets, the men of Judah and the citizens of Jerusalem. They turned their backs to me, never their faces; and though I taught them 33 so urgently, so persistently, they would not listen and learn the lesson. •They 34 have put their abominations in the Temple that bears my name to defile it. They have built the high places of Baal in the Valley of Ben-hinnom, there to 35 make their sons and daughters pass through fire in honour of Molech— something I never ordered, for it never entered my thoughts that they would do such detestable things—and so they have led Judah into sin.

"But now, and for the same reason, this is what Yahweh, the God of Israel, 36 says about this city of which you say: Sword, famine and plague will deliver it into the hands of the king of Babylon: •I mean to gather them from all the 37 countries where I have driven them in my anger, my fury and great wrath. I will bring them back to this place and make them live in safety. •Then they 38 shall be my people, and I will be their God. •I will give them a different heart and 39 different behaviour so that they will always fear me, for the good of themselves and their children after them. •I will make an everlasting covenant with them; I 40 will not cease in my efforts for their good, and I will put respect for me into their hearts, so that they turn from me no more. •It will be my pleasure to bring 41 about their good, and I will plant them firmly in this land, with all my heart and soul. •For Yahweh says this: As I have brought this great disaster on this 42 people, so I am going to bring them all the good I promise them. •People will 43 buy fields in this land of which you say: It is a wasteland without man or beast; it is given over into the power of the Chaldaeans. •People will buy fields, pay 44 money, draw up deeds and seal them, and witness them in the land of Benjamin, in the districts round Jerusalem, in the towns of Judah, of the highlands, of the Lowlands and of the Negeb. For I am going to restore their fortunes—it is Yahweh who speaks." '

Another promise of recovery for Jerusalem and Judah (LXX 40)

1 **33** Jeremiah was still confined to the Court of the Guard when the word
2 of Yahweh was addressed to him a second time, •'Yahweh, who made
the earth, who formed it and set it firm—Yahweh is his name—says this,
3 Call to me and I will answer you; I will tell you great mysteries of which you
4 know nothing. •For this is what Yahweh, the God of Israel, says about the
houses of this city and the royal palaces of Judah which are to be destroyed.
5 Against the earthworks and the palisades •they will join battle with the
Chaldaeans, only to fill the city with the corpses of those I strike down in my
anger and my wrath, of those from whom I turned my face because of all their
wickedness.

6 'But look, I will hasten their recovery and their cure; I will cure them
7 and let them know peace and security in full measure. •I will restore the fortunes
8 of Judah and Jerusalem, and build them again as they were before. •I will
cleanse them of every sin they have committed against me; the sins by which
9 they offended me and apostatised from me, all these I will forgive. •And
Jerusalem shall be my theme of joy, my honour and my boast, before all the
nations of the earth: these, when they hear of all the prosperity that I shall
grant, will be seized with fear and trembling at all the prosperity and the peace
that I provide for it.

10 'Yahweh says this: In this place of which you say, "It is a waste without
man or beast", in the towns of Judah and in the ruined streets of Jerusalem
11 where there is neither man nor beast, once more will be heard •shouts of
rejoicing and mirth, the voices of bridegroom and bride, and the singing of
those who bring thanksgiving sacrifices to the Temple of Yahweh, "Give thanks
to Yahweh Sabaoth, for Yahweh is good, for his love is everlasting". For I will
restore the fortunes of this land as they were before. Yahweh declares it!

12 'Yahweh Sabaoth says this: In this place, this waste without man or
beast, and in all its towns, once again there will be pastures for the shepherds
13 to rest their flocks. •In all the towns of the highlands, of the Lowlands
and the Negeb, in the land of Benjamin, in the districts round Jerusalem and
in the towns of Judah, once again the flocks shall pass under the hand of him
who counts them. Yahweh declares it!

The institutions of the future

14 'See, the days are coming—it is Yahweh who speaks—when I am going
to fulfil the promise I made to the House of Israel and the House of Judah:
15 'In those days and at that time,
I will make a virtuous Branch grow for David,
who shall practise honesty and integrity in the land.
16 In those days Judah shall be saved
and Israel shall dwell in confidence.
And this is the name the city will be called:
Yahweh-our-integrity.

17 For Yahweh says this: David shall never lack a male descendant to sit on
18 the throne of the House of Israel. •And the levitical priests shall never lack
a male descendant to stand in my presence and offer holocaust, to burn the
oblation and offer sacrifice every day.'

19
20 The word of Yahweh was addressed to Jeremiah, •'Yahweh says this:
If you could break my covenant with the day and my covenant with the night
21 so that day and night do not come at their due time, •then my covenant with
David my servant might also be broken and he would have no son to reign on his
throne, and so might my covenant with the levitical priests, who are my ministers.
22 As the array of heaven is past counting, the sand on the seashore beyond all

reckoning, so will I increase the heirs of David my servant and the Levites, who, with these heirs, minister to me.'

The word of Yahweh was addressed to Jeremiah, •'Have you not noticed ²³⁄₂₄ what these people say, "The two families which Yahweh chose he has now rejected"? So they despise my people, whom they no longer think of as a nation. Yahweh says this: If I have not created day and night and have not laid down 25 laws for the heavens and the earth, •why, then I reject the descendants of Jacob 26 and of David my servant and cease to choose rulers from his descendants for the heirs of Abraham, Isaac and Jacob! For I mean to restore their fortunes and take pity on them.'

E. MISCELLANEOUS PASSAGES

The fate of Zedekiah　　　　　　　　　　　　　　　　　(LXX 41:1-7)

34 The word addressed to Jeremiah by Yahweh when Nebuchadnezzar king 1 of Babylon and his whole army, with all the kingdoms of the earth under his dominion and all the peoples, were waging war on Jerusalem and its outlying towns, •'Yahweh, the God of Israel, says this: Go and speak to Zedekiah 2 king of Judah. Say this to him, "Yahweh says this: I am now handing over this city into the power of the king of Babylon, and he will burn it down. •And you 3 yourself will not escape his power but will inevitably be captured and delivered into his hands. You will see the king of Babylon face to face and speak to him personally. Then you will go to Babylon. •Even so, listen to the word of 4 Yahweh, Zedekiah king of Judah, and you will not die by the sword; •you will 5 die in peace. And as spices were burnt for your fathers, the kings who in times past preceded you, so they will also burn spices for you and raise this dirge for you: Mourn for his highness! I myself declare it—it is Yahweh who speaks." '

The prophet Jeremiah repeated all these words to Zedekiah king of Judah, 6 in Jerusalem, •while the army of the king of Babylon was attacking Jerusalem 7 and the towns of Judah which still held out, namely Lachish and Azekah, these being the only towns of Judah that still held out, since they were fortified.

The episode of the liberated slaves　　　　　　　　　　(LXX 41:8-22)

The word addressed to Jeremiah by Yahweh after King Zedekiah had made 8 a pact with all the people in Jerusalem to free their slaves: •each man was to 9 free his Hebrew slaves, men and women, and no one was any longer to keep a brother Jew in slavery. •All the nobles and all the people who had entered into 10 the pact had agreed that everyone should free his slaves, men or women, and no longer keep them as slaves: they had agreed on this and set them free. •Afterwards, 11 however, they changed their minds, recovered the slaves, men and women, whom they had set free, and reduced them to slavery again. •So the word of Yahweh 12 was addressed to Jeremiah, •'Yahweh, the God of Israel, says this: I made 13 a covenant with your ancestors when I brought them out of Egypt, out of the house of slavery; it said: •At the end of seven years each one of you is to free 14 his brother Hebrew who has sold himself to you: he may be your slave for six years, then you must send him away free. But your ancestors did not listen to me and would not pay attention. •Now, today you took a different attitude and 15 did what pleases me by proclaiming freedom for your neighbour; you made a covenant in my presence in the Temple that bears my name. •And then you changed 16 your mind and, profaning my name, each of you has recovered his slaves, men and women, whom you had sent away free to live their own lives, and has forced them to become your slaves again.

'Therefore—Yahweh says this: You have disobeyed me, by not each granting 17 freedom to his brother and his neighbour. Very well, I in my turn—it is Yahweh who speaks—leave sword, famine and plague free to deal with you;

18 I will make you an object of horror to all the kingdoms of the earth. •And these men who have infringed my covenant, who have not observed the terms of the covenant made in my presence, I will treat these men like the calf they cut in
19 two to pass between the parts of it.*ᵃ* •As for the nobles of Judah and of Jerusalem, the eunuchs and the priests, and all the people of the country who have passed
20 between the parts of the calf, •I will put them into the power of their enemies and into the power of men determined to kill them: their corpses will feed the
21 birds of heaven and the beasts of the earth. •As for Zedekiah king of Judah and his nobles, these too I will hand over to their enemies and to men determined to kill them, and to the army of the king of Babylon which has just
22 withdrawn. •Listen, I will give the order—it is Yahweh who speaks—and bring them back to this city to attack it and capture it and burn it down. I am going to make an uninhabited desert of the towns of Judah.'

The example of the Rechabites   (LXX 42)

1   2 35 The word addressed to Jeremiah by Yahweh in the days of Jehoiakim son of Josiah, king of Judah, •'Go to the clan of the Rechabites and speak to them; bring them into one of the apartments of the Temple of Yahweh and
3 offer them wine to drink'. •So I brought Jaazaniah son of Jeremiah, son of Habazziniah, with his brothers and all his sons: the whole Rechabite clan.
4 I took them to the Temple of Yahweh into the apartment of Ben-johanan son of Igdaliah, a man of God, a room near that of the officials, over the
5 apartment of Maaseiah son of Shallum, guardian of the threshold. •I then set pitchers full of wine, and some cups, before the men of the Rechabite clan and said, 'Drink some wine'.

6   They replied, 'We do not drink wine, because our ancestor Jonadab son of Rechab gave us this order: "You must never drink wine, neither you nor your
7 sons; •nor must you build houses, sow seed, plant vineyards, or own property; but you must live in tents all your lives, so that you may live long on the soil to
8 which you are alien". •We have punctiliously obeyed the orders of our ancestor, Jonadab son of Rechab, never drinking wine ourselves, nor our wives, our sons
9 or our daughters, •not building houses to live in, owning neither vineyard nor
10 field to sow, •living in tents. We have obeyed the orders of our ancestor
11 Jonadab, respecting them in every particular. •However, when Nebuchadnezzar king of Babylon invaded this country, we decided, "We must get away! We will go to Jerusalem to escape the army of the Chaldaeans and the army of Aram." So here we are, living in Jerusalem.'

12
13   Then the word of Yahweh was addressed to Jeremiah, •'Thus says Yahweh Sabaoth, the God of Israel: Go and say to the men of Judah and the inhabitants of Jerusalem, "Will you not learn the lesson and listen to my words? It is Yahweh
14 who speaks. •The word of Jonadab son of Rechab ordering his sons to drink no wine has been kept; obedient to their ancestor's command, they drink none even today. But to me, who spoke to you so urgently, so persistently, you
15 have not listened. •I have sent you all my servants the prophets so persistently, so often, to say: Each of you turn from your evil way, and amend your actions, do not follow alien gods and serve them; then you will be able to stay on the
16 soil I gave to you and your ancestors. But you would not listen to me. •The sons of Jonadab son of Rechab have kept the command their ancestor gave
17 them, but this people has not listened to me. •And so—Yahweh, the God of Sabaoth, the God of Israel, says this: I will bring down on Judah and the citizens of Jerusalem all the disasters with which I have threatened them, because I spoke to them and they would not listen, called to them and they would not answer." '
18   Then Jeremiah said to the Rechabite clan, 'Yahweh Sabaoth, the God of Israel.

34 a. The ancient ritual of covenant, Gn 15:17.

says this, "Because you have obeyed the orders of Jonadab and kept all his rules and done all that he ordered you, •for this—thus says Yahweh 19 Sabaoth, the God of Israel—Jonadab son of Rechab shall never lack a male descendant to stand in my presence" '.

IV. THE SUFFERINGS OF JEREMIAH

The scroll written in 605-604   (LXX 43)

36 In the fourth year of Jehoiakim*a* son of Josiah, king of Judah, this word 1 was addressed to Jeremiah by Yahweh, •'Take a scroll and write on it all 2 the words I have spoken to you about Jerusalem and Judah and all the nations, from the day I first spoke to you, in the time of Josiah, until today. •Perhaps 3 when the House of Judah hears of all the evil I have in mind for them, each man will turn from his evil way, and then I can forgive their misdeeds and their sin.' Jeremiah therefore summoned Baruch son of Neriah, who at his dictation wrote 4 down on the scroll all the words Yahweh had spoken to him.

Now in the fifth year of Jehoiakim son of Josiah, king of Judah, in the ninth 9 month,*b* there was a summons to a fast in the presence of Yahweh for the whole population of Jerusalem and for all the people who could come to Jerusalem from the towns of Judah. •Jeremiah then gave Baruch this order: 'As I am 5 prevented from entering the Temple of Yahweh, •you yourself must go and, 6 from the scroll you wrote at my dictation, read all the words of Yahweh to the people in his Temple on the day of the fast; read them also in the hearing of all the men of Judah who come in from the towns. •Perhaps they will offer their prayers 7 to Yahweh and each one turn from his evil way, for great is the anger and wrath with which Yahweh has threatened this people.' •Baruch son of Neriah duly 8 carried out the order that the prophet Jeremiah had given him, to read all the words of Yahweh from the book in his Temple. •He read the words of Jeremiah 10 from the book; this happened in the apartment of Gemariah, son of Shaphan the secretary, in the upper court at the entry of the New Gate of the Temple of Yahweh, where all the people could hear.

Micaiah son of Gemariah, son of Shaphan, had heard all the words of Yahweh 11 read from the book, •and he went down to the royal palace and into the 12 secretary's room. All the officials were in session there: Elishama the secretary, Delaiah son of Shemaiah, Elnathan son of Achbor, Gemariah son of Shaphan, Zedekiah son of Hananiah and all the other officials. •Micaiah reported to them 13 all the words he had heard as Baruch was reading the book to the people. •The 14 officials then by common consent sent Jehudi son of Nethaniah to Baruch, with Shelemiah son of Cushi, to give him this message, 'Come, and bring the scroll with you which you were reading to the people'. Bringing the scroll with him, Baruch son of Neriah appeared before them. •'Sit down,' they said 'and read 15 it out.' So Baruch read it to them. •When they had heard all the words they 16 turned to one another in alarm and said, 'We must certainly inform the king of all this'. •They then questioned Baruch: 'Tell us' they said 'how you came 17 to write all these words'. •'Jeremiah dictated them to me.' Baruch replied 'and 18 I wrote them down in ink in this book.' •The officials then said to Baruch, 'You 19 and Jeremiah had better go into hiding; and do not tell anyone where you are'. Whereupon they went off to the king in the palace court, depositing the scroll 20 in the room of Elishama the secretary. And they informed the king of the whole affair.

The king sent Jehudi for the scroll, and he brought it from the room of Elishama 21 the secretary and read it out to the king and all the officials standing round the king. •The king was seated in his winter apartments—it was the ninth month— 22 with a fire burning in a brazier in front of him. •Each time Jehudi had read 23 three or four columns, the king cut them off with a scribe's knife and threw

them into the fire in the brazier until the whole of the scroll had been burnt in
24 the brazier fire. •But even after hearing all these words, neither the king nor
25 any of his servants took alarm or tore their garments; •and although Elnathan
and Delaiah and Gemariah had urged the king not to burn the scroll he would
26 not listen to them. •He ordered Prince Jerahmeel and Seraiah son of Azriel and
Shelemiah son of Abdeel to arrest the scribe Baruch and the prophet Jeremiah.
But Yahweh had hidden them.

27 And then the word of Yahweh was addressed to Jeremiah, after the king
had burnt the scroll containing the words Baruch had written at the dictation
28 of Jeremiah, •'Take another scroll and write down all the words that were
29 written on the first scroll burnt by Jehoiakim king of Judah. •And as regards
Jehoiakim king of Judah, say, "Yahweh says this: You have burnt this scroll,
saying: Why have you written down: The king of Babylon will certainly come
30 and lay this country waste and leave it without man or beast? •And so, this
is what Yahweh says about Jehoiakim king of Judah: He will have no one
to sit on the throne of David, and his corpse will be tossed out to the heat of
31 the day and the frost of the night. •I will punish him, his heirs and his
servants for their misdeeds; on them, on the citizens of Jerusalem and on
the men of Judah I will bring down all the disasters with which I have
threatened them, though they have not listened." '

32 Jeremiah then took another scroll and gave it to the scribe Baruch son of
Neriah, and at the dictation of Jeremiah he wrote down all the words of the book
that Jehoiakim king of Judah had burnt, with many similar words in addition.

A verdict on Zedekiah
                                                                    (LXX 44:1-2)

37 1 Zedekiah son of Josiah became king, succeeding Coniah son of Jehoiakim:
Nebuchadnezzar king of Babylon had made him king of the land of
2 Judah. •But neither he nor his servants nor the people of the country paid any
attention to the words Yahweh spoke through the prophet Jeremiah.

Zedekiah consults Jeremiah during the respite of 588
                                                                    (LXX 44:3-10)

3 King Zedekiah sent Jehucal son of Shelemiah and the priest Zephaniah son
of Maaseiah to the prophet Jeremiah with this message, 'Intercede for us with
4 Yahweh our God'. •Now Jeremiah was still moving freely among the people:
5 he had not yet been put in prison. •Meanwhile Pharaoh's army was on the
move from Egypt and the Chaldaeans besieging Jerusalem had raised the siege
when they heard the news.

6
7 Then the word of Yahweh was addressed to the prophet Jeremiah, •'Yahweh,
the God of Israel, says this: To the king of Judah who sent you to consult
me make this reply, "Is Pharaoh's army marching to your aid? It will withdraw
8 to its own country, Egypt. •The Chaldaeans will return to attack this city;
9 they will capture it and burn it down. •Do not deceive yourselves and say:
10 The Chaldaeans are leaving us for good. They are not leaving. •Even if you cut
to pieces the whole Chaldaean army now fighting against you until there were
only the wounded left, they would stand up again, each man in his tent, to burn
this city down." '

The arrest of Jeremiah. Improvement in his treatment
                                                                    (LXX 44:11-21)

11 At the time when the Chaldaean army, threatened by the army of Pharaoh,
12 had raised the siege of Jerusalem, •Jeremiah started to leave Jerusalem and go
to the land of Benjamin, there among his own people to divide his property.
13 He was at the Benjamin Gate when a sentry on duty there, Irijah son of
Shelemiah, son of Hananiah, arrested the prophet Jeremiah. 'You are desert-
14 ing to the Chaldaeans!' he said. •'It is a lie!' Jeremiah answered. 'I am not

36 a. He had just capitulated to Nebuchadnezzar.   b. December 604.

deserting to the Chaldaeans.' But Irijah would not listen to Jeremiah and
took him under arrest to the officials. •The officials, furious with Jeremiah, had 15
him beaten and shut up in the house of Jonathan the secretary which had been
turned into a prison. •Thus Jeremiah found himself in an underground cell. 16
And there for a long time he stayed.

King Zedekiah had him sent for, and he questioned him privately in his 17
palace. 'Is there any word from Yahweh?' he asked. 'There is' Jeremiah
answered. ' "You will be handed over," he said "into the power of the king of
Babylon." ' •Jeremiah then said to King Zedekiah, 'What wrong have I done to 18
you or your servants or this people, for you to put me in prison? •Where are 19
your prophets now who prophesied, "The king of Babylon will not attack you
or this country"? •Let my lord king be pleased to listen to me now; let my 20
request meet your favour. Do not have me taken back to the house of Jonathan
the secretary, or I shall die there.' •King Zedekiah then gave an order, and 21
Jeremiah was confined in the Court of the Guard and given a loaf of bread a day
from the Street of the Bakers as long as there was bread left in the city. So
Jeremiah stayed in the Court of the Guard.

Jeremiah is thrown into the cistern. Ebed-melech intervenes   (LXX 45:1-13)

38 But Shephatiah son of Mattan, Gedaliah son of Pashhur, Jucal son of 1
Shelemiah and Pashhur son of Malchiah heard the words which Jeremiah
was saying to all the people, •'Yahweh says this, "Anyone who stays in this 2
city will die by sword, famine or plague; but anyone who leaves it and surrenders
to the Chaldaeans will live; he will escape with his life. •Yahweh says this: 3
This city will certainly be delivered into the power of the army of the king of
Babylon, who will capture it." '

These leading men accordingly spoke to the king. 'Let this man be put to 4
death: he is unquestionably disheartening the remaining soldiers in the city,
and all the people too, by talking like this. The fellow does not have the welfare
of this people at heart so much as its ruin.' •He is in your hands as you 5
know,' King Zedekiah answered 'for the king is powerless against you.' •So 6
they took Jeremiah and threw him into the well of Prince Malchiah in the
Court of the Guard, letting him down with ropes. There was no water in the
well, only mud, and into the mud Jeremiah sank.

But Ebed-melech the Cushite, a eunuch attached to the palace, heard that 7
Jeremiah had been put into the well. As the king was sitting at the Benjamin
Gate, •Ebed-melech came out from the palace and spoke to the king. •'My lord $^8_9$
king,' he said 'these men have done a wicked thing by treating the prophet
Jeremiah like this: they have thrown him into the well where he will die.'
At this the king gave Ebed-melech the Cushite the following order: 'Take 10
three men with you from here and pull the prophet Jeremiah out of the well
before he dies'. •Ebed-melech took the men with him and went into the palace 11
to the storehouse wardrobe; out of it he took some torn, worn-out rags which
he lowered on ropes to Jeremiah in the well. •Ebed-melech the Cushite then 12
said to Jeremiah, 'These torn, worn-out rags are for you to put under your
armpits to pad the ropes'. Jeremiah did this. •They then hauled Jeremiah up 13
with the ropes and pulled him out of the well. And Jeremiah stayed in the
Court of the Guard.

The last conversation between Jeremiah and Zedekiah   (LXX 45:14-28)

King Zedekiah had the prophet Jeremiah summoned to him at the third 14
entrance to the Temple of Yahweh. 'I want to ask you for a word,' the king
said to Jeremiah 'keep nothing back from me.' •Jeremiah answered Zedekiah, 15
'If I tell you, surely you will have me put to death? And if I give you advice, you
will not listen to me.' •King Zedekiah then swore this oath in secret to Jeremiah, 16
'As Yahweh lives, giver of this life of ours, I will neither have you put to death

nor handed over into the power of these men who are determined to kill you'.
17 Jeremiah then said to Zedekiah, 'Yahweh, the God of Sabaoth, the God of Israel, says this, "If you go out and surrender to the officers of the king of Babylon, your life will be safe and this city will not be burnt down; you and
18 your family will survive. •But if you do not go out and surrender to the officers of the king of Babylon, this city will be handed over into the power of the king of the Chaldaeans who will burn it down; and you yourself will not escape their
19 hands." ' •King Zedekiah then said to Jeremiah, 'I am afraid of the Jews who have already gone over to the Chaldaeans: I might be handed over to them and
20 they would ill-treat me'. •'You will not be handed over to them,' Jeremiah replied 'just listen to the voice of Yahweh, in obedience to which I have spoken, and
21 all will go well with you and your life will be safe. •But if you refuse to go,
22 this is what Yahweh has shown me: •a vision of all the women left in the palace of the king of Judah being led off to the officers of the king of Babylon and singing:

> "They have misled you, they have overreached you,
>   your fine friends!
> Are your feet sinking in the mud?
> They are up and away!"

23 Yes, all your wives and children will be led off to the Chaldaeans, and you yourself will not escape their hands, but will be a prisoner in the clutches of the king of Babylon. And as for this city, it will be burnt down.'
24 Zedekiah then said to Jeremiah, 'Do not let anyone else hear these words or
25 you will die. •If the officials hear that I have been talking to you, and come to you and say, "Tell us what you said to the king and what the king said to you;
26 keep nothing back from us, or we will put you to death", •you must reply, "I presented this request to the king: that he would not have me sent back to the house of Jonathan to die there".'
27 All the officials did in fact come to Jeremiah to question him. He told them exactly what the king had ordered him to say. They then left him in peace, since
28 no part of the conversation had been overheard. •Jeremiah stayed in the Court of the Guard until the day Jerusalem was captured.

The fall of Jerusalem: the treatment Jeremiah received   (LXX 45:28; 46:14)

Now when Jerusalem was captured...

1 **39** In the ninth year of Zedekiah king of Judah, in the tenth month,[a] Nebuchadnezzar king of Babylon came with his whole army to attack Jerusa-
2 lem and besieged it. •In the eleventh year of Zedekiah, in the fourth month,[b] a breach was made in the city wall.
3 ...all the officers of the king of Babylon marched in and took up their quarters at the Middle Gate: Nergal-sharezer, prince of Sin-magir, the chief officer, Nebus-hazban, the high official, and all the other officers of the king of Babylon...
4 Seeing this, Zedekiah king of Judah fled under cover of dark, with all the fighting men, leaving the city by way of the king's garden through the gate
5 between the two walls, and making their way towards the Arabah.[c] •The Chaldaean troops pursued them and caught up with Zedekiah in the plains of Jericho. They captured him and took him up to Nebuchadnezzar king of Babylon at Riblah
6 in the land of Hamath, who passed sentence on him. •The king of Babylon had the sons of Zedekiah slaughtered before his eyes at Riblah; the king of Babylon
7 also had all the leading men of Judah put to death. •He then put out Zedekiah's
8 eyes and, loading him with chains, carried him off to Babylon. •The Chaldaeans burnt down the royal palace and the private houses, and demolished
9 the walls of Jerusalem. •Nebuzaradan, commander of the guard, deported the

---

39 a. January-February 588.   b. August 587.   c. The Jordan valley.

remainder of the population left behind in the city, the deserters who had gone over to him, and the rest of the artisans to Babylon. •Nebuzaradan, command- 10 er of the guard, left some of the humbler people who had nothing, in the land of Judah, at the same time giving them vineyards and fields.

Nebuchadnezzar king of Babylon had given the following orders to 11 Nebuzaradan, commander of the guard, about Jeremiah: •'Take him, look 12 after him; do him no harm, but treat him as he wishes'.

Whereupon (Nebuzaradan, commander of the guard,) Nebushazban, the 13 high official, Nergal-sharezer, the chief officer, and all the officers of the king of Babylon despatched men. •...and they despatched men to take Jeremiah from the Court of the Guard, 14 and allowed him to move about freely. And so he lived among the people.

An oracle assuring the safety of Ebed-melech   (LXX 46:15-18)

While Jeremiah was confined in the Court of the Guard, the word of Yahweh 15 was addressed to him, •'Go and say to Ebed-melech the Cushite, "Yahweh, the 16 God of Israel, says this: See, I am bringing disaster, not prosperity, on this city, as I said I would. That day, when this comes true before your eyes, •I will 17 rescue you that day—it is Yahweh who speaks—and you will not be delivered into the hands of the men you fear. •I will see that you escape: you are not 18 going to fall to the sword; you will escape with your life, because you have put your trust in me—it is Yahweh who speaks."'

Further details about the treatment of Jeremiah   (LXX 47:1-6)

40 The word addressed to Jeremiah by Yahweh after Nebuzaradan, 1 commander of the guard, had released him from Ramah; there he had him singled out, chained as he was with all the other captives from Jerusalem and Judah who were being deported to Babylon. •Then taking Jeremiah aside, 2 the commander of the guard said to him, 'Yahweh your God foretold calamity for this country, •and now he has brought it. He has done what he threatened 3 to do, because you had sinned against Yahweh and would not listen to his voice; so all this has happened to you. •Look, today I am having your hands 4 unchained. If you like to come with me to Babylon, then come: I will look after you. If you do not want to come with me to Babylon, never mind. Look, you have the whole country to choose from: you may go where you please, wherever you choose. •You can, for instance, go back to Gedaliah son of Ahikam, son of Sha- 5 phan, whom the king of Babylon has appointed governor of the towns of Judah, and stay with him and live with the people; or you can go anywhere else you choose.' With that, the commander of the guard provided him with food and gave him a present and sent him on his way. •Jeremiah went to Mizpah to 6 Gedaliah son of Ahikam and stayed with him, living with the people still left in the country.

Gedaliah the governor; his assassination   (LXX 47:7-48:18)

When all the commanders of the troops, who with their men were still 7 roaming the countryside, heard that the king of Babylon had appointed Gedaliah son of Ahikam as governor of the country, making him responsible for the men, women and children, and those humbler people of the country who had not been deported to Babylon, •they went to Gedaliah at Mizpah: Ishmael son 8 of Nethaniah, Johanan son of Kareah, Seraiah son of Tanhumeth, the sons of Ephai the Netophathite, Jezaniah son of the Maacathite, they and their men. To them and to their men Gedaliah son of Ahikam, son of Shaphan, swore 9 an oath. 'Do not be afraid' he said 'of submitting to the Chaldaeans; but live in the country, and obey the king of Babylon, and all will go well with you. I for my part, as the man answerable to the Chaldaeans when they come to us, 10 am going to live here at Mizpah; but you can harvest your wine, summer fruits and oil, fill your storage jars and settle down in those towns which you care to occupy.'

11 Similarly, when all the Judaeans living in Moab and among the Ammonites, and in Edom, heard that the king of Babylon had left a remnant in Judah and had appointed Gedaliah son of Ahikam, son of Shaphan, as their governor,
12 they all came back from all the places to which they had been dispersed. On their return to the land of Judah, to Gedaliah at Mizpah, they harvested an immense quantity of wine and summer fruits.

13 Now Johanan son of Kareah, and all the army leaders still roaming in the
14 countryside, went to Gedaliah at Mizpah •and said to him, 'Are you aware that Baalis king of the Ammonites has sent Ishmael son of Nethaniah to murder
15 you?' But Gedaliah son of Ahikam would not believe them. •Johanan son of Kareah had even told Gedaliah secretly at Mizpah, 'Let me go and kill Ishmael son of Nethaniah, and no one will know who did it. Why should he murder you? It would mean that all the Judaeans who have rallied round you would be scattered
16 again. Why should the remnant of Judah perish?' •But Gedaliah son of Ahikam replied to Johanan son of Kareah, 'You must not do this; what you say about Ishmael is false'.

1 **41** But in the seventh month, Ishmael son of Nethaniah, son of Elishama, who was of royal descent, and ten men with him, came to Gedaliah son of Ahikam at Mizpah. And as they were taking their meal together, there at
2 Mizpah, •Ishmael son of Nethaniah stood up with his ten men, and attacking Gedaliah son of Ahikam, son of Shaphan, with their swords, murdered the
3 man whom the king of Babylon had made governor of the country. •And all the Judaeans who were with him at the feast, and those of the Chaldaeans who happened to be there—they were fighting men—Ishmael killed too.

4 On the day after the murder of Gedaliah, before the news had become
5 known, •eighty men arrived from Shechem, Shiloh and Samaria, with their beards shaved off, their garments torn and their bodies gashed; they had
6 oblations and incense with them to take to the Temple of Yahweh. •Ishmael son of Nethaniah left Mizpah to meet them as they approached, weeping as they
7 went. When he met them he said, 'Come to Gedaliah son of Ahikam'. •But once they were well inside the town, Ishmael son of Nethaniah slaughtered them,
8 with the help of his men, and threw them into a cistern. •There were ten of them, however, who said to Ishmael, 'Do not kill us: we have stocks of wheat and barley, oil and honey, hidden away in the fields'. So he spared them and did
9 not kill them with their brothers. •The cistern into which Ishmael threw the corpses of all the men he had killed was a large cistern which King Asa had built as a precaution against Baasha king of Israel. Ishmael son of Nethaniah
10 filled it with the bodies of his victims. •Then Ishmael led the entire remnant of the people at Mizpah away, and the royal princesses whom Nebuzaradan, commander of the guard, had left in the care of Gedaliah son of Ahikam. Ishmael son of Nethaniah set out early to cross to the Ammonites.

11 When Johanan son of Kareah and all the army leaders who were with him
12 heard about all the crimes committed by Ishmael son of Nethaniah, •mustering all their men, they set out to attack Ishmael son of Nethaniah. They caught up
13 with him at the great Pool of Gibeon. •At the sight of Johanan son of Kareah and all the army leaders with him, all the people with Ishmael were beside
14 themselves with joy. •All the people whom Ishmael had led away from Mizpah
15 turned about and rallied to Johanan son of Kareah. •Ishmael son of Nethaniah escaped from Johanan with eight of his men and fled to the Ammonites.
16 Johanan son of Kareah and all the army leaders with him then rallied the entire remnant of the people whom Ishmael son of Nethaniah had led away from Mizpah after the murder of Gedaliah son of Ahikam: men, women and children, and
17 eunuchs, whom Johanan brought back from Gibeon. •They set out, making a halt at Khan Kimham near Bethlehem. Their plan was to make for Egypt,
18 away from the Chaldaeans, of whom they were now terrified because Ishmael son of

Nethaniah had killed Gedaliah son of Ahikam whom the king of Babylon had
made governor of the country.

The flight to Egypt   (LXX 49:1-18; 50:1-3; 49:19-22; 50:4-7)

42 Then all the army leaders, with Johanan son of Kareah and Azariah 1
son of Hoshaiah, and all the people from least to greatest, approached
the prophet Jeremiah and said, 'May it please you to hear our request! Intercede 2
with Yahweh your God for all this remnant—and how few we are who once
were so many, your own eyes can now see—•so that Yahweh your God may show 3
us the way we are to go and what we must do.' •The prophet Jeremiah replied, 4
'I hear you; and I will indeed pray to Yahweh your God as you ask; and every
word Yahweh your God replies I will tell you, keeping nothing back from you'.
They in their turn said to Jeremiah, 'May Yahweh be a true and faithful 5
witness against us, if we do not follow the instructions that Yahweh your God
sends us through you. •Whether we like it or not, we mean to obey the voice of 6
Yahweh our God to whom we send you to speak for us, and by thus obeying the
voice of Yahweh our God we will prosper.'

Ten days later the word of Yahweh was addressed to Jeremiah. •He then ⁷₈
summoned Johanan son of Kareah and all the army leaders who were with
him, and all the people from least to greatest. •He said, 'Yahweh, the God of 9
Israel, to whom you delegated me to offer your request says this: •"If you are 10
willing to remain peaceably in this country, I will build you and not overthrow
you; I will plant you, not tear you up. For I am sorry for the evil I have done
you. •Do not be afraid of the king of Babylon any longer; do not fear him—it 11
is Yahweh who speaks—for I am with you to save you and deliver you from his
hands. •I will take pity on you, and move him to pity you and let you return to 12
your native soil. •But if you say: We do not want to stay in this country; if you 13
disobey the voice of Yahweh your God, •and say: No, the land of Egypt is 14
where we want to go, where we shall not see war nor hear the sound of trumpet,
nor lack for bread; that is where we want to live; •in that case, remnant of Judah, 15
listen to the word of Yahweh. Yahweh Sabaoth, the God of Israel, says this: If
you are determined to go to Egypt, and if you do go and settle there, the sword 16
you fear will overtake you, there in the land of Egypt; the famine you dread
will follow on your heels, right into Egypt; you shall die there. •All the men who 17
are determined to go to Egypt and settle there shall die by sword, famine and
plague: not one survivor will escape the disaster I mean to bring them. •Yes, 18
Yahweh Sabaoth, the God of Israel, says this: Just as my anger and my fury have
been poured out on the citizens of Jerusalem, so will my fury be poured out on
you if you go to Egypt: you will become an object of execration and horror,
a curse, a laughing-stock; and you will never see this place again." '

43 However, when Jeremiah had finished telling all the people all the words 1
of Yahweh their God, with which Yahweh had entrusted him for them
—all the words quoted above—•Azariah son of Hoshaiah, and Johanan son of 2
Kareah, and all those arrogant and apostate men, said to Jeremiah, 'You are
lying. Yahweh did not instruct you to say, "Do not go to Egypt and settle
there". •It is Baruch son of Neriah who keeps encouraging you to thwart us, 3
to hand us over into the power of the Chaldaeans, who will either put us to
death or deport us to Babylon!'

42 'Remnant of Judah!' Jeremiah answered 'Yahweh himself tells you, "Do not 19
go into Egypt". Understand this clearly: today I have given you solemn warning.
You were playing with your own lives when you made me your envoy to 20
Yahweh your God and said, "Intercede for us with Yahweh our God; tell us
what Yahweh our God orders and we will do it". •And now that I have told 21
you, you have not obeyed the voice of Yahweh your God today, or any part of
the message he gave me for you. •So understand this clearly: you are going to 22
die by sword, famine and plague in the place where you have been wanting to go
and settle.'

4 **43** Despite this, Johanan son of Kareah and all the army leaders and all the people would not obey the voice of Yahweh and stay in the
5 land of Judah. •Johanan son of Kareah and all the army leaders led off the entire remnant of Judah, those who had come back from all the nations into which
6 they had been dispersed, to live in the land of Judah: •men, women, children, the royal princesses too, and every single person entrusted to Gedaliah son of Ahikam, son of Shaphan, by Nebuzaradan, commander of the guard; they also
7 led off the prophet Jeremiah and Baruch son of Neriah. •And so, disregarding the voice of Yahweh, they reached the land of Egypt and arrived at Tahpanhes.

Jeremiah foretells the invasion of Egypt by Nebuchadnezzar (LXX 50:8-13)

8
9 At Tahpanhes the word of Yahweh was addressed to Jeremiah, •'Take some large stones and bury them in the presence of the men of Judah in the cement on the square outside the entrance of Pharaoh's palace in Tahpanhes.
10 Then say to them, "Yahweh, the God of Israel, says this: I am sending for Nebuchadnezzar, king of Babylon, my servant; he will place his throne over
11 these stones that I have buried, and spread his canopy above them. •He is coming to strike the land of Egypt:

> Those for the plague, to the plague;
> those for captivity, into captivity;
> those for the sword, to the sword!

12 He will set fire to the temples of the gods of Egypt; he will burn these gods or carry them off; as a shepherd picks his cloak clean of vermin, so will he pick
13 Egypt clean and leave without interference.[a] •He will break the obelisks of the temple of the Sun at On[b] and burn down the temples of the gods of Egypt." '

The last episode of Jeremiah's ministry: the Jews and the Queen of Heaven (LXX 51:1-30)

1 **44** The word that was addressed to Jeremiah for all the Jews living in the land of Egypt with homes in Migdol, Tahpanhes, Noph and the land of Pathros.[a]
2 'Yahweh Sabaoth, the God of Israel, says this: You have seen all the misery I have brought down on Jerusalem and the towns of Judah; today they
3 lie in ruins and uninhabited. •This was because of the wicked deeds which they committed to provoke me, offering incense and serving alien gods which neither
4 they, nor you, nor your ancestors ever knew. •I persistently sent you all my servants the prophets; I sent them to say, "Do not commit this abomination
5 that I find so hateful". •But they would not listen, would not pay attention and so turn from their wicked deeds and no longer offer incense to alien gods.
6 And so my fury and my anger overflowed, burning down the towns of Judah and the streets of Jerusalem, which were reduced to ruins and wasteland, as
7 they still are today. •And now, Yahweh, the God of Sabaoth, the God of Israel, says this: Why bring the same disaster on yourselves? Do you want to destroy all the men, women, children and babes in arms, out of Judah, and
8 leave yourselves no remnant, •by provoking me with the work of your own hands, offering incense to alien gods in the land of Egypt where you have come to settle, thus working for your own destruction, to become a curse and a
9 laughing-stock for all the nations of the earth? •Have you forgotten the crimes of your ancestors, of the kings of Judah and of their wives, your own crimes, the crimes of your own wives, committed in the land of Judah and
10 in the streets of Jerusalem? •To this day they have felt neither contrition nor

---

43 a. This successful expedition took place in 568-567.   **b.** Heliopolis.
44 a. Migdol, Tahpanhes, Noph (Memphis) are in Lower Egypt; 'the land of Pathros' is Upper Egypt.

fear; they have not observed my Law nor the statutes I proclaimed before you, as before your ancestors. •Therefore—Yahweh Sabaoth, the God of Israel, says 11 this: Now I mean to turn my face against you to bring disaster, and exterminate the whole of Judah. •The remnant of Judah who resolved to come to the land 12 of Egypt and to settle there, I will remove! they will all perish in the land of Egypt; they will fall to the sword or perish of famine, from least to greatest; by sword and famine they will die; they will be an object of execration and horror, a curse, a laughing-stock. •I will deal as severely with these who have made 13 their home in the land of Egypt, as I dealt with Jerusalem, with sword, famine and plague. •Of the remnant of Judah settled in the land of Egypt, not one 14 survivor is going to escape to return to the land of Judah where they long to live once again. For none of them are going to return, except for a few refugees.'

At this, all the men who knew that their wives offered incense to alien gods, 15 and all the women who were standing there, a large assembly (with all the people living in Pathros in the land of Egypt), answered Jeremiah as follows, 'We have no intention of listening to this word you have spoken to us in Yahweh's 16 name, •but intend to go on doing all we have vowed to do: offering incense 17 to the Queen of Heaven and pouring libations in her honour, as we used to do, we and our fathers, our kings and our leaders, in the towns of Judah and in the streets of Jerusalem: we had food in plenty then, we lived well, we suffered no disasters. •But since we gave up offering incense to the Queen of Heaven and 18 pouring libations in her honour, we have been destitute and have perished either by sword or by famine.' •The women added, 'When we offer incense 19 to the Queen of Heaven and pour libations in her honour, do you think we make cakes for her with her features on them, and pour libations to her, without our husbands' knowledge?'

To all the people, men and women; all those who had made this answer, 20 Jeremiah retorted, •'The incense you offered in the towns of Judah and in the 21 streets of Jerusalem, you, your fathers, your kings, your leaders, and the people of the country—is not this what Yahweh remembered, what came to his mind? Yahweh could no longer endure your misdeeds and your detestable practices; 22 this is why your country has today become a desert, an object of horror and a curse, uninhabited. •And this has happened because you offered incense, 23 because you sinned against Yahweh, refusing to listen to the voice of Yahweh, or to observe his Law, his statutes and his decrees; this is the cause of the disaster that has overtaken you—as is the case today.'

Then Jeremiah spoke to all the people, and particularly to all the women, 24 'Listen to the word of Yahweh: •Yahweh Sabaoth, the God of Israel, says 25 this, "You women, what your mouth promises, your hands should certainly perform! You have said: We will perform the vows we have made without fail and offer incense to the Queen of Heaven and pour libations in her honour. Very well, keep your vows, make your libations! •But listen to the word of Yahweh, 26 all you Judaeans living in the land of Egypt: I swear by my great name, Yahweh says, that my name shall be spoken no more by any man of Judah throughout the land of Egypt; not one shall say: As the Lord Yahweh lives.[b] Yes, I will watch over them for their ruin, not for their good; all the men of 27 Judah in the land of Egypt shall perish either by the sword or by famine until they are wiped out. •Yet, though few in number, those who escape the sword 28 will return to the land of Judah from the land of Egypt. Then the entire remnant of Judah who have come to settle in the land of Egypt will know whose word came true, mine or theirs.

"And here is the proof for you—it is Yahweh who speaks—that I mean to 29 deal with you in this place: so that you may know that the words with which I threaten you will come true: •Yahweh says this: I will hand the pharaoh 30 Hophra,[c] king of Egypt, over to his enemies and to those determined to kill him, just as I handed Zedekiah king of Judah over to Nebuchadnezzar king of Babylon, his enemy who was bent on killing him." '

An oracle of comfort for Baruch   (LXX 51:31-35)

1 **45** The word that the prophet Jeremiah addressed to Baruch son of Neriah
when the latter wrote these words down in a book at the dictation of
2 Jeremiah in the fourth year of Jehoiakim*ᵃ* son of Josiah, king of Judah. •This
3 is what Yahweh, the God of Israel, says about you, Baruch! •Since you have
said, "I despair, for Yahweh has added sorrow to my ordeals! I am worn out
4 with groaning, and find no relief!" •Yahweh says this, "Now I am knocking
down what I have built, tearing up what I have planted: I am going to strike
5 the whole earth. •And here you are asking for special treatment? Do not ask,
for I am now going to bring down disaster on all mankind—it is Yahweh
who speaks. As for you, I will let you escape with your own life, wherever
you may go." '

II(continued). ORACLES AGAINST THE NATIONS

B. THE ORACLES IN DETAIL

1 **46** The words of Yahweh which were addressed to the prophet Jeremiah
against the nations.

Oracles against Egypt. The defeat at Carchemish   (LXX 26,2-12)

2   On Egypt.
Against the army of Pharaoh Neco, king of Egypt, which took up position
near the river Euphrates by Carchemish,*ᵃ* when it was defeated by Nebuchadnezzar king of Babylon in the fourth year of Jehoiakim son of Josiah, king
of Judah.

3   Have buckler ready, and shield:
                 onward to battle!
4   Harness the horses:
                 into the saddle, horsemen!
                 To your ranks! On with your helmets!
                 Sharpen your spears,
                 put on your breastplates!...
5   What do I see?
                 They are panic-stricken,
                 in full retreat!
                 Their heroes, beaten back,
                 are fleeing headlong
                 with not a look behind.
                 Terror from every side!
                 —it is Yahweh who speaks.
6   The fastest cannot escape,
                 nor the bravest save himself:
                 there in the north, there by the river Euphrates,
                 they have collapsed, have fallen.

7   Who was it rose like the Nile,
                 its waters foaming like a torrent?
8   Why, Egypt rose like the Nile,
                 its waters foaming like a torrent.
                 'I will rise,' he said 'and drown the earth;

b. The worshippers of Ishtar, queen of heaven, also made a show of invoking Yahweh.
c. Hophra succeeded Neco in 588; he was dethroned and executed in 569.
45 a. 605 B.C.
46 a. 605 B.C.

sweep towns and their inhabitants away!
Charge, horses!   9
Crash on, chariots!
Advance, warriors,
you men from Cush and Put with shield in hand,
you men from Lud who bend the bow!'*b*

Now, this is the day of the Lord Yahweh,   10
a day of vengeance for his revenge on his enemies:
his sword will eat them up and have its fill,
will grow drunk with their blood.
Yes, the Lord Yahweh Sabaoth has a sacrifice to make
in the north country, by the river Euphrates.

Go up to Gilead in search of balm,   11
virgin daughter of Egypt!
You multiply remedies in vain,
nothing can cure you.
The nations have heard of your shame,   12
the dirge raised for you fills the earth:
for warrior has stumbled against warrior,
and both have fallen.

The invasion of Egypt   (LXX 26:13-28)

The word that Yahweh addressed to the prophet Jeremiah when Nebuchad- 13
nezzar king of Babylon set out to attack the land of Egypt.

Publish it in Migdol,   14
proclaim it in Noph.
Say, 'To your posts! At the ready!'
for the sword is devouring round you.
What! Has Apis*c* fled?   15
Has your Strong One not stood firm?
Yes, Yahweh has knocked him •flat!   16
He tottered, and now he has fallen down!
Then they said to each other,
'Up! Let us go back to our own people,
to the country where we were born,
far from the destroying sword!'
Give this name to Pharaoh: 17
'Much-noise-but-he-lets-the-chance-slip-by'!
As I live—it is the King who speaks   18
whose name is Yahweh Sabaoth—
someone will come, a Tabor among mountains,
a Carmel high above the sea.

Get your bundle ready for exile,   19
daughter of Egypt, so safe in your home!
Noph will be reduced to a desert,
desolate, uninhabited.
Egypt was a splendid heifer,   20
but a gad-fly from the North has settled on her.
The mercenaries she had with her, these too   21
were as sleek as fattened calves:
but they too have taken to their heels,
they all run at once and cannot hold their ground.
For on them comes the day of their disaster,
their time of reckoning.

22   Listen: a sound like a serpent hissing!
         Yes, they are coming in force
         to fall on her with their axes,
         like woodcutters,

23   they will fell her forest—it is Yahweh who speaks.
         Yes, they are past counting,
         outnumbering the locusts,
         innumerable.

24   The daughter of Egypt is put to shame,
         handed over to a people from the North.

25   Yahweh Sabaoth, the God of Israel, has said: Now I mean to punish Amon
26 of No,[d] with Pharaoh and those who put their trust in him. •I will hand him
over to those who are determined to kill him, over to Nebuchadnezzar
king of Babylon, over to his servants. But in later days, Egypt will be
inhabited again as in the past—it is Yahweh who speaks.

27   But do not be afraid, my servant Jacob,
         Israel, do not be alarmed:
         look, I will rescue you from distant countries
         and your descendants from the country where they are captive.
         Jacob will have quiet again
         and live at ease, with no one to trouble him.

28   Do not be afraid, my servant Jacob
         —it is Yahweh who speaks—for I am with you:
         I will make an end of all the nations
         where I have scattered you;
         I will not make an end of you,
         only discipline you in moderation,
         so as not to let you go entirely unpunished.

Oracle against the Philistines

(LXX 29:1-7)

1 **47** The word of Yahweh that was addressed to Jeremiah against the
2 Philistines before Pharaoh took Gaza by storm. •Yahweh says this:

         See how the waters rise from the North,
         and become an overflowing torrent,
         overflowing the country and all it contains,
         the towns and their inhabitants!
         Men shout aloud, and there is wailing
         from all the inhabitants of the country,

3   at the thunder of his stallions' hoofs,
         the crash of his chariots, the grinding of his wheels.
         Fathers forget about their children,
         their hands fall limp

4   because the day has come
         on which all the Philistines are to be destroyed,
         on which Tyre and Sidon are to be stripped
         to the last of their auxiliaries.
         Yes, Yahweh is destroying the Philistines,
         the remnant from the Isle of Caphtor.

5   A shaven scalp for Gaza!
         Silence over Ashkelon!
         Ashdod, all that is left of the Anakim,

b. Cush is Ethiopia; Put is Somaliland and the 'men from Lud' are a neighbouring African people.
c. The sacred bull of Ptah, god of Memphis.   d. Thebes, the god of which was Amon.

> how long will you gash yourselves?[a]
> Oh, sword of Yahweh,   6
> how long before you rest?
> Back into your scabbard,
> stop, keep still!
> Yet how can it rest   7
> when Yahweh has given it an order?
> Ashkelon and the sea coast,
> these are the targets assigned to it.

Oracles against Moab (LXX 31)

48 On Moab. Yahweh, the God of Israel, says this: 1

> Woe to Nebo, for it has been ravaged,
> Kiriathaim has been taken,
> all is confusion and alarm in the fortress:
> it is no longer the boast of Moab!   2
> At Heshbon[a] they plotted her downfall,
> 'Come on! Let us blot her out from the nations!'
> And you too, Madmen, you will be subdued,
> the sword is close on you.

> Hark! From the Abarim a shout,   3
> 'Devastation! Dire calamity!'
> 'Moab is shattered'   4
> the cry echoes as far as Zoar.
> Ah, slopes of Luhith,   5
> they go up them weeping.
> At the descent of Horonaim
> cries of distress are heard,
> 'Away! Flee for your lives!   6
> Run like the wild asses in the desert!'
> Yes, since you trusted in your strongholds   7
> you will be captured too.
> Chemosh[b] will go into exile,
> with all his priests and his nobles.
> The destroyer will descend on every town,   8
> not one will escape;
> the Valley will be despoiled, the Plain be plundered:
> Yahweh proclaims it!
> Give Moab a tomb,   9
> since she is totally destroyed;
> her towns are in ruins,
> with no one to live in them.

(Cursed be he who does the work of Yahweh half-heartedly! Cursed be he 10
who grudges blood to his sword!)

> From his youth Moab lived at ease,   11
> he settled on his lees,
> never having been decanted,
> never having gone into exile:
> and so he kept his own flavour,
> his aroma was unchanged.[c]

And so the days are coming—it is Yahweh who speaks—when I shall send 12
him decanters to decant him; they will empty his storage jars and break his
amphorae to bits. •Moab will blush for Chemosh then, as the House of Israel 13
blushed for Bethel[d] in whom they put their trust.

14   How can you say, 'We are heroes,
         sturdy fighting men'?

15   The destroyer of Moab has advanced on him:
         the flower of his youth goes down to the slaughter.

16   Moab's ruin is coming soon,
         his downfall comes at top speed.

17   Grieve for him, all you living near him,
         all you who knew his name.
         Say, 'Imagine it being broken, that mighty rod,
         that splendid sceptre!'

18   Come down from your glory, sit in the dung,
         daughter of Dibon, so safe in your home:
         the destroyer of Moab has advanced on you,
         he has stormed your strongholds.

19   Stand by the roadside, keep watch,
         inhabitants of Aroer.
         Question fugitive and runaway,
         ask, 'What has happened?'

20   Moab is shattered and shamed.
         Wail and shriek!
         Shout across the Arnon,
         'Moab has been laid waste!'

21 Judgement has also come on the land of the Plain, on Holon, Jahzah, Mephaath,
22,23,24 Dibon, Nebo, Beth-diblathaim, •Kiriathaim, Beth-gamul, Beth-meon, •Kerioth, Bozrah, and all the towns in the land of Moab, far and near.

25   The horn of Moab has been cut off,
         and his arm broken.

26 Make him drunk! He has set himself up against Yahweh: Moab will wallow
27 in his vomit, become a laughing-stock in his turn. •Was not Israel a laughing-stock to you? Was he caught red-handed with the thieves, for you to shake your head whenever you mention him?

28   Leave the towns, make the rocks your home,
         inhabitants of Moab.
         Learn from the dove that makes its nest
         in the walls of the gaping gorge.

29   We have heard of the pride of Moab,
         excessive pride!
         What arrogance! What pride! What conceit!
         What a haughty heart!

30   —I know all about his presumption—it is Yahweh who speaks—
         his empty boasting,
         those empty deeds of his!

31   —And so I lament for Moab,
         for all Moab I cry aloud,
         and mourn for the men of Kir-heres.ᵉ

32   More than for Jazer I weep for you,
         vine of Sibmah:
         your shoots stretched beyond the sea.

47 a. Self-inflicted wounds, like the shaven head, were a sign of mourning.
48 a. There are Hebr. puns on the similar sounds of 'Heshbob' and 'plotted'; and 'Madmen' and 'subdued'.   b. God of Moabites.   c. Moab was famous for wine.   d. The sanctuary of the Northern Kingdom, a rival to Jerusalem.   e. The capital of Moab, now Kerak.

they reached all the way to Jazer.
On your harvest, on your vintage,
the destroyer has descended.
Gladness and joy have vanished   33
from the land of Moab.
There is no longer wine in the presses,
the treader of grapes treads no more,
no more do shouts of joy ring out.

The howling of Heshbon and Elealeh can be heard as far as Jahaz. The 34
shrieks resound from Zoar to Horonaim and Eglath-shelishiyah, for the waters
of Nimrim too are now becoming desolation.
And I shall make an end—it is Yahweh who speaks—of any man in 35
Moab who offers sacrifice and incense to his god on the high places.
That is why my heart sobs like a flute for Moab, sobs like a flute for the 36
men of Kir-heres: that accumulated treasure all lost! •Yes, every head is shorn, 37
every beard cut off, gashes are on the hands of all, sackcloth round all their
loins. •On all the housetops of Moab and in its squares there is nothing but 38
lamenting, for I have broken Moab like a crock that no one wants—it is
Yahweh who speaks. •What! Broken? What! Moab so shamefully in retreat? 39
What! Moab become a laughing-stock, a thing of horror to all its neighbours?

For Yahweh says this: 40
(Here is one who hovers like an eagle,
who will spread his wings over Moab.)
The towns will be captured,   41
the strongholds seized.

(And the heart of Moab's warriors that day will be like the heart of a woman
in labour pains.)

Moab will be destroyed, no longer a people,   42
for setting itself up against Yahweh.
Terror, the pit, the snare,   43
are for you, inhabitant of Moab—
it is Yahweh who speaks:
the man who takes flight from the terror   44
shall fall into the pit,
climbing out of the pit,
he shall be caught in the snare.
Yes, these are the scourges I mean to inflict on Moab
when the year comes to punish them—
it is Yahweh who speaks.
In the shelter of Heshbon the fugitives   45
have paused, exhausted.
But a fire has come out from Heshbon,
a flame from the palace of Sihon,
consuming the brows of Moab,
the head of a turbulent brood.
Woe to you, Moab!   46
People of Chemosh, you are lost!
For your sons have been taken into exile,
and your daughters into captivity.
But I will restore the fortunes of Moab   47
in the days to come. It is Yahweh who speaks.

Thus far the judgement on Moab.

Oracle against Ammon

49 On the sons of Ammon.

> Yahweh says this:
> Has Israel no sons?
> Has he no heir?
> Why should Milcom have inherited Gad
> and his people have settled in its towns?

2
> And so the days are coming
> —it is Yahweh who speaks—
> when I will make the war cry ring out
> for Rabbath-of-the-Ammonites:
> she will become a deserted ruin,
> her daughter towns burnt down.
> Israel will then despoil his despoilers,
> Yahweh proclaims.

3
> Heshbon lament! The destroyer is on the march.
> Cry aloud, daughters of Rabbah!
> Wrap yourself in sackcloth, raise the dirge,
> walk about with your bodies gashed.
> For Milcom is going into exile,
> with all his priests and his nobles.

4
> So you boast of your valley,
> thoughtless girl!
> Confident of your resources, you say,
> 'Who will dare to attack me?'

5
> But I will bring down on you
> terror from every side;
> you shall be driven away, each man making his own way,
> with no one to rally the fugitives.

6 (But later I will restore the fortunes of the sons of Ammon. It is Yahweh who speaks.)

Oracle against Edom

7 On Edom.

> Yahweh says this:
> Is there no wisdom left in Teman?
> Have the shrewd run out of commonsense,
> has their wisdom gone stale?

8
> Away! Take to your heels! Go into hiding,
> inhabitants of Dedan!
> For I will bring down ruin on Esau,
> at the time when I must punish him.

9
> If grape-gatherers come to you,
> they will leave no gleanings behind them;
> if robbers come at night,
> they will loot to their heart's content.

10
> For I myself am despoiling Esau,
> I lay his hiding places bare
> until he has no cover left.
> His race is destroyed: it is no more!
> Of his neighbours, not one will say,

11
> 'Leave your orphans, I will keep them alive,
> your widows can rely on me'.

For Yahweh says this: Those who were not bound to drink the cup have to 12
drink it now; so why should you go unpunished? You will not go unpunished:
you too must drink! •For by my own self I have sworn it—it is Yahweh who 13
speaks: Bozrah[a] is to become an object of horror, a laughing-stock, a desert,
a curse, and all its towns ruins for ever.

> I have received a message from Yahweh,   14
> a herald has been sent throughout the nations,
> 'Muster! March against this people!
> Prepare for battle!'
> For now I will reduce you among the nations,   15
> make you despised among mankind:
> your reputation for ferocity,   16
> your pride of heart, have led you astray,
> you whose home is in the holes in the rocks,
> who cling to the topmost peaks!
> Though you made your nest high as the eagle,
> I would still fling you down again—it is Yahweh who speaks.

Edom will become a desolation; every passer-by will be appalled at it, and 17
whistle in amazement at such calamity. •As at the overthrow of Sodom and 18
Gomorrah and their neighbouring towns, no one will live there any more,
Yahweh proclaims, no man will make his home there ever again.

> See how the lion climbs from the thickets of the Jordan   19
> to a perennial pasture!
> So shall I chase them suddenly away,
> and place there whom I please.
> For who is there like me?
> Who can hale me into court?
> Name me the shepherd
> who can stand up to me.
> So now hear the plan   20
> that Yahweh has made for Edom,
> the schemes he has in mind
> for the inhabitants of Teman:
> yes, even the weakest of the flock will be dragged away.
> At such a sight their pastures will shudder with dread.
> Earth trembles at the crash of their downfall,   21
> the sound of it echoes as far as the Sea of Reeds.
> Here is someone who soars and hovers like an eagle,   22
> who will spread his wings over Bozrah.
> And the heart of Edom's warriors that day
> will be like the heart of a woman in labour pains.

Oracle against the towns of Syria   (LXX 30:29-33)

On Damascus: 23

> Hamath is in confusion, so is Arpad;[b]
> they have heard bad news.
> Their heart is faint with fear
> and cannot be calmed.
> Damascus is unmanned, she prepares for flight,   24
> she is seized with trembling

(anguish and sorrow have laid hold on her as on a woman in labour).

> What now! That famous town deserted,   25
> that city of gaiety?

26   And so in her squares her young men will fall, and all her fighting men will
perish, that day. It is Yahweh Sabaoth who speaks.

27   I will light a fire inside the walls of Damascus,
          it shall devour the palaces of Ben-hadad.

Oracle against the Arab tribes   (LXX 30:23-28)

28   On Kedar and the kingdoms of Hazor, which were conquered by Nebuchadnezzar king of Babylon. Yahweh says this:

          Up! March on Kedar,
          destroy the sons of the East!
29   Let their tents and their flocks be captured,
          their fabrics, all their gear,
          and their camels too.
          Let the shout be raised for them: 'Terror on every side!'
30   Away! Get into hiding as fast as you can,
          citizens of Hazor! It is Yahweh who speaks.
          For Nebuchadnezzar has made a plan for you,
          he has a scheme in mind for you:
31   'Up! March on a nation at its ease,
          that dwells in confidence,
          that has no gates, no bars,
          that lives in a remote place!
32   Their camels will be the plunder,
          their countless sheep the spoil.'
          I will scatter them to the winds,
          those Crop-Heads,
          and bring disaster down on them from every side,
          it is Yahweh who speaks.
33   Hazor will become a lair for jackals,
          a desert for ever.
          No one will live there any more,
          no man make his home there ever again.

Oracle against Elam   (LXX 25:14-20)

34   The word of Yahweh that was addressed to the prophet Jeremiah about
35 Elam, at the beginning of the reign of Zedekiah king of Judah. •Yahweh
Sabaoth says this:

          I am going to break the bow of Elam,
          the source of all his might.
36   I will bring four winds down on Elam
          from the four corners of the sky,

and I will scatter the Elamites to the winds: there will not be a single nation
into which the Elamites have not been driven for refuge.

37   I will make the Elamites tremble before their enemies,
          before those determined to kill them.
          I will bring down disaster on them,
          my own fierce anger.
          I will pursue them with the sword
          until I have destroyed them all.
38   I will set up my throne in Elam,
          and purge it of king and nobles.
          It is Yahweh who speaks.

49 a. The principal Edomite stronghold, N. of Petra.   **b.** Hamath is on the river Orontes,
Arpad to the N. of Aleppo.

R.E.—T

But in the days to come I will restore the fortunes of Elam. It is Yahweh 39
who speaks.

Oracle against Babylon   (LXX 27:1)

50 The word that Yahweh spoke against Babylon, against the country of 1
the Chaldaeans, through the prophet Jeremiah.

The fall of Babylon and the liberation of Israel   (LXX 27:2-20)

Publish it among the nations, proclaim it;   2
make no secret of it, say:
'Babylon is captured, Bel disgraced,
Merodach shattered.*
(Her idols are disgraced,
her Obscenities shattered.)'
For a nation is marching on her from the North,   3
to turn her country into a desert:
no one will live there any more;
man and beast have fled and gone.

In those days and at that time   4
the sons of Israel will return:
they will come weeping
in search of Yahweh their God.
They will ask the way to Zion,   5
their faces will turn in that direction:
'Come,' they say 'let us bind ourselves to Yahweh
by an everlasting covenant never to be forgotten!'

Lost sheep, such were my people;   6
their shepherds led them astray, left them wandering in the mountains;
from mountain to hill they went,
forgetful of their fold.
Whoever came across them devoured them,   7
their enemies said, 'No blame to us;
it is because they have sinned against Yahweh
their true fold and the hope of their fathers'.

Escape out of Babylon,   8
from the country of the Chaldaeans.
Go! Act like the he-goats,
be leaders of the flock.
See, I am raising a league   9
of mighty nations against Babylon.
They will come from the land of the North, will draw up the battle
        line against her:
there she will be captured;
their arrows are like a victorious warrior,
never returning empty-handed.
Chaldaea will be plundered,   10
all who plunder her will have their fill.

Rejoice, if you like! Have your triumph,   11
you plunderers of my heritage!
Be playful like calves let out to grass!
Neigh like stallions!
But your mother is covered with shame,   12
disgraced is the woman who bore you;
she is the least of nations now;

a wilderness, a parched land, a desert.

13   The fury of Yahweh will leave her uninhabited,
     she will become an empty solitude.
     All who pass by Babylon will be appalled at it,
     and whistle in amazement at such calamity.

14   Draw yourself up against Babylon, surround her,
     all you who bend the bow.
     Shoot! Do not spare your arrows.

15   Raise the war cry against her from all sides.
     She surrenders! Her bastions fall!
     Her walls collapse!
     This is the vengeance of Yahweh. Take revenge on her.
     Treat her as she has treated others.

16   Deprive Babylon of the man who sows,
     of the man who wields the sickle at harvest.
     Escape from the destroying sword,
     let everyone return to his own people,
     let everyone escape to his own country!

17   Israel was a straying sheep
     hunted by lions.

18   First, the king of Assyria devoured him; next, Nebuchadnezzar king of Babylon
     crunched his bones. •Therefore—Yahweh, the God of Israel, says this: Now
     I will punish the king of Babylon and his country as I punished the king of
     Assyria.

19   I will bring Israel back to his pastures
     to browse on Carmel and in Bashan,
     and on the highlands of Ephraim and in Gilead
     to eat his fill.

20   In those days and at that time
     you may look for Israel's iniquity, it will not be there,
     for Judah's sins, you will not find them.
     For I will pardon the remnant that I leave.

The fall of Babylon proclaimed to Jerusalem   (LXX 27:21-28)

21   March up to the land of Merathaim;
     march against it
     and against the inhabitants of Pekod;
     follow them;
     brandish the sword, let their destruction be complete,
     it is Yahweh who speaks.
     Do everything I have ordered! [b]

22   The din of battle fills the country,
     immense destruction.

23   What! Broken to pieces
     that hammer of the whole world?
     What! Babylon become a thing of horror,
     throughout the nations?

24   A snare was set for you, and you were caught
     before you knew it.

---

50 a. Bel and Marduk (Merodach) are two names of the tutelary god of Babylon.   b. The
orders are addressed to the invaders of Babylon. Merathaim is the Tigris delta region; Pekod
a region E. of Babylon.

You have been found out and overpowered,
because you defied Yahweh.

Yahweh has opened his armoury   25
and taken out the weapons of his fury.
For the Lord Yahweh has work to do
in the country of the Chaldaeans.
Fall on her, one and all,   26
break her granaries open,
pile the plunder up like heaps of grain, put her under the ban
until nothing is left of her.

Slaughter all her bulls,   27
down to the slaughter-house with them!
Woe to them, their day has come,
their time of reckoning.
Listen! Fugitives and runaways come   28
from the land of Babylon
to proclaim in Zion
the vengeance of Yahweh our God.

The sin of arrogance   (LXX 27:29-32)

Call up the archers against Babylon!   29
All you who bend the bow,
encamp round her:
leave her no way of escape.
Repay her as her deeds deserve;
treat her as she has treated others,
to repay her arrogance against Yahweh,
against the Holy One of Israel.

And so in her squares her young men will fall, and all her fighting men will 30
perish, that day. It is Yahweh who speaks.

My quarrel is with you, 'Arrogance'!   31
It is the Lord Yahweh Sabaoth who speaks:
your day has come,
the time when I must punish you.
'Arrogance' will stumble, she will fall,   32
no one will lift her up:
I will light a fire inside her towns;
it shall devour all her surroundings.

Yahweh the redeemer of Israel   (LXX 27:33-40)

Yahweh Sabaoth says this: 33
The sons of Israel are oppressed,
all those who have taken them captive hold them fast,
they will not let them go.
But their redeemer is strong: 34
Yahweh Sabaoth is his name.
He has taken up their cause:
he will bring peacefulness to the world
but trembling to the inhabitants of Babylon.

A sword for the Chaldaeans,   35
for the inhabitants of Babylon,
for her leaders and her sages!
A sword for her diviners: may they lose their wits!   36
A sword for her men of war: may they be discomfited!

37 A sword for the whole crowd of foreigners
    within her: may they be like women!
    A sword for her treasures: may they be plundered!
38 A sword for her waters: may they dry up!
For it is a country of idols: they are mad, they and their bogies.

39 Hence wild cats and jackals will live there,
    and ostriches make their home there.
    She will never be inhabited again,
    but remain uninhabited age after age.
40 As when God overthrew Sodom and Gomorrah,
    with their neighbouring towns
    —it is Yahweh who speaks—
    no one will live there any more,
    no man will make his home there ever again.

The enemy from the north and the lion of Jordan (LXX 27:41-46)

41 Now a people is coming from the North,
    a mighty nation;
    from the far ends of the earth
    great kings are stirring:
42 they fight with bow and spear,
    they are cruel and pitiless;
    their noise is like the roaring of the sea;
    they ride horses,
    each man equipped for war
    on you, daughter of Babylon.
43 But the king of Babylon has heard the news of them,
    his hands fall limp,
    anguish has seized him,
    pain like that of a woman in labour.
44 See how the lion climbs from the thickets of the Jordan
    to a perennial pasture!
    So shall I chase them suddenly away,
    and place there whom I please.
    For who is there like me?
    Who can hale me into court?
    Name me the shepherd
    who can stand up to me.
45 So now hear the plan
    that Yahweh has made for Babylon,
    the schemes he has in mind
    for the country of the Chaldaeans:
    yes, even the weakest of the flock will be dragged away.
    At such a sight their pastures will shudder with dread.
46 Earth trembles at the sound of the capture of Babylon,
    the dirge for her is heard throughout the nations.

Yahweh makes war on Babylon (LXX 28:1-19)

1 **51** Yahweh says this:
    ᵃAgainst the citizens of Leb-kamai I will rouse
    a destroying spirit;
2 I will send winnowers to Babylon to winnow her and leave her
    country bare:

51 a. Cryptogram for 'Kashdim' (Chaldaeans).

for they will beleaguer her from every side
in the day of disaster.
Let no archer bend his bow!   3
Let no man swagger in his coat of mail!
—No quarter for her young warriors!
Vow her whole army to the ban!
In the country of the Chaldaeans the slaughtered will fall,   4
in the streets of Babylon, those whom the sword runs through.
This is because their country was full of sin   5b
against the Holy One of Israel.
But Israel is not bereft   5a
of his God, Yahweh Sabaoth.

Escape out of Babylon   6
(save your lives, each one of you);
do not perish yourselves in her punishment,
for this is the time of Yahweh's vengeance:
he is paying her her reward!
Babylon was a golden cup in Yahweh's hand,   7
she made the whole world drunk,
the nations drank her wine
and then went mad.
Babylon has suddenly fallen, is broken: 8
lament for her!
Go and fetch balm for her wounds,
perhaps she can be cured!
—'We tried to cure Babylon; she has got no better.   9
Leave her alone and let us each go to his own country.'
Yes, her sentence reaches to the sky,
rises to the very clouds.
Yahweh has vindicated our integrity.   10
Come, let us tell in Zion
what Yahweh our God has done.
Sharpen the arrows,   11
fill the quivers!

Yahweh has roused the spirit of the king of the Medes,[b] because he has a plan
against Babylon to destroy it; this is the vengeance of Yahweh, the revenge
for his Temple.

Against the walls of Babylon display the standard!   12
Strengthen the guard!
Post the sentries!
Take up concealed positions!

For Yahweh made a plan, and he has treated the citizens of Babylon as he
promised he would.

Enthroned beside abundant waters,   13
rich in treasures,
you now meet your end,
the finish of your pillaging.

By his own self Yahweh Sabaoth has sworn: had I filled you with men as plentiful 14
as locusts, the war cry would still have been raised against you!

By his power he made the earth,   15
by his wisdom set the world firm,

16   by his discernment spread out the heavens.
When he thunders
there is a tumult of water in the heavens;
he raises clouds from the boundaries of earth,
makes the lightning flash for the downpour,
and brings the wind from his storehouse.

17 At this all men stand stupefied, uncomprehending,
every goldsmith blushes for the idol he has made,
since his images are nothing but delusion,
with no breath in them.

18 They are a Nothing, a laughable production,
when the time comes for them to be punished, they will vanish.

19 'The portion of Jacob' is not like these,
for he has formed everything,
and Israel is the tribe that is his heritage.
His name is Yahweh Sabaoth.

The hammer of Yahweh and the giant mountain   (LXX 28:20-20)

20 You were my mace,
a weapon of war.
With you I crushed the nations,
struck kingdoms down,

21 with you crushed horse and rider,
chariot and charioteer,

22 with you crushed man and woman,
old man and young,
youth and maid,

23 with you crushed shepherd and flock,
ploughman and team,
governors and nobles,

24 but I will let you see how I make Babylon and all the inhabitants of Chaldaea
pay for all the wrongs they have done to Zion. It is Yahweh who speaks.

25 My quarrel is with you,
Mountain of destruction
—it is Yahweh who speaks—
destroyer of the whole world!
I will stretch out my hand against you
and send you tumbling from the crags
and make you a mountain scorched.

26 Never a cornerstone will be taken from you,
never a foundation-stone either,
for you will be a desert for ever,
it is Yahweh who speaks.

The end of Babylon is imminent   (LXX 28:27-33)

27 Display the standard throughout the world,
sound the trumpet among the nations!
Prepare nations to make war on her;
summon kingdoms against her:
Ararat, Minni, Ashkenaz;c
call the roll of her enemies, officer!
Bring up the cavalry, bristling like locusts.

b. This later prose gloss names the Medes, meaning Persians; the poem speaks only of an enemy from the North.   c. Kingdoms near Armenia.

Prepare nations to make war on her: the king of Media with his governors 28
and dignitaries and the whole territory under his rule.

Then the earth trembled and writhed,   29
for Yahweh's plan against Babylon was going forward:
to change the country of Babylon
into an unpopulated desert.

The warriors of Babylon have done with fighting,   30
they have taken to their strongholds;
their strength has gone:
they are like women now.
Her houses are on fire,
her gates are shattered.
Courier follows close on courier,   31
messenger on messenger,
to tell the king of Babylon
that his city has been stormed from every side:
the fords occupied,   32
the bastions burnt down,
the fighting men thrown into panic.
For Yahweh Sabaoth, the God of Israel, says this: 33
The daughter of Babylon is like a threshing-floor
when it is being trodden:
a little while, and there the grain will lie
that has been harvested.

The vengeance of Yahweh   (LXX 28:34-40)

'He has devoured, consumed me, that king of Babylon;   34
he has left me like an empty dish,
like a dragon he has swallowed me whole,
he has filled his belly with my delicacies.'
'May her violence to me, and all my sufferings,   35
        be avenged on Babylon!'
say the people of Zion;
'On the inhabitants of Chaldaea be my blood!'
says Jerusalem.

Therefore—Yahweh says this: 36
See, I myself am taking up your cause
to make sure you are avenged.
I will dry her river up.
make her springs run dry,
and turn Babylon into a heap of stones,   37
a lair for jackals,
a thing of horror and of scorn,
with no one living in it.
Like lions they roar together,   38
they growl like lions' whelps.
Are they feverish? I will prepare them a drink   39
and make them drink until they grow drowsy
and fall into an everlasting sleep,
never to wake up;
it is Yahweh who speaks.
I will take them down to the slaughter-house like lambs,   40
like rams and he-goats.

An elegy for Babylon   (LXX 28:41-43)

41   What! Is she captured and conquered,
            the admiration of all the world?
            What! Babylon become a thing of horror,
            throughout the nations?

42   The sea has risen over Babylon,
            she sinks under its boisterous waves.

43   Her towns have been turned into desert,
            a parched land, a wilderness:
            no one lives in them,
            no man goes that way.

Yahweh punishes the idols   (LXX 28:44-57)

44   I will punish Bel in Babylon
            and take from his mouth what he has swallowed.
            In future the nations
            will stream to him no more.
            The wall of Babylon has fallen.

45   Go out of her, my people;
            save your lives, each one of you,
            from the fierce anger of Yahweh.

46 But do not be faint-hearted! Do not take fright at rumours hawked round the
country: one rumour spreads one year, next year another follows; violence rules
on earth and one tyrant cancels out another.

47   See, the days are coming
            when I am going to punish the idols of Babylon.
            Her whole country shall be put to shame,
            with all her slaughtered lying in her midst.

48   Then heaven and earth and all within them
            shall shout for joy over Babylon,
            because the destroyers from the North
            are coming against her—it is Yahweh who speaks.

49   Babylon in her turn must fall
            because of those who were slaughtered in Israel,
            just as through Babylon there fell
            men slaughtered over all the world.

50   You who have escaped her sword,
            get away, do not wait there!
            Remember Yahweh in that distant country,
            let Jerusalem be in your mind.

51   —'We were ashamed when we heard of the outrage,
            our face was covered with confusion:
            because foreigners had entered
            the holy places of the Temple of Yahweh.'

52   —See, the days are coming,
            it is Yahweh who speaks,
            when I will punish her idols,
            and the stricken shall groan throughout her country.

53   Were Babylon to scale the heavens,
            or reinforce her towering citadel,
            destroyers would still fall on her at my command,
            it is Yahweh who speaks.

54   Listen to the shouting from Babylon,
            the mighty crash from the country of the Chaldaeans!

That is Yahweh as he lays Babylon waste   55
and silences her monstrous din;
well may her waves roar like mighty waters
and their tumultuous voice resound:
for a destroyer is sweeping down on Babylon,   56
her warriors are taken captive, their bows are broken.
Yes, Yahweh is a God of retribution,
he pays in full.
I will make her nobles and her sages drink,   57
her governors, her officials and her warriors;
they shall fall into an everlasting sleep
and not wake up;
it is the King who speaks,
whose name is Yahweh Sabaoth.

Babylon razed to the ground   (LXX 28,58)

Yahweh Sabaoth says this: 58
The wide ramparts of Babylon
will be razed to the ground,
and her high gates
will be burnt down.
Thus the labouring of the peoples comes to nothing
the toiling of the nations ends in fire.

The written oracle thrown into the Euphrates   (LXX 28:59-64)

This is the order that the prophet Jeremiah gave to Seraiah son of Mahseiah 59
when the latter left for Babylon at the command of Zedekiah king of Judah,
in the fourth year of his reign. •Now Jeremiah had written down the entire 60
disaster that was to befall Babylon in a special book, all these words recorded
here as regards Babylon. •Jeremiah then said to Seraiah, 'When you reach 61
Babylon, make a point of reading out every one of these words. •Then say, 62
"Yahweh, you yourself have proclaimed that this place will be destroyed, that
no one will live here ever again, neither man nor beast, but that it will remain
desolate for ever". •When you have finished reading this book, tie a stone to it 63
and throw it into the middle of the Euphrates, •with the words, "So shall 64
Babylon sink, never to rise again from the disaster with which I am going to
overwhelm her".'
Here end the words of Jeremiah.

V. APPENDIX[a]

The destruction of Jerusalem and the pardon of Jehoiachin

52 Zedekiah was twenty-one years old when he came to the throne, and he 1
reigned for eleven years in Jerusalem. His mother's name was Hamital,
daughter of Jeremiah, from Libnah. •He did what is displeasing to Yahweh, 2
just as Jehoiakim had done. •That this happened in Jerusalem and Judah was 3
due to the anger of Yahweh, with the result that in the end he cast them
away from him.
Zedekiah rebelled against the king of Babylon. •In the ninth year of his 4
reign, in the tenth month,[b] on the tenth day of the month, Nebuchadnezzar
king of Babylon came with his whole army to attack Jerusalem; he pitched
camp in front of the city and threw up earthworks round it. •The city lay under 5
siege till the eleventh year of King Zedekiah. •In the fourth month, on the ninth 6

day of the month, when famine was raging in the city and there was no food
7 for the populace, •a breach was made in the city wall. Seeing this, the king
fled under cover of dark, with all the fighting men, leaving the city by way of
the gate between the two walls, which is near the king's garden—the Chaldaeans
8 had surrounded the city—and making his way towards the Arabah. •The
Chaldaean troops pursued the king and caught up with Zedekiah in the plains
9 of Jericho, where all his troops deserted. •The Chaldaeans captured the king
and took him to the king of Babylon at Riblah in the land of Hamath, who
10 passed sentence on him. •He had the sons of Zedekiah slaughtered before his
11 eyes; he also had all the leading men of Judah put to death at Riblah. •He then
put out Zedekiah's eyes. Loading him with chains, the king of Babylon
carried him off to Babylon where he kept him prisoner until his dying day.

12   In the fifth month, on the tenth day of the month—it was in the nineteenth
year of Nebuchadnezzar king of Babylon—Nebuzaradan, commander of the
13 guard, one of the king's ministers, entered Jerusalem. •He burnt down the
14 Temple of Yahweh, the royal palace and all the houses in Jerusalem. •The
Chaldaean troops who accompanied the commander of the guard demolished
all the walls surrounding Jerusalem.

15   Nebuzaradan, commander of the guard, deported the remainder of the
population left behind in the city, the deserters who had gone over to the king
16 of Babylon, and the remainder of the artisans. •Nebuzaradan, commander of
the guard, left some of the humbler country people as vineyard workers and
ploughmen.

17   The Chaldaeans broke up the bronze pillars from the Temple of Yahweh,
the wheeled stands and the bronze Sea that were in the Temple of Yahweh,
18 and took all the bronze away to Babylon. •They also took the ash containers,
the scoops, the knives, the sprinkling bowls, the incense boats, and all the bronze
19 furnishings used in worship. •The commander of the guard also took the bowls,
the censers, the sprinkling bowls, the ash containers, the lamp-stands, the
goblets and the saucers: everything that was made of gold and everything
20 made of silver. •As regards the two pillars, the one Sea and the twelve bronze
oxen supporting the Sea, and the wheeled stands, which King Solomon had
made for the Temple of Yahweh, there was no reckoning the weight of bronze
21 in all these objects. •As regards the pillars, the height of one pillar was eighteen
cubits, its circumference was twelve cubits, it was four fingers thick, and hollow
22 inside; •on it stood a capital of bronze, the height of the capital being five
cubits; round the capital were filigree and pomegranates, all in bronze. So also
23 for the second pillar. •There were ninety-six pomegranates which hung down,
making a hundred pomegranates round the filigree in all.

24   The commander of the guard took prisoner Seraiah the chief priest, Zephaniah
25 the priest next in rank, and the three guardians of the threshold. •In the city
he took prisoner a eunuch who was in command of the fighting men, seven of
the king's personal friends who were discovered in the city, the secretary of the
army commander, responsible for military conscription, and sixty men of
26 distinction discovered in the city. •Nebuzaradan, commander of the guard,
27 took these men and brought them to the king of Babylon at Riblah, •and at
Riblah, in the land of Hamath, the king of Babylon had them put to death.
28   Thus Judah was deported from its land. •The number of people deported
by Nebuchadnezzar was as follows. In the seventh year: three thousand and
29 twenty-three Judaeans; •in the eighteenth year of Nebuchadnezzar, eight hundred
30 and thirty-two persons were deported from Jerusalem; •in the twenty-third
year[c] of Nebuchadnezzar, Nebuzaradan, commander of the guard, deported
seven hundred and forty-five Judaeans. In all: four thousand six hundred persons.

---

52 a. An expanded version of the narrative in 2 K 24-25, partly paralleled in Jr 39.   **b.** Jan-
Feb. 588.   **c.** 582 B.C.

But in the thirty-seventh year of the exile of Jehoiachin king of Judah, in the 31 twelfth month, on the twenty-fifth day of the month, Evil-merodach king of Babylon, in the year he came to the throne, *d* pardoned Jehoiachin king of Judah and released him from prison. •He treated him kindly and allotted him 32 a seat above those of the other kings who were with him in Babylon. •So 33 Jehoiachin laid aside his prisoner's garb, and for the rest of his life always ate at the king's table. •And his upkeep was permanently ensured by the king for 34 the rest of his life day after day until his dying day.

LAMENTATIONS

FIRST LAMENTATION

1 **1**   *Aleph*   Oh, how lonely she sits,
the city once thronged with people,
as if suddenly widowed.
Though once great among the nations,
she, the princess among provinces,
is now reduced to vassalage.

2   *Beth*   She passes her nights weeping;
the tears run down her cheeks.
Not one of all her lovers
remains to comfort her.
Her friends have all betrayed her
and become her enemies.

3   *Ghimel*   Judah is exiled after her downfall
and harsh enslavement.
She dwells among the nations now,
but finds no relief there.
Her pursuers all overtake her
in places where there is no way out.

4   *Daleth*   The roads to Zion are in mourning;
no one comes to her festivals now.
Her gateways are all deserted;
her priests groan;
her virgins are grief-stricken;
she suffers bitterly.

5   *He*   Her oppressors now have the upper hand,
her enemies enjoy prosperity;
Yahweh himself has made her suffer
for her many, many sins;
her little children have left her as prisoners
driven in front of the oppressor.

6   *Waw*   From the daughter of Zion
all her glory has departed.
Her leaders were like rams
that find no pasture.
Listlessly they took the road,
driven by the drover.

7   *Zain*   Jerusalem remembers
her days of misery and distress,
when her people fell before the enemy

and no one came to help her.
Her oppressors looked at her
and laughed at her downfall.

Heth   Jerusalem has sinned grievously   8
and she has become a thing unclean.
All those who used to honour her despise her;
they have seen her nakedness.
While she herself groans
and turns her face away.

Teth   Her filth clings to the hem of her clothes.   9
She had never thought of ending like this,
sinking as low as this.
She has no one to comfort her.
'Yahweh, look on my degradation;
my enemy is triumphant.'

Yod   The oppressor has laid his hands   10
on all she treasured;
she has seen the pagans
enter her sanctuary,
men whom you had forbidden
to attend your Assembly.

Kaph   All her people groan   11
as they search for bread;
they barter their valuables for food,
to keep life in them.
'Look, Yahweh, and mark
how despised I am.'

Lamed   All you who pass this way,   12
look and see:
is any sorrow like the sorrow
that afflicts me,
with which Yahweh has struck me
on the day of his burning anger?

Mem   He has sent a fire from on high   13
down into my bones;
he has laid a snare underneath my feet;
he has brought me down;
he has left me deserted,
and ill all day long.

Nun   The yoke of my sins weighs down on me,   14
his, the hand that knotted them;
their yoke is on my neck,
he makes my energy fail.
The Lord has put me at their mercy,
I have no strength left to resist.

Samek   Yahweh has spurned   15
the bravest fighters I had;
he has summoned a host against me
to destroy the flower of my army.
In his winepress the Lord has trampled
the virgin daughter of Judah.

Ain   And that is why I weep;   16

my eyes dissolve in tears,
since the comforter who could revive me
    is far away.
My sons are in despair,
    the enemy has proved too strong.

17   *Pe*   Zion stretches out her hands;
    no one is there to comfort her.
Yahweh has summoned against Jacob
    foes from every side;
Jerusalem has become
    an unclean thing to them.

18   *Sade*   Yahweh is acting rightly,
    for I had rebelled against his order.
Listen therefore, all you nations,
    and see my sorrow.
My virgins and my young men
    have gone into exile.

19   *Qoph*   I called for help to my lovers;
    they failed me.
My priests and my elders
    were perishing inside the city,
as they searched for food
    to keep life in them.

20   *Resh*   Look, Yahweh. How great my anguish!
    My entrails shudder;
my heart turns over inside me.
    Alas! I have always been a rebel—
and now, outside, the sword has robbed me of my children,
    and inside, there is death.

21   *Shin*   Listen to my groaning;
    there is no one to comfort me.
All my enemies gloat over my disaster:
    this is your doing.
Bring the day you once foretold,
    so that they may be as I am.

22   *Tau*   Let all their wickedness come before you;
    treat them
as you have treated me
    for all my sins.
Many indeed are my groans,
    my heart is sick.

SECOND LAMENTATION

1 **2**   *Aleph*   Oh, how Yahweh in his wrath
    has brought darkness on the daughter of Zion!
He has flung the glory of Israel
    from heaven to the ground,
no more remembering his footstool[a]
    on the day of his wrath.

2 a. The Temple.

Beth	The Lord has pitilessly destroyed
	    all the homes of Jacob;
	in his displeasure he has shattered
	    the strongholds of the daughter of Judah;
	he has thrown to the ground, he has left accursed
	    the kingdom and its rulers.
		2

Ghimel	In his burning anger
	    he has broken every horn in Israel,
	withdrawn the strength of his right hand
	    at the coming of the enemy,
	and kindled in Jacob a fire
	    that burns up everything near it.
		3

Daleth	Like an enemy he has bent his bow,
	    holding his right hand steady;
	like a foe, he has slaughtered
	    everything that delights the eye;
	on the tent of the daughter of Zion
	    he has poured his anger out like fire.
		4

He	The Lord has been like an enemy;
	    he has destroyed Israel;
	he has destroyed every one of her palaces,
	    laid low her strongholds,
	and for the daughters of Judah has multiplied
	    wailing on wailing.
		5

Waw	He has wrecked his own domain like a garden,
	    shattered his own gathering place;
	Yahweh has wiped out the memory
	    of festivals and sabbaths in Zion;
	in the heat of his wrath he has repudiated
	    king and priest.
		6

Zain	The Lord has grown weary of his altar,
	    has come to loathe his sanctuary,
	and handed her palace walls
	    over to the enemy;
	from the uproar in the Temple of Yahweh
	    it might have been a day of festival.
		7

Heth	Yahweh resolved to ruin
	    the city wall of the daughter of Zion;
	with a line he measured it, and did not withdraw his hand
	    until he had completely overthrown it,
	bringing mourning on city wall and rampart;
	    now they are crumbling down together.
		8

Teth	Her gates have sunk into the ground;
	    he has shattered their bars.
	Her king, her nobles, are now with the pagans,
	    the Law is no more.
	Even her prophets receive
	    no further vision from Yahweh.
		9

Yod	Mutely they sit on the ground, the elders of the daughter of Zion; they have put dust on their heads,	10

and wrapped themselves in sackcloth.
The virgins of Jerusalem hang their heads
    down to the ground.

11   *Kaph*   My eyes wasted away with weeping,
    my entrails shuddered,
my liver spilled on the ground
    at the ruin of the daughters of my people,
as children, mere infants, fainted
    in the squares of the Citadel.

12   *Lamed*   They kept saying to their mothers,
    'Where is the bread?'
as they fainted like wounded men
    in the squares of the City,
as they poured out their souls
    on their mothers' breasts.

13   *Mem*   How can I describe you, to what compare you,
    daughter of Jerusalem?
Who can rescue and comfort you,
    virgin daughter of Zion?
For huge as the sea is your affliction;
    who can possibly cure you?

14   *Nun*   The visions your prophets had on your behalf
    were delusive, tinsel things,
they never pointed out your sin,
    to ward off your exile.
The visions they proffered you were false,
    fallacious, misleading.

15   *Samek*   All who pass your way
    clap their hands at the sight;
they whistle and shake their heads
    over the daughter of Jerusalem.
'Was this the loveliest of all,
    this, the joy of the whole world?'

16   *Pe*   Your enemies open their mouths
    in chorus against you;
they whistle and grind their teeth;
    they say, 'We have swallowed her up.
This is the day we were waiting for;
    now we can touch it, see it.'

17   *Ain*   Yahweh has accomplished his intention,
    he has carried out his word
decreed in the days of old;
    he has destroyed without pity,
giving your enemy cause to gloat over you
    and raising his horn.

18   *Sade*   Cry aloud, then, to the Lord,
    groan, daughter of Zion;
let your tears flow like a torrent,
    day and night;
give yourself no relief,
    grant your eyes no rest.

Qoph   Up, cry out in the night-time,   19
             in the early hours of darkness;
        pour your heart out like water
             before Yahweh.
        Stretch out your hands to him
             for the lives of your children.

Resh   Look, Yahweh, and consider: 20
             whom have you ever treated like this?
        Why, women have eaten their little ones,
             the children they had nursed in their arms!
        Why, priest and prophet have been slaughtered
             in the sanctuary of Yahweh!

Shin   Children and old men are lying   21
             on the ground in the streets;
        my virgins and my young men
             have fallen by the sword;
        you have killed on the day of your wrath,
             you have slaughtered pitilessly.

Tau   As though to a festival you have summoned   22
             terrors from every side;
        on the day of your wrath, no one escaped,
             no one survived.
        Those whom I had nursed and reared,
             my enemy has murdered them all.

THIRD LAMENTATION

3   *Aleph*   I am the man familiar with misery   1
             under the rod of his anger;
        I am the one he has driven and forced to walk   2
             in darkness, and without any light.
        Against me alone he turns his hand,   3
             again and again, all day long.

Beth   He has wasted my flesh and skin away,   4
             has broken my bones.
        He has made a yoke for me,   5
             has encircled my head with weariness.
        He has forced me to dwell in darkness   6
             with the dead of long ago.

Ghimel   He has walled me in; I cannot escape;   7
             he has made my chains heavy;
        and when I call and shout,   8
             he shuts out my prayer.
        He has blocked my ways with cut stones,   9
             he has obstructed my paths.

Daleth   For me he has been a lurking bear,   10
             a lion on the watch.
        He has filled my paths with briars and torn me,   11
             he has made me a thing of horror.
        He has bent his bow and taken aim,   12
             making me the target for his arrows.

13	*He*	In my back he has planted his darts, the children of his quiver.
14		I have become the laughing-stock of my whole nation, their butt all day long.
15		He has given me my fill of bitterness, he has made me drunk with wormwood.
16	*Waw*	He has broken my teeth with gravel, he has given me ashes for food.
17		My soul is shut out from peace; I have forgotten happiness.
18		And now I say, 'My strength is gone, that hope which came from Yahweh'.
19	*Zain*	Brooding on my anguish and affliction is gall and wormwood.
20		My spirit ponders it continually and sinks within me.
21		This is what I shall tell my heart, and so recover hope:
22	*Heth*	the favours of Yahweh are not all past, his kindnesses are not exhausted;
23		every morning they are renewed; great is his faithfulness.
24		'My portion is Yahweh' says my soul 'and so I will hope in him.'
25	*Teth*	Yahweh is good to those who trust him, to the soul that searches for him.
26		It is good to wait in silence for Yahweh to save.
27		It is good for a man to bear the yoke from youth onwards,
28	*Yod*	to sit in solitude and silence when the Lord fastens it on him,
29		to put his lips to the dust —perhaps there still is hope—
30		to offer his cheek to the striker, to be overwhelmed with insults.
31	*Kaph*	For the Lord does not reject mankind for ever and ever.
32		If he has punished, he has compassion so great is his kindness;
33		since he takes no pleasure in abasing and afflicting the human race.
34	*Lamed*	When all the prisoners in a country are crushed and trampled underfoot,
35		when a man's rights are overridden in defiance of the Most High,
36		when a man is deprived of justice, does not the Lord see it?
37	*Mem*	Who has only to speak to make things exist? Who commands, if not the Lord?
38		From where, if not from the mouth of the Most High, do evil and good come?

Why then should man complain?   39
     Better for him to be bold against his sins.

Nun   Let us examine our path, let us ponder it   40
     and return to Yahweh.
Let us stretch out our hearts and hands   41
     to God in heaven.
We are the ones who have sinned, who have rebelled,   42
     and you have not forgiven.

Samek   You have wrapped yourself in wrath, pursued us,   43
     slaughtered us without pity.
You have wrapped yourself in a cloud   44
     too thick for prayer to pierce.
You have reduced us to rubbish   45
     to the scourings of the nations.

Pe   Our enemies have opened their mouths   46
     in chorus against us.
Dread and pitfall have been our lot,   47
     ravage and ruin.
My eyes dissolve in torrents of tears   48
     over the ruin of the daughters of my people.

Ain   My eyes weep ceaselessly,   49
     without relief
until Yahweh looks down   50
     and sees from heaven.
My eyes have grown sore   51
     over all the daughters of my Citadel.

Sade   They hunted me, harried me like a bird,   52
     they who hate me for no reason.
They tumbled my life into a pit,   53
     they threw stones down on me.
The waters went over my head;   54
     I said, 'I am lost'.

Qoph   Yahweh, I called on your name   55
     from the deep pit.
You heard me crying, 'Do not close your ear   56
     to my prayer'.
You came near that day when I called to you;   57
     you said, 'Do not be afraid'.

Resh   You have defended the cause of my soul,   58
     you have redeemed my life.
Yahweh, you have seen the wrong done to me;   59
     grant me redress.
You have seen all their frenzy,   60
     all their plots against me.

Shin   Yahweh, you have heard their insults,   61
     all their plots against me,
my opponents slandering me   62
     under their breath all day long.
Whether they sit, or whether they stand,   63
     see, I am their butt.

64   Tau   Yahweh, repay them
                   as their deeds deserve.

65   Give them hardness of heart,
                   your curse be on them.

66   Pursue them in fury, root them out
                   from underneath your heavens.

FOURTH LAMENTATION

1 4   Aleph   Oh, how the old gold has tarnished,
                   that gold so fine!
                The sacred stones now lie scattered
                   at the corner of every street.

2   Beth   The sons of Zion, as precious
                   as finest gold,
                Oh, reckoned now no better than earthenware pots
                   made by the potter!

3   Ghimel   The very jackals give the breast,
                   and suckle their young:
                but the daughters of my people have grown cruel
                   like the ostriches of the desert.

4   Daleth   The tongue of the baby at the breast
                   sticks to his palate for thirst,
                little children go begging for bread;
                   no one spares a scrap for them.

5   He   Those who used to eat only the best,
                   now lie dying in the streets;
                those who were reared in the purple
                   claw at the rubbish heaps.

6   Waw   The crimes of the daughter of my people have outdone
                   the sins of Sodom,
                which was overthrown in a moment,
                   no time for a man to wring his hands.

7   Zain   Once her young men were brighter than snow,
                   whiter than milk;
                rosier than coral their bodies,
                   their hue as radiant as sapphire.

8   Heth   Now with faces darker than blackness itself
                   they move unrecognisable through the streets.
                The skin is shrunken against their bones,
                   dry as a stick.

9   Teth   Happy were those killed by the sword,
                   happier than those by hunger,
                spent and sinking,
                   deprived of the fruits of the fields.

10   Yod   With their own hands, tender-hearted women
                   have boiled their children;
                these have been their food
                   in the disaster that fell on the daughter of my people.

Kaph	Yahweh has indulged his fury,	11
	has poured his anger out.	
	He has lit a fire in Zion	
	that has devoured her foundations.	

Lamed   The kings of the earth never believed,   12
           nor did all the inhabitants of the world,
       that oppressor and enemy would ever penetrate
           the gates of Jerusalem.

Mem   It came through the sins of her prophets   13
           and the crimes of her priests,
       who had shed the blood of the upright
           in the heart of the city.

Nun   Through the streets like blind men, they roamed   14
           polluted with blood,
       so that no one dared to touch
           their clothes.

Samek   'Keep away! Unclean!' people shouted   15
           'Keep away! Do not touch us!'
       If they left and took refuge with the nations,
           they were not allowed to shelter there either.

Pe   The face of Yahweh dispersed them;   16
           he never spared a glance for them again.
       People respected the priests no longer,
           they paid no attention to the prophets.

Ain   And still we wore out our eyes,   17
           watching for help—in vain.
       From our towers we watched for a nation*a*
           which could not save us anyway.

Sade   Our enemies eyed our steps,   18
           and barricaded our squares.
       Our end was near,
           our days were done.

Qoph   Our pursuers were swifter   19
           than eagles in the sky;
       they dogged our steps in the mountains,
           they ambushed us in the desert.

Resh   The breath of our nostrils, Yahweh's anointed,*b*   20
           was captured in their pits,
       he of whom we said, 'Under his shadow
           we shall live among the nations'.

Shin   Rejoice, exult, daughter of Edom,   21
           as you dwell in Uz!
       To you in turn the cup will pass;
           it will make you drunk, and you will show your nakedness.

Tau   Your crime has been atoned for, daughter of Zion;   22
           he will never banish you again.
       Your crime he will punish, daughter of Edom;
           he will lay bare your sins.

FIFTH LAMENTATION

5 ¹ Yahweh, remember what has happened to us;
         look on us and see our degradation.

² Our inheritance has passed to aliens,
   our homes to barbarians.

³ We are orphans, we are fatherless;
   our mothers are like widows.

⁴ We drink our own water—at a price;
   we have to pay for what is our own firewood.

⁵ The yoke is on our necks; we are persecuted;
   we are worked to death; no relief for us.

⁶ We hold out our hands to Egypt,
   or to Assyria, just to get enough bread.

⁷ Our fathers have sinned; they are no more,
   and we ourselves bear the weight of their crimes.

⁸ Slaves*ᵃ* rule us;
   no one rescues us from them.

⁹ At peril of our lives we earn our bread,
   by risking the sword of the desert.

¹⁰ Our skin is as hot as the oven,
   such is the fever of famine.

¹¹ They have raped the women in Zion,
   the virgins in the towns of Judah.

¹² Princes have been hanged at their hands;
   the face of the old has not been respected.

¹³ Youths have toiled at the mill;
   boys have collapsed under loads of wood.

¹⁴ The elders have deserted the gateway;
   the young men have given up their music.

¹⁵ Joy has vanished from our hearts;
   our dancing has been turned to mourning.

¹⁶ The garland has fallen from our heads.
   Woe to us, because we have sinned!

¹⁷ This is why our hearts are sick;
   this is why our eyes are dim:

¹⁸ because Mount Zion is desolate;
   jackals roam to and fro on it.

¹⁹ But you, Yahweh, you remain for ever;
   your throne endures from age to age.

²⁰ You cannot mean to forget us for ever?
   You cannot mean to abandon us for good?

4 a. Egypt, ally of Judah in the reign of Zedekiah.   **b.** Zedekiah.
5 a. The Chaldaean officials.

Make us come back to you, Yahweh, and we will come back. 21
Renew our days as in times past,

unless you have utterly rejected us,   22
in an anger that knows no limit.

THE BOOK OF BARUCH

I. INTRODUCTION

Baruch and the Jews in Babylon

1 These are the words of the book written in Babylon by Baruch son of Neraiah,
2 son of Mahseiah, son of Zedekiah, son of Hasadiah, son of Hilkiah, •in
the fifth year,ᵃ on the seventh day of the month, at the time when the Chaldaeans
captured Jerusalem and burned it down.

3 Baruch read the words of this book aloud to Jeconiah son of Jehoiakim,
4 king of Judah, and to all the people who had come to hear the reading, •to the
nobles and the sons of the king, and to the elders; to the whole people, that is,
least no less than greatest, to all who lived in Babylon beside the river Sud.
5,6 On hearing it they wept, fasted and prayed before the Lord; •and they collected
7 as much money as each could afford •and sent it to Jerusalem for the priest
Jehoiakim son of Hilkiah, son of Shallum, and the other priests, and for as
8 many of the people as were with him in Jerusalem. •It was Baruch who on the
tenth day of Sivan had recovered the utensils of the house of the Lord, which
had been removed from the Temple, to take them back to the land of Judah:
these were silver utensils which Zedekiah son of Josiah, king of Judah, had had
9 made •when Nebuchadnezzar king of Babylon had deported Jeconiah from
Jerusalem to Babylon, together with the princes, the metalworkers, the men of
rank and the common people.

10 With this—they wrote—we are sending you money with which to pay for holocausts, offerings for sin, and incense; prepare oblations, and offer them on the altar
11 of the Lord our God. •Pray for the long life of Nebuchadnezzar king of Babylon,
and of his son Belshazzar, and that their days on earth may endure as the
12 heavens; •pray that the Lord may give us strength and clear understanding so
that we may lead our lives under the protection of Nebuchadnezzar king of
Babylon and of his son Belshazzar, and by our long service win their favour.
13 Also pray to the Lord our God for us, because we have sinned against him,
and the anger, the fury of the Lord, has still not yet been turned away from us.
14 Lastly, you are to read the book aloud which we send you with this and so
make public confession in the house of the Lord on the feastdayᵇ and on days
15 of solemn assembly. •You are to say:

II. THE PRAYER OF THE EXILES

Confession of sins

Integrity belongs to the Lord our God; to us the look of shame we wear
16 today, to us, the people of Judah and the citizens of Jerusalem, •to our kings
17 and princes, our priests, our prophets, as to our ancestors, •because we have

---

1 a. The year 582, probably on the anniversary of the fall of Jerusalem.   b. I.e., the feast of
Tabernacles.

sinned in the sight of the Lord, •have disobeyed him, and have not listened 18
to the voice of the Lord our God telling us to follow the commandments which
the Lord had ordained for us. •From the day when the Lord brought our ancestors 19
out of the land of Egypt until today we have been disobedient to the Lord our
God, we have been disloyal, refusing to listen to his voice. •And so the disasters, 20
and the curse which the Lord pronounced through his servant Moses the day
he brought our fathers out of Egypt to give us a land where milk and honey
flow, have seized on us, disasters we experience today. •Despite all the words 21
of those prophets whom he sent us, we have not listened to the voice of the
Lord our God, •but, each following the dictates of his evil heart, we have taken 22
to serving alien gods, and doing what is displeasing to the Lord our God.

2 And so the Lord has carried out the sentence which he passed on us, on 1
our judges who governed Israel, on our kings and leaders, on the men of
Israel and of Judah; •what he did to Jerusalem has never been paralleled under 2
the wide heavens—all this in conformity with what was written in the Law of
Moses; •we were all reduced to eating the flesh of our own sons and daughters. 3
Furthermore, he has handed them over into the power of all the kingdoms that 4
surround us, to be loathed and avoided by all the neighbouring nations among
whom he scattered them. •Instead of being masters, they found themselves 5
enslaved, because we had sinned against the Lord our God by not listening to
his voice.

Integrity belongs to the Lord our God; to us the look of shame we wear 6
today, to us, as to our ancestors. •All those disasters which the Lord pronounced 7
against us have now happened to us. •And yet we have not tried to win 8
the favour of the Lord by each one of us renouncing the dictates of his own
wicked heart; •and so the Lord has watched for the right moment to bring disaster 9
on us, since the Lord gives a just return for what we do of all that he has
ordered us to do, •and we have not listened to his voice telling us to follow 10
the commandments which the Lord had ordained for us.

The prayer

And now, Lord, God of Israel, who brought your people out of the land of 11
Egypt with a mighty hand, with signs and wonders, with great power and with
outstretched arm, to win yourself a name renowned today, •we have sinned, 12
we have been irreligious; Lord our God, we have broken all your commandments. •Let your anger turn from us since we are no more than a poor 13
remnant among the nations where you have dispersed us. •Listen, Lord, to our 14
prayer, to our entreaty; deliver us for the sake of your honour and grant us
your favour for all our captors to see it, •so that the whole world may know that 15
you are the Lord our God, since Israel and his descendants bear your name. •Look 16
down, Lord, from your holy dwelling place and give a thought to us, take
heed of us and listen, •look at us, Lord, and consider; the dead down in 17
Sheol, whose breath has been taken from their bodies, are not the ones to give
glory and due observance to the Lord; •the person overcome with affliction, 18
who goes his way bowed down and frail, with failing eyes and hungering soul,
he is the one to give you glory, Lord, and due observance.

We do not rely on the merits of our ancestors and of our kings to offer you 19
our humble plea, Lord our God. •No. You have sent down your anger and your 20
fury on us, as you promised through your servants the prophets when they said,
'The Lord says this: *Bend your necks and submit to the king of Babylon*, and you 21
will remain in the land which I gave your ancestors. •But if you do not listen to 22
the voice of the Lord and submit to the king of Babylon, •then *I will silence the* 23
shouts of rejoicing and mirth and the voices of bridegroom and bride in the towns of
Judah and in the streets of Jerusalem, and the whole land will be reduced to desert,
without inhabitants.' •But we did not listen to your voice and submit to the king 24
of Babylon, and so you carried out what you had promised through your servants

the prophets: that the bones of our kings and of our ancestors would be dragged
25 from their resting places. •They were indeed *tossed out to the heat of the day
and the frost of the night*. And people died in dreadful agony, from famine,
26 sword and plague. •And so, because of the wickedness of the House of
Israel and the House of Judah, you have made this House, that bears your
name, what it is today.

27 And yet, Lord our God, you have treated us in a way worthy of all
28 your goodness and boundless tenderness, •just as you had promised through
your servant Moses, the day you told him to write your Law in the presence of the
29 sons of Israel, and said this, •'If you do not listen to my voice, this great and
innumerable multitude will certainly be reduced to a tiny few among the nations
30 among which I shall disperse them, •and I know very well that this people
will not listen, it is so stubborn. But in the country of their exile they will take
31 all this to heart •and acknowledge that I am the Lord their God. I will give
32 them a heart and an attentive ear. •They will sing my praises in the country
33 of their exile, they will remember my name; •they will not be stubborn any
more, but, remembering what became of their ancestors who sinned in the sight
34 of the Lord, will turn from their evil deeds. •Then I will bring them back to
the land I promised on oath to Abraham, Isaac and Jacob, and make them
35 masters in it. I will increase their number: they shall not dwindle. •And I will
make an everlasting covenant with them; I will be their God and they shall
be my people. And I will never again drive my people Israel out of the land
that I have given them.'

1 3 Almighty Lord, God of Israel, a soul in anguish, a troubled heart now cries
2/3 to you: •Listen and have pity, Lord, for we have sinned in your sight. •You
4 sit enthroned for ever, while we perish continually. •Almighty Lord, God of
Israel, hear the prayer of the dead of Israel,[a] of the sons of those who have
sinned against you and have not listened to the voice of the Lord their God,
5 hence the disasters that have seized on us. •Do not call to mind the misdeeds
6 of our ancestors, but remember instead your power and your name. •You are
7 indeed the Lord our God and we long to praise you, Lord, •since you have
put respect for you in our hearts to encourage us to call on your name. We
long to praise you in our exile, for we have emptied our hearts of the evil inclin-
8 ations of our ancestors who sinned against you. •Look on us today, still in exile
where you have dispersed us as something execrable, accursed, condemned, in
punishment for all the misdeeds of our ancestors who had abandoned the Lord
our God.

III. WISDOM, THE PREROGATIVE OF ISRAEL

9 Listen, Israel, to commands that bring life;
hear, and learn what knowledge means.
10 Why, Israel, why are you in the country of your enemies,
growing older and older in an alien land,
11 sharing defilement with the dead,
reckoned with those who go to Sheol?
12 Because you have forsaken the fountain of wisdom.
13 Had you walked in the way of God,
you would have lived in peace for ever.
14 Learn where knowledge is, where strength,
where understanding, and so learn
where length of days is, where life,
where the light of the eyes and where peace.

3 a. Hyperbole: those brought near death.

But who has found out where she lives, 15
who has entered her treasure house?

Where now are the leaders of the nations 16
and those who ruled even the beasts of earth,
who had the birds of heaven at their beck and call, 17
who accumulated silver and gold
on which mankind relies,
and whose possessions had no limits,
those who displayed such artistry in silver 18
that their masterpieces beggar imagination?
They have vanished, gone down to Sheol. 19
Others have risen to their places,
more recent generations have seen the day 20
and peopled the earth in their turn:
but the way of knowledge is something they have not known,
they have not recognised the paths she treads. 21
Nor have their sons had any grasp of her,
remaining far from her way.
Nothing has been heard of her in Canaan, 22
nothing has been seen of her in Teman;
the sons of Hagar in search of worldly wisdom, 23
the merchants of Midian and Tema,
the tale-spinners and the philosophers
have none of them found the way to wisdom,
or discovered the paths she treads.

How great, Israel, is the house of God, 24
how wide his domain,
immeasurably wide, 25
infinitely lofty!
In it were born the giants, famous to us from antiquity, 26
immensely tall, expert in war;
God's choice did not fall on these, 27
he did not reveal the way to knowledge to them;
they perished for lack of wisdom, 28
perished in their own folly.

Who has ever climbed the sky and caught her 29
to bring her down from the clouds?
Who has ever crossed the ocean and found her 30
to bring her back in exchange for the finest gold?
No one knows the way to her, 31
no one can discover the path she treads.

But the One who knows all knows her, 32
he has grasped her with his own intellect,
he has set the earth firm for ever
and filled it with four-footed beasts,
he sends the light—and it goes, 33
he recalls it—and trembling it obeys;
the stars shine joyfully at their set times: 34
when he calls them, they answer, 'Here we are'; 35
they gladly shine for their creator.
It is he who is our God, 36
no other can compare with him.
He has grasped the whole way of knowledge, 37
and confided it to his servant Jacob,

to Israel his well-beloved;

38 so causing her to appear on earth
and move among men.

1 **4** This is the book of the commandments of God,
the Law that stands for ever;
those who keep her live,
those who desert her die.

2 Turn back, Jacob, seize her,
in her radiance make your way to light:

3 do not yield your glory to another,
your privilege to a people not your own.

4 Israel, blessed are we:
what pleases God has been revealed to us.

IV. THE COMPLAINTS AND HOPES OF JERUSALEM

5 Take courage, my people,
constant reminder of Israel.[a]

6 You were sold to the nations,
but not for extermination.
You provoked God;
and so were delivered to your enemies,

7 since you had angered your creator
by offering sacrifices to demons, not to God.

8 You had forgotten the eternal God who reared you.
You had also grieved Jerusalem who nursed you,

9 for when she saw the anger fall on you
from God, she said:

Listen, you neighbours of Zion:
God has sent me great sorrow.

10 I have seen my sons and daughters taken into captivity,
to which they have been sentenced by the Eternal.

11 I had reared them joyfully;
in tears, in sorrow, I watched them go away.

12 Do not, any of you, exult over me,
a widow, deserted by so many;
I suffer loneliness because of the sins of my own children,
who turned away from the Law of God,

13 who did not want to know his injunctions,
and would not follow the ways of his precepts,
or tread the paths of discipline as his justice directed.

14 Let them come here, those neighbours of Zion.
Let me remind you of the captivity of my sons and daughters
to which they have been sentenced by the Eternal:

15 how he brought a distant nation down on them,
a ruthless nation speaking a foreign language,
having neither respect for the aged,
nor pity for the child;

16 they carried off the widow's cherished sons,
they left her quite alone, bereft of her daughters.

17 For my part, how can I help you?

18 He who brought those disasters down on you,

4 a. I.e., of Jacob.

he is the one to deliver you from the hands of your enemies.
Go, my children, go your way!   19
I must stay bereft and lonely;
I have taken off the clothes of peacetime,   20
and put on the sackcloth of entreaty;
I will cry to the Eternal all my life.
Take courage, my children, call on God: 21
he will deliver you from tyranny, from the hands of your enemies;
for I look to the Eternal for your rescue,   22
and joy has come to me from the Holy One
at the mercy soon to reach you
from your saviour, the Eternal.
In sorrow and tears I watched you go away,   23
but God will give you back to me in joy and gladness for ever.
As the neighbours of Zion now witness your captivity,   24
so will they soon see you rescued by God,
who will intervene, in the great glory and splendour of the Eternal.
My children, patiently bear the anger brought on you by God.   25
Your enemy has persecuted you,
but soon you will witness his destruction
and set your foot on his neck.
My favourite children have travelled by rough roads,   26
carried off like a flock by a marauding enemy.
Take courage, my children, call on God: 27
he who brought disaster on you will remember you.
As by your will you first strayed away from God,   28
so now turn back and search for him ten times as hard;
for as he brought down those disasters on you,   29
so will he rescue you and give you eternal joy.

Take courage, Jerusalem: 30
he who gave you that name will console you.
Trouble will come to all who have ill-treated you   31
and gloated over your fall.
Trouble will come to the cities where your children were slaves;   32
trouble will come to the city which received your sons,
for just as she rejoiced at your fall   33
and was happy to see you ruined,
so shall she grieve over her own desolation.
I will deprive her of that joy known to populous cities,   34
her boasting shall be turned into mourning,
fire from the Eternal will burn in her for many a day   35
and demons will dwell in her for ages.
Jerusalem, turn your eyes to the east,   36
see the joy that is coming to you from God.
Look, the sons you watched go away are on their way home;   37
reassembled from east and west, they are on their way home
at the command of the Holy One, jubilant at the glory of God.

5   Jerusalem, take off your dress of sorrow and distress,   1
put on the beauty of the glory of God for ever,
wrap the cloak of the integrity of God around you,   2
put the diadem of the glory of the Eternal on your head:
since God means to show your splendour to every nation under heaven,   3
since the name God gives you for ever will be,   4
'Peace through integrity, and honour through devotedness'.
Arise, Jerusalem, stand on the heights   5

and turn your eyes to the east:
see your sons reassembled from west and east
at the command of the Holy One, jubilant that God has
    remembered them.

6   Though they left you on foot,
with enemies for an escort,
now God brings them back to you
like royal princes carried back in glory.

7   For God has decreed the flattening
of each high mountain, of the everlasting hills,
the filling of the valleys to make the ground level
so that Israel can walk in safety under the glory of God.

8   And the forests and every fragrant tree will provide shade
for Israel at the command of God;

9   for God will guide Israel in joy by the light of his glory
with his mercy and integrity for escort.

V. THE LETTER OF JEREMIAH

A copy of the letter which Jeremiah sent to those about to be led captive
to Babylon by the king of the Babylonians, to inform them of the instructions
which God had given him.

1 6 Because of the sins you have committed before God you are to be deported
2 to Babylon by Nebuchadnezzar king of the Babylonians. •Once you have
reached Babylon you will stay there for many years, as long as seven generations;
3 after which I shall bring you home in peace. •Now in Babylon you will see
gods made of silver, of gold, of wood, being carried shoulder-high, and filling
4 the pagans with fear. •Be on your guard. Do not imitate the foreigners, do not
5 have any fear of their gods •as you watch their worshippers flocking before and
behind them. Instead, say in your hearts, 'Master, it is you that we have to
6 worship'. •For my angel is with you; your lives will be in his care.

7   Plated with gold and silver, their tongues polished smooth by a craftsman,
8 they are counterfeit and have no power to speak. •As though for a girl fond
of finery, these pagans take gold and make crowns for the heads of their gods.
9 Sometimes, the priests actually filch gold and silver from their gods to spend
10 themselves, even using it on presents for the temple prostitutes. •They
dress up these gods of silver, gold and wood, in clothes, like human beings,
although they cannot protect themselves either from tarnish or woodworm,
11 in spite of the purple cloaks they drape them in. Their faces even have to be
12 dusted, owing to the dust of the temple which settles thick on them. •One holds
a sceptre like the governor of a province, yet is powerless to put anyone who
13 offends him to death; •another holds sword and axe in his right hand, yet is
14 powerless to defend himself against war or thieves. •From this it is evident that
they are not gods; do not be afraid of them.

15   Just as a pot in common use becomes useless once it is broken, so are these
16 gods enshrined inside their temples. •Their eyes are full of dust raised by the
17 feet of those who enter. •Just as the doors are locked on all sides on the man
who has offended the king and is under sentence of death, so the priests secure
the temples of these gods with gates and bolts and bars for fear of burglary.
18 They light more lamps than for themselves, and the gods cannot see one of them.
19 They are like one of the temple beams, gnawed away from within, so they say,
by termites which creep out of the ground and eat them, and their fine clothes
20 too. They are unaware •that their faces are blackened by the smoke that rises
21 from the temple. •Bats, swallows, birds of every kind flutter over their bodies

and heads, and cats prowl there. •From all this you can see for yourselves that 22 they are not gods: do not be afraid of them.

The gold with which they are plated is fine enough to look at, but if someone 23 does not rub off the tarnish, these gods will not do much shining on their own. They felt nothing while they were being cast. •However much was paid for them, 24 there is still no breath of life in them. •Being unable to walk, they have to be carried 25 on men's shoulders, which shows how futile they are. It is humiliating for their worshippers, too, who have to stand them up again if they fall over. •Once they 26 have been stood up, they cannot move on their own; if they tilt askew, they cannot right themselves; offerings made to them might as well be made to dead men. •Whatever is sacrificed to them, the priests re-sell and pocket the profit; 27 while their wives salt down part of it, but give nothing to the poor or to the helpless. As to the sacrifices themselves, why, women during their periods and women in childbed are not afraid to touch them! •As you can see from these 28 examples that they are not gods, do not be afraid of them.

Indeed, how can they even be called gods, when women do the offering 29 to these gods of silver, gold and wood? •In their temples, the priests stay sitting 30 down, their garments torn, heads and beard shaved and with heads uncovered; they roar and shriek before their gods as people do at funeral feasts. •The $^{31}_{32}$ priests take the robes of the gods to clothe their own wives and children. •Whether 33 these gods are treated badly or well, they are incapable of paying back either treatment; as incapable too of making or unmaking kings, •equally incapable 34 of distributing wealth or money. If anyone fails to honour a vow he has made to them, they cannot call him to account. •They can neither save a man from 35 death nor rescue the weak from the strong, •nor restore sight to the blind, nor 36 save someone in trouble, •nor take pity on a widow, nor be generous to an 37 orphan. •These wooden gods plated with gold and silver are about as much 38 use as rocks cut out of the mountain side. Humiliation awaits their worshippers. So how can anyone think or say that they are gods? 39

The Chaldaeans themselves do them no honour; if they find someone who 40 is dumb and cannot speak, they present him to Bel, entreating him for the gift of speech, as if he could hear them! •And they are incapable of drawing the 41 conclusion and abandoning those gods—such is their lack of commonsense. Women with strings round their waists sit in the streets, burning bran like incense; 42 when one of these has been picked up by a passer-by and been to bed with him, 43 she then twits her neighbour for not being singled out and for not having her string broken. •Everything going on anywhere near these gods is spurious. 44 So how can anyone think or say that they are gods?

Made by woodworkers and goldsmiths, they are only what those workmen 45 decide to make them. •The makers have not long to live themselves, so how can 46 the things they make be gods? •Their legacy to their descendants is nothing but 47 illusion and disappointment. •If war or disasters occur, the priests discuss where 48 best to hide themselves and these gods; •how can anyone fail to realise that 49 they are not gods, if they cannot save themselves from war or from disasters? And since in any case they are only made of wood plated with gold or silver, 50 it must be obvious from all this that they are spurious; and plain to everyone, to nations as to kings, that they are not gods but the work of human hands, and that there is no divine activity in them. •Can there be anyone still unconvinced 51 that they are not gods?

They can neither appoint a king over a country, nor give rain to mankind, 52 nor regulate their own affairs, nor rescue anyone who suffers a wrong; they are 53 as helpless as crows between sky and ground. •If fire falls on the temple of these 54 wooden gods plated with gold or silver, their priests fly to safety while they for their part stay there like beams, to be burnt. •They cannot put up any resistance 55 to a king or to enemies. •So how can anyone think or say that they are gods? 56

These wooden gods plated with gold or silver cannot evade thieves or 57

marauders; violent men may rob them of their gold and silver and make off with the robes they are dressed in; yet they are powerless to help even themselves.
58 Better to be a king displaying his prowess, a household pot of use to its owner, than to be these false gods; or merely the door of a house, protecting what is inside, than these false gods; or a wooden pillar in a palace than these false gods.
59 The sun, the moon and the stars, which shine and have been given work to do,
60 are obedient; •similarly, the lightning, as it flashes, is a fine sight; in the same
61 way, the wind blows across every country, •the clouds execute the order God gives them to pass over the whole earth, and the fire, sent from above to consume
62 mountain and forest, carries out its orders. •Now these gods are not their
63 equal, either in beauty or in power. •So, no one can think or say that they are gods, powerless as they are to administer justice or to do men any good.
64 Therefore, knowing that they are not gods, do not be afraid of them.
65
66 They can neither curse nor bless kings, •nor produce signs in heaven for the
67 nations, nor shine like the sun, nor shed light like the moon. •The animals are better off than they are, being able to make for cover and look after themselves.
68 There is not the slightest shred of evidence that they are gods; do not be afraid of them!
69 Their wooden gods plated with gold and silver are like a scarecrow in a melon
70 patch—protecting nothing. •Again, their wooden gods plated with gold and silver are like a thornbush in a garden—any bird may perch on it—or like
71 a corpse thrown into the dark. •From the purple and fine linen rotting on their backs you will recognise that they are not gods; and in the end, eaten away
72 themselves, they will be a disgrace to the country. •Better, then, a virtuous man who has no idols; disgrace will never come near him.

Ezekiel was a priest; he was a prophet of action who made himself a sign to Israel in elaborate symbolic miming. He was also a visionary, as the four long violently imaginative visions in the book show; these have the power of evoking size and depth and the mysteriousness of God's working. His teaching is centred on inner conversion: a new heart and a new spirit, which will be given by God. By his visions, he stands at the source of the apocalyptic tradition; for his spiritual penetration, he has been called 'the Father of Judaism'.

INTRODUCTION
TO THE BOOK OF
EZEKIEL

According to the dates given inside the book, Ezekiel's ministry as a prophet was among the exiles in Babylon between 593 and 571. Nevertheless we find in chapters 4-24 a number of reproaches and threats addressed to people living in Jerusalem, apparently before the siege; and following these, in chapters 25-32, a series of oracles against 'the nations', which belong to the same period. The remaining chapters, 33-48, plainly refer to the siege and the Exile, and indeed look forward to the future re-establishment of the nation in Palestine. Despite a certain amount of supplementary material, most of the prophecies are stamped with Ezekiel's own style and teaching, and the details of the prophet's biography remain a matter of debate and speculation.

Ezekiel was a priest; he was a prophet of action who made himself 'a sign' to Israel in elaborate symbolic miming. He was also a visionary, as the four long violently imaginative visions in the book show; these have the power of evoking size and depth and the mysteriousness of God's working. His teaching is centred on inner conversion: a new heart and a new spirit, which will be given by God. By his visions, he stands at the source of the apocalyptic tradition; for his spiritual penetration, he has been called 'the father of Judaism'.

EZEKIEL

INTRODUCTION

1 In the thirtieth year, on the fifth day of the fourth month, as I was among
the exiles on the bank of the river Chebar, heaven opened and I saw
2 visions from God. •On the fifth of the month—it was the fifth year of exile for
3 King Jehoiachin— •the word of Yahweh was addressed to the priest Ezekiel
son of Buzi, in the land of the Chaldaeans, on the bank of the river Chebar.*a*

The vision of the 'Chariot of Yahweh'

4   There the hand of Yahweh came on me. •I looked; a stormy wind blew
from the north, a great cloud with light around it, a fire from which flashes of
5 lightning darted, and in the centre a sheen like bronze at the heart of the fire. •In
the centre I saw what seemed four animals. They looked like this. They were of
6
7 human form. •Each had four faces, each had four wings. •Their legs were straight;
8 they had hooves like oxen, glittering like polished brass. •Human hands showed
9 under their wings; the faces of all four were turned to the four quarters.*b* •Their
wings touched each other; they did not turn as they moved; each one went
10 straight forward. •As to what they looked like, they had human faces, and all
four had a lion's face to the right, and all four had a bull's face to the left, and
11 all four had an eagle's face. •Their wings were spread upwards; each had two
12 wings that touched, and two wings that covered his body; •and they all went
straight forward; they went where the spirit urged them; they did not turn as
they moved.
13   Between these animals something could be seen like flaming brands or
torches, darting between the animals; the fire flashed light, and lightning
14 streaked from the fire. •And the creatures ran to and fro like thunderbolts.
15   I looked at the animals; there was a wheel on the ground by each of them, one
16 beside each of the four. •The wheels glittered as if made of chrysolite. All four
17 looked alike, and seemed to be made one inside the other. •They went forward four
18 ways and kept their course unswervingly. •Their rims seemed enormous when
19 I looked at them and all four rims had eyes all the way round. •When the animals
went forward, the wheels went forward beside them; and when the animals
20 left the ground, the wheels too left the ground. •Where the spirit urged them,
21 there the wheels went, since the spirit of the animal was in the wheels. •When
the animals moved on, they moved on; when the former halted, the latter
halted; when the former left the ground, the wheels too left the ground, since
22 the spirit of the animal was in the wheels. •Over the heads of the animals a sort
23 of vault, gleaming like crystal, arched above their heads; •under this vault
their wings stretched out to one another, and each had two covering his body.
24 I heard the noise of their wings as they moved; it sounded like rushing water,

---

1 a. There seem to be two separate introductions in vv.1-3. The second of them dates Ezekiel's
first vision in 593-592 and may be the introduction to the whole book; the other, v.1, is perhaps
the introduction to the vision of the Chariot.   **b.** They are like the Assyrian 'cherubs' whose
effigies could be seen in Babylon.

like the voice of Shaddai, a noise like a storm, like the noise of a camp; when
they halted, they folded their wings, •and there was a noise.   25

Above the vault over their heads was something that looked like a sapphire;   26
it was shaped like a throne and high up on this throne was a being that looked
like a man. •I saw him shine like bronze, and close to and all around him from 27
what seemed his loins upwards was what looked like fire; and from what seemed
his loins downwards I saw what looked like fire, and a light all round •like a   28
bow in the clouds on rainy days; that is how the surrounding light appeared.
It was something that looked like the glory of Yahweh. I looked, and prostrated
myself, and I heard a voice speaking.

The vision of the scroll[a]

2 It said, 'Son of man, stand up; I am going to speak to you'. •As he said $^1_2$
these words the spirit came into me and made me stand up, and I heard him
speaking to me. •He said, 'Son of man, I am sending you to the Israelites, to   3
the rebels who have turned against me. Till now they and their ancestors have
been in revolt against me. •The sons are defiant and obstinate; I am sending   4
you to them, to say, "The Lord Yahweh says this". •Whether they listen or   5
not, this set of rebels shall know there is a prophet among them. •And you,   6
son of man, do not be afraid of them, do not be afraid when they say, "There
are thorns all round you and scorpions under you". There is no need to be
afraid either of their words or of their looks, for they are a set of rebels.
You must deliver my words to them whether they listen or not, for they are   7
a set of rebels.

'You, son of man, listen to the words I say; do not be a rebel like   8
that rebellious set. Open your mouth and eat what I am about to give you.'
I looked. A hand was there, stretching out to me and holding a scroll. •He unrolled $^9_{10}$
it in front of me; it was written on back and front; on it was written 'lamentations,
wailings, moanings'. 3 He said, 'Son of man, eat what is given to you; eat this   1
scroll, then go and speak to the House of Israel'. •I opened my mouth; he gave   2
me the scroll to eat •and said, 'Son of man, feed and be satisfied by the scroll 3
I am giving you'. I ate it, and it tasted sweet as honey.

Then he said, 'Son of man, go to the House of Israel and tell them what   4
I have said. •You are not being sent to a nation that speaks a difficult foreign 5
language; you are being sent to the House of Israel. •Not to big nations that   6
speak difficult foreign languages, and whose words you would not understand—
if I sent you to them, they would listen to you; •but the House of Israel will not 7
listen to you because it will not listen to me. The whole House of Israel is
stubborn and obstinate. •But now, I will make you as defiant as they are, and as 8
obstinate as they are; •I am going to make your resolution as hard as a diamond 9
and diamond is harder than flint. So do not be afraid of them, do not be overawed
by them for they are a set of rebels.'

Then he said, 'Son of man, remember everything I say to you, listen closely,   10
and go to your exiled countrymen and talk to them. Tell them, "The Lord   11
Yahweh says this", whether they listen or not.'

The spirit lifted me up, and behind me I could hear a tumultuous shouting,   12
'Blessed be the glory of Yahweh in his dwelling place'. •This was the sound of the 13
animals' wings beating against each other, and the sound of the wheels beside
them; a tumultuous shouting. •The spirit lifted me up and took me; my heart,   14
as I went, overflowed with bitterness and anger, and the hand of Yahweh lay
heavy on me. •I came to Tel Abib, to the exiles beside the river Chebar where   15
they were then living; and I stayed with them for seven days like a man stunned.

The prophet as sentry

After seven days the word of Yahweh was addressed to me as follows,   16
'Son of man, I have appointed you as sentry to the House of Israel. Whenever   17

18 you hear a word from me, warn them in my Name. •If I say to a wicked man:
You are to die, and you do not warn him; if you do not speak and warn him
to renounce his evil ways and so live, then he shall die for his sin, but I will hold
19 you responsible for his death. •If, however, you do warn a wicked man and he
does not renounce his wickedness and his evil ways, then he shall die for his sin,
20 but you yourself will have saved your life. •When the upright man renounces
his integrity to do evil and I set a trap for him, he too shall die; since you failed
to warn him, he shall die for his sin and the integrity he practised will no longer
21 be remembered; but I will hold you responsible for his death. •If, however, you
warn the upright man not to sin and he abstains from sinning, he shall live,
thanks to your warning, and you too will have saved your life.'

I. BEFORE THE SIEGE OF JERUSALEM

Ezekiel is struck dumb

22 While I was there the hand of Yahweh came on me; he said, 'Get up, go out
23 into the valley; I am going to speak to you'. •I got up and went out into the
valley; the glory of Yahweh was resting there, like the glory I had seen by
24 the river Chebar, and I prostrated myself. •The spirit of Yahweh then entered me,
and made me stand up, and spoke to me.
25 He said, 'Go and shut yourself in your house. •Son of man, bonds are now
about to be laid on you; you will be bound with them and not be able to mix
26 with others. •I am going to make your tongue stick to the roof of your mouth;
27 you will be dumb; you will stop warning them, for they are a set of rebels. •When
I speak to you, I shall open your mouth and you will tell them, "The Lord
Yahweh says this". Whoever will listen, let him listen; whoever will not, let
him not; for they are a set of rebels.

The siege of Jerusalem foretold

1 4 'Son of man, take a brick and lay it in front of you; on it scratch a city,
2 Jerusalem. •You are then to besiege it, trench round it, build earthworks, pitch
3 camps and bring up battering-rams all round. •Then take an iron pan and place
it as if it were an iron wall between you and the city. Then turn to it; it is being
besieged and you are besieging it. This is a sign for the House of Israel.
4 'Lie down on your left side and take the sin of the House of Israel on
5 yourself. I am making you bear their sin for as many days as you lie there. •I myself
have set the years they will sin at a hundred and ninety days; during these you
6 are to bear the sin of the House of Israel. •And at the end of these days, you are
to lie down again on your right side and bear the sin of the House of Judah for
7 forty days. I have set the length for you as one day for one year. •And you are to
turn towards the siege of Jerusalem, lift your bare arm and prophesy against it.
8 I have laid bonds on you, and you must not turn over until the period of your
seclusion is finished.
9 'You must then take wheat, barley, beans, lentils, millet and spelt; put them
all in the same pot and make yourself some bread. You are to eat it for as many
10 days as you have been lying on your side, a hundred and ninety days. •As
regards this food you are to measure out a daily portion of twenty shekels and
11 make it last the whole day. •And you are to drink water sparingly; your drink
12 is to be the sixth of a hin and to last the whole day. •Take this food in the shape
13 of a barley cake baked where they can see you, over human dung. •And say,
"Yahweh, the God of Israel, says this: This is the way the Israelites will have to
14 eat their defiled food, wherever I disperse them among the nations".' •I then
said, 'Lord Yahweh, my soul is not defiled. From my childhood until now, I have

2 a. Probably Ezekiel's first vision; the vision of the Chariot is continued later, 3:12.

never eaten an animal that has died a natural death or been savaged; no unclean flesh has ever entered my mouth.' •'Very well,' he said 'I grant you cow's dung 15 instead of human dung; you are to bake your bread on that.' •He then said, 'Son 16 of man, I mean to destroy the stock of bread in Jerusalem; in their distress they will eat bread strictly weighed; in terror they will drink water grudgingly measured, •since bread and water will be scarce; they will all pine and waste away 17 as a result of their sins.

5 'Son of man, take a sharp blade, sharp as a barber's razor; take it and use 1 it on your head and beard. Then take scales and divide the hair you have cut off. •You are to set fire to a third in the centre of the city, while the time of the 2 siege is working itself out. Then take another third and toss it by swordpoint all round the city. The last third you are to scatter to the wind, while I unsheathe the sword behind them. •Then take a few hairs and wrap them in the folds 3 of your cloak; •and of these again take a few, and throw them on the fire and 4 burn them. From them will issue fire, and you are to say to the entire House of Israel, •"The Lord Yahweh says this: This is Jerusalem, which I have placed 5 in the middle of the nations, surrounded with foreign countries. •She is so 6 perverse that she has rebelled more against my observances than the nations, and more against my laws than the surrounding countries; for she has rejected my observances and refused to keep my laws.

Therefore, the Lord Yahweh says this: Since you are more rebellious 7 than the nations round you, since you do not keep my laws or respect my observances, and since you do not even respect the observances of the surrounding nations, •so then, the Lord Yahweh says this: I have now set myself against 8 you, I will inflict punishments upon you for all the nations to see. •On account 9 of all your filthy practices I will do things to you that I have never done before and that I will never do again. •Fathers among you will eat their 10 children, and children eat their fathers. I will inflict punishments on you and disperse what remains of you to the winds. •Therefore, as I live—it is the 11 Lord Yahweh who speaks—as sure as you have defiled my sanctuary with all your horrors and all your filthy practices, I too will reject pitilessly; I will not spare, either. •A third of your inhabitants shall die of plague or starve to death 12 inside you; a third shall fall by the sword, outside you; a third I will scatter to every wind, while I unsheathe the sword behind them. •My anger will be 13 satisfied; I mean to satisfy my fury against them and be avenged; they will know that I, Yahweh, have spoken in my jealousy, when I have exhausted my fury against them. •I mean to reduce you to a ruin, an object of contempt to sur- 14 rounding nations, in the eyes of all who pass by. •You will become an object of 15 contempt and shame, an example and a thing of horror, to all the surrounding nations, when I execute my judgements on you in anger and fury, with bitter punishments. I, Yahweh, have spoken. •Against you I mean to send the deadly 16 arrows of starvation—which will destroy you, since I shall send them to destroy you—and I will destroy your stock of bread. •Against you I mean to send famine 17 and wild animals, to rob you of your children; plague and bloodshed shall visit you. I will summon the sword against you. I, Yahweh, have spoken." '

Against the mountains of Israel

6 The word of Yahweh was addressed to me as follows, •'Son of man, turn 1/2 towards the mountains of Israel and prophesy against them. •Say, "Mountains 3 of Israel, hear the word of the Lord Yahweh. The Lord Yahweh says this to mountains and hills and ravines and valleys: Listen; I am going to summon the sword against you and destroy your high places. •Your altars will be wrecked, 4 and your incense burners smashed; your inhabitants are going to be cut to pieces and thrown down in front of your idols, •and their bones spread all round your 5 altars. •Throughout your territory the towns will be destroyed and the high 6 places wrecked, to the ruin and wrecking of your altars, the shattering and

abolition of your idols, the smashing of your incense burners and the utter
7 destruction of all your works. •Among you men will fall, and be cut to pieces;
and so you will learn that I am Yahweh.
8 But I shall spare some of you; they will escape the sword and be dispersed
9 by me among the nations. •Your survivors will remember me among the nations
where they have been deported. I shall have broken their wanton hearts for
having deserted me, and blinded their adulterous eyes for having fawned on
idols. They will loathe themselves for all the wrong they have caused by their filthy
10 practices, •and so they will learn that I am Yahweh; I have said, and I have
meant it, that I am going to inflict all these disasters on them.

The sins of Israel

11   The Lord Yahweh says this: Clap your hands, stamp your feet, and say:
Alas! for all the abominable sins of the House of Israel, which is about to
12 perish by sword, famine and plague. •Far off, they will die by plague; near at
hand they will fall by the sword; those who are spared and besieged will die of
13 hunger, since I mean to satisfy my fury against them. •You will know that I am
Yahweh when their corpses, cut to pieces, lie there among their idols, all round
their altars, on every high hill, on every mountain top, under every spreading tree,
under every leafy oak, in fact wherever they offer an appeasing fragrance to all
14 their idols. •I mean to stretch out my hand against them and reduce the
country to an empty wasteland from the desert to Riblah,[a] the length and
breadth of the country; and so they will learn that I am Yahweh." '

The end is near

$\begin{smallmatrix}1\\2\end{smallmatrix}$ **7** The word of Yahweh was addressed to me as follows, •'Son of man, say,
"The Lord Yahweh says this to the land of Israel: Finished! The end is
3 coming for the four quarters of the land. •Now all is over with you; I
mean to unleash my anger on you, and judge you as your conduct deserves and
4 force you to answer for all your filthy practices. •I mean to show you no pity,
I will not spare you; I am going to call you to account for your conduct and for
the filthy practices that you parade; and so you will learn that I am Yahweh.
5   The Lord Yahweh says this: Now disaster is going to follow on disaster.
$\begin{smallmatrix}6\\7\end{smallmatrix}$ The end is coming, the end is coming for you; it is coming now. •Now, it is
your turn, you who live in this country. The time has come, the day is near; no
8 joy now, only tumult, on the mountains. •Soon I am going to pour out my
fury on you and exhaust my anger at you; I will judge you as your conduct
9 deserves and call you to account for all your filthy practices. •I mean to show you
neither pity nor mercy, since I am going to call you to account for your conduct
and for the filthy practices which you parade; and so you will learn that I am
Yahweh, and that I strike.
10   Here is the day! It has come; your turn has come, the scourge is ready, pride
$\begin{smallmatrix}11\\12\end{smallmatrix}$ is at its peak. •Violence has risen to become the scourge of wickedness... •The
time has come and the day is near. Let neither buyer rejoice, nor seller regret,
13 for anger rages against all alike. •The seller will not recover what he has sold;
14 they will all carry on sinning and be none the stronger for it. •The trumpet will
sound, all will be ready; but no one will go into battle, since my anger rages
against all alike.

The sins of Israel

15   Outside, the sword; inside, plague and famine. Anyone who is found in
the countryside will die by the sword; anyone who is found in the city will
16 be devoured by famine and plague. •Their fugitives will run away and make
for the mountains; I shall slaughter them all like doves of the valleys, each

---

6 a. I.e., from the S. of Palestine to the most northerly point.

for his sin. •With limp hands and quaking knees, •they will put on sackcloth; ¹⁷₁₈
and shudder all over. All their faces will be red with shame and every head
will be shaved. •They will throw their silver down in the streets and their ¹⁹
gold will fill them with horror. Never again will they have enough to eat,
never again will they fill their bellies, since this has been the cause of their crimes.
They used to pride themselves on the beauty of their jewellery, out of which ²⁰
they made their loathsome images and idols. That is why I mean to make it an
object of horror to them. •I intend to hand it over to be the plunder of foreign- ²¹
ers and loot for local brigands, who will profane it. •I shall turn my face from ²²
them; my treasury will be profaned; barbarians will force their way in and
profane it.

Forge yourself a chain; for the country is filled with bloody murders, the ²³
city is full of violent crime. •I am going to summon the cruellest of the nations ²⁴
to seize their houses. I will break the pride of their grandees; their sanctuaries
will be profaned. •Anguish is on its way: they will look for peace and there ²⁵
will be none. •Disaster will follow on disaster, rumour on rumour; they will ²⁶
pester the prophet for a vision; the priest will be at a loss over the law and the
elders on how to advise. •The king will go into mourning, the prince be ²⁷
plunged in grief, the hands of the country people tremble. I mean to treat them
as their conduct deserves, and judge them as their own verdicts merit; and so
they will learn that I am Yahweh." '

A vision of the sins of Jerusalem

8 In the sixth year, on the fifth day of the sixth month,ᵃ I was sitting at home ¹
and the elders of Judah were sitting with me, when the hand of the Lord
Yahweh fell on me.

I looked and saw something that looked like a man. Downwards from what ²
seemed to be his loins he was fire; and upwards from his loins he seemed to shine
like polished bronze. •He stretched out what seemed to be a hand and took ³
me by the hair; and the spirit lifted me into the air and, in visions from God, took
me to Jerusalem, to the entrance of the inner north gate, where the idol of
Jealousy stands, provoking jealousy.ᵇ •There I saw the glory of the God of ⁴
Israel, as I had seen it in the valley. •He said, 'Son of man, raise your eyes to ⁵
the north'. I raised my eyes to the north, and there, to the north of the altar
gate, stood this statue of Jealousy at the entrance. •He said, 'Son of man, do ⁶
you see what they are doing? Do you see all the filth practised here by the House
of Israel, to drive me out of my sanctuary? You will see filthier practices yet.'

He next took me to the entrance to the court. I looked; there was a hole ⁷
in the wall. •He said, 'Son of man, break through the wall'. I broke through ⁸
the wall; there was a door. •He said, 'Go in and look at the filthy things they ⁹
are doing inside'. •I went in and looked: all sorts of images of snakes and repulsive ¹⁰
animals and all the idols of the House of Israel drawn on the wall all round.
Seventy elders of the House of Israel were standing in front of the idols, among ¹¹
them Jaazaniah son of Shaphan, each one, censer in hand; the fragrance
of incense was rising. •He said, 'Son of man, have you seen what the elders of ¹²
the House of Israel do in the dark, each in his painted room? They say, "Yahweh
cannot see us; Yahweh has abandoned the country". ' •He said, 'You will see ¹³
them at filthier practices still'.

He next took me to the entrance of the north gate of the Temple of Yahweh ¹⁴
where women were sitting, weeping for Tammuz.ᶜ •He said, 'Son of man, do you ¹⁵
see that? You will see even filthier things than that.'

He then led me to the inner court of the Temple of Yahweh. And there, ¹⁶
at the entrance to the sanctuary of Yahweh, between the porch and the altar,
there were about twenty-five men, with their backs to the sanctuary of Yahweh
and their faces turned to the east. They were bowing to the east, towards the sun.
He said to me, 'Son of man, do you see that? Is it not bad enough for the House ¹⁷

of Judah to do the filthy things that they are doing here? But they fill the country
with violence and provoke my anger further; look at them now putting that
18 branch to their nostrils. •My anger forces me to it; I will show neither pity
nor mercy. They may shout as loud as they like; I will not listen to them.'

The punishment

1 9 Then as I listened he shouted, 'Come here, you scourges of the city, and
2   bring your weapons of destruction'. •Immediately six men advanced from
the upper north gate, each holding a deadly weapon. In the middle of them was
a man in white, with a scribe's ink horn in his belt. They came in and halted
3 in front of the bronze altar. •The glory of the God of Israel rose off the cherubs
where it had been and went up to the threshold of the Temple. He called
4 the man in white with a scribe's ink horn in his belt •and said, 'Go all through
the city, all through Jerusalem, and mark a cross on the foreheads of all who
5 deplore and disapprove of all the filth practised in it'. •I heard him say to the
others, 'Follow him through the city, and strike. Show neither pity nor mercy;
6 old men, young men, virgins, children, women, kill and exterminate them all.
But do not touch anyone with a cross on his forehead. Begin at my sanctuary.'
7 So they began with the old men in front of the Temple. •He said to them, 'Defile
the Temple; fill the courts with corpses, and go'. They went out and hacked
their way through the city.

8   While they were hacking them down, I stayed behind; I fell face downwards
and exclaimed, 'Ah, Lord Yahweh, are you going to annihilate all that is left
9 of Israel as you turn your anger on Jerusalem?' •He said, 'The guilt of the House
of Israel and Judah is immense, boundless; the country is full of bloodshed, the
city overflows with wickedness, for they say, "Yahweh has abandoned the
10 country, Yahweh cannot see". •Right, then, I too will show no pity, I too will
11 not spare. I mean to call them to account for all their behaviour.' •The man
in white with the scribe's ink horn in his belt then came back and made his
report, 'I have carried out your orders'.

1 10 I looked, and I saw that above the vault over the cherubs' heads there
      was something that looked like a sapphire, and there showed above them
2 the semblance of a throne. •He then said to the man in white, 'Go under the
chariot, beneath the cherubs; take a handful of burning coal from between
the cherubs and scatter it over the city'. He went in as I watched.

3   The cherubs were on the right of the Temple as the man went in, and the
4 cloud filled the inner court. •The glory of Yahweh rose off the cherubs and
up to the threshold of the Temple; the Temple was filled with the cloud and
5 the court was filled with the brightness of the glory of Yahweh. •The noise of
the cherubs' wings could be heard even in the outer court, like the thunder of
God Almighty when he speaks.

6   When he ordered the man in white to take the fire from under the chariot,
7 between the cherubs, the man went and stopped by the wheel; •one cherub
stretched his hand towards the fire which was between the cherubs, took some
8 and put it into the hands of the man in white, who took it and went off. •I then
saw that the cherubs had what seemed to be a human hand under their wings.
9 I looked; there were four wheels at the side of the cherubs, one wheel at the side
10 of each cherub, and the wheels glittered as if made of chrysolite. •All four looked
11 alike, and seemed to be one inside the other. •They went forward four ways
and kept their course unswervingly, moving the way they faced and never swerving
12 off their course. •Their bodies, their backs, their hands, their wings, and the
13 wheels—the wheels of all four—were covered in eyes all over. •I heard that
14 the wheels were called 'galgal'. •Each cherub had four faces: the first face

8 a. September-October 592.   b. Perhaps the statue of Astarte (Ishtar) set up by Manasseh,
2 K 21:7, which would rouse the jealousy of Yahweh.   c. Adonis.

was the face of the cherub, the second face the face of a man, the third the face
of a lion, the fourth the face of an eagle. •The cherubs rose; this was the creature 15
I had seen by the river Chebar. •As the cherubs went forward, the wheels went 16
forward beside them; and the wheels did not swerve even when the cherubs
spread their wings to leave the ground. •When the former stopped, the latter 17
stopped; when the former rose, the latter rose with them, since the spirit of the
creature was in them.

The glory of Yahweh leaves the Temple

The glory of Yahweh came out from the Temple threshold and paused over 18
the cherubs. •The cherubs spread their wings and rose from the ground to leave, 19
and as I watched the wheels rose with them. They paused at the entrance to the
east gate of the Temple of Yahweh, and the glory of the God of Israel hovered
over them. •This was the creature that I had seen supporting the God of Israel 20
beside the river Chebar, and I was now certain that these were cherubs. •Each 21
had four faces and four wings and what seemed to be human hands under their
wings. •Their faces were just as I had seen them beside the river Chebar. Each 22
moved straight forward.

The sins of Jerusalem (continued)

11 The spirit lifted me up and carried me to the east gate of the Temple of 1
Yahweh, the gate that looks eastwards. There at the entrance to the gate
stood twenty-five men, among whom I saw Jaazaniah son of Azzur and Pelatiah
son of Benaiah, leaders of the people. •Yahweh said, 'Son of man, these are 2
the wicked schemers who are spreading their bad advice through this city. •They 3
say, "Shall we not soon be building houses? Here is the cooking pot and we are
the meat."ᵃ •Therefore prophesy against them, prophesy, son of man.' •The ⁴₅
spirit of Yahweh fell on me, and he said to me, 'Say, "Yahweh says this: I know
what you are saying, House of Israel, I know how insolent you are. •You have 6
filled this city with more and more corpses of murdered men, you have strewn
its streets with your victims. •And so, the Lord Yahweh says this: The corpses 7
you have thrown into it are the meat, and the city is the cooking pot; but I mean
to drive you out. •You are afraid of the sword and I will summon it against you— 8
it is the Lord Yahweh who speaks. •I shall drive you from the city and hand 9
you over to foreigners, and I shall carry out my sentence on you; •you will fall 10
by the sword on the soil of Israel; I shall execute justice on you; and so you will
learn that I am Yahweh. •This city will be no cooking pot for you, and you 11
will never be the meat inside; I am going to execute justice on you on the soil of
Israel; •and so you will learn that I am Yahweh, whose laws you have not obeyed 12
and whose observances you have not kept; instead, you have adopted the manners
of the nations round you." '

Now as I was prophesying, Pelatiah son of Benaiah dropped dead. I prostrated 13
myself and cried aloud, 'Ah, Lord Yahweh, are you going to wipe out all that
is left of Israel?'

The new covenant promised to the exiles

The word of Yahweh was then addressed to me as follows, •'Son of man, ¹⁴₁₅
your brothers, your kinsmen, the whole House of Israel, these are told by the
citizens of Jerusalem, "You have been sent away from Yahweh; it is to us that the
land was given as our domain". •Say therefore, "The Lord Yahweh says this: 16
Yes, I have sent them far away among the nations and I have dispersed them
to foreign countries; and for a while I have been a sanctuary for them in the
country to which they have gone". •Then say, "The Lord Yahweh says this: 17
I will gather you together from the peoples, I will bring you all back from the
countries where you have been scattered and I will give you the land of Israel.
They will come and will purge it of all the horrors and the filthy practices. •I will 18

19 give them a single heart and I will put a new spirit in them; •I will remove
20 the heart of stone from their bodies and give them a heart of flesh instead, •so
that they will keep my laws and respect my observances and put them into
21 practice. Then they shall be my people and I will be their God. •But those
whose hearts are set on their idols and their filthy practices I will call to account
for their conduct—it is the Lord Yahweh who speaks." '

The glory of Yahweh leaves Jerusalem

22 The cherubs then spread their wings and the wheels began to move with them,
23 while the glory of the God of Israel hovered over them. •And the glory of
Yahweh rose to leave the city and paused on the mountain to the east of the
city.
24 The spirit lifted me up in vision, in the spirit of God, and took me to
25 the Chaldaeans, away to the exiles, and so the vision I had seen faded; •and
then I told the exiles everything that Yahweh had shown me.

The mime of the emigrant

1 2 12 The word of Yahweh was addressed to me as follows, •'Son of man, you
are living with that set of rebels who have eyes and never see, ears
3 and never hear, for they are a set of rebels. •You, son of man, pack an
exile's bundle and emigrate by daylight when they can see you, emigrate from
where you are to somewhere else while they watch. Perhaps they will admit
4 then that they are a set of rebels. •You will pack your baggage like an exile's
bundle, by daylight, for them to see, and leave like an exile in the evening, making
5 sure that they are looking. •As they watch, make a hole in the wall, and go
6 out through it. •As they watch, you will shoulder your pack and go out into
the dark; you will cover your face so that you cannot see the country, since
I have made you a symbol for the House of Israel.'
7 I did as I had been told. I packed my baggage like an exile's bundle,
by daylight; and in the evening I made a hole through the wall with my hand.
I went out into the dark and shouldered my pack as they watched.
8 9 The next morning the word of Yahweh was addressed to me as follows, •'Son
of man, did not the House of Israel, did not that set of rebels, ask you what
10 you were doing? •Say, "The Lord Yahweh says this: This oracle is directed
against Jerusalem and the whole House of Israel wherever they are living".
11 Say, "I am a symbol for you; the thing I have done will be done to them; they
12 will go into exile, into banishment". •Their ruler will shoulder his pack in the
dark and go out through the wall; a hole will be made to let him out; he will
13 cover his face rather than see the country,[a] •I shall throw my net over him and
catch him in my mesh; I shall take him to Babylon, to the land of the Chaldaeans,
14 though he will not see it; and there he will die. •And all those who form his
court, his guards and all his troops, I shall scatter to all the winds and unsheathe
15 the sword behind them. •They will learn that I am Yahweh, when I scatter
16 them throughout the nations and disperse them in foreign countries. •However,
I intend to leave some of them unscathed by sword, famine and plague, to
describe all their filthy practices to the peoples among whom they will go, so
that these too may learn that I am Yahweh.'
17 18 The word of Yahweh was addressed to me as follows, •'Son of man, you are
to tremble as you eat your bread and to behave restlessly and anxiously as you
19 drink your water, •and you are to say to the people of the country, "The
Lord Yahweh says this to the citizens of Jerusalem scattered throughout
Israel: They are going to eat their bread in anxiety, and drink their water in

11 a. A proverb: 'we are as safe inside our walls as meat in a pot is safe from the fire'.
12 a. Perhaps a prophecy of two separate incidents in 2 K 25: the attempt of Zedekiah and his
army to escape, and the putting out of his eyes before he was led captive to Babylon.

fear, until the country and those who live in it are free of the violence of all its
inhabitants. •The inhabited towns are going to be destroyed and the country 20
will be reduced to desert; and so you will learn that I am Yahweh." '

Popular proverbs

The word of Yahweh was addressed to me as follows, •'Son of man, what ²¹₂₂
do you mean by this proverb common throughout the land of Israel: Days go
by and visions fade?

'Very well, tell them, "The Lord Yahweh says this: I will put an end to 23
this proverb; it shall never be heard in Israel again". Instead, tell them:

"The day is coming when every vision will come true." •From now on there 24
will be no empty vision, no deceitful prophecy in the House of Israel, •since 25
it is I, Yahweh, who will speak. What I say is said and will soon come true;
since what I pronounce I will fulfil in your own lifetime, you set of rebels—it
is the Lord Yahweh who speaks.'

The word of Yahweh was addressed to me as follows, •'Son of man, the ²⁶₂₇
House of Israel is saying, "The vision that this man sees concerns the distant
future; he is prophesying for times far ahead". •Very well, tell them, "The Lord 28
Yahweh says this: There will be no further delay in the fulfilling of any of my
words. What I say is said and will come true—it is the Lord Yahweh
who speaks." '

Against the false prophets

13 The word of Yahweh was addressed to me as follows, •'Son of man, ₂¹
prophesy against the prophets of Israel; prophesy, and say to those who
make up prophecies out of their own heads, "Hear the word of Yahweh. •The 3
Lord Yahweh says this: Woe to the foolish prophets who follow their own
spirit, without seeing anything! •Like jackals in a ruin, so are your prophets, 4
Israel.

You have never ventured into the breach; you have never bothered to 5
fortify the House of Israel, to hold fast in battle on the day of Yahweh. •They 6
have empty visions and give lying prophecies and say: It is Yahweh who speaks,
although Yahweh has not sent them; and they are still waiting for their words
to come true. •Can you deny that you have only empty visions, that you utter 7
only lying prophecies when you say: It is Yahweh who speaks, when I myself
have not spoken?

Very well, the Lord Yahweh says this: Because of your empty words and 8
lying visions, I have now set myself against you—it is the Lord Yahweh who
speaks. •I am going to stretch my hand over the prophets who have empty visions 9
and give lying predictions; they will not be admitted to the council of my people,
their names will not be entered in the Book of the House of Israel, they will not
set foot on the soil of Israel; and you will learn that I am the Lord Yahweh, •since 10
they have misled my people by saying: Peace! when there is no peace. Instead
of my people rebuilding the wall, these men come and slap on plaster. •Tell 11
these plasterers: It will rain hard, it will hail, it will blow a gale, •and down 12
will come the wall. Will not people ask: Where is the plaster you slapped on it?
Well then, the Lord Yahweh says this: I am going to unleash a stormy wind in 13
my anger, torrential rain in my wrath, hailstones in my destructive fury. •I mean 14
to shatter the wall you slapped with plaster, to throw it down and lay its foundations bare. It will fall and you will perish under it; and so you will learn that I
am Yahweh.

When I have exhausted my anger against the wall and those who plastered it, I 15
shall say to you: The wall is gone, and so are those who slapped it over with
plaster, •these prophets of Israel who prophesy about Jerusalem and have visions 16
of peace for her when there is no peace—it is the Lord Yahweh who speaks."

The false prophetesses

17 'And you, son of man, turn to the daughters of your people who make up
18 prophecies out of their own heads; prophesy against them. •Say, "The Lord
Yahweh says this: Trouble is coming to the women who sew frills round wrists,ª
who make veils for people of all sizes, the better to ensnare lives! You ensnare
19 the lives of the men of my people while looking after your own. •You dishonour
me in front of my people for a few handfuls of barley, a few bits of bread, killing
those who ought not to die and sparing those who ought not to live, lying to
my people who love to listen to lies.
20   Well then, the Lord Yahweh says this. We shall see about these frills you
use for snaring lives like birds. I intend to rip them off your arms, and free those
21 lives you try to snare like birds. •I am going to rip your veils to pieces and
rescue my people from you; they will no longer be fair game for you. And so
you will learn that I am Yahweh.
22   Since you distress with lies the heart of the upright man whom I would
never distress, and since you encourage the wicked man not to give up his wicked
23 ways and find life again, •very well, you will have no more empty visions, and
you will not make any more predictions. I mean to rescue my people from you,
and then you will learn that I am Yahweh." '

Against idolatry

1
2 **14** When some elders of Israel had come to my house and sat down with me,
3   the word of Yahweh was addressed to me as follows, •'Son of man, these
people have enshrined their own idols in their hearts, they cling to the cause
4 of their sins; am I going to let myself be consulted by them? •Well then, speak
to them; tell them this, "The Lord Yahweh says this: Every member of the
House of Israel who enshrines his own idols in his heart, or who, clinging to the
cause of his sins, comes looking for the prophet, will get his answer from me,
5 Yahweh, on account of his hundreds of idols"; •and in this way I hope to touch
the heart of the House of Israel who have deserted me in favour of a pack of idols.
6   'Say therefore to the House of Israel, "The Lord Yahweh says this: Come
7 back, renounce your idols and give up all your filthy practices; •for if any member
of the House of Israel—or even any foreigner living in Israel—deserts me to
enshrine his own idols in his heart, and, clinging to the cause of his sins, then
comes looking for the prophet to consult me, he will get his answer from me,
8 Yahweh. •I will turn against this man; I will make him an example and a
byword; I will cut him off from my people; and you will learn that I am Yahweh.
9 If the prophet is led astray and speaks, it is I, Yahweh, who have led that
prophet astray; I will stretch out my hand against him and will wipe him
10 out from my people Israel. •They will bear the weight of their faults, and the
fault of the prophet will be as grave as the fault of the man who consults him.
11 So the House of Israel will not desert me any more; it will not defile itself with
any more of these sins. They shall be my people, and I will be their God—it
is the Lord Yahweh who speaks." '

Individual responsibility

12
13   The word of Yahweh was addressed to me as follows, •'Son of man, if a
country were to sin against me by faithlessness, and if I were to stretch out my
hand against it and destroy its stock of bread and send famine to it to kill its
14 men and beasts, •and if in that country there were these three men, Noah, Danel
and Job,ª these men would have their lives spared because of their integrity
15 —it is the Lord Yahweh who speaks. •Were I to unleash wild animals on that
country to rob it of its children and reduce it to such a desert that no one would

13 a. Presumably a magical or idolatrous practice.
14 a. Danel, famous for his goodness and wisdom, is known to us from the Ras Shamra texts.

dare to cross it because of the animals, •and if these three men were in that 16
country, then, as I live—it is the Lord Yahweh who speaks—they would not be
able to save either son or daughter; they alone would be saved, and the country
would become a desert. •If I were to bring the sword into that country and 17
say: Let the sword pass through the country; I will strike down men and
beasts with it, •and if these three men were in that country, then, as I live—it 18
is the Lord Yahweh who speaks—they would not be able to save either son or
daughter; they alone would be saved. •If I were to send the plague into that 19
country and satisfy my anger with them by bloodshed, cutting off men and beasts,
if Noah and Danel and Job were in the country, as I live—it is the Lord Yahweh 20
who speaks—they would not be able to save either son or daughter, though
they would save their own lives because of their integrity.

'The Lord Yahweh says this: Now, if I do send my four dreadful scourges 21
against Jerusalem—sword, famine, wild animals and plague—to cut off its men
and beasts, •and if any survivors are left there to contrive the escape of 22
son and daughter, they will come for you to see their conduct and actions and
so be comforted in spite of the scourges I shall have brought on Jerusalem,
in spite of everything I shall have brought on her. •They will comfort you, when 23
you see their conduct and actions, and so you will learn that I have not done
all I have done against her for nothing—it is the Lord Yahweh who speaks.'

A parable of the vine

15 The word of Yahweh was addressed to me as follows: 1

'Son of man, how is the wood of the vine better   2
than wood from the branch of a forest tree?
Do people use its wood to carve it into something?   3
Do they make a peg out of it, and hang things on it?
There it is, thrown on the fire for fuel.   4
The fire burns off both ends;
the middle is charred; is it fit for carving now?
While it was intact, it was impossible to carve;   5
burned and charred, will it be now fit for carving?
Therefore, the Lord Yahweh says this: 6
As the wood of the vine among the forest trees,
which I have thrown on the fire for fuel,
so have I treated the citizens of Jerusalem.
I have turned my face against them.   7
They have escaped the fire, but the fire will devour them yet.
And you will learn that I am Yahweh, when I turn my face
against them.
I mean to reduce the country to desert, to punish their faithlessness to me   8
—it is the Lord Yahweh who speaks.'

An allegorical history of Israel

16 The word of Yahweh was addressed to me as follows, •'Son of man,   1
confront Jerusalem with her filthy crimes. •Say, "The Lord Yahweh   2 / 3
says this: By origin and birth you belong to the land of Canaan. Your father
was an Amorite and your mother a Hittite. •At birth, the very day you were 4
born, there was no one to cut your navel-string, or wash you in cleansing water,
or rub you with salt, or wrap you in napkins. •No one leaned kindly over you 5
to do anything like that for you. You were exposed in the open fields; you
were as unloved as that on the day you were born.

I saw you struggling in your blood as I was passing, and I said to you as 6
you lay in your blood: Live, •and grow like the grass of the fields. You developed, 7
you grew, you reached marriageable age. Your breasts and your hair both grew,
but you were quite naked. •Then I saw you as I was passing. Your time had come, 8

the time for love. I spread part of my cloak over you and covered your nakedness;
I bound myself by oath, I made a covenant with you—it is the Lord Yahweh
9 who speaks—and you became mine. •I bathed you in water, I washed the blood
10 off you, I anointed you with oil. •I gave you embroidered dresses, fine leather
11 shoes, a linen headband and a cloak of silk. •I loaded you with jewels, gave you
12 bracelets for your wrists and a necklace for your throat. •I gave you nose-ring
13 and earrings; I put a beautiful diadem on your head. •You were loaded with
gold and silver, and dressed in fine linen and embroidered silks. Your food was
the finest flour, honey and oil. You grew more and more beautiful; and you rose to
14 be queen. •The fame of your beauty spread through the nations, since it was
perfect, because I had clothed you with my own splendour—it is the Lord
Yahweh who speaks.

15 You have become infatuated with your own beauty; you have used your
fame to make yourself a prostitute; you have offered your services to all
16 comers... •You have taken your clothes to brighten your high places and there
17 you have played the whore... •You have taken my presents of gold and silver
18 jewellery and made yourself human images to use in your whorings. •You have
taken your embroidered clothes and put them on the images, and the oil and
19 incense which are rightly mine you have offered to them. •The bread I gave
you, the finest flour, oil and honey with which I used to feed you, you have
now offered to them as an appeasing fragrance.

20 You have even—it is the Lord Yahweh who speaks—•taken the sons and
daughters you bore me and sacrificed them as food to the images. Was it not
21 enough for you just to be a whore? •You have slaughtered my children and handed
22 them over as a burnt offering to them, •and in all your filthy practices and
your whorings you have never remembered your youth or the time when you
were quite naked and struggling in your own blood.

23 To crown your wickedness—trouble for you, it is the Lord Yahweh who
24 speaks—•you have built yourself a mound and made a high place at every cross-
25 roads. •At the beginning of every road you have built a high place to defile your
beauty there and to give your body to every comer; you have piled whoring on
26 whoring. •You have lain down for those big-membered neighbours, the Egyptians;
27 you have piled whoring on whoring to provoke me, •and now I have raised my
hand against you. I have rationed your food, I have handed you over to the
mercy of your enemies, the daughters of the Philistines, who are sick of your
28 filthy ways. •Still unsatisfied, you have prostituted yourself to the Assyrians; you
29 have played the whore and not been satisfied even then.ᵃ •You have piled whoring on whoring with Canaanite and Chaldaean, and even then not been satisfied.

30 How easily led you were—it is the Lord Yahweh who speaks—to behave
31 no better than a bold-faced whore! •When you built yourself a mound at the
beginning of every road and made a high place at every crossroads, you were
32 not, like the whore, out for money: •an adulteress welcomes strangers instead
33 of her husband; •a prostitute is paid. But you, in your whoring, have given your
presents away to all your lovers; you have offered them gifts to attract them
34 from everywhere. •In your whoring you have done the exact opposite from
other women; no one was running after you, so you went and paid them; they
did not pay you since your behaviour was so outrageous.

35
36 Well then, whore, hear the word of Yahweh. •The Lord Yahweh says this:
For having undressed and let yourself be seen naked while whoring with your
lovers and with your filthy idols, and for giving them your children's blood—
37 for all this, I am going to band together all the lovers who have pleasured you,
both those you liked and those you disliked, I am going to band them together
against you from all around; I will strip you in front of them, and let them see you

16 a. Especially in the reign of Manassch, Israel was unfaithful in adopting the foreign gods of her allies.

naked. •And I mean to punish you like women who commit adultery and murder; 38
I intend to hand you over to fury and jealousy; I will hand you over to them; they 39
will level your mound and demolish your high places; they will tear your clothes
off, take your jewels and leave you completely naked. •They will then whip 40
up the crowd against you; you will be stoned and run through with a sword;
they will set your houses on fire and execute justice on you with crowds of women 41
looking on; I will put an end to your whoring: no more paid lovers for you.
I will exhaust my fury against you. My jealousy will then leave you; I shall 42
be appeased and my anger will stop. •Since you have never remembered your 43
youth, since in all this you have done nothing but provoke me, I in my turn
intend to bring your conduct down on your own head—it is the Lord Yahweh
who speaks. Have you not been disgusting with all your filthy practices?

Now all the proverb-makers will make up a proverb about you: Like mother, 44
like daughter. •Yes; you are a true daughter of your mother, who hated her 45
husband and her children; a true sister of your sisters, who hated their husbands
and their children. Your mother was a Hittite and your father an Amorite.
Your elder sister is Samaria, who lives on your left with her daughters. Your 46
younger sister is Sodom, who lives on your right with her daughters. •You 47
have not failed to copy their behaviour; throughout your career you have
shown yourself more corrupt than they were. •As I live—it is the Lord Yahweh 48
who speaks—your sister Sodom and her daughters have not been as bad as you
and your daughters. •The crime of your sister Sodom was pride, gluttony, arro- 49
gance, complacency; such were the sins of Sodom and her daughters. They never
helped the poor and needy; •they were proud and engaged in filthy practices in 50
front of me; that is why I have swept them away as you have seen. •And yet 51
Samaria never committed half the crimes that you have.

You have done far filthier things than they did. By your filthy practices
you have made your sisters seem almost innocent, •and now you have 52
to bear the shame for all those faults of which you have cleared your sisters;
since the grossness of the sins for which you bear the guilt is more horrible
than theirs, they now appear more virtuous than you are. Be ashamed, then;
bear the shame of having put your sisters in the right.

I will restore them. I will restore Sodom and her daughters. I will restore 53
Samaria and her daughters; and, after that, I will restore you along with them,
that you may bear your shame and be ashamed of all you have done, and so 54
console them. •Your sister Sodom and her daughters will be restored to what 55
they were. Samaria and her daughters will be restored to what they were. You
and your daughters will be restored to what you were. •Did you not gloat 56
over your sister Sodom when you were still in your finery, •before you were 57
stripped naked? Now the daughters of Edom and all the women around are jeering
at you, and the daughters of the Philistines are treating you like something
beneath them, and so are all your neighbours. •You have brought it on yourself 58
by your brazenness and filth—it is the Lord Yahweh who speaks.

For the Lord Yahweh says this: I will treat you as you deserve, you who 59
have despised your oath even to the extent of breaking a covenant, •but I will 60
remember the covenant that I made with you when you were a girl, and I will
conclude a covenant with you that shall last for ever. •And you for your part 61
will remember your past behaviour and be covered with shame when I take
your elder and younger sisters and make them your daughters, although this
was not included in this covenant. •I am going to renew my covenant with you; 62
and you will learn that I am Yahweh, •and so remember and be covered with 63
shame, and in your confusion be reduced to silence, when I have pardoned you
for all that you have done—it is the Lord Yahweh who speaks."

The allegory of the eagle

17 ¹² The word of Yahweh was addressed to me as follows, •'Son of man, ask
³ them a riddle; propound a parable to the House of Israel. •Say, "The
Lord Yahweh says this:

> A large eagle,ᵃ with huge wings
> and a wide span,
> covered with speckled feathers,
> came to Lebanon.
> He took hold of the top of the cedar,
⁴
> plucked off the top branch,
> carried it off to the land of merchants,
> and set it down in a city of shopkeepers.
⁵
> Then he carried off a seedling vine,
> and planted it in fertile soil;
> by the side of a wide stream,
> as a border he set it.
⁶
> The seedling grew, and turned into a vine,
> not tall but well spread out;
> its branches grew up towards the eagle,
> its roots grew down.
> It turned into a vine;
> it sent out stems and put out sprays.
⁷
> There was another large eagle,
> with huge wings and thickly feathered.
> And now the vine twisted its roots toward him,
> stretched its branches towards him
> away from the bed where it was planted
> for him to water them.
⁸
> It was in a fertile field, by the side of a wide stream,
> that the vine had been planted,
> to grow shoots, bear fruit
> and become a noble vine."
⁹
Say, "The Lord Yahweh says this:
> Will this vine thrive?
> Will not the eagle break its roots,
> and snap up the fruit,
> so that all the new leaves will wither when they shoot?
> It will take no effort and no strong nation
> to pull it up by the roots.
¹⁰
> It is planted there; will it thrive?
> Will it not shrivel when the east wind blows?
> It will wither on the soil where it was growing." '

¹¹ The word of Yahweh was addressed to me as follows:
¹² 'Say to that set of rebels, "Do you not know what this means?" Say this,
"Listen; the king of Babylon came to Jerusalem; he carried away the king and the
¹³ princes, and took them to where he lives in Babylon. •He took a member of the
royal family and made a treaty with him, forcing him to swear loyalty, after having
¹⁴ already deported the chief men of the land, •so that the kingdom would remain
¹⁵ modest and without ambition and so maintain his treaty faithfully. •But the
prince rebelled and sent envoys to Egypt, asking for horses and a large number
of troops. Is he going to thrive? Will a man who has done this go unpunished?
¹⁶ Can he break a treaty and go unpunished? •As I live, I swear—it is the Lord
Yahweh who speaks: In Babylon, in the country of the king who put him on

17 a. Nebuchadnezzar; see interpretation in vv.12-18.

the throne, whose oath he has ignored, whose treaty he has broken, there
will he die. •Despite the pharaoh's great army and hordes of men, he will not 17
be able to save him by fighting, however many earthworks are raised, however
many trenches dug to the loss of many lives. •He has ignored the oath and broken 18
the treaty by which he was bound. He has done all this and shall not go
unpunished.

"And so, the Lord Yahweh says this: As I live, I swear: my oath which 19
he has ignored, my treaty which he has broken, I will make them both recoil
on his own head. •I mean to throw my net over him and catch him in my mesh; 20
I mean to take him to Babylon and punish him there for breaking his oath to me.
The pick of his army will fall by the sword, and the survivors be scattered to 21
all the winds. And so you will learn that I, Yahweh, have spoken.

The Lord Yahweh says this: 22

> From the top of the cedar,
> from the highest branch I will take a shoot
> and plant it myself on a very high mountain.
> I will plant it on the high mountain of Israel.   23
> It will sprout branches and bear fruit,
> and become a noble cedar.
> Every kind of bird will live beneath it,
> every winged creature rest in the shade of its branches.
> And every tree of the field will learn that I, Yahweh, am the one   24
> who stunts tall trees and makes the low ones grow,
> who withers green trees and makes the withered green.
> I, Yahweh, have spoken, and I will do it." '

Individual responsibility

18 The word of Yahweh was addressed to me as follows, •'Why do you $\frac{1}{2}$
keep repeating this proverb in the land of Israel:

> The fathers have eaten unripe grapes;
> and the children's teeth are set on edge?

'As I live—it is the Lord Yahweh who speaks—there will no longer be any 3
reason to repeat this proverb in Israel. •See now: all life belongs to me; the 4
father's life and the son's life, both alike belong to me. The man who has sinned,
he is the one who shall die.

'The upright man is law-abiding and honest; •he does not eat on the $\frac{5}{6}$
mountains[a] or raise his eyes to the idols of the House of Israel, does not seduce
his neighbour's wife or sleep with a woman during her periods. •He oppresses 7
no one, returns pledges, never steals, gives his own bread to the hungry, his clothes
to the naked. •He never charges usury on loans, takes no interest, abstains from 8
evil, gives honest judgement between man and man, •keeps my laws and sincerely 9
respects my observances—such a man is truly upright. It is Yahweh who speaks.

'But if anyone has a son prone to violence and bloodshed, who commits 10
one of these misdeeds—•even though the father never has—a son who dares 11
to eat on the mountains and to seduce his neighbour's wife, •who oppresses the 12
poor and needy, steals, fails to return pledges, raises his eyes to idols, engages in
filthy practices, •charges usury on loans and takes interest, then this son shall 13
certainly not live; having committed all these appalling crimes he will have to
die, and his blood be on his own head.

'But if he in turn has a son who, in spite of seeing all the sins that his father 14
has committed, does not imitate him, •does not eat on the mountains or raise 15
his eyes to the idols of the House of Israel, does not seduce his neighbour's
wife, •oppresses no one, takes no pledges, never steals, gives his own bread 16
to the hungry, clothes to the naked, •abstains from evil, does not charge usury 17

or take interest, respects my observances and keeps my laws, he will not die
18 for his father's sins, this son shall certainly live. •Because the father was violent,
robbed others and never did good among my people, be sure he shall die for
19 his sins. •But you object, "Why does the son not suffer for the sins of his father?"
The son, however, has been law-abiding and honest, has kept all my laws and
20 followed them, and so he shall certainly live. •The man who has sinned is the
one who must die; a son is not to suffer for the sins of his father, nor a father
for the sins of his son. To the upright man his integrity will be credited, to the
wicked his wickedness.

21   'But if the wicked man renounces all the sins he has committed, respects my
22 laws and is law-abiding and honest, he will certainly live; he will not die. •All
the sins he committed will be forgotten from then on; he shall live because of the
23 integrity he has practised. •What! Am I likely to take pleasure in the death of
a wicked man—it is the Lord Yahweh who speaks—and not prefer to see him
renounce his wickedness and live?

24   'But if the upright man renounces his integrity, commits sin, copies the
wicked man and practises every kind of filth, is he to live? All the integrity
he has practised shall be forgotten from then on; but this is because he himself
25 has broken faith and committed sin, and for this he shall die. •But you object,
"What the Lord does is unjust". Listen, you House of Israel: is what I do unjust?
26 Is it not what you do that is unjust? •When the upright man renounces his integrity
to commit sin and dies because of this, he dies because of the evil that he himself
27 has committed. •When the sinner renounces sin to become law-abiding and
28 honest, he deserves to live. •He has chosen to renounce all his previous sins;
29 he shall certainly live; he shall not die. •And yet the House of Israel objects,
"What the Lord does is unjust". Is what I do unjust, you House of Israel? Is it
30 not what you do that is unjust? •House of Israel, in future I mean to judge
each of you by what he does—it is the Lord Yahweh who speaks. Repent,
31 renounce all your sins, avoid all occasions of sin! •Shake off all the sins you have
committed against me, and make yourselves a new heart and a new spirit!
32 Why are you so anxious to die, House of Israel? •I take no pleasure in the death
of anyone—it is the Lord Yahweh who speaks. Repent and live!

A lamentation over the rulers of Israel

1 **19** 'As for you, raise a dirge for the princes of Israel. •Say:
2

"What was your mother? A lioness
surrounded by lions;
lying among the cubs
she nursed her whelps.

3   She reared one of her whelps
and it grew into a young lion;
he learnt to tear his prey;
he became a man-eater.

4   The nations combined against him;
he was caught in their pit;
they dragged him off with hooks
to the land of Egypt.[a]

5   Her expectation thwarted,
her hope dashed,
she took another of her whelps
and made a young lion of him.

6   He grew to prowl with other lions,
and grew into a young lion;

---

18 a. In sacrificial meals on the 'high places'.
19 a. King Jehoahaz, deposed and deported to Egypt in 609.

he learned to tear his prey;
he became a man-eater.
He stormed their palaces, 7
and sacked their cities;
the country and its inhabitants were alarmed
by the sound of his roars.
The nations marched out against him 8
from the surrounding provinces;
they spread their net for him;
he was caught in their pit.
They caged him with hooks 9
(they took him to the king of Babylon);
they took him into a fortress,
so that his voice could never again be heard
on the mountains of Israel. *b*

"Your mother was like a vine 10
planted beside the water,
fruitful and leafy,
because the water flowed so full.
It put out strong branches 11
that turned to royal sceptres;
they reached up, reached so high
they touched the clouds;
men admired them for their height
and their thick foliage.
But it was rooted up 12
and thrown on the ground;
the east wind dried up its fruit;
it was broken up;
its strong branch withered away;
fire consumed it all.
Now it has been transplanted into the desert, 13
the waterless country of drought;
fire has come out of its stem, 14
consumed its branches and fruit.
No more strong branch for her,
no more kingly sceptre." '

This is a dirge; it was used as such.

An account of Israel's infidelities

20 In the seventh year, on the tenth day of the fifth month,*a* some of the 1
elders of Israel came to consult Yahweh and sat down in front of me.
The word of Yahweh was addressed to me as follows, •'Son of man, speak to ²⁄₃
the elders of Israel. Say, "The Lord Yahweh says this: Have you come to
consult me?" As I live, I am not going to let myself be consulted by them—it is the
Lord Yahweh who speaks. • Are you ready to judge them? Are you ready to judge 4
them, son of man? Confront them with the filthy practices of their fathers.
Say, "The Lord Yahweh says this: On the day when I chose Israel, when I 5
raised my hand over the descendants of the House of Jacob, I told them then
in the land of Egypt; I raised my hand over them and said: I am Yahweh your
God. •On that day I raised my hand over them and swore to lead them out 6
of the land of Egypt and bring them into the land I had chosen for them, a land
where milk and honey flow, and the noblest of them all. •I said: Each one of 7
you must reject those horrors that attract you; do not pollute yourselves with

8 the idols of Egypt; I am Yahweh, your God. •But they rebelled against me and
would not listen to me. Not one of them rejected those horrors that attracted
them; they did not give up the idols of Egypt. I resolved to discharge my anger
9 on them and exhaust my fury against them in Egypt. •But respect for my
own name kept me from allowing it to be profaned in the opinion of the nations
among whom they were living, for I had given them my word that in the sight
10 of those nations I would lead my people out of the land of Egypt. •So I led
11 them out of Egypt and into the wilderness. •I gave them my laws and taught
12 them my observances, which must be practised by all who want to live. •I
even gave them my sabbaths to be a sign between me and them, so that they
13 might learn that I, Yahweh, am the one who sanctifies them. •The House of
Israel, however, rebelled against me in the wilderness; they refused to keep my
laws, they scorned my observances, which must be practised by all who wish
to live, and they profaned my sabbaths. Then I resolved to discharge my
14 anger on them in the wilderness and to destroy them. •But respect for my
own name kept me from allowing it to be profaned in the opinion of the nations,
15 in whose sight I had brought them out. •However, I did raise my hand over
them in the wilderness and swear that I would not lead them to the land which
I had given them, a land where milk and honey flow, the noblest of them all,
16 since they had scorned my observances, had refused to keep my laws and had
17 profaned my sabbaths, their hearts being so attached to idols. •In spite of this,
I took pity on them; I refrained from destroying them, and I did not kill them
all in the wilderness.

18 I said to their children in the wilderness: Do not live by your ancestors'
standards, do not practise the observances they practised, do not defile
19 yourselves with their idols. •I am Yahweh your God. Keep my laws, respect my
20 observances and practise them. •Keep my sabbaths holy; let them be a sign
between me and you, so that men may learn that I am Yahweh your God.
21 The sons, however, rebelled against me; they refused to keep my laws, they did
not respect or practise my observances, which must be practised by all who want
to live; they profaned my sabbaths. I then resolved to discharge my anger on
22 them and exhaust my fury against them in the wilderness. •But I restrained my
hand; respect for my own name kept me from allowing it to be profaned in the
23 opinion of the nations, under whose eyes I had brought them out. •Once again,
however, I raised my hand over them in the wilderness, swearing to scatter
24 them throughout the nations and disperse them in foreign countries, •because
they had not followed my observances but had rejected my laws and profaned
my sabbaths, and because they had kept their eyes fastened on their ancestors'
25 idols. •I even gave them laws that were not good and observances by which they
26 could never live; •and I polluted them with their own offerings, making them
sacrifice all their first-born; which was to punish them, so that they would learn
that I am Yahweh."

27   'For this reason, son of man, speak to the House of Israel. Say to them,
"The Lord Yahweh says this: Here is another way by which your ancestors
28 outraged me, behaving treacherously to me, •even though I led them into the land
which I had solemnly sworn to give them. There they saw all sorts of high hills,
all kinds of leafy trees, and there they performed their sacrifices and made
offerings that provoked my anger; there they laid their appeasing fragrance
29 and poured their libations. •I said to them: What is the name of the high
place where you go? And they gave, and still give it, the name of Bamah."[b]
30 Very well, say to the House of Israel, "The Lord Yahweh says this: Since you
insist on defiling yourselves by behaving like your fathers, by whoring with their
31 idols, •by offering your gifts and by burning your children as sacrifices, polluting

b. Jehoiachin, taken captive to Babylon in 597.
20 a. July-August 591.   b. There is a pun in the Hebr. words for 'high place' and 'where you go'.

yourselves with your pack of idols to this very day, how can I let you consult
me, House of Israel? As I live—it is the Lord Yahweh who speaks—I am not
going to let myself be consulted by you. •And that dream ever haunting your 32
mind will never come true, when you say: We shall be like the nations, like foreign
tribes worshipping wood and stone. •As I live I swear it—it is the Lord Yahweh 33
who speaks—I am the one who will reign over you, with a strong hand and
outstretched arm, through the discharge of my anger. •With a strong hand 34
and outstretched arm, through the discharge of my anger, I will bring you
out from the peoples and gather you together from foreign countries among
which you have been scattered. •I will lead you into the Desert of the Nations^c 35
and condemn you to your face. •As I judged your fathers in the desert of the land 36
of Egypt, so will I judge you—it is the Lord Yahweh who speaks. •I mean to 37
make you pass under my crook^d and I will bring a few of you back; •I will sort 38
out the rebels who have rebelled against me. I intend to bring them out of the
country where they are staying, but they shall not enter the land of Israel, and you
will learn that I am Yahweh. •House of Israel, the Lord Yahweh says this: 39
Go on, all of you, worship your idols, but I swear that you will hear me in the
end. You will stop profaning my Holy Name with your offerings and your idols.
For on my holy mountain, on the high mountain of Israel—it is the Lord Yahweh 40
who speaks—is where the whole House of Israel, resettled in the country, will
worship me. There I will welcome you, and there expect your presents, your
choicest gifts and all your holy offerings. •I will welcome you like an appeasing 41
fragrance when I bring you out from among the peoples; I mean to gather you
together from the foreign countries in which you have been scattered; through
you I intend to display my holiness for all the nations to see; •and you will learn 42
that I am Yahweh, when I bring you back to the soil of Israel, to the land I
solemnly swore to give to your fathers. •There you will remember your past 43
behaviour and all the misdeeds by which you have defiled yourselves, and you
will loathe yourselves for all the sins that you have committed. •Then you will 44
learn that I am Yahweh, when I treat you as respect for my own name requires,
and not as your wicked behaviour and corrupt actions deserve, House of Israel.
It is the Lord Yahweh who speaks." '

The sword of Yahweh

21 The word of Yahweh was addressed to me as follows, •'Son of man, turn ^1,2^_45,46_
to the right; utter your word towards the south, prophesy against the
forest land of the Negeb. •Say to the forest of the Negeb, "Hear the word of ^3^_47_
Yahweh. The Lord Yahweh says this: Listen; I am about to kindle a fire in
you that will burn up every green tree as well as every dry one; it will be an
unquenchable blaze and every face will be scorched by it from the Negeb to
the North. •All mankind will see that it was I, Yahweh, who kindled it, and ^4^_48_
it will not be put out." ' •I said, 'Lord Yahweh, they say of me, "What a story- ^5^_49_
teller this man is!" ' •The word of Yahweh was addressed to me as follows, ^6^_21:1_
'Son of man, turn towards Jerusalem, curse their sanctuary and prophesy ^7^_2_
against the land of Israel. •Say to the land of Israel, "Yahweh says this: Now ^8^_3_
I set myself against you; I am about to unsheathe my sword and to kill both upright
man and sinner. •My sword will leave its sheath to kill upright and sinful ^9^_4_
alike and turn against all mankind from the Negeb to the North. •All mankind is ^10^_5_
going to learn that I, Yahweh, am the one who has drawn the sword from its
sheath; it will not go back again."

'Son of man, groan as though your heart were breaking. Bitterly utter your ^11^_6_
groans where they can see you. •And if they say, "Why these groans?" reply, ^12^_7_
"The news has made all hearts sink, has numbed hands, troubled spirits, caused
knees to tremble. Now it has come, it is here; it is the Lord Yahweh
who speaks." '

The word of Yahweh was addressed to me as follows, •'Son of man, prophesy. ^13,14^_8,9_
Say, "The Lord says this". Say:

> "The sword, the sword
> sharpened and polished!

¹⁵
¹⁰
> Sharpened for slaughter,
> polished to flash like lightning...

¹⁶
¹¹
> polished only to be wielded,
> sharpened and polished to fit the slaughterer's hand!

¹⁷
¹²
> Yes, shout and howl, son of man;
> it is meant for my people,
> for all the princes of Israel, doomed like my people to the sword.

¹⁸
¹³
> So beat your breast; •this is no first attempt,
> and what would happen, were there no haughty sceptre?
> —it is the Lord Yahweh who speaks.

¹⁹
¹⁴
> Son of man, prophesy and clap your hands.
> Let the sword be twice, three times, as cruel,
> the butcher's sword,
> the great sword of slaughter, menacing all around.

²⁰
¹⁵
> To make hearts sink and to increase the number of victims
> I have posted a sword at every gate
> to flash like lightning, polished for havoc.

²¹
¹⁶
> Behind! To the right! To the left! In front!

²²
¹⁷
> And I too will clap my hands;
> I will exhaust my wrath.
> I, Yahweh, have spoken." '

The king of Babylon at the crossroads

^{23,24}
^{18,19}
The word of Yahweh was addressed to me as follows, •'Son of man, mark out two roads for the sword of the king of Babylon to come along, making both of them begin from the same country. Put up a signpost where they begin, ²⁵₂₀ showing the way to a city, •showing the sword the way to Rabbah of the ²⁶₂₁ Ammonites, and the way to Judah, to the fortress of Jerusalem. •For the king of Babylon has halted at the fork where these two roads diverge, to take the omens. He has shaken the arrows, questioned the teraphim, inspected the liver. ²⁷₂₂ Into his right hand the lot for Jerusalem falls; there he must set up battering-rams, give the word for slaughter, raise the war cry, level battering-rams against ²⁸₂₃ the gates, cast up earthworks, build entrenchments. •The citizens believe that these omens are idle, whatever oaths have been sworn. But he is evidence of ²⁹₂₄ their crimes, and these will bring about their capture. •And so, thus says the Lord Yahweh. Since you give evidence of your crimes by parading your sins and flaunting your wickedness in everything you do, and since this evidence ³⁰₂₅ is now produced against you, you will be punished. •As for you, prince of Israel, ³¹₂₆ vile criminal on the last of whose crimes the day is about to dawn, •the Lord Yahweh says this: They will take away your turban and remove your crown; ³²₂₇ everything will be changed; the low will be high and the high brought low. •To ruin, and to ruin on ruin, am I going to bring it, to such ruin as was never known before this man came who is appointed to inflict the punishment which I am determined to impose on it.

The punishment of Ammon

³³
₂₈
'Son of man, prophesy and say, "The Lord Yahweh says this: To the Ammonites with their insults, say: The sword, the sword is drawn for slaughter, ³⁴₂₉ polished to destroy, to flash like lightning—•while you have empty visions and consult lying omens—to slaughter the vile criminals on the last of whose ³⁵₃₀ crimes the day is about to dawn. •Put it back in the scabbard. In the place where you were created, in the country where you were born, there I will judge ³⁶₃₁ you; •I am going to discharge my anger on you, blow the flames of my fury

c. The Syrian desert.   d. To be counted.

against you and hand you over to barbarous men whose trade is destruction. •You $^{37}_{32}$ will be fuel to the fire, your blood will flow through the country, you will leave no memory behind you; for I, Yahweh, have spoken." '

The crimes of Jerusalem

22 The word of Yahweh was addressed to me as follows, •'Son of man, are $^1_2$ you prepared to judge? Are you prepared to judge the murderous city? Confront her with all her filthy crimes! •Say, "The Lord Yahweh says this: 3 City shedding blood inside yourself to bring your hour closer, setting up idols on your soil to defile yourself, •you have incurred guilt by the blood you have 4 shed, you have defiled yourself with the idols you have made, you have brought your hour closer, you have come to the end of your time. And so I have made you an object of scorn to the nations and a laughing-stock to every country. Near and far, they will scoff at you, the turbulent city with a tarnished name: 5 where all the princes of Israel live, each one busy shedding blood, and a law 6 to himself; •where people despise their fathers and mothers; where they ill-treat 7 the settler; where they oppress the widow and the orphan; •where you have 8 no reverence for my sanctuaries and profane my sabbaths; •where informers 9 incite to bloodshed; where there are people who eat on the mountains and couple promiscuously; •where men uncover their father's nakedness; where 10 they force women in their unclean condition; •where one man engages in filthy 11 practices with his neighbour's wife, another defiles himself with his daughter-in-law, another violates his sister, his own father's daughter; •where people take 12 bribes for shedding blood; you charge usury and interest, you rob your neighbour by extortion, you forget all about me—it is the Lord Yahweh who speaks.

Now I will clap my hands at your acts of banditry and the blood that 13 flows in you. •Will your heart be able to resist, will your hands be strong on the 14 day I call you to account? I, Yahweh, have spoken, and I will do it.

I mean to disperse you throughout the nations, to scatter you in foreign 15 countries, and to take your foulness from you. •I shall be dishonoured by 16 you in the opinion of the nations; and so you will learn that I am Yahweh." '

The word of Yahweh was addressed to me as follows, •'Son of man, the $^{17}_{18}$ House of Israel, as I see it, is base metal; they are all copper, tin, iron, lead, in the melting-pot; they are base metal. •And so, the Lord Yahweh says this: 19 Since you are all base metal, I will collect you inside Jerusalem. •As silver, 20 copper, iron, lead and tin are thrown into the melting-pot together, and the fire is stoked underneath to melt it all down, so I will collect you in my furious anger and melt you down; •I will collect you and stoke the fire of my fury 21 for you, and melt you down inside the city. •As silver is melted in the melting-pot, 22 so you will be melted down inside the city; and thus you will learn that I, Yahweh, am the one who has discharged my anger on you.'

The word of Yahweh was addressed to me as follows, •'Son of man, say $^{23}_{24}$ to her, "You are a land that has not received rain or shower on the day of anger, and whose princes are like a roaring lion tearing its prey inside her. They have 25 eaten the people, seized wealth and jewels and widowed many inside her. •Her 26 priests have violated my Law and desecrated my sanctuaries; they have drawn no distinction between sacred and profane, they have not taught people the difference between clean and unclean; they have turned their eyes away from my sabbaths and I have been dishonoured by them. •Her leaders in the city are 27 like wolves tearing their prey, shedding blood and killing people to steal their possessions. •Her prophets have whitewashed these crimes with their empty 28 visions and lying prophecies. They have said: Yahweh says this; although Yahweh has not spoken. •The people of the country have taken to extortion 29 and banditry; they have oppressed the poor and needy and ill-treated the settler for no reason. •I have been looking for someone among them to build a wall 30 and man the breach in front of me, to defend the country and prevent me from

31 destroying it; but I have not found anyone. •Hence I have discharged my anger on them; I have destroyed them in the fire of my fury. I have made their conduct recoil on their own heads—it is the Lord Yahweh who speaks." '

An allegorical history of Jerusalem and Samaria

1 23 The word of Yahweh was addressed to me as follows, •'Son of man,
2
3 there were once two women, daughters of the same mother. •They became prostitutes in Egypt, when they were girls. There their nipples were handled,
4 there their virgin breasts were first fondled. •Their names were: Oholah the elder, Oholibah her sister. They belonged to me and bore sons and daughters.
5 As regards their names, Samaria is Oholah, Jerusalem Oholibah. •Now Oholah played the whore, although she belonged to me; she lusted for her lovers, her
6 neighbours the Assyrians, •dressed in purple, governors and nobles, all of them
7 young and desirable, and skilful horsemen. •She granted them her favours—they were all the flower of the Assyrians—and she defiled herself with all the
8 idols of all those she lusted for. •She did not renounce the whoring begun in Egypt, where men had slept with her from her girlhood, fondling her virgin breast, debauching her.

9 'And that is why I have handed her over to her lovers, to those Assyrians for
10 whom she lusted. •They uncovered her nakedness, they seized her sons and daughters and put her to the sword. She became notorious among women for the justice done on her.

11 'Though her sister Oholibah saw all this, her own lust and whorings were
12 even more shameful than her sister's. •She lusted for her neighbours the Assyrians, governor and nobles, dressed in sumptuous clothes, skilful horsemen, all young
13 and desirable. •I saw that she was unchaste, that both sisters were as bad as
14 each other. •She began whoring worse than ever; no sooner had she seen wall-
15 carvings of men, paintings of Chaldaeans coloured vermilion, •men with sashes round their waists and elaborate turbans on their heads, all so imperious of
16 bearing, portraits of Babylonians from Chaldaea, •than she fell in love with them
17 at first sight and sent messengers to them in Chaldaea. •The Babylonians came to her, shared her love-bed and defiled her with their debauchery. Once defiled
18 she lost interest in them. •She flaunted her whoring, she stripped naked; then
19 I turned away from her as I had turned away from her sister. •She began whoring worse than ever, remembering her girlhood, when she had played the whore
20 in the land of Egypt, •when she had been infatuated by profligates big-membered as donkeys, ejaculating as violently as stallions.

21 'You were hankering for the debauchery of your girlhood, when they used to
22 handle your nipples in Egypt and fondle your young breasts. •And so, Oholibah, the Lord Yahweh says this: I intend to call up against you those of your lovers in whom you have lost interest; I will bring them against you from everywhere,
23 the Babylonians and all the Chaldaeans, the men of Pekod and Shoa and Koa,*a* and all the Assyrians with them, young and desirable, all governors and nobles,
24 all famous officers and horsemen. •They will advance on you from the North, with chariots and wagons, at the head of a horde of peoples. From every side they will arm against you with shield, buckler and helmet. I have told them to
25 pass sentence on you; they will pass sentence on you as they think fit. •I shall direct my jealousy against you; they will treat you with fury; they will cut off your nose and ears, and what is left of your family will fall by the sword; they will seize your sons and daughters, and what is left of you will be burnt.
26
27 They will strip off your garments and rob you of your jewels. •I mean to put an end to your debauchery and to the whorings you began in Egypt; you will not look
28 to the Egyptians any more, you will never think of them again. •For the Lord Yahweh says this: I now hand you over to those you hate, to those in whom you
29 have lost interest. •They will treat you with hatred, they will rob you of the

23 a. Peoples from the E. of Babylonia.

fruit of your labours and leave you completely naked. And thus your shameful
whoring will be exposed. Your debauchery and your whorings •are the cause 30
of these afflictions, since by playing the whore with the nations you have defiled
yourself with their idols. •As you have copied your sister's behaviour, I will 31
put her cup in your hand. •The Lord Yahweh says this: 32

> You will drink your sister's cup,
> a cup that is wide and deep,
> leading to laughter and mockery,
> so ample the draught it holds.
> You will be filled with drunkenness and sorrow.   33
> Cup of affliction and devastation,
> the cup of your sister Samaria,
> you will drink it, you will drain it;   34
> then it will be shattered to pieces
> and lacerate your breast.

I have spoken—it is the Lord Yahweh who speaks.

'And so, the Lord Yahweh says this: Since you have forgotten me 35
and have turned your back on me, you too will have to bear the weight of
your debauchery and whorings.' •And Yahweh said to me, 'Son of man, are 36
you willing to judge Oholah and Oholibah and charge them with their filthy
crimes? •They have been adulteresses, their hands are dripping with blood, 37
they have committed adultery with their idols. As for the children they had
borne me, they have made them pass through the fire to be consumed. •And 38
here is something else they have done to me: they have defiled my sanctuary
the same day and have profaned my sabbaths. •The same day as sacrificing their 39
children to their idols, they have been to my sanctuary and profaned it. Yes,
this is what they have done in my own house.

'Worse still, these men summoned from distant countries, invited by 40
messenger, arrived; you bathed and painted your eyes, put on your jewels •and 41
sat on a sumptuous bed, by which stood a table on which you had put my incense
and my oil. •The revelry of a carefree company re-echoed because of the 42
crowd of men brought in from the desert; they put bracelets on the women's
arms and magnificent crowns on their heads. •I thought: The prostitutes are 43
at work in the house of a woman worn out with adulteries. And she is still playing
the whore too, •and men keep visiting her just like a prostitute, just as they 44
went to those profligate women Oholah and Oholibah. •But upright men will 45
judge them as adulteresses and murderesses are judged, since they are adulteresses
and their hands are dripping with blood.

'The Lord Yahweh says this: Summon an assembly to deal with them, and 46
hand them over to terror and pillage; •let the assembly stone them and hack 47
them to death with the sword; let their sons and daughters be slaughtered and
their houses be set on fire. •I mean to purge the land of debauchery; all the women 48
will thus be warned, and ape your debauchery no more. •Your debauchery will 49
recoil on your own heads, and you will bear the weight of your idolatrous sins;
and so you will learn that I am the Lord Yahweh.'

A prophecy of the siege of Jerusalem

24 In the ninth year, on the tenth day of the tenth month,ᵃ the word of 1
Yahweh was addressed to me as follows, •'Son of man, write down today's 2
date, since this is the very day the king of Babylon has laid siege to Jerusalem. •So 3
pronounce a parable for this set of rebels. Say, "The Lord Yahweh says
this:

> Put the pot on the fire;
> put it on; pour water into it.
> Put cuts of meat in too,   4

> the best cuts, leg and shoulder.
> Fill it with the best bones.
5 Take the best of the flock.
> Then heap wood underneath;
> make the pot boil and bubble
> until even the bones are cooked.

6 For the Lord Yahweh says this:

> Trouble for the bloodstained city,
> that rusty cooking-pot
> whose rust can never be scoured away!
> Empty it scrap by scrap, drawing no lots.
7 For her blood is in her;
> she has put it on the naked rock;
> she has not shed it on the ground to hide it in dust.
8 To make my anger overflow, to take revenge,
> I have put her blood on the naked rock, unhidden.

9 So, the Lord Yahweh says this:

> Trouble for the bloodstained city!
> I too plan to build a great fire.
10 Heap on the wood, light it,
> cook the meat, prepare the spices,
> let the bones burn.
11 Set the pot empty to heat on the coals;
> let the bronze glow red-hot,
> the filth inside melt away,
> the rust inside be consumed.

12
13 But all that rust will not disappear in the flames. •I have tried to purge you of the filth of your debauchery, but you would not let yourself be purged of your filth. So now you will not be purged until my anger has been exhausted 14 against you. •I, Yahweh, have spoken; my word will come true; I shall act and not relent; I shall show no pity, no compassion. I intend to judge you as your conduct and actions deserve—it is the Lord Yahweh who speaks." '

The personal ordeals of the prophet

15
16 The word of Yahweh was addressed to me as follows, •'Son of man, I am about to deprive you suddenly of the delight of your eyes. But you are not 17 to lament, not to weep, not to let your tears run down. •Groan in silence, do not go into mourning for the dead, knot your turban round your head, put your sandals on your feet, do not cover your beard, do not eat common bread.' 18 I told this to the people in the morning, and my wife died in the evening, and the 19 next morning I did as I had been ordered. •The people then said to me, 'Are 20 you not going to explain what meaning these actions have for us?' •I replied, 21 'The word of Yahweh has been addressed to me as follows, •"Say to the House of Israel: The Lord Yahweh says this. I am about to profane my sanctuary, the pride of your strength, the delight of your eyes, the passion of your souls. Those of your sons and daughters whom you have left behind will fall by the 22 sword. •And you are to do as I have done; you must not cover your beards or 23 eat common bread; •you must keep your turbans on your heads and your sandals on your feet; you must not lament or weep. You shall waste away owing 24 to your sins and groan among yourselves. •Ezekiel is to be a sign for you. You are to do just as he has done. And when this happens, you will learn that I am Yahweh."

24 a. December 589–January 588.

'And, son of man, on the very day I deprive them of their sons and daughters 25 who are their strength, their pride and glory, the delight of their eyes, the joy of their hearts, •on that very day a fugitive will come and bring you news of this. 26 On that day your mouth will be opened to speak to the fugitive; you will speak 27 and not be dumb any more; you are to be a sign for them, and they will learn that I am Yahweh.'

II. ORACLES AGAINST THE NATIONS

Against the Ammonites

25 The word of Yahweh was addressed to me as follows, •'Son of man, ¹₂ turn towards the Ammonites and prophesy against them. •Say to the 3 Ammonites, "Hear the word of the Lord Yahweh. The Lord Yahweh says this:

You cried: Aha! over my sanctuary when it was profaned, and over the land of Israel when it was ravaged, and over the House of Judah when it went into exile, •and because of that I am going to hand you over to the sons of the 4 East*a*; they will pitch their camps inside your frontiers, they will settle there. They are going to eat your fruit, and drink your milk. •I intend to turn Rabbah 5 into a camel yard and the towns of Ammon into sheepfolds. And so you will learn that I am Yahweh.

The Lord Yahweh says this: Since you have clapped your hands and 6 danced for joy, inwardly full of malice against the land of Israel, •I mean to stretch 7 out my hand against you for this; I will hand you over to be looted by the peoples, obliterate you as a nation, wipe you out as a country. I will reduce you to nothing, and so you will learn that I am Yahweh.

Against Moab

The Lord Yahweh says this: 8

Since Moab and Seir*b* have said: Look at the House of Judah; it is no different from any other nation; •very well, I will strip the hillsides of Moab bare and 9 destroy her towns throughout the country, including her pride, Beth-jeshimoth, Baal-meon and Kiriath-aim.•I shall hand her over to the sons of the East, the 10 enemies of the Ammonites; I shall hand her over so that the Ammonites will not even be remembered as a nation. •Thus shall I punish Moab, and everyone 11 will learn that I am Yahweh.

Against Edom

The Lord Yahweh says this: 12

Since Edom has taken revenge on the House of Judah and committed great crimes in doing so, •very well, the Lord Yahweh says this: I will stretch 13 out my hand against Edom too and wipe out all the men and animals in the country. I shall reduce it to desert; people will be put to the sword from Teman to Dedan. •I shall unleash my revenge on Edom by means of my people Israel. 14 They will treat Edom as my anger and fury dictate, and everyone will learn that this is my vengeance—it is the Lord Yahweh who speaks.

Against the Philistines

The Lord Yahweh says this: 15

Since the Philistines have acted in revenge and taken revenge maliciously, and with persistent hatred have done their best to destroy, •very well, thus 16 speaks the Lord Yahweh: I will stretch out my hand against the Philistines; I shall destroy the Cherethites*c* and wipe out all the rest of the coastal peoples. I shall perform frightful acts of vengeance and inflict furious punishments on 17 them; and when I exact vengeance on them they will learn that I am Yahweh." '

Against Tyre

1 **26** In the eleventh year, on the first of the month,ᵃ the word of Yahweh was
addressed to me as follows:

2 'Son of man, since Tyre has jeered at Jerusalem,
"Aha! It is shattered, that gate of nations;
it is opening to me; its wealth is ruined",

3 very well, the Lord Yahweh says this:
Now, Tyre, I set myself against you.
I mean to cause many nations to surge against you
like the sea and its waves.

4 They will destroy the walls of Tyre,
they will demolish her towers;
I will sweep away her dust
and leave her a naked rock.

5 She will be a drying-ground in mid-ocean for fishing nets.
For I have spoken—it is the Lord Yahweh who speaks—
she will be the prey of the nations.

6 As for her daughters on the mainland,
these will be put to the sword,
and everyone will learn that I am Yahweh.

7 For the Lord Yahweh says this.
From the North, I am sending Nebuchadnezzar,
king of Babylon, king of kings, against Tyre
with horses and chariots and horsemen,
a horde of many races.

8 He will put your daughters
on the mainland to the sword.
He will build siege-works against you,
cast up a mound against you,
raise a siege-tower against you;

9 he will break down your walls with his battering-rams,
and demolish your towers with his siege-engines.ᵇ

10 His horses are so many their dust will hide you.
Noise of his horsemen and his chariots and wagons
will make your walls tremble as he rides through your gates
like a man entering a conquered city.

11 His horses' hoofs will trample through your streets;
he will put your people to the sword,
and throw your massive pillars to the ground.

12 Your wealth will be seized, your merchandise looted,
your walls razed, your luxurious houses shattered,
your stones, your timbers, your very dust, thrown into the sea.

13 I will stop your music and songs;
the sound of your harps will not be heard again.

14 I will reduce you to a naked rock,
and make you into a drying-ground for fishing nets,
never to be rebuilt;
for I, Yahweh, have spoken
—it is the Lord Yahweh who speaks.

15 The Lord Yahweh says this to Tyre: When they hear of your fall, the groans
of your wounded and the havoc inside your walls, will not the islands shake?

16 The rulers of the sea will all get off their thrones, lay aside their cloaks and take

25 a. The nomadic Arabs.   b. Edom.   c. Related to, and associated with, the Philistines.
26 a. The year 587-586.   b. The siege, begun by Nebuchadnezzar, lasted 13 years.

off their embroidered robes. Dressed in terror they will sit on the ground unable
to stop trembling, terrified at your fate.

'They will raise a dirge and say to you: 17

> "You are destroyed then, swept from the seas,
> city of pride,
> you who were mighty on the sea,
> you and your citizens,
> who used to terrorise
> the continent far and near.
> Now the islands are trembling   18
> on the day of your fall;
> the islands of the sea are terrified by your end."

'For the Lord Yahweh says this: 19

'When I make you as desolate as any depopulated city, when I bring up the
deep against you and the ocean covers you, •I will cast you down with those 20
who go down to the pit, down to the men of old; I will make you live in the
regions underground, in the eternal solitudes, with those who go down to the
pit, so that you can never come back and be restored to the land of the living.
I will make you an object of terror; you will not exist. People will look for you 21
and never find you again—it is the Lord Yahweh who speaks.'

A lamentation over the fall of Tyre

27 The word of Yahweh was addressed to me as follows, •'Son of man, $^1_2$
raise the dirge over Tyre. •Say to Tyre, that city standing at the edge of 3
the sea, doing business with the nations in innumerable islands, "The Lord
Yahweh says this:

> Tyre, you used to say: I am a ship
> perfect in beauty.
> Your frontiers stretched far out to sea;   4
> those who built you made you
> perfect in beauty.
> Cypress from Senir* they used   5
> for all your planking.
> They took a cedar from Lebanon
> to make you a mast.
> From the tallest •oaks of Bashan   6
> they made your oars.
> They built you a deck of cedar inlaid with ivory
> from the Kittim* isles.
> Embroidered linen of Egypt was used for your sail   7
> and for your flag.
> Purple and scarlet from the Elishah islands
> formed your deck-tent.
> Men from Sidon and from Arvad*   8
> were your oarsmen.
> Your sages, Tyre, were aboard
> serving as sailors.
> The elders and craftsmen of Gebal* were there   9
> to caulk your seams.

All the ships of the sea and the sailors in them visited you to trade with you.
Men of Persia and Lud and Put served in your army and were your warriors. 10
They hung up shield and helmet in you. They brought you glory. •The sons 11
of Arvad and their army manned your walls all round and kept watch from
your bastions. They hung their shields all round your walls and helped to make

12 your beauty perfect. •Tarshish was your client, profiting from your abundant
wealth. People paid you in silver and iron, tin and lead for your merchandise.
13 Javan, Tubal and Meshech[c] traded with you. For your merchandise they bartered
14 men and bronze implements. •The people of Beth-togarmah[f] traded you horses,
15 chargers, mules. •The sons of Dedan traded with you; many shores were your
16 clients; you were paid in ivory tusks and ebony. •Edom was your client, because
of the variety and quantity of your goods; she exchanged carbuncles, purple,
17 embroideries, fine linen, coral and rubies against your goods. •Judah and the
land of Israel also traded with you, supplying you with corn from Minnith, wax,
18 honey, tallow and balm. •Damascus was your client, because of the plentifulness
of your goods and the immensity of your wealth, furnishing you with wine from
19 Helbon and wool from Zahar. •Dan and Javan, from Uzal onwards, supplied
20 you with wrought iron, cassia and calamus in exchange for your goods. •Dedan
21 traded with you in horse-cloths. •Arabia and even the sheikhs of Kedar were
22 all your clients; they paid in lambs, rams and he-goats. •The merchants of
Sheba and Raamah traded with you; they supplied you with the best quality
23 spices, precious stones and gold against your goods. •Haran, Canneh and Eden,
24 traders of Sheba, Asshur and Chilmad[g] traded with you. •They traded rich
clothes, embroidered and purple cloaks, multi-coloured materials and strong plait-
25 ed cords in your markets. •The ships of Tarshish crossed the seas for your trade.

> Then you were rich and glorious
> surrounded by the seas.

26   Out to the open sea
> your oarsmen rowed you.
> The east wind has shattered you,
> surrounded by the seas.

27   Your riches, your goods, your cargo,
> your crew, your sailors,
> your caulkers, your commercial agents,
> all the soldiers
> you carry with you, the whole host
> who are aboard:
> all will sink surrounded by the seas
> on the day of your shipwreck.

28   When they hear the cries of your sailors
> the coasts will tremble.

29   Then the oarsmen will all desert
> their ships.
> The sailors and seafaring people
> will stay ashore.

30   They will raise their voices for you,
> and weep bitterly.
> They will throw dust on their heads,
> and roll in ashes;

31   they will shave their heads for you,
> and put sackcloth round their waists.
> They will raise a bitter dirge over you,
> in their despair;

32   they will raise a dirge and mourn for you,
> they will bewail you:
> Who could compare with haughty Tyre

27 a. Hermon.   b. Cyprus; but here it also includes other islands and coastal settlements.
c. Phoenician coastal towns.   d. Byblos.   e. Greeks.   f. Probably Armenia.   g. Towns
in the region of the Euphrates.

surrounded by the seas?
When you unloaded your goods   33
to satisfy so many peoples,
you made the kings of the earth rich
with your excess of wealth and goods.
Now you are shattered by the waves,   34
surrounded by the seas.
Your cargo and all your crew
have foundered with you.
All those who live in the distant islands   35
have been horrified at your fate.
Their kings have been panic-stricken,
their faces quite cast down.
The traders of the nations   36
have whistled at your fate,
since you have become an object of dread,
gone for ever." '

Against the king of Tyre

28 The word of Yahweh was addressed to me as follows, •'Son of man, tell $\frac{1}{2}$
the ruler of Tyre, "The Lord Yahweh says this:

Being swollen with pride,
you have said: I am a god;
I am sitting on the throne of God,
surrounded by the seas.
Though you are a man and not a god,
you consider yourself the equal of God.
You are wiser now than Danel;   3
there is no sage as wise as you.
By your wisdom and your intelligence   4
you have amassed great wealth;
you have piles of gold and silver
inside your treasure-houses.
Such is your skill in trading,   5
your wealth has continued to increase,
and with this your heart has grown more arrogant.
And so, the Lord Yahweh says this: 6
Since you consider yourself the equal of God,
very well, I am going to bring foreigners against you,   7
the most barbarous of the nations.
They will draw sword against your fine wisdom,
they will defile your glory;
they will throw you down into the pit   8
and you will die a violent death
surrounded by the seas.
Are you still going to say: I am a god,   9
when your murderers confront you?
No, you are a man and not a god
in the clutches of your murderers!
You will die like the uncircumcised   10
at the hand of foreigners.
For I have spoken—it is the Lord Yahweh who speaks." '

The fall of the king of Tyre

The word of Yahweh was addressed to me as follows, •'Son of man, $\frac{11}{12}$
raise a dirge over the king of Tyre. Say to him, "The Lord Yahweh says this:

You were once an exemplar of perfection,
full of wisdom,
perfect in beauty;

13　　you were in Eden, in the garden of God.
A thousand gems formed your mantle.
Sard, topaz, diamond, chrysolite, onyx,
jasper, sapphire, carbuncle, emerald,
the gold of which your flutes and tambourines are made,
all were prepared on the day of your creation.

14　　I had provided you with a guardian cherub;
you were on the holy mountain of God;
you walked amid red-hot coals.

15　　Your behaviour was exemplary from the day of your creation
until the day when evil was first found in you.

16　　Your busy trading
has filled you with violence and sin.
I have thrown you down from the mountain of God,
and the guardian cherub has destroyed you from amid the coals.

17　　Your heart has grown swollen with pride
on account of your beauty.
You have corrupted your wisdom
owing to your splendour.
I have thrown you to the ground;
I have made you a spectacle for other kings.

18　　By the immense number of your sins,
by the dishonesty of your trading,
you have defiled your sanctuaries.
I have brought fire out of you to consume you.
I have made you ashes on the ground
before the eyes of all who saw you.

19　　Of the nations, all who know you
are lost in amazement over you.
You are an object of terror;
gone for ever." '

Against Sidon[a]

20
21　　The word of Yahweh was addressed to me as follows, •'Son of man, turn
22　towards Sidon and prophesy against her. •Say, "The Lord Yahweh says this:

Sidon, now I set myself against you;
I will show my glory through you.
Men shall learn that I am Yahweh,
since I will execute sentence on her
and display my holiness in her.

23　　I will send the plague to her;
blood shall flow in her streets,
and in her the dead will fall
under the sword raised against her on all sides,
and so men will learn that I am Yahweh.

Israel delivered from the nations

24　　No more, for the House of Israel,
shall any of the hostile nations surrounding her

---

28 a. Sidon, a city state of Phoenicia, was a member of the alliance which led to the ruin of Judah. Jr 27:3.

be a thorn that wounds or a briar that tears;
and so men will learn that I am the Lord Yahweh.

The Lord Yahweh says this. When I gather the House of Israel from the peoples 25
among whom it is dispersed, this is how I am going to display my holiness in
the sight of the nations. They shall live on the soil that I gave to my servant
Jacob. •They shall live there in confidence, build houses, plant vineyards; they 26
shall live in confidence. When I inflict punishments on all the hostile
surrounding nations, then men will learn that I am Yahweh their God." '

Against Egypt

29 In the tenth year, on the twelfth day of the tenth month,ᵃ the word of 1
Yahweh was addressed to me as follows, •'Son of man, turn towards 2
Pharaoh king of Egypt and prophesy against him and against the whole of
Egypt. •Speak to him and say, "The Lord Yahweh says this: 3

Now I set myself against you, Pharaoh king of Egypt,
you great crocodile wallowing in your Niles,
you have said: My Niles are mine, I made them.
I am going to put hooks through your jaws, 4
make your Nile fish stick to your scales,
and pull you out of your Niles
with all your Nile fish sticking to your scales.
I shall drop you in the desert, with all your Nile fish. 5
You will fall on open ground
and not be taken up or buried.
I shall give you as food
to the beasts of the earth and the birds of heaven,
so that all the inhabitants of Egypt may learn that I am Yahweh, 6
since they have given no more support than a reed to the House
of Israel.
Whenever they grasped you, you broke in their hands 7
and cut their hands all over.
Whenever they leaned on you, you broke
and left their loins shaking.

For this reason, the Lord Yahweh says this: I am sending the sword against you, 8
to kill your men and your beasts. •Egypt will be reduced to desert and desolation, 9
and men will learn that I am Yahweh. Since he has said: The Nile is mine,
I made it, •very well, now I set myself against you and your Niles. I mean to 10
reduce Egypt to desert and desolation, from Migdol to Syene and beyond to
the frontiers of Ethiopia.ᵇ •The feet of men will not pass that way, the feet 11
of animals will not pass that way. For forty years it will remain uninhabited.
I intend to reduce the land of Egypt to a waste among wasted countries; for forty 12
years its cities will be a waste among ruined cities. And I shall scatter the
Egyptians among the nations, dispersing them throughout the peoples. •And 13
the Lord Yahweh says this: After forty years have passed, I will gather the
inhabitants of Egypt from the nations where they have been scattered. •I will 14
bring the Egyptian captives back and reinstal them in the land of Pathros,ᶜ
the land they came from. There they will constitute a weak kingdom. •Egypt 15
will be the weakest of kingdoms and no longer dominate other nations; I shall
reduce her, and she will not rule any more over the nations. •She will no longer 16
be anything for the House of Israel to trust in, but will be living evidence of
the sins of Israel at the time when Israel turned to her for help. And men will
learn that I am the Lord Yahweh." '

In the twenty-seventh year, on the first day of the first month,ᵈ the word 17
of Yahweh was addressed to me as follows:

18   'Son of man, Nebuchadnezzar king of Babylon mobilised his army for a great expedition against Tyre. Their heads have all gone bald, their shoulders are all chafed, but even so he has derived no profit from the expedition mounted
19 against Tyre either for himself or for his army. •Since this is so, the Lord Yahweh says this: I am going to hand Egypt over to Nebuchadnezzar king of Babylon. He will levy his share of riches there instead, will loot it and carry
20 off the booty to pay his army. •In reward for his efforts against Tyre I am handing the land of Egypt over to him, since he has been working for me—it is the Lord Yahweh who speaks.

21   'On that day I will cause the House of Israel to sprout a horn, and I shall allow you to open your mouth for all to hear. And so they will learn that I am Yahweh.'

Against Egypt: the day of Yahweh

$^1_2$ 30 The word of Yahweh was addressed to me as follows, •'Son of man, prophesy and say, "The Lord Yahweh says this: Howl: Alas, the day!
3 For the day is near, the day of Yahweh is near; it will be a day dark with cloud, the end of an epoch for the nations.
4   The sword will come on Egypt, and terror will visit Ethiopia when the slaughtered fall in Egypt, when her riches are carried away, when her foundations
5 are destroyed. •Cush and Put and Lud, the whole of Arabia and Cub and the sons of my covenant will fall by the sword along with them.
6   Yahweh says this:
The supports of Egypt will fall; the pride of her strength will crumble; people will fall by the sword from Migdol to Syene—it is the Lord Yahweh who speaks.
7   They will be laid waste among wasted countries; her cities will rank with
8 other ruined cities. •They will learn that I am Yahweh when I set fire to Egypt and all her supports are shattered.
9   On that day messengers despatched by me will set out in boats to shake the complacency of Ethiopia. Terror will run through her inhabitants on the
10 day of Egypt—it is coming now! •The Lord Yahweh says this: I intend to destroy the huge population of Egypt at the hand of Nebuchadnezzar king of Babylon.
11 He and his people, most barbarous of nations, will be sent to ravage the country. They will draw the sword against Egypt and fill the country with corpses.
12 I am going to dry up the arms of the Nile, hand the country over to brigands, and lay the whole country waste and everything in it, at the hand of foreigners. I, Yahweh, have spoken.
13   The Lord Yahweh says this: I mean to destroy the idols, and take the rams away from Noph.^{a} The land of Egypt will be left without a ruler. I shall
14 spread terror through the land of Egypt. •I shall lay Pathros waste, set Zoan on
15 fire, inflict my punishments on No. •I shall discharge my fury on Sin, the
16 stronghold of Egypt; I shall wipe out the crowding population of No. •I shall set fire to Egypt; Sin will be racked with anguish; there will be a flood at Nô,
17 the waters will inundate it. •The young men of On and Pi-beseth will fall by the
18 sword and the cities themselves go into captivity. •At Tahpanhes day will turn to darkness when I shatter the yoke of Egypt there, when the pride of her strength
19 ceases. A cloud will cover her, and her daughters will go into captivity. •Such will be the punishments that I am going to inflict on Egypt. And so men will learn that I am Yahweh." '
20   In the eleventh year, on the seventh day of the first month,^{b} the word of
21 Yahweh was addressed to me as follows, •'Son of man, I have broken the arm of Pharaoh king of Egypt; you can see that no one has bound up his wound

29 a. December 588-January 587.   b. From Migdol to Syene: i.e., from the N. to the S. of Egypt.   c. Upper Egypt.   d. March-April 571.
30 a. Memphis. Three of the Egyptian towns named in the following verses are more recognisable under their Greek names: Zoan as Tanis, No as Thebes, On as Heliopolis.   b. March-April 587.

to heal it, given it a bandage or a dressing to make the arm strong enough to wield the sword again. •And so, the Lord Yahweh says this: Now I set myself 22 against Pharaoh king of Egypt; I intend to break his arms, the sound one and the broken one, and make the sword drop from his hand. •I shall scatter Egypt among 23 the nations and disperse her throughout the countries. •I shall strengthen the 24 arms of the king of Babylon and put my sword in his hand. I shall break Pharaoh's arms and, confronted with his enemy, he will groan like a dying man. I shall strengthen the arms of the king of Babylon, and the arms of Pharaoh 25 will fall. And so men will learn that I am Yahweh, when I put my sword into the hands of the king of Babylon and he wields it against the land of Egypt. •I mean 26 to scatter Egypt among the nations and disperse her throughout the countries; and men will learn that I am Yahweh.'

The cedar

31 In the eleventh year, on the first day of the third month, the word of 1 Yahweh was addressed to me as follows, •'Son of man, say to Pharaoh 2 king of Egypt and to all his subjects:

"To what shall I compare you in your greatness?
Surely, to a cedar of Lebanon   3
with noble branches, thick-set needles and lofty trunk.
Its top pierces the clouds.
The waters have made it grow, the deep has made it tall,   4
pouring its rivers round the place where it is planted,
sending its streams to all the other trees.
This is why its trunk grew taller than all the other trees;   5
its branches increased in number, its boughs stretched wide,
because the plentiful waters reached it.
All the birds of heaven used to nest in its branches;   6
under its boughs all wild animals used to drop their young;
in its shade every kind of people sat.
It was beautiful in its size, in the span of its boughs;   7
its roots went deep into plentiful waters.
No cedar equalled it in the garden of God,   8
no cypress had branches such as these;
no plane tree could match its boughs,
no tree in the garden of God could rival its beauty.
I had made it lovely with branching green.   9
It was the envy of every tree in Eden, in the garden of God.

"Very well then, the Lord Yahweh says this: 10
Since it has raised itself to its full height, has lifted its top to the clouds, and has grown arrogant in its height, •I have handed it over to the prince of the 11 nations,ᵈ to do with it as its wickedness deserves; I have destroyed it. •Foreigners, 12 the most barbarous of the nations, have cut it down and felled it. On the mountains, in all the valleys, lie its branches; its broken boughs fill every ravine throughout the country; everybody in the country has left its shade and deserted it. •On the wreckage perch all the birds of heaven; all the wild animals have 13 made their dens under its branches.

In future let no tree rise in pride beside the waters, none push its top 14 through the clouds, no well-watered tree stretch its whole height towards them. For all of them are doomed to death, to the regions underground, with the common run of mankind, with those who go down to the pit.

The Lord Yahweh says this: On the day it went down to Sheol, I closed 15 the deep over it in sign of mourning. I stopped its rivers, the plentiful waters dried up; I made Lebanon dark for its sake, and all the trees of the fields wilted

16 for its sake. •With the noise when it fell I made the nations quake, as I hurled
it down to Sheol, with those who go down to the pit. In the regions underground
all the trees of Eden took comfort, all the noble and lovely trees of Lebanon
17 nourished by the waters. •And with it went down to Sheol, to the victims of
the sword, all those nations who used to live in its shade.

18   Was anyone of all the trees of Eden your equal in glory and size, for you to
be hurled with the trees of Eden down to the regions underground? With the
uncircumcised there you lie; with the victims of the sword lie Pharaoh and all
his subjects—it is the Lord Yahweh who speaks." '

The crocodile

1 **32** In the twelfth year, on the first day of the twelfth month,ᵃ the word of
2   Yahweh was addressed to me as follows, •'Son of man, raise the dirge for
Pharaoh king of Egypt. Say to him, "Young lion of nations, you have been
wiped out.

> "You were like a crocodile in the water;
>   you snorted through your nostrils,
>   you churned the water with your feet,
>   you muddied its streams.

3   "The Lord Yahweh says this:

> I am going to throw my net over you in a great concourse of nations;
>   they will drag you ashore in my net.
4 I mean to leave you on land, drop you on the ground;
>   make all the birds settle on you,
>   glut all the beasts of the earth with you,
5   lay your carcase on the mountainside,
>   fill the valleys with your offal.
6 I intend to water the country with what flows from you,
>   with your blood, on the mountainsides,
>   and the ravines will be full of it.
7 When I extinguish you I will cover the skies,
>   and darken the stars.
>   I will cover the sun with clouds
>   and the moon will not give its light.
8 I will dim every luminary in heaven for you,
>   and cover your country in darkness
>   —it is the Lord Yahweh who speaks.

9   I shall grieve the heart of many peoples when I lead your captives among
10 the nations, into countries unknown to you. •I shall stun many peoples with
shock at your fate; their kings will be panic-stricken at your fate, when I brandish
my sword before their eyes. On the day of your fall, each will tremble
11 continuously for his life. •For the Lord Yahweh says this: The sword of the
12 king of Babylon will follow you. •I shall make your throngs of subjects fall at
the swords of my warriors, who are the most barbarous of the nations. They
will annihilate the pride of Egypt, and her whole population will be destroyed.
13 I shall make all her cattle perish too on the banks of the deep waters. The feet
of men will not muddy them again, the feet of animals will not muddy them
14 again. •Then I shall calm her waters; I shall make her rivers glide like oil—it is
the Lord Yahweh who speaks.

15   When I reduce Egypt to desert and the country is stripped of its contents,
when I strike all those who live there, they will learn that I am Yahweh.

31 a. Nebuchadnezzar or one of his successors.
32 a. February-March 585.

Such is the dirge that the daughters of the nations will raise. They will 16
raise it over Egypt and her huge population. This is the dirge they will raise—
it is the Lord Yahweh who speaks." '

Egypt goes down to Sheol

In the twelfth year, on the fifteenth day of the first month, the word of 17
Yahweh was addressed to me as follows, •'Son of man, raise the dirge over 18
the huge population of Egypt; send them down, her and the daughters of the
nations in their majesty, to the regions underground, with those who go down
to the pit.

'With those who have fallen by the sword they too will fall; her strength 20
shall be totally extinguished. •In Sheol the greatest heroes will address her, 21a
"Do you excel anyone in beauty now? •Come down, make your bed with the 19
uncircumcised who have fallen by the sword." 21b

'Assyria is there with all her warriors round her tomb; all killed, all victims 22
of the sword; •their graves have been made in the deepest part of the pit, with 23
her army round her tomb, all killed, all victims of the sword, yet she once spread
terror throughout the land of the living.

'Elam is there, with all her troops round her tomb; all killed, all victims of 24
the sword, they have gone down uncircumcised to the regions underground,
yet she once spread terror throughout the land of the living. They endure the
disgrace of those who go down to the pit. •In the middle of the slaughtered 25
a bed has been made for her, with all her troops round her tomb, all of them
uncircumcised, put to the sword, yet she once spread terror throughout the land
of the living. They endure the disgrace of those who go down to the pit. They
have been put among the slaughtered.

'Meshech is there, and Tubal, with all her troops round her tomb, all of 26
them uncircumcised, put to the sword for having spread terror throughout the
land of the living. •They do not lie with the heroes who fell long ago, those 27
who went fully armed down to Sheol, who had their swords laid under their
heads and their shields put under their bones, since the heroes inspired the land
of the living with terror. •Instead, you shall lie with the uncircumcised, with 28
those who have fallen to the sword.

'Edom is there, her kings and all her princes who, despite their valour, have 29
been laid with those who have fallen by the sword. They lie with the
uncircumcised, with those who go down to the pit.

'All the princes of the North and all the Sidonians are there, having gone 30
down with the slaughtered, in spite of the terror their power inspired.
Uncircumcised they lie with those who were victims of the sword. They endure
the disgrace of those who go down to the pit.

'Pharaoh will see them and take comfort at the sight of such a host put to 31
the sword, Pharaoh and his whole army—it is the Lord Yahweh who speaks.
He who once spread terror throughout the land of the living now lies with 32
the uncircumcised, with those who were victims of the sword, Pharaoh and his
whole army. It is the Lord Yahweh who speaks.'

III. DURING AND AFTER THE SIEGE OF JERUSALEM

The prophet as sentry

33 The word of Yahweh was addressed to me as follows, •'Son of man, ½
speak to the members of your nation. Say to them, "When I send the
sword against a country, the people of that country select one of themselves
and post him as a sentry; •if he sees the sword coming against the country, 3

4 he sounds his horn to alert the people. •If someone hears the sound of the
   horn, but pays no attention, the sword will overtake him and destroy him; he
5 will have been responsible for his own death. •He has heard the sound of the
   horn and paid no attention; his death will be his own responsibility. But the
   life of someone who pays attention to the warning will be secure.
6   "If, however, the sentry has seen the sword coming but has not blown his
   horn, and so the people are not alerted and the sword overtakes them and
   destroys one of them, the latter shall indeed die for his sin, but I will hold the
   sentry responsible for his death."
7   'Son of man, I have appointed you as sentry to the House of Israel. When
8 you hear a word from my mouth, warn them in my name. •If I say to a wicked
   man: Wicked wretch, you are to die, and you do not speak to warn the wicked
   man to renounce his ways, then he shall die for his sin, but I will hold you
9 responsible for his death. •If, however, you do warn a wicked man to renounce
   his ways and repent, and he does not repent, then he shall die for his sin, but
   you yourself will have saved your life.

Conversion and perversity

10   'Son of man, say to the House of Israel, "You are continually saying: Our
   sins and crimes weigh heavily on us; we are wasting away because of them. How
11 are we to go on living?" •Say to them, "As I live—it is the Lord Yahweh
   who speaks—I take pleasure, not in the death of a wicked man, but in the turning
   back of a wicked man who changes his ways to win life. Come back, come back
   from your evil ways. Why are you so anxious to die, House of Israel?"
12   'And you, son of man, say to the members of your nation, "The integrity of an
   upright man will not save him once he has chosen to sin; the wickedness of a
   wicked man will no longer condemn him once he renounces wickedness, nor
   will an upright man live on the strength of his integrity once he has chosen
13 to sin. •If I say to an upright man: You are to live, and then, trusting in his
   own integrity, he turns to evil, all his integrity will no longer be remembered;
14 because he has sinned, he shall die. •If, however, I say to a wicked man: You
15 are to die, and he renounces his sins and does what is lawful and right, •if he
   returns pledges, restores what he has stolen, keeps the laws that give life and
16 stops committing sin—he shall live, and will not die. •All his previous sins will
   no longer be remembered—he has done what is lawful and right; he shall live.
17   "The members of your nation object: What the Lord does is unjust; but
18 it is what you do that is unjust. •When an upright man renounces his integrity
19 and commits sin, he dies for it. •And when a wicked man renounces his
20 wickedness and does what is lawful and right, because of this he lives. •You
   object: What the Lord does is unjust; but I mean to judge each of you by what
   he does, House of Israel."'

The taking of the city

21   In the twelfth year of our captivity, on the fifth day of the tenth month,[a]
   a fugitive arrived from Jerusalem and said to me, 'The city has been taken'.
22 Now the hand of the Lord had been on me the evening before the fugitive
   arrived; he had opened my mouth before the man came to me the next morning;
   my mouth had been opened and I was dumb no longer.[b]

The ravaging of the country

23
24   The word of Yahweh was then addressed to me as follows, •'Son of man,
   the people living in those ruins in the land of Israel say, "Abraham was alone
   when he was given possession of this land. Now we are many and we hold
   the country as our domain."

---

33 a. December 586-January 585.   b. See 3:22f.

'Very well, tell them, "The Lord Yahweh says this: You eat blood, you 25 raise your eyes to your idols, you shed blood; are you likely to keep possession of the land? •You rely on your swords, you engage in filthy practices, you each 26 commit adultery with your neighbour's wife; are you likely to retain possession of the land?" •Tell them this, "The Lord Yahweh says this: As I live, I swear it, 27 those in the ruins will fall to the sword, those in the countryside I will give to wild animals to devour, those in strongholds and caves will die of plague. •I intend to 28 reduce the land to desert and desolation and it will no longer take pride in its strength. The mountains of Israel will be deserted and no one will pass that way again. •And so men will learn that I am Yahweh, when I reduce the land to 29 desert and desolation on account of all their filthy practices."

The results of the preaching

'Son of man, the members of your nation are talking about you on the 30 ramparts and in doorways. They keep saying, "Come and hear the word that has come from Yahweh". •They throng towards you; my people sit down in front 31 of you and listen to your words, but they do not act on them. They cannot tell the truth and their hearts are set on dishonest gain. •As far as they are concerned, 32 you are like a love song beautifully sung to music. They listen to your words, but no one puts them into practice. •When the thing takes place—and it is 33 beginning now—they will learn that there has been a prophet among them.'

The shepherds of Israel

34 The word of Yahweh was addressed to me as follows, •'Son of man, 1 prophesy against the shepherds of Israel; prophesy and say to them, 2 "Shepherds, the Lord Yahweh says this: Trouble for the shepherds of Israel who feed themselves! Shepherds ought to feed their flock, •yet you have fed on 3 milk, you have dressed yourselves in wool, you have sacrificed the fattest sheep, but failed to feed the flock. •You have failed to make weak sheep strong, or to 4 care for the sick ones, or bandage the wounded ones. You have failed to bring back strays or look for the lost. On the contrary, you have ruled them cruelly and violently. •For lack of a shepherd they have scattered, to become the prey of any 5 wild animal; they have scattered far. •My flock is straying this way and that, 6 on mountains and on high hills; my flock has been scattered all over the country; no one bothers about them and no one looks for them.

'Well then, shepherds, hear the word of Yahweh. •As I live, I swear it—it is 7/8 the Lord Yahweh who speaks—since my flock has been looted and for lack of a shepherd is now the prey of any wild animal, since my shepherds have stopped bothering about my flock, since my shepherds feed themselves rather than my flock, •in view of all this, shepherds, hear the word of Yahweh. •The Lord 9/10 Yahweh says this: I am going to call the shepherds to account. I am going to take my flock back from them and I shall not allow them to feed my flock. In this way the shepherds will stop feeding themselves. I shall rescue my sheep from their mouths; they will not prey on them any more.

For the Lord Yahweh says this: I am going to look after my flock myself 11 and keep all of it in view. •As a shepherd keeps all his flock in view when he 12 stands up in the middle of his scattered sheep, so shall I keep my sheep in view. I shall rescue them from wherever they have been scattered during the mist and darkness. •I shall bring them out of the countries where they are; I shall gather 13 them together from foreign countries and bring them back to their own land. I shall pasture them on the mountains of Israel, in the ravines and in every inhabited place in the land. •I shall feed them in good pasturage; the high 14 mountains of Israel will be their grazing ground. There they will rest in good grazing ground; they will browse in rich pastures on the mountains of Israel. I myself will pasture my sheep, I myself will show them where to rest—it is 15 the Lord Yahweh who speaks. •I shall look for the lost one, bring back the stray, 16 bandage the wounded and make the weak strong. I shall watch over the fat and healthy. I shall be a true shepherd to them.

17 As for you, my sheep, the Lord Yahweh says this: I will judge between
18 sheep and sheep, between rams and he-goats. •Not content to graze in good pastures, you trample down the rest; not content to drink clear water, you
19 muddy the rest with your feet. •And my sheep must graze on what your feet have
20 trampled, drink what your feet have muddied. •Very well then, the Lord Yahweh says this: I myself am now about to judge between fat sheep and lean sheep.
21 Since you have butted all the weak sheep with your rumps and shoulders and
22 horns, until you have chased them away, •I am going to come and rescue my sheep from being cheated; I will judge between sheep and sheep.
23 I mean to raise up one shepherd, my servant David, and to put him in charge of them and he will pasture them; he will pasture them and be their shepherd.
24 I, Yahweh, will be their God, and my servant David shall be their ruler. I, Yahweh,
25 have spoken. •I shall make a covenant of peace with them; I shall rid the country of wild animals. They will be able to live safely in the wilderness and go to sleep
26 in the woods. •I shall settle them round my hill;[a] I shall send rain at the proper
27 time; it will be a fertile rain. •The trees of the countryside will yield their fruit and the earth its produce; they will feel safe on their own farms. And men will learn that I am Yahweh when I break their yokestraps and release them from
28 their captors. •No more will they be a prey to foreign countries, no more will they be eaten by wild animals in this country. They will live without fear and
29 no one will disturb them again. •I shall make splendid vegetation grow for them; no more will they suffer from famine in this land; no more will they have to bear
30 the insults of other nations. •And men will learn that I, their God, am with them and that they, the House of Israel, are my people—it is the Lord Yahweh who
31 speaks. •And you, my sheep, are the flock I shall pasture, and I am your God— it is the Lord Yahweh who speaks." '

Against the mountains of Edom

1
2 **35** The word of Yahweh was addressed to me as follows, •'Son of man, turn
3 towards the mountain of Seir and prophesy against it. •Say to it, "The Lord Yahweh says this: Now I set myself against you, mountain of Seir; I am stretching out my hand against you; I am going to reduce you to desert and
4 desolation, •I lay your towns in ruins, and make you a desolation, and so
5 you will learn that I am Yahweh. •Since, nourishing a long-standing hatred, you betrayed the sons of Israel to the sword during their trouble, at the time of their
6 last crime, •very well, as I live—it is the Lord Yahweh who speaks—I mean to hand you over to bloodshed, and bloodshed will pursue you. I swear it; you have
7 sinned by shedding blood, and bloodshed will pursue you. •I intend to reduce the mountain of Seir to desert and desolation, and I will eliminate everyone
8 who travels up and down the country. •I shall fill its mountains with corpses; people will fall, struck down by the sword on your hills, in your valleys, in
9 every one of your ravines. •I am going to reduce you to desolation, for ever your towns will remain uninhabited, and so you will learn that I am Yahweh.

10 Since you said to the two nations, the two countries:[a] You belong to me; we
11 are going to take possession here where Yahweh used to be: •very well, as I live —it is the Lord Yahweh who speaks—in anger and fury I will do exactly what you did because you hated them. I shall make it clear that I am punishing you
12 on their behalf; •then you will know that I, Yahweh, have overheard all the outrageous things you have said about the mountains of Israel, such as: They have

34 a. Zion.
35 a. After 587 Edom attempted to overrun not only the kingdom of Judah but the whole of Palestine.

been abandoned, they have been left for us to devour. •You have talked arrogantly 13
about me, too, you have repeatedly slandered me; I have heard! •The Lord 14
Yahweh says this: To the joy of the whole country, I am going to reduce you to
desert. •Since you rejoiced when the domain of the House of Israel became a 15
desert, I will do the same to you, mountain of Seir; you will become a desert,
and so will the whole of Edom; and so men will learn that I am Yahweh."

Oracle on the mountains of Israel

36 'Son of man, prophesy this to the mountains of Israel. Say, "Mountains 1
of Israel, hear the word of Yahweh". •The Lord Yahweh says this: Since 2
the enemy has insulted you by saying, "Aha! These eternal heights have now
become our domain", •you must prophesy. Say, "The Lord Yahweh says this: 3
Since you have been ravaged and seized on by surrounding countries, and taken
over by the rest of the nations, and made the subject of people's talk and gossip,
now, mountains of Israel, hear the word of the Lord Yahweh: The Lord Yahweh 4
says this to mountains and hills, to ravines and valleys, to abandoned ruins
and the empty plundered cities that have become the laughing-stock of all the
surrounding nations. •Yes, the Lord Yahweh says this: I swear it by the 5
fierceness of my jealousy; I am speaking to the rest of the nations and to the
whole of Edom who so exultantly and contemptuously took possession of my
country and plundered it."

'This being so, prophesy this about the land of Israel. Say to the mountains 6
and hills, to the ravines and valleys, "The Lord Yahweh says this: I am
speaking in my jealousy and rage; because you are enduring the insults of the
nations, •very well, the Lord Yahweh says this: I raise my hand and I swear 7
that the nations round you shall have their own insults to bear.

Mountains of Israel, you will grow branches and bear fruit for my people 8
Israel, who will soon return. •Yes, I am coming to you, I have turned to you; 9
you will be tilled and sown. •I shall multiply the men who live on you, the whole 10
House of Israel, yes, all. The cities will be lived in again and the ruins rebuilt.
I shall multiply the men and animals that live on you; there will be many of them 11
and they will be fertile. I shall repopulate you as you were before; I shall make you
more prosperous than you were before, and so you will learn that I am Yahweh.
Thanks to me, men will tread your soil again, my people Israel; they will have 12
you for their own domain, and never again will you rob them of their children.

The Lord Yahweh says this: Since people have said of you: You are 13
a man-eater, you have robbed your nation of its children, •very well, you will 14
eat no more men, never rob your nation of its children again—it is the Lord
Yahweh who speaks. •I shall never again let you hear the insults of the nations, 15
you will never again have to bear the taunts of the foreigners, you will never
again rob the nation of its children—it is the Lord Yahweh who speaks." '

The word of Yahweh was addressed to me as follows: •'Son of man, the ¹⁶₁₇
members of the House of Israel used to live in their own land, but they defiled
it by their conduct and actions; to me their conduct was as unclean as a woman's
menstruation. •I then discharged my fury at them because of the blood they shed 18
in their land and the idols with which they defiled it. •I scattered them among 19
the nations and dispersed them in foreign countries. I sentenced them as their
conduct and actions deserved. •And now they have profaned my holy name 20
among the nations where they have gone, so that people say of them, "These are
the people of Yahweh; they have been exiled from his land". •But I have been 21
concerned about my holy name, which the House of Israel has profaned among
the nations where they have gone. •And so, say to the House of Israel, "The 22
Lord Yahweh says this: I am not doing this for your sake, House of Israel,
but for the sake of my holy name, which you have profaned among the nations
where you have gone. •I mean to display the holiness of my great name, which has 23
been profaned among the nations, which you have profaned among them. And

the nations will learn that I am Yahweh—it is the Lord Yahweh who speaks—
24 when I display my holiness for your sake before their eyes. •Then I am going to take you from among the nations and gather you together from all the foreign
25 countries, and bring you home to your own land. •I shall pour clean water over you and you will be cleansed; I shall cleanse you of all your defilement and all
26 your idols. •I shall give you a new heart, and put a new spirit in you; I shall remove
27 the heart of stone from your bodies and give you a heart of flesh instead. •I shall put my spirit in you, and make you keep my laws and sincerely respect my
28 observances. •You will live in the land which I gave your ancestors. You shall be
29 my people and I will be your God. •I shall rescue you from all your defilement. I shall summon the corn and make it plentiful, and no more bring famines on you.
30 I shall increase the yield of fruit trees and fields so that you will no longer have
31 the ignominy of famine among the nations. •Then you will remember your evil conduct and actions. You will loathe yourselves for your sins and your filthy
32 practices. •I assure you that I am not doing this for your sake—it is the Lord Yahweh who speaks. Be ashamed and blush for your conduct, House of Israel.
33   The Lord Yahweh says this: On the day I cleanse you from all your sins,
34 I will repopulate the cities and cause the ruins to be rebuilt. •Waste land, once
35 desolate for every passer-by to see, will now be farmed again. •Everyone will say: This land, so recently a waste, is now like a garden of Eden, and the ruined cities once abandoned and levelled to the ground are now strongholds with people
36 living in them. •And the nations left round you will know that I, Yahweh, have rebuilt what was destroyed and replanted what was ruined. I, Yahweh, have spoken, and I will do it.
37   The Lord Yahweh says this: To grant them further favour, I shall encourage the House of Israel to look for me, and shall increase them like a
38 flock of men, •like a flock of sacrificial animals, like the flock in Jerusalem on her solemn feasts. And so your ruined cities will be filled with a human flock. And men will learn that I am Yahweh." '

The dry bones

1 **37** The hand of Yahweh was laid on me, and he carried me away by the spirit of Yahweh and set me down in the middle of a valley, a valley full of
2 bones. •He made me walk up and down among them. There were vast quantities of these bones on the ground the whole length of the valley; and they were quite
3 dried up. •He said to me, 'Son of man, can these bones live?' I said, 'You know,
4 Lord Yahweh'. •He said, 'Prophesy over these bones. Say, "Dry bones, hear the
5 word of Yahweh. •The Lord Yahweh says this to these bones: I am now going to
6 make the breath*a* enter you, and you will live. •I shall put sinews on you, I shall make flesh grow on you, I shall cover you with skin and give you breath, and you
7 will live; and you will learn that I am Yahweh." ' •I prophesied as I had been ordered. While I was prophesying, there was a noise, a sound of clattering; and
8 the bones joined together. •I looked, and saw that they were covered with sinews; flesh was growing on them and skin was covering them, but there was no breath
9 in them. •He said to me, 'Prophesy to the breath; prophesy, son of man. Say to the breath, "The Lord Yahweh says this: Come from the four winds, breath;
10 breathe on these dead; let them live!" ' •I prophesied as he had ordered me, and the breath entered them; they came to life again and stood up on their feet, a great, an immense army.
11   Then he said, 'Son of man, these bones are the whole House of Israel. They keep saying, "Our bones are dried up, our hope has gone; we are as good as
12 dead". •So prophesy. Say to them, "The Lord Yahweh says this: I am now going to open your graves; I mean to raise you from your graves, my people, and lead you
13 back to the soil of Israel. •And you will know that I am Yahweh, when I open

---

37 a. In Hebr. the one word *ruah* means 'breath' and 'spirit'.

your graves and raise you from your graves, my people. •And I shall put my 14
spirit in you, and you will live, and I shall resettle you on your own soil; and you
will know that I, Yahweh, have said and done this—it is the Lord Yahweh who
speaks." '

Judah and Israel in one kingdom

The word of Yahweh was addressed to me as follows, •'Son of man, take a 15 16
stick and write on it, "Judah and those Israelites loyal to him". Take another
stick and write on it, "Joseph, the wood of Ephraim, and all the House of Israel
loyal to him".

'Join one to the other to make a single piece of wood, a single stick in your 17
hand. •And when the members of your nation say, "Tell us what you mean", 18
say, "The Lord Yahweh says this: I am taking the stick of Joseph, now in the 19
hand of Ephraim, and those tribes of Israel loyal to him, and I am going to put
the stick of Judah with them. I shall make one stick out of the two, and I shall
hold them as one."

'Keep the pieces of wood you have written on in your hand where they 20
can see, •and say, "The Lord Yahweh says this: I am going to take the sons 21
of Israel from the nations where they have gone. I shall gather them together
from everywhere and bring them home to their own soil. •I shall make them into 22
one nation in my own land and on the mountains of Israel, and one king
is to be king of them all; they will no longer form two nations, nor be two
separate kingdoms. •They will no longer defile themselves with their idols and 23
their filthy practices and all their sins. I shall rescue them from all the betrayals
they have been guilty of; I shall cleanse them; they shall be my people and I will
be their God. •My servant David will reign over them, one shepherd for all; 24
they will follow my observances, respect my laws and practise them. •They will 25
live in the land that I gave my servant Jacob, the land in which your ancestors
lived. They will live in it, they, their children, their children's children, for ever.
David my servant is to be their prince for ever. •I shall make a covenant of peace 26
with them, an eternal covenant with them. I shall resettle them and increase
them; I shall settle my sanctuary among them for ever. •I shall make my home 27
above them; I will be their God, they shall be my people. •And the nations will 28
learn that I am Yahweh the sanctifier of Israel, when my sanctuary is, with them
for ever." '

Against Gog, king of Magog[a]

38 The word of Yahweh was addressed to me as follows, •'Son of man, turn 1 2
towards Gog and the country of Magog, the prince of Rosh, Meshech
and Tubal, and prophesy against him. •Say, "The Lord Yahweh says this: 3
I am against you, Gog, prince of Rosh, Meshech and Tubal. •I will turn you 4
round, fixing hooks in your jaws, and drag you and your troops along, all the
horses and well-armoured horsemen, and all that great army carrying shields
and bucklers, and wielding swords. •Persia and Cush and Put are with them, all 5
with buckler and helmet; •Gomer and all its troops, northernmost Beth- 6
togarmah and all its troops,[b] and many nations with you. •Be ready, be well 7
prepared, you and all your troops and the others rallying round you, and hold
yourself at my service.

Many days will pass before you are given orders; in years to come you will 8
march against this country. Its inhabitants will have been living undisturbed,
remote from all other peoples, since they escaped the sword and were gathered
in from various nations, here in the long-deserted mountains of Israel. •Like a 9
storm you will come up and onwards, and cover the land like a cloud, you, your
army and many nations with you.

The Lord Yahweh says this: On that day, a thought is going to enter your mind 10
and you will work out a wicked plan. •You will say: I will attack this 11

undefended country and march against this peaceful nation living undisturbed.
12 They all live in towns that have no walls or bars or gates. •To plunder them for
loot, I am going to reach out my hand towards the ruins they live in, against
this nation gathered out of other nations, these stock-breeders and tradesmen
13 who live at the navel of the earth.^c •Sheba and Dedan, the traders of Tarshish
and all its young lions will ask you: Have you come for plunder? Are you massing
your troops with a view to looting? To make off with gold and silver, seize
cattle and goods, and come away with unlimited spoil?"

14   'And so, son of man, say in prophecy to Gog, "The Lord Yahweh says this:
Is it not true that you are planning to set out at a time when my people Israel
15 is living undisturbed? •You plan to leave your home in the far north, you and
16 many nations with you, a great army of countless troops all mounted. •You plan
to invade Israel, my people. You will be like a cloud covering the earth. I myself
am going to bring you in days to come to attack my country, so that the
nations may learn what I am, when I have used you, Gog, to display my
holiness to them.

17   The Lord Yahweh says this: It was of you that I spoke in the past
through my servants the prophets of Israel, who prophesied and foretold your
18 invasion. •On the day Gog attacks the land of Israel—it is the Lord Yahweh
19 who speaks—I shall grow angry. In my anger, •my jealousy and the heat of
my fury I say it: I swear that on that day there will be a fearful quaking in the
20 land of Israel. •At my presence the fish in the sea and the birds of heaven, the
wild beasts and all the reptiles that crawl along the ground, and all men on earth,
21 will quake. Mountains will fall, cliffs crumble, walls collapse, and •I will confront
him with every sort of terror—it is the Lord Yahweh who speaks. His men will
22 turn their swords on each other, •I will punish him with plague and bloodshed
and send torrential rain, hailstones, fire and brimstone against him and his
23 hordes and against the many nations with him. •I mean to display my greatness
and holiness and to compel the many nations to acknowledge me; this is how
they will learn that I am Yahweh."

1 **39** 'Son of man, prophesy against Gog. Say, "The Lord Yahweh says this:
Now I set myself against you, Gog, prince of Rosh, Meshech and Tubal.
2 I will turn you round, lead you on, and bring you from the farthest north to
3 attack the mountains of Israel. •I will break the bow in your left hand and dash
4 the arrows out of your right. •You will be killed on the mountains of Israel, you
and all your hordes, and the nations with you. I shall make you food for carrion
5 birds and wild beasts. •You will fall in the open countryside. I have spoken—it is
6 the Lord Yahweh who speaks. •I will send fire to Magog and on those living un-
7 disturbed on islands, and they will learn that I am Yahweh. •I am going to see
that my holy name is known among my people Israel, and I will no longer allow
my holy name to be profaned; the nations shall learn that I am Yahweh, holy
in Israel.

8   All this is going to happen, all this is going to take place—it is the Lord
Yahweh who speaks. This is the day I predicted.

9   The citizens of the towns of Israel will go out and use these arms for
firewood: shields and bucklers, bows and arrows, clubs and javelins. For seven
10 years they will feed the fire with them. •Men will stop looking for wood in the
countryside or cutting it in the forest; they will be feeding the fire with arms.
They will plunder those who plundered them, and take spoil from those who
despoiled them—it is the Lord Yahweh who speaks.

11   On that day, I shall give Gog a famous spot in Israel for his grave—the valley

---

38 a. Gog cannot be identified. Among the countries of which he is called 'the prince' in v.3,
Meshech and Tubal can be recognised as nations from the far N., on the Black Sea borders,
and Gog is perhaps a type of the victorious barbarian from the N.   b. Probably the Cim-
merians.   c. Jerusalem.

of the Abarim,ᵃ on the east of the Sea—the valley that turns back the traveller—
and there Gog and his whole army will be buried, and it shall be called the Valley
of Hamon-gog. •The House of Israel will take seven months to bury them and 12
cleanse the country. •All the people of the country will dig their graves, and be 13
honoured for this on the day when I reveal my glory—it is the Lord Yahweh who
speaks. •Men will be selected to go continually up and down the country to 14
bury those left on the ground and cleanse it. For seven months they will go
searching. •If one of them sees any human bones as they go up and down the 15
country he will put a mark beside them until the gravediggers have buried them
in the valley of Hamon-gog—•the name of the town is to be Hamonah—and 16
so have cleansed the country."

'Son of man, the Lord Yahweh says this. Speak to every kind of bird and 17
to all wild beasts, "Muster, come here, meet from everywhere around for the
sacrifice I am making for you, a great sacrifice on the mountains of Israel; you
will eat flesh and drink blood. •You will eat the flesh of heroes, you will drink the 18
blood of the princes of the world. They are all rams and lambs, goats and fat
bulls of Bashan. •You will feed full on fat, drink yourselves drunk with blood, 19
at this sacrifice I am making for you. •You will glut yourselves at my table on 20
horses and chargers, on heroes and common soldiers—it is the Lord Yahweh
who speaks."

Conclusion

'That is how I shall display my glory to the nations, and all nations will feel 21
my sentence when I judge, and feel my hand when I strike them. •The House of 22
Israel will know that I am Yahweh their God, from that day forward for ever.
And the nations will learn that the House of Israel was exiled for their sin in 23
behaving so treacherously to me that I had to avert my face from them because
they had rebelled against me, and to hand them over to their enemies; and they all
perished by the sword. •I treated them as their filthy sins deserved and hid my face 24
from them. •And so, thus says the Lord Yahweh: Now I am going to bring 25
back the captives of Jacob, now I am going to take pity on the whole House of
Israel and show myself jealous for my holy name.

'They will forget the disgrace of having so often betrayed me when they were 26
living safely in their own land, with no one to disturb them. •When I bring them 27
home from the peoples, when I bring them back from the countries of their
enemies, when I reveal my holiness in them for many nations to see, •they will 28
know that I am Yahweh their God, when I rescue the captives from the pagans
and reunite them in their own country, not leaving a single one behind. •I shall 29
never hide my face from them again, since I shall pour out my spirit on the House
of Israel—it is the Lord Yahweh who speaks.'

IV. THE TORAH OF EZEKIEL

The future Temple

40 In the twenty-fifth year of our captivity, at the beginning of the year, on the 1
tenth day of the month, fourteen years after the destruction of the city,ᵃ the
hand of Yahweh came on me. •In a divine vision he took me away to the land 2
of Israel and put me down on a very high mountain, on the south of which
there seemed to be built a city. •He took me to it, and there I saw a man who 3
seemed to be made of bronze. He had a flax cord and a measuring rod in his
hand and was standing in the gateway. •The man said to me, 'Son of man, look 4
carefully, listen closely and pay attention to everything I show you, since you
have only been brought here for me to show it to you. Tell the House of
Israel everything that you see.'

The outer wall

5   The Temple was surrounded with a wall, and the man was holding a measuring rod that was six cubits long, each cubit a forearm and a handbreadth. He measured the thickness of this construction—one rod; and its height—one rod.

The east gate

6   He went to the east gate, climbed the steps and measured its threshold: one
7 rod deep. •Each guardroom one rod by one rod; and the walls between the guardrooms five cubits thick; and the threshold of the gate inwards from the
9 porch of the gate: one rod. •He measured the porch of the gate: eight cubits; its
10 jambs: two cubits; the porch of the gate was at the inner end. •There were three guardrooms on each side of the east gate, all three the same size; the walls
11 between them all the same thickness each side. •He measured the width of the entrance: ten cubits; and the width all down the gateway: thirteen cubits.
12 There was a rail in front of the guardrooms; each rail on either side was one
13 cubit. And the guardrooms on either side were six cubits square. •He measured the width of the gate from the back wall of one guardroom to the back wall of
14 the other; it was twenty-five cubits across from window to window. •He measured
15 the porch: twenty cubits; after the porch of the gate came the outer court. •From
16 the entrance end of the gate to the porch opposite: fifty cubits. •On each side of the gate there were splayed openings both in the guardrooms and in the spaces between, and there were openings all round inside the porch as well, and palm trees decorating the jambs.

The outer court

17   He took me through to the outer court that had rooms and a paved terrace
18 going all the way round; there were thirty rooms on this terrace. •This terrace, which came right up to the sides of the gates and matched their depth, is the
19 Lower Terrace. •He measured across the outer court from the lower gate to the outside of the inner court: a hundred cubits on the eastern and northern sides.

The north gate

20
21   He measured the length and breadth of the north gate of the outer court. •It had three guardrooms on each side; the thickness of the walls between them, and its porch too, all measured the same as those of the first gate: fifty cubits by
22 twenty-five cubits. •Its windows, its porch and its palm-tree decoration all measured the same as those of the east gate. There were seven steps up to it,
23 and its porch was at the inner end. •In the inner court there was, opposite the north gate, a gate like the one opposite the east gate. He measured the distance from one gate to the other: a hundred cubits.

The south gate

24   He took me to the south side where there was a south gate; he measured its guardrooms, wall-thicknesses and porch; they were of the same dimensions as
25 the others. •All round it and its porch were windows, like the other windows; it
26 measured fifty cubits by twenty-five cubits, •and it had seven steps up to it; its porch was at the inner end and had palm-tree decoration on its jambs, one on
27 each side. •The inner court had a south gate; he measured the distance southwards from one gate to the other: a hundred cubits.

The inner court. The south gate

28   He then took me into the inner court by the south gate; he measured the south
29 gate which was the same size as the others. •Its guardrooms, wall-thicknesses

39 a. The Arnon.
40 a. September-October 573.

and porch all measured the same as the others. It and its porch had windows all round. It measured fifty cubits by twenty-five cubits. • Its porch, measured, 30 in all, all round, was twenty-five cubits by five cubits. • The porch gave on to 31 the outer court. It had palm trees on its jambs, each side, and eight steps leading up to it.

The east gate

He took me to the east gate and measured it. It was the same size as the 32 others. • Its guardrooms, the thickness of its walls, its porch all measured the 33 same as the others. It and its porch had windows all round. Its area was fifty cubits by twenty-five cubits. • Its porch gave on to the outer court. There were palm 34 trees on its jambs on either side, and eight steps leading up to it.

The north gate

He took me to the north gate and measured it. • Its guardrooms, the thickness 35 36 of its walls and its porch all measured the same as the others. It had windows all round. Its area was fifty cubits by twenty-five cubits. • Its porch gave on to 37 the outer court. There were palm trees on its jambs on either side, and eight steps leading up to it.

Subsidiary buildings at the gate

There was a room entered from the porch of the gates. It was here that they 38 washed the holocaust. • And on either side of the porch of the gate there were 39 two tables for slaughtering the holocaust, the sacrifice for sin and the sacrifice of reparation. • Going northward up to the gate, there were two tables outside 40 and two more tables at the porch end of the gate. • Four tables on the inside and 41 four tables on the outside of the porch; in all, eight tables on which the sacrifices were offered. • There were also four tables of dressed stone for holocausts, a 42 cubit and a half long, a cubit and a half wide and a cubit high, on which all the things necessary for killing the holocaust and the sacrifices were put. • Rims, 43 a handbreadth broad, went all round the top, and on these tables was put the sacrificial flesh.

He took me into the inner court; there were two lodges in the inner court, 44 one at the side of the north gate, facing south, the other at the side of the south gate, facing north. • He told me, 'The lodge looking south is for the priests in 45 charge of the Temple, • and the lodge looking north is for the priests who serve 46 the altar. These are the sons of Zadok, those of the sons of Levi who approach Yahweh to serve him.'

The inner court

He measured the inner court. It was a quadrangle, a hundred cubits by a 47 hundred cubits, with the altar in front of the Temple.

The Temple. [b] The Ulam

He took me to the Ulam of the Temple and measured its door jambs—five 48 cubits each side; and the width of the entrance was fourteen cubits with a three-cubit wall each side. • The Ulam was twenty cubits by twelve cubits. There were 49 ten steps leading up to it, and there were columns by the door jambs, one on each side.

The Hekal

41 He took me into the Hekal and measured its door jambs: six cubits deep 1 on the one side, six cubits deep on the other. • The width of the entrance 2 was ten cubits. The walls each side of the entrance were five cubits on the one side and five cubits on the other. He measured its length: forty cubits; and its width: twenty cubits.

The Debir

3 He went in and measured the door jambs at the entrance: two cubits; then
4 the entrance: six cubits; and the walls each side of the entrance: seven cubits. •He
measured its length: twenty cubits; and its width measured across the end wall
of the Hekal: twenty cubits. He then said to me, 'This is the most holy place'.

The side cells

5 He measured the wall of the Temple: six cubits. The width of the side cells
6 was four cubits, all round the Temple. •The cells were one above the other,
thirty of them in three stories. The supports for the surrounding cells were fixed
into the Temple wall, so that the cells were not recessed into the wall of the
7 Temple. •The width of the cells increased, story by story, for they surrounded
8 the Temple in the stories that went right round it, and hence . . . . •Then I saw
that there was a paved terrace all round the Temple. The height of this, which
9 formed the base of the side cells, was a full rod of six cubits. •The outer wall of
the side cells was five cubits thick and the pavement formed a verandah outside
10 the cells of the Temple. •Beyond the rooms came an area twenty cubits wide
11 right round the Temple. •And for getting from the side cells on to the verandah
there was one entrance on the north side and one entrance on the south side.
The width of the verandah was five cubits right round.

The building on the west side

12 The building to the west of this surrounding area was seventy cubits by ninety
13 cubits, and the wall of the building was five cubits thick, all round. •He measured
the length of the Temple: a hundred cubits. The length of the court plus the
14 building and its walls: a hundred cubits. •The breadth of the facade of the
15 Temple with the quadrangle: a hundred cubits. •He measured the length of the
building plus the surrounding area at the back, plus the side depth of its door:
a hundred cubits.

Particulars of the Temple itself

16 The inside of the Hekal and the porches of the court, •their thresholds, the
window screens, the three sets of doors, one at each threshold, were all panelled
with wood, from floor to windows, and the windows were screened with lattice-
17 work. •From the door to the inner part of the Temple, and right round the
18 whole wall of the inner room, outside and inside, were carved •cherubs and
19 palm trees, palm trees and cherubs alternating; each cherub had two faces—•the
face of a man turned towards the palm tree one side and the face of a lion towards
20 the palm tree the other side, all round the Temple. •The cherubs and palm trees
were carved from the floor to above the entrance, as also on the wall of the hall.
21 The pillars of the Temple were square.

The wooden altar

22 In front of the Debir, there appeared to be •a wooden altar, three cubits high
and two cubits square. Its corners, base and sides were of wood. He said to me,
'This is the table in front of Yahweh'.

The doors

23 There was a double door for the Hekal, and a double door for the Debir.
24 These doors had two hinged leaves, two leaves for the one door, two leaves for
25 the other. •On them, on the doors of the Hekal, were carved cherubs and palm
trees like those carved on the walls. A wooden screen outside went across the
26 front of the Ulam. •There were screened windows with flanking palm trees on the
walls of the Ulam, and of the cells to the side of the Temple and on the screens.

b. The Temple is on the plan of Solomon's Temple, and has three parts: The Ulam or Vestibule,
the Hekal or Hall, and the Debir or Sanctuary (the 'Holy of Holies').

Outbuildings of the Temple

42 He took me northward into the court and led me to the rooms facing the 1 outer court, those to the north of the building. •They were one hundred 2 cubits long on the north side and fifty cubits wide. •On the sides facing the 3 porches of the inner court and the paving of the outer court was a gallery in front of the triple gallery. •and in front of the rooms was a walk, ten cubits broad measured 4 inwards and a hundred cubits long; their doors looked north. •The top floor 5 rooms were narrow because the galleries took up part of the width, being narrower than those on the ground floor or those on the middle floor of the building, since these were divided into three stories and had no columns such as the court 6 had. Hence they were narrower than the ground floor ones or the middle floor ones below them. •The outer wall parallel to the rooms, facing them and giving 7 on to the outer court, was fifty cubits long, •the length of the rooms facing the 8 outer court being fifty cubits, while on the side facing the Temple it was a hundred cubits. •Beneath the rooms there was an entrance from the east, leading in from 9 the outer court.

In the thickness of the wall of the court, on the south side fronting the court 10 and the building, were rooms. •A walk ran in front of them, as with the rooms 11 built on the north side; they were of the same length and breadth, and had similar design and doors in and out. •They were like the entrances of the southern 12 rooms; one entrance at the end of each walk, fronting the eastern wall, being the way in. •He said to me, 'The northern and southern rooms giving on to the court 13 are the rooms of the Debir, in which the priests who approach Yahweh will eat the most holy things. In them will be placed the most holy things: the oblation, the sacrifice for sin and the sacrifice of reparation, since this is a holy place. •Once 14 the priests have entered, they will not go out of the holy place into the outer court without leaving their liturgical vestments there, since these vestments are holy; they will put on other clothes before going near places assigned to the people.'

Measurements of the court

When he had finished measuring the inside of the Temple, he took me out to 15 the east gate and measured the whole area of the court. •He measured the east 16 side with his measuring rod: a total of five hundred cubits by the measuring rod. He then measured the north side: a total of five hundred cubits by the measuring 17 rod. •He then measured the south side: five hundred cubits by the measuring 18 rod •was the total. On the west side he measured five hundred cubits by the 19 measuring rod. •He measured the entire enclosing wall on all four sides: length 20 five hundred, breadth five hundred, separating the sacred from the profane.

The return of Yahweh

43 He took me to the gate, the one facing east. •I saw the glory of the God of $\frac{1}{2}$ Israel approaching from the east. A sound came with it, like the sound of the ocean, and the earth shone with his glory. •This vision was like the one I had 3 seen when I had come for the destruction of the city, and like the one I had seen on the bank of the river Chebar. Then I prostrated myself.

The glory of Yahweh arrived at the Temple by the east gate. •The spirit $\frac{4}{5}$ lifted me up and brought me into the inner court; I saw the glory of Yahweh fill the Temple. •And I heard someone speaking to me from the Temple while the 6 man stood beside me. •The voice said, 'Son of man, this is the dais of my throne, 7 the step on which I rest my feet. I shall live here among the sons of Israel for ever; and the House of Israel, they and their kings, will no longer defile my holy name with their whorings and the corpses of their kings, •setting their 8 threshold beside my threshold and their pillars beside my pillars, with a party wall shared by them and me. They used to defile my holy name by their filthy practices, and this is why I destroyed them in my anger. •From now on they 9 will banish their whorings and the corpses of their kings from my presence and I shall live among them for ever.

10 'Son of man, describe this Temple to the House of Israel, to shame them out
11 of their filthy practices. Let them draw up the plan, •and, if they are ashamed of their behaviour, show them the design and plan of the Temple, its exits and entrances, its shape, how all of it is arranged, the entire design and all its principles. Give them all this in writing so that they can see and take note of its
12 design and the way it is all arranged and carry it out. •This is the charter of the Temple: all the surrounding area on top of the mountain is a most holy area. Such is the charter of the Temple.'

The altar

13 Here are the dimensions of the altar, in cubits each of a cubit plus a handbreadth. The base: one cubit high and one cubit wide. The ledge all round
14 it: one span. This is the height of the altar: •from the ground level of the base up to the lower plinth, two cubits high and one cubit wide; from the lesser plinth
15 to the greater plinth, four cubits high and one cubit wide. •The altar hearth: four
16 cubits high, with four horns projecting from the hearth, •the hearth being square:
17 twelve cubits by twelve cubits; •and the square plinth: fourteen cubits by fourteen cubits; and the ledge all round: half a cubit; and the base: one cubit all round. The steps were on the east side.

The consecration of the altar

18 He said to me, 'Son of man, the Lord Yahweh says this: As regards the altar, this is how things are to be done when it has been built for the offering of
19 the holocaust and for the pouring of blood. •To those levitical priests of the race of Zadok who approach me to serve me—it is the Lord Yahweh who speaks—you
20 must give a young bull as a sacrifice for sin. •You are to take some of its blood and put it on the four horns and the four corners of the plinth and the surrounding
21 ledge. In this way you will purify it and make atonement on it. •Then take the bull of the sacrifice for sin and burn it in that part of the Temple which is cut off
22 from the sanctuary. •On the second day, you must offer an unblemished he-goat
23 as the sacrifice for sin, and the altar is to be purified again as with the bull. •When you have finished the purification you must offer a young bull without blemish
24 and an unblemished ram chosen from the flock. •You are to present them before Yahweh, and the priests will sprinkle salt on them and offer them as a holocaust
25 to Yahweh. •As a sacrifice for sin, every day for seven days you must offer a
26 he-goat, a bull and an unblemished ram from the flock, •for a week. In this way
27 the altar will be atoned for and will be purified and inaugurated. •At the end of that time, on the eighth day and afterwards, the priest is to offer your holocausts and your communion sacrifices on the altar, and I will look kindly on you—it is the Lord Yahweh who speaks.'

The use of the east gate

1 **44** He brought me back to the outer east gate of the sanctuary. It was shut.
2 Yahweh said to me, 'This gate will be kept shut. No one will open it or go through it, since Yahweh the God of Israel has been through it. And so it must
3 be kept shut. •The prince himself, however, may sit there to take his meal in the presence of Yahweh. He is to enter and leave through the porch of the gate.'

Rules of admission to the Temple

4 He led me through the north gate to the front of the Temple. I looked; I saw the glory of Yahweh filling the Temple of Yahweh, and I prostrated myself.
5 Yahweh said to me, 'Son of man, pay attention, look carefully and listen closely to everything I explain; these are all the arrangements of the Temple of Yahweh and all its laws. Be careful about which men are admitted to the Temple and
6 which are excluded from the sanctuary. •And say to the rebels of the House of

Israel, "The Lord Yahweh says this: You have gone beyond all bounds with all your filthy practices, House of Israel, •by admitting aliens, uncircumcised in 7 heart and body, to frequent my sanctuary and profane my Temple, while you offer my bread, the fat and the blood, and break my covenant with all your filthy practices. •Instead of performing your duties to me in the Holy Place, 8 you have deputed someone else to perform your duties in my sanctuary. •The 9 Lord Yahweh says this: No alien, uncircumcised in heart and body, is to enter my sanctuary, none of those aliens living among the Israelites.

The Levites

As regards the Levites who abandoned me when Israel strayed far from me 10 to follow its idols, they must bear the weight of their own sin. •They are to be 11 servants in my sanctuary, responsible for guarding the Temple gates and serving the Temple. They will kill the holocaust and the sacrifice for the people, and hold themselves at the service of the people. •Since they used to be at their service in 12 front of their idols and were an occasion of sin to the House of Israel, very well, I raise my hand against them—it is the Lord Yahweh who speaks; they must bear the weight of their sin. •They are never to approach me again to perform the 13 priestly office in my presence, or to touch my holy things and my most holy things; they must bear the disgrace of their filthy practices. •I shall give them the responsi- 14 bility of working in the Temple; I shall make them responsible for serving it and for everything to be done in it.

The priests

As regards the levitical priests, the sons of Zadok, who did their duty to me 15 in the sanctuary when the Israelites strayed far from me, they may still approach me to serve me; they may stand in my presence to offer me the fat and blood—it is the Lord Yahweh who speaks. •They may enter my sanctuary and approach 16 my table to serve me; they may perform my liturgy. •Once they enter the gates 17 of the inner court, they are to wear linen vestments; they are to wear no wool when they serve inside the gates of the inner court and in the Temple. •They are to wear 18 linen caps on their heads, and linen breeches about their loins; they are not to wear belts of . . . •When they go out to the people in the outer court, they are 19 to remove the vestments in which they have performed the liturgy and leave them in the rooms of the Holy Place, and put on other clothes, so as not to hallow the people with their vestments. •They are neither to shave their heads nor to let 20 their hair grow long, but must cut their hair to a reasonable length. •No 21 priest is to drink wine on the day he enters the inner court. •They are not to 22 marry widows or divorced women, but only virgins of the race of Israel; they may, however, marry widows, if the widow of a priest. •They are to teach my 23 people the difference between what is sacred and what is profane and make them understand the difference between what is clean and what is unclean. •They are to 24 be judges in disputes; they must judge in the spirit of my statutes; they must follow my laws and ordinances at all my feasts and keep my sabbaths holy. •They are 25 not to go near a dead man, in case they become unclean, except in these permissible cases, that is, for father, mother, daughter, son, brother or unmarried sister. •After one of them has been purified, seven days must elapse; •then, 26 27 on the day when he enters the Holy Place—enters the inner court to minister in the Holy Place—he is to offer his sacrifice for sin—it is the Lord Yahweh who speaks. •They are to have no inheritance; I myself will be their inheri- 28 tance. You are to give them no patrimony in Israel; I myself will be their patrimony. •Their food is to be the oblation, the sacrifice for sin and the 29 sacrifice of reparation. Everything in Israel put under the ban shall be for them. The best of all your first-fruits, of every sort of due and of all that you offer, 30 is to go to the priests; and the best of your dough you are also to give to the priests, so that a blessing may rest on your house. •Priests are not to eat the 31

flesh of anything that has died a natural death or been savaged, neither of a
bird nor of any other creature.

The division of the country. The portion for Yahweh

1 45 When you divide the country into portions by lot, you are to allocate
the sacred portion of the country to Yahweh: twenty-five thousand cubits
2 long and twenty thousand wide. The whole of this land is to be sacred, •and
of this an area five hundred by five hundred cubits square is to be for the
3 sanctuary, with a boundary fifty cubits wide right round. •Out of this area you
are also to measure a section twenty-five thousand by ten thousand cubits,
4 in which there shall stand the sanctuary, the Holy of Holies. •This is to be the
sacred portion of the country; it shall belong to the priests who officiate in the
sanctuary and approach Yahweh to serve him. There they are to have their houses
5 and also a district set apart for the sanctuary. •An area twenty-five thousand
by ten thousand cubits is to be kept for the Levites serving the Temple to own,
6 with towns to live in. •You are to give the city possession of an area five thousand
by twenty-five thousand cubits, near the land belonging to the sanctuary; this
is to be for the whole House of Israel.

The portion for the prince

7 The prince is to have a domain either side of the land belonging to the
Holy Place and of the land belonging to the city, and adjacent to the land belonging
to the Holy Place and the land belonging to the city, stretching westwards from
the west and eastwards from the east, its size equal to one of the portions
8 between the west and the east frontiers[a] •of the country. This is to be his
possession in Israel. Then my princes will no longer oppress my people; they
must leave the rest of the country for the House of Israel, for its tribes.
9 The Lord Yahweh says this: Let this be enough for you, princes of Israel!
Give up your violence and plundering, practise justice and integrity, crush my
10 people no more with taxation—it is the Lord Yahweh who speaks. •Have scales
11 that are fair, a fair ephah, a fair bath. •Let the ephah and bath be equal, let
the bath hold one tenth of a homer and the ephah one tenth of a homer. Let
12 the measures be based on the homer. •The shekel is to be twenty gerahs. Twenty
shekels, twenty-five shekels and fifteen shekels are to make one mina.

Offerings for worship

13 'This is the offering that you are to levy: the sixth of an ephah for every
14 homer of wheat, and the sixth of an ephah for every homer of barley. •The dues
on oil: one bath of oil out of every ten baths or out of every cor (which is equal
15 to ten baths or one homer, since ten baths equal one homer). •You are to levy
one sheep on every flock of two hundred from the patrimony of Israel for the
oblation, the holocaust and the communion sacrifice. This is to form your
16 atonement—it is the Lord Yahweh who speaks. •Let all the people of the
17 country be subject to this due for the prince of Israel. •The prince is to make
himself responsible for providing the holocausts, oblation and libation for
feasts, New Moons and sabbaths, for all the solemn festivals of the House of
Israel. He is to provide the sacrifice for sin, oblation, holocaust and communion
sacrifices atoning for the House of Israel.

The feast of the Passover

18 The Lord Yahweh says this: On the first day of the first month, you must
19 take a young bull without blemish, to purify the sanctuary. •The priest is to

45 a. This plan provides an area about seven miles square at Jerusalem for the Temple, its
precincts and towns for the priests and Levites; and on each side of it, a strip of the same width
for the prince, to the Jordan on the E. and to the Mediterranean on the W.

take blood from the sacrifice for sin and put it on the doorposts of the Temple, on the four corners of the altar plinth and on the doorposts of the gates of the inner court. •You must do the same on the seventh of the month, on behalf of anyone who has sinned through inadvertence or ignorance. This is how you are to make atonement for the Temple. •On the fourteenth day of the first month, you must celebrate the feast of the Passover. For seven days everyone is to eat unleavened loaves. •On that day, the prince must offer a bull as a sacrifice for sin, for himself and all the people in the country. •For the seven days of the feast, he must offer Yahweh a holocaust of seven bulls and seven rams without blemish, daily for a week, and one he-goat daily as a sacrifice for sin, •offering one ephah for each bull and one ephah for each ram, and a hin of oil for every ephah for the oblation. 20 21 22 23 24

The feast of Tabernacles

For the feast that falls on the fifteenth day of the seventh month, he must do the same for seven days, offering the sacrifice for sin, the holocaust, oblation and the oil. 25

The sabbath and the New Moon

46 Thus speaks the Lord Yahweh: The east gate of the inner court must be kept shut for the six working days. On the sabbath day it is to be opened, as also on the day of the New Moon; •and the prince is to go in through the porch of the outer gate and take his position by the doorposts of the gate. The priests must then offer his holocaust and his communion sacrifice. He must prostrate himself on the threshold of the gate and go out, and the gate is not to be shut again until the evening. •The people of the country are to prostrate themselves in the presence of Yahweh at the entrance to the gate on sabbaths and days of the New Moon. •The holocaust offered to Yahweh by the prince on the sabbath day is to consist of six unblemished lambs and one unblemished ram, •and an oblation of one ephah for the ram, and such oblation as he pleases for the lambs, and a hin of oil for every ephah. •On the day of the New Moon it is to consist of a young bull without blemish, six unblemished lambs and one unblemished ram, •when he must make an oblation of one ephah for the bull and one ephah for the ram, and what he pleases for the lambs, and a hin of oil for every ephah. 1 2 3 4 5 6 7

Miscellaneous regulations

When the prince goes in, he is to enter by the porch of the gate, and he must leave by the same way. •When the people of the country come into the presence of Yahweh at the solemn festivals, those who have come in by the north gate to prostrate themselves are to go out by the south gate, and those who have come in by the south gate are to go out by the north gate; no one is to turn back to leave through the gate by which he entered but is to go out on the opposite side. The prince is to come with them, coming in like them and going out like them. •On feast days and solemn festivals the oblation must be one ephah for every bull, one ephah for every ram, what he pleases for the lambs, and a hin of oil for every ephah. •When the prince offers Yahweh a voluntary holocaust or a voluntary communion sacrifice, the east gate is to be opened for him, and he is to offer his holocaust and his communion sacrifice as he does on the sabbath day; when he has gone out, the gate is to be shut after him. •Every day he must offer an unblemished lamb one year old as a holocaust to Yahweh; he must offer this every morning. •Every morning in addition he is to offer an oblation of one sixth of an ephah and one third of a hin of oil, for mixing with the flour. This is the oblation to Yahweh, an eternal law fixed in perpetuity. •The lamb, the oblation and the oil are to be offered morning after morning for ever. The Lord Yahweh says this. If the prince presents his sons with part 8 9 10 11 12 13 14 15 16

of his hereditary portion, the gift is to pass into the ownership of his sons, and
17 become their hereditary property. •If, however, he presents part of his hereditary
portion to one of his servants, it shall only belong to the man until the year of
liberation*a* and is then to revert to the prince. Only his sons may retain his hereditary
18 portion. •The prince may not take any part of the people's hereditary portion
and thus rob them of their rightful possessions; he must provide the patrimony
of his sons out of his own property, so that no member of my people is robbed
of his rightful possessions." '

19   He took me through the entrance at the side of the north gate that leads
to the rooms of the Holy Place set apart for the priests. And there before us,
20 to the west, was a space at the end. •He said to me, 'This is where the priests
are to boil the slaughtered animals for the sacrifice for sin and the sacrifice of
reparation, and where they are to bake the oblation, without having to carry
21 them into the outer court and so run the risk of hallowing the people'. •He took
me into the outer court and led me to each of its four corners; in each corner
22 of the outer court was a compound; •in other words, the four corners of the
court contained four small compounds, forty cubits by thirty, all four being
23 the same size. •Each of the four was enclosed by a wall, with hearths all round
24 the bottom of the wall. •He said, 'These are the kitchens where the Temple
servants are to boil the sacrifices offered by the people'.

The spring in the Temple

1   47 He brought me back to the entrance of the Temple, where a stream came
out from under the Temple threshold and flowed eastwards, since the
Temple faced east. The water flowed from under the right side of the Temple,
2 south of the altar. •He took me out by the north gate and led me right round
outside as far as the outer east gate where the water flowed out on the right-hand
3 side. •The man went to the east holding his measuring line and measured off a
thousand cubits; he then made me wade across the stream; the water reached
4 my ankles. •He measured off another thousand and made me wade across the
stream again; the water reached my knees. He measured off another thousand
5 and made me wade across again; the water reached my waist. •He measured
off another thousand; it was now a river which I could not cross; the stream
6 had swollen and was now deep water, a river impossible to cross. •He then
said, 'Do you see, son of man?' He took me further, then brought me back to
7 the bank of the river. •When I got back, there were many trees on each bank
8 of the river. •He said, 'This water flows east down to the Arabah and to the
9 sea; and flowing into the sea it makes its waters wholesome. •Wherever the
river flows, all living creatures teeming in it will live. Fish will be very
plentiful, for wherever the water goes it brings health, and life teems wherever
10 the river flows. •There will be fishermen on its banks. Fishing nets will be
spread from En-gedi to En-eglaim. The fish will be as varied and as
11 plentiful as the fish of the Great Sea.*a* •The marshes and lagoons, however, will
12 not become wholesome, but will remain salt. •Along the river, on either bank,
will grow every kind of fruit tree with leaves that never wither and fruit that
never fails; they will bear new fruit every month, because this water comes from
the sanctuary. And their fruit will be good to eat and the leaves medicinal.

The frontiers of the land

13   'The Lord Yahweh says this: Here are the frontiers of the territories to
be allotted between the twelve tribes of Israel, with two portions for Joseph.
14 You must share it out equally between you, since I swore to your fathers that I
15 would give them this land which now falls to you as your inheritance. •Here are

46 a. The Jubilee year, occurring every fifty years, see Lv 25:1.
47 a. The Mediterranean.

the frontiers of the land. On the north, from the Great Sea by way of Hethlon to the Pass of Hamath and on to Zedad, •Berothah, Sibraim lying between 16 the territories of Damascus and Hamath—and to Hazer-hat-ticon on the borders of Hauran. •The frontier will extend from the sea to Hazer-enon, 17 marching with the frontier of Damascus to the north of it and the frontier of Hamath also on the north; so much for the northern frontier. •On the east 18 the Jordan will serve as frontier between Hauran and Damascus, between Gilead and the land of Israel, down to the Eastern Sea*b* as far as Tamar; so much for the eastern frontier. •On the south, from Tamar southward to the waters of 19 Meribah in Kadesh, to the Wadi and the Great Sea; so much for the southern frontier. •On the west the Great Sea will serve as frontier up to the point 20 opposite the Pass of Hamath; so much for the western frontier. •You are to 21 share out this land among yourselves, between the tribes of Israel. •You are to 22 divide it into inheritances for yourselves and the aliens settled among you who have begotten children with you, since you are to treat them as citizens of Israel. They are to draw lots with you for their inheritance, with the tribes of Israel. You must give the alien his inheritance in the tribe in which he is living—it is 23 the Lord Yahweh who speaks.

The division of the land

48 'This is the list of the tribes. In the far north by way of Hethlon to the 1 Pass of Hamath, to Hazer-enon, with the frontier of Damascus lying to the north, and marching with Hamath—the land from the eastern frontier to the western frontier: Dan, one portion. •Bordering Dan, from the eastern 2 frontier to the western frontier: Asher, one portion. •Bordering Asher, from 3 the eastern frontier to the western frontier: Naphtali, one portion. •Bordering 4 Naphtali, from the eastern frontier to the western frontier: Manasseh, one portion. •Bordering Manasseh, from the eastern frontier to the western frontier: 5 Ephraim, one portion. •Bordering Ephraim, from the eastern frontier to the 6 western frontier: Reuben, one portion. •Bordering Reuben, from the eastern 7 frontier to the western frontier: Judah, one portion. •Bordering Judah, from 8 the eastern frontier to the western frontier, is the part you are to set aside, twenty-five thousand cubits wide, and as long as each of the other portions from the eastern frontier to the western frontier. The sanctuary will be in the centre of it.

'The part you must set aside for Yahweh is to be twenty-five thousand cubits 9 long and ten thousand cubits wide. •This consecrated portion is to belong to 10 the priests, being, on the north side, twenty-five thousand cubits; on the west side ten thousand cubits wide, on the east side ten thousand cubits wide and on the south side twenty-five thousand cubits long, and the sanctuary of Yahweh will be in the centre of it. •This is to belong to the consecrated priests, to those of 11 the sons of Zadok who maintained my liturgy and did not go astray with the straying Israelites, as the Levites went astray. •And so their portion is to be taken 12 out of the most holy portion of the land, near the territory of the Levites. •The 13 territory of the Levites, like the territory of the priests, is to be twenty-five thousand cubits long and ten thousand wide—the whole length being twenty-five thousand and the width ten thousand. •It will be illegal for them to sell or 14 exchange any part of it, and the domain can never be alienated, since it is consecrated to Yahweh. •As regards the remainder, an area of five thousand 15 cubits by twenty-five thousand, this is to be for the common use of the city, for houses and pastures. The city is to stand in the centre. •Here are its 16 measurements: on the north side, four thousand five hundred cubits; on the south side, four thousand five hundred cubits; on the east side, four thousand five hundred cubits; on the west side, four thousand five hundred cubits. •And 17 the city pastures are to extend two hundred and fifty cubits to the north, two hundred and fifty to the south, two hundred and fifty to the east, two hundred

18 and fifty to the west. •One strip, contiguous to the consecrated portion, must be left over, consisting of ten thousand cubits to eastward and ten thousand to westward, marching with the consecrated portion; this will bring in a revenue
19 for feeding the municipal workmen. •These municipal workpeople are to be drawn
20 from all the tribes of Israel. •The portion is to have a total area of twenty-five thousand cubits by twenty-five thousand. You are to allocate a quarter of the
21 sacred portion to form the city. •What is left over shall be for the prince, on either side of the sacred portion and of the common land belonging to the city, marching with the twenty-five thousand cubits to eastward to the eastern frontier, and marching with the twenty-five thousand cubits to westward to the western frontier—running parallel with the other portions and belonging to the prince. In the centre will be the consecrated portion and the sanctuary of
22 the Temple. •Thus, apart from the property of the Levites and the property of the city which lie inside the prince's portion, everything between the borders of Judah and the borders of Benjamin is to belong to the prince.

23   'Here are the rest of the tribes: from the eastern frontier to the western
24 frontier: Benjamin, one portion. •Bordering Benjamin, from the eastern frontier
25 to the western frontier: Simeon, one portion. •Bordering Simeon, from the
26 eastern frontier to the western frontier: Issachar, one portion. •Bordering Issachar, from the eastern frontier to the western frontier: Zebulun, one portion.
27 Bordering Zebulun, from the eastern frontier to the western frontier: Gad, one
28 portion. •The southern border of Gad will be formed by the southern frontier running through Tamar to the waters of Meribah in Kadesh, to the Wadi and
29 the Great Sea. •This is how you are to divide the land into patrimonies for the tribes of Israel; and these are to be their portions—it is the Lord Yahweh who speaks.

The gates of Jerusalem

30   'Here are the ways out of the city. On the north side, being four thousand
31 five hundred cubits long, •three gates: the gate of Reuben, the gate of Judah, the gate of Levi; the gates of the city are to be named after the tribes of Israel.
32 On the east side, being four thousand five hundred cubits long, three gates:
33 the gate of Joseph, the gate of Benjamin, the gate of Dan. •On the south side, being four thousand five hundred cubits long, three gates: the gate of Simeon,
34 the gate of Issachar, the gate of Zebulun. •On the west side, being four thousand five hundred cubits long, three gates: the gate of Gad, the gate of Asher, the
35 gate of Naphtali. •Total perimeter: eighteen thousand cubits.
   'The name of the city in future is to be: Yahweh-is-there.'

INTRODUCTION
TO THE BOOK OF
DANIEL

The book of Daniel was written between 167 and 164 B.C., during the persecution under Antiochus Epiphanes and before the Maccabean revolt. The first six chapters relate the trials and perils of Daniel's life in the service of Nebuchadnezzar. The last six describe visions granted to Daniel under successors to Nebuchadnezzar in Babylon.

The aim of the book was to sustain faith and hope among the Jews in their persecutions by showing them the triumph of Daniel over his own severe ordeals and temptations of the same kind; and to hold before them the vision of a time to come when the wrath of God would be satisfied; and the kingdom of the saints would begin under a 'Son of Man' whose reign would endure for ever.

The historical setting of the story undoubtedly disregards known facts, persons and dates and contains anachronisms in detail; the meaning of the book for its first readers was to be found in its insight into the present and the future in the purposes of God. It is the last expression of messianic prophecy in the Old Testament.

DANIEL

THE YOUNG HEBREWS
AT THE COURT OF NEBUCHADNEZZAR

1 In the third year of the reign of Jehoiakim king of Judah, Nebuchadnezzar
2 king of Babylon marched on Jerusalem and besieged it. •The Lord delivered
Jehoiakim king of Judah into his hands, with some of the furnishings of the
Temple of God. He took them away to the land of Shinar, and stored the sacred
vessels in the treasury of his own gods.

3 The king ordered Ashpenaz, his chief eunuch, to select from the Israelites
4 a certain number of boys of either royal or noble descent; •they had to be
without any physical defect, of good appearance, trained in every kind of wisdom,
well-informed, quick at learning, suitable for service in the palace of the king.
Ashpenaz himself was to teach them the language and literature of the Chaldaeans.
5 The king assigned them a daily allowance of food and wine from his own royal
table. They were to receive an education lasting for three years, after which they
6 were expected to be fit for the king's society. •Among them were Daniel,
7 Hananiah, Mishael and Azariah, who were Judaeans. •The chief eunuch gave
them other names, calling Daniel Belteshazzar, Hananiah Shadrach, Mishael
8 Meshach, and Azariah Abednego. •Daniel, who was most anxious not to defile
himself with the food and wine from the royal table, begged the chief eunuch to
9 spare him this defilement; •and by the grace of God Daniel met goodwill and
10 sympathy on the part of the chief eunuch. •But he warned Daniel, 'I am afraid
of my lord the king: he has assigned you food and drink, and if he sees you looking
thinner in the face than the other boys of your age, my head will be in danger
11 with the king because of you'. •At this Daniel turned to the guard whom the
chief eunuch had assigned to Daniel, Hananiah, Mishael and Azariah. He said,
12 'Please allow your servants a ten days' trial, during which we are given only
13 vegetables to eat and water to drink. •You can then compare our looks with
those of the boys who eat the king's food; go by what you see, and treat your
14 servants accordingly.' •The man agreed to do what they asked and put them on
15 ten days' trial. •When the ten days were over they looked and were in better
health than any of the boys who had eaten their allowance from the royal table;
16 so the guard withdrew their allowance of food and the wine they were to drink,
17 and gave them vegetables. •And God favoured these four boys with knowledge
and intelligence in everything connected with literature, and in wisdom; while
18 Daniel had the gift of interpreting every kind of vision and dream. •When the
period stipulated by the king for the boys' training was over, the chief eunuch
19 presented them to Nebuchadnezzar. •The king conversed with them, and among
all the boys found none to equal Daniel, Hananiah, Mishael and Azariah. So
20 they became members of the king's court, •and on whatever point of wisdom
or information he might question them, he found them ten times better than
21 all the magicians and enchanters in his entire kingdom. •Daniel remained there
until the first year of King Cyrus.

NEBUCHADNEZZAR'S DREAM:
THE COMPOSITE STATUE

The king questions his sages

2 In the second year of the reign of Nebuchadnezzar, Nebuchadnezzar had a ¹
series of dreams; his mind was troubled, sleep deserted him. •The king then ²
had magicians and enchanters, sorcerers and Chaldaeans *ᵃ* summoned to tell the
king what his dreams meant. They arrived and stood in the king's presence.
The king said to them, 'I have had a dream, and my mind is disturbed by a desire ³
to understand the dream'. •The Chaldaeans answered the king: ⁴
    'O king, live for ever! Tell your servants the dream, and we will reveal
its meaning for you.' •The king answered the Chaldaeans, 'This is my firm resolve: ⁵
if you cannot tell me what my dream was, and what it means, I will have you
torn limb from limb and your houses razed to the ground. •If, on the other hand, ⁶
you can tell me what I dreamt and what it means, I will give you presents,
rewards and high honour. So tell me what I dreamt and what it means.' •A ⁷
second time they said, 'Let the king tell his dream to his servants, and we will
reveal its meaning'. •But the king retorted, 'It is plain to me that you are trying ⁸
to gain time, knowing my proclaimed and firm resolve. •Your intention is ⁹
not to interpret my dream, but to make me misleading and tortuous speeches
while the time goes by. So tell me what my dream was, and I shall know whether
you can interpret it or not.' •The Chaldaeans answered the king, 'Nobody in the ¹⁰
world could find out the king's trouble; what is more, no other king, governor
or chief would think of putting such a question to any magician, enchanter or
Chaldaean. •The question the king asks is difficult, and no one can find the king ¹¹
an answer to it, except the gods, whose dwelling is not with creatures of flesh.'
At this the king flew into a rage and ordered all the Babylonian sages to be put ¹²
to death. •On publication of the decree to have the sages killed, search was made ¹³
for Daniel and his companions to have them put to death.

Daniel intervenes

    With shrewd and cautious words, however, Daniel approached Arioch, ¹⁴
commander of the king's executioners, when he was on his way to kill the Babylonian sages. •He said to Arioch, the royal marshal, 'Why has the king issued ¹⁵
such an urgent decree?' Arioch explained matters to Daniel, •and Daniel went ¹⁶
off to ask the king for a stay of execution to give him the opportunity of revealing
his interpretation to the king. •Daniel then went home and told his friends ¹⁷
Hananiah, Mishael and Azariah what had happened, •urging them to beg the ¹⁸
God of heaven to show his mercy in this mysterious affair, so that Daniel and
his friends might be spared the fate of the other Babylonian sages. •The mystery ¹⁹
was then revealed to Daniel in a night-vision, and Daniel blessed the God of
heaven. •This is what Daniel said: ²⁰

    'May the name of God
        be blessed for ever and ever,
    since wisdom and power are his alone.
    His, to control the procession of times and seasons, ²¹
        to make and unmake kings,
        to confer wisdom on the wise,
        and knowledge on those with wit to discern;
    his, to uncover depths and mysteries, ²²
        to know what lies in darkness;
        and light dwells with him.
    To you, God of my fathers, I give thanks and praise ²³
        for having given me wisdom and intelligence:

now you have shown me what we asked you,
you have revealed the king's trouble to us.'

24 So Daniel went to see Arioch whom the king had made responsible for putting
the Babylonian sages to death. On going in he said, 'Do not put the Babylonian
sages to death. Take me into the king's presence and I will reveal the meaning
25 to the king.' •Arioch lost no time in bringing Daniel to the king. 'Among the
exiles from Judah,' he said 'I have discovered a man who can reveal the meaning
26 to the king.' •The king said to Daniel (who had been given the name Belteshazzar),
27 'Can you tell me what my dream was, and what it means?' •Facing the king,
Daniel replied, 'None of the sages, enchanters, magicians or wizards has been
28 able to tell the king the truth of the mystery which the king propounded; •but
there is a God in heaven who reveals mysteries, and who has shown King Nebuchadnezzar what is to take place in the days to come. These, then, are the
dream and the visions that passed through your head as you lay in bed:
29 'O king, on your bed your thoughts turned to what would happen in the
future, and the Revealer of Mysteries disclosed to you what is to take place.
30 This mystery has been revealed to me, not that I am wiser than any other
man, but for this sole purpose: that the king should learn what it means, and
that you should understand your inmost thoughts.
31 'You have had a vision, O king; this is what you saw: a statue, a great statue
32 of extreme brightness, stood before you, terrible to see. •The head of this statue
was of fine gold, its chest and arms were of silver, its belly and thighs of bronze,
33
34 its legs of iron, its feet part iron, part earthenware. •While you were gazing, a
stone broke away, untouched by any hand, and struck the statue, struck its feet
35 of iron and earthenware and shattered them. •And then, iron and earthenware,
bronze, silver, gold all broke into small pieces as fine as chaff on the threshing-
floor in summer. The wind blew them away, leaving not a trace behind. And the
stone that had struck the statue grew into a great mountain, filling the whole
36 earth. •This was the dream; now we will explain to the king what it means.
37 You, O king, king of kings, to whom the God of heaven has given sovereignty,
38 power, strength and glory——•the sons of men, the beasts of the field, the birds
of heaven, wherever they live, he has entrusted to your rule, making you king
39 of them all—you are the golden head. •And after you another kingdom will
rise, not so great as you, and then a third, of bronze, which will rule the whole
40 world. •There will be a fourth kingdom, hard as iron, as iron that shatters and
crushes all. Like iron that breaks everything to pieces, it will crush and break
41 all the earlier kingdoms. •The feet you saw, part earthenware, part iron, are a
kingdom which will be split in two, but which will retain something of the strength
of iron, just as you saw the iron and the clay of the earthenware mixed together.
42 The feet were part iron, part earthenware: the kingdom will be partly strong and
43 partly weak. •And just as you saw the iron and the clay of the earthenware mixed
together, so the two will be mixed together in the seed of man;[b] but they will
44 not hold together any more than iron will blend with earthenware. •In the time
of these kings the God of heaven will set up a kingdom which shall never be
destroyed, and this kingdom will not pass into the hands of another race: it
45 will shatter and absorb all the previous kingdoms, and itself last for ever——just
as you saw the stone untouched by hand break from the mountain and shatter
iron, bronze, earthenware, silver and gold. The great God has shown the king
what is to take place. The dream is true, the interpretation exact.'

The king's profession of faith

46 At this, King Nebuchadnezzar fell prostrate before Daniel; he gave orders
47 for Daniel to be offered an oblation and a fragrant sacrifice. •The king said to

---

2 a. I.e., diviners; the art of divination was believed to have originated in Chaldaea.
b. Probably alluding to the intermarriage of Seleucids and Ptolemies.

Daniel, 'Your god must be the God of gods, the master of kings, and the Revealer of Mysteries, since you have been able to reveal this mystery'. •The king conferred 48 high rank on Daniel and gave him many handsome presents. He also made him governor of the whole province of Babylon and head of all the sages of Babylon. At Daniel's request, however, the king entrusted the affairs of the province of 49 Babylon to Shadrach, Meshach and Abednego; Daniel himself remained at court.

THE ADORATION OF THE GOLDEN STATUE

Nebuchadnezzar erects a golden statue

3 King Nebuchadnezzar had a golden statue made, six cubits tall and three 1 cubits wide, which he erected on the plain of Dura, in the province of Babylon. King Nebuchadnezzar then summoned the satraps, prefects, governors, 2 counsellors, treasurers, judges, men of law, and all the provincial authorities to assemble and attend the dedication of the statue erected by King Nebuchadnezzar. Then the satraps, prefects, governors, counsellors, treasurers, judges, men of 3 law and all the provincial authorities assembled for the dedication of the statue erected by King Nebuchadnezzar; and they stood there in front of the statue which King Nebuchadnezzar had erected. •The herald then made this 4 proclamation: 'Men of all peoples, nations, languages! This is required of you: the moment you hear the sound of horn, pipe, lyre, trigon, harp, bagpipe, or 5 any other instrument, you must prostrate yourselves and worship the golden statue erected by King Nebuchadnezzar. •Those who do not prostrate themselves 6 and worship shall immediately be thrown into the burning fiery furnace.' •And so, 7 the instant the people heard the sound of horn, pipe, lyre, trigon, harp, bagpipe and all the other instruments, the men of all peoples, nations and languages prostrated themselves and worshipped the statue erected by King Nebuchadnezzar.

The denunciation and condemnation of the Jews

Some Chaldaeans then came forward and laid information against the Jews. 8 They said to King Nebuchadnezzar, 'O king, live for ever! •You have issued a $^{9}_{10}$ decree, O king, to the effect that everyone on hearing the sound of horn, pipe, lyre, trigon, harp, bagpipe or any other instrument is to prostrate himself and worship the golden statue; •and that anyone who does not prostrate himself 11 and worship is to be thrown into the burning fiery furnace. •Now there are certain 12 Jews to whom you have entrusted the affairs of the province of Babylon: Shadrach, Meshach and Abednego; these men have ignored your command, O king; they do not serve your gods, and refuse to worship the golden statue you have erected.' Furious with rage, Nebuchadnezzar sent for Shadrach, Meshach and Abednego. 13 The men were immediately brought before the king. •Nebuchadnezzar addressed 14 them, 'Shadrach, Meshach and Abednego, is it true that you do not serve my gods, and that you refuse to worship the golden statue I have erected? •When 15 you hear the sound of horn, pipe, lyre, trigon, harp, bagpipe, or any other instrument, are you prepared to prostrate yourselves and worship the statue I have made? If you refuse to worship it, you must be thrown straight away into the burning fiery furnace; and where is the god who could save you from my power?' Shadrach, Meshach and Abednego replied to King Nebuchadnezzar, 'Your 16 question hardly requires an answer: •if our God, the one we serve, is able to 17 save us from the burning fiery furnace and from your power, O king, he will save us; •and even if he does not, then you must know, O king, that we will not 18 serve your god or worship the statue you have erected'. •These words infuriated 19 King Nebuchadnezzar; his expression was very different now as he looked at Shadrach, Meshach and Abednego. He gave orders for the furnace to be made seven times hotter than usual, •and commanded certain stalwarts from his army 20

to bind Shadrach, Meshach and Abednego and throw them into the burning
21 fiery furnace. •They were then bound, fully clothed, cloak, hose and headgear,
22 and thrown into the burning fiery furnace. •The king's command was so urgent
and the heat of the furnace was so fierce, that the men carrying Shadrach,
23 Meshach, and Abednego were burnt to death by the flames from the fire; •the
three men, Shadrach, Meshach and Abednego fell, still bound, into the burning
fiery furnace.

The song of Azariah in the furnace

24   And they walked in the heart of the flames, praising God and blessing the Lord.
25 Azariah stood in the heart of the fire, and he began to pray:

26   'All honour and blessing to you, Lord, God of our ancestors,
          may your name be held glorious for ever.
27   In all that you have done your justice is apparent:
          your promises are always faithfully fulfilled,
          your ways never deviate,
          your judgements are always true.
28   You have given a just sentence
          in all the disasters you have brought down on us
          and on Jerusalem, the holy city of our ancestors,
          since it is for our sins that you have treated us like this,
          fairly and as we deserved.
29   Yes, we have sinned and committed a crime by deserting you,
          yes, we have sinned gravely;
          we have not listened to the precepts of your Law,
30   we have not observed them,
          we have not done what we were told to do
          for our own good.
31   Yes, all the disasters you have brought down on us,
          all that you have done to us,
          you have been fully justified in doing.
32   You have delivered us into the power of our enemies,
          of a lawless people, the worst of the godless,
          of an unjust king, the worst in the whole world;
33   today we dare not even open our mouths,
          shame and dishonour are the lot of those who serve and worship you.
34   Oh! Do not abandon us for ever,
          for the sake of your name;
          do not repudiate your covenant,
35   do not withdraw your favour from us,
          for the sake of Abraham, your friend,
          of Isaac your servant,
          and of Israel your holy one,
36   to whom you promised descendants as countless as the stars of heaven
          and as the grains of sand on the seashore.
37   Lord, now we are the least of all the nations,
          now we are despised throughout the world, today, because of our sins.
38   We have at this time no leader, no prophet, no prince,
          no holocaust, no sacrifice, no oblation, no incense,
          no place where we can offer you the first-fruits
39   and win your favour.
          But may the contrite soul, the humbled spirit be as acceptable to you
40   as holocausts of rams and bullocks,
          as thousands of fattened lambs:
          such let our sacrifice be to you today,
          and may it be your will that we follow you wholeheartedly,

since those who put their trust in you will not be disappointed.
And now we put our whole heart into following you,   41
into fearing you and seeking your face once more.
Do not disappoint us;   42
treat us gently, as you yourself are gentle
and very merciful.
Grant us deliverance worthy of your wonderful deeds,   43
let your name win glory, Lord.
Confusion seize those who ill-treat your servants: 44
may they be covered with shame,
deprived of all their power,
and may their strength be broken.
Let them learn that you alone are God and Lord,   45
glorious over the whole earth.'

All this time the servants of the king who had thrown the men into the furnace 46
had been stoking it with crude oil, pitch, tow and brushwood •until the flames 47
rose to a height of forty-nine cubits above the furnace •and, leaping out, burnt 48
those Chaldaeans to death who were standing round it. •But the angel of the 49
Lord came down into the furnace beside Azariah and his companions; he drove
the flames of the fire outwards, •and fanned in to them, in the heart of the 50
furnace, a coolness such as wind and dew will bring, so that the fire did not even
touch them or cause them any pain or distress.

The song of the three young men

Then all three in unison began to sing, glorifying and blessing God, there 51
in the furnace, in these words:

'May you be blessed, Lord, God of our ancestors,   52
be praised and extolled for ever.
Blessed be your glorious and holy name,
praised and extolled for ever.
May you be blessed in the Temple of your sacred glory,   53
exalted and glorified above all else for ever:
blessed on the throne of your kingdom,   54
praised and exalted above all else for ever.
Blessed, you fathomer of the great depths, enthroned on the cherubs,   55
praised and glorified above all else for ever;
blessed in the vault of heaven,   56
exalted and glorified above all else for ever.

'All things the Lord has made, bless the Lord: 57
give glory and eternal praise to him.
Angels of the Lord! all bless the Lord: 58
give glory and eternal praise to him.
Heavens! bless the Lord: 59
give glory and eternal praise to him.
Waters above the heavens! bless the Lord: 60
give glory and eternal praise to him.
Powers of the Lord! all bless the Lord: 61
give glory and eternal praise to him.
Sun and moon! bless the Lord: 62
give glory and eternal praise to him.
Stars of heaven! bless the Lord: 63
give glory and eternal praise to him.
Showers and dews! all bless the Lord: 64
give glory and eternal praise to him.
Winds! all bless the Lord: 65

give glory and eternal praise to him.

66 Fire and heat! bless the Lord:
give glory and eternal praise to him.

67 Cold and heat! bless the Lord:
give glory and eternal praise to him.

68 Dews and sleets! bless the Lord:
give glory and eternal praise to him.

69 Frost and cold! bless the Lord:
give glory and eternal praise to him.

70 Ice and snow! bless the Lord:
give glory and eternal praise to him.

71 Nights and days! bless the Lord:
give glory and eternal praise to him.

72 Light and darkness! bless the Lord:
give glory and eternal praise to him.

73 Lightning and clouds! bless the Lord:
give glory and eternal praise to him.

74 Let the earth bless the Lord,
give glory and eternal praise to him.

75 Mountains and hills! bless the Lord:
give glory and eternal praise to him.

76 Every thing that grows on the earth! bless the Lord:
give glory and eternal praise to him.

77 Springs of water! bless the Lord:
give glory and eternal praise to him.

78 Seas and rivers! bless the Lord:
give glory and eternal praise to him.

79 Sea beasts and everything that lives in water! bless the Lord:
give glory and eternal praise to him.

80 Birds of heaven! all bless the Lord:
give glory and eternal praise to him.

81 Animals wild and tame! all bless the Lord:
give glory and eternal praise to him.

82 Sons of men! bless the Lord:
give glory and eternal praise to him.

83 Israel! bless the Lord:
give glory and eternal praise to him.

84 Priests! bless the Lord:
give glory and eternal praise to him.

85 Servants of the Lord! bless the Lord:
give glory and eternal praise to him.

86 Spirits and souls of the virtuous! bless the Lord:
give glory and eternal praise to him.

87 Devout and humble-hearted men! bless the Lord:
give glory and eternal praise to him.

88 Ananiah, Azariah, Mishael! bless the Lord:
give glory and eternal praise to him.
For he has snatched us from the underworld,
saved us from the hand of death,
saved us from the burning fiery furnace,
rescued us from the heart of the flame.

89 Give thanks to the Lord, for he is good,
for his love is everlasting.

90 All you who worship him, bless the God of gods,
praise him and give him thanks,
for his love is everlasting.'

The king acknowledges the miracle

Then King Nebuchadnezzar sprang to his feet in amazement. He said to his ²⁴₉₁ advisers, 'Did we not have these three men thrown bound into the fire?' They replied, 'Certainly, O king'. •'But,' he went on 'I can see four men walking about ²⁵₉₂ freely in the heart of the fire without coming to any harm. And the fourth looks like a son of the gods.'ᵃ •Nebuchadnezzar approached the mouth of the burning ²⁶₉₃ fiery furnace and shouted, 'Shadrach, Meshach and Abednego, servants of the Most High God, come out, come here!' And from the heart of the fire out came Shadrach, Meshach and Abednego. •The satraps, prefects, governors, ²⁷₉₄ and advisers of the king crowded round the three men to examine them: the fire had had no effect on their bodies: not a hair of their heads had been singed, their cloaks were not scorched, no smell of burning hung about them. Nebuchadnezzar exclaimed, 'Blessed be the God of Shadrach, Meshach and ²⁸₉₅ Abednego: he has sent his angel to rescue his servants who, putting their trust in him, defied the order of the king, and preferred to forfeit their bodies rather than serve or worship any god but their own. •I therefore decree as follows: ²⁹₉₆ Men of all peoples, nations, and languages! Let anyone speak disrespectfully of the God of Shadrach, Meshach and Abednego, and I will have him torn limb from limb and his house razed to the ground, for there is no other god who can save like this.' •Then the king showered favours on Shadrach, ³⁰₉₇ Meshach and Abednego in the province of Babylon.

THE WARNING DREAM
AND THE MADNESS OF NEBUCHADNEZZAR

Nebuchadnezzar the king, to men of all peoples, nations and languages, ³¹₉₈ throughout the world: 'May peace be always with you. •It is my pleasure to make ³²₉₉ known the signs and wonders with which the Most High God has favoured me.

> 'How great are his signs, ³³₁₀₀
> how mighty his wonders!
> His sovereignty is an eternal sovereignty,
> his empire lasts from age to age.

Nebuchadnezzar describes his dream

4 'I, Nebuchadnezzar, was living at ease at home, prosperous in my palace. 1 I had a dream; it appalled me. Dread assailed me as I lay in bed; the visions 2 that passed through my head tormented me. •So I decreed that all the sages 3 of Babylon be summoned to explain to me what the dream meant. •Magicians, 4 enchanters, Chaldaeans and wizards came, and I told them what I had dreamt, but they could not interpret it for me. •Daniel, renamed Belteshazzar after 5 my own god,ᵃ and in whom the spirit of God Most Holy resides, then came into my presence. I told him my dream:

'Belteshazzar, I said, chief of magicians, I know that the spirit of God Most 6 Holy resides in you and that no mystery puts you at a loss. This is the dream I have had; tell me what it means.

'The visions that passed through my head as I lay in bed were these: 7

> 'I saw a tree
> in the middle of the world;
> it was very tall.
> The tree grew taller and stronger, 8
> until its top reached the sky,
> and it could be seen from the ends of the earth.

9   Its foliage was beautiful, its fruit abundant,
in it was food for all.
For the wild animals it provided shade,
the birds of heaven nested in its branches,
all living creatures found their food on it.

10   I watched the visions passing through my head as I lay in bed.
Next a watcher, a holy one came down from heaven.

11   At the top of his voice he shouted,
"Cut the tree down, lop off its branches,
strip off its leaves, throw away its fruit;
let the animals flee from its shelter
and the birds from its branches.

12   But leave stump and roots in the ground
bound with hoops of iron and bronze
in the grass of the field.
Let him be drenched with the dew of heaven,
let him share the grass of the earth with the animals.

13   Let his heart turn from mankind,
let a beast's heart be given him
and seven times pass over him!

14   Such is the sentence proclaimed by the watchers,
the verdict announced by the holy ones,
that every living thing may learn
that the Most High rules over the kingship of men,
he confers it on whom he pleases,
and raises the lowest of mankind."

15   'This is the dream I had, I, Nebuchadnezzar the king. Now it is for you,
Belteshazzar, to pronounce on its meaning, since not one of the sages in my
kingdom has been able to interpret it for me; you, however, will be able to,
because the spirit of God Most Holy resides in you.'

Daniel interprets the dream

16   Daniel, known as Belteshazzar, hesitated for a moment in embarrassment.
The king said, 'Belteshazzar, do not be alarmed at the dream and its meaning'.
Belteshazzar answered, 'My lord, may the dream apply to your enemies, and its
17 meaning to your foes! •The tree you saw that grew so tall and strong that it
18 reached the sky and could be seen from the ends of the earth, •the tree with
beautiful foliage and abundant fruit, with food for all in it, providing shade for
19 the wild animals, with the birds of heaven nesting in its branches, •that tree
is yourself, O king, for you have grown tall and strong; your stature is now so
great that it reaches the sky, and your rule extends to the ends of the earth.

20   'And the watcher seen by the king, the holy one coming down from
heaven and saying, "Cut the tree down and destroy it, but leave stump and
roots in the ground, bound with hoops of iron and bronze in the grass of the
field; let him be drenched with the dew of heaven, let him share with the wild
21 animals until seven times have passed over him": •the meaning of this,
O king, this decree of the Most High passed on my lord the king, is this:

22   'You are to be driven from human society,
and live with the wild animals;
you will feed on grass like the oxen,
you will be drenched by the dew of heaven;
seven times will pass over you
until you have learnt

3 a. The protecting angel.
4 a. Bel.

> that the Most High rules over the kingship of men,
> and confers it on whom he pleases.

'And the order, "Leave the stump and roots of the tree", means that ²³ your kingdom will be kept for you until you come to understand that heaven rules all. •May it please the king to accept my advice: by virtuous actions ²⁴ break with your sins, break with your crimes by showing mercy to the poor, and so live long and peacefully.'

The dream comes true

This all happened to King Nebuchadnezzar. •Twelve months later, while ²⁵ ²⁶ strolling on the roof of the royal palace in Babylon, •the king was saying, ²⁷ 'Great Babylon! Imperial palace! Was it not built by me alone, by my own might and power to the glory of my majesty?' •The boast was not out of his ²⁸ mouth when a voice came down from heaven:

> 'King Nebuchadnezzar, these words are for you!
> Sovereignty is taken from you,
> you are to be driven from human society,   ²⁹
> and live with the wild animals;
> you will feed on grass like oxen,
> and seven times will pass over you
> until you have learnt
> that the Most High rules over the kingship of men,
> and confers it on whom he pleases.'

The words were immediately fulfilled: Nebuchadnezzar was driven from ³⁰ human society and fed on grass like oxen, and was drenched by the dew of heaven; his hair grew as long as eagle's feathers, and his nails became like bird's claws.

'When the time was over, I, Nebuchadnezzar, lifted up my eyes to heaven: ³¹ my reason returned. And I blessed the Most High,

> 'praising and extolling him who lives for ever,
> for his sovereignty is an eternal sovereignty,
> his empire lasts from age to age.
> The inhabitants of the earth count for nothing: ³²
> he does as he pleases with the array of heaven,
> and with the inhabitants of the earth.
> No one can arrest his hand
> or ask him, "What are you doing?"

'At that moment my reason returned, and, to the glory of my royal state, ³³ my majesty and splendour returned too. My counsellors and noblemen acclaimed me; I was restored to my throne, and to my past greatness even more was added. •And now I, Nebuchadnezzar, ³⁴

> 'praise and extol and glorify the King of heaven,
> his promises are always faithfully fulfilled,
> his ways are always just,
> and he has power to humble those who walk in pride.'

BELSHAZZAR'S FEAST

5 King Belshazzar^a gave a great banquet for his noblemen; a thousand of ¹ them attended, and he drank wine in company with this thousand. •As he ² sipped his wine, Belshazzar gave orders for the gold and silver vessels to be brought which his father Nebuchadnezzar had looted from the sanctuary in

Jerusalem, so that the king, his noblemen, his wives and his singing women could
3 drink out of them. •The gold and silver vessels looted from the sanctuary of the
Temple of God in Jerusalem were brought in, and the king, his noblemen,
4 his wives and his singing women drank out of them. •They drank their wine
and praised their gods of gold and silver, of bronze and iron, of wood and
5 stone. •Suddenly the fingers of a human hand appeared, and began to write
on the plaster of the palace wall, directly behind the lamp-stand; and the king
6 could see the hand as it wrote. •The king turned pale with alarm: his thigh-joints
7 went slack and his knees began to knock. •He shouted for his enchanters,
Chaldaeans and wizards. And the king said to the Babylonian sages, 'Anyone who
can read this writing and tell me what it means shall be dressed in purple, and
have a chain of gold put round his neck, and be third in rank in the kingdom'.
8 The king's sages all crowded forward, but they could neither read the writing
9 nor explain to the king what it meant. •Greatly alarmed, King Belshazzar
10 turned even paler, and his noblemen were equally disturbed. •Then the queen,
attracted by the noise made by the king and his noblemen, came into the
banqueting hall. 'O king, live for ever!' said the queen. 'Do not be alarmed,
11 do not look so pale. •In your kingdom there is a man in whom lives the spirit of
God Most Holy. In your father's days, he was known for having percipience,
intelligence and wisdom comparable to that of the gods. King Nebuchadnezzar,
your father, made him head of the magicians, enchanters, Chaldaeans and
12 wizards. •Since such a marvellous spirit, and such knowledge and intelligence
in interpreting dreams, solving enigmas and unravelling difficult problems, live
in this man Daniel, whom the king had renamed Belteshazzar, send for Daniel:
he will be able to tell you what this means.'

13 Daniel was brought into the king's presence; the king said to Daniel, 'Are you
the Daniel who was one of the Judaean exiles brought by my father the king
14 from Judah? •I am told that the spirit of God Most Holy lives in you, and
that you are known for your perception, intelligence and marvellous wisdom.
15 The sages and enchanters have already been brought to me to read this writing
and tell me what it means, but they have been unable to reveal its meaning.
16 As I am told that you are able to give interpretations and to unravel difficult
problems, if you can read the writing and tell me what it means, you shall be
dressed in purple, and have a chain of gold put round your neck, and be third
in rank in the kingdom.'

17 Then Daniel spoke up in the presence of the king. 'Keep your gifts for
yourself,' he said 'and give your rewards to others. I will read the writing to the
18 king without them, and tell him what it means. •O king, the Most High God
19 gave Nebuchadnezzar your father sovereignty, greatness, glory, majesty. •He
made him so great that men of all peoples, nations and languages shook with
dread before him: he killed whom he pleased, spared whom he pleased,
20 promoted whom he pleased, degraded whom he pleased. •But because his heart
grew swollen with pride, and his spirit stiff with arrogance, he was deposed
21 from his sovereign throne and stripped of his glory. •He was driven from the
society of men, his heart grew completely animal; he lived with the wild asses;
he fed on grass like the oxen; his body was drenched by the dew of heaven, until
he had learnt that the Most High rules over the empire of men and appoints
22 whom he pleases to rule it. •But you, Belshazzar, who are his son, you have
23 not humbled your heart, in spite of knowing all this. •You have defied the
Lord of heaven, you have had the vessels from his Temple brought to you, and
you, your noblemen, your wives and your singing women have drunk your wine
out of them. You have praised gods of gold and silver, of bronze and iron,
of wood and stone, which cannot either see, hear or understand; but you have
given no glory to the God who holds your breath and all your fortunes in his

5 a. Belshazzar ('May-Bel-protect-the-king') is a Babylonian name, and there was a historical
person bearing it; but he was not a son of Nebuchadnezzar, nor was he a king.

hands. •That is why he has sent the hand which, by itself, has written these 24
words. •The writing reads: *Mene, Mene, Tekel* and *Parsin*.ᵇ •The meaning ²⁵₂₆
of the words is this: *Mene*: God has *measured* your sovereignty and put an end
to it; •*Tekel*: you have been *weighed* in the balance and found wanting; •*Parsin*: ²⁷₂₈
your kingdom has been *divided* and given to the Medes and the *Persians*.'

At Belshazzar's order Daniel was dressed in purple, a chain of gold was put 29
round his neck and he was proclaimed third in rank in the kingdom.

That same night, the Chaldaean king Belshazzar was murdered, 6 and ³⁰₃₁ ¹
Darius the Medeᵃ received the kingdom, at the age of sixty-two.

DANIEL IN THE LION PIT

The satraps resent Daniel's promotion

It pleased Darius to appoint a hundred and twenty satraps over his kingdom ²₁
for the various parts of the kingdom, •and over them three presidents—of ³₂
whom Daniel was one—to whom the satraps were to be responsible. This was to
ensure that no harm should come to the king. • This Daniel, by virtue of the marvel- ⁴₃
lous spirit residing in him, was so evidently superior to the presidents and satraps
that the king considered appointing him to rule the whole kingdom. •The ⁵₄
presidents and satraps in consequence started hunting for some affair of state
by which they could discredit Daniel; but they could find nothing to his discredit,
and no case of negligence; he was so punctilious that they could not find a single
instance of maladministration or neglect. •These men then thought, 'We ⁶₅
shall never find a way of discrediting Daniel unless we try something to
do with the law of his God'. •The presidents and satraps then went in a body to ⁷₆
the king. 'King Darius,' they said 'live for ever! •We are all agreed, the presidents ⁸₇
of the kingdom, the prefects, satraps, counsellors and governors, that the king
should issue a decree enforcing the following regulation: whoever within the next
thirty days prays to anyone, god or man, other than to yourself O king, is to
be thrown into the lions' den. •O king, ratify the edict at once by signing ⁹₈
this document, making it unalterable, as befits the law of the Medes and the
Persians, which cannot be revoked.' •King Darius accordingly signed the ¹⁰₉
document embodying the edict.

Daniel's prayer

When Daniel heard that the document had been signed, he retired to his ¹¹₁₀
house. The windows of his upstairs room faced towards Jerusalem. Three times
each day he continued to fall on his knees, praying and giving praise to God
as he had always done. •These men came along in a body and found Daniel ¹²₁₁
praying and pleading with God. •They then came to the king and said, 'Have ¹³₁₂
you not just signed an edict forbidding any man for the next thirty days to pray
to anyone, god or man, other than to yourself O king, on pain of being thrown
into the lions' den?' 'The decision stands,' the king replied 'as befits the law
of the Medes and the Persians, which cannot be revoked.' •Then they said to ¹⁴₁₃
the king, 'O king, this man Daniel, one of the exiles from Judah, disregards both
you and the edict which you have signed: he is at his prayers three times each
day'. •When the king heard these words he was deeply distressed, and determined ¹⁵₁₄
to save Daniel; he racked his brains until sunset to find some way out. •But ¹⁶₁₅
the men came back in a body to the king and said, 'O king, remember that in
conformity with the law of the Medes and the Persians, no edict or decree can
be altered when once issued by the king'.

Daniel is thrown to the lions

The king then ordered Daniel to be fetched and thrown into the lion pit. ¹⁷₁₆
The king said to Daniel, 'Your God himself, whom you have served so faithfully,

¹⁸/₁₇ will have to save you'. •A stone was then brought and laid over the mouth of the pit; and the king sealed it with his own signet and with that of his noblemen, so that there could be no going back on the original decision about Daniel. ¹⁹/₁₈ The king returned to his palace, spent the night in fasting and refused to receive ²⁰/₁₉ any of his concubines. Sleep eluded him, •and at the first sign of dawn he was ²¹/₂₀ up, and hurried off to the lion pit. •As he approached the pit he shouted in anguished tones, 'Daniel, servant of the living God! Has your God, whom you ²²/₂₁ serve so faithfully, been able to save you from the lions?' •Daniel replied, ²³/₂₂ 'O king, live for ever! •My God sent his angel who sealed the lions' jaws, they did me no harm, since in his sight I am blameless, and I have never ²⁴/₂₃ done you any wrong either, O king.' •The king was overjoyed, and ordered Daniel to be released from the pit. Daniel was released from the pit, and ²⁵/₂₄ found to be quite unhurt, because he had trusted in his God. •The king sent for the men who had accused Daniel and had them thrown into the lion pit, they, their wives and their children: and they had not reached the floor of the pit before the lions had seized them and crushed their bones to pieces.

The king's profession of faith

²⁶/₂₅ King Darius then wrote to men of all nations, peoples and languages ²⁷/₂₆ throughout the world, 'May peace be always with you! •I decree: in every kingdom of my empire let all tremble with fear before the God of Daniel:

> 'He is the living God, he endures for ever,
> his sovereignty will never be destroyed
> and his kingship never end.
²⁸/₂₇ He saves, sets free, and works signs and wonders
> in the heavens and on earth;
> he has saved Daniel from the power of the lions.'

²⁹/₂₈ This Daniel flourished in the reign of Darius and the reign of Cyrus the Persian.

DANIEL'S DREAM: THE FOUR BEASTS

The vision of the beasts

1 **7** In the first year of Belshazzar king of Babylon, Daniel had a dream and visions that passed through his head as he lay in bed. He wrote the dream 2 down, and this is how the narrative began: •Daniel said, 'I have been seeing visions in the night. I saw that the four winds of heaven were stirring up the great ³⁄₄ sea; •four great beasts emerged from the sea, each different from the other. •The first^a was like a lion with eagle's wings; and as I looked its wings were torn off, and it was lifted from the ground and set standing on its feet like a man; 5 and it was given a human heart. •The second beast I saw^b was different, like a bear, raised up on one of its sides, with three ribs in its mouth, between its 6 teeth. "Up!" came the command "Eat quantities of flesh!" •After this I looked, and saw another beast,^c like a leopard, and with four bird's wings on its flanks; 7 it had four heads, and power was given to it. •Next I saw another vision in the visions of the night: I saw a fourth beast,^d fearful, terrifying, very strong; it had great iron teeth, and it ate, crushed and trampled underfoot what remained. It was different from the previous beasts and had ten horns.

b. The literal meaning of the words is uncertain; possibly they are the names of weights or coins—*mina, shekel* and *para* (half a *mina*) have been suggested.
6 a. He is unknown to history.
7 a. The Babylonian empire. b. The kingdom of the Medes; the author sees the Medes as the immediate successors to the Babylonians. Historically, the Persian Cyrus had already conquered Media before he captured Babylon. c. The Persian empire. d. The empire of Alexander (d.323) and his successors. The ten horns are kings of the Seleucid dynasty.

'While I was looking at these horns, I saw another horn sprouting among   8
them, a little one;ᶜ three of the original horns were pulled out by the roots to
make way for it; and in this horn I saw eyes like human eyes, and a mouth that
was full of boasts. •As I watched: 9

The vision of the 'Ancient of Days' and of the son of man

'Thrones were set in placeᶠ
and one of great age took his seat.
His robe was white as snow,
the hair of his head as pure as wool.
His throne was a blaze of flames,
its wheels were a burning fire.
A stream of fire poured out,   10
issuing from his presence.
A thousand thousand waited on him,
ten thousand times ten thousand stood before him.
A court was held
and the books were opened.

'The great things the horn was saying were still ringing in my ears, and as   11
I watched, the beast was killed, and its body destroyed and committed to the
flames. •The other beasts were deprived of their power, but received a lease   12
of life for a season and a time.

'I gazed into the visions of the night.   13
And I saw, coming on the clouds of heaven,
one like a son of man.
He came to the one of great age
and was led into his presence.
On him was conferred sovereignty,   14
glory and kingship,
and men of all peoples, nations and languages became his servants.
His sovereignty is an eternal sovereignty
which shall never pass away,
nor will his empire ever be destroyed.

The interpretation of the vision

'I, Daniel, was deeply disturbed and the visions that passed through my   15
head alarmed me. •So I approached one of those who were standing by and   16
asked him to tell me the truth about all this. And in reply he revealed to me what
these things meant. •"These four great beasts are four kings who will rise from   17
the earth. •Those who are granted sovereignty are the saints of the Most High,   18
and the kingdom will be theirs for ever, for ever and ever." •Then I asked to   19
know the truth about the fourth beast, different from all the rest, very terrifying,
with iron teeth and bronze claws, eating, crushing and trampling underfoot what
remained; •and the truth about the ten horns on its head—and why the other horn   20
sprouted and the three original horns fell, and why this horn had eyes and a mouth
that was full of boasts, and why it made a greater show than the other horns.
This was the horn I had watched making war on the saints and proving the   21
stronger, •until the coming of the one of great age who gave judgement in favour   22
of the saints of the Most High, when the time came for the saints to take over the
kingdom. •This is what he said: 23

"The fourth beast
is to be a fourth kingdom on earth,
different from all other kingdoms.
It will devour the whole earth,

trample it underfoot and crush it.

24 As for the ten horns: from this kingdom
will rise ten kings, and another after them;
this one will be different from the previous ones
and will bring down three kings;

25 he is going to speak words against the Most High,
and harass the saints of the Most High.
He will consider changing seasons and the Law,[g]
and the saints will be put into his power
for a time, two times, and half a time.[h]

26 But a court will be held and his power will be stripped from him,
consumed, and utterly destroyed.

27 And sovereignty and kingship,
and the splendours of all the kingdoms under heaven
will be given to the people of the saints of the Most High.
His sovereignty is an eternal sovereignty
and every empire will serve and obey him."

28 'Here the narrative ends.
'I, Daniel, was greatly disturbed in mind, and I grew pale; but I kept these
things to myself.'

DANIEL'S VISION: THE RAM AND THE HE-GOAT

The vision

1 **8** In the third year of King Belshazzar a vision appeared to me, Daniel,
2 after the one that originally appeared to me. •I gazed at the vision,
and as I gazed I found myself in Susa,[a] the citadel in the province of Elam;
3 gazing at the vision I found myself at the Gate of the Ulai. •I raised my eyes
to look round me, and I saw a ram standing in front of the river. It had two
horns; both were tall, but one taller than the other, and the one that rose the
higher was the second. •I saw the ram thrust westwards, northwards and
southwards. No animal could stand up to it, nothing could escape it. It did as
it pleased and grew very powerful.
5 This is what I observed: a he-goat came from the west, having covered
the entire earth but without touching the ground, and between its eyes the goat
6 had one majestic horn. •It advanced towards the ram with the two horns,
which I had seen standing in front of the river, and charged at it with all the
7 fury of its might. •I saw it reach the ram, and it was so enraged with the ram,
it knocked it down, breaking both its horns, and the ram had not the strength
to resist; it felled it to the ground and trampled it underfoot; no one was there
8 to save the ram. •Then the he-goat grew more powerful than ever, but at the
height of its strength the great horn snapped, and in its place sprouted four
majestic horns, pointing to the four winds of heaven.
9 From one of these, the small one, sprang a horn which grew to great size
10 towards south and east and towards the Land of Splendour.[b] •It grew right
up to the armies of heaven and flung armies and stars to the ground, and
11 trampled them underfoot. •It even challenged the power of that army's Prince;
it abolished the perpetual sacrifice and overthrew the foundation of his sanctuary,

---

e. Antiochus IV Epiphanes (175-163) who came to power only after getting rid of several rival
claimants.   f. For judges.   g. The hellenising policy of Antiochus Epiphanes included a
ban on observance of the sabbath and feastdays.   h. Three and a half years, the approximate
duration of the persecution under Antiochus Epiphanes; but this period of time, also expressed
as 42 months, stands for 'a temporary time of persecution with a limit set by God's providence'.
8 a. One of the royal residences of the Achmenid dynasty; the Ulai river flows through the
town.   b. Palestine.

and the army too; it put iniquity on the sacrifice and flung truth to the ground; 12
the horn was active and successful.

I heard a holy one speaking, and another who said to the speaker, 'How 13
long is this vision to be—of perpetual sacrifice, disastrous iniquity, of sanctuary
and army trampled underfoot?' •The first replied, 'Until two thousand three 14
hundred evenings and mornings have gone by: then the sanctuary shall have its
rights restored'.

The angel Gabriel interprets the vision

As I, Daniel, gazed at the vision and tried to understand it, I saw someone 15
standing before me who looked like a man. •I heard a man's voice cry over 16
the Ulai, 'Gabriel, tell him the meaning of the vision!' •He approached the 17
place where I was standing; as he approached I was seized with terror, and fell
prostrate. 'Son of man,' he said to me 'understand this: the vision shows the
time of the End.' •He was still speaking, when I fell senseless to the ground. 18
He touched me, however, and raised me to my feet. •'Come,' he said 'I will 19
tell you what is going to happen when the wrath comes to an end; this concerns
the appointed End. •As for the ram that you saw, its two horns are the 20
kings of Media and of Persia. •The hairy he-goat is the king of Javan, the large 21
horn between its eyes is the first king.ᶜ •The horn that snapped and the four 22
horns that sprouted in its place are four kingdoms rising from his nation but
not having his power.

'And at the end of their reign, when the measure of their sins is full, 23
a king will arise, a proud-faced, ingenious-minded man.
His power will gather strength—but not through power of his own— 24
he will plot incredible schemes,
he will succeed in what he undertakes,
he will destroy powerful men
and the people of the saints.
Such will be his resourcefulness of mind 25
that all his treacherous activities will succeed.
He will grow arrogant of heart,
take many unawares and destroy them.
He will challenge the power of the Prince of princes
but, no hand intervening,ᵈ shall himself be broken.
This explanation of the vision of the mornings and the evenings is true, 26
but you must keep the vision secret, for there are still many days to go.'

At this I, Daniel, lost consciousness; I was ill for several days. Then I got 27
up to discharge my duties in the king's service, keeping the vision a secret, and
not understanding what it meant.

THE PROPHECY OF THE SEVENTY WEEKS

Daniel's prayer

9 It was the first year of Darius son of Ahasuerus, who was of Median stock 1
and ruled the kingdom of Chaldaea. •In the first year of his reign I, Daniel, 2
was perusing the scriptures, counting over the number of years—as revealed
by Yahweh to the prophet Jeremiah—that were to pass before the successive
devastations of Jerusalem would come to an end, namely seventy years. •I turned 3
my face to the Lord God begging for time to pray and to plead with fasting,
sackcloth and ashes. •I pleaded with Yahweh my God and made this confession: 4
'O Lord, God great and to be feared, you keep the covenant and have kindness for those who love you and keep your commandments: •we have sinned, 5
we have done wrong, we have acted wickedly, we have betrayed your

6 commandments and your ordinances and turned away from them. •We have not listened to your servants the prophets, who spoke in your name to our kings,
7 our princes, our ancestors, and to all the people of the land. •Integrity, Lord, is yours; ours the look of shame we wear today, we, the people of Judah, the citizens of Jerusalem, the whole of Israel, near and far away, in every country to which you have dispersed us because of the treason we have committed
8 against you. •To us, Yahweh, the look of shame belongs, to our kings, our
9 princes, our ancestors, because we have sinned against you. •To the Lord our God
10 mercy and pardon belong, because we have betrayed him, •and have not listened to the voice of Yahweh our God nor followed the laws he has given us through his
11 servants the prophets. •The whole of Israel has flouted your Law and turned away, unwilling to listen to your voice; and the curse and imprecation written in the Law of Moses, the servant of God, have come pouring down on
12 us—because we have sinned against him. •He has carried out the threats which he made against us and against the princes who governed us—that he would bring so great a disaster down on us that the fate of Jerusalem would
13 find no parallel in the whole of the world. •And now all this disaster has happened to us, just as it is written in the Law of Moses; even so, we have not tried to appease Yahweh our God by renouncing our crimes and being guided by
14 your truth. •Yahweh has watched for the right moment to bring disaster on us, since Yahweh our God is just in all his dealings with us, and we have not
15 listened to his voice. •And now, Lord our God, who by your mighty hand brought us out of the land of Egypt—the renown you won then endures to
16 this day—we have sinned, we have done wrong. •Lord, by all your acts of justice turn away your anger and your fury from Jerusalem, your own city, your holy mountain, for as a result of our sins and the crimes of our ancestors,
17 Jerusalem and your own people have become a byword among all around us. •And now, our God, listen to the prayer and pleading of your servant. For your
18 own sake, Lord, let your face smile again on your desolate sanctuary. •Listen my God, listen to us; open your eyes and look on our plight and on the city that bears your name. We are not relying on our own good works but on your
19 great mercy, to commend our humble plea to you. •Listen, Lord! Lord, forgive! Hear, Lord, and act! For your own sake, my God, do not delay, because they bear your name, this is your city, this is your people.'

The angel Gabriel explains the prophecy

20   I was still speaking, still at prayer, confessing my own sins and the sins of my people Israel and placing my plea before Yahweh my God for the holy
21 mountain of my God, •still speaking, still at prayer, when Gabriel, the being I had seen originally in a vision, flew suddenly down to me at the hour of the
22 evening sacrifice. •He said to me, 'Daniel, you see me; I have come down to
23 teach you how to understand. •When your pleading began, a word was uttered, and I have come to tell you what it is. You are a man specially chosen. Grasp the meaning of the word, understand the vision:

24   'Seventy weeks are decreed[a]
        for your people and your holy city,
        for putting an end to transgression,
        for placing the seals on sin,
        for expiating crime,
        for introducing everlasting integrity,
        for setting the seal on vision and on prophecy,
        for anointing the Holy of Holies.

c. Alexander.   d. Antiochus died a natural death, see 1 M 6.
9 a. See v.25. The seventy 'weeks of years' are from Jeremiah's prophecy to the rebuilding of Jerusalem.

'Know this, then, and understand: 25
from the time this message went out:
"Return and rebuild Jerusalem"
to the coming of an anointed Prince, seven weeks
and sixty-two weeks,
with squares and ramparts restored and rebuilt,
but in a time of trouble.
And after the sixty-two weeks   26
an anointed one will be cut off—and . . . . will not be for him—
the city and the sanctuary will be destroyed
by a prince who will come.
His end will come in catastrophe
and, until the end, there will be war
and all the devastation decreed.
He will make a firm covenant with many *b*   27
for the space of a week;
and for the space of one half-week
he will put a stop to sacrifice and oblation,
and on the wing of the Temple will be the disastrous abomination *c*
until the end, until the doom assigned to the devastator.'

THE GREAT VISION

THE TIME OF WRATH

The vision of the man dressed in linen

10 In the third year of Cyrus king of Persia a revelation was made to Daniel 1
known as Belteshazzar, a true revelation of a great conflict. He grasped
the meaning of the revelation; what it meant was disclosed to him in a vision.
At that time, I, Daniel, was doing a three-week penance; •I ate no rich ²/₃
food, touched no meat or wine, and did not anoint myself, until these three
weeks were over. •On the twenty-fourth day of the first month, as I stood on 4
the bank of that great river, the Tigris, •I raised my eyes to look about me, and 5
this is what I saw:

A man dressed in linen, with a girdle of pure gold round his waist;
his body was like beryl,   6
his face shone like lightning,
his eyes were like fiery torches,
his arms and his legs had the gleam of burnished bronze,
the sound of his voice was like the noise of a crowd.

I, Daniel, alone saw the apparition; the men who were with me did not see 7
the apparition, but so great a trembling overtook them that they fled to hide.
I was left alone, gazing on this great apparition; I was powerless, my appearance 8
altered out of all recognition, what strength I had deserted me.

The apparition of the angel

I heard him speak, and at the sound of his voice I fell unconscious to the 9
ground. •I felt a hand touching me, setting my knees and my hands trembling. 10
He said, 'Daniel, you are a man specially chosen; listen carefully to the words 11
that I am going to say; stand up; I have been sent to you and here I am'. He
said this, and I stood up trembling. •He said then, 'Daniel, do not be afraid; 12
from that first day when you resolved to humble yourself before God, the better
to understand, your words have been heard; and your words are the reason why

13 I have come. •The prince of the kingdom of Persia has been resisting me for twenty-one days, but Michael,ᵃ one of the leading princes, came to my assistance.
14 I have left him confronting the kings of Persia •and have come to tell you what will happen to your people in the days to come. For here is a new vision about those days.'

15 When he had said these things to me I prostrated myself on the ground,
16 without saying a word; •then someone looking like a son of man came and touched my lips. I opened my mouth to speak, and I said to the person standing in front of me, 'My lord, anguish overcomes me at this vision, and what strength
17 I had deserts me. •How can my lord's servant speak to my lord now that
18 I have no strength left and my breath fails me?' •Once again the person like a
19 man touched me; he gave me strength. •'Do not be afraid,' he said 'you are a man specially chosen; peace be with you; play the man, be strong!' And as he spoke to me I felt strong again and said, 'Let my lord speak, you have given me strength'.

The prelude to the prophecy

20a
21a   He said then, 'Do you know why I have come to you? •It is to tell you
20b what is written in the Book of Truth. •I must go back to fight against the prince
21b of Persia: when I have done with him, the prince of Javan will come next. •In all
1 this there is no one to lend me support except Michael your prince, 11 on
2 whom I rely to give me support and reinforce me. •And now I will tell you the truth about these things.

Early struggles between Seleucids and Ptolemies

   'Three more kings are going to rise in Persia; a fourth will come and be richer than all the others, and when, thanks to his wealth, he has grown powerful, he will
3 challenge all the kingdoms of Javan. •A mighty king will rise and reign over
4 a vast empire and do whatever he pleases. •But once he has come to power his empire will be broken up and parcelled out to the four winds of heaven, though not to his descendants: it will not be ruled as he ruled it, for his sovereignty is going to be uprooted and pass to others than his own.
5   'The king of the Southᵈ will grow powerful, but one of his princesᵇ will
6 grow more powerful still with an empire greater than that of the former. •Some years later, these will form an alliance and, to ratify the agreement, the daughter of the king of the South will go to the king of the North. Her arm will not, however, retain its strength, nor his posterity endure: she will be handed over, she, her escorts and her child, and he who has had authority over her.ᶜ In due
7 time •a sprig from her roots will rise in his place, will march on the defences, force the stronghold of the king of the North, and succeed in overcoming them.
8 He will even carry off all their gods, their statues, their precious gold and silver plate to Egypt. For some years he will leave the king of the North in peace,
9 but the latter will invade the kingdom of the king of the South, then retire
10 to his own country. •His sonsᵈ will next be on the march, mustering a host of powerful forces; and heᵉ will advance, deploy, break through and march on his
11 stronghold once again. •The king of the South will fly into a rage and set out to give battle to the king of the North who will have an immense army on his
12 side, and this army will be delivered into his hands. •The army will be annihilated;

b. Probably the renegade Jews who renounced their obligations and obeyed Antiochus Epiphanes.   c. Or 'the blasphemous idol', here indicating Zeus to whom the Temple was dedicated by Antiochus. The phrasing makes an allusion to the baals denounced by the prophets. 10 a. Michael ('Who-is-like-God?') is the guardian angel of the people of God.
11 a. Ptolemy I Soter of Egypt (306-285).   b. Seleucus I Nicator (301-281).   c. Antiochus II Theos married Ptolemy II's daughter Berenice about 252.   d. Seleucus III Ceraunus (227-223) and Antiochus III the Great (223-187).   e. The following verses describe the battles of Antiochus the Great with Ptolemy IV and Ptolemy V from 220 onwards. V.15 mentions the siege of Gaza and v.16 the entry of Antiochus into Jerusalem.

he will be triumphant; he will overthrow tens of thousands; yet he will have no strength. •The king of the North will come back, having recruited an even 13 larger army than before, and finally, when the time comes, he will advance with a great army and plentiful supplies. •In those times many will rebel against 14 the king of the South; men of violence will also rebel from your own people, thus fulfilling the vision; but they will fail. •The king of the North will then 15 come and throw up siege-works to capture a strongly fortified city. The forces of the South will not stand their ground, its picked troops will not be strong enough to resist. •The invader will treat him as he pleases, no one will be able 16 to resist him: he will take his stand in the Land of Splendour, destruction in his hands. •He will consider conquering his entire kingdom, but will then make 17 a treaty with him and, to overthrow the kingdom, give him a woman's daughter;ᶠ but this will not last or be to his advantage. •He will next turn to 18 the islands and conquer many of them, but a magistrate will put a stop to his outrages in such a way that he will be unable to repay outrage for outrage.ᵍ

'He will then turn on the strongholds of his own country, but will stumble, 19 fall, and never be seen again. •In his place there will rise a man ʰwho will send an 20 extortioner to despoil the royal splendour; in a few days he will be shattered, though neither publicly nor in battle.ⁱ

Antiochus Epiphanes

'In his place there will rise a wretch: ʲ he will not be given royal honours, but will 21 insinuate himself into them in his own time and gain possession of the kingdom by intrigue. •Armies will be utterly routed and crushed by him, the prince 22 of the covenant too. ᵏ •Still conspiring, he will go from treachery to treachery, 23 ever growing stronger despite the smallness of his following. •In his own time 24 he will invade the richest provinces, acting as his fathers or his fathers' fathers never acted, distributing plunder, spoil and wealth among them, plotting his stratagems against fortresses—for a time.

'He will rouse his strength and his heart against the king of the South with 25 a great army. The king of the South will march to war with a huge and powerful army, but will offer no resistance, since he will be outwitted by trickery. •Those 26 who shared his food will ruin him; his army will be swept away, many will fall in the slaughter.

'The two kings, seated at one table, hearts bent on evil, will tell their lies; 27 but they will not have their way, for the appointed time is still to come. •He 28 will return greatly enriched to his own country, his heart set against the holy covenant; he will take action, and next return to his own country. •In due 29 time he will make his way southwards again, but this time the outcome will not be as before. •The ships of Kittimˡ will oppose him, and he will be worsted. 30 He will retire and take furious action against the holy covenant and, as before, will favour those who forsake that holy covenant.

'Forces of his will come and profane the sanctuary citadel; they will 31 abolish the perpetual sacrifice and install the disastrous abomination there. Those who break the covenant he will corrupt by his flatteries, but the people 32 who know their God will stand firm and take action. •Those of the people who 33 are learned will instruct many; for some days, however, they will be brought down by sword and flame, by captivity and by plundering. •And thus brought 34 down, little help will they receive, though many will be plotting on their side. Of the learned some will be brought down, as a result of which certain of 35 them will be purged, purified and made white—until the time of the End, for the appointed time is still to come.

'The king will do as he pleases, growing more and more arrogant, considering 36 himself greater than all the gods; he will utter incredible blasphemies against the God of gods, and he will thrive until the wrath reaches bursting point; for what has been decreed will certainly be fulfilled. •Heedless of his fathers' gods, 37

heedless of the one whom women love,[m] heedless of any god whatever, he will
38 consider himself greater than them all. Instead of them, he will honour the
god of fortresses, will honour a god unknown to his ancestors with gold and
39 silver, precious stones and valuable presents. •He will use the people of an
alien god[n] to defend the fortresses; he will confer great honours on those
who will acknowledge him, by giving them wide authority and by farming out
the land at a price.

THE TIME OF THE END

The end of the persecutor

40 'When the time comes for the End, the king of the South will try conclusions with him; but the king of the North will come storming down on him
with chariots, cavalry, and a large fleet. He will invade countries, overrun
41 them and drive on. •He will invade the Land of Splendour, and many will
fall; but Edom, Moab, and what remain of the sons of Ammon will escape
him.
42 'He will reach out to attack countries: the land of Egypt will not escape him.
43 The gold and silver treasures and all the valuables of Egypt will lie in his power.
44 Libyans and Cushites[o] will be at his feet: •but reports coming from the East
and the North will worry him, and in great fury he will set out to bring ruin and
45 complete destruction to many. •He will pitch the tents of his royal headquarters
between the sea and the mountains of the Holy Splendour. Yet he will come
to his end—there will be no help for him.

Resurrection and retribution

1 **12** 'At that time Michael will stand up, the great prince who mounts guard
over your people. There is going to be a time of great distress, unparalleled
since nations first came into existence. When that time comes, your own people
2 will be spared, all those whose names are found written in the Book. •Of those
who lie sleeping in the dust of the earth many will awake, some to everlasting
3 life, some to shame and everlasting disgrace. •The learned will shine as brightly
as the vault of heaven, and those who have instructed many in virtue, as bright
as stars for all eternity.
4 'But you, Daniel, must keep these words secret and the book sealed until
the time of the End. Many will wander this way and that, and wickedness will
go on increasing.'

The sealed prophecy

5 Then I, Daniel, looked on and saw two others standing, one on the near bank
6 of the river, one on the other. •One said to the man dressed in linen who was
standing further up the stream, 'How long until these wonders take place?'
7 I heard the man speak who was dressed in linen, standing further up the stream:
he raised his right hand and his left to heaven and swore by him who lives
for ever, 'A time and two times, and half a time; and all these things are going
to happen when he who crushes the power of the holy people meets his end'.
8 I listened but did not understand. Then I said, 'My lord, what is to be the
9 outcome?' •'Daniel,' he said 'go away: these words are to remain secret and sealed
10 until the time of the End. •Many will be cleansed, made white and purged; the

f. Antiochus, foreseeing intervention from Rome, made an alliance with Egypt and married
Ptolemy's daughter Cleopatra in 194.   g. Antiochus was defeated by Lucius Cornelius
Scipio at Magnesia in 190.   h. Seleucus IV Philopator (187-175).   i. He was assassinated.
j. Antiochus IV Epiphanes (175-165).   k. Probably the high priest Onias III.   l. I.e. 'from
across the Mediterranean'; the Roman consul landed at Alexandria.   m. Adonis.   n. Syrian
and renegade Jewish troops.   o. The peoples W. and S. of Egypt.

wicked will go on doing wrong; the wicked will never understand; the learned
will understand. •From the moment that the perpetual sacrifice is abolished 11
and the disastrous abomination erected: one thousand two hundred and
ninety days. •Blessed is he who stands firm and attains a thousand three hundred 12
and thirty-five days. •But you, go away and rest; and you will rise for your 13
share at the end of time.'

SUSANNA AND THE JUDGEMENT OF DANIEL

13 In Babylon there lived a man named Joakim. •He had married Susanna $^1_2$
daughter of Hilkiah, a woman of great beauty; and she was God-fearing,
because her parents were worthy people and had instructed their daughter in 3
the Law of Moses. •Joakim was a very rich man, and had a garden attached 4
to his house; the Jews would often visit him since he was held in greater respect
than any other man. •Two elderly men had been selected from the people that 5
year to act as judges. Of such the Lord said, 'Wickedness has come to Babylon
through the elders and judges posing as guides to the people'. •These men 6
were often at Joakim's house, and all who were engaged in litigation used to
come to them. •At midday, when everyone had gone, Susanna used to take a 7
walk in her husband's garden. •The two elders, who used to watch her every 8
day as she came in to take her walk, gradually began to desire her. •They 9
threw reason aside, making no effort to turn their eyes to heaven, and forgetting
its demands of virtue. •Both were inflamed by the same passion, but they hid their 10
desire from each other, •for they were ashamed to admit the longing to sleep 11
with her, •but they still contrived to see her every day. •One day, having parted $^{12}_{13}$
with the words, 'Let us go home, it is time for the midday meal', they went off
in different directions, •only to retrace their steps and find themselves face to 14
face again. Obliged then to explain, they admitted their desire and agreed to
look for an opportunity of surprising her alone. •So they waited for a favourable 15
moment; and one day Susanna came as usual, accompanied only by two young
maidservants. The day was hot and she wanted to bathe in the garden. •There 16
was no one about except the two elders, spying on her from their hiding place.
She said to the servants, 'Bring me some oil and balsam and shut the garden door 17
while I bathe'. •They did as they were told, shutting the garden door and going 18
back to the house by a side entrance to fetch what she had asked for;
they knew nothing about the elders, who were hiding.

Hardly were the servants gone than the two elders were there after her. 'Look,' 19
they said 'the garden door is shut, no one can see us. We want to have you, 20
so give in and let us! •Refuse, and we will both give evidence that a young 21
man was with you and that was why you sent your maids away.' •Susanna 22
sighed. 'I am trapped,' she said 'whatever I do. If I agree, that means my death;
if I resist, I cannot get away from you. •But I prefer to fall innocent into your 23
power than to sin in the eyes of the Lord.' •Then she cried out as loud as 24
she could. The two elders began shouting too, putting the blame on her, •and 25
one of them ran to open the garden door. •The household, hearing the shouting 26
in the garden, rushed out by the side entrance to see what was happening; •once 27
the elders had told their story the servants were thoroughly taken aback, since
nothing of this sort had ever been said of Susanna.

Next day a meeting was held at the house of her husband Joakim. The two 28
elders arrived, in their vindictiveness determined to have her put to death. •They 29
addressed the company: 'Summon Susanna daughter of Hilkiah and wife of
Joakim'. She was sent for, •and came accompanied by her parents, her children 30
and all her relations. •Susanna was very graceful and beautiful to look at ; •she $^{31}_{32}$
was veiled, so the wretches made her unveil in order to feast their eyes on her
beauty. •All her own people were weeping, and so were all the others who saw 33

34 her. •The two elders stood up, with all the people round them, and laid their
35 hands on the woman's head.*ᵃ* •Tearfully she turned her eyes to heaven, her
36 heart confident in God. •The elders then spoke. 'While we were walking by
ourselves in the garden, this woman arrived with two servants. She shut the
37 garden door and then dismissed the servants. •A young man who had been
38 hiding went over to her and they lay down together. •From the end of the
garden where we were, we saw this crime taking place and hurried towards
39 them. •Though we saw them together we were unable to catch the man: he
40 was too strong for us; he opened the door and took to his heels. •We did,
41 however, catch this woman and ask her who the young man was. •She refused
to tell us. That is our evidence.'

Since they were elders of the people, and judges, the assembly took their
42 word: Susanna was condemned to death. •She cried out as loud as she could,
43 'Eternal God, you know all secrets and everything before it happens ; •you
know that they have given false evidence against me. And now have I to die,
innocent as I am of everything their malice has invented against me?'

44
45 The Lord heard her cry •and, as she was being led away to die, he roused
46 the holy spirit residing in a young boy named Daniel •who began to shout,
47 'I am innocent of this woman's death!' •At which all the people turned to him and
48 asked, 'What do you mean by these words?' •Standing in the middle of the
crowd he replied, 'Are you so stupid, sons of Israel, as to condemn a daughter
49 of Israel unheard, and without troubling to find out the truth? •Go back to
the scene of the trial: these men have given false evidence against her.'

50 All the people hurried back, and the elders said to Daniel, 'Come and sit
with us and tell us what you mean, since God has given you the gifts that elders
51 have'. •Daniel said, 'Keep the men well apart from each other for I want to
52 question them'. •When the men had been separated, Daniel had one of them
brought to him. 'You have grown old in wickedness,' he said 'and now the
53 sins of your earlier days have overtaken you, •you with your unjust judgements,
your condemnation of the innocent, your acquittal of guilty men, when the Lord
54 has said, "You must not put the innocent and the just to death". •Now then,
since you saw her so clearly, tell me what tree you saw them lying under?'
55 He replied, 'Under a mastic tree'. •Daniel said, 'True enough! Your lie recoils
on your own head: the angel of God has already received your sentence from
56 him and will slash you in half.' •He dismissed the man, ordered the other to be
brought and said to him, 'Spawn of Canaan, not of Judah, beauty has seduced
57 you, lust has led your heart astray! •This is how you have been behaving with
the daughters of Israel and they were too frightened to resist; but here is a
58 daughter of Judah who could not stomach your wickedness! •Now then, tell
me what tree you surprised them under?' He replied, 'Under a holm oak'.
59 Daniel said, 'True enough! Your lie recoils on your own head: the angel of
God is waiting, with a sword to drive home and split you, and destroy the pair
of you.'

60 Then the whole assembly shouted, blessing God, the saviour of those who
61 trust in him. •And they turned on the two elders whom Daniel had convicted
62 of false evidence out of their own mouths. •As prescribed in the Law of Moses,
they sentenced them to the same punishment as they had intended to inflict on
their neighbour. They put them to death; the life of an innocent woman was spared
63 that day. •Hilkiah and his wife gave thanks to God for their daughter Susanna,
and so did her husband Joakim and all his relations, because she had been
acquitted of anything dishonourable.

64 From that day onwards Daniel's reputation stood high with the people.

---

13 a. The formal preliminary to death by stoning.

BEL AND THE DRAGON

Daniel and the priests of Bel

14 When King Astyages joined his ancestors, Cyrus of Persia succeeded him. 1
Daniel was very close to the king who thought more of him than of any 2
other of his friends. •Now in Babylon there was an idol called Bel,ᵃ to which 3
twelve bushels of the finest flour, forty sheep and six measures of wine were
offered every day. •The king took part in this cult and used to go and worship 4
the idol every day. Daniel, however, worshipped his own God.• 'Why do you 5
not worship Bel?' the king asked Daniel. 'I do not worship idols made by the
hands of men,' Daniel replied 'I worship the living God who made heaven and
earth and who has power over all living creatures.' •'You believe, then,' 6
said the king 'that Bel is not a living god? Can you not see how much he eats
and drinks every day?' •Daniel laughed. 'My king,' he said 'do not be taken in; 7
he is clay inside, and bronze outside, and has never eaten or drunk anything.'
This made the king angry; he summoned his priests, 'Tell me who eats all 8
this food,' he said 'or die. Prove to me that Bel really eats it, and I will have
Daniel put to death for blaspheming him.' •Daniel said to the king, 'Let it be as 9
you say'.

There were seventy of these priests, to say nothing of their wives and
children. •The king went to the temple of Bel, taking Daniel with him. •The ¹⁰₁₁
priests of Bel said to him, 'We are now withdrawing, as you can see;
but we will leave you, O king, to set out food and prepare the wine and leave it
there. Then you can shut the door and seal it with your own seal. If, when you
return in the morning, you do not find that everything has been eaten by Bel,
then let us be put to death; if not, then Daniel, that slanderer!' •They were 12
thinking—hence their confidence—of a secret entrance which they had made
under the table, by which they came in daily and took the offerings away.
When the priests had gone and the king had set out the food for Bel, •Daniel ¹³₁₄
made his servants bring ashes and spread them all over the temple floor, with no
other witness than the king. Then they left the building, shut the door and,
sealing it with the king's seal, went away. •That night, as usual, the priests 15
came with their wives and children; they ate and drank everything.

The king was up very early next morning; so was Daniel. •'Daniel,' said ¹⁶₁₇
the king 'are the seals intact?' 'They are intact, O king' he replied. •The king 18
then opened the door and taking one look at the table he exclaimed, 'You are
great, O Bel! There is no deception in you!' •But Daniel laughed. And restraining 19
the king from going further in, he said, 'Look at the floor and examine these
footprints'. •'I can see footprints of men, of women and of children' said the
king, •and angrily ordered the priests to be arrested, with their wives and children. 21
They showed him then the secret door through which they used to come and
remove what was on the table. •The king had them put to death and handed Bel 22
over to Daniel who destroyed both the idol and its temple.

Daniel kills the dragon

There was a big dragon in Babylon, and this was worshipped too. •The ²³₂₄
king said to Daniel, 'You are not going to tell me that this is no more than
bronze? Look, it is alive; it eats and drinks; you cannot deny that this is a
living god; worship it, then.' •Daniel replied, 'I worship the Lord my God; 25
he is the living God. With your permission, O king, without using either sword or
club I will kill this serpent.' •'You have my permission' said the king. 26
Whereupon Daniel took some pitch, some fat and some hair and boiled them 27
up together, rolled the mixture into balls and fed them to the dragon; the
dragon swallowed them and burst. Daniel said, 'Now look at the sort of thing
you worship!' •The Babylonians were furious when they heard about this and 28

began intriguing against the king. 'The king has turned Jew,' they said 'he has allowed Bel to be overthrown, and the dragon to be killed, and he has put the
29 priests to death.' •So they went to the king and said, 'Hand Daniel over to
30 us or else we will kill you, and your family'. •They pressed him so hard that the king found himself forced to hand Daniel over to them.

Daniel in the lion pit

31
32   They threw Daniel into the lion pit, and there he stayed for six days. •In the pit were seven lions, which were given two human bodies and two sheep every day; but for this period they were not given anything, to make sure they would eat Daniel.
33   Now the prophet Habakkuk was in Judaea: he had been making a stew, and breaking up bread small to put in a basket. He was on his way to the fields,
34 taking this to the harvesters, •when the angel of the Lord spoke to him, 'Take the meal you are carrying to Babylon and give it to Daniel in the lion pit'.
35 'Lord,' replied Habakkuk 'I have not even seen Babylon, and know nothing
36 about this pit.' •The angel of the Lord seized his head and carried him off by the hair to Babylon where, with a great thrust of his spirit, he set Habakkuk down
37 on the edge of the pit. •'Daniel, Daniel,' Habakkuk shouted 'take the meal
38 that God has sent you.' •And Daniel said, 'You have kept me in mind, O God;
39 you have not deserted those who love you'. •Rising to his feet he ate the meal, while the angel of God lost no time in returning Habakkuk to his own country.
40   On the seventh day the king came to lament over Daniel; on reaching the
41 pit he looked inside, and there was Daniel, quite unperturbed. •'You are great,
42 O Lord, God of Daniel,' he exclaimed 'there is no god but you!' •Then he released Daniel from the pit and had the plotters of Daniel's ruin thrown in instead, where they were instantly eaten before his eyes.

14 a. Marduk, the god of Babylon.

INTRODUCTION TO

THE MINOR PROPHETS

The twelve shorter books known as the 'Minor Prophets' appear in this edition of the Bible in their traditional order. In these introductory notes, they are treated in what is most probably their true historical order.

Amos

Amos was a shepherd, called to prophesy for a brief period in the reign of Jeroboam II, 783-743. The Northern Kingdom was prosperous, a corrupt city life had developed, and the military power of Assyria was a constant menace; in this background, the prophet from the desert condemned the social injustices of his times and preached the coming 'day of Yahweh' as a visitation of wrath from which only a remnant would be spared.

Hosea

Hosea's ministry began under Jeroboam II and continued under his successors, possibly until the fall of Samaria in 721. A key to his prophecies is Hosea's own life with his unfaithful wife, from which he was able to describe the love of Yahweh for his people, whose unfaithfulness was plain from their kings' policies of expedience, their unworthy priests, and their worship of false gods.

Micah

A contemporary of Isaiah, Micah too foresaw the ruin of Israel as the punishment for a life of religious and social corruption. Like other prophetic books, this book contains some oracles which, from their character, appear to be of a later time than that of the prophet named as the author.

Zephaniah

Zephaniah prophesied in the reign of Josiah, before the religious reform of 622 B.C. In his understanding of a 'day of retribution', Zephaniah echoes Amos; in his deep appreciation of sin as an offence against God, he anticipates Jeremiah.

Nahum

The destruction of Nineveh is foretold with great poetic power in a prophecy made shortly before the capture of that city in 612. It is seen as the vindication of God's justice.

Habakkuk

A poetic dialogue. If the oppressors who are cursed and finally routed are, as seems most likely, the Chaldaeans, the book should be dated between 605 and 597. The problem behind the prophet's questioning is that the God of goodness should choose the savage pagans as his instruments.

Haggai

The first of the post-exilic prophets. Haggai's four brief discourses urge the Jews, after the return from Babylon, to resume the work of rebuilding the Temple. They are dated precisely, in 520.

Zechariah

Chapters 1 - 8 are dated between 520 and 517, and are the work of Zechariah, the prophet of national restoration. The rest of the chapters appear to be of various dates: Greeks appear among the oppressors of Israel together with the traditional Assyrians and Egyptians, and messianic expectation is strong; parts at least can be attributed to the late 4th century.

Obadiah

This short book, half of which is a doublet of a passage in Jr 49, seems to relate to the Edomite invasion after the destruction of Jerusalem, and should be dated in the 5th century.

Malachi

'The book of my messenger'; six discourses which look forward to 'the day of Yahweh'. By its contents the book can be dated about the middle of the 5th century.

Joel

The prophet sees a disastrous plague of locusts as a 'sign', heralding the Judgement of the nations and the triumph of Yahweh and of Israel. The background is that of the post-exilic community, and the book must have been written about 400 B.C.

Jonah

A parable, written in the 4th century, but set in the remote past. It is written with a great freedom of imagination and teaches a clear lesson of God's mercy, his power, and his universality.

HOSEA

Heading

1 The word of Yahweh that was addressed to Hosea son of Beeri when Uzziah, 1
Jotham, Ahaz and Hezekiah were reigning in Judah, and Jeroboam son of
Joash in Israel.[a]

I. THE MARRIAGE OF HOSEA AND ITS SYMBOLISM

Hosea's marriage: his three children

When Yahweh first spoke through Hosea, Yahweh said this to him, 'Go, 2
marry a whore, and get children with a whore, for the country itself has
become nothing but a whore by abandoning Yahweh'.

So he went; and he took Gomer daughter of Diblaim, who conceived and 3
bore him a son. •'Name him Jezreel', Yahweh told him 'for it will not be long 4
before I make the House of Jehu pay for the bloodshed at Jezreel[b] and I put an
end to the sovereignty of the House of Israel. •When that day comes I will 5
break Israel's bow in the Valley of Jezreel.'[c]

She conceived a second time and gave birth to a daughter. 'Name her 6
Unloved' Yahweh told him. 'No more love shall the House of Israel have from
me in future, no further forgiveness. •(But my love shall go to the House of 7
Judah and through Yahweh their God I mean to save them — but not by bow
or sword or battle, horse or horseman.)'

She weaned Unloved, conceived again and gave birth to a son. •'Name $\begin{smallmatrix}8\\9\end{smallmatrix}$
him No-People-of-Mine' Yahweh said. 'You are not my people and I am not
your God.'

Yahweh and his unfaithful wife

2 Denounce your mother, denounce her, $\begin{smallmatrix}4\\2\end{smallmatrix}$
  for she is not my wife
nor am I her husband.
Let her rid her face of her whoring,
  and her breasts of her adultery,[a]
or else I will strip her naked, $\begin{smallmatrix}5\\3\end{smallmatrix}$
  expose her as on the day she was born;
I will make a wilderness of her,
  turn her into an arid land,
  and leave her to die of thirst.
I will not love her children, $\begin{smallmatrix}6\\4\end{smallmatrix}$
  since they are the children of whoring.
Yes, their mother has played the whore, $\begin{smallmatrix}7\\5\end{smallmatrix}$
  she who conceived them has disgraced herself.
'I am going to court my lovers' she said
  'who give me my bread and water,
  my wool, my flax, my oil and my drink.'[b]
She would not acknowledge, not she, $\begin{smallmatrix}10\\8\end{smallmatrix}$

that I was the one who was giving her
the corn, the wine, the oil,
and who freely gave her that silver and gold
of which they have made Baals.

¹¹/₉   That is why, when the time comes, I mean to withdraw my corn,
and my wine, when the season for it comes.
I will retrieve my wool, my flax,
that were intended to cover her nakedness;

¹²/₁₀   so will I display her shame before her lovers' eyes
and no one shall rescue her from my power.

¹⁴/₁₂   I will lay her vines and fig trees waste,
those of which she used to say,
'These are the pay my lovers gave me';
I am going to make them into thickets
for the wild beasts to ravage.

¹³/₁₁   I will put an end to all her rejoicing,
her feasts, her New Moons, her sabbaths
and all her solemn festivals.

¹⁵/₁₃   I mean to make her pay for all the days
when she burnt offerings to the Baals
and decked herself with rings and necklaces
to court her lovers,
forgetting me.
It is Yahweh who is speaking.

⁸/₆   That is why I am going to block her way with thorns,
and wall her in so that she cannot find her way;

⁹/₇   she will chase after her lovers and never catch up with them,
she will search for them and never find them.
Then she will say, 'I will go back to my first husband,
I was happier then than I am today'.

¹⁶/₁₄   That is why I am going to lure her
and lead her out into the wilderness
and speak to her heart.

¹⁷/₁₅   I am going to give her back her vineyards,
and make the Valley of Achor^c a gateway of hope.
There she will respond to me as she did when she was young,
as she did when she came out of the land of Egypt.

¹⁸/₁₆   When that day comes—it is Yahweh who speaks—
she will call me, 'My husband',
no longer will she call me, 'My Baal'.^d

¹⁹/₁₇   I will take the names of the Baals off her lips,
their names shall never be uttered again.

²⁰/₁₈   When that day comes I will make a treaty on her behalf
with the wild animals,
with the birds of heaven and the creeping things of the earth;
I will break bow, sword and battle in the country,

---

1 a. More accurately, it was under the last four kings of Israel, Menahem to Hoshea (743-724), that Hosea chiefly exercised his prophetic ministry.   **b.** It was here that Jehu massacred the descendants of Omri.   **c.** Another name for Megiddo (Armageddon), one of the great battlefields of Palestine.
2 a. Probably the amulets, tattooing and other distinctive marks of the prostitute.   **b.** The Canaanite baals were gods of fertility.   **c.** 'The Valley of Misery', one of the gorges near Jericho.   **d.** Strictly, 'my master' or 'my husband'; but the word had taken on associations with the Canaanite gods.

and make her sleep secure.
I will betroth you to myself for ever,   21/19
betroth you with integrity and justice,
with tenderness and love;
I will betroth you to myself with faithfulness,   22/20
and you will come to know Yahweh.

When that day comes—it is Yahweh who speaks—   23/21
the heavens will have their answer from me,
the earth its answer from them,
the grain, the wine, the oil, their answer from the earth,   24/22
and Jezreel his answer*ᶜ* from them.
I will sow him in the country,   25/23
I will love Unloved;
I will say to No-People-of-Mine, 'You are my people',   24
and he will answer, 'You are my God'.

Hosea takes his unfaithful wife back and tests her fidelity. The symbol explained

3 Yahweh said to me, 'Go a second time, give your love to a woman, loved 1 by her husband but an adulteress in spite of it, just as Yahweh gives his love to the sons of Israel though they turn to other gods and love raisin cakes'. So I bought her for fifteen silver shekels and a bushel-and-a-half of barley, 2 and said to her, 'For many days you must keep yourself quietly for me, not 3 playing the whore or offering yourself to others; and I will do the same for you'.

For the sons of Israel will be kept for many days without a king, without 4 a leader, without sacrifice or sacred stone, without ephod or teraphim.*ᵈ* •After- 5 wards the sons of Israel will come back; they will seek Yahweh their God and David their king; they will come trembling to Yahweh, come for his good things in those days to come.

The great future

2   And the number of the sons of Israel will be like the sand   1
           on the seashore,
which cannot be measured or counted.
In the place where they were told, 'You are no people of mine',
they will be called, 'The sons of the living God'.
The sons of Judah and of Israel will be one again   2
and choose themselves one single leader,
and they will spread far beyond their country;
so great will be the day of Jezreel.
To your brother say, 'People-of-Mine',   3
to your sister, 'Beloved'.

II. THE CRIMES AND PUNISHMENT OF ISRAEL

General corruption

4   Sons of Israel, listen to the word of Yahweh,   1
for Yahweh indicts the inhabitants of the country:
there is no fidelity, no tenderness,   2
no knowledge of God in the country,
only perjury and lies, slaughter, theft,   2
adultery and violence, murder after murder.
This is why the country is in mourning, and all who live in it pine away, 3
even the wild animals and the birds of heaven;
the fish of the sea themselves are perishing.

Against the priests

4   But let no man denounce, no man rebuke;
     it is you, priest, that I denounce.

5   Day and night you stumble along,
     the prophet stumbling with you,
     and you are the ruin of your people.

6   My people perish for want of knowledge.
     As you have rejected knowledge
     so do I reject you from my priesthood;
     you have forgotten the teaching of your God,
     I in my turn will forget your children.

7   Many as they are, all of them have sinned against me,
     they have bartered their glory for shame.

8   They feed on the sin of my people,
     they are all greedy for their iniquity.

9   But as with the people, so let it be with the priest:
     I will make them pay for their conduct,
     I will pay them out for their deeds.

10   They will eat but never be satisfied,
     they will play the whore but still be sterile,
     because they have deserted Yahweh

11   to give themselves up •to whoring.

Worship in Israel is now idolatrous and debauched

     Wine, new wine addles the wits.

12   My people consult their block of wood,
     a rod answers their questions;*a*
     for a prostituting spirit leads them astray,
     they renounce their God to play the whore.

13   They offer sacrifice on the mountain tops,
     burn their offerings on the hills,
     under oak and poplar and terebinth,
     so pleasant is their shade.
     So, although your daughters prostitute themselves
     and your sons' wives commit adultery,

14   I shall not be hard on your daughters for their whoring
     or on your sons' wives for their adultery,
     when everyone else is wandering off with whores
     and offering sacrifice with sacred prostitutes.
     Thus does a senseless people run to ruin.

A warning to Judah

15   Though you, Israel, play the whore,
     there is no need for Judah to sin too.
     Do not go to Gilgal,
     do not go up to Beth-aven,*b*
     do not take the oath, 'As Yahweh lives!'

Israel the stubborn heifer

16   Since Israel is as obstinate
     as a stubborn heifer,

e. The name Jezreel will no longer recall past crimes, see 1:4. Its true meaning is 'God sows'.
3 a. I.e., without any visible link with Yahweh: the ephod was the priest's amulet by which he determined the will of Yahweh; the teraphim a 'household god' (of unknown form).
4 a. The reference is to the sacred pole and the rod of a diviner.   b. 'House of nothing', a contemptuous name for Bethel.

how can Yahweh pasture him
like a lamb in rolling pastures?
Ephraim is wedded to idols,   17
they sprawl ·in the company of drunkards;   18
whoring is all they care about,
they barter their glory for shame.
The wind will carry them off on its wings,   19
then all their altars will bring them is disappointment.

Priests, nobles and king are the ruin of the nation

5   Listen to this, priests,   1
attend, House of Israel,
listen, royal household,
you who are responsible for justice,
for you have been a snare at Mizpah,
and a net outspread on Tabor.
They are entrenched in their deceitfulness   2
and so I am going to punish them all.
I know all about Ephraim,   3
Israel has no secrets for me;
yes Ephraim, you have played the whore,
Israel has defiled himself.
Their deeds do not allow them to return to their God,   4
since a prostituting spirit possesses them;
they do not know Yahweh.
The arrogance of Israel is his own accuser,   5
the iniquity of Ephraim knocks him down,
and down comes Judah with him.
Though they go in search of Yahweh with their sheep and oxen,   6
they do not find him;
for he has withdrawn from them.
They have proved unfaithful to Yahweh,   7
they have fathered bastards,
and now the destroyer will devour them, them and their estates.

The brothers' war

Sound the horn in Gibeah,   8
the trumpet in Ramah,
give the alarm at Beth-aven,
call Benjamin to arms!
Ephraim shall be laid waste when the day comes for punishment;   9
I pronounce certain doom for the tribes of Israel.[a]
The leaders of Judah are like men who displace the boundary mark;   10
I mean to pour my anger out on them in a flood.
Ephraim is an oppressor, he tramples on justice,   11
so set is he on his pursuit of nothingness.
Very well, I myself will be the moth of Ephraim,   12
the canker of the House of Judah.

The folly of foreign alliances

Ephraim has seen how sick he is   13
and Judah the extent of his wound,
so Ephraim has turned to Assyria,
Judah has appealed to the Great King;[b]
but he has no power to cure you
nor to heal your wound.

14   For I mean to be like a lion to Ephraim,
        like a young lion to the House of Judah;
        I, yes I, will tear to pieces, then go my way,
        I will carry off my prey, and no one can snatch it from me.

Yahweh abandons his people

15   Yes, I am going to return to my dwelling place
        until they confess their guilt and seek my face;
6:1   they will search for me in their misery.

Israel's short-lived and shallow repentance

1 **6** 'Come, let us return to Yahweh.
2   He has torn us to pieces, but he will heal us;
        he has struck us down, but he will bandage our wounds;
2/3   after a day or two he will bring us back to life,
        on the third day he will raise us
        and we shall live in his presence.
3a   Let us set ourselves to know Yahweh;
        that he will come is as certain as the dawn
5b   his judgement will rise like the light,
3b   he will come to us as showers come,
        like spring rains watering the earth.'

4   What am I to do with you, Ephraim?
        What am I to do with you, Judah?
        This love of yours is like a morning cloud,
        like the dew that quickly disappears.
5a   This is why I have torn them to pieces by the prophets,
        why I slaughtered them with the words from my mouth,
6   since what I want is love, not sacrifice;
        knowledge of God, not holocausts.

The past and present sins of Israel

7   But they have violated the covenant at Adam,
        they have proved unfaithful to me there.
8   Gilead is a town of evil-doers,
        full of bloody footprints.
9   Like so many robbers in ambush
        a band of priests commits murder on the road to Shechem—
        appalling behaviour, indeed!
10   I have seen horrors in Bethel;
        that is where Ephraim plays the whore
        and Israel defiles himself.
11   Judah, I intend a harvest for you, too,
        when I restore the fortunes of my people.

1 **7** Whenever I want to heal Israel,
        I am confronted by the guilt of Ephraim
        and the wickedness of Samaria;
        deceit is their principle of behaviour,
        thieves break into houses
        and bandits raid outside.
2   They never pause to consider
        that I know about all their wickedness;

5 a. This prophecy apparently relates to the Syro-Ephraimite war (735-734), 2 K 16-17.
b. Menahem paid tribute to Tiglath-pileser III of Assyria, 738; Ahaz appealed to the same king for help, 735.

yet their actions are all round them,
they stare me in the face.

Conspiracy the order of the day in Israel

Such is their cunning, they beguile the king,   3
and the leaders too, such is their treachery.
But they breathe fury, all of them,   4
as fiery as an oven
which the baker does not need to stoke
from the time he has kneaded the dough until it rises.
They addle the king and leaders with wine fumes   5
as he mixes with these scoundrels.
Their hearts reach oven-heat in the excitement of the plot;   6
their fury smoulders all night
and in the morning blazes like a fierce flame;
all burn at oven-heat   7
and they consume the men who rule them.
Thus have all their kings fallen,
not one of them has ever called on me.ᵃ

Israel ruined by relying on foreign powers

Ephraim mixes with the nations,   8
Ephraim is a half-baked cake.
Foreigners eat his strength away,   9
he is unconscious of it;
grey hairs are scattered on his head:
he is unconscious of it.
(The arrogance of Israel is his own accuser;   10
they will not come back to Yahweh their God;
in spite of all this they will not seek him.)
Ephraim is like a silly, witless dove,   11
calling on Egypt, turning to Assyria.
Wherever they turn, I will spread my net over them,   12
I mean to bring them down like the birds of heaven,
I will punish them for their perversity.

The ingratitude and punishment of Israel

Trouble is coming to them, for they have strayed from me!   13
Ruin on them, for they have rebelled against me!
I wanted to redeem them, but they tell lies about me.
Theirs is no heartfelt cry to me   14
when they lament on their beds.
They gash themselves for the sake of corn and wine,
yet they rebel against me.
I it was who gave strength to their arms,   15
yet all they do is make wicked plots against me.
They turn to Baal,   16
they are like a treacherous bow.
Their leaders will fall by the sword
because of their arrogant talk,
and how they will be laughed at in the land of Egypt!

Sound the alarm!

8   Put the trumpet to your lips   1
    like a watchman on duty at the house of Yahweh,
    because they have violated my covenant

	and rebelled against my Law.
2	Useless now to shout, 'God of Israel, we acknowledge you'.
3	Israel has rejected the good;
	the enemy^a will hunt him down.

Civil anarchy and idolatry

4   They have set up kings, but not with my consent,
and appointed princes, but without my knowledge.
Out of their own silver and gold they have made idols,
which are doomed to destruction.

5   I spurn your calf, Samaria,
my anger blazes against it.
(How long will it be before they purge themselves of this,

6   the sons of Israel?)
A workman made the thing,
this cannot be God!
Yes, the calf of Samaria shall go up in flames.

7   They sow the wind, they will reap the whirlwind;
their wheat will yield no ear,
the ear will yield no flour,
or, if it does, foreigners will swallow it.

Israel ruined by relying on foreign powers

8   Israel himself has been swallowed,
and is destined now to stay among the nations
like a crock that no one wants,

9   for making approaches to Assyria
—that wild ass living alone.
Ephraim is renting lovers.

10   Right; let them rent them among the nations,
I am going to disperse them this minute;
that will soon put a stop to their anointing kings and leaders.

Against the outward show of worship

11   Ephraim has built altar after altar,
they have only served him as occasion for sin.

12   Were I to write out the thousand precepts of my Law for him,
they would be paid no more attention than those of a stranger.

13   They love sacrificing; right, let them sacrifice!
They love meat; right, let them eat it!
Yahweh takes no pleasure in these.
He is now going to remember their iniquity
and punish their sins;
they will have to go back to Egypt.

Against extravagance in building

14   Israel has forgotten his Maker
and has built palaces;
Judah has built fortified town after fortified town;
right, I will rain fire on his towns,
it will devour his palaces.

---

7 a. Seven of the kings of the Northern Kingdom had been murdered by the year 737.
8 a. Assyria.

The sorrows of exile

9

Let us have no rejoicing, Israel.   1
no exulting like the other peoples;
for you have deserted God to play the whore,
you have enjoyed the prostitute's pay
on every threshing-floor.
Neither floor nor vat will nourish them,   2
the new wine will disappoint them.
They will no longer live in the land of Yahweh,   3
Ephraim will have to go back to Egypt,
and in Assyria they will eat food that is unclean.
They will pour libations of wine to Yahweh no longer,   4
nor offer sacrifice to him;
their bread will be like mourners' bread,
all those who eat it will become unclean;
for their bread will serve only for themselves,
it must not enter the house of Yahweh.
What will you do on the day of solemn festival,   5
the day of the feast of Yahweh?
Why, they will have gone, gone from the devastation.   6
Egypt will receive them, Memphis bury them,
nettles will inherit their treasures of silver,
and brambles invade their tents.

Persecution, the prophet's reward for foretelling the punishment

Now the days of reckoning have come,   7
the days of reprisals are here.
'The prophet is mad,' Israel protests 'this inspired fellow is raving.'
—Ah yes, but only because your iniquity is so great,
your apostasy so grave.
Ephraim watches the prophet's tent,   8
traps are set for him on all his paths,
in the house of his God enmity awaits him.
These men are as steeped in corruption   9
as in the days of Gibeah;
Yahweh will remember their iniquity,
he will punish their sins.

Punishment for the crime at Baal-peor

It was like finding grapes in the wilderness when I found Israel,   10
like seeing early fruit on the fig tree when I saw your fathers;
but when they reached Baal-peor they devoted themselves to shame
and became as hateful as the thing they loved.
The glory of Ephraim will fly away like a bird: 11
no giving birth, no pregnancy, no conceiving.
And if they rear sons, I will take these from them before they   12
come to manhood;
trouble for them indeed when I abandon them.
Ephraim, I see, has made his sons a prey,   13
Ephraim must lead his sons to the slaughter house.
Give them, Yahweh—what are you to give?—   14
give them wombs that miscarry, and dried-up breasts.

Punishment for the crime at Gilgal

Their wickedness appeared in full at Gilgal,[a]   15
there I came to hate them.

Because of their wicked deeds
I will drive them out of my house;
I will love them no longer,
for their leaders are all rebels.

16 Ephraim is cut down,
their roots are withered;
they will bear no fruit.
And if they bear children,
I will kill the darlings of their womb.

17 Because they have not listened to him, my God will cast them off
and they will be wanderers throughout the nations.

The destruction of Israel's cultic objects

1
10   Israel was a luxuriant vine
yielding plenty of fruit.
The more his fruit increased,
the more altars he built;
the richer his land became,
the richer he made the sacred stones.

2 Their heart is a divided heart;
very well, they must pay for it:
Yahweh is going to break their altars down
and destroy their sacred stones.

3 Then they will say,
'We have no king
because we have not feared Yahweh'.
But what can a king do for us?

4 Words, words! False oaths! Alliances!
And judgement is only a poisonous weed that thrives
in the furrows of the field.

5 The inhabitants of Samaria are trembling
for the calf of Beth-aven;
yes, its people mourn for it,
its so-called priests bewail its glory,
now this has vanished.

6 The calf itself shall be carried off to Assyria
as tribute to the Great King.
Ephraim will reap the shame,
and Israel blush for his idol.

7 Samaria has had her day.
Her king[a] is like a straw drifting on the water.

8 The idolatrous high places shall be destroyed—
that sin of Israel;
thorn and thistle will grow on their altars.
Then they will say to the mountains, 'Cover us!'
and to the hills, 'Fall on us!'

Against Gibeah

9 Ever since the days at Gibeah, Israel, you have sinned.
Things are still the same.
And will not war overtake the guilty at Gibeah?

10 I shall come and punish them.
The nations will muster against them
to punish them for their double crime.

9 a. The monarchy was instituted there, 1 S 13:7-14; 15:10-23.
10 a. The calf.

Threats and an invitation to repentance

Ephraim is a well trained heifer   11
that loves to tread the threshing-floor;
very well, I myself mean to lay the yoke on that fine neck of hers,
I am going to put Ephraim in harness,
Israel will have to plough,
Jacob must draw the harrow.
Sow integrity for yourselves,   12
reap a harvest of kindness,
break up your fallow ground:
it is time to go seeking Yahweh
until he comes to rain salvation on you.

The end of Israel

Why have you ploughed iniquity,   13
reaped injustice,
and eaten the produce, lies?
Because you have trusted in your chariots,
and in your host of warriors,
turmoil is going to break out in your towns,   14
and all your fortresses will be laid waste,
as Shalman[b] laid Beth-arbel waste
on the day of the battle,
when mothers fell, dashed to pieces, on their children.
That is what I mean to do to you, House of Israel,   15
because of your great wickedness;
and in the storm the king of Israel is going to disappear for ever.   11:1

God's love despised: his vengeance

11

When Israel was a child I loved him,   1
and I called my son out of Egypt.
But the more I called to them, the further they went from me;   2
they have offered sacrifice to the Baals
and set their offerings smoking before the idols.
I myself taught Ephraim to walk,   3
I took them in my arms;
yet they have not understood that I was the one looking after them.
I led them with reins of kindness,   4
with leading-strings of love.
I was like someone who lifts an infant close against his cheek;
stooping down to him I gave him his food.
They will have to go back to Egypt,   5
Assyria must be their king,
because they have refused to return to me.
The sword will rage through their towns,   6
wiping out their children,
glutting itself inside their fortresses.

God's love proves stronger than his vengeance

My people are diseased through their disloyalty;   7
they call on Baal,
but he does not cure them.
Ephraim, how could I part with you?   8
Israel, how could I give you up?
How could I treat you like Admah,
or deal with you like Zeboiim?[a]

My heart recoils from it,
my whole being trembles at the thought.
9   I will not give rein to my fierce anger,
I will not destroy Ephraim again,
for I am God, not man:
I am the Holy One in your midst
and have no wish to destroy.

The return from exile

10   They will follow behind Yahweh;
he will be roaring like a lion—
how he will roar!—
and his sons will come speeding from the west;
11   they will come speeding from Egypt like a bird,
speeding from the land of Assyria like a dove,
and I will settle them in their homes
—it is Yahweh who speaks.

Israel's religion and policy both alike perverse

¹²/₁₂ **12**   All round me are the lies of Ephraim
and the deceit of the House of Israel.
But God still recognises Judah,
and he is still called the people of the Holy One.
²/₁   Ephraim feeds on the wind,
forever chasing the wind from the East,
accumulating falsehood and fraud,
making treaties with Assyria,
sending oil to Egypt.

Against Jacob

³/₂   Yahweh has a case against Israel,
he will pay Jacob as his conduct merits,
and will repay him as his deeds deserve.
⁴/₃   In the very womb he supplanted his brother,
in maturity he wrestled against God.
⁵/₄   He wrestled with the angel and beat him,
he wept and pleaded with him.
He met him at Bethel
and there God spoke to him.
⁶/₅/₇/₆   Yes, Yahweh God of Sabaoth, Yahweh is his name.
Turn again, then, to your God,
hold fast to love and justice,
and always put your trust in your God.

Greed and the punishment of Israel

⁸/₇   Canaan holds fraudulent scales in his hands,
to defraud is his delight.
⁹/₈   'How rich I have become!' says Ephraim
'I have amassed a fortune.'
But he will keep nothing of all his profits,
because of the guilt that he has brought on himself.

b. Probably Salamanu, king of Moab.
11 a. Neighbouring towns of Sodom and Gomorrah in Gn 10:19; presumably overwhelmed by the same fate, according to the tradition followed here.

The prospect of reconciliation between Yahweh and Israel

I have been Yahweh, your God, since the days in the land of Egypt. ¹⁰₉
I will make you live in tents again
as on the day of Meeting.ᵃ
I will speak to the prophets, ¹¹₁₀
I will increase the visions
and through the prophets I will deal out death.

New threats

Gilead is nothing but iniquity, ¹²₁₁
they are falsehood, nothing else;
at Gilgal they sacrifice to bulls;
their altars shall be reduced to heaps of stones
in a ploughed field.

Against Jacob and Ephraim

Jacob fled to the plains of Aram, ¹³₁₂
Israel worked to win a wife,
to win a wife he looked after sheep.
But Yahweh brought Israel out of Egypt by a prophet, ¹⁴₁₃
and a prophet looked after Israel.
Ephraim has given bitter provocation ¹⁵₁₄
and Yahweh means to bring his bloodshed down on him,
his Lord will repay him for his insults.

Idolatry punished

13 When Ephraim spoke, all trembled, ₁
so great was he in Israel,
but through Baal he brought guilt on himself and perished.
And now they add sin to sin, ₂
they smelt images from their silver,
idols of their own manufacture,
smith's work, all of it.
'Sacrifice to them' they say.
Men blow kisses to calves!
Therefore they will be like morning mist, ₃
like the dew that quickly disappears,
like the chaff whirled from the threshing-floor,
like smoke escaping through the window.

The punishment for ingratitude

Yet I am Yahweh, your God since the days in the land of Egypt; ₄
you know no God but me,
there is no other saviour.
I pastured you in the wilderness; ₅
in the land of drought
I pastured them, and they were satisfied; ₆
once satisfied, their hearts grew proud,
and so they came to forget me.
Very well, I will be a lion to them, ₇
a leopard lurking by the way;
like a bear robbed of her cubs I will pounce on them, ₈
and tear the flesh round their hearts;
the dogs shall eat their flesh,
the wild beasts tear them to pieces.

The end of the monarchy

9 I mean to destroy you, Israel;
who can come to your help?

10 Your king, where is he now, to save you,[a]
where are your leaders to champion you?
Those of whom you used to say,
'Give me a king and leaders'.

11 In my anger I gave you a king
and in my wrath I take him away.

The inevitability of ruin

12 The iniquity of Ephraim is carefully hoarded,
his sin is safely stored away.

13 Pangs as of childbirth overtake him,
and a stupid child it is,
its time is up but it does not leave the womb.

14 And am I to save them from the power of Sheol?
Am I to rescue them from Death?
Where is your plague, Death?
Where are your scourges, Sheol?
I have no eyes for pity.

15 Ephraim may flourish among the reeds,
but the wind from the East will come,
the breath of Yahweh will rise from the desert
to dry his water-sources, to parch his springs,
to strip his land of all its treasures.

1 **14** Samaria must atone
for rebelling against her God.
They shall fall by the sword,
their little children be dashed to pieces,
their pregnant women disembowelled.

III. THE REPENTANCE AND RECONCILIATION OF ISRAEL. A PROMISE OF FUTURE HAPPINESS

The sincere conversion of Israel to Yahweh

2 Israel, come back to Yahweh your God;
your iniquity was the cause of your downfall.

3 Provide yourself with words
and come back to Yahweh.
Say to him, 'Take all iniquity away
so that we may have happiness again
and offer you our words of praise.

4 Assyria cannot save us,
we will not ride horses any more,[a]
or say, "Our God!" to what our own hands have made,
for you are the one in whom orphans find compassion.'

5 —I will heal their disloyalty,

---

12 a. At Sinai, Ex 5:3.
13 a. Possibly an ironic allusion to Hoshea, whose name means 'Yahweh-is-saviour'. He was imprisoned at the beginning of the siege of Samaria, see 14:1.
14 a. 'Ride horses'; possibly 'conclude an alliance with Egypt', for the sake of the mounted troops for which Egypt was famous.

I will love them with all my heart,
for my anger has turned from them.
I will fall like dew on Israel.   6
He shall bloom like the lily,
and thrust out roots like the poplar,
his shoots will spread far;   7
he will have the beauty of the olive
and the fragrance of Lebanon.
They will come back to live in my shade;   8
they will grow corn that flourishes,
they will cultivate vines
as renowned as the wine of Helbon.
What has Ephraim to do with idols any more   9
when it is I who hear his prayer and care for him?
I am like a cypress ever green,
all your fruitfulness comes from me.

Concluding admonition

Let the wise man understand these words.   10
Let the intelligent man grasp their meaning.
For the ways of Yahweh are straight,
and virtuous men walk in them,
but sinners stumble.

JOEL

1 **1** The word of Yahweh that was addressed to Joel son of Pethuel.

I. THE PLAGUE OF LOCUSTS

A. A LITURGY OF MOURNING AND ENTREATY

a. Lamentation over the ruin of the country

2   Listen to this, you elders;
    all inhabitants of the country, attend.
    Has anything like this ever happened in your day,
    or in your fathers' days?

3   Tell it to your sons,
    let your sons tell it to their sons,
    and their sons to a generation after them.

4   What the gnawer has left, the grown locust has devoured,
    what the grown locust has left, the hopper has devoured,
    what the hopper has left, the shearer has devoured.[a]

5   Awake, drunkards, and weep!
    All you who drink wine, lament
    for that new wine: it has been dashed from your lips.

6   For a nation has invaded my country,
    mighty and innumerable;
    its teeth are the teeth of lions,
    it has the fangs of a lioness.

7   It has laid waste my vines
    and torn my fig trees to pieces;
    it has stripped them clean and cut them down,
    their branches have turned white.

8   Mourn like a virgin wearing sackcloth
    for her young man betrothed to her.

9   Oblation and libation[b] have vanished
    from the house of Yahweh.
    The priests, the ministers of Yahweh,
    are in mourning.

10   Wasted lie the fields,
    the fallow is in mourning.
    For the corn has been laid waste,
    the wine fails,
    the fresh oil dries up.

1 a. The locust invasion has included insects in four distinct stages of growth.   **b.** The daily offerings from the produce of the soil: corn, wine and oil, as listed in v.10.

> Stand dismayed, you farmers,   11
> wail, you vinedressers,
> for the wheat, for the barley;
> the harvest of the field has been ruined.
> The vine has withered,   12
> the fig tree wilts away;
> pomegranate, and palm, and apple,
> every tree in the field is drooping.
> Yes, gladness has faded
> among the sons of men.

b. A call to repentance and prayer

> Priests, put on sackcloth and lament.   13
> Ministers of the altar, wail.
> Come, pass the night in sackcloth,
> you ministers of my God.
> For the house of our God has been deprived
> of oblation and libation.
> Order a fast,   14
> proclaim a solemn assembly;
> elders, call together
> all the inhabitants of the country
> to the house of Yahweh your God.
> Cry out to Yahweh,
> 'Oh, what a day!   15
> For the day of Yahweh is near,
> it comes as a devastation from Shaddai.'c

> Has not the food disappeared   16
> before our eyes?
> Have not joy and gladness vanished
> from the house of our God?
> Seeds shrivel   17
> under their clods;
> the barns are broken down,
> the granaries lie in ruins,
> for lack of harvest.
> What mourning from the beasts!   18
> The herds of cattle wander bewildered
> because they have no pasture.
> Even the flocks of sheep must bear their punishment.

> To you, Yahweh, I cry: 19
> fire has devoured the pastures on the heath,
> flame has burnt up
> every tree in the orchard.
> Even the wild beasts wait anxiously for you,   20
> for the watercourses have run dry,
> and fire has devoured the pastures on the heath.

c. The day of Yahweh and the present calamity
The alarm

2
> Sound the trumpet in Zion,   1
> give the alarm on my holy mountain!
> Let all the inhabitants of the country tremble,
> for the day of Yahweh is coming,
> yes, it is near.

2   Day of darkness and gloom,
           day of cloud and blackness.
           Like the dawn there spreads across the mountains
           a vast and mighty host,
           such as has never been before,
           such as will never be again
           to the remotest ages.

The invading army

3   In their van the fire devours,
           in their rear a flame consumes.
           The country is like a garden of Eden ahead of them
           and a desert waste behind them.
           Nothing escapes them.
4   They look like horses,
           like chargers they gallop on,
5   with a racket like the clatter of chariots
           they hurtle over the mountain tops,
           with a crackling like a blazing fire
           devouring the stubble,
           a mighty army in battle array.

6   At the sight of them the peoples are appalled
           and every face grows pale.
7   Like fighting men they press forward,
           like warriors scale the walls,
           each marching straight ahead,
           not turning from his path;
8   they never jostle each other,
           each marches straight ahead:
           arrows fly, they still press forward,
           without breaking ranks.
9   They hurl themselves at the city,
           they leap on to its walls,
           climb to the housetops,
           and make their way through windows
           like marauders.

A vision of the day of Yahweh

10   As they come on, the earth quakes,
           the skies tremble,
           sun and moon grow dark,
           the stars lose their brilliance.
11   Yahweh makes his voice heard
           at the head of his army,
           and indeed his regiments are innumerable,
           all-powerful is the one that carries out his orders,
           for great is the day of Yahweh,
           and very terrible—who can face it?

d. A call to repentance

12   'But now, now—it is Yahweh who speaks—
           come back to me with all your heart,
           fasting, weeping, mourning.'
13   Let your hearts be broken, not your garments torn,

c. There is a Hebr. pun on the word for 'devastation' and Shaddai (one of the names of God).

turn to Yahweh your God again,
for he is all tenderness and compassion,
slow to anger, rich in graciousness,
and ready to relent.
Who knows if he will not turn again, will not relent,   14
will not leave a blessing as he passes,
oblation and libation
for Yahweh your God?

Sound the trumpet in Zion!   15
Order a fast,
proclaim a solemn assembly,
call the people together,   16
summon the community,
assemble the elders,
gather the children,
even the infants at the breast.
Let the bridegroom leave his bedroom
and the bride her alcove.
Between vestibule and altar let the priests,   17
the ministers of Yahweh, lament.
Let them say,
'Spare your people, Yahweh!
Do not make your heritage a thing of shame,
a byword for the nations.
Why should it be said among the nations,
"Where is their God?" '

B. THE PRAYER ANSWERED

Then Yahweh, jealous on behalf of his land,   18
took pity on his people.

The plague ceases

Yahweh spoke in answer to his people,   19
'Now I send you
corn and wine and oil,
until you have enough.
Never again shall I make you
a thing of shame for the nations.
I will drive the invader from the north far away from you   20
and drive him into an arid, desolate land,
his vanguard to the eastern sea,
his rearguard to the western sea.
He will give off a stench,
give off a foul stink.'
(For he has done great things.)

A vision of plenty

O soil, do not be afraid;   21
be glad, rejoice,
for Yahweh has done great things.

Beasts of the field, do not be afraid;   22
the pastures on the heath are green again,
the trees bear fruit,
vine and fig tree yield abundantly.

23   Sons of Zion, be glad,
rejoice in Yahweh your God;
for he has given you
the autumn rain, since he is just,
and has poured the rains down for you,
the autumn and spring rain as before.

24   The threshing-floors will be full of grain,
the vats overflow with wine and oil.

25   'I will make up to you for the years
devoured by grown locust and hopper
by shearer and young locust,
my great army
which I sent to invade you.'

26   You will eat to your heart's content, will eat your fill,
and praise the name of Yahweh your God
who has treated you so wonderfully.
(My people will not be disappointed any more.)

27   And you will know that I am in the midst of Israel,
that I am Yahweh your God, with none to equal me.
My people will not be disappointed any more.

II. THE NEW AGE AND THE DAY OF YAHWEH

A. THE OUTPOURING OF THE SPIRIT

28 **3**   'After this
I will pour out my spirit on all mankind.
Your sons and daughters shall prophesy,
your old men shall dream dreams,
and your young men see visions.

29   Even on the slaves, men and women,
will I pour out my spirit in those days.

30   I will display portents in heaven and on earth,
blood and fire and columns of smoke.'

31   The sun will be turned into darkness,
and the moon into blood,
before the day of Yahweh dawns,
that great and terrible day.

32   All who call on the name of Yahweh will be saved,
for *on Mount Zion there will be some who have escaped,*
as Yahweh has said,
and in Jerusalem some survivors whom Yahweh will call.

B. THE JUDGEMENT OF THE NATIONS

The judgement announced

1 **4**   'For in those days and at that time,
when I restore the fortunes of Judah and Jerusalem,
2   I am going to gather all the nations
and take them down to the Valley of Jehoshaphat;
there I intend to put them on trial
for all they have done to Israel, my people and my heritage.

For *a* they have scattered them among the nations
and have divided up my land among themselves.
They have cast lots for my people;   3
they have bartered the boys for prostitutes,
have sold the girls for wine and drunk it.'

Charges against the Phoenicians and Philistines

'And you, Tyre and Sidon, what do you expect from me?   4
You too, regions of Philistia?
Do you want to take revenge on me?
If you were to take revenge on me,
I would make it recoil promptly and swiftly on your own heads.
You who have taken my silver and my gold,   5
who have carried off my rich treasures to your temples,
you who have sold to the people of Javan *b*   6
the sons of Judah and Jerusalem,
to remove them far from their own frontiers.
Now I mean to summon them from wherever you have sold them,   7
now I intend to make your crime recoil on your own heads.
I am going to sell your sons and daughters   8
into the hands of the sons of Judah,
and they will sell them to the Sabaeans, *c*
to a distant nation;
Yahweh has spoken!'

A summons to the nations

'Proclaim this among the nations.   9
"Prepare for war!
Muster the champions!
Warriors, advance,
quick march!
Hammer your ploughshares into swords,   10
your sickles into spears,
let the weakling say, 'I am a fighting man'.
Come quickly,   11
all you surrounding nations,
assemble there!"
(Yahweh, send down your champions!)

'Let the nations rouse themselves, let them march   12
to the Valley of Jehoshaphat,
for I am going to sit in judgement there
on all the nations round.
Put the sickle in: 13
the harvest is ripe;
come and tread:
the winepress is full,
the vats are overflowing,
so great is their wickedness!'

Host on host   14
in the Valley of Decision!
For the day of Yahweh is near
in the Valley of Decision!

The day of Yahweh

Sun and moon grow dark,   15
the stars lose their brilliance.

16   Yahweh roars from Zion,
   makes his voice heard from Jerusalem;
   heaven and earth tremble.

   But Yahweh will be a shelter for his people,
   a stronghold for the sons of Israel.

17   'You will learn then that I am Yahweh your God,
   dwelling in Zion, my holy mountain.
   Jerusalem will be a holy place,
   no alien will ever pass through it again.'

C. THE GLORIOUS FUTURE OF ISRAEL

18   When that day comes,
   the mountains will run with new wine
   and the hills flow with milk,
   and all the river beds of Judah
   will run with water.
   A fountain will spring from the house of Yahweh
   to water the wadi of Acacias.

19   Egypt will become a desolation,
   Edom a desert waste
   on account of the violence done to the sons of Judah
   whose innocent blood they shed in their country.

20   But Judah will be inhabited for ever,
   Jerusalem from age to age.

21   'I will avenge their blood and let none go unpunished',
   and Yahweh shall make his home in Zion.

4 a. After the siege of Jerusalem in 597, there were deportations to Babylon. There was a
further deportation in 586.   **b.** Greece.   **c.** Of S. Arabia.

AMOS

Title

1 Words of Amos who was one of the shepherds of Tekoa. The visions he had 1 about Israel in the time of Uzziah king of Judah and of Jeroboam*a* son of Joash, king of Israel, two years before the earthquake.

Introduction

He said: 2

> Yahweh roars from Zion,
> and makes his voice heard from Jerusalem;
> the shepherds' pastures mourn,
> and the crown of Carmel withers.

I. JUDGEMENT ON THE NEIGHBOURS OF ISRAEL
AND ON ISRAEL ITSELF

Damascus

Yahweh says this: 3

> For the three crimes, the four crimes,*b* of Damascus
> I have made my decree and will not relent:
> because they have thrashed Gilead with iron threshing-sledges,
> I am going to hurl fire on the House of Hazael   4
> to burn up Ben-hadad's*c* palaces;   5
> I am going to break the gate bars of Damascus,
> and cut down the one enthroned at Bikath-aven
> and the sceptred one at Beth-eden;*d*
> and the people of Aram shall go captive to Kir, says Yahweh.

Gaza and Philistia

Yahweh says this: 6

> For the three crimes, the four crimes, of Gaza
> I have made my decree and will not relent:
> because they have deported entire nations
> as slaves to Edom,
> I am going to hurl fire on the walls of Gaza   7
> to burn up her palaces.
> I am going to cut down the one enthroned at Ashdod   8
> and the sceptred one at Ashkelon;
> I am going to turn my hand against Ekron
> until the last of the Philistines is dead,
> says Yahweh.

Tyre and Phoenicia

9 Yahweh says this:

> For the three crimes, the four crimes, of Tyre
> I have made my decree and will not relent:
> because they have deported entire nations as slaves to Edom
> and have not remembered the covenant of brotherhood,

10
> I am going to hurl fire on the walls of Tyre
> to burn up her palaces.

Edom

11 Yahweh says this:

> For the three crimes, the four crimes, of Edom
> I have made my decree and will not relent:
> because he has persecuted his brother with the sword,
> stifling his pity,
> persistently nursing his fury
> and ever cherishing his rage,

12
> I am going to hurl fire on Teman*
> to burn up the palaces of Bozrah.

Ammon

13 Yahweh says this:

> For the three crimes, the four crimes, of the sons of Ammon
> I have made my decree and will not relent:
> because they have disembowelled the pregnant women of Gilead
> in order to extend their own frontiers,

14
> I am going to light a fire against the wall of Rabbah
> to burn up her palaces,
> to the sound of war-cries on the day of battle,
> amid storms on a day of hurricane;

15
> and their king shall go into exile,
> he and his princes with him,
> says Yahweh.

Moab

1 **2** Yahweh says this:

> For the three crimes, the four crimes, of Moab
> I have made my decree and will not relent:
> because they have burnt the bones of the king* of Edom for lime,

2
> I am going to hurl fire on Moab
> to burn up the palaces of Kerioth,
> and Moab shall die in tumult,
> to the sound of war cries and the blare of trumpets;

3
> I will cut down the chieftain inside her
> and slaughter all her princes with him,
> says Yahweh.

Judah

4 Yahweh says this:

1 a. Jeroboam II of Israel, 783-743. b. In the manner of the 'numerical proverbs', the two consecutive numbers indicate an indefinite number. c. King Hazael of Damascus and his son Ben-hadad III were bitter enemies of Israel. d. The two place-names (meaning 'valley of wickedness' and 'house of pleasure') stand for Damascus. e. A tribal name or place-name.
2 a. Thus ensuring the suffering of the soul.

For the three crimes, the four crimes, of Judah
I have made my decree and will not relent:
because they have rejected the Law of Yahweh
and failed to keep his precepts,
because the false gods which their ancestors followed
have led them astray,
I am going to hurl fire on Judah   5
to burn up the palaces of Jerusalem.

Israel

Yahweh says this: 6

For the three crimes, the four crimes, of Israel
I have made my decree and will not relent:
because they have sold the virtuous man for silver
and the poor man for a pair of sandals,
because they trample on the heads of ordinary people   7
and push the poor out of their path,
because father and son have both resorted to the same girl,*
profaning my holy name,
because they stretch themselves out by the side of every altar   8
on clothes acquired as pledges,
and drink the wine of the people they have fined
in the house of their god...
Yet it was I who overthrew the Amorites when they attacked,   9
men tall as cedars and strong as oaks,
I who destroyed them,
both fruit above ground
and root below.
It was I who brought you out of the land of Egypt   10
and for forty years led you through the wilderness
to take possession of the Amorite's country.
I raised up prophets from your sons   11
and nazirites from your young men.
Is this not true, sons of Israel?
—it is Yahweh who speaks.
But you have forced the nazirites to drink wine   12
and given orders to the prophets,
'Do not prophesy'.
See then how I am going to crush you into the ground   13
as the threshing-sledge crushes when clogged by straw;
flight will not save even the swift,   14
the strong man will find his strength useless,
the mighty man will be powerless to save himself.
The bowman will not stand his ground,   15
the fast runner will not escape,
the horseman will not save himself,
the bravest warriors will run away naked that day.   16
It is Yahweh who speaks.

II. ISRAEL WARNED AND THREATENED

Election and punishment

3 Listen, sons of Israel, to this oracle Yahweh speaks against you, against the 1
whole family I brought out of the land of Egypt:

2   You alone, of all the families of earth, have I acknowledged,
therefore it is for all your sins that I mean to punish you.

The prophetic call cannot be resisted

3   Do two men take the road together
if they have not planned to do so?

4   Does the lion roar in the jungle
if no prey has been found?
Does the young lion growl in his lair
if he has captured nothing?

5   Does the bird fall to the ground
if no trap has been set?
Does the snare spring up from the ground
if nothing has been caught?

6   Does the trumpet sound in the city
without the populace becoming alarmed?
Does misfortune come to a city
if Yahweh has not sent it?

7   No more does the Lord Yahweh do anything
without revealing his plans to his servants the prophets.

8   The lion roars: who can help feeling afraid?
The Lord Yahweh speaks: who can refuse to prophesy?

Samaria will perish for her corruption

9   Proclaim it in the palaces of Assyria
and in the palaces in the land of Egypt;
saying, 'Assemble on Samaria's mountain
and see what great disorder there is in that city,
what oppression is found inside her'.

10   They know nothing of fair dealing
—it is Yahweh who speaks—
they cram their palaces full by harshness and extortion.

11   Therefore, the Lord Yahweh says this:
An enemy[a] is going to invade the country,
your power will be brought low,
your palaces looted.

12   Yahweh says this:
Like a shepherd rescuing a couple of legs or a bit of an ear
from the lion's mouth,
so will these sons of Israel
be rescued, who now loll in Samaria
on the corner-pillows of their divans.

Against Bethel and domestic luxury

13   Listen, and then testify it against the House of Jacob
—it is the Lord Yahweh who speaks, the God of Sabaoth:

14   On the day I punish Israel for his crimes
I will punish the altars of Bethel;
the horns of the altar are going to be broken off
and dropped on the ground.

15   I mean to pull down both winter houses and summer houses,
the houses of ivory will be destroyed,
the houses of ebony will vanish.
It is the Lord Yahweh who speaks.

b. Sacred prostitution was a feature of Canaanite worship.
3 a. Assyria.

Against the women of Samaria

4 Listen to this word, you cows of Bashan   1
living in the mountain of Samaria,
oppressing the needy, crushing the poor,
saying to your husbands, 'Bring us something to drink!'
The Lord Yahweh swears this by his holiness: 2
The days are coming to you now
when you will be dragged out with hooks,
the very last of you with prongs.
Out you will go, each by the nearest breach in the wall,   3
to be driven all the way to Hermon.[a]
It is Yahweh who speaks.

The self-deception, obstinacy and punishment of Israel

Go to Bethel, and sin,   4
to Gilgal, and sin your hardest!
Offer your sacrifices each morning
and your tithes on the third day,
burn leavened dough as a sacrifice with praise,   5
announce your voluntary offerings, make them public,
for this is what makes you happy, sons of Israel.
It is the Lord Yahweh who speaks.

And that is why I left your teeth clean in all your towns,   6
left you without bread in all your villages;
and yet you never came back to me.
It is Yahweh who speaks.

I kept your rain back with harvest still three months away;   7
I let rain fall on one town and none on another,
one field was rained on and the next dried up because I sent it no rain;
two towns, three towns, went tottering to the next for drinking-water,   8
but their thirst had to stay unquenched;
and yet you never came back to me.
It is Yahweh who speaks.

I struck you with burning and scorching,   9
and withered your gardens and vineyards;
the locusts devoured your fig trees and olives;
and yet you never came back to me.
It is Yahweh who speaks.

I sent you a plague like Egypt's plague;   10
I slaughtered your young men with the sword,
while your horses were captured for plunder;
I filled your nostrils with the stench of your camps;
and yet you never came back to me,
It is Yahweh who speaks.

I overthrew you as God overthrew Sodom and Gomorrah,[b]   11
and you were like a brand snatched from the blaze;
and yet you never came back to me.
It is Yahweh who speaks.

This therefore, Israel, is what I plan to do to you,   12
and because I am going to do this to you,
Israel, prepare to meet your God!

Doxology

13   For he it was who formed the mountains, created the wind,
        reveals his mind to man,
        makes both dawn and dark,
        and walks on the top of the heights of the world;
        Yahweh, God of Sabaoth, is his name.

Lament for Israel

5

1   Listen to this oracle I speak against you,
        it is a dirge, House of Israel:

2   She is down and will rise no more,
        the virgin of Israel.
        There she lies all alone on her own soil,
        with no one to lift her up;

3   for thus says the Lord Yahweh to the House of Israel:
        The town which used to put a thousand in the field
        will be left with a hundred,
        and the one which used to put a hundred
        will be left with ten.

No salvation without repentance

4   For Yahweh says this to the House of Israel.
        Seek me and you shall live.

5   Do not seek Bethel,
        do not go to Gilgal,
        do not journey to Beersheba,
        since Gilgal is going to be exiled
        and Bethel brought to nothing.

6   Seek Yahweh and you shall live,
        or else he will rush like fire on the House of Joseph
        and burn it up, with none at Bethel able to put out the flames.

Doxology

8   It is he who made the Pleiades and Orion,
        who turns the dusk to dawn
        and day to darkest night.
        He summons the waters of the sea
        and pours them over the land.
        Yahweh is his name.

9   He blazes out ruin on the stronghold
        and brings destruction to the fortress.

Threats

7   Trouble for those who turn justice into wormwood,
        throwing integrity to the ground;

10   who hate the man dispensing justice at the city gate
        and detest those who speak with honesty.

11   Well then, since you have trampled on the poor man,
        extorting levies on his wheat—
        those houses you have built of dressed stone,
        you will never live in them;
        and those precious vineyards you have planted,
        you will never drink their wine.

12   For I know that your crimes are many,
        and your sins enormous:

4 a. I.e., towards Assyria.   b. Perhaps the earthquake of 1:1.

persecutors of the virtuous, blackmailers,
turning away the needy at the city gate.
No wonder the prudent man keeps silent,   13
the times are so evil.

Exhortation

Seek good and not evil   14
so that you may live,
and that Yahweh, God of Sabaoth, may really be with you
as you claim he is.
Hate evil, love good,   15
maintain justice at the city gate,
and it may be that Yahweh, God of Sabaoth, will take pity
on the remnant of Joseph.

Impending punishment

Therefore Yahweh says this,   16
the God of Sabaoth, the Lord.
In every public square there will be lamentation,
in every street wails of 'Alas! Alas!'
Peasants will be called on to lament
as well as the professional mourners
and there will be wailing in every vineyard,   17
for I am going to pass through you,
says Yahweh.

The day of Yahweh

Trouble for those who are waiting so longingly for the day of Yahweh!   18
What will this day of Yahweh mean for you?
It will mean darkness, not light,
as when a man escapes a lion's mouth,   19
only to meet a bear;
he enters his house and puts his hand on the wall,
only for a snake to bite him.
Will not the day of Yahweh be darkness, not light?   20
It will all be gloom, without a single ray of light.

Against formalism in religion

I hate and despise your feasts;   21
I take no pleasure in your solemn festivals.
When you offer me holocausts,   22
....
I reject your oblations,
and refuse to look at your sacrifices of fattened cattle.
Let me have no more of the din of your chanting,   23
no more of your strumming on harps.
But let justice flow like water,   24
and integrity like an unfailing stream.
Did you bring me sacrifice and oblation in the wilderness   25
for all those forty years, House of Israel?
Now you must shoulder Sakkuth your king   26
and Kaiwan your god,
those idols you have made for yourselves;[a]
for I mean to take you far beyond Damascus into exile,   27
says Yahweh—God of Sabaoth is his name.

Against the self-indulgent and their false sense of security

6

1 Woe to those ensconced so snugly in Zion
and to those who feel so safe on the mountain of Samaria,
those famous men of this first of nations
to whom the House of Israel goes as client.

2 Make a journey to Calneh and look,
go on from there to Hamath the great,
then down to Gath in Philistia.ᵃ
Are they any better off than these kingdoms?
Is their territory larger than yours?

3 You think to defer the day of misfortune,
but you hasten the reign of violence.

4 Lying on ivory beds
and sprawling on their divans,
they dine on lambs from the flock,
and stall-fattened veal;

5 they bawl to the sound of the harp,
they invent new instruments of music like David,

6 they drink wine by the bowlful,
and use the finest oil for anointing themselves,
but about the ruin of Josephᵇ they do not care at all.

7 That is why they will be the first to be exiled;
the sprawlers' revelry is over.

The punishment and its horrors

8 The Lord Yahweh swears it by his own self
—it is the Lord Yahweh who speaks, the God of Sabaoth.
I detest the pride of Jacob,
I hate his palaces.
I mean to abandon the cityᶜ and all it contains.

9 And if ten men are left in a single house, they shall die.

10 Only a few will escape
to carry the bones out of the house;
and if a man should say to another one in a corner of the house,
'Is there anyone left with you?'
he will reply, 'No! Hush! The name of Yahweh must not
be mentioned.'

11 For see, Yahweh himself orders it;
as he strikes, the great house falls to pieces,
the small house crumbles.

12 Do horses gallop on rocks,
do men plough the sea with oxen,
for you to change justice into poison,
and the fruit of integrity into wormwood?

13 You rejoice over Lo-debar,ᵈ
'Was it not by our own strength' you say
'that we took Karnaim?'

14 Now see, you House of Israel, how I am stirring up against you
—it is Yahweh who speaks, the God of Sabaoth—
a nation that will harry you
from the Pass of Hamath
right down to the wadi of the Arabah.ᵉ

5 a. Presumably the names are those of Babylonian gods.
6 a. Three cities already in ruins.   **b.** The impending collapse of Israel.   **c.** Samaria; possibly standing for all the towns of the Northern Kingdom   **d.** Lo-debar and Karnaim, in Transjordania, had been reconquered.   **e.** I.e., from the N. boundary to the S.

III. THE VISIONS

First vision: the locusts

7 This is what the Lord Yahweh showed me: 1
it was a swarm of locusts
at the time when the second crop was starting to grow,
a swarm of full-grown locusts, when the king's cutting was over.
They were about to devour all the greenstuff in the land,   2
but I said, 'Lord Yahweh, forgive, I beg you.
How can Jacob survive, being so small?'
And Yahweh relented;   3
'This shall not happen' said Yahweh.

Second vision: the drought

This is what the Lord Yahweh showed me: 4
the Lord Yahweh himself summoning fire in punishment;
it had devoured the great Abyss*a*
and was already encroaching on the land.
Then I said, 'Stop, Lord Yahweh, I beg you.   5
How can Jacob survive, being so small?'
And Yahweh relented;   6
'This will not happen either' said the Lord Yahweh.

Third vision: the plumb-line

This is what the Lord Yahweh showed me: 7
a man standing by a wall,
plumb-line in hand.
'What do you see, Amos?' Yahweh asked me.   8
'A plumb-line' I said.
Then the Lord said to me,
'Look, I am going to measure my people Israel by plumb-line;
no longer will I overlook their offences.
The high places of Isaac are going to be ruined,   9
the sanctuaries of Israel destroyed,
and, sword in hand, I will attack the House of Jeroboam.'

The intervention of Amaziah: Amos expelled from Bethel

Amaziah the priest of Bethel then sent word to Jeroboam king of Israel as 10
follows. 'Amos is plotting against you in the heart of the House of Israel; the
country can no longer tolerate what he keeps saying. •For this is what he says, 11
"Jeroboam is going to die by the sword, and Israel go into exile far from its
country".' •To Amos, Amaziah said, 'Go away, seer; get back to the land of 12
Judah; earn your bread there, do your prophesying there. •We want no more 13
prophesying in Bethel; this is the royal sanctuary, the national temple.' •'I was 14
no prophet, neither did I belong to any of the brotherhoods of prophets,' Amos
replied to Amaziah 'I was a shepherd, and looked after sycamores: •but it 15
was Yahweh who took me from herding the flock, and Yahweh who said, "Go,
prophesy to my people Israel". •So listen to the word of Yahweh. You say: 16

"Do not prophesy against Israel,
utter no oracles against the House of Isaac".
Very well, this is what Yahweh says,   17
"Your wife will be forced to go on the streets,
your sons and daughters will fall by the sword,
your land be parcelled out by measuring line,
and you yourself die on unclean soil
and Israel will go into exile far distant from its own land".'

Fourth vision: the basket of ripe fruit

1 This is what the Lord Yahweh showed me:
a basket of ripe fruit:

2 'What do you see, Amos?' he asked.
'A basket of ripe fruit' I said.
Then Yahweh said,
'My people Israel is ripe for destruction;
I will no longer overlook its offences.

3 The palace singing girls will wail that day
—it is the Lord Yahweh who speaks—
so many will be dead,
all thrown down anywhere. Hush!'

Against swindlers and exploiters

4 Listen to this, you who trample on the needy
and try to suppress the poor people of the country,

5 you who say, 'When will New Moon be over
so that we can sell our corn,
and sabbath, so that we can market our wheat?
Then by lowering the bushel, raising the shekel,
by swindling and tampering with the scales,

6 we can buy up the poor for money,
and the needy for a pair of sandals,
and get a price even for the sweepings of the wheat.'

7 Yahweh swears it by the pride of Jacob,
'Never will I forget a single thing you have done'.

8 Is this not the reason for the earthquakes,
for its inhabitants all mourning,
and all of it heaving, like the Nile,
then subsiding, like the river of Egypt?

Prediction of a mysterious punishment: darkness and mourning

9 'That day—it is the Lord Yahweh who speaks—
I will make the sun go down at noon,
and darken the earth in broad daylight.

10 I am going to turn your feasts into funerals,
all your singing into lamentation;
I will have your loins all in sackcloth,
your heads all shaved.
I will make it a mourning like the mourning for an only son,
as long as it lasts it will be like a day of bitterness.

Famine and drought of the word of God

11 'See what days are coming—it is the Lord Yahweh who speaks—
days when I will bring famine on the country,
a famine not of bread, a drought not of water,
but of hearing the word of Yahweh.

12 They will stagger from sea to sea,
wander from north to east,
seeking the word of Yahweh
and failing to find it.

Fresh prediction of punishment

13 That day, delicate girl
and stalwart youth shall faint from thirst.

7 a. 'The waters under the earth' from which the rain and rivers come.

All who swear by Samaria's Ashimah,   14
those who swear, "By your god's life, Dan!"[a]
and, "By your Beloved's life, Beersheba!"
these shall all fall, never to rise again.'

Fifth vision: the fall of the sanctuary

9

I saw the Lord standing at the side of the altar.   1
'Strike the capitals' he said 'and let the roof tumble down!
I mean to break their heads, every one,
and all who remain I will put to the sword;
not one shall get away,
not one escape.
Should they burrow their way down to Sheol,   2
my hand shall haul them out;
should they scale the heavens,
I will drag them down;
should they hide on Carmel's peak,   3
there I will track them down and catch them;
should they hide from my sight on the sea bed,
I will tell the Dragon to bite them there;
should they go into exile driven before their enemies,   4
I will order the sword to slaughter them there;
and my eyes will be on them
for their misfortune, not their good.'

Doxology

The Lord Yahweh of Sabaoth—   5
he touches the earth and it melts,
and all its inhabitants mourn;
it all heaves, like the Nile,
and subsides, like the river of Egypt.
He has built his high dwelling place in the heavens   6
and supported his vault on the earth;
he summons the waters of the sea
and pours them over the land.
Yahweh is his name.

No special privileges for Israel

'Are not you and the Cushites[a] all the same to me,   7
sons of Israel?—it is Yahweh who speaks.
Did not I, who brought Israel out of the land of Egypt,
bring the Philistines from Caphtor, and the Aramaeans from Kir?
Now, my eyes are turned on the sinful kingdom,   8
to wipe it off the face of the earth.

Only sinners will perish

'Yet I am not going to destroy
the House of Jacob completely—it is Yahweh who speaks.
For now I will issue orders   9
and shake the House of Israel among all the nations,
as you shake a sieve
so that not one pebble can fall on the ground.
All the sinners of my people are going to perish by the sword,   10
all those who say,
"No misfortune will ever touch us, nor even come anywhere near us".

IV. PROSPECTS OF RESTORATION
AND OF IDYLLIC PROSPERITY

11   'That day I will re-erect the tottering hut of David,
      make good the gaps in it, restore its ruins
      and rebuild it as it was in the days of old,
12   so that they can conquer the remnant of Edom
      and all the nations that belonged to me.
      It is Yahweh who speaks, and he will carry this out.

13   'The days are coming now—it is Yahweh who speaks—
      when harvest will follow directly after ploughing,
      the treading of grapes soon after sowing,
      when the mountains will run with new wine
      and the hills all flow with it.
14   I mean to restore the fortunes of my people Israel;
      they will rebuild the ruined cities and live in them,
      plant vineyards and drink their wine,
      dig gardens and eat their produce.
15   I will plant them in their own country,
      never to be rooted up again
      out of the land I have given them,
      says Yahweh, your God.'

8 a. At Dan, Jeroboam had set up a golden calf.
9 a. Ethiopians, instanced as a distant and foreign nation.

OBADIAH

Title and prologue

Vision of Obadiah: about Edom.   1a

    I have received a message from Yahweh,   1c
    a herald has been sent throughout the nations,
    'Up! Let us march against this people.
    Into battle!'

Sentence pronounced on Edom

    The Lord Yahweh says this: 1b
    Now I am going to reduce you among the nations, 2
    and make you utterly despised.

    Your pride of heart has led you astray,   3
    you whose home is in the holes in the rocks,ᵃ
    who make the heights your dwelling,
    who say in your heart,
    'Who will bring me down to the ground?'

    Though you soared like the eagle,   4
    though you set your nest among the stars,
    I would still fling you down again—it is Yahweh who speaks.

The annihilation of Edom

    If robbers came to you,   5
    or plunderers at night,
    they would steal to their heart's content.
    If grape-gatherers came to you,
    they would leave no gleanings behind them.

    How you have been pillaged!
    How Esau has been looted,   6
    his hidden treasures rifled!
    They have driven you right to the frontiers,   7
    they have misled you, all your allies.
    They have deceived you, your fine friends.
    Those who ate your bread now set traps for you,
    'He has no intelligence now'.

    When that day comes—it is Yahweh who speaks—   8
    shall I not deprive Edom of sages,
    the Mount of Esau of intelligence?

    Your warriors, Teman,ᵇ will be seized with terror 9
    until not a single one is left
    in the Mount of Esau.

The guilt of Edom

10
> For the slaughter, •for the violence
> done to your brother Jacob,^c
> shame will cover you
> and you will vanish for ever.

11
> On the day you stood by
> as strangers carried off his riches,
> as barbarians passed through his gate
> and cast lots for Jerusalem,
> you behaved like the rest of them.

12
> Do not gloat over your brother
> on the day of his misfortune.
> Do not exult over the sons of Judah
> on the day of their ruin.
> Do not play the braggart
> on the day of distress.

13
> Do not pass through the gate of my people
> on the day of its misfortune.
> Do not, in your turn, gloat over its disaster
> on the day of its misfortune.
> Do not lay a finger on its treasures
> on the day of its misfortune.

14
> Do not take your stand at the crossroads
> to cut off its fugitives.
> Do not hand over its survivors
> on the day of distress.

15
> For the day of Yahweh is near
> for all the nations.
> As you have done, so will it be done to you:
> your deeds will recoil on your own head.

The day of Yahweh. Israel revenged on Edom

16
> ^d Yes, as you have drunk on my holy mountain,
> so will all the nations drink unsparingly;
> they will drink, and drink deep,
> and will be as if they had never been.

17
> But on Mount Zion there will be some who have escaped
> —it shall become a holy place—
> and the House of Jacob will despoil
> its own despoilers.

18
> The House of Jacob shall be a fire,
> the House of Joseph^e a flame,
> the House of Esau stubble.
> They will set it alight and burn it up,
> and no member of the House of Esau shall survive.
> Yahweh has spoken.

a. The capital of Edom was named 'the Rock' (Petra).   b. Northern district of Edom.
c. The land of Judah.   d. The rest of the prophecy is addressed to Israel.   e. The Northern
Kingdom.

The new Israel

Men from the Negeb will occupy the Mount of Esau,   19
men from the Lowlands the country of the Philistines;
they will occupy the land of Ephraim and the land of Samaria,
and Benjamin will occupy Gilead.

The exiles from this army, the sons of Israel,   20
will occupy Canaanᶠ as far as Zarephath;
and the exiles from Jerusalem now in Sepharad
will occupy the towns of the Negeb.

Victorious, they will climb Mount Zion   21
to judge the Mount of Esau,
and the sovereignty shall belong to Yahweh.

f. Phoenicia; Zarephath was between Tyre and Sidon.

JONAH

Jonah rebels against his mission

¹⁄₂ 1 The word of Yahweh was addressed to Jonah son of Amittai: •'Up!' he said 'Go to Nineveh, the great city, and inform them that their wickedness has
3 become known to me.' •Jonah decided to run away from Yahweh, and to go to Tarshish.ᵃ He went down to Joppa and found a ship bound for Tarshish; he paid his fare and went aboard, to go with them to Tarshish, to get away from
4 Yahweh. •But Yahweh unleashed a violent wind on the sea, and there was such
5 a great storm at sea that the ship threatened to break up. •The sailors took fright, and each of them called on his own god, and to lighten the ship they threw the cargo overboard. Jonah, however, had gone below and lain down in
6 the hold and fallen fast asleep. •The boatswain came upon him and said, 'What do you mean by sleeping? Get up! Call on your god! Perhaps he will spare us
7 a thought, and not leave us to die.' •Then they said to each other, 'Come on, let us draw lots to find out who is responsible for bringing this evil on us'.
8 So they cast lots, and the lot fell to Jonah. •Then they said to him, 'Tell us, what is your business? Where do you come from? What is your country? What
9 is your nationality?' •He replied, 'I am a Hebrew, and I worship Yahweh, the
10 God of heaven, who made the sea and the land'. •The sailors were seized with terror at this and said, 'What have you done?' They knew that he was trying to
11 escape from Yahweh, because he had told them so. •They then said, 'What are we to do with you, to make the sea grow calm for us?' For the sea was growing
12 rougher and rougher. •He replied, 'Take me and throw me into the sea, and then it will grow calm for you. For I can see it is my fault this violent storm has
13 happened to you.' •The sailors rowed hard in an effort to reach the shore, but
14 in vain, since the sea grew still rougher for them. •They then called on Yahweh and said, 'O Yahweh, do not let us perish for taking this man's life; do not hold us guilty of innocent blood; for you, Yahweh, have acted as you have thought
15 right'. •And taking hold of Jonah they threw him into the sea; and the sea grew
16 calm again. •At this the men were seized with dread of Yahweh; they offered a sacrifice to Yahweh and made vows.

Jonah is saved

1 2 Yahweh had arranged that a great fish should be there to swallow Jonah;
and Jonah remained in the belly of the fish for three days and three nights.
2 From the belly of the fish he prayed to Yahweh, his God; he said:

3 'Out of my distress I cried to Yahweh
and he answered me;
from the belly of Sheol I cried.
and you have heard my voice.
4 You cast me into the abyss, into the heart of the sea,
and the flood surrounded me.
All your waves, your billows,
washed over me.

1 a. 'The end of the world': Tartessos in Spain.

And I said: I am cast out   5
from your sight.
How shall I ever look again
on your holy Temple?
The waters surrounded me right to my throat,   6
the abyss was all around me.
The seaweed was wrapped round my head
at the roots of the mountains.   7
I went down into the countries underneath the earth,
to the peoples of the past.
But you lifted my life from the pit,
Yahweh, my God.
While my soul was fainting within me,   8
I remembered Yahweh,
and my prayer came before you
into your holy Temple.
Those who serve worthless idols   9
forfeit the grace that was theirs.

'But I, with a song of praise,   10
will sacrifice to you.
The vow I have made, I will fulfil.
Salvation comes from Yahweh.'

Yahweh spoke to the fish, which then vomited Jonah on to the shore.   11

The conversion of Nineveh and God's pardon

3 The word of Yahweh was addressed a second time to Jonah: •'Up!' he said $\frac{1}{2}$
'Go to Nineveh, the great city, and preach to them as I told you to.' •Jonah 3
set out and went to Nineveh in obedience to the word of Yahweh. Now Nineveh
was a city great beyond compare: it took three days to cross it. •Jonah went 4
on into the city, making a day's journey. He preached in these words, 'Only
forty days more and Nineveh is going to be destroyed'. •And the people of 5
Nineveh believed in God; they proclaimed a fast and put on sackcloth, from the
greatest to the least. •The news reached the king of Nineveh, who rose from his 6
throne, took off his robe, put on sackcloth and sat down in ashes. •A procla- 7
mation was then promulgated throughout Nineveh, by decree of the king and
his ministers, as follows: 'Men and beasts, herds and flocks, are to taste nothing;
they must not eat, they must not drink water. •All are to put on sackcloth and 8
call on God with all their might; and let everyone renounce his evil behaviour
and the wicked things he has done. •Who knows if God will not change his 9
mind and relent, if he will not renounce his burning wrath, so that we do not
perish?' • God saw their efforts to renounce their evil behaviour. And God relented: 10
he did not inflict on them the disaster which he had threatened.

The grievance of the prophet and God's answer

4 Jonah was very indignant at this; he fell into a rage. •He prayed to Yahweh $\frac{1}{2}$
and said, 'Ah! Yahweh, is not this just as I said would happen when I was
still at home? That was why I went and fled to Tarshish: I knew that you were
a God of tenderness and compassion, slow to anger, rich in graciousness, relenting
from evil. •So now Yahweh, please take away my life, for I might as well be dead 3
as go on living.' •Yahweh replied, 'Are you right to be angry?' •Jonah then $\frac{4}{5}$
went out of the city and sat down to the east of the city. There he made himself
a shelter and sat under it in the shade, to see what would happen to the city.
Then Yahweh God arranged that a castor-oil plant should grow up over Jonah 6
to give shade for his head and soothe his ill-humour; Jonah was delighted with
the castor-oil plant. •But at dawn the next day, God arranged that a worm 7

8 should attack the castor-oil plant—and it withered. •Next, when the sun rose, God arranged that there should be a scorching east wind; the sun beat down so hard on Jonah's head that he was overcome and begged for death, saying,
9 'I might as well be dead as go on living'. •God said to Jonah, 'Are you right to be angry about the castor-oil plant?' He replied, 'I have every right to be
10 angry, to the point of death'. •Yahweh replied, 'You are only upset about a castor-oil plant which cost you no labour, which you did not make grow,
11 which sprouted in a night and has perished in a night. •And am I not to feel sorry for Nineveh, the great city, in which there are more than a hundred and twenty thousand people who cannot tell their right hand from their left, to say nothing of all the animals?'

MICAH

1 The word of Yahweh that was addressed to Micah of Moresheth in the time
of Jotham, Ahaz and Hezekiah, kings of Judah.
His visions of Samaria and Jerusalem.

I. ISRAEL ON TRIAL

THREAT AND CONDEMNATION

The judgement of Samaria^a

> Listen, you peoples, all of you.
> Attend, earth, and everything in it.
> Yahweh is going to give evidence against you,
> the Lord, as he sets out from his sacred palace.
> For look, Yahweh sets out from his holy place,
> he comes down, he treads the heights of earth.
> The mountains melt as he goes,
> the valleys are torn apart,
> like wax before the fire,
> like water poured out on a steep place.
>
> All this is because of the crime of Jacob,
> the sin of the House of Israel.
> What is the crime of Jacob?
> Is it not Samaria?
> What is the sin of the House of Judah?
> Is it not Jerusalem?
> I mean to make Samaria a ruin in the open country,
> a place where vines will be planted.
> I will set her stones rolling into the valley,
> I will lay her foundations bare.
> All her images are going to be shattered,
> all her earnings consumed by fire,
> all her idols broken in pieces,
> for they have been collected with prostitutes' earnings
> and prostitutes' earnings they will be again.

Lament for the lowland cities^b

> This is why I am going to mourn and lament,
> go barefoot and naked,
> howl like the jackals,
> wail like the ostriches.
> For there is no healing for the blow Yahweh strikes;
> it reaches into Judah,
> it knocks at the very door of my people,
> reaches even into Jerusalem.

10　　Do not announce it in Gath,c
　　　in . . . shed no tears.
　　　In Beth-leaphrah
　　　roll in the dust.

11　　Sound the horn,
　　　you who live in Shaphir.
　　　She has not left her city,
　　　she who lives in Zaanan.
　　　Beth-ezel is torn from its foundations,
　　　from its strong supports.

12　　What hope has she of happpiness,
　　　she who lives in Maroth?
　　　For doom has come down from Yahweh
　　　to the very gate of Jerusalem.

13　　Harness the horse to the chariot,
　　　you who live in Lachish.
　　　(This was the beginning of sin for the daughter of Zion,
　　　for Israel's crimes were to be found in you.)

14　　So you must provide a dowry
　　　for Moresheth-gath.
　　　Beth-achzib will prove a snare
　　　for the kings of Israel.

15　　The plunderer will come to you again,
　　　you who live in Mareshah.
　　　. . . to Adullam will go
　　　the glory of Israel.

16　　Off with your hair, shave your head,
　　　for the sons that were your joy.
　　　Make yourselves bald like the vulture,
　　　for they have gone from you into exile.

Against the tyranny of the rich

2

1　　Woe to those who plot evil,
　　　who lie in bed planning mischief!
　　　No sooner is it dawn than they do it
　　　—their hands have the strength for it.

2　　Seizing the fields that they covet,
　　　they take over houses as well,
　　　owner and house they confiscate together,
　　　taking both man and inheritance.

3　　So Yahweh says this:
　　　Now it is I who plot
　　　such mischief against this breed
　　　as your necks will not escape;
　　　nor will you be able to walk proudly,
　　　so evil will the time be.

4　　On that day they will make a satire on you,
　　　sing a dirge and say,
　　　'We are stripped of everything;
　　　my people's portion is measured out and shared,
　　　no one will give it back to them,
　　　our fields are awarded to our despoiler'.

1 a. Before the fall of the city in 721.　b. Twelve towns to the S.W. of Judah; one is the
prophet's home, Moresheth (1:1), and six of the others can be identified; one name is missing
from the text. The prophecy about each of the towns is a play on its name, and the whole refers
to Sennacherib's invasion of 701.　c. 2 S 1:20

Therefore you will have no one
to measure out a share
in the community of Yahweh.

5

The prophet of misfortune

'Do not rave,' they rave
'do not rave like this.
No shame is going to overtake us.
Can the House of Jacob be accursed?
Has Yahweh lost patience?
Is that his way of going to work?
Surely his words are words of kindness
for his people Israel?'
It is you who play the enemy
to my people.
From the innocent man you snatch his cloak,
on the man who thinks himself safe you inflict the damage of war.
The women of my people you drive out
from the homes they loved;
their children you rob for ever
of the honour I gave them,
'Get·up! Be off! There is no resting here.'
For a worthless thing, you exact
an extortionate pledge.
Were there a man of inspiration who would invent this lie,
'I prophesy you wine and strong drink',
he would be the prophet for a people like this.

6

7

8

9

10

11

Promises of restoration

Yes, I am going to gather all Jacob together,
I will gather the remnant of Israel,
bring them together like sheep in the fold;
like a flock in its pasture
they will fear no man.
He who walks at their head will lead the way in front of them;
he will walk at their head, they will pass through the gate
    and go out by it;
their king will go on in front of them,
Yahweh at their head.

12

13

Against the rulers who oppress the people

3 Then I said:
Listen now, you princes of the House of Jacob,
rulers of the House of Israel.
Are you not the ones who should know what is right,
you, enemies of good and friends of evil?
When they have devoured the flesh of my people
and torn off their skin
and crushed their bones;
when they have shredded them like flesh in a pot
and like meat in a cauldron,
then they will cry out to Yahweh.
But he will not answer them.
He will hide his face at that time
because of all the crimes they have committed.

1

2

3

4

Against venal prophets

5   Yahweh says this against the prophets
who lead my people astray:
So long as they have something to eat
they cry 'Peace'.
But on anyone who puts nothing into their mouths
they declare war.

6   And so the night will come to you: an end of vision;
darkness for you: an end of divination.
The sun will set for the prophets,
the day will go black for them.

7   Then the seers will be covered with shame,
the diviners with confusion;
they will all cover their lips,
because no answer comes from God.

8   Not so with me, I am full of strength
(of the breath of Yahweh),
of justice and courage
to declare Jacob's crime to his face
and Israel's to his.

To the guilty ones: prophecy of the ruin of Zion

9   Now listen to this, you princes of the House of Jacob,
rulers of the House of Israel,
you who loathe justice
and pervert all that is right,

10   you who build Zion with blood,
Jerusalem with crime.

11   Her princes pronounce their verdict for bribes,
her priests take a fee for their rulings,
her prophets make divinations for money.
And yet they rely on Yahweh. They say,
'Is not Yahweh in our midst?
No evil is going to overtake us.'

12   Because of this, since the fault is yours,
Zion will become ploughland,
Jerusalem a heap of rubble,
and the mountain of the Temple a wooded height.

II. PROMISES TO ZION

The future reign of Yahweh in Zion[a]

1   **4**   In the days to come
the mountain of the Temple of Yahweh
will be put on top of the mountains
and be lifted higher than the hills.
The peoples will stream to it,

2   nations without number will come to it; and they will say,
'Come, let us go up to the mountain of Yahweh,
to the Temple of the God of Jacob
so that he may teach us his ways
and we may walk in his paths;
since from Zion the Law will go out,

4 a. The same oracle as Is 2:2-4.

and the oracle of Yahweh from Jerusalem.'
He will wield authority over many peoples   3
and arbitrate for mighty nations;
they will hammer their swords into ploughshares,
their spears into sickles.
Nation will not lift sword against nation,
there will be no more training for war.
Each man will sit under his vine and his fig tree,   4
with no one to trouble him.
The mouth of Yahweh Sabaoth has spoken it.

For all the peoples go forward, each in the name of its god;   5
but we, we go forward in the name of Yahweh, our God,
for ever and evermore.

The gathering of the scattered flock in Zion

That day—it is Yahweh who speaks—   6
I will finally gather in the lame,
and bring together those that have been led astray
and those that have suffered at my hand.
Out of the lame I will make a remnant,   7
and out of the weary a mighty nation.
Then will Yahweh reign over them
on the mountain of Zion
from now and for ever.

And you, Tower of the Flock,   8
Ophel of the daughter of Zion,[b]
to you shall be given back your former sovereignty,
and royal power over the House of Israel.

The siege, exile, and liberation of Zion

Why are you crying aloud?   9
Is there no king within you?
Are your counsellors lost
that pains should grip you like a woman in labour?
Writhe, cry out, daughter of Zion,   10
like a woman in labour,
for now you have to leave the city
and live in the open country.
To Babylon you must go
and there you will be rescued;
there Yahweh will ransom you
out of the power of your enemies.

The pagans crushed on the threshing-floor in Zion

Now many nations   11
are mustered against you.
'Let her be desecrated,' they say
'let our eyes feast on the ruins of Zion.'
But they do not know Yahweh's thoughts,   12
they have failed to understand his purpose,
he has collected them like sheaves on the threshing floor.
Up, daughter of Zion, and thresh;   13
for I will give you horns of iron,
hoofs of bronze,
for you to trample down many peoples.

You will dedicate their plunder to Yahweh,
their treasures to the Lord of the whole earth.

The distress and glory of the Davidic dynasty

¹⁴₁ Now look to your fortifications, Fortress.
They have laid siege against us;
with a rod they strike on the cheek
the judge of Israel.

¹₂ 5 But you, (Bethlehem) Ephrathah,
the least of the clans of Judah,
out of you will be born for me
the one who is to rule over Israel;
his origin goes back to the distant past,
to the days of old.

²₃ Yahweh is therefore going to abandon them
till the time when she who is to give birth^a gives birth.
Then the remnant of his brothers will come back
to the sons of Israel.

³₄ He will stand and feed his flock
with the power of Yahweh,
with the majesty of the name of his God.
They will live secure, for from then on he will extend his power
to the ends of the land.

^{4a}_{5a}
^{5b}_{6b} He himself will be peace.
He will deliver us from Assyria should it invade our country,
should it set foot inside our frontiers.

The confidence of the people of Judah

^{4b}_{5b} As for Assyria, should it invade our country,
should it set foot on our soil,
we will raise seven shepherds against it,
eight leaders of men;

^{5a}_{6a} they will shepherd Assyria with the sword,
and the land of Nimrod with the sword blade.

The future role of the remnant among the nations

⁶₇ Then among the many peoples,
the remnant of Jacob will be
like a dew from Yahweh,
like raindrops on the grass,
putting no hope in men,
expecting nothing from mankind.

⁷₈ Then among the many peoples,
the remnant of Jacob will be
like a lion among beasts of the forest,
like a young lion among flocks of sheep
trampling as he goes,
mangling his prey which no one takes from him.

Yahweh will withdraw the temptation to rely on men

⁸₉ Let your hand be raised against your foes
and all your enemies shall be cut off.

⁹₁₀ This is how it will be, that day

b. Ophel is the district where the king lived.
5 a. Probably the 'maiden' of Isaiah's prophecy about 30 years earlier, Is 7:14.

—it is Yahweh who speaks—
I will tear away your horses from you,
and destroy your chariots;
tear the towns of your country from you,   10
bring down all your strongholds;   11
tear the charms from your hands,   11
and you will have no more soothsayers;
tear from you your images   12a
and your pillars;
tear from you your sacred poles,   13
and demolish your idols;
and no longer will you bow down   12b
before the work of your hands.
I will take revenge in anger and fury   14
on the nations that would not obey.

III. ISRAEL ON TRIAL

DENUNCIATION AND THREAT

Yahweh puts his people on trial

6   Now listen to what Yahweh is saying: 1
        Stand up and let the case begin in the hearing of the mountains
        and let the hills hear what you say.
        Listen, you mountains, to Yahweh's accusation,   2
        give ear, you foundations of the earth,
        for Yahweh is accusing his people,
        pleading against Israel:
        My people, what have I done to you,   3
        how have I been a burden to you? Answer me.
        I brought you out of the land of Egypt,   4
        I rescued you from the house of slavery;
        I sent Moses to lead you,
        with Aaron and Miriam.
        My people, remember: 5
        what did Balak plot, that king of Moab?
        What did Balaam answer, that son of Beor?
        . . . .
        . . . from Shittim to Gilgal,
        for you to know the rightness of the ways of Yahweh.
        —'With what gift shall I come into Yahweh's presence 6
        and bow down before God on high?
        Shall I come with holocausts,
        with calves one year old?
        Will he be pleased with rams by the thousand,   7
        with libations of oil in torrents?
        Must I give my first-born for what I have done wrong,
        the fruit of my body for my own sin?'
        —What is good has been explained to you, man;   8
        this is what Yahweh asks of you:
        only this, to act justly,
        to love tenderly
        and to walk humbly with your God.

Against tricksters in the city

9
> The voice of Yahweh. He is calling to the city:
> Listen, tribe, and assembly of the city

12
> whose rich men are crammed with violence,
> whose citizens are liars.

10
> Must I put up with fraudulent measure,
> or that abomination the short-weight bushel?

11
> Must I hold the man honest who measures with false scales
> and a bag of faked weights?

13
> I have therefore begun to strike you down,
> to bring you to ruin for your sins.

15
> You will sow but never reap,
> press the olive but never rub yourself with oil,
> press the grape but never drink wine from it;

14
> you will eat but never be satisfied,
> store away but never preserve—
> and what is preserved I shall give to the sword.

The example of Samaria

16
> You keep the laws of Omri
> and follow all the practices of the House of Ahab;[a]
> you are guided by their standards,
> and they force me to make a terrible example of you,
> and to turn your inhabitants into a laughing-stock,
> to suffer the scorn of the peoples.

Universal injustice

1 **7**
> I am in trouble! I have become
> like a harvester in summer time,
> like a gleaner at the vintage:
> not a single cluster to eat,
> not one of the early figs I so long for.

2
> The devout have vanished from the land:
> there is not one honest man left.
> All are lurking for blood,
> every man hunting down his brother.

3
> Their hands are skilled in evil:
> the official demands . . . ,
> the judge gives judgement for a bribe,
> the man in power pronounces as he pleases.

5
> Put no trust in a neighbour,
> have no confidence in a friend;
> to the woman who shares your bed
> do not open your mouth.

6
> For son insults father,
> daughter defies mother,
> daughter-in-law defies mother-in-law;
> a man's enemies are those of his own household.

4
> . . . among them, the best is like a briar,
> the most honest a hedge of thorn.
> Today will come their ordeal from the North,
> now is the time for their confusion.

7
> For my part, I look to Yahweh,

6 a. Omri and his son Ahab were two of the kings of Israel listed in 1 K among those who led the people into the worship of Canaanite idols.

my hope is in the God who will save me;
my God will hear me.ᵃ

IV. HOPE FOR THE FUTURE

Zion insulted by her enemy

Do not gloat over me, my enemy: 8
though I have fallen, I shall rise;
though I live in darkness,
Yahweh is my light.
I must suffer the anger of Yahweh,   9
for I have sinned against him,
until he takes up my cause
and rights my wrongs;
he will bring me out into the light
and I shall rejoice to see the rightness of his ways.
When my enemy sees it,   10
she will be covered with shame,
she who said to me, 'Where is Yahweh your God?'
My eyes will gloat over her;
she will be trampled underfoot
like mud in the streets.

An oracle of restoration

The day is coming for rebuilding your walls.   11
Your frontiers will be extended that day,
men will come to you that day   12
from Assyria as far as to Egypt,
from Tyre as far as to the river,
from sea to sea, from mountain to mountain.
The earth will become a desert   13
by reason of its inhabitants, in return for what they have done.

A prayer for the confusion of the pagans

With shepherd's crook lead your people to pasture,   14
the flock that is your heritage,
living confined in a forest
with meadow land all around.
Let them pasture in Bashan and Gilead
as in the days of old.
As in the days when you came out of Egypt   15
grant us to see wonders.
The pagans, seeing it, will be confounded   16
for all their power;
they will lay their hands to their mouths,
their ears will be deafened by it.
They will lick the dust like serpents,   17
like things that crawl on the earth.
They will come trembling from their lairs,
in terror and fear before you.

A plea for God's forgiveness

What god can compare with you: taking fault away,   18
pardoning crime,
not cherishing anger for ever
but delighting in showing mercy?

19   Once more have pity on us,
         tread down our faults,
         to the bottom of the sea
         throw all our sins.

20   Grant Jacob your faithfulness,
         and Abraham your mercy,
         as you swore to our fathers
         from the days of long ago.

7 a. Possibly the conclusion of the book of Micah; the additional poems that follow seem to date from the Exile.

NAHUM

1 Oracle on Nineveh. Book of the vision of Nahum of Elkosh. 1

PRELUDE

Psalm. The wrath of Yahweh

Aleph	Yahweh is a jealous and vengeful God,	2
	Yahweh avenges, he is full of wrath;	
	Yahweh takes vengeance on his foes,	
	he stores up fury for his enemies.	
	Yahweh is slow to anger but immense in power.	3
	Most surely Yahweh will not leave the guilty unpunished.	
Beth	In storm and whirlwind he takes his way,	
	the clouds are the dust stirred up by his feet.	
Ghimel	He rebukes the sea and drains it,	4
	he dries up all the rivers.	
Daleth	. . . Bashan and Carmel wither,	
	the green of Lebanon fades.	
He	The mountains tremble before him,	5
	the hills reel;	
Waw	the earth collapses before him,	
	the world and all who live in it.	
Zain	His fury—who can withstand it?	6
	Who can endure his burning wrath?	
Heth	His anger pours out like fire	
	and the rocks break to pieces before him.	
Teth	Yahweh is good; he is a stronghold	7
	in the day of distress;	
Yod	he calls to mind those who trust in him	
	when the flood overtakes them.	8
Kaph	Those who defy him he will destroy utterly,	
	he will pursue his foes into the darkness.	

Prophecies addressed alternately to Judah and Nineveh

to Judah	How do you imagine Yahweh?	9
	He it is who utterly destroys:	
	oppression will not lift its head a second time.	
	They will be consumed like a thicket of thorns,	10
	like dry straw, utterly.	
to Assyria	From you has sprung	11
	one who plots evil against Yahweh,	
	a man with the mind of Belial.ᵃ	
to Judah	Yahweh says this:	12
	Equipped and many though they be,	

> they are going to be cut down, annihilated.
> Though I have disciplined you,
> I will discipline you no more.

13   And now I am going to break that yoke of his that weighs
>   you down,
> and I will burst your chains.

14 *to the king of*   For you, here is Yahweh's decree:
     Nineveh   There will be no more offspring to bear your name;
> from the temple of your gods I mean to take away
> the carved and the cast image,
> and I intend to make your tomb an object of shame.

¹
15 **2** *to Judah*   See, over the mountains the messenger hurries!
> 'Peace!' he proclaims.
> Judah, celebrate your feasts,
> carry out your vows,
> for Belial will never pass through you again;
> he is utterly annihilated.

³
₂   Yes, Yahweh is restoring the vineyard of Jacob
> and the vineyard of Israel.
> For the plunderers had plundered them,
> they had broken off their branches.

THE FALL OF NINEVEH

The assault

2   A destroyer advances against you.
> Mount guard on the rampart,
> watch the road, tuck up your cloaks;
> muster all your forces.

⁴
₃   The shields of his fighting men show red,
> his warriors are dressed in scarlet;
> all the steel of the chariots flashes
> as they are thrown into battle;
> the horsemen are impatient for action;

⁵
₄   the chariots storm through the streets,
> they hurtle across the squares;
> they look like blazing flames,
> like lightning they dash to and fro.

⁶
₅   The picked troops are called out;
> the columns clash,
> they hurl themselves against the rampart,
> the mantelet is already in place.

⁷
₆   The gates that give on the river are opened,
> in the palace all is panic.

⁸
₇   The Lady[a] is carried off, taken into exile,
> her handmaids raise the dirge, with sighs
> like the moaning of doves,
> and beat their breasts.

⁹
₈   Nineveh is like a pool
> whose waters are draining away.
> 'Stop! Stop!'
> But no one turns back.

1 a. This is probably Sennacherib, 2 K 18-19.
2 a. Probably the statue of Ishtar.

'Plunder the silver! Plunder the gold!'   10
There are endless treasures,   9.
tons of valuables.
Raid and ravage and ruin!   11
Heart fails and knees give way,   10
fear is in the loins of all
and every face grows pale.

The Lion of Assyria threatened

Where is the lions' den,   12
the cave of the lion's whelps?   11
When the lion made his foray the lioness stayed behind,
the lion's cubs too; and no one molested them.
The lion clawed enough for his whelps,   13
and tore up prey for his lionesses;   12
he filled his caves with his spoil,
and his dens with the prey.
I am here! Look to yourself!—It is Yahweh Sabaoth who speaks.   14
I mean to send your chariots up in smoke;   13
the sword shall devour your lion's whelps.
I will wipe the earth clean of your plunder,
the voice of your envoys shall be heard no more.

Nineveh threatened for its crimes

3   Woe to the city soaked in blood,   1
     full of lies,
stuffed with booty,
whose plunderings know no end!
The crack of the whip!   2
The rumble of wheels!
Galloping horse,
jolting chariot,
charging cavalry,   3
flash of swords,
gleam of spears...
a mass of wounded,
hosts of dead,
countless corpses;
they stumble over the dead.
So much for all the whore's debauchery,   4
for that wonderful beauty, for that cunning witch
who enslaved nations by her debauchery
and tribes by her spells.
I am here! Look to yourself! It is Yahweh Sabaoth who speaks.   5
I mean to lift your skirts as high as your face
and show your nakedness to nations,
your shame to kingdoms.
I am going to pelt you with filth,   6
shame you, make you a public show.
And all who look on you   7
will turn their backs on you and say,
'Nineveh is a ruin'.
Could anyone pity her?
Where can I find anyone to comfort her?

The lesson of Thebes

8
>
> Are you mightier than No-amon[a]
> who had her throne beside the river,
> who had the sea for outer wall,
> the waters for rampart?

9
>
> Her strength was Ethiopia,
> Egypt too; she had no boundaries.
> Men of Put and the Libyans were her auxiliaries.

10
>
> And yet she was forced into exile,
> she went into captivity;
> her little ones, too, were dashed to pieces
> at every crossroad;
> lots were drawn for her nobles,
> all her great men were loaded with chains.

11
>
> You too will be encircled,
> you will be overwhelmed;
> you too will have to search
> for a refuge from the enemy.

Nineveh's preparations useless

12
>
> Your fortresses are all fig trees
> laden with early-ripening figs:
> shake, and they fall
> into any mouth that wants to eat them.

13
>
> Look at your people:
> your inhabitants are women.
> The gates of your country
> stand wide open to the foe;
> fire has burnt up your locking beams.

14
>
> Draw water for the siege,
> strengthen your bulwarks,
> tread the mud, tread down the clay,
> set your hand to the brick mould.

15
>
> There the fire will burn you up,
> the sword will cut you down.

The locusts fly away

>
> Increase like the locust,
> increase like the grasshopper;

16a
>
> multiply your traders
> to exceed the stars of heaven;

17a
>
> your guards are like grasshoppers,
> your scribes like a cloud of insects.
> They settle on the walls
> when the day is cold.
> The sun appears,

16b
>
> and the locusts spread their wings; they fly away,

17b
>
> they are gone, no one knows where.

A funeral lament

18
>
> Alas! •Are your shepherds asleep, then,
> king of Assyria?
> Your picked troops slumber,
> your people are scattered on the mountains

3 a. Thebes, 'the city of Amon', sacked in 663.

with no one to rally them.
There is no remedy for your wound,   19
your injury is past healing.
All who hear the news of you
clap their hands at your downfall.
For who has not felt
your unrelenting cruelty?

HABAKKUK

Title

1 1 The oracle that Habakkuk the prophet received in a vision.

I. DIALOGUE BETWEEN THE PROPHET AND HIS GOD

First complaint of the prophet: lawlessness prevails

2
How long, Yahweh, am I to cry for help
while you will not listen;
to cry 'Oppression!' in your ear
and you will not save?

3
Why do you set injustice before me,
why do you look on where there is tyranny?
Outrage and violence, this is all I see,
all is contention, and discord flourishes.

4
And so the law loses its hold,
and justice never shows itself.
Yes, the wicked man gets the better of the upright,
and so justice is seen to be distorted.

First oracle. The Chaldaeans the instrument of God's justice

5
Cast your eyes over the nations, look,
and be amazed, astounded.
For I am doing something in your own days
that you would not believe if you were told of it.

6
For now I am stirring up the Chaldaeans,
that fierce and fiery people
who march miles across country
to seize the homes of others.

7
A people feared and dreaded,
from their might proceeds their right, their greatness.

8
Their horses are swifter than leopards,
fiercer than wolves in the dark;
their horsemen gallop on,
their horsemen advance from afar,
swooping like an eagle to stoop on its prey.

9
They come for plunder, all of them,
their faces scorching like an east wind;
they scoop up prisoners like sand.

10
They are a people that scoff at kings,
and laugh at princes.

They make light of all fortresses:
they heap up earth and take them.

Then the wind changes and is gone... 11
Sinful, he who makes his own strength his god.

Second complaint of the prophet: the tyranny of the conqueror

Are not you, from ancient times Yahweh, 12
my God, my Holy One, who never dies?
Yahweh, you have made this people an instrument of justice,
set it firm as a rock in order to punish.

Your eyes are too pure to rest on wickedness, 13
you cannot look on at tyranny.
Why do you look on while men are treacherous,
and stay silent while the evil man swallows a better man than he?

You treat mankind like fishes in the sea, 14
like creeping, masterless things.

A people, these, who catch all on their hook, 15
who draw them with their net,
in their dragnet gather them,
and so, triumphantly, rejoice.

At this, they offer a sacrifice to their net, 16
and burn incense to their dragnet,
for providing them with luxury
and lavish food.

Are they then to empty their net unceasingly, 17
slaughtering nations without pity?

Second oracle: the upright man will live by faithfulness

2 I will stand on my watchtower, 1
and take up my post on my battlements,
watching to see what he will say to me,
what answer he will make to my complaints.

Then Yahweh answered and said, 2
'Write the vision down,
inscribe it on tablets
to be easily read,
since this vision is for its own time only: 3
eager for its own fulfilment, it does not deceive;
if it comes slowly, wait,
for come it will, without fail.

'See how he flags, he whose soul is not at rights, 4
but the upright man will live by his faithfulness.'

II. CURSES ON OPPRESSORS

Prelude

Wealth is indeed a treacherous thing. 5
Haughty and unable to rest is he
who is as greedy as Sheol,
who is like death, insatiable,

who assembles all the nations for his own ends,
collects all the peoples to his own advantage.

6   On him, will not all men make satires,
and turn an epigram against him?
They will say:

Five imprecations

I

Trouble is coming to the man who amasses goods that are not his,
(for how long?)
and loads himself with pledges.

7   Will not your creditors suddenly rise,
will not your duns awake?
Then you will be their victim.

8   Since you have plundered many nations,
all that remains of the peoples will plunder you;
for you have shed men's blood and ravished the country,
the city and all who live in it.

II

9   Trouble is coming to the man who grossly exploits others for
the sake of his House,
to fix his nest on high
and so evade the hand of misfortune.

10   You have contrived to bring shame on your House;
by making an end of many peoples
you have worked your own ruin.

11   For the stone from the very walls cries out,
and the beam responds from the framework.

III

12   Trouble is coming to the man who builds a town with blood
and founds a city on crime.

13   Is it not the will of Yahweh Sabaoth
that the labouring of peoples should end in fire,
and the toiling of nations come to nothing?

14   *For the country shall be filled with the knowledge of the glory of Yahweh*
as the waters swell the sea.[a]

IV

15   Trouble is coming to the man who makes his neighbours drink,
who pours his poison until they are drunk,
to look at their nakedness.

16   You are drunk with ignominy, not with glory.

Your turn now to drink and show your foreskin.
The cup from Yahweh's right hand comes round to you,
and disgrace will overshadow your glory.

17   For the violence done to Lebanon is going to overwhelm you,
so will the slaughter of terrified beasts,
for you have shed men's blood and ravished the country,
the city and all who live in it.

2 a. Is 11:9.

v

Trouble is coming to the man who says to the piece of wood,   19
   'Wake up!'
to the dumb stone, 'On your feet!'
(And that is the oracle.)
Plated it may be with gold and silver,
but not a breath of life inside it.

What is the use of a carved image, or for its maker to carve it at all?   18
It is a thing of metal, a lying oracle.
What is the use of its maker trusting this
and fashioning dumb idols?
But Yahweh is in his holy Temple: 20
let the whole earth be silent before him.

III. PLEA TO YAHWEH FOR DELIVERANCE

3 A prayer*ᵃ* of Habakkuk the prophet; tone as for dirges.   1

Yahweh, I have heard of your renown,   2
your work, Yahweh, inspires me with dread.
Repeat it in our own time,
reveal it in our time.
For all your wrath, remember to be merciful.

Eloah is coming from Teman,   3
and the Holy One from Mount Paran.*ᵇ*   *Pause*
His majesty veils the heavens,
the earth is filled with his glory.

His brightness is like the day,   4
rays flash from his hands,
that is where his power lies hidden.

Plague goes in front of him,   5
fever follows on his heels.

When he stands up hᵊ makes the earth tremble,   6
with his glance he makes the nations quake.

Then the ancient mountains are dislodged,
the everlasting hills sink down,
his pathway from of old.

I have seen the tents of Cushan terrified,   7
the pavilions of the land of Midian shuddering.*ᶜ*

Yahweh, is your anger blazing against the rivers,   8
or your fury against the sea,
that you come mounted on your horses,
on your victorious chariots?

You uncover your bow,   9
you ply its string with arrows.   *Pause*

You trench the soil with torrents;
the mountains shiver when they see you;   10
great floods sweep on their way,

the abyss[d] roars aloud,
high it lifts its hands.

11 Sun and moon stay in their houses,
avoiding the flash of your arrows,
the gleam of your glittering spear.

12 Raging, you stride the earth,
in anger you trample the nations.

13 You have marched to save your people,
to save your own anointed;
you have beaten down the wicked man's house,
bared its foundations to the rock.   *Pause*

14 With your shafts you have pierced the leader of his warriors
who stormed out with shouts of joy to scatter us,
as if they meant to devour some poor wretch in their lair.

15 You have trampled the sea with your horses,
the surge of great waters.

16 I have heard. My whole body trembles;
my lips quiver at the sound;
decay creeps into my bones,
my steps falter beneath me.

Calmly I await the day of anguish
which is dawning on the people now attacking us.

17 (For the fig tree is not going to blossom,
nor will there be any fruit on the vine,
the yield of the olive will fail,
the fields afford no food;
the sheep will vanish from the fold,
nor will there be any cattle in the stalls.)

18 But I will rejoice in Yahweh,
I will exult in God my saviour.

19 Yahweh my Lord is my strength,
he makes my feet as light as a doe's,
he sets my steps on the heights.

For the choirmaster; on stringed instruments.

3 a. The note at the end of this chapter, and the three rubrics marking pauses, show that this psalm was used in the liturgy.   **b.** Eloah is an ancient name for God. The place-names are in Edom, and the coming of Yahweh is described in terms of an advancing storm.   **c.** Midian is to the S. of Edom; Cushan appears to be the same region.   **d.** 'The waters under the earth' rise to join the rain.

ZEPHANIAH

1 The word of Yahweh that was addressed to Zephaniah son of Cushi, son of 1
Gedaliah, son of Amariah, son of Hezekiah, in the reign of Josiah son of
Amon, king of Judah.

I. THE DAY OF YAHWEH FOR JUDAH

Prelude: judgement on all creation

I mean to sweep away everything 2
off the face of the earth
—it is Yahweh who speaks.
I mean to sweep away men and beasts, 3
the birds of the air and the fish of the sea,
I mean to send the wicked staggering,
and wipe man off the face of the earth
—it is Yahweh who speaks.

Against the worship of alien gods

I am going to raise my hand against Judah 4
and against all the inhabitants of Jerusalem,
and from this place I will wipe out Baal,
to the very last vestige of him,
even to the name of his spurious priests,
those who prostrate themselves on the roofs 5
before the array of heaven,
those who prostrate themselves before Yahweh
but swear by Milcom,[a]
those who turn aside from Yahweh, 6
who do not seek Yahweh,
who will not bother with him.
Silence before the Lord Yahweh! 7
For the day of Yahweh is near.
Yes, Yahweh has prepared a sacrifice,
he has consecrated his guests.

Against the dignitaries of the court[b]

On the day of Yahweh's sacrifice, 8
I will punish the ministers,
the royal princes,
and all those who dress themselves
in foreign style.
On that day I mean to punish 9
all those who are near the throne,
those who fill the palace of their lord
with violence and deceit.

Against the merchants of Jerusalem

10   On that day—it is Yahweh who speaks—
        a shout will be raised from the Fish Gate,
        from the new town, howls,
        from the hills, a great uproar.

11   Men of the Mortar, howl!
        For the whole brood of Canaan[c] has been destroyed,
        the weighers of silver are all wiped out.

Against unbelievers

12   When that time comes
        I will search Jerusalem by torchlight,
        and punish the men
        who are stagnating on their lees,
        those who say in their hearts,
        'Yahweh has no power
        for good or for evil'.

13   Then their wealth will be given up to looting,
        their households to plundering.
        They built houses, did they? They will not live in them.
        They planted vineyards, did they? They will not drink their wine.

The day of Yahweh

14   The great day of Yahweh is near,
        near, and coming with all speed.
        How bitter the sound of the day of Yahweh,
        the day when the warrior shouts his cry of war.

15   A day of wrath, that day,
        a day of distress and agony,
        a day of ruin and of devastation,
        a day of darkness and gloom,
        a day of cloud and blackness,

16   a day of trumpet blast and battle cry
        against fortified town
        and high corner-tower.

17   I am going to bring such distress on men
        that they will grope like the blind
        (because they have sinned against Yahweh);
        their blood will be scattered like dust,
        their corpses like dung.

18   Neither their silver nor their gold
        will have any power to save them.

        On the day of the anger of Yahweh,
        in the fire of his jealousy,
        all the earth will be consumed.
        For he means to destroy, yes, to make an end
        of all the inhabitants of the earth.

Conclusion: a call to conversion

1 2   ....
        nation without desire,
2   before you are driven
        like chaff that is blown away in a day,

1 a. God of the Ammonites.   b. The regents during the minority of King Josiah.
c. 'Canaanites' is a term for the merchants.

before there descends on you
the fierce anger of Yahweh
(before there descends on you
the day of the anger of Yahweh).
Seek Yahweh,   3
all you, the humble of the earth,
who obey his commands.
Seek integrity,
seek humility:
you may perhaps find shelter
on the day of the anger of Yahweh.

II. AGAINST THE PAGANS

The enemy to the west: the Philistines

Yes, Gaza is going to be reduced to desert,   4
Ashkelon to waste.
Ashdod will be stormed in broad daylight,
and Ekron rooted out.
Woe to the members of the Confederacy of the Sea,   5
to the nation of the Cherethites!
This is the word of Yahweh against you:
I mean to bring you down, land of the Philistines,
I am going to ruin you, empty you of inhabitants;
and you will be reduced to pasture land,   6
to grazing grounds for the shepherds,
to folds for the sheep.
It will be included in the property   7
of the remnant of the House of Judah;
they will lead flocks there to pasture;
among the houses of Ashkelon they will rest at evening;
for Yahweh their God is going to deal kindly with them
and restore their fortunes.

The enemies to the east: Moab and Ammon

I have heard the taunts of Moab   8
and the insults of the sons of Ammon
as they laughed at my people,
and boasted of their own domains.
For this, as I live—it is Yahweh Sabaoth who speaks, 9
the God of Israel—
Moab shall become like Sodom
and the sons of Ammon like Gomorrah:
a realm of nettles, a heap of salt,
a desolation for ever.
What is left of my people will plunder them,
those of my nation who survive will take their heritage.
This will be the price of their pride,   10
of their taunts, of their boasts
against the people of Yahweh Sabaoth.
Full of terror will Yahweh be for them.   11
When he has utterly destroyed all the gods of the earth,
the nations will prostrate themselves before him,
each on its own soil,
all the islands of the nations.

The enemy to the south: Ethiopia[a]

12 And as for you, Ethiopians:
They will be run through with my sword.

The enemy to the north: Assyria

13 He is going to raise his hand against the north
and bring Assyria down in ruins;
he will make Nineveh a waste,
dry as the desert.

14 In the middle of her the flocks will rest;
all the beasts of the valley,
even the pelican and the heron
will roost round her cornices at night;
the owl will hoot at the window
and the raven croak on the doorstep.

. . . .

15 Is this the joyful city,
so confident on her throne,
who said in her heart,
'Here am I, with none to equal me'?
What a ruin she is now,
a lair for beasts!
All those who pass by her
whistle and shake their fists.

III. AGAINST JERUSALEM

Against the leaders of the people

1 **3** Trouble is coming to the rebellious, the defiled,
the tyrannical city!

2 She would never listen to the call,
would never learn the lesson;
she has never trusted in Yahweh,
never drawn near to her God.

3 The leaders she harbours
are roaring lions,
her judges, wolves at evening
that have had nothing to gnaw that morning;

4 her prophets are braggarts,
they are impostors;
her priests profane the holy things,
they do violence to the Law.

5 Yahweh is in her, he is just and honourable;
he never does wrong;
morning by morning he makes his law known,
each dawn unfailingly;
he knows no injustice.

The pagans punished

6 I have wiped out nations,
their corner-towers lie in ruins;
I have emptied their streets,

---

2 a. In this fragmentary oracle, 'Ethiopia' stands for Egypt, where an Ethiopian dynasty had ruled from 715 to 663.

> no one walks there;
> their towns have been sacked:
> no one left there, no more inhabitants.
> 'At least,' I used to say 'you will fear me now,   7
> you will learn the lesson;
> she cannot lose sight
> of the many times I have punished her.'
> But no, it only made them more anxious
> to see that all they did was corrupt.
>
> Therefore, expect me—it is Yahweh who speaks—   8
> on the day I stand up to make my accusation;
> for I am determined to gather the nations,
> to assemble the kingdoms,
> and to pour out my fury on you,
> the whole heat of my anger.

IV. PROMISES

Conversion of the pagans

> Yes, I will then give the peoples   9
> lips that are clean,
> so that all may invoke the name of Yahweh
> and serve him under the same yoke.
> From beyond the banks of the rivers of Ethiopia my suppliants   10
> will bring me offerings.

The humble remnant of Israel

> When that day comes   11
> you need feel no shame for all the misdeeds
> you have committed against me,
> for I will remove your proud boasters
> from your midst;
> and you will cease to strut
> on my holy mountain.
> In your midst I will leave   12
> a humble and lowly people,
> and those who are left in Israel will seek refuge in the name of Yahweh. 13
> They will do no wrong,
> will tell no lies;
> and the perjured tongue will no longer
> be found in their mouths.
> But they will be able to graze and rest
> with no one to disturb them.

Psalms of joy in Zion

> Shout for joy, daughter of Zion,   14
> Israel, shout aloud!
> Rejoice, exult with all your heart,
> daughter of Jerusalem!
> Yahweh has repealed your sentence;   15
> he has driven your enemies away.
> Yahweh, the king of Israel, is in your midst;
> you have no more evil to fear.
>
> When that day comes, word will come to Jerusalem: 16
> Zion, have no fear,

do not let your hands fall limp.

17 Yahweh your God is in your midst,
    a victorious warrior.
    He will exult with joy over you,
    he will renew you by his love;
    he will dance with shouts of joy for you
18   as on a day of festival.

Return of the exiles

I have taken away your misfortune,
    no longer need you bear the disgrace of it.
19 I am taking action here and now
    against your oppressors.
    When that time comes I will rescue the lame,
    and gather the strays,
    and I will win them praise and renown
    when I restore their fortunes.

20 When that times comes, I will be your guide,
    when that time comes, I will gather you in;
    I will give you praise and renown
    among all the peoples of the earth
    when I restore your fortunes under your own eyes,
    says Yahweh.

HAGGAI

The movement to rebuild the Temple

1 In the second year of King Darius, on the first day of the sixth month,*a* the 1
word of Yahweh was addressed through the prophet Haggai to Zerubbabel
son of Shealtiel, high commissioner of Judah, and to Joshua son of Jehozadak,
the high priest, as follows, •'Yahweh Sabaoth says this, "This people says: 2
The time has not yet come to rebuild the Temple of Yahweh. •(And the word 3
of Yahweh was addressed through the prophet Haggai, as follows:) •Is this a 4
time for you to live in your panelled houses, when this House lies in ruins?
So now, Yahweh Sabaoth says this: Reflect carefully how things have gone 5
for you. •You have sown much and harvested little; you eat but never have 6
enough, drink but never have your fill, put on clothes but do not feel warm. The
wage earner gets his wages only to put them in a purse riddled with holes. •So go to 8
the hill country, fetch wood, and rebuild the House: I shall then take pleasure
in it, and be glorified there, says Yahweh. •Yahweh Sabaoth says this: Reflect 7
carefully how things have gone for you. •The abundance you expected 9
proved to be little. When you brought the harvest in, my breath spoilt it. And
why?—it is Yahweh Sabaoth who speaks. Because while my House lies in ruins
you are busy with your own, each one of you. •That is why the sky has withheld 10
the rain and the earth withheld its yield. •I have called down drought on land 11
and hills, on wheat, on new wine, on oil and on all the produce of the ground,
on man and beast and all their labours." '

Now Zerubbabel son of Shealtiel, Joshua son of Jehozadak, the high priest, 12
and all the remnant of the people, paid attention to the voice of Yahweh their
God and to the words of the prophet Haggai, Yahweh having sent him to them.
And the people were filled with fear before Yahweh. •Haggai, the messenger of 13
Yahweh, passed on the message of Yahweh to the people, as follows, 'I am
with you—it is Yahweh who speaks'. •And Yahweh roused the spirit of 14
Zerubbabel son of Shealtiel, high commissioner of Judah, the spirit of Joshua
son of Jehozadak, the high priest, and the spirit of all the remnant of the people;
and they came and set to work on the Temple of Yahweh Sabaoth their God.
This was on the twenty-fourth day of the sixth month. 15

The glory that is to come to the Temple

In the second year of King Darius, 2 on the twenty-first day of the seventh 1
month,*a* the word of Yahweh was addressed through the prophet Haggai,
as follows, •'You are to speak to Zerubbabel son of Shealtiel, the high 2
commissioner of Judah, to Joshua son of Jehozadak, the high priest, and to all
the remnant of the people. Say this, •"Who is there left among you that saw 3
this Temple in its former glory? And how does it look to you now? Does it
seem nothing to you? •But take courage now, Zerubbabel—it is Yahweh who 4
speaks. Courage, High Priest Joshua son of Jehozadak! Courage, all you people
of the country!—it is Yahweh who speaks. To work! I am with you—it is
Yahweh Sabaoth who speaks—•and my spirit remains among you. Do not 5
be afraid! •For Yahweh Sabaoth says this: A little while now, and I am going 6
to shake the heavens and the earth, the sea and the dry land. •I will shake all 7

the nations and the treasures of all the nations shall flow in, and I will fill this
8 Temple with glory, says Yahweh Sabaoth. •Mine is the silver, mine the gold!
9 —it is Yahweh Sabaoth who speaks. •The new glory of this Temple is going to
surpass the old, says Yahweh Sabaoth, and in this place I will give peace—it is
Yahweh Sabaoth who speaks." '

The prophet consults the priests

10   On the twenty-fourth day of the ninth month, in the second year of Darius,[b]
11 the word of Yahweh was addressed to the prophet Haggai as follows, •'Yahweh
12 Sabaoth says this: Ask the priests for a decision on this question, •"If a man
carries consecrated meat in the fold of his gown and with this fold touches
bread, broth, wine, or food of any kind, does such food become holy?" ' The
13 priests answered, 'No, it does not'. •Haggai then said, 'If a man made unclean
by contact with a corpse touches any of this, does it become unclean?' The
14 priests answered, 'Yes, it does'. •Haggai then spoke out. 'It is the same with
this people,' he said 'the same with this nation as I see it—it is Yahweh who
speaks—the same with everything they turn their hands to; and what they offer
here is unclean.

A promise of agricultural prosperity

15   'Reflect carefully from today onwards. Before one stone had been laid on
16 another in the sanctuary of Yahweh, •what state were you in? A man would
come to a twenty-measure heap and there would be ten; he would come to a vat
17 to draw fifty measures and there would be twenty. •I struck with blight and
mildew and hail everything you turned your hands to. And still you would not
18 return to me—it is Yahweh who speaks. •Reflect carefully from today onwards
(from the twenty-fourth day of the ninth month, from the day the foundation
19 of the sanctuary of Yahweh was laid, think carefully) •if grain is still short
in the barn, and if vine and fig tree, pomegranate and olive, still bear no fruit.
From today onwards I intend to bless you.'

The promise to Zerubbabel

20   On the twenty-fourth day of the month the word of Yahweh was addressed
21 a second time to Haggai, as follows, •'Speak to Zerubbabel, the high commis-
22 sioner of Judah. Say this, "I am going to shake the heavens and the earth. •I will
overturn the thrones of kingdoms and destroy the power of the kings of the
nations. I will overthrow the chariots and their charioteers; horses and their
riders will be brought down; they shall fall, each to the sword of his fellow.
23 When the day comes—it is Yahweh Sabaoth who speaks—I will take you,
Zerubbabel son of Shealtiel, my servant—it is Yahweh Sabaoth who speaks—
and make you like a signet ring. For I have chosen you—it is Yahweh Sabaoth
who speaks." '

1 a. August 520.
2 a. October 520, the last day of the feast of Tabernacles.   b. December 520.

ZECHARIAH

FIRST PART

A summons to conversion

1 In the second year of Darius, in the eighth month,^a the word of Yahweh 1 was addressed to the prophet Zechariah (son of Berechiah),^b son of Iddo, as follows, •'Cry out to the remnant of this people and say to them, "Yahweh 3 Sabaoth says this: Return to me, and I will return to you, says Yahweh Sabaoth. Do not be like your ancestors, to whom the prophets in the past cried: Yahweh 4 Sabaoth says this: Turn back from your evil ways and evil deeds. But—it is Yahweh who speaks—they would not listen or pay attention to me. •Where are 5 your ancestors now? Are those prophets still alive? •Did not my words and my 6a orders, with which I charged my servants the prophets, overtake your ancestors? Yahweh was stirred to anger against your ancestors." ' •This reduced them to 2, 6b such confusion that they said, 'Yahweh Sabaoth has treated us as he resolved to do, and as our ways and deeds deserved.'

First vision: the horsemen

On the twenty-fourth day of the eleventh month (the month of Shebat), 7 in the second year of Darius,^c the word of Yahweh was addressed to the prophet Zechariah (son of Berechiah), son of Iddo, as follows, •'I saw a vision during 8 the night. It was this: a man was standing among the deep-rooted myrtles; behind him were horses, red and sorrel and black and white. •I said: What are 9 these, my lord? (And the angel who was talking to me said, "I will explain to you what they are".) •The man standing among the myrtles answered, "They 10 are those whom Yahweh has sent to patrol throughout the world". •They then 11 spoke to the angel of Yahweh standing among the myrtles; they said, "We have been patrolling the world, and see, the whole world is at peace and rest". •The 12 angel of Yahweh then spoke and said, "Yahweh Sabaoth, how long will you wait before taking pity on Jerusalem and the cities of Judah, on which you have inflicted your anger for the past seventy years?" •Yahweh then replied with very 13 consoling words to the angel who was talking to me. •The angel who was talking 14 to me then said to me, "Make this proclamation: Yahweh Sabaoth says this: I feel most jealous love for Jerusalem and Zion, •but very bitter anger against 15 the proud nations; for my part I was only a little angry, but they have overstepped all limits. •Yahweh, then, says this. I turn again in compassion to 16 Jerusalem; my Temple there shall be rebuilt—it is Yahweh Sabaoth who speaks—and the measuring line will be stretched over Jerusalem. •Make this proclamation 17 too: Yahweh Sabaoth says this: My cities are once more going to be very prosperous. Yahweh will again take pity on Zion, again make Jerusalem his very own." '

Second vision: the horns and the smiths

2 Then, raising my eyes, I saw a vision. It was this: there were four horns. 1, 18 I said to the angel who was talking to me, 'What are these horns, my lord?' 2, 19 He said to me, 'These are the horns which have scattered Judah (Israel) and Jerusalem'. •Yahweh then showed me four smiths. •And I said, 'What are 3,4, 20,21

these coming to do?' He said to me, '(Those are the horns which have so scattered Judah that no one has dared to raise his head; but) these have come to lay them low (to strike down the horns of the nations who lifted their hands against the land of Judah, in order to scatter it)'.

Third vision: the measurer

⁵/₁ Then, raising my eyes, I saw a vision. It was this: there was a man with a
⁶/₂ measuring line in his hand. •I asked him, 'Where are you going?' He said, 'To
⁷/₃ measure Jerusalem, to find out her breadth and her length'. •And then, while the angel who was talking to me stood still, another angel came forward to
⁸/₄ meet him. •He said to him, 'Run, and tell that young man this, "Jerusalem is to remain unwalled, because of the great number of men and cattle there will be
⁹/₅ in her. •But I—it is Yahweh who speaks—I will be a wall of fire for her all round her, and I will be her glory in the midst of her." '

Two exhortations to the exiles

¹⁰/₆ Up, up, and leave the land of the North (it is Yahweh who speaks)!
(For to the four winds of heaven
I have scattered you—it is Yahweh who speaks.)
¹¹/₇ Zion, up! Dweller in Babylon, flee!
¹²/₈ For Yahweh Sabaoth says this
(he whose glory has sent me here)
as regards the nations who despoiled you
(for whoever touches you touches the apple of my eye):
¹³/₉ See now, I raise my hand over them,
for them to be plunder for their slaves.
(And you will know that Yahweh Sabaoth has sent me.)
¹⁴/₁₀ Sing, rejoice,
daughter of Zion;
for I am coming
to dwell in the middle of you
—it is Yahweh who speaks.
¹⁵/₁₁ Many nations will join Yahweh,
on that day;
they will become his people.
(But he will remain among you,
and you will know that Yahweh Sabaoth has sent me to you.)
¹⁶/₁₂ But Yahweh will hold Judah
as his portion in the Holy Land,
and again make Jerusalem his very own.
¹⁷/₁₃ Let all mankind be silent before Yahweh!
For he is awaking and is coming from his holy dwelling.

Fourth vision: the investiture of Joshua

3 ₁ He[a] showed me Joshua the high priest, standing before the angel of Yahweh,
₂ with Satan standing on his right to accuse him. •The angel of Yahweh said to Satan, 'May Yahweh rebuke you, Satan, may Yahweh rebuke you, he who has made Jerusalem his very own. Is not this man a brand snatched from the
₃ fire?'[b] •Now Joshua was dressed in dirty clothes[c] as he stood before the angel
₄ₐ of Yahweh. •The angel said these words to those who stood before him, 'Take
₅ off his dirty clothes and clothe him in splendid robes of state, •and put a clean turban on his head'. They clothed him in splendid robes of state and put a clean turban on his head.[d] The angel of Yahweh was standing there and said to him,

1 a. October-November 520.   b. A gloss suggested by Is 8:2. According to Ezr 5:1 and Ne 12:16, Zechariah was the son of Iddo.   c. February 519.
3 a. Yahweh.   b. The high priest represents the Jewish people.   c. Sign of mourning or national calamity.   d. The national mourning is over.

'Look, I have taken away your iniquity from you'. •The angel of Yahweh then 4b 6
proclaimed to Joshua: •'Yahweh Sabaoth says this, "If you walk in my ways 7
and keep my ordinances, you shall govern my house, you shall watch over my
courts, and I will give you free access among those who stand here. •For this 9a
is the stone which I am placing before Joshua; on this single stone there are
seven eyes; and I myself intend to cut the inscription on it—it is Yahweh Sabaoth
who speaks.

The coming of the 'Branch'

"Now listen, High Priest Joshua, you and the friends who sit before you—for 8
you are men of good omen. I now mean to raise my servant Branch, •and 9b
I intend to put aside the iniquity of this land in a single day. •On that day—it is 10
Yahweh Sabaoth who speaks—you will entertain each other under your vine
and fig tree."'

Fifth vision: the lamp-stand and the olive trees

4 The angel who was talking to me came back and roused me as a man is 1
roused from his sleep. •And he asked me, 'What can you see?' I answered, 2
'As I look, this is what I see: there is a lamp-stand entirely of gold with a bowl
at the top of it; seven lamps are on the lamp-stand, and seven lips for the lamps
on it. •By it are two olive trees, one to the right of it and one to the left.' 3
Speaking again, I said to the angel who was talking to me, 'What do those things 4
mean, my lord?' •The angel who was talking to me replied, 'Do you not know 5
what these things mean?' I said, 'No, my lord'. •He then gave me this answer, 6a 10b 11
'These seven are the eyes of Yahweh; they cover the whole world'. •In reply
to this I asked him, 'What is the meaning of these two olive trees, to the right
and to the left of the lamp-stand?' •(Speaking again, I asked him, 'What is the 12
meaning of the two olive branches pouring the oil through the two golden
pipes?') •He replied, 'Do you not know what these things mean?' I said, 'No, 13
my lord'. •He said, 'These are the two anointed ones who stand before the 14
Lord of the whole world. ᵃ

Three sayings about Zerubbabel

'This is the word of Yahweh with regard to Zerubbabel, "Not by might and 6b
not by power, but by my spirit, says Yahweh Sabaoth.

"What are you, you great mountain? Before Zerubbabel, be a plain! He will 7
pull out the keystone to shouts of: Blessings on it, blessings on it!"'

The word of Yahweh was addressed to me as follows, •'The hands of 8 9
Zerubbabel have laid the foundation of this Temple; his hands will finish it.
(And you will learn that Yahweh Sabaoth has sent me to you.) •A day for little 10a
things, no doubt, but who would dare despise it? People will rejoice when they
see the chosen stone in the hands of Zerubbabel.'

Sixth vision: the flying scroll

5 Again I raised my eyes, and this is what I saw: a flying scroll. •The angel 1 2
who was talking to me said, 'What can you see?' I replied, 'I can see a flying
scroll; it is twenty cubits long and ten cubits broad'. •He then said to me, 3
'This is the Curse sweeping across the face of the whole country. According
to what it says, every thief will be banished; according to what it says, everyone
who swears falsely by my name will be banished. •I am going to let it loose 4
—it is Yahweh Sabaoth who speaks—to enter the house of the thief and the
house of anyone who swears falsely by my name, to settle in his house and to
consume it, timber, stone and all.'

Seventh vision: the woman in the bushel

5 The angel who was talking to me came forward and said to me, 'Raise your
6 eyes, and see what this is, moving forward'. •I said, 'What is it?' He said, 'This
is a bushel moving forward'. He went on, 'This is their iniquity throughout
7 the country'. •At this, a disc of lead was raised, and I saw a Woman sitting
8 inside the bushel. •He said, 'This is Wickedness'. And he forced her back into
9 the bushel and closed its mouth with the mass of lead. •I raised my eyes, and
this is what I saw: two women appearing. The wind caught their wings—they
had wings like a stork's; they raised the bushel midway between earth and
10 heaven. •I then said to the angel who was talking to me, 'Where are they taking
11 the bushel?' •He replied, 'They mean to build a temple for it in the land of
Shinar, and to make a plinth on which to place it'.*a*

Eighth vision: the chariots

1 6 Again I raised my eyes, and this is what I saw: four chariots coming out
between the two mountains, and the mountains were mountains of bronze.
2/3 The first chariot had red horses, the second chariot had black horses, •the
third chariot had white horses and the fourth chariot had (vigorous) piebald
4 horses. •I asked the angel who was talking to me, I said, 'What is the meaning
5 of these, my lord?' •The angel answered, 'These are going out to the four winds
6 of heaven after standing before the Lord of the whole world. •The red horses
are going out to the country of the East; the black horses are going out to the
country of the North; the white are going out to the country of the West and
7 the piebald are going out to the country of the South.' •They came out vigorously,
eager to patrol the world. He said to them, 'Go and patrol the world'. And they
8 patrolled the world. •He called me and said to me, 'See, those going northward
15 will make the spirit of Yahweh descend on the country of the North.*a* •And
those who are far away will come and rebuild the sanctuary of Yahweh. (And
you will learn that Yahweh Sabaoth has sent me to you.) (This will happen
if you listen carefully to the voice of Yahweh your God.)'

The votive crown

9/10 And the word of Yahweh was addressed to me as follows, •'Take the offerings
of the captives,*b* of Heldai, Tobijah and Jedaiah, and go to the house of Josiah
11 son of Zephaniah, who has arrived from Babylon. •Take the silver and gold,
make a crown and set it on the head of Joshua son of Jehozadak, the high
12 priest.*c* •And say this to him, "Yahweh Sabaoth says this: Here is a man whose
name is Branch; where he is, there will be a branching out (and he will rebuild
13 the sanctuary of Yahweh). •It is he who is going to rebuild the sanctuary of
Yahweh. It is he who is going to wear the royal insignia. He will sit on his throne
as ruler. And a priest shall be at his right hand. Perfect peace will reign between
14 these two; •while the crown will be a glorious memorial to Heldai, Tobijah
and Jedaiah, and to Josiah, son of Zephaniah, in the sanctuary of Yahweh." '

A question on fasting

1 7 In the fourth year of King Darius (the word of Yahweh was addressed to
Zechariah), on the fourth day of the ninth month*a* (the month of Chislev),
2/3 Bethel sent Sharezer and his men to entreat the favour of Yahweh •and to say to
the priests in the Temple of Yahweh Sabaoth, and to his prophets, 'Ought I to

4 a. Joshua, the high priest; and Zerabbabel, the High Commissioner, seen as the anointed
king.
5 a. Wickedness is banished to Babylon, where it is worshipped.
6 a. Where there are still some exiles.   b. Of the captives who have returned from captivity.
c. It is evident that the original text read 'Zerubbabel', see vv.12-13. 'Joshua son of Jehozadak'
is a 'modernisation' by a later hand.
7 a. November 518.

go on mourning and fasting in the fifth month as I have been doing for so many years past?'[b]

The nation's past surveyed

Then the word of Yahweh Sabaoth was addressed to me as follows, •'Say ⁴₅ to all the people of the country, and to the priests, "While you have been fasting and mourning in the fifth and seventh months for the past seventy years, was it for my sake you fasted so rigorously? •And when you were eating and drinking, ⁶ were not you the eaters and you the drinkers? •Do you not know the words ⁷ which Yahweh proclaimed through the prophets in the past, when Jerusalem was inhabited and secure, with her surrounding towns, and when the Negeb and the Lowlands were inhabited? (•The word of Yahweh was addressed to ⁸ Zechariah as follows: •Yahweh Sabaoth says this.) He said: Apply the law ⁹ fairly, and practise kindness and compassion towards each other. •Do not ¹⁰ oppress the widow and the orphan, the settler and the poor man, and do not secretly plan evil against one another. •But they would not pay attention; they ¹¹ turned a petulant shoulder; they stopped their ears rather than hear;• they made ¹² their hearts adamant rather than listen to the teaching and the words that Yahweh Sabaoth had sent by his spirit through the prophets in the past. This aroused great anger on the part of Yahweh Sabaoth. •And this is what happened, since ¹³ he kept calling them and they would not listen (similarly they will call and I shall not listen, says Yahweh Sabaoth): •he scattered them throughout nations ¹⁴ unknown to them; hence the country was reduced to desolation behind them, and no one came or went. They turned a land of delights into a desert." '

A prospect of messianic salvation

8 The word of Yahweh Sabaoth was addressed to me as follows: ¹

'Yahweh Sabaoth says this.   ²
I am burning with jealousy for Zion,
with great anger for her sake.

'Yahweh Sabaoth says this.   ³
I am coming back to Zion
and shall dwell in the middle of Jerusalem.
Jerusalem will be called Faithful City
and the mountain of Yahweh Sabaoth, the Holy Mountain.

'Yahweh Sabaoth says this.   ⁴
Old men and old women will again sit down
in the squares of Jerusalem;
every one of them staff in hand
because of their great age.
And the squares of the city will be full   ⁵
of boys and girls
playing in the squares.

'Yahweh Sabaoth says this.   ⁶
If this seems a miracle
to the remnant of this people (in those days),
will it seem one to me?
It is Yahweh Sabaoth who speaks.
'Yahweh Sabaoth says this.   ⁷
Now I am going to save my people
from the countries of the East
and from the countries of the West.
I will bring them back   ⁸
to live inside Jerusalem.

They shall be my people
and I will be their God
in faithfulness and integrity.

9   'Yahweh Sabaoth says this. Let your hands be strong, you who here and
now listen to these words from the mouths of the prophets who have been
prophesying since the day when the Temple of Yahweh Sabaoth had its
10 foundation laid for the rebuilding of the sanctuary. •For before the present
day men were not paid their wages and nothing was paid for the animals either;
and because of the enemy there was no security for a man to go about his business;
11 I had set every man against everyone else. •But now, with the remnant of this
12 people, I am not as I was in the past. It is Yahweh Sabaoth who speaks. •For
I mean to spread peace everywhere; the vine will give its fruit, the earth its
increase, and heaven its dew. I am going to bestow all these blessings on the
13 remnant of this people. •Just as once you were a curse among the nations, you
House of Judah (and House of Israel), so I mean to save you for you to become
a blessing. Do not be afraid; let your hands be strong.
14 For Yahweh Sabaoth says this. Just as I once resolved to inflict evil on you
when your ancestors provoked me—says Yahweh Sabaoth—and as I did not
15 then relent, •so now I have another purpose, and I intend in the present day to
confer benefits on Jerusalem and on the House of Judah. Do not be afraid.
16 'These are the things that you must do. Speak the truth to one another;
17 let the judgements at your gates be such as conduce to peace; •do not secretly
plot evil against one another; do not love false oaths; since all this is what
I hate. It is Yahweh who speaks.'

The answer to the question on fasting

18   The word of Yahweh Sabaoth was addressed to me as follows:
19   'Yahweh Sabaoth says this. The fast of the fourth month, the fast of the
fifth, the fast of the seventh and the fast of the tenth are to become gladness and
happiness and days of joyful feasting for the House of Judah.ᵃ But love the
truth and peace!

A prospect of messianic salvation

20   'Yahweh Sabaoth says this. There will be other peoples yet, and citizens of
21 great cities. •And the inhabitants of one city will go to the next and say, "Come,
let us go and entreat the favour of Yahweh, and seek Yahweh Sabaoth; I am
22 going myself". •And many peoples and great nations will come to seek Yahweh
Sabaoth in Jerusalem and to entreat the favour of Yahweh.
23   'Yahweh Sabaoth says this. In those days, ten men of nations of every language
will take a Jew by the sleeve and say, "We want to go with you, since we have
learnt that God is with you".'

---

b. The destruction of the Temple in 587 had been commemorated by a fast in the month of
July; now rebuilding has begun. The answer to this question is in ch. 8. The oracle which
follows in the next paragraph seems to have been attached merely because it too mentions
fasting, and the second fast to which it alludes was the commemoration of the murder of
Gedaliah, 2 K 25.
8 a. This answer abolishes the two fasts already mentioned, and those of the fourth and tenth
months, which commemorated the breaching of the walls and the beginning of the siege.

SECOND PART

9 An oracle.

The new promised land[a]

> Yahweh has passed
> through the land of Hadrach
> and Damascus is his dwelling place;
> for the cities of Aram belong to Yahweh
> no less than all the tribes of Israel;
> Hamath too, which borders on it,
> (Tyre) and Sidon also, despite her acumen.
> Tyre has built herself a rampart,
> has heaped up silver like dust
> and gold like the dirt of the streets.
> And now the Lord is going to take possession of her;
> he will topple her power into the sea;
> she herself will be consumed by fire.
> Seeing this, Ashkelon will be terrified,
> and Gaza be seized with trembling,
> so will Ekron, at the ruin of her prospects;
> the king will vanish from Gaza
> and Ashkelon remain unpeopled,
> but the bastard[b] will live in Ashdod!
> I mean to destroy the arrogance of the Philistine;
> I intend to take his blood out of his mouth
> and his abomination from between his teeth.[c]
> He too will become a remnant for our God
> and be like a family in Judah:
> Ekron shall be like the Jebusite.[d]
> Near my house I will take my stand
> like a watchman on guard against prowlers;
> the tyrant shall pass their way no more,
> because I have now taken notice of its distress.

The Messiah

> Rejoice heart and soul, daughter of Zion!
> Shout with gladness, daughter of Jerusalem!
> See now, your king comes to you;
> he is victorious, he is triumphant,
> humble and riding on a donkey,
> on a colt, the foal of a donkey.
> He will banish chariots from Ephraim
> and horses from Jerusalem;
> the bow of war will be banished.
> He will proclaim peace for the nations.
> His empire shall stretch from sea to sea,
> from the River to the ends of the earth.

The restoration of Israel

> As for you, because of the blood of your covenant
> I am sending back your prisoners from the pit
> (in which there is no water).
> To you, daughter of Zion,
> the hopeful captives will return.

1

2

3

4

5

6

7

8

9

10

11

12

In compensation for your days of banishment
I will give you back double.

13 For I bend my bow; it is Judah;
I make Ephraim its arrow.
I am going to brandish your children, Zion,
(against your children, Javan);[c]
I mean to make you like the sword of a hero.

14 Yahweh will appear above them
and his arrow will flash out like lightning.
(The Lord) Yahweh will sound the trumpet
and advance in the storms of the south.

15 Yahweh (Sabaoth) will protect them!
They will trample sling stones underfoot,
they will drink blood like wine,
they will be soaked in it like the horns of an altar.

16 Yahweh their God will give them victory
when that day comes;
he will pasture his people like a flock
(like the flashing jewels of a diadem)
on his land.

17 What joy and what beauty shall be theirs!
Corn will make the young men flourish,
and sweet wine the maidens.

Faithfulness to Yahweh

1 **10** Ask Yahweh for rain
at the time of the spring rains.
For it is Yahweh who sends the lightning
and gives the showers of rain;
he gives bread to man,
and grass to the cattle.

2 Because the teraphim utter futile words
and the diviners have lying visions[a]
and publish empty dreams
and voice misleading nonsense,
naturally the people stray like sheep;
they wander because they have no shepherd.

Israel's deliverance and return

3 'My anger burns against the shepherds,
and I mean to punish the he-goats.'
Yes, Yahweh (Sabaoth) will take care of his flock
(the House of Judah),
he will make it his proud steed (in battle).

4 From him will issue Cornerstone and Tent-peg,[b]
from him the Bow of battle,
from him all the Leaders.

5 Together •they will be like heroes
trampling the dirt of the streets (in battle);

---

9 a. The new Promised Land is larger than Israel and includes Aramaean, Phoenician and Philistine cities. A victorious campaign against these territories, probably that of Alexander in 333, is seen as the action of Yahweh.   **b.** A population of mixed races.   **c.** Philistines followed the pagan practice of eating meat with the blood in it, and eating the forbidden meats, such as pork.   **d.** I.e., incorporated into Israel.   **e.** This gloss refers to the conquest of the Persian empire ('Javan'—the Greeks) by Alexander.
10 a. Teraphim, often the word for a household god, here means instruments of divination.
b. Future leaders who will rise from the people.

they will fight, since Yahweh is with them,
and the riders of horses will be thrown into confusion.

And I will make the House of Judah mighty,   6
and the House of Joseph victorious.
I am going to restore them, because I have taken pity on them,
and they shall be as though I had never cast them off
(for I am Yahweh their God and I mean to answer their prayer).

Ephraim will be like a hero.   7
Their hearts will be cheered as though by wine.
Their sons will look on this in gladness,
their hearts will exult in Yahweh.

I am going to whistle to them and gather them in   8
(for I have redeemed them);
they will be as numerous as they used to be.
I have scattered them among the peoples   9
but from far away they will remember me
(they will teach their sons, and these will return).
I mean to bring them back from the land of Egypt,   10
and gather them from Assyria;
I shall lead them into the land of Gilead (and Lebanon),
and even that will not be large enough for them.
They will pass through the sea of Egypt   11
(and he will strike the waves on the sea);
all the depths of the Nile will be dried up.
The arrogance of Assyria will be cast down
and the sceptre of Egypt be taken away.

Their strength will be in Yahweh;   12
in his name they will glory:
it is Yahweh who speaks.

11   Open your gateways, Lebanon,   1
and let the fire burn down your cedars.
(Wail, cypress,   2
for felled is the cedar,
the mighty ones have been brought low!)
Wail, oaks of Bashan,
for the impenetrable forest has been felled!
The wailing of the shepherds is heard;   3
their glorious pastures have been ruined.
The roaring of the young lions is heard;
the thickets of the Jordan have been laid waste.

The two shepherds

This is how Yahweh spoke to me, 'Pasture the sheep bred for slaughter, • whose $^4_5$
buyers kill them and go unpunished, whose sellers say of them, "Blessed be
Yahweh; now I am rich!" and their shepherds handle^a them without kindness.
(For no longer am I going to show kindness to the inhabitants of the world—it is 6
Yahweh who speaks. But instead I mean to hand over every man to the next,
and to his king. They shall devastate the world and I will not deliver them
from their hands.)' • Then I began to pasture these sheep bred for slaughter for 7
the sheepdealers. I took two staves: one I called Goodwill, the other Union.
And so I began to pasture the sheep. • I dismissed the three shepherds in one 8
month.^{b} But I began to dislike the sheep, and they equally detested me. • I then 9
said, 'I am going to pasture you no longer; let those that wish to die, die; let
those that wish to perish, perish; and let those that are left devour each other's

10 flesh!' •I then took my staff, Goodwill, and broke it in half, to break the covenant
11 Yahweh had made with all the peoples.ᶜ •When it was broken, that day the
    dealers, who were watching me, realised that this had been a word of Yahweh.
12 I then said to them, 'If you think it right, give me my wages; if not, never mind'.
13 And they weighed out my wages: thirty shekels of silver.ᵈ •But Yahweh told me,
    'Throw it into the treasury, this princely sum at which they have valued me'.
    Taking the thirty shekels of silver, I threw them into the Temple of Yahweh,
14 into the treasury. •I then broke my second staff, Union, in half, to break the
    brotherhood between Judah and Israel.ᵉ
15   Next, Yahweh said to me, 'Now take the gear of an incompetent shepherd.
16 For I am now going to raise an incompetent shepherd in this country. He will
    not bother about the lost; he will not look for the stray; he will not heal the
    wounded; he will not support the weary; but he will only eat the flesh of the fat
    beasts and tear off their hoofs.

17   'Trouble is coming to the worthless shepherd
                   who deserts the flock!
                   May the sword strike his arm
                   and his right eye!
                   May his arm wither entirely,
                   may his eye be totally blinded!'

The deliverance and restoration of Jerusalem

1 **12** An oracle. The word of Yahweh about Israel. It is Yahweh who speaks,
         who spread out the heaven and founded the earth and formed the spirit
    of man within him:
2   'Look, I am going to make Jerusalem an intoxicating cup to all the surrounding
    peoples. . .
3   'When that day comes, I mean to make Jerusalem a stone to be lifted by all
    the peoples; all who try to lift it will hurt themselves severely. (And all the
4 nations of the earth will mass against her.) •When that day comes—it is Yahweh
    who speaks—I intend to strike all the horses with confusion and their riders
    with madness. (But on the House of Judah I will open my eyes.) And I will strike
5 all the horses of the peoples with blindness. •Then the clans of Judah will say
    in their hearts, "Strength for the citizens of Jerusalem is in Yahweh Sabaoth
6 their God". •When that day comes I mean to make the clans of Judah like a
    brazier burning in a pile of wood, like a flaming torch in stubble; and they will
    consume the peoples round them to right and left. And Jerusalem shall stand
7 firm in her place. •Yahweh will save the tents of Judah first to forestall the
    arrogance of the House of David and the arrogance of the citizens of Jerusalem
8 from rising to the detriment of Judah. •When that day comes, Yahweh will
    spread his protection over the citizens of Jerusalem; the one among them who
    was about to fall will be like David on that day, and the House of David will
    be like God (like the angel of Yahweh) at their head.
9   'When that day comes, I shall set myself to destroy all the nations who
10 advance against Jerusalem. •But over the House of David and the citizens of
    Jerusalem I will pour out a spirit of kindness and prayer. They will look on the
    one whom they have pierced; they will mourn for him as for an only son, and
11 weep for him as people weep for a first-born child. •When that day comes, there
    will be great mourning in Judah, like the mourning of Hadad-rimmon in the
12 plain of Megiddo. •And the country will mourn clan by clan; the clan of the
13 House of David apart, with their wives by themselves; •the clan of the House

---

11 a. Buyers and sellers are the Jewish ruling classes; the shepherds are the priests.
b. Alluding to a succession of high priests deposed.   **c.** Yahweh no longer undertakes to protect
the Jewish nation from its neighbours.   **d.** The price of a slave.   **e.** Probably the schism of
the Samaritans, who built a rival temple on Mount Gerizim in 328.

of Nathan apart, with their wives by themselves; the clan of the House of Levi
apart, with their wives by themselves; the clan of Shimei apart, with their
wives by themselves. •All the clans that remain, clan by clan, with their wives 14
by themselves. 13 When that day comes, a fountain will be opened for the House 1
of David and the citizens of Jerusalem, for sin and impurity.

'When that day comes—it is Yahweh (Sabaoth) who speaks—I am going to 2
root out the names of the idols from the country, and they shall never be
mentioned again; and I will also rid the country of the prophets, and of the
spirit of impurity. •If anyone still wants to prophesy, his father and the mother 3
who gave him birth shall say to him, "You have no right to live, since you utter
lies in the name of Yahweh". And while he is prophesying, his father and the
mother who gave him birth shall run him through. •When that day comes, 4
every prophet shall be ashamed of his prophetic vision; they will no longer put
on their hair cloaks to utter their lies, •but they will all say, "I am no prophet. 5
I am a peasant; the land has been my living ever since I was a boy." •And if 6
anyone asks him, "Then what are these wounds on your body?" he will reply,
" These I received in the house of my friends".

Invocation to the sword; the new people

'Awake, sword, against my shepherd   7
and against the man who is my companion—
it is Yahweh Sabaoth who speaks.
I am going to strike the shepherd
so that the sheep may be scattered,
and I will turn my hand against the weak.
And it will happen throughout this territory—   8
it is Yahweh who speaks—
that two-thirds in it will be cut off ('will be killed')
and the remaining third will be left.
I will lead that third into the fire,   9
and refine them as silver is refined,
test them as gold is tested.
They will call on my name
and I shall listen;
and I shall say: These are my people;
and each will say, "Yahweh is my God!"'

The eschatological battle; the splendour of Jerusalem

14 See, a day is coming for Yahweh when the spoils taken from you will 1
be divided among you. •Yahweh will gather all the nations to Jerusalem 2
for battle. The city will be taken, the houses plundered, the women ravished.
Half the city will go into captivity, but the remnant of the people will not be
cut off from the city. •Then Yahweh will take the field; he will fight against 3
these nations as he fights in the day of battle. •On that day, his feet will rest on 4
the Mount of Olives, which faces Jerusalem from the east. The Mount of Olives
will be split in half from east to west, forming a huge gorge; half the Mount
will recede northwards, the other half southwards. •And the Vale of Hinnom will 5
be filled up from Goah to Jasol; it will be blocked as it was by the earthquake
in the days of Uzziah king of Judah. Yahweh your God will come, and all the
holy ones with him.

When that day comes, there will be no more cold, no more frost. •It will $^6_7$
be a day of wonder—Yahweh knows it—with no alternation of day and night;
in the evening it will be light. •When that day comes, running waters will issue 8
from Jerusalem, half of them to the eastern sea, half of them to the western
sea; they will flow summer and winter. •And Yahweh will be king of the whole 9
world. When that day comes, Yahweh will be unique and his name unique. •The 10

entire country will be transformed into plain, from Geba to Rimmon in the Negeb. And Jerusalem will be raised higher, though still in the same place; from the Gate of Benjamin to the site of the First Gate, that is to say to the Gate of the Corner and from the Tower of Hananel to the king's winepress,

11 people will make their homes. The ban will be lifted; Jerusalem will be safe to live in.

12 And this is the plague with which Yahweh will strike all the nations who have fought against Jerusalem; their flesh will moulder while they are still standing on their feet; their eyes will rot in their sockets; their tongues will

15 rot in their mouths. •And such will be the plague on the horses and mules,

13 camels and donkeys, and all the animals to be found in that camp. •When that day comes, a great terror will fall on them from Yahweh; each man will grab

14 his neighbour's hand and they will hit out at each other. •Even Judah will fight against Jerusalem. The wealth of all the surrounding nations will be heaped together: gold, silver, clothing, in vast quantity.

16 All who survive of all the nations that have marched against Jerusalem will go up year by year to worship the King, Yahweh Sabaoth, and to keep the feast

17 of Tabernacles. •Should one of the races of the world fail to go up to Jerusalem

18 to worship the King, Yahweh Sabaoth, there will be no rain for that one. •Should the race of Egypt fail to go up and pay its visit, on it will fall the plague which Yahweh will inflict on each one of those nations that fail to go up to keep the

19 feast of Tabernacles. •Such shall be the punishment for Egypt and for all the

20 nations that fail to go up to keep the feast of Tabernacles. •When that day comes, the horse bells will be inscribed with the words, 'Sacred to Yahweh', and in the Temple of Yahweh the very cooking pots will be as fine as the sprinkling

21 bowls at the altar. •And every cooking pot in Jerusalem and in Judah shall become sacred to Yahweh Sabaoth; all who want to offer sacrifice will come and help themselves from them for their cooking; there will be no more traders in the Temple of Yahweh Sabaoth, when that day comes.

MALACHI

1

An oracle. 1
The word of Yahweh to Israel through the ministration of Malachi.[a]

The love of Yahweh for Israel

I have shown my love for you, says Yahweh. But you ask, 'How have you 2
shown your love?' Was not Esau[b] Jacob's brother?—it is Yahweh who speaks;
yet I showed my love for Jacob •and my hatred for Esau. I turned his towns into 3
a wilderness and his heritage into desert pastures. •Should Edom say, 'We 4
have been struck down but we will rebuild our ruins', this is the reply of Yahweh
Sabaoth: Let them build! I will pull down. They shall be known as Unholy
Land and Nation-with-which-Yahweh-is-angry-for-ever. •Your eyes are 5
going to see this and you will say, 'Yahweh is mighty beyond the borders
of Israel'.

An indictment of the priests

The son honours his father, the slave respects his master. If I am indeed 6
father, where is my honour? If I am indeed master, where is my respect? Yahweh
Sabaoth asks this of you, priests, you who despise my name. You ask, 'How
have we despised your name?' •By putting polluted food on my altar. You ask, 7
'How have we polluted it?' By holding the table of Yahweh in contempt. •When 8
you bring blind animals for sacrifice, is that not wrong? When you bring the
lame and the diseased, is that not wrong? Try offering them to your high commissioner, and see if he is pleased with this or receives you graciously, says Yahweh
Sabaoth. •Now try pleading with God to take pity on us (this is your own fault); 9
do you think he will receive you graciously? says Yahweh Sabaoth. •Oh, is 10
there no one among you who will shut the doors and stop you from lighting
useless fires on my altar? I am not pleased with you, says Yahweh Sabaoth;
from your hands I find no offerings acceptable. •But from farthest east to farthest 11
west my name is honoured among the nations and everywhere a sacrifice of
incense is offered to my name, and a pure offering too, since my name is
honoured among the nations, says Yahweh Sabaoth. •But you, you profane it 12
by thinking of the Lord's table as defiled and by holding in contempt the food
placed on it. •'How tiresome it all is!' you say; and you sniff disdainfully at 13
me, says Yahweh Sabaoth. You bring a stolen, lame or diseased animal, you
bring that as an offering! Am I to accept this from your hand? says Yahweh
Sabaoth. •Cursed be the rogue who owns a male which he has vowed to offer 14
from his flock, and instead sacrifices a blemished animal to me! For I am a great
king, says Yahweh Sabaoth, and my name is feared throughout the nations.
2 And now, priests, this warning is for you. •If you do not listen, if you do ½
not find it in your heart to glorify my name, says Yahweh Sabaoth, I will
send the curse on you and curse your very blessing.[a] Indeed I have already
cursed it, since there is not a single one of you who takes this to heart. •Now 3
watch how I am going to paralyse your arm and throw dung in your face—the
dung from your very solemnities—and sweep you away with it. •Then you 4

shall learn that it is I who have given you this warning of my intention to abolish
5 my covenant with Levi, says Yahweh Sabaoth. •My covenant was with him:
it stood for life and peace, and these were what I gave him; it stood for fear
6 and trembling, and he respected me and stood in awe of my name. •The teaching
of truth was in his mouth, falsehood was not to be found on his lips; he walked
7 with me in integrity and virtue; he converted many from sinning. •The
lips of the priest ought to safeguard knowledge; his mouth is where instruction
8 should be sought, since he is the messenger of Yahweh Sabaoth. •But you,
you have strayed from the way; you have caused many to stumble by your
teaching. You have destroyed the covenant of Levi, says Yahweh Sabaoth.
9 And so I in my turn have made you contemptible and vile in the eyes of the
whole people in repayment for the way you have not kept to my paths but have
shown partiality in your administration.

Mixed marriage and divorce

10   Have we not all one Father? Did not one God create us? Why, then, do we
11 break faith with one another, profaning the covenant of our ancestors? •Judah
has broken faith: a detestable thing has been done (in Israel and) in Jerusalem.
Yes, Judah has profaned the sanctuary that Yahweh loves. He has married
12 the daughter of an alien god. •The man who does this—whoever he be—may
Yahweh cut him off from the tents of Jacob and from the company of those
13 who present the offering to Yahweh Sabaoth. •And here is something else you
do: you cover the altar of Yahweh with tears, with weeping and wailing, because
14 he now refuses to consider the offering or to accept it from your hands. •And
you ask, 'Why?' It is because Yahweh stands as witness between you and the
wife of your youth, the wife with whom you have broken faith, even though
15 she was your partner and your wife by covenant. •Did he not create a single
being that has flesh and the breath of life? And what is this single being destined
for? God-given offspring. Be careful for your own life, therefore, and do not
16 break faith with the wife of your youth. •For I hate divorce, says Yahweh the
God of Israel, and I hate people to parade their sins on their cloaks, says
Yahweh Sabaoth. Respect your own life, therefore, and do not break faith like
this.

The day of Yahweh

17   You weary Yahweh with your talk. You ask, 'How do we weary him?' When
you say, 'Any evil-doer is good as far as Yahweh is concerned; indeed he likes
1 them best'; or when you say, 'Where is the God of justice now?' 3 Look, I am
going to send my messenger to prepare a way before me. And the Lord you
are seeking will suddenly enter his Temple; and the angel of the covenant
2 whom you are longing for, yes, he is coming, says Yahweh Sabaoth. •Who will be
able to resist the day of his coming? Who will remain standing when he appears?
3 For he is like the refiner's fire and the fullers' alkali. •He will take his seat
as refiner and purifier; he will purify the sons of Levi and refine them like
gold and silver, and then they will make the offering to Yahweh as it should be
4 made. •The offering of Judah and Jerusalem will then be welcomed by Yahweh
5 as in former days, as in the years of old. •I mean to visit you for the
judgement and I am going to be a ready witness against sorcerer, adulterer
and perjurer, against those who oppress the wage-earner, the widow and the
orphan, and who rob the settler of his rights—no need for you to be afraid of
me, says Yahweh Sabaoth.

1 a. 'Malachi' means 'my messenger' and is probably not a proper name.   b. The ancestor
of Edom.
2 a. The 'blessing' of the priests is the levitical revenue.

Temple tithes

No; I, Yahweh, do not change; and you, sons of Jacob, you are not ruined 6
yet! •Since the days of your ancestors you have evaded my statutes and not 7
observed them. Return to me and I will return to you, says Yahweh Sabaoth.
You ask, 'How are we to return? •Can a man cheat God?' Yet you are cheating 8
me. You ask, 'How are we cheating you?' In the matter of tithes and
dues. •The curse lies on you because you, yes you the whole nation, are cheating 9
me. •Bring the full tithes and dues to the storehouse so that there may be food 10
in my house, and then see if I do not open the floodgates of heaven for you and
pour out blessing for you in abundance. •For your sake I will lay a strict 11
injunction on the locust not to destroy the fruits of your soil nor to make the
vine in your fields barren, says Yahweh Sabaoth. •All the nations will call 12
you blessed, for you will be a land of delights, says Yahweh Sabaoth.

The triumph of the virtuous on the day of Yahweh

You say harsh things about me, says Yahweh. You ask, 'What have we said 13
against you?' •You say, 'It is useless to serve God; what is the good of keeping 14
his commands or of walking mournfully before Yahweh Sabaoth? •Now we 15
have reached the point when we call the arrogant blessed; yes, they prosper,
these evil-doers; they try God's patience and yet go free.' •This is what those 16
who fear Yahweh used to say to one another. But Yahweh took note and heard
them: a book of remembrance was written in his presence recording those who
fear him and take refuge in his name. •On the day which I am preparing, says 17
Yahweh Sabaoth, they are going to be my own special possession. I will make
allowances for them as a man makes allowances for the son who obeys him.
Then once again you will see the difference between an upright man and a wicked 18
one, between the one who serves God and the one who does not serve him.
For the day is coming now, burning like a furnace; and all the arrogant and $^{19}_{4:1}$
the evil-doers will be like stubble. The day that is coming is going to burn them
up, says Yahweh Sabaoth, leaving them neither root nor stalk. •But for you who $^{20}_{2}$
fear my name, the sun of righteousness will shine out with healing in its rays;
you will leap like calves going out to pasture. •You will trample on the wicked, $^{21}_{3}$
who will be like ashes under your feet on the day I am preparing, says Yahweh
Sabaoth.

Appendices

Remember the Law of my servant Moses to whom at Horeb I prescribed $^{22}_{4}$
laws and customs for the whole of Israel. •Know that I am going to send you $^{23}_{5}$
Elijah the prophet before my day comes, that great and terrible day. •He shall $^{24}_{6}$
turn the hearts of fathers towards their children and the hearts of children
towards their fathers, lest I come and strike the land with a curse.

THE NEW
TESTAMENT

INTRODUCTION TO
THE SYNOPTIC GOSPELS

The first three gospels are called synoptic ('with the same eye') because their narratives are all built on the same events in the life of Jesus and indeed many passages from all three of them can be placed side by side as evident parallels. From the earliest times, Matthew, Mark and Luke respectively have been named as the writers of them.

According to a tradition dating from the 2nd century, St Matthew was the first to write a gospel and he wrote 'in the Hebrew tongue'. Our Greek 'Gospel according to St Matthew' is not identified with this early Aramaic book, which is lost, though there are times when it appears to represent a more primitive text than Mark.

Some parts of the gospel story assumed a fixed and stereotyped pattern in the oral tradition founded on the preaching of the apostles; the similarity of the Passion in all four gospels suggests a common oral tradition very firmly fixed. But the relationships between the three synoptic gospels are too close and too complex to be explained by a common oral tradition underlying all of them. It is clear that Luke depends on Mark, and although it was held for a long time that Mark depends on Matthew, a number of indications now suggest the reverse. Luke and Matthew also have a number of non-Marcan passages common to both, and these probably have a common source or sources; in addition, each of these gospels includes episodes and sayings not found in the other.

Mark, said to have been Peter's interpreter, is mentioned in St Paul's letters as one of his companions, and described in Acts as a disciple from Jerusalem. Luke is also mentioned in St Paul's letters and when writing Acts incorporated parts of a first-person travel diary. Mark's gospel can be dated before A.D. 70, perhaps about 64. Our Greek Matthew and Luke are later and probably date from 70-80.

The arrangement and presentation of the historical facts in the synoptic gospels are dictated by the purposes of a written gospel: to convert, to edify, to infuse faith, to enlighten it and defend it against its opponents.

Mark

The shortest of the gospels, it is not concerned with elaborating Christ's teaching and it records few of his sayings; the real point of its message is *the manifestation of the crucified Messiah*. While on the one hand Jesus is seen by the writer as the Son of God, acknowledged by the Father and vindicating his power and his mission by miracles, on the other hand he chooses to appear to the world under the mysterious title 'Son of Man', and the gospel puts great emphasis on his apparent frustration and rejection by the people. The 'messianic secret' is a basic idea of Mark's gospel.

Matthew

This gospel is divided into five books, each consisting of a discourse introduced by painstakingly selected narrative matter which follows the same broad outline as in Mark. These are preceded by the story of the Infancy and followed by that of the Passion. The fact that this gospel reports Christ's teaching much more fully than Mark and stresses especially the theme of the 'kingdom of heaven' makes it *a dramatic account in seven acts of the coming of the kingdom*. Matthew, writing for Jewish Christians, makes a special point of demonstrating, by the use of Old Testament quotations, that *the scriptures are fulfilled* in the person and work of Jesus.

Luke

The plan of this gospel follows Mark's outline as a rule, but the narrative is controlled and edited to bring in much teaching, including the longer parables, and to omit episodes that would not interest Luke's non-Jewish readers. The originality of Luke is in *his religious mentality*: he is the faithful recorder of Christ's lovingkindness, he emphasises the necessity for prayer and he is the only one of the synoptic authors to give the Holy Spirit the prominence which we find in Paul and in Acts.

Greek style

Mark's Greek is rough, strongly Aramaic and often faulty, but it is fresh and frank. Matthew's Greek is also rather Aramaic but smoother and more correct than Mark's, though less picturesque. Luke's style is variable: excellent when he is writing independently but at other times incorporating the peculiarities of his sources; as in Acts he suits the style to the subject and occasionally he goes out of his way to give a good imitation of Septuagint Greek.

THE GOSPEL ACCORDING TO
SAINT MATTHEW

I. THE BIRTH AND INFANCY OF JESUS

● The ancestry of Jesus

1 **1** A genealogy of Jesus Christ, son of David, son of Abraham:[a]

2   Abraham was the father of Isaac,
    Isaac the father of Jacob,
    Jacob the father of Judah and his brothers,

3   Judah was the father of Perez and Zerah, Tamar being their mother,
    Perez was the father of Hezron,
    Hezron the father of Ram,

4   Ram was the father of Amminadab,
    Amminadab the father of Nahshon,
    Nahshon the father of Salmon,

5   Salmon was the father of Boaz, Rahab being his mother,
    Boaz was the father of Obed, Ruth being his mother,
    Obed was the father of Jesse;

6   and Jesse was the father of King David.

    David was the father of Solomon, whose mother had been
        Uriah's wife,

7   Solomon was the father of Rehoboam,
    Rehoboam the father of Abijah,
    Abijah the father of Asa,

8   Asa was the father of Jehoshaphat,
    Jehoshaphat the father of Joram,
    Joram the father of Azariah,

9   Azariah was the father of Jotham,
    Jotham the father of Ahaz,
    Ahaz the father of Hezekiah,

10   Hezekiah was the father of Manasseh,
    Manasseh the father of Amon,
    Amon the father of Josiah,

11   and Josiah was the father of Jechoniah and his brothers.
    Then the deportation to Babylon took place.

12   After the deportation to Babylon:
    Jechoniah was the father of Shealtiel,
    Shealtiel the father of Zerubbabel,

13   Zerubbabel was the father of Abiud,
    Abiud the father of Eliakim,
    Eliakim the father of Azor,

---

1 a. Showing the descent of Joseph, legally the father of Jesus, from Abraham and David, to whom the messianic promises were made.

Azor was the father of Zadok,   14
Zadok the father of Achim,
Achim the father of Eliud,
Eliud was the father of Eleazar,   15
Eleazar the father of Matthan,
Matthan the father of Jacob;
    and Jacob was the father of Joseph the husband of Mary;   16
    of her was born Jesus who is called Christ.

The sum of generations is therefore: fourteen from Abraham to David; 17
fourteen from David to the Babylonian deportation; and fourteen from the
Babylonian deportation to Christ.

The virginal conception of Christ

This is how Jesus Christ came to be born. His mother Mary was betrothed 18
to Joseph;[b] but before they came to live together she was found to be with child
through the Holy Spirit. •Her husband Joseph, being a man of honour and 19
wanting to spare her publicity, decided to divorce her informally. •He had 20
made up his mind to do this when the angel of the Lord appeared to him in
a dream and said, 'Joseph son of David, do not be afraid to take Mary home
as your wife, because she has conceived what is in her by the Holy Spirit. •She 21
will give birth to a son and you must name him Jesus, because he is the one who
is to save[c] his people from their sins.' •Now all this took place to fulfil the words 22
spoken by the Lord through the prophet:

> *The virgin will conceive and give birth to a son*   23
> *and they will call him Immanuel,[d]*

a name which means 'God-is-with-us'. •When Joseph woke up he did what the 24
angel of the Lord had told him to do: he took his wife to his home •and, though 25
he had not had intercourse with her, she gave birth to a son; and he named him
Jesus.

The visit of the Magi

2 After Jesus had been born at Bethlehem in Judaea during the reign of King 1
Herod,[a] some wise men came to Jerusalem from the east. •'Where is the infant 2
king of the Jews?' they asked. 'We saw his star as it rose[b] and have come to do him
homage.' •When King Herod heard this he was perturbed, and so was the whole 3
of Jerusalem. •He called together all the chief priests and the scribes of the people, 4
and enquired of them where the Christ was to be born. •'At Bethlehem in Judaea,' 5
they told him 'for this is what the prophet wrote:

> *And you, Bethlehem, in the land of Judah,*   6
> *you are by no means least among the leaders of Judah,*
> *for out of you will come a leader*
> *who will shepherd my people Israel'.[c]*

Then Herod summoned the wise men to see him privately. He asked them the 7
exact date on which the star had appeared, •and sent them on to Bethlehem. 8
'Go and find out all about the child,' he said 'and when you have found him,
let me know, so that I too may go and do him homage.' •Having listened to 9
what the king had to say, they set out. And there in front of them was the star
they had seen rising; it went forward and halted over the place where the child
was. •The sight of the star filled them with delight, •and going into the house 10/11
they saw the child with his mother Mary, and falling to their knees they did him
homage. Then, opening their treasures, they offered him gifts of gold and
frankincense and myrrh.[d] •But they were warned in a dream not to go back to 12
Herod, and returned to their own country by a different way.

The flight into Egypt. The massacre of the Innocents

13 After they had left, the angel of the Lord appeared to Joseph in a dream and said, 'Get up, take the child and his mother with you, and escape into Egypt,
14 and stay there until I tell you, because Herod intends to search for the child and do away with him'. •So Joseph got up and, taking the child and his mother
15 with him, left that night for Egypt, •where they stayed until Herod was dead. This was to fulfil what the Lord had spoken through the prophet:

> I called my son out of Egypt.[e]

16 Herod was furious when he realised that he had been outwitted by the wise men, and in Bethlehem and its surrounding district he had all the male children killed who were two years old or under, reckoning by the date he
17 had been careful to ask the wise men. •It was then that the words spoken through the prophet Jeremiah were fulfilled:

18
> A voice was heard in Ramah,
> sobbing and loudly lamenting:
> it was Rachel weeping for her children,
> refusing to be comforted
> because they were no more.[f]

From Egypt to Nazareth

19 After Herod's death, the angel of the Lord appeared in a dream to Joseph in
20 Egypt •and said, 'Get up, take the child and his mother with you and go back to
21 the land of Israel, for those who wanted to kill the child are dead'. •So Joseph got up and, taking the child and his mother with him, went back to the land of Israel.
22 But when he learnt that Archelaus[g] had succeeded his father Herod as ruler of Judaea he was afraid to go there, and being warned in a dream he left for the
23 region of Galilee.[h] •There he settled in a town called Nazareth. In this way the words spoken through the prophets were to be fulfilled:

> He will be called a Nazarene.

II. THE KINGDOM OF HEAVEN PROCLAIMED

A. NARRATIVE SECTION

The preaching of John the Baptist

1 3 In due course John the Baptist appeared; he preached in the wilderness of
2   Judaea and this was his message: •'Repent, for the kingdom of heaven[a] is
3 close at hand'. •This was the man the prophet Isaiah spoke of when he said:

> A voice cries in the wilderness:
> Prepare a way for the Lord,
> make his paths straight.[b]

4 This man John wore a garment made of camel-hair with a leather belt round his
5 waist, and his food was locusts and wild honey. •Then Jerusalem and all Judaea
6 and the whole Jordan district made their way to him, •and as they were baptised

b. In a Jewish betrothal the man was already called the 'husband' of the woman, and he could release himself from the engagement only by an act of repudiation, v. 19.   c. 'Jesus' (Hebr. Yehoshua) means 'Yahweh saves'.   d. Is. 7:14
2 a. About 5 or 4 B.C. Herod was king of Judaea, Idumaea and Samaria from 37-4 B.C.
b. 'In the east' is an alternative translation, here and in v. 9.   c. Mi 5:1   d. The wealth and perfumes of Arabia.   e. Ho 11:1   f. Jr 31:15   g. Ethnarch of Judaea, 4 B.C. to A.D. 6.
h. The territory of Herod Antipas.
3 a. 'kingdom of God'; Mt's phrase reflects the Jewish scruple against using the name of God.
b. Is 40:3

by him in the river Jordan they confessed their sins. •But when he saw a 7
number of Pharisees and Sadducees[e] coming for baptism he said to them,
'Brood of vipers, who warned you to fly from the retribution that is coming? 8
But if you are repentant, produce the appropriate fruit, •and do not presume to 9
tell yourselves, "We have Abraham for our father", because, I tell you, God can
raise children for Abraham from these stones. •Even now the axe is laid to the roots 10
of the trees, so that any tree which fails to produce good fruit will be cut down
and thrown on the fire. •I baptise you in water for repentance, but the one who 11
follows me is more powerful than I am, and I am not fit to carry his sandals; he
will baptise you with the Holy Spirit and fire. •His winnowing-fan is in his hand; 12
he will clear his threshing-floor and gather his wheat into the barn; but the chaff
he will burn in a fire that will never go out.'

Jesus is baptised

Then Jesus appeared: he came from Galilee to the Jordan to be baptised by 13
John. •John tried to dissuade him. 'It is I who need baptism from you' he said 14
'and yet you come to me!' •But Jesus replied, 'Leave it like this for the time being; 15
it is fitting that we should, in this way, do all that righteousness demands'. At this,
John gave in to him.

As soon as Jesus was baptised he came up from the water, and suddenly the 16
heavens opened and he saw the Spirit of God descending like a dove and coming
down on him. •And a voice spoke from heaven, 'This is my Son, the Beloved; 17
my favour rests on him'.

Temptation in the wilderness

4 Then Jesus was led by the Spirit out into the wilderness to be tempted by the 1
devil. •He fasted for forty days and forty nights, after which he was very 2
hungry, •and the tempter came and said to him, 'If you are the Son of God, tell 3
these stones to turn into loaves'. •But he replied, 'Scripture says: 4

> *Man does not live on bread alone*
> *but on every word that comes from the mouth of God'.[a]*

The devil then took him to the holy city and made him stand on the parapet of 5
the Temple. •'If you are the Son of God' he said 'throw yourself down; for 6
scripture says:

> *He will put you in his angels' charge,*
> *and they will support you on their hands*
> *in case you hurt your foot against a stone'.[b]*

Jesus said to him, 'Scripture also says: 7

> *You must not put the Lord your God to the test'.[c]*

Next, taking him to a very high mountain, the devil showed him all the kingdoms 8
of the world and their splendour. •'I will give you all these' he said, 'if you fall at 9
my feet and worship me.' •Then Jesus replied, 'Be off, Satan! For scripture says: 10

> *You must worship the Lord your God,*
> *and serve him alone.'[d]*

Then the devil left him, and angels appeared and looked after him. 11

Return to Galilee

Hearing that John had been arrested he went back to Galilee, •and leaving 12 13
Nazareth he went and settled in Capernaum, a lakeside town on the borders of
Zebulun and Naphtali. •In this way the prophecy of Isaiah was to be fulfilled: 14

> *Land of Zebulun! Land of Naphtali!* 15
> *Way of the sea on the far side of Jordan,*

Galilee of the nations!
16 *The people that lived in darkness*
    has seen a great light;
    on those who dwell in the land and shadow of death
    a light has dawned.[e]

17 From that moment Jesus began his preaching with the message, 'Repent, for
the kingdom of heaven is close at hand'.

The first four disciples are called

18 As he was walking by the Sea of Galilee he saw two brothers, Simon, who
was called Peter, and his brother Andrew; they were making a cast in the lake
19 with their net, for they were fishermen. •And he said to them, 'Follow me and I
20 will make you fishers of men'. •And they left their nets at once and followed him.

21 Going on from there he saw another pair of brothers, James son of Zebedee
and his brother John; they were in their boat with their father Zebedee, mending
22 their nets, and he called them. •At once, leaving the boat and their father, they
followed him.

Jesus preaches and heals the sick

23 He went round the whole of Galilee teaching in their synagogues, proclaiming
the Good News of the kingdom and curing all kinds of diseases and sickness
24 among the people. •His fame spread throughout Syria,[f] and those who were
suffering from diseases and painful complaints of one kind or another, the
possessed, epileptics, the paralysed, were all brought to him, and he cured them.
25 Large crowds followed him, coming from Galilee, the Decapolis,[g] Jerusalem,
Judaea and Transjordania.

B. THE SERMON ON THE MOUNT[a]

The Beatitudes

1 **5** Seeing the crowds, he went up the hill. There he sat down and was joined by
2   his disciples. •Then he began to speak. This is what he taught them:

3   'How happy are the poor in spirit;
               theirs is the kingdom of heaven.
4   Happy *the gentle:*[b]
               they shall have the earth for their heritage.
5   Happy those who mourn:
               they shall be comforted.
6   Happy those who hunger and thirst for what is right:
               they shall be satisfied.
7   Happy the merciful:
               they shall have mercy shown them.
8   Happy the pure in heart:
               they shall see God.
9   Happy the peacemakers:
               they shall be called sons of God.
10   Happy those who are persecuted in the cause of right:
               theirs is the kingdom of heaven.

c. Pharisees: members of a Jewish sect known for its strict observance of the Law as it was
interpreted and developed by their rabbis. Sadducees: conservatives who observed the written
form of the Law in the scriptures.
4 a. Dt 8:3   b. Ps 91:11-12   c. Dt 6:16   d. Dt 6:13   e. Is 8:23-9:1   f. I.e. Galilee and
the districts listed in v. 25.   g. The 'ten towns', a region south-east of Galilee.
5 a. In this discourse, which occupies three ch. of this gospel, Mt has included sayings which
probably originated on other occasions (cf. their parallels in Lk).   b. Or 'the lowly'; the word
comes from the Greek version of Ps 37.

R.E.—Y*

'Happy are you when people abuse you and persecute you and speak all kinds 11
of calumny against you on my account. •Rejoice and be glad, for your reward will 12
be great in heaven; this is how they persecuted the prophets before you.

Salt of the earth and light of the world

'You are the salt of the earth. But if salt becomes tasteless, what can make it 13
salty again? It is good for nothing, and can only be thrown out to be trampled
underfoot by men.

'You are the light of the world. A city built on a hill-top cannot be hidden. 14
No one lights a lamp to put it under a tub; they put it on the lamp-stand where 15
it shines for everyone in the house. •In the same way your light must shine in the 16
sight of men, so that, seeing your good works, they may give the praise to your
Father in heaven.

The fulfilment of the Law

'Do not imagine that I have come to abolish the Law or the Prophets. I have 17
come not to abolish but to complete them. •I tell you solemnly, till heaven 18
and earth disappear, not one dot, not one little stroke, shall disappear from
the Law until its purpose is achieved. •Therefore, the man who infringes even 19
one of the least of these commandments and teaches others to do the same will
be considered the least in the kingdom of heaven; but the man who keeps them
and teaches them will be considered great in the kingdom of heaven.

The new standard higher than the old

'For I tell you, if your virtue goes no deeper than that of the scribes and 20
Pharisees, you will never get into the kingdom of heaven.

'You have learnt how it was said to our ancestors: *You must not kill;*[c] and if 21
anyone does kill he must answer for it before the court. •But I say this to you: 22
anyone who is angry with his brother will answer for it before the court; if a man
calls his brother "Fool"[d] he will answer for it before the Sanhedrin;[e] and if a man
calls him "Renegade"[f] he will answer for it in hell fire. •So then, if you are bringing 23
your offering to the altar and there remember that your brother has something
against you, •leave your offering there before the altar, go and be reconciled with 24
your brother first, and then come back and present your offering. •Come to terms 25
with your opponent in good time while you are still on the way to the court with
him, or he may hand you over to the judge and the judge to the officer, and you
will be thrown into prison. •I tell you solemnly, you will not get out till you have 26
paid the last penny.

'You have learnt how it was said: *You must not commit adultery.*[c] •But I say 27
this to you: if a man looks at a woman lustfully, he has already committed 28
adultery with her in his heart. •If your right eye should cause you to sin, tear it out 29
and throw it away; for it will do you less harm to lose one part of you than to
have your whole body thrown into hell. •And if your right hand should cause 30
you to sin, cut it off and throw it away; for it will do you less harm to lose one part
of you than to have your whole body go to hell.

'It has also been said: *Anyone who divorces his wife must give her a writ of* 31
dismissal.[h] •But I say this to you: everyone who divorces his wife, except for the 32
case of fornication, makes her an adulteress; and anyone who marries a divorced
woman commits adultery.

'Again, you have learnt how it was said to our ancestors: *You must not break* 33
your oath, but must fulfil your oaths to the Lord.[i] •But I say this to you: do not 34
swear at all, either by *heaven*, since that is God's throne; •or by *the earth*, since 35
that is *his footstool;* or by Jerusalem, since that is *the city of the great king.* •Do not 36
swear by your own head either, since you cannot turn a single hair white or black.
All you need say is "Yes" if you mean yes, "No" if you mean no; anything more 37
than this comes from the evil one.

₃₈
₃₉ 'You have learnt how jt was said: *Eye for eye and tooth for tooth.*ʲ •But I say this to you: offer the wicked man no resistance. On the contrary, if anyone hits
40 you on the right cheek, offer him the other as well; •if a man takes you to law
41 and would have your tunic, let him have your cloak as well. •And if anyone
42 orders you to go one mile, go two miles with him. •Give to anyone who asks, and if anyone wants to borrow, do not turn away.

43 'You have learnt how it was said: *You must love your neighbour* and hate your
44 enemy.ᵏ •But I say this to you: love your enemies and pray for those who
45 persecute you; •in this way you will be sons of your Father in heaven, for he causes his sun to rise on bad men as well as good, and his rain to fall on honest
46 and dishonest men alike. •For if you love those who love you, what right have
47 you to claim any credit? Even the tax collectorsˡ do as much, do they not? •And if you save your greetings for your brothers, are you doing anything exceptional?
48 Even the pagans do as much, do they not? •You must therefore be perfect just as your heavenly Father is perfect.

Almsgiving in secret

1
2 **6** 'Be careful not to parade your good deeds before men to attract their notice; by doing this you will lose all reward from your Father in heaven. •So when you give alms, do not have it trumpeted before you; this is what the hypocrites do in the synagogues and in the streets to win men's admiration. I tell you
3 solemnly, they have had their reward. •But when you give alms, your left hand
4 must not know what your right is doing; •your almsgiving must be secret, and your Father who sees all that is done in secret will reward you.

Prayer in secret

5 'And when you pray, do not imitate the hypocrites: they love to say their prayers standing up in the synagogues and at the street corners for people to see
6 them. I tell you solemnly, they have had their reward. •But when you pray, *go to your private room and, when you have shut your door, pray*ᵃ to your Father who is in that secret place, and your Father who sees all that is done in secret will reward you.

How to pray. The Lord's Prayer

7 'In your prayers do not babble as the pagans do, for they think that by using
8 many words they will make themselves heard. •Do not be like them; your Father
9 knows what you need before you ask him. •So you should pray like this:

'Our Father in heaven,
may your name be held holy,
10 your kingdom come,
your will be done,
on earth as in heaven.
11 Give us today our daily bread.
12 And forgive us our debts,
as we have forgiven those who are in debt to us.
13 And do not put us to the test,
but save us from the evil one.

14 Yes, if you forgive others their failings, your heavenly Father will forgive you
15 yours; •but if you do not forgive others, your Father will not forgive your failings either.

c. Ex 20:13   **d.** Translating an Aramaic term of contempt.   **e.** The High Court at Jerusalem.
f. Apostasy was the most repulsive of all sins.   **g.** Ex 20:14   **h.** Dt 24:1   **i.** Ex 20:7
j. Ex 21:24   **k.** The quotation is from Lv 19:18; the second part of this commandment, not in the written Law, is an Aramaic way of saying 'You do not have to love your enemy'.
l. They were employed by the occupying power and this earned them popular contempt.
6 a. Not a direct quotation but an allusion to the practice common in the O.T., see 2 K 4:33.

Fasting in secret

'When you fast do not put on a gloomy look as the hypocrites do: they pull 16
long faces to let men know they are fasting. I tell you solemnly, they have
had their reward. •But when you fast, put oil on your head and wash your face, 17
so that no one will know you are fasting except your Father who sees all that is 18
done in secret; and your Father who sees all that is done in secret will reward you.

True treasures

'Do not store up treasures for yourselves on earth, where moths and 19
woodworms destroy them and thieves can break in and steal. •But store up 20
treasures for yourselves in heaven, where neither moth nor woodworms destroy
them and thieves cannot break in and steal. •For where your treasure is, there 21
will your heart be also.

The eye, the lamp of the body

'The lamp of the body is the eye. It follows that if your eye is sound, your 22
whole body will be filled with light. •But if your eye is diseased, your whole body 23
will be all darkness. If then, the light inside you is darkness, what darkness
that will be!

God and money

'No one can be the slave of two masters: he will either hate the first and love 24
the second, or treat the first with respect and the second with scorn. You cannot
be the slave both of God and of money.

Trust in Providence

'That is why I am telling you not to worry about your life and what you are to 25
eat, nor about your body and how you are to clothe it. Surely life means more than
food, and the body more than clothing! •Look at the birds in the sky. They do not 26
sow or reap or gather into barns; yet your heavenly Father feeds them. Are you
not worth much more than they are? •Can any of you, for all his worrying, add 27
one single cubit to his span of life? •And why worry about clothing? Think of the 28
flowers growing in the fields; they never have to work or spin; •yet I assure you 29
that not even Solomon in all his regalia was robed like one of these. •Now if that 30
is how God clothes the grass in the field which is there today and thrown into the
furnace tomorrow, will he not much more look after you, you men of little faith?
So do not worry; do not say, "What are we to eat? What are we to drink? How 31
are we to be clothed?" •It is the pagans who set their hearts on all these things. 32
Your heavenly Father knows you need them all. •Set your hearts on his kingdom 33
first, and on his righteousness, and all these other things will be given you as well.
So do not worry about tomorrow: tomorrow will take care of itself. Each day 34
has enough trouble of its own.

Do not judge

7 'Do not judge, and you will not be judged; •because the judgements you give $\frac{1}{2}$
are the judgements you will get, and the amount you measure out is the
amount you will be given. •Why do you observe the splinter in your brother's 3
eye and never notice the plank in your own? •How dare you say to your brother, 4
"Let me take the splinter out of your eye", when all the time there is a plank in
your own? •Hypocrite! Take the plank out of your own eye first, and then you 5
will see clearly enough to take the splinter out of your brother's eye.

Do not profane sacred things

'Do not give dogs what is holy;ᵃ and do not throw your pearls in front of pigs, 6
or they may trample them and then turn on you and tear you to pieces.

Effective prayer

7   'Ask, and it will be given to you; search, and you will find; knock, and the
8 door will be opened to you. •For the one who asks always receives; the one who
searches always finds; the one who knocks will always have the door opened to
9 him. •Is there a man among you who would hand his son a stone when he asked
10 for bread? •Or would hand him a snake when he asked for a fish? •If you, then,
11 who are evil, know how to give your children what is good, how much more will
your Father in heaven give good things to those who ask him!

The golden rule

12   'So always treat others as you would like them to treat you; that is the
meaning of the Law and the Prophets.

The two ways

13   'Enter by the narrow gate, since the road that leads to perdition is wide and
14 spacious, and many take it; •but it is a narrow gate and a hard road that leads
to life, and only a few find it.

False prophets

15   'Beware of false prophets[b] who come to you disguised as sheep but underneath
16 are ravenous wolves. •You will be able to tell them by their fruits. Can people
17 pick grapes from thorns, or figs from thistles? •In the same way, a sound tree
18 produces good fruit but a rotten tree bad fruit. •A sound tree cannot bear bad
19 fruit, nor a rotten tree bear good fruit. •Any tree that does not produce good
20 fruit is cut down and thrown on the fire. •I repeat, you will be able to tell them by
their fruits.

The true disciple

21   'It is not those who say to me, "Lord, Lord", who will enter the kingdom of
22 heaven, but the person who does the will of my Father in heaven. •When the day[c]
comes many will say to me, "Lord, Lord, did we not prophesy in your name,
23 cast out demons in your name, work many miracles in your name?" •Then
I shall tell them to their faces: I have never known you; *away from me, you evil
men!*'

24   'Therefore, everyone who listens to these words of mine and acts on them
25 will be like a sensible man who built his house on rock. •Rain came down, floods
rose, gales blew and hurled themselves against that house, and it did not fall:
26 it was founded on rock. •But everyone who listens to these words of mine and does
27 not act on them will be like a stupid man who built his house on sand. •Rain
came down, floods rose, gales blew and struck that house, and it fell; and what
a fall it had!'

The amazement of the crowds

28   Jesus had now finished what he wanted to say, and his teaching made a deep
29 impression on the people •because he taught them with authority, and not like
their own scribes.[d]

---

7 a. The meat of animals which have been offered in sacrifice in the Temple; the application is
to the parading of holy beliefs and practices in front of those who cannot understand them.
b. Lying teachers of religion.   **c.** The day of Judgement.   **d.** Doctors of the law, who but-
tressed their teaching by quotation from the scriptures and traditions.

III. THE KINGDOM OF HEAVEN IS PREACHED

A. NARRATIVE SECTION: TEN MIRACLES

Cure of a leper

8 After he had come down from the mountain large crowds followed him. 1 A leper now came up and bowed low in front of him.ᵃ 'Sir,' he said 'if you want 2 to, you can cure me.' •Jesus stretched out his hand, touched him and said, 'Of 3 course I want to! Be cured!' And his leprosy was cured at once. •Then Jesus said 4 to him, 'Mind you do not tell anyone, but go and show yourself to the priest and make the offering prescribed by Moses, as evidence for them'.

Cure of the centurion's servant

When he went into Capernaum a centurion came up and pleaded with him. 5 'Sir,' he said 'my servant is lying at home paralysed, and in great pain.' •'I will $\frac{6}{7}$ come myself and cure him' said Jesus. •The centurion replied, 'Sir, I am not 8 worthy to have you under my roof; just give the word and my servant will be cured. •For I am under authority myself, and have soldiers under me; and I say 9 to one man: Go, and he goes; to another: Come here, and he comes; to my servant: Do this, and he does it.' •When Jesus heard this he was astonished and 10 said to those following him, 'I tell you solemnly, nowhere in Israel have I found faith like this. •And I tell you that many will come from east and west 11. to take their places with Abraham and Isaac and Jacob at the feast in the kingdom of heaven; •but the subjects of the kingdomᵃ will be turned out into the dark, 12 where there will be weeping and grinding of teeth.' •And to the centurion Jesus 13 said, 'Go back, then; you have believed, so let this be done for you'. And the servant was cured at that moment.

Cure of Peter's mother-in-law

And going into Peter's house Jesus found Peter's mother-in-law in bed with 14 fever. •He touched her hand and the fever left her, and she got up and began 15 to wait on him.

A number of cures

That evening they brought him many who were possessed by devils. He cast 16 out the spirits with a word and cured all who were sick. •This was to fulfil the 17 prophecy of Isaiah:

*He took our sicknesses away and carried our diseases for us.*ᵇ

Hardships of the apostolic calling

When Jesus saw the great crowds all about him he gave orders to leave for the 18 other side.ᶜ •One of the scribes then came up and said to him, 'Master, I will 19 follow you wherever you go'. •Jesus replied, 'Foxes have holes and the birds 20 of the air have nests, but the Son of Man has nowhere to lay his head'.

Another man, one of his disciples, said to him, 'Sir, let me go and bury my 21 father first'. •But Jesus replied, 'Follow me, and leave the dead to bury their dead'. 22

The calming of the storm

Then he got into the boat followed by his disciples. •Without warning $\frac{23}{24}$ a storm broke over the lake, so violent that the waves were breaking right over the boat. But he was asleep. •So they went to him and woke him saying, 'Save us, 25 Lord, we are going down!' •And he said to them, 'Why are you so frightened, you 26 men of little faith?' And with that he stood up and rebuked the winds and the sea; and all was calm again. •The men were astounded and said, 'Whatever kind 27 of man is this? Even the winds and the sea obey him.'

The demoniacs of Gadara

28 When he reached the country of the Gadarenes on the other side, two demoniacs came towards him out of the tombs—creatures so fierce that no one 29 could pass that way. •They stood there shouting, 'What do you want with us, 30 Son of God? Have you come here to torture us before the time?'*d* •Now some 31 distance away there was a large herd of pigs feeding, •and the devils pleaded 32 with Jesus, 'If you cast us out, send us into the herd of pigs'. •And he said to them, 'Go then', and they came out and made for the pigs; and at that the whole herd 33 charged down the cliff into the lake and perished in the water. •The swineherds ran off and made for the town, where they told the whole story, including what 34 had happened to the demoniacs. •At this the whole town set out to meet Jesus; and as soon as they saw him they implored him to leave the neighbourhood.

Cure of a paralytic

¹₂ **9** He got back in the boat, crossed the water and came to his own town.*a* •Then some people appeared, bringing him a paralytic stretched out on a bed. Seeing their faith, Jesus said to the paralytic, 'Courage, my child, your sins are forgiven'. ³₄ And at this some scribes said to themselves, 'This man is blaspheming'. •Knowing what was in their minds Jesus said, 'Why do you have such wicked thoughts in 5 your hearts? •Now, which of these is easier: to say, "Your sins are forgiven", 6 or to say, "Get up and walk"? •But to prove to you that the Son of Man has authority on earth to forgive sins,'—he said to the paralytic—'get up, and pick up ⁷₈ your bed and go off home'. •And the man got up and went home. •A feeling of awe came over the crowd when they saw this, and they praised God for giving such power to men.

The call of Matthew

9 As Jesus was walking on from there he saw a man named Matthew*b* sitting by the customs house, and he said to him, 'Follow me'. And he got up and followed him.

Eating with sinners

10 While he was at dinner in the house it happened that a number of tax collectors 11 and sinners*c* came to sit at the table with Jesus and his disciples. •When the Pharisees saw this, they said to his disciples, 'Why does your master eat with 12 tax collectors and sinners?' •When he heard this he replied, 'It is not the healthy 13 who need the doctor, but the sick. •Go and learn the meaning of the words: *What I want is mercy, not sacrifice.d* And indeed I did not come to call the virtuous, but sinners.'

A discussion on fasting

14 Then John's*e* disciples came to him and said, 'Why is it that we and the 15 Pharisees fast, but your disciples do not?' •Jesus replied, 'Surely the bridegroom's attendants would never think of mourning as long as the bridegroom is still with them? But the time will come for the bridegroom to be taken away from them, 16 and then they will fast. •No one puts a piece of unshrunken cloth on to an old 17 cloak, because the patch pulls away from the cloak and the tear gets worse. •Nor do people put new wine into old wineskins; if they do, the skins burst, the wine runs out, and the skins are lost. No; they put new wine into fresh skins and both are preserved.'*f*

8 a. The Jews, natural heirs of the promises.   b. Is 53:4   c. The E. bank of Lake Tiberias. d. The day of Judgement, when the reign of God would banish all demons. 9 a. Capernaum, cf. 4:13.   b. Called Levi by Mk and Lk.   c. Social outcasts, made 'unclean' by breaking religious laws or following a disreputable profession.   d. Ho 6:6   e. John the Baptist.   f. New devotional exercises, like those which John and the Pharisees add to the religion of the old order, will not preserve it.

Cure of the woman with a haemorrhage. The official's daughter raised to life

While he was speaking to them, up came one of the officials, who bowed low 18
in front of him and said, 'My daughter has just died, but come and lay your hand
on her and her life will be saved'. •Jesus rose and, with his disciples, followed him. 19
Then from behind him came a woman, who had suffered from a haemorrhage 20
for twelve years, and she touched the fringe of his cloak, •for she said to herself, 21
'If I can only touch his cloak I shall be well again'. •Jesus turned round and saw 22
her; and he said to her, 'Courage, my daughter, your faith has restored you to
health'. And from that moment the woman was well again.
When Jesus reached the official's house and saw the flute-players, with the 23
crowd making a commotion^g he said, •'Get out of here; the little girl is not dead, 24
she is asleep'. And they laughed at him. •But when the people had been turned 25
out he went inside and took the little girl by the hand; and she stood up. •And the 26
news spread all round the countryside.

Cure of two blind men

As Jesus went on his way two blind men followed him shouting, 'Take pity 27
on us, Son of David'. •And when Jesus reached the house the blind men came 28
up with him and he said to them, 'Do you believe I can do this?' They said, 'Sir,
we do'. •Then he touched their eyes saying, 'Your faith deserves it, so let this 29
be done for you'. •And their sight returned. Then Jesus sternly warned them; 30
'Take care that no one learns about this'. •But when they had gone, they talked 31
about him all over the countryside.

Cure of a dumb demoniac

They had only just left when a man was brought to him, a dumb demoniac. 32
And when the devil was cast out, the dumb man spoke and the people were 33
amazed. 'Nothing like this has ever been seen in Israel' they said. •But the 34
Pharisees said, 'It is through the prince of devils that he casts out devils'.

The distress of the crowds

Jesus made a tour through all the towns and villages, teaching in their 35
synagogues, proclaiming the Good News of the kingdom and curing all kinds
of diseases and sickness.
And when he saw the crowds he felt sorry for them because they were harassed 36
and dejected, like sheep without a shepherd. •Then he said to his disciples, 37
'The harvest is rich but the labourers are few, so ask the Lord of the harvest to
send labourers to his harvest'.

B. THE INSTRUCTION OF THE APOSTLES

The mission of the Twelve

10 He summoned his twelve disciples, and gave them authority over unclean 1
spirits with power to cast them out and to cure all kinds of diseases and
sickness.
These are the names of the twelve apostles: first, Simon who is called Peter, 2
and his brother Andrew; James the son of Zebedee, and his brother John; •Philip 3
and Bartholomew; Thomas, and Matthew the tax collector; James the son of
Alphaeus, and Thaddaeus; •Simon the Zealot and Judas Iscariot, the one who 4
was to betray him. •These twelve Jesus sent out, instructing them as follows: 5
'Do not turn your steps to pagan territory, and do not enter any Samaritan
town; •go rather to the lost sheep of the House of Israel. •And as you go, $^6_7$
proclaim that the kingdom of heaven is close at hand. •Cure the sick, raise the 8
dead, cleanse the lepers, cast out devils. You received without charge, give without
charge. •Provide yourselves with no gold or silver, not even with a few coppers 9

10 for your purses, •with no haversack for the journey or spare tunic or footwear
or a staff, for the workman deserves his keep.

11 　'Whatever town or village you go into, ask for someone trustworthy and stay
12 with him until you leave. •As you enter his house, salute it, •and if the house
13 deserves it, let your peace descend upon it; if it does not, let your peace come back
14 to you. •And if anyone does not welcome you or listen to what you have to say,
15 as you walk out of the house or town shake the dust from your feet. •I tell you
solemnly, on the day of Judgement it will not go as hard with the land of
16 Sodom and Gomorrah as with that town. •Remember, I am sending you out
like sheep among wolves; so be cunning as serpents and yet as harmless as doves.

The missionaries will be persecuted*a*

17 　'Beware of men: they will hand you over to sanhedrins and scourge you in
18 their synagogues. •You will be dragged before governors and kings for my sake,
19 to bear witness before them and the pagans. •But when they hand you over, do
not worry about how to speak or what to say; what you are to say will be given to
20 you when the time comes; •because it is not you who will be speaking; the Spirit
of your Father will be speaking in you.

21 　'Brother will betray brother to death, and the father his child; children will
22 rise against their parents and have them put to death. •You will be hated by all
men on account of my name; but the man who stands firm to the end will be saved.
23 If they persecute you in one town, take refuge in the next; and if they persecute
you in that, take refuge in another. I tell you solemnly, you will not have gone
the round of the towns of Israel before the Son of Man comes.
24 　'The disciple is not superior to his teacher, nor the slave to his master. •It is
25 enough for the disciple that he should grow to be like his teacher, and the slave
like his master. If they have called the master of the house Beelzebul, what will
they not say of his household?

Open and fearless speech

26 　'Do not be afraid of them therefore. For everything that is now covered will
27 be uncovered, and everything now hidden will be made clear. •What I say to
you in the dark, tell in the daylight; what you hear in whispers, proclaim from
the housetops.
28 　'Do not be afraid of those who kill the body but cannot kill the soul; fear him
29 rather who can destroy both body and soul in hell. •Can you not buy two
sparrows for a penny? And yet not one falls to the ground without your Father
30 knowing. •Why, every hair on your head has been counted. •So there is no
31 need to be afraid; you are worth more than hundreds of sparrows.
32 　'So if anyone declares himself for me in the presence of men, I will declare my-
33 self for him in the presence of my Father in heaven. •But the one who disowns
me in the presence of men, I will disown in the presence of my Father in
heaven.

Jesus, the cause of dissension

34 　'Do not suppose that I have come to bring peace to the earth: it is not peace I
35 have come to bring, but a sword. •For I have come to set *a man against his father,*
a daughter against her mother, a daughter-in-law against her mother-in-law.
36 *A man's enemies will be those of his own household.*b

Renouncing self to follow Jesus

37 　'Anyone who prefers father or mother to me is not worthy of me. Anyone
38 who prefers son or daughter to me is not worthy of me. •Anyone who does not

---

g. The loud wailing of the oriental mourner.
10 a. The conditions described in vv. 17-39 are those of a later time than this first mission
of the Twelve.　　b. Mi 7:6

take his cross and follow in my footsteps is not worthy of me. •Anyone who 39
finds his life will lose it; anyone who loses his life for my sake will find it.

Conclusion

'Anyone who welcomes you welcomes me; and those who welcome me 40
welcome the one who sent me.

'Anyone who welcomes a prophet because he is a prophet will have 41
a prophet's reward; and anyone who welcomes a holy man because he is a holy
man will have a holy man's reward.

'If anyone gives so much as a cup of cold water to one of these little ones 42
because he is a disciple, then I tell you solemnly, he will most certainly not lose
his reward.'

IV. THE MYSTERY OF THE KINGDOM OF HEAVEN

A. NARRATIVE SECTION

11 When Jesus had finished instructing his twelve disciples he moved on from 1
there to teach and preach in their towns.*

The Baptist's question. Jesus commends him

Now John in his prison had heard what Christ was doing and he sent his 2
disciples to ask him, •'Are you the one who is to come, or have we got to wait for 3
someone else?' •Jesus answered, 'Go back and tell John what you hear and see; 4
the blind see again, and the lame walk, lepers are cleansed, and the deaf hear, 5
and the dead are raised to life and the Good News is proclaimed to the poor;*
and happy is the man who does not lose faith in me'. 6

As the messengers were leaving, Jesus began to talk to the people about John: 7
'What did you go out into the wilderness to see? A reed swaying in the breeze?
No? •Then what did you go out to see? A man wearing fine clothes? Oh no, those 8
who wear fine clothes are to be found in palaces. •Then what did you go out for? 9
To see a prophet? Yes, I tell you, and much more than a prophet: •he is the one 10
of whom scripture says:

> Look, I am going to send my messenger before you;
> he will prepare your way before you.*

'I tell you solemnly, of all the children born of women, a greater than John 11
the Baptist has never been seen; yet the least in the kingdom of heaven is
greater than he is. •Since John the Baptist came, up to this present time, the 12
kingdom of heaven has been subjected to violence and the violent are taking it
by storm. •Because it was towards John that all the prophecies of the prophets 13
and of the Law were leading; •and he, if you will believe me, is the Elijah who 14
was to return.* •If anyone has ears to hear, let him listen! 15

Jesus condemns his contemporaries

'What description can I find for this generation? It is like children shouting to 16
each other as they sit in the market place:

> "We played the pipes for you, 17
> and you wouldn't dance;
> we sang dirges,
> and you wouldn't be mourners".

'For John came, neither eating nor drinking, and they say, "He is possessed". 18
The Son of Man came, eating and drinking, and they say, "Look, a glutton and 19
a drunkard, a friend of tax collectors and sinners". Yet wisdom has been proved
right by her actions.'

Lament over the lake-towns

20   Then he began to reproach the towns in which most of his miracles had been worked, because they refused to repent.

21   'Alas for you, Chorazin! Alas for you, Bethsaida! For if the miracles done in you had been done in Tyre and Sidon, they would have repented long ago in
22   sackcloth and ashes. •And still, I tell you that it will not go as hard on Judgement
23   day with Tyre and Sidon as with you. •And as for you, Capernaum, did you want to be exalted as high as heaven? *You shall be thrown down to hell.*[c] For if the miracles done in you had been done in Sodom, it would have been standing yet.
24   And still, I tell you that it will not go as hard with the land of Sodom on Judgement day as with you.'

The Good News revealed to the simple. The Father and the Son

25   At that time Jesus exclaimed, 'I bless you, Father, Lord of heaven and of earth, for hiding these things from the learned and the clever and revealing them
26   to mere children. •Yes, Father, for that is what it pleased you to do. •Everything
27   has been entrusted to me by my Father; and no one knows the Son except the Father, just as no one knows the Father except the Son and those to whom the Son chooses to reveal him.

The gentle mastery of Christ

28   'Come to me, all you who labour and are overburdened, and I will give you
29   rest. •Shoulder my yoke and learn from me, for I am gentle and humble in heart,
30   *and you will find rest for your souls.*[f] •Yes, my yoke is easy and my burden light.'

Picking corn on the sabbath

1   **12** At that time Jesus took a walk one sabbath day through the cornfields. His disciples were hungry and began to pick ears of corn and eat them.
2   The Pharisees noticed it and said to him, 'Look, your disciples are doing
3   something that is forbidden on the sabbath'. •But he said to them, 'Have you
4   not read what David did when he and his followers were hungry—•how he went into the house of God and how they ate the loaves of offering which neither he nor his followers were allowed to eat, but which were for the priests alone?
5   Or again, have you not read in the Law that on the sabbath day the Temple
6   priests break the sabbath without being blamed for it? •Now here, I tell you,
7   is something greater than the Temple. •And if you had understood the meaning of the words: *What I want is mercy, not sacrifice,* you would not have condemned
8   the blameless. •For the Son of Man is master of the sabbath.'

Cure of the man with a withered hand

9
10   He moved on from there and went to their synagogue, •and a man was there at the time who had a withered hand. They asked him, 'Is it against the law to
11   cure a man on the sabbath day?' hoping for something to use against him. •But he said to them, 'If any one of you here had only one sheep and it fell down a hole
12   on the sabbath day, would he not get hold of it and lift it out? •Now a man is far more important than a sheep, so it follows that it is permitted to do good on the
13   sabbath day.' •Then he said to the man, 'Stretch out your hand'. He stretched it
14   out and his hand was better, as sound as the other one. •At this the Pharisees went out and began to plot against him, discussing how to destroy him.

Jesus the 'servant of Yahweh'

15   Jesus knew this and withdrew from the district. Many followed him and he
16
17   cured them all, •but warned them not to make him known. •This was to fulfil the prophecy of Isaiah:

---

11 a. I.e. the Jews' towns.   b. These are signs of the messianic age in the prophecies of Isaiah.
c. Ml 3:1.   d. According to the last of the prophets, Ml 3:23.   e. Is 14   f. Jr 6:16

Here is my servant whom I have chosen,   18
my beloved, the favourite of my soul.
I will endow him with my spirit,
and he will proclaim the true faith to the nations.
He will not brawl or shout,   19
nor will anyone hear his voice in the streets.
He will not break the crushed reed,   20
nor put out the smouldering wick
till he has led the truth to victory:
in his name the nations will put their hope.[a]   21

Jesus and Beelzebul

Then they brought to him a blind and dumb demoniac; and he cured him, 22 so that the dumb man could speak and see. •All the people were astounded and 23 said, 'Can this be the Son of David?' •But when the Pharisees heard this they 24 said, 'The man casts out devils only through Beelzebul,[b] the prince of devils'.

Knowing what was in their minds he said to them, 'Every kingdom divided 25 against itself is heading for ruin; and no town, no household divided against itself can stand. •Now if Satan casts out Satan, he is divided against himself; 26 so how can his kingdom stand? •And if it is through Beelzebul that I cast out 27 devils, through whom do your own experts cast them out? Let them be your judges, then. •But if it is through the Spirit of God that I cast devils out, then 28 know that the kingdom of God has overtaken you.

'Or again, how can anyone make his way into a strong man's house and 29 burgle his property unless he has tied up the strong man first? Only then can he burgle his house.

'He who is not with me is against me, and he who does not gather with me 30 scatters. •And so I tell you, every one of men's sins and blasphemies will be for- 31 given, but blasphemy against the Spirit will not be forgiven. •And anyone who 32 says a word against the Son of Man will be forgiven; but let anyone speak against the Holy Spirit and he will not be forgiven either in this world or in the next.

Words betray the heart

'Make a tree sound and its fruit will be sound; make a tree rotten and its 33 fruit will be rotten. For the tree can be told by its fruit. •Brood of vipers, how 34 can your speech be good when you are evil? For a man's words flow out of what fills his heart. •A good man draws good things from his store of goodness; a bad 35 man draws bad things from his store of badness. •So I tell you this, that for 36 every unfounded word men utter they will answer on Judgement day, •since it 37 is by your words you will be acquitted, and by your words condemned.'

The sign of Jonah

Then some of the scribes and Pharisees spoke up. 'Master,' they said 'we 38 should like to see a sign[c] from you.' •He replied, 'It is an evil and unfaithful 39 generation that asks for a sign! The only sign it will be given is the sign of the prophet Jonah. •For as Jonah *was in the belly of the sea-monster for three* 40 *days and three nights,*[d] so will the Son of Man be in the heart of the earth for three days and three nights. •On Judgement day the men of Nineveh will stand 41 up with this generation and condemn it, because when Jonah preached they repented; and there is something greater than Jonah here. •On Judgement day 42 the Queen of the South will rise up with this generation and condemn it, because she came from the ends of the earth to hear the wisdom of Solomon; and there is something greater than Solomon here.

The return of the unclean spirit

'When an unclean spirit goes out of a man it wanders through waterless 43 country looking for a place to rest, and cannot find one. •Then it says, "I will 44

return to the home I came from". But on arrival, finding it unoccupied, swept and
45 tidied, •it then goes off and collects seven other spirits more evil than itself, and
they go in and set up house there, so that the man ends up by being worse than
he was before. That is what will happen to this evil generation.'

The true kinsmen of Jesus

46 He was still speaking to the crowds when his mother and his brothers ᶜ
appeared; they were standing outside and were anxious to have a word with
48 him. •But to the man who told him this Jesus replied, 'Who is my mother?
49 Who are my brothers?' •And stretching out his hand towards his disciples he said,
50 'Here are my mother and my brothers. •Anyone who does the will of my Father
in heaven, he is my brother and sister and mother.'

B. THE SERMON OF PARABLES

Introduction

¹⁄₂ **13** That same day, Jesus left the house and sat by the lakeside, •but such
crowds gathered round him that he got into a boat and sat there. The people
3 all stood on the beach, •and he told them many things in parables.

Parable of the sower

4 He said, 'Imagine a sower going out to sow. •As he sowed, some seeds fell
5 on the edge of the path, and the birds came and ate them up. •Others fell on
patches of rock where they found little soil and sprang up straight away, because
6 there was no depth of earth; •but as soon as the sun came up they were scorched
7 and, not having any roots, they withered away. •Others fell among thorns, and
8 the thorns grew up and choked them. •Others fell on rich soil and produced their
9 crop, some a hundredfold, some sixty, some thirty. •Listen, anyone who has
ears!'

Why Jesus speaks in parables

10 Then the disciples went up to him and asked, 'Why do you talk to them in
11 parables?' •'Because' he replied 'the mysteries of the kingdom of heaven are
12 revealed to you, but they are not revealed to them. •For anyone who has will be
given more, and he will have more than enough; but from anyone who has not,
13 even what he has will be taken away. •The reason I talk to them in parables is
14 that they look without seeing and listen without hearing or understanding. •So in
their case this prophecy of Isaiah is being fulfilled:

You will listen and listen again, but not understand,
see and see again, but not perceive.
15 *For the heart of this nation has grown coarse,*
their ears are dull of hearing, and they have shut their eyes,
for fear they should see with their eyes,
hear with their ears,
understand with their heart,
and be converted
*and be healed by me.*ᵃ

16 'But happy are your eyes because they see, your ears because they hear!
17 I tell you solemnly, many prophets and holy men longed to see what you see, and
never saw it; to hear what you hear, and never heard it.

---

12 a. Is 42:1-4. 　b. 'prince Baal' often contemptuously changed (e.g. 2 K 1:2f) to 'Beelzebub'
'Lord of the flies'. 　c. A miracle to prove his authority. 　d. Jon 2:1 　e. In Hebr. and
Aramaic (and many other languages), 'brothers' is the word used for cousins or even more
distant relations of the same generation.
13 a. Is 6:9-10

The parable of the sower explained

'You, therefore, are to hear the parable of the sower. •When anyone hears ¹⁸ ¹⁹ the word of the kingdom without understanding, the evil one comes and carries off what was sown in his heart: this is the man who received the seed on the edge of the path. •The one who received it on patches of rock is the man who hears 20 the word and welcomes it at once with joy. •But he has no root in him, he does 21 not last; let some trial come, or some persecution on account of the word, and he falls away at once. •The one who received the seed in thorns is the man who 22 hears the word, but the worries of this world and the lure of riches choke the word and so he produces nothing. •And the one who received the seed in rich soil is the 23 man who hears the word and understands it; he is the one who yields a harvest and produces now a hundredfold, now sixty, now thirty.'

Parable of the darnel

He put another parable before them, 'The kingdom of heaven may be 24 compared to a man who sowed good seed in his field. •While everybody was 25 asleep his enemy came, sowed darnel all among the wheat, and made off. •When 26 the new wheat sprouted and ripened, the darnel appeared as well. •The owner's 27 servants went to him and said, "Sir, was it not good seed that you sowed in your field? If so, where does the darnel come from?" •"Some enemy has done this" 28 he answered. And the servants said, "Do you want us to go and weed it out?" But he said, "No, because when you weed out the darnel you might pull up the 29 wheat with it. •Let them both grow till the harvest; and at harvest time I shall 30 say to the reapers: First collect the darnel and tie it in bundles to be burnt, then gather the wheat into my barn." '

Parable of the mustard seed

He put another parable before them, 'The kingdom of heaven is like a mustard 31 seed which a man took and sowed in his field. •It is the smallest of all the seeds, 32 but when it has grown it is the biggest shrub of all and becomes a tree so that the birds of the air come and shelter in its branches.'

Parable of the yeast

He told them another parable, 'The kingdom of heaven is like the yeast 33 a woman took and mixed in with three measures of flour till it was leavened all through'.

The people are taught only in parables

In all this Jesus spoke to the crowds in parables; indeed, he would never speak 34 to them except in parables. •This was to fulfil the prophecy: 35

> *I will speak to you in parables*
> *and expound things hidden since the foundation of the world.*^b

The parable of the darnel explained

Then, leaving the crowds, he went to the house; and his disciples came to 36 him and said, 'Explain the parable about the darnel in the field to us'. •He said 37 in reply, 'The sower of the good seed is the Son of Man. •The field is the world; 38 the good seed is the subjects of the kingdom; the darnel, the subjects of the evil one; •the enemy who sowed them, the devil; the harvest is the end of the world; 39 the reapers are the angels. •Well then, just as the darnel is gathered up and burnt 40 in the fire, so it will be at the end of time. •The Son of Man will send his angels 41 and they will gather out of his kingdom all things that provoke offences and all who do evil, •and throw them into the blazing furnace, where there will be 42 weeping and grinding of teeth. •Then the virtuous will shine like the sun in the 43 kingdom of their Father.^c Listen, anyone who has ears!

Parables of the treasure and of the pearl

44 'The kingdom of heaven is like treasure hidden in a field which someone has found; he hides it again, goes off happy, sells everything he owns and buys the field.

45 'Again, the kingdom of heaven is like a merchant looking for fine pearls; 46 when he finds one of great value he goes and sells everything he owns and buys it.

Parable of the dragnet

47 'Again, the kingdom of heaven is like a dragnet cast into the sea that brings 48 in a haul of all kinds. •When it is full, the fishermen haul it ashore; then, sitting down, they collect the good ones in a basket and throw away those that are no 49 use. •This is how it will be at the end of time: the angels will appear and separate 50 the wicked from the just •to throw them into the blazing furnace where there will be weeping and grinding of teeth.

Conclusion

51 'Have you understood all this?' They said, 'Yes'. •And he said to them,
52 'Well then, every scribe who becomes a disciple of the kingdom of heaven is like a householder who brings out from his storeroom things both new and old'.[d]

V. THE CHURCH, FIRST-FRUITS
OF THE KINGDOM OF HEAVEN

A. NARRATIVE SECTION

A visit to Nazareth

53 When Jesus had finished these parables he left the district; •and, coming
54 to his home town,[e] he taught the people in their synagogue in such a way that they were astonished and said, 'Where did the man get this wisdom and these 55 miraculous powers? •This is the carpenter's son, surely? Is not his mother the woman called Mary, and his brothers James and Joseph and Simon and Jude? 56 His sisters, too, are they not all here with us? So where did the man get it all?' 57 And they would not accept him. But Jesus said to them, 'A prophet is only 58 despised in his own country and in his own house', •and he did not work many miracles there because of their lack of faith.

Herod and Jesus

1 **14** At that time Herod the tetrarch heard about the reputation of Jesus, •and
2 said to his court, 'This is John the Baptist himself; he has risen from the dead, and that is why miraculous powers are at work in him'.

John the Baptist beheaded

3 Now it was Herod who had arrested John, chained him up and put him in
4 prison because of Herodias, his brother Philip's[a] wife. •For John had told him,
5 'It is against the Law for you to have her'. •He had wanted to kill him but
6 was afraid of the people, who regarded John as a prophet. •Then, during the celebrations for Herod's birthday, the daughter of Herodias[b] danced before the
7 company, and so delighted Herod •that he promised on oath to give her anything
8 she asked. •Prompted by her mother she said, 'Give me John the Baptist's head,
9 here, on a dish'. •The king was distressed but, thinking of the oaths he had

b. Ps 78:2   c. The kingdom of the Son, v. 41, is succeeded by the kingdom of the Father.
d. Perhaps a saying of particular significance to Mt, a 'scribe who became a disciple'.
e. Nazareth, see 2:23.
14 a. Philip, Herod's half-brother, was still alive.   b. According to Josephus, the girl's name was Salome.

sworn and of his guests, he ordered it to be given her, •and sent and had John 10
beheaded in the prison. •The head was brought in on a dish and given to the girl 11
who took it to her mother. •John's disciples came and took the body and buried 12
it; then they went off to tell Jesus.

First miracle of the loaves

When Jesus received this news he withdrew by boat to a lonely place where 13
they could be by themselves. But the people heard of this and, leaving the towns,
went after him on foot. •So as he stepped ashore he saw a large crowd; and 14
he took pity on them and healed their sick.

When evening came, the disciples went to him and said, 'This is a lonely place, 15
and the time has slipped by; so send the people away, and they can go to the
villages to buy themselves some food'. •Jesus replied, 'There is no need for them 16
to go: give them something to eat yourselves'. •But they answered, 'All we have 17
with us is five loaves and two fish'. •'Bring them here to me' he said. •He gave ¹⁸₁₉
orders that the people were to sit down on the grass; then he took the five loaves
and the two fish, raised his eyes to heaven and said the blessing. And breaking
the loaves he handed them to his disciples who gave them to the crowds. •They 20
all ate as much as they wanted, and they collected the scraps remaining,
twelve baskets full. •Those who ate numbered about five thousand men, to say 21
nothing of women and children.

Jesus walks on the water and, with him, Peter

Directly after this he made the disciples get into the boat and go on ahead 22
to the other side while he would send the crowds away. •After sending the crowds 23
away he went up into the hills by himself to pray. When evening came, he was there
alone, •while the boat, by now far out on the lake, was battling with a heavy 24
sea, for there was a head-wind. •In the fourth watch of the nightᶜ he went towards 25
them, walking on the lake, •and when the disciples saw him walking on the lake 26
they were terrified. 'It is a ghost' they said, and cried out in fear. •But at once 27
Jesus called out to them, saying, 'Courage! It is I! Do not be afraid.' •It was Peter 28
who answered. 'Lord,' he said 'if it is you, tell me to come to you across the water.'
'Come' said Jesus. Then Peter got out of the boat and started walking towards 29
Jesus across the water, •but as soon as he felt the force of the wind, he took fright 30
and began to sink. 'Lord! Save me!' he cried. •Jesus put out his hand at once and 31
held him. 'Man of little faith,' he said 'why did you doubt?' •And as they got into 32
the boat the wind dropped. •The men in the boat bowed down before him and 33
said, 'Truly, you are the Son of God'.

Cures at Gennesaret

.Having made the crossing, they came to land at Gennesaret. •When the local ³⁴₃₅
people recognised him they spread the news through the whole neighbourhood
and took all that were sick to him, •begging him just to let them touch the fringe 36
of his cloak. And all those who touched it were completely cured.

The traditions of the Pharisees

15 Pharisees and scribes from Jerusalem then came to Jesus and said, •'Why ¹₂
do your disciples break away from the tradition of the elders?ᵃ They do not
wash their hands when they eat food.' •'And why do you' he answered 'break 3
away from the commandment of God for the sake of your tradition? •For God 4
said: *Do your duty to*ᵇ *your father and mother* and: *Anyone who curses father or
mother must be put to death.*ᶜ •But you say, "If anyone says to his father or mother: 5
Anything I have that I might have used to help you is dedicated to God", •he 6
is rid of his duty to father or mother.ᵈ In this way you have made God's word
null and void by means of your tradition. •Hypocrites! It was you Isaiah meant 7
when he so rightly prophesied:

8   *This people honours me only with lip-service,*
    while their hearts are far from me.
9   *The worship they offer me is worthless;*
    the doctrines they teach are only human regulations.'[e]

On clean and unclean

10
11   He called the people to him and said, 'Listen, and understand. •What goes into the mouth does not make a man unclean; it is what comes out of the mouth that makes him unclean.'

12   Then the disciples came to him and said, 'Do you know that the Pharisees
13   were shocked when they heard what you said?' •He replied, 'Any plant my
14   heavenly Father has not planted will be pulled up by the roots. •Leave them alone. They are blind men leading blind men; and if one blind man leads another, both will fall into a pit.'

15
16   At this, Peter said to him, 'Explain the parable for us'. •Jesus replied, 'Do
17   even you not yet understand? •Can you not see that whatever goes into the
18   mouth passes through the stomach and is discharged into the sewer? •But the things that come out of the mouth come from the heart, and it is these that make
19   a man unclean. •For from the heart come evil intentions: murder, adultery,
20   fornication, theft, perjury, slander. •These are the things that make a man unclean. But to eat with unwashed hands does not make a man unclean.'

The daughter of the Canaanite woman healed

21
22   Jesus left that place and withdrew to the region of Tyre and Sidon. •Then out came a Canaanite woman from that district and started shouting, 'Sir, Son
23   of David, take pity on me. My daughter is tormented by a devil.' •But he answered her not a word. And his disciples went and pleaded with him. 'Give
24   her what she wants,' they said 'because she is shouting after us.' •He said in
25   reply, 'I was sent only to the lost sheep of the House of Israel'. •But the woman
26   had come up and was kneeling at his feet. 'Lord,' she said 'help me.' •He replied,
27   'It is not fair to take the children's food and throw it to the house-dogs'. •She retorted, 'Ah yes, sir; but even house-dogs can eat the scraps that fall from their
28   master's table'. •Then Jesus answered her, 'Woman, you have great faith. Let your wish be granted.' And from that moment her daughter was well again.

Cures near the lake

29   Jesus went on from there and reached the shores of the Sea of Galilee, and
30   he went up into the hills. He sat there, •and large crowds came to him bringing the lame, the crippled, the blind, the dumb and many others; these they put
31   down at his feet, and he cured them. •The crowds were astonished to see the dumb speaking, the cripples whole again, the lame walking and the blind with their sight, and they praised the God of Israel.

Second miracle of the loaves

32   But Jesus called his disciples to him and said, 'I feel sorry for all these people; they have been with me for three days now and have nothing to eat. I do not
33   want to send them off hungry, they might collapse on the way.' •The disciples said to him, 'Where could we get enough bread in this deserted place
34   to feed such a crowd?' •Jesus said to them, 'How many loaves have you?' 'Seven'
35   they said 'and a few small fish.' •Then he instructed the crowd to sit down on the
36   ground, •and he took the seven loaves and the fish, and he gave thanks and broke them and handed them to the disciples who gave them to the crowds.

c. 3 to 6 a.m.
15 a. The traditional teaching, including many additions to and extensions of the Law.
b. Often translated 'honour', but the word implies a respect expressed in practical ways,
Ex 20:12.   **c.** Lv 20:9   **d.** Property dedicated in this way could not be passed to another person.   **e.** Is 29:13

They all ate as much as they wanted, and they collected what was left of the 37 scraps, seven baskets full. •Now four thousand men had eaten, to say nothing 38 of women and children. •And when he had sent the crowds away he got into the 39 boat and went to the district of Magadan.

The Pharisees ask for a sign from heaven

16 The Pharisees and Sadducees came, and to test him they asked if he would 1 show them a sign from heaven. •He replied, 'In the evening you 2 say, "It will be fine; there is a red sky", •and in the morning, "Stormy weather 3 today; the sky is red and overcast". You know how to read the face of the sky, but you cannot read the signs of the times. •It is an evil and unfaithful generation 4 that asks for a sign! The only sign it will be given is the sign of Jonah.' And leaving them standing there, he went away.

The yeast of the Pharisees and Sadducees

The disciples, having crossed to the other shore, had forgotten to take any food. 5 Jesus said to them, 'Keep your eyes open, and be on your guard against the yeast 6 of the Pharisees and Sadducees'. •And they said to themselves, 'It is because we 7 have not brought any bread'. •Jesus knew it, and he said, 'Men of little faith, 8 why are you talking among yourselves about having no bread? •Do you not yet 9 understand? Do you not remember the five loaves for the five thousand and the number of baskets you collected? •Or the seven loaves for the four thousand 10 and the number of baskets you collected? •How could you fail to understand 11 that I was not talking about bread? What I said was: Beware of the yeast of the Pharisees and Sadducees.' •Then they understood that he was telling them to be 12 on their guard, not against the yeast for making bread, but against the teaching of the Pharisees and Sadducees.[a]

Peter's profession of faith; his pre-eminence

When Jesus came to the region of Caesarea Philippi he put this question to 13 his disciples, 'Who do people say the Son of Man is?' •And they said, 'Some 14 say he is John the Baptist, some Elijah, and others Jeremiah or one of the prophets'. •'But you,' he said 'who do you say I am?' •Then Simon Peter spoke 15 up, 'You are the Christ,' he said 'the Son of the living God'. •Jesus replied, 17 'Simon son of Jonah, you are a happy man! Because it was not flesh and blood that revealed this to you but my Father in heaven. •So I now say to you: You 18 are Peter[b] and on this rock I will build my Church. And the gates of the under-world[c] can never hold out against it. •I will give you the keys of the kingdom 19 of heaven: whatever you bind on earth shall be considered bound in heaven; whatever you loose on earth shall be considered loosed in heaven.'[d] •Then he 20 gave the disciples strict orders not to tell anyone that he was the Christ.

First prophecy of the Passion

From that time Jesus began to make it clear to his disciples that he was 21 destined to go to Jerusalem and suffer grievously at the hands of the elders and chief priests and scribes, to be put to death and to be raised up on the third day. Then, taking him aside, Peter started to remonstrate with him. 'Heaven preserve 22 you, Lord;' he said 'this must not happen to you'. •But he turned and said to 23 Peter, 'Get behind me, Satan! You are an obstacle in my path, because the way you think is not God's way but man's.'

The condition of following Christ

Then Jesus said to his disciples, 'If anyone wants to be a follower of mine, 24 let him renounce himself and take up his cross and follow me. •For anyone who 25 wants to save his life will lose it; but anyone who loses his life for my sake will find it. •What, then, will a man gain if he wins the whole world and ruins his 26 life? Or what has a man to offer in exchange for his life?

27   'For the Son of Man is going to come in the glory of his Father with his angels, and, when he does, he will reward each one according to his behaviour.
28   I tell you solemnly, there are some of these standing here who will not taste death before they see the Son of Man coming with his kingdom.'ᵉ

The transfiguration

1 2 **17** Six days later, Jesus took with him Peter and James and his brother John and led them up a high mountain where they could be alone. •There in their presence he was transfigured: his face shone like the sun and his clothes
3   became as white as the light. •Suddenly Moses and Elijahᵃ appeared to them;
4   they were talking with him. •Then Peter spoke to Jesus. 'Lord,' he said 'it is wonderful for us to be here; if you wish, I will make three tents here, one for
5   you, one for Moses and one for Elijah.' •He was still speaking when suddenly a bright cloud covered them with shadow, and from the cloud there came a voice which said, 'This is my Son, the Beloved; he enjoys my favour. Listen to him.'
6 7 When they heard this, the disciples fell on their faces, overcome with fear. •But
8   Jesus came up and touched them. 'Stand up,' he said 'do not be afraid.' •And when they raised their eyes they saw no one but only Jesus.

The question about Elijah

9   As they came down from the mountain Jesus gave them this order, 'Tell
10   no one about the vision until the Son of Man has risen from the dead'. •And the disciples put this question to him, 'Why do the scribes say then that Elijah has
11   to come first?' •'True;' he replied 'Elijah is to come to see that everything is
12   once more as it should be; •however, I tell you that Elijah has come already and they did not recognise him but treated him as they pleased; and the Son of Man
13   will suffer similarly at their hands.' •The disciples understood then that he had been speaking of John the Baptist.

The epileptic demoniac

14   As they were rejoining the crowd a man came up to him and went down on
15   his knees before him. •'Lord,' he said 'take pity on my son: he is a lunatic and
16   in a wretched state; he is always falling into the fire or into the water. •I took
17   him to your disciples and they were unable to cure him.' •'Faithless and perverse generation!' Jesus said in reply 'How much longer must I be with you? How much
18   longer must I put up with you? Bring him here to me.' •And when Jesus rebuked it the devil came out of the boy who was cured from that moment.
19   Then the disciples came privately to Jesus. 'Why were we unable to cast it
20   out?' they asked. •He answered, 'Because you have little faith. I tell you solemnly, if your faith were the size of a mustard seed you could say to this mountain, "Move from here to there", and it would move; nothing would be impossible for you.'

Second prophecy of the Passion

22   One day when they were together in Galilee, Jesus said to them, 'The Son
23   of Man is going to be handed over into the power of men; •they will put him to death, and on the third day he will be raised to life again'. And a great sadness came over them.

---

16 a. Yeast, here, is regarded as adulterating pure flour.   **b.** Not, until now, a proper name: Greek *petros* (as in Engl. saltpetre) represents Aramaic *kepha*, rock.   **c.** The gates symbolise the power of the underworld to hold captives.   **d.** The keys have become the traditional insignia of Peter.   **e.** In vv. 27-28, two different sayings have been combined because both refer to the coming of the kingdom; but the first is about Judgement day, and the second is about the destruction of Jerusalem, the sign of 'the last days'.
17 a. Representing the Law and the prophets.

The Temple tax paid by Jesus and Peter

When they reached Capernaum, the collectors of the half-shekel*ᵇ* came to 24
Peter and said, 'Does your master not pay the half-shekel?' •'Oh yes' he replied, 25
and went into the house. But before he could speak, Jesus said, 'Simon, what is
your opinion? From whom do the kings of the earth take toll or tribute? From
their sons or from foreigners?' •And when he replied, 'From foreigners', Jesus 26
said, 'Well then, the sons are exempt. •However, so as not to offend these 27
people, go to the lake and cast a hook; take the first fish that bites, open its
mouth and there you will find a shekel; take it and give it to them for me and
for you.'

B. THE DISCOURSE ON THE CHURCH

Who is the greatest?

18 At this time the disciples came to Jesus and said, 'Who is the greatest in 1
the kingdom of heaven?' •So he called a little child to him and set the child 2
in front of them. •Then he said, 'I tell you solemnly, unless you change and become 3
like little children you will never enter the kingdom of heaven. •And so, the 4
one who makes himself as little as this little child is the greatest in the kingdom
of heaven.

On leading others astray

'Anyone who welcomes a little child like this in my name welcomes me. 5
But anyone who is an obstacle to bring down one of these little ones who have 6
faith in me would be better drowned in the depths of the sea with a great
millstone round his neck. •Alas for the world that there should be such obstacles! 7
Obstacles indeed there must be, but alas for the man who provides them!

'If your hand or your foot should cause you to sin, cut it off and throw it 8
away: it is better for you to enter into life crippled or lame, than to have two
hands or two feet and be thrown into eternal fire. •And if your eye should cause 9
you to sin, tear it out and throw it away: it is better for you to enter into life with
one eye, than to have two eyes and be thrown into the hell of fire.

'See that you never despise any of these little ones, for I tell you that their 10
angels in heaven are continually in the presence of my Father in heaven.*ᵃ*

The lost sheep

'Tell me. Suppose a man has a hundred sheep and one of them strays; will 12
he not leave the ninety-nine on the hillside and go in search of the stray? •I tell 13
you solemnly, if he finds it, it gives him more joy than do the ninety-nine that did
not stray at all. •Similarly, it is never the will of your Father in heaven that 14
one of these little ones should be lost.

Brotherly correction

'If your brother does something wrong, go and have it out with him alone, 15
between your two selves. If he listens to you, you have won back your brother.
If he does not listen, take one or two others along with you: *the evidence of two* 16
or three witnesses is required to sustain any charge. •But if he refuses to listen to 17
these, report it to the community;*ᵇ* and if he refuses to listen to the community,
treat him like a pagan or a tax collector.

'I tell you solemnly, whatever you bind on earth shall be considered bound in 18
heaven; whatever you loose on earth shall be considered loosed in heaven.

Prayer in common

'I tell you solemnly once again, if two of you on earth agree to ask anything 19
at all, it will be granted to you by my Father in heaven. •For where two or three 20
meet in my name, I shall be there with them.'

Forgiveness of injuries

21 Then Peter went up to him and said, 'Lord, how often must I forgive my
22 brother if he wrongs me? As often as seven times?' •Jesus answered, 'Not seven,
I tell you, but seventy-seven times.

Parable of the unforgiving debtor

23 'And so the kingdom of heaven may be compared to a king who decided
24 to settle his accounts with his servants. •When the reckoning began, they
25 brought him a man who owed ten thousand talents;ᶜ •but he had no means of
paying, so his master gave orders that he should be sold, together with his wife
26 and children and all his possessions, to meet the debt. •At this, the servant threw
himself down at his master's feet. "Give me time" he said "and I will pay the
27 whole sum." •And the servant's master felt so sorry for him that he let him go
28 and cancelled the debt. •Now as this servant went out, he happened to meet a fellow
servant who owed him one hundred denarii; ᵈ and he seized him by the throat
29 and began to throttle him. "Pay what you owe me" he said. •His fellow servant
fell at his feet and implored him, saying, "Give me time and I will pay you".
30 But the other would not agree; on the contrary, he had him thrown into prison
31 till he should pay the debt. •His fellow servants were deeply distressed when
they saw what had happened, and they went to their master and reported the
32 whole affair to him. •Then the master sent for him. "You wicked servant," he
33 said "I cancelled all that debt of yours when you appealed to me. •Were you not
bound, then, to have pity on your fellow servant just as I had pity on you?"
34 And in his anger the master handed him over to the torturers till he should pay
35 all his debt. •And that is how my heavenly Father will deal with you unless you
each forgive your brother from your heart.'

VI. THE APPROACHING ADVENT
OF THE KINGDOM OF HEAVEN

A. NARRATIVE SECTION

The question about divorce

1 **19** Jesus had now finished what he wanted to say, and he left Galilee and
2 came into the part of Judaea which is on the far side of the Jordan. •Large
crowds followed him and he healed them there.

3 Some Pharisees approached him, and to test him they said, 'Is it against the
4 Law for a man to divorce his wife on any pretext whatever?' •He answered, 'Have
5 you not read that the creator from the beginning *made them male and female* •and
that he said: *This is why a man must leave father and mother, and cling to his wife,*
6 *and the two become one body*? •They are no longer two, therefore, but one body.
So then, what God has united, man must not divide.'

7 They said to him, 'Then why did Moses command that a writ of dismissal
8 should be given in cases of divorce?' •'It was because you were so unteachable'
he said 'that Moses allowed you to divorce your wives, but it was not like this
9 from the beginning. •Now I say this to you: the man who divorces his wife—
I am not speaking of fornication—and marries another, is guilty of adultery.'

b. A tax for the upkeep of the Temple.
18 a. V. 11, at the time when verse numbers were added, consisted of a sentence which is not
now accepted as part of the original text.   b. The community of the brothers (the Church).
c. 'Millions of pounds'—about £3,000,000.   d. Under £5.

Continence

The disciples said to him, 'If that is how things are between husband and wife, 10
it is not advisable to marry'. •But he replied, 'It is not everyone who can accept 11
what I have said, but only those to whom it is granted. •There are eunuchs born 12
that way from their mother's womb, there are eunuchs made so by men and
there are eunuchs who have made themselves that way for the sake of the kingdom
of heaven. Let anyone accept this who can.'

Jesus and the children

People brought little children to him, for him to lay his hands on them and 13
say a prayer. The disciples turned them away, •but Jesus said, 'Let the little 14
children alone, and do not stop them coming to me; for it is to such as these that
the kingdom of heaven belongs'. •Then he laid his hands on them and went on 15
his way.

The rich young man

And there was a man who came to him and asked, 'Master, what good deed 16
must I do to possess eternal life?' •Jesus said to him, 'Why do you ask me about 17
what is good? There is one alone who is good. But if you wish to enter into
life, keep the commandments.' •He said, 'Which?' 'These:' Jesus replied '*You* 18
must not kill. You must not commit adultery. You must not steal. You must not
bring false witness. •*Honour your father and mother*, and: *you must love your* 19
neighbour as yourself.'[a] •The young man said to him, 'I have kept all these. What 20
more do I need to do?' •Jesus said, 'If you wish to be perfect, go and sell what you 21
own and give the money to the poor, and you will have treasure in heaven;
then come, follow me'. •But when the young man heard these words he went 22
away sad, for he was a man of great wealth.

The danger of riches

Then Jesus said to his disciples, 'I tell you solemnly, it will be hard for a 23
rich man to enter the kingdom of heaven. •Yes, I tell you again, it is easier 24
for a camel to pass through the eye of a needle than for a rich man to enter the
kingdom of heaven.' •When the disciples heard this they were astonished. 25
'Who can be saved, then?' they said. •Jesus gazed at them. 'For men' he told 26
them 'this is impossible; for God everything is possible.'

The reward of renunciation

Then Peter spoke. 'What about us?' he said to him 'We have left everything 27
and followed you. What are we to have, then?' •Jesus said to him, 'I tell you 28
solemnly, when all is made new and the Son of Man sits on his throne of glory,
you will yourselves sit on twelve thrones to judge the twelve tribes of Israel.
And everyone who has left houses, brothers, sisters, father, mother, children 29
or land for the sake of my name will be repaid a hundred times over, and also
inherit eternal life.

'Many who are first will be last, and the last, first. 30

Parable of the vineyard labourers

20 'Now the kingdom of heaven is like a landowner going out at daybreak 1
to hire workers for his vineyard. •He made an agreement with the workers 2
for one denarius a day, and sent them to his vineyard. •Going out at about the 3
third hour he saw others standing idle in the market place •and said to them, 4
"You go to my vineyard too and I will give you a fair wage". •So they went. At 5
about the sixth hour and again at about the ninth hour, he went out and did the
same. •Then at about the eleventh hour he went out and found more men standing 6
round, and he said to them, "Why have you been standing here idle all day?"
"Because no one has hired us" they answered. He said to them, "You go into 7

8 my vineyard too". •In the evening, the owner of the vineyard said to his bailiff, "Call the workers and pay them their wages, starting with the last arrivals and
9 ending with the first". •So those who were hired at about the eleventh hour came
10 forward and received one denarius each. •When the first came, they expected to
11 get more, but they too received one denarius each. •They took it, but grumbled
12 at the landowner. • "The men who came last" they said "have done only one hour, and you have treated them the same as us, though we have done a heavy day's
13 work in all the heat." •He answered one of them and said, "My friend, I am
14 not being unjust to you; did we not agree on one denarius? •Take your earnings
15 and go. I choose to pay the last-comer as much as I pay you. •Have I no right
16 to do what I like with my own? Why be envious because I am generous?" •Thus the last will be first, and the first, last.'

Third prophecy of the Passion

17   Jesus was going up to Jerusalem, and on the way he took the Twelve to one
18 side and said to them, •'Now we are going up to Jerusalem, and the Son of Man is about to be handed over to the chief priests and scribes. They will condemn
19 him to death •and will hand him over to the pagans to be mocked and scourged and crucified; and on the third day he will rise again.'

The mother of Zebedee's sons makes her request

20   Then the mother of Zebedee's sons came with her sons to make a request of
21 him, and bowed low; •and he said to her, 'What is it you want?' She said to him, 'Promise that these two sons of mine may sit one at your right hand and the
22 other at your left in your kingdom'. •'You do not know what you are asking' Jesus answered. 'Can you drink the cup that I am going to drink?' They replied,
23 'We can'. •'Very well,' he said 'you shall drink my cup,^a but as for seats at my right hand and my left, these are not mine to grant; they belong to those to whom they have been allotted by my Father.'

Leadership with service

24   When the other ten heard this they were indignant with the two brothers.
25 But Jesus called them to him and said, 'You know that among the pagans the
26 rulers lord it over them, and their great men make their authority felt. •This is not to happen among you. No; anyone who wants to be great among you must
27 be your servant, •and anyone who wants to be first among you must be your
28 slave, •just as the Son of Man came not to be served but to serve, and to give his life as a ransom for many.'

The two blind men of Jericho

29
30   As they left Jericho a large crowd followed him. •Now there were two blind men sitting at the side of the road. When they heard that it was Jesus who was
31 passing by, they shouted, 'Lord! Have pity on us, Son of David.' •And the crowd scolded them and told them to keep quiet, but they only shouted more loudly,
32 'Lord! Have pity on us, Son of David.' •Jesus stopped, called them over and
33 said, 'What do you want me to do for you?' •They said to him, 'Lord, let us
34 have our sight back'. •Jesus felt pity for them and touched their eyes, and immediately their sight returned and they followed him.

The Messiah enters Jerusalem

1   **21** When they were near Jerusalem and had come in sight of Bethphage on the
2   Mount of Olives, Jesus sent two disciples, •saying to them, 'Go to the village facing you, and you will immediately find a tethered donkey and a colt with her.

19 a. Ex 20:12-16; Dt 5:16-20   b. I.e. to govern.
20 a. Perhaps a prophecy of the martyrdom of James and John; James was certainly put to death by Herod Agrippa about 44 A.D., Ac 12:2.

Untie them and bring them to me. •If anyone says anything to you, you are to 3
say, "The Master needs them and will send them back directly".' •This took place 4
to fulfil the prophecy:

> *Say to the daughter of Zion:* 5
> *Look, your king comes to you;*
> *he is humble, he rides on a donkey*
> *and on a colt, the foal of a beast of burden.*[a]

So the disciples went out and did as Jesus had told them. •They brought 6
the donkey and the colt, then they laid their cloaks on their backs and he sat on 7
them. •Great crowds of people spread their cloaks on the road, while others 8
were cutting branches from the trees and spreading them in his path. •The crowds 9
who went in front of him and those who followed were all shouting:

> '*Hosanna*[b] to the Son of David!
> *Blessings on him who comes in the name of the Lord!*[c]
> *Hosanna* in the highest heavens!'

And when he entered Jerusalem, the whole city was in turmoil. 'Who is this?' 10
people asked, •and the crowds answered, 'This is the prophet Jesus from Nazareth 11
in Galilee'.

The expulsion of the dealers from the Temple

Jesus then went into the Temple and drove out all those who were selling and 12
buying there; he upset the tables of the money changers and the chairs of those
who were selling pigeons.[d] •'According to scripture' he said '*my house will be called* 13
a house of prayer,[e] but you are turning it into a *robbers' den*.'[f] •There were also blind 14
and lame people who came to him in the Temple, and he cured them. •At the sight 15
of the wonderful things he did and of the children shouting, 'Hosanna to the
Son of David' in the Temple, the chief priests and the scribes were indignant. •'Do 16
you hear what they are saying?' they said to him. 'Yes,' Jesus answered 'have you
never read this:

> *By the mouths of children, babes in arms,*
> *you have made sure of praise?*'[g]

With that he left them and went out of the city to Bethany where he spent the 17
night.

The barren fig tree withers. Faith and prayer

As he was returning to the city in the early morning, he felt hungry. •Seeing 18
a fig tree by the road, he went up to it and found nothing on it but leaves. 19
And he said to it, 'May you never bear fruit again'; and at that instant the fig tree
withered. •The disciples were amazed when they saw it. 'What happened to the 20
tree' they said 'that it withered there and then?' •Jesus answered, 'I tell you 21
solemnly, if you have faith and do not doubt at all, not only will you do what
I have done to the fig tree, but even if you say to this mountain, "Get up and throw
yourself into the sea", it will be done. •And if you have faith, everything you ask 22
for in prayer you will receive.'

The authority of Jesus is questioned

He had gone into the Temple and was teaching, when the chief priests and the 23
elders of the people came to him and said, 'What authority have you for acting
like this? And who gave you this authority?' •'And I' replied Jesus 'will ask you 24
a question, only one; if you tell me the answer to it, I will then tell me my
authority for acting like this. •John's baptism: where did it come from: heaven 25
or man?' And they argued it out this way among themselves, 'If we say from
heaven, he will retort, "Then why did you refuse to believe him?"; •but if we say 26
from man, we have the people to fear, for they all hold that John was a prophet'.

27 So their reply to Jesus was, 'We do not know'. And he retorted, 'Nor will I tell
you my authority for acting like this.

Parable of the two sons

28   'What is your opinion? A man had two sons. He went and said to the first,
29 "My boy, you go and work in the vineyard today". •He answered, "I will not go",
30 but afterwards thought better of it and went. •The man then went and said the
31 same thing to the second who answered, "Certainly, sir", but did not go. •Which
of the two did the father's will?' 'The first' they said. Jesus said to them, 'I tell
you solemnly, tax collectors and prostitutes are making their way into
32 the kingdom of God before you. •For John came to you, a pattern of true
righteousness, but you did not believe him, and yet the tax collectors and
prostitutes did. Even after seeing that, you refused to think better of it and
believe in him.

Parable of the wicked husbandmen

33   'Listen to another parable. There was a man, a landowner, who planted
a vineyard; he fenced it round, dug a winepress in it and built a tower; then he
34 leased it to tenants and went abroad. •When vintage time drew near he sent his
35 servants to the tenants to collect his produce. •But the tenants seized his servants,
36 thrashed one, killed another and stoned a third. •Next he sent some more servants,
37 this time a larger number, and they dealt with them in the same way. •Finally
38 he sent his son to them. "They will respect my son" he said. •But when the tenants
saw the son, they said to each other, "This is the heir. Come on, let us kill him and
39 take over his inheritance." •So they seized him and threw him out of the vineyard
40 and killed him. •Now when the owner of the vineyard comes, what will he do
41 to those tenants?' •They answered, 'He will bring those wretches to a wretched end
and lease the vineyard to other tenants who will deliver the produce to him when
42 the season arrives'. •Jesus said to them, 'Have you never read in the scriptures:

> It was the stone rejected by the builders
> that became the keystone.
> This was the Lord's doing
> and it is wonderful to see?[h]

43 I tell you, then, that the kingdom of God will be taken from you and given to
a people who will produce its fruit.'

45   When they heard his parables, the chief priests and the scribes realised he was
46 speaking about them, •but though they would have liked to arrest him they were
afraid of the crowds, who looked on him as a prophet.

Parable of the wedding feast

1 22 Jesus began to speak to them in parables once again, •'The kingdom of
2   heaven may be compared to a king who gave a feast for his son's wedding.
3 He sent his servants to call those who had been invited, but they would not come.
4 Next he sent some more servants. "Tell those who have been invited" he said
"that I have my banquet all prepared, my oxen and fattened cattle have been
5 slaughtered, everything is ready. Come to the wedding." •But they were not
6 interested: one went off to his farm, another to his business, •and the rest seized
7 his servants, maltreated them and killed them. •The king was furious. He
8 despatched his troops, destroyed those murderers and burnt their town. •Then
he said to his servants, "The wedding is ready; but as those who were invited
9 proved to be unworthy, •go to the crossroads in the town and invite everyone
10 you can find to the wedding". •So these servants went out on to the roads and

21 a. Is 62:11; Zc 9:9   b. Conventional shout of acclaim, like a cheer.   c. Ps 118:26
d. Money changers provided Temple currency, and the traders the animals, for making sacrificial
offerings.   e. Is 56:7   f. Jr 7:11   g. Ps 8:2 (LXX); Ws 10:21   h. Ps 118:22-23

collected together everyone they could find, bad and good alike; and the wedding hall was filled with guests. •When the king came in to look at the guests he noticed 11 one man who was not wearing a wedding garment, •and said to him, "How did 12 you get in here, my friend, without a wedding garment?" And the man was silent. Then the king said to the attendants, "Bind him hand and foot and throw him 13 out into the dark, where there will be weeping and grinding of teeth". •For many 14 are called, but few are chosen.'

On tribute to Caesar

Then the Pharisees went away to work out between them how to trap him 15 in what he said. •And they sent their disciples to him, together with the 16 Herodians,ᵃ to say, 'Master, we know that you are an honest man and teach the way of God in an honest way, and that you are not afraid of anyone, because a man's rank means nothing to you. •Tell us your opinion, then. Is it permissible 17 to pay taxes to Caesar or not?' •But Jesus was aware of their malice and replied, 18 'You hypocrites! Why do you set this trap for me? •Let me see the money you 19 pay the tax with.' They handed him a denarius, •and he said, 'Whose head is this? 20 Whose name?' •'Caesar's' they replied. He then said to them, 'Very well, give 21 back to Caesar what belongs to Caesar—and to God what belongs to God'. This reply took them by surprise, and they left him alone and went away. 22

The resurrection of the dead

That day some Sadducees—who deny that there is a resurrection—approached 23 him and they put this question to him, •'Master, Moses said that if a man 24 dies childless, his brother is to marry the widow, his sister-in-law, to raise children for his brother. •Now we had a case involving seven brothers; the first 25 married and then died without children, leaving his wife to his brother; •the 26 same thing happened with the second and third and so on to the seventh, •and then 27 last of all the woman herself died. •Now at the resurrection to which of those 28 seven will she be wife, since she had been married to them all?' •Jesus answered 29 them, 'You are wrong, because you understand neither the scriptures nor the power of God. •For at the resurrection men and women do not marry; no, they 30 are like the angels in heaven. •And as for the resurrection of the dead, have you 31 never read what God himself said to you: •*I am the God of Abraham, the God of* 32 *Isaac and the God of Jacob?*ᵇ God is God, not of the dead, but of the living.' And his teaching made a deep impression on the people who heard it. 33

The greatest commandment of all

But when the Pharisees heard that he had silenced the Sadducees they got 34 together •and, to disconcert him, one of them put a question, •'Master, which 35/36 is the greatest commandment of the Law?' •Jesus said, '*You must love the Lord* 37 *your God with all your heart, with all your soul,* and with all your mind. •This is 38 the greatest and the first commandment. •The second resembles it: *You must love* 39 *your neighbour as yourself.* •On these two commandments hang the whole Law, 40 and the Prophets also.'

Christ not only son but also Lord of David

While the Pharisees were gathered round, Jesus put to them this question, 41 'What is your opinion about the Christ? Whose son is he?' 'David's' they told him. 42 'Then how is it' he said 'that David, moved by the Spirit, calls him Lord, where 43 he says:

The Lord said to my Lord: 44
Sit at my right hand
and I will put your enemies
*under your feet?*ᶜ

45 'If David can call him Lord, then how can he be his son?' •Not one could think
46 of anything to say in reply, and from that day no one dared to ask him any
further questions.

The scribes and Pharisees: their hypocrisy and vanity

1
2   **23** Then addressing the people and his disciples Jesus said, •'The scribes and
3   the Pharisees occupy the chair of Moses. •You must therefore do what they
tell you and listen to what they say; but do not be guided by what they do: since
4 they do not practise what they preach. •They tie up heavy burdens and lay them
5 on men's shoulders, but will they lift a finger to move them? Not they! •Everything
they do is done to attract attention, like wearing broader phylacteries and longer
6 tassels,ª •like wanting to take the place of honour at banquets and the front
7 seats in the synagogues, •being greeted obsequiously in the market squares and
having people call them Rabbi.
8   'You, however, must not allow yourselves to be called Rabbi, since you have
9 only one Master, and you are all brothers. •You must call no one on earth your
10 father, since you have only one Father, and he is in heaven. •Nor must you allow
yourselves to be called teachers, for you have only one Teacher, the Christ.
11 The greatest among you must be your servant. •Anyone who exalts himself will
12 be humbled, and anyone who humbles himself will be exalted.

The sevenfold indictment of the scribes and Pharisees

13   'Alas for you, scribes and Pharisees, you hypocrites! You who shut up the
kingdom of heaven in men's faces, neither going in yourselves nor allowing
others to go inᵇ who want to.
15   'Alas for you, scribes and Pharisees, you hypocrites! You who travel over
sea and land to make a single proselyte, and when you have him you make him
twice as fit for hell as you are.
16   'Alas for you, blind guides! You who say, "If a man swears by the Temple,
it has no force; but if a man swears by the gold of the Temple, he is bound".
17 Fools and blind! For which is of greater worth, the gold or the Temple that
18 makes the gold sacred? •Or else, "If a man swears by the altar it has no force;
19 but if a man swears by the offering that is on the altar, he is bound". •You blind
men! For which is of greater worth, the offering or the altar that makes the
20 offering sacred? •Therefore, when a man swears by the altar he is swearing by
21 that and by everything on it. •And when a man swears by the Temple he
22 is swearing by that and by the One who dwells in it. •And when a man swears
by heaven he is swearing by the throne of God and by the One who is seated
there.
23   'Alas for you, scribes and Pharisees, you hypocrites! You who pay your tithe
of mint and dill and cumminᶜ and have neglected the weightier matters of the
Law—justice, mercy, good faith! These you should have practised, without
24 neglecting the others. •You blind guides! Straining out gnats and swallowing
camels!
25   'Alas for you, scribes and Pharisees, you hypocrites! You who clean the
outside of cup and dish and leave the inside full of extortion and intemperance.
26 Blind Pharisee! Clean the inside of cup and dish first so that the outside may
become clean as well.
27   'Alas for you, scribes and Pharisees, you hypocrites! You who are like
whitewashed tombs that look handsome on the outside, but inside are full of dead

---

22 a. Supporters of the ruling family, hoping to find a cause for denouncing Jesus to the
Romans.   **b.** Ex 3:6   **c.** Ps 110:1
23 a. Phylacteries: containers for short texts taken from the Law; they were worn on the arm
or the forehead in obedience to Ex 13:9,16 and Dt 6:8. The tassels were sewn to the corners
of the cloak.   **b.** By interpreting the Law so strictly that nobody could obey all of it.   **c.** The
law of paying tithes on crops was extended to include herbs and plants grown for flavouring.

men's bones and every kind of corruption. •In the same way you appear to people 28
from the outside like good honest men, but inside you are full of hypocrisy and
lawlessness.

'Alas for you, scribes and Pharisees, you hypocrites! You who build the 29
sepulchres of the prophets and decorate the tombs of holy men, •saying, "We 30
would never have joined in shedding the blood of the prophets, had we lived in
our fathers' day". •So! Your own evidence tells against you! You are the sons of 31
those who murdered the prophets! •Very well then, finish off the work that your 32
fathers began.

Their crimes and approaching punishment

'Serpents, brood of vipers, how can you escape being condemned to hell? 33
This is why, in my turn, I am sending you prophets and wise men and scribes: 34
some you will slaughter and crucify, some you will scourge in your synagogues
and hunt from town to town; •and so you will draw down on yourselves the blood 35
of every holy man that has been shed on earth, from the blood of Abel the Holy
to the blood of Zechariah son of Barachiah[d] whom you murdered between the
sanctuary and the altar. •I tell you solemnly, all of this will recoil on this 36
generation.

Jerusalem admonished

'Jerusalem, Jerusalem, you that kill the prophets and stone those who are 37
sent to you! How often have I longed to gather your children, as a hen gathers
her chicks under her wings, and you refused! •So be it! Your house will be left 38
to you desolate, •for, I promise, you shall not see me any more until you say: 39

Blessings on him who comes in the name of the Lord!' [e]

B. THE SERMON ON THE END

Introduction

24 Jesus left the Temple, and as he was going away his disciples came up to 1
draw his attention to the Temple buildings. •He said to them in reply, 2
'You see all these? I tell you solemnly, not a single stone here will be left
on another: everything will be destroyed.' •And when he was sitting on the 3
Mount of Olives the disciples came and asked him privately, 'Tell us, when is
this going to happen, and what will be the sign of your coming and of the end
of the world?'

The beginning of sorrows

And Jesus answered them, 'Take care that no one deceives you; •because ⁴₅
many will come using my name and saying, "I am the Christ", and they will
deceive many. •You will hear of wars and rumours of wars; do not be 6
alarmed, for this is something that must happen, but the end will not be yet.
For nation will fight against nation, and kingdom against kingdom. There will 7
be famines and earthquakes here and there. •All this is only the beginning of 8
the birthpangs.

'Then they will hand you over to be tortured and put to death; and you will 9
be hated by all the nations on account of my name. •And then many will fall 10
away; men will betray one another and hate one another. •Many false prophets 11
will arise; they will deceive many, •and with the increase of lawlessness, love in 12
most men will grow cold; •but the man who stands firm to the end will be saved. 13
'This Good News of the kingdom will be proclaimed to the whole world[a] as 14
a witness to all the nations. And then the end[b] will come.

The great tribulation of Jerusalem

15 'So when you see *the disastrous abomination*, of which the prophet Daniel
16 spoke, set up in the Holy Place (let the reader understand), •then those in
17 Judaea must escape to the mountains; •if a man is on the housetop, he must not
18 come down to collect his belongings; •if a man is in the fields, he must not
19 turn back to fetch his cloak. •Alas for those with child, or with babies at the
20 breast, when those days come! •Pray that you will not have to escape in winter
21 or on a sabbath. •For then there will be *great distress such as, until now, since*
22 the world began, there never *has* been, nor ever will be again. •And if that time
had not been shortened, no one would have survived; but shortened that time
shall be, for the sake of those who are chosen.

23 'If anyone says to you then, "Look, here is the Christ" or, "He is there",
24 do not believe it; •for false Christs and false prophets will arise and produce great
signs and portents, enough to deceive even the chosen, if that were possible.
25 There; I have forewarned you.

The coming of the Son of Man will be evident

26 'If, then, they say to you, "Look, he is in the desert", do not go there;
27 "Look, he is in some hiding place", do not believe it; •because the coming of the
Son of Man will be like lightning striking in the east and flashing far into the
28 west. •Wherever the corpse is, there will the vultures gather.

The universal significance of this coming

29 'Immediately after the distress of those days ^c the sun will be darkened, the
moon will lose its brightness, the stars will fall from the sky and the powers of
30 heaven will be shaken. •And then the sign of the Son of Man will appear
in heaven; then too all the peoples of the earth will beat their breasts; and they
will see the Son of Man coming on the clouds of heaven with power and great
31 glory.^d •And he will send his angels with a loud trumpet to gather his chosen
from the four winds, from one end of heaven to the other.

The time of this coming

32 'Take the fig tree as a parable: as soon as its twigs grow supple and its leaves
33 come out, you know that summer is near. •So with you when you see all these
34 things: know that he is near, at the very gates. •I tell you solemnly, before
35 this generation has passed away all these things will have taken place.^e •Heaven
36 and earth will pass away, but my words will never pass away. •But as for that day
and hour, nobody knows it, neither the angels of heaven, nor the Son, no one
but the Father only.

Be on the alert

37
38 'As it was in Noah's day, so will it be when the Son of Man comes. •For in
those days before the Flood people were eating, drinking, taking wives, taking
39 husbands, right up to the day Noah went into the ark, •and they suspected nothing
till the Flood came and swept all away. It will be like this when the Son of Man
40
41 comes. •Then of two men in the fields one is taken, one left; •of two women at
the millstone grinding, one is taken, one left.

42 'So stay awake, because you do not know the day when your master is coming.
43 You may be quite sure of this that if the householder had known at what time
of the night the burglar would come, he would have stayed awake and would

d. Possibly Zechariah, the last of the prophets to be killed, according to the Jewish scriptures
(2 Ch 24:20-22). **e.** Ps 118:26
24 a. The 'inhabited world' as it was known. **b.** The fall and destruction of Jerusalem. A
prophecy of this is combined, in this discourse, with descriptions of the 'last days'. **c.** Join
with v. 22. Vv. 23-28 are a digression. **d.** As foretold in Dn 7:14. **e.** Meaning the fall and
destruction of Jerusalem.

not have allowed anyone to break through the wall of his house. •Therefore, you 44 too must stand ready because the Son of Man is coming at an hour you do not expect.

Parable of the conscientious steward

'What sort of servant, then, is faithful and wise enough for the master to 45 place him over his household to give them their food at the proper time? Happy that servant if his master's arrival finds him at this employment. •I tell 46 you solemnly, he will place him over everything he owns. •But as for the 48 dishonest servant who says to himself, "My master is taking his time", •and sets 49 about beating his fellow servants and eating and drinking with drunkards, •his 50 master will come on a day he does not expect and at an hour he does not know. The master will cut him off and send him to the same fate as the hypocrites, where 51 there will be weeping and grinding of teeth.

Parable of the ten bridesmaids

25 'Then the kingdom of heaven will be like this: Ten bridesmaids took their 1 lamps and went to meet the bridegroom. •Five of them were foolish and five 2 were sensible: •the foolish ones did take their lamps, but they brought no oil, 3 whereas the sensible ones took flasks of oil as well as their lamps. •The bride- 4 groom was late, and they all grew drowsy and fell asleep. •But at midnight there 6 was a cry, "The bridegroom is here! Go out and meet him." •At this, all those 7 bridesmaids woke up and trimmed their lamps, •and the foolish ones said to 8 the sensible ones, "Give us some of your oil: our lamps are going out". •But 9 they replied, " There may not be enough for us and for you; you had better go to those who sell it and buy some for yourselves". •They had gone off to buy 10 it when the bridegroom arrived. Those who were ready went in with him to the wedding hall and the door was closed. •The other bridesmaids arrived later. 11 "Lord, Lord," they said "open the door for us." •But he replied, "I tell you 12 solemnly, I do not know you". •So stay awake, because you do not know either 13 the day or the hour.

Parable of the talents

'It is like a man on his way abroad who summoned his servants and entrusted 14 his property to them. •To one he gave five talents, to another two, to a third 15 one; each in proportion to his ability. Then he set out. •The man who had received 16 the five talents promptly went and traded with them and made five more. •The 17 man who had received two made two more in the same way. •But the man who 18 had received one went off and dug a hole in the ground and hid his master's money. •Now a long time after, the master of those servants came back and went 19 through his accounts with them. •The man who had received the five talents came 20 forward bringing five more. "Sir," he said "you entrusted me with five talents; here are five more that I have made." •His master said to him, "Well done, good 21 and faithful servant; you have shown you can be faithful in small things, I will trust you with greater; come and join in your master's happiness". •Next the man 22 with the two talents came forward. " Sir," he said "you entrusted me with two talents; here are two more that I have made." •His master said to him, "Well 23 done, good and faithful servant; you have shown you can be faithful in small things, I will trust you with greater; come and join in your master's happiness". Last came forward the man who had the one talent. "Sir," said he "I had heard 24 you were a hard man, reaping where you have not sown and gathering where you have not scattered; •so I was afraid, and I went off and hid your talent in 25 the ground. Here it is; it was yours, you have it back." •But his master answered 26 him, "You wicked and lazy servant! So you knew that I reap where I have not sown and gather where I have not scattered? •Well then, you should have deposited 27 my money with the bankers, and on my return I would have recovered my capital

28 with interest. •So now, take the talent from him and give it to the man who has
29 the five talents. •For to everyone who has will be given more, and he will have more
than enough; but from the man who has not, even what he has will be taken away.
30 As for this good-for-nothing servant, throw him out into the dark, where there
will be weeping and grinding of teeth."

The Last Judgement

31 'When the Son of Man comes in his glory, escorted by all the angels, then
32 he will take his seat on his throne of glory. •All the nations will be assembled
before him and he will separate men one from another as the shepherd separates
33 sheep from goats. •He will place the sheep on his right hand and the goats
34 on his left. •Then the King will say to those on his right hand, "Come, you whom
my Father has blessed, take for your heritage the kingdom prepared for you
35 since the foundation of the world. •For I was hungry and you gave me food;
I was thirsty and you gave me drink; I was a stranger and you made me welcome;
36 naked and you clothed me, sick and you visited me, in prison and you came to
37 see me." •Then the virtuous will say to him in reply, "Lord, when did we see
38 you hungry and feed you; or thirsty and give you drink? •When did we see you
39 a stranger and make you welcome; naked and clothe you; •sick or in prison and
40 go to see you?" •And the King will answer, "I tell you solemnly, in so far
as you did this to one of the least of these brothers of mine, you did it to me".
41 Next he will say to those on his left hand, "Go away from me, with your curse
42 upon you, to the eternal fire prepared for the devil and his angels. •For I was
hungry and you never gave me food; I was thirsty and you never gave me anything
43 to drink; •I was a stranger and you never made me welcome, naked and you
44 never clothed me, sick and in prison and you never visited me." •Then it will be
their turn to ask, "Lord, when did we see you hungry or thirsty, a stranger or
45 naked, sick or in prison, and did not come to your help?" •Then he will answer,
"I tell you solemnly, in so far as you neglected to do this to one of the least
46 of these, you neglected to do it to me". •And they will go away to eternal punishment, and the virtuous to eternal life.'

VII. PASSION AND RESURRECTION

The conspiracy against Jesus

1
2 26 Jesus had now finished all he wanted to say, and he told his disciples,
'It will be Passover, as you know, in two days' time, and the Son of Man
will be handed over to be crucified'.
3   Then the chief priests and the elders of the people assembled in the palace of
4 the high priest, whose name was Caiaphas, •and made plans to arrest Jesus by
5 some trick and have him put to death. •They said, however, 'It must not be during
the festivities; there must be no disturbance among the people'.

The anointing at Bethany

6
7   Jesus was at Bethany in the house of Simon the leper, when •a woman came
to him with an alabaster jar of the most expensive ointment, and poured it on his
8 head as he was at table. •When they saw this, the disciples were indignant; 'Why
9 this waste?' they said. •'This could have been sold at a high price and the money
10 given to the poor.' •Jesus noticed this. 'Why are you upsetting the woman?' he
said to them. 'What she has done for me is one of the good works *a* indeed!
11
12 You have the poor with you always, but you will not always have me. •When she
13 poured this ointment on my body, she did it to prepare me for burial. •I tell you
solemnly, wherever in all the world this Good News is proclaimed, what she has
done will be told also, in remembrance of her.'

26 a. As 'good works', charitable deeds were reckoned superior to almsgiving.

Judas betrays Jesus

Then one of the Twelve, the man called Judas Iscariot, went to the chief 14
priests and said, 'What are you prepared to give me if I hand him over to you?' 15
They paid him thirty silver pieces,ᵇ and from that moment he looked for an 16
opportunity to betray him.

Preparations for the Passover supper

Now on the first day of Unleavened Breadᶜ the disciples came to Jesus to 17
say, 'Where do you want us to make the preparations for you to eat the
passover?' •'Go to so-and-so in the city' he replied 'and say to him, "The Master 18
says: My time is near. It is at your house that I am keeping Passover with my
disciples." ' •The disciples did what Jesus told them and prepared the Passover. 19

The treachery of Judas foretold

When evening came he was at table with the twelve disciples. •And while they 20
were eating he said, 'I tell you solemnly, one of you is about to betray 21
me'. •They were greatly distressed and started asking him in turn, 'Not I, Lord, 22
surely?' •He answered, 'Someone who has dipped his hand into the dish with me, 23
will betray me. •The Son of Man is going to his fate, as the scriptures say he 24
will, but alas for that man by whom the Son of Man is betrayed! Better for that
man if he had never been born!' •Judas, who was to betray him, asked in his 25
turn, 'Not I, Rabbi, surely?' 'They are your own words' answered Jesus.

The institution of the Eucharist

Now as they were eating,ᵈ Jesus took some bread, and when he had said the 26
blessing he broke it and gave it to the disciples. 'Take it and eat;' he said 'this is
my body.' •Then he took a cup, and when he had returned thanks he gave it 27
to them. 'Drink all of you from this,' he said •'for this is my blood, the blood 28
of the covenant, which is to be poured out for many for the forgiveness of
sins. •From now on, I tell you, I shall not drink wine until the day I drink 29
the new wine with you in the kingdom of my Father.'

Peter's denial foretold

After psalms had been sungᵉ they left for the Mount of Olives. •Then Jesus said 30
to them, 'You will all lose faith in me this night,ᶠ for the scripture says: 31
*I shall strike the shepherd and the sheep of the flock will be scattered,*ᵍ •but after my 32
resurrection I shall go before you to Galilee'. •At this, Peter said, 'Though all 33
lose faith in you, I will never lose faith'. •Jesus answered him, 'I tell you 34
solemnly, this very night, before the cock crows, you will have disowned
me three times'. •Peter said to him, 'Even if I have to die with you, I will never 35
disown you'. And all the disciples said the same.

Gethsemane

Then Jesus came with them to a small estate called Gethsemane; and he said 36
to his disciples, 'Stay here while I go over there to pray'. •He took Peter and the 37
two sons of Zebedee with him. And sadness came over him, and great distress.
Then he said to them, 'My soul is sorrowful to the point of death. Wait here and 38
keep awake with me.' •And going on a little further he fell on his face and prayed. 39
'My Father,' he said 'if it is possible, let this cup pass me by. Nevertheless, let it
be as you, not I, would have it.' •He came back to the disciples and found them 40
sleeping, and he said to Peter, 'So you had not the strength to keep awake with
me one hour? •You should be awake, and praying not to be put to the test. The 41
spirit is willing, but the flesh is weak.' •Again, a second time, he went away and 42
prayed: 'My Father,' he said 'if this cup cannot pass by without my drinking it,
your will be done!' •And he came back again and found them sleeping, their eyes 43
were so heavy. •Leaving them there, he went away again and prayed for the 44

45 third time, repeating the same words. •Then he came back to the disciples and
said to them, 'You can sleep on now and take your rest. Now the hour has
46 come when the Son of Man is to be betrayed into the hands of sinners. •Get up!
Let us go! My betrayer is already close at hand.'

The arrest

47 He was still speaking when Judas, one of the Twelve, appeared, and with him
a large number of men armed with swords and clubs, sent by the chief priests and
48 elders of the people. •Now the traitor had arranged a sign with them. 'The one
49 I kiss,' he had said 'he is the man. Take him in charge .' •So he went straight up to
50 Jesus and said, 'Greetings, Rabbi', and kissed him. •Jesus said to him, 'My friend,
do what you are here for'. Then they came forward, seized Jesus and took him in
51 charge. •At that, one of the followers of Jesus grasped his sword and drew it; he
52 struck out at the high priest's servant, and cut off his ear. •Jesus then said, 'Put your
53 sword back, for all who draw the sword will die by the sword. •Or do you think
that I cannot appeal to my Father who would promptly send more than twelve
54 legions of angels to my defence? •But then, how would the scriptures be fulfilled
55 that say this is the way it must be?' •It was at this time that Jesus said to the
crowds, 'Am I a brigand, that you had to set out to capture me with swords
and clubs? I sat teaching in the Temple day after day and you never laid hands
56 on me.' •Now all this happened to fulfil the prophecies in scripture. Then
all the disciples deserted him and ran away.

Jesus before the Sanhedrin

57 The men who had arrested Jesus led him off to Caiaphas the high priest,
58 where the scribes and the elders were assembled. •Peter followed him at
a distance, and when he reached the high priest's palace, he went in and sat down
with the attendants to see what the end would be.
59 The chief priests and the whole Sanhedrin were looking for evidence against
60 Jesus, however false, on which they might pass the death-sentence. •But they could
not find any, though several lying witnesses came forward. Eventually two
61 stepped forward •and made a statement, 'This man said, "I have power to
62 destroy the Temple of God and in three days build it up" '. •The high priest
then stood up and said to him, 'Have you no answer to that? What is this evidence
63 these men are bringing against you?' •But Jesus was silent. And the high priest
said to him, 'I put you on oath by the living God to tell us if you are the Christ,
64 the Son of God'. •'The words are your own' answered Jesus. 'Moreover, I tell
you that from this time onward you will see the *Son of Man seated at the right
65 hand of the Power* and *coming on the clouds of heaven*.' •At this, the high priest
tore his clothes and said, 'He has blasphemed. What need of witnesses have
66 we now? There! You have just heard the blasphemy. •What is your opinion?'
They answered, 'He deserves to die'.
67 Then they spat in his face and hit him with their fists; others said as they
68 struck him, •'Play the prophet, Christ! Who hit you then?'

Peter's denials

69 Meanwhile Peter was sitting outside in the courtyard, and a servant-girl came
70 up to him and said, 'You too were with Jesus the Galilean'. •But he denied it in
71 front of them all. 'I do not know what you are talking about' he said. •When he
went out to the gateway another servant-girl saw him and said to the people there,

b. 30 shekels, the price fixed for a slave's life, Ex 21:32.   c. Unleavened bread was normally
to be eaten during the seven days which followed the Passover supper; here the writer
appears to mean the first day of the whole Passover celebration.   d. The Passover supper
itself, for which exact rules for the blessing of bread and wine were laid down. The 'eating' of
v. 21 is the first course, which came before the Passover itself.   e. The psalms of praise which
end the Passover supper.   f. 'be brought down': the regular expression for the losing of faith
through a difficulty or blow to it.   g. Zc 13:7

'This man was with Jesus the Nazarene'. •And again, with an oath, he denied 72 it, 'I do not know the man'. •A little later the bystanders came up and said to 73 Peter, 'You are one of them for sure! Why, your accent gives you away.' •Then 74 he started calling down curses on himself and swearing, 'I do not know the man'. At that moment the cock crew, •and Peter remembered what Jesus had said, 75 'Before the cock crows you will have disowned me three times'. And he went outside and wept bitterly.

Jesus is taken before Pilate

27 When morning came, all the chief priests and the elders of the people met 1 in council to bring about the death of Jesus. •They had him bound, and 2 led him away to hand him over to Pilate,*a* the governor.

The death of Judas

When he found that Jesus had been condemned, Judas his betrayer was filled 3 with remorse and took the thirty silver pieces back to the chief priests and elders. 'I have sinned;' he said 'I have betrayed innocent blood.' 'What is that to us?' 4 they replied 'That is your concern.' •And flinging down the silver pieces in the 5 sanctuary he made off, and went and hanged himself. •The chief priests picked 6 up the silver pieces and said, 'It is against the Law to put this into the treasury; it is blood-money'. •So they discussed the matter and bought the potter's field 7 with it as a graveyard for foreigners, •and this is why the field is called the Field 8 of Blood today. •The words of the prophet Jeremiah*b* were then fulfilled: *And* 9 *they took the thirty silver pieces, the sum at which the precious One was priced by children of Israel,* •*and they gave them for the potter's field, just as the Lord* 10 *directed me.*

Jesus before Pilate

Jesus, then, was brought before the governor, and the governor put to him 11 this question, 'Are you the king of the Jews?' Jesus replied, 'It is you who say it'. •But when he was accused by the chief priests and the elders he refused to 12 answer at all. •Pilate then said to him, 'Do you not hear how many charges they 13 have brought against you?' •But to the governor's complete amazement, he 14 offered no reply to any of the charges.

At festival time it was the governor's practice to release a prisoner for the 15 people, anyone they chose. •Now there was at that time a notorious prisoner 16 whose name was Barabbas. •So when the crowd gathered, Pilate said to them, 17 'Which do you want me to release for you: Barabbas, or Jesus who is called Christ?' •For Pilate knew it was out of jealousy that they had handed him over. 18 Now as he was seated in the chair of judgement, his wife sent him a message, 19 'Have nothing to do with that man; I have been upset all day by a dream I had about him'.

The chief priests and the elders, however, had persuaded the crowd to demand 20 the release of Barabbas and the execution of Jesus. •So when the governor spoke 21 and asked them, 'Which of the two do you want me to release for you?' they said, 'Barabbas'. •'But in that case,' Pilate said to them 'what am I to do with Jesus 22 who is called Christ?' They all said, 'Let him be crucified!' •'Why?' he asked 'What 23 harm has he done?' But they shouted all the louder, 'Let him be crucified!' Then Pilate saw that he was making no impression, that in fact a riot was 24 imminent. So he took some water, washed his hands in front of the crowd and said, 'I am innocent of this man's blood. It is your concern.' •And the people, 25 to a man, shouted back, 'His blood be on us and on our children!' •Then he 26 released Barabbas for them. He ordered Jesus to be first scourged*c* and then handed over to be crucified.

Jesus is crowned with thorns

27 The governor's soldiers took Jesus with them into the Praetorium and
28 collected the whole cohort round him. •Then they stripped him and made
29 him wear a scarlet cloak, •and having twisted some thorns into a crown they
put this on his head and placed a reed in his right hand. To make fun of him they
30 knelt to him saying, 'Hail, king of the Jews!' •And they spat on him and took
31 the reed and struck him on the head with it. •And when they had finished making
fun of him, they took off the cloak and dressed him in his own clothes and led
him away to crucify him.

The crucifixion

32 On their way out, they came across a man from Cyrene, Simon by name,
33 and enlisted him to carry his cross. •When they had reached a place called
34 Golgotha,ᵈ that is, the place of the skull, •they gave him wine to drink mixed
·35 with gall, which he tasted but refused to drink. •When they had finished
36 crucifying him they shared out his clothing by casting lots, •and then sat down
and stayed there keeping guard over him.
37 Above his head was placed the charge against him; it read: 'This is Jesus,
38 the King of the Jews'. •At the same time two robbers were crucified with him,
one on the right and one on the left.

The crucified Christ is mocked

39
40 The passers-by jeered at him; they shook their heads •and said, 'So you
would destroy the Temple and rebuild it in three days! Then save yourself! If
41 you are God's son, come down from the cross!' •The chief priests with the
42 scribes and elders mocked him in the same way. •'He saved others;' they said
'he cannot save himself. He is the king of Israel; let him come down from the
43 cross now, and we will believe in him. •He puts his trust in God; now let God
44 rescue him if he wants him. For he did say, "I am the son of God".' •Even the
robbers who were crucified with him taunted him in the same way.

The death of Jesus

45 From the sixth hour there was darkness over all the land until the ninth hour.ᵉ
46 And about the ninth hour, Jesus cried out in a loud voice, 'Eli, Eli, lama sabach-
47 thani?' that is, '*My God, my God, why have you deserted me?*'ᶠ • When some of
those who stood there heard this, they said, 'The man is calling on Elijah',
48 and one of them quickly ran to get a sponge which he dipped in vinegarᵍ and,
49 putting it on a reed, gave it him to drink. •'Wait!' said the rest of them 'and
50 see if Elijah will come to save him.' •But Jesus, again crying out in a loud
voice, yielded up his spirit.
51 At that, the veil of the Templeʰ was torn in two from top to bottom; the earth
52 quaked; the rocks were split; •the tombs opened and the bodies of many holy men
53 rose from the dead, •and these, after his resurrection, came out of the tombs,
54 entered the Holy City and appeared to a number of people. •Meanwhile the centurion, together with the others guarding Jesus, had seen the earthquake and all that
was taking place, and they were terrified and said, 'In truth this was a son of God.'
55 And many women were there, watching from a distance, the same

---

27 a. The Jews had to approach the Roman governor for confirmation and execution of any
sentence of death. **b.** Actually a free quotation from Zc 11:12-13. **c.** The normal prelude
to crucifixion. **d.** The Aramaic form of the name of which Calvary is the more familiar
Latin equivalent. **e.** From mid-day to 3 p.m. **f.** Ps 22:1 **g.** The rough wine drunk by
Roman soldiers. **h.** There were two curtains in the Temple; most probably this was the
inner curtain which guarded the Most Holy Place.

women who had followed Jesus from Galilee and looked after him. •Among 56
them were Mary of Magdala, Mary the mother of James and Joseph, and the
mother of Zebedee's sons.

The burial

When it was evening, there came a rich man of Arimathaea, called Joseph, 57
who had himself become a disciple of Jesus. •This man went to Pilate and asked 58
for the body of Jesus. Pilate thereupon ordered it to be handed over. •So Joseph 59
took the body, wrapped it in a clean shroud •and put it in his own new tomb 60
which he had hewn out of the rock. He then rolled a large stone across the entrance
of the tomb and went away. •Now Mary of Magdala and the other Mary were 61
there, sitting opposite the sepulchre.

The guard at the tomb

Next day, that is, when Preparation Day[i] was over, the chief priests and the 62
Pharisees went in a body to Pilate •and said to him, 'Your Excellency, we 63
recall that this impostor said, while he was still alive, "After three days I shall
rise again". •Therefore give the order to have the sepulchre kept secure until the 64
third day, for fear his disciples come and steal him away and tell the people,
"He has risen from the dead". This last piece of fraud would be worse than what
went before.' •'You may have your guard' said Pilate to them. 'Go and make 65
all as secure as you know how.' •So they went and made the sepulchre secure, 66
putting seals on the stone and mounting a guard.

The empty tomb. The angel's message

28 After the sabbath, and towards dawn on the first day of the week, Mary of 1
Magdala and the other Mary went to visit the sepulchre. •And all at once 2
there was a violent earthquake, for the angel of the Lord, descending from
heaven, came and rolled away the stone and sat on it. •His face was like lightning, 3
his robe white as snow. •The guards were so shaken, so frightened of him, that 4
they were like dead men. •But the angel spoke; and he said to the women, 5
'There is no need for you to be afraid. I know you are looking for Jesus, who was
crucified. •He is not here, for he has risen, as he said he would. Come and see 6
the place where he lay, •then go quickly and tell his disciples, "He has risen 7
from the dead and now he is going before you to Galilee; it is there you will
see him". Now I have told you.' •Filled with awe and great joy the women came 8
quickly away from the tomb and ran to tell the disciples.

Appearance to the women

And there, coming to meet them, was Jesus. 'Greetings' he said. And the 9
women came up to him and, falling down before him, clasped his feet. •Then 10
Jesus said to them, 'Do not be afraid; go and tell my brothers that they must leave
for Galilee; they will see me there'.

Precautions taken by the leaders of the people

While they were on their way, some of the guard went off into the city to tell 11
the chief priests all that had happened. •These held a meeting with the elders 12
and, after some discussion, handed a considerable sum of money to the soldiers
with these instructions, 'This is what you must say, "His disciples came during 13
the night and stole him away while we were asleep". •And should the governor 14
come to hear of this, we undertake to put things right with him ourselves and
to see that you do not get into trouble.' •The soldiers took the money and carried 15
out their instructions, and to this day that is the story among the Jews.

Appearance in Galilee. The mission to the world

Meanwhile the eleven disciples set out for Galilee, to the mountain where 16
Jesus had arranged to meet them. •When they saw him they fell down before 17

18 him, though some hesitated. •Jesus came up and spoke to them. He said, 'All
19 authority in heaven and on earth has been given to me. •Go, therefore, make
disciples of all the nations; baptise them in the name of the Father and of the
20 Son and of the Holy Spirit,ᵃ •and teach them to observe all the commands I
gave you. And know that I am with you always; yes, to the end of time.'

i. The day before the sabbath.
28 a. This formula is perhaps a reflection of the liturgical usage of the writer's own time.

THE GOSPEL ACCORDING TO
SAINT MARK

I. PRELUDE TO THE PUBLIC MINISTRY OF JESUS

The preaching of John the Baptist

1 The beginning of the Good News about Jesus Christ, the Son of God. •It is $\frac{1}{2}$
written in the book of the prophet Isaiah:

> *Look, I am going to send my messenger before you;*
> *he will prepare your way.*
> *A voice cries in the wilderness:* 3
> *Prepare a way for the Lord,*
> *make his paths straight,*[a]

and so it was that John the Baptist appeared in the wilderness, proclaiming 4
a baptism of repentance for the forgiveness of sins. •All Judaea and all the people 5
of Jerusalem made their way to him, and as they were baptised by him in the river
Jordan they confessed their sins. •John wore a garment of camel-skin, and 6
he lived on locusts and wild honey. •In the course of his preaching he said, 7
'Someone is following me, someone who is more powerful than I am, and I am
not fit to kneel down and undo the strap of his sandals. •I have baptised you 8
with water, but he will baptise you with the Holy Spirit.'

Jesus is baptised

It was at this time that Jesus came from Nazareth in Galilee and was baptised 9
in the Jordan by John. •No sooner had he come up out of the water than he 10
saw the heavens torn apart and the Spirit, like a dove, descending on him.
And a voice came from heaven, 'You are my Son, the Beloved; my favour rests 11
on you'.

Temptation in the wilderness

Immediately afterwards the Spirit drove him out into the wilderness •and he $\frac{12}{13}$
remained there for forty days, and was tempted by Satan. He was with the wild
beasts, and the angels looked after him.

II. THE GALILEAN MINISTRY

Jesus begins to preach

After John had been arrested, Jesus went into Galilee. There he proclaimed 14
the Good News from God. •'The time has come' he said 'and the kingdom of 15
God is close at hand. Repent, and believe the Good News.'

The first four disciples are called

16 As he was walking along by the Sea of Galilee he saw Simon and his brother
17 Andrew casting a net in the lake — for they were fishermen. •And Jesus said to
18 them, 'Follow me and I will make you into fishers of men'. •And at once they
left their nets and followed him.

19 Going on a little further, he saw James son of Zebedee and his brother John;
20 they too were in their boat, mending their nets. He called them at once •and,
leaving their father Zebedee in the boat with the men he employed, they went
after him.

Jesus teaches in Capernaum and cures a demoniac

21 They went as far as Capernaum, and as soon as the sabbath came he went
22 to the synagogue and began to teach. •And his teaching made a deep impression
on them because, unlike the scribes, he taught them with authority.

23 In their synagogue just then there was a man possessed by an unclean spirit,
24 and it shouted, •'What do you want with us, Jesus of Nazareth? Have you come
25 to destroy us? I know who you are: the Holy One of God.' •But Jesus said
26 sharply, 'Be quiet! Come out of him!' •And the unclean spirit threw the man into
27 convulsions and with a loud cry went out of him. •The people were so astonished
that they started asking each other what it all meant. 'Here is a teaching that is
new' they said 'and with authority behind it: he gives orders even to unclean
28 spirits and they obey him.' •And his reputation rapidly spread everywhere,
through all the surrounding Galilean countryside.

Cure of Simon's mother-in-law

29 On leaving the synagogue, he went with James and John straight to the house
30 of Simon and Andrew. •Now Simon's mother-in-law had gone to bed with fever,
31 and they told him about her straightaway. •He went to her, took her by the hand
and helped her up. And the fever left her and she began to wait on them.

A number of cures

32 That evening, after sunset, they brought to him all who were sick and those
33 who were possessed by devils. •The whole town came crowding round the door,
34 and he cured many who were suffering from diseases of one kind or another;
he also cast out many devils, but he would not allow them to speak, because they
knew who he was.[b]

Jesus quietly leaves Capernaum and travels through Galilee

35 In the morning, long before dawn, he got up and left the house, and went
36 off to a lonely place and prayed there. •Simon and his companions set out in
37 search of him, •and when they found him they said, 'Everybody is looking for
38 you'. •He answered, 'Let us go elsewhere, to the neighbouring country towns,
39 so that I can preach there too, because that is why I came'. •And he went all
through Galilee, preaching in their synagogues and casting out devils.

Cure of a leper

40 A leper came to him and pleaded on his knees: 'If you want to' he said 'you
41 can cure me'. •Feeling sorry for him, Jesus stretched out his hand and touched
42 him. 'Of course I want to!' he said. 'Be cured!' •And the leprosy left him at once
43 and he was cured. •Jesus immediately sent him away and sternly ordered him,
44 'Mind you say nothing to anyone, but go and show yourself to the priest, and
make the offering for your healing prescribed by Moses as evidence of your
45 recovery'. •The man went away, but then started talking about it freely and

---

1 a. Is 40:3   b. Throughout this gospel, Jesus never explicitly claims to be the Messiah and
he forbids others to speak of the fact.

telling the story everywhere, so that Jesus could no longer go openly into any town, but had to stay outside in places where nobody lived. Even so, people from all around would come to him.

Cure of a paralytic

2 When he returned to Capernaum some time later, word went round that he 1 was back; •and so many people collected that there was no room left, even 2 in front of the door. He was preaching the word to them •when some people 3 came bringing him a paralytic carried by four men, •but as the crowd made 4 it impossible to get the man to him, they stripped the roof over the place where Jesus was; and when they had made an opening, they lowered the stretcher on which the paralytic lay. •Seeing their faith, Jesus said to the paralytic, 'My child, 5 your sins are forgiven'. •Now some scribes were sitting there, and they thought 6 to themselves, •'How can this man talk like that? He is blaspheming. Who can 7 forgive sins but God?' •Jesus, inwardly aware that this was what they were 8 thinking, said to them, 'Why do you have these thoughts in your hearts? Which of these is easier: to say to the paralytic, "Your sins are forgiven" or to 9 say, "Get up, pick up your stretcher and walk"? •But to prove to you that the 10 Son of Man has authority on earth to forgive sins,'—•he said to the paralytic— 11 'I order you: get up, pick up your stretcher, and go off home.' •And the man 12 got up, picked up his stretcher at once and walked out in front of everyone, so that they were all astounded and praised God saying, 'We have never seen anything like this'.

The call of Levi

He went out again to the shore of the lake;ᵃ and all the people came to him, 13 and he taught them. •As he was walking on he saw Levi the son of Alphaeus, 14 sitting by the customs house, and he said to him, 'Follow me'. And he got up and followed him.

Eating with sinners

When Jesus was at dinner in his house, a number of tax collectors and sinners 15 were also sitting at the table with Jesus and his disciples; for there were many of them among his followers. •When the scribes of the Pharisee party saw him eating 16 with sinners and tax collectors, they said to his disciples, 'Why does he eat with tax collectors and sinners?' •When Jesus heard this he said to them, 'It is not the 17 healthy who need the doctor, but the sick. I did not come to call the virtuous, but sinners.'

A discussion on fasting

One day when John's disciples and the Pharisees were fasting, some people 18 came and said to him, 'Why is it that John's disciples and the disciples of the Pharisees fast, but your disciples do not?' •Jesus replied, 'Surely the bridegroom's 19 attendants would never think of fasting while the bridegroom is still with them? As long as they have the bridegroom with them, they could not think of fasting. But the time will come for the bridegroom to be taken away from them, and then, 20 on that day, they will fast. •No one sews a piece of unshrunken cloth on an old 21 cloak; if he does, the patch pulls away from it, the new from the old, and the tear gets worse. •And nobody puts new wine into old wineskins; if he does, the wine 22 will burst the skins, and the wine is lost and the skins too. No! New wine, fresh skins!'

Picking corn on the sabbath

One sabbath day he happened to be taking a walk through the cornfields, and 23 his disciples began to pick ears of corn as they went along. •And the Pharisees 24 said to him, 'Look, why are they doing something on the sabbath day that is forbidden?' •And he replied, 'Did you never read what David did in his time of 25

26 need when he and his followers were hungry—•how he went into the house of
God when Abiathar[b] was high priest, and ate the loaves of offering which only
the priests are allowed to eat, and how he also gave some to the men with him?'
27   And he said to them, 'The sabbath was made for man, not man for the
28 sabbath; •so the Son of Man is master even of the sabbath'.

Cure of the man with a withered hand

1   3 He went again into a synagogue, and there was a man there who had a withered
2   hand. •And they were watching him to see if he would cure him on the sabbath
3 day, hoping for something to use against him. •He said to the man with the
4 withered hand, 'Stand up out in the middle!' •Then he said to them, 'Is it
against the law on the sabbath day to do good, or to do evil; to save life, or to
5 kill?' But they said nothing. •Then, grieved to find them so obstinate, he looked
angrily round at them, and said to the man, 'Stretch out your hand'. He stretched
6 it out and his hand was better. •The Pharisees went out and at once began to
plot with the Herodians against him, discussing how to destroy him.

The crowds follow Jesus

7   Jesus withdrew with his disciples to the lakeside, and great crowds from
8 Galilee followed him. From Judaea, •Jerusalem, Idumaea, Transjordania and
the region of Tyre and Sidon, great numbers who had heard of all he was doing
9 came to him. •And he asked his disciples to have a boat ready for him because
10 of the crowd, to keep him from being crushed. •For he had cured so many that all
11 who were afflicted in any way were crowding forward to touch him. •And the
unclean spirits, whenever they saw him, would fall down before him and shout,
12 'You are the Son of God!' •But he warned them strongly not to make him known.

The appointment of the Twelve

13   He now went up into the hills and summoned those he wanted. So they came
14 to him •and he appointed twelve; they were to be his companions and to be sent
15
16 out to preach, •with power to cast out devils. •And so he appointed the Twelve:
17 Simon to whom he gave the name Peter, •James the son of Zebedee and John
the brother of James, to whom he gave the name Boanerges or 'Sons of Thunder';
18 then Andrew, Philip, Bartholomew, Matthew, Thomas, James the son of
19 Alphaeus, Thaddaeus, Simon the Zealot •and Judas Iscariot, the man who
was to betray him.

His relatives are concerned about Jesus

20   He went home again, and once more such a crowd collected that they could
21 not even have a meal. •When his relatives heard of this, they set out to take
charge of him, convinced he was out of his mind.

Allegations of the scribes

22   The scribes who had come down from Jerusalem were saying, 'Beelzebul is
23 in him' and, 'It is through the prince of devils that he casts devils out'. •So he called
them to him and spoke to them in parables, 'How can Satan cast out Satan?
24
25 If a kingdom is divided against itself, that kingdom cannot last. •And if
26 a household is divided against itself, that household can never stand. •Now if
Satan has rebelled against himself and is divided, he cannot stand either—it is
27 the end of him. •But no one can make his way into a strong man's house and
burgle his property unless he has tied up the strong man first. Only then can he
burgle his house.
28   'I tell you solemnly, all men's sins will be forgiven, and all their
29 blasphemies; •but let anyone blaspheme against the Holy Spirit and he will never

---

2 a. Tiberias, the 'Sea of Galilee'.   b. See 1 S 21:1-7. Abiathar was the better known as high
priest in David's reign, but Ahimelech is named in this source.

have forgiveness: he is guilty of an eternal sin.' •This was because they were saying, 'An unclean spirit is in him'.

The true kinsmen of Jesus

His mother and brothers now arrived and, standing outside, sent in a message 31 asking for him. •A crowd was sitting round him at the time the message was passed 32 to him, 'Your mother and brothers and sisters are outside asking for you'. He replied, 'Who are my mother and my brothers?' •And looking round at 33/34 those sitting in a circle about him, he said, 'Here are my mother and my brothers. Anyone who does the will of God, that person is my brother and sister and 35 mother.'

Parable of the sower

4 Again he began to teach by the lakeside, but such a huge crowd gathered 1 round him that he got into a boat on the lake and sat there. The people were all along the shore, at the water's edge. •He taught them many things in parables, 2 and in the course of his teaching he said to them, •'Listen! Imagine a sower 3 going out to sow. •Now it happened that, as he sowed, some of the seed fell on 4 the edge of the path, and the birds came and ate it up. •Some seed fell on rocky 5 ground where it found little soil and sprang up straightaway, because there was no depth of earth; •and when the sun came up it was scorched and, not having 6 any roots, it withered away. •Some seed fell into thorns, and the thorns 7 grew up and choked it, and it produced no crop. •And some seeds fell into rich 8 soil and, growing tall and strong, produced crop; and yielded thirty, sixty, even a hundredfold.' •And he said, 'Listen, anyone who has ears to hear!' 9

Why Jesus speaks in parables

When he was alone, the Twelve, together with the others who formed his 10 company, asked what the parables meant. •He told them, 'The secret of the 11 kingdom of God is given to you, but to those who are outside everything comes in parables, •so that *they may see and see again, but not perceive; may hear and* 12 *hear again, but not understand; otherwise they might be converted and be forgiven*'.[a]

The parable of the sower explained

He said to them, 'Do you not understand this parable? Then how will you 13 understand any of the parables? •What the sower is sowing is the word. •Those 14/15 on the edge of the path where the word is sown are people who have no sooner heard it than Satan comes and carries away the word that was sown in them. Similarly, those who receive the seed on patches of rock are people who, when 16 first they hear the word, welcome it at once with joy. •But they have no root 17 in them, they do not last; should some trial come, or some persecution on account of the word, they fall away at once. •Then there are others who receive 18 the seed in thorns. These have heard the word, •but the worries of this world, 19 the lure of riches and all the other passions come in to choke the word, and so it produces nothing. •And there are those who have received the seed in rich 20 soil: they hear the word and accept it and yield a harvest, thirty and sixty and a hundredfold.'

Parable of the lamp

He also said to them, 'Would you bring in a lamp to put it under a tub or 21 under the bed? Surely you will put it on the lamp-stand? •For there is nothing 22 hidden but it must be disclosed, nothing kept secret except to be brought to light. If anyone has ears to hear, let him listen to this.' 23

Parable of the measure

He also said to them, 'Take notice of what you are hearing. The amount you 24 measure out is the amount you will be given—and more besides; •for the man 25 who has will be given more; from the man who has not, even what he has will be taken away.'

Parable of the seed growing by itself

26 He also said, 'This is what the kingdom of God is like. A man throws seed on
27 the land. •Night and day, while he sleeps, when he is awake, the seed is sprouting
28 and growing; how, he does not know. •Of its own accord the land produces first
29 the shoot, then the ear, then the full grain in the ear. •And when the crop is ready, he loses no time: he starts to reap because the harvest has come.'

Parable of the mustard seed

30 He also said, 'What can we say the kingdom of God is like? What parable can
31 we find for it? •It is like a mustard seed which at the time of its sowing in the
32 soil is the smallest of all the seeds on earth; •yet once it is sown it grows into the biggest shrub of them all and puts out big branches so that the birds of the air can shelter in its shade.'

The use of parables

33 Using many parables like these, he spoke the word to them, so far as they were
34 capable of understanding it. •He would not speak to them except in parables, but he explained everything to his disciples when they were alone.

The calming of the storm

35 With the coming of evening that same day, he said to them, 'Let us cross over
36 to the other side'. •And leaving the crowd behind they took him, just as he was,
37 in the boat; and there were other boats with him. •Then it began to blow a gale
38 and the waves were breaking into the boat so that it was almost swamped. •But
39 he was in the stern, his head on the cushion, asleep. •They woke him and said to him, 'Master, do you not care? We are going down!' And he woke up and rebuked the wind and said to the sea, 'Quiet now! Be calm!' And the wind
40 dropped, and all was calm again. •Then he said to them, 'Why are you so
41 frightened? How is it that you have no faith?' •They were filled with awe and said to one another, 'Who can this be? Even the wind and the sea obey him.'

The Gerasene demoniac

5 ¹⁄₂ They reached the country of the Gerasenes[a] on the other side of the lake, •and no sooner had he left the boat than a man with an unclean spirit came out
3 from the tombs towards him. •The man lived in the tombs and no one could
4 secure him any more, even with a chain; •because he had often been secured with fetters and chains but had snapped the chains and broken the fetters, and no
5 one had the strength to control him. •All night and all day, among the tombs
6 and in the mountains, he would howl and gash himself with stones. •Catching
7 sight of Jesus from a distance, he ran up and fell at his feet •and shouted at the top of his voice, 'What do you want with me, Jesus, son of the Most High God?
8 Swear by God you will not torture me!'•—For Jesus had been saying to him,
9 'Come out of the man, unclean spirit'. •'What is your name?' Jesus asked. 'My
10 name is legion,' he answered 'for there are many of us.' •And he begged him
11 earnestly not to send them out of the district. •Now there was there on the
12 mountainside a great herd of pigs feeding, •and the unclean spirits begged
13 him, 'Send us to the pigs, let us go into them'. •So he gave them leave. With that, the unclean spirits came out and went into the pigs, and the herd of about two thousand pigs charged down the cliff into the lake, and there they were drowned.
14 The swineherds ran off and told their story in the town and in the country round
15 about; and the people came to see what had really happened. •They came to

4 a. Is 6:9-10
5 a. 'Gadarenes' in some versions.

Jesus and saw the demoniac sitting there, clothed and in his full senses—the very
man who had had the legion in him before—and they were afraid. •And those 16
who had witnessed it reported what had happened to the demoniac and what had
become of the pigs. •Then they began to implore Jesus to leave the neighbourhood. 17
As he was getting into the boat, the man who had been possessed begged to be 18
allowed to stay with him. •Jesus would not let him but said to him, 'Go home 19
to your people and tell them all that the Lord in his mercy has done for you'.
So the man went off and proceeded to spread throughout the Decapolis all that 20
Jesus had done for him. And everyone was amazed.

Cure of the woman with a haemorrhage. The daughter of Jairus raised to life

When Jesus had crossed again in the boat to the other side, a large crowd 21
gathered round him and he stayed by the lakeside. •Then one of the synagogue 22
officials came up, Jairus by name, and seeing him, fell at his feet •and pleaded 23
with him earnestly, saying, 'My little daughter is desperately sick. Do come and
lay your hands on her to make her better and save her life.' •Jesus went with him 24
and a large crowd followed him; they were pressing all round him.

Now there was a woman who had suffered from a haemorrhage for 25
twelve years; •after long and painful treatment under various doctors, she had 26
spent all she had without being any the better for it, in fact, she was getting
worse. •She had heard about Jesus, and she came up behind him through the crowd 27
and touched his cloak. •'If I can touch even his clothes,' she had told herself 28
'I shall be well again.' •And the source of the bleeding dried up instantly, and she 29
felt in herself that she was cured of her complaint. •Immediately aware that 30
power had gone out from him, Jesus turned round in the crowd and said, 'Who
touched my clothes?' •His disciples said to him, 'You see how the crowd is 31
pressing round you and yet you say, "Who touched me?" ' •But he continued 32
to look all round to see who had done it. •Then the woman came forward, 33
frightened and trembling [b] because she knew what had happened to her, and she
fell at his feet and told him the whole truth. •'My daughter,' he said 'your faith 34
has restored you to health; go in peace and be free from your complaint.'

While he was still speaking some people arrived from the house of the 35
synagogue official to say, 'Your daughter is dead: why put the Master to any
further trouble?' •But Jesus had overheard this remark of theirs and he said to 36
the official, 'Do not be afraid; only have faith'. •And he allowed no one to go 37
with him except Peter and James and John the brother of James. •So they came 38
to the official's house and Jesus noticed all the commotion, with people weeping
and wailing unrestrainedly. •He went in and said to them, 'Why all this 39
commotion and crying? The child is not dead, but asleep.' •But they laughed 40
at him. So he turned them all out and, taking with him the child's father and
mother and his own companions, he went into the place where the child lay.
And taking the child by the hand he said to her, 'Talitha, kum!' which means, 41
'Little girl, I tell you to get up'. •The little girl got up at once and began to walk 42
about, for she was twelve years old. At this they were overcome with astonishment,
and he ordered them strictly not to let anyone know about it, and told them 43
to give her something to eat.

A visit to Nazareth

6 Going from that district, he went to his home town and his disciples accompa- 1
nied him. •With the coming of the sabbath he began teaching in the synagogue 2
and most of them were astonished when they heard him. They said, 'Where did
the man get all this? What is this wisdom that has been granted him, and these
miracles that are worked through him? •This is the carpenter, surely, the son 3
of Mary, the brother of James and Joset and Jude and Simon? His sisters, too, are
they not here with us?' And they would not accept him. •And Jesus said to them, 4
'A prophet is only despised in his own country, among his own relations and

5 in his own house'; •and he could work no miracle there, though he cured a few
6 sick people by laying his hands on them. •He was amazed at their lack of faith.

The mission of the Twelve

7 He made a tour round the villages, teaching. •Then he summoned the Twelve
and began to send them out in pairs giving them authority over the unclean spirits.
8 And he instructed them to take nothing for the journey except a staff —no bread,
9 no haversack, no coppers for their purses. •They were to wear sandals but, he
10 added, 'Do not take a spare tunic'. •And he said to them, 'If you enter a house
11 anywhere, stay there until you leave the district. •And if any place does not
welcome you and people refuse to listen to you, as you walk away shake off
12 the dust from under your feet as a sign to them.' •So they set off to preach
13 repentance; •and they cast out many devils, and anointed many sick people with
oil and cured them.

Herod and Jesus

14 Meanwhile King Herod had heard about him, since by now his name was well-
known. Some were saying, 'John the Baptist has risen from the dead, and that
15 is why miraculous powers are at work in him'. •Others said, 'He is Elijah';
16 others again, 'He is a prophet, like the prophets we used to have'. •But when
Herod heard this he said, 'It is John whose head I cut off; he has risen from the
dead'.

John the Baptist beheaded

17 Now it was this same Herod who had sent to have John arrested, and had
him chained up in prison because of Herodias, his brother Philip's wife whom he
18 had married. •For John had told Herod, 'It is against the law for you to have
19 your brother's wife'. •As for Herodias, she was furious with him and wanted to
20 kill him; but she was not able to, •because Herod was afraid of John, knowing
him to be a good and holy man, and gave him his protection. When he had heard
him speak he was greatly perplexed, and yet he liked to listen to him.
21 An opportunity came on Herod's birthday when he gave a banquet for the
nobles of his court, for his army officers and for the leading figures in Galilee.
22 When the daughter of this same Herodias came in and danced, she delighted
Herod and his guests; so the king said to the girl, 'Ask me anything you like
23 and I will give it you'. •And he swore her an oath, 'I will give you anything you
24 ask, even half my kingdom'. •She went out and said to her mother, 'What shall
25 I ask for?' She replied, 'The head of John the Baptist'. •The girl hurried straight
back to the king and made her request, 'I want you to give me John the Baptist's
26 head, here and now, on a dish'. •The king was deeply distressed but, thinking
of the oaths he had sworn and of his guests, he was reluctant to break his word
27 to her. •So the king at once sent one of the bodyguard with orders to bring
28 John's head. •The man went off and beheaded him in prison; then he brought
the head on a dish and gave it to the girl, and the girl gave it to her mother.
29 When John's disciples heard about this, they came and took his body and laid
it in a tomb.

First miracle of the loaves

30 The apostles rejoined Jesus and told him all they had done and taught.
31 Then he said to them, 'You must come away to some lonely place all by yourselves
and rest for a while'; for there were so many coming and going that the apostles
32 had no time even to eat. •So they went off in a boat to a lonely place where they
33 could be by themselves. •But people saw them going, and many could guess where;
and from every town they all hurried to the place on foot and reached it before

b. According to the Law, she was unclean, and to be touched by her would be defilement.

them. •So as he stepped ashore he saw a large crowd; and he took pity on them 34
because they were like sheep without a shepherd, and he set himself to teach them
at some length. •By now it was getting very late, and his disciples came up to him 35
and said, 'This is a lonely place and it is getting very late, •so send them away, 36
and they can go to the farms and villages round about, to buy themselves
something to eat'. •He replied, 'Give them something to eat yourselves'. They 37
answered, 'Are we to go and spend two hundred denarii on bread for them to
eat?' •'How many loaves have you?' he asked 'Go and see.' And when they had 38
found out they said, 'Five, and two fish'. •Then he ordered them to get all the 39
people together in groups on the green grass, •and they sat down on the ground 40
in squares of hundreds and fifties. •Then he took the five loaves and the two fish, 41
raised his eyes to heaven and said the blessing; then he broke the loaves and
handed them to his disciples to distribute among the people. He also shared out
the two fish among them all. •They all ate as much as they wanted. •They $^{42}_{43}$
collected twelve basketfuls of scraps of bread and pieces of fish. •Those who had 44
eaten the loaves numbered five thousand men.

Jesus walks on the water

Directly after this he made his disciples get into the boat and go on ahead to 45
Bethsaida, while he himself sent the crowd away. •After saying good-bye to 46
them he went off into the hills to pray. •When evening came, the boat was far out 47
on the lake, and he was alone on the land. •He could see they were worn out 48
with rowing, for the wind was against them; and about the fourth watch of the
night he came towards them, walking on the lake. He was going to pass them by,
but when they saw him walking on the lake they thought it was a ghost and cried 49
out; •for they had all seen him and were terrified. But he at once spoke to them, 50
and said, 'Courage! It is I! Do not be afraid.' •Then he got into the boat with them, 51
and the wind dropped. They were utterly and completely dumbfounded, •because 52
they had not seen what the miracle of the loaves meant; their minds were closed.

Cures at Gennesaret

Having made the crossing, they came to land at Gennesaret and tied up. •No $^{53}_{54}$
sooner had they stepped out of the boat than people recognised him, •and started 55
hurrying all through the countryside and brought the sick on stretchers to wherever
they heard he was. •And wherever he went, to village, or town, or farm, they 56
laid down the sick in the open spaces, begging him to let them touch even the
fringe of his cloak. And all those who touched him were cured.

The traditions of the Pharisees

7 The Pharisees and some of the scribes who had come from Jerusalem gathered 1
round him, •and they noticed that some of his disciples were eating with 2
unclean hands, that is, without washing them. •For the Pharisees, and the Jews 3
in general, follow the tradition of the elders and never eat without washing their
arms as far as the elbow; •and on returning from the market place they never 4
eat without first sprinkling themselves. There are also many other observances
which have been handed down to them concerning the washing of cups and pots
and bronze dishes. •So these Pharisees and scribes asked him, 'Why do your 5
disciples not respect the tradition of the elders but eat their food with unclean
hands?' •He answered, 'It was of you hypocrites that Isaiah so rightly prophesied 6
in this passage of scripture:

> *This people honours me only with lip-service,*
> *while their hearts are far from me.*
> *The worship they offer me is worthless,* 7
> *the doctrines they teach are only human regulations.*[a]

You put aside the commandment of God to cling to human traditions.' •And $^{8}_{9}$
he said to them, 'How ingeniously you get round the commandment of God

10 in order to preserve your own tradition! •For Moses said: *Do your duty to your father and your mother*, and, *Anyone who curses father or mother must be put to*
11 *death*. •But you say, "If a man says to his father or mother: Anything I have
12 that I might have used to help you is Corban[b] (that is, dedicated to God), •then he is forbidden from that moment to do anything for his father or mother".
13 In this way you make God's word null and void for the sake of your tradition which you have handed down. And you do many other things like this.'

On clean and unclean

14 He called the people to him again and said, 'Listen to me, all of you, and
15 understand. •Nothing that goes into a man from outside can make him unclean;
16 it is the things that come out of a man that make him unclean. •If anyone has ears to hear, let him listen to this.'
17 When he had gone back into the house, away from the crowd, his disciples
18 questioned him about the parable. •He said to them, 'Do you not understand either? Can you not see that whatever goes into a man from outside cannot
19 make him unclean, •because it does not go into his heart but through his stomach
20 and passes out into the sewer?' (Thus he pronounced all foods clean.) •And he
21 went on, 'It is what comes out of a man that makes him unclean. •For it is from within, from men's hearts, that evil intentions emerge: fornication, theft, murder,
22 23 adultery, •avarice, malice, deceit, indecency, envy, slander, pride, folly. •All these evil things come from within and make a man unclean.'

III. JOURNEYS OUTSIDE GALILEE

The daughter of the Syrophoenician woman healed

24 He left that place and set out for the territory of Tyre. There he went into a house and did not want anyone to know he was there, but he could not pass
25 unrecognised. •A woman whose little daughter had an unclean spirit heard about
26 him straightaway and came and fell at his feet. •Now the woman was a pagan, by birth a Syrophoenician, and she begged him to cast the devil out of her
27 daughter. •And he said to her, 'The children should be fed first, because it is not
28 fair to take the children's food and throw it to the house-dogs'. •But she spoke up: 'Ah yes, sir,' she replied 'but the house-dogs under the table can eat the
29 children's scraps'. •And he said to her, 'For saying this, you may go home happy:
30 the devil has gone out of your daughter'. •So she went off to her home and found the child lying on the bed and the devil gone.

Healing of the deaf man

31 Returning from the district of Tyre, he went by way of Sidon towards the Sea
32 of Galilee, right through the Decapolis region. •And they brought him a deaf man who had an impediment in his speech; and they asked him to lay his hand on
33 him. •He took him aside in private, away from the crowd, put his fingers into the
34 man's ears and touched his tongue with spittle. •Then looking up to heaven he
35 sighed; and he said to him, 'Ephphatha', that is, 'Be opened'. •And his ears were opened, and the ligament of his tongue was loosened and he spoke clearly.
36 And Jesus ordered them to tell no one about it, but the more he insisted, the
37 more widely they published it. •Their admiration was unbounded. 'He has done all things well,' they said 'he makes the deaf hear and the dumb speak.'

Second miracle of the loaves

1 **8** And now once again a great crowd had gathered, and they had nothing to eat.
2 **8** So he called his disciples to him and said to them, •'I feel sorry for all these people; they have been with me for three days now and have nothing to eat.

7 a. Is 29:13   b. See note on Mt 15:6.

If I send them off home hungry they will collapse on the way; some have come ³
a great distance.' •His disciples replied, 'Where could anyone get bread to feed ⁴
these people in a deserted place like this?' •He asked them, 'How many loaves ⁵
have you?' 'Seven' they said. •Then he instructed the crowd to sit down on the ⁶
ground, and he took the seven loaves, and after giving thanks he broke them and
handed them to his disciples to distribute; and they distributed them among the
crowd. •They had a few small fish as well, and over these he said a blessing and ⁷
ordered them to be distributed also. •They ate as much as they wanted, and they ⁸
collected seven basketfuls of the scraps left over. •Now there had been about four ⁹
thousand people. He sent them away •and immediately, getting into the boat ¹⁰
with his disciples, went to the region of Dalmanutha.

The Pharisees ask for a sign from heaven

The Pharisees came up and started a discussion with him; they demanded ¹¹
of him a sign from heaven, to test him. •And with a sigh that came straight from ¹²
the heart he said, 'Why does this generation demand a sign? I tell you solemnly,
no sign shall be given to this generation.' •And leaving them again and re-em- ¹³
barking he went away to the opposite shore.

The yeast of the Pharisees and of Herod

The disciples had forgotten to take any food and they had only one loaf with ¹⁴
them in the boat. •Then he gave them this warning, 'Keep your eyes open; be ¹⁵
on your guard against the yeast of the Pharisees and the yeast of Herod'. •And ¹⁶
they said to one another, 'It is because we have no bread'. •And Jesus knew it, ¹⁷
and he said to them, 'Why are you talking about having no bread? Do you not
yet understand? Have you no perception? Are your minds closed? •Have you ¹⁸
*eyes that do not see, ears that do not hear?*ᵃ Or do you not remember? •When ¹⁹
I broke the five loaves among the five thousand, how many baskets full of scraps
did you collect?' They answered, 'Twelve'. •'And when I broke the seven loaves ²⁰
for the four thousand, how many baskets full of scraps did you collect?'
And they answered, 'Seven'. •Then he said to them, 'Are you still without ²¹
perception?'

Cure of a blind man at Bethsaida

They came to Bethsaida, and some people brought to him a blind man whom ²²
they begged him to touch. •He took the blind man by the hand and led him outside ²³
the village. Then putting spittle on his eyes and laying his hands on him, he asked,
'Can you see anything?' •The man, who was beginning to see, replied, 'I can see ²⁴
people; they look like trees to me, but they are walking about'. •Then he laid ²⁵
his hands on the man's eyes again and he saw clearly; he was cured, and he could
see everything plainly and distinctly. •And Jesus sent him home, saying, 'Do ²⁶
not even go into the village'.

Peter's profession of faith

Jesus and his disciples left for the villages round Caesarea Philippi. On the ²⁷
way he put this question to his disciples, 'Who do people say I am?' •And they ²⁸
told him. 'John the Baptist,' they said 'others Elijah; others again, one of the
prophets.' •'But you,' he asked 'who do you say I am?' Peter spoke up and said ²⁹
to him, 'You are the Christ'. •And he gave them strict orders not to tell anyone ³⁰
about him.

First prophecy of the Passion

And he began to teach them that the Son of Man was destined to suffer ³¹
grievously, to be rejected by the elders and the chief priests and the scribes, and
to be put to death, and after three days to rise again; •and he said all this quite ³²
openly. Then, taking him aside, Peter started to remonstrate with him. •But, ³³
turning and seeing his disciples, he rebuked Peter and said to him, 'Get behind
me, Satan! Because the way you think is not God's way but man's.'

The condition of following Christ

34 He called the people and his disciples to him and said, 'If anyone wants to be a follower of mine, let him renounce himself and take up his cross and follow
35 me. •For anyone who wants to save his life will lose it; but anyone who loses his
36 life for my sake, and for the sake of the gospel, will save it. •What gain, then, is
37 it for a man to win the whole world and ruin his life? •And indeed what can
38 a man offer in exchange for his life? •For if anyone in 'this adulterous and sinful generation is ashamed of me and of my words, the Son of Man will also be ashamed of him when he comes in the glory of his Father with the holy angels.'
1   **9** And he said to them, 'I tell you solemnly, there are some standing here who will not taste death before they see the kingdom of God come with power'.

The transfiguration

2   Six days later, Jesus took with him Peter and James and John and led them up a high mountain where they could be alone by themselves. There in
3   their presence he was transfigured: •his clothes became dazzlingly white, whiter
4   than any earthly bleacher could make them. •Elijah appeared to them with
5   Moses; and they were talking with Jesus. •Then Peter spoke to Jesus: 'Rabbi,' he said 'it is wonderful for us to be here; so let us make three tents, one for
6   you, one for Moses and one for Elijah'. •He did not know what to say; they were
7   so frightened. •And a cloud came, covering them in shadow; and there came
8   a voice from the cloud, 'This is my Son, the Beloved. Listen to him.' •Then suddenly, when they looked round, they saw no one with them any more but only Jesus.

The question about Elijah

9   As they came down from the mountain he warned them to tell no one what they had seen, until after the Son of Man had risen from the dead.
10 They observed the warning faithfully, though among themselves they discussed
11 what 'rising from the dead' could mean. •And they put this question to him,
12 'Why do the scribes say that Elijah has to come first?' •'True,' he said 'Elijah is to come first and to see that everything is as it should be; yet how is it that the scriptures say about the Son of Man that he is to suffer grievously and be treated
13 with contempt? •However, I tell you that Elijah has come and they have treated him as they pleased, just as the scriptures say about him.'

The epileptic demoniac

14 When they rejoined the disciples they saw a large crowd round them and
15 some scribes arguing with them. •The moment they saw him the whole crowd
16 were struck with amazement and ran to greet him. •'What are you arguing about
17 with them?' he asked. •A man answered him from the crowd, 'Master, I have
18 brought my son to you; there is a spirit of dumbness in him, •and when it takes hold of him it throws him to the ground, and he foams at the mouth and grinds his teeth and goes rigid. And I asked your disciples to cast it out and
19 they were unable to.' •'You faithless generation' he said to them in reply. 'How much longer must I be with you? How much longer must I put up with you?
20 Bring him to me.' •They brought the boy to him, and as soon as the spirit saw Jesus it threw the boy into convulsions, and he fell to the ground and
21 lay writhing there, foaming at the mouth. •Jesus asked the father, 'How
22 long has this been happening to him?' 'From childhood,' he replied •'and it has often thrown him into the fire and into the water, in order to destroy him.
23 But if you can do anything, have pity on us and help us.' •'If you can?' retorted
24 Jesus. 'Everything is possible for anyone who has faith.' •Immediately the
25 father of the boy cried out, 'I do have faith. Help the little faith I have!' •And when Jesus saw how many people were pressing round him, he rebuked the

8 a. Jr 5:21; Ezk 12:2

unclean spirit. 'Deaf and dumb spirit,' he said 'I command you: come out of him and never enter him again.' •Then throwing the boy into violent convulsions it 26 came out shouting, and the boy lay there so like a corpse that most of them said, 'He is dead'. •But Jesus took him by the hand and helped him up, and he 27 was able to stand. •When he had gone indoors his disciples asked him privately, 28 'Why were we unable to cast it out?' •'This is the kind' he answered 'that can 29 only be driven out by prayer.'

Second prophecy of the Passion

After leaving that place they made their way through Galilee; and he did 30 not want anyone to know, •because he was instructing his disciples; he was telling 31 them, 'The Son of Man will be delivered into the hands of men; they will put him to death; and three days after he has been put to death he will rise again'. But they did not understand what he said and were afraid to ask him. 32

Who is the greatest?

They came to Capernaum, and when he was in the house he asked them, 33 'What were you arguing about on the road?' •They said nothing because they 34 had been arguing which of them was the greatest. •So he sat down, called the 35 Twelve to him and said, 'If anyone wants to be first, he must make himself last of all and servant of all'. •He then took a little child, set him in front of them, 36 put his arms round him, and said to them, •'Anyone who welcomes one of 37 these little children in my name, welcomes me; and anyone who welcomes me welcomes not me but the one who sent me'.

On using the name of Jesus

John said to him, 'Master, we saw a man who is not one of us casting out 38 devils in your name; and because he was not one of us we tried to stop him'. But Jesus said, 'You must not stop him: no one who works a miracle in my name 39 is likely to speak evil of me. •Anyone who is not against us is for us. 40

Charity shown to Christ's disciples

'If anyone gives you a cup of water to drink just because you belong to Christ, 41 then I tell you solemnly, he will most certainly not lose his reward.

On leading others astray

'But anyone who is an obstacle to bring down one of these little ones who 42 have faith, would be better thrown into the sea with a great millstone round his neck. •And if your hand should cause you to sin, cut it off; it is better for you 43 to enter into life crippled, than to have two hands and go to hell, into the fire that cannot be put out. •And if your foot should cause you to sin, cut it off; it is 45 better for you to enter into life lame, than to have two feet and be thrown into hell. •And if your eye should cause you to sin, tear it out; it is better for you to 47 enter into the kingdom of God with one eye, than to have two eyes and be thrown into hell •where *their worm does not die nor their fire go out.*[a] •For everyone will 48 49 be salted with fire. •Salt is a good thing, but if salt has become insipid, how can 50 you season it again? Have salt in yourselves and be at peace with one another.'

The question about divorce

10 Leaving there, he came to the district of Judaea and the far side of the 1 Jordan. And again crowds gathered round him, and again he taught them, as his custom was. •Some Pharisees approached him and asked, 'Is it against 2 the law for a man to divorce his wife?' They were testing him. •He answered 3 them, 'What did Moses command you?' •'Moses allowed us' they said 'to draw 4 up a writ of dismissal and so to divorce.' •Then Jesus said to them, 'It was 5

because you were so unteachable that he wrote this commandment for you.
6
7 But from the beginning of creation *God made them male and female.* •*This is why*
8 *a man must leave father and mother,* •*and the two become one body.*[a] They are no
9 longer two, therefore, but one body. •So then, what God has united, man must not
10
11 divide.' •Back in the house the disciples questioned him again about this, •and
he said to them, 'The man who divorces his wife and marries another is guilty of
12 adultery against her. •And if a woman divorces her husband and marries
another she is guilty of adultery too.'

Jesus and the children

13   People were bringing little children to him, for him to touch them. The
14 disciples turned them away, •but when Jesus saw this he was indignant and said
to them, 'Let the little children come to me; do not stop them; for it is to such as
15 these that the kingdom of God belongs. •I tell you solemnly, anyone who
does not welcome the kingdom of God like a little child will never enter it.'
16 Then he put his arms round them, laid his hands on them and gave them his
blessing.

The rich young man

17   He was setting out on a journey when a man ran up, knelt before him and
put this question to him, 'Good master, what must I do to inherit eternal life?'
18 Jesus said to him, 'Why do you call me good? No one is good but God alone.
19 You know the commandments: *You must not kill; You must not commit adultery;*
You must not steal; You must not bring false witness; You must not defraud;
20 *Honour your father and mother.'* •And he said to him, 'Master, I have kept all
21 these from my earliest days'. •Jesus looked steadily at him and loved him, and
he said, 'There is one thing you lack. Go and sell everything you own and give
the money to the poor, and you will have treasure in heaven; then come, follow
22 me.' •But his face fell at these words and he went away sad, for he was a man
of great wealth.

The danger of riches

23   Jesus looked round and said to his disciples, 'How hard it is for those who
24 have riches to enter the kingdom of God!' •The disciples were astounded by
these words, but Jesus insisted, 'My children,' he said to them 'how hard it is to
25 enter the kingdom of God! •It is easier for a camel to pass through the eye of
26 a needle than for a rich man to enter the kingdom of God.' •They were more
astonished than ever. 'In that case' they said to one another 'who can be saved?'
27 Jesus gazed at them. 'For men' he said 'it is impossible, but not for God: because
everything is possible for God.'

The reward of renunciation

28   Peter took this up. 'What about us?' he asked him. 'We have left everything
29 and followed you.' •Jesus said, 'I tell you solemnly, there is no one who has left
house, brothers, sisters, father, children or land for my sake and for the sake of
30 the gospel •who will not be repaid a hundred times over, houses, brothers, sisters,
mothers, children and land—not without persecutions—now in this present time
and, in the world to come, eternal life.
31   'Many who are first will be last, and the last first.'

Third prophecy of the Passion

32   They were on the road, going up to Jerusalem; Jesus was walking on ahead
of them; they were in a daze, and those who followed were apprehensive. Once
more taking the Twelve aside he began to tell them what was going to happen
33 to him: •'Now we are going up to Jerusalem, and the Son of Man is about

9 a. Is 66:24   **10 a.** Gn 1:27; 2:24

to be handed over to the chief priests and the scribes. They will condemn him to death and will hand him over to the pagans, •who will mock him and spit at 34 him and scourge him and put him to death; and after three days he will rise again.'

The sons of Zebedee make their request

James and John, the sons of Zebedee, approached him. 'Master,' they said 35 to him 'we want you to do us a favour.' •He said to them, 'What is it you want 36 me to do for you?' •They said to him, 'Allow us to sit one at your right hand 37 and the other at your left in your glory'. •'You do not know what you are asking' 38 Jesus said to them. 'Can you drink the cup that I must drink, or be baptised with the baptism with which I must be baptised?' •They replied, 'We can'. 39 Jesus said to them, 'The cup that I must drink you shall drink, and with the baptism with which I must be baptised you shall be baptised, •but as for seats 40 at my right hand or my left, these are not mine to grant; they belong to those to whom they have been allotted'.

Leadership with service

When the other ten heard this they began to feel indignant with James and 41 John, •so Jesus called them to him and said to them, 'You know that among the 42 pagans their so-called rulers lord it over them, and their great men make their authority felt. •This is not to happen among you. No; anyone who wants to become 43 great among you must be your servant, •and anyone who wants to be first 44 among you must be slave to all. •For the Son of Man himself did not come to 45 be served but to serve, and to give his life as a ransom for many.'

The blind man of Jericho

They reached Jericho; and as he left Jericho with his disciples and a large 46 crowd, Bartimaeus (that is, the son of Timaeus), a blind beggar, was sitting at the side of the road. •When he heard that it was Jesus of Nazareth, he began to shout 47 and to say, 'Son of David, Jesus, have pity on me'. •And many of them scolded 48 him and told him to keep quiet, but he only shouted all the louder, 'Son of David, have pity on me'. •Jesus stopped and said, 'Call him here'. So they called the 49 blind man. 'Courage,' they said 'get up; he is calling you.' •So throwing off his 50 cloak, he jumped up and went to Jesus. •Then Jesus spoke, 'What do you want 51 me to do for you?' 'Rabbuni,'ᵇ the blind man said to him 'Master, let me see again.' •Jesus said to him, 'Go; your faith has saved you'. And immediately 52 his sight returned and he followed him along the road.

IV. THE JERUSALEM MINISTRY

The Messiah enters Jerusalem

11 When they were approaching Jerusalem, in sight of Bethphage and Bethany, 1 close by the Mount of Olives, he sent two of his disciples •and said to them, 2 'Go off to the village facing you, and as soon as you enter it you will find a tethered colt that no one has yet ridden. Untie it and bring it here. •If anyone says to 3 you, "What are you doing?" say, "The Master needs it and will send it back here directly".' •They went off and found a colt tethered near a door in 4 the open street. As they untied it, •some men standing there said, 'What are you 5 doing, untying that colt?' •They gave the answer Jesus had told them, and the 6 men let them go. •Then they took the colt to Jesus and threw their cloaks on its 7 back, and he sat on it. •Many people spread their cloaks on the road, others green- 8 ery which they had cut in the fields. •And those who went in front and those who 9

followed were all shouting, '*Hosanna! Blessings on him who comes in the name*
10 *of the Lord!*[a] •Blessings on the coming kingdom of our father David! *Hosanna*
11 *in the highest heavens!*' •He entered Jerusalem and went into the Temple. He
looked all round him, but as it was now late, he went out to Bethany with the
Twelve.

The barren fig tree

12
13   Next day as they were leaving Bethany, he felt hungry. •Seeing a fig tree in
leaf some distance away, he went to see if he could find any fruit on it, but when
he came up to it he found nothing but leaves; for it was not the season for figs.
14 And he addressed the fig tree. 'May no one ever eat fruit from you again' he
said. And his disciples heard him say this.

The expulsion of the dealers from the Temple

15   So they reached Jerusalem and he went into the Temple and began driving
out those who were selling and buying there; he upset the tables of the money
16 changers and the chairs of those who were selling pigeons. •Nor would he allow
17 anyone to carry anything through the Temple. •And he taught them and said,
'Does not scripture say: *My house will be called a house of prayer for all the*
18 *peoples?*[b] But you have turned it into *a robbers' den.*'[c] •This came to the ears
of the chief priests and the scribes, and they tried to find some way of doing
away with him; they were afraid of him because the people were carried away
19 by his teaching. •And when evening came he went out of the city.

The fig tree withered. Faith and prayer

20   Next morning, as they passed by, they saw the fig tree withered to the roots.
21 Peter remembered. 'Look, Rabbi,' he said to Jesus 'the fig tree you cursed has
22
23 withered away.' •Jesus answered, 'Have faith in God. •I tell you solemnly,
if anyone says to this mountain, "Get up and throw yourself into the sea", with no
hesitation in his heart but believing that what he says will happen, it will be done
24 for him. •I tell you therefore: everything you ask and pray for, believe that you
25 have it already, and it will be yours. •And when you stand in prayer, forgive
whatever you have against anybody, so that your Father in heaven may forgive
your failings too.'

The authority of Jesus is questioned

27   They came to Jerusalem again, and as Jesus was walking in the Temple, the
28 chief priests and the scribes and the elders came to him, •and they said to him,
'What authority have you for acting like this? Or who gave you authority to do
29 these things?' •Jesus said to them, 'I will ask you a question, only one; answer
30 me and I will tell you my authority for acting like this. •John's baptism: did it
31 come from heaven, or from man? Answer me that.' •And they argued it out
this way among themselves: 'If we say from heaven, he will say, "Then why did
32 you refuse to believe him?" •But dare we say from man?'—they had the people
33 to fear, for everyone held that John was a real prophet. •So their reply to Jesus
was, 'We do not know'. And Jesus said to them, 'Nor will I tell you my authority
for acting like this'.

Parable of the wicked husbandmen

1   **12** He went on to speak to them in parables, 'A man planted a vineyard; he
fenced it round, dug out a trough for the winepress and built a tower; then
2 he leased it to tenants and went abroad. •When the time came, he sent a servant
to the tenants to collect from them his share of the produce from the vineyard

b. Aramaic: 'My master'.
11 a. Ps 118:25-26   b. Is 56:7   c. Jr 7:11

But they seized the man, thrashed him and sent him away empty-handed. •Next ³₄
he sent another servant to them; him they beat about the head and treated
shamefully. •And he sent another and him they killed; then a number of others, 5
and they thrashed some and killed the rest. •He had still someone left: his beloved 6
son. He sent him to them last of all. "They will respect my son" he said. •But 7
those tenants said to each other, "This is the heir. Come on, let us kill him, and the
inheritance will be ours." •So they seized him and killed him and threw him out 8
of the vineyard. •Now what will the owner of the vineyard do? He will come and 9
make an end of the tenants and give the vineyard to others. •Have you not read 10
this text of scripture:

> *It was the stone rejected by the builders*
> *that became the keystone.*
> *This was the Lord's doing*
> *and it is wonderful to see?*ᵃ   11

And they would have liked to arrest him, because they realised that the parable 12
was aimed at them, but they were afraid of the crowds. So they left him alone
and went away.

On tribute to Caesar

Next they sent to him some Pharisees and some Herodians to catch him out 13
in what he said. •These came and said to him, 'Master, we know you are an honest 14
man, that you are not afraid of anyone, because a man's rank means nothing
to you, and that you teach the way of God in all honesty. Is it permissible to
pay taxes to Caesar or not? Should we pay, yes or no?' •Seeing through their 15
hypocrisy he said to them, 'Why do you set this trap for me? Hand me a
denarius and let me see it.' •They handed him one and he said, 'Whose head 16
is this? Whose name?' 'Caesar's' they told him. •Jesus said to them, 'Give back 17
to Caesar what belongs to Caesar—and to God what belongs to God'. This
reply took them completely by surprise.

The resurrection of the dead

Then some Sadducees—who deny that there is a resurrection—came to 18
him and they put this question to him, •'Master, we have it from Moses in 19
writing, if a man's brother dies leaving a wife but no child, the man must
marry the widow to raise up children for his brother. •Now there were seven 20
brothers. The first married a wife and then died leaving no children. •The second 21
married the widow, and he too died leaving no children; with the third it was
the same, •and none of the seven left any children. Last of all the woman herself 22
died. •Now at the resurrection, when they rise again, whose wife will she be, 23
since she had been married to all seven?'

Jesus said to them, 'Is not the reason why you go wrong, that you understand 24
neither the scriptures nor the power of God? •For when they rise from the dead, 25
men and women do not marry; no, they are like the angels in heaven. •Now 26
about the dead rising again, have you never read in the Book of Moses, in the
passage about the Bush, how God spoke to him and said: *I am the God of*
*Abraham, the God of Isaac and the God of Jacob?*ᵇ•He is God, not of the dead, 27
but of the living. You are very much mistaken.'

The greatest commandment of all

One of the scribes who had listened to them debating and had observed how 28
well Jesus had answered them, now came up and put a question to him, 'Which
is the first of all the commandments?' •Jesus replied, 'This is the first: *Listen,* 29
Israel, the Lord our God is the one Lord, •and you must love the Lord your God with 30
all your heart, with all your soul, with all your mind and *with all your strength.*ᶜ
The second is this: *You must love your neighbour as yourself.*ᵈThere is no com- 31
mandment greater than these.' •The scribe said to him, 'Well spoken, Master; 32

33 what you have said is true: that he is one and there is no other. •To love him with all your heart, with all your understanding and strength, and to love your neighbour as yourself, this is far more important than any holocaust or sacrifice.'

34 Jesus, seeing how wisely he had spoken, said, 'You are not far from the kingdom of God'. And after that no one dared to question him any more.

Christ not only son but also Lord of David

35 Later, while teaching in the Temple, Jesus said, 'How can the scribes maintain
36 that the Christ is the son of David? •David himself, moved by the Holy Spirit, said:

> The Lord said to my Lord:
> Sit at my right hand
> and I will put your enemies
> under your feet.[e]

37 David himself calls him Lord, in what way then can he be his son?' And the great majority of the people heard this with delight.

The scribes condemned by Jesus

38 In his teaching he said, 'Beware of the scribes who like to walk about
39 in long robes, to be greeted obsequiously in the market squares, •to take
40 the front seats in the synagogues and the places of honour at banquets; •these are the men who swallow the property of widows, while making a show of lengthy prayers. The more severe will be the sentence they receive.'

The widow's mite

41 He sat down opposite the treasury and watched the people putting money
42 into the treasury, and many of the rich put in a great deal. •A poor widow came
43 and put in two small coins, the equivalent of a penny. •Then he called his disciples and said to them, 'I tell you solemnly, this poor widow has
44 put more in than all who have contributed to the treasury; •for they have all put in money they had over, but she from the little she had has put in everything she possessed, all she had to live on'.

The eschatological discourse: introduction

1 **13** As he was leaving the Temple one of his disciples said to him, 'Look at the
2   size of those stones, Master! Look at the size of those buildings!' •And Jesus said to him, 'You see these great buildings? Not a single stone will be left on another: everything will be destroyed.'

3 And while he was sitting facing the Temple, on the Mount of Olives, Peter,
4 James, John and Andrew questioned him privately, •'Tell us, when is this going to happen, and what sign will there be that all this is about to be fulfilled?'

The beginning of sorrows

5 Then Jesus began to tell them, 'Take care that no one deceives you. •Many will
6
7 come using my name and saying, "I am he", and they will deceive many. •When you hear of wars and rumours of wars, do not be alarmed, this is something that
8 must happen, but the end will not be yet. •For nation will fight against nation, and kingdom against kingdom. There will be earthquakes here and there; there will be famines. This is the beginning of the birthpangs.

9 'Be on your guard: they will hand you over to sanhedrins; you will be beaten in synagogues; and you will stand before governors and kings for my sake,
10 to bear witness before them, •since the Good News must first be proclaimed to all the nations.

12 a. Ps 118:22-23   b. Ex 3:6   c. Dt 6:4-5   d. Lv 19:18   e. Ps 110:1

'And when they lead you away to hand you over, do not worry beforehand 11 about what to say; no, say whatever is given to you when the time comes, because it is not you who will be speaking: it will be the Holy Spirit. •Brother will betray 12 brother to death, and the father his child; children will rise against their parents and have them put to death. •You will be hated by all men on account of my 13 name; but the man who stands firm to the end will be saved.

The great tribulation of Jerusalem

'When you see *the disastrous abomination*^a set up where it ought not to be 14 (let the reader understand), then those in Judaea must escape to the mountains; if a man is on the housetop, he must not come down to go into the house to 15 collect any of his belongings; •if a man is in the fields, he must not turn back 16 to fetch his cloak. •Alas for those with child, or with babies at the breast, when 17 those days come! •Pray that this may not be in winter. •For in those days there $^{18}_{19}$ will be *such distress as, until now, has not been*^b equalled since the beginning when God created the world, nor ever will be again. •And if the Lord had not shortened 20 that time, no one would have survived; but he did shorten the time, for the sake of the elect whom he chose.

'And if anyone says to you then, "Look, here is the Christ" or, "Look, he 21 is there", do not believe it; •for false Christs and false prophets will arise and 22 produce signs and portents to deceive the elect, if that were possible. •You 23 therefore must be on your guard. I have forewarned you of everything.

The coming of the Son of Man

'But in those days, after that time of distress, the sun will be darkened, the 24 moon will lose its brightness, •the stars will come falling from heaven and the 25 powers in the heavens will be shaken. •And then they will see the Son of Man 26 coming in the clouds with great power and glory; •then too he will send the angels 27 to gather his chosen from the four winds, from the ends of the world to the ends of heaven.

The time of this coming

'Take the fig tree as a parable: as soon as its twigs grow supple and its leaves 28 come out, you know that summer is near. •So with you when you see these things 29 happening: know that he is near, at the very gates. •I tell you solemnly, 30 before this generation has passed away all these things will have taken place. •Heaven and earth will pass away, but my words will not pass away. 31

'But as for that day or hour, nobody knows it, neither the angels of heaven, 32 nor the Son; no one but the Father.

Be on the alert

'Be on your guard, stay awake, because you never know when the time will 33 come. •It is like a man travelling abroad: he has gone from home, and left his 34 servants in charge, each with his own task; and he has told the doorkeeper to stay awake. •So stay awake, because you do not know when the master of the 35 house is coming, evening, midnight, cockcrow, dawn; •if he comes unexpectedly, 36 he must not find you asleep. •And what I say to you I say to all: Stay awake!' 37

V. PASSION AND RESURRECTION

The conspiracy against Jesus

14 It was two days before the Passover and the feast of Unleavened Bread, and 1 the chief priests and the scribes were looking for a way to arrest Jesus by some trick and have him put to death. •For they said, 'It must not be during 2 the festivities, or there will be a disturbance among the people'.

The anointing at Bethany

3   Jesus was at Bethany in the house of Simon the leper; he was at dinner when a woman came in with an alabaster jar of very costly ointment, pure nard. She
4 broke the jar and poured the ointment on his head. •Some who were there said
5 to one another indignantly, 'Why this waste of ointment? •Ointment like this could have been sold for over three hundred denarii and the money given to the
6 poor'; and they were angry with her. •But Jesus said, 'Leave her alone. Why are you upsetting her? What she has done for me is one of the good works.
7 You have the poor with you always, and you can be kind to them whenever you
8 wish, but you will not always have me. •She has done what was in her power to
9 do: she has anointed my body beforehand for its burial. •I tell you solemnly, wherever throughout all the world the Good News is proclaimed, what she has done will be told also, in remembrance of her.'

Judas betrays Jesus

'10   Judas Iscariot, one of the Twelve, approached the chief priests with an offer
11 to hand Jesus over to them. •They were delighted to hear it, and promised to give him money; and he looked for a way of betraying him when the opportunity should occur.

Preparations for the Passover supper

12   On the first day of Unleavened Bread, when the Passover lamb was sacrificed, his disciples said to him, 'Where do you want us to go and make the preparations
13 for you to eat the passover?' •So he sent two of his disciples, saying to them, 'Go into the city and you will meet a man carrying a pitcher of water. Follow him,
14 and say to the owner of the house which he enters, "The Master says: Where
15 is my dining room in which I can eat the passover with my disciples?" •He will show you a large upper room furnished with couches, all prepared. Make the
16 preparations for us there.' •The disciples set out and went to the city and found everything as he had told them, and prepared the Passover.

The treachery of Judas foretold

17   When evening came he arrived with the Twelve. •And while they were at
18 table eating, Jesus said, 'I tell you solemnly, one of you is about to betray
19 me, one of you eating with me'. •They were distressed and asked him, one after
20 another, 'Not I, surely?' •He said to them, 'It is one of the Twelve, one who is
21 dipping into the same dish with me. •Yes, the Son of Man is going to his fate, as the scriptures say he will, but alas for that man by whom the Son of Man is betrayed! Better for that man if he had never been born!'

The institution of the Eucharist

22   And as they were eating he took some bread, and when he had said the blessing
23 he broke it and gave it to them. 'Take it,' he said 'this is my body.' •Then he took a cup, and when he had returned thanks he gave it to them, and all drank from
24 it, •and he said to them, 'This is my blood, the blood of the covenant, which is
25 to be poured out for many. •I tell you solemnly, I shall not drink any more wine until the day I drink the new wine in the kingdom of God.'

Peter's denial foretold

26   After psalms had been sung they left for the Mount of Olives. •And Jesus
27 said to them, 'You will all lose faith, for the scripture says: *I shall strike*
28 *the shepherd and the sheep will be scattered,*[a] •however after my resurrection I shall
29 go before you to Galilee'. •Peter said, 'Even if all lose faith, I will not'. •And
30 Jesus said to him, 'I tell you solemnly, this day, this very night, before

13 a. Dn 9:27, and ch. 11,12   b. Dn 12:1
14 a. Zc 13:7

the cock crows twice, you will have disowned me three times'. •But he repeated 31
still more earnestly, 'If I have to die with you, I will never disown you'. And
they all said the same.

Gethsemane

They came to a small estate called Gethsemane, and Jesus said to his disciples, 32
'Stay here while I pray'. •Then he took Peter and James and John with him. 33
And a sudden fear came over him, and great distress. •And he said to them, 'My 34
soul is sorrowful to the point of death. Wait here, and keep awake.' •And going 35
on a little further he threw himself on the ground and prayed that, if it were
possible, this hour might pass him by. •'Abba (Father)!' he said 'Everything 36
is possible for you. Take this cup away from me. But let it be as you, not I, would
have it.' •He came back and found them sleeping, and he said to Peter, 'Simon, 37
are you asleep? Had you not the strength to keep awake one hour? •You should 38
be awake, and praying not to be put to the test. The spirit is willing, but the flesh
is weak.' •Again he went away and prayed, saying the same words. •And ³⁹⁄₄₀
once more he came back and found them sleeping, their eyes were so heavy; and
they could find no answer for him. •He came back a third time and said to them, 41
'You can sleep on now and take your rest. It is all over. The hour has come. Now
the Son of Man is to be betrayed into the hands of sinners. •Get up! Let us go! 42
My betrayer is close at hand already.'

The arrest

Even while he was still speaking, Judas, one of the Twelve, came up with 43
a number of men armed with swords and clubs, sent by the chief priests and
the scribes and the elders. •Now the traitor had arranged a signal with them. 44
'The one I kiss,' he had said 'he is the man. Take him in charge, and see he is
well guarded when you lead him away.' •So when the traitor came, he went 45
straight up to Jesus and said, 'Rabbi!' and kissed him. •The others seized him 46
and took him in charge. •Then one of the bystanders drew his sword and struck 47
out at the high priest's servant, and cut off his ear.

Then Jesus spoke. 'Am I a brigand' he said 'that you had to set out to 48
capture me with swords and clubs? •I was among you teaching in the Temple day 49
after day and you never laid hands on me. But this is to fulfil the scriptures.'
And they all deserted him and ran away. •A young man who followed him had ⁵⁰⁄₅₁
nothing on but a linen cloth. They caught hold of him, •but he left the cloth 52
in their hands and ran away naked.

Jesus before the Sanhedrin

They led Jesus off to the high priest; and all the chief priests and the elders 53
and the scribes assembled there. •Peter had followed him at a distance, right 54
into the high priest's palace, and was sitting with the attendants warming himself
at the fire.

The chief priests and the whole Sanhedrin were looking for evidence against 55
Jesus on which they might pass the death-sentence. But they could not find any.
Several, indeed, brought false evidence against him, but their evidence was 56
conflicting. •Some stood up and submitted this false evidence against him, 57
'We heard him say, "I am going to destroy this Temple made by human hands, 58
and in three days build another, not made by human hands" '. •But even on 59
this point their evidence was conflicting. •The high priest then stood up before 60
the whole assembly and put this question to Jesus, 'Have you no answer to that?
What is this evidence these men are bringing against you?' •But he was silent 61
and made no answer at all. The high priest put a second question to him, 'Are
you the Christ,' he said 'the Son of the Blessed One?' •'I am,' said Jesus 'and 62
you will see *the Son of Man seated at the right hand of the Power* and *coming with
the clouds of heaven.*'ᵇ •The high priest tore his robes, 'What need of witnesses have 63

64 we now?' he said. •'You heard the blasphemy. What is your finding?' And they all gave their verdict: he deserved to die.

65   Some of them started spitting at him and, blindfolding him, began hitting him with their fists and shouting, 'Play the prophet!' And the attendants rained blows on him.

Peter's denials

66 While Peter was down below in the courtyard, one of the high priest's
67 servant-girls came up. •She saw Peter warming himself there, stared at him and
68 said, 'You too were with Jesus, the man from Nazareth'. •But he denied it.
'I do not know, I do not understand, what you are talking about' he said. And
69 he went out into the forecourt. •The servant-girl saw him and again started
70 telling the bystanders, 'This fellow is one of them'. •But again he denied it.
A little later the bystanders themselves said to Peter, 'You are one of them for
71 sure! Why, you are a Galilean.' •But he started calling down curses on himself
72 and swearing, 'I do not know the man you speak of'. •At that moment the
cock crew for the second time, and Peter recalled how Jesus had said to him,
'Before the cock crows twice, you will have disowned me three times'. And
he burst into tears.

Jesus before Pilate

1 **15** First thing in the morning, the chief priests together with the elders and scribes, in short the whole Sanhedrin, had their plan ready. They had Jesus bound and took him away and handed him over to Pilate.

2 Pilate questioned him, 'Are you the king of the Jews?' 'It is you who say it'
3 he answered. •And the chief priests brought many accusations against him.
4 Pilate questioned him again, 'Have you no reply at all? See how many accusations
5 they are bringing against you!' •But, to Pilate's amazement, Jesus made no further reply.

6 At festival time Pilate used to release a prisoner for them, anyone they asked
7 for. •Now a man called Barabbas was then in prison with the rioters who had
8 committed murder during the uprising. •When the crowd went up and began to
9 ask Pilate the customary favour, •Pilate answered them, 'Do you want me to
10 release for you the king of the Jews?' •For he realised it was out of jealousy that
11 the chief priests had handed Jesus over. •The chief priests, however, had incited
12 the crowd to demand that he should release Barabbas for them instead. •Then
Pilate spoke again. 'But in that case,' he said to them 'what am I to do with the
13
14 man you call king of the Jews?' •They shouted back, 'Crucify him!' •'Why?'Pilate
asked them 'What harm has he done?' But they shouted all the louder, 'Crucify
15 him!' •So Pilate, anxious to placate the crowd, released Barabbas for them and, having ordered Jesus to be scourged, handed him over to be crucified.

Jesus crowned with thorns

16 The soldiers led him away to the inner part of the palace, that is, the Prae-
17 torium, and called the whole cohort together. •They dressed him up in purple,
18 twisted some thorns into a crown and put it on him. •And they began saluting
19 him, 'Hail, king of the Jews!' •They struck his head with a reed and spat on him;
20 and they went down on their knees to do him homage. •And when they had finished making fun of him, they took off the purple and dressed him in his own clothes.

The way of the cross

21 They led him out to crucify him. •They enlisted a passer-by, Simon of Cyrene, father of Alexander and Rufus,ᵃ who was coming in from the country, to carry

b. Dn 7:13; Ps 110:1

15 a. Alexander and Rufus were doubtless known to the Roman circle in which Mark wrote his gospel. Cf. Rm 16:13.

his cross. •They brought Jesus to the place called Golgotha, which means the 22
place of the skull.

The crucifixion

They offered him wine mixed with myrrh, but he refused it. •Then they 23
24
crucified him, and shared out his clothing, casting lots to decide what each should
get. •It was the third hour [b] when they crucified him. •The inscription giving the 25
26
charge against him read: 'The King of the Jews'. •And they crucified two robbers 27
with him, one on his right and one on his left.

The crucified Christ is mocked

The passers-by jeered at him; they shook their heads and said, 'Aha! So you 29
would destroy the Temple and rebuild it in three days! •Then save yourself: 30
come down from the cross!' •The chief priests and the scribes mocked him among 31
themselves in the same way. 'He saved others,' they said 'he cannot save
himself. •Let the Christ, the king of Israel, come down from the cross now, for 32
us to see it and believe.' Even those who were crucified with him taunted him.

The death of Jesus

When the sixth hour came there was darkness over the whole land until the 33
ninth hour. •And at the ninth hour Jesus cried out in a loud voice, 'Eloi, Eloi, 34
lama sabachthani?' which means, *My God, my God, why have you deserted me?* [c]
When some of those who stood by heard this, they said, 'Listen, he is calling on 35
Elijah'. •Someone ran and soaked a sponge in vinegar and, putting it on a reed, 36
gave it him to drink saying, 'Wait and see if Elijah will come to take him down'.
But Jesus gave a loud cry and breathed his last. •And the veil of the Temple was 37
38
torn in two from top to bottom. •The centurion, who was standing in front of 39
him, had seen how he had died, and he said, 'In truth this man was a son of
God'.

The women on Calvary

There were some women watching from a distance. Among them were Mary 40
of Magdala, Mary who was the mother of James the younger and Joset, and
Salome. •These used to follow him and look after him when he was in Galilee. 41
And there were many other women there who had come up to Jerusalem with
him.

The burial

It was now evening, and since it was Preparation Day (that is, the vigil of the 42
sabbath), •there came Joseph of Arimathaea, a prominent member of the 43
Council, who himself lived in the hope of seeing the kingdom of God, and he
boldly went to Pilate and asked for the body of Jesus. •Pilate, astonished that 44
he should have died so soon, summoned the centurion and enquired if he was
already dead. •Having been assured of this by the centurion, he granted the 45
corpse to Joseph •who bought a shroud, took Jesus down from the cross, 46
wrapped him in the shroud and laid him in a tomb which had been hewn out
of the rock. He then rolled a stone against the entrance to the tomb. •Mary of 47
Magdala and Mary the mother of Joset were watching and took note of where
he was laid.

The empty tomb. The angel's message

16 When the sabbath was over, Mary of Magdala, Mary the mother of James, 1
and Salome, bought spices with which to go and anoint him. •And very early 2
in the morning on the first day of the week they went to the tomb, just as the
sun was rising.

They had been saying to one another, 'Who will roll away the stone for us 3

4 from the entrance to the tomb?' •But when they looked they could see that the
5 stone—which was very big—had already been rolled back. •On entering the
tomb they saw a young man in a white robe seated on the right-hand side, and
6 they were struck with amazement. •But he said to them, 'There is no need for
alarm. You are looking for Jesus of Nazareth, who was crucified: he has risen,
7 he is not here. See, here is the place where they laid him. •But you must go and
tell his disciples and Peter, "He is going before you to Galilee; it is there
8 you will see him, just as he told you".' •And the women came out and ran away
from the tomb because they were frightened out of their wits; and they said
nothing to a soul, for they were afraid...

Appearances of the risen Christ[a]

9   Having risen in the morning on the first day of the week, he appeared first to
10 Mary of Magdala from whom he had cast out seven devils. •She then went to those
who had been his companions, and who were mourning and in tears, and told
11 them. •But they did not believe her when they heard her say that he was alive
and that she had seen him.
12   After this, he showed himself under another form to two of them as they
13 were on their way into the country. •These went back and told the others, who
did not believe them either.
14   Lastly, he showed himself to the Eleven themselves while they were at table.
He reproached them for their incredulity and obstinacy, because they had refused
15 to believe those who had seen him after he had risen. •And he said to them,
16 'Go out to the whole world; proclaim the Good News to all creation. •He who
believes and is baptised will be saved; he who does not believe will be condemned.
17 These are the signs that will be associated with believers: in my name they will cast
18 out devils; they will have the gift of tongues; •they will pick up snakes in their
hands, and be unharmed should they drink deadly poison; they will lay their
hands on the sick, who will recover.'
19   And so the Lord Jesus, after he had spoken to them, was taken up into heaven:
20 there at the right hand of God he took his place, •while they, going out, preached
everywhere, the Lord working with them and confirming the word by the signs
that accompanied it.

b. 9 a.m.   c. Ps 22:1
16 a. Many MSS omit vv. 9-20 and this ending to the gospel may not have been written by
Mark, though it is old enough.

THE GOSPEL ACCORDING TO
SAINT LUKE

Prologue

1 Seeing that many others have undertaken to draw up accounts of the events 1
that have taken place among us, •exactly as these were handed down to us by 2
those who from the outset were eyewitnesses and ministers of the word, •I in my 3
turn, after carefully going over the whole story from the beginning, have decided
to write an ordered account for you, Theophilus, •so that your Excellency may 4
learn how well founded the teaching is that you have received.

I. THE BIRTH AND HIDDEN LIFE
OF JOHN THE BAPTIST AND OF JESUS

The birth of John the Baptist foretold

In the days of King Herod of Judaea there lived a priest called Zechariah 5
who belonged to the Abijah section of the priesthood, and he had a wife,
Elizabeth by name, who was a descendant of Aaron. •Both were worthy in the 6
sight of God, and scrupulously observed all the commandments and observances
of the Lord. •But they were childless: Elizabeth was barren and they were 7
both getting on in years.

Now it was the turn of Zechariah's section *a* to serve, and he was exercising 8
his priestly office before God •when it fell to him by lot, as the ritual custom 9
was, to enter the Lord's sanctuary and burn incense there. *b* •And at the hour of 10
incense the whole 'congregation was outside, praying.

Then there appeared to him the angel of the Lord, standing on the right 11
of the altar of incense. •The sight disturbed Zechariah and he was overcome with 12
fear. •But the angel said to him, 'Zechariah, do not be afraid, your prayer 13
has been heard. Your wife Elizabeth is to bear you a son and you must name
him John. *c* •He will be your joy and delight and many will rejoice at his birth, 14
for he will be great in the sight of the Lord; he must drink no wine, no strong 15
drink. *d* Even from his mother's womb he will be filled with the Holy Spirit, •and 16
he will bring back many of the sons of Israel to the Lord their God. •With the 17
spirit and power of Elijah, he will go before him *to turn the hearts of fathers
towards their children* *e* and the disobedient back to the wisdom that the virtuous
have, preparing for the Lord a people fit for him.' •Zechariah said to the angel, 18
'*How can I be sure of this?* *f* I am an old man and my wife is getting on in years.'
The angel replied, 'I am Gabriel who stand in God's presence, and I have been 19
sent to speak to you and bring you this good news. •Listen! Since you have not 20
believed my words, which will come true at their appointed time, you will be
silenced and have no power of speech until this has happened.' •Meanwhile 21
the people were waiting for Zechariah and were surprised that he stayed in the
sanctuary so long. •When he came out he could not speak to them, and they 22

realised that he had received a vision in the sanctuary. But he could only make signs to them, and remained dumb.

23
24   When his time of service came to an end he returned home. •Some time later
25 his wife Elizabeth conceived, and for five months she kept to herself. •'The Lord has done this for me' she said 'now that it has pleased him to take away the humiliation I suffered among men.'

The annunciation

26   In the sixth month the angel Gabriel was sent by God to a town in Galilee
27 called Nazareth, •to a virgin betrothed to a man named Joseph, of the House
28 of David; and the virgin's name was Mary. •He went in and said to her, 'Rejoice,
29 so highly favoured! The Lord is with you.' •She was deeply disturbed by these
30 words and asked herself what this greeting could mean, •but the angel said
31 to her, 'Mary, do not be afraid; you have won God's favour. •Listen! You are
32 to conceive and bear a son, and you must name him Jesus. •He will be great and will be called Son of the Most High. The Lord God will give him the throne
33 of his ancestor David; •he will rule over the House of Jacob for ever and his reign
34 will have no end.' •Mary said to the angel, 'But how can this come about, since
35 I am a virgin?'[g] •'The Holy Spirit will come upon you' the angel answered 'and the power of the Most High will cover you with its shadow. And so the child
36 will be holy and will be called Son of God. •Know this too: your kinswoman Elizabeth has, in her old age, herself conceived a son, and she whom people called
37 barren is now in her sixth month, •*for nothing is impossible to God.*'[h] •'I am the
38 handmaid of the Lord,' said Mary 'let what you have said be done to me.' And the angel left her.

The visitation

39   Mary set out at that time and went as quickly as she could to a town in the
40 hill country of Judah. •She went into Zechariah's house and greeted Elizabeth.
41 Now as soon as Elizabeth heard Mary's greeting, the child leapt in her womb
42 and Elizabeth was filled with the Holy Spirit. •She gave a loud cry and said, 'Of all women you are the most blessed, and blessed is the fruit of your womb.
43 Why should I be honoured with a visit from the mother of my Lord?' •For the
44 moment your greeting reached my ears, the child in my womb leapt for joy.
45 Yes, blessed is she who believed that the promise made her by the Lord would be fulfilled.'

The Magnificat

46   And Mary[i] said:

'My soul proclaims the greatness of the Lord
47   and my spirit *exults in God my saviour;*
48   because *he has looked upon his lowly hanamaid.*
Yes, from this day forward all generations will call me blessed,
49   for the Almighty has done great things for me.
Holy is his name,
50   and *his mercy reaches from age to age for those who fear him.*
51   He has shown the power of his arm,
he has routed the proud of heart.
52   *He has pulled down princes* from their thrones *and exalted the lowly.*
53   *The hungry he has filled with good things,* the rich sent empty away.

---

1 a. The 24 families of the 'sons of Aaron' were responsible in rotation for service in the Temple, and in each class or family the individual was chosen by lot. See 1 Ch 24.   b. The priest tended the brazier on the altar of incense in front of the Most Holy Place.   c. The meaning of the name is 'Yahweh is gracious'.   d. See Nb 6:1, where this abstinence is required in anyone performing a vow to the Lord.   e. Ml 3:23-24   f. Zechariah asks for a sign in a way reminiscent of Abram, Gn 15:8.   g. Lit. 'since I do not know man'.   h. Gn 8:14   i. Mary's canticle is reminiscent of Hannah's, 1 S 2:1-10. Other quotations and allusions in the Magnificat are: 1 S 1:11; Ps 103:17; Ps 111:9; Jb 5:11 and 12:19; Ps 98:3; Ps 107:9; Is 41:8-9.

He has come to the help of Israel his servant, mindful of his mercy   54
—according to the promise he made to our ancestors—   55
of his mercy to Abraham and to his descendants for ever.'

Mary stayed with Elizabeth about three months and then went back home.   56

The birth of John the Baptist and visit of the neighbours

Meanwhile the time came for Elizabeth to have her child, and she gave birth   57
to a son; •and when her neighbours and relations heard that the Lord had shown   58
her so great a kindness, they shared her joy.

The circumcision of John the Baptist

Now on the eighth day they came to circumcise the child; they were going   59
to call[^j] him Zechariah after his father, •but his mother spoke up. 'No,' she   60
said 'he is to be called John.' •They said to her, 'But no one in your family has   61
that name', •and made signs to his father to find out what he wanted him called.   62
The father asked for a writing-tablet and wrote, 'His name is John'. And they   63
were all astonished. •At that instant his power of speech returned and he spoke   64
and praised God. •All their neighbours were filled with awe and the whole affair   65
was talked about throughout the hill country of Judaea. •All those who heard   66
of it treasured it in their hearts. 'What will this child turn out to be?'
they wondered. And indeed the hand of the Lord was with him.

The Benedictus

His father Zechariah was filled with the Holy Spirit and spoke this prophecy: 67

> *'Blessed be the Lord, the God of Israel,*[^k]   68
> for he has visited his people, he has come to their rescue
> and he has raised up for us a power for salvation   69
> in the House of his servant David,
> even as he proclaimed,   70
> by the mouth of his holy prophets from ancient times,
> that he would save us from our enemies   71
> and from the hands of all who hate us.
> Thus he shows mercy to our ancestors,   72
> thus *he remembers* his holy *covenant,*[^l]
> the oath he swore   73
> to our father Abraham
> that he would grant us, free from fear,   74
> to be delivered from the hands of our enemies,
> to serve him in holiness and virtue   75
> in his presence, all our days.
> And you, little child,   76
> you shall be called Prophet of the Most High,
> for you will go before the Lord
> to prepare the way for him.
> To give his people knowledge of salvation   77
> through the forgiveness of their sins;
> this by the tender mercy of our God   78
> who from on high will bring the rising Sun to visit us,
> to give light to *those who live*   79
> *in darkness and the shadow of death,*[^m]
> and to guide our feet
> into the way of peace.'

The hidden life of John the Baptist

Meanwhile the child grew up and his spirit matured. And he lived out in   80
the wilderness until the day he appeared openly to Israel.

The birth of Jesus and visit of the shepherds

1 2 Now at this time Caesar Augustus[a] issued a decree for a census of the whole
2   world to be taken. •This census—the first[b]—took place while Quirinius was
³/₄ governor of Syria, •and everyone went to his own town to be registered. •So Joseph
      set out from the town of Nazareth in Galilee and travelled up to Judaea, to the
5   town of David called Bethlehem, since he was of David's House and line, •in
      order to be registered together with Mary, his betrothed, who was with child.
⁶/₇ While they were there the time came for her to have her child, •and she gave birth
      to a son, her first-born.[c] She wrapped him in swaddling clothes, and laid him in a
8   manger because there was no room for them at the inn. •In the countryside
      close by there were shepherds who lived in the fields and took it in turns to watch
9   their flocks during the night. •The angel of the Lord appeared to them and
      the glory of the Lord shone round them. They were terrified, •but the angel
10   said, 'Do not be afraid. Listen, I bring you news of great joy, a joy to be shared
11   by the whole people. •Today in the town of David a saviour has been born to
12   you; he is Christ the Lord. •And here is a sign for you: you will find a baby
13   wrapped in swaddling clothes and lying in a manger.' •And suddenly with the
      angel there was a great throng of the heavenly host, praising God and singing:

14   'Glory to God in the highest heaven,
                   and peace to men who enjoy his favour'.

15   Now when the angels had gone from them into heaven, the shepherds said
      to one another, 'Let us go to Bethlehem and see this thing that has happened
16   which the Lord has made known to us'. •So they hurried away and found
17   Mary and Joseph, and the baby lying in the manger. •When they saw the child
18   they repeated what they had been told about him, •and everyone who heard
19   it was astonished at what the shepherds had to say. •As for Mary, she treasured
20   all these things and pondered them in her heart. •And the shepherds went
      back glorifying and praising God for all they had heard and seen; it was exactly
      as they had been told.

The circumcision of Jesus

21   When the eighth day came and the child was to be circumcised, they gave
      him the name Jesus, the name the angel had given him before his conception.

Jesus is presented in the Temple

22   And when the day came for them to be purified[d] as laid down by the Law
23   of Moses, they took him up to Jerusalem to present him to the Lord — •observing
      what stands written in the Law of the Lord: *Every first-born male must be con-*
24   *secrated to the Lord*[e]—•and also to offer in sacrifice, in accordance with what
25   is said in the Law of the Lord, *a pair of turtledoves or two young pigeons.*[f] •Now
      in Jerusalem there was a man named Simeon. He was an upright and devout
      man; he looked forward to Israel's comforting and the Holy Spirit rested on
26   him. •It had been revealed to him by the Holy Spirit that he would not see death
27   until he had set eyes on the Christ of the Lord.[g] •Prompted by the Spirit he
      came to the Temple; and when the parents brought in the child Jesus to do for
28   him what the Law required, •he took him into his arms and blessed God; and he
      said:

---

j. The name was normally given at the time of circumcision.   k. Ps 41:13   l. Lv 26:42
m. Is 9:1
2 a. Emperor of Rome 30 B.C to 14 A.D.   b. About 8-6 B.C.   c. The term does not necessarily imply younger brothers.   d. The mother needed to be 'purified'; the child had to be
'redeemed'.   e. Ex 13:2   f. The offering of the poor, Lv 5:7.   g. 'The anointed one of God'.

The Nunc Dimittis

'Now, Master, you can let your servant go in peace,   29
just as you promised;
because my eyes have seen the salvation   30
which you have prepared for all the nations to see,   31
a light to enlighten the pagans   32
and the glory of your people Israel'.

The prophecy of Simeon

As the child's father and mother stood there wondering at the things that 33
were being said about him, •Simeon blessed them and said to Mary his mother, 34
'You see this child: he is destined for the fall and for the rising of many in Israel,
destined to be a sign that is rejected—•and a sword will pierce your own soul 35
too—so that the secret thoughts of many may be laid bare'.

The prophecy of Anna

There was a prophetess also, Anna the daughter of Phanuel, of the tribe 36
of Asher. She was well on in years. Her days of girlhood over, she had been
married for seven years •before becoming a widow. She was now eighty-four 37
years old and never left the Temple, serving God night and day with fasting
and prayer. •She came by just at that moment and began to praise God; and 38
she spoke of the child to all who looked forward to the deliverance of Jerusalem. h

The hidden life of Jesus at Nazareth

When they had done everything the Law of the Lord required, they went back 39
to Galilee, to their own town of Nazareth. •Meanwhile the child grew to maturity, 40
and he was filled with wisdom; and God's favour was with him.

Jesus among the doctors of the Law

Every year his parents used to go to Jerusalem for the feast of the Passover. 41
When he was twelve years old, they went up for the feast as usual. •When they 42/43
were on their way home after the feast, the boy Jesus stayed behind in Jerusalem
without his parents knowing it. •They assumed he was with the caravan, and 44
it was only after a day's journey that they went to look for him among their
relations and acquaintances. •When they failed to find him they went back to 45
Jerusalem looking for him everywhere.

Three days later, they found him in the Temple, sitting among the doctors, 46
listening to them, and asking them questions; •and all those who heard him 47
were astounded at his intelligence and his replies. •They were overcome 48
when they saw him, and his mother said to him, 'My child, why have
you done this to us? See how worried your father and I have been, looking for
you.' •'Why were you looking for me?' he replied 'Did you not know that I must 49
be busy with my Father's affairs?' •But they did not understand what he meant. 50

The hidden life at Nazareth resumed

He then went down with them and came to Nazareth and lived under their 51
authority. His mother stored up all these things in her heart. •And Jesus increased 52
in wisdom, in stature, and in favour with God and men.

II. PRELUDE TO THE PUBLIC MINISTRY OF JESUS

The preaching of John the Baptist

3 In the fifteenth year of Tiberius Caesar's reign,ª when Pontius Pilateᵇ was 1
governor of Judaea, Herodᶜ tetrarch of Galilee, his brother Philipᵈ tetrarch
of the lands of Ituraea and Trachonitis, Lysanias tetrarch of Abilene, •during 2
the pontificate of Annas and Caiaphas,ᵉ the word of God came to John son of

3 Zechariah, in the wilderness. •He went through the whole Jordan district pro-
4 claiming a baptism of repentance for the forgiveness of sins, •as it is written
in the book of the sayings of the prophet Isaiah:

> *A voice cries in the wilderness:*
> *Prepare a way for the Lord,*
> *make his paths straight.*
5 > *Every valley will be filled in,*
> *every mountain and hill be laid low,*
> *winding ways will be straightened*
> *and rough roads made smooth.*
6 > *And all mankind shall see the salvation of God.* ᶠ

7   He said, therefore, to the crowds who came to be baptised by him, 'Brood of
8 vipers, who warned you to fly from the retribution that is coming? •But if you are
repentant, produce the appropriate fruits, and do not think of telling yourselves,
"We have Abraham for our father" because; I tell you, God can raise children for
9 Abraham from these stones. •Yes, even now the axe is laid to the roots of the
trees, so that any tree which fails to produce good fruit will be cut down and
thrown on the fire.'

10
11   When all the people asked him, 'What must we do, then?' •he answered,
'If anyone has two tunics he must share with the man who has none, and the
12 one with something to eat must do the same'. •There were tax collectors too
13 who came for baptism, and these said to him, 'Master, what must we do?' •He
14 said to them, 'Exact no more than your rate'. •Some soldiers asked him in their
turn, 'What about us? What must we do?' He said to them, 'No intimidation!
No extortion! Be content with your pay!'

15   A feeling of expectancy had grown among the people, who were beginning
16 to think that John might be the Christ, •so John declared before them all, 'I
baptise you with water, but someone is coming, someone who is more powerful
than I am, and I am not fit to undo the strap of his sandals; he will baptise
17 you with the Holy Spirit and fire. •His winnowing-fan is in his hand to clear
his threshing-floor and to gather the wheat into his barn; but the chaff he will
18 burn in a fire that will never go out.' •As well as this, there were many other
things he said to exhort the people and to announce the Good News to them.

John the Baptist imprisoned

19   But Herod the tetrarch, whom he criticised for his relations with his brother's
20 wife Herodias and for all the other crimes Herod had committed, •added a further
crime to all the rest by shutting John up in prison.

Jesus is baptised

21   Now when all the people had been baptised and while Jesus after his own
22 baptism was at prayer, heaven opened •and the Holy Spirit descended on him
in bodily shape, like a dove. And a voice came from heaven, 'You are my Son,
the Beloved; my favour rests on you'.

The ancestry of Jesus

23   When he started to teach, Jesus was about thirty years old, being the son,
24 as it was thought, of Joseph son of Heli, •son of Matthat, son of Levi, son

h. I.e. Israel. Jerusalem is the holy city.
3 a. By Roman dating, the 15th year of Tiberius Caesar's reign was August 28 A.D. to August
29 A.D.; by the Syrian method, it was Sept.-Oct. 27 A.D. to Sept.-Oct. 28 A.D. At that time,
Jesus was between 33 and 36 years old. The mistake in calculating 'the Christian era' results
from taking Lk 3:23 as an exact statement.   b. Procurator of Judaea 26-36 A.D.   c. Herod
Antipas, tetrarch of Galilee and Peraea 4 B.C. to 39 A.D.   d. Tetrarch from 4 B.C. to 34 A.D.
e. Caiaphas was high priest from 18 to 36 A.D. His father-in-law, Annas, is associated with
him here and elsewhere; he had been high priest earlier and presumably still had great influence.
f. Is 40:3-5

of Melchi, son of Jannai, son of Joseph, •son of Mattathias, son of Amos, son 25
of Nahum, son of Esli, son of Naggai, •son of Maath, son of Mattathias, son 26
of Semein, son of Josech, son of Joda, •son of Joanan, son of Rhesa, son of 27
Zerubbabel, son of Shealtiel, son of Neri, •son of Melchi, son of Addi, son of 28
Cosam, son of Elmadam, son of Er, •son of Joshua, son of Eliezer, son of Jorim, 29
son of Matthat, son of Levi, •son of Symeon, son of Judah, son of Joseph, son 30
of Jonam, son of Eliakim, •son of Melea, son of Menna, son of Mattatha, son 31
of Nathan, son of David, •son of Jesse, son of Obed, son of Boaz, son of Sala, 32
son of Nahshon, •son of Amminadab, son of Admin, son of Arni, son of Hezron, 33
son of Perez, son of Judah, •son of Jacob, son of Isaac, son of Abraham, son 34
of Terah, son of Nahor, •son of Serug, son of Reu, son of Peleg, son of Eber, 35
son of Shelah, •son of Cainan, son of Arphaxad, son of Shem, son of Noah, 36
son of Lamech, •son of Methuselah, son of Enoch, son of Jared, son of Mahalaleel, 37
son of Cainan, •son of Enos, son of Seth, son of Adam, son of God. 38

Temptation in the wilderness

4 Filled with the Holy Spirit, Jesus left the Jordan and was led by the Spirit 1
through the wilderness, •being tempted there by the devil for forty days. 2
During that time he ate nothing and at the end he was hungry. •Then the devil 3
said to him, 'If you are the Son of God, tell this stone to turn into a loaf'. •But 4
Jesus replied, 'Scripture says: *Man does not live on bread alone*'. [a]

Then leading him to a height, the devil showed him in a moment of time all 5
the kingdoms of the world and said to him, 'I will give you all this power and 6
the glory of these kingdoms, for it has been committed to me and I give it to
anyone I choose. •Worship me, then, and it shall all be yours.' •But Jesus 7 8
answered him, 'Scripture says:

> *You must worship the Lord your God,*
> *and serve him alone*'. [b]

Then he led him to Jerusalem and made him stand on the parapet of the 9
Temple. 'If you are the Son of God,' he said to him 'throw yourself down from
here, •for scripture says: 10

> *He will put his angels in charge of you*
> *to guard you,*

and again:

> *They will hold you up on their hands* 11
> *in case you hurt your foot against a stone*'. [c]

But Jesus answered him, 'It has been said: 12

> *You must not put the Lord your God to the test*'. [d]

Having exhausted all these ways of tempting him, the devil left him, to return 13
at the appointed time.

III. THE GALILEAN MINISTRY

Jesus begins to preach

Jesus, with the power of the Spirit in him, returned to Galilee; and his 14
reputation spread throughout the countryside. •He taught in their synagogues 15
and everyone praised him.

Jesus at Nazareth

He came to Nazara, where he had been brought up, and went into the 16
synagogue on the sabbath day as he usually did. He stood up to read, [e] • and they 17

handed him the scroll of the prophet Isaiah. Unrolling the scroll he found the place where it is written:

18
> The spirit of the Lord has been given to me,
> for he has anointed me.
> He has sent me to bring the good news to the poor,
> to proclaim liberty to captives
> and to the blind new sight,
> to set the downtrodden free,
19
> to proclaim the Lord's year of favour.[f]

20 He then rolled up the scroll, gave it back to the assistant and sat down. And all
21 eyes in the synagogue were fixed on him. •Then he began to speak to them, 'This
22 text is being fulfilled today even as you listen'. •And he won the approval of all, and they were astonished by the gracious words that came from his lips.

23   They said, 'This is Joseph's son, surely?' •But he replied, 'No doubt you will quote me the saying, "Physician, heal yourself" and tell me, "We have heard all that happened in Capernaum, do the same here in your own countryside" '.
24 And he went on, 'I tell you solemnly, no prophet is ever accepted in his own country.

25   'There were many widows in Israel, I can assure you, in Elijah's day, when heaven remained shut for three years and six months and a great famine raged
26 throughout the land, •but Elijah was not sent to any one of these: he was sent
27 *to a widow at Zarephath, a Sidonian town.*[g] •And in the prophet Elisha's time there were many lepers in Israel, but none of these was cured, except the Syrian, Naaman.'

28
29   When they heard this everyone in the synagogue was enraged. •They sprang to their feet and hustled him out of the town; and they took him up to the brow
30 of the hill their town was built on, intending to throw him down the cliff, •but he slipped through the crowd and walked away.

Jesus teaches in Capernaum and cures a demoniac

31   He went down to Capernaum, a town in Galilee, and taught them on the
32 sabbath. •And his teaching made a deep impression on them because he spoke with authority.

33   In the synagogue there was a man who was possessed by the spirit of an
34 unclean devil, and it shouted at the top of its voice, •'Ha! What do you want with us, Jesus of Nazareth? Have you come to destroy us? I know who you are:
35 the Holy One of God.' •But Jesus said sharply, 'Be quiet! Come out of him!' And the devil, throwing the man down in front of everyone, went out of him
36 without hurting him at all. •Astonishment seized them and they were all saying to one another, 'What teaching! He gives orders to unclean spirits with authority
37 and power and they come out.' •And reports of him went all through the surrounding countryside.

Cure of Simon's mother-in-law

38   Leaving the synagogue he went to Simon's house. Now Simon's mother-in-law was suffering from a high fever and they asked him to do something for her.
39 Leaning over her he rebuked the fever and it left her. And she immediately got up and began to wait on them.

A number of cures

40   At sunset all those who had friends suffering from diseases of one kind or
41 another brought them to him, and laying his hands on each he cured them. •Devils

---

4 a. Dt 8:3   b. Dt 6:13   c. Ps 91:11-12   d. Dt 6:16   e. Any adult man could be permitted by the president to read the scriptures.   f. Is 61:1-2   g. 1K 17:9

too came out of many people, howling, 'You are the Son of God'. But he rebuked them and would not allow them to speak because they knew that he was the Christ.

Jesus quietly leaves Capernaum, and travels through Judaea

When daylight came he left the house and made his way to a lonely place. 42 The crowds went to look for him, and when they had caught up with him they wanted to prevent him leaving them, •but he answered, 'I must proclaim the 43 Good News of the kingdom of God to the other towns too, because that is what I was sent to do'. •And he continued his preaching in the synagogues of Judaea. 44

The first four disciples are called

5 Now he was standing one day by the Lake of Gennesaret, with the crowd 1 pressing round him listening to the word of God, •when he caught sight of two 2 boats close to the bank. The fishermen had gone out of them and were washing their nets. •He got into one of the boats—it was Simon's —and asked him to put 3 out a little from the shore. Then he sat down and taught the crowds from the boat.

When he had finished speaking he said to Simon, 'Put out into deep water 4 and pay out your nets for a catch'. •'Master,' Simon replied 'we worked hard all 5 night long and caught nothing, but if you say so, I will pay out the nets.' •And 6 when they had done this they netted such a huge number of fish that their nets began to tear, •so they signalled to their companions in the other boat to come 7 and help them; when these came, they filled the two boats to sinking point.

When Simon Peter saw this he fell at the knees of Jesus saying, 'Leave me, 8 Lord; I am a sinful man'. •For he and all his companions were completely 9 overcome by the catch they had made; •so also were James and John, sons of 10 Zebedee, who were Simon's partners. But Jesus said to Simon, 'Do not be afraid; from now on it is men you will catch'. •Then, bringing their boats back to land, 11 they left everything and followed him.

Cure of a leper

Now Jesus was in one of the towns when a man appeared, covered with 12 leprosy. Seeing Jesus he fell on his face and implored him, 'Sir,' he said 'if you want to, you can cure me.' •Jesus stretched out his hand, touched him and said, 13 'Of course I want to! Be cured!' And the leprosy left him at once. •He ordered 14 him to tell no one, 'But go and show yourself to the priest and make the offering for your healing as Moses prescribed it, as evidence for them'.

His reputation continued to grow, and large crowds would gather to hear him 15 and to have their sickness cured, •but he would always go off to some place where 16 he could be alone and pray.

Cure of a paralytic

Now he was teaching one day, and among the audience there were Pharisees 17 and doctors of the Law who had come from every village in Galilee, from Judaea and from Jerusalem. And the Power of the Lord was behind his works of healing. •Then some men appeared, carrying on a bed a paralysed man whom 18 they were trying to bring in and lay down in front of him. •But as the crowd 19 made it impossible to find a way of getting him in, they went up on to the flat roof and lowered him and his stretcher down through the tiles into the middle of the gathering, in front of Jesus. •Seeing their faith he said, 'My friend, your sins 20 are forgiven you'. •The scribes and the Pharisees began to think this over. 'Who is 21 this man talking blasphemy? Who can forgive sins but God alone?' •But Jesus, 22 aware of their thoughts, made them this reply, 'What are these thoughts you have in your hearts? •Which of these is easier: to say, "Your sins are forgiven you" 23 or to say, "Get up and walk"? •But to prove to you that the Son of Man has 24 authority on earth to forgive sins,'—he said to the paralysed man—'I order you: get up, and pick up your stretcher and go home.' •And immediately before 25 their very eyes he got up, picked up what he had been lying on and went home praising God.

26 They were all astounded and praised God, and were filled with awe, saying, 'We have seen strange things today'.

The call of Levi

27 When he went out after this, he noticed a tax collector, Levi by name, sitting
28 by the customs house, and said to him, 'Follow me'. •And leaving everything he got up and followed him.

Eating with sinners in Levi's house

29 In his honour Levi held a great reception in his house, and with them at table
30 was a large gathering of tax collectors and others. •The Pharisees and their scribes complained to his disciples and said, 'Why do you eat and drink with tax collectors
31 and sinners?' •Jesus said to them in reply, 'It is not those who are well who need
32 the doctor, but the sick. •I have not come to call the virtuous, but sinners to repentance.'

Discussion on fasting

33 They then said to him, 'John's disciples are always fasting and saying prayers, and the disciples of the Pharisees too, but yours go on eating and drinking'.
34 Jesus replied, 'Surely you cannot make the bridegroom's attendants fast while
35 the bridegroom is still with them? •But the time will come, the time for the bridegroom to be taken away from them; that will be the time when they will fast.'
36 He also told them this parable, 'No one tears a piece from a new cloak to put it on an old cloak; if he does, not only will he have torn the new one, but the piece taken from the new will not match the old. •
37 'And nobody puts new wine into old skins; if he does, the new wine will burst
38 the skins and then run out, and the skins will be lost. •No; new wine must be put
39 into fresh skins. •And nobody who has been drinking old wine wants new. "The old is good" he says.'

Picking corn on the sabbath

1 6 Now one sabbath he happened to be taking a walk through the cornfields, and his disciples were picking ears of corn, rubbing them in their hands
2 and eating them. •Some of the Pharisees said, 'Why are you doing something
3 that is forbidden on the sabbath day?' •Jesus answered them, 'So you have not
4 read what David did when he and his followers were hungry—•how he went into the house of God, took the loaves of offering and ate them and gave them to his
5 followers, loaves which only the priests are allowed to eat?' •And he said to them, 'The Son of Man is master of the sabbath'.

Cure of the man with a withered hand

6 Now on another sabbath he went into the synagogue and began to teach, and
7 a man was there whose right hand was withered. •The scribes and the Pharisees were watching him to see if he would cure a man on the sabbath, hoping to
8 find something to use against him. •But he knew their thoughts; and he said to the man with the withered hand, 'Stand up! Come out into the middle.' And he came
9 out and stood there. •Then Jesus said to them, 'I put it to you: is it against the
10 law on the sabbath to do good, or to do evil; to save life, or to destroy it?' •Then he looked round at them all and said to the man, 'Stretch out your hand'. He did
11 so, and his hand was better. •But they were furious, and began to discuss the best way of dealing with Jesus.

The choice of the Twelve

12 Now it was about this time that he went out into the hills to pray; and he spent
13 the whole night in prayer to God. •When day came he summoned his disciples

and picked out twelve of them; he called them 'apostles': •Simon whom he 14
called Peter, and his brother Andrew; James, John, Philip, Bartholomew,
Matthew, Thomas, James son of Alphaeus, Simon called the Zealot, •Judas son ¹⁵₁₆
of James,ᵃ and Judas Iscariot who became a traitor.

The crowds follow Jesus

He then came down with them and stopped at a piece of level ground where 17
there was a large gathering of his disciples with a great crowd of people from all
parts of Judaea and from Jerusalem and from the coastal region of Tyre and Sidon
who had come to hear him and to be cured of their diseases. People tormented 18
by unclean spirits were also cured, •and everyone in the crowd was trying to touch 19
him because power came out of him that cured them all.

The inaugural discourse. The Beatitudes

Then fixing his eyes on his disciples he said: 20

'How happy are you who are poor: yours is the kingdom of God.
Happy you who are hungry now: you shall be satisfied. 21
Happy you who weep now: you shall laugh.

'Happy are you when people hate you, drive you out, abuse you, denounce 22
your name as criminal, on account of the Son of Man. •Rejoice when that day 23
comes and dance for joy, for then your reward will be great in heaven. This was the
way their ancestors treated the prophets.

The curses

'But alas for you who are rich: you are having your consolation now. 24
Alas for you who have your fill now: you shall go hungry. 25
Alas for you who laugh now: you shall mourn and weep.

'Alas for you when the world speaks well of you! This was the way their 26
ancestors treated the false prophets.

Love of enemies

'But I say this to you who are listening: Love your enemies, do good to those 27
who hate you, •bless those who curse you, pray for those who treat you badly. 28
To the man who slaps you on one cheek, present the other cheek too; to the man 29
who takes your cloak from you, do not refuse your tunic. •Give to everyone who 30
asks you, and do not ask for your property back from the man who robs you.
Treat others as you would like them to treat you. •If you love those who love ³¹₃₂
you, what thanks can you expect? Even sinners love those who love them. •And if 33
you do good to those who do good to you, what thanks can you expect? For even
sinners do that much. •And if you lend to those from whom you hope to receive, 34
what thanks can you expect? Even sinners lend to sinners to get back the same
amount. •Instead, love your enemies and do good, and lend without any hope 35
of return. You will have a great reward, and you will be sons of the Most High,
for he himself is kind to the ungrateful and the wicked.

Compassion and generosity

'Be compassionate as your Father is compassionate. •Do not judge, and you ³⁶₃₇
will not be judged yourselves; do not condemn, and you will not be condemned
yourselves; grant pardon, and you will be pardoned. •Give, and there will be 38
gifts for you: a full measure, pressed down, shaken together, and running over,
will be poured into your lap; because the amount you measure out is the amount
you will be given back.'

Integrity

He also told a parable to them, 'Can one blind man guide another? Surely 39
both will fall into a pit? •The disciple is not superior to his teacher; the fully 40

41 trained disciple will always be like his teacher. •Why do you observe the splinter
42 in your brother's eye and never notice the plank in your own? •How can you say
to your brother, "Brother, let me take out the splinter that is in your eye", when
you cannot see the plank in your own? Hypocrite! Take the plank out of your
own eye first, and then you will see clearly enough to take out the splinter
that is in your brother's eye.

43 'There is no sound tree that produces rotten fruit, nor again a rotten tree that
44 produces sound fruit. •For every tree can be told by its own fruit: people do not
45 pick figs from thorns, nor gather grapes from brambles. •A good man draws what
is good from the store of goodness in his heart; a bad man draws what is bad
from the store of badness. For a man's words flow out of what fills his heart.

The true disciple

46 'Why do you call me, "Lord, Lord" and not do what I say?

47 'Everyone who comes to me and listens to my words and acts on them—I will
48 show you what he is like. •He is like the man who when he built his house dug,
and dug deep, and laid the foundations on rock; when the river was in flood it
49 bore down on that house but could not shake it, it was so well built. •But the one
who listens and does nothing is like the man who built his house on soil, with no
foundations: as soon as the river bore down on it, it collapsed; and what a ruin
that house became!'

Cure of the centurion's servant

1 7 When he had come to the end of all he wanted the people to hear, he went into
2 Capernaum. •A centurion there had a servant, a favourite of his, who was
3 sick and near death. •Having heard about Jesus he sent some Jewish elders
4 to him to ask him to come and heal his servant. •When they came to Jesus they
5 pleaded earnestly with him. 'He deserves this of you' they said •'because he is
friendly towards our people; in fact, he is the one who built the synagogue.'
6 So Jesus went with them, and was not very far from the house when the centurion
sent word to him by some friends: 'Sir,' he said 'do not put yourself to trouble;
7 because I am not worthy to have you under my roof; •and for this same reason
I did not presume to come to you myself; but give the word and let my servant
8 be cured. •For I am under authority myself, and have soldiers under me; and I say
to one man: Go, and he goes; to another: Come here, and he comes; to my
9 servant: Do this, and he does it.' •When Jesus heard these words he was
astonished at him and, turning round, said to the crowd following him, 'I tell
10 you, not even in Israel have I found faith like this'. •And when the messengers
got back to the house they found the servant in perfect health.

The son of the widow of Nain restored to life

11 Now soon afterwards he went to a town called Nain, accompanied by his
12 disciples and a great number of people. •When he was near the gate of the town
it happened that a dead man was being carried out for burial, the only son of his
mother, and she was a widow. And a considerable number of the townspeople
13 were with her. •When the Lord[a] saw her he felt sorry for her. 'Do not cry' he
14 said. •Then he went up and put his hand on the bier and the bearers stood still,
15 and he said, 'Young man, I tell you to get up'. •And the dead man sat up and
16 began to talk, and Jesus *gave him to his mother.*[b] •Everyone was filled with awe
and praised God saying, 'A great prophet has appeared among us; God has
17 visited his people'. •And this opinion of him spread throughout Judaea and all
over the countryside.

---

6 a. Or possibly 'brother of James'.
7 a. For the first time in the gospel narrative Jesus is given the title hitherto reserved for God.
b. 1 K 17:23

The Baptist's question. Jesus commends him

The disciples of John gave him all this news, and John, summoning two of his 18
disciples, •sent them to the Lord to ask, 'Are you the one who is to come, or must 19
we wait for someone else?' •When the men reached Jesus they said, 'John the 20
Baptist has sent us to you, to ask, "Are you the one who is to come or have we
to wait for someone else?" ' •It was just then that he cured many people of 21
diseases and afflictions and of evil spirits, and gave the gift of sight to many who
were blind. •Then he gave the messengers their answer, 'Go back and tell John 22
what you have seen and heard: the blind see again, the lame walk, lepers are
cleansed, and the deaf hear, the dead are raised to life, the Good News is proclaimed to the poor •and happy is the man who does not lose faith in me'. 23

When John's messengers had gone he began to talk to the people about John, 24
'What did you go out into the wilderness to see? A reed swaying in the breeze? 25
No? Then what did you go out to see? A man dressed in fine clothes?
Oh no, those who go in for fine clothes and live luxuriously are to be found at
court! •Then what did you go out to see? A prophet? Yes, I tell you, and much 26
more than a prophet: •he is the one of whom scripture says: 27

> See, I am going to send my messenger before you;
> he will prepare the way before you.ᶜ

'I tell you, of all the children born of women, there is no one greater than John; 28
yet the least in the kingdom of God is greater than he is'. •All the people who 29
heard him, and the tax collectors too, acknowledged God's plan by accepting
baptism from John; •but by refusing baptism from him the Pharisees and the 30
lawyers had thwarted what God had in mind for them.

Jesus condemns his contemporaries

'What description, then, can I find for the men of this generation? What are 31
they like? •They are like children shouting to one another while they sit in the 32
market place:

> "We played the pipes for you,
> and you wouldn't dance;
> we sang dirges,
> and you wouldn't cry".

'For John the Baptist comes, not eating bread, not drinking wine, and you 33
say, "He is possessed". •The Son of Man comes, eating and drinking, and you 34
say, "Look, a glutton and a drunkard, a friend of tax collectors and sinners".
Yet Wisdom has been proved right by all her children.' 35

The woman who was a sinner

One of the Pharisees invited him to a meal. When he arrived at the Pharisee's 36
house and took his place at table, •a woman came in, who had a bad name in 37
the town. She had heard he was dining with the Pharisee and had brought with her
an alabaster jar of ointment. •She waited behind him at his feet, weeping, and her 38
tears fell on his feet, and she wiped them away with her hair; then she covered
his feet with kisses and anointed them with the ointment.

When the Pharisee who had invited him saw this, he said to himself, 'If this 39
man were a prophet, he would know who this woman is that is touching him and
what a bad name she has'. •Then Jesus took him up and said, 'Simon, I have 40
something to say to you'. 'Speak, Master' was the reply. •'There was once a 41
creditor who had two men in his debt; one owed him five hundred denarii, the
other fifty. •They were unable to pay, so he pardoned them both. Which of them 42
will love him more?' •'The one who was pardoned more, I suppose' answered 43
Simon. Jesus said, 'You are right'.

Then he turned to the woman. 'Simon,' he said 'you see this woman? I came 44

into your house, and you poured no water over my feet, but she has poured out her
45 tears over my feet and wiped them away with her hair. •You gave me no kiss, but
46 she has been covering my feet with kisses ever since I came in. •You did not
47 anoint my head with oil, but she has anointed my feet with ointment. •For this
reason I tell you that her sins, her many sins, must have been forgiven her, or she
would not have shown such great love. It is the man who is forgiven little who
48
49 shows little love.' •Then he said to her, 'Your sins are forgiven'. •Those who
were with him at table began to say to themselves, 'Who is this man, that he even
50 forgives sins?' •But he said to the woman, 'Your faith has saved you; go in peace'.

The women accompanying Jesus

1 **8** Now after this he made his way through towns and villages preaching, and
proclaiming the Good News of the kingdom of God. With him went the
2 Twelve, •as well as certain women who had been cured of evil spirits and ailments:
Mary surnamed the Magdalene, from whom seven demons had gone out,
3 Joanna the wife of Herod's steward Chuza, Susanna, and several others who
provided for them out of their own resources.

Parable of the sower

4 With a large crowd gathering and people from every town finding their way
to him, he used this parable:
5 'A sower went out to sow his seed. As he sowed, some fell on the edge of the
6 path and was trampled on; and the birds of the air ate it up. •Some seed fell on
7 rock, and when it came up it withered away, having no moisture. •Some seed fell
8 amongst thorns and the thorns grew with it and choked it. •And some seed fell
into rich soil and grew and produced its crop a hundredfold.' Saying this he
cried, 'Listen, anyone who has ears to hear!'

Why Jesus speaks in parables

9
10 His disciples asked him what this parable might mean, •and he said, The
mysteries of the kingdom of God are revealed to you; for the rest there are only
parables, so that

they may see but not perceive,
listen but not understand.[a]

The parable of the sower explained

11
12 'This, then, is what the parable means: the seed is the word of God. •Those
on the edge of the path are people who have heard it, and then the devil comes
and carries away the word from their hearts in case they should believe and be
13 saved. •Those on the rock are people who, when they first hear it, welcome the
word with joy. But these have no root; they believe for a while, and in time of
14 trial they give up. •As for the part that fell into thorns, this is people who have
heard, but as they go on their way they are choked by the worries and riches and
15 pleasures of life and do not reach maturity. •As for the part in the rich soil, this
is people with a noble and generous heart who have heard the word and take
it to themselves and yield a harvest through their perseverance.

Parable of the lamp

16 'No one lights a lamp to cover it with a bowl or to put it under a bed. No, he
puts it on a lamp-stand so that people may see the light when they come in.
17 For nothing is hidden but it will be made clear, nothing secret but it will be
18 known and brought to light. •So take care how you hear; for anyone who has
will be given more; from anyone who has not, even what he thinks he has will
be taken away.'

c. Ml 3:1
8 a. Is 6:9

The true kinsmen of Jesus

His mother and his brothers came looking for him, but they could not get to 19 him because of the crowd. •He was told, 'Your mother and brothers are standing 20 outside and want to see you'. •But he said in answer, 'My mother and my 21 brothers are those who hear the word of God and put it into practice'.

The calming of the storm

One day, he got into a boat with his disciples and said to them, 'Let us cross 22 over to the other side of the lake'. So they put to sea, •and as they sailed he fell 23 asleep. When a squall came down on the lake the boat started taking in water and they found themselves in danger. •So they went to rouse him saying, 'Master! 24 Master! We are going down!' Then he woke up and rebuked the wind and the rough water; and they subsided and it was calm again. •He said to them, 'Where 25 is your faith?' They were awestruck and astonished and said to one another, 'Who can this be, that gives orders even to winds and waves and they obey him?'

The Gerasene demoniac

They came to land in the country of the Gerasenes, *b* which is opposite Galilee. 26 He was stepping ashore when a man from the town who was possessed by devils 27 came towards him; for a long time the man had worn no clothes, nor did he live in a house, but in the tombs. •Catching sight of Jesus he gave a shout, fell at his feet and cried out at the 28 top of his voice, 'What do you want with me, Jesus, son of the Most High God? I implore you, do not torture me.' •—For Jesus had been telling the unclean 29 spirit to come out of the man. It was a devil that had seized on him a great many times, and then they used to secure him with chains and fetters to restrain him, but he would always break the fastenings, and the devil would drive him out into the wilds. •'What is your name?' Jesus asked. 'Legion' he said—because 30 many devils had gone into him. •And these pleaded with him not to order them 31 to depart into the Abyss.*c*

Now there was a large herd of pigs feeding there on the mountain, and the 32 devils pleaded with him to let them go into these. So he gave them leave. •The 33 devils came out of the man and went into the pigs, and the herd charged down the cliff into the lake and were drowned.

When the swineherds saw what had happened they ran off and told their story 34 in the town and in the country round about; •and the people went out to see what 35 had happened. When they came to Jesus they found the man from whom the devils had gone out sitting at the feet of Jesus, clothed and in his full senses; and they were afraid. •Those who had witnessed it told them how the 36 man who had been possessed came to be healed. •The entire population of the 37 Gerasene territory was in a state of panic and asked Jesus to leave them. So he got into the boat and went back.

The man from whom the devils had gone out asked to be allowed to stay with 38 him, but he sent him away. •'Go back home,' he said 'and report all that God has 39 done for you.' So the man went off and spread throughout the town all that Jesus had done for him.

Cure of the woman with a haemorrhage. Jairus' daughter raised to life

On his return Jesus was welcomed by the crowd, for they were all there waiting 40 for him. •And now there came a man named Jairus, who was an official of the 41 synagogue. He fell at Jesus' feet and pleaded with him to come to his house, because he had an only daughter about twelve years old, who was dying. And the 42 crowds were almost stifling Jesus as he went.

Now there was a woman suffering from a haemorrhage for twelve years, 43 whom no one had been able to cure. •She came up behind him and touched 44

45 the fringe of his cloak; and the haemorrhage stopped at that instant. •Jesus said, 'Who touched me?' When they all denied that they had, Peter and his companions
46 said, 'Master, it is the crowds round you, pushing'. •But Jesus said, 'Somebody
47 touched me. I felt that power had gone out from me.' •Seeing herself discovered, the woman came forward trembling, and falling at his feet explained in front of all the
48 people why she had touched him and how she had been cured at that very moment. 'My daughter,' he said 'your faith has restored you to health; go in peace.'

49   While he was still speaking, someone arrived from the house of the synagogue official to say, 'Your daughter has died. Do not trouble the Master any further.'
50 But Jesus had heard this, and he spoke to the man, 'Do not be afraid, only have
51 faith and she will be safe'. •When he came to the house he allowed no one to go in with him except Peter and John and James, and the child's father and mother.
52 They were all weeping and mourning for her, but Jesus said, 'Stop crying; she is
53 not dead, but asleep'. •But they laughed at him, knowing she was dead. •But
54
55 taking her by the hand he called to her, 'Child, get up'. •And her spirit returned and
56 she got up at once. Then he told them to give her something to eat. •Her parents were astonished, but he ordered them not to tell anyone what had happened.

The mission of the Twelve

1   **9** He called the Twelve together and gave them power and authority over all
2   devils and to cure diseases, •and he sent them out to proclaim the kingdom of
3 God and to heal. •He said to them, 'Take nothing for the journey: neither staff, nor haversack, nor bread, nor money; and let none of you take a spare tunic.
4 Whatever house you enter, stay there; and when you leave, let it be from there.
5 As for those who do not welcome you, when you leave their town shake the
6 dust from your feet as a sign to them.' •So they set out and went from village to village proclaiming the Good News and healing everywhere.

Herod and Jesus

7   Meanwhile Herod the tetrarch had heard about all that was going on; and he was puzzled, because some people were saying that John had risen from the
8 dead, •others that Elijah had reappeared, still others that one of the ancient
9 prophets had come back to life. •But Herod said, 'John? I beheaded him. So who is this I hear such reports about?' And he was anxious to see him.

The return of the apostles. Miracle of the loaves

10   On their return the apostles gave him an account of all they had done. Then he took them with him and withdrew to a town called Bethsaida where they
11 could be by themselves. •But the crowds got to know and they went after him. He made them welcome and talked to them about the kingdom of God; and he cured those who were in need of healing.
12   It was late afternoon when the Twelve came to him and said, 'Send the people away, and they can go to the villages and farms round about to find lodging
13 and food; for we are in a lonely place here'. •He replied, 'Give them something to eat yourselves'. But they said, 'We have no more than five loaves and two
14 fish, unless we are to go ourselves and buy food for all these people'. •For there were about five thousand men. But he said to his disciples, 'Get them to sit down
15 in parties of about fifty'. •They did so and made them all sit down. •Then he took
16 the five loaves and the two fish, raised his eyes to heaven, and said the blessing over them; then he broke them and handed them to his disciples to distribute
17 among the crowd. •They all ate as much as they wanted, and when the scraps remaining were collected they filled twelve baskets.

Peter's profession of faith

18   Now one day when he was praying alone in the presence of his disciples he
19 put this question to them, 'Who do the crowds say I am?' •And they answered,

b. 'Gadarenes' in some versions.   c. The underworld.

'John the Baptist; others Elijah; and others say one of the ancient prophets come back to life'. •'But you,' he said 'who do you say I am?' It was Peter who spoke 20 up. 'The Christ of God' he said. •But he gave them strict orders not to tell 21 anyone anything about this.

First prophecy of the Passion

'The Son of Man' he said 'is destined to suffer grievously, to be rejected by the 22 elders and chief priests and scribes and to be put to death, and to be raised up on the third day.'

The condition of following Christ

. Then to all he said, 'If anyone wants to be a follower of mine, let him renounce 23 himself and take up his cross every day and follow me. •For anyone who wants 24 to save his life will lose it; but anyone who loses his life for my sake, that man will save it. •What gain, then, is it for a man to have won the whole world and to 25 have lost or ruined his very self? •For if anyone is ashamed of me and of my 26 words, of him the Son of Man will be ashamed when he comes in his own glory and in the glory of the Father and the holy angels.

The kingdom will come soon

'I tell you truly, there are some standing here who will not taste death before 27 they see the kingdom of God.'

The transfiguration

Now about eight days after this had been said, he took with him Peter and 28 John and James and went up the mountain to pray. •As he prayed, the aspect of 29 his face was changed and his clothing became brilliant as lightning. •Suddenly 30 there were two men there talking to him; they were Moses and Elijah •appearing 31 in glory, and they were speaking of his passing which he was to accomplish in Jerusalem. •Peter and his companions were heavy with sleep, but they kept awake 32 and saw his glory and the two men standing with him. •As these were leaving 33 him, Peter said to Jesus, 'Master, it is wonderful for us to be here; so let us make three tents, one for you, one for Moses and one for Elijah'.—He did not know what he was saying. •As he spoke, a cloud came and covered them with shadow; 34 and when they went into the cloud the disciples were afraid. •And a voice came 35 from the cloud saying, 'This is my Son, the Chosen One. Listen to him.' •And 36 after the voice had spoken, Jesus was found alone. The disciples kept silence and, at that time, told no one what they had seen.

The epileptic demoniac

Now on the following day when they were coming down from the mountain 37 a large crowd came to meet him. •Suddenly a man in the crowd cried out. 'Master,' 38 he said 'I implore you to look at my son: he is my only child. •All at once a spirit 39 will take hold of him, and give a sudden cry and throw the boy into convulsions with foaming at the mouth; it is slow to leave him, but when it does it leaves the boy worn out. •I begged your disciples to cast it out, and they could not.' 40 'Faithless and perverse generation!' Jesus said in reply 'How much longer must I be 41 among you and put up with you? Bring your son here.' •The boy was still moving 42 towards Jesus when the devil threw him to the ground in convulsions. But Jesus rebuked the unclean spirit and cured the boy and gave him back to his father, and everyone was awestruck by the greatness of God. 43

Second prophecy of the Passion

At a time when everyone was full of admiration for all he did, he said to his disciples, •'For your part, you must have these words constantly in your 44 mind: The Son of Man is going to be handed over into the power of men'.

45 But they did not understand him when he said this; it was hidden from them so that they should not see the meaning of it, and they were afraid to ask him about what he had just said.

Who is the greatest?

46 An argument started between them about which of them was the greatest.
47 Jesus knew what thoughts were going through their minds, and he took a
48 little child and set him by his side •and then said to them, 'Anyone who welcomes this little child in my name welcomes me; and anyone who welcomes me welcomes the one who sent me. For the least among you all, that is the one who is great.'

On using the name of Jesus

49 John spoke up. 'Master,' he said 'we saw a man casting out devils in your
50 name, and because he is not with us we tried to stop him.' •But Jesus said to him, 'You must not stop him: anyone who is not against you is for you'.

IV. THE JOURNEY TO JERUSALEM

A Samaritan village is inhospitable

51 Now as the time drew near for him to be taken up to heaven, he resolutely
52 took the road for Jerusalem •and sent messengers ahead of him. These set out,
53 and they went into a Samaritan village to make preparations for him, •but the
54 people would not receive him because he was making for Jerusalem.[a] •Seeing this, the disciples James and John said, 'Lord, do you want us to call down fire
55 from heaven to burn them up?' •But he turned and rebuked them, •and they
56 went off to another village.

Hardships of the apostolic calling

57 As they travelled along they met a man on the road who said to him, 'I will
58 follow you wherever you go'. •Jesus answered, 'Foxes have holes and the birds of the air have nests, but the Son of Man has nowhere to lay his head'.
59 Another to whom he said, 'Follow me', replied, 'Let me go and bury my
60 father first'. •But he answered, 'Leave the dead to bury their dead; your duty is to go and spread the news of the kingdom of God'.
61 Another said, 'I will follow you, sir, but first let me go and say good-bye
62 to my people at home'. •Jesus said to him, 'Once the hand is laid on the plough, no one who looks back is fit for the kingdom of God'.

The mission of the seventy-two disciples

1 **10** After this the Lord appointed seventy-two others and sent them out ahead of him, in pairs, to all the towns and places he himself was to visit.
2 He said to them, 'The harvest is rich but the labourers are few, so ask the Lord
3 of the harvest to send labourers to his harvest. •Start off now, but remember,
4 I am sending you out like lambs among wolves. •Carry no purse, no haversack,
5 no sandals. Salute no one on the road. •Whatever house you go into, let your
6 first words be, "Peace to this house!" •And if a man of peace lives there, your
7 peace will go and rest on him; if not, it will come back to you. •Stay in the same house, taking what food and drink they have to offer, for the labourer deserves
8 his wages; do not move from house to house. •Whenever you go into a town where
9 they make you welcome, eat what is set before you. •Cure those in it who are
10 sick, and say, "The kingdom of God is very near to you". •But whenever you enter

9 a. The hatred of Samaritans for Jews would show itself particularly towards those who were on pilgrimage to Jerusalem.

a town and they do not make you welcome, go out into its streets and say, •"We 11
wipe off the very dust of your town that clings to our feet, and leave it with you.
Yet be sure of this: the kingdom of God is very near." •I tell you, on that day 12
it will not go as hard with Sodom as with that town.

'Alas for you, Chorazin! Alas for you, Bethsaida! For if the miracles done 13
in you had been done in Tyre and Sidon, they would have repented long ago, sitting
in sackcloth and ashes. •And still, it will not go as hard with Tyre and Sidon at the 14
Judgement as with you. •And as for you, Capernaum, did you want to be exalted 15
high as heaven? *You shall be thrown down to hell.*

'Anyone who listens to you listens to me; anyone who rejects you rejects me, 16
and those who reject me reject the one who sent me.'

True cause for the apostles to rejoice

The seventy-two came back rejoicing. 'Lord,' they said 'even the devils 17
submit to us when we use your name.' •He said to them, 'I watched Satan fall 18
like lightning from heaven. •Yes, I have given you power to tread underfoot 19
serpents and scorpions and the whole strength of the enemy; nothing shall ever
hurt you. •Yet do not rejoice that the spirits submit to you; rejoice rather that 20
your names are written in heaven.'

The Good News revealed to the simple. The Father and the Son

It was then that, filled with joy by the Holy Spirit, he said, 'I bless 21
you, Father, Lord of heaven and of earth, for hiding these things from the learned
and the clever and revealing them to mere children. Yes, Father, for that is what
it pleased you to do. • Everything has been entrusted to me by my Father; and 22
no one knows who the Son is except the Father, and who the Father is except
the Son and those to whom the Son chooses to reveal him.'

The privilege of the disciples

Then turning to his disciples he spoke to them in private, 'Happy the eyes 23
that see what you see, •for I tell you that many prophets and kings wanted to see 24
what you see, and never saw it; to hear what you hear, and never heard it'.

The great commandment

There was a lawyer who, to disconcert him, stood up and said to him, 'Master, 25
what must I do to inherit eternal life?' •He said to him, 'What is written in the 26
Law? What do you read there?' •He replied, '*You must love the Lord your God 27
with all your heart, with all your soul, with all your strength,* and with all your
mind, *and your neighbour as yourself*'.* •'You have answered right,' said Jesus 28
'do this and life is yours.'

Parable of the good Samaritan

But the man was anxious to justify himself and said to Jesus, 'And who is 29
my neighbour?' •Jesus replied, 'A man was once on his way down from Jerusalem 30
to Jericho and fell into the hands of brigands; they took all he had, beat him
and then made off, leaving him half dead. •Now a priest happened to be travelling 31
down the same road, but when he saw the man, he passed by on the other side.
In the same way a Levite who came to the place saw him, and passed by on the 32
other side. •But a Samaritan traveller who came upon him was moved with 33
compassion when he saw him. •He went up and bandaged his wounds, pouring 34
oil and wine on them. He then lifted him on to his own mount, carried him to the
inn and looked after him. •Next day, he took out two denarii and handed them 35
to the innkeeper. "Look after him," he said "and on my way back I will make
good any extra expense you have." •Which of these three, do you think, proved 36
himself a neighbour to the man who fell into the brigands' hands?' •'The one 37
who took pity on him' he replied. Jesus said to him, 'Go, and do the same
yourself'.

Martha and Mary

38 In the course of their journey he came to a village, and a woman named
39 Martha welcomed him into her house. •She had a sister called Mary, who sat
40 down at the Lord's feet and listened to him speaking. •Now Martha who was
    distracted with all the serving said, 'Lord, do you not care that my sister is leaving
41 me to do the serving all by myself? Please tell her to help me.' •But the Lord
    answered: 'Martha, Martha,' he said 'you worry and fret about so many things,
42 and yet few are needed, indeed only one. It is Mary who has chosen the better
    part; it is not to be taken from her.'

The Lord's prayer

1   11 Now once he was in a certain place praying, and when he had finished
        one of his disciples said, 'Lord, teach us to pray, just as John taught his
2   disciples'. •He said to them, 'Say this when you pray:

        "Father, may your name be held holy,
            your kingdom come;
3   give us each day our daily bread,
            and forgive us our sins,
4   for we ourselves forgive each one who is in debt to us.
            And do not put us to the test." '

The importunate friend

5   He also said to them, 'Suppose one of you has a friend and goes to him in
6   the middle of the night to say, "My friend, lend me three loaves, •because a friend
    of mine on his travels has just arrived at my house and I have nothing to offer
7   him"; •and the man answers from inside the house, "Do not bother me. The
    door is bolted now, and my children and I are in bed; I cannot get up to give
8   it you". •I tell you, if the man does not get up and give it him for friendship's
    sake, persistence will be enough to make him get up and give his friend all he
    wants.

Effective prayer

9   'So I say to you: Ask, and it will be given to you; search, and you will find;
10 knock, and the door will be opened to you. •For the one who asks always receives;
    the one who searches always finds; the one who knocks will always have the door
11 opened to him. •What father among you would hand his son a stone when he
12 asked for bread? Or hand him a snake instead of a fish? •Or hand him a
13 scorpion if he asked for an egg? •If you then, who are evil, know how to give
    your children what is good, how much more will the heavenly Father give
    the Holy Spirit to those who ask him!'

Jesus and Beelzebul

14 He was casting out a devil and it was dumb; but when the devil had gone
15 out the dumb man spoke, and the people were amazed. •But some of them
16 said, 'It is through Beelzebul, the prince of devils, that he casts out devils'. •Others
17 asked him, as a test, for a sign from heaven; •but, knowing what they were
    thinking, he said to them, 'Every kingdom divided against itself is heading for
18 ruin, and a household divided against itself collapses. •So too with Satan: if he is
    divided against himself, how can his kingdom stand?—Since you assert that
19 it is through Beelzebul that I cast out devils. •Now if it is through Beelzebul
    that I cast out devils, through whom do your own experts cast them out? Let
20 them be your judges, then. •But if it is through the finger of God that I cast
21 out devils, then know that the kingdom of God has overtaken you. •So long as
    a strong man fully armed guards his own palace, his goods are undisturbed;

10 a. See Is 14:13,15.   b. Dt 6:5 and Lv 19:18

but when someone stronger than he is attacks and defeats him, the stronger 22 man takes away all the weapons he relied on and shares out his spoil.

No compromise

'He who is not with me is against me; and he who does not gather with me 23 scatters.

Return of the unclean spirit

'When an unclean spirit goes out of a man it wanders through waterless coun- 24 try looking for a place to rest, and not finding one it says, "I will go back to the home I came from". •But on arrival, finding it swept and tidied, •it then goes ²⁵₂₆ off and brings seven other spirits more wicked than itself, and they go in and set up house there, so that the man ends up by being worse than he was before.'

The truly happy

Now as he was speaking, a woman in the crowd raised her voice and said, 27 'Happy the womb that bore you and the breasts you sucked!' •But he replied, 28 'Still happier those who hear the word of God and keep it!'

The sign of Jonah

The crowds got even bigger and he addressed them, 'This is a wicked genera- 29 tion; it is asking for a sign. The only sign it will be given is the sign of Jonah. For just as Jonah became a sign to the Ninevites, so will the Son of Man be to this 30 generation. •On Judgement day the Queen of the South will rise up with the men 31 of this generation and condemn them, because she came from the ends of the earth to hear the wisdom of Solomon; and there is something greater than Solomon here. •On Judgement day the men of Nineveh will stand up with this 32 generation and condemn it, because when Jonah preached they repented; and there is something greater than Jonah here.

The parable of the lamp repeated

'No one lights a lamp and puts it in some hidden place or under a tub, but 33 on the lamp-stand so that people may see the light when they come in. •The lamp 34 of your body is your eye. When your eye is sound, your whole body too is filled with light; but when it is diseased your body too will be all darkness. •See to it then that 35 the light inside you is not darkness. •If, therefore, your whole body is filled with 36 light, and no trace of darkness, it will be light entirely, as when the lamp shines on you with its rays.'

The Pharisees and the lawyers attacked

He had just finished speaking when a Pharisee invited him to dine at his 37 house. He went in and sat down at the table. •The Pharisee saw this and was 38 surprised that he had not first washed before the meal. •But the Lord said to him, 39 'Oh, you Pharisees! You clean the outside of cup and plate, while inside yourselves you are filled with extortion and wickedness. •Fools! Did not he who made the 40 outside make the inside too? •Instead, give alms from what you have and then 41 indeed everything will be clean for you. •But alas for you Pharisees! You who pay 42 your tithe of mint and rue and all sorts of garden herbs and overlook justice and the love of God! These you should have practised, without leaving the others undone. •Alas for you Pharisees who like taking the seats of honour in the 43 synagogues and being greeted obsequiously in the market squares! •Alas for 44 you, because you are like the unmarked tombs that men walk on without knowing it!ᵃ

A lawyer then spoke up. 'Master,' he said 'when you speak like this you 45 insult us too.' •'Alas for you lawyers also,' he replied 'because you load on men 46 burdens that are unendurable, burdens that you yourselves do not move a finger to lift.

47 'Alas for you who build the tombs of the prophets, the men your ancestors
48 killed! •In this way you both witness what your ancestors did and approve it; they
did the killing, you do the building.

49 'And that is why the Wisdom of God said, "I will send them prophets and
50 apostles; some they will slaughter and persecute, •so that this generation will have
to answer for every prophet's blood that has been shed since the foundation
51 of the world, •from the blood of Abel to the blood of Zechariah, who was
murdered between the altar and the sanctuary". Yes, I tell you, this generation
will have to answer for it all.

52 'Alas for you lawyers who have taken away the key of knowledge! You have
not gone in yourselves, and have prevented others going in who wanted to.'

53 When he left the house, the scribes and the Pharisees began a furious attack
54 on him and tried to force answers from him on innumerable questions, •setting
traps to catch him out in something he might say.

Open and fearless speech

1 12 Meanwhile the people had gathered in their thousands so that they were
treading on one another. And he began to speak, first of all to his disciples.
'Be on your guard against the yeast of the Pharisees—that is, their hypocrisy.
2 Everything that is now covered will be uncovered, and everything now hidden
3 will be made clear. •For this reason, whatever you have said in the dark will
be heard in the daylight, and what you have whispered in hidden places will be
proclaimed on the housetops.

4 'To you my friends I say: Do not be afraid of those who kill the body and
5 after that can do no more. •I will tell you whom to fear: fear him who, after he
6 has killed, has the power to cast into hell. Yes, I tell you, fear him. •Can you
not buy five sparrows for two pennies? And yet not one is forgotten in God's
7 sight. •Why, every hair on your head has been counted. There is no need to be
afraid: you are worth more than hundreds of sparrows.

8 'I tell you, if anyone openly declares himself for me in the presence of men, the
9 Son of Man will declare himself for him in the presence of God's angels. •But
the man who disowns me in the presence of men will be disowned in the
presence of God's angels.

10 'Everyone who says a word against the Son of Man will be forgiven, but he
who blasphemes against the Holy Spirit will not be forgiven.

11 'When they take you before synagogues and magistrates and authorities,
12 do not worry about how to defend yourselves or what to say, •because when the
time comes, the Holy Spirit will teach you what you must say.'

On hoarding possessions

13 A man in the crowd said to him, 'Master, tell my brother to give me a share
14 of our inheritance'. •'My friend,' he replied 'who appointed me your judge, or
15 the arbitrator of your claims?' •Then he said to them, 'Watch, and be on your
guard against avarice of any kind, for a man's life is not made secure by what he
owns, even when he has more than he needs'.

16 Then he told them a parable: 'There was once a rich man who, having had
17 a good harvest from his land, •thought to himself, "What am I to do? I have
18 not enough room to store my crops." •Then he said, "This is what I will do:
I will pull down my barns and build bigger ones, and store all my grain and my
19 goods in them, •and I will say to my soul: My soul, you have plenty of good
things laid by for many years to come; take things easy, eat, drink, have a good
20 time". •But God said to him, "Fool! This very night the demand will be made
21 for your soul; and this hoard of yours, whose will it be then?" •So it is when
a man stores up treasure for himself in place of making himself rich in the sight
of God.'

11 a. Thus contracting legal impurity, Nb 19:16.

Trust in Providence

Then he said to his disciples, 'That is why I am telling you not to worry 22
about your life and what you are to eat, nor about your body and how you are
to clothe it. •For life means more than food, and the body more than clothing. 23
Think of the ravens. They do not sow or reap; they have no storehouses and 24
no barns; yet God feeds them. And how much more are you worth than the
birds! •Can any of you, for all his worrying, add a single cubit to his span of 25
life? •If the smallest things, therefore, are outside your control, why worry 26
about the rest? •Think of the flowers; they never have to spin or weave; yet, 27
I assure you, not even Solomon in all his regalia was robed like one of these.
Now if that is how God clothes the grass in the field which is there today and 28
thrown into the furnace tomorrow, how much more will he look after you, you
men of little faith! •But you, you must not set your hearts on things to eat and 29
things to drink; nor must you worry. •It is the pagans of this world who set their 30
hearts on all these things. Your Father well knows you need them. •No; set your 31
hearts on his kingdom, and these other things will be given you as well.

'There is no need to be afraid, little flock, for it has pleased your Father to 32
give you the kingdom.

On almsgiving

'Sell your possessions and give alms. Get yourselves purses that do not wear 33
out, treasure that will not fail you, in heaven where no thief can reach it and
no moth destroy it. •For where your treasure is, there will your heart be also. 34

On being ready for the Master's return

'See that you are dressed for action and have your lamps lit. •Be like men 35
                                                                            36
waiting for their master to return from the wedding feast, ready to open the
door as soon as he comes and knocks. •Happy those servants whom the master 37
finds awake when he comes. I tell you solemnly, he will put on an apron, sit
them down at table and wait on them. •It may be in the second watch he comes, 38
or in the third, but happy those servants if he finds them ready. •You may be 39
quite sure of this, that if the householder had known at what hour the burglar
would come, he would not have let anyone break through the wall of his house.
You too must stand ready, because the Son of Man is coming at an hour you 40
do not expect.'

Peter said, 'Lord, do you mean this parable for us, or for everyone?' •The 41
                                                                            42
Lord replied, 'What sort of steward,ᵃ then, is faithful and wise enough for the
master to place him over his household to give them their allowance of food at
the proper time? •Happy that servant if his master's arrival finds him at this 43
employment. •I tell you truly, he will place him over everything he owns. •But 44
                                                                            45
as for the servant who says to himself, "My master is taking his time coming",
and sets about beating the menservants and the maids, and eating and drinking
and getting drunk, •his master will come on a day he does not expect and at 46
an hour he does not know. The master will cut him off and send him to the same
fate as the unfaithful.

'The servant who knows what his master wants, but has not even started to 47
carry out those wishes, will receive very many strokes of the lash. •The one who 48
did not know, but deserves to be beaten for what he has done, will receive
fewer strokes. When a man has had a great deal given him, a great deal will be
demanded of him; when a man has had a great deal given him on trust, even
more will be expected of him.

Jesus and his Passion

'I have come to bring fire to the earth, and how I wish it were blazing 49
already! •There is a baptism I must still receive, and how great is my distress till 50
it is over!

Jesus the cause of dissension

51 'Do you suppose that I am here to bring peace on earth? No, I tell you, but
52 rather division. •For from now on a household of five will be divided: three
53 against two and two against three; •the father divided against the son, son
against father, mother against daughter, daughter against mother, mother-in-law
against daughter-in-law, daughter-in-law against mother-in-law.'

On reading the signs of the times

54 He said again to the crowds, 'When you see a cloud looming up in the west
55 you say at once that rain is coming, and so it does. •And when the wind is from
56 the south you say it will be hot, and it is. •Hypocrites! You know how to
interpret the face of the earth and the sky. How is it you do not know how to
interpret these times?

57
58 'Why not judge for yourselves what is right? •For example: when you go
to court with your opponent, try to settle with him on the way, or he may drag
you before the judge and the judge hand you over to the bailiff and the bailiff
59 have you thrown into prison. •I tell you, you will not get out till you have paid
the very last penny.'

Examples inviting repentance

1 **13** It was just about this time that some people arrived and told him about
the Galileans whose blood Pilate had mingled with that of their sacrifices.[a]
2 At this he said to them, 'Do you suppose these Galileans who suffered like that
3 were greater sinners than any other Galileans? •They were not, I tell you. No;
4 but unless you repent you will all perish as they did. •Or those eighteen on whom
the tower at Siloam fell and killed them? Do you suppose that they were more
5 guilty than all the other people living in Jerusalem? •They were not, I tell you.
No; but unless you repent you will all perish as they did.'

Parable of the barren fig tree

6 He told this parable: 'A man had a fig tree planted in his vineyard, and he
7 came looking for fruit on it but found none. •He said to the man who looked
after the vineyard, "Look here, for three years now I have been coming to look
for fruit on this fig tree and finding none. Cut it down: why should it be taking
8 up the ground?" •"Sir," the man replied "leave it one more year and give me
9 time to dig round it and manure it: •it may bear fruit next year; if not, then
you can cut it down." '

Healing of the crippled woman on a sabbath

10
11 One sabbath day he was teaching in one of the synagogues, •and a woman
was there who for eighteen years had been possessed by a spirit that left her
12 enfeebled; she was bent double and quite unable to stand upright. •When Jesus
saw her he called her over and said, 'Woman, you are rid of your infirmity'
13 and he laid his hands on her. And at once she straightened up, and she glorified
God.
14 But the synagogue official was indignant because Jesus had healed on the
sabbath, and he addressed the people present. 'There are six days' he said 'when
work is to be done. Come and be healed on one of those days and not on the
15 sabbath.' •But the Lord answered him. 'Hypocrites!' he said 'Is there one of
you who does not untie his ox or his donkey from the manger on the sabbath
16 and take it out for watering? •And this woman, a daughter of Abraham whom
Satan has held bound these eighteen years—was it not right to untie her bonds

---

12 a. I.e. a servant or employee with authority to act as his master's deputy in his absence.
13 a. The author expects this incident, and that mentioned in v.4, to be known to his readers;
no other evidence of them remains.

on the sabbath day?' •When he said this, all his adversaries were covered with 17
confusion, and all the people were overjoyed at all the wonders he worked.

Parable of the mustard seed

He went on to say, 'What is the kingdom of God like? What shall I compare 18
it with? •It is like a mustard seed which a man took and threw into his garden: 19
it grew and became a tree, and the birds of the air sheltered in its branches.'

Parable of the yeast

Another thing he said, 'What shall I compare the kingdom of God with? 20
It is like the yeast a woman took and mixed in with three measures of flour till 21
it was leavened all through.'

The narrow door; rejection of the Jews, call of the gentiles

Through towns and villages he went teaching, making his way to Jerusalem. 22
Someone said to him, 'Sir, will there be only a few saved?' He said to them, 23
'Try your best to enter by the narrow door, because, I tell you, many will try 24
to enter and will not succeed.

'Once the master of the house has got up and locked the door, you may find 25
yourself knocking on the door, saying, "Lord, open to us" but he will answer,
"I do not know where you come from". •Then you will find yourself saying, 26
"We once ate and drank in your company; you taught in our streets" •but he 27
will reply, "I do not know where you come from. *Away from me, all you wicked
men !"*[b]

'Then there will be weeping and grinding of teeth, when you see Abraham 28
and Isaac and Jacob and all the prophets in the kingdom of God, and yourselves
turned outside. •And men from east and west, from north and south, will come 29
to take their places at the feast in the kingdom of God.

'Yes, there are those now last who will be first, and those now first who will 30
be last.'

Herod the fox

Just at this time some Pharisees came up. 'Go away' they said. 'Leave this 31
place, because Herod means to kill you.' •He replied, 'You may go and give 32
that fox this message: Learn that today and tomorrow I cast out devils and on
the third day[c] attain my end. •But for today and tomorrow and the next day 33
I must go on, since it would not be right for a prophet to die outside Jerusalem.

Jerusalem admonished

'Jerusalem, Jerusalem, you that kill the prophets and stone those who are 34
sent to you! How often have I longed to gather your children, as a hen gathers
her brood under her wings, and you refused! •So be it! Your house will be left 35
to you. Yes, I promise you, you shall not see me till the time comes when you
say:

Blessings on him who comes in the name of the Lord !"[d]

Healing of a dropsical man on the sabbath

14 Now on a sabbath day he had gone for a meal to the house of one of the 1
leading Pharisees; and they watched him closely. •There in front of him was 2
a man with dropsy, •and Jesus addressed the lawyers and Pharisees. 'Is it 3
against the law' he asked 'to cure a man on the sabbath, or not?' •But they 4
remained silent, so he took the man and cured him and sent him away. •Then 5
he said to them, 'Which of you here, if his son falls into a well, or his ox, will
not pull him out on a sabbath day without hesitation?' •And to this they could 6
find no answer.

On choosing places at table

7 He then told the guests a parable, because he had noticed how they
8 picked the places of honour. He said this, •'When someone invites you to a
wedding feast, do not take your seat in the place of honour. A more distinguished
9 person than you may have been invited, •and the person who invited you both
may come and say, "Give up your place to this man". And then, to your em-
10 barrassment, you would have to go and take the lowest place. •No; when you
are a guest, make your way to the lowest place and sit there, so that, when your
host comes, he may say, "My friend, move up higher". In that way, everyone
11 with you at the table will see you honoured. •For everyone who exalts himself
will be humbled, and the man who humbles himself will be exalted.'

On choosing guests to be invited

12 Then he said to his host, 'When you give a lunch or a dinner, do not ask
your friends, brothers, relations or rich neighbours, for fear they repay your
13 courtesy by inviting you in return. •No; when you have a party, invite the poor,
14 the crippled, the lame, the blind; •that they cannot pay you back means that
you are fortunate, because repayment will be made to you when the virtuous
rise again.'

The invited guests who made excuses

15 On hearing this, one of those gathered round the table said to him, 'Happy
16 the man who will be at the feast in the kingdom of God!' •But he said to him,
'There was a man who gave a great banquet, and he invited a large number of
17 people. •When the time for the banquet came, he sent his servant to say to those
18 who had been invited, "Come along: everything is ready now". •But all alike
started to make excuses. The first said, "I have bought a piece of land and must
19 go and see it. Please accept my apologies." •Another said, "I have bought five
yoke of oxen and am on my way to try them out. Please accept my apologies."
20 Yet another said,"I have just got married and so am unable to come".
21 'The servant returned and reported this to his master. Then the householder,
in a rage, said to his servant, "Go out quickly into the streets and alleys of the
22 town and bring in here the poor, the crippled, the blind and the lame". •"Sir,"
said the servant "your orders have been carried out and there is still room."
23 Then the master said to his servant, "Go to the open roads and the hedgerows
24 and force people to come in to make sure my house is full; •because, I tell you,
not one of those who were invited shall have a taste of my banquet".'

Renouncing all that one holds dear

25 Great crowds accompanied him on his way and he turned and spoke to
26 them. •'If any man comes to me without hating[a] his father, mother, wife, children,
27 brothers, sisters, yes and his own life too, he cannot be my disciple. •Anyone
who does not carry his cross and come after me cannot be my disciple.

Renouncing possessions

28 'And indeed, which of you here, intending to build a tower, would not first
29 sit down and work out the cost to see if he had enough to complete it? •Otherwise,
if he laid the foundation and then found himself unable to finish the work, the
30 onlookers would all start making fun of him and saying, •"Here is a man who
31 started to build and was unable to finish". •Or again, what king marching to
war against another king would not first sit down and consider whether with
ten thousand men he could stand up to the other who advanced against him with
32 twenty thousand? •If not, then while the other king was still a long way off, he

b. Ps 6:8   c. 'after a short time'.   d. Ps 118:26
14 a. Hebraism: an emphatic way of expressing a total detachment.

would send envoys to sue for peace. •So in the same way, none of you can be 33 my disciple unless he gives up all his possessions.

On loss of enthusiasm in a disciple

'Salt is a useful thing. But if the salt itself loses its taste, how can it be 34 seasoned again? •It is good for neither soil nor manure heap. People throw it 35 out. Listen, anyone who has ears to hear!'

The three parables of God's mercy

15 The tax collectors and the sinners, meanwhile, were all seeking his company 1 to hear what he had to say, •and the Pharisees and the scribes complained. 2 'This man' they said 'welcomes sinners and eats with them.' •So he spoke this 3 parable to them:

The lost sheep

'What man among you with a hundred sheep, losing one, would not leave 4 the ninety-nine in the wilderness and go after the missing one till he found it? And when he found it, would he not joyfully take it on his shoulders •and then, ⁵⁄₆ when he got home, call together his friends and neighbours? "Rejoice with me," he would say "I have found my sheep that was lost." •In the same way, I tell you, 7 there will be more rejoicing in heaven over one repentant sinner than over ninety-nine virtuous men who have no need of repentance.

The lost drachma

'Or again, what woman with ten drachmas would not, if she lost one, light 8 a lamp and sweep out the house and search thoroughly till she found it? •And 9 then, when she had found it, call together her friends and neighbours? "Rejoice with me," she would say "I have found the drachma I lost." •In the same way, 10 I tell you, there is rejoicing among the angels of God over one repentant sinner.'

The lost son (the 'prodigal') and the dutiful son

He also said, 'A man had two sons. •The younger said to his father, "Father, ¹¹⁄₁₂ let me have the share of the estate that would come to me". So the father divided the property between them. •A few days later, the younger son got together 13 everything he had and left for a distant country where he squandered his money on a life of debauchery.

'When he had spent it all, that country experienced a severe famine, and now 14 he began to feel the pinch, •so he hired himself out to one of the local inhabitants 15 who put him on his farm to feed the pigs. •And he would willingly have filled 16 his belly with the husks the pigs were eating but no one offered him anything. Then he came to his senses and said, "How many of my father's paid servants 17 have more food than they want, and here am I dying of hunger! •I will leave 18 this place and go to my father and say: Father, I have sinned against heaven and against you; •I no longer deserve to be called your son; treat me as one of your 19 paid servants." •So he left the place and went back to his father. 20

'While he was still a long way off, his father saw him and was moved with pity. He ran to the boy, clasped him in his arms and kissed him tenderly. •Then his 21 son said, "Father, I have sinned against heaven and against you. I no longer deserve to be called your son." •But the father said to his servants, "Quick! 22 Bring out the best robe and put it on him; put a ring on his finger and sandals on his feet. •Bring the calf we have been fattening, and kill it; we are going to 23 have a feast, a celebration, •because this son of mine was dead and has come 24 back to life; he was lost and is found." And they began to celebrate.

'Now the elder son was out in the fields, and on his way back, as he drew 25 near the house, he could hear music and dancing. •Calling one of the servants 26 he asked what it was all about. •"Your brother has come" replied the servant 27

"and your father has killed the calf we had fattened because he has got him back
28 safe and sound." •He was angry then and refused to go in, and his father came
29 out to plead with him; •but he answered his father, "Look, all these years
I have slaved for you and never once disobeyed your orders, yet you never
30 offered me so much as a kid for me to celebrate with my friends. •But, for this
son of yours, when he comes back after swallowing up your property—he and
his women—you kill the calf we had been fattening."
31 'The father said, "My son, you are with me always and all I have is yours.
32 But it was only right we should celebrate and rejoice, because your brother
here was dead and has come to life; he was lost and is found." '

The crafty steward

1 **16** He also said to his disciples, 'There was a rich man and he had a steward
2 who was denounced to him for being wasteful with his property. •He called
for the man and said, "What is this I hear about you? Draw me up an account of
3 your stewardship because you are not to be my steward any longer." •Then the
steward said to himself, "Now that my master is taking the stewardship from me,
what am I to do? Dig? I am not strong enough. Go begging? I should be too
4 ashamed. •Ah, I know what I will do to make sure that when I am dismissed
from office there will be some to welcome me into their homes."
5 'Then he called his master's debtors one by one. To the first he said, "How
6 much do you owe my master?" •"One hundred measures of oil" was the reply.
The steward said, "Here, take your bond; sit down straight away and write fifty".
7 To another he said, "And you, sir, how much do you owe?" "One hundred
measures of wheat" was the reply. The steward said, "Here, take your bond and
write eighty".
8 'The master praised the dishonest steward for his astuteness.[a] For the children
of this world are more astute in dealing with their own kind than are the children
of light.'

The right use of money

9 'And so I tell you this: use money, tainted as it is, to win you friends, and
10 thus make sure that when it fails you, they will welcome you into the tents of
eternity. •The man who can be trusted in little things can be trusted in great;
11 the man who is dishonest in little things will be dishonest in great. •If then you
cannot be trusted with money, that tainted thing, who will trust you with genuine
12 riches? •And if you cannot be trusted with what is not yours, who will give
you what is your very own?
13 · 'No servant can be the slave of two masters: he will either hate the first and
love the second, or treat the first with respect and the second with scorn. You
cannot be the slave both of God and of money.'

Against the Pharisees and their love of money

14
15 The Pharisees, who loved money, heard all this and laughed at him. •He
said to them, 'You are the very ones who pass yourselves off as virtuous in
people's sight, but God knows your hearts. For what is thought highly of by men
is loathsome in the sight of God.

The kingdom stormed

16 'Up to the time of John it was the Law and the Prophets; since then, the
kingdom of God has been preached, and by violence everyone is getting in.

The Law remains

17 'It is easier for heaven and earth to disappear than for one little stroke to drop
out of the Law.

16 a. Not for his dishonesty.

Marriage indissoluble

'Everyone who divorces his wife and marries another is guilty of adultery, and 18 the man who marries a woman divorced by her husband commits adultery.

The rich man and Lazarus

'There was a rich man who used to dress in purple and fine linen and feast 19 magnificently every day. •And at his gate there lay a poor man called Lazarus, 20 covered with sores, •who longed to fill himself with the scraps that fell from 21 the rich man's table. Dogs even came and licked his sores. •Now the poor man 22 died and was carried away by the angels to the bosom of Abraham. The rich man also died and was buried.

'In his torment in Hades he looked up and saw Abraham a long way off 23 with Lazarus in his bosom. •So he cried out, "Father Abraham, pity me and 24 send Lazarus to dip the tip of his finger in water and cool my tongue, for I am in agony in these flames". •"My son," Abraham replied "remember that during 25 your life good things came your way, just as bad things came the way of Lazarus. Now he is being comforted here while you are in agony. •But that is not all: 26 between us and you a great gulf has been fixed, to stop anyone, if he wanted to, crossing from our side to yours, and to stop any crossing from your side to ours."

'The rich man replied, "Father, I beg you then to send Lazarus to my father's 27 house, •since I have five brothers, to give them warning so that they do not 28 come to this place of torment too". •"They have Moses and the prophets," 29 said Abraham "let them listen to them." •"Ah no, father Abraham," said the 30 rich man "but if someone comes to them from the dead, they will repent." •Then 31 Abraham said to him, "If they will not listen either to Moses or to the prophets, they will not be convinced even if someone should rise from the dead". '

On leading others astray

17 He said to his disciples, 'Obstacles are sure to come, but alas for the one 1 who provides them! •It would be better for him to be thrown into the sea 2 with a millstone put round his neck than that he should lead astray a single one of these little ones. •Watch yourselves! 3

Brotherly correction

'If your brother does something wrong, reprove him and, if he is sorry, forgive him. •And if he wrongs you seven times a day and seven times comes 4 back to you and says, "I am sorry", you must forgive him.'

The power of faith

The apostles said to the Lord, 'Increase our faith'. •The Lord replied, 'Were $^5_6$ your faith the size of a mustard seed you could say to this mulberry tree, "Be uprooted and planted in the sea", and it would obey you.

Humble service

'Which of you, with a servant ploughing or minding sheep, would say to him 7 when he returned from the fields, "Come and have your meal immediately"? Would he not be more likely to say, "Get my supper laid; make yourself tidy 8 and wait on me while I eat and drink. You can eat and drink yourself afterwards"? Must he be grateful to the servant for doing what he was told? •So with you: $^9_{10}$ when you have done all you have been told to do, say, "We are merely servants: we have done no more than our duty".'

The ten lepers

Now on the way to Jerusalem he travelled along the border between Samaria 11 and Galilee.ᵃ •As he entered one of the villages, ten lepers came to meet him. 12

13 They stood some way off •and called to him, 'Jesus! Master! Take pity on us.'
14 When he saw them he said, 'Go and show yourselves to the priests'. Now as they
15 were going away they were cleansed. •Finding himself cured, one of them
16 turned back praising God at the top of his voice •and threw himself at the feet
17 of Jesus and thanked him. The man was a Samaritan. •This made Jesus say,
18 'Were not all ten made clean? The other nine, where are they? •It seems that no
19 one has come back to give praise to God, except this foreigner.' •And he said to
the man, 'Stand up and go on your way. Your faith has saved you.'

The coming of the kingdom of God

20   Asked by the Pharisees when the kingdom of God was to come, he gave them
this answer, 'The coming of the kingdom of God does not admit of observation
21 and there will be no one to say, "Look here! Look there!" For, you must know,
the kingdom of God is among you.'

The day of the Son of Man

22   He said to the disciples, 'A time will come when you will long to see one of
23 the days of the Son of Man and will not see it. •They will say to you, "Look
24 there!" or, "Look here!" Make no move; do not set off in pursuit; •for as the
lightning flashing from one part of heaven lights up the other, so will be the Son
25 of Man when his day comes. •But first he must suffer grievously and be rejected
by this generation.
26   'As it was in Noah's day, so will it also be in the days of the Son of Man.
27 People were eating and drinking, marrying wives and husbands, right up to the
28 day Noah went into the ark, and the Flood came and destroyed them all. •It
will be the same as it was in Lot's day: people were eating and drinking, buying
29 and selling, planting and building, •but the day Lot left Sodom, God rained fire
30 and brimstone from heaven and it destroyed them all. •It will be the same when
the day comes for the Son of Man to be revealed.
31   'When that day comes, anyone on the housetop, with his possessions in the
house, must not come down to collect them, nor must anyone in the fields turn
32
33 back either. •Remember Lot's wife. •Anyone who tries to preserve his life will lose
34 it; and anyone who loses it will keep it safe. •I tell you, on that night two will be
35 in one bed: one will be taken, the other left; •two women will be grinding corn
37 together: one will be taken, the other left.' •The disciples interrupted. 'Where,
Lord?' they asked. He said, 'Where the body is, there too will the vultures gather'.

The unscrupulous judge and the importunate widow

1   **18** Then he told them a parable about the need to pray continually and never
2   lose heart. •'There was a judge in a certain town' he said 'who had neither
3 fear of God nor respect for man. •In the same town there was a widow who kept
on coming to him and saying, "I want justice from you against my enemy!"
4 For a long time he refused, but at last he said to himself, "Maybe I have neither
5 fear of God nor respect for man, •but since she keeps pestering me I must give
this widow her just rights, or she will persist in coming and worry me to death".'
6
7   •And the Lord said, 'You notice what the unjust judge has to say? •Now will
not God see justice done to his chosen who cry to him day and night even when
8 he delays to help them? •I promise you, he will see justice done to them, and
done speedily. But when the Son of Man comes, will he find any faith on earth?'

The Pharisee and the publican

9   He spoke the following parable to some people who prided themselves on being
10 virtuous and despised everyone else, •'Two men went up to the Temple to pray,
11 one a Pharisee, the other a tax collector. •The Pharisee stood there and said this

17 a. Making for the Jordan valley and Jericho; from there he goes up to Jerusalem.

prayer to himself, "I thank you, God, that I am not grasping, unjust, adulterous like the rest of mankind, and particularly that I am not like this tax collector here. I fast twice a week; I pay tithes on all I get." •The tax collector stood some ¹²₁₃ distance away, not daring even to raise his eyes to heaven; but he beat his breast and said, "God, be merciful to me, a sinner". •This man, I tell you, went home 14 again at rights with God; the other did not. For everyone who exalts himself will be humbled, but the man who humbles himself will be exalted.'

Jesus and the children

People even brought little children to him, for him to touch them; but 15 when the disciples saw this they turned them away. •But Jesus called the children 16 to him and said, 'Let the little children come to me, and do not stop them; for it is to such as these that the kingdom of God belongs. •I tell you solemnly, anyone 17 who does not welcome the kingdom of God like a little child will never enter it.'

The rich aristocrat

A member of one of the leading families put this question to him, 'Good 18 Master, what have I to do to inherit eternal life?' •Jesus said to him, 'Why do you 19 call me good? No one is good but God alone. •You know the commandments: 20 *You must not commit adultery; You must not kill; You must not steal; You must not bring false witness; Honour your father and mother.*' •He replied, 'I have kept 21 all these from my earliest days till now'. •And when Jesus heard this he said, 22 'There is still one thing you lack. Sell all that you own and distribute the money to the poor, and you will have treasure in heaven; then come, follow me.' •But 23 when he heard this he was filled with sadness, for he was very rich.

The danger of riches

Jesus looked at him and said, 'How hard it is for those who have riches to 24 make their way into the kingdom of God! •Yes, it is easier for a camel to pass 25 through the eye of a needle than for a rich man to enter the kingdom of God.' 'In that case' said the listeners 'who can be saved?' •'Things that are impossible ²⁶₂₇ for men' he replied 'are possible for God.'

The reward of renunciation

Then Peter said, 'What about us? We left all we had to follow you.' •He said ²⁸₂₉ to them, 'I tell you solemnly, there is no one who has left house, wife, brothers, parents or children for the sake of the kingdom of God •who will not be given 30 repayment many times over in this present time and, in the world to come, eternal life'.

Third prophecy of the Passion

Then taking the Twelve aside he said to them, 'Now we are going up to 31 Jerusalem, and everything that is written by the prophets about the Son of Man is to come true. •For he will be handed over to the pagans and will be mocked, 32 maltreated and spat on, •and when they have scourged him they will put him 33 to death; and on the third day he will rise again.' •But they could make nothing 34 of this; what he said was quite obscure to them, they had no idea what it meant.

Entering Jericho: the blind man

Now as he drew near to Jericho there was a blind man sitting at the side of the 35 road begging. •When he heard the crowd going past he asked what it was all about, 36 and they told him that Jesus the Nazarene was passing by. •So he called out, ³⁷₃₈ 'Jesus, Son of David, have pity on me'. •The people in front scolded him and told 39 him to keep quiet, but he shouted all the louder, 'Son of David, have pity on me'. Jesus stopped and ordered them to bring the man to him, and when he came up, 40

41 asked him, •'What do you want me to do for you?' 'Sir,' he replied 'let me see
42 again.' •Jesus said to him, 'Receive your sight. Your faith has saved you.'
43 And instantly his sight returned and he followed him praising God, and all the
people who saw it gave praise to God for what had happened.

Zacchaeus

$\frac{1}{2}$ **19** He entered Jericho and was going through the town •when a man whose
name was Zacchaeus made his appearance; he was one of the senior tax
3 collectors and a wealthy man. •He was anxious to see what kind of man Jesus
4 was, but he was too short and could not see him for the crowd; •so he ran ahead
and climbed a sycamore tree to catch a glimpse of Jesus who was to pass that
5 way. •When Jesus reached the spot he looked up and spoke to him: 'Zacchaeus,
6 come down. Hurry, because I must stay at your house today.' •And he hurried
7 down and welcomed him joyfully. •They all complained when they saw what
8 was happening. 'He has gone to stay at a sinner's house' they said. •But Zacchaeus
stood his ground and said to the Lord, 'Look, sir, I am going to give half my
property to the poor, and if I have cheated anybody I will pay him back four
9 times the amount'.ᵃ •And Jesus said to him, 'Today salvation has come to this
10 house, because this man too is a son of Abraham;ᵇ •for the Son of Man has come
to seek out and save what was lost'.

Parable of the pounds

11 While the people were listening to this he went on to tell a parable, because
he was near Jerusalem and they imagined that the kingdom of God was going
12 to show itself then and there. •Accordingly he said, 'A man of noble birth went
13 to a distant country to be appointed king and afterwards return.ᶜ •He summoned
ten of his servants and gave them ten pounds. "Do business with these" he told
14 them "until I get back." •But his compatriots detested him and sent a delegation
to follow him with this message, "We do not want this man to be our king".

15 'Now on his return, having received his appointment as king, he sent for those
servants to whom he had given the money, to find out what profit each had made.
$\begin{smallmatrix}16\\17\end{smallmatrix}$ The first came in and said, "Sir, your one pound has brought in ten". •"Well done,
my good servant!" he replied "Since you have proved yourself faithful in a very
18 small thing, you shall have the government of ten cities." •Then came the second
19 and said, "Sir, your one pound has made five". •To this one also he said, "And
20 you shall be in charge of five cities". •Next came the other and said, "Sir, here
21 is your pound. I put it away safely in a piece of linen •because I was afraid of you;
for you are an exacting man: you pick up what you have not put down and reap
22 what you have not sown." •"You wicked servant!" he said "Out of your own
mouth I condemn you. So you knew I was an exacting man, picking up what
23 I have not put down and reaping what I have not sown? •Then why did you not
put my money in the bank? On my return I could have drawn it out with
24 interest." •And he said to those standing by, "Take the pound from him and
25 give it to the man who has ten pounds". •And they said to him, "But, sir, he has
26 ten pounds . . ." •"I tell you, to everyone who has will be given more; but
from the man who has not, even what he has will be taken away.

27 "But as for my enemies who did not want me for their king, bring them here
and execute them in my presence." '

---

19 a. I.e. at the highest rate known to Jewish law (Ex 21:37) or the rate imposed by Roman
law on convicted thieves.   b. Although he belongs to a profession generally ranked with
pagans.   c. Probably alluding to the journey of Archelaus to Rome in 4 B.C. to have the will
of Herod the Great confirmed in his favour. A deputation of Jews followed him there to
contest his claim.

V. THE JERUSALEM MINISTRY

The Messiah enters Jerusalem

When he had said this he went on ahead, going up to Jerusalem. •Now when ²⁸
he was near Bethphage and Bethany, close by the Mount of Olives as it is called, ²⁹
he sent two of the disciples, telling them, •'Go off to the village opposite, and ³⁰
as you enter it you will find a tethered colt that no one has yet ridden. Untie it
and bring it here. •If anyone asks you, "Why are you untying it?" you are to say ³¹
this, "The Master needs it".' •The messengers went off and found everything just ³²
as he had told them. •As they were untying the colt, its owner said, 'Why are ³³
you untying that colt?' •and they answered, 'The Master needs it'. ³⁴

So they took the colt to Jesus, and throwing their garments over its back they ³⁵
helped Jesus on to it. •As he moved off, people spread their cloaks in the road, ³⁶
and now, as he was approaching the downward slope of the Mount of Olives, ³⁷
the whole group of disciples joyfully began to praise God at the top of their
voices for all the miracles they had seen. •They cried out: ³⁸

> '*Blessings on the King who comes,*
> *in the name of the Lord!*
> Peace in heaven
> and glory in the highest heavens!'

Jesus defends his disciples for acclaiming him

Some Pharisees in the crowd said to him, 'Master, check your disciples', ³⁹
but he answered, 'I tell you, if these keep silence the stones will cry out'. ⁴⁰

Lament for Jerusalem

As he drew near and came in sight of the city he shed tears over it •and said, ⁴¹
'If you in your turn had only understood on this day the message of peace! ⁴²
But, alas, it is hidden from your eyes! •Yes, a time is coming when your enemies ⁴³
will raise fortifications all round you, when they will encircle you and hem you
in on every side; •they will dash you and the children inside your walls to the ⁴⁴
ground; they will leave not one stone standing on another within you—and all
because you did not recognise your opportunity when God offered it!'

The expulsion of the dealers from the Temple

Then he went into the Temple and began driving out those who were selling. ⁴⁵
'According to scripture,' he said '*my house will be a house of prayer.*ᵈ But you ⁴⁶
have turned it into *a robbers' den.*'•

Jesus teaches in the Temple

He taught in the Temple every day. The chief priests and the scribes, with ⁴⁷
the support of the leading citizens, tried to do away with him, •but they did not ⁴⁸
see how they could carry this out because the people as a whole hung on his words.

The Jews question the authority of Jesus

20 Now one day while he was teaching the people in the Temple and ¹
proclaiming the Good News, the chief priests and the scribes came up,
together with the elders, •and spoke to him. 'Tell us' they said 'what authority ²
have you for acting like this? Or who is it that gave you this authority?' •'And ³
I' replied Jesus 'will ask you a question. Tell me: •John's baptism: did it come ⁴
from heaven, or from man?' •And they argued it out this way among themselves, ⁵
'If we say from heaven, he will say, "Why did you refuse to believe him?"; •and ⁶
if we say from man, the people will all stone us, for they are convinced that John
was a prophet'. •So their reply was that they did not know where it came from. ⁷
And Jesus said to them, 'Nor will I tell you my authority for acting like this'. ⁸

Parable of the wicked husbandmen

9 And he went on to tell the people this parable: 'A man planted a vineyard
10 and leased it to tenants, and went abroad for a long while. •When the time
came, he sent a servant to the tenants to get his share of the produce of the
vineyard from them. But the tenants thrashed him, and sent him away
11 empty-handed. •But he persevered and sent a second servant; they thrashed
12 him too and treated him shamefully and sent him away empty-handed. •He still
persevered and sent a third; they wounded this one also, and threw him out.
13 Then the owner of the vineyard said, "What am I to do? I will send them my
14 dear son. Perhaps they will respect him." •But when the tenants saw him
they put their heads together. "This is the heir," they said "let us kill him so that
15 the inheritance will be ours." •So they threw him out of the vineyard and killed
him.
16 'Now what will the owner of the vineyard do to them? •He will come and
make an end of these tenants and give the vineyard to others.' Hearing this they
17 said, 'God forbid!' •But he looked hard at them and said, 'Then what does this
text in the scriptures mean:

It was the stone rejected by the builders
that became the keystone?[a]

18 Anyone who falls on that stone will be dashed to pieces; anyone it falls on will
be crushed.'
19 But for their fear of the people, the scribes and the chief priests would have
liked to lay hands on him that very moment, because they realised that this
parable was aimed at them.

On tribute to Caesar

20 So they waited their opportunity and sent agents to pose as men devoted to
the Law, and to fasten on something he might say and so enable them to hand
21 him over to the jurisdiction and authority of the governor. •They put to him
this question, 'Master, we know that you say and teach what is right; you favour
22 no one, but teach the way of God in all honesty. •Is it permissible for us to pay
23
24 taxes to Caesar or not?' •But he was aware of their cunning and said, •'Show
25 me a denarius. Whose head and name are on it?' 'Caesar's' they said. •'Well
then,' he said to them 'give back to Caesar what belongs to Caesar—and to
God what belongs to God.'
26 As a result, they were unable to find fault with anything he had to say in
public; his answer took them by surprise and they were silenced.

The resurrection of the dead

27 Some Sadducees—those who say that there is no resurrection—approached
28 him and they put this question to him, •'Master, we have it from Moses in
writing, that if a man's married brother dies childless, the man must marry the
29 widow to raise up children for his brother. •Well then, there were seven brothers.
30
31 The first, having married a wife, died childless. •The second •and then the third
married the widow. And the same with all seven, they died leaving no children.
32
33 Finally the woman herself died. •Now, at the resurrection, to which of them
will she be wife since she had been married to all seven?'
34
35 Jesus replied, 'The children of this world take wives and husbands, •but
those who are judged worthy of a place in the other world and in the resurrection
36 from the dead do not marry •because they can no longer die, for they are the
same as the angels, and being children of the resurrection they are sons of
37 God. •And Moses himself implies that the dead rise again, in the passage

d. Is 56:7 e. Jr 7:11
20 a. Ps 118:22

about the bush where he calls the Lord *the God of Abraham, the God of Isaac and the God of Jacob.*[b] •Now he is God, not of the dead, but of the living; for 38 to him all men are in fact alive.'

Some scribes[c] then spoke up. 'Well put, Master' they said •—because they 39 40 would not dare to ask him any more questions.

Christ, not only son but also Lord of David

He then said to them, 'How can people maintain that the Christ is son of 41 David? •Why, David himself says in the Book of Psalms: 42

> *The Lord said to my Lord:*
> *Sit at my right hand*
> *and I will make your enemies* 43
> *a footstool for you.*[d]

David here calls him Lord; how then can he be his son?' 44

The scribes condemned by Jesus

While all the people were listening he said to the disciples, •'Beware of the 45 46 scribes who like to walk about in long robes and love to be greeted obsequiously in the market squares, to take the front seats in the synagogues and the places of honour at banquets, •who swallow the property of widows, while making 47 a show of lengthy prayers. The more severe will be the sentence they receive.'

The widow's mite

21 As he looked up he saw rich people putting their offerings into the 1 treasury; •then he happened to notice a poverty-stricken widow putting 2 in two small coins, •and he said, 'I tell you truly, this poor widow has put in 3 more than any of them; •for these have all contributed money they had over, 4 but she from the little she had has put in all she had to live on'.

Discourse on the destruction of Jerusalem:[a] Introduction

When some were talking about the Temple, remarking how it was adorned 5 with fine stonework and votive offerings, he said, •'All these things you are staring 6 at now—the time will come when not a single stone will be left on another: everything will be destroyed'. •And they put to him this question: 'Master,' they 7 said 'when will this happen, then, and what sign will there be that this is about to take place?'

The warning signs

'Take care not to be deceived,' he said 'because many will come using my name 8 and saying, "I am he" and, "The time is near at hand". Refuse to join them. And when you hear of wars and revolutions, do not be frightened, for this is some- 9 thing that must happen but the end is not so soon.' •Then he said to them, 'Nation 10 will fight against nation, and kingdom against kingdom. •There will be great 11 earthquakes and plagues and famines here and there; there will be fearful sights and great signs from heaven.

'But before all this happens, men will seize you and persecute you; they will 12 hand you over to the synagogues and to imprisonment, and bring you before kings and governors because of my name•—and that will be your opportunity 13 to bear witness. •Keep this carefully in mind: you are not to prepare your defence, 14 because I myself shall give you an eloquence and a wisdom that none of your 15 opponents will be able to resist or contradict. •You will be betrayed even by 16 parents and brothers, relations and friends; and some of you will be put to death. You will be hated by all men on account of my name, •but not a hair of your 17 18 head will be lost. •Your endurance will win you your lives. 19

The siege

20 'When you see Jerusalem surrounded by armies, you must realise that she will
21 soon be laid desolate. •Then those in Judaea must escape to the mountains, those
inside the city must leave it, and those in country districts must not take refuge
22 in it. •For this is the time of vengeance when all that scripture says[b] must be
23 fulfilled. •Alas for those with child, or with babies at the breast, when those days
come!

The disaster and the age of the pagans

24 'For great misery will descend on the land and wrath on this people. •They
will fall by the edge of the sword and be led captive to every pagan country; and
Jerusalem will be trampled down by the pagans until the age of the pagans is
completely over.

Cosmic disasters and the coming of the Son of Man

25 'There will be signs in the sun and moon and stars; on earth nations in agony,
26 bewildered by the clamour of the ocean and its waves; •men dying of fear as they
27 await what menaces the world, for the powers of heaven will be shaken. •And
then they will see the Son of Man coming in a cloud with power and great glory.
28 When these things begin to take place, stand erect, hold your heads high, because
your liberation[c] is near at hand.'

The time of this coming

29
30   And he told them a parable, 'Think of the fig tree and indeed every tree. •As
31 soon as you see them bud, you know that summer is now near. •So with you
when you see these things happening: know that the kingdom of God is near.
32 I tell you solemnly, before this generation has passed away all will have
33 taken place. •Heaven and earth will pass away, but my words will never pass
away.

Be on the alert

34 'Watch yourselves, or your hearts will be coarsened with debauchery and
drunkenness and the cares of life, and that day will be sprung on you suddenly,
35 like a trap. For it will come down on every living man on the face of the earth.
36 Stay awake, praying at all times for the strength to survive all that is going to
happen, and to stand with confidence before the Son of Man.'

The last days of Jesus

37   In the daytime he would be in the Temple teaching, but would spend the night
38 on the hill called the Mount of Olives. •And from early morning the people
would gather round him in the Temple to listen to him.

VI. THE PASSION

The conspiracy against Jesus: Judas betrays him

1 **22** The feast of Unleavened Bread, called the Passover, was now drawing near,
2   and the chief priests and the scribes were looking for some way of doing
away with him, because they mistrusted the people.
3   Then Satan entered into Judas, surnamed Iscariot, who was numbered among

b. Ex 3:6   **c.** Most scribes were Pharisees and believed in the resurrection of the dead
d. Ps 110:1
21 a. This passage on the End Time also includes some elements of a prophecy of the destruction of Jerusalem.   **b.** Possibly alluding to Dn 9:27.   **c.** Or 'redemption'.

the Twelve. •He went to the chief priests and the officers of the guard " to discuss 4
a scheme for handing Jesus over to them. •They were delighted and agreed to give 5
him money. •He accepted, and looked for an opportunity to betray him to them 6
without the people knowing.

Preparation for the Passover supper

The day of Unleavened Bread came round, the day on which the passover 7
had to be sacrificed, •and he sent Peter and John, saying, 'Go and make the 8
preparations for us to eat the passover'. •'Where do you want us to prepare it?' 9
they asked. •'Listen,' he said 'as you go into the city you will meet a man 10
carrying a pitcher of water. Follow him into the house he enters •and tell the 11
owner of the house, "The Master has this to say to you: Where is the dining room
in which I can eat the passover with my disciples?" •The man will show you a large 12
upper room furnished with couches. Make the preparations there.' •They set off 13
and found everything as he had told them, and prepared the Passover.

The supper

When the hour came he took his place at table, and the apostles with him. 14
And he said to them, 'I have longed to eat this passover with you before I suffer; 15
because, I tell you, I shall not eat it again until it is fulfilled in the kingdom of 16
God'.

Then, taking a cup,^{b} he gave thanks and said, 'Take this and share it among 17
you, •because from now on, I tell you, I shall not drink wine until the king- 18
dom of God comes'.

The institution of the Eucharist

Then he took some bread, and when he had given thanks, broke it and gave it 19
to them, saying, 'This is my body which will be given for you; do this as a memorial
of me'. •He did the same with the cup after supper, and said, 'This cup is the new 20
covenant in my blood which will be poured out for you.

The treachery of Judas foretold

'And yet, here with me on the table is the hand of the man who betrays me. 21
The Son of Man does indeed go to his fate even as it has been decreed, but alas for 22
that man by whom he is betrayed!' •And they began to ask one another which of 23
them it could be who was to do this thing.

Who is the greatest?

A dispute arose also between them about which should be reckoned the 24
greatest, •but he said to them, 'Among pagans it is the kings who lord it over them, 25
and those who have authority over them are given the title Benefactor. •This must 26
not happen with you. No; the greatest among you must behave as if he were the
youngest, the leader as if he were the one who serves. •For who is the greater: 27
the one at table or the one who serves? The one at table, surely? Yet here am I
among you as one who serves!

The reward promised to the apostles

'You are the men who have stood by me faithfully in my trials; •and now 28
29
I confer a kingdom on you, just as my Father conferred one on me: •you will 30
eat and drink at my table in my kingdom, and you will sit on thrones to judge the
twelve tribes of Israel.

Peter's denial and repentance foretold

'Simon, Simon! Satan, you must know, has got his wish to sift you all like 31
wheat; •but I have prayed for you, Simon, that your faith may not fail, and once 32
you have recovered, you in your turn must strengthen your brothers.' •'Lord,' 33

34 he answered 'I would be ready to go to prison with you, and to death.' •Jesus replied, 'I tell you, Peter, by the time the cock crows today you will have denied three times that you know me'.

A time of crisis

35 He said to them, 'When I sent you out without purse or haversack or sandals,
36 were you short of anything? •'No' they said. He said to them, 'But now if you have a purse, take it; if you have a haversack, do the same; if you have no sword, sell
37 your cloak and buy one, •because I tell you these words of scripture have to be fulfilled in me: *He let himself be taken for a criminal.*[c] Yes, what scripture says
38 about me is even now reaching its fulfilment.' •'Lord,' they said 'there are two swords here now.' He said to them, 'That is enough!'

The Mount of Olives

39 He then left to make his way as usual to the Mount of Olives, with the
40 disciples following. •When they reached the place he said to them, 'Pray not to be put to the test'.
41 Then he withdrew from them, about a stone's throw away, and knelt down
42 and prayed. •'Father,' he said 'if you are willing, take this cup away from me.
43 Nevertheless, let your will be done, not mine.' •Then an angel appeared to
44 him, coming from heaven to give him strength. •In his anguish he prayed even more earnestly, and his sweat fell to the ground like great drops of blood.
45 When he rose from prayer he went to the disciples and found them sleeping
46 for sheer grief. •'Why are you asleep?' he said to them. 'Get up and pray not to be put to the test.'

The arrest

47 He was still speaking when a number of men appeared, and at the head of them the man called Judas, one of the Twelve, who went up to Jesus to kiss him.
48
49 Jesus said, 'Judas, are you betraying the Son of Man with a kiss?' •His followers,
50 seeing what was happening, said, 'Lord, shall we use our swords?' •And one of
51 them struck out at the high priest's servant, and cut off his right ear. •But at this Jesus spoke. 'Leave off!' he said 'That will do!' And touching the man's ear he healed him.
52 Then Jesus spoke to the chief priests and captains of the Temple guard and elders who had come for him. 'Am I a brigand' he said 'that you had to set out
53 with swords and clubs? •When I was among you in the Temple day after day you never moved to lay hands on me. But this is your hour; this is the reign of darkness.'

Peter's denials

54 They seized him then and led him away, and they took him to the high
55 priest's house. Peter followed at a distance. •They had lit a fire in the middle of
56 the courtyard and Peter sat down among them, •and as he was sitting there by the blaze a servant-girl saw him, peered at him, and said, 'This person was with
57 him too'. •But he denied it. 'Woman,' he said 'I do not know him.' •Shortly
58 afterwards someone else saw him and said, 'You are another of them'. But Peter
59 replied, 'I am not, my friend'. •About an hour later another man insisted,
60 saying, 'This fellow was certainly with him. Why, he is a Galilean.' •'My friend,' said Peter 'I do not know what you are talking about.' At that instant,
61 while he was still speaking, the cock crew, •and the Lord turned and looked straight at Peter, and Peter remembered what the Lord had said to him, 'Before
62 the cock crows today, you will have disowned me three times'. •And he went outside and wept bitterly.

---

22 a. The Temple police, chosen from among the Levites. **b.** Luke distinguishes the Passover and the cup of vv. 15-18 from the bread and the cup of vv. 19-20. **c.** Is 53:12

Jesus mocked by the guards

Meanwhile the men who guarded Jesus were mocking and beating him. 63
They blindfolded him and questioned him. 'Play the prophet' they said. 'Who 64
hit you then?' •And they continued heaping insults on him. 65

Jesus before the Sanhedrin

When day broke there was a meeting of the elders of the people, attended 66
by the chief priests and scribes. He was brought before their council, •and they 67
said to him, 'If you are the Christ, tell us'. 'If I tell you,' he replied 'you will not
believe me, •and if I question you, you will not answer. •But from now on, the ⁶⁸₆₉
Son of Man will be *seated at the right hand* of the Power *of God.'ᵈ* •Then they 70
all said, 'So you are the Son of God then?' He answered, 'It is you who say I am'.
'What need of witnesses have we now?' they said. 'We have heard it for ourselves 71
from his own lips.' 23 The whole assembly then rose, and they brought him 1
before Pilate.

Jesus before Pilate

They began their accusation by saying, 'We found this man inciting our 2
people to revolt, opposing payment of the tribute to Caesar, and claiming to be
Christ, a king'. •Pilate put to him this question, 'Are you the king of the Jews?' 3
'It is you who say it' he replied. •Pilate then said to the chief priests and the crowd, 4
'I find no case against this man'. •But they persisted, 'He is inflaming the people 5
with his teaching all over Judaea; it has come all the way from Galilee, where he
started, down to here'. •When Pilate heard this, he asked if the man were a 6
Galilean; •and finding that he came under Herod's jurisdiction he passed him 7
over to Herod who was also in Jerusalem at that time.

Jesus before Herod

Herod was delighted to see Jesus; he had heard about him and had 8
been wanting for a long time to set eyes on him; moreover, he was hoping to see
some miracle worked by him. •So he questioned him at some length; but without 9
getting any reply. •Meanwhile the chief priests and the scribes were there, violently 10
pressing their accusations. •Then Herod, together with his guards, treated him 11
with contempt and made fun of him; he put a rich cloakᵃ on him and sent him
back to Pilate. •And though Herod and Pilate had been enemies before, they 12
were reconciled that same day.

Jesus before Pilate again

Pilate then summoned the chief priests and the leading men and the people. 13
'You brought this man before me' he said 'as a political agitator. Now I have 14
gone into the matter myself in your presence and found no case against the man
in respect of all the charges you bring against him. •Nor has Herod either, since 15
he has sent him back to us. As you can see, the man has done nothing that
deserves death, •so I shall have him flogged and then let him go.' •But as one ¹⁶₁₈
man they howled, 'Away with him! Give us Barabbas!' •(This man had been 19
thrown into prison for causing a riot in the city and for murder.)

Pilate was anxious to set Jesus free and addressed them again, •but they ²⁰₂₁
shouted back, 'Crucify him! Crucify him!' •And for the third time he spoke 22
to them, 'Why? What harm has this man done? I have found no case against
him that deserves death, so I shall have him punished and then let him go.' •But 23
they kept on shouting at the top of their voices, demanding that he should be
crucified. And their shouts were growing louder.

Pilate then gave his verdict: their demand was to be granted. •He released ²⁴₂₅
the man they asked for, who had been imprisoned for rioting and murder, and
handed Jesus over to them to deal with as they pleased.

The way to Calvary

26   As they were leading him away they seized on a man, Simon from Cyrene,
who was coming in from the country, and made him shoulder the cross and
27 carry it behind Jesus. •Large numbers of people followed him, and of women
28 too,[b] who mourned and lamented for him. •But Jesus turned to them and said,
'Daughters of Jerusalem, do not weep for me; weep rather for yourselves and for
29 your children. •For the days will surely come when people will say, "Happy are
those who are barren, the wombs that have never borne, the breasts that have
30 never suckled!" •Then they will begin to *say to the mountains,"Fall on us!"; to the*
31 *hills, "Cover us!"*[c] •For if men use the green wood like this, what will happen
32 when it is dry?' •Now with him they were also leading out two other criminals
to be executed.

The crucifixion

33   When they reached the place called The Skull, they crucified him there and the
34 two criminals also, one on the right, the other on the left. • Jesus said, 'Father,
forgive them; they do not know what they are doing'. Then they cast lots to
share out his clothing.

The crucified Christ is mocked

35   The people stayed there watching him. As for the leaders, they jeered at him.
'He saved others,' they said 'let him save himself if he is the Christ of God, the
36 Chosen One.' •The soldiers mocked him too, and when they approached to offer
37
38 him vinegar •they said, 'If you are the king of the Jews, save yourself'. •Above
him there was an inscription: 'This is the King of the Jews'.

The good thief

39   One of the criminals hanging there abused him. 'Are you not the Christ?'
40 he said. 'Save yourself and us as well.' •But the other spoke up and rebuked him.
'Have you no fear of God at all?' he said. 'You got the same sentence as he did,
41 but in our case we deserved it: we are paying for what we did. But this man has
42 done nothing wrong. •Jesus,' he said 'remember me when you come into your
43 kingdom.' •'Indeed, I promise you,' he replied 'today you will be with me in
paradise.'

The death of Jesus

44   It was now about the sixth hour and, with the sun eclipsed, a darkness came
45 over the whole land until the ninth hour. •The veil of the Temple was torn right
46 down the middle; •and when Jesus had cried out in a loud voice, he said, 'Father,
into your hands I commit my spirit'?[d] With these words he breathed his last.

After the death

47   When the centurion saw what had taken place, he gave praise to God and
48 said, 'This was a great and good man'. •And when all the people who had gathered
for the spectacle saw what had happened, they went home beating their breasts.
49   All his friends stood at a distance; so also did the women who had accompanied
him from Galilee, and they saw all this happen.

The burial

50   Then a member of the council arrived, an upright and virtuous man named
51 Joseph. •He had not consented to what the others had planned and carried out.
He came from Arimathaea, a Jewish town, and he lived in the hope of seeing the

d. Ps 110:1
23 a. Ceremonial dress of a prince.   **b.** The Talmud records that noblewomen of Jerusalem
used to give soothing drinks to condemned criminals.   **c.** Ho 10:8   **d.** Ps 31:5

kingdom of God. •This man went to Pilate and asked for the body of Jesus. 52
He then took it down, wrapped it in a shroud and put him in a tomb which was 53
hewn in stone in which no one had yet been laid. •It was Preparation Day and 54
the sabbath was imminent.

Meanwhile the women who had come from Galilee with Jesus were following 55
behind. They took note of the tomb and of the position of the body.

Then they returned and prepared spices and ointments. And on the sabbath 56
day they rested, as the Law required.

VII. AFTER THE RESURRECTION

The empty tomb. The angel's message

24 On the first day of the week, at the first sign of dawn, they went to the 1
tomb with the spices they had prepared. •They found that the stone had 2
been rolled away from the tomb, •but on entering discovered that the body of the 3
Lord Jesus was not there. •As they stood there not knowing what to think, two 4
men in brilliant clothes suddenly appeared at their side. •Terrified, the women 5
lowered their eyes. But the two men said to them, 'Why look among the dead
for someone who is alive? •He is not here; he has risen. Remember what he told 6
you when he was still in Galilee: •that the Son of Man had to be handed over 7
into the power of sinful men and be crucified, and rise again on the third day.'
And they remembered his words. 8

The apostles refuse to believe the women

When the women returned from the tomb they told all this to the Eleven and 9
to all the others. •The women were Mary of Magdala, Joanna, and Mary the 10
mother of James. The other women with them also told the apostles, •but this 11
story of theirs seemed pure nonsense, and they did not believe them.

Peter at the tomb

Peter, however, went running to the tomb. He bent down and saw the binding 12
cloths but nothing else; he then went back home, amazed at what had happened.

The road to Emmaus

That very same day, two of them were on their way to a village called Emmaus, 13
seven miles[a] from Jerusalem, •and they were talking together about all that had 14
happened. •Now as they talked this over, Jesus himself came up and walked by 15
their side; •but something prevented them from recognising him. •He said to 16 17
them, 'What matters are you discussing as you walk along?' They stopped short,
their faces downcast.

Then one of them, called Cleopas, answered him, 'You must be the only 18
person staying in Jerusalem who does not know the things that have been
happening there these last few days'. •'What things?' he asked. 'All about Jesus 19
of Nazareth' they answered 'who proved he was a great prophet by the things
he said and did in the sight of God and of the whole people; •and how our chief 20
priests and our leaders handed him over to be sentenced to death, and had him
crucified. •Our own hope had been that he would be the one to set Israel free. 21
And this is not all: two whole days have gone by since it all happened; •and some 22
women from our group have astounded us: they went to the tomb in the early
morning, •and when they did not find the body, they came back to tell us they 23
had seen a vision of angels who declared he was alive. •Some of our friends 24
went to the tomb and found everything exactly as the women had reported, but
of him they saw nothing.'

Then he said to them, 'You foolish men! So slow to believe the full message 25
of the prophets! •Was it not ordained that the Christ should suffer and so enter 26

27 into his glory?' •Then, starting with Moses and going through all the prophets, he explained to them the passages throughout the scriptures that were about himself.

28 When they drew near to the village to which they were going, he made as if
29 to go on; •but they pressed him to stay with them. 'It is nearly evening' they said
30 'and the day is almost over.' So he went in to stay with them. •Now while he was with them at table, he took the bread and said the blessing; then he broke it and
31 handed it to them. •And their eyes were opened and they recognised him; but he
32 had vanished from their sight. •Then they said to each other, 'Did not our hearts burn within us as he talked to us on the road and explained the scriptures to us?'
33 They set out that instant and returned to Jerusalem. There they found the
34 Eleven assembled together with their companions, •who said to them, 'Yes, it is
35 true. The Lord has risen and has appeared to Simon.' •Then they told their story of what had happened on the road and how they had recognised him at the breaking of bread.

Jesus appears to the apostles

36 They were still talking about all this when he himself stood among them
37 and said to them, 'Peace be with you!' •In a state of alarm and fright, they thought
38 they were seeing a ghost. •But he said, 'Why are you so agitated, and why are
39 these doubts rising in your hearts? •Look at my hands and feet; yes, it is I indeed. Touch me and see for yourselves; a ghost has no flesh and bones as you can see
40
41 I have.' •And as he said this he showed them his hands and feet. •Their joy was so great that they still could not believe it, and they stood there dumbfounded;
42 so he said to them, 'Have you anything here to eat?' •And they offered him a piece
43 of grilled fish, •which he took and ate before their eyes.

Last instructions to the apostles

44 Then he told them, 'This is what I meant when I said, while I was still with you, that everything written about me in the Law of Moses, in the Prophets and
45 in the Psalms, has to be fulfilled'. •He then opened their minds to understand the
46 scriptures, •and he said to them, 'So you see how it is written that the Christ would
47 suffer and on the third day rise from the dead, •and that, in his name, repentance for the forgiveness of sins would be preached to all the nations, beginning
48 from Jerusalem. •You are witnesses to this.
49 'And now I am sending down to you what the Father has promised. Stay in the city then, until you are clothed with the power from on high.'

The ascension

50 Then he took them out as far as the outskirts of Bethany, and lifting up his
51 hands he blessed them. •Now as he blessed them, he withdrew from them and
52 was carried up to heaven. •They worshipped him and then went back to
53 Jerusalem full of joy; •and they were continually in the Temple praising God.

---

24 a. The identity of the village is disputed.

INTRODUCTION TO
THE GOSPEL AND LETTERS OF
SAINT JOHN

Date, authorship and form of the gospel

Tradition almost unanimously names John the apostle, the son of Zebedee, as the author. Before A.D. 150 the book was known and used by Ignatius of Antioch, Papias, Justin and the author of the *Odes of Solomon*, and the first explicit testimony is by Irenaeus, c. 180: 'Last of all John, too, the disciple of the Lord who leant against his breast, himself brought out a gospel while he was in Ephesus'. The gospel itself has much supporting evidence, apart from its claim to be the work of an eye-witness who was a beloved disciple of the Lord: its vocabulary and style betray its semitic origin, it is familiar with Jewish customs and with the topography of Palestine, and its author is evidently a close friend of Peter.

It was published not by John himself but by his disciples after his death, and it is possible that in this gospel we have the end-stage of a slow process that has brought together not only component parts of different ages but also corrections, additions and sometimes more than one revision of the same discourse. The arrangement of the gospel is not always easy to explain, but it is clear that the author attaches special importance to the Jewish liturgical feasts which punctuate his narrative; the following analysis can be made:

Prologue (1:1-18)
I. *First week* of the messianic ministry, ending with the first miracle at Cana (1:19–2:11)
II. *First Passover* with accompanying events, ending with the second miracle at Cana (2:12–4:54)
III. *Sabbath 'of the paralytic'* (5:1–47)
IV. *The Passover 'of the bread of life'* and its discourse (6:1–71)
V. *The feast of Tabernacles* and the man born blind (7:1–10:21)
VI. *The feast of Dedication* and the raising of Lazarus (10:22–11:54)
VII. *Week of the Passion* and the crucifixion Passover (11:55–19:42)
VIII. *The resurrection* and week of appearances (20:1–29)
IX. *Appendix:* the Church and Christ's return (ch. 21)

This division suggests that Christ not only fulfilled the Jewish liturgy but in doing so brought it to an end.

Special characteristics of the gospel

The fourth gospel is concerned to bring out the significance of all that Christ did and said. The things that he did were 'signs', and the meaning of them, hidden at first, could be understood only after his glorification; the things he said had a deeper meaning not perceived at the time but understood only after the Spirit who spoke in the name of the risen Christ had come to 'lead' his disciples 'into all truth'. The gospel is revelation at this stage of development.

The whole of John's thought is dominated by the mystery of the Incarnation, from the Prologue with which the book opens. Here the revelation of Christ's glory, which in the synoptic gospels is associated primarily with his return at the end of time, has a new interpretation: judgement is working here and now in the soul, and eternal life (John's counterpart to the 'kingdom' of the synoptic gospels) is made to be something actually present, already in the possession of those who have faith. God's victory over evil, his salvation of the world, is already guaranteed by Christ's resurrection in glory.

The letters

The three letters are like the gospel in style and doctrine. The first, an encyclical letter to the Christian communities of 'Asia', summarises the whole content of John's religious experience and develops themes from the gospel, for churches threatened with disintegration under the impact of the early heresies. The second letter was written to a church in answer to some who had denied the reality of the Incarnation. The third, which is probably the earliest in date, was written to settle a dispute on jurisdiction in one of the churches acknowledging John's authority.

THE GOSPEL ACCORDING TO SAINT JOHN

PROLOGUE

1
In the beginning was the Word:
the Word was with God
and the Word was God.   1

He was with God in the beginning.   2
Through him all things came to be,   3
not one thing had its being but through him.
All that came to be had life in him   4
and that life was the light of men,
a light that shines in the dark,   5
a light that darkness could not overpower.[a]

A man came, sent by God.   6
His name was John.
He came as a witness,   7
as a witness to speak for the light,
so that everyone might believe through him.
He was not the light,   8
only a witness to speak for the light.

The Word was the true light   9
that enlightens all men;
and he was coming into the world.
He was in the world   10
that had its being through him,
and the world did not know him.
He came to his own domain   11
and his own people did not accept him.
But to all who did accept him   12
he gave power to become children of God,
to all who believe in the name of him
who was born not out of human stock   13
or urge of the flesh
or will of man
but of God himself.
The Word was made flesh,   14
he lived among us,[b]
and we saw his glory,
the glory that is his as the only Son of the Father,
full of grace and truth.

John appears as his witness. He proclaims: 15

'This is the one of whom I said:
He who comes after me
ranks before me
because he existed before me'.

16 Indeed, from his fulness we have, all of us, received—
yes, grace in return for grace,
17 since, though the Law was given through Moses,
grace and truth have come through Jesus Christ.
18 No one has ever seen God;
it is the only Son, who is nearest to the Father's heart,
who has made him known.

I. THE FIRST PASSOVER

A. THE OPENING WEEK

The witness of John

19 This is how John appeared as a witness. When the Jews[c] sent priests and
20 Levites from Jerusalem to ask him, 'Who are you?' •he not only declared, but
21 he declared quite openly, 'I am not the Christ'. •'Well then,' they asked 'are you
22 Elijah?'[d] 'I am not' he said. 'Are you the Prophet?'[e] He answered, 'No'. •So they
said to him, 'Who are you? We must take back an answer to those who sent us.
23 What have you to say about yourself?' •So John said, 'I am, as Isaiah prophesied:

a voice that cries in the wilderness:
Make a straight way for the Lord'.[f]

24
25 Now these men had been sent by the Pharisees, •and they put this further
question to him, 'Why are you baptising if you are not the Christ, and not Elijah,
26 and not the prophet?' •John replied, 'I baptise with water; but there stands
27 among you—unknown to you—•the one who is coming after me; and I am
28 not fit to undo his sandal-strap'. •This happened at Bethany, on the far side of
the Jordan, where John was baptising.
29 The next day, seeing Jesus coming towards him, John said, 'Look, there is
30 the lamb of God that takes away the sin of the world. •This is the one I spoke
of when I said: A man is coming after me who ranks before me because he
31 existed before me. •I did not know him myself, and yet it was to reveal him to
32 Israel that I came baptising with water.' •John also declared, 'I saw the Spirit
33 coming down on him from heaven like a dove and resting on him. •I did not
know him myself, but he who sent me to baptise with water had said to me,
"The man on whom you see the Spirit come down and rest is the one who is
34 going to baptise with the Holy Spirit". •Yes, I have seen and I am the witness
that he is the Chosen One of God.'

The first disciples

35 On the following day as John stood there again with two of his disciples,
36 Jesus passed, and John stared hard at him and said, 'Look, there is the lamb of
37
38 God'. •Hearing this, the two disciples followed Jesus. •Jesus turned round, saw
them following and said, 'What do you want?' They answered, 'Rabbi,'—which
39 means Teacher—'where do you live?' •'Come and see' he replied; so they went

1 a. Or 'grasp', in the sense of 'enclose' or 'understand'. **b.** 'pitched his tent among us'.
c. In Jn this usually indicates the Jewish religious authorities who were hostile to Jesus; but
occasionally the Jews as a whole. **d.** Whose return was expected, Ml 3:23-24. **e.** The
Prophet greater than Moses who was expected as Messiah, on an interpretation of Dt 18:15.
f. Is 40:3

and saw where he lived, and stayed with him the rest of that day. It was about the tenth hour.*

One of these two who became followers of Jesus after hearing what John had 40 said was Andrew, the brother of Simon Peter. •Early next morning, Andrew 41 met his brother and said to him, 'We have found the Messiah'—which means the Christ—•and he took Simon to Jesus. Jesus looked hard at him and said, 42 'You are Simon son of John; you are to be called Cephas'—meaning Rock.

The next day, after Jesus had decided to leave for Galilee, he met Philip and 43 said, 'Follow me'. •Philip came from the same town, Bethsaida, as Andrew and 44 Peter. •Philip found Nathanael *h* and said to him, 'We have found the one 45 Moses wrote about in the Law, the one about whom the prophets wrote: he is Jesus son of Joseph, from Nazareth'. •'From Nazareth?' said Nathanael 'Can 46 anything good come from that place?' 'Come and see' replied Philip. •When 47 Jesus saw Nathanael coming he said of him, 'There is an Israelite who deserves the name, incapable of deceit'. •'How do you know me?' said Nathanael. 48 'Before Philip came to call you,' said Jesus 'I saw you under the fig tree.' •Na- 49 thanael answered, 'Rabbi, you are the Son of God, you are the King of Israel'. Jesus replied, 'You believe that just because I said: I saw you under the fig tree. 50 You will see greater things than that.' •And then he added, 'I tell you most 51 solemnly, you will see heaven laid open and, above the Son of Man, the angels of God ascending and descending'.

The wedding at Cana

2 Three days later there was a wedding at Cana in Galilee. The mother of 1 Jesus was there, •and Jesus and his disciples had also been invited. •When ⅔ they ran out of wine, since the wine provided for the wedding was all finished, the mother of Jesus said to him, 'They have no wine'. •Jesus said, 'Woman, why 4 turn to me? My hour has not come yet.' •His mother said to the servants, 5 '*Do whatever he tells you*'.*•*There were six stone water jars standing there, meant 6 for the ablutions that are customary among the Jews: each could hold twenty or thirty gallons. •Jesus said to the servants, 'Fill the jars with water', and they 7 filled them to the brim. •'Draw some out now' he told them 'and take it to the 8 steward.' •They did this; the steward tasted the water, and it had turned into 9 wine. Having no idea where it came from—only the servants who had drawn the water knew—the steward called the bridegroom •and said, 'People generally 10 serve the best wine first, and keep the cheaper sort till the guests have had plenty to drink; but you have kept the best wine till now'.

This was the first of the signs given by Jesus: it was given at Cana in Galilee. 11 He let his glory be seen, and his disciples believed in him. •After this he went 12 down to Capernaum with his mother and the brothers, but they stayed there only a few days.

B. THE PASSOVER

The cleansing of the Temple

Just before the Jewish Passover Jesus went up to Jerusalem, •and in the ¹³⁄₁₄ Temple he found people selling cattle and sheep and pigeons, and the money changers sitting at their counters there. •Making a whip out of some cord, he 15 drove them all out of the Temple, cattle and sheep as well, scattered the money changers' coins, knocked their tables over •and said to the pigeon-sellers, 'Take 16 all this out of here and stop turning my Father's house into a market'. •Then his 17 disciples remembered the words of scripture: *Zeal for your house will devour me.*ᵇ The Jews intervened and said, 'What sign can you show us to justify what you 18 have done?' •Jesus answered, 'Destroy this sanctuary, and in three days I will 19 raise it up'. •The Jews replied, 'It has taken forty-six years to build this 20

21 sanctuary:ᶜ are you going to raise it up in three days?' •But he was speaking of
22 the sanctuary that was his body, •and when Jesus rose from the dead, his disciples
remembered that he had said this, and they believed the scripture and the words
he had said.

23   During his stay in Jerusalem for the Passover many believed in his name
24 when they saw the signs that he gave, •but Jesus knew them all and did not trust
25 himself to them; •he never needed evidence about any man; he could tell what
a man had in him.

C. THE MYSTERY OF THE SPIRIT REVEALED
TO A MASTER IN ISRAEL

The conversation with Nicodemus

$\frac{1}{2}$ **3** There was one of the Pharisees called Nicodemus, a leading Jew, •who came
to Jesus by night and said, 'Rabbi, we know that you are a teacher who comes
from God; for no one could perform the signs that you do unless God were with
3 him'. •Jesus answered:

> 'I tell you most solemnly,
> unless a man is born from above,
> he cannot see the kingdom of God'.

4 Nicodemus said, 'How can a grown man be born? Can he go back into his
5 mother's womb and be born again?' •Jesus replied:

> 'I tell you most solemnly,
> unless a man is born through water and the Spirit,
> he cannot enter the kingdom of God:
6   what is born of the flesh is flesh;
>   what is born of the Spirit is spirit.
7   Do not be surprised when I say:
>   You must be born from above.
8   The wind blows wherever it pleases;
>   you hear its sound,
>   but you cannot tell where it comes from or where it is going.
>   That is how it is with all who are born of the Spirit.'

$\frac{9}{10}$ 'How can that be possible?' asked Nicodemus. •'You, a teacher in Israel,
and you do not know these things!' replied Jesus.

11   'I tell you most solemnly,
>   we speak only about what we know
>   and witness only to what we have seen
>   and yet you people reject our evidence.
12   If you do not believe me
>   when I speak about things in this world,
>   how are you going to believe me
>   when I speak to you about heavenly things?
13   No one has gone up to heaven
>   except the one who came down from heaven,
>   the Son of Man who is in heaven;
>   and the Son of Man must be lifted up
14   as Moses lifted up the serpent in the desert,

g. 4 p.m.   h. Probably the Bartholomew of the other gospels.
2 a. Gn 41:55   b. Ps 69:9   c. Reconstruction work on the Temple began in 19 B.C. This
is therefore the Passover of 28 A.D.

so that everyone who believes may have eternal life in him.   15
Yes, God loved the world so much   16
that he gave his only Son,
so that everyone who believes in him may not be lost
but may have eternal life.
For God sent his Son into the world   17
not to condemn the world,
but so that through him the world might be saved.
No one who believes in him will be condemned;   18
but whoever refuses to believe is condemned already,
because he has refused to believe
in the name of God's only Son.
On these grounds is sentence pronounced: 19
that though the light has come into the world
men have shown they prefer
darkness to the light
because their deeds were evil.
And indeed, everybody who does wrong   20
hates the light and avoids it,
for fear his actions should be exposed;
but the man who lives by the truth   21
comes out into the light,
so that it may be plainly seen that what he does is done in God.'

II. JOURNEYS IN SAMARIA AND GALILEE

John bears witness for the last time

After this, Jesus went with his disciples into the Judaean countryside and   22
stayed with them there and baptised. •At the same time John was baptising at 23
Aenon[a] near Salim, where there was plenty of water, and people were going
there to be baptised. •This was before John had been put in prison.   24
Now some of John's disciples had opened a discussion with a Jew about   25
purification, •so they went to John and said, 'Rabbi, the man who was with   26
you on the far side of the Jordan, the man to whom you bore witness, is baptising
now; and everyone is going to him'. •John replied: 27

'A man can lay claim
only to what is given him from heaven.

'You yourselves can bear me out: I said: I myself am not the Christ; I am   28
the one who has been sent in front of him.

'The bride is only for the bridegroom;   29
and yet the bridegroom's friend,
who stands there and listens,
is glad when he hears the bridegroom's voice.
This same joy I feel, and now it is complete.
He must grow greater,   30
I must grow smaller.
He who comes from above   31
is above all others;
he who is born of the earth
is earthly himself and speaks in an earthly way.
He who comes from heaven
bears witness to the things he has seen and heard,   32
even if his testimony is not accepted;
though all who do accept his testimony   33

are attesting the truthfulness of God,
since he whom God has sent
speaks God's own words:
God gives him the Spirit without reserve.
The Father loves the Son
and has entrusted everything to him.
Anyone who believes in the Son has eternal life,
but anyone who refuses to believe in the Son will never see life:
the anger of God stays on him.'

The saviour of the world revealed to the Samaritans

1 When Jesus heard that the Pharisees had found out that he was making
2 and baptising more disciples than John—•though in fact it was his disciples
3 who baptised, not Jesus himself—•he left Judaea and went back to Galilee.
4 This meant that he had to cross Samaria.
5 On the way he came to the Samaritan town called Sychar,ᵃ near the land
6 that Jacob gave to his son Joseph. •Jacob's well is there and Jesus, tired by the
7 journey, sat straight down by the well. It was about the sixth hour.ᵇ •When
a Samaritan woman came to draw water, Jesus said to her, 'Give me a drink'.
⁸₉ His disciples had gone into the town to buy food. •The Samaritan woman said
to him, 'What? You are a Jew and you ask me, a Samaritan, for a drink?'—Jews,
10 in fact, do not associate with Samaritans—•Jesus replied:

'If you only knew what God is offering
and who it is that is saying to you:
Give me a drink,
you would have been the one to ask,
and he would have given you living water'.

11 'You have no bucket, sir,' she answered 'and the well is deep: how could
12 you get this living water? •Are you a greater man than our father Jacob who
13 gave us this well and drank from it himself with his sons and his cattle?' •Jesus
replied:

'Whoever drinks this water
will get thirsty again;
14 but anyone who drinks the water that I shall give
will never be thirsty again:
the water that I shall give
will turn into a spring inside him, welling up to eternal life'.

15 'Sir,' said the woman 'give me some of that water, so that I may never get
16 thirsty and never have to come here again to draw water.' •'Go and call your
17 husband' said Jesus to her 'and come back here.' •The woman answered, 'I have
18 no husband'. He said to her, 'You are right to say, "I have no husband"; •for
although you have had five, the one you have now is not your husband. You
¹⁹₂₀ spoke the truth there.' •'I see you are a prophet, sir' said the woman. •'Our
fathers worshipped on this mountain,ᶜ while you say that Jerusalem is the place
21 where one ought to worship.' •Jesus said:

'Believe me, woman, the hour is coming
when you will worship the Father
neither on this mountain nor in Jerusalem.
22 You worship what you do not know;
we worship what we do know;

3 a. A tradition locates Aenon ('Springs') in the Jordan valley 7 m. from Scythopolis.
4 a. Either Shechem (Aramaic: Sichara), or Askar at the foot of Mt Ebal. 'Jacob's Well'
is not mentioned in Gn.   b. Noon.   c. Gerizim, the mountain on which the Samaritans
built a rival to the Jerusalem Temple; it was destroyed by Hyrcanus, 129 B.C.

for salvation comes from the Jews.
But the hour will come—in fact it is here already—   23
when true worshippers will worship the Father in spirit and truth:
that is the kind of worshipper
the Father wants.
God is spirit,   24
and those who worship
must worship in spirit and truth.'

The woman said to him, 'I know that Messiah—that is, Christ—is coming; 25
and when he comes he will tell us everything'. •'I who am speaking to you,' 26
said Jesus 'I am he.'

At this point his disciples returned, and were surprised to find him speaking 27
to a woman, though none of them asked, 'What do you want from her?' or,
'Why are you talking to her?' •The woman put down her water jar and hurried 28
back to the town to tell the people, •'Come and see a man who has told me 29
everything I ever did; I wonder if he is the Christ?' •This brought people out of 30
the town and they started walking towards him.

Meanwhile, the disciples were urging him, 'Rabbi, do have something to 31
eat'; •but he said, 'I have food to eat that you do not know about'. •So the 32
33
disciples asked one another, 'Has someone been bringing him food?' •But Jesus 34
said:

'My food
is to do the will of the one who sent me,
and to complete his work.
Have you not got a saying: 35
Four months and then the harvest?
Well, I tell you:
Look around you, look at the fields;
already they are white, ready for harvest!
Already •the reaper is being paid his wages,   36
already he is bringing in the grain for eternal life,
and thus sower and reaper rejoice together.
For here the proverb holds good: 37
one sows, another reaps;
I sent you to reap   38
a harvest you had not worked for.
Others worked for it;
and you have come into the rewards of their trouble.'

Many Samaritans of that town had believed in him on the strength of the 39
woman's testimony when she said, 'He told me all I have ever done', •so, when 40
the Samaritans came up to him, they begged him to stay with them. He stayed
for two days, and •when he spoke to them many more came to believe; •and 41
42
they said to the woman, 'Now we no longer believe because of what you told us;
we have heard him ourselves and we know that he really is the saviour of the
world'.

The cure of the nobleman's son

When the two days were over Jesus left for Galilee. •He himself had declared 43
44
that there is no respect for a prophet in his own country, •but on his arrival the 45
Galileans received him well, having seen all that he had done at Jerusalem
during the festival which they too had attended.

He went again to Cana in Galilee, where he had changed the water into wine. 46
Now there was a court official there whose son was ill at Capernaum •and, 47
hearing that Jesus had arrived in Galilee from Judaea, he went and asked him
to come and cure his son as he was at the point of death. •Jesus said, 'So you will 48

49 not believe unless you see signs and portents!' •'Sir,' answered the official 'come
50 down before my child dies.' •'Go home,' said Jesus 'your son will live.' The man
51 believed what Jesus had said and started on his way; •and while he was still on
52 the journey back his servants met him with the news that his boy was alive. •He
asked them when the boy had begun to recover. 'The fever left him yesterday'
53 they said 'at the seventh hour.' •The father realised that this was exactly the time
when Jesus had said, 'Your son will live'; and he and all his household believed.
54   This was the second sign given by Jesus, on his return from Judaea to Galilee.

III. THE SECOND FEAST AT JERUSALEM

The cure of a sick man at the Pool of Bethzatha

1 5 Some time after this there was a Jewish festival, and Jesus went up to Jeru-
2   salem. •Now at the Sheep Pool in Jerusalem there is a building, called Beth-
3 zatha in Hebrew, consisting of five porticos; •and under these were crowds of
4 sick people—blind, lame, paralysed—waiting for the water to move; •for at
intervals the angel of the Lord came down into the pool, and the water was
disturbed, and the first person to enter the water after this disturbance was cured
5 of any ailment he suffered from. •One man there had an illness which had lasted
6 thirty-eight years, •and when Jesus saw him lying there and knew he had been in
7 this condition for a long time, he said, 'Do you want to be well again?' •'Sir,'
replied the sick man 'I have no one to put me into the pool when the water is
disturbed; and while I am still on the way, someone else gets there before me.'
8/9 Jesus said, 'Get up, pick up your sleeping-mat and walk'. •The man was cured
at once, and he picked up his mat and walked away.
10   Now that day happened to be the sabbath, •so the Jews said to the man who
had been cured, 'It is the sabbath; you are not allowed to carry your sleeping-
11 mat'. •He replied, 'But the man who cured me told me, "Pick up your mat and
12 walk" '. •They asked, 'Who is the man who said to you, "Pick up your mat and
13 walk"?' •The man had no idea who it was, since Jesus had disappeared into the
14 crowd that filled the place. •After a while Jesus met him in the Temple and said,
'Now you are well again, be sure not to sin any more, or something worse may
15 happen to you'. •The man went back and told the Jews that it was Jesus who
16 had cured him. •It was because he did things like this on the sabbath that the
17 Jews began to persecute Jesus. •His answer to them was, 'My Father goes on
18 working, and so do I'. •But that only made the Jews even more intent on killing
him, because, not content with breaking the sabbath, he spoke of God as his own
Father, and so made himself God's equal.
19   To this accusation Jesus replied:

'I tell you most solemnly,
the Son can do nothing by himself;
he can do only what he sees the Father doing:
and whatever the Father does the Son does too.

20   For the Father loves the Son
and shows him everything he does himself,
and he will show him even greater things than these,
works that will astonish you.

21   Thus, as the Father raises the dead and gives them life,
so the Son gives life to anyone he chooses;

22   for the Father judges no one;
he has entrusted all judgement to the Son,

23   so that all may honour the Son
as they honour the Father.
Whoever refuses honour to the Son
refuses honour to the Father who sent him.

I tell you most solemnly,   24
whoever listens to my words,
and believes in the one who sent me,
has eternal life;
without being brought to judgement
he has passed from death to life.
I tell you most solemnly,   25
the hour will come—in fact it is here already—
when the dead will hear the voice of the Son of God,
and all who hear it will live.
For the Father, who is the source of life,   26
has made the Son the source of life;
and, because he is the Son of Man,   27
has appointed him supreme judge.
Do not be surprised at this,   28
for the hour is coming
when the dead will leave their graves
at the sound of his voice:
those who did good   29
will rise again to life;
and those who did evil, to condemnation.
I can do nothing by myself;   30
I can only judge as I am told to judge,
and my judging is just,
because my aim is to do not my own will,
but the will of him who sent me.

'Were I to testify on my own behalf,   31
my testimony would not be valid;
but there is another witness who can speak on my behalf,   32
and I know that his testimony is valid.
You sent messengers to John,   33
and he gave his testimony to the truth:
not that I depend on human testimony;   34
no, it is for your salvation that I speak of this.
John was a lamp alight and shining   35
and for a time you were content to enjoy the light that he gave.
But my testimony is greater than John's: 36
the works my Father has given me to carry out,
these same works of mine
testify that the Father has sent me.
Besides, the Father who sent me   37
bears witness to me himself.
You have never heard his voice,
you have never seen his shape,
and his word finds no home in you   38
because you do not believe
in the one he has sent.

'You study the scriptures,   39
believing that in them you have eternal life;
now these same scriptures testify to me,
and yet you refuse to come to me for life!   40
As for human approval, this means nothing to me.   41
Besides, I know you too well: 42
you have no love of God in you.
I have come in the name of my Father   43

and you refuse to accept me;
if someone else comes in his own name
you will accept him.

44 How can you believe,
since you look to one another for approval
and are not concerned
with the approval that comes from the one God?
45 Do not imagine that I am going to accuse you before the Father:
you place your hopes on Moses,
and Moses will be your accuser.
46 If you really believed him
you would believe me too,
since it was I that he was writing about;
47 but if you refuse to believe what he wrote,
how can you believe what I say?'

IV. ANOTHER PASSOVER, THE BREAD OF LIFE

The miracle of the loaves

1,2 6 Some time after this, Jesus went off to the other side of the Sea of Galilee—
or of Tiberias—and a large crowd followed him, impressed by the signs he
3 gave by curing the sick. •Jesus climbed the hillside, and sat down there with his
4 disciples. •It was shortly before the Jewish feast of Passover.
5 Looking up, Jesus saw the crowds approaching and said to Philip, 'Where
6 can we buy some bread for these people to eat?' •He only said this to test Philip;
7 he himself knew exactly what he was going to do. •Philip answered, 'Two hundred
8 denarii would only buy enough to give them a small piece each'. •One of his
9 disciples, Andrew, Simon Peter's brother, said, •'There is a small boy here
10 with five barley loaves and two fish; but what is that between so many?' •Jesus
said to them, 'Make the people sit down'. There was plenty of grass there, and
11 as many as five thousand men sat down. •Then Jesus took the loaves, gave
thanks, and gave them out to all who were sitting ready; he then did the same with
12 the fish, giving out as much as was wanted. •When they had eaten enough he
said to the disciples, 'Pick up the pieces left over, so that nothing gets wasted'.
13 So they picked them up, and filled twelve hampers with scraps left over from the
14 meal of five barley loaves. •The people, seeing this sign that he had given, said,
15 'This really is the prophet who is to come into the world'. •Jesus, who could see
they were about to come and take him by force and make him king, escaped
back to the hills by himself.

Jesus walks on the waters

16,17 That evening the disciples went down to the shore of the lake and •got into
a boat to make for Capernaum on the other side of the lake. It was getting
18 dark by now and Jesus had still not rejoined them. •The wind was strong, and
19 the sea was getting rough. •They had rowed three or four miles when they saw
Jesus walking on the lake and coming towards the boat. This frightened them,
20,21 but he said, 'It is I. Do not be afraid.' •They were for taking him into the boat,
but in no time it reached the shore at the place they were making for.

The discourse in the synagogue at Capernaum

22 Next day, the crowd that had stayed on the other side saw that only one boat
had been there, and that Jesus had not got into the boat with his disciples, but
23 that the disciples had set off by themselves. •Other boats, however, had put in
24 from Tiberias, near the place where the bread had been eaten. •When the

people saw that neither Jesus nor his disciples were there, they got into those
boats and crossed to Capernaum to look for Jesus. •When they found him on 25
the other side, they said to him, 'Rabbi, when did you come here?' •Jesus ans- 26
wered:

> 'I tell you most solemnly,
> you are not looking for me
> because you have seen the signs
> but because you had all the bread you wanted to eat.
> Do not work for food that cannot last,   27
> but work for food that endures to eternal life,
> the kind of food the Son of Man is offering you,
> for on him the Father, God himself, has set his seal.'

Then they said to him, 'What must we do if we are to do the works that God 28
wants?' •Jesus gave them this answer, 'This is working for God: you must 29
believe in the one he has sent'. •So they said, 'What sign will you give to show us 30
that we should believe in you? What work will you do? •Our fathers had manna 31
to eat in the desert; as scripture says: *He gave them bread from heaven to eat.*ᵃ

Jesus answered: 32

> 'I tell you most solemnly,
> it was not Moses who gave you bread from heaven,
> it is my Father who gives you the bread from heaven,
> the true bread;
> for the bread of God   33
> is that which comes down from heaven
> and gives life to the world'.

'Sir,' they said 'give us that bread always.' •Jesus answered:
    34
    35

> 'I am the bread of life.
> He who comes to me will never be hungry;
> he who believes in me will never thirst.
> But, as I have told you,   36
> you can see me and still you do not believe.
> All that the Father gives me will come to me,   37
> and whoever comes to me
> I shall not turn him away;
> because I have come from heaven,   38
> not to do my own will,
> but to do the will of the one who sent me.
> Now the will of him who sent me   39
> is that I should lose nothing
> of all that he has given to me,
> and that I should raise it up on the last day.
> Yes, it is my Father's will   40
> that whoever sees the Son and believes in him
> shall have eternal life,
> and that I shall raise him up on the last day.'

Meanwhile the Jews were complaining to each other about him, because he 41
had said, 'I am the bread that came down from heaven'. •Surely this is Jesus 42
son of Joseph' they said. 'We know his father and mother. How can he now say,
"I have come down from heaven"?' •Jesus said in reply, 'Stop complaining to 43
each other.

> 'No one can come to me   44
> unless he is drawn by the Father who sent me,
> and I will raise him up at the last day.

45 It is written in the prophets:
    They will all be taught by God,[b]
    and to hear the teaching of the Father,
    and learn from it,
    is to come to me.

46 Not that anybody has seen the Father,
    except the one who comes from God:
    he has seen the Father.

47 I tell you most solemnly,
    everybody who believes has eternal life.

48 I am the bread of life.

49 Your fathers ate the manna in the desert
    and they are dead;

50 but this is the bread that comes down from heaven,
    so that a man may eat it and not die.

51 I am the living bread which has come down from heaven.
    Anyone who eats this bread will live for ever;
    and the bread that I shall give
    is my flesh, for the life of the world.'

52 Then the Jews started arguing with one another: 'How can this man give
53 us his flesh to eat?' they said. •Jesus replied:

    'I tell you most solemnly,
    if you do not eat the flesh of the Son of Man
    and drink his blood,
    you will not have life in you.

54 Anyone who does eat my flesh and drink my blood
    has eternal life,
    and I shall raise him up on the last day.

55 For my flesh is real food
    and my blood is real drink.

56 He who eats my flesh and drinks my blood
    lives in me
    and I live in him.

57 As I, who am sent by the living Father,
    myself draw life from the Father,
    so whoever eats me will draw life from me.

58 This is the bread come down from heaven;
    not like the bread our ancestors ate:
    they are dead,
    but anyone who eats this bread will live for ever.'

59
60 He taught this doctrine at Capernaum, in the synagogue. •After hearing it,
    many of his followers said, 'This is intolerable language. How could anyone
61 accept it?' •Jesus was aware that his followers were complaining about it and
62 said, 'Does this upset you? •What if you should see the Son of Man ascend to
    where he was before?

63   'It is the spirit that gives life,
        the flesh has nothing to offer.
        The words I have spoken to you are spirit
        and they are life.

64 'But there are some of you who do not believe.' For Jesus knew from the outset
65 those who did not believe, and who it was that would betray him. •He went on,

6 a. Ex 16:4f   b. Is 54:13

'This is why I told you that no one could come to me unless the Father allows him'. •After this, many of his disciples left him and stopped going with him.   66

Peter's profession of faith

Then Jesus said to the Twelve, 'What about you, do you want to go away too?'   67
Simon Peter answered, 'Lord, who shall we go to? You have the message of   68
eternal life, • and we believe; we know that you are the Holy One of God.'   69
Jesus replied, 'Have I not chosen you, you Twelve? Yet one of you is a devil.'   70
He meant Judas son of Simon Iscariot, since this was the man, one of the Twelve,   71
who was going to betray him.

V. THE FEAST OF TABERNACLES

Jesus goes up to Jerusalem for the feast and teaches there

7 After this Jesus stayed in Galilee; he could not stay in Judaea, because the   1
Jews were out to kill him.
As the Jewish feast of Tabernacles drew near, •his brothers[a] said to him,   2/3
'Why not leave this place and go to Judaea, and let your disciples[b] see the works
you are doing; •if a man wants to be known he does not do things in secret; since   4
you are doing all this, you should let the whole world see'. •Not even his brothers,   5
in fact, had faith in him. •Jesus answered, 'The right time for me has not come yet,   6
but any time is the right time for you, •The world cannot hate you, but it does   7
hate me, because I give evidence that its ways are evil. •Go up to the festival   8
yourselves: I am not going to this festival, because for me the time is not ripe
yet.' • Having said that, he stayed behind in Galilee.   9
However, after his brothers had left for the festival, he went up as well, but   10
quite privately, without drawing attention to himself. •At the festival the Jews   11
were on the look-out for him: 'Where is he?' they said. •People stood in groups   12
whispering[c] about him. Some said, 'He is a good man'; others, 'No, he is leading
the people astray'. •Yet no one spoke about him openly, for fear of the Jews.   13
When the festival was half over, Jesus went to the Temple and began to   14
teach. •The Jews were astonished and said, 'How did he learn to read? He has   15
not been taught.' •Jesus answered them: 16

'My teaching is not from myself:
it comes from the one who sent me;
and if anyone is prepared to do his will,   17
he will know whether my teaching is from God
or whether my doctrine is my own.
When a man's doctrine is his own   18
he is hoping to get honour for himself;
but when he is working for the honour of one who sent him,
then he is sincere
and by no means an impostor.
Did not Moses give you the Law?   19
And yet not one of you keeps the Law!

'Why do you want to kill me?' •The crowd replied, 'You are mad! Who wants   20
to kill you?' •Jesus answered, 'One work I did, and you are all surprised by it.   21
Moses ordered you to practise circumcision—not that it began with him, it goes   22
back to the patriarchs—and you circumcise on the sabbath. •Now if a man   23
can be circumcised on the sabbath so that the Law of Moses is not broken,
why are you angry with me for making a man whole and complete on a sabbath?
Do not keep judging according to appearances; let your judgement be according   24
to what is right.'

The people discuss the origin of the Messiah

25 Meanwhile some of the people of Jerusalem were saying, 'Isn't this the man
26 they want to kill? •And here he is, speaking freely, and they have nothing to
say to him! Can it be true the authorities have made up their minds that he is
27 the Christ? •Yet we all know where he comes from, but when the Christ appears
no one will know where he comes from.'ᵈ

28 Then, as Jesus taught in the Temple, he cried out:

'Yes, you know me and you know where I came from.
Yet I have not come of myself:
no, there is one who sent me and I really come from him,
and you do not know him,
29 but I know him
because I have come from him
and it was he who sent me.'

30 They would have arrested him then, but because his time had not yet come
no one laid a hand on him.

Jesus foretells his approaching departure

31 There were many people in the crowds, however, who believed in him; they
were saying, 'When the Christ comes, will he give more signs than this man?'
32 Hearing that rumours like this about him were spreading among the people,
the Pharisees sent the Temple police to arrest him.
33 Then Jesus said:

'I shall remain with you for only a short time now;
then I shall go back to the one who sent me.
34 You will look for me and will not find me:
where I am
you cannot come.'

35 The Jews then said to one another, 'Where is he going that we shan't be
able to find him? Is he going abroad to the people who are dispersed among
36 the Greeks and will he teach the Greeks? •What does he mean when he says:

"You will look for me and will not find me:
where I am,
you cannot come"?'

The promise of living water

37 On the last day and greatest day of the festival, Jesus stood there and cried
out:

'If any man is thirsty, let him come to me!
38 Let the man come and drink •who believes in me!'

As scripture says, From his breast shall flow fountains of living water.ᵉ
39 He was speaking of the Spirit which those who believed in him were to receive;
for there was no Spirit as yet because Jesus had not yet been glorified.

Fresh discussions on the origin of the Messiah

40 Several people who had been listening said, 'Surely he must be the prophet',
41 and some said, 'He is the Christ', but others said, 'Would the Christ be from

7 a. In the wide sense, as in Mt 12:46: relations of his own generation.   b. Those in Jerusalem
and Judaea.   c. Or 'In the crowds there was whispering about him'.   d. Although the
prophecy that the Messiah would be born in Bethlehem was well known, it was commonly
believed that he would appear suddenly from some secret place.   e. Life-giving water for
Zion was a theme of the readings from scripture on the feast of Tabernacles (Zc 14:8, Ezk 47:1f);
the liturgy included prayers for rain and the commemoration of the miracle of Moses and the
water, Ex 17.

Galilee? •Does not scripture say that the Christ must be descended from David 42
and come from the town of Bethlehem?' •So the people could not agree about 43
him. •Some would have liked to arrest him, but no one actually laid hands on 44
him.

The police went back to the chief priests and Pharisees who said to them, 45
'Why haven't you brought him?' •The police replied, 'There has never been 46
anybody who has spoken like him'. •'So' the Pharisees answered 'you have been 47
led astray as well? •Have any of the authorities believed in him? Any of the 48
Pharisees? •This rabble knows nothing about the Law—they are damned.' 49
One of them, Nicodemus—the same man who had come to Jesus earlier—said to 50
them, •'But surely the Law does not allow us to pass judgement on a man without 51
giving him a hearing and discovering what he is about?' •To this they answered, 52
'Are you a Galilean too? Go into the matter, and see for yourself: prophets do
not come out of Galilee.'

The adulterous woman[f]

They all went home, 8 and Jesus went to the Mount of Olives. ⁵³₁

At daybreak he appeared in the Temple again; and as all the people came 2
to him, he sat down and began to teach them.

The scribes and Pharisees brought a woman along who had been caught 3
committing adultery; and making her stand there in full view of everybody,
they said to Jesus, 'Master, this woman was caught in the very act of committing 4
adultery, •and Moses has ordered us in the Law to condemn women like this to 5
death by stoning. What have you to say?' •They asked him this as a test, looking 6
for something to use against him. But Jesus bent down and started writing on
the ground with his finger. •As they persisted with their question, he looked 7
up and said, 'If there is one of you who has not sinned, let him be the first to
throw a stone at her'. •Then he bent down and wrote on the ground again. 8
When they heard this they went away one by one, beginning with the eldest, 9
until Jesus was left alone with the woman, who remained standing there. •He 10
looked up and said, 'Woman, where are they? Has no one condemned you?'
'No one, sir' she replied. 'Neither do I condemn you,' said Jesus 'go away, and 11
don't sin any more.'

Jesus, the light of the world

When Jesus spoke to the people again, he said: 12

> 'I am the light of the world;
> anyone who follows me will not be walking in the dark;
> he will have the light of life'.

A discussion on the testimony of Jesus to himself

At this the Pharisees said to him, 'You are testifying on your own behalf; 13
your testimony is not valid'. •Jesus replied: 14

> 'It is true that I am testifying on my own behalf,
> but my testimony is still valid,
> because I know
> where I came from and where I am going;
> but you do not know
> where I come from or where I am going.
> You judge by human standards; 15
> I judge no one,
> but if I judge, 16
> my judgement will be sound,
> because I am not alone:
> the one who sent me is with me;
> and in your Law it is written 17

18 I may be testifying on my own behalf,
but the Father who sent me is my witness too.'

19 They asked him, 'Where is your Father?' Jesus answered:

'You do not know me, nor do you know my Father;
if you did know me, you would know my Father as well'.

20 He spoke these words in the Treasury, while teaching in the Temple. No one arrested him, because his time had not yet come.

The unbelieving Jews warned

21 Again he said to them:

'I am going away; you will look for me
and you will die in your sin.
Where I am going, you cannot come.'

22 The Jews said to one another, 'Will he kill himself? Is that what he means by
23 saying, "Where I am going, you cannot come"?' •Jesus went on:

'You are from below;
I am from above.
You are of this world;
I am not of this world.
24 I have told you already: You will die in your sins.
Yes, if you do not believe that I am He,
you will die in your sins.'

25 So they said to him, 'Who are you?' Jesus answered:

'What I have told you from the outset.
26 About you I have much to say
and much to condemn;
but the one who sent me is truthful,
and what I have learnt from him
I declare to the world.'

27 They failed to understand that he was talking to them about the Father.
28 So Jesus said:

'When you have lifted up the Son of Man,
then you will know that I am He
and that I do nothing of myself:
what the Father has taught me
is what I preach;
29 he who sent me is with me,
and has not left me to myself,
for I always do what pleases him'.

30 As he was saying this, many came to believe in him.

Jesus and Abraham

31 To the Jews who believed in him Jesus said:

'If you make my word your home
you will indeed be my disciples,
32 you will learn the truth
and the truth will make you free'.

---

f. The author of this passage is not John; the oldest MSS do not include it or place it elsewhere.
The style is that of the Synoptics.

They answered, 'We are descended from Abraham and we have never been 33
the slaves of anyone; what do you mean, "You will be made free"?' •Jesus replied: 34

'I tell you most solemnly,
everyone who commits sin is a slave.
Now the slave's place in the house is not assured, 35
but the son's place is assured.
So if the Son makes you free, 36
you will be free indeed.
I know that you are descended from Abraham; 37
but in spite of that you want to kill me
because nothing I say has penetrated into you.
What I, for my part, speak of 38
is what I have seen with my Father;
but you, you put into action
the lessons learnt from your father.'

They repeated, 'Our father is Abraham'. Jesus said to them: 39

'If you were Abraham's children,
you would do as Abraham did.
As it is, you want to kill me 40
when I tell you the truth
as I have learnt it from God;
that is not what Abraham did.
What you are doing is what your father does.' 41

'We were not born of prostitution,'ᵃ they went on 'we have one father: God.'
Jesus answered: 42

'If God were your father, you would love me,
since I have come here from God; yes, I have come from him;
not that I came because I chose,
no, I was sent, and by him.
Do you know why you cannot take in what I say? 43
It is because you are unable to understand my language.
The devil is your father, 44
and you prefer to do
what your father wants.
He was a murderer from the start;
he was never grounded in the truth;
there is no truth in him at all:
when he lies
he is drawing on his own store,
because he is a liar, and the father of lies.
But as for me, I speak the truth 45
and for that very reason,
you do not believe me.
Can one of you convict me of sin? 46
If I speak the truth, why do you not believe me?
A child of God 47
listens to the words of God;
if you refuse to listen,
it is because you are not God's children.'

The Jews replied, 'Are we not right in saying that you are a Samaritan and 48
possessed by a devil?' Jesus answered:

'I am not possessed; 49
no, I honour my Father,
but you want to dishonour me.

50 Not that I care for my own glory,
there is someone who takes care of that and is the judge of it.
51 I tell you most solemnly,
whoever keeps my word
will never see death.'

52 The Jews said, 'Now we know for certain that you are possessed. Abraham
is dead, and the prophets are dead, and yet you say, "Whoever keeps my word
53 will never know the taste of death". •Are you greater than our father Abraham,
54 who is dead? The prophets are dead too. Who are you claiming to be?' •Jesus
answered:

'If I were to seek my own glory
that would be no glory at all;
my glory is conferred by the Father,
by the one of whom you say, "He is our God"
55 although you do not know him.
But I know him,
and if I were to say: I do not know him,
I should be a liar, as you are liars yourselves.
But I do know him, and I faithfully keep his word.
56 Your father Abraham rejoiced
to think that he would see my Day;
he saw it and was glad.'

57 The Jews then said, 'You are not fifty yet, and you have seen Abraham!'
58 Jesus replied:

'I tell you most solemnly,
before Abraham ever was,
I Am'.

59 At this they picked up stones to throw at him;[b] but Jesus hid himself and left
the Temple.

The cure of the man born blind

9 ¹ ² As he went along, he saw a man who had been blind from birth. •His disciples
asked him, 'Rabbi, who sinned, this man or his parents, for him to have been
3 born blind?' •'Neither he nor his parents sinned,' Jesus answered 'he was born
blind so that the works of God might be displayed in him.

4 'As long as the day lasts
I must carry out the work of the one who sent me;
the night will soon be here when no one can work.
5 As long as I am in the world
I am the light of the world.'

6 Having said this, he spat on the ground, made a paste with the spittle, put
7 this over the eyes of the blind man. •and said to him, 'Go and wash in the Pool
of Siloam[a] (a name that means 'sent'). So the blind man went off and washed
himself, and came away with his sight restored.

8 His neighbours and people who earlier had seen him begging said, 'Isn't
9 this the man who used to sit and beg?' •Some said, 'Yes, it is the same one'.
Others said, 'No, he only looks like him'. The man himself said, 'I am the man'.
10 11 So they said to him, 'Then how do your eyes come to be open?' •The man called
Jesus' he answered 'made a paste, daubed my eyes with it and said to me, "Go

8 a. By 'prostitution' the prophets often mean religious infidelity, cf. Ho 1:2.   b. Stoning was
the penalty for blasphemy. Cf. 10:33.
9 a. Water from this pool was drawn during the feast of Tabernacles to symbolise the waters of
blessing.

and wash at Siloam"; so I went, and when I washed I could see.' •They asked, 12
'Where is he?' 'I don't know' he answered.

They brought the man who had been blind to the Pharisees. •It had been a $\begin{smallmatrix}13\\14\end{smallmatrix}$
sabbath day when Jesus made the paste and opened the man's eyes, •so when 15
the Pharisees asked him how he had come to see, he said, 'He put a paste on
my eyes, and I washed, and I can see'. •Then some of the Pharisees said, 'This 16
man cannot be from God: he does not keep the sabbath'. Others said, 'How
could a sinner produce signs like this?' And there was disagreement among them.
So they spoke to the blind man again, 'What have you to say about him yourself, 17
now that he has opened your eyes?' 'He is a prophet' replied the man.

However, the Jews would not believe that the man had been blind and had 18
gained his sight, without first sending for his parents and •asking them, 'Is this 19
man really your son who you say was born blind? If so, how is it that he is now
able to see?' •His parents answered, 'We know he is our son and we know he 20
was born blind, •but we don't know how it is that he can see now, or who 21
opened his eyes. He is old enough: let him speak for himself.' •His parents 22
spoke like this out of fear of the Jews, who had already agreed to expel from the
synagogue anyone who should acknowledge Jesus as the Christ. •This was why 23
his parents said, 'He is old enough; ask him'.

So the Jews again sent for the man and said to him, 'Give glory to God!^{b} 24
For our part, we know that this man is a sinner.' •The man answered, 'I don't 25
know if he is a sinner; I only know that I was blind and now I can see'. •They 26
said to him, 'What did he do to you? How did he open your eyes?' •He replied, 27
'I have told you once and you wouldn't listen. Why do you want to hear it all
again? Do you want to become his disciples too?' •At this they hurled abuse 28
at him: 'You can be his disciple,' they said 'we are disciples of Moses: •we 29
know that God spoke to Moses, but as for this man, we don't know where he
comes from'. •The man replied, 'Now here is an astonishing thing! He has 30
opened my eyes, and you don't know where he comes from! •We know that God 31
doesn't listen to sinners, but God does listen to men who are devout and do his
will. •Ever since the world began it is unheard of for anyone to open the eyes 32
of a man who was born blind; •if this man were not from God, he couldn't do 33
a thing.' •'Are you trying to teach us,' they replied 'and you a sinner through 34
and through, since you were born!' And they drove him away.

Jesus heard they had driven him away, and when he found him he said to 35
him, 'Do you believe in the Son of Man?' •'Sir,' the man replied 'tell me who 36
he is so that I may believe in him.' •Jesus said, 'You are looking at him; he is 37
speaking to you'. • The man said, 'Lord, I believe', and worshipped him. 38
Jesus said: 39

'It is for judgement
that I have come into this world,
so that those without sight may see
and those with sight turn blind'.

Hearing this, some Pharisees who were present said to him, 'We are not blind, 40
surely?' •Jesus replied: 41

'Blind? If you were,
you would not be guilty,
but since you say, "We see",
your guilt remains.

The good shepherd

10 'I tell you most solemnly, anyone who does not enter the sheepfold 1
through the gate, but gets in some other way is a thief and a brigand.
The one who enters through the gate is the shepherd of the flock; •the $\frac{2}{3}$
gatekeeper lets him in, the sheep hear his voice, one by one he calls his

4 own sheep and leads them out. •When he has brought out his flock, he goes
5 ahead of them, and the sheep follow because they know his voice. •They never
follow a stranger but run away from him: they do not recognise the voice of
strangers.'

6 Jesus told them[a] this parable but they failed to understand what he meant
by telling it to them.

7 So Jesus spoke to them again:

'I tell you most solemnly,
I am the gate of the sheepfold.
8 All others who have come
are thieves and brigands;
but the sheep took no notice of them.
9 I am the gate.
Anyone who enters through me will be safe:
he will go freely in and out
and be sure of finding pasture.
10 The thief comes
only to steal and kill and destroy.
I have come
so that they may have life
and have it to the full.
11 I am the good shepherd:
the good shepherd is one who lays down his life for his sheep.
12 The hired man, since he is not the shepherd
and the sheep do not belong to him,
abandons the sheep and runs away
as soon as he sees a wolf coming,
and then the wolf attacks and scatters the sheep;
13 this is because he is only a hired man
and has no concern for the sheep.
14 I am the good shepherd;
I know my own
and my own know me,
15 just as the Father knows me
and I know the Father;
and I lay down my life for my sheep.
16 And there are other sheep I have
that are not of this fold,
and these I have to lead as well.
They too will listen to my voice,
and there will be only one flock,
and one shepherd.
17 The Father loves me,
because I lay down my life
in order to take it up again.
18 No one takes it from me;
I lay it down of my own free will,
and as it is in my power to lay it down,
so it is in my power to take it up again;
and this is the command I have been given by my Father.'

19
20 These words caused disagreement among the Jews. •Many said, 'He is
21 possessed, he is raving; why bother to listen to him?' •Others said, 'These are
not the words of a man possessed by a devil: could a devil open the eyes of the
blind?'

b. I.e. putting the man on oath.
10 a. The Pharisees.

VI. THE FEAST OF DEDICATION

Jesus claims to be the Son of God

It was the time when the feast of Dedication was being celebrated in Jerusalem. 22
It was winter, •and Jesus was in the Temple walking up and down in the Portico 23
of Solomon. •The Jews gathered round him and said, 'How much longer are 24
you going to keep us in suspense? If you are the Christ, tell us plainly.' •Jesus 25
replied:

> 'I have told you, but you do not believe.
> The works I do in my Father's name are my witness;
> but you do not believe, 26
> because you are no sheep of mine.
> The sheep that belong to me listen to my voice; 27
> I know them and they follow me.
> I give them eternal life; 28
> they will never be lost
> and no one will ever steal them from me.
> The Father who gave them to me is greater than anyone, 29
> and no one can steal from the Father.
> The Father and I are one.' 30

The Jews fetched stones to stone him, •so Jesus said to them, 'I have done 31
many good works for you to see, works from my Father; for which of these 32
are you stoning me?' •The Jews answered him, 'We are not stoning you for doing 33
a good work but for blasphemy: you are only a man and you claim to be God'.
Jesus answered: 34

> 'Is it not written in your Law:
> *I said, you are gods?* [b]
>
> So the Law uses the word gods 35
> of those to whom the word of God was addressed,
> and scripture cannot be rejected.
> Yet you say to someone the Father has consecrated and sent 36
>   into the world,
> "You are blaspheming",
> because he says, "I am the Son of God".
> If I am not doing my Father's work, 37
> there is no need to believe me;
> but if I am doing it, 38
> then even if you refuse to believe in me,
> at least believe in the work I do;
> then you will know for sure
> that the Father is in me and I am in the Father.'

They wanted to arrest him then, but he eluded them. 39

Jesus withdraws to the other side of the Jordan

He went back again to the far side of the Jordan to stay in the district where 40
John had once been baptising. •Many people who came to him there said, 'John 41
gave no signs, but all he said about this man was true'; •and many of them 42
believed in him.

The resurrection of Lazarus

11 There was a man named Lazarus who lived in the village of Bethany with 1
the two sisters, Mary and Martha, and he was ill.—•It was the same 2
Mary, the sister of the sick man Lazarus, who anointed the Lord with
ointment and wiped his feet with her hair. •The sisters sent this message to 3

4 Jesus, 'Lord, the man you love is ill'. •On receiving the message, Jesus said,
'This sickness will end not in death but in God's glory, and through it the Son
of God will be glorified'.

5
6   Jesus loved Martha and her sister and Lazarus, •yet when he heard that
7 Lazarus was ill he stayed where he was for two more days •before saying to the
8 disciples, 'Let us go to Judaea'. •The disciples said, 'Rabbi, it is not long since
9 the Jews wanted to stone you; are you going back again?' •Jesus replied:

> 'Are there not twelve hours in the day?
> A man can walk in the daytime without stumbling
>   because he has the light of this world to see by;
10 > but if he walks at night he stumbles,
>   because there is no light to guide him.'

11   He said that and then added, 'Our friend Lazarus is resting, I am going to
12 wake him'. •The disciples said to him, 'Lord, if he is able to rest he is sure to get
13 better'. •The phrase Jesus used referred to the death of Lazarus, but they thought
14
15 that by 'rest' he meant 'sleep', so •Jesus put it plainly, 'Lazarus is dead; •and
for your sake I am glad I was not there because now you will believe. But let
16 us go to him.' •Then Thomas—known as the Twin—said to the other disciples,
'Let us go too, and die with him'. •

17   On arriving, Jesus found that Lazarus had been in the tomb for four days
18
19 already. •Bethany is only about two miles from Jerusalem, •and many Jews had
20 come to Martha and Mary to sympathise with them over their brother. •When
Martha heard that Jesus had come she went to meet him. Mary remained sitting
21 in the house. •Martha said to Jesus, 'If you had been here, my brother would
22 not have died, •but I know that, even now, whatever you ask of God, he will
23
24 grant you'. •'Your brother' said Jesus to her 'will rise again.' •Martha said,
25 'I know he will rise again at the resurrection on the last day'. •Jesus said:

> 'I am the resurrection.
> If anyone believes in me, even though he dies he will live,
26 > and whoever lives and believes in me
> will never die.
> Do you believe this?'

27 'Yes, Lord,' she said 'I believe that you are the Christ, the Son of God, the one
who was to come into this world.'

28   When she had said this, she went and called her sister Mary, saying in a low
29 voice, 'The Master is here and wants to see you'. •Hearing this, Mary got up
30 quickly and went to him. •Jesus had not yet come into the village; he was still
31 at the place where Martha had met him. •When the Jews who were in the house
sympathising with Mary saw her get up so quickly and go out, they followed
her, thinking that she was going to the tomb to weep there.

32   Mary went to Jesus, and as soon as she saw him she threw herself at his
33 feet, saying, 'Lord, if you had been here, my brother would not have died'. •At
the sight of her tears, and those of the Jews who followed her, Jesus said in great
34 distress, with a sigh that came straight from the heart, •'Where have you put
35
36 him?' They said, 'Lord, come and see'. •Jesus wept; •and the Jews said, 'See
37 how much he loved him!' •But there were some who remarked, 'He opened the
38 eyes of the blind man, could he not have prevented this man's death?' •Still
sighing, Jesus reached the tomb: it was a cave with a stone to close the opening.
39 Jesus said, 'Take the stone away'. Martha said to him, 'Lord, by now he will
40 smell; this is the fourth day'. •Jesus replied, 'Have I not told you that if you
41 believe you will see the glory of God?' •So they took away the stone. Then
Jesus lifted up his eyes and said:

b. Ps 82:6

'Father, I thank you for hearing my prayer. I knew indeed that you always hear me, but I speak for the sake of all these who stand round me, so that they may believe it was you who sent me.' 42

When he had said this, he cried in a loud voice, 'Lazarus, here! Come out!' 43 The dead man came out, his feet and hands bound with bands of stuff and a 44 cloth round his face. Jesus said to them, 'Unbind him, let him go free'.

The Jewish leaders decide on the death of Jesus

Many of the Jews who had come to visit Mary and had seen what he did 45 believed in him, •but some of them went to tell the Pharisees what Jesus had 46 done. •Then the chief priests and Pharisees called a meeting. 'Here is this man 47 working all these signs' they said 'and what action are we taking? •If we let 48 him go on in this way everybody will believe in him, and the Romans will come and destroy the Holy Place and our nation.' •One of them, Caiaphas, the 49 high priest that year, said, 'You don't seem to have grasped the situation at all; you fail to see that it is better for one man to die for the people, than for the 50 whole nation to be destroyed'. •He did not speak in his own person, it was as 51 high priest that he made this prophecy that Jesus was to die for the nation— and not for the nation only, but to gather together in unity the scattered children 52 of God. •From that day they were determined to kill him. •So Jesus no longer 53/54 went about openly among the Jews, but left the district for a town called Ephraim, in the country bordering on the desert, and stayed there with his disciples.

VII. THE LAST PASSOVER

A. BEFORE THE PASSION

The Passover draws near

The Jewish Passover drew near, and many of the country people who had 55 gone up to Jerusalem to purify themselves •looked out for Jesus, saying to one 56 another as they stood about in the Temple, 'What do you think? Will he come to the festival or not?' •The chief priests and Pharisees had by now given their 57 orders: anyone who knew where he was must inform them so that they could arrest him.

The anointing at Bethany

12 Six days before the Passover, Jesus went to Bethany, where Lazarus 1 was, whom he had raised from the dead. •They gave a dinner for him 2 there; Martha waited on them and Lazarus was among those at table. •Mary 3 brought in a pound of very costly ointment, pure nard, and with it anointed the feet of Jesus, wiping them with her hair; the house was full of the scent of the ointment. •Then Judas Iscariot—one of his disciples, the man who was to betray 4 him—said, •'Why wasn't this ointment sold for three hundred denarii, and the 5 money given to the poor?' •He said this, not because he cared about the poor, 6 but because he was a thief; he was in charge of the common fund and used to help himself to the contributions. •So Jesus said, 'Leave her alone; she had to 7 keep this scent for the day of my burial. •You have the poor with you always, 8 you will not always have me.'

Meanwhile a large number of Jews heard that he was there and came not 9 only on account of Jesus but also to see Lazarus whom he had raised from the dead. •Then the chief priests decided to kill Lazarus as well, •since it was on his 10/11 account that many of the Jews were leaving them and believing in Jesus.

The Messiah enters Jerusalem

12 The next day the crowds who had come up for the festival heard that Jesus
13 was on his way to Jerusalem. •They took branches of palm and went out to
meet him, shouting, '*Hosanna! Blessings on* the King of Israel, *who comes in the*
14 *name of the Lord.*'*ᵃ* •Jesus found a young donkey and mounted it—as scripture
15 says: • *Do not be afraid, daughter of Zion; see, your king is coming, mounted on*
16 *the colt of a donkey.*ᵇ •At the time his disciples did not understand this, but later,
after Jesus had been glorified, they remembered that this had been written
17 about him and that this was in fact how they had received him. •All who had
been with him when he called Lazarus out of the tomb and raised him from the
18 dead were telling how they had witnessed it; •it was because of this, too, that
the crowd came out to meet him: they had heard that he had given this sign.
19 Then the Pharisees said to one another, 'You see, there is nothing you can do;
look, the whole world is running after him!'

Jesus foretells his death and subsequent glorification

20 Among those who went up to worship at the festival were some Greeks.ᶜ
21 These approached Philip, who came from Bethsaida in Galilee, and put this
22 request to him, 'Sir, we should like to see Jesus'. •Philip went to tell Andrew,
and Andrew and Philip together went to tell Jesus.
23 Jesus replied to them:

'Now the hour has come
for the Son of Man to be glorified.
24 I tell you, most solemnly,
unless a wheat grain falls on the ground and dies,
it remains only a single grain;
but if it dies,
it yields a rich harvest.
25 Anyone who loves his life loses it;
anyone who hates his life in this world
will keep it for the eternal life.
26 If a man serves me, he must follow me,
wherever I am, my servant will be there too.
If anyone serves me, my Father will honour him.
27 Now my soul is troubled.
What shall I say:
Father, save me from this hour?
But it was for this very reason that I have come to this hour.
28 Father, glorify your name!'

A voice came from heaven, 'I have glorified it, and I will glorify it again'.
29 People standing by, who heard this, said it was a clap of thunder; others
30 said, 'It was an angel speaking to him'. •Jesus answered, 'It was not for my sake
that this voice came, but for yours.

31 'Now sentence is being passed on this world;
now the prince of this world is to be overthrown.ᵈ
32 And when I am lifted up from the earth,
I shall draw all men to myself.'

33
34 By these words he indicated the kind of death he would die. •The crowd
answered, 'The Law has taught us that the Christ will remain for ever. How can
35 you say, "The Son of Man must be lifted up"? Who is this Son of Man?' •Jesus
then said:

12 a. Ps 118:26   **b.** Zc 9:9f   **c.** The 'God-fearing men' of Ac 10:2: converts who observed
certain specific Mosaic observances.   **d.** Satan.

'The light will be with you only a little longer now.
Walk while you have the light,
or the dark will overtake you;
he who walks in the dark does not know where he is going.
While you still have the light,   36
believe in the light
and you will become sons of light.'

Having said this, Jesus left them and kept himself hidden.

Conclusion: the unbelief of the Jews

Though they had been present when he gave so many signs, they did not 37
believe in him; •this was to fulfil the words of the prophet Isaiah: *Lord, who* 38
could believe what we have heard said, and to whom has the power of the Lord
been revealed?• •Indeed, they were unable to believe because, as Isaiah says 39
again: • *He has blinded their eyes, he has hardened their heart, for fear they should* 40
see with their eyes and understand with their heart, and turn to me for healing.[f]

Isaiah said this when he saw his glory,[g] and his words referred to Jesus. 41

And yet there were many who did believe in him, even among the leading 42
men, but they did not admit it, •through fear of the Pharisees and fear of being
expelled from the synagogue: •they put honour from men before the honour 43
that comes from God.

Jesus declared publicly: 44

'Whoever believes in me
believes not in me
but in the one who sent me,
and whoever sees me, 45
sees the óne who sent me.
I, the light, have come into the world, 46
so that whoever believes in me
need not stay in the dark any more.
If anyone hears my words and does not keep them faithfully, 47
it is not I who shall condemn him,
since I have come not to condemn the world,
but to save the world:
he who rejects me and refuses my words 48
has his judge already:
the word itself that I have spoken
will be his judge on the last day.
For what I have spoken does not come from myself; 49
no, what I was to say, what I had to speak,
was commanded by the Father who sent me,
and I know that his commands mean eternal life. 50
And therefore what the Father has told me
is what I speak.'

B. THE LAST SUPPER

Jesus washes his disciples' feet

13 It was before the festival of the Passover, and Jesus knew that the hour 1
had come for him to pass from this world to the Father. He had always
loved those who were his in the world, but now he showed how perfect his
love was.

They were at supper, and the devil had already put it into the mind of 2
Judas Iscariot son of Simon, to betray him. •Jesus knew that the Father had 3
put everything into his hands, and that he had come from God and was returning

4 to God, •and he got up from table, removed his outer garment and, taking a
5 towel, wrapped it round his waist; •he then poured water into a basin and
began to wash the disciples' feet[a] and to wipe them with the towel he was wearing.

6   He came to Simon Peter, who said to him, 'Lord, are you going to wash my
7 feet?' •Jesus answered, 'At the moment you do not know what I am doing, but
8 later you will understand'. •'Never!' said Peter 'You shall never wash my feet.'
Jesus replied, 'If I do not wash you, you can have nothing in common with me'.
9 'Then, Lord,' said Simon Peter 'not only my feet, but my hands and my head
10 as well!' •Jesus said, 'No one who has taken a bath needs washing, he is clean
11 all over. You too are clean, though not all of you are.' •He knew who was
going to betray him, that was why he said, 'though not all of you are'.

12   When he had washed their feet and put on his clothes again he went back
13 to the table. 'Do you understand' he said 'what I have done to you? •You call
14 me Master and Lord, and rightly; so I am. •If I, then, the Lord and Master,
15 have washed your feet, you should wash each other's feet. •I have given you
an example so that you may copy what I have done to you.

16   'I tell you most solemnly,
                    no servant is greater than his master,
                    no messenger is greater than the man who sent him.

17   'Now that you know this, happiness will be yours if you behave accordingly.
18 I am not speaking about all of you: I know the ones I have chosen; but what
scripture says must be fulfilled: *Someone who shares my table rebels against me*.[b]

19   'I tell you this now, before it happens,
                    so that when it does happen
                    you may believe that I am He.
20   I tell you most solemnly,
                    whoever welcomes the one I send welcomes me,
                    and whoever welcomes me welcomes the one who sent me.'

The treachery of Judas foretold

21   Having said this, Jesus was troubled in spirit and declared, 'I tell you most
22 solemnly, one of you will betray me'. •The disciples looked at one another,
23 wondering which he meant. •The disciple Jesus loved was reclining next
24
25 to Jesus; •Simon Peter signed to him and said, 'Ask who it is he means', •so
26 leaning back on Jesus' breast he said, 'Who is it, Lord?' •'It is the one' replied
Jesus 'to whom I give the piece of bread that I shall dip in the dish.' He dipped
27 the piece of bread and gave it to Judas son of Simon Iscariot. •At that instant,
after Judas had taken the bread, Satan entered him. Jesus then said, 'What you
28 are going to do, do quickly'. •None of the others at table understood the reason
29 he said this. •Since Judas had charge of the common fund, some of them thought
Jesus was telling him, 'Buy what we need for the festival', or telling him to give
30 something to the poor. •As soon as Judas had taken the piece of bread he went
out. Night had fallen.

31   When he had gone Jesus said:

                    'Now has the Son of Man been glorified,
                    and in him God has been glorified.
32   If God has been glorified in him,
                    God will in turn glorify him in himself,[c]
                    and will glorify him very soon.

---

e. Is 53:1   f. Is 6:9f   g. Isaiah's vision in the Temple, Is 6:4, interpreted as a prophetic
vision of Christ's glory.

13 a. The dress and the duty are those of a slave.   b. Ps 41:9   c. I.e. the Father will take
the Son of Man to himself in glory.

Farewell discourses

'My little children,   33
I shall not be with you much longer.
You will look for me,
and, as I told the Jews,
where I am going,
you cannot come.
I give you a new commandment: 34
love one another;
just as I have loved you,
you also must love one another.
By this love you have for one another,   35
everyone will know that you are my disciples.'

Simon Peter said, 'Lord, where are you going?' Jesus replied, 'Where I am 36
going you cannot follow me now; you will follow me later'. •Peter said to him, 37
'Why can't I follow you now? I will lay down my life for you.' •'Lay down your 38
life for me?' answered Jesus. 'I tell you most solemnly, before the cock crows
you will have disowned me three times.

14 'Do not let your hearts be troubled.   1
Trust in God still, and trust in me.
There are many rooms in my Father's house;   2
if there were not, I should have told you.
I am going now to prepare a place for you,
and after I have gone and prepared you a place,   3
I shall return to take you with me;
so that where I am
you may be too.
You know the way to the place where I am going.'   4

Thomas said, 'Lord, we do not know where you are going, so how can we 5
know the way?' •Jesus said: 6

'I am the Way, the Truth and the Life.
No one can come to the Father except through me.
If you know me, you know my Father too.
From this moment you know him and have seen him.'   7

Philip said, 'Lord, let us see the Father and then we shall be satisfied'. 8
'Have I been with you all this time, Philip,' said Jesus to him 'and you still do 9
not know me?

'To have seen me is to have seen the Father,
so how can you say, "Let us see the Father"?
Do you not believe   10
that I am in the Father and the Father is in me?
The words I say to you I do not speak as from myself:
it is the Father, living in me, who is doing this work.
You must believe me when I say   11
that I am in the Father and the Father is in me;
believe it on the evidence of this work, if for no other reason.
I tell you most solemnly,   12
whoever believes in me
will perform the same works as I do myself,
he will perform even greater works,
because I am going to the Father.
Whatever you ask for in my name I will do,   13
so that the Father may be glorified in the Son.

14 If you ask for anything in my name,
I will do it.

15 If you love me you will keep my commandments.

16 I shall ask the Father,
and he will give you another Advocate[a]
to be with you for ever,

17 that Spirit of truth
whom the world can never receive
since it neither sees nor knows him;
but you know him,
because he is with you, he is in you.

18 I will not leave you orphans;
I will come back to you.

19 In a short time the world will no longer see me;
but you will see me,
because I live and you will live.

20 On that day
you will understand that I am in my Father
and you in me and I in you.

21 Anybody who receives my commandments and keeps them
will be one who loves me;
and anybody who loves me will be loved by my Father,
and I shall love him and show myself to him.'

22 Judas[b]—this was not Judas Iscariot—said to him, 'Lord, what is all this
23 about? Do you intend to show yourself to us and not to the world?' •Jesus
replied:

'If anyone loves me he will keep my word,
and my Father will love him,
and we shall come to him
and make our home with him.

24 Those who do not love me do not keep my words.
And my word is not my own:
it is the word of the one who sent me.

25 I have said these things to you
while still with you;

26 but the Advocate, the Holy Spirit,
whom the Father will send in my name,
will teach you everything
and remind you of all I have said to you.

27 Peace[c] I bequeath to you,
my own peace I give you,
a peace the world cannot give, this is my gift to you.
Do not let your hearts be troubled or afraid.

28 You heard me say:
I am going away, and shall return.
If you loved me you would have been glad to know that I am
going to the Father,
for the Father is greater than I.

29 I have told you this now before it happens,
so that when it does happen you may believe.

30 I shall not talk with you any longer,
because the prince of this world is on his way.

14 a. Greek *parakletos*: advocate or counsellor or protector. b. 'Judas, brother of James' in
Lk 6:16 and Ac 1:13; the Thaddaeus of Mt 10:3 and Mk 3:18. c. The customary Jewish
farewell.

He has no power over me,
but the world must be brought to know that I love the Father   31
and that I am doing exactly what the Father told me.
Come now, let us go.

The true vine

15   'I am the true vine,   1
and my Father is the vinedresser.
Every branch in me that bears no fruit   2
he cuts away,
and every branch that does bear fruit he prunes
to make it bear even more.
You are pruned already,   3
by means of the word that I have spoken to you.
Make your home in me, as I make mine in you.   4
As a branch cannot bear fruit all by itself,
but must remain part of the vine,
neither can you unless you remain in me.
I am the vine,   5
you are the branches.
Whoever remains in me, with me in him,
bears fruit in plenty;
for cut off from me you can do nothing.
Anyone who does not remain in me   6
is like a branch that has been thrown away
—he withers;
these branches are collected and thrown on the fire,
and they are burnt.
If you remain in me   7
and my words remain in you,
you may ask what you will
and you shall get it.
It is to the glory of my Father that you should bear much fruit,   8
and then you will be my disciples.
As the Father has loved me,   9
so I have loved you.
Remain in my love.
If you keep my commandments   10
you will remain in my love,
just as I have kept my Father's commandments
and remain in his love.
I have told you this   11
so that my own joy may be in you
and your joy be complete.
This is my commandment: 12
love one another,
as I have loved you.
A man can have no greater love   13
than to lay down his life for his friends.
You are my friends,   14
if you do what I command you.
I shall not call you servants any more,   15
because a servant does not know
his master's business;
I call you friends,
because I have made known to you
everything I have learnt from my Father.

16   You did not choose me,
no, I chose you;
and I commissioned you
to go out and to bear fruit,
fruit that will last;
and then the Father will give you
anything you ask him in my name.

17   What I command you
is to love one another.

The hostile world

18   'If the world hates you,
remember that it hated me before you.

19   If you belonged to the world,
the world would love you as its own;
but because you do not belong to the world,
because my choice withdrew you from the world
therefore the world hates you.

20   Remember the words I said to you:
A servant is not greater than his master.
If they persecuted me,
they will persecute you too;
if they kept my word,
they will keep yours as well.

21   But it will be on my account that they will do all this
because they do not know the one who sent me.

22   If I had not come,
if I had not spoken to them,
they would have been blameless;
but as it is they have no excuse for their sin.

23   Anyone who hates me hates my Father.

24   If I had not performed such works among them
as no one else has ever done,
they would be blameless;
but as it is, they have seen all this,
and still they hate both me and my Father.

25   But all this was only to fulfil the words written in their Law:
They hated me for no reason.[a]

26   When the Advocate comes,
whom I shall send to you from the Father,
the Spirit of truth who issues from the Father,
he will be my witness.

27   And you too will be witnesses,
because you have been with me from the outset.

16
1   'I have told you all this
so that your faith may not be shaken.

2   They will expel you from the synagogues,
and indeed the hour is coming
when anyone who kills you will think he is doing a holy duty for God

3   They will do these things
because they have never known either the Father or myself.

4   But I have told you all this,
so that when the time for it comes
you may remember that I told you

15 a. Ps 35:19

The coming of the Advocate

'I did not tell you this from the outset,
because I was with you;
but now I am going to the one who sent me.   5
Not one of you has asked, "Where are you going?"
Yet you are sad at heart because I have told you this.   6
Still, I must tell you the truth: 7
it is for your own good that I am going
because unless I go,
the Advocate will not come to you;
but if I do go,
I will send him to you.
And when he comes,   8
he will show the world how wrong it was,
about sin,
and about who was in the right,
and about judgement:
about sin: 9
proved by their refusal to believe in me;
about who was in the right: 10
proved by my going to the Father
and your seeing me no more;
about judgement: 11
proved by the prince of this world being already condemned.
I still have many things to say to you   12
but they would be too much for you now.
But when the Spirit of truth comes   13
he will lead you to the complete truth,
since he will not be speaking as from himself
but will say only what he has learnt;
and he will tell you of the things to come.
He will glorify me,   14
since all he tells you
will be taken from what is mine.
Everything the Father has is mine;   15
that is why I said:
All he tells you
will be taken from what is mine.

Jesus to return very soon

'In a short time you will no longer see me,   16
and then a short time later you will see me again.'

Then some of his disciples said to one another, 'What does he mean, "In a 17
short time you will no longer see me, and then a short time later you will see me
again" and, "I am going to the Father"? •What is this "short time"? We don't 18
know what he means.' •Jesus knew that they wanted to question him, so he 19
said, 'You are asking one another what I meant by saying: In a short time you
will no longer see me, and then a short time later you will see me again.

'I tell you most solemnly,   20
you will be weeping and wailing
while the world will rejoice;
you will be sorrowful,
but your sorrow will turn to joy.
A woman in childbirth suffers,   21
because her time has come;

but when she has given birth to the child she forgets the suffering
in her joy that a man has been born into the world.

22 So it is with you: you are sad now,
but I shall see you again, and your hearts will be full of joy,
and that joy no one shall take from you.

23 When that day comes,
you will not ask me any questions.
I tell you most solemnly,
anything you ask for from the Father
he will grant in my name.

24 Until now you have not asked for anything in my name.
Ask and you will receive,
and so your joy will be complete.

25 I have been telling you all this in metaphors,
the hour is coming
when I shall no longer speak to you in metaphors;
but tell you about the Father in plain words.

26 When that day comes
you will ask in my name;
and I do not say that I shall pray to the Father for you,

27 because the Father himself loves you
for loving me
and believing that I came from God.

28 I came from the Father and have come into the world
and now I leave the world to go to the Father.'

29 His disciples said, 'Now you are speaking plainly and not using metaphors!
30 Now we see that you know everything, and do not have to wait for questions to
31 be put into words; because of this we believe that you came from God.' •Jesus
answered them:

'Do you believe at last?

32 Listen; the time will come—in fact it has come already—
when you will be scattered, each going his own way
and leaving me alone.
And yet I am not alone,
because the Father is with me.

33 I have told you all this
so that you may find peace in me.
In the world you will have trouble,
but be brave:
I have conquered the world.'

The priestly prayer of Christ

17 After saying this, Jesus raised his eyes to heaven and said:

1 'Father, the hour has come:
glorify your Son
so that your Son may glorify you;

2 and, through the power over all mankind^a that you have given him,
let him give eternal **life** to all those you have entrusted to him.

3 And eternal life is this:
to know you,
the only true God,
and Jesus Christ whom you have sent.

17 a. Lit. 'all flesh'.

I have glorified you on earth   4
and finished the work
that you gave me to do.
Now, Father, it is time for you to glorify me   5
with that glory I had with you
before ever the world was.
I have made your name known   6
to the men you took from the world to give me.
They were yours and you gave them to me,
and they have kept your word.
Now at last they know   7
that all you have given me comes indeed from you;
for I have given them   8
the teaching you gave to me,
and they have truly accepted this, that I came from you,
and have believed that it was you who sent me.
I pray for them;   9
I am not praying for the world
but for those you have given me,
because they belong to you:
all I have is yours   10
and all you have is mine,
and in them I am glorified.
I am not in the world any longer,   11
but they are in the world,
and I am coming to you.
Holy Father,
keep those you have given me true to your name,
so that they may be one like us.
While I was with them,   12
I kept those you had given me true to your name.
I have watched over them and not one is lost
except the one who chose to be lost,[b]
and this was to fulfil the scriptures.
But now I am coming to you   13
and while still in the world I say these things
to share my joy with them to the full.
I passed your word on to them,   14
and the world hated them,
because they belong to the world
no more than I belong to the world.
I am not asking you to remove them from the world,   15
but to protect them from the evil one.
They do not belong to the world   16
any more than I belong to the world.
Consecrate them in the truth;   17
your word is truth.
As you sent me into the world,   18
I have sent them into the world,
and for their sake I consecrate myself   19
so that they too may be consecrated in truth.
I pray not only for these,   20
but for those also
who through their words will believe in me.
May they all be one.   21
Father, may they be one in us,

as you are in me and I am in you,
so that the world may believe it was you who sent me.

22 I have given them the glory you gave to me,
that they may be one as we are one.

23 With me in them and you in me,
may they be so completely one
that the world will realise that it was you who sent me
and that I have loved them as much as you loved me.

24 Father,
I want those you have given me
to be with me where I am,
so that they may always see the glory
you have given me
because you loved me
before the foundation of the world.

25 Father, Righteous One,
the world has not known you,
but I have known you,
and these have known
that you have sent me.

26 I have made your name known to them
and will continue to make it known,
so that the love with which you loved me may be in them,
and so that I may be in them.'

C. THE PASSION

The arrest of Jesus

1 18 After he had said all this Jesus left with his disciples and crossed the
Kedron valley. There was a garden there, and he went into it with his
2 disciples. •Judas the traitor knew the place well, since Jesus had often met his
3 disciples there, •and he brought the cohort[a] to this place together with a detachment of guards sent by the chief priests and the Pharisees, all with lanterns and
4 torches and weapons. •Knowing everything that was going to happen to him,
5 Jesus then came forward and said, 'Who are you looking for?' •They answered,
'Jesus the Nazarene'. He said, 'I am he'. Now Judas the traitor was standing
6 among them. •When Jesus said, 'I am he', they moved back and fell to the ground.
7 He asked them a second time, 'Who are you looking for?' They said, 'Jesus the
8 Nazarene'. •'I have told you that I am he' replied Jesus. 'If I am the one you
9 are looking for, let these others go.' •This was to fulfil the words he had spoken,
'Not one of those you gave me have I lost'.

10 Simon Peter, who carried a sword, drew it and wounded the high priest's ser-
11 vant, cutting off his right ear. The servant's name was Malchus. •Jesus said to
Peter, 'Put your sword back in its scabbard; am I not to drink the cup that the
Father has given me?'

Jesus before Annas and Caiaphas. Peter disowns him

12 The cohort and its captain and the Jewish guards seized Jesus and bound
13 him. •They took him first to Annas, because Annas was the father-in-law of
14 Caiaphas, who was high priest that year. •It was Caiaphas who had suggested
to the Jews, 'It is better for one man to die for the people'.

15 Simon Peter, with another disciple, followed Jesus. This disciple, who was
16 known to the high priest, went with Jesus into the high priest's palace, •but

b. Lit. 'the son of perdition'.
18 a. A detachment from the Roman garrison in Jerusalem.

Peter stayed outside the door. So the other disciple, the one known to the high priest, went out, spoke to the woman who was keeping the door and brought Peter in. •The maid on duty at the door said to Peter, 'Aren't you another of 17 that man's disciples?' He answered, 'I am not'. •Now it was cold, and the servants 18 and guards had lit a charcoal fire and were standing there warming themselves; so Peter stood there too, warming himself with the others.

The high priest questioned Jesus about his disciples and his teaching. •Jesus $^{19}_{20}$ answered, 'I have spoken openly for all the world to hear; I have always taught in the synagogue and in the Temple where all the Jews meet together; I have said nothing in secret. •But why ask me? Ask my hearers what I taught: they know 21 what I said.' •At these words, one of the guards standing by gave Jesus a slap 22 in the face, saying, 'Is that the way to answer the high priest?' •Jesus replied, 'If 23 there is something wrong in what I said, point it out; but if there is no offence in it, why do you strike me?' •Then Annas sent him, still bound, to Caiaphas 24 the high priest.

As Simon Peter stood there warming himself, someone said to him, 'Aren't 25 you another of his disciples?' He denied it saying, 'I am not'. •One of the high 26 priest's servants, a relation of the man whose ear Peter had cut off, said, 'Didn't I see you in the garden with him?' •Again Peter denied it; and at once a cock 27 crew.

Jesus before Pilate

They then led Jesus from the house of Caiaphas to the Praetorium.*b* It was 28 now morning. They did not go into the Praetorium themselves or they would be defiled*c* and unable to eat the passover. •So Pilate came outside to them and 29 said, 'What charge do you bring against this man?' They replied, •'If he were 30 not a criminal, we should not be handing him over to you'. •Pilate said, 'Take 31 him yourselves, and try him by your own Law'. The Jews answered, 'We are not allowed to put a man to death'. •This was to fulfil the words Jesus had spoken 32 indicating the way he was going to die.

So Pilate went back into the Praetorium and called Jesus to him, 'Are you 33 the king of the Jews?' he asked. •Jesus replied, 'Do you ask this of your own 34 accord, or have others spoken to you about me?' •Pilate answered, 'Am I a Jew? 35 It is your own people and the chief priests who have handed you over to me: what have you done?' •Jesus replied, 'Mine is not a kingdom of this world; if 36 my kingdom were of this world, my men would have fought to prevent my being surrendered to the Jews. But my kingdom is not of this kind.' •'So you are a 37 king then?' said Pilate. 'It is you who say it' answered Jesus. 'Yes, I am a king. I was born for this, I came into the world for this: to bear witness to the truth; and all who are on the side of truth listen to my voice.' •'Truth?' said Pilate 38 'What is that?'; and with that he went out again to the Jews and said, 'I find no case against him. •But according to a custom of yours I should release one 39 prisoner at the Passover; would you like me, then, to release the king of the Jews?' •At this they shouted: 'Not this man,' they said 'but Barabbas'. Barabbas 40 was a brigand.

19 Pilate then had Jesus taken away and scourged; •and after this, the soldiers $^{1}_{2}$ twisted some thorns into a crown and put it on his head, and dressed him in a purple robe. •They kept coming up to him and saying, 'Hail, king of the 3 Jews!'; and they slapped him in the face.

Pilate came outside again and said to them, 'Look, I am going to bring 4 him out to you to let you see that I find no case'. •Jesus then came out wearing 5 the crown of thorns and the purple robe. Pilate said, 'Here is the man'. •When 6 they saw him the chief priests and the guards shouted, 'Crucify him! Crucify him!' Pilate said, 'Take him yourselves and crucify him: I can find no case against him'. 'We have a Law,' the Jews replied 'and according to that Law he ought to die, 7 because he has claimed to be the Son of God.'

8
9
When Pilate heard them say this his fears increased. •Re-entering the Praetorium, he said to Jesus, 'Where do you come from?' But Jesus made no answer.
10 Pilate then said to him, 'Are you refusing to speak to me? Surely you know I
11 have power to release you and I have power to crucify you?' •'You would have
no power over me' replied Jesus 'if it had not been given you from above; that
is why the one who handed me over to you has the greater guilt.'

Jesus is condemned to death

12   From that moment Pilate was anxious to set him free, but the Jews shouted,
'If you set him free you are no friend of Caesar's; anyone who makes himself
13 king is defying Caesar'. •Hearing these words, Pilate had Jesus brought out, and
seated himself on the chair of judgement at a place called the Pavement, in
14 Hebrew Gabbatha. •It was Passover Preparation Day, about the sixth hour.ᵃ
15 'Here is your king' said Pilate to the Jews. •'Take him away, take him away!'
they said. 'Crucify him!' 'Do you want me to crucify your king?' said Pilate.
16 The chief priests answered, 'We have no king except Caesar'. •So in the end Pilate
handed him over to them to be crucified.

The crucifixion

17   They then took charge of Jesus, •and carrying his own cross he went out
of the city to the place of the skull or, as it was called in Hebrew, Golgotha,
18 where they crucified him with two others, one on either side with Jesus in the
19 middle. •Pilate wrote out a notice and had it fixed to the cross; it ran: 'Jesus
20 the Nazarene, King of the Jews'. •This notice was read by many of the Jews,
because the place where Jesus was crucified was not far from the city, and the
21 writing was in Hebrew, Latin and Greek. •So the Jewish chief priests said to
Pilate, 'You should not write "King of the Jews", but "This man said: I am King
22 of the Jews" '. •Pilate answered, 'What I have written, I have written'.

Christ's garments divided

23   When the soldiers had finished crucifying Jesus they took his clothing and
divided it into four shares, one for each soldier. His undergarment was seamless,
24 woven in one piece from neck to hem; •so they said to one another, 'Instead of
tearing it, let's throw dice to decide who is to have it'. In this way the words
of scripture were fulfilled:

> They shared out my clothing among them.
> They cast lots for my clothes.ᵇ

This is exactly what the soldiers did.

Jesus and his mother

25   Near the cross of Jesus stood his mother and his mother's sister, Mary the
26 wife of Clopas, and Mary of Magdala. •Seeing his mother and the disciple
he loved standing near her, Jesus said to his mother, 'Woman, this is your son'.
27 Then to the disciple he said, 'This is your mother'. And from that moment the
disciple made a place for her in his home.

The death of Jesus

28   After this, Jesus knew that everything had now been completed, and to
fulfil the scripture perfectly he said:

> 'I am thirsty'.ᶜ

b. The judicial court of the Roman procurator.   c. By entering the house of a pagan.
Cf. Lk 7:6.
19 a. On Preparation Day, the Passover supper was made ready for eating after sunset. The
sixth hour is midday, by which time all leaven had to be removed from the house; during the
feast only unleavened bread was eaten.   b. Ps 22:18   c. Ps 22:15

A jar-full of vinegar stood there, so putting a sponge soaked in the vinegar on 29 a hyssop stick they held it up to his mouth. •After Jesus had taken the vinegar 30 he said, 'It is accomplished'; and bowing his head he gave up his spirit.

The pierced Christ

It was Preparation Day, and to prevent the bodies remaining on the cross 31 during the sabbath—since that sabbath was a day of special solemnity—the Jews asked Pilate to have the legs broken[d] and the bodies taken away. •Consequently 32 the soldiers came and broke the legs of the first man who had been crucified with him and then of the other. •When they came to Jesus, they found he was already 33 dead, and so instead of breaking his legs •one of the soldiers pierced his side 34 with a lance; and immediately there came out blood and water. •This is the 35 evidence of one who saw it —trustworthy evidence, and he knows he speaks the truth—and he gives it so that you may believe as well. •Because all this happened 36 to fulfil the words of scripture:

> Not one bone of his will be broken;[e]

and again, in another place scripture says: 37

> They will look on the one whom they have pierced.[f]

The burial

After this, Joseph of Arimathaea, who was a disciple of Jesus—though a 38 secret one because he was afraid of the Jews—asked Pilate to let him remove the body of Jesus. Pilate gave permission, so they came and took it away. Nicodemus came as well—the same one who had first come to Jesus at night-time 39 —and he brought a mixture of myrrh and aloes, weighing about a hundred pounds. •They took the body of Jesus and wrapped it with the spices in linen 40 cloths, following the Jewish burial custom. •At the place where he had been 41 crucified there was a garden, and in this garden a new tomb in which no one had yet been buried. •Since it was the Jewish Day of Preparation and the tomb 42 was near at hand, they laid Jesus there.

VIII. THE DAY OF CHRIST'S RESURRECTION

The empty tomb

20 It was very early on the first day of the week and still dark, when Mary 1 of Magdala came to the tomb. She saw that the stone had been moved away from the tomb •and came running to Simon Peter and the other disciple, 2 the one Jesus loved. 'They have taken the Lord out of the tomb' she said 'and we don't know where they have put him.'

So Peter set out with the other disciple to go to the tomb. •They ran together, $\frac{3}{4}$ but the other disciple, running faster than Peter, reached the tomb first; •he bent 5 down and saw the linen cloths lying on the ground, but did not go in. •Simon 6 Peter who was following now came up, went right into the tomb, saw the linen cloths on the ground, •and also the cloth that had been over his head; this was 7 not with the linen cloths but rolled up in a place by itself. •Then the other disciple 8 who had reached the tomb first also went in; he saw and he believed. •Till this 9 moment they had failed to understand the teaching of scripture, that he must rise from the dead. •The disciples then went home again.   10

The appearance to Mary of Magdala

Meanwhile Mary stayed outside near the tomb, weeping. Then, still weeping, 11 she stooped to look inside, •and saw two angels in white sitting where the body 12 of Jesus had been, one at the head, the other at the feet. •They said, 'Woman, 13

why are you weeping?' 'They have taken my Lord away' she replied 'and I
14 don't know where they have put him.' •As she said this she turned round and
15 saw Jesus standing there, though she did not recognise him. •Jesus said, 'Woman,
why are you weeping? Who are you looking for?' Supposing him to be the
gardener, she said, 'Sir, if you have taken him away, tell me where you have put
16 him, and I will go and remove him'. •Jesus said, 'Mary!' She knew him then
17 and said to him in Hebrew, 'Rabbuni!'—which means Master. •Jesus said to
her, 'Do not cling to me, because I have not yet ascended to the Father. But
go and find the brothers, and tell them: I am ascending to my Father and your
18 Father, to my God and your God.' •So Mary of Magdala went and told the
disciples that she had seen the Lord and that he had said these things to her.

Appearances to the disciples

19 In the evening of that same day, the first day of the week, the doors were
closed in the room where the disciples were, for fear of the Jews. Jesus came
20 and stood among them. He said to them, 'Peace be with you', •and showed
them his hands and his side. The disciples were filled with joy when they saw
21 the Lord, •and he said to them again, 'Peace be with you.

> 'As the Father sent me,
> so am I sending you.'

22 After saying this he breathed on them and said:

> 'Receive the Holy Spirit.
23 For those whose sins you forgive,
> they are forgiven;
> for those whose sins you retain,
> they are retained.'

24 Thomas, called the Twin, who was one of the Twelve, was not with them
25 when Jesus came. •When the disciples said, 'We have seen the Lord', he answered, 'Unless I see the holes that the nails made in his hands and can put my
finger into the holes they made, and unless I can put my hand into his side,
26 I refuse to believe'. •Eight days later the disciples were in the house again and
Thomas was with them. The doors were closed, but Jesus came in and stood
27 among them. 'Peace be with you' he said. •Then he spoke to Thomas, 'Put
your finger here; look, here are my hands. Give me your hand; put it into my
28 side. Doubt no longer but believe.' •Thomas replied, 'My Lord and my God!'
29 Jesus said to him:

> 'You believe because you can see me.
> Happy are those who have not seen and yet believe.'

CONCLUSION

30 There were many other signs that Jesus worked and the disciples saw, but
31 they are not recorded in this book. •These are recorded so that you may believe
that Jesus is the Christ, the Son of God, and that believing this you may have life
through his name.

---

d. To hasten death.   **e.** Two texts are here combined: Ps 34:20 and Ex 12:46. The allusion
is both to God protecting the good man, and to the ritual for preparing the Passover lamb.
f. Zc 12:10

APPENDIX[a]

The appearance on the shore of Tiberias

21 Later on, Jesus showed himself again to the disciples. It was by the Sea 1 of Tiberias, and it happened like this: •Simon Peter, Thomas called the 2 Twin, Nathanael from Cana in Galilee, the sons of Zebedee and two more of his disciples were together. •Simon Peter said, 'I'm going fishing'. They replied, 3 'We'll come with you'. They went out and got into the boat but caught nothing that night.

It was light by now and there stood Jesus on the shore, though the disciples 4 did not realise that it was Jesus. •Jesus called out, 'Have you caught anything, 5 friends?' And when they answered, 'No', •he said, 'Throw the net out to starboard 6 and you'll find something'. So they dropped the net, and there were so many fish that they could not haul it in. •The disciple Jesus loved said to Peter, 'It is 7 the Lord'. At these words 'It is the Lord', Simon Peter, who had practically nothing on, wrapped his cloak round him and jumped into the water. •The 8 other disciples came on in the boat, towing the net and the fish; they were only about a hundred yards from land.

As soon as they came ashore they saw that there was some bread there, and 9 a charcoal fire with fish cooking on it. •Jesus said, 'Bring some of the fish you 10 have just caught'. •Simon Peter went aboard and dragged the net to the shore, 11 full of big fish, one hundred and fifty-three of them; and in spite of there being so many the net was not broken. •Jesus said to them, 'Come and have breakfast'. 12 None of the disciples was bold enough to ask, 'Who are you?'; they knew quite well it was the Lord. •Jesus then stepped forward, took the bread and gave it 13 to them, and the same with the fish. •This was the third time that Jesus showed 14 himself to the disciples after rising from the dead.

After the meal Jesus said to Simon Peter, 'Simon son of John, do you love 15 me more than these others do?' He answered, 'Yes Lord, you know I love you'. Jesus said to him, 'Feed my lambs'. •A second time he said to him, 'Simon son 16 of John, do you love me?' He replied, 'Yes, Lord, you know I love you'. Jesus said to him, 'Look after my sheep'. •Then he said to him a third time, 'Simon 17 son of John, do you love me?' Peter was upset that he asked him the third time, 'Do you love me?' and said, 'Lord, you know everything; you know I love you'. Jesus said to him, 'Feed my sheep.

'I tell you most solemnly, 18
when you were young
you put on your own belt
and walked where you liked;
but when you grow old
you will stretch out your hands,
and somebody else will put a belt round you
and take you where you would rather not go.'

In these words he indicated the kind of death by which Peter would give glory 19 to God. After this he said, 'Follow me'.

Peter turned and saw the disciple Jesus loved following them—the one who 20 had leaned on his breast at the supper and had said to him, 'Lord, who is it that will betray you?' •Seeing him, Peter said to Jesus, 'What about him, Lord?' 21 Jesus answered, 'If I want him to stay behind till I come, what does it matter 22 to you? You are to follow me.' •The rumour then went out among the brothers 23 that this disciple would not die. Yet Jesus had not said to Peter, 'He will not die', but, 'If I want him to stay behind till I come'.

Conclusion

24   This disciple is the one who vouches for these things and has written them down, and we know that his testimony is true.

25   There were many other things that Jesus did; if all were written down, the world itself, I suppose, would not hold all the books that would have to be written.

---

21 a. Added either by the evangelist or by a disciple of his.

INTRODUCTION TO
THE ACTS OF THE APOSTLES

St Luke's Gospel and The Acts of the Apostles are the two volumes of a single work that today we should call 'a history of the rise of Christianity'. The two books are inseparably linked by their Prologues and by their style. From the text of Acts it is evident that the author was a Christian of the apostolic age, either a thoroughly hellenised Jew or more probably a well-educated 'Greek' with a thorough knowledge of the Septuagint and of Jewish culture and traditions. No other name has ever been suggested than that of Luke, the close friend of Paul, who according to an ancient tradition was a Syrian from Antioch, a doctor and a convert from paganism.

Acts is in the form of a single continuous narrative. It begins with the birth and growth of the primitive Christian community in Jerusalem and tells of the founding of the community in Antioch by hellenist Jews and the conversion of St Paul; it goes on to show the spread of the Church outside Palestine through the missionary travels of Paul and ends with his captivity in Rome in A.D. 61-63. The narrative can be seen to be made up of separate episodes of varying lengths, all containing a great deal of circumstantial detail and commonly joined to each other by editorial formulae.

For the later journeys of Paul, Luke appears to have his own notes; the rest of the book confirms the claim made in the Prologue of the first volume (Lk 1:1-4) that the author collected a large quantity of evidence from a variety of sources. In the editing of this, and the chronological arranging of it, a certain amount of repetition, fusion and anomalies in the order of incidents was unavoidable, but the basic reliability of the work may be seen by checking Luke's account of Paul's missionary activities with Paul's own letters, which were not among his sources. The historical worth of Acts is high, since it not only includes a major section which is an eye-witness account of the events described, but gives much detailed factual information which we should otherwise lack. Although Luke, like any other classical historian, took the freedom to reconstruct speeches which he had not himself heard, there is every evidence that he went back to true sources and treated them with respect: notice, for instance, the archaisms and semitisms left in the reported speeches of Peter and Stephen, and the remarkable distinction between the simple theological background of the earliest Christian sermons and that of Paul's later teaching. It is also to be noticed that he can include a speech which failed to convince its hearers.

Thus Acts is a principal source for much of our knowledge of life in the earliest Christian communities, of the first impact made by the Christian faith on pagan nations, of the primitive beginnings of church organisation, of the early developments of Christology, of the personalities of the apostolic age. Luke is, however, not interested in presenting a formal history of the spread of Christianity. What he is interested in is: 1. The spiritual energy inside Christianity that motivates its expansion, and 2. the spiritual doctrine that he can show by object lessons with the facts at his disposal.

THE ACTS
OF THE APOSTLES

Prologue

1 In my earlier work,[a] Theophilus, I dealt with everything Jesus had done and ·taught from the beginning ·until the day he gave his instructions to the apostles he had chosen through the Holy Spirit, and was taken up to heaven. He had shown himself alive to them after his Passion by many demonstrations: for forty days he had continued to appear to them and tell them about the kingdom of God. ·When he had been at table with them, he had told them not to leave Jerusalem, but to wait there for what the Father had promised. 'It is' he had said 'what you have heard me speak about: ·John baptised with water but you, not many days from now, will be baptised with the Holy Spirit.'

The ascension

Now having met together,[b] they asked him, 'Lord, has the time come? Are you going to restore the kingdom to Israel?' ·He replied, 'It is not for you to know times or dates that the Father has decided by his own authority, ·but you will receive power when the Holy Spirit comes on you, and then you will be my witnesses not only in Jerusalem but throughout Judaea and Samaria, and indeed to the ends of the earth'.

As he said this he was lifted up while they looked on, and a cloud took him from their sight. ·They were still staring into the sky when suddenly two men in white were standing near them ·and they said, 'Why are you men from Galilee standing here looking into the sky? Jesus who has been taken up from you into heaven, this same Jesus will come back in the same way as you have seen him go there.'

I. THE JERUSALEM CHURCH

The group of apostles

So from the Mount of Olives, as it is called, they went back to Jerusalem, a short distance away, no more than a sabbath walk; ·and when they reached the city they went to the upper room where they were staying; there were Peter and John, James and Andrew, Philip and Thomas, Bartholomew and Matthew, James son of Alphaeus and Simon the Zealot, and Jude son of James.[c] ·All these joined in continuous prayer, together with several women, including Mary the mother of Jesus, and with his brothers.[d]

The election of Matthias

One day Peter stood up to speak to the brothers[e]—there were about a hundred and twenty persons in the congregation: ·'Brothers, the passage of scripture had to be fulfilled in which the Holy Spirit, speaking through David,

foretells the fate of Judas, who offered himself as a guide to the men who
17 arrested Jesus—•after having been one of our number and actually sharing this
18 ministry of ours. •As you know, he bought a field with the money he was paid
for his crime. He fell headlong and burst open, and all his entrails poured out.
19 Everybody in Jerusalem heard about it and the field came to be called the Bloody
20 Acre, in their language Hakeldama. •Now in the Book of Psalms it says:

> Let his camp be reduced to ruin,
> Let there be no one to live in it.[f]

And again:

> Let someone else take his office.[g]

21 'We must therefore choose someone who has been with us the whole time that
22 the Lord Jesus was travelling round with us, •someone who was with us right
from the time when John was baptising until the day when he was taken up from
us—and he can act with us as a witness to his resurrection.'

23   Having nominated two candidates, Joseph known as Barsabbas, whose
24 surname was Justus, and Matthias, •they prayed, 'Lord, you can read everyone's
25 heart; show us therefore which of these two you have chosen •to take over this
ministry and apostolate, which Judas abandoned to go to his proper place'.
26 They then drew lots for them, and as the lot fell to Matthias, he was listed as
one of the twelve apostles.

Pentecost

1 2 When Pentecost day came round, they had all met in one room, •when
2   suddenly they heard what sounded like a powerful wind from heaven, the
3 noise of which filled the entire house in which they were sitting; •and something
4 appeared to them that seemed like tongues of fire; these separated and came
to rest on the head of each of them. •They were all filled with the Holy Spirit,
and began to speak foreign languages as the Spirit gave them the gift of speech.

5   Now there were devout men living in Jerusalem from every nation under
6 heaven, •and at this sound they all assembled, each one bewildered to hear these
7 men speaking his own language. •They were amazed and astonished. 'Surely'
8 they said 'all these men speaking are Galileans? •How does it happen that each
9 of us hears them in his own native language? •Parthians, Medes and Elamites;
10 people from Mesopotamia, Judaea and Cappadocia, Pontus and Asia, •Phrygia
and Pamphylia, Egypt and the parts of Libya round Cyrene; as well as visitors
11 from Rome—•Jews and proselytes[a] alike—Cretans and Arabs; we hear them
12 preaching in our own language about the marvels of God.' •Everyone was
amazed and unable to explain it; they asked one another what it all meant.
13 Some, however, laughed it off. 'They have been drinking too much new wine'
they said.

Peter's address to the crowd

14   Then Peter stood up with the Eleven and addressed them in a loud voice:
'Men of Judaea, and all you who live in Jerusalem, make no mistake about
15 this, but listen carefully to what I say. •These men are not drunk, as you
16 imagine; why, it is only the third hour of the day.[b] •On the contrary, this is
what the prophet[c] spoke of:

17   In the days to come —it is the Lord who speaks—
         I will pour out my spirit on all mankind.

1 a. The gospel according to Luke.   b. This verse takes up the narrative broken off in
Lk 24:49.   c. 'Son' (of Alphaeus, of James) is not in the Greek. This Jude is not the Jude
'brother' of Jesus, Mt 13:55 and Mk 6:3, and brother of James (Jude 1). Nor is it likely that
'James of Alphaeus' was James brother of the Lord.   d. Cousins, as in the gospels.   e. The
term for Christians, usually the laity as distinct from apostles and elders.   f. Ps 69:25
g. Ps 109:8
2 a. Converts from paganism.   b. About 9 a.m.   c. Joel. See Jl 3:1-5.

> Their sons and daughters shall prophesy,
> your young men shall see visions,
> your old men shall dream dreams.
> Even on my slaves, men and women, 18
> in those days, I will pour out my spirit.
> I will display portents in heaven *above* 19
> and *signs* on earth *below*.
> The sun will be turned into darkness 20
> and the moon into blood
> before the great Day of the Lord dawns.
> All who call on the name of the Lord will be saved. 21

'Men of Israel, listen to what I am going to say: Jesus the Nazarene was a 22 man commended to you by God by the miracles and portents and signs that God worked through him when he was among you, as you all know. •This 23 man, who was put into your power by the deliberate intention and foreknowledge of God, you took and had crucified by men outside the Law.*d* You killed him, but God raised him to life, freeing him from the pangs of Hades; for it was 24 impossible for him to be held in its power since, •as David says of him: 25

> *I saw the Lord before me always,*
> *for with him at my right hand nothing can shake me.*
> *So my heart was glad* 26
> *and my tongue cried out with joy;*
> *my body, too, will rest in the hope*
> *that you will not abandon my soul to Hades* 27
> *nor allow your holy one to experience corruption.*
> *You have made known the way of life to me,* 28
> *you will fill me with gladness through your presence.*ᶜ

'Brothers, no one can deny that the patriarch David himself is dead and 29 buried: his tomb is still with us. •But since he was a prophet, and knew that 30 God *had sworn him* an oath *to make one of his descendants succeed him on the throne,*ᶠ •what he foresaw and spoke about was the resurrection of the Christ: 31 he is the one who was *not abandoned to Hades*, and whose body did not *experience corruption*. •God raised this man Jesus to life, and all of us are witnesses to that. 32 Now raised to the heights by God's right hand, he has received from the Father 33 the Holy Spirit, who was promised, and what you see and hear is the outpouring of that Spirit. •For David himself never went up to heaven; and yet these 34 words are his.

> *The Lord said to my Lord:*
> *Sit at my right hand*
> *until I make your enemies*
> *a footstool for you.*ᵍ 35

'For this reason the whole House of Israel can be certain that God has made 36 this Jesus whom you crucified both Lord and Christ.'

The first conversions

Hearing this, they were cut to the heart and said to Peter and the apostles, 37 'What must we do, brothers?' •'You must repent,' Peter answered 'and every 38 one of you must be baptised in the name of Jesus Christ for the forgiveness of your sins, and you will receive the gift of the Holy Spirit. •The promise that was 39 made is for you and your children, and for all *those who are far away, for all those whom the Lord our God will call to himself.*ʰ •He spoke to them for a long 40 time using many arguments, and he urged them, 'Save yourselves from this perverse generation'. •They were convinced by his arguments, and they accepted 41 what he said and were baptised. That very day about three thousand were added to their number.

The early Christian community

42 These remained faithful to the teaching of the apostles, to the brotherhood, to the breaking of bread and to the prayers.

43 The many miracles and signs worked through the apostles made a deep impression on everyone.

44 45 The faithful all lived together and owned everything in common; •they sold their goods and possessions and shared out the proceeds among themselves according to what each one needed.

46 They went as a body to the Temple every day but met in their houses for the
47 breaking of bread; they shared their food gladly and generously; •they praised God and were looked up to by everyone. Day by day the Lord added to their community those destined to be saved.

The cure of a lame man

1 3 Once, when Peter and John were going up to the Temple for the prayers at
2 the ninth hour,ᵃ •it happened that there was a man being carried past. He was a cripple from birth; and they used to put him down every day near the Temple entrance called the Beautiful Gate so that he could beg from the people
3 going in. •When this man saw Peter and John on their way into the Temple he
4 begged from them. •Both Peter and John looked straight at him and said, 'Look
5 at us'. •He turned to them expectantly, hoping to get something from them,
6 but Peter said, 'I have neither silver nor gold, but I will give you what I have:
7 in the name of Jesus Christ the Nazarene, walk!' •Peter then took him by the hand and helped him to stand up. Instantly his feet and ankles became firm,
8 he jumped up, stood, and began to walk, and he went with them into the Temple,
9 walking and jumping and praising God. •Everyone could see him walking and
10 praising God, •and they recognised him as the man who used to sit begging at the Beautiful Gate of the Temple. They were all astonished and unable to explain what had happened to him.

Peter's address to the people

11 Everyone came running towards them in great excitement, to the Portico of Solomon, as it is called, where the man was still clinging to Peter and John.
12 When Peter saw the people he addressed them, 'Why are you so surprised at this? Why are you staring at us as though we had made this man walk by our
13 own power or holiness? •You are Israelites, and it is *the God of Abraham, Isaac and Jacob, the God of our ancestors, who has glorified his servant*ᵇ Jesus, the same Jesus you handed over and then disowned in the presence of Pilate after Pilate
14 had decided to release him. •It was you who accused the Holy One, the Just
15 One, you who demanded the reprieve of a murderer •while you killed the prince of life. God, however, raised him from the dead, and to that fact we are the
16 witnesses; •and it is the name of Jesus which, through our faith in it, has brought back the strength of this man whom you see here and who is well known to you. It is faith in that name that has restored this man to health, as you can all see.

17 'Now I know, brothers, that neither you nor your leaders had any idea what
18 you were really doing; •this was the way God carried out what he had foretold,
19 when he said through all his prophets that his Christ would suffer. •Now you
20 must repent and turn to God, so that your sins may be wiped out, •and so that the Lord may send the time of comfort. Then he will send you the Christ
21 he has predestined, that is Jesus, •whom heaven must keep till the universal restoration comes which God proclaimed, speaking through his holy prophets.

---

d. The Romans.   **e.** Ps 16:8-11; quoted according to the LXX.   **f.** 2 S 7:12 and Ps 132:11.
g. Ps 110:1   **h.** Is 57:19
3 a. The time of evening sacrifice.   **b.** Ex 3:6,15 and Is 52:13

Moses, for example, said: *The Lord God will raise up a prophet like myself for you,* 22
from among your own brothers; you must listen to whatever he tells you. •*The* 23
*man who does not listen to that prophet is to be cut off from the people.*ᶜ •In fact, 24
all the prophets that have ever spoken, from Samuel onwards, have predicted
these days.

'You are the heirs of the prophets, the heirs of the covenant God made with 25
our ancestors when he told Abraham: *in your offspring all the families of the earth*
*will be blessed.*ᵈ •It was for you in the first place that God raised up his servant 26
and sent him to bless you by turning every one of you from your wicked
ways.'

Peter and John before the Sanhedrin

4 While they were still talking to the people the priests came up to them, accom- 1
panied by the captain of the Temple and the Sadducees.ᵃ •They were extremely 2
annoyed at their teaching the people the doctrine of the resurrection from the
dead by proclaiming the resurrection of Jesus. •They arrested them, but as it 3
was already late, they held them till the next day. •But many of those who had 4
listened to their message became believers, the total number of whom had now
risen to something like five thousand.

The next day the rulers, elders and scribesᵇ had a meeting in Jerusalem •with ⁵₆
Annas the high priest, Caiaphas, Jonathan, Alexander and all the members
of the high-priestly families. •They made the prisoners stand in the middle and 7
began to interrogate them, 'By what power, and by whose name have you men
done this?' •Then Peter, filled with the Holy Spirit, addressed them, 'Rulers of 8
the people, and elders! •If you are questioning us today about an act of kindness 9
to a cripple, and asking us how he was healed, •then I am glad to tell you all, 10
and would indeed be glad to tell the whole people of Israel, that it was by the
name of Jesus Christ the Nazarene, the one you crucified, whom God raised
from the dead, by this name and by no other that this man is able to stand up
perfectly healthy, here in your presence, today. •This is *the stone rejected* by you 11
*the builders, but which has proved to be the keystone.*ᶜ •For of all the names in the 12
world given to men, this is the only one by which we can be saved.'

They were astonished at the assurance shown by Peter and John, considering 13
they were uneducated laymen; and they recognised them as associates of Jesus;
but when they saw the man who had been cured standing by their side, they could 14
find no answer. •So they ordered them to stand outside while the Sanhedrin had 15
a private discussion. •'What are we going to do with these men?' they asked. 16
'It is obvious to everybody in Jerusalem that a miracle has been worked through
them in public, and we cannot deny it. •But to stop the whole thing spreading 17
any further among the people, let us caution them never to speak to anyone in
this name again.'

So they called them in and gave them a warning on no account to make 18
statements or to teach in the name of Jesus. •But Peter and John retorted, 'You 19
must judge whether in God's eyes it is right to listen to you and not to God. •We 20
cannot promise to stop proclaiming what we have seen and heard.' •The court 21
repeated the warnings and then released them; they could not think of any way
to punish them, since all the people were giving glory to God for what
had happened. •The man who had been miraculously cured was over forty years 22
old.

The apostles' prayer under persecution

As soon as they were released they went to the community and told them 23
everything the chief priests and elders had said to them. •When they heard it 24
they lifted up their voice to God all together. 'Master,' they prayed 'it is you
who made heaven and earth and sea, and everything in them; •you it is who said 25
through the Holy Spirit and speaking through our ancestor David, your servant:

> *Why this arrogance among the nations,*
> *these futile plots among the peoples?*
>
> 26 *Kings on earth setting out to war,*
> *princes making an alliance,*
> *against the Lord and against his Anointed.* [d]

27 'This is what has come true: in this very city Herod and Pontius Pilate *made an alliance* with the pagan *nations* and the *peoples* of Israel, against your holy
28 servant Jesus whom you *anointed*,[e] •but only to bring about the very thing that you
29 in your strength and your wisdom had predetermined should happen. •And now, Lord, take note of their threats and help your servants to proclaim your
30 message with all boldness, •by stretching out your hand to heal and to work
31 miracles and marvels through the name of your holy servant Jesus.' •As they prayed, the house where they were assembled rocked; they were all filled with the Holy Spirit and began to proclaim the word of God boldly.

The early Christian community

32 The whole group of believers was united, heart and soul; no one claimed for his own use anything that he had, as everything they owned was held in common.
33 The apostles continued to testify to the resurrection of the Lord Jesus with great power, and they were all given great respect.
34 None of their members was ever in want, as all those who owned land or
35 houses would sell them, and bring the money from them, •to present it to the apostles; it was then distributed to any members who might be in need.

The generosity of Barnabas

36 There was a Levite of Cypriot origin called Joseph whom the apostles surnamed
37 Barnabas (which means 'son of encouragement'). •He owned a piece of land and he sold it and brought the money, and presented it to the apostles.

The fraud of Ananias and Sapphira

1 5 There was another man, however, called Ananias. He and his wife, Sapphira,
2 agreed to sell a property; •but with his wife's connivance he kept back part of
3 the proceeds, and brought the rest and presented it to the apostles. •'Ananias,' Peter said 'how can Satan have so possessed you that you should lie to the Holy Spirit
4 and keep back part of the money from the land? •While you still owned the land, wasn't it yours to keep, and after you had sold it wasn't the money yours to do with as you liked? What put this scheme into your mind? It is not to men that
5 you have lied, but to God.' •When he heard this Ananias fell down dead. This
6 made a profound impression on everyone present. •The younger men got up, wrapped the body in a sheet, carried it out and buried it.
7 About three hours later his wife came in, not knowing what had taken place.
8 Peter challenged her, 'Tell me, was this the price you sold the land for?' 'Yes,'
9 she said 'that was the price.' •Peter then said, 'So you and your husband have agreed to put the Spirit of the Lord to the test! What made you do it? You hear those footsteps? They have just been to bury your husband; they will carry you out,
10 too.' •Instantly she dropped dead at his feet. When the young men came in they found she was dead, and they carried her out and buried her by the side of her
11 husband. •This made a profound impression on the whole Church and on all who heard it.

c. Dt 18:18,19   d. Gn 12:3
4 a. The Sadducees (see note on Mt 3:7) are always represented as denying the doctrine of the resurrection, e.g. Ac 23.   b. I.e. the Sanhedrin, explained for the non-Jewish reader.
c. Ps 118:22   d. Ps 2:1-2   e. I.e. made the Christ, the anointed Messiah.

The general situation

They all used to meet by common consent in the Portico of Solomon. •No one 12b
else ever dared to join them, but the people were loud in their praise •and the 14
numbers of men and women who came to believe in the Lord increased steadily.
So many signs and wonders were worked among the people at the hands of the 12a
apostles •that the sick were even taken out into the streets and laid on beds and 15
sleeping-mats in the hope that at least the shadow of Peter might fall across some
of them as he went past. •People even came crowding in from the towns round 16
about Jerusalem, bringing with them their sick and those tormented by unclean
spirits, and all of them were cured.

The apostles' arrest and miraculous deliverance

Then the high priest intervened with all his supporters from the party of the 17
Sadducees. Prompted by jealousy, •they arrested the apostles and had them put 18
in the common gaol.
But at night the angel of the Lord opened the prison gates and said as he led 19
them out, •'Go and stand in the Temple, and tell the people all about this new 20
Life'. •They did as they were told; they went into the Temple at dawn and 21
began to preach.

A summons to appear before the Sanhedrin

When the high priest arrived, he and his supporters convened the Sanhedrin
—this was the full Senate of Israel—and sent to the gaol for them to be brought.
But when the officials arrived at the prison they found they were not inside, so 22
they went back and reported, •'We found the gaol securely locked and the warders 23
on duty at the gates, but when we unlocked the door we found no one inside'.
When the captain of the Temple and the chief priests heard this news they 24
wondered what this could mean. •Then a man arrived with fresh news. 25
'At this very moment' he said 'the men you imprisoned are in the Temple.
They are standing there preaching to the people.' •The captain went with his 26
men and fetched them. They were afraid to use force in case the people stoned
them.
When they had brought them in to face the Sanhedrin, the high priest 27
demanded an explanation. •'We gave you a formal warning' he said 'not to 28
preach in this name, and what have you done? You have filled Jerusalem with
your teaching, and seem determined to fix the guilt of this man's death on us.'
In reply Peter and the apostles said, 'Obedience to God comes before obedience 29
to men; •it was the God of our ancestors who raised up Jesus, but it was you 30
who had him executed by hanging on a tree.[a] •By his own right hand God has 31
now raised him up to be leader and saviour, to give repentance and forgiveness
of sins through him to Israel. •We are witnesses to all this, we and the Holy 32
Spirit whom God has given to those who obey him.' •This so infuriated them 33
that they wanted to put them to death.

Gamaliel's intervention

One member of the Sanhedrin, however, a Pharisee called Gamaliel, who was 34
a doctor of the Law and respected by the whole people,[b] stood up and asked
to have the men taken outside for a time. •Then he addressed the Sanhedrin, 35
'Men of Israel, be careful how you deal with these people. •There was Theudas 36
who became notorious not so long ago. He claimed to be someone important,
and he even collected about four hundred followers; but when he was killed,
all his followers scattered and that was the end of them. •And then there was 37
Judas the Galilean, at the time of the census, who attracted crowds of supporters;
but he got killed too, and all his followers dispersed. •What I suggest, therefore, 38
is that you leave these men alone and let them go. If this enterprise, this movement
of theirs, is of human origin it will break up of its own accord; •but if it does in 39

fact come from God you will not only be unable to destroy them, but you might find yourselves fighting against God.'

40 His advice was accepted; •and they had the apostles called in, gave orders for them to be flogged, warned them not to speak in the name of Jesus and
41 released them. •And so they left the presence of the Sanhedrin glad to have had the honour of suffering humiliation for the sake of the name.
42 They preached every day both in the Temple and in private houses, and their proclamation of the Good News of Christ Jesus was never interrupted.

II. THE EARLIEST MISSIONS

The institution of the Seven

1 6 About this time, when the number of disciples was increasing, the Hellenists made a complaint against the Hebrews:[a] in the daily distribution their own
2 widows were being overlooked. •So the Twelve called a full meeting of the disciples and addressed them, 'It would not be right for us to neglect the word
3 of God so as to give out food; •you, brothers, must select from among yourselves seven men of good reputation, filled with the Spirit and with wisdom; we will
4 hand over this duty to them, •and continue to devote ourselves to prayer and
5 to the service of the word'. •The whole assembly approved of this proposal and elected Stephen, a man full of faith and of the Holy Spirit, together with Philip, Prochorus, Nicanor, Timon, Parmenas, and Nicolaus of Antioch, a convert to
6 Judaism. •They presented these to the apostles, who prayed and laid their hands on them.[b]
7 The word of the Lord continued to spread: the number of disciples in Jerusalem was greatly increased, and a large group of priests made their submission to the faith.

Stephen's arrest

8 Stephen was filled with grace and power and began to work miracles and
9 great signs among the people. •But then certain people came forward to debate with Stephen, some from Cyrene and Alexandria who were members of the synagogue called the Synagogue of Freedmen,[c] and others from Cilicia and Asia.
10 They found they could not get the better of him because of his wisdom, and
11 because it was the Spirit that prompted what he said. •So they procured some men to say, 'We heard him using blasphemous language against Moses and against
12 God'. •Having in this way turned the people against him as well as the elders and scribes, they took Stephen by surprise, and arrested him and brought him
13 before the Sanhedrin. •There they put up false witnesses to say, 'This man
14 is always making speeches against this Holy Place and the Law. •We have heard him say that Jesus the Nazarene is going to destroy this Place and alter the
15 traditions that Moses handed down to us.' •The members of the Sanhedrin all looked intently at Stephen, and his face appeared to them like the face of an angel.

Stephen's speech

1
2 7 The high priest asked, 'Is this true?' •He replied, 'My brothers, my fathers, listen to what I have to say. The God of glory appeared to our ancestor Abraham,
3 while he was in Mesopotamia before settling in Haran, •*and said to him, "Leave*

---

5 a. The phrase recalls Dt 21:23.   b. Gamaliel I, a Pharisee of the school of Hillel; he was Paul's teacher.
6 a. 'Hellenists': Jews from outside Palestine; they had their own synagogues in Jerusalem, where the scriptures were read in Greek. The 'Hebrews' were Palestinian Jews and in their synagogues scriptures were read in Hebrew.   b. 'and they prayed and laid their hands on them'; probably meaning the apostles, handing over their duties as in v.3.   c. Probably the descendants of Jews carried off to Rome, 63 B.C. and sold as slaves but later released.

*your country and your family and go to the land I will show you".*ᵃ •So he left 4
Chaldaea and settled in Haran; and after his father died God made him leave ,
Haran and come to this land where you are living today. •God did not give him 5
a single square foot of this land to call his own, yet he promised to *give it to him
and after him to his descendants, childless*ᵇ though he was. •The actual words God 6
used when he spoke to him are that *his descendants would be exiles in a foreign land,
where they would be slaves and oppressed for four hundred years.* •*But I will pass* 7
judgement on the nation that enslaves them" God said "*and after this they will leave,
and worship me in this* place."ᶜ •Then he made the covenant of circumcision: so 8
when his son Isaac was born he circumcised him on the eighth day. Isaac did the
same for Jacob, and Jacob for the twelve patriarchs.

'The patriarchs were *jealous of Joseph and sold him into slavery in Egypt.*ᵈ But 9
*God was with him,*ᵉ •and rescued him from all his miseries by making him wise 10
enough to attract the attention of Pharaoh king of Egypt, who *made him governor
of Egypt*ᶠ and put him in charge of the royal household. •*Then a famine came* that 11
caused much suffering *throughout Egypt and Canaan,* and our ancestors could
find nothing to eat. •When Jacob *heard that there was grain for sale in Egypt,* 12
he sent our ancestors there on a first visit, •but it was on the second that *Joseph* 13
made himself known to his brothers, and told Pharaoh about his family. •Joseph 14
then sent for his father Jacob and his whole family, a total of *seventy-five people.*
Jacob went down into Egypt and after he and our ancestors had died there, 15
their bodies were brought back to Shechem and buried in the tomb that Abraham 16
had bought and paid for from the sons of Hamor, the father of Shechem.

'As the time drew near for God to fulfil the promise he had solemnly made 17
to Abraham, our nation in Egypt *grew larger and larger,* •until a new king came 18
*to power in Egypt who knew nothing of*ᵍ Jos⸱ ph. •*He exploited* our race, and ill- 19
treated our ancestors, forcing them to expose their babies to prevent their
surviving. •It was at this period that Moses was born, *a fine child* and favoured 20
by God. He was looked after for three months in his father's house, •and after 21
he had been exposed, *Pharaoh's daughter* adopted him and *brought him up
as her own son.* •So Moses was taught all the wisdom of the Egyptians and 22
became a man with power both in his speech and his actions.

'At the age of forty he decided to visit *his countrymen, the sons of Israel.* •When ²³₂₄
he saw one of them being ill-treated he went to his defence and rescued the man by
killing the Egyptian. •He thought his brothers realised that through him God 25
would liberate them, but they did not. •The next day, when he came across 26
some of them fighting, he tried to reconcile them. 'Friends,' he said 'you are
brothers; why are you hurting each other?' •But *the man who was attacking his* 27
fellow countryman pushed him aside. '*And who appointed you*' he said '*to be our
leader and judge? •Do you intend to kill me as you killed the Egyptian yesterday?*' 28
Moses fled when he heard thisʰ and *he went to stay in the land of Midian,* where 29
he became the father of two sons.

'Forty years later, *in the wilderness* near Mount Sinai, *an angel appeared to him* 30
in the flames of a bush that was on fire. •Moses was amazed by what he saw. 31
As he went nearer to look at it the voice of the Lord was heard, •"*I am the God of* 32
your ancestors, the God of Abraham, Isaac and Jacob". Moses trembled and *did not
dare to look any more.* •The Lord said to him, "*Take off your shoes; the place where* 33
you are standing is holy ground. •I have seen the way my people are ill-treated in 34
*Egypt, I have heard their groans, and I have come down to liberate them. So come
here and let me send you into Egypt.*"

'It was the same Moses that they had disowned when they said, "*Who* 35
appointed you to be our leader and judge?" who was now sent to be both leader
and redeemer through the angel who had appeared to him in the bush. •It was 36
Moses who, after performing *miracles and signs in Egypt,* led them out across the
Red Sea and *through the wilderness for forty years.*ⁱ •It was Moses who told the 37
sons of Israel, "*God will raise up a prophet like myself for you from among*

38 *your own brothers*".[j] •When they held the assembly in the wilderness it was only
through Moses that our ancestors could communicate with the angel who had
spoken to him on Mount Sinai; it was he who was entrusted with words of life
39 to hand on to us. •This is the man that our ancestors refused to listen to: they
40 pushed him aside, *turned back to Egypt* in their thoughts, •*and said to Aaron,*
"*Make some gods to be our leaders; we do not understand what has come over this*
41 *Moses who led us out of Egypt*"[k] •It was then that *they made a bull calf and offered*
sacrifice to the idol. They were perfectly happy with something they had made
42 for themselves. •God turned away from them and abandoned them to the
worship of the army of heaven,[l] as scripture says in the book of the prophets:

> *Did you bring me victims and sacrifices in the wilderness*
> *for all those forty years, you House of Israel?*
43 > *No, you carried the tent of Moloch on your shoulders*
> *and the star of the god Rephan,*
> *those idols that you had made to adore.*
> *So now I will exile you even further than Babylon.*[m]

44   'While they were in the desert our ancestors possessed the Tent of Testimony
that had been constructed according to the instructions God gave Moses, telling
45 him to *make an exact copy of the pattern*[n] he had been shown. •It was handed
down from one ancestor of ours to another until Joshua brought it into the
country we had conquered from the nations which were driven out by God as
46 we advanced. Here it stayed until the time of David. •He won God's favour and
47 asked permission *to have a temple built for* the House of *Jacob,* •though it was
48 *Solomon* who actually *built God's house*[o] for him. •Even so the Most High does
not live in a house that human hands have built: for as the prophet says:

> *With heaven my throne*
49 > *and earth my footstool,*
> *what house could you build me,*
> *what place could you make for my rest?*
50 > *Was not all this made by my hand?*[p]

51   'You stubborn people, with your pagan hearts and pagan ears. You are always
52 resisting the Holy Spirit, just as your ancestors used to do. •Can you name
a single prophet your ancestors never persecuted? In the past they killed those
who foretold the coming of the Just One, and now you have become his
53 betrayers, his murderers. •You who had the Law brought to you by angels are
the very ones who have not kept it.'
54   They were infuriated when they heard this, and ground their teeth at him.

The stoning of Stephen. Saul as persecutor

55   But Stephen, filled with the Holy Spirit, gazed into heaven and saw the glory
56 of God, and Jesus standing at God's right hand. •'I can see heaven thrown open'
57 he said 'and the Son of Man standing at the right hand of God.' •At this all the
members of the council shouted out and stopped their ears with their hands; then
58 they all rushed at him, •sent him out of the city and stoned him. The wit-
59 nesses[q] put down their clothes at the feet of a young man called Saul. •As they
were stoning him, Stephen said in invocation, 'Lord Jesus, receive my spirit'.
60 Then he knelt down and said aloud, 'Lord, do not hold this sin against them';
1 and with these words he fell asleep. 8 Saul entirely approved of the killing.

7 a. Gn 12:1   b. Gn 15:2   c. Gn 15:2,13,14; Ex 3:12   d. Gn 37   e. Gn 39
f. Gn 41. Other direct quotations and allusions in this paragraph are from Gn 42-50
g. O.T. quotations from here to v. 35 are from Ex 1-3.   h. In Ex 2:15 Moses runs away
because he is afraid of Pharaoh.   i. Nb 14:33   j. Dt 18:15,18   k. Ex 32:1,23 and 32:4,6
l. The stars and planets.   m. Am 5:25-27 (LXX)   n. Ex 25:40   o. 1 K 6:2   p. Is 66:1-2
q. By the Law, the accusers had to begin the execution of the sentence.

That day a bitter persecution started against the church in Jerusalem, and everyone[a] except the apostles fled to the country districts of Judaea and Samaria.

There were some devout people, however, who buried Stephen and made 2 great mourning for him.

Saul then worked for the total destruction of the Church; he went from house 3 to house arresting both men and women and sending them to prison.

Philip in Samaria

Those who had escaped went from place to place preaching the Good News. 4 One of them was Philip who went to a Samaritan town and proclaimed the 5 Christ to them. •The people united in welcoming the message Philip preached, 6 either because they had heard of the miracles he worked or because they saw them for themselves. •There were, for example, unclean spirits that came shrieking 7 out of many who were possessed, and several paralytics and cripples were cured. As a result there was great rejoicing in that town.   8

Simon the magician

Now a man called Simon had already practised magic arts in the town and 9 astounded the Samaritan people. He had given it out that he was someone momentous, •and everyone believed what he said; eminent citizens and ordinary 10 people alike had declared, 'He is the divine power that is called Great'. •They 11 had only been won over to him because of the long time he had spent working on them with his magic. •But when they believed Philip's preaching of the Good 12 News about the kingdom of God and the name of Jesus Christ, they were baptised, both men and women, •and even Simon himself became a believer. 13 After his baptism Simon, who went round constantly with Philip, was astonished when he saw the wonders and great miracles that took place.

When the apostles in Jerusalem heard that Samaria had accepted the word 14 of God, they sent Peter and John to them, •and they went down there, and 15 prayed for the Samaritans to receive the Holy Spirit, •for as yet he had not come 16 down on any of them: they had only been baptised in the name of the Lord Jesus. Then they laid hands on them, and they received the Holy Spirit.   17

When Simon saw that the Spirit was given through the imposition of hands 18 by the apostles, he offered them some money. •'Give me the same power' he said 19 'so that anyone I lay my hands on will receive the Holy Spirit.' •Peter answered, 20 'May your silver be lost forever, and you with it, for thinking that money could buy what God has given for nothing! •You have no share, no rights, in this: 21 God can see how your heart is warped. •Repent of this wickedness of yours, and 22 pray to the Lord; you may still be forgiven for thinking as you did; •it is plain 23 to me that you are trapped in the bitterness of gall and the chains of sin.' 'Pray to the Lord for me yourselves' Simon replied ' so that none of the things 24 you have spoken about may happen to me.'

Having given their testimony and proclaimed the word of the Lord, they went 25 back to Jerusalem, preaching the Good News to a number of Samaritan villages.

Philip baptises a eunuch

The angel of the Lord spoke to Philip saying, 'Be ready to set out at noon 26 along the road that goes from Jerusalem down to Gaza, the desert road'. •So he 27 set off on his journey. Now it happened that an Ethiopian had been on pilgrimage to Jerusalem; he was a eunuch and an officer at the court of the kandake, or queen, of Ethiopia, and was in fact her chief treasurer. •He was now on his way 28 home; and as he sat in his chariot he was reading the prophet Isaiah. •The 29 Spirit said to Philip, 'Go up and meet that chariot'. •When Philip ran up, he 30 heard him reading Isaiah the prophet and asked, 'Do you understand what you are reading?' •'How can I' he replied 'unless I have someone to guide me?' So 31 he invited Philip to get in and sit by his side. •Now the passage of scripture he 32 was reading was this:

Like a sheep that is led to the slaughter-house,
like a lamb that is dumb in front of its shearers,
like these he never opens his mouth.

33 *He has been humiliated and has no one to defend him.*
Who will ever talk about his descendants,
since his life on earth has been cut short ! [b]

34 The eunuch turned to Philip and said, 'Tell me, is the prophet referring to
35 himself or someone else?' •Starting, therefore, with this text of scripture Philip
proceeded to explain the Good News of Jesus to him.

36 Further along the road they came to some water, and the eunuch said, 'Look,
38 there is some water here; is there anything to stop me being baptised?[c] •He
ordered the chariot to stop, then Philip and the eunuch both went down into
39 the water and Philip baptised him. •But after they had come up out of the water
again Philip was taken away by the Spirit of the Lord, and the eunuch never
40 saw him again but went on his way rejoicing. •Philip found that he had reached
Azotus and continued his journey proclaiming the Good News in every town as
far as Caesarea.

The conversion of Saul

1 9 Meanwhile Saul was still breathing threats to slaughter the Lord's disciples.
2 He had gone to the high priest •and asked for letters addressed to the
synagogues in Damascus, that would authorise him to arrest and take to Jerusalem
any followers of the Way, men or women, that he could find.

3 Suddenly, while he was travelling to Damascus and just before he reached
4 the city, there came a light from heaven all round him. •He fell to the ground,
and then he heard a voice saying, 'Saul, Saul, why are you persecuting me?'
5 'Who are you, Lord?' he asked, and the voice answered, 'I am Jesus, and you
6 are persecuting me. •Get up now and go into the city, and you will be told what
7 you have to do.' •The men travelling with Saul stood there speechless, for
8 though they heard the voice they could see no one. •Saul got up from the ground,
but even with his eyes wide open he could see nothing at all, and they had to lead
9 him into Damascus by the hand. •For three days he was without his sight, and
took neither food nor drink.

10 A disciple called Ananias who lived in Damascus had a vision in which he
11 heard the Lord say to him, 'Ananias!' When he replied, 'Here I am, Lord', •the
Lord said, 'You must go to Straight Street and ask at the house of Judas for
someone called Saul, who comes from Tarsus. At this moment he is praying,
12 having had a vision of a man called Ananias coming in and laying hands on him
to give him back his sight.'

13 When he heard that, Ananias said, 'Lord, several people have told me about
14 this man and all the harm he has been doing to your saints in Jerusalem. •He has
only come here because he holds a warrant from the chief priests to arrest
15 everybody who invokes your name.' •The Lord replied, 'You must go all the
same, because this man is my chosen instrument to bring my name before pagans
16 and pagan kings and before the people of Israel; •I myself will show him how
17 much he himself must suffer for my name'. •Then Ananias went. He entered
the house, and at once laid his hands on Saul and said, 'Brother Saul, I have been
sent by the Lord Jesus who appeared to you on your way here so that you may
18 recover your sight and be filled with the Holy Spirit'. •Immediately it was as
though scales fell away from Saul's eyes and he could see again. So he was
19 baptised there and then, •and after taking some food he regained his strength.

---

8 a. The persecution seems to have been directed principally against the Hellenists.
b. Is 53:7-8, quoted from the LXX version. **c.** At the time when verse numbers were introduced, there was a gloss, numbered v. 37, at this point.

Saul's preaching at Damascus

After he had spent only a few days with the disciples in Damascus, ·he began 20 preaching in the synagogues, 'Jesus is the Son of God'. ·All his hearers were 21 amazed. 'Surely' they said 'this is the man who organised the attack in Jerusalem against the people who invoke this name, and who came here for the sole purpose of arresting them to have them tried by the chief priests?' ·Saul's power 22 increased steadily, and he was able to throw the Jewish colony at Damascus into complete confusion by the way he demonstrated that Jesus was the Christ.

Some time passed,[a] and the Jews worked out a plot to kill him, ·but news of $^{23}_{24}$ it reached Saul. To make sure of killing him they kept watch on the gates day and night, ·but when it was dark the disciples took him and let him down from 25 the top of the wall, lowering him in a basket.

Saul's visit to Jerusalem

When he got to Jerusalem he tried to join the disciples, but they were all 26 afraid of him: they could not believe he was really a disciple. ·Barnabas, 27 however, took charge of him, introduced him to the apostles, and explained how the Lord had appeared to Saul and spoken to him on his journey, and how he had preached boldly at Damascus in the name of Jesus. ·Saul now started to go 28 round with them in Jerusalem, preaching fearlessly in the name of the Lord. But after he had spoken to the Hellenists, and argued with them, they became 29 determined to kill him. ·When the brothers knew, they took him to Caesarea, 30 and sent him off from there to Tarsus.

A lull

The churches throughout Judaea, Galilee and Samaria were now left in peace, 31 building themselves up, living in the fear of the Lord, and filled with the consolation of the Holy Spirit.

Peter cures a paralytic at Lydda

Peter visited one place after another and eventually came to the saints living 32 down in Lydda. ·There he found a man called Aeneas, a paralytic who had been 33 bedridden for eight years. ·Peter said to him, 'Aeneas, Jesus Christ cures you: 34 get up and fold up your sleeping mat'. Aeneas got up immediately; ·everybody 35 who lived in Lydda and Sharon saw him, and they were all converted to the Lord.

Peter raises a woman to life at Jaffa

At Jaffa there was a woman disciple called Tabitha, or Dorcas in Greek,[b] 36 who never tired of doing good or giving in charity. ·But the time came when she 37 got ill and died, and they washed her and laid her out in a room upstairs. ·Lydda 38 is not far from Jaffa, so when the disciples heard that Peter was there, they sent two men with an urgent message for him, 'Come and visit us as soon as possible'.

Peter went back with them straightaway, and on his arrival they took him 39 to the upstairs room, where all the widows stood round him in tears, showing him tunics and other clothes Dorcas had made when she was with them. ·Peter 40 sent them all out of the room and knelt down and prayed. Then he turned to the dead woman and said, 'Tabitha, stand up'. She opened her eyes, looked at Peter and sat up. ·Peter helped her to her feet, then he called in the saints and 41 widows and showed them she was alive. ·The whole of Jaffa heard about it and 42 many believed in the Lord.

Peter stayed on some time in Jaffa, lodging with a leather-tanner called Simon. 43

Peter visits a Roman centurion

10 One of the centurions of the Italica cohort stationed in Caesarea was 1 called Cornelius. ·He and the whole of his household were devout and 2 God-fearing, and he gave generously to Jewish causes and prayed constantly to God.

3   One day at about the ninth hour he had a vision in which he distinctly saw
4 the angel of God come into his house and call out to him, 'Cornelius!' •He stared
at the vision in terror and exclaimed, 'What is it, Lord?' 'Your offering of prayers
5 and alms' the angel answered 'has been accepted by God. •Now you must send
6 someone to Jaffa and fetch a man called Simon, known as Peter, •who is lodging
7 with Simon the tanner whose house is by the sea.' •When the angel who said
this had gone, Cornelius called two of the slaves and a devout soldier of his staff,
8 told them what had happened, and sent them off to Jaffa.

9   Next day, while they were still on their journey and had only a short distance
to go before reaching Jaffa, Peter went to the housetop at about the sixth hour
10 to pray. •He felt hungry and was looking forward to his meal, but before it was
11 ready he fell into a trance •and saw heaven thrown open and something like a big
12 sheet being let down to earth by its four corners; •it contained every possible
13 sort of animal and bird, walking, crawling or flying ones. •A voice then said
14 to him, 'Now, Peter; kill and eat!' •But Peter answered, 'Certainly not, Lord;
15 I have never yet eaten anything profane or unclean'. •Again, a second time, the
voice spoke to him, 'What God has made clean, you have no right to call
16 profane'. •This was repeated three times, and then suddenly the container was
drawn up to heaven again.

17   Peter was still worrying over the meaning of the vision he had seen, when the
men sent by Cornelius arrived. They had asked where Simon's house was and
18 they were now standing at the door, •calling out to know if the Simon known as
19 Peter was lodging there. •Peter's mind was still on the vision and the Spirit had
20 to tell him, 'Some men have come to see you. •Hurry down, and do not hesitate
21 about going back with them; it was I who told them to come.' •Peter went down
22 and said to them, 'I am the man you are looking for; why have you come?' •They
said, 'The centurion Cornelius, who is an upright and God-fearing man, highly
regarded by the entire Jewish people, was directed by a holy angel to send for you
23 and bring you to his house and to listen to what you have to say'. •So Peter
asked them in and gave them lodging.

   Next day, he was ready to go off with them, accompanied by some of the
24 brothers from Jaffa. •They reached Caesarea the following day, and Cornelius
was waiting for them. He had asked his relations and close friends to be there,
25 and as Peter reached the house Cornelius went out to meet him, knelt at his feet
26 and prostrated himself. •But Peter helped him up. 'Stand up,' he said 'I am only
27 a man after all!' •Talking together they went in to meet all the people assembled
28 there, •and Peter said to them, 'You know it is forbidden for Jews to mix with
people of another race and visit them, but God has made it clear to me that
29 I must not call anyone profane or unclean. •That is why I made no objection
to coming when I was sent for; but I should like to know exactly why you
30 sent for me.' •Cornelius replied, 'Three days ago I was praying in my house
at the ninth hour, when I suddenly saw a man in front of me in shining robes.
31 He said, "Cornelius, your prayer has been heard and your alms have been
32 accepted as a sacrifice in the sight of God; •so now you must send to Jaffa and
fetch Simon known as Peter who is lodging in the house of Simon the tanner, by
33 the sea". •So I sent for you at once, and you have been kind enough to come.
Here we all are, assembled in front of you to hear what message God has given
you for us.'

Peter's address in the house of Cornelius

34   Then Peter addressed them: 'The truth I have now come to realise' he said
35 'is that God does not have favourites, •but that anybody of any nationality who
fears God and does what is right is acceptable to him.

36   'It is true, God sent his word to the people of Israel, and it was to them that

---

9 a. Three years, according to Ga 1:17-18.   b. I.e. 'Gazelle'.

the good news of peace was brought[a] by Jesus Christ—but Jesus Christ is Lord of all men. •You must have heard about the recent happenings in Judaea; about 37 Jesus of Nazareth and how he began in Galilee, after John had been preaching baptism. •*God had anointed him with the Holy Spirit*[b] and with power, and because 38 God was with him, Jesus went about doing good and curing all who had fallen into the power of the devil. • Now I, and those with me, can witness to everything 39 he did throughout the countryside of Judaea and in Jerusalem itself: and also to the fact that they killed him by hanging him on a tree, • yet three days afterwards 40 God raised him to life and allowed him to be seen, • not by the whole people 41 but only by certain witnesses God had chosen beforehand. Now we are those witnesses—we have eaten and drunk with him after his resurrection from the dead—• and he has ordered us to proclaim this to his people and to tell them 42 that God has appointed him to judge everyone, alive or dead. • It is to him that 43 all the prophets bear this witness: that all who believe in Jesus will have their sins forgiven through his name.'

Baptism of the first pagans

While Peter was still speaking the Holy Spirit came down on all the listeners. • 44 Jewish believers who had accompanied Peter were all astonished that the gift 45 of the Holy Spirit should be poured out on the pagans too, • since they could 46 hear them speaking strange languages and proclaiming the greatness of God. Peter himself then said, • 'Could anyone refuse the water of baptism to these 47 people, now they have received the Holy Spirit just as much as we have?' • He 48 then gave orders for them to be baptised in the name of Jesus Christ. Afterwards they begged him to stay on for some days.

Jerusalem: Peter justifies his conduct

11 The apostles and the brothers in Judaea heard that the pagans too had 1 accepted the word of God, • and when Peter came up to Jerusalem the 2 Jews criticised him · • and said, 'So you have been visiting the uncircumcised 3 and eating with them, have you?' • Peter in reply gave them the details point by 4 point: • 'One day, when I was in the town of Jaffa,' he began 'I fell into a trance as 5 I was praying and had a vision of something like a big sheet being let down from heaven by its four corners. This sheet reached the ground quite close to me. I watched it intently and saw all sorts of animals and wild beasts—everything 6 possible that could walk, crawl or fly. • Then I heard a voice that said to me, "Now, 7 Peter; kill and eat!" • But I answered: Certainly not, Lord; nothing profane or 8 unclean has ever crossed my lips. • And a second time the voice spoke from 9 heaven, "What God has made clean, you have no right to call profane". • This 10 was repeated three times, before the whole of it was drawn up to heaven again.

'Just at that moment, three men stopped outside the house where we were 11 staying; they had been sent from Caesarea to fetch me, • and the Spirit told me 12 to have no hesitation about going back with them. The six brothers here came with me as well, and we entered the man's house. • He told us he had seen an angel 13 standing in his house who said, "Send to Jaffa and fetch Simon known as Peter; he has a message for you that will save you and your entire household". 14

'I had scarcely begun to speak when the Holy Spirit came down on them 15 in the same way as it came on us at the beginning, • and I remembered that the 16 Lord had said, "John baptised with water, but you will be baptised with the Holy Spirit". • I realised then that God was giving them the identical thing he gave to us 17 when we believed in the Lord Jesus Christ; and who was I to stand in God's way?'

This account satisfied them, and they gave glory to God. 'God' they said 'can 18 evidently grant even the pagans the repentance that leads to life.'

Foundation of the church of Antioch

Those who had escaped during the persecution that happened because of 19 Stephen travelled as far as Phoenicia and Cyprus and Antioch,[a] but they usually

20 proclaimed the message only to Jews. •Some of them, however, who came from Cyprus and Cyrene, went to Antioch where they started preaching to the Greeks,
21 proclaiming the Good News of the Lord Jesus to them as well. •The Lord helped them, and a great number believed and were converted to the Lord.
22 The church in Jerusalem heard about this and they sent Barnabas to Antioch.
23 There he could see for himself that God had given grace, and this pleased him, and he urged them all to remain faithful to the Lord with heartfelt devotion;
24 for he was a good man, filled with the Holy Spirit and with faith. And a large number of people were won over to the Lord.
25 26 Barnabas then left for Tarsus to look for Saul, •and when he found him he brought him to Antioch. As things turned out they were to live together in that church a whole year, instructing a large number of people. It was at Antioch that the disciples were first called 'Christians'.

Barnabas and Saul sent as deputies to Jerusalem

27 While they were there some prophets[b] came down to Antioch from Jerusalem,
28 and one of them whose name was Agabus, seized by the Spirit, stood up and predicted that a famine would spread over the whole empire. This in fact happened
29 before the reign of Claudius came to an end.[c] •The disciples decided to send relief, each to contribute what he could afford, to the brothers living in Judaea.
30 They did this and delivered their contributions to the elders in the care of Barnabas and Saul.

Peter's arrest and miraculous deliverance[a]

1 2 3 12 It was about this time that King Herod started persecuting certain members of the Church. •He beheaded James the brother of John, •and when he
4 saw that this pleased the Jews he decided to arrest Peter as well. •This was during the days of Unleavened Bread, and he put Peter in prison, assigning four squads of four soldiers each to guard him in turns. Herod meant to try Peter in public
5 after the end of Passover week. •All the time Peter was under guard the Church prayed to God for him unremittingly.
6 On the night before Herod was to try him, Peter was sleeping between two soldiers, fastened with double chains, while guards kept watch at the main
7 entrance to the prison. •Then suddenly the angel of the Lord stood there, and the cell was filled with light. He tapped Peter on the side and woke him. 'Get up!'
8 he said 'Hurry!'—and the chains fell from his hands. •The angel then said, 'Put on your belt and sandals'. After he had done this, the angel next said, 'Wrap
9 your cloak round you and follow me'. •Peter followed him, but had no idea that what the angel did was all happening in reality; he thought he was seeing a vision.
10 They passed through two guard posts one after the other, and reached the iron gate leading to the city. This opened of its own accord; they went through it and had walked the whole length of one street when suddenly the angel left him.
11 It was only then that Peter came to himself. 'Now I know it is all true' he said. 'The Lord really did send his angel and has saved me from Herod and from all that the Jewish people were so certain would happen to me.'
12 As soon as he realised this he went straight to the house of Mary the mother
13 of John Mark,[b] where a number of people had assembled and were praying. •He
14 knocked at the outside door and a servant called Rhoda came to answer it. •She recognised Peter's voice and was so overcome with joy that, instead of opening

10 a. Is 52:7   b. Is 61:1
11 a. Antioch on the Orontes, capital of Syria.   b. Christian prophets, inspired speakers, generally ranked second to the apostles in the lists of the persons 'gifted by the Spirit'.   c. Claudius reigned until 54 A.D.
12 a. Herod Agrippa I was king of Judaea and Samaria, 41-44 A.D. This episode, though fitted in the book between 11:30 and 12:25, must have taken place before Barnabas and Saul visited Jerusalem.   b. Mark is mentioned in ch. 12,13 and 15: also in Col 4 and Phm 24 and 2 Tim 4. Tradition names him as author of the second gospel.

the door, she ran inside with the news that Peter was standing at the main entrance. They said to her, 'You are out of your mind', but she insisted that it was true. 15 Then they said, 'It must be his angel!' •Peter, meanwhile, was still knocking, 16 so they opened the door and were amazed to see that it really was Peter himself. With a gesture of his hand he stopped them talking, and described to them how 17 the Lord had led him out of prison. He added, 'Tell James and the brothers'. Then he left and went to another place.

When daylight came there was a great commotion among the soldiers, who 18 could not imagine what had become of Peter. •Herod put out an unsuccessful 19 search for him; he had the guards questioned, and before leaving Judaea to take up residence in Caesarea he gave orders for their execution.

The death of the persecutor

Now Herod was on bad terms with the Tyrians and Sidonians. However, they 20 sent a joint deputation which managed to enlist the support of Blastus, the king's chamberlain, and through him negotiated a treaty, since their country depended for its food supply on King Herod's territory. •A day was fixed, and Herod, 21 wearing his robes of state and enthroned on a dais, made a speech to them. The people acclaimed him with, 'It is a god speaking, not a man!', •and at 22 23 that moment the angel of the Lord struck him down, because he had not given the glory to God. He was eaten away with worms and died.

Barnabas and Saul return to Antioch

The word of God continued to spread and to gain followers. •Barnabas and 24 25 Saul completed their task and came back from Jerusalem, bringing John Mark with them.

III. THE MISSION OF BARNABAS AND PAUL
THE COUNCIL OF JERUSALEM

The mission sent out

13 In the church at Antioch the following were prophets and teachers: Barnabas, Simeon called Niger, and Lucius of Cyrene, Manaen, who had 1 been brought up with Herod the tetrarch, and Saul. •One day while they were 2 offering worship to the Lord and keeping a fast, the Holy Spirit said, 'I want Barnabas and Saul set apart for the work to which I have called them'. •So it was 3 that after fasting and prayer they laid their hands on them and sent them off.

Cyprus: the magician Elymas

So these two, sent on their mission by the Holy Spirit, went down to Seleucia 4 and from there sailed to Cyprus. •They landed at Salamis and proclaimed the 5 word of God in the synagogues of the Jews; John acted as their assistant.

They travelled the whole length of the island, and at Paphos they came in 6 contact with a Jewish magician called Bar-jesus. •This false prophet was one 7 of the attendants of the proconsul Sergius Paulus who was an extremely intelligent man. The proconsul summoned Barnabas and Saul and asked to hear the word of God, •but Elymas Magos—as he was called in Greek—tried to stop them 8 so as to prevent the proconsul's conversion to the faith. •Then Saul, whose other 9 name is Paul, looked him full in the face •and said, 'You utter fraud, you 10 impostor, you son of the devil, you enemy of all true religion, why don't you stop twisting the straightforward ways of the Lord? •Now watch how the hand 11 of the Lord will strike you: you will be blind, and for a time you will not see the sun.' That instant, everything went misty and dark for him, and he groped about to find someone to lead him by the hand. •The proconsul, who had watched 12 everything, became a believer, being astonished by what he had learnt about the Lord.

They arrive at Antioch in Pisidia

13 Paul and his friends went by sea from Paphos to Perga in Pamphylia where
14 John left them to go back to Jerusalem. •The others carried on from Perga till they
reached Antioch in Pisidia. Here they went to synagogue on the sabbath and took
15 their seats. •After the lessons from the Law and the Prophets had been read,
the presidents of the synagogue sent them a message: 'Brothers, if you would
like to address some words of encouragement to the congregation, please do so'.
16 Paul stood up, held up a hand for silence and began to speak:

Paul's preaching before the Jews

17 'Men of Israel, and fearers of God, listen! •The God of our nation Israel
chose our ancestors, and made our people great when they were living as foreigners
18 in Egypt; then by divine power he led them out, •and for about forty years *took*
19 *care of them in the wilderness.* •*When he had destroyed seven nations in Canaan,*
20 *he put them in possession*ᵃ of their land •for about four hundred and fifty years.
21 After this he gave them judges, down to the prophet Samuel. •Then they
demanded a king, and God gave them Saul son of Kish, a man of the tribe of
22 Benjamin. After forty years, he deposed him and made David their king, of
whom he approved in these words, "*I have selected David son of Jesse, a man after*
23 *my own heart, who will carry out my whole purpose*".ᵇ •To keep his promise, God
24 has raised up for Israel one of David's descendants, Jesus, as Saviour, •whose
coming was heralded by John when he proclaimed a baptism of repentance for the
25 whole people of Israel. •Before John ended his career he said, "I am not the one
you imagine me to be; that one is coming after me and I am not fit to undo his
sandal".

26 'My brothers, sons of Abraham's race, and all you who fear God, this message
27 of salvation is meant for you. •What the people of Jerusalem and their rulers
did, though they did not realise it, was in fact to fulfil the prophecies read on every
28 sabbath. •Though they found nothing to justify his death, they condemned him
29 and asked Pilate to have him executed. •When they had carried out everything
that scripture foretells about him they took him down from the tree and buried
30/31 him in a tomb. •But God raised him from the dead, •and for many days he
appeared to those who had accompanied him from Galilee to Jerusalem: and
it is these same companions of his who are now his witnesses before our people.

32 'We have come here to tell you the Good News. It was to our ancestors that
33 God made the promise but •it is to us, their children, that he has fulfilled it,
by raising Jesus from the dead. As scripture says in the first psalm: *You are my*
34 *son: today I have become your father.* •The fact that God raised him from the
dead, never to return to corruption, is no more than what he had declared: *To*
35 *you I shall give the sure and holy things promised to David.*ᶜ •This is explained by
36 another text: *You will not allow your holy one to experience corruption.*ᵈ •Now when
David in his own time had served God's purposes he died; he was buried with
37 his ancestors and has certainly *experienced corruption.* •The one whom God has
raised up, however, has not *experienced corruption.*

38 'My brothers, I want you to realise that it is through him that forgiveness of
your sins is proclaimed. Through him justification from all sins which the Law
39 of Moses was unable to justify •is offered to every believer.
40 'So be careful—or what the prophets say will happen to you.

41   *Cast your eyes around you, mockers;*
          be amazed, and perish !
          For I am doing something in your own days
          *that you would not believe if you were to be told of it.*ᵉ

13 a. Dt 1:31; 7:1   **b.** 1 S 13:14   **c.** Is 55:3   **d.** Ps 16:9   **e.** Hab 1:5

As they left they were asked to preach on the same theme the following 42 sabbath. •When the meeting broke up many Jews and devout converts joined 43 Paul and Barnabas. and in their talks with them Paul and Barnabas urged them to remain faithful to the grace God had given them.

Paul and Barnabas preach to the pagans

The next sabbath almost the whole town assembled to hear the word of God. 44 When they saw the crowds, the Jews, prompted by jealousy, used blasphemies 45 and contradicted everything Paul said. •Then Paul and Barnabas spoke out 46 boldly. 'We had to proclaim the word of God to you first, but since you have rejected it, since you do not think yourselves worthy of eternal life, we must turn to the pagans. •For this is what the Lord commanded us to do when he said: 47

I have made you a light for the nations,
so that my salvation may reach the ends of the earth.'f

It made the pagans very happy to hear this and they thanked the Lord for his 48 message; all who were destined for eternal life became believers. •Thus the 49 word of the Lord spread through the whole countryside.

But the Jews worked upon some of the devout women of the upper 50 classes and the leading men of the city and persuaded them to turn against Paul and Barnabas and expel them from their territory. •So they shook the dust 51 from their feet in defiance and went off to Iconium; •but the disciples were filled 52 with joy and the Holy Spirit.

Iconium evangelised

14 At Iconium they went to the Jewish synagogue, as they had at Antioch, 1 and they spoke so effectively that a great many Jews and Greeks became believers.

Some of the Jews, however, refused to believe, and they poisoned the minds 2 of the pagans against the brothers.a

Accordingly Paul and Barnabas stayed on for some time, preaching fearlessly 3 for the Lord; and the Lord supported all they said about his gift of grace, allowing signs and wonders to be performed by them.

The people in the city were divided, some supported the Jews, others the 4 apostles, •but eventually with the connivance of the authorities a move was 5 made by pagans as well as Jews to make attacks on them and to stone them. When the apostles came to hear of this, they went off for safety to Lycaonia where, 6 in the towns of Lystra and Derbe and in the surrounding country, •they preached 7 the Good News.

Healing of a cripple

A man sat thereb who had never walked in his life, because his feet were 8 crippled from birth; •and as he listened to Paul preaching, he managed to catch 9 his eye. Seeing that the man had the faith to be cured, •Paul said in a loud voice, 10 'Get to your feet—stand up', and the cripple jumped up and began to walk.

When the crowd saw what Paul had done they shouted in the language of 11 Lycaonia, 'These people are gods who have come down to us disguised as men'. They addressed Barnabas as Zeus, and since Paul was the principal speaker they 12 called him Hermes.c •The priests of Zeus-outside-the-Gate, proposing that all 13 the people should offer sacrifice with them, brought garlanded oxen to the gates. When the apostles Barnabas and Paul heard what was happening they tore their 14 clothes,d and rushed into the crowd, shouting, •'Friends, what do you think you 15 are doing? We are only human beings like you. We have come with good news to make you turn from these empty idols to the living God who made heaven and earth and the sea and all that these hold. •In the past he allowed each nation 16 to go its own way; •but even then he did not leave you without evidence of himself 17

in the good things he does for you: he sends you rain from heaven, he makes your
18 crops grow when they should, he gives you food and makes you happy.' •Even
this speech, however, was scarcely enough to stop the crowd offering them
sacrifice.

The mission is disrupted

19   Then some Jews arrived from Antioch and Iconium, and turned the people
against the apostles. They stoned Paul and dragged him outside the town,
20 thinking he was dead. •The disciples came crowding round him but, as they did
so, he stood up and went back to the town. The next day he and Barnabas went
off to Derbe.

21   Having preached the Good News in that town and made a considerable number
22 of disciples, they went back through Lystra and Iconium to Antioch. •They put
fresh heart into the disciples, encouraging them to persevere in the faith. 'We
all have to experience many hardships' they said 'before we enter the kingdom
23 of God.' •In each of these churches they appointed elders, and with prayer and
fasting they commended them to the Lord in whom they had come to believe.

24
25   They passed through Pisidia and reached Pamphylia. •Then after proclaiming
26 the word at Perga they went down to Attalia •and from there sailed for Antioch,
where they had originally been commended to the grace of God for the work
they had now completed.

27   On their arrival they assembled the church and gave an account of all that
God had done with them, and how he had opened the door of faith to the pagans.
28 They stayed there with the disciples for some time.

Controversy at Antioch

1 **15** Then some men came down from Judaea[a] and taught the brothers, 'Unless
you have yourselves circumcised in the tradition of Moses you cannot be
2 saved'. •This led to disagreement, and after Paul and Barnabas had had a long
argument with these men it was arranged that Paul and Barnabas and others of
the church should go up to Jerusalem and discuss the problem with the apostles
and elders.

3   All the members of the church saw them off, and as they passed through
Phoenicia and Samaria they told how the pagans had been converted, and this
4 news .was received with the greatest satisfaction by the brothers. •When they
arrived in Jerusalem they were welcomed by the church and by the apostles and
elders, and gave an account of all that God had done with them.

Controversy at Jerusalem

5   But certain members of the Pharisees' party who had become believers
objected, insisting that the pagans should be circumcised and instructed to keep
6
7 the Law of Moses. •The apostles and elders met to look into the matter, •and
after the discussion had gone on a long time, Peter stood up and addressed them.

Peter's speech

'My brothers,' he said 'you know perfectly well that in the early days God
made his choice among you: the pagans were to learn the Good News from me
8 and so become believers. •In fact God, who can read everyone's heart, showed his
9 approval of them by giving the Holy Spirit to them just as he had to us •God
made no distinction between us and them, since he purified their hearts by faith.
10 It would only provoke God's anger now, surely, if you imposed on the disciples
the very burden that neither we nor our ancestors were strong enough to support?

---

f. Is 49:6, quoted freely from the LXX.
14 a. This sentence is a parenthesis. V.3 continues from v.1.   b. In Lystra.   c. Mercury,
the messenger or herald of the gods.   d. Conventional sign of despair.
15 a. In the allusion to this incident in Ga, they are said to have come 'from James', Ga 2:12.

Remember, we believe that we are saved in the same way as they are: through 11 the grace of the Lord Jesus.'

This silenced the entire assembly, and they listened to Barnabas and Paul 12 describing all the signs and wonders God had worked through them among the pagans.

James' speech

When they had finished it was James who spoke. 'My brothers,' he said 13 'listen to me. •Simeon[b] has described how God first arranged to enlist a people 14 for his name out of the pagans. •This is entirely in harmony with the words of the 15 prophets, since the scriptures say:

> After that I shall return 16
> and rebuild the fallen House of David;
> I shall rebuild it from its ruins
> and restore it.
> Then the rest of mankind, 17
> all the pagans who are consecrated to my name,
> will look for the Lord,
> says the Lord who made this •known so long ago.[c] 18

'I rule, then, that instead of making things more difficult for pagans who 19 turn to God, •we send them a letter telling them merely to abstain from anything 20 polluted by idols,[d] from fornication,[e] from the meat of strangled animals and from blood. •For Moses has always had his preachers in every town, and is 21 read aloud in the synagogues every sabbath.'

The apostolic letter

Then the apostles and elders decided to choose delegates to send to Antioch 22 with Paul and Barnabas; the whole church concurred with this. They chose Judas known as Barsabbas and Silas,[f] both leading men in the brotherhood, and gave them this letter to take with them: 23

'The apostles and elders, your brothers, send greetings to the brothers of pagan birth in Antioch, Syria and Cilicia. •We hear that some of our members have 24 disturbed you with their demands and have unsettled your minds. They acted without any authority from us, •and so we have decided unanimously to elect 25 delegates and to send them to you with Barnabas and Paul, men we highly respect who have dedicated their lives to the name of our Lord Jesus Christ. •Accord- $^{26}_{27}$ ingly we are sending you Judas and Silas, who will confirm by word of mouth what we have written in this letter. •It has been decided by the Holy Spirit and by 28 ourselves not to saddle you with any burden beyond these essentials: •you 29 are to abstain from food sacrificed to idols, from blood, from the meat of strangled animals and from fornication. Avoid these, and you will do what is right. Farewell.'

The delegates at Antioch

The party left and went down to Antioch, where they summoned the whole 30 community and delivered the letter. •The community read it and were delighted 31 with the encouragement it gave them. •Judas and Silas, being themselves prophets, 32 spoke for a long time, encouraging and strengthening the brothers. •These two 33 spent some time there, and then the brothers wished them peace and they went back to those who had sent them. •Paul and Barnabas, however, stayed on in 35 Antioch, and there with many others they taught and proclaimed the Good News, the word of the Lord.

IV. PAUL'S MISSIONS

Paul separates from Barnabas and recruits Silas

36 On a later occasion Paul said to Barnabas, 'Let us go back and visit all the towns where we preached the word of the Lord, so that we can see how
37 the brothers are doing'. •Barnabas suggested taking John Mark, •but Paul was not
38 in favour of taking along the very man who had deserted them in Pamphylia and had refused to share in their work.
39 After a violent quarrel they parted company, and Barnabas sailed off with
40 Mark to Cyprus. •Before Paul left, he chose Silas to accompany him and was commended by the brothers to the grace of God.

Lycaonia: Paul recruits Timothy

41 He travelled through Syria and Cilicia, consolidating the churches.
1 **16** From there he went to Derbe, and then on to Lystra. Here there was a disciple called Timothy, whose mother was a Jewess who had become a
2 believer; but his father was a Greek. •The brothers at Lystra and Iconium spoke
3 well of Timothy, •and Paul, who wanted to have him as a travelling companion, had him circumcised. This was on account of the Jews in the locality where everyone knew his father was a Greek.
4 As they visited one town after another, they passed on the decisions reached by the apostles and elders in Jerusalem, with instructions to respect them.
5 So the churches grew strong in the faith, as well as growing daily in numbers.

The crossing into Asia Minor

6 They travelled through Phrygia and the Galatian country, having been told
7 by the Holy Spirit not to preach the word in Asia. •When they reached the frontier of Mysia they thought to cross it into Bithynia, but as the Spirit of Jesus would
8 not allow them, •they went through Mysia and came down to Troas.
9 One night Paul had a vision: a Macedonian appeared and appealed to him
10 in these words, 'Come across to Macedonia and help us'. •Once he had seen this vision we lost no time in arranging a passage to Macedonia, convinced that God had called us to bring them the Good News.

Arrival at Philippi

11 Sailing from Troas we made a straight run for Samothrace; the next day for
12 Neapolis, •and from there for Philippi, a Roman colony and the principal city
13 of that particular district of Macedonia. After a few days in this city •we went along the river outside the gates as it was the sabbath and this was a customary place for prayer.*a* We sat down and preached to the women who had come to the
14 meeting. •One of these women was called Lydia, a devout woman from the town of Thyatira who was in the purple-dye trade. She listened to us, and the Lord
15 opened her heart to accept what Paul was saying. •After she and her household had been baptised she sent us an invitation: 'If you really think me a true believer in the Lord,' she said 'come and stay with us'; and she would take no refusal.

Imprisonment of Paul and Silas

16 One day as we were going to prayer, we met a slave-girl who was a soothsayer
17 and made a lot of money for her masters by telling fortunes. •This girl started following Paul and the rest of us and shouting, 'Here are the servants of the Most
18 High God; they have come to tell you how to be saved!' •She did this every day

---

b. Semitic form of Simon Peter's name. c. Am 9:11,12, quoted according to the LXX.
d. I.e. which has been offered in sacrifice to false gods. e. Perhaps all the irregular marriages listed in Lv 18. f. Silas, also mentioned in Ac 18; 1 Th, 2 Th, 2 Co, 1 P.
16 a. There was no synagogue in this Latin city; the Jews met by the river for ritual ablutions.

afterwards until Paul lost his temper one day and turned round and said to the spirit, 'I order you in the name of Jesus Christ to leave that woman'. The spirit went out of her then and there.

When her masters saw that there was no hope of making any more money 19 out of her, they seized Paul and Silas and dragged them to the law courts in the market place •where they charged them before the magistrates and said, 'These 20 people are causing a disturbance in our city. They are Jews •and are advocating 21 practices which it is unlawful for us as Romans to accept or follow.'ᵇ •The crowd 22 joined in and showed its hostility to them, so the magistrates had them stripped and ordered them to be flogged. •They were given many lashes and then thrown 23 into prison, and the gaoler was told to keep a close watch on them. •So, following 24 his instructions, he threw them into the inner prison and fastened their feet in the stocks.

The miraculous deliverance of Paul and Silas

Late that night Paul and Silas were praying and singing God's praises, while 25 the other prisoners listened. •Suddenly there was an earthquake that shook the 26 prison to its foundations. All the doors flew open and the chains fell from all the prisoners. •When the gaoler woke and saw the doors wide open he drew his sword 27 and was about to commit suicide, presuming that the prisoners had escaped. •But 28 Paul shouted at the top of his voice, 'Don't do yourself any harm; we are all here'.

The gaoler called for lights, then rushed in, threw himself trembling at the 29 feet of Paul and Silas, •and escorted them out, saying, 'Sirs, what must I do to be 30 saved?' •They told him, 'Become a believer in the Lord Jesus, and you will be 31 saved, and your household too'. •Then they preached the word of the Lord to 32 him and to all his family. •Late as it was, he took them to wash their wounds, 33 and was baptised then and there with all his household. •Afterwards he took 34 them home and gave them a meal, and the whole family celebrated their conversion to belief in God.

When it was daylight the magistrates sent the officers with the order: 'Release 35 those men'. •The gaoler reported the message to Paul, 'The magistrates have 36 sent an order for your release; you can go now and be on your way'. •'What!' 37 Paul replied 'They flog Roman citizens in public and without trial and throw us into prison, and then think they can push us out on the quiet! Oh no! They must come and escort us out themselves.'

The officers reported this to the magistrates, who were horrified to hear the 38 men were Roman citizens. •They came and begged them to leave the town. 39 From the prison they went to Lydia's house where they saw all the brothers and 40 gave them some encouragement; then they left.

Thessalonika: difficulties with the Jews

17 Passing through Amphipolis and Apollonia, they eventually reached 1 Thessalonika, where there was a Jewish synagogue. •Paul as usual introduced himself and for three consecutive sabbaths developed the arguments from 2 scripture for them, •explaining and proving how it was ordained that the Christ 3 should suffer and rise from the dead. 'And the Christ' he said 'is this Jesus whom I am proclaiming to you.' •Some of them were convinced and joined Paul and 4 Silas, and so did a great many God-fearing people and Greeks, as well as a number of rich women.

The Jews, full of resentment, enlisted the help of a gang from the market place, 5 stirred up a crowd, and soon had the whole city in an uproar. They made for Jason's house, hoping to find them there and drag them off to the People's Assembly; •however, they only found Jason and some of the brothers, and these 6 they dragged before the city council, shouting, 'The people who have been turning the whole world upside down have come here now; •they have been 7 staying at Jason's. They have broken every one of Caesar's edicts by claiming

8 that there is another emperor, Jesus.' •This accusation alarmed the citizens
9 and the city councillors •and they made Jason and the rest give security before
setting them free.

Fresh difficulties at Beroea

10 When it was dark the brothers immediately sent Paul and Silas away to Beroea,
11 where they visited the Jewish synagogue as soon as they arrived. •Here the Jews
were more open-minded than those in Thessalonika, and they welcomed the word
very readily; every day they studied the scriptures to check whether it was true.
12 Many Jews became believers, and so did many Greek women from the upper
classes and a number of the men.
13 When the Jews of Thessalonika heard that the word of God was being preached
by Paul in Beroea as well, they went there to make trouble and stir up the people.
14 So the brothers arranged for Paul to go immediately as far as the coast, leaving
15 Silas and Timothy behind. •Paul's escort took him as far as Athens, and went
back with instructions for Silas and Timothy to rejoin Paul as soon as they could.

Paul in Athens

16 Paul waited for them in Athens and there his whole soul was revolted at the
17 sight of a city given over to idolatry. •In the synagogue he held debates with the
Jews and the God-fearing, but in the market place he had debates every day with
18 anyone who would face him. •Even a few Epicurean and Stoic philosophers
argued with him. Some said, 'Does this parrot know what he's talking about?'
And, because he was preaching about Jesus and the resurrection, others said,
'He sounds like a propagandist for some outlandish gods'.[a]
19 They invited him to accompany them to the Council of the Areopagus, where
they said to him, 'How much of this new teaching you were speaking about are
20 we allowed to know? •Some of the things you said seemed startling to us and we
21 would like to find out what they mean.' •The one amusement the Athenians and
the foreigners living there seem to have, apart from discussing the latest ideas,
is listening to lectures about them.
22 So Paul stood before the whole Council of the Areopagus and made this
speech:

Paul's speech before the Council of the Areopagus

'Men of Athens, I have seen for myself how extremely scrupulous you are
23 in all religious matters, •because I noticed, as I strolled round admiring your
sacred monuments, that you had an altar inscribed: To An Unknown God. Well,
the God whom I proclaim is in fact the one whom you already worship without
knowing it.
24 'Since the God who made the world and everything in it is himself Lord of
heaven and earth, he does not make his home in shrines made by human hands.
25 Nor is he dependent on anything that human hands can do for him, since he can
never be in need of anything; on the contrary, it is he who gives everything—
26 including life and breath—to everyone. •From one single stock he not only
created the whole human race so that they could occupy the entire earth, but he
decreed how long each nation should flourish and what the boundaries of its
27 territory should be. •And he did this so that all nations might seek the deity
and, by feeling their way towards him, succeed in finding him. Yet in fact he is not
28 far from any of us, •since it is in him that we live, and move, and exist,[b] as indeed
some of your own writers have said:

"We are all his children".[c]

b. The Jews had no right to proselytise Romans.
17 a. They assumed that *Anastasis* ('Resurrection') was the name of a goddess.   b. Expression suggested by the poet Epimenides.   c. From the *Phainomena* of Aratus.

'Since we are the children of God, we have no excuse for thinking that the 29
deity looks like anything in gold, silver or stone that has been carved and designed
by a man.

'God overlooked that sort of thing when men were ignorant, but now he is 30
telling everyone everywhere that they must repent, •because he has fixed a day 31
when the whole world will be judged, and judged in righteousness, and he has
appointed a man to be the judge. And God has publicly proved this by raising
this man from the dead.'

At this mention of rising from the dead, some of them burst out laughing; 32
others said, 'We would like to hear you talk about this again'. •After that Paul 33
left them, •but there were some who attached themselves to him and became 34
believers, among them Dionysius the Areopagite and a woman called Damaris,
and others besides.

Foundation of the church of Corinth

18 After this Paul left Athens and went to Corinth, •where he met a Jew $\frac{1}{2}$
called Aquila whose family came from Pontus. He and his wife Priscilla*
had recently left Italy because an edict of Claudius had expelled all the Jews from
Rome.* Paul went to visit them, •and when he found they were tentmakers, of the 3
same trade as himself, he lodged with them, and they worked together. •Every 4
sabbath he used to hold debates in the synagogues, trying to convert Jews as well
as Greeks.

After Silas and Timothy had arrived from Macedonia, Paul devoted all his 5
time to preaching, declaring to the Jews that Jesus was the Christ. •When they 6
turned against him and started to insult him, he took his cloak and shook it out
in front of them, saying, 'Your blood be on your own heads; from now on I can
go to the pagans with a clear conscience'. •Then he left the synagogue and moved 7
to the house next door that belonged to a worshipper of God called Justus.
Crispus, president of the synagogue, and his whole household, all became believers 8
in the Lord. A great many Corinthians who had heard him became believers and
were baptised. •One night the Lord spoke to Paul in a vision, 'Do not be afraid 9
to speak out, nor allow yourself to be silenced: •I am with you. I have so many 10
people on my side in this city that no one will even attempt to hurt you.' •So Paul 11
stayed there preaching the word of God among them for eighteen months.

The Jews take Paul to court

But while Gallio was proconsul of Achaia,* the Jews made a concerted attack 12
on Paul and brought him before the tribunal. •'We accuse this man' they said 13
'of persuading people to worship God in a way that breaks the Law.' •Before 14
Paul could open his mouth, Gallio said to the Jews, 'Listen, you Jews. If this were
a misdemeanour or a crime, I would not hesitate to attend to you; •but if it is 15
only quibbles about words and names, and about your own Law, then you must
deal with it yourselves—I have no intention of making legal decisions about things
like that.' •Then he sent them out of the court, •and at once they all turned on $^{16}_{17}$
Sosthenes, the synagogue president, and beat him in front of the court house.
Gallio refused to take any notice at all.

Return to Antioch and departure for the third journey

After staying on for some time, Paul took leave of the brothers and sailed for 18
Syria,* accompanied by Priscilla and Aquila. At Cenchreae he had his hair cut
off, because of a vow he had made.

When they reached Ephesus, he left them, but first he went alone to the 19
synagogue to debate with the Jews. •They asked him to stay longer but he declined, 20
though when he left he said, 'I will come back another time, God willing'. Then 21
he sailed from Ephesus.

He landed at Caesarea, and went up to greet the church. Then he came down 22

23 to Antioch •where he spent a short time before continuing his journey through the Galatian country and then through Phrygia, encouraging all the followers.

Apollos

24   An Alexandrian Jew named Apollos now arrived in Ephesus. He was an
25 eloquent man, with a sound knowledge of the scriptures, and yet, •though he had been given instruction in the Way of the Lord and preached with great spiritual earnestness and was accurate in all the details he taught about Jesus, he had only
26 experienced the baptism of John. •When Priscilla and Aquila heard him speak boldly in the synagogue, they took an interest in him and gave him further instruction about the Way.
27   When Apollos thought of crossing over to Achaia, the brothers encouraged him and wrote asking the disciples to welcome him. When he arrived there he was
28 able by God's grace to help the believers considerably •by the energetic way he refuted the Jews in public and demonstrated from the scriptures that Jesus was the Christ.

The disciples of John at Ephesus

1 **19** While Apollos was in Corinth, Paul made his way overland as far as
2   Ephesus, where he found a number of disciples. •When he asked, 'Did you receive the Holy Spirit when you became believers?' they answered, 'No,
3 we were never even told there was such a thing as a Holy Spirit'. •'Then how
4 were you baptised?' he asked. 'With John's baptism' they replied. •'John's baptism' said Paul 'was a baptism of repentance; but he insisted that the people should believe in the one who was to come after him—in other words Jesus.'
5
6 When they heard this, they were baptised in the name of the Lord Jesus, •and the moment Paul had laid hands on them the Holy Spirit came down on them,
7 and they began to speak with tongues and to prophesy.•There were about twelve of these men.

Foundation of the church of Ephesus

8   He began by going to the synagogue, where he spoke out boldly and argued
9 persuasively about the kingdom of God. He did this for three months, •till the attitude of some of the congregation hardened into unbelief. As soon as they began attacking the Way in front of the others, he broke with them and took his
10 disciples apart to hold daily discussions in the lecture room of Tyrannus. •This went on for two years, with the result that people from all over Asia,*a* both Jews and Greeks, were able to hear the word of the Lord.

The Jewish exorcists

11
12 So remarkable were the miracles worked by God at Paul's hands •that handkerchiefs or aprons which had touched him were taken to the sick, and they were cured of their illnesses, and the evil spirits came out of them.
13   But some itinerant Jewish exorcists tried pronouncing the name of the Lord Jesus over people who were possessed by evil spirits; they used to say, 'I command
14 you by the Jesus whose spokesman is Paul'. •Among those who did this were
15 seven sons of Sceva, a Jewish chief priest. •The evil spirit replied, 'Jesus
16 I recognise, and I know who Paul is, but who are you?' •and the man with the evil spirit hurled himself at them and overpowered first one and then another, and handled them so violently that they fled from that house naked and badly
17 mauled. •Everybody in Ephesus, both Jews and Greeks, heard about this episode;

18 a. Also called Prisca, Rm 16:3; 1 Co 16:19; 2 Tm 4:19.   **b.** This edict was issued in 49 or 50.   **c.** In 52, according to an inscription from Delphi.   **d.** To Antioch.
19 a. I.e. the region round Ephesus, including the seven towns of Rv 1:11.

they were all greatly impressed, and the name of the Lord Jesus came to be held in great honour.

Some believers, too, came forward to admit in detail how they had used spells 18 and a number of them who had practised magic collected their books and made 19 a bonfire of them in public. The value of these was calculated to be fifty thousand silver pieces.

In this impressive way the word of the Lord spread more and more widely 20 and successfully.

V. A PRISONER FOR CHRIST

Paul's plans

When all this was over Paul made up his mind to go back to Jerusalem through 21 Macedonia and Achaia. 'After I have been there' he said 'I must go on to see Rome as well.' •So he sent two of his helpers, Timothy and Erastus, ahead of 22 him to Macedonia, while he remained for a time in Asia.

Ephesus: the silversmiths' riot

It was during this time that a rather serious disturbance broke out in connection 23 with the Way. •A silversmith called Demetrius, who employed a large number 24 of craftsmen making silver shrines of Diana, •called a general meeting of his own 25 men with others in the same trade. 'As you men know,' he said 'it is on this industry that we depend for our prosperity. •Now you must have seen and heard 26 how, not just in Ephesus but nearly everywhere in Asia, this man Paul has persuaded and converted a great number of people with his argument that gods made by hand are not gods at all. •This threatens not only to discredit our trade, but 27 also to reduce the sanctuary of the great goddess Diana to unimportance. It could end up by taking away all the prestige of a goddess venerated all over Asia, yes, and everywhere in the civilised world.' •This speech roused them to fury, and they 28 started to shout, 'Great is Diana of the Ephesians!' •The whole town was in an 29 uproar and the mob rushed to the theatre dragging along two of Paul's Macedonian travelling companions, Gaius and Aristarchus. •Paul wanted to 30 make an appeal to the people, but the disciples refused to let him; •in fact, some 31 of the Asiarchs,[b] who were friends of his, sent messages imploring him not to take the risk of going into the theatre.

By now everybody was shouting different things till the assembly itself had 32 no idea what was going on; most of them did not even know why they had been summoned. •The Jews pushed Alexander to the front, and when some of the 33 crowd shouted encouragement he raised his hand for silence in the hope of being able to explain things to the people. •When they realised he was a Jew, they all 34 started shouting in unison, 'Great is Diana of the Ephesians!' and they kept this up for two hours. •When the town clerk eventually succeeded in calming the 35 crowd, he said, 'Citizens of Ephesus! Is there anybody alive who does not know that the city of the Ephesians is the guardian of the temple of great Diana and of her statue that fell from heaven? •Nobody can contradict this and there is no 36 need for you to get excited or do anything rash. •These men you have brought 37 here are not guilty of any sacrilege or blasphemy against our goddess. •If Deme- 38 trius and the craftsmen he has with him want to complain about anyone, there are the assizes and the proconsuls; let them take the case to court. •And if you want 39 to ask any more questions you must raise them in the regular assembly. •We could 40 easily be charged with rioting for today's happenings: there was no ground for it all, and we can give no reason for this gathering.' •When he had finished this 41 speech he dismissed the assembly.

Paul leaves Ephesus

1 **20** When the disturbance was over, Paul sent for the disciples and, after speaking words of encouragement to them, said good-bye and set out for 2 Macedonia. •On his way through those areas he said many words of encourage-3 ment to them and then made his way into Greece, •where he spent three months. He was leaving by ship for Syria[a] when a plot organised against him by the Jews 4 made him decide to go back by way of Macedonia. •He was accompanied by Sopater, son of Pyrrhus, who came from Beroea; Aristarchus and Secundus who came from Thessalonika; Gaius from Doberus, and Timothy, as well as Tychicus 5 and Trophimus who were from Asia. •They all went on to Troas where they 6 waited for us. •We ourselves left Philippi by ship after the days of Unleavened Bread and met them five days later at Troas, where we stopped for a week.

Troas: Paul raises a dead man to life

7 On the first day of the week[b] we met to break bread. Paul was due to leave the next day, and he preached a sermon that went on till the middle of the night. 8 9 A number of lamps were lit in the upstairs room where we were assembled, •and as Paul went on and on, a young man called Eutychus who was sitting on the window-sill grew drowsy and was overcome by sleep and fell to the ground three 10 floors below. He was picked up dead. •Paul went down and stooped to clasp the 11 boy to him. 'There is no need to worry,' he said 'there is still life in him.' •Then he went back upstairs where he broke bread and ate and carried on talking till 12 he left at daybreak. •They took the boy away alive, and were greatly encouraged.

From Troas to Miletus

13 We were now to go on ahead by sea, so we set sail for Assos, where we were to take Paul on board; this was what he had arranged, for he wanted to go by road. 14 15 When he rejoined us at Assos we took him aboard and went on to Mitylene. •The next day we sailed from there and arrived opposite Chios. The second day we touched at Samos and, after stopping at Trogyllium, made Miletus the next day. 16 Paul had decided to pass wide of Ephesus so as to avoid spending time in Asia, since he was anxious to be in Jerusalem, if possible, for the day of Pentecost.

Farewell to the elders of Ephesus

17 18 From Miletus he sent for the elders of the church of Ephesus. •When they arrived he addressed these words to them:

'You know what my way of life has been ever since the first day I set foot 19 among you in Asia, •how I have served the Lord in all humility, with all the 20 sorrows and trials that came to me through the plots of the Jews. •I have not hesitated to do anything that would be helpful to you; I have preached to you, 21 and instructed you both in public and in your homes, •urging both Jews and Greeks to turn to God and to believe in our Lord Jesus.

22 'And now you see me a prisoner already in spirit; I am on my way to Jeru-23 salem, but have no idea what will happen to me there, •except that the Holy Spirit, in town after town, has made it clear enough that imprisonment and persecution 24 await me. •But life to me is not a thing to waste words on, provided that when I finish my race I have carried out the mission the Lord Jesus gave me—and that was to bear witness to the Good News of God's grace.

25 'I now feel sure that none of you among whom I have gone about proclaiming 26 the kingdom will ever see my face again. •And so here and now I swear that my

b. Local leaders of the official state worship.
20 a. Taking to Jerusalem the proceeds of the collection, Rm 15:25. b. The day was reckoned in the Jewish fashion; the Lord's day began on the evening of Saturday and it was then that this meeting was held.

conscience is clear as far as all of you are concerned, •for I have without faltering 27
put before you the whole of God's purpose.

'Be on your guard for yourselves and for all the flock of which the Holy Spirit 28
has made you the overseers, to feed the Church of God which he bought with
his own blood. •I know quite well that when I have gone fierce wolves will invade 29
you and will have no mercy on the flock. •·Even from your own ranks there will 30
be men coming forward with a travesty of the truth on their lips to induce the
disciples to follow them. •So be on your guard, remembering how night and day 31
for three years I never failed to keep you right, shedding tears over each one of
you. •And now I commend you to God, and to the word of his grace that has 32
power to build you up and to give you your inheritance among all the sanctified.

'I have never asked anyone for money or clothes; •you know for yourselves $^{33}_{34}$
that the work I did earned enough to meet my needs and those of my companions. •I did this to show you that this is how we must exert ourselves to support 35
the weak, remembering the words of the Lord Jesus, who himself said, "There is
more happiness in giving than in receiving". '

When he had finished speaking he knelt down with them all and prayed. •By $^{36}_{37}$
now they were all in tears; they put their arms round Paul's neck and kissed him;
what saddened them most was his saying they would never see his face again. 38
Then they escorted him to the ship.

The journey to Jerusalem

21 When we had at last torn ourselves away from them and put to sea, we set 1
a straight course and arrived at Cos; the next day we reached Rhodes, and
from there went on to Patara. •Here we found a ship bound for Phoenicia, so we 2
went on board and sailed in her. •After sighting Cyprus and leaving it to port, 3
we sailed to Syria and put in at Tyre, since the ship was to unload her cargo there.
We sought out the disciples and stayed there a week. Speaking in the Spirit, 4
they kept telling Paul not to go on to Jerusalem, •but when our time was up we set 5
off. Together with the women and children they all escorted us on our way till we
were out of the town. When we reached the beach, we knelt down and prayed;
then, after saying good-bye to each other, we went aboard and they returned 6
home.

The end of our voyage from Tyre came when we landed at Ptolemais, where 7
we greeted the brothers and stayed one day with them. •The next day we left and 8
came to Caesarea. Here we called on Philip the evangelist, one of the Seven, and
stayed with him. •He had four virgin daughters who were prophets. •When we $^{9}_{10}$
had been there several days a prophet called Agabus arrived from Judaea •to see 11
us. He took Paul's girdle, and tied up his own feet and hands, and said, 'This
is what the Holy Spirit says, "The man this girdle belongs to will be bound like
this by the Jews in Jerusalem, and handed over to the pagans" '. •When we heard 12
this, we and everybody there implored Paul not to go on to Jerusalem. •To 13
this he replied, 'What are you trying to do—weaken my resolution by your tears?
For my part, I am ready not only to be tied up but even to die in Jerusalem for
the name of the Lord Jesus.' •And so, as he would not be persuaded, we gave up 14
the attempt, saying, 'The Lord's will be done'.

Paul's arrival in Jerusalem

After this we packed and went on up to Jerusalem. •Some of the disciples $^{15}_{16}$
from Caesarea accompanied us and took us to the house of a Cypriot with whom
we were to lodge; he was called Mnason and had been one of the earliest disciples.

On our arrival in Jerusalem the brothers gave us a very warm welcome. •The $^{17}_{18}$
next day Paul went with us to visit James, and all the elders were present. •After 19
greeting them he gave a detailed account of all that God had done among the
pagans through his ministry. •They gave glory to God when they heard this. 20
'But you see, brother,' they said 'how thousands of Jews have now become

21 believers, all of them staunch upholders of the Law, and •they have heard that
you instruct all Jews living among the pagans to break away from Moses,
authorising them not to circumcise their children or to follow the customary
22 practices. •What is to be done? Inevitably there will be a meeting of the whole
23 body, since they are bound to hear that you have come. •So do as we suggest.
24 We have four men here who are under a vow; •take these men along and be
purified with them and pay all the expenses connected with the shaving of their
heads.ᵃ This will let everyone know there is no truth in the reports they have heard
25 about you and that you still regularly observe the Law. •The pagans who have
become believers, as we wrote when we told them our decisions, must abstain from
things sacrificed to idols, from blood, from the meat of strangled animals and
from fornication.'
26 So the next day Paul took the men along and was purified with them, and he
visited the Temple to give notice of the time when the period of purification would
be over and the offering would have to be presented on behalf of each of them.

Paul's arrest

27 The seven days were nearly over when some Jews from Asia caught sight of
28 him in the Temple and stirred up the crowd and seized him, •shouting, 'Men of
Israel, help! This is the man who preaches to everyone everywhere against our
people, against the Law and against this place. Now he has profaned this Holy
29 Place by bringing Greeks into the Temple.' •They had, in fact, previously seen
Trophimus the Ephesian in the city with him, and thought that Paul had brought
him into the Temple.
30 This roused the whole city; people came running from all sides; they seized
Paul and dragged him out of the Temple, and the gates were closed behind them.
31 They would have killed him if a report had not reached the tribune of the cohortᵇ
32 that there was rioting all over Jerusalem. •He immediately called out soldiers
and centurions, and charged down on the crowd, who stopped beating Paul when
33 they saw the tribune and the soldiers. •When the tribune came up he arrested
Paul, had him bound with two chains and enquired who he was and what he had
34 done. •People in the crowd called out different things, and since the noise made
it impossible for him to get any positive information, the tribune ordered Paul
35 to be taken into the fortress. •When Paul reached the steps, the crowd became
36 so violent that he had to be carried by the soldiers; •and indeed the whole mob
was after them, shouting, 'Kill him!'
37 Just as Paul was being taken into the fortress, he asked the tribune if he could
38 have a word with him. The tribune said, 'You speak Greek, then? •So you are
not the Egyptian who started the recent revolt and led those four thousand cut-
39 throatsᶜ out into the desert?' •'I?' said Paul 'I am a Jew and a citizen of the well-
known city of Tarsus in Cilicia. Please give me permission to speak to the people.'
40 The man gave his consent and Paul, standing at the top of the steps, gestured to
the people with his hand. When all was quiet again he spoke to them in Hebrew. ᵈ

Paul's address to the Jews of Jerusalem

1 22 'My brothers, my fathers, listen to what I have to say to you in my defence.'
2 When they realised he was speaking in Hebrew, the silence was even greater
3 than before. •'I am a Jew,' Paul said 'and was born at Tarsus in Cilicia. I was
brought up here in this city. I studied under Gamaliel and was taught the exact
observance of the Law of our ancestors. In fact, I was as full of duty towards God
4 as you are today. •I even persecuted this Way to the death, and sent women as
5 well as men to prison in chains •as the high priest and the whole council of elders
can testify, since they even sent me with letters to their brothers in Damascus.

21 a. For the duration of a nazirite vow, the hair was not to be cut. Discharge from the vow,
on fulfilment, had to be celebrated with expensive sacrifices.   b. Commanding officer of
the Roman garrison.   c. Nationalist extremists.   d. I.e. Aramaic.

When I set off it was with the intention of bringing prisoners back from there to Jerusalem for punishment.

'I was on that journey and nearly at Damascus when about midday a bright 6 light from heaven suddenly shone round me. •I fell to the ground and heard a voice 7 saying, "Saul, Saul, why are you persecuting me?" •I answered: Who are you, 8 Lord? and he said to me, "I am Jesus the Nazarene, and you are persecuting me". •The people with me saw the light but did not hear his voice as he spoke 9 to me. •I said: What am I to do, Lord? The Lord answered, "Stand up and go 10 into Damascus, and there you will be told what you have been appointed to do". The light had been so dazzling that I was blind and my companions had to take 11 me by the hand; and so I came to Damascus.

'Someone called Ananias, a devout follower of the Law and highly thought 12 of by all the Jews living there, •came to see me; he stood beside me and said, 13 "Brother Saul, receive your sight". Instantly my sight came back and I was able to see him. •Then he said, "The God of our ancestors has chosen you to know 14 his will, to see the Just One and hear his own voice speaking, •because you are 15 to be his witness before all mankind, testifying to what you have seen and heard. And now why delay? It is time you were baptised and had your sins washed away 16 while invoking his name."

'Once, after I had got back to Jerusalem, when I was praying in the Temple, 17 I fell into a trance •and then I saw him. "Hurry," he said "leave Jerusalem at 18 once; they will not accept the testimony you are giving about me." •Lord, 19 I answered, it is because they know that I used to go from synagogue to synagogue, imprisoning and flogging those who believed in you; •and that when the 20 blood of your witness *a* Stephen was being shed, I was standing by in full agreement with his murderers, and minding their clothes. •Then he said to me, "Go! I am 21 sending you out to the pagans far away." '

Paul the Roman citizen

So far they had listened to him, but at these words they began to shout, 'Rid 22 the earth of the man! He is not fit to live!' •They were yelling, waving their 23 cloaks and throwing dust into the air, •and so the tribune had him brought into 24 the fortress and ordered him to be examined under the lash, to find out the reason for the outcry against him. •But when they had strapped him down Paul said 25 to the centurion on duty, 'Is it legal for you to flog a man who is a Roman citizen and has not been brought to trial?' •When he heard this the centurion went and 26 told the tribune; 'Do you realise what you are doing?' he said 'This man is a Roman citizen'. •So the tribune came and asked him, 'Tell me, are you a 27 Roman citizen?' 'I am' Paul said. •The tribune replied, 'It cost me a large sum to 28 acquire this citizenship'. 'But I was born to it' said Paul. •Then those who were 29 about to examine him hurriedly withdrew, and the tribune himself was alarmed when he realised that he had put a Roman citizen in chains.

His appearance before the Sanhedrin

The next day, since he wanted to know what precise charge the Jews were 30 bringing, he freed Paul and gave orders for a meeting of the chief priests and the entire Sanhedrin; then he brought Paul down and stood him in front of them.

23 Paul looked steadily at the Sanhedrin and began to speak, 'My brothers, 1 to this day I have conducted myself before God with a perfectly clear conscience'. •At this the high priest Ananias ordered his attendants to strike him 2 on the mouth. •Then Paul said to him, 'God will surely strike you, you 3 whitewashed wall! How can you sit there to judge me according to the Law, and then break the Law by ordering a man to strike me?' •The attendants said, 'It is 4 God's high priest you are insulting!' •Paul answered, 'Brothers, I did not realise 5 it was the high priest, for scripture says: *You must not curse a ruler of your people*'. *a*

6   Now Paul was well aware that one section was made up of Sadducees and the other of Pharisees, so he called out in the Sanhedrin, 'Brothers, I am a Pharisee and the son of Pharisees. It is for our hope in the resurrection of the dead that
7 I am on trial.' •As soon as he said this a dispute broke out between the Pharisees
8 and Sadducees, and the assembly was split between the two parties. •For the Sadducees say there is neither resurrection, nor angel, nor spirit, while the
9 Pharisees accept all three. •The shouting grew louder, and some of the scribes from the Pharisees' party stood up and protested strongly, 'We find nothing wrong
10 with this man. Suppose a spirit has spoken to him, or an angel?' •Feeling was running high, and the tribune, afraid that they would tear Paul to pieces, ordered his troops to go down and haul him out and bring him into the fortress.
11   Next night, the Lord appeared to him and said, 'Courage! You have borne witness for me in Jerusalem, now you must do the same in Rome.'

The conspiracy of the Jews against Paul

12   When it was day, the Jews held a secret meeting at which they made a vow
13 not to eat or drink until they had killed Paul. •There were more than forty who
14 took part in this conspiracy, •and they went to the chief priests and elders, and told them, 'We have made a solemn vow to let nothing pass our lips until we have
15 killed Paul. •Now it is up to you and the Sanhedrin together to apply to the tribune to bring him down to you, as though you meant to examine his case more closely; we, on our side, are prepared to dispose of him before he reaches you.'
16   But the son of Paul's sister heard of the ambush they were laying and made
17 his way into the fortress and told Paul, •who called one of the centurions and
18 said, 'Take this young man to the tribune; he has something to tell him'. •So' the man took him to the tribune, and reported, 'The prisoner Paul summoned me and
19 requested me to bring this young man to you; he has something to tell you'. •Then the tribune took him by the hand and drew him aside and asked, 'What is it you
20 have to tell me?' •He replied, 'The Jews have made a plan to ask you to take Paul down to the Sanhedrin tomorrow, as though they meant to inquire more closely
21 into his case. •Do not let them persuade you. There are more than forty of them lying in wait for him, and they have vowed not to eat or drink until they have got rid of him. They are ready now and only waiting for your order to be given.'
22 The tribune let the young man go with this caution, 'Tell no one that you have given me this information'.

Paul transferred to Caesarea

23   Then he summoned two of the centurions and said, 'Get two hundred soldiers ready to leave for Caesarea by the third hour of the night with seventy cavalry and
24 two hundred auxiliaries; •provide horses for Paul, and deliver him unharmed
25
26 to Felix the governor'.ᵇ •He also wrote a letter in these terms: •'Claudius Lysias
27 to his Excellency the governor Felix, greetings. •This man had been seized by the Jews and would have been murdered by them but I came on the scene with my troops and got him away, having discovered that he was a Roman citizen.
28 Wanting to find out what charge they were making against him, I brought him
29 before their Sanhedrin. •I found that the accusation concerned disputed points of their Law, but that there was no charge deserving death or imprisonment.
30 My information is that there is a conspiracy against the man, so I hasten to send him to you, and have notified his accusers that they must state their case against him in your presence.'
31   The soldiers carried out their orders; they took Paul and escorted him by night
32 to Antipatris. •Next day they left the mounted escort to go on with him and
33 returned to the fortress. •On arriving at Caesarea the escort delivered the letter
34 to the governor and handed Paul over to him. •The governor read the letter

22 a. *Martyr:* the word had not yet acquired its restricted meaning.
23 a. Ex 22:27   b. Antoninus Felix, procurator of Judaea from 52 to 59-60.

and asked him what province he came from. Learning that he was from Cilicia he said, •'I will hear your case as soon as your accusers are here too'. Then he 35 ordered him to be held in Herod's praetorium.

The case before Felix

24 Five days later the high priest Ananias came down with some of the 1 elders and an advocate named Tertullus, and they laid information against Paul before the governor. •Paul was called, and Tertullus opened for the 2 prosecution, 'Your Excellency, Felix, the unbroken peace we enjoy and the reforms this nation owes to your foresight •are matters we accept, always 3 and everywhere, with all gratitude. •I do not want to take up too much of your 4 time, but I beg you to give us a brief hearing. •The plain truth is that we find 5 this man a perfect pest; he stirs up trouble among Jews the world over, and is a ringleader of the Nazarene sect. •He has even attempted to profane the Temple. 6 We placed him under arrest, intending to judge him according to our Law, •but 7 the tribune Lysias intervened and took him out of our hands by force, •ordering 8 his accusers to appear before you; if you ask him*a* you can find out for yourself the truth of all our accusations against this man.' •The Jews supported him, 9 asserting that these were the facts.

When the governor motioned him to speak, Paul answered: 10

Paul's speech before the Roman governor

'I know that you have administered justice over this nation for many years, and I can therefore speak with confidence in my defence. •As you can verify for 11 yourself, it is no more than twelve days since I went up to Jerusalem on pilgrimage, •and it is not true that they ever found me arguing with anyone or 12 stirring up the mob, either in the Temple, in the synagogues, or about the town; neither can they prove any of the accusations they are making against me now. 13

'What I do admit to you is this: it is according to the Way which they describe 14 as a sect that I worship the God of my ancestors, retaining my belief in all points of the Law and in what is written in the prophets; •and I hold the same hope 15 in God as they do that there will be a resurrection of good men and bad men alike. •In these things, I, as much as they, do my best to keep a clear conscience 16 at all times before God and man.

'After several years I came to bring alms to my nation and to make offerings; 17 it was in connection with these that they found me in the Temple; I had been 18 purified, and there was no crowd involved, and no disturbance. •But some Jews 19 from Asia . . .—these are the ones who should have appeared before you and accused me of whatever they had against me. •At least let those who are present 20 say what crime they found me guilty of when I stood before the Sanhedrin, •unless 21 it were to do with this single outburst, when I stood up among them and called out: It is about the resurrection of the dead that I am on trial before you today.'

Paul's captivity at Caesarea

At this, Felix, who knew more about the Way than most people, adjourned 22 the case, saying, 'When Lysias the tribune has come down I will go into your case'. •He then gave orders to the centurion that Paul should be kept under arrest 23 but free from restriction, and that none of his own people should be prevented from seeing to his needs.

Some days later Felix came with his wife Drusilla who was a Jewess.*b* He sent 24 for Paul and gave him a hearing on the subject of faith in Christ Jesus. •But when 25 he began to treat of righteousness, self-control and the coming Judgement, Felix took fright and said, 'You may go for the present; I will send for you when I find it convenient'. •At the same time he had hopes of receiving money from Paul, 26 and for this reason he sent for him frequently and had talks with him.

When the two years*c* came to an end, Felix was succeeded by Porcius Festus 27 and, being anxious to gain favour with the Jews, Felix left Paul in custody.

Paul appeals to Caesar

25 1 Three days after his arrival in the province, Festus went up to Jerusalem 2 from Caesarea. •The chief priests and leaders of the Jews informed him of 3 the case against Paul, urgently •asking him to support them rather than Paul, and to have him transferred to Jerusalem. They were, in fact, preparing an ambush 4 to murder him on the way. •But Festus replied that Paul would remain in custody 5 in Caesarea, and that he would be going back there shortly himself. •'Let your authorities come down with me' he said 'and if there is anything wrong about the man, they can bring a charge against him.'

6 After staying with them for eight or ten days at the most, he went down to Caesarea and the next day he took his seat on the tribunal and had Paul brought 7 in. •As soon as Paul appeared, the Jews who had come down from Jerusalem surrounded him, making many serious accusations which they were unable to 8 substantiate. •Paul's defence was this, 'I have committed no offence whatever 9 against either Jewish law, or the Temple, or Caesar'. •Festus was anxious to gain favour with the Jews, so he said to Paul, 'Are you willing to go up to Jerusalem 10 and be tried on these charges before me there?' •But Paul replied, 'I am standing before the tribunal of Caesar and this is where I should be tried. I have done the 11 Jews no wrong, as you very well know. •If I am guilty of committing any capital crime, I do not ask to be spared the death penalty. But if there is no substance in the accusations these persons bring against me, no one has a right to surrender 12 me to them. I appeal to Caesar.' •Then Festus conferred with his advisers and replied, 'You have appealed to Caesar; to Caesar you shall go'.

Paul appears before King Agrippa

13 Some days later King Agrippa and Bernice *a* arrived in Caesarea and paid 14 their respects to Festus. •Their visit lasted several days, and Festus put Paul's case before the king. 'There is a man here' he said 'whom Felix left behind in 15 custody, •and while I was in Jerusalem the chief priests and elders of the Jews 16 laid information against him, demanding his condemnation. •But I told them that Romans are not in the habit of surrendering any man, until the accused confronts his accusers and is given an opportunity to defend himself against the 17 charge. •So they came here with me, and I wasted no time but took my seat on 18 the tribunal the very next day and had the man brought in. •When confronted with him, his accusers did not charge him with any of the crimes I had expected; 19 but they had some argument or other with him about their own religion and about 20 a dead man called Jesus whom Paul alleged to be alive. •Not feeling qualified to deal with questions of this sort, I asked him if he would be willing to go to 21 Jerusalem to be tried there on this issue. •But Paul put in an appeal for his case to be reserved for the judgement of the august emperor, so I ordered him to be 22 remanded until I could send him to Caesar.' •Agrippa said to Festus, 'I should like to hear the man myself'. 'Tomorrow' he answered 'you shall hear him.'

23 So the next day Agrippa and Bernice arrived in great state and entered the audience chamber attended by the tribunes and the city notables; and Festus 24 ordered Paul to be brought in. •Then Festus said, 'King Agrippa, and all here present with us, you see before you the man about whom the whole Jewish community has petitioned me, both in Jerusalem and here, loudly protesting 25 that he ought not to be allowed to remain alive. •For my own part I am satisfied that he has committed no capital crime, but when he himself appealed to the 26 august emperor I decided to send him. •But I have nothing definite that I can write to his Imperial Majesty about him; that is why I have produced him before you all, and before you in particular, King Agrippa, so that after the examination

24 a. Lysias. b. Youngest daughter of Herod Agrippa. c. The maximum length of protective custody; Felix was breaking the law by continuing to detain Paul.
25 a. Agrippa, Bernice and Drusilla (24:24) were children of Herod Agrippa I.

I may have something to write. •It seems to me pointless to send a prisoner 27
without indicating the charges against him.'

26 Then Agrippa said to Paul, 'You have leave to speak on your own behalf'. 1
And Paul held up his hand and began his defence:

Paul's speech before King Agrippa

'I consider myself fortunate, King Agrippa, in that it is before you I am to 2
answer today all the charges made against me by the Jews, •the more so because 3
you are an expert in matters of custom and controversy among the Jews. So I beg
you to listen to me patiently.

'My manner of life from my youth, a life spent from the beginning among 4
my own people and in Jerusalem, is common knowledge among the Jews. •They 5
have known me for a long time and could testify, if they would, that I followed
the strictest party in our religion and lived as a Pharisee. •And now it is for my 6
hope in the promise made by God to our ancestors that I am on trial, •the promise 7
that our twelve tribes, constant in worship night and day, hope to attain. For
that hope, Sire, I am actually put on trial by Jews! •Why does it seem incredible 8
to you that God should raise the dead?

'As for me, I once thought it was my duty to use every means to oppose the 9
name of Jesus the Nazarene. •This I did in Jerusalem; I myself threw many of the 10
saints into prison, acting on authority from the chief priests, and when they were
sentenced to death I cast my vote against them. •I often went round the 11
synagogues inflicting penalties, trying in this way to force them to renounce their
faith; my fury against them was so extreme that I even pursued them into foreign
cities.

'On one such expedition I was going to Damascus, armed with full powers 12
and a commission from the chief priests, •and at midday as I was on my way, 13
your Majesty, I saw a light brighter than the sun come down from heaven. It
shone brilliantly round me and my fellow travellers. •We all fell to the ground, 14
and I heard a voice saying to me in Hebrew, "Saul, Saul, why are you persecuting
me? It is hard for you, kicking like this against the goad."ᵃ •Then I said: Who 15
are you, Lord? And the Lord answered, "I am Jesus, and you are persecuting
me. •But get up and stand on your feet, for I have appeared to you for this 16
reason: to appoint you as my servant and as witness of this vision in which you
have seen me, and of others in which I shall appear to you. •*I shall deliver you* 17
from the people and *from the pagans, to whom I am sending you* •*to open their* 18
eyes, so that they may turn *from darkness to light,*ᵇ from the dominion of Satan
to God, and receive, through faith in me, forgiveness of their sins and a share
in the inheritance of the sanctified."

'After that, King Agrippa, I could not disobey the heavenly vision. •On the ¹⁹₂₀
contrary I started preaching, first to the people of Damascus, then to those of
Jerusalem and all the countryside of Judaea, and also to the pagans, urging them
to repent and turn to God, proving their change of heart by their deeds. •This 21
was why the Jews laid hands on me in the Temple and tried to do away with me.
But I was blessed with God's help, and so I have stood firm to this day, testifying 22
to great and small alike, saying nothing more than what the prophets and Moses
himself said would happen: •that the Christ was to suffer and that, as the first 23
to rise from the dead, he was to proclaim that light now shone for our people and
for the pagans too.'

His hearers' reactions

He had reached this point in his defence when Festus shouted out, 'Paul, you 24
are out of your mind; all that learning of yours is driving you mad'. •'Festus, 25
your Excellency,' answered Paul 'I am not mad: I am speaking nothing but the
sober truth. •The king understands these matters, and to him I now speak with 26
assurance, confident that nothing of all this is lost on him; after all, these things
were not done in a corner. •King Agrippa, do you believe in the prophets? I know 27

28 you do.' •At this Agrippa said to Paul, 'A little more, and your arguments would
29 make a Christian of me'. •'Little or more,' Paul replied 'I wish before God
that not only you but all who have heard me today would come to be as I am
—except for these chains.'
30 At this the king rose to his feet, with the governor and Bernice and those who
31 sat there with them. •When they had retired they talked together and agreed,
32 'This man is doing nothing that deserves death or imprisonment'. •And Agrippa
remarked to Festus, 'The man could have been set free if he had not appealed to
Caesar'.

The departure for Rome

1 **27** When it had been decided that we should sail for Italy, Paul and some
other prisoners were handed over to a centurion called Julius, of the
2 Augustan cohort. •We boarded a vessel from Adramyttium bound for ports on the
Asiatic coast, and put to sea; we had Aristarchus with us, a Macedonian of
3 Thessalonika. •Next day we put in at Sidon, and Julius was considerate enough
to allow Paul to go to his friends to be looked after.
4 From there we put to sea again, but as the winds were against us we sailed
5 under the lee of Cyprus, •then across the open sea off Cilicia and Pamphylia,
6 taking a fortnight to reach Myra in Lycia. •There the centurion found an Alexandrian ship leaving for Italy and put us aboard.
7 For some days we made little headway, and we had difficulty in making
Cnidus. The wind would not allow us to touch there, so we sailed under the lee
8 of Crete off Cape Salmone •and struggled along the coast until we came to a place
called Fair Havens, near the town of Lasea.

Storm and shipwreck

9 A great deal of time had been lost, and navigation was already hazardous
since it was now well after the time of the Fast,[a] so Paul gave them this warning,
10 'Friends, I can see this voyage will be dangerous and that we run the risk of losing
11 not only the cargo and the ship but also our lives as well'. •But the centurion
took more notice of the captain and the ship's owner than of what Paul was
12 saying; •and since the harbour was unsuitable for wintering, the majority were
for putting out from there in the hope of wintering at Phoenix—a harbour in
Crete, facing south-west and north-west.
13 A southerly breeze sprang up and, thinking their objective as good as reached,
14 they weighed anchor and began to sail past Crete, close inshore. •But it was not
long before a hurricane, the 'north-easter' as they call it, burst on them from across
15 the island. •The ship was caught and could not be turned head-on to the wind,
16 so we had to give way to it and let ourselves be driven. •We ran under the lee of
a small island called Cauda and managed with some difficulty to bring the ship's
17 boat under control. •They hoisted it aboard and with the help of tackle bound
cables round the ship; then, afraid of running aground on the Syrtis banks, they
18 floated out the sea-anchor and so let themselves drift. •As we were making very
19 heavy weather of it, the next day they began to jettison the cargo, •and the third
20 day they threw the ship's gear overboard with their own hands. •For a number
of days both the sun and the stars were invisible and the storm raged unabated
until at last we gave up all hope of surviving.
21 Then, when they had been without food for a long time, Paul stood up among
the men. 'Friends,' he said 'if you had listened to me and not put out from Crete,
22 you would have spared yourselves all this damage and loss. •But now I ask you
not to give way to despair. There will be no loss of life at all, only of the ship.
23 Last night there was standing beside me an angel of the God to whom I belong

26 a. Greek proverbial expression for useless resistance. b. Quotations from Jr 1; Is 42;
Is 9.
27 a. 'the Fast', the feast of Atonement, was kept about the time of the autumn equinox;
winter was coming on.

and whom I serve, •and he said, "Do not be afraid, Paul. You are destined to 24
appear before Caesar, and for this reason God grants you the safety of all who
are sailing with you." •So take courage, friends; I trust in God that things will 25
turn out just as I was told; •but we are to be stranded on some island.' 26

On the fourteenth night we were being driven one way and another in the 27
Adriatic,*b* when about midnight the crew sensed that land of some sort was near.
They took soundings and found twenty fathoms; after a short interval they 28
sounded again and found fifteen fathoms. •Then, afraid that we might run 29
aground somewhere on a reef, they dropped four anchors from the stern and
prayed for daylight. •When some of the crew tried to escape from the ship and 30
lowered the ship's boat into the sea as though to lay out anchors from the bows,
Paul said to the centurion and his men, 'Unless those men stay on board you 31
cannot hope to be saved'. •So the soldiers cut the boat's ropes and let it drop 32
away.

Just before daybreak Paul urged them all to have something to eat. 'For 33
fourteen days' he said 'you have been in suspense, going hungry and eating
nothing. •Let me persuade you to have something to eat; your safety is not in 34
doubt. Not a hair of your heads will be lost.' •With these words he took some 35
bread, gave thanks to God in front of them all, broke it and began to eat. •Then 36
they all plucked up courage and took something to eat themselves. •We were 37
in all two hundred and seventy-six souls on board that ship. •When they had 38
eaten what they wanted they lightened the ship by throwing the corn overboard
into the sea.

When day came they did not recognise the land, but they could make out 39
a kind of bay with a beach; they planned to run the ship aground on this if they
could. •They slipped the anchors and left them to the sea, and at the same time 40
loosened the lashings of the rudders; then, hoisting the foresail to the wind, they
headed for the beach. •But the cross-currents carried them into a shoal and the 41
vessel ran aground. The bows were wedged in and stuck fast, while the stern began
to break up with the pounding of the waves.

The soldiers planned to kill the prisoners for fear that any should swim off 42
and escape. •But the centurion was determined to bring Paul safely through, and 43
would not let them do what they intended. He gave orders that those who could
swim should jump overboard first and so get ashore, •and the rest follow either 44
on planks or on pieces of wreckage. In this way all came safe and sound to land.

Waiting in Malta

28 Once we had come safely through, we discovered that the island was 1
called Malta. •The inhabitants treated us with unusual kindness. They 2
made us all welcome, and they lit a huge fire because it had started to rain and
the weather was cold. •Paul had collected a bundle of sticks and was putting 3
them on the fire when a viper brought out by the heat attached itself to his hand.
When the natives saw the creature hanging from his hand they said to one 4
another, 'That man must be a murderer; he may have escaped the sea, but divine
vengeance would not let him live'. •However, he shook the creature off into the 5
fire and came to no harm, •although they were expecting him at any moment 6
to swell up or drop dead on the spot. After they had waited a long time without
seeing anything out of the ordinary happen to him, they changed their minds
and began to say he was a god.

In that neighbourhood there were estates belonging to the prefect of the 7
island, whose name was Publius. He received us and entertained us hospitably
for three days. •It so happened that Publius' father was in bed, suffering from 8
feverish attacks and dysentery. Paul went in to see him, and after a prayer he laid
his hands on the man and healed him. •When this happened, the other sick 9
people on the island came as well and were cured;•they honoured us with many 10
marks of respect, and when we sailed they put on board the provisions we
needed.

From Malta to Rome

11 At the end of three months we set sail in a ship that had wintered in the
12 island; she came from Alexandria and her figurehead was the Twins. •We put in
13 at Syracuse and spent three days there; •from there we followed the coast up to
Rhegium. After one day there a south wind sprang up and on the second day we
14 made Puteoli,ª •where we found some brothers and were much rewarded by
staying a week with them. And so we came to Rome.
15 When the brothers there heard of our arrival they came to meet us, as far as
the Forum of Appius and the Three Taverns. When Paul saw them he thanked
16 God and took courage. •On our arrival in Rome Paul was allowed to stay in
lodgings of his own with the soldier who guarded him.

Paul makes contact with the Roman Jews

17 After three days he called together the leading Jews. When they had assembled,
he said to them, 'Brothers, although I have done nothing against our people or
the customs of our ancestors, I was arrested in Jerusalem and handed over to
18 the Romans. •They examined me and would have set me free, since they found
19 me guilty of nothing involving the death penalty; •but the Jews lodged an objection, and I was forced to appeal to Caesar, not that I had any accusation to make
20 against my own nation. •That is why I have asked to see you and talk to you,
for it is on account of the hope of Israel that I wear this chain.'
21 They answered, 'We have received no letters from Judaea about you, nor has
any countryman of yours arrived here with any report or story of anything to
22 your discredit. •We think it would be as well to hear your own account of
your position; all we know about this sect is that opinion everywhere condemns it.'

Paul's declaration to the Roman Jews

23 So they arranged a day with him and a large number of them visited him at his
lodgings. He put his case to them, testifying to the kingdom of God and trying
to persuade them about Jesus, arguing from the Law of Moses and the prophets.
24 This went on from early morning until evening, •and some were convinced by
25 what he said, while the rest were sceptical. •So they disagreed among themselves
and, as they went away, Paul had one last thing to say to them, 'How aptly the
Holy Spirit spoke when he told your ancestors through the prophet Isaiah:

26   *Go to this nation and say:*
        You will hear and hear again but not understand,
        see and see again, but not perceive.
27   *For the heart of this nation has grown coarse,*
        their ears are dull of hearing and they have shut their eyes,
        for fear they should see with their eyes,
        hear with their ears,
        understand with their heart,
        and be converted
        *and be healed by me.*ᵇ

28 'Understand, then, that this salvation of God has been sent to the pagans
they will listen to it.'

Epilogue

30 Paul spent the whole of the two yearsᶜ in his own rented lodging. He welcomed
31 all who came to visit him, •proclaiming the kingdom of God and teaching the
truth about the Lord Jesus Christ with complete freedom and without hindrance
from anyone.

b. The term includes the seas between Greece, Italy and Africa.
28 a. Pozzuoli, on the Gulf of Naples.   b. Is 6:9-10   c. See note on 24:27

INTRODUCTION TO
THE LETTERS OF SAINT PAUL

Paul was born about A.D. 10, of a Jewish family living among 'the Greeks' at Tarsus, a Roman municipality in Cilicia. He was educated as a Pharisee in Jerusalem. He was converted to belief in Christ about A.D. 34, and many particulars of his life as an apostle can be found in his letters and in Acts. The letters may be dated from A.D. 50-65. Paul was imprisoned in Rome, A.D. 61-63, and set free for want of evidence; a second imprisonment in Rome ended, according to a very ancient tradition, in martyrdom by execution, probably in the year 67.

Paul's letters show him as a man of sensitive temperament and warm emotions, completely dedicated to the spreading of the 'Good News' that Christ by his death and resurrection was proved to be the one universal saviour of Jew and 'Greek' alike. Crises and controversies led him to explain the message of the gospel in ways adapted to the needs of his readers and so to bring into play his remarkable powers of theological analysis and his grasp of profundities. His letters, in a fluent Greek which was his second mother-tongue, were generally a response to a particular situation in a particular church, and although some passages in them were obviously written after long and careful thought, more often the style suggests spontaneity and urgency. The letters were usually dictated, and then signed by Paul with a short personal greeting.

The order in which the letters are printed in this Bible is the traditional one which arranges them in order of diminishing length. If they are read in the order in which they were written, the development in Paul's theological thinking can be seen as he finds expression for further depths and implications in the gospel.

1 and 2 Thessalonians. A.D. 50-51

1 Thessalonians was written from Corinth, when Paul's companion Timothy had come back from a second visit to Thessalonika and reported to Paul on the state of the church there. Besides a series of practical recommendations, it includes Paul's teaching on death and the 'second coming' of Christ, expressed in the terms of contemporary apocalyptic writing.

2 Thessalonians, written about a year later, shows that Paul's thought on the same subject had deepened. Parts of the two letters show some close correspondences, and some critics have doubted the authenticity of 2 Thessalonians. However, the earliest authorities accepted them as both by Paul.

1 and 2 Corinthians. A.D. 57

Corinth, a great and populous port, was a magnet to every sort of philosophy and religion and was also a notorious centre of immorality. Paul's
converts in the city were particularly in need of instruction and guidance,
both about the Good News itself and about the Christian life which it
implied. Paul appears to have written four letters to the church in Corinth,
of which we now have only two.

His first letter to Corinth has not survived, and the earliest we have was
written from Ephesus sometime near Easter, 57. Shortly afterwards, Paul
had to pay a brief visit to Corinth in which he had to take painful disci-
plinary measures, and when later he sent a representative to Corinth
instead of going himself, the Corinthians did not accept his authority, and
Paul wrote a third letter which was very severe. In Macedonia, towards the
end of 57, Paul heard from Titus that the 'severe letter' had had the desired
effect, and then he wrote the letter which we know as 2 Corinthians.

However, 2 Corinthians is not a single consistent letter; it has been
suggested that it includes part of the lost first letter (2 Co 6:14–7:1) and
part of the 'severe letter' (2 Co 10-13).

The two letters to the Corinthians contain much information about
urgent problems that faced the church and the important decisions which
were made to meet them: questions of morality, about the liturgy and the
holding of assemblies, the recognition of spiritual gifts and the avoidance of
contamination from pagan religions. It was Paul's religious genius to turn
what might have remained textbook cases of conscience into the means of
exploring the profound doctrines of Christian liberty, the sanctification of
the body, the supremacy of love, and union with Christ.

Galatians. Romans. A.D. 57-58

These two letters analyse the same problem, but while Galatians is Paul's
immediate response to a particular situation, Romans is more like a systematic treatise and gives a methodical arrangement to all the new ideas that
had emerged from the argument.

Paul had not himself founded the church at Rome. It was a mixed
community in which there was a danger that Jewish and non-Jewish
converts might look down on each other, and Paul, before visiting the
church, sent this considered examination of how Judaism and Christianity
were related to one another, using the ideas which he had developed in the
Galatian crisis and further refining them. In both these letters we can see
Paul correcting the unbalance of the Greek outlook which relied too
exclusively on human reason, just as in earlier letters he had corrected the
unbalance of the Jewish outlook which relied too heavily on the Law.

Philippians. A.D. 56-57

This is a letter without a lot of doctrinal exposition in it, giving some news
to his converts at Philippi and warning them of some enemies who had
worked against Paul elsewhere and might turn to them next. At the time of
writing, Paul was under arrest, but it is unlikely that this letter was written
from Rome during his imprisonment there in 61-63 and it may have been
written from Ephesus.

Ephesians. Colossians. Philemon. A.D. 61-63

All three letters are closely related and were written while Paul was under arrest in Rome. It appears that the relation between Ephesians and Colossians is like that between Romans and Galatians. The news of a crisis at Colossae led Paul to write a letter to the Christians there against the growing belief and trust in celestial and cosmic powers. Paul accepts these powers as the angels of Jewish tradition, but he shows that in the great scheme of salvation they have only a preparatory and subordinate part and now there is a new order in which Christ is all. About the same time, he wrote a fuller and more systematic treatment of the same ideas and this is the letter that we know as 'Ephesians' though it was probably written for circulation through all the churches.

Some critics have questioned the authorship of both these letters, and particularly of Ephesians, since it seems to borrow ideas from Colossians and not always to digest them smoothly. But we know nothing of any other person capable of writing them; in parts of them, Paul is at his most personal and characteristic, and they represent a further reconsideration of themes which he had already explored in his earlier letters.

The short letter to Philemon is a personal message which was written in Paul's own handwriting.

1 Timothy. Titus. 2 Timothy. A.D. 65

These are letters of advice and instruction to two of Paul's most loyal followers in their work of organising and leading the communities to which he had sent them. It is possible that 1 Timothy and Titus were written from Macedonia about A.D. 65, but by the time he wrote 2 Timothy, Paul was a prisoner in Rome awaiting death. From the details of his recent movements given in this letter, this must have been a second imprisonment, and not that of 61-63.

Hebrews. A.D. 67

The question who wrote this letter to Jewish Christians has been a subject of debate from the earliest times. It is ranked with Paul's letters in importance, its doctrine has Pauline overtones, and it was written from Italy, perhaps from Rome; but while there may be a strong presumption that its author had come under the influence of Paul, the letter can hardly be attributed to Paul himself.

It is a sustained argument from Old Testament texts, to keep its readers firm under persecution. The theme is that the ineffectual sacrifices of the levitical priests are replaced by the one uniquely efficacious sacrifice of Christ, and that his priesthood is of an altogether higher order than that of the Jewish priests, derived from Aaron.

ROMANS

THE LETTER OF PAUL
TO THE CHURCH IN ROME

Address

1 ¹ From Paul, a servant of Christ Jesus who has been called to be an apostle,
2 and specially chosen to preach the Good News that God •promised long
ago through his prophets in the scriptures.

3 This news is about the Son of God who, according to the human nature he
4 took, was a descendant of David: •it is about Jesus Christ our Lord who, in the
order of the spirit, the spirit of holiness that was in him, was proclaimed Son
5 of God in all his power through his resurrection from the dead. •Through him
we received grace and our apostolic mission to preach the obedience of faith
6 to all pagan nations in honour of his name. •You are one of these nations, and
7 by his call belong to Jesus Christ. •To you all, then, who are God's beloved in
Rome, called to be saints, may God our Father and the Lord Jesus Christ send
grace and peace.

Thanksgiving and prayer

8 First I thank my God through Jesus Christ for all of you and for the way in
9 which your faith is spoken of all over the world. •The God I worship spiritually
by preaching the Good News of his Son knows that I never fail to mention you
10 in my prayers, •and to ask to be allowed at long last the opportunity to visit
11 you, if he so wills. •For I am longing to see you either to strengthen you by
12 sharing a spiritual gift with you, •or what is better, to find encouragement
13 among you from our common faith. •I want you to know, brothers, that I have
often planned to visit you—though until now I have always been prevented—
in the hope that I might work as fruitfully among you as I have done among the
14 other pagans. •I owe a duty to Greeks ᵃ just as much as to barbarians, to the
15 educated just as much as to the uneducated, •and it is this that makes me want
to bring the Good News to you too in Rome.

SALVATION BY FAITH
I. JUSTIFICATION

The theme stated

16 For I am not ashamed of the Good News: it is the power of God saving all
17 who have faith—Jews first, but Greeks as well—•since this is what reveals the
justice of God to us: it shows how faith leads to faith, or as scripture says:
*The upright man finds life through faith.*ᵇ

1 a. When contrasted with 'barbarians' (as here), 'Greeks' means the inhabitants of the
hellenic world, including the Romans; when contrasted with 'Jews', it means the pagans in
general.   **b.** Hab 2:4

God's anger against the pagans

The anger of God is being revealed from heaven against all the impiety and 18
depravity of men who keep truth imprisoned in their wickedness. •For what can 19
be known about God is perfectly plain to them since God himself has made it
plain. •Ever since God created the world his everlasting power and deity— 20
however invisible—have been there for the mind to see in the things he has
made. That is why such people are without excuse: •they knew God and yet 21
refused to honour him as God or to thank him; instead, they made nonsense
out of logic and their empty minds were darkened. •The more they called 22
themselves philosophers, the more stupid they grew, •until *they exchanged the* 23
glory^c of the immortal God for a worthless imitation, *for the image* of mortal man,
of birds, of quadrupeds and reptiles. •That is why God left them to their filthy 24
enjoyments and the practices with which they dishonour their own bodies,
since they have given up divine truth for a lie and have worshipped and served 25
creatures instead of the creator, who is blessed for ever. Amen!

That is why God has abandoned them to degrading passions: why their women 26
have turned from natural intercourse to unnatural practices •and why their 27
menfolk have given up natural intercourse to be consumed with passion for each
other, men doing shameless things with men and getting an appropriate reward
for their perversion.

In other words, since they refused to see it was rational to acknowledge God, 28
God has left them to their own irrational ideas and to their monstrous behaviour.
And so they are steeped in all sorts of depravity, rottenness, greed and malice, 29
and addicted to envy, murder, wrangling, treachery and spite. •Libellers, 30
slanderers, enemies of God, rude, arrogant and boastful, enterprising in sin,
rebellious to parents, •without brains, honour, love or pity. •They know what $\frac{31}{32}$
God's verdict is: that those who behave like this deserve to die—and yet they
do it; and what is worse, encourage others to do the same.

The Jews are not exempt from God's anger

2 So no matter who you are, if you pass judgement you have no excuse. 1
In judging others you condemn yourself, since you behave no differently
from those you judge. •We know that God condemns that sort of behaviour 2
impartially: •and when you judge those who behave like this while you are 3
doing exactly the same, do you think you will escape God's judgement? •Or are 4
you abusing his abundant goodness, patience and toleration, not realising that
this goodness of God is meant to lead you to repentance? •Your stubborn refusal 5
to repent is only adding to the anger God will have towards you on that day of
anger when his just judgements will be made known. •*He will repay each one as* 6
his works deserve.^d •For those who sought renown and honour and immortality 7
by always doing good there will be eternal life; •for the unsubmissive who 8
refused to take truth for their guide and took depravity instead, there will be
anger and fury. •Pain and suffering will come to every human being who employs 9
himself in evil—Jews first, but Greeks as well; •renown, honour and peace will 10
come to everyone who does good—Jews first, but Greeks as well. •God has 11
no favourites.

The Law will not save them

Sinners who were not subject to the Law will perish all the same, without 12
that Law; sinners who were under the Law will have that Law to judge them.
It is not listening to the Law but keeping it that will make people holy in the 13
sight of God. •For instance, pagans who never heard of the Law but are led 14
by reason to do what the Law commands, may not actually 'possess' the Law,
but they can be said to 'be' the Law. •They can point to the substance of the 15

Law engraved on their hearts—they can call a witness, that is, their own
conscience—they have accusation and defence, that is, their own inner mental
16 dialogue.*^b* •...on the day when, according to the Good News I preach, God,
through Jesus Christ, judges the secrets of mankind.

17   If you call yourself a Jew, if you really trust in the Law and are proud of
18 your God, •if you know God's will through the Law and can tell what is right,
19 if you are convinced you can guide the blind and be a beacon to those in the
20 dark, •if you can teach the ignorant and instruct the unlearned because your Law
21 embodies all knowledge and truth, •then why not teach yourself as well as the
22 others? You preach against stealing, yet you steal; •you forbid adultery, yet you
23 commit adultery; you despise idols, yet you rob their temples. •By boasting about
24 the Law and then disobeying it, you bring God into contempt. •As scripture
says: *It is your fault that the name of God is blasphemed among the pagans.*

Circumcision will not save them

25   It is a good thing to be circumcised if you keep the Law; but if you break the
26 Law, you might as well have stayed uncircumcised. •If a man who is not
circumcised obeys the commandments of the Law, surely that makes up for not
27 being circumcised? •More than that, the man who keeps the Law, even though
he has not been physically circumcised, is a living condemnation of the way you
disobey the Law in spite of being circumcised and having it all written down.
28 To be a Jew is not just to look like a Jew, and circumcision is more than a physical
29 operation. •The real Jew is the one who is inwardly a Jew, and the real circumcision is in the heart—something not of the letter but of the spirit. A Jew like that
may not be praised by man, but he will be praised by God.

God's promises will not save them

1   **3** Well then, is a Jew any better off? Is there any advantage in being circum-
2   cised? •A great advantage in every way. First, the Jews are the people to
3 whom God's message was entrusted. •What if some of them were unfaithful?
4 Will their lack of fidelity cancel God's fidelity? •That would be absurd. God will
always be true even though *everyone* proves to be *false;*^a so scripture says: *In all*
5 *you say your justice shows, and when you are judged you win your case.*^b •But if our
lack of holiness makes God demonstrate his integrity, how can we say God is
6 unjust when—to use a human analogy—he gets angry with us in return? •That
7 would be absurd, it would mean God could never judge the world. •You might
as well say that since my untruthfulness makes God demonstrate his truthfulness
8 and thus gives him glory, I should not be judged to be a sinner at all. •That
would be the same as saying: Do evil as a means to good. Some slanderers have
accused us of teaching this, but they are justly condemned.

All are guilty

9   Well: are we any better off? Not at all: as we said before, Jews and Greeks
10 are all under sin's dominion. •As scripture says:

>   *There is not a good man left, no, not one;*
11 >   *there is not one who understands,*
>   *not one who looks for God.*
12 >   *All have turned aside, tainted all alike;*
>   *there is not one good man left, not a single one.*
13 >   *Their throats are yawning graves;*
>   *their tongues are full of deceit.*
>   *Vipers' venom is on their lips,*
14 >   *bitter curses fill their mouths.*

c. Ps 106:20
2 a. Ps 6:12   b. This verse follows on from v.13
3 a. Ps 116:11   b. Ps 51:4 (LXX)

Their feet are swift when blood is to be shed,   15
wherever they go there is havoc and ruin.   16
They know nothing of the way of peace,   17
there is no fear of God before their eyes.[c]   18

Now all this that the Law says is said, as we know, for the benefit of those   19
who are subject to the Law, but it is meant to silence everyone and to lay the
whole world open to God's judgement; •and this is because *no one can be justified* 20
in the sight of[d] God by keeping the Law: all that law does is to tell us what is
sinful.

B. FAITH AND THE JUSTICE OF GOD

The revelation of God's justice

God's justice that was made known through the Law and the Prophets has   21
now been revealed outside the Law, •since it is the same justice of God that   22
comes through faith to everyone, Jew and pagan alike, who believes in Jesus
Christ. •Both Jew and pagan sinned and forfeited God's glory, •and both are   23/24
justified through the free gift of his grace by being redeemed in Christ Jesus
who was appointed by God to sacrifice his life so as to win reconciliation through   25
faith. In this way God makes his justice known; first, for the past, when sins went
unpunished because he held his hand, •then, for the present age, by showing   26
positively that he is just, and that he justifies everyone who believes in Jesus.

What faith does

So what becomes of our boasts? There is no room for them. What sort of   27
law excludes them? The sort of law that tells us what to do? On the contrary,
it is the law of faith, •since, as we see it, a man is justified by faith and not   28
by doing something the Law tells him to do. •Is God the God of Jews alone and   29
not of the pagans too? Of the pagans too, most certainly, •since there is only one   30
God, and he is the one who will justify the circumcised because of their faith
and justify the uncircumcised through their faith. •Do we mean that faith makes   31
the Law pointless? Not at all: we are giving the Law its true value.

C. THE EXAMPLE OF ABRAHAM

Abraham justified by faith

4 Apply this to Abraham, the ancestor from whom we are all descended.   1
If Abraham was justified as a reward for doing something, he would really   2
have had something to boast about, though not in God's sight •because scripture   3
says: *Abraham put his faith in God, and this faith was considered as justifying him.*[a]
If a man has work to show, his wages are not considered as a favour but as his   4
due; •but when a man has nothing to show except faith in the one who justifies   5
sinners, then his faith is considered as justifying him. •And David says the same: 6
a man is happy if God considers him righteous, irrespective of good deeds:

Happy those whose crimes are forgiven,   7
whose sins are blotted out;
happy the man whom the Lord considers sinless.[b]   8

Justified before circumcision

Is this happiness meant only for the circumcised, or is it meant for others as   9
well? Think of Abraham again: *his faith,* we say, *was considered as justifying him,*
but when was this done? When he was already circumcised or before he had been   10

11 circumcised? It was before he had been circumcised, not after; •and when he was *circumcised* later it was only *as a sign* and guarantee that the faith he had before his circumcision justified him. In this way Abraham became the ancestor of all
12 uncircumcised believers, so that they too might be considered righteous; •and ancestor, also, of those who though circumcised do not rely on that fact alone, but follow our ancestor Abraham along the path of faith he trod before he had been circumcised.

Not justified by obedience to the Law

13 The promise of inheriting the world was not made to Abraham and his descendants on account of any law but on account of the righteousness which
14 consists in faith. •If the world is only to be inherited by those who submit to
15 the Law, then faith is pointless and the promise worth nothing. •Law involves the possibility of punishment for breaking the law—only where there
16 is no law can that be avoided. •That is why what fulfils the promise depends on faith, so that it may be a free gift and be available to all of Abraham's descendants, not only those who belong to the Law but also those who belong
17 to the faith of Abraham who is the father of all of us. •As scripture says: *I have made you the ancestor of many nations*ᶜ—Abraham is our father in the eyes of God, in whom he put his faith, and who brings the dead to life and calls into being what does not exist.

Abraham's faith, a model of Christian faith

18 Though it seemed Abraham's hope could not be fulfilled, he hoped and he believed, and through doing so he did become *the father of many nations* exactly
19 as he had been promised: *Your descendants will be as many as the stars.*ᵈ •Even the thought that his body was past fatherhood—he was about a hundred years
20 old—and Sarah too old to become a mother, did not shake his belief. •Since God had promised it, Abraham refused either to deny it or even to doubt it, but drew
21 strength from faith and gave glory to God, •convinced that God had power
22 to do what he had promised. •This is the faith that was '*considered as justi-*
23 *fying him*'. •Scripture however does not refer only to him but to us as well
24 when it says that his faith was thus 'considered'; •our faith too will be 'considered'
25 if we believe in him who raised Jesus our Lord from the dead, •Jesus who was *put to death for our sins*ᵉ and raised to life to justify us.

II. SALVATION

Faith guarantees salvation

1 5 So far then we have seen that, through our Lord Jesus Christ, by faith we are
2 judged righteous and at peace with God, •since it is by faith and through Jesus that we have entered this state of grace in which we can boast about
3 looking forward to God's glory. •But that is not all we can boast about; we can
4 boast about our sufferings. These sufferings bring patience, as we know, •and
5 patience brings perseverance, and perseverance brings hope, •and this hope is not deceptive, because the love of God has been poured into our hearts by the
6 Holy Spirit which has been given us. •We were still helpless when at his appointed
7 moment Christ died for sinful men. •It is not easy to die even for a good man— though of course for someone really worthy, a man might be prepared to die—
8 but what proves that God loves us is that Christ died for us while we were still
9 sinners. •Having died to make us righteous, is it likely that he would now fail
10 to save us from God's anger? •When we were reconciled to God by the death of

c. Quotations from Ps 14, Ps 5, Ps 140, Ps 10, Is 59, Ps 36.   d. Ps 143:2
4 a. Gn 15:6   b. Ps 32:1-2   c. Gn 17:5 (the same chapter to which allusion is made in v. 11, above).   d. Gn 15:5   e. Is 53:5,6

his Son, we were still enemies; now that we have been reconciled, surely we may count on being saved by the life of his Son? •Not merely because we have been 11 reconciled but because we are filled with joyful trust in God, through our Lord Jesus Christ, through whom we have already gained our reconciliation.

A. DELIVERANCE FROM SIN AND DEATH AND LAW

Adam and Jesus Christ

Well then, sin *entered the world* through one man, and through sin death, and 12 thus death has spread through the whole human race because everyone has sinned. •Sin existed in the world long before the Law was given. There was no 13 law and so no one could be accused of the sin of 'law-breaking', •yet death reigned 14 over all from Adam to Moses, even though their sin, unlike that of Adam, was not a matter of breaking a law.

Adam prefigured the One to come, •but the gift itself considerably outweighed 15 the fall. If it is certain that through one man's fall so many died, it is even more certain that divine grace, coming through the one man, Jesus Christ, came to so many as an abundant free gift. •The results of the gift also outweigh the results of 16 one man's sin: for after one single fall came judgement with a verdict of condemnation, now after many falls comes grace with its verdict of acquittal. •If it is 17 certain that death reigned over everyone as the consequence of one man's fall, it is even more certain that one man, Jesus Christ, will cause everyone to reign in life who receives the free gift that he does not deserve, of being made righteous. Again, as one man's fall brought condemnation on everyone, so the good act of 18 one man brings everyone life and makes them justified. •As by one man's disobed- 19 ience many were made sinners, so by one man's obedience many will be made righteous. •When law came, it was to multiply the opportunities of falling, 20 but however great the number of sins committed, grace was even greater; •and 21 so, just as sin reigned wherever there was death, so grace will reign to bring eternal life thanks to the righteousness that comes through Jesus Christ our Lord.

Baptism

6 Does it follow that we should remain in sin so as to let grace have greater 1 scope? •Of course not. We are dead to sin, so how can we continue to live 2 in it? •You have been taught that when we were baptised in Christ Jesus we were 3 baptised in his death; •in other words, when we were baptised we went into 4 the tomb with him and joined him in death, so that as Christ was raised from the dead by the Father's glory, we too might live a new life.

If in union with Christ we have imitated his death, we shall also imitate him 5 in his resurrection. •We must realise that our former selves have been crucified 6 with him to destroy this sinful body and to free us from the slavery of sin. •When 7 a man dies, of course, he has finished with sin.

But we believe that having died with Christ we shall return to life with him: 8 Christ, as we know, having been raised from the dead will never die again. Death 9 has no power over him any more. •When he died, he died, once for all, to sin, 10 so his life now is life with God; •and in that way, you too must consider yourselves 11 to be dead to sin but alive for God in Christ Jesus.

Holiness, not sin, to be the master

That is why you must not let sin reign in your mortal bodies or command 12 your obedience to bodily passions, •why you must not let any part of your body 13 turn into an unholy weapon fighting on the side of sin; you should, instead, offer yourselves to God, and consider yourselves dead men brought back to life; you should make every part of your body into a weapon fighting on the side of God; •and then sin will no longer dominate your life, since you are living by 14 grace and not by law.

The Christian is freed from the slavery of sin

15 Does the fact that we are living by grace and not by law mean that we are
16 free to sin? Of course not. •You know that if you agree to serve and obey a
master you become his slaves. You cannot be slaves of sin that leads to death
17 and at the same time slaves of obedience that leads to righteousness. •You were
once slaves of sin, but thank God you submitted without reservation to the
18 creed you were taught. •You may have been freed from the slavery of sin, but only
19 to become 'slaves' of righteousness. •If I may use human terms to help your
natural weakness: as once you put your bodies at the service of vice and immorality, so now you must put them at the service of righteousness for your sanctification.

The reward of sin and the reward of holiness

20
21 When you were slaves of sin, you felt no obligation to righteousness, •and
what did you get from this? Nothing but experiences that now make you blush,
22 since that sort of behaviour ends in death. •Now, however, you have been set
free from sin, you have been made slaves of God, and you get a reward leading
23 to your sanctification and ending in eternal life. •For the wage paid by sin is
death; the present given by God is eternal life in Christ Jesus our Lord.

The Christian is not bound by the Law

1 **7** Brothers, those of you who have studied law will know that laws affect
2 a person only during his lifetime. •A married woman, for instance, has legal
obligations to her husband while he is alive, but all these obligations come to
3 an end if the husband dies. •So if she gives herself to another man while her
husband is still alive, she is legally an adulteress; but after her husband is dead
her legal obligations come to an end, and she can marry someone else without
4 becoming an adulteress. •That is why you, my brothers, who through the body
of Christ are now dead to the Law, can now give yourselves to another husband,
5 to him who rose from the dead to make us productive for God. •Before our
conversion[a] our sinful passions, quite unsubdued by the Law, fertilised our
6 bodies to make them give birth to death. •But now we are rid of the Law, freed
by death from our imprisonment, free to serve in the new spiritual way and not
the old way of a written law.

The function of the Law

7 Does it follow that the Law itself is sin? Of course not. What I mean is that
I should not have known what sin was except for the Law. I should not for
instance have known what it means to covet if the Law had not said *You shall
8 not covet*. •But it was this commandment that sin took advantage of to produce
all kinds of covetousness in me, for when there is no Law, sin is dead.
9 Once, when there was no Law, I[b] was alive; but when the commandment
10 came, sin came to life •and I died: the commandment was meant to lead me to
11 life but it turned out to mean death for me, •because sin took advantage of the
commandment to mislead me, and so sin, through that commandment, killed me.
12
13 The Law is sacred, and what it commands is sacred, just and good. •Does
that mean that something good killed me? Of course not. But sin, to show itself
in its true colours, used that good thing to kill me; and thus sin, thanks to the
commandment, was able to exercise all its sinful power.

The inward struggle

14 The Law, of course, as we all know, is spiritual; but I am unspiritual; I have
15 been sold as a slave to sin. •I cannot understand my own behaviour. I fail to carry
16 out the things I want to do, and I find myself doing the very things I hate. •When

7 a. 'While we were in the flesh'.   b. Rhetorical figure; Paul speaks in the person of mankind.

I act against my own will, that means I have a self that acknowledges that the Law is good, •and so the thing behaving in that way is not my self but sin living 17 in me. •The fact is, I know of nothing good living in me—living, that is, in my 18 unspiritual self—for though the will to do what is good is in me, the performance is not, •with the result that instead of doing the good things I want to do, I carry 19 out the sinful things I do not want. •When I act against my will, then, it is not 20 my true self doing it, but sin which lives in me.

In fact, this seems to be the rule, that every single time I want to do good 21 it is something evil that comes to hand. •In my inmost self I dearly love God's 22 Law, but •I can see that my body follows a different law that battles against 23 the law which my reason dictates. This is what makes me a prisoner of that law of sin which lives inside my body.

What a wretched man I am! Who will rescue me from this body doomed to 24 death? •Thanks be to God through Jesus Christ our Lord! 25

In short, it is I who with my reason serve the Law of God, and no less I who serve in my unspiritual self the law of sin.

B. THE CHRISTIAN'S SPIRITUAL LIFE

The life of the spirit

8 The reason, therefore, why those who are in Christ Jesus are not condemned, 1 is that the law of the spirit of life in Christ Jesus has set you free from the 2 law of sin and death. •God has done what the Law, because of our unspiritual 3 nature,ᵃ was unable do do. God dealt with sin by sending his own Son in a body as physical as any sinful body, and in that body God condemned sin. •He did 4 this in order that the Law's just demands might be satisfied in us, who behave not as our unspiritual nature but as the spirit dictates.

The unspiritual are interested only in what is unspiritual, but the spiritual 5 are interested in spiritual things. •It is death to limit oneself to what is unspiritual; 6 life and peace can only come with concern for the spiritual. •That is because to 7 limit oneself to what is unspiritual is to be at enmity with God: such a limitation never could and never does submit to God's law. •People who are interested 8 only in unspiritual things can never be pleasing to God. •Your interests, however, 9 are not in the unspiritual, but in the spiritual, since the Spirit of God has made his home in you. In fact, unless you possessed the Spirit of Christ you would not belong to him. •Though your body may be dead it is because of sin, but if Christ 10 is in you then your spirit is life itself because you have been justified; •and if the 11 Spirit of him who raised Jesus from the dead is living in you, then he who raised Jesus from the dead will give life to your own mortal bodies through his Spirit living in you.

So then, my brothers, there is no necessity for us to obey our unspiritual 12 selves or to live unspiritual lives. •If you do live in that way, you are doomed to 13 die; but if by the Spirit you put an end to the misdeeds of the body you will live.

Children of God

Everyone moved by the Spirit is a son of God. •The spirit you received ¹⁴/₁₅ is not the spirit of slaves bringing fear into your lives again; it is the spirit of sons, and it makes us cry out, 'Abba, Father!'ᵇ •The Spirit himself and our spirit 16 bear united witness that we are children of God. •And if we are children we 17 are heirs as well: heirs of God and coheirs with Christ, sharing his sufferings so as to share his glory.

Glory as our destiny

I think that what we suffer in this life can never be compared to the glory, 18 as yet unrevealed, which is waiting for us. •The whole creation is eagerly 19

20 waiting for God to reveal his sons. •It was not for any fault on the part of creation that it was made unable to attain its purpose, it was made so by God;
21 but creation still retains the hope •of being freed, like us, from its slavery to
22 decadence, to enjoy the same freedom and glory as the children of God. •From the beginning till now the entire creation, as we know, has been groaning in
23 one great act of giving birth; •and not only creation, but all of us who possess the first-fruits of the Spirit, we too groan inwardly as we wait for our bodies
24 to be set free. •For we must be content to hope that we shall be saved—our
25 salvation is not in sight, we should not have to be hoping for it if it were—•but, as I say, we must hope to be saved since we are not saved yet—it is something we must wait for with patience.

26   The Spirit too comes to help us in our weakness. For when we cannot choose words in order to pray properly, the Spirit himself expresses our plea in a way
27 that could never be put into words, •and God who knows everything in our hearts knows perfectly well what he means, and that the pleas of the saints expressed by the Spirit are according to the mind of God.

God has called us to share his glory

28   We know that by turning everything to their good God co-operates with all those who love him, with all those that he has called according to his purpose.
29 They are the ones he chose specially long ago and intended to become true
30 images of his Son, so that his Son might be the eldest of many brothers. •He called those he intended for this; those he called he justified, and with those he justified he shared his glory.

A hymn to God's love

31   After saying this, what can we add? With God on our side who can be against
32 us? •Since God did not spare his own Son, but gave him up to benefit us all, we may be certain, after such a gift, that he will not refuse anything he can give.
33
34 Could anyone accuse those that God has chosen? When God acquits, •could anyone condemn? Could Christ Jesus? No! He not only died for us—he rose from the dead, and there at God's right hand he stands and pleads for us.

35   Nothing therefore can come between us and the love of Christ, even if we are troubled or worried, or being persecuted, or lacking food or clothes, or being
36 threatened or even attacked. •As scripture promised: *For your sake we are being*
37 *massacred daily, and reckoned as sheep for the slaughter.*[c] •These are the trials through which we triumph, by the power of him who loved us.

38   For I am certain of this: neither death nor life, no angel, no prince, nothing
39 that exists, nothing still to come, not any power, •or height or depth,[d] nor any created thing, can ever come between us and the love of God made visible in Christ Jesus our Lord.

C. THE PLACE OF ISRAEL

The privileges of Israel

1   **9** What I want to say now is no pretence; I say it in union with Christ—it is the truth—my conscience in union with the Holy Spirit assures me of it too.
2 What I want to say is this: my sorrow is so great, my mental anguish so endless,
3 I would willingly be condemned[a] and be cut off from Christ if it could help my
4 brothers of Israel, my own flesh and blood. •They were adopted as sons, they were given the glory and the covenants; the Law and the ritual were drawn up

8 a. 'flesh'.   b. The prayer of Christ in Gethsemane.   c. Ps 44:11   d. 'powers', 'heights' and 'depths' are probably cosmic forces hostile to mankind.
9 a. *Anathema,* cursed and excommunicated.

for them, and the promises were made to them. •They are descended from the 5
patriarchs and from their flesh and blood came Christ who is above all, God for
ever blessed! Amen.

God has kept his promise

Does this mean that God has failed to keep his promise? Of course not. 6
Not all those who descend from Israel are Israel; •not all the descendants of 7
Abraham are his true children. Remember: *It is through Isaac that your name will* 8
be carried on,[b] •which means that it is not physical descent that decides who are
the children of God; it is only the children of the promise who will count as the
true descendants. •The actual words in which the promise was made were: *I shall* 9
visit you at such and such a time, *and Sarah will have a son.*[c] •Even more to the 10
point is what was said to Rebecca when she was pregnant by our ancestor Isaac,
but before her twin children were born and before either had done good or evil. 11
In order to stress that God's choice is free, •since it depends on the one who 12
calls, not on human merit, Rebecca was told: *the elder shall serve the younger,*[d]
or as scripture says elsewhere: *I showed my love for Jacob and my hatred for Esau.*[e] 13

God is not unjust

Does it follow that God is unjust? Of course not. •Take what God said to ¹⁴₁₅
Moses: *I have mercy on whom I will, and I show pity to whom I please.*[f] •In other 16
words, the only thing that counts is not what human beings want or try to do,
but the mercy of God. •For in scripture he says to Pharaoh: *It was for this I raised* 17
you up, to use you as a means of showing my power and to make my name known
throughout the world.[g] •In other words, when God wants to show mercy he does, 18
and when he wants to harden someone's heart he does so.

You will ask me, 'In that case, how can God ever blame anyone, since no one 19
can oppose his will?' •But what right have you, a human being, to cross-examine 20
God? *The pot has no right to say to the potter: Why did you make me this shape?*[h]
Surely a potter can do what he likes with the clay? It is surely for him to decide 21
whether he will use a particular lump of clay to make a special pot or an ordinary
one?

Or else imagine that although God is ready to show his anger and display 22
his power, yet he patiently puts up with the people who make him angry,
however much they deserve to be destroyed. •He puts up with them for the sake 23
of those other people, to whom he wants to be merciful, to whom he wants to
reveal the richness of his glory, people he had prepared for this glory long ago.
Well, we are those people; whether we were Jews or pagans we are the ones he 24
has called.

All has been foretold in the Old Testament

That is exactly what God says in Hosea: *I shall say to a people that was not* 25
mine, 'You are my people', and to a nation I never loved, 'I love you'. •Instead of 26
being told, 'You are no people of mine', they will now be called the sons of the living
God.[i] •Referring to Israel Isaiah had this to say: *Though Israel should have as* 27
many descendants as there are grains of sand on the seashore, only a remnant will
be saved, •for without hesitation or delay the Lord will execute his sentence on the 28
earth.[j] •As Isaiah foretold: *Had the Lord of hosts not left us some descendants we* 29
should now be like Sodom, we should be like Gomorrah.[k]

From this it follows that the pagans who were not looking for righteousness 30
found it all the same, a righteousness that comes of faith, •while Israel, looking 31
for a righteousness derived from law failed to do what that law required. •Why 32
did they fail? Because they relied on good deeds instead of trusting in faith. In
other words, they *stumbled over the stumbling-stone*[l] •mentioned in scripture: 33
See how I lay in Zion a stone to stumble over, a rock to trip men up—only those
who believe in him will have no cause for shame.[m]

Israel fails to see that it is God who makes us holy

1,2 **10** Brothers, I have the very warmest love for the Jews, and I pray to God for them to be saved. •I can swear to their fervour for God, but their zeal is
3 misguided. •Failing to recognise the righteousness that comes from God, they try to promote their own idea of it, instead of submitting to the righteousness of
4 God. •But now the Law has come to an end with Christ, and everyone who has faith may be justified.

The testimony of Moses

5 When Moses refers to being justified by the Law, he writes: *those who keep*
6 *the Law will draw life from it.*[a] •But the righteousness that comes from faith says this: Do not tell yourself you have to bring Christ down—as in the text: *Who*
7 *will go up to heaven?*[b] •or that you have to bring Christ back from the dead—as
8 in the text: *Who will go down to the underworld?* •On the positive side it says: *The word,* that is the faith we proclaim, *is very near to you, it is on your lips and*
9 *in your heart.* •If your lips confess that Jesus is Lord and if you believe in your
10 heart that God raised him from the dead, then you will be saved. •By believing from the heart you are made righteous; by confessing with your lips you are
11 saved. •When scripture says: *those who believe in him will have no cause for shame,*[c]
12 it makes no distinction between Jew and Greek: all belong to the same Lord who
13 is rich enough, however many ask his help, •*for everyone who calls on the name of the Lord will be saved.*[d]

Israel has no excuse

14 But they will not ask his help unless they believe in him, and they will not believe in him unless they have heard of him, and they will not hear of him unless
15 they get a preacher, •and they will never have a preacher unless one is sent, but as scripture says: *The footsteps of those who bring good news is a welcome sound.*[e]
16 Not everyone, of course, listens to the Good News. As Isaiah says: *Lord, how many*
17 *believed what we proclaimed?*[f] •So faith comes from what is preached, and what is preached comes from the word of Christ.
18 Let me put the question: is it possible that they did not hear? Indeed they did; in the words of the psalm, *their voice has gone out through all the earth, and*
19 *their message to the ends of the world.*[g] •A second question: is it possible that Israel did not understand? Moses answered this long ago: *I will make you jealous of people who are not even a nation; I will make you angry with an irreligious people.*[h]
20 Isaiah said more clearly: *I have been found by those who did not seek me, and have*
21 *revealed myself to those who did not consult me;*[i] •and referring to Israel he goes on: *Each day I stretched out my hand to a disobedient and rebellious people.*

The remnant of Israel

1 **11** Let me put a further question then: is it possible that *God has rejected his people?*[a] Of course not. I, an Israelite, descended from Abraham through
2 the tribe of Benjamin, •could never agree that God had rejected his people, the people he chose specially long ago. Do you remember what scripture says of
3 Elijah—how he complained to God about Israel's behaviour? •*Lord, they have killed your prophets and broken down your altars. I, and I only, remain, and they*
4 *want to kill me.*[b] •What did God say to that? *I have kept for myself seven*
5 *thousand men who have not bent the knee to Baal.*[c] •Today the same thing
6 has happened: there is a remnant, chosen by grace. •By grace, you notice, nothing therefore to do with good deeds, or grace would not be grace at all!
7 What follows? It was not Israel as a whole that found what it was seeking,

b. Gn 21:12　**c.** Gn 18:10　**d.** Gn 25:23　**e.** Ml 1:2-3　**f.** Ex 33:19　**g.** Ex 9:16
h. Is 29:16　**i.** Ho 2:25 and 2:1　**j.** Is 10:22:23　**k.** Is 1.9　**l.** Is 8:14　**m.** Is 28:16
10 a. Lv 18:5　**b.** This quotation, and the two following, are a free rendering of Dt 30:12-14.
c. Is 28:16　**d.** Jl 3:5　**e.** Is 52:7　**f.** Is 53:1　**g.** Ps 19:4　**h.** Dt 32:21　**i.** Is 65:1,2
11 a. Ps 94:14　**b.** 1 K 19:10.14　**c.** 1 K 19:18

but only the chosen few. The rest were not allowed to see the truth; •as scripture 8
says: *God has given them a sluggish spirit, unseeing eyes and inattentive ears, and
they are still like that today.*ᵈ •And David says: *May their own table prove a trap* 9
for them, a snare and a pitfall—let that be their punishment; •*may their eyes be* 10
*struck incurably blind, their backs bend for ever.*ᵉ

The Jews to be restored in the future

Let me put another question then: have the Jews fallen for ever, or have they 11
just stumbled? Obviously they have not fallen for ever: their fall, though, has
saved the pagans in a way the Jews may now well emulate. •Think of the extent 12
to which the world, the pagan world, has benefited from their fall and defection—
then think how much more it will benefit from the conversion of them all. •Let 13
me tell you pagansᶠ this: I have been sent to the pagans as their apostle, and I am
proud of being sent, •but the purpose of it is to make my own people envious 14
of you, and in this way save some of them. •Since their rejection meant the 15
reconciliation of the world, do you know what their admission will mean? Nothing
less than a resurrection from the dead!

The Jews are still the chosen people

A whole batch of bread is made holy if the first handful of dough is made 16
holy; all the branches are holy if the root is holy. •No doubt some of the branches 17
have been cut off, and, like shoots of wild olive, you have been grafted among
the rest to share with them the rich sap provided by the olive tree itself, •but still, 18
even if you think yourself superior to the other branches, remember that you do
not support the root; it is the root that supports you. •You will say, 'Those 19
branches were cut off on purpose to let me be grafted in!' True, •they were cut off, 20
but through their unbelief; if you still hold firm, it is only thanks to your faith.
Rather than making you proud, that should make you afraid. •God did not 21
spare the natural branches, and he is not likely to spare you. •Do not forget 22
that God can be severe as well as kind: he is severe to those who fell, and he is
kind to you, but only for as long as he chooses to be, otherwise you will find
yourself cut off too, •and the Jews, if they give up their unbelief, grafted back in 23
your place. God is perfectly able to graft them back again; •after all, if you were 24
cut from your natural wild olive to be grafted unnaturally on to a cultivated olive,
it will be much easier for them, the natural branches, to be grafted back on the
tree they came from.

The conversion of the Jews

There is a hidden reason for all this, brothers, of which I do not want you 25
to be ignorant, in case you think you know more than you do. One section of
Israel has become blind, but this will last only until the whole pagan world has
entered, •and then after this the rest of Israel will be saved as well. As scripture 26
says: *The liberator will come from Zion, he will banish godlessness from Jacob.*
*And this is the covenant I will make with them when I take their sins away.*ᵍ 27

The Jews are enemies of God only with regard to the Good News, and 28
enemies only for your sake; but as the chosen people, they are still loved by God,
loved for the sake of their ancestors. •God never takes back his gifts or revokes 29
his choice.

Just as you changed from being disobedient to God, and now enjoy mercy 30
because of their disobedience, •so those who are disobedient now—and only 31
because of the mercy shown to you—will also enjoy mercy eventually. •God has 32
imprisoned all men in their own disobedience only to show mercy to all mankind.

A hymn to God's mercy and wisdom

How rich are the depths of God—how deep his wisdom and knowledge— 33
and how impossible to penetrate his motives or understand his methods!

³⁴
³⁵ *Who could ever know the mind of the Lord? Who could ever be his counsellor?* • *Who*
³⁶ *could ever give him anything or lend him anything?*[h] •All that exists comes from him;
all is by him and for him. To him be glory for ever! Amen.

EXHORTATION

Spiritual worship

1 **12** Think of God's mercy, my brothers, and worship him, I beg you, in a way
that is worthy of thinking beings, by offering your living bodies as a holy
2 sacrifice, truly pleasing to God. •Do not model yourselves on the behaviour
of the world around you, but let your behaviour change, modelled by your new
mind. This is the only way to discover the will of God and know what is good,
what it is that God wants, what is the perfect thing to do.

Humility and charity

3 In the light of the grace I have received I want to urge each one among you
not to exaggerate his real importance. Each of you must judge himself soberly by
4 the standard of the faith God has given him. •Just as each of our bodies has
5 several parts and each part has a separate function, •so all of us, in union with
6 Christ, form one body, and as parts of it we belong to each other. •Our gifts
differ according to the grace given us. If your gift is prophecy, then use it as your
7 faith suggests; •if administration, then use it for administration; if teaching,
8 then use it for teaching. •Let the preachers deliver sermons, the almsgivers give
freely, the officials be diligent, and those who do works of mercy do them
cheerfully.
⁹
¹⁰ Do not let your love be a pretence, but sincerely prefer good to evil. •Love
each other as much as brothers should, and have a profound respect for each
11 other. •Work for the Lord with untiring effort and with great earnestness of
12 spirit. •If you have hope, this will make you cheerful. Do not give up if trials
13 come; and keep on praying. •If any of the saints are in need you must share with
them; and you should make hospitality your special care.

Charity to everyone, including enemies

¹⁴
¹⁵ Bless those who persecute you: never curse them, bless them. •Rejoice with
16 those who rejoice and be sad with those in sorrow. •Treat everyone with equal
kindness; never be condescending but make real friends with the poor. Do not
17 allow yourself to become self-satisfied. •Never repay evil with evil but let everyone
18 see that you are interested only in the highest ideals. •Do all you can to live at
19 peace with everyone. •Never try to get revenge; leave that, my friends, to God's
anger. As scripture says: *vengeance is mine—I will pay them back,*[a] the Lord
20 promises. •But there is more: *If your enemy is hungry, you should give him food,*
21 *and if he is thirsty, let him drink. Thus you heap red-hot coals on his head.*[b] •Resist
evil and conquer it with good.

Submission to civil authority

1 **13** You must all obey the governing authorities. Since all government comes
2 from God, the civil authorities were appointed by God, •and so anyone who
resists authority is rebelling against God's decision, and such an act is bound
3 to be punished. •Good behaviour is not afraid of magistrates; only criminals
have anything to fear. If you want to live without being afraid of authority, you
4 must live honestly and authority may even honour you. •The state is there to
serve God for your benefit. If you break the law, however, you may well have

d. Is 29:10   e. Ps 69:22f   f. Converts from paganism.   g. Is 27:9   h. Is 40:13
12 a. Dt 32:35   b. Pr 25:21-22

fear: the bearing of the sword has its significance. The authorities are there to
serve God: they carry out God's revenge by punishing wrongdoers. •You must 5
obey, therefore, not only because you are afraid of being punished, but also
for conscience' sake. •This is also the reason why you must pay taxes, since all 6
government officials are God's officers. They serve God by collecting taxes.
Pay every government official what he has a right to ask—whether it be direct 7
tax or indirect, fear or honour.

Love and law

Avoid getting into debt, except the debt of mutual love. If you love your fellow 8
men you have carried out your obligations. •All the commandments: *You shall* 9
not commit adultery, you shall not kill, you shall not steal, you shall not covet, ^a
and so on, are summed up in this single command: *You must love your neighbour*
as yourself.^b •Love is the one thing that cannot hurt your neighbour; that is why 10
it is the answer to every one of the commandments.

Children of the light

Besides, you know 'the time' has come: you must wake up now: our salvation 11
is even nearer than it was when we were converted. •The night is almost over, it 12
will be daylight soon—let us give up all the things we prefer to do under cover
of the dark; let us arm ourselves and appear in the light. •Let us live decently 13
as people do in the daytime: no drunken orgies, no promiscuity or licentiousness,
and no wrangling or jealousy. •Let your armour be the Lord Jesus Christ; forget 14
about satisfying your bodies with all their cravings.

Charity towards the scrupulous

14 If a person's faith is not strong enough, welcome him all the same without 1
starting an argument. •People range from those who believe they may eat 2
any sort of meat to those whose faith is so weak they dare not eat anything
except vegetables. •Meat-eaters must not despise the scrupulous. On the other 3
hand, the scrupulous must not condemn those who feel free to eat anything they
choose, since God has welcomed them. •It is not for you to condemn someone 4
else's servant: whether he stands or falls it is his own master's business; he will
stand, you may be sure, because the Lord has power to make him stand. •If 5
one man keeps certain days as holier than others, and another considers all days
to be equally holy, each must be left free to hold his own opinion. •The one who 6
observes special days does so in honour of the Lord. The one who eats meat also
does so in honour of the Lord, since he gives thanks to God; but then the man
who abstains does that too in honour of the Lord, and so he also gives God thanks.
The life and death of each of us has its influence on others; •if we live, we live ⁷⁄₈
for the Lord; and if we die, we die for the Lord, so that alive or dead we belong
to the Lord. •This explains why Christ both died and came to life, it was so that 9
he might be Lord both of the dead and of the living. •This is also why you should 10
never pass judgement on a brother or treat him with contempt, as some of you
have done. We shall all have to stand before the judgement seat of God; •as 11
scripture says: *By my life—it is the Lord who speaks—every knee shall bend before*
me, and every tongue shall praise God.^a •It is to God, therefore, that each of us 12
must give an account of himself.

Far from passing judgement on each other, therefore, you should make up 13
your mind never to be the cause of your brother tripping or falling. •Now I am 14
perfectly well aware, of course, and I speak for the Lord Jesus, that no food is
unclean in itself; however, if someone thinks that a particular food is unclean,
then it is unclean for him. •And indeed if your attitude to food is upsetting your 15
brother, then you are hardly being guided by charity. You are certainly not free
to eat what you like if that means the downfall of someone for whom Christ died.
In short, you must not compromise your privilege, •because the kingdom ¹⁶⁄₁₇

of God does not mean eating or drinking this or that, it means righteousness and
18 peace and joy brought by the Holy Spirit. •If you serve Christ in this way you
19 will please God and be respected by men. •So let us adopt any custom that leads
20 to peace and our mutual improvement; •do not wreck God's work over a
question of food. Of course all food is clean, but it becomes evil if by eating it
21 you make somebody else fall away. •In such cases the best course is to abstain
from meat and wine and anything else that would make your brother trip or
fall or weaken in any way.

22   Hold on to your own belief, as between yourself and God —and consider
the man fortunate who can make his decision without going against his conscience.
23 But anybody who eats in a state of doubt is condemned, because he is not in good
faith; and every act done in bad faith is a sin.

1 **15** We who are strong have a duty to put up with the qualms of the weak
2   without thinking of ourselves. •Each of us should think of his neighbours and
3 help them to become stronger Christians. •Christ did not think of himself: the words
4 of scripture—*the insults of those who insult you fall on me*[a]—apply to him. •And
indeed everything that was written long ago in the scriptures was meant to teach
us something about hope from the examples scripture gives of how people who
5 did not give up were helped by God. •And may he who helps us when we refuse
to give up, help you all to be tolerant with each other, following the example
6 of Christ Jesus, •so that united in mind and voice you may give glory to the God
and Father of our Lord Jesus Christ.

An appeal for unity

7   It can only be to God's glory, then, for you to treat each other in the same
8 friendly way as Christ treated you. •The reason Christ became the servant of
circumcised Jews was not only so that God could faithfully carry out the promises
9 made to the patriarchs, •it was also to get the pagans to give glory to God for
his mercy, as scripture says in one place: *For this I shall praise you among the*
10 *pagans and sing to your name.*[b] •And in another place: *Rejoice, pagans, with his*
11 *people,*[c] •and in a third place: *Let all the pagans praise the Lord, let all the peoples*
12 *sing his praises.*[d] •Isaiah too has this to say: *The root of Jesse will appear, rising*
up to rule the pagans, and in him the pagans will put their hope.[e]
13   May the God of hope bring you such joy and peace in your faith that the
power of the Holy Spirit will remove all bounds to hope.

EPILOGUE

Paul's ministry

14   It is not because I have any doubts about you, my brothers; on the contrary
I am quite certain that you are full of good intentions, perfectly well instructed
15 and able to advise each other. •The reason why I have written to you, and put
some things rather strongly, is to refresh your memories, since God has given me
16 this special position. •He has appointed me as a priest of Jesus Christ, and I am
to carry out my priestly duty by bringing the Good News from God to the pagans,
and so make them acceptable as an offering, made holy by the Holy Spirit.
17   I think I have some reason to be proud of what I, in union with Christ Jesus,
18 have been able to do for God. •What I am presuming to speak of, of course, is
only what Christ himself has done to win the allegiance of the pagans, using
19 what I have said and done •by the power of signs and wonders, by the power of
the Holy Spirit. Thus. all the way along, from Jerusalem to Illyricum,[f] I have

---

13 a. From the Commandments in Ex 20 and Dt 17.   **b.** Lv 19:18
14 a. Is 45:23
15 a. Ps 69:9   **b.** Ps 18:50   **c.** Dt 32:43 (LXX)   **d.** Ps 117:1   **e.** Is 11:10; 11:1   **f.** The
two extremes of Paul's missionary journeys.

preached Christ's Good News to the utmost of my capacity. •I have always, 20 however, made it an unbroken rule never to preach where Christ's name has already been heard. The reason for that was that I had no wish to build on other men's foundations; •on the contrary, my chief concern has been to fulfil the 21 text: *Those who have never been told about him will see him, and those who have never heard about him will understand.*[9]

Paul's plans

That is the reason why I have been kept from visiting you so long, •though 22 23 for many years I have been longing to pay you a visit. Now, however, having no more work to do here, •I hope to see you on my way to Spain and, after 24 enjoying a little of your company, to complete the rest of the journey with your good wishes. •First, however, I must take a present of money to the saints in 25 Jerusalem, •since Macedonia and Achaia have decided to send a generous 26 contribution to the poor among the saints at Jerusalem. •A generous contribution 27 as it should be, since it is really repaying a debt: the pagans who share the spiritual possessions of these poor people have a duty to help them with temporal possessions. •So when I have done this and officially handed over what has been raised, 28 I shall set out for Spain and visit you on the way. •I know that when I reach you 29 I shall arrive with rich blessings from Christ.

But I beg you, brothers, by our Lord Jesus Christ and the love of the Spirit, 30 to help me through my dangers by praying to God for me. •Pray that I may 31 escape the unbelievers in Judaea, and that the aid I carry to Jerusalem may be accepted by the saints. •Then, if God wills, I shall be feeling very happy when 32 I come to enjoy a period of rest among you. •May the God of peace be with you 33 all! Amen.

Greetings and good wishes

16 I commend to you our sister Phoebe,[a] a deaconess of the church at 1 Cenchreae. •Give her, in union with the Lord, a welcome worthy of saints, 2 and help her with anything she needs: she has looked after a great many people, myself included.

My greetings to Prisca and Aquila, my fellow workers in Christ Jesus, •who 3 4 risked death to save my life:[b] I am not the only one to owe them a debt of gratitude, all the churches among the pagans do as well. •My greetings also 5 to the church that meets at their house.

Greetings to my friend Epaenetus, the first of Asia's gifts to Christ; greetings 6 to Mary who worked so hard for you; •to those outstanding apostles Andronicus 7 and Junias, my compatriots and fellow prisoners who became Christians before me; •to Ampliatus, my friend in the Lord; •to Urban, my fellow worker in 8 9 Christ; to my friend Stachys; •to Apelles who has gone through so much for 10 Christ; to everyone who belongs to the household of Aristobulus; •to my 11 compatriot Herodion; to those in the household of Narcissus who belong to the Lord; •to Tryphaena and Tryphosa, who work hard for the Lord; to my friend 12 Persis who has done so much for the Lord; •to Rufus, a chosen servant of 13 the Lord, and to his mother who has been a mother to me too. •Greetings to 14 Asyncritus, Phlegon, Hermes, Patrobas, Hermas, and all the brothers who are with them; •to Philologus and Julia, Nereus and his sister, and Olympas and all 15 the saints who are with them. •Greet each other with a holy kiss. All the churches 16 of Christ send greetings.

A warning and first postscript

I implore you, brothers, be on your guard against anybody who encourages 17 trouble or puts difficulties in the way of the doctrine you have been taught. Avoid them. •People like that are not slaves of Jesus Christ, they are slaves of their 18 own appetites, confusing the simple-minded with their pious and persuasive arguments. •Your fidelity to Christ, anyway, is famous everywhere, and that 19

makes me very happy about you. I only hope that you are also wise in what is
20 good, and innocent of what is bad. •The God of peace will soon crush Satan
beneath your feet. The grace of our Lord Jesus Christ be with you.

Last greetings and second postscript

21 Timothy, who is working with me, sends his greetings; so do my compatriots,
22 Jason and Sosipater. •I, Tertius, who wrote out this letter, greet you in the Lord.
23 Greetings from Gaius, who is entertaining me and from the whole church that
meets in his house. Erastus, the city treasurer, sends his greetings; so does our
brother Quartus.

Doxology

25 Glory to him who is able to give you the strength to live according to the
Good News I preach, and in which I proclaim Jesus Christ, the revelation of a
26 mystery kept secret for endless ages, •but now so clear that it must be broadcast
to pagans everywhere to bring them to the obedience of faith. This is only what
scripture has predicted, and it is all part of the way the eternal God wants things
27 to be. •He alone is wisdom; give glory therefore to him through Jesus Christ
for ever and ever. Amen.

g. Is 52:15
16 a. Probably the bearer of the letter.   **b.** Probably in Ephesus, either at the time of the
riot described in Ac 19 or during Paul's imprisonment there.

1 CORINTHIANS

THE FIRST LETTER OF PAUL
TO THE CHURCH AT CORINTH

INTRODUCTION

Address and greetings. Thanksgiving

1 I, Paul, appointed by God to be an apostle, together with brother Sosthenes, 1 send greetings •to the church of God in Corinth, to the holy people of Jesus 2 Christ, who are called to take their place among all the saints everywhere who pray to our Lord Jesus Christ; for he is their Lord no less than ours. •May God 3 our Father and the Lord Jesus Christ send you grace and peace.

I never stop thanking God for all the graces you have received through 4 Jesus Christ. •I thank him that you have been enriched in so many ways, especial- 5 ly in your teachers and preachers; •the witness to Christ has indeed been strong 6 among you •so that you will not be without any of the gifts of the Spirit while 7 you are waiting for our Lord Jesus Christ to be revealed; •and he will keep you 8 steady and without blame until the last day, the day of our Lord Jesus Christ, because God by calling you has joined you to his Son, Jesus Christ; and God 9 is faithful.

I. DIVISIONS AND SCANDALS

A. FACTIONS IN THE CORINTHIAN CHURCH

Dissensions among the faithful

All the same, I do appeal to you, brothers, for the sake of our Lord Jesus 10 Christ, to make up the differences between you, and instead of disagreeing among yourselves, to be united again in your belief and practice. •From what 11 Chloe's people have been telling me, my dear brothers, it is clear that there are serious differences among you. •What I mean are all these slogans that you have, 12 like: 'I am for Paul', 'I am for Apollos', 'I am for Cephas',*a* 'I am for Christ'. Has Christ been parcelled out? Was it Paul that was crucified for you? Were you 13 baptised in the name of Paul? •I am thankful that I never baptised any of you 14 after Crispus and Gaius •so none of you can say he was baptised in my name. 15 Then there was the family of Stephanas, of course, that I baptised too, but no one 16 else as far as I can remember.

The true wisdom and the false

For Christ did not send me to baptise, but to preach the Good News, and 17 not to preach that in the terms of philosophy*b* in which the crucifixion of Christ cannot be expressed. •The language of the cross may be illogical to those who 18

are not on the way to salvation, but those of us who are on the way see it as God's
19 power to save. •As scripture says: *I shall destroy the wisdom of the wise and bring*
20 *to nothing all the learning of the learned.* •*Where are the philosophers now? Where
   are the scribes?*[c] Where are any of our thinkers today? Do you see now how God
21 has shown up the foolishness of human wisdom? •If it was God's wisdom that
   human wisdom should not know God, it was because God wanted to save
   those who have faith through the foolishness of the message that we preach.
22/23 And so, while the Jews demand miracles and the Greeks look for wisdom, •here
   are we preaching a crucified Christ; to the Jews an obstacle that they cannot
24 get over, to the pagans madness, •but to those who have been called, whether
25 they are Jews or Greeks, a Christ who is the power and the wisdom of God. •For
   God's foolishness is wiser than human wisdom, and God's weakness is stronger
   than human strength.

26   Take yourselves for instance, brothers, at the time when you were called:
   how many of you were wise in the ordinary sense of the word, how many were
27 influential people, or came from noble families? •No, it was to shame the wise
   that God chose what is foolish by human reckoning, and to shame what is strong
28 that he chose what is weak by human reckoning; •those whom the world thinks
   common and contemptible are the ones that God has chosen—those who are
29 nothing at all to show up those who are everything. •The human race has nothing
30 to boast about to God, •but you God has made members of Christ Jesus and by
   God's doing he has become our wisdom, and our virtue, and our holiness, and
31 our freedom. •As scripture says: *if anyone wants to boast, let him boast about
   the Lord.*[d]

1 2 As for me, brothers, when I came to you, it was not with any show of oratory
2   or philosophy, but simply to tell you what God had guaranteed. •During
   my stay with you, the only knowledge I claimed to have was about Jesus, and
3 only about him as the crucified Christ. •Far from relying on any power of my
4 own, I came among you in great 'fear and trembling'[a] •and in my speeches and
   the sermons that I gave, there were none of the arguments that belong to philo-
5 sophy; only a demonstration of the power of the Spirit. •And I did this so that
   your faith should not depend on human philosophy but on the power of God.

6   But still we have a wisdom to offer those who have reached maturity: not
   a philosophy of our age, it is true, still less of the masters of our age, which
7 are coming to their end. •The hidden wisdom of God which we teach in our
   mysteries is the wisdom that God predestined to be for our glory before the ages
8 began. •It is a wisdom that none of the masters of this age have ever known, or
9 they would not have crucified the Lord of Glory; •we teach what scripture calls:
   *the things that no eye has seen and no ear has heard, things beyond the mind of man,
   all that God has prepared for those who love him.*[b]

10   These are the very things that God has revealed to us through the Spirit, for
11 the Spirit reaches the depths of everything, even the depths of God. •After all,
   the depths of a man can only be known by his own spirit, not by any other man,
   and in the same way the depths of God can only be known by the Spirit of God.
12 Now instead of the spirit of the world, we have received the Spirit that comes
13 from God, to teach us to understand the gifts that he has given us. •Therefore
   we teach, not in the way in which philosophy is taught, but in the way that the
14 Spirit teaches us: we teach spiritual things spiritually. •An unspiritual person
   is one who does not accept anything of the Spirit of God: he sees it all as nonsense;
   it is beyond his understanding because it can only be understood by means of the
15 Spirit. •A spiritual man, on the other hand, is able to judge the value of everything,
16 and his own value is not to be judged by other men. •As scripture says: *Who*

---

1 a. Peter.   b. 'wisdom', the term used by Paul for the human wisdom of philosophy and
rhetoric.   c. Quotations from Is 29:14, Ps 33:10 and Is 33:18 (LXX).   d. Jr 9:22-23
2 a. A scriptural cliché frequently used by Paul.   b. A free combination of Is 64:3 and
Jr 3:16.

can know the mind of the Lord, so who can teach him? But we are those who have
the mind of Christ.

3 Brothers, I myself was unable to speak to you as people of the Spirit: I treated 1
you as sensual men, still infants in Christ. •What I fed you with was milk, 2
not solid food, for you were not ready for it; and indeed, you are still not ready
for it •since you are still unspiritual. Isn't that obvious from all the jealousy 3
and wrangling that there is among you, from the way that you go on behaving
like ordinary people? •What could be more unspiritual than your slogans, 'I am 4
for Paul' and 'I am for Apollos'?

The place of the Christian preacher

After all, what is Apollos and what is Paul? They are servants who brought 5
the faith to you. Even the different ways in which they brought it were assigned
to them by the Lord. •I did the planting, Apollos did the watering, but God 6
made things grow. •Neither the planter nor the waterer matters: only God, who 7
makes things grow. •It is all one who does the planting and who does the watering, 8
and each will duly be paid according to his share in the work. •We are fellow 9
workers with God; you are God's farm, God's building.

By the grace God gave me, I succeeded as an architect and laid the foundations, 10
on which someone else is doing the building. Everyone doing the building must
work carefully. •For the foundation, nobody can lay any other than the one 11
which has already been laid, that is Jesus Christ. •On this foundation you can 12
build in gold, silver and jewels, or in wood, grass and straw, •but whatever the 13
material, the work of each builder is going to be clearly revealed when the day
comes. That day will begin with fire, and the fire will test the quality of each man's
work. •If his structure stands up to it, he will get his wages; •if it is burnt down, 14
15
he will be the loser, and though he is saved himself, it will be as one who has gone
through fire.

Didn't you realise that you were God's temple and that the Spirit of God was 16
living among you? •If anybody should destroy the temple of God, God 17
will destroy him, because the temple of God is sacred; and you are that temple.

Conclusions

Make no mistake about it: if any one of you thinks of himself as wise, in the 18
ordinary sense of the word, then he must learn to be a fool before he really can be
wise. •Why? Because the wisdom of this world is foolishness to God. As scripture 19
says: *The Lord knows wise men's thoughts: he knows how useless they are;*
or again: *God is not convinced by the arguments of the wise.* •So there is 20
21
nothing to boast about in anything human: •Paul, Apollos, Cephas, the world, 22
life and death, the present and the future, are all your servants; •but you belong 23
to Christ and Christ belongs to God.

4 People must think of us as Christ's servants, stewards entrusted with the 1
mysteries of God. •What is expected of stewards is that each one should be 2
found worthy of his trust. •Not that it makes the slightest difference to me 3
whether you, or indeed any human tribunal, find me worthy or not. I will not
even pass judgement on myself. •True, my conscience does not reproach me at 4
all, but that does not prove that I am acquitted: the Lord alone is my judge.
There must be no passing of premature judgement. Leave that until the Lord 5
comes: he will light up all that is hidden in the dark and reveal the secret intentions
of men's hearts. Then will be the time for each one to have whatever praise he
deserves, from God.

Now in everything I have said here, brothers, I have taken Apollos and 6
myself as an example (remember the maxim: 'Keep to what is written'); it is not
for you, so full of your own importance, to go taking sides for one man against
another. •In any case, brother, has anybody given you some special right? What 7
do you have that was not given to you? And if it was given, how can you boast

8 as though it were not? •Is it that you have everything you want—that you are rich already, in possession of your kingdom, with us left outside? Indeed I wish
9 you were really kings, and we could be kings with you! •But instead, it seems to me, God has put us apostles at the end of his parade, with the men sentenced to death; it is true—we have been put on show in front of the whole universe,
10 angels as well as men. •Here we are, fools for the sake of Christ, while you are the learned men in Christ; we have no power, but you are influential; you are
11 celebrities, we are nobodies. •To this day, we go without food and drink and
12 clothes; we are beaten and have no homes; •we work for our living with our own hands. When we are cursed, we answer with a blessing; when we are hounded,
13 we put up with it; •we are insulted and we answer politely. We are treated as the offal of the world, still to this day, the scum of the earth.

An appeal

14 I am saying all this not just to make you ashamed but to bring you, as my
15 dearest children, to your senses. •You might have thousands of guardians in Christ, but not more than one father and it was I who begot you in Christ Jesus
16/17 by preaching the Good News. •That is why I beg you to copy me •and why I have sent you Timothy, my dear and faithful son in the Lord: he will remind you of the way that I live in Christ, as I teach it everywhere in all the churches.

18 When it seemed that I was not coming to visit you, some of you became self-
19 important, •but I will be visiting you soon, the Lord willing, and then I shall want to know not what these self-important people have to say, but what they
20/21 can do, •since the kingdom of God is not just words, it is power. •It is for you to decide: do I come with a stick in my hand or in a spirit of love and goodwill?

B. INCEST IN CORINTH

1 5 I have been told as an undoubted fact that one of you is living with his father's wife.[a] This is a case of sexual immorality among you that must be unparal-
2 leled even among pagans. •How can you be so proud of yourselves? You should be in mourning. A man who does a thing like that ought to have been expelled
3 from the community. •Though I am far away in body, I am with you in spirit, and have already condemned the man who did this thing as if I were actually
4 present. •When you are assembled together in the name of the Lord Jesus, and I am spiritually present with you, then with the power of our Lord Jesus
5 he is to be handed over to Satan so that his sensual body may be destroyed and his spirit saved on the day of the Lord.

6 The pride that you take in yourselves is hardly to your credit. You must know
7 how even a small amount of yeast is enough to leaven all the dough, •so get rid of all the old yeast, and make yourselves into a completely new batch of bread, unleavened as you are meant to be. Christ, our passover, has been sacrificed;
8 let us celebrate the feast, then, by getting rid of all the old yeast of evil and wick-edness, having only the unleavened bread of sincerity and truth.[b]

9 When I wrote in my letter to you not to associate with people living immoral
10 lives, •I was not meaning to include all the people in the world who are sexually immoral, any more than I meant to include all usurers and swindlers or idol-worshippers. To do that, you would have to withdraw from the world altogether.
11 What I wrote was that you should not associate with a brother Christian who is leading an immoral life, or is a usurer, or idolatrous, or a slanderer, or a drunk-
12 ard, or is dishonest; you should not even eat a meal with people like that. •It is

c. Is 40:13
3 a. Jb 5:13   b. Ps 94:11
5 a. Stepmother. Lv 18:8 forbids sexual relations with 'your father's wife'.   b. See note *a* to Jn 19, on the Passover practice.

not my business to pass judgement on those outside. Of those who are inside, you can surely be the judges. •But of those who are outside, God is the judge. 13 *You must drive out this evil-doer from among you.*^c

C. RECOURSE TO THE PAGAN COURTS

6 How dare one of your members take up a complaint against another in the 1 lawcourts of the unjust^a instead of before the saints? •As you know, it is the 2 saints who are to 'judge the world'; and if the world is to be judged by you, how can you be unfit to judge trifling cases? •Since we are also to judge angels, it follows 3 that we can judge matters of everyday life; •but when you have had cases of that 4 kind, the people you appointed to try them were not even respected in the Church. •You should be ashamed: is there really not one reliable man among 5 you to settle differences between brothers •and so one brother brings a court 6 case against another in front of unbelievers? •It is bad enough for you to have 7 lawsuits at all against one another: oughtn't you to let yourselves be wronged, and let yourselves be cheated? •But you are doing the wronging and the cheating, 8 and to your own brothers.

You know perfectly well that people who do wrong will not inherit the 9 kingdom of God: people of immoral lives, idolaters, adulterers, catamites, sodomites, •thieves, usurers, drunkards, slanderers and swindlers will never 10 inherit the kingdom of God. •These are the sort of people some of you were 11 once, but now you have been washed clean, and sanctified, and justified through the name of the Lord Jesus Christ and through the Spirit of our God.

D. FORNICATION

'For me there are no forbidden things';^b maybe, but not everything does good. 12 I agree there are no forbidden things for me, but I am not going to let anything dominate me. •Food is only meant for the stomach, and the stomach for food; 13 yes, and God is going to do away with both of them. But the body—this is not meant for fornication; it is for the Lord, and the Lord for the body. •God, 14 who raised the Lord from the dead, will by his power raise us up too.

You know, surely, that your bodies are members making up the body of 15 Christ; do you think I can take parts of Christ's body and join them to the body of a prostitute? Never! •As you know, a man who goes with a prostitute is one 16 body with her, since *the two,* as it is said, *become one flesh.* •But anyone who is 17 joined to the Lord is one spirit with him.

Keep away from fornication. All the other sins are committed outside the 18 body; but to fornicate is to sin against your own body. •Your body, you know, 19 is the temple of the Holy Spirit, who is in you since you received him from God. You are not your own property; •you have been bought and paid for. That is 20 why you should use your body for the glory of God.

II. ANSWERS TO VARIOUS QUESTIONS

A. MARRIAGE AND VIRGINITY

7 Now for the questions about which you wrote. Yes, it is a good thing for 1 a man not to touch a woman; •but since sex is always a danger, let each 2 man have his own wife and each woman her own husband. •The husband must 3 give his wife what she has the right to expect, and so too the wife to the husband. The wife has no rights over her own body; it is the husband who has them. In the 4 same way, the husband has no rights over his body; the wife has them. •Do not 5 refuse each other except by mutual consent, and then only for an agreed time, to leave yourselves free for prayer; then come together again in case Satan should

6 take advantage of your weakness to tempt you. •This is a suggestion, not a rule:
7 I should like everyone to be like me, but everybody has his own particular gifts from God, one with a gift for one thing and another with a gift for the opposite.
8 There is something I want to add for the sake of widows and those who are
9 not married: it is a good thing for them to stay as they are, like me, •but if they cannot control the sexual urges, they should get married, since it is better to be married than to be tortured.
10 For the married I have something to say, and this is not from me but from
11 the Lord: a wife must not leave her husband — •or if she does leave him, she must either remain unmarried or else make it up with her husband—nor must a husband send his wife away.
12 The rest is from me and not from the Lord. If a brother has a wife who is an unbeliever, and she is content to live with him, he must not send her away;
13 and if a woman has an unbeliever for her husband, and he is content to live with
14 her, she must not leave him. •This is because the unbelieving husband is made one with the saints through his wife, and the unbelieving wife is made one with the saints through her husband. If this were not so, your children would be
15 unclean, whereas in fact they are holy. •However, if the unbelieving partner does not consent, they may separate; in these circumstances, the brother or
16 sister is not tied: God has called you to a life of peace. •If you are a wife, it may be your part to save your husband, for all you know; if a husband, for all you know, it may be your part to save your wife.
17 For the rest, what each one has is what the Lord has given him and he should continue as he was when God's call reached him. This is the ruling that I give
18 in all the churches. •If anyone had already been circumcised at the time of his call, he need not disguise it, and anyone who was uncircumcised at
19 the time of his call need not be circumcised; •because to be circumcised or uncircumcised means nothing: what does matter is to keep the commandments
20 of God. •Let everyone stay as he was at the time of his call. •If, when you were
21 called, you were a slave, do not let this bother you; but if you should have the
22 chance of being free, accept it. •A slave, when he is called in the Lord, becomes the Lord's freedman, and a freeman called in the Lord becomes Christ's slave.
23 You have all been bought and paid for; do not be slaves of other men. •Each
24 one of you, my brothers, should stay as he was before God at the time of his call.
25 About remaining celibate, I have no directions from the Lord but give my
26 own opinion as one who, by the Lord's mercy, has stayed faithful. •Well then, I believe that in these present times of stress this is right: that it is good for a man
27 to stay as he is. •If you are tied to a wife, do not look for freedom; if you are
28 free of a wife, then do not look for one. •But if you marry, it is no sin, and it is not a sin for a young girl to get married. They will have their troubles, though, in their married life, and I should like to spare you that.
29 Brothers, this is what I mean: our time is growing short. Those who have
30 wives should live as though they had none, •and those who mourn should live as though they had nothing to mourn for; those who are enjoying life should live as though there were nothing to laugh about; those whose life is buying things
31 should live as though they had nothing of their own; •and those who have to deal with the world should not become engrossed in it. I say this because the world as we know it is passing away.
32 I would like to see you free from all worry. An unmarried man can devote
33 himself to the Lord's affairs, all he need worry about is pleasing the Lord; •but a married man has to bother about the world's affairs and devote himself to

c. Dt 13:6
6 a. The pagan magistrates of Corinth.   b. Probably one of Paul's own sayings which has been misapplied by false teachers: this section of the letter is directed against the libertines, who had been teaching that sexual intercourse was as necessary for the body as food and drink.

pleasing his wife: •he is torn two ways. In the same way an unmarried woman, 34
like a young girl, can devote herself to the Lord's affairs; all she need worry
about is being holy in body and spirit. The married woman, on the other hand,
has to worry about the world's affairs and devote herself to pleasing her husband.
I say this only to help you, not to put a halter round your necks, but simply to 35
make sure that everything is as it should be, and that you give your undivided
attention to the Lord.

Still, if there is anyone who feels that it would not be fair to his daughter to 36
let her grow too old for marriage, and that he should do something about it, he
is free to do as he likes: he is not sinning if there is a marriage. •On the other 37
hand, if someone has firmly made his mind úp, without any compulsion and
in complete freedom of choice, to keep his daughter as she is, he will be doing
a good thing. •In other words, the man who sees that his daughter is married 38
has done a good thing but the man who keeps his daughter unmarried has done
something even better.*

A wife is tied as long as her husband is alive. But if the husband dies, she is 39
free to marry anybody she likes, only it must be in the Lord. •She would be 40
happier, in my opinon, if she stayed as she is—and I too have the Spirit of God,
I think.

B. FOOD OFFERED TO IDOLS

General principles

8 Now about food sacrificed to idols. 'We all have knowledge'; yes, that is so, 1
but knowledge gives self-importance—it is love that makes the building grow.
A man may imagine he understands something, but still not understand anything 2
in the way that he ought to. •But any man who loves God is known by him 3
Well then, about eating food sacrificed to idols:* we know that idols do not really 4
exist in the world and that there is no god but the One. •And even if there were 5
things called gods, either in the sky or on earth—where there certainly seem to
be 'gods' and 'lords' in plenty—•still for us there is one God, the Father, from 6
whom all things come and for whom we exist; and there is one Lord, Jesus Christ,
through whom all things come and thróugh whom we exist.

The claims of love

Some people, however, do not have this knowledge. There are some who 7
have been so long used to idols that they eat this food as though it really
had been sacrificed to the idol, and their conscience, being weak, is defiled
by it. •Food, of course, cannot bring us in touch with God: we lose nothing 8
if we refuse to eat, we gain nothing if we eat. •Only be careful that you 9
do not make use of this freedom in a way that proves a pitfall for the weak.
Suppose someone sees you, a man who understands, eating in some temple 10
of an idol; his own conscience, even if it is weak, may encourage him
to eat food which has been offered to idols. •In this way your knowledge 11
could become the ruin of someone weak, of a brother for whom Christ
died. •By sinning in this way against your brothers, and injuring their weak 12
consciences, it would be Christ against whom you sinned. •That is why, 13
since food can be the occasion of my brother's downfall, I shall never eat meat
again in case I am the cause of a brother's downfall.

Paul invokes his own example

9 I, personally, am free: I am an apostle and I have seen Jesus our Lord. You 1
are all my work in the Lord. •Even if I were not an apostle to others, I should 2
still be an apostle to you who are the seal of my apostolate in the Lord. •My 3
answer to those who want to interrogate me is this: •Have we not every right 4
to eat and drink?* •And the right to take a Christian woman round with us, 5
like all the other apostles and the brothers of the Lord and Cephas?

⁶⁄₇ Are Barnabas and I the only ones who are not allowed to stop working? •Nobody ever paid money to stay in the army, and nobody ever planted a vineyard and refused to eat the fruit of it. Who has there ever been that kept a flock and did not feed on the milk from his flock?

8 These may be only human comparisons, but does not the Law itself say the
9 same thing? •It is written in the Law of Moses: *You must not put a muzzle on the*
10 *ox when it is treading out the corn.*[b] Is it about oxen that God is concerned, •or is there not an obvious reference to ourselves? Clearly this was written for our sake to show that the ploughman ought to plough in expectation, and the thresher to
11 thresh in the expectation of getting his share. •If we have sown spiritual things
12 for you, why should you be surprised if we harvest your material things? •Others are allowed these rights over you and our right is surely greater? In fact we have never exercised this right. On the contrary we have put up with anything rather
13 than obstruct the Good News of Christ in any way. •Remember that the ministers serving in the Temple get their food from the Temple and those serving at the
14 altar can claim their share from the altar itself. •In the same sort of way the Lord directed that those who preach the gospel should get their living from the gospel.

15 However, I have not exercised any of these rights, and I am not writing all this to secure this treatment for myself. I would rather die than let anyone take
16 away something that I can boast of. •Not that I do boast of preaching the gospel, since it is a duty which has been laid on me; I should be punished if I did not
17 preach it! •If I had chosen this work myself, I might have been paid for it, but
18 as I have not, it is a responsibility which has been put into my hands. •Do you know what my reward is? It is this: in my preaching, to be able to•offer the Good News free, and not insist on the rights which the gospel gives me.

19 So though I am not a slave of any man I have made myself the slave of
20 everyone so as to win as many as I could. •I made myself a Jew to the Jews, to win the Jews; that is, I who am not a subject of the Law made myself a subject of the Law to those who are the subjects of the Law, to win those who are subject
21 to the Law. •To those who have no Law, I was free of the Law myself (though not free from God's law, being under the law of Christ) to win those who have
22 no Law. •For the weak I made myself weak. I made myself all things to all men in
23 order to save some at any cost; •and I still do this, for the sake of the gospel, to have a share in its blessings.

24 All the runners at the stadium are trying to win, but only one of them gets
25 the prize. You must run in the same way, meaning to win. •All the fighters at the games go into strict training; they do this just to win a wreath that will wither
26 away, but we do it for a wreath that will never wither. •That is how I run, intent
27 on winning; that is how I fight, not beating the air. •I treat my body hard and make it obey me, for, having been an announcer myself, I should not want to be disqualified.

A warning, and the lessons of Israel's history

1 **10** I want to remind you, brothers, how our fathers were all guided by a cloud
2 above them and how they all passed through the sea. •They were all
3 baptised into Moses in this cloud and in this sea; •all ate the same spiritual
4 food •and all drank the same spiritual drink, since they all drank from the
5 spiritual rock that followed them as they went, and that rock was Christ. •In spite of this, most of them failed to please God and their corpses littered the desert.

---

7 a. 'daughter' is not the only possible word; this passage has been read as alluding to the practice of a man and a woman living together under vows of chastity; a practice for which there is evidence of a later date.
8 a. At feasts and public ceremonies, portions of the food were 'sacrificed' and went to the gods, the priests and the donors; the whole of the food was regarded as dedicated, whether it was eaten at a ceremonial meal or part of it sold in the markets.
9 a. At the expense of the Christian congregations. b. Dt 25:4

These things all happened as warnings[a] for us, not to have the wicked lusts 6
for forbidden things that they had. •Do not become idolaters as some of them 7
did, for scripture says: *After sitting down to eat and drink, the people got up to
amuse themselves.*[b] •We must never fall into sexual immorality: some of them did, 8
and twenty-three thousand met their downfall in one day. •We are not to put 9
the Lord to the test: some of them did, and they were killed by snakes. •You 10
must never complain: some of them did, and they were killed by the Destroyer.

All this happened to them as a warning, and it was written down to be a lesson 11
for us who are living at the end of the age. •The man who thinks he is safe must 12
be careful that he does not fall. •The trials that you have had to bear are no 13
more than people normally have. You can trust God not to let you be tried
beyond your strength, and with any trial he will give you a way out of it and the
strength to bear it.

Sacrificial feasts. No compromise with idolatry

This is the reason, my dear brothers, why you must keep clear of idolatry. 14
I say to you as sensible people: judge for yourselves what I am saying. •The 15 16
blessing-cup that we bless is a communion with the blood of Christ, and the
bread that we break is a communion with the body of Christ. •The fact that there 17
is only one loaf means that, though there are many of us, we form a single body
because we all have a share in this one loaf. •Look at the other Israel, the race, 18
where those who eat the sacrifices are in communion with the altar. •Does this 19
mean that the food sacrificed to idols has a real value, or that the idol itself is
real? •Not at all. It simply means that the sacrifices that they offer *they sacrifice to* 20
demons who are not God.[c] I have no desire to see you in communion with
demons. •You cannot drink the cup of the Lord and the cup of demons. You 21
cannot take your share at the table of the Lord and at the table of demons. •Do 22
we want to make the Lord angry; are we stronger than he is?

Food sacrificed to idols. Practical solutions

'For me there are no forbidden things', but not everything does good. True, 23
there are no forbidden things, but it is not everything that helps the building to
grow. •Nobody should be looking for his own advantage, but everybody for the 24
other man's. •Do not hesitate to eat anything that is sold in butchers' shops: 25
there is no need to raise questions of conscience; •for *the earth and everything* 26
that is in it belong to the Lord.[d] •If an unbeliever invites you to his house, go if 27
you want to, and eat whatever is put in front of you, without asking questions
just to satisfy conscience. •But if someone says to you, 'This food was offered 28
in sacrifice', then, out of consideration for the man that told you, you should
not eat it, for the sake of his scruples; •his scruples, you see, not your own. Why 29
should my freedom depend on somebody else's conscience? •If I take my share 30
with thankfulness, why should I be blamed for food for which I have thanked
God?

Conclusion

Whatever you eat, whatever you drink, whatever you do at all, do it for the 31
glory of God. •Never do anything offensive to anyone—to Jews or Greeks or to 32
the Church of God; •just as I try to be helpful to everyone at all times, not 33
anxious for my own advantage but for the advantage of everybody else, so that
they may be saved.
Take me for your model, as I take Christ. 1

11

C. DECORUM IN PUBLIC WORSHIP

Women's behaviour at services

You have done well in remembering me so constantly and in maintaining 2
the traditions just as I passed them on to you. •However, what I want you to 3

understand is that Christ is the head of every man, man is the head of woman,
4 and God is the head of Christ. •For a man to pray or prophesy with his head
5 covered is a sign of disrespect to his head.ᵈ •For a woman, however, it is a sign
of disrespect to her headᵇ if she prays or prophesies unveiled; she might as well
6 have her hair shaved off. •In fact, a woman who will not wear a veil ought to have
her hair cut off. If a woman is ashamed to have her hair cut off or shaved, she
ought to wear a veil.

7 A man should certainly not cover his head, since he is the image of God and
8 reflects God's glory; but woman is the reflection of man's glory. •For man did
9 not come from woman; no, woman came from man; •and man was not created
10 for the sake of woman, but woman was created for the sake of man. •That is the
argument for women's covering their heads with a symbol of the authority
11 over them, out of respect for the angels.ᶜ •However, though woman cannot do
12 without man, neither can man do without woman, in the Lord; •woman may
come from man, but man is born of woman—both come from God.

13 Ask yourselves if it is fitting for a woman to pray to God without a veil;
14 and whether nature itself does not tell you that long hair on a man is nothing
15 to be admired, •while a woman, who was given her hair as a covering, thinks
long hair her glory?

16 To anyone who might still want to argue: it is not the custom with us, nor in
the churches of God.

The Lord's Supper

17 Now that I am on the subject of instructions, I cannot say that you have done
18 well in holding meetings that do you more harm than good. •In the first place,
I hear that when you all come together as a community, there are separate
19 factions among you, and I half believe it—•since there must no doubt be separate
20 groups among you, to distinguish those who are to be trusted. •The point is,
when you hold these meetings, it is not the Lord's Supperᵈ that you are eating,
21 since when the time comes to eat, everyone is in such a hurry to start his own
22 supper that one person goes hungry while another is getting drunk. •Surely you
have homes for eating and drinking in? Surely you have enough respect for the
community of God not to make poor people embarrassed? What am I to say to
you? Congratulate you? I cannot congratulate you on this.

23 For this is what I received from the Lord, and in turn passed on to you: that
24 on the same night that he was betrayed, the Lord Jesus took some bread, •and
thanked God for it and broke it, and he said, 'This is my body, which is for you;
25 do this as a memorial of me'. •In the same way he took the cup after supper,
and said, 'This cup is the new covenant in my blood. Whenever you drink it, do
26 this as a memorial of me.' •Until the Lord comes, therefore, every time you eat
27 this bread and drink this cup, you are proclaiming his death, •and so anyone
who eats the bread or drinks the cup of the Lord unworthily will be behaving
unworthily towards the body and blood of the Lord.

28 Everyone is to recollect himself before eating this bread and drinking this
29 cup; •because a person who eats and drinks without recognising the Body
30 is eating and drinking his own condemnation. •In fact that is why many of you
31 are weak and ill and some of you have died. •If only we recollected ourselves,
32 we should not be punished like that. •But when the Lord does punish us like that,
it is to correct us and stop us from being condemned with the world.

33 So to sum up, my dear brothers, when you meet for the Meal, wait for one
34 another. •Anyone who is hungry should eat at home, and then your meeting
will not bring your condemnation. The other matters I shall adjust when I come.

10 a. Lit. 'types'; events prefiguring in the history of Israel the spiritual realities of the
messianic age.　b. Ex 32:6　c. Dt 32:17　d. Ps 24:1
11 a. His leader, a Greek pun.　b. Her husband, who is her head; she is claiming equality.
c. The guardians of due order in public worship.　d. The *agapē*, or love feast, preceding the
liturgical meal.

Spiritual gifts

12 Now my dear brothers, I want to clear up a wrong impression about ¹ spiritual gifts. •You remember that, when you were pagans, whenever ² you felt irresistibly drawn, it was towards dumb idols? •It is for that reason that ³ I want you to understand that on the one hand no one can be speaking under the influence of the Holy Spirit and say, 'Curse Jesus', and on the other hand, no one can say, 'Jesus is Lord' unless he is under the influence of the Holy Spirit.

The variety and the unity of gifts

There is a variety of gifts but always the same Spirit; •there are all sorts of ⁴₅ service to be done, but always to the same Lord; •working in all sorts of different ⁶ ways in different people, it is the same God who is working in all of them. •The ⁷ particular way in which the Spirit is given to each person is for a good purpose. One may have the gift of preaching with wisdom given him by the Spirit; another ⁸ may have the gift of preaching instruction given him by the same Spirit; •and ⁹ another the gift of faith given by the same Spirit; another again the gift of healing, through this one Spirit; •one, the power of miracles; another, prophecy; ¹⁰ another the gift of recognising spirits; another the gift of tongues and another the ability to interpret them. •All these are the work of one and the same Spirit, ¹¹ who distributes different gifts to different people just as he chooses.

The analogy of the body

Just as a human body, though it is made up of many parts, is a single unit ¹² because all these parts, though many, make one body, so it is with Christ. •In ¹³ the one Spirit we were all baptised, Jews as well as Greeks, slaves as well as citizens, and one Spirit was given to us all to drink.

Nor is the body to be identified with any one of its many parts. •If the foot ¹⁴₁₅ were to say, 'I am not a hand and so I do not belong to the body', would that mean that it stopped being part of the body? •If the ear were to say, 'I am not ¹⁶ an eye, and so I do not belong to the body', would that mean that it was not a part of the body? •If your whole body was just one eye, how would you hear anything? ¹⁷ If it was just one ear, how would you smell anything?

Instead of that, God put all the separate parts into the body on purpose. •If ¹⁸₁₉ all the parts were the same, how could it be a body? •As it is, the parts are many ²⁰ but the body is one. •The eye cannot say to the hand, 'I do not need you', nor can ²¹ the head say to the feet, 'I do not need you'.

What is more, it is precisely the parts of the body that seem to be the weakest ²² which are the indispensable ones; •and it is the least honourable parts of the ²³ body that we clothe with the greatest care. So our more improper parts get decorated •in a way that our more proper parts do not need. God has arranged ²⁴ the body so that more dignity is given to the parts which are without it, •and so ²⁵ that there may not be disagreements inside the body, but that each part may be equally concerned for all the others. •If one part is hurt, all parts are hurt with ²⁶ it. If one part is given special honour, all parts enjoy it.

Now you together are Christ's body; but each of you is a different part of it. ²⁷ In the Church, God has given the first place to apostles, the second to prophets, ²⁸ the third to teachers; after them, miracles, and after them the gift of healing; helpers, good leaders, those with many languages. •Are all of them apostles, ²⁹ or all of them prophets, or all of them teachers? Do they all have the gift of miracles, •or all have the gift of healing? Do all speak strange languages, and ³⁰ all interpret them?

The order of importance in spiritual gifts. Love

Be ambitious for the higher gifts. And I am going to show you a way that is ³¹ better than any of them.

1,2 **13** If I have all the eloquence of men or of angels, but speak without love, I am simply a gong booming or a cymbal clashing. •If I have the gift of prophecy, understanding all the mysteries there are, and knowing everything, and if I have faith in all its fulness, to move mountains, but without love, then

3 I am nothing at all. •If I give away all that I possess, piece by piece, and if I even let them take my body to burn it, but am without love, it will do me no good whatever.

4 Love is always patient and kind; it is never jealous; love is never boastful
5 or conceited; •it is never rude or selfish; it does not take offence, and is not
6 resentful. •Love takes no pleasure in other people's sins but delights in the truth;
7 it is always ready to excuse, to trust, to hope, and to endure whatever comes.

8 Love does not come to an end. But if there are gifts of prophecy, the time will come when they must fail; or the gift of languages, it will not continue for ever; and knowledge—for this, too, the time will come when it must fail.
9,10 For our knowledge is imperfect and our prophesying is imperfect; •but once
11 perfection comes, all imperfect things will disappear. •When I was a child, I used to talk like a child, and think like a child, and argue like a child, but now I am
12 a man, all childish ways are put behind me. •Now we are seeing a dim reflection in a mirror; but then we shall be seeing face to face. The knowledge that I have now is imperfect; but then I shall know as fully as I am known.

13 In short, there are three things that last: faith, hope and love; and the greatest of these is love.

Spiritual gifts: their respective importance in the community

1,2 **14** You must want love more than anything else; but still hope for the spiritual gifts as well, especially prophecy. •Anybody with the gift of tongues speaks to God, but not to other people; because nobody understands him when he
3 talks in the spirit about mysterious things. •On the other hand, the man who prophesies does talk to other people, to their improvement, their encouragement
4 and their consolation. •The one with the gift of tongues talks for his own benefit, but the man who prophesies does so for the benefit of the community.
5 While I should like you all to have the gift of tongues, I would much rather you could prophesy, since the man who prophesies is of greater importance than the man with the gift of tongues, unless of course the latter offers an interpretation so that the church may get some benefit.

6 • Now suppose, my dear brothers, I am someone with the gift of tongues, and I come to visit you, what use shall I be if all my talking reveals nothing new, tells
7 you nothing, and neither inspires you nor instructs you? •Think of a musical instrument, a flute or a harp: if one note on it cannot be distinguished
8 from another, how can you tell what tune is being played? •Or if no one can be sure which call the trumpet has sounded, who will be ready for the attack?
9 It is the same with you: if your tongue does not produce intelligible speech, how
10 can anyone know what you are saying? You will be talking to the air. •There are any number of different languages in the world, and not one of them is meaning-
11 less, •but if I am ignorant of what the sounds mean, I am a savage to the man
12 who is speaking, and he is a savage to me. •It is the same in your own case: since you aspire to spiritual gifts, concentrate on those which will grow to benefit the community.

13 That is why anybody who has the gift of tongues must pray for the power
14 of interpreting them. •For if I use this gift in my prayers, my spirit may be praying
15 but my mind is left barren. •What is the answer to that? Surely I should pray not only with the spirit but with the mind as well? And sing praises not only with
16 the spirit but with the mind as well? •Any uninitiated person will never be able to say Amen to your thanksgiving, if you only bless God with the spirit, for he
17 will have no idea what you are saying. •However well you make your thanks-
18 giving, the other gets no benefit from it. •I thank God that I have a greater gift

of tongues than all of you, •but when I am in the presence of the community 19
I would rather say five words that mean something than ten thousand words
in a tongue.

Brothers, you are not to be childish in your outlook. You can be babies as 20
far as wickedness is concerned, but mentally you must be adult. •In the written 21
Law it says: *Through men speaking strange languages and through the lips of
foreigners, I shall talk to the nation, and still they will not listen to me, says the
Lord.*[a] •You see then, that the strange languages are meant to be a sign not for 22
believers but for unbelievers, while on the other hand, prophecy is a sign not for
unbelievers but for believers. •So that any uninitiated people or unbelievers, 23
coming into a meeting of the whole church where everybody was speaking in
tongues, would say you were all mad; •but if you were all prophesying and an 24
unbeliever or uninitiated person came in, he would find himself analysed and
judged by everyone speaking; •he would find his secret thoughts laid bare, 25
and then fall on his face and worship God, declaring that *God is among you
indeed.*[b]

Regulating spiritual gifts

So, my dear brothers, what conclusion is to be drawn? At all your meetings, 26
let everyone be ready with a psalm or a sermon or a revelation, or ready to use
his gift of tongues or to give an interpretation; but it must always be for the
common good. •If there are people present with the gift of tongues, let only two or 27
three, at the most, be allowed to use it, and only one at a time, and there must
be someone to interpret. •If there is no interpreter present, they must keep quiet 28
in church and speak only to themselves and to God. •As for prophets, let two 29
or three of them speak, and the others attend to them. •If one of the listeners 30
receives a revelation, then the man who is already speaking should stop. •For 31
you can all prophesy in turn, so that everybody will learn something and
everybody will be encouraged. •Prophets can always control their prophetic 32
spirits, •since God is not a God of disorder but of peace. 33

As in all the churches of the saints, •women are to remain quiet at meetings 34
since they have no permission to speak; they must keep in the background as
the Law itself lays it down. •If they have any questions to ask, they should ask 35
their husbands at home: it does not seem right for a woman to raise her voice
at meetings.

Do you think the word of God came out of yourselves? Or that it has come 36
only to you? •Anyone who claims to be a prophet or inspired ought to recognise 37
that what I am writing to you is a command from the Lord. •Unless he recognises 38
this, you should not recognise him.

And so, my dear brothers, by all means be ambitious to prophesy, do not 39
suppress the gift of tongues, •but let everything be done with propriety and in order. 40

III. THE RESURRECTION OF THE DEAD

The fact of the resurrection

15 Brothers, I want to remind you of the gospel I preached to you, the gospel 1
that you received and in which you are firmly established; •because the 2
gospel will save you only if you keep believing exactly what I preached to you—
believing anything else will not lead to anything.

Well then, in the first place, I taught you what I had been taught myself, 3
namely that Christ died for our sins, in accordance with the scriptures; •that he 4
was buried; and that he was raised to life on the third day, in accordance with
the scriptures; •that he appeared first to Cephas and secondly to the Twelve. 5
Next he appeared to more than five hundred of the brothers at the same time, 6
most of whom are still alive, though some have died; •then he appeared to 7

8 James, and then to all the apostles; •and last of all he appeared to me too; it was as though I was born when no one expected it.

9 I am the least of the apostles; in fact, since I persecuted the Church of God,
10 I hardly deserve the name apostle; •but by God's grace that is what I am, and the grace that he gave me has not been fruitless. On the contrary, I, or rather
11 the grace of God that is with me, have worked harder than any of the others; •but what matters is that I preach what they preach, and this is what you all believed.

12 Now if Christ raised from the dead is what has been preached, how can
13 some of you be saying that there is no resurrection of the dead? •If there is no
14 resurrection of the dead, Christ himself cannot have been raised, •and if Christ has not been raised then our preaching is useless and your believing it is useless;
15 indeed, we are shown up as witnesses who have committed perjury before God,
16 because we swore in evidence before God that he had raised Christ to life. •For
17 if the dead are not raised, Christ has not been raised, •and if Christ has not been
18 raised, you are still in your sins. •And what is more serious, all who have died in
19 Christ have perished. •If our hope in Christ has been for this life only, we are the most unfortunate of all people.

20 But Christ has in fact been raised from the dead, the first-fruits of all who
21 have fallen asleep. •Death came through one man and in the same way the
22 resurrection of the dead has come through one man. •Just as all men die in Adam,
23 so all men will be brought to life in Christ; •but all of them in their proper order: Christ as the first-fruits and then, after the coming of Christ, those who belong
24 to him. •After that will come the end, when he hands over the kingdom to God the Father, having done away with every sovereignty, authority and power.
25
26 For he must be king *until he has put all his enemies under his feet*[a] •and the last of the enemies to be destroyed is death, for everything is to be *put under his feet*.
27 —Though when it is said that *everything is subjected*, this clearly cannot include
28 the One who subjected everything to him. •And when everything is subjected to him, then the Son himself will be subject in his turn to the One who subjected all things to him, so that God may be all in all.

29 If this were not true, what do people hope to gain by being baptised for the dead? If the dead are not ever going to be raised, why be baptised on their
30 behalf? •What about ourselves? Why are we living under a constant threat?
31 I face death every day, brothers, and I can swear it by the pride that I take in you
32 in Christ Jesus our Lord. •If my motives were only human ones, what good would
33 it do me to fight the wild animals at Ephesus? •You say: *Let us eat and drink today; tomorrow we shall be dead*.[b] You must stop being led astray: 'Bad friends
34 ruin the noblest people'.[c] •Come to your senses, behave properly, and leave sin alone; there are some of you who seem not to know God at all; you should be ashamed.

The manner of the resurrection

35 Someone may ask, 'How are dead people raised, and what sort of body do they
36 have when they come back?' •They are stupid questions. Whatever you sow in the
37 ground has to die before it is given new life •and the thing that you sow is not what is going to come; you sow a bare grain, say of wheat or something like that,
38 and then God gives it the sort of body that he has chosen: each sort of seed gets its own sort of body.

39 Everything that is flesh is not the same flesh: there is human flesh, animals'
40 flesh, the flesh of birds and the flesh of fish. •Then there are heavenly bodies and there are earthly bodies; but the heavenly bodies have a beauty of their own and
41 the earthly bodies a different one. •The sun has its brightness, the moon a different brightness, and the stars a different brightness, and the stars differ from each

14 a. A free version of Is 28:11-12.   b. Is 45:14
15 a. Ps 110:1   b. Is 22:13   c. This quotation from Menander's *Thais* may have become a proverb.

other in brightness. •It is the same with the resurrection of the dead: the thing 42
that is sown is perishable but what is raised is imperishable; •the thing that is 43
sown is contemptible but what is raised is glorious; the thing that is sown is weak
but what is raised is powerful; •when it is sown it embodies the soul, when it is 44
raised it embodies the spirit.

If the soul has its own embodiment, so does the spirit have its own embodiment.
The first *man*, Adam, as scripture says, *became a living soul*; but the last Adam 45
has become a life-giving spirit. •That is, first the one with the soul, not the spirit, 46
and after that, the one with the spirit. •The first man, being from the earth, is 47
earthly by nature; the second man is from heaven. •As this earthly man was, so 48
are we on earth; and as the heavenly man is, so are we in heaven. •And we, who 49
have been modelled on the earthly man, will be modelled on the heavenly man.

Or else, brothers, put it this way: flesh and blood cannot inherit the kingdom 50
of God: and the perishable cannot inherit what lasts for ever. •I will tell you 51
something that has been secret: that we are not all going to die, but we shall all
be changed. •This will be instantaneous, in the twinkling of an eye, when the 52
last trumpet sounds. It will sound, and the dead will be raised, imperishable,
and we shall be changed as well, •because our present perishable nature must 53
put on imperishability and this mortal nature must put on immortality.

A hymn of triumph. Conclusion

When this perishable nature has put on imperishability, and when this 54
mortal nature has put on immortality, then the words of scripture will come
true: *Death is swallowed up in victory.* • *Death, where is your* victory? *Death, where* 55
is your sting?[d] •Now the sting of death is sin, and sin gets its power from the Law. 56
So let us thank God for giving us the victory through our Lord Jesus Christ. 57

Never give in then, my dear brothers, never admit defeat; keep on working 58
at the Lord's work always, knowing that, in the Lord, you cannot be labouring
in vain.

CONCLUSION

Commendations. Greetings

16 Now about the collection made for the saints: you are to do as I told the 1
churches in Galatia to do. •Every Sunday, each one of you must put 2
aside what he can afford, so that collections need not be made after I have come.
When I am with you, I will send your offering to Jerusalem by the hand 3
of whatever men you give letters of reference to; •if it seems worth while for me 4
to go too, they can travel with me.

I shall be coming to you after I have passed through Macedonia—and I am 5
doing no more than pass through Macedonia—•and I may be staying with you, 6
perhaps even passing the winter, to make sure that it is you who send me on my
way wherever my travels take me. •As you see, I do not want to make it only 7
a passing visit to you and I hope to spend some time with you, the Lord permit-
ting. •In any case I shall be staying at Ephesus until Pentecost •because a big 8/9
and important door has opened for my work and there is a great deal
of opposition.

If Timothy comes, show him that he has nothing to be afraid of in you: like 10
me, he is doing the Lord's work, •and nobody is to be scornful of him. Send 11
him happily on his way to come back to me; the brothers and I are waiting for
him. •As for our brother Apollos, I begged him to come to you with the brothers 12
but he was quite firm that he did not want to go yet and he will come as soon
as he can.

Be awake to all the dangers; stay firm in the faith; be brave and be strong. 13
Let everything you do be done in love. 14

15 There is something else to ask you, brothers. You know how the Stephanas family, who were the first-fruits of Achaia, have really worked hard to help the
16 saints. •Well, I want you in your turn to put yourselves at the service of people
17 like this, and anyone who helps and works with them. •I am delighted that Stephanas, Fortunatus and Achaicus have arrived; they make up for your
18 absence. •They have settled my mind, and yours too; I hope you appreciate men like this.
19 All the churches of Asia send you greetings. Aquila and Prisca, with the church that meets at their house, send you their warmest wishes, in the Lord.
20 All the brothers send you their greetings. Greet one another with a holy kiss.
21 This greeting is in my own hand—Paul.
22 If anyone does not love the Lord, a curse on him. 'Maran atha.'[a]
23 The grace of the Lord Jesus be with you.
24 My love is with you all in Christ Jesus.

d. A free version; see Ho 13:14.
16 a. Aramaic. 'The Lord is coming', or 'Lord, come'.

2 CORINTHIANS

THE SECOND LETTER OF PAUL
TO THE CHURCH AT CORINTH

INTRODUCTION

Address and greetings. Thanksgiving

1 From Paul, appointed by God to be an apostle of Christ Jesus, and from 1
Timothy, one of the brothers, to the church of God at Corinth and to all the
saints in the whole of Achaia. •Grace and peace to you from God our Father and 2
the Lord Jesus Christ.

Blessed be the God and Father of our Lord Jesus Christ, a gentle Father and 3
the God of all consolation, •who comforts us in all our sorrows, so that we can 4
offer others, in their sorrows, the consolation that we have received from God
ourselves. •Indeed, as the sufferings of Christ overflow to us, so, through Christ, 5
does our consolation overflow. •When we are made to suffer, it is for your 6
consolation and salvation. When, instead, we are comforted, this should be a
consolation to you, supporting you in patiently bearing the same sufferings as
we bear. •And our hope for you is confident, since we know that, sharing our 7
sufferings, you will also share our consolations.

For we should like you to realise, brothers, that the things we had to undergo 8
in Asia were more of a burden than we could carry, so that we despaired of
coming through alive. •Yes, we were carrying our own death warrant with us, 9
and it has taught us not to rely on ourselves but only on God, who raises the
dead to life. •And he saved us from dying, as he will save us again; yes, that is our 10
firm hope in him, that in the future he will save us again. •You must all join in the 11
prayers for us: the more people there are asking for help for us, the more will be
giving thanks when it is granted to us.

I. SOME RECENT EVENTS REVIEWED

Why Paul changed his plans

There is one thing we are proud of, and our conscience tells us it is true: that 12
we have always treated everybody, and especially you, with the reverence and
sincerity which come from God, and by the grace of God we have done this
without ulterior motives. •There are no hidden meanings in our letters besides 13
what you can read for yourselves and understand. •And I hope that, although 14
you do not know us very well yet, you will have come to recognise, when the day
of our Lord Jesus comes, that you can be as proud of us as we are of you.

Because I was so sure of this, I had meant to come to you first, so that you 15
would benefit doubly; •staying with you before going to Macedonia and coming 16
back to you again on the way back from Macedonia, for you to see me on my way
to Judaea. •Do you think I was not sure of my own intentions when I planned 17

this? Do you really think that when I am making my plans, my motives are ordinary human ones, and that I say Yes, yes, and No, no, at the same time?

18
19 I swear by God's truth, there is no Yes and No about what we say to you. •The Son of God, the Christ Jesus that we proclaimed among you—I mean Silvanus

20 and Timothy and I—was never Yes and No: with him it was always Yes, •and however many the promises God made, the Yes to them all is in him. That is

21 why it is 'through him' that we answer Amen to the praise of God. •Remember it is God himself who assures us all, and you, of our standing in Christ, and has

22 anointed us, •marking us with his seal and giving us the pledge, the Spirit, that we carry in our hearts.

23 By my life, I call God to witness that the reason why I did not come to Corinth

24 after all was to spare your feelings. •We are not dictators over your faith, but are fellow workers with you for your happiness; in the faith you are steady enough.

1 **2** Well then, I made up my mind not to pay you a second distressing visit.

2 I may have hurt you, but if so I have hurt the only people who could give me any

3 pleasure. •I wrote as I did to make sure that, when I came, I should not be distressed by the very people who should have made me happy. I am sure you all

4 know that I could never be happy unless you were. •When I wrote to you, in deep distress and anguish of mind, and in tears, it was not to make you feel hurt but to let you know how much love I have for you.

5 Someone has been the cause of pain; and the cause of pain not to me, but to

6 some degree—not to overstate it—to all of you. •The punishment already imposed

7 by the majority on the man in question is enough; •and the best thing now is to give him your forgiveness and encouragement, or he might break down from so

8 much misery. •So I am asking you to give some definite proof of your love for

9 him. •What I really wrote for, after all, was to test you and see whether you are

10 completely obedient. •Anybody that you forgive, I forgive; and as for my forgiving anything—if there has been anything to be forgiven, I have forgiven

11 it for your sake in the presence of Christ. •And so we will not be outwitted by Satan—we know well enough what his intentions are.

From Troas to Macedonia. The apostolate: its importance

12 When I went up to Troas to preach the Good News of Christ, and the door

13 was wide open for my work there in the Lord, •I was so continually uneasy in mind at not meeting brother Titus there, I said good-bye to them and went on to Macedonia.

14 Thanks be to God who, wherever he goes, makes us, in Christ, partners of his triumph,[a] and through us is spreading the knowledge of himself, like a sweet smell,

15 everywhere. •We are Christ's incense to God for those who are being saved and

16 for those who are not; •for the last, the smell of death that leads to death, for the first the sweet smell of life that leads to life. And who could be qualified for work

17 like this? •At least we do not go round offering the word of God for sale, as many other people do. In Christ, we speak as men of sincerity, as envoys of God and in God's presence.

1 **3** Does this sound like a new attempt to commend ourselves to you? Unlike other people, we need no letters of recommendation either to you or from

2 you, •because you are yourselves our letter, written in our hearts, that anybody

3 can see and read, •and it is plain that you are a letter from Christ, drawn up by us, and written not with ink but with the Spirit of the living God, not on stone tablets but on the tablets of your living hearts.

4
5 Before God, we are confident of this through Christ: •not that we are qualified in ourselves to claim anything as our own work: all our qualifications come from

6 God. •He is the one who has given us the qualifications to be the administrators of this new covenant, which is not a covenant of written letters but of the Spirit:

2 a. Like a victorious general making his ceremonial entry into Rome.

the written letters bring death, but the Spirit gives life. •Now if the administering 7
of death, in the written letters engraved on stones, was accompanied by such a
brightness that the Israelites could not bear looking at the face of Moses, though
it was a brightness that faded, •then how much greater will be the brightness that 8
surrounds the administering of the Spirit! •For if there was any splendour in 9
administering condemnation, there must be very much greater splendour in
administering justification. •In fact, compared with this greater splendour, the 10
thing that used to have such splendour now seems to have none; •and if what 11
was so temporary had any splendour, there must be much more in what is going
to last for ever.

Having this hope, we can be quite confident; •not like Moses, who put a veil ¹²₁₃
over his face so that the Israelites would not notice the ending of what had to
fade.ᵃ •And anyway, their minds had been dulled; indeed, to this very day, that 14
same veil is still there when the old covenant is being read, a veil never lifted, since
Christ alone can remove it. •Yes, even today, whenever Moses is read, the veil is 15
over their minds. •It will not be removed until they turn to the Lord. •Now this ¹⁶₁₇
Lord is the Spirit, and where the Spirit of the Lord is, there is freedom. •And 18
we, with our unveiled faces reflecting like mirrors the brightness of the Lord, all
grow brighter and brighter as we are turned into the image that we reflect; this
is the work of the Lord who is Spirit.

4 Since we have by an act of mercy been entrusted with this work of adminis- 1
tration, there is no weakening on our part. •On the contrary, we will have 2
none of the reticence of those who are ashamed, no deceitfulness or watering
down the word of God; but the way we commend ourselves to every human
being with a conscience is by stating the truth openly in the sight of God. •If our 3
gospel does not penetrate the veil, then the veil is on those who are not on the
way to salvation; •the unbelievers whose minds the god of this world has blinded, 4
to stop them seeing the light shed by the Good News of the glory of Christ, who
is the image of God. •For it is not ourselves that we are preaching, but Christ 5
Jesus as the Lord, and ourselves as your servants for Jesus' sake. •It is the same 6
God that said, 'Let there be light shining out of darkness', who has shone in our
minds to radiate the light of the knowledge of God's glory, the glory on the face
of Christ.

The trials and hopes of the apostolate

We are only the earthenware jars that hold this treasure, to make it clear 7
that such an overwhelming power comes from God and not from us. •We are in 8
difficulties on all sides, but never cornered; we see no answer to our problems,
but never despair; •we have been persecuted, but never deserted; knocked down, 9
but never killed; •always, wherever we may be, we carry with us in our body 10
the death of Jesus, so that the life of Jesus, too, may always be seen in our body.
Indeed, while we are still alive, we are consigned to our death every day, for the 11
sake of Jesus, so that in our mortal flesh the life of Jesus, too, may be openly
shown. •So death is at work in us, but life in you. 12

But as we have the same spirit of faith that is mentioned in scripture— 13
*I believed, and therefore I spoke*ᵃ—we too believe and therefore we too speak,
knowing that he who raised the Lord Jesus to life will raise us with Jesus in our 14
turn, and put us by his side and you with us. •You see, all this is for your benefit, 15
so that the more grace is multiplied among people, the more thanksgiving there
will be, to the glory of God.

That is why there is no weakening on our part, and instead, though this outer 16
man of ours may be falling into decay, the inner man is renewed day by day.
Yes, the troubles which are soon over, though they weigh little, train us for the 17
carrying of a weight of eternal glory which is out of all proportion to them. •And 18
so we have no eyes for things that are visible, but only for things that are
invisible; for visible things last only for a time, and the invisible things are
eternal.

1 5 For we know that when the tent that we live in on earth is folded up, there
   is a house built by God for us, an everlasting home not made by human hands,
2 in the heavens. •In this present state, it is true, we groan as we wait with longing
3 to put on our heavenly home over the other; •we should like to be found wearing
4 clothes and not without them. •Yes, we groan and find it a burden being still
   in this tent, not that we want to strip it off, but to put the second garment over it
5 and to have what must die taken up into life. •This is the purpose for which
   God made us, and he has given us the pledge of the Spirit.
6 We are always full of confidence, then, when we remember that to live in the
7 body means to be exiled from the Lord, •going as we do by faith and not by sight
8 —we are full of confidence, I say, and actually want to be exiled from the body
9 and make our home with the Lord. •Whether we are living in the body or exiled
10 from it, we are intent on pleasing him. •For all the truth about us will be brought
   out in the law court of Christ, and each of us will get what he deserves for the
   things he did in the body, good or bad.

The apostolate in action

11 And so it is with the fear of the Lord in mind that we try to win people over.
   God knows us for what we really are, and I hope that in your consciences you
12 know us too. •This is not another attempt to commend ourselves to you: we are
   simply giving you reasons to be proud of us, so that you will have an answer ready
   for the people who can boast more about what they seem than what they are.
13 If we seemed out of our senses, it was for God; but if we are being reasonable
14 now, it is for your sake. •And this is because the love of Christ overwhelms us
   when we reflect that if one man has died for all, then all men should be dead;
15 and the reason he died for all was so that living men should live no longer for
   themselves, but for him who died and was raised to life for them.
16 From now onwards, therefore, we do not judge anyone by the standards of the
   flesh. Even if we did once know Christ in the flesh, that is not how we know him
17 now. •And for anyone who is in Christ, there is a new creation; the old creation
18 has gone, and now the new one is here. •It is all God's work. It was God who
   reconciled us to himself through Christ and gave us the work of handing on this
19 reconciliation. •In other words, God in Christ was reconciling the world to
   himself, not holding men's faults against them, and he has entrusted to us the
20 news that they are reconciled. •So we are ambassadors for Christ; it is as though
   God were appealing through us, and the appeal that we make in Christ's name
21 is: be reconciled to God. •For our sake God made the sinless one into sin, so
1 that in him we might become the goodness of God. 6 As his fellow workers, we
2 beg you once again not to neglect the grace of God that you have received. •For
   he says: *At the favourable time, I have listened to you; on the day of salvation
   I came to your help.*[a] Well, now is the favourable time; this is the day of salvation.
3 We do nothing that people might object to, so as not to bring discredit on our
4 function as God's servants. •Instead, we prove we are servants of God by great
5 fortitude in times of suffering: in times of hardship and distress; •when we are
6 flogged, or sent to prison, or mobbed; labouring, sleepless, starving. •We prove
   we are God's servants by our purity, knowledge, patience and kindness; by a
7 spirit of holiness, by a love free from affectation; •by the word of truth and by
   the power of God; by being armed with the weapons of righteousness in the right
8 hand and in the left, •prepared for honour or disgrace, for blame or praise; taken
9 for impostors while we are genuine; •obscure yet famous; said to be dying and
10 here are we alive; rumoured to be executed before we are sentenced; •thought
   most miserable and yet we are always rejoicing; taken for paupers though we make
   others rich, for people having nothing though we have everything.

3 a. See Ex 34:33.
4 a. Ps 116:10
6 a. Is 49:8

Paul opens his heart. A warning

Corinthians, we have spoken to you very frankly; our mind has been opened 11
in front of you. •Any constraint that you feel is not on our side; the constraint 12
is in your own selves. •I speak as if to children of mine: as a fair exchange, open 13
your minds in the same way.

Do not harness yourselves in an uneven team with unbelievers. Virtue is no 14
companion for crime. Light and darkness have nothing in common. •Christ is 15
not the ally of Beliar, nor has a believer anything to share with an unbeliever.
The temple of God has no common ground with idols, and that is what we 16
are—the temple of the living God. We have God's word for it: *I will make
my home among them and live with them; I will be their God and they shall be my
people.*[b] •Then *come away from them and keep aloof, says the Lord. Touch nothing* 17
that is unclean,[c] *and I will welcome you* •*and be your father, and you shall be my* 18
sons and daughters, says the Almighty Lord.[d]

7 With promises like these made to us, dear brothers, let us wash off all that 1
can soil either body or spirit, to reach perfection of holiness in the fear of God.

Keep a place for us in your hearts. We have not injured anyone, or ruined 2
anyone, or exploited anyone. •I am not saying this to put any blame on you; 3
as I have already told you, you are in our hearts—together we live or together
we die. •I have the very greatest confidence in you, and I am so proud of you that 4
in all our trouble I am filled with consolation and my joy is overflowing.

Paul in Macedonia; he is joined by Titus

Even after we had come to Macedonia, however, there was no rest for this 5
body of ours. Far from it; we found trouble on all sides: quarrels outside, mis-
givings inside. •But God comforts the miserable, and he comforted us, by the 6
arrival of Titus, •and not only by his arrival but also by the comfort which he 7
had gained from you. He has told us all about how you want to see me, how sorry
you were, and how concerned for me, and so I am happier now than I was before.

But to tell the truth, even if I distressed you by my letter, I do not regret it. 8
I did regret it before, and I see that that letter did distress you, at least for a time;
but I am happy now—not because I made you suffer, but because your suffering 9
led to your repentance. Yours has been a kind of suffering that God approves,
and so you have come to no kind of harm from us. •To suffer in God's way 10
means changing for the better and leaves no regrets, but to suffer as the world
knows suffering brings death. •Just look at what suffering in God's way has 11
brought you: what keenness, what explanations, what indignation, what alarm!
Yes, and what aching to see me, what concern for me, and what justice done!
In every way you have shown yourselves blameless in this affair. •So then, though 12
I wrote the letter to you, it was not written for the sake either of the offender
or of the one offended; it was to make you realise, in the sight of God, your own
concern for us. •That is what we have found so encouraging. 13

With this encouragement, too, we had the even greater happiness of finding
Titus so happy; thanks to you all, he has no more worries; •I had rather boasted 14
to him about you, and now I have not been made to look foolish; in fact, our
boasting to Titus has proved to be as true as anything that we ever said to you.
His own personal affection for you is all the greater when he remembers how 15
willing you have all been, and with what deep respect you welcomed him. •I am 16
very happy knowing that I can rely on you so completely.

II. ORGANISATION OF THE COLLECTION

Why the Corinthians should be generous

8 Now here, brothers, is the news of the grace of God which was given in the 1
churches in Macedonia; •and of how, throughout great trials by suffering, 2
their constant cheerfulness and their intense poverty have overflowed in a wealth

3 of generosity. •I can swear that they gave not only as much as they could afford,
4 but far more, and quite spontaneously, •begging and begging us for the favour
5 of sharing in this service to the saints •and, what was quite unexpected, they
offered their own selves first to God and, under God, to us.

6   Because of this, we have asked Titus, since he has already made a beginning,
7 to bring this work of mercy to the same point of success among you. •You
always have the most of everything—of faith, of eloquence, of understanding, of
keenness for any cause, and the biggest share of our affection—so we expect
8 you to put the most into this work of mercy too. •It is not an order that I am
giving you; I am just testing the genuineness of your love against the keenness of
9 others. •Remember how generous the Lord Jesus was: he was rich, but he
10 became poor for your sake, to make you rich out of his poverty. •As I say, I am
only making a suggestion; it is only fair to you, since you were the first, a year
11 ago, not only in taking action but even in deciding to. •So now finish the work
and let the results be worthy, as far as you can afford it, of the decision you made
12 so promptly. •As long as the readiness is there, a man is acceptable with whatever
13 he can afford; never mind what is beyond his means. •This does not mean that
to give relief to others you ought to make things difficult for yourselves: it is
14 a question of balancing •what happens to be your surplus now against their
present need, and one day they may have something to spare that will supply
15 your own need. That is how we strike a balance: •as scripture says: *The man who
gathered much had none too much, the man who gathered little did not go short.*[a]

The delegates recommended to the Corinthians

16   I thank God for putting into Titus' heart the same concern for you that I have
17 myself. •He did what we asked him; indeed he is more concerned than ever, and
18 is visiting you on his own initiative. •As his companion we are sending the
19 brother who is famous in all the churches for spreading the gospel. •More than
that, he happens to be the same brother who has been elected by the churches
to be our companion on this errand of mercy that, for the glory of God, we have
20 undertaken to satisfy our impatience to help. •We hope that in this way there
21 will be no accusations made about our administering such a large fund; •for *we*
22 *are trying to do right* not only *in the sight of God* but *also* in the sight of *men.*[b] •To
accompany these, we are sending a third brother, of whose keenness we have
often had proof in many different ways, and who is particularly keen about this,
23 because he has great confidence in you. •Titus, perhaps I should add, is my own
colleague and fellow worker in your interests; the other two brothers, who are
24 delegates of the churches, are a real glory to Christ. •So then, in front of all the
churches, give them a proof of your love, and prove to them that we are right
to be proud of you.

1 **9** There is really no need for me to write to you on the subject of offering
2   your services to the saints, •since I know how anxious you are to help; in
fact, I boast about you to the Macedonians, telling them, 'Achaia has been ready
3 since last year'. So your zeal has been a spur to many more. •I am sending the
brothers all the same, to make sure that our boasting about you does not prove
to have been empty this time, and that you really are ready as I said you would
4 be. •If some of the Macedonians who are coming with me found you unprepared,
we should be humiliated—to say nothing of yourselves—after being so confident.
5 That is why I have thought it necessary to ask these brothers to go on to you
ahead of us, and make sure in advance that the gift you promised is all ready,
and that it all comes as a gift out of your generosity and not by being extorted
from you.

b. Lv 26:11-12   c. Is 52:11   d. Is 43:6
8 a. Ex 16:18   b. Pr 3:4 (LXX)

Blessings to be expected from the collection

Do not forget: thin sowing means thin reaping; the more you sow, the more 6 you reap. •Each one should give what he has decided in his own mind, not 7 grudgingly or because he is made to, for *God loves a cheerful giver.*^a •And there 8 is no limit to the blessings which God can send you—he will make sure that you will always have all you need for yourselves in every possible circumstance, and still have something to spare for all sorts of good works. •As scripture says: *He* 9 *was free in almsgiving, and gave to the poor: his good deeds will never be forgotten.*^b

The one who provides *seed for the sower and bread for food* will provide you with 10 all the seed you want and make *the harvest of your good deeds* a larger one, •and, 11 made richer in every way, you will be able to do all the generous things which, through us, are the cause of thanksgiving to God. •For doing this holy service 12 is not only supplying all the needs of the saints, but it is also increasing the amount of thanksgiving that God receives. •By offering this service, you show 13 them what you are, and that makes them give glory to God for the way you accept and profess the gospel of Christ, and for your sympathetic generosity to them and to all. •And their prayers for you, too, show how they are drawn to you on 14 account of all the grace that God has given you. •Thanks be to God for his inex- 15 pressible gift!

III. PAUL'S APOLOGIA

Paul's reply to accusations of weakness

10 This is a personal matter; this is Paul himself appealing to you by the 1 gentleness and patience of Christ—I, the man who is so humble when he is facing you, but bullies you when he is at a distance. •I only ask that I do not 2 have to bully you when I come, with all the confident assurance I mean to show when I come face to face with people I could name who think we go by ordinary human motives. •We live in the flesh, of course, but the muscles that we fight 3 with are not flesh. •Our war is not fought with weapons of flesh, yet they are 4 strong enough, in God's cause, to demolish fortresses. We demolish sophistries, and the arrogance that tries to resist the knowledge of God; every thought is 5 our prisoner, captured to be brought into obedience to Christ. •Once you have 6 given your complete obedience, we are prepared to punish any disobedience.

Face plain facts. Anybody who is convinced that he belongs to Christ must 7 go on to reflect that we all belong to Christ no less than he does. •Maybe I do 8 boast rather too much about our authority, but the Lord gave it to me for building you up and not for pulling you down, and I shall not be ashamed of it. •I do not 9 want you to think of me as someone who only frightens you by letter. •Someone 10 said, 'He writes powerful and strongly-worded letters but when he is with you you see only half a man and no preacher at all'. •The man who said that can 11 remember this: whatever we are like in the words of our letters when we are absent, that is what we shall be like in our actions when we are present.

His reply to the accusation of ambition

We are not being so bold as to rank ourselves, or invite comparison, with 12 certain people who write their own references. Measuring themselves against themselves, and comparing themselves to themselves, they are simply foolish. We, on the other hand, are not going to boast without a standard to measure 13 against: taking for our measure the yardstick which God gave us to measure with, which is long enough to reach to you. •We are not stretching further than 14 we ought; otherwise we should not have reached you, as we did come all the way to you with the gospel of Christ. •So we are not boasting without any measure, 15 about work that was done by other people; in fact, we trust that, as your faith grows, we shall get taller and taller, when judged by our own standard. •I mean, 16

we shall be carrying the gospel to places far beyond you, without encroaching on
17 anyone else's field, not boasting of the work already done. •*If anyone wants to*
18 *boast, let him boast of the Lord.*[a] •It is not the man who commends himself that
can be accepted, but the man who is commended by the Lord.

Paul is driven to sound his own praises

1 11 I only wish you were able to tolerate a little foolishness from me. But of
2 course: you are tolerant towards me. •You see, the jealousy that I feel
for you is God's own jealousy: I arranged for you to marry Christ so that I might
3 give you away as a chaste virgin to this one husband. •But the serpent, with his
cunning, seduced Eve, and I am afraid that in the same way your ideas may get
4 corrupted and turned away from simple devotion to Christ. •Because any new-
comer has only to proclaim a new Jesus, different from the one that we preached,
or you have only to receive a new spirit, different from the one you have already
received, or a new gospel, different from the one you have already accepted—and
5 you welcome it with open arms. •As far as I can tell, these arch-apostles have
6 nothing more than I have. •I may not be a polished speechmaker, but as for
knowledge, that is a different matter; surely we have made this plain, speaking
on every subject in front of all of you.
7   Or was I wrong, lowering myself so as to lift you high, by preaching the
8 gospel of God to you and taking no fee for it? •I was robbing other churches
9 living on them so that I could serve you. •When I was with you and ran out of
money, I was no burden to anyone; the brothers who came from Macedonia
provided me with everything I wanted. I was very careful, and I always shall be,
10 not to be a burden to you in any way, •and by Christ's truth in me, this cause
11 of boasting will never be taken from me in the regions of Achaia. •Would I do that
12 if I did not love you? God knows I do. •I intend to go on doing what I am doing
now—leaving no opportunity for those people who are looking for an opportunity
13 to claim equality with us in what they boast of. •These people are counterfeit
14 apostles, they are dishonest workmen disguised as apostles of Christ. •There is
nothing unexpected about that; if Satan himself goes disguised as an angel of light,
15 there is no need to be surprised when his servants, too, disguise themselves as the
servants of righteousness. They will come to the end that they deserve.
16   As I said before, let no one take me for a fool; but if you must, then treat me
17 as a fool and let me do a little boasting of my own. •What I am going to say now
is not prompted by the Lord, but said as if in a fit of folly, in the certainty that
18 I have something to boast about. •So many others have been boasting of their
19 worldly achievements, that I will boast myself. •You are all wise men and can
20 cheerfully tolerate fools, •yes, even to tolerating somebody who makes slaves of
you, makes you feed him, imposes on you, orders you about and slaps you in the
21 face. •I hope you are ashamed of us for being weak with you instead!
     But if anyone wants some brazen speaking—I am still talking as a fool—then
22 I can be as brazen as any of them, and about the same things. •Hebrews, are they?
23 So am I. Israelites? So am I. Descendants of Abraham? So am I. •The servants
of Christ? I must be mad to say this, but so am I, and more than they: more,
because I have worked harder, I have been sent to prison more often, and whipped
24 so many times more, often almost to death. •Five times I had the thirty-nine
25 lashes from the Jews; •three times I have been beaten with sticks; once I was
stoned; three times I have been shipwrecked and once adrift in the open sea for
26 a night and a day. •Constantly travelling, I have been in danger from rivers and
in danger from brigands, in danger from my own people and in danger from
pagans; in danger in the towns, in danger in the open country, danger at sea and
27 danger from so-called brothers. •I have worked and laboured, often without
sleep; I have been hungry and thirsty and often starving; I have been in the cold

9 a. Pr 22:8 (LXX)   b. Ps 112:9
10 a. Jr 9:23

without clothes. •And, to leave out much more, there is my daily preoccupation: 28
my anxiety for all the churches. •When any man has had scruples, I have had 29
scruples with him; when any man is made to fall, I am tortured.

If I am to boast, then let me boast of my own feebleness. •The God and Father 30 31
of the Lord Jesus—bless him for ever—knows that I am not lying. •When I was 32
in Damascus, the ethnarch of King Aretas put guards round the city to catch
me, •and I had to be let down over the wall in a hamper, through a window, in 33
order to escape.

12 Must I go on boasting, though there is nothing to be gained by it? But 1
I will move on to the visions and revelations I have had from the Lord.
I know a man in Christ who, fourteen years ago, was caught up—whether still in 2
the body or out of the body, I do not know; God knows—right into the third
heaven.ᵃ •I do know, however, that this same person—whether in the body or 3
out of the body, I do not know; God knows—•was caught up into paradise and 4
heard things which must not and cannot be put into human language. •I will 5
boast about a man like that, but not about anything of my own except my weaknesses. •If I should decide to boast, I should not be made to look foolish, because 6
I should only be speaking the truth; but I am not going to, in case anyone should
begin to think I am better than he can actually see and hear me to be.

In view of the extraordinary nature of these revelations, to stop me from 7
getting too proud I was given a thorn in the flesh, an angel of Satan to beat me
and stop me from getting too proud! •About this thing, I have pleaded with the 8
Lord three times for it to leave me, •but he has said, 'My grace is enough for 9
you: my power is at its best in weakness'. So I shall be very happy to make my
weaknesses my special boast so that the power of Christ may stay over me, •and 10
that is why I am quite content with my weaknesses, and with insults, hardships,
persecutions, and the agonies I go through for Christ's sake. For it is when I am
weak that I am strong.

I have been talking like a fool, but you forced me to do it: you are the ones 11
who should have been commending me. Though I am a nobody, there is not
a thing these arch-apostles have that I do not have as well. •You have seen done 12
among you all the things that mark the true apostle, unfailingly produced: the
signs, the marvels, the miracles. •Is there anything of which you have had less than 13
the other churches have had, except that I have not myself been a burden on
you? For this unfairness, please forgive me. •I am all prepared now to come to 14
you for the third time, and I am not going to be a burden on you: it is you I want,
not your possessions. Children are not expected to save up for their parents, but
parents for children. •I am perfectly willing to spend what I have, and to be 15
expended, in the interests of your souls. Because I love you more, must I be loved
the less?

All very well, you say: I personally put no pressure on you, but like the cunning 16
fellow that I am, I took you in by a trick. •So we exploited you, did we, through 17
one of the men that I have sent to you? •Well, Titus went at my urging, and I sent 18
the brother that came with him. Can Titus have exploited you? You know that
he and I have always been guided by the same spirit and trodden in the same
tracks.

Paul's fears and anxieties

All this time you have been thinking that our defence is addressed to you, 19
but it is before God that we, in Christ, are speaking; and it is all, my dear
brothers, for your benefit. •What I am afraid of is that when I come I may find 20
you different from what I want you to be, and you may find that I am not as you
would like me to be; and then there will be wrangling, jealousy, and tempers
roused, intrigues and backbiting and gossip, obstinacies and disorder. •I am 21
afraid that on my next visit, my God may make me ashamed on your account
and I shall be grieving over all those who sinned before and have still not repented
of the impurities, fornication and debauchery they committed.

1 **13** This will be the third time I have come to you. *The evidence of three, or at*
2 *least two, witnesses is necessary to sustain the charge.*[a] •I gave warning when
I was with you the second time and I give warning now, too, before I come, to
those who sinned before and to any others, that when I come again, I shall have
3 no mercy. •You want proof, you say, that it is Christ speaking in me: you have
4 known him not as a weakling, but as a power among you? •Yes, but he was
crucified through weakness, and still he lives now through the power of God.
So then, we are weak, as he was, but we shall live with him, through the power
of God, for your benefit.

5 Examine yourselves to make sure you are in the faith; test yourselves. Do
you acknowledge that Jesus Christ is really in you? If not, you have failed the
6 test, •but we, as I hope you will come to see, have not failed it. •We pray to God
7 that you will do nothing wrong: not that we want to appear as the ones who have
8 been successful—we would rather that you did well even though we failed. •We
9 have no power to resist the truth; only to further it. •We are only too glad to be
weak provided you are strong. What we ask in our prayers is for you to be made
10 perfect. •That is why I am writing this from a distance, so that when I am with
you I shall not need to be strict, with the authority which the Lord gave me for
building up and not for destroying.

CONCLUSION

Recommendations. Greetings. Final good wishes

11 In the meantime, brothers, we wish you happiness; try to grow perfect; help
one another. Be united; live in peace, and the God of love and peace will be with
you.
12 Greet one another with the holy kiss. All the saints send you greetings.
13 The grace of the Lord Jesus Christ, the love of God and the fellowship of the
Holy Spirit be with you all.

12 a. I.e. the highest heaven.
13 a. Dt 19:15

GALATIANS

THE LETTER OF PAUL
TO THE CHURCH IN GALATIA

Address

1 From Paul to the churches of Galatia, and from all the brothers who are here ¹₂
with me, an apostle who does not owe his authority to men or his appointment
to any human being but who has been appointed by Jesus Christ and by God the
Father who raised Jesus from the dead. •We wish you the grace and peace of 3
God our Father and of the Lord Jesus Christ, •who in order to rescue us from 4
this present wicked world sacrificed himself for our sins, in accordance with
the will of God our Father, •to whom be glory for ever and ever. Amen. 5

A warning

I am astonished at the promptness with which you have turned away from the 6
one who called you and have decided to follow a different version of the Good
News. •Not that there can be more than one Good News; it is merely that some 7
troublemakers among you want to change the Good News of Christ; •and let 8
me warn you that if anyone preaches a version of the Good News different from
the one we have already preached to you, whether it be ourselves or an angel
from heaven, he is to be condemned. •I am only repeating what we told you 9
before: if anyone preaches a version of the Good News different from the one
you have already heard, he is to be condemned. •So now whom am I trying to 10
please—man, or God? Would you say it is men's approval I am looking for?ᵃ If
I still wanted that, I should not be what I am—a servant of Christ.

I. PAUL'S APOLOGIA

God's call

The fact is, brothers, and I want you to realise this, the Good News I 11
preached is not a human message •that I was given by men, it is something 12
I learnt only through a revelation of Jesus Christ. •You must have heard of 13
my career as a practising Jew, how merciless I was in persecuting the Church of
God, how much damage I did to it, •how I stood out among other Jews of my 14
generation, and how enthusiastic I was for the traditions of my ancestors.
Then God, who had specially *chosen* me while I was *still in my mother's* 15
*womb,*ᵇ called me through his grace and chose •to reveal his Son in me, so that 16
I might preach the Good News about him to the pagans. I did not stop to discuss
this with any human being, •nor did I go up to Jerusalem to see those who were 17
already apostles before me, but I went off to Arabiaᶜ at once and later went
straight back from there to Damascus. •Even when after three years I went up 18
to Jerusalem to visit Cephas and stayed with him for fifteen days, •I did not see 19
any of the other apostles; I only saw James, the brother of the Lord, •and I 20

21 swear before God that what I have just written is the literal truth. •After that
22 I went to Syria and Cilicia, •and was still not known by sight to the churches of
23 Christ in Judaea, •who had heard nothing except that their one-time persecutor
24 was now preaching the faith he had previously tried to destroy; •and they gave
glory to God for me.

The meeting at Jerusalem

1 2 It was not till fourteen years had passed that I went up to Jerusalem again.
2   I went with Barnabas and took Titus with me. •I went there as the result of \
a revelation, and privately I laid before the leading men the Good News as I
proclaim it among the pagans; I did so for fear the course I was adopting or had
3 already adopted would not be allowed. •And what happened? Even though Titus
4 who had come with me is a Greek, he was not obliged to be circumcised. •The
question came up only because some who do not really belong to the brotherhood
have furtively crept in to spy on the liberty we enjoy in Christ Jesus, and want
5 to reduce us all to slavery. •I was so determined to safeguard for you the true
meaning of the Good News, that I refused even out of deference to yield to
6 such people for one moment. •As a result, these people who are acknowledged
leaders—not that their importance matters to me, since God has no favourites—
7 these leaders, as I say, had nothing to add to the Good News as I preach it. •On
the contrary, they recognised that I had been commissioned to preach the Good
News to the uncircumcised just as Peter had been commissioned to preach it to
8 the circumcised. •The same person whose action had made Peter the apostle of
9 the circumcised had given me a similar mission to the pagans. •So, James,
Cephas and John, these leaders, these pillars, shook hands with Barnabas and
me as a sign of partnership: we were to go to the pagans and they to the
10 circumcised.ᵃ •The only thing they insisted on was that we should remember to
help the poor, as indeed I was anxious to do.

Peter and Paul at Antioch

11   When Cephas came to Antioch, however, I opposed him to his face, since
12 he was manifestly in the wrong. •His custom had been to eat with the pagans,ᵇ
but after certain friends of James arrived he stopped doing this and kept away
13 from them altogether for fear of the group that insisted on circumcision. •The
other Jews joined him in this pretence, and even Barnabas felt himself obliged
to copy their behaviour.
14   When I saw they were not respecting the true meaning of the Good News,
I said to Cephas in front of everyone, 'In spite of being a Jew, you live like the
pagans and not like the Jews, so you have no right to make the pagans copy
Jewish ways'.

The Good News as proclaimed by Paul

15
16   'Though we were born Jews and not pagan sinners, •we acknowledge that
what makes a man righteous is not obedience to the Law, but faith in Jesus
Christ. We had to become believers in Christ Jesus no less than you had, and
now we hold that faith in Christ rather than fidelity to the Law is what justifies
17 us, and that *no one can be justified*ᶜ by keeping the Law. •Now if we were to
admit that the result of looking to Christ to justify us is to make us sinners like
the rest, it would follow that Christ had induced us to sin, which would be
18 absurd. •If I were to return to a position I had already abandoned, I should be
19 admitting I had done something wrong. •In other words, through the Law I am

1 **a.** Probably a rejoinder to an accusation by the judaisers that Paul was trying to make the
pagans' conversion easy by not insisting on circumcision.   **b.** Is. 49:1   **c.** Probably the
kingdom of the Nabataean Arabs, to the S. of Damascus.
2 **a.** The distinction is geographical rather than racial; when Paul went among the Gentiles
the resident Jews were his first concern.   **b.** Converts from paganism.   **c.** Ps 143:2

dead to the Law, so that now I can live for God. I have been crucified with
Christl, •and I live now not with my own life but with the life of Christ who 20
lives in me. The life I now live in this body I live in faith: faith in the Son of
God who loved me and who sacrificed himself for my sake. •I cannot bring 21
myself to give up God's gift: if the Law can justify us, there is no point in the
death of Christ.'

II. DOCTRINAL MATTERS

Justification by faith

3 Are you people in Galatia mad? Has someone put a spell on you, in spite 1
of the plain explanation you have had of the crucifixion of Jesus Christ?
Let me ask you one question: was it because you practised the Law that you 2
received the Spirit, or because you believed what was preached to you? •Are you 3
foolish enough to end in outward observances what you began in the Spirit?
Have all the favours you received been wasted? And if this were so, they would 4
most certainly have been wasted. •Does God give you the Spirit so freely and 5
work miracles among you because you practise the Law, or because you believed
what was preached to you?

Take Abraham for example: *he put his faith in God, and this faith was* 6
considered as justifying him.^a •Don't you see that it is those who rely on faith who 7
are the sons of Abraham? •Scripture foresaw that God was going to use faith 8
to justify the pagans, and proclaimed the Good News long ago when Abraham
was told: *In you all the pagans will be blessed.*^b •Those therefore who rely on 9
faith receive the same blessing as Abraham, the man of faith.

The curse brought by the Law

On the other hand, those who rely on the keeping of the Law are under a 10
curse, since scripture says: *Cursed be everyone who does not persevere in observing*
everything prescribed in the book of the Law.^c •The Law will not justify anyone 11
in the sight of God, because we are told: *the righteous man finds life through faith.*^d
The Law is not even based on faith, since we are told: *The man who practises* 12
these precepts finds life through practising them.^e • Christ redeemed us from the 13
curse of the Law by being cursed for our sake, since scripture says: *Cursed be*
everyone who is hanged on a tree.^f •This was done so that in Christ Jesus the 14
blessing of Abraham might include the pagans, and so that through faith we might
receive the promised Spirit.

The Law did not cancel the promise

Compare this, brothers, with what happens in ordinary life. If a will has 15
been drawn up in due form, no one is allowed to disregard it or add to it. •Now 16
the promises were addressed to Abraham *and to his descendants*—notice, in
passing, that scripture does not use a plural word as if there were several
descendants, it uses the singular: to his posterity, which is Christ. •But my 17
point is this: once God had expressed his will in due form, no law that came
four hundred and thirty years later could cancel that and make the promise
meaningless. •If you inherit something as a legal right, it does not come to you 18
as the result of a promise, and it was precisely in the form of a promise that God
made his gift to Abraham.

The purpose of the Law

What then was the purpose of adding the Law? This was done to specify 19
crimes, until the posterity came to whom the promise was addressed. The Law
was promulgated by angels,^g assisted by an intermediary. •Now there can only 20
be an intermediary between two parties, yet God is one. •Does this mean that 21
there is opposition between the Law and the promises of God? Of course not.

We could have been justified by the Law if the Law we were given had been
22 capable of giving life, •but it is not: scripture makes no exceptions when it says
that sin is master everywhere. In this way the promise can only be given through
faith in Jesus Christ and can only be given to those who have this faith.

The coming of faith

23   Before faith came, we were allowed no freedom by the Law; we were being
24 looked after till faith was revealed. •The Law was to be our guardian until the
25 Christ came and we could be justified by faith. •Now that that time has come
26 we are no longer under that guardian, •and you are, all of you, sons of God
27 through faith in Christ Jesus. •All baptised in Christ, you have all clothed
28 yourselves in Christ, •and there are no more distinctions between Jew and
Greek, slave and free, male and female, but all of you are one in Christ Jesus.
29 Merely by belonging to Christ you are the posterity of Abraham, the heirs he
was promised.

Sons of God

1   4 Let me put this another way: an heir, even if he has actually inherited
everything, is no different from a slave for as long as he remains a child.
2 He is under the control of guardians and administrators until he reaches the
3 age fixed by his father. •Now before we came of age we were as good as slaves to
4 the elemental principles of this world,*ᵃ* •but when the appointed time came,
5 God sent his Son, born of a woman, born a subject of the Law, •to redeem the
6 subjects of the Law and to enable us to be adopted as sons. •The proof that you
are sons is that God has sent the Spirit of his Son into our hearts: the Spirit
7 that cries, 'Abba, Father', •and it is this that makes you a son, you are not a
slave any more; and if God has made you son, then he has made you heir.
8   Once you were ignorant of God, and enslaved to 'gods' who are not really
9 gods at all; •but now that you have come to acknowledge God—or rather, now
that God has acknowledged you—how can you want to go back to elemental
10 things like these, that can do nothing and give nothing, and be their slaves? •You
11 and your special days and months and seasons and years! •You make me feel I
have wasted my time with you.

A personal appeal

12   Brothers, all I ask is that you should copy me as I copied you. You have
13 never treated me in an unfriendly way before; •even at the beginning, when that
14 illness gave me the opportunity to preach the Good News to you, •you never
showed the least sign of being revolted or disgusted by my disease that was such
a trial to you; instead you welcomed me as an angel of God, as if I were Christ
15 Jesus himself. •What has become of this enthusiasm you had? I swear that you
16 would even have gone so far as to pluck out your eyes and give them to me. •Is it
17 telling you the truth that has made me your enemy? •The blame lies in the way
they have tried to win you over: by separating you from me, they want to win
18 you over to themselves. •It is always a good thing to win people over—and
19 I do not have to be there with you—but it must be for a good purpose, •my
children! I must go through the pain of giving birth to you all over again, until
20 Christ is formed in you. •I wish I were with you now so that I could know exactly
what to say; as it is, I have no idea what to do for the best.

The two covenants: Hagar and Sarah

²¹₂₂   You want to be subject to the Law? Then listen to what the Law says. •It
says, if you remember, that Abraham had two sons, one by the slave-girl, and one

---

3 a. Gn 15:6   b. Gn 12:3   c. Dt 27:26   d. Hab 2:4   e. Lv 18:5   f. Dt 21:23   g. In
Jewish tradition angels were present at Sinai; the 'intermediary' is Moses.
4 a. The principles that make up the physical universe; Paul has related the Law to 'outward
observances', 3:3.

by his free-born wife. •The child of the slave-girl was born in the ordinary way; 23
the child of the free woman was born as the result of a promise. •This can be 24
regarded as an allegory: the women stand for the two covenants. The first who
comes from Mount Sinai, and whose children are slaves, is Hagar—•since Sinai 25
is in Arabia—and she corresponds to the present Jerusalem that is a slave like
her children. •The Jerusalem above, however, is free and is our mother, •since ²⁶₂₇
scripture says: *Shout for joy, you barren women who bore no children! Break into
shouts of joy and gladness, you who were never in labour. For there are more sons of
the forsaken one than sons of the wedded wife.*[b] •Now you, my brothers, like Isaac, 28
are children of the promise, •and as at that time the child born in the ordinary 29
way persecuted the child born in the Spirit's way, so also now. •Does not 30
scripture say: *Drive away that slave-girl and her son; this slave-girl's son is not to
share the inheritance with the son*[c] of the free woman? •So, my brothers, we are 31
the children, not of the slave-girl, but of the free-born wife.

III. EXHORTATION

Christian liberty

5 When Christ freed us, he meant us to remain free. Stand firm, therefore, 1
and do not submit again to the yoke of slavery. •It is I, Paul, who tell you 2
this: if you allow yourselves to be circumcised, Christ will be of no benefit to
you at all. •With all solemnity I repeat my warning: Everyone who accepts 3
circumcision is obliged to keep the whole Law. •But if you do look to the Law 4
to make you justified, then you have separated yourselves from Christ, and have
fallen from grace. •Christians are told by the Spirit to look to faith for those 5
rewards that righteousness hopes for, •since in Christ Jesus whether you are 6
circumcised or not makes no difference—what matters is faith that makes its
power felt through love.

You began your race well: who made you less anxious to obey the truth? 7
You were not prompted by him who called you! •The yeast seems to be spreading ⁸₉
through the whole batch of you. •I feel sure that, united in the Lord, you will 10
agree with me, and anybody who troubles you in future will be condemned,
no matter who he is. •As for me, my brothers, if I still preach circumcision,[a] 11
why am I still persecuted? If I did that now, would there be any scandal of the
cross? •Tell those who are disturbing you I would like to see the knife slip. 12

Liberty and charity

' My brothers, you were called, as you know, to liberty; but be careful, or this 13
liberty will provide an opening for self-indulgence. Serve one another, rather, in
works of love, •since the whole of the Law is summarised in a single command: 14
Love your neighbour as yourself.[b] •If you go snapping at each other and tearing 15
each other to pieces, you had better watch or you will destroy the whole
community.

Let me put it like this: if you are guided by the Spirit you will be in no danger 16
of yielding to self-indulgence, •since self-indulgence is the opposite of the Spirit, 17
the Spirit is totally against such a thing, and it is precisely because the two are
so opposed that you do not always carry out your good intentions. •If you are 18
led by the Spirit, no law can touch you. •When self-indulgence is at work the 19
results are obvious: fornication, gross indecency and sexual irresponsibility;
idolatry and sorcery; feuds and wrangling, jealousy, bad temper and quarrels; 20
disagreements, factions, •envy; drunkenness, orgies and similar things. I warn 21
you now, as I warned you before: those who behave like this will not inherit the
kingdom of God. •What the Spirit brings is very different: love, joy, peace, 22
patience, kindness, goodness, trustfulness, •gentleness and self-control. There 23

24 can be no law against things like that, of course. •You cannot belong to Christ Jesus unless you crucify all self-indulgent passions and desires.

25
26   Since the Spirit is our life, let us be directed by the Spirit. •We must stop being conceited, provocative and envious.

On kindness and perseverance

1 6 Brothers, if one of you misbehaves, the more spiritual of you who set him right should do so in a spirit of gentleness, not forgetting that you may be
2 tempted yourselves. •You should carry each other's troubles and fulfil the
3 law of Christ. •It is the people who are not important who often make the
4 mistake of thinking that they are. •Let each of you examine his own conduct; if you find anything to boast about, it will at least be something of your own, not
5 just something better than your neighbour has. •Everyone has his own burden to carry.

6   People under instruction should always contribute something to the support of the man who is instructing them.

7   Don't delude yourself into thinking God can be cheated: where a man sows,
8 there he reaps: •if he sows in the field of self-indulgence he will get a harvest of corruption out of it; if he sows in the field of the Spirit he will get from it a
9 harvest of eternal life. •We must never get tired of doing good because if we
10 don't give up the struggle we shall get our harvest at the proper time. •While we have the chance, we must do good to all, and especially to our brothers in the faith.

Epilogue

11   Take good note of what I am adding in my own handwriting and in large
12 letters. •It is only self-interest that makes them want to force circumcision on
13 you—they want to escape persecution for the cross of Christ—•they accept circumcision but do not keep the Law themselves; they only want you to be
14 circumcised so that they can boast of the fact. •As for me, the only thing I can boast about is the cross of our Lord Jesus Christ, through whom the world is
15 crucified to me, and I to the world. •It does not matter if a person is circumcised
16 or not; what matters is for him to become an altogether new creature. •Peace and mercy to all who follow this rule, who form the Israel of God.

17   I want no more trouble from anybody after this; the marks on my body are
18 those of Jesus. •The grace of our Lord Jesus Christ be with your spirit, my brothers. Amen.

b. Is 54:1   **c.** Gn 21:10
5 a. As Paul's enemies were apparently claiming.   **b.** Lv 19:18

EPHESIANS

THE LETTER OF PAUL
TO THE CHURCH AT EPHESUS

Address and Greetings

1 From Paul, appointed by God to be an apostle of Christ Jesus, to the saints 1
who are faithful to Christ Jesus: •Grace and peace to you from God our 2
Father and from the Lord Jesus Christ.

I. THE MYSTERY OF SALVATION AND OF THE CHURCH

God's plan of salvation

Blessed be God the Father of our Lord Jesus Christ, 3
who has blessed us with all the spiritual blessings of heaven in Christ.
Before the world was made, he chose us, chose us in Christ, 4
to be holy and spotless, and to live through love in his presence,
determining that we should become his adopted sons, through 5
    Jesus Christ
for his own kind purposes,
to make us praise the glory of his grace, 6
his free gift to us in the Beloved,
in whom, through his blood, we gain our freedom, the forgiveness 7
    of our sins.
Such is the richness of the grace
which he has showered on us 8
in all wisdom and insight.
He has let us know the mystery of his purpose, 9
the hidden plan he so kindly made in Christ from the beginning
to act upon when the times had run their course to the end: 10
that he would bring everything together under Christ, as head,
everything in the heavens and everything on earth.
And it is in him that we were claimed as God's own, 11
chosen from the beginning,
under the predetermined plan of the one who guides all things
as he decides by his own will;
chosen to be, 12
for his greater glory,
the people who would put their hopes in Christ before he came.
Now you too, in him, 13
have heard the message of the truth and the good news of your
    salvation,
and have believed it;

and you too have been stamped with the seal of the Holy Spirit
of the Promise,

14   the pledge of our inheritance
which brings freedom for those whom God has taken for his own,
to make his glory praised.

The triumph and the supremacy of Christ

15   That will explain why I, having once heard about your faith in the Lord Jesus,
16 and the love that you show towards all the saints, •have never failed to remember
17 you in my prayers and to thank God for you. •May the God of our
Lord Jesus Christ, the Father of glory, give you a spirit of wisdom and perception
18 of what is revealed, to bring you to full knowledge of him. •May he enlighten
the eyes of your mind so that you can see what hope his call holds for you, what
19 rich glories he has promised the saints will inherit •and how infinitely great is
the power that he has exercised for us believers. This you can tell from the strength
20 of his power •at work in Christ, when he used it to raise him from the dead and
21 to make him sit at his right hand, in heaven, •far above every Sovereignty,
Authority, Power, or Domination,^a or any other name that can be named, not
22 only in this age but also in the age to come. •*He has put all things under his feet,*^b
23 and made him, as the ruler of everything, the head of the Church; •which is his
body, the fullness of him who fills the whole creation.

Salvation in Christ a free gift

¹₂ 2 And you were dead, through the crimes and the sins •in which you used to live
when you were following the way of this world, obeying the ruler who governs
3 the air,^a the spirit who is at work in the rebellious. •We all were among them
too in the past, living sensual lives, ruled entirely by our own physical desires
and our own ideas; so that by nature we were as much under God's anger as the
4 rest of the world. •But God loved us with so much love that he was generous
5 with his mercy: •when we were dead through our sins, he brought us to life
6 with Christ—it is through grace that you have been saved—•and raised us up
with him and gave us a place with him in heaven, in Christ Jesus.
7   This was to show for all ages to come, through his goodness towards us in
8 Christ Jesus, how infinitely rich he is in grace. •Because it is by grace that you
have been saved, through faith; not by anything of your own, but by a gift from
9 God; •not by anything that you have done, so that nobody can claim the credit.
10 We are God's work of art, created in Christ Jesus to live the good life as from the
beginning he had meant us to live it.

Reconciliation of the Jews and the pagans with each other and with God

11   Do not forget, then, that there was a time when you who were pagans
physically, termed the Uncircumcised by those who speak of themselves as the
12 Circumcision by reason of a physical operation, •do not forget, I say, that
you had no Christ and were excluded from membership of Israel, aliens with
no part in the covenants with their Promise; you were immersed in this world,
13 without hope and without God. •But now in Christ Jesus, you that used to be
so far apart from us have been brought very close, by the blood of Christ.
14 For he is the peace between us, and has made the two into one and broken
down the barrier which used to keep them apart, actually destroying in his
15 own person the hostility •caused by the rules and decrees of the Law. This
was to create one single New Man in himself out of the two of them and by
16 restoring peace •through the cross, to unite them both in a single Body and
17 reconcile them with God. In his own person he killed the hostility. •Later he
came to bring the good news of peace, *peace to you who were far away and peace*

1 a. Orders of the angelic hierarchy in Jewish literature.   b. Ps 8:6
2 a. Satan.

to those who were near at hand. [b] •Through him, both of us have in the one Spirit 18 our way to come to the Father.

So you are no longer aliens or foreign visitors: you are citizens like all the 19 saints, and part of God's household. •You are part of a building that has the 20 apostles and prophets [c] for its foundations, and Christ Jesus himself for its main cornerstone. •As every structure is aligned on him, all grow into one holy temple 21 in the Lord; •and you too, in him, are being built into a house where God lives, 22 in the Spirit.

Paul, a servant of the mystery

3 So I, Paul, a prisoner of Christ Jesus for the sake of you pagans.... •You have ¹⁄₂ probably heard how I have been entrusted by God with the grace he meant for you, •and that it was by a revelation that I was given the knowledge of the 3 mystery, as I have just described it very shortly. •If you read my words, you will 4 have some idea of the depths that I see in the mystery of Christ. •This mystery 5 that has now been revealed through the Spirit to his holy apostles and prophets was unknown to any men in past generations; •it means that pagans now share 6 the same inheritance, that they are parts of the same body, and that the same promise has been made to them, in Christ Jesus, through the gospel. •I have 7 been made the servant of that gospel by a gift of grace from God who gave it to me by his own power. •I, who am less than the least of all the saints, have been 8 entrusted with this special grace, not only of proclaiming to the pagans the infinite treasure of Christ •but also of explaining how the mystery is to be 9 dispensed. Through all the ages, this has been kept hidden in God, the creator of everything. Why? •So that the Sovereignties and Powers should learn 10 only now, through the Church, how comprehensive God's wisdom really is, exactly according to the plan which he had had from all eternity in Christ Jesus 11 our Lord. •This is why we are bold enough to approach God in complete 12 confidence, through our faith in him; •so, I beg you, never lose confidence just 13 because of the trials that I go through on your account: they are your glory.

Paul's prayer

This, then, is what I pray, kneeling before the Father, •from whom every ¹⁴₁₅ family, [a] whether spiritual or natural, takes its name:

Out of his infinite glory, may he give you the power through his Spirit 16 for your hidden self to grow strong, •so that Christ may live in your hearts 17 through faith, and then, planted in love and built on love, •you will with all 18 the saints have strength to grasp the breadth and the length, the height and the depth; •until, knowing the love of Christ, which is beyond all knowledge, 19 you are filled with the utter fullness of God.

Glory be to him whose power, working in us, can do infinitely more than we 20 can ask or imagine; •glory be to him from generation to generation in the Church 21 and in Christ Jesus for ever and ever. Amen.

II. EXHORTATION

A call to unity

4 I, the prisoner in the Lord, implore you therefore to lead a life worthy of your 1 vocation. •Bear with one another charitably, in complete selflessness, 2 gentleness and patience. •Do all you can to preserve the unity of the Spirit by the 3 peace that binds you together. •There is one Body, one Spirit, just as you were all 4 called into one and the same hope when you were called. •There is one Lord, one 5 faith, one baptism, •and one God who is Father of all, over all, through all and 6 within all.

Each one of us, however, has been given his own share of grace, given as 7 Christ allotted it. •It was said that he would: 8

When he ascended to the height, he captured prisoners,
he gave gifts to men.ᵃ

9   When it says, 'he ascended', what can it mean if not that he descended right
10 down to the lower regions of the earth? •The one who rose higher than all the
11 heavens to fill all things is none other than the one who descended. •And to
some, his gift was that they should be apostles; to some, prophets; to some,
12 evangelists; to some, pastors and teachers; •so that the saints together make
13 a unity in the work of service, building up the body of Christ. •In this way we
are all to come to unity in our faith and in our knowledge of the Son of God, until
we become the perfect Man, fully mature with the fullness of Christ himself.

14   Then we shall not be children any longer, or tossed one way and another and
carried along by every wind of doctrine, at the mercy of all the tricks men play
15 and their cleverness in practising deceit. •If we live by the truth and in love, we
16 shall grow in all ways into Christ, who is the head •by whom the whole body
is fitted and joined together, every joint adding its own strength, for each
separate part to work according to its function. So the body grows until it has
built itself up, in love.

The new life in Christ

17   In particular, I want to urge you in the name of the Lord, not to go on living
18 the aimless kind of life that pagans live. •Intellectually they are in the dark,
and they are estranged from the life of God, without knowledge because they
19 have shut their hearts to it. •Their sense of right and wrong once dulled, they
have abandoned themselves to sexuality and eagerly pursue a career of indecency
20
21 of every kind. •Now that is hardly the way you have learnt from Christ, •unless
you failed to hear him properly when you were taught what the truth is in Jesus.
22 You must give up your old way of life; you must put aside your old self, which
23 gets corrupted by following illusory desires. •Your mind must be renewed by a
24 spiritual revolution •so that you can put on the new self that has been created in
God's way, in the goodness and holiness of the truth.

25   So from now on, there must be no more lies: *You must speak the truth to one*
26 *another,ᵇ* since we are all parts of one another. •*Even if you are angry, you must not*
27 *sin:ᶜ* never let the sun set on your anger •or else you will give the devil a foothold.
28 Anyone who was a thief must stop stealing; he should try to find some useful
manual work instead, and be able to do some good by helping others that are
29 in need. •Guard against foul talk; let your words be for the improvement of
30 others, as occasion offers, and do good to your listeners, •otherwise you will
only be grieving the Holy Spirit of God who has marked you with his seal for
31 you to be set free when the day comes. •Never have grudges against others, or
lose your temper, or raise your voice to anybody, or call each other names,
32 or allow any sort of spitefulness. •Be friends with one another, and kind,
forgiving each other as readily as God forgave you in Christ.

1
2   **5** Try, then, to imitate God, as children of his that he loves, •and follow Christ
by loving as he loved you, giving himself up in our place *as a fragrant offering •*
3 *and a sacrifice to God.ᵃ* •Among you there must be not even a mention of
fornication or impurity in any of its forms, or promiscuity: this would
4 hardly become the saints! •There must be no coarseness, or salacious talk and
5 jokes—all this is wrong for you; raise your voices in thanksgiving instead. •For
you can be quite certain that nobody who actually indulges in fornication
or impurity or promiscuity—which is worshipping a false god—can inherit
6 anything of the kingdom of God. •Do not let anyone deceive you with empty

b. Is 57:19   c. The N.T. prophets.
3 a. A pun on the words 'Father' and 'family' (clan or tribe) is lost in translation; traces of
it survive in *paternity* and *patriotism*.
4 a. Ps 68:18   b. Zc 8:16   c. Ps 4:4 (LXX)
5 a. Ex 29:18

arguments: it is for this loose living that God's anger comes down on those who rebel against him. •Make sure that you are not included with them. •You were darkness once, but now you are light in the Lord; be like children of light, •for the effects of the light are seen in complete goodness and right living and truth. Try to discover what the Lord wants of you, •having nothing to do with the futile works of darkness but exposing them by contrast. •The things which are done in secret are things that people are ashamed even to speak of; •but anything exposed by the light will be illuminated •and anything illuminated turns into light. That is why it is said:[b]

> Wake up from your sleep,
> rise from the dead,
> and Christ will shine on you.

So be very careful about the sort of lives you lead, like intelligent and not like senseless people. •This may be a wicked age, but your lives should redeem it. And do not be thoughtless but recognise what is the will of the Lord. •Do not drug yourselves with wine, this is simply dissipation; be filled with the Spirit. Sing the words and tunes of the psalms and hymns when you are together, and go on singing and chanting to the Lord in your hearts, •so that always and everywhere you are giving thanks to God who is our Father in the name of our Lord Jesus Christ.

The morals of the home

Give way to one another in obedience to Christ. •Wives should regard their husbands as they regard the Lord, •since as Christ is head of the Church and saves the whole body, so is a husband the head of his wife; •and as the Church submits to Christ, so should wives to their husbands, in everything. •Husbands should love their wives just as Christ loved the Church and sacrificed himself for her •to make her holy. He made her clean by washing her in water with a form of words, •so that when he took her to himself she would be glorious, with no speck or wrinkle or anything like that, but holy and faultless. •In the same way, husbands must love their wives as they love their own bodies; for a man to love his wife is for him to love himself. •A man never hates his own body, but he feeds it and looks after it; and that is the way Christ treats the Church, •because it is his body—and we are its living parts. •*For this reason, a man must leave his father and mother and be joined to his wife, and the two will become one body.*[c] •This mystery has many implications; but I am saying it applies to Christ and the Church. •To sum up; you too, each one of you, must love his wife as he loves himself; and let every wife respect her husband.

6 Children, be obedient to your parents in the Lord—that is your duty. •The first commandment that has a promise attached to it is: *Honour your father and mother,* •and the promise is: *and you will prosper and have a long life in the land.*[a] And parents, never drive your children to resentment but in bringing them up correct them and guide them as the Lord does.

Slaves, be obedient to the men who are called your masters in this world, with deep respect and sincere loyalty, as you are obedient to Christ: •not only when you are under their eye, as if you had only to please men, but because you are slaves of Christ and wholeheartedly do the will of God. •Work hard and willingly, but do it for the sake of the Lord and not for the sake of men. •You can be sure that everyone, whether a slave or a free man, will be properly rewarded by the Lord for whatever work he has done well. •And those of you who are employers, treat your slaves in the same spirit; do without threats, remembering that they and you have the same Master in heaven and he is not impressed by one person more than by another.

The spiritual war

¹⁰
¹¹ Finally, grow strong in the Lord, with the strength of his power. •Put God's
¹² armour on so as to be able to resist the devil's tactics. •For it is not against human
enemies that we have to struggle, but against the Sovereignties and the Powers
who originate the darkness in this world, the spiritual army of evil in the heavens.
¹³ That is why you must rely on God's armour, or you will not be able to put up any
resistance when the worst happens, or have enough resources to hold your
ground.
¹⁴ So stand your ground, with *truth buckled round your waist*, and *integrity*
¹⁵ *for a breastplate*,ᵇ •wearing for shoes on your feet *the eagerness to spread the*
¹⁶ *gospel of peace*ᶜ •and always carrying the shield of faith so that you can use it to
¹⁷ put out the burning arrows of the evil one. •And then you must accept *salvation*
from God to be your helmet and receive the word of God from the Spirit to use
as a sword.
¹⁸ Pray all the time, asking for what you need, praying in the Spirit on every
possible occasion. Never get tired of staying awake to pray for all the saints;
¹⁹ and pray for me to be given an opportunity to open my mouth and speak
²⁰ without fear and give out the mystery of the gospel •of which I am an ambassador
in chains; pray that in proclaiming it I may speak as boldly as I ought to.

Personal news and final salutation

²¹ I should like you to know, as well, what is happening to me and what I am
doing; my dear brother Tychicus, my loyal helper in the Lord, will tell you
²² everything. •I am sending him to you precisely for this purpose, to give you
news about us and reassure you.
²³ May God the Father and the Lord Jesus Christ grant peace, love and faith to
²⁴ all the brothers. •May grace and eternal life be with all who love our Lord
Jesus Christ.

---

b. Presumably a quotation from a Christian hymn.   c. Gn 2:24
6 a. Ex 20:12   **b.** Is 59:17   **c.** Is 40:9

PHILIPPIANS

THE LETTER OF PAUL
TO THE CHURCH AT PHILIPPI

Address

1 From Paul and Timothy, servants of Christ Jesus, to all the saints in Christ 1
Jesus, together with their presiding elders and deacons.ᵃ •We wish you the 2
grace and peace of God our Father and of the Lord Jesus Christ.

Thanksgiving and prayer

I thank my God whenever I think of you; and •every time I pray for all of you, I ³₄
pray with joy,ᵇ •remembering how you have helped to spread the Good Newsᶜ 5
from the day you first heard itᵈ right up to the present. •I am quite certain that 6
the One who began this good work in you will see that it is finished when the Day
of Christ Jesus comes. •It is only natural that I should feel like this towards 7
you all, since you have shared the privileges which have been mine: both my
chains and my work defending and establishing the gospel. You have a permanent
place in my heart, •and God knows how much I miss you all, loving you as Christ 8
Jesus loves you. •My prayer is that your love for each other may increase more 9
and more and never stop improving your knowledge and deepening your
perception •so that you can always recognise what is best. This will help you to 10
become pure and blameless, and prepare you for the Day of Christ, •when you 11
will reach the perfect goodness which Jesus Christ produces in us for the glory
and praise of God.

Paul's own circumstances

I am glad to tell you, brothers, that the things that happened to meᶠ have 12
actually been a help to the Good News.

My chains, in Christ, have become famous not only all over the Praetoriumᵍ but 13
everywhere, •and most of the brothers have taken courage in the Lord from these 14
chains of mine and are getting more and more daring in announcing the Messageʰ
without any fear. •It is true that some of them are doing it just out of rivalry 15
and competition, but the rest preach Christ with the right intention, •out of 16
nothing but love, as they know that this is my invariable way of defending the
gospel. •The others, who proclaim Christ for jealous or selfish motives, do not 17
mind if they make my chains heavier to bear. •But does it matter? Whether 18
from dishonest motives or in sincerity, Christ is proclaimed; and that makes me
happy; •and I shall continue being happy, because I know *this will help to save* 19
me, thanks to your prayers and to the help which will be given to me by the
Spirit of Jesus. •My one hope and trust is that I shall never have to admit defeat, 20
but that now as always I shall have the courage for Christ to be glorified in my
body,ⁱ whether by my life or by my death. •Life to me, of course, is Christ, but 21
then death would bring me something more; •but then again, if living in this 22
body means doing work which is having good results—I do not know what

body means doing work which is having good results—I do not know what
23 I should choose. •I am caught in this dilemma: I want to be gone and be with
24 Christ, which would be very much the better, •but for me to stay alive in this
25 body is a more urgent need for your sake. •This weighs with me so much that I feel
sure I shall survive and stay with you all, and help you to progress in the faith
26 and even increase your joy in it; •and so you will have another reason to give
praise to Christ Jesus on my account when I am with you again.

Fight for the faith

27 Avoid anything in your everyday lives that would be unworthy of the gospel
of Christ, so that, whether I come to you and see for myself, or stay at a distance
and only hear about you, I shall know that you are unanimous in meeting the
28 attack with firm resistance, united by your love for the faith of the gospel •and
quite unshaken by your enemies. This would be the sure sign that they will lose
29 and you will be saved. It would be a sign from God •that he has given you the
30 privilege not only of believing in Christ, but of suffering for him as well. •You and
I are together in the same fight as you saw me fighting before and, as you will
have heard, I am fighting still.

Preserve unity in humility

1 2 If our life in Christ means anything to you, if love can persuade at all,
2 or the Spirit that we have in common, or any tenderness and sympathy, •then
be united in your convictions and united in your love, with a common purpose
and a common mind. That is the one thing which would make me completely
3 happy. •There must be no competition among you, no conceit; but everybody
is to be self-effacing. Always consider the other person to be better than yourself,
4 so that nobody thinks of his own interests first but everybody thinks of other
5 people's interests instead. •In your minds you must be the same as Christ Jesus:[a]

6   His state was divine,
                    yet he did not cling
                    to his equality with God
7   but emptied himself
                    to assume the condition of a slave,
                    and became as men are;
                    and being as all men are,
8   he was humbler yet,
                    even to accepting death,
                    death on a cross.
9   But God raised him high
                    and gave him the name
                    which is above all other names
10   so that *all beings*
                    in the heavens, on earth and in the underworld,
                    should bend the knee[b] at the name of Jesus
11   and that every tongue should acclaim
                    Jesus Christ as Lord,
                    to the glory of God the Father.

Work for salvation

12 So then, my dear friends, continue to do as I tell you, as you always have;
not only as you did when I was there with you, but even more now that I am no
13 longer there; and work for your salvation 'in fear and trembling'. •It is God,

---

1 a. Jb 13:16 (LXX)
2 a. Vv. 6-11 are a hymn, though whether composed or only quoted by Paul is uncertain.
b. Is 45:23

for his own loving purpose, who puts both the will and the action into you. Do all that has to be done without complaining or arguing •and then you will $^{14}_{15}$ be innocent and genuine, *perfect children of God among a deceitful and underhand brood,*[c] and you will shine in the world like bright stars •because you are offering 16 it the word of life. This would give me something to be proud of for the Day of Christ, and would mean that I had not run in the race and exhausted myself for nothing. •And then, if my blood has to be shed as part of your own sacrifice 17 and offering—which is your faith[d]—I shall still be happy and rejoice with all of you, •and you must be just as happy and rejoice with me.   18

The mission of Timothy and Epaphroditus

I hope, in the Lord Jesus, to send Timothy to you soon, and I shall be 19 reassured by having news of you. •I have nobody else like him here, as whole- 20 heartedly concerned for your welfare: •all the rest seem more interested in 21 themselves than in Jesus Christ. •But you know how he has proved himself by 22 working with me on behalf of the Good News like a son helping his father. That is why he is the one that I am hoping to send you, as soon as 23 I know something definite about my fate. •But I continue to trust, in the Lord, 24 that I shall be coming soon myself.

It is essential, I think, to send brother Epaphroditus back to you. He was sent 25 as your representative to help me when I needed someone to be my companion in working and battling, •but he misses you all and is worried because you heard 26 about his illness. •It is true that he has been ill, and almost died, but God took 27 pity on him, and on me as well as him, and spared me what would have been one grief on top of another. •So I shall send him back as promptly as I can; you will 28 be happy to see him again, and that will make me less sorry. •Give him a most 29 hearty welcome, in the Lord; people like him are to be honoured. •It was for 30 Christ's work that he came so near to dying, and he risked his life to give me the 3 help that you were not able to give me yourselves   1
Finally, my brothers, rejoice in the Lord.[a]

The true way of Christian salvation

It is no trouble to me to repeat what I have already written to you, and as far 2 as you are concerned, it will make for safety. •Beware of dogs! Watch out for 3 the people who are making mischief. Watch out for the cutters.[b] •We are the real people of the circumcision, we who worship in accordance with the Spirit of God; we have our own glory from Christ Jesus without having to rely on a 4 physical operation. •If it came to relying on physical evidence, I should be fully qualified myself. Take any man who thinks he can rely on what is physical: I am even better qualified. •I was born of the race of Israel and of the tribe of Benjamin, 5 a Hebrew born of Hebrew parents, and I was circumcised when I was eight days old. As for the Law, I was a Pharisee; •as for working for religion, I was a 6 persecutor of the Church; as far as the Law can make you perfect, I was faultless. But because of Christ, I have come to consider all these advantages that I had 7 as disadvantages. •Not only that, but I believe nothing can happen that will 8 outweigh the supreme advantage of knowing Christ Jesus my Lord. For him I have accepted the loss of everything, and I look on everything as so much rubbish if only I can have Christ •and be given a place in him. I am no longer trying for 9 perfection by my own efforts, the perfection that comes from the Law, but I want only the perfection that comes through faith in Christ, and is from God and based on faith. •All I want is to know Christ and the power of his resurrection 10 and to share his sufferings by reproducing the pattern of his death. •That is the 11 way I can hope to take my place in the resurrection of the dead. •Not that I have 12 become perfect yet: I have not yet won, but I am still running, trying to capture the prize for which Christ Jesus captured me. •I can assure you my brothers, 13 I am far from thinking that I have already won. All I can say is that I forget the

14 past and I strain ahead for what is still to come; •I am racing for the finish, for
15 the prize to which God calls us upwards to receive in Christ Jesus. •We who are
    called 'perfect' must all think in this way. If there is some point on which you
16 see things differently, God will make it clear to you; •meanwhile, let us go forward
    on the road that has brought us to where we are.

17   My brothers, be united in following my rule of life. Take as your models
    everybody who is already doing this and study them as you used to study us.
18 I have told you often, and I repeat it today with tears, there are many who are
19 behaving as the enemies of the cross of Christ. •They are destined to be lost.
    They make foods into their god and they are proudest of something they ought
20 to think shameful; the things they think important are earthly things. •For us,
    our homeland is in heaven, and from heaven comes the saviour we are waiting
21 for, the Lord Jesus Christ, •and he will transfigure these wretched bodies of ours
    into copies of his glorious body. He will do that by the same power with which
    he can subdue the whole universe.

1 4 So then, my brothers and dear friends, do not give way but remain faithful
      in the Lord. I miss you very much, dear friends; you are my joy and my
    crown.

Last advice

2   I appeal to Evodia and I appeal to Syntyche to come to agreement with each
3 other, in the Lord; •and I ask you, Syzygus,ᵃ to be truly a 'companion' and to
    help them in this. These women were a help to me when I was fighting to defend
    the Good News—and so, at the same time, were Clement and the others who
    worked with me. Their names are written in the book of life.
4   I want you to be happy, always happy in the Lord; I repeat, what I want is
5 your happiness. •Let your tolerance be evident to everyone: the Lord is very
6 near. •There is no need to worry; but if there is anything you need, pray for it,
7 asking God for it with prayer and thanksgiving, •and that peace of God, which
    is so much greater than we can understand, will guard your hearts and your
8 thoughts, in Christ Jesus. •Finally, brothers, fill your minds with everything that
    is true, everything that is noble, everything that is good and pure, everything that
    we love and honour, and everything that can be thought virtuous or worthy
9 of praise. •Keep doing all the things that you learnt from me and have been
    taught by me and have heard or seen that I do. Then the God of peace will be
    with you.

Thanks for help received

10   It is a great joy to me, in the Lord, that at last you have shown some concern
    for me again; though of course you were concerned before, and only lacked an
11 opportunity. •I am not talking about shortage of money: I have learnt to manage
12 on whatever I have, •I know how to be poor and I know how to be rich too.
    I have been through my initiation and now I am ready for anything anywhere:
13 full stomach or empty stomach, poverty or plenty. •There is nothing I cannot
14 master with the help of the One who gives me strength. •All the same, it was
15 good of you to share with me in my hardships. •In the early days of the
    Good News, as you people of Philippi well know, when I left Macedonia, no other
16 church helped me with gifts of money. You were the only ones; •and twice
17 since my stay in Thessalonika you have sent me what I needed. •It is not your
    gift that I value; what is valuable to me is the interest that is mounting up in
18 your account. •Now for the time being I have everything that I need and more:
    I am fully provided now that I have received from Epaphroditus the offering

---

c. Dt 32:5   **d.** Libations were common to Greek and Jewish sacrifices.
3 a. Paul's conclusion is interrupted by a long postscript.   **b.** A contemptuous reference to
the circumcisers comparing circumcision with self-inflicted gashes in pagan cults.
4 a. 'Companion' is the meaning of the proper name Syzygus.

that you sent, *a sweet fragrance*—the sacrifice that God accepts and finds pleasing. •In return my God will fulfil all your needs, in Christ Jesus, as lavishly 19 as only God can. •Glory to God, our Father, for ever and ever. Amen.   20

Greetings and final wish

My greetings to every one of the saints in Christ Jesus. The brothers who are 21 with me send their greetings. •All the saints send their greetings, especially those 22 of the imperial household.^b •May the grace of the Lord Jesus Christ be with 23 your spirit.

b. I.e. in the service of the emperor.

COLOSSIANS

THE LETTER OF PAUL

TO THE CHURCH AT COLOSSAE

PREFACE

Address

1 From Paul, appointed by God to be an apostle of Christ Jesus, and from our
2 brother Timothy •to the saints in Colossae, our faithful brothers in Christ:
Grace and peace to you from God our Father.

Thanksgiving and prayer

3   We have never failed to remember you in our prayers and to give thanks for
4 you to God, the Father of our Lord Jesus Christ, •ever since we heard about
your faith in Christ Jesus and the love that you show towards all the saints
5 because of the hope which is stored up for you in heaven. It is only recently that
you heard of this, when it was announced in the message of the truth. The Good
6 News •which has reached you is spreading all over the world and producing the
same results as it has among you ever since the day when you heard about God's
7 grace and understood what this really is. •Epaphras, who taught you, is one of
8 our closest fellow workers and a faithful deputy for us as Christ's servant, •and
it was he who told us all about your love in the Spirit.
9   That will explain why, ever since the day he told us, we have never failed to
pray for you, and what we ask God is that through perfect wisdom and spiritual
10 understanding you should reach the fullest knowledge of his will. •So you will
be able to lead the kind of life which the Lord expects of you, a life acceptable
to him in all its aspects; showing the results in all the good actions you do and
11 increasing your knowledge of God. •You will have in you the strength, based on
12 his own glorious power, never to give in, but to bear anything joyfully, •thanking
the Father who has made it possible for you to join the saints and with them
to inherit the light.
13   Because that is what he has done: he has taken us out of the power of darkness
14 and created a place for us in the kingdom of the Son that he loves, •and in him,
we gain our freedom, the forgiveness of our sins.

I. FORMAL INSTRUCTION

Christ is the head of all creation

15   He is the image of the unseen God
          and the first-born of all creation,
16   for in him were created

all things in heaven and on earth:
everything visible and everything invisible,
Thrones, Dominations, Sovereignties, Powers—
all things were created through him and for him.
Before anything was created, he existed,   17
and he holds all things in unity.
Now the Church is his body,   18
he is its head.

As he is the Beginning,
he was first to be born from the dead,
so that he should be first in every way;
because God wanted all perfection   19
to be found in him
and all things to be reconciled through him and for him,   20
everything in heaven and everything on earth,
when he made peace
by his death on the cross.

The Colossians have their share in salvation

Not long ago, you were foreigners and enemies, in the way that you used to 21
think and the evil things that you did; •but now he has reconciled you, by his 22
death and in that mortal body. Now you are able to appear before him holy,
pure and blameless—•as long as you persevere and stand firm on the solid base 23
of the faith, never letting yourselves drift away from the hope promised by the
Good News, which you have heard, which has been preached to the whole human
race, and of which I, Paul, have become the servant. •

Paul's labours in the service of the pagans

It makes me happy to suffer for you, as I am suffering now, and in my own   24
body to do what I can to make up all that has still to be undergone by Christ for
the sake of his body, the Church. •I became the servant of the Church when God 25
made me responsible for delivering God's message to you, •the message which 26
was a mystery hidden for generations and centuries and has now been revealed to
his saints. •It was God's purpose to reveal it to them and to show all the rich glory 27
of this mystery to pagans. The mystery is Christ among you, your hope of glory:
this is the Christ we proclaim, this is the wisdom in which we thoroughly train 28
everyone and instruct everyone, to make them all perfect in Christ. •It is for 29
this I struggle wearily on, helped only by his power driving me irresistibly.

Paul's concern for the Colossians' faith

2 Yes, I want you to know that I do have to struggle hard for you, and for 1
those in Laodicea, and for so many others who have never seen me face to
face. •It is all to bind you together in love and to stir your minds, so that your 2
understanding may come to full development, until you really know God's
secret •in which all the jewels of wisdom and knowledge are hidden.   3
I say this to make sure that no one deceives you with specious arguments. 4
I may be absent in body, but in spirit I am there among you, delighted to find you 5
all in harmony and to see how firm your faith in Christ is.

II. A WARNING AGAINST SOME ERRORS

Live according to the true faith in Christ, not according to false teaching

You must live your whole life according to the Christ you have received— 6
Jesus the Lord; •you must be rooted in him and built on him and held firm by the 7
faith you have been taught, and full of thanksgiving.

8   Make sure that no one traps you and deprives you of your freedom by some
secondhand, empty, rational philosophy based on the principles of this world
instead of on Christ.

Christ alone is the true head of men and angels

9   In his body lives the fullness of divinity, and in him you too find your own
10 fulfilment, •in the one who is the head of every Sovereignty and Power.^a

11   In him you have been circumcised, with a circumcision not performed by
human hand, but by the complete stripping of your body of flesh. This is cir-
12 cumcision according to Christ. •You have been buried with him, when you
were baptised; and by baptism, too, you have been raised up with him through
13 your belief in the power of God who raised him from the dead. •You were dead,
because you were sinners and had not been circumcised: he^b has brought you
to life with him, he has forgiven us all our sins.

14   He has overridden the Law, and cancelled every record of the debt that we
15 had to pay; he has done away with it by nailing it to the cross;^c •and so he got
rid of the Sovereignties and the Powers, and paraded them in public, behind him
in his triumphal procession.^d

Against the false asceticism based on 'the principles of this world'

16   From now onwards, never let anyone else decide what you should eat or drink,
17 or whether you are to observe annual festivals, New Moons or sabbaths. •These
18 were only pale reflections of what was coming: the reality is Christ. •Do not be
taken in by people who like grovelling to angels and worshipping them; people
like that are always going on about some vision they have had, inflating them-
19 selves to a false importance with their worldly outlook. •A man of this sort
is not united to the head, and it is the head that adds strength and holds the
whole body together, with all its joints and sinews—and this is the only way in
which it can reach its full growth in God.

20   If you have really died with Christ to the principles of this world, why do you
21 still let rules dictate to you, as though you were still living in the world? •'It is
forbidden to pick up this, it is forbidden to taste that, it is forbidden to touch
22 something else'; •all these prohibitions are only concerned with things that
perish by their very use—an example of *human doctrines and regulations!*^e
23 It may be argued that true wisdom is to be found in these, with their self-imposed
devotions, their self-abasement, and their severe treatment of the body; but once
the flesh starts to protest, they are no use at all.

Life-giving union with the glorified Christ

1 **3** Since you have been brought back to true life with Christ, you must look for
the things that are in heaven, where Christ is, sitting at God's right hand.
2 Let your thoughts be on heavenly things, not on the things that are on the earth,
3 because you have died, and now the life you have is hidden with Christ in God.
4 But when Christ is revealed—and he is your life—you too will be revealed in all
your glory with him.

III. EXHORTATION

General rules of Christian behaviour

5   That is why you must kill everything in you that belongs only to earthly life:
fornication, impurity, guilty passion, evil desires and especially greed, which is
6 the same thing as worshipping a false god; •all this is the sort of behaviour that

---

2 a. I.e. over the highest orders of angels.   **b.** God the Father.   **c.** Destroying our death
warrant.   **d.** The tradition was that the Law was brought down to Moses by angels.
e. Is 29:13

makes God angry. •And it is the way in which you used to live when you were 7
surrounded by people doing the same thing, •but now you, of all people, must 8
give all these things up: getting angry, being bad-tempered, spitefulness, abusive
language and dirty talk; •and never tell each other lies. You have stripped off 9
your old behaviour with your old self, •and you have put on a new self which will 10
progress towards true knowledge the more it is renewed in the image of its
creator; •and in that image there is no room for distinction between Greek 11
and Jew, between the circumcised or the uncircumcised, or between barbarian
and Scythian, slave and free man. There is only Christ: he is everything and he
is in everything.

You are God's chosen race, his saints; he loves you, and you should be clothed 12
in sincere compassion, in kindness and humility, gentleness and patience. •Bear 13
with one another; forgive each other as soon as a quarrel begins. The Lord has
forgiven you; now you must do the same. •Over all these clothes, to keep them 14
together and complete them, put on love. •And may the peace of Christ reign 15
in your hearts, because it is for this that you were called together as parts of one
body. Always be thankful.

Let the message of Christ, in all its richness, find a home with you. Teach 16
each other, and advise each other, in all wisdom. With gratitude in your hearts
sing psalms and hymns and inspired songs to God; •and never say or do anything 17
except in the name of the Lord Jesus, giving thanks to God the Father through
him.

The morals of the home and household

Wives, give way to your husbands, as you should in the Lord. •Husbands, 18
19
love your wives and treat them with gentleness. •Children, be obedient to your 20
parents always, because that is what will please the Lord. •Parents, never drive 21
your children to resentment or you will make them feel frustrated.

Slaves, be obedient to the men who are called your masters in this world; 22
not only when you are under their eye, as if you had only to please men, but
wholeheartedly, out of respect for the Master. •Whatever your work is, put 23
your heart into it as if it were for the Lord and not for men, •knowing that the 24
Lord will repay you by making you his heirs. It is Christ the Lord that you are
serving; •anyone who does wrong will be repaid in kind and he does not favour 25
one person more than another. 4 Masters, make sure that your slaves are given 1
what is just and fair, knowing that you too have a Master in heaven.

The apostolic spirit

Be persevering in your prayers and be thankful as you stay awake to pray. 2
Pray for us especially, asking God to show us opportunities for announcing the 3
message and proclaiming the mystery of Christ, for the sake of which I am in
chains; •pray that I may proclaim it as clearly as I ought. 4

Be tactful with those who are not Christians and be sure you make the best 5
use of your time with them. •Talk to them agreeably and with a flavour of wit, 6
and try to fit your answers to the needs of each one.

Personal news

Tychicus will tell you all the news about me. He is a brother I love very much, 7
and a loyal helper and companion in the service of the Lord. •I am sending him 8
to you precisely for this purpose: to give you news about us and to reassure you.
With him I am sending Onesimus, that dear and faithful brother who is a fellow 9
citizen of yours. They will tell you everything that is happening here.

Greetings and final wishes

Aristarchus, who is here in prison with me, sends his greetings, and so does 10
Mark, the cousin of Barnabas—you were sent some instructions about him;

11 if he comes to you, give him a warm welcome—•and Jesus Justus adds his greetings. Of all those who have come over from the Circumcision, these are the only ones actually working with me for the kingdom of God. They have been a great

12 comfort to me. •Epaphras, your fellow citizen, sends his greetings; this servant of Christ Jesus never stops battling for you, praying that you will never lapse but

13 always hold perfectly and securely to the will of God. •I can testify for him that

14 he works hard for you, as well as for those at Laodicea and Hierapolis. •Greetings from my dear friend Luke, the doctor, and also from Demas.

15 Please give my greetings to the brothers at Laodicea and to Nympha and the

16 church which meets in her house. •After this letter has been read among you, send it on to be read in the church of the Laodiceans; and get the letter from

17 Laodicea for you to read yourselves. •Give Archippus this message, 'Remember the service that the Lord wants you to do, and try to carry it out'.

18 Here is a greeting in my own handwriting—PAUL. Remember the chains I wear. Grace be with you.

1 THESSALONIANS

THE FIRST LETTER OF PAUL
TO THE CHURCH IN THESSALONIKA

Address

1 From Paul, Silvanus and Timothy, to the Church in Thessalonika which is in 1
God the Father and the Lord Jesus Christ; wishing you grace and peace.

Thanksgiving and congratulations

We always mention you in our prayers and thank God for you all, •and ⅔
constantly remember before God our Father how you have shown your faith in
action, worked for love and persevered through hope, in our Lord Jesus Christ.

We know, brothers, that God loves you and that you have been chosen, 4
because when we brought the Good News to you, it came to you not only as 5
words, but as power and as the Holy Spirit and as utter conviction. And you
observed the sort of life we lived when we were with you, which was for your
instruction, •and you were led to become imitators of us, and of the Lord; and 6
it was with the joy of the Holy Spirit that you took to the gospel, in spite of the
great opposition all round you. •This has made you the great example to all 7
believers in Macedonia and Achaia •since it was from you that the word of the 8
Lord started to spread—and not only throughout Macedonia and Achaia, for
the news of your faith in God has spread everywhere. We do not need to tell other
people about it: •other people tell us how we started the work among you, how 9
you broke with idolatry when you were converted to God and became servants
of the real, living God; •and how you are now waiting for Jesus, his Son, whom 10
he raised from the dead, to come from heaven to save us from the retribution
which is coming.

Paul's example in Thessalonika

2 You know yourselves, my brothers, that our visit to you has not proved 1
ineffectual.

We had, as you know, been given rough treatment and been grossly insulted 2
at Philippi, and it was our God who gave us the courage to proclaim his Good
News to you in the face of great opposition. •We have not taken to preaching 3
because we are deluded, or immoral, or trying to deceive anyone; •it was God 4
who decided that we were fit to be entrusted with the Good News, and when we
are speaking, we are not trying to please men but God, *who can read* our *inmost
thoughts.*[a] •You know very well, and we can swear it before God, that never at 5
any time have our speeches been simply flattery, or a cover for trying to get money;
nor have we ever looked for any special honour from men, either from you or 6
anybody else, •when we could have imposed ourselves on you with full weight, 7
as apostles of Christ.

Instead, we were unassuming. Like a mother feeding and looking after her own
8 children, •we felt so devoted and protective towards you, and had come to love
you so much, that we were eager to hand over to you not only the Good News
9 but our whole lives as well. •Let me remind you, brothers, how hard we used to
work, slaving night and day so as not to be a burden on any one of you while
10 we were proclaiming God's Good News to you. •You are witnesses, and so
is God, that our treatment of you, since you became believers, has been impeccably
11 right and fair. •You can remember how we treated every one of you as a father
12 treats his children, •teaching you what was right, encouraging you and appealing
to you to live a life worthy of God, who is calling you to share the glory of his
kingdom.

The faith and the patience of the Thessalonians

13 Another reason why we constantly thank God for you is that as soon as you
heard the message that we brought you as God's message, you accepted it for what
it really is, God's message and not some human thinking; and it is still a living
14 power among you who believe it. •For you, my brothers, have been like the
churches of God in Christ Jesus which are in Judaea, in suffering the same
15 treatment from your own countrymen as they have suffered from the Jews, •the
people who put the Lord Jesus to death, and the prophets too. And now they have
been persecuting us, and acting in a way that cannot please God and makes them
16 the enemies of the whole human race, •because they are hindering us from
preaching to the pagans and trying to save them. They never stop trying *to finish
off the sins they have begun*,[b] but retribution is overtaking them at last.

Paul's anxiety

17 A short time after we had been separated from you—in body but never in
thought, brothers—we had an especially strong desire and longing to see you face
18 to face again, •and we tried hard to come and visit you; I, Paul, tried more than
19 once, but Satan prevented us. •What do you think is our pride and our joy? You
are; and you will be *the crown* of which we shall be *proudest* in the presence of our
20 Lord Jesus when he comes; •you are our pride and our joy.

Timothy's mission to Thessalonika

1 3 When we could not bear the waiting any longer, we decided it would be best
2 to be left without a companion at Athens, and •sent our brother Timothy,
who is God's helper in spreading the Good News of Christ, to keep you firm and
3 strong in the faith •and prevent any of you from being unsettled by the present
4 troubles. As you know, these are bound to come our way: •when we were with
you, we warned you that we must expect to have persecutions to bear, and that
5 is what has happened now, as you have found out. •That is why, when I could
not stand waiting any longer, I sent to assure myself of your faith: I was afraid
the Tempter[a] might have tried you too hard, and all our work might have been
wasted.

Paul thanks God for good reports of the Thessalonians

6 However, Timothy is now back from you and he has given us good news of
your faith and your love, telling us that you always remember us with pleasure
7 and want to see us quite as much as we want to see you. •And so, brothers, your
faith has been a great comfort to us in the middle of our own troubles and sorrows;
8/9 now we can breathe again, as you are still holding firm in the Lord. •How can we
thank God enough for you, for all the joy we feel before our God on your account?
10 We are earnestly praying night and day to be able to see you face to face again and
make up any shortcomings in your faith.
11 May God our Father himself, and our Lord Jesus Christ, make it easy for us

2 a. Jr 11:20   b. 2 M 6:14
3 a. I.e. 'the one who puts you to the test'.

to come to you. •May the Lord be generous in increasing your love and make you 12
love one another and the whole human race as much as we love you. •And may 13
he so confirm your hearts in holiness that you may be blameless in the sight of our
God and Father when our Lord Jesus Christ comes *with all his saints.*

Live in holiness and charity

4 Finally, brothers, we urge you and appeal to you in the Lord Jesus to make 1
more and more progress in the kind of life that you are meant to live: the life
that God wants, as you learnt from us, and as you are already living it. •You 2
have not forgotten the instructions we gave you on the authority of the Lord Jesus.

What God wants is for you all to be holy. He wants you to keep away from 3
fornication, •and each one of you to know how to use the body that belongs to 4
him[a] in a way that is holy and honourable, •not giving way to selfish lust like *the* 5
pagans who do not know God.[b] •He wants nobody at all ever to sin by taking advan- 6
tage of a brother in these matters; the Lord always punishes sins of that sort, as
we told you before and assured you. •We have been called by God to be holy, 7
not to be immoral; •in other words, anyone who objects is not objecting to a 8
human authority, but to God, *who gives you his* Holy *Spirit.*[c]

As for loving our brothers, there is no need for anyone to write to you about 9
that, since you have learnt from God yourselves to love one another, •and in fact 10
this is what you are doing with all the brothers throughout the whole of
Macedonia. However, we do urge you, brothers, to go on making even greater
progress •and to make a point of living quietly, attending to your own business 11
and earning your living, just as we told you to, •so that you are seen to 12
be respectable by those outside the Church, though you do not have to depend
on them.

The dead and the living at the time of the Lord's coming

We want you to be quite certain, brothers, about those who have died,[d] to make 13
sure that you do not grieve about them, like the other people who have no hope.
We believe that Jesus died and rose again, and that it will be the same for those 14
who have died in Jesus: God will bring them with him. •We can tell you this from 15
the Lord's own teaching, that any of us who are left alive until the Lord's coming
will not have any advantage over those who have died. •At the trumpet of God, 16
the voice of the archangel will call out the command and the Lord himself will
come down from heaven; those who have died in Christ will be the first to rise,
and then those of us who are still alive will be taken up in the clouds, together 17
with them, to meet the Lord in the air. So we shall stay with the Lord for ever.
With such thoughts as these you should comfort one another.   18

Watchfulness while awaiting the coming of the Lord

You will not be expecting us to write anything to you, brothers, about 'times 1
and seasons', •since you know very well that the Day of the Lord is going to 2
come like a thief in the night. •It is when people are saying, 'How quiet and 3
peaceful it is' that the worst suddenly happens, as suddenly as labour pains come
on a pregnant woman; and there will be no way for anybody to evade it.

But it is not as if you live in the dark, my brothers, for that Day to overtake 4
you like a thief. •No, you are all sons of light and sons of the day: we do not belong 5
to the night or to darkness, •so we should not go on sleeping, as everyone else 6
does, but stay wide awake and sober. •Night is the time for sleepers to sleep and 7
drunkards to be drunk, •but we belong to the day and we should be sober; let us 8
put on faith and love for a *breastplate,* and the hope of *salvation* for a *helmet.*
God never meant us to experience the Retribution, but to win salvation through 9
our Lord Jesus Christ, •who died for us so that, alive or dead, we should still live 10
united to him. •So give encouragement to each other, and keep strengthening one 11
another, as you do already.

Some demands made by life in community

12 We appeal to you, my brothers, to be considerate to those who are working
13 amongst you and are above you in the Lord as your teachers. •Have the greatest
respect and affection for them because of their work.

14 Be at peace among yourselves. •And this is what we ask you to do, brothers:
warn the idlers, give courage to those who are apprehensive, care for the weak and
15 be patient with everyone. •Make sure that people do not try to take revenge;
16 you must all think of what is best for each other and for the community. •Be
17
18 happy at all times; •pray constantly; •and for all things give thanks to God,
because this is what God expects you to do in Christ Jesus.
19
20 Never try to suppress the Spirit •or treat the gift of prophecy with contempt;
21
22 think before you do anything—hold on to what is good •and *avoid every* form of
evil.

Closing prayer and farewell

23 May the God of peace make you perfect and holy; and may you all be kept
safe and blameless, spirit, soul and body, for the coming of our Lord Jesus Christ.
24 God has called you and he will not fail you.
25 Pray for us, my brothers.
26
27 Greet all the brothers with the holy kiss. •My orders, in the Lord's name,
are that this letter is to be read to all the brothers.
28 The grace of our Lord Jesus Christ be with you.

4 a. Lit. 'the vessel that is his': either his own body or his wife's.　**b.** Jr 10:25; Ps 79:6
c. Ezk 37:14　**d.** Lit. 'those who are sleeping'.

2 THESSALONIANS

THE SECOND LETTER OF PAUL
TO THE CHURCH IN THESSALONIKA

Address

1 From Paul, Silvanus and Timothy, to the Church in Thessalonika which is in 1
God our Father and the Lord Jesus Christ; •wishing you grace and peace 2
from God the Father and the Lord Jesus Christ.

Thanksgiving and encouragement. The Last Judgement

We feel we must be continually thanking God for you, brothers; quite rightly, 3
because your faith is growing so wonderfully and the love that you have for one
another never stops increasing; •and among the churches of God we can take 4
special pride in you for your constancy and faith under all the persecutions and
troubles you have to bear. •It all shows that God's judgement is just, and the 5
purpose of it is that you may be found worthy of the kingdom of God; it is for the
sake of this that you are suffering now.

God will very rightly repay with injury those who are injuring you, •and reward $\frac{6}{7}$
you, who are suffering now, with the same peace as he will give us, when the Lord
Jesus appears from heaven with the angels of his power. •He will come *in flaming* 8
fire to impose the penalty on *all who do not acknowledge God*[a] and *refuse to accept*
the Good News of our Lord Jesus. •It will be their punishment to be lost eter- 9
nally, excluded *from the presence of the Lord and from the glory of his strength
on that day* when he comes *to be glorified among his saints* and *seen in his glory*[b] 10
by all who believe in him; and you are believers, through our witness.

Knowing this, we pray continually that our God will make you worthy of his 11
call, and by his power fulfil all your desires for goodness and complete all that
you have been doing through faith; •because in this way *the name* of our Lord 12
Jesus Christ *will be glorified* in you and you in him, by the grace of our God and the
Lord Jesus Christ.

The coming of the Lord and the prelude to it

2 To turn now, brothers, to the coming of our Lord Jesus Christ and how we 1
shall all be gathered round him: •please do not get excited too soon or 2
alarmed by any prediction or rumour or any letter claiming to come from us,
implying that the Day of the Lord has already arrived. •Never let anyone 3
deceive you in this way

It cannot happen until the Great Revolt has taken place and the Rebel, the
Lost One, has appeared. •This is the Enemy, the one who claims to be so much 4
greater than all that men call 'god', so much greater than anything that is worshipped,•that *he enthrones himself* in *God's* sanctuary and claims that he is God.
Surely you remember me telling you about this when I was with you? •And you $\frac{5}{6}$
know, too, what is still holding him back from appearing before his appointed
time. •Rebellion is at its work already, but in secret, and the one who is holding 7
it back has first to be removed •before the Rebel appears openly. The Lord 8

will kill him with the breath of his mouth[a] and will annihilate him with his glorious appearance at his coming.

9 But when the Rebel comes, Satan will set to work: there will be all kinds of
10 miracles and a deceptive show of signs and portents, •and everything evil that can deceive those who are bound for destruction because they would not grasp
11 the love of the truth which could have saved them. •The reason why God
12 is sending a power to delude them and make them believe what is untrue •is to condemn all who refused to believe in the truth and chose wickedness instead.

Encouragement to persevere

13 But we feel that we must be continually thanking God for you, brothers whom the Lord loves, because God chose you from the beginning to be saved by the
14 sanctifying Spirit and by faith in the truth. •Through the Good News that we brought he called you to this so that you should share the glory of our Lord Jesus
15 Christ. •Stand firm, then, brothers, and keep the traditions that we taught you,
16 whether by word of mouth or by letter. •May our Lord Jesus Christ himself, and God our Father who has given us his love and, through his grace, such inexhaust-
17 ible comfort and such sure hope, •comfort you and strengthen you in everything good that you do or say.

1 **3** Finally, brothers, pray for us; pray that the Lord's message may spread
2 quickly, and be received with honour as it was among you; •and pray that we may be preserved from the interference of bigoted and evil people, for faith is not
3 given to everyone. •But the Lord is faithful, and he will give you strength and
4 guard you from the evil one, •and we, in the Lord, have every confidence that
5 you are doing and will go on doing all that we tell you. •May the Lord turn your hearts towards the love of God and the fortitude of Christ.

Against idleness and disunity

6 In the name of the Lord Jesus Christ, we urge you, brothers, to keep away from any of the brothers who refuses to work or to live according to the tradition we passed on to you.
7 You know how you are supposed to imitate us: now we were not idle when
8 we were with you, •nor did we ever have our meals at anyone's table without paying for them; no, we worked night and day, slaving and straining, so as not to
9 be a burden on any of you. •This was not because we had no right to be, but in order to make ourselves an example for you to follow.
10 We gave you a rule when we were with you: not to let anyone have any food if
11 he refused to do any work. •Now we hear that there are some of you who are living in idleness, doing no work themselves but interfering with everyone else's.
12 In the Lord Jesus Christ, we order and call on people of this kind to go on quietly working and earning the food that they eat.
13 My brothers, never grow tired of doing what is right. •If anyone refuses to obey
14 what I have written in this letter, take note of him and have nothing to do with
15 him, so that he will feel that he is in the wrong; •though you are not to regard him as an enemy but as a brother in need of correction.

Prayer and farewell wishes

16 May the Lord of peace himself give you peace all the time and in every way. The Lord be with you all.
17 From me, PAUL, these greetings in my own handwriting, which is the mark
18 of genuineness in every letter; this is my own writing. •May the grace of our Lord Jesus Christ be with you all.

1 a. God's *coming in fire* is quoted from Is 66:15; the penalty on *those who do not acknow-ledge him* is a quotation from Jr 10:25.   **b.** Quotations from Is 2:10-17; 49:3; 66:5.
2 a. Is 11:4

1 TIMOTHY

THE FIRST LETTER
FROM PAUL TO TIMOTHY

Address

1 From Paul, apostle of Christ Jesus appointed by the command of God our 1
saviour and of Christ Jesus our hope, •to Timothy, true child of mine in the 2
faith; wishing you grace, mercy and peace from God the Father and from Christ
Jesus our Lord.

Suppress the false teachers

As I asked you when I was leaving for Macedonia, please stay at Ephesus, to 3
insist that certain people stop teaching strange doctrines •and taking notice of 4
myths and endless genealogies; these things are only likely to raise irrelevant
doubts instead of furthering the designs of God which are revealed in faith.
The only purpose of this instruction is that there should be love, coming out 5
of a pure heart, a clear conscience and a sincere faith. •There are some people 6
who have gone off the straight course and taken a road that leads to empty
speculation; •they claim to be doctors of the Law but they understand neither 7
the arguments they are using nor the opinions they are upholding.

The purpose of the Law

We know, of course, that the Law is good, but only provided it is treated 8
like any law, •in the understanding that laws are not framed for people who 9
are good. On the contrary, they are for criminals and revolutionaries, for the
irreligious and the wicked, for the sacrilegious and the irreverent; they are for
people who kill their fathers or mothers and for murderers, •for those who are 10
immoral with women or with boys or with men, for liars and for perjurers—and
for everything else that is contrary to the sound teaching •that goes with the 11
Good News of the glory of the blessed God, the gospel that was entrusted to me.

Paul on his own calling

I thank Christ Jesus our Lord, who has given me strength, and who judged 12
me faithful enough to call me into his service •even though I used to be 13
a blasphemer and did all I could to injure and discredit the faith. Mercy, however,
was shown me, because until I became a believer I had been acting in ignorance;
and the grace of our Lord filled me with faith and with the love that is in Christ 14
Jesus. •Here is a saying that you can rely on and nobody should doubt: that 15
Christ Jesus came into the world to save sinners. I myself am the greatest of them;
and if mercy has been shown to me, it is because Jesus Christ meant to make 16
me the greatest evidence of his inexhaustible patience for all the other people
who would later have to trust in him to come to eternal life. •To the eternal 17
King, the undying, invisible and only God, be honour and glory for ever and
ever. Amen.

Timothy's responsibility

18   Timothy, my son, these are the instructions that I am giving you: I ask you
to remember the words once spoken over you by the prophets, and taking them
19 to heart to fight like a good soldier •with faith and a good conscience for your
weapons. Some people have put conscience aside and wrecked their faith in
20 consequence. •I mean men like Hymenaeus and Alexander, whom I have handed
over to Satan to teach them not to be blasphemous.

Liturgical prayer

1 2 My advice is that, first of all, there should be prayers offered for everyone
2   —petitions, intercessions and thanksgiving—•and especially for kings and
others in authority, so that we may be able to live religious and reverent lives
3 in peace and quiet. •To do this is right, and will please God our saviour: •he
4
5 wants everyone to be saved and reach full knowledge of the truth. •For there
is only one God, and there is only one mediator between God and mankind,
6 himself a man, Christ Jesus, •who sacrificed himself as a ransom for them all.
7 He is the evidence of this, sent at the appointed time, and •I have been named
a herald and apostle of it and—I am telling the truth and no lie—a teacher of
the faith and the truth to the pagans.

8   In every place, then, I want the men to lift their hands up reverently
in prayer, with no anger or argument.

Women in the assembly

9   Similarly, I direct that women are to wear suitable clothes and to be dressed
quietly and modestly, without braided hair or gold and jewellery or expensive
10 clothes; their adornment is •to do the sort of good works that are proper for
11 women who profess to be religious. •During instruction, a woman should be
12 quiet and respectful. •I am not giving permission for a woman to teach or to
13 tell a man what to do. A woman ought not to speak, •because Adam was
14 formed first and Eve afterwards, •and it was not Adam who was led astray but
15 the woman who was led astray and fell into sin. •Nevertheless, she will be saved
by childbearing, provided she lives a modest life and is constant in faith and
love and holiness.

The elder-in-charge

1 3 Here is a saying that you can rely on: To want to be a presiding elder[a] is to
2   want to do a noble work. •That is why the president must have an impeccable
character. He must not have been married more than once, and he must be
3 temperate, discreet and courteous, hospitable and a good teacher; •not a heavy
drinker, nor hot-tempered, but kind and peaceable. He must not be a lover of
4 money. •He must be a man who manages his own family well and brings his
5 children up to obey him and be well-behaved: •how can any man who does not
understand how to manage his own family have responsibility for the church
6 of God? •He should not be a new convert, in case pride might turn his head
7 and then he might be condemned as the devil was condemned. •It is also
necessary that people outside the Church should speak well of him, so that he
never gets a bad reputation and falls into the devil's trap.

Deacons

8   In the same way, deacons must be respectable men whose word can be
trusted, moderate in the amount of wine they drink and with no squalid greed
9 for money. •They must be conscientious believers in the mystery of the faith.
10 They are to be examined first, and only admitted to serve as deacons if there
11 is nothing against them. •In the same way, the women must be respectable,

3 a. The word *episcopos* used here by Paul had not yet acquired the same meaning as 'bishop'.

not gossips but sober and quite reliable. •Deacons must not have been married 12
more than once, and must be men who manage their children and families
well.• Those of them who carry out their duties well as deacons will earn a 13
high standing for themselves and be rewarded with great assurance in their
work for the faith in Christ Jesus.

The Church and the mystery of the spiritual life

At the moment of writing to you, I am hoping that I may be with you soon; 14
but in case I should be delayed, I wanted you to know how people ought to behave 15
in God's family—that is, in the Church of the living God, which upholds the
truth and keeps it safe. •Without any doubt, the mystery of our religion is very 16
deep indeed:

> He was made visible in the flesh,
> attested by the Spirit,
> seen by angels,
> proclaimed to the pagans,
> believed in by the world,
> taken up in glory.

False teachers

4 The Spirit has explicitly said that during the last times there will be some 1
who will desert the faith and choose to listen to deceitful spirits and doctrines
that come from the devils; •and the cause of this is the lies told by hypocrites 2
whose consciences are branded as though with a red-hot iron:ᵃ •they will say 3
marriage is forbidden, and lay down rules about abstaining from foods which
God created to be accepted with thanksgiving by all who believe and who know
the truth.ᵇ •Everything God has created is good, and no food is to be rejected, 4
provided grace is said for it: •the word of God and the prayer make it holy. 5
If you put all this to the brothers, you will be a good servant of Christ Jesus and 6
show that you have really digested the teaching of the faith and the good doctrine
which you have always followed. •Have nothing to do with godless myths and 7
old wives' tales. Train yourself spiritually. •'Physical exercises are useful enough, 8
but the usefulness of spirituality is unlimited, since it holds out the reward of
life here and now and of the future life as well'; •that is a saying that you can 9
rely on and nobody should doubt it. •I mean that the point of all our toiling and 10
battling is that we have put our trust in the living God and he is the saviour of
the whole human race but particularly of all believers. •This is what you are to 11
enforce in your teaching.

Do not let people disregard you because you are young, but be an example 12
to all the believers in the way you speak and behave, and in your love, your faith
and your purity. •Make use of the time until I arrive by reading to the people, 13
preaching and teaching. •You have in you a spiritual gift which was given to 14
you when the prophets spoke and the body of elders laid their hands on you;
do not let it lie unused. •Think hard about all this, and put it into practice, and 15
everyone will be able to see how you are advancing. •Take great care about what 16
you do and what you teach; always do this, and in this way you will save both
yourself and those who listen to you.

Pastoral practice

5 Do not speak harshly to a man older than yourself, but advise him as you 1
would your own father; treat the younger men as brothers •and older women 2
as you would your mother. Always treat young women with propriety, as if they
were sisters.

Widows

Be considerate to widows; I mean those who are truly widows. •If a widow ³⁄₄
has children or grandchildren, they are to learn first of all to do their duty to

their own families and repay their debt to their parents, because this is what
5 pleases God. •But a woman who is really widowed and left without anybody
can give herself up to God and consecrate all her days and nights to petitions
6 and prayer. •The one who thinks only of pleasure is already dead while she
7 is still alive: •remind them of all this, too, so that their lives may be blameless.
8 Anyone who does not look after his own relations, especially if they are living
with him, has rejected the faith and is worse than an unbeliever.

9   Enrolment as a widow is permissible only for a woman at least sixty years
10 old who has had only one husband. •She must be a woman known for her good
works and for the way in which she has brought up her children, shown hospitality to strangers and washed the saints' feet, helped people who are in trouble
11 and been active in all kinds of good work. •Do not accept young widows because
if their natural desires get stronger than their dedication to Christ, they want
12 to marry again, •and then people condemn them for being unfaithful to their
13 original promise. •Besides, they learn how to be idle and go round from house
to house; and then, not merely idle, they learn to be gossips and meddlers in
other people's affairs, and to chatter when they would be better keeping quiet.
14 I think it is best for young widows to marry again and have children and a home
to look after, and not give the enemy any chance to raise a scandal about them;
15/16 there are already some who have left us to follow Satan. •If a Christian woman
has widowed relatives, she should support them and not make the Church bear
the expense but enable it to support those who are genuinely widows.

The elders

17   The elders who do their work well while they are in charge are to be given
double consideration, especially those who are assiduous in preaching and
18 teaching. •As scripture says: *You must not muzzle an ox when it is treading out*
19 *the corn;*[a] and again: *The worker deserves his pay.*[b] •Never accept any accusation
20 brought against an elder unless it is supported *by two or three witnesses.* •If any
21 of them are at fault, reprimand them publicly, as a warning to the rest. •Before
God, and before Jesus Christ and the angels he has chosen, I put it to you as a
duty to keep these rules impartially and never to be influenced by favouritism.
22 Do not be too quick to lay hands on any man, and never make yourself an
accomplice in anybody else's sin; keep yourself pure.

23   You should give up drinking only water and have a little wine for the sake
of your digestion and the frequent bouts of illness that you have.

24   The faults of some people are obvious long before anyone makes any
complaint about them, while others have faults that are not discovered until
25 afterwards. •In the same way, the good that people do can be obvious; but even
when it is not, it cannot be hidden for ever.

Slaves

1 **6** All slaves 'under the yoke' must have unqualified respect for their masters,
so that the name of God and our teaching are not brought into disrepute.
2 Slaves whose masters are believers are not to think any the less of them because
they are brothers; on the contrary, they should serve them all the better,
since those who have the benefit of their services are believers and dear to
God.

The true teacher and the false teacher

This is what you are to teach them to believe and persuade them to do.
3 Anyone who teaches anything different, and does not keep to the sound teaching

4 a. Like runaway slaves.   b. The rejection of marriage was to be one of the hallmarks of
Gnosticism; dietary regulations were more specifically Jewish.
5 a. Dt 25:4   b. Not traceable in the O.T.; but this is also to be found in Lk 10:7 where,
again, it may be a quotation.

which is that of our Lord Jesus Christ, the doctrine which is in accordance with true religion, •is simply ignorant and must be full of self-conceit—with a craze 4 for questioning everything and arguing about words. All that can come of this is jealousy, contention, abuse and wicked mistrust of one another; •and unending 5 disputes by people who are neither rational nor informed and imagine that religion is a way of making a profit. •Religion, of course, does bring 6 large profits, but only to those who are content with what they have. •We brought 7 nothing into the world, and we can take nothing out of it; •but as long as we 8 have food and clothing, let us be content with that. •People who long to be rich 9 are a prey to temptation; they get trapped into all sorts of foolish and dangerous ambitions which eventually plunge them into ruin and destruction. •'The love 10 of money is the root of all evils' and there are some who, pursuing it, have wandered away from the faith, and so given their souls any number of fatal wounds.

Timothy's vocation recalled

But, as a man dedicated to God, you must avoid all that. You must aim to 11 be saintly and religious, filled with faith and love, patient and gentle. •Fight the 12 good fight of the faith and win for yourself the eternal life to which you were called when you made your profession and spoke up for the truth in front of many witnesses. •Now, before God the source of all life and before Jesus Christ, 13 who spoke up as a witness for the truth in front of Pontius Pilate, I put to you the duty •of doing all that you have been told, with no faults or failures, until 14 the Appearing of our Lord Jesus Christ,

> who at the due time will be revealed   15
> by God, the blessed and only Ruler of all,
> the King of kings and the Lord of lords,
> who alone is immortal,   16
> whose home is in inaccessible light,
> whom no man has seen and no man is able to see:
> to him be honour and everlasting power. Amen.

Rich Christians

Warn those who are rich in this world's goods that they are not to look down 17 on other people; and not to set their hopes on money, which is untrustworthy, but on God who, out of his riches, gives us all that we need for our happiness. Tell them that they are to do good, and be rich in good works, to be generous 18 and willing to share—•this is the way they can save up a good capital sum for 19 the future if they want to make sure of the only life that is real.

Final warning and conclusion

My dear Timothy, take great care of all that has been entrusted to you. Have 20 nothing to do with the pointless philosophical discussions and antagonistic beliefs of the 'knowledge' which is not knowledge at all; •by adopting this, some 21 have gone right away from the faith. Grace be with you.

2 TIMOTHY

THE SECOND LETTER
FROM PAUL TO TIMOTHY

Greeting and thanksgiving

1 From Paul, appointed by God to be an apostle of Christ Jesus in his design
2 to promise life in Christ Jesus; •to Timothy, dear child of mine, wishing you
grace, mercy and peace from God the Father and from Christ Jesus our Lord.
3 Night and day I thank God, keeping my conscience clear and remembering
my duty to him as my ancestors did, and always I remember you in my prayers;
4 I remember your tears •and long to see you again to complete my happiness.
5 Then I am reminded of the sincere faith which you have; it came first to live in
your grandmother Lois, and your mother Eunice, and I have no doubt that it
is the same faith in you as well.

The gifts that Timothy has received

6 That is why I am reminding you now to fan into a flame the gift that God
7 gave you when I laid my hands on you. •God's gift was not a spirit of timidity,
8 but the Spirit of power, and love, and self-control. •So you are never to be
ashamed of witnessing to the Lord, or ashamed of me for being his prisoner;
but with me, bear the hardships for the sake of the Good News, relying on the
9 power of God •who has saved us and called us to be holy—not because of
anything we ourselves have done but for his own purpose and by his own grace.
This grace had already been granted to us, in Christ Jesus, before the beginning
10 of time, •but it has only been revealed by the Appearing of our saviour Christ
Jesus. He abolished death, and he has proclaimed life and immortality through
11 the Good News; •and I have been named its herald, its apostle and its teacher.
12 It is only on account of this that I am experiencing fresh hardships here
now;[a] but I have not lost confidence, because I know who it is that I have put
my trust in, and I have no doubt at all that he is able to take care of all that
I have entrusted to him until that Day.
13 Keep as your pattern the sound teaching you have heard from me, in the
14 faith and love that are in Christ Jesus. •You have been trusted to look after
something precious; guard it with the help of the Holy Spirit who lives in us.
15 As you know, Phygelus and Hermogenes and all the others from Asia refuse
16 to have anything more to do with me. •I hope the Lord will be kind to the
family of Onesiphorus, because he has often been a comfort to me and has never
17 been ashamed of my chains. •On the contrary, as soon as he reached Rome, he
18 really searched hard for me and found out where I was. •May it be the Lord's
will that he shall find the Lord's mercy on that Day. You know better than
anyone else how much he helped me at Ephesus.

1 a. The second imprisonment at Rome.

How Timothy should face hardships

2 Accept the strength, my dear son, that comes from the grace of Christ Jesus. 1
You have heard everything that I teach in public; hand it on to reliable 2
people so that they in turn will be able to teach others.

Put up with your share of difficulties, like a good soldier of Christ Jesus. 3
In the army, no soldier gets himself mixed up in civilian life, because he must 4
be at the disposal of the man who enlisted him; •or take an athlete—he cannot 5
win any crown unless he has kept all the rules of the contest; •and again, it is 6
the working farmer who has the first claim on any crop that is harvested. •Think 7
over what I have said, and the Lord will show you how to understand it all.

Remember the Good News that I carry, 'Jesus Christ risen from the dead, 8
sprung from the race of David'; •it is on account of this that I have my own 9
hardships to bear, even to being chained like a criminal—but they cannot chain
up God's news. •So I bear it all for the sake of those who are chosen, so that 10
in the end they may have the salvation that is in Christ Jesus and the eternal
glory that comes with it.

Here is a saying that you can rely on: 11

> If we have died with him, then we shall live with him.
> If we hold firm, then we shall reign with him.   12
> If we disown him, then he will disown us.
> We may be unfaithful, but he is always faithful,   13
> for he cannot disown his own self.

The struggle against the immediate danger from false teachers

Remind them of this; and tell them in the name of God that there is to be 14
no wrangling about words: all that this ever achieves is the destruction of those
who are listening. •Do all you can to present yourself in front of God as a man 15
who has come through his trials, and a man who has no cause to be ashamed
of his life's work and has kept a straight course with the message of the truth.
Have nothing to do with pointless philosophical discussions—they only lead 16
further and further away from true religion. •Talk of this kind corrodes like 17
gangrene, as in the case of Hymenaeus and Philetus, •the men who have gone 18
right away from the truth and claim that the resurrection has already taken
place. Some people's faith cannot stand up to them.

However, God's solid foundation stone is still in position, and this is the 19
inscription on it: 'The Lord knows those who are his own'ᵃ and 'All who call on
the name of the Lord'ᵇ must avoid sin'.

Not all the dishes in a large house are made of gold and silver; some are 20
made of wood or earthenware: some are kept for special occasions and others
are for ordinary purposes. •Now, to avoid these faults that I am speaking about 21
is the way for anyone to become a vessel for special occasions, fit for the Master
himself to use, and kept ready for any good work.

Instead of giving in to your impulses like a young man, fasten your attention 22
on holiness. faith, love and peace, in union with all those who call on the Lord
with pure minds. •Avoid these futile and silly speculations, understanding that 23
they only give rise to quarrels; •and a servant of the Lord is not to 24
engage in quarrels, but has to be kind to everyone, a good teacher, and patient.
He has to be gentle when he corrects people who dispute what he says, never 25
forgetting that God may give them a change of mind so that they recognise the
truth and •come to their senses, once out of the trap where the devil caught 26
them and kept them enslaved.

The dangers of the last days

3 You may be quite sure that in the last days there are going to be 1
some difficult times. •People will be self-centred and grasping; boastful, 2
arrogant and rude; disobedient to their parents, ungrateful, irreligious; •heartless 3

and unappeasable; they will be slanderers, profligates, savages and enemies of
4 everything that is good; •they will be treacherous and reckless and demented
5 by pride, preferring their own pleasure to God. •They will keep up the outward
appearance of religion but will have rejected the inner power of it. Have nothing
to do with people like that.

6   Of the same kind, too, are those men who insinuate themselves into families
in order to get influence over silly women who are obsessed with their sins and
7 follow one craze after another •in the attempt to educate themselves, but can
8 never come to knowledge of the truth. •Men like this defy the truth just as
Jannes and Jambres defied Moses:ᵃ their minds are corrupt and their faith
9 spurious.•But they will not be able to go on any longer: their foolishness, like
that of the other two, must become obvious to everybody.

10   You know, though, what I have taught, how I have lived, what I have aimed
11 at; you know my faith, my patience and my love; my constancy •and the
persecutions and hardships that came to-me in places like Antioch, Iconium and
Lystra—all the persecutions I have endured; and the Lord has rescued me from
12 every one of them. •You are well aware, then, that anybody who tries to live
13 in devotion to Christ is certain to be attacked; •while these wicked impostors
will go from bad to worse, deceiving others and deceived themselves.

14   You must keep to what you have been taught and know to be true; remember
15 who your teachers were, •and how, ever since you were a child, you have known
the holy scriptures—from these you can learn the wisdom that leads to salvation
16 through faith in Christ Jesus. •All scripture is inspired by God and can profit-
ably be used for teaching, for refuting error, for guiding people's lives and
17 teaching them to be holy. •This is how the man who is dedicated to God
becomes fully equipped and ready for any good work.

A solemn charge

1 **4** Before God and before Christ Jesus who is to be judge of the living and the
dead, I put this duty to you, in the name of his Appearing and of his kingdom:
2 proclaim the message and, welcome or unwelcome, insist on it. Refute falsehood,
correct error, call to obedience—but do all with patience and with the intention
3 of teaching. •The time is sure to come when, far from being content with sound
teaching, people will be avid for the latest novelty and collect themselves a whole
4 series of teachers according to their own tastes; •and then, instead of listening
5 to the truth, they will turn to myths. •Be careful always to choose the right
course; be brave under trials; make the preaching of the Good News your life's
work, in thoroughgoing service.

Paul in the evening of his life

6   As for me, my life is already being poured away as a libation, and the time
7 has come for me to be gone. •I have fought the good fight to the end; I have run
8 the race to the finish; I have kept the faith; •all there is to come now is the
crown of righteousness reserved for me, which the Lord, the righteous judge,
will give to me on that Day; and not only to me but to all those who have longed
for his Appearing.

Final advice

9
10   Do your best to come and see me as soon as you can. •As it is, Demas has
deserted me for love of this life and gone to Thessalonika, Crescens has gone
11 to Galatia and Titus to Dalmatia; •only Luke is with me. Get Mark to come
12 and bring him with you; I find him a useful helper in my work. •I have sent
13 Tychicus to Ephesus. •When you come, bring the cloak I left with Carpus in

2 a. Nb 16:5,26   b. Is 26:13
3 a. In Jewish tradition, the leaders of the Egyptian magicians and disciples of Balaam.

Troas, and the scrolls, especially the parchment ones. •Alexander the copper- 14
smith has done me a lot of harm; *the Lord will repay him for what he has done.*ᵃ
Be on your guard against him yourself, because he has been bitterly contesting 15
everything that we say.

The first time I had to present my defence, there was not a single witness to 16
support me. Every one of them deserted me—may they not be held accountable
for it. •But the Lord stood by me and gave me power, so that through me the 17
whole message might be proclaimed for all the pagans to hear; and so I was
*rescued from the lion's mouth.*ᵇ •The Lord will rescue me from all evil attempts 18
on me, and bring me safely to his heavenly kingdom. To him be glory for ever
and ever. Amen.

Farewells and final good wishes

Greetings to Prisca and Aquila, and the family of Onesiphorus. •Erastus 19
remained at Corinth, and I left Trophimus ill at Miletus. •Do your best to come 20 21
before the winter.

Greetings to you from Eubulus, Pudens, Linus, Claudia and all the brothers.
The Lord be with your spirit. Grace be with you. 22

TITUS

THE LETTER FROM PAUL TO TITUS

Address

1 1 From Paul, servant of God, an apostle of Jesus Christ to bring those whom
God has chosen to faith and to the knowledge of the truth that leads to true
2 religion; •and to give them the hope of the eternal life that was promised so long
3 ago by God. He does not lie •and so, at the appointed time, he revealed his
decision, and, by the command of God our saviour, I have been commissioned to
4 proclaim it. •To Titus, true child of mine in the faith that we share, wishing you
grace and peace from God the Father and from Christ Jesus our saviour.

The appointment of elders

5 The reason I left you behind in Crete was for you to get everything organised
6 there and appoint elders in every town, in the way that I told you: •that is, each
of them must be a man of irreproachable character; he must not have been married
more than once, and his children must be believers and not uncontrollable or
7 liable to be charged with disorderly conduct. •Since, as president, he will be God's
representative, he must be irreproachable: never an arrogant or hot-tempered
8 man, nor a heavy drinker or violent, nor out to make money; •but a man who
is hospitable and a friend of all that is good; sensible, moral, devout and
9 self-controlled; •and he must have a firm grasp of the unchanging message of the
tradition, so that he can be counted on for both expounding the sound doctrine
and refuting those who argue against it.

Opposing the false teachers

10 And in fact you have there a great many people who need to be disciplined,
who talk nonsense and try to make others believe it, particularly among those
11 of the Circumcision. •They have got to be silenced: men of this kind ruin whole
families, by teaching things that they ought not to, and doing it with the vile motive
12 of making money. •It was one of themselves, one of their own prophets, who
13 said,[a] 'Cretans were never anything but liars, dangerous animals and lazy': •and
that is a true statement. So you will have to be severe in correcting them, and
14 make them sound in the faith •so that they stop taking notice of Jewish myths
and doing what they are told to do by people who are no longer interested in the
truth.

15 To all who are pure themselves, everything is pure; but to those who have been
corrupted and lack faith, nothing can be pure—the corruption is both in their
16 minds and in their consciences. •They claim to have knowledge of God but the
things they do are nothing but a denial of him; they are outrageously rebellious
and quite incapable of doing good.

1 a. Attributed to the Cretan poet Epimenides of Knossos.

Some specific moral instruction

2 It is for you, then, to preach the behaviour which goes with healthy doctrine. ¹ The older men should be reserved, dignified, moderate, sound in faith and ² love and constancy. •Similarly, the older women should behave as though they ³ were religious, with no scandalmongering and no habitual wine-drinking—they are to be the teachers of the right behaviour •and show the younger women how ⁴ they should love their husbands and love their children, •how they are to be ⁵ sensible and chaste, and how to work in their homes, and be gentle, and do as their husbands tell them, so that the message of God is never disgraced. •In the ⁶ same way, you have got to persuade the younger men to be moderate •and in ⁷ everything you do make yourself an example to them of working for good: when you are teaching, be an example to them in your sincerity and earnestness •and ⁸ in keeping all that you say so wholesome that nobody can make objections to it; and then any opponent will be at a loss, with no accusation to make against us. Tell the slaves that they are to be obedient to their masters and always do what ⁹ they want without any argument; •and there must be no petty thieving—they ¹⁰ must show complete honesty at all times, so that they are in every way a credit to the teaching of God our saviour.

The basis of the Christian moral life

You see, God's grace has been revealed, and it has made salvation possible for ¹¹ the whole human race •and taught us that what we have to do is to give up every- ¹² thing that does not lead to God, and all our worldly ambitions; we must be self-restrained and live good and religious lives here in this present world, •while ¹³ we are waiting in hope for the blessing which will come with the Appearing of the glory of our great God and saviour Christ Jesus.ᵃ •He sacrificed himself for ¹⁴ us in order to *set us free from all wickedness*ᵇ and *to purify a people so that it could be his very own*ᶜ and would have no ambition except to do good.

, Now this is what you are to say, whether you are giving instruction or ¹⁵ correcting errors; you can do so with full authority, and no one is to question it.

General instruction for believers

3 Remind them that it is their duty to be obedient to the officials and represent- ¹ atives of the government; to be ready to do good at every opportunity; •not ² to go slandering other people or picking quarrels, but to be courteous and always polite to all kinds of people. •Remember, there was a time when we too were ³ ignorant, disobedient and misled and enslaved by different passions and luxuries; we lived then in wickedness and ill-will, hating each other and hateful ourselves.

But when the kindness and love of God our saviour for mankind were revealed, ⁴ it was not because he was concerned with any righteous actions we might have ⁵ done ourselves; it was for no reason except his own compassion that he saved us, by means of the cleansing water of rebirth and by renewing us with the Holy Spirit which he has so generously poured over us through Jesus Christ our saviour. ⁶ He did this so that we should be justified by his grace, to become heirs looking ⁷ forward to inheriting eternal life. •This is doctrine that you can rely on. ⁸

Personal advice to Titus

I want you to be quite uncompromising in teaching all this, so that those who now believe in God may keep their minds constantly occupied in doing good works. All this is good, and will do nothing but good to everybody. •But avoid ⁹ pointless speculations, and those genealogies, and the quibbles and disputes about the Law—these are useless and can do no good to anyone. •If a man disputes ¹⁰ what you teach, then after a first and a second warning, have no more to do with him: •you will know that any man of that sort has already lapsed and condemned ¹¹ himself as a sinner.

Practical recommendations, farewells and good wishes

12   As soon as I have sent Artemas or Tychicus to you, lose no time in joining
13 me at Nicopolis, where I have decided to spend the winter. •See to all the travelling
      arrangements for Zenas the lawyer and Apollos, and make sure they have every-
14 thing they need. •All our people are to learn to occupy themselves in doing good
      works for their practical needs as well, and not to be entirely unproductive.
15   All those who are with me send their greetings. Greetings to those who love
      us in the faith. Grace be with you all.

PHILEMON

THE LETTER FROM PAUL TO PHILEMON

Address

From Paul, a prisoner of Christ Jesus and from our brother Timothy; to our 1
dear fellow worker Philemon, •our sister Apphia, our fellow soldier Archippus 2
and the church that meets in your house; •wishing you the grace and the peace 3
of God our Father and the Lord Jesus Christ.

Thanksgiving and prayer

I always mention you in my prayers and thank God for you, •because I hear 4/5
of the love and the faith which you have for the Lord Jesus and for all the saints.
I pray that this faith will give rise to a sense of fellowship that will show you all 6
the good things that we are able to do for Christ. •I am so delighted, and com- 7
forted, to know of your love; they tell me, brother, how you have put new heart
into the saints.

The request about Onesimus

Now, although in Christ I can have no diffidence about telling you to do 8
whatever is your duty, •I am appealing to your love instead, reminding you that 9
this is Paul writing, an old man now and, what is more, still a prisoner of Christ
Jesus. •I am appealing to you for a child of mine, whose father I became while 10
wearing these chains: I mean Onesimus. •He was of no use to you before, but he 11
will be useful[a] to you now, as he has been to me. •I am sending him back to you, 12
and with him—I could say—a part of my own self. •I should have liked to keep 13
him with me; he could have been a substitute for you, to help me while I am in the
chains that the Good News has brought me. •However, I did not want to do 14
anything without your consent; it would have been forcing your act of kindness,
which should be spontaneous. •I know you have been deprived of Onesimus for 15
a time, but it was only so that you could have him back for ever, •not as a slave 16
any more, but something much better than a slave, a dear brother; especially
dear to me, but how much more to you, as a blood-brother as well as a brother
in the Lord. •So if all that we have in common means anything to you, welcome 17
him as you would me; •but if he has wronged you in any way or owes 18
you anything, then let me pay for it. •I am writing this in my own handwriting: 19
I, Paul, shall pay it back—I will not add any mention of your own debt to me,
which is yourself. •Well then, brother, I am counting on you, in the Lord; put 20
new heart into me, in Christ. •I am writing with complete confidence in your 21
compliance, sure that you will do even more than I ask.

A personal request.   Good wishes

There is another thing: will you get a place ready for me to stay in? I am hoping 22
through your prayers to be restored to you.

Epaphras, a prisoner with me in Christ Jesus, sends his greetings; •so do my 23/24
colleagues Mark, Aristarchus, Demas and Luke.

May the grace of our Lord Jesus Christ be with your spirit. 25

a. A pun—'Onesimus' means 'useful'.

THE LETTER TO THE

HEBREWS

A LETTER ADDRESSED
TO A JEWISH-CHRISTIAN COMMUNITY

PROLOGUE

The greatness of the incarnate Son of God

1 At various times in the past and in various different ways, God spoke to our
2 ancestors through the prophets; but •in our own time, the last days, he has
spoken to us through his Son, the Son that he has appointed to inherit everything
3 and through whom he made everything there is. •He is the radiant light of God's
glory and the perfect copy of his nature, sustaining the universe by his powerful
command; and now that he has destroyed the defilement of sin, he has gone to
4 take his place in heaven at the right hand of divine Majesty. •So he is now as far
above the angels as the title which he has inherited is higher than their own name.

I. THE SON IS GREATER THAN THE ANGELS

Proof from the scriptures

5 God has never said to any angel: *You are my Son, today I have become your*
6 *father;*[a] or: *I will be a father to him and he a son to me.*[b] •Again, when he brings the
7 First-born into the world, he says: *Let all the angels of God worship him.*[c] •About
8 the angels, he says: *He makes his angels winds and his servants flames of fire,*[d] •but
to his Son he says: *God, your throne shall last for ever and ever;* and: *his royal*
9 *sceptre is the sceptre of virtue; •virtue you love as much as you hate wickedness.*
This is why God, your God, has anointed you with the oil of gladness, above all your
10 *rivals.*[e] •And again: *It is you, Lord, who laid earth's foundations in the beginning,*
11 *the heavens are the work of your hands; •all will vanish, though you remain, all*
12 *wear out like a garment; •you will roll them up like a cloak, and* like a garment
they will be changed. But yourself. you never change and your years are unending.[f]
13 God has never said to any angel: *Sit at my right hand and I will make your enemies*
14 *a footstool for you.*[g] •The truth is they are all spirits whose work is service, sent to
help those who will be the heirs of salvation.

An exhortation

1 2 We ought, then, to turn our minds more attentively than before to what we
2 have been taught, so that we do not drift away. •If a promise that was made
through angels[a] proved to be so true that every infringement and disobedience

1 a. Ps 2:7   b. 2 S 7:14   c. Dt 32:43   d. Ps 104:4   e. Ps 45:6-7   f. Ps 102:25-27
g. Ps 110:1
2 a. The Law.

brought its own proper punishment, •then we shall certainly not go unpunished 3
if we neglect this salvation that is promised to us. The promise was first announced
by the Lord himself, and is guaranteed to us by those who heard him;
God himself confirmed their witness with signs and marvels and miracles of all 4
kinds, and by freely giving the gifts of the Holy Spirit.

Redemption brought by Christ, not by angels

He did not appoint angels to be rulers of the world to come, and that world is 5
what we are talking about. •Somewhere there is a passage that shows us this. It 6
runs: *What is man that you should spare a thought for him, the son of man that you
should care for him? •For a short while you made him lower than the angels; you* 7
crowned him with glory and splendour. • You have put him in command of every- 8
thing.[b] Well then, if he has *put him in command of everything,* he has left nothing
which is not under his command. At present, it is true, we are not able to see that
everything has been put under his command, •but we do see in Jesus one who was 9
for a short while made lower than the angels and is now *crowned with glory and
splendour* because he submitted to death; by God's grace he had to experience
death for all mankind.

As it was his purpose to bring a great many of his sons into glory, it was appro- 10
priate that God, for whom everything exists and through whom everything exists,
should make perfect, through suffering, the leader who would take them to their
salvation. •For the one who sanctifies, and the ones who are sanctified, are of the 11
same stock; that is why he openly calls them *brothers* •in the text: *I shall announce* 12
your name to my brothers, praise you in full assembly;[c] or the text: •*In him I hope*; 13
or the text: *Here I am with the children whom God has given me.*[d]

Since all the *children* share the same blood and flesh, he too shared equally 14
in it, so that by his death he could take away all the power of the devil, who had
power over death, •and set free all those who had been held in slavery all their 15
lives by the fear of death. •For it was not the angels that he took to himself; he 16
took to himself *descent from Abraham.*[e] •It was essential that he should in this way 17
become completely like his brothers so that he could be a compassionate and
trustworthy high priest of God's religion, able to atone for human sins. •That is, 18
because he has himself been through temptation he is able to help others who are
tempted.

II. JESUS THE FAITHFUL AND MERCIFUL HIGH PRIEST

Christ higher than Moses

3 That is why all you who are holy brothers and have had the same heavenly 1
call should turn your minds to Jesus, the apostle and the high priest of our
religion. •He was *faithful* to the one who appointed him, just like *Moses,* who 2
stayed faithful *in all his house;* •but he has been found to deserve a greater glory 3
than Moses. It is the difference between the honour given to the man that built
the house and to the house itself. •Every house is built by someone, of course; 4
but God built everything that exists. •It is true that Moses was *faithful in the* 5
house of God, as a servant, acting as witness to the things which were to be
divulged later; •but Christ was faithful as a son, and as the master in the house. 6
And we are his house, as long as we cling to our hope with the confidence that we
glory in.

How to reach God's land of rest

The Holy Spirit says: *If only you would listen to him today; •do not harden* 7
your hearts, as happened in the Rebellion, on the Day of Temptation in the 8
wilderness, •when your ancestors challenged me and tested me, though they had 9
seen what I could do •for forty years. That was why I was angry with that generation 10

11 *and said: How unreliable these people who refuse to grasp my ways! •And so, in*
12 *anger, I swore that not one would reach the place of rest I had for them.*[a] •Take care,
brothers, that there is not in any one of your community a wicked mind, so unbe-
13 lieving as to turn away from the living God. •Every day, as long as this 'today'
lasts, keep encouraging one another so that none of you is *hardened* by the lure of
14 sin, •because we shall remain co-heirs with Christ only if we keep a grasp on our
15 first confidence right to the end. •In this saying: *If only you would listen to him*
16 *today; do not harden your hearts, as happened in the Rebellion,* •those who
rebelled after they had *listened* were all the people who were brought out of Egypt
17 by Moses. •And those who made God *angry for forty years* were the ones who
18 sinned and whose *dead bodies were left lying in the wilderness.*[b] •Those that he
swore would never reach the place of rest he had for them were those who had been
19 disobedient. •We see, then, that it was because they were unfaithful that they
were not able to reach it.

1   4 Be careful, then: the promise of *reaching the place of rest he had for them* still
2   holds good, and none of you must think that he has come too late for it. •We
received the Good News exactly as they did; but hearing the message did them no
3 good because they did not share the faith of those who listened. •We, however,
who have faith, shall reach a place of rest, as in the text: *And so, in anger, I swore*
that not one would reach the place of rest I had for them. God's work was undoubt-
4 edly all finished at the beginning of the world; •as one text says, referring to the
5 seventh day: *After all his work God rested on the seventh day.*[a] •The text we are
6 considering says: *They shall not reach the place of rest I had for them.* •It is established, then, that there would be some people who would reach it, and since those
7 who first heard the Good News failed to reach it through their disobedience, •God
fixed another day when, much later, he said 'today' through David in the text
already quoted: *If only you would listen to him today; do not harden your hearts.*
8 If Joshua had led them into this place of rest, God would not later on have spoken
9 so much of another day. •There must still be, therefore, a place of rest reserved
10 for God's people, the seventh-day rest, •since to *reach the place of rest* is to *rest*
11 *after your work,* as God did after his. •We must therefore do everything we can
to *reach this place of rest,* or some of you might copy this example of disobedience
and be lost.

The word of God and Christ the priest

12   The word of God is something alive and active: it cuts like any double-edged
sword but more finely: it can slip through the place where the soul is divided from
the spirit, or joints from the marrow; it can judge the secret emotions and
13 thoughts. •No created thing can hide from him; everything is uncovered and open
to the eyes of the one to whom we must give account of ourselves.

14   Since in Jesus, the Son of God, we have the supreme high priest who has gone
through to the highest heaven, we must never let go of the faith that we have
15 professed. •For it is not as if we had a high priest who was incapable of feeling
our weaknesses with us; but we have one who has been tempted in every way that
16 we are, though he is without sin. •Let us be confident, then, in approaching the
throne of grace, that we shall have mercy from him and find grace when we are in
need of help.

Jesus the compassionate high priest

1   5 Every high priest has been taken out of mankind and is appointed to act for
2   men in their relations with God, to offer gifts and sacrifices for sins; and so
2 he can sympathise with those who are ignorant or uncertain because he too lives

b. Ps 8:4-6 (LXX)   **c.** Ps 22:22   **d.** This, and the previous text, are from Is 8:17-18.
e. Is 41:8-9
3 a. Ps 95   **b.** Nb 14:29
4 a. Gn 2:2

in the limitations of weakness. •That is why he has to make sin offerings for ³
himself as well as for the people. •No one takes this honour on himself, but each ⁴
one is called by God, as Aaron was. •Nor did Christ give himself the glory of ⁵
becoming high priest, but he had it from the one who said to him: *You are my*
*son, today I have become your father,*ᵃ •and in another text: *You are a priest of* ⁶
*the order of Melchizedek, and for ever.*ᵇ •During his life on earth, he offered up ⁷
prayer and entreaty, aloud and in silent tears, to the one who had the power to
save him out of death, and he submitted so humbly that his prayer was heard.
Although he was Son, he learnt to obey through suffering; •but having been ⁸ ⁹
made perfect, he became for all who obey him the source of eternal salvation
and was acclaimed by God with the title of high priest *of the order of Melchizedek.* ¹⁰

III. THE AUTHENTIC PRIESTHOOD OF JESUS CHRIST

Christian life and theology

On this subject we have many things to say, and they are difficult to explain ¹¹
because you have grown so slow at understanding. •Really, when you should by ¹²
this time have become masters, you need someone to teach you all over again the
elementary principles of interpreting God's oracles; you have gone back to needing
milk, and not solid food. •Truly, anyone who is still living on milk cannot digest ¹³
the doctrine of righteousness because he is still a baby. •Solid food is for mature ¹⁴
men with minds trained by practice to distinguish between good and bad.

The author explains his intention

6 Let us leave behind us then all the elementary teaching about Christ and ¹
concentrate on its completion, without going over the fundamental doctrines
again: the turning away from dead actions and towards faith in God; •the teaching ²
about baptisms and the laying-on of hands; the teaching about the resurrection
of the dead and eternal judgement. •This, God willing, is what we propose to do. ³
 As for those people who were once brought into the light, and tasted the gift ⁴
from heaven, and received a share of the Holy Spirit, •and appreciated the good ⁵
message of God and the powers of the world to come •and yet in spite of this ⁶
have fallen away—it is impossible for them to be renewed a second time. They
cannot be repentant if they have wilfully crucified the Son of God and openly
mocked him. •A field that has been well watered by frequent rain, and gives the ⁷
crops that are wanted by the owners who grew them, is given God's blessing;
but one that grows brambles and thistles is abandoned, and practically cursed. ⁸
It will end by being burnt.

Words of hope and encouragement

But you, my dear people—in spite of what we have just said, we are sure you ⁹
are in a better state and on the way to salvation. •God would not be so unjust ¹⁰
as to forget all you have done, the love that you have for his name or the services
you have done, and are still doing, for the saints.ᵃ •Our one desire is that every ¹¹
one of you should go on showing the same earnestness to the end, to the perfect
fulfilment of our hopes, •never growing careless, but imitating those who have the ¹²
faith and the perseverance to inherit the promises.
When God made the promise to Abraham, he *swore by his own self,* since it ¹³
was impossible for him to swear by anyone greater: •*I will shower blessings on* ¹⁴
*you and give you many descendants.*ᵇ •Because of that, Abraham persevered and ¹⁵
saw the promise fulfilled. •Men, of course, swear an oath by something greater ¹⁶
than themselves, and between men, confirmation by an oath puts an end to all
dispute. •In the same way, when God wanted to make the heirs to the promise ¹⁷
thoroughly realise that his purpose was unalterable, he conveyed this by an oath;
so that there would be two unalterable things in which it was impossible for God ¹⁸

to be lying, and so that we, now we have found safety, should have a strong
19 encouragement to take a firm grip on the hope that is held out to us. •Here we
have an anchor for our soul, as sure as it is firm, and reaching right *through
20 beyond the veil*[c] •where Jesus has entered before us and on our behalf, to become
a high *priest of the order of Melchizedek, and for ever.*

A. CHRIST'S PRIESTHOOD HIGHER THAN LEVITICAL
PRIESTHOOD

Melchizedek[a]

1 7 You remember that *Melchizedek, king of Salem, a priest of God Most High,*
went to meet Abraham who was on his way back after defeating the kings, and
2 *blessed him;* •and also that it was to him that Abraham gave *a tenth of all that
he had.* By the interpretation of his name, he is, first, 'king of righteousness' and
3 also *king of Salem,* that is, 'king of peace'; •he has no father, mother or ancestry,
and his life has no beginning or ending; he is like the Son of God. He remains
a priest for ever.

Melchizedek accepted tithes from Abraham

4   Now think how great this man must have been, if the patriarch *Abraham paid
5 him a tenth of the treasure he had captured.*[b] •We know that any of the descendants
of Levi who are admitted to the priesthood are obliged by the Law to take tithes
from the people, and this is taking them from their own brothers although they
6 too are descended from Abraham. •But this man, who was not of the same
descent, took his tenth from Abraham, and he gave his blessing to the holder of
7 the promises. •Now it is indisputable that a blessing is given by a superior to an
8 inferior. •Further, in the one case it is ordinary mortal men who receive the
9 tithes and in the other, someone who is declared to be still alive. •It could be said
that Levi himself, who receives tithes, actually paid them, in the person of
10 Abraham, •because he was still in the loins of his ancestor when *Melchizedek
came to meet him.*

From levitical priesthood to the priesthood of Melchizedek

11   Now if perfection had been reached through the levitical priesthood because
the Law given to the nation rests on it, why was it still necessary for a
new priesthood to arise, one *of the same order as Melchizedek*[c] not counted as being
12 'of the same order as' Aaron? •But any change in the priesthood must mean a
change in the Law as well.
13   So our Lord, of whom these things were said, belonged to a different tribe,
14 the members of which have never done service at the altar; •everyone knows he
came from Judah, a tribe which Moses did not even mention when dealing with
priests.

The abrogation of the old Law

15   This[d] becomes even more clearly evident when there appears a second
16 Melchizedek, who is a priest •not by virtue of a law about physical descent, but
17 by the power of an indestructible life. •For it was about him that the prophecy
18 was made: *You are a priest of the order of Melchizedek, and for ever.* •The

5 a. Ps 2:7   b. Ps 110:4
6 a. The same phrase is used in Rm and 2 Co about a collection of money made for the
church in Jerusalem.   b. Gn 22   c. Lv 16:2
7 a. Gn 14, from which the following quotation is made, is silent about any ancestors or
descendants of Melchizedek, and about 'the beginning and ending' of his life.   b. The regular
tithe paid to levitical priests was a tenth.   c. Ps 110:4   d. What has been said in v. 12.

earlier commandment is thus abolished, because it was neither effective nor useful, since the Law could not make anyone perfect; but now this commandment is 19 replaced by something better—the hope that brings us nearer to God.

Christ's priesthood is unchanging

What is more, this was not done without the taking of an oath. The others, 20 indeed, were made priests without any oath; •but he with an oath sworn by the 21 one who declared to him: *The Lord has sworn an oath which he will never retract: you are a priest, and for ever.*[c] •And it follows that it is a greater covenant for 22 which Jesus has become our guarantee. •Then there used to be a great number of 23 those other priests, because death put an end to each one of them; •but this one, 24 because he remains *for ever*, can never lose his priesthood. •It follows, then, that 25 his power to save is utterly certain, since he is living for ever to intercede for all who come to God through him.

The perfection of the heavenly high priest

To suit us, the ideal high priest would have to be holy, innocent and 26 uncontaminated, beyond the influence of sinners, and raised up above the heavens; •one who would not need to offer sacrifices every day, as the other high 27 priests do for their own sins and then for those of the people, because he has done this once and for all by offering himself. •The Law appoints high priests who are 28 men subject to weakness; but the promise on oath, which came after the Law, appointed the Son who is made perfect *for ever.*

B. THE SUPERIORITY OF THE WORSHIP, THE SANCTUARY AND THE MEDIATION PROVIDED BY CHRIST THE PRIEST

The new priesthood and the new sanctuary

8 The great point of all that we have said is that we have a high priest 1 of exactly this kind. He has his place *at the right* of the throne of divine Majesty in the heavens, •and he is the minister of the sanctuary and of the true 2 *Tent* of Meeting which *the Lord*, and not any man, *set up.*[a] •It is the duty of every 3 high priest to offer gifts and sacrifices, and so this one too must have something to offer. •In fact, if he were on earth, he would not be a priest at all, since there 4 are others who make the offerings laid down by the Law •and these only maintain 5 the service of a model or a reflection of the heavenly realities. For Moses, when he had the Tent to build, was warned by God who said: *See that you make everything according to the pattern shown you on the mountain.*[b]

Christ is the mediator of a greater covenant

We have seen that he has been given a ministry of a far higher order, and to 6 the same degree it is a better covenant of which he is the mediator, founded on better promises. •If that first covenant had been without a fault, there would have 7 been no need for a second one to replace it. •And in fact God does find fault with 8 them; he says:

> *See, the days are coming—it is the Lord who speaks—*
> *when I will establish a new covenant*
> *with the House of Israel and the House of Judah,*
> *but not a covenant like the one I made with their ancestors*   9
> *on the day I took them by the hand*
> *to bring them out of the land of Egypt.*
> *They abandoned that covenant of mine,*
> *and so I on my side deserted them. It is the Lord who speaks.*
> *No, this is the covenant I will make*   10

> *with the House of Israel*
> *when those days arrive—it is the Lord who speaks.*
> *I will put my laws into their minds*
> *and write them on their hearts.*
> *Then I will be their God*
> *and they shall be my people.*

11   *There will be no further need for neighbour to try to teach neighbour,*
>   *or brother to say to brother,*
>   *'Learn to know the Lord'.*
>   *No, they will all know me,*
>   *the least no less than the greatest,*
12   *since I will forgive their iniquities*
>   *and never call their sins to mind.*[c]

13   By speaking of a *new* covenant, he implies that the first one is already old. Now anything old only gets more antiquated until in the end it disappears.

Christ enters the heavenly sanctuary

1   9 The first covenant also had its laws governing worship, and its sanctuary,
2   a sanctuary on this earth. •There was a tent which comprised two compartments: the first, in which the lamp-stand, the table and the presentation
3   loaves were kept, was called the Holy Place; •then beyond the second veil, an
4   innermost part which was called the Holy of Holies •to which belonged the gold altar of incense, and the ark of the covenant, plated all over with gold. In this were kept the gold jar containing the manna, Aaron's branch that grew the buds,
5   and the stone tablets of the covenant. •On top of it was the throne of mercy, and outspread over it were the glorious cherubs. This is not the time to go into greater detail about this.

6   Under these provisions, priests are constantly going into the outer tent to
7   carry out their acts of worship, •but the second tent is entered only once a year, and then only by the high priest who must go in by himself and take the blood to
8   offer for his own faults and the people's. •By this, the Holy Spirit is showing that no one has the right to go into the sanctuary as long as the outer tent remains
9   standing; •it is a symbol for this present time. None of the gifts and sacrifices offered under these regulations can possibly bring any worshipper to perfection
10 in his inner self; •they are rules about the outward life, connected with foods and drinks and washing at various times, intended to be in force only until it should be time to reform them.

11   But now Christ has come, as the high priest of all the blessings which were to come. He has passed through the greater, the more perfect tent, which is better
12 than the one made by men's hands because it is not of this created order; •and he has entered the sanctuary once and for all, taking with him not the blood of goats and bull calves, but his own blood, having won an eternal redemption for us.
13 The blood of goats and bulls and the ashes of a heifer are sprinkled on those who have incurred defilement and they restore the holiness of their outward lives;
14 how much more effectively the blood of Christ, who offered himself as the perfect sacrifice to God through the eternal Spirit, can purify our inner self from dead actions so that we do our service to the living God.

Christ seals the new covenant with his blood

15   He brings a new covenant, as the mediator, only so that the people who were called to an eternal inheritance may actually receive what was promised: his death
16 took place to cancel the sins that infringed the earlier covenant. •Now wherever
17 a will is in question, the death of the testator must be established; •indeed, it only

e. Ps 110:4
8 a. Nb 24:6 (LXX)   b. Ex 25:40   c. Jr 31:31-34

becomes valid with that death, since it is not meant to have any effect while the
testator is still alive. •That explains why even the earlier covenant needed 18
something to be killed in order to take effect, •and why, after Moses had 19
announced all the commandments of the Law to the people, he took the calves'
blood, the goats' blood and some water, and with these he sprinkled the book
itself and all the people, using scarlet wool and hyssop; •saying as he did so: *This* 20
is the blood of the covenant that God has laid down for you.[a] •After that, he sprinkled 21
the tent and all the liturgical vessels with blood in the same way. •In fact, 22
according to the Law almost everything has to be purified[b] with blood; and if
there is no shedding of blood, there is no remission. •Obviously, only the copies 23
of heavenly things can be purified in this way, and the heavenly things themselves
have to be purified by a higher sort of sacrifice than this. •It is not as though 24
Christ had entered a man-made sanctuary which was only modelled on the real
one; but it was heaven itself, so that he could appear in the actual presence of God
on our behalf. •And he does not have to offer himself again and again, like the 25
high priest going into the sanctuary year after year with the blood that is not his
own, •or else he would have had to suffer over and over again since the world 26
began. Instead of that, he has made his appearance once and for all, now at the
end of the last age, to do away with sin by sacrificing himself. •Since men only 27
die once, and after that comes judgement, •so Christ, too, offers himself only once 28
to take the faults of many on himself,[c] and when he appears a second time, it will
not be to deal with sin but to reward with salvation those who are waiting for
him.

SUMMARY: CHRIST'S SACRIFICE SUPERIOR TO THE SACRIFICES OF THE MOSAIC LAW

The old sacrifices ineffective

10 So, since the Law has no more than a *reflection* of these realities, and no 1
finished picture of them, it is quite incapable of bringing the worshippers to
perfection, with the same sacrifices repeatedly offered year after year. •Otherwise, 2
the offering of them would have stopped, because the worshippers, when they had
been purified once, would have no awareness of sins. •Instead of that, the sins are 3
recalled year after year in the sacrifices. •Bulls' blood and goats' blood are useless 4
for taking away sins, •and this is what he said, on coming into the world: 5

> *You who wanted no sacrifice or oblation,*
> *prepared a body for me.*
> *You took no pleasure in holocausts or sacrifices for sin;* 6
> *then I said,* 7
> *just as I was commanded in the scroll of the book,*
> *'God, here I am! I am coming to obey your will.'*[a]

Notice that he says first: *You did not want* what the Law lays down as the things 8
to be offered, that is: *the sacrifices, the oblations, the holocausts and the sacrifices*
for sin, and *you took no pleasure* in them; •and then he says: *Here I am! I am* 9
coming to obey your will. He is abolishing the first sort to replace it with the
second. •And this *will* was for us to be made holy by the *offering* of his *body* made 10
once and for all by Jesus Christ.

The efficacy of Christ's sacrifice

All the priests stand at their duties every day, offering over and over again 11
the same sacrifices which are quite incapable of taking sins away. •He, on the 12
óther hand, has offered one single sacrifice for sins, and then taken his place for
ever, *at the right hand of God,* •where he is now waiting *until his enemies are made* 13
into a footstool for him.[b] •By virtue of that one single offering, he has achieved 14

15 the eternal perfection of all whom he is sanctifying. •The Holy Spirit assures us of this; for he says, first:

16
> *This is the covenant I will make with them*
> *when those days arrive;* [c]

and the Lord then goes on to say:

> *I will put my laws into their hearts*
> *and write them on their minds.*

17
> *I will never call their sins to mind,*
> *or their offences.*

18 When all sins have been forgiven, there can be no more sin offerings.

IV. PERSEVERING FAITH

The Christian opportunity

19 In other words, brothers, through the blood of Jesus we have the right to enter
20 the sanctuary, •by a new way which he has opened for us, a living opening
21 through the curtain, that is to say, his body. •And we have the *supreme high priest*
22 over all *the house of God.* •So as we go in, let us be sincere in heart and filled with
faith, our minds sprinkled and free from any trace of bad conscience and our
23 bodies washed with pure water. •Let us keep firm in the hope we profess, because
24 the one who made the promise is faithful. •Let us be concerned for each other,
25 to stir a response in love and good works. •Do not stay away from the meetings
of the community, as some do, but encourage each other to go; the more so as you
see the Day drawing near.

The danger of apostasy

26 If, after we have been given knowledge of the truth, we should deliberately
27 commit any sins, then there is no longer any sacrifice for them. •There will be
left only the dreadful prospect of judgement and of *the raging fire* that is to *burn*
28 *rebels.* [d] •Anyone who disregards the Law of Moses is ruthlessly *put to death on the*
29 *word of two witnesses or three;* [e] •and you may be sure that anyone who tramples
on the Son of God, and who treats *the blood of the covenant* which sanctified him
as if it were not holy, and who insults the Spirit of grace, will be condemned to a
30 far severer punishment. •We are all aware who it was that said: *Vengeance is*
31 *mine; I will repay.* [f] And again: *The Lord will judge his people.* •It is a dreadful thing
to fall into the hands of the living God.

Motives for perseverance

32 Remember all the sufferings that you had to meet after you received the
33 light, in earlier days; •sometimes by being yourselves publicly exposed to insults
and violence, and sometimes as associates of others who were treated in the same
34 way. •For you not only shared in the sufferings of those who were in prison, but
you happily accepted being stripped of your belongings, knowing that you owned
35 something that was better and lasting. •Be as confident now, then, since the reward
36 is so great. •You will need endurance to do God's will and gain what he has
promised.

37
> Only *a little while now, a very little while,*
> *and the one that is coming will have come; he will not delay.* [g]

38
> *The righteous man will live by faith,*
> *but if he draws back, my soul will take no pleasure in him.* [h]

---

9 a. Ex 24:8   b. Many instances are given in Lv.   c. Is 53:12
10 a. Ps 40:6-8 (LXX)   b. Ps 110   c. From the long quotation from Jr 31 made in ch. 8.
d. Is 26:11 (LXX)   e. Dt 17:6   f. Dt 32:35-36   g. Is 26:20 (LXX)   h. Hab 2:3-4 (LXX)

You and I are not the sort of people who *draw back*, and are lost by it; we are 39
the sort who keep *faithful* until our souls are saved.

The exemplary faith of our ancestors

11 Only faith can guarantee the blessings that we hope for, or prove the 1
existence of the realities that at present remain unseen. •It was for faith 2
that our ancestors were commended.

It is by faith that we understand that the world was created by one word from 3
God, so that no apparent cause can account for the things we can see.

It was because of his faith that Abel offered God a better sacrifice than Cain, 4
and for that he was declared to be righteous when *God* made acknowledgement
of *his offerings*. Though he is dead, he still speaks by faith.

It was because of his faith that Enoch was taken up and did not have to 5
experience death: *he was not to be found because God had taken him.*[a] This was
because before his assumption it is attested that *he had pleased God.* •Now it is 6
impossible to please God without faith, since anyone who comes to him must
believe that he exists and rewards those who try to find him.

It was through his faith that Noah, when he had been warned by God of 7
something that had never been seen before, felt a holy fear and built an ark to save
his family. By his faith the world was convicted, and he was able to claim the
rightousness which is the reward of faith.

It was by faith that Abraham obeyed the call to *set out* for a country that was 8
the inheritance given to him and his descendants, and that *he set out* without
knowing where he was going. •By faith he arrived, *as a foreigner*, in the Promised 9
Land, and lived there as if in a strange country, with Isaac and Jacob, who were
heirs with him of the same promise. •They lived there in tents while he looked 10
forward to a city founded, designed and built by God.

It was equally by faith that Sarah, in spite of being past the age, was made able 11
to conceive, because she believed that he who had made the promise would be
faithful to it. •Because of this, there came from one man, and one who was 12
already as good as dead himself, *more descendants than could be counted, as many
as the stars of heaven or the grains of sand on the seashore.*[b]

All these died in faith, before receiving any of the things that had been 13
promised, but they saw them in the far distance and welcomed them, recognising
that they were only *strangers and nomads on earth.* •People who use such terms 14
about themselves make it quite plain that they are in search of their real homeland.
They can hardly have meant the country they came from, since they had the 15
opportunity to go back to it; •but in fact they were longing for a better homeland, 16
their heavenly homeland. That is why God is not ashamed to be called their God,
since he has founded the city for them.

It was by faith that Abraham, *when put to the test, offered up Isaac.*[c] He offered 17
to sacrifice his only son even though the promises had been made to him •and he 18
had been told: *It is through Isaac that your name will be carried on.*[d] •He was 19
confident that God had the power even to raise the dead; and so, figuratively
speaking, he was given back Isaac from the dead.

It was by faith that this same Isaac gave his blessing to Jacob and Esau for the 20
still distant future. •By faith Jacob, when he was dying, blessed each of Joseph's 21
sons, *leaning on the end of his stick as though bowing to pray.*[e] •It was by faith that, 22
when he was about to die, Joseph recalled the Exodus of the Israelites and made
the arrangements for his own burial.

It was by faith that Moses, when he was born, *was hidden by his parents for* 23
three months; they defied the royal edict when they *saw* he was such a *fine* child.
It was by faith that, *when he grew to manhood*, Moses refused to be known as the 24
son of Pharaoh's daughter •and chose to be ill-treated in company with God's 25
people rather than to enjoy for a time the pleasures of sin. •He considered that 26
the insults offered to the Anointed were something more precious than all the

27 treasures of Egypt, because he had his eyes fixed on the reward. •It was by faith
that he left Egypt and was not afraid of the king's anger; he held to his purpose
28 like a man who could see the Invisible. •It was by faith that he kept *the Passover*
and sprinkled *the blood* to prevent *the Destroyer* from touching any of the first-
29 born sons of Israel. •It was by faith they crossed the Red Sea as easily as dry land,
while the Egyptians, trying to do the same, were drowned.
30   It was through faith that the walls of Jericho fell down when the people had
31 been round them for seven days. •It was by faith that Rahab the prostitute
welcomed the spies and so was not killed with the unbelievers.
32   Is there any need to say more? There is not time for me to give an account
of Gideon, Barak, Samson, Jephthah, or of David, Samuel and the prophets.
33 These were men who through faith conquered kingdoms, did what is right and
34 earned the promises. They could keep a lion's mouth shut, •put out blazing fires
and emerge unscathed from battle. They were weak people who were given
35 strength, to be brave in war and drive back foreign invaders. •Some came back
to their wives from the dead, by resurrection; and others submitted to torture,
36 refusing release so that they would rise again to a better life. •Some had to bear
37 being pilloried and flogged, or even chained up in prison. •They were stoned,
or sawn in half,ᶠ or beheaded; they were homeless, and dressed in the skins of
sheep and goats; they were penniless and were given nothing but ill-treatment.
38 They were too good for the world and they went out to live in deserts and
39 mountains and in caves and ravines. •These are all heroes of faith, but they did
40 not receive what was promised, •since God had made provision for us to have
something better, and they were not to reach perfection except with us.

The example of Jesus Christ

1 **12** With so many witnesses in a great cloud on every side of us, we too, then,
should throw off everything that hinders us, especially the sin that clings
2 so easily, and keep running steadily in the race we have started. •Let us not lose
sight of Jesus, who leads us in our faith and brings it to perfection: for the sake of
the joy which was still in the future, he endured the cross, disregarding the
shamefulness of it, and *from now on has taken his place at the right* of God's throne.
3 Think of the way he stood such opposition from sinners and then you will not
4 give up for want of courage. •In the fight against sin, you have not yet had to
keep fighting to the point of death.

God's fatherly instruction

5   Have you forgotten that encouraging text in which you are addressed as sons?
My son, when the Lord corrects you, do not treat it lightly; but do not get discouraged
6 *when he reprimands you.* •*For the Lord trains the ones that he loves and he punishes*
7 *all those that he acknowledges as his sons.*ᵃ •Suffering is part of your *training;*
God is treating you as his *sons.* Has there ever been any *son* whose father did not
8 *train* him? •If you were not getting this training, as all of you are, then you would
9 not be *sons* but bastards. •Besides, we have all had our human fathers who
punished us, and we respected them for it; we ought to be even more willing to
10 submit ourselves to our spiritual Father, to be given life. •Our human fathers
were thinking of this short life when they punished us, and could only do what
they thought best; but he does it all for our own good, so that we may share his
11 own holiness. •Of course, any punishment is most painful at the time, and far
from pleasant; but later, in those on whom it has been used, it bears fruit in peace
12
13 and goodness. •So *hold up your limp arms and steady your trembling knees*ᵇ •and
*smooth out the path you tread;*ᶜ then the injured limb will not be wrenched, it will
grow strong again.

11 a. Gn 5:24   b. Gn 22:17, also quoted in Ex 32.   c. Gn 22:1-14   d. Gn 21:12   e. Gn
47:31   f. Some aprocryphal books say that this was how King Manasseh had Isaiah executed.
12 a. Ps 3:11-12 (LXX)   b. Is 35:3   c. Pr 4:26 (LXX)

Unfaithfulness is punished

Always be wanting peace[d] with all people, and the holiness without which no 14
one can ever see the Lord. •Be careful that no one is deprived of the grace of God 15
and that no *root of bitterness should begin to grow and make trouble;*[e] this can poison
a whole community. •And be careful that there is no immorality, or that any of 16
you does not degrade religion like Esau, *who sold his birthright* for one single
meal. •As you know, when he wanted to obtain the blessing afterwards, he was 17
rejected and, though he pleaded for it with tears, he was unable to elicit a change
of heart.

The two covenants

What you have come to is nothing known to the senses: not a *blazing fire,*[f] 18
or a *gloom* turning to *total darkness,* or a *storm;* •or *trumpeting thunder* or the 19
great voice speaking which made everyone that heard it beg that no more should
be said to them. •They were appalled at the order that was given: *If even an animal* 20
touches the mountain, it must be stoned. •The whole scene was so terrible that 21
Moses said: *I am afraid,*[g] and was trembling with fright. •But what you have come 22
to is Mount Zion and the city of the living God, the heavenly Jerusalem where the
millions of angels have gathered for the festival, •with the whole Church in which 23
everyone is a 'first-born son' and a citizen of heaven. You have come to God
himself, the supreme Judge, and been placed with the spirits of the saints who have
been made perfect; •and to Jesus, the mediator who brings a new covenant and a 24
blood for purification which pleads more insistently than Abel's. •Make sure that 25
you never refuse to listen when he speaks. The people who refused to listen to the
warning from a voice on earth could not escape their punishment, and how shall
we escape if we turn away from a voice that warns us from heaven? •That time 26
his voice made the earth shake, but now he has given us this promise: *I shall make*
the earth shake once more and not only the earth but *heaven as well.*[h] •The words 27
once more show that since the things being shaken are created things, they are
going to be changed, so that the unshakeable things will be left. •We have 28
been given possession of an unshakeable kingdom. Let us therefore hold on to the
grace that we have been given and use it to worship God in the way that he finds
acceptable, in reverence and fear. •For our *God* is a *consuming fire.*[i] 29

APPENDIX

Final recommendations

13 Continue to love each other like brothers, •and remember always to ¹⁄₂
welcome strangers, for by doing this, some people have entertained angels
without knowing it. •Keep in mind those who are in prison, as though you were 3
in prison with them; and those who are being badly treated, since you too are in
the one body. •Marriage is to be honoured by all, and marriages are to be kept 4
undefiled, because fornicators and adulterers will come under God's judgement.
Put greed out of your lives and be content with whatever you have; God himself 5
has said: *I will not fail you or desert you,*[a] •and so we can say with confidence: 6
With the Lord to help me, I fear nothing: what can man do to me?[b]

Faithfulness

Remember your leaders, who preached the word of God to you, and as you 7
reflect on the outcome of their lives, imitate their faith. •Jesus Christ is the same 8
today as he was yesterday and as he will be for ever. •Do not let yourselves 9
be led astray by all sorts of strange doctrines: it is better to rely on grace for inner
strength than on dietary laws which have done no good to those who kept them.
We have our own altar from which those who serve the tabernacle have no right 10
to eat. •The bodies of the animals *whose blood is brought into the sanctuary* by the 11

12 high priest *for the atonement of sin are burnt outside the camp,*ᶜ •and so Jesus too
13 ·suffered outside the gate to sanctify the people with his own blood. •Let us go to
14 him, then, *outside the camp,* and share his degradation. •For there is no eternal
15 city for us in this life but we look for one in the life to come. •Through him,
let us offer God an unending *sacrifice of praise,*ᵈ a verbal sacrifice that is offered
16 every time we acknowledge his name. •Keep doing good works and sharing your
resources, for these are sacrifices that please God.

Obedience to religious leaders

17   Obey your leaders and do as they tell you, because they must give an account
of the way they look after your souls; make this a joy for them to do, and not a
18 grief—you yourselves would be the losers. •We are sure that our own conscience
is clear and we are certainly determined to behave honourably in everything we
19 do; pray for us. •I ask you very particularly to pray that I may come back to you
all the sooner.

EPILOGUE

News, good wishes and greetings

20   I pray that the God of peace, *who brought* our Lord Jesus *back*ᵉ from the dead
*to become the great Shepherd of the sheep*ᶠ *by the blood that sealed an eternal*
21 *covenant,*ᵍ •may make you ready to do his will in any kind of good action; and
turn us all into whatever is acceptable to himself through Jesus Christ, to whom
be glory for ever and ever, Amen.
22   I do ask you, brothers, to take these words of advice kindly; that is why I have
written to you so briefly.
23   I want you to know that our brother Timothy has been set free. If he arrives
24 in time, he will be with me when I see you. •Greetings to all your leaders and to
25 all the saints. The saints of Italy send you greetings. •Grace be with you all.

---

d. Ps 34:14   e. Dt 29:17   f. The quotations in vv. 18-20 are from Ex 19 (recalled in Dt 4).
g. Dt 9:19   h. Hg 2:6, probably influenced also by Ps 68:8.   i. Dt 4:24
13 a. Dt 31:6   b. Ps 118:6; Ps 27:1   c. Lv 16:27   d. Ps 50:14   e. Is 63:11   f. Ezk
34:23   g. Ezk 37:26

INTRODUCTION TO
THE LETTERS TO ALL CHRISTIANS

Seven letters not written by Paul are included in the New Testament and these, because they were addressed to the Church at large, have been known as 'the catholic epistles'. The three of them attributed to John have been briefly introduced in the introductory note to John's Gospel.

James

The traditional attribution of this letter to 'James, the brother of the Lord', is supported by internal evidence. Though it was written in Greek, the letter is full of hebraisms and its style of argument is characteristically semitic, and it was clearly intended for Jewish converts so familiar with the Old Testament that they would understand allusions to it without direct quotation. It is more a sermon than a letter and consists largely of moral exhortations, laying particular stress on the practical 'good works' expected of Christians and re-presenting much of the Jewish Wisdom tradition. It takes a different point of view from Paul's on the problem of relating faith to works, and may either be earlier than Galatians-Romans and written as early as A.D. 49, or it may be a rejoinder to what Paul had written and be placed at 57 or 58.

Jude

This is also a letter to Jewish Christians, probably written between A.D. 70 and 80. It denounces certain false teachers and threatens them with the punishments promised by Jewish tradition, and it quotes from apocryphal Jewish writings.

1 Peter. 2 Peter

1 Peter has from the earliest times been accepted as written by the apostle, though it may not have been first composed as a single letter. It is addressed to Christian churches largely made up of converts from paganism, and is in quite good Greek, perhaps through the help of the disciple Silvanus mentioned in it as secretary. The letter reflects a time of trial through which the churches were passing and contains much practical teaching under the dominating theme of fortitude in persecution.

2 Peter seems to date from later than Peter's death, though the writer may have had some claim to represent Peter and was possibly a disciple of his. One possibility is that he filled out one of Peter's writings by adopting the letter of Jude to make a chapter (ch. 2).

THE LETTER OF
JAMES

Address and greetings

1 From James, servant of God and of the Lord Jesus Christ. Greetings to the twelve tribes of the Dispersion.^a

Trials a privilege

2 My brothers, you will always have your trials but, when they come, try to treat
3 them as a happy privilege;^b •you understand that your faith is only put to the
4 test to make you patient, •but patience too is to have its practical results so that
you will become fully-developed, complete, with nothing missing.

5 If there is any one of you who needs wisdom, he must ask God, who
6 gives to all freely and ungrudgingly; it will be given to him. •But he must ask
with faith, and no trace of doubt, because a person who has doubts is like the
7 waves thrown up in the sea when the wind drives. •That sort of person, in two
8 minds, wavering between going different ways, must not expect that the Lord
will give him anything.

9 It is right for the poor brother to be proud of his high rank, •and the rich
10 one to be thankful that he has been humbled, because riches last no longer than
11 *the flowers in the grass;* •the scorching sun comes up, and *the grass withers, the*
flower falls;^c what looked so beautiful now disappears. It is the same with the rich
man: his business goes on; he himself perishes.

12 *Happy the man who stands firm^d* when trials come. He has proved himself,
and will win the prize of life, the crown that the Lord has promised to those who
love him.

Temptation

13 Never, when you have been tempted, say, 'God sent the temptation'; God
cannot be tempted to do anything wrong, and he does not tempt anybody.
14 Everyone who is tempted is attracted and seduced by his own wrong desire.
15 Then the desire conceives and gives birth to sin, and when sin is fully grown, it too
has a child, and the child is death.

16 Make no mistake about this, my dear brothers: •it is all that is good,
17 everything that is perfect, which is given us from above; it comes down from the
Father of all light; with him there is no such thing as alteration, no shadow of a
18 change. •By his own choice he made us his children by the message of the truth
so that we should be a sort of first-fruits of all that he had created.

1 a. In O.T. days the 'Dispersion' (*diaspora*) meant the Jews who had emigrated from their
own country. The writer is using it here to mean the Jewish-Christians, living in the Graeco-
Roman world.   b. 'happy privilege' is a pun on the greeting formula in v. 1.   c. Is 40:6-7
d. Dn 12:12

True religion

Remember this, my dear brothers: be *quick to listen*[e] but *slow* to speak and 19
slow to rouse your temper; •God's righteousness is never served by man's anger; 20
so do away with all the impurities and bad habits that are still left in you—accept 21
and submit to the word which has been planted in you and can save your souls.
But you must do what the word tells you, and not just listen to it and deceive 22
yourselves. •To listen to the word and not obey is like looking at your own features 23
in a mirror and then, •after a quick look, going off and immediately forgetting 24
what you looked like. •But the man who looks steadily at the perfect law of 25
freedom and makes that his habit—not listening and then forgetting, but actively
putting it into practice—will be happy in all that he does.

Nobody must imagine that he is religious while he still goes on deceiving 26
himself and not keeping control over his tongue; anyone who does this has the
wrong idea of religion. •Pure, unspoilt religion, in the eyes of God our Father 27
is this: coming to the help of orphans and widows when they need it, and keeping
oneself uncontaminated by the world.

Respect for the poor

2 My brothers, do not try to combine faith in Jesus Christ, our glorified Lord, 1
with the making of distinctions between classes of people. •Now suppose a man 2
comes into your synagogue,[a] beautifully dressed and with a gold ring on, and at
the same time a poor man comes in, in shabby clothes, •and you take notice of the 3
well-dressed man, and say, 'Come this way to the best seats'; then you tell the
poor man, 'Stand over there' or 'You can sit on the floor by my foot-rest'. •Can't 4
you see that you have used two different standards in your mind, and turned
yourselves into judges, and corrupt judges at that?

Listen, my dear brothers: it was those who are poor according to the world 5
that God chose, to be rich in faith and to be the heirs to the kingdom which he
promised to those who love him. •In spite of this, you have no respect for anybody 6
who is poor. Isn't it always the rich who are against you? Isn't it always their
doing when you are dragged before the court? •Aren't they the ones who insult 7
the honourable name to which you have been dedicated? •Well, the right thing 8
to do is to keep the supreme law of scripture: *you must love your neighbour as
yourself;*[b] •but as soon as you make distinctions between classes of people, you are 9
committing sin, and under condemnation for breaking the Law.

You see, if a man keeps the whole of the Law, except for one small point 10
at which he fails, he is still guilty of breaking it all. •It was the same person who 11
said, '*You must not commit adultery*' and '*You must not kill*'.[c] Now if you commit
murder, you do not have to commit adultery as well to become a breaker of the
Law. •Talk and behave like people who are going to be judged by the law of 12
freedom, •because there will be judgement without mercy for those who have 13
not been merciful themselves; but the merciful need have no fear of judgement.

Faith and good works

Take the case, my brothers, of someone who has never done a single good 14
act but claims that he has faith. Will that faith save him? •If one of the brothers 15
or one of the sisters is in need of clothes and has not enough food to live on,
and one of you says to them, 'I wish you well; keep yourself warm and 16
eat plenty', without giving them these bare necessities of life, then what good is
that? •Faith is like that: if good works do not go with it, it is quite dead. 17

This is the way to talk to people of that kind: 'You say you have faith and I 18
have good deeds; I will prove to you that I have faith by showing you my good
deeds—now you prove to me that you have faith without any good deeds to show.
You believe in the one God—that is creditable enough, but the demons have the 19
same belief, and they tremble with fear. •Do realise, you senseless man, that faith 20
without good deeds is useless. •You surely know that Abraham our father was 21

22 justified by his deed, because he *offered his son Isaac on the altar?*[d] •There you see it: faith and deeds were working together; his faith became perfect by what he did.

23 This is what scripture really means when it says: *Abraham put his faith in God, and this was counted as making him justified;*[e] and that is why he was called 'the friend of God'.

24 You see now that it is by doing something good, and not only by believing,
25 that a man is justified. •There is another example of the same kind: Rahab the prostitute, justified by her deeds because she welcomed the messengers and
26 showed them a different way to leave. •A body dies when it is separated from the spirit, and in the same way faith is dead if it is separated from good deeds.

Uncontrolled language

1 **3** Only a few of you, my brothers, should be teachers, bearing in mind that those of us who teach can expect a stricter judgement.

2 After all, every one of us does something wrong, over and over again; the only man who could reach perfection would be someone who never said anything
3 wrong—he would be able to control every part of himself. •Once we put a bit into the horse's mouth, to make it do what we want, we have the whole animal
4 under our control. •Or think of ships: no matter how big they are, even if a gale is driving them, the man at the helm can steer them anywhere he likes by
5 controlling a tiny rudder. •So is the tongue only a tiny part of the body, but it can proudly claim that it does great things. Think how small a flame can set fire to a
6 huge forest; •the tongue is a flame like that. Among all the parts of the body, the tongue is a whole wicked world in itself: it infects the whole body; catching fire
7 itself from hell, it sets fire to the whole wheel of creation. •Wild animals and birds,
8 reptiles and fish can all be tamed by man, and often are; •but nobody can tame the
9 tongue—it is a pest that will not keep still, full of deadly poison. •We use it to bless the Lord and Father, but we also use it to curse men who are made in God's
10 image: •the blessing and the curse come out of the same mouth. My brothers,
11 this must be wrong—•does any water supply give a flow of fresh water and salt
12 water out of the same pipe? Can a fig tree give you olives, my brothers, or a vine give figs? No more can sea water give you fresh water.

Real wisdom and its opposite

13 If there are any wise or learned men among you, let them show it by their good
14 lives, with humility and wisdom in their actions. •But if at heart you have the bitterness of jealousy, or a self-seeking ambition, never make any claims for
15 yourself or cover up the truth with lies —•principles of this kind are not the wisdom that comes down from above: they are only earthly, animal and
16 devilish. •Wherever you find jealousy and ambition, you find disharmony, and
17 wicked things of every kind being done; •whereas the wisdom that comes down from above is essentially something pure; it also makes for peace, and is kindly and considerate; it is full of compassion and shows itself by doing good; nor is
18 there any trace of partiality or hypocrisy in it. •Peacemakers, when they work for peace, sow the seeds which will bear fruit in holiness.

Disunity among Christians

1 **4** Where do these wars and battles between yourselves first start? Isn't it precisely
2 in the desires fighting inside your own selves? •You want something and you haven't got it; so you are prepared to kill. You have an ambition that you cannot satisfy; so you fight to get your way by force. Why you don't have what you
3 want is because you don't pray for it; •when you do pray and don't get it, it

e. Si 5:11
2 a. Jewish Christians may still have been attending synagogues, or the writer may have adopted this word for the Christian assembly. **b.** Lv 19:18 **c.** Ex 20 **d.** Gn 22:9 **e.** Gn 15:6

is because you have not prayed properly, you have prayed for something to indulge your own desires.

You are as unfaithful as adulterous wives; don't you realise that making 4 the world your friend is making God your enemy? Anyone who chooses the world for his friend turns himself into God's enemy. •Surely you don't think scripture 5 is wrong when it says: the spirit which he sent to live in us wants us for himself alone? •But he has been even more generous to us, as scripture says: *God opposes* 6 *the proud but he gives generously to the humble.*ª •Give in to God, then; resist the 7 devil, and he will run away from you. •The nearer you go to God, the nearer he 8 will come to you. Clean your hands, you sinners, and clear your minds, you waverers. •Look at your wretched condition, and weep for it in misery; be 9 miserable instead of laughing, gloomy instead of happy. •Humble yourselves 10 before the Lord and he will lift you up.

Brothers, do not slander one another. Anyone who slanders a brother, or 11 condemns him, is speaking against the Law and condemning the Law. But if you condemn the Law, you have stopped keeping it and become a judge over it. There is only one lawgiver and he is the only judge and has the power to acquit 12 or to sentence. Who are you to give a verdict on your neighbour?

A warning for the rich and the self-confident

Here is the answer for those of you who talk like this: 'Today or tomorrow, 13 we are off to this or that town; we are going to spend a year there, trading, and make some money'. •You never know what will happen tomorrow: you are no 14 more than a mist that is here for a little while and then disappears. •The most 15 you should ever say is: 'If it is the Lord's will, we shall still be alive to do this or that'. •But how proud and sure of yourselves you are now! Pride of this kind is 16 always wicked. •Everyone who knows what is the right thing to do and doesn't 17 do it commits a sin.

5 Now an answer for the rich. Start crying, weep for the miseries that are 1 coming to you. •Your wealth is all rotting, your clothes are all eaten up by 2 moths. •All your gold and your silver are corroding away, and the same corrosion 3 will be your own sentence, and eat into your body. It was a burning fire that you stored up as your treasure for the last days. •Labourers mowed your fields, and 4 you cheated them—listen to the wages that you kept back, calling out; realise that the cries of the reapers have reached the ears of the Lord of hosts. •On earth 5 you have had a life of comfort and luxury; in the time of slaughter you went on eating to your heart's content. •It was you who condemned the innocent and 6 killed them; they offered you no resistance.

A final exhortation

Now be patient, brothers, until the Lord's coming. Think of a farmer: how 7 patiently he waits for the precious fruit of the ground until it has had the autumn rains and the spring rains! •You too have to be patient; do not lose heart, 8 because the Lord's coming will be soon. •Do not make complaints against one 9 another, brothers, so as not to be brought to judgement yourselves; the Judge is already to be seen waiting at the gates. •For your example, brothers, in sub- 10 mitting with patience, take the prophets who spoke in the name of the Lord; remember it is those who had endurance that we say are the blessed ones. You 11 have heard of the patience of Job, and understood the Lord's purpose, realising that *the Lord is kind and compassionate.*ª

Above all, my brothers, do not swear by heaven or by the earth, or use any 12 oaths at all. If you mean 'yes', you must say 'yes'; if you mean 'no', say 'no'. Otherwise you make yourselves liable to judgement.

If any one of you is in trouble, he should pray; if anyone is feeling happy, he 13 should sing a psalm. •If one of you is ill, he should send for the elders 14 of the church, and they must anoint him with oil in the name of the Lord and pray over him. •The prayer of faith will save the sick man and the Lord will raise 15

16 him up again; and if he has committed any sins, he will be forgiven. •So confess
your sins to one another, and pray for one another, and this will cure you; the
17 heartfelt prayer of a good man works very powerfully. •Elijah was a human
being like ourselves—he prayed hard for it not to rain, and no rain fell for
18 three-and-a-half years; •then he prayed again and the sky gave rain and the earth
gave crops.

19   My brothers, if one of you strays away from the truth, and another brings
20 him back to it,•he may be sure that anyone who can bring back a sinner from
the wrong way that he has taken will be saving a soul from death and *covering
up a great number of sins.*[b]

4 a. Pr 3:34 (LXX)
5 a. Ps 103:8   b. Pr 10:12

1 PETER

THE FIRST LETTER OF PETER

Address. Greetings

1 Peter, apostle of Jesus Christ, sends greetings to all those living among 1
foreigners in the Dispersion of Pontus, Galatia, Cappadocia, Asia and
Bithynia, who have been chosen, •by the provident purpose of God the Father, 2
to be made holy by the Spirit, obedient to Jesus Christ and sprinkled with his
blood. Grace and peace be with you more and more.

Introduction. The salvation of Christians

Blessed be God the Father of our Lord Jesus Christ, who in his great mercy 3
has given us a new birth as his sons, by raising Jesus Christ from the dead, so that
we have a sure hope •and the promise of an inheritance that can never be spoilt 4
or soiled and never fade away, because it is being kept for you in the heavens.
Through your faith, God's power will guard you until the salvation which has 5
been prepared is revealed at the end of time. •This is a cause of great joy for you, 6
even though you may for a short time have to bear being plagued by all sorts of
trials; •so that, when Jesus Christ is revealed, your faith will have been tested and 7
proved like gold—only it is more precious than gold, which is corruptible even
though it bears testing by fire—and then you will have praise and glory and
honour. •You did not see him, yet you love him; and still without seeing him, 8
you are already filled with a joy so glorious that it cannot be described, because
you believe; •and you are sure of the end to which your faith looks forward, that 9
is, the salvation of your souls.

The hope of the prophets

It was this salvation that the prophets were looking and searching so hard for; 10
their prophecies were about the grace which was to come to you. •The Spirit of 11
Christ which was in them foretold the sufferings of Christ and the glories that
would come after them, and they tried to find out at what time and in
what circumstances all this was to be expected. •It was revealed to them that the 12
news they brought of all the things which have now been announced to you, by
those who preached to you the Good News through the Holy Spirit sent from
heaven, was for you and not for themselves. Even the angels long to catch a
glimpse of these things.

A call to sanctity and watchfulness

Free your minds, then, of encumbrances; control them, and put your trust 13
in nothing but the grace that will be given you when Jesus Christ is revealed.
Do not behave in the way that you liked to before you learnt the truth; make 14
a habit of obedience: •be holy in all you do, since it is the Holy One who has 15
called you, •and scripture says: *Be holy, for I am holy.*[a] 16
If you are acknowledging as your Father one who has no favourites and judges 17
everyone according to what he has done, you must be scrupulously careful as long

18 as you are living away from your home. •Remember, the ransom that was *paid*
   to free you[b] from the useless way of life your ancestors handed down was not paid
19 in anything corruptible, neither in *silver* nor gold, •but in the precious blood of a
20 lamb without spot or stain, namely Christ; •who, though known since before
   the world was made, has been revealed only in our time, the end of the ages, for
21 your sake. •Through him you now have faith in God, who raised him from the
   dead and gave him glory for that very reason—so that you would have faith and
   hope in God.

Love

22 You have been obedient to the truth and purified your souls until you can
   love like brothers, in sincerity; let your love for each other be real and from the
23 heart—•your new birth was not from any mortal seed but from the everlasting
24 word of the living and eternal God. •*All flesh is grass and its glory like the wild*
25 *flower's. The grass withers, the flower falls,* •*but the word of the Lord remains for*
   ever.[c] What is this word? It is the Good News that has been brought to you.

Integrity

1 2 Be sure, then, you are never spiteful, or deceitful, or hypocritical, or envious
2   and critical of each other. •You are new born, and, like babies, you should
   be hungry for nothing but milk—the spiritual honesty which will help you to
3 grow up to salvation—•now that you have *tasted the goodness of the Lord.*[a]

The new priesthood

4 He is the living stone, rejected by men but chosen by God and precious to him;
5 set yourselves close to him •so that you too, the holy priesthood that offers the
   spiritual sacrifices which Jesus Christ has made acceptable to God, may be living
6 stones making a spiritual house. •As scripture says: *See how I lay in Zion a precious*
   cornerstone that I have chosen and *the man who rests his trust on it will not be disap-*
7 *pointed.*[b] •That means that for you who are believers, it is precious; but for
8 unbelievers, *the stone rejected by the builders has proved to be the keystone,*[c] •*a*
   stone to stumble over, a rock to bring men down.[d] They stumble over it because they
   do not believe in the word; it was the fate in store for them.

9 But you are *a chosen race, a royal priesthood, a consecrated nation, a people set*
   apart[e] to sing the praises of God who called you out of the darkness into his
10 wonderful light. •Once you were *not a people*[f] at all and now you are the People
   of God; once you were *outside the mercy* and now *you have been given mercy.*

The obligations of Christians: towards pagans

11 I urge you, my dear people, while you are *visitors and pilgrims*[g] to keep your-
12 selves free from the selfish passions that attack the soul. •Always behave
   honourably among pagans so that they can see your good works for themselves
   and, when the day of reckoning comes, give thanks to God for the things which
   now make them denounce you as criminals.

Towards civil authority

13 For the sake of the Lord, accept the authority of every social institution: the
14 emperor, as the supreme authority, •and the governors as commissioned by him
15 to punish criminals and praise good citizenship. •God wants you to be good
16 citizens, so as to silence what fools are saying in their ignorance. •You are slaves
   of no one except God, so behave like free men, and never use your freedom as an
17 excuse for wickedness. •Have respect for everyone and love for our community;
   fear God and honour the emperor.

---

1 a. Lv 19:2   b. Is 52:3   c. Is 40:6-8
2 a. Ps 34:8   b. Is 28:16   c. Ps 18:22   d. Is 8:14   e. Is 43:20-21   f. Ho 1:9; the two
other quotations in this sentence are allusive references to Ho 2.   g. Ps 39:12

Towards masters

Slaves must be respectful and obedient to their masters, not only when they 18
are kind and gentle but also when they are unfair. •You see, there is some merit 19
in putting up with the pains of unearned punishment if it is done for the sake of
God •but there is nothing meritorious in taking a beating patiently if you have 20
done something wrong to deserve it. The merit, in the sight of God, is in bearing
it patiently when you are punished after doing your duty.

This, in fact, is what you were called to do, because Christ suffered for you 21
and left an example for you to follow the way he took. •He had not done anything 22
wrong, and *there had been no perjury in his mouth*.[h] •He was insulted and did not 23
retaliate with insults; when he was tortured he made no threats but he put his
trust in the righteous judge. •He was *bearing our faults* in his own body on the 24
cross, so that we might die to our faults and live for holiness; *through his wounds
you have been healed.* You had *gone astray like sheep* but now you have come •
back to the shepherd and guardian[i] of your souls.

In marriage

3 In the same way, wives should be obedient to their husbands. Then, if there 1
are some husbands who have not yet obeyed the word, they may find themselves won over, without a word spoken, by the way their wives behave, •when 2
they see how faithful and conscientious they are. •Do not dress up for show: 3
doing up your hair, wearing gold bracelets and fine clothes; •all this should be 4
inside, in a person's heart, imperishable: the ornament of a sweet and gentle
disposition—this is what is precious in the sight of God. •That was how the holy 5
women of the past dressed themselves attractively—they hoped in God and were
tender and obedient to their husbands; •like Sarah, who was obedient to Abraham, 6
and called him her *lord.* You are now her children, as long as you live good lives
and do not give way to fear or worry.

In the same way, husbands must always treat their wives with consideration 7
in their life together, respecting a woman as one who, though she may be the
weaker partner, is equally an heir to the life of grace. This will stop anything
from coming in the way of your prayers.

Towards the brothers

Finally: you should all agree among yourselves and be sympathetic; love the 8
brothers, have compassion and be self-effacing. •Never pay back one wrong 9
with another, or an angry word with another one; instead, pay back with a
blessing. That is what you are called to do, so that you inherit a blessing yourself.
Remember: *Anyone who wants to have a happy life and to enjoy prosperity must* 10
banish malice from his tongue, deceitful conversation from his lips; •he must never 11
yield to evil but must practise good; he must seek peace and pursue it. •Because the 12
*face of the Lord frowns on evil men, but the eyes of the Lord are turned towards the
virtuous.*[a]

In persecution

No one can hurt you if you are determined to do only what is right; •if you $^{13}_{14}$
do have to suffer for being good, you will count it a blessing. *There is no need to
be afraid or to worry about them.*[b] •Simply reverence the *Lord*[c] Christ in your 15
hearts, and always have your answer ready for people who ask you the reason for
the hope that you all have. •But give it with courtesy and respect and with a clear 16
conscience, so that those who slander you when you are living a good life in Christ
may be proved wrong in the accusations that they bring. •And if it is the will of 17
God that you should suffer, it is better to suffer for doing right than for doing
wrong.

The resurrection and 'the descent into hell'

18   Why, Christ himself, innocent though he was, had died once for sins, died for the guilty, to lead us to God. In the body he was put to death, in the spirit he was
19 raised to life, •and, in the spirit, he went to preach to the spirits in prison.
20 Now it was long ago, when Noah was still building that ark which saved only a small group of eight people 'by water', and when God was still waiting patiently,
21 that these spirits refused to believe. •That water is a type of the baptism which saves you now, and which is not the washing off of physical dirt but a pledge made to God from a good conscience, through the resurrection of Jesus Christ,
22 who has entered heaven and is at God's right hand, now that he has made the angels and Dominations and Powers his subjects.

4   Think of what Christ suffered in this life, and then arm yourselves with the same resolution that he had: anyone who in this life has bodily suffering has
2 broken with sin, •because for the rest of his life on earth he is not ruled by human
3 passions but only by the will of God. •You spent quite long enough in the past living the sort of life that pagans live, behaving indecently, giving way to your passions, drinking all the time, having wild parties and drunken orgies and
4 degrading yourselves by following false gods. •So people cannot understand why you no longer hurry off with them to join this flood which is rushing down to
5 ruin, and then they begin to spread libels about you. •They will have to answer
6 for it in front of the judge who is ready to judge the living and the dead. •And because he is their judge too, the dead had to be told the Good News as well, so that though, in their life on earth, they had been through the judgement that comes to all humanity, they might come to God's life in the spirit.

The revelation of Christ is close

7   Everything will soon come to an end, so, to pray better, keep a calm and sober
8 mind. •Above all, never let your love for each other grow insincere, since *love*
9 *covers over many a sin.*[a] •Welcome each other into your houses without grumbling.
10 Each one of you has received a special grace, so, like good stewards responsible
11 for all these different graces of God, put yourselves at the service of others. •If you are a speaker, speak in words which seem to come from God; if you are a helper, help as though every action was done at God's orders; so that in everything God may receive the glory, through Jesus Christ, since to him alone belong all glory and power for ever and ever. Amen.

Recapitulation

12   My dear people, you must not think it unaccountable that you should be tested
13 by fire. There is nothing extraordinary in what has happened to you. •If you can have some share in the sufferings of Christ, be glad, because you will enjoy a much
14 greater gladness when his glory is revealed. •It is a blessing for you when they insult you for bearing the name of Christ, because it means that you have the
15 Spirit of glory, the Spirit of God resting on you. •None of you should ever deserve
16 to suffer for being a murderer, a thief, a criminal or an informer; •but if anyone of you should suffer for being a Christian, then he is not to be ashamed of it; he
17 should thank God that he has been called one. •The time has come for the judgement to begin at the household of God; and if what we know now is only the beginning, what will it be when it comes down to those who refuse to believe God's
18 Good News? •*If it is hard for a good man to be saved, what will happen to the wicked*
19 *and to sinners?*[b] •So even those whom God allows to suffer must trust themselves to the constancy of the creator and go on doing good.

---

h. This quotation, and the others in this paragraph, are from Is 53.   i. *episcopos.*
3 a. Ps 34:12-16   b. Is 8:12-13 (LXX)   c. Pr 3:25
4 a. Pr 10:12   b. Pr 11:31 (LXX)

Instructions: to the elders

5 Now I have something to tell your elders: I am an elder myself, and a witness 1 to the sufferings of Christ, and with you I have a share in the glory that is to be revealed. •Be the shepherds of the flock of God that is entrusted to you: 2 watch over it, not simply as a duty but gladly, because God wants it; not for sordid money, but because you are eager to do it. •Never be a dictator over any 3 group that is put in your charge, but be an example that the whole flock can follow. •When the chief shepherd appears, you will be given the crown of 4 unfading glory.

To the faithful

To the rest of you I say: do what the elders tell you, and all wrap yourselves 5 in humility to be servants of each other, because *God refuses the proud and will always favour the humble.*[a] •Bow down, then, before the power of God now, and he 6 will raise you up on the appointed day; •*unload all your worries on to him,*[b] since 7 he is looking after you. •*Be calm but vigilant,* because your enemy the devil is 8 prowling round like a roaring lion, looking for someone to eat. •Stand up to him, 9 strong in faith and in the knowledge that your brothers all over the world are suffering the same things. •You will have to suffer only for a little while: the God of 10 all grace who called you to eternal glory in Christ will see that all is well again: he will confirm, strengthen and support you. •His power lasts for ever and ever. Amen. 11

Last words. Greetings

I write these few words to you through Silvanus, who is a brother I know I can 12 trust, to encourage you never to let go this true grace of God to which I bear witness.

Your sister in Babylon, who is with you among the chosen, sends you 13 greetings; so does my son, Mark.

Greet one another with a kiss of love. 14

Peace to you all who are in Christ.

5 a. Pr 3:34 (LXX)   b. Ps 55:22

2 PETER

THE SECOND LETTER OF PETER

Greetings

1 From Simeon Peter, servant and apostle of Jesus Christ; to all who treasure the same faith as ourselves, given through the righteousness of our God and ² saviour Jesus Christ. •May you have more and more grace and peace as you come to know our Lord more and more.

A call to Christian living, and its reward

3 By his divine power, he has given us all the things that we need for life and for true devotion, bringing us to know God himself, who has called us by his own ⁴ glory and goodness. •In making these gifts, he has given us the guarantee of something very great and wonderful to come: through them you will be able to share the divine nature and to escape corruption in a world that is sunk in vice. ⁵ But to attain this, you will have to do your utmost yourselves, adding goodness ⁶ to the faith that you have, understanding to your goodness, •self-control to your understanding, patience to your self-control, true devotion to your patience, ⁷ kindness towards your fellow men to your devotion, and, to this kindness, love. ⁸ If you have a generous supply of these, they will not leave you ineffectual or unproductive: they will bring you to a real knowledge of our Lord Jesus Christ. ⁹ But without them a man is blind or else short-sighted; he has forgotten how ¹⁰ his past sins were washed away. •Brothers, you have been called and chosen: work all the harder to justify it. If you do all these things there is no danger that you will ¹¹ ever fall away. •In this way you will be granted admittance into the eternal kingdom of our Lord and saviour Jesus Christ.

The apostolic witness

12 That is why I am continually recalling the same truths to you, even though you ¹³ already know them and firmly hold them. •I am sure it is my duty, as long as ¹⁴ I am in this tent, to keep stirring you up with reminders, •since I know the time for taking off this tent is coming soon, as our Lord Jesus Christ foretold to me. ¹⁵ And I shall take great care that after my own departure you will still have a means to recall these things to memory.
16 It was not any cleverly invented myths that we were repeating when we brought you the knowledge of the power and the coming of our Lord Jesus Christ; ¹⁷ we had seen his majesty for ourselves. •He was honoured and glorified by God the Father, when the Sublime Glory itself spoke to him and said, 'This is my Son, ¹⁸ the Beloved; he enjoys my favour'. •We heard this ourselves, spoken from heaven, when we were with him on the holy mountain.ᵃ

The value of prophecy

19 So we have confirmation of what was said in prophecies; and you will be right to depend on prophecy and take it as a lamp for lighting a way

1 a. At the transfiguration; Mt 17, Mk 9, Lk 9.

through the dark until the dawn comes and the morning star rises in your minds. At the same time, we must be most careful to remember that the interpretation 20 of scriptural prophecy is never a matter for the individual. •Why? Because no 21 prophecy ever came from man's initiative. When men spoke for God it was the Holy Spirit that moved them.

False teachers

2 As there were false prophets in the past history of our people, so you too will 1 have your false teachers, who will insinuate their own disruptive views and disown the Master who purchased their freedom. They will destroy themselves very quickly; •but there will be many who copy their shameful behaviour and the 2 Way of Truth will be brought into disrepute on their account. •They will eagerly 3 try to buy you for themselves with insidious speeches, but for them the Condemnation, pronounced so long ago, is at its work already, and Destruction is not asleep. •When angels sinned, God did not spare them: he sent them down to the 4 underworld and consigned them to the dark underground caves to be held there till the day of Judgement. •Nor did he spare the world in ancient times: it was 5 only Noah he saved, the preacher of righteousness, along with seven others, when he sent the Flood over a disobedient world. •The cities of Sodom and Gomorrah, 6 these too he condemned and reduced to ashes; he destroyed them completely, as a warning to anybody lacking reverence in the future; •he rescued Lot, however, 7 a holy man who had been sickened by the shameless way in which these vile people behaved—•for that holy man, living among them, was outraged in his good soul 8 by the crimes that he saw and heard of every day. •These are all examples of how 9 the Lord can rescue the good from the ordeal, and hold the wicked for their punishment until the day of Judgement, •especially those who are governed by 10 their corrupt bodily desires and have no respect for authority.

The punishment to come

Such self-willed people with no reverence are not afraid of offending against the glorious ones, •but the angels in their greater strength and power make no 11 complaint or accusation against them in front of the Lord. •All the same, these 12 people who only insult anything that they do not understand are not reasoning beings, but simply animals born to be caught and killed, and they will quite certainly destroy themselves by their own work of destruction, •and get their 13 reward of evil for the evil that they do. They are unsightly blots on your society: men whose only object is dissipation all day long, and they amuse themselves deceiving you even when they are your guests at a meal; •with their eyes always 14 looking for adultery; men with an infinite capacity for sinning, they will seduce any soul which is at all unstable. Greed is the one lesson their minds have learnt. They are under a curse. •They have left the right path and wandered off to follow 15 the path of Balaam son of Beor, who thought he could profit best by sinning, until he was called to order for his faults. The dumb donkey put a stop to that 16 prophet's madness when it talked like a man. •People like this are dried-up rivers,. 17 fogs swirling in the wind, and the dark underworld is the place reserved for them. With their high-flown talk, which is all hollow, they tempt back the ones who 18 have only just escaped from paganism, playing on their bodily desires with debaucheries. •They may promise freedom but they themselves are slaves, slaves 19 to corruption; because if anyone lets himself be dominated by anything, then he is a slave to it; •and anyone who has escaped the pollution of the world once 20 by coming to know our Lord and saviour Jesus Christ, and who then allows himself to be entangled by it a second time and mastered, will end up in a worse state than he began in. •It would even have been better for him never to have 21 learnt the way of holiness, than to know it and afterwards desert the holy rule that was entrusted to him. •What he has done is exactly as the proverb rightly 22 says: *The dog goes back to his own vomit*[a] and: When the sow has been washed, it wallows in the mud.

The Day of the Lord; the prophets and the apostles

1,2 3 My friends, this is my second letter to you, and in both of them I have tried to awaken a true understanding in you by giving you a reminder: •recalling to you what was said in the past by the holy prophets and the commandments of the Lord and saviour which you were given by the apostles.

3 We must be careful to remember that during the last days there are bound to be people who will be scornful, the kind who always please themselves what 4 they do, and they will make fun of the promise •and ask, 'Well, where is this coming? Everything goes on as it has since the Fathers died, as it has since it 5 began at the creation.' •They are choosing to forget that there were heavens at the beginning, and that the earth was formed by the word of God out of 6 water and between the waters, •so that the world of that time was destroyed by 7 being flooded by water. •But by the same word, the present sky and earth are destined for fire, and are only being reserved until Judgement day so that all sinners may be destroyed.

8 But there is one thing, my friends, that you must never forget: that with the Lord, 'a day' can mean a thousand years, and *a thousand years is like a day*.[a]
9 The Lord is not being slow to carry out his promises, as anybody else might be called slow; but he is being patient with you all, wanting nobody to be lost and 10 everybody to be brought to change his ways. •The Day of the Lord will come like a thief, and then with a roar the sky will vanish, the elements will catch fire and fall apart, the earth and all that it contains will be burnt up.

Conclusion and doxology

11 Since everything is coming to an end like this, you should be living holy and 12 saintly lives •while you wait and long for the Day of God to come, when the sky 13 will dissolve in flames and the elements melt in the heat. •What we are waiting for is what he promised: the new heavens and new earth, the place where right-14 eousness will be at home. •So then, my friends, while you are waiting, do your 15 best to live lives without spot or stain so that he will find you at peace. •Think of our Lord's patience as your opportunity to be saved: our brother Paul, who is so dear to us, told you this when he wrote to you with the wisdom that is his special 16 gift. •He always writes like this when he deals with this sort of subject, and this makes some points in his letter hard to understand; these are the points that uneducated and unbalanced people distort, in the same way as they distort the rest 17 of scripture—a fatal thing for them to do. •You have been warned about this, my friends; be careful not to get carried away by the errors of unprincipled 18 people, from the firm ground that you are standing on. •Instead, go on growing in the grace and in the knowledge of our Lord and saviour Jesus Christ. To him be glory, in time and in eternity. Amen.

2 a. Pr 26:11
3 a. Ps 90:4

1 JOHN

THE FIRST LETTER OF JOHN

INTRODUCTION

The incarnate Word

1 Something which has existed since the beginning,
that we have heard,
and we have seen with our own eyes;
that we have watched
and touched with our hands:
the Word, who is life—
this is our subject.
That life was made visible: 2
we saw it and we are giving our testimony,
telling you of the eternal life
which was with the Father and has been made visible to us.
What we have seen and heard   3
we are telling you
so that you too may be in union with us,
as we are in union
with the Father
and with his Son Jesus Christ.
We are writing this to you to make our own joy complete.   4

I. WALK IN THE LIGHT

This is what we have heard from him,   5
and the message that we are announcing to you:
God is light; there is no darkness in him at all.
If we say that we are in union with God *a*   6
while we are living in darkness,
we are lying because we are not living the truth.
But if we live our lives in the light,   7
as he is in the light,
we are in union with one another,
and the blood of Jesus, his Son,
purifies us from all sin.

First condition: break with sin

If we say we have no sin in us,   8
we are deceiving ourselves
and refusing to admit the truth;
but if we acknowledge our sins,   9

then God who is faithful and just
will forgive our sins and purify us
from everything that is wrong.

10 To say that we have never sinned
is to call God a liar
and to show that his word is not in us.

1 2 I am writing this, my children,
to stop you sinning;
but if anyone should sin,
we have our advocate with the Father,
Jesus Christ, who is just;

2   he is the sacrifice that takes our sins away,
and not only ours,
but the whole world's.

Second condition: keep the commandments, especially the law of love

3   We can be sure that we know God
only by keeping his commandments.

4   Anyone who says, 'I know him',
and does not keep his commandments,
is a liar,
refusing to admit the truth.

5   But when anyone does obey what he has said,
God's love comes to perfection in him.
We can be sure
that we are in God

6   only when the one who claims to be living in him
is living the same kind of life as Christ lived.

7   My dear people,
this is not a new commandment that I am writing to tell you,
but an old commandment
that you were given from the beginning,
the original commandment which was the message brought to you.

8   Yet in another way, what I am writing to you,
and what is being carried out in your lives as it was in his,
is a new commandment;
because the night is over
and the real light is already shining.

9   Anyone who claims to be in the light
but hates his brother
is still in the dark.

10   But anyone who loves his brother is living in the light
and need not be afraid of stumbling;

11   unlike the man who hates his brother and is in the darkness,
not knowing where he is going,
because it is too dark to see.

Third condition: detachment from the world

12   I am writing to you, my own children,
whose sins have already been forgiven through his name;

13   I am writing to you, fathers,
who have come to know the one
who has existed since the beginning;

---

1 a. In the translation, 'God' or 'Christ' has been used in several places, where the Greek has a simple pronoun, in order to make the writer's meaning clear.

I am writing to you, young men,
who have already overcome the Evil One;
I have written to you, children,   14
because you already know the Father;
I have written to you, fathers,
because you have come to know the one
who has existed since the beginning;
I have written to you, young men,
because you are strong and God's word has made its home in you,
and you have overcome the Evil One.
You must not love this passing world   15
or anything that is in the world.
The love of the Father cannot be
in any man who loves the world,
because nothing the world has to offer   16
—the sensual body,
the lustful eye,
pride in possessions—
could ever come from the Father
but only from the world;
and the world, with all it craves for,   17
is coming to an end;
but anyone who does the will of God
remains for ever.

Fourth condition: be on guard against the enemies of Christ

Children, these are the last days;   18
you were told that an Antichrist must come,
and now several antichrists have already appeared;
we know from this that these are the last days.
Those rivals of Christ came out of our own number, but they had   19
    never really belonged;
if they had belonged, they would have stayed with us;
but they left us, to prove that not one of them
ever belonged to us.
But you have been anointed by the Holy One,   20
and have all received the knowledge.
It is not because you do not know the truth that I am writing to you 21
but rather because you know it already
and know that no lie can come from the truth.
The man who denies that Jesus is the Christ—   22
he is the liar,
he is Antichrist;
and he is denying the Father as well as the Son,
because no one who has the Father can deny the Son,   23
and to acknowledge the Son is to have the Father as well.
Keep alive in yourselves what you were taught in the beginning: 24
as long as what you were taught in the beginning is alive in you,
you will live in the Son
and in the Father;
and what is promised to you by his own promise   25
is eternal life.
This is all that I am writing to you about the people who are   26
    trying to lead you astray.
But you have not lost the anointing that he gave you,   27
and you do not need anyone to teach you;

the anointing he gave teaches you everything;
you are anointed with truth, not with a lie,
and as it has taught you, so you must stay in him.

28 Live in Christ, then, my children,
so that if he appears, we may have full confidence,
and not turn from him in shame
at his coming.

29 You know that God is righteous—
then you must recognise that everyone whose life is righteous
has been begotten by him.

II. LIVE AS GOD'S CHILDREN

1 3 Think of the love that the Father has lavished on us,
by letting us be called God's children;
and that is what we are.
Because the world refused to acknowledge him,
therefore it does not acknowledge us.

2 My dear people, we are already the children of God
but what we are to be in the future has not yet been revealed;
all we know is, that when it is revealed
we shall be like him
because we shall see him as he really is.

First condition: break with sin

3 Surely everyone who entertains this hope
must purify himself, must try to be as pure as Christ.

4 Anyone who sins at all
breaks the law,
because to sin is to break the law.

5 Now you know that he appeared in order to abolish sin,
and that in him there is no sin;

6 anyone who lives in God does not sin,
and anyone who sins
has never seen him or known him.

7 My children, do not let anyone lead you astray:
to live a holy life
is to be holy just as he is holy;

8 to lead a sinful life is to belong to the devil,
since the devil was a sinner from the beginning.
It was to undo all that the devil has done
that the Son of God appeared.

9 No one who has been begotten by God sins;
because God's seed remains inside him,
he cannot sin when he has been begotten by God.

Second condition: keep the commandments, especially the law of love

10 In this way we distinguish the children of God
from the children of the devil:
anybody not living a holy life
and not loving his brother
is no child of God's.

11 This is the message
as you heard it from the beginning:
that we are to love one another;

not to be like Cain, who belonged to the Evil One   12
and cut his brother's throat;
cut his brother's throat simply for this reason,
that his own life was evil and his brother lived a good life.
You must not be surprised, brothers, when the world hates you;   13
we have passed out of death and into life,   14
and of this we can be sure
because we love our brothers.
If you refuse to love, you must remain dead;   15
to hate your brother is to be a murderer,
and murderers, as you know, do not have eternal life in them.
This has taught us love—   16
that he gave up his life for us;
and we, too, ought to give up our lives for our brothers.
If a man who was rich enough in this world's goods   17
saw that one of his brothers was in need,
but closed his heart to him,
how could the love of God be living in him?
My children,   18
our love is not to be just words or mere talk,
but something real and active;
only by this can we be certain   19
that we are children of the truth
and be able to quieten our conscience in his presence,
whatever accusations it may raise against us,   20
because God is greater than our conscience and he knows everything.
My dear people,   21
if we cannot be condemned by our own conscience,
we need not be afraid in God's presence,
and whatever we ask him,   22
we shall receive,
because we keep his commandments
and live the kind of life that he wants.
His commandments are these: 23
that we believe in the name of his Son Jesus Christ
and that we love one another
as he told us to.
Whoever keeps his commandments   24
lives in God and God lives in him.
We know that he lives in us
by the Spirit that he has given us.

**Third condition: be on guard against the enemies of Christ
and against the world**

4 It is not every spirit, my dear people, that you can trust;   1
test them, to see if they come from God;
there are many false prophets, now, in the world.
You can tell the spirits that come from God by this: 2
every spirit which acknowledges that Jesus the Christ has come
     in the flesh
is from God;
but any spirit which will not say this of Jesus   3
is not from God,
but is the spirit of Antichrist,
whose coming you were warned about.
Well, now he is here, in the world.

4   Children,
     you have already overcome these false prophets,
     because you are from God and you have in you
     one who is greater than anyone in this world;

5   as for them, they are of the world,
     and so they speak the language of the world
     and the world listens to them.

6   But we are children of God,
     and those who know God listen to us;
     those who are not of God refuse to listen to us.
     This is how we can tell
     the spirit of truth from the spirit of falsehood.

III. LOVE AND FAITH

Love

7   My dear people,
     let us love one another
     since love comes from God
     and everyone who loves is begotten by God and knows God.

8   Anyone who fails to love can never have known God,
     because God is love.

9   God's love for us was revealed
     when God sent into the world his only Son
     so that we could have life through him;

10   this is the love I mean:
     not our love for God,
     but God's love for us when he sent his Son
     to be the sacrifice that takes our sins away.

11   My dear people,
     since God has loved us so much,
     we too should love one another.

12   No one has ever seen God;
     but as long as we love one another
     God will live in us
     and his love will be complete in us.

13   We can know that we are living in him
     and he is living in us
     because he lets us share his Spirit.

14   We ourselves saw and we testify
     that the Father sent his Son
     as saviour of the world.

15   If anyone acknowledges that Jesus is the Son of God,
     God lives in him, and he in God.

16   We ourselves have known and put our faith in
     God's love towards ourselves.
     God is love
     and anyone who lives in love lives in God,
     and God lives in him.

17   Love will come to its perfection in us
     when we can face the day of Judgement without fear;
     because even in this world
     we have become as he is.

18   In love there can be no fear,
     but fear is driven out by perfect love:

because to fear is to expect punishment,
and anyone who is afraid is still imperfect in love.
We are to love, then,   19
because he loved us first.
Anyone who says, 'I love God',   20
and hates his brother,
is a liar,
since a man who does not love the brother that he can see
cannot love God, whom he has never seen.
So this is the commandment that he has given us,   21
that anyone who loves God must also love his brother.

5

Whoever believes that Jesus is the Christ   1
has been begotten by God;
and whoever loves the Father that begot him
loves the child whom he begets.
We can be sure that we love God's children   2
if we love God himself and do what he has commanded us;
this is what loving God is—   3
keeping his commandments;
and his commandments are not difficult,   4
because anyone who has been begotten by God
has already overcome the world;
this is the victory over the world—
our faith.

Faith

Who can overcome the world?   5
Only the man who believes that Jesus is the Son of God:
Jesus Christ who came by water and blood,^a   6
not with water only,
but with water and blood;
with the Spirit as another witness—
since the Spirit is the truth—
so that there are three witnesses,   7
the Spirit, the water and the blood,   8
and all three of them agree.
We accept the testimony of human witnesses,   9
but God's testimony is much greater,
and this is God's testimony,
given as evidence for his Son.
Everybody who believes in the Son of God   10
has this testimony inside him;
and anyone who will not believe God
is making God out to be a liar,
because he has not trusted
the testimony God has given about his Son.
This is the testimony: 11
God has given us eternal life
and this life is in his Son;
anyone who has the Son has life,   12
anyone who does not have the Son does not have life.

Conclusion

I have written all this to you   13
so that you who believe in the name of the Son of God
may be sure that you have eternal life.

ENDING

Prayer for sinners

14 We are quite confident that if we ask him for anything,
and it is in accordance with his will,
he will hear us;

15 and, knowing that whatever we may ask, he hears us,
we know that we have already been granted what we asked of him.

16 If anybody sees his brother commit a sin
that is not a deadly sin,
he has only to pray, and God will give life to the sinner
—not those who commit a deadly sin;
for there is a sin that is death,
and I will not say that you must pray about that.

17 Every kind of wrong-doing is sin,
but not all sin is deadly.

Summary of the letter

18 We know that anyone who has been begotten by God
does not sin,
because the begotten Son of God protects him,
and the Evil One does not touch him.

19 We know that we belong to God,
but the whole world lies in the power of the Evil One.

20 We know, too, that the Son of God has come,
and has given us the power
to know the true God.
We are in the true God,
as we are in his Son, Jesus Christ.
This is the true God,
this is eternal life.

21 Children, be on your guard against false gods.

---

5 a. The water and the blood from the side of Jesus, Jn 19:34, are here used as figures of his 'coming' to all Christians, through the water of baptism and through his sacrificial death.

2 JOHN

THE SECOND LETTER OF JOHN

From the Elder: my greetings to the Lady, the chosen one,*a* and to her 1
children, she whom I love in the truth—and I am not the only one, for so do all
who have come to know the truth—•because of the truth that lives in us and will 2
be with us for ever. •In our life of truth and love, we shall have grace, mercy and 3
peace from God the Father and from Jesus Christ, the Son of the Father.

The law of love

It has given me great joy to find that your children have been living the life of 4
truth as we were commanded by the Father. •I am writing now, dear lady, not to 5
give you any new commandment, but the one which we were given at the beginning, and to plead: let us love one another.

To love is to live according to his commandments: this is the commandment 6
which you have heard since the beginning, to live a life of love.

The enemies of Christ

There are many deceivers about in the world, refusing to admit that Jesus 7
Christ has come in the flesh. They are the Deceiver; they are the Antichrist.
Watch yourselves, or all our work will be lost and not get the reward it deserves. 8
If anybody does not keep within the teaching of Christ but goes beyond it, he 9
cannot have God with him: only those who keep to what he taught can have the
Father and the Son with them. •If anyone comes to you bringing a different 10
doctrine, you must not receive him in your house or even give him a greeting.
To greet him would make you a partner in his wicked work. 11

There are several things I have to tell you, but I have thought it best not to 12
trust them to paper and ink. I hope instead to visit you and talk to you personally,
so that our joy may be complete.

Greetings to you from the children of your sister,*b* the chosen one. 13

---

1 a. The local church to which the letter is addressed.   **b.** The local church from which the
letter is sent.

3 JOHN

THE THIRD LETTER OF JOHN

1 From the Elder: greetings to my dear friend Gaius, whom I love in the truth.
2 My dear friend, I hope everything is going happily with you and that you are as
3 well physically as you are spiritually. •It was a great joy to me when some brothers.
came and told of your faithfulness to the truth, and of your life in the truth.
4 It is always my greatest joy to hear that my children are living according to
the truth.
5 My friend, you have done faithful work in looking after these brothers, even
6 though they were complete strangers to you. •They are a proof to the whole
Church of your charity and it would be a very good thing if you could help them
7 on their journey in a way that God would approve. •It was entirely for the sake
of the name that they set out, without depending on the pagans for anything;
8 it is our duty to welcome men of this sort and contribute our share to their work
for the truth.

Beware of the example of Diotrephes

9 I have written a note for the members of the church, but Diotrephes, who
10 seems to enjoy being in charge of it, refuses to accept us. •So if I come I shall
tell everyone how he has behaved, and about the wicked accusations he has been
circulating against us. As if that were not enough, he not only refuses to welcome
our brothers, but prevents the other people who would have liked to from doing
11 it, and expels them from the church. •My dear friend, never follow such a bad
example, but keep following the good one; anyone who does what is right is a
child of God, but the person who does what is wrong has never seen God.

Commendation of Demetrius

12 Demetrius has been approved by everyone, and indeed by the truth itself.
We too will vouch for him and you know that our testimony is true.

Epilogue

13 There were several things I had to tell you but I would rather not trust them
14 to pen and ink. •However, I hope to see you soon and talk to you personally.
15 Peace be with you; greetings from your friends; greet each of our friends by name.

THE LETTER OF
JUDE

Address

From Jude, servant of Jesus Christ and brother of James; to those who are 1
called, to those who are dear to God the Father and kept safe for Jesus Christ,
wishing you all mercy and peace and love. 2

The reason for this letter

My dear friends, at a time when I was eagerly looking forward to writing to 3
you about the salvation that we all share, I have been forced to write to you
now and appeal to you to fight hard for the faith which has been once and for all
entrusted to the saints. •Certain people have infiltrated among you, and they 4
are the ones you had a warning about, in writing, long ago, when they were
condemned for denying all religion, turning the grace of our God into immorality,
and rejecting our only Master and Lord, Jesus Christ.

The false teachers: the certainty of their punishment

I should like to remind you—though you have already learnt it once and for 5
all—how the Lord rescued the nation from Egypt, but afterwards he still
destroyed the men who did not trust him. •Next let me remind you of the angels 6
who had supreme authority but did not keep it and left their appointed sphere;[a]
he has kept them down in the dark, in spiritual chains, to be judged on the great
day. •The fornication of Sodom and Gomorrah and the other nearby towns was 7
equally unnatural, and it is a warning to us that they are paying for their crimes
in eternal fire.

Their violent language

Nevertheless, these people are doing the same: in their delusions they not 8
only defile their bodies and disregard authority, but abuse the glorious angels
as well. •Not even the archangel Michael, when he was engaged in argument 9
with the devil about the corpse of Moses, dared to denounce him in the language
of abuse; all he said was, 'Let the Lord correct you'. •But these people abuse 10
anything they do not understand; and the only things they do understand—just
by nature like unreasoning animals—will turn out to be fatal to them.

Their vicious behaviour

May they get what they deserve, because they have followed Cain; they have 11
rushed to make the same mistake as Balaam and for the same reward; they have
rebelled just as Korah did—and share the same fate. •They are a dangerous 12
obstacle to your community meals, coming for the food and quite shamelessly
only looking after themselves. They are like clouds blown about by the winds and
bringing no rain, or like barren trees which are then uprooted in the winter and so
are twice dead; •like wild sea waves capped with shame as if with foam; or like 13
shooting stars bound for an eternity of black darkness. •It was with them in 14

mind that Enoch, the seventh patriarch from Adam, made his prophecy when he
said, 'I tell you, the Lord will come with his saints in their tens of thousands,
15 to pronounce judgement on all mankind and to sentence the wicked for all the
wicked things they have done, and for all the defiant things said against him by
16 irreligious sinners'. •They are mischief-makers, grumblers governed only by
their own desires, with *mouths full of boastful talk*, ready with flattery for other
people when they see some advantage in it.

A warning

17 But remember, my dear friends, what the apostles of our Lord Jesus Christ
18 told you to expect. •'At the end of time,' they told you 'there are going to be
people who sneer at religion and follow nothing but their own desires for
19 wickedness.' •These unspiritual and selfish people are nothing but mischief-
makers.

The duties of love

20 But you, my dear friends, must use your most holy faith as your foundation
21 and build on that, praying in the Holy Spirit; •keep yourselves within the love
of God and wait for the mercy of our Lord Jesus Christ to give you eternal life.
22/23 When there are some who have doubts, reassure them; •when there are some
to be saved from the fire, pull them out; but there are others to whom you must
be kind with great caution, keeping your distance even from outside clothing
which is contaminated by vice.

Doxology

24 Glory be to him who can keep you from falling and bring you safe to his
25 glorious presence, innocent and happy. •To God, the only God, who saves us
through Jesus Christ our Lord, be the glory, majesty, authority and power, which
he had before time began, now and for ever. Amen.

a. Briefly mentioned in Gn 6:1-2, but elaborated in *The Book of Enoch*.

INTRODUCTION TO
THE BOOK OF REVELATION

A 'Revelation' (called *Apocalypse*, from the Greek term) is a distinct literary form; apocalyptic writing was very popular in some Jewish circles at the beginning of the Christian era. The framework of a Revelation is always a vision of hidden supernatural events; the language in which the vision is described is richly symbolic and so allusive that the message can be interpreted in more ways than one.

Thus the Book of Revelation is not to be accepted simply as an allegory which can be directly translated into other terms. It contains the author's vision of heaven and of the vindication of the Christian martyrs in the world to come, but it must be understood first and foremost as a tract for the times, written to increase the hope and determination of the Church on earth in a period of disturbance and bitter persecution, and prophesying the certain downfall and destruction of the Roman imperial power. The imagery, largely drawn from the Old Testament, especially Daniel, allows the author to allude to the enemy, Rome, under the disguise of the old enemy, Babylon; and to present the happenings of his own day, seen by their reflections in the heavens, as recapitulations or fulfilments of the great events of Israel's past.

The text contains difficulties: there are repetitions and interruptions, and there are passages out of context. One promising hypothesis is that the strictly prophetic part of the book is made up of two different 'apocalypses' written at different times and later conflated. The author cannot be identified with the author of the Gospel according to John, but we can say that the book was written inside the evangelist's immediate circle and is pervaded by his doctrine. Its date is generally estimated as A.D. 95, but there are some who believe that parts, at least, were composed as early as Nero's time, shortly before A.D. 70.

THE BOOK OF
REVELATION

Prologue

1 This is the revelation given by God to Jesus Christ so that he could tell his
servants about the *things which are* now *to take place*[a] very soon; he sent his
2 angel to make it known to his servant John, •and John has written down
everything he saw and swears it is the word of God guaranteed by Jesus Christ.
3 Happy the man who reads this prophecy, and happy those who listen to him, if
they treasure all that it says, because the Time is close.

I. THE LETTERS TO THE CHURCHES OF ASIA

Address and greeting[b]

4 From John, to the seven churches of Asia: grace and peace to you from him
who is, who was, and who is to come, from the seven spirits in his presence before
5 his throne, •and from Jesus Christ, *the faithful witness, the First-born* from the
dead, *the Ruler of the kings of the earth.* He loves us and has washed away our
6 sins with his blood, •and made us a *line of kings, priests to serve* his God and
7 Father; to him, then, be glory and power for ever and ever. Amen. •It is he who
is coming on the clouds; everyone will see him, even *those who pierced
him,* and *all the races of the earth will mourn over him.* This is the truth. Amen.
8 'I am the Alpha and the Omega' says the Lord God, who is, who was, and who
is to come, the Almighty.

The beginning of the vision

9 My name is John, and through our union in Jesus I am your brother and share
your sufferings, your kingdom, and all you endure. I was on the island of Patmos[c]
10 for having preached God's word and witnessed for Jesus; •it was the Lord's day
and the Spirit possessed me, and I heard a voice behind me, shouting like
11 a trumpet, •'Write down all that you see in a book, and send it to the seven
churches of Ephesus, Smyrna, Pergamum, Thyatira, Sardis, Philadelphia and
12 Laodicea'. •I turned round to see who had spoken to me, and when I turned
13 I saw seven golden lamp-stands •and, surrounded by them, a figure *like a Son
14 of man,*[d] dressed in a long robe tied at the waist with a *golden girdle.* •*His head*
and *his hair* were *white as white wool* or as snow, *his eyes* like a *burning* flame,
15 *his feet like burnished bronze* when it has been refined in a furnace, and *his voice*

---

1 a. Dn 2:28   **b.** This section contains many O.T. allusions to the time of the Messiah.
The five direct quotations printed in italic are from: Ps 89:37,27; Is 55:4; Ex 19:6; Dn 7:13;
and Zc 12:10,14.   **c.** Patmos (10m. × 5m.) was used by the Romans as a penal colony.   **d.** The
messianic figure in Dn; the descriptive quotations which follow are from Dn 7 and 10.

like the sound of the ocean.[e] •In his right hand he was holding seven stars, out of 16 his mouth came a sharp sword, double-edged, and his face was like the sun shining with all its force.

When I saw him, I fell in a dead faint at his feet, but he touched me with his 17 right hand and said, 'Do not be afraid; it is I, *the First and the Last;* I am the Living One, •I was dead and now I am to live for ever and ever, and I hold the 18 keys of death and of the underworld. •Now write down all that you see of present 19 happenings and *things that are still to come.*[f] •The secret of the seven stars you 20 have seen in my right hand, and of the seven golden lamp-stands is this: the seven stars are the angels of the seven churches, and the seven lamp-stands are the seven churches themselves.

1. Ephesus

2 'Write to the angel of the church in Ephesus and say, "Here is the message 1 of the one who holds the seven stars in his right hand and who lives surrounded by the seven golden lamp-stands: •I know all about you: how hard 2 you work and how much you put up with. I know you cannot stand wicked men, and how you tested the impostors who called themselves apostles and proved they were liars. •I know, too, that you have patience, and have suffered for my 3 name without growing tired. •Nevertheless, I have this complaint to make; 4 you have less love now than you used to. •Think where you were before you fell; 5 repent, and do as you used to at first, or else, if you will not repent, I shall come to you and take your lamp-stand from its place. •It is in your favour, nevertheless, 6 that you loathe as I do what the Nicolaitans are doing. •If anyone has ears 7 to hear, let him listen to what the Spirit is saying to the churches: those who prove victorious I will feed *from the tree of life set in* God's *paradise.*"[a]

2. Smyrna

'Write to the angel of the church in Smyrna and say, "Here is the message of 8 *the First* and *the Last*, who was dead and has come to life again: •I know the trials 9 you have had, and how poor you are—though you are rich— and the slanderous accusations that have been made by the people who profess to be Jews but are really members of the synagogue of Satan. •Do not be afraid of the sufferings 10 that are coming to you: I tell you, the devil is going to send some of you to prison *to test you*, and you must face an ordeal for *ten days.*[b] Even if you have to die, keep faithful, and I will give you the crown of life for your prize. •If anyone has 11 ears to hear, let him listen to what the Spirit is saying to the churches: for those who prove victorious there is nothing to be afraid of in the second death."

3. Pergamum

'Write to the angel of the church in Pergamum and say, "Here is the message 12 of the one who has the sharp sword, double-edged: •I know where you live, 13 in the place where Satan is enthroned, and that you still hold firmly to my name, and did not disown your faith in me even when my faithful witness, Antipas, was killed in your own town, where Satan lives.[c]

Nevertheless, I have one or two complaints to make: some of you are 14 followers of Balaam, who taught Balak to set a trap for the Israelites so that they committed adultery by eating food that had been sacrificed to idols; •and 15 among you, too, there are some as bad who accept what the Nicolaitans teach. You must repent, or I shall soon come to you and attack these people with the 16 sword out of my mouth. •If anyone has ears to hear, let him listen to what the 17 Spirit is saying to the churches: to those who prove victorious I will give the hidden manna and a white stone[d]—a stone with *a new name* written on it, known only to the man who receives it."

4. Thyatira

'Write to the angel of the church in Thyatira and say, "Here is the message 18 of the Son of God who has eyes like a burning flame and feet like burnished

19 bronze: •I know all about you and how charitable you are; I know your faith and
devotion and how much you put up with, and I know how you are still making
20 progress. •Nevertheless, I have a complaint to make: you are encouraging the
woman Jezebel[e] who claims to be a prophetess, and by her teaching she is luring
my servants away to commit the adultery of eating food which has been sacrificed
21 to idols. •I have given her time to reform but she is not willing to change her
22 adulterous life. •Now I am consigning her to bed, and all her partners in adultery
to troubles that will test them severely, unless they repent of their practices;
23 and I will see that her children die, so that all the churches realise that it is I who
search heart and loins and give each one of you what your behaviour deserves.[f]
24 But on the rest of you in Thyatira, all of you who have not accepted this teaching
or learnt the secrets of Satan, as they are called, I am not laying any special
25
26 duty; •but hold firmly on to what you already have until I come. •To those who
prove victorious, and keep working for me until the end, *I will give* the
27
28 authority over *the pagans*[g] •which I myself have been given by my Father, *to rule
them with an iron sceptre and shatter them like earthenware.* And I will give him
29 the Morning Star.[h] •If anyone has ears to hear, let him listen to what the Spirit
is saying to the churches."

5. Sardis

1 3 'Write to the angel of the church in Sardis and say, "Here is the message
of the one who holds the seven spirits of God and the seven stars: I know all
2 about you: how you are reputed to be alive and yet are dead. •Wake up; revive
what little you have left: it is dying fast. So far I have failed to notice anything in
3 the way you live that my God could possibly call perfect, •and yet do you
remember how eager you were when you first heard the message? Hold on to that.
Repent. If you do not wake up, I shall come to you like a thief, without telling
4 you at what hour to expect me. •There are a few in Sardis, it is true, who have
kept their robes from being dirtied, and they are fit to come with me, dressed
5 in white. •Those who prove victorious will be dressed, like these, in white robes;
I shall not blot their names out of the book of life, but acknowledge their names
6 in the presence of my Father and his angels. •If anyone has ears to hear, let him
listen to what the Spirit is saying to the churches."

6. Philadelphia

7 'Write to the angel of the church in Philadelphia and say, "Here is the message
of the holy and faithful one who *has the key of David,* so that *when he opens,*
8 *nobody can close, and when he closes, nobody can open:*[a] •I know all about you;
and now I have opened in front of you a door that nobody will be able to close—
and I know that though you are not very strong, you have kept my commandments
9 and not disowned my name. •Now I am going to make the synagogue of
Satan—those who profess to be Jews, but are liars, because they are no such
thing—I will make them come and *fall at your feet*[b] and admit that *you are* the
10 people *that I love.*[c] •Because you have kept my commandment to endure trials,
I will keep you safe in the time of trial which is going to come for the whole world,
11 to test the people of the world. •Soon I shall be with you: hold firmly to what
12 you already have, and let nobody take your prize away from you. •Those who
prove victorious I will make into pillars in the sanctuary of my God, and they
will stay there for ever; I will inscribe on them the name of my God and the

e. Ezk 43:2   f. Dn 2:28
2 a. Gn 2:9   b. I.e. of short duration.   c. I.e. 'where emperor-worship is practised.'
d. The manna hidden by Jeremiah (2 M 2:4-8), to be the food of those who are saved in the
heavenly kingdom; the white stone is a badge or token of admittance or membership.
e. By this name the writer is indicating a prophetess of the Nicolaitan sect.   f. Jr 11:20
g. Ps 2:8-9   h. Symbol of power and thus of the resurrection.
3 a. Is 22:22   b. Is 45:14   c. Is 43:4

name of the city of my God, the new Jerusalem which comes down from my God
in heaven, and my own new name as well. •If anyone has ears to hear, let him 13
listen to what the Spirit is saying to the churches."

7. Laodicea

'Write to the angel of the church in Laodicea and say, "Here is the message of 14
the Amen, the faithful, the true witness, the ultimate source of God's creation:
I know all about you: how you are neither cold nor hot. I wish you were one or 15
the other, •but since you are neither, but only lukewarm, I will spit you out of my 16
mouth. •You say to yourself, 'I am rich, I have made a fortune, and have 17
everything I want', never realising that you are wretchedly and pitiably poor, and
blind and naked too. •I warn you, buy from me the gold that has been tested in 18
the fire to make you really rich, and white robes to clothe you and cover your
shameful nakedness, and eye ointment to put on your eyes so that you are able
to see. •I *am* the one *who reproves and disciplines all those he loves:*[a] so repent 19
in real earnest. •Look, I am standing at the door, knocking. If one of you hears 20
me calling and opens the door, I will come in to share his meal, side by side with
him. •Those who prove victorious I will allow to share my throne, just as I was 21
victorious myself and took my place with my Father on his throne. •If anyone has 22
ears to hear, let him listen to what the Spirit is saying to the churches."'

II. THE PROPHETIC VISIONS

A. THE PRELUDE TO THE GREAT DAY

God entrusts the future of the world to the Lamb

4 Then, in my vision, I saw a door open in heaven and heard the same voice 1
speaking to me, the voice like a trumpet, saying, 'Come up here: I will show
you *what is to come* in the future'. •With that, the Spirit possessed me and I saw 2
a throne standing in heaven, and the *One* who was *sitting on the throne*, •and 3
the Person sitting there looked like a diamond and a ruby. There was a rainbow
encircling the throne, and this looked like an emerald.[a] •Round the throne in a 4
circle were twenty-four thrones, and on them I saw twenty-four elders sitting,
dressed in white robes with golden crowns on their heads. •Flashes of lightning 5
were coming from the throne, and the sound of peals of thunder, and in front
of the throne there were seven flaming lamps burning, the seven Spirits of
God. •Between the throne and myself was a sea that seemed to be made of glass, 6
like crystal. *In the centre,* grouped round the throne itself, were *four animals*[b]
with many eyes, in front and behind. •*The first* animal was like *a lion, the second* 7
like *a bull, the third* animal had *a human face,* and *the fourth* animal was like
a flying *eagle.* •*Each* of the four animals had *six wings* and *had eyes all the way* 8
round as well as inside; and day and night they never stopped singing:

> '*Holy, Holy, Holy*
> *is the Lord God, the Almighty;*
> he was, he is and he is to come'.

Every time the animals glorified and honoured and gave thanks to the One sitting 9
on the throne, *who lives for ever and ever,* •the twenty-four elders prostrated 10
themselves before him to worship the One *who lives for ever and ever,* and threw
down their crowns in front of the throne, saying, •'You are our Lord and our 11
God, you are worthy of glory and honour and power, because you made all the
universe and it was only by your will that everything was made and exists'.

5 I saw that in the right hand of the One sitting on the throne there was *a scroll* 1
that had writing on back and front[a] and was sealed with seven seals. •Then 2
I saw a powerful angel who called with a loud voice, 'Is there anyone worthy

3 to open the scroll and break the seals of it?' •But there was no one, in heaven or on the earth or under the earth, who was able to open the scroll and read it.
4
5 I wept bitterly because there was nobody fit to open the scroll and read it, •but one of the elders said to me, 'There is no need to cry: *the Lion* of the tribe *of Judah, the Root*[b] of David, has triumphed, and he will open the scroll and the seven seals of it'.

6   Then I saw, standing between the throne with its four animals and the circle of the elders, a Lamb that seemed to have been sacrificed; it had seven horns, and it had seven eyes, which are the seven Spirits God has *sent out all over the*
7 *world.*[c] •The Lamb came forward to take the scroll from the right hand of the
8 One sitting on the throne, •and when he took it, the four animals prostrated themselves before him and with them the twenty-four elders; each one of them was holding a harp and had a golden bowl full of incense made of the prayers
9 of the saints. •They sang a new hymn:

'You are worthy to take the scroll
and break the seals of it,
because you were sacrificed, and with your blood
you bought men for God
of every race, language, people and nation
10   and made them *a line of kings and priests,*[d]
to serve our God and to rule the world'.

11   In my vision, I heard the sound of an immense number of angels gathered round the throne and the animals and the elders; there were *ten thousand times*
12 *ten thousand of them*[e] and *thousands upon thousands,* •shouting, 'The Lamb that was sacrificed is worthy to be given power, riches, wisdom, strength, honour,
13 glory and blessing'. •Then I heard all the living things in creation—everything that lives in the air, and on the ground, and under the ground, and in the sea, crying, 'To the One who is sitting on the throne and to the Lamb, be all praise,
14 honour, glory and power, for ever and ever'. •And the four animals said, 'Amen'; and the elders prostrated themselves to worship.

The Lamb breaks the seven seals

1   6 Then I saw the Lamb break one of the seven seals, and I heard one of the
2   four animals shout in a voice like thunder, 'Come'. •Immediately a white horse appeared, and the rider on it was holding a bow; he was given the victor's crown and he went away, to go from victory to victory.
3   When he broke the second seal, I heard the second animal shout, 'Come'.
4 And out came another horse, bright red, and its rider was given this duty: to take away peace from the earth and set people killing each other. He was given a huge sword.
5   When he broke the third seal, I heard the third animal shout, 'Come'. Immediately a black horse appeared, and its rider was holding a pair of scales;
6 and I seemed to hear a voice shout from among the four animals and say, 'A ration of corn for a day's wages, and three rations of barley for a day's wages, but do not tamper with the oil or the wine'.
7   When he broke the fourth seal, I heard the voice of the fourth animal shout,
8 'Come'. •Immediately another horse appeared, deathly pale, and its rider was called Plague, and Hades followed at his heels.
    They were given authority over a quarter of the earth, *to kill by the sword, by famine, by plague and wild beasts.*[a]

d. Pr 3:12
4 a. For many of the descriptive details in this scene the writer draws on Ezk 1 and 10 and Is 6.   b. The angels or 'principles' which direct the physical world. Since Irenaeus, these four creatures have been used as symbols of the four evangelists.
5 a. Ezk 2:9   b. Gn 49:9; Is 11:10   c. Zc 4:10   d. Is 61:6   e. Dn 7:10
6 a. Ezk 14:21

When he broke the fifth seal, I saw underneath the altar the souls of all the 9
people who had been killed on account of the word of God, for witnessing to it.
They shouted aloud, 'Holy, faithful Master, how much longer will you wait 10
before you pass sentence and take vengeance for our death on the inhabitants
of the earth?' •Each of them was given a white robe, and they were told to be 11
patient a little longer, until the roll was complete and their fellow servants and
brothers had been killed just as they had been.

In my vision, when he broke the sixth seal, there was a violent earthquake 12
and the sun went as black as coarse sackcloth; the moon turned red as blood all
over, •and *the stars of the sky fell*[b] on to the earth *like figs* dropping from a fig 13
tree when a high wind shakes it; •the *sky disappeared like a scroll rolling up* and all 14
the mountains and islands were shaken from their places. •Then all the earthly 15
rulers, the governors and the commanders, the rich people and the men of
influence, the whole population, slaves and citizens, took to the mountains *to hide
in caves and among the rocks.*[c] •*They said to the mountains*[d] and the rocks, '*Fall on us* 16
and hide us away from the One who sits on the throne and from the anger of
the Lamb. •For *the Great Day of his anger* has come, *and who can survive it?*'[e] 17

God's servants will be preserved

7 Next I saw four angels, standing at *the four corners of the earth,*[a] holding the 1
four winds of the world back to keep them from blowing over the land or the
sea or in the trees. •Then I saw another angel rising where the sun rises, carrying 2
the seal of the living God; he called in a powerful voice to the four angels
whose duty was to devastate land and sea, •'Wait before you do any damage on 3
land or at sea or to the trees, until we have put the *seal on the foreheads*[b] of the
servants of our God'. •Then I heard how many were sealed: a hundred and forty- 4
four thousand,[c] out of all the tribes of Israel.

From the tribe of Judah, twelve thousand had been sealed; from the tribe of 5
Reuben, twelve thousand; from the tribe of Gad, twelve thousand; •from the 6
tribe of Asher, twelve thousand; from the tribe of Naphtali, twelve thousand;
from the tribe of Manasseh, twelve thousand; •from the tribe of Simeon, twelve 7
thousand; from the tribe of Levi, twelve thousand; from the tribe of Issachar,
twelve thousand; •from the tribe of Zebulun, twelve thousand; from the tribe of 8
Joseph, twelve thousand; and from the tribe of Benjamin, twelve thousand were
sealed.

The rewarding of the saints

After that I saw a huge number, impossible to count, of people from every 9
nation, race, tribe and language; they were standing in front of the throne and in
front of the Lamb, dressed in white robes and holding palms in their hands.
They shouted aloud, •'Victory to our God, who sits on the thone, and to the 10
Lamb!' •And all the angels who were standing in a circle round the throne, 11
surrounding the elders and the four animals, prostrated themselves before
the throne, and touched the ground with their foreheads, worshipping God
with these words, 'Amen. Praise and glory and wisdom and thanksgiving and 12
honour and power and strength to our God for ever and ever. Amen.'

One of the elders then spoke, and asked me, 'Do you know who these people 13
are, dressed in white robes, and where they have come from?' •I answered him, 14
'You can tell me, my lord'. Then he said, 'These are the people who have been
through the great persecution,[d] and because they have washed their robes white
again in the blood of the Lamb, •they now stand in front of God's throne and 15
serve him day and night in his sanctuary; and the One who sits on the throne will
spread his tent over them. •*They will never hunger or thirst* again; *neither the* 16
sun nor scorching wind will ever plague them, •because the Lamb who is at the 17
throne *will be their shepherd and will lead them to springs of living water;*[e] and God
will wipe away all tears from their eyes.'[f]

The seventh seal

1 8 The Lamb then broke the seventh seal, and there was silence in heaven for about half an hour.[a]

The prayers of the saints bring the coming of the Great Day nearer

2 Next I saw seven trumpets being given to the seven angels who stand in the 3 presence of God. •Another angel, who had a golden censer,[b] came and stood at the altar.[c] A large quantity of incense was given to him to offer with the prayers 4 of all the saints on the golden altar that stood in front of the throne; •and so from the angel's hand the smoke of the incense went up in the presence of God 5 and with it the prayers of the saints. •Then the angel took the censer and *filled it with the fire* from the altar, which he then threw down on to the earth; immediately there came peals of thunder and flashes of lightning, and the earth shook.

The first four trumpets

6 The seven angels that had the seven trumpets now made ready to sound them. 7 The first blew his trumpet and, with that, hail and fire, mixed with blood, were dropped on the earth; a third of the earth was burnt up, and a third of all trees, 8 and every blade of grass was burnt. •The second angel blew his trumpet, and it was as though a great mountain, all on fire, had been dropped into the sea: a third 9 of the sea turned into blood, •a third of all the living things in the sea were 10 killed, and a third of all ships were destroyed. •The third angel blew his trumpet, and a huge star fell from the sky, burning like a ball of fire, and it fell on a third 11 of all rivers and springs; •this was the star called Wormwood, and a third of all water turned to bitter wormwood, so that many people died from drinking it. 12 The fourth angel blew his trumpet, and a third of the sun and a third of the moon and a third of the stars were blasted, so that the light went out of a third of them and for a third of the day there was no illumination, and the same with the night.

13 In my vision, I heard an eagle, calling aloud as it flew high overhead, 'Trouble, trouble, trouble, for all the people on earth at the sound of the other three trumpets which the three angels are going to blow'.

The fifth trumpet

1 9 Then the fifth angel blew his trumpet, and I saw a star[a] that had fallen from heaven on to the earth, and he was given the key to the shaft leading down 2 to the Abyss.[b] •When he unlocked the shaft of the Abyss, *smoke poured up* out of the Abyss *like the smoke from a huge furnace*[c] so that the sun and the sky were 3 darkened by it, •and out of the smoke dropped locusts which were given the 4 powers that scorpions have on the earth: •they were forbidden to harm any fields or crops or trees and told only to attack any men who were without God's 5 seal on their foreheads. •They were not to kill them, but to give them pain for 6 five months, and the pain was to be the pain of a scorpion's sting. •When this happens, *men will long for death and not find it anywhere;*[d] they will want to die and death will evade them.

7 To look at, these locusts were *like horses armoured for battle;*[e] they had things 8 that looked like gold crowns on their heads, and faces that seemed human, •and

b. Is 34:4   c. Ho 10:8   d. Is 2:10,18,19   e. Jl 2:11; 3:4
7 a. Ezk 7:2   b. Ezk 9:4 (see also Is 44:5).   c. Twelve (the sacred number) squared and multiplied by a thousand, representing the totality of the faithful.   d. Under Nero. e. Is 49:10   f. Is 25:8
8 a. An awed silence; the 'coming of Yahweh' is preceded by silence in the prophetic writings. b. In the shape of a shovel: the flat incense-vessel was also used for carrying live coals from the altar on which offerings were burnt.   c. The altar of incense.
9 a. A fallen angel.   b. Where fallen angels were imprisoned, to be released only to their final punishment.   c. Ex 19:18   d. Jb 3:21   e. The descriptive details in vv. 7-9 owe much to Jl 1 and 2.

hair like women's hair, and *teeth like lions' teeth*. •They had body-armour like 9
iron breastplates, and the noise of their wings sounded like a great charge of
horses and chariots into battle. •Their tails were like scorpions', with stings, 10
and it was with them that they were able to injure people for five months. •As 11
their leader they had their emperor, the angel of the Abyss, whose name in
Hebrew is Abaddon, or Apollyon*j* in Greek.

That was the first of the troubles; there are still two more to come.   12

The sixth trumpet

The sixth angel blew his trumpet, and I heard a voice come out of the four 13
horns of the golden altar in front of God. •It spoke to the sixth angel with the 14
trumpet, and said, 'Release the four angels that are chained up at the great river
Euphrates'. •These four angels had been put there ready for this hour of this 15
day of this month of this year, and now they were released to destroy a third of
the human race. •I learnt how many there were in their army: twice ten thousand 16
times ten thousand mounted men. •In my vision I saw the horses, and the riders 17
with their breastplates of flame colour, hyacinth-blue and sulphur-yellow; the
horses had lions' heads, and fire, smoke and sulphur were coming out of their
mouths. •It was by these three plagues, the fire, the smoke and the sulphur coming 18
out of their mouths, that the one third of the human race was killed. •All the 19
horses' power was in their mouths and their tails: their tails were like snakes,
and had heads that were able to wound. •But the rest of the human race, who 20
escaped these plagues, refused either to abandon *the things they had made with
their own hands*g—the *idols made of gold, silver, bronze, stone and wood*h that can
neither see nor hear nor move—or to stop worshipping devils. •Nor did they give 21
up their murdering, or witchcraft, or fornication or stealing.

The imminence of the last punishment

10 Then I saw another powerful angel coming down from heaven, wrapped in 1
a cloud, with a rainbow over his head; his face was like the sun, and his legs
were pillars of fire. •In his hand he had a small scroll, unrolled; he put his right foot 2
in the sea and his left foot on the land •and he shouted so loud, it was *like a lion* 3
roaring. At this, seven claps of thunder made themselves heard •and when the 4
seven thunderclaps had spoken, I was preparing to write, when I heard a voice
from heaven say to me, 'Keep the words of the seven thunderclaps secret and do
not write them down'. •Then the angel that I had seen, standing on the sea 5
and the land, *raised his right hand to heaven,*a •and *swore by the One who lives* 6
for ever and ever, *and made heaven and all that is in it*, and *earth and all it bears*,
and *the sea and all it holds*,b 'The time of waiting is over; •at the time when the 7
seventh angel is heard sounding his trumpet, God's secret intention will be
fulfilled, just as he announced in the Good News told to *his servants the prophets*'.

The seer eats the small scroll

Then I heard the voice I had heard from heaven speaking to me again. 'Go,' 8
it said 'and take that open scroll out of the hand of the angel standing on sea
and land.' •I went to the angel and asked him to give me the small scroll, and 9
he said, 'Take it and eat it; it will turn your stomach sour, but in your mouth it
will taste as sweet as honey'. •So I took it out of the angel's hand, and swallowed 10
it; it was as sweet as honey in my mouth, but when I had eaten it my stomach
turned sour. •Then I was told, 'You are to prophesy again, this time about 11
many different nations and countries and languages and emperors'.

The two witnesses

11 Then I was given a long cane as a measuring rod, and I was told, 'Go and 1
measure God's sanctuary, and the altar, and the people who worship there;
but leave out the outer court and do not measure it, because it has been handed 2

3 over to pagans—they will trample on the holy city for forty-two months.ᵃ •But
I shall send my two witnesses to prophesy for those twelve hundred and sixty days,
4 wearing sackcloth. •These are the *two olive trees*ᵇ and the two lamps *that stand*
5 *before the Lord of the world.*ᶜ •Fire can come from their mouths and consume
their enemies if anyone tries to harm them; and if anybody does try to harm
6 them he will certainly be killed in this way. •They are able to lock up the sky so
that it does not rain as long as they are prophesying; they are able to turn water
into blood and strike the whole world with any plague as often as they like.
7 When they have completed their witnessing, the beast that comes out of the
8 Abyss *is going to make war on them and overcome them*ᵈ and kill them. •Their
corpses will lie in the main street of the Great City known by the symbolic
9 names Sodom and Egypt, in which their Lord was crucified.ᵉ •Men out of every
people, race, language and nation will stare at their corpses, for three-and-a-half
10 days, not letting them be buried, •and the people of the world will be glad about
it and celebrate the event by giving presents to each other, because these two
prophets have been a plague to the people of the world.'
11   After the three-and-a-half days, *God breathed life into them and they stood up,*ᶠ
12 and everybody who saw it happen was terrified; •then they heard a loud voice
from heaven say to them, 'Come up here', and while their enemies were watching,
13 they went up to heaven in a cloud. •Immediately, there was a violent earthquake,
and a tenth of the city collapsed; seven thousand personsᵍ were killed in the
earthquake, and the survivors, overcome with fear, could only praise the God
of heaven.

The seventh trumpet

14   That was the second of the troubles; the third is to come quickly after it.
15   Then the seventh angel blew his trumpet, and voices could be heard shouting
in heaven, calling, 'The kingdom of the world has become the kingdom of our
16 Lord and his Christ, and he will reign for ever and ever'. •The twenty-four elders,
enthroned in the presence of God, prostrated themselves and touched the ground
17 with their foreheads worshipping God •with these words, 'We give thanks to
you, Almighty Lord God, He-Is-and-He-Was, for using your great power and
18 beginning your reign. •*The nations were seething with rage*ʰ and now the time has
come for your own anger, and for the dead to be judged, and for your servants
the prophets, for the saints and for all who worship you, small or great, to be
rewarded. The time has come to destroy those who are destroying the earth.'
19   Then the sanctuary of God in heaven opened, and the ark of the covenant
could be seen inside it. Then came flashes of lightning, peals of thunder and an
earthquake, and violent hail.

The vision of the woman and the dragon

1   **12** Now a great sign appeared in heaven: a woman, adorned with the sun,
standing on the moon, and with the twelve stars on her head for a crown.
2/3 She was pregnant, and in labour, crying aloud in the pangs of childbirth. •Then
a second sign appeared in the sky, a huge red dragon which had seven heads
4 and ten horns, and each of the seven heads crowned with a coronet. •Its tail
dragged a third of *the stars from the sky and dropped them to the earth,*ᵃ and the

f. 'Destruction'.   g. Is 17:8   h. Dn 5:4
10 a. Dt 32:40   b. Ne 9:6
11 a. This period, taken from Dn, is used as the symbol for any time of persecution.   b. Zc
4:3,14, where they symbolise Joshua and Zerubbabel; here they probably represent Peter and
Paul.   c. 2 K 1:10   d. Dn 7:21   e. The 'Great City' or 'Babylon' in this book is Rome,
whose actions were identified with Sodom's rejection of God's messengers and Egypt's oppression of God's people. The words 'in which their Lord was crucified' may be a gloss, or may be
justified by the responsibility of the Roman authority for the crucifixion.   f. Ezk 37:5,10
g. That is, a great number of all classes.   h. Ps 2:1,5
12 a. Dn 8:10

dragon stopped in front of the woman as she was having the child, so that he could eat it as soon as it was born from its mother. •The woman brought *a male child* 5 *into the world*, the son who was *to rule all the nations with an iron sceptre*,[b] and the child was taken straight up to God and to his throne, •while the woman escaped 6 into the desert, where God had made a place of safety ready, for her to be looked after in the twelve hundred and sixty days.

And now war broke out in heaven, when Michael with his angels attacked the 7 dragon. The dragon fought back with his angels, •but they were defeated and 8 driven out of heaven. •The great dragon, the primeval serpent, known as the 9 devil or Satan, who had deceived all the world, was hurled down to the earth and his angels were hurled down with him. •Then I heard a voice shout from 10 heaven, 'Victory and power and empire for ever have been won by our God, and all authority for his Christ, now that the persecutor, who accused our brothers day and night before our God, has been brought down. •They have triumphed 11 over him by the blood of the Lamb and by the witness of their martyrdom, because even in the face of death they would not cling to life. •Let the heavens 12 rejoice and all who live there; but for you, earth and sea, trouble is coming— because the devil has gone down to you in a rage, knowing that his days are numbered.'

As soon as the devil found himself thrown down to the earth, he sprang 13 in pursuit of the woman, the mother of the male child, •but she was given a huge 14 pair of eagle's wings to fly away from the serpent into the desert, to the place where she was to be looked after for *a year and twice a year and half a year*.[c] So the serpent vomited water from his mouth, like a river, after the woman, 15 to sweep her away in the current, •but the earth came to her rescue; it opened 16 its mouth and swallowed the river thrown up by the dragon's jaws. •Then the 17 dragon was enraged with the woman and went away to make war on the rest of her children, that is, all who obey God's commandments and bear witness for Jesus.

The dragon delegates his power to the beast

I was standing on the seashore. 13 Then I saw *a beast emerge from the sea:*[a] 1⁸₁ it had seven heads and ten horns, with a coronet on each of its ten horns, and its heads were marked with blasphemous titles.[b] •I saw that the beast *was like* 2 *a leopard*, with paws like *a bear* and a mouth like *a lion*;[c] the dragon had handed over to it his own power and his throne and his worldwide authority. •I saw that 3 one of its heads seemed to have had a fatal wound but that this deadly injury had healed and, after that, the whole world had marvelled and followed the beast. They prostrated themselves in front of the dragon because he had given the beast 4 his authority; and they prostrated themselves in front of the beast, saying, 'Who can compare with the beast?[d] How could anybody defeat him?' •For forty-two 5 months the beast was allowed *to mouth its boasts*[e] and blasphemies and to do whatever it wanted; •and it mouthed its blasphemies against God, against his 6 name, his heavenly Tent and all those who are sheltered there. •It was allowed 7 *to make war against the saints and conquer them, and given power* over every race, people, language and nation; •and all people of the world will worship it, that 8 is, everybody whose name has not been written down since the foundation of the world in the book of life of the sacrificial Lamb. •If anyone has ears to hear, 9 let him listen: •*Captivity for those who are destined for captivity; the sword for* 10 *those who are to die by the sword.*[f] This is why the saints must have constancy and faith.

The false prophet as the slave of the beast

Then I saw a second beast;[g] it emerged from the ground; it had two horns 11 like a lamb, but made a noise like a dragon. •This second beast was servant to 12 the first beast, and extended its authority everywhere, making the world and

all its people worship the first beast, which had had the fatal wound and had
13 been healed. •And it worked great miracles, even to calling down fire from
14 heaven on to the earth while people watched. •Through the miracles which it
was allowed to do on behalf of the first beast, it was able to win over the people
of the world and persuade them to put up a statue in honour of the beast that
15 had been wounded by the sword and still lived. •It was allowed to breathe
life into this statue, so that the statue of the beast was able to speak, and to have
16 *anyone who refused to worship the statue of the beast*[h] put to death. •He compelled
everyone—small and great, rich and poor, slave and citizen—to be branded on
17 the right hand or on the forehead, •and made it illegal for anyone to buy or sell
anything unless he had been branded with the name of the beast or with the
number of its name.
18   There is need for shrewdness here: if anyone is clever enough he may interpret
the number of the beast: it is the number of a man, the number 666.[i]

The companions of the Lamb

1 **14** Next in my vision I saw Mount Zion, and standing on it a Lamb who
had with him a hundred and forty-four thousand people, all with his name
2 and his Father's name written on their foreheads. •I heard a sound coming
out of the sky like the sound of the ocean or the roar of thunder; it seemed to be
3 the sound of harpists playing their harps. •There in front of the throne they were
singing a new hymn in the presence of the four animals and the elders, a hymn
that could only be learnt by the hundred and forty-four thousand who had been
4 redeemed from the world. •These are the ones who have kept their virginity[a]
and not been defiled with women; they *follow* the Lamb wherever he goes;
they have been redeemed from amongst men to be *the first-fruits for God*[b] and
5 for the Lamb. •They never *allowed a lie to pass their lips*[c] and no fault can be
found in them.

Angels announce the day of Judgement

6   Then I saw another angel, flying high overhead, sent to announce the Good
News of eternity to all who live on the earth, every nation, race, language and
7 tribe. •He was calling, 'Fear God and praise him, because the time has come for
him to sit in judgement; worship *the maker of heaven and earth and sea*[d] and every
water-spring'.
8   A second angel followed him, calling, '*Babylon has fallen, Babylon the Great has
fallen,*[e] Babylon which gave the whole world *the wine of* God's *anger* to drink'.
9   A third angel followed, shouting aloud, 'All those who worship the beast and
10 his statue, or have had themselves branded on the hand or forehead, •will be made
to drink the wine of God's fury which is ready, undiluted, in his cup of anger;
in *fire and brimstone*[f] they will be tortured in the presence of the holy angels and
11 the Lamb •and *the smoke* of their torture *will go up for ever*[g] and ever. There will
be no respite, *night or day*, for those who worshipped the beast or its statue
12 or accepted branding with its name.' •This is why there must be constancy in the
13 saints who keep the commandments of God and faith in Jesus. •Then I heard
a voice from heaven say to me, 'Write down: Happy are those who die in the
Lord! Happy indeed, the Spirit says; now they can rest for ever after their work,
since their good deeds go with them.'

b. Ps 2:9   c. Dn 7:25. Cf. 11:3.
13 a. Dn 7:3   b. Seven heads represent a succession of seven Roman emperors; ten crowned
horns are ten subject kings.   c. Dn 7:4-6   d. A parody of the name Michael, 'Who-can-
compare-with-God?'   e. Dn 7:8,11   f. Jr 15:2   g. Also called 'the false prophet', 16:13;
19:20; 20:10.   h. Dn 3:5-7,15   i. Codes and riddles were made in both Greek and Hebr.
by using numbers for letters, according to their order in the alphabet. Some commentators
have claimed that 666 is the total of the number-values of 'Nero Caesar'.
14 a. As so often in the O.T., 'virginity' stands for faithfulness, and 'adultery' or 'fornication'
for idolatry.   b. Jr 2:2-3   c. Zp 3:13   d. Ex 20:11   e. Is 21:9. The *wine of* God's *anger*
is a phrase from Is 51:17, also used in Jr 25:15f.   f. Gn 19:28   g. Is 34:9-10

The harvest and vintage of the pagans

Now in my vision I saw a white *cloud* and, *sitting on it, one like a son of man* 14 with a gold crown on his head and a sharp sickle in his hand. •Then another angel 15 came out of the sanctuary, and shouted aloud to the one sitting on the cloud, '*Put your sickle in* and reap: harvest time has come and *the harvest* of the earth *is ripe*'.[h] •Then the one sitting on the cloud set his sickle to work on the earth, and 16 the earth's harvest was reaped.

Another angel, who also carried a sharp sickle, came out of the temple in 17 heaven, •and the angel in charge of the fire left the altar and shouted aloud to 18 the one with the sharp sickle, 'Put your sickle in and cut all the bunches off the vine of the earth; all its grapes are ripe'. •So the angel set his sickle to work on 19 the earth and harvested the whole vintage of the earth and put it into a huge winepress, the winepress of God's anger, •outside the city, where it was trodden 20 until the blood that came out of the winepress was up to the horses' bridles as far away as sixteen hundred furlongs.

The hymn of Moses and the Lamb

15 What I saw next, in heaven, was a great and wonderful sign: seven angels 1 were bringing the seven plagues that are the last of all, because they exhaust the anger of God. •I seemed to see a glass lake suffused with fire, and 2 standing by the lake of glass, those who had fought against the beast and won, and against his statue and the number which is his name. They all had harps from God, •and they were singing the hymn of Moses, the servant of God, 3 and of the Lamb:

'How great and wonderful are all your works,
Lord God Almighty;
just and true are all your ways,
King of nations.
Who would not revere and *praise your name, O Lord?* 4
You alone are holy,
and all the pagans will come and adore you
for the many acts of justice you have shown.'[a]

The seven bowls of plagues

After this, in my vision, the sanctuary, the Tent of the Testimony, opened 5 in heaven, •and out came the seven angels with the seven plagues, wearing pure 6 white linen, fastened round their waists with golden girdles. •One of the four 7 animals gave the seven angels seven golden bowls filled with the anger of God who lives for ever and ever. •*The smoke from the glory* and the power *of God* 8 *filled the temple so that no one could go into it*[b] until the seven plagues of the seven angels were completed.

16 Then I heard a voice from the sanctuary shouting to the seven angels, 1 'Go, and empty the seven bowls of God's anger over the earth'.

The first angel went and emptied his bowl over the earth; at once, on all the 2 people who had been branded with the mark of the beast and had worshipped its statue, there came disgusting and virulent sores.

The second angel emptied his bowl over the sea, and it turned to blood, like 3 the blood of a corpse, and every living creature in the sea died.

The third angel emptied his bowl into the rivers and water-springs and they 4 turned into blood. •Then I heard the angel of water say, 'You are the holy 5 He-Is-and-He-Was, the Just One, and this is a just punishment: •they spilt the 6 blood of the saints and the prophets, and blood is what you have given them to drink; it is what they deserve'. •And I heard the altar itself say, 'Truly, Lord 7 God Almighty, the punishments you give are true and just'.

8   The fourth angel emptied his bowl over the sun and it was made to scorch
9 people with its flames; •but though people were scorched by the fierce heat of it,
they cursed the name of God who had the power to cause such plagues, and
they would not repent and praise him.

10   The fifth angel emptied his bowl over the throne of the beast and its whole
empire was plunged into darkness. Men were biting their tongues for pain,
11 but instead of repenting for what they had done, they cursed the God of heaven
because of their pains and sores.

12   The sixth angel emptied his bowl over the great river Euphrates; all the water
13 dried up so that a way was made for the kings of the East[a] to come in. •Then
from the jaws of dragon and beast and false prophet I saw three foul spirits come;
14 they looked like frogs •and in fact were demon spirits, able to work miracles,
going out to all the kings of the world to call them together for the war of the
15 Great Day of God the Almighty.—•This is how it will be: I shall come like
a thief. Happy is the man who has stayed awake and not taken off his clothes
16 so that he does not go out naked and expose his shame.—•They called the
kings together at the place called, in Hebrew, Armageddon.[b]

17   The seventh angel emptied his bowl into the air, and a voice shouted from
18 the sanctuary, 'The end has come'. •Then there were flashes of lightning and
peals of thunder and the most violent earthquake *that anyone has ever seen since
19 there have been* men *on the earth*.[c] •The Great City was split into three parts
and the cities of the world collapsed; Babylon the Great was not forgotten:
20 God made her drink the full winecup of his anger. •Every island vanished and
21 the mountains disappeared; •and hail, with great hailstones weighing a talent
each, fell from the sky on the people. They cursed God for sending a plague
of hail; it was the most terrible plague.

B. THE PUNISHMENT OF BABYLON

The famous prostitute

1 **17** One of the seven angels that had the seven bowls came to speak to me,
and said, 'Come here and I will show you the punishment given to the
2 famous prostitute[a] who rules *enthroned beside abundant waters*,[b] •the one with
whom all the kings of the earth have committed fornication, and who has made
3 all the population of the world drunk with the wine of her adultery'.[c] •He took
me in spirit to a desert, and there I saw a woman riding a scarlet beast which
had seven heads and ten horns and had blasphemous titles written all over it.
4 The woman was dressed in purple and scarlet, and glittered with gold and jewels
and pearls, and she was holding a gold winecup filled with the disgusting filth
5 of her fornication; •on her forehead was written a name, a cryptic name:
'Babylon the Great, the mother of all the prostitutes and all the filthy practices
6 on the earth'. •I saw that she was drunk, drunk with the blood of the saints,
and the blood of the martyrs of Jesus; and when I saw her, I was completely
7 mystified. •The angel said to me, 'Don't you understand? Now I will tell you
the meaning of this woman, and of the beast she is riding, with the seven heads
and the ten horns.

h. Jl 4:13; Am 8:2
15 a. This hymn is nearer to the Psalms than to the Song of Moses in Ex 15. The two direct
quotations are from Jr 10 and Ps 86; the opening of it is reminiscent of Ps 92 and 98.
b. 1 K 8:10-11
16 a. Of Parthia, the savage enemy dreaded by the Roman world.   b. 'Megiddo mountains';
Josiah's defeat at Megiddo, 2 K 23:29f, made this place a symbol of military disaster, cf.
Zc 12:11.   c. Dn 12:1
17 a. Rome.   b. Jr 51:13, a literal description of Babylon, here applied metaphorically, as
the author explains in v. 15.   c. I.e. the idolatry of emperor-worship.

The symbolism of the beast and the prostitute

'The beast you have seen once was and now is not;[d] he is yet to come up 8 from the Abyss, but only to go to his destruction. And the people of the world, whose names have not been written since the beginning of the world in the book of life, will think it miraculous when they see how the beast once was and now is not and is still to come. •Here there is need for cleverness, for a shrewd mind; 9 the seven heads are the seven hills, and the woman is sitting on them.

'The seven heads are also seven emperors. Five of them have already gone, 10 one is here now, and one is yet to come; once here, he must stay for a short while. The beast, who once was and now is not, is at the same time the eighth and one of 11 the seven, and he is going to his destruction.

'*The ten horns are ten kings*[e] who have not yet been given their royal power 12 but will have royal authority only for a single hour and in association with the beast. •They are all of one mind in putting their strength and their powers at the 13 beast's disposal, •and they will go to war against the Lamb; but the Lamb is 14 *the Lord of lords and the King of kings,*[f] and he will defeat them and they will be defeated by his followers, the called, the chosen, the faithful.'

The angel continued, 'The waters you saw, beside which the prostitute was 15 sitting, are all the peoples, the populations, the nations and the languages. •But 16 the time will come when the ten horns and the beast will turn against the prostitute, and *strip off her clothes and leave her naked;*[g] then they will eat her flesh and burn the remains in the fire. •In fact, God influenced their minds to do 17 what he intended, to agree together to put their royal powers at the beast's disposal until the time when God's words should be fulfilled. •The woman you 18 saw is the great city which has authority over all the rulers on earth.'

An angel announces the fall of Babylon

18 After this, I saw another angel come down from heaven, with great 1 authority given to him; *the earth was lit up with his glory.*[a] •At the top of 2 his voice he shouted, '*Babylon has fallen,* Babylon the Great has fallen, and has become *the haunt of devils*[b] and a lodging for every foul spirit and dirty, loathsome bird. •All the nations have been intoxicated by the wine of her prostitution; 3 every king in the earth has committed fornication with her, and every merchant grown rich through her debauchery.'

The people of God summoned away

A new voice spoke from heaven; I heard it say, 'Come out, my people, away 4 from her, so that you do not share in her crimes and have the same plagues to bear. •*Her sins have reached up to heaven,*[c] and God has her crimes in mind: 5 *she is to be paid in her own coin.*[d] She must be paid double the amount she exacted. 6 She is to have a doubly strong cup of her own mixture. •Every one of her shows 7 and orgies is to be matched by a torture or a grief. *I am the queen on my throne, she says to herself,*[e] and *I am no widow* and shall never be in mourning. •For that, 8 *within a single day*, the plagues will fall on her: disease and mourning and famine. She will be burnt right up. The Lord God has condemned her, and he has great power.'

The people of the world mourn for Babylon

There will be mourning and weeping for her by the kings of the earth who 9 have fornicated with her and lived with her in luxury. They see the smoke as she burns, •while they keep at a safe distance from fear of her agony. They will 10 say:

> 'Mourn, mourn for this great city,
> Babylon, so powerful a city,
> doomed as you are within a single hour'.

11 There will be weeping and distress over her among all the traders of the earth
12 when there is nobody left to buy their cargoes of goods; •their stocks of gold
and silver, jewels and pearls, linen and purple and silks and scarlet; all the
13 sandalwood, every piece in ivory or fine wood, in bronze or iron or marble; •the
cinnamon and spices, the myrrh and ointment and incense; wine, oil, flour and
corn; their stocks of cattle, sheep, horses and chariots, their slaves, their human
cargo.
14 'All the fruits you had set your hearts on have failed you; gone for ever, never
to return, is your life of magnificence and ease.'
15 The traders who had made a fortune out of her will be standing at
16 a safe distance from fear of her agony, mourning and weeping. •They will be
saying:

> 'Mourn, mourn for this great city;
> for all the linen and purple and scarlet that you wore,
> for all your finery of gold and jewels and pearls;
17 > your riches are all destroyed within a single hour'.

All the captains and seafaring men, sailors and all those who make a living
18 from the sea will be keeping a safe distance, •watching the smoke as she burns,
19 and crying out, 'Has there ever been a city as great as this!' •They will throw dust
on their heads and say, with tears and groans:

> 'Mourn, mourn for this great city
> whose lavish living has made a fortune
> for every owner of a sea-going ship;
> ruined within a single hour.

20 'Now heaven, celebrate her downfall, and all you saints, apostles and prophets:
God has given judgement for you against her.'
21 Then a powerful angel picked up a boulder like a great millstone, and as he
hurled it into the sea, he said, 'That is how the great city of Babylon is going
to be hurled down, never to be seen again.

22 > 'Never again in you, Babylon,
> will be heard the song of harpists and minstrels,
> the music of flute and trumpet;
> never again will craftsmen of every skill be found
> or *the sound of the mill[1]* be heard;
23 > never again will shine *the light of the lamp*,
> never again will be heard
> *the voices of bridegroom and bride*.
> Your traders were the princes of the earth,
> all the nations were under your spell.

24 In her you will find the blood of prophets and saints, and all the blood that was
ever shed on earth.'

Songs of victory in heaven

1 **19** After this I seemed to hear the great sound of a huge crowd in heaven,
2 singing, 'Alleluia! Victory and glory and power to our God! •He judges
fairly, he punishes justly, and he has condemned the famous prostitute who
corrupted the earth with her fornication; he has avenged his servants that she
3 killed'. •They sang again, 'Alleluia! *The smoke* of her *will go up for ever* and
4 ever.' •Then the twenty-four elders and the four animals prostrated themselves

---

d. The popular belief that Nero would return from the dead at the head of a Parthian army
accounts for this parody of the divine title.   e. Dn 7:24; here they are kings of the satellite
nations.   f. Dn 10:17   g. Ezk 16:37f
18 a. Ezk 43:2 . b. Is 34:11f   c. Jr 51:9   d. Jr 50:15   e. Is 47:8   f. Jr 25:10

and worshipped God seated there on his throne, and they cried, 'Amen, Alleluia'.

Then a voice came from the throne; it said, 'Praise our God, you servants 5 of his and *all who, great or small, revere him*'. •And I seemed to hear the voices 6 of a huge crowd, like the sound of the ocean or the great roar of thunder, answering, 'Alleluia! The reign of the Lord our God Almighty has begun; •let us 7 be glad and joyful and give praise to God, because this is the time for the marriage of the Lamb. •His bride is ready, and she has been able to dress herself in dazzling 8 white linen, because her linen is made of the good deeds of the saints.' •The 9 angel said, 'Write this: Happy are those who are invited to the wedding feast of the Lamb', and he added, 'All the things you have written are true messages from God'. •Then I knelt at his feet to worship him, but he said to me, 'Don't 10 do that: I am a servant just like you and all your brothers who are witnesses to Jesus. It is God that you must worship.' The witness Jesus gave is the same as the spirit of prophecy.

C. THE DESTRUCTION OF THE PAGAN NATIONS

The first battle of the End

And now I saw heaven open, and a white horse appear; its rider was called 11 Faithful and True; he is *a judge with integrity*,[a] a warrior for justice. •His eyes 12 were flames of fire, and his head was crowned with many coronets; the name written on him was known only to himself, •*his cloak was soaked in blood.*[b] He is 13 known by the name, The Word of God. •Behind him, dressed in linen of dazzling 14 white, rode the armies of heaven on white horses. •From his mouth came a sharp 15 sword to strike the pagans with; he is the one *who will rule them with an iron sceptre*,[c] and tread out the wine of Almighty God's fierce anger. •On his cloak and 16 on his thigh[d] there was a name written: *The King of kings and the Lord of lords.*

I saw an angel standing in the sun, and he shouted aloud to all the birds that 17 were flying high overhead in the sky, 'Come here. *Gather together at the great feast*[e] that God is giving. •*There will be the flesh* of kings for you, and the flesh of 18 great generals and heroes, the flesh of horses and their riders and of all kinds of men, citizens and slaves, small and great.'

Then I saw the beast, with all the kings of the earth and their armies, gathered 19 together to fight the rider and his army. •But the beast was taken prisoner, 20 together with the false prophet who had worked miracles on the beast's behalf and by them had deceived all who had been branded with the mark of the beast and worshipped his statue. These two were thrown alive into the fiery lake of burning sulphur. •All the rest were killed by the sword of the rider, which 21 came out of his mouth, and *all the birds were gorged with their flesh.*

The reign of a thousand years

20 Then I saw an angel come down from heaven with the key of the Abyss 1 in his hand and an enormous chain. •He overpowered the dragon, that 2 primeval serpent which is the devil and Satan, and chained him up for a thousand years. •He threw him into the Abyss, and shut the entrance and sealed it over him, 3 to make sure he would not deceive the nations again until the thousand years had passed. At the end of that time he must be released, but only for a short while.

Then I saw some thrones, and I saw *those who are given the power to be judges*[a] 4 take their seats on them. I saw the souls of all who had been beheaded for having witnessed for Jesus and for having preached God's word, and those who refused to worship the beast or his statue and would not have the brand-mark on their foreheads or hands; they came to life, and reigned with Christ for a thousand years. •This is the first resurrection; the rest of the dead did not come to life 5 until the thousand years were over. •Happy and blessed are those who share 6 in the first resurrection; the second death cannot affect them but they will be priests of God and of Christ and reign with him for a thousand years.

The second battle of the End

7 When the thousand years are over, Satan will be released from his prison
8 and will come out to deceive all the nations in the four quarters of the earth, *Gog and Magog,*[b] and mobilise them for war. His armies will be as many as the
9 sands of the sea; •they will come swarming over the entire country and besiege the camp of the saints, which is the city that God loves. But *fire will come down*
10 *on them from heaven*[c] and consume them. •Then the devil, who misled them, will be thrown into the lake of fire and sulphur, where the beast and the false prophet are, and their torture will not stop, day or night, for ever and ever.

The punishment of the pagans

11 Then I saw a great white throne and the One who was sitting on it. In his
12 presence, earth and sky vanished, leaving no trace. •I saw the dead, both great and small, standing in front of his throne, while the book of life was opened, and *other books opened* which were the record of what they had done in their lives, by which the dead were judged.
13
14 The sea gave up all the dead who were in it; •Death and Hades were emptied of the dead that were in them; and every one was judged according to the way in which he had lived. Then Death and Hades were thrown into the burning
15 lake. This burning lake is the second death; •and anybody whose name could not be found written in the book of life was thrown into the burning lake.

D. THE JERUSALEM OF THE FUTURE

The heavenly Jerusalem

1 **21** Then I saw *a new heaven and a new earth;*[a] the first heaven and the first
2 earth had disappeared now, and there was no longer any sea. •I saw the holy city, and the new Jerusalem, coming down from God out of heaven, as
3 beautiful as a bride all dressed for her husband. •Then I heard a loud voice call from the throne, 'You see this city? Here God lives among men. He will make *his home among them; they shall be his people,*[b] and he will be their God; his name
4 is *God-with-them.* •*He will wipe away all tears from their eyes;*[c] there will be no more death, and no more mourning or sadness. The world of the past has gone.'
5 Then the One sitting on the throne spoke: 'Now I am making the whole of creation new' he said. 'Write this: that what I am saying is sure and will come
6 true.' •And then he said, 'It is already done. I am the Alpha and the Omega, the Beginning and the End. I will give water from the well of life free to anybody
7 who is thirsty; •it is the rightful inheritance of the one who proves victorious;
8 and *I will be his God* and *he a son to me.*[d] •But the legacy for cowards, for those who break their word, or worship obscenities, for murderers and fornicators, and for fortune-tellers, idolaters or any other sort of liars, is the second death in the burning lake of sulphur.'

The messianic Jerusalem

9 One of the seven angels that had the seven bowls full of the seven last plagues came to speak to me, and said, 'Come here and I will show you the bride that the
10 Lamb has married'. •*In the spirit, he took me to the top of an enormous high mountain*[e] and showed me Jerusalem, the holy city, coming down from God out
11 of heaven. •It *had all the radiant glory of God*[f] and glittered like some precious

---

19 a. Is 11:4   b. Is 63:1   c. Ps 2:9   d. I.e. the place where he wears his sword; so, perhaps, 'on his sword'.   e. Ezk 39:17
20 a. Dn 7:22   b. Ezk 38:2   c. Ezk 38:22
21 a. Is 65:17   b. Ezk 37:27   c. Is 8:8 and 25:8   d. 2 S 7:14   e. Ezk 40:2   f. Is 60:1-2

jewel of crystal-clear diamond. •The walls of it were of a great height, and had 12
twelve gates; at each of the twelve gates there was an angel, and over the gates
were written the names *of the twelve tribes of Israel; •on the east there were three* 13
*gates, on the north three gates, on the south three gates, and on the west three gates.*ᵍ
The city walls stood on twelve foundation stones, each one of which bore the 14
name of one of the twelve apostles of the Lamb.

The angel that was speaking to me was carrying a gold measuring rod 15
to measure the city and its gates and wall. •The plan of the city is perfectly 16
square, its length the same as its breadth. He measured the city with his rod and
it was twelve thousand furlongs in length and in breadth, and equal in height.
He measured its wall, and this was a hundred and forty-four cubits high—the 17
angel was using the ordinary cubit. •The wall was built of diamond, and the city 18
of pure gold, like polished glass. •The foundations of the city wall were faced 19
with all kinds of precious stone: the first with diamond, the second lapis lazuli,
the third turquoise, the fourth crystal, •the fifth agate, the sixth ruby, the seventh 20
gold quartz, the eighth malachite, the ninth topaz, the tenth emerald, the eleventh
sapphire and the twelfth amethyst. •The twelve gates were twelve pearls, each 21
gate being made of a single pearl, and the main street of the city was pure gold,
transparent as glass. •I saw that there was no temple in the city since the Lord 22
God Almighty and the Lamb were themselves the temple, •and the city did not 23
need the sun or the moon for light, since it was lit by the radiant glory of God
and the Lamb was a lighted torch for it. •*The pagan nations will live by its light*ʰ 24
and the kings of the earth will bring it their treasures. •*The gates of it will never* 25
be shut by day—and there will be no night there—•and *the nations will come,* 26
bringing their treasure and their wealth. •Nothing unclean may come into it: no 27
one who does what is loathsome or false, but only those who are listed in the
Lamb's book of life.

22 Then the angel showed me the river of life, rising from the throne of God 1
and of the Lamb and flowing crystal-clear •down the middle of the city 2
street. *On either side of the river were the trees of life, which bear twelve crops*
of fruit in a year, one in each month, and the leaves of which are the cure for the
*pagans.*ᵃ

*The ban will be lifted.*ᵇ The throne of God and of the Lamb will be in its place 3
in the city; his servants will worship him, •they will see him face to face, and his 4
name will be written on their foreheads. •It will never be night again and they 5
will not need lamplight or sunlight, because the Lord God will be shining on them.
They will reign for ever and ever.

The angel said to me, 'All that you have written is sure and will come true: 6
the Lord God who gives the spirit to the prophets has sent his angel to reveal
to his servants *what is soon to take place.* •Very soon now, I shall be with you 7
again.' Happy are those who treasure the prophetic message of this book.

I, John, am the one who heard and saw these things. When I had heard 8
and seen them all, I knelt at the feet of the angel who had shown them to me,
to worship him; •but he said, 'Don't do that: I am a servant just like you and 9
like your brothers the prophets and like those who treasure what you have written
in this book. It is God that you must worship.'

This, too, he said to me, 'Do not keep the prophecies in this book a secret, 10
because the Time is close. •Meanwhile let the sinner go on sinning, and 11
the unclean continue to be unclean; let those who do good go on doing good,
and those who are holy continue to be holy. •Very soon now, I shall be with you 12
again, *bringing the reward to be given to every man according to what he*
*deserves.*ᶜ •I am the Alpha and the Omega, *the First and the Last*, the Beginning 13
and the End. •Happy are those who will have washed their robes clean, so that 14
they will have the right to feed on the tree of life and can come through the gates
into the city. •These others must stay outside: dogs, fortune-tellers, and forni- 15
cators, and murderers, and idolaters, and everyone of false speech and false life.'

EPILOGUE

16   I, Jesus, have sent my angel to make these revelations to you for the sake of the churches. I am of David's line, the root of David and the bright star of the morning.

17   The Spirit and the Bride say, 'Come'. Let everyone who listens answer, 'Come'. *Then let all who are thirsty come:*[a] all who want it may *have the water* of life, *and have it free.*

18   This is my solemn warning to all who hear the prophecies in this book: if anyone adds anything to them, God will add to him every plague mentioned in the

19   book; •if anyone cuts anything out of the prophecies in this book, God will cut off his share of the tree of life and of the holy city, which are described in the book.

20   The one who guarantees these revelations repeats his promise: I shall indeed *be with you* soon. Amen; come, Lord Jesus.

21   May the grace of the Lord Jesus be with you all. Amen.

g. Ezk 48:31-35   h. Is 60:3
22 a. Ezk 47:12   b. Zc 14:11   c. Ps 62:12   d. Is 55:1